The **Rough Guide** to

China

written and researched by

David Leffman, Simon Lewis and Jeremy Atiyah

with additional contributions by

Simon Farnham, Mark South and Martin Zatko

NEW YORK • LONDON • DELHI

www.roughguides.com

Contents

◀◀ View of Pudong from The Bund, Shanghai ◀ Rice terraces, Longji Titian, Guangxi

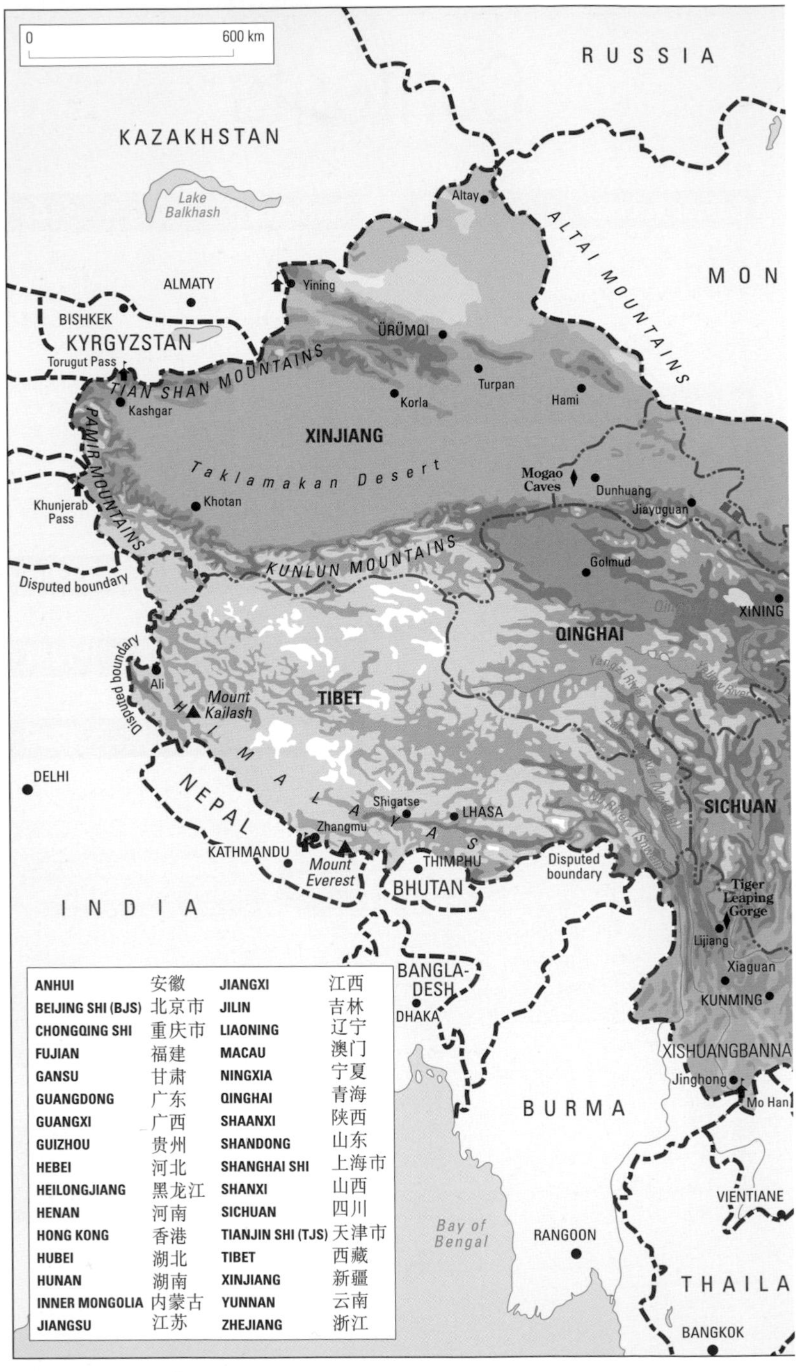

ANHUI	安徽	JIANGXI	江西
BEIJING SHI (BJS)	北京市	JILIN	吉林
CHONGQING SHI	重庆市	LIAONING	辽宁
FUJIAN	福建	MACAU	澳门
GANSU	甘肃	NINGXIA	宁夏
GUANGDONG	广东	QINGHAI	青海
GUANGXI	广西	SHAANXI	陕西
GUIZHOU	贵州	SHANDONG	山东
HEBEI	河北	SHANGHAI SHI	上海市
HEILONGJIANG	黑龙江	SHANXI	山西
HENAN	河南	SICHUAN	四川
HONG KONG	香港	TIANJIN SHI (TJS)	天津市
HUBEI	湖北	TIBET	西藏
HUNAN	湖南	XINJIANG	新疆
INNER MONGOLIA	内蒙古	YUNNAN	云南
JIANGSU	江苏	ZHEJIANG	浙江

Lake Baikal
Irkutsk
Ulan Ude
Manzhouli
Heihe
Amur River
Yichun
Qiqihar
HEILONGJIANG
HARBIN
ULAAN BAATUR
GOLIA
Gobi Desert
INNER MONGOLIA
CHANGCHUN
Jilin
JILIN
Erlianhot
SHENYANG
Changbai Shan Nature Reserve
NORTH KOREA
Jinzhou
LIAONING
SEA OF JAPAN
HOHHOT
Great Wall
HEBEI
Chengde
Dandong
Yellow River
BJS
PYONGYANG
Datong
BEIJING
Tangshan
Dalian
Wutai Shan
TJS
TIANJIN
Bay of Bohai
SEOUL
YINCHUAN
TAIYUAN
SHIJIAZHUANG
Yantai
SOUTH KOREA
NINGXIA
SHANXI
JI'NAN
Tai Shan
LANZHOU
Yan'an
Qingdao
YELLOW SEA
Yuncheng
Anyang
SHANDONG
Terracotta Army
GANSU
ZHENGZHOU
JIANGSU
XI'AN
Kaifeng
Xuzhou
Hongze Hu
Jiuzhaigou Scenic Reserve
SHAANXI
Song Shan
Tai Hu
JAPAN
Huai River
HENAN
Songpan
NANJING
Wudang Shan
Xiangfan
HEFEI
SHANGHAI
PACIFIC OCEAN
Suzhou
Wolong Panda Reserve
CHONGQING SHI
HUBEI
ANHUI
SHANGHAI SHI
WUHAN
Huang Shan
Three Gorges Dam
HANGZHOU
Ningbo
CHENGDU
Emei Shan
CHONGQING
Poyang Hu
ZHEJIANG
Leshan
Jingdezhen
Yangzi River
Wulingyuan Scenic Reserve
EAST CHINA SEA
Dongting Hu
NANCHANG
Fanjing Shan
HUNAN
CHANGSHA
JIANGXI
FUJIAN
GUIZHOU
Heng Shan
FUZHOU
GUIYANG
TAIPEI
Guilin
Ganzhou
Liuzhou
Xiamen
Li River
Meizhou
TAIWAN
Hong Shui River
GUANGDONG
YUNNAN
NANNING
GUANGZHOU
Wuzhou
Zhuhai
Shenzhen
GUANGXI
Hekou
Youyi Guan
HONG KONG
MACAU
Beihai
HANOI
HAIKOU
SOUTH CHINA SEA
HAINAN
Wuzhi Shan
LAOS
VIETNAM
Sanya
ND
PHILIPPINES
MANILA
metres
6000
5000
4000
3000
2000
1000
500
200
0

Introduction to China

China has grown up alone and aloof, cut off from the rest of Eurasia by the Himalayas to the southwest and the Siberian steppe to the north. For the last three millennia, while empires, languages and peoples in the rest of the world rose, blossomed and disappeared without trace, China has been busy largely recycling itself. The ferocious dragons and lions of Chinese statuary have been produced for 25 centuries or more, and the script still used today reached perfection at the time of the Han dynasty, two thousand years ago. Until the late nineteenth century, the only foreigners China saw – apart from occasional ruling elites of Mongol and Manchu origin, who quickly became assimilated – were visiting merchants from far-flung shores or uncivilized nomads from the wild steppe: peripheral, unimportant and unreal.

Today, the negative stories surrounding China – the runaway pollution, the oppression of dissidents, and imperialist behaviour towards Tibet and other minority regions – are only part of the picture. As the Communist Party moves ever further from hard-line political doctrine and towards economic pragmatism, China is undergoing a huge commercial and creative upheaval. Hong Kong-style city skylines are rearing up across the country, and tens of millions of people are finding jobs that earn them a spending power their parents could never have known. Whatever the reasons you are attracted to China, the sheer pace of change, visible in every part of Chinese life, will ensure that your trip is a unique one.

The first thing that strikes visitors to the country is the extraordinary density of its **population**. In central and eastern China, villages, towns and cities seem to sprawl endlessly into one another along the grey arteries of busy expressways. These are the **Han Chinese** heartlands, a world of chopsticks, tea, slippers, grey skies, shadow-boxing, teeming crowds, chaotic train stations, smoky temples, red flags and the smells of soot and frying tofu. Move west or north away from the major cities, however, and the population thins out as it begins to vary: indeed, large areas of the People's Republic are inhabited not by the "Chinese", but by scores of distinct **ethnic minorities**, ranging from animist hill tribes to urban Muslims. Here, the **landscape** begins to dominate: green paddy fields and misty hilltops in the southwest, the scorched, epic vistas of the old Silk Road in the northwest, and the magisterial mountains of Tibet.

While travel around the country itself is exhausting rather than difficult, it would be wrong to pretend that it is an entirely easy matter to

▲ Going to market Dali, Yunnan

Fact file

- With an **area** of 9.6 million square kilometres, China is the fourth largest country in the world – practically the same size as the United States – and the most populous nation on earth, with around 1.3 billion people. Of these, 92% are of the **Han** ethnic group, with the remainder comprising about sixty minorities such as Mongols, Uyghurs and Tibetans. The main **religions** are Buddhism, Taoism and Christianity (Confucianism has died out as a religious system, but its tenets remain embedded in the Chinese psyche), though the country is officially atheist. A third of China comprises fertile river plains, and another third arid deserts, plateaux or mountains. China's longest river is the **Yangzi** (6275km) and the highest peak is **Qomolongma** – Mount Everest (8850m) – on the Nepalese border.
- China is a one-party state run by the **Chinese Communist Party**, the sole political organization, which is divided into Executive, Legislative and Judicial branches. The chief of state (President) and the head of government (Premier) are elected for five-year terms at the National People's Congress. After decades of state planning, the economy is now mixed, with state-owned enterprises on the decline and free-market principles ubiquitous. China's main **exports** are clothing, textiles, tea and fossil fuels, and its main trading partners are the US, Japan, South Korea and Europe.

The Beijing Olympics

The **2008 Olympic Games** are scheduled for August 8 to August 24. Most events are being held in Beijing, although football, sailing and the new 10km marathon swimming will take place in Qingdao and Shanghai, with the equestrian events set for Hong Kong. There are seven million tickets, including nearly three million for the opening and closing ceremonies; the most expensive cost ¥5000, but there are plenty of cheap seats, too. In the run up to the games, the official logo, a dancing character called "Jing", can be seen all over China, as can the cuddly mascots – the five "friendlies", each representing one colour of the Olympic rings (the red one is the most popular).

Face-conscious China is treating the games as its coming-out party, an excuse to show its new prominence on the international stage. Accordingly, the preparations have been lavish. The torch relay, the longest ever, goes from Greece to Beijing via Mount Everest – where a highway has been constructed for the purpose. In the capital, as well as showcase facilities such as Herzog and de Meuron's National Olympic Stadium (the "Birds' Nest") and the National Swimming Centre (the "Water Cube"), new parks and subway lines have been constructed. In an effort to deal with the cities appalling pollution, factories have been moved to the suburbs; before the Games, cars will be banned from Beijing's gridlocked streets. In the run up to the events, the local press has been even more tightly managed than usual, though protests over issues such as Tibetan Independence and human rights remain a possibility.

For more on Beijing's Olympic Games, including how to get hold of tickets, see box on p.77 .

▲ The National Olympic Stadium

penetrate modern China. The main tourist highlights – the Great Wall, the Forbidden City, the Terracotta Army, and Yangzi gorges – are relatively few considering the vast size of the country, and much of China's historic architecture has been deliberately destroyed in the rush to modernize. Added to this are the frustrations of travelling in a land where few people speak English, the writing system is alien and foreigners are regularly viewed as exotic objects of intense curiosity – though overall you'll find that the Chinese, despite a reputation for curtness, are generally hospitable and friendly.

Where to go

As China has opened up in recent years, so the emphasis on tourism has changed. Many well-known cities and sights have become so developed that their charm has vanished; while in remoter regions – particularly Tibet, Yunnan and the northwest – previously restricted or "undiscovered" places have become newly accessible. The following outline is a selection of both "classic" China sights and less-known attractions, which should come in handy when planning a schedule.

Inevitably, **Beijing** is on everyone's itinerary, and the Great Wall and the splendour of the Forbidden City are certainly not to be missed; the capital also offers some of the country's best food and nightlife. **Chengde**, too, just north of Beijing, has some stunning imperial buildings, constructed by emperors when this was their favoured retreat for the summer.

South of the capital, the **Yellow River valley** is the cradle of Chinese civilization, where remnants of the dynastic age lie scattered in a unique landscape of loess terraces. The cave temples at **Datong** and **Luoyang** are magnificent, with huge Buddhist sculptures staring out impassively across their now industrialized settings. Of the historic capitals, **Xi'an** is the most obvious destination, where the celebrated Terracotta Army still stands guard over the tomb of Emperor Qin Shi Huang. Other ancient towns include sleepy **Kaifeng** in Henan and **Qufu**, the birthplace of Confucius, in Shandong, both offering architectural treasures and an intimate, human scale that's missing in the large cities. The area is also well

▲ Nightclub in Beijing

Wildlife

Although China's varied geography and climate have created a wealth of wildlife habitats, the country's vast human population has put pressure on the environment, bringing some high-profile creatures to the edge of extinction. Most famous of these is the giant panda, which survives in pockets of high-altitude bamboo forest across the southwest. A few Siberian tigers haunt the northeastern highlands, while the critically endangered South China tiger numbers just thirty wild individuals. Less well-known rarities include the snub-nosed golden monkey, white-headed langur and Chinese alligator, all of which are possible – with a lot of luck – to see in the wild. Birdlife can be prolific, with freshwater lakes along the Yangzi and in western Guizhou, along with the vast saline Qinghai Lake, providing winter refuge for hosts of migratory wildfowl – including rare Siberian and black-necked cranes.

supplied with holy mountains, providing both beautiful scenery and a rare continuity with the past: **Tai Shan** is perhaps the grandest and most imperial of the country's pilgrimage sites; **Song Shan** in Henan sees followers of the contemporary kung-fu craze making the trek to the Shaolin Si, where the art originated; and **Wutai Shan** in Shanxi features some of the best-preserved religious sites in the country.

Dominating China's east coast near the mouth of the Yangzi, **Shanghai** is the mainland's most Westernized city, a booming port where the Art Deco monuments of the old European-built Bund – the riverside business centre – rub shoulders with a hyper-modern metropolis, crowned with two of the world's tallest skyscrapers. It's interesting to contrast Shanghai's cityscape with that of rival business hub **Hong Kong**, off China's south coast. With its colonial heritage and refreshingly cosmo-

▼ Temple, Hong Kong

▲ Rush hour in Shanghai

politan outlook, there's almost nothing Hong Kong cannot offer in the way of tourist facilities, from fine beaches to great eating, drinking and nightlife. Nearby **Macau** is also worth a visit, if not for its casinos, then for its Baroque churches and Portuguese cuisine.

In the southwest of the country, Sichuan's **Chengdu** and Yunnan's **Kunming** remain two of China's most interesting and easy-going provincial capitals, and the entire region is, by any standards, exceptionally diverse, with landscapes encompassing everything from snowbound summits and alpine lakes to steamy tropical jungles. The karst (limestone peak) scenery is particularly renowned, especially along the Li River between **Yangshuo** and **Guilin** in Guangxi. In Sichuan, pilgrims flock to see the colossal Great Buddha at **Leshan**, and to ascend the holy mountain of **Emei Shan**; to the east, the city of **Chongqing** marks the start of river trips down the **Yangzi**, Asia's longest river, through the **Three Gorges**. As Yunnan and Guangxi share borders with Vietnam, Laos and Burma, while Sichuan rubs up against Tibet, it's not surprising to find that the region is home to near extinct wildlife and dozens of ethnic autonomous regions; the attractions of the latter range from the traditional Bai town of **Dali**, the Naxi town of **Lijiang** and the Dai villages of **Xishuangbanna** in Yunnan, to the Khampa heartlands of western Sichuan, to the exuberant festivals and textiles of Guizhou's Miao and the wooden architecture of Dong settlements in Guangxi's north.

The huge area of China referred to as the Northwest is where the people thin out and real wilderness begins. Inner Mongolia, just hours from Beijing, is already at the frontiers of Central Asia; here you can follow in the footsteps of Genghis Khan by going horse-riding on the endless grasslands

Chinese script

Chinese characters are simplified images of what they represent, and their origins as pictograms can often still be seen, even though they have become highly abstract today. The earliest-known examples of Chinese writing are predictions that were cut into "oracle bones" over three thousand years ago during the Shang dynasty, though the characters must have been in use long before as these inscriptions already amount to a highly complex writing system. As the characters represent concepts, not sounds, written Chinese cuts through the problem of communication in a country with many different dialects. However, learning characters is a never-ending job – though you only need to recognize a couple of thousand for everyday use. Foreigners learning Mandarin use the modern *pinyin* transliteration system of accented Roman letters – used throughout this book – to help memorize the sounds. For more on language, see p.1207.

of the steppe. To the south and west, the old **Silk Road** heads out of Xi'an right to and through China's western borders, via **Jiayuguan**, terminus of the Great Wall of China, and the lavish Buddhist cave art in the sandy deserts of **Dunhuang**.

West of here lie the mountains and deserts of vast Xinjiang, where China blends into old Turkestan and where simple journeys between towns become modern travel epics. The oasis cities of **Turpan** and **Kashgar**, with their bazaars and Muslim heritage, are the main attractions, though the blue waters of **Tian Chi**, offering alpine scenery in the midst of searing desert, are deservedly popular. Beyond Kashgar, travellers face some of the most

▼ Lijiang, Yunnan

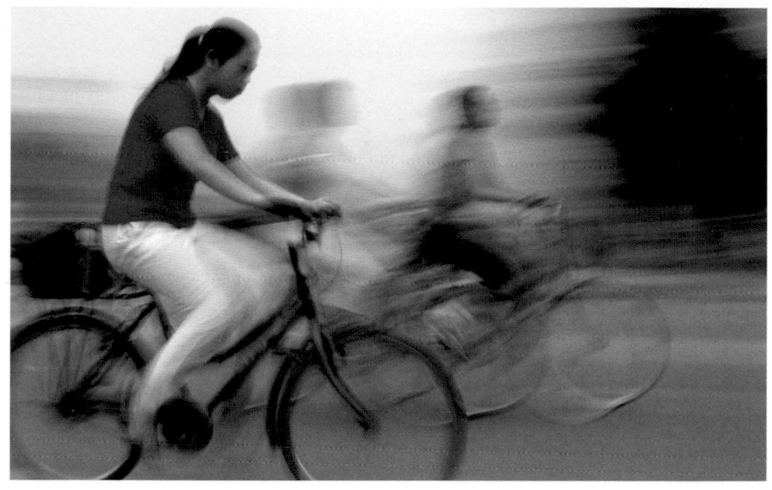

▲ Cyclists in Xi'an

adventurous routes of all, over the Khunjerab and Torugut passes to Pakistan and Kyrgyzstan respectively.

Tibet remains an exotic destination, especially if you come across the border from Nepal or brave the long road in from Golmud in Qinghai province. Despite fifty years of Chinese rule, coupled with a mass migration of Han Chinese into the region, the manifestations of Tibetan culture remain intact – the Potala Palace in **Lhasa**, red-robed monks, lines of pilgrims turning prayer wheels, butter sculptures and gory frescoes decorating monastery halls. And Tibet's mountain scenery, which includes **Mount Everest**, is worth the trip in itself, even if opportunities for independent travel are more restricted than elsewhere in China.

When to go

China's **climate** is extremely diverse. The **south** is subtropical, with wet, humid summers (April–Sept), when temperatures can approach 40°C, and a typhoon season on the southeast coast between July and September. Though it is often still hot enough to swim in the sea in December, the short winters (Jan–March), can be surprisingly chilly.

Central China, around Shanghai and the Yangzi River, has brief, cold winters, with temperatures dipping below zero, and long, hot, humid summers. It's no surprise that three Yangzi cities – Chongqing, Wuhan and Nanjing – are proverbially referred to as China's three "furnaces". Rainfall

Urban pollution

A reliance on coal for power and heating, factories spewing untreated waste into the atmosphere, growing numbers of vehicles, and the sheer density of the urban population all conspire to make Chinese cities some of the most polluted on earth. Black sludge fills canals and streams; buildings are mired by soot; blue sky is only a memory; the population seem permanently stricken with bronchitis; and acid rain withers plants. In summer, the worst spots are the Yangzi valley "furnaces" of Nanjing, Chongqing and Wuhan; winter in Xi'an, on the other hand, features black snow.

The Chinese government is finally beginning to take pollution seriously, especially with the Beijing Olympics in 2008: in the capital at least, factories are being relocated and elderly, fume-belching minibuses have been scrapped or foisted on other cities.

here is high all year round. Farther north, the **Yellow River basin** marks a rough boundary beyond which central heating is fitted as standard in buildings, helping to make the region's harsh winters a little more tolerable. Winter temperatures in Beijing rarely rise above freezing from December to March, and biting winds off the Mongolian plains add a vicious wind-chill factor. In summer, however, temperatures here can be well over 30°C. In **Inner Mongolia** and **Manchuria**, winters are at least clear and dry, but tempera-

▲ Li River, Guangxi

tures remain way below zero, while summers can be uncomfortably warm. **Xinjiang** gets fiercely hot in summer, though without the humidity of the rest of the country, and winters are as bitter as anywhere else in northern China. **Tibet** is ideal in midsummer, when its mountain plateaux are pleasantly warm and dry; in winter, however, temperatures in the capital, Lhasa, frequently fall below freezing.

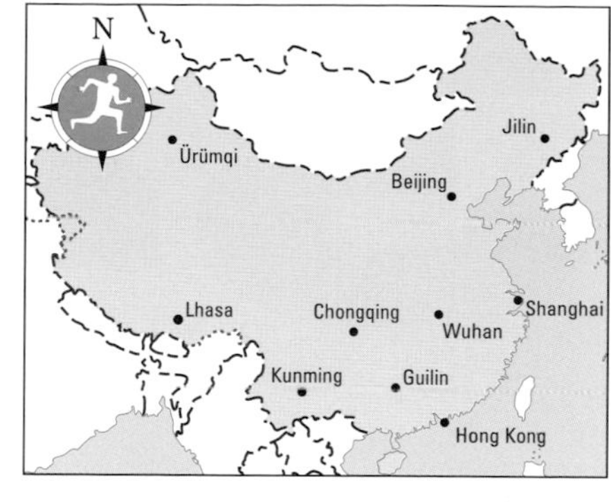

Overall, the **best time to visit** China is **spring** or **autumn**, when the weather is at its most temperate. In the spring, it's best to start in the south and work north or west as summer approaches; in the autumn, start in the north and work south.

	Jan	Feb	Mar	Apr	May	Jun	Jul	Aug	Sep	Oct	Nov	Dec
Beijing												
max/min (°C)	1/-10	4/-8	11/-1	21/7	27/13	31/18	31/21	30/20	26/14	20/6	9/-2	3/-8
rainfall mm	4	5	8	17	35	78	243	141	58	16	11	3
Chongqing												
max/min (°C)	9/5	13/7	18/11	23/16	27/19	29/22	34/24	35/25	28/22	22/16	16/12	13/8
rainfall mm	15	20	38	99	142	180	142	122	150	112	48	20
Guilin												
max/min (°C)	16/8	17/10	20/14	25/19	29/23	31/25	32/26	32/26	31/24	27/19	23/15	19/12
rainfall mm	33	56	97	160	206	193	160	178	84	43	38	37
Hong Kong												
max/min (°C)	18/13	17/13	19/16	24/19	28/23	29/26	31/26	31/26	29/25	27/23	23/18	20/15
rainfall mm	33	46	74	137	292	394	381	367	257	114	43	31
Jilin												
max/min (°C)	-6/-18	-2/-14	6/-6	16/3	23/10	29/16	31/21	29/19	24/11	16/3	5/-6	-4/-15
rainfall mm	8	8	18	28	69	84	183	170	64	36	28	15
Kunming												
max/min (°C)	20/8	22/9	25/12	28/16	29/18	29/19	28/19	28/19	28/18	24/15	22/12	20/8
rainfall mm	8	18	28	41	127	132	196	198	97	51	56	15
Lhasa												
max/min (°C)	7/-10	9/-7	12/-2	16/1	19/5	24/9	23/9	22/9	21/7	17/1	13/-5	9/-9
rainfall mm	0	13	8	5	25	64	122	89	66	13	3	0
Shanghai												
max/min (°C)	8/1	8/1	13/4	19/10	25/15	28/19	32/23	32/23	28/19	23/14	17/7	12/2
rainfall mm	48	58	84	94	94	180	147	142	130	71	51	36
Ürümqi												
max/min (°C)	-11/-22	-8/-19	-1/-11	16/2	22/8	26/12	28/14	27/13	21/8	10/-1	-1/-11	-8/-13
rainfall mm	15	8	13	38	28	38	18	25	15	43	41	10
Wuhan												
max/min (°C)	8/1	9/2	14/6	21/13	26/18	31/23	34/26	34/26	29/21	23/16	17/9	11/3
rainfall mm	46	48	97	152	165	244	180	97	71	81	48	28

34 things not to miss

It's not possible to see everything that China has to offer in one trip – and we don't suggest you try. What follows, in no particular order, is a selective taste of the country's highlights: stunning scenery, distinctive cuisine, exuberant festivals and monumental architecture. They're arranged in five colour-coded categories, which you can browse through to find the very best things to see and experience. All highlights have a page reference to take you straight into the guide, where you can find out more.

01 **Mount Everest** Page **1136** • The sight of the mountain towering above ensures you won't regret the long journey up to Base Camp.

02 **798 Art District** Page **111** • Rub shoulders with China's bohemians at this chic warren of art galleries housed in that most postmodern of venues – an old state-run factory.

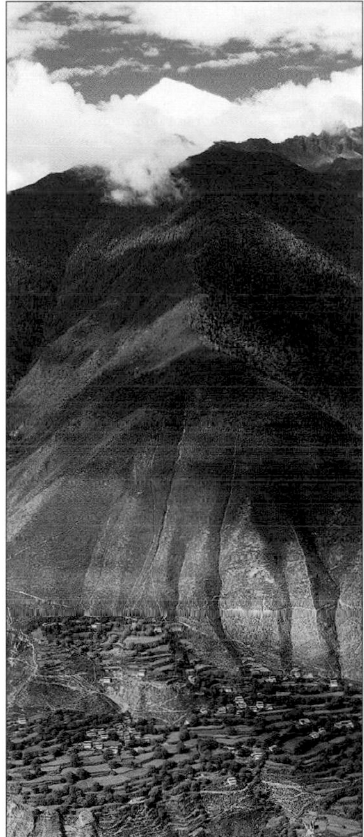

03 **Meili Xue Shan** Page **827** • A wilderness area that offers great hiking, superlative views and a glimpse of the Tibetan world.

04 **The Forbidden City** Page **99** • Once centre of the Chinese imperial universe and off limits to the hoi polloi, the emperor's impressive palace complex in Beijing is now open to all.

05 **Hotpot** Page **123** • Sear your tastebuds on this classic, chilli-rich Sichuanese dish, now popular all over the country.

06 The Silk Road Page **950** • Abandoned cities here, such as Jiaohe, hint at the former importance of this ancient trading route.

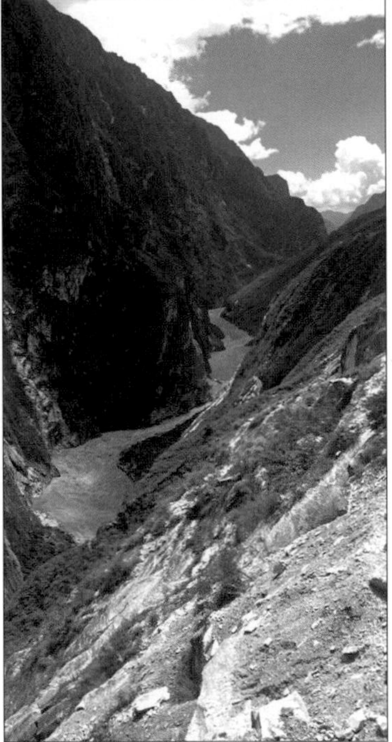

07 Tiger Leaping Gorge Page **918** • One of China's great hikes, along a ridge above a dramatic gorge, with attractive homestays along the way.

08 Dim sum Page **582** • The classic Cantonese breakfast; there's no better place to try it than Guangzhou.

09 The Jokhang, Lhasa Page **1104** • Stuffed with gorgeous statuary and perpetually wreathed in juniper smoke and incense, this temple is one of the holiest in Tibet.

10 Bird-watching, Cao Hai Page **772** • Being punted around this shallow lake after rare birdlife is a wonderfully restful experience.

11 Mogao Caves Page **1009** • These thousand-year-old man-made caves on the old Silk Road contain China's most impressive Buddhist heritage.

12 Kashgar's Sunday Market Page **1070** • Crowds from all over Central Asia descend to trade livestock, carpets, knives and clothes at this weekly event.

13 Hong Kong's skyline Page **670** • The drive of generations of the former colony's inhabitants is writ large in this electrifying cityscape.

14 The Bund, Shanghai Page **360** • An elegant parade of colonial architecture, nestling incongruously at the heart of Shanghai's gaudy modernity.

15 Sichuanese teahouses Page **871** • Relaxed places to gossip, read or socialize for the price of a cup of tea.

16 Sisters' Meal festival Page **764** • Join tens of thousands of locals in Taijiang, Guizhou, as they participate in this annual three-day showcase of ethnic Miao culture.

17 Tai Shan Page **317** • The taxing ascent of this holy peak in Shandong is rewarded with some immaculate temples and pavilions.

18 Minority villages, Yunnan Page **843** • The Xishuangbanna region, bordering Laos and Burma, is home to a range of ethnic groups with very different cultures and lifestyles.

19 Jiayuguan fort Page **1006** • A famously lonely outpost overlooking the desert at the western tail of the Great Wall.

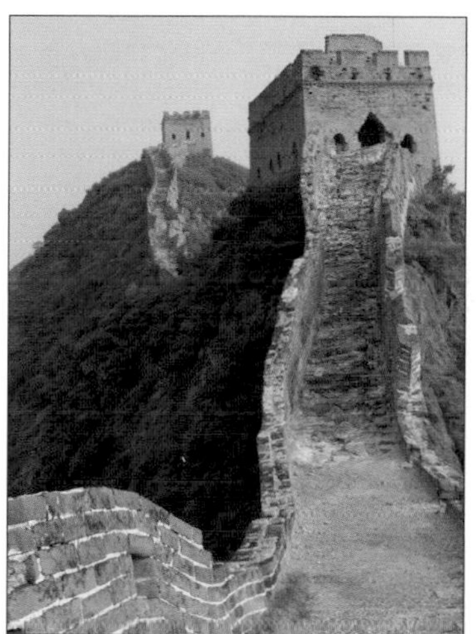

20 The Great Wall Page **141** • Once the division between civilizations, this monumental barrier is still awe-inspiring.

21 Confucius Temple Page **328** • This lavish complex in Confucius's home town of Qufu shows the esteem in which China's great sage was held.

22 The Yungang Caves, Datong Page **237** • Giant but detailed Buddhist sculptures were carved into caves and grottoes around 500AD in an amazing demonstration of faith.

23 Changbai Shan Nature Reserve Page **210** • Well worth a visit – though you'd have to be exceptionally lucky to spot its rare Siberian tigers.

25 Yonghe Gong, Beijing Page **116** • This charismatic Tibetan temple is an explosion of ornament and colour.

26 Acrobats Page **133** • "Ooh" and "aah" at the thrills and spills of China's talented acrobats – Beijing or Shanghai are the best places to check out a performance.

24 The Great Buddha (Dafo), Leshan Page **893** • You'll feel a mere speck as you gaze up at the world's largest carved Buddha.

27 The Terracotta Army Page **278** • Near the old capital of Xi'an, these 2200-year-old, life-size soldiers guard the tomb of China's first emperor.

28 Chengde Page **172** • The emperors' former retreat from the heat of summer holds a string of pretty temples.

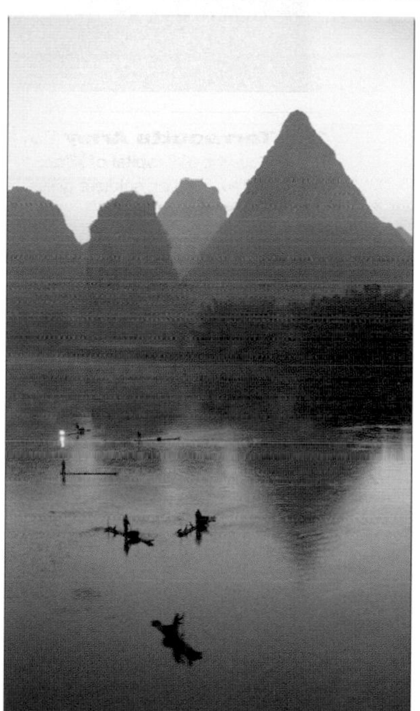

29 Li River scenery Page **721** • Take a boat trip here to admire the weird, contorted peaks of the sort you'll see on Chinese scroll paintings.

30 Labrang Monastery, Xiahe Page **998** • One of the most important Tibetan Buddhist monasteries, a riot of lavishly decorated halls, butter sculptures and ragged pilgrims.

31 A cruise down the Yangzi River Page **912** • Enjoy awesome scenery and a wealth of historic sights, despite rising water levels caused by the controversial Three Gorges Dam.

32 Beijing duck Page **123** • A northern Chinese culinary speciality and absolutely delicious – crisp skin and juicy meat eaten in a pancake.

33 Harbin Ice Festival Page **218** • "Lurid" and "outrageous" don't begin to describe the bizarre sculptures here – everything from life-size ice castles to fantastical snowy tableaux.

34 Dali Page **800** • The capital of the Bai ethnic group is now a charming backpackers' oasis and host to the colourful Spring Fair festival.

Basics

Basics

Getting there

China's most important long-haul international gateways are Beijing, Hong Kong, Guangzhou and Shanghai, though many other Chinese cities are served by international flights, operated mainly by airlines based in East Asia. There are also well-established overland routes into China – including road and rail links from its Southeast Asian neighbours, as well as the alluring Trans-Siberian Express from Moscow.

Fares to Hong Kong are at their highest during the fortnight before Christmas, the fortnight before Chinese New Year (see p.52) and from mid-June to early October. The cheapest time to fly there is the months of February (after Chinese New Year), May and November. For Beijing and Shanghai, peak season is generally summertime. Note also that flying on weekends is slightly more expensive; price ranges quoted below assume midweek travel.

If China is only one stop on a much longer journey, you might want to consider buying a **Round-the-World** (**RTW**) ticket (around £1000/US$2000). Some travel agents can sell you an "off-the-shelf" RTW ticket that will have you touching down in about half a dozen cities (Hong Kong is on many itineraries); others will have to assemble one for you, which can be tailored to your needs but is apt to be more expensive.

Flights from the UK and Ireland

You can fly **direct** to China from London Heathrow with Air China, Virgin, British Airways and Cathay Pacific to either Beijing (10hr), Hong Kong (12hr) or Shanghai (11hr), and the budget carrier Oasis flies from Gatwick to Hong Kong. Other airlines flying via a change of planes in a hub city include Aeroflot, Air France, KLM, Singapore, Swiss and Thai. Flying to China from other UK airports or from the Republic of Ireland involves either catching a connecting flight to London or flying via the airline's hub city.

From the UK, the lowest available **fares** to Beijing or Shanghai from London start from around £400 in low season, rising to £800 in high season; to Hong Kong, the corresponding range is about £350–700, with Oasis usually the cheapest. Less popular airlines such as Air China and Aeroflot offer competitive fares, while British Airways often run special offers or promotions.

Flights from the US and Canada

From North America, there are more flights to **Hong Kong** than to other Chinese destinations, though there's no shortage of flights to Beijing and Shanghai and there are some direct services to Guangzhou. Airlines flying **direct** include Air Canada, Air China, Cathay Pacific, United, Northwest Airlines and China Eastern. You can also choose to fly to a Chinese provincial city – Chinese, Japanese, Korean and Hong Kong airlines offer services to cities throughout China via their respective hubs. It takes around thirteen hours' **flying time** to reach Beijing from the West Coast; add seven hours or more to this if you start from the East Coast (including a stopover on the West Coast en route). New routes over the North Pole shave off a couple of hours flying time; so far, that's only Air Canada's Toronto and Continental's Newark flights to Beijing.

Round-trip fares to Hong Kong, Beijing and Shanghai are broadly comparable: in low season, expect to pay US$850–1200/CDN$1300–1500 from the West Coast (Los Angeles, San Francisco, Vancouver), or US$1000–1200/CDN$1400–2000 from the East Coast (New York, Montréal, Toronto). To get a good fare during high season it's important to buy your ticket as early as possible, in which case you probably won't pay more than US$200/CDN$320 above what you would have paid in low season.

Flights from Australia, New Zealand and South Africa

The closest entry point into China from Australia and New Zealand is Hong Kong, though from Australia it's also possible to fly direct to Guangzhou, Shanghai and Beijing. It's not a problem to fly elsewhere in China from either country if you catch a connecting flight along the way, though this can involve a long layover in the airline's hub city.

From eastern Australia, some of the cheapest fares to Hong Kong are with Cathay Pacific (A$750–1000), China Airlines, EVA Airlines or Singapore Airlines; to Shanghai (A$950–1100) with Royal Brunei, Singapore or Japanese Airlines (JAL); to Guangzhou (A$1000–1150) with Singapore, Malaysian Airlines, JAL and Air China; and to Beijing (A$950–1100) with Singapore, JAL, Malaysian or China Eastern. Cathay, Qantas, Air China and China Eastern fly direct; other trips require a stopover in the airline's hub city. **From Perth**, fares to the above destinations are A$100 or so more expensive.

Flights **from New Zealand** are limited and therefore expensive: about the best deal is on Air New Zealand or Singapore Airlines from Auckland to Hong Kong (NZ$1800). Air New Zealand, Malaysian Airlines and

Fly less – stay longer! Travel and climate change

Climate change is the single biggest issue facing our planet. It is caused by a build-up in the atmosphere of carbon dioxide and other greenhouse gases, which are emitted by many sources – including planes. Already, flights account for around 3–4 percent of human-induced global warming: that figure may sound small, but it is rising year on year and threatens to counteract the progress made by reducing greenhouse emissions in other areas.

Rough Guides regard travel, overall, as a global benefit, and feel strongly that the advantages to developing economies are important, as are the opportunities for greater contact and awareness among peoples. But we all have a responsibility to limit our personal "carbon footprint". That means giving thought to how often we fly and what we can do to redress the harm that our trips create.

Flying and climate change

Pretty much every form of motorized travel generates CO_2, but planes are particularly bad offenders, releasing large volumes of greenhouse gases at altitudes where their impact is far more harmful. Flying also allows us to travel much further than we would contemplate doing by road or rail, so the emissions attributable to each passenger are greater. For example, one person taking a return flight between Europe and California produces the equivalent impact of 2.5 tonnes of CO_2 – similar to the yearly output of the average UK car.

Less harmful planes may evolve but it will be decades before they replace the current fleet – which could be too late for avoiding climate chaos. In the meantime, there are limited options for concerned travellers: to reduce the amount we travel by air (take fewer trips, stay longer!), to avoid night flights (when plane contrails trap heat from Earth but can't reflect sunlight back to space), and to make the trips we do take "climate neutral" via a carbon offset scheme.

Carbon offset schemes

Offset schemes run by **climatecare.org**, **carbonneutral.com** and others allow you to "neutralize" the greenhouse gases that you are responsible for releasing. Their websites have simple calculators that let you work out the impact of any flight. Once that's done, you can pay to fund projects that will reduce future carbon emissions by an equivalent amount (such as the distribution of low-energy light-bulbs and cooking stoves in developing countries). Please take the time to visit our website and make your trip climate neutral.

Ⓦ **www.roughguides.com/climatechange**

other carriers also fly via other Southeast Asian hub cities to Hong Kong and elsewhere in China.

From South Africa, South African Airlines have direct flights to Hong Kong (14hr), which will cost around US$2500/ZAR17,000 in high season.

Airlines, agents and operators

Many airlines and discount travel websites offer you the opportunity to book your tickets, hotels and holiday packages online, cutting out the costs of agents and middlemen; these are worth going for, as long as you don't mind the inflexibility of non-refundable, non-changeable deals. There are some bargains to be had on auction sites, too, if you're prepared to bid keenly. Almost all airlines have their own websites, offering flight tickets that can sometimes be just as cheap, and are often more flexible.

Online booking

ⓦ **www.expedia.co.uk** (in UK), ⓦ **www.expedia.com** (in US) ⓦ **www.expedia.ca** (in Canada)
ⓦ **www.flychina.com** (in US)
ⓦ **www.lastminute.com** (in US)
ⓦ **www.opodo.co.uk** (in UK)
ⓦ **www.orbitz.com** (in US)
ⓦ **www.travelocity.co.uk** (in UK), ⓦ **www.travelocity.com** (in US), ⓦ **www.travelocity.ca** (in Canada)
ⓦ **www.zuji.com.au** (in Australia), ⓦ **www.zuji.co.nz** (in New Zealand)

Airlines

Aeroflot UK ⓣ020/7355 2233, US ⓣ1-888/340 6400, Canada ⓣ1-416/642-1653, Australia ⓣ02/9262 2233, ⓦwww.aeroflot.co.uk; ⓦwww.aeroflot.com.

Air Canada UK ⓣ0871/220 1111, Republic of Ireland ⓣ01/679 3958, US & Canada ⓣ1-888/247-2262, Australia ⓣ1300/655 767, New Zealand ⓣ0508/747 767; ⓦwww.aircanada.com.

Air China UK ⓣ020/7744 0800, US ⓣ1-800-9828/802, Canada ⓣ416-581/8833, Australia ⓣ02/9232 7277; ⓦwww.airchina.com.cn.

Air France UK ⓣ0870/142 4343, US ⓣ1-800/237-2747, Canada ⓣ1-800/667-2747, Australia ⓣ1300/390 190, South Africa ⓣ086/1340 340; ⓦwww.airfrance.com.

Air New Zealand UK ⓣ0800/028 4149, US ⓣ1800-262/1234, Canada ⓣ1800-663/5494, Australia ⓣ13 24 76, New Zealand ⓣ0800/737 000; ⓦwww.airnz.co.nz.

Alitalia UK ⓣ0870/544 8259, Republic of Ireland ⓣ01/677 5171, US ⓣ1-800/223-5730, Canada ⓣ1-800/361-8336, New Zealand ⓣ09/308 3357, South Africa ⓣ011/721 4500; ⓦwww.alitalia.com.

All Nippon Airways (ANA) UK ⓣ0870/837 8866, Republic of Ireland ⓣ1850/200 058, US and Canada, ⓣ1-800/235-9262; ⓦwww.anaskyweb.com.

American Airlines UK ⓣ0845/7789 789, Republic of Ireland ⓣ01/602 0550, US ⓣ1-800/433-7300, Australia ⓣ1800/673 486, New Zealand ⓣ0800/445 442; ⓦwww.aa.com.

Asiana Airlines UK ⓣ0207/514 0201/8, US ⓣ1-800/227-4262, Australia ⓣ02/9767 4343: ⓦwww.flyasiana.com.

Atlantic Airways UK ⓣ020/7823 4242, ⓦwww.atlantic.fo.

Austrian Airlines UK ⓣ0870/124 2625, Republic of Ireland ⓣ1800/509 142, USⓣ1-800/843-0002, Canada ⓣ1888-8174/444, Australia ⓣ1800/642 438 or 02/9251 6155; ⓦwww.aua.com.

British Airways UK ⓣ0870/850 9850, Republic of Ireland ⓣ1890/626 747, US and Canada ⓣ1-800/AIRWAYS, Australia ⓣ1300/767 177, New Zealand ⓣ09/966 9777, South Africa ⓣ011/441 8000; ⓦwww.ba.com.

Cathay Pacific UK ⓣ020/8834 8888, US ⓣ1-800/233-2742, Canada ⓣ1-800/2686-868, Australia ⓣ13 17 47, New Zealand ⓣ09/379 0861, South Africa ⓣ011/700 8900; ⓦwww.cathaypacific.com.

China Airlines US ⓣ1-917/368-2003, UK ⓣ020/7436 9001, Australia ⓣ02/9231 5500, New Zealand ⓣ09/308 3364; ⓦwww.china-airlines.com.

China Southern Airlines US ⓣ1-888/338-8988, Australia ⓣ02/9231 1988; ⓦwww.cs-air.com.

China Eastern Airlines UK ⓣ0870/760 6232, US ⓣ1626-1583/1500, Canada ⓣ1604-6898/998, Australia ⓣ02/9290 1148; ⓦwww.chinaeastern.co.uk.

Continental Airlines UK ⓣ0845/607 6760, Republic of Ireland ⓣ1890/925 252, US and Canada ⓣ1-800/523-3273, Australia ⓣ02/9244 2242, New Zealand ⓣ09/308 3350, International ⓣ1800/231 0856; ⓦwww.continental.com.

Emirates UK ⓣ0870/243 2222, US and Canada ⓣ1-800/777-3999, Australia ⓣ03/9940 7807, New Zealand ⓣ05/0836 4728, South Africa ⓣ086/136 3728; ⓦwww.emirates.com.

EVA Air UK ⓣ020/7380 8300, US and Canada ⓣ1-800/695-1188, Australia ⓣ02/8338 0419, New Zealand ⓣ09/358 8300; ⓦwww.evaair.com.

Finnair UK ⓣ0870/241 4411, Republic of Ireland ⓣ01/844 6565, US ⓣ1-800/950-5000, Australia ⓣ02/9244 2299, South Africa ⓣ011/339 4865/9; ⓦwww.finnair.com.
Gulf Air UK ⓣ0870/777 1717, Republic of Ireland ⓣ0818/272 828, Australia ⓣ1300/366 337, South Africa ⓣ011/268 8909; ⓦwww.gulfairco.com.
JAL (Japan Air Lines) UK ⓣ0845/774 7700, Republic of Ireland ⓣ01/408 3757, US and Canada ⓣ1-800/525-3663, Australia ⓣ02/9272 1111, New Zealand ⓣ09/379 9906, South Africa ⓣ011/214 2560; ⓦwww.jal.com or ⓦwww.japanair.com.
KLM (Royal Dutch Airlines) See Northwest/KLM. UK ⓣ0870/507 4074, Republic of Ireland ⓣ1850/747 400, US and Canada ⓣ1-800/225-2525, Australia ⓣ1300/392 192, New Zealand ⓣ09/921 6040, South Africa ⓣ011/961 6727; ⓦwww.klm.com.
Korean Air UK ⓣ0800/413 000, Republic of Ireland ⓣ01/799 7990, US and Canada ⓣ1-800/438-5000, Australia ⓣ02/9262 6000, New Zealand ⓣ09/914 2000; ⓦwww.koreanair.com.
LufthanSouth Africa UK ⓣ0870/837 7747, Republic of Ireland ⓣ01/844 5544, US ⓣ1-800/3995-838, Canada ⓣ1-800/563-5954, Australia ⓣ1300/655 727, New Zealand ⓣ0800-945 220, South Africa ⓣ086/1842 538; ⓦwww.lufthansa.com.
Malaysia Airlines UK ⓣ0870/607 9090, Republic of Ireland ⓣ01/6761 561, US ⓣ1-800/5529-264, Australia ⓣ13 26 27, New Zealand ⓣ0800/777 747, South Africa ⓣ011/880 9614; ⓦwww.malaysia-airlines.com.
Malev Hungarian Airlines UK ⓣ0870/909 0577, Republic of Ireland ⓣ01/844 4303, US ⓣ1-212/566-9944, Canada ⓣ1-416/944-0093; ⓦwww.malev.hu.
Northwest/KLM UK ⓣ0870/507 4074, US ⓣ1-800/225-2525, Australia ⓣ1300/767 310; ⓦwww.nwa.com.
PIA (Pakistan International Airlines) UK ⓣ0800/587 1023, US and Canada ⓣ1-800/578-6786; ⓦwww.piac.com.pk.
Qantas Airways UK ⓣ0845/774 7767, Republic of Ireland ⓣ01/407 3278, US and Canada ⓣ1-800/227-4500, Australia ⓣ13 13 13, New Zealand ⓣ0800/808 767 or 09/357 8900, South Africa ⓣ011/441 8550; ⓦwww.qantas.com.
Qatar Airways UK ⓣ0870/770 4215, US ⓣ1-877/777-2827, Canada ⓣ1-888/366-5666, Australia ⓣ386/054 855, South Africa ⓣ011/523 2928; ⓦwww.qatarairways.com.
Royal Brunei UK ⓣ020/7584 6660, Australia ⓣ1300/721 271, New Zealand ⓣ09/977 2209; ⓦwww.bruneiair.com.
Royal Jordanian UK ⓣ020/7878 6300, US ⓣ1-800/223-0470, Canada ⓣ1-800/363-0711, Australia ⓣ02/9244 2701, New Zealand ⓣ03/365 3910; ⓦwww.rja.com.jo.
Royal Nepal Airlines US ⓣ1-800/266-3725, ⓦwww.royalnepal.com.
SAS (Scandinavian Airlines) UK ⓣ0870/6072 7727, Republic of Ireland ⓣ01/844 5440, US and Canada ⓣ1-800/221-2350, Australia ⓣ1300/727 707; ⓦwww.scandinavian.net.
Singapore Airlines UK ⓣ0844/800 2380, Republic of Ireland ⓣ01/671 0722, US ⓣ1-800/742-3333, Canada ⓣ1-800/663-3046, Australia ⓣ13 10 11, New Zealand ⓣ0800/808 909, South Africa ⓣ011/880 8560 or 011/880 8566; ⓦwww.singaporeair.com.
Swiss UK ⓣ0845/601 0956, Republic of Ireland ⓣ1890/200 515, US ⓣ1-877/3797-947, Canada ⓣ1-877/559-7947, Australia ⓣ1300/724 666, New Zealand ⓣ09/977 2238, South Africa ⓣ086/004 0506; ⓦwww.swiss.com.
Thai Airways UK ⓣ0870/606 0911, US ⓣ1-212/949-8424, Australia ⓣ1300/651 960, New Zealand ⓣ09/377 3886, South Africa ⓣ011/455 1018; ⓦwww.thaiair.com.
United Airlines UK ⓣ0845/844 4777, US ⓣ1-800/UNITED-1, Australia ⓣ13 17 77; ⓦwww.united.com.
US Airways UK ⓣ0845/600 3300, Republic of Ireland ⓣ1890/925 065, US and Canada ⓣ1-800/428-4322; ⓦwww.usair.com.
Vietnam Airlines UK ⓣ0870/224 0211, US ⓣ1-415/677-0888, Canada ⓣ1-416/599-2888, Australia ⓣ02/9283 9658; ⓦwww.vietnamairlines.com.
Virgin Atlantic UK ⓣ0870/380 2007, US ⓣ1-800/821-5438, Australia ⓣ1300/727 340, South Africa ⓣ011/340 3400; ⓦwww.virgin-atlantic.com.

Specialist tour operators

Absolute Asia US ⓣ1-800/736-8187, ⓦwww.absoluteasia.com. Numerous tours of China lasting from between 6 and 23 days, in first-class accommodation, such as the 14-day "Art and History of China" tour.
Adventure Center US ⓣ1-800/228-8747 or 510/654-1879, ⓦwww.adventure-center.com. Dozens of tours in China and Tibet, from a week-long whizz around the highlights to a month of walking, hiking and biking expeditions.
Adventures Abroad US ⓣ1-800/665-3998 or 360/775-9926, ⓦwww.adventures-abroad.com. Small-group specialists with tours through China and Mongolia.

Asian Pacific Adventures US ⓣ1-800/825-1680 or 818/886-5190, ⓦwww.asianpacificadventures.com. Numerous tours of China, focusing on southwestern ethnic groups and often-overlooked rural corners.

Backroads US ⓣ1-800/GO-ACTIVE or 510/527-1555, ⓦwww.backroads.com. Cycling and hiking between Beijing and south China's Guangdong province.

Birdfinders UK ⓣ01258/839066, ⓦwww.birdfinders.co.uk. Several trips per year to find rare and endemic species in mainland China and Tibet.

Birding Worldwide Australia ⓣ03/9899 9303, ⓦwww.birdingworldwide.com.au. Organizes group trips to China – including Tibet – for those wanting to glimpse typical, unique and rare bird species.

China Holidays UK ⓣ020/74872999, ⓦwww.chinaholidays.co.uk. Aside from mainstream packages to the Three Gorges, Shanghai and Guilin, they also run a "Taste of China" gastronomic tour sampling food between Beijing and Hong Kong.

CTS Horizons UK ⓣ020/7836 9911, ⓦwww.ctshorizons.com. The China Travel Service's UK branch, offering an extensive range of tours including very cheap off-season hotel-and-flight packages to Beijing, and tailor-made private tours.

Exodus UK ⓣ020/8675 5550, ⓦwww.exodus.co.uk. Offers some interesting and unusual overland itineraries in the wilds of Tibet, Inner Mongolia and the Northwest; the three-week tours are particularly good value

Explore Worldwide UK ⓣ01252/760 000, ⓦwww.explore.co.uk. Big range of small-group tours and treks, including Tibet tours and trips along the Yangzi. Some supplements for single travellers.

Geographic Expeditions US ⓣ1-800/777-8183 or 415/922-0448, ⓦwww.geoex.com. Adventurous travel amongst the ethnic groups of Guizhou, Tibet, western Sichuan, Xinjiang and Xishuangbanna, as well as more straightforward trips around Shanghai and Beijing.

Intrepid Travel UK ⓣ020/8960 6333, Australia ⓣ1300/360 667 or 03/9473 2626, ⓦwww.intrepidtravel.com. Small-group tours with the emphasis on cross-cultural contact and low-impact tourism; visits some out-of-the-way corners of China.

Imaginative Traveller UK ⓣ020/8742 8612, ⓦwww.imaginative-traveller.com. An emphasis on the unusual, with cycling tours, a panda trek in Sichuan and a Kathmandu–Lhasa–Kathmandu overland trip.

Magic of the Orient UK ⓣ01293/537700, ⓦwww.magic-of-the-orient.com. Tailor-made holidays, sometimes off the beaten track, in Yunnan and along the Yangzi.

Mir Corp US ⓣ206-624-7289, ⓦwww.mircorp.com. Specialists in Trans-Siberian rail travel, for small groups as well as individual travellers.

Mountain Travel Sobek USⓣ1-888/MTSOBEK or 510/687-6235, ⓦwww.mtsobek.com. Adventure tours to Yunnan, the Yangzi and along the Silk Road.

Pacific Delight Tours US ⓣ1-800/221-7179 or 212/818-1781, ⓦwww.pacificdelighttours.com. City breaks, cruises along the Li River and Yangzi, plus a range of tours to Tibet, the Silk Road and western Yunnan.

Regent Holidays UK ⓣ0117/921 1711, ⓦwww.regent-holidays.co.uk. Offers interesting Trans-Siberian packages for individual travellers in either direction and with different possible stopover permutations.

REI Adventures US ⓣ1-800/622-2236, ⓦwww.rei.com/travel. Cycling and hiking tours throughout China.

The Russia Experience UK ⓣ020/8566 8846, ⓦwww.trans-siberian.co.uk. Besides detailing their Trans Siberian packages, their website is a veritable mine of information about the railway.

Sundowners Australia ⓣ03/9672 5300, ⓦwww.sundownerstravel.com. Tours of the Silk Road, plus Trans-Siberian rail bookings.

Travel Indochina Australia ⓣ1300/138 755, ⓦwww.travelindochina.com.au Covers the obvious China sights but goes a bit beyond them, too; also arranges cross-border visas for Thailand, Laos, Vietnam and Cambodia.

World Expeditions UK ⓣ020/8870 2600, ⓦwww.worldexpeditions.co.uk, Australia ⓣ1300/720 000, ⓦwww.worldexpeditions.com.au, New Zealand ⓣ0800/350 354; ⓦwww.worldexpeditions.co.nz. Offers cycling and hiking tours in rural areas.

Overland routes

China has a number of **land borders** open to foreign travellers. When planning your trip, remember that Chinese visas must be used within three months of their date of issue, and so you may have to apply for one en route. Visas are obtainable in the capitals of virtually all European and Asian countries, and are likely to take several days to be issued (see p.59 for embassy addresses). Note that most nationalities can fly to Hong Kong without a visa, and easily pick one up there.

Via Russia and Mongolia

One of the classic overland routes to China is through Russia on the so-called **Trans-Siberian Express**. As a one-off trip, the rail journey is a memorable way to begin or end a stay in China; views of stately birch forests, misty lakes and arid plateaus help time pass much faster than you'd think, and there are frequent stops during which you can wander the station platform, purchasing food and knick-knacks – packages (see below) include more lengthy stopovers. The trains are comfortable and clean: second-class compartments contain four berths, while first-class have two and even boast a private shower.

There are actually two rail lines from Moscow to Beijing: the **Trans-Manchurian**, which runs almost as far as the Sea of Japan before turning south through Dongbei (Manchuria) to Beijing; and the **Trans-Mongolian**, which cuts through Mongolia from Siberia. The Manchurian train takes about six days, the Mongolian train about five. The latter is more popular with foreigners, Trans-Mongolian Chinese Train #4 being the preferred service – a scenic route that rumbles past Lake Baikal and Siberia, the grasslands of Mongolia, and the desert of northwest China, skirting the Great Wall along the way. At the Mongolia/China border, you can watch as the undercarriage is switched to a different gauge. The one drawback of this route is that you will need an additional visa for Mongolia.

Meals are included while the train is in China. In Mongolia, the dining car accepts payment in both Chinese and Mongolian currency; while in Russia, US dollars or Russian roubles can be used. It's worth having small denominations of US dollars as you can change these on the train throughout the journey, or use them to buy food from station vendors along the way – though experiencing the cuisine and people in the dining cars is part of the fun. Bring instant noodles and snacks as a backup, plenty of film, and that great long novel you've always wanted to read.

Tickets and packages

Booking tickets needs some advance planning, especially during the popular summer months. Sorting out travel arrangements from abroad is also a complex business – you'll need transit visas for Russia, as well as for Mongolia if you intend to pass through there, and if you plan on reaching or leaving Moscow by rail via Warsaw, you'll have to get a transit visa for Belarus, too. It's therefore advisable to use an experienced **travel agent** who can organize all tickets, visas and stopovers if required, in advance. Visa processing is an especially helpful time saver, given the queues and paperwork required for visas along the route. One firm offering these services as well as rail packages that you can book from abroad is Monkey Business (Ⓦwww.monkeyshrine.com), who have offices in Hong Kong and Beijing; for details of companies **at home** that can sort out Trans-Siberian travel, see the lists of specialist travel agents earlier in this section. If you want to book a ticket yourself, reckon on paying the equivalent of at least US$200 for second-class travel from Moscow to Beijing. For information on taking the train **from Beijing**, see p.83.

Via the Central Asian republics

From Russia, you can also theoretically reach China through several Central Asian countries, though the obstacles can occasionally be insurmountable; contact the in-country agents listed below, or Trans-Siberian operators listed earlier in this section, for up-to-date practicalities.

The main cities of **Kazakhstan** and **Kyrgyzstan** – Almaty and Bishkek – are both still linked by daily trains to Moscow (3 days), though getting Russian transit visas and booking berths on these trains is not easy. Kyrgyzstan-based Asia Silk Travel (Ⓦwww.centralasiatravel.com) or Kyrgyz Concept (Ⓦeng.concept.kg) are good sources of background information, including visa requirements, and can make bookings. It is also possible to get into Central Asia via **Turkmenistan**, and thence to the rest of Central Asia, via northeastern Iran or from Azerbaijan across the Caspian Sea, thus bypassing Russia completely. Ayan Travel, based in the Turkmenistan capital, Ashgabat (Ⓦwww.ayan-travel.com), are the people to contact for this stage of the journey.

Once in the region, crossing into China from Kazakhstan is straightforward – there are comfortable twice-weekly trains from Almaty to Ürümqi, which take 35 hours and cost about US$80 for a berth in a four-berth compartment. There are also cheaper, faster, less comfortable buses (US$60; about 24hr). From Bishkek in Kyrgyzstan, Kashgar in the northwestern Chinese province of Xinjiang is only eleven hours' drive away (about US$55), and the two cities are linked by buses in summer months. Foreigners, however, have had difficulties in trying to use these and have usually had to resort to expensive private transport, run by local tour operators to help them across (see p.1068 in the Guide). You may well be expected to bribe the border guards US$20 or so.

From Pakistan and Nepal

The routes across the Himalayas to China are among the toughest in Asia. The first is from Pakistan into Xinjiang province over the **Karakoram Highway**, along one of the branches of the ancient Silk Road. This requires no pre-planning, except for the fact that it is open only from May to October, and closes periodically due to landslides. Check your government's travel advice as the area is home to some fundamentalist militants and attacks on Westerners have been known. The Karakoram Highway actually starts at Rawalpindi (the old city outside the capital Islamabad), and in theory you can get from here to Kashgar in four days on public buses. From Rawalpindi, first take one of the daily minibuses that run the arduous fifteen-hour trip up the Indus gorge to the village of Gilgit, where you'll have to spend a night. From Gilgit, the next destination is the border town of Sust, a five-hour journey. There are a couple of daily buses on this route. Once in Sust, immediately book your ticket to Kashgar for the next morning – it costs 1450 rupees (about US$35). A few travellers have managed to talk their way into being issued a visa at the border, but you're strongly advised to have one already. The route is popular with cyclists, but there's no guarantee that you will be allowed to bike across the border; you'll probably have to load your bike on a bus for this part of the trip. For more on crossing the Chinese border here, see p.1074.

Another popular route is travelling **from Nepal into Tibet**, but Nepal's political situation can be volatile, and you should check your government's travel advice on the latest situation – practical details are covered on p.1093. It's advisable to arrive in Nepal with a Chinese visa already in your passport, as the Chinese Embassy in Nepal will only issue group visas. From India itself there are, for political reasons, no border crossings to China. For years, the authorities have discussed opening a bus route from Sikkim to Tibet, north from Darjeeling, but despite both sides working on the road, the border has yet to be opened.

From Vietnam

Vietnam has three border crossings with China – **Dong Dang**, 60km northeast of Hanoi; **Lao Cai,** 150km northwest; and the little-used **Mong Cai**, 200km south of Nanning. All three are open daily between 8.30am and 5pm. Note that officious Chinese customs officials at this border occasionally confiscate guidebooks, including this one (see p.59); bury it at the bottom of your bag.

A **direct train** service from Hanoi is advertised as running all the way to **Beijing** (60hr), passing through **Kunming**, **Nanning** and **Guilin**. In practice, though, you'll have to leave the train at Dong Dang, walk across the border, and catch a minibus to the Chinese railhead, 15km away at Pingxiang, to catch the connecting train. Alternatively, there are good rail and road connections from Hanoi to Lang Son, from where a minibus can take you the last 5km to Dong Dang. Similarly, there are daily trains from Hanoi to Lao Cai, eleven hours' away in Vietnam's mountainous and undeveloped northwest (near the pleasant resort of Sa Pa), from where you can cross into Yunnan province at Hekou, and catch the daily train to Kunming. From Mong Cai, there are regular buses to Nanning.

From Laos and Burma (Myanmar)

Crossing into China **from Laos** also lands you in Yunnan, this time at Bian Mao Zhan in the Xishuangbanna region. Formalities are very relaxed and unlikely to cause any problems, though take some hard cash as you can't change traveller's cheques on the

Chinese side. It's 220km on local buses north from here to the regional capital, Jinghong, with a likely overnight stop in the town of Mengla along the way (see p.853).

Entering China **from Burma** (Myanmar) is a possibility, too, with the old Burma Road cutting northeast from Rangoon (Yangon) to Lashio and the crossing at Wanding in Yunnan, just south of Ruili. At present, this border is open only to groups travelling with a tour agency, which will sort out all the necessary paperwork in Yangon. Be aware that border regulations here are subject to change.

Getting around

Public transport is comprehensive and good value in China: you can fly to all regional capitals and many cities; the rail network extends to every region; and you can reach China's remotest corners on local buses. Tibet is the one area where there are widespread restrictions on independent travel (see p.1094 for more details), though a few other localities around the country are officially off- limits to foreigners.

However, getting around a crowded country with over a billion people often requires planning, patience and stamina. This is especially true for long-distance journeys, where you'll find travelling in as much comfort as you can afford saves a lot of undue stress. **Tours** are one way of taking the pressure off, and may be the only practical way of getting out to certain sights.

Public holidays – especially either side of the three "Golden Weeks" (see p.51) – are rotten times to travel, as half China is on the move between family and workplace: ticket prices rise (legally, by no more than fifteen percent, though often by up to fifty), bus- and train-station crowds swell insanely, and even flights become scarce.

By rail

China's rail network is vast and efficient, and the safest, most reliable way to get around. The country's leaders invest billions of yuan annually on the network, considering a healthy transport infrastructure as essential to economic growth – and political cohesion. Recent years have seen some impressive developments: a rail line over (and through) the mountains between eastern China and **Tibet** completed in 2005, with pressurized carriages to cope with the altitude; and the country's first ultra-fast "**bullet**" trains, which began operation in eastern China in 2007.

Food, though expensive and ordinary, is always available on trains, either as polystyrene boxes of rice and stir-fries wheeled around along with snacks, or in the restaurant car between the soft-sleeper section and the rest of the train. You can also buy snacks from vendors at train stations during the longer station stops.

Timetables and tickets

Booths outside train stations sell national **train timetables** in book form and single sheets covering local services, which are often also printed on the back of city maps. These are all in Chinese only, and can be very complex (even Chinese people have trouble with the books); you need to be able to recognize the characters for both where you are and your destination, then memorize the train number and how many services there are, in case your first choice isn't available. Two good **online train schedules** in English are Ⓦwww.chinahighlights.com/china-trains/index.htm and Ⓦwww.ravelchinaguide.com/china-trains.

Tickets – always **one way** – show the date of travel and destination, along with the train number, carriage, and seat or berth number. They become available up to five days in advance, though demand frequently outstrips supply. **Station ticket offices** are almost all computerized, and while queues can tie you up for an hour or more of jostling, you'll generally get what you're after if you have some flexibility. At the counter, state your destination, the day you'd like to travel, and the class you want, and have some alternatives handy. If you can't speak Chinese, get someone to write things down for you before setting out, as staff rarely speak English, though you may strike it lucky in big cities. In cities, you'll also find **downtown advance purchase offices**, where you pay a small commission (around ¥5 per ticket); it makes sense to try these places first as train stations are often located far from city centres. The easiest option – especially if you don't speak Chinese – is to book tickets through an **agent**, such as a hotel travel service, though you'll pay a commission of ¥30 or more per ticket. At present, the best way to **book tickets online**, and have them delivered to your hotel door in major Chinese cities, is through Ⓦwww.chinatripadvisor.com – you'll pay a surcharge of about 25 percent.

If you've bought a ticket but decide not to travel, you can get most of the fare **refunded** by returning the ticket to a ticket office at least two hours before departure. The process is called *tuipiao* and there's sometimes a window especially for this at stations.

Ticket classes

There are four **ticket classes**: soft sleeper, hard sleeper, soft seat and hard seat, not all necessarily available on each train. **Soft sleeper** (*ruanwo*) costs around the same as flying, and gets you a berth in a four-person compartment with a soft mattress, fan, optional radio and a choice of Western- or Chinese-style toilets. **Hard sleeper** (*yingwo*), about two-thirds the price of *ruanwo*, is the best value. Carriages are divided into twenty sets of three-tiered **bunks**; the lowest bunk is the most expensive, but gets used as communal seating during the day and you may appreciate being able to withdraw to a higher level. The end tier of bunks is closest to night-lights and the connecting space between carriages, where smokers congregate. Each set of six bunks has its own vacuum flask of boiled water (topped up from the urn at the end of each carriage) – bring your own mugs and tea. Every carriage also has a toilet and washbasin, which can become unsavoury. There are fairly spacious **luggage racks**, though make sure you chain your bags securely while you sleep.

In either sleeper class, on boarding the carriage you will have your ticket exchanged for a metal tag by the attendant. The tag is swapped back for your ticket (so you'll be able to get through the barrier at the station) about half an hour before you arrive at your destination; you'll be woken up whatever hour of the day or night this happens to be.

Soft seat (*ruanzuo*) is increasingly available on services whose complete route takes less than a day. Seats are around the cost of an express-bus fare, have plenty of legroom and are well padded. More common is **hard seat** (*yingzuo*), which costs around half the soft-seat fare but is only recommended for relatively short journeys, as things can get crowded and excruciatingly uncomfortable. The basic hard-seat setup is a padded three-person bench offering just enough room to sit, with every available inch of floor space crammed with travellers who were unable to book a seat. You'll often be the focus of intense and unabashed speculation from peasants and labourers who can't afford to travel in better style – the best way to cope is to join in as best you can, whether you can speak Chinese or not.

Finally, if there's nothing else available, you can buy an **unreserved ticket** (*wuzuo*, literally "no seat"), which doesn't give you an assigned seat but lets you board the hard-seat section of the train – though you might have to stand for the entire journey if you can't upgrade on board.

Types of train

The different **types of train** each have their own code of timetables. **High-speed** services include the new D-class, or "bullet trains", which travel up to 250kph; followed by the Z-, T- and K-class trains, which can

Sample train fares

The fares below are for one-way travel on express trains. As always in China, the faster services are more expensive.

	Hard seat	Hard sleeper	Soft sleeper
From Beijing			
Guangzhou	¥205	¥553	¥756
Hong Kong	¥215	¥595	¥925
Shanghai	¥135	¥375	¥515
Xi'an	¥140	¥390	¥531
From Xi'an			
Guangzhou	¥220	¥607	¥830
Turpan	¥215	¥585	¥805
Ürümqi	¥225	¥625	¥842

still reach 150–200kph. These all have modern fittings with text tickers at the carriages' end scrolling through the temperature, arrival time at next station and speed. **No-smoking rules** are often vigorously enforced.

Ordinary trains (*putong che*) have a number only and range from those with clean carriages and able to top 100kph, to ancient plodders with cigarette-burned linoleum floors and grimy windows that are destined for the scrapheap. A few busy, short-haul express services, such as the Shenzhen–Guangzhou train, have **double-decker carriages**.

Boarding the train

Turn up at the station with time to spare before your train leaves. All luggage has to be passed through **x-ray machines** at the station entrance to check for dangerous goods such as firecrackers – though there's rarely anyone paying any attention to the monitors. Carry **film** through separately to avoid the possibility of it getting damaged. You then need to work out which **platform** your train leaves from – most stations have electronic departure boards in Chinese, or you can show your ticket to station staff who will point you in the right direction. Passengers are not allowed onto the platform until the train is in and ready to leave, which can result in some mighty stampedes out of the crowded waiting rooms when the gates open. Carriages are **numbered** on the outside, and your ticket is checked by a guard as you board. Once on the train, you can **upgrade** any ticket at the controller's booth, in the hard-seat carriage next to the restaurant car (usually #8), where you can sign up for beds or seats as they become available.

By bus and minibus

While cities and major towns usually have a train station, getting from these out to other places – whether rural Yunnan or simply an interesting village near Shanghai – usually requires a **bus**. Finding the right bus station isn't always easy though; even small towns often have both a central **main bus station** and several outlying **depots** handling specific destinations (located on the side of town in which traffic is heading).

Bus station **timetables** – except the new electronic ones – can be ignored; ask station staff about schedules and frequencies, though they generally can't speak English. **Tickets** are easy to buy: ticket offices at main stations are often computerized, queues are seldom bad, and – with the exception of back-road routes, which might only run every other day – you don't need to book in advance. In country towns, you sometimes buy tickets on board the bus. **Destinations** are always displayed in Chinese characters on the front of the vehicle.

There are various **types of buses**, though there's not always a choice available for particular routes and if there is, station staff will assume that as a foreigner you'll want the fastest, most comfortable service –

which will also be the most expensive. **Ordinary buses** (*putong che*) are cheap and basic, with lightly padded seats; they're never heated or air-conditioned, so dress accordingly. Seats can be cramped and luggage racks tiny; you'll have to put anything bulkier than a satchel on the roof or your lap, or beside the driver. They tend to stop off frequently, so don't count on an average speed of more than 50kph. **Express buses** (*kuai che*) are the most expensive and have good legroom, comfy seats that may well recline, air-conditioning and video – usually playing the latest kung fu, pop or karaoke releases. Bulky luggage gets locked away in the belly of the bus, a fairly safe option as these buses operate on a speedy point to point basis, with no stops en route. Formerly common, **sleeper buses** (*wopu che*) have cramped, basic bunks instead of seats, minimal luggage space and a poor safety record, and are not recommended if there is any alternative. The final option is **minibuses** (*xiao che* or *bao che*) seating up to twenty people, common on routes of less than 100km or so. Prices vary around the country, but they typically cost a little more than the same journey by ordinary bus. They can be extremely cramped, however, and often circuit the departure point for ages until they have filled up.

Downsides to bus travel include the possibility of rough roads; drivers who spend the journey chatting on their mobile phone or coast downhill in neutral, with the engine off; and the fact that vehicles are obliged to use the horn before overtaking anything – earplugs are recommended. Take some **food** along, too, because although buses usually pull up at inexpensive roadhouses at mealtimes, they have been known to plough on for a full 24 hours without stopping. Only the most upmarket coaches have **toilets**; drivers stop every few hours or if asked to do so by passengers (roadhouse toilets are some of the worst in the country, however).

By plane

China's **airlines** link all major cities. The main operators are Air China (Ⓦwww.airchina.com.cn/en/index.jsp), China Southern (Ⓦwww.cs-air.com/en) and China Eastern (Ⓦwww.ce-air.com), which – along with smaller regional companies – are overseen by the Civil Aviation Administration of China, or **CAAC**. Flying is a luxury worth considering for long distances as prices compare with soft-sleeper train travel but journey times are obviously far less, planes are generally modern and well maintained and service is good.

Buying tickets from the local CAAC office, hotel desk or tour agent is easy, and there seem to be enough flights along popular routes to cope with demand. Agents often give substantial discounts on advertised fares, especially if you book a day or two in advance. Competitive fares are available if you buy your ticket online at Ⓦwww.elong.com; there's a button on the website for English. In major Chinese cities, they can also deliver the ticket (for free) a few hours after you book it, and you pay the ticket price to the delivery boy. You'll need to provide a phone number to confirm the booking.

Timetables are displayed at airline offices and agent desks, and often on the back of city maps. **Fares** are based on one-way travel (so a return ticket is the price of two one-way tickets) and include all **taxes**. As an illustration, from Beijing, expect to pay at least ¥620 to Xi'an; ¥690 to Shanghai; ¥935 to Chengdu; ¥1055 to Guangzhou; ¥1190 to Kunming, ¥1440 to Ürümqi and ¥1800 to Hong Kong.

Airlines frequently provide an **airport bus** running to and from the airport. As these can be 30km or more from city centres, it's worth finding out if a bus is available, if not already mentioned in this guide. **Check-in time** for all flights is two hours before departure.

By car

Driving a car across China is an appealing idea, but an experience currently forbidden to foreign tourists (though foreign residents can take a driving test). It is possible, however, to **rent vehicles** for local use in **Beijing**, **Shanghai** and **Hong Kong**, from rental companies at the airports. You need an international driving licence and a credit card to cover the deposit. Special licence plates make these rental vehicles easily identifiable to Chinese police, so don't try taking them beyond the designated boundaries. Rates are about ¥300 a day plus petrol.

The mainland Chinese drive **on the right**, although in practice drivers seem to drive wherever they like – through red lights, up one-way streets, even on the left. They use their horns instead of the brake, and lorries and buses plough ahead regardless while smaller vehicles get out of the way. The exception is in Hong Kong, where they drive on the left, and actually take traffic regulations seriously.

Elsewhere, the only option is to rent a **taxi**, **minibus** or Chinese **Jeep**, complete **with driver**. Prices are set by negotiating and average ¥400 a day, and you'll be expected to provide lunch for the driver. It's cheapest to approach drivers directly, though if you can't speak Chinese your accommodation should be able to help, and some tour operators run vehicles, too – and might include the services of an interpreter. In Tibet, renting a Jeep with a driver is pretty much the only way to get to many destinations (see p.1094).

Ferries

River and sea journeys are on the decline in China, with **passenger ferries** being made redundant by new and faster roads and rail lines. One of the world's great river journeys remains, however, namely the **Yangzi**, which is navigable for thousands of kilometres between the Sichuanese port of Chongqing and Yichang in Hubei, a journey that takes you through the mighty **Three Gorges** – though the spectacle has been lessened by the construction of the giant Three Gorges Dam. Another favourite is the day-cruise down the **Li River** between Guilin and Yangshuo in southwestern Guangxi province, past a forest of pointy mountains looking just like a Chinese scroll painting. By **sea**, there are **passenger ferries** between Hong Kong and Macau; between Guangxi and Hainan Island; and from ports in Shandong and Shanghai to neighbouring South Korea and Japan.

Conditions on board are greatly variable, but on overnight trips there's always a choice of **classes** – sometimes as many as six – which can range from a bamboo mat on the floor, right through to private cabins. Don't expect anything too impressive, however; many mainland services are cramped and overcrowded, and cabins, even in first class, are grimly functional.

Cycling

China has the highest number of **bicycles** of any country in the world, with about a quarter of the population owning one (despite a rising trend towards mopeds, motorbikes and cars). Few cities have any hills and some have **bike lanes**, though many of the bigger cities are in the process of banning bicycles from main roads in order to free them up for cars.

Rental shops or booths are common around train stations, where you can rent a set of wheels for ¥5–10 a day. You will need to leave a deposit (¥200–400) and/or some form of ID, and you're fully responsible for anything that happens to the bike while it's in your care, so check brakes, tyre pressure and gears before renting. Most rentals are bog-standard black rattletraps – the really de luxe models feature working bells and brakes. There are **repair shops** all over the place should you need a tyre patched or a chain fixed up (around ¥2). If the bike sustains any serious damage, it's up to the parties involved to sort out responsibility and payment on the spot. To **avoid theft**, always use a **bicycle chain** or lock – they're available everywhere – and in cities, leave your vehicle in one of the ubiquitous designated **parking areas**, where it will be guarded by an attendant for a few yuan.

An alternative to renting is to **buy a bike**, a sensible option if you're going to be based anywhere for a while. All department stores sell them: a heavy, unsophisticated machine will only set you back about ¥200; whereas a mountain bike will be upwards of ¥500. A **folding bike** (around ¥350) is a great idea, as you can cycle around all day and when you're tired, put it in the boot of a taxi; and, of course, you can take it from one destination to another on the bus. You can also **bring your own bike** into China; international airlines usually insist that the front wheel is removed, deflated and strapped to the back, and that everything is thoroughly packaged. Inside China, airlines, trains and ferries all charge to carry bikes, and the ticketing and accompanying paperwork can be baffling. Where possible, it's easier to stick to long-distance buses and stow it for free on the roof, no questions asked. Another option is to see China on a **specialized bike tour** such as those offered by Bike China (Ⓦwww.bikechina.com) or Cycle China (Ⓦwww.cyclechina.com); though by no means cheap, these can be an excellent start to a longer stay in China. For adventurous mountain biking, the best place to head is Yunnan, in the southwest; challenging tours are offered by Haiwei Trails (Ⓦwww.haiweitrails.com).

Tours

Tour operators – whether just a desk at a hotel or a proper organization – always offer excursions, from local city sights to river cruises and multi-day cross-country trips. While you always pay for the privilege, sometimes these tours are good value: travel, accommodation and food – usually plentiful and excellent – are generally included, as might be the services of an interpreter and guide. And in some cases,

tours are the most practical (if not the only) way to see something really worthwhile, saving endless bother organizing local transport and accommodation.

On the downside, there are disreputable operators who'll blatantly overcharge for mediocre services, foist guides on you who can't speak local dialects or are unhelpful and spend three days on what could better be done in an afternoon. It always pays to make exhaustive **enquiries** about the exact nature of the tour, such as exactly what the price includes and the departure/return times, before handing any money over.

As regards **adventure tours**, it's worth checking out **WildChina** (Ⓦwww.wildchina.com), which is based in-country and runs excursions around the nation's fringes for individuals and groups, with trekking and hiking a focus of many trips, though some tours have an architectural or cultural emphasis.

City transport

All Chinese cities have some form of **public transit system**. An increasing number have (or are building) **light-rail systems** and underground **metros**; elsewhere, the **city bus** is the transport focus. These are cheap and run from around 6am to 9pm or later, but – Hong Kong's apart – are usually slow and crowded. Pricier **private minibuses** often run the same routes in similar comfort but at greater speed; they're either numbered or have their destination written up at the front.

Taxis are always available in larger towns and cities; main roads, transit points and tourist hotels are good places to find them. They either cost a fixed rate within certain limits – ¥5 seems normal – or about ¥8 to hire and then ¥1–3 per kilometre. You'll also find (motorized- or cycle-) **rickshaws** and **motorbike taxis** outside just about every mainland bus and train station, whose highly erratic rates are set by bargaining beforehand.

Accommodation

Although Chinese hotels are often lacking in character – old family-run institutions of the kind that can be found all over Asia and Europe are rare – there is an increasing range of choice, especially in the large cities, where you can find foreigner-friendly hostels, budget motels and hotels ranging from drab urban models to upmarket international chains.

Price is not a good indicator of quality, however, with a good deal of overlap between the various places – a motel double room, for example, is often cheaper than a hotel and better value than a hostel. The Chinese hospitality industry is on a steep learning curve, so new places are often vastly better than old ones.

Security in accommodation is reasonably good, although you would be foolish to leave money or valuables lying about in your room. If you lock things inside your bag before going out, you are unlikely to have problems.

Finding a room

Increasingly, **booking ahead** is a routine procedure for all hostels and motels – which tend to get booked out in advance – and more modern hotels, where you'll often get an automatic discount for doing so. You can book by phone, through the accommodation's own website if there is one, or by using a **dedicated accommodation-booking website** such as elong (Ⓦwww.elong.com) or China Trip (Ⓦwww.ctrip.com), both of which have English-language content and offer massive discounts on selected mid-range to upmarket hotel rates. Budget travellers should

临时住宿登记表

REGISTRATION FORM FOR TEMPORARY RESIDENCE

请用正楷填写 Please write in block letters

英文性 Surname	英文名 First name	性别 Sex
中文姓名 Name in Chinese	国籍 Nationality	出生日期 Date of birth
证件种类 Type of certificate (eg "Passport")	证件号码 Certificate no.	签证种类 Type of visa
签证有效期 Valid date of visa	抵店日期 Date of arrival	离店日期 Date of departure
由何处来 From	交通工具 Carrier	往何处 To
永久地址 Permanent address		停留事由 Object of stay
职业 Occupation		
接待单位 Received by		房号 Room no.

check out hostel booking services such as hostel bookers (ⓦwww.hostelbookers.com). Staff on airport buses usually hand out elong or China Trip discount cards and booklets listing special offers. Sometimes, the local CITS can also wrangle excellent discounts for you.

For other hotels, however, the concept of booking ahead may be alien, and you won't make much headway without spoken Chinese – though it's a good idea to call (or to ask someone to call for you) to see if vacancies exist before lugging your bag across town. Be aware that even at these places **room rates** displayed at reception often turn out to be merely the starting point in negotiations. Staff are almost always amenable to **bargaining** and it's not unusual to get thirty percent off the advertised price, even more perhaps in low season or where there's plenty of competition. Always ask to see the room first.

If you haven't booked ahead, time things so that you reach your destination in broad daylight, then deposit your bag at a left-luggage office at the train or bus station and check out possible accommodation options. New arrivals at city bus and train stations are often besieged by **touts** wanting to lead them to a hotel where they'll receive a commission for bringing guests in; these people are generally OK, but you do need to be very clear about how much you're willing to pay before being dragged all over town.

If you find yourself being turned away by cheaper hotels, they probably haven't obtained **police permission** to take foreigners, and would face substantial fines for doing so. The situation is dependent on the local authorities, and can vary not just from province to province, but also from town to town. Nothing is ever certain in China, however: being able to speak Chinese greatly improves your chances, as does being able to write your name in Chinese on the register (or having it printed out so the receptionist can do this for you) – in which case the authorities need never know that a foreigner stayed.

Checking in and out

The **checking-in process** involves filling in a detailed **form** giving details of your name, age, date of birth, sex and address, places where you are coming from and going to, how many days you intend staying and your visa and passport numbers. Upmarket hotels have English versions of these forms, and might fill them in for you, but hotels unaccustomed to foreigners usually have them in Chinese only, and might never have seen a foreign passport before – which explains the panic experienced by many hotel receptionists when they see a foreigner walk in the door. There's an example of this form in English and Chinese opposite to help smooth difficulties.

You are always asked to **pay in advance**, including a **deposit**, which may amount to twice the price of the room. Assuming you haven't broken anything – make sure everything works properly when you check in – deposits are generally refunded; just don't lose the receipt.

In cheaper places, you won't get a **key** from reception; instead, you'll get a piece of paper that you take to the appropriate **floor attendant** who will give you a room card and open the door for you whenever you come in. You can usually ask to keep the key, though again you'll have to pay a refundable deposit of ¥10–20. If your room has a **telephone**, disconnect it to avoid being woken by prostitutes calling up through the night.

Check-out time is noon, though you can ask to keep the room until later for a proportion of the daily rate. Make sure you come to an arrangement for this before check-out time, however, as there have been reports of staff telling guests to sort this out after check-out time, then refusing to refund their room deposit claiming that they have overstayed. Conversely, if you have to leave very early in the morning (to catch transport, for instance), you may be unable to find staff to refund your deposit, and might also encounter locked front doors or compound gates. This is most of a problem in rural areas, though often the receptionist sleeps behind the desk and can be woken up if you make enough noise.

Hotels

The different Chinese words for hotel are vague indicators of the status of the place – see the "Language" section (p.1217) for the *pinyin* and Chinese characters. Sure signs of upmarket pretensions are the modern-sounding **dajiulou** or **dajiudian**, which translate as something like "big wine bar". The term **binguan** is similarly used for smart new establishments, though it is also the name given to the older government-run hotels, many of which have now been renovated; foreigners can nearly always stay in these. **Fandian** (literally "restaurant") is used indiscriminately for top-class hotels as well as humble and obscure ones. Reliably downmarket – and rarely accepting foreigners – is **zhaodaisuo** ("guesthouse"), while the humblest of all is **lüguan** ("inn"), where you might occasionally get to stay in some rural areas. These cheaper places are often simply signed **zhusu** ("accommodation").

Accommodation price codes

The accommodation listed in this book has been given one of the following price codes, which represent the price of the cheapest **double room**. In the cheaper hotels that have **dormitories** or that rent out individual beds in small rooms, we give the price of a bed in yuan.

It should generally be noted that in the **off season** – from October to June, excluding holidays such as Christmas and Chinese New Year – prices in tourist hotels are more flexible, and often lower, than during the peak summer months.

Note that the price codes do not take into account the **service charge** of fifteen percent added to bills in all mid-range and upmarket hotels.

❶ Under ¥50	❹ ¥140–199	❼ ¥450–599
❷ ¥50–79	❺ ¥200–299	❽ ¥600–800
❸ ¥80–139	❻ ¥300–449	❾ Over ¥800

Whatever type of hotel you are staying in, there are two things you can rely on: one is a pair of plastic or paper **slippers** under the bed, which you use for walking to the bathroom, and the other is a vacuum flask of drinkable **hot water** that can be refilled any time by the floor attendant – though upmarket places tend to provide electric kettles instead. **Breakfast** is sometimes included in the price; nearly all hotels, even fairly grotty ones, will have a restaurant where at least a Chinese breakfast of buns, pickles and congee is served between 7 and 9am.

Upmarket

In the larger cities, you'll find **upmarket** four- or five-star hotels. Conditions in such hotels are comparable to those anywhere in the world, with all the usual **international facilities** on offer – such as swimming pools, gyms and business centres – though the finer nuances of service will sometimes be lacking. Prices for standard doubles in these places are upwards of ¥800 (❾ in our price-code scheme) and go as high as ¥1500, with a fifteen-percent **service charge** on top; the use of credit cards is routine. In **Hong Kong** and **Macau**, the top end of the market is similar in character to the mainland, though prices are higher and service more efficient – price codes for these areas are found on p.656.

Even if you cannot afford to stay in the upmarket hotels, they can still be pleasant places to escape from the hubbub, and nobody in China blinks at the sight of a stray foreigner roaming around the foyer of a smart hotel. As well as air-conditioning and clean toilets, you'll find **cafés and bars** (sometimes showing satellite TV), telephone and fax facilities and seven-days-a-week money changing (though this is seldom available to non-guests).

Mid-range

Many urban Chinese hotels built nowadays are **mid-range**, and practically every town in China has at least one hotel of this sort. Most rooms in these places are twin bed (*shuangrenfang*) or single (*danrenfang*); if you want a double bed, ask for a single with a "large bed" (*dachuan*). The **quality** of mid-range places is the hardest to predict from the price: an old hotel with cigarette-burned carpets, leaking bathrooms and grey bedsheets might charge the same as a sparkling new establishment next door (newer places are generally better, as a rule).

In remote places, you should get a twin or double in a mid-range place for ¥100–250, but expect to pay at least ¥300 in any sizeable city. Some mid-range hotels built during the dawn of tourism in 1980s, however, might retain older, **cheaper wings**. These are often well maintained, if threadbare, and cost ¥100–200 for a double with bathroom, and might even have dorm beds for as low as ¥25 (see "Budget hotels" below).

Budget hotels

Cheap hotels, with doubles costing less than ¥100, vary in quality from the dilapidated to the perfectly comfortable. In many cities, they're commonly located near the train or bus stations, though they may need persuading to take foreigners. Where they do, you'll notice that the Chinese routinely **rent beds** rather than rooms – doubling up with one or more strangers – as a means of saving money. Foreigners are seldom allowed to share rooms with Chinese people, but if there are three or four foreigners together it's often possible for them to share one big room; otherwise you might have to negotiate a price for the whole room.

Motels

The last few years has seen an explosion in urban **motels**, which for the first time offer clean, modern, good-value places to stay right in city centres. Having originated in Shanghai, there are three nation-wide chains at present: **Motel168** (ⓦwww.motel168.com); **Jinjiang Inn** (ⓦwww.jj-inn.com); and **Home Inn** (ⓦwww.homeinns.com), all of whom offer small but not cramped double rooms with showers, phones, TV and Internet portal from about ¥160. Generally, they're a very good deal and need to be booked in advance both because of their popularity and because you'll only get the cheapest rooms this way – prices are otherwise fixed. The English-language pages on their websites are not always up to date, but staff at reception usually speak a little English if you call ahead.

Hostels and guesthouses

There's a rapidly expanding network of **youth hostels** across China, most of whom are affiliated with the IYHA. Contact details for individual hostels are given through the guide, and **booking ahead** is always advisable. The Chinese youth hostel website isn't up to speed with the situation, and there's better info and easier booking available through the international IYHA site or Ⓦwww.hostelbookers.com. IYHA members get a small discount, usually ¥10, and you can join at any mainland hostel for ¥60.

Hong Kong, Macau and a few regions of China (mostly in southwestern provinces) also have a number of **privately run guesthouses** in everything from family mansions to Mongolian tents, whose variety comes as a relief after the dullness of mainland accommodation. Prices for double rooms in these guesthouses are generally cheaper than in hotels in most of eastern China, and very cheap dormitories are also plentiful.

Youth hostel associations

China

YHA China Ⓣ020/87345080, Ⓕ87345428, Ⓦwww.yhachina.com/english.

International

International Youth Hostel Association (IYHA) Ⓦwww.hihostels.com.

UK and Ireland

Youth Hostel Association (YHA) Ⓣ0870/770 8868, Ⓦwww.yha.org.uk.
Scottish Youth Hostel Association Ⓣ01786/891 400, Ⓦwww.syha.org.uk.
Irish Youth Hostel Association Ⓣ01/830 4555, Ⓦwww.irelandyha.org.
Hostelling International Northern Ireland Ⓣ028/9031 5435, Ⓦwww.hini.org.uk.

US and Canada

Hostelling International-American Youth Hostels Ⓣ301/495-1240, Ⓦwww.hiayh.org.
Hostelling International Canada Ⓣ1-800/663-5777, Ⓦwww.hihostels.ca.

Australia and New Zealand

Australia Youth Hostels Association Ⓣ02/9565 1699, Ⓦwww.yha.com.au.
Youth Hostelling Association New Zealand Ⓣ0800/278 299 or 03/379 9970, Ⓦwww.yha.co.nz.

University accommodation

In some cities with limited alternatives, **university accommodation** might be an option, though as youth hostels continue to proliferate and campuses are huge and often remote from arrival points or sights, they're not always such a good choice. Once at the campus, you need to locate the "Foreigners' Guesthouse" (*Waibing Zhaodaisuo*) or the "Foreign Experts' Building" (*Waiguo Zhuanjia Lou*), designed primarily to accommodate foreign students or teachers. These buildings act like simple hotels and you have to fill in all the usual forms. Expect to pay around ¥50 a night, though some places are now charging tourists substantially more. Sometimes, you'll find yourself sharing with a resident foreign student who may be less than gracious about having you – but this happens only if the student concerned has paid for only one of the two beds in their room, so you needn't feel guilty about it.

Camping and pilgrims' inns

Camping is only really feasible in the wildernesses of western China – in parts of Tibet, Sichuan, Yunnan, Qinghai, Xinjiang, Gansu and Inner Mongolia – where you are not going to wake up under the prying eyes of thousands of local villagers. Don't bother actually trying to get permission for it – this is the kind of activity that the Chinese authorities do not really have any clear idea about, so if asked they will certainly answer "no". The only kind of regular, authorized camping in China is by the nomadic Mongolian and Kazakh peoples of the steppe who have their own felt tents (*mengu bao*), which tourists can stay in under certain circumstances (see p.948).

An alternative to camping is staying at **pilgrims' inns** at important monasteries and lamaseries, an experience well worth trying once. Facilities range from cheap and basic cells designed for roaming clergy where you'll pay around ¥30, to tourist-standard rooms with toilets and heating costing over ¥100 at popular locations such as Emei Shan in Sichuan. Such places always offer vegetarian meals for an additional fee.

Food and drink

The Chinese love to eat, and from market-stall buns and soup, right through to the intricate variations of regional cookery, China boasts one of the world's greatest cuisines. Unfortunately, the inability to order effectively sees many travellers missing out, and they leave convinced that the bland stir-fries and dumplings served up in the cheapest canteens are all that's available. With a bit of effort, however, you can eat well whatever your budget and ability with the language.

Meals are considered social events, and the process is accordingly geared to a group of diners sharing a variety of different dishes with their companions. Fresh ingredients are available from any market stall, though unless you're living long term in the country there are few opportunities to cook for yourself.

Ingredients and cooking methods

In the south, **rice** as grain, noodles, or dumpling wrappers is the staple, replaced in the cooler north by **wheat**, formed into buns or noodles. Keep an eye out for **lamian** – literally "pulled noodles" – a Muslim treat made as you wait by pulling out ribbons of dough between outstretched arms, and serving them in a spicy soup (see p.1036).

Meat is held to be invigorating and, ideally, forms the backbone of any meal. **Pork** is the most common meat used, except in areas with a strong Muslim tradition where it's replaced with **mutton** or **beef**. **Fowl** is considered especially good during old age or convalescence, and was quite a luxury in the past, though today most rural people in central and southern China seem to own a couple of **chickens**, and the countryside is littered with **duck** and **geese** farms. **Fish and seafood** are highly regarded and can be expensive – partly because local pollution means that they often have to be imported – as are rarer **game** meats.

Eggs – duck, chicken or quail – are a popular nationwide snack, often flavoured by hard-boiling in a mixture of tea, soy sauce and star anise. There's also the so-called "thousand-year-old" variety, preserved for a few months in ash and straw – they look gruesome, with translucent brown albumen and green yolks, but actually have a delicate, brackish flavour. **Dairy products** serve limited purposes in China. Goat's cheese and yoghurt are eaten in parts of Yunnan and the Northwest, but milk is considered fit only for children and the elderly and is not used in cooking.

Vegetables accompany nearly every Chinese meal, used in most cases to balance tastes and textures of meat, but also appearing as dishes in their own right. Though the selection can be very thin in some parts of the country, there's usually a wide range on

For a comprehensive menu reader and useful phrases for ordering food and drink, see p.1220. For more on Chinese food, see the *Chinese cuisine* colour section.

offer, from leafy greens to water chestnuts, mushrooms, bamboo shoots, seaweed and radish – even thin, transparent "glass" noodles, made out of pea starch, which the Chinese regard as vegetables, too.

Soya beans are ubiquitous in Chinese cooking, being a good source of protein in a country where meat has often been a luxury. The beans themselves are small and green when fresh, and are sometimes eaten this way in the south. More frequently, however, they are salted and used to thicken sauces, fermented to produce **soy sauce**, or boiled and pressed to make white cakes of **tofu** (bean curd). Fresh tofu is flavourless and as soft as custard, though it can be pressed further to create a firmer texture, deep-fried until crisp, or cooked in stock and used as a meat substitute in vegetarian cooking. Regional variations abound: in the west, tofu is served heavily spiced; in Hunan, they grow mould on it (rather like cheese); in the south, it's stuffed with meat; northerners make it spongy by freezing it; and everywhere it gets used in soup. The skin that forms on top of the liquid while tofu is being made is itself skimmed off, dried, and used as a wrapping for spring rolls and the like.

Seasonal availability is smoothed over by a huge variety of **dried**, **salted** and **pickled vegetables**, meats and seafood, which often characterize local cooking styles. There's also an enormous assortment of regional **fruit**, great to clean the palate or fill a space between meals.

Breakfast, snacks and street food

Breakfast is not usually a big event by Chinese standards, more something to line the stomach for a few hours. Much of the country is content with a bowl of **zhou** rice porridge (also known as congee) flavoured with pickles and eaten with plain buns, or **doujiang** (sweetened soya milk) accompanied by a fried dough stick. Another favourite is a plain soup with noodles or **wuntun** dumplings and perhaps a little meat. Guangdong and Hong Kong are the exceptions, where the traditional breakfast of **dim sum** (also known as **yum cha**) involves a selection of tiny buns, dumplings and dishes served with tea.

Other **snacks and street food** are served through the day from small, early-opening **stalls** located around markets, train and bus stations. These serve grilled chicken wings; kebabs; spiced noodles; baked yams and potatoes; boiled eggs; various steamed or stewed dishes dished up in earthenware **sandpots**; grilled corn and – in places such as Beijing and Sichuan – countless local treats. Also common are **steamed buns**, which are either stuffed with meat or vegetables (*baozi*) or plain (*mantou*, literally "bald heads"). The buns originated in the north and are especially warming on a winter's day; a sweeter Cantonese variety is stuffed with barbecued pork. Another northern snack now found everywhere is the ravioli-like **jiaozi**, again with a meat or vegetable filling and either fried or steamed; **shuijiao** are boiled *jiaozi* served in soup. Some small restaurants specialize in *jiaozi*, containing a bewildering range of fillings and always sold by weight.

Restaurants and eating out

The cheapest **hole-in-the-wall canteens** are necessarily basic, with simple food costing a few yuan a serve and often much better than you'd expect from the furnishings. Proper **restaurants** are usually bright, busy places whose preferred atmosphere is *renao*, or "hot and noisy", rather than the often quiet norm in the West. Prices at these places obviously vary a lot, but even expensive-looking establishments charge only ¥15–50 for a main dish, and servings tend to be generous. Restaurants are often divided up by floor, with the cheapest, most public area on the ground floor and more expensive, private booths with waitress service upstairs.

While the cheaper places might have long hours, **restaurant opening times** are early and short: breakfast lasts from around 6–9am; lunch 11am–2pm; and dinner from around 5–9pm, after which the staff will be yawning and sweeping the debris off the tables around your ankles.

Ordering and dining

Pointing is all that's required at street stalls and small restaurants, where the ingredients are displayed out the front in buckets, bundles and cages; canteens usually have the fare laid out or will have the selection scrawled illegibly on strips of paper or a board hung on the wall. You either tell the cook directly what you want or buy chits from a cashier, which you exchange at the kitchen hatch for your food and sit down at large communal tables or benches.

When you enter a **proper restaurant** you'll be escorted to a chair and promptly given a pot of tea, along with pickles and nuts in upmarket places. The only tableware provided is a spoon, a bowl and a pair of chopsticks, and at this point the Chinese will ask for boiling water and a bowl to wash it all in – not usually necessary, but something of a ritual. Unless you're in a big tourist destination, **menus** will be Chinese-only and the restaurant staff will probably be unable to speak English, though fortunately there's a growing trend in **photo menus** – in fact, some regional Chinese dishes have such obscure names that even non-local Chinese have to ask what they are. Alternatively, have a look at what other diners are eating – the Chinese are often delighted that a foreigner wants to eat Chinese food, and will indicate the best food on their table.

If this fails, you might be escorted through to the kitchen to make your choice by pointing at the raw ingredients. You need to get the idea across here if you want different items cooked together (say *yikuair*), otherwise you might end up with separate plates of nuts, meat and vegetables when you thought you'd ordered a single dish of chicken with cashews and green peppers. Note also that unless you're specific about how you want your food prepared, it inevitably arrives stir-fried.

When **ordering**, unless eating a one-dish meal like Beijing duck or a hotpot, try to select items with a **range of tastes and textures**; it's also usual to include a soup. In cheap places, servings of noodles or rice are huge, but as they are considered basic stomach fillers, quantities decline the more upmarket you go. Note that dishes such as *jiaozi* and some seafood, as well as fresh produce, are **sold by weight**: a *liang* is 50g, a *banjin* 250g, a *jin* 500g, and a *gongjin* 1kg.

Dishes are all **served** at once, placed in the middle of the table for diners to share. With some poultry dishes you can crunch up the smaller bones, but anything else is spat out on to the tablecloth or floor, more or less discreetly depending on the establishment – watch what others are doing. **Soups** tend to be bland and are consumed last (except in the south where they may be served first or as part of the main meal) to wash the meal down, the liquid slurped from a spoon or the bowl once the noodles, vegetables or meat in it have been picked out and eaten. **Desserts** aren't a regular feature in China, though in the south, sweet soups and buns are eaten (the latter not confined to main meals), particularly at festive occasions.

Resting your chopsticks together across the top of your bowl means that you've **finished** eating. After a meal, the Chinese don't hang around to talk over drinks as in the West, but get up straight away and leave. In canteens, you'll **pay** up front, while at restaurants you ask for the bill and pay either the waiter or at the front till. **Tipping** is not expected in mainland China, though in Hong Kong you generally leave around ten percent.

Western and international food

There's a fair amount of **Western and international food** available in China, though supply and quality vary. Hong Kong, Shanghai and Beijing have the best range, with some excellent restaurants covering everything from Russian to Brazilian cuisine, and there are international food restaurants in every Chinese city of any size, with Korean and Japanese the best represented. Elsewhere, upmarket hotels may have Western restaurants, serving expensive but huge **buffet breakfasts** of scrambled egg, bacon, toast, cereal and coffee; and there's a growing number of **cafés** in many cities, especially ones with large foreign expat populations. **Burger**, **fried-chicken** and **pizza** places are ubiquitous, including domestic chains such as *Dicos* alongside *McDonald's*, *KFC* and *Pizza Hut*.

Drink

Water is easily available in China, but never drink what comes out of the tap. **Boiled water** is always on hand in hotels and trains, either provided in large vacuum flasks or an urn, and you can buy **bottled spring water** at station stalls and supermarkets – read the labels and you'll see some unusual substances (such as radon) listed, which you'd probably want to avoid.

Tea

Tea has been known in China since antiquity and was originally drunk for medicinal reasons. Although its health properties are still important, and some food halls sell nourishing or stimulating varieties by the bowlful, over the centuries a whole **social culture** has sprung up around this beverage, spawning **teahouses** that once held the same place in Chinese society that the local pub or bar does in the West. Plantations of neat rows of low tea bushes adorn hillsides across southern China, while the brew is enthusiastically consumed, from the highlands of Tibet – where it's mixed with barley meal and butter – to every restaurant and household between Hong Kong and Beijing.

Often the first thing you'll be asked in a restaurant is *he shenme cha* – "what sort of tea would you like?" Chinese tea comes in red, green and flower-scented **varieties**, depending on how it's processed; only Hainan produces Indian-style **black** tea. Some regional kinds, such as *pu'er* from Yunnan, Fujian's *tie guanyin*, Zhejiang's *longjing* or Sichuan's *zhuye qing*, are highly sought after; indeed, after locals in Yunnan decided that banks weren't paying enough interest, they started investing in *pu'er* tea stocks, causing prices to soar.

Though tea is never drunk with milk and only very rarely with sugar, the manner in which it's **served** also varies from place to place: sometimes it comes in huge mugs with a lid, elsewhere in dainty cups served from a miniature pot; there are also formalized **tea rituals** in parts of Fujian and Guangdong. When drinking in company, it's polite to top up others' cups before your own, whenever they become empty; if someone does this for you, lightly tap your first two fingers on the table to show your thanks. If you've had enough, leave your cup full, and in a restaurant take the lid off or turn it over if you want the pot refilled during the meal.

It's also worth trying some **Muslim** *babao cha* or **Eight Treasures Tea**, which involves dried fruit, nuts, seeds, crystallized sugar and tea heaped into a cup with the remaining space filled with hot water, poured with panache from an immensely long-spouted copper kettle. It's becoming widely available in upmarket restaurants everywhere, and is sometimes sold in packets from street stalls.

Alcohol

The popularity of **beer** – *pijiu* – in China rivals that of tea, and, for men, is the preferred mealtime beverage (drinking alcohol in public is considered improper for Chinese women, though not for foreigners). The first brewery was set up in the northeastern port of Qingdao by the Germans in the nineteenth century, and now, though the Tsingtao label is widely available, just about every province produces at least one brand of four-percent Pilsner. Sold in litre bottles, it's always drinkable, often pretty good, and is actually cheaper than bottled water. Draught beer is becoming available across the country.

Watch out for the term "**wine**" on English menus, which usually denotes **spirits**, made from rice (*mijiu*), sorghum or millet (*baijiu*). Serving spirits to guests is a sign of hospitality, and they're always used for toasting at banquets. Again, local home-made varieties can be quite good, while mainstream brands – especially the expensive, nationally famous Moutai and Wuliangye – are pretty vile to the Western palate. **Imported beers and spirits** are sold in large department stores and in city bars, but are always expensive. China does actually have a couple of commercial **vineyards** producing the mediocre Great Wall and Dynasty labels, more of a status symbol than an attempt to rival Western growers. Far better are the local pressings in Xinjiang province, where the population of Central Asian descent takes its grapes seriously.

Western-style bars are found not only in Hong Kong and Macau, but also in the major mainland cities. These establishments serve both local and imported beers and spirits, and are popular with China's middle class as well as foreigners. Mostly, though, the Chinese drink alcohol only with their meals – all restaurants serve at least local beer and *baijiu*.

Soft drinks

Canned drinks, usually sold unchilled, include various lemonades and colas. **Fruit juices** can be unusual and refreshing, however, flavoured with chunks of lychee, lotus and water chestnuts. **Coffee** is grown and drunk in Yunnan and Hainan, and imported brews are available in cafés; you can buy instant powder in any supermarket. **Milk** is sold in powder form as baby food, and increasingly in bottles for adult consumption as its benefits for invalids and the elderly become accepted wisdom. Sweetened **yoghurt drinks**, available all over the country in little packs of six, are a popular treat for children, though their high sugar content won't do your teeth much good on a regular basis.

The media

The Chinese news agency, Xinhua, is a state-run organization that supplies both the national print and TV media. Most content is Party-controlled and censored, though there is a growing openness about social issues as long as no fingers are pointed towards the central government. Some stories about corrupt local officials, armed confrontations between developers, peasants being forced off their land, or the appalling conditions of coal-mine workers do occasionally get through the net, though both journalists and editors take a risk reporting such things: several doing so have been jailed by the government or even beaten to death by the thugs they were trying to expose.

Newspapers and magazines

The national **Chinese-language newspaper** is the *People's Daily* (with an online English edition at Ⓦenglish.peopledaily.com.cn), though all provincial capitals and many major cities produce their own dailies with a local slant. **Lifestyle magazines** have really taken off in the last few years, and newsagent stalls sag under the weight of publications covering fashion, teen, interior furnishings and countless other subjects.

The only **English-language newspaper** on the mainland is the *China Daily* (Ⓦwww.chinadaily.com.cn), which is scarce outside Beijing. As well as the predictably mind-numbing stories of economic success the paper also has a Beijing listings section and articles on uncontroversial aspects of Chinese culture. Other official English-language publications such as *Beijing Review* and *Business Beijing* are glossy titles, again very difficult to get hold of outside the capital, with articles on investment opportunities and the latest state successes, as well as interesting places to visit.

A good range of English-language newspapers and magazines is published in **Hong Kong**, including the *South China Morning Post*, the *Hong Kong Standard*, the *Eastern Express* and the *Far Eastern Economic Review*. Asian editions of a number of international magazines and newspapers are also produced here – *Time*, *Newsweek*, the *Asian Wall Street Journal* and *USA Today*, for example. These have so far remained openly critical of Beijing on occasion, despite the former colony's changeover to Chinese control.

Several cities also have free **English-language magazines aimed at expats** containing listings of local venues and events, plus classifieds and feature articles; they're monitored by the authorities, though this doesn't stop them sailing quite close to the wind at times. In large cities, you'll also find copies of (generally uncensored) imported publications such as *Time, Newsweek* and the *Far Eastern Economic Review*.

Television and radio

Chinese **television** comprises a dozen or so channels run by the state television company, **CCTV**, plus a host of regional stations; not all channels are available across the country. Most of the content comprises news, flirty game shows, travel and wildlife documentaries, soaps and historical dramas, and bizarre song-and-dance extravaganzas featuring performers in fetishistic, tight-fitting military outfits entertaining party officials with rigor-mortis faces. Tune in to **CCTV 1** for news; **CCTV 5** is dedicated to sport; **CCTV 6** shows films (with at least one war feature a day, in which the Japanese are shown getting mightily beaten); **CCTV 9** broadcasts an **English-language** mix of news, documentaries and travel shows; while **CCTV 11** concentrates on Chinese opera. The **regional stations** are sometimes more adventurous, with a current trend for hard-hitting investigative reporting and reality TV shows, and there's a growing availability of **cable and satellite stations** – the latter often foreign – which seem to enjoy comparatively little censorship.

On the **radio** you're likely to hear the latest soft ballads, or versions of Western pop songs sung in Chinese. For **news from home**, you'll need to bring a **shortwave radio** with you; see the websites of the **BBC World Service** (Ⓦwww.bbc.co.uk/worldservice), **Radio Canada** (Ⓦwww.rcinet.ca), the **Voice of America** (Ⓦwww.voa.gov) and **Radio Australia** (Ⓦwww.abc.net.au/ra) for schedules and frequencies.

Festivals

China celebrates many secular and religious festivals, three of which – the Spring Festival (Chinese New Year), Labour Day and National Day – are known as "Golden Weeks" and involve nationwide holidays where the entire population are encouraged to spend money by travelling and shopping, thus supporting the economy. Avoid travel yourself during these times, however, as the country's transport network becomes severely overloaded.

Most festivals take place according to dates in the **Chinese lunar calendar**, in which the first day of the month is the time when the moon is at its thinnest, with the full moon marking the middle of the month. By the Gregorian calendar used in the West, such festivals fall on a different day every year – check online for the latest dates. Most festivals celebrate the turning of the seasons or auspicious dates, such as the eighth day of the eighth month (eight is a lucky number in China), and are times for gift giving, family reunion and feasting. In the countryside, lanterns are lit and **firecrackers** (banned in the cities) are set off. It's always worth visiting temples on festival days, when the air is thick with incense, and people queue up to kowtow to altars and play games that bring good fortune, such as trying to hit the temple bell by throwing coins.

Aside from the following national festivals, China's **ethnic groups** punctuate the year with their own ritual observances, which are described in the relevant chapters of the Guide. In Hong Kong, all the national Chinese festivals are celebrated.

Spring Festival (Chinese New Year)

The **Spring Festival** is two weeks of festivities marking the beginning of the lunar **New Year**, usually in late January or early February. In Chinese astrology, each year is associated with one of twelve animals, and the passing into a new phase is a momentous occasion. The festival sees China at its most colourful, with shops and houses decorated with good-luck messages, and stalls and shops selling paper money, drums and costumes. The first day of the festival is marked by a family feast at which *jiaozi* (dumplings) are eaten, sometimes with coins hidden inside. To bring luck, people dress in red clothes (red being a lucky colour) and eat fish, since the Chinese script for fish resembles the script for "surplus", something everyone wishes to enjoy during the year. Firecrackers are let off almost constantly to scare ghosts away and, on the fifth day, to honour **Cai Shen**, god of wealth (in the cities, where fireworks are banned, people play recordings of explosions as a substitute). Another ghost-scaring tradition is the pasting up of images of door gods at the threshold. Outside the home, New Year is celebrated at **temple fairs**, which feature acrobats, drummers and clouds of smoke as the Chinese light incense sticks to placate the gods. The celebrations end with the **lantern festival**, when the streets are filled with multicoloured paper lanterns, a tradition dating from the Han dynasty. Many places also have flower festivals and street processions with paper dragons and other animals parading through the town. It's customary at this time to eat *tang yuan*, glutinous rice balls stuffed with sweet sesame paste.

A holidays and festivals calendar

January/February Two-week-long Spring Festival (see box above).

February Tiancang Festival On the twentieth day of the first lunar month, Chinese peasants celebrate Tiancang, or Granary Filling Day, in the hope of ensuring a good harvest later in the year.

March Guanyin's Birthday Guanyin, the Bodhisattva of Mercy, and probably China's most popular deity, is celebrated on the nineteenth day of the second lunar month.

April 5 Qingming Festival This festival, also referred to as Tomb Sweeping Day, is the time to visit the graves of ancestors and burn ghost money in honour of the departed.

April 13–15 Dai Water Splashing Festival Anyone on the streets of Xishuangbanna, in Yunnan province, is fair game for a soaking.

May 1 Labour Day Now just the main day of a week-long national holiday when everyone goes on the move.

May 4 Youth Day Commemorating the student demonstrators in Tian'anmen Square in 1919, which gave rise to the Nationalist "May Fourth Movement". It's marked in most cities with flower displays.

June 1 Children's Day Most schools go on field trips, so if you're visiting a popular tourist site, be prepared for mobs of kids in yellow baseball caps.

June/July Dragon-boat Festival On the fifth day of the fifth lunar month, dragon-boat races are held in memory of the poet Qu Yuan, who drowned himself in 280 BC. Some of the most famous venues for this festival in the country are Yueyang in Hunan province, and Hong Kong. The traditional food to accompany the celebrations is zongzi (lotus-wrapped rice packets).

August/September Ghost Festival The Chinese equivalent of Halloween, this is a time when ghosts from hell are supposed to walk the earth. It's not celebrated so much as observed; it's regarded as an inauspicious time to travel, move house or get married.

September/October Moon Festival On the fifteenth day of the eighth month of the lunar calendar, the Chinese celebrate the Moon Festival, also known as the Mid-Autumn Festival, a time of family reunion that is celebrated with fireworks and lanterns. Moon cakes, containing a rich filling of sugar, lotus-seed paste and walnut, are eaten, and plenty of spirits consumed. In Hong Kong, the cakes sometimes contain salted duck-egg yolks.

September/October Double Ninth Festival Nine is a number associated with yang, or male energy, and on the ninth day of the ninth lunar month such qualities as assertiveness and strength are celebrated. It's believed to be a good time for the distillation (and consumption) of spirits.

September 28 Confucius Festival The birthday of Confucius is marked by celebrations at all Confucian temples. It's a good time to visit Qufu, in Shandong province, when elaborate ceremonies are held at the temple there.

October 1 National Day Another anchor for a week-long holiday when everyone has time off to celebrate the founding of the People's Republic. TV is even more dire than usual as it's full of programmes celebrating Party achievements.

December 25 Christmas This is marked as a religious event only by the faithful, but for everyone else it's an excuse for a feast and a party.

Sport and outdoor activities

In 2008, of course, China hosts the Olympics, and athletic passion has become almost a patriotic duty. But the most visible forms of exercise are fairly timeless; head to any public space in the morning and you'll see citizens going through all sorts of martial-arts routines, playing ping pong and street badminton, even ballroom dancing. Sadly though, facilities for organized sport are fairly limited.

The Chinese are good at "small ball" games such as squash and badminton, and, of course, table tennis, at which they are world champions, but admit room for improvement in the "big ball" games, such as **football**. Nevertheless, Chinese men follow foreign football avidly, particularly foreign teams with Chinese players, such as (at the time of writing) Manchester City. English, Spanish and German league games are shown on CCTV5. There's also a national obsession amongst students for **basketball**, which predates the recent rise to international fame of NBA star **Yao Ming**, who plies his trade for the Houston Rockets.

If China has an indigenous "sport", however, it's the **martial arts** – not surprising, perhaps, in a country whose history is littered with long periods of civil conflict. Today, there are hundreds of Chinese martial-arts styles, usually taught for exercise rather than for fighting – see p.1172 for more.

As for **outdoor activities**, hiking for its own sake has yet to catch on, though tourists have plenty of opportunities for step-aerobic-type exercise up long, steep staircases ascending China's many **holy mountains**. Snow sports have become popular in Dongbei, which has several **ski resorts**, while the wilds of Yunnan and Sichuan, along with Qinghai and Tibet, are drawing increasing numbers of adventurous young city-born Chinese – always dressed in the latest outdoor gear – to **mountaineering** and four-wheel-drive expeditions.

Culture and etiquette

The Chinese are, on the whole, pragmatic, materialistic and garrulous. Many of the irritations experienced by foreigners – the sniggers and the unhelpful service – can almost invariably be put down to nervousness and the language barrier, rather than hostility. Visitors who speak Chinese will encounter an endless series of delighted and amazed interlocutors wherever they go, invariably asking about their country of origin, their job and the reason they are in China.

If you're **invited** to someone's home, take along a **gift** – a bottle of spirits, some tea or an ornamental trinket are good choices (anything too utilitarian could be considered patronizing) – though your hosts won't impolitely open this in front of you. **Restaurant bills** are not shared out between the guests but instead people will go to great lengths to pay the whole amount themselves. Normally this honour will fall to the person perceived as the most senior, and as a foreigner dining with Chinese you should make some effort to stake your claim, though it is probable that someone else will grab the bill before you do. Attempting to pay a "share" of the bill will embarrass your hosts.

Privacy

The Chinese have almost no concept of **privacy** – even public toilets are built with partitions so low that you can chat with your neighbour while squatting. All leisure activities including visits to natural beauty spots or holy relics are done in large noisy groups, and the desire of some Western tourists to be "left alone" is variously interpreted by locals as eccentric, arrogant or even sinister.

Exotic foreigners inevitably become targets for **blatant curiosity**. People stare and point, voices on the street shout out "helloooo" twenty times a day, or – in rural areas – people even run up and jostle for a better look, exclaiming loudly to each other, *laowai, laowai* ("foreigner"). This is not usually intended to be aggressive or insulting, though the cumulative effects of such treatment can be annoying and alienating. One way to render yourself human again is to address the onlookers in Chinese, if you can.

Spitting and smoking

Various other forms of behaviour perceived as antisocial in the West are considered perfectly normal in China. Take the widespread habit of **spitting**, for example, which can be observed in buses, trains, restaurants and even inside people's homes. Outside the company of urban sophisticates, it would not occur to people that there was anything disrespectful in delivering a powerful spit while in conversation with a stranger. **Smoking**, likewise, is almost universal among men, and any attempt to stop others from lighting up is met with incomprehension. As in many countries, handing out cigarettes is a basic way of establishing goodwill, and non-smokers should be apologetic about turning down offered cigarettes.

Clothing

Chinese clothing styles lean towards the casual, though surprisingly for such an apparently conservative-minded country, summertime **skimpy clothing** is common in all urban areas, particularly among women (less so in the countryside). Even in potentially sensitive Muslim areas, many Han Chinese girls insist on wearing miniskirts and see-through blouses. Although Chinese men commonly wear short trousers and expose their midriffs in hot weather, Western men who do the same should note that the bizarre sight of hairy flesh in public – chest or legs – will instantly become the focus of giggly gossip. The generally relaxed approach to clothing applies equally when visiting temples, though in **mosques** men and women alike should cover their bodies above the wrists and ankles. As for

beachwear, bikinis and briefs are in, but nudity has yet to make its debut.

Casual clothing is one thing, but **scruffy clothing** is quite another. If you want to earn the respect of the Chinese – useful for things like getting served in a restaurant or checking into a hotel – you need to make some effort with your appearance. While the average Chinese peasant might reasonably be expected to have wild hair and wear dirty clothes, a rich foreigner doing so will arouse a degree of contempt.

Meeting people

When **meeting people** it's useful to have a name or **business card** to flash around – Chinese with business aspirations hand them out at every opportunity, and are a little crestfallen if you can't produce one in return. It's polite to take the proffered card with both hands and to have a good look at it before putting it away. If you don't speak Chinese but have your name in Chinese printed on them, they also become useful when checking in to hotels that are reluctant to take foreigners, as the staff can then copy your name into the register.

Shaking hands is not a Chinese tradition, though it is fairly common between men. Bodily contact in the form of embraces or back-slapping can be observed between same-sex friends, and these days, in cities, a boy and a girl can walk round arm in arm and even kiss without raising an eyebrow. **Voice level** in China seems to be pitched several decibels louder than in most other countries, though this should not necessarily be interpreted as a sign of belligerence.

Sex and gender issues

Women travellers in China usually find incidence of **sexual harassment** less of a problem than in other Asian countries. Chinese men are, on the whole, deferential and respectful. A more likely complaint is being ignored, as the Chinese will generally assume that any man accompanying a woman will be doing all the talking. Women on their own visiting remote temples or sights need to be on their guard – don't assume that all monks and caretakers have impeccable morals. As ever, it pays to be aware of how local women dress and behave accordingly: miniskirts and heels may be fine in the cosmopolitan cities, but fashions are much more conservative in the countryside.

Prostitution, though illegal, has made a big comeback – witness all the "hairdressers", saunas and massage parlours, every one of them a brothel. Single foreign men are likely to be approached inside hotels; it's common practice for prostitutes to phone around hotel rooms at all hours of the night. Bear in mind that the consequence of a Westerner being caught with a prostitute may be unpleasant, and that AIDS is on the increase.

Homosexuality is increasingly tolerated by the authorities and people in general, though public displays may get you in trouble outside the more cosmopolitan cities. There are gay bars in most major cities, especially Beijing and Shanghai.

Dating a local won't raise many eyebrows in these relaxed times, though displays of mixed-race public affection certainly will.

Shopping

China is a good place for shopping, especially for tourist souvenirs, clothes, fake goods and computer software. Even small villages usually have markets, often specializing in just one thing – groceries, clothes or antiques, for example – while larger cities will also have big department stores, shopping malls and even international supermarket chains.

Prices in stores will be fixed, but **discounts** are common: they're marked by a number between one and nine and the character for *zhe* (discount), indicating the percentage of the original price you have to pay – "8 *zhe*", for example, means that the item is on sale at eighty percent of its original price. At **markets**, however, you're expected to **bargain** for goods unless prices are displayed, though even here there's some latitude. If you can speak Chinese, hang around for a while to get an idea what others are paying, or just ask at a few stalls selling the same things; Chinese shoppers usually state the price they're willing to pay, rather than beginning low and working up to it after haggling. Don't become obsessed about saving every last yuan; being charged more than locals and getting ripped off from time to time is almost inevitable.

Souvenirs popular with foreign tourists include "chops" (stone seals with your name engraved in characters on the base); all manner of reproduction antiques, from porcelain to furniture; mementoes of Mao and the Cultural Revolution – Little Red Books and cigarette lighters that chime "*The East is Red*"; T-shirts and "old-style" Chinese clothes; scroll paintings; and ethnic jewellery and embroideries. Chinese tourists also look for things like local teas, "purple sand" teapots and bright tack. Pretty much the same selection is sold at all tourist sites, irrespective of relevancy. For **real antiques**, you need specialist stores or markets – some are listed in the guide – where anything genuine is meant to be marked with a wax seal and requires an export licence to take out of the country. The Chinese are clued-up, avid collectors, so don't expect to find any astounding bargains.

Clothes are a very good deal in China, with brand stores such as Giordano, Baleno, Meters/Bonwe and Yishion selling smart-casual wear, and specialist stores stocking outdoors and hiking gear – all for a fraction of what you'd pay at home. Fashion-concious cities such as Shanghai and Hong Kong also have **factory outlet** stores, selling last year's designs at low prices. **Sizes** bear no relationship to what it says on the label, so always try things on before buying them. Silk and other **fabrics** are also good value, if you're into making your own clothes. **Shoes** are inexpensive, too, though sizes are relatively limited.

Just about every market and bookstore in China has a range of **music CDs** of everything from Beijing punk to Beethoven, plus **VCDs** and **DVDs** of martial-arts movies (often subtitled – check on the back), vintage and recent foreign films, instructional martial-arts or language courses, and computer software. While extremely cheap at ¥2–25, most of this is **pirated** (the discs may be confiscated at customs when you get home). Note also that Chinese DVD films may be region-coded for Asia, so check the label and whether your player at home will handle them. There are no such problems with CDs or VCDs.

Travel essentials

Children

Children in China are, thanks to the one-child policy, usually indulged and pampered, and foreigners travelling with children can expect to receive lots of attention from curious locals – and the occasional admonition that the little one should be wrapped up warmer.

While **formula and nappies** might be available in modern, big city supermarkets such as Carrefour, elsewhere you'll need to bring a supply (and any **medication** if required) with you – local kids don't use nappies, just pants with a slit at the back, and when baby wants to go, mummy points him at the gutter. Similarly, changing facilities and baby-minding services are virtually unknown on the mainland outside high-end international hotels. Don't breast-feed in public.

Hong Kong is the only part of China where children are specifically catered to by attractions such as Ocean World and Disneyland; elsewhere, the way that most Chinese tourist sites are decked up like fairground rides makes them attractive for youngsters in any case. Things to watch for include China's poor levels of **hygiene** (keeping infants' and toddlers' hands clean can be a full-time occupation), spicy or just unusual food, plus the **stress levels** caused by the ambient crowds, pollution and noise found in much of the country – though it often seems to affect parents worse than children.

Costs

China is an **expensive** place to travel compared with the rest of Asia. Though food and transport are good value, accommodation is usually expensive for what you get. Actual prices vary considerably between regions: Hong Kong and Macau are as costly as Europe or the US; the developed eastern provinces are expensive by Chinese standards; while the further west you go, the more prices fall.

By doing everything cheaply and sticking mostly to the less expensive interior provinces, you can survive on £20/US$40/¥300 a day; travel a bit more widely and in better comfort and you're looking at £40/US$80/¥600 a day; while travelling in style and visiting only key places along the east coast, you could run up daily expenses of £80/US$160/¥1200 and above.

It used to be government policy to **surcharge** foreigners for public transport and admission fees for sights. Though the practice is officially banned, you might still be sold the most expensive option for these things, without being informed of less costly alternatives; take comfort in the fact that Chinese tourists suffer the same treatment. **Discount rates** for pensioners and students are available for many entry fees, however; students generally need a Chinese student card, though ISIC cards sometimes work; pensioners can often just use their passports to prove they are over 60 (women) or 65 (men). Note that high-end restaurants and hotels add a ten- or fifteen-percent **service charge** to the bill.

Crime and personal safety

While the worst that happens to most visitors to China is that they have their pocket picked on a bus or get **scammed** (see box, p.58), you do need to take care. Passports and money should be kept in a concealed money belt, and it's a good idea to keep some foreign notes – perhaps around US$200 – separately from the rest of your cash, together with your traveller's-cheque receipts, insurance policy details and photocopies of your passport and visa. Be wary on **buses**, the favoured haunt of **pickpockets**, and **trains**, particularly in hard-seat class and on overnight journeys. Take a chain and padlock to secure your luggage in the rack.

Hotel rooms are on the whole secure, dormitories much less so, though often it's your fellow travellers who are the problem here. Most hotels should have a safe, but it's not unusual for things to go missing from these.

Scams

There's been a recent rise in professional **con artists** targeting tourists – especially in places such as Shanghai, Beijing and Guilin – with variations on the following scam. A sweet-looking young couple, a pair of girls, or perhaps a kindly old man, will ask to practise their English or offer to show you round. Having befriended you – which may take hours – they will suggest some refreshment, and lead you to a teahouse, art gallery or restaurant. After eating or drinking, you will be presented with a bill for thousands of yuan, your new "friends" will vanish or pretend to be shocked, and some large gentlemen will appear. It's hard to believe just how convincing these people can be – only eat or drink with a stranger if you know how much you're expected to pay.

On the street, try not to be too ostentatious with flashy jewellery or watches, and be discreet when taking out your cash. Wandering around cities late at night is as bad an idea in China as anywhere else; similarly, walking alone across the countryside is ill-advised, particularly in remote regions. If anyone does try to rob you, try to stay calm but don't resist.

You may see stress-induced **street confrontations**, though these rarely result in violence, just a lot of shouting. Another irritation, particularly in the southern cities, are gangs of **child beggars**, organized by a nearby adult. They target foreigners and can be very hard to shake off; handing over money usually results in increased harassment.

The police

The **police**, known as the **Public Security Bureau** or **PSB** (*gong'an ju* in Chinese), are recognizable by their dark blue uniforms and caps, though there are a lot more around than you might at first think, as plenty are undercover. They have much wider powers than most Western police forces, including establishing the guilt of criminals – trials are used only for deciding the sentence of the accused (though this is changing and China now has the beginnings of an independent judiciary). If the culprit is deemed to show proper remorse, this will result in a more lenient sentence.

The PSB also have the job of looking after foreigners, and you'll most likely have to seek them out for **visa extensions**, reporting theft or losses, and obtaining permits for otherwise closed areas of the country (mostly in Tibet). On occasion, they might seek you out; it's common for the police to call round to your hotel room if you're staying in an out-of-the-way place – they usually just look at your passport and then move on.

While individual police can go out of their way to help foreigners, the PSB itself has all the problems of any police force in a country where corruption is widespread, and it's best to minimize contact with them.

Emergency numbers

Police ⓣ110
Fire ⓣ119
Ambulance ⓣ120
Though you are generally better off taking a taxi to the nearest hospital than calling for an ambulance.

Offences to avoid

With adjacent opium-growing areas in Burma and Laos, and a major Southeast Asian distribution point in Hong Kong, China has a massive **drug problem**. Heroin use has become fairly widespread in the south, particularly in depressed rural areas, and ecstasy is used in clubs and discos. In the past, the police have turned a blind eye to foreigners with drugs, as long as no Chinese are involved, but you don't want to test this out. On the annual UN anti-drugs day in June, China regularly holds mass **executions** of convicted drug offenders.

Visitors are not likely to be accused of **political crimes**, but foreign residents, including teachers or students, may find themselves expelled from the country for talking about politics or religion. The Chinese they talk to will be treated less leniently. In Tibet, and at sensitive border areas, censorship is taken much more seriously; **photographing** military installations (which can include major road bridges), instances of police brutality or gulags is not a good idea.

Electricity

The electricity supply runs on 220 volts, with the most common type of **plug** a dual flat prong, except in Hong Kong, where they favour the UK-style square triple prong. Adaptors are widely available from neighbourhood hardware stores.

Entry requirements

All foreign nationals require a **visa** to enter mainland China, available worldwide from Chinese embassies and consulates and through specialist tour operators and visa agents, and online. However, they're easiest to obtain **in Hong Kong** – often without the documentation insisted on by overseas agents – if you're planning to come that way (see box, p.650).

Visas must be used within three months of issue, and **cost** US$30–100 depending on the visa type, the length of stay, the number of entries allowed, and your nationality. Your passport must be valid for at least another six months from your planned date of entry into China, and have at least one blank page for visas. You'll be asked your **occupation** – it's not wise to admit to being a journalist, photographer or writer, as you might be called in for an interview. At times of political sensitivity you may be asked for a copy of any air tickets and hotel bookings in your name.

Single-entry tourist visas (L) are generally valid for a month from date of entry, but the authorities will usually grant a request for a two- or three-month visa if asked, though they might only issue visas of short duration at times of heavy tourist traffic. A **business visa** (F) is valid for between three months and two years and can be either multiple or single entry; to apply, you'll need an official invitation from a government-recognized Chinese organization (except in Hong Kong, where you can just buy one). **Twelve-month work visas** (Z) again require an invitation, plus a **health certificate**.

Students intending to study in China for less than six months need an invitation or letter of acceptance from a college there and they'll be given an F visa. If you're intending study for longer than six months, there is an additional form, available from Chinese embassies and online, and you will also need a health certificate; then you'll be issued with an X visa, which allows you to stay and study for up to a year.

You're allowed to **import** into China up to 400 cigarettes, 2l of alcohol, 20fl (590 ml) of perfume and up to 50g of gold or silver. You can't take in more than ¥6000, and foreign currency in excess of US$5000 or the equivalent must be declared. It's illegal to import **printed or filmed matter** critical of the country, but this is currently only a problem with Chinese border guards at crossings from Vietnam, who have recently begun confiscating guidebooks to China that contain maps showing Taiwan as a separate country (such as this one); keep them buried in the bottom of your bags.

Chinese embassies and consulates

Australia 15 Coronation Drive, Yarralumla, Canberra, ACT 2600 ⓣ02/6273 4780, ⓦwww.au.china-embassy.org. Also consulates at 77 Irving Rd, Toorak, Victoria (visa & passport enquiries ⓣ03/9804 3683); 539 Elizabeth St, Surry Hills (ⓣ02/9698 7929); 39 Dunblane St, Camperdown, New South Wales (ⓣ02/8595 8000); and 45 Brown St, East Perth (ⓣ02/9222 0321).

Canada 515 St Patrick St, Ottawa, Ontario K1N 5H3 ⓣ1-613/234-2682, ⓦwww.chinaembassycanada.org. Visas can also be obtained from the consulates in Calgary, Toronto and Vancouver.

Ireland 40 Ailesbury Rd, Dublin 4 ⓣ01/269 1707.

New Zealand 2–6 Glenmore St, Wellington ⓣ04/474 9631, plus a consulate in Auckland ⓣ09/525 1589; ⓦwww.chinaconsulate.org.nz.

South Africa 965 Church Street, Arcadia, Pretoria ⓣ012/342 4194, ⓦwww.chinese-embassy.org.za.

UK 31 Portland Place, London W1B 1QD ⓣ020/7631 1430, plus a consulate at Denison House, 71 Denison Rd, Rusholme, Manchester M14 5RX ⓣ0161/224 7443; ⓦwww.chinese-embassy.org.uk.

USA 2300 Connecticut Ave NW, Washington DC 20008 ⓣ1-202/328-2517, ⓦwww.chinese-embassy.org. Also consulates in Chicago, Houston, Los Angeles, New York and San Francisco.

Visa extensions

Visa extensions are handled by the **Public Security Bureau** (**PSB**), so you can apply for one in any reasonably sized town – the department will be called something like "Aliens' Entry Exit Section". The cost, and the amount of hassle you'll have, varies greatly depending on where you are and your nationality.

A **first extension**, valid for a month, is easy to obtain and will cost around ¥160. However, the particular PSB office may decide to levy extra charges on top, or even waive the fee completely. In some small towns, the process takes ten minutes; in cities, it can take up to a week. The worst place to apply is Tibet (you'll be given a week's extension at most); next worst are Beijing and then Shanghai.

A **second or third extension** is harder to get – in major cities, you will probably be turned away. PSB offices in small towns are a much better bet, and you'd be unlucky to come away without some kind of extension, though it may only be for ten or twenty days. You will be asked your reasons for wanting an extension – simply saying you want to spend more time in this wonderful country usually goes down well, or you could cite illness or transport delays. Don't admit to being low on funds. Fourth or even fifth extensions are possible, but you'll need to foster connections with a PSB office. Ask advice from a local independent travel agent – they often have the right sort of contacts. In Shanghai and Beijing, it is possible to get extra extensions from a visa agent – they advertise in the back of expat magazines.

Don't overstay your visa even for a few hours – the fine is ¥500 a day, and if you're caught at the airport with an out-of-date visa, the hassle that follows may mean you miss your flight.

Health

No vaccinations are required to visit China, except for yellow fever if you're coming from an area where the disease is endemic. It's worth taking a **first-aid kit** with you, particularly if you will be travelling extensively outside the cities, where getting hold of the appropriate medicines might be difficult. Include bandages, plasters, painkillers, oral rehydration solution, medication to counter diarrhoea, vitamin pills and antiseptic cream. A sterile set of hypodermics may be advisable, as re-use of hypodermics does occur in China. Note there is widespread ignorance of sexual health issues, and AIDS and STDs are widespread – always practise **safe sex**.

The most common health hazard in China is the **cold and flu infections** that strike down a large proportion of the population in the winter months. **Diarrhoea** is also common, usually in a mild form while your stomach gets used to unfamiliar food, but also sometimes with a sudden onset accompanied by stomach cramps and vomiting, which indicates **food poisoning**. In both instances, get plenty of rest, drink lots of water, and in serious cases replace lost salts with **oral rehydration solution** (**ORS**); this is especially important with young children. Take a few sachets with you, or make your own by adding half a teaspoon of salt and three of sugar to a litre of cool, previously boiled water. While down with diarrhoea, avoid milk, greasy or spicy foods, coffee and most fruit, in favour of bland foodstuffs such as rice, plain noodles and soup. If symptoms persist, or if you notice blood or mucus in your stools, consult a doctor as you may have **dysentery**.

To avoid stomach complaints, eat at places that look busy and clean and stick to fresh, thoroughly cooked food. Shellfish is a potential hepatitis A risk, and best avoided. Fresh fruit you've peeled yourself is safe; other uncooked foods may have been washed in unclean water. **Don't drink untreated tap water** – boiled or bottled water is widely available.

Hepatitis A is a viral infection spread by contaminated food and water, which causes an inflammation of the liver. The less common **hepatitis B** virus can be passed on through unprotected sexual contact, transfusions of unscreened blood, and dirty needles. Hepatitis symptoms include yellowing of the eyes and skin, preceded by lethargy, fever, and pains in the upper right abdomen.

Typhoid and cholera are spread by contaminated food or water, generally in localized epidemics. Symptoms of **typhoid** include headaches, high fever and constipation, followed by diarrhoea in the later stages. The disease is infectious and requires immediate medical treatment. **Cholera** begins with sudden but painless onset of watery diarrhoea, later combined with vomiting, nausea and muscle cramps. Rapid dehydration rather than the infection itself is the main danger, and should be treated with constant oral rehydration solutions if you can't get immediate medical help.

Summer outbreaks of **malaria** and **dengue fever** occur across southern China, usually in localized areas. Symptoms are similar – severe headaches, joint pains, fever and shaking – though a rash might also appear with dengue. There's no cure for dengue fever, whereas malaria can be prevented and controlled with medication; both require immediate medical attention to ensure that there are no complications. You can minimize your chances of being bitten by mosquitoes in the first place by wearing light-coloured, full-length clothing and insect repellent in the evenings when mosquitoes are active.

In tropical China, the **temperature and humidity** can take a couple of weeks to adjust to. High humidity can cause **heat rashes**, **prickly heat** and **fungal infections**. Prevention and cure are the same: wear loose clothes made of natural fibres, wash frequently and dry-off thoroughly afterwards. Talcum or anti-fungal powder and the use of mild antiseptic soap help, too.

Don't underestimate the strength of the sun in the tropics, desert regions such as Xinjiang or high up on the Tibetan Plateau. Sunscreen is not easily available in China. Signs of **dehydration** and **heatstroke** include a high temperature, lack of sweating, a fast pulse and red skin. Reducing your body temperature with a lukewarm shower will provide initial relief.

Plenty of places in China – Tibet and the north in particular – also get very **cold** indeed. Watch out here for **hypothermia**, where the core body temperature drops to a point that can be fatal. Symptoms are a weak pulse, disorientation, numbness, slurred speech and exhaustion. To prevent the condition, wear lots of layers and a hat (most body heat is lost through the head), eat plenty of carbohydrates, and stay dry and out of the wind. To treat hypothermia, get the victim into shelter, away from wind and rain, give them hot drinks – but not alcohol – and easily digestible food, and keep them warm. Serious cases require immediate hospitalization.

High altitude, in regions such as Tibet and parts of Xinjiang, Sichuan and Yunnan, prevents the blood from absorbing oxygen efficiently, and can lead to **altitude sickness**, also known as **AMS** (acute mountain sickness). Most people feel some symptoms above 3500m, which include becoming easily exhausted, headaches, shortness of breath, sleeping disorders and nausea; they're intensified if you ascend to altitude rapidly, for instance by flying direct from coastal cities to Lhasa. Relaxing for the first few days, **drinking** plenty of water, and taking painkillers will ease symptoms. Having acclimatized at one altitude you should still ascend slowly, or you can expect the symptoms to return.

If for any reason the body fails to acclimatize to altitude, serious conditions can develop including **pulmonary oedema** (characterized by severe breathing trouble, a cough and frothy white or pink sputum), and **cerebral oedema** (causing severe headaches, loss of balance, other neurological symptoms and eventually coma). The only treatment for these is **rapid descent**: in Tibet, this means flying out to Kathmandu or Chengdu without delay. If symptoms have been serious, or persist afterwards, seek immediate medical treatment.

Hospitals, clinics and pharmacies

Medical facilities in China are best in major cities with large expat populations, where there are often high-standard clinics, and the hotels may even have resident doctors. Elsewhere, larger cities and towns have hospitals, and for minor complaints there are plenty of pharmacies that can suggest remedies, though don't expect English to be spoken.

Chinese hospitals use a mix of Western and Traditional Chinese Medicine approaches, and sometimes charge high prices for simple drugs and use procedures that aren't necessary – they'll put you on a drip just to administer antibiotics – so always ask for a second opinion from a Western-trained doctor if you're worried (your embassy should be able to recommend one if none is suggested in the Guide). In an **emergency**, you're better off taking a cab than waiting for an ambulance – it's quicker and will work out much cheaper. There's virtually **no health care** in China even for its citizens; expect to pay around ¥500 as a consultation **fee**.

Pharmacies are marked by a green cross. Be wary of backstreet pharmacies, as **counterfeit drugs** are common (check for spelling mistakes in the packaging or instructions).

Medical resources for travellers

In the UK and Ireland

MASTA (Medical Advisory Service for Travellers Abroad) UK ⓣ0870/606 2782, ⓦwww.masta-travel-health.com. Forty clinics across the UK.

Tropical Medical Bureau Republic of Ireland ⓣ1850/487674, ⓦwww.tmb.ie.

In the US and Canada

Canadian Society for International Health ⓦwww.csih.org. Extensive list of travel health centres in Canada.

CDC ⓣ1-877/394-8747, ⓦwww.cdc.gov. Official US government travel-health site.

International Society for Travel Medicine ⓦwww.istm.org. A full list of clinics worldwide specializing in travel health.

In Australia, New Zealand and South Africa

Netcare Travel Clinics ⓦwww.travelclinic.co.za. Travel clinics in South Africa.

Travellers' Medical & Vaccination Centre ⓦwww.tmvc.com.au. Website lists travellers' medical and vaccination centres throughout Australia and New Zealand.

Insurance

With medical cover expensive in China you'd be wise to have **travel insurance**. There's little opportunity for dangerous sports in the country (unless crossing the road counts) so a standard policy should be sufficient.

Rough Guides has teamed up with **Columbus Direct** to offer you travel insurance that can be tailored to suit your needs. Products include a low-cost backpacker option for long stays; a short-break option for city getaways; a typical holiday package option; and others. There are also annual multi-trip policies for those who travel regularly. Different sports and activities (trekking, skiing, etc) can usually be covered if required.

See our **website** (ⓦwww.roughguides.com/website/shop) for eligibility and purchasing options. Alternatively, UK residents should call ⓣ08700/339988; Australians should call ⓣ1300/669 999 and New Zealanders should call ⓣ0800/559911. All other nationalities should call ⓣ+44 8708/902843.

Internet

Internet bars with high-speed connections are everywhere in China, from big cities – where some seat hundreds of people – to rural villages. They're invariably full of network-gaming teenagers, and are usually slightly hidden away off main roads, rarely on ground floors. **Signs** are only ever in Chinese – see the Language section, p.1219, for the "net bar" characters. They're generally open 24hrs and **cost** ¥2–5/hour, though you may have to pay a ¥10 deposit and each bar has its own setup: sometimes you're given a card with a password to use on any available machine, sometimes the staff log you in at a particular terminal. Technically, you are supposed to show your passport before being allowed near a computer, though this rule will only be enforced in big cities.

All large hotels have **business centres** where you can get online, but this is expensive, especially in the classier places (around ¥30/hr). Better value are the **backpacker hostels**, where getting online costs around ¥5/hr or is free. But the best deal is to tote a **laptop** – cities such as Beijing, Shanghai, Xi'an and Chengdu have cafés with free **Wi-Fi**, and motel chains (and even some youth hostels) have ADSL sockets in their rooms.

In an attempt to keep control of news and current affairs availability, China's Internet censors have set up the dryly named "**Great Firewall**", which blocks access to any websites that are deemed undesirable by the state – you'll likely find the BBC, flickr and wikipedia blocked, for example. To get around it, you need to use a **web proxy** such as "Anonymouse" (http://anonymouse.org/anonwww.html), which doesn't require you to install any software (just access the website and then use it like a normal browser); or TOR (http://tor.eff.org), which requires about 4.5MB and works well with Firefox. Proxies are not always effective and also slow down computer operation.

Laundry

Big city hotels, and youth hostels all over, offer a **laundry service** for anything between ¥10 and ¥100; alternatively, some hostels have self-service facilities or you can use your room sink (every corner store in China sells **washing powder**). Otherwise, ask at accommodation either for the staff to wash your clothes or for the nearest **laundry**, where they usually charge by dry weight. Laundromats are virtually unknown in China.

Living in China

It is becoming increasingly easy for foreigners to live in China full time, whether as a student, a teacher or for work. Anyone planning to stay more than six months is required to pass a **medical** (from approved clinics) proving that they don't have any venereal disease – if you do have a VD, expect to be deported and your passport endorsed with your ailment.

Many mainland cities – including Beijing, Shanghai, Guangzhou, Kunming and Chengdu – have no restrictions on where foreigners can **reside**, though either you or your landlord must register with the local PSB. **Property rental** is inexpensive if you avoid purpose-built foreign enclaves – two-bedroom flats cost upwards of ¥600 a month, though ¥5000 and above is more likely in a city like Shanghai. The easiest way to find accommodation is to go through an **agent**, who will generally charge one month's rent as a fee. There are plenty who advertise in expat magzines and online.

Teaching

There are **schemes** in operation to place **foreign teachers** in Chinese educational institutions – contact your nearest Chinese embassy (see p.59 for addresses) for details. Some employers ask for a TEFL qualification, though a degree, or simply the ability to speak the language as a native, is usually enough.

The standard **teaching salary** for a foreigner is ¥3500 per month for a bachelor's degree, ¥4000 for a master's degree and ¥5000 for a doctorate. This isn't enough to put much away, but you should also get subsidized on-campus accommodation, plus a fare to your home country, one way for a single semester and a return for a year's work. The workload is usually fourteen hours a week and, if you work a year you get paid through the winter holiday. Most teachers find their students keen, hard-working, curious and obedient, and report that it was the contact with them that made the experience worthwhile. That said, avoid talking about religion or politics in the classroom as this can get them into trouble. You'll earn more – up to ¥150/hr – in a **private school**, though be aware of the risk of being ripped off by a commercial agency (you might be given more classes to teach than you'd signed up for, for example). Check out the institution thoroughly before committing yourself.

Studying

Many universities in China now host substantial populations of **Western students**, especially in Beijing, Shanghai and Xi'an. Indeed, the numbers of foreigners at these places are so large that in some ways you're shielded from much of a "China experience", and you may find smaller centres like Chengdu and Kunming offer both a mellower pace of life and more contact with Chinese outside the campus.

Most foreign students come to China to study **Mandarin**, though there are many additional options available – from martial arts to traditional opera or classical literature – once you break the language barrier. Courses cost from the equivalent of US$2400 a year, or US$800 a semester. Hotel-style campus accommodation costs around US$10 a day; most people move out as soon as they speak enough Chinese to rent a flat.

Your first resource is the nearest Chinese embassy, which can provide a list of contact details for Chinese universities offering the courses you are interested in; most universities also have English-language **websites**. Be aware, however, that promotional material may have little bearing on what is actually provided; though teaching standards are good, university administration departments are often confused or misleading places. Ideally, visit the campus first and be wary of paying course fees up front until you've spoken to a few students.

Working

There is plenty of **work** available for foreigners in mainland Chinese cities, where a whole section of expat society get by as actors, cocktail barmen, Chinglish correctors, models, freelance writers and so on. To really make any money here, however, you need to either be employed by a foreign company or start your own business.

China's vast markets and WTO membership present a wealth of **commercial opportunities** for foreigners. However, anyone wanting to do business here should do thorough research beforehand. The difficulties are formidable – red tape and shady business practices abound. Remember that the Chinese do business on the basis of mutual trust and pay much less attention to contractual terms or legislation. Copyright and trademark laws are often ignored, and any successful business model will be immediately copied. You'll need to develop your *guanxi* – connections – assidiously, and cultivate the virtues of patience, propriety and bloody-mindedness.

Mail

The Chinese mail service is fast and efficient, with letters taking a day to reach destinations in the same city, two or more days to other destinations in China, and up to several weeks to destinations abroad. **Overseas postage rates** are fairly expensive and vary depending on weight, destination and also – not so surprising given China's size – where you are in the country. An **Express Mail Service (EMS)** operates to most countries and to most destinations within China; besides cutting delivery times, the service ensures the letter or parcel is sent by registered delivery.

Main post offices are open daily between about 8am and 8pm; smaller offices may keep shorter hours or close at weekends. As well as at post offices, you can post letters in green **postboxes**, though these are rare outside big cities.

To send **parcels**, turn up with the goods you want to send and the staff will sell you a box and pack them in for ¥15 or so. Once packed, but before the parcel is sealed, it must be checked at the customs window and you'll have to complete masses of paperwork, so don't be in a hurry. If you are sending valuable goods bought in China, put the receipt or a photocopy of it in with the parcel, as it may be opened for customs inspection farther down the line.

Poste restante services are available in any city. Mail is kept for several months, and you'll need to present ID when picking it up. Have letters addressed to you c/o Poste Restante, GPO, street, town or city, province. Check under both your surname and given names, as mail can easily be misfiled.

Maps

Street maps are available in China from street kiosks, hotel shops and bookshops for almost every town and city. Most are in Chinese only, showing bus routes, hotels, restaurants and tourist attractions; local bus, train and flight timetables are often printed on the back as well. The same vendors also sell pocket-sized provincial **road atlases**, again in Chinese only.

Some of the major cities and tourist destinations also produce **English-language** maps, available at upmarket hotels, principal tourist sights, or tour operators' offices. In Hong Kong and Macau, the local tourist offices provide free maps, which are adequate for most visitors' needs.

Countrywide maps, which you should buy before you leave home, include the excellent 1:4,000,000 map from GeoCenter, which shows relief and useful sections of all neighbouring countries, and the Collins 1:5,000,000 map. One of the best maps of Tibet is *Stanfords Map of South-Central Tibet; Kathmandu–Lhasa Route Map*.

Money

The mainland **Chinese currency** is formally called **yuan** (¥), more colloquially known as **renminbi** (RMB, literally "the people's money") or **kuai**. One yuan breaks down into ten **jiao**, also known as **mao**. **Paper money** was invented in China and is still the main form of exchange, available in ¥100, ¥50, ¥20, ¥10, ¥5 and ¥1 notes, with a similar selection of mao. One mao, five mao, and ¥1 **coins** are increasingly common, though people in rural areas may never have seen them before. China suffers regular outbreaks of **counterfeiting** – everyone checks their change for watermarks, metal threads, and the feel of the paper.

The yuan floats within a narrow range set by a basket of currencies, keeping Chinese exports cheap (much to the annoyance of the US). At the time of writing, the **exchange rate** was approximately ¥7.5 to US$1, ¥15 to £1, ¥10 to €1, ¥7 to CAN$1, ¥6 to A$1, ¥5.5 to NZ$1 and ¥1.1 to ZAR1

Hong Kong's currency is the Hong Kong **dollar** (HK$), divided into one hundred cents, while in **Macau** they use **pataca** (usually written MOP$), in turn broken down into 100 avos. Both currencies are worth slightly less than the yuan, but while Hong Kong dollars are accepted in Macau and southern China's Special Economic Zones and can be exchanged internationally, neither yuan nor pataca is any use outside the mainland or Macau respectively. Tourist hotels in Beijing, Shanghai and Guangzhou also sometimes accept payment in Hong Kong or US dollars.

Banks and ATMs

Banks in major Chinese cities are sometimes open seven days a week, though **foreign exchange** is usually only available Monday to Friday, approximately between 9am and noon and again from 2 to 5pm. All banks are closed for the first three days of the Chinese New Year, with reduced hours for the following eleven days, and at other holiday times. In Hong Kong, banks are generally open Monday to Friday from 9am to 4.30pm, until 12.30pm on Saturday, while in Macau they close thirty minutes earlier.

Cirrus, Visa and Plus **cards** can be used to make cash withdrawals from **ATMs** operated by the Bank of China, the Industrial and Commercial Bank of China, China Construction Bank and Agricultural Bank of China, as long as they display the relevant logo. In major east-coast cities, almost every one of these banks' ATMs will work with foreign cards, but elsewhere it's likely that only the main branch of the Bank of China will have a suitable machine. Note that most ATMs are inside banks or shopping centres, so close when they do, though some are accessible 24 hours a day. The maximum for each withdrawal is ¥2500; your bank back home will charge a **fee** on each withdrawal, either a fixed rate or a percentage of the transaction. Keep your **exchange receipts** and when you leave you can change your yuan into dollars or sterling at any branch of the Bank of China.

Traveller's cheque and foreign currency

Traveller's cheque are a convenient way to carry your funds around, as they can be replaced if lost or stolen – for which contingency it's worth keeping a list of the serial numbers separate from the cheques. They also attract a slightly better rate of exchange than cash, though you'll have to pay a fee when you buy them. Available through banks and travel agents, they can be cashed only at branches of the Bank of China and at tourist hotels.

It's also worth taking along a small quantity of **foreign currency** – such as US, Canadian or Australian dollars, or British pounds or euros – as cash is more widely exchangeable than traveller's cheque. Don't try to change money on the **black market** as you'll almost certainly get ripped off.

Credit cards and wiring money

China is basically a cash economy, and **credit cards**, such as Visa, American Express and MasterCard, are only accepted at big tourist hotels and the fanciest restaurants, and by some tourist-oriented shops; there is usually a four-percent handling charge. It's straightforward to obtain cash advances on a Visa card at many Chinese banks (however, the commission is a steep three percent). Visa card holders can also get cash advances using ATM machines bearing the "Plus" logo.

It's possible to **wire money** to China through Western Union (Ⓦwww.westernunion.com); funds can be collected from one of their agencies, in post offices and the Agricultural Bank of China – check their website Ⓦwww.abchina.com for further information.

Opening hours

China officially has a **five-day week**, though this only really applies to government offices, which open Monday to Friday approximately 8am to noon and again from 1 to 5pm. Generalization is difficult, though: post offices open daily, as do many shops, often keeping long, late hours, especially in big cities. Although banks *usually* close on Sundays – or for the whole weekend – even this is not always the case.

Tourist sights open every day, usually between 8am and 5pm and without a lunch break. Most public **parks** open from about 6am. **Museums** tend to have more restricted hours, often closing one day a week. If you arrive at an out-of-the-way place that seems to be closed, however, don't despair – knocking or poking around will often turn up a drowsy doorkeeper. Conversely, you may find other places locked and deserted when they are supposed to be open.

For dates of public holidays, see p.52.

Phones

Everywhere in China has an **area code**, which must be used when phoning from outside that locality; these are given for all telephone numbers throughout the Guide. **Local calls** are free from land lines, and **long-distance** China-wide calls are ¥0.3 a minute. International calls cost from ¥3.5 a minute (much cheaper if you use an IP internet phone card – see below).

Card phones, widely available in major cities, are the cheapest way to make domestic long-distance calls (¥0.2 for 3min), and can also be used for international calls (under ¥10 for 3min). They take **IC Cards**, which come in units of ¥20, ¥50 and ¥100. There's a fifty-percent discount after 6pm and on weekends. You will be cut off when your card value drops below the amount needed for the next minute. A cheaper option is the **IP card**, which can be used with any phone, and comes in ¥100 units. You dial a local number, then a PIN, then the number you're calling. Rates are as low as ¥2.4 per minute to the US and Canada, ¥3.2 to Europe.

Both IC and IP cards are sold from corner stores, mobile-phone emporiums, and from street hawkers (usually outside the mobile-phone emporiums) all over the country. Note, however, that these cards can only be used in the places you buy them – move to another city and you'll have to buy a new card.

Mobile coverage in China is excellent and comprehensive; they use the GSM system. Assuming your phone is unlocked and compatible, you can use local **SIM cards**, available from any China Mobile shop or

Dialling codes

To **call mainland China** from abroad, dial your international access code (Ⓣ00 in the UK and the Republic of Ireland, Ⓣ011 in the US and Canada, Ⓣ0011 in Australia, Ⓣ00 in New Zealand and Ⓣ27 in South Africa), then 86 (China's country code), then area code (minus initial zero) followed by the number.

To call **Hong Kong**, dial your international access code followed by Ⓣ852, then the number; and for **Macau**, dial your international access code, then Ⓣ853 and then the number.

Phoning abroad from China

To call abroad from mainland China, Hong Kong or Macau, dial Ⓣ00, then the country code (see below), then the area code minus initial zero (if any), followed by the number.

UK Ⓣ44	Ireland Ⓣ353	Australia Ⓣ61
New Zealand Ⓣ64	US & Canada Ⓣ1	South Africa Ⓣ27

street kiosk, in your home handset (you will have a new number). SIM cards **cost** upwards of ¥80 depending on how "lucky" the number is – favoured sixes and eights bump up the cost, unlucky fours make it cheaper. They come with ¥50 of time, which you extend with ¥100 prepaid cards. Making and receiving domestic calls this way costs ¥0.6 per minute; an international call will cost around ¥8 a minute, though often you can only send texts overseas. You can also **rent** mobile phones – look for the ads in expat magazines or ask at your hotel. The cheapest phones to buy will cost around ¥400; make sure the staff change the operating language into English for you.

Photography

Photography is a popular pastime among the Chinese, and all big towns and cities have photo stores selling the latest cameras (especially Hong Kong – see p.692), where you can also download your digital images onto disc for around ¥30, though prints are expensive at ¥1 each. Camera batteries, film and memory cards are fairly easy to obtain in city department stores. **Film processing** is becoming harder to arrange; it's probably best to take it home with you.

Many temples **prohibit photography** inside buildings (antiques thieves have been known to use photographs to plan robberies), and you should avoid taking pictures of anything to do with the military, or that could be construed as having strategic value – including ordinary structures such as bridges in sensitive areas along borders, in Tibet, etc.

Time

China occupies a single time zone, eight hours ahead of GMT, thirteen hours ahead of US Eastern Standard Time, sixteen hours ahead of US Pacific Time and two hours behind Australian Eastern Standard Time. There is no daylight saving.

Tourist information

The **Internet** is your best source of information before you travel, as Chinese tourist offices overseas mostly sell packages and have little to offer individual travellers. Once you reach the mainland, you'll find the **CITS** (China International Travel Service) and alternatives such as the **CTS** (China Travel Service) everywhere from large cities to obscure hamlets. While they all book flight and train tickets, local tours and accommodation, their value to independent travellers varies from office to office – some are extremely clued-up and helpful, others totally indifferent and uninformed. Don't take it for granted that anyone will speak English at these places. Other sources of information on the ground include accommodation staff or tour desks – especially at youth hostels – and backpacker cafés in destinations such as Dali and Yangshuo that see heavy numbers of foreign tourists.

Cities with large expat populations (including Beijing, Shanghai, Chengdu and Guangzhou) have English-language **magazines** with bar, restaurant and other **listings**. These are usually distributed free in bars and upmarket hotels, and often have accompanying websites.

Hong Kong and Macau both have efficient and helpful tourist information offices, and several free listings magazines; see p.652 and p.699 for more on these.

Chinese tourist offices abroad

Australia 11th Floor, 234 George St, Sydney, New South Wales 2000 ⓣ 02/9252 9838, ⓦ www.cnto.org.au.

Canada 480 University Ave, Suite 806, Toronto, Ontario M5G 1V2 ⓣ 0416/599-6636, ⓦ www.tourismchina-ca.com.

UK 71 Warwick Rd, London SW5 9HB ⓣ 020/7373 0888.

USA 350 Fifth Ave, Suite 6413, Empire State Building, New York, NY 10118 toll-free ⓣ 1-888/760-8218, ⓔ ny@cnto.org; 550 North Brand Blvd, Suite 910, Glendale, CA 91203 toll free ⓣ 1-800/670-2228, ⓔ la@cnto.org.

Travel advice

Australian Department of Foreign Affairs ⓦ www.dfat.gov.au, ⓦ www.smartraveller.gov.au.

British Foreign & Commonwealth Office ⓦ www.fco.gov.uk.

Canadian Department of Foreign Affairs ⓦ www.dfait-maeci.gc.ca.

Irish Department of Foreign Affairs ⓦ www.foreignaffairs.gov.ie.

New Zealand Ministry of Foreign Affairs ⓦwww.mft.govt.nz.
South African Department of Foreign Affairs ⓦwww.dfa.gov.za/consular/travel_advice.htm.
US State Department ⓦwww.travel.state.gov.

China online

China ⓦwww.china.org.cn. Magazine with state-approved news, but also regular features on archeology, living in China, film and travel.
China expat ⓦwww.chinaexpat.com. Though aimed at foreign residents, this is a useful English-language resource for anyone in the country, with a wide range of China-related articles and plenty of links.
Danwei ⓦwww.danwei.org. English-language commentary on the daily goings-on in the Chinese media, with excellent thumbnails of what China-wide papers and magazines are about.
International Campaign for Tibet ⓦwww.savetibet.org. An authoritative source of current news from Tibet.
Managing the Dragon ⓦwww.managingthedragon.com. Blog commentary on economic subjects from investor-who-lost-millions Jack Perkowski (who has since bounced back).
Olympics ⓦen.beijing2008.cn. Official English-language website for the 2008 Olympics.
Peking Duck ⓦwww.pekingduck.org. Acerbic, sometimes insightful commentary from one of China's most productive expat bloggers.
Sinomania ⓦwww.sinomania.com. A California-based site with links to current Chinese news stories and a good popular-music section, with MP3s available.
Travel China ⓦwww.travelchinaguide.com. Unusual in covering obscure places and small-group tours, as well as the normal run of popular sites and booking links.
Youku ⓦwww.youku.com. One of the many "Youtube"-style clones in China, with a similar range of content (all in Chinese).
Zhongwen ⓦwww.zhongwen.com. A handy online Chinese/English dictionary.

Travellers with disabilities

Mainland China makes few provisions for disabled travellers, though operators offering China tours for the disabled include the Kunming-based ⓦwww.travel-to-china.net, and Beijing-based ⓦwww.tour-beijing.com and ⓦwww.beijing.etours.cn. In Hong Kong, contact the Hong Kong Tourist Association (ⓦwww.hkta.org) for their free booklet, *Hong Kong Access Guide for Disabled Visitors*.

Guide

Guide

CHAPTER 1

Highlights

* **Forbidden City** Imperial magnificence on a grand scale and the centre of the Chinese universe for six centuries. See p.99

* **Temple of Heaven** This classic Ming-dynasty building, a picture in stone of ancient Chinese cosmogony, is a masterpiece of architecture and landscpae design. See p.104

* **798 Art District** This huge complex of galleries and studios provides the focus for a thriving contemporary arts scene. See p.111

* **Nanluogu Xiang** Artsy alley of laid-back cafés, restaurants and bars, at the centre of a charming neighbourhood. See p.116

* **Summer Palace** Escape the city in this serene and elegant park, dotted with imperial architecture. See p.120

* **Hotpot** A northern Chinese classic, a stew of sliced lamb, tofu, cabbage and anything else you fancy boiled up at your table. Specialist restaurants abound, but *Dong Lai Shun Fan Zhuang* is one of the best. See p.126

* **Acrobatics** The style may be vaudeville, but the stunts, performed by some of the world's greatest acrobats, are breathtaking. See p.133

* **The Great Wall** One of the world's most extraordinary engineering achievements, the old boundary between civilizations is China's must-see. See p.140

▲ The Forbidden City

1

Beijing and around

The brash modernity of **BEIJING** (the name means "Northern Capital") comes as a surprise to many visitors. Traversed by motorways (it's the proud owner of more than a hundred flyovers) and spiked with high-rises, this vivid metropolis is China at its most dynamic. For a thousand years, the drama of China's **imperial history** was played out here, with the emperor sitting enthroned at the centre of the Chinese universe, and though today the city is a very different one, it remains spiritually and politically the heart of the country. Between the swathes of concrete and glass, you'll find some of the lushest temples, and certainly the grandest remnants of the imperial age. Unexpectedly, some of the country's most pleasant scenic spots lie within the scope of a day-trip, and, just to the north of the city, one of the world's most famous sights, the long and lonely **Great Wall**, winds between hilltops.

First impressions of Beijing are of an almost inhuman vastness, conveyed by the sprawl of apartment buildings, in which most of the city's population of fifteen million are housed, and the eight-lane motorways that slice it up. It's a notion that's reinforced on closer acquaintance, from the magnificent **Forbidden City**, with its stunning wealth of treasures, the concrete desert of **Tian'anmen Square** and the gargantuan buildings of the modern executive around it, to the rank after rank of office complexes that line its mammoth roads. Outside the centre, the scale becomes more manageable, with parks, narrow alleyways and ancient sites such as the **Yonghe Gong**, the **Observatory** and, most magnificent of all, the **Temple of Heaven**, offering respite from the city's oppressive orderliness and rampant reconstruction. In the suburbs beyond, the two **summer palaces** and the **Western Hills** have been favoured retreats since imperial times.

Beijing is an invaders' city, the capital of oppressive foreign dynasties – the Manchu and the Mongols – and of a dynasty with a foreign ideology – the Communists. As such, it has assimilated a lot of outside influence, and today has an international flavour reflecting its position as the capital of a major commercial power. As the front line of China's grapple with **modernity**, it is being ripped up and rebuilt at a furious pace – attested by the cranes that skewer the skyline and the white character *chai* ("demolish") painted on old buildings. Students in the latest fashions while away their time in Internet cafés, hip-hop has overtaken the clubs, businessmen are never without their laptops, and schoolkids carry mobile phones in their lunchboxes. Rising incomes have led not just to a brash consumer-capitalist society Westerners will feel very familiar with, but also to a revival of older **Chinese culture** – witness the re-emergence of the teahouse as a genteel meeting place and the interest in imperial cuisine. In the evening, you'll see large groups of the older generation performing the

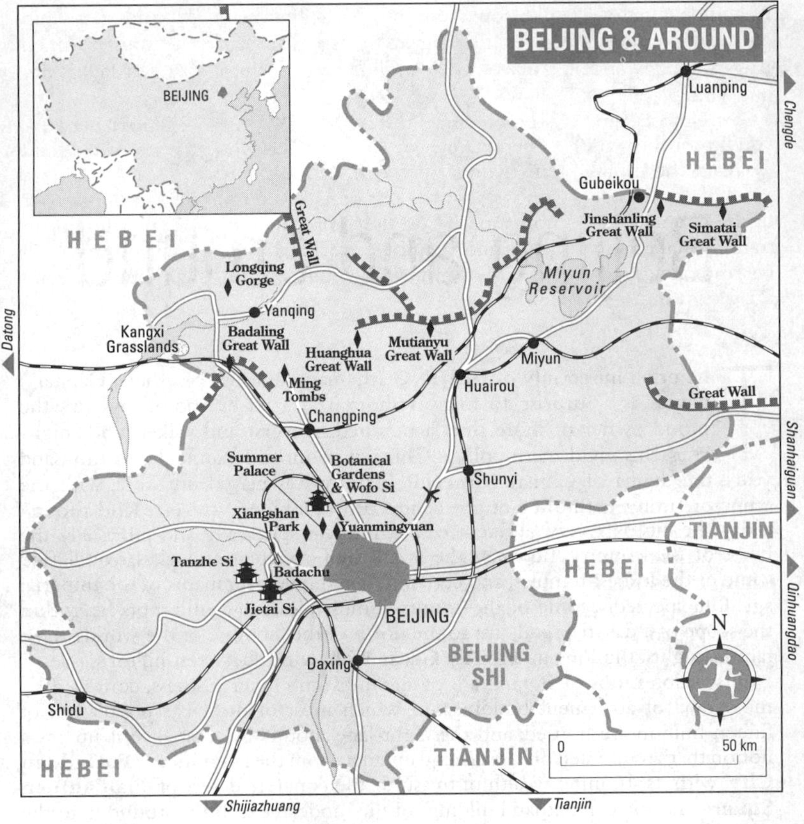

yangkou (loyalty dance), Chairman Mao's favourite dance universally learned a few decades ago, and in the *hutongs*, the city's twisted grey stone alleyways, men sit with their pet birds and pipes as they always have done.

Beijing is a city that almost everyone enjoys. For new arrivals, it provides a gentle introduction to the country, and for travellers who've been roughing it round rural China, the creature comforts on offer are a delight. But it's essentially a private city, whose surface is difficult to penetrate; sometimes, it seems to have the superficiality of a theme park. Certainly, there is something mundane about the way tourist groups are efficiently shunted around, from hotel to sight and back to hotel, with little contact with everyday reality. To get deeper into the city, wander what's left of the labyrinthine *hutongs*, "fine and numerous as the hairs of a cow" (as one Chinese guidebook puts it), and check out the little antique markets, the residential shopping districts, the smaller, quirkier sights, and the parks, some of the best in China, where you'll see Beijingers performing *tai ji* and hear birdsong – just – over the hum of traffic. Take advantage, too, of the city's burgeoning nightlife and see just how far the Chinese have gone down the road of what used to be called spiritual pollution.

If the Party had any control over it, no doubt Beijing would have the best climate of any Chinese city; as it is, it has one of the worst. The **best time to visit** is in autumn, between September and October, when it's dry and clement.

In winter, it gets very cold, down to minus 20°C, and the mean winds that whip off the Mongolian plains feel like they're freezing your ears off. Summer (June–Aug) is muggy and hot, up to 30°C, and the short spring (April & May) is dry but windy.

Getting to Beijing is no problem: as the centre of China's **transport** network you'll probably wind up here sooner or later, whether you want to or not, and to avoid the capital seems wilfully perverse. On a purely practical level, it's a good place to stock up on visas for the rest of Asia, and to arrange transport out of the country – most romantically, on the Trans-Siberian or Trans-Mongolian trains. To take in its superb sights requires a week, by which time you may well be ready to move on to China proper; Beijing is a fun place, but make no mistake, it in no way typifies the rest of the nation.

Some history

It was in Tian'anmen, on October 1, 1949, that Chairman Mao Zedong hoisted the red flag to proclaim officially the **foundation of the People's Republic**. He told the crowds that the Chinese had at last stood up, and defined liberation as the final culmination of a 150-year fight against foreign exploitation.

The claim, perhaps, was modest. Beijing's **recorded history** goes back a little over three millennia, to beginnings as a trading centre for Mongols, Koreans and local Chinese tribes. Its predominance, however, dates to the mid-thirteenth century, and the formation of **Mongol China** under Genghis and later **Kublai Khan**. It was Kublai who took control of the city in 1264, and who properly established it as a capital, replacing the earlier power centres of Luoyang and Xi'an. Marco Polo visited him here, working for a while in the city, and was clearly impressed with the level of sophistication; he observed in *The Travels*:

> So great a number of houses and of people, no man could tell the number
> I believe there is no place in the world to which so many merchants come, and dearer things, and of greater value and more strange, come into this town from all sides than to any city in the world

The **wealth** came from the city's position at the start of the Silk Road, and Polo described "over a thousand carts loaded with silk" arriving "almost each day", ready for the journey west out of China. And it set a precedent in terms of style and grandeur for the Khans, later known as emperors, with Kublai building himself a palace of astonishing proportions, walled on all sides and approached by great marble stairways.

With the accession of the **Ming dynasty**, who defeated the Mongols in 1368, the capital temporarily shifted to present-day Nanjing, but Yongle, the second Ming emperor, returned, building around him prototypes of the city's two greatest **monuments** – the Imperial Palace and Temple of Heaven. It was in Yongle's reign, too, that the basic **city plan** took shape, rigidly symmetrical, extending in squares and rectangles from the palace and inner-city grid to the suburbs, much as it is today.

Subsequent, post-Ming history is dominated by the rise and eventual collapse of the Manchus – the **Qing dynasty**, northerners who ruled China from Beijing from 1644 to the beginning of the twentieth century. The capital was at its most prosperous in the first half of the eighteenth century, the period in which the Qing constructed the legendary **Summer Palace** – the world's most extraordinary royal garden, with two hundred pavilions, temples and palaces, and immense artificial lakes and hills – to the north of the city. With the central Imperial Palace, this was the focus of endowment and the symbol of

Chinese wealth and power. However, in 1860, the Opium Wars brought British and French troops to the walls of the capital, and the Summer Palace was first looted and then burned by the British, more or less entirely to the ground.

While the imperial court lived apart, within what was essentially a separate walled city, conditions for the civilian population, in the capital's suburbs, were starkly different. Kang Youwei, a Cantonese visiting in 1895, described this dual world:

> **No matter where you look, the place is covered with beggars. The homeless and the old, the crippled and the sick with no one to care for them, fall dead on the roads. This happens every day. And the coaches of the great officials rumble past them continuously.**

The indifference, rooted according to Kang in officials throughout the city, spread from the top down. From 1884, using funds meant for the modernization of the nation's navy, the Empress Dowager Cixi had begun building a new Summer Palace of her own. The empress's project was really the last grand gesture of **imperial architecture** and patronage – and like its model was also badly burned by foreign troops, in another outbreak of the Opium War in 1900. By this time, with successive waves of occupation by foreign troops, the empire and the imperial capital were near collapse. The **Manchus abdicated** in 1911, leaving the Northern Capital to be ruled by warlords. In 1928, it came under the military dictatorship of Chiang Kaishek's **Guomindang**, being seized by the **Japanese** in 1939, and at the end of **World War II**, the city was controlled by an alliance of Guomindang troops and American marines.

The **Communists** took Beijing in January 1949, nine months before Chiang Kaishek's flight to Taiwan assured final victory. The **rebuilding of the capital**, and the erasing of symbols of the previous regimes, was an early priority. The city that Mao Zedong inherited for the Chinese people was in most ways primitive. Imperial laws had banned the building of houses higher than the official buildings and palaces, so virtually nothing was more than one storey high. The roads, although straight and uniform, were narrow and congested, and there was scarcely any industry. The new plans aimed to reverse all but the city's sense of ordered planning, with Tian'anmen Square at its heart – and initially, through the early 1950s, their inspiration was Soviet, with an emphasis on heavy industry and a series of poor-quality high-rise housing programmes.

In the zest to be free from the past and create a modern, people's capital, much of **Old Beijing** was destroyed, or co-opted: the Temple of Cultivated Wisdom became a wire factory and the Temple of the God of Fire produced electric light bulbs. In the 1940s, there were eight thousand temples and monuments in the city; by the 1960s, there were only around a hundred and fifty. Even the city walls and gates, relics mostly of the Ming era, were pulled down and their place taken by ring roads and avenues.

Much of the city's **planning policy** was disastrous, creating more problems than it solved. In 1969, when massive restoration was needed above ground, Mao instead launched a campaign to build a network of subterranean tunnels as shelter in case of war. Millions of man-hours went into constructing a useless labyrinth, built by hand, that would be no defence against modern bombs and served only to lower the city's water table. Most of the traditional courtyard houses, which were seen to encourage individualism, were destroyed. In their place went anonymous concrete buildings, often with inadequate sanitation and little running water. After the destruction of all the capital's dogs in 1950, it was the turn of sparrows in 1956. A measure designed to preserve grain, its only effect was to lead to an increase in the insect population. To combat this, all the grass was pulled up, which in turn led to dust storms in the windy winter months.

More destruction was to follow during the **Cultural Revolution**. Under Mao's guidance, Beijing's students organized themselves into a political militia

The Beijing Olympics

The only developing country with the resources to host the Olympics, and the narrow loser of the 2000 bid, Beijing was a natural choice for the **2008 Olympic Games**, though its lousy human-rights record caused plenty of protest at the nomination.

▲The mascots of the Beijing Olympics

The focus of the games is the new **Olympic Forest Park**, a vast arcadia in the far north of the city, along the old imperial axis (round about where the Yuan-dynasty city gates once stood). Its focus is Herzog and de Meuron's futuristic 90-000 seater **National Olympic Stadium**, whose massive external lattice of intertwined beams have earned it the nickname "the Bird's Nest". Though the retractable roof was scrapped in an effort to keep costs down, it still looks like it will cost almost half a billion dollars. Nearby, the **National Swimming Centre** is an equally stunning translucent block swathed in an energy-saving skin that looks like bubble wrap (this one is nicknamed "the Water Cube"). The eight-kilometre north–south corridor leading to the Olympic Forest Park has been reconstructed by Albert Speer Junior (the son of Hitler's favourite architect) as a green strip of parkland, playgrounds and walkways.

Nothing is being left to chance; **Olympic preparatory measures** include attempts to teach cabbies English, replacing "Chinglish" signs and improving the manners of the populace – public spitters are fined and the eleventh of every month is "Queing Awareness" day. High-quality "Olympic food" is being produced for the Olympic Village to ensure athletes don't get food poisioning. You can be pretty sure that stray cats and dogs and beggars will vanish from Beijing's streets just before the opening ceremony. The most serious threat to a successful games is the city's terrible **pollution**, so in the months before the Olympics traffic will be strictly controlled, with more than a million cars banned from entering the city. In order to guarantee at least some clear skies, a few days before the games the clouds over the city will be seeded (done with silver iodide fired from rockets) to force them to rain.

The **games will take place** from August 8 to August 24, with the opening ceremony beginning eight seconds past 8.08pm (eight being a fortuitous number to the Chinese) at the National Olympic Stadium. There are seven million tickets, including nearly three million for the opening and closing ceremonies; the most expensive cost ¥5000, but there are plenty of cheap seats at ¥200 or so. To get **tickets**, book online at Ⓦwww.tickets.beijing2008.cn or go to one of the thousand or so appointed branches of the Bank of China (call Ⓣ8610 952008 for locations). As for **accommodation**, rooms are likely to be ten times more expensive than normal, and booked to capacity months in advance – you can rent aparments at Ⓦwww.homestaybeijing2008.com. All public transport to the Olympic sites will be free, and you can check out bus routes by calling Ⓣ96166 and pressing "3" for English. For more information, check out the official website, Ⓦwww.beijing-2008.org.

– the **Red Guards**, who were sent out to destroy the Four Olds: old ideas, old culture, old customs and old habits. They attacked anything redolent of capitalism, the West or the Soviet Union; few of the capital's remaining ancient buildings escaped destruction. Things improved with the death of Mao and the accession of pragmatic Deng Xiaoping and his fellow moderates, who embraced capitalism, though not, as shown by the massacre at Tian'anmen Square and the surrounding events of 1989, freedom (see p.96).

Today, as the showcase city of the face-conscious People's Republic, and host to the 2008 **Olympic Games**, Beijing has become the recipient of a huge amount of investment. Infrastructure has vastly improved, with six new subway lines, and a light-rail system opening soon. Some US$12 billion has been spent on green projects, including a 125-kilometre tree belt around the city to curb the winter sandstorms that rage in from the Gobi Desert, the adoption of strict European vehicle-emission standards, and the relocation of polluting factories to the suburbs. Parks and verges have been prettified, fetid canals cleaned, and public facilities are better than anywhere else in China – the public toilets just west of Tian'anmen Square are the most expensive in the country, costing more than a million yuan. Historic sites have been opened, renovated, or, it sometimes appears, invented. With lots of money washing around for prestige projects, and no geographical constraints or old city to preserve, Beijing has become an architect's playground; huge, weirdly shaped buildings are popping up across the city – most notably, Paul Andreu's National Grand Theatre (nicknamed the "Egg") and Rem Koolhaas's double-z-shaped CCTV (the "Twisted Doughnut Building").

The city gleams like never before, but what little character Beijing had is fast disappearing as old city blocks and *hutongs* are demolished. Now, the city's main problems are the pressures of **migration** and **traffic** – car ownership has rocketed, and the streets are nearing gridlock. Despite all the green projects, the air quality is appalling, with only sixty clean-air days in 2007.

Orientation, arrival and information

There's no doubt that Beijing's initial culture shock owes much to the artificiality of the city's **layout**. The main streets are huge, wide and dead straight, aligned east–west or north–south, and extend in a series of widening rectangles across the whole thirty square kilometres of the inner capital.

The pivot of the ancient city was a north–south road that led from the entrance of the Forbidden City to the city walls. This remains today as **Qianmen Dajie**, though the main axis has shifted to the east–west road that divides Tian'anmen Square and the Forbidden City and, like all major boulevards, changes its name every few kilometres along its length. It's generally referred to as **Chang'an Jie**.

Few traces of the old city remain except in the **street names**, which look bewilderingly complex but are not hard to figure out once you realize that they are compounds of a name, plus a direction – *bei, nan, xi, dong* and *zhong* (north, south, west, east and middle) – and the words for inside and outside – *nei* and *wai* – which indicate the street's position in relation to the old city walls that enclosed the centre. Central streets often also contain the word *men* (gate), which indicates that they once had a gate in the wall along their length.

The **ring roads**, freeways arranged in concentric rectangles centring on the Forbidden City, are rapid-access corridors. The first, running round Tian'anmen

Square, is nominal, but the second and third, Erhuan Lu and Sanhuan Lu, are useful, cutting down on journey times but extending the distance travelled and therefore much liked by taxi drivers. The fourth and fifth are too out of the way to be of much interest to visitors. While most of the sights are in the city centre, most of the modern buildings – hotels, restaurants, shopping centres and flashy office blocks – are along the ring roads.

You'll soon become familiar with the experience of barrelling along a motorway in a bus or a taxi while identical blocks flicker past, not knowing which direction you're travelling in, let alone where you are. To get some sense of **orientation**, take fast mental notes on the more obvious and imposing landmarks: the Great Hall of the People in Tian'anmen Square; the *Beijing Hotel*, at the south end of Wangfujing; the oddly shaped *International Hotel* on Dongchang'an Jie; and farther east on the same road, the Friendship Store and World Trade Centre.

Arrival

The first experience most visitors have of China is the smooth ride along the motorway, lined with hoardings and jammed with cars, that leads from the airport into Beijing. Unless you arrive by train, it's a long way into the centre from either the bus stations or the airport, and even when you get into downtown you're still a good few kilometres from most hotels, which tend to cluster between the second and third ring roads. It's a good idea to hail a **taxi** from the centre to get you to your final destination rather than tussle with the buses, as the public transport system is confusing at first and the city layout rather alienating. Walking to your hotel isn't really an option, as distances are always long, exhausting at the best of times and unbearable with luggage.

By plane

The showcase **Beijing Capital Airport** was opened in 1999 on October 1, the fiftieth birthday of Communist rule. Twenty-nine kilometres northeast of the centre, it serves both international and domestic flights. There are a couple of banks and an ATM on the right as you exit through customs, and commission rates are the same as everywhere else. Get some small change if you're planning to take any buses. The CAAC office sells tickets for onward domestic flights.

Beijing arrival

Beijing	北京	*běijīng*
Beijing Capital Airport	北京首都机场	*běijīng shǒudū jīchǎng*
Bus Stations		
Deshengmen	德胜门公共汽车站	*déshèngmén gōnggòng qìchēzhàn*
Dongzhimen	东直门公共汽车站	*dōngzhímén gōnggòng qìchēzhàn*
Haihutun	海户屯公共汽车站	*hǎihùtún gōnggòng qìchēzhàn*
Zhaogongkou	赵公口公共汽车站	*zhàogōngkǒu gōnggòng qìchēzhàn*
Train Stations		
Beijing Zhan	北京站	*běijīng zhàn*
Xi Zhan	西站	*xī zhàn*
Xizhimen Zhan	西直门站	*xīzhímén zhàn*
Yongdingmen Zhan	永定门站	*yǒngdìngmén zhàn*

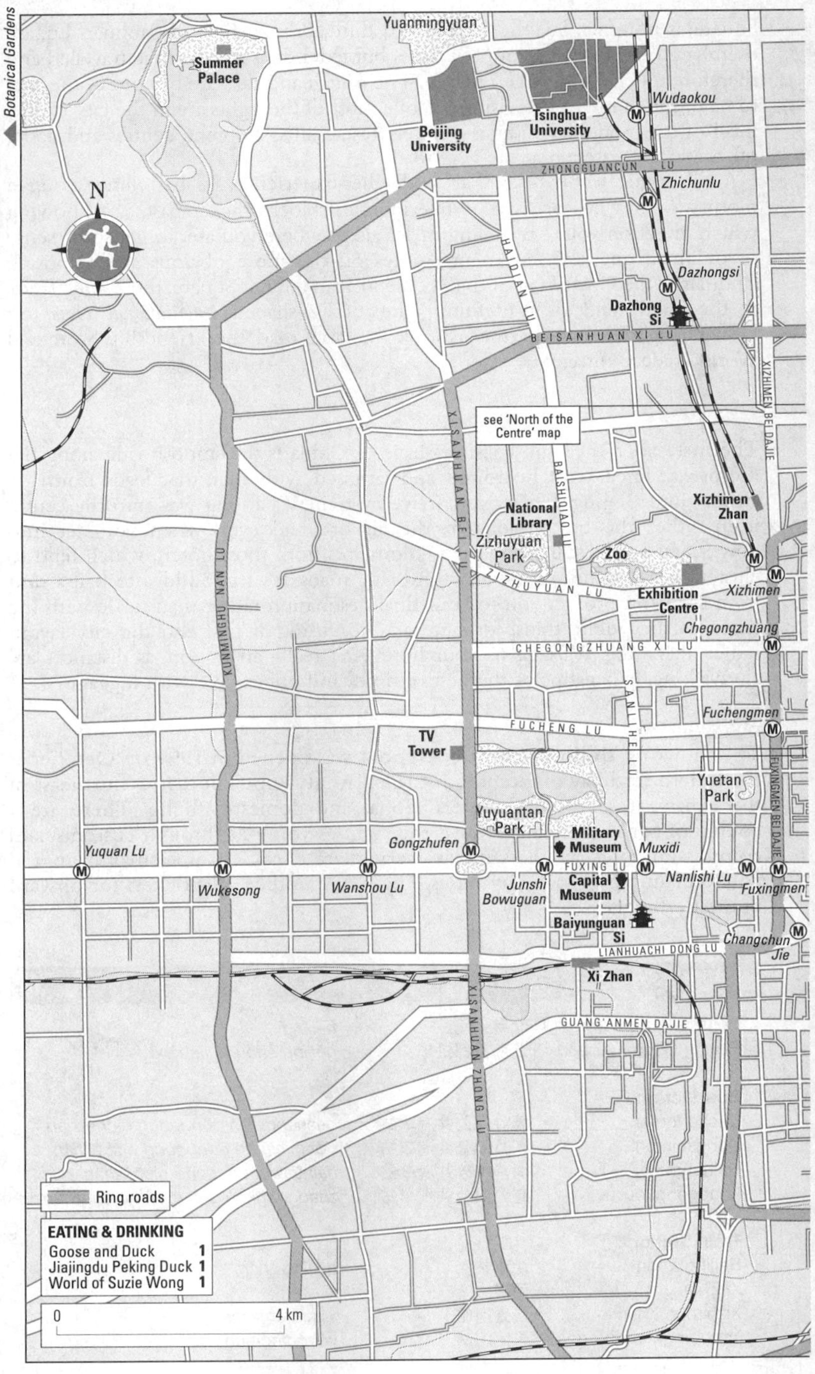
Botanical Gardens
Yuanmingyuan
Summer Palace
Beijing University
Tsinghua University
Wudaokou
ZHONGGUANCUN LU
Zhichunlu
HAIDIAN LU
Dazhongsi
Dazhong Si
BEISANHUAN XI LU
XIZHIMEN BEI DAJIE
XISANHUAN BEI LU
see 'North of the Centre' map
BAISHIQIAO LU
Xizhimen Zhan
National Library
Zizhuyuan Park
Zoo
ZIZHUYUAN LU
Exhibition Centre
Xizhimen
Chegongzhuang
CHEGONGZHUANG XI LU
KUNMINGHU NAN LU
SANLIHE LU
Fuchengmen
FUCHENG LU
TV Tower
FUXINGMEN BEI DAJIE
Yuetan Park
Yuyuantan Park
Military Museum
Gongzhufen
Muxidi
Yuquan Lu
FUXING LU
Nanlishi Lu
Junshi Bowuguan
Capital Museum
Fuxingmen
Wukesong
Wanshou Lu
Baiyunguan Si
Changchun Jie
LIANHUACHI DONG LU
Xi Zhan
GUANG'ANMEN DAJIE
XISANHUAN ZHONG LU
Ring roads
EATING & DRINKING
Goose and Duck 1
Jiajingdu Peking Duck 1
World of Suzie Wong 1
0
4 km

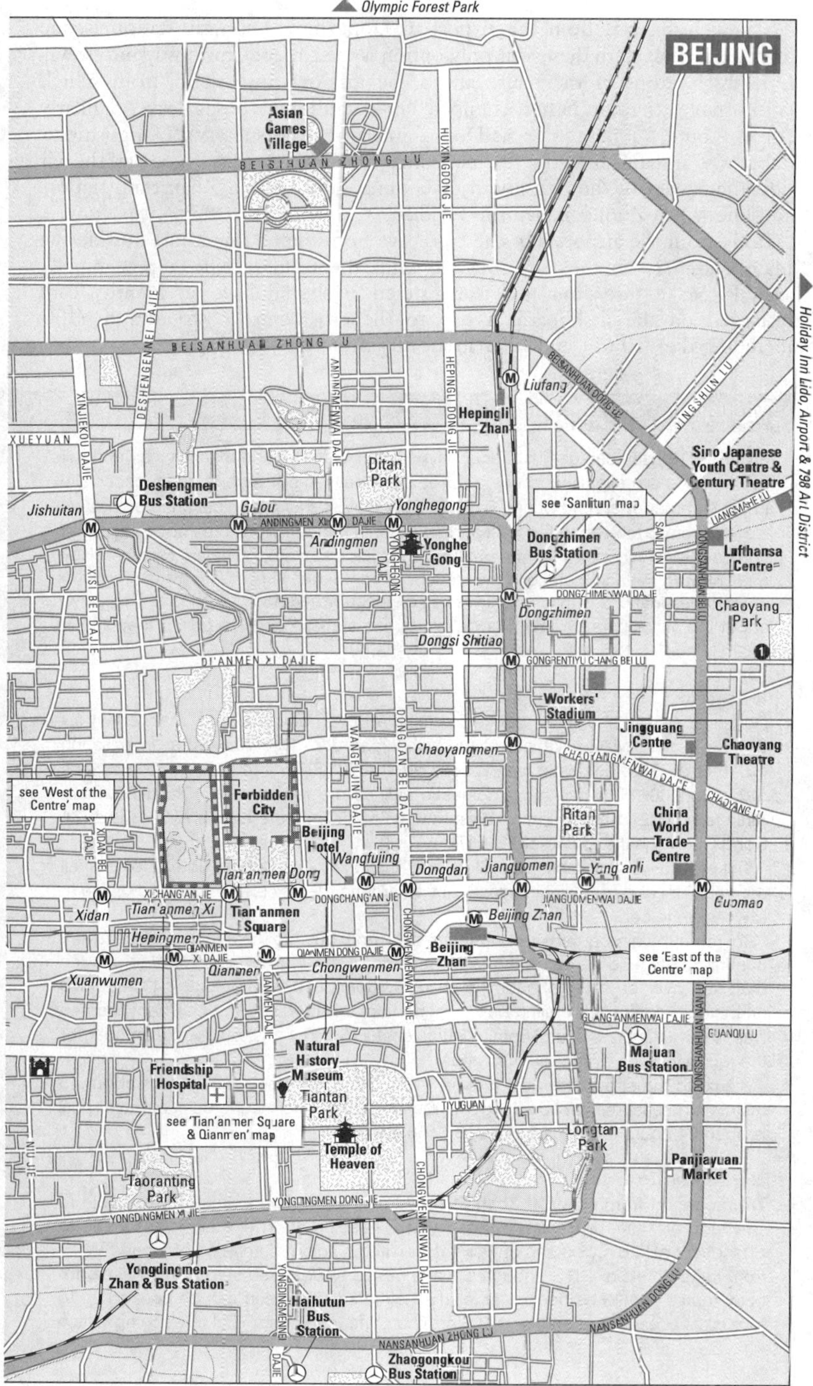
BEIJING
Olympic Forest Park
Holiday Inn Lido, Airport & 798 Art District
Asian Games Village
Beijing Zhan
Deshengmen Bus Station
Jishuitan
Gulou
Andingmen
Yonghegong
Yonghe Gong
Ditan Park
Liufang
Hepingli Zhan
Sino Japanese Youth Centre & Century Theatre
see 'Sanlitun' map
Dongzhimen Bus Station
Lufthansa Centre
Dongzhimen
Chaoyang Park
Dongsi Shitiao
Workers' Stadium
Jingguang Centre
Chaoyang Theatre
Chaoyangmen
see 'West of the Centre' map
Forbidden City
Beijing Hotel
Wangfujing
Ritan Park
China World Trade Centre
Tian'anmen Dong
Dongdan
Jianguomen
Yong'anli
Guomao
Xidan
Tian'anmen Xi
Tian'anmen Square
Hepingmen
Qianmen
Chongwenmen
Xuanwumen
see 'East of the Centre' map
Majuan Bus Station
Natural History Museum
Friendship Hospital
Tiantan Park
Temple of Heaven
see 'Tian'anmen Square & Qianmen' map
Longtan Park
Panjiayuan Market
Taoranting Park
Yongdingmen Zhan & Bus Station
Haihutun Bus Station
Zhaogongkou Bus Station
BEISIHUAN ZHONG LU
BEISANHUAN ZHONG LU
BEISANHUAN DONG LU
HUIXINGDONG JIE
HEPINGLI DONG JIE
ANDINGMENWAI DAJIE
DESHENGMENNEI DAJIE
XINJIEKOU DAJIE
XUEYUAN
JINGSHUN LU
ANDINGMEN XI DAJIE
YONGHEGONG DAJIE
SANLITUN LU
LIANGMAHE LU
DONGSANHUAN BEI LU
DONGZHIMENWAI DAJIE
XISI BEI DAJIE
DI'ANMEN XI DAJIE
GONGRENTIYUCHANG BEI LU
DONGDAN BEI DAJIE
WANGFUJING DAJIE
CHAOYANGMENWAI DAJIE
CHAOYANG LU
XIDAN BEI DAJIE
XICHANG'AN JIE
DONGCHANG'AN JIE
JIANGUOMENWAI DAJIE
CHONGWENMENNEI DAJIE
QIANMEN XI DAJIE
QIANMEN DONG DAJIE
QIANMEN DAJIE
GUANG'ANMENWAI DAJIE
GUANQU LU
DONGSANHUAN NAN LU
TIYUGUAN LU
NIU JIE
CHONGWENMENWAI DAJIE
YONGDINGMEN XI JIE
YONGDINGMEN DONG JIE
YONGDINGMENNEI DAJIE
NANSANHUAN DONG LU
NANSANHUAN ZHONG LU

A new **light rail** from the airport to Dongzhimen subway station is due imminently, but until then your only option is the airport expressway into town. Directly in front of the main exit is the **airport bus** stand, from which comfortable, though rather cramped, air-conditioned buses leave regularly (¥16). Route #1 buses stop at Dongzhimen (for the subway), Dongsishitiao, Yabao Lu and finish at the Airline Office in Xidan. Line #2 goes to the far north and west of the city, line 3 to Guomao and Bejiing Zhan train station, and line #4 to Zhongguancun in Haidian.

Taxis from the airport into the city leave from the taxi rank just outside the main entrance, on the left; don't go with the hustlers who approach new arrivals. Make sure your taxi is registered; it should have an identity card displayed on the dashboard. A trip to the city centre costs around ¥100, including the ¥10 toll, and takes about fifty minutes.

Moving on from Beijing

From Beijing, you can get just about anywhere in China via the extensive air and rail system. You'd be advised to buy a ticket a few days in advance, though, especially in the summer or around Spring Festival. Few visitors travel long distance by **bus** as it's less comfortable than the train and takes longer, though it has the advantage that you can usually just turn up and get on, as services to major cities are frequent. Buy a ticket from the ticket office in the station, or on the bus itself. Tianjin and Chengde are two destinations within easy travelling distance, where the bus and the train have about the same journey time. For details of bus stations and the points they serve, see "By bus", p.84.

By plane

Domestic **flights** should be booked at least a day in advance. The main outlet for **tickets** is the Aviation Office, at 15 Xichang'an Jie (daily 7am–8pm; information ⓣ010/66017755, domestic reservations ⓣ010/66013336, international reservations ⓣ010/66016667), where most domestic airlines are represented. China Southern Airlines is at 227 Chaoyangmen Dajie (ⓣ010/65533624), and Xinhua Airlines is at 2A Dong Chang'an Jie (ⓣ010/65121587).

Tickets are also available from CITS (see "Listings", p.141), from hotels (for a small commission) and from airline agents dotted around the city (see p.138) and online at ⓦwww.elong.com.

To get to the airport, **airport buses** run daily from outside the Aviation Office (every 30min; 5.30am–7pm), from the northwest side of the *International Hotel* (cross the road and look for the sign; hourly; 6.30am–4.30pm), and from outside a ticket office on the east side of Wangfujing Dajie, just north of the intersection with Chaoyangmen Dajie (every 30min; 5.30am–6pm). Tickets cost ¥16 and you should allow an hour for the journey, twice this in the rush hour.

A **taxi** to the airport will cost around ¥100, and the journey should take about 45 minutes, at least half an hour longer in rush hour. The information desk at the airport is open 24 hours for enquiries (ⓣ010/64563604).

By domestic train

Trains depart from either **Xi Zhan**, if you're heading south or west, for example to Chengdu or Xi'an, or **Beijing Zhan**, if you're heading north or east, for example to Shanghai or Harbin. You can buy **tickets** – with an added surcharge of around ¥40 – from large hotels or CITS, though it's little hassle to do it yourself direct. Tickets for busy routes should be booked at least a day in advance, and can be booked up to four days ahead. Buy tickets at Beijing Zhan; the Foreigners' Ticket Booking Office

By train

Beijing has two main **train stations**. **Beijing Zhan**, the central station, just south of Dongchang'an Jie, is where trains from destinations north and east of Beijing arrive. There are **left-luggage** lockers as well as a main luggage office here (see p.140 for details). From Beijing Zhan, the only hotel within walking distance is the uninspiring *International*. Most arrivals will need to head straight to the **bus terminus**, about 100m east of the station, the **metro stop** at the northwestern edge of the concourse, or to the **taxi rank**, over the road and 50m east. The waiting taxis are supervised by an official with a red armband who makes sure the queue is orderly and that drivers flip their meters on. Don't get a cab from the station concourse, as none of the drivers here will use their meters. Travellers from the south and west of the capital will arrive at the west station, **Xi Zhan**, Asia's largest rail terminal, at

is in the soft-sleeper waiting room at the back of the station, on the left side as you enter, and is signposted in English. It's open daily 5.30 to 7.30am, 8am to 6.30pm and 7 to 11pm. There's a timetable in English on the wall. At Xi Zhan, the Foreigners' ticket office is on the second floor and is open 24hrs. You can also get tickets from separate ticket outlets – as these are little known, there are never any queues. There's one on the first floor in the Wangfujing Department Store at 225 Wangfujing Dajie (daily 9–11am & 1–4pm) and another in the Air China ticket office in the China World Trade Centre at 1 Jianguomenwai Dajie (daily 8am–6pm). For train information (in Chinese only), phone ⓣ010/65129525.

Trans-Siberian and Trans-Mongolian trains

The International Train Booking Office (Mon–Fri 8.30am–noon & 1.30–5pm; ⓣ010/65120507) is the best thing about the *International Hotel* at 9 Jianguomenwai Dajie. Here you can buy **tickets to Moscow and Ulaan Baatur** with the minimum of fuss (they also take Internet bookings – ⓦwww.cits.net/travel/reservation/train.jsp – though you have to pay by bank transfer). Out of season, few people make the journey, but in summer there may well not be a seat for weeks. Allow yourself a week or two for dealing with embassy bureaucracy. After putting down a ¥100 deposit on the ticket at the booking office, you'll be issued with a reservation slip. Take this with you to the embassy when you apply for visas and the process should be fairly painless. A Russian transit visa, valid for a week, costs around US$50, with a surcharge for certain nationalities (mostly African and South American). Transit visas for Mongolia are valid for one week and cost US$30; tourist visas valid for a month cost US$40. You can also buy tickets at the Foreigners' Ticket Booking Office in Beijing Zhan (see above) though they aren't much good on visa advice.

Chinese train #3, which follows the **Trans-Mongolian route**, leaves every Wednesday from Beijing Zhan and takes five and a half days. A bunk in a second-class cabin with four beds – which is perfectly comfortable – costs around US$387. The Russian train #19, which follows the **Trans-Siberian route**, leaves on Saturdays from Beijing Zhan and takes six days. The cheapest bunk here is around US$457. A Mongolian train leaves for Ulaan Baatur every Tuesday and costs around US$108 for one bed in a four-bed berth.

The **tour company** Monkey Business can organize your trip, though you pay a lot more than the ticket price. Their office is room 35 of the *Red House Hotel* off Dongzhimenwai Dajie (see "Accommodation", p.92). A second-class ticket costs almost US$700 (including visas), for which you also get an info pack and a ride to the station. Their other packages include stopovers in Ulaan Baatur, Lake Baikal and Irkutsk.

the head of the Beijing–Kowloon rail line. A prestige project, the station is ten times the size of Beijing Zhan. The left-luggage office is on the second floor, but at ¥5 an hour, it's expensive. Bus #122 runs between the two main stations, or, if you're heading south to the budget hotels, you can take bus #52 to Qianmen and get another bus from there. However, it's probably easier to take a **taxi** from the taxi rank.

Beijing does have more stations, though you are unlikely to arrive at them unless you have come on a suburban train from, for example, the Great Wall at Badaling or Shidu. Beijing North, also known as **Xizhimen Zhan**, is at the northwestern edge of the second ring road, on the metro. Beijing South, or **Yongdingmen Zhan**, is in the south of the city, just inside the third ring road, with a bus terminus outside.

By bus

The **bus system** in Beijing is extensive, but complicated, as there are many terminuses, each one serving buses from only a few destinations. **Dongzhimen**, on the northeast corner of the second ring road, connected by metro, is the largest bus station and handles services from Shenyang and the rest of Dongbei. **Deshengmen**, also called Beijiao, the north station serving Chengde and Datong, is just north of the second ring road, on the route of bus #55, which will take you to Xi'anmen Dajie, west of Beihai Park. **Haihutun**, in the south, at the intersection of the third ring road, Nansanhuan Zhong Lu, and Yongdingmenei Dajie, is for buses from Tianjin and cities in southern Hebei. **Private minibuses** are more likely to terminate outside one of the two main train stations.

Information and maps

A large fold-out **map** of the city is vital. There is a wide variety available at all transport connections and from street vendors, hotels and bookshops. The best map to look out for, labelled in English and Chinese, and with bus routes, sights and hotels marked, is the *Beijing Tour Map*. Fully comprehensive A-Z map books are available from bookshops and street vendors outside Beijing Zhan metro stop, but only in Chinese.

Beijing Travel Service (BTS) is an official **tourist information service** with a few central offices (see p.141 for details). They're mostly interested in selling tours and handing out leaflets.

There are a number of English-language publications that will help you get the best out of the city. The *China Daily* (¥1), available from the Friendship Store, the Foreign Language Bookstore and the bigger hotels, has a listings section detailing cultural events. *Beijing This Month* covers the same ground,

Warning: scams

Spend any time in tourist areas of the capital and you will inevitably be approached by youths claiming to be **art students** or **asking to practise their English**. Their aim is to get you to visit a bogus art gallery or teahouse, and pay ridiculous prices for a few cups of tea or for prints purporting to be paintings. They'll go to astonishing lengths to befriend foreigners.

Though there are plenty around, don't use **cycle-rickshaws**. Drivers will almost certainly overcharge foreigners, even take them places they don't want to go and then demand more money. An exception are the accredited tourist rickshaws – whose drivers wear company waistcoats – that whisk visitors around the Houhai Lakes.

with light features aimed at tourists. Much more useful are the **free magazines** aimed at the large expat community, which contain up-to-date and fairly comprehensive entertainment and restaurant listings. Look for *City Weekend* (Ⓦwww.cityweekend.com) and *That's Beijing* (Ⓦwww.thatsbeijing.com). Both have listings sections including club nights, art happenings and gigs, with addresses written in *pinyin* and Chinese; you can pick up copies of all three magazines in most bars and other expat hang-outs. Anyone intending to live here should get hold of the fat *Insiders Guide to Beijing*, published by the Middle Kingdom Press, which includes plenty of information on finding places to live and doing business. It's available in the Friendship Store.

City transport

The scale of the city militates against taking "bus number 11" – Chinese slang for walking – almost anywhere, and most of the main streets are so straight that going by foot soon gets tedious. The **public transport system** is extensive but somewhat oversubscribed; most visitors tire of the heaving buses pretty quickly and take rather more taxis than they'd planned. The **metro** is speedy but not yet quite extensive enough. **Cycling** is a good alternative, though, with plenty of rental outlets in the city.

Buses

Even though every one of the city's two-hundred-odd **bus and trolleybus services** runs about once a minute, you'll find getting on or off at busy times hard work (rush hours are 7–9am & 4.30–6pm). The **fare** for ordinary buses is ¥1. There are also five comfortable double-decker bus services, costing ¥2 a trip. **Tourist buses** – which look like ordinary buses but have route numbers written in green – make regular trips (mid-April to mid-Oct) between the city centre and certain out-of-town attractions; we've listed useful routes in the text.

Services generally run from 5.30am to 11pm every day, though some are 24-hour. Buses numbered in the 200s only provide night services. All routes are efficiently organized and easy to understand – an important factor, since stops tend to be a good kilometre apart. Buses numbered in the 800s are modern, air-conditioned, and actually quite pleasant, but more expensive, with fares starting at ¥3 and going up to ¥10.

A word of warning – be very wary of **pickpockets** on buses. Skilful thieves target Westerners, and especially backpackers, looking not just for money but coveted Western passports.

Clean, efficient, and very fast, the **metro** is an appealing alternative to the bus, though it is very crowded during rush hours. Mao Zedong ordered its construction in 1966, and more than 20km were open within three years, but until 1977 it was reserved for the use of senior cadres only, apparently because it was too close to the underground defence network.

The metro operates daily from 5.30am to 11pm, and entrances are marked by a logo of a square inside a "G" shape. **Tickets** cost ¥3 per journey; buy them from the ticket offices at the top of the stairs above the platforms. It's worth buying a few at once to save queuing every time you use the system. The tickets are undated slips of paper and an attendant at the station takes one from you before you get on to the platform. All stops are marked in *pinyin*, and announced in English and Chinese over an intercom when the train pulls in, though the system is not taxing to figure out, as there are only a few lines.

Useful bus routes

Bus routes are indicated by red or blue lines on all good maps; a dot on the line indicates a stop, the tiny characters next to it the stop's name – which you need to know for the conductor to work out your fare. Trying to show the poor man a dot on a map in a swaying, crammed bus is nigh impossible; fortunately, the *Beijing Tour Map* has stops marked in *pinyin*. The following are some of the most useful services:

Bus #1 and double-decker #1 From Xi Zhan east along the main thoroughfare, Chang'an Jie.

Double-decker #2 From the north end of Qianmen Dajie, north to Dongdan, the Yonghe Gong and the Asian Games Village.

Double-decker #4 From Beijing Zoo to Qianmen via Fuxingmen.

Bus #5 From Deshengmen, on the second ring road in the northwest of the city, south down the west side of the Forbidden City and Tian'anmen to Qianmen Dajie.

Bus #15 From Beijing Zoo down Xidan Dajie past Liulichang, ending at the Tianqiao area just west of Yongdingmennei Dajie, close to Tiantan Park.

Bus #20 From Beijing Zoo to Yongdingmen Zhan, south of Taoranting Park.

Bus #52 From Xi Zhan east to Lianhuachi Qiao, Xidan Dajie, Tian'anmen Square, then east along Chang'an Jie.

Trolleybus #103 From Beijing Zhan, north up the east side of the Forbidden City, west along Fuchengmennei Dajie, then north up Sanlihe Lu to Beijing Zoo.

Trolleybus #104 From Beijing Zhan to Hepingli Zhan in the north of the city, via Wangfujing.

Trolleybus #105 From the northwest corner of Tiantan Park to Xidan Dajie, then west to Beijing Zoo.

Trolleybus #106 From Yongdingmen Zhan to Tiantan Park and Chongwenmen, then up to Dongzhimennei Dajie.

Bus #300 Circles the third ring road.

Bus #332 From Beijing Zoo to Beida (University and the Summer Palace).

Luxury Bus #802 From Xi Zhan to Panjiayuan Market in the southeast.

Luxury Bus #808 From just northwest of Qianmen to the Summer Palace.

A **loop line** runs around the city, making useful stops at Beijing Zhan, Jianguomen (under the flyover, close to the Ancient Observatory and the Friendship Store), Yonghe Gong (50m north of the temple of the same name), and Qianmen, at the northern end of Qianmen Dajie. The **east–west line** runs from the western to the eastern suburbs; useful stops are Junshi Bowugaun (Military Museum), Tian'anmen (west and east) and Wangfujing. There are interchanges at Fuxingmen and Jianguomen. The new third line, bafflingly called **Line 13**, serves the far north of the city. In fact, it's an overground light rail, though the stations use the metro logo. You can get onto it from the loop line at Xizhimen or Dongzhimen, though you have to leave the station, walk a short distance and buy a new ticket to do so. The only useful stations for tourists are Dazhong Si (for the Great Bell Temple) and Wudaokou (for Beijing University and the summer palaces).

So many lines are **under construction** that the present pleasingly minimalist subway map will soon look like a plate of noodles. **Line #5**, which should be complete by the time you read this, will run north–south with interchanges at Yonghe Gong, Dongdan and Chongwenmen. North–south running **line #4** might be finished in time for the Olympics – but don't bet on it. It'll be handy

BEILING SUBWAY & TRANSPORT CONNECTIONS

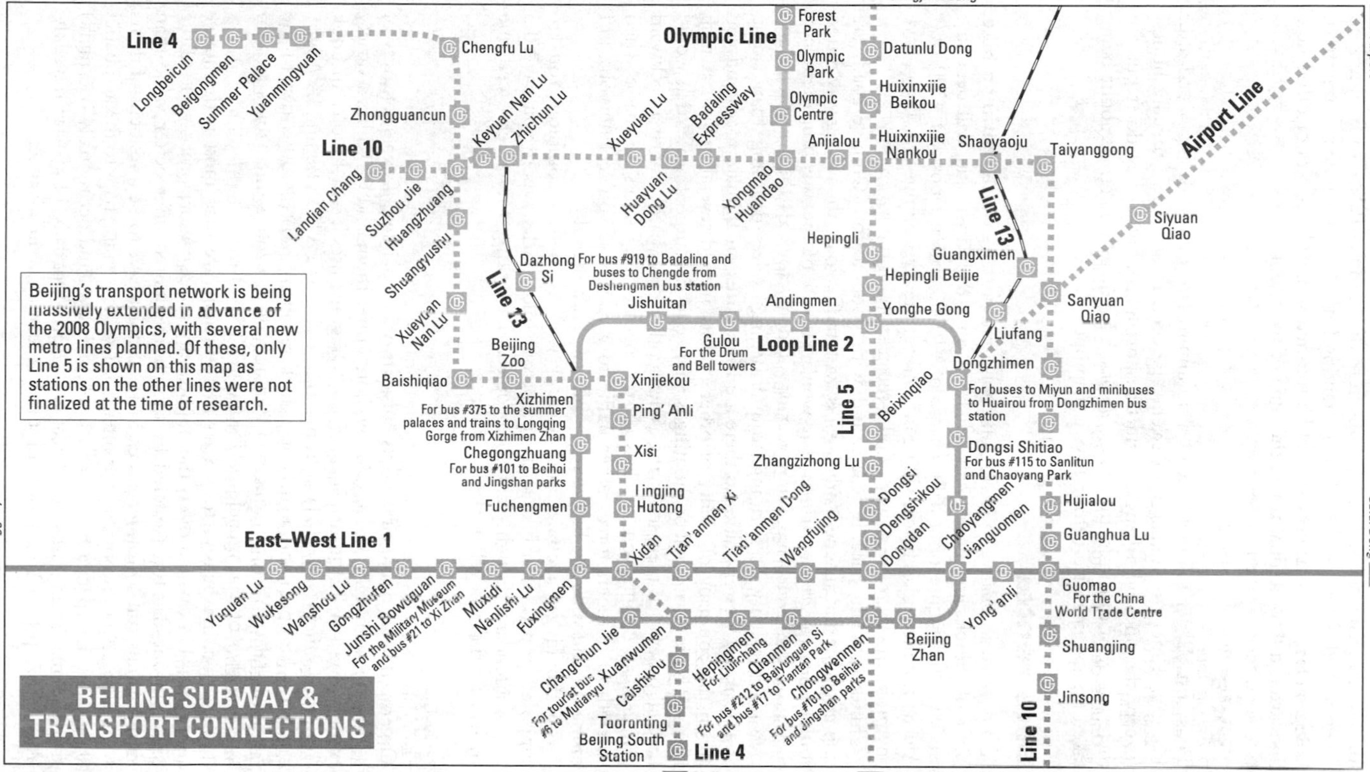

Beijing's transport network is being massively extended in advance of the 2008 Olympics, with several new metro lines planned. Of these, only Line 5 is shown on this map as stations on the other lines were not finalized at the time of research.

Songjiazhuang
Airport
Pingguoyuan
Shui Dong
Majialou
Taipingzhuang Bei

Line 4
Longbeicun
Beigongmen
Summer Palace
Yuanmingyuan
Chengfu Lu
Olympic Line
Forest Park
Olympic Park
Olympic Centre
Datunlu Dong
Huixinxijie Beikou
Huixinxijie Nankou
Anjialou
Shaoyaoju
Taiyanggong
Airport Line
Siyuan Qiao
Line 10
Landian Chang
Suzhou Jie
Huangzhuang
Zhongguancun
Keyuan Nan Lu
Zhichun Lu
Xueyuan Lu
Badaling Expressway
Huayuan Dong Lu
Xongmao Huandao
Shuangyushu
Xueyuan Nan Lu
Line 13
Dazhong Si
For bus #919 to Badaling and buses to Chengde from Deshengmen bus station
Hepingli
Hepingli Beijie
Guangximen
Line 13
Sanyuan Qiao
Liufang
Jishuitan
Andingmen
Yonghe Gong
Gulou
For the Drum and Bell towers
Loop Line 2
Beijing Zoo
Baishiqiao
Xizhimen
For bus #375 to the summer palaces and trains to Longqing Gorge from Xizhimen Zhan
Xinjiekou
Ping' Anli
Xisi
Chegongzhuang
For bus #101 to Beihai and Jingshan parks
Lingjing Hutong
Fuchengmen
Line 5
Beixinqiao
Zhangzizhong Lu
Dongsi
Dengshikou
Dongdan
Dongzhimen
For buses to Miyun and minibuses to Huairou from Dongzhimen bus station
Dongsi Shitiao
For bus #115 to Sanlitun and Chaoyang Park
Chaoyangmen
Jianguomen
Hujialou
Guanghua Lu
East–West Line 1
Yuquan Lu
Wukesong
Wanshou Lu
Gongzhufen
Junshi Bowuguan
For the Military Museum and bus #21 to Xi Zhan
Muxidi
Nanlishi Lu
Fuxingmen
Xidan
Tian'anmen Xi
Tian'anmen Dong
Wangfujing
Yong'anli
Guomao
For the China World Trade Centre
Shuangjing
Jinsong
Line 10
Changchun Jie
For tourist bus #6 to Mutianyu
Xuanwumen
Caishikou
Taoranting
Beijing South Station
Line 4
Hepingmen
For Liulichang
Qianmen
For bus #212 to Baiyunguan Si and bus #17 to Tiantan Park
Chongwenmen
For bus #101 to Beihai and Jingshan parks
Beijing Zhan

for tourists seeing the sights, as it runs from the Summer Palace to Beijing Zoo down to Xidan and then south to Taoranting Park. A light-rail lie running from Dongzhimen to the airport should be finished soon. The routes of other new lines were still to be finalized at the time of writing.

Taxis

Taxis cost ¥2 per kilometre, with a minimum fare of ¥10. Using a taxi after 11pm will incur a surcharge of twenty percent. Drivers are generally honest (except the ones who hang around transport links), but if they don't put the meter on, you can insist by saying "*da biao*". If you're concerned about being taken on an expensive detour, have a map open on your lap.

Bike rental

As a positive alternative to relying on public transport, it's worth **renting a bike**. Most of the cheaper hotels rent out bikes on a daily basis and will negotiate weekly rates. Figure on a daily charge of ¥10–50 and a deposit of ¥200–500. Always test the brakes before riding off, and get the tyres pumped up. If you have any problems, there are plenty of bike-repair stalls on the pavement.

Chinese cycling pace is sedate, and with good reason. Chinese roads are unpredictable and at times fairly lawless, with traffic going the wrong way round roundabouts, aggressive trucks that won't get out of the way, impatient taxi drivers in the cycle lane, buses veering suddenly towards the pavement, and jaywalkers aplenty. Still, riding around Beijing is less daunting than riding around many Western cities, as there are **bike lanes** on all main roads and you are in the company of plenty of other cyclists, indeed several million at rush hours. Ringing your bell or shouting is rarely effective; urgent noises that would have all other road users scurrying aside in other cities hardly merit a backward glance here. At junctions, cyclists cluster together then cross en masse when strength of numbers forces other traffic to give way. If you feel nervous, just dismount and walk the bike across – plenty of Chinese do.

You should get a **chain and lock** as well, as theft is common. You are supposed to park your bike at the numerous **bike parks**, where you pay ¥0.3 to the attendant, though plenty of people don't, risking a rarely enforced fine by leaving their bicycle locked to railings.

Tours

Organized tours of the city and its outskirts offer a painless, if expensive, way of seeing the main sights quickly. All big hotels offer them, and CITS has a variety of one- and two-day tour packages, on "Dragon Buses", which you can book from their offices (see p.141) or from a BTS office (see p.141). Beijing By Night, a trip to the opera and a meal at a duck restaurant, costs ¥330; a trip to the Summer Palace, Yonghe Gong and Beijing Zoo is ¥260. Similar tours are run by two other official agencies: CTS and CYTS.

One good, inexpensive tour that's more imaginative than most is the *hutong* tour (see p.114), which offers the opportunity to see a more private side of the city. The one-day tours offered by the cheaper hotels offer better value than similar jaunts run by classier places, and you don't have to be a resident of theirs to go along. All the youth hostels offer good-value evening trips to the acrobatics shows and the opera a few times a week, and day- (and occasionally overnight) trips to Simatai and Jinshanling Great Wall (April–Oct daily; Nov–March weekly; ¥60–80; see p.144). You must book these at least a day in advance.

Accommodation

Affordable **accommodation** options in Beijing are much improved of late. There are now plenty of well-run, cheap, well-located hotels and youth hostels – budget travellers no longer have to congregate in soulless suburban dormitories but can stay right in the centre of town. At the **cheapest places**, you can expect a bed in a clean but cramped dorm, and all the facilities will be communal. Double rooms almost always come with attached bathrooms. All hostels offer a ¥10 discount for international youth hostel members, and can sell you membership cards for ¥60. In **three-star** places and above, rooms are more spacious, and there are usually facilities such as satellite TV, swimming pools and saunas. Pretty much every hotel has a hairdresser, a restaurant and a business centre. **Luxury hotels** are of an international standard and are

Beijing accommodation

Bamboo Garden	竹园宾馆	*zhúyuán bīnguǎn*
Beijing	北京饭店	*běijīng fàndiàn*
Beiwei and Tianqiao	北纬饭店	*běiwěi fàndiàn*
Chongwenmen	崇文门饭店	*chóngwénmén fàndiàn*
Downtown Backpackers	东堂青年旅舍	*dōngtáng qīngnián lǚshè*
Drum Tower Youth Hostel	鼓楼青年旅舍	*gǔlóu qīngnián lǚshè*
Far East International Youth Hostel	远东国际青年旅舍	*yuǎndōng guójì qīngnián lǚshè*
Great Wall Sheraton	长城饭店	*chángchéng fàndiàn*
Guxiang 20	古巷20号商务会	*gǔ xiàng èr shí hào shāngwùhuì*
Hademen	哈德门饭店	*hădémén fàndiàn*
Haoyuan	好园宾馆	*hǎoyuán bīnguǎn*
Holiday Inn Crowne Plaza	国际艺苑皇冠饭店	*guójì yìyuàn huángguān fàndiàn*
Hutong	胡同人文化旅馆	*hútóngrén wénhuà lǚguǎn*
Jianguo	建国饭店	*jiànguó fàndiàn*
Jianguo Qianmen	建国前门饭店	*jiànguó qiánmén fàndiàn*
Jinglun	京伦饭店	*jīnglún fàndiàn*
Kempinski	凯宾斯基饭店	*kǎibīnsījī fàndiàn*
Lama Temple Youth Hostel	雍和国际青年旅舍	*yōnghé guójì qīngnián lǚshè*
Lüsongyuan	侣松园宾馆	*lǚsōngyuán bīnguǎn*
New Otani	长富宫饭店	*chángfùgōng fàndiàn*
Novotel Xin Qiao	诺富特新桥宾馆	*nuòfùtè xīnqiáo bīnguán*
Peninsula Palace	王府饭店	*wángfǔ fàndiàn*
Red Capital Residence	新红资客栈	*Xīnhóngzī kèzhàn*
Red House	瑞秀宾馆	*ruìxiù bīnguǎn*
Red Lantern House	红灯笼宾馆	*hóngdēnglóng bīnguǎn*
Saga Youth Hostel	实佳青年旅舍	*shíjiā qīngnián lǚshè*
Sleepy Town Inn	丽舍什刹海国际青年旅店	*lìshě shíshāhǎi guójì qīngnián lǚdiàn*
St Regis	国际俱乐部饭店	*guójìjùlèbù fàndiàn*
Youyi Hostel	天坛体育宾馆	*tiāntántǐyù bīnguǎn*
Zhaolong International Youth Hostel	兆龙青年旅舍	*zhàolóngqīngnián lǚshè*

generally foreign run and managed, and sometimes offer discounts of up to seventy percent off season.

Hotels in **Qianmen** are close to the centre in a shabby but characterful area. Most of the mid-range and high-class hotels are **east of the centre**, strung out along the international shopping streets of Wangfujing and Jianguomen or clustered around metro stations. Further north, the **Sanlitun district** has some good accommodation options for all budgets, with plenty of places to eat and drink nearby. The most characterful places to stay are those hidden in the *hutongs* **north of the centre** around Houhai and Nanluogu Xiang, close to good eating and nightlife options; there's something here for all budgets. Beijing being the size it is, proximity to a metro station is a big advantage.

Except at the cheapest places, you should always **haggle** politely for a room – rack rates are only an indication, and hardly anyone pays those any more. You can often get a worthwhile discount if you book on the Internet (try ⓦwww.sinohotels.com or ⓦwww.egochina.com) a few days in advance, or try the airport reservations' counter when you arrive.

Qianmen

See map p.95

Beiwei and Tianqiao 13 Xijing Lu ⓣ010/63012266, ⓕ010/63011366. This Sino-Japanese joint-venture consists of two buildings, one very upmarket, one not; the inexpensive section (Beiwei) looks like a barracks compared to the battleship-like superior section (Tianqiao) next door. Bus #20 from the main station will get you to Yongdingmennei Dajie, from where the hotel is a 1km walk west. ⑤–⑧

Far East International Youth Hostel 113 Tieshuxie Jie, Qianmenwai ⓣ010/63018811. A great little place, in a traditional courtyard house. The four- and six-bed dorms are clean and have sinks. There's a kitchen, washing machine and an elegant lounge. It's sunk in one of the city's last earthy *hutong* districts, 1km from Qianmen. The easiest way to find the hostel is to walk south from Hepingmen metro stop and turn left just before the first big junction with Zhushikou Dajie. Then follow the *hutong* and take the first left. Rooms in the new block over the road, are rather musty; come for the dorms. Dorms ¥55, rooms ⑤

Jianguo Qianmen 175 Yong'an Lu ⓣ010/63016688, ⓕ010/63013883. Big, popular three-star hotel with its own theatre, which nightly shows a version of Beijing Opera, mostly to visiting tour groups (see p.132). ⑨

East of the centre

See map p.109

Beijing 33 Dongchang'an Jie ⓣ010/65137766, ⓦwww.chinabeijinghotel.com. The most central hotel, just east of Tian'anmen Square, and one of the most recognizable buildings in Beijing. The view from the top floors of the west wing, over the Forbidden City, is superb. But it's pricey, renovations have expunged the historic feel, and service is not up to scratch. The cheapest rooms are US$180.

Chongwenmen 2 Chongwenmen Xi Dajie ⓣ010/65122211, ⓕ010/65122122. This hotel is a little cramped for space, but well located, close to the Chongwenmen metro stop on the loop line. Rack rates are comparatively high, so barter. ⑧

Cote Cour SL 70 Yanyue Hutong, Dongcheng Qu ⓣ010/65128021, ⓦwww.hotelcotecoursl.com. This new fourteen-room courtyard-style boutique hotel, in the middle of the city but in a quiet *hutong*, is recommended, if you would rather pay for style and character than lavish facilities. You'll have to reserve in advance. Wangfujing subway stop. ⑧

Hademen 2a Chongwenmenwai Dajie ⓣ010/67012244, ⓕ010/67016865. This two-star place is a little rambling, and staff speak no English, but as one of the few moderately priced, central hotels, close to the Chongwenmen metro stop, it's worth considering. ⑧

Haoyuan 53 Shijia Hutong ⓣ010/65125557, ⓕ010/65253179. A sedate little courtyard hotel just half a kilometre from Wangfujing but very quiet. Rooms are small but cosy and with Ming-style furniture. Head north up Dongdan Bei Dajie and take the last alley to the right before the intersection with Dengshikou Dajie. The hotel is 200m down here on the left, marked by two red lanterns. Often full; book ahead. ⑦

Holiday Inn Crowne Plaza 48 Wangfujing Dajie ⓣ010/65133388. Well-established hotel with artsy pretensions (there's an on-site gallery) that's handy for the shops. US$250.

Jianguo 5 Jianguomen Dajie, next to Yong'an Li metro stop ⓣ010/65002233, ⓦwww.hoteljianguo.com. Well run and good looking, with many of the rooms arranged around cloistered gardens, this place is deservedly very popular with regular visitors. The restaurant, *Justine's*, has some of the best French food in the city. US$200.

Jinglun (Hotel Beijing-Toronto) 3 Jianguomenwai Dajie ⓣ010/65002266, ⓕ010/65002022. Bland-looking from the outside, this Japanese-run place is very comfortable and plush inside. A standard double is US$150.

New Otani 26 Jianguomenwai Dajie ⓣ010/65125555, ⓕ010/65139810. You can get seriously pampered in this five-star, modern, Japanese-run mansion, one of the most luxurious in Beijing, though the fee for the privilege, at least US$212 a night, is hefty.

Novotel Xin Qiao 2 Dong Jiao Min Xiang ⓣ010/65133366, ⓦwww.novotel.com. A decent chain hotel, well located right by Chongwenmen metro stop, that's the best within its range if you want comfort, reliability and familiarity. 8

Peninsula Palace 8 Jingyu Hutong ⓣ010/65128899, ⓦbeijing.peninsula.com. A discreet and well-located upmarket place with a good shopping centre; now regularly voted the city's top place to stay. US$300.

Saga Youth Hostel 9 Shijia Hutong, off Chaoyangmen Nan Xiaojie ⓣ010/65272773. In a quiet *hutong* off a busy street, and just walkable from the main train station. It's signposted off Chaoyangmen Nan Xiao Jie, just beyond the stop for bus #24. The hostel is clean and utilitarian, with a tour office, bike rental, Internet access, a kitchen and a washing machine. Unusually, some of the otherwise plain dorms have TVs. Dorm beds ¥60, 4

St Regis 21 Jianguomenwai Dajie ⓣ010/64606688, ⓕ010/64603299. One of the most expensive hotels in the city, choice of visiting nobs such as President George W. Bush; rooms have a butler thrown in, who'll unpack your suitcase for you. Rooms start at US$265.

North of the centre

See map pp.112–113

Bamboo Garden 24 Xiaoshiqiao Hutong ⓣ010/64032229, ⓦwww.bbgh.com.cn. A quiet, charming courtyard hotel in a *hutong* close to the Drum and Bell towers. Quiet gardens are its best feature. A recent renovation has added to its charm. 7

Downtown Backpackers 85 Nanluogu Xiang ⓣ010/84002429. Possibly the best backpacker place, with a location on artsy Nanluogu Xiang, Beijing's trendiest *hutong*, that can't be beat; you won't be short of eating and nightlife options. There are a couple of single rooms and doubles, which get rapidly booked up. The plumbing can be a bit noisy in winter. Six-bed dorms ¥60, 3

Drum Tower Youth Hostel 51 Jiugulou Dajie, ⓣ010/64037702. A great location, spartan but clean rooms, friendly staff and a mellow rooftop patio make this hostel on a main road worth considering. There's a self-service kitchen and all the facilities you might expect but no free Internet (¥8/hr). It's a 10min walk south from Gulou subway station. Dorms ¥50, 3

Guxiang 20 20 Nanluogu Xiang ⓣ010/64005566. A promising new hotel, well located on trendy Nanluogu Xiang, done out in opium-den chic. The best doubles have four-poster beds, and there's a tennis court on the roof. It doesn't maintain much presence on the street and looks rather clubby. Rooms are surprisingly inexpensive, making this a great mid-range choice; though they may put their prices up as they become established. 5

Hutong 71 Xiaoju'er Hutong, ⓣ010/84025238. Another hotel taking advantage of the area's gentrification. This courtyard just off Nanluogu Xiang is quiet and cosy, and unlike some similar hotels, just about gets enough natural light. There's a small bar and free Wi-Fi. All in all, some of the best cheap rooms in the city. 4

Lama Temple Youth Hostel 56 Beixinqiao Toutiao ⓣ010/64028663 First *hutong* north of the Dongzhimennei and Yonghegong Dajie intersection, a few minutes south of Yonghe Gong subway stop; look for the yellow sign at the *hutong* entrance. Well-located courtyard hostel just south of the Yonghe Gong. Rooms are spacious but dark and there's a large common room with DVD collection. Staff are keen. For meals, it's handy both for Ghost Street and Nanluogu Xiang. Dorms, ¥60, rooms 4

Lüsongyuan 22 Banchang Hutong ⓣ010/64040436, ⓕ010/64030418. A charismatic courtyard hotel converted from a Qing-dynasty mansion, with stylish and elegant rooms. Pleasant gardens, too. It's popular with tour groups, so you'll probably have to book ahead in season (April–Sept). It's well located in an alley off Nanluogu Xiang. Take bus #104 from the station and get off at Beibingmasi bus stop. Walk south for 50m and you'll see a sign in English pointing down an alley to the hotel. 7

Red Capital Residence 9 Dongsi Liu Tiao ⓣ010/84035308, ⓦwww.redcapitalclub.com.cn. This little hotel is an old state guesthouse, and the five rooms are tricked out with Cultural Revolution artefacts for the latest in post-communist ironic consumption. The courtyard rock formation hides the entrance to a bomb shelter turned bar. It's more a novelty than a luxury experience, but as Beijing's most original boutique hotel, it's very popular and you'll have to book in advance. It's difficult to see from outside; look for the red doors and the little "9". ❽

Red Lantern House No.5 Zhengjue Hutong, Xinjie Kou ⓣ010/63015433. A converted courtyard house in a quiet *hutong*, close to *JJs Disco* and the Houhai bar area. The courtyard with its jumble of lanterns and ornaments, is quite something. The alley is east off Xinjie Kou, its entrance marked by a Dairy Queen. Offers bike rental, Internet and laundry. Bus #22 from Beijing Zhan. Two- to four-bed dorms ¥45–60, rooms ❸, breakfast included.

Sleepy Town Inn 103 Deshengmennei Dajie ⓣ010/64069954, ⓦwww.sleepyinn.com.cn. This homely place has friendly staff and a great location, beside a canal just off Houhai Lake, but few facilities. Dorms are good value. It's a 10min walk from Jishuitan subway stop. Four- to eight-bed dorms ¥60, ❺

Sanlitun

See map p.128

Great Wall Sheraton 6 Dongsanhuan Bei Lu ⓣ010/65005566, ⓦwww.sheraton.com/beijing. A very swish, five-star modern compound out on the third ring road. US$160.

Kempinski Lufthansa Centre, 50 Liangmaqiao Lu ⓣ010/64653388, ⓦwww.kempinski-beijing.com. Off the third ring road on the way to the airport, this five-star place is a little out of the way, though with a huge shopping complex attached and an expat satellite town of bars and restaurants nearby, there's no shortage of diversions on site. ❾

Red House 10 Chunxiu Jie ⓣ010/64167500, ⓦwww.redhouse.com.cn. Head down Dongzhimenwai Dajie, take the turning opposite *Pizza Hut* and look for the big red-brick building. Decent rooms, a good location and discount rates for long stayers make this a long-standing favourite. ❼

Youyi Hostel Off Sanlitun Lu ⓣ010/64172632, ⓦwww.poachers.com.cn. This place behind the *Poacher's Inn*, just off the Sanlitun bar strip, is clean, though staff are a bit stand-offish. There are dorms, but most of the rooms are doubles – all facilities are communal. There's free laundry and the price includes breakfast. To find it, head north up Sanlitun Lu from Gongren Tuyuchang Bei Lu, and turn left after 200m, at the sign for the *Cross Bar*. Then follow the road round to the left and it's on the right. Dorm beds ¥70, ❹

Zhaolong International Youth Hostel 2 Gongrentiyuchang Bei Lu ⓣ010/65972299. Behind the swanky *Zhaolong Hotel*. Another clean and ably managed hostel, a short stumble from the bars on Sanlitun Lu. Offers free laundry, bike rental and Internet access. Dorm beds ¥60–70, rooms ❹

The City

Beijing requires patience and planning to do it justice. Wandering aimlessly around without a destination in mind will rarely be rewarding. The place to start is **Tian'anmen Square**, geographical and psychic centre of the city, where a cluster of important sights can be seen in a day, although the **Forbidden City**, at the north end of the square, deserves a day, or even several, all to itself. **Qianmen**, a noisy market area south of here, is a bit more alive, and ends in style with one of the city's highlights, the **Temple of Heaven** in Tiantan Park. The giant motorway, **Chang'an Jie**, zooming east–west across the city, is a corridor of high-rises with a few museums, shopping centres and even the odd ancient site worth tracking down. **Wangfujing Dajie**, running off Chang'an Jie, is the capital's main shopping street. Scattered in the **north** of the city, a section with a more traditional and human feel, are some magnificent **parks**, **palaces and temples**, some of them in the *hutongs*; while, to the east, the **Sanlitun** area is a ghetto of expat services including some good upscale restaurants and plenty of bars. An expedition to the outskirts is amply rewarded by the **Summer Palace**, the best place to get away from it all.

Beijing sights		Continued...
798 Art District	798艺术区	*qī jiǔ bā yìshùqū*
Ancient Observatory	古观象台	*gǔguānxiàngtái*
Asian Games Village	亚运村	*yàyùncūn*
Baita Si	白塔寺	*bátǎ sì*
Baiyun Guan	白云观	*báyún guàn*
Beihai Park	北海公园	*běihǎi gōngyuán*
Beijing University	北京大学	*běijīng dàxúe*
Beijing Zoo	北京动物园	*běijīng dòngwùyuán*
Capital Museum	首都博物馆	*shǒudū bówùguǎn*
China Art Gallery	中国美术馆	*zhōngguó měishùguǎn*
Confucius Temple	孔庙	*kǒng miào*
Dazhong Si	大钟寺	*dàzhōng sì*
Ditan Park	地坛公园	*dìtán gōngyuán*
Exhibition Centre	展览中心	*zhǎnlǎn zhōng xīn*
Forbidden City	故宫	*gùgōng*
Great Hall of the People	人民大会堂	*rénmín dàhuìtáng*
Guangji Si	广济寺	*guǎngjì sì*
Gulou (Drum Tower)	鼓楼	*gǔ lóu*
Jingshan Park	景山公园	*jǐngshān gōngyuán*
Lu Xun Museum	鲁迅博物馆	*lǔxùn bówùguǎn*
Mao Memorial Hall	毛主席纪念堂	*máozhǔxí jìniantáng*
Military Museum	军事博物馆	*jūnshì bówùguǎn*
Museum of Ancient Architecture	古代建筑博物馆	*gǔdài jiánzhù bówùguǎn*
Museum of Chinese History	中国历史博物馆	*zhōngguó lìshǐ bówùguǎn*
Museum of the Chinese Revolution	中国革命博物馆	*zhōngguó gémìng bówùguǎn*
Museum of Urban Planning	规划博物馆	*guīhuà bówùguǎn*
Nan Luogu Xiang	南锣鼓巷	*nán luó gǔ xiàng*
National Opera House	中国国家大剧院	*zhōngguó guójiā dà jùyuàn*
National Swimming Centre	国家游泳中心	*guójiā yóuyǒng zhōngxīn*
Natural History Museum	自然博物馆	*zìrán bówùguǎn*
Niu Jie	牛街	*niújiē*
Olympic Park	北京奥林匹克公园	*běijīng àolínpǐkè gōngyuán*
Olympic Stadium	奥林匹克体育馆	*àolínpǐkè tǐyùguǎn*
Prince Gong's Palace	恭王府	*gōngwángfǔ*
Qianmen	前门	*qiánmén*
Qinghua University	清华大学	*qīnghuá dàxué*
Ritan Park	日坛公园	*rìtán gōngyuán*
Song Qingling's Residence	宋庆龄故居	*sòngqìnglíng gùjū*
Summer Palace	颐和园	*yíhéyuán*
Taoranting Park	陶然亭公园	*táorántíng gōngyuán*
Temple of Heaven	天坛	*tiāntán*
Tian'anmen	天安门	*tiān'ānmén*
Tian'anmen Square	天安门广场	*tiān'ānmén guǎngchǎng*
TV Tower	电视塔	*diànshì tǎ*
Working Peoples' Culture Palace	劳动人民文化宫	*láodong rénmín wénhuàgōng*
World Trade Centre	国际贸易中心	*guójì màoyì zhōngxīn*

Beijing sights		
Xu Beihong Museum	徐悲鸿纪念馆	*xúbēihóng jìniànguǎn*
Yonghe Gong	雍和宫	*yōng hé gōng*
Yuanmingyuan	圆明园	*yuán míng yuán*
Zheng Yang Men	正阳门	*zhèng yáng mén*
Zhonglou (Bell Tower)	钟楼	*zhōng lóu*
Zhongnanhai	中南海	*zhōng nán hǎi*
Zhong Shan Park	中山公园	*zhōngshān gōngyuán*
Zizhuyuan Park	紫竹院公园	*zǐzhúyuàn gōngyuán*

Tian'anmen Square and the Forbidden City

The first stop for any visitor to Beijing is **Tian'anmen Square**. Physically at the city's centre, symbolically it's the heart of China, and the events it has witnessed have shaped the history of the People's Republic from its inception. Chairman Mao lies here in his marble **memorial hall**, with the **Great Hall of the People** to the west and the **Museum of the Chinese Revolution** to the east. Monumental architecture that's much, much older lies just to the north – China's Imperial Palace, the **Forbidden City**, now open to all. Paul Andreu's striking dome-shaped **National Grand Opera House**, just to the west, is a high-visibility example of the city planners' ambitions to create a modern, cosmopolitan world capital – and you can see the designs for plenty more such prestige projects at the **Museum of Urban Planning**, just south of the square.

Tian'anmen Square

Covering more than forty hectares, **Tian'anmen Square** must rank as the greatest public square on earth. It's a modern creation, in a city that traditionally had no squares, as classical Chinese town planning did not allow for places where crowds could gather. Tian'anmen only came into being when imperial

▲ Tian'anmen Square

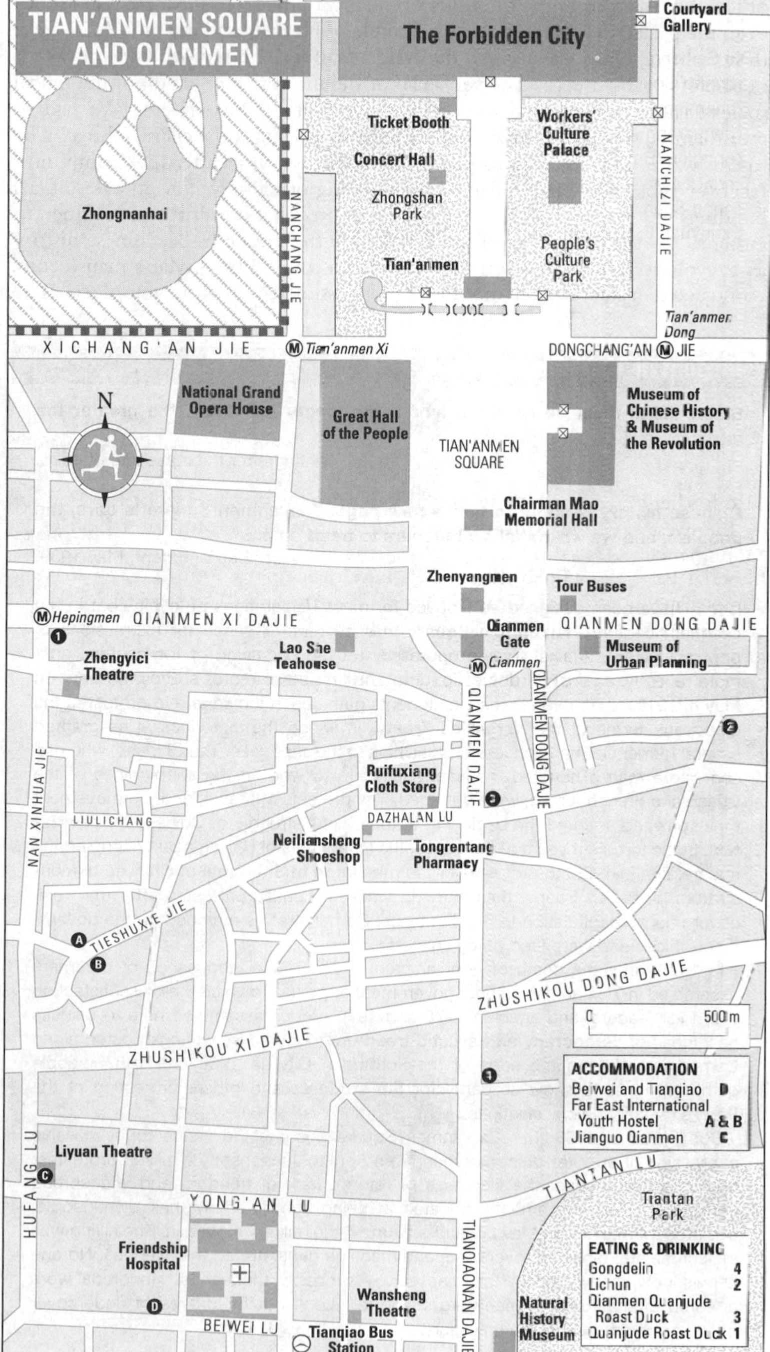
TIAN'ANMEN SQUARE AND QIANMEN
The Forbidden City
Courtyard Gallery
Ticket Booth
Concert Hall
Zhongshan Park
Tian'anmen
Workers' Culture Palace
People's Culture Park
Zhongnanhai
NANCHANG JIE
NANCHIZI DAJIE
XICHANG'AN JIE
Tian'anmen Xi
Tian'anmen Dong
DONGCHANG'AN JIE
N
National Grand Opera House
Great Hall of the People
TIAN'ANMEN SQUARE
Museum of Chinese History & Museum of the Revolution
Chairman Mao Memorial Hall
Zhenyangmen
Tour Buses
Hepingmen
QIANMEN XI DAJIE
QIANMEN DONG DAJIE
Qianmen Gate
Qianmen
Museum of Urban Planning
Zhengyici Theatre
Lao She Teahouse
QIANMEN DAJIE
QIANMEN DONG DAJIE
NAN XINHUA JIE
Ruifuxiang Cloth Store
LIULICHANG
DAZHALAN LU
Neiliansheng Shoeshop
Tongrentang Pharmacy
TIESHUXIE JIE
ZHUSHIKOU DONG DAJIE
ZHUSHIKOU XI DAJIE
0
500m
ACCOMMODATION
Beiwei and Tianqiao D
Far East International Youth Hostel A & B
Jianguo Qianmen C
Liyuan Theatre
HUFANG LU
TIANTAN LU
Tiantan Park
YONG'AN LU
Friendship Hospital
TIANQIAONAN DAJIE
EATING & DRINKING
Gongdelin 4
Lichun 2
Qianmen Quanjude Roast Duck 3
Quanjude Roast Duck 1
Wansheng Theatre
Natural History Museum
BEIWEI LU
Tianqiao Bus Station
Architecture Museum
Temple of Heaven

offices were cleared from either side of the great processional way that led south from the palace to Qianmen and the Temple of Heaven, and the broad east–west thoroughfare, Chang'an Jie, had the walls across its path removed. In the words of one of the architects: "The very map of Beijing was a reflection of the feudal society, it was meant to demonstrate the power of the emperor. We had to transform it, we had to make Beijing into the capital of socialist China." The square was not enlarged to its present size until ten years after the Communist takeover, when the Party ordained the building of ten new Soviet-style official buildings in ten months. These included the three that dominate Tian'anmen to either side – the Great Hall of the People, and the museums of Chinese history and revolution. In 1976, a fourth was added in the centre – Mao's mausoleum, constructed (again in ten months) by an estimated million volunteers. The

Dissent in Tian'anmen Square

Blood debts must be repaid in kind – the longer the delay, the greater the interest.

Lu Xun, writing after the massacre of 1926.

Chinese history is about to turn a new page. Tian'anmen Square is ours, the people's, and we will not allow butchers to tread on it.

Wuer Kaixi, student, May 1989.

It may have been designed as a space for mass declarations of loyalty, but in the twentieth century **Tian'anmen Square** was as often a venue for expressions of popular dissent; against foreign oppression at the beginning of the century, and, more recently, against its domestic form. The first mass protests occurred here on May 4, 1919, when three thousand students gathered in the square to protest at the disastrous terms of the **Versailles Treaty**, in which the victorious allies granted several former German concessions in China to the Japanese. The Chinese, who had sent more than a hundred thousand labourers to work in the supply lines of the British and French forces, were outraged. The protests of May 4, and the movement they spawned, marked the beginning of the painful struggle of Chinese modernization. In the turbulent years of the 1920s, the inhabitants of Beijing again occupied the square, first in 1925, to protest over the **massacre in Shanghai** of Chinese demonstrators by British troops, then in 1926, when the public protested after the weak government's capitulation to the Japanese. Demonstrators marched on the government offices and were fired on by soldiers.

In 1976, after the death of popular premier Zhou Enlai, thousands of mourners assembled in Tian'anmen without government approval, to voice their dissatisfaction with their leaders, and again in 1978 and 1979 groups assembled here to discuss new ideas of **democracy and artistic freedom**, triggered by writings posted along Democracy Wall on the edge of the Forbidden City. In 1986 and 1987, people gathered again to show solidarity for the **students** and others protesting at the Party's refusal to allow elections.

But it was in **1989** that Tian'anmen Square became the venue for a massive expression of **popular dissent**, when, from April to June, nearly a million protesters demonstrated against the slowness of reform, lack of freedom and widespread corruption. The government, infuriated at being humiliated by their own people, declared martial law on May 20, and on **June 4** the military moved in. The killing was indiscriminate; tanks ran over tents and machine guns strafed the avenues. No one knows how many died in the massacre – probably thousands. Hundreds were arrested afterwards and many are still in jail. Look out for droves of undercover police on the massacre's anniversary.

square is lined with railings (for crowd control), and you can enter or leave only via the gaps at either end or in the middle. Bicycles are not permitted, and the streets either side are one way; the street on the east side is for traffic going south, the west side for northbound traffic.

Tian'anmen Square unquestionably makes a strong impression, but this concrete plain dotted with worthy statuary and bounded by monumental buildings can seem inhuman. Together with the bloody associations it has for many visitors, it often leaves people cold, especially Westerners unused to such magisterial representations of political power. For many Chinese tourists, though, the square is a place of **pilgrimage**. Crowds of peasants flock to see the corpse of Chairman Mao, others quietly bow their heads before the **Monument to the Heroes**, a thirty-metre-high obelisk commemorating the victims of the revolutionary struggle. Among the visitors is the occasional monk, and the sight of robed Buddhists standing in front of the uniformed sentries outside the Great Hall of the People makes a striking juxtaposition. Others come just to hang out or to fly kites, but the atmosphere is not relaxed and a ¥5 fine for spitting and littering is rigorously enforced. At dawn, the flag at the northern end of the square is raised in a military ceremony and lowered again at dusk, which is when most people come to see it, though foreigners complain that the regimentation of the crowds is oppressive and reminds them of school. After dark, the square is at its most appealing and, with its sternness softened by mellow lighting, it becomes the haunt of strolling families and lovers.

For an overview of the square, head to the south gate, **Zhenyangmen** (daily 9am–4pm; ¥3), similar to Tian'anmen (the north gate) and 40m high, which gives a good idea of how much more impressive the square would look if Mao's mausoleum hadn't been stuck in the middle of it.

The Museum of Urban Planning

Beijing's newest attraction, just off Qianmen Dong Dajie, is the six-storey, marble-faced Museum of Urban Planning (Tues–Sun 9am–5pm; ¥30). Along with a host of rather banal displays and presentations on Beijing's bright urban future, a fascinating model shows the city as it used to look in imperial times when every significant building was part of an awesome, grand design. The star attraction, though, is an enormous diorama of Beijing that takes up the entire top floor: it illustrates what the place will look like once it's finished being ripped up and redesigned in 2020. Visitors can wander Gulliver-like around the amazingly detailed mock-up. You might even catch some locals coming to see just what their home is being bulldozed for.

The Chairman Mao Memorial Hall

At the centre of the centre of China lies a corpse that nobody dare remove.

Tiziano Terzani, *Behind the Forbidden Door*

The **Chairman Mao Memorial Hall** (daily 8.30–11am; Oct–April also Mon, Wed & Fri 2–4pm), home to the pickled corpse of the architect of modern China, is an ugly building, looking like a school gym, which contravenes the principles of *feng shui* (geomancy), presumably deliberately, by interrupting the line from the palace to Qianmen and by facing north. Mao himself wanted to be cremated, and the erection of the mausoleum was apparently no more than a power ploy by his would-be successor, Hua Guofeng. In 1980, Deng Xiaoping said it should never have been built, although he wouldn't go so far as to pull it down.

After depositing your bag at the offices on the eastern side, you join the orderly queue of Chinese on the northern side. This advances surprisingly quickly, and takes just a couple of minutes to file through the chambers in silence – photography is banned and the atmosphere reverent – any joking around will cause deep offence. Mao's corpse is draped with a red flag within a crystal coffin. Mechanically raised from a freezer every morning, it looks unreal, like wax or plastic. It is said to have been embalmed with the aid of Vietnamese technicians who had recently worked on Ho Chi Minh (rumour has it that Mao's left ear fell off and had to be stitched back on). Once through the marble halls, you're herded past a splendidly wide array of tacky Chairman Mao souvenirs.

Great Hall of the People and the museums

Taking up almost half the west side of the square is the **Great Hall of the People**. This is the venue of the National People's Congress, and hundreds of black Audis with tinted windows are parked outside when it's in session. When it isn't, it's open to the public (daily 8.30am–3pm; ¥20; buy tickets and leave bags at the office on the south side). What you see on the mandatory route is a selection of the 29 reception rooms – all looking like the lobby of a Chinese three-star hotel, with badly fitted red carpet and armchairs lined up against the walls.

On the other side of the square, there are two **museums** (daily 8.30am–4.30pm) housed in the same building: the **Museum of Chinese History**, covering everything up to 1919, and the less interesting **Museum of the Revolution**. Both are full of propaganda; the latter often closing for refits (for twelve years during the Cultural Revolution, for example) as its curators are faced with the Kafkaesque dilemma of constantly having to reinvent history according to the latest Party line. At the time of writing, both museums are closed, presumably to be refitted in time for the Olympics; it will be interesting to see once the Museum of Chinese History reopens whether its huge collection of exhibits are still divided up according to a Marxist view of history, into "primitive", "slave", "feudal" and "semi-colonial". In the meantime, a temporary waxworks show (¥10) has models of superstar Communists, if that's your idea of entertainment.

Tian'anmen and towards the Forbidden City

Tian'anmen, the "Gate of Heavenly Peace" (daily 8am–5pm; ¥30, students ¥10), is the main entrance to the Forbidden City. The boxy gatehouse is familiar across the world, and occupies an exalted place in Chinese communist iconography, appearing on banknotes, coins, stamps and indeed virtually any piece of state paper you can imagine. As such, it's a prime object of pilgrimage, with many visitors milling around waiting to be photographed in front of the large **portrait of Mao** (one of the very few still on public display), which hangs over the central passageway. From the reviewing platform above, Mao delivered the liberation speech on October 1, 1949, declaring that "the Chinese people have now stood up". For the pricey entrance fee you can climb up to this platform yourself, where security is tight – all visitors have to leave their bags, are frisked and have to go through a metal detector before they can ascend. Inside, the fact that most people cluster around the souvenir stall selling official certificates of their trip reflects the fact that there's not much to look at.

Once through Tian'anmen, you find yourself on a long walkway, with the moated palace complex and massive Wumen gate directly ahead (this is where you buy your ticket to the Forbidden City). The two parks either side,

Zhongshan and the People's Culture Park (both daily 6am–9pm), are great places to chill out away from the rigorous formality nearby. The **Workers' Culture Palace** (¥5), on the eastern side, which was symbolically named in deference to the fact that only with the Communist takeover in 1949 were ordinary Chinese allowed within this central sector of their city, has a number of modern exhibition halls (sometimes worth checking) and a scattering of original fifteenth-century structures, most of them Ming or Qing ancestral temples. The hall at the back often holds prestigious art exhibitions. The western **Zhongshan Park** (¥1) boasts the remains of the Altar of Land and Grain, a biennial sacrificial site with harvest functions closely related to those of the Temple of Heaven (see p.104).

The Forbidden City

The Gugong, or Imperial Palace, is much better known by its unofficial title, the **Forbidden City**, a reference to its exclusivity. Indeed, for the five centuries of its operation, through the reigns of 24 emperors of the Ming and Qing dynasties, ordinary Chinese were forbidden from even approaching the walls of the palace. The complex, with its maze of eight hundred buildings and reputed nine thousand chambers, was the symbolic and literal heart of the capital, and of the empire, too. From within, the **emperors**, the Sons of Heaven, issued commands with absolute authority to their millions of subjects.

Although the earliest structures on the Forbidden City site began with Kublai Khan during the Mongol dynasty, the **plan** of the palace buildings is essentially Ming. Most date to the fifteenth century and the ambitions of Emperor Yongle, the monarch responsible for switching the capital back to Beijing in 1403. The halls were laid out according to geomantic theories – in accordance to the *yin* and *yang*, the balance of negative and positive – and since they stood at the exact centre of Beijing, and Beijing was considered the centre of the universe, the harmony was supreme. The palace complex constantly reiterates such references, alongside personal symbols of imperial power such as the dragon and phoenix (emperor and empress) and the crane and turtle (longevity of reign).

After the Manchu dynasty fell in 1911, the Forbidden City began to fall into disrepair, exacerbated by looting of artefacts and jewels by the Japanese in the 1930s and again by the Nationalists, prior to their flight to Taiwan, in 1949. A programme of **restoration** has been under way for decades, and today the complex is in better shape than it was for most of the last century.

To do it justice, you should plan to spend a day here, though you can wander the complex for a week and keep discovering new aspects. The central halls, with their wealth of imperial pomp, may be the most magnificent buildings, but for many visitors it's the side rooms, with their displays of the more intimate accoutrements of court life, that bring home the realities of life for the inhabitants of this, the most gilded of cages.

Visiting the Forbidden City

The complex is open to visitors daily 8.30am–5pm in summer, 8.30am–4.30pm in winter, with last admission an hour before closing (¥40, ¥60 including the special exhibitions). Note that the entrance is quite a way after Tian'anmen; just keep on past the souvenir stalls till you can't go any further; as well as the main entrance under Tian'anmen, you can also come in through the smaller north and east gates. You have the freedom of most of the hundred-hectare site, though not all of the buildings, which are labelled in English. The ticket has a

Life inside the Forbidden City

The emperors rarely left the Foribidden City – perhaps with good reason. Their lives, right up to the fall of the Manchu in the twentieth century, were governed by an extraordinarily developed taste for luxury and excess. It is estimated that a single meal for a Qing emperor could have fed several thousand of his impoverished peasants, a scale obviously appreciated by the last influential occupant, the Empress Dowager Cixi (see box, p.121), who herself would commonly order preparation of a hundred and eight dishes at a single sitting. Sex, too, provided startling statistics, with the number of Ming-dynasty **concubines** approaching ten thousand. At night, the emperor chose a girl from his harem by picking out a tablet bearing her name from a pile on a silver tray. She would be delivered to the emperor's bedchamber naked but for a yellow cloth wrapped around her, and carried on the back of a servant, since she could barely walk with her bound feet.

The only other men allowed into the palace were **eunuchs**, to ensure the authenticity of the emperor's offspring. In daily contact with the royals, they often rose to considerable power, but this was bought at the expense of their dreadfully low standing outside the confines of the court. Confucianism held that disfiguration of the body impaired the soul, and eunuchs were buried apart from their ancestors in special graveyards outside the city. In the hope that they would still be buried "whole", they kept and carried around their testicles in bags hung on their belts. They were usually recruited from the poorest families – attracted by the rare chance of amassing wealth other than by birth. Eunuchry was finally banned in 1924 and the remaining 1500 eunuchs were expelled from the palace. An observer described them "carrying their belongings in sacks and crying piteously in high-pitched voices".

map on the back, which also shows where the exhibitions are. If you want detailed explanation of everything you see, you can tag on to one of the numerous tour groups or buy one of the many specialist books on sale. The audio tour (¥30), available by the main gate, is also worth considering – though if you do this, it's worth retracing your steps afterwards for an untutored view. Useful **bus routes** serving the Forbidden City are #5 from Qianmen, and #54 from Beijing Zhan, or you could use #1, which passes the complex on its journey along Chang'an Jie. You can get to the back gate, opposite Jingshan Park, on bus #101, #103 or #109. The nearest **metros** are Tian'anmen west and east. If you're in a **taxi**, you can save yourself the walk across Tian'anmen Square by asking to be dropped at the east gate.

From Wumen to Taiheman

The **Wumen** (Meridian Gate) itself is the largest and grandest of the Forbidden City gates and was reserved for the emperor's sole use. From its vantage point, the Sons of Heaven would announce the new year's calendar to their court and inspect the army in times of war. It was customary for victorious generals returning from battle to present their prisoners here for the emperor to decide their fate. He would be flanked, on all such imperial occasions, by a guard of elephants, the gift of Burmese subjects.

Passing through the Wumen you find yourself in a vast paved court, cut east–west by the **Jinshui He**, the Golden Water Stream, with its five marble bridges, decorated with carved torches, a symbol of masculinity. Beyond is a further ceremonial gate, the **Taihemen**, Gate of Supreme Harmony, its entrance guarded by a magisterial row of lions, and beyond this a still greater courtyard where the principal imperial audiences were held. Within this space the entire court, up to one hundred thousand people, could be accommodated. They would have made their way in through the lesser side gates – military men from the west, civilian officials from the east – and waited in total silence as the emperor ascended his throne. Then, with only the Imperial Guard remaining standing, they kowtowed nine times.

The ceremonial halls

The main **ceremonial halls** stand directly ahead, dominating the court. Raised on a three-tiered marble terrace is the first and most spectacular of the three, the **Taihedian**, Hall of Supreme Harmony. This was used for the most important state occasions, such as the emperor's coronation or birthdays and the nomination of generals at the outset of a campaign, and last saw action in an armistice ceremony in 1918. A marble pavement ramp, intricately carved with dragons and flanked by bronze incense burners, marks the path along which the emperor's chair was carried. His golden dragon throne stands within.

Moving on, you enter the **Zhonghedian**, Hall of Middle Harmony, another throne room, where the emperor performed ceremonies of greeting to foreigners and addressed the imperial offspring (the product of several wives and numerous concubines). The hall was used, too, as a dressing room for the major Taihedian events, and it was here that the emperor examined the seed for each year's crop.

The third of the great halls, the **Baohedian**, Hall of Preserving Harmony, was used for state banquets and imperial examinations, graduates from which were appointed to positions of power in what was the first recognizably bureaucratic civil service. Its galleries, originally treasure houses, display various finds from the site, though the most spectacular, a vast block carved with dragons and clouds, stands at the rear of the hall. This is a Ming creation, reworked in the eighteenth century, and it's among the finest carvings in the palace. It's certainly the largest – a 250-tonne chunk of marble transported here from well outside the city by flooding the roads in winter to form sheets of ice.

The imperial living quarters

To the north, paralleling the structure of the ceremonial halls, are the three principal palaces of the **imperial living quarters**. Again, the first chamber, the **Qianqinggong**, Palace of Heavenly Purity, is the most extravagant. It was originally the imperial bedroom – its terrace is surmounted by incense burners in the form of cranes and tortoises (symbols of immortality) – though it later became a conventional state room. Beyond, echoing the Zhonghedian in the ceremonial complex, is the **Jiaotaidian**, Hall of Union, the empress's throne room; and finally the **Kunninggong**, Palace of Earthly Tranquillity, where the emperor and empress traditionally spent their wedding night. By law the emperor had to spend the first three nights of his marriage, and the first day of Chinese New Year, with his wife. This last palace is a bizarre building, partitioned in two. On the left is a large sacrificial room with its vats ready to receive offerings (1300 pigs a year under the Ming). The wedding chamber is a small room, off to one side, painted entirely in red, and covered with decorative emblems symbolizing fertility and joy. It was last pressed into operation in 1922 for the child wedding of Pu Yi, the last emperor, who, finding it "like a melted red wax candle", decided that he preferred the Yangxinciang and went back there.

The **Yangxindiang**, or Mind Nurture Palace, is one of a group of palaces to the west where emperors spent most of their time. Several of the palaces retain their furniture from the Manchu times, most of it eighteenth century; in one, the **Changchungong** (Palace of Eternal Spring), is a series of paintings illustrating the Ming novel, *The Story of the Stone*. To the east is a similarly arranged

Exhibitions in the Forbidden City

The Forbidden City is increasingly being devoted to museum space – fifty thousand square metres today and, in a few years, four hundred thousand. It's growing into one of the best museums in China, and after appreciating the palace itself, it's worth visiting a second time just to take in the exhibits. There's a strip of exhibition halls on the western side of the complex and a few more in the northeast: all exhibitions are free unless specified otherwise. Check out what's on at ⓦwww.dpm.com.cn; new exhibitions are opening all the time.

In the western galleries you'll find exhibits detailing aspects of **Qing dynasty life** – insignia, weapons, musical instruments, the life of concubines and so on – but the most gorgeous relics, including exquisite lacquerware and carvings of jade, wood, bamboo and ivory are in the Hall of Treasures at the northern end. The shows in the northeast corner of the palace are mainly of **pottery** and **porcelain**, but check the **painting gallery**, whose show is changed monthly. Just north of this, in the Yangxindiang and Leshoutang, a hall just north of it, is a large show of **jewellery** (¥10). The first hall houses mostly gold, silver and jade tableware and tea and wine utensils. There are also gold chimes, seals, books and a pagoda that was used to store any hair that fell out, on brushing, from the imperial head of Emperor Qianlong's mother. The second hall holds the costumes and utensils the emperor and empress used. Particularly impressive is a huge jade carving illustrating a Taoist immortal taming the waves. It weighs over five tonnes and reputedly took ten years to carve.

The show of **clocks** and **watches** in Fengxiandian, the eastern palace quarters, is a real crowd-pleaser (¥10). On display is the result of one Qing emperor's passion for liberally ornamented Baroque timepieces, most of which are English and French, though the rhino-sized water clock by the entrance is Chinese. There's even one with a mechanical scribe that can write eight characters. Some clocks are wound to demonstrate their workings at 11am and 2pm.

group of palaces, adapted as **museum galleries** for displays of bronzes, ceramics, paintings, jewellery and Ming and Qing arts and crafts. The atmosphere here is much more intimate, and you can peer into well-appointed chambers full of elegant furniture and ornaments, including English clocks decorated with images of English gentlefolk, which look very odd among the jade trees and ornate fly whisks.

Moving away from the palace chambers – and by this stage something of a respite – the Kunningmen leads out from the Inner Court to the **Imperial Garden**. There are a couple of cafés here (and toilets) amid a pleasing network of ponds, walkways and pavilions, the classic elements of a Chinese garden. At the centre is the **Qinandian**, Hall of Imperial Peace, dedicated to the Taoist god of fire, Xuan Wu. You can exit here into Jingshan Park, which provides an overview of the complex – see p.112.

South of Tian'anmen

The **Qianmen** area, to the south of Tian'anmen, offers a tempting antidote to the prodigious grandeurs of the Forbidden City – and a quick shift of scale. The lanes and *hutongs* here comprise a **traditional shopping quarter**, full of small, specialist stores, which, to a large extent, remain grouped according to their particular trades – though how much character will survive the present huge demolitions is debatable. Down Qianmen Dajie, once the Imperial Way, now a clogged road clustered with small shops, the **Natural History** and

Architecture museums are worth a browse, and **Tiantan**, the ravishing Temple of Heaven, perfectly set in one of Beijing's best parks, is an example of imperial architecture at its finest.

Qianmen

The entry to this quarter is marked by the imposing, fifteenth-century, double-arched **Qianmen** gate just south of Tian'anmen Square. Before the city's walls were demolished, this sector controlled the entrance to the inner city from the outer, suburban sector. Shops and places of entertainment were banned from the former in imperial days, and they became concentrated in the Qianmen area.

Qianmen Dajie, the quarter's biggest street, runs immediately south from the gate; off to either side are trading streets and *hutongs*, with intriguing traditional pharmacies and herbalist shops, dozens of clothes shops, silk traders and an impressive array of side stalls and cake shops selling fresh food and cooked snacks. For a rather sanitized taste of the district's old delights, visit the Lao She Teahouse, which puts on daily shows of acrobatics and opera (see p.133).

Dazhalan Lu

Cramped **Dazhalan Lu** is the oldest and most interesting of the Qianmen lanes leading west off Qianmen Dajie; the lane's entrance is marked by a white arch opposite the *Qianmen Roast Duck* restaurant on the east side of the road. This was once a major theatre street, now it's a hectic shopping district, with mostly teashops and clothing stores occupying the genteel old buildings. At no. 24, Tongrengtang, a famous **Traditional Chinese Medicine store**, has shelves full of deer horn, bear-heart capsules and the like, and a formidable array of aphrodisiacs. At the end of the street, marked by a scattering of Chinese-only hotels, was the old red-light district, formerly containing more than three hundred brothels. This is one of the last substantial networks of **hutongs** left in the city, and it's certainly worth wandering (or, better, biking) down random alleyways, though expect to get lost – at least, for a while.

Liulichang Jie

Turning north at the western end of Dazhalan, then heading west along a *hutong*, then north and west again, brings you to **Liulichang Jie**, parallel to Dazhalan Jie. Liulichang, whose name literally means "Glaze factory street", after the erstwhile factories here making glazed tiles for the roofs of the Forbidden City, has been rebuilt as a heritage street, using Ming-style architecture; today, it's full of **curio stores** – remember to bargain hard.

The Natural History and Architecture museums

It's a long and boring thirty-minute walk from the northern end of Qianmen Dajie down to the **Natural History Museum** (daily 8.30am–5pm; ¥15), a few blocks farther south; take bus #17 or #20. After halls of stuffed wildlife and plastic dinosaurs, check out the gruesome exhibition in the building to the left of the entrance: pickled human legs, arms, brains and foetuses are arranged around the stars of the show, two adult corpses – a woman wearing socks, gloves and a hood, and a man with all his skin removed, leaving just the fingernails and lips. You can recover in the sedate environs of the **Museum of Architecture** (daily 9am–5pm; ¥15) a short walk to the southwest. Look for the red arch south off Beiwei Lu; the ticket office is just beyond here and the museum itself is further down the road on the right. This was once the Xiannong Temple, where the emperor ritually ploughed a furrow to ensure a good harvest. You can see the gold-plated plough he used in the Hall of Worship. The Hall of Jupiter has a fantastically ornate ceiling and cutaway models of famous buildings from all over the country. Anyone who has ever wondered how a *dougong* works – those ornate interlocking brackets seen on temples – can satisfy their curiosity here. A model of the city as it appeared in 1949, before the Communists ripped it up, shows how the imperial buildings that remain today are fragments from an awesome grand design.

The Temple of Heaven

Set in its own large and tranquil park about 2km south of Tian'anmen along Qianmen Dajie, **Tiantan**, otherwise known as the **Temple of Heaven** (daily 8.30am–8pm, buildings close at 5pm; ¥30 for a ticket that includes access to all buildings; just the park low season ¥10, high season ¥15), is widely regarded as the high point of Ming design. For five centuries it was at the very heart of imperial ceremony and symbolism, and for many modern visitors its architectural unity and beauty remain more appealing – and on a much more accessible scale – than the Forbidden City. There are various bus routes to Tiantan: bus #106 runs from Dongzhimen to the north entrance; #54 passes the west gate on its way from Beijing Zhan; #17 passes the west gate on its way from Qianmen; and #41 from Chongwenmen stops close to the east gate.

The temple was begun during the reign of Emperor Yongle and completed in 1420. It was conceived as the prime meeting point of Earth and Heaven, and symbols of the two are integral to its plan. Heaven was considered round, and Earth square, thus the round temples and altars stand on square bases, while the whole park has the shape of a semicircle sitting beside a square. The intermediary between Earth and Heaven was of course the **Son of Heaven**, the emperor, and the temple was the site of the most important ceremony of the imperial-court calendar, when the emperor prayed for the year's harvests at the **winter solstice**. Purified by three days of fasting, he made his way to the park on the day before the solstice, accompanied by his court in all its magnificence. On arrival, he would meditate in the Imperial Vault, ritually conversing with the gods on the details of government, before spending the night in the Hall of Prayer for Good Harvests. The following day, amid exact and numerological ritual, the emperor performed animal sacrifices before the Throne of Heaven at the Round Altar.

It was forbidden for the commoners of old Beijing to catch a glimpse of the great annual procession to the temple and they were obliged to bolt their windows and remain, in silence, indoors. The Tiantan complex remained sacrosanct until it was thrown open to the people on the first Chinese National Day of the Republic in October 1912. Two years after this, the infamous General Yuan Shikai performed the solstice ceremonies himself, as part of his attempt to be proclaimed emperor. He died before the year was out.

The temple buildings

Although you're more likely to enter the actual park from the north or the west, to properly appreciate the religious ensemble it's best to skirt round to the south entrance, the Zhaohen Gate, from where you can follow the ceremonial route up through the complex. The main pathway from Zhaozhen leads straight to the **Round Altar**, consisting of three marble tiers representing Man, Earth and (at the summit) Heaven. The tiers themselves are composed of blocks in various multiples of nine, which the Chinese saw as cosmologically the most powerful odd number, representing both Heaven and Emperor. The top terrace now stands bare, but the spot at its centre, where the Throne of Heaven was placed, was considered to be the middle of the Middle Kingdom – the very centre of the earth. Various acoustic properties are claimed for the surrounding tiers, and from this point it is said that all sounds are channelled straight upwards. To the east of the fountain, which was reconstructed after fire damage in 1740, are the ruins of a group of buildings used for the preparation of sacrifices.

Directly ahead, the **Imperial Vault of Heaven** is an octagonal structure made entirely of wood, with a dramatic roof of dark blue, glazed tiles. It is preceded by the so-called **Echo Wall**, said to be a perfect whispering gallery, although the unceasing cacophony of tourists trying it out makes it impossible to tell.

The principal temple building – the **Hall of Prayer for Good Harvests**, at the north end of the park – amply justifies all this build up. It is, quite simply, a wonder. Made entirely of wood, without the aid of a single nail, the circular structure rises from another three-tiered marble terrace, to be topped by three blue-tiled roofs of harmonious proportions. Four compass-point pillars support the vault (in representation of the seasons), enclosed in turn by twelve outer pillars (for the months of the year and the watches of the day). The dazzling colours of the interior, surrounding the central dragon motif, make the pavilion seem ultramodern; it was, in fact, entirely rebuilt, faithful to the Ming design, after the original was destroyed by lightning in 1889. The official explanation for this appalling omen was that it was divine punishment meted out on a sacrilegious caterpillar, which was on the point of reaching the golden ball on the hall's apex when the lightning struck. Thirty-two court dignitaries were executed for allowing this to happen.

Niu Jie and the Muslim Quarter

Some 3km southwest of Qianmen, **Niu Jie** (Ox Street) is a cramped thoroughfare in the city's **Muslim Quarter**. The street, a *hutong* leading off Guang'anmenwai Dajie, on the route of bus #6 from the north gate of Tiantan Park, is lined with offal stalls and vendors selling fried dough rings, rice cakes and *shaobang* (muffins). The white hats and the beards worn by the men are what most obviously set these Hui minority people apart from the Han Chinese – there are nearly two hundred thousand of them in the capital. The focus of the street is the **mosque** at its southern end (daily 8am–5pm; ¥10), an attractive building colourfully decorated in Chinese style with abstract decorations and text in Chinese and Arabic over the doors. You won't get to see the handwritten copy of the Koran, dating back to the Yuan dynasty, without special permission, or be allowed into the main prayer hall if you're not a Muslim, but you can inspect the courtyard, where a copper cauldron, used to cook food for the devotees, sits near the graves of two Persian imams who came here to preach in the thirteenth century.

West of the centre

Heading west from Tian'anmen Square along **Xichang'an Jie**, the giant motorway that runs east–west across the city, you pass a string of grandiose buildings, the headquarters of official and corporate power. Though most of the sites and amenities are elsewhere, western Beijing has enough of interest to kill a day or two. There's a good shopping district, **Xidan**, the **Military Museum** and the **Capital Museum**, and the pleasant **Baiyun Guan** to chill out in.

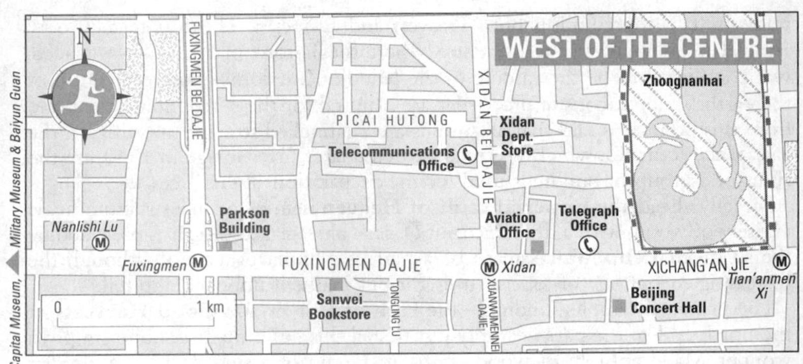

Zhongnanhai to Xidan

West along Xichang'an Jie, the first major building you pass is, on the left, the new **National Grand Opera House**. Designed by French architect Paul Andreu and nicknamed, for obvious reasons, the "Egg", the glass-and-titanium dome houses a concert hall, two theatres and a 2500-seat opera house. Visitors enter through a tunnel under the lake outside. Though it wasn't open to the public at the time of writing, it had hosted one soloist – ex-president and opera enthusiast Jiang Zemin. Critics have already labelled it a white elephant, but it makes an undeniably striking contrast to the surrounding, somewhat po-faced, monumentalism.

You may not realize it, but on the north side of the road you are passing the **Communist Party Headquarters**, the **Zhongnanhai**. Armed sentries stand outside the gates, ensuring that only invited guests actually get inside. This is perhaps the most important and historic building in the country, base since 1949 of the Central Committee and the Central People's Government, and Mao and Zhou Enlai both worked here. Before the Communist takeover it was home to the Empress Dowager Cixi.

Just west, the **Aviation Office**, the place to buy tickets and catch the airport bus, stands on the site of Democracy Wall, and over the road looms the **Beijing Concert Hall**, recessed a little from the street, another uninspiring construction. **Xidan**, the street heading north from the next junction, *is* worth exploring, at least along its initial few blocks, though not at weekends, when it's heaving with people. This is where the locals shop, and the area is a dense concentration of **department stores**. The choice is less esoteric and the shopping experience less earthy than in Qianmen, but if you want to know what the kids are wearing this season, this is the place to go.

It takes persistence to continue much beyond this point, though you might be spurred on by the sight of the **Parkson Building** on the north side of the next main junction, a shopping centre for seriously rich Chinese. On the fifth floor of the south building is an exhibition hall (daily 9.30am–4.30pm; ¥15, students ¥4) with the air of an exclusive private collection, showing "masterpieces" from the craftwork factories across China – similar to the stuff you'll see in the Friendship Store but of much better quality. Though it's all terribly kitsch – a Red Army meeting in ivory, for example – the craftsmanship in evidence is astonishing. If you're peckish, there's a giant food court on the sixth floor.

A kilometre west of here, on the south side of the street and not far from Muxidi subway stop, the new **Capital Museum** (Tues–Sun 9am–5pm; ¥30;

Ⓦwww.capitalmuseum.org.cn/en) is easy to miss, despite its size – from the outside, it rather resembles the bank headquarters that precede it. Inside, the architecture is much more interesting; a bronze cylinder shoots down through the roof as if from heaven. The layout is simple: exhibition halls concering the city are in the cube, cultural relics in the cylinder. The ground-floor gallery in the **cylinder** holds Ming and Qing paintings, mostly landscapes. The calligraphy upstairs can be safely missed unless you have a special interest, but the bronzes on level three are pretty interesting: a sinister third-century BC owl-headed dagger, for example, or the strangely modern-looking three-legged cooking vessels decorated with geometrical patterns – which are more than three thousand years old. The display of jade on the fourth floor is definitely worth lingering over; some astonishing workmanship has gone into the buckles, boxes and knick-knacks here; the white quail-shaped vessels are particularly lovely. The **cube** of exhibition halls on the building's west side can be travelled round rather faster. The bottom level hosts a confusing show on the history of Beijing – there aren't enough English captions to make any sense of the exhibition whatsoever – while the models of historical buildings on the next level up can be skipped in favour of the show-stealing Buddhist figurines on the top floor. As well as depictions of serene, long-eared gentlemen, there are some very esoteric lamaist figures from Tibet; the Goddess Marici, for example, comes with her own pig-drawn chariot, and other fierce deities have lion heads or many arms.

The stern Soviet-looking **Military Museum** on Fuxing Lu (daily 8am–4.30pm; ¥15) is more exciting than its name suggests; it does its job of impressing you with China's military might and achievements very well. Catch bus #1, which terminates close by, or the metro to Junshi Bowuguan. On entering, you are confronted with giant paintings celebrating martial valour, then an enormous rocket standing proud at the centre of the high main hall. Exhibits stake out the history of the **People's Liberation Army**, with heavy emphasis, inevitably, on the war against the Nationalists and the Japanese. Curiosities include, in the rear courtyard, a somewhat miscellaneous group of old aircraft – among them the shells of two American spy planes (with Nationalist markings) shot down in the 1950s. Upstairs, there's an exhibition on the Korean War and a "Friendship Hall", which displays gifts from other countries; competition for the most tasteless is fierce, but the gold machine gun from Lebanon just about steals it.

The TV Tower and Baiyun Guan

There's little reason to continue west from here – you can visit the four-hundred-metre-high **TV Tower** on Xisanhuan Lu (daily 8am–5pm), which offers a spectacular view over the city, but it costs a steep ¥50. It's more worthwhile to head a little south to the **Baiyun Guan**, the White Cloud Temple (daily 8am–5.30pm; ¥10), just off Baiyun Lu and signposted in English. You can get here on bus #212 from Qianmen, or bus #40 from Nansanhuan Lu. Once the most influential Taoist centre in the country, the temple has been extensively renovated after a long spell as a military barracks and is now the location for the China Taoism Association. There are thirty resident monks, and it's become a popular place for pilgrims, with a busy, thriving feel to it, in some ways preferable to the more touristy lamaist temple, the Yonghe Gong (see p.116). There are three monkeys depicted in relief sculptures around the temple, and it is believed to be lucky to find all three: the first is on the gate, easy to spot as it's been rubbed black, and the other two are in the first courtyard. Though laid out in a similar way to a Buddhist temple, it has a few unusual features, such as the three gateways at the entrance, symbolizing the three worlds of Taoism – Desire,

Substance and Emptiness. The attached bookshop has only one text in English, the *Book of Changes*, but plenty of tapes and lucky charms. The place is at its most colourful during the New Year temple fair (see "Festivals", p.52).

East of the centre

As you head east from Tian'anmen Square, you enter the upmarket, commercial eastern side of the city. Here you'll find **Wangfujing**, the oldest shopping street in the city, and still one of the best, though these days the international zone of Jianguomen, further east, is rather more glamorous. It's not all mindless materialism; the **China Art Gallery**, at the north end of Wangfujing, and the **Ancient Observatory** on Jiangguomen are welcoming oases of culture. Further north, **Sanlitun** remains a raucous nightlife zone, though it has some civilized parts. It's a long way northeast from here towards the airport, but the **798 Art District**, an abandoned factory complex now full of art galleries, is the city's newest must-see.

Wangfujing Dajie

Wangfujing Dajie (head north from the *Beijing Hotel* on Dongchang'an Jie) is where the capital gets down to the business of **shopping** in earnest. But it does have some decent sights as well, and it's short enough to stroll along its length. For a century the haunt of quality stores, on the western side of the street are plenty of small stores selling clothes. Just before the crossroads with Dong'anmen Jie is the Foreign Languages Bookstore, the largest in China and a good resource for travellers (see p.137 for more details). On the other side of the street, the Sun Dong'an Plaza is a glitzy mall; you're better off going for a snack or to change money at the Bank of China (ground floor; Mon–Fri 9am–noon & 1.30–5pm) than to buy any of the very pricey, mostly designer clothes on sale, though the basement stalls are worth a browse if you're after tea or souvenirs. In the evening, check out the street food on sale at the **Dong'anmen Night Market**, which runs west off the northern end of the street (see p.124).

On the eastern side of the street, a number of **hutongs** lead into a quiet area well away from the bustle of the main street. The ten brothers of a Ming-dynasty emperor used to live here, so that he could keep a wary eye on them, and you can still see their palace at the end of Shuaifuyuan Hutong, now converted into a medical college. Continuing east through the *hutongs*, you'll reach **Dongdan Bei Dajie**, parallel to Wangfujing, which is rapidly becoming a shopping centre to rival it, full of clothing boutiques.

The China Art Gallery

When you're tired of shopping, head north to the **China Art Gallery** (Tues–Sun 9am–4pm; entrance fee varies ¥2–20), at the top end of Wangfujing, on the route of bus #2, which runs north–south between Qianmen and Andingmen Dajie, or trolleybus #104, which runs between Andingmennei Dajie and Beijing Zhan. A huge and draughty building, it usually holds several shows at once, though there's no permanent collection. Shows in the past have included specialist women's and minority exhibitions, and even a show of socialist realist propaganda, put up not to inspire renewed vigour but as a way to consider past follies – revolutionary imagery has long had its day and Chinese painting is enjoying a renaissance. You can see the work of the Bejing art colleges in July, when they hold their degree shows here. Check the listings magazines (see p.85) for what's on.

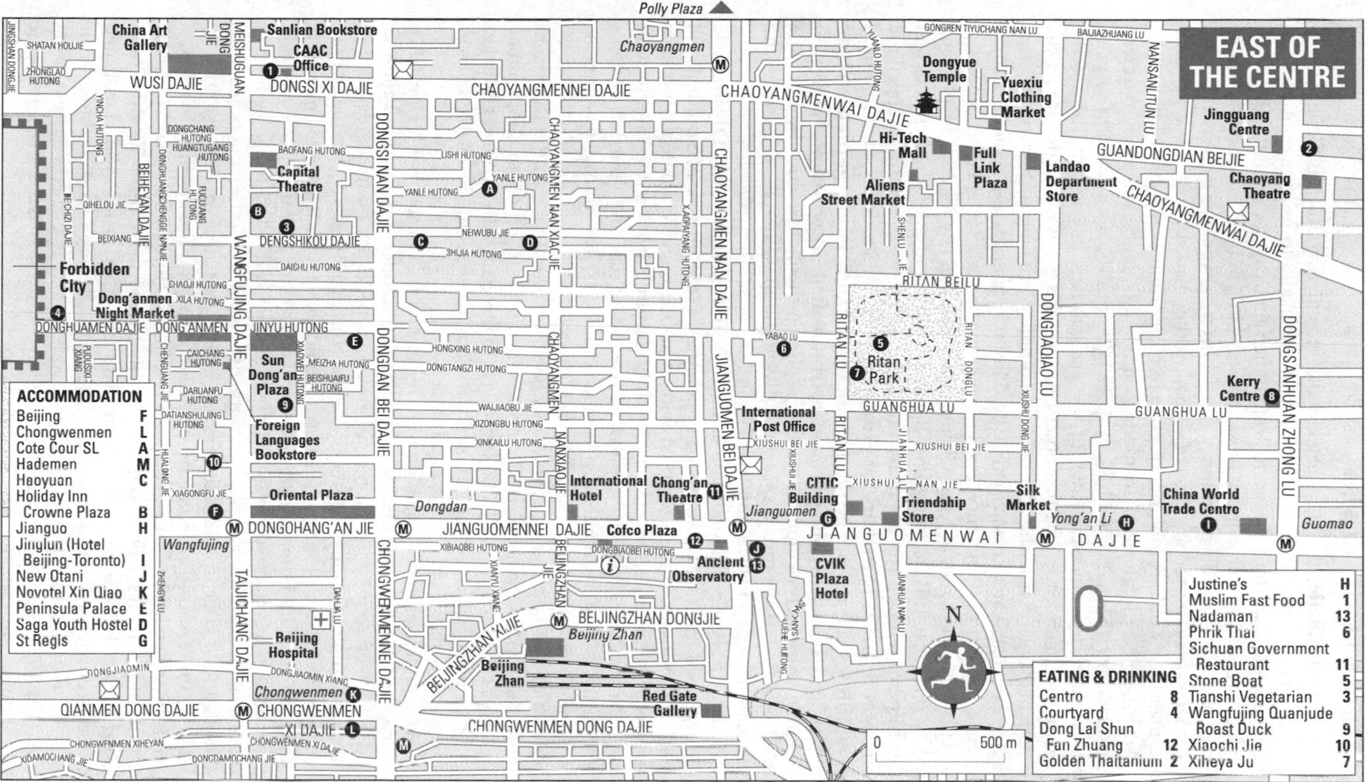

EAST OF THE CENTRE
ACCOMMODATION
Beijing F
Chongwenmen L
Cote Cour SL A
Hademen M
Haoyuan C
Holiday Inn Crowne Plaza B
Jianguo H
Jinglun (Hotel Beijing-Toronto) I
New Otani J
Novotel Xin Qiao K
Peninsula Palace E
Saga Youth Hostel D
St Regis G
EATING & DRINKING
Centro 8
Courtyard 4
Dong Lai Shun Fan Zhuang 12
Golden Thaitanium 2
Justine's H
Muslim Fast Food 1
Nadaman 13
Phrik Thai 6
Sichuan Government Restaurant 11
Stone Boat 5
Tianshi Vegetarian 3
Wangfujing Quanjude Roast Duck 9
Xiaochi Jie 10
Xiheya Ju 7
Polly Plaza
China Art Gallery
Sanlian Bookstore
CAAC Office
Chaoyangmen
Dongyue Temple
Yuexiu Clothing Market
Jingguang Centre
Hi-Tech Mall
Full Link Plaza
Landao Department Store
Chaoyang Theatre
Aliens Street Market
Capital Theatre
Forbidden City
Dong'anmen Night Market
Sun Dong'an Plaza
Foreign Languages Bookstore
Oriental Plaza
Ritan Park
Kerry Centre
International Post Office
International Hotel
Chang'an Theatre
CITIC Building
Friendship Store
Silk Market
China World Trade Centre
Dongdan
Jianguomen
Yong'an Li
Guomao
Wangfujing
Cofco Plaza
Ancient Observatory
CVIK Plaza Hotel
Beijing Hospital
Beijing Zhan
Red Gate Gallery
Chongwenmen
WUSI DAJIE
DONGSI XI DAJIE
MEISHUGUAN DONG JIE
CHAOYANGMENNEI DAJIE
CHAOYANGMENWAI DAJIE
GONGREN TIYUCHANG NAN LU
BAIJIAZHUANG LU
NANSANLITUN LU
GUANDONGDIAN BEIJIE
YUANLO HUTONG
DONGSI NAN DAJIE
CHAOYANGMEN NAN XIAOJIE
CHAOYANGMEN NAN DAJIE
XIAOPAIYANG HUTONG
BAOFANG HUTONG
LISHI HUTONG
YANLE HUTONG
NEIWUBU JIE
3HIJIA HUTONG
DENGSHIKOU DAJIE
DAIJCHU HUTONG
SHATAN HOUJIE
ZHONGLAO HUTONG
JINGSHAN DONGJIE
YINCHA HUTONG
DONGCHANG HUTONG
HUANGTUGANG HUTONG
BEIHEYAN DAJIE
DONGHUANGCHENGGE NANJIE
FUCUANG HUTONG
QIHELOU JIE
BEICHIZI DAJIE
BEIXIANG
SHAOJI HUTONG
XILA HUTONG
DONGHUAMEN DAJIE
DONG'ANMEN
JINYU HUTONG
WANGFUJING DAJIE
XIAOWEI HUTONG
MEIZHA HUTONG
BEISHUAIFU HUTONG
CAICHANG HUTONG
CHENGUANG JIE
PUDUSIXI XIANG
DARUANFU HUTONG
DATIANSHUIJING HUTONG
HUALONG JIE
XIAGONGFU JIE
DONGDAN BEI DAJIE
HONGXING HUTONG
DONGTANGZI HUTONG
WAIJIAOBU JIE
XIZONGBU HUTONG
XINKAILU HUTONG
NANXIAOJIE
SHENLU JIE
RITAN BEILU
RITAN LU
RITAN DONGLU
YABAO LU
GUANGHUA LU
DONGDAQIAO LU
DONGSANHUAN ZHONG LU
XIUSHUI BEI JIE
XIUSHUI DONG JIE
XIUSHUI NAN JIE
XIUSHUI JIE
JIANHUA LU
JIANHUA NAN LU
JIANGUOMEN BEI DAJIE
DONGCHANG'AN JIE
JIANGUOMENNEI DAJIE
JIANGUOMENWAI DAJIE
XIBIAOBEI HUTONG
DONGBIAOBEI HUTONG
XIANYU XIANG
BEIJINGZHAN JIE
BEIJINGZHAN DONGJIE
BEIJINGZHAN XIJIE
SAN CANG
YUEHE HUTONG
TAIJICHANG DAJIE
CHONGWENMENNEI DAJIE
DAHUA LU
ZHENGYI LU
DONGJIAOMIN XIANG
DONGJIAOMIN
QIANMEN DONG DAJIE
CHONGWENMEN XI DAJIE
CHONGWENMEN XIHEYAN
XIDAMOCHANG JIE
DONGDAMOCHANG JIE
CHONGWENMEN DONG DAJIE
0 500 m
N

Jianguomen Dajie

Jianguomen Dajie, the strip beyond the second ring road, is Beijing's rich quarter, a ritzy area with an international flavour thanks to its large contingent of foreigners and staff from the weird Jianguomen embassy compound. Eating and staying around here will soon sap most travellers' budgets (first-time tourists can be heard here expressing disappointment that China is as expensive as New York), but the wide variety of shopping offered – good clothes markets, the Friendship Store, and malls that wouldn't look out of place in Hong Kong – will suit all pockets.

An unexpected survivor marooned amid the high-rises, the **Ancient Observatory** (Mon–Fri 9–11.30am & 1–4.30pm; ¥10) is a charming surprise, tucked in the southwest corner of the Jianguomen intersection, beside the Jianguomen metro stop. The first observatory on this site was founded under the orders of Kublai Khan, the astronomers' commission being to reform the then faulty calendar. Later it was staffed by Muslim scientists, as medieval Islamic science enjoyed pre-eminence, but, bizarrely, in the early seventeenth century it was placed in the hands of Jesuit Christian missionaries. The Jesuits, a small group led by one Matteo Ricci, arrived in Beijing in 1601 and astonished citizens and the emperor with a series of precise astronomical forecasts. They re-equipped the observatory and remained in charge through to the 1830s. Today, the building is essentially a shell, and the best features of the complex are the **garden**, a placid retreat, and the eight Ming-dynasty **astronomical instruments** sitting on the roof, stunningly sculptural armillary spheres, theodolites and the like. The small attached **museum**, displaying early astronomy-influenced pottery and navigational equipment, is an added bonus.

Turn up Ritan Lu and you'll hit the **Jianguomenwai Diplomatic Compound**, the first of two embassy complexes (the other is at Sanlitun, well northeast of here), a giant toytown with neat buildings in ordered courtyards and frozen sentries on red and white plinths. **Ritan Park** is a five-minute walk from Jianguomen Dajie. It's popular with embassy staff and courting couples, who make use of its numerous secluded nooks. It also hosts a few upscale restaurants and the lovely *Stone Boat Bar* (see p.129).

North of the park you enter the city's Russian zone, where all the shop signs are in the Cyrillic alphabet; to the north, Shenlu Jie is full of fur shops aimed squarely at the Russian moll. The street ends in the giant **Aliens Street Market** (9.30am–6pm), a chaotic mall of gaudy trinkets, fakes and questionable fashion, thronging with Russian tourists and traders.

Back on Jianguomen Dajie, continuing west you'll reach the **Friendship Store**, the Chinese state's idea of a shopping centre, once the only kind allowed, and now overtaken by its commercial competitors. Its top floors are devoted to the usual range of goods – clothes, jewellery and paintings – but its lower floor is of more use, with a foreign exchange (open daily), a supermarket selling plenty of foreign goodies, an information desk where you can pick up the *China Daily*, and a bookshop. On the other side of the road, the CVIK Plaza (daily 9am–9pm) is a more modern shopping centre with five floors of clothes and accessories. There's a food court in the basement and a Bank of China on the first floor.

The main reason to continue beyond here is to head for the **Silk Market**, a giant six-storey mall of fake goods (see p.138), just north of Yong'an Li subway stop. From here, it's a dull couple of kilometres to the **China World Trade Centre** just before the intersection with the third ring road. Dedicated consumers who make it here are rewarded with Beijing's most exclusive mall, boasting four gleaming storeys of pricey goods, as well as a basement ice-skating rink. The Wellcome Supermarket here is one of the best supermarkets in the city, though – unsurprisingly – it's not cheap.

Chaoyangmen Dajie and Sanlitun

North of Jianguomenwai Dajie, the Ming-dynasty **Dongyue Temple** (Tues–Sun 8am–5pm; ¥10), a short walk from Ritan Park or Chaoyangmen metro stop, is an intriguing place. Pass under the Zhandaimen archway and you enter a courtyard holding around thirty annexes, each of which deals with a different aspect of Taoist life, the whole making up a sort of surreal spiritual bureaucracy. There's the "Department of Suppressing Schemes", "Department of Wandering Ghosts", even a "Department for Fifteen Kinds of Violent Death". In each, a statue of Taoist deity Lao Zi holds court over brightly painted figures, many with monstrous animal heads, too many limbs and the like. The temple shop sells red tablets for worshippers to sign and leave outside the annexes as petitions to the spiritual officials. Departments dealing with longevity and wealth are predictably popular, but so, tellingly, is the "Department for Official Morality".

Not far north of here is the **Poly Plaza**, at Dongsi Shitiao metro stop. It's mostly offices, but at the back lies a small **museum** (Mon–Sat 9.30am–4.30pm; ¥50), which, though comparatively pricey, has one of the most select collections of antiquities in the capital. In the Hall of Ancient Bronzes you'll find four of the twelve bronze animals that were looted from the Old Summer Palace (see p.120); all were bought in the west by patriotic businessmen, and their return was much heralded. The second hall displays ancient Buddha statues.

East of here is the **Sanlitun** bar district (see map, p.128). By night, it's raucous and gaudy, but during the day beguilingly civilized, with many small cafés and restaurants that are good for people-watching. As well as drinking, there are plenty of opportunities to eat and shop here.

798 Art District

Although it's out on the way to the airport, the **798 Art District**, a collection of art galleries, boutiques and cafés, is the latest hotspot for the arty crowd; take bus #915, #918 or #934 from Dongzhimen Station. Originally, it was an electronics factory; when that closed down in the 1990s artists moved in and converted the airy, light, and above all, cheap spaces into studios. As the Chinese art market blossomed, galleries followed, then shops and cafés.

There are exhibition openings every week, and every art form is well represented – though with such a lot of it about, it varies in quality. The most established **galleries** are Beijing Commune, Marcella Gallery, the huge Beijing Tokyo Art Projects and White Space (see p.135). There's a good English-language art bookstore, Timezone 8, and plenty of places for food; for crepes, try *Vincent's*, and for a cappuccino, the *At Café*.

North of the centre

The area north of the Forbidden City has a scattered collection of sights, many of them remnants of the imperial past, when this area was the home of princes, dukes and monks. Beyond the imperial parks of **Jingshan** and **Beihai** is the one part of the city that is truly a pleasure to walk around – the well-preserved

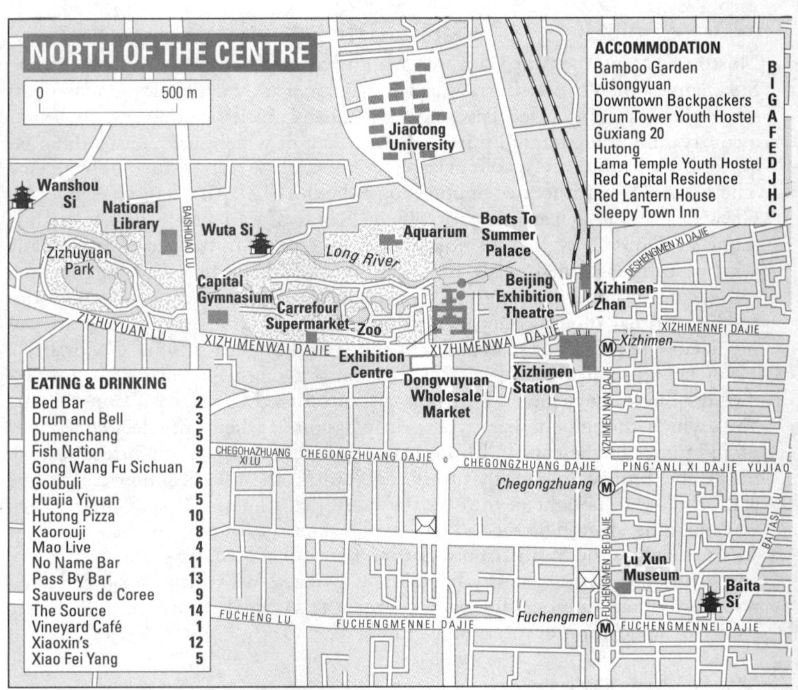

hutong district around **Houhai**. Tucked away here you'll find **Prince Gong's Palace**, **Song Qingling's residence** and the **Bell** and **Drum towers**, all within strolling distance of one another.

A few kilometres east of here, you'll find the appealing **Nanluogu Xiang**, a street where the artsy set hang out, and, right next to the Yonghe Gong metro stop, the **Yonghe Gong** Tibetan lamasery – one of Beijing's most colourful (and popular) attractions. While you're in the vicinity, don't miss the peaceful, and unjustly ignored, **Confucius Temple** and **Ditan Park**, within easy walking distance of one another.

West of this area, you'll find a number of little **museums** – the homes of two twentieth-century cultural icons, **Lu Xun** and **Xu Beihong** now hold exhibitions of their works, while the **Baita Si** functions as a museum of religious relics as well as a place of pilgrimage.

Jingshan and Beihai parks

Jingshan Park (daily 6am–10pm; ¥3) is a natural way to round off a trip to the Forbidden City. An artificial mound, it was created by the digging of the palace moat, and served as a windbreak and a barrier to malevolent spirits (believed to emanate from the north) for the imperial quarter of the city. It takes its name, meaning Coal Hill, from a coal store once sited here. Its history, most momentously, includes the suicide of the last Ming emperor, **Chong Zhen**, in 1644, who hanged himself here from a locust tree after rebel troops broke into the

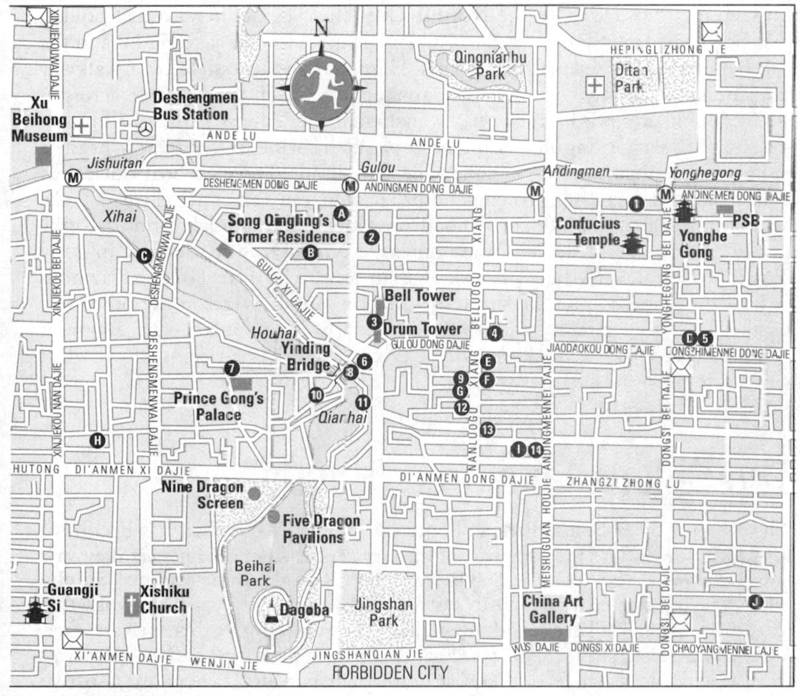

imperial city. The spot, on the eastern side of the park, is easy to find as it is signposted everywhere (underneath signs pointing to a children's playground), though the tree that stands here is not the original.

It's the **views** from the top of the hill that make this park such a compelling target: they take in the whole extent of the Forbidden City – giving a revealing perspective – and a fair swath of the city outside, a deal more attractive than at ground level. To the west is Beihai with its fat snake lake; in the north, Gulou and Zhonglou (the Drum and Bell towers); and to the northeast, the Yonghe Gong.

Almost half of **Beihai Park** (daily 6am–8pm; ¥5, buildings ¥10), a few hundred metres west of Jingshan on the route of bus #5 from Qianmen, is water – and a favourite ice-skating spot in the winter months. The park was supposedly created by Kublai Khan, long before any of the Forbidden City structures were conceived, and its scale is suitably ambitious: the lake was man-made, an island being created in its midst with the excavated earth. Emperor Qianlong oversaw its landscaping into a classical garden, and Mao's widow, the ill-fated Jiang Qing, was a frequent visitor here. Today, its elegance is marred by funfairs and shops among the willows and red-columned galleries, though it's still a grand place to retreat from the city and recharge. Most of the buildings (daily 6am–4pm) lie on the central island, whose summit is marked by a white dagoba, built in the mid-seventeenth century to celebrate a visit by the Dalai Lama, a suitable emblem for a park that contains a curious mixture of religious buildings, storehouses for cultural relics and imperial garden architecture.

Just inside the south gate, the **Round City** encloses a courtyard that holds a jade bowl, said to have belonged to Kublai Khan. The white jade Buddha in the hall behind was a present from Burma. The **island** is accessible by a walkway from here. It's dotted with religious architecture, which you'll come across as you scramble around the rocky paths, including the **Yuegu Lou**, a hall full of steles, and the giant **dagoba** sitting on top with a shrine to the demon-headed, multi-armed lamaist deity, Yamantaka, nestling inside. There's a boat dock near here, where you can rent rowing **boats**, or you can rent duck-shaped pedal boats from near the south gate – good ways to explore the lake and its banks. On the north side of the lake, the impressive **Nine Dragon Screen**, in good condition, is one of China's largest at 27m long. The Five Dragon Pavilions nearby are supposedly in the shape of a dragon's spine. Over on the other side of the lake, the gardens and rockeries here were popular with Emperor Qianlong, and it's easy to see why – even when the place is crowded at weekends, the atmosphere is tranquil.

The Shicha lake area (Houhai)

The area north of Beihai Park, colloquially known as **Houhai**, has become a heritage zone, and it's the only part of the city centre where the *hutong* alleyways have been preserved at any scale. The area centres on the three artificial **Shicha lakes**, created during the Yuan dynasty, and the port for a canal network that served the capital. The choked, grey alleys show Beijing's other, private, face; here you'll see cluttered courtyards and converted palaces, and come across small open spaces where old men sit with their pet birds. There are also two giant old buildings, the Bell and Drum towers, hidden away among the alleys. The area has been prettified, with touristy venues being built and rickshaw tours running from outside the Bell Tower, but it retains its charm, at least for the moment. It's also become one of Beijing's hipper hang-outs, with plenty of

▲ A hutong near Houhai

bars and restaurants along the lakeside (see p.129). The best way to get around is certainly by **bike**. Traffic is light and you're free to dive into any alley you fancy, though you're almost certain to get lost – in which case, cycle around until you come to one of the lakes, the only big landmarks around. The best point of entry is the *hutong* nearest the northern entrance to Beihai Park – to get here by bus, take trolleybus #111 from Dongdan Bei Dajie, or bus #13 from the Yonghe Gong.

Prince Gong's Palace and around

Residence of the last Qing emperor's father, **Prince Gong's Palace** (daily 9am–4.30pm; ¥20) is the best-kept courtyard house in the city. To get here, follow the curving alley north from Beihai Park's north entrance – Qianhai Hu (the southernmost lake) will be on your right – then take the first left, then the first right on to Qianhai Xi Jie. If you're trying to reach the palace directly by bus, you'll have to get off on Dianmen Xi Dajie and walk the same route. The attractive, leafy garden of the palace is split into discreet compounds and imaginatively landscaped. The largest hall hosts irregular performances of **Beijing Opera** – though you'll have to time your arrival with that of the tour groups, at around 11am, 4pm and 7.30pm, to witness these. There are plenty of other **old palaces** in the area, as this was once something of an imperial pleasure ground and home to a number of high officials and distinguished eunuchs. The Palace of Tao Beile, now a school, is just west of here on Liuyin Jie. Doubling back and heading north along the lakeside, you'll come to the humpbacked Yinding Bridge, at the point where the lake is narrowest. Over the bridge is the excellent *Kaorouji Restaurant* (see p.127), which boasts good views over the lake. Opposite, you'll find the *Buddha Bar* (among many others), a great place to sit outside with a coffee.

Song Qingling's Former Residence and the Drum and Bell towers

From Yinding Bridge, head north along the lakeside and loop around to the west and you'll reach **Song Qingling's Former Residence** (Tues–Sun 9am–4.30pm; ¥20), another Qing mansion, with a delicate, spacious garden. Song Qingling, the wife of Sun Yatsen, commands great respect in China and an exhibition inside details her busy life in a dry, admiring tone. From here, an alley will take you on to Gulou Xi Dajie, a major street, at the eastern end of which squats the **Drum Tower** (Gulou; daily 9am–4.30pm; ¥10), a fifteenth-century Ming creation. From this vantage point drums were beaten to mark dusk and to call imperial officials to meetings. Every half-hour between 10am and noon and from 2 to 4pm a troupe of drummers whacks cheerfully away at the giant drums inside. They're not, to be blunt, very artful, but it's still an impressive sight. The building's twin, the **Bell Tower** (Zhonglou; same times and prices), is at the other end of the plaza. Originally Ming, it was destroyed by fire and rebuilt in the eighteenth century. It still has its original bell, which used to be rung at dawn. These towers stand on the city's main north–south axis – head directly south, going round Jingshan Park, and past the Forbidden City, and you'll eventually come to Qianmen Dajie, a route followed by bus #5.

Xu Beihong Museum

Just outside the *hutong* quarter, but easily combined with a visit to Houhai, the **Xu Beihong Museum** (Tues–Sun 9–11am & 1.30–4.30pm; ¥5) at 53 Xinjiekou Bei Dajie, on the route of bus #22 from Qianmen or #38 from the east end of Fuchingmennei Dajie, and five minutes' walk north of Jishuitan metro stop, is definitely worth the diversion. The son of a wandering portraitist, Xu Beihong (1895–1953) did for Chinese art what his contemporary Lu Xun did for literature. Xu had to look after his whole family from the age of 17 after his father died, and spent much of his early life in semi-destitution before receiving the acclaim he deserved. His extraordinary facility is well in evidence here in seven halls that display a huge collection of his work, including many of the ink paintings of horses he was most famous for, but also oil paintings in a Western style, which he produced when studying in France, and large-scale allegorical images that allude to events in China at the time. However, the images that are easiest to respond to are his delightful sketches and studies, in ink and pencil, often of his son.

Nanluogu Xiang

There aren't, to be frank, too many streets in Beijing that could be called appealing, so this north–south *hutong* is a little oasis. Dotted with laid-back cafés, boutiques and restaurants, it has become a playground for the city's bobos (bourgeois-bohemians). Still, there are enough open-air mahjong games, rickety stores, and old men sitting out with their caged birds to maintain that ramshackle, backstreet Beijing charm. If there seems to be a surfeit of bright and beautiful young things, that's because of the drama school just around the corner. All in all, it's a great place to idle over a cappuccino; *Xiao Xin's* and the *Pass by Bar* (see p.125 and 130) are recommended venues.

Yonghe Gong and around

Though it is a little touristy, the colourful **Yonghe Gong**, Tibetan Lama Temple (daily 9am–5pm; ¥25), is well worth a visit; it couldn't be much easier to reach – Yonghe Gong metro stop is right next door. It was built towards the end of the seventeenth century as the residence of Prince Yin Zhen. In 1723, when the prince became the Emperor Yong Zheng and moved into the Forbidden City, the temple was retiled in imperial yellow and restricted thereafter to religious use. It became a lamasery in 1744, housing monks from Tibet and also from Inner Mongolia, over which it had a presiding role, supervising the election of the Mongolian Living Buddha, who was chosen by lot from a gold urn. After the civil war in 1949, the Yonghe Gong was declared a national monument and for thirty years was closed; remarkably, it escaped the ravages of the Cultural Revolution.

Visitors are free to wander through the prayer halls and ornamental gardens, though the experience is largely aesthetic rather than spiritual. As well as the amazing *mandalas* hanging in side halls, there is some notable statuary. In the Third Hall, the **Pavilion of Eternal Happiness**, are *nandikesvras*, representations of Buddha having sex. Once used to educate the emperors' sons, the statues are now completely covered by drapes. The **Hall of the Wheel of Law**, behind it, has a gilded bronze statue of the founder of the Yellow Hat Sect and paintings that depict his life, while the thrones next to it are for the Dalai Lamas when they used to come here to teach. In the last, grandest hall – the **Wanfu Pavilion** – an eighteen-metre-high statue of the Maitreya Buddha, is made from a single trunk of sandalwood, a gift for Emperor Qianlong from the seventh Dalai Lama. The wood is Tibetan and it took three years to ship it to Beijing.

The lamasery also functions as an active **Tibetan Buddhist centre**, though it's used basically for propaganda purposes, to show China guaranteeing and respecting the religious freedom of minorities. It's questionable how genuine the monks you see wandering around are – at best, they're state-approved.

Confucius Temple and Ditan Park

Opposite the Yonghe Gong, on the west side, is a quiet *hutong* lined with little shops selling religious tapes, incense and images. This street, one of the city's oldest, has been home to scholars since the Yuan dynasty and is lined with *pailous*, decorative arches, which once graced many of Beijing's streets – they were torn down in the 1950s as a hindrance to traffic. On the right, about 100m down, the **Confucius Temple** (daily 8.30am–5pm; ¥10) will be worth a look when the extensive renovations are finished in 2008. The best thing to do here is sit on a bench in the peaceful courtyard, among ancient, twisted trees, and enjoy the silence.

Returning to the Yonghe Gong and heading north, **Ditan Park** (daily 6am–9pm; ¥1, buildings ¥5) is just 100m away, more interesting as a place to wander among the trees and spot the odd *tai ji* performance than for its small **museum** (¥5) holding the emperor's sedan chair and the enormous altar at which he performed sacrifices to the earth.

Around Fuchengmennei Dajie

Heading west from the south end of Beihai Park along Wenjin Dajie, you'll come to **Fuchengmennei Dajie**, just off Xidan Dajie, the area's shopping district. A couple of places along here make it worth a nose around on the way to the deservedly popular Summer Palace. Bus #101 from the north exit of the Forbidden City, and #13 from the Yonghe Gong, traverse the street. The **Guangji Si**, headquarters of the China Buddhist Association, is a working Buddhist temple near its eastern end, on the north side of the road, with an important collection of painting and sculpture. There's no entrance fee and visitors are free to look around. Farther west along the street you'll come to a temple on the north side that's been converted into a school – the spirit wall now forms one side of a public lavatory. Beyond this, the massive white dagoba of the **Baita Si** (Tues–Sun 9am–5pm; ¥10) becomes visible, rising over the rooftops of a labyrinth of *hutongs*; the only access is from Fuchengmennei Dajie. Shaped like an upturned bowl with an ice-cream cone on top, the 35-metre-high dagoba was built to house relics in the Yuan dynasty and designed by a Nepalese architect. The temple is worth a visit just for the small Buddha statues, mostly Tibetan, housed in one hall. Another hall holds a collection of bronze luohans, including one with a beak, small bronze Buddhas and other, weirder lamaist figures, together with silk and velvet priestly garments, which were unearthed from under the dagoba in 1978. Just outside the temple there's a tasty pancake stall.

Lu Xun Museum

Continue west and, just before the giant intersection with Fuchengmen Bei Dajie, you'll see Xisantiao Hutong to the north, which leads to the **Lu Xun Museum** (Tues–Sun 9am–4pm; ¥10), a large and extensively renovated courtyard house. Lu Xun (1881–1936) is widely accepted as the greatest modern Chinese writer, who gave up a promising career in medicine to write books (see p.1206).

A hater of pomposity, he might feel a little uneasy in his house now, where the atmosphere is of uncritical admiration. His possessions have been preserved like relics, incidentally giving a good idea of what Chinese interiors looked like at the beginning of the last century, and there's a photo exhibition of his life, lauding his achievements. A bookshop in the eastern building sells English translations of his work, including his most popular book, *The True Story of Ah Q*.

Beijing Zoo

Beijing Zoo (daily 7.30am–5pm; ¥15), on Xizhimenwei Dajie, marks the edge of the inner city. There's a metro stop, Xizhimen, 1km east of the zoo, and a bus terminus just south of it; bus #7, which you can catch from Fuchingmennei Dajie, terminates here. Xizhimen Zhan (Beijing North train station) is north of the metro stop. The zoo itself, flanked on either side by the monumental Capital Gymnasium and Soviet-built Exhibition Centre, is not a great attraction unless you really need to see a panda. You can join the queues to have your photo taken sitting astride a plastic replica, then push your way through to glimpse the living variety – kept in relatively palatial quarters and highly familiar through ritual diplomatic mating exchanges over the last decades. While the pandas lie on their backs in their luxury pad, waving their legs in the air, other animals, less cute or less endangered, slink, pace or flap around their miserable cells. Much the best part of the rest of the zoo is the new **aquarium**, though it's a bit pricey (¥100, ¥50 children).

Wuta Si and Wanshou Si

Past the zoo, head north up Baishiqiao Lu, take the first right and follow the canal, and ten minutes' walk will bring you to the **Wuta Si** (daily 9am–4.30pm; ¥10). The central hall is radically different from any other sacred building you'll see in the capital. Completed in 1424, it's a stone cube decorated on the outside with reliefs of animals, Sanskrit characters, and Buddha images – each has a different hand gesture – and topped with five layered, triangular spires. It's visibly Indian in influence, and is said to be based on a temple in Bodhgaya, where Buddha gained enlightenment. There are 87 steps to the top (¥5), where you can inspect the spire carvings at close quarters – including elephants and Buddhas, and, at the centre of the central spire, a pair of feet. The new halls behind the museum are home to statues of bulbous-eyed camels, docile-looking tigers, puppy-dog lions and the like, all collected from the spirit ways of tombs and long-destroyed temples.

From here it's a half-hour stroll following the river west back to Baishiqiao Lu, through the bamboo groves of **Zizhuyuan Park**, and out of the park's northwest exit to the **Wanshou Si** (daily 9am–4.30pm; ¥20). This Ming temple, a favourite of Empress Dowager Cixi's, is now a small museum of ancient art, with five exhibition halls of Ming and Qing relics, mostly ceramics.

The summer palaces and far northwest

In the northwest corner of the city is a cluster of attractions that improve the further out you go. The **Dazhong Si** is worth a poke around on the way to or from more alluring destinations, and the nearby districts of Haidian and Zhongguancun are known for hi-tech shopping and youth culture.

Though it's eclipsed by its newer neighbour, **Yuanmingyuan**, the old Summer Palace, is worth checking out for the sobering history it attests to. Nearby **Yiheyuan**, usually known in English as *the* Summer Palace, is an excellent place to get away from the city smog – a recommended escape, summer or winter.

Dazhong Si

The **Dazhong Si** (Great Bell Temple; Tues–Sun 8am–4.30pm; ¥15) is one of Beijing's most interesting little museums, showcasing several hundred **bronze bells** from temples all over the country. It's stuck out on Beisanhuan Lu, the north section of the third ring road, a long way from the centre; buses #302 and #367 go right past, or you can take the metro to Dazhongsi stop and walk 200m west. The best way to visit is on the way to or from the Summer Palace.

The bells here are considerable works of art, their surfaces enlivened with embossed texts in Chinese and Tibetan, abstract patterns, and images of storks and dragons. The odd, scaly, dragon-like creature shown perching on top of each bell is a *pulao*, a legendary animal supposed to shriek when attacked by a whale (the wooden hammers used to strike the bells are carved to look like whales). The smallest bell here is the size of a goblet; the largest, a Ming creation called the **King of Bells**, is as tall as a two-storey house. Hanging in the back hall, it is, at fifty tonnes, the biggest and oldest surviving bell in the world, and can reputedly be heard up to 40km away. You can climb up to a platform above it to get a closer look at some of the 250,000 Chinese characters on its surface, and join Chinese visitors in trying to throw a coin into the small hole in the top. The method of its construction and the history of Chinese bell-making are explained by displays, with English captions, in side halls. Audio tapes and CDs on sale of the bells in action are more interesting than they might appear: the shape of Chinese bells dampens vibrations, so they only sound for a short time and can be effectively used as instruments.

Haidian

It's not an obvious tourist attraction, but the whole of **Haidian district**, northwest of the third ring road, west of the Wudaokou metro stop, bears mentioning: here you'll find the more underground bars and clubs, and on

Zhongguangcun Lu, nicknamed Electronics Street, a hi-tech zone of computer shops. In the north of the area, on the way to the Summer Palace, you'll pass **Beijing University** (or "Beida" as it's known colloquially), China's most prestigious university. Originally established and administered by the Americans at the beginning of the twentieth century, it stood in Jingshan Park and was moved to its present site in 1953. Now busy with new contingents of foreign students from the West, it was half-deserted during the Cultural Revolution when both students and teachers, regarded as suspiciously liberal, were dispersed for "re-education". The pleasant campus, with its old buildings and quiet, well-maintained grounds, makes it nicer than most of the city's parks. The technical college, Tsinghua, is not far from here, to the east, though it's much less attractive. Around the gates of both universities you'll find small, inexpensive **restaurants**, **bars** and **Internet cafés** catering for the students.

Yuanmingyuan

Beijing's original Summer Palace, the **Yuanmingyuan** (daily 9am–6pm; ¥15), is a thirty-minute walk north of Beida, or take bus #375 from Xizhimen metro stop, bus #331 from Wudaokou metro stop, or bus #322 from Beijing Zoo. Built by the Qing emperor Kangxi in the early eighteenth century, the palace, nicknamed "China's Versailles" by Europeans, once boasted the largest royal gardens in the world – with some two hundred pavilions and temples set around a series of lakes and natural springs. Marina Warner recreates the scene in *The Dragon Empress*:

Scarlet and golden halls, miradors, follies and gazebos clustered around artificial hills and lakes. Tranquil tracts of water were filled with fan-tailed goldfish with telescopic eyes, and covered with lotus and lily pads; a superabundance of flowering shrubs luxuriated in the gardens; antlered deer wandered through the grounds; ornamental ducks and rare birds nestled on the lakeside.

Today, however, there is little to hang your imagination upon. In 1860, the entire complex was burnt and destroyed by British and French troops, ordered by the Earl of Elgin to make the imperial court "see reason" during the Opium Wars. There are plenty of signs to remind you of this, making Yuanmingyuan a tiresome monument to contemporary Chinese xenophobia. The park extends over 350 hectares but the only really identifiable ruins are the **Hall of Tranquillity** in the northeastern section. The stone and marble remains of fountains and columns hint at how fascinating the original must once have been, with its marriage of European Rococo decoration and Chinese motifs. The government is jazzing the place up with a programme of restoration and construction, but this remains an attraction wholly eclipsed by the new Summer Palace.

The Summer Palace

Yiheyuan, *the* **Summer Palace** (daily 8am–7pm, buildings close at 4pm; ¥40), is certainly worth the effort to seek out. This is one of the loveliest spots in Beijing, a vast public park where the latter-day imperial court would decamp during the hottest months of the year. The site is perfect, surrounded by hills, cooled by the lake (which takes up two-thirds of the park's area) and sheltered

Empress Dowager Cixi

The notorious Cixi entered the imperial palace at 15 as Emperor Xianfeng's **concubine**, quickly becoming his favourite and bearing him a son. When the emperor died in 1861, she became regent, ruling in place of her infant boy. For the next 25 years, she in effect ruled China, displaying a mastery of intrigue and court politics. When her son died of syphilis, she installed her nephew as puppet regent imprisoned him, and retained her authority. Her fondness of extravagant gestures (every year she had ten thousand caged birds released on her birthday) drained the state's coffers, and her deeply conservative policies were inappropriate for a time when the nation was calling out for reform.

With foreign powers taking great chunks out of China's borders on and off during the nineteenth century, Cixi was moved to respond in a typically misguided fashion. Impressed by the claims of the xenophobic **Boxer Movement** (whose Chinese title translated as "Righteous and Harmonious Fists"), Cixi let them loose on all the foreigners in China in 1899. The Boxers laid siege to the foreign legation's compound in Beijing for nearly two months before a European expeditionary force arrived and, predictably, slaughtered the agitators. Cixi and the emperor escaped the subsequent rout of the capital by disguising themselves as peasants and fleeing the city. On her return, Cixi clung to power, attempting to delay the inevitable fall of her dynasty. One of her last acts, before she died in 1908, was to arrange for the murder of her puppet regent.

by garden landscaping. The impressive temples and pleasure houses are spread out along the lakeside and connected by a suitably majestic gallery.

The quickest route to Yiheyuan is to take a taxi from Xizhimen or Wudaokou metro stop (¥15). Alternatively, take the same buses that go to Yuanmingyuan and get off a few stops later, at the terminus, or take bus #808 from Qianmen. There's also an interesting boat service from the back of the Exhibition Centre, which is just east of the zoo. The boats operate daily between 9am and 3pm, leaving when full, and cost ¥40 single and ¥70 return.

There have been summer imperial pavilions at Yiheyuan since the eleventh century, although the present layout is essentially eighteenth century, created by the Manchu emperor Qianlong. However, the key character associated with the palace is the **Empress Dowager Cixi**, (see box above) – Yiheyuan was very much her pleasure ground. She rebuilt the palaces in 1888 and determinedly restored them in 1902 after foreign troops had ransacked them. Her ultimate flight of fancy was the construction of a magnificent marble boat from the very funds intended for the Chinese navy. Whether her misappropriations had any real effect on the empire's path is hard to determine, but it certainly speeded the decline, with China suffering heavy naval defeats during the war with Japan. To enjoy the site, however, you need know very little of its history – like Beihai, the park, its lake and pavilions form a startling visual array, like a traditional landscape painting brought to life.

The palaces

The **palaces** are built to the north of the lake, on and around Wanshou Shan (Longevity Hill), and many remain intimately linked with Cixi – anecdotes about whom are staple fare of the numerous guides. Most visitors enter through the **East Gate**, where the buses stop, above which is the main palace compound, including the **Renshoudian** (Hall of Benevolence and Longevity), a majestic hall where the empress and her predecessors gave audience. It contains much of the original nineteenth-century furniture, including an imposing throne. Beyond, to the right, is the **Deheyuan** (Palace of Virtue and Harmony), dominated by a three-storey **theatre**, complete with trap doors for the appearances and disappearances of the actors. Theatre was one of Cixi's main passions and she sometimes took part in performances, dressed as Guanyin, the goddess of mercy. The next major building along the path is the **Yulantang** (Jade Waves Palace). This is where the child emperor Guangxu was kept in captivity for ten years, while Cixi exercised his powers. Just to the west is the dowager's own principal residence, the **Leshoutang** (Hall of Joy and Longevity), which houses Cixi's hardwood throne, and the table where she took her notorious 108-course meals. The chandeliers were China's first electric lights, installed in 1903 and powered by the palace's own generator.

Kunming lake

From here to the northwest corner of the lake runs the **Long Gallery**, the nine-hundred-metre covered way, painted with mythological scenes and flanked by various temples and pavilions. It is said that no pair of lovers can walk through without emerging betrothed. Near the west end of the gallery is the infamous **marble boat**, completed by Cixi with purloined naval cash and regarded by her acolytes as a suitably witty and defiant gesture. Close by, and the tourist focus of this site, is a jetty with **rowing boats** for rent (¥10 per hour). Boating on the lake is a popular pursuit, with locals as much as foreigners, and well worth the money. You can dock again below Wanshou Shan and row out to the two **bridges** – the Jade Belt on the western side and Seventeen Arched on the east. In winter, the Chinese skate on the lake here, an equally spectacular sight, and skates are available for rent.

Eating, drinking, nightlife, entertainment and shopping

You're spoilt for choice when it comes to food in Beijing. Splurging in classy **restaurants** is a great way to spend your evenings, as prices in even the most luxurious places are very competitive and a lot more affordable than their equivalent in the West. Beijing has a great deal of entertainment options, too, with a lively arts scene, and it's well worth seeking them out; remember you won't have much opportunity outside the capital. There is a promising **bar and club scene** worth sampling, if just for the strange cultural juxtapositions it throws up. If you want to check out a Chinese disco or indigenous rock band, this is the place to do it, and again, a night on the town won't break your budget. **Shopping** is another diverting pastime, with the best choice of souvenirs and consumables in the country; in particular, Beijing still has a collection of intriguing little markets offering an appealing and affordable alternative to the new giant malls.

Eating

Nowhere else on the Chinese mainland can compete with the culinary wealth of Beijing: every style of **Chinese food** is available, plus just about any Asian and most world cuisines. Amongst all this abundance it's sometimes easy to forget that **Beijing** has its own culinary tradition – specialities well worth trying are **Beijing duck** (*Beijing kaoya*) and **Mongolian hotpot**. Beijing duck appears in Chinese restaurants worldwide and consists of small pieces of meat that you dip in plum sauce, then wrap with chopped onions in a pancake. It's very rich and packs a massive cholesterol count. Mongolian hotpot is healthier, a poor man's fondue, involving a large pot of boiling stock, usually heated from

Beijing restaurants and cafés

Berena's Bistro	伯瑞娜	*bó ruì nà*
Bookworm	书虫	*shū chóng*
Courtyard	四合院	*sìhéyuàn*
Damofang	大磨坊面包	*dàmòfáng miànbāo*
Dong'anmen Night Market	东华门夜市	*dōnghuámén yèshì*
Dong Lai Shun Fan Zhuang	东来顺饭庄	*dōngláishùn fànzhuāng*
Dumenchang	独门冲	*dú mén chōng*
Fish Nation	鱼邦	*yú bāng*
Golden Thaitanium	泰合金	*tàihéjīn*
Gong Wang Fu Sichuan	恭王府四川饭店	*gōngwángfǔ sìchuān fàndian*
Gongdelin	功德林素菜馆	*gōngdélín sùcàiguǎn*
Goubuli	狗不理	*gǒubùlǐ*
Huajia Yiyuan	花家怡园	*huā jiā yí yuán*
Hutong Pizza	胡同批萨	*hútóng pīsà*
Jiajingdu Peking Duck	嘉靖都烤鸭店	*jiājìngdū kǎoyādiàn*
Kaorouji	烤肉季	*kǎoròujì*
Lichun	利群烤鸭店	*lìqún kǎoyādiàn*
Muslim Fast Food	回民快餐店	*huímín kuàicān diàn*
Nadaman	滩万	*tān wàn*
One Thousand and One Nights	一千零一夜	*yī qiān ling yī yè*
Pass By Bar	过客酒吧	*guòkè jiǔbā*
Phrik Thai	泰辣椒	*tàilàjiāo*
Qianmen Quanjuce Roast Duck	前门全聚德烤鸭店	*qiánmén quánjùdé kǎoyādiàn*
Quanjude Roast Duck	全聚德烤鸭店	*quánjùdé kǎoyādiàn*
Sauveurs De Coree	韩香馆	*hán xiāng guǎn*
Serve the People	为人民服务	*wèirénmín fúwù*
Sichuan Government Restaurant	四川酒楼	*sìchuān jiǔlóu*
Sorabol	萨拉伯尔	*sàlābó'ěr*
The Source	都江源	*dū jiāng yuán*
Tianshi Vegetarian	绿色天食	*lǜsè tiānshí*
Trattoria	意大利威尼斯餐厅	*yìdàlì wēinísī cāntīng*
Vineyard Café	葡萄院儿	*pútao yuàn'er*
Wangfujing Quanjude Roast Duck	王府井全聚德烤鸭店	*wángfǔjǐng quánjùdé kǎoyādian*
Xiao Fei Yang	小肥羊	*xiǎo féi yáng*
Xiaochi Jie	小吃街	*xiǎo chī jiē*
Xiaoxin's	小新的店	*xiǎo xīn de diàn*
Xiheya Ju	羲和雅居	*xīhé yǎjū*

underneath the table, into which you dip strips of mutton, cabbage and noodles, then, if you're really committed, drink the rest as soup.

There's ample opportunity to eat **Western food** in Beijing, though it generally costs a little more than Chinese. If you really want the comforts of the familiar, try international places such as the *Hard Rock Café* – everything just like at home, including the prices. **Japanese** and **Korean** cuisine is mainly available from restaurants in upmarket hotels, though it's possible to eat both without breaking your budget, and they're well worth trying. Chinese fast food is a canteen-style serving, usually of noodles in a polystyrene packet, which you find in department stores or buy from street stalls; **street food**, mostly noodle dishes, is widely available, though not in the centre, where vendors are shooed away by the police – your best bet is at one of the designated night markets. Avoid the ice-cream vendors who hang around the parks as their home-made wares are of a dubious standard.

These days, **supermarkets** sell plenty of Western food. The CRC Supermarket in the base of the China World Trade Centre is impressive, though Western goods cost at least twenty percent more here than they do at home. The same is true of the supermarkets in the Friendship Store and Lufthansa Centre. For hard-to-find Western food such as olives, head to *Jenny Lou*'s outside the west gate of Chaoyang Park.

Breakfast, snacks and fast food

Many visitors find the Chinese **breakfast** of dumplings and glutinous rice served in canteens bland and unappealing, but *jian bing guozi*, the classic Beijing breakfast snack – vegetables wrapped in an omelette wrapped in a pancake – deftly assembled by street vendors in thirty seconds, is definitely worth trying (¥3). Most hotels offer some form of Western breakfast, or alternatively, head for a branch of *Damofang* for cheap croissants or *Starbucks* for cake and a caffeine jolt. For cheap and filling **suppers**, try street food like *huntun*, basically wonton soup, and *xianr bing* – stuffed pancake – or the diverse varieties of noodles. You'll find plenty of street food at the **night markets**, which begin operating around 5pm and start to shut down around 10pm. They're at their best in summer.

It's also worth knowing that every mall and shopping centre has a **food court**, sometimes in the basement but usually on the top floor, which offer inexpensive meals from a variety of outlets. You have to buy a plastic card at a central booth, which is debited at the counter when you order. Good food courts can be found at the Parkson Building on Fuxingmennei Dajie, in the Xidan Department Store, and, on Wangfujing, on the top floor of the Sun Dong'an Plaza and basement of the Oriental Plaza.

Damofang Qianmen Xi Dajie; basement of the Lufthansa Centre; Level 2, Sun Dong'an Plaza, Wangfujing. This good little French bakery chain has affordable pizzas, fresh croissants and cakes.

Dong'anmen Night Market Dong'anmen Dajie, off Wangfujing Dajie. Stalls set up along the street offering *xiaochi* (literally, "small food") from all over China. Nothing is more than a few yuan, except the odd delicacy such as scorpion on a stick for ¥10.

Goubuli 155 Dianmenwai Dajie, just south of the Drum Tower. A branch of the Tianjin institution, this place sells delicious dumplings (*baozi*) for a few yuan. You can eat them here – the downstairs canteen is cheaper than upstairs – or take them home, as most of the customers do. See map pp.112–113.

Kempi Deli First Floor, *Kempinski Hotel*, Lufthansa Centre, 50 Liangmaqiao Lu. Deserves a mention for producing the city's best bread and pastries. Prices halve after 8pm. See map p.128.

Xiaochi Jie Xiagongfu Jie, running west off the southern end of Wangfujing Dajie. This alley is lined with stalls where pushy vendors sell exotica at fixed prices. It's the perfect place to sample food to freak the folks back home: skewers of fried scorpions, silkworm pupae, crickets and sparrows are all available for less than ¥10 – though none of them, in truth, tastes of much. You can also get good noodles and seafood for a few yuan. See map p.109.

Cafés

As well as the places listed below, note that some bars are also great places to linger over a cappuccino, notably *Pass By Bar* (see p.130), *Drum and Bell* (see p.130) and *Stone Boat* (see p.129). All those, and the places below, have free Wi-Fi.

Bookworm Sanlitun Nan Jie, back of building 4 ⓦ www.beijingbookworm.com. This bistro cum café cum lending library raises the tone of the whole area. There's a programme of events and lectures; check the website. A good place to muse. See map p.128.

Sculpting in Time 7 Weigongcun Lu, outside the southern gate of the Beijing Insititute of Technology. A casual, attractive café with a largely student clientele. Fit in by drinking lattes, browsing the book collection and gazing thoughtfully out of the window. They serve good muffins and pasta dishes here, too.

Starbucks First Floor, China World Trade Centre, Jianguomenwai Dajie; 1 Jianguomenwai Dajie (east side of the Friendship Store); COFCO Plaza, 8 Jianguomennei Dajie; Chaoyangmenwai Dajie, opposite the Dongyue Temple; Forbidden City, near the north entrance; Sun Dong'an Plaza (basement) and Oriental Plaza (first floor) on Wangfujing Dajie; north side of Xidan Plaza, Xidan. The coffee colonizers have overtaken *McDonald's* as the most potent symbol of Westernization. A medium-sized cup of their caffeinated mud is ¥15.

Vineyard Café 31 Wudaoying Hutong, south of Yonghe Gong Bridge. Good Western wine and food, including pizzas. Cross the second ring road onto Yonghe Gong Dajie and take the first *hutong* on the right. Good brunches; combine with a trip to the Yonghe Gong. Closed Mon. See map pp.112–113.

Xiaoxin's 103 Nanluogu Xiang. A cosy staple of artsy Nanluogu Xiang with a limited menu but a tasty cheesecake (¥18). See map pp.112–113.

Restaurants

All the expensive **hotels** have several well-appointed restaurants, where the atmosphere is sedate but prices are sometimes not as high as you might expect; look out for their special offers, advertised in the city's listings magazines. Local restaurants, though, are cheaper and livelier. Expect to eat earlier than you would in Western cities: lunch is around noon and dinner around 6 or 7pm. Few places stay open after 11pm. Restaurants sometimes have two **dining rooms**, which are priced differently – though the food comes from the same kitchen. The cheapest one is usually the open-plan area on the first floor. Telephone numbers have been included in the reviews below only for the more expensive and popular restaurants where **reservations** are advisable.

Qianmen

The places listed below are marked on the map on p.95.

Gongdelin 158 Qianmen Nan Dajie. This odd vegetarian restaurant serves Shanghai dishes with names like "the fire is singeing the snowcapped mountains". The food comprises mostly meat imitations that taste eerily genuine. Try the fish dishes and "dragons' eyes" made of tofu and mushroom. Service and surroundings are a bit lacklustre.

Lichun 11 Bei Xiang Hutong ⓣ 010/67025681. Deep in a *hutong*, this place is tough to find but offers good duck at half the price of the chains (¥80). From Qianmen metro stop, walk east along Qianmen Dong Dajie and take the first right into Zhengyi Lu, and at the end turn right. Then follow the English sign to the "Lijun Roast Duck Restaurant" – left, left and it's on the left. You'll probably have to ask. The restaurant is in a shabby old courtyard house, and it's small, so you'd be wise to reserve beforehand.

Qianmen Quanjude Roast Duck 32 Qianmen Dajie ⓣ 010/67011379. "The Great Wall and Roast Duck, try both to have a luck", says a ditty by the entrance to this Beijing institution. It's massive, professional and proficient, if obvious and touristy, though there's nothing wrong with the food. Tour groups are shepherded upstairs, but the ground floor is more atmospheric. A whole duck (which feeds two) costs ¥168.

Quanjude Roast Duck 14 Qianmen Xi Dajie ⓣ 010/63018833. The size of this giant eatery – seating more than two thousand – has earned it its "Super Duck" moniker. Prices the same as at the Qianmen branch.

East of the centre

Unless otherwise stated, the places listed below are marked on the map on p.109.

Courtyard 95 Donghuamen Dajie, outside the east gate of the Forbidden City ⓣ010/65268883, ⓦwww.courtyardbeijing.com. Listed in *Condé Nast Traveller* as one of the world's fifty best restaurants, this elegant, modish place specializes in fusion cuisine – continental food with a Chinese twist – which will set you back ¥250 or so. There's a contemporary art gallery downstairs (see p.135) and a cigar lounge upstairs. Daily 6pm–1am.

Dong Lai Shun Fan Zhuang Xiaoyangmao Jie, just off Jianguomennei Dajie. A great place to sample hotpot; it's inexpensive, with a very good reputation among locals and an English menu. Stick to the staples – glass noodles, veg, tofu and lots of thinly sliced meat – for a good feed. It's just around the corner from the Ancient Observatory. Around ¥50 per person.

Golden Thaitanium Dongsanhuan Bei Lu, next to the Chaoyang Theatre. Tasty, very spicy and inexpensive Thai food in a relaxed setting. There's a picture menu. Combine with a trip to the acrobatics at the theatre next door (see p.133) for a pleasant evening out; they stay open after the performance finishes at 9pm.

Jiajingdu Peking Duck 8 Hot Spring Chamber, Chaoyang Park West Gate ⓣ010/65918008, ⓦwww.afunti.com.cn. This place is pure theatre; you sit in what looks like an imperial hall, and the emperor and his concubines come out to greet you. It might be bizarre but the imperial fantasy is done with admirable thoroughness and the banquets are pretty good – though the duck is the last of many courses, so arrive hungry. Only set meals, starting at ¥200. See map pp.80–81.

Justine's Jianguo Hotel, 5 Jianguomenwai Dajie. An elegant French restaurant with the best wine list in the capital. Try the lobster soup or grilled lamb. Around ¥150 per person.

Muslim Fast Food Head up Wangfujing and just past the crossroads with Wusi Dajie there's a *hutong* full of clothes stalls on the east side of the road. Walk down here about 200m and you'll come to a little square – the restaurant is on the south side, opposite a *McDonald's* (look for the white writing on a green background). This technicolour canteen might not look like much, but the food is both delicious and cheap. Point to the dishes that take your fancy from the wide selection on display at the counters, plenty of vegetarian options among them. The sweets are especially good.

Nadaman Floor 3, *China World Hotel*, China World Trade Centre ⓣ010/65052266. Discreet, simple and seriously expensive Japanese restaurant with a set menu priced at ¥300 per person. Most of the ingredients are flown in from Japan.

Phrik Thai Gateway Building, 10 Yabao Lu ⓣ010/65925236. Elegant Thai restaurant popular with expats. Try the red curry and chicken satay.

Sichuan Government Restaurant Gongyun Tou Tiao, off Jianguomennei Dajie. This is the best place for Sichuan food in Beijing, serving the homesick bureaucrats who work in the same building. Head north up the alley that passes the east side of the Chang'an Theatre and after 200m there's an alley to the right with a public toilet opposite. Fifty metres down the alley a set of green and gold gates on the left marks the entrance to the Sichuan Government Building. Pass through the gates and the restaurant is on the left. There's no English menu, but it's superb and inexpensive, and very spicy.

Tianshi Vegetarian Restaurant 57 Dengshi Xikou, just off Wangfujing. All dishes in this bright, modern restaurant are tuber-, legume- or grain-based, low in calories and cholesterol-free, although, this being China, most of it is presented as a meat imitation: try the "chicken" or "eel". About ¥50 per head. No alcohol is served.

Wangfujing Quanjude Roast Duck 13 Shuaifuyuan Hutong ⓣ010/65253310. Smaller than the others in the chain, with a full roast duck costing ¥160. This one earned its unfortunate nickname, the "Sick Duck", thanks to the proximity of a hospital.

Xiheya Ju Inside Ritan Park, at the northeast corner ⓣ010/65067643. Sichuan food in an imitation Qing-dynasty mansion. Try the *ganbian rou si*, dried beef fried with celery and chilli. There's also a Western menu. You'll pay around ¥60 per head.

North of the centre

The places listed below are marked on the map on pp.112–113.

Fish Nation Nanluogu Xiang. You wouldn't guess from the decor, but this is an English restaurant, with a surprisingly authentic fish'n'chips for ¥40. Shame about the lacklustre service, but there's a good balcony.

Gong Wang Fu Sichuan Restaurant 14 Liuyin Jie, just north of Prince Gong's Palace ⓣ010/66156924. Fiery Sichuan food in a lavishly re-created traditional setting with bamboo chairs and a lot of rosewood – but with pop art on the walls. Sees plenty of tourist traffic, so there's an English menu and they'll tone down the spices if asked. Around ¥60 per head.

Huajia Yiyuan 235 Dongzhimen Neidajie. This secluded courtyard restaurant, with

Ghost Street

Dongzhimennei Dajie, nicknamed Ghost Street (Gui Jie), is lined with dozens of restaurants, all festooned with red lanterns and neon, to make for a colourful and boisterous scene, especially on weekends. Take the subway to Yonghe Gong and walk south for ten minutes.

Note that staff will likely speak little or no English; though few establishments have an English menu, plenty have a picture menu. Many venues specialize in hotpot and *shuixhuyu* (spicy Sichuan-style fish served in oil on a heated metal tray). You can't go too far wrong just picking somewhere busy, but recommended is famous hotpot brand **Xiao Fei Yang** (209 Dongzhimen Neidajie, north side), which sources its mutton from Mongolia, and Beijing-duck restaurant **Huajia Yiyuan** (see above). For spicy fish, try **Dumenchang** (208 Dongzhimen Neidajie, south side).

caged song birds and pleasant outdoor seating, is an excellent place to sample Beijing duck, a bargain at ¥88. It's a few doors east of the *Lama Temple Youth Hostel*.

Hutong Pizza 9 Yindingqiao ⓣ010/66175916. A charming little courtyard restaurant serving up good, square pizzas. It's sunk in an alley; go to the *hutong* directly opposite *Kaorouji* and follow the signs.

Kaorouji 14 Qianhai Dong Yuan ⓣ010/64045921. In the *hutongs* close to the Drum Tower, this Muslim place takes advantage of its great lakeside location with big windows and, in summer, balcony tables. The beef and barbecued lamb dishes are recommended. From the Drum Tower, continue south down Di'anmenwai Dajie, then take the first *hutong* on the right; the restaurant is a short walk down here, just before the lake bridge. Around ¥60 a head. Daily 11am–2pm & 5–8.30pm.

Sauveurs de Coree 29 Nanluogu Xiang ⓣ010/64016083. If you're new to spicy Korean cuisine, go for one of the set meals at this little Korean bistro, which start at ¥50 for *bibimbap*. Finish with iced cinnamon tea.

The Source 14 Banchang Hutong ⓣ010/64003736, ⓦwww.yanclub.com. Foreigner-friendly Sichuan set meals, starting at ¥120 per person, in a courtyard restaurant next to the *Lüsongyuan Hotel*.

Sanlitun

The places listed below are marked on the map on p.128.

Berena's Bistro 6 Gongti Dong Lu. English-speaking waiters, good service and decent Sichuan food make this a favourite with local expats. Try *gongbao jiding* – pepper chicken.

Lufthansa Centre Beisanhuan Dong Lu. There are plenty of upmarket restaurants in this shopping complex, including the *Trattoria* (ⓣ010/64653388 ext 5707), for Italian food, and the *Brauhaus* (ⓣ010/64653388 ext 5732), for German fare – their pork and sauerkraut meal for two (¥135) is about as cheap as it gets around here. In the basement, *Sorabol* (ⓣ010/64651845) specializes in Korean cuisine.

One Thousand and One Nights 21 Gongrentiyuchang Bei Lu, 200m west of Sanlitun Jiu Ba Jie. Beijing's first Middle Eastern restaurant. Try the hummus as a starter and the baked chicken for a main course, but leave enough room for some baklava, which you can also buy at their sweet shop 100m east of the restaurant. It's open till very late, but some dishes sell out early.

Serve the People 1 Sanlitun Xiwujie. Trendy Thai restaurant, going for a Soviet look, presumably ironically. Thai staples such as green curry and *tom yam* seafood soup are all worth sampling, and you can ask them to tone down the spices if you want.

Drinking, nightlife and entertainment

Beijing offers much more than the karaoke and bland hotel bars you'll find in many other Chinese cities. Huge **clubs** are packed every night with young, affluent Chinese, and more sophisticated **Western-style nightclubs** feature the latest DJs flown in from the West or Japan. The fashion amongst modern urbanites, however, is for **bars**. Originally aimed at the city's foreign community, they are now patronized as much by locals.

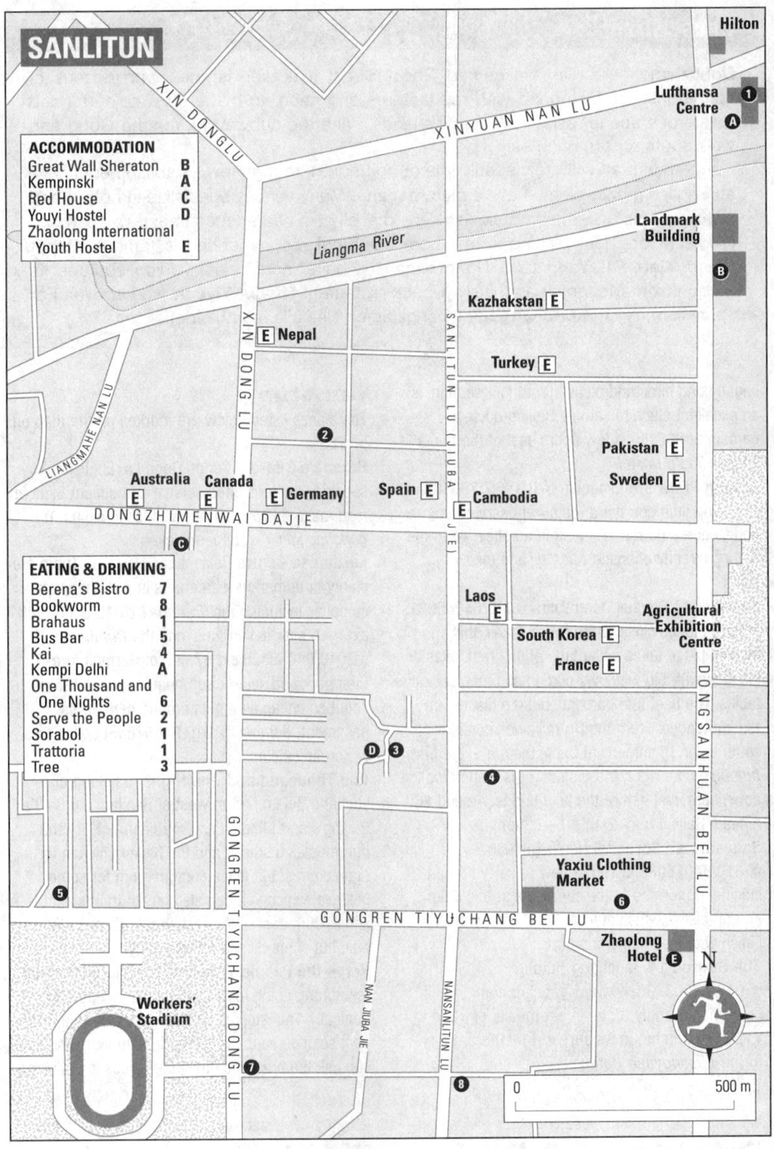

The city's bars have given a boost to its **music scene**, providing much-needed venues. Meanwhile, most visitors take in at least a taste of **Beijing Opera** and the excellent Chinese **acrobats** – both of which seem pretty timeless. In contrast, the contemporary theatrical scene is changing fast as home-grown dramatists experiment with foreign forms. Cinemas might be full of Hollywood products but there is plenty of opportunity to catch the

Beijing bars and clubs

Baby Face	娃娃脸	*wá wá liǎn*
Bed Bar	床吧	*chuáng bā*
Bus Bar	车吧	*chē bā*
Club Banana	巴那那俱乐部	*bānànà jùlèbù*
Centro	炫酷酒廊	*xuànkù jiǔláng*
China Doll	中国娃娃	*zhōngguó wáwa*
Drum and Bell	鼓钟咖啡馆	*gǔzhōng kāfēiguǎn*
Goose and Duck	鹅和鸭	*éhéyā*
Kai	开吧	*kāibā*
Stone Boat	石舫酒吧	*shífǎng jiǔbā*
Tree	树酒吧	*shù jiǔbā*
Vics	威克斯	*wēikèsī*
What? Bar	什么酒吧	*shénme jiǔbā*
World of Suzie Wong	苏西黄酒吧	*sūxīhuáng jiǔbā*

serious and fairly controversial movies emerging from a new wave of younger film-makers.

Bars

Plenty of **bars** are clustered around **Sanlitun Lu**, also called Jiu Ba Jie (literally, "Bar Street"), all within staggering distance of one another. To get here take any bus east from Dongsi Shitiao metro stop. An alternative bar scene exists around the prettified **Shicha lakes** (known locally as "Houhai") where lounge bars now proliferate the way pondweed once did. There are other small bar scenes around Nanluogu Xiang, a kilometre or so from here, and at Chaoyang Park West Gate. A Tsingtao beer is generally ¥15 or more. Phone numbers for those bars that have regular live music have been included below. For up-to-the-minute bar reviews, check the expat mags.

Sanlitun and east of the centre

Just inside the northeast section of the third ring road, this busy area can be reached by taking the subway to Dongsi Shitiao, then bus #113 east; get off at the third stop. The main strip – **Sanlitun Lu** – is sometimes called **Jiuba Jie**. Unless otherwise stated, the places listed below are marked on the map on p.128.

Bus Bar On the edge of the car park by the north gate of the Workers' Stadium. A cheap and cheerful bar made out of two buses welded together and decorated with graffiti. ¥5 tequilas and gangster rap bring in plenty of passengers.

Centro First Floor, *Kerry Centre Hotel*, 1 Guanghua Lu. Slinky lounge bar whose cocktails will cost the best part of a red bill. Dress up.

Kai Sanlitun Bei Jie, behind 3.3 Mall. A raucous little dive bar, popular with foreigners for its ¥10 beers.

Stone Boat Southwest corner of Ritan Park, by the lake ⓣ010/65019986. A stubby pier shaped like a boat – the sort of thing you would expect to find in the Summer Palace – has been sympathetically converted into a great little venue, with a good tea and wine list and live music on summer evenings. Recommended at any time of day. See map p.109.

Tree 43 Sanlitun Nan Lu, behind 3.3 Mall ⓣ010/64151954, ⓦwww.treebeijing.com. Cosy, relaxed and understated bar, with a good selection of Belgian white beers and great pizza. Free Wi-Fi.

Around Chaoyang Park

Bus #113 comes here from Dongsi Shitiao subway – get off at the fourth stop. The places listed here are marked on the map on pp.80–81.

Goose and Duck Outside the park's west gate Ⓦwww.gdclub.net.cn. A faux-British pub run by an American, this is the place to play pool and darts, watch sports on TV and pick up anti-fashion and hick-hair tips. Tuck your shirt into your jeans then order a Guiness and a shepherd's pie. Two drinks for the price of one 4–8pm.

World of Suzie Wong Outside the park's west gate, above the *Mirch Masala* restaurant – look for the discreet yellow neon sign outside Ⓦwww.suziewong.com.cn. Striking neo-Oriental decor – think lacquer and rose petals. Dancing downstairs and a cocktail bar above. Though named after a fictional Hong Kong prostitute, this is a classy place, so dress up. Bit of a meat market, though.

North of the centre

As well as the obvious strip that runs alongside of **Houhai**, there are plenty of mellower venues sunk in the *hutongs* all around. To reach the area, take bus #107 from Dongzhimen subway stop, get off at the north entrance to Beihai Park and walk north around the lake.

The places listed here are marked on the map on pp.112–113.

Bed Bar 17 Zhangwang Hutong Ⓣ010/84001554. Courtyard-style nightspot, rather hidden away from the action and all the better for it. Serves tapas.

Drum and Bell 41 Zhonglouwan Hutong Ⓣ010/84033600. A great location between the Drum and Bell towers, with welcoming staff. The rooftop patio is great in summer.

No Name Bar 3 Qianhai Dongyuan, just east of the *Kaorouji* restaurant. A hippy-ish café/bar that thinks it's special because it doesn't have a sign. Look for the red walls and the out-of-control foliage. This was the first lakeside bar, and its trendy anonymity and bric-a-braccy interior design has informed every other one in the area. They also serve Yunnan cuisine.

Pass By Bar 108 Nan Luo Guo Xiang, off Di'anmen Dong Dajie Ⓣ010/84038004. A renovated courtyard house turned cosy bar/restaurant that's popular with backpackers and students. There are lots of books and pictures of China's far-flung places to peruse, and well-travelled staff to chat to, if you can get their attention. Pretty good pizzas.

Clubs

Chinese **clubs** are pretty slick these days – gone are the days when everything stopped at 10pm for a raffle – with hip-hop and house music proving crowd-pleasers. All places listed here have a cover charge, given in our reviews, which generally increases at weekends. As well as the venues below, there is a concentration of hip big clubs around the west gate of the Workers' Stadium.

If you just want to dance, and aren't too prissy about the latest music, see the bar reviews above for venues with their own dance floor; *Suzie Wong's* is a popular choice.

Babyface 6 Gongti Xi Lu, Workers' Stadium West Gate. Big, brash and bold, for those who need lasers and breakbeat in their life. Steaming dance floor. Regularly hosts international DJs and has just been ranked as one of the world's top fifty clubs by *DJ Magazine*. ¥40 cover, more on weekends.

China Doll Tongli Studios, second floor, Sanlitun Jie. Despite the name, this slinky place has an undersea theme; popular with sharks, exotic tropicals and bottom feeders. No cover, but pricey drinks.

Club Banana Scitech Hotel, 22 Jianguomenwai Dajie. Big, brash and in your face, this mega club has three sections – techno, funk and chill-out – and features go-go girls, karaoke rooms and an enthusiastic, young clientele. Mon–Thurs & Sun 8.30pm–4am, Fri & Sat 8.30pm–5am. ¥20, weekends ¥40.

Vics Inside the Workers' Stadium's north gate, next to the *Outback* steakhouse. Eighties LA decor, a sweaty dance-floor and a less-than-zero ambience of numb dissipation. The low cover charge and cheapish drinks (bottled beer ¥15) make it popular with students and embassy brats. Women get in free on Wed and get free drinks till midnight. Thurs is ragga/reggae night. Hip-hop, R&B and techno all weekend. Daily 7pm–6am. ¥30 except Thurs, when it's free to get in.

Entertainment and art

There's always a healthy variety of **cultural events** taking place in the city. Check the *China Daily* for listings on officially approved events. For the best rundown of street-level happenings, including gigs, try to track down a copy of *That's Beijing*, available at expat bars and restaurants.

Live music

To hear traditional Chinese music, visit the concert halls, or the Sanwei Bookstore (see p.133) on a Saturday night. Western classical music is popular and can be heard at any of the concert halls. Mainstream Chinese pop is hard to avoid, much as you may want to, as it pumps out of shops and restaurants.

Beijing Concert Hall 1 Beixinhua Jie, just off Xichang'an Jie ⓣ010/66055812. Sates the considerable appetite in the capital for classical music, with regular concerts by Beijing's resident orchestra, and visiting orchestras from the rest of China and overseas. Ticket prices vary. You can get tickets at the box office or at the CVIK Plaza.

Fobidden City Concert Hall Zhongshan Park, Xichang'an Jie ⓣ010/65598285. A stylish new hall, with performances of Western and Chinese classical music.

Poly Plaza Theatre Poly Plaza, 14 Dongzhimen Nan Dajie ⓣ010/65001188. A gleaming hall that hosts diverse performances of jazz, ballet, classical music, opera and modern dance for the city's cultural elite. Tickets are on the pricey side, usually starting at ¥100.

Workers' Stadium Gongren Tiyuchang Bei Lu. Giant gigs, mostly featuring Chinese pop stars, though Vanessa Mae and Bjork have also played here.

Film

There are plenty of cinemas showing Chinese films and dubbed Western films, usually action movies. Just ten Western films are picked by the government for release every year. Despite such restrictions, these days most Beijingers have an impressive knowledge of world cinema, thanks to the prevalence of cheap pirated DVDs.

Some of the largest **screens** in Beijing, showing mainstream Chinese and foreign films, are the old Dahua Cinema at 82 Dongdan Bei Dajie (ⓣ010/65274420, ⓦwww.dhfilm.cn), Star City in the Oriental Plaza Mall (BB65, 1 Dongchang'an Jie; ⓣ010/85186778, ⓦwww.xfilmcity.com); the Xin Dong'an Cinema on the fifth floor of the Sun Dong'an Plaza on Wangfujing (ⓣ010/65281988, ⓦwww.xfilmcity.com) and the UME Huaxing Cinema at

Beijing rock

Beijing has a vibrant **rock** scene. Good local bands to look out for are The Retros, Joyside and Queen Sea Big Shark, all of whom sing some songs in English. Most decent bands are on Modern Sky and Badhead records. You can check the scene out at *Mao Live*, 111 Gulou Dong Dajie, at the north end of Nanluogu Xiang (ⓣ010/64025080, ⓦwww.maolive.com), at *D22* at 242 Chengfu Lu – come out of Wudaokou metro stop and walk towards the Beijing University East Gate (ⓣ010/62653177, ⓦwww.d22beijing.com) and at *What Bar*, 72 Beichang Jie, just north of the west gate of the Forbidden City. Tickets at all venues cost around ¥30.

If you're here in May, check out the annual **Midi rock festival** (ⓦwww.midifestival.com) in Haidian Park, just west of Beijing University campus. In 2007, there were four stages and almost two hundred bands played. Plenty of local talent is on display, along with a few foreign acts. You can even camp, for the full-on "Chinese Glastonbury" experience. Tickets are ¥100 for the four-day event, ¥50 for one day.

Beijing entertainment

Beijing Concert Hall	音乐厅	*yīnyuè tīng*
Beijing Exhibition Centre	展览中心	*zhǎnlǎn zhōng xīn*
Capital Theatre	首都剧场	*shǒudū jùchǎng*
Chang'an Theatre	长安大剧场	*cháng'ān dàjùchǎng*
Chaoyang Theatre	朝阳剧场	*cháoyáng jùchǎng*
Courtyard Gallery	四合院画廊	*sìhéyuàn huàláng*
Dahua Cinema	大华电影院	*dàhuá diànyǐngyuàn*
Experimental Theatre for Dramatic Arts	国家话剧院	*guójiā huàjùyuàn*
Forbidden City Concert Hall	中山公园音乐厅	*zhōngshān gōngyuán yīnyuètīng*
Lao She Tea House	老舍茶馆	*lǎoshě cháguǎn*
Liyuan Theatre	梨园剧场	*líyuán jùchǎng*
Mao Live	光芒	*guāng máng*
Poly Plaza Theatre	保利大厦国际剧院	*bǎolìdàshà guójìjùyuàn*
Puppet Theatre	中国木偶剧院	*zhōngguó mù'ǒu jùyuàn*
Red Gate Gallery	红门画廊	*hóngmén huàláng*
Sanwei Bookstore	三味书屋	*sānwèi shūwū*
Star City	星城亮马国际公寓	*xīngchéng liàngmǎ guójì gōngyù*
Tianqiao Tea House	天桥乐茶园	*tiānqiáolè cháyuán*
UME Huaxing Cinema	华星国际影城	*huáxīng guójì yǐngchéng*
Wanfung	云峰画廊	*yúnfēng huàláng*
Wansheng Theatre	万胜剧场	*wànshèng jùchǎng*
Workers' Stadium	工人体育场	*gōngrén tǐyùchǎng*
Xin Dong'an Cinema	新东安影院	*xīndōng'ān yǐngyuàn*
Xin Rong Theatre	鑫融剧院	*xīnróng jùyuàn*
Zhengyici Theatre	正义祠剧场	*zhèngyìcí jùchǎng*

44 Kexueyuan Nan Lu, Haidian, next to the Shuang Yu Shopping Centre, just off the third ring road (Ⓣ010/62555566) – which has the biggest screen. Tickets cost ¥50 or more. There are usually two showings of foreign movies, one dubbed into Chinese, the other subtitled; ring to check.

The best serious film venue though, is **Cherry Lane Movies**, usually housed at the Peking Opera Photo Studio, Kent Centre, 29 Liangmaqiao Lu, 2km east of the *Kempinski Hotel* (Ⓣ010/65224046, Ⓦwww.cherrylanemovies.com.cn; check as the venue changes occasionally). Screenings, which include obscure and controversial underground Chinese films, usually with English subtitles, take place every Friday at 7.30pm (¥50), followed by a discussion, sometimes featuring the director or cast members.

Traditional opera

Beijing Opera (*jing xi*; see p.1187) is the most celebrated of the country's three hundred and fifty or so regional styles – a unique combination of song, dance, acrobatics and mime, with some similarities to Western pantomime.

Chang'an Theatre 7 Jianguomennei Dajie Ⓣ010/65101309. Tickets from ¥20 up to ¥800 for front seats and a duck dinner. An hour-long performance with a lot of acrobatics.

Liyuan Theatre First floor of the *Jianquo Qianmen*, 175 Yong'an Lu. Nightly performances begin at 7.30pm. There's a ticket office in the front courtyard of the hotel (daily 9–11am, noon–4.45pm & 5.30–8pm). Tickets cost ¥30–150; the more expensive seats are at tables at the front where you can sip tea and nibble pastries during the performance. In season, you'll need to book tickets a day or two in advance. The opera shown is enlivened with some martial arts and slapstick.

Zhengyici Theatre 220 Xiheyan Dajie, Qianmen Ⓣ010/63033104. The only surviving wooden

Beijing Opera theatre left, and worth a visit just to check out the architecture. Nightly performances begin at 7.30pm, last two hours and cost ¥150. Dinner – duck, of course – costs an additional ¥110. Check the *China Daily* for listings.

Drama and dance

Spoken drama was only introduced into Chinese theatres in the twentieth century. But the **theatre**, along with most of China's cinemas, was closed down for almost a decade during the Cultural Revolution, during which only eight "socially improving" plays were allowed to be performed. The People's Art Theatre Company reassembled in 1979. As well as drama, good old-fashioned **song-and-dance** extravaganzas are very popular, though a little glitzy for many foreigners' tastes.

Beijing Exhibition Theatre 135 Xizhimenwai Dajie ⓣ010/68354455. For the glitzier type of show. Musicals at ¥50–100 a ticket are a lot cheaper than at home.

Capital Theatre 22 Wangfujing Dajie ⓣ010/65253677. Home to the People's Art Theatre Company, this is the most prestigious, and largest, theatre. Tickets cost at least ¥60.

The Experimental Theatre For Dramatic Arts 45 Mao'er Hutong, just north of the Bell Tower ⓣ010/64031099. Known for putting on modern and avant-garde performances. Tickets from ¥40.

Puppet Theatre A, Section 1, Anhua Xi Li, Bei Sanhuan Lu (third ring road), opposite the Sogo Department Store ⓣ010/64254798. Daily shows at 6.30pm for ¥20. The skilled puppeteers here produce shows pitched at a family audience.

Acrobatics and martial arts

Certainly the most accessible and exciting of the traditional Chinese entertainments, **acrobatics** covers anything from gymnastics and animal tricks to magic and juggling. Professional acrobats have existed in China for two thousand years and the tradition continues at the main training school, Wu Qiao in Hebei province, where students begin training at the age of 5. The style may be vaudeville, but performances are spectacular, with truly awe-inspiring feats.

Chaoyang Theatre 36 Dongsanhuan Bei Lu ⓣ010/65072421. The easiest place to see a display. Shows are nightly (7.15–8.30pm; ¥180, it can be cheaper if you book through your hotel). There are plenty of souvenir stalls in the lobby – buy after the show rather than in the interval, as prices go down.

Wansheng Theatre 95 Tianqiao Market, Qianmen. Nightly performances begin at 7.15pm and cost ¥100–150.

Xin Rong Theatre 16 Baizhifang Xi Jie ⓣ010/83559285, ⓦwww.kungfushow.com. A nightly kungfu show. Performances begin at 7.30pm; tickets start at ¥70.

Teahouse theatres

A few **teahouse theatres**, places to sit and snack and watch performances of Beijing Opera, sedate music and martial arts, have reappeared in the capital.

Lao She Teahouse 3rd Floor, Dawancha Building, 3 Qianmen Xi Dajie ⓣ010/63036830, ⓦwww.laosheteahouse.com. You can watch a variety show of opera, martial arts and acrobatics (¥40–130) here. Performances are at 2.30pm and 7.40pm and last an hour and a half; the afternoon performances are cheaper.

Tianqiao Happy Teahouse 113 Tianqiao Nan Dajie (performances at 7pm; closed Mon; ⓣ010/63040617). A tourist trap that gives a colourful taste of the surface aspects of Chinese culture (¥180). Even the staff are in costume.

Sanwei Bookstore Teahouse 60 Fuxingmennei Dajie ⓣ010/66013204, opposite the *Minzu Hotel*. The haunt of expats and arty Chinese, you can hear performances of light jazz on Fri and Chinese folk music on Sat (8.30–10pm).

▲ Acrobats at the Chaoyang Theatre

Contemporary art

Beijing is the centre for the vigorous **Chinese arts scene** and there are plenty of interesting new galleries opening up. The best place to find out about new shows is in the expat magazines. For mainstream art, visit the China Art Gallery, but for a taste of the more exciting contemporary scene, put on some black clothes and check out the 798 Art District, also known as Dashanzi, up towards the airport (see p.111). Some of the most reputable galleries here are the Beijing Commune (Ⓣ010/86549428, Ⓦwww.beijingcommune.com), White Space (Ⓣ010/84562054, Ⓦwww.alexanderochs-galleries.de), Star Gallery (Ⓣ010/84560591, Ⓦwww.stargallery.com) and Beijing Tokyo Art Projects (Ⓣ010/84573245, Ⓦwww.tokyo-gallery.com).

Courtyard Gallery 95 Donghuamen Dajie Ⓣ010/65268882, Ⓦwww.courtyard-gallery.com. Located in an old courtyard house opposite the east gate of the Forbidden City. There's also a cigar shop and a very classy restaurant here.

The Red Gate Gallery Dongbianmen Watchtower, Chongwenmen Dajie Ⓣ010/65251005, Ⓦwww.redgategallery.com. One of the best places to see contemporary art, with a high profile. The gallery is housed in a beautiful restored watchtower.

Wanfung 136 Nanchizi Dajie Ⓣ010/65233320, Ⓦwww.wanfung.com.cn. In the old archive building of the Forbidden City, showing established contemporary artists, sometimes from abroad. Can be chintzy.

Shopping

Beijing has a good reputation for shopping, with the widest choice of anywhere in China. **Clothes** are particularly inexpensive, and are one reason for the city's high number of Russians, as smuggling them across the northern border is a lucrative trade. There's also a wide choice of **antiques and handicrafts**, but don't expect to find any bargains or particularly unusual items as the markets are well picked over. Be aware that just about everything that is passed off as antique is fake. Good souvenir buys are **art materials**, particularly brushes and blocks of ink; **chops** carved with a name; small **jade** items; and handicraft items such as **kites**, painted snuff bottles and papercuts.

There are four main shopping districts: **Wangfujing**, popular and mainstream; **Xidan**, characterized by giant department stores; **Dongdan**, which mainly sells brand-name clothes; and **Qianmen**, perhaps the area that most rewards idle browsing, with a few oddities among the cheap shoes and clothes stores. In addition, and especially aimed at visitors, **Liulichang** is a good place to get a lot of souvenir buying done quickly. For general goods, check the **department stores**, which sell a little of everything, and provide a good index of current Chinese taste. The Beijing Department Store, on Wangfujing, and the Xidan Department Store on Xidan Dajie are prime examples, or check out the newer Landao Department Store, on Chaoyangmenwai Dajie. The Parkson Building, west of Xidan on Fuchenqmennei Dajie, is the plushest. Rising living standards for some are reflected in the new giant **malls**, where everything costs as much as it does in the West. Try the Sun Dong'an Plaza, on Wangfujing, the Sea-Sky Plaza, on Chaoyangmenwai Dajie, or the CVIK, COFCO or China World Trade Centre plazas on Jianguomen if you don't get enough of this at home.

Shops are open daily from 8.30am to 8pm (7pm in winter), with large shopping centres staying open till 9pm.

Beijing shopping

Aliens Street Market	老番街	*lǎo fān jiē*
Arts and Crafts Store	工艺美术商店	*gōngyìměishù shāngdiàn*
Beijing Curio City	北京古玩城	*běijīng gǔwánchéng*
Beijing Silk Shop	北京丝绸商店	*běijīng sīchóu shāngdiàn*
Dongwuyuan Wholesale Market	动物园服装批发市场	*dòngwùyuán fúzhuāng pīfā shìchǎng*
Five Colours Earth	五色土	*wǔ sè tǔ*
Foreign Languages Bookstore	外交书店	*wàijiāo shūdiàn*
Friendship Store	友谊商店	*yǒuyí shāngdiàn*
Hongqiao Department Store	红桥百货中心	*hóngqiáo bǎihuò zhōngxīn*
Liulichang	琉璃厂	*liúlí chǎng*
Mingxing Clothing Store	明星服饰商店	*míngxīngfúshì shāngdiàn*
Neiliansheng Shoeshop	合格证鞋店	*hé gé zhèng xiédiàn*
Panjiayuan Market	潘家园市场	*pānjiāyuán shìchǎng*
Parkson Building	百盛购物中心	*bǎishèng gòuwù zhōngxīn*
PLA Official Factory Outlet	军需批发门市部	*jūnxū ménshì pīfābù*
Ruifuxiang Clothes Store	瑞蚨祥服装商店	*ruìfúxiáng fúzhuāng shāngdiàn*
Sanlian Bookstore	三联书店	*sānlián shūdiàn*
Silk Market	秀水街	*xiùshǔi jīe*
Sun Dong'an Plaza	新东安	*xīdōng'ān*
Timezone 8	现代书店	*xiàn dài shū diàn*
Yansha Outlets Mall	燕莎奥特莱斯购物中心	*yànshān àotèláisī go4uwù zhōngxīn*
Yaxiu Clothing Market	雅秀市场	*yǎxiù shìchǎng*
Yuexi Clothing Market	越秀市场	*yuèxiù shìchǎng*

Antiques, souvenirs and carpets

If you're a serious antique hunter, go to Tianjin, where the choice is more eclectic and prices cheaper (see p.154). That said, there's no shortage of **antique stores** and **markets** in Beijing offering opium pipes, jade statues, porcelain Mao figures, mahjong sets and Red Guard alarm clocks. Almost all of the old stuff is fake, though; even copies of Mao's Little Red Book are new, and aged with tea.

Arts and Crafts Store 293 Wangfujing. A good if predictable selection of expensive *objets d'art*.

Beijing Curio City Dongsanhuan Nan Lu, west of Huawei Bridge. A giant mall of more than 250 stalls. Visit on a Sun, when other antique traders come and set up in the streets around. The mall includes a section for duty-free shopping; take your passport and a ticket out of the country along and you can buy goods at the same reduced price as at the airport. Daily 9.30am–6.30pm.

Friendship Store Jianguomenwai Dajie. Tourist souvenirs with a wide range of prices, but more expensive than the markets. Large carpet section.

Hongqiao Department Store Opposite the northeast corner of Tiantan Park. The giant, cramped and humid Hongqiao Department Store can be wearying but has some good bargains. The top floor sells antiques and curios; one stall is given over solely to Cultural Revolution kitsch. The stalls share space, oddly, with a pearl and jewellery market. The second floor sells clothes and accessories and the first is the place to go for small electronic items, including such novelties as watches that speak the time in Russian when you whistle at them.

Liulichang East of Qianmen Dajie (see p.103). This has the densest concentration of curio stores, with a great choice, particularly of art materials and chops, though prices are steep.

Lufthansa Centre Liangmaqiao Lu. A section in this giant mall sells expensive antiques and carpets.

Panjiayuan Market On Panjia Lu, just south of Jinsong Zhong Jie. Beijing's biggest antique market, well worth browsing around, even if you have no intention to buy, for the sheer range of secondhand goods, sometimes in advanced stages of decay, on sale. Open weekdays, but it's at its biggest and best at weekends between 6am and 3pm.

Books

Beijing can claim a better range of **English-language literature** than anywhere else in China. If you're starting a trip of any length, stock up here. The expensive hotels all have bookstores with fairly decent collections, though at off-putting prices. You'll also find copies of foreign **newspapers and magazines**, such as *Time* and *Newsweek*, sold for around ¥40.

Foreign Languages Bookstore 235 Wangfujing Dajie. It might not look like much, but this is the largest foreign-language bookshop in China. Downstairs are textbooks and translations of Chinese classics, and the products of Beijing Foreign Language Press, while the third floor sells pricey imported books, including plenty of modern novels. Mon–Sat 9am–7pm.

Friendship Store Jianguomenwai Dajie. As well as a wide variety of books on all aspects of Chinese culture, the bookshop within the store sells foreign newspapers (¥80), a few days out of date. It's all very expensive, though. Daily 9am–8.30pm.

Sanlian Bookstore Wangfujing Dajie (100m beyond the intersection with Chaoyangmennei Dajie, on the east side of the road; look for a blue glass building slightly recessed from the street). This is the most pleasant bookshop in Beijing, though its selection of English fiction, in the basement, is much less extensive than that of the Foreign Languages Bookstore to the south. Upstairs, there are a huge variety of art books. Mon–Sat 9am–6pm.

Timezone 8 4 Jiuxianqiao, 798 Dashanzi Art Area. This chic art bookstore with attached café is the most civilized venue in that bobo playground, the 798 Art District. Tote an Apple Mac to really fit in. Free Wi-Fi. Daily 8.30am–9pm.

Clothes

Clothes are a bargain in Beijing; witness all the Russians buying in bulk. The best place to go is Jianguomen Dajie, where the Friendship Store and the CVIK Plaza offer something for every budget (see p.110). The Silk Market is a giant six-storey mall for knock-offs of branded clothes. Bear in mind that if you're particularly tall or have large feet, you'll have difficulty finding clothes and shoes to fit you. For Chinese street fashion, head to Xidan, and, for designer creations, to the malls.

Aliens Street Market Yabao Lu, south of the Fullink Plaza. This huge mall is where the Russians come, en masse. There's a vast range of goods, but it's particularly worth picking over for clothes and accessories.

Beijing Silk Shop 5 Zhubaoshi Jie, just west of Qianmen Dajie. Located just inside the first *hutong* to the west as you head south down Qianmen Dajie, this is the best place in Beijing to buy quality silk clothes in Chinese styles, with a wider selection and keener prices than any of the tourist stores. The ground floor sells silk fabrics, while clothes can be bought upstairs.

Dongwuyuan Wholesale Market Xizhimenwai Daijie, south of the zoo. This giant indoor market is full of stalls selling very cheap clothes, shoes and accessories to locals in the know. You'll have to bargain, and there won't be anything in any large sizes, but it's one of the city's best places to pick up a few cut-price outfits.

Five Colours Earth 10 Dongzhimen Nan Dajie. Interesting and unusual collections, often incorporating fragments of old embroidery, by a talented local designer. Not too expensive either; you can pick up a coat for ¥500.

Mingxing Clothing Store 133 Wangfujing Dajie. Well-made Chinese-style garments, such as *cheongsams* and *qipaos*.

Neiliansheng Shoeshop Western end of Dazhalan, Qianmen. Look for the giant shoe in the window. All manner of handmade flat, slip-on shoes and slippers in traditional designs, starting from ¥100 or so – great gifts.

PLA Official Factory Outlet Dongsanhuan Bei Lu, about 1km north of the China World Trade Centre. As well as military outfits, they stock such oddments as wrist compasses, canteens and police hats. There's also a huge selection of military footwear and chunky fur-lined coats. Bus #300 from Guomao metro stop.

Ruifuxiang Clothes Store 5 Dazhalan, off Qianmen Dajie; also at 190 Wangfujing Dajie. Silk and cotton fabrics and a good selection of shirts and dresses. Mon–Sat 8.30am–8pm.

Silk Market Xiushui Jie, off Jianguomenwai Dajie, very near Yong'anli metro stop. This huge six-storey mall for tourists has electronics, jewellery and souvenirs, but its main purpose is to profit through flouting international copyright laws, with hundreds of stalls selling fake designer labels. You'll need to bargain hard; you shouldn't pay more than ¥80 for a pair of jeans, or ¥70 for trainers. There are also a few tailors – pick out your material, then bargain, and you can get a suit made in 24hr for ¥800 or so. Vendors are tiresomely pushy.

Yansha Outlets Mall 9 Dongsihuannan Jie, the southern end of the eastern section of the fourth ring road ⓣ010/67395678. A huge outlet for genuine designer clothes and bags, all old lines, at discounts of between thirty and fifty percent.

Yaxiu Clothing Market 58 Gongrentiyuchang Bei Lu. A two-storey mall of stalls selling designer fakes. Not yet overrun with tourists, so the shopping experience and the prices are better than at the Silk Market.

Yuexiu Clothing Market 99 Chaoyangmennei Dajie. A new market with a little bit of everything and a great deal of fake clothes. Not many foreigners get here as yet, so the prices are a little more competitive, though you'll still have to barter.

Listings

Airline offices The following foreign airlines have offices in Beijing: Aeroflot, First floor, *Jinglun Hotel*, 3 Jianguomenwai Dajie ⓣ010/65002412; Air Canada, Room C201, Lufthansa Centre, 50 Lianmaqiao Lu ⓣ010/64682001; Air China, Xidan Aviation Office, 15 Chang'an Xi Lu ⓣ800/8101111; Air France, Room 1606–1611, Building 1, Kuntai International Mansion, 12A Chaowai Dajie ⓣ400/8808808; Air Ukraine, *Poly Plaza Hotel*, Dongsi Shitiao ⓣ010/65010282; Alitalia, Room 141, *Jianguo Hotel*, 5 Jianguomenwai Dajie ⓣ010/65918468; All Nippon Airways, Fazhan Dasha, Room N200, 5 Dongsanhuan Bei Lu ⓣ010/65909174; Asiana Airlines, 12th floor, Building A, Jiacheng Plaza, 18 Xiaguangli ⓣ010/64684000; Austrian Airlines, Room 603, Lufthansa Centre, 50 Liangmaqiao Lu ⓣ010/64622161; British Airways, Room 210, SCITECH Tower, 22 Jianguomenwai Dajie ⓣ010/65124070; Canadian Airlines, Room C201, 50 Liangmaqiao Lu ⓣ010/64637901; China Southern Airlines, Building A, AVIC Building, 2 Dongsanhuan Nan Lu ⓣ010/9503333; Continental Airlines, 500 Sunflower Tower, 37 Maizidian Jie ⓣ010/85726686; Dragonair, Room 1710, Office Tower 1, Henderson Centre, 18 Jianguomennei Dajie ⓣ010/65182533; El Al, Room 2906, Jing Guang Centre, Hujia Lou, Chaoyang ⓣ010/65014512; Finnair, Room 204, SCITECH Tower, 22 Jianguomenwai Dajie ⓣ010/65127180; Garuda Indonesia, Poly Plaza, 14 Dongzhimen Nan Dajie ⓣ010/64157658; Japan Airlines, 1/F Changfugong Office Building, 26A Jianguomenwai Dajie ⓣ400/8880808; KLM, 1609–1611 Kuntai International Building, Chaoyangmenwai Dajie ⓣ400/8808222; Korean Air, 1602 Hyundai Motor Building, 38 Xiaoyun Lu ⓣ400/6588888; Lufthansa, Room S101, Lufthansa Centre, 50 Liangmaqiao Lu ⓣ010/64688838; Malaysia Airlines, Lot 115A/B, Level 1, West Wing, China World Trade Centre, 1 Jianguomenwai Dajie ⓣ010/65052681; Mongolian Airlines, China Golden Bridge Plaza, 1A Jianguomenwai Dajie ⓣ010/65079297; Northwest Airlines, 501B, West Wing, China World Trade Centre, 1 Jianguomenwai Dajie ⓣ400/8140081; Pakistan Airlines, Room 106A, China World Trade Centre, 1 Jianguomenwai Dajie ⓣ010/65052256; Qantas, Lufthansa Centre, B7–8, Tenth floor, West Tower, LG Twin Tower, B12 Jianguomenwai Dajie ⓣ010/65679006; SAS Scandinavian Airlines, Room 430, Beijing Sunflower Tower, 37 Maizidian Jie ⓣ010/85276100;

Shanghai Airlines, Nanzhuyuan Yiqu, Building 3, Beijign Capital International Airport ☎010/64569019; Singapore Airlines, Room 801, Tower 2, China World Trade Centre, 1 Jianguomenwai Dajie ☎010/65052233; Swissair, Room 612, SCITECH Tower, 22 Jianguomenwai Dajie ☎010/65123555; Thai International, Room 303, W3 Tower, Oriental Plaza ☎010/85150088; United Airlines, Lufthansa Centre, 50 Liangmaqiao Lu ☎010/64631111; Vietnam Airlines, S121 Lufthansa Centre, 50 Liangmaqiao Lu ☎010/64638448.

Banks and exchange The Commercial Bank (Mon–Fri 9am–noon & 1–4pm) in the CITIC Building at 19 Jianguomenwai Dajie, next to the Friendship Store, has the widest service, and the only place that will let you change money into non-Chinese currencies (useful for travellers taking the train to Russia). The main branch of the Bank of China (Mon–Fri 9am–noon & 1.30–5pm) is at 8 Yabuo Lu, off Chaoyangmen Dajie, just north of the International Post Office, but it doesn't do anything the smaller branches won't. You'll find other branches in the CVIK Plaza (Mon–Fri 9am–noon & 1–6.30pm), the China World Trade Centre (Mon–Fri 9am–5pm, Sat 9am–noon), the Sun Dong'an Plaza (Mon–Fri 9.30am–noon & 1.30–5pm) and the Lufthansa Centre (Mon–Fri 9–noon & 1–4pm). A foreign-exchange office (daily 9am–6.30pm) inside the entrance to the Friendship Store is one of the few places you can change money at the weekend at the standard rate. If you have applied for a visa and only have a photocopy of your passport, some hotels and the Hong Kong and Shanghai Bank in the *Jianguo Hotel* will reluctantly advance cash on traveller's cheques; most banks won't. There are ATM machines in every mall, usually in the basement, and in four- and five-star hotels.

Bike rental Pretty much all the hotels rent out bikes, at ¥20–50 a day, depending on how classy the hotel is.

Courier service DHL has a 24hr office at 2 Jiuxian Qiao in the Chaoyang district ☎010/64662211. More convenient are the offices in the *New Otani Hotel* (daily 8am–8pm; ☎010/65211309) and at L115, China World Trade Centre (daily 8am–8pm).

Embassies Visa departments usually open for a few hours every weekday morning (phone for exact times and to see what you'll need to take); you'll need a Chinese-speaker on standby as not all will have someone who speaks English. Remember that they'll take your passport off you for as long as a week sometimes, and it's very hard to change money without it, so stock up on cash before applying for any visas. You can get passport-size photos from an annexe just inside the front entrance of the Friendship Store. Some embassies require payment in US dollars; you can change traveller's cheques for these at the CITIC Building (see "Banks and exchange" above). Most embassies are either around Sanlitun in the northeast or in Jianguomenwai compound, north of and parallel to Jianguomenwai Dajie: Australia, 21 Dongzhimenwai Dajie, Sanlitun ☎010/65322331; Azerbaijan, 7-2-5-1 Tayuan Building ☎010/65324614; Canada, 19 Dongzhimenwai Dajie, Sanlitun ☎010/65323536; France, 3 Dong San Jie, Sanlitun ☎010/65321331; Germany, 5 Dongzhimenwai Dajie, Sanlitun ☎010/65322161; India, 1 Ritan Dong Lu, Sanlitun ☎010/65321856; Ireland, 3 Ritan Dong Lu, Sanlitun ☎010/65322691; Japan, 7 Ritan Lu, Jianguomenwai ☎010/65322361; Kazakhstan, 9 Dong Liu Jie, Sanlitun ☎010/65326183; Kyrgyzstan, 2-4-1 Tayuan Building ☎010/65326458; Laos, 11 Dong Si Jie, Sanlitun ☎010/65321224; Mongolia, 2 Xiushui Bei Jie, Jianguomenwai ☎010/65321203; Myanmar (Burma), 6 Dongzhimenwai Dajie, Sanlitun ☎010/65321425; New Zealand, 1 Ritan Dong'er Jie, Sanlitun ☎010/65322731; North Korea, Ritan Bei Lu, Jianguomenwai ☎010/65321186; Pakistan, 1 Dongzhimenwai Dajie, Sanlitun ☎010/65322660; Russian Federation, 4 Dongzhimen Bei Zhong Jie, south off Andingmen Dong Dajie ☎010/65322051; South Korea, Floors 3 & 4, China World Trade Centre ☎010/65053171; Thailand, 40 Guanghua Lu, Jianguomenwai ☎010/65321903; UK, 11 Guanghua Lu, Jianguomenwai ☎010/65321961; Ukraine, 11 Dong Lu Jie, Sanlitun ☎010/65324014; US, 3 Xiushui Bei Jie, Jianguomenwai ☎010/65323831; Uzbekistan, 7 Beixiao Jie, Sanlitun ☎010/65326305; Vietnam, 32 Guanghua Lu, Jianguomenwai ☎010/65321155.

English corner Sun in Zizhuyuan Park.

Hospitals and clinics Most big hotels have a resident medic. If you need a hospital, the following have foreigners' clinics where some English is spoken: Sino-Japanese Friendship Hospital on Heping Dajie ☎010/64221122 (daily 8–11.30am & 1–4.30pm); Friendship Hospital at 95 Yongan Lu, west of Tiantan Park ☎010/63014411; Beijing Hospital at 15 Dahua Lu. For a service run by and for foreigners, try the International Medical Centre at S106 in the Lufthansa Centre, Dong Sanhuan Bei Lu ☎010/64651561, or the Hong Kong International Clinic on the third floor of the Swissotel Hong Kong Macao Centre, Dongsi Shitiao ☎010/65012288 ext 2346 (daily 9am–9pm). For real emergencies, the AEA International offers a comprehensive and expensive service at 14 Liangmahe Lu, not far from the Lufthansa Centre (clinic ☎010/64629112, emergencies ☎010/64629100).

Internet access Beijing is one of the few places in China that doesn't abound in Internet cafés, thanks to a mass closure a few years ago. Those still open are heavily regulated – you will be asked to show your passport before being allowed near a computer. One of the few central Internet cafés is the Qianyi on the third floor of "The Station", the shopping centre on the east side of Qianmen; note that there are actually two cafés up here, a cheap one (¥7/hr) and a pricey one (¥20/hr), and the obnoxious owners turn foreigners away from the cheap one. There's a much cheaper one (¥3/hr; open 24hr) on Ping'an Dajie, oppsite the entrance to Nanluogu Xiang. All hotels have business centres with Internet available, but it can be ridiculously expensive, especially in the classier places. Your best option is to head for a backpacker hotel or hostel, where Internet access is generally ¥5 an hour or so.

Kids Attractions popular with kids include the Beijing Aquarium (see p.118) or the Puppet Theatre (see p.133). There's an amusement park inside Chaoyang Park (daily 8.30am–6pm) with lots of rides – though it's no Disneyland – or they could try ice-skating on the basement level 2 of the China World Trade Centre (daily 10am–10pm except Tues and Thurs 10am–5.50pm and Sun 10am–8pm; ¥30 an hour) – though be aware that the Chinese kids are very good. Baggily attired skateboarders show off their moves in the plaza at the corner of Xidan Bei Dajie and Xichang'an Jie.

Language courses You can do short courses (from two weeks to two months) in Mandarin Chinese at Beijing Foreign Studies University, 2 Xi Erhuan Lu ⓣ010/68468167; at the Bridge School in Jianguomenwai Dajie ⓣ010/64940243, which offers evening classes; or the Cultural Mission at 7 Beixiao Jie in Sanlitun ⓣ010/65323005, where most students are diplomats. For courses in Chinese lasting six months to a year, apply to Beijing International School at Anzhenxili, Chaoyang ⓣ010/64433151; Beijing University in Haidian ⓣ010/62751230; or Beijing Normal University, at 19 Xinjiekouwai ⓣ010/62207986. Expect to pay around US$1000 in tuition fees per semester.

Left luggage There's a left-luggage office in the foreigners' waiting room at the back of Beijing Zhan, with lockers for ¥5 or ¥10 a day depending on size, though as these are often full, you are better off going to the main left-luggage office (daily 5am–midnight; ¥5 a day) at the east side of the station. The left-luggage office at Xi Zhan is downstairs on the left as you enter and costs ¥10 a day.

Libraries The Beijing National Library, at 39 Baishiqiao Lu, just north of Zizhuyuan Park (Mon–Fri 8am–5pm; ⓣ010/68415566), is one of the largest in the world, with more than ten million volumes, including manuscripts from the Dunhuang Caves and a Qing-dynasty encyclopedia. The oldest texts are Shang-dynasty inscriptions on bone. You'll need to join before they let you in. To take books out, you need to be resident in the city, but you can turn up and get a day pass that lets you browse around. An attached small cinema shows Western films in English at weekends; phone for details. The Library of the British Embassy, on Floor 4 of the Landmark Building at 8 Dong Sanhuan Bei Lu, has a wide selection of books and magazines and anyone can wander in and browse.

Mail The International Post Office is on Chaoyangmen Dajie (Mon–Sat 8am–6pm), just north of the intersection with Jianguomen Dajie. This is where poste restante letters (addressed poste restante, GPO, Beijing) end up, dumped in a box; you have to rifle through them all and pay ¥1.5 for the privilege (you'll also need to bring your passport for identification). Letters are only kept for one month, after which the officious staff are quick to send them back. It's also possible to rent a PO Box here, and there's a packing service for parcels and a wide variety of stamps on sale. Other convenient post offices are in the basement of the China World Trade Centre; on Xi Chang'an Jie; just east of the Concert Hall; and at the north end of Xidan Dajie. All are open Mon–Sat 9am–7pm. EMS can be sent from any post office.

Pharmacies There are large pharmacies at 136 Wangfujing and 42 Dongdan Bei Dajie, or you could try the famous Tongrentang Medicine Store on Dazhalan (see p.103), which also has a doctor for on-the-spot diagnosis. For imported non-prescription medicines, try Watsons at the *Holiday Inn Lido*, Shoudujichang Lu, (daily 9am–9pm), in the northeast of the city, or at the Full Link Plaza on Chaoyangmenwai Dajie (daily 10am–9pm).

PSB The Foreigners' Police, at 2 Andingmen Dong Dajie (Mon–Fri 8am–noon & 1.30–4pm; ⓣ010/84015292), will give you a first visa extension for a fee of ¥160. It will take them up to a week to do it, so make sure you've got plenty of cash before you go as you can't change money without your passport. Apply for a second extension and you'll be told to leave the country: don't, just leave Beijing and apply elsewhere. The nearest place with a friendly PSB office, where your visa will be extended on the spot, is Chengde (see p.172); you can make it there and back in a day. If you have an emergency and require urgent assistance, dial ⓣ110 or ⓣ010/550100, and have a Chinese-speaker handy to help you.

Spectator sports Beijing's football team, Guo An, plays at the massive Workers' Stadium in the northeast of the city, off Gongren Tiyuchang Bei Lu (bus #110 along Dongdaqiao), usually every other Sunday afternoon at 3.30pm. There's a timetable outside the ticket office, which is just east of the north gate of the stadium. Tickets are cheap (¥15), and you buy them at the ground on the day. Basketball is almost as popular and has thrown up the unlikely hero Yao Ming, a 6'11" Inner Mongolian who plays for the Houston Rockets in the US's NBA. Beijing's Ao Shen team play at the Workers' Stadium.
Swimming pool Try the Olympic-size pool in the Asian Games Village, Anding Lu (daily 8am–9pm; ¥50), on the route of trolleybus #108 from Chongwenmennei Dajie, which also boasts some of the city's fiercest showers.
Travel agents CITS is at 103 Fuxingmennei Dajie (daily 8.30–11.30am & 1.30–4.30pm; ⓣ010/66011122. They offer expensive tours, a tour guide and interpreter service, and advance ticket booking for trains, planes and ferries (from Tianjin), with a commission of around ¥20 added. Other CITS offices are in the *Beijing Hotel*, 33 Dongchang'an Jie ⓣ010/65120507 and the *New Century Hotel* (ⓣ010/68491426), opposite the zoo. Good private alternatives to the state monolith, geared at corporate groups, include China Swan International Tours on the 4th floor of the Longhui Building, 1 Nanguang Nanli, Dongsanhuan Lu (ⓣ010/67316393, ⓦwww.china-swan.com) and BTG International at 206 Beijing Tourism Building (ⓣ010/96906798, ⓦwww.btgtravel.cn). For adventure travel within China, contact Wildchina, Room 801, Oriental Place, 9 Dongfang Dong Lu Dongsanhuan Bei Lu (ⓣ010/64656602, ⓦwww.wildchina.com). Beijing's most unusual tour agency is Koryo Tours at Room 43, Red House Hotel, 10 Taiping Zhuang (ⓣ010/64167544, ⓦwww.koryogroup.com), who arrange visits (heavily controlled, of course) to the paranoid hermit kingdom of North Korea. Expect to pay at least US$2000 for the privilege. The Tourism Hotline ⓣ010/65130828 is open 24hr for enquiries and complaints.

Around Beijing

There are plenty of scenic spots and places of interest scattered in the plains and hills around the capital, and no visit would be complete without a trip to the **Great Wall**, accessible in three places within easy journey time of Beijing. The **Ming Tombs**, another remnant of imperial glory, are often combined with a trip to the nearby wall. In addition, the **Western Hills** shouldn't be overlooked, and if you're in the capital for any length of time, this large stretch of densely wooded parkland provides an invigorating breather from the pressures of the city. Further out, the **Jietai** and **Tanzhe temples** are pretty in themselves and, unlike the city's other temples, they're attractively situated.

The Great Wall

This is a Great Wall and only a great people with a great past could have a great wall and such a great people with such a great wall will surely have a great future.

Richard M. Nixon

Stretching from Shanhaiguan, by the Yellow Sea, to Jiayuguan Pass in the Gobi Desert, the **Great Wall** is an astonishing feat of engineering. The practice of building walls along China's northern frontier began in the fifth century BC and continued until the sixteenth century. Over time, this discontinuous array of fortifications and ramparts came to be known as **Wan Li Changcheng** (literally, "Long Wall of Ten Thousand Li", *li* being a Chinese measure of

Around Beijing

Badachu	八大处	*bādàchù*
Badaling Great Wall	八达岭	*bādálǐng*
Biyun Si	碧云寺	*bìyún sì*
Botanical Gardens	植物园	*zhíwù yuán*
Great Wall	长城	*chángchéng*
Huanghua Great Wall	黄花长城	*huánghuā chángchéng*
Huairou	怀柔	*huáiróu*
Jietai Si	戒台寺	*jiètái sì*
Jinshanling Great Wall	金山岭长城	*jīnshānlǐng chángchéng*
Longqing Gorge	龙庆峡	*lóngqìng xiá*
Miyun Reservoir	密云水库	*mìyún shuǐkù*
Mutianyu Great Wall	慕田峪	*mùtiányù*
Shisan Ling	十三陵	*shísān líng*
Simatai Great Wall	司马台	*sīmǎtái*
Tanzhe Si	潭柘寺	*tánzhé sì*
Western Hills	西山	*xīshān*
Wofo Si	卧佛寺	*wòfó sì*
Xiangshan	香山公园	*xiāngshān gōngyuán*

distance roughly equal to 500m), or "the Great Wall" to English-speakers. Even the most-visited section at **Badaling**, constantly overrun by Chinese and foreign tourists, is still easily one of China's most spectacular sights. The section at **Mutianyu** is somewhat less crowded; distant **Simatai** and **Jinshanling** are much less so, and far more beautiful. To see the wall in all its crumbly glory, head out to **Huanghua**. For other trips to unreconstructed sections, check out Ⓦwww.wildwall.com or contact Beijing Hikers at Ⓦwww.beijinghikers.com.

Some history

The Chinese have walled their cities since earliest times and during the Warring States period (around the fifth century BC) simply extended the practice to separate rival territories. The Great Wall's origins lie in these fractured lines of fortifications and in the vision of the first Emperor **Qin Shi Huang** who, having unified the empire in the third century BC, joined and extended the sections to form one continuous defence against barbarians.

Under subsequent dynasties, whenever insularity rather than engagement drove foreign policy, the wall continued to be maintained and, in response to shifting regional threats, grew and changed course. It lost importance under the Tang, when borders were extended north, well beyond it. The Tang was in any case an outward-looking dynasty that kept the barbarians in check far more cheaply, by fostering trade and internal divisions. With the emergence of the insular Ming, however, the wall's upkeep again became a priority, and from the fourteenth to the sixteenth century military, technicians worked on its reconstruction, and the Ming wall is the one that you see today.

The seven-metre-high, seven-metre-thick wall, with its 25,000 battlements, served to bolster Ming sovereignty for a couple of centuries. It restricted the movement of the nomadic peoples of the distant, non-Han minority regions, preventing plundering raids. Signals made by gunpowder blasts, flags and smoke swiftly sent news of enemy movements to the capital. In the late sixteenth century, a couple of huge Mongol invasions were repelled, at Jinshanling and Badaling. But a wall is only as strong as its guards, and by the seventeenth century the Ming royal house was corrupt and its armies weak;

the wall was little hindrance to the invading Manchus. After they had established their own dynasty, the Qing, they let the wall fall into disrepair. Slowly it crumbled away, useful only as a source of building material – demolitions of old *hutongs* in Beijing have turned up bricks from the wall, marked with the imperial seal.

Now, this great monument to state paranoia is great business – the restored sections are besieged daily by rampaging hordes of tourists – and is touted by the government as a source of national pride. Its image adorns all manner of products, from wine to cigarettes, and is even used – surely rather inappropriately – on visa stickers.

Badaling

The best-known section of the wall is at **Badaling**, 70km northwest of Beijing (daily 8am–4.30pm; ¥45). It was the first section to be restored (in 1957) and opened up to tourists. Here the wall is 6m wide, with regularly spaced watchtowers dating from the Ming dynasty. It follows the highest contours of a steep range of hills, forming a formidable defence, such that this section was never attacked directly but instead taken by sweeping around from the side after a breach was made in the weaker, low-lying sections.

Badaling may be the easiest part of the wall to get to from Beijing, but it's also the most packaged. At the entrance, a giant tourist circus – a plethora of restaurants and souvenir stalls – greets you. As you ascend to the wall, you pass a train museum (¥5), a cable car (¥30) and the **Great Wall Museum** (included in the main ticket). The wall museum, with plenty of aerial photos, models and construction tools, is worth a browse, though it's more interesting visited on the way down.

Once you're up on the wall, flanked by guard rails, it's hard to feel that there's anything genuine about the experience. Indeed, the wall itself is hardly original here, as the "restorers" basically rebuilt it wholesale on the ancient foundations. To get the best out of this part of the wall you need to walk – you'll quickly lose the crowds and, generally, things get better the further you go. You come to unreconstructed sections after heading 1km north (left) or 2km south (right). That's as far as you are allowed to go; guards posted here will turn you back.

Practicalities

As well as CITS, all the more expensive Beijing hotels (and a few of the cheaper ones) run **tours** to Badaling, usually with a trip to the Ming Tombs thrown in. If you come with a tour, you'll arrive in the early afternoon, when the place is at its busiest, spend an hour or two at the wall, then return, which really gives you little time for anything except the most cursory of jaunts and the purchase of an "I climbed the Great Wall" T-shirt. It's just as easy, and cheaper, to travel under your own steam. The easiest way to get here is on bus #919 from Deshengmen (a 2min walk east from Jishuitan subway stop) – there's an ordinary service (2hr; ¥3) and a much quicker air-con luxury bus (1hr; ¥10). Or there are plenty of tourist buses (outward journeys daily 6–10am; every 20min; ¥36–50): routes #1, #3 and #5 leave from Qianmen, #2 from the #103 terminus at Beijing Zhan, and #4 from outside the zoo. The journey to Badaling on one of these takes about an hour and a half, and the buses visit the Ming Tombs (see p.146) on the way back. Returning to Beijing shouldn't be a problem, as tourist buses run until about 6pm.

Mutianyu

A two-kilometre section, the **Mutianyu Great Wall**, 90km northeast of the city (daily 8am–5pm; ¥35), is more appealing to most foreign visitors than Badaling, as it has rather fewer tourist trappings. Passing along a ridge through some lush, undulating hills, this part of the wall is well endowed with guard towers, built in 1368 and renovated in 1983.

From the entrance, steep steps lead up to the wall; you can get a cable car up (¥35) though it's not far to walk. The stretch of wall you can traverse here is about 3km long (barriers in both directions stop you continuing any further). The atmospheric *Mutianyu Great Wall Guesthouse* (Ⓣ010/69626867; ③), situated in a reconstructed watchtower 500m before the eastern barrier, is a good place for a quiet overnight stay, though be aware it has no plumbing; you have to call ahead.

Minibuses for Mutianyu leave from Dongzhimen and Xizhimen stations every morning (¥10 one way), but they take in photo stops and dubious amusement parks along the way. Alternatively, you can get tourist bus #6 (mid-April to mid-Oct, weekends only, outward journeys daily 7–8.30am; ¥50) from the south cathedral, near Xuanwumen metro stop, or the #42 bus station, just south of Dongsi Shitiao metro stop; they'll wait around at the site for an hour or two before heading back to Beijing. Returning by other means shouldn't be a hassle provided you do so before 6pm, as plenty of minibuses wait in the car park to take people back to the city. If you can't find a minibus back to Beijing, get one to the town of **Huairou**, from where you can get regular bus #916 back to the capital – the last bus leaves at 6.30pm.

Simatai

Peaceful and semi-ruined, **Simatai** (daily 8am–4pm; ¥40), 110km northeast of the city, is the most unspoilt section of the Great Wall around Beijing. With the wall snaking across purple hills that resemble crumpled velvet from afar, and blue mountains in the distance, it fulfils the expectations of most visitors more than the other sections, though it gets a little crowded at weekends. Most of this section is unrenovated, dating back to the Ming dynasty, and sporting a few late innovations such as spaces for cannon, with the inner walls at right angles to the outer wall to thwart invaders who breached the first defence.

From the car park, a winding path takes you up to the wall, where most visitors turn right. Regularly spaced watchtowers allow you to measure your progress uphill along the ridge. If you're not scared of heights you can take the cable car to the eighth tower (¥20). The walk over the ruins isn't an easy one, and gets increasingly precipitous after about the tenth watchtower. The views are sublime, though. After about the fourteenth tower (2hr on), the wall peters out and the climb becomes quite dangerous, and there's no point going any further.

Turning left when you first reach the wall, you can do the popular hike to Jinshanling in three hours (see opposite). Most people though, do the walk in the other direction, as it's more convenient to finish up in Simatai.

Practicalities

The journey out from the capital to Simatai takes about three hours. **Tours** run from the backpacker hotels and hostels for around ¥150, generally once or twice a week in the off season, daily in the summer, and sometimes offer overnight stays. Most other hotels can arrange transport, too, though expect to pay a little more.

You can travel here independently, but considering the logistical hassles and expense, this is only worth doing if you want to stay for a night or two. To get

At all the less touristy places, each tourist or group of tourists will be followed along the wall by a villager selling drinks and postcards, for at least an hour; if you don't want to be pestered, make it very clear from the outset that you are not interested in anything they are selling – though after a few kilometres you might find that ¥5 can of coke very welcome.

here under your own steam, catch a direct Simatai bus from Dongzhimen bus station (buses leave 7–9am; ¥40) or take bus #980 to Miyun and negotiate for a minibus or taxi to take you the rest of the way (you shouldn't have to pay more than ¥40). Between mid-April and mid-October tourist bus #12 heads to Simatai from the #42 bus station south of Dongsi Shitiao metro stop (buses leave 6–8am; ¥50), and from opposite Xuanwumen subway stop; buses return between 4 and 6pm. A rented **taxi** will cost about ¥350, there and back including a wait.

The *Simatai Youth Hostel*, by the entrance, has dingy **rooms** for ¥160 and hard beds in an eight-bed dorm for ¥70. There's hot water for two hours a day. You'll get rather better value if you head off with one of the locals who hang around the car park; they will charge ¥70 or so for a spare room in their house, though facilities will be simple, the only hot water being available by the bucket. As for **eating**, avoid the youth hostel's overpriced restaurant and head to one of the nameless places at the side of the car park, whose owners can whip up some very creditable dishes; if you're lucky, they'll have some locally caught wild game in stock.

To get from Simatai back to Beijing, you can either get a taxi to Miyun (¥70 or so, after some negotiaton; from Miyun, the last public bus back to Beijing is at 4pm), or wait till the tourist buses start to leave at 4pm.

Jinshanling

Jinshanling (¥30), 10km west of Simatai, is one of the least-visited and best-preserved parts of the wall, with jutting obstacle walls and oval watchtowers,

▲ The Great Wall between Jinshanling and Simatai

some with octagonal or sloping roofs. It's not easy to reach without your own transport, but there are plenty of tours out here from the hostels (¥180); they'll drop you off here in the morning and pick you up at Simatai in the afternoon. Otherwise, a taxi from Miyun (see above for routes) will cost around ¥100.

Turn left when you hit the wall and it's a three-hour walk to Simatai along an unreconstructed section. You won't meet many other tourists, and will experience something of the wall's magnitude: a long and lonely road that unfailingly picks the toughest line between peaks. Take the hike seriously, as you are scrambling up and down steep, crumbly inclines, and you need to be sure of foot. Watch, too, for loose rocks dislodged by your companions. When you reach Simatai there's a ¥30 toll at the suspension bridge.

Finally, if you head right when you get onto the wall at Jinshanling, you quickly reach an utterly abandoned and overgrown section. After about four hours' walk along here you'll reach a road that cuts through the wall, and from here you can flag a bus back to Beijing. This is only recommended for the intrepid.

Huanghua

The section of the wall at **Huanghua** (¥25), 60km north of Beijing, is completely unreconstructed. It's a good example of Ming defences, with wide ramparts, intact parapets and beacon towers. You can hike along the wall for as long as you like, though some sections are a bit of a scramble. It's not too hard to get here: backpacker hotels have started taking tours, otherwise take bus #916 from Dongzhimen bus station to Huairou (¥8), and catch a minibus taxi from there (around ¥10; agree the fare before setting off, as the driver may try to overcharge foreigners). You'll be dropped off on a road that cuts through the wall. The section to the left is too hard to climb, but the section on the right, past a little reservoir, shouldn't present too many difficulties for the agile; indeed, the climb gets easier as you go, with the wall levelling off along a ridge.

The wall here is attractively ruined – so watch your step – and its course makes for a pleasant walk through some lovely countryside. Keep walking the wall for about 2km, to the seventh tower, and you'll come to steps that lead south down the wall and onto a stony path. Follow this path down past an ancient barracks to a pumping station, and you'll come to a track that takes you south back to the main road, through a graveyard and orchards. When you hit the road you're about 500m south of where you started. Head north and after 150m you'll come to a bridge where taxis (¥10) and buses to Huairou congregate. The last bus from Huairou to Beijing is at 6.30pm.

The Ming Tombs

After their deaths, all but three of the sixteen Ming-dynasty emperors were entombed in giant underground vaults, the **Shisan Ling** (literally, "Thirteen Tombs", usually called the **Ming Tombs** in English). Two of the tombs, Chang Ling and Ding Ling, were restored in the 1950s; the latter was also excavated. The tombs are located in and around a valley 40km northwest of Beijing. The location, chosen by the third Ming emperor, Yongle, for its landscape of gentle hills and woods, is undeniably one of the loveliest around the capital, the site marked above ground by grand halls and platforms. That said, the fame of the tombs is overstated in relation to the actual interest of their site, and unless you've a strong archeological bent, a trip here isn't worth making for its own sake. The tombs are, however, very much on the tour circuit, being conveniently placed on the way to Badaling Great Wall (see p.143). The site also makes a nice place to picnic, especially if you just feel like taking a break from the city and its more tangible sights. To get the most out of the place, it's best not to stick to the tourist route between the car park and Ding Ling, but to spend a day here and hike around the smaller tombs farther into the hills. You'll need a map to do this – you'll find one on the back of some Beijing city maps, or you can buy one at the site (¥6).

The easiest way to get to the Ming Tombs is to take any of the **tourist buses** that go to Badaling (see p.143), which visit the tombs on the way to and from Beijing. You can get off here, then rejoin another tourist bus later either to continue to Badaling or to return to the city. To get there on ordinary public transport, take bus #845 from Xizhimen to the terminus at Changping, then get bus #345 the rest of the way. All buses drop you at a car park in front of one of the tombs, Ding Ling, where you buy your entrance ticket (¥35).

The Spirit Way and Chang Ling

The approach to the Ming Tombs, the seven-kilometre **Spirit Way**, is Shisan Ling's most exciting feature, well worth backtracking along from the ticket office. The road commences with the **Dahongmen** (Great Red Gate), a triple-entranced triumphal arch, through the central opening of which only the emperor's dead body was allowed to be carried. Beyond, the road is lined with colossal stone statues of animals and men. Startlingly larger than life, they all date from the fifteenth century and are among the best surviving examples of Ming sculpture. Their precise significance is unclear, although it is assumed they were intended to serve the emperors in their next life. The animals depicted include the mythological *qilin* – a reptilian beast with deer's horns and a cow's tail – and the horned, feline *xiechi*; the human figures are stern, military mandarins. Animal statuary reappears at the entrances to several of the tombs, though the structures themselves are something of an anticlimax.

At the end of the Spirit Way stands **Chang Ling** (daily 8.30am–5pm; ¥35), which was the tomb of Yongle himself, the earliest at the site. There are plans to excavate the underground chamber, an exciting prospect since the tomb is contemporary with some of the finest buildings of the Forbidden City in the capital. At present, the enduring impression above ground is mainly one of scale – vast courtyards and halls, approached by terraced white marble. Its main feature is the Hall of Eminent Flowers, supported by huge columns consisting of individual tree trunks, which, it is said, were imported all the way from Yunnan in the south of the country.

Ding Ling

The main focus of the area is **Ding Ling** (daily 8.30am–5pm; ¥35), the underground tomb-palace of Emperor Wanli, who ascended the throne in 1573 at the age of 10. Reigning for almost half a century, he began building his tomb when he was 22, in line with common Ming practice, and hosted a grand party within on its completion. The mausoleum, a short distance east of Chang Ling, was opened up in 1956 and found to be substantially intact, revealing the emperor's coffin, flanked by those of two of his empresses, and floors covered with scores of trunks containing imperial robes, gold and silver and even the imperial cookbooks. Some of the treasures are displayed in the tomb, a huge, musty stone vault, undecorated but impressive for its scale; others have been replaced by replicas. It's a cautionary picture of useless wealth accumulation, as pointed out by the tour guides.

The Western Hills

Like the Summer Palace (see p.120), the **Western Hills** are somewhere to escape urban life for a while, though they're more of a rugged experience. Thanks to their coolness at the height of summer, the hills have long been favoured as a restful retreat by religious men and intellectuals, as well as politicians in modern times – Mao lived here briefly, and the Politburo assembles here in times of crisis.

The hills are divided into three parks, the nearest to the centre being the **Botanical Gardens**, 3.5km due west of the Summer Palace. Two kilometres farther west, **Xiangshan** is the largest and most impressive of the parks, but just as pretty is **Badachu**, its eight temples strung out along a hillside 2.5km to the south of Xiangshan.

The hills take roughly an hour to reach on public transport. You can explore two of the parks in one day, but each deserves a day to itself. For a weekend escape and some in-depth exploration of the area, the *Xiangshan Hotel*, close to the main entrance of Xiangshan Park, is a good base (Ⓣ010/62591166; ❻). A startling sight, the light, airy hotel is one of the city's more innovative buildings, something between a temple and an airport lounge. It was designed by Bei Yuming (more usually known as I.M. Pei in the West), who also designed the pyramid at the Louvre in Paris and the Bank of China building at Xidan.

The Botanical Gardens

The **Botanical Gardens** (daily 6am–8pm; ¥5) are accessible by bus #333 from the Summer Palace (see p.120). Two thousand varieties of trees and plants are arranged in formal gardens (labelled in English), at their prettiest in summer, though the terrain is flat and the landscaping is not as original as in the older parks. The impressive new conservatory (¥50) has desert and tropical environments and a lot of fleshy foliage from Yunnan. The main path leads after 1km to the **Wofo Si** (daily 8am–4.30pm; ¥5), whose main hall houses a huge reclining Buddha, more than 5m in length and cast in copper. With two giant feet protruding from the end of his painted robe, and a pudgy, baby-face, calm in repose, he looks rather cute, although he is not actually sleeping but dying – about to enter nirvana. Suitably huge shoes, presented as offerings, are on display around the hall. Behind the temple is a bamboo garden, from which paths wind off into the hills. One heads northwest to a pretty cherry valley, just under 1km away, where Cao Xueqiao is supposed to have written *The Dream of Red Mansions* (see p.1206).

Xiangshan Park

Two kilometres west of the gardens lies **Xiangshan Park** (Fragrant Hills; daily 7am–6pm; ¥5; same buses as for the Botanical Gardens, stopping at the main entrance), a range of hills dominated by Incense Burner Peak in the western corner. It's at its best in the autumn (before the sharp November frosts), when the leaves turn red in a massive profusion of colour. Though busy at weekends, the park is too large to appear swamped, and is always a good place for a hike and a picnic.

Northeast from here, the **Zhao Miao** (Temple of Brilliance), one of the few temples in the area that escaped vandalism by Western troops in 1860 and 1900, was built by Qianlong in 1780 in Tibetan style, designed to make visiting Lamas feel at home. From here, follow the path west up to the peak (1hr) from where, on clear days, there are magnificent views down towards the Summer Palace and as far as distant Beijing. You can hire a horse to take you down again for ¥20, the same price as the cable car. Both drop you on the northern side of the hill, by the north entrance, a short walk from the superb **Biyun Si** (Azure Clouds Temple), just outside the park gate. A striking building, it's dominated by a north Indian-style dagoba and topped by extraordinary conical stupas. Inside, rather bizarrely, a tomb holds the hat and clothes of Sun Yatsen – his body was held here for a while before being moved in 1924. The giant main hall is now a maze of corridors lined with *arhats*, five hundred in all, and it's a magical place. The benignly smiling golden figures are all different – some have two heads or sit on animals, one is even pulling his face off – and you may see monks moving among them and bowing to each.

Badachu

Badachu, or the Eight Great Sights (daily 8am–5pm; ¥10), is a forested hill 10km south of Xiangshan Park and accessible on bus #347 from the zoo. Along the path that snakes around the hill are eight **temples**, fairly small affairs, but quite attractive on weekdays, when they're not busy. The new pagoda at the base of the path holds a Buddha tooth, which once sat in the fourth temple. The third, a nunnery, is the most pleasant, with a teahouse in the courtyard. There's a statue of the rarely depicted thunder deity inside, boggle-eyed and grimacing. As well as the inevitable cable car (¥20), it's also possible to slide down the hill on a metal track (¥40).

Tanzhe Si and Jietai Si

Due west of Beijing, two splendid temples sit in the wooded country outside the industrial zone that rings the city. Though **Tanzhe Si** and **Jietai Si** are relatively little visited by tourists, foreign residents rate them as among the best places to escape the city smoke. Take a picnic and make a day of it, as getting there and back can be time-consuming.

Tourist bus #7 visits both temples (mid-April to mid-Oct outward journeys 7–8.30am; ¥38 return), giving you ninety minutes at each, before returning to Qianmen. Otherwise, you could ride the east–west metro line all the way to its western terminus at Pingguoyuan, then catch bus #931 (¥3; this bus has two routes, so make sure the driver knows where you're going) to Tanzhe Si. From here you'll be able to find a taxi on to Jietai Si (¥20), from where you'll have to get a cab back to the city. Or you can save yourself some hassle by hiring a taxi to visit both temples, which should cost around ¥250 if you start from the city centre.

Tanzhe Si

Forty kilometres west of the city, **Tanzhe Si** (daily 8am–6pm; ¥35) occupies the most beautiful and serene temple site anywhere near the city. It's Beijing's largest and one of the oldest, first recorded in the third century as housing a thriving community of monks. Wandering through the complex, past terraces of stupas, you reach an enormous central courtyard, with an ancient towering ginkgo that's more than a thousand years old (christened the "King of Trees" by Emperor Qianlong) at its heart. Across the courtyard, a second, smaller tree, known as "The Emperor's Wife", is supposed to produce a new branch every time a new emperor is born. From here you can take in the other temple buildings, on different levels up the hillside, or look round the lush bamboo gardens, whose plants are supposed to cure all manner of ailments. The spiky *zhe* (Cudrania) trees near the entrance apparently "reinforce the essence of the kidney and control spontaneous seminal emission".

Jietai Si

Twelve kilometres back along the road to Beijing, **Jietai Si** (daily 8am–6pm; ¥35) is a complete contrast to the Tanzhe Si: sitting on a hillside surrounded by forbiddingly tall, red walls it looks more like a fortress than a temple. It's an extremely atmospheric, peaceful place, made slightly spooky by its dramatically shaped pines – eccentric-looking, venerable trees growing in odd directions. Indeed, one, leaning out at an angle of about thirty degrees, is pushing over a pagoda on the terrace beneath it. In the main hall is an enormous Liao-dynasty platform of white marble, 3m high and intricately carved with figures – monks, monsters (beaked and winged) and saints – at which novice monks were ordained. Another, smaller hall, holds a beautiful wooden altar that swarms with relief dragons.

Aviation Museum

Out in the sticks 60km north of the city, the **Aviation Museum** is a fascinating place (daily 8.30am–5.30pm; ¥40; bus #912 from Andingmen metro stop). This enormous museum contains over three hundred aircraft, displayed in a giant hangar inside a hollow mountain and on a concourse. These range from the copy of the Wright brothers' plane flown by Feng Ru, a pioneering Chinese aviator, in 1909, to Gulf War helicopter gunships. As well as plenty of fighter planes, many of which saw action in the Korean War, the bomber that flew in China's first atom-bomb test is here, as is Mao's personal jet (with his teacup and frilly cushions still inside) and the plane that scattered the ashes of the deceased Zhou Enlai, which is covered with wreaths and tributes. But unless you have a special interest in aircraft, it's the sight of archaic downed machines en masse, like the setting for a J.G. Ballard story, that makes the place memorable.

Longqing Gorge

There's not a great deal of lush countryside around Beijing; one exception is **Longqing Gorge** (¥40), a local recreation spot at the edge of a reservoir some 90km northwest of the capital, the place to come for outdoor pursuits such as canoeing, horse riding and rock climbing, all of which can be arranged when you arrive. The main attraction, though, is the **Ice Festival** held on the shore of the reservoir (late Jan & Feb, sometimes into March), at which groups of sculptors compete to create the most impressive sculpture. The enormous results depict cartoon characters, dragons, storks and figures from Chinese popular culture; with coloured lights inside for a gloriously tacky psychedelic effect, they look great at night.

There are two ways to reach the gorge by public **transport**: either tourist bus #8 (mid-April to mid-Oct and during Ice Festival) from the #328 bus terminus near Andingmen metro stop, or train #575 from Xizhimen Zhan (daily at 8.30am; 2hr 30min). Unfortunately, the **hotels** around the reservoir are expensive and a bit dirty, and their rooms are especially pricey during the festival – though you needn't feel compelled to stay, as there are buses back to Beijing until 10pm at least. The nearest decent hotel in this area is the *Yanqing Guesthouse* in **Yanqing**, a few kilometres to the south (ⓣ010/69142363; ❸).

Travel details

Trains

Beijing Zhan to: Baotou (daily; 14hr); Beidaihe (3 daily; 5hr); Changchun (daily; 8hr); Chengde (4 daily; 4hr); Dalian (2 daily; 11hr); Dandong (daily; 12hr); Datong (twice daily; 7hr); Fuzhou (daily; 32hr); Hangzhou (daily; 22hr); Harbin (daily; 12hr); Hohhot (2 daily; 12hr); Ji'nan (daily; 7hr); Lhasa (twice daily; 48hr; requires travel permit); Nanjing (daily; 13hr); Qingdao (daily; 18hr); Shanghai (5 express daily; 12hr); Shanhaiguan (3 daily; 4hr); Shenyang (8 daily; 9hr); Tai'an (twice daily; 8hr); Tianjin (frequent; 1hr 30min); Yantai (daily; 14hr).
Xi Zhan to: Changsha (daily; 20hr); Chengdu (3 daily; 25hr); Chongqing (twice daily; 24hr); Guangzhou (8 daily; 20hr); Guilin (3 daily; 22hr); Guiyang (4 daily; 35hr); Hong Kong (daily; 29hr); Lanzhou (4 daily; 27hr); Luoyang (6 daily; 12hr); Kunming (daily; 48hr); Nanchang (5 daily; 22hr); Nanning (daily; 40hr); Shijiazhuang (daily; 4hr); Taiyuan (daily; 10hr); Ürümqi (daily; 40hr); Xi'an (daily; 12hr); Yichang (daily; 19hr); Zhanjiang (daily; 40hr); Zhengzhou (4 daily; 8hr). As well as the above, there are weekly services from Xi Zhan to Moscow and Ulaan Baatur; see p.83 for details.

Buses

There is little point travelling to destinations far from Beijing by bus; the journey takes longer than the train and is far less comfortable. The following destinations are within bearable travelling distance. Services are frequent, usually hourly during the day, with a few sleeper buses travellling at night. Note that there are also private bus services to Tianjin and Chengde from outside the main train station, Beijing Zhan.

Deshengmen bus station to: Chengde (4hr); Datong (10hr).
Dongzhimen bus station to: Shenyang (18hr).
Haihutun bus station to: Shijiazhuang (10hr); Tianjin (2hr).
Majuan bus station to: Beidaihe (9hr); Shanhaiguan (9hr; express service takes 5hr).

Flights

Beijing to: Baotou (1hr 30min); Beihai (4hr); Changchun (1hr 45min); Changsha (2hr); Chengdu (2hr 30min); Chifeng (3hr); Chongqing (2hr 40min); Dalian (1hr 20min); Dandong (1hr 20min); Fuzhou (2hr 50min); Guangzhou (3hr); Guilin (3hr); Guiyang (4hr 45min); Haikou (3hr 45min); Hangzhou (1hr 50min); Harbin (2hr); Hefei (2hr); Hohhot (1hr 10min); Hong Kong (3hr); Huangshan (2hr); Huangyan (2hr 40min); Jiamusi (2hr); Jilin (1hr 50min); Ji'nan (1hr); Jingjinag (2hr 30min); Jinzhou (1hr 20min); Kunming (3hr 30min); Lanzhou (2hr 20min); Lhasa (4hr); Lianyungang (5hr 30min); Linyi (2hr 30min); Liuzhou (2hr 45min); Luoyang (1hr 40min); Mudanjiang (1hr 50min); Nanchang (2hr); Nanjing (1hr 45min); Nanning (3hr 30min); Nantong (2hr 30min); Nanyang (1hr 30min); Ningbo (2hr 20min); Qingdao (1hr 15min); Qiqihar (2hr); Sanya (5hr 20min); Shanghai (1hr 50min); Shantou (3hr); Shenyang (1hr); Shenzhen (3hr 10min); Taiyuan (1hr 10min); Tongliao (1hr 45min); Urumqi (3hr 50min); Weifang (1 hr); Wenzhou (2hr 20min) Wuhan (2hr); Wuyishan (1hr 45min); Xiamen (2hr 50min); Xi'an (1hr 30min); Xining (2hr 30min); Xuzhou (1 hr 15min); Yanan (1hr 20min); Yanji (2hr); Yantai (1hr); Yibin (3hr 45min); Yinchuan (2hr); Zhangjiajie (3hr); Zhengzhou (1hr 20min); Zhuhai (3hr 30min).

CHAPTER 2

Highlights

* **Tianjin** Glimpse dilapidated colonial architecture and browse the souvenir markets of this huge city. See p.154

* **Beidaihe beachfront** Once the pleasure preserve of colonists, then Communists, the summer sands are now chock-a-block with the bikinis of the masses. See p.167

* **Shanhaiguan** A dusty relic of a walled city on the Bohai Gulf, where you can follow the Great Wall to where it disappears dramatically into the sea and sleep near the First Pass Under Heaven. See p.168

* **Chengde** The summer playground of emperors, whose many palaces and temples have been restored to the delight of Beijing day-trippers. See p.172

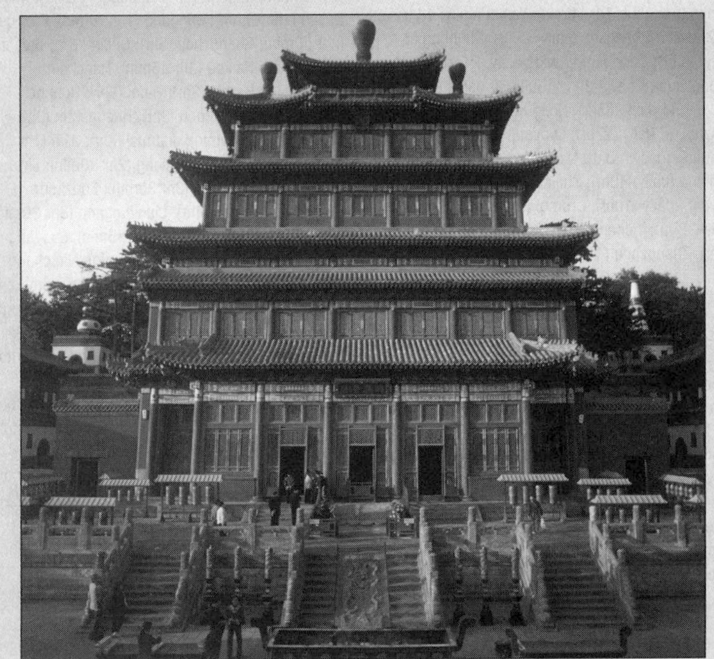

▲ The Bishu Shanzhuang in Chengde

2

Hebei and Tianjin

Hebei is a somewhat anonymous province, with two great cities, Beijing and Tianjin, at its heart but administratively outside its domain. In the south, a landscape of flatlands is spotted with heavy industry and mining towns – China at its least glamorous – which are home to the majority of the province's seventy million inhabitants. Most travellers pass through here on their way to or from the capital, though few stop. However, the bleak, sparsely populated tableland to the north, rising from the **Bohai Gulf**, holds more promise. For most of its history this marked China's northern frontier, and was the setting for numerous battles with invading forces; both the **Mongols** and the **Manchus** swept through here. The mark of this bloody history remains in the form of the **Great Wall**, winding across lonely ridges.

The first sections of the wall were built in the fourth century AD, along the Hebei–Shanxi border, by the small state of Zhongshan, in an effort to fortify its borders against aggressive neighbours. Two centuries later, Qin Shi Huang's Wall of Ten Thousand Li (see p.1144) skirted the northern borders of the province. The parts of the wall visible today, however, are the remains of the much younger and more extensive Ming-dynasty wall, begun in the fourteenth century as a deterrent against the Mongols. You can see the wall where it meets the sea at **Shanhaiguan**, a relaxing little fortress town only a day's journey from Beijing. If you're in the area, don't miss the intriguing seaside resort of **Beidaihe**, along the coast to the south, whose beaches and seafood outlets play host to hordes of summertime vacationers and dwindling numbers of Communist Party elite. Well north of the wall, the town of **Chengde** is the province's most visited attraction, an imperial base set amid the wild terrain of the Hachin Mongols and conceived on a grand scale by the eighteenth-century emperor Kangxi, with temples and monuments to match. All three towns are popular spots with domestic tourists, particularly Beijingers snatching a weekend away from the capital's bustle and stress, and part of the interest of going is in seeing the Chinese at their most carefree. Though the Chinese like their holiday spots the way they like their restaurants – *renao* (literally "hot and noisy") – it's easy to beat the crowds and find some great scenery.

Tianjin, an industrial giant, long ago outgrew its role as the region's capital, and is now a separate municipality. A former concession town with a distinctly Western stamp, it's worth a day-trip from Beijing to see its unique medley of unkempt nineteenth-century European architecture and modern office towers, which loom over the quieter parts of the city.

Good roads link towns in Hebei with Tianjin and Beijing, making long-distance buses a viable alternative to trains. The express buses that run

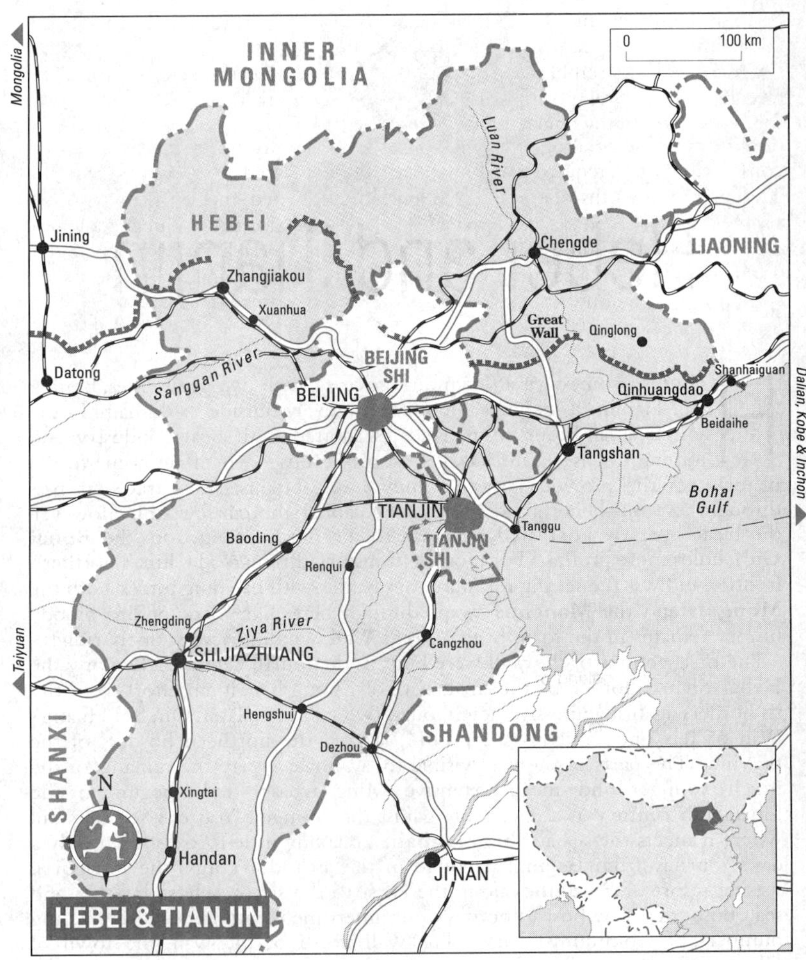

between Beijing and Qinhuangdao, a port town near Shanhaiguan, are often more convenient than the trains which, though regular, often run at inconvenient times of day.

Tianjin

And there were sections of the city where different foreigners lived – Japanese, White Russians, Americans and Germans – but never together, and all with their own separate habits, some dirty, some clean. And they had houses of all shapes and colours, one painted in pink, another with rooms that jutted out at every angle like the backs and fronts of Victorian dresses, others with roofs like pointed hats and wood carvings painted white to look like ivory.

Amy Tan, *The Joy Luck Club*

Massive and dynamic, **TIANJIN** is China's third-largest city, located near the coast some 80km east of Beijing. The city has few actual sights; it's the streetscapes – an assemblage of ageing nineteenth- and early twentieth-century foreign architecture, mostly European, juxtaposed with the concrete and glass monoliths of wealthy contemporary China – that are its most engrossing attraction. Locals say, not altogether with pride, that the city has become a massive construction site, requiring a new map to be printed every three months. Though wide swaths of the city are being redeveloped, much of the colonial architecture has been placed under protection – look for the distinctive plaques on the relevant buildings. Feng Jicai, one of China's best-known writers and a Tianjin resident, led a campaign to preserve the old city, noting, "Once a nation has lost its own culture, it faces a spiritual crisis more dreadful than that brought on by material poverty. If you regard a city as having a spirit, you will respect it, safeguard it, and cherish it. If you regard it as only matter, you will use it excessively, transform it at will, and damage it without regret." Contemporary Tianjin

Tianjin

Tianjin	天津	*tiānjīn*
Ancient Culture St	古文化街	*gǔwénhuà jiē*
Antique Market	旧货市场	*jiùhuò shìchǎng*
Dabei Yuan	大悲院	*dàbēi yuàn*
Drum Tower	鼓楼	*gǔlóu*
Earthquake Memorial	抗震纪念碑	*kàngzhèn jìniànbēi*
Fine Art Museum	艺术博物馆	*yìshù bówùguǎn*
Mosque	清真寺	*qīngzhēn sì*
Passenger ferry booking office	港客轮运输	*gǎngkèlún yùnshū*
Wanghailou Church	望海楼教堂	*wànghǎilóu jiàotáng*
Xikai Catholic Church	西开教堂	*xīkāi jiàotáng*
Zhongxin Park	中心公园	*zhōngxīn gōngyuán*
Zhou Enlai Memorial Hall	周恩来纪念馆	*zhōu'ēnlái jìniànguǎn*
Accommodation		
Astor Hotel	利顺德饭店	*lìshùndé fàndiàn*
Friend	富蓝特大酒店	*fùlántè dàjiǔdiàn*
Friendship	友谊宾馆	*yǒuyí bīnguǎn*
Hyatt Regency	凯酒店	*kǎiyuè jiǔdiàn*
Jinfang Hotel	津纺宾馆	*jīnfǎng bīnguǎn*
Kedu	客都大酒店	*kèdū dàjiǔdiàn*
Longmen Guesthouse	龙门旅店	*lóngmén lǚdiàn*
Nankai University	南开大学	*nánkāi dàxué*
Tianjin Number One	天津第一饭店	*tiānjīn dìyī fàndiàn*
Tianjin University	天津大学	*tiānjīn dàxué*
Xinfang	新纺宾馆	*xīnfǎng bīnguǎn*
Eating		
Erduoyan Fried Cake Shop	耳朵眼炸糕店	*ěrduǒyǎn zhágāodiàn*
Food Street	食品街	*shípǐnjiē*
Goubuli Stuffed Dumpling Restaurant	狗不理包子铺	*gǒubùlǐ bāozipù*
Guifaxiang	桂发祥麻花	*guìfāxiáng máhuā*
Kiessling's	起士林西式餐厅	*qǐshìlín xīshì cāntīng*
Suiyuan	随园酒家	*suíyuán jiǔjiā*
Tanggu	塘沽	*tánggū*
International Seamens' Club	国际海员俱乐部	*guójì hǎiyuán jùlèbù*
New Harbour Ferry Terminal	新港客运站	*xīngǎng kèyùnzhàn*

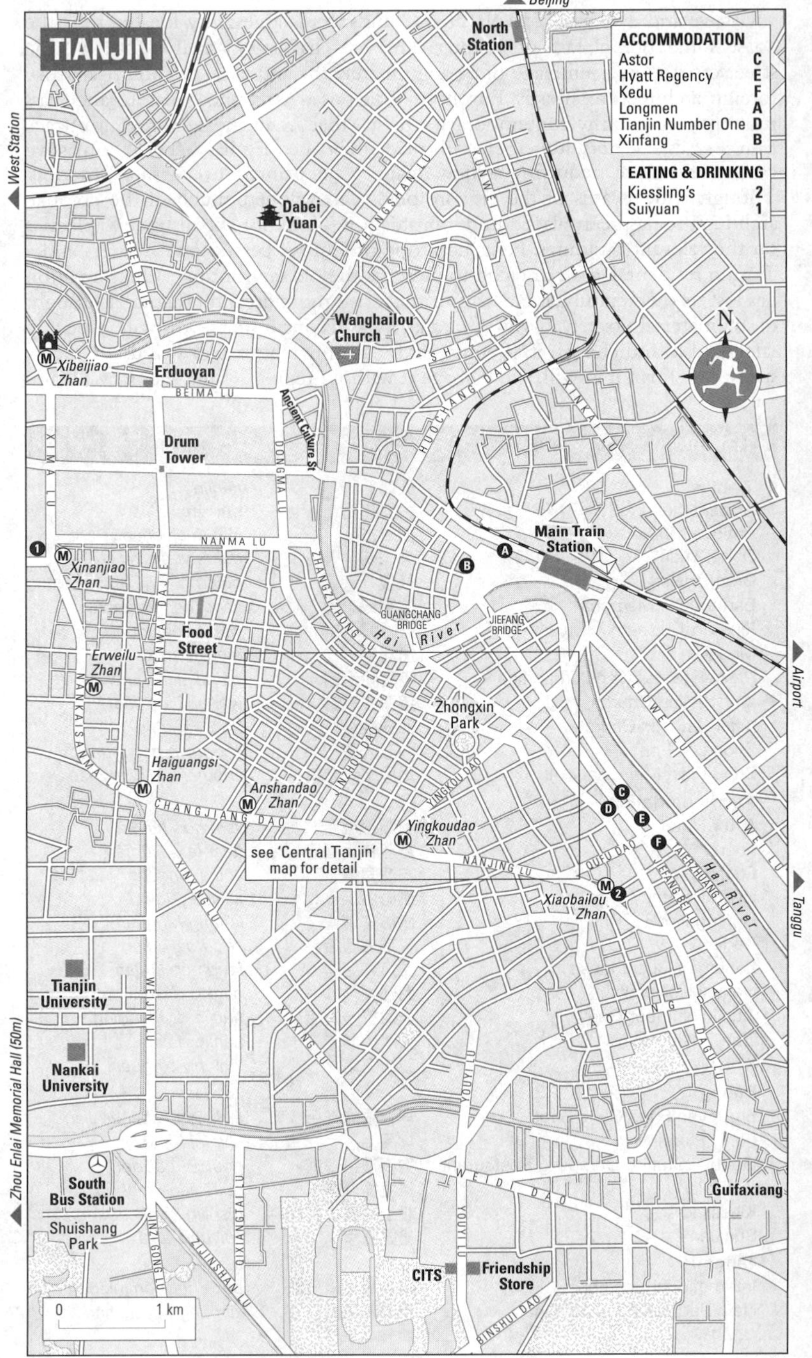

TIANJIN
ACCOMMODATION
Astor C
Hyatt Regency E
Kedu F
Longmen A
Tianjin Number One D
Xinfang B
EATING & DRINKING
Kiessling's 2
Suiyuan 1
Beijing
West Station
Airport
Tanggu
Zhou Enlai Memorial Hall (50m)
North Station
Dabei Yuan
Wanghailou Church
Xibeijiao Zhan
Erduoyan
Drum Tower
Main Train Station
Xinanjiao Zhan
Food Street
Erweilu Zhan
Zhongxin Park
Haiguangsi Zhan
Anshandao Zhan
Yingkoudao Zhan
see 'Central Tianjin' map for detail
Xiaobailou Zhan
Tianjin University
Nankai University
South Bus Station
Shuishang Park
Guifaxiang
CITS
Friendship Store
GUANGCHANG BRIDGE
JIEFANG BRIDGE
Hai River
BEIMA LU
NANMA LU
XIMA LU
DONGMA LU
HEBEI DAJIE
HONGSHAN LU
JINWEI LU
SHIZILIN DAJIE
HUOCHANG DAO
XINKAI LU
ZHANGZHONG LU
NANMENWAI DAJIE
NANKAI SANMA LU
CHANGJIANG DAO
XINXING LU
NANJING LU
YINGKOU DAO
QUFU DAO
JIEFANG BEILU
TAIERZHUANG LU
LIUWEI LU
SHAOXING DAO
DAGU LU
WEIJIN LU
YOUYI LU
WEIDI DAO
JINZI GONG LU
JIANSHAN LU
QIXIANGTAI LU
BINSHUI DAO
0
1 km
N

is an illustration of the latter, an unwieldy fusion of Beijing's bustle and Shanghai's Bund, though delivered without the character of either.

Nevertheless, Tianjin has architecture and shopping opportunities, especially for antiques, that just about justify a day-trip from the capital. The journey takes just over an hour by express train, a journey on which you may well be joined by young Beijingers coming to shop for clubwear, older residents in search of curios, and businesspeople shuttling between deals.

Though today the city is given over to industry and commerce, it was as a **port** that Tianjin first gained importance. When the Ming emperor Yongle moved the capital from Nanjing to Beijing, Tianjin became the dock for vast quantities of imperial tribute rice, transported here from all over the south through the Grand Canal. In the nineteenth century, the city caught the attention of the seafaring Western powers, who used the boarding of an English ship by Chinese troops as an excuse to declare war. With well-armed gunboats, they were assured of victory, and the Treaty of Tianjin, signed in 1856, gave the Europeans the right to establish nine concessionary bases on the mainland, from which they could conduct trade and sell opium.

These separate **concessions**, along the banks of the Hai River, were self-contained European fantasy worlds: the French built elegant chateaux and towers, while the Germans constructed red-tiled Bavarian villas. The Chinese were discouraged from intruding, except for servants, who were given pass cards. Tensions between the indigenous population and the foreigners exploded in the **Tianjin Incident** of 1870, when a Chinese mob attacked a French-run orphanage and killed the nuns and priests in the belief that the Chinese orphans were being kidnapped for later consumption. Twenty Chinese were beheaded as a result, and the prefect of the city was banished. A centre for secretive anti-foreign movements, the city had its genteel peace interrupted again by the **Boxer Rebellion** in 1900 (see p.1150), after which the foreigners levelled the walls around the old Chinese city to enable them to keep an eye on its residents.

Arrival and city transport

The city's huge **main train station** is well organized, and conveniently located just north of the Hai River; the town centre is just under 2km to the south (take bus #24). There are two other stations in town: **North**, where you are likely to arrive if you have come from northeast China; and **West**, which is on the main line between Beijing and destinations farther south. Trains terminating in Tianjin may call at one of the other stations before reaching the main station. The most stylish way to arrive is on the double-decker T-class trains (¥30–40 one way), which leave Beijing every hour, starting before 7am, and take eighty minutes. Public **buses** from Beijing also arrive at the main train station, as do most of the private ones – though the bus trip is comparatively long at nearly three hours (¥20). For details on trains out of Tianjin, see p.164. If you've arrived from Beijing by train and don't fancy returning this way, you could look for the line of unmarked VW Santanas in front of Tianjin's main station; these leave when full and take ninety minutes (¥50 per person).

The only buses serving Tianjin's large international **airport**, 15km east of the city, are Air China shuttles coinciding with their flights; a taxi into the centre from the airport should cost around ¥30. If you arrive by **ferry**, you'll find yourself in the port of **Tanggu**, a dull appendage of the city. Buses that take you into the city centre from here congregate around the passenger ferry terminal, and drop you at the **South bus station** near Shuishang Park. The train is faster, taking just under an hour, but Tanggu South station is inconveniently situated about 2km west of the ferry terminal.

Moving on by ferry from Tanggu

Much of Tianjin's port activity has shifted to Tanggu, 50km east. Every Monday morning a ferry sails from here to Kobe in Japan. The cheapest ticket, which gets you a *tatami* mat in a dormitory, costs ¥1600. Another ferry goes to Inchon in South Korea, with departures every Thursday and Sunday; the cheapest tickets are ¥888, rising to ¥1950 for the most comfortable berths. Note that for international ferries you have to check in two hours before departure. CITS in Tianjin sells tickets for international trips, which usually depart at 11am. A domestic ferry departs for Dalian at 7pm daily from March to October, alternate days the rest of the year (weather depending). Tickets start at ¥155, and can be bought at 1 Pukou Dao (T022/24406543), a small street west off Taierzhuang Lu, near Tianjin's *Astor Hotel*.

Frequent minibuses to Tanggu run from outside Tianjin's main station. Public buses leave from the South bus station, or you can catch the #151 which leaves from a small street opposite the main station: cross the bridge to the west, turn left, then take the second right and walk about 100m down the street. Many northbound trains out of Tianjin stop in Tanggu, half an hour away. Those heading to or from Beijing can take direct buses, avoiding the need to stop in Tianjin.

Tanggu itself is at least as expensive as Tianjin. One fairly cheap place to stay is the *International Seamen's Club* (T022/65770518; 5), just north of the passenger terminal; alternatively, port officials have been known to help foreigners find dormitory accommodation in the area.

City transport

Downtown and the old concession areas are just small enough to explore on foot, which is fortunate, as the **bus** network is both complicated and overcrowded, though bus maps are available around the train stations. Some useful routes include the **#24**, which runs from the West station into town, then doubles back on itself and terminates at the main station; **#1**, which runs from the North station into town, terminating at Zhongxin Park, the northern tip of the downtown area; and **#50**, which meanders into town from the main train station and takes you close to the Xikai Catholic Church. Bus fares in are a standard ¥1.5 throughout the city centre.

An alternative to the fiendish bus system is the **subway** (from ¥2 per journey), which runs south from the West train station, stopping near the Drum Tower and along Nanjing Lu, which is close to the main downtown shopping area. **Taxis** are plentiful – ¥10 is sufficient for most journeys around town.

Accommodation

There are few inexpensive hotels in Tianjin, though hotels do regularly slash their prices outside peak travel periods, so be sure to ask for a discounted rate and keep pressing until you get one. If you're travelling on a tight budget, the foreign student residences at Tianjin and Nankai universities, in the south of town (bus #8 from the main train station), are good options, at ¥150 or so for a comfortable double. Of the handful of cut-rate flophouses lining the back of the shopping centre on the train station's western concourse, with signboards in Chinese, the best is the *Longmen Guesthouse* (T022/24307611; 2).

Astor 33 Tai'er Zhuang Lu T022/23311688, F23316282. Located in a stylish British mansion more than 100 years old, this hotel misses no opportunity to remind you of its history: portraits of warlords line the walls, and there are museum-style displays everywhere, including such priceless items as the first Chinese-made light bulbs the hotel ever used. Service standards, however, can be almost amateur. 8

Friend 231 Xinhua Lu ⓣ 022/83326399, ⓕ 23125446. Very friendly, clean, and a bargain by Tianjin standards. Across the street from the *Friendship*'s East Building, and much more welcoming. ❺

Friendship 94 Nanjing Lu ⓣ 022/23310372, ⓕ 23310616. A modern building opposite the Earthquake Memorial, south of the town centre, and home to comfy rooms. The cheapest ones are around the corner in the East Building on Xinhua Lu, though these are rather bland. From the main building's entrance turn left, walk to the first intersection, turn left, and the East Building is 50m ahead on the left. East building ❺ main building ❼

Hyatt Regency 219 Jiefang Bei Lu ⓣ 022/23301234, ⓕ 23311234. The only one of Tianjin's main hotels to combine top-drawer prices with first-class service, though rooms are slightly smaller than regular patrons of the chain might be used to. ❽

Kedu Jiefang Bei Lu. Base yourself among the big spenders while paying rock-bottom prices – a Tianjin rarity – at this little money-saver, located just south of the *Hyatt* above the Bank of China. ❷

Tianjin Number One Jiefang Bei Lu ⓣ 022/23309988, ⓕ 23123000. A nice, rambling old colonial building with high ceilings, wide halls and Art Deco touches, though the reception can be more than a little frosty. ❻

Xinfang 10 Sanjing Lu ⓣ 022/24463555, ⓕ 24468480. Basic, tidy hotel to the west of the main railway station. From the arrival exit, walk straight past the bus stop and taxi stand to the seven-storey building directly across Sanjing Road. ❹

The City

The part of the city of interest to visitors – the dense network of ex-concession streets south and west of the central train station, and south of the Hai River – is fairly compact. Many *pinyin* street signs help in navigating the central grid of streets, as do plenty of distinctive landmarks, notably the T-shaped pedestrianized shopping district of **Binjiang Dao** and **Heping Lu** at Tianjin's heart.

The **old city** was strictly demarcated into national zones, and each section of the city centre has retained a hint of its old flavour. The area northwest of the main train station, on the west side of the Hai River, was the old Chinese city. Running from west to east along the north bank of the river were the Austrian, Italian, Russian and Belgian concessions, though most of the old buildings here have been destroyed. Unmistakable are the chateaux of the French concession, which now make up the downtown district just south of the river, and the haughty mansions the British built east of here. Farther east, also south of the river, the architecture of an otherwise unremarkable district has a sprinkling of stern German constructions. For a waterside view of the entire town all the way to Tanggu, there are marathon daily **boat rides** – popular with Chinese tourists – departing in the morning from the kiosk across from the main train station, just west of Jiefang Bridge (8hr; ¥78).

Downtown Tianjin

The majority of Tianjin's colonial buildings are clustered in the grid of streets on the southern side of the river. From the main train station, you can approach it via Jiefang Bridge, built by the French in 1903, which leads south along Jiefang Bei Lu to an area given an oddly Continental feel by the pastel colours and wrought-iron scrollwork balconies of the French concession. This is at its most appealing around the glorified roundabout known as **Zhongxin Park**. At 77 Jiefang Bei Lu, the pink **Fine Art Museum** (daily 8.30am–noon & 1.30–5pm; ¥10), a slightly pompous old building, has a broad collection of paintings, kites, Chinese New Year prints and *ni ren*, literally "mud men", clay figurines which became a popular local craft in the nineteenth century. Their greatest exponent was a skilled caricaturist named Zhang who made copies of opera stars and other notables. Some of his work is on show here; unfortunately, none of his depictions of Tianjin's foreigners, which got him into trouble with the authorities, is displayed.

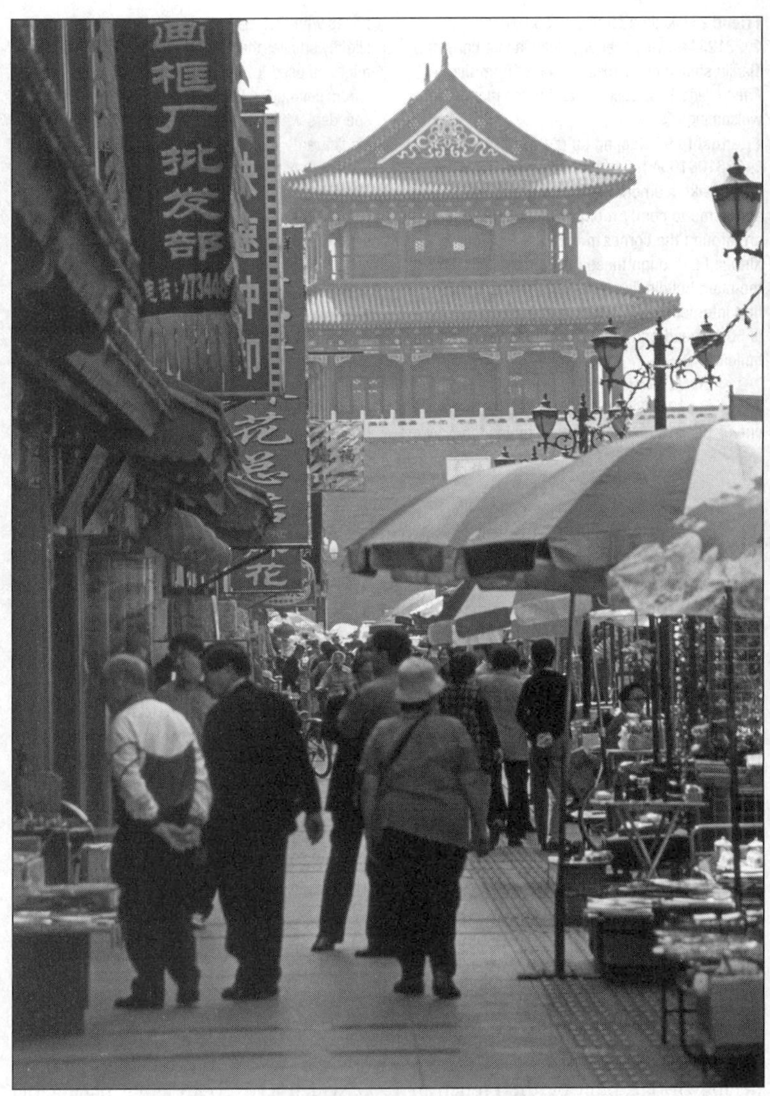

▲ Tianjin's old city

Zhongxin Park marks the southeastern end of the main **shopping district**, an area bounded by Dagu Lu, Jinzhou Dao and Chifeng Dao; Heping Lu and Binjiang Dao are the two busiest streets. Though stuffed with intrepid shoppers (as fashionably dressed as a Beijing crowd), these narrow tree-lined streets have a pleasingly laid-back feel, as traffic is light, and Heping Lu and Binjiang Dao are pedestrianized and lined with sculptures and benches. There are plenty of places for a snack hereabouts. It's hard to avoid Western fast-food chains, though a more traditional form of fast food is available at *Goubuli* (see p.163). Electric trolleybuses run the length of the shopping area (¥2).

The antique market

Just west of here is a shopping district of a very different character, the **antique market** (daily 8am–5pm), centred on Shandong Lu but spilling over into side alleys. A great attraction even if you have no intention of buying, the alleys are lined with dark, poky shops, pavement vendors with their wares spread out in front of them on yellowed newspapers, and stallholders waving jade and teapots in the faces of passers-by. The market expands and contracts according to the time of year (small in winter, big in summer) but it's always at its largest on Sundays, swelled by Beijingers here for the weekend. It's generally cheaper than any in the capital, though you will have to look hard for a bargain.

The variety of goods on display is astonishing: among the standard jade jewellery, ceramic teapots, fans and perfume bottles are Russian army watches, opium pipes, snuffboxes, ornate playing cards, old photographs, pornographic paintings and rimless sunglasses. Look out for the stalls selling picture postcards of revolutionary dramas depicting synchronized ballet dancers performing graceful, mid-air leaps with hand grenades. Bargaining is mandatory; be aware that some of the stuff is fake.

Around Nanjing Lu

At the southern end of Binjiang Dao, the **Xikai Catholic Church** (daily 5.30am–4.30pm) is a useful landmark and one of the most distinctive buildings in the city, with its odd facade of horizontal brown and orange brick stripes topped with three green domes. The diffuse zone of unremarkable buildings east of here, around Nanjing Lu, is notable only for the **Earthquake Memorial** opposite the *Friendship Hotel*. More tasteful than most Chinese public statuary, this hollow pyramid commemorates the 250,000 people who died in the 1976 earthquake in Tangshan, a city to the northeast.

North of the centre

The main sight in the northern part of the city, best reached by taxi, is the **Dabei Yuan**, located on a narrow alleyway off Zhongshan Lu (daily 9am–4.30pm; ¥4). Tianjin's major centre for Buddhist worship, it's easy to find as the alleys all around are crammed with stalls selling a colourful mix of religious knick-knacks: incense, tapes of devotional music, mirror-glass shrines, and ceramic Buddhas with flashing lights in their eyes. Large bronze vessels full of water stand outside the buildings, a fire precaution that has been in use for centuries. Outside the first hall, which was built in the 1940s, the devout wrap their arms around a large bronze incense burner before lighting incense sticks and kowtowing. In the smaller, rear buildings – seventeenth-century structures extensively restored after the Tangshan earthquake – you'll see the temple's jovial resident monks, while small antique wood and bronze Buddhist figurines are displayed in a hall in the west of the complex.

The stern **Wanghailou Church** (formerly the Notre Dame des Victoires cathedral) stands not far south of Dabei Yuan, over Shizilin Dajie on the north bank of the river. Built in 1904, it has an austere presence thanks to the use of dark stone and is the third church to stand on this site – the first was destroyed in the massacre of 1870, a year after it was built, and the second was burnt down in 1900 in the Boxer Rebellion. It's possible to visit during the week, but the Sunday-morning Chinese-language services (7am) make a stop here much more interesting.

Ancient Culture Street

A short walk southwest of Wanghailou Church, the more prosaic **Ancient Culture Street** runs off Beima Lu just west of the river, its entrance marked by a colourful arch. Like Liulichang Jie in Beijing, this is a re-creation of a nineteenth-century Chinese street – minus the beggars and filth and plus the neon "OK Karaoke" signs – designed as a tourist shopping mall. It's fake but undeniably pretty, with carved balconies and columns decorating the facade of red and green wooden shops topped with curling, tiled roofs. The shops sell pricey antiques and souvenirs, and there's an especially large range of teapots. The first shop on the right after the arch sells fifteen-centimetre-high clay figurines, in the style of Tianjin's master Zhang. Look out, too, for the stalls selling *chatang*, soup made with millet and sugar; the stallholders attract customers by demonstrating their skill at pouring boiling soup from a long, dragon-shaped spout into four bowls all held in one hand. About halfway down the street is the entrance to the heavily restored **Sea Goddess Temple** (daily 9am–5pm; ¥3), originally built in 1326 and supposedly the oldest building in Tianjin. There's an exhibition of local crafts in the side halls.

The Drum Tower and around

Just west of Ancient Culture Street, the recently built, characterless **Drum Tower** (daily 9am–4.30pm, ¥10) stands in what was once a quiet network of *hutongs* demarcated by four "horse" (*ma*) streets – **Beima**, **Nanma**, **Dongma** and **Xima**. The original *hutongs* have been swept away, replaced by new pseudo-*hutongs* packed to the rooflines with shops selling souvenirs and antiques, making this one of China's most concentrated tourist shopping areas. The main outlet of the famous **Erduoyan Fried Cake Shop** (see below) is located a short walk north of the Drum Tower development, though the confections and history are poorly showcased by the grubby building.

The **mosque**, farther west off Dafeng Lu, is an active place of worship, and you're free to wander around the buildings, though only Muslims may enter the prayer halls. It's a fine example of Chinese Muslim architecture, with some striking wood carvings of floral designs in the eaves and around the windows.

Zhou Enlai Memorial Hall

Southwest of the centre is the massive **Zhou Enlai Memorial Hall** (daily 9am–5pm; ¥10), paying tribute to Tianjin's most famous resident. A bunker perched on the northern edge of Shuishang Park, the hall features a few wax figures, Zhou's aeroplane and limousine, and scattered English explanations of his achievements, though it's not so much an analysis of the difficulties in being Chairman Mao's right-hand man as a paean to his marriage to fellow comrade Deng Yingchao. Try not to crack up when reading the description of the couple's bond: "Cherishing the same ideals, following the same path, and comrade-in-arms affection tied them in love relations." The events around the Cultural Revolution, from which Zhou's legacy derives most of its strength, are curtly summarized thus: "He frustrated the attempts of the Gang of Four." To get here, take bus #8 from the main station and get off at Shuishang Park near the statue of Nie Zhongjie, a general who is depicted on horseback.

Eating

Make sure you don't leave Tianjin without sampling some of its famous cakes and pastries. The **Erduoyan Fried Cake Shop** specializes in rice-powder cakes fried in sesame oil; don't be put off by the name, which means "ear hole". There are branches around the city, but the oldest is at Beimen Dajie, just north of the Drum Tower. Another Tianjin chain is the **Guifaxiang** shop, 568 Dagu Lu, renowned for its fried dough twists (*mahua*), a delicious local speciality that makes a good gift – the assistants will wrap and box them for you.

Downtown, the side streets around Heping Lu (close to Zhongxin Park) are home to local restaurants that are often worth sampling, particularly the lively *Goubuli* (yet another Tianjin chain). Heping Lu itself is rife with Western fast-food chains.

Food Street East of Nanmenwai Dajie, on Qingyi Dajie. A cheerful two-storey mall, this is still the best place to eat in Tianjin, though standards have slipped a little over the years, and a *McDonald's* now anchors the ground floor. Yet with over twenty restaurants on each level, there's something to suit all budgets and tastes. Upstairs, try the *Zhejiang Restaurant* for Zhejiang cuisine, the *Da Jin Haiwei* for Tianjin seafood, *Penglaichun* for Shandong dishes, and *Haidefu* for Sichuan. A local favourite is the bustling branch of *Goubuli* for *baozi*, also on the second floor. Between the restaurants are stalls and shops selling cakes, biscuits, dried fruit, nuts, chocolates and dead ducks.

Goubuli Stuffed Dumpling Restaurant Convenient if you're shopping around Binjiang Dao, this famous Tianjin restaurant has grown from a poky little store to the flagship of a chain with branches in the US and across Asia. Dumplings plus assorted condiments in an airline-food-style tray cost a very reasonable ¥13. The name, which means "dogs wouldn't believe it", is thought to be a reference either to the ugliness of the original proprietor or to the low-class status of dumplings. The flagship is at 77 Shandong Lu and marked on the map, though there are less attractive branches around the city.

Kiessling's 333 Zhejiang Lu, just off Nanjing Lu. Formerly Austrian-owned, this restaurant has been around for nearly 100 years, and the cafeteria upstairs still serves Western fare: breaded fish fillets, mashed potatoes, pasta and so forth. The beer hall and dining room on the top level is worth a stop, if only for their home-brewed dark beer.

Suiyuan Huanghe Dao, just west of Xima Lu. A good selection of Shandong-style dishes for around ¥50 per head.

Listings

Airlines Air China's main office is at 103 Nanjing Lu (daily 8am–4.30pm; ☎022/23301543). Airport shuttles (¥10) only run to Tianjin's airport in time for departures of scheduled Air China flights. More convenient are the regular shuttles making the run to and from Beijing's airport (4am, 5am, then 6am–5.30pm every 2hr or so; ¥70).

Banks and exchange The main office of the Bank of China is in a grand colonial edifice at 80 Jiefang Bei Lu (daily 8am–5pm).

Bookshops The Foreign Language Bookstore is at 130 Chifeng Dao.

Internet access Internet cafés are scattered along Baidi Lu, which runs along the west sides of Tianjin and Nankai universities.

Mail and telephones A post office occupies the building just east of the train station (daily 9am–6.30pm), and there's a 24hr telecom facility here too.

PSB 30 Tangshan Dao.

Shopping As well as the clothing and antique markets in the city centre, Tianjin is renowned for its handmade rugs and carpets, featuring bright, complex, abstract patterns. They're not cheap, and are best bought directly from the factories in the suburbs. Tianjin is also noted for its kites and its bright woodblock prints of domestic subjects, pinned up for good luck at Chinese New Year; the latter are made and sold at the Yangliuqing Picture Studio, which has an outlet on Ancient Culture St, and another at 111 Sanhe Dao (a small alley west of Youyi Lu and a 15min walk north of the Friendship Store). The Tianjin Antique Company, located fairly centrally at 161 Liaoning Lu (daily 9am–5pm; ⓣ022/27110308), has a wide selection of antique jade, embroidery, calligraphy and carvings. For pricier souvenirs, try the four-storey Friendship Store, which has a good supermarket, opposite CITS at 21 Youyi Lu.

Trains The majority of trains leave from the main station. A few trains to the northeast leave only from the North station, and some trains to southern destinations, such as Shanghai, that don't originate in Tianjin, call only at the West station. At the time of writing, the last express train back to Beijing left daily at around 7pm; latecomers will be pushed into a shared taxi (around ¥70 per person). Tickets for Beijing are on sale at a special English-labelled kiosk to the right of the escalators of the main station. You can also buy your return ticket on the train from Beijing. To avoid the queues when buying train tickets from the main station, try the soft-sleeper ticket office – go up the escalator, turn left towards the soft-sleeper waiting room, and the office is discreetly located on the left.

Travel agents CITS is at 22 Youyi Lu (ⓣ022/28358866 ext 102), opposite the Friendship Store. They don't impart much information, but they will book train and boat tickets for onward travel.

Beidaihe to Shanhaiguan

On the **Bohai Gulf**, 300km east of Beijing, lies the rather bizarre seaside resort of **Beidaihe**. The coastline, reminiscent of the Mediterranean – rocky, sparsely vegetated, erratically punctuated by beaches – was originally patronized a

Beidaihe to Shanhaiguan

Beidaihe	北戴河	*běidàihé*
Lianfengshan Park	联峰山公园	*liánfēngshān gōngyuán*
Pigeon Nest Park	鸽子窝公园	*gēziwō gōngyuán*
Accommodation and eating		
Diplomatic Missions Guesthouse	外交人员宾馆	*wàijiāo rényuán bīnguǎn*
Friendship	友谊宾馆	*yǒuyí bīnguǎn*
Jinhai Hotel	金海宾馆	*jīnhǎi bīnguǎn*
Jinshan Hotel	金山宾馆	*jīnshān bīnguǎn*
Kiessling's	起士林餐厅	*qǐshìlín cāntīng*
Tiger Rock	老虎石宾馆	*lǎohǔshí bīnguǎn*
Nandaihe	南戴河	*nándàihé*
Qinhuangdao	秦皇岛	*qínhuángdǎo*
Haiyue Hotel	海岳大厦	*hǎiyuè dàshà*
Shanhaiguan	山海关	*shānhǎiguān*
First Pass Under Heaven	天下第一关	*tiānxià dìyīguān*
Great Wall Museum	长城搏物馆	*chángchéng bówùguǎn*
Jiao Shan	角山	*jiǎo shān*
Lao Long Tou	老龙头	*lǎolóng tóu*
Longevity Mountain	长寿山	*chángshòu shān*
Mengjiangnü Miao	孟姜女庙	*mèngjiāngnǚ miào*
Yansai Hu	燕塞湖	*yànsài hú*
Accommodation and eating		
Cai Pu	菜铺	cài pù
Dongfang	东方宾馆	*dōngfāng bīnguǎn*
Hua Rong	华荣	*huáróng*
Jiaozi Wang	老王头饺子馆	*lǎowángtóu jiǎoziguǎn*
Jingshan	京山宾馆	*jīngshān bīnguǎn*
Juchunyuan Chaguan	朱春园茶馆	*jūchūnyuán cháguǎn*
Sitiao Baozi	四条包子	*sìtiáo bāozi*

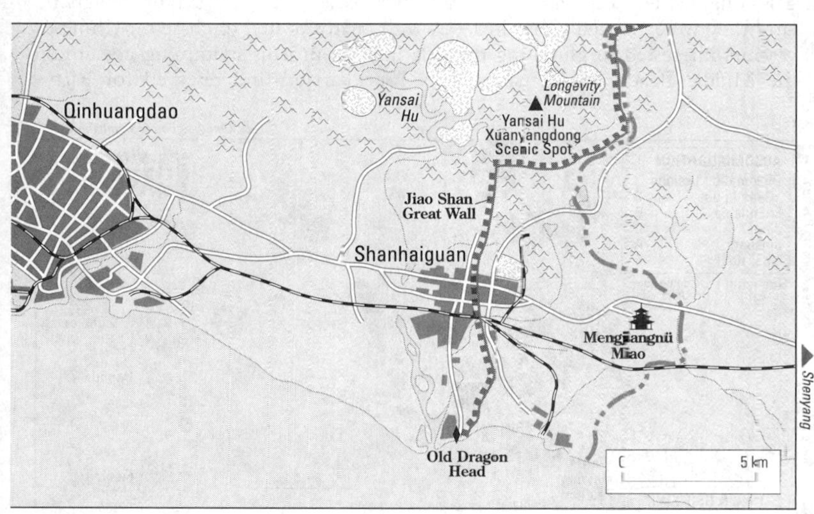

hundred years ago by European diplomats, missionaries and businessmen, who can only have chosen it out of homesickness. They built villas and bungalows here, and reclined on verandas sipping cocktails after indulging in the new bathing fad. After the Communist takeover, the village became a pleasure resort for Party bigwigs, reaching its height of popularity in the 1970s when seaside trips were no longer seen as decadent and revisionist. Though you'll still see serious men in uniforms and sunglasses licking lollipops, and black Audis with tinted windows (the Party cadre car) cruising the waterfront, most of Beidaihe's visitors nowadays are ordinary, fun-loving tourists, usually well-heeled Beijingers. In high season, when the temperature is steady around the mid-20s Celsius and the water warm, it's a fun place to spend the day.

Only 25km or so to the northeast, **Shanhaiguan** makes a good base if you're touring the area – far cheaper than Beidaihe, and with year-round appeal. The central area is small enough to walk around, and though the town is rapidly being redeveloped, it can still be a peaceful stop, particularly if you can nab a room inside the city wall. The surrounding countryside contains some fine sturdy fortifications and remnants of the **Great Wall**.

This part of the Bohai Gulf is more easily reached from Beijing on the express-bus service to **QINHUANGDAO** than by train. Midway between Beidaihe and Shanhaiguan, Qinhuangdao is an industrial city and charmless modern port. Once you're in the area, it's straightforward to get around by **bus**; local bus services are frequent, usually hourly during the day. Buses #6 and #34 shuttle between Beidaihe and Qinhuangdao (¥3), while buses #25 and #33 run the Qinhuangdao–Shanhaiguan route (same fare). Qinhuangdao used to boast a passenger-ferry service to Dalian, though this wasn't in service at the time of writing. If you do get stuck in Qinhuangdao, you could do worse than stay at the *Haiyue Hotel*, 159 Yingbin Lu (☎0335/3065760; ④); walk south from the train station concourse and the hotel is on the west side of the road.

Beidaihe and around

It wasn't so long ago that **BEIDAIHE** had strict rules ordering where individuals could bathe, according to their rank. West Beach was reserved for foreigners after they were granted access in 1979, with guards posted to chase off Chinese voyeurs interested in glimpsing their daringly bourgeois swimming costumes; the Middle Beach was demarcated by rope barriers and reserved for Party

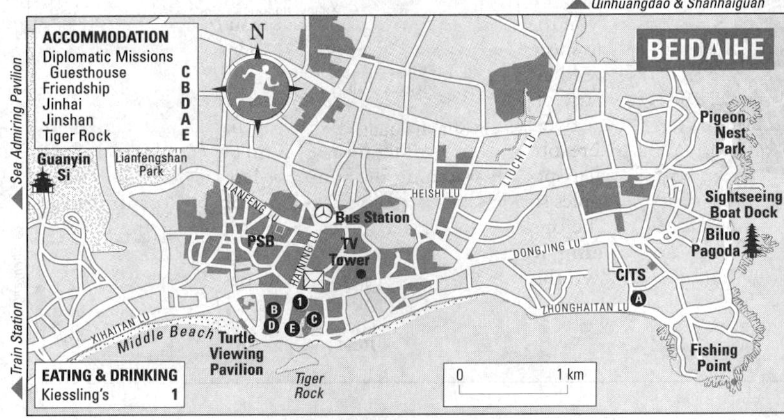

officials, with a sandy cove – the best spot – set out for the higher ranks. Dark swimsuits were compulsory, to avoid the illusion of nudity. These days the barriers have gone, along with the inhibitions of the urban Chinese (skimpy bikinis are fashionable now), and the contemporary town is a fascinating mix of the austerely communist and the gaudy kitsch of any busy seaside resort.

The Town

Much of Beidaihe shuts down during colder months; in high season, the streets along the seafront are at their liveliest – most buildings are either restaurants, with crabs and prawns bobbing about in buckets outside, or shops selling Day-Glo swimsuits, inflatables, snorkelling gear, souvenirs and even sculptures of chickens made of shells and raffia. Away from the sea, up the hill, the tree-lined streets are much quieter, and many of the buildings are guesthouses, though this is also where you find the **villas** of the Party elite, guarded by discreet soldiers. It's rumoured that every Politburo member once had a residence here, and many probably still do. All around are huge, chunky buildings, often with absurd decorative touches – Roman columns, fake totem poles, Greek porticoes – grafted onto their ponderous facades. These are work-unit hotels and sanatoriums for heroes of the people – factory workers, soldiers and the like – when they are granted the privilege of a seaside holiday.

On the far western side of town, 500m back from the beach, **Lianfengshan Park** is a hill of dense pines with picturesque pavilions and odd little caves, a good place to wander and get away from the crowds for a while. Atop the hill is the **Sea Admiring Pavilion**, which has good views of the coast. Also here is a quiet temple, **Guanyin Si**.

The beaches

On Beidaihe's three beaches, stirring revolutionary statues of lantern-jawed workers and their wives and children stand among the throngs of bathers. **Middle Beach**, really many small beaches with rocky outcrops in between, is the most convenient and popular. The promenade at the back is lined with soft-drink vendors, photo stalls, hoopla games and bathing huts that look like moon dwellings from a 1950s science-fiction movie. You can get your photograph taken atop a stuffed tiger, in a cardboard speedboat, or dressed up like an emperor. **West Beach** is more of the same, but a little quieter. East of the resort, stretching 15km to Qinhuangdao, is **East Beach** (take bus #6 or #34), popular with cadres and sanatorium patients for its more sedate atmosphere. The beach is long enough for you to be able to find a spot where you can be alone, though much of the muddy shoreline isn't very attractive. At low tide its wide expanse is dotted with seaweed collectors in rubber boots.

At the southern tip of East Beach is **Pigeon Nest Park** (bus #21 from Zhonghaitan Lu), a twenty-metre-high rocky outcrop named for the seagulls fond of perching here, obviously by someone who wasn't skilled in bird identification. It's a popular spot for watching the sunrise. Mao sat here in 1954 and wrote a poem, "Ripples sifting sand/Beidaihe", which probably loses something in translation. Just before Pigeon Nest Park, the bus stops near the dock for Beidaihe's **sightseeing boats**, which in season leave regularly during the day to chug up and down the somewhat underwhelming coast (1hr; ¥32).

Practicalities

Beidaihe's **train station** is inconveniently located 15km out of town; bus #5 will take you from here into the centre. If you arrive at night, there'll be private minibuses and taxis waiting; bargain hard to get the fare down below ¥50. If you plan on visiting both Beidaihe and Shanhaiguan, it's far more convenient and interesting to base yourself in Shanhaiguan, where the accommodation is cheaper and the train station close to the hotels, and visit Beidaihe either as a day-trip or on the way to or from Beijing. From Beidaihe's **bus station**, it's a fifteen-minute walk downhill to Middle Beach.

Taxis around town cost ¥10, but Beidaihe is small enough to get around easily on foot. The Beidaihe **CITS** is located in a nondescript building at 4 Jinshanzui Lu (ⓣ0335/4041748), though those arriving by bus will find it more convenient to use the tourist information booth near the bus station.

Accommodation and eating

Beidaihe's accommodation is most in demand between May and August; at other times of year, room prices are often slashed to half their summer high. More and more of Beidaihe's many **hotels** are opening their doors to foreigners. One of the best is the *Diplomatic Missions Guesthouse* at 1 Baosan Lu (ⓣ0335/4041287, ⓕ4041807; ❽), a quiet street ten minutes' walk north of Middle Beach. It's a stylish complex of thirteen villas set among gardens of cypress and pine, with a karaoke bar, a nightclub, a tennis court, a gym and a good outdoor restaurant featuring barbecues in the summer. Other good options include *Tiger Rock* (ⓣ0335/4041373; ❺) and the *Jinhai* (ⓣ0335/4030048; ❻), both well located right next to the beach, but a little bland and characterless; similar, but farther north on Haining Lu, is the small *Friendship* (ⓣ0335/4041176; ❻), and further away in a pleasant, quiet cove on Zhonghaitan Lu is the *Jinshan*, a three-star complex with a pool (ⓣ0335/4041338; ❼).

Foodwise, Beidaihe is noted for its crab, cuttlefish and scallops. Try one of the innumerable small **seafood** places on Haining Lu, where you order by pointing to the tastiest looking thing scuttling or slithering around the bucket, or *Kiessling's*, on Dongjing Lu near the *Diplomatic Missions Guesthouse*. Originally Austrian, this restaurant has been serving the foreign community for most of the last century, and still has a few Western dishes on its reasonably priced menu – Western diners are even offered knives and forks. It's an ideal place for breakfast, offering good pastries and bread.

Around Beidaihe

The countryside around Beidaihe has been designated as a **nature reserve** and is a stopping-off point for Siberian and red-crowned cranes migrating to Dongbei in May; Beidaihe's CITS is a useful point of contact for birders.

Fifteen kilometres west along the coast, **NANDAIHE** is a tourist resort constructed to take advantage of Beidaihe's popularity. With 3km of beach and a few parks and viewpoints, it's the same sort of thing as Beidaihe but more regimented and artificial, and is thus best visited as a day-trip; frequent minibuses come here from the Beidaihe bus station. The main attraction in Nandaihe is **Golden Beach** to the west, where you can go "sand sliding" down the steep sand dunes on a rented sledge – great fun, but remember to keep your feet and elbows in the air. Foreigners can stay here at the *Nandaihe Beach House* resort complex (ⓣ0335/4042807; ❺).

Shanhaiguan and beyond

A town at the northern tip of the Bohai Gulf, **SHANHAIGUAN**, "the Pass Between the Mountains and the Sea", was originally built during the Ming dynasty as a fortress to defend the eastern end of the **Great Wall**. The wall crosses the Yanshan Mountains to the north, forms the east wall of the town

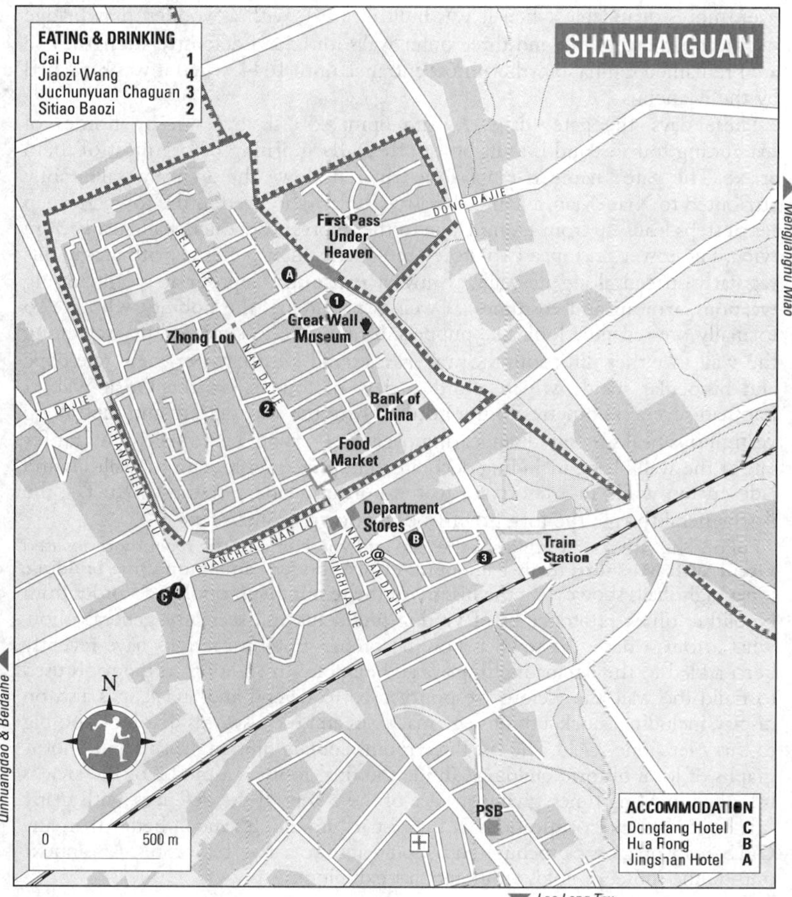

and meets the sea a few kilometres to the south. Far from being a solitary castle, Shanhaiguan originally formed the centre of a network of defences: smaller forts, now nothing but ruins, existed to the north, south and east, and beacon towers were dotted around the mountains. The town's obvious tourist potential is now being tapped, and at the time of writing the area bounded by the wall had been almost entirely levelled in preparation for a full-scale makeover; according to locals this will look "very pretty" in the near future, and they may well be right. The best thing to do here is rent a bike and spend a day or two exploring.

The Town

Shanhaiguan is still arranged along its original plan of straight boulevards following the points of a compass, intersected with a web of alleys. Dominating the town is a fortified gatehouse in the east wall, the **First Pass Under Heaven**, which for centuries was the entrance to the Middle Kingdom from the barbarian lands beyond. An arch topped by a two-storey tower, the gate makes its surrounding buildings look puny in comparison; it must have looked even more formidable when it was built in 1381, with a wooden drawbridge over a moat 18m wide, and three outer walls for added defensive strength. The arch remained China's northernmost entrance until 1644, when it was breached by the Manchus.

These days, the gate (daily 7.30am–6pm; ¥50) is overrun by hordes of marauding tourists, and is at its best in the early morning before most of them arrive. The gate's name is emblazoned in red above the archway, calligraphy attributed to Xiao Xian, a Ming-dynasty scholar who lived in the town. A steep set of steps leads up from Dong Dajie to the impressively thick wall, nearly 30m wide. The tower on top, a two-storey, ten-metre-high building with arrow slits regularly spaced along its walls, is now a **museum**, appropriately containing weapons, armour and costumes, as well as pictures of the nobility, who are so formally dressed they look like puppets. It's possible to stroll a little way along the wall in either direction; the wall is scattered with pay-per-view telescope and binocular stands, which afford a view of tourists on the Great Wall at Jiaoshan several kilometres to the north, where the wall zigzags and dips along vertiginous peaks before disappearing over the horizon. There's plenty of tat for sale at the wall's base, including decorated chopsticks, hologram medallions and jade curios, while in a courtyard to the northern side, a statue of Xu Da, the first general to rule the fort, frowns sternly down on the scene.

Follow the city wall south from the gate and you come to the recently renovated **Great Wall Museum** (daily 8am–6pm; ¥10). A modern, imitation Qing building, it has eight halls showcasing the history of the region in chronological order from Neolithic times; photographs of visiting presidents and secretary-generals show what a tourist draw the town is now becoming. English captions have recently been added to the fascinating displays and exhibits. In addition to the tools used to build the wall, the vicious weaponry used to defend and attack it is also on display, including mock-ups of siege machines and broadswords that look too big to carry, let alone wield. The last three rooms contain dioramas, plans and photographs of local historic buildings. Inside the final room is a model of the area as it looked in Ming times, giving an idea of the extent of the defences, with many small outposts and fortifications in the district around. It's much better than any CITS map or glossy brochure and should inspire a few bike rides. An annexe outside the museum holds temporary art exhibitions.

Practicalities

Whether you arrive by **train** or **bus**, you'll be greeted by an eager mob of taxi and motor-rickshaw drivers; the ¥5 flag fall covers a ride to any destination in town. **Local buses** from Qinhuangdao and Beidaihe run along Guancheng Nan Lu, with a stop just outside the southern city gate. Before reconstruction of the area got underway, **bikes** could be rented from shops along Nan Dajie (¥10/day, ¥100 deposit) – these are almost guaranteed to return post-mess.

One decent **hotel** – ideally located near the First Pass Under Heaven – avoided the wrecking balls swung liberally around the old city. The palatial *Jingshan Hotel* (☎0335/5051130; ⑤) was built to imitate a Qing mansion, with high ceilings, decorative friezes, curling roofs and red brick walls and balconies. Rooms, equipped with television and fan, are off a series of small courtyards. More hotels are sure to open in due course, but until then you can choose from a number of options between the train station and the south wall. The friendly *Dongfang Hotel* (☎0335/5151111; ⑤), facing the south wall on Guancheng Nan Lu, offers four-person dorms (summer only) and doubles; further down the price scale is the *Hua Rong* (☎0335/5022661; ③), which has perfectly adequate rooms and amiable owners, though suffers from an occasional lack of hot water.

As for **eating**, the *Jingshan*'s fancy restaurant serves up huge dishes at reasonable prices, and has that Hebei rarity – an English-language menu. Facing the First Pass Under Heaven is *Cai Pu*, which serves much of the same fare. For delicious, plump, steamed Chinese ravioli, there's *Jiaozi Wang*, next to the *Dongfang Hotel*. *Sitiao Baozi* on Nan Dajie once turned humble pork and vegetarian *baozi* into the centrepiece of a good meal, but whether it will resurface after the area's reconstruction remains to be seen. Those arriving by train can fall straight into *Juchunyuan Chaguan*, a cheap, friendly eatery opposite the lemon clocktower on the west side of the station.

The Great Wall beyond Shanhaiguan

You'll see plenty of tourist **minibuses** grouped around the major crossroads in town and at the station, all serving the sights outside Shanhaiguan. Public **buses** also travel these routes, but if you have the time you're best off travelling by **bike**: the roads are quiet, the surrounding countryside is strikingly attractive and there are any number of pretty places off the beaten track where you can escape the crowds.

Intrepid hikers could try and make it to **Yansai Hu**, a lake in the mountains directly north of Shanhaiguan, or to **Longevity Mountain**, a hill of rugged stones east of the lake, where many of the rocks have been carved with the character *shou* (longevity). There's also a mountain pool here, a good place for a quiet swim.

Lao Long Tou

Follow the remains of the Great Wall south and after 4km you'll reach **Lao Long Tou** (Old Dragon Head, after a large stone dragon's head that used to look out to sea here; daily 7.30am–5pm; ¥50), the point at which the wall hits the coast. Bus #24 heads here from Xinghua Jie, near Shanhaiguan's train station. A miniature fortress with a two-storey temple in the centre stands right at the end of the wall, but unfortunately everything here has been so reconstructed it all looks brand new, and the area is surrounded by a rash of tourist development. The rather dirty beaches either side of the wall are popular bathing spots.

Walk a few minutes past the restaurants west of Lao Long Tou and you'll come to the old British Army **barracks**, on the right; this was the beachhead for the Eight Allied Forces in 1900, when they came ashore to put down the Boxers. A plaque here reminds visitors to "never forget the national humiliation and invigorate the Chinese nation". Do your part by taking care not to trample the lawn.

Mengjiangnü Miao

Some 6.5km northeast of town is **Mengjiangnü Miao** (daily 7.30am–5pm; ¥25), a temple dedicated to a legendary woman whose husband was press-ganged into one of the Great Wall construction squads. He died from exhaustion, and she set out to search for his body to give him a decent burial, weeping as she walked along the wall. So great was her grief, it is said that the wall crumbled in sympathy, revealing the bones of her husband and many others who had died in its construction. The temple is small and elegant, with good views of the mountains and the sea. Statues of the lady herself and her attendants sit looking rather prim inside. To get here, take bus #23 from outside Shanhaiguan's south gate.

Jiao Shan

A couple of kilometres to the north of Shanhaiguan, it's possible to hike along the worn remains of the Great Wall all the way to the mountains. Head north along Bei Dajie and out of town, and after about 10km you'll come to a reconstructed section known as **Jiao Shan** (daily 8am–4pm; ¥25), passing the ruins of two forts – stone foundations and earthen humps – along the way. A steep path from the reconstructed section takes you through some dramatic scenery into the Yunshan Mountains, or you can cheat and take the cable car (¥15, ¥30 return).

The further along the wall you go the better it gets – the crowds peter out, the views become more dramatic, and once the reconstructed section ends, you're left standing beside – or on top of – the real, crumbly thing. Head a few kilometres further east and you'll discover a trio of passes in the wall, and a beacon tower that's still in good condition. You can keep going into the mountains for as long as you like, so it's worth getting here early and making a day of it. A pedicab or taxi back into town from Jiao Shan's car park costs ¥5.

Chengde

CHENGDE, a country town 250km northeast of Beijing, sits in a river basin on the west bank of the Wulie River, surrounded by the Yunshan mountain range. It's a quiet, unimportant place, rather bland in appearance, but on its outskirts are some of the most magnificent examples of imperial architecture in China, remnants from its glory days as the **summer retreat** of the Manchu emperors. Gorgeous temples punctuate the cabbage fields around town, and a palace-and-park hill complex, **Bishu Shanzhuang**, covers an area nearly as large as the town itself. In recent years Chengde has once more become a summer haven, justly popular with weekending Beijingers escaping the hassles of the capital.

Chengde

Chengde	承德	*chéngdé*
Anyuan Miao	安远庙	*ānyuǎn miào*
Arhat Hill	罗汉山	*luóhàn shān*
Frog Crag	蛤蟆石	*háma shí*
Bishu Shanzhuang	避暑山庄	*bìshǔ shānzhuāng*
Palace	正宫	*zhèng gōng*
Pule Si	普乐寺	*pǔlè sì*
Puning Si	普宁寺	*pǔníng sì*
Puren Si	溥仁寺	*pǔrén sì*
Putuozongcheng Miao	普陀宗乘之庙	*pǔtuó zōngchéng zhīmiào*
Shuxiang Si	殊像寺	*shūxiàng sì*
Sledgehammer Rock	棒锺山	*bàngzhōng shān*
Xumifushouzhi Miao	须弥福寿之庙	*xūmífúshòu zhīmiào*
Accommodation and eating		
Chengde Plaza	承德大厦	*chéngdé dàshà*
Fangyuan	芳园居	*fāngyuánjū*
Mountain Villa	山庄宾馆	*shānzhuāng bīnguǎn*
Qianlong Jiaoziguan	乾隆饺子馆	*qiánlóng jiǎoziguǎn*
Qiwanglou	倚望楼宾馆	*yǐwànglóu bīnguǎn*
Shang Ke Tang	上客堂宾馆	*shàng kè táng bīnguǎn*
Yi Yuan	易园宾馆	*yì yuán bīnguǎn*
Yunshan Fandian	云山饭店	*yúnshān fàndiàn*

Some history

Originally called "Rehe", the town was discovered by the Qing-dynasty emperor **Kangxi** at the end of the seventeenth century, while marching his troops to the Mulan hunting range to the north. He was attracted to the cool summer climate and the rugged landscape, and built small lodges here from which he could indulge in a fantasy Manchu lifestyle, hunting and hiking like his northern ancestors. The building programme expanded when it became diplomatically useful to spend time north of Beijing, to forge closer links with the troublesome Mongol tribes. Kangxi, perhaps the ablest and most enlightened of his dynasty, was known more for his economy – "The people are the foundation of the kingdom; if they have enough then the kingdom is rich" – than for such displays of imperial grandeur. Chengde, however, was a thoroughly pragmatic creation, devised as an effective means of defending the empire by overawing Mongol princes with splendid audiences, hunting parties and impressive military manoeuvres. He firmly resisted all petitions to have the Great Wall repaired, saying this would be an unnecessary burden on the people, and noting that the Wall was a poor means of control, too, as it had posed no obstacle to the founders of his dynasty only a few years before.

Construction of the first palaces started in 1703. By 1711 there were 36 palaces, temples, monasteries and pagodas set in a great walled park, its ornamental pools and islands dotted with beautiful pavilions and linked by bridges. Craftsmen from all parts of China were invited to work on the project; Kangxi's grandson, **Qianlong** (1736–96), added another 36 imperial buildings during his reign, which was considered to be the heyday of Chengde.

In 1786, the **Panchen Lama** was summoned from Tibet by Qianlong for his birthday celebrations. This was an adroit political move to impress the followers of Lamaist Buddhism. The Buddhists included a number of minority groups who were prominent thorns in the emperor's side, such as Tibetans, Mongols, Torguts, Eleuths, Djungars and Kalmucks. Some accounts (notably not Chinese) tell how Qianlong invited the Panchen Lama to sit with him on the Dragon Throne, which was taken to Chengde for the summer season. He was certainly feted with honours and bestowed with costly gifts and titles, but the greatest impression on him and his followers must have been made by the replicas of the Potala and of his own palace, constructed at Chengde to make him feel at home – a munificent gesture, and one that would not have been lost on the Lamaists. However, the Panchen Lama's visit ended questionably when he succumbed to smallpox, or possibly poison, in Beijing and his coffin was returned to Tibet with a stupendous funeral cortege.

The first **British Embassy** to China, under Lord Macartney, visited Qianlong's court in 1793. Having suffered the indignity of sailing up the river to Beijing in a ship whose sails were painted with characters reading "Tribute bearers from the vassal king of England", they were somewhat disgruntled to discover that the emperor had decamped to Chengde for the summer. However, they made the 150-kilometre journey there, in impractical European carriages, arriving at Chengde in September 1793. They were well received by the emperor, despite Macartney's refusal to kowtow, and Qianlong's disappointment with their gifts, supplied by the opportunist East India Company. Qianlong, at the height of Manchu power, was able to hold out against the British demands, refusing to grant any of the treaties requested and remarking, in reply to a request for trade: "We possess all things. I set no value on objects strange or ingenious, and have no use for your country's manufactures." His letter to the British monarch concluded, magnificently, "O king, Tremblingly Obey and Show No Negligence!"

Chengde gradually lost its imperial popularity when the place came to be seen as unlucky after emperors Jiaqing and Xianfeng died here in 1820 and 1860 respectively. The buildings were left empty and neglected for most of the twentieth century, but largely escaped the ravages of the Cultural Revolution. Restoration, in the interests of tourism, began in the 1980s and is ongoing.

Arrival and transport

The train journey from Beijing to Chengde takes four hours on the fastest trains (¥75) through verdant, rolling countryside, hugging the Great Wall awhile before arriving at the **train station** in the south of town. Travelling from Beijing by bus is equally spectacular and takes about the same time, though you run greater risk of traffic and weather delays. Buses from Beijing (¥50) terminate

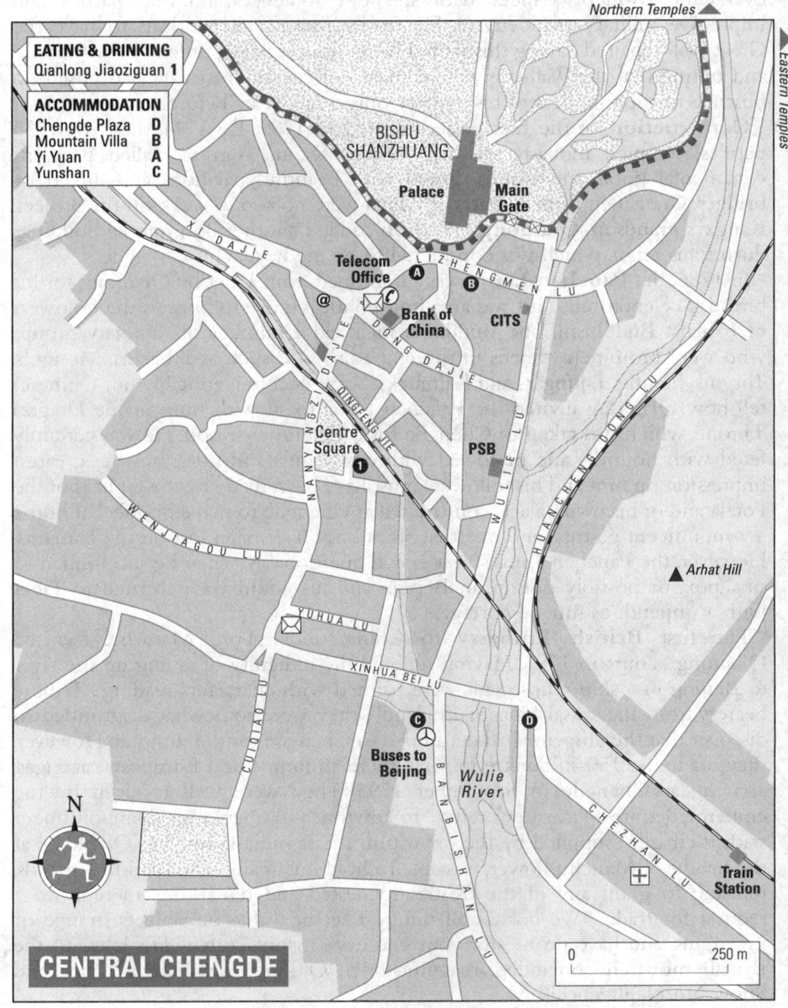

just outside the *Yunshan Hotel*. Touts wait in ambush at the train station, and can be useful if you already have a hotel in mind, as you won't be charged for the ride there; however, they will hassle you to take a minibus tour with them. Onward train tickets can be booked, with a ¥30 surcharge, from **CITS** on Wulie Lu (Ⓣ0314/2027483) or from any of the hotels.

Getting around Chengde by public transport isn't easy, as **local buses** are infrequent and always crammed. Buses #5 and #11, which go from the train station to Bishu Shanzhuang, and bus #6, from there to the Puning Si, are the most useful. **Taxis** are easy to find, but the drivers are often unwilling to use their meters – a ride around town should cost ¥5, or ¥10 to an outlying temple. At peak hours during the summer, the main streets are so congested that it's quicker to walk. The town itself is just about small enough to cover on foot.

If your time is limited, consider a minibus **tour** to cram in all the sights. It's occasionally possible to arrange an English-speaking day-tour through CITS, though it's much easier to go through one of the larger hotels. Chinese tours, which leave sporadically from outside the train station, are slightly cheaper. A day-long organized tour is something of a trial of endurance, however, and the tours tend to overlook the less spectacular temples, which are also the most peaceful. Probably the best way to see everything in a short time is to take a minibus or a bike around the temples one day and explore the mountain resort the next. If you're travelling in a group you can charter a taxi or a minibus for around ¥150 a day (bargain hard) and create your own itinerary.

Accommodation

There are plenty of hotels in Chengde town itself, plus a couple of expensive places inside Bishu Shanzhuang. Rates are highly negotiable; the price codes below apply to the peak summer season and weekends. At other times you can get discounts of up to two-thirds.

Chengde Plaza Chezhan Lu Ⓣ0314/2083808, Ⓕ2024319. This recently renovated fifteen-storey block is convenient for the station, but in an uninteresting area of town. ❽

Mountain Villa 127 Xiaonanmen (entrance on Lizhengmen Lu) Ⓣ0314/2025588. This grand, well-located complex has huge rooms, high ceilings and a cavernous, gleaming lobby, and is extremely popular with tour groups. The large rooms in the main building are nicer but a little more expensive than those in the ugly building round the back, and there are some very cheap rooms in the basement. Buses #5 or #11 from the train station will get you here. ❺

Qiwanglou Around the corner and uphill from the Bishu Shanzhuang main entrance Ⓣ0314/2024385. A well-run hotel in a pleasing imitation Qing-style building, the grounds make for an interesting walk even if you're not staying here. ❽

JShang Ke Tang Puning Si Ⓣ0314/2058888. This interesting hotel's staff wear period clothing and braided wigs befitting the adjoining Puning temple, and glide along the dim bowels of the complex to lead you to appealingly rustic rooms. ❼

Yi Yuan Lizhengmen Lu. Just around the corner from the *Mountain Villa*, this sprawling complex has gloomy rooms but is cheap year round and extremely convenient for Bishu Shanzhuang. ❷

Yunshan 2 Banbishan Lu Ⓣ0314/2055588, Ⓕ20558855. This modern block was once popular with tour groups, before being trumped by the *Mountain Villa*. The second-floor restaurant is good, the plushest in town, and not too expensive. A 10min walk from the train station. ❽

The Town

Bishu Shanzhuang lies in the north of the town, while farther north and to the east, on the other side of the river, stand Chengde's eight imposing **temples**. The majority of Chengde's one-million-strong population live in a semi-rural suburban sprawl to the south of the centre, leaving the city itself fairly small-scale

– its new high-rises yet to obscure the view of distant mountains and fields. However, hundreds of thousands of visitors come here each year, and on summer weekends in particular, the town can be packed with tourists, and its main artery, **Nanyingzi Dajie**, clogged with traffic. The street is much more pleasant in the evening, when a **night market** stretches all the way down it. In addition to snacks, many vendors sell antiques and curios that are generally cheaper than in Beijing or Tianjin, but you'll have to bargain hard (and don't expect everything to be genuine).

Bishu Shanzhuang

Surrounded by a ten-kilometre wall and larger than the Summer Palace in Beijing, **Bishu Shanzhuang** (also referred to as the Mountain Resort) occupies the northern third of the town's area (daily: summer 7am–5.30pm; winter 8am–4.30pm; ¥90 combined ticket for the park and the palace). This is where, in the summer months, the Qing emperors lived, feasted, hunted, and occasionally dealt with affairs of state. The palace buildings just inside the main entrance are unusual for imperial China as they are low, wooden and unpainted – simple but elegant, in contrast to the opulence and grandeur of Beijing's palaces. It's said that Emperor Kangxi wanted the complex to mimic a Manchurian village, to show his disdain for fame and wealth, though with 120 rooms and several thousand servants he wasn't exactly roughing it. The same principle of idealized naturalness governed the design of the park. With its twisting paths and streams, rockeries and hills, it's a fantasy re-creation of

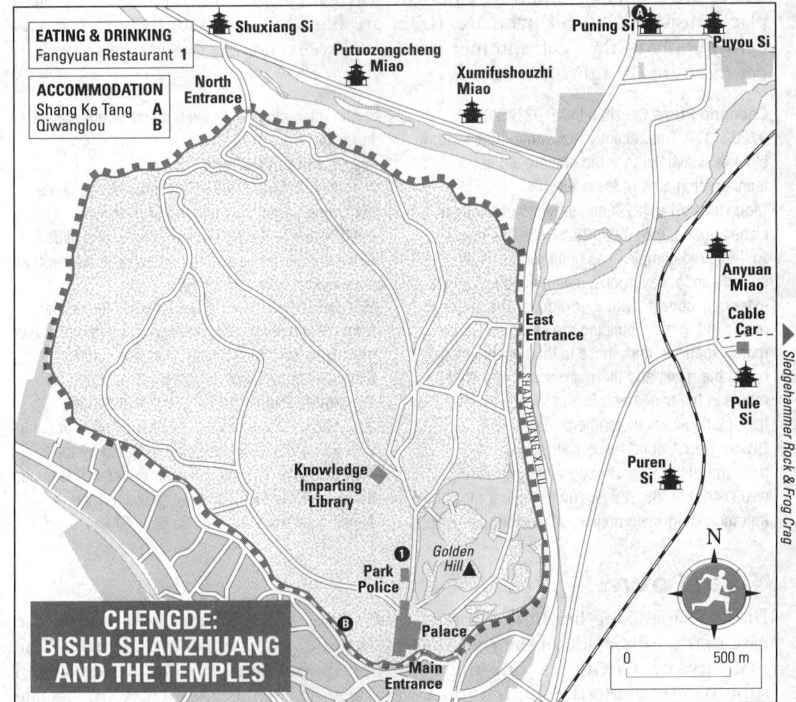

CHENGDE: BISHU SHANZHUANG AND THE TEMPLES

the rough northern terrain and southern Chinese beauty spots that the emperors would have seen on their tours of inspection. The whole is an attempt to combine water, buildings and plants in graceful harmony. Lord Macartney noted its similarity to the "soft beauties" of an English manor park of the Romantic style.

Covering the whole park and its buildings takes at least a day, and an early start is recommended. It's at its nicest in the early morning anyway, when a vegetable market sets up just outside the front gate, and old people practise *tai ji* or play Go by the palace. The park is simply too big to get overcrowded, and if you head north beyond the lakes, you're likely to find yourself alone.

The palace

The **main gate**, Lizhengmen, is in the south wall, off Lizhengmen Lu. The **palace quarter**, just inside the complex to the west of the main gate, is built on a slope, facing south, and consists of four groups of dark wooden buildings spread over an area of 100,000 square metres. The first, southernmost group, the Front Palace, where the emperors lived and worked, is the most interesting, as many of the rooms have been restored to their full Qing elegance, decked out with graceful furniture and ornaments. Even the everyday objects are impressive: brushes and ink stones on desks, ornate fly whisks on the arms of chairs, little jade trees on shelves. Other rooms house displays of ceramics, books and exotic martial-art weaponry. The Qing emperors were fine calligraphers, and examples of their work appear throughout the palace.

There are 26 buildings in this group, arranged south to north in nine successive compounds, which correspond to the nine levels of heaven. The main gate leads into the **Outer Wumen**, where high-ranking officials waited for a single peal of a large bell, indicating that the emperor was ready to receive them. Next is the **Inner Wumen**, where the emperor would watch his officers practise their archery. Directly behind, the **Hall of Frugality and Sincerity** is a dark, well-appointed room made of cedarwood, imported at great expense from south of the Yangzi River by Qianlong, who had none of his grandfather Kangxi's scruples about conspicuous consumption. Topped with a curved roof, the hall has nine bays, and patterns on the walls include symbols of longevity and good luck. The **Four Knowledge Study Room**, behind, was where the emperor did his ordinary work, changed his clothes and rested. A vertical scroll on the wall outlines the knowledge required of a gentleman, as written in the Chinese classics: he must be aware of what is small, obvious, soft and strong. It's more spartanly furnished, a little more intimate and less imposing than the other rooms.

The main building in the **Rear Palace** is the **Hall of Refreshing Mists and Waves**, the living quarters of the imperial family, and beautifully turned out in period style. It was in the west room here that Emperor Xianfeng signed the humiliating Beijing Treaty in the 1850s, giving away more of China's sovereignty and territory after their defeat in the Second Opium War. The **Western Apartments** are where the notorious Cixi, better known as the Dowager Empress (see p.121), lived when she was one of Xianfeng's concubines. A door connects the apartments to the hall, and it was through here that she eavesdropped on the dying emperor's last words of advice to his ministers, intelligence she used to force herself into power. The courtyard of the Rear Palace has a good **souvenir shop**, inside an old Buddhist tower reached by climbing a staircase by the rockery.

The other two complexes are much smaller. The **Pine and Crane Residence**, a group of buildings parallel to the front gate, is a more subdued version of the

Front Palace, home to the emperor's mother and his concubines. In the **Myriad Valleys of Rustling Pine Trees**, to the north of here, Emperor Kangxi read books and granted audiences, and Qianlong studied as a child. The group of structures southwest of the main palace is the **Ahgesuo**, where male descendants of the royal family studied during the Manchurian rule; lessons began at 5am and finished at noon. A boy was expected to speak Manchu at 6, Chinese at 12, be competent with a bow by the age of 14, and marry at 16.

The grounds

The best way to get around the **lake area** of the park – a network of pavilions, bridges, lakes and waterways – is to rent a **rowing boat** (¥20 an hour). Much of the architecture here is a direct copy of southern Chinese buildings. In the east, the **Golden Hill**, a cluster of buildings grouped on a small island, is notable for a hall and tower modelled after the Golden Hill Monastery in Zhenjiang, Jiangsu Province. The **Island of Midnight and Murmuring Streams**, roughly in the centre of the lake, holds a three-courtyard compound which was used by Kangxi and Qianlong as a retreat, while the compound of halls, towers and pavilions on **Ruyi Island**, the largest, was where Kangxi dealt with affairs of state before the palace was completed.

Just beyond the lake area, on the western side of the park, is the grey-tiled **Wenjinge**, or Knowledge Imparting Library, surrounded by rockeries and pools for fire protection. From the outside, the structure appears to have two storeys. In fact there are three – a central section is windowless to protect the books from the sun. A fine collection is housed in the building, including *The Four Treasures*, a 36,304-volume Qing-dynasty encyclopedia, but sadly you can't go inside.

A vast expanse of **grassland** extends from the north of the lake area to the foothills of the mountains, comprising Wanshun Wan (Garden of Ten Thousand Trees) and Shima Da (Horse Testing Ground). Genuine Qing-dynasty **yurts** sit here, the largest an audience hall where Qianlong received visiting dignitaries from ethnic minorities.

The hilly area in the northwest of the park has a number of rocky valleys, gorges and gullies with a few tastefully placed lodges and pagodas. The deer, which graze on tourist handouts, were reintroduced after being wiped out by imperial hunting expeditions.

The temples and Sledgehammer Rock

The **temples** (daily 8am–5.30pm) in the foothills of the mountains around Chengde were built in the architectural styles of different ethnic nationalities, so that wandering among them is rather like being in a religious theme park. This isn't far from the original intention, as they were constructed by Kangxi and Qianlong less to express religious sentiment than as a way of showing off imperial magnificence, and also to make envoys from anywhere in the empire feel more at home. Though varying in design, all the temples share **Lamaist features** – Qianlong found it politically expedient to promote Tibetan and Mongolian Lamaism as a way of keeping these troublesome minorities in line.

The temples are now in varying states of repair, having been left untended for decades. Originally there were twelve, but two have been destroyed and another two are dilapidated. Present restoration work is being paid for by the high entrance fees charged in the large temples.

The best way to see the temples is to **rent a bicycle** (ask at your hotel; the *Qiwanglou* and *Mountain Villa* have bikes to rent): the roads outside the town are quiet, it's hard to get lost and you can dodge the tour groups. One workable itinerary would be to see the northern cluster in the morning and return to town for lunch (it's impossible to cross the river to the eastern temples from outside town); in the afternoon, head east for the Pule Si, then take the cable car up to **Sledgehammer Rock**, a bizarre hilltop protuberance that dominates the eastern horizon of the town. Before you head back to the centre, you may want to check out the small, peaceful Anyuan and Puren temples, good places to chill out with a book.

The northern temples

Just beyond the northern border of Bishu Shanzhuang are five temples that were once part of a string of nine. Three of these deserve special attention but the **Puning Si** (Temple of Universal Peace; ¥40) is a must, if only for the awe-inspiring statue of Guanyin, the largest wooden statue in the world. This is the only working temple in Chengde, with shaven-headed Mongolian monks manning the altars and trinket stalls, though the atmosphere is not especially spiritual. Undergoing restoration at the time of writing, the temple is usually clamorous with day-trippers, some of whom seem to take outrageous liberties, judging by the sign that says "No shooting birds in the temple area". There are rumours that the monks are really paid government employees working for the tourist industry, though the vehemence with which they defend their prayer mats and gongs from romping children suggests otherwise.

The Puning Si was built in 1755 to commemorate the Qing victory over Mongolian rebels at Junggar in northwest China, and is based on the oldest Tibetan temple, the Samye. Like traditional Tibetan buildings, it lies on the slope of a mountain facing south, though the layout of the front is typically Han, with a gate hall, stele pavilions, a bell and a drum tower, a Hall of Heavenly Kings, and the Mahavira Hall. In the **Hall of Heavenly Kings**, the statue of a fat, grinning monk holding a bag depicts Qi Ci, a tenth-century character with a jovial disposition, who is believed to be a reincarnation of the Buddha. Four gaudy *devarajas* (guardian demons) glare down at you with bulging eyeballs from niches in the walls. In the **West Hall** are statues of Buddha Manjusri, Avalokiteshvara and Samantabhadra. In the **East Hall**, the central statue, flanked by *arhats*, depicts Ji Gong, a Song-dynasty monk who was nicknamed Crazy Ji for eating meat and being almost always drunk, but who was much respected for his kindness to the poor.

The rear section of the temple, separated from the front by a wall, comprises 27 Tibetan-style rooms laid out symmetrically, with the **Mahayana Hall** in the centre. Some of the buildings are actually solid (the doors are false), suggesting that the original architects were more concerned with appearances than function. The hall itself is dominated by the 23-metre-high wooden **statue of Guanyin**, the Goddess of Mercy. She has 42 arms with an eye in the centre of each palm, and three eyes on her face, which symbolize her ability to see into the past, present and future. The hall has two raised entrances, and it's worth looking at the statue from these upper viewpoints as they reveal new details, such as the eye sunk in her belly button, and the little Buddha sitting on top of her head.

On the thirteenth day of the first lunar month (Jan or Feb), the monks observe the ritual of "**catching the ghost**", during which a ghost made of dough is placed on an iron rack while monks dressed in white dance around it, then divide it into pieces and burn it. The ritual is thought to be in honour of a ninth-century Tibetan Buddhist, Lhalung Oaldor, who assassinated a king who had ordered the destruction of Tibetan Buddhist temples, books and priests. The wily monk entered the palace on a white horse painted black, dressed in a white coat with a black lining. After killing the king, he washed the horse and turned the coat inside out, thus evading capture from the guards who did not recognize him.

Recently restored, the **Xumifushouzhi Miao** (Temple of Sumeru Happiness and Longevity; ¥40), just southwest of Puning Si, was built in 1780 in Mongolian style for the ill-fated sixth Panchen Lama when he came to Beijing to pay his respects to the emperor. The centrepiece is the **Hall of Loftiness and Solemnity**, its finest feature the eight sinuous gold dragons sitting on the roof, each weighing over a thousand kilograms.

The Putuozongcheng Miao and Shuxiang Si

Next door to the Xumifushouzhi Miao, the magnificent **Putuozongcheng Miao** (Temple of Potaraka Doctrine; ¥30) was built in 1771 and is based on the Potala Palace in Lhasa. Covering 220,000 square metres, it's the largest temple in Chengde, with sixty groups of halls, pagodas and terraces. The grand terrace forms a Tibetan-style facade screening a Chinese-style interior, although many of the windows on the terrace are fake, and some of the whitewashed buildings around the base are merely filled-in shapes. Inside, the West Hall is notable for holding a rather comical copper statue of the Propitious Heavenly Mother, a fearsome woman wearing a necklace of skulls and riding side-saddle on a mule. According to legend, she vowed to defeat the evil demon Raksaka, so she first lulled him into a false sense of security – by marrying him and bearing him two sons – then swallowed the moon and in the darkness crept up on him and turned him into a mule. The two dancing figures at her feet are her sons; their ugly features betray their paternity. The **Hall of All Laws Falling into One**, at the back, is worth a visit for the quality of the decorative religious furniture on display. Other halls hold displays of Chinese pottery and ceramics and Tibetan religious artefacts, an exhibition slanted to portray the gorier side of Tibetan religion and including a drum made from two children's skulls. The roof of the temple has a good view over the surrounding countryside.

It's very easy to walk or cycle between the two westernmost temples, and even on to Puning Si if necessary, though this last section is busy, tedious and best navigated by taxi. Between the first two, a west-to-east course is recommended – you'll see the temples on your left, the fortress on your right, and Sledgehammer Rock's rocky finger in the distance.

The eastern temples

The three **eastern temples** are easily accessible off a quiet road that passes through dusty, rambling settlements, 3–4km from the town centre. From Lizhengmen Lu, cross over to the east bank of the river and head north.

The **Puren Si** (Temple of Universal Benevolence) is the first one you'll reach and the oldest in the complex, but it has been closed to tourists. It was built by Kangxi in 1713, as a sign of respect to the visiting Mongolian nobility, who came to congratulate the emperor on the occasion of his sixtieth birthday.

The **Pule Si** (Temple of Universal Happiness; ¥30) farther north was built in 1766 by Qianlong as a place for Mongol envoys to worship, and its style is an odd mix of Han and Lamaist elements. The Lamaist back section, a triple-tiered terrace and hall, with a flamboyantly conical roof and lively, curved surfaces, steals the show from the more sober, squarer Han architecture at the front. The ceiling of the back hall is a wood and gold confection to rival the Temple of

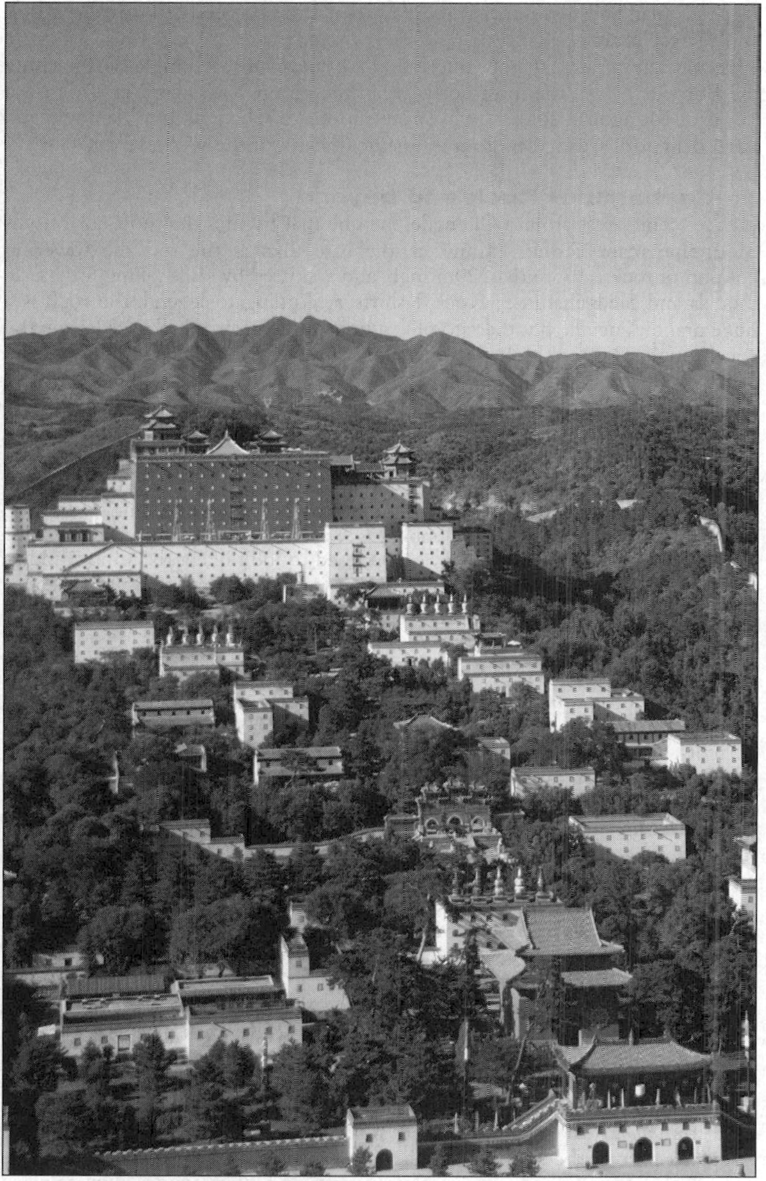

▲ Putuozongcheng Miao

Heaven in Beijing. Glowing at its centre is a mandala of Samvara, a Tantric deity, in the form of a cross. The altar beneath holds a Buddha of Happiness, a life-size copper image of sexual congress; more cosmic sex is depicted in two beautiful mandalas hanging outside. In the courtyard, prayer flags flutter while prayer wheels sit empty and unturned. Outside the temple, the view from the car park is spectacular, and just north is the path that leads to **Sledgehammer Rock** and the cable car.

Recently renovated, the less interesting **Anyuan Miao** (Temple of Appeasing the Borders; ¥30) is the most northerly of the group. It was built in 1764 for a troop of Mongolian soldiers who were moved to Chengde by Qianlong, and has a delightful setting on the tree-lined east bank of the Wulie River.

Sledgehammer Rock and beyond

Of the scenic areas around Chengde, the one that inspires the most curiosity is **Sledgehammer Rock**. Thinner at the base than at the top, the towering column of rock is more than 20m high, and is skirted by stalls selling little scale models and Sledgehammer Rock T-shirts. According to legend, the rock is a huge dragon's needle put there to plug a hole in the peak, which was letting the sea through. The rock's obviously phallic nature is tactfully not mentioned in tourist literature, but is acknowledged in local folklore – should the rock fall, it is said, it will have a disastrous effect on the virility of local men.

Sledgehammer Rock (¥20) is a couple of kilometres on foot from the Pule Si, or there's a **cable car** option (¥40), offering impressive views. On the south side of the rock, at the base of a cliff, is **Frog Crag**, a stone that vaguely resembles a sitting frog – the two-kilometre walk here is pleasant, if the frog itself disappoints. Other rocky highlights within walking distance are **Arhat Hill**, on the eastern side of the river, supposed to look like a reclining Buddha, and **Monk's Headgear Peak**, 4km south of town, the highest point in the area and best reached by bike – head south down Chezhan Lu.

Eating and drinking

Chengde is located in Hebei's most fertile area, which mainly produces maize and sorghum but also yields excellent local chestnuts, mushrooms and apricots. This fresh produce, plus the culinary legacy of the imperial cooks, means you can eat very well here. The town is also noted for its **wild game**, particularly deer (*lurou*), hare (*yetou*) and pheasant (*shanji*), and its medicinal **juice drinks**: almond juice is said to be good for asthma; date and jujube juice for the stomach; and *jinlianhua* (golden lotus) juice for a sore throat. Date and almond are the sweetest and most palatable. Local **cakes**, such as the glutinous Feng family cakes, once an imperial delicacy but now a casual snack, can be found in the stalls on Yuhua Lu and Qingfeng Jie. Rose cakes – a sweet, crisp pastry cake and a particular favourite of Qianlong – are sold in Chengde's department stores.

There are plenty of **restaurants** catering to tourists on Lizhengmen Lu, around the main entrance to Bishu Shanzhuang. The small places west of the *Mountain Villa* hotel are fine, if a little pricey, and lively on summer evenings, when rickety tables are put on the pavement outside. A meal for two should cost about ¥60, and plenty of diners stay on drinking well into the evening. The best *jiaozi* in town are served at *Qianlong Jiaoziguan*, just off Centre Square, a park at the heart of the shopping district. Nearby, **Qingfeng Jie** is an old, charmingly seedy street of restaurants and salons, and is a great place to have a satisfying *shaguo* – a veggie claypot costs ¥6, a meat-based one ¥10. Inside Bishu Shanzhuang itself, the *Fangyuan* offers imperial cuisine, including such exotica as "Pingquan Frozen Rabbit", in an attractive environment.

Travel details

Trains

Beidaihe to: Beijing (7 daily; 2hr 40min–4hr 50min); Qinhuangdao (frequent; 20min); Shanhaiguan (frequent; 40min); Shenyang (2 daily; 5hr 20min); Tianjin (7 daily; 3–6hr).
Chengde to: Beijing (8 daily; 4hr–6hr 30min); Dandong (daily; 17hr 30min); Shenyang (2 daily; 12hr 30min or 13hr 20min); Tianjin (daily; 9hr).
Qinhuangdao to: Beidaihe (frequent; 20min); Beijing (frequent; 3hr–6hr 15min); Shanhaiguan (frequent; 20min); Shenyang (frequent; 3hr 40min–7hr); Tianjin (frequent; 3hr–4hr 15min).
Shanhaiguan to: Beidaihe (frequent; 1hr); Beijing (frequent; 2hr 40min–5hr 40min); Qinhuangdao (frequent; 15min); Shenyang (frequent; 4hr–6hr 30min); Tianjin (frequent; 3–4hr).
Tianjin to: Beidaihe (7 daily; 3hr–6hr 40min); Beijing (11 daily express services; 1hr 20min); Chengde (daily; 9hr); Guangzhou (3 daily; 26hr); Jilin (3 daily; 15hr 30min–18hr); Qinhuangdao (frequent; 3–4hr 15min); Shanghai (10 daily; 11hr–19hr 30min); Shanhaiguan (frequent; 3–4hr); Xi'an (3 daily; 17hr–22hr).

Buses

Beidaihe to: Beijing (4hr); Qinhuangdao (20min); Shanhaiguan (40min); Tianjin (3hr 30min).
Chengde to: Beijing (4–5hr); Tianjin (4hr).
Qinhuangdao to: Beidaihe (20min); Beijing (5hr); Shanhaiguan (20min); Tianjin (4hr).
Shanhaiguan to: Beidaihe (40min); Beijing (5hr 20min); Qinhuangdao (20min); Tianjin (4hr 30min).
Tianjin to: Beidaihe (3hr 30min); Beijing (2hr); Chengde (4hr); Qinhuangdao (4hr); Shanhaiguan (4hr 20min).

Ferries

Tianjin (Tanggu) to: Dalian (March–Oct daily; rest of year every other day; 13–15hr); Inchon (South Korea; 2 weekly; 26hr); Kobe (Japan; weekly; 51hr).

Flights

Qinhuangdao to: Dalian (3 weekly; 1hr).
Tianjin to: Changsha (4 weekly; 1hr 40min); Chengdu (daily; 2hr 20min); Dalian (daily; 50min); Fuzhou (3 weekly; 3hr 50min); Guangzhou (4 daily; 3hr); Guilin (2 weekly; 4hr 30min); Haikou (daily; 3hr 15min); Hangzhou (5 weekly; 1hr 30min); Harbin (daily; 3hr); Hong Kong (daily; 3hr 15min); Kunming (8 weekly; 3hr 20min); Nanjing (daily; 1hr 40min); Ningbo (daily; 3hr 10min); Qingdao (daily; 1hr); Shanghai (daily; 1hr 45min); Shenyang (3 weekly; 1hr 20min); Shenzhen (daily; 2hr 45min); Taiyuan (daily; 1hr); Wuhan (7 weekly; 2hr 30min); Xiamen (5 weekly; 2hr 30min); Xi'an (daily; 2hr); Zhengzhou (daily; 1hr 10min).

CHAPTER 3

Highlights

* **The Imperial Palace, Shenyang** Pre-empting Beijing's Forbidden City, this was the historical seat of the Manchus before they seized the capital. See p.192

* **Old Yalu Bridge, Dandong** Walk halfway to North Korea on this structure, bombed by the US during the Korean War. See p.204

* **Puppet Emperor's Palace, Changchun** The second act of the "last emperor" Puyi's life was played out here, where he was installed by the Japanese as leader of Manchuria. See p.207

* **Changbai Shan** The northeast's loveliest nature reserve – see the crater lake and root around for wild ginseng, though beware of North Korean border guards. See p.210

* **Winter ice festivals** Most Manchurian metropolises have one, but Harbin's is the biggest and best, carvings by international artists. See p.218

* **Zhalong Nature Reserve** Bird-watchers flock to the reedy lakes west of Harbin where the red-crowned crane and thousands of its cousins breed. See p.222

▲ Tian Chi, Changbai Shan Nature Reserve

3

Dongbei

Dongbei – or more evocatively Manchuria – may well be the closest thing to the "real" China that visitors vainly seek in the well-travelled central and southern parts of the country. Not many foreign tourists get up to China's northernmost arm, however, due to its reputation as an inhospitable wasteland: "Although it is uncertain where God created paradise", wrote a French priest when he was here in 1846, "we can be sure he chose some other place than this." Yet, with its immense swaths of fertile fields and huge resources of **mineral wealth**, Dongbei is metaphorically a treasure house. Comprising **Liaoning**, **Jilin** and **Heilongjiang** provinces, it is economically and politically among the most important regions of China, and the area has been fiercely contested for much of its history by Manchus, Nationalists, Russians, Japanese and Communists.

With 4000km of sensitive border territory alongside North Korea and Russia, Dongbei is one of China's most vulnerable regions strategically, and also one of the country's most sensitive, with worker protests common and a widening gap between haves and have-nots that is threatening to become a chasm. In the heady days of a planned economy, Dongbei's state-owned enterprises produced more than a third of the country's heavy machinery, half its coal and oil and most of its automobiles and military equipment. Since market reforms, however, **lay-offs** have been rampant, with unofficial statistics suggesting fifty percent unemployment in some areas.

Tourism has become Dongbei's leading growth industry. The region is cashing in on its colourful history, seen most vividly in the preservation of long-ignored Russian and Japanese colonial architecture, some of which you can actually stay in. In Liaoning, the thriving port of **Dalian** sports cleaned-up beaches, a cliffside drive, a restored Russian and Japanese neighbourhood and China's best football club. The country's window on North Korea is **Dandong**, featuring a promenade on the Yalu River and an incredible Korean War museum. China's other Forbidden City – the restored Manchu Imperial Palace – and the tombs of the men who established the Qing dynasty draw tourists to Liaoning's otherwise bland capital, **Shenyang**. To the north in Jilin province, **Jilin** city is famed for the ice-coated trees that line its riverfront in winter, and there are ski resorts on the outskirts of town. In the provincial capital, **Changchun**, the Puppet Emperor's Palace memorializes Puyi's reign as "emperor" of the Japanese state Manchukuo. Evidence of Heilongjiang province's border with Russia can be seen throughout its capital, **Harbin**: a restored central shopping district preserves the city's old architecture, while a history museum set in an Orthodox cathedral ensures China's northernmost metropolis is known for more reasons than its world-famous **Ice Festival**.

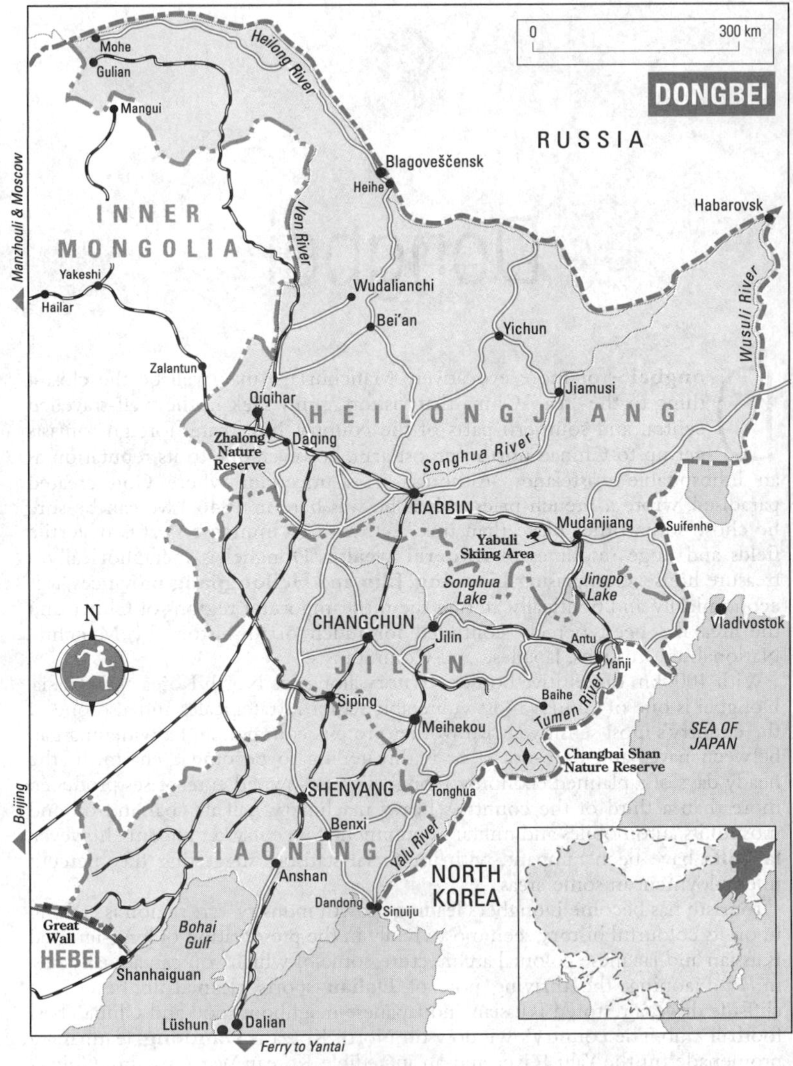

Visitors to these parts tend to come for quite specific reasons. Dongbei's geography, a terrain of fertile plains, rugged mountains and forests, is itself an attraction, and keen **hunters**, **hikers** and **bird-watchers** will all find places to indulge their passions. Although long derided by Han Chinese as "the land beyond the pale", the region "outside" the Great Wall is home to several protected reserves, most famously the mountainous **Changbai Shan Nature Reserve** in Jilin province near the Korean border, where a huge lake, Tian Chi, nestles in jaw-dropping scenery. **Zhalong Nature Reserve**, in Heilongjiang, is a summer breeding ground for thousands of species of birds, including the rare red-crowned crane. Foreign **students** find an environment free of thick accents and perfect for practising Chinese, and fans of recent Chinese **history** couldn't choose a better place to visit: Dongbei's past one hundred years of domestic and international conflicts have heavily influenced the shape of the PRC today. Those interested in the **Russo-Japanese War** can follow the route of the Japanese advance; if you can find them, bring copies of Jack London's *Reports*, which contain the columns he wrote on assignment for the *San Francisco Examiner*, and *Thirty Years in Moukden* by Dugald Christie. **Puyi**'s autobiography, *From Emperor to Citizen*, lends insight to Manchukuo, and Ha Jin's *Ocean of Words* shows what life was like patrolling the Heilongjiang–Siberian border in the tense 1970s. CITS has special-interest **tours** to the region, though independent local firms provide better service and a wider selection of trips.

Dongbei's **climate** is one of extremes: in summer, it is hot, and in winter it is very, very cold, with temperatures as low as -30°C and howling Siberian gales. But the whole of winter brings excellent, cheap **skiing**, **sledding** and **skating**, while a trip up here in January has the added attraction of **ice festivals** in Jilin and Harbin.

Thanks to Dongbei's export-based economy, there's an efficient **rail** system between the cities and an extensive **highway** network. The region's **food** is heavily influenced by neighbouring countries, and every town has a cluster of Korean, Japanese and, up north, Russian restaurants. The cuisine is also diverse, ranging from fresh crabs in Dalian and *luzi yu* river fish in Dandong, to mushroom dishes and fresh bread in Harbin, to silkworms in the countryside (a mushy, pasty-tasting local delicacy).

Some history

The history of Manchuria proper begins with **Nurhaci**, a tribal leader who in the sixteenth century united the warring tribes of the northeast against the corrupt central rule of Ming-dynasty Liaoning. He introduced an alphabet based on the Mongol script, administered Manchu law and, by 1625, had created a firm and relatively autonomous government that was in constant confrontation with the Chinese. Subsequently, Dorgun was able to go a stage further, marching on Beijing with the help of the defeated Ming general Wu Sangui. In 1644, the **Qing dynasty** was proclaimed and one of Nurhaci's grandsons, Shunzhi, became the first of a long line of Manchu emperors, with his uncle Dorgun as regent.

Keen to establish the Qing over the whole of China, the first **Manchu emperors** – Shunzhi, Kangxi and Qianlong – did their best to assimilate Chinese customs and ideas. They were, however, even more determined to protect their homeland, and so the whole of the northeast was closed to the rest of China. This way they could guard their monopoly on the valuable **ginseng trade**, and keep the agricultural Han Chinese from ploughing up their land, a practice that often resulted in the desecration of the graves of the Manchus' ancestors. But isolationism was a policy that could not last forever, and the eighteenth century saw increasing migration into Manchuria. By 1878, these laws had been rescinded, and the Chinese were moving into the region by the million, escaping the flood-ravaged plains of the south for the fertile northeast.

All this time, Manchuria was much coveted by its neighbours. The **Sino-Japanese War** of 1894 left the Japanese occupying the Liaodong Peninsula in the south of Liaoning province, and the only way the Chinese could regain it was by turning to **Russia**, also hungry for influence in the area. The deal was that the Russians be allowed to build a rail line linking Vladivostok to the main body of Russia, an arrangement that in fact led to a gradual and, eventually, complete occupation of Manchuria by the imperial Russian armies. This was a bloody affair, marked by atrocities and brutal reprisals, and was followed in 1904 by a Japanese declaration of war in an attempt to usurp the Russians' privileges for themselves.

The Russo–Japanese War ended in 1905 with a convincing Japanese victory, though Japan's designs on Manchuria didn't end there. The Japanese population had almost doubled in the last sixty years, and this, coupled with a disastrous economic situation at home and an extreme militaristic regime, led to their invasion of the region in 1932, establishing the puppet state of **Manchukuo**. This regime was characterized by instances of horrific and violent oppression – not least the secret germ-warfare research centre in Pingfang, where experiments were conducted on live human subjects. Rice was reserved for the Japanese, and it was a crime for the locals to eat it. It was only with the establishment of a united front between the **Communists** and the **Guomindang** that Manchuria was finally rid of the Japanese, in 1945, although it was some time (and in spite of a vicious campaign backed by both Russia and the USA against the Communists) before Mao finally took control of the region.

Recent history is dominated by relations with **Russia**. In the brief romance between the two countries in the 1950s, Soviet experts helped the Chinese build efficient, well-designed factories and workshops in exchange for the region's agricultural products. These factories, such as the plant that produces the Liberation Truck in Changchun, remain some of the best in the area today. In the 1960s, relations worsened, the Soviets withdrew their technical support, and bitter **border disputes** began, notably around the Wusuli (Ussuri) River, where hundreds of Russian and Chinese troops died fighting over an insignificant island in the world's first military confrontation between communist states. An extensive network of nuclear shelters was constructed in northeastern cities. Following the collapse of the Soviet Union, military build-ups around the border areas and state paranoia have lessened, and the shelters have been turned into underground shopping centres. Russian faces can again be seen on the streets, often **traders**, legal and otherwise, buying up consumer goods to take over the border now that Russia's own manufacturing industry has almost collapsed.

Shenyang

SHENYANG, the capital of Liaoning province and unofficial capital of the northeast, is both a railway junction and banking centre that's served as host to the Manchus, Russians, Japanese, Nationalists and then Communists. An hour's flight from Beijing, the city likens itself to the capital; any cabby here will delight in telling you that they have the only other Imperial Palace in China.

Shenyang does indeed resemble the capital, but only in its wide, characterless avenues walled by Soviet-style matchbox buildings and glassy bank towers. In fact, the most remarkable thing about Shenyang is that it isn't remarkable at all. All the ingredients for an interesting visit are here: China's other Forbidden City, constructed by Manchus before their takeover of the Ming dynasty; a stunning monument to Chairman Mao built during the frenzied height of the Cultural Revolution; the tombs of two former emperors; architecture left over from Japan's occupation, including one of China's loveliest hotels. The list goes on and on. And a list is what Shenyang feels like, a collection of curios out of context in their industrial surroundings, with little to detain you for more than a brief stop.

Shenyang

Shenyang	沈阳	*shěnyáng*
Botanical Garden	世博园	*shì bó yuán*
East Tomb	东陵	*dōng líng*
Imperial Palace	沈阳故宫	*shěnyáng gùgōng*
Liaoning Provincial Museum	辽宁省博物馆	*liáoníngshěng bówùguǎn*
Long-distance bus station	快速客运站	*kuàisù kèyùnzhàn*
North Pagoda	北塔	*běi tǎ*
North Tomb	北陵	*běi líng*
September 18 History Museum	九一八历史博物馆	*jiǔyībā lìshǐ bówùguǎn*
Zhongshan Square	中山广场	*zhōngshān guǎngchǎng*
Accommodation and eating		
Chinese Folk Custom Restaurant	华夏民族村	*huáxià mínzúcūn*
City Central Youth Hostel	城市青年旅馆	*chéngshì qīngnián lǚguǎn*
Handu Korean BBQ	韩都烧烤	*hándū shāokǎo*
Holiday Inn	假日饭店	*jiàrì fàndiàn*
Intercontinental	沈阳洲际酒店	*shěnyáng zhōujì jiǔdiàn*
Laobian	老边饺子馆	*lǎobiān jiǎoziguǎn*
Liaoning Hotel	辽宁宾馆	*liáoníng bīnguǎn*
New World Hotel	新世界宾馆	*xīnshìjiè bīnguǎn*
Peace Hotel	和平宾馆	*hépíng bīnguǎn*
Phoenix Hotel	凤凰饭店	*fènghuáng fàndiàn*
Railway Hotel	沈阳铁路大厦	*shěnyáng tiělù dàshà*
Strollers Bar	流浪者酒吧	*liúlàngzhě jiǔbā*
Traders Hotel	商贸饭店	*shāngmào fàndiàn*
World and View Vegetarian	素食馆	*sù shí guǎn*

Though well known in China as an important power base for the more radical hardline factions in Chinese politics (Mao's nephew, Yuanxin, was deputy Party secretary here until he was thrown in jail in 1976), Shenyang had its real heyday in the early seventeenth century. The city (then known as Mukden) was declared first capital of the expanding **Manchu empire** by Nurhaci. He died in 1626, as work on his palace was just beginning, and was succeeded by his eighth son, **Abahai**, who consolidated and extended Manchu influence across northern China. When the Manchus, having defeated the resident Ming, moved to Beijing in 1644 and established the Qing dynasty, Shenyang declined steadily in importance. The city began to take on its modern, industrial role with the arrival of the Russians in the nineteenth century, who made it the centre of their rail-building programme. Years later, the puppets of the Japanese state also set up shop here, exploiting the resources of the surrounding region and building an industrial infrastructure whose profits and products were sent home to Japan.

Arrival and city transport

Shenyang's international **airport**, the busiest in the northeast, lies 20km south of the city. It's linked to the CAAC office in the centre by an airport bus (¥15), while a taxi into town should cost around ¥100 – make sure you agree a price before setting off.

Five lines converge on Shenyang's two main **train stations**. If you've come from Beijing or farther south, you'll arrive first at the **South station**, the larger and more central one. The newer **North station**, serving destinations to the

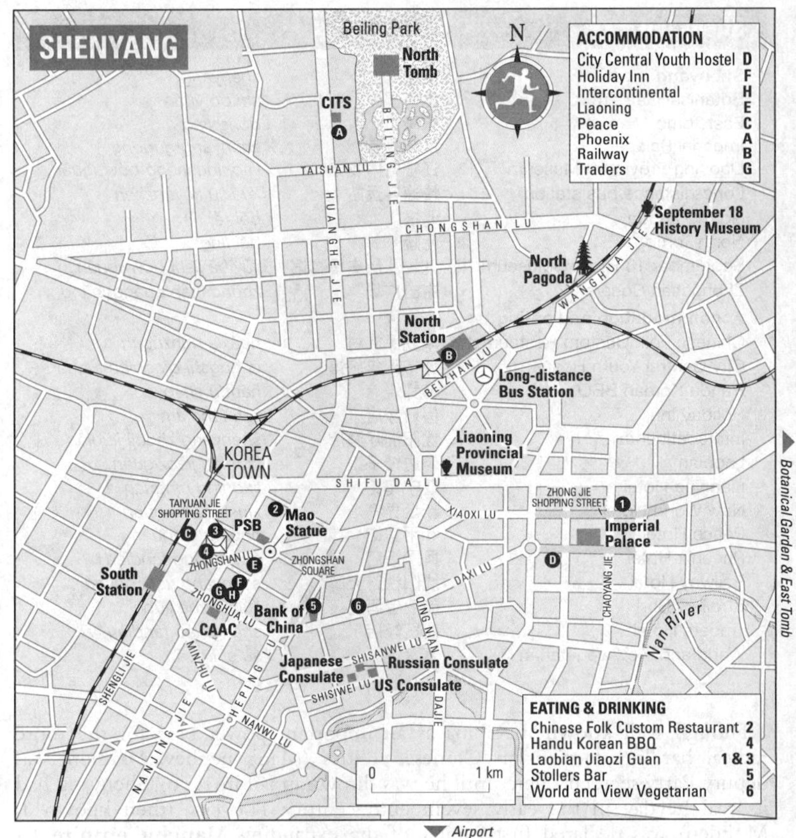

north (and the terminus for Beijing trains, which continue here from the South station), is out of the centre; take trolleybus #5 from here to Zhongshan Square and the South station (also served from here by bus #203). The North station has an upstairs ticket booth, while the booking office for the South station is in a large hall to the left as you face the station. Tickets for services leaving from the North station can be bought from the South station, and vice versa; you may need to double-check which station the train you want actually leaves from. The gleaming, futuristic **long-distance bus station** (referred to locally as the express-bus station) is near the North station. To get into the centre from here, catch one of the many minibuses plying the route, or take a taxi (¥10).

If you're entering the city by train and planning on **moving on** immediately to a major city by bus, get off at the North station, where coaches depart from the east side of the concourse to Beijing (7–8hr) and Dalian (5hr). For Jilin (4hr), Changchun (3hr) and Harbin (6hr) services, walk one block south to the long-distance bus station.

Shenyang is very spread out and trying to walk anywhere is frustrating, especially as bikes have been directed to use the pavements to help alleviate traffic congestion. **Taxis** are widely available, comprised of new VW Santanas. The flagfall is ¥8 for 3km; a taxi to or between most of the sights is around ¥20, though getting to the East Tomb from the South station costs about ¥50. Alternatively, the **local bus** and trolleybus system is extensive and not too crowded. Bus maps can be bought outside the stations.

From December to February, the town hosts the increasingly popular **Shenyang International Ice and Snow Festival**, which is held at Qipanshan, 17km outside town.

Accommodation

Shenyang's **hotels** cater mainly to business travellers, and most respectable establishments in the city centre don't look kindly on haggling over rates. Several no-frills travellers' hotels are gathered around Zhonghua Lu in front of the South station.

City Central Youth Hostel 103 Shenyang Jie. Ⓣ024/24844868, Ⓦwww.chinayha.com. Shenyang's only real backpacker-friendly accommodation. Rooms are clean and staff are friendly, though largely clueless. Dorm ¥40. ④

Holiday Inn 204 Nanjing Beilu Ⓣ024/23341888, Ⓦwww.holiday-inn.com. New high-rise in the heart of town, featuring Shenyang's best health club, the entrance is just off Nanjing Lu at the northwestern corner of the building. Rates are slashed in the winter months. ⑧

Intercontinental 208 Nanjing Beilu Ⓣ024/23341999, Ⓦwww.interconti.com. The *Holiday Inn*'s big brother is just that little bit more luxurious, but may be cheaper than its neighbour if you happen to catch one of the frequent special offers, which cut rates by forty percent. ⑥

Liaoning 97 Zhongshan Lu Ⓣ024/23839104, Ⓕ23839103. This historic lodging, constructed by the Japanese in 1927, overlooks the Chairman Mao statue on Zhongshan Square. Rooms are spacious and light. Stop over if only for a look at how things were eighty years ago – the fittings and furnishings are remarkably well preserved. ⑥

Peace 104 Shengli Beijie Ⓣ024/23833033, Ⓕ23837389. Conveniently near the South train station. No longer the backpacker hangout it once was, this is now more of a mid-range business hotel. Newly renovated rooms are smart, and prices have gone up accordingly, but staff are still friendly and its travel service can organize train and plane tickets. ⑤

Phoenix 109 Huanghe Nan Dajie Ⓣ024/86105858, Ⓦwww.phoenixhotel.com.cn. Plush behemoth near Beiling Park, recently refurbished but retaining that old communist group-tour vibe. ⑥

Railway Located inside the North train station Ⓣ024/62231888, Ⓕ62232888. Nothing special, but an adequate place to crash if arriving late or departing early. ③

Traders 68 Zhonghua Lu Ⓣ024/23412288, Ⓦwww.shangri-la.com. One of the nicest places to stay in Shenyang with good-sized, well-looked-after, international-standard rooms, and rates that include laundry, airport transport and breakfast. ⑧

The City

Shenyang has some great examples of uncompromising Soviet-style building, and you may well find yourself staying in one. The giant **Mao statue** in **Zhongshan Square** at the city's centre, erected in 1969, is by far the most distinctive landmark, its base lined with strident, blocky peasants, Daqing oilmen, PLA soldiers and students, though the Little Red Books they were waving have mostly been chipped off. Above them, the monolithic Mao stands wrapped in an overcoat, a bald superman whose raised hand makes him look as if he's directing the traffic that swarms around him. Head in the direction he's facing, and you'll hit the city's **shopping district**, centred around Zhongshan Lu, Zhonghua Lu and Taiyuan Jie, which abound with department stores.

The **Liaoning Provincial Museum** (Tues–Sun 9am–4pm; ¥20), in the heart of the downtown area, is one of the largest museums in the northeast, the exhibits including paintings, copperware, pottery and porcelain. Perhaps most interesting are the fragments of oracle bones, inscribed with characters and used for divination; these feature some of the earliest extant examples of written

Chinese. South of here, the Nan River marks the southern boundary of the downtown area, with the larger Hun River just beyond.

The Imperial Palace

More rewarding than the city centre are the Manchu structures on the outskirts of Shenyang, starting with the **Imperial Palace** (daily 8.30am–6pm; ¥50), begun in 1626, a miniature replica of Beijing's Forbidden City. It's located at the pleasant centre of the old city in the east of town, itself worth pacing around for a few hours (bus #237 comes here from the South station). The complex divides into three sections. The first, the Cong Zhen Dian, is a low, wooden-fronted hall where the Qing dynasty was proclaimed and which was used by ministers to discuss state affairs. Beyond here, in the second courtyard, stands the Phoenix Tower, most formal of the ceremonial halls, and the Qing Ning Lou, which housed bedrooms for the emperor and his concubines. In the eastern section of the complex, the Da Zheng Dian is a squat, octagonal, wooden structure in vivid red and lacquered gold, with two pillars cut with writhing golden dragons in high relief. Here the emperor Shunzhi was crowned before seizing Beijing – and the empire – in 1644. Just in front stand ten square pavilions, the Shi Wang, once used as offices by the chieftains of the Eight Banners (districts) of the Empire, and now housing a collection of bizarrely shaped swords and pikes. Take time to wander away from the groups amid the side palaces, most of which have been restored in the past few years. Note the Manchu dragons in bas-relief, unique to this palace.

The tombs

From the Imperial Palace, bus #213 will get you to the **North Tomb** (daily 9am–4.30pm; ¥30) in **Beiling Park** (park entry ¥6), or you can take bus #220 direct from the South station. The tomb is where Abahai is buried, and though it was his father Nurcahi who was the real pioneering imperialist, Abahai certainly got the better tomb. The well-preserved complex, constructed in 1643, is entered through a gate to the south, either side of which are pavilions; the easternmost was for visiting emperors to wash and refresh themselves, the

▲ Imperial Palace

westernmost for sacrifices of pigs and sheep. A drive flanked with statues of camels, elephants, horses and lions leads to the Long En Hall, which contains an altar for offerings and the spirit tablets of the emperor and his wife. Their tree-covered burial mounds are at the rear, where you'll also find a fine dragon screen. Winter in Beiling Park sees snow sculptures, ice skates available for rent (¥10), as well as *pali* (¥30 for large ones), wooden sleds with blades on the bottom, which you move using two metal ski poles while seated.

The more restrained **East Tomb** (daily 7am–6pm; ¥30), built in 1629 as the last resting place of Nurhaci, is set among conifers next to **Dongling Park** (daily 9am–4.30pm; ¥2) in the east of the city. Buses #168 and #218 come here from the stop one block north and one block east of the Imperial Palace. The tomb is less monumental in layout than Abahai's and shows more signs of age, but it's still an impressive structure, with fortified walls and a three-storey tower. One hundred and eight steps (the number of beads on a Buddhist rosary) lead into the main gate, while all around the tomb are walking trails into the woods covering Mount Tianzhu – a hill, really.

The rest of the city

Aside from the major imperial relics, Shenyang's other sights are something of a disappointment. Of the four pagodas and four temples that once stood at the limits of the city, one on each side, the only one in a reasonable state is the **North Pagoda** (daily 9am–4.30pm), a short walk north of the long-distance bus station. The pagoda contains a sky and earth Buddha (Tiandifu), a carnal image of twin Buddhas rarely found in Chinese temples; to see it, you'll have to trouble the lone attendant to unlock the gate. Not far away, the **September 18 History Museum** at 46 Wanghua Nanjie (daily 8.30am–4.30pm) focuses on Japan's invasion of Shenyang in 1931, telling the story through a predictable array of black-and-white photos, maps and rusty weapons. It's a "patriotic education base", so the tone of the Chinese-only captions is easy to guess. Bus #213 from the North Tomb stops here, and also near the North Pagoda.

A half-hour bus ride outside town, **Shenyang Botanical Garden** (daily 9am–6pm; ¥50; bus #168), site of the 2006 International Horticultural Exposition, is a vast area featuring formal gardens from all over China. Some of the sub-Disney attempts at foreign gardens are a little cringe-inducing, but overall it makes for a good escape from the dust of the city.

Eating and drinking

Eating in Shenyang is a bit of a letdown, though there are some tasty bargains in the Korea Town area on Shifu Da Lu. Another option is the *Handu Korean BBQ*, 62 Kunming Beijie. Dinner here is good value starting at around ¥50 for two, and you can wash it down with *zaocha*, a sweet, fruity tea that goes well with platefuls of beef. It's easily spotted as it's almost next door to a *USA Beef Noodle King*, signed in English. Shenyang's most famous restaurant is *Laobian Jiaozi Guan* at 55 Shengli Beijie, whose excellent *jiaozi* cost ¥5 for a *liang*; try their speciality, and a Dongbei favourite, pork and chives. They have another branch at 6 Zhong Jie, a popular shopping street that dates back to 1636, but the service here is poor. The most authentic Western bar in town is *Strollers Bar* at 36 Bei Wujing Jie, near the junction with Shiyi Weilu. Beers start from ¥20; food, including T-bone steak and French onion soup, ranges between ¥35 and ¥60. They also have big screen football. Slightly less authentic, but tasty and with added kitsch value is the *Chinese Folk Custom Restaurant*, which serves up ethnic dishes from around China at 11 Bei Wumalu, just north of Mao's statue on

Zhongshan Square. The curiously titled *World and View Vegetarian* on the north side of Shiyi Weilu near the junction with Bei Yijing Jie is the place to go if meat is off your menu.

Listings

Airlines CAAC is at 117 Zhonghua Lu (☎024/89392520; daily 8am–6pm). Plane tickets can also be bought from hotels or from CITS.
Banks and exchange Bank of China, 253 Shifu Da Lu (Mon–Fri 8.30am–5.30pm, Sat & Sun 9am–3.30pm).
Consulates The Japanese, Russian and US consulates are all in the same road, Shisiwei Lu, in the south of the city. Reports on whether Russian visas can be obtained easily here aren't encouraging; it's better to apply in Beijing.
Internet access Walk from the South station down Zhonghua Lu, and a block past *KFC*, at no. 25, is a 24hr Internet café – look for the orchid sign reading *wangba*, then head upstairs to the second floor. Amid the shopping lanes just north of here, *Wanghe Internet Café*, 72 Beier Malu, also stays open around the clock.
Mail and telephones Shenyang's main post office is at 32 Zhongshan Lu (Mon–Fri 8am–6pm), and has a 24hr telephone/fax service.
PSB On Zhongshan Lu, by the Mao statue (Mon–Fri 8am–5pm).
Travel agents The CITS office at 113 Nan Huanghe Dajie (☎024/86131251), one building north of the *Phoenix Hotel*, is the central branch for Liaoning province, though they offer speciality tours of the northeast only to large groups (20 or more). The travel service in the *Peace Hotel* is friendlier and more accommodating.

Dalian and around

A modern, sprawling city on the Yellow Sea, **DALIAN** is one of China's most cosmopolitan cities, partly because it has changed hands so often. As the only **ice-free port** in the region it was eagerly sought by the foreign powers that held sway over China in the nineteenth century. The Japanese gained the city in 1895, only to lose it a few years later to the Russians, who saw it as an alternative to ice-bound Vladivostok. In 1905, after decisively defeating the Russian navy, the Japanese wrested it back and remained in control for long enough to complete the construction of the port facilities and city grid – still visible in the many traffic circles and axial roads. After World War II, the Soviet Union occupied the city for ten years, finally withdrawing when Sino-Soviet relations improved.

The "foreign devils" are still here, though they're now invited: Dalian has been designated a Special Economic Zone, one of China's "open-door" cities with regulations designed to attract overseas investment. Today, Dalian is busier than ever, the funnel for Dongbei's enormous natural and mineral wealth and an industrial producer in its own right, specializing in petrochemicals and shipbuilding. Unlike most Chinese metropolises, the city boasts green spaces and an excellent traffic control system, both the handiwork of the high-flying former mayor turned national commerce minister **Bo Xilai**. Locals seem to admire him as much as they do Dalian's football team, **Shide** (formerly Wanda), which has been the champion of the Chinese league more times than not in recent years, and contributed six players to the country's 2002 World Cup squad, facts that explain the large sculptures of footballs you'll see around, including a massive one crowning Laodong Park.

Still, Dalian manages to be a leisurely place, popular with tourists who come here for the scenic spots and **beaches** outside the city, to recover their health in sanatoriums and to gorge themselves on seafood. The city also boasts easy connections to the historical port of **Lüshun**. Tourists looking for relics from

Dalian and around

Dalian	大连	*dàlián*
Forest Zoo	森林动物园	*sēn lín dōngwùyuán*
Fujiazhuang Beach	傅家庄公园浴场	*fùjiāzhuāng gōngyuán yùchǎng*
Heishijiao	黑石礁	*hēishí jiāo*
Modern Museum	现代博物馆	*xiàndài bówùguǎn*
Old Russian Quarter	老俄罗斯风景区	*lǎoéluósī fēngjǐngqū*
Renmin Square	人民广场	*rénmín guǎngchǎng*
Sun Asia Ocean World Aquarium	圣亚海洋世界	*shèngyà hǎiyáng shìjiè*
Tiger Beach	老虎滩	*lǎohǔ tān*
Xinghai Beach	星海公园浴场	*xīnghǎi gōngyuán yùchǎng*
Yanwoling Park	燕窝岭公园	*yànwōlǐng gōngyuán*
Zhongshan Square	中山广场	*zhōngshān guǎngchǎng*
Accommodation, eating and drinking		
Dalian Binguan	大连宾馆	*dàlián bīnguǎn*
Dalian Binhai	大连滨海大厦酒店	*dàlián bīnhǎi dàshà jiǔdiàn*
Friendship Hotel	友谊饭店	*yǒuyí fàndiàn*
Furama Hotel	富丽华大酒店	*fùlìhuá dàjiǔdiàn*
Home Inn	如家酒店	*rújiā jiǔdiàn*
Huanan Youth Hostel	华南国际青年旅舍	*huánán guójìqīngnián lǚshè*
Huayue	海悦酒店	*hǎi yuè jiǔdiàn*
Meeting Place Bar	互情酒吧	*hùqíng jiǔbā*
Noah's Ark	诺亚方舟酒吧	*nuòyǎ fāngzhōu jiǔbā*
Pizza King	比萨王	*bǐsà wáng*
Ramada	九州华美达酒店	*jiǔzhōu huáměidá jiǔdiàn*
Tiantian Yugang Jiulou	天天渔港酒楼	*tiāntiānyúgǎng jiǔlóu*
Tianyuan Vegetarian	天缘素食店	*tiānyuán sùshídiàn*
Xintiandi	新天地	*xīn tiān dì*
Zhongshan Hotel	中山饭店	*zhōngshān fàndiàn*
Lüshun	旅顺	*lǚshùn*
Japanese Russian Imperial Prison Site	日俄监狱旧址	*rì'é jiānyù jiùzhǐ*

Dalian's colonial past will be disappointed, however: unlike other treaty ports such as Shanghai, Dalian is looking firmly forward to the future, it's skyline still very much a work in progress

Arrival and transport

Dalian sits at the southern tip of the Liaodong Peninsula, filling a piece of land that's shaped like a tiger's head – the result, local legend has it, of a mermaid flattening the animal into land as punishment for eating the fiancé of a beautiful girl. The city has four main sections: **Zhongshan Square**, at the tiger's eye; **Renmin Square**, at his ear; the **beaches**, at his mouth and throat, and **Heishijiao** (Black Coral Reef) across the Malan River to the west of town.

A taxi to or from the **airport**, 10km northeast of the city, should cost ¥25, or there's a regular airport bus (¥5) to and from Shengli Square. The main **train station** (there are three in total) and **passenger-ferry terminal** (for services to Yantai) are within 1km of Zhongshan Square. **Long-distance buses** pick up and drop off passengers around Shengli Square, outside the train station – if you're on an express bus from Beijing, you'll probably be dropped here – while the main bus station is located at the terminus of bus #201, around 1km to the

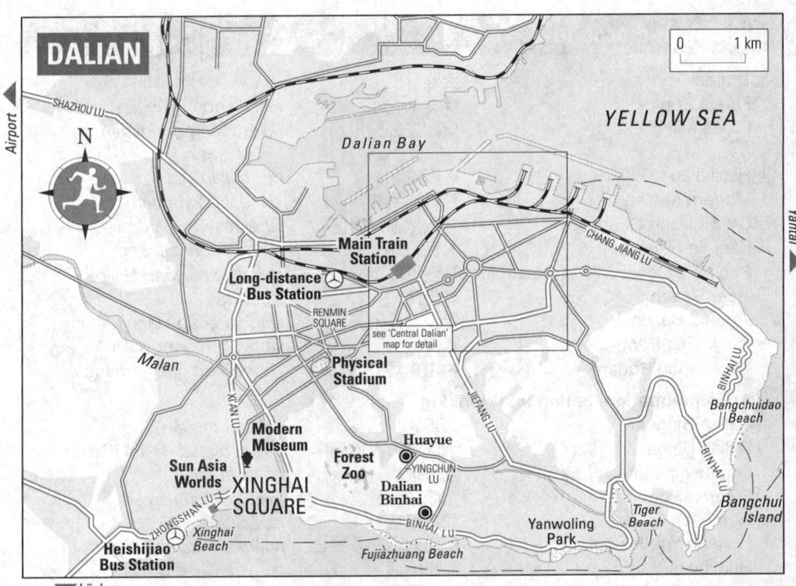

west. You'll need to check where to board your bus when you buy your ticket. There's also a further regional bus station on Zhongshan Lu near Xinghai Beach in Heishijiao, from where buses to Lüshun depart.

As the city centre is compact, the minimum ¥8 fare in a **taxi** will get you to most places. Alternatively, the tram line, #202 (¥1), runs north–southwest roughly along Zhongshan Lu, beginning in the shopping area around the north end of Xi'an Lu, a couple of kilometres west of the train station, before passing Xinghai Square and terminating at Heishijiao.

Accommodation

Dalian is choked with five-star **hotels** – *Holiday Inn*, *Ramada*, *Swissotel*, *Kempinski* and *Shangri-la* can all be found here – but budget options amenable to foreigners are thin on the ground. In tune with the city's aspirations of becoming an upscale tourism and business centre, hotel rates have rocketed. The only good news accommodation-wise is that, being a beach town, rates out of season are usually half those in summer – be sure to bargain wherever you go, as the supply of hotel rooms exceeds demand.

Dalian Binguan 4 Zhongshan Square ⓣ0411/82633111, ⓦwww.dl-hotel.com. A stylish old place, built by the Japanese in 1927, but it's really only the location and history that make it worthy of consideration; service is indifferent at best, and beyond the lobby – which features a fascinating panoramic shot of the square in the 1920s – the building is showing its age. ❻

Dalian Binhai 2 Binhai Lu ⓣ0411/82406666, ⓕ82400873. The location is the most noteworthy thing about this two-star affair, overlooking Fujiazhuang Beach. ❺

Friendship Third Floor, 91 Renmin Lu ⓣ0411/82634121, ⓦwww.dlfsh.cn. Above the Friendship Store, close to the passenger-ferry terminal, and newly renovated. ❻

Furama 60 Renmin Lu ⓣ0411/82630888, ⓦwww.furama.com.cn. A very upscale Japanese hotel, this place has every imaginable facility, a lobby big enough for Shide to play in and palatial rooms. ❾

Home Inn 92 Renmin Lu ⓣ0411/39858588, ⓦwww.homeinns.com. Budget Chinese hotel chain offering tidy, moderately priced rooms near the centre, but service is distinctly no-frills. ⑤

Huayue 1 Yingchun Lu ⓣ0411/82588666, ⓕ82588732. One of the former youth hostels, the renamed and renovated building now bills itself a business hotel. This means the carpets are new but there are few useful facilities, so the trip out from the station (buses #404, #702 or minibus #525; taxi ¥15) is no longer nearly so justified. That said, you can still bag yourself a bed here for under ¥100. ③

Ramada 18 Shengli Square ⓣ0411/82808888, ⓦwww.ramada.com. Four-star luxury in the heart of town next to the train station, overlooking Shengli Square. ⑧

Xintiandi Train Station, East Exit ⓣ81234530/62891001. Actually attached to the train station itself, this recently opened option feels temporary and has paper-thin walls, but rooms are clean, modern, convenient and cheap. ③

The City

The hub of Dalian is **Zhongshan Square**, really a circle, whose spokes are some of the most interesting streets in the city. Japanese and Russian buildings, German cars, *KFC* and *McDonald's*, girls in miniskirts, and Western dance music blaring from the shops give the area an international flavour. The main **shopping** streets are Shanghai Lu and Tianjin Jie, which at the time of writing were being converted from simple stalls into massive malls. Continue northwest

on Shanghai Lu and cross the railroad tracks to reach the **old Russian quarter**. This neighbourhood used to house Russia's gentry, though today each peeling mansion is home to several families. The pedestrian street takes you past restored pistachio-coloured facades and street vendors selling Russian cigarettes, lighters, vodka and Soviet pins. It's hardly an authentic colonial avenue, but step west into one of the lanes, and you've gone back a century. Ask nicely and you may even get to see inside the homes.

Follow Zhongshan Lu west past **Shengli Square**, the train station, and the meandering shopping lanes of Qing Er Jie to reach **Renmin Square**, large, grassy and lit with footlights at night. It's a long walk from the train station, but several buses ply the route, among them #15, #702 and #801. The neighbourhoods to the south of the square retain their Russian colonial architecture and narrow, tree-lined streets, making for excellent wandering.

South of the train station is the Japanese-designed **Laodong Park** (¥3). The hilly neighbourhood across the street east of here, **Nanshan**, was once home to the Japanese community; now, the cream-coloured, red-roofed villas are being renovated by nouveau riche Chinese.

The beaches

Dalian's main attraction, its **beaches**, are clean, sandy and packed in the summertime. All are free; near Xinghai Beach, there's also an unusual attraction in the futuristic **Modern Museum**.

The beaches are hugged by Dalian's scenic drive, **Binhai Lu**, which winds past the villas of Party bigwigs as well as Shide stars. Bus #801 (spring and summer only; ¥20) from the train station circles the entire town and serves all the beaches, though some are reached more directly by trams or other buses from the centre, detailed below. A taxi from the city centre will cost ¥30.

Bangchuidao and Tiger beaches

Bangchuidao beach, next to a golf course, was formerly reserved for cadres but is now open to the public. Highly developed **Tiger Beach**, next along the coast to the west, can be reached from town on buses #2, #4, #402 or #801. Here, **Laohutan Ocean Park** (¥60, 7.30am–5.30pm) seems to cover the entire bay area. Basically a funfair, a mind-boggling array of combination tickets (up to ¥210) are available covering attractions inside the park, such as the dolphin show and coral hall, and others nearby including **Bird Singing Woods** (¥30), a giant aviary housing more than 2000 birds. One of Dalian's two former youth hostels can also be found here: *Boat 104*, a warship, is now a tourist attraction in its own right (daily 7.30am–5.30pm; ¥20) but the Hostelling International logos remain. Tandem and mountain-bikes are available to rent along the waterfront for ¥20 an hour, and there are boat trips out to Bangchui Island and beyond (from ¥60); routes and prices are posted at ticket kiosks.

Yanwoling Park, Fujiazhuang Beach and Dalian Forest Zoo

From Tiger Beach, it's a beautiful, if strenuous, seven-kilometre hike along Binhai Lu to **Fujiazhuang Beach**. The turquoise sea stretches before you to the south, while the north side of the road is green year round with trees and new grass. You cross Beida Bridge, a suspended beauty, before winding 3km up to **Yanwoling Park** (daily dawn–dusk; ¥10). Once you're past the statue made of shells of a little boy with seagulls, there's a profusion of maintained trails and stairs to take you down to the sea. One particularly nice hike, signed in English, ends up at Sunken Boat Rock, a cove where starfish cling to rocks and the only sounds are those of the waves. Don't attempt to swim here, however, as a strong current 50m out has claimed lives.

Continuing 4km west on Binhai Lu, you wind downhill to **Fujiazhuang Beach** (daily dawn–dusk), sheltered from the wind in a rocky bay and less developed than Tiger Beach. You can charter speedboats from here to outlying islands, while a trip west to Xinghai Beach and back costs around ¥40 depending on your bargaining skills. At the back of the beach are plenty of good, open-air **seafood** restaurants; expect to pay around ¥80 for a meal for two.

A couple of kilometres northwest along Binhai Lu, you'll come to **Dalian Forest Zoo** (daily 8am–5pm; adults ¥120, students/OAPs ¥60, children under 1.3m free). Naturally, the stars of the show here are the pandas, with both giant and smaller red varieties represented, though the big cats and performing parrots are also popular.

The Modern Museum and Xinghai Beach

On the northwest shoulder of the massive **Xinghai Square** (tram #202 comes here from Xi'an Lu), beside the Malan River, the **Modern Museum** (daily 9am–5pm; ¥30) showcases Dalian's idealized future. Visitors can drive unclogged mock streets, steer an oil tanker into the port on a simulator or ride a flying carpet through pollution-free skies. The museum (the brainchild of former mayor Bo Xilai, like so much in Dalian) isn't all pie in the sky – UN awards attest to the success of the city's ongoing urban revamp.

Xinghai Beach (daily 7am–9pm) is a long walk or short tram ride southwest along Zhongshan Lu from the Modern Museum (take bus #202 three stops to the Medical University). Besides the usual fairground rides, souvenir stands and restaurants, the beach features a trio of attractions in the form of **Sun Asia Ocean World** (9am–4pm; ¥100), **Sun Asia Polar World** (same hours; ¥80) and **Sun Asia Coral World** (same hours; ¥50). Combination tickets for two or more of the "worlds" offer a money-saving option of sorts. Ocean World boasts a 118-metre underwater tunnel in the main tank, while Polar World has Kaka, the largest polar bear in China. West of the park is **Heishijiao**, the jumping-off point for Lüshun (see p.200).

Eating, drinking and entertainment

Dalian is full of **restaurants**, especially around Shengli Square, and just south and west of here on the pedestrian streets bordered by Qing Er Jie and Jiefang Lu. For simple, affordable fare, head south from Zhongshan Square toward the University of Foreign Languages: Yan'an Lu is lined with restaurants. There's a stretch of **Korean BBQ joints** along Gao Er Ji Lu, a block south of Renmin Square; simply follow the smoke and bustle, and the touts out front will wave you in. More conveniently, there's a similar option close to the train station on Changjiang Lu.

For **seafood** away from the beaches, don't miss one of Dalian's many branches of *Tiantian Yugang Jiulou*. The one near the university, at 20 Jilin Jie, is usually packed with people enjoying draught beer and fresh steamed crab; dinner for two with drinks comes to around ¥150. You'll have to shell and eat the thing with chopsticks, so wear clothes you don't mind getting splattered with crab. There's also a more central branch at 10 Renmin Lu.

There are passable pizzas and other Western food at *Pizza King* on Youhao Lu, or if you're craving something a bit different, the enormous *Zhongshan Hotel* at 3 Jiefang Lu, just south of Shengli Square, has an **Indian restaurant** on the fifth floor and a **Russian restaurant** on the thirty-eighth. Both have live music and dance performances. Vegetarians can head for the hard-to-find *Tianyuan Vegetarian,* just past the small but colourful Songshan Temple a short way along Tangshan Jie, for a fix of cheap meat-alike tofu dishes (Ⓣ0411/83673110).

Dalian has lots of **bars**; among the liveliest is the reliable *Meeting Place Bar*, 12 Renmin Lu. It has tattooed, English-speaking bartenders, live rock music, bottled beers from around the world and the requisite Russian prostitutes. Immediately next door is *Remix,* which claims the mantle of no.1 hip-hop club in town; boasting two foreign Djs, *Wave Bar,* on Youhao Square, is the biggest challenger to the crown. *Noah's Ark*, at 32 Wusi Lu, across the street from Renmin Square, is another long-standing favourite for live music; look for the wooden wagon out front.

Listings

Banks and exchange The Bank of China is at 9 Zhongshan Square (Mon–Fri 8.30am–noon & 1–5pm). Outside office hours you can change money and traveller's cheques at the *Dalian Binguan* opposite.

Buses From the long-distance bus station, there are buses to Shenyang, Dandong and other provincial towns. Tickets can be bought the night before to avoid queues. More convenient are the luxury buses to Shenyang and Beijing, which depart throughout the day from the north and east sides of Shengli Square; tickets can be bought on the bus.

Ferries Services have been greatly reduced, with Yantai now the travel hub for the province. The ferry to Yantai itself is a full day faster than the train, and cheaper (6hr; ¥100–800). From Yantai, there are frequent bus connections to Qingdao (4hr). Tickets can be bought in advance from the passenger-ferry terminal on Yimin Jie in the northeast of the city, or from one of the many windows both at and around the train station.

Football From late March until October, the Physical Stadium, just southwest of Renmin Square on Wusi Lu, is the venue for Dalian Shide matches. Good seats go for ¥40 – buy tickets at the stadium itself.

Internet access Many Internet cafés can be found in the area surrounding the University of Foreign Languages, south of Zhongshan Square.

Mail and telephones The post office (Mon–Sat 8am–6pm) is next to the main train station, and there's a 24hr telecom office next door.

PSB Centrally located on the northeast side of Zhongshan Square (daily 8am–4.30pm).

Trains Tickets are easy to buy at the main train station. The ticket windows are on the ground floor, outside and to the left of the station's main entrance.

Travel agents CITS, 2F, *Central Plaza Hotel*, 145 Zhongshan Lu (Ⓣ0411/83691159, Ⓦwww.citsdl.com; daily 8.30am–4.30pm). Most hotels also have their own ticketing and tour offices, or can point you in the direction of a preferred partner.

Lüshun

The port city of **LÜSHUN**, 40km south of Dalian, makes up for the latter's lack of attention to the past. It was near Lüshun that the Japanese shocked the world by defeating the Russians in a naval battle in 1904. This was the beginning of a bloody campaign that ended in Shenyang, where the tsar at last surrendered in 1905. Northeast China was subsequently in the hands of the Japanese, who ruled the region for the next forty years.

For tourists interested in the **Russo-Japanese War**, the chief attraction is the town's prison camp turned museum, commemorating those who were interned here.

The Town

Lüshun is a quiet place, largely unchanged from its colonial role as Port Arthur, with one main square fronted by Japanese-style buildings. The highlight is the **Japanese Russian Imperial Prison Site**, on a small hill in the north of town (daily 9am–5pm; ¥15), a five-minute taxi ride from the bus station. Half the camp was built by the Russians in 1902 as a prison for

Chinese; from 1905 to 1945 it was enlarged by Japan, who used it to hold Chinese, Russians and Japanese dissidents opposed to the emperor. Finally, the Communists used the prison to hold Chinese – you can still read, under the neat squares of burgundy paint attempting to block it out, "Mao Ze Dong Live Forever!" The prison also has a torture room, a gallows with skeletons of victims on display, and a 1914 Model T Ford that belonged to the Japanese warden, in front of which you can have your picture taken for ¥15. A **Tomb for Russian Martyrs**, in memory of the soldiers who died to liberate the city in 1945, is located west of the prison.

Rows of cannon and other fortifications left by the Japanese sit atop **Baiyu Shan** (¥16), a hill overlooking the Yellow Sea near the centre of town. It's not a long walk from the bus station, but the uphill hike is considerable.

Practicalities

Buses from Dalian's Heishijiao bus station make the hour-long run to Lüshun (every 15min; ¥10). From Dalian's centre, take trolleybus #202 or buses #28 or #406, and get off at the *KFC* on the north side of Zhongshan Lu; the bus station is across the road, 50m ahead on your left. The road between Dalian and Lüshun is lined with old Japanese villas since turned into farmhouses or stables.

Taxis around Lüshun charge a minimum of ¥5, covering the trip from the bus station to the prison, for example, while a trip up to Baiyun Shan is ¥16. There are no **restaurants** near Lüshun's sights; however, fruit and noodles can be bought around the bus station and the area fronting the central square.

Dandong

Once an obscure port tucked away in the corner of Liaoning province at the confluence of the Yalu River and the Yellow Sea, pleasant **DANDONG** is now

Dandong

Dandong	丹东	*dāndōng*
Museum to Commemorate Aiding Korea Against US Aggression	抗美援朝纪念馆	*kàngměi yuáncháo jìniànguǎn*
Old Yalu Bridge	鸭绿断桥	*yālù duànqiáo*
Wenhua Square	文化广场	*wénhuà guǎngchǎng*
Yalu River Park	鸭绿江公园	*yālùjiāng gōngyuán*
Accommodation, eating and drinking		
An Dong Great World	安东大世界	*āndōng dàshìjiè*
Dantie Dajiudian	丹铁大酒店	*dāntiě dàjiǔdiàn*
Donghai Village	东海渔村	*dōnghǎi yúcūn*
Europaer	欧罗巴	*ōuluóbā*
Hong Kong Coffee House	香港咖啡厅	*xiānggǎng kāfēitīng*
Huashipai	华士派	*huáshìpài*
Jiangbin Hotel	江滨酒店	*jiāngbīn jiǔdiàn*
Kaixuan Hotel	凯旋宾馆	*kǎixuán bīnguǎn*
Sunlight Bar	阳光酒吧	*yáng guāng jiǔ bā*
Yalu River Guesthouse	鸭绿江大厦	*yālùjiāng dàshà*
Yinghua Dajiudian	樱花大酒店	*yīnghuā dàjiǔdiàn*
Zhonglian Hotel	中联大酒店	*zhōnglián dàjiǔdiàn*

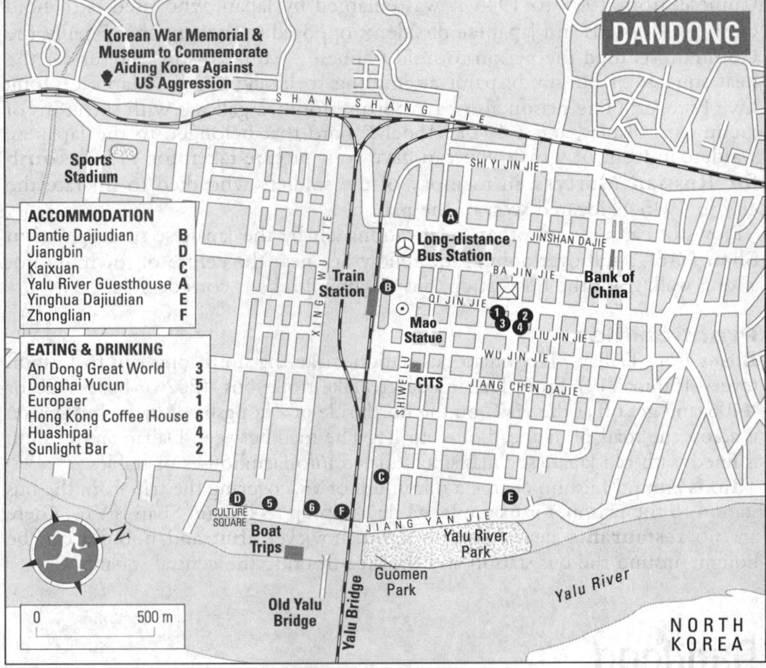

a popular weekend destination for Chinese, who come to gaze across the border into North Korea – the listless Korean city of **Sinuiju** (Xinyizhou in Chinese) lies on the other side of the Yalu River. South Koreans, too, come to look across at their northern neighbour, while foreigners from further afield visit also to see the massive memoria and museum dedicated to the defence of China's communist neighbour against imperialists during the Korean War. All in all, Dandong makes a worthwhile weekend trip out of Beijing or a stopover while touring the sooty northeast, as well as a convenient departure point for the Changbai Shan Nature Reserve (see p.210).

It's intended that an ambitious highway and undersea-tunnel network will pass through Dandong, allowing trains to travel from Beijing, through Korea, all the way to Tokyo. Any plans involving North Korea are, however, speculative at best. For years there has been talk of making Sinuiju a free-trade zone, but while Chinese entrepreneurs are setting up small-scale markets on the other side of the Yalu, the far shore's economy remains moribund.

Arrival and information

Arriving at Dandong **train station**, or at the **long-distance bus station** just to the north, puts you right in the centre of town, a gleaming marble-paved square featuring a statue of Mao Zedong, about 1km north of the Yalu River. Dandong has a small **airport** 14km southwest of town and there's a **ferry terminal** 38km away, where vessels from South Korea dock. **Taxis** in Dandong charge a minimum of ¥5, which is sufficient for rides around town.

Most facilities, such as the **post office** (daily 8am–5.30pm), can be found along (or just off) Qi Jing Jie, the main road running east from the station and site of a bustling **night market**. There are also branches of Bank of China and a post office down on the waterfront at Culture Square. US, Hong Kong and Japanese money can also be changed at the *Yalu River Guesthouse*.

Accommodation

Dantie Dajiudian Train Station Square ⓣ0415/2307777. Situated within the station itself, this is convenient if arriving late or leaving early, and recent renovations mean rooms are not (yet) too shabby. ❸

Jiangbin Culture Square ⓣ0415/3153784. Has a business hotel facade but the interior is shabby, and the bordelloish decor can be just a bit too seedy for some. However, get an odd-numbered room on the fifth floor or above and you'll have almost the same view as the *Zhonglian*, at a fraction of the price. ❺

Kaixuan 9 Shiwei Lu ⓣ0415/2125566. North of the Yalu Bridge, the *Kaixuan* has clean triples from ¥80 per bed, including breakfast, though for ¥20 more its probably worth getting a room to yourself. ❸

Yalu River Guesthouse 87 Jiuwei Lu ⓣ0415/2125901, ⓦwww.yaluriverhotel.cn. A Sino-Japanese effort – though the rooms have seen better days they are more than adequate, even coming equipped with satellite TV. Staff are helpful, and the ticket service is able to deal with onward travel requests. ❻

Yinghua Dajiudian 2 Liuwei Lu ⓣ0414/2100999. Boasting views across the river, and large rooms all equipped with broadband Internet access, this place is a decent and reasonably priced bet if you're on a business trip. ❺

Zhonglian 62 Binjiang Zhonglu ⓣ0415/3170666, ⓦwww.zlhotel.com.cn. The poshest accommodation in town, this waterfront hotel looks out across the bombed-out bridge towards North Korea. As well as smart rooms with great views, the lobby travel service is exceedingly helpful in booking tickets. ❼

The City

Dandong remains small enough to feel human in scale, and the tree-lined main streets are uncrowded, clean and prosperous. A strong **Korean influence** can be felt in the city: vendors along the riverfront promenade sell North Korean stamps, bearing slogans in Korean such as "Become human gun bombs!", and North Korean TV is on view in Dandong hotels.

Moving on from Dandong

Dandong is well connected to northeast China, with **trains** arriving and departing daily. Tickets are easy enough to get from the train station, and can also be booked through CITS (ⓣ0415/2123688, ⓦwww.ddcits.com), just north of the Shiwei Lu/Jiang Chen Dajie intersection. There are **flights** to Sanya, Shanghai and Shenzhen; CITS can book you tickets or most hotels will either be able to book tickets for you or point you in the right direction. If you're planning to head off to the **Changbai Shan Nature Reserve**, you'll need to get the 6.30am or 8.50am bus to **Tonghua** (8–10hr; ¥60); buy a ticket the night before from the efficient booking office at the bus station. VW Santanas heading to **Shenyang** ply for passengers on the west side of the station concourse (¥70/person), which works out faster than taking the train.

CITS run a ten-day **tour**, which takes in Sinuiju, Pyongyang and Mount Kumgang in **North Korea**, but these tours aren't cheap and Westerners are unlikely to be accepted. If you're desperate to visit North Korea, it's better to arrange a tour with the Beijing-based Koryo Tours (ⓦwww.koryogroup.com), run by Englishman Nick Bonner.

▲ A boat trip passes under the new Yalu Bridge

On foot, the nearest you can get to the North Korean soil without a visa is halfway across the river, on the **Old Yalu Bridge** (daily 8.30am–5pm; ¥15) in the south of town, next to the new bridge. The Koreans have dismantled their half but the Chinese have left theirs as a memorial, replete with thirty framed photos of its original construction by the Japanese in 1911, when the town was called Andong. The bridge ends at a tangled mass of metal resulting from the American bombing in 1950 in response to the Chinese entering the Korean War. Several viewing platforms, with picnic tables, are on site, along with Chinese entrepreneurs who charge ¥1 for a few minutes' staring at Sinuiju through a telescope.

From 8am, **boats** set out from all along Dandong's promenade, by the bridge, on thirty-minute trips across the river (costing ¥20 in a large boat that leaves when full, or ¥35 per person for a zippy six-seater). The boats take you into North Korean waters to within a few metres of shore, where you can do your part for international relations by waving at the teenage soldiers shouldering automatic rifles. Photography is allowed, but most foreign tourists keep their cameras packed away: there isn't much to see on Sinuiju's desultory shore, save for some rusting ships and languid civilians. If you've an interest in visiting Sinuiju, it's best to check the current situation with Dandong's CITS (see box, p.203), though they'll most likely say that all foreigners are forbidden from joining their North Korean tour.

The Dandong side of the river is a boomtown in comparison. The riverside by the bridges is the most scenic area, full of strolling tourists, particularly in the early evening. Nearby is **Yalu River Park**, where you can drive bumper cars and pay ¥1 to sit on a patch of downy green grass. At the western end of the riverside promenade, **Culture Square** is a well-lit local evening hangout.

The Museum to Commemorate Aiding Korea Against US Aggression

Built in 1993, the huge, macabre **Museum to Commemorate Aiding Korea Against US Aggression** (daily 8.00am–4.30pm; ¥40) feels like a relic of the Cold War. It has nine exhibition halls on the Korean War, full of maps, plans, dioramas, machine guns, hand grenades, photographs (almost all of which are captioned in English), and sculptures of lantern-jawed Chinese and Korean soldiers. A few large plaques in each hall spell out, in English and Chinese, the basic theme of each room – tending to be along the lines of "the Americans were terrible aggressors, China heroically won the war after stepping in to help its Korean brothers and sisters." The trifling detail that the North Koreans kicked off the war by invading the South is conspicuous by its absence.

In a field behind the museum, a collection of Chinese and captured US aircraft and artillery are on display, while a paintball area, assault course and fighter plane simulator help crank up the fun factor a little bit further. Purchase another ticket (¥15) and you can climb up inside the huge memorial next to the museum – surrounded by statues of burly Chinese soldiers trampling US army helmets underfoot – for a view over Dandong and into North Korea. This ticket also gains you entry to a slightly bizarre display of replica terracotta warriors underneath the base of the monument.

The museum is in the northwest of the city and can be reached on buses #1, #3, #4 or #5 from the station; get off by the sports stadium and walk north for five minutes. If you've developed a thirst by the time you arrive, note the ice-cold Coca-Colas for sale at the entrance to the compound, next to Jiang Zemin's large plaque swearing eternal North Korean–Sino friendship.

Eating

Restaurants in Dandong cater to masses of weekenders craving freshwater fish and Korean dishes. Try the local *luzi yu*, a river fish, at *Donghai Yucun* no. 42, Block E (promenade buildings are labelled with letters), west of the Yalu Bridge. All dishes here are served with glutinous rice, soup, bread and dumplings, and a feast for two is a bargain at ¥30. In fact, restaurants stretch the length of the promenade, many following the popular northern style of having plates of food out ready for you to choose from, which saves a lot of time messing around with menus. For an alternative start to your morning, you can check out the latest North Korean TV news at *Hong Kong Coffee House*, no. 32, Block D, where strong Korean coffee is ¥20.

In the centre, a clutch of restaurants nestle around the junctions of Liuwei Lu, Qi Jin Jie and Liu Jin Jie. There are Western dishes available at *Europaer* and *Huashipai,* both serving pizzas from ¥30 and steak for about ¥50, while *An Dong Great World*, opposite *Huashipai*, is a posh *dim sum* restaurant that stays open late, though check the price of each plate as you order or you could be in for a nasty surprise when the bill comes. For cheaper, local and Korean dishes, there is another string of restaurants along San Jin Jie, running north from its junction with Shiwei Lu.

For a **beer**, choices are limited, though there are plenty of coffee shops dotted around that also serve alcohol. The *Sunlight Bar* at the corner of Liu Weilu and Qi Jin Jie, is always a reliable if uninspiring backup.

Changchun and Jilin

The cities of **Jilin province** took the brunt of Japanese, Russian and Chinese communist planning more than anywhere in China. This was a result of Jilin's vast mineral reserves, deposits of coal and iron ore that

Changchun and Jilin

Changchun	长春	*chángchūn*
Chunyi Hotel	春谊宾馆	*chūnyí bīnguǎn*
Geological Palace	地质宫博物馆	*dìzhìgōng bówùguǎn*
Jindu Hotel	金都饭店	*jīndū fàndiàn*
Postal Hotel	邮政宾馆	*yóuzhèng bìnguàn*
Puppet Emperor's Palace	伪皇宫	*wěihuáng gōng*
Rail Station Hotel	铁路宾馆	*tiělù bīnguǎn*
Shangri-La Hotel	香格里拉饭店	*xiānggélǐlā fàndiàn*
Weiduoqian Lamian	味多千拉面	*wèiduōqiān lāmiàn*
Wenhua Square	文化广场	*wénhuà guǎngchǎng*
Xiangyangtun Restaurant	向阳屯饭店	*xiàngyángtún fàndiàn*
Jilin	吉林	*jílín*
Angel Hotel	天使宾馆	*tiānshǐ bīnguǎn*
Beida Hu Ski Park	北大湖滑雪场	*běidàhú huáxuěchǎng*
Beishan Park	北山公园	*běishān gōngyuán*
Catholic Church	天主堂	*tiānzhǔ táng*
Changchun Hotel	长春宾馆	*chángchūn bīnguǎn*
Dongfang Jiaozi Wang	东方饺子王	*dōngfāng jiǎoziwáng*
Dongguan Hotel	东关宾馆	*dōngguān bīnguǎn*
Jiangbei Park	江北公园	*jiāngběi gōngyuán*
Jiangnan Park	江南公园	*jiāngnán gōngyuán*
Jilin Fandian	吉林饭店	*jílín fàndiàn*
Jilin International Hotel	吉林国际大酒店	*jílín guójì dàjiǔdiàn*
Jinchi Binguan	金池宾馆	*jīnchí bīnguǎn*
Shenzhou Hotel	神州大酒店	*shénzhōu dà jiǔdiàn*
Songhua Hu	松花湖	*sōnghuā hú*
Songhuahu Ski Park	松花湖滑雪场	*sōnghuā hú huáxuěchǎng*
Zhuque Shan	朱雀山	*zhūquè shān*

transformed the area into a network of sprawling industrial hubs, and, for thirteen years, the seat of the Manchukuo government. The closing of state-owned factories has resulted in massive lay-offs, but not all is glum, as tourism has crept in as one of the few growth industries in Jilin. Roads have been improved, the rail network is thorough and easy to use, most hotels are delighted to see foreigners, and winter brings low-cost **skiing and sledding**. Popular with both domestic and South Korean tourists is the **Changbai Shan Nature Reserve** (see p.210), a swath of mountain and forest boasting breathtaking scenery in the far eastern section of the province, along the North Korean border. The most convenient jumping-off point for Changbai Shan is **Jilin**, a pleasant little city with little by way of sights, but great winter sports. Some 90km to the west, **Changchun** is the provincial capital and former capital of Manchukuo. The city retains much imperial architecture and design, with straight boulevards and squares throughout.

Jilin province is famous in its own country for **er ren zhuan**, a form of theatre closer to vaudeville than Beijing opera, incorporating dancing, singing, baton-twirling, costume changes and soliloquies. A typical performance sees a man and woman regaling the audience with a humorous tale of their courtship and love. Tape recordings of the genre are available at stores, and you may be able to get into a performance with translation via CITS, or you could just ask a cabby or local to point you to a theatre.

Changchun

CHANGCHUN has a historical notoriety deriving from its role as Hsinking, capital of Manchukuo, the Japanese-controlled state from 1932 to 1945 that had Xuantong (better known as Puyi) as its emperor. Now a huge, sprawling industrial city, it's also renowned for its many colleges, its movie studio and the **Number One Automobile Factory**, producer of the ubiquitous Liberation Truck and Red Flag sedans, though in these joint-venture days the majority of the city's auto production focuses on Volkswagen Santanas.

A good, but long, introduction to the city is to stroll south from the train station down the main artery, Renmin Dajie, past Japan's former Kwangtung Army Headquarters (identifiable by its spiky eaves) to Renmin Square and then west to Wenhua Square. The latter is the second-largest square in the world (after Tian'anmen), and was to be the site of Puyi's palace. Today, it's a large paved expanse with statues of a muscular naked man, standing with his arms raised in liberation, and a reclining naked woman marking its centre. All that remains of the planned palace are its foundations, topped by the so-called **Geological Palace** (daily 8.30am–4.30pm; ¥10). Inside, rows upon rows of minerals attest to Jilin's abundant resources. Bored school groups come to life when they see the pair of dinosaur skeletons, including a "Manchusaurus".

The Puppet Emperor's Palace

Changchun's only notable attraction is the **Puppet Emperor's Palace** (daily: summer 8.30am–4.20pm, winter 8.30am–3.40pm; ¥80), in the east of the city on the route of buses #10, #125, #264 and #268 from the train station. In 1912, at the age of 8, Puyi ascended to the imperial throne in Beijing, at the behest of the dying Dowager Cixi. Although forced to abdicate that same year by the Republican government, he retained his royal privileges, continuing to reside as a living anachronism in the Forbidden City. Outside, the new republic was coming to terms with democracy and the twentieth century, and Puyi's life, circumscribed by court ritual, seems a fantasy in comparison. In 1924, he was expelled by Nationalists uneasy at what he represented, but the Japanese protected him and eventually found a use for him here in Changchun as a figure who lent a symbolic legitimacy to their rule. After the war, he was re-educated by the Communists and lived the last years of his life as a gardener. His story was the subject of Bernardo Bertolucci's lavish film, *The Last Emperor*.

Like its former occupant, the palace is really just a shadow of Chinese imperial splendour, a poor miniature of Beijing's Forbidden City but, in its defence, it does boast a swimming pool and horse racing track (¥10), both of which its ancient forebear lacks. This luxurious retreat, though, was only meant to be temporary, until his grand abode proper was completed at Culture Square.

The **Museum of North East China's Occupation by Japan** (¥20) on the same site, documents Japan's brutal invasion and rule. On a lighter note, be sure to see the restored **Japanese garden**, one of Changchun's most tranquil spots.

Practicalities

Numerous flights connect Changchun with every major city in China. A bus from the **airport** (40min; ¥20), 10km northwest of town, drops you outside the **CAAC Hotel** (☎0431/82988888) at 480 Jiefang Dalu, about 3km south of the train station. Both **train** and **bus stations** are in the north of town, with frequent connections to the rest of the northeast. At the bus station, there are also VWs for intercity journeys – negotiate a price and wait for the car to fill with passengers, and you're off. Fares aren't that much higher than taking the bus, and you'll arrive at least an hour earlier. Do expect, however, to have to change vehicles at some point on the journey. Taxis within the city have a ¥5 flag fall.

The **Bank of China** (Mon–Fri 8.30am–4.30pm) is not far from the *Shangri-La*, at 1 Tongzhi Lu. **CITS** (Ⓣ0431/86909076) is further south, at 1296 Xinmin Dajie, while the **PSB** is at 99 Renmin Dajie. The **post office** (daily 8.30am–4.30pm) is just to the left as you exit the train station. A good **Internet café** can be found on the fifth floor of the building opposite the *Shangri-La* hotel on Xi'an Dalu, while there's a 24-hour one at 47 Tongzhi Jie, across from the Foreign Language Bookstore.

Accommodation, eating and drinking

The most convenient **place to stay** is the *Rail Station Hotel*, right at the train station (Ⓣ0431/82703627; ④), but slightly smarter rooms at a similar price are available at the *Postal Hotel* a little further along (Ⓣ0431/82987888; ④). Directly across from the station's south exit, the *Chunyi Hotel* (Ⓣ0431/82096888, Ⓕ88960171; ④) is the province's oldest inn. Built in 1909 by the Japanese, it lacks the charm of similar properties in Shenyang and Dalian, but is good value for cleanliness, location and price. Rooms have cable TV and hot water, and rates include breakfast. The *Shangri-La* at 569 Xi'an Da Lu (Ⓣ0431/88981818, Ⓦwww.shangri-la.com; ⑨) is right in the centre of the new commercial district and serves as the town's five-star option. They take credit cards and keep free maps of Changchun's sights in the lobby. Nearby, the *Jindu Hotel* (Ⓣ0431/88482888, Ⓕ888482999; ⑥) at 1077 Xi'an Da Lu is a well-located, smart business hotel.

The city's main **bar** and **restaurant** area lies between Tongzhi Jie and Renmin Dajie, sandwiched between the zoo and art institute. Here, noodle shops, cafés and pubs pack the three east–west roads: Longli, Guilin and Xikang Lu. Directly across from the *Shangri-La*, *Weiduoqian Lamian* does excellent Xinjiang-style hand-pulled noodles. Consider, too, *Xiangyangtun*, a branch of the Beijing restaurant recalling the privations of the Great Leap Forward. The menu includes griddle cakes, greens fried in batter, and even fried scorpions, all of which represent the depths Chinese cooking sank to during lean years. These dishes are merely foils, however, to hearty and well-prepared Dongbei meat and vegetable dishes: here you can sample the region's beloved stewed cabbage (*suan baicai*), which is to Dongbei what duck is to Beijing. To reach *Xiangyangtun*, walk south on Tongzhi Jie from the *Shangri-La* and turn left at Dong Chaoyang Lu; the restaurant is on the left-hand side, at no. 3.

Jilin and around

Known as Kirin during the Manchukuo time, **JILIN** is split in two by the **Songhua River**, with the downtown area spread along its northern shore. The **promenade** along the river was finished in 1998, making for a pretty walk, especially in winter, when the trees are coated in frost – a phenomenon, known as *shugua* in Chinese, that results from condensation from the city's hydroelectric dam at **Songhua Hu** (¥10). It's Jilin's claim to fame, along with an **ice festival** in January and three neighbouring **parks** for **skiing and sledding**. This makes winter the ideal time to visit Jilin, though the parks – Beishan, Jiangnan and Jiangbei – are nice enough in summer. Beishan, in the west of town at the terminus of bus routes #7 and #107, is the best known of the three (¥5). It's filled with pathways and temples, the most interesting of which is **Yuhuangge** (Jade Emperor's Temple), where rows of fortune-tellers gather out front.

A reminder of the past, Jilin's **Catholic church** is the town's prettiest building, built in 1917 at 3 Songjiang Lu the road bordering the river promenade. Next door is a hospice for the elderly, which explains why the median age of a Jilin Catholic appears to be 80.

Practicalities

Jilin's small **airport** is located 33km northwest of town; a **taxi** into the centre will cost ¥50. Taxi fares begin at ¥5, which covers most rides within town. The central **train and bus stations** are around 2km north of the river; but note that departing from Changchun offers many more destination options. If you're going to Changbai Shan, it's worthwhile talking to the **CITS** office (Ⓣ0432/2435819, Ⓕ2430690) in the lobby of the *Dongguan Hotel*. The main **Bank of China** (daily 8am–5pm) and **post office** (8am–5pm) are across from each other on opposite sides of Jilin Dajie, just north of the bridge, church and *Dongguan Hotel*. For **Internet access**, Chongqing Jie, a road that runs diagonally northeast from the post office to the train station, has several places to choose from near the intersection with Shanghai Lu.

The *Dongguan Hotel*, at 2 Jiang Wan Lu (Ⓣ0432/2160188; ④), is cavernous and frayed but puts you smack in the city centre. More comfortable is the *Jilin International* at 20 Zhongxing Jie (Ⓣ0432/6129818, Ⓕ2553788; ⑤), right in front of the train station. Next door, the budget *Jinchi Binguan* (Ⓣ0432/6110258; ③) at 18 Zhongxing Lu is shabby but convenient. A smarter in-town choice is the *Angel Hotel*, 2 Nanjing Jie (Ⓣ0432/2481848; ④), near the Catholic Church, off the main north–south road, Jilin Dajie. Where Tianjin Lu meets the river, at 1 Songjiang Donglu, the new *Shenzhou Hotel* (Ⓣ0432/2161000, Ⓦwww.jlszhotel.com; ⑤) is about the smartest Jilin has to offer.

Chongqing Jie is lined with good **restaurants**, including a "Dumpling King", *Dongfang Jiaozi Wang*, south of the *Jilin International*.

Around Jilin

Twenty kilometres east of Jilin is **Songhua Hu**, a deep, very attractive lake, set in a large forested park and surrounded by hills. A taxi to this popular local beauty spot should cost about ¥40, and there are rowing boats for rent. In 1992, an off-duty soldier reported being attacked by a dragon while boating here – it's a risk you'll just have to take. Unlike most Chinese scenic attractions, Songhua Hu seems big enough to absorb the impact of all its visitors, and even on weekends it's possible to escape to some quiet, peaceful spot.

At the lake's southern end is the huge **Fengman Dam**, a source of great local pride. Although in recent years the Songhua River's level has dropped by half (a result of extensive tree felling in its catchment area), the river floods every year, and at least a couple of the dam's four sluice gates have to be opened. With ruthless Chinese pragmatism, cities in Dongbei have been graded in order of importance in the event that the annual floods ever become uncontrollable. Jilin is judged more important than Harbin, so if the river does ever flood disastrously, Jilin will be spared and Harbin submerged.

Local ski areas

In winter, the area around the lake is great for skiing and sledding, and ski packages are available through Jilin's tourist agencies. Closest to Jilin city, on bus routes #9 and #33, is **Zhuque Shan**, a park long known for its hiking and temples but now also for its skiing. It's 14km outside Jilin; a metered taxi costs ¥35 from the train station. After you're dropped off, you have to walk 1km to the park, though entrepreneurs on horseback or dogsled will take you in for

¥10. You then buy an entrance ticket (daily dawn–dusk; ¥5). There are two small slopes here, one for sledding and one for skiing. The sleds are two downhill skis nailed together with a piece of raised plywood, and really fly if you get a running start and bellyflop. It's ¥20 for a day of sledding, or ¥40 for skiing (¥100 deposit required). There's a good **restaurant** that seats guests on a *kang*, a heated raised platform that provides a nice vantage point over the hill. Foreigners are a rarity here, and the staff and patrons a lot of fun. Skiing lessons are free; just look helpless and a staffer will come to the rescue.

Jilin also has two first-class ski areas, replete with chairlifts – though transport and lift tickets plus equipment rental at **Songhua Hu Huaxue Chang** (ⓣ0432/4697666) and **Beida Hu Huaxue Chang** (ⓣ0432/4202168) are respectively double and triple the cost of Zhuque Shan. To get to the Songhua Hu resort, take bus #9 or #33 to the small district of **Fengman** (30min) and continue by taxi, or get a taxi all the way from Jilin city (26km) for about ¥50. Transport to the bigger Beida Hu ski area, 56km southeast of Jilin, is easiest by taxi (¥120), though in winter months hourly buses also make the trip (1hr 30min; ¥20).

Changbai Shan Nature Reserve

The Changbai mountains run northeast to southwest along the Chinese–Korean border for over a thousand kilometres. With long, harsh winters and humid summers, this is the only mountain range in east Asia to possess alpine tundra, and its highest peak, Baitou Shan (2744m), is the tallest mountain on the eastern side of the continent. The huge lake, **Tian Chi**, high in the Changbai mountains, is one of the highlights of Dongbei, as is the surrounding area, the beautiful **Changbai Shan Nature Reserve**. With jagged peaks emerging from swaths of lush pine forest, this is remote, backwater China, difficult to access even after recent improvements in infrastructure. Heading a little off the tourist track into the wilderness is the way to get the most out of the area, though you'll need to come well prepared with all-weather gear, whatever the time of year.

Changbai Shan Nature Reserve		
Changbai Shan	长白山	*chángbái shān*
Athlete's Village	运动员村宾馆	*yùndòngyuáncūn bīnguǎn*
Cuckoo Villas	杜鹃山庄	*dùjuān shānzhuāng*
Heaven Springs Hotel	天上温泉宾馆	*tiānshàng wēnquán bīnguǎn*
International Tourist Hotel	长白山国际旅游宾馆	*chángbáishān guójìlǚyóu bīnguǎn*
Tian Chi	天池	*tiānchí*
Tonghua	通化	*tōnghuà*
Underground Forest	地下森林	*dìxià sēnlín*
Yanji	延吉	*yánjí*
Baihe	白河	*báihé*
Hongda Binguan	宏达宾馆	*hóngdá bīnguǎn*
Ding Jia Hongda Binguan	丁家宏达宾馆	*dīngjiāhóng bīnguǎn*
Xinda Binguan	信达宾馆	*xìndá bīnguǎn*
Yongxu Binguan	永旭宾馆	*yǒngxù bīnguǎn*
Changbai Shan Nature Reserve	长白山自然保护区	*chángbáishān zìrán beohùqū*

Established in 1961, the nature reserve covers more than 800 square kilometres of luxuriant forest, most of which lies 500 to 1100m above sea level. At the base of the range, the land is dense with huge Korean pines, which can grow up to 50m tall, and mixed broadleaf forest. The rare Manchurian fir is also found here. Higher altitudes are home to the Changbai Scotch pine, recognizable by its yellow bark, and the Japanese yew. As the climate becomes colder and damper higher up, the spruces and firs get hardier before giving way to a layer of sub-alpine grassland with colourful alpine plants and tundra. Animal species on the reserve include the leopard, lynx, black bear and **Siberian tiger**, all now protected, though decades of trapping have made them a rarity. Notable bird species include the golden-rumped swallow, orioles and the ornamental red crossbill. The area is rich in medicinal plants, too, and has been a focus of research since the eleventh century. The Chinese regard the region as the best place in the country for **ginseng** and deer antlers, both prized in traditional remedies, and the reserve's rare lichens have recently been investigated as a treatment for cancer.

Visitors, mostly domestic tourists, South Koreans and Japanese, come here in great numbers, and a tourist village has grown up on the mountain, with the result that the scenery and atmosphere are somewhat marred by litter, souvenir stalls and hawkers. Not all visitors are here for the landscape – plenty come to search for herbs, and many of the Japanese are here to catch butterflies (to keep) and ants (to eat). When the day-trippers have left, though, the reserve is peaceful, and there are opportunities to hike far from the crowds.

The **weather** in the region is not kind and can change very suddenly. In summer, torrential rain is common, and at any time of year cloud and mist can

Ginseng

Ginseng has been collected as a medicinal plant for millennia, and the first Chinese pharmacopoeia, written in the first century, records its ability to nourish the five internal organs, sharpen intelligence, strengthen *yin* (female energy) and invigorate *yang* (male energy).

It is the ginseng **root** that is prized. It's quite conceivable to search for weeks and not find a single specimen, and ginseng hunters have even disappeared, the combination of which has given rise to a host of **superstitions**. The roots are said to be guarded by snakes and tigers, and legend has it that if a hunter should dream of a laughing, white-bearded man or a group of dancing fairies, he must get up, remain silent, and walk off into the forest. His colleagues must follow without speaking to him, and he will lead them to a root.

Changbai ginseng is regarded as the finest in China. Ginseng hunters in Changbai work in summer, when the plant can be spotted by its red berries. One way to find it is to listen for the call of the Bangchui sparrow, which becomes hoarse after eating ginseng seeds. When a ginseng is found, a stick is planted in the ground and a red cloth tied to it: according to tradition, the cloth stops the ginseng child – the spirit of the root – from escaping.

Ginseng generally grows in the shade of the Korean pine, and it is said that a plant of real medicinal value takes fifty years to mature. The plants are low-growing, with their roots pointing upwards in the topsoil. Digging one out is a complex, nail-biting operation, because if any of the delicate roots are damaged, the value of the whole is severely diminished. Roots are valued not just by weight, but by how closely the root system resembles a human body, with a head and four limbs. If you find a wild root, you're rich, as Changbai ginseng sells for ¥1000 a gram. Artificially reared ginseng is worth a fraction of this.

make it impossible to see ten yards ahead of you, let alone the grandeur of Tian Chi lake. Chinese-speakers can call the park's tourist office (ⓣ0433/5710778) to check on conditions. Given the climate, the **best time to visit** is between June and September; at other times, heavy snows can close roads and transport can be limited.

Reaching the reserve

Changbai Shan is a long way from anywhere, and the easiest way to get there is by booking one of the three-day, two-night **tours** arranged through CITS in Jilin (see p.209). These cost ¥600–1000, including park entrance fees and accommodation, and stop at all the must-sees, including Tian Chi.

At the base of the mountain, **Baihe** village is the rail terminus for Changbai Shan. The most convenient approach is from the north via bus **from Jilin** to Baihe (4hr; ¥50). **From Changchun**, train #N188/189 departs daily at 2.46pm, arriving in Baihe at 5.40am the next day. You can also approach **from Dandong** to the south: two daily buses depart before 9am for **Tonghua** (7hr; ¥60), arriving in plenty of time to catch the 9.45pm night train to Baihe, which gets in at 4.30am; if you miss that, there's a morning train that leaves at 7.30am and arrives in Baihe at 2pm. Approaching from **Beijing**, there is a daily overnight train to Tonghua, which departs at 3pm and arrives in Tonghua at 7.15am the next day.

The train is also the best overland route **back out** of the Changbai Shan region, with daily direct trains **to Shenyang** and **Beijing.** There are also four buses daily from Baihe to **Yanji**, in China's **Korean Autonomous Prefecture,** from where you can transfer west to **Jilin** and **Changchun**, or north towards **Harbin.**

Baihe

Once a logging village in its own right, **BAIHE** is now little more than a staging post for tourists visiting Changbai Shan Nature Reserve, 20km away. There are accommodation options around the train and bus stations and in the commercial area, called **Erhao Baihe Zhen**. Around the train station, the *Hongda Binguan* (ⓣ0433/5718637; ❶–❷) runs a virtual cartel, with places to stay on both sides of the station car park: the *Hongda* itself is on the right as you get off the train and the cheaper *Ding Jia*, (same phone) where you can get a bed for around ¥20, on the left.

Arrival at the station is bedlam; you can collect your thoughts over a steaming cup of tea in the *Yanleyuan Restaurant*, also in the car park square.

If the spartan budget options around the station don't suit, it's only a ¥5 taxi ride to Erdao Baihe Zhan, where there are a string of smarter establishments to choose from. The *Landmark Resort* (ⓣ0433/5712422; ❺) is not as tacky as it sounds and has smart, clean rooms, while, directly opposite, the newly renovated *Xinda Binguan* (ⓣ0433/5720111; ❹) is probably the best value in this part of town. At the top of the street, the *Yongxu Binguan* (ⓣ0433/5720111; ❺) does not really give enough to justify its higher rates but off season there is a surplus of rooms, so bargaining can pay significant dividends.

The reserve

The undisputed jewel of the reserve, it is surely only a matter of time before **Tian Chi**, a hugely dramatic volcanic crater lake 5km across, encircled by angular crags, gushing waterfalls and snow-capped peaks, takes its place alongside Beijing's Forbidden City and Xi'an's Terracotta Army as one of

China's must-see wonders. The effort of climbing the 1000 or so concrete steps to reach the lake, not to mention all the trouble of just getting to the reserve in the first place, is forgotten as you cross the boulder-strewn snow field towards what must be one of the most spectacular views anywhere in the world.

Of the other specific sights in the reserve, **Small Tian Chi** is almost laughable when compared to its larger sibling, but the **Underground Forest** – a tree-filled canyon – is an unexpected wonder.

Despite its remoteness, in summer Changbai Shan averages around 10,000 visitors a day – and as you're herded from one beauty spot to the next, it's easy to feel the outdoors experience has been diluted a bit. Getting away from the crowds along the beaten path is the key to a rewarding visit. Head off on your own and you can quickly be swallowed up in the wilderness, but be careful around Tian Chi; the lake straddles the Chinese–North Korean **border** – if you stray across, you're liable to arrest and charges of espionage. At the height of the Cultural Revolution, Chairman Mao ordered that the line be demarcated, but it isn't clearly marked on the ground.

Reserve practicalities

The **bus** trip from Baihe to the main gate of the reserve takes 45min (¥35), and regular tourist buses run up and down the mountain during the summer months. The last buses return to Baihe around 4pm. Alternatively, you can charter a **taxi** from anywhere in Baihe, which should cost around ¥80 for a round trip to the gates of the reserve and back – don't pay the full amount until you have been safely returned to where you came from.

Entry to the reserve (daily 7.30am–6pm) costs ¥100, half-price for students and other groups spelled out in minute detail at the ticket office. However, there's an additional ¥45 fee for using the parks "eco" buses (or ¥80 if you opt for a decidedly non-eco 4WD), which, considering it is 16km from the entrance to Tian Chi (¥25), all uphill, is an unavoidable option.

Among the cluster of new **hotels** inside the park are *Athletes' Village* (Ⓣ0433/5746066; ❻) and *Cuckoo Villas* (Ⓣ0433/5746099; ❺), which represent the cheap to mid-range options. At the upper end of the spectrum, and popular with the many Korean tour groups who visit, are the *International Tourist Hotel* (Ⓣ0433/5746001; ❽), which has rooms with views of a waterfall, and the *Heaven Springs Hotel* (Ⓣ0433/5822157; ❽), which has a hot-spring swimming pool, filled by sulphurous waters bubbling up from beneath the mountains.

Harbin and beyond

The capital of Heilongjiang province, **HARBIN** is probably the northernmost location that's of interest to visitors, the last major city before you hit the sub-Siberian wilderness and its scattering of oil and mining towns. It's worth a visit for its **winter Ice Festival** alone, but it's also one of the few northern cities with a distinctive character, the result of colonialism and cooperation with nearby Russia.

Harbin was a small fishing village on the Songhua River until world history intervened. In 1896, the Russians obtained a contract to build a rail line from Vladivostok through Harbin to Dalian, and the town's population swelled to include 200,000 foreigners. More Russians arrived in 1917, this time White Russian refugees fleeing the Bolsheviks, and many stayed on. In 1932, the city was briefly captured by the Japanese forces invading Manchuria, then in 1945 it fell again to the Russian army, who held it for a year before Stalin and Chiang Kaishek finally came to an agreement. Harbin reverted to the Chinese, though when the Russians withdrew, they took with them most of the city's industrial plant. Things haven't been totally peaceful since – Harbin was the scene of fierce factional fighting during the Cultural Revolution, and when relations with the Soviet Union deteriorated, the inhabitants looked anxiously north as fierce border skirmishes took place.

Not surprisingly, the city used to be nicknamed "**Little Moscow**", and though much of the old architecture has been replaced with sterile blocks and skyscrapers, corners of Harbin still look like the last threadbare outpost of imperial Russia. Leafy boulevards are lined with European-style buildings painted in pastel shades, and bulbous onion domes dot the skyline. The city's

Harbin and beyond

Harbin	哈尔滨	*hāěrbīn*
Chairman Mao Memorial	毛主席纪念馆	*máozhǔxí jìniànguǎn*
Dongdazhi Jie	南岗教堂	*nángǎng jiàotáng*
Flood Control Monument	防洪纪念碑	*fánghóng jìniànbēi*
Harbin Amusement Park	哈尔滨游乐园	*hā'érbīn yóulèyuán*
Harbin Architecture and Art Centre	哈尔滨建筑艺术馆	*hā'ěrbīn jiànzhù yìshùguǎn*
Ice Festival	冰灯节	*bīngdēngjié*
Provincial Museum	黑龙江博物馆	*hēilóngjiāng bówùguǎn*
Songhua River	松花江	*sōnghuā jiāng*
Stalin Park	斯大林公园	*sīdàlín gōngyuán*
Sun Island	太阳岛	*tàiyáng dǎo*
Temple of Bliss	吉乐寺	*jílè sì*
Tiger Park	东北虎林园	*dōngběihǔ línyuán*
Zhaolin Park	兆林公园	*zhàolín gōngyuán*
Zhongyang Dajie	中央大街	*zhōngyāng dàjiē*
Accommodation, eating and drinking		
Beibei	北北大酒店	*běiběi dàjiǔdiàn*
Blues Bar	布蓝斯酒吧	*bùlánsī jiǔbā*
Dahe	大和美食日本菜	*dàhé měishí rìběncài*
Dongcai Dumpling King	东才饺子王	*dōngcái jiǎoziwáng*
Gloria Plaza	饥莱花园大酒店	*jīcài huāyuán dàjiǔdiàn*
Holiday Inn	哈尔滨万达假日饭店	*hāěrbīn wàndájiàrì fàndiàn*
Hongda	宏达宾馆	*hóngdá bīnguǎn*
Huamei	华梅饭店	*huáméi fàndiàn*
Huangjin	黄金宾馆	*huángjīn bīnguǎn*
Longmen	龙门大厦	*lóngmén dàshà*
Longyun	龙运宾馆	*lóngyùn bīnguǎn*
Modern	马达尔宾馆	*mǎdá'ěr bīnguǎn*
Portman	波特曼西餐厅	*bōtèmàn xīcāntīng*
Russia 1914	俄罗斯１９１４	*éluósī yījiǔyīsì*
Shangri-La	香格里拉大饭店	*xiānggélǐlā dàfàndiàn*
Pingfang	平方	*píngfāng*
Qiqihar	齐齐哈尔	*qíqíhāěr*
Hecheng Binguan	鹤城宾馆	*hèchéng bīnguǎn*
Hubin Binguan	湖滨宾馆	*húbīn bīnguǎn*
Huimin Fandian	回民饭店	*huímínfàndiàn*
Zhalong Nature Reserve	扎龙自然保护区	*zhālóng zìrán bǎohùqū*
Yabuli Ski Resort	亚布力滑雪场	*yàbùlì huáxuěchǎng*

past is celebrated with a restored shopping street, **Zhongyang Dajie**, as well as in a Russian cathedral that now houses a photographic history of Harbin. There are several Russian restaurants, and the locals have picked up on some of their neighbour's customs: as well as a taste for ice cream and pastries, the residents have a reputation as the hardest drinkers in China. On the outskirts of the city is a stark reminder of one of the country's blackest periods – during

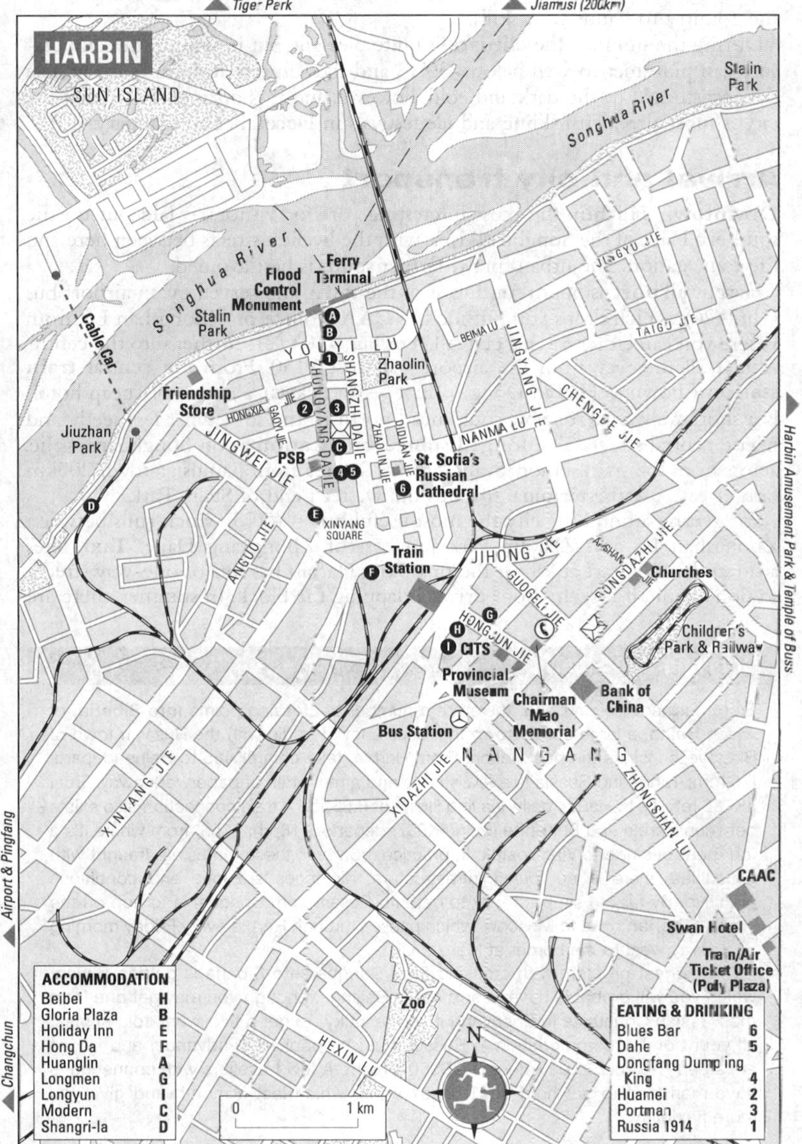

World War II, the former village, now suburb, of **Pingfang** was home to **Unit 731**, a Japanese military research base where prisoners of war were used as human guinea pigs.

Outside Harbin, tourist sites are limited, and journeys can be arduous, though new highways and trains have shortened travel times. Ornithologists will be interested in the **Zhalong Nature Reserve**, and particularly its rare red-crowned cranes, accessed from the mundane town of **Qiqihar**. If you're keen on skiing, you'll find **Yabuli**, the resort southwest of Harbin, the best place in the country to flaunt your skills.

During the summer, the **climate** is quite pleasant, but in winter the temperature can plummet to well below -30°C, and the sun sets at 4pm. Local people are accustomed to the dark and cold, however, and it is during winter that the city is most alive, with skiing and ice festivals in December and January.

Arrival and city transport

Downtown Harbin, the most interesting part for visitors, is laid out on the southern bank of the Songhua River, with the liveliest streets between here and the train station. The urban sprawl farther south is best avoided.

Harbin **airport** is 50km southwest of the town, and served by an airport bus (1hr; ¥20), which drops you outside the **CAAC** office on Zhongshan Lu, from where you can either catch a taxi (¥12) or bus #103 (¥1) further into the centre. A taxi all the way from the airport will cost ¥150. From the central **train station** (shown as Harbin Dong – "East" – on tickets), a clutch of cheap hotels is a short walk away, or you could head north to the somewhat less seedy and hectic central streets. The **long-distance bus station** is on Songhuajiang Jie, across from the train station. Summertime **ferries** from Jiamusi, a town 200km farther east, use the terminal towards the western end of Stalin Park.

For getting around the city, the most useful **bus** is #103, which runs between Zhongshan Lu and Zhaolin Park just east of Zhongyang Dajie. **Taxi** fares around the city start at ¥8 for the first 3km; Harbin has lots of one-way streets, so don't panic if it seems your driver is lapping the block. In summer, there are

Crossing into Siberia

From northern Heilongjiang, there are a number of crossing points **into Siberia**, of which **Heihe**, a large border town that sees a lot of traffic with the Russian town of Blagoveščensk, is the best option. From Harbin, take train #K485 to Heihe (departs 6.54pm; 12hr), and Russia is a few strides and a mountain of paperwork away. Train #K486 returns to Harbin daily, leaving Heihe at 6.53pm. A train connection also exists between Harbin and **Suifenhe** (train #K607; departs 7.18pm; 11hr), from where it's a four-hour bus ride to Vladivostok. In practice, however, these routes are fraught with difficulties; there is no tourist infrastructure, distances are long and conditions primitive. By far the simplest way to get into Russia from Dongbei is to hop on the **Trans-Siberian train** to Moscow, which passes through Harbin every Friday morning on its way west to the border at Manzhouli.

The biggest problem with crossing from Dongbei into Siberia is getting a **visa**, which you will probably have to sort out in Beijing, although you may get one from the Russian Consulate in Shenyang if you're lucky. To get a two-week tourist visa, all your hotel accommodation in Russia must be booked in advance, and prices are steep – expect to pay at least US$50 a night. A few travellers with connections have managed to get hold of business visas, which last a month and give you more flexibility.

small boats (¥2–30) across the Songhua, or you can take the ferry (¥5). Good English **maps** of the city are sold in the gift shop at the *Holiday Inn*; alternatively, the *Hongda* sells detailed Chinese-only versions, and a less detailed tourist plan is available free at the *Shangri-La*.

Accommodation

Harbin is one of the less expensive cities of the northeast for accommodation. The choice of **hotels** is better than elsewhere in the region, and the prices almost reasonable. Always ask the front desk if they can lower the price a bit – they usually will, even at the high-end hotels.

The hotels around Zhongyang Dajie are the best option if you're staying for any length of time. There's a cluster around the train station – and the train station itself possesses one of the cheapest places to stay in the form of the grim *Station Hotel* – but the area is noisy, dirty and crowded. One interesting feature of this area, however, is the row of women sitting in glass-fronted boxes behind the *Longyun Hotel* who bang their combs on the glass as you pass by. The women are, in fact, masseuses, and quote a price of ¥50 for a 45-minute rub, though you can bargain this down.

Beibei Directly across from the train station ⓣ0451/82570960, ⓕ82570972. Formerly a seedy dive called the *Beiyuan*, the *Beibei* has been reincarnated and refurbished under new management – the hot water now works, but rates remain reasonable. ❸

Gloria Plaza 259 Zhongyang Dajie ⓣ0451/8670000, ⓕ86770088. Smart four-star affair excellently located at the top of Zhongyang Dajie looking out across the river towards Sun Island. As with the *Holiday Inn*, discounts can make this a comfortably affordable option. ❼

Holiday Inn 90 Jingwei Jie ⓣ0451/84887205, ⓦwww.holiday-inn.com/harbinchn. Fading a bit, but good value for its location at the head of Zhongyang Dajie, as well as the very helpful English-speaking staff. Year-round discounts can dramatically cut rates. ❼

Hongda 2 Shangzhi Dajie ⓣ0451/84637582, ⓕ87680577. Clean, friendly and cheap, and just a 5min walk from Zhongyang Lu. Breakfast included. ❸

Huangjin 261 Zhongyang Dajie ⓣ0451/55569977. Right next to the *Gloria Plaza*, this offers an excellent location, especially given the price – which is thoroughly negotiable – but don't expect too many creature comforts. ❸

Longmen 85 Hongqi Jie ⓣ0451/86791999. A grand old place built in 1901 as the *Chinese Eastern Railway Hotel*, this restored gem is a snapshot of Harbin's bicultural past. If you don't stay here, pop in to admire the woodwork, sculptures, and English-language captions on the photographs – and ask to see the suite, used by the warlord Zhang Xueliang and later by Chairman Mao. The ordinary rooms are pleasant, and the staff top-notch. Bargaining can lower rates to under ¥300. ❻

Longyun ⓣ0451/82830102, ⓕ53634937. A clean, modern place a few doors to the right of the *Beibei* as you exit the train station. ❸

Modern 89 Zhongyang Dajie ⓣ0451/84884199, ⓕ84614997. The name is a misnomer, as this place was built in 1906 and survives as Harbin's oldest hotel. An elegant building on one of the city's busiest streets, it's bursting with character, with European- and Russian-style restaurants and 160 rooms. From Zhongyang Dajie, you enter via the lobby of a bank. ❼

Shangri-La 555 Youyi Lu ⓣ0451/84858888, ⓦwww.shangri-la.com. Harbin's only five-star hotel overlooks Stalin Park, Zhongyang Dajie and Zhaolin Park, making it the best place to stay during the Ice Festival. Book early. ❾

The City and around

Harbin is more a recreational centre than a cultural Mecca, a place to shop and explore the streets. A good starting point is the **Daoli** district, in the triangle outlined by **Diduan Jie** and **Jingwei Jie**, where there are plenty of brand-name clothing boutiques, fur shops and department stores. The smaller streets and alleys around here are the best places to see the city's **Russian architecture**, with its

Harbin festivals

In compensation for the cruel winter weather, the annual **Ice Festival**, centred on Zhaolin Park, is held from January 5 to February 5 – though with the influx of tourists, the dates extend each year. At this time, the park becomes a fairy-tale landscape with magnificent sculptures – sometimes entire buildings, complete with slides, stairways, arches and bridges – made of ice, carved with chainsaws and picks, and often with coloured lights inside them to heighten the psychedelic effect. Sculptors, some of them teenagers, work in -20°C December weather, earning ¥20 for a twelve-hour day. Highlights of past festivals have included detailed replicas of St Paul's Cathedral and life-size Chinese temples, though these days cartoon characters outnumber more traditional Chinese subject matter. Over on Sun Island, a snow sculpture display is held, the highlights of which are the toboggan and snow-tube pistes. It's as much fun watching ecstatic Chinese bounce down the slopes as it is sledding. You can walk across the river yourself or take a horse-drawn carriage for ¥10. Festival's end is marked with fireworks and pickaxes; visitors are encouraged to destroy the icy artwork by hand.

In summer, Harbin hosts a classical and traditional **music festival** from the middle to the end of July, during which orchestras and smaller groups play in the city's eight theatres.

decaying stucco facades and elegant balconies. There's an extensive market selling women's clothes off Xinyang Square, while the best large department stores are on Diduan Jie and **Zhongyang Dajie**.

Shops along the latter road have all been restored, with plaques out front in English detailing their past lives as colonial homes and stores. Make sure you go in the department store at no. 107, if only to see its spectacular skylight and rendition of a section from Michelangelo's Sistine Chapel mural, which hangs on the back wall. Across the street is another beautiful structure, the Jiaoyu Bookstore, well worth exploring. There are numerous good restaurants and bars along Zhongyang Dajie, which is paved with cobblestones and closed to cars. At the north end, a modern shopping mall, including a Walmart, rather encroaches on the atmosphere, but can be useful for locating Western "essentials". In winter, ice sculptures line the street, while summer sees pavement cafés set up.

The cathedral and around

The most beautiful and interesting sight in Harbin has to be the Russian Orthodox **cathedral** (formerly St Sofia's, built in 1907) on Zhaolin Jie. Turn east off Zhongyang Dajie on to Xi Shi Er Dao, and carry on until you hit Government Square, which fronts a new department store; the church is right behind the store. Set in its own square and restored to all its onion-domed glory, the cathedral now houses the **Harbin Architecture and Art Centre** (daily 8.30am–5pm; ¥25), with an interesting photographic survey of Harbin's history as a Russian railway outpost. Additional photos are available via touch-screen computers inside, although the captions, like those throughout the hall, are in Chinese.

Due to frosty relations with the Soviet Union in the 1960s and 70s (subject of Ha Jin's excellent *Ocean of Words*, a book of short stories by a former PLA soldier who was based on the Siberian border), Harbin also boasts a network of **underground bomb shelters** turned marketplaces. You can enter from the train station and walk all the way to Dongdazhi Jie and beyond. The markets sell a huge selection of goods, from pirated video discs to leather jackets.

▲ A sculpture at Harbin's Ice Festival

Along Dongdazhi Jie

Heading southeast from the train station, when they aren't filming historical dramas here you can enter a Russian-era mansion, the mansard-roofed **Chairman Mao Memorial** (daily 9am–4pm; ¥6), named for its most famous post-Revolution guest. The home is at the junction of Hongjun Jie and Dongdazhi Jie, next to the *Sinoway Hotel*. Diagonally across the street, at 48-50 Hongjun Jie, is the faded **Provincial Museum** (daily 9am–4pm; ¥10). Entered through an anonymous set of doors lacking any English signage between a sports shop and a shoe shop, the museum's collection has certainly seen better days. With virtually no English explanations, there would be no reason to visit were it not for the dinosaur, mammoth and woolly rhino skeletons secreted away upstairs. Just beyond, the junction with **Guogeli Jie** (formerly called Fendou Lu) is an up-and-coming area for drinking and shopping. One spin-off of improved Sino-Indian relations is the mall here called India Street, where bemused Indian shopkeepers sell trinkets and curry to camera-wielding Chinese tourists.

Out from the centre, there are some nice old working **churches** in the Nangang District. At 25 Dongdazhi Jie is a German Lutheran chapel built in 1914, while just a little further on at no. 268 you can peek inside an onion-domed Russian Orthodox building.

Continuing along Dongdazhi, you'll eventually come to a long street market, hawking the usual collection of clothes, shoes and DVDs. This in turn leads to the **Temple of Bliss** (daily 8am–4pm; ¥10), itself surrounded by tourist shops and stalls. Built in the 1920s, the Buddhist complex includes an architecturally impressive seven-tiered pagoda, and the smattering of monks suggests there is at least some genuinely religious, as well as mercantile, activity. At the end of all this lies **Harbin Amusement Park**, its huge ferris wheel dwarfing the only in-town competition – a significantly smaller effort in Zhaolin Park.

Along the river

The **riverbank** area is another worthwhile district to explore, starting from the **Flood Control Monument** at the bottom of Zhongyang Dajie. Built in 1958, the monument commemorates the many thousands who have died in the Songhua floods, and has been updated to mark the horrible floods in the summers of 1989 and 1998. The square here is a popular hangout for local people, who gather to feed pigeons and fly kites, as is **Stalin Park**, a strip of land along the east bank of the river that's particularly lively on weekends. People come to what must be China's last public memorial to Stalin in order to wash their clothes, meet and chat, even bathe in the river – the last is not a good idea, as mercury levels in the water are so high that fish can no longer survive in it. Others cluster around palm-readers and storytellers who relate old Chinese folk legends. Just southeast of the monument, **Zhaolin Park**, unremarkable in summer, is host to the spectacular winter **Ice Festival** (see box, p.218).

In winter, the **Songhua River** freezes solid and you can take a horse carriage, rent a go-kart or walk across – the ice is so thick it will support a fully loaded bus or lorry and gets used as a road. In summer, ferries (¥5) leave from near the Flood Control Monument for the northern bank and the busy resort and sanatorium village of **Taiyang (Sun) Island** (daily 8.30am–4.30pm; ¥10). You can also access Sun Island by **cable car** (¥50 one way). The island is an enormous park and leisure complex, with lakes for boating, swimming pools and fairground rides, as well as a **Tiger Park** (9am–4pm; ¥50); supposedly a refuge and breeding centre for the critically endangered Siberian tiger, this place smells more of commerce than conservation as park staff encourage visitors (for a small fee) to release domestic livestock to be stalked, slain and eaten by the animals.

Pingfang: unit 731

Harbin's most notorious and macabre attraction lies out in the suburbs, a forty-minute bus journey southwest of the centre, in **PINGFANG.** This was the home of a secret Japanese research establishment during World War II, now open to the public as a grisly **museum** (daily 9–11.30am & 1–3.30pm; ¥20). Here prisoners of war were injected with deadly viruses, dissected alive, and frozen or heated slowly until they died. More than three thousand people from China, Russia and Mongolia were murdered by troops from unit 731 of the Japanese army. After the war, the Japanese tried to hide all evidence of the base, and its existence only came to light through the efforts of Japanese investigative journalists. It was also discovered that, as with scientists in defeated Nazi Germany, the Americans gave the Japanese scientists immunity from prosecution in return for their research findings.

Near the terminus of bus #338, which you can catch one street west of Harbin's central train station square, the museum mostly comprises photographs labelled in Chinese. Looking at the displays, which include a painting of bound prisoners being used as bomb targets, it's easy to understand why many Chinese mistrust Japan to this day.

Eating, drinking and nightlife

Away from expensive regional delicacies such as bear paw and deer muzzle, available in upmarket hotels, **food** in Harbin is good value. Influenced by Russian cuisine, local cooking is characterized by the exceptionally heavy use of garlic – and a lot of potato. A favourite local dish is *xiaoji dunmogu* (chicken and stewed mushrooms). In summer and during the busy winter periods, tented areas resembling outdoor German beer halls spring up on the fringes of Zhongyang Dajie. They're a great spot to enjoy piping-hot barbecued skewers and a stein or two of ice-cold Harbin beer.

For **bars**, try Guogeli Jie east of the train station, or along the river, where drinking establishments tend to have a Russian theme. Top draw as regards **nightlife** is *Blues Bar* at 100 Dicuan Jie, where Russian and Chinese students – plus a rogues' gallery of older folk – dance the night away on weekends.

Restaurants and cafés

Dahe 60 Xi 14 Dao Jie. Reasonably priced Japanese restaurant serving all the favourites, from steaming bowls of udon noodles to well-sculpted plates of sashimi.

Dongfang Dumpling King 39 Zhongyang Dajie. The place to be seen in Harbin, with a wait for a table often required. The dumplings here are so good, you may be loath to leave. Everyone else seems to linger for another draught beer, another plate of food.

Huamei 112 Zhongyang Jie. A Harbin institution, food here is basic but good – the stroganoff comes particularly highly recommended – and unless you go for caviar, it won't break the bank.

Portman 53 Xi Qidao Jie. A European-style pub and grill with a heavily Russian-influenced menu.

Russia 1914 57 Xi Toudao Jie. The perfect place for afternoon tea, with an atmosphere to match – you can almost imagine yourself back in the early 1900s. Main meals are also served, but if you're just after a little something, it's hard to beat a cup of tea with Russian bread and jam.

Listings

Airlines The CAAC sales office is at 99 Zhongshan Lu (Ⓣ0451/82651188); airport buses run from outside every 20min (1hr; ¥20). If you're leaving the city by plane, allow an hour to get to the airport through the traffic.

Banks and exchange The Bank of China is on Zhongshan Lu (Mon–Fri 8am–noon & 1–5pm). The foreign-exchange counter is upstairs but get your passport photocopied downstairs first before you start queuing. You can also change money at its branch at 37 Zhaolin Jie (same hours).

Internet access There are plenty of Internet cafes throughout town, including one directly opposite the train station, next door to the *Longyun*; another across the street from the *Hongda* at 4 Shangzhu Dajie; and several on side streets running off Zhongyang Dajie.

Mail The main post office is at 51 Jianshe Jie (Mon–Sat 8am–6pm).

PSB 26 Duan Jie, off Zhongyang Dajie (Mon–Fri 8–11am & 2–5pm).

Telephones There's a telecom office (24hr) on Guogeli Jie, east of the train station.

Travel agents CITS (Ⓣ0451/53633151, Ⓦwww.hljcits.com), at 68 Hongjun Jie, is friendly and dependable, and the similarly titled CTIS (Ⓣ0451/53665858), round the corner from the railway station at 14 Songhuajiang Jie, specializes in tours across the province. Out near the CAAC office, Swan Travel (Ⓣ0451/88870333), in the grounds of the *Swan Hotel*, 95 Zhongshan Lu, can arrange ski trips and tours to areas farther north, including specialist hunting, fishing, skiing and bird-watching trips. All the above are able to organize ski packages to Yabuli, but with transport to the resort so plentiful, and accommodation at the slopes only available through *Windmill Village* (Ⓣ0451/53455088, Ⓦwww.yabuliski.com), it can be just as easy to arrange independently.

Qiqihar and the Zhalong Nature Reserve

Four hours' bus ride west of Harbin, **QIQIHAR** is one of the northeast's oldest cities, and still a thriving industrial centre. Alas, it's more fun to say the city's

Dongbei's minority communities

After forcing **minority communities** to embrace official communist culture during the 1950s and 60s, the Chinese government now takes a more enlightened – if somewhat patronizing – approach to the minority nations of the north. The **Manchu** people, spread across Inner Mongolia and Dongbei, are the most numerous and assimilated. Having lived so long among the Han, they are now almost identical, though Manchus tend to be slightly taller, and Manchu men have more facial hair. Manchus are noted for an elaborate system of etiquette and will never eat dog, unlike their Korean neighbours, who love it. The "three strange things" that the southern Chinese say are found in the northeast are all Manchu idiosyncrasies: paper windows pasted outside their wooden frame, babies carried by their mothers in handbags and women smoking in public (the latter, of course, can be a habit of Han and every other ethnicity in large cities).

In the inhospitable northern margins of Dongbei live small communities such as the **Hezhen**, one of the smallest minority nations in China with an estimated 1400 members. Inhabiting the region where the Songhua, Heilong and Wusuli (Ussuri) rivers converge, they're known to the Han Chinese as the "Fish Tribe", and their culture and livelihood centre around fishing. Indeed, they're the only people in the world to make clothes out of fish skin: the fish is gutted, descaled, then dried and tanned and the skins sewn together to make light, waterproof coats, shoes and gloves. More numerous are the **Daur**, 120,000 of whom live along the Nenjiang River. They are fairly seamlessly assimilated these days, but still retain distinctive marriage and funerary traditions, and have a reputation for being superb at hockey, a form of which they have played since the sixth century.

However, perhaps the most distinctive minority are the **Oroqen**, a tribe of nomadic hunters living in patrilineal clan communes called *wulileng* in the northern sub-Siberian wilderness. Although they have recently adopted a more settled existence, their main livelihood still comes from deer-hunting, while household items, tools and canoes are made from birch bark by Oroqen women. Clothes are fashioned from deer hide, and include a striking hat made of a roe deer head, complete with antlers and leather patches for eyes, which is used as a disguise in hunting.

name aloud than to stay here for more than a day. The only place of marginal interest is a big park, **Longsha Gongyuan** (¥2), in the south of town, accessible via the main north–south artery, Longhua Lu, which begins in front of the train station; buses #1 and #2 ply the route.

The main reason to come to Qiqihar is to visit the **Zhalong Nature Reserve** (¥20), 30km outside town. This marshy plain abounds in shallow reedy lakes and serves as the summer breeding ground of thousands of species of birds, including white storks, whooper swans, spoonbills, white ibis and – the star attractions – nine of the world's fifteen species of **crane**. Most spectacular of these is the endangered red-crowned crane, a lanky black-and-white bird over a metre tall, with a scarlet bald patch. It has long been treasured in the East as a paradigm of elegance – the Japanese call it the Marsh God – and is a popular symbol of longevity, as birds can live up to sixty years. The birds mate for life, and the female only lays one or two eggs each season, over which the male stands guard. The best time to visit the reserve is from April to June, when the migrants have just arrived, though the viewing season extends through September. Walking around the reserve, although not forbidden, is not encouraged by the keepers, or the murderous swarms of mosquitoes – come prepared. Binoculars are a good idea, too. Dedicated ornithologists might like to spend a few days here, but for most people an afternoon crouched in the reedbeds will be enough.

Practicalities

Buses to the reserve (1hr; ¥5) leave from Qiqihar's **bus station**, 1km south down Longhua Lu, on the left, and also from in front of the **train station**. A taxi will cost ¥130 return, depending on how long you make the driver wait around. Splendid though the birds are, it can be difficult to fill the hours the bus timetable obliges you to spend in Qiqihar, so consider devoting part of your visit to the flat-bottomed-boat **tour** that leaves from the reserve entrance; book through CITS (☎0452/2474646) at the *Hubin Hotel*.

Visitors to Zhalong have to stay in nearby Qiqihar. The two tourist **hotels** are the two-star *Hecheng* (☎0452/2712908; ❺) and *Hubin* (☎0452/2713124; ❺). They're in the same compound at 4 Wenhua Dajie, on the route of bus #15 from the train station. The *Huimin Fandian*, across the street from the station on the left as you exit, is a good place to eat; a bowl of Muslim-style pulled noodles is ¥3.

Yabuli

Regarded as the premier ski resort in China, **YABULI** is the place to be for Heilongjiang's **International Ski Festival**, which takes place from December 5 to January 5. The resort's 3,800-metre piste spreads across the southern side of Guokui (literally Pot-lid) Mountain (1300m), 194km southeast of Harbin. There's also a 2.5-kilometre steel **toboggan run**, built in 1996 when the resort hosted the Asian Winter Games. Six lifts shuttle an average of 10,000 skiers per day during the winter months. Although popular, a visit to Yabuli should come with at least a couple of provisos: the pistes are nowhere near as good as those in Europe, North America or Japan, and neither are they as cheap to ski. If you're after a proper skiing holiday, this is not the place, and if you just want a couple of hours' fun, the slopes cropping up outside Beijing and many of the other northern cities offer much better value for money and are far less hassle to get to.

In Yabuli, ski season runs from October to March and lift tickets and gear rental costs ¥200 for two hours, ¥300 for a half day and ¥600 for a full day. Private skiing lessons also run on a sliding scale; with English-speaking instructors at a premium, expect to pay ¥150 for an hour.

In winter, resort buses depart frequently from in front of Harbin's **train station** (3hr; ¥80). The only place to stay at Yabuli is the *Windmill Village Resort* (☎0451/53455088; ❻–❾), which has a wide variety of rooms, almost all of which are overpriced. Packages covering travel, accommodation and skiing can be booked at CITS and other travel agents in Harbin and throughout China.

Travel details

Trains

Changchun to: Beijing (12 daily; 6–15hr); Dandong (2 daily; 9hr); Harbin (32 daily; 2–3hr); Jilin (11 daily; 1hr 30min–2hr); Shenyang (42 daily; 2–4hr); Tonghua (2 daily; 6-8hr).

Dalian to: Beijing (2 daily; 10-11hr); Dandong (daily; 10hr 30min); Harbin (6 daily; 9–13hr) Shenyang (30 daily; 3hr 30min–6hr).

Dandong to: Beijing (2 daily; 14–21 hr); Changchun (2 daily; 9hr); Dalian (daily; 11 hr); Shenyang (10 daily; 3–5hr).

Harbin to: Beijing (10 daily; 10–18hr); Changchun (32 daily; 2–3hr); Daqing (27 daily; 1hr 30min–3hr); Jilin (2 daily; 5–6hr); Moscow (weekly; 6 days); Qiqihar (21 daily; 3–4hr); Shanghai (daily; 31hr); Shenyang (33 daily; 5–7hr).
Jilin to: Beijing (2 daily; 11–17hr); Changchun (11 daily; 1hr 30min–2hr); Dalian (3 daily; 13hr–15hr); Harbin (4 daily; 5–6hr); Shenyang (12 daily; 5hr–9hr 30min).
Qiqihar to: Bei'an (3 daily; 4hr); Beijing (4 daily; 15–20hr); Hailar (6 daily; 7hr 30min–13hr), Harbin (21 daily; 3–4hr).
Shenyang to: Beijing (32 daily; 4hr–17hr); Changchun (46 daily; 2–4hr); Dalian (31 daily; 3hr 30min–6hr); Dandong (9 daily; 3hr 30min–6hr); Harbin (32 daily; 3–7hr); Jilin (11 daily; 5hr–11hr 30min); Tonghua (3 daily; 6–7hr).
Tonghua to: Baihe (3 daily; 6hr 30min–8hr); Beijing (daily; 15hr 30min); Changchun (2 daily; 7–8hr); Shenyang (4 daily; 6hr–7hr 30min).

Buses

Bus connections are comprehensive and can be picked up to all major towns from the bus station or in front of the train station. For some stretches, buses are faster and more convenient than trains, especially from Harbin to the west and south; Changchun to Jilin and Shenyang; and Shenyang to Dalian. Away from the major cities, however, roads turn rough and the journeys arduous.

Ferries

Dalian to: Tanggu (for Tianjin; daily or alternate days; 13–15hr); Weihai (2 daily; 8hr); Yantai (4 daily; 6hr).
Dandong to: Inchon (South Korea; 3 weekly; 20hr).
Harbin to: Jiamusi (daily in summer; 18hr).

Flights

Besides the domestic services listed, some useful international connections serve this part of China, including flights from Changchun to Seoul; from Dalian to Fukuoka, Hiroshima, Nagoya, Osaka, Seoul, Tokyo and Vladivostok; and from Shenyang to Bangkok, Osaka, Pyongyang, Seoul and Tokyo.
Changchun to: Beijing (11 daily; 1hr 30min); Chengdu (5 weekly; 5hr); Chongqing (3 weekly; 4hr 40min); Dalian (4 daily; 1hr 10min); Fuzhou (2 weekly; 4hr 20min); Guangzhou (daily; 5hr 40min); Hangzhou (daily; 2hr 50min); Hong Kong (2 weekly; 4hr 30min); Ji'nan (daily; 1hr 55min); Kunming (3 weekly; 6hr); Nanjing (daily; 2hr 15min); Qingdao (daily; 1hr 35min); Shanghai (3 daily; 2hr 30min); Shenzhen (3 daily; 5hr); Xiamen (8 weekly; 5hr); Xi'an (3 weekly; 4hr 10min); Yanji (2 daily; 1hr); Yantai (daily; 2hr 25min).
Dalian to: Beijing (12 daily; 1hr 10min); Changchun (3 daily; 1hr); Changsha (2 daily; 3hr 40min); Chengdu (2 daily; 3hr 40min); Chongqing (4 weekly; 3hr); Fuzhou (daily; 3hr 30min); Guangzhou (3 daily; 3hr 15min); Guilin (2 weekly; 4hr 25min); Haikou (daily; 3hr 35min); Hangzhou (2 daily; 2hr); Harbin (3 daily; 1hr 25min); Hefei (weekly; 1hr 50min); Hong Kong (daily; 3hr 25min); Jilin (3 weekly; 1hr 20min); Ji'nan (2 daily; 1hr); Kunming (daily; 5hr); Luoyang (3 weekly; 1hr 40min); Nanjing (3 daily; 1hr 30min); Ningbo (daily; 1hr 50min); Qingdao (5 daily; 40min); Qinhuangdao (3 weekly; 1hr); Sanya (3 weekly; 6hr 30min); Shanghai (7 daily; 1hr 30min); Shenyang (daily; 50min); Shenzhen (3 daily; 4hr 50min); Taiyuan (daily; 3hr 30min); Tianjin (2 daily; 1hr); Wenzhou (daily; 2hr); Wuhan (8 weekly; 3hr); Xiamen (2 daily; 3hr 35min); Xi'an (daily; 2hr 20min); Yanji (daily; 2hr 30min); Yantai (daily; 35min); Zhengzhou (9 weekly; 1hr 45min).
Dandong to: Sanya (3 weekly; 6hr 25min); Shanghai (3 weekly; 2hr 20min); Shenzhen (3 weekly; 5hr 35min).
Harbin to: Beijing (13 daily; 1hr 50min); Chengdu (daily; 5hr 50min); Chongqing (4 weekly; 3hr 50min); Dalian (4 daily; 1hr 20min); Fuzhou (daily; 4hr 25min); Guangzhou (2 daily; 5hr 35min); Guiyang (3 weekly; 5hr 35min); Haikou (4 weekly; 5hr 30min); Hangzhou (daily; 3hr 10min); Hong Kong (4 weekly; 4hr 40min); Ji'nan (daily; 2hr 10min); Kunming (daily; 7hr); Nanjing (daily; 3hr 50min); Ningbo (4 weekly; 3hr); Qingdao (4 daily; 1hr 50min); Sanya (4 weekly; 7hr); Shanghai (7 daily; 2hr 40min); Shenyang (2 daily; 55min); Shenzhen (daily; 5hr); Tianjin (daily 3hr); Wenzhou (5 weekly; 4hr 30min); Wuhan (daily; 4hr); Xiamen (2 daily; 5hr); Xi'an (daily; 3hr); Zhengzhou (7 weekly; 3hr 40min).
Jilin to: Beijing (4 weekly; 1hr 40min); Dalian (3 weekly; 1hr 20min); Guangzhou (2 weekly; 6hr 35min); Shanghai (2 weekly; 2hr 30min).
Qiqihar to: Beijing (3 weekly; 1hr 50min); Guangzhou (2 weekly; 5hr 55min); Shanghai (2 weekly; 2hr 50min).
Shenyang to: Beijing (7 daily; 1hr 15min); Changsha (daily; 3hr); Chengdu (daily; 4hr 30min); Chongqing (daily; 3hr 15min); Dalian (daily; 50min); Fuzhou (daily; 2hr 50min); Guangzhou (3 daily; 3hr 45min); Guiyang (3 weekly; 4hr 40min); Haikou (daily; 5hr 30min); Hangzhou (daily; 2hr 20min); Harbin (2 daily; 1hr); Hefei (4 weekly; 1hr 45min); Hohhot (3 weekly; 1hr 30min); Hong Kong

(4 weekly; 4hr 35min); Ji'nan (daily; 1hr 20min); Kunming (2 daily; 5hr 10min); Lanzhou (7 weekly; 3hr 10min); Nanjing (6 weekly; 1hr 50min); Ningbo (daily; 2hr 10min); Qingdao (2 daily; 1hr 10min); Sanya (daily; 5hr 30min); Shanghai (8 daily; 2hr); Shantou (2 weekly; 4hr); Shenzhen (4 daily; 4hr); Shijiazhuang (4 weekly; 1hr 40min); Taiyuan (2 daily; 1hr 40min); Tianjin (8 weekly; 1hr 20min); Ürümqi (3 weekly; 6hr 30min); Wenzhou (daily 2hr 35min); Wuhan (daily; 3hr 25min); Xiamen (2 daily; 3hr 10min); Xi'an (daily; 2hr 30min); Yanji (2 daily; 1hr 10min); Yantai (daily; 1hr); Zhengzhou (daily; 2hr); Zhuhai (2 weekly; 6hr 30min).

CHAPTER 4 Highlights

✱ **Yungang Caves** See glorious Buddhist statuary from the fifth century, nestling in grottoes near Datong. See p.237

✱ **Walking Wutai Shan** The least developed of China's four Buddhist mountains is actually five flat peaks, perfect for independent exploration. See p.241

✱ **Pingyao** An intact Ming-era walled city, home to winding back alleys and a number of atmospheric hotels and guesthouses. See p.250

✱ **The Terracotta Army** No visit to China is complete without a peek at these warrior figurines, guarding the tomb of Qin Shi Huang near Xi'an. See p.278

✱ **Longmen Caves, Luoyang** Walk along a riverside promenade past caves peppering limestone cliff faces, containing more than 100,000 Buddhist carvings. See p.294

▲ The Terracotta Army

4

The Yellow River

The central Chinese provinces of **Shanxi**, **Shaanxi**, **Henan** and **Shandong** are linked and dominated by the **Yellow River** (*huánghé*), which has played a vital role in their history, geography and fortunes. The river is often likened to a dragon, a reference not just to its sinuous course, but also to its uncontrollable nature – by turns benign and malevolent. It provides much-needed irrigation to an area otherwise arid and inhospitable, but as its popular nickname, "China's Sorrow", hints, its floods and changes of course have repeatedly caused devastation, and for centuries helped to keep the delta region in Shandong one of the poorest areas in the nation.

The river's modern name is a reference to the vast quantities of yellow silt – **loess** – it carries, which has clogged and confused its course throughout history, and which has largely determined the region's geography. Loess is a soft soil, prone to vertical fissuring, and in Shanxi and northern Shaanxi it has created one of China's most distinctive landscapes, plains scarred with deep, winding crevasses, in a restricted palette of browns. In southern Shaanxi and Henan, closer to the river, the landscape is flat as a pancake and about the same colour. It may look barren, but where irrigation has been implemented the loess becomes **rich and fertile**, easily tillable with the simplest of tools. It was in this soil, on the Yellow River's flood plain, that Chinese civilization first took root (see p.230).

Of the four provinces, **Shanxi** is the poor relation, relatively underdeveloped and with the least agreeable climate and geography (temperatures regularly drop to -10°C in winter). But it does have some great attractions, most notably the **Yungang cave temples**, and a very beautiful holy mountain, **Wutai Shan**. Dotted around the small towns along the single rail line leading south to the Yellow River plain are quirky temples and villages that seem stuck in the nineteenth century. **Shaanxi** province is more of the same, yet its wealthy and historically significant capital city, **Xi'an**, is one of China's biggest tourist destinations, with as many temples, museums and tombs as the rest of the region put together, and the **Terracotta Army** deservedly ranking as one of China's premier sights. The city is also home to a substantial **Muslim** minority, whose cuisine is well worth sampling. Within easy travelling distance of here, following the Yellow River east, are two more holy mountains, **Hua Shan** and **Song Shan** (home of the legendary **Shaolin temple**), and the city of **Luoyang** in **Henan**, with the superb **Longmen cave temples** and **Baima Si** just outside. Henan's capital, **Zhengzhou**, is most important as a transport nexus, though just east is the appealing lakeside town of **Kaifeng**, a small place with little grandeur but a strong local character. East again lies **Shandong**, a province with less of a distinctive identity, but home to more small and

intriguing places: **Qufu**, the birthplace of Confucius, with its giant temple and mansion; **Tai Shan**, the most popular holy mountain in the area; and the coastal city of **Qingdao**, which offers a couple of beaches and a ferry service to South Korea.

With generally good transport infrastructure, a well-developed tourist industry and an agreeable climate outside the winter months, **travel** in the region presents few difficulties, although the rail network in Shanxi and northern Shaanxi is noticeably sparse. Sadly, the capricious nature of the river makes river travel impossible in the region. All towns, cities and tourist areas have accommodation catering for a wide range of budgets, with a glut of youth hostels in the most popular destinations.

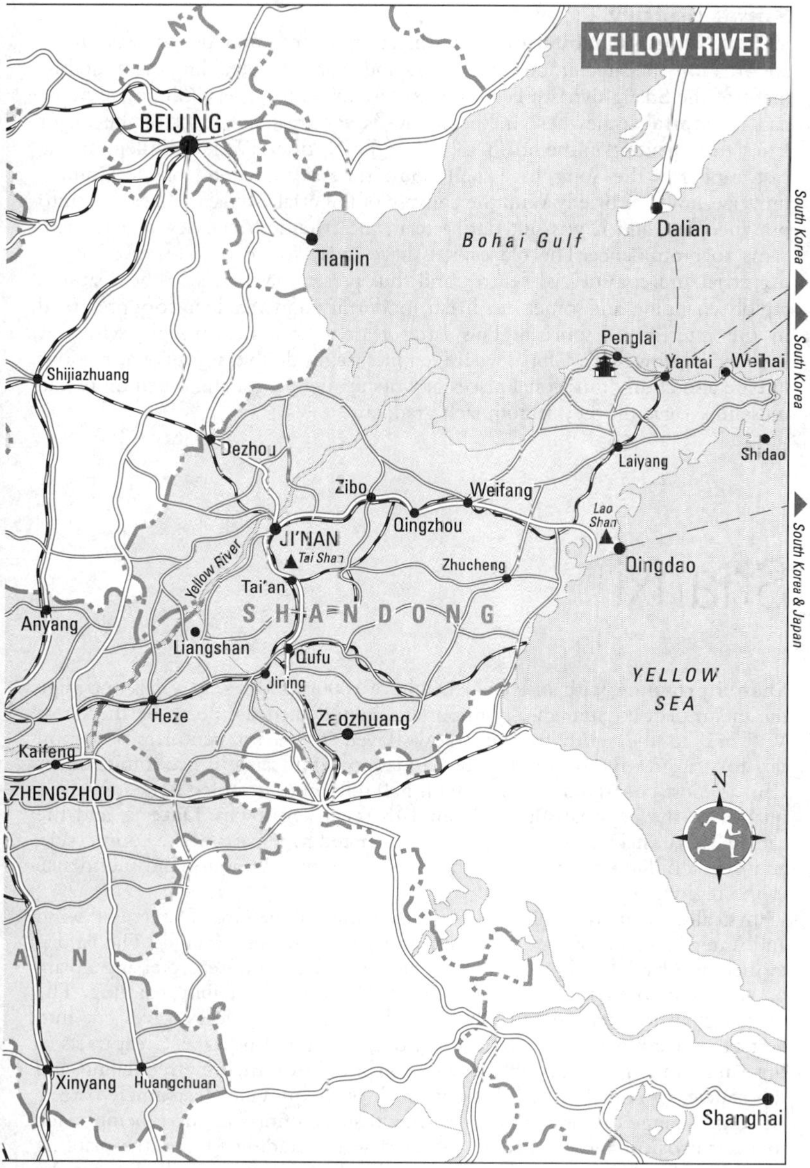

Some history

Sites of **Neolithic habitation** along the river are common, but the first major conurbation appeared around three thousand years ago, heralding the establishment of the Shang dynasty. For the next few millennia, every Chinese dynasty had its **capital** somewhere in the Yellow River area, and most of the major cities, from Datong in the north, capital of the Northern Wei, to Kaifeng in the east, capital of the Song, have spent some time as the centre of the Chinese universe, however briefly. With the collapse of imperial China, the area sank into provincialism, and it was not until late in the twentieth century that it again came to prominence. The old capitals have today found new leases of life as industrial and commercial centres, and thus present two sides to the visitor: a rapidly changing, and sometimes harsh, modernity; and a static history, preserved in the interests of tourism. This latter feature contrasts strongly with, for instance, southwestern China, where temples might double as tourist attractions but are also clearly functional places of worship; here, most feel much more like museums – even if they seldom lack grandeur.

Shanxi

Shanxi province, with an average height of 1000m above sea level, is one huge mountain plateau. Strategically important, bounded to the north by the Great Wall and to the south by the Yellow River, it was for centuries a bastion territory against the northern tribes. Today, its significance is economic: this is China's most **coal-rich** province, with 500 million tons mined here annually, a quarter of the national supply. Around the two key towns, **Datong** and the capital **Taiyuan**, open-cast mining has obliterated large parts of the countryside, and over a million people had to be recently rehoused due to land subsidence in the region.

Physically, Shanxi is dominated by the proximity of the Gobi Desert, and wind and water have shifted sand, dust and silt right across the province. The land is farmed, as it has been for millennia, by slicing the hills into steps, creating a plain of ribbed hillocks that look like the realization of a cubist painting. The dwellings in this terrain often have mud walls, or are simply caves cut into vertical embankments, seemingly a part of the strange landscape. Great tracts of this land, though, are untillable, due to **soil erosion** caused by tree felling, and the paucity of rainfall, which has left much of the province fearsomely barren, an endless range of dusty hills cracked by fissures. Efforts are now being made to arrest **erosion** and the advance of the desert, including a huge tree-planting campaign. Sometimes, you'll even see wandering dunes held in place by immense nets of woven straw.

While Shanxi's cities are generally functional and laminated in coal dust, once you get beyond them – sometimes not even very far – things improve dramatically. Tourism staff in the province call the province a "museum above the ground", a reference to the many unrestored but still intact **ancient buildings** that dot the region, some from dynasties almost unrepresented elsewhere in China. Just outside Datong, the **Yungang cave temples** are one of China's

Cave houses

A common sight among the folds and fissures of the dry loess plain of northern Shanxi (and neighbouring Shaanxi) are **cave dwellings**, a traditional form of housing that's been in use for nearly two thousand years. Hollowed into the sides of hills terraced for agriculture, they house more than eighty million people, and are eminently practical – cheap, easy to make, naturally insulated and long-lasting. In fact, a number of intact caves in Hejin, on the banks of the Yellow River in the west of the province, are said to date back to the Tang dynasty. Furthermore, in a region where flat land has to be laboriously hacked out of the hillside, caves don't take up land that could be cultivated.

The **facade** of the cave is usually a wooden frame on a brick base. Most of the upper part consists of a wooden lattice – designs of which are sometimes very intricate – faced with white paper, which lets in plenty of light, but preserves the occupants' privacy. Tiled eaves above protect the facade from rain damage. Inside, the **single-arched chamber** is usually split into a bedroom at the back and a living area in front, furnished with a *kang*, whose flue leads under the bed and then outside to the terraced field that is the roof – sometimes, the first visible indication of a distant village is a set of smoke columns rising from the crops.

Such is the popularity of cave homes that prosperous cave dwellers often prefer to build themselves a new courtyard and another cave rather than move into a house. Indeed, in the suburbs of towns and cities of northern Shaanxi, **new concrete apartment buildings** are built in imitation of caves, with three windowless sides and an arched central door. It is not uncommon even to see soil spread over the roofs of these apartments with vegetables grown on top.

major Buddhist art sites, easily taken in en route between Beijing and Hohhot in Inner Mongolia. Not quite as accessible, **Wutai Shan** is a holy mountain on the northeastern border with Hebei, with an unusually devout atmosphere and beautiful alpine scenery. Farther south, all within a bus ride of the towns spread along the rail line between Taiyuan and Xi'an, are a host of little places worth a detour, the highest profile of which is **Pingyao**, an old walled town preserved entirely from its Qing-dynasty heyday as a banking centre. West of here and surprisingly time-consuming to reach, the Yellow River presents its fiercest aspect at **Hukou Falls**, as its chocolate-coloured waters explode out of a short, tight gorge.

Datong and around

Gritty, polluted and unattractive, there would seem to be little reason to visit **DATONG**, Shanxi's "northern capital", situated near the border with Inner Mongolia. Two huge coal-fired power stations sit in the outskirts, one of which supplies electricity for Beijing, the other for the whole of Shanxi province, and their fallout covers the streets, buildings and population in grime. However, several ancient sites mark the city's glory days as the capital of two non-Han Chinese dynasties, and it's certainly worth stopping here for a day.

The Turkic **Toba** people took advantage of the internal strife afflicting central and southern China to establish their own dynasty, the **Northern Wei** (386–534 AD), taking Datong as their capital in 398 AD. Though the period was one of discord and warfare, the Northern Wei became fervent Buddhists and commissioned a magnificent series of **cave temples** at Yungang, just west of

Datong and around

Datong	大同	*dàtóng*
Drum Tower	鼓楼	*gǔlóu*
Huayuan Si	华严寺	*huáyán sì*
Nine Dragon Screen	九龙壁	*jiǔlóng bì*
Shanhua Si	善化寺	*shànhuà sì*
Yungang Caves	云冈石窟	*yúngāng shíkū*
Bus stations		
North Bus Station	汽车北站	*qìchē běizhàn*
Xinnan Bus Station	新南站	*xīnnán zhàn*
Yantong Xi Lu Depot	长途汽车站	*chángtú qìchēzhàn*
Accommodation		
Feitian Binguan	飞天宾馆	*fēitiān bīnguǎn*
Huangcheng Fandian	皇城饭店	*huángchéng fàndiàn*
Huayuan Dajiudian	花园大酒店	*huāyuán dàjiǔdiàn*
Lüguan	旅馆	*lǚguǎn*
Yuzeyuan Binguan	玉泽缘宾馆	*yùzéyuán bīnguǎn*
Yungang International	云冈国际酒店	*yún gāng guójì jiǔdiàn*
Restaurants		
Deyue Lou	得月楼	*déyuè lóu*
Meizhou Xiao Chi	眉州小吃	*méizhōu xiǎochī*
Mujia Zhai	穆家寨	*mùjiāzhài*
Yonghe	永和大酒店	*yǒnghé dàjiǔdiàn*
Hunyuan	浑源	*húnyuán*
Hanging Temple	悬空寺	*xuánkōng sì*
Heng Shan	恒山	*héngshān*
Heng Shan Binguan	恒山宾馆	*héngshān bīnguǎn*
Yingxian	应县	*yìngxiàn*
Jincheng Binguan	金城宾馆	*jīnchéng bīnguǎn*
Wood Pagoda	应县木塔	*yìngxiàn mùtǎ*

the city. Over the course of almost a century, more than a thousand grottoes were completed, containing over fifty thousand statues, before the capital was moved south to Luoyang, where construction began on the similar Longmen Caves (see p.294).

A second period of greatness came with the arrival of the Mongol **Liao dynasty**, also Buddhists, who made Datong their capital in 907. Their rule lasted two hundred years, leaving behind a small legacy of statuary and some fine temple architecture, notably in the **Huayan** and **Shanhua temples** in town, and a **wooden pagoda**, the oldest in China, in the nearby town of **Yingxian**. Datong remained important to later Chinese dynasties for its strategic position just inside the Great Wall, south of Inner Mongolia, and the tall **city walls** date from the early Ming dynasty. Though most visitors today are attracted by the Buddhist sites, Datong is the closest city to **Heng Shan**, one of the five holy mountains of Taoism, whose most spectacular building, the **Hanging Temple**, is firmly on the tour agenda. It's also possible to use Datong as the jumping-off point for an excursion to the Buddhist centre of **Wutai Shan** (see p.241).

Arrival, information and transport

Downtown Datong, bounded by square walls, is split by **Da Bei Jie** and **Da Xi Jie**, two busy, dead-straight shopping streets on north–south and

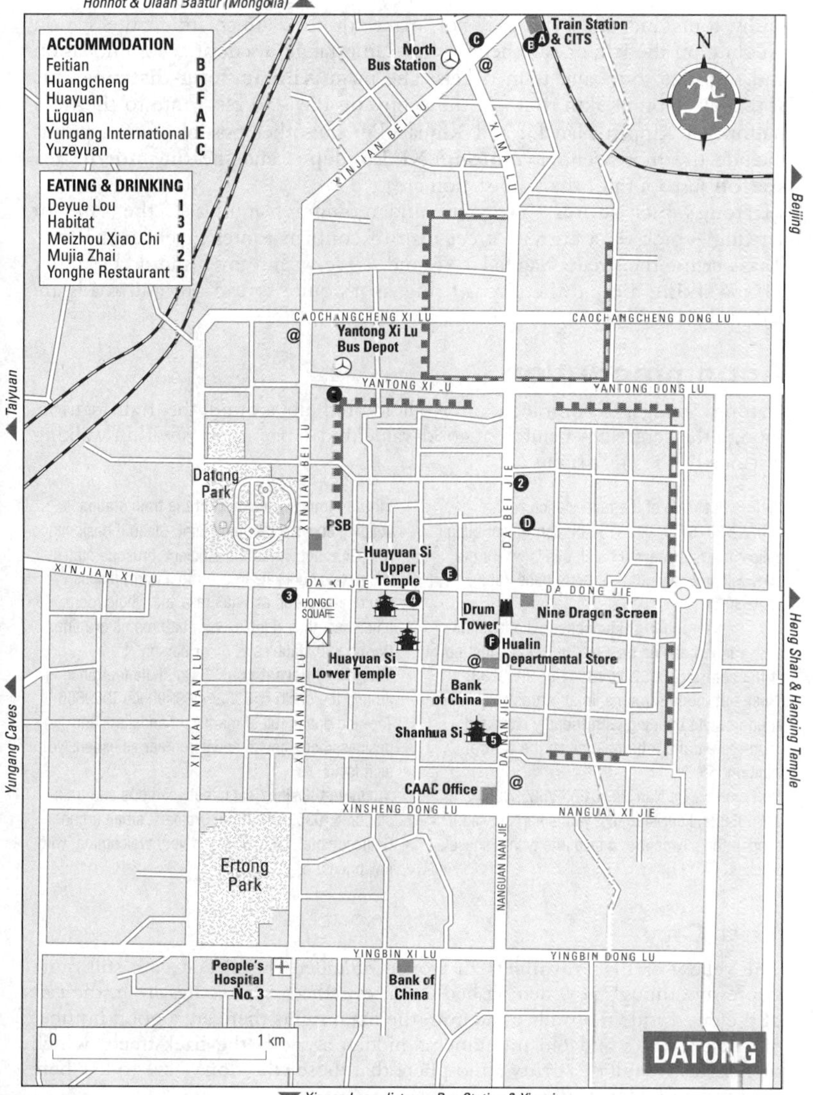

east–west axes, which intersect at the heart of the city, close to all the central attractions.

Datong's **airport** is 15km away; the airport bus service was uncertain at the time of writing and you might have to take a taxi into town (¥50). The **train station** is on the city's northern edge, at the end of Xinjian Bei Lu, around 2.5km from the centre – city bus #4 runs from here down Da Bei Jie before heading west along Da Xi Jie. You may be grabbed on arrival by a representative of the helpful station **CITS office** (6.30am–6.30pm; ⓣ0352/7124882 or 1350/9723056, ⓦwww.datongcits.com), at first indistinguishable from other pushy touts and taxi drivers; if not, make for their office inside the station building on the left, or call them – they can arrange discount accommodation and organize tours and train tickets. The main **Xinnan long-distance bus station** is around 5km south of the centre on the #30 bus route to the train station via Xinjian Nan Lu and Xinjian Bei Lu; other possible arrival points include the more central **Yantong Xi Lu depot** and the tiny **north bus station** just south of the train station area.

Datong's **bus routes** (¥1) were undergoing replanning at the time of writing – pick up a current street map to confirm routes given in the text. **Taxis** cruise the streets; flag fall is ¥5, and a ride within town should be under ¥10. **Walking** around the city is tiring, as it's quite spread out and roads are tediously straight.

Accommodation

Datong's budget accommodation is all located up around the train station, though the centre has a clutch of good-value mid-range options within walking distance of the city's sights.

Feitian East side of the train-station square ⓣ0352/2815117, ⓕ2813483. Convenient budget option in a fairly decent hotel; this is where the CITS will probably put you. Dorm beds ¥35, doubles ④

Huangcheng Huangcheng Jie, a small lane heading east off Da Bei Jie, just north of the centre ⓣ0352/2048444 or 2059788. Small but modern rooms, in an attractive, antique-style building with friendly staff and a good restaurant; a bargain given the central location. ⑤

Huayuan 59 Da Nan Jie ⓣ0352/5865825, ⓕ5865824. Four-star joint with smart service, bang in the city centre; a favourite with Chinese officials. ⑧

Lüguan Immediately east of the train station building above a fast-food joint. Clean if basic place with 24hr hot water and efficient, brusque staff. You're fairly unlikely to get into a dorm unless you're in a group and can take the whole room; otherwise, their doubles with bathrooms are fine. Dorms ¥30, doubles ¥75 per person.

Yungang International 38 Da Xi Jie (entrance is around the back) ⓣ0352/5869999, ⓕ5869666. Top-end option full of marble, chandeliers and businessmen, though nowhere near as expensive as it looks. ⑥

Yuzeyuan Xinjian Bei Lu, between bus and train station ⓣ0352/2807889. Ordinary, small urban Chinese hotel, fairly new and very welcoming, with low prices. ③

The City

The yellow earthen **ramparts** that once bounded the old city are still quite impressive, though now demolished in places – the best stretches are in the east of the city. Inside the walls, aside from the main sights there are a good number of small temples and old monuments hidden away in the backstreets, which themselves are full of a gritty atmosphere that those who don't have to live here might just find appealing.

The Drum Tower and Nine Dragon Screen

Just south of the crossroads of Da Xi Jie and Da Bei Jie, at the heart of the city, Datong's three-storey **Drum Tower** dates back to the Ming dynasty. You can't go inside, but it makes a useful landmark. A little way east on the south side of Da Dong Jie, the **Nine Dragon Screen** (7.30am–7.30pm; ¥10) is the largest of several similar Ming dynasty screens around the city; a lively forty-five-metre-long relief of nine sinuous dragons depicted in 426 multicoloured glazed tiles, rising from the waves and cavorting among suns. The only other dragon screens of this age are in Beijing, the main difference here being that these dragons have only four claws, indicating the dwelling of a prince, not an emperor (whose dragons had five claws). Originally, the screen stood directly in front of a palace, destroyed in the fifteenth century, as an unpassable obstacle to evil spirits, which, it was thought, could only travel in straight lines. A long, narrow pool in front of the screen is meant to reflect the dragons and give the illusion of movement when you look into its rippling surface.

Huayan Si

A few minutes west of the crossroads and south off Da Xi Jie, **Huayuan Jie** has been redeveloped recently in an "antique" style, though the shops lining the street sell only the usual tourist knick-knacks. A short way down are the remaining buildings of **Huayan Si**, originally a large temple dating back to 1062 AD during the Liao dynasty and now forming two complexes. The **Upper Temple** (daily 8am–6.30pm; ¥20), the first one you come to, is a little shabby, but its twelfth-century **Main Hall** is one of the largest in China, and is unusual for facing east – it was originally built by a sect that worshipped the sun. The roof is superb, a Tang-style design with two vertical "horns" fashioned to look like lions doing handstands. The cavernous interior has some wonderful Ming statuary including twenty life-size guardians, gently inclined as if listening attentively, but the main draw is the Qing-dynasty **frescoes** completely covering the walls, depicting Buddha's attainment of nirvana – sadly, the lighting is poor.

Turn right out of the entrance to this complex and you come to the **Lower Temple** (daily 8am–6.30pm; ¥20), notable for its rugged-looking hall, a rare Liao-dynasty construction from 1038, complete with contemporary statues. Halls surrounding the front courtyard form a **museum** of regional discoveries spanning the Liao, Jin, Khitan and Yuan eras.

Shanhua Si

South of the Drum Tower on Da Nan Jie and tucked away behind the *Yonghe* restaurant is the **Shanhua Si** (daily 8am–6pm; ¥20). A temple has stood here since the Tang dynasty, though what you see is a Ming restoration of a Jin structure. The buildings, with little decoration, thick russet walls and huge, chunky wooden brackets in the eaves, have a solid presence very different from the delicate look of later Chinese temples, and are impressive for their obvious age alone – one dates from 1154. The Jin-dynasty statues in the main hall, five Buddhas in the centre with 24 *lokapalas* (divine generals) lined up on either side, are exceptionally finely detailed. One of the outlying courtyards sports a **five dragon screen**, relocated from a monastery that once stood to the south of the city.

Eating and drinking

Datong is far enough north for **mutton hotpot** to figure heavily in the local cuisine, along with potatoes, which you can buy, processed into a starchy jelly and seasoned with sauces, from street stalls. Other typically northern dishes available are *zongyi* (glutinous rice dumplings) and *yuanxiao* (sweet dumplings).

There are plenty of inexpensive dumpling places up around the train-station area, with a clutch next to the north bus station. For hotpot, try the Muslim-run *Deyue Lou* on Yantong Xi Lu, across from the bus station, or *Mujia Zhai* on Da Bei Jie, where ¥30 buys enough meat and vegetables for two. *Meizhou Xiao Chi* is a great Sichuan-style snack house close to Huayan Si on Huayuan Jie, where almost everything is less than ¥5 and there are photos to help you order; while the *Yonghe Restaurant*, in front of Shanhua Si on Da Nan Jie, has a hotpot

Moving on from Datong

The **CAAC office** (☎0352/2052777 or 2043388) is on 1 Nanguan Nan Jie (daily 8.30am–5pm), with several flights weekly each to Beijing, Shanghai and Guangzhou. Ask here about an airport bus. **Train tickets** are straightforward enough to buy at the station, or at the advance-ticket office (8am–12.30pm & 2.30–6pm) at the corner of Nanguan Nan Jie and Nanguan Xi Jie. At the back of the station opposite the door, there's a comfortable waiting room (¥5) with armchairs and TV.

The main **long-distance bus station** is the Xinnan station south of town on the #30 bus route, for services to Taiyuan and Yingxian. Try the Yantong Xi Lu depot for departures to **Hunyuan**, **Baotou** and **Beijing**; the north bus station for Wutai Shan; and the train station forecourt for shared taxis and minibuses to Beijing or Taiyuan.

section, a snack section, and a restaurant specializing in Sichuanese and Cantonese cooking at around ¥60 a head. For a **drink**, the expat-oriented *Habitat* on Xinjian Nan Lu, across from Hongqi Square, has beer for ¥10, though there's little atmosphere except at weekends. Datong's latest **clubs** can be found near the Drum Tower, on Da Nan Jie and Da Xi Jie.

Listings

Banks and exchange The only place to cash traveller's cheques is at the main Bank of China (Mon–Fri 8am–6pm) on Yingbin Xi Lu; there's a small branch with an ATM at the southern end of Da Nan Jie.

Hospital People's Hospital No. 3 is in the south of the city on Yingbin Xi Lu, just west of the crossroads with Xinjian Nan Lu.

Internet access There's a net bar just south of the *Feitian* in the train station area, and one just west of the Hualin Department Store in the basement of a shopping centre.

Left luggage There's a left-luggage office outside the train station on the western side of the concourse (¥5).

Mail and telephones The large Russian-looking stately building fronting Hongqi Square, south of Da Xi Jie, houses both the post office (daily 8am–6pm) and a 24hr telecom office. Droves of women stand about selling cut-rate IC and IP phone cards.

PSB The police station (Mon–Sat 8.30am–noon & 2.30–6pm) is on Xinjian Bei Lu, 200m north of the post office; take along a Mandarin-speaker, since they're not particularly heedful to traveller needs.

Travel agents The train station CITS office (see "Arrival" section on p.232) is the city's most foreigner-friendly, able to book train and plane tickets for a ¥10–50 mark-up depending on ticket class. They also offer day-trips for ¥100 per person, or ¥225 including all entry fees and lunch, to Yungang Caves and the Hanging Temple; the Hanging Temple and Wooden Pagoda; and the caves and city temples.

Around Datong

The sights outside the city are far more diverting than those within. Apart from the **Yungang Caves**, several ancient buildings dotted around in nearby country towns are also worth checking out. Roads are sometimes bumpy and often blocked in winter, when transport times can double, but at least journeys are enlivened by great views: the lunar emptiness of the fissured landscape is broken only occasionally by villages whose mud walls seem to grow out of the raw brown earth. Some of the villages in the area still have their **beacon towers**, left over from when this really was a wild frontier.

Some **maps** of Datong include plans of Hunyuan and Yingxian, together with area maps showing the roads, so are worth picking up before you go. Getting around to all the sites on teeth-rattling public buses can be time-consuming, so consider taking a **CITS tour** – see Datong "Listings" above for details.

▲ The Yungang Caves

The Yungang Caves

Just 16km west of Datong, the monumental **Yungang Caves** (daily 8am–6.30pm; ¥60), a set of Buddhist grottoes carved into the side of a sandstone cliff, are a must. Built around 400 AD at a time of Buddhist revival, the caves were the first and grandest of the three major Buddhist grottoes (the latter two being the Longmen Caves in Luoyang and the Mogao Caves in Gansu) they also remain the best preserved. Access is straightforward: take **bus #3-2** (every 10–15min; ¥2)

Building the Yungang Caves

Construction of the Yungang Caves began in 453 AD, when Datong was the capital of the Northern Wei dynasty, and petered out around 525, after the centre of power moved to Luoyang. The caves were made by first hollowing out a section at the top of the cliff, then digging into the rock, down to the ground and out, leaving two holes, one above the other. As many as forty thousand craftsmen worked on the project, coming from as far as India and Central Asia, and there is much foreign influence in the **carvings**: Greek motifs (tridents and acanthus leaves), Persian symbols (lions and weapons), and bearded figures, even images of the Hindu deities Shiva and Vishnu, are incorporated among the more common dragons and phoenixes of Chinese origin. The soft, rounded modelling of the **sandstone figures** – China's first stone statues – lining the cave interiors has more in common with the terracotta carvings of the Mogao Caves near Dunhuang in Gansu, begun a few years earlier, than with the sharp, more linear features of Luoyang's later limestone work. In addition, a number of the seated Buddhas have sharp, almost Caucasian noses.

The caves' present condition is misleading, as originally the cave entrances would have been covered with wooden facades, and the sculptures would have been faced with plaster and brightly painted; the larger sculptures are pitted with regular holes, which would once have held wooden supports on which the plaster face was built. Over the centuries, some of the caves have inevitably suffered from weathering, though there seems to have been little vandalism, certainly less than at Luoyang.

from the train station, which travels via Xinjian Bei Lu and Xinjian Nan Lu and then heads out to the caves.

Arranged in three **clusters** (east, central and west) and numbered east to west from 1 to 51, the caves originally spread across an area more than 15km long, though today just a kilometre-long fragment survives. If it's spectacle you're after, just wander at will, but to get an idea of the changes of style and the accumulation of influences, you need to move sequentially between the three clusters. The earliest group is caves 16–20, followed by 7, 8, 9 and 10, then 5, 6 and 11 – the last to be completed before the court moved to Luoyang. Then followed 4, 13, 14 and 15, with the caves at the eastern end – 1, 2 and 3 – and cave 21 in the west, carved last. Caves 22–50 are smaller and less interesting.

The eastern caves

The easternmost late caves are slightly set apart from, and less spectacular than, the others. **Caves 1 and 2** are constructed around a single square central pillar, elaborately carved in imitation of a wooden stupa but now heavily eroded, around which devotees perambulated. **Cave 3**, 25m deep, is the largest in Yungang; an almost undecorated cavern, it may once have been used as a lecture hall. The three statues at the west end, a ten-metre-high Buddha and his two attendants, are skillfully carved and in good condition. The rounded fleshiness of their faces, with double chins and thick, sensuous lips, hints at their late construction, as they are characteristic of Tang-dynasty images. In **cave 4**, which again has a central pillar carved with images of Buddha, there's a well-preserved, cross-legged Maitreya Buddha on the west wall.

The central caves

The most spectacular caves are numbers 5–13, dense with **monumental sculpture**. Being suddenly confronted and dwarfed by a huge, seventeen-metre-high Buddha as you walk into **cave 5**, his gold face shining softly in the half-light, is an awesome, humbling experience. Other Buddhas of all sizes, a heavenly gallery, are massed in niches, which honeycomb the grotto's gently curving walls, and two Bodhisattvas stand attentive at his side.

Cave 6, though very different, is just as arresting. A wooden facade built in 1652 leads into a high, square chamber dominated by a thick central pillar carved with Buddhas and Bodhisattvas in deep relief, surrounded by flying Buddhist angels and musicians. The vertical grotto walls are alive with images, including reliefs depicting incidents from the **life of the Buddha** at just above head height, which were designed to form a narrative when read walking clockwise around the chamber. Easy-to-identify scenes at the beginning include the birth of the Buddha from his mother's armpit, and Buddha's father carrying the young infant on an elephant. The young prince's meeting with a fortune-teller – here an emaciated man with a sharp goatee, who (the story goes) predicted he would become an ascetic if confronted by disease, death and old age – is shown on the north side of the pillar. In an attempt to thwart this destiny, his father kept him in the palace all through his youth. Buddha's first trip out of the palace, which is depicted as a schematic, square Chinese building, is shown on the east wall of the cave, as is his meeting with the grim realities of life, in this case a cripple with two crutches.

Caves 7 and 8 are a pair, both square, with two chambers, and connected by an arch lined with angels and topped with what looks like a sunflower. The figures here, such as the six celestial worshippers above the central arch, are more Chinese in style than their predecessors in caves 16–20, perhaps indicating the presence of craftsmen from Gansu, which the Wei conquered in 439 AD.

Two figures on either side of the entrance to cave 8 are some of the best carved and certainly the most blatantly foreign in the complex: a five-headed, six-armed Shiva sits on a bird on the left as you enter, while on the right, a three-headed Vishnu sits on a bull. These Indian figures have distinctly Chinese features, however, and the bird, a garuda in Hindu mythology, is identical to the Chinese phoenix.

The columns and lintels at the entrances of **caves 9, 10 and 12** are awash with sculptural detail in faded pastel colours: Buddhas, dancers, musicians, animals, flowers, angels and abstract, decorative flourishes (which bear a resemblance to Persian art). Parts of cave 9 are carved with imitation brackets to make the interior resemble a wooden building. The tapering columns at the entrance to cave 12 are covered with tiny Buddhas, but look out for the cluster of musicians with strange-looking instruments depicted behind them.

The outstretched right arm of the fifteen-metre-high Buddha inside **cave 13** had to be propped up for stability, so his sculptors ingeniously carved the supporting pillar on his knee into a four-armed mini-Buddha. The badly eroded sculptures of **caves 14 and 15** are stylistically some way between the massive figures of the early western caves and the smaller reliefs of the central caves.

The western caves

Compared to the images in the central caves, the figures in these, the **earliest caves** (16–20) are simpler and bolder, and though they are perhaps more crudely carved, they are at least as striking. The **giant Buddhas**, with round faces, sharp noses, deep eyes and thin lips, are said to be the representations of five emperors. Constructed between 453 and 462 AD, under the supervision of the monk Tan Hao, all are in the same pattern of an enlarged niche containing a massive Buddha flanked by Bodhisattvas. The Buddha in **cave 16**, whose bottom half has disintegrated, has a knotted belt high on his chest, Korean-style. The Buddhas were carved from the top down, and when the sculptors of the Buddha in **cave 17** reached ground level they needed to dig down to fit his feet in. The same problem was solved in **cave 18** by giving the Buddha shortened legs. Despite the stumpy limbs, this is still one of the finest sculptures in the complex, in which charming details, including the rows of tiny Bodhisattvas carved into his robe, are set off by strong sweeping forms, such as the simplified planes of his face. The fourteen-metre-high Buddha in **cave 20**, sitting open to the elements in a niche that once would have been protected by a wooden canopy, is probably the most famous, and certainly the most photographed. The figure is characteristic of Northern Wei art, with the folds of his garments expressed by an ordered pattern, and his physiognomy and features formed by simple curves and straight lines. His huge ears almost touch his shoulders.

The small caves 21–51, the least spectacular of the set, are not much visited, but the ceiling of **cave 50** is worth a look for its flying elephants, which also appear in **cave 48**, and in **caves 50 and 51** there are sculptures of acrobats.

Heng Shan and the Hanging Temple

Heng Shan (8am–6pm; ¥60) is a range of peaks around 80km southeast of Datong near the town of **Hunyuan**, and is one of China's five main Taoist mountains. Its history as a religious centre stretches back more than two thousand years, and plenty of emperors have put in an appearance here to climb the highest peak, Xuanwu (2000m), a trend begun by the very first emperor, Qin Shi Huang. From the base of the mountain, an easy climb takes you to Heng Shan's main temple, **Hengzong Si**, via switchbacking paths through other smaller temples, about a thirty-minute walk up and twenty minutes down (a cable-car round trip costs ¥42). Heng shan's peak lies another forty minutes uphill from Hengzong Si, and might be the quietest place left on the mountain.

The **Hanging Temple** (daily 7am–6pm; ¥60) is on the valley road that runs up to Heng Shan, and you'll probably stop here first if you're on a tour. Clinging to the side of a sheer cliff face, the temple (its name literally translates as "Temple Suspended in the Void") is anchored by wooden beams set into the rock. There's been a temple on this site since the Northern Wei, though the buildings were periodically destroyed by the flooding of the Heng River (now no longer there, thanks to a dam upstream), occasioning the temple to be rebuilt higher and higher each time. What with souvenir stalls and a terraced garden below, the temple is a little disappointing at first, but it's a great deal more atmospheric once you're inside the rickety, claustrophobic structure. Tall, narrow stairs and plank walkways connect the six halls – natural caves and ledges with wooden facades – in which shrines exist to Confucianism, Buddhism and Taoism, all of whose major figures are represented in nearly eighty statues in the complex, made from bronze, iron and stone.

Practicalities

Buses to Hunyuan (1hr; ¥27) depart Datong's Yantong Xi Lu depot every fifteen minutes from 6.30am until 6pm. From here, catch a public tourist bus (¥2) to the base of the temple area. Transportation gets more difficult to arrange in low travel seasons, when it might make more sense to book a taxi for the round trip from Hunyuan (around ¥50 including waiting time).

To return to Hunyuan from the Hanging Temple or Heng Shan, be prepared to haggle with the vehicles for hire, which start at ¥20. The last bus back to Datong leaves Hunyuan at 6pm, though note that in summer it's possible to stay the night in Hunyuan and get a ride on to Wutai Shan on the morning bus from Datong (assuming that the pass is open): you can book seats through the *Hengshan Binguan* in Hunyuan.

Be warned, **restaurants** at Heng Shan and especially the Hanging Temple are a ridiculous rip-off – bring your own food if you're just here for the day.

The Wood Pagoda

At the centre of the small town of **YINGXIAN**, 75km south of Datong, the stately **Wood Pagoda** (daily 8am–6pm; ¥42), built in 1056 in the Liao dynasty, is one of the oldest wooden buildings in China, a masterful piece of structural engineering that looks solid enough to stand here for another millennium. The "Woody Tower", as the English sign explains, reaches nearly 70m high and is octagonal in plan, with nine internal storeys, though there are only six layers of eaves on the outside. At present, you can climb up as far as the second storey, though it's fairly certain that the structure will soon be closed off in the interests of conservation.

The first storey is taller than the rest with extended eaves held up by columns forming a cloister around a mud-and-straw wall. The original pagoda was constructed without nails, though there are plenty in the floors nowadays. The ceilings and walls of the spacious internal halls are networks of beams held together with huge, intricate **wooden brackets**, called *dougongs*, of which there are nearly sixty different kinds. Interlocking, with their ends carved into curves and layered one on top of another, these give the pagoda a burly, muscular appearance, and as structural supports they perform their function brilliantly – the building has survived seven earthquakes.

Originally, each storey had a statue inside, but now only one remains, an eleven-metre-tall Buddha with facial hair and stretched-out earlobes – characteristic of northern ethnic groups, such as the Khitan, who came to power in Shanxi during the Liao dynasty (916–1125 AD). During a recent renovation, a cache of **treasures** was found buried underneath the pagoda, including Buddhist sutras printed using woodblocks dating back to the Liao.

Buses to Yingxian from Datong (¥16) take two hours and leave from the Xinnan long-distance bus station. **Yingxian's bus station** is on the western section of the town's main east–west road, about 1km southwest of the pagoda. You can stay the night in Yingxian at the *Jinchen Binguan*, at 18 Xinjian Nan Lu, about 2km south of the pagoda on the main north–south road (Ⓣ0349/5022013; ❸). From Yingxian, there are buses to Hunyuan, about 50km away, for Heng Shan and the Hanging Temple; these leave every hour until 5pm – also the time of the last bus back to Datong. Alternatively, if you start early you can just about manage to see both the Hanging Temple and the Wood Pagoda by public transport in one (long) day.

Wutai Shan

One of China's four Buddhist mountains, the five flat peaks of **Wutai Shan** – the name means "Five-terrace Mountain" – rise around 3000m above sea level in the northeastern corner of Shanxi province, near the border with Hebei. The

Wutai Shan

Wutai Shan	五台山	*wǔtái shān*
Taihuai	台怀	*táihuái*
Bishan Si	碧山寺	*bìshān sì*
Dailuo Ding	黛螺顶	*dàiluó dǐng*
Foguang Si	佛光寺	*fóguāng sì*
Jinge Si	金阁寺	*jīngé sì*
Longquan Si	龙泉寺	*lóngquán sì*
Luohou Si	罗寺	*luóhóu sì*
Nanchan Si	南禅寺	*nánchán sì*
Nanshan Si	南山寺	*nánshān sì*
Shancai Si	山财寺	*shāncái sì*
Ta Yuan Si	塔院寺	*tǎyuàn sì*
Xiantong Si	显通寺	*xiǎntōng sì*
Yanqing Si	延庆寺	*yánqìng sì*
Yuanzhao Si	圆照寺	*yuánzhào sì*
Zhenhai Si	镇海寺	*zhènhǎi sì*
Accommodation and eating		
Cuiyan	翠岩宾馆	*cuìyán bīnguǎn*
Hongyun	鸿运宾馆	*hóngyùn bīnguǎn*
Jiaotong	交通宾馆	*jiāotōng bīnguǎn*
Number Five Hostel	第五招待所	*dìwǔ zhāodàisuǒ*
Quan Sucai	全素菜	*quán sùcài*
Ruyi Fanfu	如意饭府	*rúyì fànfǔ*
Xinjian	新建宾馆	*xīnjiàn bīnguǎn*
Dong Ye	东冶	*dōng yě*
Shahe	沙河	*shāhé*

long bus ride here is rewarded with fresh air, superb scenery, some fascinating temple architecture and a spiritual (if not always peaceful) tone.

Though increasingly accessible today, the mountain's formerly remote location has always given it a degree of protection, and many of Wutai Shan's forty temples have survived the centuries intact. The monastic village of **Taihuai** is the focus, which sits in a depression surrounded by the five holy peaks; highlights are the ninth-century **revolving bookcase** of the Tayuan Si and the **two ancient temples**, the Song-dynasty Foguang and the Tang-dynasty Nanchan. All the temples today are working and full of resident clergy, despite an escalating number of tour groups trudging around them in peak season – though it must be said, you'll also see a surprising number of ordinary Chinese people here as **pilgrims**, thumbing rosaries and prostrating themselves on their knees as they clamber up the temples' steep staircases.

Some history

Wutai Shan was an early bastion of Buddhism in China, a religious centre at least since the reign of Emperor Ming Di (58–75 AD). At that time, a visiting Indian monk had a vision in which he met **Manjusri** (**Wenshu**), the Buddhist incarnation of Wisdom, who is usually depicted riding a blue lion and carrying a manuscript (to represent a sutra) and a sword to cleave ignorance. By the time of the Northern Wei, Wutai Shan was a prosperous Buddhist centre, important enough to be depicted on a mural at the Dunhuang Caves in Gansu. The mountain reached its height of popularity in the Tang dynasty, when there were more than two hundred temples scattered around its peaks, in which monks devoted themselves to the study of the *Avatamsaka* sutra, which contained references to "a pure and fresh mountain in the northeast" where Manjusri once resided, identified with Wutai Shan. In the fifteenth century, the founder of the **Yellow Hat order**, now the dominant Buddhist sect in Tibet, came to the area to preach; Manjusri is particularly important in Tibetan and Mongolian Buddhism, and Wutai Shan remains an important pilgrimage place for Lamaists.

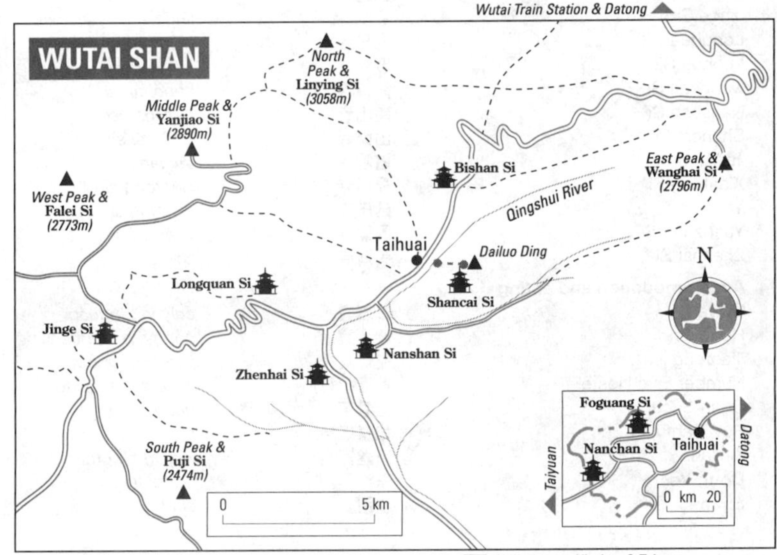

Practicalities

Getting to Wutai Shan is straightforward, though access can be restricted outside the warmer months. Your target is **Taihuai**, also known as "Wutai Shan" (but not "Wutai", another township): the nearest **train station** is ninety minutes away at **Shahe**, a stop on the Beijing–Taiyuan line and connected through the day to Taihuai by taxis and shuttle buses. By **bus**, you can get here in summer from Datong's north long-distance bus station (4hr 30min; ¥60), though the road crosses a high pass, which can see it closed at short notice by snow; and more reliably from Taiyuan's east bus station (5hr; ¥56). However you arrive, you'll be turfed off the bus at some point to pay the mountain's **entry** fee (¥75).

To avoid the crowds, the **best time to visit** is between October and April, though you will have to come prepared for some low temperatures and possible blizzards. Whatever the time of year, don't **hike** off into the hills around Taihuai without some warm, weatherproof gear, food and water, and a torch, even though in good weather the trails here present no special difficulties. Allow plenty of time for hikes, as the paths are hard to find in the dark and even in summer the temperature drops sharply at sundown.

Taihuai

TAIHUAI is a strip of tourist facilities and temples spread along about a kilometre of road, overlooked by high, dark brown hills. **Orientation** is easy: uphill along the road is north, with the main batch of temples, which have all expanded into one another, immediately to the west, and a smaller group of pavilions studding the steep hillside to the east across a river.

The most obvious first place to head for – it's easily spotted west of the road behind the *Cui Yuan Binguan* – is the fifty-metre-tall, Tibetan-style **White Stupa** of the **Ta Yuan Si** (¥5). The stupa is a staggering sight against the temple's dark grey roofs, a bulbous, whitewashed peak hung with 250 bells whose chiming can be heard across the valley on a windy day. The largest of many such bottle-shaped pagodas on Wutai Shan, it testifies to the importance of the mountain to Lamaism, which is also represented by the tall **wooden poles** with bronze caps standing inside many of the temple's entrances. Inside

▲ Ta Yuan Si

a hall behind the pagoda, a Ming-dynasty, two-storey library was built to house a bizarre and beautiful revolving **wooden bookcase**, much older than the rest of the complex. Its 33 layers of shelves, split into cubbyholes and painted with decorative designs, hold volumes of sutras in Tibetan, Mongolian and Chinese. Not far from **Shanhai Lou**, the chunky main gate of the temple – which you can climb for views – is the **Chairman Mao Memorial Hall** (¥2), whose placement at the heart of one of Buddhism's most sacred sights is in decidedly poor taste.

Just north of Ta Yuan Si's entrance, **Luohou Si** (¥4) is a Ming-dynasty reconstruction of a Tang temple. Crowds gather to gawk at the spinning round wooden altar in the main hall with a wave design at its base supporting a large wooden lotus with movable petals. A mechanism underneath opens the petals to reveal four Buddhas sitting inside the flower.

The **Xiantong Si** (¥5), just uphill from the Ta Yuan Si, reputedly dates back to 68 AD, and so is one of the oldest Buddhist sites in China. The main sights here are the whitewashed **Beamless Hall**, built in brick to resemble a wooden structure; and the dazzling five-metre-high **Bronze Palace**, constructed entirely of the metal and recently gilded. Its walls and doors are covered with animal and flower designs on the outside and rank upon rank of tiny Buddhas on the inside, along with an elegant bronze Manjusri Buddha sitting on a human-faced lion. The grounds also house an interesting sundial, which uses zodiac animals to depict the hours.

Sitting on the hill behind Luohou Si, via a splendid statue of Manjusri surrounded by *arhats* and clouds at the **Yuanzhao Si**, and atop a stone staircase of 108 steps, is the **Pusa Ding** (¥5). This Ming and Qing complex once accommodated emperors Kangxi and Qianlong, hence the yellow roof tiles and dragon tablet on the stairway, both indicating imperial patronage. This is a great destination for a first day in town, as it affords an aerial view of the valley and is a good way to warm up for longer hikes to higher temples.

Practicalities

Buses and taxis terminate on the main road in Taihuai; this is where to come to catch **transport out**, which leaves for Taiyuan, Datong and northeasterly Shahe (for the train) from about 7am until early afternoon. It's worth checking with drivers the day before you want to leave about times, but put off buying tickets until you depart. In summer, it might be possible to arrange transport to Datong via Heng Shan and the Hanging Temple; ask at your accommodation or at the **CITS**, next to the *Cui Yuan Binguan* (Ⓣ0350/6545288). However, CITS – along with the **Bank of China**, about 500m downhill on the main road – doesn't seem to open out of season.

A good budget **place to stay** near the centre of town is the *Number Five Hostel* (Ⓣ0350/6545373; ❸), near where the buses drop off (avoid the eastern "karaoke wing"). Alternatively, there are a string of clean, tiled basic hotels uphill from here, such as the *Jiaotong* (Ⓣ0350/6545840), *Hongyun* (Ⓣ0350/6545378) and *Xinjian* (Ⓣ0350/65455063), all charging around ¥100 per person in season, or half this at other times. A more upmarket option is the *Cui Yuan Binguan* (Ⓣ0350/6545388; ❹), downhill from the bus area on the corner of the lane leading towards Ta Yuan Si.

Taihuai's **restaurants** are plentiful but the food is mediocre and expensive – ¥5 for rice, ¥5 for tea and around ¥20 for a simple stir-fry. *Ruyi Fanfu*, near the bus area, is slightly better than most, but a pleasant exception is the vegetarian *Quan Suzai*, on the main road just uphill from the *Cui Yuan Binguan*, still pricey but with real cuisine.

Outlying temples

Few tourists get very far out of Taihuai; it's certainly worth the effort, however, as not just the temples, but also the views and the scenery, are gorgeous. The following are all within an easy day's hike from Taihuai, though you can also hire a "**tour taxi**" at the central car park for any combination of sights, ranging from ¥48 for a ten-stop tour to ¥165 for eight of the farthest sights. Posted rates to hire a car are ¥380 for a half-day, though you can probably negotiate fares well below that on the street.

For an excellent view of Taihuai, **Dailuo Ding**, the hillside overlooking the town to the east, is well worth a trip; you can walk up the steep stone staircase in about twenty minutes or take a cable car most of the way (¥25 ascent, ¥23 descent). At the top is **Shancai Si** (¥4), a tiny but beautiful temple with unpretentious halls dedicated to Manjusri.

The **Nanshan Si** (¥4) sits in a leafy spot halfway up Yangbai Shan, a hilltop 5km south of Taihuai. It's again approached by a steep flight of stairs, its entrance marked by a huge screen wall of cream-coloured brick. More decorated brickwork inside, including fake brackets and images of deities in flowing robes, is the temple's most distinctive feature. Eighteen Ming images of *lohans* in the main hall are unusually lifelike and expressive; one gaunt figure is sleeping with his head propped up on one knee, his skin sagging over his fleshless bones. Two kilometres southwest of here, the **Zhenhai Si** (¥4), sitting at an altitude of 1600m just off the road, seems an odd place to build a temple celebrating the prevention of floods, although legend has it that Manjusri tamed the water of the spring that now trickles past the place. During the Qing dynasty, a monk called Zhang Jia, reputed to be the living Buddha, stayed here; he is commemorated with a small pagoda south of the temple.

The **Longquan Si** (¥4) is on the west side of the Qingshui River, 5km southwest of Taihuai, just off the main road, and easily accessible by bus from town. Its highlight is the decorated **marble entranceway** at the top of 108 steps, whose surface is densely packed with images of dragons, phoenixes and foliage buried in a mass of abstract pattern. The rest of the temple seems sedate in comparison, though the Puji Pagoda inside is a similar confection – a fat stupa carved with guardians, surmounted by a fake wooden top and guarded by an elaborate railing. Both structures are fairly late, dating from the beginning of the twentieth century.

The **Bishan Si** (¥4), 2km north of the town, was originally used as a reception house for monks and *upasaka* (lay Buddhists). The Ming building holds many Qing sculptures, including a white jade Buddha donated by Burmese devotees.

The far temples and the peaks

Too far to reach on foot, the following temples and peaks are all served by minibuses or taxis from Taihuai, organized yourself or through the hotels. Preserved from vandalism by their inaccessibility, the temple complexes include some of the oldest buildings in the country.

The **Jinge Si** (¥4) is 10km southwest of Taihuai, and worth the trip for an impressive seventeen-metre-tall Guanyin inside – the largest statue at Wutai Shan. Some of the original Tang structure remains in the inscribed base of the pillars. Ask if you can stay in their **pilgrims' accommodation**, a useful base from which to walk the trails behind the complex.

The superb Nanchan Si and Foguang Si require a considerable diversion to reach. The **Nanchan Si** (¥5) is about 60km southwest of Taihuai, a little way off the road from Taiyuan, near the county town of **Wutai**. Tour buses from

Taiyuan sometimes stop here on their way into Taihuai; otherwise, you can catch a bus to Wutai, then get a motor-rickshaw to the village of **Dong Ye**. A large sign here points the way, but it's another 7km along a rough road to the complex. The temple's small **main hall**, built in 782, is the oldest wooden hall in China, a perfectly proportioned building whose columns and walls slope gently inwards, the sturdiness given by its thick, carved, wooden brackets nicely offset by the slight curves of its wide, flaring roof. Two inward-curving peaks sit at the ends of the roof ridge – all features characteristic of very early Chinese architecture. The hall of the Jin-dynasty **Yanqing Si**, accessible by a short path behind the Nanchan Si and included in the ticket price, is somewhat dilapidated but notable for quirky architectural detail, particularly the carved demons' heads, which sit atop the two columns on either side of its main entrance.

The **Foguang Si** (¥10), 40km west of Taihuai, is a museum complex of more than a hundred buildings, mostly late, but including Wutai Shan's second Tang-dynasty hall, built in 857, whose eaves are impressive for the size and complexity of their interlocking *dougongs*. The walls inside the hall are decorated with lively Tang and Song paintings of Buddhist scenes; most of the images are of saintly figures sitting sedately, but a few ferocious demons are shown, dragging emaciated bodies behind them. To get here, catch a **morning bus** (¥10) from Taihuai to **Doucun,** where you'll be dropped at the junction near a large sign pointing the way to Foguang. It's a five-kilometre walk from here along a dusty road to the temple, or you can negotiate an onward round trip with a vehicle for around ¥150.

The peaks

The five flat **peaks** around Taihuai, north, south, east, west and middle, are all approximately 15km away and considerably higher than Taihuai, with the tallest at over 3000m above sea level. On each summit sits a small temple, and pilgrims endeavour to visit each one, a time-consuming process even with the help of minibuses that go some way up each mountain. In the past, the truly devout took up to two years to reach all the temples on foot, but today most visitors make do with looking at the silhouette of the summit temples through the telescopes of entrepreneurs in town. Set off in any direction out of Taihuai for a rewarding walk, although the **South Peak** is regarded as the most beautiful, its slopes described in a Ming poem as "bedecked with flowers like a coloured silk blanket".

Taiyuan and around

TAIYUAN, industrial powerhouse and the capital of Shanxi province, is a busy transport hub, with rail and road connections north to Wutai Shan, Datong and Beijing, and south to Pingyao and Xi'an. There's not much in the way of essential viewing in town, though spending the night here in transit is no great hardship.

Taiyuan sits in the "invasion corridor" between the barbarian lands to the north and the Chinese heartland around the Yellow River to the south, and as a result has suffered throughout history from invaders and the fallout from dynastic collapse. The Mongolian Huns invaded first in 200 BC, later ousted by the Turkic Tobas who founded the Northern Wei in the fourth century. During the Tang dynasty, the city enjoyed a brief period of prosperity as an important frontier town, before becoming one of the major battlefields during the Five

Taiyuan and around		
Taiyuan	太原	*tàiyuán*
Chongshan Si	崇善寺	*chóngshàn sì*
Chunyang Gong	纯阳宫	*chúnyáng gōng*
Shuangta Si	双塔寺	*shuāngtǎ sì*
Wen Miao	文化庙	*wénhuá miào*
Wuyi Square	五一广场	*wǔyī guǎngchǎng*
Bus Stations		
East Bus Station	客运东站	*kèyùn dōngzhàn*
Yingze Dajie Station	长途汽车站	*chángtú qìchēzhàn*
Jiannan Station	建南汽车站	*jiànnán qìchēzhàn*
Accommodation		
Gang Wan	港湾大酒店	*gǎngwān dàjiǔdiàn*
Guofang	国防宾馆	*guófáng bīnguǎn*
Tielu	铁路宾馆	*tiělù bīnguǎn*
Yingze	迎泽宾馆	*yíngzé bīnguǎn*
Yinhai	银海宾馆	*yínhǎi bīnguǎn*
Yuyuan	豫园宾馆	*yùyuán bīnguǎn*
Eating		
Duowei Jiaozi Guan	多味饺子馆	*duōwèi jiǎozi guǎn*
Hongbin Lou	鸿宾楼	*hóngbīn lóu*
Hua'an Beef in Hot Pot	华安肥牛迎泽店	*húa'ān féiniú yíngzédiàn*
Shanshuijian	山水间	*shānshuǐjiān*
Jinci Si	晋祠寺	*jìncí sì*

Dynasties (907–979), a period of strife following the Tang's collapse. In 976, the expanding Song dynasty razed the city to the ground.

More recently, Taiyuan was governed by the fierce but reform-minded warlord Yan Xishan between 1912 and 1949, though he was unable to stop the Japanese exploiting the area's rich **coalfields** from 1940. Industrialization began in earnest after the Communist takeover and today it is the factories that dominate, relentlessly processing the region's coal and mineral deposits.

Arrival, transport and accommodation

Taiyuan is a huge, sprawling place, though fortunately most of the transit points and attractions, along with plenty of accommodation, are within striking distance of the city centre along **Yingze Dajie**, which cuts east–west across town.

The **airport** is 15km southeast of the city (a ¥70 ride away by taxi). The huge **train station**, on the Beijing–Xi'an line, is conveniently located at the eastern end of Yingze Dajie; it's fairly clean and efficient, though with the usual chaos of buses and stalls outside. There are several **long-distance bus stations**: the one at the eastern end of Yingze Dajie handles express services from Datong; the east bus station, 1.5km east of the train station on Wulongkou Jie is where you'll wind up coming from Wutai Shan (catch bus #615 to Yingze Dajie); and Jiannan station, 3km south of the centre, is the Pingyao terminus (catch bus #201 north to the train station).

Useful **city buses** include the #1 and #611, both of which run the length of Yingze Dajie. **Taxis** cost ¥8 to hire, though a ride across town will cost at least twice this.

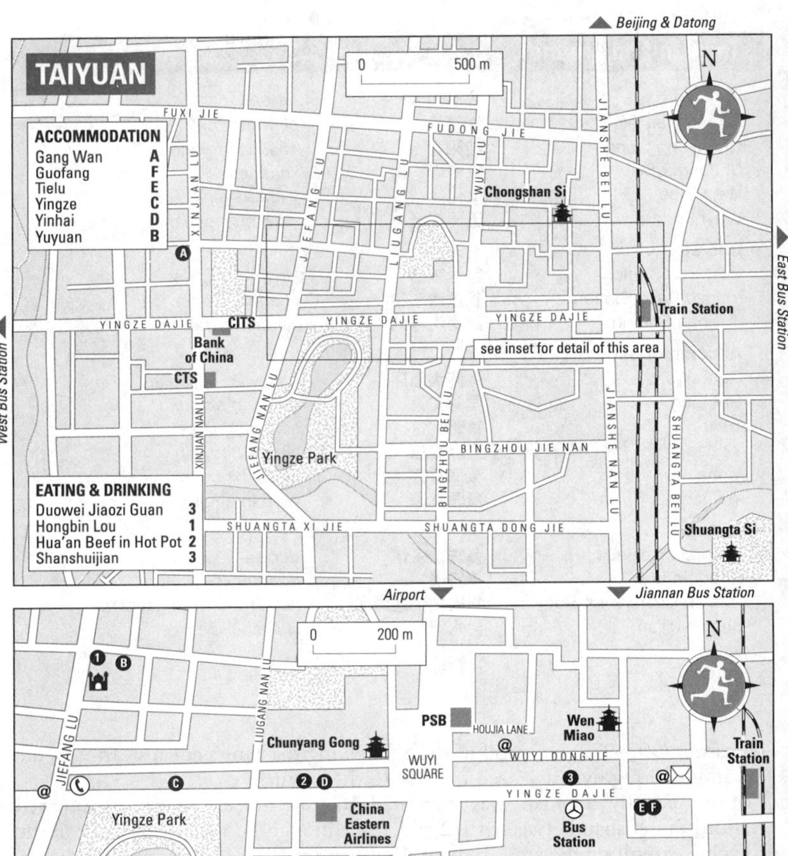

Moving on from Taiyuan

The main **airline office** is China Eastern, west of Wuyi Square on Yingze Dajie. **Buses** leave from all over, but useful options include frequent express coaches to Datong from the Yingze Dajie station (3hr 30min; ¥71); buses to Wutai Shan/Taihuai from the east bus station between 8am and 5pm (5hr; ¥56); and through the day to Pingyao from the Jiannan station (2hr; ¥25). Dozens of north–south **trains** pass through Taiyuan daily, and getting a sleeper is seldom a problem, even at the last minute. Note, however, that for Datong, buses are much faster, and even Pingyao is usually quicker by road.

Accommodation

Taiyuan's accommodation places are spread right across town, with the cheaper options up near the train station.

Gang Wan 87 Xinjian Lu ⓣ0351/8225655 or 82225699. Ordinary but clean and quiet mid-range Chinese urban hotel, a bit far from transit points but probably better for it. Attached restaurant is good. ❺

Guofang 12 Yingze Dajie ⓣ0351/8822209, ⓕ4124029. Rooms are small and tend towards the grotty end of the spectrum; avoid ones facing the street as they get lit up at night by flashing neon signs. However, the price is fine. Dorms ¥30, ❸

Tielu 11 Yingze Dajie ⓣ0351/4040624. Railway-run budget option next door to the *Guofang*, cleaner and tidier though no more upmarket. Doubles with/without bathroom ❸/❷

Yingze 189 Yingze Dajie ⓣ0351/8828888, ⓦshanxiyingzehotel.com. This stylish four-star hotel has its own café, bookshop and tour company, and is thick with visiting dignitaries and upmarket domestic tourists. ❾

Yinhai 145 Yingze Dajie ⓣ0351/4037569, ⓕ4048879. Set back off the street next to a bank, this odd little place is clean and quiet, though unused to foreign guests. Haggle over the rate and you can get a good deal here. ❺

Yuyuan Kaihuasi Jie, just east off Jiefang Lu ⓣ0351/8323333, ⓕ2024433. A good, if slightly expensive mid-range option, set in a quiet street in an interesting part of town. ❸

The City

A huge stainless-steel sculpture of three noble workers with exaggerated angular features stands outside Taiyuan's train station, and sets the tone for the main city street, **Yingze Dajie**, beyond. Somewhere between a boulevard and a freeway, it's along Yingze Dajie that the city tries its best to live up to its status as provincial capital, with a sprinkling of neon and new buildings. For a more interesting wander, however, it's worth exploring the roads north off it between parallel **Fudong Jie**, full of market activity and shopping complexes.

About 1km west down Yingze Dajie, **Wuyi Square** is a concrete plaza marked by a huge sculpture of a man playing a flute, a deer, and a woman with pneumatic breasts; it's lit up in fluorescent green at night. Just west of here, **Chunyang Gong** (daily 9am–5pm; ¥5) is a Ming temple complex of small, multistorey buildings and interconnected courtyards dedicated to the Taoist deity Lü Dongbin, currently housing a motley collection of artefacts. Similarly, attractive Ming buildings at **Wen Miao** (daily 9am–noon & 2.30–5pm; ¥2), a Confucius Temple east of here off Jianshe Bei Lu, are more interesting than its displays of relics, which include a few Shang bronzes and a large collection of Buddhist sutras.

Northeast of Wuyi Square, reached along alleys that grow shabbier the farther you go, the **Chongshan Si** (daily 8am–6pm; ¥2) is worth the fifteen-minute walk – look for the fortune-tellers who congregate outside. The temple contains a display of scrolls and books – sutras printed in the Song, Yuan and Ming dynasties, some in Tibetan – and a number of woodcut illustrations.

A tour of the city's ancient buildings is completed with a look at the two fifty-metre-tall pagodas of the **Shuangta Si** (daily 8am–8pm; ¥20), south of the train station off Shuangta Bei Lu. These were built by a monk called Fu Deng in the Ming dynasty, under the orders of the emperor, and today have become a symbol of the city. You can climb the thirteen storeys for a panoramic view of Taiyuan.

Eating

The cheapest places to get a feed are the stalls in streets north of Yingze Dajie, such as Jiefang Lu and Liugang Lu, the latter clogged at night by people selling kebabs, candied fruit on sticks and cut buns stuffed with red-stewed beef. Yingze Dajie itself has a good smattering of **restaurants**, from cheap and efficient dumpling houses such as *Duowei Jiaozi Guan*, opposite the bus station, to upmarket spots such as *Shanshuijian* and *Hua'an Beef in Hot Pot*, both offering Mongolian-style hotpot and nowhere near as expensive as they appear – count on ¥30 a head. Another excellent area is in the vicinity of the **old Mosque** on

Jiefang Lu, where there are several inexpensive Muslim noodle houses and the *Hongbin Lou* restaurant, where you can get a whole roast duck with pancakes and soup for ¥68 (¥34 for half), along with cold dishes served on trolleys.

Listings

Banks and exchange The main Bank of China is at 288 Yingze Dajie (Mon–Fri 8am–5.30pm, Sat & Sun 8am–5pm), with another branch with an ATM west of Wuyi Square on Yingze Dajie.
Internet access There's a net bar just west of the post office on Yingze Dajie.
Mail and telephones There's a major post office facing the train station on the corner with Yingze Dajie. The telecom area, with a row of card phones and phone-card hawkers, is at the corner of Yingze Dajie and Jiefang Lu.
PSB The PSB office is at 9 Houjia Lane (daily 8am–noon & 2.30–5.30pm) on the northeastern corner of Wuyi Square.
Travel agents CITS is next to the main Bank of China on Yingze Dajie (☎0351/4063562). The CTS office on Xinjian Nan Lu (☎351/4946300) is well worth the effort to get to, since the helpful English-speaking staff can arrange discounts on accommodation and a variety of excursions.

Jinci Si

About 25km southwest of Taiyuan, **Jinci Si** (daily 8.30am–6pm; ¥40) contains perhaps the finest Song-dynasty buildings in the country, though the complex is oriented towards tourism rather than worship. **Buses** #804, #848 and #856 from the train station judder out there through a stark industrial zone, dropping you amongst a charmless fair of souvenir stalls and ragged camels, by a river at the base of a mountain.

A temple has stood on the site since the Northern Wei, and today's buildings are a diverse collection from various dynasties. The open space just inside the gate was once used as a theatre, with the richly ornamented Ming stage, the **Water Mirror Platform**, at its centre. Over the bridge behind the stage, four Song-dynasty iron figures of warriors, apparently guardians of the local river, stand on a platform; inscriptions on their chests record their dates of construction. The **Hall of Offerings** beyond and, behind that, the **Hall of the Holy Mother** originated in the Jin period as shrines to the mother of Prince Shuyu, founder of the dynasty. They were rebuilt in the Song and today are two of the largest buildings from that dynasty still extant. The Hall of the Holy Mother is the highlight, its facade a mix of decorative flourishes and the sturdily functional, with wooden dragons curling around the eight pillars that support the ridge of its upward-curving roof. The hall's interior is equally impressive, with some delicate-looking Song-dynasty female figures, posed naturalistically, some with broomsticks, jugs and seals, attendants to a central image of a gracious-looking Holy Mother.

Pingyao and around

As one of the few towns in China comprising virtually only traditional eighteenth- and nineteenth-century buildings, **Pingyao**, 100km south of Taiyuan, is certainly worth a visit. Though many people only stop off here for the day in transit between Taiyuan and Xi'an, the town's charismatic hotels – set in old courtyard mansions – plus a couple of very fine rural **temples** and some impressive **fortified clan villages** in the area, all call out for a longer stay.

There are plentiful **buses** to Pingyao from Taiyuan, with one fast bus daily direct from Xi'an. Pingyao is also a stop on the Taiyuan–Xi'an **train** line.

Pingyao and around

Pingyao	平遥	*píngyáo*
City God Temple	城隍庙	*chénghuáng miào*
City tower	市楼	*shìlóu*
Confucian temple	文庙	*wénmiào*
County yamen	平遥县衙门	*píngyáoxiàn yámén*
Hui Wu Lin martial arts hall	汇武林博物馆	*huìwǔlín bówùguǎn*
Kuixing tower	奎星楼	*kuíxīnglóu*
Residence of Lei Lütai	雷履泰故居	*léilǚtài gùjū*
Rishengchang	日升昌	*rìshēngchāng*
Accommodation		
Dejuyuan	德居源客栈	*déjūyuán kèzhàn*
Dongfushun	东副顺民俗栈	*dōngfùshùn mínsúzhàn*
Harmony	和义昌客栈	*héyìchāng kèzhàn*
Jixian	集贤客栈	*jíxián kèzhàn*
Runzeyuan	润泽苑民俗客栈	*rùnzéyuàn mínsú kèzhàn*
Tianyuankui	天元奎客栈	*tiānyuánkuí kèzhàn*
Yamen	衙门官舍	*yámén guānshè*
Yide	一得客栈	*yīdé kèzhàn*
Around Pingyao		
Jiexiu	介休	*jièxiū*
Qiaojia Dayuan	乔家大院	*qiáojiā dàyuàn*
Shuanglin Si	双林寺	*shuānglín sì*
Wangjia Dayuan	王家大院	*wángjiā dàyuàn*
Zhenguo Si	镇国寺	*zhènguó sì*

Pingyao

PINGYAO reached its zenith in the Ming dynasty, when it was a prosperous **banking centre**, one of the first in China, and its wealthy residents constructed luxurious **mansions**, adding **city walls** to defend them. In the course of the twentieth century, however, the town slid rapidly into provincial obscurity, which kept it largely unmodernized. Inside the town walls, Pingyao's narrow streets, lined with elegant Qing architecture – no neon, no white tile, no cars – are a revelation, harking back to the nineteenth-century heyday. Few buildings are higher than two storeys; most are small shops much more interesting for their appearance than their wares, with ornate wood and painted glass lanterns hanging outside, and intricate wooden latticework holding paper rather than glass across the windows.

Entry to the town itself is free, but to visit the attractions you have to buy an **all-inclusive ticket** (¥120), which covers nineteen of the city buildings, plus the walls. It's valid for two days, but you need to get it validated for the second day the afternoon before at the north gate.

Orientation, arrival and information

Massive, fifteen-hundred-metre-long **walls** enclose Pingyao on four sides, each pierced by at least one gate. Inside, the four **main streets** – Bei Dajie, Xi Dajie, Dong Dajie and Nan Dajie – are arranged along compass points, a typical *feng shui*-influenced design that the Chinese compare to the markings on a tortoise shell. Nan Dajie, the southern axis, actually slopes downward ever so slightly, as it used to transport the city's sewage out of the figurative tortoise's rear end. The central streets are closed to cars in daylight hours,

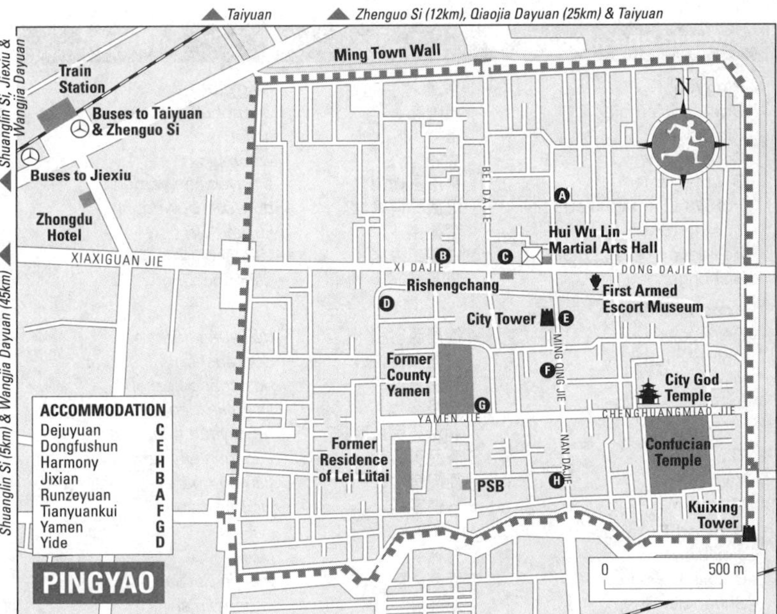

though are usually so congested with bicycles and pedestrians that the back alleys make an attractive diversion.

Pingyao's tiny **train station** is just northwest of the walls in a grubby, shambolic bit of town, which is also where **buses** set down and congregate. If you're just here for the day, several businesses outside the train station offer to look after luggage for you. It's only a ten-minute walk to accommodation, but if your bags are heavy a swarm of **bicycle rickshaws** and **electric buggies** will offer to carry you – ¥5 is a decent fare.

Note that Pingyao has **no banks** capable of foreign-currency transactions. If you need money, some hotels cash foreign notes but otherwise you'll have to catch a bus 30km to **Jiexiu**, get off at the train station and head 1km down Nan He Yan Jie opposite, where you'll find a Bank of China and an ATM on the corner with Jinrong Lu.

Moving on from Pingyao

Unless you're heading to Taiyuan – in which case, catch a direct **bus** from outside the train station – you'll probably need to leave Pingyao by train, though there's also an **express bus** to Xi'an, which you can book through some of the following accommodation or the *Zhongdu Binguan* just across from the train station. **Trains** head to Taiyuan (2hr; the bus is faster), Beijing (12hr), Xi'an (11hr) and Linfen (2hr 30min), and seats, at least, are easy enough to buy yourself at the station, where some staff speak a little English. Sleepers are harder to get, though accommodation in Pingyao have sorted out a system where they book your ticket through Beijing or Xi'an and then get a photocopy of it, which you use in place of the real thing – it sounds like a scam, but reports say that it works. Expect a ¥40 fee per ticket for this.

Accommodation

Staying overnight in Pingyao is a must: all the following places are housed in atmospheric mansions with stone courtyards, wooden window screens, traditional furniture and beds raised up on platforms. Although offering much the same in the way of decor, prices vary quite a lot – you'll pay most along Xi Dajie for some reason. Just be aware that lodgings can fill up quickly – especially at weekends or during holidays – and it's always best to book in advance.

Dejuyuan 43 Xi Dajie ⓣ0354/5685266, ⓦwww.pydjy.net. Tends to draw larger groups, and often has live-music performances in the courtyard. Staff very helpful. Various-sized doubles ❹–❻

Dongfushun 38 Nan Dajie ⓣ0354/5686003, ⓕ5685005. Occupies a superb location in a restored 200-year-old home near the Bell Tower, with inexpensive rooms. ❸

Harmony 165 Nan Dajie ⓣ0354/5684952 or 135/93085633. Hostel with good facilities – bike rental, Internet and booking service – and offering free pick-up from the station if booked in advance. Dorms ¥35, ❸

Jixian 87 Xi Dajie ⓣ0354/5683458 or 137/53421144. Former silk merchant's house and a bit more dolled up with silk draperies than most, especially in the bedrooms. Good deal for this location. ❺

Runzeyuan 3 Hongshengmiao Jie, about 100m north of the post office and to the east ⓣ0354/5681777, ⓦpykz518.com. A family-run place, not as smartened up as other accommodation in town, and no English spoken, but their most expensive rooms are still cheaper than a double anywhere else, and are beautifully decorated. ❷–❸

Tianyuankui 73 Nan Dajie ⓣ0354/5680069 ⓦwww.pytyk.com. This is the liveliest of the central guesthouses, though can get a bit noisy when the town is busy. ❺

Yamen 68 Yamen Jie ⓣ0354/5683539 ⓕ5683975. An IYHA hostel offering the best value in town, given that rooms are spacious, the building is lovely, there's free Internet and tour advice, inexpensive bike rental, and staff can't be faulted for helping you out. Dorms ¥35, ❸

Yide 16 Sha Xiang, just south off Xi Dajie ⓣ0354/5685988, ⓦwww.yide-hotel.com. Eighteenth-century building hidden at the end of a quiet lane and surrounded by several other courtyard homes. Rooms are cosy, and the restaurant is worth a look in itself. ❺

The Town

Pingyao is a great place to get lost in the lattice of narrow backstreet alleys, especially by night when the glow from nearby houses shows the way – though small kids stay off the street after dark, haunted by their parents' tales of returning Ming-era **ghosts** who, it's said, navigate the unchanged alleys with ease.

Just inside the arch of the West Gate on Xi Dajie are steps leading up to the Ming **town walls** (daily 8am–6.30pm), 12m high and crenellated, with a watchtower along every 50m of their six-kilometre length. You can walk all the way around them in two hours, and get a good view into some of the many courtyards inside the walls (and, more incongruously, at an army training base outside them, where you can watch recruits practising drills and throwing fake hand grenades). The structures where the wall widens out are *mamian* (literally, horse faces), where soldiers could stand and fight. At the southeast corner of the wall, the **Kuixing Tower**, a tall, fortified pagoda with a tiled, upturned roof, is a rather flippant-looking building in comparison to the martial solidity of the battlements.

It's also possible to climb the **City Tower** (¥5) on central Ming Qing Jie, a charming little building that provides a fantastic rooftop view of the old city. The eave decoration includes colourful reliefs of fish and portly merchants, and guardian statues of Guanyin and Guandi face north and south, respectively.

At the western end of Dong Dajie, you can look around the **Rishengchang** (daily 9am–5pm), a bank established in 1824, the first in the country and one of the first places in the world where cheques were used. During the Qing,

▲ Pingyao

more than four hundred financial houses operated in Pingyao, handling over eighty million ounces of silver annually. After the Boxer Rebellion, Dowager Empress Cixi came here to ask for loans to pay the high indemnities demanded by the Eight Allied Forces. Soon after, the court defaulted, then abdicated, and the banks dried up. Hong Kong and Shanghai took over Pingyao's mantle, rendering the city an isolated backwater.

There are many, many other **museums** in town (all included in the entry price and open around 8am–6pm), but after visiting a few you'll find the exhibits are repetitive and nowhere near as interesting as the buildings themselves, which are probably much like your accommodation. Still, they give a good excuse to wander, and some – like the two **armed escort museums** and former **Hui Wu Lin martial arts training hall** – are, given the need to protect the city's financial reserves from banditry, also relevant to Pingyao's history. Worthwhile exceptions include the **Former County Yamen** (daily 8am–6.30pm), a massive complex on Yamen Jie, which housed the town's administrative bureaucracy (the prisons were in use until the 1960s); the **Former Residence of Lei Lütai** (daily 8am–7pm), Rishengchang's founder; the ramshackle **City God Temple** on Chenghuang Miao Jie; and the large **Confucian Temple**, also on Chenghuang Miao Jie.

Eating

Eating in Pingyao is quite fun, with a score of restaurants along Ming Qing Jie offering a similar run of tasty, well-presented **local dishes**, though prices – at around ¥20 per dish – are tourist inflated. Things to look for include salted, five-spiced beef; wild greens; yams; flat "mountain noodles" (served on their edges in a steamer); and "cat's ear noodles" (triangular flecks of dough flicked into boiling water). For **Western food**, try either of the hostels, both of which have pretty decent kitchens and inexpensive coffee. For cheap **Chinese staples**, head to the western end of Xi Dajie, or the streets between the West Gate and the train station.

Listings

Bike rental Bikes are available from some of the guesthouses, and agencies with English signs along Xi Dajie (¥10 per day, ¥100 deposit).
Clinics There's a helpful clinic at 43 Dong Dajie (☎0354/5683732).
Mail The post office is at 1 Xi Dajie (daily 8am–6pm).
PSB At 110 Zhoubi Nan Jie, near the Former County Yamen. They might be willing to extend a visa, but it would be better to do this in Taiyuan.
Shopping Anywhere along Ming Qing Jie and the first section of Xi Dajie that isn't a restaurant or hotel will be selling souvenirs – lacquerware, papercuts, embroideries and the usual run of "new antiques", along with martial-arts weaponry. Prices are good after haggling.

Around Pingyao

Two **temples** near Pingyao – one full of superb statues, the other interesting for its age – are easy to visit from town. Further afield, a couple of Ming-dynasty **fortified mansions** standing starkly amongst the surrounding hills would be even more impressive if you hadn't seen Pingyao first, but are anyway worth the minimal effort it takes to reach them.

Shuanglin Si

The **Shuanglin Si** (daily 8am–6pm; ¥25) stands 5km southwest of Pingyao, just off the main road to Jiexiu – cycle, catch a Jiexiu-bound bus from near the train station, or haggle with a taxi (try ¥25 for the round trip with wait). Originally built in the Northern Wei, the present buildings, ten halls arranged around three courtyards, are Ming and Qing.

The complex looks more like a fortress from the outside, being protected by high walls and a gate. Once you're inside, the fine architecture pales beside the contents of the halls, a treasury of 1600 coloured terracotta and wood **sculptures** dating from the Song to the Qing dynasties. They're arranged in tableaux, with backgrounds of swirling water or clouds, turning the dusty wooden halls into rich grottoes. Some of the figures are in bad shape but most still have a good deal of their original paint, although it has lost its gaudy edge. It's worth hiring a **guide** (ask at your accommodation), as each hall and each row of statues has intriguing elements, such as the statue of the husband and wife who lived here and protected the temple during the Cultural Revolution.

The horsemen dotted in vertical relief around the **Wushung Hall**, the first on the right, illustrate scenes from the life of Guandi, the god of war, but the figures in most of the halls are depictions of Buddha or saints and guardians. The **eighteen arhats** in the **second hall**, though unpainted, are eerily lifelike, and somewhat sinister in the gloom with their bulging foreheads, long tapering fingernails and eyes of black glass that follow you round the room. In the **third hall**, the walls are lined with elegant twenty-centimetre-high Bodhisattvas inclined towards a set of larger Buddha figures at the centre like so many roosting birds. The statue of **Guanyin** – sitting in a loose, even provocative, pose – is probably a reflection of the confidence and pride Pingyao enjoyed during its economic heyday.

Zhenguo Si

Out in the fields 12km northeast of Pingyao – catch bus #9 from outside the train station – **Zhenguo Si** (daily 8am–6pm; ¥20) is a quiet, forgotten place, fronted by gnarled old trees. It's surprising then to find one of China's **oldest wooden buildings** here: the Wanfo Hall was built in 963 AD and looks like it hasn't been touched since, with an amazingly complex system of brackets holding the roof up and full of contemporary, Indian-influenced statuary. At the rear, the upper hall has some Qing frescoes of the life of Buddha, all set in a Chinese context, while the Ming-dynasty **Dizang Hall** is a riot of paintings of the King of Hell and his demons handing out punishments to sinners.

Wangjia Dayuan and Qiaojia Dayuan

Wangjia Dayuan – the Wang Family Mansion (daily 8am–5pm; ¥66) – is more like a huge, fortified castle than a private residence. Some 45km southwest of Pingyao, it's reached via the town of **Jiexiu**: catch a Jiexiu bus from outside Pingyao's train station (1hr; ¥5), then minibus #11 from Jiexiu's train station to the mansion (30min; ¥4). Set amongst stark brown hills, the location, the enormous scale and – especially – the details of the mansion buildings are all astounding, with high brick walls surrounding an intricate and vast collection of interconnected Qing-dynasty courtyards, halls (around a thousand), gardens, galleries, triumphal archways and screens, all built in carved grey stone along a rigidly symmetrical plan. The Wangs settled here at the end of the Mongol dynasty and built this complex in the early nineteenth century, after the family struck it rich not only in commerce but also political appointments; the infamous **Empress Dowager Cixi** stayed a night here whilst fleeing to Xi'an after the Boxer Rebellion in 1901. The complex is in two sections, joined by a stone bridge over a gully, and you could easily spend half a day here getting lost amongst the architecture.

The similar but much more comfortably scaled **Qiaojia Dayuan** – the Qiao Family Mansion (daily 8am–5pm; ¥66) – lies 25km northeast of Pingyao near the hamlet of **Leguan Zhen**. Check with accommodation about transport, or cast around for buses outside the train station to Leguan Zhen (1hr; ¥4) and then get a motor-rickshaw (¥10). The mansion was used as a setting by Zhang Yimou for his film *Raise the Red Lantern*, in which the labyrinthine layout of the place symbolizes just how restricted life was for women in classical China.

Between Pingyao and Xi'an

The small towns between Pingyao and Xi'an give access to some interesting places, somewhat off the regular routes but not too hard to reach. About 140km south of Pingyao, **Linfen** is a transit point for **Hukou Falls**, which, though regarded by the Chinese as one of their premier beauty spots, fall short of the hype. Farther south, the town of **Yuncheng** is a springboard to the **Guan Di Miao**, a fine Qing-dynasty temple popular with the Taiwanese, and for the town of **Ruicheng** and the nearby **Yongle Gong**, a Taoist temple with some excellent murals, from where Xi'an is only a four-hour bus ride away.

Between Pingyao and Xi'an		
Linfen	临纷	*línfēn*
Hukou Falls	壶口瀑布	*húkǒu pùbù*
Hukou Guesthouse	壶口招待所	*húkǒu zhāodàisuǒ*
Pingyang Hotel	平阳宾馆	*píngyáng bīnguǎn*
Ruicheng	芮成	*ruìchéng*
Ruicheng Binguan	芮成宾馆	*ruìchéng bīnguǎn*
Yongle Gong	永乐宫	*yǒnglè gōng*
Yuncheng	运城	*yùnchéng*
Guan Di Miao	关帝庙	*guāndì miào*
Jiezhou	解州	*jièzhōu*

Linfen and the Hukou Falls

Poetically described by CITS as "giant dragons fighting in a river", **Hukou Falls** (¥60), 150km west of the rail town of **Linfen**, is the Yellow River at its most impressively turbulent. At Jinshan Gorge, the 400-metre-wide river is suddenly forced into a twenty-metre gap and tumbles down a cliff, where the fierce torrent squirts spray high into the air; the hiss of the water can be heard 2km away, which is what gives it the name "*hukou*", meaning kettle spout. A popular spot with the Chinese, the falls are impressive – especially when the summer rains have swollen the river – but it's a long way to go, and, with souvenir stalls aplenty, is not exactly a wilderness experience.

Your first target is **LINFEN**, a curious place whose centre is built like a mini-Beijing, with a replica Tian'anmen Square, Temple of Heaven and Great Wall, and even a park containing a scale topographic model of the whole country, where visitors can play Godzilla, stomping on towns they dislike. The **train station**, just three hours down the line from Pingyao, is in the west of town. Check with the CITS (ⓣ0357/3330281), on the south side of the train-station plaza, to see if they have a tour running or can recommend where to pick up a **tourist minibus**; otherwise, take bus #11 from the train station to the **Yaomiao bus station** in the southwest of town and take a long-distance bus to **Jixian** (¥45), from where local buses make the run to the falls – a six-hour trip in all from Linfen. There's **accommodation** in Linfen at the *Pingyang Hotel*, at 58 Jiefang Nan Lu (ⓣ0357/2086666; ❸), rooms range from the very basic to the rather plush; and at the falls themselves, in the adequate *Hukou Guesthouse* (❸).

Yuncheng and the Guan Di Miao

YUNCHENG, 140km south of Linfen, is the last major town before Xi'an on the train line south from Datong, and is the starting point for bus trips west and south to the Guan Di Miao, Ruicheng and the Yongle Gong. The **train station**, with a statue of Guan Di outside, is in the northwest of town, at the end of Zhan Nan Lu, while the **central bus station** is 2km east, linked by bus #1 (¥1). You can get buses to just about everywhere between Datong and Xi'an from here, including Ruicheng (2.5hr; ¥15); Xi'an itself is just a four-hour ride away (¥68).

The *Railway Hotel* (ⓣ0359/2068899, ⓕ8659168; ❸), to the right as you exit the train station, is a friendly, comfortable place. On the left as you exit the station, the *Xinfeng Hotel* (ⓣ0359/2067888, ❸, dorm beds from ¥18–35) is clean and also accepts foreigners. The *Huanghe Hotel* (ⓣ0359/2023135; ❹), right from the station concourse at the end of Zhan Dong Lu, has a wide range of rooms and a decent restaurant.

Guan Di Miao

About 20km southwest of Yuncheng, the **Guan Di Miao** (daily 8am–6.30pm; ¥48, ¥20 to ascend main hall), the finest temple to the god of war in China, sits in the small country town of **JIEZHOU**, accessible by bus #11 (¥3.50) from opposite Yuncheng's train station concourse. Contemporary Jiezhou, known locally as Haizhou, doesn't look like much – the bus drops you in a muddy square lined with a few stalls and pool tables, which makes the massive temple complex on its western side look quite out of proportion. However, this was the birthplace of **Guan Di** (aka Guan Yu), a general of the Three Kingdoms period (220–280 AD; see box, p.453) who epitomized all the classical martial virtues, which included finally choosing execution over betraying his oath brother, Liu Bei. Later deified as god of war, his temple (founded in 589 AD, though the present structure is eighteenth century) is appropriately robust, looking more like a castle, with high battlements and thick wooden doors. Among the images on the wooden arch at the entrance is a victorious jouster gleefully carrying off the loser's head and the martial theme is carried into the interior, with much smiting of enemies going on in the superb Qing-dynasty **friezes** and stone carvings in the eaves. Look, too, for a small hall with a sculpture of his **horse** inside, which died of sorrow after Guan Di was executed.

Ruicheng and the Yongle Gong

The bus journey from Yuncheng to **RUICHENG**, 75km south near the Yellow River, is an easy trip over the Zhongtiao Mountains, an ochre landscape of loess soil, limestone peaks, cornfields and orchards. Buses arrive at the long-distance **bus station** just west of Ruicheng's main, central intersection. The utilitarian *Ruicheng Binguan* is nearby, behind the eastern side of the central square (Ⓣ0359/3030611, Ⓕ3030659; ❹), though with frequent bus links to Yuncheng and Xi'an, you can probably drop in on the town for a few hours and be on your way.

Yongle Gong

The **Yongle Gong**, Palace of Eternal Joy (daily 8.30am–6pm; ¥50), is a major Taoist temple, 4km north of Ruicheng at the terminus of bus #2, most notable for its excellent murals. Its name derives from the position it once held in the village of Yongle, farther south on the banks of the Yellow River. It was moved brick by brick in 1959, when the dam at Sanmenxia was built and Yongle disappeared beneath the water.

There are **three halls**, three sides of which are covered in vivid **murals**. In the **first hall**, the three major gods of Taoism, sitting on thrones, are surrounded by the pantheon of minor deities, looking like emperors surrounded by courtiers. Each figure is over 2m tall, brightly painted and concisely outlined, but although great attention is paid to an exact rendering of the details of facial expression and costume, the images have no depth. The figures, four deep, are flat, like staggered rows of playing cards. Some have the faces of monsters, others have beards that reach almost to their waists and in which every hair is painted; one man has six eyes. In the **second hall**, elegant robed figures disport themselves in finely observed walled courtyards and temple complexes set among misty, mountainous landscapes. These are images from the life of **Lü Dongbin**, one of the eight Taoist immortals who was born at Yongle, arranged in panels like a comic strip. The murals in the **third hall**, showing the life of a Taoist priest, are unfortunately damaged and little remains visible.

Shaanxi and Henan

The provinces of **Shaanxi** and **Henan** are both remarkable for the depth and breadth of their history. The region itself is dusty, harsh and unwelcoming, with a climate of extremes: in winter, strong winds bring yellow dust storms, while summer is hot and officially the rainy season. But, thanks to the Yellow River, this was the cradle of Chinese history, and for millennia the centre of power for a string of dynasties, the remains of whose capital cities are strung out along the southern stretch of the plain.

Of these ancient cities, none is more impressive than thriving **Xi'an**, now the capital of Shaanxi province and perhaps the most cosmopolitan city in China outside the eastern seaboard. It also retains copious evidence of its former glories – most spectacularly in the tomb guards of the great emperor Qin Shi Huang, the renowned **Terracotta Army**, but also in a host of temples and

The Yellow River

The **Yellow River** flows for 6000km through nine provinces, from the Tibetan plateau in the west, through Inner Mongolia, turning abruptly south to mark the border between Shanxi and Shaanxi, and then east through the flood plains of Henan and Shandong to the Bohai Gulf. The upriver section provides much-needed irrigation and power, but in the latter half of its journey the river causes as much strife as it alleviates. The problem is the vast quantity of **silt** the river carries along its twisted length – 1.6 billion tonnes a year – whose choking nature has confused its course throughout history. Sometimes, the river has flowed into the sea near Beijing, at other times it has flowed into the lower Yangzi valley, and its unpredictable swings have always brought chaos. From 1194 to 1887, there were fifty major Yellow River **floods**, with three hundred thousand people killed in 1642 alone. A disastrous flood in 1933 was followed in 1937 by another tragedy – this time man-made – when Chiang Kaishek used the river as a weapon against the advancing Japanese, breaching the dykes to cut the rail line. A delay of a few weeks was gained at the cost of hundreds of thousands of Chinese lives.

Attempts to enhance the river's potential for creation rather than destruction began very early, at least by the eighth century BC, when the first **irrigation canals** were cut. In the fifth century BC, the Zheng Guo Canal irrigation system stretched an impressive 150km; it's still in use today. But the largest scheme was the building of the 1800-kilometre **Grand Canal** in the sixth century, which connected the Yellow and the Yangzi rivers and was used to carry grain to the north. It was built using locks to control water level, an innovation that did not appear in the West for another four hundred years. The more predictable Yangzi soon became the county's main highway for food and trade, leading to a decline in the Yellow River area's wealth.

Dykes, too, have been built since ancient times, and in some eastern sections the river bottom is higher than the surrounding fields, often by as much as 5m. Dyke builders are heroes around the Yellow River, and every Chinese knows the story of Da Yu (Yu the Great), the legendary figure responsible for battling the capricious waters. It is said that he mobilized thousands of people to dredge the riverbed and dig diversionary canals after a terrible flood in 297 BC. The work took thirteen years, and during that period Yu never went home. At work's end, he sank a bronze ox in the waters, a talisman to tame the flow. A replica of the ox guards the shore of Kunming Lake in Beijing's Summer Palace. Today, **river control** continues on a massive scale. To stop flooding the riverbed is dredged, diversion channels are cut and reservoirs constructed on the river's tributaries. Land around the river has been forested to help prevent erosion and so keep the river's silt level down.

For most of its course, the river meanders across a flat flood plain with a horizon sharp as a knife blade. Two good places to see it are at the **Yellow River Viewing Point** in Kaifeng and from the **Yellow River Park** outside Zhengzhou. To see the river in a more tempestuous mood, take a diversion to **Hukou Falls** (see p.257), farther north on the Shaanxi–Shanxi border.

museums. The whole region is crowded with buildings that reflect the development of **Chinese Buddhism** from its earliest days; one of the finest is the **Baima Si** in **Luoyang**, a city farther east, thought by the ancient Chinese to be the centre of the universe. The **Longmen Caves**, just outside the city, are among the most impressive works of art in China, but also rewarding are excursions in the area around, where two holy mountains, **Hua Shan** and **Song Shan**, one Buddhist, one Taoist, offer a welcome diversion from the monumentality of the cities. **Zhengzhou**, farther east, the capital of Henan, has less of interest beyond a good museum but the nearby former Song-dynasty capital of **Kaifeng** is a pretty and quiet little place, though little remains of its past thanks to its proximity to the treacherous Yellow River. If you've had enough of the relics of ancient cultures, get a glimpse of recent history at **Yan'an** in northern Shaanxi, the isolated base high in the loess plateau to which the Long March led Mao in 1937.

Xi'an

The capital of Shaanxi province, **XI'AN** is a manufacturing city of five million inhabitants and holds a key position in the fertile plain between the high loess plateau of the north and the Qingling Mountains to the south. Though prone to heavy **pollution**, it's one of the more pleasant Chinese cities, the de facto capital of China's west and more prosperous than anywhere in inland China except Chengdu. Its tourism industry, of course, means Xi'an is already far more developed than the surrounding area, a fact suggested by the large numbers of rural migrants who hang around at informal labour markets near the city gates. Xi'an is also a primer in **Chinese history**, as between 1000 BC and 1000 AD it served as the **imperial capital** for eleven dynasties. You'll find a wealth of important sites and relics hereabouts: **Neolithic Banpo**, the **Terracotta Army** of the Qin emperor, the Han and Tang **imperial tombs**, and, in the city itself, two Tang-dynasty **pagodas**, the **Bell and Drum towers** and the **Ming city walls**, as well as two excellent **museums** holding a treasury of relics from the most glamorous parts of Chinese history. Xi'an is also very popular with **foreign residents**, and many come here to study, as the colleges are regarded as some of the best places to learn Chinese outside of Beijing.

Some history

Three thousand years ago, the western Zhou dynasty, known for their skilled bronzework, built their capital at **Fenghao**, a few miles west of Xi'an – one of their chariot burials has been excavated nearby. When Fenghao was sacked by northwestern tribes, the Zhou moved downriver to **Luoyang** and, as their empire continued to disintegrate into warring chiefdoms, the nearby Qin kingdom expanded. In 221 BC, the larger-than-life **Qin Shi Huang** united the Chinese in a single empire, the Qin, with its capital at **Xianyang**, just north of Xi'an. The underground **Terracotta Army**, intended to guard his tomb, are this tyrant's inadvertent gift to today's tourist prosperity.

His successors, the **Han**, also based here, ruled from 206 BC to 220 AD. Near-contemporaries of Imperial Rome, they ruled an empire of comparable size and power. Here in Xi'an was the start of the **Silk Road**, along which, among many other things, Chinese silk was carried to dress Roman senators and their wives at the court of Augustus. There was also a brisk trade with south and west Asia;

Xi'an

Xi'an	西安	*xī'ān*
Andingmen Gate	安定门	*āndìngmén*
Anyuan Gate	安远门	*ānyuǎnmén*
Baxian Gong	八仙宫	*bāxiān gōng*
Beilin Museum	碑林博物馆	*bēilín bówùguǎn*
Bell Tower	钟楼	*zhōng lóu*
Big Goose Pagoda	大雁塔	*dàyàn tǎ*
Changlemen	长乐门	*chánglèmén*
Dacien Si	大慈恩寺	*dàcíēn sì*
Daxingshan Si	大兴善寺	*dàxīngshàn sì*
Drum Tower	鼓楼	*gǔlóu*
Great Mosque	大清真寺	*dàqīngzhēn sì*
Shaanxi History Museum	陕西历史博物馆	*shǎnxīlìshǐ bówùguǎn*
Small Goose Pagoda	小雁塔	*xiǎoyàn tǎ*
Tang Dynasty Arts Museum	唐代艺术馆	*tángdài yìshùguǎn*
West Mosque	西清真寺	*xīqīngzhēn sì*
Yongning gate	永宁门	*yǒngníngmén*
Bus Stations		
Chengnan Depot	城南汽车站	*chéngnán qìchēzhàn*
East Bus Station	客运东站	*kèyùn dōngzhàn*
Main Bus Station	省汽车站	*shěng qìchēzhàn*
Shichang Depot	市长途汽车站	*shìchángtú qìchēzhàn*
Accommodation		
3e	商务酒店	*shāngwù jiǔdiàn*
Bell Tower	钟楼饭店	*zhōnglóu fàndiàn*
Hang Tan Inn	潢唐旅舍	*huángtáng lǚshè*
Hyatt Regency	凯悦饭店	*kǎiyuè fàndiàn*
Jiefang	解放饭店	*jiěfàng fàndiàn*
Jinjiang Inn	锦江之星旅馆	*jǐnjiāng zhīxīng lǚguǎn*
Qixian	七仙旅舍	*qīxiān lǚshè*
Renmin	雅商人民大厦	*yǎshāng rénmín dàshà*
Royal Garden	皇城花园酒店	*huángchéng huāyuán jiǔdiàn*
Shuyuan	书院旅舍	*shūyuàn lǚshè*
Wuyi	五一饭店	*wǔyī fàndiàn*
Xiangzimen	湘子门国际青年旅舍	*xiāngzǐmén guójì qīngnián lǚshè*
Restaurants		
Anjia Shaocai	安家炒菜	*ānjiā chǎocài*
Daqinghua Jiaozi	大清花饺子	*dàqīnghuā jiǎozi*
King Town	秦唐一号中国餐馆	*qíntáng yīhào zhōngguó cānguǎn*
Laosunjia	老孙家	*lǎosūnjiā*
Shanghai Renjia	上海人家	*shànghǎi rénjiā*
Sushi	回转寿司店	*huízhuǎn shòusīdiàn*
Tang Dynasty	唐乐宫	*tánglè gōng*
Tongshengxiang	同盛祥	*tóngshèngxiáng*
Wuyi	五一饭店	*wǔyī fàndiàn*
Xi'an	西安宾馆	*xīān bīnguǎn*
Xi'an Roast Duck	西安烤鸭店	*xīān kǎoyādiàn*

Han China was an outward-looking empire. The emperors built themselves a new, splendid and cosmopolitan capital a few miles northwest of Xi'an, which they called **Chang'an** – Eternal Peace. Its size reflected the power of their empire, and records say that its walls were 17km round with twelve great gates. When the dynasty fell, Chang'an was destroyed. Their **tombs** remain, though, including Emperor Wu's mound at **Mao Ling**.

It was not until 589 that the **Sui** dynasty reunited the warring kingdoms into a new empire, but their dynasty hardly lasted longer than the time it took to build a new capital near Xi'an, called **Da Xingcheng** – Great Prosperity. The **Tang**, who replaced them in 618, took over the capital, overlaying it with their own buildings in a rational grid plan that became the model not only for many other Chinese cities, but also the contemporary Japanese capital Hei'an (now Kyoto). During this time, the city became one of the biggest in the world, with over a million inhabitants.

The Tang period was a **golden age** for China's arts, and ceramics, calligraphy, painting and poetry all reached new heights. Its sophistication was reflected in its religious tolerance – not only was this a great period for **Buddhism**, with monks busy translating the sutras that the adventurous monk **Xuan Zong** had brought back from India, but the city's **Great Mosque** dates from the Tang, and

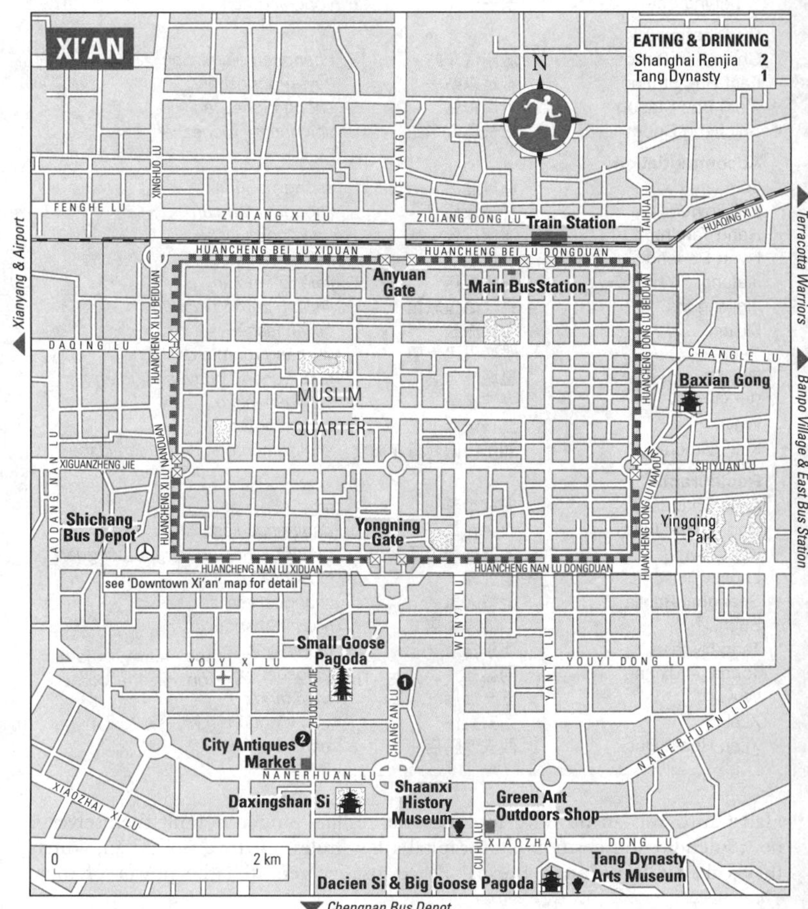

one of the steles in the Provincial Museum bears witness to the founding of a chapel by Nestorian Christians.

After the fall of the Tang, Xi'an went into a long **decline**. It was never again the imperial capital, though the Ming emperor Hong Wu rebuilt the city as a gift for his son; today's great walls and gates date from this time. Occasionally, though, the city did continue to provide a footnote to history. When the Empress Dowager Cixi had to flee Beijing after the Boxer Rebellion, she set up her court here for two years. In 1911, during the uprising against the Manchu Qing dynasty, the Manchu quarter in Xi'an was destroyed and the Manchus massacred. And in 1936, Chiang Kaishek was arrested at Huaqing Hot Springs nearby in what became known as the Xi'an Incident (see box, p.278).

Orientation, arrival and city transport

Xi'an is easy to get around, as the layout of today's city closely follows the ordered **grid plan** of the ancient one, with straight, wide streets running along the compass directions. The **centre** is bounded by city walls, with a bell tower marking the crossroads of the four main streets, Bei Dajie, Nan Dajie, Dong Dajie and Xi Dajie – north, south, east and west streets. Another major street runs south from the train station, where it's called Jiefang Lu, across the city, crossing Dong Dajie where it changes its name to Heping Lu, then to Yanta Lu outside the walls, and continues all the way to the Big Goose Pagoda in the **southern outskirts**, where many of the city's sights are. The only exception to the grid plan of the central streets is the **Muslim Quarter**, northwest of the Bell Tower, around whose unmarked winding alleys it's easy (and not necessarily unpleasurable) to get lost.

The **modern city**, extending far beyond the confines of the walls, in general adheres to the same ordered pattern, with two large highways forming ring roads, the innermost of which goes around the outside of the city walls.

Arrival

Xi'an's **airport**, 40km northwest of the city, is connected to town by regular **airport buses** (6am–8pm; ¥25), which drop passengers off at the *Melody Hotel*, just west of the Bell Tower. A taxi costs ¥100, and it's best to negotiate

Moving on from Xi'an

Air tickets can be arranged through all accommodation; if hostels try to charge mark-ups, go elsewhere. The **airport bus** (¥25) leaves from outside the *Melody Hotel* on Xi Dajie on the hour from 6am to 7pm, and takes around an hour; buy tickets on board. Taxis hang around the same place; they'll take four people for ¥100 and will stick solo passengers in with others to make up numbers. There's a **hotel** in the basement of the airport charging ¥100 for two hours if you need a rest and brush-up.

Train tickets are a nightmare to get at the station; either use your accommodation (hostels charge around ¥40 a ticket) or one of several **advance-ticket offices** scattered around, where the fee is only ¥5. There's a massive one at the corner of Jiefang Lu and Xiwu Lu (8am–midnight), labelled "Shaanxi Xi'an Railway Ticket E-Business Co. Ltd"; and another smaller branch on Shangqin Lu between Dongqi Lu and Dongliu Lu.

Heading out by **bus**, it's likely that the main station at the top of Jiefang Lu will have what you need, though staff are pretty brusque. There are masses of transport here towards Luoyang, Zhengzhou, Yan'an and Taiyuan, though other directions might be better served by train – or plane, if you're heading further afield; flying is almost half the price of a soft sleeper.

DOWNTOWN XI'AN

ACCOMMODATION	
3e	J
Bell Tower	G
Hang Tan Inn	E
Hyatt Regency	I
Jiefang	A
Jinjiang Inn	D
Qixian (Seven Sages)	B
Renmin (Sofitel/Mercure)	C
Royal Garden	H
Shuyuan	L
Wuyi	F
Xiangzimen	K

EATING & DRINKING	
Anjia Shaocai	1
Daqinghua Jiaozi	8
King Town	7
Laosunjia	5
Music Man	9
Sushi Restaurant	4
Tongshengxiang	2
Wuyi	E
Xi'an	6
Xi'an Roast Duck	3

the fare in advance rather than risk being taken a long way round on the meter. At the airport, there are several ATMs upstairs in the departures area, but none in arrivals.

The busy **train station**, in the northeast corner of town, just outside the city walls, is a major stop on routes from Zhengzhou, Beijing, Chengdu and Lanzhou. City buses leave from the tangled north end of Jiefang Lu, just south of the station – buses #206, #205, #201 and #610 (aka tourist bus #8) will get you to the Bell and Drum tower area. Taxis congregate on the western side of the station concourse.

The main **bus station** faces the train station at the top of Jiefang Lu (same buses into town as for the train station). Other major depots include the **east bus station**, 2km outside the walls, on Changle Lu (catch bus #13 to the main bus station or a taxi to accommodation); the **Shichang depot**, just outside the south-western corner of the walls (bus #15 to the Drum Tower); and the Chengnan depot, about 3km south of the walls on Zhuque Dajie (taxi is your best bet).

City transport

The largest concentration of **city buses** is found outside the train station at the northern end of Jiefang Lu. There are other clusters just outside the South Gate, and at the southern end of Yanta Lu, just north of the Big Goose Pagoda. Normal buses cost ¥1, fancier ones with air conditioning ¥2. **Bus #610** (aka **tourist bus #8**) is particularly useful, as it links most of the sights. Otherwise, there are plenty of green **taxis** cruising the streets, and they can be hailed anywhere. Most destinations within the city walls are within the ¥6 flag fall.

As the streets are wide and flat, **cycling** is a good way to get around. All the main streets have cycle lanes, controlled at major intersections by officials with flags. There are, however, few bike parks, and most people risk a (rarely enforced) ¥10 fine by leaving their bikes padlocked to railings. Make sure you have a good security chain, especially if your bike is anything other than a downbeat Flying Pigeon. For **rental places**, see p.273.

Xi'an also has a **metro** under construction, a controversial project considering the city's complex archeology. Two lines totalling 23.5km of track are due for completion around 2011, one running north–south, the other east–west.

City **maps** (¥5), some in English, are available everywhere and are worth picking up immediately, as bus routes are continually amended.

Accommodation

Xi'an is firmly on the tourist itinerary, and **accommodation** abounds, ranging from a slew of inexpensive hostels through a couple of good-value motel options and on to upmarket international hotel chains. As plenty of these are located within the city walls, close to the most interesting bits of Xi'an and with easy access to the tourist sights, there seems little point in staying outside, in the drabber, more modern parts of town. It's a good idea to **book ahead**, especially for the hostels, all of which offer Internet, laundry, food and beer, and tour desks, though bear in mind that the motels are probably better value for doubles, if a touch more expensive.

Hostels

Hang Tan Inn 211 Xi Dajie, just west of the Parkson building and next to a branch of Watson's Pharmacy ☎029/87287772. Bus #205 from the train station stops outside. Not as pretty as some of the other hostels, but staff are helpful, it's right next to the Muslim Quarter, and it has the best-value laundry and Western breakfasts in town. Dorms ¥30, ④

Qixian (Seven Sages) 1 Beixin Lu ☎029/87444087 or 81709181. Grey brick courtyard building formerly used as headquarters of the 8th Route Army in the 1930s. Rooms are clean and simple with modern bathrooms, and though a little distant from the centre it's close to the bus and train stations. Dorms ¥30, 3

Shuyuan Just inside and 20m west of the city wall's South Gate ⓣ029/87287721, ⓦwww.hostelxian.com. From the train station, take bus #603 or #608 to the South Gate. An excellent location, with a front door facing the city walls and the building based on a traditional courtyard plan. Avoid the overflow basement rooms at all costs, however: they're damp, windowless cells. Dorm beds ¥30–50, 4

Xiangzimen 16 Xiangzi Miao Jie ⓣ029/62867888, ⓕ62867999. Bus #603 or #608 from the train station to the South Gate. Beautiful old courtyard mansion with wooden fittings – there's nothing else like this closer than Pingyao. The downstairs doubles, however, are decent but windowless and claustrophobic; better to try one of the other rooms. Dorms ¥30, 4

Motels

3e 54 Nan Dajie ⓣ029/87513131. Bus #603 or #608 from the train station. Clean and tidy motel above a nightclub (though it seems to be adequately soundproofed), a real bargain given the location halfway between the Bell Tower and South Gate. The staff are mathematically inept, however, and this can lead to problems at checkout time. 4

Jinjiang Inn 110 Jiefang Lu ⓣ029/87452288, ⓦwww.jj-inn.com. The town's outstanding bargain for a double or twin, with the lowest rates cheaper than some of the backpacker doubles; rooms are simple, smart and modern, with an Internet socket for your laptop. 4

Hotels

Bell Tower 110 Nan Dajie ⓣ029/87600000, ⓦwww.belltowerhtl.com. Massively popular with tour groups, this smart hotel has a great location opposite the southwest corner of the Bell Tower, right in the centre of town. 9

Hyatt Regency 158 Dong Dajie, just east of Heping Lu ⓣ029/87691234, ⓕ87696799. This well-located, steel-and-concrete fortress has a plush interior, populated by tour groups and business folk alike. 9

Jiefang 181 Jiefang Lu ⓣ029/87698888, ⓦwww.xiantourismgroup.com. Huge warren of rooms with brusque, offhand staff – best considered for transit reasons only. 5

Renmin (Sofitel/Mercure) 319 Dongxin Jie ⓣ029/87928888, ⓦwww.sofitel.com. New wings are the usual modern effort, though the bulbous facade of the older central core, built in the 1950s to house Russian advisers, has some character. Staff are all bilingual. 9

Royal Garden 334 Dong Dajie ⓣ029/87690000, ⓦwww.hotelroyalgardenxian.com. Another Chinese-owned upmarket tour-group standby, and with an interesting restaurant that often has unusual specials, such as medicinal dishes. 9

Wuyi 351 Dong Dajie ⓣ029/87681098, ⓕ87213824. Take bus #611 from the station. In a superb location tucked behind its dumpling shop in the centre of town, this little hotel has character and is good value, as well as housing an excellent restaurant. Deservedly popular and often full. 5

The City

Xi'an successfully integrates its architectural heritage with the modern city, its imposing walls and ancient geometric street plan, centring on the Bell Tower, giving it a distinct identity. **Downtown Xi'an**, inside the walls, is just about compact enough to get around on foot, with enough sights to fill a busy day and where the city's prosperity is most evident, in the variety and prices of goods in the shops on **Dong Dajie**, the main shopping street. **Nan Dajie**, to the south, is another shopping district, southeast of which you'll find the **Beilin Museum**, which holds a massive collection of steles, next to the **city walls**, more imposing remnants of Imperial China. Contrast is provided by the **Muslim Quarter** northwest of the Drum Tower, which preserves a different side of old China in its labyrinth of alleys centring on the **Great Mosque**.

The area south of the Ming-dynasty city walls is scattered with architecture from the Han and Tang dynasties. The excellent **Shaanxi History Museum** and the small **Daxingshan Si** sit between the two **Goose pagodas** and their temples, which are some of Xi'an's oldest – and certainly the most distinctive – buildings.

The most useful **bus** for sightseeing is #610, also labelled as tourist bus #8 in Chinese, which runs from the train station via Bei Xin Jie, Bei Dajie, the Bell and Drum towers, then south off Xi Dajie down Guangji Jie to Small Goose Pagoda, Daxingshan Si, the History Museum and on to the Big Goose Pagoda.

Downtown Xi'an

In the heart of town, the **Bell Tower** (daily 8am–9pm; ¥20, or ¥30 including the Drum Tower) stands at the centre of the crossroads where the four main streets meet. The original tower was raised two blocks west of here in 1384, at the centre of the Tang-dynasty city; the present triple-eaved wooden structure standing on a brick platform was built in 1582 and restored in 1739. You can enter only via the subway on Bei Dajie, where you buy your ticket and where you must leave any large bags. Inside is an exhibition of chimes and a bronze bell (not the original). A balcony all the way around the outside provides a view of the city's traffic.

Just west of the Bell Tower is the **Drum Tower** (daily 8am–6pm, till 10pm summer; ¥20, or ¥30 including the Bell Tower). It's a triple-eaved wooden building atop a fifty-metre-long arch straddling the road. You enter up steps on the eastern side, to find a row of drums that used to be banged at dusk, a complement to the bell in the Bell Tower, which heralded the dawn.

The Muslim Quarter

North of the Drum Tower, the scale of Xi'an's streets constricts, and the narrow alleys lined with cramped half-timbered, two-storey buildings feel more like a village than a sprawling provincial capital. This is the **Muslim Quarter**, for centuries the centre for Xi'an's thirty thousand Hui people, said to be descended from eighth-century Arab soldiers. **Beiyuanmen**, the street that runs north from the Drum Tower gate, is flagstoned and lined with Muslim restaurants, all packed out and lively in the evening. **Huajue Xiang**, a narrow, covered alley heading west off Beiyuanmen (30m or so north of the Drum

▲The Bell Tower at right

Tower), is one long line of tourist souvenir stalls and a great place to shop for gifts, though with the exception of a couple of places selling Muslim hats, rugs and crockery, nothing feels particularly relevant. Bargain hard, as asking prices are sometimes absurd.

After Huajue Xiang curves to the north, you'll arrive at the spiritual heart of the district, the **Great Mosque** (daily 8am–6pm; ¥12), the entrance facing a small intersection of alleys. The largest mosque in China, it was originally established in 742, then rebuilt in the Qing dynasty and heavily restored. An east–west facing complex that integrates Arabic features into a familiar Chinese design, it's a calm place, untouched by the hectic atmosphere of the streets outside. On either side of the stone arch at the entrance are two **steles** by two of the most famous calligraphers in China, Mi Fei of the Song dynasty and Dong Qichang of the Ming. The attractive courtyard beyond, which holds a minaret in the form of an octagonal pagoda at its centre, is lined with wooden buildings featuring abstract eave decorations – the usual figurative designs being inappropriate for a mosque. Also here are freestanding steles bearing inscriptions in Chinese, Persian and Arabic. The **main prayer hall**, just beyond the two fountains, has a turquoise roof and some fine carvings on the doors and eaves.

The Muslim Quarter extends west from here nearly to the city wall, though the widening of Xi Dajie has encroached on the far end of the quarter. There are a couple of targets: the **produce market**, including antique and pet stalls, in the streets north off Miaohou Jie (the western extension of Xiyang Shi Jie); and the small **West Mosque**, at the end of Miaohou Jie. Streets along the way are full of poky dumpling shops with rows of street stalls in front, selling daily necessities, **sweets** such as steamed "eight treasure pudding" (glutinous rice cooked in a tiny wooden pot and dusted with sugar and sesame), mutton cooked on skewers while you wait, and nuts, seeds and preserved fruits heaped on plates outside tiny shop fronts.

The Beilin Museum

Heading south from the Bell Tower along Nan Dajie, a street of department stores and offices, you come to Yongning, the huge **south gate**. A turn east takes you along **Shuyuanmen**, a pleasant, cobbled street of souvenir shops, art stores and antique shops traversing the heart of Beilin, a touristy artists' quarter.

About 500m east along here, after a quick curve to the south, is an access point for the city walls and the **Beilin Museum** (daily 8.30am–6.30pm; ¥30), a converted Confucian temple. Aside from an annexe on the west side, which holds an exhibition of chronologically arranged **Buddhist images** where you can follow the evolution of styles over the centuries, the museum's main focus is six halls containing more than a thousand **steles**. The **first hall** contains the twelve Confucian classics – texts outlining the Confucian philosophy – carved onto 114 stone tablets, a massive project ordered by the Tang emperor Wenzong in 837 as a way of ensuring the texts were never lost or corrupted by copyists' errors. The **second hall** includes the **Daqing Nestorian tablet**, on the left as you go in, recognizable by a cross on the top, which records the arrival of a Nestorian priest in Chang'an in 781 and gives a rudimentary description of Christian doctrine. Condemned as heretical in the West for its central doctrine of the dual nature of Christ, both human and divine, and for refusal to see the Virgin Mother as the Mother of God, Nestorianism spread to Turkey and the East as its priests fled persecution, and was the first Christian doctrine to appear in China. In the **third hall**, one stele is inscribed with a **map of Chang'an** at the height of its splendour, when the walls were extensive enough to include the Big Goose Pagoda within their perimeter. Rubbings are often being made in the

fourth hall, where the most carved drawings are housed; thin paper is pasted over a stele and a powdered ink applied with a flat stone wrapped in cloth. Among the steles is an image called the "God of Literature Pointing the Dipper", with the eight characters that outline the Confucian virtues – regulate the heart, cultivate the self, overcome selfishness and return propriety – cleverly made into the image of a jaunty figure. "To point the dipper" meant to come first in the exams on Confucian texts, which controlled entry to the civil service.

The city walls

Imposing enough to act as a physical barrier between the city centre and the suburbs, Xi'an's **city walls** (daily: summer 7am–9.30pm; rest of year 8am–6pm; ¥40) were originally built of rammed earth in 1370 on the foundation of the walls of the Tang-dynasty imperial city, though they took their modern form in 1568, when they were faced with brick. Recently restored, the walls are the most distinctive feature of the modern city, forming a twelve-metre-high rectangle whose perimeter is nearly 14km in length. Some 18m wide at the base, they're capped with crenellations, a watchtower at each corner and a fortress-like gate in the centre of each side. Originally, the city would have been further defended with a moat and drawbridges, but today the area around the walls is a thin strip of parkland, created after a major restoration in 1983.

You can **ascend** the wall from the **four main gates**: Yongning to the south, Anyuan to the north, Changlemen to the east and western Andingmen. An **electric shuttle** runs around (¥50 for the circuit, or ¥5 to the next of fifteen stations), but more fun are the **rentable bikes** (¥20 per 100min, just enough time to get around; you can't bring your own bike up here) – if prepared with food and drinks, you can spend the better part of a day exploring Xi'an from the wall.

The Small Goose Pagoda and the Daxingshan Si

The **Xiaoyan Ta** or **Small Goose Pagoda** (daily 8am–6pm; ¥18, plus ¥10 to climb the pagoda) is southwest of the Yongding gate on Youyi Xi Lu. A 45-metre-tall, delicate construction, founded in the Tang dynasty in 707 to store sutras brought back from India, the pagoda sits in what remains of the Jianfu Si. Two of the pagoda's original fifteen storeys were damaged in an earthquake, leaving a rather abrupt jagged top to the roof, to which you can ascend for a view of the city. A shop at the back of the complex sells Shaanxi folk arts.

Just south of here on Xingshan Xijie, in Xinfeng Park, accessible down a narrow market street, the small **Daxingshan Si** (daily 8am–5pm; ¥20) is usually overlooked by visitors, but is worth a visit. This is the only working Buddhist temple in Xi'an; it was destroyed in the Tang persecution of Buddhism, and thus today's buildings are mainly Qing. Monks in baggy orange trousers will write your name on a prayer sheet in the main hall for a donation.

Shaanxi History Museum

One of the city's major highlights, the **Shaanxi History Museum** (March–Nov 8.30am–6pm, ¥50; Dec–Feb 9am–5.30pm, ¥35) is an impressive modern building within walking distance of the Daxingshan Si and the Big Goose Pagoda. The exhibition halls are spacious, well laid out, and have English captions, displaying to full advantage a magnificent collection of more than three thousand relics.

The **lower floor**, which contains a general survey of the development of civilization until the Zhou dynasty, holds mostly weapons, ceramics and simple ornaments – most impressive is a superb set of Western Zhou and Shang **bronze**

vessels covered in geometric designs suggestive of animal shapes, used for storing and cooking ritual food. Two **side halls** host themed exhibitions. The **western hall** holds bronzes and ceramics, in which the best-looking artefacts are Tang. Large numbers of ceramic **funerary objects** include superbly expressive and rather vicious-looking camels, guardians, dancers, courtiers and warriors, glazed and unglazed. The **eastern hall** holds a display of Tang **gold and silver**, mainly finely wrought images of dragons and tiny, delicate flowers and birds, and an exhibition of Tang **costume and ornament**. The hall's introduction states that Tang women led "brisk and liberated lives", though it's hard to imagine how when you see the wigs arranged to show their complex, gravity-defying hair-dos, and the tall, thin wooden soles on their shoes.

The two **upstairs galleries** display relics from the Han through the Qing dynasties; notable are the Han ceramic funerary objects, particularly the model houses.

The Dacien Si, Big Goose Pagoda and Tang Dynasty Arts Museum

The **Dacien Si** (daily 8am–6.30pm; ¥25), in the far south of town, 4km from the city walls at the end of Yanta Lu, is the largest temple in Xi'an. The original, destroyed in 907, was even bigger: founded in 647, it had nearly two thousand rooms, and a resident population of more than three hundred monks. The surrounding area is a bit of a circus nowadays, with the armies of souvenir sellers dwarfed by a crowd-pulling **musical fountain**, arranged in steps, which fills the northern approach to the temple. The main entrance, however, is to the south, and once inside the walls the atmosphere is much calmer, though still oriented towards tourism rather than worship, even though there are resident monks here.

The most famous person associated with the temple is **Xuan Zang**, the Tang monk who made a pilgrimage to India and returned with a trove of sacred Buddhist texts (see box, p.1040). At his request, the Dayan Ta, or **Big Goose Pagoda** (daily 8am–6.20pm; ¥20) was built of brick at the centre of the temple as a fireproof store for his precious sutras. More impressive than its little brother, the Big Goose Pagoda is sturdy and angular, square in plan, and more than 60m tall. As you go in, look for a famous **tablet** on the right showing Xuan Zang dwarfed by his massive bamboo backpack, rubbings of which are sold all over the city. At either side of the south entrance, stone tablets hold calligraphy by two Tang emperors, surrounded by bas-relief dragons and flying angels; over the lintel of the west door is a fine Tang carving of Buddha and his disciples sitting in a Chinese building. The pagoda has **seven storeys**, each with large windows (out of which visitors throw money for luck). The view from the north windows is the most impressive for the rigorous geometry of the streets below, though it's hard to believe that when built the temple was at least 3km inside the Tang city.

A short walk east of here, the **Tang Dynasty Arts Museum** (daily 8.30am–5.30pm; ¥5) is not as good as it could be, considering the wealth of relics from this age, regarded as the high point of Chinese arts. Nevertheless, it does contain some excellent pieces, mostly pottery horses and camels and tricoloured glazed figures, including among the usual range of warriors and courtiers a couple of stuffy-looking bureaucrats in elaborate costumes. The exhibits are dated but have no English captions.

The Baxian Gong

The **Baxian Gong** (¥3), Xia'an's largest Taoist temple, lies in a shabby area east of the city walls – probably the easiest way to get here is to catch bus #203 east along Dong Dajie, get off at the first stop outside the walls, and head north with a map. It's said to be sited over the wine shop where **Lü Dongbin**, later one of the Eight Immortals (see p.502), was enlightened by Taoist master Han Zhongli. Containing an interesting collection of steles, including pictures of local scenic areas and copies of complex ancient medical diagrams of the human body, the temple is the setting for a popular **religious festival** on the first and fifteenth day of every lunar month. However, it is probably of most interest to visitors for the **antique market** that takes place outside every Wednesday and Sunday (see below).

Shopping

Xi'an is an excellent place to pick up souvenirs and antiques, which are generally cheaper and more varied than in Beijing, though prices have to be bartered down and the standard of goods, especially from tourist shops, is sometimes shoddy. Be aware that many apparent "antiques" – however dusty and worn – are reproductions. Shopping is also an enjoyable evening activity, since the markets and department stores are open until 10pm – the Muslim Quarter and Beilin make for an entertaining stroll under the stars, where the nocturnal hawkers sell everything from dinner to souvenir silk paintings.

Artwork

Xi'an has a strong artistic pedigree, and the **paintings** available here are much more varied in style than those you see elsewhere in China. As well as the widespread line and wash paintings of legendary figures, flowers and animals, look for bright, simple **folk paintings**, usually of country scenes. A traditional Shaanxi art form, appealing for their decorative, flat design and lush colours, these images were popular in China in the 1970s for their idealistic, upbeat portrayal of peasant life. A good selection is sold in a shop just behind the Small Goose Pagoda and in the temple compound, as well as outside the Banpo Museum (see p.276). For **rubbings** from steles, much cheaper than paintings and quite striking, try the Big Goose Pagoda and Shuyuanmen, especially around the Beilin Museum, which is also a great area to find **calligraphy and paintings**. The underground pedestrian route at the South Gate includes an interesting diversion down an old bomb shelter tunnel to Nan Shang Jie, where **papercuts** are for sale.

Strong competition means you can pick up a painting quite cheaply if you're prepared to **bargain** – a good, sizeable work can be had for less than ¥150. However, beware the bright young things who introduce themselves as art students whose class happens to be having an exhibition. They're essentially touts who will lead you to a room full of mediocre work at inflated prices.

Souvenirs

Beiyuanmen and Huajue Xiang, the alley that runs off to the Great Mosque, are the places to go for **small souvenirs**, engraved chopsticks, teapots, chiming balls and the like. Clusters of stalls and vendors swarm around all the tourist sights, and are often a nuisance, though the stalls around the Great Mosque are worth checking out – you'll see curved Islamic *shabaria* knives among the Mao watches and other tourist knick-knacks. Some stalls sell small figures of terracotta soldiers in a mesh basket; you can bargain them down to just a few yuan, but the figures aren't fired properly, and will leave your hands black whenever you touch them. For better quality, buy them from a department store or more upmarket souvenir shop.

For a personalized souvenir, try the **seal engravers** along Shuyuanmen, where you'll also find a variety of **artists' materials** – calligraphy sets and the like.

Antiques

The best place to go for **antiques** is the **City Antiques Market**, about a block south of the Small Goose Pagoda on Zhuque Dajie – bus #18, from the wall end of Zhuque Dajie, stops nearby. This is pretty good, with some genuine antiques and oddities (such as old military gear) at reasonable prices, and Mao-era artwork with price tags that show the dealers here know how much these things sell for overseas. Another good place is the market outside **Baxian Gong**, which is biggest on Wednesdays and Sundays; many vendors are villagers from the outlying regions who look as if they are clearing out their attics. You can find some unusual items here, such as books and magazines dating from the Cultural Revolution containing rabid anti-Western propaganda, Qing vases, opium pipes, and even rusty guns.

Clothes and books

A range of good-value **clothes** is sold on Dong Dajie, with a wide selection of name-brand stores. The best **bookshop** is also here, the Foreign Languages Bookstore, whose tiny entrance is just east of the *Wuyi* hotel and restaurant. They have many books in English about China and Xi'an in particular, along with translations of Chinese classics and a large selection of Victorian and early twentieth-century English-language novels.

Eating

Xi'an is a great place to eat, though the best of the **local food** is fairly rough and ready, most enjoyably consumed in the Muslim Quarter's hectic, open-fronted restaurants. Here you'll find *liang fen* (cold, translucent noodles shaved off a block of beanstarch jelly and served with a spicy sauce), *hele* (buckwheat noodles) and *mianpi* (flat noodles made of refined wheat dough), with a choice of dressings including one made from sesame paste; and huge rounds of flat bread, which make an excellent accompaniment to a handful of grilled mutton skewers. The most widely touted Xi'an dish, however, is *paomo*, basically a meat soup poured over a bowlful of tiny bread cubes; there are both lamb (*yangrou paomo*) and beef (*niurou paomo*) versions.

Restaurants

Anjia Shaocai Beiyuanmen. One of the busiest, nosiest and cleanest of many similar Muslim restaurants on this street, with excellent kebabs, cold noodles and vegetable dishes. They also serve beer, unlike some of the stricter establishments. Getting all your food served at the same time takes some doing though, as kebabs are grilled in huge batches.

Daqinghua Jiaozi Wuyuemiaomen, facing up Dachejia Gang. First-rate Dongbei restaurant decked in hefty yellow pine furniture with cannons and sabres as decor. *Jiaozi* are not what they do best; go for the whole stewed pork leg, cold spiced *mu'er* fungus, steamed bitter gourd and sweetcorn with peas. They often give you complimentary soup and honeyed potatoes. Even with beer, four people can fill up here for under ¥100.

King Town 176 Dongmu Tuoshi. Smart, excellent Sichuanese restaurant, with a casual snack area at street level and a more formal restaurant upstairs where you can pay over ¥50 a head.

Laosunjia Xiyang Shi Jie in the Muslim Quarter, and also at 364 Dong Dajie. *Yangrou paomo* is the house speciality here; you'll be given a hunk of bread, which you break into little pieces and drop into a bowl – a time-consuming process, but it gets you hungry. The bowl, marked with a numbered clothes peg, is then taken to the kitchen and piled with shredded meat and noodles, and it's all served with cloves of pickled garlic and chilli paste for you to tip in as required. The Xiyang Shi Jie branch is down to earth, the Dong Dajie one more refined but three times the price.

Shanghai Renjia Zhuque Dajie, just north of the antiques market. An easy walk from the Small Goose Pagoda. Seafood, stews, and other Shanghai and Jiangnan food.

Sushi Restaurant 223 Dong Dajie. Authentic and reasonably priced sushi bar. You can either sit and select from the conveyor belt, or order pricier options from one of the booths.

Tang Dynasty 75 Chang'an Beicajie. Speciality dumplings and a daily Cantonese lunch buffet. Dinner is an imperial-style banquet (arrive 6.30–7pm) followed by a 90min cultural show, which will set you back ¥410, or ¥200 if you only want a cocktail with the performance (8pm). Tickets can be bought in advance from the theatre lobby on the ground floor, though some accommodation can get you in at a discounted rate.

Tongshengxiang In the block of restaurants behind and just west of the Bell Tower, Xi Dajie. This multistoreyed Muslim place is famous for its *paomo* and *tangbao* (soup buns).

Wuyi 351 Dong Dajie. There's a row of windows selling steamed buns outside, with a similar counter inside offering a huge range of local snacks, from noodles to soups, meats and vegetable dishes – pick up a tray, point to what you want, pay at the till and then sit down and eat. Great for a Chinese breakfast or a light meal, with most dishes under ¥10.

Xi'an 298 Dong Dajie. A restaurant famed as the place where the plotters of the Xi'an Incident (see p.278) met to form their plan to kidnap Chiang Kaishek. The downstairs canteen is alright, with set breakfasts and lunch buffets for ¥10–22 (the *Wuyi* is better), but the upstairs restaurant is excellent, with banquet dishes such as Gourd-shaped Chicken. It's not cheap though: expect ¥60 a head.

Xi'an Roast Duck 368 Dong Dajie, and also on the corner of Jiefang Lu and Dong Si Lu. This otherwise unassuming, two-floor restaurant is usually crowded at lunch. Cafeteria-style downstairs, dining room upstairs. A whole duck (enough for 2/3 people) costs around ¥65.

Drinking and nightlife

Though not as lively as Beijing or Shanghai, Xi'an's large student population and general prosperity make it more exciting at night than most other Chinese cities. The easiest place to start is the **bar street** area on **Defu Lu**, just north of the *Xiangzimen* hostel, which is lined with Western-style pubs. Just outside the South Gate, in an amusement park, is *Music Man*, a fun bar with occasional live music.

Tuesday is the most popular night to go out, when women get in free to all the **discos**. A favourite spot with foreign students is *1+1* on Dong Dajie – the music is a typical mix of hip-hop and techno. Things are a lot better after 10.30pm, when the music gets faster and only the serious clubbers are left.

Listings

Bike rental Hostels rent out bikes around ¥20 a day, with a deposit of up to ¥200.

Banks and exchange Convenient branches of the Bank of China with ATMs are marked on the "Downtown Xi'an" map. You can also exchange cash at the business centres of the larger hotels and many other banks.

Cinema There's a big complex at 379 Dong Dajie, where they show the occasional dubbed foreign action-movie, a change from all the home-grown action movies.

Guides If you're looking for a guide, contact English-speaking Frank Che (Ⓣ029/81909165, Ⓔchexing_2000@yahoo.com), who is especially good at organizing trips to try and see wild pandas around the reserve at Foping.

Hospital The Provincial Hospital is on Youyi Xi Lu, just west of the intersection with Lingyuan Lu.

Internet access Hostels all offer free net access. The best netbar in town is on the fifth floor of the Parkson Building on Xi Dajie – enter via the external glass lift underneath the huge gateway at the mouth of Beiguang Jie. You get armchairs to slouch in, and the equipment is hi-tech and fast for ¥2 an hour. There's another, more ordinary one, up next to the main bus station.

Mail and telephones The central post office (8am–8pm) faces the Bell Tower at the intersection of Bei Dajie and Dong Dajie. The "Telecom district", with phone emporiums and card sellers, is around the intersection of Bei Dajie and Xixin Jie.

Massage There's a centre staffed by blind masseuses at 118 Beiyuanmen, in the Muslim Quarter – look for the English sign on the west side of the street. ¥50 will get you an hour of excellent pressure-point manipulation.

PSB At 138 Xi Dajie (Mon–Sat 8am–noon & 3–5pm).

Travel agents All hostels can book you on local tours, and some act as agents for Yangzi ferries, too; you don't have to be staying with them either. Hotels and motels also have tour desks, though you're likely to be bundled in with Chinese-speaking groups if you use them. The main office of CITS is at 48 Chang'an Lu (daily 8am–6pm; ⓣ029/85399999), and can arrange tours and hires out minibuses seating 5–6 for ¥400 a day.

Around Xi'an

You could spend days on excursions around Xi'an: look at any tourist map and the area is dense with attractions. People swarm to see the **Terracotta Army** and **Banpo Museum** at least, though two recommended attractions off the tour-group itinerary are the **Famen Si**, with a superb museum attached – which is a little too remote for most visitors – and the exhausting but highly scenic holy mountain of **Hua Shan**.

The easiest way to see the sights around Xi'an is to get up early and take one of the many **tours** on offer. There are two routes: the popular **eastern route** covers the Huaqing Pool and the Lintong Museum, the Terracotta Army, the Tomb of Qin Shi Huang and the Banpo Museum; the **western route**, going to the Imperial Tombs and the Famen Si, is less popular as more travel time is involved, and it's more expensive (it's also harder to find anyone running it off season). Bear in mind that the best tours leave by 8am.

The ticket booths in front of the *Jiefang* hotel – with boards outside showing the route and the price – are the civilized faces of the seething mass of **private tour buses** fighting to exit the car park east of the train-station square. Tours should cost about ¥40 for the east route, ¥60 for the west. Tour operators on the western route often skip the remote Famen Si despite advertising it on their signs: check before you go.

Hotels and hostels also organize tours, usually with breakfast, transport, admission and guide thrown in for upwards of ¥160 per person depending on destination. **CITS** normally deals with tour groups rather than individuals, but

Around Xi'an

Banpo Museum	半坡博物馆	*bànpō bówùguǎn*
Famen Si	法门寺	*fǎmén sì*
Huaqing Pool	华清池	*huáqīng chí*
Mao Ling	茂陵	*màolíng*
Princess Yong Tai's Tomb	永泰墓	*yǒngtài mù*
Qian Ling	乾陵	*qián líng*
Qin Shi Huang's Tomb	秦始皇陵	*qínshǐhuáng líng*
Terracotta Army	兵马俑	*bīngmǎ yǒng*
Xianyang	咸阳	*xiányáng*
Xianyang Museum	咸阳博物馆	*xiányáng bówùguǎn*
Zhao Ling	昭陵	*zhāo líng*
Hua Shan	华山	*huáshān*
East Peak Guesthouse	东峰饭店	*dōngfēng fàndiàn*
Hua Shan station	华山站	*huáshānzhàn*
Yuquan Si	玉泉寺	*yùquán sì*

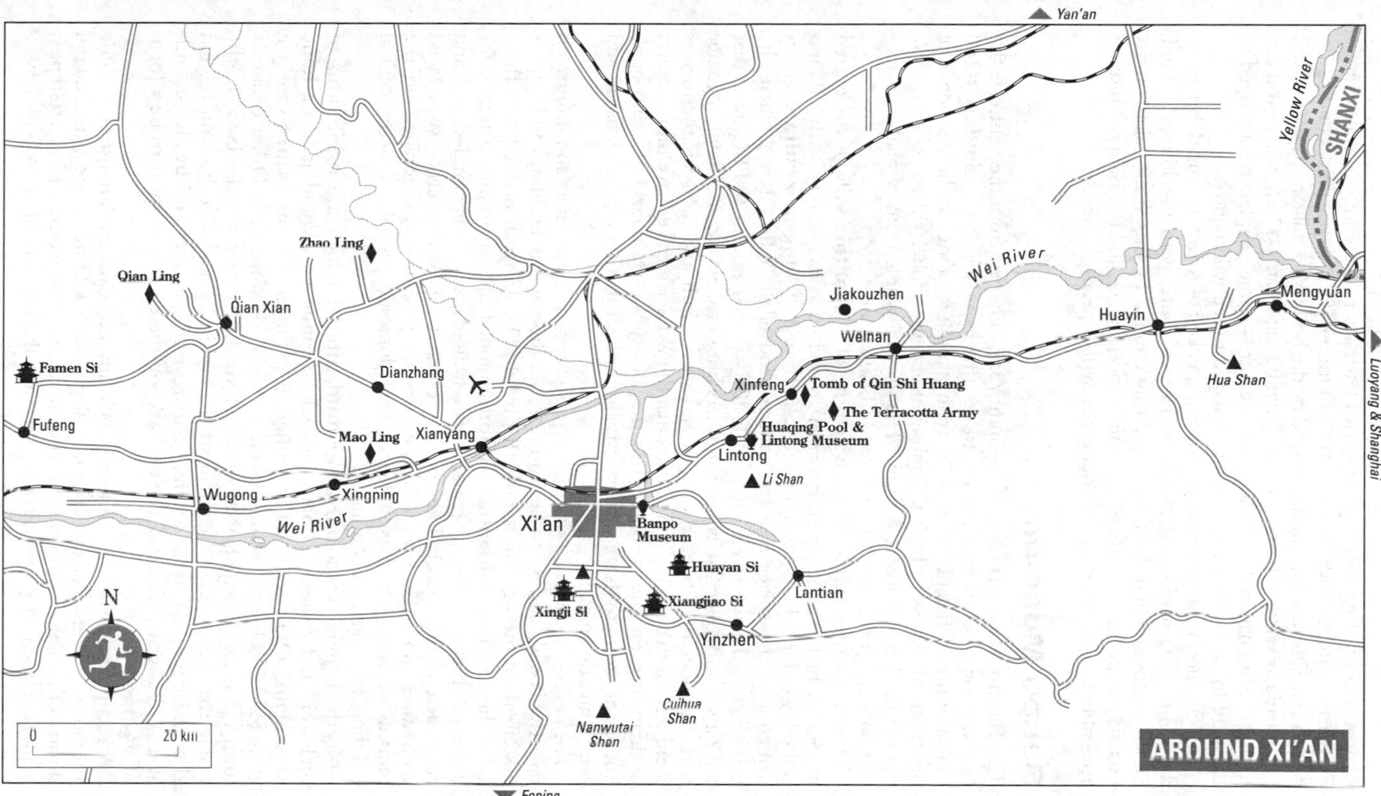
AROUND XI'AN
Yan'an
Luoyang & Shanghai
Foping
SHANXI
Yellow River
Wei River
Mengyuan
Hua Shan
Huayin
Welnan
Jiakouzhen
Tomb of Qin Shi Huang
The Terracotta Army
Xinfeng
Huaqing Pool &
Lintong Museum
Lintong
Li Shan
Banpo
Museum
Xi'an
Huayan Si
Xiangjiao Si
Xingji Si
Lantian
Yinzhen
Cuihua
Shan
Nanwutai
Shan
Xianyang
Dianzhang
Mao Ling
Xingping
Zhao Ling
Qian Ling
Qian Xian
Famen Si
Fufeng
Wugong
N
0
20 km

it's worth contacting them to see what their current rates are – you can rent a six-person minibus with driver from them from ¥400 a day, again depending on destination. One unusual option offered by the hostels is a full day-trip southwest to a **panda reserve** at Foping in the Qingling mountains (¥160), where you can see captive animals and tour the research centre - some people have arranged to stay here for a few days and actually managed to see wild pandas.

The cheapest option – though not the quickest – is to take **local buses** to the sights. This works best along the eastern route, with the Huaqing Pool, Lintong Museum and the Terracotta Army covered by **bus #306** (aka **tourist bus #5**) from the east side of the train station square, and the Banpo Museum accessible by city buses. See accounts below for specific details.

Banpo Museum

The **Banpo Museum** (daily 8am–5pm; ¥35), 8km east from the centre, is the first stop on most eastern tours – to get there yourself, catch city **bus #240** from the top of Jiefang Lu near the train station; it's about an hour's ride. The ticket affords access to both the museum and the model village (same hours), though the latter is a waste of time. The site as a whole is not visually spectacular, so some imagination is required to bring it alive.

The Banpo Museum is the excavated site of a **Neolithic village**, discovered in 1953, which was occupied between around 4500 BC and 3750 BC. Banpo is the biggest and best-preserved site so far found of **Yangshao culture**, and is named after the village near the eastern bend of the Yellow River where the first relics of this type were found. A history written around 300 BC states that the Yangshao people "knew their mothers but not their fathers. Living together with the deer they tilled the earth and wove cloth and between themselves there was no strife." This, and the fact that the women's graves have more objects in them than the men's, implies that the society was **matriarchal**. From bone hooks and stone tools unearthed, it is also known that they farmed, fished and kept domestic animals.

The covered excavation site is a lunar landscape of pits, craters and humps, on raised walkways, and it can be hard to relate these to the buildings and objects described on the signs in whimsical English. The village is divided into three areas; the first is a **residential section** bounded by a surrounding trench for defence, which includes the remains of 46 houses, round or pyramid-shaped and constructed half underground around a central fire pit with walls of wood faced with mud and straw. Around the houses are pits, used for storage, and the remains of pens, which would have held domestic animals. A larger, central building was used as a communal hall.

North of here was a **burial ground**, around which are exhibitions of skeletons and funerary objects, mostly ceramic bowls and jade or bone ornaments. One grave, of a young girl, buried in an earthenware jar, contained 76 objects, including jade earrings and stone balls. Other ceramics found at the site, which were made in **six kilns** here, are displayed in the **museum wing**. They are surprisingly sophisticated, made by hand of red clay and decorated with schematic images of fish, deer and heads, or with abstract patterns, sometimes with marks on the rim that appear to be a form of writing.

A compound of huts outside the museum, the **Culture Village** is a crude attempt to reconstruct the original village – a Neolithic theme park entered through the nether regions of an enormous fibreglass woman. Little attempt is made at authenticity beyond trying to cover the fire extinguishers with leaves.

Huaqing Pool and the Lintong Museum

Huaqing Pool (daily 8am–5pm; ¥40, students ¥20) is at the foot of Li Shan, 30km east of Xi'an on the road to the Terracotta Army. **Bus #306** (**tourist bus #5**) runs out here every few minutes from the east side of the train-station square. Its **springs**, with mineral-rich water emerging at a constant and agreeable 43°C, have been attracting people for nearly 2500 years, including many emperors. Qin Shi Huang had a residence here, as did the Han emperors, but its present form, a complex of **bathing houses and pools**, was created in the Tang dynasty. The first Tang emperor, Tai Zong, had a palace at Huaqing, but it was under his successor, **Xuan Zong**, who spent much of the winter here in the company of his favourite concubine, **Yang Guifei** (see box, below), that the complex reached its height of popularity as an imperial pleasure resort.

Nowadays, Huaqing is a collection of classical buildings, a little less romantic than it sounds – the buildings are nothing special, and the site is always thronged with day-trippers. The old **imperial bathhouses**, at the back of the complex, must once have looked impressive, but today they just resemble half-ruined, drained swimming pools. The largest is **Lotus Pool**, more than a hundred metres square, once reserved for the use of Xuan Zong; a little smaller is **Crabapple Pool**, for concubine Yang. As well as the pools, there are a few halls, now housing souvenir shops, and a small **museum**, where fragments of Qin and Tang architectural detail – roof tiles and decorated bricks – hint at past magnificence. A **marble boat**, at the edge of Jiulong Pond, on the left as you enter, was constructed in 1956. The **Huaqing Hot Spring Bathhouse** behind it offers you the chance to bathe in the waters; for a steep ¥70 you are shut in a room that looks like a mid-range hotel room (complete with a photo of a glossy tropical paradise on the wall and little plastic bottles of shampoo) with a bath and a shower. Better is the **public bathhouse** at the front of the complex, on the left of the gate as you go in, where you can bathe in a communal pool for ¥20; you'll need to take your own towel and soap.

The Lintong Museum

The **Lintong Museum** (daily 8am–6pm; ¥25) nearby provides a rewarding diversion while visiting Huaqing Pool; turn right out of the pool complex, then run a gauntlet of souvenir sellers for 150m and you'll see the museum on your right. Though small and relatively expensive, it's worth it for a varied collection that includes silver chopsticks and scissors, a bronze jar decorated with human faces, a crossbow and numerous Han funerary objects, including ceramic figures of horses, dogs, ducks and pigs. The best exhibit, a **Tang reliquary** unearthed

Xuan Zong and Yang Guifei

The tale of Emperor Xuan Zong and his concubine Yang Guifei is one of the great Chinese **tragic romances**, the equivalent to the Western Antony and Cleopatra, and is often depicted in art and drama, most famously in an epic by the great Tang poet Bai Juyi. Xuan Zong took a fancy to Yang Guifei – originally the concubine of his son – when he was over 60, and she was no spring chicken. They fell in love, but his infatuation with her, which led to his neglect of affairs of state, was seen as harmful to the empire by his officials, and in part led to the rebellion of the disgruntled General **An Lushan**. As An Lushan and his troops approached the capital, the emperor and his retinue were forced to flee southwest into Sichuan; along the way, his army mutinied and demanded Yang Guifei's **execution**. In despair, she hanged herself.

The Xi'an Incident

Huaqing Pool's modern claim to fame is as the setting for the **Xi'an Incident** in 1936, when **Chiang Kaishek** was arrested by his own troops and forced to sign an alliance with the Communists. The story is a little more complicated than this. As Japanese troops continued to advance into China, Chiang insisted on pursuing his policy of national unification – meaning the destruction of the Communists before all else. In December 1936, he flew to Xi'an to overlook another extermination campaign. The area was under the control of **Marshal Zhang Xueliang** and his Manchurian troops. Although GMD supporters, they, like many others, had grown weary of Chiang's policies, fuelled by the fact that their Manchurian homeland was now occupied by the Japanese. In secret meetings with Communist leaders, Zhang had been convinced of their genuine anti-Japanese sentiments, and so, on the morning of December 12, Nationalist troops stormed Chiang's headquarters at the foot of Li Shan, capturing most of the headquarters staff. The great leader himself was eventually caught halfway up the slope in a house at the back of the complex, behind the pools – a neo-Grecian pavilion on the lower slopes of the mountain marks the spot. Still in his pyjamas and without his false teeth, he had bolted from his bed at the sound of gunfire. Chiang was forced to pay a heavy ransom but was otherwise unharmed, his captors allowing him to remain in control of China provided that he allied with the Communists against the Japanese. Nowadays, tourists line up at the pavilion to don GMD uniforms and have their pictures taken.

nearby, is in the second of the three rooms. Inside a stone stupa about a metre high, decorated with images of everyday life, was found a silver coffin with a steep sloping roof, fussily ornamented with silver spirals, strings of pearls and gold images of monks on the side. Inside this, a gold coffin a few inches long held a tiny glass jar with a handful of dust at the bottom. These delicate relics, and the dust, optimistically labelled "ashes of the Buddha", though crudely exhibited in what look like Perspex lunchboxes, are more interesting than anything at Huaqing Pool.

The Terracotta Army and Tomb of Qin Shi Huang

The **Terracotta Army** – probably the highlight of a trip to Xi'an – and the Tomb of Qin Shi Huang, which it guards, are 28km east of Xi'an, just beyond Huaqing Pool. Plenty of tours come here, giving you two hours at the army and twenty minutes at the tomb. Alternatively, it's easy enough to get here by yourself on **bus #306** (¥7) from the east side of the Xi'an train station; the journey takes an hour. More expensive, but a little quicker, are the **minibuses** (¥26) that leave from the same place. You get dropped off in a vast car park at the start of a newly built tourist complex of industrial proportions whose main purpose seems to be to channel visitors through a kilometre-long gauntlet of overpriced restaurants and souvenir stalls. The food is diabolical, and it's best to eat before you go.

The Terracotta Army

No records exist of the **Terracotta Army** (daily 8am–6pm; ¥90, winter ¥65; audio-guides ¥20 plus ¥200 deposit), which was set to guard Qin Shi Huang's tomb over two thousand years ago, and was only discovered by peasants sinking a well in 1974. Three rectangular vaults were found, constructed of earth with brick floors and timber supports. Today, **hangars** have been built over the

Qin Shi Huang

Though only 13 when he ascended the throne of the western state of Qin in 246 BC, within 25 years **Qin Shi Huang** had managed to subjugate all the quarrelsome eastern states, thus becoming the first emperor of a **unified China**. "As a silkworm devours a mulberry leaf, so Qin swallowed up the kingdoms of the Empire", or so the first-century BC historian Sima Qian put it. During his eleven years as the sole monarch of the Chinese world, Qin Shi Huang set out to transform it, hoping to create an empire that his descendants would continue to rule for "ten thousand years". His reign was marked by centralized rule, and often **ruthless tyranny**. As well as standardizing weights and measures (even the width of cartwheels) and ordering a unified script to be used, the First Emperor decreed that all books, except those on the history of the Qin and on such practical matters as agriculture, be destroyed, along with the scholars who produced them. It was only thanks to a few Confucian scholars, who hid their books away, that any literature from before this period has survived. Qin Shi Huang himself favoured the strict philosophy of "legalism", a system of thought that taught that human nature was intrinsically bad, and must be reined in by the draconian laws of the state.

As well as overseeing the construction of roads linking all parts of the empire, mainly to aid military operations, Qin Shi Huang began the construction of the **Great Wall**, a project that perhaps more than any of his harsh laws and high taxes turned the populace, drummed into constructing it, against him. Ambitious to the end, Qin Shi Huang died on a journey to the east coast seeking the legendary island of the immortals and the secret drug of longevity they held. His entourage concealed his death – easy to do as he lived in total seclusion from his subjects – and on their return installed an easily manipulated prince on the throne. The empire soon disintegrated into civil war, and within a few years Qin Shi Huang's capital at Xianyang had been destroyed, his palace burnt and his tomb ransacked.

It is possible that Qin Shi Huang, seen as an archetypal tyrant, has been harshly judged by history, as the story of his reign was written in the Han dynasty, when an eastern people whom he subjugated became ascendant. They are unlikely to have been enamoured of him, and the fact that the Terracotta Army faces east, the direction that Qin Shi Huang thought threats to his empire would come from, indicates the animosity that existed. The outstanding artistry of the terracotta figures has revised the accepted view of the Qin dynasty as a time of unremitting philistinism, and his reign has been reassessed since their discovery. Mao Zedong, it is said, was an admirer of his predecessor in revolution.

excavated site so that the ranks of soldiers – designed never to be seen, but now one of the most popular tourist attractions in China – can be viewed in situ. You can take photos, but are not meant to use tripods or flash.

Vault 1

Vault 1 is the largest, and about a fifth of the area has been excavated, revealing more than a **thousand figures** (out of an estimated eight thousand) ranked in battle formation and assembled in a grid of six-metre-deep corridors. Facing you as you enter the hangar, this is one of the most memorable sights in China; you can inspect the static soldiers at closer range via raised walkways running around their perimeter. Averaging 1.8m in height, the figures are hollow from the thighs up; head and hands were modelled separately and attached to the mass-produced bodies. Each soldier has **different features** and expressions and wears marks of rank; some believe that each is a portrait of a real member of the ancient Imperial Guard. Their hair is tied in buns and they are wearing knee-length battle tunics; the figures on the outside originally wore leather armour, now decayed. Traces of **pigment** show that their dress was once bright yellow, purple and green, though it's grey now. Originally, the troops carried real bows, swords, spears and crossbows, more than ten thousand of which have been found. The metal weapons, made of sophisticated alloys, were still sharp when discovered, and the arrowheads contained lead to make them poisonous.

A central group of **terracotta horses** is all that remains of a set of chariots. These wore harnesses with brass fittings and have been identified as depicting a breed from Gansu and Xinjiang. Each has six teeth, an indication that they are in their prime.

Vaults 2 and 3

Vault 2 is a smaller, L-shaped area, still under excavation; it's thought to hold more warriors than vault 1. The four groups here – crossbowmen, charioteers, cavalry and infantry – display more variety of posture and uniform than the figures in the main vault, though a large number of smashed and broken figures make the scene look more like the aftermath of a battle than the preparation for one. Four exceptional figures found here are exhibited at the side: a kneeling **archer**, a **cavalryman** leading a horse, an **officer** with a stylish goatee and the magnificent figure of a **general**, 2m tall, wearing engraved armour and a cap with two tails. Also on show are some of the weapons discovered at the site, including a huge bronze battle-axe.

The much smaller **vault 3**, where 68 figures and a chariot have been found, seems to have been battle headquarters. Armed with ceremonial *shu*, a short bronze mace with a triangular head, the figures are not in battle formation but form a guard of honour. Animal bones found here provide evidence of ritual sacrifices, which a real army would have performed before going into battle. A photo exhibition of plaster replicas gives some idea of how the figures would have been painted. At times, you'll find a half-blind peasant signing postcards in the shop at vault 2; this is **Yang Zhifa**, the man who discovered it all in 1974.

The rest of the site

At the side of vault 2 is a small **museum** where two magnificent **bronze chariots**, found in 1982 near Qin Shi Huang's tomb, are displayed in glass cases. They're about half actual size. The front one, depicting the Imperial Fleet leader's chariot, has four horses and a driver, and is decorated with dragon, phoenix and cloud designs, with a curved canopy and a gold-and-silver harness. Behind the driver is a large compartment featuring a silver door-latch and windows that open and close. The chariot at the back was the emperor's and has seats and beds in the rear. Both chariots were made with astonishing attention to detail; even the driver's knuckles, nails and fingerprints are shown. Another museum holds small artefacts found around the area, including a skull with an arrowhead still embedded in it, and a few kneeling pottery attendants, the only **female figures** depicted.

The Tomb of Qin Shi Huang

The **Tomb of Qin Shi Huang** (daily 8am–5pm; ¥25) is now no more than an artificial hill, nearly 2km west of the Terracotta Army – there's no transport so you'll have to walk. The burial mound was originally at the southern end of an inner sanctuary with walls 2.5km long, itself the centre of an outer city stretching for 6km, none of which remains. There's not much to see here; hassled at every step by souvenir sellers, you can walk up stone steps to the top of the hill, where you have a view of fields scraped bare for agriculture.

According to accounts by **Sima Qian** in his *Historical Records*, written a century after the entombment, 700,000 labourers took 36 years to create an imperial city below ground, a complex full of wonders: the heavens were depicted on the ceiling of the central chamber with pearls, and the geographical divisions of the earth were delineated on a floor of bronze, with the seas and rivers represented by pools of mercury and made to flow with machinery. Automatic crossbows were set to protect the many gold and silver relics. Abnormally high quantities of **mercury** have recently been found in the surrounding soil, suggesting that at least parts of the account can be trusted. Secrecy was maintained, as usual, by killing most of the workmen. The tomb has yet to be excavated; digs in the surrounding area have revealed the inner and outer walls, ten gates and four watchtowers.

North and west of the city

Except for the museum at **Xianyang**, the tombs, temples and museums in the north and west of Xi'an are a little far out to be visited conveniently. Trying to get around yourself is tricky, as the only place served by regular **country buses** is Xianyang, though it's also possible to get to Qian Ling and Famen Si independently. **Tours** start early and get back late, with the sights thinly spread out in a long day of travelling across stark loess plains, but the museums are stimulating and it's good to get the feel of the tombs from which so many museum treasures come, even though most are little more than great earth mounds. The farthest sight, the **Famen Si**, is also the most rewarding.

Xianyang

XIANYANG, now a nondescript city 60km southeast of Xi'an (buses from the main long-distance bus station take 1hr 30min), was the centre of China a couple of millennia ago, the site of the capital of **China's first dynasty**, the Qin. Little evidence remains of the era, however, except a flat plain in the east of the city that was once the site of Qin Shi Huang's palace. Relics found here, mostly unspectacular architectural details of more interest to archeologists – roof tiles, water pipes, bricks and so on – are in the **city museum** on Zhongshan Lu (daily 8am–5.30pm; ¥20), a converted Confucian temple. From the Xianyang bus station, the museum is about 2km away: turn left on to Xilan Lu, then immediately left on to Shengli Anding Lu, which turns into Zhongshan Lu when it crosses Leyu Lu – the museum is on Zhongshan Lu, on the left. Star of the collection is a **miniature terracotta army** unearthed from a tomb, probably of a high official, 20km away, a lot less sinister than the real thing as each of the nearly three thousand terracotta figures is about 50cm high. The mass-produced figures are of two types, cavalry and infantry, some of which have heavy armour and a cap, others have light armour and a bun hairstyle. Some also still have traces of their original bright paint scheme, which show that the designs on their shields varied widely. The warriors are fairly crude, but the horses are well done.

The Imperial Tombs

The area around Xi'an was the location of multiple ancient capitals spanning multiple dynasties over more than a thousand years; the result is one of the richest archeological areas in China. The many **Imperial Tombs** scattered along the Wei River valley to the west of Xi'an are largely Han- and Tang-dynasty structures, less touristy than other sites in Xi'an, and a good way to escape the eastbound crowds and see a bit of the countryside.

Mao Ling

The resting place of the fifth Han emperor, Wu Di (157–87 BC), **Mao Ling** (daily 8am–5pm; ¥20), 40km west of Xi'an, is the largest of the twenty Han tombs in the area. It's a great green mound against the hills, which took more than fifty years to construct and contains, among many treasures, a full **jade burial suit** – jade was believed to protect the corpse from decay and therefore enhanced the possibilities of longevity of the soul. A dozen **smaller tombs** nearby belong to the emperor's court and include those of his favourite concubine and his generals, including the brilliant strategist **Huo Qubing** who fought several campaigns against the northern tribes (the Huns) and died at the age of 24. A small **museum** displays some impressive relics, including many massive stone sculptures of animals that once lined the tombs' spirit ways, simplified figures that look appealingly quirky; look for the frogs and a cow, and the horse trampling a demonic-looking Hun with its hooves, a macabre subject made to look almost comical.

Qian Ling

Qian Ling (daily 8am–5pm; ¥30) is 80km northwest of Xi'an, and usually the second tomb tour after Mao Ling. To get here under your own steam, take tour bus line #2 (3hr; ¥28) from the east side of the Xi'an train station. This hill tomb, on the slopes of Liang Shan, is where **Emperor Gao Zong** and his empress **Wu Zetian** were buried in the seventh century.

The **Imperial Way** leading to the tombs is formed from two facing rows of carved stone figures of men and flying horses, and with two groups of (now headless) mourners – guest princes and envoys from tribute states, some with their names on their backs. The tall stele on the left praises Gao Zong; opposite is the uninscribed **Wordless Stele**, erected by the empress to mark the supreme power that no words could express.

Seventeen **lesser tombs** are contained in the southeast section of the area. Among the five excavated since 1960 here is the **tomb of Prince Zhang Huai**, second son of Gao Zong, forced to commit suicide by his mother Wu Zetian during one of her periodic purges of those opposing her rise to power. At this tomb you walk down into a vault frescoed with army and processional scenes, a lovely tiger with a perm in the dip on either side. One fresco shows

Empress Wu Zetian

The rise to power of **Empress Wu Zetian** is extraordinary. Originally the **concubine** of Emperor Gao Zong's father, she emerged from her mourning to win the affections of his son, bear him sons in turn, and eventually marry him. As her husband ailed, her power over the administration grew until she was strong enough, at his death, to usurp the throne. Seven years later she was declared empress in her own right, and ruled until being forced to abdicate in favour of her son shortly before her death in 705 AD. Her reign was notorious for intrigue and bloodshed, but even her critics admit that she chose the right ministers for the job, often solely through merit. The heavy negative historical criticism against her may be solely because she was a woman, as the idea of a female in a position of authority is entirely contrary to Confucian ethics (her title was "Emperor", there being no female equivalent for so exalted a position). For example, one historian described her as a whore for taking male lovers (while any male emperor would be expected to number his concubines in the hundreds), and the stone mourners along the Imperial Way leading to her tomb were decapitated by unknown later generations. For more about Wu Zetian, see also Chapter 12 "Sichuan and Chongqing", p.883.

the court's welcome to visiting foreigners, with a hook-nosed Westerner depicted. There are also vivid frescoes of polo playing and, in the **museum** outside, some Tang pottery horses.

Princess Yong Tai's tomb (¥20) is the finest here – she was the emperor's granddaughter. Niches in the wall hold funeral offerings, and the vaulted roof still has traces of painted patterns. The passage walls leading down the ramp into the tomb are covered with murals of animals and guards of honour. The court ladies are still clear, elegant and charming after 1300 years, displaying Tang hairstyles and dress. At the bottom is the great tomb in black stone, lightly carved with human and animal shapes. Some 1300 gold, silver and pottery objects were found here and are now in Xi'an's Shaanxi History museum. At the mouth of the tomb is the traditional **stone tablet** into which the life story of the princess is carved – according to this, she died in childbirth at the age of 17, but some records claim that she was murdered by her grandmother, the empress Wu Zetian. The **Shun mausoleum** of Wu's own mother is small, but it's worth a look for the two unusually splendid granite figures that guard it, a three-metre-high lion and an even bigger unicorn.

Zhao Ling

At **Zhao Ling** (daily 8am–6pm; ¥21), east of Qian Ling and 70km northwest of Xi'an, nineteen **Tang tombs** include that of Emperor Tai Zong. Begun in 636 AD, this took thirteen years to complete. Tai Zong introduced the practice of building his tomb into the hillside instead of as a tumulus on an open plain. From the main tomb, built into the slope of Jiuzou, a great cemetery fans out southeast and southwest, which includes 167 lesser tombs of the imperial family, generals and officials. A small **museum** displays stone carvings, murals and pottery figures from the smaller tombs.

Famen Si

The extraordinary **Famen Si** (daily 8am–6pm; ¥28, relics ¥32), 120km west of Xi'an, home of the finger bone of the Buddha, and the nearby **museum** containing an unsurpassed collection of Tang-dynasty relics, are worth the long trip it takes to get out here. The easiest way is to catch **tour bus #2** (3hr; ¥18) at the Xi'an train station, across the concourse on the east side in front of the *Jiefang* hotel; it also stops at Qian Ling. Hostels charge ¥700 for an eight-person **minibus** to the temple, which isn't such a bad deal. Otherwise, take the hourly **bus to Fufeng** from Xi'an's long-distance bus station (4hr), from where you can catch a minibus to the temple (20min).

In 147 AD, King Asoka of India, to atone, it is said, for his warlike life, distributed precious **Buddhist relics** (*sarira*) to Buddhist colonies throughout Asia. One of the earliest places of Buddhist worship in China, the Famen Si was built to house his gift of a **finger**, in the form of three separate bones. The temple enjoyed great fame in the Tang dynasty, when Emperor Tuo Bayu began the practice of having the bones temporarily removed and taken to the court at Chang'an at the head of a procession repeated every thirty years; when the emperor had paid his respects, the finger bones were closed back up in the **crypt** underneath the temple stupa, together with a lavish collection of offerings. After the fall of the Tang, the vault was forgotten about until the protective stupa above collapsed in 1981, revealing the most astonishing array of Tang precious objects, and at the back, concealed inside box after box, the legendary finger of the Buddha.

Today, the temple is a popular place of pilgrimage. The stupa and crypt have been rebuilt, with a **shrine** holding the finger at the crypt's centre. A praying

▲ Famen Si

monk is always in attendance, sitting in front of the finger, next to the safe in which it is kept at night (if it's not being exhibited elsewhere, as happens periodically). Indeed, the temple's monks are taking no chances, and the only entrance to the crypt is protected by a huge metal door of the kind usually seen in a bank. You can see into the original crypt – at 21m long, the largest of its kind ever discovered in China – though there's not much to see in there now.

The museum

The **museum** west of the temple houses the well-preserved Tang relics found in the crypt, and is certainly one of the best small museums in China. Exhibits are divided into sections according to their material, with copious explanations in English. On the lower floor, the **gold and silver** is breathtaking for the quality of its workmanship: especially notable are a silver incense burner with an internal gyroscope to keep it upright; a silver tea basket, the earliest physical evidence of tea-drinking in China; and a gold figure of an elephant-headed man. Some unusual items on display are twenty **glass plates and bottles**, some Persian, with Arabic designs, some from the Roman Empire including a bottle made in the fifth century. Glassware, imported along the Silk Road, was more highly valued than gold at the time, as none was made in China. Also in the crypt were a thousand volumes of Buddhist **sutras**, pictures of which are shown, and 27,000 **coins**, the most unusual of which, made of tortoiseshell, are on display here. An **annexe** holds the remains of the silk sheets that all the relics were wrapped up in, together with an exhibition on its method of manufacture.

At the centre of the main room is a gilded **silver coffin**, which held one of the finger bones, itself inside a copper model of a stupa, inside a marble pagoda. Prominent upstairs is a gold and silver **monk's staff**, which, ironically, would have been used for begging alms, but the main display here is of the **caskets** that the other two finger bones were found in – finely made boxes of diminishing size, of silver, sandalwood, gold and crystal, which sat inside each other, while the finger bones themselves were in tiny jade coffins.

South of the city

In the wooded hilly country south of Xi'an, a number of important **temples** serve as worthy focal points for a day's excursion. The **Xingjiao Si**, 24km southeast of the city on a hillside by the Fan River, was founded in 669 AD to house the ashes of the travelling monk Xuan Zang (see p.1040), whose remains are underneath a square stupa at the centre of the temple. The two smaller stupas either side mark the tombs of two of his disciples. Beside the stupa, a pavilion holds a charming and commonly reproduced stone carving of Xuan Zang looking cheery despite being laden down under a pack. Little remains of the **Huayan Si**, on the way to the Xingjiao Si, except two small brick pagodas, one of which holds the remains of the monk Dushun, one of the founders of Zen Buddhism. The **Xingji Si**, 5km west of here, has a ten-storey pagoda, which covers the ashes of Shandao, founder of the Jingtu sect.

No tours visit the temples, but the sites are accessible by **bus #215**, which leaves from just outside Xian's south gate. Ride right to the last stop, then take a rickshaw to the temples; you'll have to negotiate a return trip.

Hua Shan

The five peaks of **Hua Shan**, 120km east of Xi'an (¥70 entrance fee) were originally known as Xiyue (Western Mountain), because it is the westernmost of the five sacred Taoist mountains. It's always been a popular place for pilgrimage, though these days people puffing up the steep, narrow paths or enjoying the dramatic views from the peaks are more likely to be tourists.

There's a Chinese saying, "There is one path and one path only to the summit of Hua Shan", meaning that sometimes the hard way is the only way. This isn't so true today, perhaps, what with a **cable car** (¥110 return) running from the east gate – note that the ride doesn't go to the peak, but does put you above the toughest climbs. The original, arduous **old route** begins at the **west gate** and **Yuquan Si** (Jade Spring Temple), dedicated to the tenth-century monk Xiyi who lived here as a recluse. From here, every few hundred metres you'll come across a wayside refreshment place offering stone seats, a burner, tea, soft drinks, maps and souvenirs – the higher you go, the more attractive the knobbly walking sticks on sale seem. In summer, you'll be swept along in a stream of Chinese, mostly young couples, dressed in their fashionable, but often highly impractical, holiday finest, including high-heeled shoes.

Known as the "**Eighteen Bends**", the deceptively easy-looking climb up the gullies in fact winds for about two hours before reaching the flight of narrow stone steps that ascend to the first summit, **North Peak** (1500m). The mountain was formerly dotted with temples, and there are still half a dozen. Many people turn back at this point, although you can continue to **Middle Peak** next, then East, West and South peaks (each at around 2000m), which make up an **eight-hour circuit trail**.

Though the summits aren't that high, the gaunt rocky cliffs, twisted pines and rugged slopes certainly look like genuine mountains as they swim in and out of the mist trails. It's quite possible to ascend and descend the mountain in a single day, especially if you use the cable car. The going is rough in places and a few of the upper paths require a head for heights, with chain handrails, wooden galleries and rickety ladders attached at difficult points. Some people arrive in the evening and climb by moonlight in order to see the **sunrise** over the Sea of Clouds from Middle or East Peak.

Practicalities

As Hua Shan lies between Xi'an and Luoyang, you can take in the mountain en route between the two cities, as an excursion from Xi'an, or on the way to Xi'an from Ruicheng in Shanxi. **Tour bus #1** from Xi'an's train-station concourse takes two hours to get to the east gate and cable car (¥28). The last buses back to Xi'an leave from each gate at around 5.30pm, but walk to the main road and you'll find private minibuses leaving as late as 8pm. A **day-tour** organized by hostels in Xi'an, including transport, cable car, entry and breakfast, costs ¥310 per person, or you can rent an eight-person minibus through them for ¥700.

You can also get here by **train** to Hua Shan station (aka Mengyuan), a village about 20km to the east of either of the mountain gates. From the station, **public buses** (¥3) will drop you at Yuquan Jie, the street that runs uphill to Yuquan Si and the hiking trail. **Private minibuses** follow the same route, but go straight to Yuquan Si (¥5). A taxi should cost ¥15–20 to either gate from the train station, and ¥10 to make the trip between the gates if you find yourself in the wrong place. If you plan to climb at night, be sure to take some warm clothes and a flashlight with spare batteries.

There are several **places to stay** (typically ❸, dorm beds ¥40) on Yuquan Jie: the *Huaiying Dajiudian* (❸, dorm bed ¥30) is a popular staging point for night ascents. There are also **basic hotels** about every 5km along the circuit route, where a bed should cost about ¥30, but you'll have to bargain. Don't expect light or heat at these places, and if you plan to stay the night on the mountain it's a good idea to take your own sleeping bag. These places are at least easy to find, though, and hotel touts waylay travellers along the route. There's a more upmarket place on top of the East Peak, the *East Peak Guesthouse* (❸), catering to the sun watchers.

The nicest thing to be said about the **food** near the east gate and on the mountain is that it's palatable. It's also more expensive the higher you go. If you're on a tight budget, stock up beforehand. There is a small **convenience store** just uphill from the *Huaiying*, and plenty of noodle restaurants nearby as well.

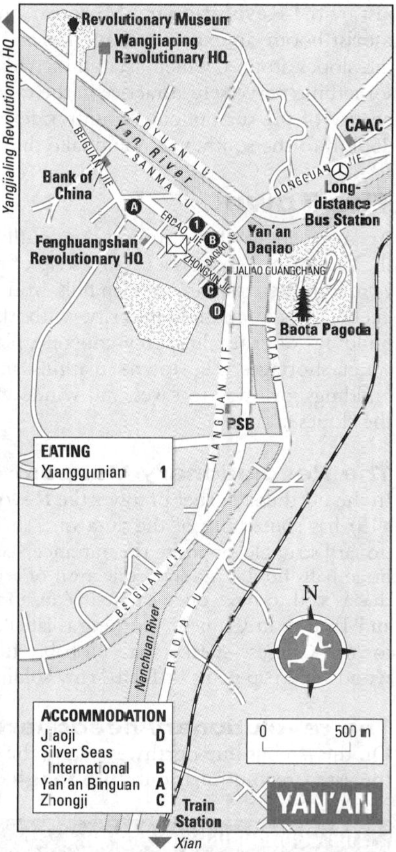

Yan'an

YAN'AN, set deep in the bleakly attractive dry loess hills of northern Shaanxi, is closer in appearance and temperament to Shaanxi's industrial cities than the ancient capitals of the Yellow River plain. The town is a quiet backwater, and as you walk its dour streets it's hard to imagine that, as the **headquarters of the Communist Party** in the 1930s and early 1940s, this was once a major revolutionary pilgrimage site second only to Mao's birthplace at Shaoshan. In the changed political climate, with enthusiasm for the Party no longer compulsory, it's now hardly different from any other northern town, rarely visited except by groups of PLA soldiers and the odd ideologue.

There's nothing spectacular about the sights, unless the fact that Mao and Co were once here is enough to inspire awe by itself. The three **revolutionary Communist headquarters** sites are dusty and feel a little forlorn despite their historical importance. The Yangjialing headquarters is the site of the first Central Committee meeting, and is the most popular tourist destination in Yan'an. Some insight into China's modern history is given not

Yan'an

Yan'an	延安	*yán'ān*
Baota Pagoda	延安塔	*yánān tă*
Fenghuangshan Revolutionary HQ	凤凰山革命旧址	*fènghuángshān gémìng jiùzhǐ*
Revolutionary Museum	延安革命纪念馆	*yán'ān gémìng jìniànguǎn*
Wangjiaping Revolutionary HQ	王家坪革命旧址	*wángjiāpíng gémìng jiùzhǐ*
Yangjialing Revolutionary HQ	杨家岭革命旧址	*yángjiālǐng gémìng jiùzhǐ*
Accommodation		
Jiaoji	延安交际宾馆	*yánān jiāojì bīnguǎn*
Silver Seas International Hotel	银海国际大饭店	*yínhǎi guójì dàjiǔdiàn*
Yan'an Binguan	延安宾馆	*yánān bīnguǎn*
Zhongji	中际大厦	*zhōngjì dàshà*

just by the **Revolutionary Museum**, but by the town centre, built during the tourist boom, an example of utilitarian 1950s and 1960s **architecture**, and by the slopes around, which are full of traditional Shaanxi **cave houses**. There is something perversely attractive in the town's grimness, which, together with the beauty of the surrounding countryside, makes it worth a day-trip from Xi'an, 250km to the south; you could take the overnight train up and a bus back.

The Town

Arranged in a Y-shape around the confluence of the east and west branches of the Yan River, Yan'an is a narrow strip of brutal breeze-block architecture, about 7km long, hemmed in by steep hills. Ironically, the centre conforms to Cold War clichés of communist austerity, with streets lined with identical apartment buildings of crumbling grey concrete, plagued by frequent electricity cuts and water shortages. The town's margins are much more attractive, as the dour buildings give way to caves, and windowless houses built to look like caves, on the slopes around.

The Revolutionary Museum

In the northeast corner of town, the **Revolutionary Museum** (daily 8am–6pm; ¥15) has something of the aura of a shrine, and a sculpture depicting revolutionary struggle, opposite the entrance, has offerings of money in front of it. The huge halls hold a massive collection of artefacts, including a stuffed white horse that is said to have once carried Mao, and translations of books by Lenin, Stalin and Trotsky in Chinese. Nothing is labelled in English, though; of most interest to non-Chinese-speakers are probably the propaganda pictures, which include wood- and papercuts of Red Army soldiers helping peasants in the fields.

The revolutionary headquarters

On the #3 bus line northwest along the river is the most impressive, and most touristed, revolutionary site, the **Yangjialing Revolutionary Headquarters**

The Communists in Yan'an

The arrival of the Communists in Yan'an in October 1935 marked the end of the **Long March**, an astonishing and now semi-mythical journey in which eighty thousand men, women and children of the Red Army fled their mountain bases in Jiangxi province to escape encirclement and annihilation at the hands of the Nationalists (see box, p.526).

When Mao finally arrived in Yan'an there were only about five thousand still with him, but here they met up with northern Communists who had already established a soviet. Gradually, stragglers and those who had been sent on missions to other parts arrived to swell their numbers. The **Yan'an soviet** came to control a vast tract of the surrounding country, with its own economy and banknotes to back the new political system. Soldiers in China usually lived parasitically off the peasants unfortunate enough to be in their way; but Mao's troops, trained to see themselves as defenders of the people, were under orders to be polite and courteous and pay for their supplies. **Mao** wrote some of his most important essays here, including much that was later included in the Little Red Book. As well as most of the major political personalities of Communist China, a number of distinguished foreigners came here, too, including Edgar Snow, whose book *Red Star Over China* includes descriptions of life in Yan'an, and Norman Bethune, the Canadian surgeon who died in the service of the Red Army. Both are memorialized at the Fenghuangshan Revolutionary Headquarters.

(daily 8am–5.30pm; ¥10). Set in a picturesque gulley, these grounds were home to the Communist leaders in the early 1940s, a time when Mao began to look beyond fighting off the Japanese and Guomindang, and conceptualized what a Communist Chinese state would be like. The first Central Committee meeting was held in an almost chapel-like hall, with wooden benches and the lyrics to the great revolutionary song *The East is Red* posted on the front wall. Cut into the hillside above are the residences of Mao, Zhou Enlai, Liu Shaoqi and Zhu De, with plaques marking where The Great Helmsman had a certain conversation, or cultivated vegetables. You half expect to see a tomb with a stone rolled aside.

Back in town, the **Wangjiaping Revolutionary Headquarters** (daily 7am–7pm; ¥10) is a compound of low buildings, just around the corner from the Revolutionary Museum. Turn immediately left as you leave the museum compound and walk 200m to the access road – look for the large traffic sign over the road. The simple, low buildings of white plaster over straw, mud and brick, typical of traditional local architecture, are elegant structures, with wooden lattice windows faced with paper, sometimes incorporating the communist star into their design. Mao and company lived and worked here in the late 1940s. The complex has a rather monastic feel – the arched rooms, with cups sitting on the table and bedding still on the beds, have the simplicity of monks' cells, and the main hall is reminiscent of a prayer hall.

At the end of a side road off Zhongxin Jie between the post office and *Yan'an Binguan*, the unassuming **Fenghuangshan Revolutionary Headquarters** (daily 8am–5.30pm; ¥7) served as the initial residence of the Communists. In 1937 and 1938, the two main rooms in the western courtyard functioned as Mao's bedroom and study, and still house his wooden bed, desk with chairs and a latrine – as well as a collection of letters and photos of Communist officers, all of which are labelled in Chinese only. Two souvenir shops sell reproductions of anything to do with the period – mostly tacky offerings including singing Mao lighters.

Baota Pagoda

Standing on a hill in the southeast corner of town, on the east bank of the river, the Ming-dynasty **Baota Pagoda** (daily 6am–9pm; ¥21, plus ¥10 to ascend the nine flights of stairs) is sometimes used as a symbol of the Communist Party. High above the town and reached by a twisty road, the pagoda commands an impressive view of its angular planes and the ragged hills, pocked with caves, beyond. Outside, tourists can pose for photographs dressed up in the blue and grey military uniforms of the first Communist soldiers, complete with red armband and wooden gun.

Practicalities

The **train station** is in the far south of town, a long way from anything interesting. **Bus #2**, which heads up through the centre of town near the accommodation, is the most useful service to catch from here. **Long-distance buses**, which are faster than the train arrive either at the train-station concourse or the **bus station**, about 1km east of the town centre. A service from Linfen in Shanxi and Yulin in the north, close to the border with Inner Mongolia, also arrives here.

Yan'an is notorious for its **lodging restrictions** on foreigners, though things seem to have eased recently. The towering *Silver Seas International Hotel* (Ⓣ0911/2139999; ❸) is well located in the centre of town on Daqiao Jie, and is a finer choice than the ageing *Yan'an Binguan* (Ⓣ0911/2113122; ❺) in the north end of town. Better budget options include the *Zhongji* (Ⓣ0911/2315666; ❹–❺), at 25 Zhongxin Jie 50m up from Hualiao Guangchang; and the *Jiaoji* on Nanguan Xie (Ⓣ0911/2113862; ❸). **Eating out** in Yan'an can be a problem if you want anything more sophisticated than a bowl of noodles, though there is a *KFC* on Hualiao Guangchang, with a sushi place upstairs in the same building, and a Sichuan restaurant in the alley across the street. Still, don't miss the *Xianggumian* noodle shop on Bei'er Xiang.

To **move on to Xi'an**, there are three daily trains, one in the early afternoon and two in the evening, the best overnight train being #4761 (8hr; ¥76). Hard-sleeper tickets are sold only from the first window of the station ticket office (officially daily 6–7am, 3.30–5pm & 8–9.30pm, but they're often closed). If you arrived from Xi'an by train or are heading for Xi'an for the first time, consider getting the bus, as the views of loess and cave dwellings en route are incredible. Express services to Xi'an leave from the bus station every 30min, beginning at 5.30am and finishing at noon (6hr; ¥69).

Luoyang and around

LUOYANG, in the middle reaches of the Yellow River valley, has been occupied since Neolithic times and served as China's capital at various points from the Zhou through to 937 AD. Confucius once studied here, and this is where

Luoyang and around

Luoyang	洛阳	*luòyáng*
Luoyang Museum	洛阳博物馆	*luòyáng bówùguǎn*
Wancheng Park	王成公园	*wángchéng gōngyuán*
Bus Stations		
Jinyuan Bus Station	锦远汽车站	*jǐnyuǎn qìchēzhàn*
Main Bus Station	洛阳汽车站	*luòyáng qìchēzhàn*
Accommodation		
Fangda Business Hotel	芳达商务酒店	*fāngdá shāngwù jiǔdiàn*
Luoyang Air Hotel	洛阳航空大厦	*luòyáng hángkōng dàshà*
Luoyang Lüshe	洛阳旅舍	*luòyáng lǚshè*
Luoyang Mingyuan Youth Hostel	明苑国际青年旅舍	*míngyuàn guójì qīngnián lǚshè*
Luoyang Youth Hostel	洛阳国际青年旅舍	*luòyáng guójì qīngnián lǚshè*
Peony	牡丹大酒店	*mǔdān dàjiǔdiàn*
Qunying Star Vogue Hotel	群英之皇的尚酒店	*qúnyīng zhīhuǎngde jiǔdiàn*
Yinyan	银燕酒店	*jǐnyàn jiǔdiàn*
Restaurants		
Deheng Kaoya Dian	德恒烤鸭店	*déhéng kaōyā diàn*
Laoluo Tangmian Guan	老雒汤面馆	*lǎoluò tāngmián guǎn*
Palace	宫邸	*gōng dǐ*
Sichuan Fandian	四川饭店	*sìchuān fàndiàn*
Tianxiang	天香饭店	*tiānxiāng fàndiàn*
Around Luoyang		
Baima Si	白马寺	*báimǎ sì*
Guanlin Miao	关林庙	*guānlín miào*
Longmen Caves	龙门石窟	*lóngmén shíkū*
Museum of Ancient Tombs	洛阳古墓博物馆	*luòyáng gǔmù bówùguǎn*

Buddhism first took root in China in 68AD. While the industrial and drab modern city itself retains no atmosphere of past glories, the outlying fields are dotted with earthern **tomb mounds** of former officials and wealthy citizens, and there are two outstanding Buddhist sites nearby: the **Longmen Caves**, one of China's three major rock art galleries; and the venerable **Baima Si**. The city also makes a good base for day-trips to Song Shan and Shaolin Si (see p.299).

Arrival and city transport

Luoyang is spread between the rail line in the north and the Luo River to the south. The centre of town is about halfway between, focused along Zhongzhou Zhong Lu, which runs diagonally east–west across the city. Both Jiefang Lu and Jinguyuan Lu run down from the train station to the centre.

Luoyang **airport**, 20km north of town, is tiny and served by bus #83 to the train station. The massive **train station**, a major intersection on China's north–south and east–west lines, is in the town's northern extremity where Jiefang Lu and Jinguyuan Lu converge, a busy and unattractive area that nonetheless offers good budget accommodation. The **bus stations** are here, too: most services use the big one east of the train-station square at the top of Jinguyuan Lu, but there's also the Jinyuan depot, west of the train station, which handles inter-provincial destinations.

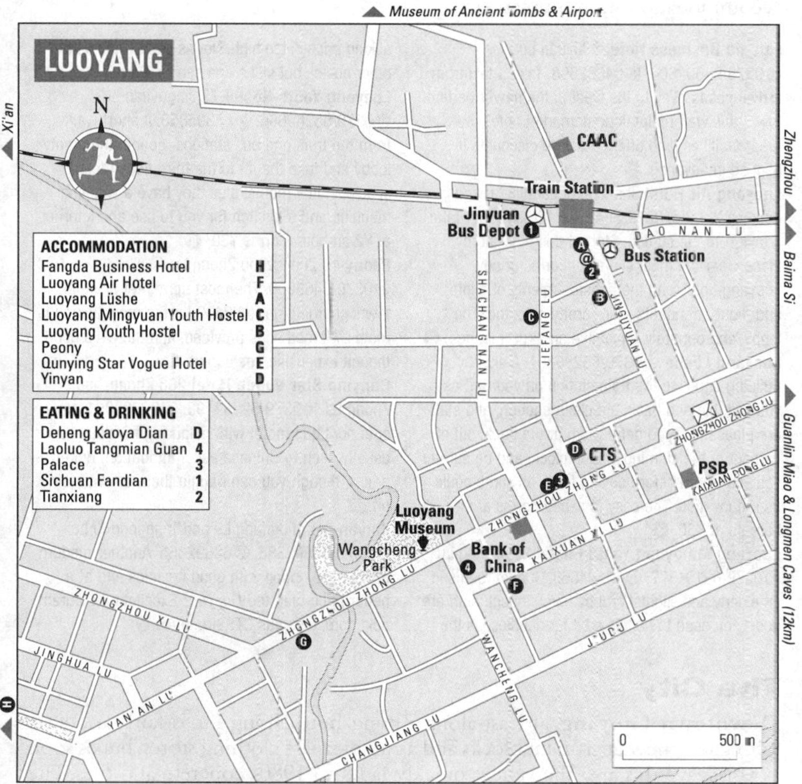

Moving on from Luoyang

The #83 bus runs to the **airport** in under an hour from the west side of the train-station square. For tickets, CAAC are at 196 Dao Bei Lu (Ⓣ0379/3935301), 200m north of the station, and there's also a China Southern office on Zhongzhou Zhong Lu, just east of Jiefang Lu. **Trains** head west to Xi'an and east to Zhengzhou, north to Taiyuan and south into Hubei province, and the station is pretty orderly, with ticket windows open from 7.40am to 1pm, 1.40–5.20pm and 5.30pm–midnight. **Buses** leave through the day from the main station to Xi'an, Dengfeng, Zhengzhou and beyond, though the ticket office can be a bit of a scrum. Touts for **Shaolin Si buses** hang around outside the main bus station at the corner of Jinguyuan Lu, and are not shy of grabbing customers.

The train-station area is also the place to pick up **city buses**, including those to Baima Si and the Longmen Caves (see accounts for details). **Taxis**, which can be hailed on the streets, are plentiful, with a ¥6 flag fall.

Accommodation

Basing yourself in one of the budget options near Luoyang's train station isn't such a bad idea, as there are good connections to the sights and transport out once you've finished. However, the centre of town is cleaner, though the accommodation more upmarket.

Fangda Business Hotel 6 Xiyuan Lu Ⓣ0379/64682600, Ⓕ64682698. Take a taxi from arrival points. Way to the west in the newer parts of town, this well-maintained upmarket hotel has great facilities, and offers massive discounts if booked in advance. ❼

Luoyang Air Hotel Junction of Fanglin Lu and Kaixuan Xi Lu Ⓣ0379/3944668, Ⓕ3915552. Take a taxi from the station. Staff at this nine-storey place wear the most stylish uniforms of any Luoyang hotel, and the guests – plenty of pilots and flight attendants – are pretty chic, too. The lobby, appropriately, looks like an airport lounge. ❺

Luoyang Lüshe Ⓣ0379/65295381. A shabby building opposite the train station on your left as you exit, big and basic but clean enough, and staff are pleasant. Try to get a room at the back, out of earshot of the chiming station clock, and be sure to see your room before paying for it, as some could use renovation. The cosy four-bed dorms are a bargain at ¥30, ❷

Luoyang Mingyuan Youth Hostel 20 Jiefang Lu Ⓣ0379/63191377, Ⓕ63194668. Budget rooms in an elderly and slightly grubby hotel, though staff are good. You need to haggle a bit for doubles, as the asking price is too high. Not as good value as the other hostel, but still a fine choice. Dorms ¥30, ❹

Luoyang Youth Hostel 72 Jinguyuan Lu Ⓣ0379/65260666, Ⓕ63305858. A short walk from the train and bus stations; go into the empty lobby and take the lift to the third floor. Clean, spacious, tidy rooms, plus they have a washing machine and a kitchen for you to use and Internet at ¥2 an hour. Dorms ¥30, ❸

Peony 15 Zhongzhou Zhong Lu Ⓣ & Ⓕ0379/6468000. The most upmarket place in town, charging up to ¥2400 for the most luxurious rooms. All mod cons provided, and there's a good, though expensive, restaurant. ❽

Qunying Star Vogue Hotel 266 Zhongzhou Zhong Lu Ⓣ0379/62983198, Ⓕ62683001. New, cute boutique motel with colourful, frivolous decor usually alien to Chinese accommodation. Relatively pricey, though you can haggle them down a fair bit. ❻

Yinyan Cnr of Jiefang Lu and Tanggong Xi Lu Ⓣ0379/63892388, Ⓕ63892355. Another modern, motel-style option with good facilities and at a better price than the *Qunying*. Excellent restaurant next door, too, plus CTS are here. ❺

The City

Downtown Luoyang, at least along Zhongzhou Zhong Lu, is fairly modern, with glossy new apartment blocks and a run of smart clothing stores, but as soon as you leave this area the veneer quickly fades to 1980s concrete and tiles. The

Luoyang's peonies

It's said that in 800 AD the Tang Empress Wu Zetian, enraged that the **peonies**, alone among flowers, disobeyed her command to bloom in the snow, banished them from her capital at Chang'an. Many were transplanted to Luoyang (the secondary capital) where they flourished, and have since become one of the city's most celebrated attractions, the subject of countless poems and cultivation notes. Luoyang now boasts over 150 varieties of peony, which have found their way onto every available patch or scrap of ground – a splendid sight when they flower in spring. The peony motif is also everywhere in the city, from trellises to rubbish bins.

sole two sights are located along Zhongzhou Zhong Lu, around 2km southwest of the station – catch bus #40 down Jiefang Lu, or #50 down Jinguyuan Lu. **Wangcheng Park** (daily 5.30am–9.30pm; ¥3), at its best in April when the peonies are blooming, is a popular recreation spot at dawn, and overlies the site of the **Zhou capital**, though none of the walls, palaces, temples or marketplace remains are on show.

Most of what has been left of the city's dynastic importance is gathered into the **Luoyang Museum** (daily 9am–5.30pm; ¥20), just east of the park, a surprisingly bright and well-captioned exhibition inside a grubby building. The area around Luoyang entered the Bronze Age before the rest of China, so the **Shang bronzes** are especially extensive; look, too, for an endearing **jade tiger** from the Zhou, as well as some Indian-influenced **Wei statuary**, and a model farm from a Han tomb with a sow and her row of piglets. As usual, the Tang wins hands down for pottery, with their multicoloured, expressive camels and several hook-nosed, pointy-chinned foreigners, and for **gold and silver**, where their ornate decorative objects show the influence of Persian and Roman styles.

Eating

As far as **restaurants** go, the Sichuanese have landed and taken over Luoyang, though there are a couple of places where dishes don't arrive smothered in chillies. For cheap noodles and dumplings, try the snack stalls near the station. There's also a knot of **cafés** at the south end of Shachang Nan Lu, near the junction with Kaixuan Xi Lu.

Deheng Kaoya Dian Tanggong Xi Lu, next to the *Yingyan* hotel. Famous roast-duck restaurant with smart antique-style furnishings but not especially expensive – a whole duck is around ¥60.

Laoluo Tangmian Guan Wangcheng Lu, just south of the park and museum. Good, old-style place for snacks and light meals; downstairs canteen and more formal rooms above. Not expensive in any case.

Palace Cnr of Jiefang Lu and Zhongzhou Zhong Lu. New restaurant-bar offering eclectic mix of Sichuanese, pizza and Japanese dishes, plus lots of beer. A bit pricey for what you get but good atmosphere.

Sichuan Fandian West side of the road, at the top end of Jiefang Lu. One of a clutch of cheap restaurants, this is a surprisingly good, noisy joint where dishes are around the ¥10 mark.

Tianxiang 56 Jingyuyuan Lu. Crowded, smoky and inexpensive Sichuanese restaurant, very popular and with decent food. They have an English menu of sorts, too. Part of a hotel of the same name.

Listings

Banks and exchange The Bank of China is on the corner of Zhongzhou Zhong Lu and Shangchang Nan Lu (daily 8am–5pm).

Mail The post office is tucked on the north side of Zhongzhou Zhong Lu, near the junction with Jinguyuan Lu (Mon–Sat 8am–6pm).

Telephones There's a 24hr telecom building next to the post office, on Jinguyuan Lu.
Travel agents and tours If your accommodation can't help out, the CTS are in the *Yinyan* hotel on Tanggong Xi Lu (Ⓣ0379/65372020, mob 13592058448). A standard day-tour of the sights in the vicinity of town, including Baima Si and Shaolin Si, costs around ¥55.
PSB The PSB is at 1 Kaixuan Xi Lu (Mon–Sat 8am–noon & 2–6pm), with gory pictures of traffic accidents displayed outside.

Around Luoyang

The main destination around Luoyang lies south at the **Longmen Caves** – however little you know about Buddhism or about sculpture, you cannot help but be impressed by the scale and complexity of the work here and by the extraordinary contrast between the power of the giant figures and the intricate delicacy of the miniatures. Nearby, you can also visit **Guanlin Miao**, a memorial temple to Three Kingdom hero Guan Di. The other major sight is the Buddhist temple of **Baima Si**, which lies east of the city; and there's also an interesting, if not very well-presented, **Museum of Ancient Tombs** northwest of Luoyang, where you can see the interiors of the mounds that dot the local fields. All these can be visited on **public buses** from Luoyang, and you could pack the lot into one very busy day. Alternatively, all but the museum are served by private **tourist minibuses**, which run from outside the station. Note that if you're heading east to Song Shan or Zhengzhou after Luoyang, Baima Si is on the way and makes a good spot to break the journey; day-tours to Shaolin Si tend to stop off here, too.

The Longmen Caves

A UNESCO World Heritage Site, the **Longmen Caves** (daily 7.30am–5.30pm; ¥80) are a spectacular parade of Buddhist figurines and reliefs. **Bus #81** (¥1.50) runs here from the east side of the train station via Jingguyuan Lu, turning east onto Zhongzhou Zhong Lu and then south down Dingding Lu and Longmen Lu to its terminus at the caves; the journey can take up to an hour, though it's only 12km south of town. A metered **taxi** ride will be around ¥30. The roadhead is a kilometre short of the caves, and if you don't fancy a walk through the souvenir stalls, head down to the river and follow it to the entrance. The site is very busy in the summer, overrun with tourists posing in the empty niches for photos, and also very hot and exposed – try to visit early on.

Over the years, 1350 caves, 750 niches and 40 pagodas containing 110,000 statues were carved out of the limestone cliffs bordering the **Yi River**. The carvings, stretching 1km and mostly found on the west bank, were commissioned by emperors, the imperial family, other wealthy families wanting to buy good fortune, generals hoping for victory, and religious groups. The **Toba Wei** began the work in 492 AD, when they moved their capital to Luoyang from Datong, where they had carved the Yungang Caves. At Longmen, they adapted their art to the different requirements of a harder, limestone surface. Three sets of caves, **Guyang**, **Bingyang** and **Lianhua**, date from this early period. Work continued for five hundred years and reached a second peak under the **Tang**, particularly under Empress Wu Zetian, a devoted adherent of Buddhism.

There's a clearly visible progression from the early style brought from Datong, of simple, rounded, formally modelled holy figures, to the complex and elaborate, but more linear, Tang carvings, which include women and court characters. In general, the Buddhas are simple, but the sculptors were able to show off with the attendant figures and the decorative flourishes around the edges of the caves. Also discernible are traces of vandalism and looting (lots of missing heads and hands), which began with the anti-Buddhist movement in the ninth century, was continued by souvenir-hunting Westerners in the nineteenth and twentieth centuries, and culminated in (surprisingly muted) attacks by Red Guards during the Cultural Revolution.

A tour of the caves

The caves have been beautifully renovated and feature English labelling. Starting from the entrance at the northern end and moving south down the group, the following are the largest and most important carvings, which stand out due to their size. The three **Bingyang caves** are early; the central one, commissioned by Emperor Xuan Wu to honour his parents, supposedly took 800,000 men working from 500 to 523 AD to complete it. The eleven statues of Buddha inside show northern characteristics – long features, thin faces, splayed fishtail robes – and traces of Greek influence. The side caves, completed under the Tang, are more natural and voluptuous, carved in high relief. **Wanfo** (Cave of Ten Thousand Buddhas), just south of here, was built in 680 by Gao Zong and his empress Wu Zetian, and has fifteen thousand Buddhas carved in tiny niches, each one different and the smallest just 2cm high. **Lianhua** (Lotus Flower Cave) is another early one, dating from 527, and named after the beautifully carved lotus in its roof; while at **Moya Sanfo** you can see an incomplete trinity, abandoned when the Tang dynasty began to wobble. But by far the most splendid is **Fengxian** (Ancestor Worshipping Cave), where an overwhelming seated figure of Vairocana Buddha, 17m high with two-metre-long ears, sits placidly overlooking the river, guarded by four warrior attendants (though the westerly two are almost completely gone) who are grinding malevolent spirits underfoot. **Medical Prescription Cave**, built in 575, details several hundred cures for everything from madness to the common cold. **Guyang** is the earliest of all, begun in 495, where you can still see traces of the vivid paintwork that originally gave life to these carvings. There's a central Buddha and nineteen of the "Twenty Pieces", important examples of ancient calligraphy.

From the end of the west bank you can cross the bridge to the east side, for a good view of the caves peppering the opposite bank like rabbit warrens. Up the hill is the **Tomb of Bai Juyi**, the famous Tang poet, who spent his last years in Luoyang as the Retired Scholar of the Fragrant Hill.

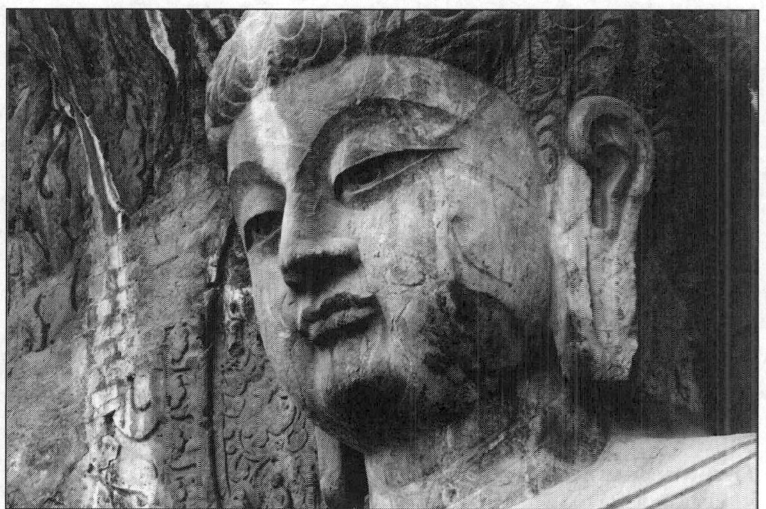

▲Vairocana Buddha, Fengxian Cave

Guanlin Miao

On its way back to Luoyang from the Longmen Caves, bus #81 stops 7km south of town outside the red-walled **Guanlin Miao** (daily 8am–5pm; ¥30) a complex dedicated to **Guan Di** – also known as Guang Gong and Guan Yu – loyal general of Liu Bei of the Three Kingdoms period (for more about which, see the box on p.453). He was captured and executed by the King of Wu who sent his head to Cao Cao, King of Wei, hoping in this way to divert on to the Wei any revenge that might be coming. Cao Cao neatly sidestepped this grisly game of pass-the-parcel by burying the head with honour in a tomb behind the temple, now a wooded, walled mound.

Despite its military theme, the temple is beautiful and rather peaceful, the elegant Ming buildings highly carved and richly decorated. Especially fine are the carved stone lionesses lining the path to the Main Hall. Each has a different expression and a different cub, some riding on their mother's back, some hiding coyly behind her paws. In the first hall, look carefully at the eaves for rather comical images of Guan Di fighting – he's the one on the red horse, a faithful animal called **Red Hare** – and leading an army engaged in sacking a city engulfed by carved wooden flames. Inside, stands a seven-metre-tall statue of the general, resplendent in technicolour ceremonial robes with a curtain of beads hanging from his hat.

The Baima Si

Historic, leafy **Baima Si** (White Horse Temple; daily 7.30am–5.30pm; ¥40), 12km east of Luoyang at the end of the #56 bus route from the train station (¥1.5), is attractive for its ancient buildings and devotional atmosphere. You'll be dropped either on the side of the road or at the car park, from where it's a dash through a gauntlet of souvenir shops to the ticket window.

Founded in 68 AD, the Baima Si has some claim to being the first Buddhist temple in China. Legend says that the Emperor Mingdi of the Eastern Han dreamed of a golden figure with the sun and moon behind its head. Two monks sent to search for the origin of the dream reached India and returned riding white horses with two Indian monks in tow, and a bundle of sutras. This temple was built to honour them, and its layout is in keeping with the legend: there are two stone horses, one on either side of the entrance, and the tombs of the two monks, earthen mounds ringed by round stone walls, lie in the first courtyard.

Home to a thriving community of monks, the Baima Si is primarily a place of worship, and over-inquisitive visitors are tactfully but firmly pointed in the right direction. Inside the temple, you'll find this a placid place, its silence only pricked by the sound of gongs or the tapping of stonemasons carving out a stele. Beyond the Hall of Celestial Guardians, the **Main Hall** holds a statue of Sakyamuni flanked by the figures of Manjusri and Samantabhadra. Near the Great Altar is an ancient bell weighing more than a tonne; as in the days when there were over ten thousand Tang monks here, it is still struck in time with the chanting. The inscription reads: "The sound of the Bell resounds in Buddha's temple causing the ghosts in Hell to tremble with fear". Behind the Main Hall is the **Cool Terrace** where, it is said, the original sutras were translated. Offerings of fruit on the altars, multicoloured cloths hanging from the ceilings, and lighted candles in bowls floating in basins of water, as well as the heady gusts of incense issuing from the burners in the courtyards, indicate that, unlike other temples in the area, this is the genuine article.

The Museum of Ancient Tombs

In a patch of open land around 6km northwest of the city (catch bus #83 from the east side of the train station), the **Museum of Ancient Tombs** (daily

8am–5pm; ¥20) contains the relocated brick interiors of two dozen tomb mounds from the Luoyang area dating from the Western Han to Northern Song. Most had been robbed, and the museum is very neglected, but it does give a more human view of the times when compared with Longmen's overwhelming scale.

The tombs are arranged underground around a central atrium, into which you descend from beside souvenir stalls (there are no signs, but the helpful stall-holders will point the way). Each are entered through a short tunnel, and are very small – you can barely stand in a couple – but decorated brickwork and frescoes liven the whole thing up. Best, however, is **Jing Ling**, the tomb of Xuan Wu of the Northern Wei, which stands just outside the museum grounds – again, there's no sign but you can't miss the huge earth hillock. This hasn't been relocated, and you descend a fifty-metre-long ramp into Xuan Wu's tomb chamber – guarded by two sneering demons – where his sarcophagus remains in situ.

Song Shan

The seventy peaks of the **Song Shan** range stretch over 64km across Dengfeng county, midway between Luoyang and Zhengzhou. When the Zhou ruler Ping moved his capital to Luoyang in 771 BC, it was known as Zhong Yue, Central Peak – being at the axis of the **five sacred Taoist mountains**, with Hua Shan to the west, Tai Shan to the east, Heng Shan to the south and another Heng Shan to the north. The mountains, thickly clad with trees, rise from narrow, steep-sided rocky valleys and appear impressively precipitous, though with the highest peak, Junji, at just 1500m, they're not actually very lofty. When the summits emerge from a swirling sea of cloud, though, and the slopes are dressed in their brilliant autumn colours, they can certainly look the part.

Given its importance to Taoism, it's ironic that the busiest sight at Song Shan today is in fact the **Shaolin Si**, a Buddhist temple famed not just as one of the earliest dedicated to the Chan (Zen) sect, but also where **Chinese kung fu** is said to have originated. A major Taoist temple survives, too, in the **Zhongye Miao**, though it's by no means as busy. The mountain ranges themselves are

Song Shan		
Song Shan	嵩山	*sōngshān*
Dengfeng	登封	*dēngfēng*
Bus station	登封客运站	*dēngfēng kèyùnzhàn*
Gaocheng Observatory	观星台	*guānxīng tái*
Gaotian Jiudian	高天酒店	*gāotiān jiǔdiàn*
Shaolin Binguan	少林宾馆	*shàolín bīnguǎn*
Shaolin bus station	少林寺车站	*shàolínsì chēzhàn*
Songyang Academy	嵩阳书院	*sōngyáng shūyuàn*
Songyue Temple Pagoda	嵩岳寺塔	*sōngyuèsì tǎ*
Zhongyue Miao	中岳庙	*zhōngyuè miào*
Shaolin Si	少林寺	*shàolín sì*
Qianfo Hall	千佛殿	*qiānfó diàn*
Ta Lin	塔林	*tǎlín*
White Robe Hall	白衣殿	*báiyī diàn*
Zen International Hotel	禅居国际饭店	*chánjū guójì fàndiàn*

another draw, with numerous paths meandering around the valleys, passing temples, pagodas and guard towers, and some wonderful views. Unlike at other holy mountains, there is no single set path, and, as the slopes are not steep and the undergrowth is sparse, you can set out in any direction you like. Song Shan's sights aren't close to one another, so you won't be able to do more than one or two a day and count on getting back to Dengfeng before nightfall.

You can visit Song Shan on a **day-trip** from either **Luoyang** or **Zhengzhou**, though it's more satisfying – and certainly less rushed – to base yourself in the town of **Dengfeng**, from where you can explore Shaolin Si, Zhongye Miao and a couple of other nearby sites at your own pace. Note that buses from Luoyang pass Shaolin on the way to Dengfeng, so you can always get off here first. **Maps** of the area are included on the back of local maps of Zhengzhou (available in Zhengzhou, and possibly Luoyang), or can be bought from shops at Dengfeng and Shaolin.

Dengfeng and around

DENGFENG is a small market town stretched along a valley at the heart of the Song Shan range, 13km east of Shaolin. Zhongyue Dajie is the main street, running east–west across town, with a centre of sorts around its intersection with north–south Songshan Lu – though all the central grid of streets are equally busy. The Zhengzhou–Luoyang highway runs parallel with Zhongyue Dajie and two blocks south as Shaolin Dadao. One attraction are the numerous **martial-arts schools**, both actually in Dengfeng itself and lining the road between here and Shaolin – there's one where the road from Luoyang and Shaolin meets Zhongyue Dajie, where you can watch students training outside in the afternoons.

Dengfeng's **bus station** is about 3km southeast where the road from Zhengzhou hits the edge of town; bus #1 or #3 will get you to Zhongyue Dajie (¥1) or a taxi costs about ¥5. Arriving by local bus from Shaolin Si, you'll get dropped off at the **Shaolin bus station** towards the western end of Zhongyue Dajie; if you're coming on a long-distance bus from Luoyang, ask to be dropped off at the junction of the highway and Zhongyue Dajie, as you're fairly close to accommodation here. The two best **places to stay** in town are the motel-like *Shaolin Binguan* at 66 Zhongyue Dajie (ⓣ0371/60161616, ⓦwww.shaolinhotel.cn; ❻), a great place amenable to bargaining; and the *Gaotian Jiudian* further east at 166 Zhongyue Dajie (ⓣ0371/2885200, ⓕ2885201; ❹). If you're on a tight budget, it's cheaper to stay around Shaolin Si (see opposite). For **food**, there are numerous dumpling places scattered around, or head to the frenetic **night market** in the lane directly facing the *Shaolin* hotel for street food.

To head **to Shaolin Si** from town, walk west (uphill) along Zhongyue Dajie and look for buses marked "Shaolin" in Chinese hanging around outside the little bus station compound. Buses run from dawn until dusk and the ¥2 ride takes about twenty minutes. A taxi will cost ¥25 each way.

Zhongyue Miao

The **Zhongyue Miao** (daily 8am–6pm; ¥30), on the eastern edge of Dengfeng on the #2 bus route from Shaolin Dadao, is a huge Taoist temple founded as long ago as 220 BC, though the buildings here today date from the Ming. Inside, it's an attractive place, with spacious, wooded courtyards and brilliantly coloured buildings standing out against the grey and green of the mountain behind. If you've just come from crowded Shaolin, the quiet, calm atmosphere of this working Taoist monastery is particularly striking.

A series of gateways, courtyards and pavilions leads to the **Main Hall** where the emperor made sacrifices to the mountain. The Junji Gate, just before the hall, has two great sentries, nearly 4m high, brightly painted and flourishing their weapons. The courtyard houses gnarled old cypresses, some of them approaching the age of the temple itself, and there are four Song-dynasty **iron statues** of guardian warriors in martial poses on the eastern side. The **Bedroom Palace** behind the Main Hall is unusual for having a shrine that shows a deity lying in bed. Contemporary worshippers tend to gravitate to the back of the complex, where you may see people burning what look like little origami hats in the iron burners here, or practising *qi gong*, exercises centring around control of the breath.

If you go to the back of the complex, past the monks' quarters on the right, you come to the temple's back exit, where you are charged ¥2 for the privilege of walking 200m up stone steps to a little **pagoda** on a hill behind the temple. From here, paths take you through pinewoods to the craggy peaks of the mountain, a worthwhile afternoon's excursion and a rare chance for solitude; the only other person you are likely to see is the odd shepherd.

Other sights around Dengfeng

Three kilometres north of Dengfeng at the top end of Songshan Lu, the **Songyang Academy** consists of a couple of lecture halls, a **library** and a memorial hall, founded in 484 AD, which was one of the great centres of learning under the Song. Many famous scholars from history lectured here, including Sima Guang and Cheng Hao. In the courtyard are two enormous cypresses said to be three thousand years old, as well as a stele from the Tang dynasty. The path beyond climbs to Junji Peak and branches off to the **Songyue Temple Pagoda**, 5km north of Dengfeng. Built at the beginning of the sixth century by the Northern Wei, this 45-metre structure is both the oldest pagoda and the oldest complete brick building in China, rare for having twelve sides.

Around 12km southeast of Dengfeng, the **Gaocheng Observatory** was built in 1279 and designed by Gui Shou Jing to calculate the solstices. It's a fascinating, sculptural-looking building, an almost pyramidal tower with a long straight wall marked with measurements running along the ground behind it. A round trip by taxi should cost about ¥40, including waiting time.

Shaolin Si

Around 13km west of Dengfeng, through rugged, mountainous countryside and a main road lined with martial-arts schools, **Shaolin Si** (daily 8am–6pm; ¥100) is the place of legends. This is the temple where the sixth-century founder of Buddhism's Chan (Zen) sect, **Bodhidarma**, consolidated his teachings in China; and also where – surprisingly given Buddhism's peaceful doctrines – **Chinese kung fu** is said to have originated. Today, it's a tourist black spot, packed with noisy groups and commercial enterprises, and a complete non-starter if you're seeking any form of spiritual enlightenment – though as an entertaining look into modern China's kung fu cult, it's a lot of fun. In September, the place is particularly busy, filling up with martial-arts enthusiasts from all over the world who come to attend the international **Wushu Festival**.

The original Shaolin Si was built in 495 AD. Shortly afterwards, the Indian monk **Bodhidarma** (known as **Da Mo** in China) came to live here after visiting the emperor in Nanjing, then crossing the Yangzi on a reed (depicted in a tablet at the temple). As the temple has been burned down on several occasions – most recently in 1928, by the warlord Shi Yousan – the buildings you see here today are mostly reconstructions in the Ming style, built over the last twenty years. Despite this, and the incredible density of tourists, the temple and surroundings are beautiful, and the chance to see some impressive martial-art displays here make it well worth the trip.

The temple and around

All transport drops you at the mouth of a long plaza lined with souvenir shops selling a startling array of weapons, from swords to throwing stars and poleaxes. The **ticket office** is hidden away on the left just before the huge stone archway; included in the price is entry to a kung fu show, which you shouldn't miss. Once through the gates, walk downhill where the road passes two huge open areas packed in the morning and afternoons with hundreds of **martial-arts students** in tracksuits, arranged in small groups and practising jumps, throws, kicks and weapons routines. Just on from here and to the right is the **kung fu show hall**, with performance times (around 5 daily) posted outside. The half-hour performance is a cut-down version of the stage show that regularly tours the world, with demonstrations of Shaolin's famous stick fighting and animal-style kung fu, all pretty electrifying if you haven't seen it before.

On from here, it's about 500m to the **temple entrance** and a walkway past rows of steles commemorating visits by foreign kung fu schools (look, too, for

Shaolin kung fu

Kung fu was first developed at the Shaolin Si as a form of gymnastics to counterbalance the immobility of meditation. The monks studied the movement of animals and copied them – the way snakes crawled, tigers leapt and mantises danced – and coordinated these movements with meditational breathing routines. As the temple was isolated it was often prey to bandits, and gradually the monks turned their exercises into a form of self-defence.

The monks owed their strength to rigorous **discipline**. From childhood, monks trained from dawn to dusk, every day. To strengthen their hands, they thrust them into sacks of beans, over and over; when they were older, into bags of sand. To strengthen their fists, they punched a thousand sheets of paper glued to a wall; over the years, the paper wore out and the young monks punched brick. To strengthen their legs, they ran around the courtyard with bags of sand tied to their knees, and to strengthen their heads, they hit them with bricks.

Only after twenty years of such exercises could someone consider themselves proficient in kung fu, by which time they were able to perform incredible **feats**, examples of which you can see illustrated in the murals at the temple and in photographs of contemporary martial-arts masters in the picture books on sale in the souvenir shops. Apart from such commonplaces as breaking concrete slabs with their fists and iron bars with their heads, the monks can balance on one finger, take a sledgehammer blow to the chest, and hang from a tree by the neck. Their **boxing routines** are equally extraordinary, their animal qualities clearly visible in the vicious clawing, poking, leaping and tearing that they employ. One comic-looking variation that requires a huge amount of flexibility is **drunken boxing**, where the performer twists, staggers and weaves as if inebriated – useful training given that Shaolin monks are allowed alcohol.

However, the monks were not just fighters, and their art was also intended as a technique to reach the goal of inner peace, with monks spending as many hours **meditating and praying** as in martial training. They obeyed a moral code, which included the stricture that only fighting in self-defence was acceptable, and killing your opponent was to be avoided if possible. These rules became a little more trees here with holes drilled in the bark by kung fu practioners' fingers). At the end is a boxy pavilion housing two fearsome demon statues that tower overhead, fists raised, past which is the first courtyard. On the right here are two large glassed-in tablets from 728 AD, raised by the emperor **Taizong** after thirteen of Shaolin's monks had aided him against the rebel Wang Shichang; in gratitude, he passed an edict allowing monks at the temple to eat meat and drink wine. Another stele over towards the left has a wonderful, single brush-stroke image of Da Mo. The temple's succession of halls are quite small and simple, but two at the rear of the complex are worth attention: **Qianfo Hall**, whose brick floor is dented from where the monks used to stamp during their kung fu training; and the **White Robe Hall**, where Ming-dynasty **murals** covering two walls depict Taizong being saved by the monks.

The **Ta Lin**, 200m farther up the hill past the temple entrance, is where hundreds of stone pagodas, memorials to past monks, are tightly grouped together in a "forest". Up to 10m tall, and with a stepped, recessed top, these golden stone structures look particularly impressive against the purple mountain when snow is on the ground. The earliest dates to 791 AD and commemorates a monk named Fawan, while the forest is still being added to as monks die.

Beyond here the mountain can be ascended by cable car or stone steps, but there is not much to see except the **cave** where Bodhidarma supposedly

flexible over the centuries as emperors and peasants alike sought their help in battles, and the Shaolin monks became legendary figures for their interventions on the side of righteousness. Well-known Chinese tales include the story of the monk who fought a thousand enemies with a stick while pretending to be drunk, and the tale of the cook who kept a horde at bay with a poker at the temple gates while the other monks continued their meditations undisturbed.

The monks were at the height of their power in the Tang dynasty, though they were still a force to be reckoned with in the Ming, when **weapons** were added to their discipline – most famously their athletic stick routine. However, the temple was sacked during the 1920s and again in the 1960s during the Cultural Revolution, when the teaching of kung fu in China was **banned** and Shaolin's monks persecuted and dispersed. Things picked up again in the 1980s, when, as a result of Jet Li's enormously popular first film *Shaolin Temple*, there was a **resurgence** of interest in the art. The old masters were allowed to teach again, and the government realized that the temple was better exploited as a tourist resource than left to rot.

Evidence of the popularity of kung fu in China today can be seen not just at the tourist circus of the Shaolin Si, but in any cinema, where **kung fu films**, often concerning the exploits of Shaolin monks, make up a large proportion of the entertainment on offer. Many young Chinese today want to study kung fu, and to meet demand numerous **schools** have opened around the temple. Few of them want to be monks, though – the dream of many is to be a movie star.

Inevitably, such attention and exploitation has taken its toll on Shaolin Si's original purpose as a Buddhist monastery. While the monks here are undoubtably skilled fighters, the temple's primary drive today is less towards the spiritual and more about the travelling shows and protecting commercial interests – they are currently pursuing efforts to trademark the very name "Shaolin", in order to capitalize on its use by everything from martial-arts outfits to beer companies. For a good account of what it's like to live and train here, and the challenges that the modern temple faces, read *American Shaolin* by Matthew Polly (see "Books", p.1201).

passed a nine-year vigil, sitting motionless facing a wall in a state of illumination (the mystic knowledge of the Nothingness of Everything). You can save yourself some effort by paying a few yuan to look at it from the road through a high-powered telescope.

Practicalities

Besides minibuses from Dengfeng, transport and day-tours run to the temple from Luoyang and Zhengzhou, either of which is around ninety minutes away. You can **stay** beside the temple at the modern and comfortable *Zen International Hotel* (Ⓣ0371/6275666, Ⓕ62745555; ❻), behind the kung fu show hall, where you'll get better rates than advertised by booking in advance. Far cheaper are the host of identical, simple hotels near the bus park on the road towards Dengfeng, such as the *Farmhouse Fragrant Hotel*, *Shaolin Village Hotel* and *Tianfu Hotel* (beds ¥50–75; ❸). They all have **restaurants**, but the best place to eat is the *Zen International*'s restaurant, which offers huge vegetarian lunch buffets at ¥25 a head. Otherwise, there's not much to eat in the area beyond a few stallholder-sold snacks along the main path.

To **train** at the temple, contact either Robert Huang (Ⓣ0371/61156090, Ⓔrobert0213@sohu.com), or the Training Department's Director, Yan Zhijun (Ⓣ0371/62865877, ⒺDFYanZhiJun@tom.com). Finally, if you're planning to head off into the hills for a **walk** – a nice prospect on a sunny day – take plenty of water along with you.

Zhengzhou and around

Close to the south bank of the Yellow River, **ZHENGZHOU** lies almost midway between Luoyang to the west and Kaifeng to the east. The walled town that existed here 3500 years ago was probably an early capital of the Shang dynasty, and excavations have revealed bronze foundries, bone-carving workshops and sacrificial altars. Nowadays, Zhengzhou is the capital of Henan province,

Zhengzhou and around		
Zhengzhou	郑州	*zhèngzhōu*
Chenghuang Miao	城隍庙	*chénghuáng miaò*
Erqi Pagoda	二七塔	*èrqī tǎ*
Henan Provincial Museum	河南省博物馆	*hénánshěng bówùguǎn*
Renmin Park	人民公园	*rénmín gōngyuán*
Accommodation		
Crowne Plaza	中州皇冠假日酒店	*zhōngzhōu huángguān jiàrì jiǔdiàn*
Home Inn	如家酒店	*rújiā jiǔdiàn*
Jinjiang Inn	锦江之星旅馆	*jǐnjiāng zhīxīng lǚguǎn*
Sofitel	索菲特国际饭店	*suǒfēitè guójì fàndiàn*
Tian'e	天鹅宾馆	*tiān'é bīnguǎn*
Zhengzhou	郑州饭店	*zhèngzhōu fàndiàn*
Eating		
Huayuchuan	华豫川酒家	*huáyúchuān jiǔjiā*
Kaoya Dian	烤鸭店	*kǎoyādiàn*
Wenxin Canyin	温馨餐饮	*wēnxīn cānyǐn*
Yellow River Park	黄河公园	*huánghé gōngyuán*

though this owes nothing to its past and everything to its position astride the meeting of the north–south (Beijing–Guangzhou) and west–east (Xi'an–Shanghai) rail lines. As the most important **rail junction** in China, Zhengzhou has a population of more than three million – and the industry to match.

The modern city is basically a business and transport centre, with no major tourist sights outside the **museum**, which is worth a couple of hours. Fortunately, there are some decent hotels and restaurants, as the place is difficult to avoid if you're travelling in central China. From here, Kaifeng and Luoyang are easily accessible, and you can take a bus trip to Song Shan.

Orientation, arrival and city transport

Zhengzhou **airport** lies well to the east of the city; a taxi into the centre should cost ¥70, while hourly **CAAC buses** cost ¥15 and deliver to the Aviation Building on Jinshui Lu, from where bus #26 will get you to the train station. The **train station** is fronted by a bustling square and faces the main **long-distance bus station**, though there are also the usual run of other depots scattered around the city's edges.

Leaving Zhengzhou

The main **CAAC ticket office** is at 3 Jinshui Lu (open 24hr; ⓣ0371/5991111), where the airport bus departs from. **Train tickets** can be hard to buy at the station due to the overwhelming crowds – there are advance-booking booths open 8am–noon and 2.30–5pm up near the museum on Huayuan Lu, again on Huayuan Lu north of the Jinshui Lu intersection, and inside the regional bus station on Erma Lu, 500m north of the train station; see the map for locations. You can also book plane and train tickets through some accommodation, or from **Henan Tourism**, west of the *Crowne Plaza* on Jinshui Lu (ⓣ0371/65959892 or 68262900). **Bus tickets** to all major regional destinations are easy to get at the horde of windows surrounding the main bus station; **day-trips to Shaolin** leave from in front of the train station around 8am, when you'll find minibuses lined up.

There are two clusters of **city bus terminals** on either side of the square outside the train station. **Taxis** have a ¥7 minimum charge, and congregate along the north side of the train-station square. **Maps** in Chinese with details of bus routes are available outside the train station (¥4).

Accommodation

If you've only come to Zhengzhou in transit, it makes sense to stay around the train-station area, where there's plenty of inexpensive, decent accommodation, though it can get noisy. There are also a couple of motel and upmarket hotel options further out, in less crowded settings.

Crowne Plaza 115 Jinshui Lu ⓣ0371/65950055, ⓦwww.crowneplaza.com. Located in the east of town in an uninteresting cluster of five-star lodging, the *Crowne Plaza* has all mod cons imaginable, including a pool. A lobby of cream-coloured marble gives the hotel a palatial look. ❾

Home Inn 68 Chengdong Lu ⓣ0371/66380188, ⓦwww.homeinns.com. You can't miss this bright yellow, friendly motel, where smart modern doubles go for as little as ¥179. Bus #33 from the station stops nearby. ❹–❺

Jinjiang Inn 96 Chengdong Lu ⓣ0371/66305388, ⓦwww.jj-inn.com. Another excellent-value motel option, even cheaper than the nearby *Home Inn*. Bus #33 from the station stops nearby. ❹

Sofitel 289 Chengdong Lu ⓣ0371/65950088, ⓦwww.sofitel.com. The most comfortable, and newest, of Zhengzhou's five-stars. ❾

Tian'e ⓣ0371/66768599, ⓕ66768977. One of several budget hotels occupying the large, blocky Zhongyuan Dasha building directly opposite the train station. There's an enormous stack of budget rooms with an eccentric atmosphere and a wide variety of prices. Huge, cheap doubles come complete with fly swat and spittoon. Dorms ¥50, ❹

Zhengzhou 8 Xinglong Jie ⓣ0371/66760038, ⓕ66760469. Ahead and on the left as you leave the train station. A huge, fairly modern hotel with hundreds of rooms, which are well furnished and spacious, if a little under-maintained. Bargain and they drop the rate considerably. ❻

The City

Today, Zhengzhou is an entirely modern city, rebuilt virtually from scratch after heavy bombing in the war against Japan. There are few old sights, none of them of great importance, but the city has a good feel to it, even if there's little to see amongst the broad avenues lined with shopping malls and boutiques.

The hub of downtown Zhengzhou is the **Erqi Pagoda** (daily 8.30am–6pm; ¥5), a twin-towered, seven-storey structure built to commemorate those killed in a 1923 Communist-led rail strike that was put down with great savagery by the warlord Wu Pei Fu. To the north, **Renmin Park** is where to head if you need some space; there's paving everywhere but also plenty of trees.

East of the Erqi Pagoda, there's a remnant of **old Zhengzhou** in its ancient **city walls**, rough earthen ramparts 10m high, originally built more than two thousand years ago. There's a path along the top, and you can walk for about 3km along the south and east sections (the west section has been destroyed by development), descending to cross the main roads along the way. Planted with trees, the walls are now used by the locals as a short cut and a park, full of courting couples, kids who slide down the steep sides on metal trays, and old men who hang their cagebirds from the trees and sit around fires cooking sweet potatoes. Indeed, the charm of the wall comes from the way it has been incorporated by the inhabitants – it doesn't seem to occur to anyone to treat it as a historical monument. While you're in the area, **Chenghuang Miao** (daily 8am–6pm), on the north side of Shangcheng Lu, is the most interesting of Zhengzhou's temples, with well-observed images of birds decorating the eaves of the first hall, underneath roof sculptures of dragons and phoenixes. Murals in the modern Main Hall owe much to 1950s socialist realism, and surround a sculpture of a stern-looking Chenghuang, magisterial defender of city folk, who sits flanked by two attendants.

Henan Provincial Museum

A giant stone pyramid at the northern end of Jingqi Lu, the modern **Henan Provincial Museum** (daily 8.30am–6.15pm; ¥20; English audio-guide ¥30, plus ¥500 or your passport as a deposit; bus #32 from the south side of the train-station area) boasts an outstanding collection of relics unearthed in the region, dating back to when Henan was the cradle of Chinese civilization. Moving clockwise, each hall covers a particular stage of regional history, beginning with the stone age: look for **oracle bones** inscribed with the ancestors of modern Chinese script unearthed from **Anyang**, 200km north of Zhengzhou, site of China's Shang dynasty capital; and some outstanding **bronzes**, from the Shang to Tang periods, including large tripods and tiny animal figures used as weights. By far the most interesting pieces, however, are the **Han pottery**, with scale models of houses showing defensive walls and towers, models of domestic animals, and huge numbers of human figurines – dancers, musicians, soldiers, court ladies – all leaving the impression that the Han were an articulate, fun-loving people who liked to show off.

Eating, drinking and entertainment

Zhengzhou has abundant **eating options**. Around the train station there are plenty of small **noodle and snack restaurants**, all much the same, and enormous numbers of shops selling travellers' nibbles – walnuts, oranges and dates – which testify to the great number of people passing through here every day. For something a bit smarter, there's the popular *Huayuchuan* restaurant at 59 Erqi Lu, a Sichuanese chain with a photo menu and well-presented dishes such as tea-smoked duck and garlic pork costing around ¥20; and the *Kaoya Dian* just up the road, which is where to get Beijing-style roast duck. Another good option is the *Wenxin Canyin*, a regional restaurant up near the museum on Jinqi Lu, packed out at lunchtime. Pricey Shandong cuisine can be had at the *Jingya*, more or less opposite the *Sofitel*. For **coffee**, head to *Jienong Coffee*, across from the park entrance on Erqi Lu.

For an evening **drink**, there are numerous bars ranging from raucous to catatonic along Jinqi Lu and the surrounding area, where you pay ¥100 for eight beers. The *Happy Bar* has its moments, though *Miubiao* on Jinliu Lu is much livelier.

Listings

Banks and exchange The main Bank of China is on Jinshui Lu; the closest branch to southern accommodation is on Dong Dajie – both have ATMs.
Mail and telephones The principal post office is next to the train station on the south side (Mon–Fri 8am–8pm), with a 24hr telecom office next door.
PSB The visa section is at 70 Erqi Lu (Mon–Fri 8.30am–noon & 3–6pm; ⓣ0371/69620359).

The Yellow River Park

Twenty-eight kilometres north of Zhengzhou, at the terminus of bus #16, which leaves from Minggong Lu just outside Zhengzhou's train station, the **Yellow River Park** (daily 8am–6pm; ¥30) is really a stretch of typical Chinese countryside, incorporating villages and allotments, that you have to pay to get into because it has a view of the Yellow River. There's a pretty hill, Mang Shan, but none of the sights listed on the map that you can buy at the entrance – dilapidated temples and statues, including a huge image of Yu the Great – is worth it. You can spend an afternoon here walking around the hills at the back of the park, or riding – there are plenty of men hiring out horses, and an escorted trot around the hills for an hour or two should cost about ¥20. From the hilltops you have a good view over the river and the plain of mud either side of it. It's hard to imagine that in 1937, when Chiang Kaishek breached the dykes 8km from the city to prevent the Japanese capturing the rail line, the Yellow River flooded this great plain, leaving more than a million dead and countless more homeless.

Kaifeng

Located on the alluvial plains in the middle reaches of the Yellow River 70km east of Zhengzhou, **KAIFENG** is an ancient capital with a history stretching back over three thousand years. However, unlike other ancient capitals in the area, the city hasn't grown into an industrial monster, and remains pleasingly compact, with most of its sights in a fairly small area within the walls. While not an especially attractive town, its low-key ambience and sprinkling of older temples and pagodas encourage a wander, and the longer you stay, the more you register the town's distinctive local character. In all, this a worthwhile place to spend a couple of days, especially if you've grown weary of the scale and pace of most Chinese cities.

Some history

First heard of as a Shang town around 1000 BC, Kaifeng's heyday was during the Song dynasty between 960 and 1127 AD, when the city became the political, economic and cultural centre of the empire. A famous five-metre-long horizontal **scroll** by Zhang Azheduan, *Qingming Shang He* (*Along the River at the Qingming Festival*), now in the Forbidden City in Beijing, unrolls to show views of the city at this time, teeming with life, crammed with people, boats, carts and animals. It was a great age for painting, calligraphy, philosophy and poetry, and Kaifeng was famed for the quality of its textiles and embroidery and for its production of ceramics and printed books. It was also the home of the first mechanical timepiece in history, Su Song's **astronomical clock tower** of 1092, which worked by the transmission of energy from a huge water wheel.

Kaifeng

Kaifeng	开封	*kāifēng*
Baogong Hu	包公湖	*bāogōng hú*
Fan Pagoda	繁塔	*fán tǎ*
Iron Pagoda Park	铁塔公园	*tiětǎ gōngyuán*
Kaifeng Museum	开封博物馆	*kāifēng bówùguǎn*
Longting Park	龙亭公园	*lóngtíng gōngyuán*
Memorial Temple to Lord Bao	包公祠	*bāogōng cí*
Qingming Park	清明上河园	*qīngmíng shànghéyuán*
Shanshanguan Guild Hall	陕山甘会馆	*shǎnshāngān huìguǎn*
Shudian Jie	书店街	*shūdiàn jiē*
Song Jie	宋都御街	*sòngdū yùjiē*
Xiangguo Si	相国寺	*xiàngguó sì*
Yangjia Hu	杨家湖	*yángjiā hú*
Yanqing Guan	延庆观	*yánqìng guàn*
Yellow River Viewing Point	黄河公园	*huánghé gōngyuán*
Yuwangtai Park	禹王台公园	*yǔwángtái gōngyuán*
Bus Stations		
East Bus Station	长青汽车站	*chángqīng qìchēzhàn*
Main Bus Station	开封汽车站	*kāifēng qìchēzhàn*
West Bus Station	汽车西站	*qìchē xīzhàn*
Accommodation		
Bianjing	汴京饭店	*biànjīng fàndiàn*
Dajintai	大金台旅馆	*dàjīntái lǚguǎn*
Dongjing	东京大饭店	*dōngjīng dàfàndiàn*
Henan	河南酒店	*hénán jiǔdiàn*
Kaifeng	开封宾馆	*kāifēng bīnguǎn*
Restaurants		
Diyi Lou	第一楼	*dìyīlóu*
Gulou Jiaozi Guan	鼓楼饺子馆	*gǔlóu jiǎoziguǎn*
Songxiang Chuan Jiujia	宋像川酒家	*sòngxiàngchuān jiǔjiā*
Xinxin Fanlou	新新饭楼	*xīnxīn fànlóu*

Some of this artistic heritage survives – the nearby town of Zhuxian Zhen is still known for its **New Year woodblock prints** – but Kaifeng's Golden Age ended suddenly in 1127 when Jurchen invaders overran the city. Just one royal prince escaped to the south, to set up a new capital out of harm's reach at Hangzhou beyond the Yangzi, though Kaifeng itself never recovered. What survived has been damaged or destroyed by repeated **flooding** since – between 1194 and 1887 there were more than fifty severe incidents, including one fearful occasion when the dykes were breached during a siege and at least 300,000 people are said to have died, among which were many of Kaifeng's **Jewish community**.

Orientation, arrival and city transport

Central Kaifeng, bounded by walls roughly 3km long at each side, is fairly small, and most places of interest lie within walking distance of one another. **Zhongshan Lu** is the main north–south thoroughfare, while **Sihou Jie**, which changes its name to Gulou Jie at the centre and Mujiaqiao Jie in the east, is the main east–west road. The town is crisscrossed by canals, once part of a network that connected it to Hangzhou and Yangzhou in ancient times.

Kaifeng's Jews

The origins of Kaifeng's **Jewish community** are something of a mystery. A Song-dynasty stele now in the Kaifeng Museum records that they arrived here in the Zhou dynasty, nearly three thousand years ago, which seems doubtful. It's more likely their ancestors came here from central Asia around 1000 AD, when trade links between the two areas were strong, a supposition given some weight by the characteristics they share with Persian Jews, such as their use of a Hebrew alphabet with 27 rather than 22 letters. The community was never large, but it seems to have flourished until the nineteenth century, when – perhaps as a result of disastrous floods, including one in 1850 that destroyed the synagogue – the Kaifeng Jews almost completely died out. The synagogue, which stood at the corner of Pingdeng Jie and Beixing Jie, on the site of what is now a **hospital**, was never rebuilt, and no trace of it remains today.

A number of families in Kaifeng trace their lineage back to the Jews, and, following the atmosphere of greater religious tolerance in contemporary China, have begun practising again. You can see a few relics from the synagogue in the museum, including three steles that once stood outside it, but most, such as a *Torah* in Chinese now in the British Museum, are in collections abroad.

The **train station**, on the Xi'an–Shanghai line, is in a dull, utilitarian area outside the walls, about 2km south of the centre. The main long-distance **bus station** is here, too, though you might also wind up at the smaller west or east bus stations, near the southern walls – all are on **city bus routes**; or bargain with a rickshaw or taxi for a ride to accommodation (¥5–10). **Maps** of Kaifeng cost around ¥3 at arrival points.

Accommodation

Despite Kaifeng's small size, it has several good-value **hotels**, though bargain motels have yet to put in an appearance. The *Dajintai* is the budget hotel of choice.

Bianjing Corner of Dong Dajie and Beitu Jie ⓣ0378/2886699, ⓕ2882449. Bus #3 from the train station. A large, pink-and-white wedding cake of a place, which recent renovations have given pretensions to luxury. ❺

Dajintai Gulou Dajie ⓣ0378/2552888. On the route of bus #4. In the heart of the night market and most interesting section of town, this is the best budget place to stay, and not unduly noisy. Haggle hard as they're quite stubborn as regards discounts. Dorm beds ¥60, ❸

Dongjing 14 Yingbin Lu ⓣ0378/3989388, ⓕ3938861. A short walk from the west bus station, and buses #1 and #9 come here from the train station. This compound of buildings, set in a park just inside the walls in the south of the city, looks like a health sanatorium, and is suitably quiet, low-key and comfortable, with a good range of services, including a post office. ❹

Henan 23 Sihou Jie ⓣ0378/5999888 or 5999886. New urban Chinese number right in the centre. ❺

Leaving Kaifeng

The nearest **airport** to Kaifeng is Zhengzhou; buy air tickets at the CAAC office at the southwest corner of Zhongshan Lu and Sihou Jie (8am–7pm; ⓣ0378/5955555). The **train station** is small and not too hard to figure out; buy tickets here or through CITS or CTS if your accommodation can't help. Most **buses** departing for major destinations leave from the main station, though if you're heading to Zhengzhou or Heze (for connections to Qufu in Shandong) try the west station first.

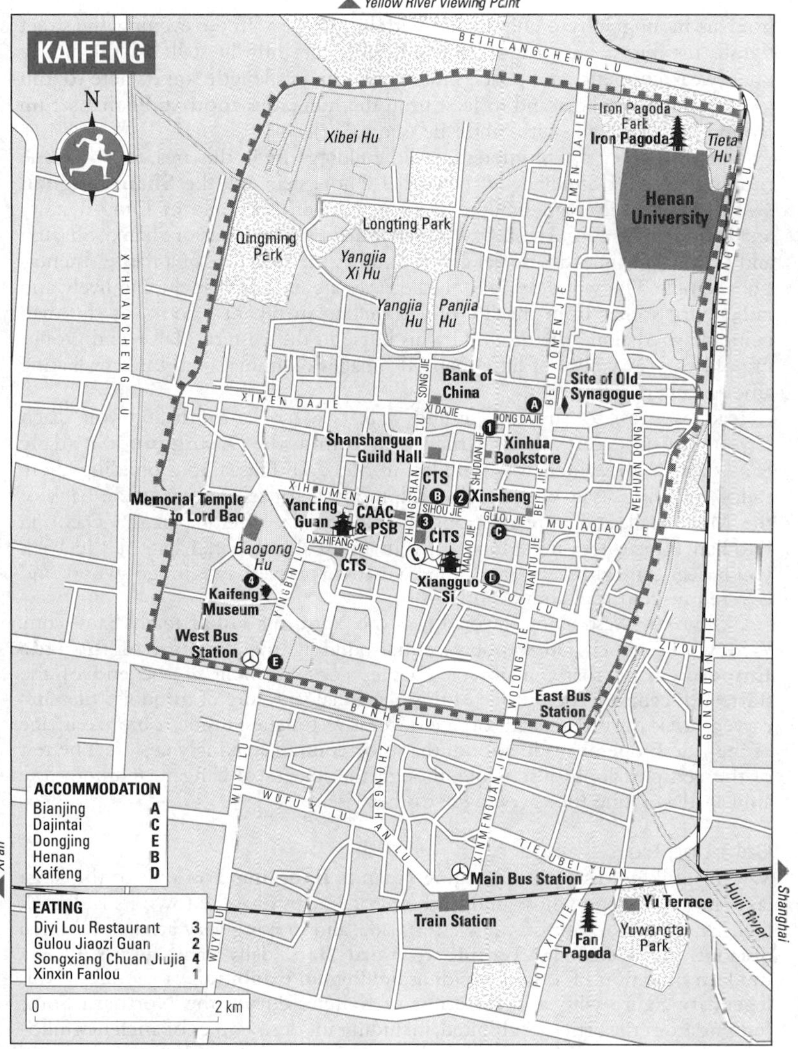

Kaifeng 66 Ziyou Lu ⓣ0378/5955589 ext 6119, ⓦwww.kaifengbinguan.com. Bus #9 from the train station. This central, three-star hotel in a large, attractive compound off the street is where most tour groups end up. It has four buildings and a range of rooms, including triples and quads. Comfortable without being ostentatious, and surprisingly inexpensive. 5

The Town

The **town walls**, tamped earth ramparts, have been heavily damaged and there's no path along them, but they do present a useful landmark. **Shudian Jie** – Bookshop Street – is at the centre of town, a scruffy run of two-storey imitation Qing buildings with fancy balconies. Many shops here do indeed sell books, from art monographs to pulp fiction with lurid covers. In the evening, the street transforms into a busy **night market**, when brightly lit stalls selling mostly underwear, cosmetics and plastic kitchenware line its length, somewhere to join the locals for a wander and to feast from the numerous **food stalls** that set up around the crossroads with Sihou Jie (see p.312).

Some of Kaifeng's most interesting old buildings are in this area, too. In a lane running west off Shudian Jie to parallel Zhongshan Lu, the **Shanshanguan Guild Hall** (daily 8am–6.30pm; ¥20) is a superb example of Qing-dynasty architecture at its most lavish. It was established by merchants of Shanxi, Shaanxi and Gansu provinces as a social centre and has the structure of a flashy, ostentatious temple. The woodcarvings on the eaves are excellent, including lively and rather wry scenes from the life of a travelling merchant – look for the man being dragged along the ground by his horse in the Eastern Hall – and groups of gold bats (a symbol of luck) beneath images of animals and birds frolicking among bunches of grapes.

Head back on to Shudian Jie and walk two blocks south and you reach Ziyou Lu, just east along which you'll find the **Xiangguo Si** (daily 8am–6pm; ¥30), which was founded in 555 AD. The simple buildings here today are Qing style, with a colourful, modern frieze of *arhat* at the back of the Main Hall, and an early Song-dynasty bronze Buddha in the Daxiong Baodian (Great Treasure House). In an unusual octagonal hall at the back you'll see a magnificent four-sided Guanyin carved in ginkgo wood and covered in gold leaf, about 3m high.

A kilometre west, along Ziyou Lu, is the **Yanqing Guan** (daily 8am–7pm; ¥15), whose rather odd, knobbly central building, the **Pavilion of the Jade Emperor**, is all that remains of a larger complex built at the end of the thirteenth century. The outside of this octagonal structure of turquoise tiles and carved brick is overlaid with ornate decorative touches; inside, a bronze image of the Jade Emperor sits in a room that is by contrast strikingly austere. The rest of the complex looks just as old, though the images of kangaroos among the animals decorating the eaves suggest otherwise.

Baogong Hu

Within walking distance of Yanqing Guan is **Baogong Hu**, one of the large lakes inside Kaifeng whose undisturbed space helps give the town its laid-back feel. On a promontory on the western side, and looking very attractive from a distance, the **Memorial Temple to Lord Bao** (daily 7am–7pm; ¥20) is a modern imitation of a Song building holding an exhibition of the life of this legendary figure who was Governor of Kaifeng during the Northern Song. Judging from the articles exhibited, including modern copies of ancient guillotines, and the scenes from his life depicted in paintings and waxworks, Lord Bao was a harsh but fair judge, who must have had some difficulty getting through doors if he really wore a hat and shoes like the ones on display. A substantial mansion on the south side of the lake, the **Kaifeng Museum** (daily 8.30–11.30am & 2.30–5.30pm; ¥10), holds steles recording the history of Kaifeng's Jewish community that used to stand outside the synagogue, and a good exhibition of local folk art.

Song Jie, Yangjia Hu, Qingming and Longting parks

At the north end of Zhongshan Lu and under a stone archway, **Song Jie** is a street of antique-style tourist shops built over the site of the Song-dynasty Imperial Palace. The shops sell handmade paper, paintings, reproduction classical scrolls and, around Chinese New Year, brightly coloured woodblock prints of animals and legendary figures, which people paste on their doors for good luck. In the winter, when the tourists have gone, many of the shops switch to selling household goods.

Song Jie runs up to a large **plaza** full of people strolling and flying kites, beyond which **Yangjia Hu** was originally part of the imperial gardens but is now at the centre of a large warren of carnival-like tourist traps arranged around the lakeshore. At **Qingming Park** (daily 9am–5.30pm; ¥30), west of the lake, you can walk through a realized version of *Qingming Shang He*, wandering to your heart's content past costumed courtesans and ingratiating shopkeepers. **Longting Park** (daily 6am–6.30pm; ¥35), across the causeway and on the northern shore of Yangjia Hu, has a somewhat desolate feel, though it makes for good people-watching when the crowds are out.

Iron Pagoda Park

From the centre of town, buses #1 and #3 go to the far northeast corner of the city walls, to **Iron Pagoda Park** (daily 7am–7pm; ¥20), which is only accessible off Beimen Dajie. At its centre you'll find the 13-storey, 56-metre-high **Iron Pagoda** that gives it its name, a striking Northern Song (1049 AD) construction so named because its surface of glazed tiles gives the building the russet tones of rusted iron. Its base, like all early buildings in Kaifeng, is buried beneath a couple of metres of silt deposited during floods. Most of the tiles hold relief images, usually of the Buddha, but also of Buddhist angels, animals and abstract patterns. You can climb up the inside, via a gloomy spiral staircase, for an extra ¥10.

Outside the walls

Three kilometres southeast of the city centre – a cab is the best way to get here, as it's a dusty, drab walk – **Yuwangtai Park** (daily 7am–7pm; ¥10) surrounds the **Yu Terrace**, an earthen mound now thought to have been a music terrace, that was once the haunt of Tang poets. The park, dotted with pavilions and commemorative steles, is pleasant in summer when the many flower gardens are in bloom.

Not far from here, its top visible from the park, the **Fan Pagoda** (7am–7pm; ¥5) is not in a park as maps say, but sits between a car repair yard and a set of courtyards in a suburbia of labyrinthine alleyways. The only approach is from the western side. The fact that the local inhabitants tie their washing lines to the wall around the base and peel sweetcorn in the courtyard adds to the charm of the place. Built in 997 AD and the oldest standing building in Kaifeng this dumpy hexagonal brick pagoda was once 80m tall and had nine storeys; three remain today, and you can ascend for a view of rooftops and factories. The carved bricks on the outside are good, though the bottom few layers are new after vandalism in the Cultural Revolution.

From a bus station on the west side of Beimen Dajie, opposite the entrance to the Iron Pagoda Park, it's worth catching bus #6 to the **Yellow River Viewing Point**, 11km north of town, especially if you haven't seen the river before. From the pavilion here you can look out onto a plain of silt that stretches to the horizon, across whose dramatic emptiness the syrupy river meanders. Beside the pavilion is an **iron ox**, which once stood in a now submerged temple. It's a cuddly looking beast with a horn on its head that makes it look like a rhino sitting on its hind legs. An inscription on the back reveals its original function – a charm to ward off floods, a tradition begun by the legendary flood-tamer Da Yu (see p.259).

Eating

The best **place to eat** is the **night market** on Shudian Jie, where the food as well as the ambience is good. Here you'll find not just the usual staples such as *jiaozi*, made in front of you, and skewers of mutton cooked by Uyghur pedlars, but also a local **delicacy** consisting of hot liquid **jelly**, into which nuts, berries, flowers and fruit are poured. You can spot jelly stalls by the huge bronze kettle they all have with a spout in the form of a dragon's head.

For **dumplings**, don't miss the *Gulou Jiaozi Guan*, in a mock Qing structure at the corner of Gulou Jie and Shudian Jie. As for **restaurants**, *Xinxin Fanlou*, at the north end of Shudian Jie near the intersection with Dong Dajie, is a busy Muslim place selling *baozi* at ¥5 a steamer and roast duck for just ¥30. The *Diyi Lou Restaurant*, 43 Sihou Jie is a smart spot famous for its *baozi* but in autumn also serves delicious little river crabs stir-fried with chillies, which you eat whole, shells and all – dinner for two with drinks should come to around ¥60. If you need lunch down near the museum, *Songxiang Chuan Jiujia* is a good, straightforward Sichuanese restaurant just on the corner of Yingbin Lu. At the Mid-Autumn Festival, look out for Kaifeng's unique **mooncakes** – the usual thickness but a foot wide.

Listings

Banks and exchange The main Bank of China is in a Song-style building on the corner of Xi Dajie and Song Jie, with another branch on Zhongshan Lu. Both have ATMs.
Bookshops Shudian Jie is lined with shops catering to most tastes. The Xinhua Bookstore, on the east side of the street just north of Xi Dajie, has a limited selection of English books, but they do sell good maps.
Internet access A large, clean Internet bar (24hr; ¥1.5/hr) is just down the alley behind the PSB office.
Mail and telephones There's a large, efficient post office on Ziyou Lu (Mon–Fri 8am–noon & 2.30–6pm), with a 24hr telecom office next door.
PSB The main police station is on Zhongshan Lu. The section that deals with visas is windows #3 and #4, where the staff are so laid-back they're almost hip; a visa extension (¥120) can take 10min.
Shopping Kaifeng is a good place to find paintings and calligraphy, among the best buys in China – the obvious thing to pick up is a full-size reproduction of *Qingming Shang He*, which shoudln't set you back more than ¥50. Try the shops on Song Jie and stalls at the night market on Shudian Jie.
Travel agents The CTS are directly opposite Yangning Guan on Dazhifang Jie (ⓣ0378/3931861 or 3268689). The CITS are across from the PSB on Zhongshan Lu (ⓣ0378/5650712, ⓕ5650711); the only thing you'll possibly need them for is buying train tickets.

Shandong

Shandong province, a fertile plain through which the Yellow River completes its journey, was once one of the poorest regions of China, overpopulated and at the mercy of the river, whose course has continually shifted, bringing chaos with every move. However, the fertility of the flood plain means that human settlements have existed here for more than six thousand years, with **Neolithic remains** found at two sites, Dawenkou and Longshan, indicating a sophisticated agricultural society. In the Warring States Period (720–221 BC), Shandong included the states of Qi and Lu, and the province is well endowed with **ancient tombs and temples**, the best of which are to be found on **Tai Shan**, China's holiest Taoist mountain near the centre of the province. A second major religious site is the magnificent temple complex at **Qufu**, home of the province's most illustrious son, **Confucius**.

Shandong's recent history, though, has been dominated by **foreign influence** and its ramifications. In 1897, the Germans arrived, occupying first the port of **Qingdao** and then the capital, **Ji'nan**, their influence spreading further as they built a rail system across the province. Resentment at this interference, exacerbated by floods and an influx of refugees from the south, combined at the turn of the twentieth century to make Shandong the setting for the **Boxer Rebellion** (see p.1150). Today, however, there's little evidence of those times besides a flotsam of crumbling German architecture in Qingdao, and the main thrust is towards rapid industrialization and the exploitation of natural resources: Qingdao and the neighbouring ports of **Yantai** and **Penglai** are amongst the busiest in the country, and the recently developed **Shengli oilfield**, in the northeast, is China's second largest, the first tappings from reserves under the Bohai Sea.

As far as tourists are concerned, there's little reason to stray from the well-developed areas around Tai Shan and Qufu, though the port cities offer **ferries** to South Korea and elsewhere in China and, despite a sparse rail network, highways are good and bus services frequent. Another bonus is the friendliness of the people, who are proud of their reputation for hospitality, a tradition that goes right back to Confucius, who declared in *The Analects*, "Is it not a great pleasure to have guests coming from afar?"

Ji'nan

The capital of Shandong and a busy industrial city with three million inhabitants, **JI'NAN** is a bright and modern place with wide boulevards and gleaming towers, the province's major transit point and communication centre. There's not much to do here, however, and the city is best thought of as a stop on the way to or from Qufu and Tai'an.

Ji'nan stands on the site of one of China's **oldest settlements**, and pottery unearthed nearby has been dated to over four thousand years ago. It later became a military outpost and marketplace, expanding greatly during the Ming dynasty, when the city walls were built – they're no longer standing but you can see where they were on any map by the moats that once surrounded them. Ji'nan is famous in China for its **natural springs**, clear blue upwellings that are set amongst several urban parks and must rank as some of the cleanest water available in any Chinese city. The main sights here are the **provincial museum** and the steep hillside at **Qianfo Shan**, both at the city's southern limits and a good way to fill in time in transit.

Arrival, city transport and information

Ji'nan's **airport**, with international connections to Japan, South Korea and Hong Kong, is 40km east of the city. A private company operates airport shuttles (6am–6pm; ¥20; 30min ride), which drop you outside the airline ticket office opposite the *Sofitel Silver Plaza* hotel. Taxis from the airport into the city cost ¥100. The large and noisy main **train station**, at the junction of the Beijing– Shanghai line, and the line that goes east to Yantai and Qingdao, is in the northwest of town. The **long-distance bus station** is nearly 2km due north of the train station, with bus #84 running between the two, though you could also wind up at the **Lianyun bus station** on the train-station square, which has connections to cities within Shandong.

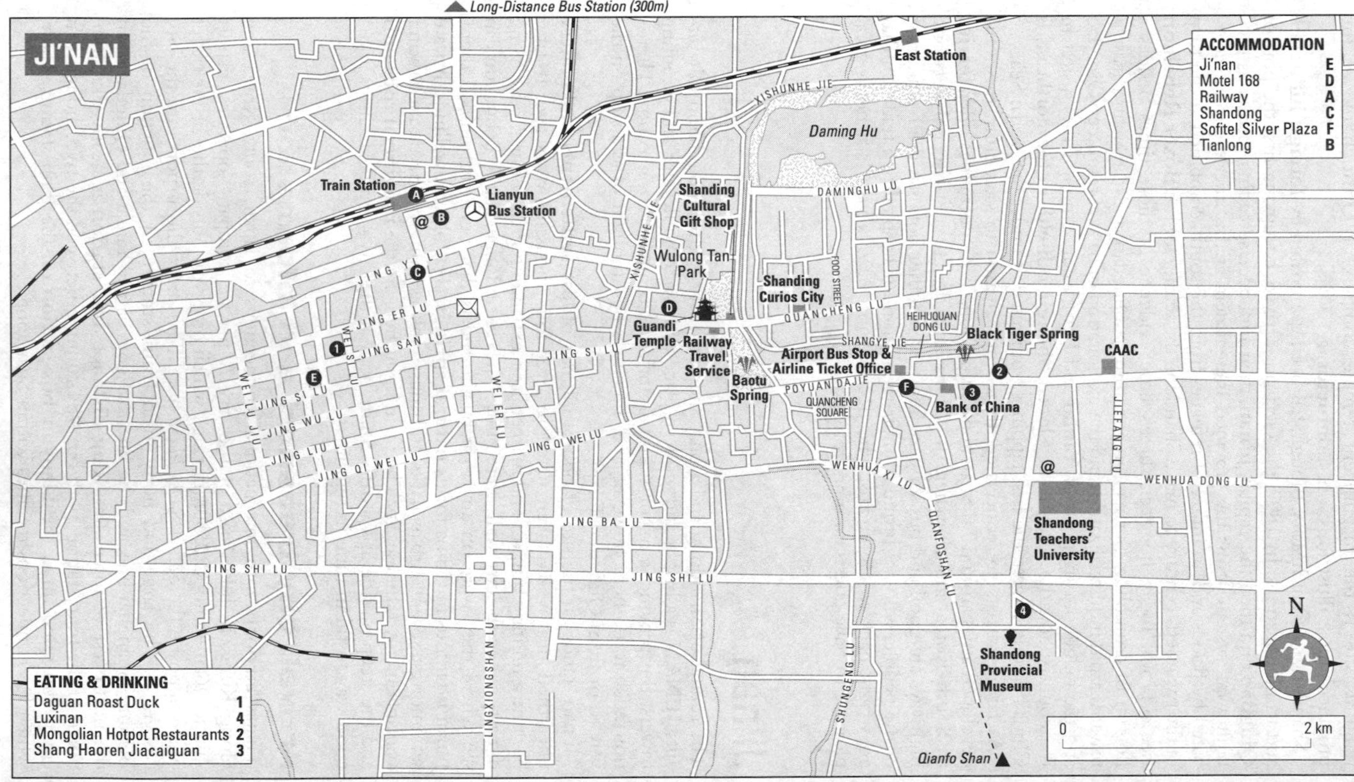
JI'NAN
Long-Distance Bus Station (300m)
ACCOMMODATION
Ji'nan E
Motel 168 D
Railway A
Shandong C
Sofitel Silver Plaza F
Tianlong B
EATING & DRINKING
Daguan Roast Duck 1
Luxinan 4
Mongolian Hotpot Restaurants 2
Shang Haoren Jiacaiguan 3
East Station
Train Station
Lianyun Bus Station
Daming Hu
XISHUNHE JIE
DAMINGHU LU
Shanding Cultural Gift Shop
Wulong Tan Park
Shanding Curios City
FOOD STREET
QUANCHENG LU
HEIHUQUAN DONG LU
Black Tiger Spring
CAAC
Guandi Temple
Railway Travel Service
Baotu Spring
Airport Bus Stop & Airline Ticket Office
SHANGYE JIE
POYUAN DAJIE
QUANCHENG SQUARE
Bank of China
JIEFANG LU
WENHUA XI LU
WENHUA DONG LU
QIANFOSHAN LU
Shandong Teachers' University
Shandong Provincial Museum
Qianfo Shan
SHUNGENG LU
LINGXIONGSHAN LU
JING YI LU
JING ER LU
JING SAN LU
JING SI LU
JING WU LU
JING LIU LU
JING QI WEI LU
JING BA LU
JING SHI LU
WEI SI LU
WEI ER LU
WEI LU JIU
N
0
2 km

Ji'nan

Ji'nan	济南	*jì'nán*
Baotu Spring Park	趵突泉公园	*bàotū quán gōngyuán*
Black Tiger Spring	黑虎泉	*hēihǔ quán*
Daming Hu	大明湖	*dàmíng hú*
Guangong Temple	关公庙	*guāngōng miào*
Qianfo Shan	千佛山	*qiānfóshān*
Quancheng Square	泉城广场	*quánchéng guǎngchǎng*
Shandong Provincial Museum	山东省博物馆	*shāndōngshěng bōwùguǎn*
Wulong Tan Park	五龙潭公园	*wǔlóngtán gōngyuán*
Bus Stations		
Lianyun Bus Station	汽车联运站	*qìchē liányùnzhàn*
Long distance Bus Station	长途汽车站	*chángtú qìchēzhàn*
Accommodation		
Ji'nan Hotel	济南大酒店	*jìnán dàjiǔdiàn*
Motel 168	莫泰连锁旅店	*mòtài liánsuǒ lǚdiàn*
Railway Hotel	铁道大酒店	*tiědào dàjiǔdiàn*
Shandong	山东宾馆	*shāndōng bīnguǎn*
Sofitel Silver Plaza	索菲特银座大酒店	*suǒfēitè yínzuò dàjiǔdián*
Tianlong	天龙大酒店	*tiānlóng dàjiǔdiàn*
Eating		
Daguan Roast Duck	大观烤鸭店	*dàguān kǎoyādiàn*
Luxinan	鲁西南风味楼	*lǔxīnán fēngwèilóu*
Shang Haoren Jiacaiguan	上好人家菜馆	*shàghǎo rénjiā càiguǎn*

Many of the city's **bus routes** begin from the train station, and **taxis** are cheap, the ¥6 basic fare just about covering trips around the city centre – these are your best option in most cases for reaching accommodation on arrival.

Accommodation

Ji'nan's **hotel** situation is a little limited, with foreigners excluded from the cheapest places. The train-station touts are OK, but make it very clear how much you're willing to pay if you don't want an endless run-around, and avoid the *Hongya*, whose staff are masters at finding reasons not to refund your room deposit.

Ji'nan Hotel 240 Jing San Lu ⓣ0531/87938981, ⓕ87932906. Bus #9 from the train station. Solid but characterless place in quiet grounds, though a long way from anywhere. ❹

Motel 168 Puli Jie ⓣ0531/86168168 or 81679999, ⓦwww.motel168.com. Clean, friendly and well located, with all rooms under ¥200 this is the city's bargain place to stay and is often full – book ahead. ❹

Moving on from Ji'nan

The main **CAAC office** is at 95 Jiefang Lu (8am–5.30pm; ⓣ0531/86988777), though it's far easier to get your tickets and airport shuttles from the airline ticket office across from the *Sofitel*. **Train tickets** are not hard to get at the station, though there's also the large Railway Travel Service opposite Wulong Tan Park (ⓣ0531/81817171; 8.30am–5pm), which can also reserve flights. For **buses** to Qingdao, Tai'an and Qufu, try the Lianyun bus station before heading out to the main long-distance station, though you'll probably need this for travel outside the province.

Railway Hotel On the train-station square ⓣ0531/86328888. Three-star, comfy place attached to the station front, convenient for transport. ❻

Shandong Jingyi Lu, about 500m south of the train-station area ⓣ86057881, ⓦwww.jnsdhotel.com. Elderly building with reasonably maintained rooms and grumpy staff but the cheapest deal in town for foreigners after you haggle over the rates. Beds ¥50, ❹

Sofitel Silver Plaza 66 Luoyuan Dajie ⓣ0531/86068888, ⓦwww.sofitel.com. The pinnacle of luxury in Ji'nan, right in the heart of the city with views of Quancheng Square. Rates often discounted by half or more. ❾

Tianlong On the train-station square ⓣ0531/86328888. Sister to the adjacent *Railway Hotel* and slightly cheaper, this modern place often has respectable discounts. ❺

The City

Ji'nan is pretty spread out, though there's something of a downtown focus around the oblong vastness of **Quancheng Square**, surrounded by shopping precincts and close to several of the city's parks. Immediately west, **Baotu Spring** (7am–5.30pm; ¥40) is enclosed in a pleasant park, but the entrance fee is absurd; better head just north to **Wulong Tan Park** (7am–5.30pm; ¥5), whose springs – now enclosed in goldfish-filled ponds – were mentioned in the *Spring and Autumn Annals*, government texts of 694 BC. Just outside the south gate is a tiny **Guandi Temple**, noted as the site where eunuch An Dehai, manipulative confidant of the Qing Empress Dowager Cixi, was executed by governor Ding Baozhen (after whom the Sichuanese dish "Gongbao Jiding" is named). In the east of the park is a modern hall to one of China's most famous female poets, **Li Qingzhao**, who was born in 1084 in Ji'nan – it contains extracts from her work and paintings by well-known contemporary artists.

Just over a kilometre north of Quancheng Square on the route of bus #11 from the train station, **Daming Hu** (daily 6am–6pm; ¥15) is surrounded by some quaint gardens, pavilions and bridges, and the lake is edged with willow trees and sprinkled with water lilies. About the same distance east, behind a wall on Heihuquan Dong Lu, the famous **Black Tiger Spring** (open all day; free) rises from a subterranean cave and emerges through tiger-headed spouts into a canal that once formed the old city's moat. People come here to fill up jerrycans from the spring and play in the water.

Qianfo Shan and the Shandong Provincial Museum

A scenic spot worth a trip is **Qianfo Shan** (daily 8am–6pm; ¥30), to the south of the city, on the route of bus #K54, which leaves from a terminus in the southwest corner of Daming Hu; the journey is about 5km. The mountainside is leafy and tracked with winding paths, the main one lined with painted opera masks. Most of the original statues that once dotted the slopes, freestanding images of Buddhas and Bodhisattvas, were destroyed by Red Guards, but new ones are being added, largely paid for by donations from Overseas Chinese. It's quite a climb to the summit (2hr), but the sculptures, and the view, get better the higher you go. Behind the **Xingguo Si** near the top are some superb sixth-century Buddhist carvings.

Near the mountain, and accessible on the same bus, the **Shandong Provincial Museum** (Mon–Fri 8.30–noon & 2–6pm, Sat & Sun 9am–4.30pm; ¥10) contains a number of fine Buddhist carvings as well as exhibits from the excavations at Longshan and Dawenkou, two nearby Neolithic sites noted for the delicate black pottery unearthed there. The remains date back to 5000 to 2000 BC. There's also a 22-metre-long Ming-dynasty **wooden boat**, excavated from the marshes southwest near Liangshan (setting for China's Robin Hood epic, *Outlaws of the Marsh*) and, in the basement, a huge and well-presented collection of Han **pictorial tomb reliefs** and Tang-dynasty tombstones.

Eating

To fill up inexpensively, there are plenty of noodle places around the train station, with the *Daguan Roast Duck* **restaurant** on Wei Si Lu not too far away if you fancy something more substantial. South of Black Tiger Spring on Poyuan Dajie you'll find a string of **Mongolian hotpot restaurants**, easily identifiable by the copper funnel hotpots outside. For local-style dining, both the smart and comfortable *Shang Haoren Jiacaiguan* restaurant at 9 Poyuan Dajie and the *Luxinan*, down near the museum at 150 Lishan Lu, serve Shandong fare, along with Beijing-style food.

Listings

Banks and exchange The Bank of China is on Poyuan Dajie, just east of the *Sofitel* (Mon–Fri 8.30am–5pm).
Bookshops The Foreign Language Bookstore is on Chaoshan Jie southwest of the *Sofitel*.
Internet access There's net access on the third floor of the Tianlong department store on the train-station square.
Mail and telephones Ji'nan's main post office is a red-brick building on Wei Er Lu just west of Jing Er Lu (8am–4.30pm). There's a 24hr telecom office inside.
Shopping There are two good spots for antiques and souvenirs on Quancheng Lu: Shandong Curios City in a mock-Ming shopping complex; and the higher-end Shandong Cultural Gift Shop at the southeastern corner of Wulong Tan Park.

Tai'an and Tai Shan

Tai Shan is not just a mountain, it's a god. Lying 100km south of Ji'nan, it's the easternmost and holiest of China's five holy Taoist mountains (the other four being Hua Shan, the two Heng Shans and Song Shan), and has been worshipped by the Chinese for longer than recorded history. It is justifiably famed for its scenery and the ancient buildings strung out along its slopes. Once host to emperors and the devout, it's now Shandong's biggest tourist attraction: the ascent is engrossing and beautiful – and very hard work.

The small town of **Tai'an** lies at the base of the mountain, and for centuries has prospered from the busy traffic of pilgrims coming to pay their respects to the mountain. You'll quickly become aware just how popular the pilgrimage is – on certain holy days ten thousand people might be making their way to the peak, and year round the town sees over half a million visitors.

Tai'an

TAI'AN is unremarkable but not unpleasant. It's just small enough to cover on foot, though few people pay it much attention; the town is overshadowed, literally, by the great mountain just to the north. Dongyue Dajie is the largest street, a corridor of high-rises running east–west across town. Qingnian Lu, the main **shopping street**, runs off its eastern end. The trailhead is reached on Hongmen Lu, which is flanked by a string of souvenir shops selling gnarled walking sticks made from tree roots, and shoes. Just south of Daizhong Dajie, in the north, are some busy **market streets** selling medicinal herbs that grow on the mountain, such as ginseng, the tuber of the multiflower knotweed, and Asian puccoon, along with strange vegetables, bonsai trees and potted plants.

Tai'an and Tai Shan

Tai'an	泰安	*tài'ān*
Dai Miao	岱庙	*dài miào*
Accommodation		
Lijing Hotel	丽景宾馆	*lìjǐng bīnguǎn*
Roman Holiday	罗马假日商务酒店	*luómǎ jiàrì shāngwù jiǔdiàn*
Tai'an Binguan	泰安宾馆	*tài'ān bīnguǎn*
Taishan Binguan	泰山宾馆	*tàishān bīnguǎn*
Yulong Binguan	裕隆宾馆	*yùlóng bīnguǎn*
Restaurants		
A Dong Jiachangcai	阿东家常菜	*ādōng jiāchángcài*
Maojia Fandian	毛家饭店	*máojiā fàndiàn*
Renzhong Shifu	人众食府	*rénzhòng shífǔ*
Tai Shan	泰山	*tàishān*
Bixia Ci	碧霞祠	*bìxiá cí*
Cablecar station	索道站	*suǒdào zhàn*
Dou Mu Convent	斗母宫	*dòumǔ gōng*
Hongmen Gong	红门宫	*hóngmén gōng*
Horse Turn Back Ridge	回马岭	*huímǎ lǐng*
Nantianmen Binguan	南天门宾馆	*nántiānmén bīnguǎn*
Pavilion of the Teapot Sky	壶天阁	*hútiān gé*
Puzhao Si	普照寺	*pǔzhào sì*
Sheng Xian Fang	升仙房	*shēngxiān fáng*
Stone Sutra Ravine	经石谷	*jīngshí gǔ*
Wangmu Chi	王母池	*wángmǔ chí*
Yitianmen	一天门	*yītiānmén*
Yuhuang Si	玉皇寺	*yùhuáng sì*
Yunbu Qiao	云步桥	*yúnbù qiáo*
Zhongtianmen	中天门	*zhōngtiānmén*
Zhongtianmen Hotel	中天门宾馆	*zhōngtiānmén bīnguǎn*

Arrival and information

Tai'an's **train station** is on the Ji'nan–Shanghai line, and exiting into the square outside you'll be greeted by a mob of eager taxi drivers. The minimum fare of ¥5 is sufficient for rides around town, with no more than ¥7 required to reach the mountain. There is a helpful **tourist info office** (24hr) in front of the train-station exit (bypass the uninformative tourist office *inside* the station) that sells a useful English map of the area (¥5). **Long-distance buses** from Ji'nan and Qufu terminate at the **Tai'an bus station** on Sanlizhuang Lu, south of the train station, though it's possible you'd end up at the Tai Shan depot just east of the train station. Both the train station and the Tai'an bus station have **left-luggage** facilities charging about ¥2 per day. Most of Tai'an's **city buses** run along Dongyue Dajie, just north of the station: bus #3 links both the western and eastern trailheads; #14 also goes to the eastern trailhead via Daizhong Dajie.

The **post office** is on Dongyue Dajie (Mon–Fri 8am–6pm), near the junction with Qingnian Lu. The main **Bank of China** is located at 48 Dongyue Dajie, though a small branch with an ATM is uphill from the *Taishan Binguan*. The helpful English-speaking branch of **CITS** is a bit out of the way, just off Nanhe Xi Lu (ⓣ0538/8223259). There is an **Internet** café just uphill from the *Taishan Binguan*, another not far to the south on Dai Zhong Dajie, and a third opposite the *Yulong Binguan* on Longtan Lu.

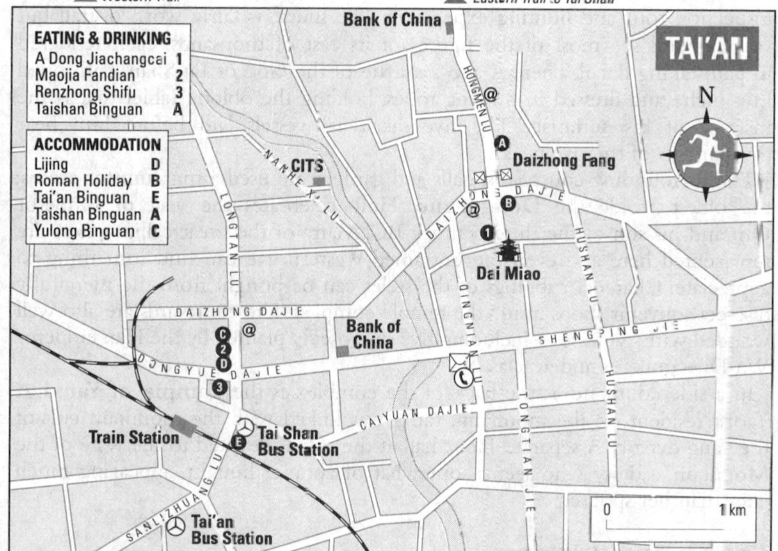

Accommodation

There's a mess of **places to stay** around the arrival points, and you might get in to the bedrock places – they're signed in Chinese only – if you speak some Chinese. Otherwise, two of the cheaper options likely to take foreigners are the *Tai'an Binguan*, across from the train station on Sanlizhuang Lu (ⓣ0538/6911111; ④); and *Yulong Binguan* at 17 Longtan Lu (ⓣ0538/8218164; ③), both with worn but clean doubles, which solo travellers might wrangle to half price. In the same area but a different price bracket, the *Lijing Hotel* at 1 Longtan Lu (ⓣ0538/8538888; ⑤) has an attached café. The other group of hotels is up between Dai Miao and the eastern trail on Hongmen Lu: the comfy, motel-like *Roman Holiday* at 18 Hongmen Lu (ⓣ0538/6279999, ⓕ6278889; ⑤) immediately offers discounts; while the five-storey *Taishan Binguan* (ⓣ0538/8224678, ⓕ8221432; ⑥) is one of the best-run places in town, smart but casual.

There's also **accommodation on Tai Shan** itself, but it's expensive for what you get – see the mountain account for details.

Dai Miao

Dai Miao (daily 8am–5pm; ¥20), the temple where emperors once made sacrifices to the mountain, is the traditional starting point for the procession up Tai Shan. It's a magnificent structure, with yellow-tiled roofs, red walls and towering old trees, one of the largest temples in the country and one of the most celebrated. Though it appears an ordered whole, the complex is really a blend of buildings from different belief systems, with veneration of the mountain as the only constant factor.

The Main Hall, **Tiankuangdian** (Hall of the Celestial Gift), is matched in size only by halls in the Forbidden City and at Qufu. The hall's construction started as early as the Qin dynasty (221–206 BC), though expansion and renovation have gone on ever since, particularly during the Tang and Song dynasties. Inside is a huge **mural** covering three of the walls, a Song-dynasty masterpiece depicting the Emperor Zhen Zong as the God of Tai Shan on an inspection tour and hunting expedition. The mural is fairly worn overall but you can still see most of the figures of its cast of thousands, each rendered in painstaking detail. There is also a **statue** of the God of Tai Shan, enthroned in a niche and dressed in flowing robes, holding the oblong tablet that is the insignia of his authority. The five sacrificial vessels laid before him bear the symbols of the five peaks.

The surrounding courtyards, halls and gardens are used a museum for **steles**; the oldest, inside the **Dongyuzuo Hall**, celebrates the visit of Emperor Qin and his son in the third century BC. Many of the great calligraphers are represented here and even the untrained Western eye can find something to appreciate. Charcoal rubbings of the steles can be bought from the mercifully discreet souvenir shops inside the temple complex. The courtyards are also well wooded with cypresses – including five supposedly planted by the Han emperor Wu Di – ginkgos and acacias.

In a side courtyard at the back of the complex is the **Temple of Yanxi**. A Taoist resident on the mountain, Yanxi was linked with the mountain cult of the Tang dynasty. A separate Taoist hall at the rear is devoted to the Wife of the Mountain, a deity who seems somewhat of an afterthought, appearing much later than her spouse.

Eating and drinking

A speciality of **Tai'an cuisine** is red-scaled carp, fresh from pools on the mountain and fried while it's still alive. Other dishes from the mountain include chicken stewed with *siliquose pelvetia* (a fungus only found within 2m of the ancient pine trees around the Nine Dragon Hill), coral herb and hill lilac. The best place to try these things is in the *Taishan Binguan*, where a meal for two, with vegetable and meat dishes as well as drinks, should come to around ¥80. If this is too much, *A Dong Jiachangcai*, further south on Hongmen Lu, is a popular, busy place serving staples. Down near the train station, *Renzhong Shifu* is a cheap joint with an English menu, sort of, and tasty stir-fries; while ✱ *Maojia Fandian* is a more upmarket place offering excellent Hunanese food, such as chilli-smoked meat and dry-fried beans (complete with photo menu), at around ¥20 a main.

Tours

Apart from trips up the mountain, which you'd be better off doing under your own steam, CITS runs two **tours** that are worth considering. The **Buyang Village Tour** is a chance to visit a real, dusty, ramshackle Chinese village and get a taste of rural life. You can go fishing with the locals or try your hand at making dumplings, and if you're really interested you can stay the night at a farmer's house. You'll need to get a group of four or five together, and the tour costs ¥120 per person, dinner included.

Another tour (¥50 per person) is by taxi to the **Puzhao Si** to see an old Taoist monk, a *qi gong* master who can apparently swallow needles and thread them with his tongue. Don't expect a performing clown – he only does his stuff when he feels like it. This tour gets mixed reactions, and some visitors have reported feeling intrusive.

Tai Shan

More so than any other holy mountain, **Tai Shan** was the haunt of emperors, and owes its obvious glories – the temples and pavilions along its route – to the patronage of the imperial court. From its summit, a succession of emperors surveyed their empires, made sacrifices and paid tribute. Sometimes, their retinues stretched right from the top to the bottom of the mountain, 8km of pomp and ostentatious wealth. In 219 BC, Emperor Qin Shi Huang had **roads** built all over the mountain so that he could ride here in his carriage under escort of the royal guards when he was performing the grand ceremonies of *feng* (sacrifices to heaven) and *chan* (offerings to earth). Various titles were offered to the mountain by emperors keen to bask in reflected glory. As well as funding the temples, emperors had their visits and thoughts recorded for posterity on steles here, and men of letters carved poems and tributes to the mountain on any available rockface. Shandong-native Confucius is also said to have made a trip here, and there is a temple in his honour in the shadow of the highest peak.

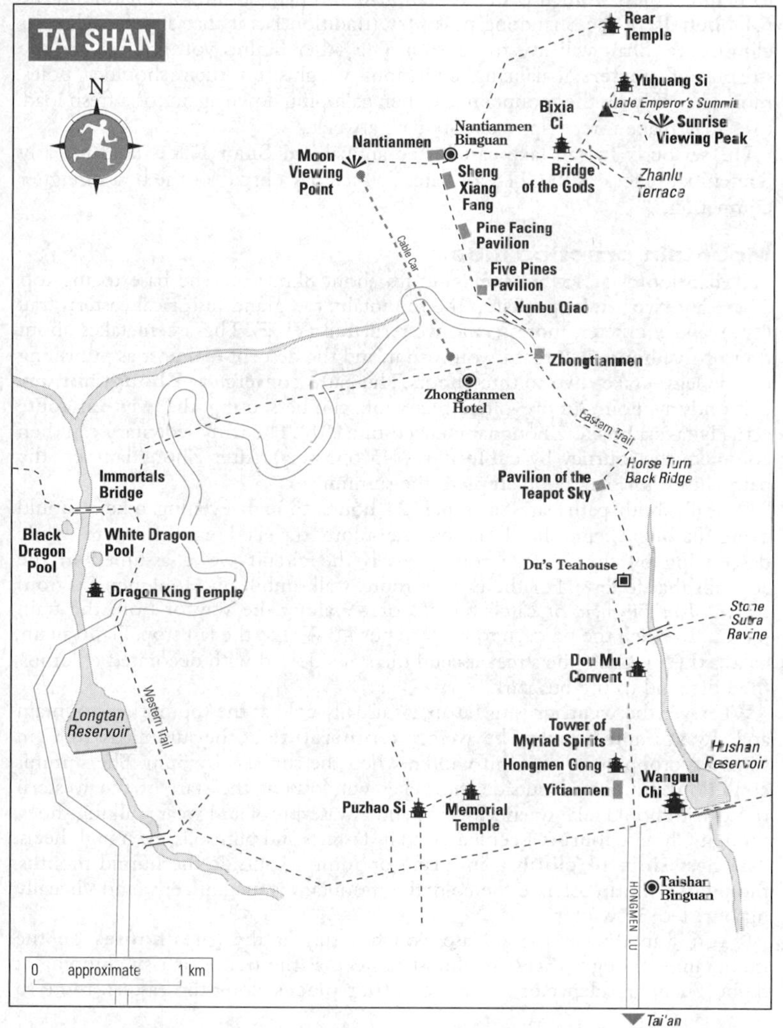

In recent years, this huge open-air museum has mutated into a religious theme park, and the path is now thronged with a constant procession of **tourists**. There are photo booths, souvenir stalls, soft-drinks vendors and teahouses. You can get your name inscribed on a medal, get your photograph taken and buy medicinal herbs from vendors squatting on walls. Halfway up, there's a **bus station** and **cable car**. Yet Tai Shan retains an atmosphere of grandeur; the buildings and the mountain itself are magnificent enough to survive their trivialization.

It is surprising, though, to see that numbering among the hordes of tourists are a great many genuine **pilgrims**. Taoism, after a long period of communist proscription, is again alive and flourishing, and you're more than likely to see a bearded Taoist monk on the way up. Women come specifically to pray to **Bixia Yuan Jun**, the Princess of the Rosy Clouds, a Taoist deity believed to be able to help childless women conceive. Tai Shan also plays an important role in the **folk beliefs** of the Shandong peasantry (tradition has it that anyone who has climbed Tai Shan will live to be 100). The other figures you will see are the streams of **porters**, balancing enormous weights on their shoulder poles, moving swiftly up the mountain and then galloping down again for a fresh load; they may make three trips a day, six days a week.

The seriously fit can take part in the annual **Tai Shan Race**, held in early September (check with CITS for dates), which has a prize for the best foreigner competing.

Mountain practicalities

Tai Shan looms at 1545m high, and it's about 8km from the base to the top. There are **two main paths** up the mountain: the grand historical eastern trail (¥80), and a quieter, more scenic western trail (¥102). The ascent takes about four or five hours, half that if you rush it, and the descent – almost as punishing on the legs – takes two to three hours. The paths converge at **Zhongtianmen**, the midway point (more often than not, climbers using the western route actually take a **bus** to Zhongtianmen, costing ¥18). The truly sedentary can then complete the journey by **cable car** (¥45 one way). After Zhongtianmen, the path climbs for over 6000 **steps** to the summit.

Offically, both path gates are open 24 hours, though evening hikers should bring flashlights and head up by the more travelled eastern route while descending by the western route; this is the circuit we've assumed in the account that follows. For the eastern route, walk uphill on Hongmen Lu from the *Taishan Binguan*, or catch bus #3 or #9 along the way or from the train station. To reach the western route, take bus #3 (¥1) to the last stop, Tianwaicun, or a taxi (¥7). Cross the street, ascend the stairs dotted with decorated columns, then descend to the bus park.

Whatever the **weather** is in Tai'an, it's usually cold at the top of the mountain and always unpredictable. The average **temperature** at the summit is 18°C in summer, dropping to -9°C in winter, when the sun sets by 5pm. The summit conditions are posted outside the ticket windows at the start of the western route. You should take warm clothing and a waterproof and wear walking shoes, though Chinese tourists ascend dressed in T-shirts and plimsolls, even high heels. The **best time to climb** is in spring or autumn, outside the humid months, though if you can tolerate the cold, the mountain is magnificent (and virtually untouristed) in winter.

If you want to see the sunrise, you can stay at the **guesthouses** on the mountain – though prices are almost as steep as the trail – or risk climbing at night. There are plenty of affordable **eating places** along the eastern route to

Zhongtianmen, but it's a good idea to take your own **food** as well, as the fare on offer past the midway point is unappealing and gets more expensive the higher you go.

The ascent

Using the **eastern trail**, your ascent will begin from **Daizhong Fang**, a stone arch to the north of the Dai Miao in Tai'an. North of the arch and on the right is a pool, **Wangmu Chi**, and a small and rather quaint-looking nunnery, from

▲ The route up Tai Shan

where you can see the whimsically named Hornless Dragon Pool and Combing and Washing River. In the main hall of the nunnery is a statue of Xiwang Mu, Queen Mother of the West, the major female deity in Taoism.

Yitianmen to Zhongtianmen

About 500m up is the official start of the path at **Yitianmen** (First Heavenly Gate). This is followed by a Ming arch, said to mark the spot where Confucius began his climb, and the **Hongmen Gong** (Red Gate Palace), where emperors used to change into sensible clothes for the ascent, and where you buy your ticket, which includes insurance. Built in 1626, Hongmen Gong is the first of a series of temples dedicated to the Princess of the Rosy Clouds. It got its name from the two red rocks to the northwest, which together resemble an arch.

There are plenty of buildings to distract you around here. Just to the north is the Tower of Myriad Spirits, and just below that the Tomb of the White Mule is said to be where the mule that carried the Tang emperor Xuan up and down the mountain finally dropped dead, exhausted. Xuan made the mule a posthumous general and at least it got a decent burial. The next group of buildings is the former **Dou Mu Convent**, a hall for Taoist nuns. Its date of founding is uncertain, but it was reconstructed in 1542. Today, there are three halls, a drum tower, a bell tower and an ancient, **gnarled tree** outside, which is supposed to look like a reclining dragon. Like all the temple buildings on the mountain, the walls are painted with a blood-red wash, here interspersed with small grey bricks.

North of here, a path veers east off the main route for about a kilometre to the **Stone Sutra Ravine** where the text of the Buddhist Diamond Sutra has been carved on the rockface. This is one of the most prized of Tai Shan's many calligraphic works, and makes a worthwhile diversion as it's set in a charming, quiet spot. Back on the main path, don't miss **Du's Teahouse**, built on the spot where, more than a thousand years ago, General Cheng Yao Jing Tang planted four pines, three of which are still alive. The teahouse and everything in it is quaintly built out of polished tree roots, and the "maiden tea" is excellent, and a speciality of this mountain area.

After a tunnel of cypress trees, and the **Pavilion of the Teapot Sky** (so called because the peaks all around supposedly give the illusion of standing in a teapot), you see a sheer cliff rising in front of you, called **Horse Turn Back Ridge**. This is where Emperor Zhen Zong had to dismount because his horse refused to go any farther. Not far above is **Zhongtianmen** (Halfway Gate to Heaven), the midpoint of the climb. There are some good views here, though the **cable car** will be the most welcome sight if you're flagging. The pleasant *Zhongtianmen Hotel* is situated here (Ⓣ0538/8226740; ❺), plus a collection of dull restaurants. Confusingly, you have to descend two staircases and then follow the road round to continue the climb.

Zhongtianmen to the top

The next sight is **Yunbu Qiao** (Cloud Stepping Bridge), after which you arrive at **Five Pines Pavilion**, where the first Qin emperor took shelter from a storm under a group of pines. The grateful emperor then promoted the lucky pine trees to ministers of the fifth grade. From here you can see the lesser peaks of Tai Shan: the Mountain of Symmetrical Pines, the Flying Dragon Crag and Hovering Phoenix Ridge.

Farther up you pass under **Sheng Xian Fang** (Archway to Immortality), which, according to mountain myth, assures your longevity and provides the viewpoint that inspired Tang poet Li Bai to write: "In a long breath by the heavenly gate, the fresh wind comes from a thousand miles away", though by this point most climbers are long past being able to appreciate poetry, let alone compose it.

The **final section** of the climb is the hardest, as the stone stairs are steep and narrow, and ascend almost vertically between two walls of rocks (often through thick white mist) – almost everyone by this point is unashamedly grasping the handrails as they haul themselves upwards. And then suddenly you're at the top on **Tian Jie** (Heaven Street), a tourist strip where you can buy "I climbed Tai Shan" T-shirts, slurp a pot noodle and get your picture taken dressed as an emperor. There are a couple of **restaurants** here, **hotels** and a few **shops**. This thriving little tourist village represents a triumph of the profit motive over the elements; it's often so misty you can hardly see from one souvenir stall to the next. If you want to **stay the night**, try and negotiate a discount at the wildly overpriced *Nantianmen Binguan* (Ⓣ0538/8330988, dorm beds ¥70, ❽), which also has a restaurant.

The **Bixia Ci**, on the southern slopes of the summit, is the final destination for most of the bona fide pilgrims, and offerings are made to a bronze statue of the princess in the main hall. It's a working temple and its guardians enforce strict rules about where the merely curious are allowed to wander. It's also a splendid building, the whole place tiled with iron to resist wind damage, and all the decorations are metal, too. The bells hanging from the eaves, the mythological animals on the roof, and even the two steles outside are bronze. From 1759 until the fall of the Qing, the emperor would send an official here on the eighteenth day of the fourth lunar month each year to make an offering. Just below is a small **shrine to Confucius**, at the place where he was supposed to have commented, "the world is small".

At the **Yuhuang Si** (Jade Emperor Temple), you have truly arrived at the **highest point** of the mountain, and a rock with the characters for "supreme summit" and "1545m" carved on it stands within the courtyard. In Chinese popular religion, which mixes Taoism and Confucianism with much earlier beliefs, the Jade Emperor is the supreme ruler of heaven, depicted in an imperial hat with bead curtains hanging down his face. Outside the temple is the **Wordless Monument**, thought to have been erected by Emperor Wu more than two thousand years ago. The story goes that Wu wanted to have an inscription engraved that would do justice to his merits. None of the drafts he commissioned came up to scratch, however, so he left the stele blank, leaving everything to the imagination.

Southeast of here is the peak for **watching the sunrise** (4.45am in June, 7am in December). It was here that the Song emperor performed the *feng* ceremony, building an altar and making sacrifices to heaven. On a clear day, you can see 200km to the coast, and at night you can see the lights of Ji'nan. There are numerous **trails** from here to fancifully named scenic spots – Fairy Bridge, Celestial Candle Peak, and the like. If the weather is good, it's a great place for aimless wandering.

The descent

The best way down is along the **western trail**, which is longer, quieter and has some impressive views. It starts at Zhongtianmen, loops round and joins the main trail back at the base of the mountain. Midway is the **Black Dragon Pool**, a dark, brooding pond, home of the Tai Shan speciality dish, red-scaled carp, once so precious that the fish was used as tribute to the court. Near the bottom, the **Puzhao Si** (Temple of Universal Clarity) is a pretty, mostly Qing, temple complex. It's east of the western trail, though access is via the road that runs around the base of the mountain.

Qufu and around

QUFU, a small town in the south of Shandong, easily accessible by bus or train from Tai'an, 100km north, and Ji'nan, 180km away, is of immense historical and cultural importance. **Confucius** (Kong Zi) was born here around 551 BC, and, having spent his life teaching his moral code – largely unappreciated by his contemporaries – was buried just outside the town, in what became a sacred burial ground for his clan, the Kong. His teachings caught on after his death, however, and despite periodic purges (most recently during the Cultural Revolution), they have become firmly embedded in the Chinese psyche. All around the town is architectural evidence of the esteem in which he was held by successive dynasties – most monumentally by the Ming, who were responsible for the two dominant sights, the **Confucius Temple** and the **Confucius Mansion**, whose scale seems more suited to Beijing. For more on Confucius and Confucianism, see "Contexts" p.1164.

Qufu is an interesting place to stop over for a few days, with plenty to see concentrated in an area small enough to walk around. As a major tourist destination, however, you'll have to expect the usual crowds and hustles – especially around the end of September, **on Confucius's birthdate** in the lunar calendar, when a **festival** is held here and reconstructions of many of the original rituals are performed. If it all gets too much, there are places to escape amidst old buildings, trees and singing birds, such as the **Confucian Forest** to the north, though it might help, too, to remember the words of the master himself: "A gentleman understands what is moral, a base man understands only what is profitable."

Arrival, information and city transport

The **train station**, on a spur of the Shanghai–Xi'an line, is 5km east at the end of the #5 bus route. This runs into town past the **long-distance bus station**, from where you can get transport to Heze (for Kaifeng), Ji'nan,

Qufu and around		
Qufu	曲阜	*qǔfǔ*
Bell Tower	钟楼	*zhōng lóu*
Confucian Forest	孔林	*kǒng lín*
Confucius Mansion	孔府	*kǒng fǔ*
Confucius Temple	孔庙	*kǒng miào*
Drum Tower	鼓楼	*gǔlóu*
Hall of Great Achievements	大成殿	*dàchéng diàn*
Hall of Poetry and Rights	侍社堂	*shīshè táng*
Yan Miao	颜庙	*yán miào*
Zhougong Miao	周公庙	*zhōugōng miào*
Accommodation and eating		
Great Wall	长城宾馆	*chángchéng bīnguǎn*
Huaqiao	华侨宾馆	*huáqiáo bīnguǎn*
Kongfuyan Dajiudian	孔府宴大酒店	*kǒngfǔyań dàjiǔdiàn*
Queli	阙里宾舍	*quèlǐ bīnshè*
Yingshi	影视宾馆	*yǐngshì bīnguǎn*
Yonghe Doujiang	永和豆浆	*yǒnghé dóujiāng*
Yulong	裕隆大饭店	*yùlóng dàfàndiàn*

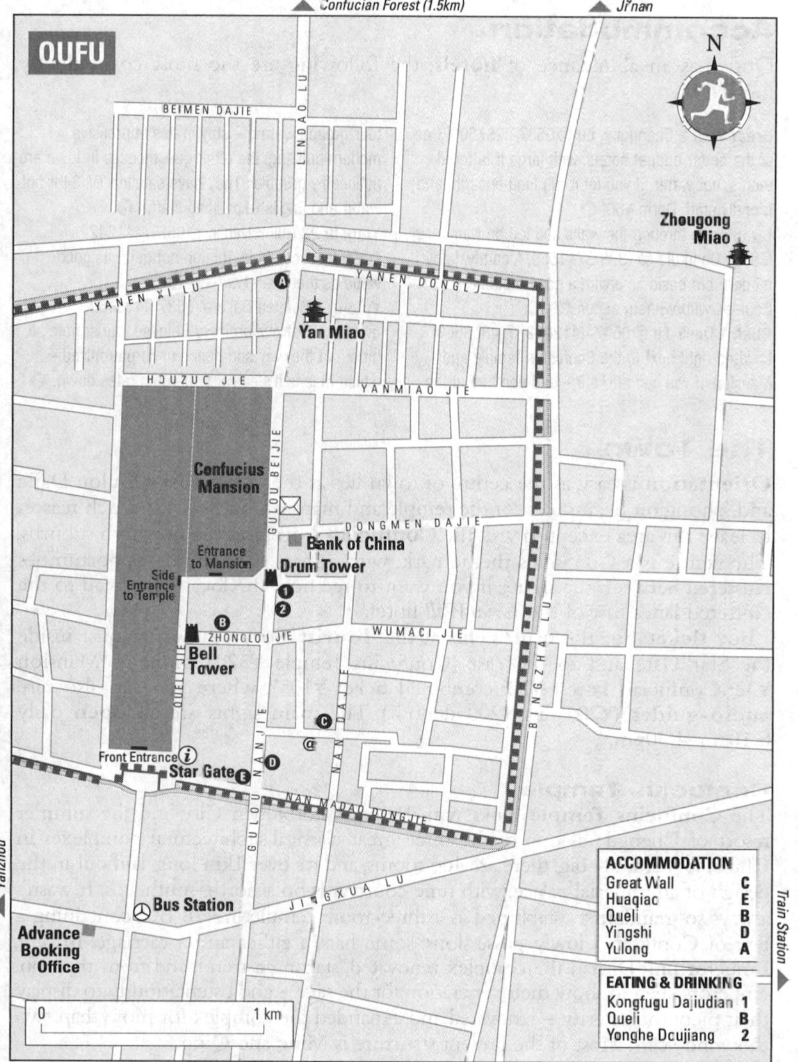

Tai'an, Qingdao, Yantai and Zhengzhou. Train and airline ticket **booking** counters (the nearest airport is Ji'nan's) are southwest across the street from the bus station.

Once in town, the only **city bus** you'll need is the #1, which runs up Gulou Beijie to the Confucian Forest. Otherwise, grab a **cycle-rickshaw**, whereby the passenger is slung low in the front, giving an uninterrupted dog's-eye view of the street. A ride anywhere in town should cost ¥3–5. There are also horse-drawn gypsy-style **carts**, strictly for tourists, so not cheap. A **taxi** in town will start at ¥6.

Accommodation

Qufu has an abundance of **hotels**; the following are the most conveniently located.

Great Wall 2 Changqing Lu ⓣ0537/2287500. One of the better budget hotels, with large if tattered rooms, hot water (if you let it run long enough) and friendly staff. Dorm ¥60, ❸

Huaqiao In through the walls and left on Nan Madao Dong Jie ⓣ1395/3711550. A comfy, fairly modern but basic hotelwith a good restaurant. Doubles with/without aircon ❷–❹

Queli 1 Queli Jie ⓣ0537/4412022, ⓕ4866660. Located right next to the Confucius Temple and Mansion. If you can afford it – and don't mind the tour-group swarms – stay in this impressive modern building: the other guesthouses in town are noticeably grubbier. They have satellite TV, 24hr hot water and English-speaking staff. ❻

Yingshi 22 Gulou Nanjie ⓣ0537/4412422. Perfectly acceptable, though not quite as good value as the *Great Wall*. ❷–❹

Yulong 1 Beimen Dajie ⓣ0537/4413469, ⓕ4413209. New, ordinary Chinese tourist hotel, a bit out of the way and hence underpatronized – which means it's easier to bargain rates down. ❺

The Town

Orientation is easy, as the centre of town lies at the crossroads of Gulou Dajie and Zhonglou Jie, just east of the temple and mansion. There's not much reason to leave this area except to visit the **Confucian Forest** in the northern suburbs. The centre is a Confucius theme park, with a mass of shopping opportunities clustered between the sights; if you want to see how the locals live, head to the cluttered lanes east of the *Great Wall* hotel.

Buy **tickets** for the main sights at the **Tourist Service Centre**, just inside the Star Gate and to the east (Confucius Temple ¥52; Confucius Mansion ¥32; Confucian Forest ¥22; combined ticket ¥105), where you can also hire **audio-guides** (¥20, plus ¥200 deposit). The main sights are all **open** daily 8.10am–4.30pm.

Confucius Temple

The **Confucius Temple** ranks with Beijing's Forbidden City and the summer resort of Chengde as one of the three great classical architectural complexes in China. It's certainly big: there are 466 rooms, and it's over 1km long, laid out in the design of an imperial palace, with nine courtyards on a north–south axis. It wasn't always so grand, first established as a three-room temple in 478 BC, containing a few of Confucius's lowly possessions: some hats, a zither and a carriage. In 539, Emperor Jing Di had the complex renovated, starting a trend, and from then on, emperors keen to show their veneration for the sage – and ostentatiously to display their piety to posterity – renovated and expanded the complex for more than two thousand years. Most of the present structure is Ming and Qing.

Entering the complex

The temple's main approach is in the southern section of the temple wall, and this is the best place to enter if you want an ordered impression of the complex (there is also an entrance on Queli Lu, just west of the mansion). Through the gate, flanked by horned creatures squatting on lotus flowers, first views are of clusters of wiry cypresses and monolithic steles, some sitting on the backs of carved *bixi*, stoic-looking turtle-like creatures, in an overgrown courtyard. A succession of gates leads into a courtyard holding the magnificent **Kui Wen Pavilion**, a three-storey wooden building constructed in 1018 with a design unique in Chinese classical architecture – a triple-layered roof with curving eaves and four layers of crossbeams. It was renovated in 1504 and has since withstood an earthquake undamaged, an

Confucianism in modern China

When the **Communists** came to power they saw **Confucianism** as an archaic, feudal system and an **anti-Confucius campaign** was instigated, which came to a climax during the Cultural Revolution. Now, however, Conservatives frightened by the pace of change, the growing generation gap, and the new materialism of China, are calling for a **return to Confucian values** of respect and selflessness, just as their nervous counterparts in the West preach a return to family values. Confucian social morality – obeying authority, regarding family as the seat of morality, and emphasizing the mutual benefits of friendship – is sometimes hailed as one of the main reasons for the success of East Asian economies, just as Protestantism provided the ideological complement to the growth of the industrialized West.

Most of the Confucian buildings in Qufu have been recently renovated, but this is strictly in the interests of **tourism**, not worship. Confucianism as a moral force was thought to have died, yet the ability of Chinese traditions to survive modernization and suppression always surprises observers. As one Chinese visitor commented, "Confucius is the one Chinese leader who never let the people down."

event recorded on a tablet on the terrace. To the east and west, the two pavilions are abstention lodges where visiting emperors would fast and bathe before taking part in sacrificial ceremonies.

The **thirteen stele pavilions** in the courtyard beyond are worth checking out, containing 53 tablets presented by emperors to commemorate their visits, and gifts of land and funds for renovations made to the Kong family. The earliest are Tang and the latest are from the Republican period. Continuing north, you come to **five gates** leading off in different directions. The eastern ones lead to the hall where sacrifices were offered to Confucius's ancestors, the western to the halls where his parents were worshipped, while the central Gate of Great Achievements leads to a large pavilion, the **Apricot Altar**. Tradition has it that Confucius taught here after travelling the country in search of a ruler willing to implement his ideas. The cypress just inside the gate was supposed to have been planted by Confucius himself, and its state of health is supposed to reflect the fortunes of the Kongs.

The Hall of Great Achievements

The Hall of Great Achievements, behind the Apricot Altar, is the temple's grandest building, its most striking feature being 28 **stone pillars** carved with bas-relief dragons, dating from around 1500. Each pillar has nine gorgeous dragons, coiling around clouds and pearls towards the roof. There is nothing comparable in the Forbidden City in Beijing, and when emperors came to visit, the columns were covered with yellow silk to prevent imperial jealousy. Originally, the temple was solely dedicated to the worship of Confucius, but in 72 AD, Emperor Liu Zhuang offered sacrifices to his 72 disciples, too. Five hundred years later, Zhen Guan of the Tang dynasty issued an edict decreeing that 22 eminent Confucians should also be worshipped. Emperors of later dynasties (not wishing to be outdone) added more, and there are presently 172 "eminent worthies".

Behind the main hall is the inner hall for the worship of **Confucius's wife, Qi Guan**, who also, it seems, merited deification through association (though Confucian values placed women way down the social hierarchy, with wives less important than their sons, and daughters-in-law less important than anybody). The phoenixes painted on its columns and ceiling are symbols of female power, in the same way as the dragon symbolizes masculinity.

Beyond is the **Hall of the Relics of the Sage**, where 120 carved stone plates made in the sixteenth century from Song paintings depict scenes from Confucius's life. They begin with Confucius's mother praying for a son, and end with his disciples mourning at his grave. The workmanship is excellent but the light in the room is dim and you'll have to squint.

The Hall of Poetry and Rites and the Lu Wall

The **eastern axis** of the temple is entered here, through the **Gate of the Succession of the Sage** next to the Hall of Great Achievements. Here is the **Hall of Poetry and Rites** where Confucius was supposed to have taught his son, Kong Li, to learn poetry from the *Book of Odes* in order to express himself, and ritual from the *Book of Rites* in order to strengthen his character.

A solitary wall in the courtyard is the famous **Lu Wall**, where Kong Fu, a ninth-generation descendant of Confucius, hid the sage's **books** when Qin Shi Huang, the first emperor (see p.1144), persecuted the followers of Confucius and burned all his books. Several decades later, Liu Yu, prince of Lu and son of the Emperor Jing Di, ordered Confucius's dwelling to be demolished in order to build an extension to his palace, whereupon the books were found, which led to a schism between those who followed the reconstructed version of his last books, and those who followed the teachings in the rediscovered originals. In the east wall of the temple, near the Lu Wall, an unobtrusive gate leads to the legendary **site of Confucius's home**, sandwiched between the spectacular temple and the magnificent mansion, a tiny square of land, just big enough to have held a couple of poky little rooms.

The western section

The **western section** is entered through the Gate of He Who Heralds the Sage, by the Hall of Great Achievements. A paved path leads to a high brick terrace on which stands the five-bay, green-tiled **Hall of Silks and Metals** and the **Hall of He Who Heralds the Sage**, built to venerate Confucius's father, **Shu Lianghe**. He was originally a minor military official who attained posthumous nobility through his son. Behind is, predictably, the Hall of the Wife of He Who Heralds the Sage, dedicated to Confucius's mother.

Confucius Mansion

The First Family Under Heaven – the descendants of Confucius – lived continuously at the **Confucius Mansion**, accessible off Queli Jie in the centre of town, for more than 2500 years, spanning 74 generations. The opulence and size of the mansion testifies to the power and wealth of the **Kong clan** and their head, the **Yansheng Duke**. Built on a north–south axis, the mansion is loosely divided into living quarters, an administrative area and a garden. In the east is a temple and ancestral hall, while the western wing includes the reception rooms for important guests and the rooms where the rites were learned.

Intricate and convoluted, this complex of twisting alleyways and over 450 rooms (most of them sixteenth century) has something decidedly eccentric about it. Inside the complex lies a central courtyard lined with long, narrow buildings, which were once administrative offices; now they hold a few trinket shops. The **Gate of Double Glory** to the north was opened only on ceremonial occasions or when the emperor dropped in. To its east and west are **old administrative departments**, modelled after the six ministries of the imperial government: the Department of Rites was in charge of ancestor worship; the Department of Seals concerned with jurisdiction and edicts; then followed

The Yansheng Duke and the Kong family

The status of the **Yansheng Duke** – the title given to Confucius's direct male descendant – rose throughout imperial history as emperors granted him increasing **privileges and hereditary titles**; under the Qing dynasty, he enjoyed the unique privilege of being permitted to ride a horse inside the Forbidden City and walk along the Imperial Way inside the palace. Emperors presented the duke with large areas of sacrificial fields (so called because the income from the fields was used to pay for sacrificial ceremonies), as well as exempting him from taxes.

As a family, the Kongs remained close-knit, practising a severe interpretation of **Confucian ethics**. For example, any young family member who offended an elder was fined two taels of silver and battered twenty times with a bamboo club. Strict rules governed who could go where within the house, and when a fire broke out in the living quarters in the last century it raged for three days as only twelve of the five hundred hereditary servants were allowed to go into the area to put it out. A female family member was expected to obey her father, her husband and her son. One elderly Kong general, after defeat on the battlefield, cut his throat for the sake of his dignity. When the news reached the mansion, his son hanged himself as an expression of filial piety. After discovering the body, his wife hanged herself out of female virtue. On hearing this, the emperor bestowed the family with a board, inscribed "A family of faithfulness and filiality".

The Kong family enjoyed the good life right up until the beginning of the twentieth century. **Decline** set in rapidly with the downfall of imperial rule, and in the 1920s the family was so poor that when wine was required for entertaining a guest, the servants bought it out of their own pocket, as a favour to their masters. In 1940, the last of the line, **Kong Decheng**, fled to Taiwan during the Japanese invasion, breaking the tradition of millennia. His sister, **Kong Demao**, penned *In the House of Confucius*, a fascinating account of life lived inside this strange family chained to the past; it's available in foreign-language bookstores. Half of Qufu now claims descent from the Kongs, who are so numerous there is an entire local telephone directory dedicated to the letter K.

Music, Letters and Archives, Rent Collection and Sacrificial Fields. Beyond the Gate of Double Glory, the **Great Hall** was where the Yansheng Duke sat on a wooden chair covered with a tiger skin and proclaimed edicts. The flags and arrow tokens hanging on the walls are symbols of authority. Signs next to them reading "Make way!" were used to clear the roads of ordinary people when the duke left the mansion.

The next hall was where the duke held examinations in music and rites, and beyond it lies the **Hall of Withdrawal**, where he took tea. The hall contains two sedan chairs; the green one was for trips outside the mansion, the red one for domestic use.

The residential apartments

The **residential apartments** of the mansion are to the north, accessible through gates that would once have been heavily guarded; no one could enter of their own accord under pain of death. Tiger-tail cudgels, goose-winged pitchforks and golden-headed jade clubs used to hang here to drive the message home. Even the water-carrier was not permitted, and emptied the water into a stone trough outside that runs through the apartment walls. On a screen inside the gates is a painting of a *tan*, an imaginary animal shown eating treasures and greedily eyeing the sun. Feudal officials often had this picture painted in their homes as a warning against avarice.

The first hall is the seven-bay **Reception Hall**, where relatives were received, banquets held and marriage and funeral ceremonies conducted. Today, the only remnants of its once-salubrious past are several golden throne chairs and ornate staffs. Directly opposite the Reception Hall, the **central eastern room** contains a set of furniture made from tree roots, presented to the mansion by Emperor Qianlong – an original imperial decree lies on the table. Elsewhere in the central eastern room, check out the dinner service; it contains 404 pieces, including plates shaped like fish and deer, for consumption of the appropriate animals. Banquets for honoured guests could stretch to 196 courses.

Past the outbuildings and through a small gate, you reach the **Front Main Building**, an impressive two-storey structure in which are displayed paintings and clothes. The eastern central room was the home of **Madame Tao**, wife of Kong Lingyi, the seventy-sixth duke. Their daughter, Kong Demao, lived in the far eastern room, while Kong Lingyi's concubine, Wang, originally one of Tao's handmaids, lived in the inner western room. It doesn't sound like an arrangement designed for domestic bliss; indeed, whenever the duke was away, Madame Tao used to beat Wang with a whip she kept for the purpose. When Wang produced a male heir, Tao poisoned her. A second concubine, Feng, was kept prisoner in her rooms by Tao until she died.

The duke himself lived in the **rear building**, which has been left as it was when the last duke fled to Taiwan. Behind that is the garden where, every evening, flocks of **crows** come to roost noisily. Crows are usually thought to be inauspicious in China, but here they are welcome, and said to be the crow soldiers of Confucius, who protected him from danger on his travels. To the southeast of the inner east wing is a four-storey building called the **Tower of Refuge**, a planned retreat in the event of an uprising or invasion. The first floor was equipped with a movable hanging ladder, and a trap could be set in the floor. Once inside, the refugees could live for weeks on dried food stores.

The temple

In the east of the complex you'll find the family temple, the Ancestral Hall and residential quarters for less important family members. The **temple** is dedicated to the memory of Yu, wife of the seventy-second duke, and daughter of Emperor Qianlong. The princess had a mole on her face, which, it was predicted, would bring disaster unless she married into a family more illustrious than either the nobility or the highest of officials. The Kongs were the only clan to fulfil the criteria, but technically the daughter of the Manchu emperor was not allowed to marry a Han Chinese. This inconvenience was got around by first having the daughter adopted by the family of the Grand Secretary Yu, and then marrying her to the duke as Yu's daughter. Her dowry included twenty villages and several thousand trunks of clothing.

The rest of town

Not far to the east of the gate of the Confucius Mansion is the Ming **Drum Tower**, which forms a pair with the **Bell Tower** on Queli Jie. The drum was struck to mark sunset, the bell to mark sunrise, and at major sacrificial ceremonies they would be sounded simultaneously. You can't go inside either.

A little way northeast of the Confucius Mansion is the **Yan Miao** (8am–5pm; ¥10), a smaller temple dedicated to Yan Hui, who was regarded as Confucius's greatest disciple and sometimes called "The Sage Returned". A temple has been situated here since the Han dynasty, though the present structure is Ming. It's attractive, quieter than the Confucius Temple, and contains some impressive architectural details, such as the dragon pillars on the main hall, and a dragon head embedded in the roof. The eastern building now contains a display of locally excavated Neolithic and Zhou pottery.

The **Zhougong Miao** (7.30am–4.30pm; ¥5) in the northeast of town is dedicated to a Zhou-dynasty duke, a statue of whom stands in the main hall, together with his son Bo Qin and Bo Qin's servant. Legend has it that Bo Qin was a rasher man than his father, and the duke, worried that his son would not act sensibly in state matters, inscribed a pithy maxim from his own political experience on a slate and directed the servant to carry it on his back. Whenever Bo Qin was about to do something foolish, the ever-present servant would turn his back so Bo Qin would think again. The open terrace before the hall, where sacrifices were made to the duke, contains a striking stone incense burner carved with coiling dragons.

The Confucian Forest

The **Confucian Forest** is in the suburbs 3km north of the town centre, reachable by cycle-rickshaw or bus #1 up Gulou Nanjie. You can hire **bikes** (¥5) at the gates, which is good because the area is really too large to explore thoroughly on foot. The forest is the **burial ground** of the Kongs and, like the temple, it expanded over the centuries from something simple and austere to a grand complex, in this case centring around a single grave – **the tomb of Confucius**. In the Song dynasty, the place was planted with trees, and in 1331 a wall was built around it. Pavilions and halls were added in the Ming dynasty and large-scale reconstructions made in 1730 when Yong Zhen constructed some impressive memorial archways. Confucian disciples collected exotic trees to plant here, and there are now more than a hundred thousand different varieties. Today, it's an atmospheric place, sculptures half concealed in thick undergrowth, tombstones standing aslant in groves of ancient trees and wandering paths dappled with sunlight. A great place to spend an afternoon, it's one of the few famous scenic spots in China that it's possible to appreciate unaccompanied by crowds.

Running east from the chunky main gate, the imperial carriageway leads to a gateway and an arched stone bridge, beyond which is the spot where Confucius and his son are buried. The **Hall of Deliberation**, just north of the bridge, was where visitors put on ritual dress before performing sacrifices. An avenue, first of chop carvers and souvenir stalls, then of carved stone animals, leads to the **Hall of Sacrifices**, and behind that to a small grassy mound – the **grave**. Just to the west of the tomb, a hut, looking like a potting shed, was where Confucius's disciples each spent three years watching over the grave. Confucius's son is buried just north of here. His unflattering epitaph reads: "He died before his father without making any noteworthy achievements."

According to legend, before his death Confucius told his disciples to bury him at this spot because the *feng shui* was good. His disciples objected, as there was no river nearby. Confucius told them that a river would be dug in the future. After the first Qin emperor, Qin Shi Huang, unified China, he launched an anti-Confucian campaign, burning books and scholars, and tried to sabotage the grave by ordering a river to be dug through the cemetery, thus inadvertently perfecting it.

Eating, drinking and nightlife

Local specialities include fragrant rice and boiled **scorpions** soaked in oil. The Kong family also developed its own **cuisine**, featuring dishes such as "Going to the Court with the Son" (pigeon served with duck) and "Gold and Silver Fish" (a white and a yellow fish together). It's possible to sample this refined cuisine at the *Queli* hotel and the *Kongfugu Dajiudian* near the Drum Tower, though count on up to ¥200 per head. There are also many smaller places around town offering much cheaper **set menus** of these things: six dishes and a soup at ¥30 per person, eight dishes and soup ¥60 and so on. They all have boards outside listing their prices.

For simpler fare, the *Yonghe Doujiang* outlet on Gulou Nanjie is open 24 hours, and is a reliable place for rice and noodle dishes or an early-morning soy milk. At night, Wumaci Dajie fills up with open-air **food stalls**, offering tasty-looking hotpots and stews. The food's not bad and the atmosphere is lively, though make sure you know the price before you order anything. Otherwise, backstreets such as Nan Dajie, east of the *Great Wall* hotel, are thick with hole-in-the-wall noodle and stir-fry places, where you can fill up for under ¥10.

Don't expect much **nightlife** in town, and think hard before going to the **Confucius Six Arts City** to see the atrocious revue *Confucius' Dream* (daily April–Oct 8pm; ¥40), advertised all over town. It's doubtful the great sage's mind was filled with feather-headdress-wearing dancing girls and fan-waving martial-arts experts as he slept, as this show depicts.

Shopping

There are plenty of **stalls and shops** selling **tourist gimmicks** all through the town. Unsurprisingly, the Confucian connection has been exploited to the hilt, with Confucius fans, beer, sweets and something called the "Confucius Treasure Box", which claims to include an acorn from the Confucian Forest and sand from the great sage's grave. Pick up a **book** of translated **Confucian sayings** at the *Queli* hotel, but beware price tags covering the actual printed price on these. While steering clear of Confucian paraphernalia, it's worth checking out the **chops** (which can be carved with your name in a few minutes), rubbings taken from the steles in the temple and locally crafted pistachio carvings. Get your **scorpion essence** – a local product, advertised as a general tonic – in the department stores on Wumaci Jie.

Qingdao and around

The eastern Shandong port city of **QINGDAO** sprang to prominence in 1897, when Germany's **Kaiser Wilhelm**, wanting to extend his country's sphere of influence in the East, **annexed** the city after two German missionaries were murdered here during the **Boxer Rebellion** (see p.1150). Following the Kaiser's hysterical speech (which coined the phrase "Yellow Peril"), the feeble Manchu court ceded the territory for 99 years, along with the right to build the Shandong rail lines. Qingdao made an ideal deep-water base for the German navy, and while they were here they established a **brewery** producing the now world-famous Tsingtao Beer (Tsingtao is the old transliteration of Qingdao). However, the city was forcibly taken off Germany in 1914 by the **Japanese** and later gifted to Japan at the Treaty of Versailles, an event that led to nation-wide demonstrations – the beginning of the May Fourth Movement (see Contexts, p.1151). Qingdao was returned to China in 1922.

Modern Qingdao is still a very important **port**, China's fourth largest, but the **old town**, which once was a museum piece of red-roofed Bavarian architecture,

Qingdao and around

Qingdao	青岛	*qīngdǎo*
Catholic Church	天主教堂	*tiānzhǔ jiàotáng*
Gospel Church	基督教堂	*jīdū jiàotáng*
Lu Xun Park	鲁迅公园	*lǔxùn gōngyuán*
Navy Museum	海军博物馆	*hǎijūn bówùguǎn*
Qingdao Museum	青岛市博物馆	*qīngdǎoshì bówùguǎn*
Qingdao Olympic Marina	青岛国际帆船中心	*qīngdǎo guójì fānchuán zhōngxīn*
Tsingtao Museum and Bar	青岛啤酒博物馆	*qīngdǎo píjiǔ bówùguǎn*
Yingbin Hotel	迎宾馆	*yíngbīnguǎn*
Transit Points		
Old Train Station	青岛火车站	*qīngdǎo huǒchēzhàn*
Passenger Ferry Terminal	大港客运站	*dàgǎng kèyùnzhàn*
Sifang Train Station	四方站	*sìfāng zhàn*
Accommodation		
Holiday Inn	颐中假日酒店	*yízhōng jiàrì jiǔdiàn*
Home Inn	如家酒店	*rújiā jiǔdiàn*
Huiquan Dynasty	汇泉王朝大酒店	*huìquán wángcháo dàjiǔdiàn*
Oceanwide Elite	泛海名人酒店	*fànhǎi míngrén jiǔdiàn*
Qingdao Kaiyue Youth Hostel	青岛凯越国际青年旅馆	*qīngdǎo kǎiyuè guójì qīngnián lǚguǎn*
Renquan	人□宾馆	*rénquán bīnguǎn*
Zhanqiao	栈桥宾馆	*zhànqiáo bīnguǎn*
Eating		
Beifang Shuijiao	北方水饺	*běifāng shuǐjiǎo*
Bestejahre	百事特雅大厦	*bǎishìtèyǎ dàshà*
Chunhelou	春和楼饭店	*chūnhélóu fàndiàn*
Lao Shan	崂山	*láoshān*

is today being run down and neglected as a huge, modern industrial city cut by multi-lane highways sprouts 5km to the east; pretty much the only reason to head this way is for the year-round **ferry connections** to South Korea and Japan. While you're here, though, there are some decent white-sand **beaches** dotted along the shoreline – indeed, the city has been chosen to host the sailing events of the **2008 Summer Olympics** – and a worthwhile day-trip east to **Lao Shan**, one of China's famous peaks.

Arrival, information and city transport

The **old town**, in the southwest side of the city, is fairly close to the beaches and most transit points. North–south **Zhongshan Lu** is the main shopping district here, with a mesh of roads and lanes spread either side.

The **airport**, 30km to the northeast, is served by an **airport bus** (¥15) to the *Haitian Dajiudian*, still 5km east of the city – cross the road and catch bus #26 to its terminus off Taiping Lu. A taxi the whole way is at least ¥100. The old train station is being restored until June 2008, and for now the nearest place to arrive by rail is 5km north, at **Sifang train station**, a grotty area near where there's also a clutch of **long-distance bus stations** – bus #5 runs from the area down to the seafront at Taiping Lu. There's also a **bus depot** down near the old train station, within walking distance to accommodation. The

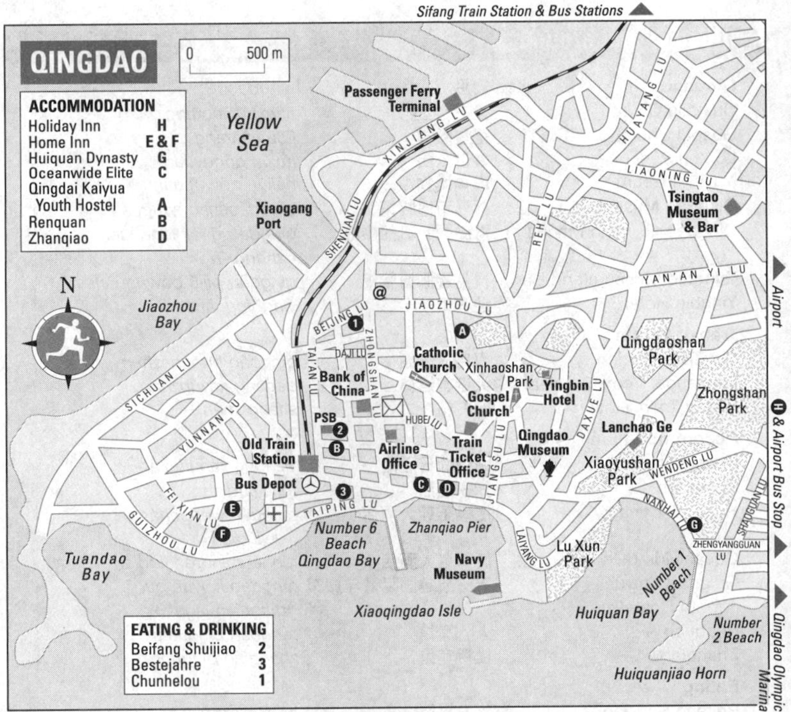

passenger-ferry terminal is again north of the old town – turn right out of the terminal and catch bus #303 to the old train-station area, or #8 to Zhongshan Lu. **Taxis** start at ¥10, though expect to pay double this to get to the eastern part of town.

Moving on from Qingdao

There's an **airlines office** at 29 Zhongshan Lu (☎0532/2895577); the airport bus leaves from outside the *Haitian Dajiudian* in the modern, eastern part of town, between 6am and 9pm. **Trains** (up until June 2008, departing from Sifang station) run east to Yantai, and west to Ji'nan and beyond. There's an **advance-ticket office** inside a compound shared with a carwash on Yishui Lu (an eastern continuation of Hubei Lu); otherwise, ask at accommodation or head to the station. For **buses**, try the depot south of the old train station first, which has departures to Yantai, Beijing, Shanghai, Ji'nan and Xi'an.

There are also international ferries from the **passenger-ferry terminal** on Xinjiang Lu to Inchon (17hr; ¥750–1090) and Gunsan (22hr; ¥810–3070), South Korea; and to Shimonoseki, Japan (36hr; ¥1100–7920), with multiple departures each week in the high season. **Tickets** can be bought in advance. There are five classes (special, first, second, third and fourth), with severe gradations in price as you move down the scale. Third class is about the same level of comfort as hard sleeper on a train and is probably best unless you're particularly loaded or skint. For **Dalian**, you'll need to get a ferry from Yantai, three hours north by bus.

Accommodation

Qingdao's old town has abundant **accommodation**, and though the city's newest, flashest places are much further east, there's a good range here. Pick of the low- to mid-price bunch are the *Home Inn* motel, one of several in town, and the youth hostel.

Holiday Inn 76 Xianggang Zhong Li ⓣ0532/8571888, ⓦwww.ichotelsgroup.com. Luxury high-rise on the modern east side of town, with all mod cons. ⑨

Home Inn 52 Danxian Lu, just off Guizhou Lu ⓣ0532/82669000, ⓦwww.homeinns.com. Usual good value offered by this new, clean motel chain – book ahead if possible. There's another branch nearby at 62 Fuzhou Lu, if they're full here. ④

Huiquan Dynasty 9 Nanhai Lu ⓣ0532/82999888, ⓕ82871122. A well-located four-star hotel – the beach is directly opposite. ⑨

Oceanwide Elite 29 Taiping Lu ⓣ0532/82996699, ⓦwww.oweh.com. In an excellent location opposite Zhanqiao Pier, this immaculate four-star hotel has an impressive interior and all the facilities you'd expect. ⑨

Qingdao Kaiyua Youth Hostel 31 Jining Lu ⓣ0532/82845450, ⓦwww.yhaqd.com. Situated near some of the town's older colonial quarters, and inside what was once a church, this is a lovely place to stay, and the staff can organize all watersports plus kite-flying activities. Dorms ¥30, standard doubles ③, family rooms ⑤

Renquan 64 Hunan Lu ⓣ0532/82967166 or 82967188. Neat, unpretentious Chinese hotel, though very hard to get discounts and better value is to be had at the *Home Inn*. ⑤

Zhanqiao 31 Taiping Lu ⓣ0532/82888666, ⓕ82870936. Elderly place but with heaps of character, from the wood-panelled lobby upwards Sun Yatsen stayed here once, too. ⑦ or ⑧ for sea views.

The City

The main thing to do in Qingdao is to wander through the **old German town**, where some quiet back lanes retain a century-old ambience, or to head down to the **waterfront**, where besides the beaches there's an offbeat museum.

Anchoring the old German town is the fine **Catholic Church** (Mon–Sat 8am–5pm, Sun noon–5pm; ¥5), whose distinctive double spires can be seen from all over the western parts of the city. The streets east of here are interesting, some cobbled, many lined with pink buildings with black iron balconies overlooking the street; there's also the 1908 **Gospel church**, built of solid stone and with a dark blue tin clocktower, on Jiangsu Lu. East again, the **Yingbin Hotel** on Longshan Lu (daily 8.30am–4.30pm; ¥15) is an incredible, Disney-style fortress built in 1905. It's worth a tour, as the German Governor-General, the warlord Yuan Shikai and Chairman Mao have lodged here in their time. South of here, the **Qingdao Museum** on Daxue Lu (Tues–Sun 8.30am–5pm; ¥15) is housed in a beautiful, temple-like building, which in the 1930s was the headquarters of the sinister-sounding Red Swastika Association, a welfare institute. There's a collection of paintings here from the Yuan through to Qing dynasties, and four large **Buddhas** dating back to 500–527 AD, slim striking figures with bulbous, smiling heads, one hand pointing upward to heaven, the other down to the earth.

One last essential sight is the **Tsingtao Museum and Bar**, around 1.5km northeast of the Gospel Church at 56 Dengzhou Lu (ⓣ0532/8383 3437; daily 8.30am-4.30pm; ¥50). Though the museum itself is pretty tame, the ticket includes three glasses of beer, and the **bar** here will let you buy more.

The waterfront

Qingdao's **beaches**, with fine white sand, are busy places in the summer, when holidaymakers come to promenade or just slump and look out to sea against a

▲ Beach at Qingdao

backdrop of pine trees. **Kite flying** is popular, too – some of the country's best kites are made at the nearby city of Weifang.

Closest to the old town, **Number 6 beach** is at the bottom of Zhongshan Lu; it's small but has the liveliest social scene, with crowds promenading along **Zhanqiao Pier** and numerous little stalls lining Taiping Lu selling gaudy swimsuits and cheap souvenirs. Follow the bay around east of the pier and you reach the **Navy Museum** (daily 8am–5pm; ¥30), where a decommissioned **submarine** and a **destroyer** sit in the water. You're required to leave cameras at the ticket booth, which seems a little oversensitive as both exhibits are virtually antiques. The submarine is the most interesting, its narrow, dark rooms arrayed with masses of chunky old valves, dials, levers and knobs, many of them bearing Russian markings.

East along Laiyang Lu is pleasant **Lu Xun Park** (¥5), a strip of pine trees and benches above the rocky coast, and then the old town ends abruptly with a flurry of high-rises and paved plazas at **Number 1 beach**, the biggest (580m long) and best. In season, it's packed, swarming with ice-cream vendors, trinket stalls and a rash of photographers. There are beachball-shaped changing huts, showers, multicoloured beach umbrellas, and designated swimming areas marked out with buoys and protected by shark nets. The water, however, is like Chinese soup – murky and warm, with unidentifiable things floating in it – so swimming is not recommended. If it feels too crowded here, head east to the more sheltered **number 2 and 3 beaches**, popular with the older, sanatorium-dwelling crowd. At the eastern end of Number 2 beach stands the **former German Governor's Residence**, a grand castle looking out to sea.

Around 3km east of here, the **Qingdao Olympic Marina** is an ¥80 million complex built to host the sailing events for the 2008 Olympics – it's best reached by taxi from the old town, as you have to change buses several times.

Eating, drinking and nightlife

Qingdao has ample **restaurants** to choose from. The speciality is, unsurprisingly, seafood; mussels and crabs here are particularly good. There are plenty of small, noisy and busy **seafood places** in the streets leading down to the coast, where competition means that standards are high and, with some exceptions, costs are reasonably low.

The Bestejahre building, just across Taiping Lu from Number 6 beach, houses a café, pizzeria, dumpling restaurant and a Japanese place. *Chunhelou*, at 146 Zhongshan Lu, is a famous, busy spot with generous portions and highly recommended spicy chicken. For *jiaozi* and northern fare, head to *Beifang Shuijiao* at the corner of Henan and Hubei streets, where they have an English menu and two can eat well for ¥40.

Strangely, **nightlife** isn't as exciting here as might be expected, and it's easier to find a convenience store with draught beer than it is to find a pub with it on tap. The best place to be in the early evening is around Zhanqiao Pier, where everyone goes for a stroll after eating.

Listings

Banks and exchange The main Bank of China, which has an ATM, is at 62 Zhongshan Lu (Mon–Fri 8.30am–5pm, Sat–Sun 9.30am–4pm).

Bookshops The relatively well-stocked Foreign Language Bookstore is at 10 Henan Lu, just south of Hubei Lu.

Internet access A large, comfortable Internet café (¥2 per hr) is at the corner of Zhongshan Lu and Jiaozhou Lu.

Mail and telephones The main post office and telecom building is about halfway along Zhongshan Lu (Mon–Sat 8am–6pm).

PSB The PSB is at 29 Hubei Lu (Mon–Sat 8am–noon & 2–7pm), not far from the old train station.

Lao Shan

The **Lao Shan** area, 400 square kilometres of rugged, mountainous coast 40km east of Qingdao, is an easy day-trip from the city. **Minibus tours** (¥65) depart in the early morning from Taiping Lu, west of the pier; **public buses** #304 & #802 (¥8) leave frequently from the east side of the old train-station site, dropping you at **Wu Kou**, the easternmost part of the area. Plenty of other buses come here from other parts of Qingdao, plus there are paths, cable cars and shuttle buses between the sights, so getting around and back to town afterwards is not a problem. It's definitely worth getting a **map**, however – quite detailed spreads of Lao Shan are printed on the back of most city maps.

Lao Shan is a good place to **hike** around, as the whole area is dotted with caves, springs and waterfalls amid striking scenery, and with a bit of effort it's possible to lose the crowds and trinket stalls. Writers have been inspired by the landscape for centuries – *Strange Stories from a Chinese Studio* by the Qing-dynasty author **Pu Songling** (see "Books", p.1206) was written here – and have left noble graffiti in the form of poems and sage reflections, cut into rocks all round the area. Jiushui Valley here is also the source of **Lao Shan mineral water**, which gives Tsingtao beer its taste; it's one of the few Chinese mineral waters that doesn't taste of swimming pools.

Around the mountain

On a clear day, the **coastal road route** from Qingdao is spectacular, winding precariously along clifftops. On the way you'll pass the **Stone Old Man**, a ten-metre-high rock standing in the sea, said to be the petrified body of a man who turned to stone after his daughter was kidnapped by Longwang, the King of the East Sea.

You'll be charged ¥50 entrance (¥30 off season) near **Lao Shan village**, after which there are various routes out to the sights. One of these, heading southeast, takes you to a village at the foot of Lao Shan, from where a pathway of stone steps, constructed a century ago by the enterprising German Lao Shan Company to cater for their compatriots' weakness for alpine clambering, runs all the way to the summit and then back down a different route on the other side. The **path** climbs past gullies and woods, streams and pools, and the ascent takes about two hours. There's a temple halfway up, where you can fortify yourself with fruit and tea for the final haul. At the **summit**, 1133m above sea level, a ruined temple now houses a meteorological station. The view is great, and gets even better as you descend by the alternative route back to the village.

Other scenic spots have a religious connection. On **Naloyan Shan**, 2km northeast of Lao Shan, is a cave in which the Naloyan Buddha was said to have meditated, and on the coast just north of here the **Baiyun Cave** was once the home of a famous monk, Tian Baiyun. Ever since, it has been seen as an auspicious place to meditate. **Mingxia Cave**, 3km farther south down the coast, on the slopes of Kunyu Shan, was written about by a famous Taoist, Qiu Changchun. Inside the cave are stones that reflect the rays of the morning sun, and the flat area outside is a good vantage point from which to watch the sunset.

Well worth a visit is the **Taiqing Gong** (¥15), a temple to the south of Lao Shan, by the coast, and close to the boat dock. It's the oldest and grandest of Lao Shan's temples, consisting of three halls set amid old trees – some dating back to the Han and Tang dynasties – and flower gardens. Outside the first hall are two camellias about which Pu Songling wrote a story. There are nine other temples nearby, which, though smaller, are quiet, peaceful places.

Yantai and around

YANTAI, on the Yellow Sea in northern Shandong, 240km northeast of Qingdao, is a somewhat battered-looking seaside town, with a burgeoning port. It's the poor relation of Qingdao, and consequently lost out in the bidding to stage the 2008 Olympic sailing competition despite having better maritime conditions. Like Qingdao, the main reason to visit the area is to pick up **ferries** to Dalian and Korea, either from here or **Weihai**, 80km east. The same distance to the west, restored fortifications at **Penglai** make for a quirky half-day trip.

Yantai means "smoke mound", the name deriving from the ancient practice of lighting fires on the headland to warn of imminent Japanese invasion or (more likely) approaching pirates. Prior to 1949, it was a fishing port called **Chefoo**, and its recent history, like that of Qingdao, is closely bound up with European colonialism. In 1862, Chefoo was made a **British treaty port** as a prize of the Opium War. Thirty years later the **Germans** arrived, wishing to extend their influence on the peninsula. After World War I, it was the turn of the **Americans**, who used the port as a summer station for their entire Asian

Yantai and around

Yantai	烟台	*yāntái*
Changchu Wine Museum	张□酒文博物馆	*zhāngjí jiǔwén bōwùguǎn*
Number 2 Beach	第二海水浴场	*dì'èr hǎishuǐ yùchǎng*
Passenger ferry terminal	港客运站	*gǎngkè yùnzhàn*
Yantai Museum	烟台博物馆	*yāntái bówùguǎn*
Yantaishan Park	烟台山公园	*yāntáishān gōngyuán*
Accommodation and eating		
Niutou Guan	牛头馆	*niútóu guǎn*
Sanzhan Binguan	三站宾馆	*sānzhàn bīnguǎn*
Tiedao Dasha	铁道大厦	*tiědào dàshà*
Yaxiya Dajiudian	亚细亚大酒店	*yàxìyà dàjiǔdiàn*
Yingpeng Binguan	鹰鹏宾馆	*yíngpéng bīnguǎn*
Penglai	蓬莱	*pénglái*
Penglai Fortress	蓬莱海洋台	*pénglái hǎiyángtái*
Weihai	威海	*wēihǎi*
Passenger Ferry Terminal	港客运站	*gǎngkè yùnzhàn*
Qing Quan Hotel	清泉大酒店	*qīngquán dàjiǔdiàn*
Weihaiwei Hotel	威海威大酒店	*wēihǎiwēi dàjiǔdiàn*

fleet, and then the **Japanese**, who set up a trading establishment here. However, all this foreign influence has not left a distinctive mark – most of the town is of much more recent origin, a product of the rapid industrialization that has taken place since 1949. Yantai is also known for its **wine**, produced in vineyards set up by Singaporean Chinese in 1893, who learned their skills from French soldiers stationed here.

The City

Away from the transit points along scruffy Beima Lu, Yantai is quite a modern, bustling place, with a busy shopping district on **Nan Dajie** south of the port. **Yantai Museum**, east along Nan Dajie (daily 8am–5pm; ¥10), is housed in a beautiful old guild hall, set up for the use of merchants and shipowners. The main building here is the **Tian Hou Miao**, a temple to the southern Chinese sea goddess (for more on whom, see Chapter 9 "Hong Kong and Macau"), who sailors trust to guide ships to safety. The temple itself was brought from Fujian by ship in 1864 and is a unique example of southern architecture in northern China, with its richly carved wooden roof beams, eaves and panels illustrating historical scenes, and sweeping, pronged roofline fancifully ornamented with mythical figures in wood, stone and glazed ceramics. The whole temple complex is set in a little garden with pools and a stage (the goddess is said to have been fond of plays).

A twenty-minute walk northeast, the **Chanchu Wine Museum** on Dama Lu (daily 9am–5pm; ¥30, or ¥50 including wine tasting) is worth a look, not so much for the humdrum historical exhibits but because – almost uniquely in China – they produce a grape wine that is better than just drinkable. Make sure you descend in to the vast **cellar** where, sitting proud and beribboned amongst lesser casks, are the three-century-old "Barrel Kings", each holding fifteen tons. You can have a go at bottling in cellar 4, or make your way straight to the **bar** in cellar 5 for your samples – the twelve-year-old red is excellent, as is their brandy, both of which are on sale in the museum shop.

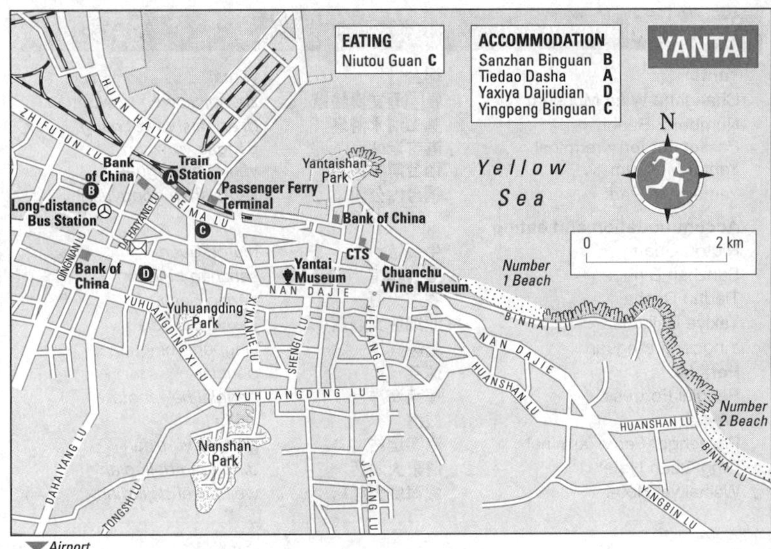

After this you've pretty well exhausted Yantai's attractions, though the **seafront** is pleasant on a good day. **Yantaishan Park** (¥8), marking the eastern edge of the port area, features a steep hill where the locals used to keep an eye out for pirates, latticed with twisting paths, pavilions, a couple of former European consulates and an old Japanese military camp. The city's two **beaches** are both east of here, but they're not great – littered, windy and hemmed in by unattractive buildings. Number 2 beach, the farther of the two, is the better, though the water is very polluted.

Practicalities

Yantai's **airport** is 15km south of the city; bus #9 runs from here to the train station, or a taxi will cost around ¥50. The other arrival points are fairly closely grouped in the northwest of town: on Beima Lu, the **train station**, on lines to Qingdao and Ji'nan, is just west of the **port**, which handles ferries from Dalian and Inchon. **Buses** mostly use the main station about a kilometre west of the train station on Qingnian Lu, though sometimes you get dropped in the train-station forecourt.

Taxis are plentiful and cost ¥5, with ¥15 enough to journey to the far eastern beaches. Bus #10 is the most useful around the city, travelling east from the train station along Beima Lu, and then heading east along the coast. The **post office** (Mon–Fri 8am–6pm) is on Nan Dajie, while the main **Bank of China** (Mon–Fri 8am–noon & 2–5pm) with an ATM is on the corner of Qingnian Lu and Nan Dajie.

Leaving Yantai, you can book **train, rail and ferry tickets** at the relevant offices or through CTS (☎0535/6231539, 6216533 or 6611582), west of the wine museum on Beima Lu. The **CAAC office** is on Da Haiyang Lu (☎0535/6669777), near the train station; bus #9 to the airport leaves from the train station. **Train tickets** are easy to get at the station, which is well organized, with helpful staff; the **bus station** has regular departures to Penglai, Weihai and most other places in Shandong, though the further you're going the fewer services there are. **Ferries** to Inchon in South Korea (16hr; ¥960) leave several times a week, while those to Dalian (4hr; ¥160) leave several times a day; the port ticket office is open daily 9 to 11.30am and 1 to 4pm.

Accommodation and eating

The rail and port areas are flooded with **hotels** charging just ¥100 for a double, though not all will take foreigners. The *Tiedao Dasha*, immediately west of the train station (ⓣ0535/2961188, ⓕ6261391; ❸), has small rooms but is otherwise a good budget choice and not too noisy despite the location; otherwise, the *Yingpeng Binguan*, opposite the port at 59 Beima Lu (ⓣ0535/620655, ⓕ6260755; ❹) is just what you need after a long ferry ride – clean, friendly and good value, with a coffee shop attached. The *Sanzhan Binguan*, at 13 Qingnian Lu, diagonally across from the bus station (ⓣ0535/6269058, ⓕ6250955; ❺) is a mid-range hotel that gives big reductions; while the *Yaxiya Dajiudian*, 116 Nan Dajie (ⓣ0535/6588888, ⓦwww.asiahotel.cn; ❼) is a business-standard hotel selling golfing supplies in its shop and with a big café-restaurant out front.

For **eating**, the 24hr noodle and dumpling place next to the *Tiedao*, and a Korean barbecue place called the *Niutou Guan* next to the *Yingpeng*, make the best alternatives to dining at your accommodation, or you can try the street stalls in the back lanes between Beima Lu and Nan Dajie.

Penglai

Before the Chinese tourist industry discovered Shangri-la, beautiful places would be described as a "**Penglai fairyland**", thanks, rather oddly, to a former coastal fortress and mirage 80km west of Yantai. Buses from Yantai's bus station (¥16) depart every twenty minutes between 6am and 6pm to **PENGLAI**; turn left out of the bus depot here and the **Penglai Fortress** (daily 8am–5pm; ¥70) is 150m away. With its walkable two-kilometre stretch of wall topped with cannons, this defence station was founded in Song times and then greatly expanded in 1553 by **Qi Jiguang**, who was trying to stop Japanese pirates from raiding the coastline. Once in through the entrance, make your way to the **Ancient Ships Hall** for a look at the wooden hull from a 28-metre-long Yuan vessel, then climb the wall and walk to the end, where a rocky, wooded headland is crowned by a complex of small, interlocked **temples** and the **Puzhao tower**, a little lighthouse built in 1868. There are great views out to where the Yellow Sea becomes the Bohai Gulf around a group of islands, which have now been turned into wind farms and sport a forest of tall white turbines. The view from here is also famous for the **Penglai mirage**, which locals claim appears every few decades. Accounts of it vary widely, from a low-lying sea mist to an island in the sky, complete with people, trees and vehicles.

Weihai

The port of **WEIHAI**, 80km east of Yantai, has nothing specific to recommend it to tourists, but you might end up here on the thrice-weekly **ferry from Korea** – going the other way, tickets for Inchon (14hr; ¥750–1380) can be booked at the port and some accommodation in town. Weihai's **long-distance bus station** is a ten-minute taxi ride from the port, with services to Beijing (¥150) and Shanghai (¥200) every afternoon, and departures through the day to Yantai (1hr; ¥17) and Qingdao. **Accommodation** options include the upmarket *Weihaiwei Dasha*, at 32 Haigang Lu, at the corner of Kunming Lu and

Xinwei Lu (Ⓣ0631/5285888, Ⓕ5285777; ❽), and the cheaper *Qing Quan Hotel*, two blocks west at 5 Gongyuan Lu (Ⓣ0631/5224112; ❺). The **Bank of China**, where you can change traveller's cheques, is a few minutes farther west along Kunming Lu from the *Weihaiwei Dasha*.

Travel details

Trains

Datong to: Baotou (many daily; 6hr); Beijing (many daily; 6–7hr); Hohhot (13 daily; 4hr 20min); Lanzhou (1 daily; 21hr); Linfen (3 daily; 11hr); Taiyuan (5 daily; 7hr); Xi'an (1 daily; 17hr).
Hua Shan to: Xi'an (daily; 2hr); Yuncheng (4 daily; 1hr 40min).
Ji'nan to: Beijing (14 daily; 5–8hr); Qingdao (daily; 6–7hr); Qufu (daily; 2hr); Shanghai (15 daily; 10–15hr); Taishan (daily; 1hr); Yantai (7 daily; 9hr).
Kaifeng to: Shanghai (8 daily; 12hr); Xi'an (13 daily; 8hr); Yanzhou (7 daily; 5hr 30min); Zhengzhou (daily; 50min).
Linfen to: Taiyuan (daily; 4hr 30min); Xi'an (5 daily; 6–7hr); Yuncheng (10 daily; 2hr 30min).
Luoyang to: Beijing (10 daily; 8–11hr); Shanghai (5 daily; 14–16hr); Xi'an (daily; 5hr); Zhengzhou (daily; 1hr 30min).
Qingdao to: Beijing (2 daily; 11hr 30min); Ji'nan (daily; 6–7hr); Shenyang (2 daily; 22hr); Tianjin (4 daily; 10–13hr); Yantai (1 daily; 3hr 30min).
Qufu Ji'nan (daily; 2hr); Taishan (daily; 1hr).
Taishan to: Beijing (6 daily; 8–10hr); Ji'nan (daily; 1hr); Qufu (daily; 1hr).
Taiyuan to: Beijing (6 daily; 8–10hr); Datong (5 daily; 7hr); Linfen (daily; 4hr 30min); Luoyang (1 daily; 12hr); Pingyao (daily; 2hr); Shijiazhuang (11 daily; 5hr); Xi'an (5 daily; 10–12hr); Yuncheng (9 daily; 5–8hr); Zhengzhou (4 daily; 11hr 30min–13hr).
Xi'an to: Baoji (daily; 2hr); Beijing (10 daily; 12hr 30min); Datong (1 daily; 17hr); Guangzhou (2 daily; 26hr); Hua Shan (daily; 2hr); Lanzhou (daily; 9hr); Linfen (5 daily; 6–7hr); Luoyang (daily; 5hr); Taiyuan (5 daily; 10–12hr); Shanghai (7 daily; 16–21hr); Ürümqi (9 daily; 31–40hr); Xining (4 daily; 13hr); Yan'an (3 daily; 7–8hr); Yuncheng (4 daily; 4hr); Zhengzhou (daily; 7hr).
Yantai to: Beijing (1 daily; 15hr 20min); Ji'nan (7 daily; 9hr); Qingdao (1 daily; 3hr 30min).
Yuncheng to: Linfen (10 daily; 2hr 30min); Taiyuan (9 daily; 5–8hr); Xi'an (4 daily; 4hr).
Zhengzhou to: Beijing (daily; 6hr 30min); Guangzhou (11 daily; 16hr); Luoyang (daily; 1hr 30min); Shanghai (11 daily; 10–13hr); Shijiazhuang (daily; 2hr 30min–3hr 30min); Taiyuan (4 daily; 11hr 30min–13hr); Xi'an (many daily; 7hr).

Buses

Datong to: Taiyuan (3hr 30min); Wutai Shan (6hr).
Dengfeng to: Luoyang (1hr 20min); Zhengzhou (1hr 30min).
Ji'nan to: Beijing (5hr 30min); Qingdao (4hr 30min); Qufu (2hr 30min); Tai'an (1hr 30min).
Kaifeng to: Heze (for Qufu or Ji'nan; 3hr); Zhengzhou (1hr 30min).
Linfen to: Pingyao (3hr); Taiyuan (3hr); Yuncheng (3hr).
Luoyang to: Dengfeng (1hr 20min); Ruicheng (4hr); Xi'an (4hr 30min); Yuncheng (4hr); Zhengzhou (2hr).
Pingyao to: Linfen (3hr); Taiyuan (2 hr); Xi'an (7hr).
Qufu to: Qingdao (6hr); Heze (for Kaifeng; 3hr); Ji'nan (2hr 30min); Tai'an (1hr).
Tai'an to: Beijing (7hr); Ji'nan (1hr 30min); Qufu (1hr); Zhengzhou (7hr).
Taiyuan to: Datong (3hr 30min); Pingyao (2hr); Shijiazhuang (3hr 30min); Wutai Shan (4hr); Yuncheng (7hr).
Weihai to: Beijing (13hr); Qingdao (4hr); Shanghai (16hr); Yantai (1hr).
Xi'an to: Hua Shan (2hr 30min); Luoyang (4hr); Pingyao (7hr); Ruicheng (3hr); Yan'an (6hr); Yuncheng (4hr); Zhengzhou (6hr).
Yantai to: Beijing (12hr); Ji'nan (5hr); Qingdao (3hr 30min); Weihai (1hr).
Yuncheng to: Linfen (3hr); Ruicheng (2hr); Taiyuan (4hr 30min); Xi'an (3hr).
Zhengzhou to: Dengfeng (1hr 30min); Kaifeng (1hr 30min); Luoyang (2hr 30min).

Ferries

Qingdao to: Gunsan (South Korea; 3 weekly; 17hr); Inchon (South Korea; 3 weekly; 22hr); Shimonoseki (Japan; 2 weekly; 36hr).
Weihai to: Inchon (South Korea; 3 weekly; 14hr).
Yantai to: Dalian (daily; 4hr); Inchon (South Korea; several weekly; 16hr).

Flights

Among international connections from this part of China, there are flights from Ji'nan (Seoul, Singapore), Qingdao (Fukuoka, Osaka, Seoul,

Singapore, Tokyo), Xi'an (Bangkok, Fukuoka, Nagoya, Niigata, Seoul, Tokyo).

Datong to: Beijing (3 weekly; 50min); Guangzhou (3 weekly; 2hr 50min); Shanghai (2 weekly; 2hr 20min).

Ji'nan to: Beijing (4–5 daily; 1hr); Chengdu (2–3 daily; 2hr 20min); Chongqing (1–2 daily; 2hr); Guangzhou (4 daily; 2hr 30min); Hong Kong (3 weekly; 2hr 50min); Kunming (2–3 daily; 2hr); Nanjing (1–4 daily; 65min); Shanghai (10 daily; 1hr); Wenzhou (2–3 daily; 1hr 40min); Xi'an (2 daily; 1hr 35min); Yantai (daily; 50min).

Luoyang to: Beijing (daily; 50min); Guangzhou (daily; 2hr); Kunming (3 weekly; 2hr); Shanghai (daily; 50min); Shenzhen (4 weekly; 3hr 20min).

Qingdao to: Beijing (14 daily; 55min); Chengdu (2–3 daily; 2hr 30min); Chongqing (2 weekly; 2hr 30min); Guangzhou (3–4 daily; 3hr); Guilin (2 weekly; 3hr); Hangzhou (8 daily; 1hr 20min); Hong Kong (1–2 daily; 3hr 20min); Kunming (2 daily; 3hr 30min); Lanzhou (4 weekly; 3hr 40min); Nanjing (3–5 daily; 65min); Shanghai (12 daily; 1hr 15min); Xi'an (1–2 daily; 1hr 50min); Zhengzhou (daily; 1hr 15min).

Taiyuan to: Beijing (5 daily; 1hr); Chengdu (3 weekly; 2hr); Chongqing (1–2 daily; 1hr 40min); Guangzhou (6 daily; 2hr 40min); Nanjing (4 weekly; 1hr 50min); Shanghai (4 daily; 1hr 45min); Tianjin (1–2 daily; 1hr); Xi'an (1–3 daily; 55min); Zhengzhou (daily; 55min).

Xi'an to: Beijing (18 daily; 1hr 30min); Chengdu (9 daily; 50min); Chongqing (5–6 daily; 1hr); Dalian (1–4 daily; 2hr); Dunhuang (2 daily; 2hr 50min); Guangzhou (8 daily; 2hr); Guilin (2–3 daily; 1hr 40min); Hong Kong (daily; 2hr 30min); Ji'nan (2 daily; 1hr 30min); Kunming (2–3 daily; 2hr); Lanzhou (7 daily; 1hr 10min); Nanjing (2 daily; 1hr 50min); Qingdao (1–2 daily; 1hr 40min); Shanghai (8 daily; 1hr 50min); Taiyuan (1–3 daily; 1hr).

Yantai to: Beijing (4 daily; 1hr 15min); Guangzhou (daily; 3hr); Hong Kong (2 weekly; 3hr 30min); Ji'nan (daily; 50min); Nanjing (4 weekly; 1hr 20min); Shanghai (2–4 daily; 1hr 30min).

Zhengzhou to: Beijing (7 daily; 65min); Chengdu (2–3 daily; 1hr 40min); Chongqing (1–2 daily; 1hr 20min); Guangzhou (4 daily; 2hr); Hong Kong (daily; 2hr 35min); Kunming (3–4 daily; 2hr 35min); Lanzhou (3 weekly; 1hr 30min); Nanjing (4 weekly; 1hr); Qingdao (daily; 1hr 15min); Shanghai (7 daily; 1hr 40min); Taiyuan (daily; 50min).

CHAPTER 5 Highlights

* **The Bund** Fusty colonial architecture and brash modernity stare each other down over the Huangpu River. See p.360

* **Huangpu boat trips** Get out on the river for a sense of the maritime industry that's at the heart of the city's success. See p.366

* **Jinmao Tower observation platform** The view from the top floor of Shanghai's finest building is simply awesome. See p.368

* **Shanghai Museum** A candidate for the best museum in the country, with a wide range of exhibits housed in a building that's shaped like an ancient Chinese pottery vessel. See p.371

* **Moganshan Art District** Fascinating new arts venue full of trendy art galleries and studios. See p.373

* **Yu Yuan** An elegant Chinese garden with opportunities to snack and sip tea in the vicinity. See p.374

* **Shanghai nightlife** Glamorous, raucous, vacuous and often very decadent. See p.389

▲ The Bund

5

Shanghai and around

After years of stagnation, the great metropolis of **SHANGHAI** is undergoing one of the fastest economic expansions the world has ever seen. Nearly a third of China's exports come from the area and it attracts almost a quarter of all the country's foreign investment, more than any single developing country. As Shanghai begins to recapture its position as East Asia's leading business city, a status it last held before World War II, the skyline is filling with skyscrapers; there are three thousand now, more than New York, and another two thousand are coming soon. Gleaming shopping malls, luxurious hotels and prestigious arts centres are rising alongside. Shanghai's 21 million residents enjoy the highest incomes on the mainland, and there's plenty for them to splash out on; witness the rash of celebrity restaurants and designer flagship stores. In short, it's a city with a swagger, bursting with nouveau riche exuberance and élan.

And yet, for all the modernization, Shanghai is still known in the West for its infamous role as the base of **European imperialism** in mainland China. Whichever side you were on, life in Shanghai then was rarely one of moderation. China's most prosperous city, in large part European- and American-financed, Shanghai introduced Asia to electric light, boasted more cars than the rest of the country put together, and created for its rich citizens a world of European-style mansions, tree-lined boulevards, chic café society, horse-racing and exclusive gentlemen's clubs. Alongside, and as much part of the legend, lay a city of singsong girls, warring gangsters and millions living in absolute poverty.

When the Communists marched into Shanghai in May 1949, they took control of the most important business and trading centre in Asia, an international port where vast fortunes were made. For most of the communist period, the central government in Beijing deliberately ran Shanghai down, siphoning off its surplus to other parts of the country, to the point where the city came to resemble a living museum, housing the largest array of **Art Deco architecture** in the world and frozen in time since the 1940s. Parts of the city still resemble a 1920s vision of the future, a grimy metropolis of monolithic Neoclassical facades, threaded with overhead cables and walkways, and choked by vast crowds and rattling trolleybuses.

Yet the Shanghainese never lost their ability to make waves for themselves. The present boom dates back to 1990, with the opening of the "New Bund" – the Special Economic Zone across the river in Pudong. Ever since, the city has enjoyed double-digit growth, and what was once a sleepy suburb of rice fields now looks like a city of the future, quite literally – when sci-fi film *Code 46* was shot here, no CGI was used.

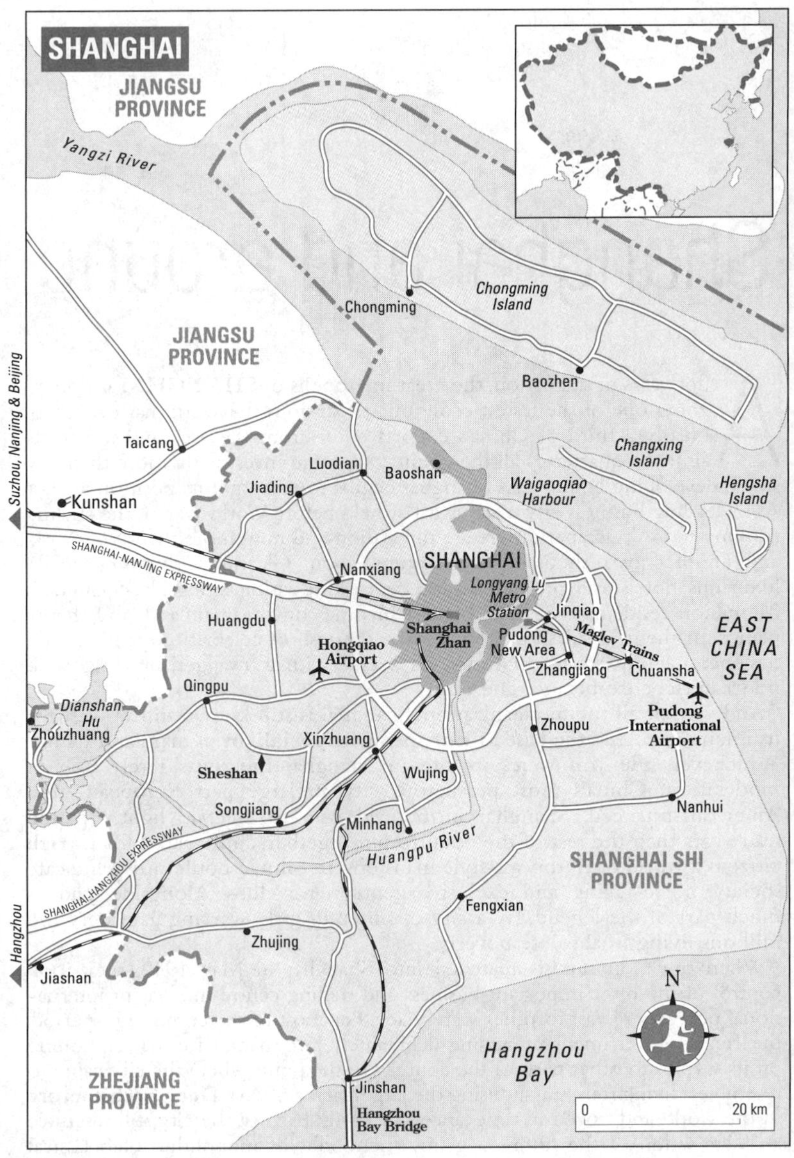

Not that the old Shanghai is set to disappear overnight. Most of the urban area was partitioned between foreign powers until 1949, and their former embassies, banks and official residences still give large sections of Shanghai an early twentieth-century European flavour. It's still possible to make out the boundaries of what used to be the foreign concessions, with the bewildering tangle of alleyways of the old Chinese city at its heart. Only along the Huangpu waterfront, amid the stolid grandeur of the **Bund**, is there some sense of space – and here you feel the past more strongly than ever. It's ironic that the relics of hated foreign imperialism are now protected as city monuments.

Like Hong Kong, its model for economic development, Shanghai does not brim with obvious attractions. Besides the Shanghai Museum, the Suzhou-reminiscent gardens of Yu Yuan, and the Huangpu River cruise, there are few obvious tourist attractions with broad appeal. But the beauty of visiting Shanghai lies in less obvious pleasures: Shanghai is one of the few Chinese cities that rewards aimless wandering, and it's fascinating to stroll the Bund, explore the pockets of colonial architecture in the former French Concession, or get lost in the alleys of the old city. The place absolutely excels in all materialistic pleasures, so make sure you sample the exploding restaurant and nightlife scenes, and budget some time for serious shopping. Perhaps the greatest fascination is in simply absorbing the splendour of a city so extravagantly on the up.

Some history

Contrary to Western interpretations, Shanghai's history did not begin with the founding of the British Concession in the wake of the First Opium War. Located at the confluence of the Yangzi River, the Grand Canal and the Pacific Ocean, Shanghai served as a major commercial port from the Song dynasty, channelling the region's extensive cotton crop to Beijing, the hinterland and Japan. By the Qing dynasty, vast **mercantile guilds**, often organized by trade and bearing superficial resemblance to their Dutch counterparts, had established economic and, to some extent, political control of the city. Indeed, the British only chose to set up a treaty port in Shanghai because, in the words of East India Company representative Hugh Lindsay, "the city had become the principal emporium of Eastern Asia" by the 1840s.

After the **Opium Wars**, the British moved in under the Treaty of Nanking in 1842, to be rapidly followed by the French in 1847. These two powers set up the first **foreign concessions** in the city – the British along the Bund and the area to the north of the Chinese city, the French in an area to the southwest, on the site of a cathedral a French missionary had founded two centuries earlier. Later the Americans (in 1863) and the Japanese (in 1895) came to tack their own areas onto the British Concession, which expanded into the so-called International Settlement. Traders were allowed to live under their own national laws, policed by their own armed forces, in a series of privileged enclaves that were leased indefinitely. By 1900, the city's favourable position, close to the main trade route to the major silk- and tea-producing regions, had allowed it to develop into a sizeable port and manufacturing centre. At this time, it was largely controlled by the "Green Gang", the infamous Chinese crime syndicate founded in the 1700s by unemployed boatmen, which by the 1920s ran the city's vast underworld. Businessmen and criminals who flouted the Green Gang's strict code of behaviour were subject to "knee-capping" punishment – having every visible tendon severed with a fruit knife before being left to die on a busy pavement.

Shanghai's cheap workforce was swollen during the Taiping Uprising (see box, p.419) by those who took shelter from the slaughter in the foreign settlements, and by peasants attracted to the city's apparent prosperity. Here China's first urban proletariat emerged, and the squalid living conditions, outbreaks of unemployment and glaring abuses of Chinese labour by foreign investors made Shanghai a natural breeding ground for **revolutionary politics**. The Chinese Communist Party was founded in the city in 1921, only to be driven underground by the notorious massacre of hundreds of strikers in 1927.

Inevitably, after the Communist takeover, the bright lights dimmed. The foreign community may have expected "business as usual", but the new regime was determined that Shanghai should play its role in the radical reconstruction of China. The worst slums were knocked down to be replaced by apartments, the gangsters and prostitutes were taken away for "re-education", and foreign capital was ruthlessly taxed if not confiscated outright (although Chiang Kaishek did manage to spirit away the gold reserves of the Bank of China to Taiwan, leaving the city broke). For 35 years, Western influences were forcibly suppressed.

Even since 1949, the city has remained a centre of radicalism – Mao, stifled by Beijing bureaucracy, launched his Cultural Revolution here in 1966. Certain Red Guards even proclaimed a Shanghai Commune, before the whole affair descended into wanton destruction and petty vindictiveness. After Mao's death, Shanghai was the last stronghold of the Gang of Four in their struggle for the succession, though their planned coup never materialized. During China's opening up, many key modernizing officials in the central government came from the Shanghai area; Jiang Zemin and Zhu Rongji were both former mayors of the city. Though today, the central government is trying to clip Shanghai's wings – in 2007 both the mayor and the Party secretary were arrested for corruption – the Shanghai clique remains influential.

As well as an important power base for the ruling party, Shanghai has always been the most fashion-conscious and **outward-looking** city in China, its people by far the most highly skilled labour force in the country, and renowned for their quick wit and entrepreneurial skills. Many Shanghainese fled to Hong Kong after 1949 and oversaw the colony's economic explosion, while a high proportion of Chinese successful in business elsewhere in the world emigrated from this area. Even during the Cultural Revolution, Western "excesses" like curled hair and holding hands in public survived in Shanghai. Despite the incomprehensibility of the local Shanghainese dialect to other Chinese, it has always been easier for visitors to communicate with the locals here than anywhere else in the country, because of the excellent level of English spoken and the familiarity with foreigners and foreignness.

Orientation, arrival, information and city transport

Shanghai is a surprisingly compact place, considering its enormous population, and it's not hard to find your way around on foot – though you'll certainly need buses or taxis for crossing from one quarter to the next. The area of most interest to visitors is bordered to the east by the **Huangpu River** (which flows from south to north), and to the north by the **Suzhou Creek** (which flows from west to east). A good place to get your bearings is at the southwestern corner of the junction of these two rivers, at the entrance to the small Huangpu Park. To the north, across the iron Waibaidu Bridge over Suzhou Creek, is the area of the old Japanese Concession. South from Huangpu Park, along the western bank of the Huangpu River, runs the **Bund** – in Chinese, officially **Zhongshan Lu**, unofficially **Wai Tan**. The Bund is in turn overlooked from the east bank by the Oriental Pearl TV Tower, the city's most conspicuous landmark, in the **Pudong** Special Economic Zone.

A hundred metres south from Huangpu Park, the Bund is met by **Nanjing Lu**, one of the city's premier shopping streets, which runs west, past the

Shanghai: arrival and transport

Shanghai	上海	*shànghǎi*
Airport Express	飞机场特快汽车	*fēijīchǎng tèkuài qìchē*
Gongpinglu Wharf	公平路码头	*gōngpínglù mǎtóu*
Hongqiao Airport	虹桥机场	*hóngqiáo jīchǎng*
International Passenger Quay	国际客运码头	*guójì kèyùn mǎtóu*
Maglev train	磁悬浮列车	*cíxuánfú lièchē*
Pudong International Airport	浦东国际机场	*pǔdōng guójì jīchǎng*
Shanghai Metro	上海地铁	*shànghǎi dìtiě*
Shanghai Zhan	上海火车站	*shànghǎi huǒchēzhàn*
Shanghai West Station	上海西站	*shànghǎi xīzhàn*

northern edge of Renmin Park in the centre of the city. (Like all the east–west routes, Nanjing Lu takes its name from that of a city; north–south roads are named after provinces.) A few blocks to the south of Nanjing Lu is another major east–west thoroughfare, Yan'an Lu, which, to the east, leads into a tunnel under the Huangpu River. South of here, just west of the Bund, is the oval-shaped area corresponding to the **Old City**. The most important of the north–south axes is Xizang Lu, cutting through the downtown area just east of **Renmin Park**. Heading south, Xizang Lu runs down to an intersection with **Huaihai Lu**, Shanghai's other main shopping boulevard, which heads west into the heart of the **former French Concession**.

Arrival

Arriving by **air**, you'll touch down either at the new Pudong International Airport, 40km east of the city along the mouth of the Yangzi River, or at the old Hongqiao Airport, 15km west of the city. Pudong handles most international flights, with the smaller Hongqiao servicing domestic flights.

The most romantic way to get into town from Pudong is on the world's only commercial **Maglev train** (daily 8.30am–5.30pm; every 20min), suspended above the track and propelled by the forces of magnetism. It whizzes from Pudong to Longyang Lu metro station in the eastern suburbs in eight minutes, accelerating to 430kph in the first four minutes, then immediately starting to decelerate. As you near top speed – there's a digital speedometer in each cabin – the view from the windows becomes an impressionistic blur. Tickets cost ¥50 one way, ¥40 if you show a plane ticket. Never mind that the Maglev terminal is a few minutes' walk from the airport, and that Longyang Lu metro is still a long way from the centre of town – you may never get another chance to go this fast on land.

A taxi from Pudong to the Bund should cost around ¥140, to Nanjing Xi Lu around ¥120, or you can board an airport bus. There are stops opposite the exit gates, and eight routes to choose from, with departures every fifteen minutes; tickets cost around ¥20. Remember to use the loo in the Arrivals Hall before you board as the journey into town takes around an hour and a half. Bus #2 is generally the most useful as it goes to the Jing'an metro stop in the city centre. Bus #1 goes to Hongqiao Airport; bus #3 goes to the *Galaxy Hotel*, in the Hongqiao business district in the west of the city, and then to Xujiahui; bus #4 goes to Hongkou Stadium, in the north; bus #5 goes to Shanghai Zhan train station; bus #6 goes to Zhonghsan Park, bus #7 to the south railway station, in the southern suburbs. The only one with a drop off in Pudong is bus #5 (Dongfang Hospital).

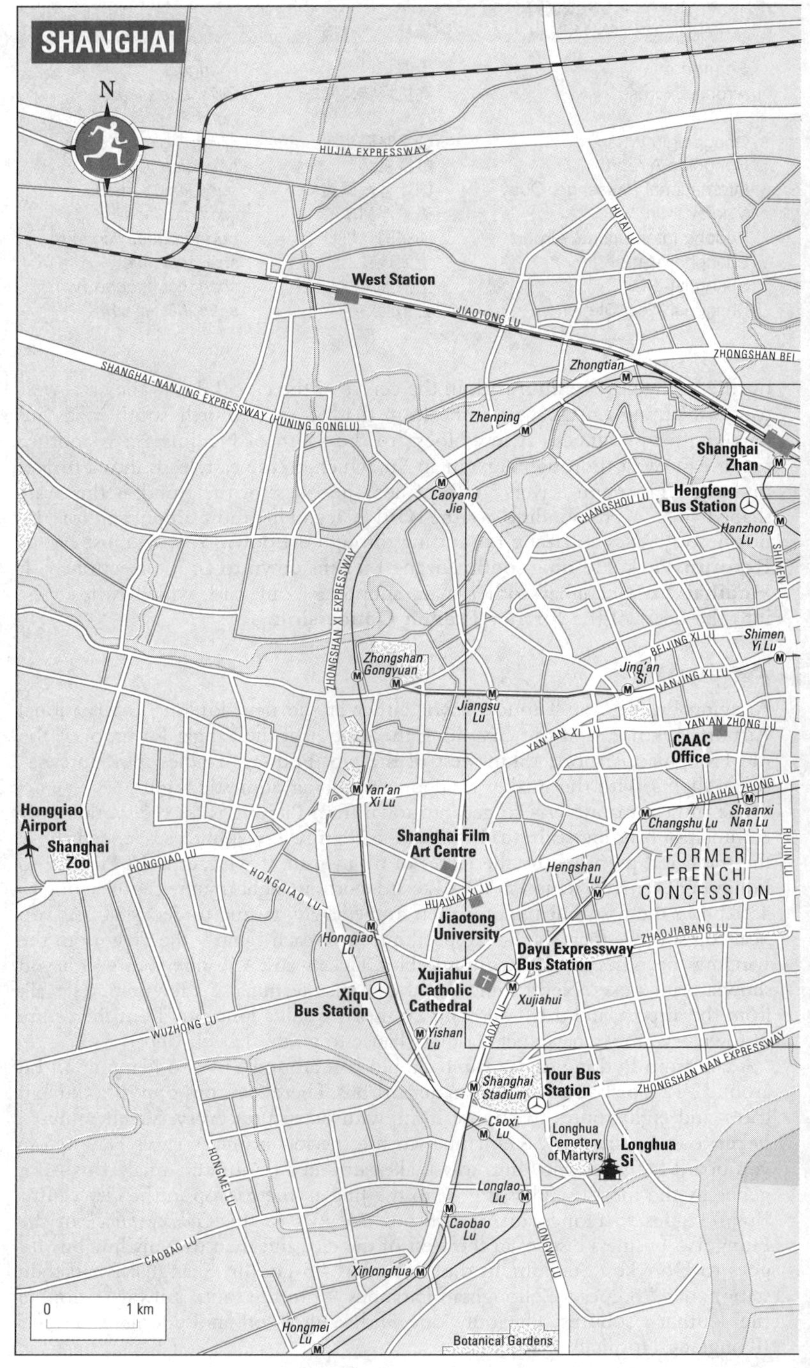

SHANGHAI
N
HUJIA EXPRESSWAY
HUTAI LU
West Station
JIAOTONG LU
ZHONGSHAN BEI
SHANGHAI-NANJING EXPRESSWAY (HUNING GONGLU)
Zhongtian
Zhenping
Shanghai Zhan
Caoyang Jie
CHANGSHOU LU
Hengfeng Bus Station
Hanzhong Lu
SHIMEN LU
ZHONGSHAN XI EXPRESSWAY
Shimen Yi Lu
BEIJING XI LU
Zhongshan Gongyuan
Jing'an Si
NANJING XI LU
Jiangsu Lu
YAN'AN ZHONG LU
YAN' AN XI LU
CAAC Office
Yan'an Xi Lu
HUAIHAI ZHONG LU
Hongqiao Airport
Shanghai Zoo
Changshu Lu
Shaanxi Nan Lu
Shanghai Film Art Centre
RUIJIN LU
FORMER FRENCH CONCESSION
HONGQIAO LU
Hengshan Lu
HUAIHAI XI LU
Jiaotong University
Hongqiao Lu
ZHAOJIABANG LU
Dayu Expressway Bus Station
Xujiahui Catholic Cathedral
Xiqu Bus Station
Xujiahui
CAOXI LU
WUZHONG LU
Yishan Lu
ZHONGSHAN NAN EXPRESSWAY
Shanghai Stadium
Tour Bus Station
Caoxi Lu
Longhua Cemetery of Martyrs
Longhua Si
HONGMEI LU
Longlao Lu
Caobao Lu
CAOBAO LU
LONGWU LU
Xinlonghua
0
1 km
Hongmei Lu
Botanical Gardens

5 SHANGHAI AND AROUND

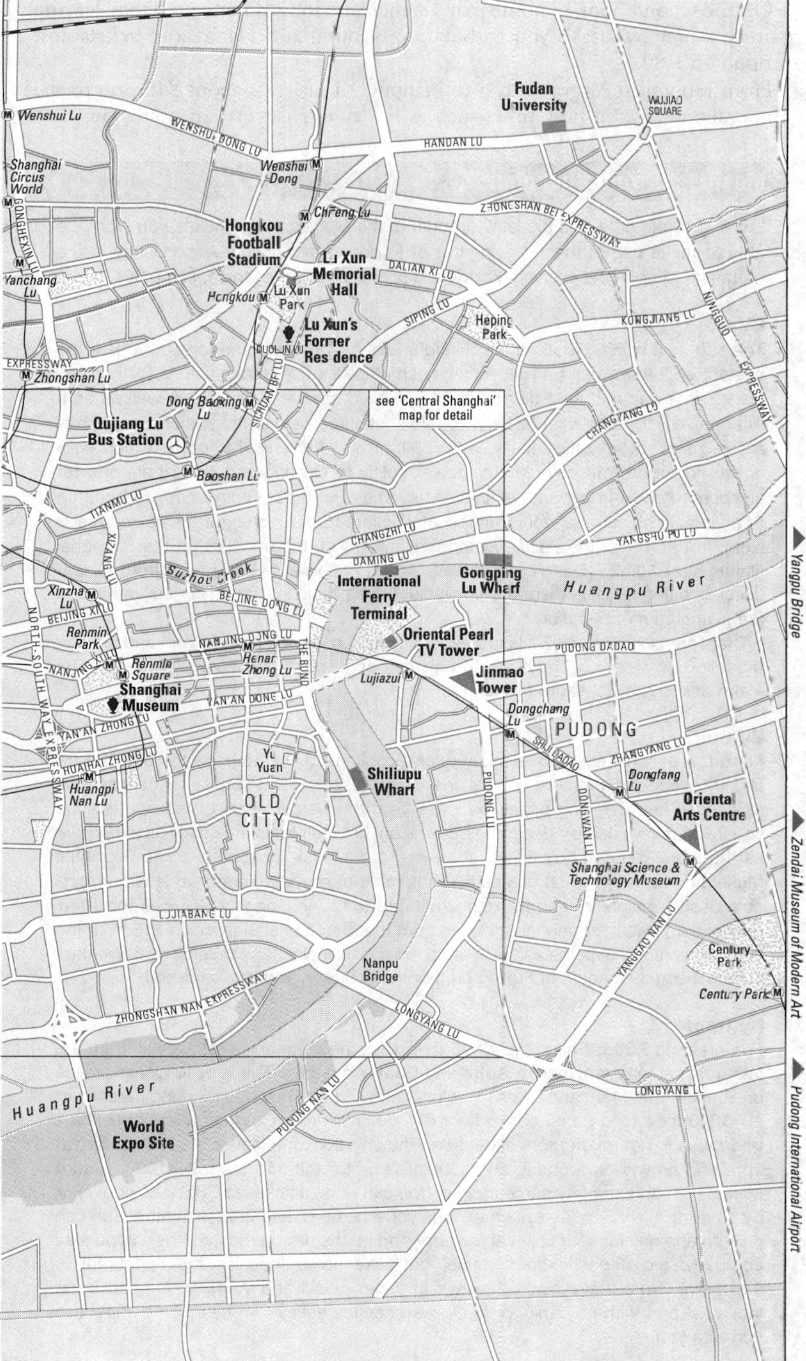
Fudan University
WUJIAO SQUARE
Wenshui Lu
WENSHUI DONG LU
HANDAN LU
Shanghai Circus World
Wenshui Dong
Chifeng Lu
ZHONGSHAN BEI EXPRESSWAY
GONGHEXIN LU
Hongkou Football Stadium
Lu Xun Memorial Hall
DALIAN XI LU
Yanchang Lu
Hongkou
Lu Xun Park
Lu Xun's Former Residence
SIPING LU
Heping Park
KONGJIANG LU
GUOQING EXPRESSWAY
DUOLUN LU
EXPRESSWAY
Zhongshan Lu
Dong Baoxing Lu
see 'Central Shanghai' map for detail
SICHUAN BEI LU
Qujiang Lu Bus Station
CHANGYANG LU
Baoshan Lu
TIANMU LU
XIZANG LU
CHANGZHI LU
YANGSHU PU LU
DAMING LU
Suzhou Creek
International Ferry Terminal
Gongping Lu Wharf
Huangpu River
Xinzha Lu
BEIJING XI LU
BEIJING DONG LU
NORTH-SOUTH WAY EXPRESSWAY
Renmin Park
NANJING DONG LU
Oriental Pearl TV Tower
PUDONG DADAO
NANJING XI LU
Renmin Square
Henan Zhong Lu
THE BUND
Lujiazui
Jinmao Tower
Shanghai Museum
YAN'AN DONG LU
YAN'AN ZHONG LU
Dongchang Lu
PUDONG
SHIJI DADAO
Yu Yuan
ZHANGYANG LU
HUAIHAI ZHONG LU
Shiliupu Wharf
Dongfang Lu
Huangpi Nan Lu
OLD CITY
PUDONG LU
DONGWAN LU
Oriental Arts Centre
Shanghai Science & Technology Museum
LUJIABANG LU
YANGGAO NAN LU
Century Park
Nanpu Bridge
ZHONGSHAN NAN EXPRESSWAY
LONGYANG LU
Huangpu River
PUDONG NAN LU
World Expo Site
Yangpu Bridge
Zendai Museum of Modern Art
Pudong International Airport

On the second floor, opposite exit 18, there are long-distance coaches, leaving hourly, which will take you to Suzhou, Nanjing and Hangzhou; tickets cost around ¥50–80.

From Hongqiao Airport, a taxi to Nanjing Xi Lu costs about ¥45, and to the Bund about ¥60; on busy times such as Friday nights, you can wait more than

Moving on from Shanghai

Leaving by air, note that the limited hours of the Maglev trains means you won't be able to make use of them if flying out of Pudong International Airport early in the morning or late in the evening. For details of airline offices in town, see p.394.

By train

The soft-seat waiting room in the Shanghai Zhan (enter from the forecourt, near the eastern end; there's an English sign) has an office that sells train tickets (daily 7am–9pm; same-day and next-day travel only) – hard seat and sleeper as well as soft. Alternatively, the *Longmen Hotel*, a couple of minutes west of the station square, has a foreigners' ticket office (daily 7am–5.30pm & 6–9pm) in the lobby, which sells tickets for up to four days in advance – mainly to Nanjing and Hangzhou, and for sleepers to a few important destinations such as Beijing or Guangzhou. To book up to a week in advance of your journey, buy tickets from a hotel (for a small commission); from CTS, in the *Pacific Hotel* on Nanjing Xi Lu; from CITS, in the Shanghai Centre or at 2 Jinling Dong Lu (both daily 8.30–11.30am & 1–4.45pm); or from a train-ticket booking office – there are convenient ones at 121 Xizang Nan Lu and inside Longyang Lu metro station.

There are five excellent Z-class sleepers to Beijing leaving around 7pm and arriving the following morning. Trains are soft-sleeper only and cabins have air-con and TVs – and at ¥500, It's cheaper than flying.

By bus

For a few destinations, buses might offer a convenient way to leave the city: they're slightly cheaper than trains, and it's easy to get a seat. Private buses for destinations in Jiangsu and Zhejiang provinces leave from the western part of the train-station square, and from nearby Hengfeng bus station, but their fares are nearly as expensive as the train. You can buy tickets there or from a kiosk just south of the Shanghai Museum. The Qiujiang Lu bus station has more reasonable fares, yet less comfortable buses, mainly leaving for Hangzhou and towns in Jiangsu. Services for a few destinations within Shanghai Shi leave from the Xiqu bus station (bus #113 from the train station) or a nameless bus stop on Shanxi Nan Lu, outside the Wenhua Guangchang, just south of Fuxing Lu. For these buses, you pay on board.

By boat

For ferries to **Putuo Shan**, see p.395. Two shipping companies sail weekly from the international ferry terminal, to **Kobe** and **Osaka** in Japan. The ferry to Osaka leaves on Tuesdays at 11am and takes two nights, arriving on Thursday morning; fares start at ¥1270 for a roll-up bed on the floor of a common room, though a bunk in a four-bed cabin is not much more expensive. The ship to Kobe leaves every Saturday at 1pm and arrives on Monday at 10.30am; fares for this trip start at ¥1300. Return tickets cost an extra fifty percent or so. You can book a ticket at CITS (see above) or by emailing ⓔzhangyz@suzhaohao.com; you'll be given a reference number and can pick up and pay for your ticket at the ferry port on the day. Ferries, run by a Japanese company, are perfectly comfortable, but take some food as the restaurant is expensive. Note that when you arrive in Japan you'll find yourself dumped in an industrial port with no banks or foreign exchanges nearby, so take some Japanese yen with you.

an hour for a taxi at the rank – walk to departures and pick up one that's just dropped someone off, or get on any bus for a couple of stops and hail one there. Buses leave from the car park: bus #1 goes to Pudong International Airport, the airport shuttle goes to Jing'an Temple metro stop in the city centre, bus #925 goes to Renmin Square and bus #941 goes to the Shanghai Zhan. Each of these bus rides from Hongqiao can take up to an hour depending on traffic.

By train

The main **train station – Shanghai Zhan** – is to the north of Suzhou Creek. Its vast concrete forecourt is a seething mass of encamped peasants at all hours, and it's not a particularly safe place to hang around at night. City buses are not an easy way to get out of the station area; you're better off taking metro line #1 or a taxi, the latter not likely to cost more than ¥15–20. There's an official rank outside the station and no trouble with drivers hustling foreigners. Another station in the remote northwest of town, **Shanghai West**, is the terminus for a few long-distance trains, such as the train from Inner Mongolia. This is linked to the metro and taxi rank at the main station by bus #106. The south station has services to Hangzhou.

By bus and boat

Hardly any tourists arrive in Shanghai by **bus**, and one good reason to avoid doing this is that you might be dropped in the remote outskirts of the city. Some services use the **bus station** on Qiujiang Lu, close to the Baoshan Lu metro station, a few private buses terminate at the train station itself, or you may arrive at nearby at Hengfeng station over the road from the Hanzhong Lu metro station, but generally speaking it's pot luck where you end up.

An enjoyable way to arrive in Shanghai is by **boat**, whether from Japan, Korea or the towns along the coast or inland up the Yangzi. The Yangzi ferries and coastal boats to and from Ningbo and Putuo Shan sail south right past the Bund to the **Shiliupu wharf** linked by bus #55 to the northern end of the Bund. Coastal boats to and from Qingdao and Fuzhou use the **Gongping Lu wharf**, which is only about twenty minutes' walk to the northeast of the Bund or a short ride on bus #135, while boats from Japan and South Korea dock at the **International Passenger Quay**, about ten minutes' walk east of the Waibaidu Bridge.

Information

You can pick up glossy free leaflets, containing basic tourist information, at the upmarket hotels and at the airport. Much more useful, though, are the free magazines aimed at the expat community, such as *City Weekend* (Ⓦwww.cityweekend.com.cn/shanghai), *Hint* (Ⓦwww.hintmagazinesh.com). *Time Out Shanghai* and the once great but now rather pedestrian *That's Shanghai* (Ⓦwww.thatsshanghai.com); they're free, and you can pick them up at most expat hangouts. All have listings sections including restaurants, club nights and art happenings, with addresses written in *pinyin* and Chinese, but no maps. Smart Shanghai (Ⓦwww.smartshanghai.com) is an excellent listings website that includes maps and user-submitted reviews.

The city's official tourism body, the tourist bureau, publishes the English-language papers *Travel China: Shanghai Edition* and *Shanghai Today*, both with an emphasis on news and less on restaurant and nightlife listings.

Various glossy English-language **maps** are available, including the *Shanghai Official Tourist Map*, which is paid for by advertising and is issued free in hotels

Useful Shanghai bus routes

North–south

#18 (trolleybus) From Lu Xun Park, across Suzhou Creek and along Xizang Lu.

#41 Passes Tianmu Xi Lu, in front of Shanghai Zhan and goes down through the former French Concession to Longhua Cemetery.

#64 From Shanghai Zhan, along Beijing Lu, then close to Shiliupu wharf on the south of the Bund.

#65 From the top to the bottom of Zhongshan Lu (the Bund), terminating in the south at the Nanpu Bridge.

East–west

#19 (trolleybus) From near Gongping Lu wharf in the east, passing near the *Pujiang Hotel* and roughly following the course of Suzhou Creek to Yufo Si.

#20 From Jiujiang Lu (just off the Bund) along Nanjing Dong Lu, past Jing'an Si, then on to Zhongshan Gongyuan in the west of the city.

#42 From Guangxi Lu (just off the Bund), then along Huaihai Lu in the former French Concession.

#135 From Yangpu Bridge in the east of the city to the eastern end of Huaihai Lu, via the Bund.

and from the tourist kiosk in the Renmin Square metro station. Additionally, bus routes can be found on the *Shanghai Communications Map*, which is widely available from street vendors, though this has street names in Chinese only.

City transport

The clean, efficient **Shanghai metro** (daily 5.50am–11pm) currently comprises four lines, with more under construction. All stations have plenty of English signage, and as there are really only two useful lines for visitors it is easy to find your way around. Line #1 runs north–south with useful stops at Shanghai Zhan, Renmin Square, Changshu Lu (for the former French Concession), Xujiahui and Shanghai Stadium. Line #2 runs east–west with stops at Jing'an Temple, Nanjing Lu, and, in Pudong, Lujiazui and the Science and Technology Museum. These two lines intersect at the enormous Renmin Square station (take careful note of the wall maps here to see which exit you should leave at). Overground commuter lines #3 and #4, serving the suburbs, are of less interest to visitors. Tickets cost ¥3–7 depending on the distance travelled and are bought from ticket machines, which also sell a card valid for multiple journeys (¥50).

Local buses run everywhere from around 4am to 10.30pm, but they are crowded (especially during rush hour) and slow, stops are far apart, and few lines travel from one side of the city to the other. Fares are ¥2; buy your ticket from the conductor onboard.

Taxis are very easy to get hold of and, if you're not on a very tight budget, they are often the most comfortable way to get around – fares usually come to ¥20–40 for rides within the city, with a flag fall of ¥11 (¥14 at night). Few drivers speak English, so it helps to have your destination written in Chinese. The only hassle you're likely to suffer is from drivers who take you on unnecessarily long detours, but if you sit in the front seat and hold a map on your lap they usually behave themselves. Drivers also ask if you want to use the elevated expressway – *zou gao jia* – at busy times; it'll be quicker but tends to involve slightly greater distances and is thus more expensive.

Accommodation

Accommodation in Shanghai is plentiful, and in places highly stylish, but prices are higher than elsewhere in China. The **grand old-world hotels** that form so integral a part of Shanghai's history cost at least US$150 per night these days, and for comfort and elegance have been overtaken by new arrivals, such as the clutch of boutique hotels.

If you want to be near the centre of the action, go for somewhere around Renmin Park or the Bund, and there are options here for all budgets. For style and panache, head to the genteel former French Concession, where attractive mid-range hotels are close to upmarket dining and nightlife. For the latest in corporate chic, Pudong has the fanciest options, but the area is rather dull. If you're simply looking for somewhere that's good value and convenient, stay in the outskirts near a metro station. Many travellers arrive in Shanghai assuming there is only one really **budget** option in the entire city, the *Pujiang* – well, not any more, it's gone upmarket. In its place a host of good options have opened up. At all but the cheapest hotels, rack rates should not be taken seriously; it's almost always possible to bargain the rate down, by as much as two-thirds off season.

Shanghai accommodation		
24K Hotel	24K国际连锁酒店	*24K guójì liánsuǒjiǔ diàn*
88 Xintiandi	88 新天地	*bā shí bā xīntiāndì*
Captain Hostel	船长酒店	*chuánzhǎng jiǔdiàn*
Dorure	都伦国际大酒店	*dūlún guójì dàjiǔdiàn*
Dong Hu	东湖宾馆	*dōnghú bīnguǎn*
Grand Hyatt Pudong	浦东金茂凯悦大酒店	*pǔdōng jīnmàokǎiyuè dàjiǔdiàn*
Hengshan Moller Villa	衡山马勒墅饭店	*héngshān mǎ lè shù fàndiàn*
Jinjiang	锦江饭店	*jǐnjiāng fàndiàn*
JW Marriott	明天广场JW万怡酒店	*míngtiān guǎngchǎng JW wànyí jiǔdiàn*
Metropole	新城饭店	*xīnchéng fàndiàn*
Mingtown Hikers Hostel	明堂上海旅行者国际青年旅馆	*míngtáng shànghǎi lǚxíngzhé guójì qīngnián lǚguǎn*
Mingtown Etour Hostel	上海明堂新易途国际青年旅	*shànghǎi míngtáng xīnyìtú guójì qīngnián lǚguǎn*
Okura Garden	上海花园饭店	*shànghǎi huāyuán fàndiàn*
Old House Inn	上海老时光餐厅酒吧	*shànghǎi lǎoshíguāng cāntīng jiǔbā*
Peace	和平饭店	*hépíng fàndiàn*
Pudong Shangri-La	浦东香格里拉大酒店	*pǔdōng xiānggélǐlā dà jiǔdiàn*
Pujiang	浦江饭店	*pǔjiāng fàndiàn*
Radisson New World	新世界丽笙大酒店	*xīnshìjiè lìshēng dàjiǔdiàn*
Ruijin Guesthouse	瑞金宾馆	*ruìjīn bīnguǎn*
Seagull	海鸥饭店	*hǎi'ōu fàndiàn*
Shanghai Mansions	上海大厦	*shànghǎi dàshà*
Taiyuan Villa	太原别墅	*tàiyuán biéshù*
Westin	威斯汀大酒店	*weī sī tīng dà jiǔdiàn*
YMCA Hotel	青年会宾馆	*qīngniánhuì bīnguǎn*

The Bund and around

Captain Hostel 37 Fuzhou Lu ⓣ021/63235053, ⓦwww.captainhostel.com.cn. Doubles at this place just off the Bund are pricey, but it's of most interest for its clean, cheap dorms, all made to look like cabins. Staff are dressed in sailor suits – though it hasn't made them any jollier. The *Captain Bar* on the sixth floor has great views of Pudong (see p.389). Internet access is ¥10/hr, bike rental ¥2/hr (guests only), and there's free use of the washing machine. Dorm beds ¥50, ❼

Metropole 180 Jiangxi Lu ⓣ021/63213030. Just off the Bund and dating from 1931, this is one of the more affordable of the older hotels, but like them it suffers from uninspired renovation and old-fashioned service. There's a great Art Deco lobby and exterior, but the rooms are plain. ❽

Mingtown Hikers Hostel 450 Jiangxi Zhong Lu ⓣ021/63297889. Very well located just north of the Bund, this cheap-and-cheerful hostel has a self-catering kitchen, wireless Internet and a lively bar. Henan Zhong Lu metro stop. Four- and six-bed dorms ¥45; rooms with shared bathrooms ❶, en-suite rooms ❹

Peace Junction of the Bund and Nanjing Dong Lu ⓣ021/63216888, ⓦwww.shanghaipeacehotel.com. Occupying both sides of the road, this was formerly the *Cathay Hotel*, the most famous hotel in Shanghai and still well worth a visit to admire the lobby's Art Deco interiors. The long list of illustrious previous guests includes Charlie Chaplin and Noel Coward; these days though, its glories have faded, and rooms are poky and cluttered with chintz. Despite the prices – doubles start at ¥880 – the service is definitely not up to it. Come for a nose around, but don't stay. ❾

Pujiang 15 Huangpu Lu ⓣ021/63246388, ⓦwww.pujianghotel.com. Located across the Waibaidu Bridge north of the Bund and slightly to the east, opposite the blue Russian Consulate building. Formerly the *Astor Hotel*, and dating back to 1846, this is a pleasingly old-fashioned place with creaky wooden floors and high ceilings, and the antiquated look of a Victorian school. ❼

Seagull 60 Huangpu Lu ⓣ021/63251500. Pink-uniformed staff and a kitsch lobby make this place look camp, but it offers recently refurbished rooms with a great view of the Huangpu for less than you pay elsewhere. The area is not very exciting, but you're only a few minutes from the Bund. ❾

Shanghai Mansions (Broadway Mansions); 20 Suzhou Bei Lu ⓣ021/63246260. This is the huge, ugly lump of a building on the north bank of Suzhou Creek, visible from the north end of the Bund. Rooms get pricier the higher up you go. ❾

Pudong

Grand Hyatt Jinmao Tower, 88 Shijia Dadao ⓣ021/50491234, ⓦwww.shanghai.hyatt.com. Taking up the top floors of the magnificent Jinmao Tower, the *Hyatt* is the world's tallest hotel. There's no doubt, the place is fantastic – awesome views, great design, lots of lucky numbers (555 rooms, 88 storeys) – but, it has to be said, the area is hardly interesting. *Cloud Nine* (see p.390), the world's highest bar, is on the top floor. ❾

Pudong Shangri-La 33 Fucheng Lu ⓣ021/68828888, ⓦwww.shangri-la.com/shanghai. The other monster hotel in Pudong, with almost a thousand rooms. Popular with upscale business travellers for comfort, convenience and of course, the views through the huge windows. Home to the fabulous *Jade on 36* restaurant (see p.389). ❾

The former French Concession

88 Xintiandi 380 Huangpi Bei Lu ⓣ021/53838833, ⓦwww.88intiandi.com. Fifty-room boutique hotel at the edge of the yuppie fantasy land that is the Xintiandi complex. The best rooms have a view of the lake. There's a pool, and guests can use the adjacent spa and fitness centre. The no-smoking floors are a nice touch. Convenient for Huangpi Nan Lu metro stop. ❾

Dong Hu 70 Donghu Lu, one block north of Huaihai Zhong Lu ⓣ021/64158158, ⓦwww.donghuhotel.com. Make sure you get a room in the old building, and not the dull new block over the road. The good location and the pleasant gardens make this one of the best hotels in its price range. ❾

Hengshan Moller Villa 30 Shaanxi Nan Lu ⓣ021/62478881, ⓦwww.mollervilla.com. Describing itself as a boutique heritage hotel, the main building here is a gorgeous Scandinavian gothic fantasy built in the 1930s. You can stay in the villa's well-appointed rooms, with their balconies and fireplaces, but they're expensive; most rooms are in a three-storey block just behind. ❾

Jinjiang 59 Maoming Lu ⓣ021/62582582, ⓦwww.jinjianghotels.com. A vast place in the former French Concession, with many wings, much history and good facilities (see p.377). Perhaps it's a trifle old-fashioned, and has been overtaken by slick new competitors, but it's well located, just north of Shanxi Nan Lu metro stop, off busy Huaihai Zhong Lu. 9

The Nine 9 Jianguo Xi Lu, by Taiyuan Lu ⓣ021/64719950. A select boutique hotel in an old villa, with the feel of a private club; there are only five rooms, all tricked out with antiques. It's very discreet and there's not even a sign – look for the sturdy gates. Good dinners at the long table. Phone reservations (well in advance) are essential. 9

Okura Garden 58 Maoming Nan Lu ⓣ021/64151111, ⓦwww.gardenhotelshanghai.com. Japanese-managed luxury mansion; the grounds are lovely, and the lobby, which used to be the Cercle Sportif French Club, has some great Art Deco detailing; but the rooms, in a giant new monolith looming at the back, are a little nondescript. 9

Old House Inn 16 Lane 351, Huashan Lu, by Changshu Lu ⓣ021/62486118, ⓦwww.oldhouse.cn. A small guesthouse in a sympathetically restored *shikumen* house. The dozen rooms are comfortable, though the corridors are authentically poky. Free Wi-Fi. You'll need to book in advance. 8

Ruijin Guesthouse 118 Ruijin Er Lu (main entrance on Fuxing Lu) ⓣ021/64725222, ⓦwww.ruijinhotelsh.com. Cosy and exclusive Tudor-style villas in manicured gardens. The lavish *Face Bar* (see p.377) is an additional bonus. It's not quite the fabulous destination it could be thanks to occasionally lacklustre service, but is still recommended. Ask for Building One, where Mao used to stay. 9

Taiyuan Villa 106 Taiyuan Lu, by Yongjia Lu ⓣ021/64716688. If you don't mind a 10min walk to the nearest metro, this historic villa set in lovely grounds in a quiet street in the former French Concession is certainly one of the best places to stay in this price range. Dark wood panelling in the rooms adds to the period charm. 9

Around Renmin Square

24K Hotel 155 Weihai Lu ⓣ021/51181222 555 Fuzhou Lu ⓣ021/51503588, ⓦwww.24khotels.com. Chirpy design, clean, and much cheaper than the competition. Some English is spoken. Free Wi-Fi ,and there's even a machine that dispenses medicines in the lobby. 5

JW Marriot Tomorrow Square, 399 Nanjing Xi Lu ⓣ021/53594969, ⓦwww.marriott.com. Housed in the top floors of one of Shanghai's most uncompromising landmarks (something like an upraised claw), this swanky venue is both well located and has magnificent views, making it one of the finest top-end destinations. 9

Mingtown Etour Hostel 57 Jiangxi Zhong Lu ⓣ021/63277766.This is the best of the cheapies, being very well located – tucked in the alleyway behind Tomorrow Square, right beside Renmin Park – yet quiet and surprisingly affordable. Everything centres on a relaxing courtyard. Rooms vary, so ask to see a few – one or two have balconies. Bathrooms are shared between two or three rooms. Internet is free, but there are only two computers. Dorms ¥45, rooms 4

Radisson New World 88 Nanjing Xi Lu ⓣ021/63599999, ⓦwww.radisson.com. A new and swish venue that has quickly become popular, offering a convenient location right at the corner of bustling Nanjing Lu, and, in general, a slick upscale experience. 9

Westin 88 Henan Zhong Lu ⓣ021/63351888, ⓦwww.westin.com/shanghai. Chinese luxury hotels usually try to impress with either a water feature or palm trees in the lobby; the over-the-top Westin goes for both, and then, as if that weren't enough to declare its intentions, the building has a crown on top. Rooms aren't so flashy, which is a good thing; ask for one with a view. Good on-site restaurants and spa. 9

YMCA Hotel 123 Xizang Nan Lu ⓣ021/63261040, ⓦwww.ymcahotel.com. Bright, practical and central; no frills and it has seen better days. The four-bed dorms are on the pricey side (you can do better elsewhere), but the rooms are cheap considering the location. Dorms ¥100, rooms 6

The North

Dorure 1885 Sichuan Bei Lu ⓣ021/56969999, ⓦwww.dorurehotel.com. This smart international business hotel is at the end of Duolun Culture Street, so the area is charming and quiet and there are some nice cafés, shops and an art gallery nearby; though it's a little far from the centre of town, the East Baoxing Lu metro stop is a 2min walk away. The place itself is new and well designed, and staff are keen. One of the best mid-range options. 7

The City

Although most parts of Shanghai that you are likely to visit lie to the west of the **Huangpu River** and its colonial riverfront, the **Bund**, by far the most easily recognizable landmark in the city is on the east side – the rocket-like Oriental Pearl TV Tower, so high its antenna is often shrouded in mist. The best way to check out both banks of the Huangpu River and their sights is to take a splendid **Huangpu River tour**.

Nanjing Lu, reputedly the busiest shopping street in China, runs through the heart of downtown Shanghai. Headed at its eastern end by the famous **Peace Hotel**, the road leads west to **Renmin Park**, which today houses the excellent **Shanghai Museum** as well as a couple of decent art galleries. The other main sights lie about 1500m south of Nanjing Lu in the **Old City**, the longest continuously inhabited part of Shanghai, with the **Yu Yuan** – a fully restored classical Chinese garden – and bazaars at its heart. To the southwest of here lies the marvellous **former French Concession**, with its cosmopolitan cooking traditions, European-style housing and revolutionary relics. The energetic eating and nightlife centre of Shanghai, **Huaihai Lu**, serves as the area's main artery.

Farther out from the centre remains a scattering of sights. Just west of Shanghai Zhan is the fascinating Moganshan Art District, an old factory full of art galleries and studios. North of Suzhou Creek is the interesting **Lu Xun Park**, with its monuments to the great twentieth-century writer, Lu Xun, while Duolun Culture Street, with its quirky museums and shops, is a lovely place to while away an afternoon. Finally, in the far west are two of Shanghai's most important surviving religious sites: the **Longhua Si** and the **Yufo Si**.

The Bund and the Huangpu River

Shanghai's original signature skyline, and the first stop for any visitor, is **the Bund**, a strip of grand colonial edifices on the west bank of the Huangpu River, facing the flashy skyscrapers of Pudong on the opposite shore. Since 1949, it's been known officially as Zhongshan Lu, but it's better known among locals as Wai Tan (literally "Outside Beach"). Named after an old Anglo-Indian term, "bunding" (the embanking of a muddy foreshore), the Bund was old Shanghai's commercial heart, with the river on one side, the offices of the leading banks and trading houses on the other. During Shanghai's riotous heyday it was also a hectic working harbour, where anything from tiny sailing junks to ocean-going freighters unloaded under the watch of British – and later American and Japanese – warships. Everything arrived here, from silk and tea to heavy industrial machinery. Amidst it all, wealthy foreigners disembarked to pick their way to one of the grand hotels through crowds of beggars, hawkers, black marketeers, shoeshine boys, overladen coolies and even funeral parties – Chinese too poor to pay for the burial of relatives would launch the bodies into the river in boxes decked in paper flowers.

Today, it's the most exclusive chunk of real estate in China, with pretensions to becoming the nation's Champs-Elysées; the world's most luxurious brands have set up shop here and there are a clutch of celebrity restaurants (though if you just want to eat, rather than have a gourmet experience, choice is rather limited).

Grand designs: Chinese architecture

Though much of urban China has been ripped up and rebuilt in the last fifty years, there are enough beautiful ancient buildings left, mostly temples and palaces, to illustrate three thousand years of illustrious architectural history. There is a remarkable consistency across centuries – marked by a historical adherence to the rules of *feng shui* – with only minor variations by dynasty, and it doesn't take a visitor long to grasp the fundamentals of Chinese design.

Monumental architecture

Traditional temples and palaces follow a basic **building structure**: the foundations form a raised platform of earth, brick or stone. Columns rest on separate bases with their heads linked by beams running lengthways and across; above this, beams are raised on posts set on the beam below to create an interlocking structure that rises to the point of the roof – here, posts at the centre support the roof ridge. The arrangement produced a characteristic **curved roofline** with upcurled eaves, felt to confer good luck. **Cantilevered brackets**, introduced in the eighth century, allowed the curving eaves to extend well beyond the main pillars and acquire decorative value. Though scale and space were ultimately limited by a lack of arches (essential in supporting the massive walls found in European cathedrals), this structural design was solid enough to allow the use of heavy **ceramic roof tiles**.

▲ Xian's Bell Tower sports classic curved rooflines

These features reached a peak of elegance and sophistication during the **Tang and Song** eras. Though little survives intact from this time, later restorations of Tang edifices, such as the temples at Wudang Shan in Hubei province, or Xi'an's central Bell Tower, convey something of the period's spirit. Two **regional styles** also developed: **northern** architecture was comparatively restrained and sober, while that from the **south** exaggerated curves and ornamentation; Guangdong's Foshan Ancestral Temple is a classic of the latter type. Inside both, however, spaces between the columns were filled by screens providing different combinations of wall, door and latticework, which could be removed or changed to order the spaces within.

Imperial buildings were distinguished by four-sided roofs, high platforms, wide staircases and by special yellow glazed tiles for the roofs.

Domestic architecture

Domestic architecture shares many guiding principles of temple and palace design, with curved rooflines, and the use of *feng shui*-influenced spirit walls or mirrors, the latter placed over external doorways to repulse demons. Older homes with these basic features can be found all over the country, but in many cases, practical considerations – principally the climate – created distinctive **local styles**, most obvious in a basic north–south divide. **Northern** China's intensely cold winters and hot summers spawned solidly insulated brick

◀ Dong wind-and-rain bridge, Guangxi

walls, while more stable, subtropical **southern** temperatures encourage the use of open eaves, internal courtyards and wooden lattice screens to allow air to circulate freely.

Rural areas are good places to find some of the more traditional or unusual types of residential architecture. Striking examples exist in the mountainous border areas between Guizhou and Guangxi provinces, where ethnic **Dong** and **Miao** build huge, two- or three-storey wooden houses from local cedar. The Dong are further known for their wooden **drum towers** and **wind-and-rain bridges**. Another ethnic group building distinctive houses is the **Hakka**, a Han subgroup, whose immense stone circular clan or family mansions – some of which can accommodate hundreds of people – were built for defensive purposes in their Guangdong–Fujian homelands. Extreme adaptation to local conditions can be seen in Shaanxi province, where **underground homes**, cool in summer and warm in winter, have been excavated in prehistoric sedimentary soils deposited by the Yellow River.

Feng shui

Whatever the scale of a building project, the Chinese consider divination using **feng shui** an essential part of the initial preparations. Literally meaning "wind and water", *feng shui* is a form of **geomancy**, which assesses how buildings must be positioned so as not to disturb the spiritual attributes of the surrounding landscape. This reflects **Taoist cosmology**, which believes that the disruption of a single element can cause potentially dangerous alterations to the whole. It's vital, therefore, that sites – whether for peasant homes or entire cities such as Beijing – be favourably orientated according to points on the compass and protected from local "unlucky directions" by other buildings, walls, hills, mountain ranges, water or even a Terracotta Army.

Geomancy compass ▶

▲ National Grand Theatre, Beijing

Modern architecture

Under the Communists, a brutally functional **Soviet style** became the urban norm, requiring that everything from factories to hotels be built as identical drab, characterless grey boxes. Since China opened up to the Western world and capitalism in the 1980s, however, there's been a move towards a more "international" look, as seen in the concrete-and-glass high-rises going up across the country. Here you'll often see attempts to marry the traditional Chinese idiom with current needs, and in a few cases you'll see apartment buildings surrounded by walled compounds and topped with curled roof tiles.

In recent years, with a great deal of money and resources washing around (and few planning restrictions), the Chinese urban landscape is being ripped up and reconstructed yet again. Eye-catching, prestige projects by the world's most expensive architects have been springing up, particularly in **Beijing** – with the purpose of presenting it as a dynamic, hip city in time for the Olympics in 2008 – and **Shanghai**.

Four great modern buildings

CCTV Building, Beijing Designed by the radical Dutch firm OMA, this is a truly bizarre structure, a double "Z" with a hole in the middle and no right angles, nicknamed "the Twisted Doughnut".

National Grand Theatre, Beijing Also known as "the Egg", the National Grand Theatre – three halls under a dome floating at the centre of an artificial lake – has been designed by French architect Paul Andreu.

National Olympic Stadium, Beijing Designed by Herzog and de Meuron to resemble a bird's nest, this looks set to be the most popular of the new eyebrow raisers.

Xintiandi, Shanghai Complex of accommodation and restaurants in Shanghai that is a rare example of an extravagant architectural gesture that's still recognizably Chinese, a collection of *shikumen*, houses with stone gateways, painstakingly reconstructed with original materials.

◀ Xintiandi, Shanghai

▲ Tai ji in Huangpu Park, The Bund

Before tackling the Bund proper, have a look at the Main Post Office, just north of it, built in 1931, and easily recognizable by its clocktower. It's the only Bund building that has never been used for anything but its original function. It houses the **Shanghai Post Museum** (Wed, Thurs, Sat & Sun 9am–4pm; ¥10) on the third floor, which is more interesting than it sounds. The collection of letters and stamps is only mildly diverting, but the new atrium is very impressive, and the view of the Bund from the grassed-over roof is superb.

The northern end of the Bund starts from the confluence of the Huangpu and Suzhou Creek, by **Waibaidu Bridge**, and runs south for 1500m to Jinling Dong Lu, formerly Rue du Consulat. At the outbreak of the Sino-Japanese War in 1937, the bridge formed a no-man's-land between the Japanese-occupied areas north of Suzhou Creek and the **International Settlement** – it was guarded at one end by Japanese sentries, the other by British. Today, though most ships dock farther downstream, the waterways are still well-used thoroughfares, and the Bund itself is a popular place for an after-dinner stroll or morning exercises, while tourists from all over China patrol the waterfront taking photos of each other against the backdrop of the Oriental Pearl TV Tower.

The first building south of the bridge was one of the cornerstones of British interests in old Shanghai, the **former British Consulate**, once ostentatiously guarded by magnificently dressed Sikh soldiers. The blue building just to the northeast of here across the Suzhou Creek still retains its original function as the **Russian Consulate**. Right on the corner of the two waterways, **Huangpu Park** was another British creation, the British Public Gardens, established on a patch of land formed when mud and silt gathered around a wrecked ship. Here, too, there were Sikh troops, ready to enforce the rules that forbade Chinese from entering, unless they were servants accompanying their employer. After protests, the regulations were relaxed to admit "well-dressed" Chinese, who had to apply for a special entry permit. Though it's firmly established in the Chinese popular imagination as a symbol of Western racism, there's no evidence that there ever was a sign here reading "no dogs or Chinese allowed". These days,

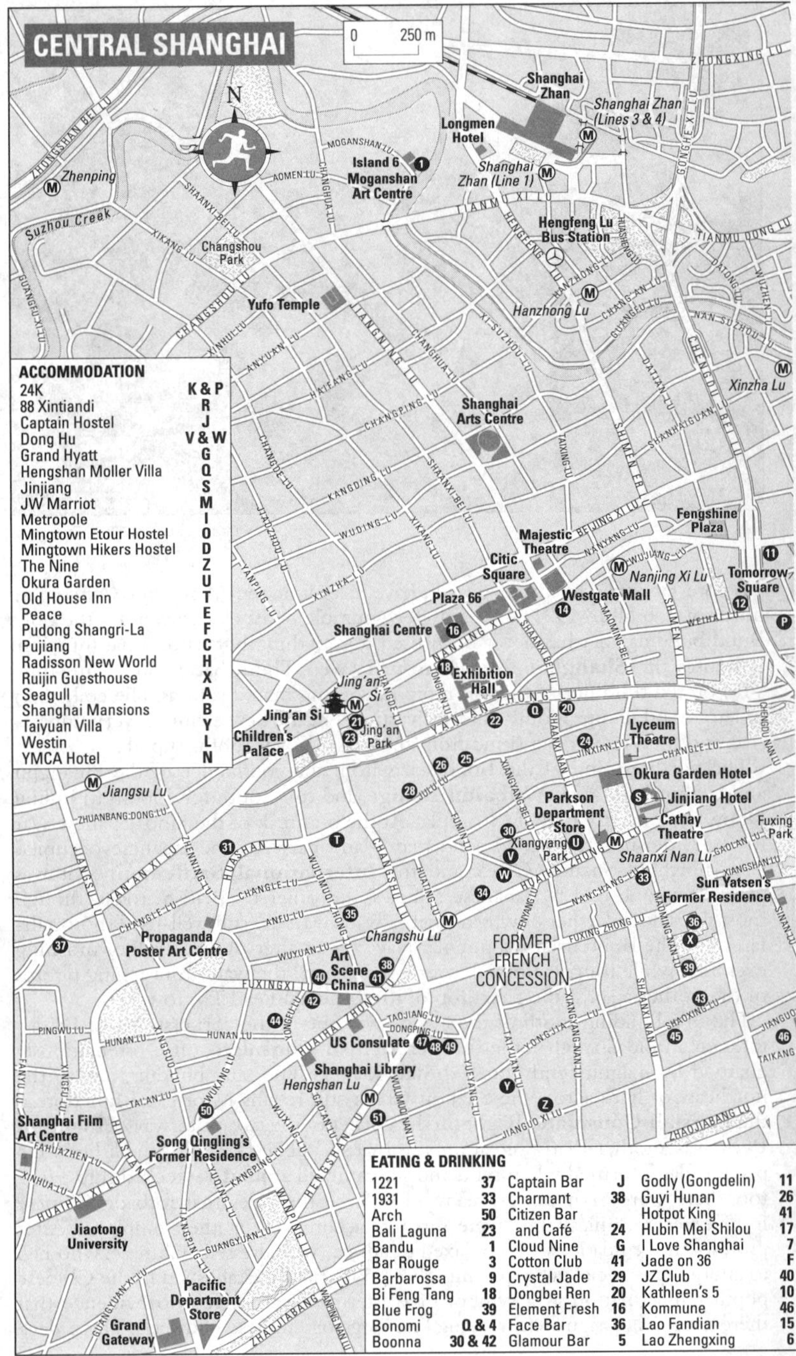
CENTRAL SHANGHAI
0 250 m
N
ACCOMMODATION
24K K & P
88 Xintiandi R
Captain Hostel J
Dong Hu V & W
Grand Hyatt G
Hengshan Moller Villa Q
Jinjiang S
JW Marriot M
Metropole I
Mingtown Etour Hostel O
Mingtown Hikers Hostel D
The Nine Z
Okura Garden U
Old House Inn T
Peace E
Pudong Shangri-La F
Pujiang C
Radisson New World H
Ruijin Guesthouse X
Seagull A
Shanghai Mansions B
Taiyuan Villa Y
Westin L
YMCA Hotel N
EATING & DRINKING
1221 37
1931 33
Arch 50
Bali Laguna 23
Bandu 1
Bar Rouge 3
Barbarossa 9
Bi Feng Tang 18
Blue Frog 39
Bonomi Q & 4
Boonna 30 & 42
Captain Bar J
Charmant 38
Citizen Bar and Café 24
Cloud Nine G
Cotton Club 41
Crystal Jade 29
Dongbei Ren 20
Element Fresh 16
Face Bar 36
Glamour Bar 5
Godly (Gongdelin) 11
Guyi Hunan 26
Hotpot King 41
Hubin Mei Shilou 17
I Love Shanghai 7
Jade on 36 F
JZ Club 40
Kathleen's 5 10
Kommune 46
Lao Fandian 15
Lao Zhengxing 6
Shanghai Zhan
Shanghai Zhan (Lines 3 & 4)
Longmen Hotel
Island 6
Moganshan Art Centre
Shanghai Zhan (Line 1)
Zhenping
Suzhou Creek
Changshou Park
Hengfeng Lu Bus Station
Hanzhong Lu
Yufo Temple
Xinzha Lu
Shanghai Arts Centre
Fengshine Plaza
Majestic Theatre
Citic Square
Nanjing Xi Lu
Tomorrow Square
Plaza 66
Westgate Mall
Shanghai Centre
Exhibition Hall
Jing'an Si
Jing'an Park
Children's Palace
Lyceum Theatre
Okura Garden Hotel
Jinjiang Hotel
Cathay Theatre
Fuxing Park
Parkson Department Store
Xiangyang Park
Shaanxi Nan Lu
Sun Yatsen's Former Residence
Jiangsu Lu
Changshu Lu
Propaganda Poster Art Centre
Art Scene China
FORMER FRENCH CONCESSION
US Consulate
Shanghai Library
Hengshan Lu
Shanghai Film Art Centre
Song Qingling's Former Residence
Jiaotong University
Pacific Department Store
Grand Gateway
ZHONGXING LU
TIANMU DONG LU
TIANMU XI LU
MOGANSHAN LU
AOMEN LU
CHANGHUA LU
ZHONGSHAN BEI LU
SHAANXI BEI LU
XIKANG LU
GUANGFU XI LU
CHANGSHOU LU
XINHUI LU
JIANGNING LU
ANYUAN LU
HAIFANG LU
CHANGPING LU
KANGDING LU
WUDING LU
XINZHA LU
CHANGDE LU
JIAOZHOU LU
YANPING LU
NANJING XI LU
BEIJING XI LU
NANYANG LU
WUJIANG LU
WEIHAI LU
YAN'AN ZHONG LU
JULU LU
CHANGLE LU
JINXIAN LU
HUAIHAI ZHONG LU
NANCHANG LU
FUXING ZHONG LU
FUXING XI LU
HUASHAN LU
ANFU LU
WUYUAN LU
WULUMUQI ZHONG LU
YONGFU LU
HUNAN LU
PINGWU LU
XINGGUO LU
TAOJIANG LU
DONGPING LU
YONGJIA LU
SHAOXING LU
JIANGUO XI LU
ZHAOJIABANG LU
HENGSHAN LU
WANPING LU
KANGPING LU
GUANGYUAN LU
GUANGYUAN XI LU
TIANPING LU
YUQING LU
WUXING LU
GAO'AN LU
TAIYUAN LU
YUEYANG LU
XIANGYANG NAN LU
SHAANXI NAN LU
MAOMING NAN LU
CHENGDU BEI LU
SHIMEN ER LU
SHIMEN YI LU
HUAIHAI XI LU
FAHUAZHEN LU
XINHUA LU
FANYU LU
TAI'AN LU
WUKANG LU
ZHUANBANG DONG LU
YAN'AN XI LU
ZHENNING LU
JIANGSU LU
FUMIN LU
HUATING LU
CHANGSHU LU
FENYANG LU
GAOLAN LU
XIANGSHAN LU
SINAN LU
TAIKANG LU
JIANGUO LU
DATIAN LU
TAIXING LU
SHANHAIGUAN LU
XI SUZHOU LU
HENGFENG LU
HANZHONG LU
CHANG'AN LU
GUANGFU LU
NAN SUZHOU LU
DATONG LU
WUZHEN LU
GONGHE XIN LU
HUASHENG LU
TONGREN LU
MAOMING BEI LU
CHENGDU NAN LU

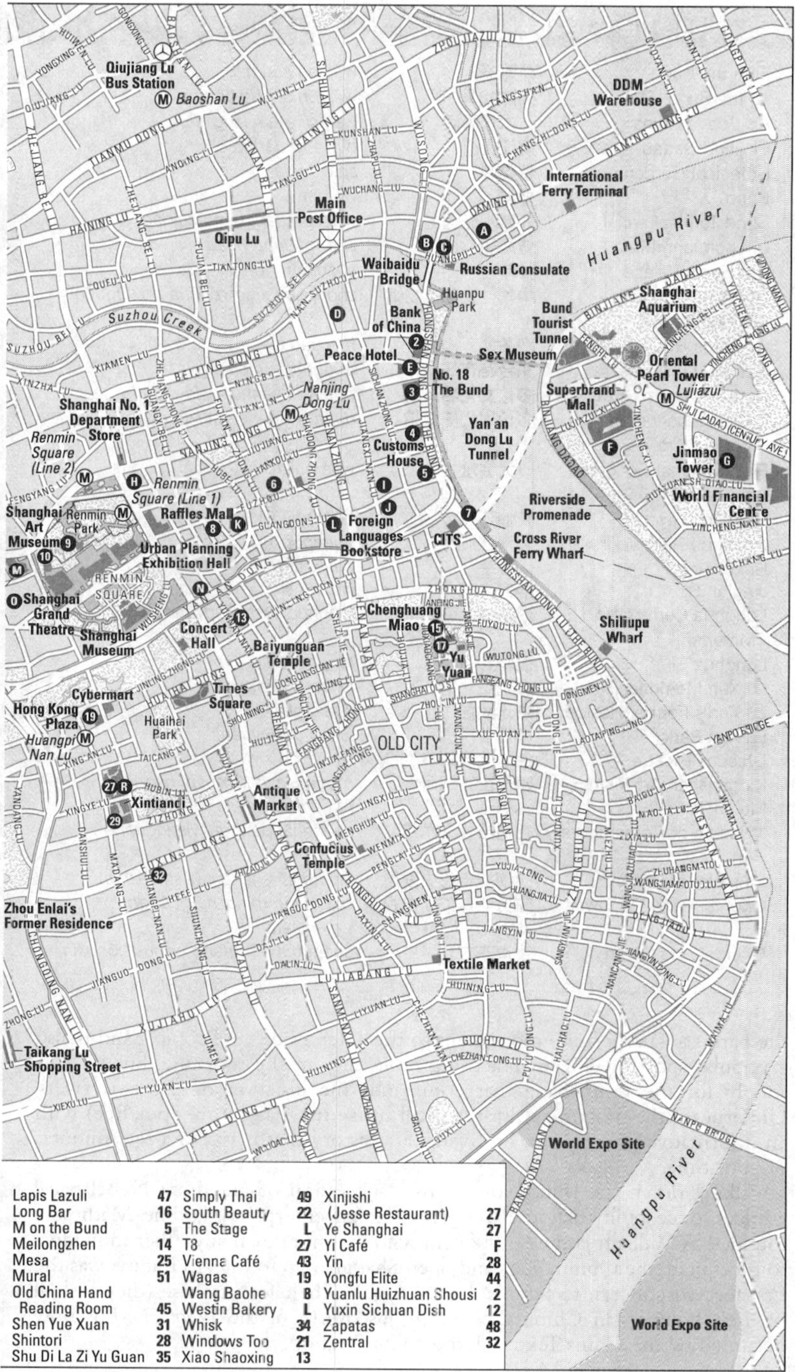

Lapis Lazuli	47	Simply Thai	49	Xinjishi	
Long Bar	16	South Beauty	22	(Jesse Restaurant)	27
M on the Bund	5	The Stage	L	Ye Shanghai	27
Meilongzhen	14	T8	27	Yi Café	F
Mesa	25	Vienna Café	43	Yin	28
Mural	51	Wagas	19	Yongfu Elite	44
Old China Hand		Wang Baohe	B	Yuanlu Huizhuan Shousi	2
Reading Room	45	Westin Bakery	L	Yuxin Sichuan Dish	12
Shen Yue Xuan	31	Whisk	34	Zapatas	48
Shintori	28	Windows Too	21	Zentral	32
Shu Di La Zi Yu Guan	35	Xiao Shaoxing	13		

Shanghai: The City and around

3 on the Bund	外滩3号	*wài tān sān hào*
18 the Bund	外滩18号	*wài tān shí bā hào*
Art Scene China	艺术景画廊	*yìshùjǐng huàláng*
Binjiang Dadao	滨江大道	*bīnjiāng dàdào*
Botanical Gardens	植物园	*zhíwù yuán*
Bund	外滩	*wàitān*
Bund Tourist Tunnel	外滩观光隧道	*wàitān guānguāng suìdào*
Chenghuang Miao	城皇庙	*chénghuáng miào*
Children's Palace	少年宫	*shàonián gōng*
China Sex Culture Exhibition	中华性文化博物馆	*zhōnghuá xìngwénhuà bówùguǎn*
Customs House	海关楼	*hǎiguān lóu*
Dongtai Lu Market	东台路市场	*dōngtáilù shìchǎng*
Duolun Culture Street	多伦文化名人街	*duō lún wénhuà míngrén jiē*
Duolun Museum of Modern Art	多伦现代美术馆	*duōlún xiàndài měishùguǎn*
First National Congress of the CCP	一大会址	*yídà huìzhǐ*
Huangpu River	黄浦江	*huángpǔ jiāng*
Huangpu River Tour	黄浦江旅游	*huángpǔjiāng lǚyóu*
Huxin Ting	湖心亭	*húxīn tíng*
Jing'an Si	静安寺	*jíng'ān sì*
Longhua Cemetery Of Martyrs	龙华烈士陵园	*lónghuá lièshì língyuán*
Longhua Si	龙华寺	*lónghuá sì*
Lu Xun Memorial Hall	鲁迅纪念馆	*lǔxùn jìniànguǎn*
Lu Xun's Former Residence	鲁迅故居	*lǔxùn gùjū*
Lu Xun Park	鲁迅公园	*lǔxùn gōngyuán*
Lyceum Theatre	兰心大戏院	*lánxīn dà xìyuàn*
Moganshan Art District	莫干山路50号	*mògānshān lù wǔshí hào*
Mu'en Tang	沐恩堂	*mù'ēn táng*
Museum of Contemporary Art	上海当代艺术馆	*shànghǎi dāngdài yìshùguǎng*
Museum of History	上海城市历史发展	*shànghǎi chéngshì lìshǐ fāzhǎn*
Oriental Pearl TV Tower	东方明珠广播电视塔	*dōngfāng míngzhū guǎngbō diànshìtā*
Oriental Arts Centre	上海东方艺术中心	*shànghǎi dōngfāng yìshù zhōngxīn*

the park contains a stone monument to the "Heroes of the People", and is also a popular spot for citizens practising *tai ji* early in the morning, but it's best simply for the promenade that commands the junction of the two rivers. Underneath the monument lurks a small **museum** (daily 9am–4pm; free) with an informative presentation on Shanghai's history that is worth a few minutes of your time.

Walking down the Bund, you'll pass a succession of grandiose Neoclassical edifices, once built to house the great foreign enterprises. Jardine Matheson, founded by William Jardine – the man who did more than any other individual to precipitate the Opium Wars and open Shanghai up to foreign trade – was the first foreign concern to buy land in Shanghai. Their former base (they lost all of their holdings in China after 1949), just north of the *Peace Hotel*, is now occupied by the China Textiles Export Corporation.

Pudong	浦东新区	*pŭdōng xīnqū*
Propaganda Poster Centre	宣传画黏画艺术中心	*xuānchuánhuà niánhuà yìshù zhōng xīn*
Renmin Park	人民公园	*rénmín gōngyuán*
Renmin Square	人民广场	*rénmín guăngchăng*
Science and Technology Museum	上海科技馆	*shànghăi kē jì guăn*
Shanghai Centre	上海商城	*shànghăi shāngchéng*
Shanghai Exhibition Centre	上海展览中心	*shànghăi zhănlăn zhōngxīn*
Shanghai Grand Theatre	上海大剧院	*shànghăi dà jù yuàn*
Shanghai Museum	上海博物馆	*shànghăi bówùguăn*
Shanghai Urban Planning Hall	上海城市规划展示馆	*shànghăi chéngshì guīhuà zhănshìguăn*
Shanghai zoo	上海动物园	*shànghăi dòngwùyuán*
She Shan	佘山	*shéshān*
Shiji Dadao	世纪大道	*shìjì dàdào*
Shikumen Open House Museum	石库门民居陈列馆	*shíkùmén mínjū chénlièguăn*
Song Qingling's Former Residence	宋庆龄故居	*sòngqìnglíng gùjū*
Sun Yatsen Memorial Residence	孙中山故居	*sūnzhōngshān gùjū*
The Old City	南市区	*nánshì qū*
Tung Feng Hotel	东风饭店	*dōngfēng fàndiàn*
Tomorrow Square	明天广场	*míngtiān guăngchăng*
Waibaidu Bridge	外白渡桥	*wàibáidù qiáo*
Xiangyang Market	襄阳服饰市场	*xiāngyáng fúshì shìchăng*
Xintiandi	新天地	*xīntiāndì*
Xujiahui Cathedral	徐家汇天主教堂	*xújiāhuì tiānzhŭ jiàotáng*
Yu Yuan	豫园	*yùyuán*
Yufo Si	玉佛寺	*yùfó sì*
Zendai Museum of Modern Art	证大现代艺术馆	*zhèngdà xiàndài yìshùguăn*
Zhou Enlai's Former Residence	周恩来故居	*zhōu'ēnlái gùjū*
Zhouzhuang	周庄	*zhōuzhuāng*

The Peace Hotel and the Bank of China

Straddling the eastern end of Nanjing Lu is one of the most famous hotels in China, the **Peace Hotel**, formerly the *Cathay Hotel*. The hotel's main building (on the north side of Nanjing Lu) is a relic of another great trading house, **Sassoon's**, and was originally known as Sassoon House. Like Jardine's, the Sassoon business empire was built on opium trading, but by the early years of the last century, the family fortune had mostly been sunk into Shanghai real estate, including the *Cathay*. The place to be seen in prewar Shanghai, it offered guests a private plumbing system fed by a spring on the outskirts of town, marble baths with silver taps, and vitreous china lavatories imported from Britain. Noel Coward is supposed to have stayed here while writing *Private Lives*. Sassoon lived long enough to see his hotel virtually destroyed by the Japanese, including his rooftop private apartment, with 360-degree views and dark oak panelling (it has

Huangpu River tours

One highlight of a visit to Shanghai, and the easiest way to view the edifices of the Bund, is to take one of the Huangpu River tours. These leave a wharf near the end of Nanjing Dong Lu. You can book tickets at the jetty (daily 8am–4.30pm).

The hour-long round trip south to the Yanpu Bridge costs ¥45, while the slightly longer trip to Nanpu Bridge costs ¥65 and takes two hours, but the classic cruise here is the three-hour-long, sixty-kilometre journey to the mouth of the **Yangzi** and back. There are departures daily at 9am and 2pm, and tickets cost between ¥90 and ¥120, with the higher prices offering armchairs, a higher deck, tea and snacks. On this, you're introduced to the vast amount of shipping that uses the port, and you'll also be able to inspect all the paraphernalia of the shipping industry, from sampans and rusty old Panamanian-registered freighters to sparkling Chinese navy vessels. You'll also get an idea of the colossal construction that is taking place on the eastern shore, before you reach the mouth of the Yangzi River itself, where the wind kicks in and it feels like you're almost in open sea. There are also two-hour-long **night cruises**, with boats departing at 7 and 8.30pm (¥78; ¥150 with buffet dinner). Note that tours do not run in foggy or windy weather (for current information, call ⓣ021/63744461).

Finally, it's also possible to take boat tours from a wharf in Pudong (see opposite).

recently been restored), but also long enough to get most of his money away to the Bahamas. The *Peace* today is worth a visit for a walk around the lobby and upper floors to take in the faded Art Deco elegance.

Next door to the *Peace*, at no. 19 on the Bund, the **Bank of China** was designed in the 1920s by Shanghai architectural firm Palmer & Turner, who brought in a Chinese architect to make the building "more Chinese" after construction was complete. The architect placed a Chinese roof onto the Art Deco edifice, creating a delightful juxtaposition of styles, an idea that is being endlessly and much less successfully copied across the nation today.

Number 18 The Bund was originally the Chartered Bank of India and Australia, but today is home to the city's ritziest shops, given gravitas by the building's Italian marble columns. If you want to spot Chinese celebrities (assuming you can recognize them), this is the place to be seen. As well as top-end retail outlets such as Younik (see p.392) and Cartier, the building houses an arts space and two ventures run by the Michelin-starred Pourcell brothers – the *Sens & Bund* restaurant and swanky *Bar Rouge* (see p.389) above, which has a fantastic roof terrace with views of Pudong.

The Customs House and points south

Further down the Bund, the **Customs House** is one of the few buildings to have retained its original function, though its distinctive clocktower was adapted to chime *The East is Red* at six o'clock every morning and evening during the Cultural Revolution (the original clockwork has since been restored). The clocktower was modelled on Big Ben, and after its completion in 1927, local legend had it that the chimes that struck each fifteen minutes confused the God of Fire: believing the chimes were a firebell, the god decided Shanghai was suffering from too many conflagrations, and decided not to send any more. You can step into the downstairs lobby for a peek at some faded mosaics of maritime motifs on the ceiling.

Right next to this, and also with an easily recognizable domed roofline, the former headquarters of the **Hong Kong and Shanghai Bank** (built in 1921) has one of the most imposing of the Bund facades. Each wall of the marble octagonal entrance originally boasted a mural depicting the Bank's eight primary locations: Bangkok, Calcutta, Hong Kong, London, New York, Paris, Shanghai and Tokyo. It's considered lucky to rub the noses of the bronze lions that stand guard outside. The small door north of the main entrance will get you to the second-floor *Bonomi* café (see p.384), a good place for a break.

Cross Fuzhou Lu and you'll come to some very posh addresses. Most of number five (officially "**Five on the Bund**") is home to the Huaxia Bank but on Guangdong Lu you'll find the entrance to the building's upscale restaurant, *M on the Bund* (see p.385). Opened in 1999, it kicked off the zone's present revival. A little further down, **Three on the Bund** is perhaps the most luxurious of the new developments: there's an Armani flagship store, Evian spa and three swish restaurants, including *Whampoa Club*.

The east bank of the Huangpu: Pudong district

Historically, **Pudong** has been known as the "wrong side of the Huangpu" – before 1949, the area was characterized by unemployed migrants, prostitution, murders, and the most appalling living conditions in the city. It was here that bankrupt gamblers would *tiao huangpu*, commit suicide by drowning themselves in the river. Shanghai's top gangster, Du Yuesheng, more commonly known as "Big-eared Du", learned his trade growing up in this rough section of town. In 1990, however, fifteen years after China's economic reforms started, it was finally decided to grant the status of Special Economic Zone (SEZ) to this large tract of mainly agricultural land, a decision which, more than any other, is now fuelling Shanghai's rocket-like economic advance. The skyline has since been completely transformed from a stream of rice paddies into a sea of cranes, and ultimately a maze of skyscrapers that seemingly stretches east as far as the eye can see.

The bustling street life that so animates the rest of Shanghai is striking by its absence, but if you know where you're going, Pudong can be very rewarding. There are two areas that are really interesting; the first is the battery of skyscrapers in Lujiazui, just across the water from the Bund, where you'll find the bulbous Oriental Pearl TV Tower and the elegant Jinmao Tower, both of which offer sublime views across the city. Several museums have been plonked here, to take advantage of the huge crowds of Chinese tourists who flock to the Pearl TV Tower. Of these, the Museum of History is fun, and the China Sex Culture Exhibition is intriguing.

From Liujiazui, the eight-lane Century Avenue zooms for 4km to one of the city's few spacious green spaces, Century Park, where you'll find the Science and Technology Museum, the Oriental Arts Centre and, further out, the Zendai Museum of Modern Art.

Getting to Pudong

The simplest way to reach the area is to catch the metro, which whooshes passengers from Renmin Square to downtown Pudong in less than three minutes; otherwise, several minibuses cross under the river using the Yan'an Dong Lu tunnel. For a more picturesque trip, catch the very frequent double-decker **ferry** from the Bund opposite the eastern end of Jinling Lu (¥1). The lower deck gives a better feel for how crowded these waterways are. There's also a **Tourist Tunnel** under the river (entrance in the metro opposite Beijing Dong Lu; ¥20 one way, ¥30 return), in which you're driven past a silly light show.

Lujiazui

Lujiazui is, above all, an area of **commerce**, with few activities of interest to the visitor besides giving your neck a good workout as you gaze upwards at the skyline. Ascending the 457-metre-high **Oriental Pearl TV Tower** (daily 8am–9.30pm; ¥70 to go to the top bauble) to admire the giddying views has become a mandatory pilgrimage for most Chinese visitors to Shanghai, despite the ridiculously high entrance fee and long queue for the lift.

You can get a similar view for less by ascending to the observation platform at the top of the **Jinmao Tower** (daily 7am–9.30pm; ¥50; enter from the building's north side), although there are also great (free) views to be had by going in the front door (in the east) and up to the hotel lobby on the 54th floor, where you can take advantage of the *Hyatt*'s comfy, window-side chairs. But to observe the panorama in style, put on your best clothes and pay a night-time trip to the hotel bar *Cloud Nine*, on the eighty-seventh floor of the same building (see p.390).

The riverside promenade, **Binjiang Dadao**, is close enough to the Huangpo to hear the slap of the water, and it's the only place in Liujiazui where a walk

▲ Jinmao Tower

can feel rewarding. The north end of the promenade is close to the exit of the Bund Tourist Tunnel, and it's here where you will find the absorbing **China Sex Culture Exhibition** (daily 8am–10pm; ¥20), the private collection of a single-minded academic, Liu Dalin. As well as plenty of rather twee pornographic images and jade phalluses, there is a "widow's pillow" – a headrest with a secret dildo compartment – a tool for expanding anuses, a knife used to turn men into eunuchs, and a saddle with a wooden stump for punishing adulterous women. It's the only museum of its kind in China and corporate Pudong seems an incongruous place to put it.

Century Park and around

Shiji Dadao (Century Boulevard) runs arrow-straight for 4km to Century Park, one of Shanghai's largest green spaces. The simplest way to get here is on the metro; the Shanghai Science and Technology Museum stop (labelled in English) is three stops east of Lujiazui, and just north of the park. There are some striking new buildings here, not high-rises for once, foremost among which is the **Science and Technology Museum** itself (daily 9am–5pm; ¥60, students ¥45), though it's rather too big perhaps, as the cavernous halls make some of the twelve exhibitions look threadbare – there isn't much English explanation or quite enough interactivity. The section on space exploration is good – a big topic in China right now, with the nation fully intending to get to the moon as soon as possible – with real spacesuits, models of spacecraft and the like, and in the section on robots you can take on a robotic arm at archery and play a computer at Go. The most interesting sections, however, are the cinemas: the space theatre (every 40min; ¥40) shows astronomical films; the two IMAX domes in the basement (hourly 10.30am–4.30pm; ¥40) show cartoons; while the IWERKS dome on the first floor (every 40min; ¥30) is an attempt to take the concept of immersive realism even further – as well as surround sound and images there are moving seats, and water and wind effects.

Just north of the museum, the **Oriental Arts Centre** is a magnificent, glass-faced, flower-shaped building that houses a concert hall, opera theatre, exhibition space and performance hall – they're the petals. It was designed by French architect Paul Andrea, who also created the new opera house in Beijing. Locals complain that it's a white elephant – it cost more than a billion yuan, has huge maintainence costs and doesn't get a great deal of use (see p.392).

From here it's a pleasant ten-minute stroll along a pedestrian walkway to **Century Park** (though the park also has its own metro stop). The park is spacious, the air is clean and it's possible to feel that you have escaped the city. You can hire a tandem bike (¥20/hr) – sadly you're not allowed to ride your own bicycle – and pedalos are available to rent on the central lake (25¥/hr).

Nanjing Lu and around

Stretching west from the Bund through the heart of Shanghai lie the main commercial streets of the city, among them one of the two premier shopping streets, **Nanjing Lu**, with its two major parallel arteries, **Fuzhou Lu** and **Yan'an Lu**. In the days of the foreign concessions, expatriates described Nanjing Lu as a cross between Broadway and Oxford Street. It was also at this time that Nanjing Lu and Fuzhou Lu housed numerous teahouses that functioned as the city's most exclusive brothels. Geisha-like *shuyu* (singer/storyteller girls) would saunter from teahouse to teahouse, performing classical plays and scenes from operas, and host banquets for guests. In a juxtaposition symbolic

Warning: the tea scam

Foreigners in tourist areas of Shanghai will inevitably be approached by young girls and sweet-looking couples claiming to be art students or asking to practise their English. They are very skilled scam artists, and their aim is to befriend you, then coax you into visiting a bogus art gallery or teahouse. After a few cups of tea, you'll be presented with a bill for hundreds or even thousands of yuan, your new friends will disappear and some large gentlemen will appear. Never drink with a stranger unless you've seen a price list.

of prewar Shanghai's extremes, strings of the lowest form of brothel, nicknamed *dingpeng* ("nail sheds" because the sex, at ¥0.3, was "as quick as driving nails"), lay just two blocks north of Nanjing Dong Lu, along Suzhou Creek. The street was dubbed "Blood Alley" for the nightly fights between sailors on leave who congregated here.

Nanjing Dong Lu

On its eastern stretch, **Nanjing Dong Lu**'s garish neon lights and window displays are iconic; come here in the evening to appreciate the lightshow in its full tacky splendour. But the shopping is not what it once was, with the emphasis now firmly on cheap rather than chic.

Number 635 was once the glorious **Wing On** emporium, and diagonally opposite was the **Sincere**. These were not just stores: inside, there were restaurants, rooftop gardens, cabarets and even hotels. The **Shanghai Department Store** near Guizhou Lu at no. 800, once the largest in China, is still going, and is still a place of pilgrimage for out-of-towners, but it's nothing like as spectacular as it was. Off the circular overhead walkway at the junction between Nanjing Dong Lu and Xizang Zhong Lu, just northeast of Renmin Park, is the grandest of the district's department stores, the venerable **Shanghai No. 1 Store**.

If you're looking for cheap clothes, you'll be spoilt for choice, but for something distinctly Chinese you'll have to look a bit harder. Your best bet for curiosities is to head to the **Shanghai First Food Store** at the west end of the street, at no. 720. The Chinese often buy food as a souvenir, and this busy store sells all kinds of locally made gift-wrapped sweets, cakes and preserves, as well as tea and tasty pastries.

Renmin Square

Its perimeters defined by the city's main arteries – Xizang, Nanjing and Yan'an roads – **Renmin Square**, or People's Square, is the modern heart of Shanghai. The area of Renmin Square was originally the site of the Shanghai racecourse, built by the British in 1862. The races became so popular among the foreign population that most businesses closed for the ten-day periods of the twice-yearly meets. They soon caught on with the Chinese, too, so that by the 1920s the Shanghai Race Club was the third wealthiest foreign corporation in China. It was converted into a sports arena in 1941 by Chiang Kaishek, who thought gambling immoral. During World War II the stadium served as a holding camp for prisoners and as a temporary mortuary; afterwards, most of it was levelled, and while the north part was landscaped to create Renmin Park, the rest was paved to form a dusty concrete parade ground for political rallies. Only the racecourse's clubhouse survives, as the venue for the Shanghai Art Museum.

There's an impressive clutch of sights, with the Shanghai Museum, Museum of Urban Planning, Shanghai Art Museum and little Museum of Contemporary Art all within walking distance of each other. Add to that an unexpectedly peaceful park, and you have one of Shanghai's most rewarding destinations.

The easiest way to get here is on the metro, as Renmin Square is at the interchange of lines #1 and #2.

The Shanghai Museum

The unmistakeable pot-shaped **Shanghai Museum** (daily 9am–5pm; ¥20, students ¥5; audio-guide ¥40, with ¥400 deposit) is one of the city's highlights, with a fantastic, well-presented collection. On the ground floor, the gallery of ancient **bronzes** holds cooking vessels, containers and weapons, many covered with intricate geometrical designs that reference animal shapes – check out the cowrie container from the Western Han dynasty, with handles shaped like stalking tigers. Most of the exhibits in the sculpture gallery next door are of religious figures – boggle-eyed temple guardians, serene Buddhas and the like, including a row of huge, fearsome Tang-dynasty heads. Tang-dynasty figurines again steal the show in the first-floor ceramics gallery, in the form of multi-coloured ferocious-looking beasties placed to guard tombs.

On the second floor, skip the calligraphy and carved seals unless you have a special interest and investigate the **painting** gallery, which shows some amazingly naturalistic Ming-dynasty images of animals. The colourful top-floor exhibition dedicated to Chinese **minority peoples** is the museum highlight. One wall is lined with spooky lacquered masks from Tibet and Guizhou, while nearby are colourfully decorated boats from the Taiwanese minority, the Gaoshan. The silver ceremonial headdresses of southwest China's Miao people are breathtaking for their intricacy, if rather impractical to wear. Elaborate abstract designs turn the Dai lacquered tableware into art. In the section on traditional costumes, look out for the fish-skin suit made by the Hezhen people of Dongbei, in the far north.

Shanghai Urban Planning Exhibition Hall and Shanghai Grand Theatre

It's revealing of the Shanghai mindset that one of the city's grandest museums is dedicated not to the past but the future: the **Shanghai Urban Planning Exhibition Hall** (daily 9am–5pm; ¥40) is interesting for its insight into the grand ambitions and the vision of the city planners, though if you're not keen on slick propaganda presentations it can be safely skipped. Most worthy of note is the tennis-court-sized model of the city on the second floor, showing what it will (hopefully) look like in 2020. There's no room in this brave new world for shabby little alleyways; it's a parade ground of skyscrapers and apartment blocks in which, according to this model, the whole of the Old City (see p.374) is doomed. Look out for the giant ferris wheel at the northern end of the Bund. Other as yet unbuilt structures are shown in transparent plastic.

Continuing west from here, past frumpy City Hall, brings you to the impressive **Shanghai Grand Theatre**, distinguished by its convex roof and transparent walls and pillars (see p.392). If you're just passing, there's a café on site, and a good shop sells reasonably priced DVDs and CDs.

Shanghai Art Museum

Past the Grand Theatre, turning right along Huangpi Bei Lu will bring you to the **Shanghai Art Museum** (Tues–Sun 9am–5pm, no entry after 4pm; ¥20;

Ⓦ www.cnarts.net/shanghaiart), whose distinctive clocktower was once nicknamed "Little Ben". You can see hints of its former function as the racecourse clubhouse in the equestrian detailing on the balustrades. There's no permanent exhibition, but its shows of contemporary art are always worth a wander round, and it's a must during the Biennale every other autumn (see p.391), when it's full of work by the hottest international artists and you'll have to queue to get in. The third-floor café is okay but you'd be better off heading up to *Kathleen's 5* restaurant (see p.385) on the top floor for afternoon tea and fantastic views over the square.

Renmin Park

Just east of the Art Museum is the north gate to lovely **Renmin Park**. It's surprisingly quiet, with rocky paths winding between shady groves and alongside ponds – the only sign that you are in the heart of a modern city is the skyscrapers looming above the treetops. Crossing the lotus pond brings you to the glass-walled **Museum of Contemporary Art** (MoCA; 10am–6pm; ¥20, students free; Ⓦ www.mocashanghai.org). This attractive, privately funded museum has no permanent collection but its themed shows are imaginatively curated, and the museum holds regular talks and tours; check the website for details.

Nanjing Xi Lu

The historic **Pacific** and **Park hotels** stand on Nanjing Xi Lu opposite Renmin Park. The *Park Hotel*, for many years the tallest building in Shanghai, once had a reputation for superb food as well as for its dances, when the roof would be rolled back to allow guests to cavort under the stars. Latterly, Mao Zedong always stayed here when he was in Shanghai. Today, however, it has been stripped of most of its old-world charm. The *Pacific Hotel*, by contrast, a few metres to the east of the *Park*, is still worth having a look at, both for its mighty and ostentatious facade and for the fabulous plaster reliefs in the lobby.

The western end of Nanjing Xi Lu was known to "Shanghailanders" (the Europeans who made their homes here) as Bubbling Well Road, after a spring that used to gush at the far end of the street. Then, as today, it was one of the smartest addresses in the city, leading into tree-lined streets where Westerners' mock-Tudor mansions sheltered behind high walls. Now it's also the location of a number of luxury hotels, including the **Shanghai Centre**, an ultra-modern complex of luxury shops, restaurants and residential flats centred around the five-star *Portman Hotel*.

Opposite the Shanghai Centre, the gigantic Stalinist wedding cake that is the **Exhibition Hall** is worth seeing for its colossal ornate entrance, decorated with columns patterned with red stars and capped by a gilded spire. Constructed by the Russians in 1954, it was originally known as the Palace of Sino-Soviet Friendship and housed a permanent exhibition of industrial products from the Shanghai area – in recent years, it has become a venue for trade fairs, most notably (and ironically, considering its history) the yearly "Millionaires Fair".

Also at this end of Nanjing Xi Lu, a few hundred metres west of the Shanghai Centre, **Jing'an Si** (daily 5am–5pm; ¥5) is a small active temple nestling beside the tiny Jing'an Park and under looming high-rises. Building work first began on the temple during the Three Kingdoms period, and its apparent obscurity belies its past as the richest Buddhist foundation in the city, headed by legendary abbot Khi Vehdu, who combined his abbotly duties with a gangster lifestyle. The abbot and his seven concubines were shadowed by White Russian bodyguards, each carrying a leather briefcase lined with bulletproof steel, to be used as a shield in case of attack. Today, the temple is the primary place of ancestral worship in the city, although an equal number of people come to pray for more material reasons – worshippers eagerly throw coins into incense burners, in the hope that the gods will bestow financial success. Bus #20 runs here from Renmin Square, while a stop on metro line #2 lies underneath.

Yufo Si

Three kilometres north of the Jing'an Si is the **Yufo Si**, the **Jade Buddha Temple** (daily, 8am–5pm; ¥15), a much more interesting and attractive complex. The pretty temple buildings have flying eaves, complicated brackets and intricate roof and ceiling decorations. It's a lively place of worship, with gusts of incense billowing from the central burner, and worshippers kowtowing before effigies and tying red ribbons to the branches of trees, decorative bells and the stone lions on the railings.

The star attractions here, though, are the relics. Two jade Buddhas were brought here from Burma in the 1882, and the temple was built to house them. The larger, at nearly 2m tall, sits in its own separate building in the north of the temple, and costs an extra ¥10 to see. It was carved from a single block of milky-white jade and is encrusted with agate and emerald. The second statue, in the Western Hall, is a little smaller, around a metre long, but easier to respond to. It shows a recumbent Buddha, at the point of dying (or rather entering nirvana), with a languid expression on his face, like a man dropping off after a good meal.

The central Great Treasure Hall holds three huge figures of the past, present and future Buddhas, as well as the temple drum and bell. The gods of the twenty heavens, decorated with gold leaf, line the hall like guests at a celestial cocktail party, and a curvaceous copper Guanyin stands at the back. It's all something of a retreat from the material obsessions outside, but it's still Shanghai; religious trinkets, such as fake money for burning and Buddhas festooned with flashing lights, are for sale everywhere and the monks are doing a roaring trade flogging blessings.

Moganshan Art District

An old factory beside Suzhou Creek in the north of the city, 3km northeast of the Yufo Temple, **Moganshan Art District** is a complex of studios and galleries that makes up the city's biggest arts scene. The nearest metro stop to Moganshan is at Shanghai Zhan, a ten-minute walk away; otherwise, you'll have to take a taxi.

Attracted by cheap rents, artists took over the abandoned buildings at 50 Moganshan Lu and used them as studios. Then the art galleries moved in, and now the design studios and cafés and more commercial galleries are arriving. What makes it so fascinating – at the moment – is the way the area is both shabby and sophisticated, jumbling together paint-spattered artists, slick dealers, pretentious fashionistas and baffled locals. Most of the smaller galleries double as studios and there's something for all tastes, so expect to spend at least a morning poking around.

Note that many of the galleries are closed on Mondays, and that there's a map on the wall to the right of the entrance. Of the 35 or so **galleries**, one of the biggest is Eastlink (daily 10am–5.30pm; ⓣ021/62769932, ⓦwww.eastlinkgallery.cn) on the fifth floor of Building 6; it's the oldest gallery here, resolutely resisting commercial pressures to water down its content. Another heavy hitter is ShangART (daily 10am–6pm; ⓣ021/63593923, ⓦwww.shangartgallery.com), housed in buildings 16 and 18. The most credible gallery is the Bizart Centre on the fourth floor of Building 7 (Mon–Sat 11am–6pm; ⓣ021/62775358, ⓦwww.biz-art.com); it's a not-for-profit gallery that promotes Chinese and foreign contemporary art, with an artist-in-residence programme. The ArtSea Studio and Gallery, on the second floor of Building 9 (Wed–Sun 10am–6pm; ⓣ021/62278380) is the best photography gallery.

The Old City

The **Old City** is that strange oval on the map, circumscribed by two roads, Renmin Lu and Zhonghua Lu, which follow the old path of the city walls. The **Old City** never formed part of the International Settlement and was known by the foreigners who lived in Shanghai, somewhat contemptuously, as the **Chinese City**. Based on the original **walled city** of Shanghai, which dated back to the eleventh century, the area was reserved in the nineteenth and early twentieth centuries as a ghetto for vast numbers of Chinese who lived in conditions of appalling squalor, while the foreigners carved out their living space around them. The easiest approach from Nanjing Dong Lu is to walk due south along Henan Lu or Sichuan Lu.

Tree-lined ring roads had already replaced the original walls and moats as early as 1912, and sanitation has obviously improved vastly since the last century, but to cross the boundaries into the Old City is still to enter a different world. The twisting alleyways are a haven of free enterprise, bursting with makeshift markets selling fish, vegetables, cheap trinkets, clothing and food. Ironically, for a tourist entering the area, the feeling is like entering a Chinatown in a Western city. The centre of activity today is an area known locally as **Chenghuang Miao** (after a local temple), surrounding the two most famous and crowded tourist sights in the whole city, the Yu Yuan and the *Huxin Ting* teahouse, both located right in the middle of a new, touristy bazaar that caters to the Chinese visitors who pour into the area. "Antiques", scrolls and kitsch souvenirs feature prominently, and there are also lots of good places to eat Shanghainese *dianxin*, some more reasonable than others (see "Restaurants", p.385).

Yu Yuan

A classical Chinese garden featuring pools, walkways, bridges and rockeries, the **Yu Yuan** (Jade Garden; daily 8.30am–5.30pm; ¥40) was created in the sixteenth century by a high official in the imperial court in honour of his father. The Yu Yuan is less impressive than the gardens of nearby Suzhou, but given that it predates the relics of the International Settlement by some three hundred years, the Shanghainese are understandably proud of it. Despite fluctuating fortunes, the garden has surprisingly survived the passage of the centuries. It was spared from its greatest crisis – the Cultural Revolution – apparently because the anti-imperialist "Little Sword Society" had used it as their headquarters in 1853 during the Taiping Uprising. Garden connoisseurs today will appreciate the whitewashed walls topped by undulating dragons made of tiles, and the huge, craggy and indented rock in front of the Yuhua Tang (Hall of Jade Magnificence). During the Lantern Festival on the fifteenth day of the traditional New

Year, ten thousand lanterns (and an even larger number of spectators) brighten up the garden.

After visiting the garden, you can check out the delightful **Huxin Ting** (Heart of Lake Pavilion; daily 8am–9pm), a two-storey teahouse on an island at the centre of an ornamental lake, reached by a zigzagging bridge. The Queen of England and Bill Clinton, among other illustrious guests, have dropped in for tea. These days it's a bit pricey at ¥50 for a limitless cup of tea, but you're welcome to poke about.

The antique markets

If you're in Chenghuang Miao early on Sunday morning (8–11am is the best time, though trade continues into mid-afternoon), you can visit a great **Sunday market** on Fuyou Lu, the small street running east–west along the northern edge of Yu Yuan. The market has a raw, entrepreneurial feel about it; all sorts of curios and antiques – mostly fakes – ranging from jade trinkets to Little Red Books can be found here, though you'll have to bargain fiercely if you want to buy.

Just outside the Old City, in a small alley called Dongtai Lu leading west off Xizang Nan Lu, is the largest permanent **antique market** in Shanghai (daily 10am–4pm), and possibly in all China. Even if you're not interested in buying, this is a fascinating area to walk around. The range is vast, from old Buddhas, coins, vases and teapots to mahjong sets, renovated furniture and Cultural Revolution badges. As with all antique markets in China, the vast majority of goods are fake.

The former French Concession

Established in the mid-nineteenth century, the **former French Concession** lay to the south and west of the International Settlement, abutting the Chinese City. Despite its name, it was never particularly French: before 1949, in fact, it was a low-rent district mainly inhabited by Chinese and White Russians. Other Westerners looked down on the latter as they were obliged to take jobs that, it was felt, should have been left to the Chinese.

The French Concession was notorious for its lawlessness and the ease with which police and French officials could be bribed, in contrast to the well-governed areas dominated by the British. This made it ideal territory for gangsters, including the king of all Shanghai mobsters, Du Yuesheng, the right-hand man of Huang Jinrong. For similar reasons, **political activists** also operated in this sector – the first meeting of the Chinese Communist Party took place here in 1921, and both Zhou Enlai and Sun Yatsen, the first provisional President of the Republic of China after the overthrow of the Qing dynasty, lived here. The preserved former homes of these two in particular (see below) are worth visiting simply because, better than anywhere else in modern Shanghai, they give a sense of how the Westerners, and the Westernized, used to live.

Certain French characteristics have lingered here, in the local chic and in a taste for bread and sweet cakes – exemplified in **Huaihai Lu**, the main street running through the heart of the area. Not as crowded as Nanjing Lu, Huaihai Lu is considerably more upmarket, particularly in the area around **Maoming Lu** and **Shanxi Lu**, where fashion boutiques, extremely expensive department stores and excellent cake shops abound.

▲ Cyclists in the former French Concession

Xintiandi

Although it might seem like an obvious idea, the **Xintiandi** development, which comprises two blocks of renovated and rebuilt *shikumen* converted into a genteel open-air mall, was the first of its kind in China. It has met with such success that now town planners all over the country are studying its winning formula. Paved and pedestrianized, with narrow lanes (*longtang*) opening out onto a central plaza, Xintiandi is a great place to wind down or linger over a coffee, with upscale restaurants (see p.387) and shops (see p.392) and plenty of outside seating for people-watching. The easiest way to get here is to take the metro to Huangpi Nan Lu and walk south for five minutes.

Shikumen Open House Museum

The **Shikumen Open House Museum** (daily 10am–10pm; ¥20), at the bottom end of Xintiandi north block, does an excellent job of evoking early twentieth-century Chinese gentility. This reconstruction of a typical *shikumen* is filled with everyday objects – typewriters, toys, a four-poster bed and the like – so it doesn't look as bare as the "former residences" elsewhere in the city. A top-floor display details how Xintiandi came about, admitting that most of it was built from scratch. A quote on the wall is perhaps more revealing than was intended: "Foreigners find it Chinese and Chinese find it foreign."

The First National Congress of the Chinese Communist Party

On the east side of the complex, at the junction of Xingye Lu and Huangpi Nan Lu, you'll find, rather incongruously, one of the shrines of Maoist China, the **First National Congress of the Chinese Communist Party** (daily 9am–5pm, last admission 4pm; ¥3). The official story of this house is that on July 23, 1921, thirteen representatives of the Communist cells that had developed all over China, including its most famous junior participant, Mao Zedong, met here to discuss the formation of a national party. The meeting was discovered by a French police agent (it was illegal to hold political meetings in the French Concession), and on July 30 the delegates fled north to nearby Zhejiang province, where they resumed their talks in a boat on Nan Hu. Quite how much of this really happened is unclear, but it seems probable that there were in fact more delegates than the record remembers – the missing names would have been expunged according to subsequent political circumstances. There's a little exhibition hall downstairs, where relics from the period such as maps, money and a British policeman's uniform and truncheon are more interesting than the comically outdated propaganda rants. The last room has a waxwork diorama of Mao and his fellow delegates.

The former residences

From Xintiandi it's a short walk to Sinan Lu, where you'll find the **Former Residence of Sun Yatsen**, the first president of the Chinese Republic, and his wife, Song Qingling (daily 9am–4.30pm; ¥8). The dry exhibition of the man's books and artefacts is nothing special, but just as an example of an elegantly furnished period house it is worth a look.

Head south down Sinan Lu and you enter a smart neighbourhood of old houses. Five minutes' walk brings you to one you can get into, the **Former Residence of Zhou Enlai** at no. 73 (daily 9am–4pm; ¥2). Zhou was Mao's right-hand man, but he has always been looked on with rather more affection than the Chairman. When he lived here he was head of the Shanghai Communist Party, and as such was kept under surveillance from a secret outpost over the road. There's not, in truth, a great deal to see, beyond a lot of hard beds on a nice wooden floor. The house has a terrace at the back with rattan chairs and polished wooden floors, and its garden, with hedges and ivy-covered walls, could easily be a part of 1930s suburban London.

Ruijin Lu and Maoming Lu

Heading west, the south section of **Ruijin Er Lu** is busy and cramped but there's a wonderful escape in the form of the stately **Ruijin Guesthouse**, just south of Fuxing Zhong Lu. This Tudor-style country manor was home in the early twentieth century to the Morris family, owners of the *North China Daily News*; Mr Morris raised greyhounds for the Shanghai Race Club and the former Canidrome dog track across the street. The house, having miraculously escaped severe damage during the Cultural Revolution because certain high-ranking officials used it as their private residence, has now been turned into a pleasant inn. Even if you're not a guest, you're free to walk around the spacious, quiet grounds, where it's hard to believe you're in the middle of one of the world's most hectic cities. Check out the sumptuous *Face Bar* (see p.390).

The two plush hotels north of here, the *Okura Garden* (see p.359) and the *Jinjiang* (see p.359), are worth a visit for glimpses of past luxuries. The *Okura*, originally the French Club, or Cercle Sportif Français, was taken over by the Americans during World War II and converted by the egalitarian communists into the People's Cultural Palace. Anyone can wander round the lovely gardens and go in to look at the sumptuous ceiling design of stained glass on the ballroom.

The *Jinjiang* compound opposite includes the former **Grosvenor Residence** complex, the most fashionable and pricey address in pre-World War II Shanghai. The Grosvenor has recently been modernized, but the *VIP Club* still retains much of its 1920s architecture and *Great Gatsby* ambience. Non-guests might be able to sneak a peek by taking the elevator to the top floor of the Old Wing of the *Jinjiang*, where the club is located, although gaining entrance to one of the twenty astonishingly beautiful refurbished Art Deco VIP mansion rooms on the floors directly below (a snip at US$800 per night), might prove slightly more difficult. Never mind; visit the excellent and much more affordable *Yin* restaurant instead (see p.389).

If you keep walking up Maoming Nan Lu you come to the Art Deco **Lyceum Theatre**, built in 1931 and once home to the British Amateur Dramatic Club. It now holds nightly acrobatic shows (see p.391).

Around Changshu Lu

West of Changshu Lu metro station you really get a good idea of what the French Concession is all about. Many of the villas here have been converted to embassy properties (the more sensitive are guarded by soldiers with fixed bayonets) and there are also plenty of upmarket, expat-oriented restaurants, a fair few beauty salons and, oddly, not that many shops. It's more a place to soak up atmosphere on a sunny day than to take in specific sights.

Fuxing Xi Lu is a discreetly charming street, typical of the area, with a winning combination of artsiness, idiosyncratic low-rise buildings and coffee stops. **Art Scene China**, an art gallery inside a restored villa, in an alley just off the southern side of the street, is always worth popping into. Their stable of artists produces painterly, tasteful work that's neither trendy nor gaudy. Have a look at the workshop of Shanghai Trio, next door, for cute bags. A little further up are cafés *Urban Tribe* (see p.384) and *Boonna* (see p.384); and the prestigious *Yongfu Elite* (see p.390), a great place for a pre-dinner cocktail, is just around the corner, too.

A pleasant ten-minute stroll away on Huashan Lu, the **Propaganda Poster Centre** (daily 9.30am–4.30pm; ¥20; ⓣ021/62111845) is an abrupt change of tone, providing a fascinating glimpse into communist China – you will not come across a more vivid evocation of the bad old days of Marx and Mao. To find the place, present yourself to the security guard at the entrance to 868 Huashan Lu. He'll give you a name card with a map on the back showing you which building in the complex beyond to head for – the centre is a basement flat in building 4. The walls are covered with Chinese socialist-realist posters, over three thousand examples arranged chronologically from the 1950s to the 1970s, which the curator will talk you round, whether or not you understand his Chinese. There are, fortunately, English captions. With slogans like "the Soviet Union is the stronghold of world peace" and "hail the over-fulfillment of steel production by ten million tons" and images of sturdy, lantern-jawed peasants and soldiers defeating big-nosed, green-skinned imperialists or riding tractors into a glorious future, the black-and-white world view of communism is dramatically realized.

Former Residence of Song Qingling

Some twenty minutes' walk southwest from Hengshan Lu metro station, at 1843 Huaihai Xi Lu, is the **Former Residence of Song Qingling** (daily 9–11am & 1–4.30pm; ¥8). As the wife of Sun Yatsen, Song Qingling was part of a bizarre family coterie – her sister Song Meiling was married to Chiang Kaishek and her brother, known as T.V. Soong, was finance minister to Chiang. Once again, the house is a charming step back into a residential Shanghai of the past, and although this time the trappings on display – including her official limousines parked in the garage – are largely post-1949, there is some lovely wood panelling and lacquerwork inside the house. Song Qingling lived here on and off from 1948 until her death in 1981.

Western Shanghai

In the west of the city, sights are too distant from one another to walk between. The main attractions are two **temples**, the rambling old Longhua Si to the southwest, and Yufo Si, which has superb statuary, to the northwest.

Due west from the city there is less to see; if you follow Nanjing Lu beyond Jing'an Si, it merges into Yan'an Lu, which (beyond the city ring road) eventually turns into Hongqiao Lu, the road that leads to the airport. Shortly before the airport it passes **Shanghai Zoo** (daily 6.30am–4.30pm; ¥20), a massive affair with more than two thousand animals and birds caged in conditions that, while not entirely wholesome, are better than in most Chinese zoos. The stars, inevitably, are the giant pandas. The zoo grounds used to serve as one of pre-1949 Shanghai's most exclusive golf courses. Next door, at 2409 Hongqiao Lu, stands the mansion that once functioned as the **Sassoons' home**, and which originally boasted a fireplace large enough to roast an ox; the central room, since renovated, resembled a medieval castle's Great Hall. Victor Sassoon, who used this mansion as a weekend residence (his other pad was the top-floor apartment of the *Peace Hotel*), only allowed for the design of two small bedrooms because he wanted to avoid potential overnight guests. It has served since as a Japanese naval HQ, a casino and as the private villa of the Gang of Four, but now suffers the relative ignominy of being rented out as office space. Bus #57 from the western end of Nanjing Lu will bring you out here. The side gate is sometimes open if you wish to take a peek.

The Xujiahui Catholic Cathedral

The **Xujiahui Catholic Cathedral** in the southwest of the city is one of many places of public worship that have received a new lease of life in recent years. Built in 1846 on the grave of Paul Xu Guangqi, Matteo Ricci's personal assistant and first Jesuit convert, it was closed for more than ten years during the Cultural Revolution, reopening in 1979. Most of the cathedral library's 200,000 volumes, as well as the cathedral's meteorological centre (built at the same time as the cathedral and now housing the Shanghai Municipal Meteorology Department), survive in the grounds.

Longhua Cemetery of Martyrs and Longhua Si

Southeast of the Xujiahui Cathedral, **Longhua Cemetery of Martyrs** (daily 6.30am–4pm; cemetery ¥1, exhibition hall ¥5) is a park commemorating those who died fighting for the cause of Chinese communism in the decades leading up to the final victory of 1949. In particular, it remembers those workers, activists and students massacred in Shanghai by Chiang Kaishek in the 1920s – the site of the cemetery is said to have been the main execution ground. In the centre is a glass-windowed, pyramid-shaped **exhibition hall** with a bombastic memorial to 250 communist martyrs who fought Chiang's forces. The cemetery is a short walk south from the terminus of bus #41, which you can catch from Huaihai Zhong Lu near Shanxi Nan Lu, or from Nanjing Xi Lu near the Shanghai Centre.

Right next to the Cemetery of Martyrs is one of Shanghai's main religious sites, the **Longhua Si** (daily 5.30am–4pm; ¥10), and its associated tenth-century pagoda. The **pagoda** itself is an octagonal structure about 40m high (until the feverish construction of bank buildings along the Bund in the 1910s, the pagoda was the tallest edifice in Shanghai), its seven brick storeys embellished with wooden balconies and red-lacquer pillars. After a long period of neglect (Red Guards saw it as a convenient structure to plaster with banners), an ambitious re-zoning project has spruced up the pagoda and created the tea gardens, greenery and shop stalls that now huddle around it.

Though there has been a temple on the site since the third century, the halls are only around a century old. It's the most active Buddhist site in the city, and a centre for training monks. On the right as you enter is a bell tower, where you can strike the bell for ¥10 to bring you good luck. On Chinese New Year, a monk bangs the bell 108 times, supposedly to ease the 108 "mundane worries" of Buddhist thought.

Botanical Gardens

Taking bus #56 south down the main road, Longwu Lu, just to the west of the Longhua Si site, will bring you to the **Botanical Gardens** (daily 7am–4pm; ¥15). More than nine thousand plants are on view in the gardens, including two pomegranate trees that are said to date from the reign of Emperor Qianlong in the eighteenth century; despite their antiquity, they still bear fruit. Look out, too, for the orchid chamber, where more than a hundred different varieties are on show.

North of Suzhou Creek

North across the Waibaidu Bridge from the Bund, you enter an area that, before the war, was the Japanese quarter of the International Settlement, and which since 1949 has been largely taken over by housing developments. The obvious interest lies in the Lu Xun Park area (also known as Hongkou Park), and its monuments to the political novelist Lu Xun, although the whole district is lively and architecturally interesting.

From East Baoxing road metro station, on line #3, it's a short walk to **Duolun Lu**, a heritage street of antique and bric-a-brac shops housed in elegant imitation Qing buildings. The best thing about it is the *Old Movie Café*, charmingly decorated with film posters, and the seven-storey **Duolun Museum of Modern Art** (Tues–Sun 10am–6pm; ¥10). There's no permanent show; check Ⓦ www.duolunart.com to see what's on.

Lu Xun Park (daily 6am–7pm), five minutes' stroll north of here, is one of the best places for observing Shanghainese at their most leisured. Between 6 and 8am, the masses undergo their daily *tai ji* workout; later in the day, amorous couples frolic on paddle boats in the park lagoon and old men teach their grandkids how to fly kites. The park is also home to the pompous **Tomb of Lu Xun**, complete with a seated statue and an inscription in Mao's calligraphy, which was erected here in 1956 to commemorate the fact that Lu Xun had spent the last ten years of his life in this part of Shanghai. The tomb went against Lu Xun's own wishes to be buried simply in a small grave in a western Shanghai cemetery. The novelist is further commemorated in the **Lu Xun Memorial Hall** (daily 9–11am & 1.30–4pm; ¥8), also in the park, to the right of the main entrance. Exhibits include original correspondence, among them letters and photographs from George Bernard Shaw.

A block southeast of the park on Shanyin Lu (Lane 132, House 9), the **Former Residence of Lu Xun** (daily 9am–4pm; ¥8) is worth going out of your way to see, especially if you have already visited the former residences of Zhou Enlai and Sun Yatsen in the French Concession (see p.377). The sparsely furnished house where Lu Xun and his wife and son lived from 1933 until his death in 1936 offers a fascinating glimpse into typical Japanese housing of the period – a good deal smaller than their European counterparts, but still surprisingly comfortable.

Outside the city

Shanghai Shi (Shanghai Municipality) covers approximately two thousand square kilometres, comprising ten counties and extending far beyond the limits of the city itself. Surprisingly, very little of this huge area is ever visited by foreign tourists, though there are a couple of interesting sights. Most can be visited by tour bus – services leave from 1111 Caoxi Bei Lu, near Shanghai Stadium.

The most obvious of these is **She Shan** (daily 7.30am–4pm; ¥5), about 30km southwest of the city. Such is the flatness of the surrounding land that the hill, which only rises about 100m, is visible for miles around; it's crowned by a huge and thoroughly impressive **basilica**, a legacy of the nineteenth-century European missionary work. The hill has been under the ownership of a **Catholic** community since the 1850s, though the present church was not built until 1925. Services take place only on Christian festivals; nevertheless, it's a pleasant walk up the hill at any time of year (or you can take the cable car if you prefer), past bamboo groves and the occasional ancient pagoda. Also on the hill is a meteorological station and an old observatory, which contains a small exhibition room displaying an ancient earthquake-detecting device – a dragon with steel balls in its mouth, which is so firmly set in the ground that only movement of the earth itself, from the vibrations of distant earthquakes, can cause the balls to drop out. The more balls drop, the more serious the earthquake. To reach She Shan, take a bus from the Wenhua Guangchang bus stop or the Xiqu bus station (see p.354), or take tour bus #1B (¥12).

Zhouzhuang

Another 20km west, just across the border in Jiangsu province, is the huddle of Ming architecture that comprises the small canal town of **ZHOUZHUANG** (¥120). Buses make the run from the tour-bus stop by Shanghai Stadium (1hr 30min; buses leave between 7 and 10am and return at around 4.30pm). Lying astride the large Jinghang Canal connecting Suzhou and Shanghai, Zhouzhuang grew prosperous from the area's brisk grain, silk and pottery trade during the Ming dynasty. Many rich government officials, scholars and artisans moved here and constructed beautiful villas, while investing money into developing the stately stone bridges and tree-lined canals that now provide the city's main attractions. Chinese tour groups invade Zhouzhuang in droves on weekends, but if you come on a weekday you should be able to appreciate the town in its serene, original splendour. There are no shortage of **places to eat**, all offering the local speciality of pig's trotters in sauce, which you can buy packaged up from souvenir stalls. It's possible to travel by speedboat from here to another canal town farther in Jiangsu, **Tongli** (see p.410), from where frequent buses complete the journey to Suzhou.

Eating, drinking, nightlife, entertainment and shopping

Food in Shanghai is fantastic; though there are fairly few options to eat cheap street food, most forms of international cuisine are widely available and there are plenty of classy **restaurants**. You're similarly spoilt for choice when it comes to entertainment; the arts scene has got considerably livelier of late, with a number of new arts centres and plenty of new galleries offering something for all tastes. The **bar and club scene** is excellent; though Beijing is the place to go for live music, Shanghai has the edge when it comes to clubbing. **Shopping** is another diverting pastime, with the best choice of souvenirs and consumables in the country; in particular, Shanghai has the best fashion stores in China.

Eating

If you are arriving from other areas of China, be prepared to be astounded by the excellent **diversity** of food in Shanghai, with most Chinese regional cuisines represented, as well as an equally impressive range of foreign cuisine, including Brazilian, Indian, Japanese and European. It's hard to believe that up until the early 1990s, simply getting a table in Shanghai was a cutthroat business.

Compared to, for example, Sichuan or Cantonese, **Shanghai cuisine** is not particularly well known or popular among foreigners. Most of the cooking is done with added ginger, sugar and Shaoxing wine, but without heavy spicing. There are some interesting dishes, especially if you enjoy exotic seafood. Fish and shrimps are considered basic to any respectable meal, and eels and crab may appear as well. In season (Oct–Dec), you may get the chance to try *dazha* crab, the most expensive and, supposedly, the most delicious. Inexpensive **snack food** is easily available in almost any part of the city at any time of night or day – try *xiao long bao*, a local dumpling speciality.

Breakfast, cafés and fast food

Mcdonalds, *KFC* and their ilk are everywhere; but rather better (and certainly healthier) are Asian fast-food chains *Yoshinoya* and *Ajisen* (for noodles). Every mall and shopping centre has a cluster of **fast-food restaurants**, either in the basement or on the top floor. A good one is in the basement of Raffles Mall on Fuzhou Lu; Megabite on the sixth floor is a huge food court.

Shanghai eating

1221	一二二一酒家	*yī èr èr yī jiǔjiā*
1931	一九三一饭店	*yījiǔsānyī fàndiàn*
Arch	玖间酒吧	*jiǔ jiān jiǔbā*
Bali Laguna	巴厘岛	*bā lǐ dǎo*
Bandu	半度音乐	*bàn dù yīnyuè*
Barbarossa	芭芭露莎	*bā bā lù shā*
Bi Feng Tang	避风塘	*bì fēng táng*
Bonomi	波诺米饭店	*bōnuòmǐ fàndiàn*
Charmant	小城故事	*xiǎochéng gùshì*
Citizen Bar and Café	天台餐厅	*tiāntái cāntīng*
Crystal Jade	翡翠酒家	*fěicuì jiǔjiā*
Dongbei Ren	东北人	*dōng běi rén*
Element Fresh	新元素	*xīn yuán sù*
Godly (Gongdelin)	功德林素食馆	*gōngdélín sùshíguǎn*
Guyi Hunan	古意湘味浓	*gǔ yì xiāng wèi nóng*
Hotpot King	来福楼	*láifú lóu*
Hubin Mei Shilou	湖滨美食楼	*húbīn měishílóu*
Kathleen's 5	赛马餐饮屋	*sài mǎ cānyǐnwū*
Kommune	公社酒吧	*gōngshè jiǔbā*
Lao Fandian	老饭店	*lǎo fàndiàn*
Lao Zhengxing	老振兴餐馆	*lǎo zhen xìng cānguǎn*
Lapis Lazuli	藏龙坊	*cáng lóng fāng*
M on the Bund	米氏西餐厅	*mǐshì xīcāntīng*
Meilongzhen	梅龙镇酒家	*méi lóng zhèn*
Mesa	梅萨	*méi sà*
Old China Hand Reading room	汉源书屋	*hàn yuán shū wū*
Old Film Café	老电影咖啡吧	*lǎo diàn yǐng kāfēibā*
Shen Yue Xuan	申粤轩饭店	*shēnyuè xuān fàndiàn*
Shintori	新都里餐厅	*xīndūlǐ cāntīng*
Shu Di La Zi Yu Guan	蜀地辣子鱼馆	*shǔdìlàzǐ yúguǎn*
Simply Thai	天泰餐厅	*tiāntài cāntīng*
South Beauty	俏江南	*qiào jiāng nán*
Vienna Café	维也纳咖啡馆	*wéi yě nà kāfēiguǎn*
Wagas	沃歌斯	*wò gē sī*
Wang Baohe	王宝和酒家	*wáng bǎo hé jiǔjiā*
Whisk	威斯忌	*weì sī jì*
Xiao Shaoxing	小绍兴饭店	*xiǎo shàoxīng fàndiàn*
Xinjishi (Jesse)	新吉士餐厅	*xīn jí shì cāntīng*
Ye Shanghai	夜上海	*yè shàng hǎi*
Yin	音	*yīn*
Yuanlu Huizhuan Shousi	元绿回转寿司	*yuán lǜ huí zhuǎn shòusī*
Yuxin Sichuan Dish	渝信川菜	*yúxìn chuāncài*
Zentral	膳趣饭店	*shànqù fàndiàn*

Shanghai, it needs to be noted, does **cafés** very well. As any tourist itinerary here involves lots of fairly unstructured wandering around, visitors might find themselves spending more time than they thought people-watching over a cappuccino. All the cafés listed below have free Wi-Fi.

Finally, many visitors find the Chinese breakfast of glutinous rice and fried dough sticks unpalatable; fortunately, there are plenty of places for a good western breakfast – best are *Wagas*, *Zentral* and *Element Fresh* (see below).

Arch 439 Wukang Lu, on the corner of Huaihai Zhong Lu. This stylish café is well loved by the media set. Good burgers (¥40), cheesecake (¥25) and smoothies (¥35). It's more like a bar at night, with a decent range of European beers. Daily 10.30am–2am.

Bandu 50 Moganshan Lu, near Changhua Lu. The best of the Moganshan Art District (see p.373) cafés, this intimate hideaway hosts performances of Chinese folk music every Saturday at 8pm. Daily 11am–11pm.

Barbarossa 231 Nanjing Xi Lu, inside Renmin Park. This mellow, onion-domed Arabian fantasy is beautifully situated by the lotus pond in Renmin Park. It's also a bar and a restaurant, but don't eat here as the food is overpriced. Makes a great pitstop for anyone doing the sights in nearby Renmin Square. Daily 10.30am–2am.

Bonomi Room 226, 12 Zhongshan Dong Yi Lu; *Hengshan Moller Villa*, 30 Shaanxi Nan Lu, just north of Julu Lu. This stylish Italian chain is a winner thanks to their fantastic locations. The one on the Bund, secreted on the second floor of the former HSBC, feels like a secret club, and there's a nice terrace, too. The branch inside the *Hengshan Moller Villa* (see p.358) also has a lovely terrace, overlooking the garden. You won't mind paying ¥25 for a coffee with views like this. Daily 8am–10pm.

Boonna I and II 88 Xinle Lu; 57 Fuxing Xi Lu. Writing a business plan on an Apple iMac is not mandatory at these artsy little cafés but would certainly help you fit in. The paintings and photos are all for sale. Afternoon tea is ¥28.

Citizen Bar and Café 222 Jinxian Lu ⓣ021/62581620. A great continental-style café tucked away in a gentrified neighbourhood. A good brunch place, with a wide choice of bar snacks, and a very civilized venue for a pre-dinner cocktail and a slice of apple pie. Daily 11am–1am.

Element Fresh Shanghai Centre (east side), 1376 Nanjing Xi Lu daily 7am–11pm; fourth floor, KWah Centre, 1028 Huaihai Zhong Lu daily 7am–11pm; Unit 2, second floor, Headquarters Building, 168 Xi Zang Zhong Lu (by Renmin Square) daily 7am–7pm; ⓦwww.elementfresh.com. This airy, informal bistro is the best place in town for a Western breakfast (note that they're open early), with plenty of options both hearty and healthy; it won't cost you more than ¥50 and includes limitless coffee. The branch near Renmin Square, inside an office block south of Fuzhou Lu, is a good place for a light lunch.

Kommune 210 Taikang Road, Building 7, near Sinan Lu. Hip café hidden at the heart of Taikang Lu Shopping Street (see p.393) – head north up the alley, take the first left and it's just there. Very popular with the designer set, especially for weekend brunch, when the courtyard outside fills up. Deli sandwiches for ¥38. Daily 9am–10pm.

Old China Hand Reading Room 27 Shaoxing Lu, by Shanxi Nan Lu ⓣ021/64732526. Bookish but not fusty, this is the place to come for leisured reflection. There's a huge collection of tomes to peruse or buy, many printed by the café press, which specializes in coffee-table books about French Concession architecture. Daily 10am–midnight.

Old Film Café 123 Duolun Lu, by Sichuan Bei Lu ⓣ021/5696 4763. If you're in the area, this charming old house full of period detail and wallpapered with old film ads is great for refreshments. Film buffs will be excited by the possibility of screening their fine collection of old Chinese and Russian films – just ask the owner.

Starbucks House 18, North Block Xintiandi, Lane 181 Taicang Lu, by Madang Lu; Binjiang Da Dao Fu Du Duan. The coffee colonizers have spread all over the city, so you're never far from an overpriced shot of caffeinated mud. The two stores above are the best, notable for having pleasant outdoor seating.

Vienna Café 25 Shaoxing Lu, near Ruijin Lu ⓦwww.viennashanghai.com. Popular and charming Austrian-style French Concession café, almost managing that *fin-de-siècle* vibe. You can't fault their strudel or *Kaiserchmarn* – pancake served with apple sauce. Daily 8am–8pm.

Wagas Shop G107, Hong Kong World Plaza, 300 Huaihai Zhong Lu; CITIC Square basement, 1168 Nanjing Xi Lu, near Jiangning Lu. Good-looking yet wholesome food, decor and staff at this New York-style deli. Order their Western breakfast before 10am and it's half-price (only ¥27) – and add coffee for ¥10. Smoothies and frappés for just over ¥30; wraps and sandwiches are a little more. Daily 7:30am–11pm.

Westin Bakery The Westin Shanghai Bund Centre, 88 Henan Zhong Lu. This bakery, tucked at the back of the over-the-top *Westin* hotel lobby (see p.359), deserves a mention for being understated and good value (unlike the hotel). Tasty cakes, tarts and coffees. Treat yourself to a lychee vodka truffle (¥7).

Whisk 1250 Huaihai Lu, near Changhsu Lu metro stop. Minimalist decor and a chocolate-themed menu. They do meals, but they're undistinguished – come for the speciality hot chocolate or one of the many varieties of velvety chocolate-cake naughtiness. Daily 8.30am–11.30pm.

Zentral 567 Huangpi Lu, corner of Fuxing Zhong Lu ⓦwww.zentral.com.cn. Tasteful health-food restaurant behind Xintiandi. Good burgers (¥38) and smoothies, including a hangover special (¥35). Daily 8am–10pm.

Restaurants

The traditions of Shanghai's cosmopolitan past are still dimly apparent in the city's **restaurants**. Many of the old establishments have continued to thrive, and although the original wood-panelled dining rooms are succumbing to modernization year by year, the growth of private enterprise ensures that the choice of venues is now wider than ever.

Restaurants are more expensive in Shanghai than elsewhere in China, although **prices** remain reasonable by international standards; most dishes at Chinese restaurants are priced around ¥35, and even many upmarket Western restaurants have meal specials that come to less than ¥90. The reviews give phone numbers for those places where **reservations** are advisable. Restaurant opening hours are the same as the rest of the country, though generally speaking expat places are open a little later; places with unusually long hours are marked.

The Bund, Nanjing Dong Lu, Renmin Park and around

The **Bund** itself has a number of upmarket restaurants in some of the old Art Deco buildings, most notably *M on the Bund*.

Godly (Gongdelin) 445 Nanjing Xi Lu. A vegetarian restaurant with templey decor, specializing in fake meat dishes. It's all rather hit and miss; try the meatballs, roast duck, crab and ham, but avoid anything meant to taste like fish or pork, and be wary of ordering just vegetables, as they'll turn up too oily. Staff could be livelier. Around ¥60 per head.

Kathleen's 5 Fifth floor, Shanghai Art Museum, 325 Nanjing Xi Lu ⓣ021/63272221. Great location – an elegant glass box on top of the old Shanghai Art Museum building, with views over Renmin Square. The Western food is not quite as inspiring, but the three-course lunch sets (¥140) are decent value, as is the afternoon tea set (¥50). Try the crab-meat tower – which includes avocado and mango – as a starter and follow with the cod or lamb. Good for a date.

Lao Zhengxing 556 Fuzhou Lu. This unassuming restaurant is perennially popular for its light, non-greasy Shanghai cuisine. Good for seafood and famous for herring; try "squirrel fish", and a selection of dumplings. Around ¥50 per person.

M on the Bund Seventh floor, 5 Wai Tan, entrance at Guang Dong Lu ⓣ021/63509988. Worth eating at for the extraordinary view overlooking the Bund. Some complain that as a fine-dining experience it isn't all that great, but the Mediterranean-style cuisine is some of the classiest (and most expensive) food in town, and the set lunch (¥118) is good value. If you're going to splash out, try the grilled salmon and finish with pavlova.

The Stage Westin Level 1, The Westin Shanghai Bund Center, 88 Henan Zhong Lu, near Guangdong Lu ⓣ021/ 335 0577. The "it" place for a buffet brunch – ¥200 for as much as you can eat and drink, including champagne and caviar. Come hungry and not too hung over, and pig out. 6am–12am.

Wang Baohe 603 Fuzhou Lu ⓣ021/63223673. *Wang Baohe* bills itself as the "king of crabs and ancestor of wine". It's been around for more than 200 years, so it must be doing something right, and is famous for its hairy crab set meals, which start at ¥200 per person.

Yuanlu Huizhuan Shousi Convenient, bright and friendly Japanese restaurant with sushi on a conveyor belt; each plate is priced between ¥9 and ¥18.

Yuxin Sichuan Dish Third floor, 333 Chengdu Bei Lu ⓣ021/52980438. Super spicy Sichuan food in a no-nonsense dining hall. Very popular with families and the white-collar crowd, so reservation is recommended. Go for the *kou shui ji* (saliva chicken) and *sha guo yu* (fish pot) and work on developing a face as red as the peppers. Little English is spoken, but there's a picture menu

The Old City

The Yu Yuan area has traditionally been an excellent place for **snacks** – *xiao long bao* and the like – eaten in unpretentious surroundings. Although the quality is generally superb and prices very low, there is a drawback, in the long lines that form at peak hours. Try to come outside the main eating times of 11.30am to 1.30pm, or after 5.30pm. Among the snack bars in the alleys around Yu Yuan, perhaps the best is *Lubolang* with a large variety of dumplings and noodles. Very

▲ Xiao long bao dumplings

close to the Yu Yuan entrance is the *Hubin Mei Shilou*, which serves a delicious sweet bean *changsheng zhou* (long-life soup). The *Lao Fandian*, just north of Yu Yuan at 242 Fuyou Lu, is one of the most famous restaurants in town for local Shanghai food, though prices are slightly inflated. For quick bites, check out the satay, noodle and corn-on-the-cob stands lining the street bordering the western side of Yu Yuan bazaar.

The former French Concession and western Shanghai

This is the area where most expats eat and correspondingly where prices begin to approach international levels. The compensation is that you'll find menus in English, and English will often be spoken, too. For travellers tired of Chinese food, Huaihai Lu and Maoming Lu brim with **international cuisine**. Many excellent **Shanghainese** and **Sichuanese restaurants** also cluster in the alleys around Huaihai Lu, at prices much lower than for international food. Huaihai Lu itself is lined with fast-food joints, bakeries and snack stalls.

Xintiandi on Taicang Lu is an "olde worlde" renovated courtyard complex of fancy cafés, bars and over 25 restaurants (pick up the handy map at the entrance), all rather pricey – you won't get away with paying much less than ¥100 a head.

1221 1221 Yan'an Xi Lu, by Pan Yu Lu. A little out of the way, a 10min walk east of Yan'an Lu metro stop (though bus #71 stops right outside), this is one of the city's best and most creative Shanghainese restaurants, attracting a mix of locals and expatriates. The drunken chicken and *xiang su ya* (fragrant crispy duck) are excellent, as are the onion cakes. Good choice for vegetarians, too.

1931 112 Maoming Nan Lu, just south of Huaihai Zhong Lu ⓣ021/64725264. The right mix of Shanghainese, Japanese and Southeast Asian cuisines and reasonably priced, good-sized portions characterize this civilized little place. ¥150 per person.

Bali Laguna 189 Huashan Lu, inside Jing'an Park, near Yan'an Lu ⓣ021/6248 6970, ⓦwww.balilaguna.com. A popular, classy Indonesian restaurant beautifully situated in quiet Jing'an Park. Good place for a date. The seafood curry (¥88) is served inside a pineapple. ¥140 per person.

Bi Feng Tang 1333 Nanjing Xi Lu, by Tongren Lu; 175 Changle Lu. This cheap and tasty Cantonese fast-food diner makes a great last spot on a night out (though beware the merciless lighting). There's a picture menu, and you can't go far wrong with their many *dim sum* and dumpling options. Finish off with custard tarts. Open 24hr.

Charmant 1414 Huaihai Zhong Lu ⓣ021/64318027. Great Taiwanese place – convenient, cheap, functioning as much as a café as a restaurant – that's open till the early hours, handy after a night of drinking in the former French Concession. Daily 11.30am–4am.

Crystal Jade Unit 12A–B, second floor, Building 7, South Block, Xintiandi ⓣ021/63858752; B110 Hong Kong Plaza, 300 Huaihai Zhong Lu. Great Hong Kong food, sophisticated looks and down-to-earth prices make this *the* place to eat in Xintiandi, and the best place in town for *dim sum*. Try the barbecued pork – and leave room for mango pudding. The second branch in the Hong Kong Plaza is not as swanky, but is less busy. Cheaper than it looks, at around ¥80 per head.

Dongbei Ren 1 Shanxi Nan Lu, by Yan'an Zhong Lu ⓣ021/52289898. Hale and hearty, the way those sturdy *dongbei ren* – northeasterners – like it. It's all meat and potatoes, much like Scottish fare (must be something to do with the cold). Try the dumplings, lamb skewers and braised pork shank. ¥60 a head.

Guyi Hunan 89 Fumin Lu, near Julu Lu ⓣ021/62495628. The spicy Hunan cuisine packs them in at this stylish place. Take a few people to get a good range of dishes – including spare ribs or fish with beans and scallions – and make sure you reserve. About ¥80 per head.

Hotpot King Second floor, 146 Huaihai Zhong Lu, by Fuxing Xi Lu ⓣ021/64736380. English menus, understanding staff and tasteful decor make this an accessible way to sample a local favourite. Order lamb, glass noodles, mushrooms and tofu (at the least) and chuck them into the pot in the middle of the table. Perfect for winter evenings. ¥70 per person. Daily 11am–4am.

Lapis Lazuli 9 Dongping Lu, near Hengshan Lu ⓣ021/64731021. Pleasant, clubby hideaway, very stylish if a bit dark, serving reasonably priced continental food. The intimate outdoor terrace makes this a great place for a date on a summer evening. Try the seafood risotto. About ¥100 per head.

Meilongzhen 22, Lane 1081, Nanjing Xi Lu ⓣ021/62535353. A Shanghai restaurant with a dash of Sichuan spiciness; it's very popular, so be sure to reserve. It's tucked behind Nanjing Lu, but you can't miss the colourful arched doorway. Go for twice-cooked pork, drink eight-treasure tea – check out the long-spouted kettles – and finish off with a sugar-roasted banana. ¥90 per person.

Mesa 748 Julu Lu, near Fumin Lu ⓣ021/6289 9108. Fine dining, Western style, in a stylish converted factory. Try the carpaccio of beef or seared duck breast but leave room for the dessert tasting platter. Service could be a tad better but they're trying. The bar upstairs, *Manifesto* is handy. ¥300 per person, weekend buffet brunch (11.30am–5pm) is good value at ¥150. Daily 10am–late.

Shen Yue Xuan 849 Hua Shan Lu ⓣ021/62511166. The best Cantonese place in Shanghai, with scrumptious *dim sum* at lunchtime and pleasant, if cavernous, decor. In warmer weather, you can dine al fresco in the garden, a rarity for a Cantonese restaurant. Dinner for two comes to around ¥120 per head drinks included.

Shintori 288 Wulumuqi Nan Lu, three blocks south of Hengshan Lu t021/64672459. Take someone you want to impress to this nouvelle Japanese trendsetter: the buffet will set you back around ¥300. Entertaining presentation will give you something to talk about, though you'd better order

Shanghai drinking, nightlife and entertainment

Bars and clubs		
Blue Frog	蓝蛙	*lán wā*
Cloud Nine	九重天酒吧	*jiǔchóngtiān jiǔbā*
Cotton Club	棉花俱乐部	*miánhuā jùlèbù*
I Love Shanghai	我爱上海	*wǒ ài shànghǎi*
JZ Club	爵士	*jué shì*
Long Bar	长吧	*chángbā*
Mural	摩砚	*mó yàn*
Windows Too	蕴德诗酒吧	*yùndéshī jiǔbā*
Yongfu Elite	雍福会	*yōng fú huì*
Entertainment venues and art galleries		
Art Scene China	艺术景画廊	*yìshùjǐng huàláng*
Broadband International Cineplex	万裕国际影城-	*wànyù guójì yǐngchéng*
Lyceum	心大院	*lánxīn dàxìyuàn*
Majestic Theatre	美琪大剧院	*Měiqí dàjùyuàn*
Oriental Arts Centre	上海东方艺术中心	*shànghǎi dōngfāng yìshù zhōngxīn*
Paradise Warner International City	永华电影城	*yǒnghuá diànyǐng chéng*
Shangart	香格纳画廊	*xiānggénà huàláng*
Shanghai Centre	上海商城剧院	*shànghǎi shāngchéng jùyuàn*
Shanghai Circus World	上海马戏城	*shànghǎi mǎxì chéng*
Shanghai Concert Hall	上海音乐厅	*shànghǎi yīnyuètīng*
Shanghai Grand Theatre	上海大剧院	*shànghǎi dàjùyuàn*
Shanghai Film Art Centre	上海影院中心	*shànghǎi yǐngyuàn zhōngxīn*
Shanghai Symphony Orchestra Hall	上海交响乐团演奏厅	*shànghǎi jiāoxiǎngyuètuán yǎnzòutīng*
UME International Cineplex	新天地国际影城	*xīntiāndì guójì yǐngchéng*

a lot or you'll be bitching about the small portions. Finish with green tea tiramisu (¥60).

Shu Di La Zi Yu Guan 187 Anfu Lu, on the corner with Wulumuqi Zhong Lu. Never mind the tacky decor and concentrate on the excellent, inexpensive Sichuan and Hunanese cuisine. A big pot of Sichuan spicy fish is a must, but also recommended is *zhu xiang ji* (bamboo fragrant chicken) and old fave, *mala doufu* (spicy tofu).

Simply Thai 5-C Dong Ping Lu ⓣ021/64459551. The best of the city's Thai joints, with good, eclectic dishes and a smart but informal setting, including a leafy courtyard. Try the stir-fried asparagus and fish cakes. The Xintiandi branch is not nearly as good.

South Beauty 881 Yan'an Lu, opposite the Exhibition Hall ⓣ021/62475878. Upmarket Sichuan food in what looks like an English country house. Speciality of the house is beef in boiling oil – cooked at your table. ¥200 per person.

T8 House 8, North Block, Xintiandi, Taicang Road ⓣ021/6355 8999. Fine continental-style dining, courtesy of an Austrailian chef, in an elegant reconstruction of a courtyard house. Reserve, and ask for one of the booths at the back. Leave room for their chocolate-addiction dessert platter. ¥400 a head.

Xiao Shaoxing Yunnan Lu (east side), immediately north of Jinling Dong Lu. Famous in Shanghai for its *bai qie ji*, chicken simmered in wine, although adventurous diners might also wish to sample the blood soup or chicken feet.

Xinjishi (Jesse Restaurant) 41 Tianping Lu; Shop 9, North Block, Xintiandi, 181 Taicang Lu ⓣ021/6336 4746 ⓦwww.xinjishi.com. The decor is a bit tatty at the tiny, original branch on Tianping Lu, but there's nothing wrong with the tasty homestyle cooking, with dishes from all over the country. Go for the red cooked pork and other local faves. The new branch at Xintiandi, with its traditional styling, looks better, but the food is not quite as good. Daily 11am–2pm, 5–9.30pm.

Ye Shanghai House 6, North Block, Xintiandi, 338 Huangpi Nan Lu. Shanghai cuisine in an upmarket pastiche of colonial grandeur – so lots of red lanterns and dark wood. A good introduction to local tastes – particularly recommended are the drunken chicken, prawns with chilli sauce and the many crab dishes. Around ¥200 per person.

Yin 59 Maoming Nan Lu ⓣ021/54665070. Hardwood floors and screens create an intimate atmosphere, and the food is similarly tasteful, well thought through and understated. No MSG is used, and all dishes – Shanghai staples – are light and not oily. A great place to sample local cuisine such as eggplant pancakes. Set menu is ¥100 per person. There's no sign; go to the alley that parallels Maoming Nan Lu, and it's the grand wooden doors opposite the back of Shanghai Tang.

Pudong

There's nothing particularly mid-range around **Lujiazui**; either head to a mall for the cheap and cheery food court, or a hotel for a fabulous, if pricey, culinary experience.

Jade on 36 36th floor, Tower 2, *Pudong Shangri-La*, 33 Fucheng Lu ⓣ021/68828888, ⓦwww.shangri-la.com. Celebrity chef Paul Pairet's gimmicky food contrasts with the grandiloquence of the venue, which has an amazing view of the Bund. There are lots of foams and sorbets, and odd combinations abound – a foie gras lollipop and a sardine mousse, for example. There are only set menus, which start at ¥480.

Yi Café L2, Tower 2, *Pudong Shangri-La*, 33 Fucheng Lu ⓣ021/68828888, ⓦwww.shangri-la.com. This slickly designed place is the best of the hotel buffets. All you can eat – and there's an enormous choice, with ten show kitchens – for ¥268 plus fifteen-percent service charge. Go hungry. Very popular for Sunday brunch (11am–2pm). Daily 6am–1am.

Drinking and nightlife

Western-style **bars** are found mostly in the Huaihai Lu area, nearly all of which serve food, and some of which have room for dancing. Bars tend to cluster in districts; Julu Lu, Tongren Lu and Maoming Nan Lu each have a dense concentration of venues, though some have a sleazy edge. There are also plenty of rather more upmarket places for a drink in Xintiandi.

You'll find the full range of drinks available, though beer is usually bottled rather than draught and prices are on the high side; reckon on ¥30–60 per drink in most places. This hasn't stopped the development of a jumping, occasionally sleazy, nightlife, though the scene is patently focused on expats and the moneyed Chinese elite. The **club** scene will be eerily familiar to anyone who's been clubbing in any Western capital – you won't hear much in the way of local sounds – but at least door prices are much cheaper, never more than ¥100. One Chinese innovation is the addition of karaoke booths at the back; another, much less welcome, is the annoying practice of having to pay to sit at a table. Most places have international DJs, and plenty of famous faces have popped in for a spin of the decks. Wednesday is (usually) ladies' night, Thursday is hip-hop night, and, of course, the weekends are massive. Note that there are also dance floors in *Windows Too* and *Zapatas*, reviewed in "Bars".

Bars

Bar Rouge 7F, Bund 18, 18 Zhongshan Dong Yi Lu, near Dianchi Lu. The terrace has unrivalled views over the Bund. ¥50 cover on weekends and you won't get much change from a red bill for a drink.

Blue Frog 207 Maoming Nan Lu, by Fuxing Lu; 86 Tongren Lu. A cultivated frog among the sleazy toads of Maoming Lu – so no over-friendly bar girls, but there is a good Western food list, an intimate upstairs lounge and a talkative crowd and you won't leave feeling the need for a shower.

Captain Bar Sixth floor, 37 Fuzhou Lu, by Sichuan Zhong Lu. This relaxed venue scores for its terrace with a great view of Pudong. It sits atop a backpacker hotel (see p.358), though most guests are put off by the prices – draught beer ¥40.

Cloud Nine 87th floor, *Grand Hyatt*, Jinmao Tower, 88 Shiji Dadao, Pudong ⓣ021/50491234. The highest bar in the world, on the 87th floor of the *Grand Hyatt* in the Jinmao Tower (see p.358). Inside, it's all rather dark and metallic, but the view is astonishing. Be smart – pick a cloudless day, and arrive soon after opening time (6pm) to bag one of the coveted window-side tables facing Puxi. ¥120 minimum spend per person, which will only get you one cocktail.

Cotton Club 1416 Huaihai Zhong Lu, near Fuxing Xi Lu ⓣ021/64377110. A long-running, relaxed jazz club with none of that bristling Shanghai attitude. Music gets going at 9.30pm, a bit later at weekends.

Face Bar Building Four, *Ruijin Guesthouse,* 118 Ruijin Er Lu. Very civilized, largely thanks to the venue, a lovely old villa in the manicured grounds of the *Ruijin Guesthouse.* It's quiet, the lighting is low, the decor is opium-den chic and the crowd is smart, casual and loaded. Cocktails ¥65. Happy Hour 5–8pm.

Glamour Bar Sixth floor, *M on the Bund*, 20 Guangdong Lu, by Zhonghsan Dong Yi Lu ⓦwww.m-theglamourbar.com. Pink, frivolous and fabulous, this is Shanghai's destination *du jour* for poseurs. Good view of the Bund though, and there's a schedule of cultural events. Cocktails from ¥65 (great mojitos).

I Love Shanghai 155 East Zhongshan Er Lu, at the intersection with Jin Ling Dong Lu ⓦwww.iloveshanghailounge.com. Friendly Bund bar; the decor is undistinguished, but it's cheaper than in any of the more glamorous venues nearby – and with less attitude. Tuesday is ladies' night – free drinks for girls till midnight; Saturday is a ¥100 open bar. Beers from ¥30.

JZ Club 46 Fuxing Lu, near Yongfu Lu ⓦwww.jzclub.cn. A popular venue, dark but not smoky, with live jazz every night from 10pm. Pricey drinks (starting at ¥45) but there's no cover.

Long Bar 2F, Shanghai Centre, 1376 Nanjing Xi Lu. Comfy expat bar, for networking and post-work drinks. Beers from ¥35.

Mural 697 Yongjia Lu, near Hengshan Lu ⓦwww.muralbar.com. Cheap and cheery basement venue, incongruously decorated like a Buddhist cave, popular for its ¥100 open bar on Friday nights.

Windows Too J104, Jingan Si Plaza, 1699 Nanjing Xi Lu, by Hua Shan Lu. Packs them in nightly thanks to a revolutionary idea – affordable beer, at ¥10 a bottle. Popular with the bottom of the Shanghai foreigner food chain – students, teachers and backpackers. Commercial hip-hop on the decks, a ¥50 cover on the weekend. No posing, no attitude, no class.

Yongfu Elite 200 Yongfu Lu, by Hunan Lu. A private member's club now open to the public, this fabulously opulent villa has vintage everything; heaven forbid that you spill a drink. Sip cocktails (which start at ¥60) on the veranda under the gaze of the garden's huge Buddha statue, and feel like a film star.

Zapatas 5 Hengshan Road, near Dongping Road ⓦwww.zapatas-shanghai.com. No self-respecting Mexican anarchist would be seen dead in the company of this lascivious frat-house crowd. Never mind, it's a heaving party on their Monday and Wednesday "free margaritas for the ladies before midnight" special. You enter through the garden of *Sasha's*, the nearby restaurant.

Clubs

Attica 11F, 15 Zhongshan Dong Er Lu, near Jin Ling Dong Lu ⓦwww.attica-shanghai.com The trendiest club in town, with an awesome view of Pudong from the terrace for when the dance floors (one house/techno, one R&B) get too sweaty. ¥100 cover gets you one drink; girls get in free before midnight. Doesn't really get going till 1am; then it's party central till 5am.

Bonbon 2F Yunhai Tower, 1329 Huaihai Zhong Lu ⓦwww.clubbonbon.com.The home of *Gods Kitchen*, *Bonbon* is packed with a young crowd, even on weekdays; Tuesdays are popular. Hip-hop on Thursdays. Cover charge ¥40–100.

Mint 2F, 333 Tongren Road near Beijing Road ⓦwww.mintclub.com.cn. Popular, pocket-sized, lounge-style house-music venue. International guest DJs on the weekends. Happy Hour 6–8pm, but it doesn't really get going till after midnight. Cover charge ¥50 on weekends.

Entertainment

Most visitors take in an **acrobatics show** and perhaps the **opera**, but equally worthy of note are the flourishing contemporary art and music scenes. The **Shanghai Arts Festival** (ⓦwww.artsbird.com) is held from mid-October to mid-November – though you'd be forgiven for not noticing it, arts programming does much better during the festival, with lot of visiting shows. For listings of big cultural spectaculars such as visiting ballet troupes, check the *China Daily*, but for the lowdown on punk gigs, underground art shows and the like, get an up-to-date expat magazine such as *City Weekend* or check the website Ⓦwww.smartshanghai.com.

The simplest way to get **tickets** is at the box office before the show starts, or a few days earlier if there's any danger that it will sell out. You can also buy tickets from the booking centre behind the Westgate Mall on Nanjing Xi Lu.

The contemporary art scene can be conveniently checked out at the Moganshan Art District; see p.373 for more. The next **Shanghai Biennale**, held in venues all over town, is in 2008 (Ⓦwww.shanghaibiennale.com).

Acrobatics

There are three main venues for the perennially popular **acrobatics**; the Shanghai Circus World in the far north of the city (2266 Gonghe Xin Lu; performances daily 7.30pm; tickets ¥50–580; Ⓣ021/66527750, Ⓦwww.era-shanghai.com) puts on a nightly show "ERA: the Intersection of Time", but never mind the daft name, this is a good old-fashioned spectacular, in a specially built dome. The shows at the Shanghai Centre's theatre (1376 Nanjing Xi Lu, by Xikang Lu; performances daily at 7.30pm; tickets ¥100–200; Ⓣ021/62798948, Ⓦwww.shanghaicentre.com) and the Lyceum (57 Maoming Nan Lu; performances daily 7.30pm; tickets ¥150–250; Ⓣ021/62565544) are lighter on the glitz but full of breathtaking feats.

Cinema

China's first **movie studios** were in Shanghai, in the 1930s (see contexts, p.1191 for more), and you can see old classics such as *Sister Flower* and *The Goddess* – both surprisingly hard-hitting naturalistic tragedies – at the *Old Film Café* (see p.384). The studios might have gone but, increasingly, you can find Shanghai depicted on film, most succesfully in Lou Ye's tragic love story *Suzhou Creek* (2002). The city has been used as an exotic backdrop by foreign film-makers; parts of *Mission Impossible III* were set here, and Michael Winterbottom filmed sci-fi actioner *Code 46* in Pudong.

Two cinemas that show foreign blockbusters in their original languages are the UME International Cineplex (fifth floor, South Block, Xintiandi; tickets from ¥50; Ⓣ021/6373333, an English schedule follows the Chinese when you call, Ⓦwww.ume.com) and the Paradise Warner International City (sixth floor, Grand Gateway, 1 Hongqiao Lu, Xujiahui; tickets from ¥50; Ⓣ021/64076622, Ⓦwww.paradisewarner.com). They also show all the latest Chinese releases, though in Mandarin Chinese only, as does Shanghai's other giant multiplex, the Broadband International Cineplex (sixth floor, Times Square, 99 Huaihai Lu, near Huangpi Nan Lu metro station; tickets from ¥50; Ⓣ021/63910363, Ⓦwww.swy99.com). The only vaguely art-house cinema, which shows at least some non-mainstream content, is the Shanghai Film Art Centre (160 Xinhua Lu, near Panyu Lu; tickets from ¥45 Ⓣ021/62804088, Ⓦwww.filmcenter.com.cn).

Music

A number of new world-class venues are sating local demand for **classical music** and imported **musicals**. The Shanghai Cultural Information and Booking Centre has a comprehensive website with the schedules of all the most popular venues (Ⓦ www.culture.sh.cn/English, reservations on Ⓣ 021/62172426), as has the China Ticket Online (Ⓦ shdx.piao.com.cn/en_piao, reservations Ⓣ 021/63744968). At both, tickets can be booked over the phone then delivered to your hotel or home at no extra charge, provided you book more than three days before the performance. Ticket prices vary, but you can expect to pay around ¥100, three times that for the best seats.

Shanghai doesn't have much of a rock scene – you'll have to go to Bejing for that – but **jazz** is perennially popular; check out *JZ* and the *Cotton Club* (see bars, p.390).

Majestic Theatre 66 Jiangning Lu, near Nanjing Xi Lu Ⓣ 021/62174409. When built in 1941 this was one of Asia's best theatres. Usually musicals, but with some English-language drama.

Oriental Arts Centre 425 Dingxiang Lu, near Century Avenue Ⓣ 021/68541234. There's no doubt that this is one of Asia's most important concert venues but at present this fantastic, forty-thousand-square-metre behemoth (see p.369) struggles to fill its schedule. Hosts a little bit of everything, but comes into its own as a concert venue as the acoustics are superb.

Shanghai Concert Hall 523 Yan'an Dong Lu, near Xizang Zhong Lu Ⓣ 021/63862836. This lovely old building was moved 60m east in 2003, at tremendous cost, to get it away from the din of Yan'an Lu. Today, it's the premier venue for classical music. Tickets from ¥80.

Shanghai Grand Theatre 300 Renmin Dadao Ⓣ 021/63273094. Lovely building that puts on popular contemporary dramas, operas and classical ballets, and plays host to most of the visiting musicals. Regular performances by the in-house Shanghai Symphony Orchestra.

Shopping

The shopping is great in Shanghai, and it's a rare visitor who doesn't end up having to buy another bag to keep all their new goodies in. The Shanghainese love luxury goods, and it's not uncommon to find young women spending several months' salary on a handbag, but all those glitzy brand names that give the streets such a lot of their shine are not good value; high-end goods and international brands are generally twenty percent more expensive than they

▲ Fake handbags for sale

would be in the West. Ignore them, and instead plunge into the fascinating world of the backstreet boutiques and markets.

There are several **fake markets** catering largely to foreigners (all open daily 9am–8pm). As well as clothes, there are trainers, sunglasses, bags and watches on sale. The biggest and most convenient is the Fengshine Plaza at 580 Nanjing Xi Lu (Renmin Square metro). The Yatai Xinyang Fashion & Gift market is in the Science and Technology Museum metro station, its entrance close to the ticketing machines. Qipu Road Market at 183 Qipu Lu is just north east of the Bund. Not everything is a copy; some of this stuff, mainly the jeans and trainers, is made in the same factories as the real thing. You'll have to bargain harder here than anywhere else in the city; the pushy vendors commonly start at ten or twenty times the real price, and it pays to shop around as plenty of people are selling the same thing.

Sartorial elegance is something of a local obsession, so you're spoilt for choice if you're looking for **clothes**. If you want to see international designer clothes in showpiece stores head to Plaza 66 or the Bund. The chicest shopping is to be had in the former French Concession; central Huaihai Zhong Lu itself is full of familiar brands, but the streets off it – such as Nanchang, Shanxi Nan Lu and Maoming Lu – are full of fascinating little boutiques, which make this the place to forage for fashionable gear.

Getting **tailored** clothes is a recommended Shanghai experience, as it will cost so much less than at home and the artisans are skilled (provided you're clear about exactly what you're after) and quick. At the textile market at 399 Lujiabang Lu (Old City, near Liushui Lu; daily 10am–7pm) on-site tailors will make you a suit for around ¥500, including material (you'll have to barter a bit), which will take a couple of days. If you're looking for a tailored *qipao*, your best bet is to head to one of the dozen or so specialist stores on Maoming Nan Lu, just south of Huaihai Lu. One highly skilled local tailor is Yaya, who has a tiny shop next to the German Consulate at 253 Yongfu Lu (Ⓣ021/64745324; Tues–Sun 1–8pm). She specializes in copying dresses; give her a picture and she'll make a great replica for around ¥700.

For designer clothes at bargain basement prices, head to a **factory overstock** shop. These will be unpromising from the outside, possibly won't have a name, and will usually carry their own lines in the window, with the good stuff hung rather negligently on a rail at the back. The place to start looking is Ruijin Er Lu, at the intersection with Huaihai Zhong Lu. Head south down the street then turn onto Nanchang Lu – look in any clothes shop that's busy on the way. A second concentration of these stores is on Fuxing Zhong Lu, east of Baoqing Lu. Or find your way to a branch of overstock chain Hot Wind (Ⓦwww.hotwind.net): there are convenient ones at 358 Huaihai Zhong Lu (by Huangpi Nan Lu metro station exit three); 127 Ruijin Yi Lu; and 106 Ruijin Yi Lu. They put their own label over the original – you have to scrape it off with a fingernail.

The place to start looking for interesting crafts and souvenirs is Taikang Lu Shopping Street, an alleyway of boutiques and galleries. Notable here is the Tian Zi Fang leather workshop at number 15, lane 210, which sells bags and belts; Cholon at 108, number 3, which sells Vietnamese knick-knacks and homeware; and Jooi Design at Studio 201, the International Artist Factory, which has some great cushion covers and embroidered evening bags. Otherwise, if you're looking to do some souvenir shopping in a hurry, head to the bazaar around the Yu Yuan.

The best places to shop for **electronic goods** are the giant tech-souks Cybermart (282 Huahai Zhong Lu, at its intersection with Huangpi Nan Lu), Metro City (111 Zhaojiabang Lu, by Caoxi Bei Lu, in the basement of the mall shaped like a giant bubble, Xujiahui metro) and Pacific Digital Plaza (117 Zhaojiabang Lu; Xujiahui metro). Obscure brand laptops, MP3 players, memory sticks, RAM, and low-end accessories such as headphones can be very cheap. Shop around, as many of the stalls sell the same things, and barter (though this isn't the fake market; you'll get at most fifteen percent off the asking price). Test everything thoroughly, and remember that for the majority of this stuff the warranty is not valid internationally.

For **books**, head to Charterhouse, in the basement of Times Square at 93 Hauihai Zhong Lu, whose good selections of imported English-language books cost a little more than they would at home. The Foreign Languages Bookstore at 390 Fuzhou Lu is a useful resource, with plenty of English-language guides and the like; the novels, published by Chinese publishers, are cheap.

Listings

Airlines China Eastern Airlines (domestic ⓣ021/62475953; international ⓣ021/62472255) is in the CAAC building at 200 Yan'an Xi Lu, while Shanghai Airlines lies at 212 Jiangning Lu ⓣ021/62558888. The following foreign carriers have offices in Shanghai (if no address is given, the airline is in the Shanghai Centre, 1376 Nanjing Xi Lu): Aeroflot, *Donghu Hotel*, Donghu Lu ⓣ021/64158158; Air China, 2555 Zhongshan Bei Lu ⓣ021/62570000; Air France, Hongqiao Airport ⓣ021/62688817; Air Macan All Nippon ⓣ021/62797000; Ansett Australia, 19th Floor, 918 Huaihai Zhong Lu ⓣ021/64155208; Asiania, 2000 Yan An Xi Lu ⓣ021/62709900; Air Macau, *Equatorial Hotel*, 65 Yan'an Xi Lu ⓣ021/62481110; Austrian Airlines, Room 303, *Equatorial Hotel*, 65 Yan'an Xi Lu ⓣ021/62491202; China Eastern Airlines, Yan'an Xi Lu ⓣ021/62471960; Dragonair ⓣ021/62798099; Japan Airlines, *Rui Jin Hotel* ⓣ021/64723000; Korean Air, 2099 Yan'an Lu ⓣ021/62758649; Lufthansa, *Hilton Hotel* ⓣ021/62481100; Malaysia Airlines ⓣ021/62798607; Northwest Airlines ⓣ021/62798088; Qantas ⓣ021/62798660; Singapore Airlines ⓣ021/62798008; Swissair ⓣ021/62797381; Thai Airways ⓣ021/62487766; United Airlines ⓣ021/62798009; Virgin, Suite 221, second floor, 12 The Bund ⓣ021/63236409.

American Express Room 206, Shanghai Centre, 1376 Nanjing Xi Lu (Mon–Fri 9am–5.30pm; ⓣ021/62798082).

Banks and exchange The head office of the Bank of China is at 23 Zhongshan Lu (The Bund), next to the *Peace Hotel* (Mon–Fri 9am–noon & 1.30–4.30pm, Sat 9am–noon). Next door is a Citibank ATM machine with 24hr access.

Consulates Australia, CITIC Square, 1168 Nanjing Xi Lu ⓣ021/52925500; Austria, Qihua Tower, 1375 Huaihai Zhong Lu ⓣ021/64740268; Canada, Room 604 West Tower, Shanghai Centre, 1376 Nanjing Xi Lu ⓣ021/62798400; Denmark, Floor 6, 1375 Huaihai Lu ⓣ021/64314301; France, 689 Guangdong Lu, near Yunnan Zhong Lu 021/61032200; Germany, 181 Yongfu Lu ⓣ021/64336951; Holland, #1403, 250 Hua Shan Lu ⓣ021/62480000; India, Room 1008, Shanghai International Trade Center, 2200 Yan'an Lu ⓣ021/62758885; Ireland, 700A Shanghai Centre, 1376 Nanjing Xi Lu ⓣ021/62798729; Israel, #55, Floor 7, Lou Shan Guan Lu ⓣ021/62098008; Italy, Floor 11, Qihua Tower, 1375 Huaihai Zhong Lu ⓣ021/64716980; Japan, 8 Wanshan Lu ⓣ62780788; New Zealand, Floor 15, Qihua Tower, 1375 Huaihai Lu ⓣ021/64711108; Poland, 618 Jianguo Lu ⓣ021/64339288; Russia, 20 Huangpu Lu ⓣ021/63242682; Singapore, 400 Wulumuqi Zhong Lu ⓣ021/64331362; South Korea, Floor 4, 2200 Yan'an Lu ⓣ021/62196420; Sweden, 6A Qihua Tower, 1375 Huaihai Zhong Lu ⓣ021/64741311; Thailand, 3F, 7 Zhongshan Dong Lu ⓣ021/63219371; UK, Room 301, Shanghai Centre, 1376 Nanjing Xi Lu ⓣ021/62797650; USA, 1469 Huaihai Zhong Lu ⓣ021/64336880.

Football During the football season (winter) you can watch Shanghai's main team, Shenhua (ⓦwww.shenhua.com.cn) play every other Sun at 3.30pm at the gleaming 35,000-seat Hongkou Football Stadium, 444 Dongjianwan Lu, in the north of town. Tickets are ¥30 and can be bought at the ground on the day.

Hospitals A number of the city's hospitals have special clinics for foreigners, including the Huadong Hospital at 221 Yan'an Xi Lu (ⓣ021/62483180) and the Hua Shan Hospital at 12 Wulumuqi Lu (go to the eighth floor; ⓣ02162489999 ext 2531). You'll find top-notch medical care at World Link Medical and Dental Centres in Suite 203 of the Shanghai Centre West Tower at 1376 Nanjing Xi Lu (ⓣ021/62797688, ⓦwww.worldlink-shanghai.com), but they are pricey at ¥700 per consultation.

Internet access Net bars are dotted around the backstreets (¥3/hr; 24hr); you'll need to show your passport before you're let near a computer. There's a handy Internet office in the basement of the Shanghai Library at 1555 Huaihai Zhong Lu (daily 8.30am–8pm; ¥4/hr).

Mail The main post office is at 1 Sichuan Bei Lu, just north of and overlooking Suzhou Creek (see p.361). A stately Art Deco edifice, it offers a very efficient parcel service; the express option can get packages to Britain or the US within two days. Poste restante arrives at the Bei Suzhou Lu office across the street – each separate item is recorded on a little slip of cardboard in a display case near the entrance. Both the main post office and the poste restante service are open daily 9am–7pm. Branch post offices dot the city, with convenient locations along Nanjing Dong Lu, Huaihai Zhong Lu, in the Portman Centre, and near the Huangpu River ferry jetties at the corner of Jinling Dong Lu and Sichuan Bei Lu.

PSB 210 Hankou Lu, near the corner of Henan Zhong Lu. For visa extensions, go to 1500 Minsheng Lu, in Pudong, near Yinchun Lu (Science and Technology Museum metro stop; Mon–Fri 9am–11.30pm & 1.30–4.30pm). The visa office is on the third floor.

Telephones International calls are most easily and cheaply made with phone cards. Otherwise, you can call from the second floor of the main post office at 1 Sichuan Bei Lu, or at the China Telecom office three stores down from the north building of the *Peace Hotel* on 30 Nanjing Dong Lu (open 24hr). The large, English-speaking staff can deal with most requests.

Travel agents CITS has a helpful office at 66 Nanjing Dong Lu (ⓣ021/63233384, ⓕ63290295), providing travel and entertainment tickets, with a small commission added on. There's another CITS branch at 1277 Beijing Xi Lu (ⓣ021/62898899), as well as a transport ticket office just off the Bund at 2 Jinling Dong Lu. All branches daily 8.30am–5pm. Most hotels have travel agencies offering the same services.

Travel details

Trains

Shanghai Station to: Beijing (8 daily; 12hr); Changsha (3 daily; 19hr); Changzhou (17 daily; 2–3hr); Chengdu (twice daily; 40–45hr); Chongqing (daily; 44hr); Fuzhou (twice daily; 21hr); Guangzhou (3 daily; 24hr); Guilin (3 daily; 27hr); Hangzhou (16 daily; 2–3hr); Harbin (daily; 33hr); Hefei (5 daily; 9hr); Hong Kong (daily; 24hr); Huangshan (daily; 12hr); Kunming (daily; 48–58hr); Lanzhou (twice daily; 30hr); Nanchang (daily; 12hr); Nanjing (frequent; 3–4hr); Nanning (twice daily; 15hr); Ningbo (6 daily; 6–9hr); Qingdao (daily; 20hr); Shaoxing (6 daily; 3–5hr); Shenyang (daily; 28hr); Suzhou (23 daily; 1hr); Tai'an (for Qufu; 4 daily; 11hr); Tianjin (4 daily; 16hr); Ürümqi (daily; 51hr); Wuxi (16 daily; 1hr); Xiamen (daily; 26hr); Xi'an (7 daily; 17hr); Xining (daily; 41hr); Xuzhou (7 daily; 9hr); Zhenzhou (daily; 15hr); Zhenjiang (16 daily; 3hr).

Shanghai West Station to: Baotou (twice daily; 34hr); Hohhot (twice daily; 31hr).

Buses

Shanghai to: Hangzhou (frequent; 3hr); Lianyungang (5 daily; 8hr); Nanjing (frequent; 4hr); Shaoxing (6 daily; 4hr); Suzhou (frequent; 1hr); Wenzhou (3 daily; 12hr); Wuxi (35 daily; 3hr); Yangzhou (13 daily; 5hr); Zhouzhuang (4 daily; 1hr 30min).

Ferries

Shanghai to: Inchon (South Korea; weekly; 22hr); Kobe (Japan; 1 weekly; 38hr); Osaka (Japan; 1 weekly; 36hr); Putuo Shan (4 daily; 4–12hr).

Flights

Shanghai to: Baotou (twice weekly; 2hr 50min); Beijing (16 daily; 1hr 50min); Changsha (5 daily; 4hr); Changchun (4 daily; 2hr 45min); Chengdu (12 daily; 2hr 45min); Chongqing (8 daily; 2hr 30min) Dalian (5 daily; 1hr 30min); Fuzhou (11 daily; 1hr 30 min); Guangzhou (10 daily; 2hr); Guilin (4 daily; 2hr 20min); Haikou (4 daily; 3hr); Harbin (2–4 daily; 2hr 40min); Hefei (4 daily; 1hr); Hohhot (3 weekly; 2hr 20min); Hong Kong (19 daily; 2hr 10min); Huangshan (3 daily; 1hr); Kunming (9 daily; 3hr); Lanzhou (1–2 daily; 3hr); Lhasa (twice weekly; 6hr); Lijiang (daily; 4hr 30min); Macau (twice daily; 2hr 20 min); Nanning (twice daily; 3hr); Ningbo (daily; 40min); Qingdao (daily; 1hr 20min); Shenzhen (daily; 2hr); Taiyuan (daily; 2hr); Tianjin (8 daily; 1hr 30min); Ürümqi (4 daily; 5hr); Wenzhou (1–3 daily; 1hr); Wuhan (3 daily; 1hr); Xiamen (3 daily; 1hr 30min); Xi'an (7 daily; 2hr 15min); Xining (daily; 4hr); Yichang (twice daily; 1hr 30min).

CHAPTER 6

Highlights

* **The Grand Canal** The original source of the region's wealth, and a construction feat to rival the Great Wall. See p.400

* **Suzhou** A striking medley of tree-lined canals, ramshackle homes, old stone bridges and hi-tech factories. See p.401

* **Tongli** This quiet, charming town of winding lanes and canals holds some lovely old buildings. See p.410

* **Fuzi Miao, Nanjing** A bustling consumer cornucopia, hot, noisy and earthy. See p.419

* **Xi Hu, Hangzhou** You will get great vistas from this beautiful lake, best appreciated by cycling the area. See p.431

* **Moganshan** An old colonial hill resort that has become fashionable as a summer retreat – it's a great spot for a brisk hike. See p.437

* **Shaoxing** Charismatic backwater once home to some cultural heavyweights, such as the writer Lu Xun, whose elegant mansion – now a museum – offers a glimpse into a vanished world. See p.438

* **Putuo Shan** A tranquil island of Buddhist temples and beaches. See p.443

▲ Fragrant Isle, Zhuozheng Yuan, Suzhou

6

Jiangsu and Zhejiang

China's original heartland may have been the dusty Yellow River basin, but it was the greenness and fertility of the **Yangzi River estuary** that drew the Chinese south, and provided them with the wealth and power needed to sustain a huge empire. The provinces of **Jiangsu** and **Zhejiang**, which today flank the metropolitan area of Shanghai, have played a vital part in the cultural and economic development of China for the last two thousand years. No tour of eastern China would be complete without stopovers in some of their classic destinations.

The story begins in the sixth century BC when the area was part of the state of Wu and had already developed its own distinct culture. The flat terrain, the large crop yield and the superb communications offered by coastal ports and navigable waterways enabled the principal towns of the area to develop quickly into important **trading centres**. These presented an irresistible target for the expanding Chinese empire under the Qin dynasty, and in 223 BC the region was annexed, immediately developing into one of the economic centres of the empire. After the end of the Han dynasty in the third century AD, several regimes established short-lived capitals in southern cities; however, the real boost for southern China came when the Sui (589–618 AD) extended the **Grand Canal** to link the Yangzi with the Yellow River and, ultimately, to allow trade to flow freely between here and the northern capitals. With this, China's centre of gravity took a decisive shift south. Under later dynasties, Hangzhou and then Nanjing became the greatest cities in China.

Visiting the region, you find yourself in a world of **water**. The whole area is intensively drained, canalized, irrigated and farmed, and the rivers, canals and lakes which web the plain give it much of its character. The traditional way to travel here was by **boat**, though passenger traffic has diminished in all but the most touristed areas. One local service inland survives, between Suzhou and Hangzhou.

The powerful commercial cities of the waterways have long acted as counterweights to the bureaucratic tendencies of Beijing. Both **Hangzhou** and **Nanjing** have served as capitals of China, the latter having been Sun Yatsen's capital during the brief years of the Chinese Republic after the overthrow of the Qing dynasty. Marco Polo called Hangzhou "the most beautiful and magnificent city in the world", and its Xi Hu (West Lake), still recognizable from classic scroll paintings, is deservedly rated as one of the most scenic spots in China. **Suzhou** too, should not be missed, for the bustle of life along the canals that crisscross its centre, and the peace of its famous **gardens**.

These and other cities in the region have also developed as manufacturing centres, enjoying the boom that has put Jiangsu and Zhejiang at the forefront

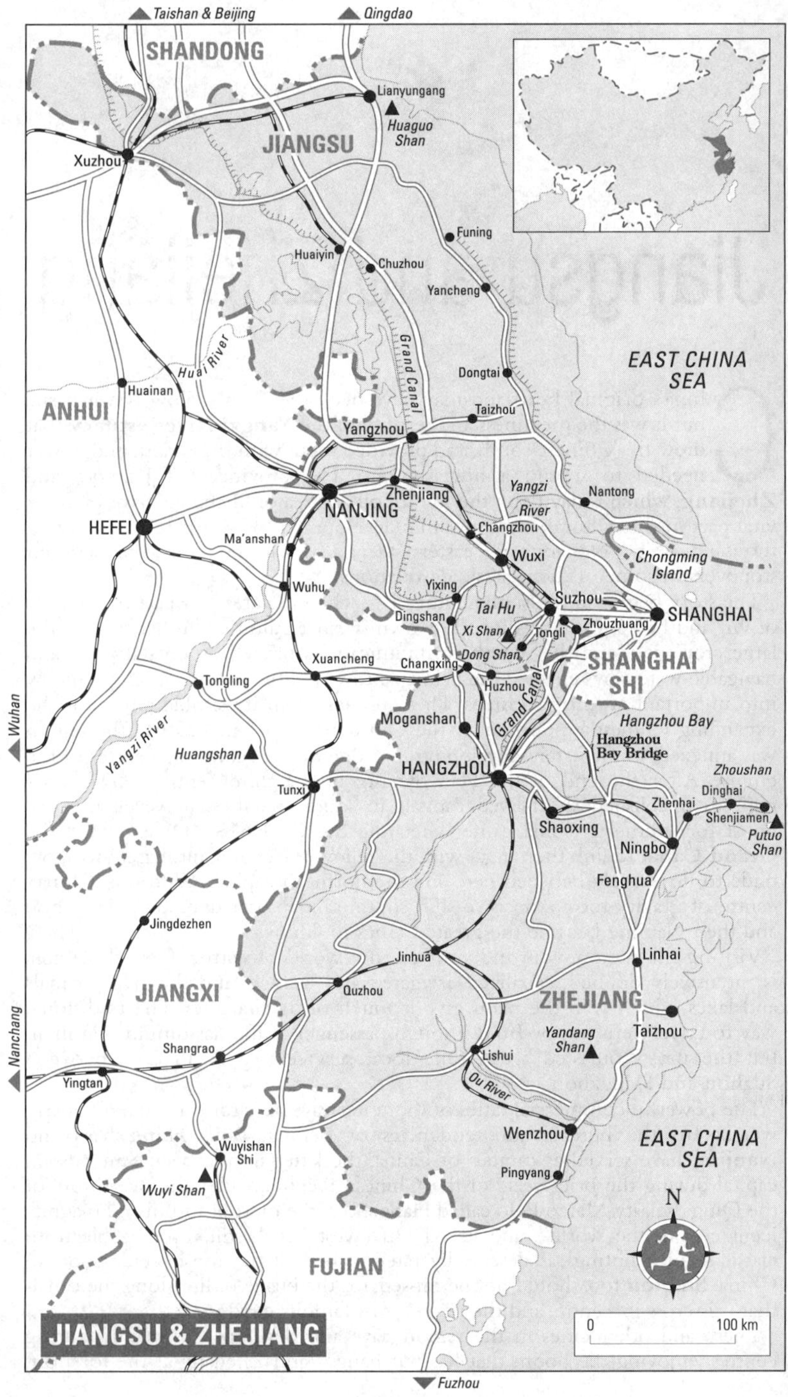
Taishan & Beijing
Qingdao
SHANDONG
Lianyungang
Huaguo Shan
JIANGSU
Xuzhou
Funing
Huaiyin
Chuzhou
Yancheng
Grand Canal
Huai River
Dongtai
EAST CHINA SEA
Huainan
ANHUI
Taizhou
Yangzhou
Zhenjiang
Yangzi River
Nantong
NANJING
HEFEI
Changzhou
Ma'anshan
Wuxi
Chongming Island
Wuhu
Yixing
Suzhou
Tai Hu
SHANGHAI
Dingshan
Zhouzhuang
Xi Shan
Tongli
Dong Shan
SHANGHAI SHI
Xuancheng
Changxing
Tongling
Huzhou
Grand Canal
Hangzhou Bay
Moganshan
Wuhan
Hangzhou Bay Bridge
Huangshan
Yangzi River
HANGZHOU
Zhoushan
Tunxi
Dinghai
Zhenhai
Shenjiamen
Putuo Shan
Shaoxing
Ningbo
Fenghua
Jingdezhen
Jinhua
Linhai
Quzhou
JIANGXI
ZHEJIANG
Taizhou
Yandang Shan
Nanchang
Shangrao
Lishui
Yingtan
Ou River
Wenzhou
EAST CHINA SEA
Wuyishan Shi
Pingyang
Wuyi Shan
N
FUJIAN
0
100 km
JIANGSU & ZHEJIANG
Fuzhou

of economic development in China. The downside to relative prosperity in China is chronic overpopulation. Well over 120 million people live in Jiangsu, Shanghai and Zhejiang, and it can seem that the area has been built over from end to end. You'll be hard-pressed to find much that might be classed as countryside here, with the exceptions of the area around charming **Shaoxing**, and, above all, the sacred Buddhist island of **Putuo Shan**, where superb beaches and monasteries are set deep in wooded hillsides.

Most visitors come here are on expensive package tours, and there are few facilities, such as foreigners' dormitories, for independent travellers. **Accommodation** is on the expensive side, with the cheapest hotels dipping only slightly below ¥200 for a double room – though youth hostels are an option in Hangzhou, Nanjing and Suzhou. **Transport** connections are decent, however: comfortable modern buses run along the many intercity expressways, and are often the best way to make relatively short trips, while train connections are also good.

The area around the Yangzi, despite being low-lying and far from the northern plains, is unpleasantly cold and damp in winter, and unbearably hot and sticky during the summer months when most people choose to visit – Nanjing's age-old reputation as one of the "three furnaces" of China is well justified. If possible, try to visit in **spring** (mid-April to late May), during which a combination of rain showers, sunshine and low humidity gives the terrain a splash of green as well as putting smiles on the faces of residents emerging from the harsh winter.

Jiangsu

Jiangsu is a long, narrow province hugging the coast south of Shandong. Low-lying, flat and wet, it is one of China's most fertile and long-inhabited areas. Today, much of it is industrial sprawl, which is why it's one of China's richest areas, but there are a few gems among all the new factory towns; provincial capital **Nanjing** is one of the great historical cities of China while **Suzhou** is an ancient city famous throughout China for its gardens and silk production.

The traditional route across Jiangsu is the **Grand Canal**, which was once navigable all the way from Hangzhou in Zhejiang province to Beijing, and is still very much alive in the sections that flow through southern Jiangsu. The province's other great water highway – the **Yangzi River** – connects Nanjing with Shanghai, ensuring that trade from both east and west continues to bring wealth to the region.

Jiangsu **cuisine** tends to be on the sweet side and is characterized by an emphasis on flavour rather than texture, and by the use of wine in cooking. That said, one of the best-known dishes, *yanshui ya* (brine duck), has none of these qualities. The duck is first pressed and salted, then steeped in brine and baked; the skin should be creamy-coloured and the flesh red and tender. Other Jiangsu dishes worth trying include *majiang yaopian* (pig's intestines), *jiwei xia* (a lake crustacean vaguely resembling a lobster, but much better tasting, locals affirm) and *paxiang jiao* (a type of vegetable that resembles banana leaves).

The Grand Canal

The **Grand Canal** (Da Yun He), at 1800km the longest canal on earth, ranks alongside the Great Wall of China as the country's greatest engineering achievement. The first sections were dug about 400 BC, probably for military purposes, but the historic task of linking the Yellow and the Yangzi rivers was not achieved until the early seventh century AD under the Sui emperor Yang Di, when as many as six million men may have been pressed into service for its construction.

Locals like to point out that whereas the Great Wall was designed to stop contact and communication, the canal was made to further it. The original function of the canal was specifically to join the fertile rice-producing areas of the Yangzi with the more heavily populated but barren lands of the north, and to alleviate the effects of regular crop failures and famine. Following its completion, however, the canal became a vital element in the expansion of **trade** under the Tang and Song, benefiting the south as much as the north. Slowly the centre of political power drifted south – by 800 AD the Yangzi basin was taking over from the Yellow River as the chief source of the empire's finances, a transformation that would bring an end to the long domination of the old northern capitals, and lead to Hangzhou and Nanjing becoming China's most populous and powerful cities. A Japanese monk, Ennin, who travelled in China from 836 to 847 AD, described the traffic on the water:

Two water buffalo were tied to more than forty boats, with two or three of the latter joined to form a single raft and with these connected in line by hawsers. Since it was difficult to hear from head to stern there was great shouting back and forth. . . . Boats of the salt bureau passed laden with salt, three or four or five boats bound side by side and in line, following one another for several tens of li.

By the twelfth century, the provinces of Jiangsu and Zhejiang had become the economic and political heart of China. The Song dynasty moved south and established a capital at **Hangzhou** and the Ming emperors subsequently based themselves in **Nanjing**. During this period, and for centuries afterwards, the canal was constantly maintained and the banks regularly built up. A Western traveller, Robert Morrison, journeying as late as 1816 from Tianjin all the way down to the Yangzi, described the sophisticated and frequent locks and noted that in places the banks were so high and the country around so low that from the boat it was possible to look down on roofs and treetops.

Not until early in the twentieth century did the canal seriously start falling into **disuse**. Contributing factors included the frequent flooding of the Yellow River, the growth of coastal shipping and the coming of the rail lines. Unused, much of the canal rapidly silted up. But since the 1950s its value has once more been recognized, and renovation undertaken. The stretch **south of the Yangzi**, running from Zhenjiang through Changzhou, Wuxi and Suzhou (and on to Hangzhou in Zhejiang province), is now navigable all year round, at least by flat-bottomed barges and the cruisers built for the tourist trade. Although most local **passenger boat services** along the canal have been dropped, the surviving services between Hangzhou and Suzhou will probably give you enough of a taste. It's fascinating rather than beautiful – as well as the frenetic loading and unloading of barges, you'll see serious pollution and heavy industry. **North of the Yangzi**, the canal is seasonably navigable virtually up to Jiangsu's northern border with Shandong, and major works are going on to allow bulk carriers access to the coal-producing city of Xuzhou. Beyond here, towards the Yellow River, sadly the canal remains impassable.

Suzhou and around

Famous for its gardens and its silk, the ancient and moated city of **SUZHOU**, just sixty minutes from Shanghai by train, lies at the point where the rail line meets the Grand Canal, about 30km to the east of Tai Hu. The town itself is built on a network of interlocking canals whose waters feed the series of renowned **classical gardens** that are Suzhou's pride and glory.

He Lu, semi-mythical ruler of the Kingdom of Wu, is said to have founded Suzhou in 600 BC as his capital, but it was the arrival of the **Grand Canal** more than a thousand years later that marked the beginning of the city's prosperity. The **silk trade** too was established early here, flourishing under the Tang and thoroughly booming when the whole imperial court moved south under the Song. To this day, silk remains an important source of Suzhou's income.

With the imperial capital close by at Hangzhou, Suzhou attracted an overspill of scholars, officials and merchants, bringing wealth and patronage with them. In the late thirteenth century, Marco Polo reported "six thousand bridges, clever merchants, cunning men of all crafts, very wise men called Sages and great natural physicians". These were the people responsible for carving out the intricate gardens that now represent Suzhou's primary attractions. When the first Ming emperor founded his capital at Nanjing, the city continued to enjoy a privileged position within the orbit of the court and to flourish as a centre for the production of wood block and the weaving of silk. The business was transformed by the gathering of the workforce into great sheds in a manner not seen in the West until the coming of the Industrial Revolution three centuries later.

Until recently, Suzhou's good fortune had been to avoid the ravages of history, despite suffering brief periods of occupation by the Taipings (see p.419) in the 1860s and by the Japanese during World War II. The 2500-year-old city walls, however, which even in 1925 were still an effective defence against rampaging warlords, were almost entirely demolished after 1949, and the parts of the **old city** that still survive – moats, gates, tree-lined canals, stone bridges, cobblestoned streets and whitewashed old houses – are disappearing fast. Suzhou is now a boom town, with industrial areas springing up all round the outskirts. But its centre retains enough of its original character to merit a visit of several days, while in the immediate vicinity of the city are a number of places which make easy day- or half-day trips, with **Tai Hu** (see p.410) a straightforward excursion slightly further afield.

Arrival and city transport

Lying within a rectangular moat formed by canals, the historic town's clear grid of streets and waterways makes Suzhou a relatively easy place in which to get your bearings. **Renmin Lu**, the main street, bulldozes south through the centre from the **train station**, which is just to the north of the moat. The traditional commercial centre of the city lies around **Guanqian Jie**, halfway down Renmin Lu, an area of cramped, animated streets thronged with small shops, teahouses and restaurants.

Nearly all travellers arrive by **train**, Suzhou being on the main Shanghai–Nanjing rail line. Buses #1 and #20 take you into town from just east of the train station. Some private **minibuses**, for example services to and from Wuxi and points on Tai Hu, also use the train-station square as their terminus.

Suzhou and around

Suzhou	苏州	*sūzhōu*
Beisi Ta	北寺塔	*běisì tā*
Canglang Ting	沧浪亭	*cānglàng tíng*
Museum of Opera and Theatre	戏曲博物馆	*xìqǔ bówùguǎn*
Ou Yuan	耦园	*ǒuyuán*
Pan Men	盘门	*pánmén*
Ruiguang Ta	瑞光塔	*ruìguāng tǎ*
Shi Lu	石路	*shílù*
Shizi Lin	狮子林	*shīzi lín*
Shuang Ta	双塔	*shuāng tǎ*
Silk Museum	丝绸博物馆	*sīchóu bówùguǎn*
Suzhou Museum	苏州博物馆	*sūzhōu bówùguǎn*
Wangshi Yuan	网狮园	*wǎngshī yuán*
Wumen Qiao	吴门桥	*wúmén qiáo*
Xuanmiao Guan	玄妙观	*xuánmiào guàn*
Yi Yuan	怡园	*yíyuán*
Zhuozheng Yuan	拙政园	*zhuózhèng yuán*
Accommodation		
Bamboo Grove	竹辉饭店	*zhúhuī fàndiàn*
Dongwu	东吴饭店	*dōngwú fàndiàn*
Lexiang	乐乡饭店	*lèxiāng fàndiàn*
Motel 168	莫泰连锁旅店	*mò tài lián suǒ lǚ diàn*
Nanlin	南林饭店	*nánlín fàndiàn*
New Century	新世纪大酒店	*xīnshìjì dàjiǔdiàn*
Sheraton	喜来登大酒店	*xǐláidēng dàjiǔdiàn*
Suzhou	苏州饭店	*sūzhōu fàndiàn*
Suzhou Friendship	苏州友谊宾馆	*sūzhōu yǒuyí bīnguǎn*
Suzhou International Youth Hostel	苏州国际青年旅社	*sūzhōu guójì qīngnián lǚshè*
Eating		
Dasanyuan	大三元	*dà sǎn yuán*
Deyuelou	得月	*déyuè lóu*
Dianyun Fanzhuang	滇云饭庄	*diānyún fànzhuāng*
Korea Restaurant	汉城韩国料理	*hànchénghánguó liàolǐ*
Laozhenxing	老振兴餐馆	*lǎozhenxīng cānguǎn*
Scarlet's	乱世佳人	*luànshì jiārén*
Songhelou Caiguan	松鹤楼	*sōnghèlóu*
Suco Coffee	苏卡咖啡	*sūkǎ kāfēi*
Xinjiang Yakexi	新疆亚克西酒楼	*xīnjiāng yǎkèxī jiǔlóu*
Around Suzhou		
Baodai Qiao	宝带桥	*bǎodài qiáo*
Lingyan Shan	灵岩山	*língyán shān*
Tianchi Shan	天池山	*tiānchí shān*
Tianping Shan	天平山	*tiānpíng shān*
Tongli	同里	*tónglǐ*
Tai Hu	太湖	*tàihú*
Ferry Pier	陆巷码头	*lùxiàng mǎtóu*
Dong Shan	东山	*dōngshān*
Longtou Shan	龙头山	*lóngtóu shān*
Zijin An	紫金庵	*zǐjīn' ān*
Xi Shan	西山	*xīshān*
Donghe	东河	*dōnghé*
Linwu Cave	林屋古洞	*línwūgǔdòng*

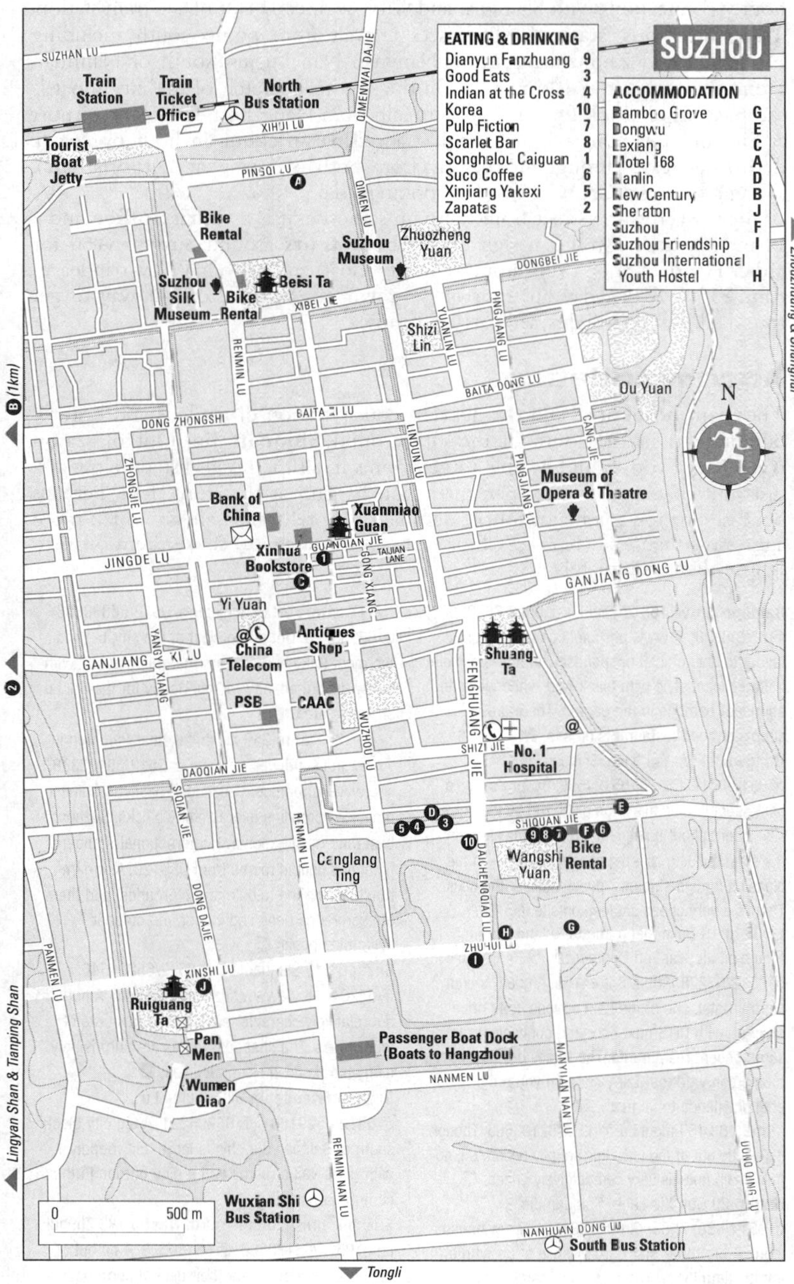
SUZHOU
EATING & DRINKING
Dianyun Fanzhuang 9
Good Eats 3
Indian at the Cross 4
Korea 10
Pulp Fiction 7
Scarlet Bar 8
Songhelou Caiguan 1
Suco Coffee 6
Xinjiang Yakexi 5
Zapatas 2
ACCOMMODATION
Bamboo Grove G
Dongwu E
Lexiang C
Motel 168 A
Nanlin D
New Century B
Sheraton J
Suzhou F
Suzhou Friendship I
Suzhou International Youth Hostel H
Train Station
Train Ticket Office
North Bus Station
Tourist Boat Jetty
Bike Rental
Suzhou Museum
Zhuozheng Yuan
Suzhou Silk Museum
Beisi Ta
Shizi Lin
Ou Yuan
Museum of Opera & Theatre
Bank of China
Xuanmiao Guan
Xinhua Bookstore
Yi Yuan
Antiques Shop
China Telecom
Shuang Ta
PSB
CAAC
No. 1 Hospital
Canglang Ting
Wangshi Yuan
Ruiguang Ta
Pan Men
Wumen Qiao
Passenger Boat Dock (Boats to Hangzhou)
Wuxian Shi Bus Station
South Bus Station
SUZHAN LU
XIHUI LU
PINSQI LU
QIMENWAI DAJIE
QIMEN LU
DONGBEI JIE
XIBEI JIE
RENMIN LU
YUANLIN LU
PINGJIANG LU
BAITA DONG LU
BAITA XI LU
DONG ZHONGSHI
LINDUN LU
CANG JIE
ZHONGJIE LU
GUANQIAN JIE
TAIJIAN LANE
GONG XIANG
JINGDE LU
GANJIANG DONG LU
GANJIANG XI LU
YANGYU XIANG
FENGHUANG JIE
WUZHOU LU
SHIZI JIE
DAOQIAN JIE
SIQIAN JIE
SHIQUAN JIE
DAICHENGQIAO LU
DONG DAJIE
ZHUHUI LU
PANMEN LU
XINSHI LU
NANMEN LU
NANYUAN NAN LU
RENMIN NAN LU
QING DONG LU
NANHUAN DONG LU
0 500 m
N
B (1km)
2
Lingyan Shan & Tianping Shan
Zhouzhuang & Shanghai
Tongli

6

JIANGSU AND ZHEJIANG

Suzhou has two main bus stations. The **north bus station**, which has half-hourly connections with Shanghai and Wuxi, is directly east of the train station. The **south bus station**, which sees arrivals from points south including Hangzhou and Zhouzhuang, is on Nanyuan Nan Lu just south of Nanhuan Dong Lu. Just east of Renmin Lu on the southern stretch of the city moat is the **passenger dock** for canal boats to and from Hangzhou. There's no airport at Suzhou (the nearest is at Shanghai, accessible in about an hour by coach; departures leave throughout the day from both of Shanghai's airports; ¥52), though there is a CAAC office for bookings (see p.409).

Directly across the street from the train station exit is a **tourist office** and a small jetty where you can sign up for **boat tours** around Suzhou (¥60 for either Hanshan Si or a ride around the city moat) and to Tongli (day-trip leaves 8am; ¥150). A one-day bus tour of the town can be an excellent way to get round all the main sights; see p.410 for more.

Accommodation

The main **hotel** area, and the heaviest concentration of gardens and historic buildings, is in the south of the city, around **Shiquan Jie**. Out of season (Oct–May), you should be able to get rooms in all the hotels listed below at a discount of ten to twenty percent if you bargain at the front desk. Perhaps because Suzhou is a major tourist destination, hotel touts here are much more aggressive than elsewhere in China – the best strategy to shake them off is to ignore them completely.

Bamboo Grove 168 Zhuhui Lu ⓣ0512/65205601, ⓕ65208778, ⓦwww.bg-hotel.com. A tour-group favourite, this efficient Japanese-run four-star hotel imitates local style with black-and-white walls and abundant bamboo in the garden. There are a couple of good restaurants on site. ⑨

Dongwu 24 Wu Ya Chang, Shiquan Jie ⓣ0512/65193681, ⓕ65194590. By far Suzhou's best budget hotel, this large place run by the university is central but quiet, and offers rooms either in the main building or – the cheaper option – in the pleasant foreign students' guesthouse at the back. There's a very cheap canteen on site too. ④

Lexiang 18 Dajin Xiang, the third lane south of Guanqian Jie, east off Renmin Lu ⓣ0512/65228888, ⓕ65244165. A good, friendly, central hotel, one of the best options in its price bracket, with CITS next door and convenient for some decent restaurants. The three- or four-bed rooms can work out fairly cheap if you bring enough friends to fill them. ⑦

Motel 168 16 Pingqi Lu ⓣ0512/82106666. Though it's a little out of the way, this chirpily decorated, no-frills chain hotel is very competitively priced. ③

Nanlin 20 Gun Xiu Fang, Shiquan Jie ⓣ0512/68017888, ⓕ68015818, ⓦwww.nanlin.com. A big three-star garden-style affair with an immaculate lobby. The new wing has luxury rooms, while the old wing still offers reasonably priced doubles and triples. ⑨

New Century 23 Guangji Lu ⓣ0512/65338888, ⓕ65335798. Out in the west of the city, beyond the moat (take bus #7 from the train station), with nicely decorated, airy rooms. Handy for the Shi Lu shopping area. ⑦

Sheraton 259 Xinshi Lu, near Pan Men in the southwest of town ⓣ0512/65103388, ⓦwww.sheraton.com/suzhou. A pastiche Chinese mansion sprawling over two city blocks, Suzhou's best (and most expensive) international-standard hotel has double rooms from US$120. A stream runs through the middle of the grounds, and there are serene gardens and indoor and outdoor swimming pools. ⑧

Suzhou 345 Shiquan Jie ⓣ0512/65204646, ⓕ65204015, ⓦwww.suzhou-hotel.com. A huge but relatively characterless place, a favourite of tour groups. The cheapest rooms are surprisingly dingy but do have clean facilities. ⑧

Suzhou Friendship 349 Zhuhui Lu ⓣ0512/65291601, ⓕ65206221. A big city block south of Shiquan Jie, this is large and friendly, with good-value rooms and a nice garden in the central atrium. ⑥

Suzhou International Youth Hostel 186 Zhuhui Lu ⓣ0512/65180266, ⓕ65180366. A bit out of the way, but worth it for their decent dorm beds. Rooms, however are far better at the *Dongwu*. Free Wi-Fi and laundry. Dorm beds ¥45, ⑤

The City

Among the Chinese, Suzhou is one of the most highly favoured tourist destinations in the country, and the city is packed with visitors from far and wide. This can make for a festive atmosphere, but it also means that you are rarely able to appreciate the **gardens** in the peace for which they were designed. The three most famous gardens – Wangshi Yuan, Shizi Lin and Zhuozheng Yuan – attract a stream of visitors year round, but many of the equally beautiful yet lesser-known gardens, notably Canglang Ting and Ou Yuan, are comparatively serene and crowd-free. The best strategy is to visit as much of the three popular gardens as possible before 10am and spend the rest of the day in the smaller gardens. If you can, choose a day with blue sky and a hint of cloud – the gardens need contrast, light and shade, clear shadow and bold reflection. They can be appreciated at any time of year, although springtime brings more blossom and brighter colours. The gardens are open daily; note that during the summer and the major public holidays, entry fees are slightly higher than given below

You can enjoy Suzhou by simply **roaming**. Stray from the main streets and you'll come across pagodas, temples, lively shopping districts and hectic canal traffic. Distances are a bit too large to rely purely on walking, but **cycling** is an excellent alternative as the terrain is pretty flat (see p.409 for bike rental).

Suzhou's gardens

Gardens, above all, are what Suzhou is all about. They have been laid out here since the Song dynasty, a thousand years ago, and in their Ming and Qing heyday it is said that the city had two hundred of them. Some half-dozen major gardens have now been restored, as well as a number of smaller ones. Elsewhere in China you'll find grounds – as at Chengde or the Summer Palace outside Beijing – laid out on a grand scale, but the gardens of Suzhou are tiny in comparison, often in small areas behind high compound walls, and thus are far closer to the true essence of a Chinese garden.

Chinese gardens do not set out to improve upon a slice of nature or to look natural, which is why many Western eyes find them hard to accept or enjoy. They are a serious art form, the garden designer working with rock, water, buildings, trees and vegetation in subtly different combinations; as with painting, sculpture and poetry, the aim is to produce for contemplation the **balance**, **harmony**, **proportion** and **variety** which the Chinese seek in life. The wealthy scholars and merchants who built Suzhou's gardens intended them to be enjoyed either in solitude or in the company of friends over a glass of wine and a poetry recital or literary discussion. Their designers used little pavilions and terraces to suggest a larger scale, undulating covered walkways and galleries to give a downward view, and intricate interlocking groups of rock and bamboo to hint at, and half conceal, what lies beyond. Glimpses through delicate lattices, tile-patterned openings or moon gates, and reflections in water created cunning perspectives which either suggested a whole landscape or borrowed outside features (such as external walls of neighbouring buildings) as part of the design, in order to create an illusion of distance.

Among the essential features of the Suzhou gardens are the white pine trees, the odd-shaped rocks from Tai Hu and the stone tablets over the entrances. The whole was completed by animals – there are still fish and turtles in some ponds today. **Differences in style** among the various gardens arise basically from the mix and balance of the ingredients; some are dominated by water, others are mazes of contorted rock, yet others are mainly inward-looking, featuring pavilions full of strange furniture. Almost everything you see has some symbolic significance – the pine tree and the crane for long life, mandarin ducks for married bliss, for example.

Beisi Ta and the Suzhou Silk Museum

A few minutes' walk south down Renmin Lu from the train station, the **Beisi Ta** (North Temple Pagoda; daily 7.45am–5pm; ¥35) looms up unmistakeably. On the site of the residence of the mother of Wu Kingdom king Sun Quan, the Beisi Ta was first built in the third century AD, and rebuilt in 1582. The pagoda is, at 76m, the tallest Chinese pagoda south of the Yangzi, though it retains only nine of its original eleven storeys. Climbing it gives an excellent view over some of Suzhou's more conspicuous features – the Shuang Ta, the Xuanmiao Guan, and, in the far southwest corner, the Ruiguang Ta. There's also a very pleasant teahouse on site.

Virtually opposite, also on Renmin Lu, is the **Suzhou Silk Museum** (daily 9am–5.30pm; ¥10), one of China's better-presented museums, labelled in English throughout. Starting from the legendary inventor of silk, Lei Zu, the concubine of the equally legendary emperor Huang Di, it traces the history of silk production and its use from 4000 BC to the present day. There are displays of looms and weaving machines, and reproductions of early silk patterns, but the most riveting display – and something of a shock – is the room full of silkworms munching mulberry leaves and spinning cocoons, and copulating moths.

Suzhou Museum, Zhuozheng Yuan and Shizi Lin

The town seems proud of the new **Suzhou Museum** (daily 8.15am–4.15pm; ¥20), at the intersection of Dongbei Lu and Qimen Lu; you'll see pictures of it everywhere. Designed by China's premier "starchitect", IM Pei, it is by far the most successful of the many attempts to update Suzhou's characteristic white wall and black beam style. The collection, though small, is pretty good too, and there are plenty of English captions. Some exquisitely delicate china and jade pieces are on show in the first two galleries; look out for the ugly toad carved out of jasper. In the painting gallery the Ming image of a duckling will raise a smile, but the museum's highlight is the craft gallery, which holds some fantastically elaborate carvings of Buddhist scenes in bamboo roots.

Just next door lies the largest of the Suzhou gardens, covering forty thousand square metres, the **Zhuozheng Yuan** (Humble Administrator's Garden; ¥70). It's based on water and set out in three linked sections: the eastern part (just inside the entrance) consists of a small lotus pond and pavilions; the centre is largely water, with two small islands connected by zigzag bridges, while the western part has unusually open green spaces. Built at the time of the Ming by an imperial censor, Wang Xianchen, who had just resigned his post, the garden was named by its creator as an ironic lament on the fact that he could now administer nothing but gardening.

A couple of minutes south of the Zhuozheng Yuan is another must-see garden, the **Shizi Lin** (Lion Grove; daily 7.30am–4.30pm; ¥30). Tian Ru, the monk who laid this out in 1342, named it in honour of his teacher, Zhi Zheng, who lived on Lion Rock Mountain, and the rocks of which it largely consists are supposed to resemble lions in all shapes and sizes. Once chosen, these strange water-worn rocks were submerged for decades in Tai Hu to be further eroded. Part of the rockery takes the form of a convoluted labyrinth, from the top of which you emerge occasionally to gaze down at the water reflecting the green trees and grey stone. Qing emperors Qianlong and Kangxi were said to be so enamoured of these rockeries that they had the garden at the Yuanmingyuan Palace in Beijing modelled on them.

Xuanmiao Guan and Yi Yuan

Moving south from here, you arrive at the **Xuanmiao Guan** (Taoist Temple of Mystery; daily 7.30am–4.30pm; ¥10), just north of Guanqian Jie and rather incongruously at the heart of the modern city's consumer zone. Founded originally during the Jin dynasty in the third century AD, the temple has been destroyed, rebuilt, burnt down and put back together many times during its history. For centuries it was the scene of a great bazaar where travelling showmen, acrobats and actors entertained the crowds. Nowadays the complex, still an attractive, lively place, basically consists of a vast entrance court full of resting locals with, at its far end, a hall of Taoist deities and symbols; it's all encircled by a newly constructed park.

A few minutes south of Guanqian Jie, on the northwest corner of the Renmin Lu and Ganjiang Lu junction, is one of the lesser gardens, **Yi Yuan** (Joyous Garden; daily 7.30am–11pm; ¥15), laid out by official Gu Wenbin. Late Qing-dynasty, and hence considerably newer than the others, it is supposed to encompass all the key features of a Chinese garden; unusually, it also has formal flowerbeds and arrangements of coloured pebbles.

The Museum of Opera and Theatre and Ou Yuan

A ten-minute walk along narrow lanes due east from Guanqian Jie, the unusual and memorable **Museum of Opera and Theatre** stands on Zhongzhangjia Xiang (daily 8.30am–4.30pm; ¥8). The rooms are filled with costumes, masks, musical instruments, and even a full-sized model orchestra, complete with cups of tea, though the building itself is the star, a Ming-dynasty theatre made of latticed wood. The Suzhou area is the historical home of the 5000-year-old **Kun Opera** style, China's oldest operatic form – Beijing Opera has existed for a mere 3000 years. Kun is distinguished by storytelling and ballad singing, though it can be hard to follow as it is performed in the all-but-unintelligible (even if you speak Chinese) Suzhou dialect. The curators are gold mines of information on the art form as well as on the degradation that opera performers had to endure during the Cultural Revolution – but you'll need to speak Chinese to engage them in conversation.

A five-minute walk northeast of the museum, abutting the outer moat and along a canal, is the **Ou Yuan** (daily 8am–5pm; ¥15), whose greatest asset is its comparative freedom from the loudhailer-toting tour groups that crowd the other gardens. Here a series of hallways and corridors opens onto an intimate courtyard, with a pond in the middle surrounded by abstract rock formations and several relaxing teahouses. The surrounding area houses some of the loveliest architecture, bridges and canals in Suzhou.

Shuang Ta and Canglang Ting

Several blocks east of Renmin Lu and immediately south of Ganjiang Lu, the **Shuang Ta** (Twin Pagodas; daily 7am–4.30pm; ¥4) are matching slender towers built during the Song dynasty by a group of successful candidates in the imperial examinations who wanted to honour their teacher. Too flimsy to climb the pagodas sprout from a delightful patch of garden. At the other end is a teahouse crowded in summer with old men fanning themselves against the heat.

A kilometre or so farther southwest of here, just beyond Shiquan Jie the undervisited but intriguing **Canglang Ting** (Dark Blue Wave Pavilion; daily 8am–5pm; ¥15) is the oldest of the major surviving gardens, at the corner of Renmin Lu and Zhuhui Lu. Originally built in the Song dynasty by scholar Su Zimei around 1044 AD, it's approached through a grand stone bridge and ceremonial marble archway. The central mound inside is designed to look like a forested hill. In the south of the garden (away from the entrance) stands the curious Five Hundred Sage Temple lined with stone tablets recording the names and achievements of great statesmen, heroes and poets of Suzhou.

Wangshi Yuan

Wangshi Yuan (Master of the Nets Garden; daily 7.30am–5pm; ¥30) is on Shiquan Jie, a short walk west from the *Suzhou Hotel* and down a narrow alleyway on the left. So named because the owner, a retired official, decided he wanted to become a fisherman, this tiny and intimate garden was started in 1140, but was later abandoned and not restored to its present layout until 1770. Considered by garden connoisseurs to be the finest of them all, it boasts an attractive central lake, minuscule connecting halls, pavilions with pocket-handkerchief courtyards and carved wooden doors – and rather more visitors than it can cope with. The garden is said to be best seen on moonlit nights, when the moon can be seen three times over from the Moon-watching Pavilion – in the sky, in the water and in a mirror. The garden's other main features are its delicate latticework and fretted windows, through which you can catch a series of glimpses – a glimmer of bamboo, dark interiors, water and a miniature rockery framed in the three windows of a study. Outside the dead winter months Wangshi Yuan plays host to nightly arts performances.

Pan Men and around

In the far southwestern corner of the moated area is one of the city's most pleasant areas, centred around **Pan Men** (Coiled Gate) and a stretch of the original city wall, built in 514 BC by King Helu of the Wu Kingdom; the gate is the only surviving one of eight that once surrounded Suzhou. The best approach to this area is from the south, via **Wumen Qiao**, a delightful high-arched bridge (the tallest in Suzhou) with steps built into it; it's a great vantage point for watching the canal traffic (bus #7 from the train station passes the southern edge of the moat). Just inside Pan Men sits the dramatic **Ruiguang Ta** (¥6), a thousand-year-old pagoda now rebuilt from ruins, once housing a rare Buddhist pearl stupa (since moved to the Suzhou Museum).

Eating, drinking and entertainment

Suzhou cooking, with its emphasis on fish from the nearby lakes and rivers, is justly renowned; specialities include *yinyu* ("silver fish") and *kaobing* (grilled

▲ Wumen Qiao

pancakes with sweet filling). The town is well stocked with **restaurants** for all budgets – in addition to those reviewed below, flanking *Songhelou* on Taijian Lane are four other restaurants of repute: the *Dasanyuan*, *Deyuelou*, *Wangsi* and *Laozhengxing*, all of which claim more than 100 years of history, are big, busy and good for a splurge on local dishes, with foreigner-friendly staff and menus.

The town holds little in the way of **nightlife** – the younger set escapes to Shanghai for serious nights out. That said, there is a slew of touristy bars scattered along Shiquan Jie near Wangshi Yuan; the best are *Pulp Fiction*, 200m west of the *Suzhou Hotel*, the next door *Scarlet Bar*, and the Shanghai chain *Zapatas* at 158 Xinggang Lu (a pedestrianized strip of bars and shops), in the west of the city. For the latest on new bar and restaurant openings, check Ⓦ www.whatsoninsuzhou.com.

The best entertainment in town is the nightly **opera extravaganza** at Wangshi Yuan (spring–autumn 7.30–10pm; ¥80 including admission to garden), featuring eight displays of the most prominent forms of Chinese performing arts, from Beijing Opera to folk dancing and storytelling.

Restaurants

Dianyun Fanzhuang 519 Shiquan Jie. A friendly, inexpensive place for rice noodles and other Yunnan specialties – sit by the window for a view of the tourists. Open 24hr.

Good Eats Cafe 694 Shiquan Jie. An American café that's open till 4am; go for the hot dogs rather than the fish and chips.

Indian at the Cross 758 Shiquan Jie. Relatively cheap curries and friendly staff. Daily 11am–2pm & 5–11pm.

Korea Restaurant 579 Daichengqiao Lu, at the Shiquan Jie intersection. One of the best of a host of unimaginatively named Korean restaurants, with good barbecued beef cooked at the table.

Songhelou Caiguan On Taijian Lane, 200m east of Renmin Lu. The most famous restaurant in town – it claims to be old enough to have served Emperor Qianlong. The menu is elaborate and long on fish and seafood (crab, eel, squirrel fish and the like), though not cheap at around ¥150 a head. There are four good places nearby on Taijian Lane; see above.

Suco Coffee 357 Shiquan Jie. A café with excellent smoothies, and they'll recommend a brand of Chinese tea according to your star sign. Wireless and comfy seating make for a good place to linger.

Xinjiang Yakexi 768 Shiquan Jie. Xinjiang comfort food – pulled noodles with vegetables (*latiaozi*) and naan bread, among others – in a bright dining room bustling with local Uyghurs and tourists. Open late.

Listings

Airlines The main CAAC reservations and ticketing office is at 943 Renmin Lu, a few minutes' walk south of Ganjiang Lu (daily 8am–7pm; Ⓣ 0512/65104881).

Banks and exchange The Bank of China head office is on Renmin Lu right in the centre of town, just north of Guanqian Jie (daily 8.15am–5.15pm).

Bike rental Many gift shops along Shiquan Jie rent bikes; check those just west of the *Suzhou Hotel* main gate. They charge ¥15–25 for a day with a deposit of a few hundred yuan (or a passport). A couple of storefronts just north of the Silk Museum also rent bikes, as does the Youth Hostel (see p.404; ¥20/day).

Boats A nightly boat service operates between Suzhou and Hangzhou in both directions, taking around 10hr, with a bar and karaoke on board. The incoming boat arrives around 7am, and the outbound boat leaves at 5.30pm; fares range from ¥80 to ¥150. Buy tickets at the dock at the passenger boat dock, or at the ticket window (daily 8am–8pm) 50m south of Xuanmiao Guan, on the west side of Gong Xiang.

Bookshops The Xinhua bookstore at 166 Guanqian Jie has a small selection of classic novels.

Hospital The No. 1 Hospital is at the junction of Fenghuang Jie and Shizi Jie.

Internet access The most pleasant place to get online is an unnamed net bar on Shizi Jie east of the hospital. Alternatively, try the Jinpo Net bar next to China Telecom at 333 Renmin Lu. Places are constantly opening and closing along Shiquan Jie, so check with your hotel for the latest information.

Mail Suzhou's main post office (daily 8am–8pm) is at the corner of Renmin Lu and Jingde Lu.

PSB On Renmin Lu, at the junction with the small lane Dashitou Xiang.

Shopping There are numerous opportunities to shop for silk in Suzhou, although be aware of outrageous prices, especially in the boutiques along Shiquan Jie and Guanyin Jie and the night market on Shi Lu. Bargain hard, as these sellers can quote prices up to ten times the going rate. The King Silk Store next to the Silk Museum has a good selection, including great duvets starting at just over ¥300. The Antique Store (daily 9.30am–9.30pm) along Renmin Lu at Ganjiang Dong Lu is the place to find old furniture, while paintings and embroidery are on hand in a pavilion near the corner of Renmin Lu and Baita Xi Lu and in the shops along Shiquan Jie.

Tours Minibus tours of Suzhou, on which you get ferried to the sights, often without any commentary, depart from the train-station square at 7.30am and return at 4.30pm, and cost ¥15 exclusive of admission charges. Air-conditioned bus tours to Suzhou sights or to surrounding areas such as Tongli can be booked at CITS (or other travel services).

Trains The train ticket office is located in a separate building to the left of the station as you emerge. There's also a convenient ticket window 50m south of Xuanmiao Guan on the west side of Gong Xiang (daily 8am–8pm). CITS and most hotels will book tickets for a commission.

Travel agents CITS is next to the *Lexiang Hotel* on Dajing Xiang (☎0512/65155207). Nearly all hotels have their own travel agencies.

Around Suzhou

TONGLI (¥60), 23km from Suzhou, is a superb example of a town built on water – every house backs on to canals, there are 49 stone bridges and nearly all movement takes place by boat. You can reach this small town by minibus from either bus station for ¥7. Tongli's main street has become very touristy, with overpriced souvenir stands and restaurants, but a little exploration along the back alleys will reveal canals shaded by stately bridges, overhanging willows, lazing elderly folk, putt-putting barges and rural splendour. The top sight here is the UNESCO-listed **Tuisi Yuan** (daily 7.45am–5.30pm; ¥25), a late Qing garden that rather resembles Suzhou's Ou Yuan. It was built by disillusioned retired official Ren Lansheng in 1886 as a place to retreat and meditate – though you'll have to come in the early morning, before the tour groups arrive, if that is your intention. Nearby, you'll find the **Jiayin Hall** (daily 9am–5.15pm; ¥2), the austere two-storey home of Liu Yazi, a Nationalist actor and entertainer renowned for his eccentric collection of gauze caps. Finally, few visitors can resist popping into the **Sex Museum** (daily 8am–5.30pm; ¥2) just around the corner from the Tuisi Garden. Set up by single-minded sexologist Liu Dalin, the collection of ancient dildoes and love beads, foot-binding tools, graphic bronzes, erotic scroll paintings and the like are all presented with explanations of their historical context. It's all rather less titillating and more informative than you might expect.

Fifteen and eighteen kilometres respectively west from Suzhou, **Lingyan Shan** and **Tianping Shan** both offer tremendous views and together make a good day's outing on a bicycle. At Lingyan Shan (daily 7.30am–5.30pm; ¥10) you climb stone steps past a bell tower to reach a walled enclosure with a temple hall, a seven-storey pagoda and a well. Tianping Shan (daily 8am–5pm; ¥10), 3km beyond, was already a well-known beauty spot under the Song, the hillside cut with streams and dotted with strange rock formations. Wooded paths meander up to the summit past pavilions and small gardens, and in autumn the maples which cover the slopes seem to blaze. Adventurous types can hike from Tianping Shan along a three- to four-kilometre trail that follows a hillcrest to **Tianchi Shan** (¥5), another temple complex set in more remote, scenic surroundings.

Thirty-five kilometres west of Suzhou lies the enormous **Tai Hu**, one of the largest freshwater lakes in China. It's a popular focus for a day out, though

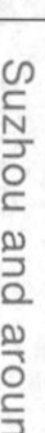

▲Tongli

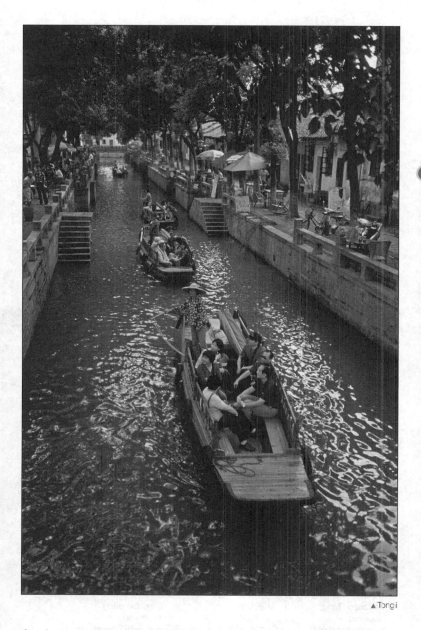

there's not much to do but wander the wooded hills around the shore. From Suzhou train station, take a minibus to rural Dongshan (1hr), which sits at the end of a long promontory. Here, you can pop into the lovely **Zijin An** (Purple Gold Nunnery; daily 7.30am–5pm; ¥20), notable for its ancient statuary and location in a secluded wood surrounded by sweet-smelling orange groves. Then it's an easy hike up to Longtou Shan, or Dragon's Head Mountain. If the peak's not shrouded, there are stunning views of the surrounding tea plantations and the lake. Head back to Dongshan and walk northwest and you'll come to the pier for ferries to the nearby island of **Xishan** (¥5). There are plenty of woods to wander through before returning to Dongshan for a minibus back to Suzhou.

Nanjing

NANJING, formerly known in the West as Nanking, is one of China's greatest cities. Its very name, "Southern Capital", stands as a direct foil to the "Northern Capital" of Beijing, and the city is still considered the rightful capital of China by many Overseas Chinese, particularly those from Taiwan. Today, it's a prosperous city, benefiting both from its proximity to Shanghai and from its gateway position on the **Yangzi River**, which stretches away west deep into China's interior. With broad, tree-lined boulevards and balconied houses within Ming walls and gates, Nanjing is also one of the most attractive of the major Chinese cities, and although it has become rather an expensive place to visit, it offers a fairly cosmopolitan range of tourist facilities, as well as a wealth of historic sites that can easily fill several days' exploration.

Nanjing

Nanjing	南京	*nánjīng*
Bailuzhou	白鹭洲	*báilù zhōu*
Chaotian Gong	朝天宫	*cháotiān gōng*
City Wall	城市墙	*chéngshì qiáng*
Dujiang Jinianbei	渡江纪念碑	*dùjiāng jìniànbēi*
Fuzi Miao	夫子庙	*fūzǐ miào*
Gugong Park	故宫公园	*gùgōng gōngyuán*
Gulou	鼓楼	*gǔlóu*
Jinghai Si	静海寺	*jìnghǎi sì*
Linggu Si	灵谷寺	*línggǔ sì*
Meiyuan Xincun	梅园新村	*méiyuán xīncūn*
Memorial to the Nanjing Massacre	南京大屠杀纪念馆	*nánjīngdàtúshā jìniànguǎn*
Ming Xiaoling	明孝陵	*míngxiào líng*
Mochou Hu Park	莫愁湖公园	*mòchóuhú gōngyuán*
Nanjing Museum	南京博物馆	*nánjīng bówùguǎn*
Presidential Palace	总统府	*zǒngtǒng fǔ*
Qinhuai River	秦淮河	*qínhuái hé*
Qixia Si	栖霞寺	*qīxiá sì*
Shixiang Lu	石象路	*shíxiàng lù*
Taiping Heavenly Kingdom History Museum	太平天国历史博物馆	*tàipíngtiānguólìshǐ bówùguǎn*
Tianchao Gong	天朝宫	*tiāncháo gōng*
Xinjiekou	新街口	*xīnjiē kǒu*
Xuanwu Hu Park	玄武湖公园	*xuánwǔhú gōngyuán*
Yangzi River Bridge	长江大桥	*chángjiāng dàqiáo*
Yuejiang Lou	阅江楼	*yuèjiāng lóu*
Yuhuatai Park	雨花台公园	*yǔhuātái gōngyuán*
Zhonghua Men	中华门	*zhōnghuá mén*
Zhongshan Ling	中山陵	*zhōngshān líng*

Some history

Occupying a strategic site on the south bank of the Yangzi River in a beautiful setting of lakes, river, wooded hills and crumbling fortifications, Nanjing has had an important role from the earliest times, though not until 600 BC were there the beginnings of a walled city. By the time the Han empire broke up in 220 AD, Nanjing was the capital of half a dozen local dynasties, and when the Sui reunited China in 589, the building of the **Grand Canal** began considerably to increase the city's economic importance. Nanjing became renowned for its forges, foundries and weaving, especially for the veined **brocade** made in noble houses and monasteries. During the Tang and Song periods, the city rivalled nearby Hangzhou as the wealthiest in the country, and in 1368 the first emperor of the Ming dynasty decided to establish Nanjing as the **capital** of all China.

Although Nanjing's claims to be the capital would be usurped by the heavily northern-based Qing dynasty, for centuries thereafter anti-authoritarian movements associated themselves with movements to restore the old capital. For eleven years in the mid-nineteenth century, the **Taiping rebels** (see box, p.419) set up the capital of their Kingdom of Heavenly Peace at Nanjing. The siege and final recapture of the city by the foreign-backed Qing armies in 1864 was one of the saddest and most dramatic events in China's history. After the Opium

Zhongshan Men	中山门	*zhōngshān mén*
Zhongyang Men	中央门	*zhōngyāng mén*
Zijin Shan	紫金山	*zǐjīn shān*
Accommodation		
Central	中心大酒店	*zhōngxīn dàjiǔdiàn*
Daqiao	大桥饭店	*dàqiáo fàndiàn*
Fuzi Miao Youth Hostel	夫子庙国际青年旅社	*fūzǐmiào guójì qīngnián lǚshè*
Grand Metro	古南都基酒店	*gǔnán dūjī jiǔdiàn*
Hongqiao	虹桥饭店	*hóngqiáo fàndiàn*
Jin's Inn	金一村大方巷店	*jīnyīcūn dàfāngxiàngdiàn*
Mandarin Garden	状元大酒店	*zhuàngyuán dàjiǔdiàn*
Sheraton Kingsley	金丝利喜来登酒店	*jīnsīlì xǐláidēng jiǔdiàn*
Shuangmenlou	双门楼宾馆	*shuāngménlóu bīnguǎn*
Xihuamen	西华门饭店	*xīhuámén fàndiàn*
Xuanwu	玄武饭店	*xuánwǔ fàndiàn*
Zhanyuan Youth Hostel	瞻园国际青年旅舍	*zhānyuán guójì qīngnián lǚshè*
Zhongshan	中山大厦	*zhōngshān dàshà*
Eating and drinking		
Bella Napoli	贝拉那波利意大利餐厅	*bèilā nàbōlì yìdàlì cāntīng*
Blue Marlin	蓝枪鱼西餐厅	*lánqiāngyú xīcāntīng*
Daniang Shuijiao	大娘水饺	*dàniáng shuǐjiǎo*
Jiangsu	江苏饭店	*jiāngsū fàndiàn*
Lao Zhengxing	老正兴菜馆	*lǎozhèngxīng càiguǎn*
Scarlet's	乱世佳人	*luànshì jiārén*
Shanghai Tan	上海滩	*shànghǎi tān*
Shizi Qiao	狮子桥	*shīzi qiáo*
Swede & Kraut	老外乐	*lǎowài lè*
Xiao Ren Ren	云中食品店	*yúnzhōng shípǐndiàn*

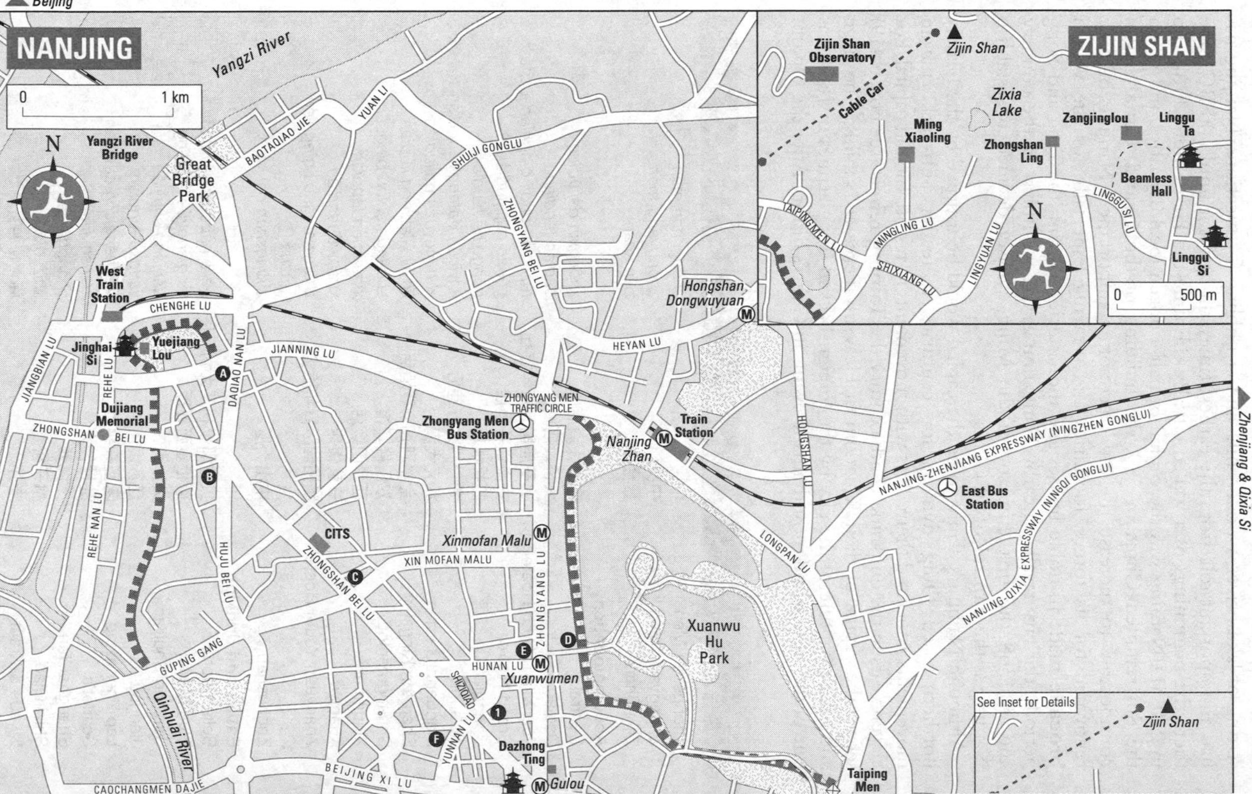
NANJING
0 1 km
N
Beijing
Yangzi River
Yangzi River Bridge
Great Bridge Park
BAOTAIQIAO JIE
YUAN LI
SHUIJI GONGLU
ZHONGYANG BEI LU
West Train Station
CHENGHE LU
Yuejiang Lou
Jinghai Si
JIANGBIAN LU
REHE LU
DAQIAO NAN LU
JIANNING LU
A
Dujiang Memorial
ZHONGSHAN BEI LU
B
REHE NAN LU
HUJU BEI LU
CITS
ZHONGSHAN BEI LU
C
XIN MOFAN MALU
Xinmofan Malu
ZHONGYANG MEN TRAFFIC CIRCLE
Zhongyang Men Bus Station
ZHONGYANG LU
D
E
HUNAN LU
Xuanwumen
GUPING GANG
Qinhuai River
SHIZIQIAO
1
F
YUNNAN LU
Dazhong Ting
BEIJING XI LU
CAOCHANGMEN DAJIE
Gulou
Hongshan Dongwuyuan
HEYAN LU
Train Station
Nanjing Zhan
HONGSHAN LU
Xuanwu Hu Park
LONGPAN LU
Taiping Men
NANJING-ZHENJIANG EXPRESSWAY (NINGZHEN GONGLU)
East Bus Station
NANJING-QIXIA EXPRESSWAY (NINGQI GONGLU)
Zhenjiang & Qixia Si
See Inset for Details
Zijin Shan
ZIJIN SHAN
Zijin Shan Observatory
Cable Car
Zijin Shan
Zixia Lake
Ming Xiaoling
Zhongshan Ling
Zangjinglou
Linggu Ta
Beamless Hall
LINGGU SI LU
Linggu Si
TAIPINGMEN LU
MINGLING LU
SHIXIANG LU
LINGYUAN LU
N
0 500 m

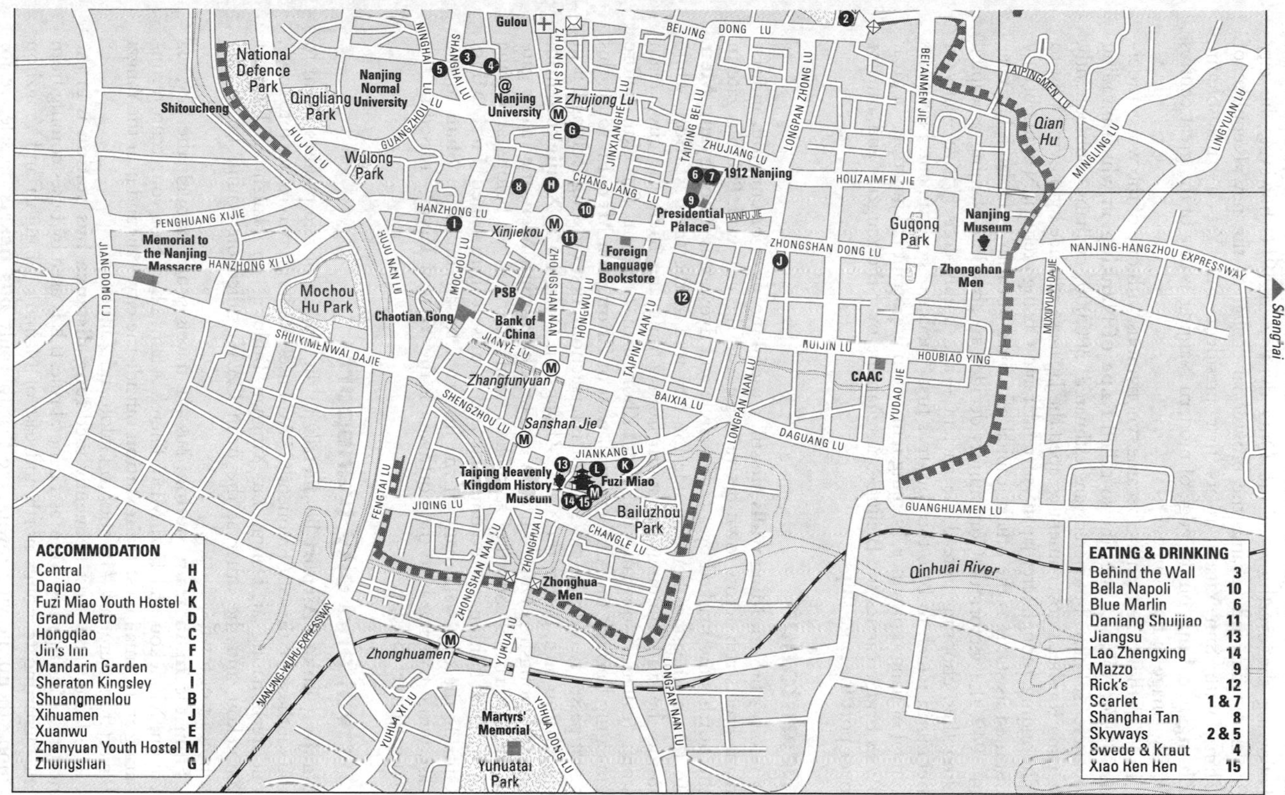
ACCOMMODATION
Central H
Daqiao A
Fuzi Miao Youth Hostel K
Grand Metro D
Hongqiao C
Jin's Inn F
Mandarin Garden L
Sheraton Kingsley I
Shuangmenlou B
Xihuamen J
Xuanwu E
Zhanyuan Youth Hostel M
Zhongshan G
EATING & DRINKING
Behind the Wall 3
Bella Napoli 10
Blue Marlin 6
Daniang Shuijiao 11
Jiangsu 13
Lao Zhengxing 14
Mazzo 9
Rick's 12
Scarlet 1 & 7
Shanghai Tan 8
Skyways 2 & 5
Swede & Kraut 4
Xiao Ren Ren 15
Shanghai
Airport
Gulou
Beijing Dong Lu
Bei'anmen Jie
Taipingmen Lu
Qian Hu
Mingling Lu
Lingyuan Lu
National Defence Park
Shitoucheng
Qingliang Park
Nanjing Normal University
Nanjing University
Ninghai Lu
Shanghai Lu
Zhongshan Lu
Zhujiong Lu
Jinxianghe Lu
Taiping Bei Lu
Longpan Zhong Lu
Zhujiang Lu
1912 Nanjing
Houzaimen Jie
Huju Lu
Guangzhou Lu
Wulong Park
Changjiang Lu
Presidential Palace
Hanfu Jie
Hanzhong Lu
Fenghuang Xijie
Xinjiekou
Gugong Park
Nanjing Museum
Zhongshan Dong Lu
Nanjing-Hangzhou Expressway
Memorial to the Nanjing Massacre
Hanzhong Xi Lu
Jiangdong Lu
Mochou Hu Park
Huju Nan Lu
Mochou Lu
Foreign Language Bookstore
Zhongshan Nan Lu
Hongwu Lu
PSB
Chaotian Gong
Bank of China
Zhongchan Men
Muxuyuan Dajie
Shuiximenwai Dajie
Jianye Lu
Taiping Nan Lu
Ruijin Lu
Houbiao Ying
CAAC
Zhangfunyuan
Longpan Nan Lu
Baixia Lu
Yudao Jie
Shengzhou Lu
Sanshan Jie
Daguang Lu
Jiankang Lu
Taiping Heavenly Kingdom History Museum
Fuzi Miao
Fengtai Lu
Jiqing Lu
Bailuzhou Park
Guanghuamen Lu
Changle Lu
Qinhuai River
Zhonghua Lu
Zhonghua Men
Nanjing-Wuhu Expressway
Zhonghuamen
Yuhua Lu
Yuhua Xi Lu
Martyrs' Memorial
Yuhua Dong Lu
Yunuatai Park

War, the **Treaty of Nanking** which ceded Hong Kong to Britain was signed here in 1841, and Nanjing itself also suffered the indignity of being a treaty port. Following the overthrow of the Qing dynasty in 1911, however, the city flowered again and became the provisional capital of the new Republic of China, with Sun Yatsen as its first president. Sun Yatsen's mausoleum, **Zhongshan Ling**, on the edge of modern Nanjing, is one of the great centres of pilgrimage of the Chinese.

In 1937, the name Nanjing became synonymous with one of the worst atrocities of World War II, after the so-called **Rape of Nanking**, in which invading Japanese soldiers butchered an estimated 300,000 civilians. Subsequently, Chiang Kaishek's government escaped the Japanese advance by moving west to Chongqing, though after Japan's surrender and Chiang's return, Nanjing briefly resumed its status as the official capital of China. Just four years later, however, in 1949, the victorious Communists decided to abandon Nanjing as capital altogether, choosing instead the ancient – and highly conservative – city of Beijing in which to base the country's first "modern" government. Nowadays capital of Jiangsu province, Nanjing remains an important rail junction – a great 1960s bridge carries the Beijing–Shanghai line over the Yangzi – and a major river port for large ships.

Orientation

The city's broken Ming **walls** are still a useful means of orientation, and the main streets run across town between gates in the city wall. The big gate in the north, now marked by a traffic circle and flyovers, is **Zhongyang Men**. To the northeast of here, outside the city wall, is the **train station**, while inside the wall, running due south from Zhongyang Men, the city's main street (called Zhongyang Lu, then Zhongshan Lu) runs for 8km before emerging through the southern wall west of **Zhonghua Men**. En route, this street passes two of the city's major intersections, first crossing Beijing Lu in the **Gulou** area, before traversing Zhongshan Dong Lu at **Xinjiekou**, from where Zhongshan Dong Lu runs east to **Zhongshan Men**, the major gate in the eastern wall. South of Xinjiekou (a kilometre or two before Zhonghua Men) is a fashionable commercial and tourist centre called **Fuzi Miao**. Outside the city wall, many of the historic sites are on **Zijin Shan** to the east, while fringing it to the northwest is the **Yangzi River**, crossed by the Yangzi River Bridge.

Arrival and city transport

Nanjing Lukou Airport lies literally in the middle of rice paddies 42km to the southeast of the city. Frequent CAAC buses (¥25) run two routes into town, one terminating at Tianjin Lu Xinghan Building on Hanzhong Lu near Xinjiekou, and the other at the main CAAC office on Ruijin Lu, in the southeast of town.

From the **main train station**, bus #1 travels south through the city, via Gulou, Xinjiekou and Fuzi Miao. There's a faint chance of your train terminating at the small **west train station** outside the city walls and near the Yangzi River; from here bus #16 goes to Gulou and Xinjiekou.

The largest and most frequently used **long-distance bus station** is in the north, at **Zhongyang Men**; as a general rule, this is used by buses coming from and departing to points north and east of Nanjing (Shanghai and Yangzhou among them). Leaving town, note that the only **bus tickets** on sale are for same- or next-day departures.

Accommodation

Outside the summer months, you should be able to bargain to get a ten- to twenty-percent discount on rooms.

Central 75 Zhongshan Lu, west side ⓣ025/84733888, ⓕ84733999. A 5min walk north of Xinjiekou, this is one of the most luxurious places in town. ⑨

Daqiao 255 Jianning Lu, at the junction with Daqiao Nan Lu ⓣ025/88801544, ⓕ8809255. A friendly, if overpriced, place with singles and doubles, about 1km from the west train station. Bus #10 comes here from the train station or Zhongyang Men. ⑥

Fuzi Miao Youth Hostel 68 Pingjiangfu Jie ⓣ025/86624133. Brightly coloured, no-frills place that's popular with Chinese backpackers. Facilities are good, with bike rental (¥20/day), free Internet and a pool table. Six- and eight-bed dorms have their own bathrooms and are pretty good value, but rooms are a little pricey. Try for one with a view of the river. ③

Grand Metro Hotel 22-1 Xuanwumen ⓣ025/83280000, ⓕ83280111. A low-key hotel with neat, inviting rooms and an excellent location at Xuanwu Hu, within walking distance of the Shizi Qiao food street. ⑤

Hongqiao 202 Zhongshan Bei Lu, just north of Xinmofan Malu ⓣ025/83400888, ⓕ83420756. Bus #13 comes here from the train station. A pleasant hotel with very comfortable, spotless doubles. ⑦

Jin's Inn 26 Yunnan Lu ⓣ025/83755666. There are several of these good-value budget hotels around town but this is the best located, being central and handy for the best bars. Rooms might be small but they're neat and comfortable and have free Internet. ③

Mandarin Garden 9 Zhuang Yuan Jing ⓣ025/52202555, ⓕ52201876. A stylish place with hundreds of rooms and five-star amenities. It's right in the heart of lively Fuzi Miao, on a small lane facing the southern end of Taiping Lu. ⑨

Sheraton Kingsley 185 Hanzhong Lu, two blocks west of Xinjiekou ⓣ025/86668888, ⓕ86504293, ⓦwww.sheraton.com/nanjing. As plush and luxurious as its sister hotels all over the world. Doubles from ¥1660. ⑨

Shuangmenlou 185 Huju Bei Lu, near the intersection with Zhongshan Bei Lu ⓣ025/58800888 ext 80, ⓕ58826298. Surrounded by large gardens, this is a perfectly decent place popular with tour groups, though a little far from the interesting parts of town. ⑦

Xihuamen 202 Longpan Zhong Lu ⓣ025/84596221. About 2km east of Xinjiekou. Quite an attractive place set in gardens, and with perfectly decent rooms. ⑥

Xuanwu 193 Zhongyang Lu, just north of Hunan Lu ⓣ025/83358888 ext 10, ⓕ83369800. A huge place with good views over Xuanwu Hu Park, this has pretensions to being a luxury hotel, and almost makes it. ⑨

Zhanyuan Youth Hostel 80 Zhanyuan Lu, Fuzi Miao ⓣ025/66850566. A basic hostel well located in the heart of things at Fuzi Miao – though that can make it noisy at night. There's a bar on the top floor and free wireless. Rooms are pricey, and you can do better elsewhere, but the four- to eight-bed dorms, which start at ¥45, are good value. ③

Zhongshan 200 Zhongshan Lu, at the corner of Zhujiang Lu, midway between Gulou and Xinjiekou ⓣ025/83361888, ⓕ83377228. Spacious and elegantly furnished rooms, with a disco and a travel agency on the premises. ⑧

The City

Nanjing is huge, and a thorough exploration of all its sights would take several days. Among the three major **downtown** focal points, Xinjiekou and Fuzi Miao are the most interesting areas for simply wandering, with historic buildings, pedestrianized shopping streets canals and some good restaurants. A number of bus routes, including #1, #16, #26 and #33, pass through or near these two districts as well as Gulou.

The **north** of the city takes in the enormous **Xuanwu Hu Park** and the **Yangzi River** area, while to the **west** are a number of smaller parks, including the Ming **Chaotian Gong** and the **Memorial to the Victims of the Nanjing Massacre**. The **east** and the **south** contain some of the best-preserved relics of Nanjing's mighty Ming **city wall**, as well as the excellent **Nanjing Museum**. However, the most interesting area of all for tourists is the green hill beyond the city walls to the east of the city, **Zijin Shan**, with its wealth of historical and cultural relics. If you only have a day or two to spare, you should at least try and see Zijin Shan, the Nanjing Museum, the city wall and the **Presidential Palace**, the former seat of government under both the nineteenth-century Taipings and the Nationalists.

Gulou

The **Gulou** area, around the junction between Zhongyang Lu, Zhongshan Lu and Beijing Lu, is the administrative centre in the heart of old Nanjing. When Nanjing became a Treaty Port in the mid-nineteenth century the foreign consulates were all based here, though today it comprises mostly traffic jams overlooked by offices. There are just a couple of relics from earlier times, both rather lost in the bustle. One, immediately west of the main traffic circle, is the 600-year-old Gulou itself (daily 8am–5pm; ¥5), a small, solid **drum tower** on a grassy mound in the road, entered through a traditional-style gateway. Historically, a drum used to call the watch from here seven times a day, and sound warnings at times of danger; now the interior holds exhibits of amateur paintings, while the tower itself has been semi-converted into a teahouse. A ghastly legend surrounds the fourteenth-century bell sitting outside – it's said that the emperor ordered the bell be fused by the blood of a virgin. The two daughters of the city's blacksmith apparently threw themselves into the furnace so that their father could obey the emperor and thus escape the death penalty.

The other sight by Gulou is the **Dazhong Ting** (Great Bell Pavilion), immediately northeast of the junction behind the China Telecom building, sitting in a well-kept garden and also home to a pleasant teahouse. Enter just south of the *McDonald's*.

Xinjiekou

Nearly 2km due south of Gulou along Zhongshan Lu lies the geographical centre of Nanjing, **Xinjiekou**. At its heart is a huge traffic circle adorned by a statue of Sun Yatsen.

About fifteen minutes' walk from Xinjiekou and a short block north, on Changjiang Lu (running into Hanfu Jie), the **Presidential Palace** (daily 8am–5pm; ¥30) is located in the Suzhou-esque garden, Xu Yuan. Both palace and garden were built more than six hundred years ago for a Ming prince, and were subsequently turned into the seat of the provincial governor under the Qing. In 1853 the building was seized by the armies of the Taiping Heavenly Kingdom and converted into the headquarters of Taiping leader Hong Xiuquan. After the overthrow of the Qing, it became the Guomindang government's Presidential Palace. It was from here, in the early decades of the twentieth century, that first Sun Yatsen and later Chiang Kaishek governed China. Visiting the palace today, you'll see exhibitions on the Taiping Uprising and the life and times of Sun and Chiang.

West on Jianye Lu (bus #4 from Fuzi Miao) is the former Ming palace, the **Chaotian Gong**, now containing the tiny **Municipal Museum** (daily 8am–5pm; ¥30), home to a few excellent bronzes. Built in 1384, the Chaotian Gong was used by nobles to worship their ancestors, as well as for audiences with the emperor – hence the name Chaotian, meaning Worshipping Heaven. Later it became a seat of learning and a temple to Confucius. The large square that houses the palace, bounded by a high vermilion wall on one side and a gateway protected by tigers on the other, is supposedly the site of the ancient Ye Cheng (Foundry City), built in the fifth century BC. During the Han dynasty, peasants gathered here to offer sacrifices to heaven or ask for a fruitful harvest. Antiques, mostly fake, are for sale in the market in the front courtyard.

Fuzi Miao

Two kilometres south of Xinjiekou, near the terminus of bus #1, is the **Fuzi Miao** (Temple of Confucius) area, which begins south of Jiankang Lu and harbours a noisy welter of street vendors, boutiques, arcades and restaurants. On a hot day, nothing beats slurping on a *lüdou shatou*, a drink made of green beans with shaved ice (¥3), sold at streetside stalls.

The central **Temple of Confucius** (daily 8am–9.30pm; ¥15) resembles a theme park inside, complete with mannequins in period costume. The temple is hardly worth bothering about, but there is an attractive waterfront area along the canal here (where the Tang poet Liu Yuxi composed his most famous poem, *Wuyi Lane*), along which you can pick up **leisure boats** (electric ¥20, paddle ¥10; 30min) that trundle south to Zhonghua Men. Cross the canal in front of the temple, and a short walk southeast will bring you to a small park, **Bailuzhou** (Egret Isle). This ancient corner of the city remained the Chinese quarter after the arrival of the Manchu Qing dynasty in the seventeenth century, and there are still a few traditional houses.

Ten minutes' walk west of the Temple of Confucius and right on the small Zhanyuan Lu, just east of Zhonghua Lu, is the **Taiping Heavenly Kingdom History Museum** (daily 8am–4.30pm; ¥10), well worth a visit. The sad but fascinating story of the Taiping Uprising is told here in pictures and relics, with English captions. The building itself was the residence of Xu Da, a Ming prince, and became the home of one of the rebel generals during the uprising.

Zhonghua Men and Yuhuatai Park

Zhonghua Men in the far south is now largely bereft of its wall and isolated in the middle of a traffic island, just inside the river moat on the bus #16 route from Xinjiekou and Gulou. This colossal gate actually comprises four gates, one inside another, and its seven enclosures were designed to hold three thousand men in case of enemy attack, making it one of the biggest of its kind in China.

The Taiping Uprising

One of the consequences of the weakness of the Qing dynasty in the nineteenth century was the extraordinary **Taiping Uprising**, an event that would lead to the slaughter of millions, and which has been described as the most colossal civil war in the history of the world. The Taipings were led by **Hong Xiuquan**, failed civil-service candidate and Christian evangelist, who, following a fever, declared himself to be the younger brother of Jesus Christ. In 1851, he assembled 20,000 armed followers at **Jintian village**, near Guiping in Guangxi Province, and established the **Taiping Tianguo**, or Kingdom of Heavenly Peace. This militia routed the local Manchu forces, and by the following year were sweeping up through Hunan into central China. They **captured Nanjing** in 1853, but though the kingdom survived another eleven years, this was its last achievement. Poorly planned expeditions failed to take Beijing or win over western China, and Hong's leadership – originally based on the enfranchisement of the peasantry and the outlawing of opium, alcohol and sexual discrimination – devolved into paranoia and fanaticism. After a gigantic struggle, **Qing forces** finally managed to unseat the Taipings when Western governments sent in assistance, most notably in the person of Queen Victoria's personal favourite, Charles "Chinese" Gordon.

Despite the rebellion's ultimately disastrous failure and its overtly Christian message, the whole episode is seen as a precursor to the arrival of communism in China. Indeed, in its fanatical rejection of Confucianism and the incredible damage it wrought on buildings and sites of historic value, it finds curious echoes in Mao Zedong's Cultural Revolution.

Today you can walk through the central archway and climb up two levels, passing arched recesses which are used for displays and snack stalls, and are beautifully cool in summer. Up above, there's a tremendous view of the gates with the city spread out beyond.

The road south, across the Qinhuai River, between Zhonghua Men and Yuhuatai Park, is an interesting stretch lined with two-storey wooden-fronted houses, many with balconies above, while below are small shops and workshops. The trees lining the pavement provide shade as well as room to hang birdcages, pot plants and laundry. Just beyond, the road reaches a small hill, now a park known as **Yuhuatai** (daily 6am–6.45pm; ¥25). In legend it was here that a fifth-century Buddhist monk delivered sermons so moving that flowers rained down from the sky upon him. You still see Chinese tourists grubbing around here for the multicoloured pebbles called *yuhuashi* (literally rain-flower stones), associated with the legend. Sadly, the hill also has other, less pleasant connotations. After 1927 it was used as an execution ground, and the Guomindang is said to have murdered vast numbers of people here. The spot is now marked by a **Martyrs' Memorial**, a colossal composite of nine thirty-metre-high figures, worth seeing as a prime example of gigantic Chinese Socialist Realism. The park itself is pleasantly laid out on a slope thickly forested with pine trees. You can climb the four-storey pagoda on the hillock behind the memorial for excellent views of Nanjing.

Around the Yangzi River

The far northwest of town in the area of the **Yangzi River** offers a modicum of interest. The **Nanjing Treaty Museum**, located in **Jinghai Si** (daily 8am–4.30pm; ¥6), lies very near the west train station off Rehe Lu. It was in this temple that the British and Chinese negotiated the first of the many unequal treaties in the wake of the Opium War in 1843 (the treaty was later signed on a British naval ship in Nanjing harbour). Unfortunately, the museum's detailed exposition of fractious Sino-British relations throughout the nineteenth and twentieth centuries is in Chinese only, but the temple is pleasant to stroll around nonetheless. It was originally built in the Ming dynasty by Emperor Chengzu to honour the Chinese Muslim naval hero **Zhenghe**, who led the Chinese fleet on exploratory voyages to East Africa and the Persian Gulf; you'll see his name commemorated throughout the city.

The streets around Jinghai Si, the west train station (bus #16 from Gulou and Xinjiekou) and the port, just beyond the city wall, are atmospheric, with their crumbling alleys and smelly fish markets. A huge stone monument, **Dujiang Jinianbei**, marks the junction between Rehe Lu and Zhongshan Bei Lu; it was erected in memory of the crossing of the river from the north and the capture of Nanjing by the Communists in 1949.

If you're in this area you should definitely take a look at the 1500-metre-long **double-decker bridge** over the Yangzi, still a source of great pride to the Chinese who built it under their own steam after the Russians pulled out in 1960. Before the bridge was built, it took ninety minutes to ferry trains and road vehicles across the river. For a great view of the structure and the banks of the Yangzi, head for **Great Bridge Park** (daily 7am–4.30pm) on the eastern bank; you can ride in an lift up to a raised platform above the upper (road) deck of the bridge, for ¥4. Bus #15 heads to the park from Zhongyang Men and Gulou.

Wulong and Mochou Hu parks and the Nanjing Massacre memorial

The west and southwest of the city hold a few minor sights and one major attraction. Arguably the best of the small parks here is the tiny **Wulong Park**

Nanjing's city walls

Though Nanjing was walled as many as 2500 years ago, the present **city wall** is basically the work of the first Ming emperor, who extended and strengthened the earlier walls in 1369–73. His wall, built of brick and more than 32km long, followed the contours of the country, skirting Xuanwu Hu in the north, fringing Xijin Shan in the east, and tracing the Qinhuai River (which doubled as a moat) to the west and south. The wall was mainly paid for by rich families resettled here by the emperor: one third of it was "donated" by a single native of Wuxiang in Zhejiang province. Its construction employed 200,000 conscripts, who ensured that the bricks were all the same size and specification, each one bearing the names of the workman and overseer. They were held together, to an average height of 12m and a thickness of 7m, by a mixture of lime and glutinous rice paste.

The original structure, of red rock in places, is still plainly visible along a three-hundred-metre section of the wall at the so-called **Shitoucheng**, in the west of the city between Caochangmen Dajie and Fenghuang Jie. You can see it from bus #18, which runs outside the walls between Xinjiekou and the west train station.

off Guangzhou Lu (daily 7am–9pm; ¥4), often full of old musicians who gather to sing opera and play traditional instruments. Farther south, just across the narrow Qinhuai River, lies the entrance to **Mochou Hu Park** (daily 5.30am–10pm; ¥10), which is only worth the entrance fee during weekdays – at weekends, it's invaded by hordes of schoolchildren. An open-air stage juts out into the lake here, with a substantial teahouse behind. Among the clutch of pavilions and walkways is the **Square Pavilion**, with a statue of the legendary maiden, Mochou, after whom the lake is named: her name means "sorrow-free" because her sweet singing could soothe away all unhappiness. Ming emperor Zhu Yuanzhang once played a pivotal game of chess with his first general in the **Winning Chess Building**, next to the Square Pavilion.

West of the park is the must-see **Memorial to the Nanjing Massacre** (Tues–Sun 8.30am–4.30pm; free). This grim, gravelly garden includes a gruesome display of victims' skulls and bones, half-buried in the dirt, as well as a clearly labelled (in English) photographic account of the sufferings endured by the Chinese at the hands of the Japanese army during World War II.

Xuanwu Hu Park

North of the centre, to the east of Zhongyang Lu and south of the train station, the enormous **Xuanwu Hu Park** (daily 5am–9pm; ¥20) comprises mostly water, with hills on three sides and the city wall skirting the western shore. Formerly a resort for the imperial family and once the site of a naval inspection by Song emperor Xiaowu, it became a park in 1911 and is a pleasant place to mingle with the locals who come here en masse at weekends. The lake contains five small **islets** linked by causeways and bridges, with restaurants, teahouses, pavilions, rowing boats, paddle boats, places to swim, an open-air theatre and a zoo. The southern end of the park contains one of the better-preserved reaches of the city wall. Xuanwu Gate, on Zhongyang Lu about 1km north of Gulou (bus #1), is the most convenient way to enter the park.

The Nanjing Museum and Zhongshan Men

On Zhongshan Dong Lu about 3km east of Xinjiekou (buses #5 and #9 from Xinjiekou; #20 from Gulou), the huge **Nanjing Museum** (daily 9am–4pm; ¥20) is one of the best provincial museums in China, especially in terms of clarity of explanations – nearly everything is labelled in English. Highlights include some superb silk-embroidered sedan chairs and several heavy cast bronzes, dating from as early as the Western Zhou (1100–771 BC). The jade and lacquerwork sections, as well as the model Fujian trading ships, are also well worth seeing.

A short walk east of the museum is **Zhongshan Men**, the easternmost gate of the ancient city walls. You can climb to the top of the wall here, and walk along a little way to the north before the structure crumbles into a small lake, Qian Hu. It's surprisingly spacious and peaceful on the top and affords excellent views.

Zijin Shan

Not far outside Zhongshan Men is **Zijin Shan** (Purple Gold Mountain), named after the colour of its rocks. Traditionally, the area has been a cool and shady spot to escape the furnace heat of Nanjing's summer, with fragrant woods and stretches of long grass, but also here are the three most visited sites in Nanjing. Of these, the centrepiece, right in the middle of the hill, is **Zhongshan Ling**, the magnificent mausoleum of China's first president, Sun Yatsen. To the east of Zhongshan Ling is the **Linggu Si** complex, and to the west are the ancient **Ming Xiaoling**, tombs of the Ming emperors who ruled China from Nanjing.

Visiting the three main sites on Zijin Shan can easily take a full day. Bus #9 goes to Zhongshan Ling via Linggu Si from Xinjiekou, while bus #20 heads to Ming Xiaoling from Gulou. Private minibuses and a host of private operators also make the trek from the train station square. Perhaps the best way to visit all three without backtracking is to catch a bus from town to either Ming Xiaoling or Linggu Si, and then walk to the other two sites. Various half-day **bus tours** are also available from town; ask at any travel service or upmarket hotel. If you're interested in an overview of the whole mountain, you can ride the **cable car** to the peak from a station about 1km east of Taiping Men, the gate by the southern end of Xuanwu Hu Park (one way ¥25, return ¥45).

Linggu Si

Starting from the eastern side of the hill, farthest from the city, the first if least interesting sight on Zijin Shan is the collection of buildings around **Linggu Si** (daily 8am–5pm; ¥15 entry to the site). If you arrive here by bus, the main building in front of you is the so-called **Beamless Hall**. Completed in 1381, and much restored since, it's unusual for its large size and particularly for its self-supporting brick arch construction, with five columns instead of a central beam. The hall was used to store Buddhist sutras before the Taiping rebels made it a fortress; now it's an exhibition hall.

A couple of minutes' walk southeast from the Beamless Hall is the Linggu Si itself, a very much smaller and much restored version of its original self – and still attended by yellow-robed monks. North of the hall stands a small pavilion surrounded by beautiful cypresses and pines, and north of this again is the **Linggu Ta**, an octagonal, nine-storey, sixty-metre-high pagoda, dating back to the 1930s and built, rather extraordinarily, as a monument to Guomindang members killed in the fighting against insurgent Communists in 1926–27. It's well worth climbing up for the views over the surrounding countryside.

Although the Linggu buildings and Zhongshan Ling are connected by a shuttle bus, there's also a delightful footpath through the wood between the two, leading northwest from the Linggu buildings. On the way, you'll pass one or two more buildings, including the **Zangjinglou** (Buddhist Library) at the top of a grand stairway, which now houses the rather dull **Sun Yatsen Museum**, a collection of pictures with explanations in Chinese.

Zhongshan Ling

Dr Sun Yatsen, the first president of post-imperial China, is the only hero revered by Chinese jointly on both sides of the Taiwan Straits. The former leader's mausoleum, the **Zhongshan Ling** (daily 6.30am–6.30pm; ¥40), with its famous marble stairway soaring up the hillside, is one of the most popular sites in the country for Chinese tourists. Walking up the steps is worth it for the great views back down the stairs and across the misty hills to the south.

An imposing structure of white granite and blue tiles (the Nationalist colours), set off by the green pine trees, the mausoleum was completed in 1929, four years after Sun Yatsen's death. From the large bronze statue at the bottom, 392 marble steps lead up to the Memorial Hall, dominated by a five-metre-tall seated white marble figure of the great man himself. Beyond the marble figure is the burial chamber with another marble effigy lying on the stone coffin, from where, according to unsubstantiated rumours, the bones were removed to Taiwan by fleeing Guomindang leaders in 1949. The Guomindang ideals – Nationalism, Democracy and People's Livelihood – are carved above the entrance to the burial chamber in gold on black marble.

Ming Xiaoling

A walk of half an hour or so along the road west from Zhongshan Ling brings you to the **Ming Xiaoling** (daily 8am–5.30pm; ¥50), the burial place of Zhu Yuanzhang, founder of the Ming dynasty and the only one of its fourteen emperors to be buried at Nanjing (his thirteen successors are all buried in Beijing; see p.146). So colossal was the task of moving earth and erecting the stone walls that it took two years and a hundred thousand soldiers and conscripts to complete the tomb in 1383. Although the site was originally far larger than the Ming tombs near Beijing, its halls and pavilions, and 22-kilometre-long enclosing vermilion wall, were mostly destroyed by the Taipings. Today what remains is a walled collection of trees, stone bridges and dilapidated gates leading to the lonely mound at the back containing the (as yet unexcavated) burial site of the emperor and his wife, as well as the fifty courtiers and maids of honour who were buried alive to keep them company.

The Ming Xiaoling actually comprises two parts, the tomb itself and the approach to the tomb, known as Shandao (Sacred Way) or, more commonly, **Shixiang Lu** (Stone Statue Road; daily 8am–6.30pm; ¥10) – which leads to the tomb at an oblique angle as a means of deterring evil spirits, who can only travel in straight lines. It's a strange and magical place to walk through, the road lined with twelve charming pairs of stone animals – including lions, elephants and camels – and four pairs of officials. Most people visit the tomb first and the approach afterwards, simply because the road from Zhongshan Ling arrives immediately outside the tomb entrance. To reach the Sacred Way from the tomb entrance, follow the road right (with the tomb behind you) and then round to the left for about fifteen minutes.

Next to Ming Xiaoling is the entrance to **Zixia Hu** (daily 7am–6pm; ¥10), a small lake whose wooded surroundings are perfect for a stroll at any time of year. In summer, the lake is open for swimming, although you should avoid the weekends when the place is full of locals escaping the heat of the city.

One more sight here is the **Zijin Shan Observatory** (¥15), built in 1929 high on one of the three peaks where the Taipings formerly had a stronghold. For fresh air and good views of Nanjing, try to find a minibus heading this way.

Eating

Nanjing has a wide selection of local, regional Chinese and foreign foods, often at much more reasonable prices than their counterparts in nearby Shanghai. It's an especially great place to sample **Jiangsu cuisine**, the best areas for which are north of Gulou along Zhongyang Lu and northwest along Zhongshan Bei Lu.

The presence of a heavy contingent of foreign students in the city, as well as a growing population of expatriate and home-grown business people, ensures a scattering of highly **Westernized restaurants and bars**, which are not necessarily expensive. Xinjiekou and Fuzi Miao are generally good districts to browse for restaurants, but for a staggering variety of Asian food – including just about every kind of Chinese cuisine, plus Indian, Japanese and Thai – head for the constellation of restaurants at the pedestrianized **Shizi Qiao**, off Hunan Lu to the west of Xuanwu Hu Park. Phone numbers are given for popular places that might need booking.

Behind the Wall 150 Shanghai Lu. Head a few metres uphill along the alley here, called Nan Xiu Cun, and go up the nondescript staircase on the left, which leads to the patio entrance. Great Mexican-style food, especially the quesadillas and enchiladas. In decent weather, the patio is perfect for quiet lunches and livelier evening barbecues.

Bella Napoli 75 Zhongshan Dong Lu, just east from Xinjiekou. Good if slightly overpriced Italian food; the pizzas are a better bet than the pasta.

Daniang Shuijiao Under the Xinjiekou Department Store, and reached from the pavement facing the traffic circle, this popular chain serves up more than forty varieties of cheap and filling *shuijiao*, most for under ¥5 each.

Jiangsu 26 Jiankang Lu, just east of Zhonghua Lu. One of the most upmarket places to try Jiangsu food – brine duck is a speciality.

Lao Zhengxing 119 Gongyuan Jie, near Fuzi Miao. A favourite of GMD officials in the 1930s, this is a lively place with interesting local dishes, backing onto the river.

Shanghai Tan On a small alley directly behind the *Central Hotel*, off Guanjia Qiao ⓣ025/84700010. Excellent Shanghainese cuisine with the odd Jiangsu dish (notably *yanshui ya*) thrown in. The seafood is especially good. Very popular with locals.

Skyways Bakery & Deli 3–6 Hankou Xi Lu, west off Shanghai Lu. The best deli sandwiches in China are served here, though the range of fillings isn't vast: they bake their own baguettes, ciabatta and cookies, and have a caseful of handmade confections and cakes. There's another branch just west of Taiping Men. Daily 9am–9.30pm.

Swede & Kraut 14 Nan Xiu Cun, off Shanghai Lu ⓣ025/86638798. Sharing management with *Skyways*, this does by far the best Western food in the city, and isn't too pricey either. The pasta and bread are all home-made. The lasagne and fettucini especially are scrumptious, and the steaks are great, too.

Xiao Ren Ren 97 Gongyuan Jie, Fuzi Miao. Friendly place designed in the style of a traditional teahouse, with musicians serenading patrons. You can try a selection of local delicacies for just ¥40.

Drinking and entertainment

Nanjing **nightlife** is nowhere near as varied as Shanghai's, though there are a few bars and discos that see a regular mix of foreigners and Chinese. The bars are generally pretentious and stiff – for a laid-back drink it's better to hang out at *Behind the Wall*. Clubs are inexpensive for foreigners (for whom cover charges are generally waived) and beers can be as cheap as ¥10 per bottle. For a civilized night out, the 1912 Nanjing complex is the local answer to Shanghai's Xintiandi, a pedestrianized zone of restored buildings now housing upscale bars and restaurants.

Nanjing's cultural life is sadly lagging far behind Shanghai's, though your visit might coincide with infrequent acrobatics or Chinese opera performances somewhere in town. The expat-oriented **listings** magazine *Map* can be found at most bars and restaurants geared up for foreign custom – *Henry's Home* at the southern end of Shizi Qiao can be relied on to carry it.

Blue Marlin At the north end of the 1912 Nanjing complex, Taiping Bei Lu. Above the restaurant is a dance floor and terrace with occasional Latin dance nights. Staff are often willing to plug your iPod into their sound system.

Mazzo South end of the 1912 Nanjing complex. Good service and comfortable seating make this a nice spot to wind down after *Scarlet*. When the music's good (it's distinctly variable), *Mazzo* is also a great place to dance.

Rick's 413 Changbai Lu. A three-level club, with a bar at street level, and dance floor and lounge above. Like the other clubs in Nanjing, hope for a good DJ when you go.

Scarlet 34-1 Hubei Lu, an alley south of Yunnan Lu; a second branch is at the northern end of the 1912 Nanjing complex. Two-storey bar that's the late night venue of choice with most expat residents, with the occasional Western DJ playing dance sounds and rock. Daily until 2am.

Listings

Airlines The main CAAC reservations and ticketing office is at 52 Ruijin Lu in the southeast of town (daily 7.30am–10pm; ⓣ025/84499378). China Eastern Airlines' head office is at the corner of Changbai Jie and Zhongshan Dong Lu (daily 8.30am–5.30pm; ⓣ025/84454325).

Banks and exchange The Bank of China head office (daily 8.30am–5pm), with a 24hr ATM, is a few hundred metres due south of Xinjiekou on Zhongshan Nan Lu.

Bookshops The best selection of English-language books is in the Foreign Language Bookstore on Zhongshan Dong Lu, 700m east of Xinjiekou.

Hospitals The most central hospital is the Gulou Hospital, on Zhongshan Lu just south of the Gulou intersection.

Internet access A multitude of Internet places are scattered around the Nanjing University area. There's also a Net bar on the street running along the Gulou post office building's south side.

Mail and telephones Nanjing's main post office (daily 8am–6.30pm), offering international phone and fax calls as well as postal services, faces the Gulou traffic circle. There's also a post office at 19 Zhongshan Lu, just north of Xinjiekou.

Travel agents Nearly all hotels have their own travel agencies. CITS is at 202 Zhongshan Bei Lu (Mon–Fri 8.30am–noon & 2–5pm, Sat & Sun 9am–4pm; ⓣ025/83538564, ⓕ83538561), a couple of kilometres northwest of Gulou.

Zhejiang

ZHEJIANG, one of China's smallest provinces but also one of the wealthiest, is made up of two quite different areas. The northern part shares its climate, geography, history and the Grand Canal with Jiangsu – the land here is highly cultivated, fertile and netted with waterways, hot in summer and cold in winter. The south, however, mountainous and sparsely populated in the interior, thriving and semitropical on the coast, has much more in common with Fujian province.

Recent excavations have shown, contrary to expectations, that the Yangzi delta had Neolithic settlements every bit as old as those in the Yellow River valley. At Hemudu on the Shaoxing-Ningbo plain, settled farmers were growing rice and building solid, precisely structured two-storey houses as far back as seven thousand years ago, when rhinoceros and elephant still roamed the land. For millennia thereafter the region remained prosperous but provincial, politically in the shadow of the more populous Yellow River basin in northern China. The eventual economic shift to the south slowly worked to the region's advantage, however. The Grand Canal was built and, finally, in the twelfth century AD, the imperial court of the Song moved south and set up capital in Hangzhou. For more than two centuries, northern Zhejiang enjoyed a spell of unprecedented power, which ended only when the capital moved back to Beijing.

The whole province has an attractive, prosperous air. **Hangzhou**, the terminus of the Grand Canal, is one of the greenest, most attractive cities in China, with a famous lake, former resort of emperors, and is still a centre for silk, tea and paper-making. Nearby **Shaoxing**, a charming small town threaded by canals, offers the chance to tour its beautiful surroundings by boat. Off the coast, and accessible from Shanghai, **Putuo Shan** is a Buddhist island with more temples than cars; as fresh, green and tranquil as eastern China gets.

Hangzhou and around

HANGZHOU, capital of the province, southern terminus of the Grand Canal, and one of China's most established tourist attractions, lies in the north of Zhejiang at the head of Hangzhou Bay. The canal has been the instrument of the city's prosperity and fortunes, ensuring it was a place of great wealth and culture for more than a thousand years. As is often the case in China, the modern city is

Hangzhou and around

Hangzhou	杭州	*hángzhōu*
Bai Di	白堤	*báidī*
Baopu Daoist Compound	包朴道院	*bāopǔ dàoyuàn*
Baoshu Ta	保淑塔	*bǎoshū tǎ*
Feilai Feng	飞来峰	*fēilái fēng*
Gu Shan	孤山	*gūshān*
Huanglong Dong Park	黄龙洞公园	*huánglóngdòng gōngyuán*
Hupaomeng Quan	虎跑梦泉	*hǔpǎomèng quán*
Huqingyu Tang Museum of Chinese Medicine	胡庆余堂中药博物馆	*húqìngyútáng zhōngyào bówùguǎn*
Jinci Si	净慈寺	*jìngcí sì*
Lingyin Si	灵隐寺	*língyǐn sì*
Liuhe Ta	六和塔	*liùhé tǎ*
Longjing	龙井	*lóngjǐng*
Nine Creeks and Eighteen Gullies Road	九溪十八涧	*jiǔxī shíbājiàn*
Passenger Boat Dock	市客运码头	*shì kèyùn mǎtóu*
Santanyinyue	三潭印月	*sāntán yìnyuè*
Su Di	苏堤	*sūdī*
Xi Hu	西湖	*xīhú*
Xiling Seal Engravers' Society	西泠印社	*xīlíng yìnshè*
Yuefei Mu	岳飞墓	*yuèfēi mù*
Zhejiang Museum	浙江博物馆	*zhèjiāng bówùguǎn*
Zhongshan Park	中山公园	*zhōngshān gōngyuán*
Accommodation		
Chinese Academy of Art	中国美术学院国际教育学院	*zhōngguó měishù xuéyuàn guójì jiàoyù xuéyuàn*
Dahua	大华饭店	*dàhuá fàndiàn*
Dongpo	东坡宾馆	*dōngpō bīnguǎn*

not of much interest in itself, but **Xi Hu** – the lake around which Hangzhou curls – and its shores still offer wonderful Chinese vistas of trees, hills, flowers, old causeways over the lake, fishing boats, pavilions and pagodas. No tour of China would be complete without appreciating the lake's stunning natural beauty – still largely intact despite the ever-increasing flood of tourists – and its subsequent impact on the evolution of Chinese literature and culture.

The city is particularly busy at weekends and in summer, when it's packed with trippers escaping from the concrete jungle of Shanghai. This has pushed up hotel prices, but it also brings advantages: there are plenty of restaurants, the natural environment is being protected and the bulk of the Taiping destruction to the temples and gardens on the lakeside has been repaired. Most of the places to see can be visited on foot or by bicycle.

Finally, much further afield, the old colonial hill resort of **Moganshan** is today making a comeback as a place for city slickers to escape the heat.

Some history

Apart from the fact that **Yu the Great**, tamer of floods, is said to have moored his boats here, Hangzhou has little in the way of a legendary past or ancient history, for the simple reason that the present site, on the east shore of Xi Hu,

Foreign Students' Building, Zhejiang University	浙大西溪校区留学生楼	*zhédà xīxī xiàoqū liúxuéshēng lóu*
Holiday Wuyang	五洋假日酒店	*wǔyáng jiàrì jiǔdiàn*
Huaqiao	华侨饭店	*huáqiáo fàndiàn*
Mingtown Garden Youth Hostel	名堂杭州国际青年旅舍	*míngtáng hángzhōu guójì qīngnián lǚshè*
Mingtown Youth Hostel	华美达广场杭州海华大酒店	*huáměidá guǎngchǎng hángzhōu hǎihuá dàjiǔdiàn*
Ramada Plaza Hangzhou Haihua	华美达广场杭州海华大酒店	*huáměidá guǎngchǎng hángzhōu hǎihuá dàjiǔdiàn*
Shangri-la	香格里拉饭店	*xiānggélǐlā fàndiàn*
Xinqiao	新桥饭店	*xīnqiáo fàndiàn*
Xinxin	新新饭店	*xīnxīn fàndiàn*
Zhejiang University Guesthouse	浙江大学招待所	*zhèjiāng dàxué zhāodàisuǒ*
Zhonghua	中华饭店	*zhōnghuá fàndiàn*
Eating and drinking		
JZ Club	黄楼	*huáng lóu*
Kuiyuan Guan	奎元馆	*kuíyuán guǎn*
Louwailou	楼外楼	*lóuwài lóu*
Tianwaitian	天外天	*tiānwài tiān*
Traveller Bar	旅行者俱乐部	*lǚ xíng zhě jù lè bù*
Vienna Coffee House	维也纳咖啡厅	*wéiyěnà kāfēitīng*
Zhiweiguan	知味观	*zhīwèi guàn*
Around Hangzhou		
Du Yuesheng Villa	杜月笙别墅	*dùyuèshēng biéshù*
Moganshan	莫干山	*mògān shān*
Songliang Shanzhuang	松梁山庄	*sōngliáng shānzhuāng*
Yinshan Jie	荫山街	*yīnshān jiē*

was originally under water. Xi Hu itself started life as a wide shallow **inlet** off the bay, and it is said that Emperor Qin Shihuang sailed in from the sea and moored his boats on what is now the northwestern shore of the lake. Only around the fourth century AD did river currents and tides begin to throw up a barrier of silt, which eventually resulted in the formation of the lake.

However, Hangzhou rapidly made up for its slow start. The first great impetus came from the building of the **Grand Canal** at the end of the sixth century, and Hangzhou developed with spectacular speed as the centre for trade between north and south, the Yellow and Yangzi river basins. Under the **Tang dynasty** it was a rich and thriving city, but its location between lake and river made it vulnerable to the fierce equinox tides in Hangzhou Bay. When Tang-dynasty governors were building locks and dykes to control the waters round Hangzhou, a contemporaneous writer, describing the beginning of a sea wall in 910 AD, explained that "archers were stationed on the shore to shoot down the waves while a poem was recited to propitiate the King of Dragons and Government of the Waters; the waves immediately left the wall and broke on the opposite bank so the work could go on." The problem of **floods** – and the search for remedies – was to recur down the centuries.

During the **Song dynasty**, Hangzhou received its second great impetus when the encroachment of the Tartars from the north destroyed the northern capital of Kaifeng and sent remnants of the imperial family fleeing south in search of a new base. The result of this upheaval was that from 1138 until 1279 Hangzhou became the **imperial capital**. There was an explosion in the silk and brocade industry, and indeed in all the trades that waited upon the court and their wealthy friends. Marco Polo, writing of Hangzhou towards the end of the thirteenth century, spoke of "the City of Heaven, the most beautiful and magnificent in the world. It has ten principal market places, always with an abundance of victuals, roebuck, stags, harts, hares, partridge, pheasants, quails, hens and ducks, geese... all sorts of vegetables and fruits... huge pears weighing ten pounds apiece. Each day a vast quantity of fish is brought from the ocean. There is also an abundance of lake fish." So glorious was the reputation of the city that it rapidly grew overcrowded. On to its sandbank Hangzhou was soon cramming more than a million people, a population as large as that of Chang'an (Xi'an) under the Tang, but in a quarter of the space – tall wooden buildings up to five storeys high were crowded into narrow streets, creating a ghastly fire hazard.

Hangzhou ceased to be a capital city after the Southern Song dynasty was finally overthrown by the Mongols in 1279, but it remained an important centre of commerce and a place of luxury, with **parks and gardens** outside the ramparts and hundreds of boats on the lake. In later years, the Ming rulers repaired the city walls and deepened the Grand Canal so that large ships could go all the way from Hangzhou to Beijing. Two great Qing emperors, Kangxi and Qianlong, frequented the city and built villas, temples and gardens by the lake. Although the city was largely destroyed by the **Taiping Uprising** (see p.419), it recovered surprisingly quickly, and the **foreign concessions** established towards the end of the century stimulated the growth of new industries alongside traditional silk- and brocade-manufacturing. Since 1949 the city's population has grown to around one million, much the same as under the Song.

Arrival, information and transport

Hangzhou has two halves; to the east and north is **downtown**, with its shops and tourist facilities, while to the west and south the **lake** offers greenery and

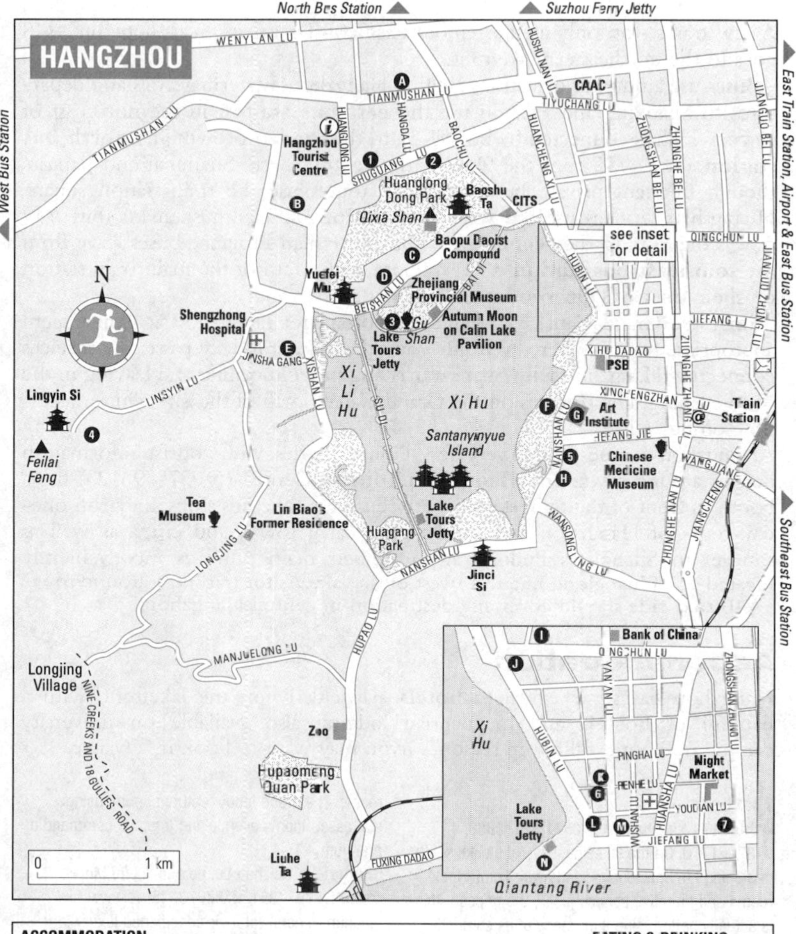

ACCOMMODATION

- Chinese Academy of Art G
- Dahua N
- Dongpo K
- Foreign Students' Building, Zhejiang University A
- Holiday Wuyang H
- Huaqiao J
- Mingtown Garden Youth Hostel E
- Mingtown Youth Hostel F
- Ramada Plaza Hangzhou Haihua I
- Shangri-La D
- Xinqiao M
- Xinxin C
- Zhejiang University Guesthouse B
- Zhonghua L

EATING & DRINKING

- JZ Club 5
- Kuiyuan Guan 7
- Louwailou 3
- Tianwaitian 4
- Traveller Bar 1
- Vienna Coffee House 2
- Zhiweiguan 6

scenic spots. The area around the Jiefang Lu/Yan'an Lu intersection (including the lake front and the small streets just to the north) is the commercial centre of town where you can shop, stay, eat and catch buses round the lake. On the outskirts of the city, the **Qiantang River**, Hangzhou's gateway to the sea, flows well to the south and west, while the **Grand Canal** runs across to meet it from the north; many travellers to Hangzhou never see either of them.

Hangzhou's **airport** is 15km north of town, and connected by CAAC bus (¥5) to the main CAAC office on Tiyuchang Lu. The **train station** is 2km east of the city centre. Reaching the lake from here on foot takes about forty minutes; otherwise, take bus #7 direct to the lake or #151 as far as Yan'an Lu.

A few trains stop only at the remote **east train station**; from here, bus #48 goes to the northeastern lakefront.

Buses use a number of stations ringing Hangzhou. Eastern arrivals and departures to Shaoxing and Fuzhou use the **east bus station** in the northeast of town, which is connected by bus #K35 to the centre of town. The **north bus station** (bus #155 runs the 9km to the centre) serves Shanghai and Jiangsu, though frequent private buses on these routes use the train-station square. Huangshan services use the **west bus station** on Tianmushan Lu (bus #49 travels the 8km to the centre). Wenzhou and Fujian Province buses leave from the **southeast bus station**, a five-minute walk south of the main train station on the corner of Dongbao Lu and Qiutao Lu.

Since the Grand Canal has been so important for Hangzhou, it would seem appropriate to arrive here by **boat** – and there are still daily passenger services connecting Hangzhou with Suzhou, arriving in the morning and leaving in the early evening. The **dock** is on the Grand Canal north of the city centre, accessible on bus #155.

Hangzhou is one of the very few Chinese cities with tourist information booths around town. The **Hangzhou Tourist Centre** (ⓣ0571/96123) has a booth in front of the train station, between the public bus stops; they run one-day tours of Hangzhou and surrounding canal towns and cities, as well as shuttles to Shanghai's Pudong airport. Their main office is inconveniently located at 3 Huanglong Lu, northwest of the lake. As for transport around town, a ¥10 **taxi** ride should cover any destination in central Hangzhou.

Accommodation

Hangzhou has some excellent **hotels**, particularly on the lakefront, with a handful of **hostels** and inexpensive lodging also available on university campuses. Rooms fill fast in season, so you may want to book in advance.

Hotels

Dahua 171 Nanshan Lu ⓣ0571/87181888, ⓕ87061770. On the lakeside, several blocks south of Jiefang Lu. Spacious grounds with comfortable rooms and attentive service justify the prices – this is actually better value than many of its competitors. Mao Zedong and Zhou Enlai stayed here whenever they were in town. ❽

Dongpo 52 Renhe Lu ⓣ0571/87069769, ⓕ87024266. Smart rooms, a beautiful six-storey central atrium and friendly staff make this just about the best deal in Hangzhou. ❺

Holiday Wuyang 109 Qingbo Lu, along Xi Hu ⓣ0571/87655678, ⓕ87655888. Recently renovated and in a promising location, near the lake but tucked away on a side street. ❽

Huaqiao 39 Hubin Lu ⓣ0571/87074401, ⓕ87074978. This four-star offering has good if slightly overpriced rooms, in a great location on the lakefront just south of Qingchun Lu. ❼

Ramada Plaza Hangzhou Haihua 298 Qingchun Lu ⓣ0571/87215888, ⓕ87215108, ⓦwww.ramadainternational.com. One of the more upmarket offerings from this international hotel chain, with luxurious and tastefully designed rooms. The grand lobby features an imposing staircase. Rooms overlooking the lake command a premium. ❾

Shangri-La Beishan Lu, next to Yuefei Mu ⓣ0571/87977951, ⓕ87073545, ⓦwww.shangri-la.com. Total air-conditioned luxury in beautiful, secluded grounds, overhung by trees, on the northern shore of the lake. There's an expensive but scrumptious breakfast buffet. ❾

Xinqiao 226 Jiefang Lu, on the corner of Yan'an Lu ⓣ0571/87076688, ⓕ87071428. One of the town's plushest hotels, in an absolutely central location. ❽

Xinxin 58 Beishan Lu ⓣ0571/87999090, ⓕ87051898. Standard, mildly worn rooms in one of the nicest locations in town, overlooking the northern shore of the lake. ❽

Zhonghua 55 Youdian Lu ⓣ0571/87027094, ⓕ87077089. Very central, between the lakefront and Yan'an Lu, this place offers good single and double rooms. ❻

University and hostel lodgings

Chinese Academy of Art 218 Nanshan Lu ⓣ0571/87164713. Inside the left gate as you face the main building: take the first doorway to your left just inside the gate and go to the third floor of building no. 9. The International College here is a well-located place to stay, quieter than the hostels, plus you get to hang out with art students. No dorms. ❹

Foreign Students' Building, Zhejiang University Tianmushan Lu ⓣ0571/88273784. There are sometimes a few spare beds or double rooms, with communal showers available here. To find it, head to the university's Xixi campus, turn right inside the main gate, then proceed west for 5min to building no. 3. No dorms. ❷

 **Mingtown Garden Hostel** 4 Zhaogong Causeway, ⓣ0571/87895883. This mellow hostel is in a refurbished villa at the west side of the lake. Perhaps a little far out for convenience but, with a leafy garden and lake views, it's a nice place just to hang out and relax. Dorm beds ¥40, ❸

Mingtown Youth Hostel 101 Nanshan Lu ⓣ0571/87918948, f87922018. Down an alley directly across from the Chinese Academy of Art, with a range of rooms, including a few with lake views and private bathroom. Take bus #2 from the train station. Dorm beds ¥40, ❸

Zhejiang University Guesthouse 16 Zheda Lu ⓣ0571/87951211. Just off Yugu Lu near the *Lingfeng Hotel*, take bus #16 from the lakeside. Good value, though with a strong institutional feel. ❹

The City

Unusually for a Chinese city, the municipality of Hangzhou encompasses large areas of greenery that might normally be classified as countryside. This is mainly thanks to **Xi Hu** itself – so central and dominant a role has the lake played in the city's history that even today a trip right round its shores does not feel like an excursion out of the city.

Within the lake are various **islands** and causeways, while the shores are home to endless **parks** holding Hangzhou's most famous individual sights, ranging from the extravagant and historic **Yuefei Mu** (Tomb of Yuefei) to the ancient hillside Buddhist carvings of **Feilai Feng** and its associated temple, the **Lingyin Si**, one of China's largest and most renowned. Farther afield, beautiful tea plantations nestle around the village of **Longjing**, while south down to the **Qiantang River** are excellent walking opportunities.

With most of Hangzhou's sights located on or near the lakeshore, you'll find that the ideal way to get between them is by **bike**; otherwise you can use local buses or simply walk. It's possible to walk round the lake's entire circumference in one day, but you wouldn't have time to do justice to all the sights en route.

Xi Hu

A voyage on this lake offers more refreshment and pleasure than any other experience on earth...

Marco Polo

Xi Hu forms a series of landscapes with rock, trees, grass and lakeside buildings all reflected in the water and backed by luxuriant wooded hills. The lake itself stretches just over 3km from north to south and just under 3km from east to

Boat trips on Xi Hu

One of the loveliest things to do in Hangzhou is take a boat trip on the lake. Tourist boats (¥45, including entrance fees for Santanyinyue) launch from the two lake tour jetties and head directly for the **islands**. Then there are the freelance boatmen in small canopied boats, who fish for tourists along major lakeside gathering points, especially the causeways, and charge ¥80 for an hour for up to six people. You can also take out a boat of your own – either electric putt-putters for four people (¥30/30min; ¥200 deposit), or paddle boats (¥15–20/30min).

west, though the surrounding parks and associated sights spread far beyond this. On a sunny day the colours are brilliant, but even with grey skies and choppy waters, the lake views are soothing and tranquil; for the Chinese they are also laden with literary and historic associations. Although the crowds and hawkers are sometimes distracting, the area is so large that you can find places to escape the hubbub. A good time to enjoy the lake is sunrise, when mellow *tai ji* practitioners hone their craft against a backdrop of early-morning mists.

As early as the Tang dynasty, work was taking place to control the waters of the lake with dykes and locks, and the two **causeways** that now cross sections of the lake, Bai Di across the north and Su Di across the west, originated in these ancient embankments. Mainly used by pedestrians and cyclists, the causeways offer instant escape from the noise and smog of the built-up area to the east. Strolling the causeways at any time, surrounded by clean, fresh water and flowering lilies, is a pleasure and a favourite pursuit of Chinese couples. The western end of Bai Di supposedly offers the best vantage point over the lake.

Bai Di and Gu Shan

Bai Di is the shorter and more popular of the two causeways, about 1500m in length. Starting in the northwest of the lake near the *Shangri-La Hotel*, it runs along the outer edge of Gu Shan before crossing back to the northeastern shore, enclosing a small strip known as Beili Hu (North Inner Lake). The little island of **Gu Shan** in the middle of the causeway is one of Hangzhou's highlights, a great place to relax under a shady tree. Bursting with chrysanthemum blossoms in the spring and sprinkled with pavilions and pagodas, this tiny area was originally landscaped under the Tang, but the present style dates from the Qing, when Emperor Qianlong built himself a palace here, surrounded by the immaculate **Zhongshan Park**. Part of the palace itself, facing south to the centre of the lake, is now the **Zhejiang Provincial Museum** (Mon noon–4pm, Tues–Sun 9am–4pm; free), a huge place with clear English captions throughout and a number of different wings. The main building in front of the entrance houses historical relics, including some superb bronzes from the eleventh to the eighth century BC. Another hall centres on coin collections and has specimens of the world's first banknotes, dating to the Northern Song; you'll get an appreciation of the deep conservatism of Chinese society from its coinage, which remained fundamentally unchanged for two thousand years from the Han to the Qing dynasties. New galleries outside hold displays of painting and Tibetan Buddha statues.

The curious **Xiling Seal Engravers' Society** (daily 9am–5pm; ¥5), founded in 1904, occupies the western side of the hill, next to the *Louwailou Restaurant*. Its tiny park encloses a pavilion with a pleasant blend of steps, carved stone tablets, shrubbery, and nearby a small early Buddhist stupa; drop by here in summer and you can often see the engravers at work. On the southeastern side of the hill by the water is another of Qianlong's buildings, the **Autumn Moon on a Calm Lake Pavilion**, which is the perfect place to watch the full moon. It's a teahouse now, very popular after sunset and full of honeymooners. The low stone **Duan Qiao** (Broken Bridge), at the far eastern end of the causeway, gets its name because winter snow melts first on the hump of the bridge, creating the illusion of a gap.

Su Di and Santanyinyue Island

The longer causeway, **Su Di**, named after the Song-dynasty poet-official Su Dong Po, who was governor of Hangzhou, starts from the southwest corner of the lake and runs its full length to the northern shore close to Yuefei Mu.

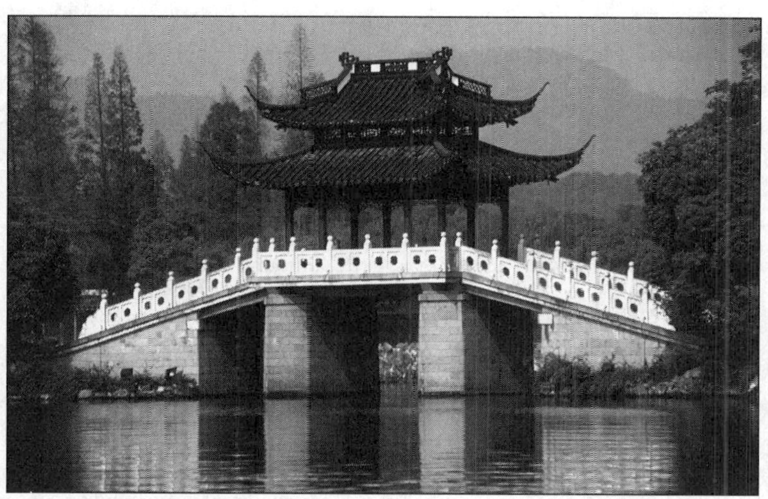

▲ Su Di bridge, Xi Hu

Consisting of embankments planted with banana trees, weeping willows and plum trees, linked by six stone-arch bridges, the causeway encloses a narrow stretch of water, **Xili Hu** (West Inner Lake). East of the causeway and in the southern part of the lake is the largest of the islands here, **Xiaoying**, built up in 1607. It's better known as **Santanyinyue** (Three Flags Reflecting the Moon) after the three "flags" in the water – actually stone pagodas, said to control the evil spirits lurking in the deepest spots of the lake. Bridges link across from north to south and east to west so that the whole thing seems like a wheel with four spokes, plus a central hub just large enough for a pavilion, doubling as a shop and a restaurant. The ¥20 admission fee to get onto the island is usually included if you take one of the tourist boat rides here.

The lakeshore

The account here assumes you start from the northeast of the lake on Beishan Lu and head anticlockwise, in which case the seven-storey **Baoshu Ta** on Baoshi Shan is the first sight you'll encounter. Looming up on the hillside to your right, the pagoda is a 1933 reconstruction of a Song-dynasty tower, and a nice place to walk to along hillside tracks. From Beishan Lu a small lane leads up behind some buildings to the pagoda. Tracks continue beyond, and you can climb right up to **Qixia Shan** (Mountain Where Rosy Clouds Linger) above the lake. About halfway along this path you'll see a yellow-walled monastery with black roofs lurking below to your left, the **Baopu Daoist Compound**. It's well worth a stop, especially in the late afternoon, if only because you might be able to discreetly watch one of the frequent ancestral worship ceremonies that are held here, with priests clad in colourful garb and widows clutching long black necklaces to pay tribute to their husbands. If you climb the stairs, you will find several smaller halls where old men practise their calligraphy and young women play the *pipa*.

Back on the path along the ridge above the monastery, you can stroll past **Chuyang** (Sunrise Terrace), traditionally the spot for watching the spring sun rise over the lake and Gu Shan. If you continue west, you'll eventually reach some steep stone stairs which will bring you back down to the road, close to the Yuefei Mu at the northwest end of the lake, next to the *Shangri-La Hotel*.

Yuefei Mu and Huanglong Dong Park

The **Yuefei Mu** (Tomb of Yuefei; daily 7.30am–5.30pm; ¥25) is one of Hangzhou's big draws, the twelfth-century Song general Yuefei being considered a hero in modern China thanks to his unquestioning patriotism. Having emerged victorious from a war against barbarian invaders from the north, Yuefei was falsely charged with treachery by a jealous prime minister, and executed at the age of 39. Twenty years later, the subsequent emperor annulled all charges against him and had him reburied here with full honours. Walk through the temple to reach the tomb itself – a tiny bridge over water, a small double row of stone men and animals, steles, a mound with old pine trees and four cast-iron statues of the villains, kneeling in shame with their hands behind their backs. The calligraphy on the front wall of the tomb reads, "Be loyal to your country".

Immediately west of Yuefei's tomb is a lane leading away from the lake and north into the hills behind. Thirty minutes' walk along here eventually leads to the **Huanglong Dong Park** (Yellow Dragon Cave Park; daily 6.30am–4pm; ¥15), to the north of Qixia Shan. The park can also be approached from the roads to the north of here, south of Hangzhou University. The main area of the park is charmingly secretive, sunk down between sharply rising hills with a pond, teahouses, a shrine to Yue Lao (the Chinese god of arranging marriages), cherry blossoms in the early spring, and a pavilion where musicians perform traditional music.

Huagang Park, Jinci Si and the Museum of Chinese Medicine

On a promontory in the southwestern corner of the lake, the small Song-era **Huagang Park** contains a pond full of enormous fish, and there are also wonderful stretches of grass and exotic trees under which to relax. East of here, by the southern shore of Xi Hu, is another temple, **Jinci Si** (daily 7.30am–5pm; ¥10), which has been fully restored; tourist buses #1 and #2 run past.

Finally, a kilometre east of the lake is the **Huqingyu Tang Museum of Chinese Medicine** (daily 8am–5pm; ¥10), which traces the complicated history of Chinese medicine from its roots several thousand years ago. The museum is housed in a traditional medicine shop, an architectural gem hidden down a small alley off Hefang Jie. On Hefang Jie itself, look for the white wall with seven large characters and turn down the first alley along its west side; the museum is on the right after about 30m.

Feilai Feng and Lingyin Si

Three kilometres west, away from the lake (bus #7 from Yuefei Mu to its terminus), Hangzhou's most famous sights are scattered around **Feilai Feng** (daily 5.30am–5.30pm; ¥25). The hill's bizarre name – "The Hill that Flew Here" – derives from the tale of an Indian Buddhist devotee named Hui Li who, upon arrival in Hangzhou, thought he recognized the hill from one back home in India, and asked when it had flown here. Near the entrance is the **Ligong Pagoda**, constructed for him. If you turn left shortly after entering the site, you'll come to a surprisingly impressive group of fake rock carvings, replicas of giant Buddhas from all over China. To the right of the entrance you'll find a snack bar and beautiful views over the neighbouring tea plantations up the hill.

The main feature of Feilai Feng is the hundreds of **Buddhist sculptures** carved into its limestone rocks. These date from between the tenth and fourteenth centuries and are the most important examples of their type to be found south of the Yangzi. Today the little Buddhas and other figurines are dotted about everywhere, moss-covered and laughing among the foliage. It's possible to follow trails right up to the top of the hill to escape the tourist hubbub.

Deep inside the Feilai Feng tourist area you'll eventually arrive at **Lingyin Si** (Temple of the Soul's Retreat; daily 7.30am–4.30pm; ¥20), one of the biggest temple complexes in China. Founded in 326 AD by Hui Li, who is buried nearby, it was the largest and most important monastery in Hangzhou and once had three thousand monks, nine towers, eighteen pavilions and 75 halls and rooms. Today it is an attractive working temple with daily services, usually in the early morning or after 3pm.

In the 1940s the temple was so badly riddled with woodworm that the main crossbeams collapsed onto the statues; the eighteen-metre-high Tang statue of Sakyamuni is a replica, carved in 1956 from 24 pieces of camphorwood. Elsewhere in the temple, the old frequently brushes against the new – the **Hall of the Heavenly King** contains four large and highly painted Guardians of the Four Directions made in the 1930s, while the Guardian of the Buddhist Law and Order, who shields the Maitreya, was carved from a single piece of wood eight hundred years ago.

Southwest of the lake

Down in the southwestern quarter of the lake, in the direction of the village of Longjing, the dominant theme is **tea production**: gleaming green tea bushes sweep up and down the land, and old ladies pester tourists into buying fresh tea leaves. Fittingly, this is where you'll find the **Tea Museum** (daily 8am–5pm; free), a smart place with lots of captions in English, covering themes such as the history of tea and the etiquette of tea drinking. There are displays on different varieties of tea, cultivation techniques, the development of special teaware, and finally, reconstructed tearooms in various ethnic styles, such as Tibetan and Yunnanese. Bus #27 from Pinghai Lu in the town centre comes here; get off more or less opposite the former *Zhejiang Hotel*, then head southwest to the museum along a small lane just to the north of, and parallel to, the main road.

A couple of kilometres further southwest, the village of **LONGJING** ("Dragon Well"), with tea terraces rising on all sides behind the houses, is famous as the origin of **Longjing tea**, perhaps the finest variety of green tea produced in China. Depending on the season, a stroll around here affords glimpses of leaves in different stages of processing – being cut, sorted or dried. You'll be pestered to sit at an overpriced teahouse or to buy leaves when you get off the bus – have a good look around first, as there is a very complex grading system and a huge range in quality and price. The **Dragon Well** itself is at the end of the village, a group of buildings around a spring, done up in a rather touristy fashion. Bus #27 runs to Longjing from the northwestern lakeshore, near Yuefei Mu; alternatively, you can actually hike up here from the Qiantang River (see below).

South of the lake

The area to the south and southwest of Xi Hu, down to the Qiantang River, is full of trees and gentle slopes. Of all the parks in this area, perhaps the nicest is the **Hupaomeng Quan** (Tiger Running Dream Spring; daily 8am–5pm; ¥15). Bus #504 and tourist bus #5 both run here from the city centre, down the eastern shore of the lake, while tourist bus #3 passes close by on the way down from Longjing. The spring – according to legend, originally found by a ninth-century Zen Buddhist monk with the help of two tigers – is said to produce the purest water around, the only water that serious connoisseurs use for brewing the best Longjing teas. For centuries, this has been a popular site for hermits to settle and is now a large forested area dotted with teahouses, shrines, waterfalls and pagodas.

A few more stops south on bus #308 takes you to the 1000-year-old **Liuhe Ta** (daily 7am–5.30pm; ¥20, tower ¥10), a pagoda occupying a spectacular site overlooking the Qiantang River, a short way west of the rail bridge. The story goes that a Dragon King used to control the tides of the river, wreaking havoc on farmers' harvests. Once a particularly massive tide swept away the mother of a boy named Liuhe to the Dragon King's lair. Liuhe threw pebbles into the river, shaking the Dragon Palace violently, which forced the Dragon King to return his mother to him and to promise never again to manipulate the tides. In appreciation villagers built the pagoda, a huge structure of wood and brick, hung with 104 large iron bells on its upturned eaves. Today, ironically, the pagoda is a popular vantage point from which to view the dramatic **tidal bores** during the autumn equinox.

Twenty minutes' walk upriver west from the pagoda, at the #4 bus terminus, a lane known as **Nine Creeks and Eighteen Gullies** runs off at right angles to the river and up to Longjing. This is a delightful narrow way, great for a bike ride or a half-day stroll, following the banks of a stream and meandering through paddy fields and tea terraces with hills rising in swelling ranks on either side. Halfway along the road, a restaurant serving excellent tea and food straddles the stream where it widens into a serene lagoon.

Eating, drinking and nightlife

As a busy resort for local tourists, Hangzhou has plenty of good **places to eat**, though there's nothing like the cosmopolitan range of either Shanghai or Nanjing. The wedge-shaped neighbourhood between Hubin Lu and Yan'an Lu is home to a number of Chinese restaurants and fast-food joints. Touristy Hefang Jie is also a good spot to make for, with a variety of Chinese restaurants and snacks.

Many Chinese tourists make it a point to visit one of the famous historical restaurants in town: both *Louwailou* (Tower Beyond Tower) and *Tianwaitian* (Sky Beyond Sky) serve local specialities at reasonable prices, while a third, *Shanwaishan* (Mountain Beyond Mountain), has garnered a bad reputation over the years. All three restaurants were named after a line in Southern Song poet Lin Hejin's most famous poem: "Sky beyond sky, Mountain beyond mountain and tower beyond tower/Could song and dance by West Lake be ended anyhow?"

As for **nightlife**, there's a good scene in Hangzhou if you know where to look. Nanshan Lu and Shuguang Lu are the best bar strips. The *JZ Club* on 6 Liuyin Lu, off Nanshan Lu (Ⓣ0571/87028293; Ⓦwww.jzclub.com), is a very urbane place for a drink, with a good sound system and drink list and live jazz every night. Legendary Bejing rocker Cui Jian has been known to show up at *Traveller Bar*, 176 Shuguang Lu, and run through a few numbers; when he's not around the house rock band do a pretty good job.

Restaurants and cafés

Kuiyuan Guan Jiefang Lu, just west of Zhongshan Zhong Lu (go through the entrance with Chinese lanterns hanging outside, and it's on the left, upstairs). Specializes in more than forty noodle dishes for all tastes, from the mundane (beef noodle soup) to the acquired (pig intestines and kidneys). Also offers a range of local seafood delicacies.

Louwailou Gu Shan Island. The best-known restaurant in Hangzhou, whose specialities include *dongpo* pork, fish-shred soup and beggar's chicken (a whole chicken cooked inside a ball of mud, which is broken and removed at your table). Lu Xun and Zhou Enlai, among others, have dined here. Standard dishes cost ¥30–45.

Tianwaitian At the gate to Feiliai Feng and Lingyin Si. Chinese tourists flock here to sample the fresh seafood, supposedly caught from Xi Hu. Not as good as *Louwailou* though. Dishes are ¥40–55 each.

Vienna Coffee House 91 Shugang Lu. A branch of the famous Shanghai café, and a little slice of *fin-de-siècle* Austria. Coffee is pricey at ¥Y38; the cakes are better value at around ¥Y25. try the tiramisu. Free Wi-Fi.

Zhiweiguan Renhe Lu, half a block east of the lake. In a very urbane atmosphere, with piped Western classical music, you can enjoy assorted *dianxin* by the plate for around ¥20, including *xiao long bao* (small, fine stuffed dumplings) and *mao erduo* (fried, crunchy stuffed dumplings). The *huntun tang* (wonton soup) and *jiu miao* (fried chives) are also good.

Listings

Airlines The main CAAC reservations and ticketing office is at 390 Tiyuchang Lu in the north of town (daily 7.30am–8pm; reservations ⓣ0571/86662391; domestic flight schedules ⓣ0571/85151397). CAAC buses to the airport (5.45am–8pm; ¥15) leave here every 30min.

Banks and exchange The Bank of China head office is at 140 Yan'an Bei Lu (daily 8am–5pm), immediately north of Qingchun Lu.

Bike rental Hangzhou's Freedom Network Bike Rental is one of the best operations of its kind in China, with locations around the lake and the option to return your bike to any of their outlets. One convenient outlet is the small corner office at 175 Nanshan Lu (ⓣ0571/87131718), in a freestanding grey building 200m south of Jiefang Lu. Rentals cost ¥10/hr or ¥50/day, with a ¥400 deposit.

Hospitals The most central is the Shengzhong, on Lingyun Lu, west of the lake.

Internet access There are a number of poky Internet places on Zhongshan Zhong Lu just north of Hefang Jie, as well as outside the gates of both universities.

Mail The main post office is just north of the train station on Huancheng Dong Lu.

PSB For visa extensions, enquire at the PSB in the centre of town, on the southwest corner of the junction between Jiefang Lu and Yan'an Lu.

Shopping The most touristed concentration of souvenir outlets – selling silk, tea and crafts – is along Hefang Jie. An L-shaped night market bends around the western end of Renhe Lu, with street sellers peddling a proletarian jumble of wares, ranging from watches to DVDs to Little Red Books. The ritziest brand names are all on Hubin Lu, right on the waterfront.

Trains The main train station contains a very convenient soft-seat ticket office for foreigners (daily 8am–7pm) on the north side of the station building at street level, left as you enter the station. An equally convenient soft-seat waiting room (daily 6am–midnight) is just around the corner on the station's front facade. The main ticket hall is on the second level; there's also a ticket window next to the tourist info booth.

Travel agents CITS is on the north shore of the lake, on a hillock above the junction of Beishan Lu and Baoshu Lu. Walk through the main gate and the office is a couple of minutes' walk ahead to the left (ⓣ0571/85059033, ⓕ85059052; daily 8.30am–5pm). Nearly all Hangzhou hotels have their own travel agencies, usually more helpful than CITS.

Around Hangzhou: Moganshan

The hill station of **MOGANSHAN**, 60km north of Huangzhou, was popular before World War II with the fast foreign set and has recently reprised its former role as a resort to escape the stifling summer heat. The old European-style villas and po-faced communist-style sanatoriums are being restored and turned into guesthouses, bars and cafes. There's little to do here but wander the incongruously European-looking village, hike in the bamboo woods and enjoy the views. It's lovely; but get here sooner rather than later, before it all gets overdeveloped.

You can get here by **bus** from Hangzhou's north bus station, which will drop you off at the base of the mountain in Wukang; a taxi the rest of the way costs around ¥30, and there's a fee of ¥80 for entering the resort. Moganshan has a surfeit of faded, Chinese-style two-star **accommodation**, fine if you just want a bed, from ¥150; try the *Songliang Shanzhuang*, at the south end of the main road, *Yinshan Jie* (Ⓣ0572/803381) or the higher *Baiyun Hotel* (Ⓣ0572/8033382; Ⓦwww.mogan-mountain.com. The *Du Yuesheng Villa*, once owned by the gangster himself (see p.367) and now operated by the Radisson chain (Ⓣ0572/3033601; ⑨) is upmarket but a little overpriced with rooms at ¥1100. For **food**, Yinshan Jie is lined with restaurants offering local specialities such as wild game; recommended is the bar-cum-restaurant at the *Moganshan Lodge* (Ⓣ0572/8033011; Ⓦwww.moganshanlodge.com) in a wing of the *Songliang Shanzhuang*. The helpful owners will point you in the right direction for good local walks. Note that there are no **ATMs** in town, so arrive with enough money to last your stay.

Shaoxing and around

Located south of Hangzhou Bay in the midst of a flat plain crisscrossed by waterways and surrounded by low hills, **SHAOXING** is one of the oldest cities in Zhejiang, having established itself as a regional centre in the fifth century BC. During the intervening centuries – especially under the Song, when the imperial court was based in neighbouring Hangzhou – Shaoxing remained a flourishing city, though the lack of direct access to the sea has always kept it out of the front line of events.

For the visitor, Shaoxing is a quieter and more intimate version of Suzhou, combining attractive little sights with great opportunities for boating round classic Chinese countryside. It's a small city that seems to have played a disproportionate role in Chinese culture – some of the nation's more colourful characters came from here, including the mythical tamer of floods Yu the Great, the wife-murdering Ming painter Xin Wei, the female revolutionary hero Qiu Jin, and the great twentieth-century writer Lu Xun, all of whom have left their mark on the city.

Near Shaoxing is **Jian Hu**, a lake whose unusual clarity has made the city known throughout China for its alcohol. Most famous are the city's sweet

Shaoxing and around

Shaoxing	绍兴	*shàoxīng*
Bazi Qiao	八子桥	*bāzǐ qiáo*
Cang Qiao Heritage Street	仓桥直街	*cāngqiáo zhíjiē*
Fushan Park	府山公园	*fǔshān gōngyuán*
Lu Xun's Former Residence	鲁迅故居	*lǔxùn gùjū*
Lu Xun Memorial Hall	鲁迅纪念馆	*lǔxùn jìniànguǎn*
Qingteng Shuwu	青滕书屋	*qīngténg shūwū*
Qiu Jin's Former Residence	秋瑾故居	*qiūjǐn gùjū*
Sanwei Shuwu	三味书屋	*sānwèi shūwū*
Xi Jie	西街	*xī jiē*
Yingtian Pagoda	应天塔	*yìngtiān tǎ*
Accommodation and eating		
Shaoxing Caiguan	绍兴菜馆	*shàoxīng càiguǎn*
Shaoxing Fandian	绍兴饭店	*shàoxīng fàndiàn*
Shaoxing Laotai Men	绍兴老台门旅店	*shàoxīng lǎotáimén lǚdiàn*
Dong Hu	东湖	*dōnghú*
Lanting	兰亭	*lántíng*
Yu Ling	禹陵	*yǔlíng*

yellow rice wine, made from locally grown glutinous rice, and its ruby-coloured **n,'er hong wine**, traditionally the tipple brides sipped to toast their new husbands – it was bought when the bride was born, and buried in the backyard to age.

Arrival, information and accommodation

Shaoxing's **train station** is in the far north of town – the rail line that comes through here is a spur running between Hangzhou and the city of Ningbo. Bus #2 runs from here along Jiefang Lu to the southern end of the city. If you're coming from Hangzhou or Ningbo by bus, you'll probably arrive at the Keyun Zhongxin, a **bus station** in the far northeast of town, in which case take bus #3 to the city centre.

The main **Bank of China** is on Renmin Xi Lu (daily 7.30am–5.30pm). **CITS** at 288 Zhongxing Zhong Lu (☎0575/5200079) can arrange tours of the surrounding area as well as book onward travel.

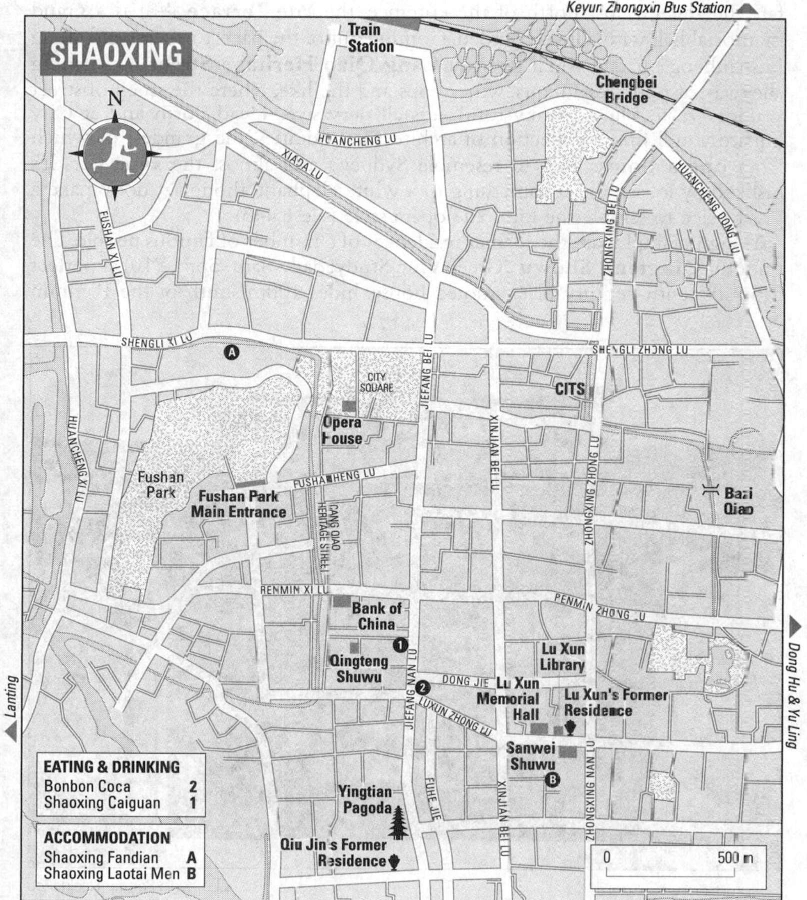

The most upmarket **hotel** in town is the Ming-style *Shaoxing Fandian* on Shengli Lu (ⓣ0575/5155888; ❼), a huge and charming place in grounds so large that you can travel around them by boat. It's a couple of hundred metres west of Jiefang Lu – bus #30 heads there from the train station. Otherwise, consider the *Shaoxing Laotai Men*, housed in an old courtyard building on Lu Xun Zhong Lu; it's all rather rickety, but with its period fittings has something of the feel of a country inn (❸).

The City and around

Although Shaoxing's immediate centre comprises a standard shopping street, elsewhere there are running streams, black-tiled whitewashed houses, narrow lanes divided by water, alleys paved with stone slabs, and back porches housing tiny kitchens that hang precariously over canals. **Fushan Park** (daily 8am–4.30pm), in the west of town south of the *Shaoxing Hotel*, is as good a place as any to get your bearings, with a view over the town's canals and bridges from the top. The main entrance to the park is on Fushanheng Lu – look for the prominent archway guarding its eastern end next to the north–south thoroughfare, Jiefang Lu. Just north of the entrance, the **Yue Terrace** (¥8) is a grand memorial hall with a lovely garden. Coming out of the park, turn east and along Fushanheng Lu, and you'll arrive at **Cang Qiao Heritage Street**, a charming alleyway of poky restaurants, wine shops and the like, where the smell of street vendors' *chou dofu* – "stinky tofu" – is all pervasive. Head north and at City Square you'll find a collection of architectural oddities, the grandest of which is an **opera house** built to resemble Sydney's and almost the same size. It's disliked by locals, and is something of a white elephant, though it does make a great place to sample the local Yue opera style (see p.443).

Along Jiefang Lu are the former residences of a number of famous people. The tranquil **Qingteng Shuwu** (Green Vine Study; daily 8am–5pm; ¥10), a perfect little sixteenth-century black-roofed house, hides 100m south of the Renmin

▲ Lu Xun's Former Residence

Lu intersection on a small alley, Houguan Xiang, west off the main road. The serenity of the place belies the fact that it was once the home of eccentric Ming painter and dramatist Xu Wei (1521–93), who is notorious for having murdered his wife.

Another 500m south down Jiefang Lu from here, the **Yingtian Pagoda** (daily 8am–5pm; ¥5) crowns a low hill, Tu Shan. Part of a temple founded by the Song, burnt down by the Taiping rebels and subsequently rebuilt, the pagoda repays the stiff climb with splendid views over the town's canals. The black roof tiles, visible a block to the south, belong to the former residence of the radical woman activist **Qiu Jin**, which is situated on a small lane, Hechang Tang (daily 8am–5pm; ¥15). Born here in 1875, Qiu Jin studied in Japan before returning to China and joining Sun Yatsen's clandestine revolutionary party. After editing several revolutionary papers in Shanghai and taking part in a series of abortive coups, she was captured and executed in Hangzhou in 1907 by Qing forces.

East off Jiefang Lu, down Luxun Lu, are several sights associated with the writer **Lu Xun** (see p.1206), all open daily from 8am to 5pm; a combined ticket to see them all costs ¥120. Lu Xun's childhood and early youth were spent in Shaoxing, and local characters populate his books. Supposedly, he based his short story *Kong Yi Ji*, about a village idiot who failed the imperial exams and was thus ostracized from mainstream society, in part on observations in a bar that used to stand on this street. A few minutes farther east from the **Lu Xun Memorial Hall**, beyond the plain **Lu Xun Library**, you'll find **Lu Xun's Former Residence**, now converted into a **Folk Museum**. If you've seen the high, secretive outer walls so many compounds have, you'll find it a refreshing change to get to look at the spacious interior and numerous rooms inside a traditional house; drop in here for a wander through the writer's old rooms and for a stroll in his garden. Immediately across the road from the museum is the **Sanwei Shuwu**, the small school where Lu Xun was taught as a young boy. In the one room to see, there's a small desk on which you'll find a smooth stone and a bowl of water, in former times the only available tools for calligraphy students too poor to buy ink and paper. Visitors are supposed to write their names in water on the stone for luck.

One further sight definitely worth seeking out in Shaoxing predates Lu Xun by several hundred years. A couple of hundred metres to the north of the Lu Xun buildings, in the east of the town – in the heart of one of Shaoxing's most picturesque and traditional neighbourhoods – is the most famous of all the town's old bridges, **Bazi Qiao** (Character Eight Bridge). This thirteenth-century piece of engineering, which acquired its name because it looks like the Chinese character for the number eight, is still very much in use. A small alley called Baziqiao Zhi Jie runs east off Zhongxing Zhong Lu to the bridge.

Dong Hu

Easily accessible from town, the photogenic **Dong Hu** (East Lake; daily 7am–5.30pm; ¥40) is a twenty-minute ride away on the #1 bus route. Despite appearances, the lake is not a natural one. In the seventh century the Sui rulers quarried the hard green rock east of Shaoxing for building, and when the hill streams were dammed, the quarry became a lake to which, for picturesque effect, a causeway was added during the Qing. The cliff face and lake are now surrounded by a maze of streams, winding paths, pagodas and stepping-stone bridges. Once inside the site, you can rent a little three-person boat (¥40) to take you around the various caves, nooks and crannies in the cliff face. You can choose to be dropped on the opposite shore, from where a flight of steps leads up to a path running to the clifftop, offering superb views over the surrounding paddy fields.

The last bus back to Shaoxing leaves around 5.30pm, though you can take a **boat** back instead (45min; ¥45 per boat after bargaining), or continue through the network of waterways on to Yu Ling (see below). This is a great trip (1hr 20min; ¥65 per boat after bargaining) in a long, slim, flat-bottomed vessel, the boatman steering with a paddle and propelling the boat with his bare feet on the loom of the long oar.

Yu Ling and Lanting

Yu Ling (Tomb of Yu; daily 8am–4pm; ¥50), 6km southeast of Shaoxing and linked to town by bus #2, is a heaped-up chaos of temple buildings in a beautiful setting of trees, mossy rocks and mountains. Yu, the legendary founder of the Xia dynasty, around 2000 BC, earned his title "Tamer of Floods" by tossing great rocks around and dealing with the underwater dragons who caused so many disasters. It took him eight years to control a great flood in the Lower Yangzi. The first temple was probably built around the sixth century AD, while the actual tomb, which seems to predate the temple, may be Han dynasty. The temple today, most recently restored in the 1930s, contains a large painted figure of Yu and scores of inscribed tablets. Outside, the tall, roughly shaped tombstone is sheltered by an elegant open pavilion. The vigorous worshipping you'll see inside the temple shows what a revered figure Yu still is in modern China.

Another wonderfully rural excursion from Shaoxing is 11km southwest to **Lanting**, the Orchid Pavilion (daily 7.30am–5pm; ¥40), named when Goujian, a Yue Kingdom king, planted an orchid on this site almost three thousand years ago. The fourth-century poet and calligrapher Wang Xizhi allegedly composed the *Orchid Pavilion Anthology* here, today considered to be one of the masterpieces of Chinese poetry. Wang held a party with 41 friends, sitting along a creek and floating cups full of wine along it. When a cup stopped, the person sitting nearest either had to drink from the cup or compose a poem. Wang later composed the *Anthology* as a preface to all the poems. Today Lanting is considered a shrine, a place of resonance for all Chinese serious about calligraphy and poetry. Inside Wang's ancestral shrine, located on a small island in the middle of spacious gardens, you can watch artists and calligraphers work. Lanting is on the #3 bus route from Jiefang Lu (45min), but you'll have to ask locals where to get off.

Finally, **Anchang**, 10km west of town, on bus route #118 from Jiefang Lu, is a kilometre-long strip of traditional buildings alongside a canal. This makes for a pleasant stroll – and of course you can always take a boat (¥5). It's a sleepy and untouristy backwater, though all around lie modern textile factories.

Eating, drinking and entertainment

You'll find a few **restaurants** around the northern half of Jiefang Bei Lu. The restaurant in the *Shaoxing Hotel* is good, serving several dishes in the local Shaoxing *mei* (charcoal-grilled) style, but note that the menu is in Chinese only. Dried freshwater fish is a great speciality in Shaoxing, as is the yellow rice wine that's these days more commonly used for cooking than drinking – *shaoxing ji* (Shaoxing chicken) is a classic dish prepared with it. To sample local cuisine in upscale surroundings, visit the *Shaoxing Caiguan*. The menu has no English but plenty of pictures. While walking around town you might be struck by the huge number of stalls selling that malodorous staple of Chinese street life, *chou doufu* (smelly tofu). The recipe was allegedly created by a Shaoxing woman who, tired of her limited cooking prowess, decided to experiment by throwing a variety of spices into a wok with some tofu.

For entertainment, head to the opera house on City Square, which has performances of the local **Yue opera** – considerably softer and more melodious than Beijing opera – every evening at 7.30pm (¥50–160; Ⓦ www.sxdjy.com). Of the **bars**, the best is *Bonbon Coca* on Qian Wang Si, an alley off Jiefang Nan Lu, which has live music most nights.

Putuo Shan

A few hours by boat from Shanghai lies the island of **Putuo Shan**, just twelve square kilometres in area and divided by a narrow channel from the much larger Zhoushan Island. Putuo Shan is also a peak that rises to 300m at one end of the island, one of the four Chinese mountains sacred to Buddhism. Undoubtedly one of the most charming places in eastern China, the island has no honking cars or department stores, only endless vistas of blue sea, sandy beaches and lush green hills dotted with ancient monasteries, making it an ideal place to escape the noise, traffic and dirt of the big cities, with endless opportunities for walking. Although bursts of local tourists at weekends and in summer threaten the serenity, you should still be able to avoid the hordes if you schedule your visit on a weekday or in the off season; the best times to come are April, May, September and October, when the weather is warm and the island isn't especially busy. And bring some walking shoes; you'll get much more out of the place if you walk between the attractions rather than taking the tour buses.

Over the years more than a hundred monasteries and shrines were built at Putuo Shan, with magnificent halls and gardens to match. At one time there

Putuo Shan		
Putuo Shan	普陀山	*pǔtuó shān*
Chaoyang Dong	潮阳洞	*cháoyáng dòng*
Chaoyin Dong	潮音洞	*cháoyīn dòng*
Dasheng An	大乘庵	*dàshèng' ān*
Duobao Pagoda	多宝塔	*duōbǎo tǎ*
Fanyin Dong	梵音洞	*fányīn dòng*
Fayu Si	法雨寺	*fǎyǔ sì*
Foding Shan	佛顶山	*fódǐng shān*
Guanyin Leap	观音跳	*guānyīn tiào*
Huiji Si	慧济寺	*huìjì sì*
Hundred Step Sands	百步沙	*bǎibù shā*
Puji Si	普济寺	*pǔjì sì*
Shenjiamen	沈家门	*shěnjiā mén*
Thousand Step Sands	千步沙	*qiānbù shā*
Zizhu Si	紫竹寺	*zǐzhú sì*
Accommodation		
Fu Quan	福泉山庄	*fúquán shānzhuāng*
Putuoshan Hotel	普陀山大酒店	*pǔtuóshān dàjiǔdiàn*
Putuo Shanzhuang	普陀山庄宾馆	*pǔtuóshānzhuāng bīnguǎn*
Ronglai Yuan	融来院	*rónglái yuàn*
Sanshengtang	三圣堂饭店	*sānshèngtáng fàndiàn*
Xilai Xiaozhuang	息来小庄宾馆	*xīlái xiǎozhuāng bīnguǎn*
Xilin	锡麟饭店	*xīlín fàndiàn*

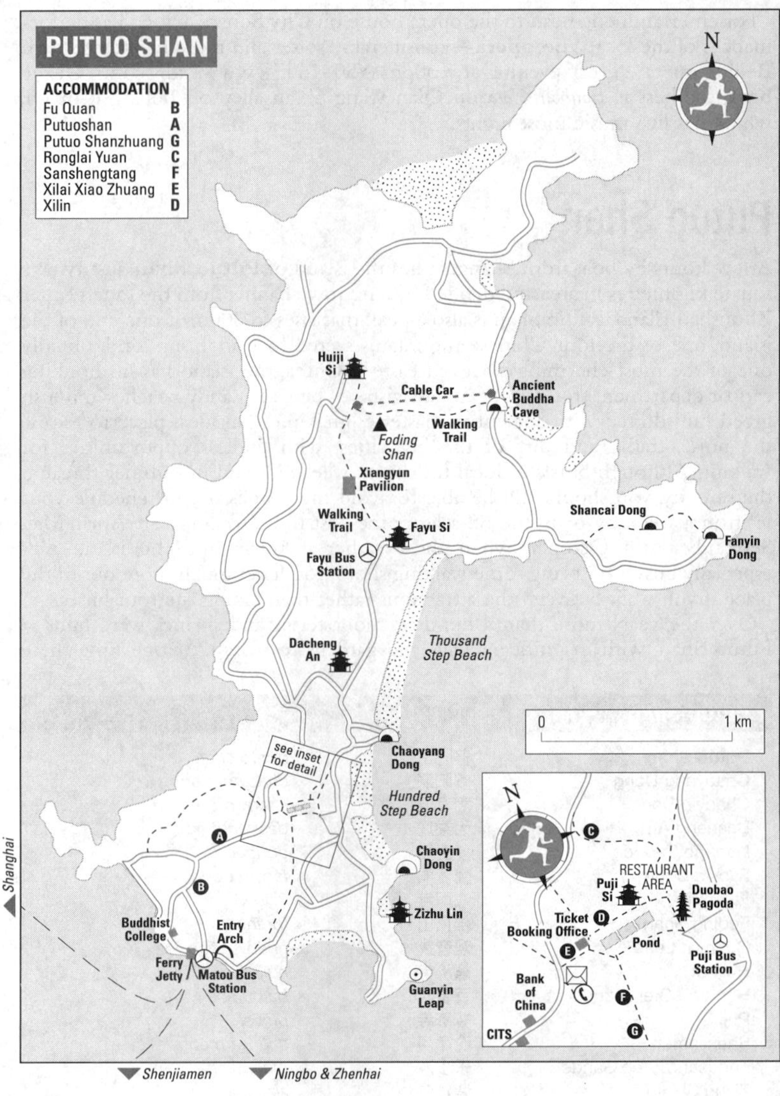

were four thousand monks squeezed onto the island, and even as late as 1949 the Buddhist community numbered around two thousand. Indeed, until that date secular structures were not permitted on the island, and nobody lived here who was not a monk. Although there was a great deal of destruction on Putuo Shan during the Cultural Revolution, many treasures survived, some of which are in the Zhejiang Provincial Museum in Hangzhou (see p.432). Restoration continues steadily, and the number of monks has grown from only 29 in the late 1960s to several hundred. Three principal monasteries survive – **Puji**, the oldest and most central; **Fayu**, on the southern slopes; and **Huiji**, at the summit.

Putuo Shan has been attracting Buddhist pilgrims from all over northeast Asia for at least a thousand years, and there are many tales accounting for the island's status as the centre of the **cult of Guanyin**, Goddess of Mercy. According to one, the goddess attained enlightenment here; another tells how a Japanese monk named Hui'e, travelling home with an image of the goddess, took shelter here from a storm and was so enchanted by the island's beauty that he stayed, building a shrine on the spot. With the old beliefs on the rise again, many people come specifically to ask Guanyin for favours, often to do with producing children or grandchildren. The crowds of Chinese tourists carry identical yellow cotton bags which are stamped with symbols of the goddess at each temple, sometimes in exchange for donations.

Access to the island

Boats to Putuo Shan run frequently from **Shanghai** (see p.395). Leaving Putuo Shan, the last ferry back to Shanghai goes at 4.30pm (¥90). There are also several fast ferries to **Shanghai**, plus one or two slow overnight departures (¥90–350). The slow boat back to Shanghai is worth considering, chugging into the city just after sunrise and providing an absorbing and memorable view of the awakening metropolis. Second-class on the overnight Shanghai boat affords a tolerably comfortable berth in a three- or four-bed cabin with a washbasin.

Putuo Shan is also linked several times a day with **Shenjiamen** on neighbouring Zhoushan Island, a half-hour boat ride away (¥18). Shenjiamen is an interesting place to spend a few hours, and there are frequent bus connections with Ningbo, via the bridge to the mainland.

Arrival

The island is long and thin, with the **ferry jetty**, where all visitors arrive, in the far south; a ¥120 fee is payable when you set foot on the island. There's a helpful hotel booking counter here, which will also drop you off at the accommodation you choose. About 1km north from here is the main "town", a tiny collection of hotels, shops and restaurants, with a recognizable central square around three ponds, dotted with trees and faced to the north by Puji Si. There are only a few roads, travelled by a handful of minibuses (¥4–6) that connect the port with Puji Si and other sights farther north.

Upon arrival, you can reach the town by following either the road heading west or the one east from the jetty, or by picking up a bus from the car park just east of the arrival gate. The westerly route is slightly shorter and takes you past most of the modern buildings and facilities on the island, including the **Bank of China** (daily 8–11am & 1–4.30pm) and the **CITS** office. A little farther north, up a small lane to the left just before the *Xilin Hotel*, is the **post office** and **China Telecom** office, while in the central square, at the northwestern corner, you'll find a **ticket office** where you can book domestic flights out of Ningbo or Shanghai. The eastern route from the jetty takes you through a ceremonial arch symbolizing the entrance to the mountain and then on to a path that cuts away to the left a few minutes later, with the imposing statue of Guanyin standing on a promontory point straight ahead. When you need to **move on** from Putuo Shan, you can buy tickets for outbound boats from any of the island's hotels or at the jetty office (daily 6am–6pm).

Accommodation

There are several delightful **hotels** on Putuo Shan, including a number of converted monasteries, but be warned that in the peak summer months, and especially during the weekend stampede out of Shanghai, you may face a trek around town to find an empty room, not to mention very expensive rates. The price codes in the reviews represent peak season, outside of which rates fall sharply. Another option, often the only one for budget travellers, is to stay in a private house, standard practice for Chinese tourists on Putuo Shan though technically illegal for foreigners, so use your discretion. It's not hard to find people with houses to let – they congregate at the jetty pier, and you should be able to bargain them down to around ¥100–150 per person, depending on the season. A third option, pursued especially by younger foreign travellers, is to crash on one of the island's two beaches for the night.

Fu Quan Not far from the jetty ⓣ0580/6092069. The sign is only in Chinese and easy to miss. Basic but agreeable rooms. ⑤

Putuoshan Hotel On the main west road from the jetty to the town ⓣ0580/6092828, ⓕ6091818. Very easy to spot, thanks to its spacious grounds and opulent design, this is the best hotel on the island, with prices to match. Furniture in the classier rooms and the vegetarian restaurant is in traditional Chinese style. ⑦

Putuo Shanzhuang Just south of the *Sansheng-tang* ⓣ0580/6091530, ⓕ6091228. A beautiful, relatively isolated and extremely comfortable option set on the wooded hillside opposite Puji Si. ⑦

Ronglai Yuan Guesthouse In the middle of town ⓣ0580/6091262, ⓕ6091235. Walk past Puji Si to its eastern end, through an arch, then turn left (north) up the first alley. The alley first bends slightly to the right, then seriously to the left (the hotel is actually directly behind Puji Si). Foreigners aren't allowed to stay in the main building, a converted ancient monastery overhung by giant trees, but can use the small annexe across the street, where the rooms are comfortable enough, if slightly cramped. The genteel owner speaks no English but is always helpful. ⑦

Sanshengtang ⓣ0580/6091277, ⓕ6091140. On the eastern route from the jetty to town, this is just a couple of minutes due south of the centre on a small path. It's quite an attractive place, styled like a temple, but they tend to surcharge foreigners by fifty percent. ⑤

Xilai Xiao Zhuang ⓣ0580/6091505 ext 501, ⓕ6091023. A plain concrete block that's nonetheless a very comfortable hotel, and the first choice for many Chinese tour groups. You'll pass it at the northern end of the west route just before you reach the centre of town. ⑨

Xilin Right on the central square, to the west of Puji Si ⓣ0580/6091303, ⓕ6091199. Features an entrance that makes it look like a temple, plus a good restaurant; you may be able to persuade them to waive their foreigners' surcharge. ⑦

The island

The three main temples on the island are in extremely good condition, recently renovated, with yellow-ochre walls offsetting the deep green of the mature trees in their forecourts. This is particularly true of **Puji Si** (daily 6am–9pm; ¥5), right in the centre of the island, built in 1080 and enlarged by successive dynasties. Standing among magnificent camphor trees, it boasts a bridge lined with statues and an elegantly tall pagoda with an enormous iron bell.

South of here and just to the east of the square ponds is the five-storey **Duobao Pagoda**. Built in 1334 using stones brought over from Tai Hu in Jiangsu province, it has Buddhist inscriptions on all four sides. Twenty minutes' walk farther south down on the southeastern corner of the island is a cave, **Chaoyin Dong**. The din of crashing waves here is remarkable, thought to resemble the call of Buddha (and hence this was a popular spot for monks to commit suicide in earlier days). The neighbouring **Zizhu Si** (Purple Bamboo Temple; daily 6am–6pm; ¥5 including admission to Chaoyin Dong) is one of the less touristed temples on the island and, for that reason alone, a good spot to observe the monks' daily rituals.

On the island's southern tip is Putuo's most prominent sight, the **Guanyintiao** (Guanyin Leap; daily 7am–5pm; ¥6), a headland from which rises a spectacular 33-metre-high bronze-plated statue of the Goddess of Mercy, visible

▲Puji Si, Putuo Shan

from much of the island. In her left hand, Guanyin holds a steering wheel, symbolically protecting fishermen (not to mention travelling monks like Hui'e) from violent seastorms. The pavilion at the base of the statue holds a small exhibit of wooden murals recounting how Guanyin aided Putuo villagers and fishermen over the years, while in a small room directly underneath the statue sit four hundred statues representing the various spiritual incarnations of Guanyin. The view from the statue's base over the surrounding islands and fishing boats is sublime, especially on a clear day. A small memorial plaque on the coast between Guanyintiao and Chaoyin Dong marks the spot where Hui'e made landfall while escaping a violent storm.

North of the town

The two temples in the northern half of the island, Huiji Si and Fayu Si, make for a pleasant day-trip from town. They're conveniently connected to the southern half by minibuses departing from the bus stop just southeast of the central square, and there are minibuses between the temples as well.

Huiji Si stands near the top of **Foding Shan**, whose summit provides spectacular views of the sea and the surrounding islands. You can hike up or use the **cable car** from the minibus stand (daily 7am–5pm; ¥25 up, ¥15 down). The temple itself (daily 6.30am–5pm; ¥5), built mainly between 1793 and 1851, occupies a beautiful site just to the northwest of the summit, surrounded by green tea plantations. The halls stand in a flattened area between hoary trees and bamboo groves, the greens, reds, blues and gold of their enamelled tiles gleaming magnificently in the sunshine. There's also a vegetarian restaurant here.

You can head down along a marked path towards the third major temple, Fayu Si, the whole walk taking about an hour. Shortly after setting off, you'll see a secondary track branching away to the left towards the **Ancient Buddha Cave**, a delightfully secluded spot by a sandy beach on the northeastern coast of the island; give yourself a couple of hours to get there and back. Back on the main path, the steep steps bring you to the **Xiangyun Pavilion**, where you can rest and drink tea with the friendly monks.

Thirty minutes farther on you'll reach the **Fayu Si** (daily 6.30am–5.30pm; ¥5), another superb collection of more than two hundred halls amid huge green trees, built up in levels against the slope during the Ming. With the mountain behind and the sea just in front, it's a delightful place to sit in peaceful contemplation. The Daxiong Hall has been brilliantly restored, and the Dayuan Hall has a unique beamless arched roof and a dome, around the inside of which squirm nine carved wooden dragons. This hall is said to have been moved here from Nanjing by Emperor Kangxi in 1689. Its great statue of **Guanyin**, flanked by monks and nuns, is the focal point of the goddess's birthday celebrations in early April, when thousands of pilgrims and sightseers crowd onto the island for chanting and ceremonies that last all evening.

Occasional minibuses head out along the promontory immediately east of Fayu Si to **Fanyin Dong** (daily 8am–4.30pm; ¥5), a cave whose name derives from the resemblance of the sound of crashing waves to Buddhist chants. The cave is set in the rocky cliff, with a small shrine actually straddling a ravine. Walking around on the promontory is a pleasure given the absence of crowds and the difficulty of getting lost.

You'll appreciate Putuo's beauty much more by making the trip to Huiji Si and Fayu Si **on foot** via the two excellent **beaches** that line the eastern shore: Qianbu Sha (Thousand Step Beach; ¥12 until 5pm, free afterwards) and Baibu Sha (Hundred Step Beach; ¥10 until 5pm, free afterwards). In summer, it's possible to bring a sleeping bag and camp out on either beach – be sure to bring all your supplies from town as there are no stores or restaurants nearby. The beaches are separated by a small headland hiding the **Chaoyang Dong**. Just inside this little cave there's a teahouse and a seating area overlooking the sea, while from the top of the headland itself you'll get great views. One kilometre south of Fayu Si and directly across from Wanbu Sha, the **Dacheng An** (daily 8am–5.30pm; ¥1) is a nunnery notable for the reclining Buddha downstairs in the main hall, and the thousands of tiny seated Buddhas upstairs.

Eating

Eating is not likely to be the highlight of your trip to Putuo Shan – most food must be brought in from the mainland, and is therefore expensive. The lane running northeast away from Puji Si as well as the road between the jetty departure and arrival points both have a string of dingy-looking eating houses which specialize in **seafood** ranging from fish to molluscs and eel, though they also do standard dishes and noodles. Otherwise, all the main temples have simple vegetarian restaurants and there's a more upscale vegetarian place attached to the *Putuoshan Hotel*.

Travel details

Trains

Hangzhou to: Beijing (4 daily; 10–22hr); Guangzhou (3 daily; 25hr); Nanchang (9 daily; 10–12hr); Nanjing (frequent; 6hr 30min–8hr); Shanghai (frequent; 2–3hr); Shaoxing (frequent; 50min); Suzhou (frequent; 3–4hr).

Nanjing to: Beijing (8 daily; 11–16hr); Chengdu (4 daily; 32–36hr); Fuzhou (3 daily; 20–24hr); Hangzhou (frequent; 5hr 30min–7hr 30min); Ma'anshan (frequent; 1hr 30min); Shanghai (frequent; 3–5hr); Suzhou (frequent; 2hr 30min–4hr); Wenzhou (3 daily; 15–16hr); Wuhu (frequent; 2hr); 2hr); Xi'an (10 daily; 13–19hr).

Shaoxing to: Hangzhou (frequent; 50min); Ningbo (frequent; 1hr 30min); Shanghai (7 daily; 4–5hr).
Suzhou to: Hangzhou (frequent; 3–4hr); Nanjing (frequent; 2hr 30min–4hr); Shanghai (frequent; 45min–1hr 20min).

Buses

There are frequent departures on many of the routes listed below, though if your journey is a lengthy one, it's advisable to try to set off before noon.
Hangzhou to: Huang Shan (4hr); Nanjing (4hr); Shanghai (2hr 30min); Shaoxing (1hr 30min); Suzhou (2hr); Wenzhou (4hr 30min).
Nanjing to: Huang Shan (5hr); Hangzhou (5hr); Hefei (7hr); Qingdao (12hr); Shanghai (4–5hr); Suzhou (3–4hr); Wenzhou (12hr); Wuhan (19hr).
Shaoxing to: Hangzhou (1hr 30min).
Suzhou North station to: Dingshan (3hr); Nanjing (3hr); Shanghai (1–2hr).
South station to: Hangzhou (4hr); Tongli (1hr); Zhouzhuang (2hr).

Ferries

Hangzhou to: Suzhou (daily; 10hr).
Putuo Shan to: Shanghai (several daily; 4hr express, 10hr overnight); Shenjiamen (at least 7 daily; 30min); Zhenhai (several daily; 2hr 30min).
Suzhou to: Hangzhou (daily; 10hr).

Flights

Hangzhou to: Beijing (frequent; 2hr); Chengdu (5 daily; 2hr 30min); Fuzhou (3 daily; 1hr); Guangzhou (frequent; 2hr); Guilin (2 daily; 2hr); Hong Kong (5 daily; 2hr); Kunming (4 daily; 2hr); Qingdao (6 daily; 1hr 30min); Shanghai (2 daily; 20min); Shenzhen (10 daily; 2hr); Wenzhou (1–3 daily; 40min); Xiamen (4–5 daily; 1hr 10min); Xi'an (3–4 daily; 2hr).
Nanjing to: Beijing (frequent; 1hr 30min); Chengdu (4–5 daily; 2hr 20min); Chongqing (3–4 daily; 2hr 20min); Dalian (3–4 daily; 1hr 30min); Fuzhou (daily; 1hr); Guangzhou (7 daily; 2hr); Guilin (1–3 daily; 2hr); Haikou (3 daily; 2hr 25min); Hong Kong (4 daily; 2hr 20min); Kunming (4 daily; 2hr 40min); Ningbo (2–3 daily; 1hr); Qingdao (3–5 daily; 1hr); Shenzhen (6 daily; 2hr); Wenzhou (daily; 1hr); Xiamen (4–5 daily; 1hr 40min); Xi'an (2 daily; 2hr).

CHAPTER 7 Highlights

* **Yixian** An amazing collection of antique Ming villages, used atmospherically in Zhang Yimou's film *Raise the Red Lantern*. **See p.468**

* **Huang Shan** Arguably China's most scenic mountain, wreathed in narrow stone staircases, contorted trees and cloud-swept peaks. **See p.468**

* **Hubei Provincial Museum, Wuhan** On show here are 2000-year-old relics from the tombs of aristocrats, including a lacquered coffin and an orchestra of 64 giant bronze bells. **See p.480**

* **Shennongjia Forest Reserve** Wild and remote mountain refuge of the endangered golden monkey and (allegedly) the enigmatic *ye ren*, China's yeti. **See p.488**

* **Wudang Shan** Temple-covered mountains at the heart of Taoist martial-art mythology; it's said this is where *tai ji* originated. **See p.490**

* **Jingdezhen** China's porcelain capital for the last six centuries, with a fine ceramic history museum and busy street markets. **See p.521**

▲ Practising tai ji on Wudang Shan

The Yangzi basin

Having raced out of Sichuan through the narrow Three Gorges, the **Yangzi** (here known as the **Chang Jiang**) widens, slows down, and loops through its flat, low-lying middle reaches, swelled by lesser streams and rivers which drain off the highlands surrounding the four provinces of the Yangzi basin: **Anhui**, **Hubei**, **Hunan** and **Jiangxi**. As well as watering one of China's key rice- and tea-growing areas, this stretch of the Yangzi has long supported trade and transport; back in the thirteenth century, Marco Polo was awed by the "innumerable cities and towns along its banks, and the amount of shipping it carries, and the bulk of merchandise that merchants transport by it". The fact that rural fringes away from the river – including much of Anhui and Jiangxi provinces – remain some of the least developed regions in central China may be redressed by the completion around 2008 of the mighty **Three Gorges Dam** on the border between Hubei and Chongqing, whose hydroelectric output powers a local industrial economy to rival that of the east coast.

The river basin itself is best characterized by the flat expanses of China's two largest freshwater lakes: **Dongting**, which pretty well marks the border between Hunan and Hubei, and **Poyang**, in northern Jiangxi, famed for porcelain produced at nearby **Jingdezhen**. Riverside towns such as **Wuhu** in Anhui are also interesting as working ports, where it's still possible to see traditional river industries – fish farming, grain, rice and bamboo transportation – existing alongside newer ventures in manufacturing. Strangely enough, while all four regional capitals are located near water, only **Wuhan**, in Hubei, is actually on the Yangzi itself, a privileged position which has turned the city into central China's liveliest urban conglomeration. By contrast, the other provincial capitals – **Changsha** in Hunan, Anhui's **Hefei** and Jiangxi's **Nanchang** – seem somewhat dishevelled, though long settlement has left a good deal of **history** in its wake, from well-preserved Han-dynasty tombs to whole villages of Ming-dynasty houses, and almost everywhere you'll stumble over sites from the epic of the **Three Kingdoms**, making the tale essential background reading (see box, p.453). Many cities also remain studded with hefty European buildings, a hangover from their being forcibly opened up to foreign traders as **Treaty Ports** in the 1860s, following the Second Opium War. Perhaps partly due to these unwanted intrusions, the Yangzi basin can further claim to be the **cradle of modern China**: Mao Zedong was born in Hunan; Changsha, Wuhan and Nanchang are all closely associated with Communist Party history; while the mountainous border between Hunan and Jiangxi was both a Red refuge during right-wing purges in the late 1920s and the starting point for the subsequent Long March to Shaanxi.

Away from the river, wild mountain landscapes make for some fine **hiking**, the pick of which is undoubtedly at **Huang Shan** in southern Anhui, followed by Hubei's remote **Shennongjia Forest Reserve**, and **Wulingyan Scenic Reserve** (known locally as **Zhangjiajie)** in Hunan's far west. Pilgrims also have a selection of Buddhist and Taoist **holy mountains** to scale on seemingly unending stone-flagged staircases – Hubei's **Wudang Shan** is outstanding – and less dedicated souls can find pleasant views at the mountain resort town of **Lu Shan** in Jiangxi. As an alternative to the better-known Huang Shan, Anhui's **Jiuhua Shan** has many advantages: it's lower (the highest peak is a little over 1300m), the walking is considerably easier, and there's plenty of interest beyond the scenery.

In theory, **getting around** isn't a problem. **Rail** lines from all over China cross the region, and **buses** and swifter, pricier minibuses link cities to the remotest of corners. **Ferries**, once the principal mode of transport, have been superseded, and passenger services are now limited to the stretch between Wuhan and Chongqing. Autumn is probably the most pleasant time of year, though even winters are generally mild, but near-constant rains and consequential lowland **flooding** plague the summer months. In 1998, the worst floods in

Sanguo: The Three Kingdoms

The empire, long divided, must unite; long united, must divide. Thus it has ever been.

So, rather cynically, begins one of China's best-known stories, the fourteenth-century historical novel **Romance of the Three Kingdoms**. Covering 120 chapters and a cast of thousands, the story touches heavily on the Yangzi basin, which, as a buffer zone between the Three Kingdoms, formed the backdrop for many major battles and key events. Some surviving sites are covered in this chapter and elsewhere in the guide.

The *Romance of the Three Kingdoms* is essentially fictionalized, though well founded in historical fact. Opening in 168 AD, the tale recounts the decline of the Han empire, how China was split into three states by competing warlords, and the subsequent (short-lived) reunification of the country in 280 AD under a new dynasty. The main action began in 189 AD. At this point, the two protagonists were the villainous **Cao Cao** and the virtuous **Liu Bei**, whose watery character was compensated for by the strength of his spirited sworn brothers **Zhang Fei** and **Guan Yu** – the latter eventually becoming enshrined in the Chinese pantheon as the red-faced god of war and healing. Having put down the Yellow Turban taoist secret society uprising in 184 AD in the name of the emperor, both Cao and Liu felt their position threatened by the other; Cao was regent to the emperor **Xian**, but Liu had a remote blood tie to the throne. Though both claimed to support the emperor's wishes, Cao and Liu began fighting against each other, with Cao being defeated in Hubei at the **Battle of the Red Cliffs** (208 AD) after Liu engaged the aid of the wily adviser **Zhuge Liang**, who boosted Liu's heavily outnumbered forces by enlisting the help of a third warlord, **Sun Quan**.

Consolidating their positions, each of the three formed a private kingdom: Cao Cao retreated north to the Yellow River basin where he established the state of **Wei** around the ailing imperial court; Sun Quan set up **Wu** farther south along the lower Yangzi; while Liu Bei built a power base in the riverlands of Sichuan, the state of **Shu**. The alliance between Shu and Wu fell apart when Sun Quan asked Guan Yu to betray Liu. Guan refused and was assassinated by Sun in 220 AD. At this point Cao Cao died, and his ambitious son, **Cao Pi**, forced the emperor to abdicate and announced himself head of a new dynasty. Fearing retaliation from the state of Shu after Guan Yu's murder, Sun Quan decided to support Cao Pi's claims, while over in Shu, Liu Bei also declared his right to rule.

Against Zhuge Liang's advice, Liu marched against Wu to avenge Guan Yu's death but his troops mutinied, killing Zhang Fei. Humiliated, Liu withdrew to **Baidicheng** in the Yangzi Gorges and died. With him out of the way, Cao Pi attacked Sun Quan, who was therefore forced to renew his uncomfortable alliance with Shu – now governed by Zhuge Liang – to keep the invaders out of his kingdom. By 229 AD, however, things were stable enough for Sun Quan to declare himself as a rival emperor, leaving Zhuge to die five years later fighting the armies of Wei. Wei was unable to pursue the advantage, as a coup against Cao Pi started a period of civil war in the north, ending around 249 AD when the **Sima clan** emerged victorious. Sun Quan died soon afterwards, while Shu abandoned all claim to the empire. Wei's Sima clan founded a new dynasty, the **Jin**, in 265 AD, finally overpowering Wu and uniting China in 280 AD.

living memory claimed four thousand lives, wiped out entire villages, isolated cities and destroyed millions of hectares of crops, with a similar disaster only narrowly averted in 2002.

Anhui

Despite government hopes that it will one day become a wealthy corridor between the coast and interior, **Anhui** largely lives up to its tradition as eastern China's poorest province. It has a long history, however, not all of it bad: million-year-old remains of the proto-human *Homo erectus* have been found here, while Shang-era copper mines in southern Anhui fuelled China's Bronze Age. The province later became well known for its artistic refinements, from decorative Han tombs through to Song-dynasty porcelain and Ming architecture.

All this, however, has been a struggle against Anhui's unfriendly geography. Arid and eroded, the north China plains extend into its upper third as far as the **Huai River**, and while the south is warmer and wetter, allowing for tea and tobacco cultivation, the fertile wooded hills soon climb to rugged mountains, and not much in the way of food can be grown there. But it is the **Yangzi** itself that ensures Anhui's poverty by regularly inundating the province's low-lying centre, which would otherwise produce a significant amount of crops. Until recently, a lack of bridges across the river also created a very physical division, separating the province's mountainous south from its more settled regions. Despite improvements in infrastructure since the 1990s, including the expansion of highways and railways, Anhui seems to remain, rather unfairly, as economically retarded as ever.

For the visitor, this isn't all bad news. Neither **Hefei** – the provincial capital – nor the north have much beyond their history; yet there are compensations for Anhui's lack of development south of the Yangzi. Here, superlative mountain landscapes at **Huang Shan** and the collection of Buddhist temples at **Jiuhua Shan** have been pulling in sightseers for centuries, and there's a strong cultural tradition stamped on the area, with a substantial amount of antique rural architecture surviving intact around **Tunxi**. A riverside reserve near **Xuancheng** protects the **Chinese alligator**, one of the world's most endangered animals, though another local species, the **Yangzi river dolphin**, is now believed to be extinct.

Flooding aside (and there's a near guarantee of this affecting bus travel during the summer months), the main problem with finding your way around Anhui is that many towns have a range of aliases, and can be differently labelled on maps and timetables. **Rail lines** connect Hefei to Nanjing through **Wuhu** – Anhui's major port – with other lines running west towards Changsha, north to Xi'an and Beijing, and south from Tunxi to Jiangxi.

Hefei

Nestled in the heart of the province but generally overlooked in the rush to cross the Yangzi and reach Huang Shan, Anhui's capital, **HEFEI**, gets few chance visitors. An unimportant backwater until developed as a modest industrial base after 1949, Hefei's sole points of interest consist of a couple of **historical sites** and an unusually thorough **museum**. However, it's a comfortable place to spend a couple of days, relatively untouched by the ugly building mania sweeping the rest of the country and dignified by a number of important science and technology colleges.

Hefei

Hefei	合肥	*héféi*
Bao Gong Ci	包公祠	*bāogōng cí*
Baohe Park	包河公园	*bāohé gōngyuán*
Li Hongzhang Ju	李鸿章居	*lǐhóngzhāng jū*
Mingjiao Si	明教寺	*míngjiào sì*
Provincial Museum	省博物馆	*shěng bówùguǎn*
Three Kingdoms	三国	*sān guó*
Xiaoyaojin Park	逍遥津公园	*xiāoyáojīn gōngyuán*
Accommodation and eating		
Donghai	东海饭店	*dōnghǎi fàndiàn*
Fuhao	富豪饭店	*fùháo fàndiàn*
Hao Xiang Lai	豪享来	*háoxiáng lái*
Holiday Inn	古井假日饭店	*gǔjǐng jiàrì fàndiàn*
Huaqiao	华侨饭店	*huáqiáo fàndiàn*
Jindatang	金大糖宾馆	*jīndàtáng bīnguǎn*
Motel 168	莫泰连锁旅店	*mòtàiliánsuǒ lǚdiàn*
Ri Yue Ming	日月明大食堂	*rìyuèmíng dàshítáng*
Xiao Fei Yang	小肥羊	*xiǎo féi yáng*
Xinya	新亚大酒店	*xīnyà dàjiǔdiàn*

Arrival and information

Luogang airport is about 11km from the city, and is connected by an airport bus to the **CAAC office** on Meiling Dadao, whose entrance doubles as a florist's (daily 8am–10pm; ⓣ0551/2886626, ⓕ2885553). The **train station** is 3km northeast of the centre at the end of Shengli Lu – bus #119 runs down Shengli Lu and into town along Changjiang Lu – with lines servicing Bozhou, Shanghai, Guangzhou, Chengdu, Xiamen and Beijing. Train and air tickets are available with a minimal commission charged at 2/8 Chang Hong Zhong Lu.

Hefei's **main bus station**, on Mingguang Lu, handles traffic to all over Anhui and to adjacent provincial capitals, though there are just as many services from the chaotic clutch of **minibus depots** nearby on Shengli Lu – leaving, you'll have to hunt around stations for the right vehicle.

Changjiang Lu is Hefei's main street, with all essential services in its vicinity, including a huge **Bank of China** (Mon–Fri 8.30am–5pm), a **post office** (daily 8am–6pm) with telephones and upstairs **Internet bar**, and a **hospital** with English-speaking doctors at the junction with Tongchang Lu. For **information** and **tours**, the **CYTS** (ⓣ0551/2206555, ⓔinbound@cyts.ah.cn) is housed on the tenth floor of the *Holiday Inn*. The Xinhua Bookstore on Changjiang Lu has some **books** in English – including translated Chinese novels – on the second floor, as does the Foreign Languages Bookshop on Huaihe Lu. The **PSB** is on Shouchun Lu, a few blocks north of Changjiang Lu.

Accommodation

Hefei has a range of unremarkable places to stay. Spoken Chinese may get you into one of the budget **hostels** (dorm beds around ¥35) near the long-distance bus stations.

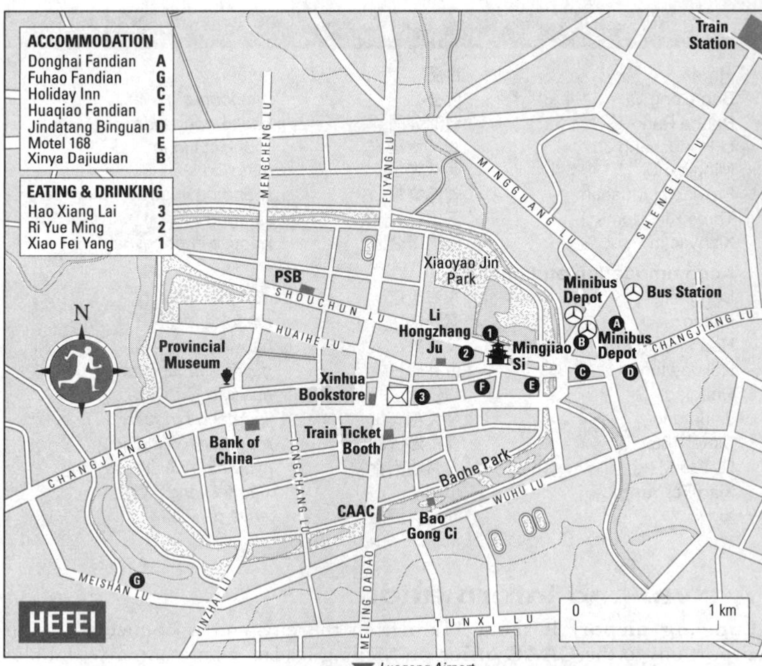

Donghai Fandian Mingguang Lu ⓣ0551/4693004. The best-value budget accommodation in town, with small, comfortable doubles and larger twin rooms. ❸

Fuhao Fandian Meishan Lu ⓣ0551/2218888, ⓕ2817583. The budget wing of the four-star *Anhui Fandian*, located around the back. Rooms are sparsely furnished but well looked after. ❹

Holiday Inn 1104 Changjiang Lu ⓣ0551/2206666, ⓦwww.ichotelsgroup.com. The usual range of facilities, along with a surprisingly good and inexpensive 24hr noodle bar. Foreign exchange counter for guests only. ❽

Huaqiao Fandian 98 Changjiang Lu ⓣ0551/2652221,ⓕ2642861. Also known as the *Anhui Overseas Chinese Hotel*, this is arguably overpriced, but has decent facilities and the rate includes a light breakfast. ❻

Jindatang Binguan 1071 Changjiang Lu ⓣ0551/4696272. Good-value place with smart, comfortable rooms, and reasonable service, though some travellers have reported an over-zealous "massage" service. ❹

Motel 168 1 Baohe Lu, ⓣ0551/2161111. Easy to find with Its massive neon sign, *168* is part of a growing chain and provides a nice break from the cookie-cutter rooms of most Chinese hotels. Stylish, good-value digs, unfortunately not yet matched by the quality of service. ❹

Xinya Dajiudian Near the bus stations on Shengli Lu ⓣ0551/2203388, ⓕ2203333. The upmarket lobby belies worn furnishings upstairs, but the rooms are large, everything works, and the staff are happy to have you. ❹

The City

Ringed by parkland and canals – the remains of Ming-dynasty moats – downtown Hefei resembles a suburban high street more than a provincial capital. The **Provincial Museum** on Mengcheng Lu (Tues–Sun 8.30am–5pm; ¥10) provides sound evidence for Anhui's contributions to Chinese culture. A walk-through plaster cave leads on to a cast of the **Homo erectus cranium** from Taodian in the south of the province, proudly displayed in an oversized glass case, while splinters of more immediate history emerge in a few Stone Age items and an exceptional Shang bronze urn decorated with tiger and dragon motifs. Also interesting are the carved blocks taken from **Han-dynasty mausoleums** – Chinese-speakers might be able to decipher the comments about the Cao family (of *Three Kingdoms* fame) incised into the bricks of their Bozhou tomb by construction labourers. Farther on, there's a special exhibition of the "**Four Scholastic Treasures**" for which the province is famed: high-quality ink sticks, heavy carved inkstones, weasel-hair writing brushes and multicoloured papers.

Across town, modern shopping plazas along the busy, pedestrian eastern half of Huaihe Lu seem an unlikely location for **Mingjiao Si** (daily 8am–5.30pm; ¥10), a restored sixteenth-century temple, whose fortress-like walls front the unpretentious halls and peach garden. The temple occupies a *Three Kingdoms* site where the northern leader **Cao Cao** drilled his crossbowers during the winter of 216–217 AD. Earlier, his general Zhang Liao had routed Wu's armies at the bloody battle of **Xiaoyao Jin** – the site is now an unexciting **park** directly north of the temple – where Sun Quan, the leader of Wu, had to flee on horseback by leaping the bridgeless canal. A glassed-in **well** in the temple's main courtyard reputedly dates from this time, and definitely looks ancient, a worn stone ring set close to the ground, deeply scored over the centuries by ropes being dragged over the rim. Just west of Mingjiao Si, **Li Hongzhang Ju** (daily 8.30am–5.30pm; ¥15) is a similarly anachronistic Qing-era mansion, whose surrounding grey brick wall hides a series of tastefully decorated courtyards and halls embellished with opulently carved wooden furniture.

Down at the southeastern side of town, **Baohe Park** is a nice strip of lakeside willows and arched bridges off Wuhu Lu, where the **Bao Gong Ci** (Lord Bao Memorial Hall; ¥20) identifies Hefei as the birthplace of Bao, the famous Song-dynasty administrator, later governor of Kaifeng. Lord Bao's ability to uncover the truth in complex court cases, and his proverbially unbiased rulings, are the subject of endless tales – he also often appears as a judge in paintings of Chinese hell. Along with gilded statues, a **waxworks** brings a couple of well-known stories to life: look for Lord Bao's dark face, improbably "winged" hat, and the **three axes** – shaped as a dragon, tiger and dog – he had made for summary executions; the implement used was chosen according to the status of the condemned.

Eating, drinking and entertainment

There are plenty of cheap **stalls and canteens** where you can fill up on stir-fries, noodle soups and **river food** – especially little crabs and snails – east of the museum on Huaihe Lu. Recent development in Hefei has seen the loss of a few local favourites, but the *Xiao Fei Yang* (Little Sheep) hotpot restaurant at 8 Shouchun Lu is as popular as ever, with great staff offering the usual hotpot fare at around ¥50 per head for a couple. Across the road at 73 Shouchun Lu, *Ri Yue Ming* offers the whole gamut of Chinese cuisine from ¥10–200 per dish, with a clean, visible kitchen and staff that seem perplexed by foreign faces. The usual plethora of Western-style fast-food outlets are available along Changjiang Lu and Huaihe Lu, or for a steak meal (¥25 upwards) try *Hao Xiang Lai* near the *Huaqiao Fandian* on Changjiang Lu.

For an evening out, Hefei has something of a reputation for **stage productions** – there are at least two indigenous opera styles and a local acrobatic troupe. Ask at CYTS as to whether there are performances at the Guixiangyuan theatre on Changjiang Lu (tickets cost around ¥100 for a 1hr 30min show).

Northern Anhui

Cynics say that northern Anhui's high points are its roads, which run on flood-proof embankments a few metres above the green, pancake-flat paddy fields. Certainly, about the only geographic features are **rivers** such as the **Huai He**, setting for the rather drab industrial and grain centre of **Bangbu**. The **battle of Huai Hai** took place nearby in 1948, when a million Guomindang and PLA combatants fought a decisive encounter in which the guerrilla-trained Communists overran Chiang Kaishek's less flexible forces. A demoralized GMD surrendered in Beijing in January the next year, and though war resumed when the two sides couldn't agree on terms, it was largely a mopping-up operation by the Communists against pockets of GMD control.

All this is mainly background for what you'll see along the way, but historians, town planners and anyone interested in Traditional Chinese Medicine will find a smattering of attractions at **Shouxian** – feasible as a day-trip from Hefei – and **Bozhou**, which is worth a day's scrutiny on the long haul into or out of the province. There are **minibuses** throughout the day from Hefei's Shengli Lu depots to Bozhou or Shouxian; make sure with the latter that you don't end up getting herded aboard a bus bound for the more familiar tourist destination of Shexian (the local pronunciation is very similar).

Shouxian

About 100km north of Hefei, **SHOUXIAN** was a regional capital back in 241BC, during the Warring States Period, and is now a small country seat surrounded by over 6km of dykes and Ming-era **stone walls,** which can be climbed for views. Minibuses from Hefei drop you at the virtually defunct bus station about 700m south of the walls; the road bends around to enter the town through the **south gate**'s triple arch, before following Shouxian's die-straight main road through the best surviving example of a Song-dynasty street plan in China. There are a couple of specific sights – an old **theatre** on the eastern axis, and the ruinous **Bao'en Monastery** hidden in the southwestern quarter – but there's more fun in just wandering the tiny back lanes, where you'll frequently come across buildings with dated wooden lintels and bronze detailing on doors. Shouxian was also the home of the Han-dynasty philosopher **Liu An**, who supposedly invented bean curd; there's an annual September **Tofu Festival** in his honour.

A couple of inexpensive **guesthouses** (¥70) lie along Shouxian's main street, but foreigners are a rare sight in town and attract so much attention that you

Northern Anhui		
Bangbu	蚌埠	*bàngbù*
Bozhou	亳州	*bózhōu*
Chinese Medicinal Products Marketplace	中药材交易中心	*zhōngyàocái jiāoyìzhōngxīn*
Dixia Yunbing Dao	地下运兵道	*dìxià yùnbīngdào*
Gujing Dajiudian	古井大酒店	*gǔjǐng dàjiǔdiàn*
Gu Qian Zhuang	古钱庄	*gǔqián zhuāng*
Huaxi Lou	花戏楼	*huāxì lóu*
Fuyang	阜阳	*fǔyáng*
Huainan	淮南	*huáinán*
Shouxian	寿县	*shòuxiàn*
Bao'en Monastery	报恩寺	*bàoēn sì*

may feel more comfortable moving on. For destinations further afield than Hefei, catch a minibus-taxi (¥4) from outside the bus station 20km east to the monochrome coal-mining centre of **Huainan**, from where there are irregular buses to Nanjing, Shanghai, Wuhan and **Fuyang**, on the way to Bozhou. There's a clutch of average eateries on the main street.

Bozhou

BOZHOU lies in Anhui's northwestern corner, around five hours from Hefei or three from Shouxian, the journey taking in scenes of river barges loading up with coal, red-brick villages surrounded by pollarded willows, and a level horizon pierced by kiln chimneys. The city's fame rests on its being the largest marketplace in the world for **traditional medicines**; as the birthplace of **Hua Mulan**, heroine of Chinese legend and Disney animation (though there are no monuments to her here…yet); and as the ancestral home of the *Three Kingdoms*, **Cao Cao**. Portrayed in the *Romance of the Three Kingdoms* as a self-serving villain whose maxim was "Better to wrong the world than have it wrong me", he was nonetheless a brilliant general and respectable poet, whose claims to rule China were just as legitimate as those of his arch-rival, Lu Bei. At any rate, nobody in Bozhou seems ashamed of the connection.

Bozhou's grimy, squalid main streets may have you wondering why you made the journey, but it's worth persevering. About 3km southeast of the centre, the eastern end of Zhan Qian Lu (the train station approach road) sets up from Monday to Friday as a **medicinal market**, attracting something in the region of 60,000 traders daily from all over China and Southeast Asia. The main **Chinese Medicinal Products Marketplace** here is a huge building on the south side of the road, packed to the roof in places with bales of dried plants, fungi – including the bizarre caterpillar fungus, or *cordyceps* – and animals (or bits of them), the rest of the space taken up by enthusiastic crowds. The market's activity and strangely reassuring smell alone justify the trip to town.

The rest of Bozhou is for history buffs. On the south side of Renmin Zhong Lu, **Dixia Yunbing Dao** (¥12) is a one-hundred-metre-long subterranean **tunnel** Cao Cao had installed so his troops could take an invading army by surprise; the arched, claustrophobic brick passages are totally unexpected at street level. North from here, Renmin Bei Jie forms the congested heart of Bozhou's **Muslim** community, full of noodle, bread and mutton kebab vendors, and containing a couple of small **mosques**; the street ends where it passes through the city's solid stone **north gate**. Beyond, the area between Heping Lu and the river is filled by a quiet net of nineteenth-century lanes, a procession of small, whitewashed shops and home industries. **Gu Qian Zhuang** (Old Bank; ¥5) on Nanjing Gang here served its original function between 1825 and 1949 and provides great views of surrounding grey-tiled roofs from an upstairs balcony, though otherwise it's rather bare.

Bozhou's architectural masterpiece is **Huaxi Lou** (¥20), a seventeenth-century guild-temple **theatre** some 500m north of Gu Qian Zhuang at the river end of Nanjing Gang. Sporting skilfully carved brick and wood embellishments, the theatre is named after the Han-dynasty doctor **Hua Tuo**, the first person credited with using anaesthetics during surgery, who was bumped off by Cao Cao after refusing to become the warlord's personal physician. Check out the painted friezes surrounding the stage, where several well-known *Three Kingdoms* set pieces are depicted, including Zhuge Liang's celebrated "Empty City Stratagem": having no troops to defend the key stronghold of Xicheng, Zhuge opened the gates and sat in surrender on the battlements while his men swept the road below. Knowing his cunning, the invading general, Sima Yi, suspected some elaborate trap and fled. The theatre's rear hall contains a collection of Neolithic stone axes and Eastern Han artefacts unearthed nearby, including a **jade burial suit** made of 2400 tiles belonging to Cao Cao's father, Cao Song, who was ignominiously killed by rebels while hiding in a toilet.

Practicalities

Bozhou's centre is a two-kilometre-wide grid just south of the slow-flowing **Wo He**, the main roads being the east–west Renmin Lu and the north–south Qiaoling Lu that intersect on the eastern side of town. The **train station** is about 3km southeast – best reached by taxi – and has a few services down to Hefei each day. An alternative rail option is to catch a minibus south to **Fuyang** (around 1hr 30min), which is on the Beijing–Jiujiang and Hefei–Zhengzhou lines. The two adjacent **bus stations** on Qiaoling Lu mostly serve Hefei, Fuyang or local destinations, with a few battered and elderly long-distance buses to adjoining provinces.

The intersection of Renmin Lu and Qiaoling Lu, about 500m south of the bus stations, marks a heap of **accommodation** options. The three-star *Gujing Dajiudian* (Ⓣ0558/5521298; ❺) has some pretensions to comfort with the usual cloned Chinese-hotel rooms replete with bad carpets and loose fittings. The **Bank of China** is also on the crossroads, with the main **post office** 500m west on Renmin Zhong Lu. Hotpot and noodle stalls abound, and the *Gujing Dajiudian*'s **restaurant** offers tasty, if pricey, fare.

The Yangzi: Ma'anshan and Xuancheng

The Yangzi flows silt-grey and broad for 350km across Anhui's lower third, forming a very visible geographic boundary. An indication of the province's chronic underdevelopment is the fact that as recently as 1995 the only way to cross the river was by ferry, though it's now bridged in the east at **Wuhu** and roughly halfway along at **Tongling**. A reserve at the latter was at the forefront of apparently unsuccessful efforts to save the light grey *baiji*, or **Yangzi river dolphin**, from a catastrophic decline – a study in 2007 failed to find any of the animals, though they were common as recently as the 1970s – linked to the growth of industrial pollution, river traffic and net fishing on the Yangzi. The species seems doomed to linger on only in Tongling's **Baiji beer**, which has the dolphin's Latin name, *Lipotes vexillifer*, stamped on the bottle cap.

The Yangzi: Ma'anshan and Xuancheng		
Ma'anshan	马鞍山	*mǎ'ān shān*
Cuiluo Shan	翠螺山	*cuìlúo shān*
Great Wall Hotel	长城宾馆	*chángchéng bīnguǎn*
Xuancheng	宣城	*xuānchéng*
Chinese Alligator Breeding Centre	扬子鳄养殖场	*yángzǐè yǎngzhíchǎng*
Xuanzhou Binguan	宣州宾馆	*xuānzhōu bīnguǎn*
Tongling	铜岭	*tónglǐng*
Wuhu	芜湖	*wúhú*
Yangzi River	长江	*chángjiāng*
River dolphins	白鲫河	*báijì hé*

Most of the riverside towns are unashamedly functional and don't really justify special trips. **Ma'anshan** and **Xuancheng** offer a modicum of interest in their associations with Tang-dynasty poet Li Bai and the breeding of Chinese alligators, respectively.

Ma'anshan

On the Wuhu–Nanjing rail line, **MA'ANSHAN** is notable for cliffside scenery 7km south at **Cuiluo Shan** (¥40), reached on a twenty-minute crawl through the town's industrial hinterland on bus #4 from the bus or train station. A vast expanse of parkland, Cuiluo Shan is dotted with a series of halls and pavilions commemorating the itinerant Tang-dynasty romantic poet **Li Bai** (aka Tai Bai, see p.1206). Inspired by the scenery at **Caishiji**, considered first among the Yangzi's three famous rock outcrops, Li Bai wrote many of his works here, and it was nearby that he drowned in 762 AD after drunkenly falling out of a boat while trying to touch the moon's reflection. His **tomb** lies amid ancient pines and willows at the foot of Qing Shan.

Ma'anshan's **bus and train stations** are both fairly central on Hongqi Lu, which leads down to the town centre (head left out of the bus station or right out of the train station), set around Yushan Lake Park. You can stay at the *Great Wall Hotel* (Ⓣ0555/2479888 ④), a fifteen-minute walk from the stations down Hongqi Lu and then left along the edge of Yushan Lake on Hubei Lu. The **Bank of China** and **post office** are both on Hubei Lu.

Xuancheng

Chinese-speakers interested in wildlife should make the trip to **XUANCHENG**, two hours by bus to the southeast of Wuhu across low hills patterned by tea plantations – confusingly, you pass another Wuhu, the county town, halfway there. Xuancheng is also reachable by train, as it's on the Hefei–Tunxi (Huang Shan) rail line. An untidy but friendly place, the town is associated with the production of high-quality handmade art paper (though this actually comes from **Jiangxian**, 55km to the southwest), but is worth visiting for the **Chinese alligator breeding centre** (daily 8am–5pm; ¥30) that lies several kilometres to the south. Wild populations of these timid alligators are few and confined to Anhui, with their habitat ever more encroached upon. Since the 1990s, a worldwide project coordinated by the US Bronx Zoo has boosted their captive numbers here to ten thousand. The centre offers the opportunity to get very close to the alligators and, as inappropriate as it may seem, to enjoy the taste of their meat in its restaurant. To reach the centre, you can negotiate with the minibus drivers at the crossroads near the bus station, or ask travel companies in Tunxi or Hefei to phone ahead and arrange a visit for you.

Surrounded by small rivers, Xuancheng is about 2km across, with the **train station** on the eastern side and the main **bus station** to the southwest. For **accommodation**, there's the *Xuanzhou Binguan* on Zhuangyuan Lu (Ⓣ0563/3022957; ④), near the bus station.

Jiuhua Shan

A place of worship for fifteen hundred years, **Jiuhua Shan** (Nine Glorious Mountains) has been one of China's sacred Buddhist mountains ever since the Korean monk **Jin Qiaojue** (believed to be the reincarnation of the Bodhisattva

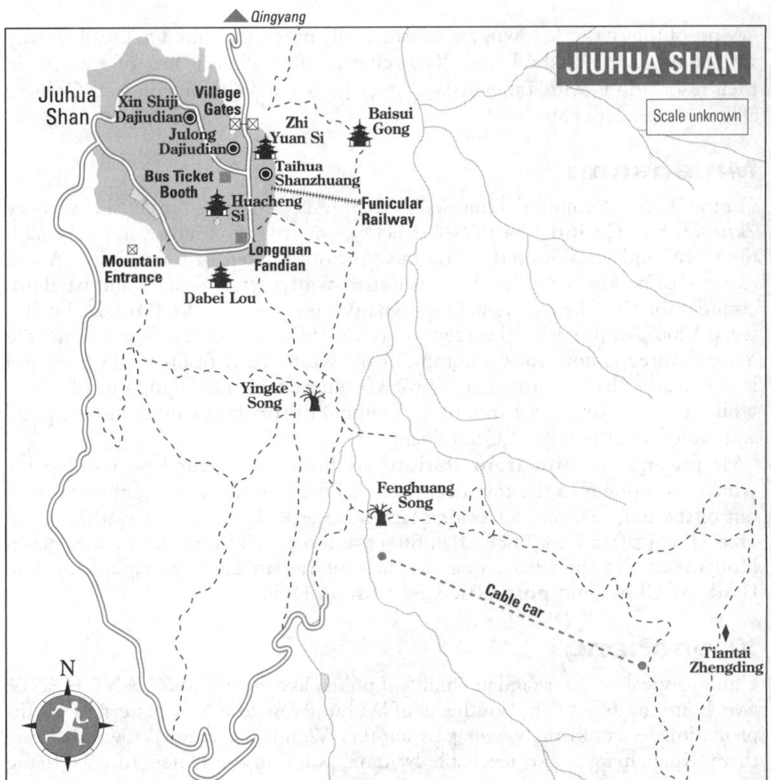

Dizang, whose doctrines he preached) died here in a secluded cave in 794 AD. Today, there are more than sixty temples – some founded back in the ninth century – containing a broad collection of sculptures, religious texts and early calligraphy, though there are also plenty of visitors (many of them overseas Chinese and Koreans) and some outsized building projects threatening to overwhelm Jiuhua Shan's otherwise human scale. Even so, an atmosphere of genuine devotion is clearly evident in the often austere halls with their wisps of incense smoke and distant chanting.

Practicalities

Though it's 60km south of the Yangzi and remote from major transport centres, Jiuhua Shan is straightforward to reach, with direct **buses** at least from Hefei, Tangkou, Taiping (Huang Shan), Tongling and Guichi. Other traffic might drop you 25km to the northeast at **Qingyang**, from where mountain minibuses (¥8) leave when full throughout the day; in case you arrive late, there's a cheap **hotel** attached to the bus station here.

The twisting Jiuhua Shan road passes villages scattered amidst the moist green of rice fields and bamboo stands, white-walled houses built of bricks interlocked in a "herringbone" pattern, with some inspiring views of bald, spiky peaks above and valleys below. The road ends at picturesque **Jiuhua Shan**

Jiuhua Shan		
Jiuhua Shan	九华山	*jiǔhuá shān*
Baisui Gong	百岁宫	*bǎisuì gōng*
Cable-car station	索道站	*suǒdào zhàn*
Dabei Lou	大悲楼	*dàbēi lóu*
Fenghuang Song	凤凰松	*fènghuáng sōng*
Funicular Railway	缆车站	*lǎnchē zhàn*
Huacheng Si	化城寺	*huàchéng sì*
Tiantai Zhengding	天台正顶	*tiāntái zhèngdǐng*
Yingke Song	迎客松	*yíngkè sōng*
Zhiyuan Si	执园寺	*zhíyuán sì*
Accommodation		
Julong Dajiudian	聚笼大酒店	*jùlóng dàjiǔdiàn*
Taihua Shanzhuang	太华山庄	*tàihuá shānzhuāng*
Xin Shiji Dajiudian	新世纪大酒店	*xīnshìjì dàjiǔdiàn*
Qingyang	青阳	*qīngyáng*

Village, where the mountain's accommodation, and the most famous temples, huddle around a couple of cobbled streets and squares, all hemmed in by encircling hills. Upon arrival at the village **gates** you'll have to pay Jiuhua Shan's **entry fee** (March–Nov ¥90; Dec–Feb ¥80). From here the road runs up past a host of market stalls selling postcards, trinkets, and waterproof **maps** and umbrellas for the frequently sodden weather.

About 100m along, the road divides around the village in a two-kilometre circuit; a booth selling onward **bus tickets** is just down on the right here, while the core of the village lies straight ahead. Long-distance transport to Hefei, Nanjing, Tangkou, Taiping, Tunxi and Shanghai congregates first thing in the morning near the booth, or you can pick up frequent minibuses to Qingyang and look for connections there.

You'll be grabbed on arrival and offered all manner of **accommodation**, most of it decent value. For more upmarket facilities try *Julong Dajiudian* to the right of the village gates behind an illuminated fountain (Ⓣ0566/5011022, Ⓦwww.jiuhuashan.com.cn; ⑥), although they won't bargain and rooms are damp. On the other side of the street, Zhiyuan Si has extremely bare beds (¥30) designed for itinerant monks, which may be available to tourists. Up the main street on the left, look for steps and an English sign above a car park for *Taihua Shanzhuang* (Ⓣ0566/5011340, Ⓔjhswwx@163.com; ④), a hospitable guesthouse with constant hot water, and a very helpful travel service, although they don't speak English. For cheaper lodgings head up the hill past the bus ticket booth, where there are several small hotels such as *Xin Shiji Dajiudian* (Ⓣ0566/501174; ③) with simple, shabby rooms, as well as a few more expensive options. Numerous **places to eat** offer everything from cheap buns to expensive game dishes.

On Jiuhua Shan

Just inside the village gates, **Zhiyuan Si** (¥5) is an imposing Qing monastery built with smooth, vertical walls, upcurving eaves and a yellow-tiled roof nestled up against a cliff. Despite a sizeable exterior, the numerous little halls are cramped and stuffed with sculptures, including a fanged, bearded and hooknosed thunder god bursting out of its protective glass cabinet just inside the gate. Head for the main hall, in which a magnificently gilded **Buddhist**

trinity sits solemnly on separate lotus flowers, blue hair dulled by incense smoke, and ringed by *arhats*. This makes quite a setting for the annual **temple fair**, held in Dizang's honour on the last day of the seventh lunar month, when the hall is packed with worshippers, monks and tourists. Make sure you look behind the altar, where Guanyin statuettes ascend right to the lofty wooden roof beams.

If you follow the main road around through the village, the next temple of note you come to is the new and garish **Dabei Lou** (¥6), which sports some hefty carved stonework; more or less opposite, **Huacheng Si** (¥8) is the mountain's oldest surviving temple, in part possibly dating right back to the Tang, though comprehensively restored. The stone entrance is set at the back of a large cobbled square whose centrepiece is a deep pond inhabited by some gargantuan goldfish. Inside, Huacheng's low-ceilinged, broad main hall doubles as a **museum**, with paintings depicting the life of Jin Qiaojue from his sea crossing to China (accompanied only by a faithful hound) to his death at the age of 90, and the discovery of his miraculously preserved corpse three years later.

To the peaks

The mountain's official "entrance" is marked by a huge ornamental gateway and temple about 500m past Dabei Lou on the main road, though well-concealed, smaller flagstoned paths ascend from behind Zhiyuan Si and at the corners of the main road in the village. There's also a **funicular railway** from the main street near *Longquan Fandian* to the ridge above (¥45). Using these access points, you can do a good, easy **circuit walk** on the ridges just above the village in about an hour, or extend this to a full **day's hike** up around Jiuhua's higher peaks – though again, you can save time by using minibuses and the cable car for part of the way. To get on the circuit, walk past Dabei Lou to where the road bends sharply right. Steps ascend from here to a temple complex whose entrance-hall atrium contains some gruesomely entertaining, life-size sculptures of **Buddhist hell**. These are so graphic that it's hard not to feel that the artists enjoyed their task of depicting sinners being skewered, pummelled, strangled, boiled and bisected by demons, the virtuous looking down, doubtless exceedingly thankful for their salvation. Beyond the temple, a few minutes' walk brings you to a meeting of several paths at **Yingke Song** (Welcoming Guest Pine). Bear left and it's a couple of kilometres past several pavilions and minor temples to steep views down onto the village from **Baisui Gong** (¥8), a plain, atmospheric monastery whose interior is far from weatherproof, with clouds drifting in and out of the main hall. A rear room contains the mummy of the Ming priest **Wu Xia**, best known for compiling the **Huayan sutras** in gold dust mixed with his own blood; his tiny body is displayed seated in prayer, grotesquely covered in a thick, smooth skin of gold leaf. Steps descend from Baisui Gong to Zhiyuan Si, or you can take the **funicular railway** down to the main street.

To reach the upper peaks, turn right at Yingke Song, and you've a two-hour climb ahead of you via **Fenghuang Song** (Phoenix Pine), more temples, wind-scoured rocks, and superb scenery surrounding the summit area at **Tiantai Zhengding** (Heavenly Terrace). There's also a **cable car** from Fenghuang Song to just below the peaks (¥40). The truly indolent can catch a minibus from the entrance gate to the Fenghuang Song terminus, opposite Dabei Lou in the village; these buses are included in the Jiuhua Shan entry fee. Witnessing the sunrise from here, **Li Bai**, the Tang man of letters, was inspired to bestow Jiuhua Shan with its name by the sight of the major pinnacles rising up out of clouds. In future years, this will also be the place to follow the progress of China's most grandiose religious building project: a 99-metre-high **statue of Dizang** is planned for the mountain, which if completed will be the largest Buddha sculpture in the world.

Tunxi, Shexian and Yixian

The most obvious reason to stop in **Tunxi**, down near Anhui's southernmost borders, is because of the town's transport connections to **Huang Shan**, 50km off to the northwest (see p.468): Tunxi has the closest airport and train station to the mountain, while many long-distance buses pass through here as well. However, if you've even the slightest interest in classical Chinese **architecture**, then Tunxi and its environs are worth checking out in their own right. Anhui's isolation has played a large part in preserving a liberal sprinkling of seventeenth-century monuments and homes in the area, especially around **Shexian** and **Yixian**. The guide fees and other costs associated with spending a day at Yixian make Shexian a better bet if you're on a tight budget.

Any exploration of Shexian and its surroundings will reveal a host of traditional Ming and Qing architectural features, most notably the **paifang** or ornamental archway – there are over eighty of these in She county alone. Of wood or stone, *paifang* can be over 10m in height, and are finely carved, painted or tiled, the central beam often bearing a moral inscription. They were constructed for a variety of reasons, foremost among which, cynics would argue, was the ostentatious display of wealth. This aside, the gateways were built to celebrate or reward virtuous behaviour, family success, important historical

Tunxi, Shexian and Yixian		
Tunxi	屯溪	*túnxī*
Cheng Dawei's House	程大位居	*chéngdàwèi jū*
Cheng Family House	程氏三宅	*chéngshì sānzhái*
Huang Shan Shi	黄山市	*huángshānshì*
Lao Jie	老街	*lǎojiē*
Accommodation and eating		
Hehuachi Zaochi Yitiao Jie	荷花池早吃一条街	*héhuāchí zǎochī yìtiáojiē*
Huashan Binguan	华山宾馆	*huáshān bīnguǎn*
Huaxi Fandian	花溪饭店	*huāxī fàndiàn*
Huochezhan Tielu	火车站铁路招待所	*huǒchēzhàn tiělù zhāodàisuǒ*
Jingwei	经纬酒店	*jīngwěi jiǔdiàn*
Zengtong	政通宾馆	*zhèngtōng bīnguǎn*
Shexian	歙县	*shèxiàn*
Doushan Jie	斗山街	*dǒushān jiē*
Nan Lou	南楼	*nánlóu*
Tangyue Arches	堂越牌坊	*tángyuè páifāng*
Xuguo Archway	许国石坊	*xǔguó shífāng*
Yanghe Men	阳和门	*yánghé mén*
Yixian	黟县	*yíxiàn*
Hongcun	宏村	*hóngcūn*
Nanping	南屏村	*nánpíng cūn*
Xidi	西递	*xīdì*

events or figures, and to reflect prevailing values such as filial piety; as such, they provide a valuable insight into the mores of the time.

Tunxi

An old trading centre, **TUNXI** (aka **Huang Shan Shi**) is set around the junction of two rivers, with the original part of town along the north bank of the **Xin'an Jiang** at the intersection of Huang Shan Lu and Xin'an Lu, and a newer quarter focused around the train and bus stations a kilometre or so to the northeast. If you've time to spare, try tracking down two **Ming-dynasty houses** in Tunxi's eastern backstreets (neither is well marked). The more easterly house – that of the mathematician Cheng Dawei – is in a sorry state of repair, but both it and the Cheng family house are classic examples of the indigenous **Huizhou style**, of which you'll find plenty more at Shexian or Yixian. Their plan, of two floors of galleried rooms based around a courtyard, proved so popular that it became the benchmark of urban domestic architecture in central and eastern China.

For more, head down to Tunxi's historic, flagstoned **Lao Jie** (Old Street), a westerly continuation of Huang Shan Xi Lu. Here, 500m of **Ming shops** running parallel to the river have been nicely restored, selling local teas, medicinal herbs and all manner of artistic materials and "antiques" – inkstones, brushes, Mao badges, decadent advertising posters from the 1930s, and carved wooden panels prised off old buildings. A few genuine businesses stand out, notably an apothecary sporting 1920s timber decor, and several small **dumpling houses** filled with local clientele. You'll also see characteristic **horse-head gables** rising out below the rooflines in steps. These originated as fire baffles between adjoining houses, stopping the spread of flames from building to building, but eventually became somewhat decorative affairs.

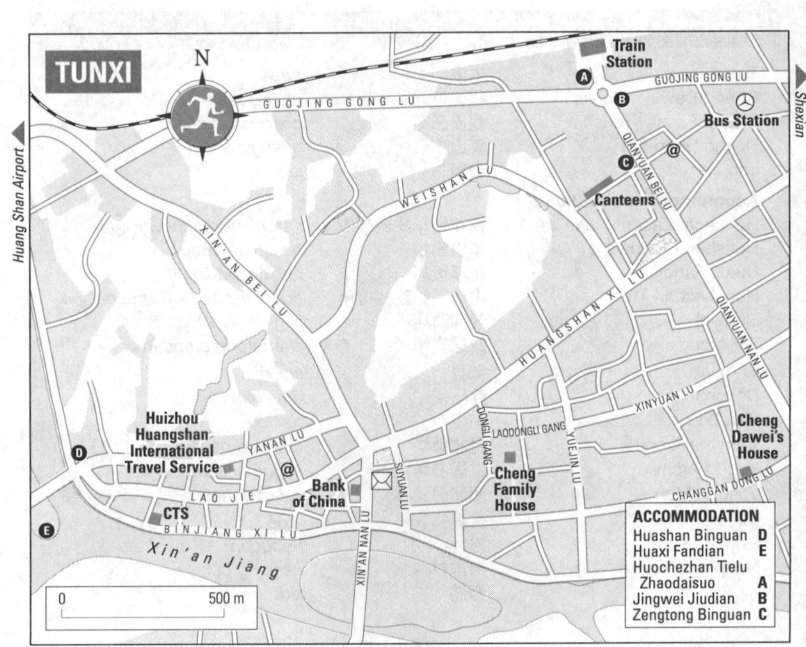

Practicalities

A taxi into the centre from busy **Huang Shan airport**, around 10km west of town, should cost around ¥15 on the meter. The **train station** is at the northern city limits on the end of Qianyuan Bei Lu; there are connections to Hefei (via Xuancheng and Wuhu), Nanchang, Shanghai, Xiamen and Beijing, along with useful, though ploddingly slow, trains southwest to Jingdezhen. Tangkou minibuses prowl the station forecourt, while Tunxi's **bus station** occupies an entire block 250m east, off Guojing Gong Lu, with frequent services for Shexian, Yixian, Tangkou and Taiping, and long-distance departures to Jiuhua Shan, Wuhu, Hefei, Shanghai, Jiujiang, Nanchang and even Guangzhou. A couple of **city buses** run around Tunxi: from the train station, #6 takes a back road into town, while #12 follows Huang Shan Xi Lu southwest from the bus station – either route is a twenty-minute walk.

A knot of convenient, if mostly dull and overpriced, places to **stay** surrounds the train station, the best of which are the smart *Jingwei Jiudian* (ⓣ0559/2345188, ⓕ2345098; ⑥), which out of season offers fifty-percent discounts; and the nearby *Zengtong Binguan* (ⓣ0559/2112968; ⑥) with comfortable, modern rooms. The *Huochezhan Tielu Zhaodaisuo* (ⓣ0559/2113699; ④) is immediately to the right out of the train station and has acceptable, tidy rooms. Near the old town and next to the bridge on Yanan Lu is the smart *Huashan Binguan* (ⓣ0559/2328888; ③); on the opposite side of the river the *Huaxi Fandian* is quiet and pleasant (ⓣ0559/2328000, ⓕ2514990; ⑦). There are numerous small **restaurants** around the Xin'an Lu/Lao Jie intersection. Near the train station, cheap eats can be found at the string of canteens on Hehuachi Zaochi Yitiao Jie, off Qianyuan Lu.

Most services are around the Huang Shan Lu/Xin'an Lu intersection, where, along with markets and department stores, you'll find a **Bank of China** (Mon–Fri 8am–5.30pm) and the main **post office** (Mon–Fri 8am–8pm). For **information**, **plane tickets**, and **permits** for Yixian, try the riverside CTS at 1 Binjiang Xi Lu (ⓣ0559/2522649, ⓕ2522635) or the Huizhou Huangshan International Travel Service Yanan Lu (ⓣ0559/3384556). The latter has day-tours to Shexian and to Yixian. There are a couple of **Internet** places, one just off Lao Jie and another in the small street on the other side of Qianyuan Bei Lu from Hehuachi Zaochi Yitiao Jie.

Shexian

Anhui owes a good deal to **SHEXIAN**, an easy forty-minute **minibus** ride 25km northeast of Tunxi up the Xin'an River and once the regional capital – the name "Anhui" is a telescoping of Anqing (a Yangzi town in the southwest) and **Huizhou**, Shexian's former name. The region blossomed in the seventeenth century after local salt merchants started raising elaborate town houses and intricately carved stone archways, some of which survive today, in a showy display of their wealth. The province's opera styles were formalized here, and the town became famous for *hui* inkstones and fine-grained *she* ink sticks, the latter still considered China's best. One of Shexian's charms is that most buildings are still in everyday use, not tarted up for tourism, and there's a genuinely old-world ambience to soak up.

Shexian's **bus station** is out on the highway, where disembarking passengers get hassle from "guides" and motor-rickshaw drivers. You don't need them: take the bridge over the river and carry straight on past 100m of uninspiring, concrete-and-tile buildings; at the end of the road turn right, then first left, and you're walking up **Jiefang Jie**, off which run the narrow lanes that comprise the older part of town. To the sides you'll see the restored **Nan Lou** and **Yanghe Men** gate towers; straight ahead, however, Jiefang Jie runs under the smaller but highly decorative **Xuguo archway**, one of the finest in the region. Nearby are souvenir stalls and a **bookshop**, where you should pick up a **map** of Shexian (about ¥3) with all the streets and points of interest marked. You could just walk at random, snacking on traditional "pressed buns", but for a detailed look, seek out **Doushan Jie**, a street full of well-preserved Huizhou-style homes, around which you can tour with a Chinese-speaking guide (¥8). When you've had enough, return to the station and get a Tunxi-bound minibus to drop you off around 5km down the highway, then walk or catch a motorbike-rickshaw for the last 3km to where the **Tangyue arches** (¥50, Chinese-speaking guide included) form a strange spectacle of seven ornamental gates standing isolated in a row in a field, albeit with the usual tourist restaurants and shops close at hand.

Yixian and around

You need a **police permit** (¥50, most easily arranged through agents in Tunxi for an extra ¥20) to stop off in **YIXIAN**, 60km due west of Tunxi. The town itself is a stepping stone to surrounding villages, for which you'll have to charter a minibus (about ¥30 per stop) and pay fees for compulsory guides (¥10 per person in a group, up to ¥50 if you're on you own) and admission. **Xidi** (entry ¥60) is the pick of these, and hence the most visited, a particularly attractive place comprising some 120 eighteenth-century houses set along a riverbank, now turned into a large antiques market. There are endless examples of carved gilded wooden screens and panels inside the houses, as well as thin line paintings on front walls showing pairs of animals or "double happiness" characters. Mirrors placed above the three-tiered door lintels reflect bad luck or reveal a person's true character – a useful tool for judging the nature of strangers. **Hongcun** is another fine spot, whose street plan resembles (with some imagination) the body of a buffalo, complete with horns, body and legs, while **Nanping** was used as a set in Zhang Yimou's disturbing film *Judou*. Combined admission for both Hongcun and Nanping is ¥60.

Huang Shan

Rearing over southern Anhui, **Huang Shan** – the Yellow Mountains – are among eastern China's greatest sights. It's said that once you've ascended their peaks you will never want to climb another mountain, and certainly the experience is staggeringly scenic, with pinnacles emerging from thick bamboo forests, above which rock faces dotted with ancient, contorted pine trees growing from narrow ledges disappear into the swirling mists. These views often seem familiar, for Huang Shan's landscape has left an indelible impression on Chinese art, and painters are a common sight on the paths, huddled in padded jackets and sheltering their work from the incipient drizzle beneath umbrellas – the more serious of them spend months at a time up here.

As a pilgrimage site trodden by emperors and Communist leaders alike, Huang Shan is regarded as sacred in China, and it's the ambition of every Chinese to conquer it at least once in their lifetime. Consequently, don't expect to climb alone: noisy multitudes swarm along the neatly paved paths, or crowd out the three cable-car connections to the top. All this can make the experience depressingly like visiting an amusement park, but then you'll turn a corner and

Huang Shan

Huang Shan	黄山	*huángshān*
Bai'e Feng	白鹅峰	*bái'é fēng*
Banshan Si	半山寺	*bànshān sì*
Beginning-to-Believe Peak	始信峰	*shǐxìn fēng*
Cable-car Station	索道站	*suǒdào zhàn*
Ciguang Shi	慈光阁	*cíguāng gé*
Feilai Shi	飞来石	*fēilái shí*
Guangming Ding	光明顶	*guāngmíng dǐng*
Jiyu Bei	鲫鱼背	*jìyú bèi*
Paiyun Ting	排云亭	*páiyún tíng*
Tiandu Feng	天都峰	*tiāndū fēng*
Yingke Song	迎客松	*yíngkèsōng*
Yungu Si	云谷寺	*yúngǔ sì*
Yuping Lou	玉屏楼	*yùpíng lóu*
Accommodation and eating		
Beihai Binguan	北海宾馆	*běihǎi bīnguǎn*
Paiyun Ting Binguan	排云亭宾馆	*páiyúntíng bīnguǎn*
Shilin Dajiudian	石林大酒店	*shílín dàjiǔdiàn*
Tianhai Binguan	天海宾馆	*tiānhǎi bīnguǎn*
Xihai Fandian	西海饭店	*xīhǎi fàndiàn*
Taiping	太平	*tàipíng*
Tangkou	汤口	*tāngkǒu*
Dazhong Fandian	大众饭店	*dàzhòng fàndiàn*
Hongdashi Jiudian	洪大师酒店	*hóngdàshī jiǔdiàn*
Zhounan Dajiudian	洲楠大酒店	*zhōunán dàjiǔdiàn*
Wenquan	温泉	*wēnquán*
Huangshan Binguan	黄山宾馆	*huángshān bīnguǎn*
Taoyuan Binguan	桃源宾馆	*táoyuán bīnguǎn*
Wenquan Dajiudian	温泉大酒店	*wēnquán dàjiǔdiàn*

come face to face with a huge, smooth monolith topped by a single tree, or be confronted with views of a remote square of forest growing isolated on a rocky platform. Nature is never far away from reasserting itself here.

Accessing Huang Shan

Transport pours into the Huang Shan region from all over eastern China. There are direct buses from Shanghai, Hangzhou and Nanjing, as well as Jiuhua Shan, Wuhu, Hefei and other places within Anhui. Much of this, and all rail and air traffic, passes through **Tunxi** (aka Huang Shan Shi; see p.466), with regular shuttle buses (¥13) connecting the train and bus stations here with Huang Shan's main gateway at **Tangkou**, 50km northwest of Tunxi on the mountain's southern foothills. Alternatively, **Taiping** is a lesser-used access point to the north of the mountain on the Jiuhua Shan–Tangkou road. Be aware that some long-distance buses go directly to Tangkou or Taiping, and might refer to these towns as "Huang Shan" on their timetables.

Tangkou is the starting point for Huang Shan's two **hiking trails** and parallel **cable cars** (daily 8am–4.30pm; April–Oct ¥65, Nov–March ¥55). An additional cable car (same prices) is accessed from Taiping by catching a minibus from the main-street bus station for the 22-kilometre ride to the terminus at **Songgu**. Note that **queues** for peak-bound cable cars can be quite long (there's usually

less of a wait to go down), and that services are suspended during windy weather. The Huang Shan **entry fee** (April–Oct ¥200, Nov–March ¥120) is payable at the start of the trails or at the cable-car ticket offices. The cable cars take upwards of twenty minutes; you'll need between two and eight hours to walk up, depending on whether you follow the easier **eastern route** or the lengthy and demanding **western route**. Once at the top, there's a half-day of relatively easy hiking around the peaks. Ideally, plan to spend two or three days on the mountain to allow for a steady ascent and circuit, though it's quite feasible to see a substantial part of Huang Shan in a full day.

There's **accommodation** (mostly fairly expensive) and **food** available in Tangkou, Taiping and on the mountain itself, but you'll need to come prepared for steep paths, rain and winter snow – all an essential part of the experience. Note that in winter, hotels either dramatically drop their prices or close shop until spring. Hiring guides and porters is something of an extravagance, as paths are easy to follow and accommodation in Tangkou and Taiping will store surplus gear; just bring a daypack, suitable footwear and something warm for the peak.

There are branches of the **Bank of China** in Tangkou, Wenquan and on the mountaintop, and there's an **Internet café** in Tangkou.

Tangkou and Wenquan

Two hours from Tunxi, **TANGKOU** is an unattractive jumble of narrow lanes, hotels and restaurants on the **Taohua Gully**, where roads from Wuhu, Tunxi and Jiuhua Shan meet. From here another road runs up the mountain to further accommodation 3km along at **Wenquan**, where the road divides and continues to the two trailheads.

Minibuses from Tunxi and Jiuhua Shan collect and drop off at Tangkou's central bridge, while the **long-distance bus stop** is 1km up the Wenquan road, by Huang Shan's official entrance. Tangkou's **places to stay** are of most interest to late arrivals: just off the main road, the *Hongdashi Jiudian* (ⓣ0559/5562577; ❻) has clean, comfortable rooms, as does the *Zhounan Dajiudian* (ⓣ0559/5562387; ❻) next door. Alternatively, ask around to find the cheaper Chinese-oriented *Dazhong* (ⓣ0559/5562453; ❺, dorm beds ¥80).

The cheapest places to eat a filling noodle or *baozi* breakfast are at tables under the bridge, with a host of canteens all around the town, whose owners will drag you in as you walk past. Some have bilingual menus offering arresting delights such as squirrel hotpot and scrambled mountain frog, and more conventional soya-braised bamboo shoots and fungi – if there's no price on the menu, agree the cost in advance to avoid being ripped off. You can also pick up umbrellas, walking sticks, warm clothes and mountain **maps** from hawkers and stalls around Tangkou. **Heading up** the mountain, minibuses wait on the Wenquan road, where you'll have to bargain hard for reasonable fares – around ¥5 to Wenquan and ¥10 to the eastern route at **Yungu Si**.

Wenquan

About 3km uphill from Tangkou where the mountain's two main ascent routes diverge, **WENQUAN** is altogether a nicer prospect, surrounded by pine and bamboo forest and perched above the clear blue **Taoyuan Stream** and a noisy waterfall. The first thing you'll see here is the arched bridge over the gully, where the road heads on 8km to the eastern route's trailhead; follow the footpath upstream and it's about half an hour to **Ciguang Ge**, the Merciful Light Pavilion, at the start of the western route. A minibus to either trailhead from Wenquan costs ¥5.

Wenquan's **places to stay** are on either side of the stream. The smartest is the nearside *Taoyuan Binguan* (ⓣ0559/5585666, ⓕ5585288; ❽), while below the bridge the *Wenquan Dajiudian* (ⓣ0559/5562198, ⓕ5562788; ❻) is fine if you avoid the damp, cheaper rooms. Across the bridge, the red-roofed *Huangshan Binguan* (ⓣ0559/5585818, ⓕ5585816; ❻) has tiny rooms but is relatively inexpensive and amenable to bargaining. Near the *Huangshan Binguan*, the trail-weary can take advantage of a **thermal bathhouse** (¥35, or ¥80 for a private spa), though it's a bit grotty. **Eat** at your accommodation, or head down to Tangkoua and take your pick of one of the ordinary eateries there.

Huang Shan hikes

Huang Shan barely rises above 1870m, but as you struggle up either of the staircases on the trails it can begin to feel very high indeed. The **eastern route** is by far the easier; the road from Wenquan ends at **Yungu Si** (Cloud Valley Temple), where a **cable car** can whisk you to the summit area at **Bai'e Feng** in twenty minutes – once you've queued two hours or so for your turn. Alternatively, you can climb the steps to Bai'e Feng in under three hours, though the forest canopy tends to block views and the path is thick with **porters** ferrying laundry, rubbish and building materials up and down the slopes.

In contrast, the exceptional landscapes on the fifteen-kilometre **western route** are accompanied by up to eight hours of exhausting legwork – though you can shorten things by catching another gondola between the trailhead at Ciguang Ge and Yuping Lou. There are around two thousand steps from the Ciguang Ge to **Banshan Si**, the misleadingly named Midway Monastery, after which things start to get interesting as you continue up an increasingly steep and narrow gorge, its sides overgrown with witch hazel, azaleas and wild plum. The rocks are huge, their weirdly contorted figures lending some credence to the usual gamut of names hailing from ancient times, and the broken hillside is riddled with caves. A steep, hour-long detour from Banshan – not a climb for those nervous of heights – follows steps cut into the cliffs up to **Tiandu Feng** (Heavenly City Peak), where **Jiyu Bei** (Kingfish Ridge), a narrow, ten-metre-long path extending over a precipice towards distant pinnacles surrounded by clouds, provides Huang Shan's most spectacular views.

Back on the main track, the beautifully positioned **Yuping Lou** (Jade Screen Pavilion) is the true halfway house at around three hours into the journey. The vegetation thins out here, exchanged for bare rocks with only the occasional

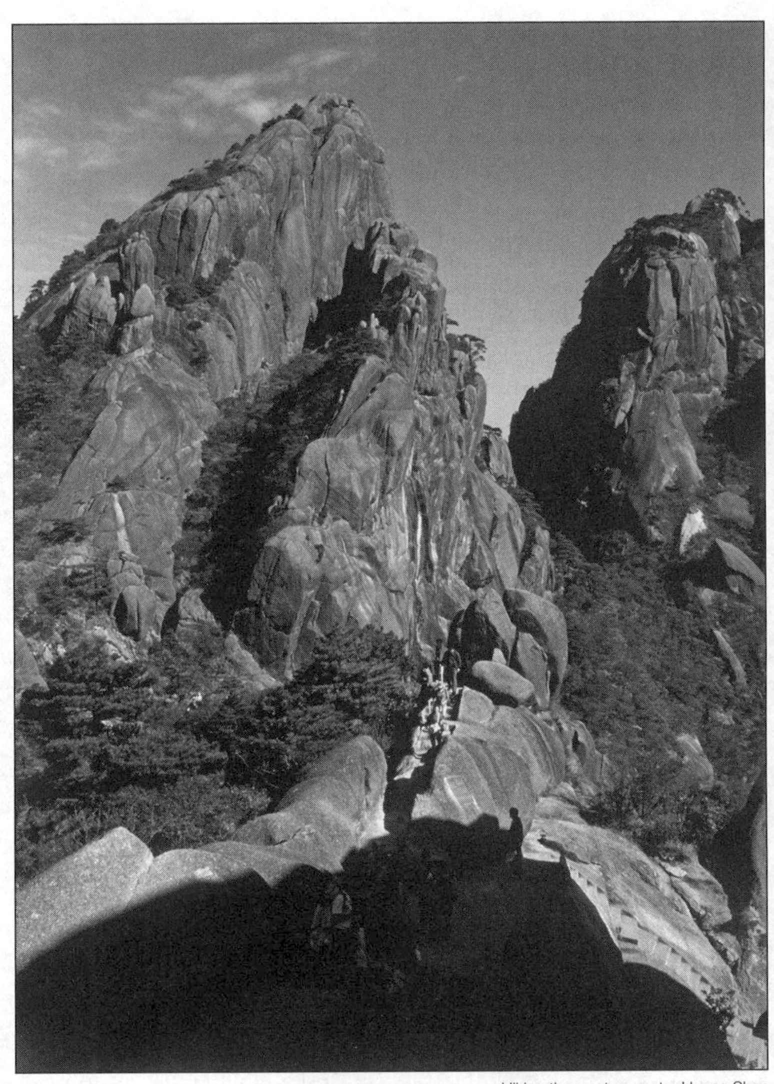

▲ Hiking the western route, Huang Shan

wind-contorted tree, one of which, **Yingke Song** (Welcoming Guest Pine), has been immortalized in countless scroll paintings, photographs, cigarette packets and beer labels. The steps wind on up to a pass where more strange rocks jut out of the mist; bear right for the climb to Huang Shan's apex at **Lianhua Feng** (Lotus Flower Peak; 1864m) or press on to **accommodation** at *Tianhai Binguan* (Ⓣ0559/5562201; ¥430). From here, it's just a short climb to where you finally reach the peak circuit at **Guangming Ding** (Brightness Summit), with a TV tower and weather station off to the right, and **Feilai Shi** (the "Rock Flown From Afar") ahead.

The peak circuit

It takes around three hours to **circuit the peaks**. North (anticlockwise) from the eastern steps and Bai'e Feng cable-car terminus, the first stop is where a track leads out to **Shixin Feng** (Beginning-to-Believe Peak). This cluster of rocky spires makes a wonderful perch to gaze down to lowland woods and rivers, with white-rumped swifts and pine and rock silhouettes moving in and out of shifting silver clouds. Tour groups concentrate on the higher levels, so the lower stairs are more peaceful.

From here, the path continues round to the first of a few accommodation options, including the comfortable *Beihai Binguan* (Ⓣ0559/5582555, Ⓕ5581996; ❽, dorm beds ¥150), where there's also a **Bank of China** with, incredibly, an ATM. Crowds congregate each morning on the terrace nearby to watch the **sunrise** over the "northern sea" of clouds, one of the most stirring sights on the mountain. The views are good even without the dawn, and the area tends to be busy all day. Straight ahead, a side track leads to the cosy *Shilin Dajiudian* (Ⓣ0559/5584040, Ⓦwww.shilin.com; ❾, dorm beds ¥150), which even has copies of the *China Daily*; while another twenty minutes on the main path brings you to the well-placed *Xihai Fandian* (Ⓣ0559/5588888, Ⓦwww.hsxihaihotel.com; ❽), the perfect spot to sip drinks on the terrace and watch, in its turn, the sun setting over the "western cloud sea".

It's another ten minutes or so from *Xihai* to where the track splits at the mountain's least expensive accommodation, the *Paiyun Ting Binguan* (Ⓣ0559/5581558, Ⓔhspyl@sohu.com; ❼). Ahead is the **Taiping cable-car station** down to Songgu (see p.469). Stay on the main track for **Paiyun Ting**, the Cloud-dispelling Pavilion; on a clear day you'll see a steep gorge squeezed between jagged crags below, all covered in pine trees and magnolias. More views await farther round at the lonely tower of **Feilai Shi**, which after rain looks across at cascades dropping off lesser peaks seemingly into infinity. Beyond here, the path undulates along the cliff edge to where the western steps descend on the right (below the TV tower and weather station), and then winds back to the Bai'e Feng cable car.

Hubei

HUBEI is Han China's agricultural and geographic centre, mild in climate and well watered. Until 280 BC this was the independent state of **Chu**, whose sophisticated bronzeworking skills continue to astound archeologists, but for the last half-millennium the province's eastern bulk, defined by the low-lying **Jianghan plain** and spliced by waterways draining into the Yangzi and Han rivers, has become an intensely cultivated maze of rice fields so rich that, according to tradition, they alone are enough to supply the national need. More recently, Hubei's central location and mass of transport links into neighbouring regions saw the province becoming the first in the interior to be heavily industrialized. The colossal **Three Gorges hydroelectric dam** upstream from **Yichang** (see p.484), car manufacturing – up and running with the help of foreign investment – and long-established iron and steel plants provide a huge source of income for central China.

As the "Gateway to Nine Provinces", skirted by mountains and midway along the Yangzi between Shanghai and Chongqing, Hubei has always been of great strategic importance, and somewhere that seditious ideas could easily spread to the rest of the country. The central regions upriver from the capital, **Wuhan**, feature prominently in the *Romance of the Three Kingdoms*, with the ports of **Jingzhou** and **Chibi** retaining their period associations, while Wuhan itself thrives on industry and river trade, and played a key role in China's early twentieth-century revolutions. In the west, the ranges that border Sichuan contain the holy peak of **Wudang Shan**, alive with Taoist temples and martial-arts lore, and the remote and little-visited **Shennongjia Forest Reserve**, said to be inhabited by China's yeti.

Wuhan

One way or another, almost anyone travelling through central China has to pass through **WUHAN**, Hubei's sprawling capital. The name is a portmanteau label for the original settlements of **Wuchang**, **Hankou** and **Hanyang**, separate across the junction of the Han and Yangzi rivers, but given some sense of unity by three massive interconnecting bridges. The city's sheer size, bustle and obvious regional economic importance lend atmosphere, even if Wuhan is more of an administrative and social centre than a tourist magnet. Nonetheless it's an upbeat, characterful metropolis, and Hankou's former role as a **foreign concession** has left a whole quarter of colonial European heritage in its wake, while the **Provincial Museum** in Wuchang is one of China's best. There are also a couple of temples and historical monuments to explore, some connected to the

Wuhan

Wuhan	武汉	*wu3hàn*
Hankou	汉口	*hànkǒu*
Hanyang	汉阳	*hànyáng*
Wuchang	武昌	*wǔchāng*
The City		
Changchun Guan	长春观	*chángchūn guàn*
Customs House	武汉海关	*wǔhàn hǎiguān*
Electric special #1	电一专路	*diànyī zhuānlù*
Flood Control Monument	防洪纪念碑	*fánghóng jìniànbēi*
Great Changjiang Bridge	长江大桥	*chángjiāng dàqiáo*
Gui Shan Park	龟山公园	*guīshān gōngyuán*
Guiyuan Si	归元寺	*guīyuán sì*
Guqin Tai	古琴塔	*gǔqíntǎ*
Hong Ge	红阁	*hónggé*
Hubei Provincial Museum	湖北省博物馆	*húběishěng bówùguǎn*
She Shan	蛇山	*shéshān*
Tianhe Airport	天河飞机场	*tiānhé fēijīchǎng*
Workers' Cultural Palace	工人文化宫	*gōngrén wénhuàgōng*
Wuhan Museum	武汉博物馆	*wǔhàn bówùguǎn*
Wuhan University	武汉大学	*wǔhàn dàxué*
Yangzi Ferry Terminal	武汉港客运站	*wǔhàngǎng kèyùnzhàn*
Yellow Crane Tower	黄鹤塔	*huánghè tǎ*

1911 revolution that ended two thousand years of imperial rule. On the downside, Wuhan has a well-deserved reputation – along with Chongqing and Nanjing – as one of China's three summer "furnaces": between May and September you'll find the streets melting and the gasping population surviving on a diet of watermelon and iced treats.

Arrival and city transport

Wuhan spreads more than 10km across, and with an extensive choice of transit points – there are two train stations and at least three long-distance bus stations – it's important to know where you're arriving before you get here; train and bus timetables usually spell out the district where services arrive, rather than just "Wuhan". Most people stay on the northern bank of the Yangzi in **Hankou**, which, as the city's trade and business centre, contains the best of the services and accommodation. South across the smaller Han River is lightly industrial **Hanyang**, while **Wuchang** recedes southeast of the Yangzi into semi-rural parkland.

Tianhe airport sits 30km to the north of Wuhan along a good road, with a **bus link** (¥15, every 15 minutes) from here to the China Southern airline office on Hangkong Lu in Hankou. **Rail** services from the north tend to terminate at Hankou's train station, up in the north of the city along Fazhan Dadao, while those from the south favour Wuchang's station, on the other side of town on Zhongshan Lu. Arriving by bus, you could end up at any one of the major **long-distance bus stations** – on Jiefang Dadao in downtown Hankou, on Hanyang Dadao in Hanyang, or near Wuchang's train station on Zhongshan Lu – irrespective of where you're coming from; there are also several private bus depots outside the Yangzi ferry terminal and along Yanhe Dadao in Hankou. At

Zhongshan Park	中山公园	*zhōngshān gōngyuán*
Accommodation		
Guansheng Yuan	冠生园大酒店	*guānshēngyuán dàjiǔdiàn*
Hanghai	航海宾馆	*hánghǎi bīnguǎn*
Holiday Inn	天安假日酒店	*tiānānjiàri jiǔdiàn*
Jianghan	江汉饭店	*jiānghàn fàndiàn*
Jinlun	金轮宾馆	*jīnlún bīnguǎn*
Kunlun Victory	昆仑胜利饭店	*kūnlún shènglì fàndiàn*
Linjiang	临江饭店	*línjiāng fàndiàn*
Mengtian Hu	明天湖宾馆	*míngtiānhú bīnguǎn*
New Oriental Empire	新东方帝豪酒店	*xīndōngfāng dìháo jiǔdiàn*
Xuangong	璇宫饭店	*xuángōng fàndiàn*
Eating and drinking		
Bordeaux Bar	波尔图酒吧	*bōěrtú jiǔbā*
Changchun Sucai Guan	长春素菜馆	*chángchūn sùcàiguǎn*
Da Zhonghua	大中华	*dà zhōnghuá*
Dezhuang Huoguo Guangchang	德庄火锅广场	*dézhuāng huǒguō guǎngchǎng*
Si Li Mei	四李美	*sìlǐměi*
Yangrou Meiwei	羊肉美味	*yangrou meiwei*
Yonghe Dawang	永和大王	*yǒnghé dàwáng*

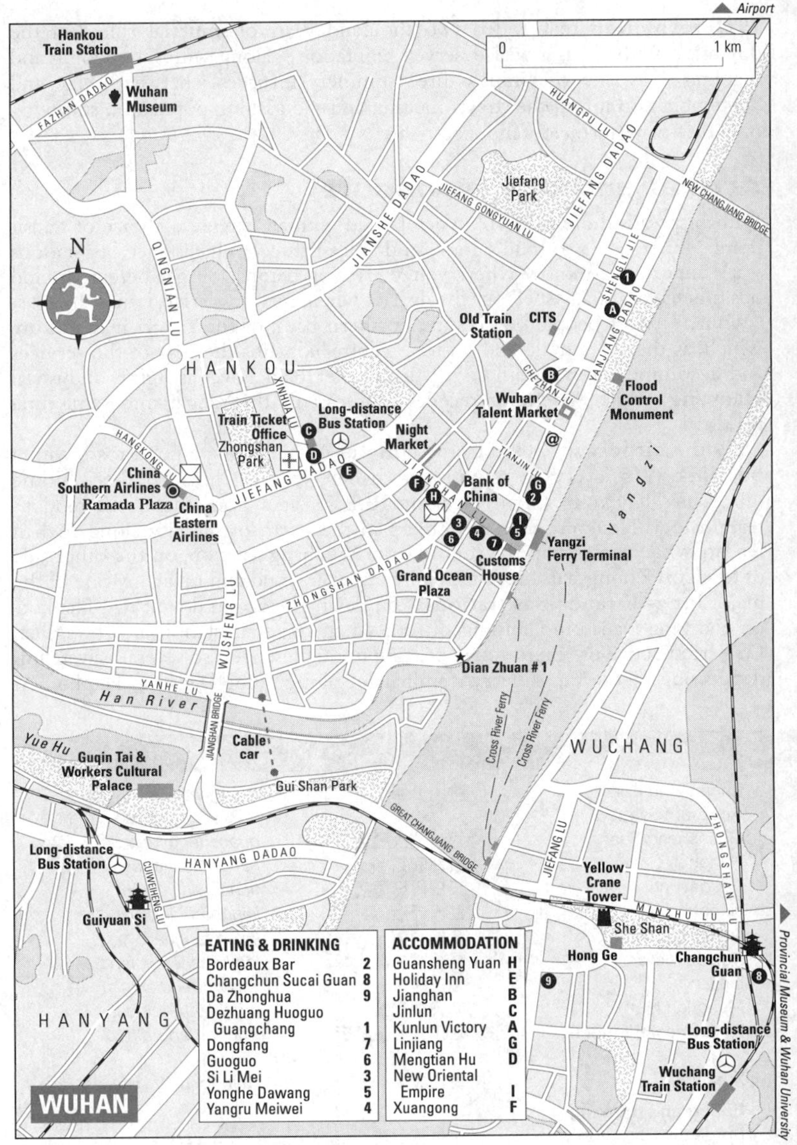

least there's no confusion with **Yangzi ferries** – passengers arrive at the ferry **terminal** on Yanjiang Dadao in Hankou.

City transport

Wuhan is too large to consider walking everywhere, though the overloaded **bus and trolleybus** systems seldom seem to be much quicker, and stops can be widely separated. The main **city-bus terminuses** are at Hankou and

Useful bus routes

The most convenient bus for sightseeing is the **Dian Zhuan** (Electric Special) **#1**, not to be confused with any other #1 bus or trolleybus – the characters for *dian zhuan* are displayed either side of the number. It runs from Yanhe Dadao in Hankou, via Hanyang and the Great Changjiang Bridge, and then links the Yellow Crane Tower with Changchun Guan and the Provincial Museum. Other noteworthy services are:

#38 From Hankou train station through the downtown concession area, terminating along the river on Yanjiang Dadao near the Flood Control Monument.

#503 From Wuchang train station to the Yangzi ferry terminal.

#507 Between Hankou and Wuchang train stations, via the Yangzi ferry terminal, taking 45–90 minutes, depending on traffic.

#595 Connects Hankou train station with the Yangzi ferry terminal.

Wuchang train stations, and beside the Yangzi ferry terminal on Yanjiang Dadao. Staff are on hand at each of these to help you find the right vehicle. Services are at least regular and cheap – it only costs ¥2 between Wuchang and Hankou stations – and crawl out to almost every corner of the city between around 6am and 10pm.

Taxis are ubiquitous and, at ¥8 for the first 2km, not too expensive. For short hops, haggle with the **motorbike** and **motor-rickshaw** drivers who prowl the bus and train depots. During daylight hours, there are **passenger ferries** across the Yangzi between the southern end of Hankou's Yanjiang Dadao and Wuchang's city-bus terminus, below and just north of the Changjiang Bridge; trips cost ¥1.5 and take about twenty minutes.

Maps of Wuhan showing transport routes can be picked up at bus and train stations, but shop around first, as many are either painfully detailed or almost abstract. **Bicycles** are difficult to rent and not overly used, partly because of Wuhan's size, but also because of unpredictably enforced regulations banning them from being ridden across the bridges (though many still are).

Accommodation

Much of Wuhan's **hotel** accommodation is upmarket, but there are a couple of inexpensive options, and mid-range places can be good value. The biggest selection – a sprinkling of which are reviewed below – is in **Hankou**. In Wuchang, the noisy *Hanghai* (Ⓣ027/88740122; ④), on Zhongshan Lu opposite the train station, is only recommended if you arrive late in the day; bus #507 to Hankou runs past the door.

Guansheng Yuan 109 Jianghan Lu Ⓣ027/82779069, Ⓔguansy@public.wh.hb.cn. Located beside a department store of the same name and just south of the *Xuangong* hotel. Nothing glamorous, but central and the right price. Often full. ④

Holiday Inn 868 Jiefang Dadao Ⓣ027/85867888, Ⓦwww.ichotelsgroup.com. Reliable comfort and level of service and surprisingly good rates can be found at this smart international hotel. ⑦

Jianghan 245 Shengli Jie Ⓣ027/82811600, Ⓦwww.jhhotel.com. Wuhan's best, a renovated French colonial mansion, with porphyry floors and wooden panelling throughout the lobby, fairly luxurious rooms and bilingual staff. ⑧

Jinlun Xinhua Lu Ⓣ027/85807060, Ⓕ85778420. Excellent-value, comfortable twins, with friendly staff, and well located for the Hankou bus station. ③

Kunlun Victory 11 Siwei Lu Ⓣ027/82732780, Ⓕ82721106. Hidden away behind a high wall and difficult to locate, this is a modern, five-storey block with much the same facilities as the nearby *Jianghan*, but none of the panache. ⑦

Linjiang 1 Tianjin Lu Ⓣ 027/68826135, Ⓕ68825200. An army-owned hotel with a colonial facade (in 1924, this was the Asian Kerosene

Company building), just up the road from the Yangzi ferry terminal. Reasonably priced rooms for town, and good service; discounts are available. 5

Mengtian Hu West of Hankou's bus station, on Jiefang Dadao ⓣ027/85796368. Some of the cheapest doubles in town, with shared facilities and certainly past their best; nevertheless, they're still a good deal, as are the slightly pricier en-suite rooms. 3

New Oriental Empire 136 Yanjiang Dadao ⓣ027/82212005. Another colonial frontage and mid-range urban hotel interior; a notch above the nearby *Linjiang*. 6

Xuangong 57 Jianghan Lu ⓣ027/6882258, ⓦwww.xuangonghotel.com. A gloomy but very atmospheric 1920s concession building with comfortable rooms; the entrance is on a side street to the west of the main road. Rates are often hugely reduced. 7

Hankou

Presently the largest of Wuhan's districts, **Hankou** was a simple fishing harbour until it opened as a **treaty port** in 1861 – a move greatly resented by the Chinese, who took to stoning any foreigners bold enough to walk the streets. Consequently, the Chinese were barred from the riverside concession area, which over the following decades was developed in a grand style, complete with a racetrack and a **Bund** (flood-preventing embankments built by the British in the 1860s) lined with Neoclassical European architecture housing banks, embassies and company headquarters.

The twentieth century was not kind to the city, however. On October 10, 1911, a **bomb** exploded prematurely at the Hankou headquarters of a revolutionary group linked to **Sun Yatsen**'s Tongmen Hui, a society keen on dismantling imperial rule in China and replacing it with a democratic government. imperial troops executed the ringleaders, sparking a savage, citywide **uprising against the Manchus**, which virtually levelled Hankou and soon spread across China. The last emperor, Pu Yi, was forced to abdicate and a Republican government under Sun Yatsen was duly elected in Nanjing the following year. The foreign concession was rebuilt, but anti-Western riots broke out in 1925 and again in 1927, leading to the **handing back** of Hankou's concession areas to China. A few months afterwards, the Guomindang stormed through on their Northern Expedition and returned briefly in 1937 to establish a national government in town before being forced farther west by the Japanese. Thirty years later, Hankou saw more fighting, this time between the PLA and various Red Guard factions, who had been slugging it out over differing interpretations of Mao's Cultural Revolution.

The district

Bursting with traffic and crowds, Hankou is a place to walk, shop, eat, spend money and watch modern Chinese doing the same. The main thoroughfare is **Zhongshan Dadao**, a packed, three-kilometre-long stretch of restaurants, stores and shopping plazas. Surprisingly, given the city's history, Hankou's **colonial quarter** survives almost in its entirety, restored during a big clean-up project in 2001. Aside from the racetrack, now watery **Zhongshan Park** near the corner of Jiefang Dadao and Qingnian Lu, the colonial core lies mostly between the eastern half of Zhongshan Dadao and the river. The best sections are along the former Bund, renamed **Yanjiang Dadao**, and **Jianghan Lu**. The two roads converge at the mighty **Customs House**, a solid Renaissance edifice with imposing grey-stone portico and Corinthian capitals. The Bund itself is still visible; in 1954, the Communists erected a **Flood Control Monument**, a tall obelisk embellished with Mao's portrait, in Binjiang Park. Many buildings in the area have plaques in English outlining their history; some to look for include the unusual seven-storey Art Deco/modernist exterior of the former **Siming Bank** at 45 Jianghan Lu, and the brick "Wuhan Talent Market" on Yanjiang Dadao – once the **US Consulate**. The **Bank of China**, at the intersection of Jianghan Lu and Zhongshan Dadao, retains its period interior of wooden panelling and chandeliers, while Hankou's **old train station** on Chezhan Lu sports a derelict French Gothic shell surrounded by a mass of seedy shops and stalls.

If you're up near Hankou's train station, drop in to the **Wuhan Museum** (daily 9am–5pm; ¥20), which houses an outstanding collection of antique bronzes, porcelain, jade and scrolls of painting and calligraphy. In particular, there's a wonderful Ming-dynasty painting of the Yueyang Tower in Hunan (see p.507), with a view of gnarled pines and boats riding a turbulent Yangzi; and a 1700-year-old, fifteen-centimetre-wide bronze mirror decorated with scenes from the Han-dynasty collection of Chinese mythology, the *Book of Songs*.

Hanyang

From Hankou, you can cross the Han River into Hanyang either by bus over the short Jianghan Bridge or the **cable car** (¥40) between Yanhe Dadao and eastern Hanyang's **Gui Shan Park**. Settled as far back as 600 AD, Hanyang remained insignificant until the late nineteenth century when the viceroy **Zhang Zhidong** built China's first large-scale steel foundry here as part of the "Self-Strengthening Movement" – a last-ditch effort to modernize China during the twilight years of the Qing dynasty.

Hanyang remains Wuhan's principal manufacturing sector; its distinctly shabby streets are dotted with small-scale industries. The Jianghan Bridge runs south to a huge **roundabout** below the western end of Gui Shan Park, from whose hills the Xia king Yu is said to have quelled floods four thousand years ago. West of the roundabout, **Guqin Tai** (Ancient Lute Platform; ¥15) was the haunt of legendary strummer **Yu Boya**, who played over the grave of his friend Zhong Ziqi and then smashed his instrument because the one person able to appreciate his music was dead. Infrequent gatherings at the adjacent Workers' Cultural Palace are worth a look; here, bands perform traditional tunes to a slumbering, elderly audience.

Guiyuan Si (daily 8.30am–5pm; ¥10) is a busy Buddhist monastery a couple of streets southwest of the roundabout on Cuiweiheng Lu, behind Hanyang's long-distance bus station. There's an authoritarian atmosphere to the place, emphasized by blocky, black-and-white brick buildings, though the temple's **scripture collection** – which includes a complete seven-thousand-volume set of the rare *Longcan Sutra* – has made it famous among Buddhist circles. Of more general interest are several hundred individually styled saintly statues in the Arhat Hall as well as the statue of Sakyamuni in the main hall, a gift from Burma in 1935, carved from a single block of white jade.

Wuchang

Wuchang, on the right bank of the Yangzi, was founded as Sun Quan's walled capital of Wu during the Three Kingdoms period. Tang rulers made the city a major port, which, under the Mongols, became the administrative centre of a vast region covering present-day Hunan, Hubei, Guangdong and Guangxi provinces.

During the 1910 insurrection, Wuchang hosted appalling scenes when ethnic Han troops mutinied under a banner proclaiming "Long live the Han,

Exterminate the Manchu" and accordingly slaughtered a Manchu regiment and over eight hundred civilians here. The city and its bureaucracy survived however, and nowadays Wuchang comprises government offices and the huge **Wuhan University** campus. Highlights include the Taoist **Changchun Guan**, the **Yellow Crane Tower** – the greatest of the Yangzi's many riverside pavilions – and the **Provincial Museum**, close to the lakeside scenery of Dong Hu.

Yellow Crane Tower and around

The road from Hanyang to Wuchang crosses the **Great Changjiang Bridge**, before whose construction in 1957 all traffic – rail included – had to be ferried 1500m across the river. On the far side, Wuluo Lu curves around She Shan (Snake Hill), which, along with the river, is overlooked by the bright tiles and red wooden columns of the fifty-metre-high **Yellow Crane Tower** (¥50). It's no less magnificent for being an entirely modern Qing-style reproduction, situated 1km from where the original third-century structure burned down in 1884. Legend has it that She Shan was once home to a Taoist Immortal who paid his bills at a nearby inn by drawing a picture of a crane on the wall, which would fly down at intervals and entertain the guests. A few years later the Immortal flew off on his creation, and the landlord, who doubtless could afford it by then, built the tower in his honour. Climb the internal staircases to the top floor to see Wuhan and the Yangzi at their best.

On the southern slopes of She Shan, **Hong Ge** is a handsome colonial-style red-brick mansion which housed the Hubei Military Government during the 1910 uprising. A bronze statue of Sun Yatsen stands in front, though at the time of the uprising he was abroad raising funds. Follow Wuluo Lu east for 1km from here and you'll be standing outside the russet walls of **Changchun Guan** (¥5), a Taoist complex which made its name through the Yuan-dynasty luminary **Qiu Chuzi**, who preached here and later founded his own sect. Only partially open to the public, the halls are simply furnished with statues of the Three Purities, the Jade Emperor and other Taoist deities. A side wing has been co-opted as a pharmacy, where Chinese-speakers can have their vital signs checked by a traditional doctor and buy medicines collected, according to the staff, on Wudang Shan. There's also a martial-arts training area, with rusty poleaxes and swords displayed on racks. Next door, Changchun's **vegetarian restaurant** is well worth visiting at lunchtime (see opposite).

Hubei Provincial Museum

From the Yellow Crane Tower, it's around twenty minutes by bus to the **Hubei Provincial Museum** (daily 8.30am – noon & 1.30–5pm; ¥30) on Donghu Lu. The museum's display of items unearthed from the Warring States Period's **tomb of the Marquis Yi** deserves a good hour of your time – especially if you're planning on visiting similar collections at Jingzhou (see p.484) and Changsha (see p.494).

The marquis died in 433 BC and was buried in a huge, multi-layered, wooden lacquered coffin at nearby Suizhou, then a major city of the state of **Zeng**. His corpse was accompanied by fifteen thousand bronze and wooden artefacts, twenty-one women and one dog. The museum's comprehensive English explanations of contemporary history and photos of the 1978 excavation put everything in perspective. Don't miss the impressive orchestra of **64 bronze bells**, ranging in weight from a couple of kilos to a quarter of a tonne, found in the waterlogged tomb – the largest such set ever discovered – along with the wooden frame from which they once hung in rows. Played with hand-held rods, each bell can produce two notes depending on where it is struck. The knowledge of metals and casting required to achieve this initially boggled modern researchers, who took five years to make duplicates. Souvenir shops outside sell pricey **recordings** of period tunes played on the bells, and there are brief **performances** every hour or so in the museum's auditorium. More than a hundred other musical instruments are also on display, including stone chimes, drums, flutes and zithers, along with spearheads and a very weird brazen crane totem sprouting antlers – an inscription suggests that this was the marquis's steed in the afterlife.

Eating and drinking

Cooking in Wuhan reflects the city's position midway between Shanghai and Chongqing, and restaurants here offer a good balance of Eastern-style steamed and braised dishes – particularly **fish and shellfish** – along with some seriously spicy Sichuanese food. There's also a strong **snacking** tradition in town, and many places specialize in designer dumplings: various types of *shaomai*; *tangbao*, soup buns stuffed with jellied stock which burst messily as you bite them, much to the amusement of other diners; and *doupi*, sticky rice packets stuffed with meat and rolled up in a beanpaste skin.

Hankou has the best of the **restaurants**, which are concentrated along Zhongshan Dadao and its offshoots. Even the formal places are inexpensive, and many have first-floor canteens where you can eat local staples very cheaply. An increasing number of Western-style **cafés and bars** – many livening up after dark – are springing up along Yanjiang Dadao and Jianghan Lu. The *Holiday Inn*'s ground-floor coffee shop offers chocolate and cream confections from ¥12 a piece, or you can pay ¥26 per person for afternoon tea. There's also a stack of **cake shops** at the river end of Jianghan Lu.

Restaurants

Hankou

Bordeaux Bar Just west of the *Linjiang* hotel on Yanjiang Dadao. One of many such café-bars in the area, replete with pavement tables and nicely dimmed lighting inside. The Western-style pasta and steak dishes, along with an eclectic range of Chinese fare, are expensive.

Dezhuang Huoguo Guangchang Corner of Yanjiang Dadao and Sanyang Lu. If you're craving northern-style hotpot, this is the place to come – big, bright, noisy and inexpensive.

Dongfang Near the Customs House on Jianghan Lu. A comfortable and popular place to take a breather from all that strenuous shopping and tuck into some tasty hotpots (¥25).

Guoguo Jiaotong Lu. Seethingly popular canteen serving excellent, inexpensive dumplings. Order at the counter and then wait in line.

Si Li Mei Zhongshan Dadao. It's easy to miss the entrance to this place, which is wedged in amongst modern shpfronts. Another place to try river food and *tangbao*.

Yangrou Meiwei Just over the road from Guoguo down the side of the old tenement block, this is just one of a range of small eateries that serve up the whole range of local delicaces with all the flavour at just a fraction of the cost of the restaurants.

Yonghe Dawang Across from the ferry terminal on Yanjiang Dadao, and elsewhere. Open around the clock, this restaurant chain's logo looks suspiciously like *KFC*'s but the food is very different: big bowls of beef noodle soup or *doujiang*, steamed buns and fried rice.

Wuchang

Changchun Sucai Guan Wulou Lu. Vegetarian restaurant with Ming decor and a resolutely Chinese menu. The "beef" and "chicken" are made from bean-curd sheets, "prawns" from bean starch, and so on. Portions are huge (ask for small servings if you want to try a variety), liberally laced with chillies and aniseed, and very tasty. Mains from ¥15 or so.

Da Zhonghua Pengliuyang Lu. A four-storey establishment long known for its classic and innovative ways with fish – try the lake fish with red berry sauce. Noodles and soups are served on the first floor; the third floor is a general dining room, with a teahouse right on top. Most dishes under ¥30.

Listings

Banks and exchange Bank of China, Zhongshan Dadao, Hankou (Mon–Sat 8.30am–5pm).
Bookshops The Xinhua bookstore, just west of the Jianghan Lu/Zhongshan Dadao intersection, Hankou, has plenty of maps and some English titles, including abridged texts of Chinese classics.
Cinema There are screens in Hankou at Warner Village in Walmart near the Mingcheng Plaza on Zhongshan Dadao, and near the former US Consulate on Yanjiang Dadao.
Hospitals The Tongji, east of the Jiefang Dadao/ Qingnian Lu crossroads in Hankou, is considered Wuhan's best. Another good place to go for acupuncture and massage is the hospital attached to the Hubei Traditional Medicine College, just north of She Shan, Wuchang.
Internet access In Hankou, there are Internet bars on the second floor of the cinema complex on Yanjiang Dadao, and east of the *Holiday Inn* on Jiefang Dadao. In Wuchang there's one on Wulou Lu, west of Zhongshan Lu.
Left luggage There are booths charging ¥2 a bag at the bus (daily 8am–8pm) and train stations (24hr).
Mail and telephones The main post offices, with IDD phones, are on Zhongshan Dadao and at the junction of Hangkong Lu and Qingnian Lu, Hankou (daily 8am–6pm). There is no GPO as such, so ensure that poste-restante mail addresses use the street name and "Hankou", or it could end up anywhere in the city.
Markets and shopping For "antique" souvenirs, try the shops at the Hubei Provincial Museum, Wuchang. Hankou's old concession area, north of Zhongshan Dadao, has the liveliest market activity, mostly revolving around fruit and vegetables. Like most Chinese cities, Hankou is a very good place to buy clothes – try the new Grand Ocean Plaza or the Walmart Super Centre, both on Zhongshan Dadao, or numerous smaller shops nearby, many with unfortunate names such as the "Ebola" clothes shop on Zhongshan Dadao.
Pharmacies In addition to smaller places elsewhere, Hankou's Hangkong Lu has a string of pharmacies stocking traditional and modern medicines, the biggest of which is the Grand Pharmacy, or, according to the English sign, the "Ark of Health".
Travel agents These abound around the Yangzi ferry terminal and the Hankou long-distance bus station. Alternatively, CITS here are a well-informed, English-, German- and French-speaking agency which can organize Three Gorges cruises and trips to Shennongjia and Wudang Shan; they're located just north of the *Jianghan Hotel* at 909 Zhongshan Dadao, Hankou (☎027/82787386).

Up the Yangzi: Wuhan to Yichang

The flat, broad river plains west of Wuhan don't seem too exciting at first, but historic remains lend solid character to towns along the way. It takes around 36 hours to navigate upstream from Wuhan via **Chibi** and **Jingzhou** to **Yichang**, from where the exciting journey through the Yangzi Gorges and on to Chongqing begins. As most boats don't stop along the way, if you want to see anything it's more convenient – and far quicker – to use the Wuhan–Jingzhou–Yichang **expressway**, which bypasses Chibi but cuts the journey time to Yichang down to less than four hours.

Chibi

The first place of any significance along the river, about 80km southwest of Wuhan, **CHIBI** (Red Cliffs) was the setting f or the most important battle of the Three Kingdoms period, the confrontation at which the competing states defined their final boundaries. It was here in 208 AD that the northern armies of Wei, led by Cao Cao, descended on the combined southern forces of Liu Bei and Sun Quan. Though heavily outnumbered, the southerners had brought two remarkable strategists along – **Zhuge Liang** and **Pang Tong** – who took full advantage of Cao's decision to launch a naval assault across the river. Misled by Pang Tong's spies, Cao chained his ships together on the north bank while

Up the Yangzi: Wuhan to Yichang

Chibi	赤壁	*chìbì*
Baifeng Terrace	拜风台	*bàifēng tái*
Feng Chu An	风雏庵	*fēngchú ān*
Nanping Shan	南屏山	*nánpíng shān*
Wangjiang Pavilion	望江亭	*wàngjiāng tíng*
Wuhou Palace	武侯宫	*wǔhóu gōng*
Jingzhou	荆州	*jīngzhōu*
Jingzhou Museum	荆州博物馆	*jīngzhōu bówùguǎn*
Kaiyuan Guan	开元观	*kāiyuán guàn*
Puqi	蒲圻	*púqí*
Shashi	沙市	*shāshì*
Yichang	宜昌	*yíchāng*
Dagong Bridge Transit Terminal	大公桥水路客运站	*dàgōngqiáo shuǐlù kèyùnzhàn*
Gezhou Dam	葛洲坝	*gězhōu bà*
Heping Jiari Jiudian	和平假日酒店	*hépíng jiàrì jiǔdiàn*
Huangbao Canting	环保餐厅	*huánbǎo cāntīng*
Hydrofoil Port	高速客轮中心	*gāosù kèlún zhōngxīn*
Qing Zhou Cai	青粥菜	*qīngzhōu cài*
Sanxia Airport	三峡机场	*sānxiá jīchǎng*
Taohualing Binguan	桃花岭宾馆	*táohuālǐng bīnguǎn*
Three Gorges Dam site	三峡大坝区	*sānxiá dàbàqū*
Xing Gui Zu	新贵族	*xīn guì zú*
Yichang International Hotel	宜昌国际大酒店	*yíchāng guójì dàjiǔdiàn*
Yunji Fandian	云集饭店	*yúnjí fàndiàn*
Zili Lu	自立路	*zìlì lù*

preparing for the attack, and Zhuge Liang – allegedly using Taoist magic – created an unseasonal southeasterly wind and sent a flotilla of burning hulks across the Yangzi, completely incinerating Cao's armada and permanently imprinting the colour of flames on the cliffs. Despite Cao Cao's defeat, neither of the other armies had the strength to pursue him, nor to take on each other in a final engagement that could have seen China unified, instead of plunged into civil war for most of the following five centuries.

To reach Chibi, clearly visible from the river, take a train or bus to **Chibi Shi** (also known as **Puqi**) about two-thirds of the way between Wuhan and Yueyang in Hunan, from where it's a ninety-minute local bus ride to the site, locally known as **Sanguo Chibi** to distinguish it from Chibi Shi. A flight of steps on the right near the bus stop leads up Jinluan Hill to **Feng Chu An**, a whitewashed hall where Pang Tong studied military strategy and so conceived the plan that defeated Cao. Back below, following the main road to the left brings you to **Nanping Shan**, where two stone lions up on the hill flank the entrance to **Wuhou Palace** and **Baifeng Terrace**. Four statues here commemorate Zhuge Liang and Liu Bei, along with Liu Bei's oath brothers, Guan Yu and Zhang Fei. Farther on towards the river, the small **Wangjiang Pavilion** is a former guard post, which still commands broad views of the terraced paddy fields below. Spears, arrowheads and pottery shards in a gloomy museum nearby offer proof that the legends have a historical basis. The cliffs overlooking the Yangzi's southern bank just outside town are embellished with the two characters for "*chibi*", supposedly carved by the triumphant Wu general, **Zhou Yu**.

Jingzhou Shi and around

Around 240km west of Wuhan on the highway to Yichang, or the best part of a day upstream by ferry from Chibi, **JINGZHOU SHI** lies on the north bank of the Yangzi, where the Wuhan–Yichang expressway joins the highway up to Xiangfan in northern Hubei. The city is divided into two separate districts: while the easterly section of **Shashi** is an indifferent modern port, the **Jingzhou** district, 10km west, is ringed by around 8km of moats and well-maintained, seven-metre-high **battlements**, built by the *Three Kingdoms* hero Guan Yu, who commanded Shu's eastern defences here. Even earlier, the now vanished city of **Jinan**, immediately north of Jingzhou, was the capital of the state of Chu until its destruction by the Qin armies around 278 BC.

From Shashi's long-distance bus station on Taqiao Lu, city bus #1 runs west into Jingzhou through the **east gate**, trundles down past Jingzhou's own long-distance bus station on Jing Nan Lu, turns into **Jingzhong Lu** and finally terminates by the **west gate**. Walls aside, there's not much to be impressed with in this forty-minute trawl, but walk 100m back along Jingzhong Lu from the bus stop and you'll be outside **Jingzhou Museum** (daily 8.30am–4.30pm; ¥20). Skip the lifeless main building, full of dusty cases of unidentified pots and blurred photos, and instead walk around to the back, where ¥10 gets you into the "Treasure Display" (same hours), a fantastic collection of Western Han **tomb remains**. These were found a few kilometres north at **Fenghuang Shan**, the site of Jinan, which former residents turned into a cemetery after the city's destruction in order to be buried alongside their ancestors. More than 180 tombs dating from the Qin era to the end of the Western Han (221 BC–24 AD) have been found, an impressive range for a single site; the exhibition here focuses on Tomb 168 – that of a court official named **Sui**. In many regards the items on display are similar to those in Wuhan's provincial museum (see p.480) – the house-like sarcophagi and copious lacquerwork, for example – but the bonus here is Sui's astoundingly well-preserved **corpse**, along with some comfortingly practical household items and wooden miniatures of his servants; either he wasn't powerful enough to have his real attendants buried with him, or else this trend had gone out of style. *Romance of the Three Kingdoms* aficionados should go next door to **Kaiyuan Guan**, a tiny, elderly temple dedicated to Guan Yu and set among overgrown gardens.

There are buses both ways along the expressway until early evening from either Jingzhou's or Shashi's **long-distance bus stations**, with at least eight additional services north to Xiangfan throughout the day. There's **accommodation** (❸) in the vicinity of both bus stations.

Yichang and the Three Gorges Dam

You might well end up spending a night at **YICHANG**, a transport terminus on the Yangzi 120km west from Jingzhou; Yichang marks the start of routes north to Shennongjia (see p.488), and is positioned on the rail line between Xi'an and Hunan. A commercial centre under the Han, it later became an important, if remote, treaty port, fading during the twentieth century. The recent blossoming of Yangzi tourism and the building of the Three Gorges Dam just upstream has got the place kicking again, though in Yichang itself you're limited to seeking out scattered remnants of the colonial era (for instance, the **church** just east off Yunji Lu) or taking in the animated evening river scenery, complete with moored water traffic and crowds flying kites, gorging themselves on shellfish at nearby street restaurants, or just cooling off with an ice cream.

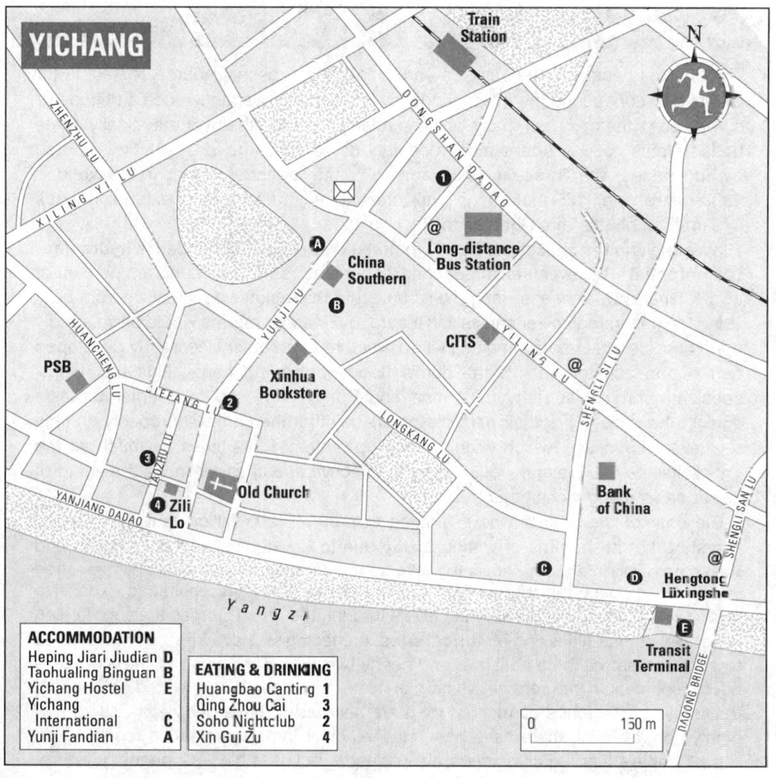

The **Three Gorges Dam** (¥105), the world's most ambitious hydropower project, is about 35km west of Yichang at **Sandouping**. A perspex-roofed bus takes you to a viewing platform overlooking the locks, ship-lift and the dam itself. Although, as most of the dam is underwater, you may wonder why you came in the first place. To reach the site, catch bus #4 in front of the train station on (northbound) Yunji Lu for nine stops, then bus #8 (¥10) to the dam – all in all, this takes about an hour and a half. The driver will tell you where to get off. From here, you can continue along the road for fifteen minutes to the ticket office or take one of the waiting taxis for ¥5. At the office you'll buy your ticket and be directed onto one of the tour buses that will take you to the three viewing areas for a rather under-whelming ninety minutes. If you're travelling on a Yangzi cruise boat, the dam may be included on your itinerary, or may be an optional extra, which can make for an easier visit.

Practicalities

Yichang stretches along the Yangzi's northern bank for around 5km, directly below the relatively small **Gezhou dam** (¥25). Arriving at **Sanxia airport**, 10km east of town, you'll need to catch a taxi into the centre (¥60). The **train station** is at the north side of town atop a broad flight of steps leading down to the intersection of Dongshan Dadao and **Yunji Lu**, while the main **long-distance bus station** is 500m to the east. Buses might terminate south across

The Three Gorges Dam

Through the centuries, the Yangzi's unruly nature has been a source of trauma for China, and conquering the river's tendency to flood extravagantly once a decade or so has been the dream of many Chinese rulers; by 2009, the river may finally come under human control. After almost a century of planning (the idea was first mooted by Sun Yatsen), the **Three Gorges Dam** will be the largest of its kind in the world, a 1983-metre-long, 185-metre-high wall creating an artificial lake extending back 670km through the Three Gorges to Chongqing.

Investment in the project has been promoted on the back of the dam's **hydroelectric potential** – the eventual output of its 26 generators will be around ten percent of all of China's power needs – and the income that the region would receive from both using the generated power and selling it abroad. Financial returns would undoubtedly bring considerable improvements in infrastructure to an otherwise poorly developed part of the country. Yet it's the dam's **flood-controlling** capabilities that blunt-speaking Communist Party front man Zhu Rongji has used to counter protests against the project. For their part, dissenters say that the dam will probably do little to prevent flooding – which occurs along downstream tributaries as much as the Yangzi itself – and claim it would be more effective and cheaper to build a string of lesser dams along these other rivers.

The cost of the project was estimated at around ¥205 billion, but had already overshot that at the time of writing, partly due to developers pocketing funds and then employing inferior materials to make up the shortfall – a practice which resulted in **cracks** appearing in the wall and locks in winter 2001, necessitating expensive repairs. In addition, increased water levels through the Three Gorges are submerging dozens of communities and **historical sites**. Archeologists have frantically scrambled to excavate as much as possible, and nearly two million residents of the area have been relocated, a programme which has itself been costly (aggravated by the fact that some of the funds earmarked for it are believed to have been embezzled) and highly controversial; there have been clashes involving transmigrants resettling on other people's lands. Ecologically, the project is indefensible – Chongqing, one of China's most heavily industrial cities, pours its effluent directly into the new lake, while even the Chinese government admits that siltation will make the dam unusable within seventy years unless they come up with a solution.

town at the riverside **Dagong Bridge Transit Terminal**, which is also where **Yangzi ferries** pull in. Arrival by **hydrofoil** from Chongqing lands you about 5km northwest of town where bus #3 awaits. The train station and Dagong Bridge area are connected by buses #3 and #4 available at Yunji Lu and the waterfront. A **taxi** costs a fixed ¥5 in to the city centre.

Yichang's **accommodation** is generally a little overpriced in summer, but is a bargain out of season. The *Heping Jiari Jiudian* (Ⓣ0717/6254000; ❺) offers comfortable rooms close to the ferry terminal, while nearby is a more upmarket affair, the *Yichang International Hotel* on the corner of Yanjiang Dadao and Shengli Si Lu (Ⓣ0717/6222888, Ⓦwww.ycinthotel.com; ❻), which has its own brewery, a revolving restaurant and 24-hour café. Equally smart is the *Taohualing Binguan* (Ⓣ0717/6236666, Ⓔthlhotel@yc.cninfo.net; ❼), set in quiet grounds off Yunji Lu. A little further up at 8 Yunji Lu is the *Yunji Fandian* (Ⓣ0717/6443104, Ⓕ6448151; ❹), which has some twin rooms and newer, more comfortable, doubles, some of which enjoy views over the park behind. Alternatively, there's the no-frills **hostel** (❶) on the third floor of the terminal building, dorm beds ¥30.

There are some good, cheap local eateries on Guo Yuan Yi Lu, first left if left out of the bus station. Try the *Huangbao Canting*, a friendly, family-run

▲ Three Gorges Dam

business with all its fresh ingredients temptingly on display for your perusal; the *suantai larou* (garlic shoots and smoked pork) is particularly good. The southern Chinese medicinal favourite *zhou* – so-called rice "porridge" – is available in abundance at *Qing Zhou Cai* at the southern end of Yunji Lu with dishes ranging from ¥3 to ¥30, or you can head to one of the zhou shops on Zili Lu where you won't pay more than ¥5 for any of the varieties on offer. The liver and spinach is a good pick-me-up. For Western fare, try the *Xin Gui Zu* coffee and steak house, also at the southern end of Yunji Lu where steak set meals start at ¥28. As far as nightlife is concerned, the city's heartbeat is the *Soho Nightclub* on Yunji Lu, just north of the junction with Jiefang Lu. Live acts and loud music pack this place out most nights, though service is appalling as the bar staff spend

Moving on from Yichang

Leaving Yichang, you can arrange plane, ferry and train **tickets** at accommodation tour desks; the one at the *Yichang International Hotel* is the best for foreigners. They also book **tours** of the Three Gorges, Shennongjia, and Zhangjiajie, as do CITS on Yiling Lu (Ⓣ0717/6220837, Ⓕ6220973) – a fairly helpful bunch – and Hengtong Lüxingshe (Ⓣ0717/6222714, Ⓕ6224860) next to the Dagong Bridge Transit Terminal.

Ferry departure times upstream to Chongqing are posted on a board beside the Dagong Bridge Terminal booking office – see p.907 for more about classes and conditions. The **hydrofoil** up through the Three Gorges to Chongqing (11hr; ¥480) departs daily at 7am from above the Gezhou Dam, 5km northwest of town – catch bus #3 or a taxi.

Yichang's **long-distance bus station** has an English-speaking information desk, a **left-luggage** office which stays open until 8pm, and departures to almost everywhere between Chongqing and Shanghai. Xingshan, Xiangfan, Jingzhou and Wuhan are also reachable by minibuses from the bus-station forecourt.

The airport is a ¥60 taxi ride east of town, with flights to Beijing, Chongqing, Guangzhou and Shanghai. China Southern's office (Ⓣ0717/6251538) is opposite the Yunji Fandian on Yunji Lu. If you're travelling by train, it's a smooth ride up to Xiangfan and points north, or south to Zhangjiajie in Hunan; it's easy enough to acquire tickets at the new station.

most of their time playing drinking games with the more moneyed patrons. Er Ma Lu, west of the Old Church, is home to a collection of coffee shops and bars that are home to a trickle of local custom. The main **Bank of China** is on Shengli Si Lu, while the **post office** is at the junction of Yunji Lu and Yiling Lu. There are **Internet cafés** on Yiling Lu with a much more comfortable one just south of there on Yiling Lu.

Shennongjia Forest Reserve

Hidden away 200km northwest of Yichang in Hubei's far west, **Shennongjia Forest Reserve** encloses a rugged chain of mountains, culminating in the 3053-metre-high **Da Shennongjia**, the tallest peak in central China. Botanically, this is one of the country's richest corners, famed for its plantlife ever since the Taoist immortal and legendary Xia king **Shennong** – also credited with introducing mankind to farming, medicine and tea – scoured these heights for herbs. More recently, the botanist **Ernest Wilson** found several new species for London's Kew Gardens here in the early twentieth century. Intriguingly, Shennongjia has since hosted sightings of the **Chinese wild man**, whose existence seems far from impossible in this stronghold of ancient plants – but even if he eludes you, there's a good chance of seeing endangered **golden monkeys** here.

Excluded from many tourist agendas, Shennongjia is easy to reach from Yichang – three days is sufficient for a quick return trip – though most of the region is actually **off limits to foreigners**. Chinese maps highlight the central **Shennongjia town** (known locally as **Songbai** or **Songbo**) as an access point: arrive here and you will be arrested, fined and booted out by the PSB. Unless the authorities have a change of heart (enquire at Yichang's PSB or CITS about this), it isn't possible for foreigners to continue north to Shiyan and Wudang Shan, however easy this appears on a map. If you stick to the open area around the village of **Muyu Zhen**, however, you'll have a trouble-free trip; just

Shennongjia Forest Reserve

Muyu Zhen	木鱼镇	*mùyú zhèn*
Shennong Resort	神农山庄	*shénnóng shānzhuāng*
Songbai	松柏	*sōngbǎi*
Xingshan	兴山	*xīngshān*
Yumingshan Binguan	玉名山宾馆	*yùmíngshān bīnguǎn*
Shennongjia Forest Reserve	神农架林区	*shénnóngjià línqū*
Banbi Yan	板壁岩	*bǎnbì yán*
Dalong Tan	大龙潭	*dàlóng tán*
Fengjing Ya	风京垭	*fēngjīng yà*
Jinhou Ling	金猴岭	*jīnhóu lǐng*
Reserve Gates	鸭子口	*yāzi kǒu*
Xiaolong Tan	小龙潭	*xiǎolóng tán*
Wildlife		
Giant salamander	娃娃鱼	*wáwá yú*
Golden monkey	金丝猴	*jīnsīhóu*
Golden pheasant	红胸锦鸟	*hóngxiōng jǐnniǎo*
Temminck's tragopan	红胸角雉	*hóngxiōng juézhì*

remember that its altitude makes the region very cold in winter, and the reserve can be **snowbound** between November and May.

To Muyu Zhen and the reserve

Minibuses from outside Yichang's bus station leave every thirty minutes between dawn and mid-afternoon for the four-hour run to **XINGSHAN** (¥45), most of this on a decent road climbing through well-farmed, increasingly mountainous country overloaded with hydroelectric stations. Xingshan itself is an unpleasant industrial town; turn right out of the bus station and walk 100m up to a crossroads and you'll find battered **minibuses** to Muyu Zhen (¥10) waiting to fill up with passengers for the final two-hour stretch up the Songbai road.

MUYU ZHEN – also known as **Muyu** or **Yuzhen** – is a service centre 17km south of the reserve, a 500-metre-long street of small stores, guesthouses and canteens leading off the main road. It's a good base for a quick visit, though there's cheaper accommodation inside the reserve if you're planning on staying a while. Muyu's **hotels** are surprisingly upmarket: at the far end of the street, the *Yumingshan Binguan* (☎0719/3453088; ❺) has spacious doubles and a fair restaurant. The exclusive *Shennong Resort* (☎0719/3452513; ❻) is clearly visible on the hill above. For **maps and tours** of the reserve, drop into Muyu's **Forestry Office Travel Service,** about 100m before *Yumingshan Binguan* – look for the "Shennongjia Natural Reserve" sign on the left. Some staff here speak English, and can advise on the best places to find unusual plants and animals – hiring a car and interpreter for the day will cost ¥400. To reach the reserve on your own, either flag down Songbai-bound buses on the main road (note that the reserve gates here are as far up this road as foreigners are allowed to travel) or bargain with the Xingshan minibus drivers for a charter (about ¥50 to the reserve gates, or ¥300 for the day), who otherwise run **back to Xingshan** until the afternoon.

Around the reserve

The steep and twisting Songbai road continues north of Muyu Zhen to a checkpoint marking the **reserve gates**, where you hand over the ¥60 entry fee and add your name to the list of the few foreigners who make it here each year. From here, 6km of gravel track runs southwest up a once-logged valley to the couple of wooden Forestry Department buildings that comprise **XIAOLONG TAN**, a place to get **beds** (¥50), meals and close-up views of golden monkeys – if any have been brought to the "animal hospital" here. There's also a **Wild Man museum**, where paintings, newspaper clippings, maps and casts of footprints document all known encounters with the gigantic, shaggy, red-haired *ye ren*, first seen in 1924. The creature was most recently spotted in June 2003 by a party of six, including a local reporter, who described the beast as being 1.65 metres tall, of greyish hue, with shoulder-length hair and a footprint measuring some twelve inches.

There are some good **walking tracks** around Xiaolong Tan, though you'll need advice from Forestry staff on current conditions. One route (much of it along a vehicle track) climbs south, for around 2.5km, to a forest of China firs on the slopes of **Jinhou Ling** (Golden Monkey Peak), a prime spot to catch family groups of **golden monkeys** foraging first thing in the morning. Favouring green leaves, stems, flowers and fruit, the monkeys live through the winter on **lichen** and moss, which cover the trees here. The males especially are a tremendous sight, with reddish-gold fur, light blue faces, huge lips and no visible nose. A far rougher trail continues to the top of the mountain in four hours, which you'd be ill-advised to tackle without a guide. Alternatively, a more relaxed, 3km stroll north of Xiaolong Tan is **Dalong Tan**, a cluster of run-down huts by a stream (reputedly inhabited by giant salamanders), from where there's an undemanding eight-kilometre walk up the valley to **Guanyin Cave**. Most of this is through open country, which gets plenty of wildflowers in the spring; birders can spot **golden pheasants** and the splendidly coloured, grouse-like **tragopans**.

Worth the scenery alone, the gravel road from Xiaolong Tan curves westwards up the valley, climbing almost continually along the ridges and, in clear weather, affords spectacular views. On the way, you'll cross Da Shennongjia, though the rounded peak is barely noticeable above the already high road. Better are the cliffscapes about 10km along at **Fengjing Ya** and **Jinzi Yanya**, and the "forest" of limestone spires where the road finally gives up the ghost 17km due west of Xiaolong Tan at **Banbi Yan**.

Wudang Shan

Hubei's river plains extend well into the province's northwest, where they reluctantly cede to mountain ranges butting up against Henan, Shaanxi and Sichuan. The region's peaks are steeped in legends surrounding **Wudang Shan**, the Military Mountain, known for its Taoist temples and fighting style. An easy ascent, coupled with the mountain's splendid scenery and the availability of transport from Wuhan, Xi'an and Yichang, make the journey worthwhile.

Wudang Shan's 72 pinnacles have, since Tang times, been liberally covered in **Taoist temples**. Those that survived a wave of thirteenth-century revolts were restored following proclamations for the development of religion under the Ming emperor **Cheng Zi** in 1413 – the work took three hundred thousand labourers ten years to complete – and the mountain is currently enjoying another bloom of religious fervour, with many of the temples emerging fabulously decorated and busy after decades of neglect.

Wudang Shan is also famous for its **martial arts**, which command as much respect as those of Henan's Shaolin Si (see p.299). It's said that the Song-dynasty monk **Zhang Sanfeng** developed Wudang boxing – from which *tai ji* is derived – after watching a fight between a snake and a magpie, which revealed to him the essence of *neijia*, an internal force used (in typical Taoist manner) to control "action" with "non-action". Fighting skills would also have come in handy considering the vast number of **outlaws** who've inhabited these mountains over the centuries. The rebel peasant **Li Zicheng** ammassed his forces and eventually deposed the last Ming emperor from here – there's a tablet recording the suppression of the Red Turbans on the mountain by Qing troops in 1856. More recently, the Communist **Third Front Army** found sanctuary here in 1931, after their march from Hong Lake in southern Hubei.

On a more peaceful note, Wudang Shan was also the retreat of Emperor **Zhen Wu**, who cultivated his longevity in these mountains during the fifteenth century, and whose portly statues grace many local temples. His **birthday** is celebrated locally on the third day of the third lunar month, a good time to visit the mountain. Wudang's valuable plants later attracted the attention of the sixteenth-century pharmacologist **Li Shizhen**, who included four hundred local species among the 1800 listed in his *Materia Medica*, still a important reference work on the medicinal use of Chinese herbs.

Wudang Shan

Shiyan	十堰	*shíyàn*
Wudang Shan Town	武当山市镇	*wǔdāngshān shìzhèn*
Taishan Miao	泰山庙	*tàishān miào*
Xuanwu Jiudian	玄武酒店	*xuánwǔ jiǔdiàn*
Yuxu Gong	玉虚宫	*yùxū gōng*
Wudang Shan	武当山	*wǔdāng shān*
Feisheng Rock	飞升岩	*fēishēng yán*
Huangjing Hall	皇经堂	*huángjīng táng*
Huanglong Dong	黄龙洞	*huánglóng dòng*
Jindian Gong	金殿宫	*jīndiàn gōng*
Lang Mei Xian Ci	榔梅仙祠	*lángméi xiāncí*
Nanyan Binguan	南岩宾馆	*nányán bīnguǎn*
Nanyan Gong	南岩宫	*nányán gōng*
Santian Men	三天门	*sāntiān mén*
Taihe Gong	太和宫	*tàihé gōng*
Zixiao Gong	紫霄宫	*zǐxiāo gōng*
Xiangfan	襄樊	*xiāngfán*

Wudang Shan town

About 120km west of **Xiangfan**, a manufacturing town and transport hub on the Hanshui River, road and rail converge at the small market town of **WUDANG SHAN**, with the mountain range rising immediately to the south. There are buses here until late afternoon and daily trains from Xiangfan, or you can leave transport 25km farther west at the city of **Shiyan** and catch a minibus back to Wudang Shan (¥10) from opposite Shiyan's train station.

Wudang Shan town is just a few muddy backstreets south of the 500-metre-long main road. *Xuanwu Jiudian* (☎0719/5666013; ❸), on the main street opposite the bus station, is the pick of the **accommodation**, with some cheap rooms and more expensive refurbished twins, as well as a decent restaurant. You'll also find the **Bank of China** and a supermarket in town.

If you're at a loose end, look south into the backstreets beside the bus station, and you'll see a road which passes under a railway arch; follow it down and on the left before the arch you'll find **Taishan Miao** (¥2), a small temple museum whose eccentric exhibits include a hefty bronze model of Jindian Gong (see opposite), and an illustrated medical scroll describing how the phases of the moon affect different organs. Heading on under the railway arch brings you to **Yuxu Gong** (¥2), the largest temple complex at Wudang Shan before it burnt down in 1745; it's now just a few vegetated pavilions, staircases and wells scattered around a flagstoned area the size of a couple of soccer pitches.

The mountain

It's possible to **hike** from town to the summit in about eight hours – the footpath starts near the train station – though most people catch one of the ubiquitous **minibuses** (¥10) to the roadhead three-quarters of the way up near Nanyan Gong. There's a stop at the **park gates** outside town to pay the inevitable entrance fee (around ¥147, including entry to temples on the mountain and a refundable deposit of ¥20 on safe return of yourself), then drivers tear up past stark fields, outlying temples and martial-arts schools to where the road ends amid a cluster of hotels, sword shops and parked vehicles. You can buy **maps** of the area here. Bear in mind that if you're

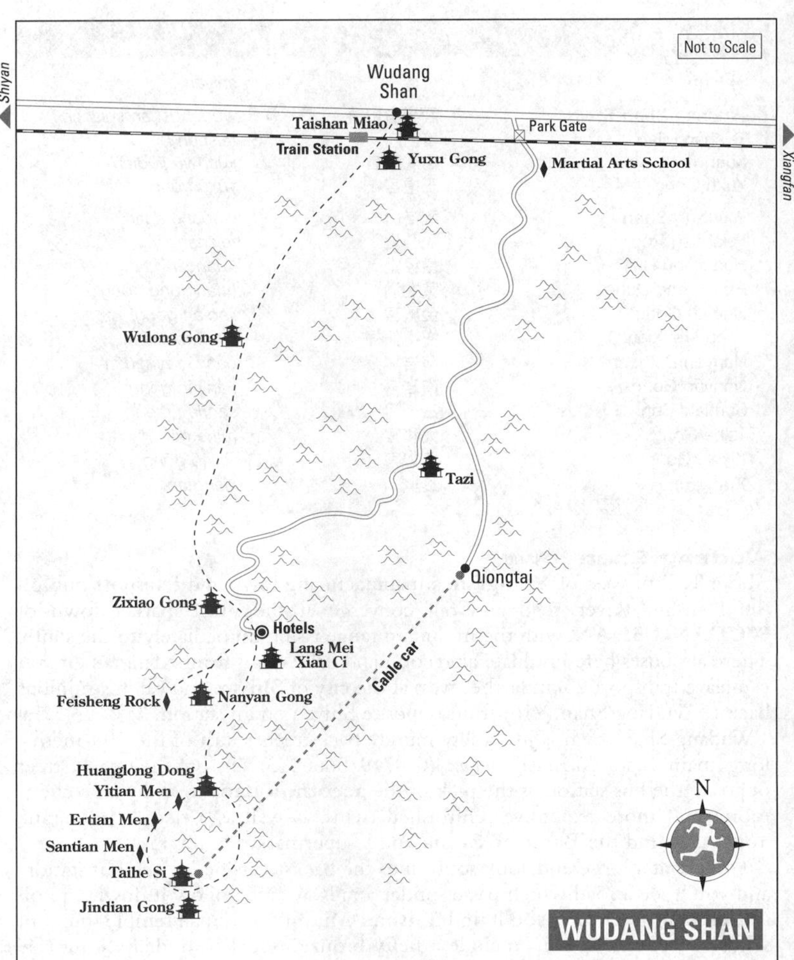

visiting between December and March the road may be snowbound, in which case minibuses won't run, and you'll have to walk the whole lot or try to bargain with a motorbike taxi to take you as far as possible. Another option is to take a minibus (¥70) to the cable car at Qiongtai (¥80 return), which then speeds you up to the summit.

Places to stay are generally expensive for what they offer, and you'll need to thoroughly check out the room and availability of hot water before bargaining. There are several smaller, cheap hotels, though their hot-water situation tends to be sketchy. Reasonable deals can be found at the large *Nanyan Binguan* (Ⓣ0719/5689182; ❹) at the very end of the road, or, slightly lower down, *Baihui Shanzhuang* (Ⓣ0719/5689191; ❺). There's also a **hostel** (dorm beds ¥25) just outside the temple gates on Tianzhu Peak; Chinese-speakers will find the monks' company well worth enduring the spartan facilities.

Nanyan Gong and Zixiao Gong

A path from the hotel area leads, via several Tang-dynasty ruins and long views down onto the plains, to **Nanyan Gong**, perched fortress-like on a precipice. The halls are tiny and austere, carved as they are out of the cliff face, but the main sight here is **Dragon Head Rock**, a two-metre-long slab sculpted with swirls and scales, which projects straight out over the void. Before it was walled off, countless people lost their lives trying to walk to the end with a stick of incense. Carry on past the temple to **Feisheng Rock** for far safer views of the scenery.

About 3km downhill from the end of the road – you'll have seen it in passing – is **Zixiao Gong**, the Purple Cloud Palace, an impressively huge early-Ming temple complex whose pattern of successively higher platforms appears to mimic the structure of the hills above. Pleasantly active with monks, tourists and the occasional mendicant traveller, the place is becoming the mountain's most important single monastery. Through the gates, a broad stone staircase climbs between boxy Tang pavilions housing massive stone tortoises to the **main hall**, whose exterior is lightened by the graceful sweep of its tiled roof. Inside is a rare wooden spiral cupola and a benevolent statue of the Yellow Emperor; surrounding courtyards are sometimes used for martial-arts displays.

Tianzhu

It takes around two hours to walk from the hotel area to the top of **Tianzhu Peak** (the highest here, at 1600m) along a comfortably paved path (a waterproof or umbrella may come in handy as protection against Wudang Shan's famously unpredictable weather). One way to keep your mind off the flight of steps is by watching out for the colourful variety of birds in the forest, including boisterous red-billed magpies with graceful blue tails, and magnificent golden pheasants. You'll soon arrive at **Lang Mei Xian Ci**, a small shrine dedicated to Zhang Sanfeng and his contribution to Chinese martial arts – there's a statue of him along with a cast-iron halberd in one hall, and Chinese-only accounts of his development of Wudang boxing in adjoining rooms.

Halfway up to Tianzhu the path divides at **Huanglong Dong** (Yellow Dragon Cave) to form an eventual circuit via the peak; continue straight ahead for the least taxing walk with superb views through the canopy of cloud-swept, apparently unscalable cliffs. A surprisingly short time later you'll find yourself on top of them, outside the encircling wall which has turned Tianzhu and its temples into a well-defended citadel. Inside, the Ming-dynasty **Taihe Si** is impressive for the atmosphere of grand decay enclosed by the thick green tiles and red walls of **Huangjing Hall**, where monks stand around the cramped stone courtyards or pray in the richly decorated, peeling rooms squeezed inside. From here you can ascend the unbelievably steep **Jiuliandeng** (Nine-section Staircase) to where the mountain is literally crowned by **Jindian Gong** (Golden Palace Temple), a tiny shrine with a gilded bronze roof embellished with cranes and deer, whose interior is filled by a statue of armour-clad Zhen Wu sitting behind a desk in judgement. Views from the front terrace (clearest in the morning) look down from the top of the world, with sharp crags dropping away through wispy clouds into the forest below. For an alternative descent, follow the stairs off Jindian Gong's rear terrace, which return to Huanglong Dong down some very rickety steps via **Santian Men**, the Three Sky Gates.

Hunan

For many travellers, their experience of **Hunan** is a pastiche of the tourist image of rural China – a view of endless muddy tracts or paddy fields rolling past the train window, coloured green or gold depending on the season. But the bland countryside, or rather the peasants farming it, has greatly affected the country's recent history. Hunan's most famous peasant son, **Mao Zedong**, saw the crushing poverty inflicted on local farmers by landlords and a corrupt government, and the brutality with which any protests were suppressed. Though Mao is no longer accorded his former god-like status, monuments to him litter the landscape around the provincial capital **Changsha**, which is a convenient base for exploring the areas where he spent his youth. By contrast, the historical town of **Yueyang** in northern Hunan, where the Yangzi meanders past **Dongting Hu**, China's second largest lake, offers more genteel attractions. Both Hunan and Hubei – literally "south of the lake" and "north of the lake" respectively – take their names from this vast expanse of water, which is intricately linked to the origins of **dragon-boat racing**. South of Changsha, **Heng Shan** houses a pleasant assortment of mountain temples, while **Wulingyuan Scenic Reserve** in the far west boasts inspiringly rugged landscapes. A few hours south of here lies the picturesque historic town of **Fenghuang**, where you'll find remnants of the **Southern Great Wall**.

Changsha and around

There's little evidence to show that the site of **CHANGSHA**, Hunan's tidy, nondescript capital, has in fact been inhabited for three thousand years, though it has long been an important river town and, prior to Qin invasions in 280 BC, was the southern capital of the kingdom of **Chu**. Changsha was declared a treaty port in 1903, though Europeans found that the Hunanese had a very short fuse (something other Chinese already knew): after the British raised the market price of rice during a famine in 1910, the foreign quarter was totally destroyed by rioting. The Guomindang torched most of what was left in 1938, following their "scorched earth" policy as they fled the Japanese advance, and recent modernization has claimed the rest. While ancient sites and objects occasionally surface nearby – such as Shang-era bronze wine jars, and the magnificently preserved contents of three **Han burial mounds** – their presence is swamped by busy clover-leaf intersections, grey concrete facades and other trappings of modern urban China.

Primarily, though, Changsha is known for its links with **Mao**. He arrived here at the age of eighteen from his native Shaoshan as nationwide power struggles erupted following the Manchu dynasty's fall in 1911 and decided to put aside his university studies to spend six months in the local militia. After Mao returned to university in 1913, Changsha became a breeding ground for secret political societies and intellectuals; by 1918 there was a real movement for Hunan to become an independent state. For a time, this idea found favour with the local warlord **Zhao Hendi**, though he soon turned violently on his supporters. Mao, then back in Shaoshan heading a Communist Party branch and leading peasant protests, was singled out and fled to Guangzhou in 1925 to take up a teaching post at the Peasant Movement Training Institute. Within three years he would return to Hunan to organize the abortive **Autumn Harvest Uprising** and establish guerrilla bases in rural Jiangxi.

Mao was by no means the only young Hunanese caught up in these events, and a number of his contemporaries later surfaced in the Communist government: **Liu Shaoqi**, Mao's deputy until he became a victim of the Cultural Revolution; four Politburo members under Deng Xiaoping, including the former CCP chief, **Hu Yaobang**; and **Hua Guofeng**, Mao's lookalike and briefly empowered successor. Today, several of Changsha's formal attractions involve the Chairman, though there are also some parks to wander around, and a fascinating **Provincial Museum**. Possible day-trips from Changsha include Mao's birthplace at **Shaoshan**, 90km to the southwest, and the famous tower at **Yueyang** (see p.501), 120km to the north, both of which are easily reached by local rail.

Arrival and city transport

The bulk of Changsha is spread east of the **Xiang River**, and the city's name – literally "Long Sand" – derives from a narrow midstream bar, now called **Juzi**

Changsha and around

Changsha	长沙	*chángshā*
Aiwan Ting	爱晚亭	*àiwǎn tíng*
Hunan Provincial Museum	湖南省博物馆	*húnánshěng bówùguǎn*
Hunan University	湖南大学	*húnán dàxué*
Juzi Dao	桔子岛	*júzi dǎo*
Martyrs' Park	烈士公园	*lièshì gōngyuán*
Qingshui Tang	清水潭	*qīngshuǐ tán*
Wangxiang Ting	望乡亭	*wàngxiāng tíng*
Yuelu Academy	岳麓书院	*yuèlù shūyuàn*
Yuelu Shan	岳麓山	*yuèlù shān*
Accommodation		
Civil Aviation	民航大酒店	*mínháng dàjiǔdiàn*
Didu	地都大酒店	*dìdū dàjiǔdiàn*
Dolton	通程国际大酒店	*tōngchéng guójì dàjiǔdiàn*
Lianjing Jiudian	联京酒店	*liánjīng jiǔdiàn*
Milkyway Hotel	银河大酒店	*yínhé dàjiǔdiàn*
Purple Gold Dragon	紫金龙大酒店	*zǐjīnlóng dàjiǔdiàn*
Taicheng	泰成大酒店	*tàichéng dàjiǔdiàn*
Eating		
Chaozhou Caiguan	潮州菜馆	*cháozhōu càiguǎn*
Dong Lai Shun	东来顺	*dōnglái shùn*
Fire Palace	火宫饭店	*huǒgōng fàndiàn*
Gaximu Canting	咖稀穆餐厅	*jiāxīmù cāntīng*
Laobaixing Canting	老百姓餐厅	*lǎobǎixìng cāntīng*
Xinhua Lou	新华楼	*xīnhuá lóu*
Shaoshan	韶山	*sháoshān*
Dishui Dong	滴水洞	*dīshuǐ dòng*
Mao Ancestral Temple	毛氏宗祠	*máoshì zōngcí*
Mao Zedong Exhibition Hall	毛泽东纪念馆	*máozédōng jìniànguǎn*
Mao's Family Home	毛泽东故居	*máozédōng gùjū*
Shaoshan Binguan	韶山宾馆	*sháoshān bīnguǎn*

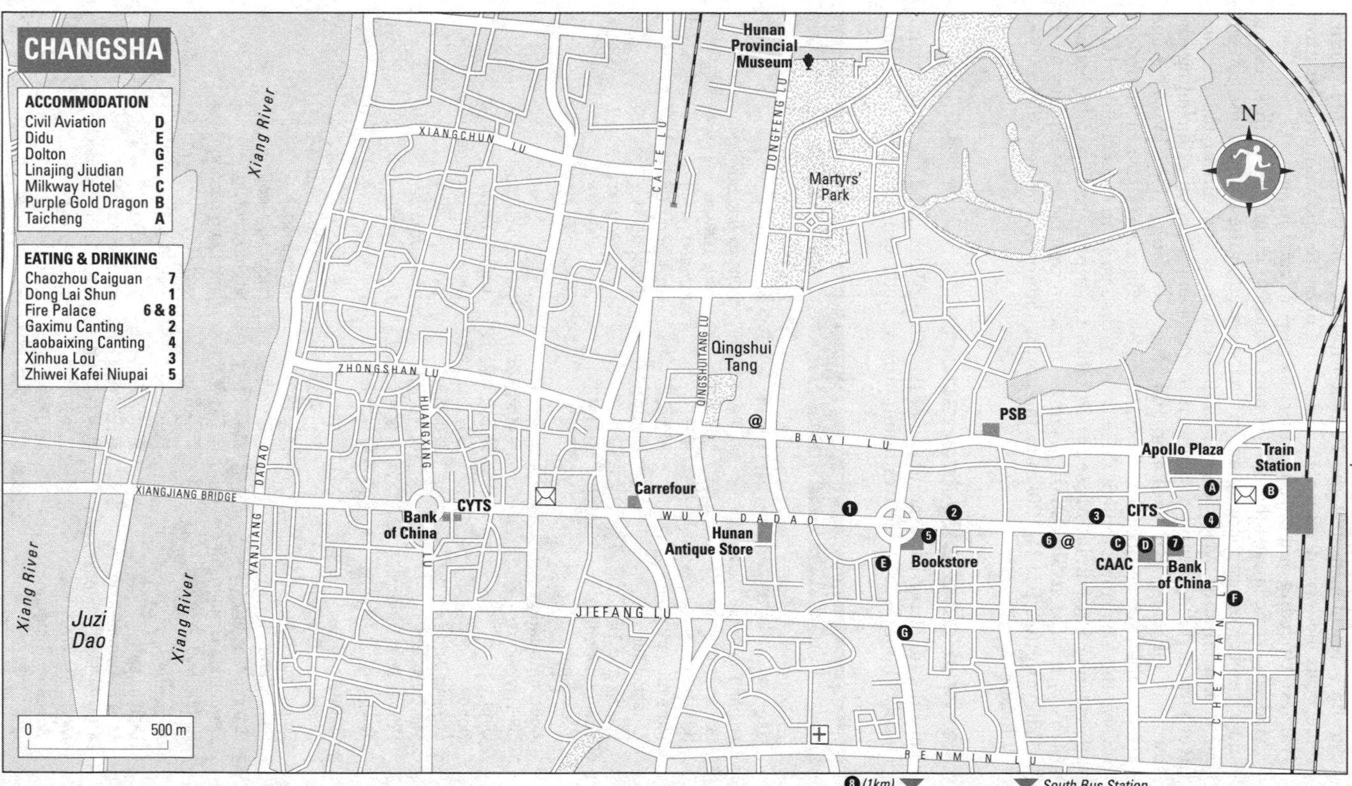
CHANGSHA
ACCOMMODATION
Civil Aviation D
Didu E
Dolton G
Linajing Jiudian F
Milkway Hotel C
Purple Gold Dragon B
Taicheng A
EATING & DRINKING
Chaozhou Caiguan 7
Dong Lai Shun 1
Fire Palace 6 & 8
Gaximu Canting 2
Laobaixing Canting 4
Xinhua Lou 3
Zhiwei Kafei Niupai 5
Hunan Provincial Museum
Martyrs' Park
Qingshui Tang
PSB
Apollo Plaza
Train Station
CITS
CAAC
Bank of China
Bookstore
Hunan Antique Store
Carrefour
CYTS
Bank of China
Xiang River
Xiang River
Xiang River
Juzi Dao
XIANGCHUN LU
CAI'E LU
DONGFENG LU
QINGSHUITANG LU
ZHONGSHAN LU
HUANGXING LU
BAYI LU
WUYI DADAO
XIANGJIANG BRIDGE
YANJIANG DADAO
JIEFANG LU
CHEZHAN LU
RENMIN LU
West Bus Station & Hunan University
Airport & East Bus Station
South Bus Station
8 (1km)
0 500 m
N

Moving on from Changsha

There are **flights** from Changsha to Hefei, Yichang, Zhangjiajie, Shanghai, Beijing, and everywhere else between Hong Kong and Ürümqi. Between 7am and 9pm there are half-hourly buses to the airport from the **airline office**, west of the *Civil Aviation* hotel on Wuyi Dadao (daily 6.30am–8pm; ⓣ0731/4112222).

Leaving by **bus**, try the east bus station for eastern destinations, the west for western ones, and the south for southern – though the train is a better option for almost all travel. **Trains** head north from Changsha to Yueyang and Hubei province; west to Guizhou, Jishou and Zhangjiajie; east to Nanchang in Jiangxi; and south via Hengyang to Guangdong and Guangxi. There's also a special tourist train daily to Shaoshan. Currently, the fastest train to Zhangjiajie is #T358, which leaves at 6.15am and takes a mere five hours. Ticket offices are on the south side of the square (daily 6am–11pm).

Dao, Tangerine Island. The river itself is spanned by the lengthy Xiangjiang Bridge, which links the city to the west-bank suburbs, **Yuelu Academy** and parkland. **Wuyi Dadao** is Changsha's main drag and forms an unfocused downtown district as it runs broad and straight for 4km across the city.

The **airport**, 15km east of town, is connected to the airline offices on Wuyi Dadao by a **shuttle bus** (¥15). Changsha's **train station** is conveniently central at the eastern end of Wuyi Dadao, but the three main **long-distance bus stations** are all several kilometres out of town in the suburbs, and you could easily wind up at any of them; to reach the train station, catch **city bus** #126 from the east bus station (4km), bus #302 from the west bus station (8km), or bus #7 from the south bus station (10km).

Changsha's **city buses** run between about 6am and 9pm and almost all originate, or at least stop, at the train-station square. Chinese **maps** of the city, with the **bus routes** clearly marked, are easily picked up from street vendors at arrival points, which are also good places to hail a **taxi**.

Accommodation

Due to tight controls, **hotels** in Changsha that accept foreigners are, almost without exception, fairly expensive. The university aside, the following have restaurants and train- and flight-booking agents.

Civil Aviation 47 Wuyi Dadao ⓣ07312/391888, ⓕ2915800. A well-run and tidy airlines-owned operation, though reception staff are seemingly harassed and brusque. ❹

Didu 80 Shaoshan Lu ⓣ0731/4451555, ⓕ4454483. Inexpensive lodgings in a restored but now tatty 1930s building. Not listed as a foreigners' hotel but – at time of writing – had no qualms about letting them stay. Buses along Wuyi Dadao stop nearby. ❸

Dolton 159 Shaoshan Lu ⓣ0731/4168888, ⓦwww.dolton-hotel.com. The height of luxury in Changsha, a hugely opulent sprawl of marble and chandeliers, with five-star service. Worth a visit, if only to meet the over-enthusiastic doorman. ❾

Lianjing Jiudian 290 Chezhan Lu, ⓣ0731/2169218. Friendly, but slightly run-down affair, just around the corner from the train station. Warm and cheap. ❷

Milkyway Hotel 59 Wuyi Dadao ⓣ0731/4111818, ⓕ4116905. Don't be fooled by the tacky glass and chrome exterior, as the inside has had a complete overhaul. State of the art, neo-Qing decor and attentive staff make for a very pleasant stay. ❺

Purple Gold Dragon ⓣ0731/2279999, ⓕ2279978. Situated right next to the train-station exit, this popular place is good value and usually full, so it might be advisable to ring ahead if you want to flop straight into bed on arrival. ❺

Taicheng Chezhan Lu, opposite the train station ⓣ0731/2331111. This newish place has passable, standard rooms, with more comfortable ones available for not a lot more. ❸

The City

While there's little in Changsha to absorb between the sites, it's a clean, well-ordered city and people are noticeably friendly – don't be surprised if you acquire a guide while walking around. If the city's streets seem unusually empty and you're wondering where Changsha's crowds hang out, head down to the main **shopping district** west of the centre at the junction of Wuyi Dadao and **Huangxing Lu**. The latter is pedestrianized between Jiefang Lu and Chengnan Lu, to the south, and the area is loaded with shopping plazas, Western fast-food chains, and groups of teenagers orbiting between the two.

Qingshui Tang

North of Wuyi Dadao, on Bayi Lu, is **Qingshui Tang** (Clearwater Pool; daily 8am–4.45pm; ¥10; bus #113 stops outside), Mao's former home in Changsha and the site of the first local Communist Party offices. A white marble statue of Mao greets you at the gate, and the garden walls are covered with stone tablets carved with his epigrams. Near the pool itself is a scruffy vegetable patch and the reconstructed room in which Mao and his second wife, **Yang Kaihui** (daughter of Mao's stoical and influential teacher, Yang Changji), lived after moving here from Beijing following their marriage in 1921. There's also a display of peasant tools – a grindstone, thresher, carrypole and baskets – and a short history of Chinese agriculture. On the same grounds, a brightly tiled **museum** contains a low-key but interesting collection of historical artefacts, including a clay tomb figurine of a bearded horseman and a cannon that was used to defend the city against Taiping incursions in 1852. These pieces lead to a depressing photographic record of Guomindang atrocities and eulogies to Mao, Zhou Enlai and others. The three red flags here are those of the Party, the PLA and the nation.

Martyrs' Park and Hunan Provincial Museum

From Qingshui Tang, follow Qingshuitang Lu north and then turn east for 500m to the gates of **Martyrs' Park** (free). Though it's often crowded, plenty of shade, lakes as well as ornamental gardens, bridges and pagodas make the park a nice place to stroll. But the main reason to head up this way is to visit **Hunan Provincial Museum** (daily 9am–6pm; ¥20; bus #126, from the station via Wuyi Dadao, stops outside), whose entrance is on Dongfeng Lu at the park's northwestern corner. One of Changsha's highlights, the museum is dedicated solely to the Han-era tomb of **Xin Zui**, the Marquess of Dai. Xin Zui died around 160 BC, and her subterranean tomb – roughly contemporary with similar finds at Jingzhou (see p.484) and Wuhan (see p.474) – was one of three discovered in 1972 during construction work at **Mawangdui**, about 4km northeast (the others contained her husband and son). Thanks to damp-proof rammed walls of clay and charcoal, a triple wooden sarcophagus, and wrappings of linen and silk, the Marquess' **body** was so well preserved that modern pathologists were able to determine that she suffered from tuberculosis, gallstones, arteriosclerosis and bilharzia when she died at age 50. The sarcophaguses are in a side hall, while access to the mummy (after sealing your dusty shoes in plastic bags) is through a basement display of **embroideries**, lacquered bowls and coffins, musical instruments, wooden tomb figures and other funerary offerings. Taoist texts written on silk were also found in the tomb, and one piece illustrating **qigong postures** is on display. Xin Zui herself lies in a fluid-filled tank below several inches of perspex, a gruesome white doll covered from chin to thigh, with her internal organs displayed in jars.

Around the river

When crossing the river, gaze down upon semi-rural, midstream **Juzi Dao**, which was settled by the local European community after the events of 1910. Some of their former homes are still standing, though one-time mansions are now partitioned into family apartments. Legend has it that Mao regularly used to swim to shore from the southern tip of the island, a feat he repeated on his 65th birthday as one of his famous river crossings.

On the other side of the river, **Hunan University**'s campus sits south of **Yuelu Shan**, a famous breezy hilltop and beauty spot, reached from the train station on bus #202, which crosses the bridge and heads south to terminate at a square dominated by a Mao statue below **Yuelu Academy**. Paths flanked by food and souvenir stalls lead from here to the park gates (¥20), then meander uphill, making for forty minutes' stroll through pleasant woodland to **Wangxiang Ting**, a pavilion with views over the city. On the way, the small **Aiwan Ting** (Loving the Dusk Pavilion), built in 1792, was one of Mao's youthful haunts, and there's a tablet here bearing his calligraphy. The pavilion's name derives from the verse *Ascending the Hills* by the soulful Tang poet Du Mu:

A stony path winds far up cool hills
Towards cottages hidden deep amongst white clouds
Loving the maple trees at dusk I stop my cart
To sit and watch the frosted leaves
Redder than February flowers

A little west of here, **Lushan Si** dates from the Western Jin dynasty (263–316 AD), making it one of the oldest monasteries in Hunan; the enormous yew tree immediately in front of the temple is said to be of a similar age.

Eating, drinking and entertainment

A predilection for strong flavours and copious chillies places **Hunanese food** firmly inside the Western Chinese cooking belt – Mao himself claimed that it was the fiery food that made locals so (politically) red. Pungent **regional specialities** include air-cured and **chilli-smoked meat**; *dong'an* chicken, in which the shredded, poached meat is seasoned with a vinegar-soy dressing; *gualiang fen*, a gelatinous mass of cold, shaved rice noodles covered in a spicy sauce; *chou doufu* (literally "stinking tofu"), a fermented bean-curd dish which actually tastes good; and a mass of less spicy snacks – preserved eggs, pickles, buns and dumplings – that form the regular fare in town. Canteens around the train station are unusually good for these things, as are several upmarket but still inexpensive restaurants.

There's a plethora of **Western-style cafés** with the usual run of set meals and fresh brews, especially along the eastern end of Wuyi Dadao: try *Zhiwei Kafei Niupai*, near the Xinhua bookstore.

For unknown reasons, tropical **betel nut** (the areca palm's stimulating seed pod) is a popular pick-me-up here, sold either boiled and sliced for chewing, or powdered in cigarettes.

Restaurants

Chaozhou Caiguan Wuyi Dadao. Big, mid-range southern Chinese restaurant with a penchant for seafood.

Dong Lai Shun Wuyi Dadao. Muslim restaurant specializing in lamb hotpots served with pickled garlic dip; their meat is meticulously selected and tasty.

Fire Palace There are two branches of this riotously good restaurant: on Shaoshan Lu (bus #7, #202 or #104 from outside the train station), and Wuyi Dadao. The original on Shaoshan Lu is the best, and a busier, noisier, and more thoroughly enjoyable place to wolf down Hunanese food would be hard to imagine. Get an order card off the waitress, request some dark Baisha beer, and stop trolleys loaded with small plates of goodies as they pass. Stay off the à la carte menu and you'll only pay ¥2–12 a plate at either branch.
Gaximu Canting Wuyi Dadao. Another great Muslim eatery, this one a bit more upmarket and comfortable, but affordable nevertheless. There's a choice of *lamian* (stretched noodles), hefty meat skewers or dumplings. Dishes from ¥5.
Laobaixing Canting Junction of Wuyi Dadao and Chezhan Zhong Lu. This is a no-nonsense people's eatery reminiscent of the Communist canteens from revolutionary days gone by. The ¥6–7 fried rice and soup specials are great value.
Xinhua Lou Eastern end of Wuyi Dadao. Another excellent place for local dishes, with trolleys of smoked tofu and meats, crisp cold vegetables dressed in sesame oil, black-skinned-chicken soup, preserved eggs, and a huge range of dumplings being wheeled around between 6.30am and 1.30am. ¥2–10 a dish.

Listings

Banks and exchange The principal Bank of China is near the train station on Wuyi Dadao (Mon–Sat 8am–noon & 2.30–5pm). Upmarket hotels such as the *Dolton* also change traveller's cheques, and might not mind whether you're staying or not.
Bookshops Xinhua Bookstore, at the intersection of Wuyi Dadao and Shaoshan Lu, has a good selection of art books – including some on painting techniques – but slim pickings in English.
Hospital Changsha Number 2 Medical College, Renmin Lu ⓣ0731/5550400 or 5550511.
Internet access There are Internet cafés throughout the city, generally charging ¥3 an hour; a convenient option is the one on the second floor of the *Sanjiu Chunyun* hotel, while there are others near the CAAC on Wuyi Dadao and near the entrance to Qingshui Tang on Bayi Lu.
Left luggage Both the train and bus stations have left-luggage offices.
Mail and telephones The most convenient post office – with parcel post and international phones – is in the train-station square.
PSB The Foreign Affairs Department of the PSB is on Bayi Lu at its junction with Chengdao Lu (Mon–Fri 8am–noon & 2.30–5.30pm; ⓣ0731/4590788).
Shopping As you'll appreciate after visiting the Provincial Museum, Changsha has long had a reputation for silk embroidery, which you can buy at various stores along Wuyi Dadao.
Travel agents CITS are at 46 Wuyi Dadao (ⓣ0731/2280184, ⓕ2296270), and can organize tours. You can also book Chinese-oriented tours to all the aforementioned places of interest, for between ¥135–300 at the Hunan Shida Travel Service (ⓣ0731/4131177) at 1 Wuyi Dadao, opposite the train station.

Shaoshan

Mao Zedong's birthplace, the hamlet of **SHAOSHAN**, lies 90km to the southwest of Changsha, a fine day-trip from the provincial capital through the Hunanese countryside. Established as a pilgrimage site for idolatrous Red Guards during the Cultural Revolution, Shaoshan today seethes with Chinese tourists, who – following a low point in Mao's reputation through the 1980s – have started to flock back to visit the Great Helmsman's hometown. The best way to get here is on the **special train** from Changsha, which departs daily at 6.45am for the three-hour journey (¥101 return; returns from Shaoshan at 4.55pm). Alternatively, **tour buses** leave from the square outside the train station ticket office at 7am (guided day-tour ¥135).

Shaoshan contains two settlements: a knot of hotels and services that have sprung up around the railhead and long-distance bus depot, and **Shaoshan Dong**, the village itself, some 6km distant. Patriotic jingles and a large portrait of Mao greet **arrivals** at the train station, as do **minibuses** heading up to the village. Unless you're planning to stay overnight or are hungry – in which case there's a cheap **hotel** (❸) and several **restaurants** ahead and round to the right near the bus depot – you should hop on the first minibus. The first place to disembark is just before the village proper outside **Mao's Family Home** (daily 8am–5pm; free), a compound of bare adobe buildings next to a lotus-filled pond, where Mao was born on December 26, 1893. The home is neatly preserved, with a few pieces of period furniture, the odd photograph, and wonderfully turgid English explanations completing the spartan furnishings. Here he led a thoroughly normal childhood, one of four children in a relatively wealthy peasant household that comfortably survived the terrible famines in Hunan during the first decade of the twentieth century. Though a rebellious youth, it was not until he moved to Changsha in his late teens that he became politicized.

Just up the road is the huge **village square** where, next to a bronze statue of an elderly Mao and a swarm of souvenir stalls, stands the **Mao Zedong Exhibition Hall** (daily 8am–5pm; ¥15). Photos and knick-knacks here chart Mao's career, though today there's a great distinction between Mao the heroic revolutionary and the character who inflicted the Great Leap Forward – the disastrous movement which was meant to bring Chinese industrial output up to Western levels – and Cultural Revolution on his country. The exhibition reflects this: noticeable omissions include the Little Red Book, and just about any mention of the years between 1957 and his funeral in 1976. Next door to the museum is the former **Mao Ancestral Temple** (free), now a memorial to the leader's early work among the peasants here.

After his Great Leap Forward had begun to falter, Mao returned to Shaoshan in 1959 to interview peasants on the movement's shortcomings. He can't have liked what he heard; on his final visit in 1966 at the start of the Cultural Revolution, he kept himself aloof near the reservoir in a secret retreat, poetically named **Dishui Dong** (Dripping Water Cave; ¥30), to which you can catch a minibus. Alternatively, the elegant pavilion atop **Shaoshan peak** overlooks the local landscape – not really typical, given the amount of tourist revenue, but a nice scene of healthy fields and bamboo thickets.

There are a few restaurants and **places to stay** in Shaoshan village around the square, including the *Shaoshan Binguan* in the square itself, with a jumble of very ordinary rooms around an ornamental pool (Ⓣ0732/5685262; ❻).

Yueyang and Dongting Hu

YUEYANG, a major riverside city on the Beijing–Guangzhou rail line and stop for Yangzi ferries, lies 160km southwest of Wuhan and 120km north of Changsha. The city also lies on the eastern shores of **Dongting Hu**, China's second largest freshwater lake, covering 2500 square kilometres. Fringed with reeds and lotus ponds, villages farming rich cane and paddy fields surround the lake; many locals also earn a livelihood from fishing. Despite accelerating tourism and an unpleasantly down-at-heel new city springing up in the background, the impressive **Yueyang Tower** – frequently packed with Chinese tourists – and historical links to the nationwide sport of **dragon-boat racing** make Yueyang a reasonable place to spend the day in transit between Changsha and Wuhan.

Yueyang's main street, **Baling Lu**, runs west for 5km, bare, broad and numbingly straight right up to **Nanyuepo docks** on the lakeshore. Here it's crossed by **Dongting Lu**, with the Yueyang Tower and most of the services close to this junction. On Dongting Bei Lu, the **Yueyang Tower** (daily: summer 7am–6.25pm;

Yueyang and Dongting Hu

Yueyang	岳阳	*yuèyáng*
Chenglingji	城陵矶	*chénglíng jī*
Junshan Dao	君山岛	*jūnshān dǎo*
Miluo River	汨罗江	*mìluó jiāng*
Nanyuepo Docks	南越码头	*nányuè mǎtóu*
Yueyang Docks	岳阳楼客运站	*yuèyánglóu kèyùnzhàn*
Yueyang Tower	岳阳楼	*yuèyáng lóu*
Yunmeng Hotel	云梦宾馆	*yúnmèng bīnguǎn*
Dongting Hu	洞庭湖	*dòngtínghú*

winter 7.30am–5.55pm; ¥46) rises from walled ramparts overlooking Dongting Hu, but the site was originally a mere platform where the *Three Kingdoms* general **Lu Su** reviewed his troops. It was through Lu's diplomacy that the armies of his native Wu and those of Shu were united against the overwhelming forces of Wei, who were subsequently defeated in 208 AD at the Battle of the Red Cliffs (p.482). A tower was first built here in 716, but the current timber edifice, 20m tall, is of Qing design. Three upward-curving, yellow-glazed roofs are supported by huge, blood-red pillars of *nanmu* (southernwood); with its screens, eaves and crossbeams decorated with animal carvings, the tower makes a striking and brilliant spectacle. You can climb up and take in grand views of the lake, which quickly whip up into a stormy sea scene at the first breath of wind.

Flanking the tower are two lesser pavilions: **Xianmei Ting** (Immortal's Plum) – named after the delicately etched blossom design on a Ming stone tablet within – and **Sanzui Ting** (Thrice Drunk). This recalls the antics of **Lu Dongbin**, one of the Taoist Eight Immortals, who regularly visited the pavilion to down a wine gourd or two; there's a comic painting of this inside, warts and all, and an overflowing votive box. Lu is also credited with populating Dongting

Dragon boats

The former state of **Chu**, which encompassed northern Hunan, was under siege in 278 BC from the first stirrings of the ambitious Qin armies, who later brought all of China under their control. At the time, Dongting was the haunt of the exiled poet-governor **Qu Yuan**, a victim of palace politics but nonetheless a great patriot of Chu. Hearing of the imminent invasion, Qu picked up a heavy stone and drowned himself in the nearby **Miluo River** rather than see his beloved state conquered. Distraught locals raced to save him in their boats, but were too late. They returned later to scatter *zongzi* (packets of meat and sticky rice wrapped up in reeds and lotus leaves) into the river as an offering to Qu Yuan's spirit.

The **Dragon Boat Festival**, held throughout China on the fifth day of the fifth lunar month (June or July), commemorates the rowers' hopeless rush – though many historians trace the tradition of food offerings and annual boat races to long before Qu's time. At any rate, it's a festive rather than mournful occasion, with the consumption of huge quantities of steamed *zongzi* and keen **competition** between local dragon-boat teams, who can be seen practising in their narrow, powerful crafts months before the event to the steady boom of a pacing drum. It's a lively spectator sport, with crowds cheering the rowers along, but you need to be up early to get the most from the ceremonies (for example, the dedication of the dragon-headed prows) as the race itself lasts only a few minutes. In Yueyang, the race is staged on the Miluo River south of town; contact CITS for details.

Hu with shoals of silvery fish by tossing woodshavings into the water. **Xiao Qiao**, the wife of another historic general, lies buried at the northern end of the surrounding gardens, the grassy mound honoured by a tablet bearing the calligraphy of the renowned Song-dynasty poet, **Su Dongpo**.

Stores in Yueyang sell the incredibly expensive **silver needle tea**, the main produce of **Junshan Dao**, an island half an hour away by boat across the lake. Said to impart longevity, the tea was once paid in tribute to the emperor, and has tips that look like pale green twists; pour boiling water over them, inhale the musty vapour and watch them bob up and down in the glass. A spoonful of the tea sells for around ¥5.

Practicalities

Yueyang's **bus and train stations** are on opposite sides of a huge, multi-level roundabout 3km east down Baling Lu, along which you can catch **city bus** #22 to the lake and then north along Dongting Bei Lu to the Yueyang Tower – pick up a **map** on arrival. **Yangzi ferries** stop 17km north of the city at **Chenglingji**, where bus #1 connects with the train station.

The English-speaking **CITS** (daily 9–11.30am & 2–5pm; ⓣ0730/8232010), located inside the *Yunmeng Hotel* on Yunmeng Lu, can arrange tours to lakeside sights. There's a **post office** on Baling Lu towards the bus and train stations (daily 8am–6pm), and a **Bank of China** to the right from the train station on Zhanqian Lu. There's a range of places to stay around the bus and train stations and the Yueyang Tower, though it isn't worth overnighting here except during the Dragon Boat Festival.

Heng Shan

Some 120km south of Changsha, the **Heng Shan region** is one of China's holiest sites. Spread over 80km or so, the ranges form scores of low peaks dressed in woodland with a smattering of **Buddhist and Taoist temples**, some of which were established more than 1300 years ago. It's somewhere to relax and admire the scenery (frosted in winter, golden in autumn and misty year-round), either tackling the easy walks between shrines on foot, or resorting to local transport to ascend the heights.

Confusingly, it's **Nanyue**, not the nearby Hengshan Town, which marks the starting point up into the hills. Early-morning **buses** from Changsha or

Heng Shan		
Heng Shan	衡山	*héngshān*
Danxia Si	丹霞寺	*dānxiá sì*
Huangting Si	黄庭寺	*huángtíng sì*
Shangfeng Si	上封寺	*shàngfēng sì*
Xuandu Si	玄都寺	*xuándū sì*
Zhurong Gong	祝融殿	*zhùróng diàn*
Zushi Gong	祖师宫	*zǔshī gōng*
Nanyue	南岳	*nányuè*
Nanyue Damiao	南岳大庙	*nányuè dàmiào*
Zhusheng Si	祝圣寺	*zhùshèng sì*
Hengyang	衡阳	*héngyáng*

Shaoshan take around three hours to reach Nanyue via **Xiangtan**. If you're coming up from the south by road or rail from Shaoguan in Guangdong province or Guilin in Guangxi, the nearest city is **Hengyang**, where minibuses to Nanyue leave for the hour-long trip from the depot on Jiefang Lu – bus #1 connects Hengyang's nightmarishly busy **train station** with this depot, which is across the river. Alternatively, leave the train farther on at **Hengshan Town**, where regular minibuses cover the twenty-kilometre trip west to Nanyue.

Nanyue

Banners strung across the highway welcome visitors to **NANYUE** (South Mountain), a small but expanding village of old flagstoned streets and new hotels set around Nanyue Damiao and Zhusheng Si, the two largest and most architecturally impressive temple complexes in the area. The Changsha–Hengyang highway runs along the eastern side of the village, with the **bus station** at its southern (Hengyang) end, where map sellers, rickshaw drivers and hotel touts descend on new arrivals. Midway along the highway an ornamental **stone archway** forms the "entrance" to the village proper and leads through to the main street, Dongshan Lu. Here you'll find a mass of **restaurants**, whose staff will call you over as you pass – as always, avoid overcharging by establishing prices before you order. Many of these places also offer basic **accommodation** for about ¥35 a bed, but there are plenty of easy-to-find **hotels** in the vicinity (4).

Off Dongshan Lu, streets lead through the old village centre to **Nanyue Damiao** (¥15). The site has served as a place of worship since at least 725 AD – some say that it was sanctified in Qin times – but the older buildings succumbed to fire long ago and were replaced in the nineteenth century by a smaller version of Beijing's Forbidden City. It's a lively place, freshly painted, echoing with bells and thick with smoke from incense and detonating firecrackers – there are actually furnaces in the courtyards to accommodate the huge quantities offered up by the crowds. Seventy-two pillars, representing Heng Shan's peaks, support the massive wooden crossbeams of the **main hall**'s double-staged roof, and gilt phoenixes loom above the scores of kneeling worshippers paying homage to Taoist and Buddhist deities. Other halls in the surrounding gardens are far more humble but boast detailed carvings along their eaves and exterior alcoves.

Far quieter, with fewer tourists and more monks in evidence, is the monastery **Zhusheng Si**, a short walk left out of the temple gates. A purely Buddhist site originating around the same time as Nanyue, the entire monastery – whose name translates as "Imperial Blessings" – was reconstructed for the anticipated visit of **Emperor Kangxi** in 1705, but he never showed up. The smaller scale and lack of pretence here contrast with Nanyue's extravagances, though there's a series of five hundred engravings of Buddhist *arhat*s set into the wall of the rear hall, and a fine multi-faced and many-handed likeness of **Guanyin** to seek out among the charming courtyards.

In the hills

There's a good day's walking to be had between Nanyue and **Zhurong Gong**, a hall perched 15km from town on Heng Shan's 1290-metre apex. Even major temples along the way are small and unassuming, requiring little time to explore, and tracks are easy, so around eight hours should be sufficient for a return hike along the most direct route – though you'd need at least ten hours to see everything on the mountain. **Minibuses** run between Nanyue and Shangfeng Si, below the summit, in under an hour (¥10). **Food stalls** lurk at strategic points, so there's no need to carry much beyond something to keep out any seasonally inclement weather at the top.

Take the main road through Nanyue to the park gates behind Nanyue Damiao, where the **admission fee** (¥102) covers entry to all temples and includes a bilingual **map** of the mountain. The first two hours are spent passing occasional groups of descending tourists and black-clad Taoist mendicants, as the road weaves past rivers and patches of farmland before reaching the temple-like **Martyrs' Memorial Hall**, built to commemorate those killed during the 1911 revolution. Entering pine forests shortly thereafter, you'll find **Xuandu Si**, which marks the halfway point (it's also known as the Midway Monastery) and is Hunan's Taoist centre, founded around 700 AD. Even so, an occasional Buddhist saint graces side shrines, but the best feature is the unusually domed ceiling in the second hall, watched over by a statue of Lao Zi holding a pill of immortality.

The rest of the ascent passes a handful of functioning, day-to-day temples with monks and nuns wandering around the gardens – **Danxia Si** and **Zushi Gong** are larger than most – before arriving outside **Shangfeng Si**'s red timber halls, which mark the minibus terminus. Overpriced **hotels** cater to those hoping to catch the dawn from the **sunrise-watching terrace**, a short walk away below a radio tower. On a cloudy day, it's more worthwhile pushing on for a further twenty minutes to the summit, where **Zhurong Gong**, a tiny temple built almost entirely of heavy stone blocks and blackened inside from incense smoke, looks very atmospheric as it emerges from the mist. For the descent, there's always the bus, or an alternative track (shown on local maps) from Xuandu Si which takes in Lingzhi spring, the Mirror Grinding Terrace and the bulky Nantai Monastery, before winding back to town past the quiet halls of **Huangting Si**, another sizeable Taoist shrine.

Wulingyuan (Zhangjiajie)

Hidden away in the northwestern extremities of Hunan, **Wulingyuan Scenic Reserve** (widely known as **Zhangjiajie**) protects a mystical landscape of sandstone shelves and fragmented limestone towers, often misted in low clouds and scored by countless streams, with practically every horizontal surface hidden under a primeval, subtropical green mantle. Among the 550-odd tree species (twice Europe's total) within its 370 square kilometres are rare dove trees, ginkgos and **dawn redwoods**, the last identified by their stringy bark and feathery leaves; now popular as an ornamental tree, until 1948 they were believed to be extinct. The **wildlife** list is impressive, too, including civets, giant salamanders, monkeys and gamebirds. The region is also home to several million ethnic **Tujia**, said by some to be the last descendants of western China's mysterious prehistoric Ba kingdom. On the downside, despite the UNESCO World Heritage listing, a total fire ban (smoking included) and a generous number of erosion-resistant paths, Wulingyuan is beginning to suffer from its popularity – more accessible parts of the reserve are often almost invisible under hordes of litter-hurling tour groups, and the admission fee has reached an exorbitant ¥160.

Practicalities

Most visitors base themselves on the southern boundaries of the reserve at **Zhangjiajie village**, where there's certainly enough to keep you occupied for a few days. It's also possible to organize extended walks north to **Tianzi Mountain**, or east to the **Suoxi Valley**. There are villages and stalls along the

Wulingyuan (Zhangjiajie)

Wulingyuan Scenic Reserve	武陵源风景区	*wǔlíngyuán fēngjǐngqū*
Baofeng Hu	宝峰湖	*bǎofēng hú*
Bewitching Terrace	迷魂台	*míhún tái*
Black Dragon Village	黑龙寨	*hēilóng zhài*
Huanglong Dong	黄龙洞	*huánglóng dòng*
Huangshi Village	黄石寨	*huángshí zhài*
Immortals' Bridge	仙人桥	*xiānrén qiáo*
Shentangwan	神堂湾	*shéntáng wān*
Suoxi Village	索溪峪镇	*suǒxīyù zhèn*
Ten-li Corridor	十里画廊	*shílǐ huàláng*
Tianzi Shan village	天子山镇	*tiānzǐ shānzhèn*
Zhangjiajie Shi	张家界市	*zhāngjiājiè shī*
Wuling Binguan	武陵宾馆	*wǔlíng bīnguǎn*
Zhangjiajie village	张家界国家森林公园管理处	*zhāngjiājiè guójiā sēnlín gōngyuán guǎnlǐchù*
Minsu Shanzhuang	民俗山庄	*mínsú shānzhuāng*
Xiangdian Shanzhuang	香殿山庄	*xiāngdiàn shānzhuāng*

way supplying accommodation and food, but take water and snacks on long journeys. You'll need comfortable walking shoes and the right seasonal dress – it's humid in summer, cold from late autumn, and the area is often covered in light snow early in the year.

Note that **accommodation prices** double at weekends and holidays, when crowds are at their worst and train tickets are in short supply; if you can, try to avoid these times. If you're on a Chinese package **tour** to Wulingyuan, beware if they try to sting you an extra ¥50–100 based on a supposedly higher foreigners' entrance fee to the reserve: there's no discriminatory pricing here. If the tour staff won't back down, tell them you'll pay the surcharge yourself at the gates.

Zhangjiajie Shi

ZHANGJIAJIE SHI is the regional hub, 33km south of the reserve. The **bus station** is fairly central, but the **train station** and ticket office are a further 9km south, and the **airport** is a similar distance to the west. **Minibuses** prowl arrival points for the hour-long journey to the reserve at either Zhangjiajie village (¥6) or Suoxi (¥10).

It's only worth staying here if you arrive too late to get the last bus to the park (around 7pm). There are a host of mediocre hotels in town – the *Wuling Binguan* is the best of these (Ⓣ0744/82226302; ⑥).

Leaving, there are regular buses covering the journey to Changsha and down to Jishou for Fenghuang. **Trains** are faster; there are direct services east to Changsha, north to Yichang in Hubei, and south to Jishou and Liuzhou in Guangxi. For Guizhou and points west you'll have to change trains at the junction town of **Huaihua**, four hours to the southwest – sleeper tickets out of Huaihua are virtually impossible to buy at the station, but you can usually upgrade on board. You can also **fly** from Zhangjiajie Shi to Changsha and a half-dozen other provincial capitals.

Zhangjiajie village and around

ZHANGJIAJIE village is simply a couple of streets in the valley at the reserve entrance, overflowing with **map** and souvenir retailers, pricey **restaurants**

(meat dishes are particularly expensive), a **post office** and **places to stay**. Note that in winter many of these places close and those that remain open may have water shortages. You can ask around about basic places to stay within the reserve, which are recommended if you want to get away from it all.

The best-value hotel in the village is the Tujia-run *Minsu Shanzhuang* (☎0744/5719188; ❹), a wooden building at the bottom of town. Farther up is the village's best hotel, the *Xiangdian Shanzhuang* (☎0744/5712266; ❼) Its travel service is fairly helpful with general hiking advice, and can arrange **white-water rafting** day tours in the Suoxi Valley (¥250 per person).

The reserve

With a dense forest of tall, eroded karst pinnacles splintering away from a high plateau, Zhangjiajie's scenery is awesomely poetic – even Chinese tour groups are often hushed by the spectacle. The road through the village leads downhill past a throng of Tujia selling medicinal flora and cheap plastic ponchos at the **reserve entrance**, where you buy your ticket (¥160). You also have your thumbprint scanned to allow for re-entrance during the two days the ticket is valid. There are also **bicycles** for rent – of dubious quality for many of the tracks.

The left path here follows a four-hour circuit along a short valley up to **Huangshi village**, on the edge of a minor, island-like plateau surrounded by views of the area. There's also a cable car to the top (¥45). The right path offers several options, the shortest of which (again, around 4hr) runs along **Golden Whip Stream**, branching off to the right and returning to base through a particularly dense stand of crags below two facing outcrops known as the **Yearning Couple** (engraved tablets along the path identify many other formations). Alternatively, bearing left after a couple of kilometres – consult a map – takes you up past **Bewitching Terrace** into the **Shadao Valley**. From here, basic trails continue through magnificent scenery around the western edge of the plateau to **Black Dragon village**, then circuit back to the park gates. This is a lengthy day's walk, and you won't see many other tourists along the way.

Suoxi Valley and Tianzi Shan

With much of the same facilities as Zhangjiajie, **SUOXI village** makes a good base for exploring the east and north of the reserve. Set in the **Suoxi Valley**, it's 10km as the crow flies from Zhangjiajie but the better part of a day away on foot, though it's possible to get between the two by local bus. Attractions here include groups of rhesus monkeys and relatively open riverine gorges where it's possible to **cruise** – or even go white-water rafting – between the peaks. Around the two-kilometre-long **Baofeng Hu**, a lake accessed by a ladder-like staircase from the valley floor, there's a chance of encountering golden pheasants, the grouse-like tragopans and **giant salamanders** – secretive, red-blotched monsters which reach 2m in length; considered a great delicacy, they're sometimes seen in the early mornings around Baofeng's shore. There's also **Huanglong Dong** (Yellow Dragon Cave), a few kilometres east of Suoxi, a mass of garishly lit limestone caverns linked by a subterranean river, and **Hundred Battle Valley**, where the Song-dynasty Tujia king, Xiang, fought imperial forces.

The **Tianzi Shan** region, which basically covers the north of the park, is named after an isolated 1250-metre-high peak, and contains most of Wulingyuan's caves. It's probably best visited from Suoxi village, where there's a possible circuit of 30km setting off along the **Ten-li Corridor**. High points include the mass of lookouts surrounding **Shentangwan**, a valley thick with needle-like rocks where Xiang is said to have committed suicide after his eventual defeat, and **Immortals' Bridge**, next to the peak itself, an unfenced, narrow strip of rock bridging a deep valley. Instead of returning to Suoxi, you can continue past the mountain to **TIANZI SHAN village**, spend the night in the guesthouse there, and then either hike south to Zhangjiajie or leave Wulingyuan by catching a bus first to **Songzhi** (45km) and then on to **Dayong** (another 60km).

Fenghuang and around

Two hours south of Zhangjiajie by road or rail is **Jishou**, the jumping-off point for the charming town of **FENGHUANG**, with its stilted houses, flagstoned streets and communities of **Miao** and **Tujia** peoples. Fenghuang is a great place to unwind for a couple of days: it's relatively unspoilt (though note that in summer it can be packed out with Chinese visitors), its twelve-hundred-year history is evident in architecture, and the renovated **Southern Great Wall** can be explored in the vicinity. The narrow, labyrinthine streets provide plenty of opportunity to temporarily lose yourself in space and time; you might even find yourself alone amid centuries of history—a rarity in China.

Arrival and information

After arriving in Jishou by train, take a bus or a taxi (¥4) over the bridge to the **bus station** on Wuling Lu, just off the main Tuan Jie Lu. From here there are plenty of Fenghuang buses until 6pm or so (¥12). If you are coming from Yichang you will arrive at 10pm and will need to stay overnight. There are a smattering of accommodation options near the train station, with the *Jin Lai*

Fenghuang and around		
Fenghuang	凤凰	*fènghuáng*
Bingo	边各	*biāngè*
Dongling Canteen	东岭餐宿	*dōnglǐng cānsù*
Fengtian Binguan	凤天宾馆	*fèngtiān bīnguǎn*
Government Hotel	政府宾馆	*zhèngfǔ bīnguǎn*
Guyun Binguan	古韵宾馆	*gǔyún bīnguǎn*
Hong Qiao	虹桥	*hóngqiáo*
International Youth Hostel	青年旅馆	*qīngnián lǚguǎn*
Jinyuan Jiangbian Binguan	金源江边宾馆	*jīnyuán jiāngbiān bīnguǎn*
Meng Yuan Binguan	梦源宾馆	*mèngyuán bīnguǎn*
Shen Congwen's residence	沈从文故居	*shěncóngwén gùjū*
Shen Congwen's tomb	沈从文墓地	*shěncóngwén mùdì*
Shui Shang Lou	水上楼	*shuǐshàng lóu*
Soul Café	素咖啡馆	*sù kāfēiguǎn*
Xiong Xiling's residence	熊希龄故居	*xióngxīlíng gùjū*
Around Fenghuang		
Alaying	阿拉营	*ālāyíng*
Huangsi Qiao	黄丝桥	*huángsīqiáo*
Jinlai Hotel	金来宾馆	*jīnlái bīnguǎn*
Southern Great Wall	南方长城	*nánfāng chángchéng*

Hotel, 4 Guangming Dong Lu (☎0743/8721188; ❸) providing the best mix of value and facilities in the area. Alternatively, you can fly into Tongren, in Sichuan, and get a bus (3–4hr) to Fenghuang. Flight destinations from **Tongren** in neigbouring Sichuan are increasing on an almost daily basis, so check with a travel agent for availability, although flying into the town does take some of the romance out of the venture.

Buses from Jishou initially drop you at Nanhua Lu bridge into the jaws of hungry hotel touts. If you stay on a minute more until the bus stops, you can get off at the bus station in Ku Yuan Lu, where you'll get less hassle. You can then walk to the west gate (Xi Men) and into the old town. **Bike hire** is available for ¥10–15 per day in Wenhua Square near the West Gate, where you can also find a couple of well-stocked **shops** selling fairly priced local handicrafts. There are two **Internet cafés** on the south side of Hong Qiao, as well as a **travel agent** who can arrange **tickets** for onward travel. The **PSB** is based just off Nanhua Lu near the *Government Hotel*, where you will also find a couple of shops offering international **telephone services**. The **post office** and **hospital** (☎0743/3221058) are in the new town on Jian She Lu between the West and South gates to the old town.

Accommodation

Fenghuang International Youth Hostel ☎0743/3260546, @www.yhachina.com. Young staff's lack of experience is tempered by low prices and willingness to let you join them for their evening meal for a mere ¥5. Dormbeds ¥15. ❸

Fengtian Hotel 8 Nanhua Lu ☎0743/3501000. Newly built four-star affair, tastefully furnished, with 24hr hot water and heating to boot. A nice way to treat yourself if you have been enduring unheated guesthouses. ❼

Government Hotel Xi Men Po, off Nanhua Lu ☎0743/3224091. Formerly the last word in luxury here, this hotel has passed its prime but is a good landmark and straddles the old and new towns nicely. ❺

Guyun Binguan 52 Lao Cai Jie, near the old city wall by the river ☎0743/3500077, Ⓕ3500066.

Rising from the ashes of an old courtyard dwelling, this slightly upmarket riverside establishment has plenty of character but unfortunately little in the way of atmosphere. ⑤

Jinyuan Jiangbian Binguan 94 Lao Gong Shao ⓣ13974346711. Ideally situated by the river, just below the Nanhua bridge, this traditional style, family-run hotel boasts good views, but icy rooms outside summer. ②

Mengyuan Binguan Hostel Ku Yuan Lu, just off Nanhua Lu ⓣ0743/6122941. Easily the best budget option outside of the old town and handily situated by the bus station. Spotless rooms, hot water and a good on-site restaurant make this a viable option. ③

The Town

Fenghuang is a small, easily navigable place largely south of the Tuo River, which runs roughly west to east. The old town is bounded on its north side by the river, with a restored section of the city's Ming **walls** running along the riverbank, punctuated from west to east by the splendid Nanhua, North and East **gates**, in that order; these respectively give way to a road bridge, a wooden footbridge and adjacent stepping stones, and **Hong Qiao**, a 300-year-old covered bridge. The principal thoroughfare, **Dongzheng Jie**, is a pedestrianized alley squeezing its way northeast between the old houses through the centre to the East gate and Hong Qiao. To the west and south Nanhua Lu and Jianshe Lu delimit the old town respectively, the latter curling north from the southeast corner of town to end up at Hong Qiao.

Fenghuang is the hometown of many important Chinese, including **Xiong Xiling**, an ethnic Miao who, after the collapse of the Qing dynasty, became the first premier of China's republican government under Yuan Shikai. You can visit his **former home** near the North Gate (daily 8am–5.30pm), a simple affair preserved as it was and holding a few photos, including those of his three wives, with some English captions.

Shen Congwen (1902–88), one of China's greatest writers and also Miao, was from Fenghuang and many of his stories centre on the Miao people and the landscapes of Western Hunan (*Recollections of West Hunan* is available in English, published by Chinese Literature). In 1949, Shen's writing was banned in both mainland China and Taiwan after he failed to align with either, and this effectively ended his career, although his works have enjoyed a revival of late. His **former residence** can be found just off Dongzheng Jie (daily 8am–5.30pm), while his **tomb** is pleasantly located twenty minutes' stroll east along the south bank at Tingtao Shan. The epitaph on the jagged gravestone translates as "Thinking in my way you can understand me. And thinking in my way you can understand others". There is one ticket for all places of interest in the town that can be bought at any of the locations for ¥98 and lasts for three days.

For a different view of the town you could do as the Chinese do and take a **bamboo raft** from the North gate for a forty-minute river ride (¥30 per person), which includes stopping to listen to three girls marooned on a raft who bang a drum and sing soundbites from folk songs before exchanging cheeky repartee with tourists.

Eating, drinking and nightlife

There is plenty to eat in Fenghuang, although much of it is overpriced; wild animals cater to the more outlandish tastes of Chinese tourists. Should you feel adventurous, there are a clutch of these restaraunts by the East Gate Tower at the junction of Lao Cai Jie and Bian Jie. *Shui Shang Lou* has a location and atmosphere that's hard to beat: diners walk through a doorway lined with live, caged animals and other stuff resembling **roadkill**, all awaiting the pot. There's

street food aplenty on the north side of Hong Qiao, where you can stuff your face for just a few Yuan. For something a little more laid-back try the *Soul Café* on Hui Long Ge, north of the river by the water wheel where they serve up **fantastic coffee**, and cheesecake to die for. On the same stretch is a gaggle of **friendly bars** where, in the evenings, you can see the Chinese really let their hair down. If you fancy a quieter night, walk over by the pagoda to a place called *Bingo* that is full of fun hideyholes, fascinating *objets d'art*, and has a good selection of **pizzas and pastas**. For **breakfast** try the *Dong Ling* canteen, also over by the pagoda, where you can watch locals tuck into all sorts of indigenous morning treats accompanied by copious amounts of chillies.

Around Fenghuang

The pretty countryside near Fenghuang has some easily accessible and worthwhile sights, the nearest being the **Southern Great Wall**, which, astonishingly, wasn't recognized for what it was until 2000. Originally constructed in 1554 as a defence against the Miao, the wall ran for around 190km from Xiqueying in Western Hunan to Tongren in Guizhou. There are several hundred metres of intact wall at a site 13km from Fenghuang, the journey to which takes around half an hour by bus from a roundabout at the western end of Jianshe Lu. A ticket to the site (¥45) grants you access to the newly renovated wall, which, while not as rugged as its northern counterpart, is nevertheless impressive and significantly less visited; if you come in winter you'll probably have the place to yourself.

Ten kilometres from the wall, **Huangsi Qiao** (Huang's Silk Bridge) is another ancient settlement, which prospered after Huang, a silk merchant, decided to build a bridge to attract people to the town. A smaller version of Fenghuang, with attractive stilted houses, the town is only half a kilometre across and has gate towers to the north, east and west. You can get here by bus from the wall or Fenghuang (¥3, 30 minutes).

If you want to see more of the Miao or acquire some of their handicrafts, you could head to **Alaying**, 7km west of the Great Wall, where market days (on dates ending with a 2 or 7, as is the local practice) attract the surrounding villagers. Buses leave for Alaying from the western end of Jianshe Lu in Fenghuang (¥5, one hour).

Jiangxi

Stretched between the Yangzi in the north and a mountainous border with Guangdong in the south, **Jiangxi province** has always been a bit of a backwater. Though it has been inhabited for some four thousand years, the first major influx of settlers came as late as the Han dynasty, when its interior offered sanctuary for those dislodged by warfare. The northern half benefited most from these migrants, who began to farm the great plain around China's largest freshwater lake, **Poyang Hu**. A network of rivers covering the province drains into Poyang, and when the construction of the Grand Canal created a route through Yangzhou and the lower Yangzi in the seventh century, Jiangxi's capital, **Nanchang**, became a key point on the great north–south link of inland waterways. The region then enjoyed a long period of quiet prosperity, until coastal shipping and the opening up of treaty ports took business away in the 1840s. The next century saw a complete reversal of Jiangxi's fortunes: the population halved as millions fled competing warlords and, during the 1920s and 1930s, there was protracted fighting between the Guomindang and Communist forces concentrated in the southern **Jinggang Shan** ranges, which eventually led to an evicted Red Army starting on their **Long March** across China.

Despite the troubles, things picked up quickly after the Communist takeover, and a badly battered Nanchang licked its wounds and reinvented itself as a revolutionary city and centre of modern heavy industry. More traditionally, access provided by Poyang and the Yangzi tributaries benefits the hilly areas to the east, where **Jingdezhen** retains its title as China's porcelain capital. North of the lake, **Jiujiang** is a key Yangzi port on the doorsteps of Anhui and Hubei, while the nearby mountain area of **Lu Shan**, also easily visited from Nanchang, offers a pleasant reminder of Jiangxi's better days, when it served as a summer retreat for Chinese literati and colonial servants.

Nanchang

Hemmed in by hills, **NANCHANG** sits on Jiangxi's major river, the **Gan Jiang**, some 70km south of where it flows into Poyang Hu. Built on trade, today Nanchang has its position as a rail hub for central-southern China to thank for its character; unfortunately, this mostly reflects its steel and chemical industries and an overbearing, incomplete reconstruction since the 1950s. First impressions of a grey and noisy place afflicted by the usual stifling summer temperatures are slightly moderated by the handful of resurrected older monuments, and the sheer enthusiasm with which locals have grasped free-market principles, crowding every alley with stalls.

Nanchang saw little action until the twentieth century, when the Guomindang army occupied the city in December 1926. At the time, the military was still an amalgam of Nationalist and Communist forces, but when Chiang Kaishek broke his marriage of convenience with the Communists the following year, all left-wing elements were expelled from the Party. On August 1, 1927, **Zhou Enlai** and **Zhu De**, two Communist GMD officers, mutinied in Nanchang and took control of the city with thirty thousand troops. Though they were soon forced to flee into Jiangxi's mountainous south, the day is celebrated as the foundation of the **People's Liberation Army**, and the red PLA flag still bears the Chinese characters "8" and "1" (*bayi*) for the month and day.

Arrival, transport and accommodation

Nanchang sprawls away from the east bank of the Gan Jiang into industrial complexes and wasteland, but the centre is a fairly compact couple of square kilometres between the river and **Bayi Dadao**, which runs north through the heart of the city from the huge **Fushan roundabout** and past **Renmin Square**, becoming **Yangming Lu** as it turns east over the Bayi Bridge.

Arriving at **Changbei International Airport**, forty minutes north of the centre, you'll need to take a taxi into town (¥100). Other transit points are more central. Nanchang's **train station** is 700m east of the Fushan roundabout at the end of Zhanqian Lu; locals consider the huge square hole through the station

Nanchang

Nanchang	南昌	nánchāng
August 1 Uprising Museum	八一纪念馆	bāyī jìniànguǎn
Bada Shanren Museum	八大山人纪念馆	bādàshānrén jìniànguǎn
Bayi Monument	八一纪念塔	bāyī jìniàntǎ
Bayi Park	八一公园	bāyī gōngyuán
Changbei International Airport	昌北国际机场	chāngběi guójì jīchǎng
Provincial Museum	省博物馆	shěng bówùguǎn
Renmin Square	人民广场	rénmín guǎngchǎng
Shengjin Ta	绳金塔	shéngjīn tǎ
Taxia Si	塔下寺	tǎxià sì
Tengwang Pavilion	滕王阁	téngwáng gé
Youmin Si	佑民寺	yòumín sì
Zhu De's Former Residence	朱德旧居	zhūdé jiùjū
Accommodation		
Gloria Plaza	凯莱大酒店	kǎilái dàjiǔdiàn
Hua Guang Binguan	华光宾馆	huáguāng bīnguǎn
Jiangnan Fandian	江南饭店	jiāngnán fàndiàn
Jiaotong	交通宾馆	jiāotōng bīnguǎn
Jiujiu Long	九九隆大酒店	jiǔjiǔlóng dàjiǔdiàn
Ruidu	瑞都大酒店	ruìdū dàjiǔdiàn
Youzheng Dasha	邮政大厦	yóuzhèng dàshà
Eating and drinking		
Aosit	奥斯汀	àosītīng
Denver 1857	丹佛酒吧	dānfó jiǔbā
Hao Xiang Lai	豪享来	háoxiǎng lái
Hunan Wangcai Guan	湖南王菜馆	húnánwáng càiguǎn
Little Sheep Hotpot	小肥羊火锅	xiǎoféiyáng huǒguō
Ming Dynasty	明朝铜鼎煨汤府	míngcháo tóngdǐng wèitāngfǔ
Ren Kouwei Tang	人口味堂	rénkǒuwèi táng
Xinghuacun	杏花村	xìnghuā cūn

facade bad *feng shui*, allowing the city's wealth to escape down the tracks. Some buses from Lu Shan, Jinggang Shan and farther afield terminate here, but the main **long-distance bus station** is 1km away on Bayi Dadao. **Taxis** (¥6 standing charge) cruise downtown arrival points, while **city bus** #2 runs from the train station along Bayi Dadao and then makes a circuit of the central area, passing or coming close to all the hotels.

Accommodation

There's a good range of accommodation in town, much of it pretty close to the train and bus stations.

Gloria Plaza 88 Yanjiang Bei Lu ⓣ0791/5738855, ⓦwww.gphnanchang.com. Modern, international-style joint-venture hotel, the most foreigner-friendly in Nanchang and worth visiting for its Western food (see p.517). ❾

Hua Guang Binguan 58 Xiangshan Bei Lu ⓣ0791/6777222. New and friendly venture in the heart of town. Clean, stylish rooms and corridors oddly lit with electric blue light. ❸

Jiangnan Fandian 142 Bayi Dadao ⓣ0791/7101800. Excellent facilities for the price bracket. Clean rooms and attentive, friendly staff. ❸

Jiaotong Just north of the bus station, on Bayi Dadao ⓣ & ⓕ0791/6256918. Clean, well-maintained block of standard hotel rooms, nothing fancy but well priced. Solo travellers might be able to wrangle a half-price double. ❸

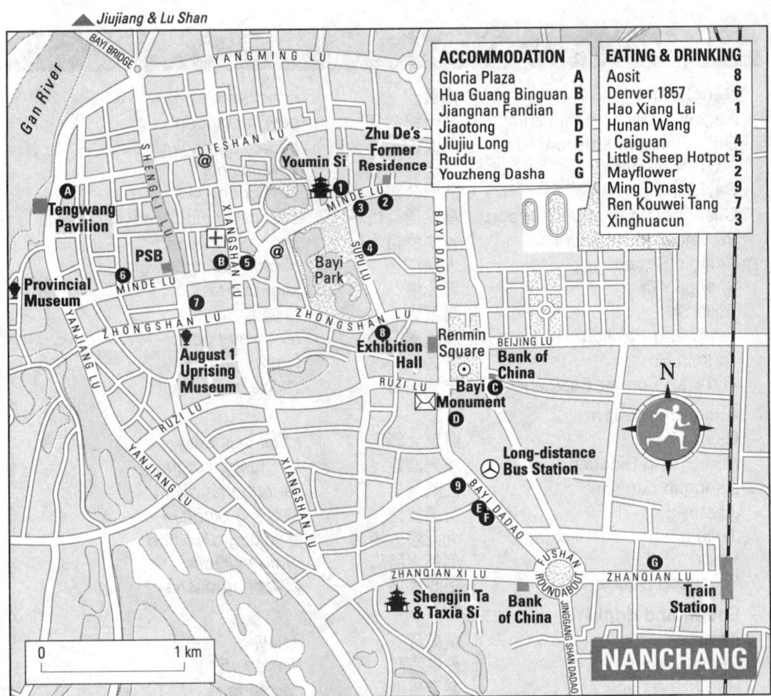

Jiujiu Long 122 Bayi Dadao ⓣ0791/8866555, ⓕ6295299. Smart three-star venture, good value, with attentive staff. ④

Ruidu 399 Guangchang Lu ⓣ0791/6201888, ⓕ62019999. An upmarket place, nicely located on the southeast corner of Renmin Square. ⑦

Youzheng Dasha 86 Zhanqian Lu ⓣ & ⓕ0791/7037900. Post-office-run hotel, cheap and convenient for departure points if not wonderfully appealing. Dorm beds ¥50, ④

The City

Despite slow modernization and a few antiques rising from the rubble, Nanchang's architecture mostly reflects the Civil War years and later Soviet-inspired industrialization. Much of this, such as the overbearing **Exhibition Hall**, is concentrated around the enormous **Renmin Square**, and the strangely shaped red and white stone **Bayi Monument** at the southern end. West of here, **Zhongshan Lu** runs through the core of Nanchang's bustling shopping district, with the water and greenery of **Bayi Park** to the north and, further along, the **August 1 Uprising Museum** (daily 8am–5.30pm; ¥25). Formerly a hotel, this was occupied by the embryonic PLA as their 1927 General Headquarters, and is now of interest mainly as the most complete example of Nanchang's colonial architecture. As a museum, however, it's dull – three floors stuffed with period furniture, weapons, and maps labelled in Chinese. North from here, **pedestrianized** Shengli Lu provides more opportunities to window-shop.

Opposite the top end of Bayi Park and set back off Minde Lu, **Youmin Si** (¥2) is a Buddhist temple dating back to 503 AD, which – perhaps because of

Moving on from Nanchang

You can **fly** from Nanchang to Beijing, Shanghai, Guangzhou and a handful of other cities. Zhanqian Lu is teeming with airline agents, and most hotels can book flights. China Eastern (☎0791/8514195) is on Beijing Lu.

Nanchang lies on the Kowloon–Beijing **train** line and just off the Shanghai–Kunming line, with connections through easterly Yingtan down into Fujian province. Sleeper tickets are pretty easy to obtain, but prepare for some mighty queues; alternatively, the airline agents on Zhanqian Lu also sell train tickets at a slight mark-up. If you're heading to southern Jiangxi, note that "Jinggang Shan" railhead is not Ciping, but a small town 120km further east.

The **bus** station looks huge and crowded, but the ticket office is user-friendly and there's no problem getting seats. Minibuses and smart coaches operate throughout the day along fast expressways to Jiujiang, Lu Shan and Jingdezhen, with daily services within Jiangxi to Jinggang Shan and Ganzhou, and further afield to Wuyi Shan in Fujian and destinations across central China.

the city's revolutionary associations – Nanchang's Red Guards were especially diligent in wrecking during the 1960s. The three restored halls include a striking, ten-metre-high **standing Buddha statue**, which rises out of a lotus flower towards a cupola decorated with a coiled golden dragon. East of here, the austere-looking traditional grey brick house on the corner of Huayuanjiao Jie is **Zhu De's former residence** (daily 8am–5.30pm; ¥2). Inside you'll find a series of Chinese-captioned photographs of Zhu De and Zhou Enlai, Zhu's bedroom and a few personal effects, including his gun.

It might all sound a bit heavy, but in fact Nanchang has a very youthful feel at street level. The city's colonial history has left a legacy of drinking and dancing among the locals, who enjoy a good night on the tiles as much as their not-so-distant Shanghai cousins. Nanchang is also a very clean place, especially after its dedication as "Hygenic city" by the central government at the end of 2006.

Tengwang Pavilion and the Provincial Museum

The mighty **Tengwang Pavilion** (summer 7.30am–5.30pm; winter 8am–4.30pm; ¥50) overlooks the river on Yanjiang Lu, 1km or so west of Youmin Si. There have been 26 multistoreyed towers built on this site since the first was raised more than a thousand years ago in memory of a Tang prince; the current "Song-style" building was only completed in 1989. Nonetheless, it's impressive to look at: a huge pile isolated by a grey-paved square and a monumental stone base, each floor lightened by a broadly flared roof supported by interlocking wooden beams. The six-storey interior is a letdown, with the upper-level balconies offering views of a drab cityscape. However, it's worth catching the lift (¥1) to the top floor at weekends, when a tiny indoor **theatre** hosts traditional dances and music sessions; with luck, there may even be a performance of local opera.

South of the pavilion, bridges off Yanjiang Lu cross an inlet to the **Provincial Museum** (Tues–Sun 8.30am–5.30pm; ¥10), a weird, futuristic-looking construction with green glass towers and knife-like side wings. The buildings feel almost deserted, though the collection covers everything from dinosaurs to Jingdezhen **porcelain**.

Southern Nanchang

West of the Fushan roundabout off Zhanqian Lu (bus #5 passes by on its route between the roundabout and Xiangshan Lu), you'll find **Shengjin Ta** (daily 8am–

▲ Tengwang Pavilion

5.30pm; ¥10) which, legend has it, holds the key to Nanchang's survival – apparently the city will fall if the seven-storey pagoda is ever destroyed. The warning is still taken fairly seriously, despite the fact that Shengjin has been knocked down several times, the last time being in the early eighteenth century. At any rate, the pagoda itself is only of moderate interest, but the restored architecture of the surrounding streets and a few **teahouses**, which Nanchang was once famous for – down-to-earth, open-fronted establishments patronized by gregarious old men watching the world go by – make this market quarter worth a wander.

For an easy reprieve from the city, catch bus #20 from Yanjiang Lu 5km south to the **Bada Shanren Museum** (Tues–Sun 8.30am–4.30pm; ¥20), a white-washed Ming-era compound set in parkland. This was the haunt of the painter Zhu Da, also known as Bada Shanren, a wandering Buddhist monk of royal descent who came to live in this former temple in 1661 and was later buried here. He is said to have painted in a drunken frenzy – his pictures certainly show great spontaneity. There are a number of originals displayed inside, and some good reproductions on sale.

Eating, drinking and nightlife

Nanchang's **eating** options cover quite a broad range, from dumpling houses and spicy Hunanese restaurants to the regional **Gan cooking** – lightly sauced fresh fish, crayfish, snails and frogs. **Soups** are something of a Jiangxi favourite – egg and pork soup is a typical breakfast – along with communal affairs served up in huge pots at the table. Restaurants are spread all over the city, though the streets around Bayi Park seem to have the highest concentration. All the usual Western fast-food chains are here and there's an increasing number of coffee shops, which also serve some Western and Chinese fare. Minde Lu hosts several **bars and nightclubs**. Try the cosy *Denver 1857* for a drink, or the *Mayflower* if you want to dance as well.

Restaurants

Aosit Second floor, 102 Zhongshan Lu. A young and happy eatery that's clear and easy to use; just point to what you want from the boards on the wall. Hot and cold dishes and set meals range from ¥2–30.

Hao Xiang Lai Minde Lu. Good-value, sizzling pepper steaks for ¥25; plus delicious Chinese snacks, biscuits and dumplings wheeled around *dim sum*-style, from ¥3 a plate.

Hunan Wang Caiguan Supu Lu. Popular, mid-range spicy Hunanese restaurant overlooking Bayi Park.

Little Sheep Hotpot 495 Minde Lu. Spicy hotpots from around ¥30 per person.

Ming Dynasty Bayi Dadao, next to the *Jiangnan Fandian*. The big bronze cauldron standing outside marks this as a Jiangxi-style soup restaurant. Individual pots from ¥18 or three- to four-person pots from ¥30.

Ren Kouwei Tang Shengli Lu. Bustling dumpling house, one of several in the area. You order from the range of plastic cards behind the cashier, or point to whatever others are eating. Individual clay-pot casseroles, cold meats, buns and vegetables from ¥2–10.

Xinghuacun Minde Lu. Three-storey, mid-range restaurant serving good Jiangxi fare, including, of course, soups.

Listings

Bank and exchange The main Bank of China is on Zhanqian Xi Lu just off the Fushan roundabout, and there's another large branch in the south-eastern corner of Renmin Square (both Mon–Fri 8am–5.30pm).

Hospital First City Hospital, Xiangshan Lu ⓣ0791/6784813.

Internet access There are Internet bars scattered across the city, including one on Xiangshan Lu near the intersection with Dieshan Lu and another just west of Bayi Park on Minde Lu.

Left luggage Offices at train and bus stations open roughly 6am–7pm.

Mail and telephones The main post office and the telecommunications building (both daily 8am–6pm) are near each other at the corner of Bayi Dadao and Ruzi Lu.

PSB On Shengli Lu, just north of Minde Lu (ⓣ0791/6742000; daily 8am–noon & 2.30–5.30pm).

Shopping Nanchang Department Store, the city's largest and best-stocked department store, hides behind a 1950s frontage west of Renmin Square along Zhongshan Lu. Zhongshan Lu itself and the pedestrianized southern stretch of Shengli Lu are rife with clothing stores and boutiques. A good supermarket is Walmart, on the second floor of the shopping centre at the northern end of Renmin Square. For a big range of porcelain, chops and paintings, try the Jiangxi Antique Store on Minde Lu.

Travel agents Most accommodation places have travel desks where you can book train and plane tickets.

Jiujiang and Lu Shan

Set on the Yangzi 150km north of Nanchang, **Jiujiang** had its heyday in the nineteenth century as a treaty port, and now serves mostly as a jumping-off point for tourists exchanging the torrid lowland summers for nearby cool hills at **Lu Shan**. Trains on the Kowloon–Beijing line stop at Jiujiang,

Jiujiang and Lu Shan

Jiujiang	九江	*jiǔjiāng*
Bailu Binguan	白鹿宾馆	*báilù bīnguǎn*
Gantang Hu	甘棠湖	*gāntáng hú*
Huifeng Binguan	荟丰宾馆	*huìfēng bīnguǎn*
Xinhua Binguan	新华宾馆	*xīnhuá bīnguǎn*
Xunyang Lou	寻阳楼	*xúnyáng lóu*
Yanshui Pavilion	烟水亭	*yānshuǐ tíng*
Guling	牯岭	*gǔlǐng*
Guling Fandian	牯岭饭店	*gǔlǐng fàndiàn*
Lushan Binguan	庐山宾馆	*lúshān bīnguǎn*
Lushan Dasha	庐山饭店	*lúshān dàshà*
Lushan Fandian	庐山大厦	*lúshān fàndiàn*
Lushan Villas	庐山别墅	*lúshān biéshù*
Mei Villa	美庐别墅	*měilú biéshù*
Lu Shan	庐山	*lúshān*
Botanical Garden	植物园	*zhíwù yuán*
Lulin Hu	芦林湖	*lúlín hú*
People's Hall	人民剧院	*rénmín jùyuàn*
Ruqin Hu	如琴湖	*rúqín hú*
Xianren Dong	仙人洞	*xiānrén dòng*
Wucheng	武城	*wùchéng*

while fast buses from Nanchang run throughout the day to both Jiujiang and Lu Shan.

Jiujiang

Small but always an important staging post for river traffic, **JIUJIANG** (Nine Rivers) is appropriately named, situated as it is on the south bank of the Yangzi near where Poyang Hu disgorges itself in a maze of streams. The town grew wealthy during the Ming dynasty through trade in Jingdezhen porcelain, which was distributed all over China from here. Largely destroyed during the Taiping Uprising, Jiujiang was rebuilt as a treaty port in the 1860s, and today – despite catastrophic flooding through the town centre in 1998 – it's enjoying a low-scale renaissance, with its docks and adjacent streets busy from dawn to dusk.

The west side of town between the Yangzi and **Gantang Hu** is the most interesting area, a collection of narrow streets packed with small stores selling bright summer clothing, porcelain and home-made hardware utensils. Completely occupying a tiny islet in the lake is the picturesque **Yanshui Pavilion** (daily 8am–8pm; ¥10), its tastefully proportioned Ming pavilion commemorating the Tang poet-official **Li Bai**, who was responsible for the causeway and the restored moon-shaped sluice gate.

On Binjiang Lu northeast of Gantang Hu, **Xunyang Lou** (daily 9am till late; ¥6) is an "antique" wooden wine house facing Anhui and Hubei provinces across the Yangzi. Built in 1986 to replace a previous Tang-dynasty structure, it was the setting for a scene in **Outlaws of the Marsh** (aka *The Water Margin*), China's own Robin Hood legend. This lively story, set mostly farther east in Zhejiang province, involved 108 rebel heroes who were often more bloodthirsty than the oppressive Song-dynasty officials they fought – the tale was one of Mao's favourites. The wine house was where the future outlaws' leader Song Jiang imprudently wrote some revolutionary verses on the back wall after downing too much wine; condemned to death, he was dramatically rescued at the last moment. Those familiar with the tale will recognize porcelain figurines of Song Jiang, "Black Whirlwind" Liu Kei (the original axe-wielding maniac) and the other heroes in the lobby. The upstairs **restaurant** is worth visiting at lunchtime for *dongpo rouding* (steamed and braised pork belly), river fish, "Eight Treasure" duck, scrambled eggs and green pepper, or *sunyang dabing* (a pancake invented by one of the outlaws).

Practicalities

Jiujiang's centre is laid out in the narrow space between the north shore of Gantang Hu and the Yangzi: **Xunyang Lu** runs west from the top of the lake out to the highway, while parallel **Binjiang Lu** is 100m farther north and follows the riverbank.

The **train station** is 3km southeast of the centre at the bottom end of Gantang Hu – catch #1 to the bus station – and has quick links to Nanchang and Hefei. The **long-distance bus station** is 1500m east down Xunyang Lu, with buses back to Nanchang until 7pm, or earlier for Lu Shan, and others to Wuhan and Nanjing. On Xunyang Lu between here and the lake you'll find a **Bank of China** (Mon–Fri 8am–5pm), and Jiujiang's most convenient **accommodations**. For value, the *Xinhua Binguan* (Ⓣ0792/8989222, Ⓕ8989999; ❺) is the one to look for, slightly past its prime but comfortable nevertheless. Nearby, the ultra-modern *Huifeng Binguan* (Ⓣ0792/8986000; ❻) has chrome fittings and enormous glass-screened bathrooms. More traditional rooms are available at *Bailu Binguan* (Ⓣ0792/8980888, Ⓕ8980866; ❺), a smart place patronized by tour groups.

Summer evenings are too humid to spend indoors, so everyone heads down Xunyang Lu to window-shop and eat at one of the **pavement cafés** on Gantang's north shore. There, they can admire the views of Lu Shan while gorging on fish and crayfish hotpots, sautéed frogs and piles of freshwater snails. There are a number of restaurants, along with cheap street food, in the lanes between the lake and the river; the *Chuanwang* serves tasty, moderately priced hotpots. If you like Chinese spirits, crack open a bottle of Jiuling Jiu, the local firewater, which comes with a clay seal – once opened, you'll have to drink the lot.

Lu Shan

Lu Shan's cluster of wooded hills rises to a sudden 1474m from the level shores of Poyang Hu, its heights a welcome relief from the Yangzi basin's steamy summers. Once covered in temples, Lu Shan was developed in the mid-nineteenth century by **Edward Little**, a Methodist minister turned property speculator, as a resort area for European expatriates. The Chinese elite moved in after the Europeans lost their grip on the region; **Chiang Kaishek** built a summer residence and training school for Guomindang officials here in the 1930s, and Lu Shan hosted one of the key meetings of the Maoist era twenty years later. Nowadays, the place is overrun with proletariat holidaymakers who pack out the restaurants and troop along the paths to enjoy the clean air; former mansions have been converted into hotels and sanatoriums for their benefit. Crowds reach plague proportions between spring and autumn, so winter – though very cold – can be the best season to visit, and a weekend's walking is enough for a good sample of the scenery.

Guling

The thirty-kilometre trip from Jiujiang takes around an hour and a half on the sharply twisting road, with sparkling views back over the great lake and its junction with the Yangzi. There's a pause at the top gates for passengers to pay the steep **entry fee** (¥100), then it's a short way to **GULING** township in Lu Shan's northeastern corner, whose handful of quaintly cobbled streets, European stone villas and bungalows are the base for further exploration. The one attraction in town is the **Mei Villa** on He Xi Lu (daily 8.30am–5pm; ¥15), former residence of Chiang Kaishek (though it's named after his wife, Song Meiling) and of interest simply because its exhibition is one of the few in China to so much as mention the Generalissimo.

Buses arrive on He Dong Lu immediately after emerging from a tunnel into town (though minibuses from Jiujiang might terminate anywhere). Fifty metres downhill on the right is a pedestrian mall leading through to Guling Jie. Most essential services are either in the mall or on Guling Jie: souvenir shops selling **maps**, a **post office**, **Bank of China** (though larger hotels are a better bet for exchanging travellers cheques) and a **market** selling vegetables, bananas, peaches and lychees.

Leaving Lu Shan is fairly simple, but it's essential to book long-distance tickets the day before departure. Regular buses head to Jiujiang, Nanchang and beyond; if you can't find direct services, go first to Jiujiang for Wuhan and points east, and Nanchang for southern or westerly destinations.

Accommodation and eating

Summers are very busy – arrive early on in the day to ensure a room – and expensive, with hotel-owners raising their rates (price codes below apply to summer) and refusing to bargain. Rates tumble during winter months, when it gets cold enough to snow, so check the availability of heating and hot water.

There are plenty of **restaurants** in Guling, mostly good value, and some post their menus and prices outside. For local flavours – mountain fungus and fish – try the stalls and open restaurants around the market, or the *Wurong Canting*, above a teashop in the mall.

Guling Fandian 104 He Dong Lu ⓣ0792/8282200, ⓕ8282209. The two wings of this hotel face each other across the road about 100m downhill from the bus stop. Rooms in the newer building are much smarter and thus pricier. ❻

Lushan Binguan 446 He Xi Lu ⓣ0792/8295203, ⓕ8282843. Ten minutes farther on past the *Guling*, this is a heavy stone mansion with pleasant, comfortable rooms, good-value suites and a fine restaurant. ❽

Lushan Dasha 506 He Xi Lu ⓣ0792/8282806. Another 5min from the *Lushan Binguan*, a regimental exterior betrays this hotel as the former Guomindang Officers' Training Centre; rooms are well furnished and comfortable. ❼

Lushan Hotel At the bus-stop end of Guling Jie ⓣ0792/8281813. Acceptable rooms near the centre of town. ❺

Lushan Villas ⓣ0792/8282927, ⓕ8282387. Nice quiet location off He Xi Lu and next to Meilu Villa. The rooms are in a group of renovated cottage villas named after different historic figures, and there are two excellent restaurants on site. ❽

Into the hills

Covering some 300 square kilometres, Lu Shan's **highlands** form an elliptical platform tilted over to the southwest, comprising a central region of lakes surrounded by pine-clad hills, with superb rocks, waterfalls and views along the vertical edges of the plateau. Freelance minibuses cruise Guling Lu and usually charge a flat fee of ¥10 per person to any site in Lu Shan, while tour buses cover a variety of places on day-trips from the long-distance bus arrival stop.

For an easy walk out from town (3hr there and back), follow the road downhill to the southwest from Guling Lu and the Jiexin Garden to the far end of **Ruqin Hu**, where you can pick up the **Floral Path**. This gives impressive views of the Jinxui Valley as it winds along Lu Shan's western cliff edge past **Xianren Dong**, the Immortal's Cave, once inhabited by an ephemeral Taoist monk and still an active shrine, complete with a slowly dripping spring.

The most spectacular scenery can be found on Lu Shan's southern fringes. Proper exploration requires a fair day's hike, so even hardened walkers take advantage of transport into the area. About an hour's stroll down He Xi Lu and then left takes you past the unpleasantly crowded **People's Hall** (daily 8am–5pm; ¥15), site of the 1959 Central Committee meeting at which Marshal Peng Dehui openly criticized the Great Leap Forward, and was subsequently denounced as a "Rightist" by Mao – events which ultimately sparked the Cultural Revolution. Next is **Lulin Hu**, a nice lakeside area with its attractive Dragon Pools and elderly Three Treasure trees over to the west. Due east of here – about 5km by road but less along walking tracks – is China's only sub-alpine **botanical garden**, the finest spot in Lu Shan to watch the sunrise. Admittedly, clear days are a rarity on Lu Shan, whose peaks are frequently obscured by mist; the local brew is suitably known as "Cloud Fog Tea".

Jingdezhen

JINGDEZHEN, across Poyang Hu from Nanchang and not far from the border with Anhui province, is a scruffy city whose streets labour under the effects of severe pollution caused by the numerous **porcelain factories** dotted throughout the centre. The city has been producing ceramics for at least two thousand years, and thanks to local geography and national politics, ceramics remain its chief source of income and the reason Jingdezhen figures on tourist itineraries. You'll find a day-trip here worthwhile even without a special interest in porcelain – though given the filthy air, only ceramics buffs will want to hang around longer.

The city lies in a river valley rich not only in clay suitable for firing but also in the feldspar needed to turn it into porcelain; when the Ming rulers developed a taste for fine ceramics in the fourteenth century, the capital was at Nanjing, conveniently close to Jingdezhen. An **imperial kiln** was built in 1369, and its wares became so highly regarded – "as white as jade, as thin as paper, as bright as a mirror, as tuneful as a bell" – that Jingdezhen retained official favour even after the Ming court shifted to Beijing fifty years later.

As demand grew, workshops experimented with new **glazes** and a classic range of decorative styles emerged: *qinghua*, blue and white; *jihong*, rainbow; *doucai*, a blue and white overglaze; and *fencai*, multicoloured *famille rose*. The first examples reached Europe in the seventeenth century and became so popular

Jingdezhen

Jingdezhen	景德镇	*jǐngdézhèn*
Ancient Porcelain Workshop	古窑瓷厂	*gǔyáo cíchǎng*
Jinsheng Dajiudian	金盛大酒店	*jīnshèng dàjiǔdiàn*
Longzhu Ge	龙珠阁	*lóngzhū gé*
Museum of Ceramic History	陶瓷历史博物馆	*táocí lìshǐ bówùguǎn*
Zhongjin Dajiudian	中锦大酒店	*zhōngjǐn dàjiǔdiàn*
Yingtan	鹰潭	*yīngtán*

that the English word for China clay – kaolin – derives from its source nearby at **Gaoling**. Factories began to specialize in **export ware** shaped and decorated in European-approved forms, which reached the outside world via the booming Canton markets: the famous **Nanking Cargo**, comprising 150,000 pieces salvaged from the 1752 wreck of the Dutch vessel *Geldermalsen* and auctioned in 1986, was one such shipment. Foreign sales on this scale petered out after European ceramic technologies improved at the end of the eighteenth century, but Jingdezhen survived by sacrificing innovation for more Ford-like production-line manufacturing. Today the town's scores of private and state-owned kilns employ some fifty thousand people.

The Town

The only available vistas of Jingdezhen are from the four-storey **Longzhu Ge** on Zhonghua Bei Lu (daily 8.30am–5.30pm; ¥15), a pleasant construction in wood and orange tiles along the lines of Hunan's Yueyang Tower, which also contains a small porcelain museum. From the top, the town's smoggy horizon, a patchwork of paddy fields and tea terraces, is liberally pierced by tall, thin smokestacks, which fire up by late afternoon.

But porcelain, not views, makes Jingdezhen worth a visit and the town is geared towards selling. There are a few tourist shops, but it's more fun – and affordable – to head to the **markets** on Jiefang Lu south of the central square, where you'll find pavements clogged by stacks of everything that has ever been made in porcelain, in or out of fashion: metre-high vases, life-sized dogs, Western- and Chinese-style crockery, antique reproductions including yellow and green-glazed Tang camels, ugly statuettes of Buddhist and historical figures, and simple porcelain pandas for the mantelpiece. It's a surreal sight, as are the Chinese visitors buying them by the cartload.

The Museum of Ceramic History

To experience the manufacturing side of things, either try to join a CITS **factory tour**, or visit the **Museum of Ceramic History** (daily 9am–5pm; ¥50). Normally the museum is a bit quiet, but if a big tour party is expected, the workshops get fired up and it's much more entertaining.

The museum is out of town on the west side of the river – take bus #3 from Zhushan Lu to its terminus on Cidu Dadao, then cross the road and head under the ornamental arch opposite. A fifteen-minute walk through fields leads to a surprising collection of antique buildings divided into two sections. A Ming mansion houses the **museum** itself, and its ornate crossbeams, walled gardens and gilt eave screens are far more interesting than the second-rate **ceramics display**, though this covers everything from 1000-year-old kiln fragments through to the Ming's classic simplicity and overwrought, multicoloured extravagances of the late nineteenth century. Next door, another walled garden conceals the **Ancient Porcelain Workshop**, complete with a Confucian temple and working pottery, where the entire process of throwing, moulding and glazing takes place. Out back is a rickety two-storey **kiln**, packed with all sizes of the unglazed yellow pottery sleeves commonly seen outside local field kilns – these shield each piece of porcelain from damage in case one explodes during the firing process.

Practicalities

It's only three hours to Jingdezhen from Nanchang, using the route following the Jiujiang expressway clockwise around the lake. Arriving from Fujian, you can catch a train to the copper-mining town of **Yingtan**, and continue by bus

▲ Classical Jingdezhen porcelain

for three hours to Jingdezhen (half this for the train, changing in Yingtan itself). It's also easy to get here by bus or train from Tunxi in Anhui, and there are trains from Nanjing and Shanghai.

The town is concentrated on the east bank of the **Chang Jiang** – not the Yangzi, but a lesser river of the same name. **Zhushan Lu** runs east from the river for a kilometre through to where roads converge at central **Guangchang**, a broad, paved square where children fly kites in windy weather. The **train station** is 1500m southeast of Guangchang on Tongzhan Lu, while the **long-distance bus station** is 3km west across the river – bus #28 connects the two via Zhushan Lu and Guangchang.

For factory tours or ticket booking there's a CITS (Mon–Sat 9am–5.30pm; ⓣ0798/8629999) in the *Binjiang Hotel* by the river on Zhushan Xi Lu. You'll find the **Bank of China** on the way into town on Ma'anshan Lu; the main **post office** is west of the river on Zhushan Lu, and there's a small **Internet bar** (¥2) on Ma'anshan Lu near the junction with Tongzhan Lu.

It's just as well that many visitors treat Jingdezhen as a day-trip, as **accommodation** prospects are mediocre. The best option near the train station is *Zhongjin Dajiudian* on Tongzhan Lu (ⓣ0798/7020777; ❹); around Guangchang, try the comfortable, welcoming *Jinsheng Dajiudian* on the north side of Zhushan Zhong Lu (ⓣ0798/8207818; ❺), west off the square. **Food stalls** offering hotpots and stir-fries can be found east of Guangchang along Tongzhan Lu.

Southern Jiangxi

When Zhou Enlai and Zhu De were driven out of Nanchang after their abortive uprising, they fled to the **Jinggang Shan** ranges, 300km southwest along the mountainous border with Hunan. Here they met up with Mao, whose **Autumn Harvest Uprising** in Hunan had also failed, and the remnants of the two armies joined to form the first real PLA divisions. Their initial base was near the country town of **Ciping**, and, though they declared a Chinese Soviet Republic in 1931 at the Fujian border town of **Ruijin**, Ciping was where the Communists stayed until forced out by the Guomindang in 1934.

Jinggang Shan is reasonably accessible thanks to new roads, though it doesn't attract a large number of tourists. This makes it a pleasant proposition, as there is some good forest scenery and a few hiking trails. Ciping is an eight-hour **bus** trip from Nanchang via the ancient river town of **Ji'an**, whose landmark **Yunzhang Ge** (Cloud Sect Pavilion) is built out on a wooded midstream island. You can also get into the region **by train**, disembarking either at the southern city of **Ganzhou**, or east at **Taihe**, sometimes described as the Jinggang Shan station – either way, you've still got at least 90km to cover by bus.

Ciping and Jinggang Shan

Also known as Jinggang Shan Shi, **CIPING** is, at least in scale, nothing more than a village. Completely destroyed by artillery bombardments during the 1930s, it was rebuilt after the Communist takeover as one enormous revolutionary relic,

Southern Jiangxi		
Ciping	茨坪	*cípíng*
Former Revolutionary Headquarters	革命旧居群	*gémìng jiùjūqún*
Jinggang Shan Binguan	井岗山宾馆	*jǐnggāngshān bīnguǎn*
Martyrs' Tomb	烈士纪念堂	*lièshì jìniàntáng*
Revolutionary Museum	井岗山博物馆	*jǐnggāngshān bówùguǎn*
Jinggang Shan	井岗山	*jǐnggāng shān*
Wulong Tan	五龙潭	*wǔlóng tán*
Wuzhi Feng	五指峰	*wǔzhǐ fēng*
Ganzhou	赣州	*gànzhōu*
Bajing Park	八境公园	*bājìng gōngyuán*
Ganzhou Fandian	赣州饭店	*gànzhōu fàndiàn*
Ji'an	吉安	*jí'ān*

though recent greening projects have lightened the heavily heroic architecture and monuments, giving the place a dated rural charm. The main streets form a two-kilometre elliptical circuit, the lower half of which is taken up with a lake surrounded by grassy gardens – much appreciated by straying cattle – and a tiny amusement park, complete with a real MiG-style fighter plane to play on.

Ciping's austere historical monuments can be breezed through fairly quickly, as it's the surrounding hills that best recreate a feeling of how Communist guerrillas might have lived. Five minutes west of the bus station at the top end of town is the squat, angular **Martyrs' Tomb**, positioned at the top of a broad flight of stairs and facing the mountains that the fighters it commemorates died defending. Farther round at the **Revolutionary Museum** (daily 8am–4pm; ¥15), where signs ban smoking, spitting and laughter, the exhibition consists almost entirely of maps showing battlefields and troop movements up until 1930, after which the Communists suffered some heavy defeats. Paintings of a smiling Mao preaching to peasant armies face cases of the spears, flintlocks and mortars that initially comprised the Communist arsenal. On a more mundane level, a group of mud-brick rooms across the park at the **Former Revolutionary Headquarters** (daily 8am–4pm; ¥15) gives an idea of what Ciping might originally have looked like and, as the site of where Mao and Zhu De coordinated their guerrilla activities and the start of the **Long March**, is the town's biggest attraction as far as visiting cadres are concerned.

Practicalities

Ciping's **bus station** is on the northeastern side of the circuit, served by buses from Nanchang and Ganzhou, and also Hengyang in Hunan province, from where there are transport links into southern and central China. There are a host of budget and mid-range **places to stay** near the bus station. Alternatively, take the first street down the hill on the right, which leads through Ciping's tourist market (a collection of white-tiled shops selling local teas, cloud-ear fungus and bamboo roots carved into faces) to the *Jinggang Shan Binguan* (ⓣ0796/6552272, ⓕ6552221; ❼), favoured by visiting officials but otherwise a bit grey. There's a **CITS** office here (Mon–Sat 9am–5.30pm; ⓣ0796/6552504). Just past the Former Revolutionary Headquarters is a large **Bank of China** only too happy to change traveller's cheques (Mon–Fri 9–11.30am & 2–5pm).

Jinggang Shan

Having waded through the terribly serious displays in town, it's nice to escape from Ciping into Jinggang Shan's surprisingly wild **countryside**. Some of the peaks provide glorious views of the sunrise, or more frequent mists, and there are colourful plants, natural groves of pine and bamboo, deep green temperate cloud forests, and hosts of butterflies and birds. If you want a day-tour of all the local sights, ask CITS to arrange a jeep and driver or use the minibuses that leave from the station.

One problem with **walking** anywhere is that maps of the footpaths are pretty vague, and locals can be shy of foreigners, running off should you stop to ask directions. One of the nicest areas to explore, and relatively easy to find, is **Wulong Tan** (Five Dragon Pools), about 8km north along the road from the Martyrs' Tomb. A footpath from the roadhead leads past some poetically pretty waterfalls dropping into the pools (of which there are actually eight) between a score of pine-covered peaks. The same distance south is **Jinggang Shan** itself, also known as **Wuzhi Feng**, apex of the mountains at 1586m. Follow the road out of town past the Bank of China, then turn right and take the concrete "driveway" uphill past company housing and on to a dirt road. About ten

The Long March

In 1927, Chiang Kaishek, the new leader of the Nationalist Guomindang (GMD) government, began an obsessive war against the 6-year-old Chinese Communist Party, using a union dispute in Shanghai as an excuse to massacre their leadership. Driven underground, the Communists set up half a dozen remote rural bases, or soviets, across central China. The most important of these were the **Fourth Front army** in northern Sichuan, under the leadership of **Zhang Guotao**; the **Hunan soviet**, controlled by the irrepressible peasant general **He Long**; and the main **Jiangxi soviet** in the Jinggang Mountains, led by **Mao Zedong** and **Zhu De**, the Communist Commander-in-Chief.

Initially poorly armed, the Jiangxi soviet successfully fought off GMD attempts to oust them, acquiring better weapons in the process and swelling their ranks with disaffected peasantry and defectors from the Nationalist cause. But they overestimated their position and in 1933, abandoning Mao's previously successful guerrilla tactics, they were drawn into several disastrous pitched battles. Chiang, ignoring Japanese incursions into Manchuria in his eagerness to defeat the Communists, blockaded the mountains with a steadily tightening ring of bunkers and barbed wire, systematically clearing areas of guerrillas with artillery bombardments. Hemmed in and facing eventual defeat, the **First Front army**, comprising some eighty thousand Red soldiers, decided to break through the blockade in October 1934 and retreat west to team up with the Hunan soviet – marking the beginning of the **Long March**.

Covering a punishing 30km a day on average, the Communists moved after dark whenever possible so that the enemy would find it difficult to know their exact position; even so, they faced daily skirmishes. One thing in their favour was that many putative GMD divisions were, in fact, armies belonging to local warlords who owed a token allegiance to Chiang Kaishek, and had no particular reason to fight once it became clear that the Red Army was only crossing their territory. But after incurring severe losses during a battle at the **Xiang River** near Guilin in Guangxi, the marchers found their progress north impeded by massive GMD forces, and were obliged to continue west to Guizhou, where they took the town of **Zunyi** in January 1935. With their power structure in disarray and with no obvious options left, an emergency meeting of the Communist Party hierarchy was called – the **Zunyi Conference**. Mao emerged as the undisputed leader of the Party, with a mandate to "go north to fight the Japanese" by linking up with Zhang Guotao in Sichuan. In subsequent months they circled through Yunnan and Guizhou, trying to shake off the GMD, routing twenty

minutes later this forks; go left down to the bridge, cross over and carry on past a huge quarry, where machinery turns boulders into gravel, and on to a **tunnel** leading into the hillside. Ignore the tunnel and follow the steps above up through a small patch of forest full of ginger, ferns and moss-covered trees, to more stairs ascending to Wuzhi Feng's sharp and lightly wooded summit. The last bit of the track is slippery and not overly used, giving a rare opportunity to be on your own, musing on how the Communists must have found things and watching the trees and waterfalls below sliding in and out of the clouds. Examine the bushes and you'll find some extraordinary insects: multicoloured crickets, scarabs with orange antennae, and huge, bushy caterpillars.

Ganzhou

Five hours south of Jinggang Shan on the Kowloon–Beijing rail line, **GANZHOU** lies on the subtropical side of Jiangxi's mountain ranges, only a short hop from the Guangdong border. The town makes an interesting regiments of the Guangxi provincial army at the **Loushan Pass** in the process; they then suddenly moved up into Sichuan to cross the Jinsha River and, in one of the most celebrated and heroic episodes of the march, took the **Luding Bridge** across the Dadu River (see p.933). Now they had to negotiate **Daxue Shan** (Great Snowy Mountains), where hundreds died from exhaustion, exposure and altitude sickness before the survivors met up on the far side with the Fourth Front army.

The meeting between these two major branches of the Red Army was tense. Mao, with Party backing, wanted to start resistance against the Japanese, but Zhang, who felt that his better-equipped forces and better education gave him superiority, wanted to found a Communist state in Sichuan's far west. Zhang eventually capitulated, and he and Mao took control of separate columns to cross the last natural barrier they faced, the **Aba grasslands** in northern Sichuan. But here, while Mao was bogged down by swamps, hostile nomads and dwindling food reserves, Zhang's column suddenly retreated to **Garzê**, where Zhang set up an independent government. Mao and what remained of the First Front struggled through southern Gansu, where they suffered further losses through Muslim supporters of the GMD, finally arriving in Communist-held **Yan'an**, Shaanxi province, in October 1935. While the mountains here were to become a Communist stronghold, only a quarter of those who started from Jiangxi twelve months before had completed the 9500-kilometre journey. For his part, Zhang was soon harried out of western Sichuan by Chiang's forces, and after meeting up with He Long, he battled through to Shaanxi, adding another twenty thousand to the Communist ranks. Here he made peace with Mao in October 1936, but later defected to the GMD.

Immediately after the Long March, Mao admitted that in terms of losses and the Red Army's failure to hold their original positions against the Nationalists, the Guomindang had won. Yet in a more lasting sense, the march was an incredible success, uniting the Party under Mao and defining the Communists' aims, while changing the Communists' popular image from simply another rebel group opposing central authority into one of a determined and patriotic movement. After Zunyi, Mao turned the march into a deliberate propaganda mission to spread the Communist faith among the peasantry, opening up prisons in captured GMD towns and promoting tolerance and cooperation with minority groups (though not always successfully). As Mao said, "Without the Long March, how could the broad masses have learned so quickly about the existence of the great truth which the Red Army embodies?"

few hours' break in your journey, and is very different in feel from elsewhere in Jiangxi.

Ganzhou was formerly a strategic port guarding the routes between central and southern China; the town sits on a triangular peninsula where two rivers, the Gong Shui and Zhang Shui, combine to form the **Gan Jiang**, which flows north from here all the way to Nanchang and Poyang Hu. During the 1930s, Chiang Kaishek's son was governor here, doubtless keeping a close watch on the events at Jinggang Shan, and a surprising amount survives from these times. The peninsula's northern end is enclosed by several kilometres of **stone battlements**: at the very tip, **Bajing Park** (¥8) is an untidy arrangement of willows and ponds enlivened by **Bajing Tai**, a platform and tower whose rusting cannon no longer threaten barges negotiating the river junction below. Exiting the park, you can follow the walls southeast down Zhongshan Lu through 1930s streets to the old **east gate**, still with a functioning portcullis; on the far side is a small market, where people fish midstream with cast nets and **cormorants**, and villagers wheel their bicycles to the far bank across a low **pontoon**

bridge. Originally built by chaining punts across the river and laying a wooden decking on top (though the mid-section floats are steel), these bridges were common through the region until the 1950s, as they were cheap to make and easily removable in times of flooding or war. Look back from the middle at the steep walls and appreciate Ganzhou's defences – it wouldn't have taken much time to cut the bridge, drop the portcullis and load the cannon.

Back inside the city, if you head more or less southwest you'll see older architecture, including narrow side streets of Qing houses, colonial-style colonnaded shop fronts along the main roads, a couple of small temples and a pagoda – nothing of great importance but atmospheric all the same, though demolitions have started to take their toll.

Practicalities

The town is a small place by Chinese standards, whose centre is only a couple of kilometres across. The town's centrepiece is **Nanmen Guangchang**, South Gate Square: from here, **Wenqing Lu** runs north through the centre to Bajing Park and the river, lined with clothes shops and restaurants, while **Hongqi Lu** is the town's east–west transport artery.

The **long-distance bus station** is on Bayi Si Dadao, 3km from the centre at the southeastern corner of town, a relentlessly unappealing area. The **train station** is farther out in the same direction; from either station, bus #2 will get you to Nanmen Guangchang. **Leaving**, trains head to Jinggang Shan, Nanchang, Jiujiang, Wuhan, Hefei and well beyond, with useful buses south to Shaoguan and Guangzhou in Guangdong province.

The main **Bank of China** is halfway up Wenqing Lu and a **post office** can be found on Nanmen Guangchang. There are a few cheap **hotels** north of the bus station on Bayi Si Dadao, but you're better off forking out for a decent room at the *Ganzhou Fandian*, near Nanmen Guangchang at 29 Hongqi Dadao (Ⓣ0797/8280188; ❺) – it's not as expensive as you'd think from the exterior. As for **eating**, head up Wenqing Lu: there's Western-style food and coffee upstairs at *Spring of Taipei*, about 100m along on the west side; 500m along at the intersection with Qingnian Lu you'll find extremely popular hotpots at *Wuzhou Kuaican*, and buns, soya milk and snacks at *Yonghe Doujiang*.

Travel details

Trains

Changsha to: Beijing (14 daily; 14–19hr 30min); Guangzhou (38 daily; 7hr 30min–11hr); Guilin (5 daily; 7–10hr); Guiyang (4 daily; 13hr 30min); Hengyang (40 daily; 2–3hr); Nanchang (daily; 7hr); Shaoshan (daily; 3hr); Shenzhen (7 daily; 9–13hr); Wuhan (41 daily; 3hr 30min–5hr); Yueyang (35 daily; 1hr 30min–2hr 30min); Zhangjiajie (5 daily; 5–6hr).

Ganzhou to: Beijing (daily; 22hr); Guangzhou (3 daily; 8–10hr); Hefei (3 daily; 11–13hr); Jinggang Shan (daily; 1hr 40min); Jiujiang (13 daily; 6–8hr 30min); Nanchang (17 daily; 4hr 30min–6hr); Shenzhen (3 daily; 9hr); Wuhan (daily; 14hr).

Hefei to: Beijing (4 daily; 10–15hr); Bozhou (9 daily; 4hr 30min); Ganzhou (3 daily; 11–13hr); Jingdezhen (2 daily; 9hr 30min); Jiujiang (4 daily; 5hr); Nanchang (5 daily; 6–7hr); Nanjing (5 daily; 4–5hr 30min); Shanghai (3 daily; 7–9hr); Tunxi (3 daily; 6hr 30min–7hr 30min); Wuhu (10 daily; 2–3hr); Xian (3 daily; 15hr 30min–17hr).

Jingdezhen to: Hefei (2 daily; 9–10hr 30min); Nanchang (3 daily; 4hr 30min–6hr); Shanghai (daily; 16hr 30min); Tunxi (11 daily; 3hr 30min).

Jiujiang to: Ganzhou (13 daily; 6–8hr 30min); Hefei (4 daily; 4–5hr); Nanchang (26 daily; 1hr 30min–2hr 30min); Shanghai (daily; 17hr 30min).

Nanchang to: Beijing (7 daily; 13hr 30min–18hr 30min); Changsha (daily; 7hr); Fuzhou (6 daily; 12–13hr 30min); Ganzhou (17 daily; 4hr 30min–6hr); Guangzhou (6 daily; 11–14hr); Hefei (5 daily; 6–7hr); Jingdezhen (4 daily; 5–6hr); Jinggang Shan

(8 daily; 3hr); Jiujiang (26 daily; 1hr 30min–3hr); Shanghai (7 daily; 13–16hr); Shenzhen (6 daily; 10–15hr); Tunxi (2 daily; 9hr 30min); Wuhan (14 daily; 6–10hr); Xiamen (4 daily; 17–21hr); Yingtan (frequent; 2–3hr).
Tunxi to: Beijing (daily; 19hr 30min); Hefei (3 daily; 6–7hr); Jingdezhen (11 daily; 3–5hr); Nanchang (daily; 9hr); Nanjing (9 daily; 6–10hr); Shanghai (2 daily; 11–12hr 30min).
Wuhan to: Beijing (15 daily; 10–15hr 30min); Changsha (frequent; 3hr 30min–5hr); Ganzhou (daily; 14hr); Guangzhou (frequent; 11–15hr); Nanchang (14 daily; 5hr 30min–10hr 30min); Shiyan (8 daily; 5–10hr 30min); Wudang Shan (daily; 7hr 30min); ; Yueyang (frequent; 2–3hr 30min); Xi'an (6 daily; 13hr 30min–19hr); Xiangfan (12 daily; 3–6hr 30min).
Wuhu to: Hefei (10 daily; 2hr); Ma'anshan (daily; 40min); Nanjing (18 daily; 2–4hr); Shanghai (4 daily; 5–9hr).
Xiangfan to: Shiyan (19 daily; 2–6hr 30min); Wudang Shan (3 daily; 2hr–5hr 30min); Wuhan (12 daily; 3hr 30min–6hr 30min); Yichang (8 daily; 4hr); Zhangjiajie (2 daily; 7–9hr 30min).
Yichang to: Beijing (daily; 20hr); Xi'an (daily; 16hr 30min); Xiangfan (8 daily; 4hr); Zhangjiajie (daily; 5hr 30min).
Yueyang to: Changsha (35 daily; 1hr 30min–2hr 30min); Wuhan (29 daily; 2–3hr 30min).
Zhangjiajie to: Changsha (5 daily; 5–6hr); Huaihua (for connections to Guiyang or Changsha; 8 daily; 4–6hr 30min); Jishou (for Fenghuang; 6 daily; 2hr); Xiangfan (2 daily; 7hr 30min–10hr 30min); Yichang (daily; 6hr).

Buses

Changsha to: Heng Shan (3hr); Jiujiang (13hr); Nanchang (6hr); Wuhan (4hr); Yichang (6hr); Yueyang (3hr); Zhangjiajie (7hr).
Ciping (Jinggang Shan Shi) to: Ganzhou (5hr); Hengyang (8hr); Taihe (for Jinggang Shan; 2hr); Nanchang (8hr).
Hefei to: Bozhou (5hr); Huainan (2hr); Jiuhua Shan (5hr); Jiujiang (5hr); Ma'anshan (3hr); Nanchang (6hr); Nanjing (3hr); Shouxian (2hr); Tongling (3hr); Tunxi (5hr); Wuhan (6hr); Wuhu (2hr).
Jingdezhen to: Jiujiang (1–2hr); Nanchang (3hr); Tunxi (3hr 30min); Yingtan (3hr).
Jiuhua Shan to: Hefei (5hr); Qingyang (30min); Taiping (3hr); Tangkou (4hr); Tongling (2hr); Wuhu (3hr).
Jiujiang to: Changsha (13hr); Jingdezhen (1–2hr); Hefei (5hr); Lu Shan (1hr 30min); Nanchang (2hr); Wuhan (4hr).
Jishou to: Fenghuang (1hr 30min).
Nanchang to: Ciping (8hr); Changsha (6hr); Hefei (6hr); Jingdezhen (3hr); Jinggang Shan (6hr); Jiujiang (2hr); Lu Shan (4hr); Wuhan (6hr); Yingtan (2hr 30min).
Tunxi to: Hefei (5hr); Jingdezhen (3hr 30min); Jiuhua Shan (5hr); Nanjing (6hr); Shanghai (12hr); Shexian (1hr); Tangkou (1hr); Tongling (4hr); Wuhu (3hr); Yixian (2hr).
Wuhan to: Changsha (4hr); Hefei (6hr); Jingzhou (3hr 30min); Jiujiang (4hr); Nanchang (6hr); Xiangfan (5hr); Yichang (4hr); Yueyang (4hr).
Wuhu to: Hefei (2hr); Jiuhua Shan (3hr); Ma'anshan (1hr); Nanjing (3hr); Tunxi (3hr); Tongling (2hr); Xuancheng (2hr).
Xiangfan to: Jingzhou (4hr 30min); Wudang Shan (2hr); Wuhan (5hr); Yichang (5hr).
Yichang to: Changsha (6hr); Jingzhou (1hr 30min); Jiujiang (12hr); Wuhan (4hr); Xiangfan (5hr); Xing Shan (4hr).
Zhangjiajie to: Changsha (7hr); Jishou (for Fenghuang; 2hr).

Ferries

Wuhan to: Chongqing (daily; 5 days).
Yichang to: Chongqing (daily; 11hr by hydrofoil, otherwise 2–4 days).

Flights

Changsha to: Beijing (6 daily; 2hr); Chongqing (2 daily; 1hr 15min); Guangzhou (3 daily; 1hr); Hefei (daily; 1hr 35min); Hong Kong (7 weekly; 1hr 30min); Shanghai (6 daily; 1hr 30min); Shenzhen (6 daily; 1hr 10min); Tianjin (5 weekly; 1hr 40min); Zhangjiajie (daily; 40min).
Hefei to: Beijing (3 daily; 1hr 40min); Changsha (daily; 1hr 35min); Guangzhou (3 daily; 1hr 50min); Nanchang (2 weekly; 1hr); Shenzhen (2 daily; 2hr); Tunxi (daily; 40min); Xiamen (daily; 1hr 35min); Xi'an (daily; 1hr 30min).
Nanchang to: Beijing (5 daily; 2hr); Chengdu (daily; 2hr); Guangzhou (3 daily; 1hr 10min); Hefei (2 weekly; 1hr); Kunming (daily; 2hr); Shanghai (5 daily; 1hr); Tunxi (2 weekly; 50min).
Tunxi (Huang Shan) to: Beijing (2 weekly; 2hr); Guangzhou (2 daily; 1hr 30min–3hr 10min); Hefei (daily; 40min); Nanchang (2 weekly; 50min); Shanghai (daily; 1hr).
Wuhan to: Beijing (7 daily; 1hr 50min); Guangzhou (5 daily; 1hr 30min); Hong Kong (daily; 1hr 50min); Shanghai (10 daily; 1hr 15min).
Yichang to: Beijing (daily; 2hr); Chongqing (daily; 1hr 20min); Guangzhou (daily; 1hr 45min); Shanghai (2 weekly; 1hr 30min).
Zhangjiajie to: Changsha (daily; 40min).

CHAPTER 8

Highlights

- **Wuyi Shan** Dramatic gorges and great hiking trails amongst some of the finest scenery in southern China. See p.538
- **Gulangyu Islet** Uniquely relaxing island sporting vehicle-free streets, European-style colonial mansions, and sea views. See p.553
- **Hakka mansions** These circular mud-brick homes, sometimes housing upwards of five hundred people, are China's most distinctive traditional architecture. See p.555
- **Cantonese food** Sample China's finest cuisine, from *dim sum* to roast goose, in one of Guangzhou's restaurants. See p.580
- **Chaozhou** Old town with Ming-dynasty walls, some great street life, the famous Kaiyuan Si – and more good food. See p.609
- **Hainan Island** Soak up the sun, swim, surf and watch Chinese and Russians at play on the country's best beaches. See p.620

▲ The Thirty-Six Peaks, Wuyi Shan

8

Fujian, Guangdong and Hainan Island

There's something very self-contained about the provinces of **Fujian**, **Guangdong** and **Hainan Island**, which occupy 1200km or so of China's convoluted southern seaboard. Though occasionally taking centre stage in the country's history, the provinces share a sense of being generally isolated from mainstream events by the mountain ranges surrounding Fujian and Guangdong, physically cutting them off from the rest of the empire. Forced to look seawards, the coastal regions have a long history of contact with the outside world, continually importing – or being forced to endure – foreign influences and styles. This is where Islam entered China, and porcelain and tea left it along the **Maritime Silk Road**; where the mid-nineteenth-century theatricals of the Opium Wars, colonialism, the Taiping Uprising and the mass overseas exodus of southern Chinese were played out; and where today you'll find China's most Westernized cities. Conversely, the interior mountains enclose some of the country's wildest, most remote corners, parts of which were virtually in the Stone Age within living memory.

Possibly because its specific attractions are thinly spread, the region receives scant attention from visitors. Huge numbers do pass through Guangdong, in transit between the mainland and Hong Kong and Macau, but only because they have to, and few look beyond the overpowering capital, Guangzhou. Yet while the other two regional capitals – **Fuzhou** in Fujian, and Hainan's **Haikou** – share Guangzhou's modern veneer, all three also hide temples and antique architecture that have somehow escaped developers, while other cities and towns have managed to preserve their old, character-laden ambience intact. The pick of these are the Fujian port of **Xiamen**, its streets almost frozen in time since the start of the twentieth century, and **Chaozhou** in eastern Guangdong, a staunchly conservative place consciously preserving its traditions in the face of the modern world.

Indeed, a sense of local tradition and of being different from the rest of the country pervades the whole region, though this feeling is rarely expressed in any tangible way. **Language** is one difference you will notice, however, as the main dialects here are Cantonese and Minnan, whose rhythms are recognizably removed from Mandarin, even if you can't speak a word of Chinese. Southern pronunciation is also very distinct: "h" and "k" replace "f" and "j" respectively, for instance, so that "Fujian" comes out as "Hokkian" in local parlance. Less

obvious are specific **ethnic groups**, including the **Hakka**, a widely spread Han subgroup whose mountainous Guangdong–Fujian heartland is dotted with fortress-like mansions; the Muslim **Hui**, who form large communities in Guangzhou, coastal Hainan and in **Quanzhou** in Fujian; and the **Li**, Hainan's animistic, original inhabitants.

While a quick look around much of the coastal areas here leaves a gloomy impression of uncontrolled development and its attendant ills (some cities seem to consist of nothing but beggars and building sites), most of this is actually contained within various **Special Economic Zones** (SEZs), specifically created in the mid-1980s as a focus for heavy investment and industrialization. Beyond their boundaries lurk some respectably wild – and some nicely tamed – corners where you can settle back and enjoy the scenery. Over in western Guangdong, the city of **Zhaoqing** sits beside some pleasant lakes and hills, while the **Wuyi Shan** range in northeastern Fujian contains the region's lushest, most picturesque mountain forests. Way down south lie the country's best **beaches** – encouraging the tourist industry to hype Hainan as "China's Hawaii" – and there's also a limited amount of hiking to try, through the island's interior highlands.

Anyone wanting to stop off and explore will find plentiful local and long-distance **transport**, though **accommodation** can be expensive and suffers additional seasonal price hikes in Guangzhou. The **weather** is nicest in spring and autumn, as summer storms from June to August bring daily doses of heavy humidity, thunder and afternoon downpours on the coast, while the higher reaches of the Guangdong–Fujian border can get very cold in winter.

Fujian

FUJIAN, on China's southeastern coast, is well off the beaten track for most Western travellers, which is a pity because the province possesses not only a wild mountainous interior, but also a string of old ports, including **Xiamen**, China's most relaxed coastal city. From Hong Kong, the well-trodden routes head directly west towards Guilin, or north to Shanghai, but a detour to Xiamen makes an excellent introduction to mainland China – boats from Hong Kong come here, as does a spur of China's rail network.

Culturally and geographically, the province splits into distinct halves. One is made up of large, historical seaports and lush, semitropical coastal stretches, whose sophisticated population enjoy warm sun and blossoming trees even in January. The other is the rugged, mountainous and largely inaccessible interior, freezing cold in winter, home to around 140 different local dialects and with a history of poverty and backwardness: when the Red Army arrived in the 1960s they found communities unaware that the Qing dynasty had been overthrown; and even today, the area is wild enough to harbour the last few populations of the **South China tiger**. However, while inland Fujian knew very little of China, contacts between the coastal area and the outside world had been flourishing for centuries. In the Tang dynasty, the port of **Quanzhou** was considered on a par with Alexandria as the most international port in the world, and teemed with Middle Eastern traders, some of whose descendants still live in the area today. So much wealth was brought into the ports here that a population explosion led to mass emigration, and large parts of the Malay Peninsula, the Philippines and Taiwan were colonized by Fujianese. In the early eighteenth century this exodus of able-bodied subjects became so drastic that the imperial court in distant Beijing tried, ineffectually, to ban it.

Today the interior of Fujian remains largely unvisited and unknown, with the exception of the scenic **Wuyi Shan** area in the northwest of the province, and the **Hakka regions** around southwesterly **Yongding**. The coast, however, is booming, with colossal investment pouring in from both Hong Kong and, in particular, neighbouring **Taiwan**, many of whose citizens originate from the province and speak the same dialect, Minnan Hua. The cities of **Fuzhou** and Xiamen are among the wealthiest in the country, particularly Xiamen, with its clean beaches, charming streets and shopping arcades. The proximity of Taiwan accounts not only for the city's rapid economic development and the proliferation of first-class tourist facilities, but also for the occasional outbreak of tension. During Taiwanese elections, mainland authorities often hold large-scale military exercises just off the Taiwan coast as a gentle reminder to the Taiwanese not to vote for separatist candidates – a tactic which usually backfires, as demonstrated by the back-to-back election victories of pro-independence Chen Shui-Bian in 2000 and 2004. And while cross-straits business manages to smooth over the cracks somewhat, the hundreds of missiles pointing from the mainland to Taiwan remain.

Getting around Fujian has become easier in recent years, with an extremely fast **coastal expressway** linking the main cities with neighbouring Zhejiang and Guangdong provinces. To reach the interior wilds of Wuyi Shan, you're better off catching a **train**, with separate lines from Fuzhou, Quanzhou and Xiamen; Fuzhou also has a decent link through to Jiangxi province, and there's another track west to Meizhou in Guangdong from Xiamen and Quanzhou. Otherwise, train travel within or beyond the province is circuitous and very slow.

Fuzhou

Capital of Fujian Province, **FUZHOU** is a comfortably modern and clean city, with shiny business skyscrapers looming over the main roads. An important trading centre for more than a thousand years, it was visited by Marco Polo during the Yuan dynasty. In the fifteenth century, Fuzhou shipbuilders earned themselves the distinction of having built the world's largest ocean-going ship, the *Baochuan*, sailed by the famous Chinese navigator Zheng He, who used it to travel all around Asia and Africa. One thing Polo noted when he was here was the high-profile presence of Mongol armies to suppress any potential uprisings; the city is no less well defended today, forming the heart of Fujian's military opposition to Taiwan. There's precious

Fuzhou		
Fuzhou	福州	*fúzhōu*
Bai Ta	白塔	*báitǎ*
Changle Airport	长乐机场	*chánglè jīchǎng*
Fuzhou Provincial Museum	福建省博物馆	*fújiànshěng bówùguǎn*
Gu Shan	鼓山	*gǔshān*
Lin Zexu Memorial Hall	林则徐纪念馆	*línzéxú jìniànguǎn*
Mao Zedong Statue	毛塑像	*máo sùxiàng*
Min River	闽江	*mǐnjiāng*
Wu Ta	乌塔	*wūtǎ*
Wuyi Square	五一广场	*wǔyī guǎngchǎng*
Xi Hu Park	西湖公园	*xīhú gōngyuán*
Yu Shan	于山	*yúshān*
Accommodation and eating		
Best Western	最佳西方财富酒店	*zuìjiāxīfāngcáifù jiǔdiàn*
Cang Jin Zhai	仓锦斋	*cāngjǐn zhāi*
Foreign Trade Centre	外宾中心酒店	*wàibīnzhōngxīn jiǔdiàn*
Galaxy Garden	银河花园大饭店	*yínhéhuāyuán dàfàndiàn*
Hao Ke Lai	豪客来	*háokè lái*
Haoyun	好运宾馆	*hǎoyùn bīnguǎn*
Juchunyuan	聚春园大酒店	*jùchūnyuán dàjiǔdiàn*
Minhang	民航大厦	*mínháng dàshà*
Minjiang	闽江饭店	*mīnjiāng fàndiàn*
Nanyang	南洋饭店	*nányáng fàndiàn*
Wenquan	温泉大饭店	*wēnquán dàfàndiàn*
Xinglong Sheng	兴隆盛酒店	*xīnglóngshèng jiǔdiàn*
Yushan	于山宾馆	*yúshān bīnguǎn*

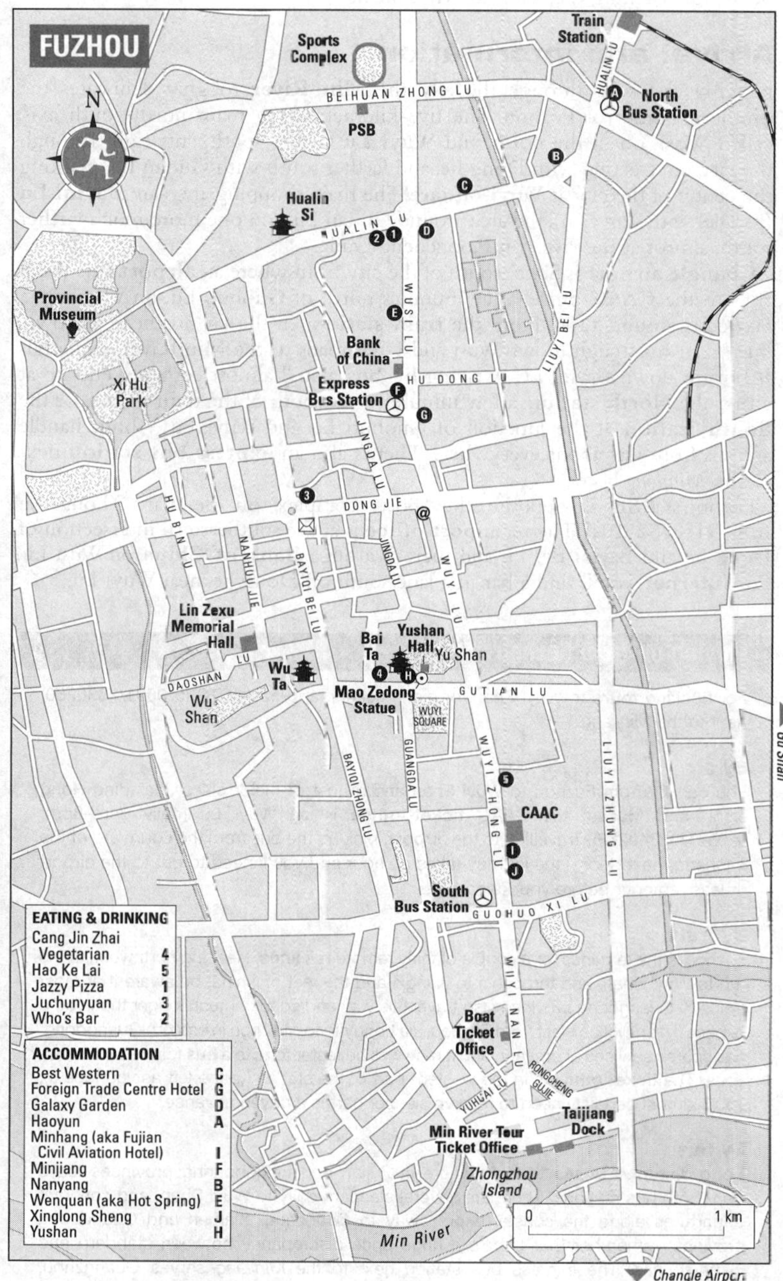
FUZHOU
N
Sports Complex
Train Station
HUALIN LU
BEIHUAN ZHONG LU
North Bus Station
PSB
Hualin Si
HUALIN LU
WUSI LU
LIUYI BEI LU
Provincial Museum
Bank of China
HU DONG LU
Express Bus Station
Xi Hu Park
JINGDA LU
DONG JIE
HU BIN LU
NANHOU JIE
BAYIQI BEI LU
JINGDA LU
WUYI LU
Lin Zexu Memorial Hall
Bai Ta
Yushan Hall
Yu Shan
DAOSHAN LU
Wu Ta
Mao Zedong Statue
GUTIAN LU
Wu Shan
WUYI SQUARE
Gu Shan
BAYIQI ZHONG LU
GUANGDA LU
WUYI ZHONG LU
LIUYI ZHONG LU
CAAC
South Bus Station
GUOHUO XI LU
WUYI NAN LU
Boat Ticket Office
RONGCHENG GUJIE
YUHUAI LU
Taijiang Dock
Min River Tour Ticket Office
Zhongzhou Island
Min River
0
1 km
Changle Airport
EATING & DRINKING
Cang Jin Zhai Vegetarian 4
Hao Ke Lai 5
Jazzy Pizza 1
Juchunyuan 3
Who's Bar 2
ACCOMMODATION
Best Western C
Foreign Trade Centre Hotel G
Galaxy Garden D
Haoyun A
Minhang (aka Fujian Civil Aviation Hotel) I
Minjiang F
Nanyang B
Wenquan (aka Hot Spring) E
Xinglong Sheng J
Yushan H

little to detain casual visitors, and the city is probably best used as a springboard for reaching the wilds of Wuyi Shan.

Arrival and information

Flowing east–west through the city, the **Min River** roughly delineates the southern border of Fuzhou. The five-kilometre-long main north–south axis, called **Wusi Lu** in the north, and **Wuyi Lu** farther south, cuts right through the city, intersecting with Dong Jie, and farther south with Gutian Lu, marking the centre of the city at **Wuyi Square**. The main shopping areas are **Bayiqi Lu** (parallel with Wuyi Lu), the area around Gutian Lu, and one more much farther south, almost at the river, on Rongcheng Gujie.

Changle airport is 50km south of the city, from where an **airport bus** (¥20) runs to the CAAC office, a few minutes north of Guohuo Lu, on Wuyi Lu; a taxi costs around ¥100. From the **train station**, in the far northeast of town, bus #51 runs straight down Wusi and Wuyi roads to the Min River, while bus #20 runs down Bayiqi Lu. Arriving **by bus**, you'll almost certainly end up at either the **North station**, a few minutes' walk south of the train station, or the **South station** at the junction of Guohuo Lu and Wuyi Lu – both handle arrivals from just about everywhere. There's also an **express bus station** next to the *Minjiang* hotel.

Fuzhou's **PSB** is opposite the sports complex on Beihuan Zhong Lu (①0591/87821104). The main **post office** is at the southeastern intersection of Dong Jie and Bayiqi Bei Lu and there is a huge **Bank of China** on Wusi Lu. For **Internet**, you'll find a bar in a lane south off Dong Jie, near Wuyi Lu.

Moving on from Fuzhou

For booking **tours** to Wuyi Shan, or plane tickets, approach CTS (①0591/7536250) next to the *Minjiang*.

By air

You can **fly** from Fuzhou to Wuyi Shan and a host of major cities, including Hong Kong and Macau; the CAAC **ticket office** is on Wuyi Lu (daily 8am–8pm; ①0591/83340268). Travelling to the **airport**, pick up the bus from the courtyard of the *Minhang*, next door – the journey takes an hour and you'll need to get to the airport at least an hour before your departure.

By train

Fuzhou is the terminus for a couple of fairly remote **rail lines**. Heading northwest, trains run to Wuyi Shan, and through into Jiangxi and the rest of China; be aware that most trains to Guangdong province also travel this way and so take much longer than you'd expect. The new line west from Fuzhou, via Longyan to Meizhou in eastern Guangdong, has sparse services at present, and it may well be faster to take a bus for these destinations. The **ticket office** is in the western part of the station (to the left as you face it); you'll almost certainly need to reserve sleeper berths a day in advance.

By bus

Long-distance buses to everywhere in Fujian and neighbouring provinces leave from both bus stations. There are several sleepers daily to Wuyi Shan, and constant departures along the coastal expressway to Quanzhou, Xiamen and Guangdong province; remember that there's a huge price discrepancy between standard and luxury buses. The express bus station next to the *Minjiang* serves Guangzhou, Shanghai and a few other distant destinations.

Accommodation

Most of Fuzhou's **accommodation** is upmarket, with a few budget options that can usually be persuaded to take foreigners, most notably around the train and North bus stations.

Best Western 220 Hualin Lu ⓣ0591/87523388, ⓦwww.bwfortunehotel.com. A new arrival in town, offering quality business rooms at competitive, flexible rates. Good location, impossible to miss. 6
Foreign Trade Centre Wusi Lu ⓣ0591/88199998, ⓕ87550358. One of the top choices, but so large it tends to feel rather lonely and empty most of the time. North wing 6, South wing 7
Galaxy Garden Corner of Hualin Lu and Wusi Lu ⓣ0591/87831888, ⓕ87843662. Business-oriented hotel with smart furnishings and attentive staff. 5
Haoyun Beside the North bus station ⓣ0591/87580888. One of many budget hotels in the vicinity. Beds from ¥38. 3
Minhang (aka Fujian Civil Aviation Hotel) Next to CAAC, Wuyi Zhong Lu ⓣ0591/83343988, ⓕ83341978. CAAC-run hotel with spacious, comfortable and clean rooms. A fair deal. 3
Minjiang Wusi Lu ⓣ0591/87557895, ⓔmjht@pub2.fz.fj.cn. Mid-range hotel with sound rooms, well placed just south of Hu Dong Lu next to the express bus station. 5
Nanyang Hualin Lu ⓣ0591/87579699, ⓕ87577085. A convenient location near the train and North bus stations. Rooms a bit frayed for the price, but staff are helpful. 4
Wenquan (aka Hot Spring) Wusi Lu ⓣ0591/87851818, ⓦwww.hshfz.com. A smart hotel with a cavernous interior full of top-name designer shops. Service is excellent, as you'd expect for the price. 7
Xinglong Sheng Wuyi Zhong Lu ⓣ0591/83371037, ⓕ83370779. A good-value place near the South bus station, with clean, pleasant, slightly tattered rooms and friendly staff. 2
Yushan Yushan Lu, off Gutian Lu ⓣ0591/83351668, ⓕ83357694. ⓦwww.yushan-hotel.com. This hotel enjoys a fine location just below Yu Shan and next to Bai Ta, with large, wooden-floored rooms and helpful staff. 5

The City

Almost totally devoid of formal sights – though many small, nondescript temples are secreted between more modern structures – Fuzhou is centred around **Wuyi Square**, an open expanse dominated by a statue of Mao Zedong looking south. This statue commemorates the Ninth Congress of the Chinese Communist Party in 1969, an event that ratified Maoism as the "state religion" of China, and named the mysterious Lin Biao (subsequently disgraced) as official heir to Mao's throne. Just behind Mao's statue, the large modern building, **Yushan Hall**, is sometimes used for exhibitions – climbing up a path to the west of it lands you at the gates of **Yu Shan** (Jade Hill), a nice place for a stroll. The main sight here is the 1000-year-old **Bai Ta**, a whitewashed pagoda located beside a temple, and a small exhibition of the contents of a local Song-dynasty tomb, which includes the preserved bodies of a man and a woman and some silk garments.

West from Yu Shan is **Bayiqi Lu**, a busy, crowded avenue at the heart of Fuzhou's shopping district. On the far side is another small hill, Wu Shan. The flat summit, fringed with banyan trees, is capped by a small temple and **Wu Ta**, a black granite pagoda dating back to the same era as the white Bai Ta, and containing some attractive statuary. North from here on the corner of Daoshan Lu and Nanhou Jie, you'll find the **Lin Zexu Memorial Hall** (daily 8.30am–12.30pm & 1–5pm; ¥10), a quiet, attractive couple of halls and courtyards with funereal statues of animals. Lin Zexu (1785–1850) is fondly remembered as the patriotic Qing-dynasty official who fought against the importation of opium by foreigners – even writing persuasive letters to Queen Victoria on the subject – though his destruction of thousands of chests of the drug in 1840 sparked the first Opium War and, rather unfairly, he was exiled to Xinjiang.

Running north from behind Yushan Hall is **Jingda Lu**, Fuzhou's second shopping street. A far more intimate affair than Wuyi Lu, Jingda is home to hundreds of clothing boutiques selling a variety of designer- (some genuine) and Chinese-brand garments. While not quite up to Shanghai shoppers' standards, prices are lower and there is the odd hidden gem waiting to be found.

The northwest of the city is dominated by **Xi Hu Park** (daily 7am–9pm; ¥4), whose entrance is along southerly Hu Bin Lu – you can get here on bus #1 or #2 from the southern end of Bayiqi Lu, or #810 from the train station. The park, mostly comprising an artificial lake formed by excavations some seventeen hundred years ago, is a good spot to go boating or stroll with the masses on a hot day. Within the grounds, staff at the newly rebuilt but largely ignored **Fuzhou Provincial Museum** (daily 10.30am–5pm; ¥10) will be delighted to see you. The highlight of their collection, among thousands of pieces of porcelain and examples of primitive iron tools, is a 3500-year-old coffin-boat removed from a Wuyi Shan cave.

Gu Shan

Fuzhou's most-touted tourist attraction is **Gu Shan** (Drum Mountain), about 9km east of the city. To get here, catch one of the regular **minibuses** from the Nanmen terminus on Guangda Lu, just west of Wuyi Square (¥8); it's an attractive 45-minute journey through forested hills, with sweeping views as the road starts climbing. The Gu Shan area offers woodland walks as well as scattered sights, including the 1000-year-old, heavily restored **Yongquan Si**, which gets phenomenally crowded at weekends. One way to escape the crowds is to climb the 2500 stone steps (allow around an hour; your knees will want plenty of rests) behind the temple to the wooded summit of Gu Shan.

Eating and drinking

For such a major city, Fuzhou suffers a serious lack of **restaurants**, outside of those in the hotels, though Western and Chinese fast-food chains are everywhere. For **snacks**, hole-in-the-wall operations surround transit points, while street vendors peddle small, bagel-like *gua bao* ("cut buns"), stuffed with vegetables or a slice of spiced, steamed pork. Otherwise, the highest concentration of places to eat is along downtown Dong Jie. You'll find popular hotpot places like the restaurant in the *Juchunyuan*, which does all-you-can-eat for ¥48. Another place for inexpensive, good and varied food in a comfortable setting is a branch of *Hao Ke Lai*, which serves Sichuan-style cold spiced meats and vegetables, along with soups, noodles, spring rolls and local buns, all at a few yuan a serve – look for the yellow and green sign spelling out "Houcaller" on Wuyi Zhong Lu. Vegetarians can eat meat-free at *Cang Jin Zhai*, not far from Yu Shan; a rare Buddhist-themed restaurant that also indulges customers wishing to smoke and drink beer. Steak houses abound, while for something Italian try *Jazzy Pizza* at the junction of Haulin Lu and Wusi Lu. For **nightlife**, head for the bars and clubs on Dong Jie, and the loosely Western-style *Who's Bar*, on Hualin Lu, a little beyond the junction with Wusi Lu.

Wuyi Shan

Away in the northeast of the province, 370km from Fuzhou and close to the Fujian–Jiangxi border, the **WUYI SHAN** area contains some of the most impressive scenery in southern China. It's the only inland part of Fujian

Wuyi Shan		
Wuyi Shan Scenic District	武夷山风景区	*wǔyíshān fēngjǐng qū*
Chishi	赤石	*chìshí*
Chongyang Stream	崇阳溪	*chóngyáng xī*
Dawang Feng	大王峰	*dàwáng fēng*
Dujia Qu	度假区	*dùjiàqū*
Jiuqu River	九曲溪	*jiǔqǔ xī*
Shuilian Cave	水帘洞	*shuǐlián dòng*
Tianyou Feng	天游峰	*tiānyóu fēng*
Wuyigong	武夷宫	*wǔyí gōng*
Wuyishan Shi	武夷山市	*wǔyíshān shì*
Xingcun	腥村	*xīng cūn*
Yingzui Yan	鹰嘴岩	*yīngzuǐ yán*
Accommodation		
Aihu Binguan	矮胡宾馆	*ǎihú bīnguǎn*
Gu Yue	古越山庄	*gǔyuè shānzhuāng*
Hualong	花龙大酒店	*huālóng dàjiǔdiàn*
Wuyi Mountain Villa	武夷山庄	*wǔyíshān zhuāng*
Yue Hong	悦宏酒店	*yue hong jiudian*

regularly visited by tourists, and consists of two principal parts: the **Jiuqu River**, which meanders at the feet of the mountains, and the **Thirty-Six Peaks**, which rise up from the river, mostly to its north. With peaks protruding from low-lying mists, the scenery is classic Chinese scroll-painting material, and the park, dotted with small, attractive villages, can be a tremendous place to relax for a few days, offering clean mountain air and leisurely walks through a landscape of lush green vegetation, deep red sandstone mountains, soaring cliff faces, rock pools, waterfalls and caves. Despite the remoteness, Wuyi is surprisingly full of tourists – especially Taiwanese – in high summer, so a visit off season might be preferable, when you'll also see the mountaintops cloaked with snow. Note that as Wuyi Shan has developed into a major attraction, it is losing some of its charm, and tourists have become regarded as fair game for some serious overcharging.

Practicalities

The sixty-square-kilometre site is bordered by the **Jiuqu** (Nine-Twisting) **River** to the south, which runs its crooked course for some 8km between **Xingcun** village to the west, and the main village in the area, **WUYIGONG** to the east – where it joins the **Chongyang Stream** running from north to south and demarcates the park's eastern border. There is a strip of tourist hotels, restaurants, shops, and bus- and plane-ticket booking offices, along with a **Bank of China** (daily 8am–5.30pm), immediately east of the stream, just before the bridge. Over the bridge 1km or so, Wuyigong lies in the cleft between the junction of the two waterways and contains a bus stop and some hotels.

Most transport arrives 15km north of the park at **WUYISHAN SHI** the regional town. You can get here by **train** from Fuzhou, Quanzhou or Xiamen, or by **sleeper bus** (¥80) from Fuzhou. The alternative is to **fly** from Fuzhou (¥380 each way), Xiamen and other cities across China; **Wuyi airport** is at the village of **Chishi**, a few kilometres to the northeast of the scenic area and to the south of Wuyishan Shi. Frequent minibuses connect Wuyishan Shi and the

Bamboo-raft trips

The traditional way to appreciate Wuyi Shan is to take a two-hour **bamboo-raft trip** along the Jiuqu River. Rafts leave daily between 7.30am and around 4pm all year round, from the small village of **Xingcun**, which you can reach on public buses from Wuyi Shan Shi and Wuyigong (both ¥2.5). On arrival, locals will happily point you towards the river where boatmen wait to pick up tourists. Tickets cost ¥100 and rafts only set off when they have the necessary six people. Be prepared to be pushed, tugged, shouted at and generally cajoled into taking the final seat on a raft that is waiting to leave – even if you are travelling in a pair. At busy times the river becomes a noisy bamboo conveyor-belt, but, although it is hardly the tranquil experience it may once have been, from the first crook in the meandering river right up to the ninth, you'll still have stupendous gorge scenery all the way. Watch out for the odd, boat-shaped **coffins** in caves above the fourth crook; they are said to be 4000 years old, and appear similar to those in Gongxian and along the Little Three Gorges in Sichuan (see p.901 and p.915).

airport with Wuyigong. Fuzhou's CTS (see p.536) also runs **tour buses** direct to Wuyigong.

Accommodation and eating

Dujia Qu, as the new development east of the river is known, holds a plethora of identikit **places to stay**, many with delusions of grandeur. However, prices are almost infinitely flexible (especially outside of summer or weekends), and,

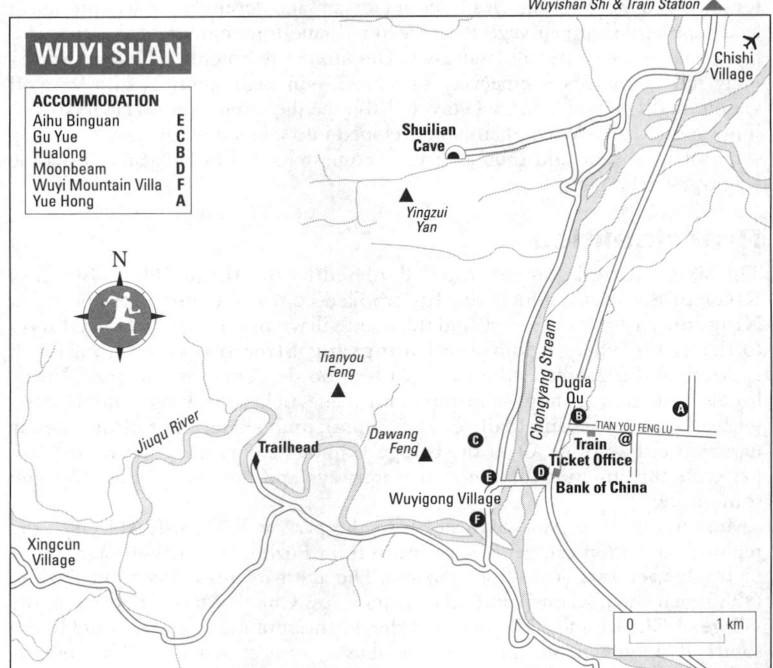

although being a foreigner will definitely count against you, hard bargaining can result in prices of ¥80-100 even in hotels with claimed rack rates of more than ¥400.

Generally, the further south you go on the hotel strip and the further away from the main road you venture, the cheaper the accommodation gets; the *Moonbeam* (Ⓣ0599/5253618; ❸), with its lightly tattered rooms, is one to try if you're looking for a deal, while the newer, cleaner *Yue Hong Hotel* (Ⓣ0599/5252942; ❹) can be similarly flexible, although the bar across the road can be deafening. Along the main road, the *Hualong* (Ⓣ0599/5252999; Ⓦwww.hualonghotel.cn; ❻) is one of the more established names. It's better to cross the river for quieter, more pleasant options: the *Gu Yue* (Ⓣ0599/5252916; ❸) and *Aihu Binguan* (Ⓣ0599/5252263; ❹) are reasonably priced and away from the bustle of Dujia. Towards Wuyigong, the *Wuyi Mountain Villa* (Ⓣ0599/5251888, Ⓕ5252567; ❼) is an upmarket place with a marvellous setting, resting hard under Dawang Feng and built around a Suzhou-style ornamental garden. **Wuyishan Shi** itself also has several options on Zhanqian Lu near the train station, from the budget *Aihu*, not to be confused with its far nicer namesake in the mountain proper (Ⓣ0559/5196293; ❷) to the smarter *Dengfeng* (Ⓣ0599/5101558; ❻) over the road, though there's no point in staying here unless you absolutely have to.

Foodwise, it's the local Shilin bullfrogs that make **Wuyi cuisine** special; along with other popular dishes such as bamboo shoots and fungus, they're served almost everywhere, along with pheasant, rabbit and other game such as venison and what some restaurateurs claim to be bear. Many places have vegetables and meat on show outside which makes ordering as easy as pointing, but to avoid any nasty shocks – overcharging is rife – check the price of each dish as you order.

The Thirty-Six Peaks

A series of trails head north into the mountains from the main trailhead area at the base of **Tianyou Feng** (Heavenly Tour Peak), about halfway between Xingcun and Wuyigong. Minibuses, motorcycle taxis and taxis all run here. It costs a steep ¥62–111 to enter the trails, depending on how much of the area you want to see. The **mountains** look quite large and imposing, but in fact are relatively easy to climb. The summit of Tianyou Feng is no more than a thirty-minute clamber away from the ticket office. The best time to get up here is early morning, when you can catch the sunrise and watch the mists clear to reveal the nine crooks in the Jiuqu River. A number of tiny pavilions and **tea gardens** on the lower slopes can provide sustenance on the way up. **Tea** is a big deal in Fujian, and Wuyi Shan is famous as the original home of **Oolong**, one of the few types known by name in the West. Leaves for Oolong are picked when mature, then processed by alternate bruising, fermenting and airing before being fire-dried to create the distinctive taste; one of the best varieties is the widely available *tie guanyin cha*, or Iron Buddha Tea.

Another peak well worth the ascent is **Dawang Feng** (King of Peaks) at the easternmost end of the river, north of Wuyigong, and more of a gentle walk than a climb (2hr). If you have time, try to get to the **Shuilian Cave**, about 6km north of the river; you can walk along easy trails or take a minibus from the Tianyou Feng area or from Wuyigong. The cave is about halfway up a cliff of red sandstone, down which a large waterfall cascades in the summer months. You can sit in the adjacent teahouse, cut out of the rock, while the waterfall literally crashes down beside you. The walk between the cave and river passes tea plantations, more teahouses and all kinds of little sights, including **Yingzui Yan** (Eagle Beak Crag), whose main point of interest is the walkways leading to a set of caves where, during the Taiping Uprising, local bigwigs fled to escape persecution.

Quanzhou and around

I tell you that for one shipload of pepper which may go to Alexandria or to other places, to be carried into Christian lands, there come more than one hundred of them to this port.

Thus wrote Marco Polo when he visited **QUANZHOU**, then called Zaytoun (from the Arabic word for olive, symbol of peace and prosperity), in the late thirteenth century. At this time, Quanzhou was a great port, one of the two largest in the world, exploiting its deep natural harbour and sitting astride trade routes that reached southeast to Indonesian Maluku, and west to Africa and

Quanzhou and around		
Quanzhou	泉州	*quánzhōu*
Cheng Tian Si	承天寺	*chéngtiān sì*
Fuwen Miao	府文庙	*fǔwén miào*
Guandi Miao	关帝庙	*guāndì miào*
Kaiyuan Si	开元寺	*kāiyuán sì*
Maritime Museum	海外交通史博物馆	*hǎiwàijiāotōngshǐ bówùguǎn*
Qingjing Mosque	清净寺	*qīngjìng sì*
Qingyuan Shan	清源山	*qīngyuán shān*
Sheng Mu	伊斯兰教圣墓	*yīsī lánjiào shèngmù*
Tianhou Gong	天后宫	*tiānhòu gōng*
Yuanmiao Guan	元妙观	*yuánmiào guàn*
Accommodation, eating and drinking		
Blue & Sea	蓝海餐厅	*lánhǎi cāntīng*
Coffee Language	尚典啡茶语	*shàngdiǎnfēi cháyǔ*
Dawin Café Coffee Shop	达文咖啡店	*dáwén kāfēidiàn*
Great Wall	长城宾馆	*chángchéng bīnguǎn*
Happy-Tom	快乐汤姆	*kuàilè tāngmǔ*
Huaqiao Zhijia	华侨之家	*huáqiáo zhījiā*
Jianfu	建福商务酒店	*jiànfú shāngwù jiǔdiàn*
Jinquan	金泉酒店	*jīnquán jiǔdiàn*
Jinzhou	金州大酒店	*jīnzhōu dàjiǔdiàn*
Korean Restaurant	度彼岸韩国料理	*dùbǐàn hánguó liàolǐ*
Luye Shangwu Kuaican	录野商务快餐	*lùyě shāngwù kuàicān*
Noble Family Steakhouse	贵族世家牛排	*guìzúshìjiā niúpái*
Qing Qi Sheng Chadian	请其神茶店	*qdngqíshén chádiàn*
Qiwei Yazai	奇味鸭仔	*qíwèi yāzǎi*
Quanzhou	泉州酒店	*quánzhōu jiǔdiàn*
Three Virtues Vegetarian	三德素食馆	*sāndé sùshíguàn*
Anping Bridge	安平桥	*ānpíng qiáo*
Chongwu	崇武古城	*chóngwǔ gǔchéng*
Shishi	石狮	*shíshī*
Sisters-in-law Tower	姑嫂塔	*gūsǎo tǎ*

Europe. It became uniquely cosmopolitan, with tens of thousands of Arabs and Persians settling here, some of them to make colossal fortunes – the Arabs of Quanzhou are also believed responsible for introducing to the West the Chinese inventions of the compass, gunpowder and printing.

The Song and Yuan dynasties saw the peak of Quanzhou's fortunes, when the old Silk Road through northwestern China into Central Asia was falling prey to banditry and war, deflecting trade seawards along the **Maritime Silk Road**. Polo was by no means the only European to visit Quanzhou around this time: the Italian **Andrew Perugia**, Quanzhou's third Catholic bishop, died here in 1332, having supervised the building of a cathedral; and fourteen years later the great Moroccan traveller **Ibn Battuta** saw the port bustling with large junks. But by the Qing era, the city was suffering from overcrowding and a decaying harbour, and an enormous **exodus** began, with people seeking new homes in Southeast Asia. According to Chinese government statistics, there are more than two million Quanzhounese living abroad today – which compares to just half a million remaining in the entire municipal area. Despite these depredations of history, Quanzhou today retains several reminders of its glorious past, and it's certainly worth a stopover between Fuzhou and Xiamen.

Arrival and information

You'll most likely arrive in Quanzhou by **bus** along the coastal expressway between Xiamen and Fuzhou. The imposing new **long-distance bus station** is in the southeast of town, 3km east down Quanxiu Jie from Wenling Lu.

Orange bus #15 from outside will take you back northwest up to Wenling Lu; get off when you see the giant stone column on the roundabout, the Great Ocean department store, or *McDonald's*, and you'll be in the bottom right hand corner of the map on p.543. Quanzhou's **train station** is about 5km east down Dong Hu Jie; bus #23 from outside will get you to the old long-distance bus station, a handy landmark. There's also an **airport** about 20km southeast of town, from which you'll need to take a taxi (¥30–50). The **Bank of China** (Mon–Fri 8am–5.30pm) is on Nanjun Lu, while the enormous **post office** (Mon–Sat 8am–8pm) is on Wenling Lu. There are several **Internet cafés** in the lane north of the Qingjing Mosque and more on Haogouqian Lu near the *Quanzhou* hotel.

Moving on from Quanzhou, there are frequent daytime buses from the new long-distance bus station to Xiamen (¥15–40) and Fuzhou (¥35–70), and to practically anywhere in southern China, from Ningbo and Hangzhou in the north, to Guangzhou and Shenzhen in the south. If you're catching a night bus, note that the left luggage office closes at 8pm sharp – anything still inside at the end of the day will stay locked there until morning. By train, there's a morning departure to Wuyi Shan, and slow services to Longyan, Yongding and Meizhou; a couple of **ticket offices** in town, just north of the *Great Wall* hotel on Wenling Lu and opposite the *Jinquan Dajiudian* save trekking out to the station. In addition, most hotels, and the **CTS office** near the *Jinquan* on Daxi Jie, can make travel bookings for a small fee.

Accommodation

Quanzhou does not offer budget accommodation for foreigners, but the following hotels are all good value.

Great Wall Wenling Lu ⓣ0595/22171688, ⓕ2288965. Excellent value, good location and friendly staff. ❸

Huaqiao Zhijia Southern end of Wenling Lu ⓣ0595/22175395, ⓕ22175385. Spacious and comfortable rooms, if slightly threadbare. ❸

Jinquan (aka Golden Fountain) Baiyuan Lu ⓣ0595/22171361, ⓕ22281676. Situated on a small road leading south from Daxi Jie, this is the budget wing of the adjacent *Huaqiao Dasha*, offering good-quality, clean en-suite twins and doubles. ❹

Jinzhou Around the corner from the old long-distance bus station, on Quanxiu Lu ⓣ0595/22586788, ⓕ22581011. Reasonably smart and comfortable place, and quite convenient for the new bus station. ❸

Quanzhou Zhuangfu Xiang ⓣ0595/22289958, ⓦwww.quanzhouhotel.com. A ludicrous Neoclassical white-and-gold monstrosity, right in the centre of town, just west of Zhongshan Zhong Lu. Rooms are of an international standard but, disappointingly, they do not live up to the absurd grandeur of the hotel's exterior. Old wing ❼, new wing ❽

The town and around

Quanzhou is a small, prosperous town, located entirely on the northeast bank of the Jin River, and the majority of its sights can be reached on foot. The two major north–south streets are Zhongshan Lu and Wenling Lu. The town centre falls mainly between these two, with the oldest part of town to the west and up along the northern section of Zhongshan Lu, where you'll find attractively restored, colonial-era arcaded streets, lined with trees and packed with pedestrians and cyclists. As in Fuzhou, there are plenty of minor temples scattered around, perhaps the best of which is **Tianhou Gong**, a large airy hall at the southern end of Zhongshan Lu, dedicated to southeastern China's most popular deity, the Heavenly Empress.

One of the town centre's most interesting areas lies north off **Tumen Jie**, Quanzhou's main east–west street, which sports a surprisingly well-integrated collection of genuine antique buildings and modern shops with traditional flourishes. Heading northwest up Tumen Jie from its junction with Wenling Lu, you'll first encounter **Guandi Miao**, a splendid and busy temple on the junction with Mingquan Lu, dedicated to the Three Kingdoms' hero turned god of war and healing, Guan Yu (see p.453). The temple's roofline is typically florid and curly, and the atmospheric interior – guarded by life-sized statues of soldiers on horseback – features low-ceilinged halls, smoke-grimed statues and wall engravings showing scenes from Guan Yu's life.

Almost the next building along, the granite-built **Qingjing Mosque** (daily 8am–5.30pm; ¥3) provides firm evidence of just how established the Arabs became in medieval Quanzhou. Founded by Arab settlers in 1009 and rebuilt by Persian Muslims three centuries later, Qingjing ranks as one of the oldest mosques in China and is highly unusual in being Middle Eastern in design, though only parts of the original buildings survive. The tall gate tower is said to be an exact copy of a Damascus original, its leaf-shaped archway embellished with fourteenth-century Arabic calligraphy and designs, while parts of the walls and supporting pillars of the original prayer hall stand alongside. A side room has a detailed account of the Arab presence in Quanzhou, with an English translation; the small tiled building next door is the modern prayer hall. The "Houcheng Tourism and Culture Street" behind the mosque is not as hokey as it sounds, containing some original buildings, many of which are now antique and souvenir shops.

West between Qingjing Mosque and Zhongshan Lu, an ornamental gateway leads north to a broad paved square, at the back of which is a Confucian temple, **Fuwen Miao**. This isn't of great importance, but the square is dotted with freshly restored examples of Quanzhou's **traditional domestic architecture**, all built of granite blocks and characteristic red bricks marked with dark chevrons, the roof ridges pulled up into projecting forks.

Other attractions include the newly renovated **Yuan Miao Guan**, a Taoist temple shoehorned between buildings on **Zhuangyuan Jie**, which has nothing to particularly recommend it over Guandi Miao but offers a fascinating insight into the painstaking workmanship and effort still expended in renovating these temples. **Cheng Tian Si,** a Buddhist monastery a little further southeast along Nanjun Lu, provides a wonderful oasis of calm in the heart of the city.

Kaiyuan Si

Quanzhou's most impressive historical remains are at **Kaiyuan Si**, a huge, restful temple dotted with magnificent trees in the northwest of town on Xi Jie (daily 7.30am–5.30pm; ¥10). Bus #2 runs up here from the old long-distance bus station, but it's much more interesting to follow the backstreets from the Tumen Jie/Zhongshan Lu intersection, through narrow lanes lined with elderly homes. Founded in 686 AD, Kaiyuan was built, legend has it, after the owner of a mulberry grove dreamed a Buddhist monk asked him to erect a place of worship on his land. "Only if my mulberry trees bear lotus flowers", replied the owner dismissively – whereupon the lotus flowers duly appeared. In memory of this, an ancient mulberry in the temple courtyard bears the sign "Mulberry Lotus Tree". The two five-storey **stone pagodas** were added in the thirteenth century, apart from these, the whole complex was rebuilt during the Ming dynasty after being destroyed by fire.

The temple is highly regarded architecturally, not least for its details, which include one hundred stone columns supporting the roof of the **main hall**, most of which are carved with delicate musicians holding instruments or sacrificial objects. Surviving everything from earthquakes to the Red Guards, the unimaginably solid pagodas are also carved on each of their eight sides with two images of the Buddha; inside, one of them has forty Buddhist stories inscribed on its walls. The temple grounds also hold a special **exhibition hall** (¥2) housing the hull of a twelfth- or thirteenth-century **wooden sailing vessel** found in 1974 (a series of photos detail the stages of the excavation), still with the herbs and spices it had been carrying, preserved in its hold.

The Maritime Museum

Across on the northeast side of town on Dong Hu Lu, the **Maritime Museum** (Tues–Sun 8.30am–5.30pm; ¥10; bus #19 from the long-distance bus station) recalls Quanzhou's trading history and illustrates how advanced Chinese shipbuilders were, compared to their European contemporaries. Two floors of exhibits track the development of Chinese boatbuilding, reaching as far back as the Warring States period (around 500 BC). A corner devoted to the "Recovery of Taiwan from the Greedy Grasp of the Dutch Invaders and the Development of Foreign Trade" reinterprets **Koxinga**'s exploits (see p.547) in a modern light, but the museum's heart is its hundreds of lovingly made **wooden models**, illustrating everything from small, coastal junks to Zheng He's mighty *Baochuan* – possibly the largest wooden vessel ever made – and ornate pleasure boats used by the wealthy for touring China's famous lakes and rivers.

While you're here, don't miss the first-floor collection of **tombstones** dating back to Quanzhou's heyday. Most of these are Muslim, but you'll also find those of Italians and Spaniards, Nestorian Christians from Syria, and the fourteenth-century Bishop, Andrew Perugia. In the back, stone pillars, lintels and statues show that there were also Hindus and Manichaeans (followers of a Persian religion that drew on Christianity, Jainism and Buddhism) in Quanzhou, each with their own places of worship – further proof of the city's cosmopolitan heritage.

Qingyuan Shan and Sheng Mu

A few sites just outside the town warrant the effort of reaching them on local buses. The **Qingyuan Shan** scenic area is 3km to the north, with good views over Quanzhou from small crags and pavilions, though most people come out here for the huge stone **Laojun Yan**, a Song-dynasty sculpture of Laozi which is said to aid longevity if you climb onto its back and rub noses. Bus #3 comes up here from Tumen Jie and Zhongshan Zhong Lu.

East of the town centre on Donghu Jie, **Sheng Mu** is a Muslim cemetery housing the graves of two of Mohammed's disciples sent to China in the seventh century to do missionary work – and so presumably the first Muslims in China. There's little to see, but it's a peaceful, semi-forested place; catch bus #7 from Wenling Lu to the Sheng Mu stop. The entrance can be seen to the south of the road – when you glimpse a stone archway, take the alley leading towards it.

Around Quanzhou

About 60km east of Quanzhou, **CHONGWU** is an old walled city built entirely of stone, now nicely restored as a huge museum piece. The adjacent new town has one of southern China's largest fishing fleets, with just about every man employed in this industry – the women work in local stone quarries, carting huge rocks around on carrypoles and wearing characteristic blue jackets and wide-brimmed straw hats. Slightly closer to the southeast is the town of **SHISHI** (Stone Lion), from where you can pick up a ride for the 5km to the beautiful **Sisters-in-law Tower**, another Song-dynasty monument, overlooking the sea. Finally, 30km south, just off the expressway to Xiamen and outside the town of Anhai, the spectacular two-kilometre-long, 800-year-old **Anping Bridge** actually crosses a section of sea.

Eating and drinking

Food options around the new **long-distance bus station** include the ¥38 all-you-can-eat pizza paradise that is *Happy-Tom* and the more urbane *Dawin Café Coffee Shop*. **In town**, northern Zhongshan Lu, the area around Kaiyuan Si, and backstreets off Tumen Jie are thick with cheap noodle stalls and canteens. Light meals can be had at the spotless, good-value *Blue & Sea* canteen, next to the *Jinzhou*, for around ¥15, but for something slightly more upmarket, try a barbecue at the *Korean Restaurant* (best enjoyed if there is a group of you), near the *Great Wall* on Wenling Jie, or head north of the Bank of China on Nanjun Lu to *Qiwei Yazai*, which specializes in roast duck. The *Jianfu*, near the *Huaqiao Zhijia* hotel at the southern end of Wenling Lu, serves weekend all-you-can-eat breakfast *dim sum* (¥15 a person) on the fifth floor.

For Western food, there are the ubiquitous fast-food chains, along with several **cafés** along Tumen Jie that serve sandwiches and grills. Try *Noble Family Steakhouse* at the corner with Wenling Lu, or *Coffee Language* just south of Guandi Miao. The *Quanzhou* hotel also has its own Western-style restaurant. For something more traditional, *Qing Qi Sheng Chadian* **teahouse** is in an old brick home, in the lane directly behind Qingjing Mosque.

Vegetarians should head for the *Lu Ye Shang Wu Kuai Can*, directly north of the mosque on Tumen Jie, or the more upmarket *Three Virtues Vegetarian Restaurant* near Cheng Tian Si monastery at 124 Nanjun Lu.

Xiamen

XIAMEN, traditionally known in the West as **Amoy**, is smaller and much prettier than the provincial capital Fuzhou. It also offers more to see, its streets and buildings, attractive shopping arcades and bustling seafront boasting a nineteenth-century European flavour. One of China's most tourist-friendly cities, Xiamen is, in addition, the cleanest and, perhaps, most tastefully renovated city you'll see anywhere in the country, giving it the feel of a holiday resort, despite the occasional seedy, fishy backstreet. Compounding the resort atmosphere is the little island of **Gulangyu**, a ten-minute ferry ride to the southwest, the old colonial home of Europeans and Japanese, whose mansions still line the island's traffic-free streets – staying here is highly recommended.

Some history

Xiamen was founded in the mid-fourteenth century and grew in stature under the Ming dynasty, becoming a **thriving port** by the seventeenth century, influenced by a steady and rather secretive succession of Portuguese, Spanish and Dutch fortune-hunters. When invading Manchu armies poured down from the north in the seventeenth century, driving out the Ming, Xiamen became a centre of resistance for the old regime. The pirate and self-styled **Prince Koxinga** (also known as Zheng Chenggong) led the resistance before being driven out to set up his last stronghold in Taiwan – incidentally, deposing the Dutch traders who were based there – where he eventually died before Taiwan, too, was taken by the Manchus. Koxinga's exploits have been heavily romanticized and reinterpreted over the years, and today his recapturing of Taiwan from

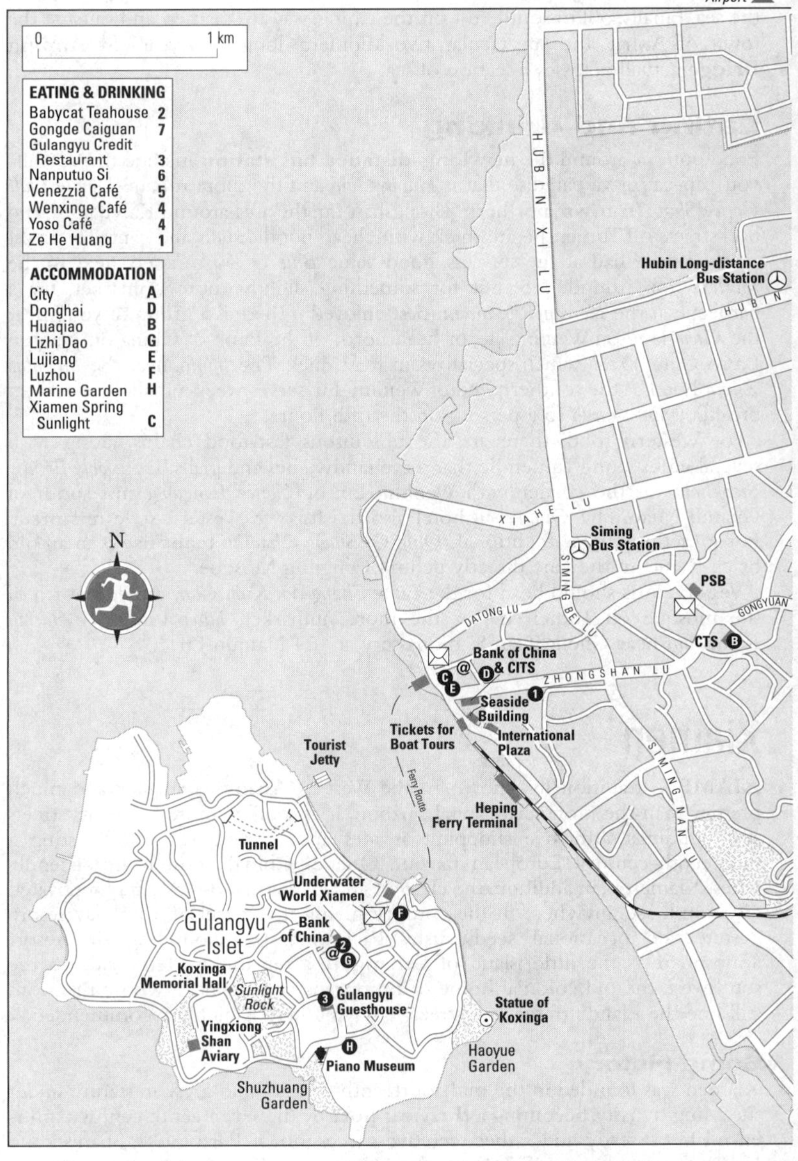

unfriendly forces is used both to justify China's claims on its neighbour, and also to provide an example of how to pursue those claims.

A couple of hundred years later, the **British** arrived, increasing trade and establishing their nerve centre on Gulangyu; the manoeuvre was formalized with the Treaty of Nanjing in 1842. By the start of the twentieth century, Xiamen, with its offshore foreigners, had become a relatively prosperous

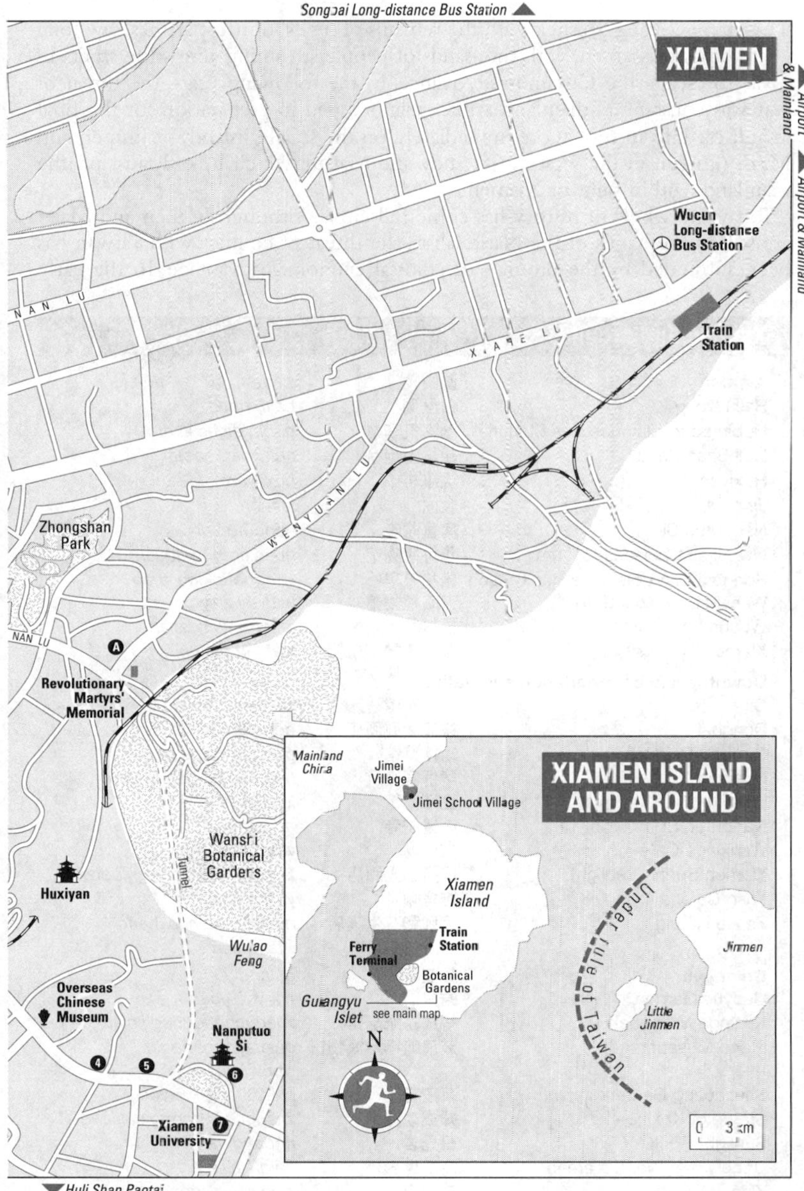

community, supported partly by a steady turnover in trade and by the trickling back of wealth from the city's emigrants who, over the centuries, had continued to swell in numbers. This happy state of affairs continued until the **Japanese invasion** at the beginning of World War II.

The end of the war did not bring with it a return to the good old days, however. The **arrival of the Communists** in 1949, and the final escape to

Taiwan by Chiang Kaishek with the remains of his Nationalist armies, saw total chaos around Xiamen, with thousands of people streaming across the straits in boats to escape the Communist advance. In the following years, the threat of war was constant, as mainland armies manoeuvred in preparation for the final assault on Taiwan, and, more immediately, on the smaller islands of Jinmen and Mazu (known in the West as Quemoy and Matsu), which lie only just off the mainland, within sight of Xiamen.

Today the wheel of history has come full circle. Although Jinmen and Mazu are still in the hands of the Nationalists, the threat of conflict with Taiwan has been subsumed by the promise of colossal economic advantage. In the early

Xiamen and around

Xiamen	厦门	*xiàmén*
Bailu Dong	白鹿洞	*báilù dòng*
Hubin Long-distance Bus Station	湖宾气车站	*húbīn qìchē zhàn*
Huli Shan Paotai	胡里山炮台	*húlǐ shān pàotái*
Huxiyan	虎溪岩	*hǔxī yán*
Jinmen	金门	*jīnmén*
Nanputuo Si	南普陀寺	*nánpǔtuó sì*
Overseas Chinese Museum	华侨博物馆	*huáqiáo bówùguǎn*
Songbai Long-distance Bus Station	松柏气车站	*songbai qiche zhan*
Wanshi Botanical Gardens	万石植物馆	*wànshí zhíwùguǎn*
Wucun Long-distance Bus Station	捂村气车站	*wǔcūn qìchēzhàn*
Xiamen University	厦门大学	*xiàmén dàxué*
Downtown accommodation and eating		
City	厦门宾馆	*xiàmén bīnguǎn*
Donghai	东海大厦酒店	*dōnghǎi dàshà jiǔdiàn*
Gongde Caiguan	功德莱馆	*gōngdé càiguǎn*
Huaqiao	华侨宾馆	*huáqiáo bīnguǎn*
Lujiang	鹭江宾馆	*lùjiāng bīnguǎn*
Nanputuo Si	南普陀寺	*nánpǔtuó sì*
Wenxinge Café	文心阁	*wénxīngé*
Xiamen Spring Sunlight	厦门春光酒店	*xiàmén chūnguāng jiǔdiàn*
Yoso Café	雅舍咖啡	*yǎshè kāfēi*
Ze He Huang	黄则和花生汤店	*huángzéhé huāshēng tāngdiàn*
Gulangyu	鼓浪屿	*gǔlàng yǔ*
Haoyue Garden	皓月园	*hàoyuè yuán*
Koxinga Memorial Hall	郑成功纪念馆	*zhèngchénggōng jìniànguǎn*
Piano Museum	鼓浪屿钢琴博物馆	*gǔlàngyǔ gāngqín bówùguǎn*
Shuzhuang Garden	菽庄花园	*shūzhuāng huāyuán*
Statue of Koxinga	郑成功塑像	*zhèngchénggōng sùxiàng*
Sunlight Rock	日光岩	*rìguāng yán*
Underwater World Xiamen	海底世界	*hǎidǐ shìjiè*
Yingxiong Shan	英雄山	*yīngxióng shān*
Accommodation and eating		
Babycat Teahouse	小猫茶馆	*xiǎomāo cháguǎn*
Gulangyu Guesthouse	鼓浪屿宾馆	*gǔlàngyǔ bīnguǎn*
Lizhi Dao	丽之岛酒店	*lìzhīdǎo jiǔdiàn*
Luzhou	绿洲酒店	*lǜzhōu jiǔdiàn*
Marine Garden	海上花园酒店	*hǎishàng huāyuán jiǔdiàn*

1980s, Xiamen was declared one of China's first **Special Economic Zones** and, like Shenzhen on the border with Hong Kong, the city is still reaping the benefits, with a booming economy and ambitious workers flocking from all over China – including prosperous towns and cities on the east coast – in search of a better life. Indeed, Xiamen's pleasant climate, healthy economy and relatively sympathetic urban development mean that it is regularly voted the city in China with the best all-round standard of living.

Arrival and city transport

Joined to the mainland by a five-kilometre-long causeway, the island on which Xiamen stands is located inside a large inlet on the southeastern coast of Fujian. The built-up area occupies the western part of the island, which faces the mainland, while the eastern part faces onto Taiwanese Jinmen Island. The areas of most interest are the **old town** in the far southwest, and **Gulangyu Islet** just offshore. The remainder of the city is the Special Economic Zone, which stretches away to the east and the north, and to the causeway back to the mainland.

The main north–south road, passing through the centre of the old town, is **Siming Lu**, which is crossed from east to west by **Zhongshan Lu**, the main

Moving on from Xiamen

Xiamen is well placed for bus and plane connections, though rail lines – as usual in Fujian – are a bit unsatisfactory You've also the option of catching a boat to Hong Kong.

By bus

With three long-distance bus stations – Hubin, Songbai and Wucun – Xiamen has frequent departures to **Fuzhou** and **Quanzhou** between about 6am and 10pm; several daily to **Longyan** and **Yongding**; and services at least daily to **Guangzhou** and **Shantou**. The problem is knowing which bus leaves from where. Fortunately, bus-station staff are sympathetic, giving times and instructions on how to get to the right departure point, whether you're at the right station or not. With this in mind, the Siming Bus Station in town is the easiest place to start, even though, if you're after a long-distance service, the bus you want is unlikely to actually leave from here.

CTS operates a rival private service, with buses leaving directly form their office on Xinhua Lu next to the *Huaqiao* hotel.

By air

Flights link Xiamen with Wuyi Shan, Fuzhou, Guangzhou and several other cities in eastern China; see Listings, p.555, for airline offices and travel agents.

By train

Rail lines run north from Xiamen to **Wuyi Shan** and **Jiangxi province**, and west into **Guangdong province** via **Longyan**. Services to Fuzhou are very circuitous; it's much faster to take the bus. Buying tickets is not too problematic, though queues are often lengthy (ticket office daily 8.10am–noon, 1.40–6.10pm & 7.20–9.30pm).

By boat

There's a weekly (monthly in winter) service to **Hong Kong** from the Heping Ferry Terminal (daily 8–11.15am & 2.30–5.15pm; ⓣ0592/2022517); berths for the eighteen-hour trip cost anything from ¥335 to ¥2180, depending on whether you want a dorm bed, shared cabin or private suite. As yet, there's no regular service to Jinmen Island in Taiwan; group vessels are chartered as necessary and the option isn't open to Westerners.

shopping street. Xiamen's **train station**, connected by city buses #3 and #7, is on **Xiahe Lu**, about 4km east from the seafront. There are several **long-distance bus stations**; you'll most likely end up either 2km northeast of the centre on Hubin Nan Lu (exit the station, turn right and it's 100m to the stop for city bus #23 to the seafront), or about 200m north of the train station at the Wucun bus station. The most central arrival point is the **Heping Ferry Terminal**, served by boats from Hong Kong. Twelve kilometres to the north of town, Xiamen's **airport** is connected to the waterfront area by bus #27.

Buses cover the city and are fast, regular and cheap – rides cost ¥1–2. **Taxis** are also plentiful, costing upwards of ¥8 to hire. Vendors sell city **maps** (¥6) near the Gulangyu ferry terminal and outside the stations.

Accommodation

There's a good choice of accommodation in Xiamen, from mid-range to luxurious. Some of the nicest hotels (and the cheapest one that takes foreigners) are on **Gulangyu Islet**, although you'll have to carry your own luggage here, as there are no buses or taxis. The wonderful peace and quiet of the island more than compensate for this, however. Wherever you stay, make a point of bargaining – off-season discounts can slash as much as forty percent off advertised rates.

Downtown Xiamen

City 16 Huyuan Lu ⓣ0592/2053333, ⓦwww.cityhotelxm.com. A modern, ultra-smart place to stay, built up a hillside and overhung by trees, yet not too remote. ❼

Donghai (aka East Ocean) 1 Zhongshan Lu ⓣ0592/2021111, ⓕ2033264. ⓦwww.easy-inn.cn. In a good location, behind the *Lujiang*, with nice rooms. ❺

Huaqiao Xinhua Lu ⓣ0592/2660888, ⓦwww.xmhqhotel.com.cn. Very smart, modern and well-serviced hotel, with airline agents and CTS conveniently located outside. ❼

Lujiang 54 Lujiang Lu ⓣ0592/2022922, ⓦwww.Lujiang-Hotel.com. Occupying a prime site on the seafront in a well-maintained colonial building, this is an excellent hotel, and the ideal place to stay for views over Gulangyu Islet. The cheaper twins are rather small. ❻

Xiamen Spring Sunlight Haihou Lu ⓣ0592/2665558, ⓕ2071665. Good value, given the location directly opposite the Gulangyu ferry terminal. Behind its colonial-style facade the interior is modern, spotless and a little bland. ❺

Gulangyu Islet

Lizhi Dao (aka Beautiful Island) 133 Longtou Lu ⓣ0592/2063309, ⓦwww.lzd-hotel.com. Very convenient, if suffering minor damp problems; the cheapest rooms are small and airless, but get one with a window and it's fair value. ❸

Luzhou Longtou Lu ⓣ0592/2065390, ⓕ2065843. Straight ahead and just on the left as you leave the ferry – a clean, ordinary Chinese hotel facing a green lawn. Nice views from the more expensive rooms, which also have wooden floors. ❹

Marine Garden 27 Tianwei Lu ⓣ0592/2062588, ⓦwww.MarineGardenHotel.com. Just above Shuzhuang Garden, this plush, mildly garish faux-colonial place has quality rooms, a pool, tennis court and good views over the beach. ❼

The City

The main pleasure in Xiamen, apart from visiting Gulangyu Islet, is simply walking the streets of the old city. At the western end of Zhongshan Lu, where the **seafront** opens up, you'll see the island of Gulangyu right in front, across the water. You can organize boat trips around Jinmen from various places, including the waterfront opposite Zhongshan Lu, Heping Ferry Terminal and Gulangyu. Prices start at ¥100 for an hour and forty minutes – for good views of the Guomindang front line, bring binoculars. For a cheaper trip, go to the Gulangyu ferry terminal, from where there are tours that circle Gulangyu before dropping you on the island (30min; ¥15).

Southeast and east from the town centre there's a thin scattering of tourist sights. On Siming Nan Lu, about 2km south of Zhongshan Lu, you'll find the **Overseas Chinese Museum** (Tues–Sun 9.30am–4pm; ¥10). This houses collections presented by the huge Fujianese diaspora around the world, including pottery and some exceptional bronzes going back as far as the Shang dynasty. Another kilometre farther southeast (bus #1 to Xiada, Xiamen University) is the **Nanputuo Si** (daily 5am–6pm; ¥3), a temple complex established more than a thousand years ago on the southern slopes of Wulao Feng. This is one of China's most organized, modern-looking Buddhist temples, its roofs a gaudy jumble of flying dragons, human figures and multicoloured flowers, and containing among its collection of treasures a set of tablets carved by resistance fighters at the time of the early Qing, recording Manchu atrocities. Inside the main hall, behind the Maitreya Buddha, is a statue of Wei Tuo, the deity responsible for Buddhist doctrine, who holds a stick pointing to the ground – signifying that the monastery is wealthy and can provide board and lodging for itinerants. The temple today is very active and has a **vegetarian restaurant** (see p.555).

Immediately south of Nanputuo stands **Xiamen University**, and a few laid-back cafés that cater to students and the odd expat. From here you can cut through to Daxue Lu, the coastal road, which runs past attractive sandy beaches. A kilometre or so southwest is **Huli Shan Paotai** (Huli Mountain Gun Emplacement), at the terminus of bus #2. This nineteenth-century hunk of German heavy artillery had a range of 10km and was used during the Qing dynasty to fend off foreign imperialists. You can rent binoculars here to look across to **Jinmen**, which lies less than 20km to the west.

A lengthy hike (at least 2hr) from the grounds of Nanputuo takes you up and over the forested Wulao Shan behind the temple – you can also get there on bus #17 from the little street outside Nanputuo's entrance. Either way, you'll arrive at **Wanshi Botanical Gardens** (daily 6.30am–6.30pm; ¥40), and its 4000 varieties of plant life including a redwood tree brought here by President Nixon on his official visit to China. From the botanical gardens' north (main) gate, you cross a rail line to reach the **Revolutionary Martyrs' Memorial**, about 1500m west of the town centre, near the #4 bus route. Southwest of here, along the rail line, is the **Huxiyan** (Tiger Stream Rock) on your right, built up high on a rocky hillside. If you climb up you'll find a great little temple nestling amid a pile of huge boulders; slip through the cave to one side and climb the rock-hewn steps to the top of the largest. Right up on the hilltop, a second small temple, **Bailu Dong**, commands spectacular views over the town and the sea.

Gulangyu Islet

Gulangyu Islet was Xiamen's foreign concession until World War II, and architecturally it remains more or less intact from that time. In summer and at weekends, the island and its accommodation are packed, but with battery-powered golf-buggies (¥10 for a short journey, ¥50 for a round-island trip) being the only vehicles allowed on the island, the atmosphere is always restful, and exploring can easily fill up a day. Gulangyu's narrow tangle of streets can be confusing, but the compactness of the island (it's less than two square kilometres in size) means this isn't really a problem. Though it's not worth walking a complete circuit of the island – the northwest is very exposed and has nothing to see – any stroll through the streets will uncover plenty of architectural attractions, especially along Fuzhou Lu and Guxin Lu, overhung with flowers and blossom all through the year.

The **boat** to the island runs from 5.30am until just after midnight from the pier across from the *Lujiang*, the short ride offering delightful views of the waterways. On the outbound journey the lower deck is free, while the upper deck is ¥1, and on the way back the lower and upper decks cost ¥8 and ¥9 respectively. The **island centre** – a knot of small shopping streets with a **Bank of China**, a **post office**, a few **restaurants** and plenty of shops hawking tourist tat – is ahead as you disembark from the ferry. Diagonally to your right a splendid bronze sculpture of a giant octopus marks the entrance to **Underwater World Xiamen** (daily 9.30am–4.30pm; ¥70, children and students ¥40), with walk-through aquariums, seal displays, penguins, turtles and a massive whale skeleton. Past here, follow Sanming Lu northwest and you'll come to the mouth of a **tunnel**, built in the 1950s when the threat of military confrontation with Taiwan seemed imminent, which burrows right underneath the hill to Gulangyu's northern end on Neicuo Ao Lu. From here, try and find your way back to the jetty through the back lanes – an excellent half-hour walk.

If you head southeast from the jetty, you'll pass a number of grand old buildings, including the former British and German consulates. The road continues on to the island's rocky eastern headland, now enclosed by **Haoyue Garden** (¥15), containing a gigantic granite **statue of Koxinga** dressed in grand military attire and staring meaningfully out towards Taiwan, the island he once heroically recaptured from foreign colonialists. Shortly beyond the garden, the road heads west towards the middle of the island, bringing you to a sports ground, with the old colonial **Gulangyu Guesthouse** facing onto it. President Nixon stayed here on his 1972 trip, and it was, until recently, the haunt of Chinese VIPs. There has been no public access to the inside for years, but rumour has it the middle of the three buildings has its original 1920s decor and furniture intact, with dark wooden panelling, a billiard hall and a terrace with rattan chairs. For a closer glimpse of colonial life, the **Huaijiugu Langyu Museum** (daily 8am–6pm; ¥35), up the alley on the north end of the sports ground, is not quite as grand as the guesthouse, but it gives you an idea of what life might once have been like.

Due south, on the southern shore, the flower-filled **Shuzhuang Garden** (daily 6.30am–8pm; ¥30) boasts some nicely shaded areas for taking tea right by the sea. The **Piano Museum**, inside the garden, is a reflection of the island's history with the instrument; foreigners began to teach locals here at the start of the twentieth century and the island has produced some of China's finest pianists – if you stay, chances are you'll hear the tinkling of ivories drifting across the hills. The museum contains over a hundred pianos from Austria, France, Germany and Britain, including the odd Steinway.

The clean, sandy **beach** running west from the park is very tempting for swimming when it's not too packed. It's overlooked to the north by the **Sunlight Rock** (daily 6am–8pm; ¥60 includes cable-car ride), the highest point on Gulangyu (93m) and something of a magnet for the large numbers of local tourists who ride up to the platform for the views right over the entire island. At the foot of the rock (and covered by the same entrance ticket) is the **Koxinga Memorial Hall**, which contains various relics, including Koxinga's own jade belt and bits of his "imperial" robe; there are no English captions. Follow the path along the coast from here – a beautiful walk on a bright day – and you pass below **Yingxiong Shan**, the top of which is enclosed in netting as an open-air **aviary** (included in Sunlight Rock ticket price), thick with tropical pigeons, egrets and parrots. You can buy a **multi-ticket** for entry to Haoyue and Shuzhuang Gardens, Sunlight Rock and Yingxiong Shan for ¥80.

Eating and drinking

Xiamen has plenty of places to eat fresh **fish and seafood**, particularly oysters, crabs and prawns. Head for the restaurants around Gulangyu's market area – the curiously titled *Gulangyu Credit Restaurant* is particularly popular with Chinese tourists – or the backstreets behind the *Donghai*, but make sure you establish a price in advance: the seafood is usually sold by weight, not per portion. Otherwise the city centre has plenty of places to eat: for **peanut buns and soups** (another regional speciality) check out *Ze He Huang*, a crowded, noisy canteen on Zhongshan Lu. Nanputuo Si's **vegetarian restaurant** is expensive for what you get, with set meals at ¥30–80, depending on the number of dishes you want; across from the temple and near Xiamen University, *Gongde Caiguan* is a cheaper, vegetarian option. Nearby, a clutch of student-oriented **cafés** on Nanhua Lu near the campus offer Chinese and Western food, beers and cocktails, in a relaxed atmosphere with outdoor seating – try *Yoso*, *Wenxinge*, or *Venezzia*. On **Gulangyu**, around the corner from the Lizhi Dao, the contemporary Taiwan-style *Babycat* teahouse – a relaxed coffee shop and café – has simple Western food, Internet access and a resident feline.

Listings

Airlines Air China, *Huguang Dasha*, Hubin Dong Lu ⓣ0592/5084382; Dragon Air, 8 Jianye Lu ⓣ0592/5117702; China Eastern, 311 Siming Nan Lu ⓣ0592/2028936; Malaysian Airlines, *Crowne Plaza* ⓣ0592/2023333; Philippine Airlines, *Marco Polo Hotel*, Jianye Lu ⓣ0592/2394729; Silk Air, International Plaza ⓣ0592/2053257; Thai Airways, International Plaza ⓣ0592/2261688.

Banks and exchange There are branches of the Bank of China on Gulangyu Islet and on Zhongshan Lu, back from the seafront (Mon–Fri 8.30am–noon & 2.30–5pm, Sat 8am–12.30pm).

Consulates Philippines, near the geographic centre of Xiamen on Lianhua Bei Lu (ⓣ0592/5130355).

Internet access There are several Internet bars in the lane directly north of the *Donghai*, parallel with Datong Lu; *Babycat* teahouse has wireless as well as one fixed terminal.

Mail and telephones Xiamen's main post office, where IDD telephone calls can also be made, is on the seafront, just north of the *Xiamen Spring Sunlight*, and there's another large branch on Xinhua Lu, south of the junction with Siming Dong Lu.

PSB Across from the Post Office on Gongyuan Nan Lu ⓣ0592/2262203.

Travel agents CTS, *Huaqiao Hotel*, Xinhua Lu ⓣ0592/2025602; Xiamen Tourism Group, *Lujiang* ⓣ0592/2029933.

Southwestern Fujian: the Hakka homelands

Fujian's hilly southwestern border with Guangdong is an area central to the **Hakka**, a Han subgroup known to locals as *kejia* (guest families) and to nineteenth-century Europeans as "China's gypsies". Originating in the Yangzi basin during the third century and dislodged ever southward by war and revolution, the Hakka today form large communities both here and in Hong Kong and Hainan island. They managed to retain their original languages and customs by remaining aloof from their neighbours in the lands in which they settled, a habit that caused resentment and led to their homes being well defended. While towns up this way are mostly unattractive low-level industrial settlements, the countryside is pretty in spring, and villages and hamlets around the focal city of **Yongding** sport fortress-like **Hakka mansions** built of stone and adobe. The largest are four or five storeys high, circular, and house entire clans.

If you can't find direct transport from coastal Fujian, aim first for **LONGYAN**, a small city 170km northwest of Xiamen, where roads and separate rail lines from Fuzhou, Quanzhou and Xiamen converge to head west to Meizhou in

Southwestern Fujian

Yongding	永定	*yǒngdìng*
Dongfu Jiudian	东府酒店	*dōngfǔ jiǔdiàn*
Jiari Lüguan	假日旅馆	*jiàrì lǚguǎn*
Tianhe Lüguan	天河旅馆	*tianhé lǚguǎn*
Chengqi	乘启	*chéngqǐ*
Hukeng	湖坑	*húkēng*
Zhencheng Lou	振城楼	*zhènchéng lóu*
Longyan	龙岩	*lóngyán*
Yuchang Lou	裕昌	*yùcha1ng léu*

Guangdong (see p.614). From the **train station** on the eastern edge of town, catch bus #14 over three bridges to Longzhou Xi Lu and the **long-distance bus station**, 2km away and just south of Longyan's centre. Here you'll be mobbed by minibus drivers for the final sixty-kilometre, hour-long run southwest to Yongding (¥10), through several Hakka towns marked by large, mud-brick mansions and inevitably surrounded by cement factories.

Yongding and around

Set on the edge of a flat river basin, **YONGDING** is an old town, today recast as a heavily built-up, typically ugly place, whose residents are nevertheless very friendly towards the few foreigners who make it up here. The road from Longyan ends up at a **roundabout**, where you'll find the **bus station** and decent, if forgettable and slightly noisy, **accommodation** options. The best of these is the *Dongfu Jiudian* (Ⓣ0957/5830668; ❸), which has clean, pleasant rooms and helpful staff; the nearby *Jiari Lüguan* (❷) and *Tianhe Lüguan* (Ⓣ0597/5835769; ❷) aren't quite as comfortable. From the roundabout, the main street runs north over the river and into town; on the far bank, Huangcheng Dong Lu forks left after 100m into a market area, while steps on the right climb a ridge to a park, with views across town and the countryside. If you carry straight on you'll reach the Bank of China. **Places to eat** surround the bus station and main streets; you'll find all sorts of rice noodles, snacks, and **kourou**, a Hakka dish made from slices of soya-braised pork belly on a bed of

▲ Hakka tulou

bitter kale. **Leaving**, there are daily buses to Meizhou in Guangdong, and Xiamen, as well as minibuses through the day back to Longyan, and at least as far east as Hukeng village.

Hukeng and Zhencheng Lou

An hour's bus ride east of Yongding, **Zhencheng Lou** is considered to be the most perfect **Hakka roundhouse** or *tulou*. This century-old home forms the well-maintained, if slightly sterile, centrepiece of the **Zhencheng Village tourist attraction** (¥50): plain and forbidding on the outside, the huge outer wall encloses three storeys of galleried rooms looking inwards to a central courtyard where guests were entertained, and which contained the clan shrine. The galleries are vertically divided into eight segments by thick **fire walls**, a plan that intentionally turns the building into a giant **bagua**, Taoism's octagonal symbol. This powerful design occurs everywhere in the region, along with demon-repelling **mirrors** and other Taoist motifs. An almost disastrous consequence of roundhouse design – which from above looks like a ring – was that (so locals say) the first US satellite photos of the region identified the houses as missile silos.

The tourist village is nice enough in itself, with other, more "authentic", houses (still lived in) laid out along a small stream. Those worth investigating include a 1920s schoolhouse; **Fuyu Lou**, the old *yamen* building; **Rushen**, one of the smallest multistorey roundhouses; and **Kuijiu**, a splendid, 160-year-old square-sided Hakka mansion, its interior like a temple squeezed into a box.

To get to Zhengcheng from Yongding, jump on one of the regular direct buses (1hr; ¥16), which will drop you outside a row of guesthouses a few hundred metres from Zhengcheng Lou itself. Guesthouse owners will meet you from the bus, offering modern rooms (❶–❷) or the chance to stay in the impressive but very basic **Huangxin Lou** opposite (❶). Mr Li at the *Backpacker's Station* is particularly hospitable. From Zhengcheng it's easy to organize trips (reckon on around ¥100 for a full day, but be prepared to haggle) to surrounding *tulou*, including **Chengqi Lou,** the largest roundhouse of them all, built in 1709, with more than 300 rooms housing more than 400 people; **Tianhe Lüguan,** a remote and remarkably active grouping of five large houses – including three roundhouses, one square walled house and one oval – that date back between two and three hundred years and still house around 600 people; and **Yuchang Lou,** the oldest and, at more than 21 metres, the tallest of the roundhouses. Yuchang's five storeys have stood since 1309, despite a drunken 15° lean in its uprights.

Moving on from Zhengcheng, you could take one of several daily buses to Yongding and Longyan from where it's a short skip into **Guangdong**. Alternatively, three daily direct buses head to **Xiamen**, 160km south on the Fujian coast (4hr 30min; ¥63). All leave from the unofficial-looking bus station opposite the **Zhencheng Village tourist attraction** bus park.

Guangdong

Halfway along **Guangdong**'s eight-hundred-kilometre coastline, rivers from all over the province and beyond disgorge themselves into the South China Sea, through the tropically fertile **Pearl River Delta**, one of China's most densely cultivated and developed areas. Perched right at the delta's northern apex and adjacent to both Hong Kong and Macau, the provincial capital **Guangzhou** provides many travellers with their first taste of mainland China. It's not everyone's favourite city, but once you've found your bearings among the busy roads and packed shopping districts, Guangzhou's world-famous **food** merits a stop, as does an assortment of museums, parks and monuments. The Pearl River Delta itself has a few patches of green and some history to pick up in passing, but the major targets are the cities of **Shenzhen** and **Zhuhai**, modern, purpose-built economic buffer zones at the crossings into Hong Kong and Macau.

Farther afield, the rest of the province is more picturesque, with a mass of sights, from Buddhist temples to Stone Age relics, to slow you down around **Shaoguan**, up north by the Hunan and Jiangxi borders. Over in the east near Fujian, the ancient town of **Chaozhou** has well-preserved Ming architecture peppered amongst a warren of narrow streets, while nearby **Meizhou** is a useful stepping stone to the ethnic Hakka heartland, set in the beautiful surrounding countryside. On the way west into Guangxi province, **Zhaoqing** sports pleasant, formalized lakes and hilly landscapes, while those heading towards Hainan need to aim for the ferry port of **Hai'an**, down in Guangdong's southwestern extremities.

Guangdong has a generous quantity of rail and road traffic, and **getting around** is none too difficult, though often requires some advance preparation. **Rail lines** run north through Shaoguan and up into Hunan and central China, east to Meizhou, Shantou and Fujian, and west through Zhaoqing to Zhanjiang and Guangxi. **River travel** was, until recently, a highlight of the province, though the only easy excursions left are the fast hydrofoils between the Pearl River Delta towns and Hong Kong, and a day-cruise from the northern town of **Qingyuan** to some riverside temples. As for the **climate**, summers can be sweltering across the province, with typhoons along the coast, while winter temperatures get decidedly nippy up in the northern ranges – though it's more likely to be miserably wet than to snow, except around the highest mountain peaks.

Guangzhou

It was not so long ago that **GUANGZHOU**, once known to the Western world as **Canton**, was dismissed as a nightmare caricature of Hong Kong, one of the most dizzyingly overcrowded, polluted and chaotic places to daunt a newcomer to the country. While the city is still hardly somewhere to come for peace and relaxation, recent improvements have wrought great **changes**: an expanding **metro network** and multi-layered flyovers are relieving traffic congestion; the waterfront area has been paved and flowerbeds dug wherever possible; old buildings have been scrubbed and restored to public view by demolishing the badly constructed 1950s concrete boxes which obscured them; and the city's **nightlife** is snowballing.

True, Guangzhou's **sights** remain relatively minor, though a fascinating 2000-year-old tomb and palace site complement the obligatory round of temples. Yet the city is an enjoyable place, especially if you love to dine out. The Cantonese are compulsively garrulous, turning Guangzhou's two famous obsessions – **eating** and **business** – into social occasions, and filling streets, restaurants and buildings with the sounds of Yueyu, the Cantonese language. And while the newer districts pass as a blur of chrome and concrete from the inside of your taxi, make your way around on foot through the back lanes and you'll discover a very different city, one of flagstoned residential quarters, tiny collectors' markets, laundry strung on lines between buildings, and homes screened away behind barred wooden gates. Guangzhou has also long been the first place where foreign influences have seeped into the country, often through returning Overseas Chinese, and this is where to watch for the latest fashions and to see how China will interpret alien styles.

It may seem, though, what with the **biannual Trade Fair**, that the emphasis here is towards business rather than tourism – and it's certainly true that commerce is Guangzhou's lifeblood, an ethos inspiring train-station pickpockets and company CEOs alike. In purely practical terms, however, while the city is expensive compared with some parts of China, it's far **cheaper** than Hong Kong, particularly in regard to **onward travel**. Airfares into China are considerably less from Guangzhou than what you'd pay just south of the border, allowing big savings even after you factor in transport from Hong Kong and a night's accommodation.

Some history

Legend tells how Guangzhou was founded by **Five Immortals** riding five rams, each of whom planted a sheaf of rice symbolizing endless prosperity – hence Guangzhou's nickname, **Yang Cheng** (Goat City). Myths aside, a settlement called **Panyu** had sprung up here by the third century BC, when a rogue Qin commander founded the **Nanyue Kingdom** and made it his capital. Remains of a contemporary **shipyard** uncovered in central Guangzhou during the 1970s suggest that the city had contact with foreign lands even then: there were merchants who considered themselves Roman subjects here in 165 AD, and from Tang times, vessels travelled to Middle Eastern ports, introducing **Islam** into China and exporting porcelain to Arab colonies in distant Kenya and Zanzibar. By 1405, Guangzhou's population of foreign traders and Overseas Chinese was so large that the Ming emperor Yongle founded a special quarter for them. When xenophobia later closed the rest of China to outsiders, Guangzhou became the country's main link with the rest of the world.

Restricted though it was, this contact with other nations proved to be Guangzhou's – and China's – undoing. From the eighteenth century, the **British East India Company** used the city as a base from which to purchase silk, ceramics and tea, but became frustrated at the Chinese refusal to accept trade goods instead of cash in return. To even accounts, the company began to import **opium** from India; addiction and demand followed, making colossal profits for the British and the **Co Hong**, their Chinese distributors, but rapidly depleting imperial stocks of silver. In 1839 the Qing government sent the incorruptible Commissioner **Lin Zexu** to Guangzhou with a mandate to stop the drug traffic, which he did by blockading the foreigners into their waterfront quarters and destroying their opium stocks. Britain declared war, and, with a navy partly funded by the opium traders, forced the Chinese to cede five ports (including Guangzhou and Hong Kong) to British control under the **Nanking Treaty** of 1842.

Unsurprisingly, the following century saw Guangzhou develop into a revolutionary cauldron. It was here during the late 1840s that Hong Xiuquan formulated his **Taiping Uprising** (see p.419), and sixty years later the city hosted a premature attempt by **Sun Yatsen** to kick out China's Qing rulers. When northern China was split by warlords through the 1920s, Sun Yatsen chose Guangzhou as his **Nationalist capital**, while a youthful Mao Zedong and Zhou Enlai flitted in and out between mobilizing rural peasant groups. At the same time, anger at continuing colonial interference in China was channelled by **unionism**, the city's workers becoming notoriously well

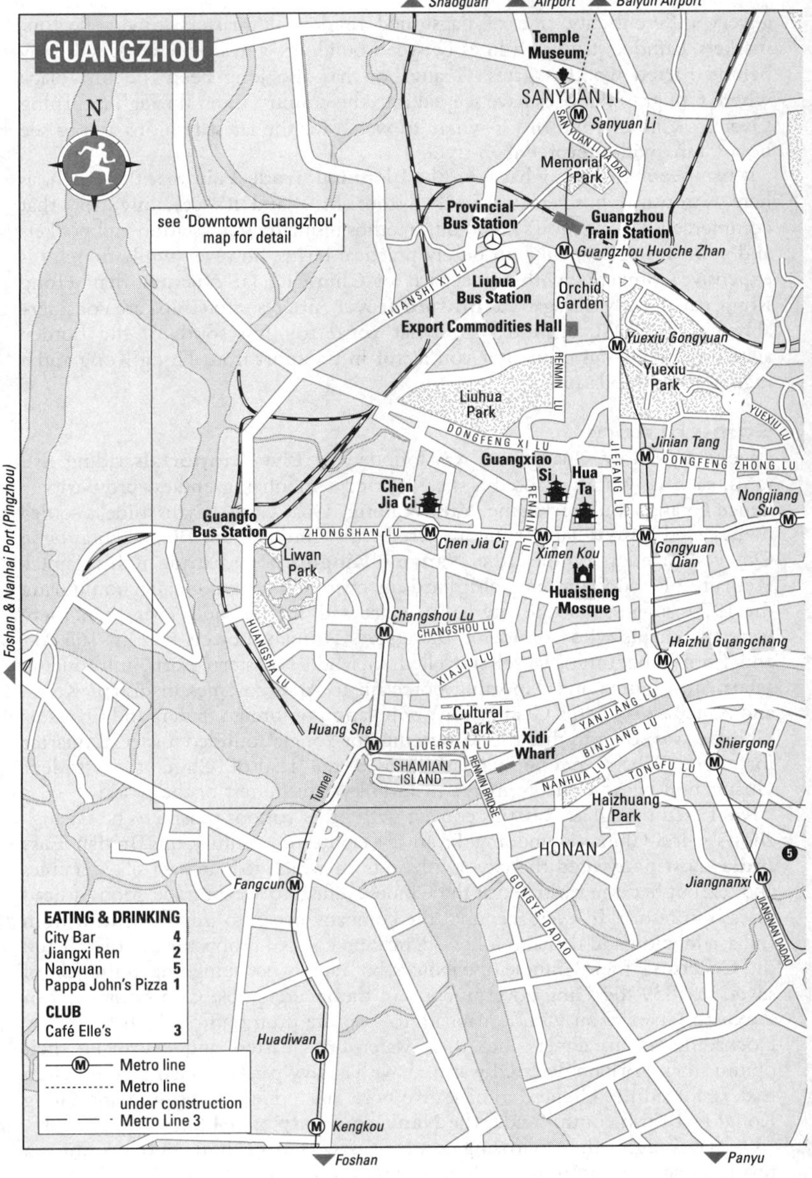

organized and prone to rioting in the face of outrages perpetrated by the Western powers. However, many of Guangzhou's leftist youth subsequently enrolled in militias and went north to tackle the warlords in the **Northern Expedition**, and so became victims of the 1927 **Shanghai Massacre**, Chiang Kaishek's suppression of the Communists (see p.1151). A Red uprising in Guangzhou that same year, in December, failed, leaving the city's population

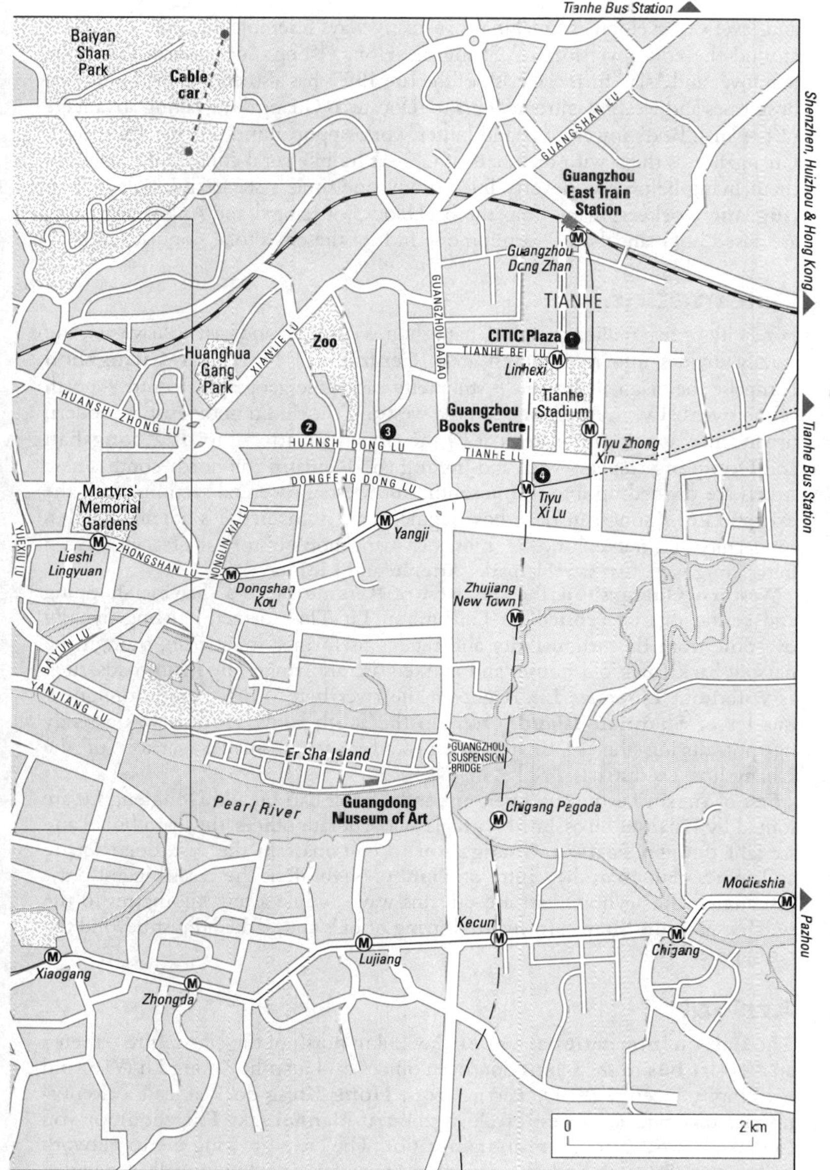

totally demoralized. Controlled by the Japanese during the war, and the Guomindang afterwards, residents became too apathetic to liberate themselves in 1949, and had to wait for the PLA to do it for them.

Few people would today describe the Cantonese as apathetic, at least when it comes to **business** acumen. Unlike many large, apparently modern Chinese cities, Guangzhou enjoys real wealth and solid infrastructure, its river location and level of development making it in many ways resemble a grittier, rougher-around-the-edges version of Shanghai. Hong Kong's downturn since the handover and Asian financial crisis of the late 1990s has also encouraged southern businesses and wealthy entrepreneurs to relocate to Guangzhou, taking advantage of the mainland's lower costs and better work opportunities. At the same time, Guangzhou is thick with members of China's mobile rural community, many of them living below the poverty line. At any one time, a staggering one million **migrant workers**, many from the backblocks of Jiangxi and Anhui provinces, are based in Guangzhou – forming one fifth of the city's total population.

Orientation

For a city of five million people, Guangzhou is compact and easy to navigate, and readily divides into five uneven areas. **Central** and **Northern Guangzhou** comprise the original city core – still pretty much the geographic centre – north of the river between Renmin Lu in the west and Yuexiu Lu in the east. A modern urban landscape predominates, cut by the city's main arterial roads: **Zhongshan** and **Dongfeng** run east–west, and **Jiefang** and **Renmin** run north–south. These streets are divided up into north, south, east, west and central sections, with the exception of Zhongshan Lu, whose segments are numbered. It's not all relentless modernity and traffic, however: most of Guangzhou's historical sites are located here, along with two sizeable parks, **Yuexiu** and **Liuhua**.

Western Guangzhou, the area west of Renmin Lu, is a thriving shopping and eating district centred on Changshou Lu. This formed a Ming-dynasty overflow from the original city and retains its former street plan, though the narrow back lanes, old houses and markets are also ringed by main roads, such as waterfront **Liuersan Lu**. Right on the river here is the former foreigners' quarter of **Shamian Island**. Over on the south bank, **Honan** was a seedy hotspot during the 1930s, though nowadays it's a smaller version of the Changshou Lu districts.

East of Yuexiu Lu the city opens up, and Zhongshan Lu and Dongfeng Lu are joined by Huanshi Lu as, lined with glassy corporate offices, they run broad and straight through **Eastern Guangzhou** to culminate in the vast, open square and sports stadium at the centre of **Tianhe**. Nightlife is the east's biggest draw – many of Guangzhou's bars are out this way – while a few kilometres to the north is **Baiyun Shan**, a formalized string of hills and parkland just beyond the city proper.

Arrival

The **Baiyun international airport** lies 20km north of the city centre – there's an **airport bus** to the China Southern offices on Huanshi Zhong Lu (¥16) and taxis into the centre (¥100). Ferries **from Hong Kong** dock at least a twenty-minute taxi ride southwest of Guangzhou at **Nanhai** (aka Pingzhou), or you can take bus #275 to the main train station. The city's growing metro network will, eventually, reach both the airport and ferry terminal but, initially scheduled to be open by 2007, when this will actually happen is anyone's guess.

Currently, the city has two major **train stations**, although a third, planned to be Asia's largest, is due to be operational by the end of 2008. The new station is under construction in Zhongcun, Shibi Town, in the city's Panyu district, around 17km south of the city centre. Designed to handle 78 million passengers in its first year of operation, rising to 116 million when fully up and running, the station will have fifteen platforms – up from the main station's current four – and as well as handling trains to all parts of the country, will also be linked to the city's metro system. At the northern end of Renmin Lu, **Guangzhou train station** is the most confrontational place to arrive, the vast **square** outside perpetually seething with passengers, hawkers and hustlers. Mainline services from most central, northern and western destinations terminate here. New arrivals exit on the west side of the square, convenient for the metro; for Shamian, take it south three stops to Gongyuan Qian interchange, then catch line #1 south to Huang Sha. **Taxis** and most **city buses** wait over on the east side; buses #5 and #31 will take you down to the Cultural Park near Shamian Island.

Guangzhou's second rail terminus is **Guangzhou East train station**, 5km east of the centre at Tianhe. This is where trains from Shenzhen terminate, along with the Kowloon Express, services from Shantou, Meizhou and western Fujian, and a growing quantity of traffic from central China. From the basement, catch metro line #1 direct to the Huang Sha stop for Shamian Island; for Guangzhou train station, take bus #271 or the metro, changing at Gongyuan Qian. A taxi to the centre costs ¥30–40.

There are several major long-distance bus stations. West of Guangzhou train station on Huanshi Xi Lu, the **provincial bus station** handles arrivals from almost everywhere in the country, with more local traffic often winding up across the road at one of the number of depots that comprise **Liuhua station**. Buses from eastern Guangdong and central China might terminate out in the

Guangzhou arrival and downtown metro stops

Guangzhou	广州	*guǎngzhōu*
Arrival		
Baiyun Airport	白云机场	*báiyún jīchǎng*
Guangfo Bus Station	广佛车站	*guǎngfó chēzhàn*
Guangzhou East Train Station	东方火车站	*guǎngzhōu chēzhàn*
Guangzhou Train Station	广州火车站	*guǎngzhōu huǒchēzhàn*
Liuhua Bus Station	流花车客运站	*liúhuāchē kèyùnzhàn*
Metro	地铁	*dìtiě*
Nanhai (Pingzhou) Ferry Termina	南海（平洲）码头	*nánhǎi (píngzhōu)mǎtóu*
Provincial Bus Station	省汽车客运站	*shěngqìchē kèyùnzhàn*
Tianhe Bus Station	天河客运站	*tiānhé kèyùnzhàn*
Useful Metro Stops		
Changshou Lu	长寿路	*chángshòu lù*
Chen Jia Ci	陈家祠	*chénjiā cí*
Dongshan Kou	东山口	*dōngshān kǒu*
Gongyuan Qian	公园前	*gōngyuán qián*
Guangzhou Dong Zhan	广州东站	*guǎngzhōu dōngzhàn*
Guangzhou Train Station	广州火车站	*guǎngzhōu huǒchēzhàn*
Haizhu Guangchang	海珠广场	*hǎizhū guǎngchǎng*
Huang Sha	黄沙	*huángshā*
Jinian Tang	纪念堂	*jìniàntáng*
Lieshi Lingyuan	烈士陵园	*lièshì língyuán*
Nongjiang Suo	农讲所	*nóngjiǎng suǒ*
Shiergong	市二宫	*shìèrgōng*
Yuexiu Park	越秀公园	*yuèxiù gōngyuán*
Tiyu Xi Lu	西门口	*xīmén kǒu*
Tiyu Zhong Xin	体育西路	*tǐyù xīlù*
Ximen Kou	体育中小	*tǐyù zhōngxiǎo*
Yangji	杨箕	*yángjī*

northeastern suburbs at **Tianhe bus station**; from here your best bet for reaching the centre is to catch either the shuttle bus to the provincial bus station, or a taxi to Guangzhou East train station and city transport from there – though Tianhe bus station will ultimately also be on a metro line.

City transport and information

Getting around Guangzhou isn't difficult, though the city is too big to walk everywhere, and bicycles are not recommended because of heavy traffic. Where possible, it's best to plump for Guangzhou's speedy **metro**. At the time of writing, four lines serve almost all of central Guangzhou, with the considerable exception of the commercial district around the *Garden* hotel, where construction on a new line is ongoing. Of the two most central lines, line #1 runs diagonally across the city from Guangzhou East train station at Tianhe, through the centre along Zhongshan Lu, then turns south at Chen Jia Ci, past Shamian Island and across the river. Line #2 runs south from Sanyuan Li via Guangzhou train station, interchanging with line #1 at Gongyuan Qian, then crossing the

Moving on from Guangzhou

Leaving Guangzhou requires advance planning, and you'll generally need a few days to arrange tickets or at least check out the options, especially for the train.

By air

With an **airport** designed to rival Hong Kong's, with considerably cheaper fares, Guangzhou is well connected by air to all major cities in China, many in Southeast Asia and increasingly more worldwide. The regional airline, China Southern (Ⓣ020/950333), has its headquarters just east of the train station, with its well-organized ticket office upstairs (daily 9am–6pm). See "Listings", p.587, for international airline offices and travel agents. Airport buses (¥10–30) leave from outside China Southern (every 20min 5am–11pm), or there are taxis (¥100). The metro is not scheduled to reach the airport until 2010.

By train

Demand for train tickets out of Guangzhou is very high. Tickets become available three days before departure, but sleepers sell out swiftly, as do even hard seats on popular lines. There are several **advance-ticket offices** around town, where there's no commission and the queues are usually shorter than at the stations: the most convenient are down near the river at the northeastern corner of the Guangzhou Qiyi Lu/Yide Lu intersection; and west of the *Garden* hotel on Huanshi Zhong Lu. CITS Travel, 618 Jie Fang Bei Lu, just north of Gongyuan Qian metro station or CTS, next to the *Landmark,* can also be helpful with booking rail and flight tickets.

Paying an **agent** can cut out so much bother that it's money well spent, despite the service fees involved – upwards of ¥50 a ticket. Most agents, however, deal only with major destinations like Shanghai, Beijing, Hong Kong, Guilin and Xi'an.

Guangzhou train station (bus #5 or #31 from the south of the city) handles all destinations except Kowloon and the Shantou line, though points east are better served from the Guangzhou East station. The **ticket hall** is at the eastern end of the station; crowds are horrendous here at peak times, when entry is through guarded gateways that are closed off when the interior becomes too chaotic. Otherwise, you'll generally get what you want if you've a flexible schedule and are prepared to queue for an hour, though staff can be positively hostile.

Guangzhou East train station (bus #271 from the first floor at Liuhua bus station, or the metro to Guangzhou Dong Zhan), at time of writing, handles the Kowloon river and heading east to Pazhou. Line #2 should connect to the airport in the future, and plans are also afoot for a line from Tianhe bus station to Panyu, as well as a link from line #1 out to Foshan (see p.596) via the ferry port at Nanhai. **Metro stations** can be hard to locate at street level, but sometimes they will be signposted from nearby roads; keep an eye out for the logo, rather like a "Y" made up of two red (or yellow) lines on a white (or yellow) background. **Fares** are ¥2–7, according to the number of stops from your starting point. Carriages have bilingual route maps, and each stop is announced in Mandarin and English.

If you can't get somewhere by metro, you'll find yourself using Guangzhou's cheap and slow **bus and trolleybus** network, which covers most of the city from ¥1 a ride. **Taxis** are plentiful and can be hailed in the street. Fares start at ¥7, but larger vehicles charge more – all have meters. Drivers rarely try any scams, though the city's complex traffic flows can sometimes make it seem that you're heading in the wrong direction. If you're travelling solo and feeling confident, **motorcycle taxis** are a cheaper way of getting door to door, but you'll probably have to haggle.

Express (12 daily 8.35am–9.20pm; ¥198–293), Shenzhen traffic (50 daily 6.30am–10.20pm; ¥70) – mostly fast, double-decker trains – eastern lines to Shantou and Fujian, and an increasing number of services north through central China. While it is likely to retain the Shenzhen services, other intercity services will be moved to the new station 17km south of the town centre (see p.562).

By bus

Leaving Guangzhou by bus can be the cheapest of all exit options, and more comfortable than the average hard-seat experience if you have any distance to travel. Fast, relatively expensive **express buses** are very much the rage at present – especially around the Pearl River Delta and along the expressway to eastern Guangdong – so if money is your prime consideration, check to see whether there are any ordinary buses (*putong che*) to your destination.

The **provincial bus station** on Huanshi Xi Lu, diagonally opposite the main station, is always full of people, but tickets are easy to get – and there are at least daily departures to everywhere in Guangdong, and as far afield as Guizhou, Anhui, Hainan and Fujian provinces.Destinations within 100km or so of Guangzhou – including all Delta towns, Qingyuan and Huizhou – are covered from the **Liuhua bus station**, also on Huanshi Xi Lu. Buses for Shantou, Meizhou and points east mostly depart from the new **Tianhe bus station**, about 7km east of town. You can buy tickets for these at the provincial bus station – they'll stamp your ticket on the back for a free shuttle bus to the Tianhe station, which takes around thirty minutes.

Express buses to **Hong Kong** and **Macau** run by CTS and others depart from various hotels between 5.30am and 8pm; buy tickets at the departure points. For **Kowloon** – either Hong Kong Airport (3hr; around ¥255) or Kowloon Tong MTR (3hr; around ¥115) – try the *China Marriott* (26 daily), *Landmark* (16 daily), or *White Swan* (5 daily). For **Macau** (3hr 30min; ¥75), the *Landmark* has nine departures daily.

By boat

Guangzhou's **ferry port** is southwest of the city at **Nanhai** (Pingzhou), about halfway to Foshan (see p.596), with two daily speedboats to the China–Hong Kong City Terminal in Hong Kong (2hr 30min; ¥170). To get there, either take the free shuttle bus if you're staying in one of the city's smarter hotels, a taxi, or bus #275 from the main train station.

Maps of varying detail and quality are sold for around ¥5 by hawkers at the train and bus stations, and at numerous bookshops, hotels and stalls around the city. The current favourite is *The Tour Map of Guangzhou*, which has many of the sights marked in English, and is kept fairly up to date – though no maps illustrate all of Guangzhou's two-hundred-plus bus routes. For Guangzhou's eating, drinking and bar scene, as well as other expat-related and tourist information, there are a number of English-language **websites**: try Ⓦwww.guangzhou.asiaxpat.com, Ⓦwww.thatsgz.com or Ⓦwww.cityweekend.com.cn/guangzhou, or pick up a copy of the *That's PRD* magazine available at most restaurants on Shamian Island.

Accommodation

Guangzhou's business emphasis means that true budget accommodation is limited – even Hong Kong has a better range – so resign yourself to this and plan your finances accordingly. Prices can more than **double** during the three-week trade fairs each April and October, when beds will be in short supply, and can be discounted by as much as fifty percent in winter, when fewer visitors are about. Every hotel has some sort of travel-booking service, while smarter places have their own banks, post offices, restaurants and shops, and are likely to accept international credit cards.

For anything more than an overnight stop, **Shamian Island** is the best place to hole up. Whatever your budget, it's a pleasant spot with well-tended parks, a bit of peace, and plenty of good places to eat. Otherwise, there are several relatively inexpensive Chinese-style hotels in **central Guangzhou**, mostly near the river-front, and upmarket accommodation in the city's **north and eastern** quarters, where you will also find a few budget options near Guangzhou train station.

Shamian Island

The places reviewed below are marked on the map on p.578.

Customs Hotel Shamian Dajie Ⓣ020/81102388, Ⓕ81818552, Ⓦwww.gzchotel.com. Upmarket hotel aimed at Chinese businessmen, inside a former Customs House – though the interior is strictly modern. ❻

Guangzhou Youth Hostel Shamian Si Jie Ⓣ020/81218606, Ⓕ81219079. Across from the lavish *White Swan*, this is one of Guangzhou's cheapest options – there's usually a waiting list for spare beds here, which are distributed at noon. The dorms are a bit damp, but other rooms are modern and clean. There's a left-luggage office and a transport booking service. Despite the name, not an actual IYHF hostel. Dorm beds ¥50, ❹

Overseas Chinese Activity Centre Shamian Dajie Ⓣ020/81218218. Identifiable by the faded Bank of China sign above the door, this place is under-patronized, so they're eager for business and try hard to please. Furnishings are pretty straightforward, in keeping with its reasonable price. ❹

Shamian Shamian Nan Jie Ⓣ020/81218288, Ⓦwww.gdshamianhotel.com. Now part of the *Unotel* chain, which operates another eight hotels in the city (Ⓦwww.unotel.com.cn). The cheaper rooms here are small and mostly windowless, but otherwise this is a very snug and comfortable option, with Internet in every room, just around the corner from the youth hostel. ❺

Victory (aka Shengli) Shamian Bei Jie and Shamian Si Jie Ⓣ020/81216688, Ⓦwww.vhotel.com. Formerly the *Victoria* in colonial days, this is a good-value upmarket choice, with two separate buildings; the annexe (on Si Jie) is a little cheaper, though you may have to walk to the main building for breakfast. There's a good restaurant and store with a coffee bar and trove of imported Western foods. Fifty-percent discounts are available outside of peak season. Bei Jie building ❽, Si Jie building ❼

White Swan Shamian Nan Jie Ⓣ020/81886968, Ⓦwww.whiteswanhotel.com. Once Guangzhou's most upmarket place to stay, this hotel is probably still the city's most famous and prestigious, and a favourite with US citizens in town to adopt Chinese orphans. You'll find a waterfall in the lobby, river views, an on-site bakery and countless other services – some reserved for the use of guests alone. ❽

Guangzhou accommodation

Aiqun	爱群大酒店	*àiqún dàjiǔdiàn*
Baigong	白宫酒店	*báigōng jiǔdiàn*
Beijing	北京大酒店	*běijīng dàjiǔdiàn*
China Marriott	中国大酒店	*zhōngguó dàjiǔdiàn*
CITS Hotel Guangdong	广东国旅酒店	*guǎngdōng guólv jiǔdiàn*
Customs Hotel	海关会议接待中心	*hǎiguān huìyì jiēdài zhōngxīn*
Dongfang	东方宾馆	*dōngfāng bīnguǎn*
Garden	花园酒店	*huāyuán jiǔdiàn*
Guangdong Guesthouse	广东宾馆	*guǎngdōng bīnguǎn*
Guangzhou Youth Hostel	广州青年招待所	*guǎngzhōu qīngnián zhāodàisuǒ*
Holiday Inn	文化假日酒店	*wénhuà jiàrì jiǔdiàn*
Landmark	华厦大酒店	*huáxià dàjiǔdiàn*
Liuhua	流花宾馆	*liúhuā bīnguǎn*
Overseas Chinese Activity Centre	广东省侨胞活动中心	*guǎngdōngshěng qiáobāo huódòng zhōngxīn*
Shamian	沙面宾馆	*shāmiàn bīnguǎn*
Victory	胜利宾馆	*shènglì bīnguǎn*
White Swan	白天鹅宾馆	*báitiān'é bīnguǎn*
Yishu	艺术宾馆	*yìshù bīnguǎn*

Central Guangzhou

The places reviewed below are marked on the map on pp.570–571.

Aiqun Yanjiang Lu ⓣ020/81866668, ⓕ81883519. Slightly gloomy (or possibly atmospheric) 1930s monumental mansion block with good river views and snooty staff; this was the tallest pre-liberation building in Guangzhou. Fair-value doubles and singles available. ❺

Baigong 13–17 Renmin Nan Lu ⓣ020/81925999, ⓦwww.baigong-hotel.com. Classic urban hotel. Rooms are past their best and can be noisy, but it's also tidy, friendly and excellent value for the location. ❹

Beijing 105 Xihao Er Lu ⓣ020/62793388, ⓕ81883799. Another typical inner-city Chinese hotel – smart lobby, slightly tarnished rooms, huge restaurant and, of course, a karaoke hall. Also has a travel booking centre. Easily confused with the similarly priced *New Beijing* across the street. ❸

Guangdong Guesthouse Jiefang Bei Lu ⓣ020/83332950, ⓦwww.ggh.com.cn. A huge complex of square concrete wings, Sinocized with green tiling and flared eaves. Quite comfortable, but fading around the edges. ❻

King Long Hotel 505 Huifu Dong Lu ⓣ020/83190988, ⓕ83312307. A modern neon-signed hotel above the *Lemon House* Vietnamese restaurant, this is not bad value for the central location but can be a bit noisy. Also rents rooms by the hour. ❹

Landmark 8 Qiaoguang Lu ⓣ020/83355988, ⓦwww.hotel-landmark.com.cn. Four-star business centre between a busy roundabout and the river. ❼

Northern and eastern Guangzhou

The places reviewed below are marked on the map on pp.570–571.

China Marriott Liuhua Lu ⓣ020/86666888, ⓦwww.marriotthotels.com. Five-star labyrinth of red marble corridors opposite the Export Commodities Hall, with upmarket shopping malls and places to eat. You almost need a map to get around and are expected to pay in foreign currency, but rooms are good. ❾

CITS Hotel Guangdong 179 Huanshi Xi Lu ⓣ020/86666889, ⓕ86679787, ⓔgdtourist@fm365.com. Right next to the China Southern office and Guangzhou train station, this CITS-managed, IYHF-affiliated affair lacks almost all facilities associated with a youth hostel – it's basically just a cheap hotel – and is popular with budget travellers.

Dorm beds ¥60 for IYHF members, ¥95 non-members, ❸

Dongfang 120 Liuhua Lu ⓣ020/86669900, ⓦwww.dongfanghotel-gz.com. Literally in the *Marriott*'s shadow, this is another self-contained five-star maze with a dazzling number of restaurants housed in smartly remodelled 1950s buildings. ❽

Garden 368 Huanshi Dong Lu ⓣ020/83338989, ⓦwww.thegardenhotel.com.cn. The city's most opulent accommodation, this classier version of the *White Swan* – there's even a waterfall – is its superior in every respect but the setting. Pool and gym free for guests. ❾

Holiday Inn Guangming Lu ⓣ020/87766999, ⓦwww.holiday-inn-guangzhou.com. Usual international-standard facilities, including a cinema. ❽

Liuhua 194 Huanshi Xi Lu ⓣ020/86668800, ⓦwww.lh.com.cn. Trusty but ageing hotel close to the train station, with a broad range of rooms – the cheaper ones are not such good value, however. ❼

Yishu (aka Art Hotel) Renmin Bei Lu ⓣ020/86670255, ⓕ86670266. Tucked back from the street just north of the undistinguished *Friendship Hotel*; look for the English name on a gateway out front and follow the driveway to the hotel. Nothing exceptional, with worn carpets and basic bathrooms, but inexpensive, given its busy location near to the Export Commodities Hall. ❹

The city centre

Central Guangzhou is basically a two-kilometre-wide band running north from the river between Renmin Lu and Yuexiu Lu. As remnants of the **Nanyue Kingdom** illustrate, this was the core of the city from its very foundation around 220 BC, and sports a host of historical monuments from this time right up to the 1930s. Most of these are located south of Dongfeng Lu, a mixed, rather scruffy mesh of old and new roads, alleys and businesses.

Around the Pearl River to Wuxian Guan

Yanjiang Lu, the northern promenade along the **Pearl River**, was paved in 2001 as part of a civic smartening campaign coinciding with Guangzhou hosting the China National Games. Lined with trees and a smattering of colonial-era buildings – such as the **Customs House** and **Aiqun Hotel** – it's a good place just to mill about on hot summer evenings.

If you follow Yanjiang Lu to its eastern end you'll find yourself crossing to **Er Sha Island**, the focus of much upmarket housing development and home to the **Guangdong Museum of Art** (Tues–Sun 9am–5pm; ¥15; ⓦwww.gdmoa.com). The museum holds one of China's largest collections of contemporary art, along with special exhibitions reflecting the country's shifting political and social conditions.

Back in the centre, north from the river, **Yide Lu** is stuffed with small shops selling toys, dried marine produce – jellyfish, shark's fin, fish maw and whole salted mackerel – along with sacks of nuts and candied fruit. Set north off the road at the back of a court, the **Sacred Heart Church** – also known as the Stone House – is a Gothic-style cathedral completed in 1888, impressive for its size and unexpected presence, though it's not generally open to the public. Three streets up from here on Huifu Xi Lu is **Wuxian Guan** (Five Immortals' Temple). Closed for renovation at time of writing, the temple is due to open again by 2008 – whether the more ancient of the temple's artefacts will survive the refit is a matter of some debate. Dating from 1377, the original wooden building isn't much to write home about, but there are some obviously ancient statues around the place: weathered guardian lions flank the way in, and there are some stylized Ming sculptures at the back, looking like giant chess pieces. The Five Immortals – three men and two women – are depicted too, riding their goatly steeds as they descend through the clouds to found Guangzhou. Also impressive is a fourteenth-century **bell tower** behind the temple, in which hangs a three-metre-high, five-tonne bronze bell, silent since receiving the

Guangzhou sights

Baiyun Shan	白云山	*báiyún shān*
Chen Jia Ci	陈家祠	*chénjiā cí*
Cultural Park	文化公园	*wénhuà gōngyuán*
Customs House	广州海关	*guăngzhōu hăiguān*
Dafo Si	大佛寺	*dàfó sì*
Er Sha Island	二沙岛	*èrshādăo*
Export Commodities Hall	中国出口商品交易会	*zhōngguó chūkŏushāngpĭn jiāoyìhuì*
Five Rams Statue	五羊石像	*wŭyáng shíxiàng*
Guangdong Museum of Art	广东美术馆	*guăngdōng mĕishùguăn*
Guangming Theatre	光明剧院	*guāngmíng jùyuàn*
Guangxiao Si	光孝寺	*guāngxiào sì*
Guangzhou Zoo	广州动物园	*guăngzhōu dòngwùyuán*
Haizhuang Park	海幢公园	*hăizhuàng gōngyuán*
Honan	河南	*hénán*
Hua Ta	花塔	*huātă*
Huaisheng Mosque	怀圣清真寺	*huáishèng qīngzhēn sì*
Hualin Si	华林寺	*huálín sì*
Huanghua Gang Park	黄花岗公园	*huánghuā găng gōngyuán*
Islamic Cemetery	清真古墓	*qīngzhēn gŭmù*
Liuhua Park	流花公园	*liúhuā gōngyuán*
Liurong Si	六榕寺	*liùróng sì*
Martyrs' Memorial Gardens	烈士陵园	*lièshì língyuán*
Nanyue Tomb	西汉南越王墓	*xīhàn nányuèwángmù*
Orchid Garden	兰圃	*lánpŭ*
Pearl River	珠江	*zhūjiāng*
Peasant Movement Training Institute	农民运动讲习所	*nóngmín yùndòng jiăngxísuŏ*
Provincial Museum	省博物馆	*shĕng bówùguăn*
Qian Chu Si	千处寺	*qiānchù sì*
Qingping Market	清平市场	*qīngpíng shìchăng*
Red Cross Hospital	红十字会医院	*hóngshízìhuì yīyuàn*
Sacred Heart Church	圣心大教堂	*shèngxīn dàjiàotáng*
Sanyuan Gong	三元宫	*sānyuán gōng*
Sanyuan Li	三元里	*sānyuán lĭ*
Shamian Island	沙面岛	*shāmiàn dăo*
Shamian Park	沙面公园	*shāmiàn gōngyuán*
Sun Yatsen Memorial Hall	中山纪念堂	*zhōngshān jìniàn táng*
Wuxian Guan	五仙观	*wŭxiān guàn*
Xidi Wharf	西堤码头	*xīdī mătóu*
Yuexiu Park	越秀公园	*yuèxiù gōngyuán*
Zhenhai Lou	镇海楼	*zhènhăi lóu*

blame for a plague which broke out shortly after its installation in 1378 – it has been called the "Forbidden Bell" ever since.

Huaisheng Mosque, Liurong Si and Guangxiao Si

A few blocks north of Wuxian Guan, the modern thoroughfare of **Zhongshan Lu** runs within striking distance of three of Guangzhou's most important **temples** – Ximen Kou or Gongyuan Qian are the closest **metro** stops. South of Zhongshan Liu Lu on Guangta Lu, **Huaisheng Mosque** and its grey, conical tower, **Guangta**, loom over a surrounding wall which bars entry to non-Muslims.

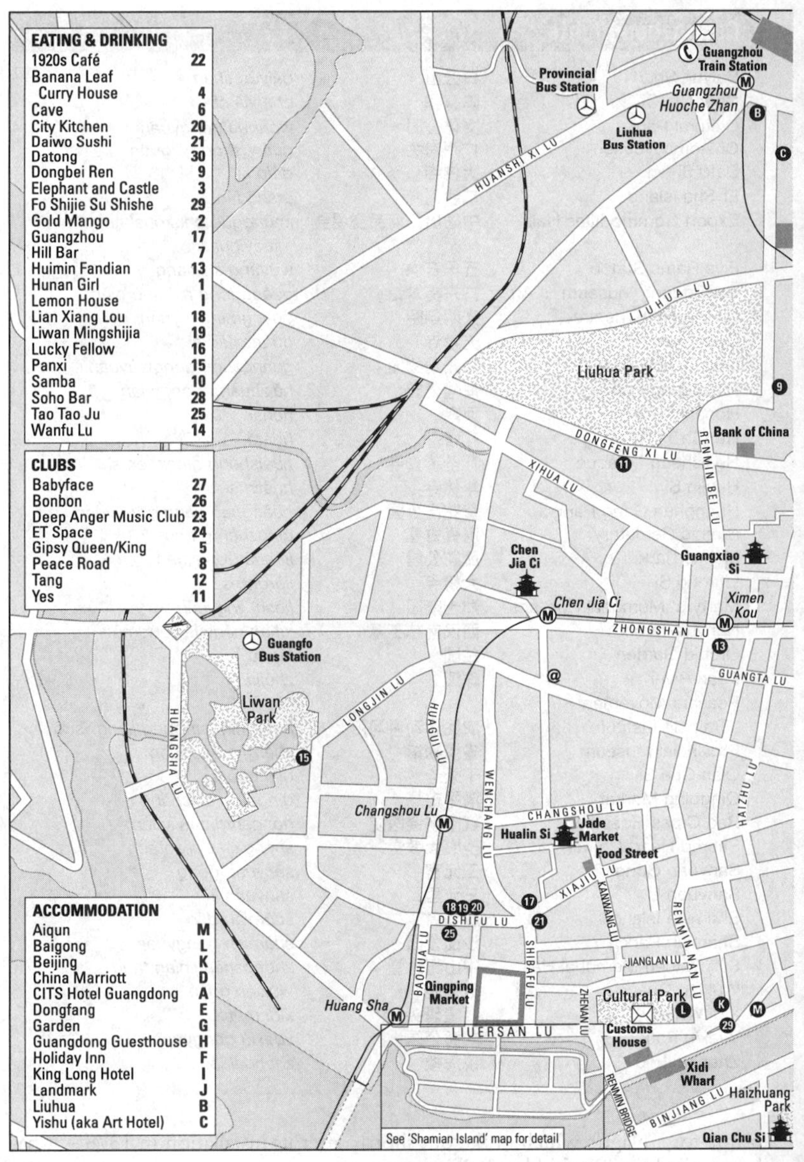

Looking like a lighthouse, Guangta is possibly the world's oldest minaret outside Mecca and something of a stylistic fossil, said by some to have been built by Abu Waqas in the seventh century (see p.575). During the fifteenth century, Huaisheng's environs were known as **Fanfang**, the foreigners' quarter; today there's a smattering of halal canteens and restaurants in the vicinity, including the famous *Huimin Fandian* (see p.581).

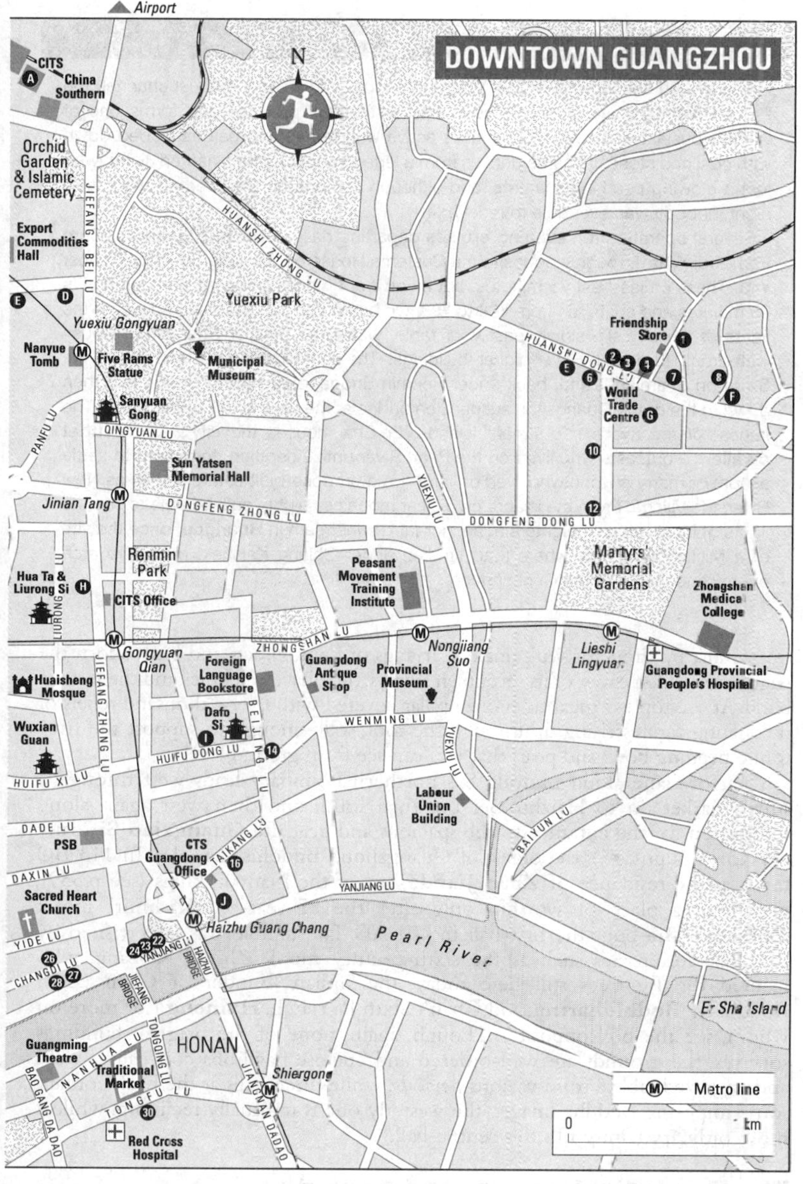

Liurong Si (Temple of the Six Banyan Trees; daily 8am–5pm; ¥5; Flower Pagoda ¥10) lies north of the mosque on Liurong Lu, and is associated with the dissident poet-governor **Su Dongpo**, who named the temple on a visit in 1100 and drew the characters for "Liu Rong" on the two stone steles just inside the gates. Very little of the temple itself survives, and the site is better known for the 57-metre-high **Hua Ta** (Flower Pagoda), a contemporary structure enshrining relics brought

Pearl River cruises

Oily grey and second only to the Yangzi in importance as an industrial channel, the **Pearl River** (Zhu Jiang) originates in eastern Yunnan province and forms one of China's busiest waterways, continually active with ferries and barges loaded down with coal and stone. Its name derives from a legend about a monk named Jiahu, who lost a glowing pearl in its waters, and although it shone on the riverbed night after night, nobody was ever able to recover it.

Several operators run **evening cruises** departing daily between 7.20 and 9.20pm from **Xidi Wharf**, roughly opposite the Customs House on Yanjiang Lu – tickets cost ¥48. These cruises last 75 minutes, but if you want dinner on board, the duration is 90 minutes and costs run from ¥88 to ¥98. On board you can sit back and watch the lights of the city slip slowly past your table, with fine views of Guangzhou's busy waterfront, flanked by ever-higher buildings. The route takes you past the *White Swan* on Shamian Island, back under Renmin Bridge, past Haizhu Bridge and then down to the grand Guangzhou suspension bridge at the far end of Er Sha Island. The largest of the river's mid-stream islands, Er Sha, houses the city's former **boat dwellers** – outcasts who lived on the Pearl River until Liberation, forbidden to settle ashore or marry anyone who lived on land – in a purpose-built estate known as New Riverside Village. From the island, on a clear moonless night you'll be able to see the lights of international freighters at anchor far downstream in **Huangpu**, once the site of a Military Academy where Mao studied under Chiang Kaishek, his future arch enemy and leader of the Guomindang.

from India by Emperor Wu's uncle. Carvings of lions, insects and birds adorn the pagoda's wooden eaves; of its seventeen storeys, nine have balconies and the rest are blind. At the top is a gigantic bronze pillar covered with over a thousand reliefs of meditating figures rising up through the roof, solid enough to support the five-tonne begging bowl and pearl that you can see from ground level.

A narrow lane along Liurong Si's northern boundary leads west through a street market on to Haizhu Bei Lu. Turn south and then west again along Jinghui Lu for the entrance to the spacious and peaceful **Guangxiao Si** (daily 6.30am–5.30pm; ¥5), the oldest of Guangzhou's Buddhist temples. In 113 BC this was the residence of **Zhao Jiande**, last of the Nanyue kings (see p.559), becoming a place of worship only after the 85-year-old Kashmiri monk **Tanmo Yeshe** built the first hall in 401 AD. The temple was later visited by Buddhist luminaries such as the sixth-century monk Zhiyao Sanzang, who planted the fig trees still here today; the Indian founder of Chan (Zen) Buddhism, **Bodhidharma**; and Chan's Sixth Patriarch, **Huineng** (for more on whom, see the box opposite). Though, again, none of the original buildings survives, the grounds are well-ordered and enclose pavilions concealing wells and engraved tablets from various periods, while three halls at the back contain some imposing Buddha images; the westerly one is unusually reclining, while a more ordinary trinity fills the central hall.

The Provincial Museum and around

Around 1500m east of Wuxian Guan on Wenming Lu is the **Provincial Museum** (daily 9am–5pm; ¥15), entry to which is through a gateway just around the corner on Yuexiu Lu. Walking here from Wuxian Guan, you'll pass the small and unassuming **Dafo Si**, the Big Buddha Temple, and the frenetically crowded shopping district along **Beijing Lu**; coming straight up from the river, look for the yellow 1920s **Labour Union Building** on Yuexiu Lu, later appropriated, somewhat cynically, as the Guomindang headquarters.

Chan Buddhism

Chan – known in Japan as **Zen** – believes that an understanding of the true nature of being can be achieved by sudden **enlightenment**, sparked by everyday, banal conversations or events. In this it differs from other forms of Buddhism, with their emphasis on the need for years of study of ritual and religious texts; though also using meditation and parables to achieve its ends, Chan therefore puts enlightenment within the grasp of even the most secular individual.

The founder of Chan was **Bodhidharma** (known as **Damo** in China), who arrived in Guangzhou from India around 520 AD intending to enrich China's rather formal, stodgy approach to Buddhism with his more lateral slant. After baffling the emperor with his teachings, Bodhidharma ended up at **Shaolin Si** in Henan; while there, exercises he taught the monks, to balance their long hours of meditation, are believed to have formed the basis of Chinese **kung fu** (see p.1172 & p.300). Shaolin subsequently became the centre for Chan Buddhism, spreading from there across China and into Japan and Korea.

Chan's most famous exponent was its Sixth Patriarch, **Huineng** (638–713). Huineng was from Guangzhou, but as a youth heard a wandering monk reciting sutras and was so impressed that he went to **Huangmei** in central China specifically to study Chan under the Fifth Patriarch, Hong Ren. Scorned by his fellow students for his rough southern manners, Huineng nonetheless demonstrated such a deep understanding of Chan that within a mere eight months he had achieved enlightenment on hearing the **Diamond Sutra** (which teaches how to recognize and dispense with illusions), and had been elected by Hong Ren to succeed him as patriarch, though the matter was kept secret at the time. Returning south to Guangzhou in 676, Huineng settled incognito at **Guangxiao Si**, where one day he heard two monks watching a flag and debating whether it was the wind or the flag that was moving. As they couldn't reach a decision, Huineng volunteered that neither was right, it was the mind that moved. His statement so stunned everyone present that he was invited to lecture, thereby revealing himself as the Sixth Patriarch (Hong Ren having died in the meantime). Huineng apparently spent his later years at **Nanhua Si** near Shaoguan in northern Guangdong.

The similar-looking buildings inside the Provincial Museum grounds are those of the former **Zhongshan University**; the writer **Lu Xun** lectured here and his life is outlined in photographs. A more modern structure houses the museum proper; its best features are a **natural history display**, incorporating an innovative walk-through "jungle" with spotlit creatures hidden in the undergrowth, as well as several rooms of exquisitely fine porcelain, carved jade and Ming household ornaments. The lack of visitors and explanatory notes somewhat deadens it all, but it's remarkable to see such a high standard of exhibits.

Thanks to the subsequent career of its dean, Mao Zedong, Guangzhou's **Peasant Movement Training Institute**, on Zhongshan Lu (Tues–Sun 9am–4.30pm; ¥5), is the city's most frequented revolutionary site. It still looks like the Confucian Academy it was for six hundred years, before **Peng Pai**, a "rich peasant" from Guangdong, established the Institute in 1924 with Guomindang permission and 38 students. The school lasted just over two years, with Mao, Zhou Enlai and Peng Pai taking the final classes in August 1926, eight months before the Communist and Guomindang alliance ended violently in Shanghai. There's actually little to see; most poignant are the photographs of alumni who failed to survive the Shanghai Massacre and the subsequent **1927 Communist Uprising** in Guangzhou.

The scene of the latter event lies farther east along Zhongshan Lu at the **Martyrs' Memorial Gardens** (daily 6am–9pm; ¥3). It was near here, on December 11, 1927, that a small Communist force under **Zhang Teilai** managed to take the Guangzhou Police Headquarters, announcing the foundation of the **Canton Commune**. Expected support never materialized, however, and on the afternoon of the second day, Guomindang forces moved in; five thousand people were killed outright or later executed for complicity. Despite their history, the gardens are quite a jolly place and as well as the evocatively titled Blood Spilled Pavilion are also home to a boating lake, children's playground and roller-rink.

Northern Guangzhou

The area north between Dongfeng Lu and Guangzhou train station is primarily occupied by two huge **parks**, Liuhua and Yuexiu, the impressive **Nanyue Tomb**, and the sole memento of a colonial-era confrontation further out beyond the station at **Sanyuan Li**.

Yuexiu Park

Yuexiu Park (daily 6am–9pm; ¥15) is China's biggest urban park, encompassing more than ninety hectares of sports courts, historic monuments, teahouses and shady groves. On the way here you'll pass a couple of notable buildings, most visibly the large rotunda and blue-tiled roof of the **Sun Yatsen Memorial Hall** on Dongfeng Zhong Lu (daily 8am–6pm; ¥5 or Y10 with entrance to the adjoining exhibition hall), built on the spot where the man regarded by Guomindang and Communists alike as the father of modern China took the presidential oath in 1912. Inside it's a plain auditorium with seating for two thousand people, occasionally used as a concert hall. Far less obvious is **Sanyuan Gong** (Three Purities Temple; daily 8am–5pm; ¥1) in the street immediately behind. Its entrance can be found by simply heading for the gaggle of hawkers touting brightly wrapped packs of ghost money and incense. This is actually the largest Taoist temple in Guangzhou, and the oldest too – it was first consecrated in 319 – though the current arrangement of dark, spartan halls occupied by statues of Taoist deities is Qing. Gloomy furnishings aside, it's a busy place of worship, and there are a few splashes of red and gold in the painted bats, cranes and other Taoist motifs scattered around.

The park

While there are entrances at all points of the compass, Yuexiu's **front gate** is on Jiefang Bei Lu, a ten-minute walk north of San Yuan Gong. To the north of the porcelain dragons here are **Beixiu Hu** and the **Garden of Chinese Idiom**, where many strange stone and bronze sculptures lurk in the undergrowth, illustrating popular sayings. Head south, and you'll wind up at the much-photographed **Five Rams Statue**, commemorating the myth of Guangzhou's foundation – at least one of these is definitely not a ram, however.

Roughly in the middle of the park atop a hill, paths converge at **Zhenhai Lou**, the "Gate Tower Facing the Sea", a wood and rendered-brick building that once formed part of the Ming city walls. Today it houses the **Municipal Museum** (daily 9am–5pm; ¥10), three floors of locally found exhibits ranging from Stone Age pottery fragments and ivory from Africa found in a Han-dynasty tomb, to fifth-century coins from Persia, a copy of *Good Words for Exhorting the World* (the Christian tract which inspired the Taiping leader, Hong Xiuquan), and nineteenth-century cannons tumbled about in the courtyard (two made by the German company, Krupp). A statue of Lin Zexu and letters from him to the Qing emperor documenting his disposal of the British opium stocks always draws big crowds of tongue-clicking Chinese.

The Nanyue Tomb and Liuhua Park

Five hundred metres north of Yuexiu Park's Jiefang Bei Lu entrance (and accessible on bus #5 or via the Yuexiu Gongyuan metro stop) is the looming, red sandstone facade of the **Nanyue Tomb** (daily 9am–5.30pm, last admission 4.45pm; ¥12). Discovered in 1983 during foundation-digging for a residential estate, this houses the 2000-year-old site of the tomb of **Zhao Mo**, grandson of the Nanyue Kingdom's founder Zhao Tuo, and really deserves an hour of your time – there's another English-language **video** and a mass of exhibits.

Zhao Mo made a better job of his tomb than running his kingdom, which disintegrated shortly after his death: excavators found the tomb stacked with gold and priceless trinkets. They're on view in the museum, including a **burial suit** made from more than a thousand tiny jade tiles (jade was considered to prevent decay), and the ash-like remains of slaves and concubines immured with him. Several artefacts show Central Asian influence in their designs, illustrating how even at this early stage in Guangzhou's history there was contact with non-Chinese peoples. It's all fascinating and expertly presented, particularly worthwhile if you plan to visit contemporary grave sites in the Yangzi Basin or at Xi'an. Incidentally, Zhao Tuo's tomb still awaits discovery, though rumours of its fabulous treasures had eager excavators turning Guangzhou inside out as long ago as the Three Kingdoms period (220–280 AD).

West of the Nanyue Tomb between Liuhua Lu and Renmin Bei Lu, **Liuhua Park** (daily 6am–10pm; ¥5) is a large expanse of lakes, purpose-built in 1958 and pleasant enough during the week, though hellishly crowded at weekends. Liuhua means "Flowing Flowers", a name said to date back to the Han period when palace maids tossed petals into a nearby stream while dressing their hair.

To Guangzhou train station

About 1km south of Guangzhou train station and surrounded by business hotels on Liuhua Lu and Renmin Lu, the **Export Commodities Hall** is the venue each April and October for the city's **Trade Fair**, first held in 1957 to encourage Western investments. This isn't the most pleasant area of town but there is one oasis of peace and quiet: Guangzhou's delightful, though fairly small, **Orchid Garden**, off Jiefang Bei Lu (Mon–Fri 8am–6pm, Sat & Sun 8am–7pm; ¥8, ¥20 including tea in the central pavilion). Besides orchids, there are ponds surrounded by tropical ferns and lilies, winding stone paths, palms and giant figs with drooping aerial roots, and pink-flowering azaleas. Apart from the filtered traffic noise, it's hard to believe that the city lies just outside. Along the western edge of the garden, Guangzhou's **Islamic Cemetery** contains the tomb of **Abu Waqas**, a seventh-century missionary who brought Islam to China. The details are a little sketchy, however, as Abu Waqas supposedly died around 629, three years before Mohammed, and the Quran wasn't collated for another generation afterwards. The cemetery was recently closed to non-Muslims, though it can be glimpsed from inside the garden through a screen of bamboos.

Sanyuan Li

For a return to earth after the Orchid Garden, continue up Jiefang Bei Lu for 1km after it crosses Huanshi Lu to **Sanyuan Li**. A recently redeveloped part of the city, 150 years ago this was a separate village outside Guangzhou, and it was here that the **Sanyuan Li Anti-British Movement** formed in 1841 after the British stormed into the area during the First Opium War. Following months of abuse from the invaders, local workers and peasants rose under the farmer **Wei Shaoguang** and attacked the British camp, killing around twenty soldiers in an indecisive engagement before being dispersed by heavy rain. A **temple** on the north side of San Yuan Li Dadao, not far from Sanyuan Li metro exit B, was built in 1860 on the sight of the battle and now houses a small **museum** (daily 9am–5pm; ¥2) exhibiting the peasants' armoury of farm tools and ceremonial weapons – don't take the captions, the turgid product of later propaganda, too seriously. A park featuring a **memorial** to the resistance (daily 5.45am–6pm; ¥2) is also nearby, a few minutes' walk east from the metro (Exit A1).

Western Guangzhou

Western Guangzhou, the area west of Renmin Lu and south of Dongfeng Xi Lu, features a charismatic warren of back roads and lanes around Changshou Lu, all stuffed to overflowing with market activity, restaurants and shops, which empty down near the waterfront opposite **Shamian Island**, a quiet haven of colonial mood and huge trees. North of the river, Zhongshan Lu continues westwards through the area, cut by a score of roads running south to parallel **Liuersan Lu**, along the river; south, the main roads are Nanhua Lu and Tongfu Lu.

Chen Jia Ci

Zhongshan Lu's western arm cuts through a new, relatively tidy district before eventually heading over a tributary of the Pearl River and out of the city towards Foshan. About 2.5km from the Jiefang Lu intersection, a pedestrian walkway across the road leads to gardens outside **Chen Jia Ci** (Chen Clan Academy; daily 8.30am–5.30pm, last admission 5pm; ¥10). The story of its founding is unusual; subscriptions were invited from anyone named **Chen** – one of the most common Cantonese surnames – and the money raised went to build this complex, part ancestor temple where Chens could worship, part school where they could receive an education. Though belittled today by tea-rooms and souvenir stalls, the buildings remain impressive, forming a series of rooms arranged around open courtyards, all decorated by the most garish tiles and gorgeously carved screens and stonework that money could buy in the 1890s. Have a good look at the extraordinary brick reliefs under the eaves, both inside and out. One of the first, on the right as you enter, features an opera being performed to what looks like a drunken horse, which lies squirming on the floor with mirth. Other cameos feature stories from China's "noble bandit" saga, *Outlaws of the Marsh*, and some of the sights around Guangzhou.

Changshou Lu and around

Below Zhongshan Lu, the ring of part of the old city walls can be traced along **Longjin Lu** in the north, and **Dishifu Lu** and others to the south – you'll actually cross a low mound marking their foundations if you enter the area off Zhongshan Lu down Huagui Lu. Though a couple of wide, modern main roads barge through, most of this district, with east–west **Changshou Lu** at its core, retains its Ming-dynasty street plan and a splash of early twentieth-century architecture, making for excellent random walks. In addition to some of Guangzhou's biggest shopping plazas and a crowd of markets spreading into each other south from Changshou Lu right down to the river, several **famous restaurants** are here, and the area is particularly busy at night.

Shops and markets selling jade run all the way from the pedestrian square on Xiajiu Lu right up to Changshou Lu, culminating in two multistorey jade shopping malls newly built either side of the **Hualin Si** Buddhist temple (daily 9am–5.30pm; ¥3), founded as a modest nunnery by the Brahman prince **Bodhidharma** in 527 (see box, p.573). After his Chan teachings caught on in the seventeenth century, the main hall was enlarged to house five hundred *arhat* sculptures ranged along the cross-shaped aisles, and Hualin remains the most lively temple in the city – during festivals you'll be crushed, deafened and blinded by the crowds, firecrackers and incense smoke.

From here, the best thing you can do is throw away your map and roam unaided southwards through the maze of alleys and Qing-era homes (some of which are protected historic relics), most likely emerging in the vicinity of the *Guangzhou* restaurant. Two streets lined with restored 1920s facades and pedestrianized at the weekends lie here – **Dishifu Lu** to the west and **Xiajiu Lu** to the east – and places to eat and shop are legion, the pavements always crammed to capacity. South again off Xiajiu Lu, you enter the upper reaches of the infamous **Qingping Market**, with each intersecting east–west lane forming dividing lines for the sale of different goods: dried medicines, spices and herbs, fresh vegetables, livestock, birds and fish. Once one of China's most confronting – not to say gory – markets, this has been scaled down considerably in recent years with the removal of rare animals and large-scale streetside butchering, though it remains a lively and busy affair, amply illustrating the Cantonese demand for fresh and unusual food.

You exit Qingping onto **Liuersan Lu**, a recently widened road given a stack of flyovers to relieve chronic traffic congestion, lined with palms, flowerbeds, and fake colonial frontages mirroring the real thing opposite on Shamian Island. "Liuersan" means "6, 23", referring to June 23, 1925, when fifty people were shot by colonial troops during a demonstration demanding, among other things, the return of Shamian Island to Chinese control. East along Liuersan, the **Cultural Park** (daily 6am–9.30pm; ¥3), in the heart of the city's electronics market district, is a rather bland area of paving and benches, where gangs of children queue for their turn on arcade games and fairground rides, and theatre and sound stages host weekend performances of anything from local rock to opera. The park also hosts Guangzhou's annual **Food Festival** at the end of November (¥10).

Shamian Island

It's just a short hop across Liuersan Lu and a muddy canal (or head to Huang Sha metro, then cross the bridge) on to **Shamian Island**, but the pace changes instantly, and Guangzhou's busiest quarter is exchanged for its most genteel. A tear-shaped sandbank about 1km long and 500m wide, Shamian was leased to European powers as an Opium War trophy, the French getting the eastern end and the British the rest. Here the colonials recreated their own backyards, planting the now massive **trees** and throwing up solid, Victorian-style **villas**, banks, embassies, churches and tennis courts – practically all of which are still standing. Iron gates on the bridges once excluded the Chinese from Shamian (as the Chinese had once forbidden foreigners to enter within Guangzhou's city walls), leaving the Europeans in self-imposed isolation from the bustle across the water. Shamian retains that atmosphere today, a quiet bolt hole for many long-term travellers in the city. There's restricted traffic flow, and the well-tended architecture, greenery and relative peace make it a refreshing place to visit, even if you're not staying or sampling the restaurants and bars.

The main thoroughfare is east–west **Shamian Dajie**, with five numbered streets running south across the island. Wandering around, you'll find buildings have largely been restored to their original appearance – most were built between the 1860s and early twentieth century – with plaques sketching their

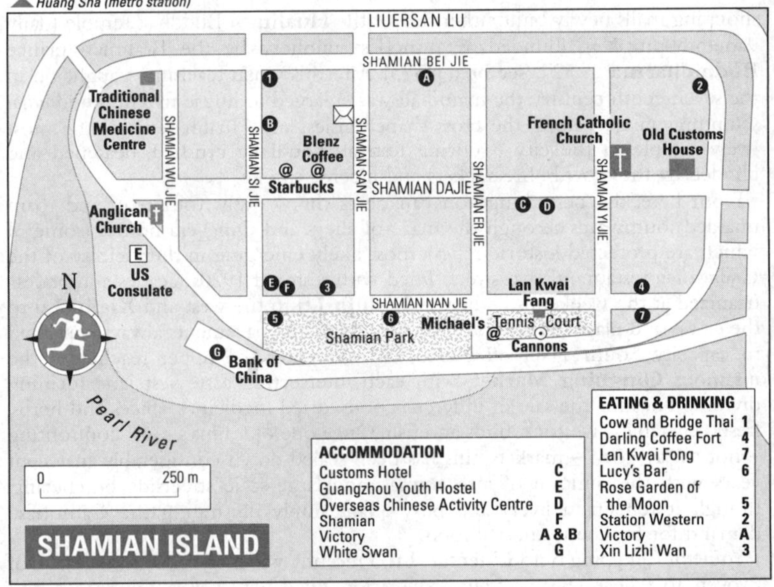

history. Though sharing such a tiny area, the British and French seemingly kept themselves to themselves, building separate bridges, churches and customs houses; nothing is particularly worth searching out, but it's all great browsing. Next to the atypically modern *White Swan* hotel on the **Shamian Nan Jie** esplanade, a focus of sorts is provided by **Shamian Park**, where two **cannons**, cast in nearby Foshan during the Opium Wars, face out across the river, and you might catch Cantonese opera rehearsals here on Saturday afternoons. The island's waterfront area is also the venue for Guangzhou's major Spring Festival **fireworks display**, held on the first night at around 9pm; the best seats are at the *White Swan*'s riverside buffet, but failing that you can join half of the city in the surrounding streets – or watch from your room at the *Youth Hostel*.

Honan

Honan, the area immediately south of the river between westerly **Gongye Dadao** and **Jiangnan Dadao**, 1500m further east, can be reached on any of **three bridges**: Renmin Bridge, which connects Liuersan Lu with Gongye Dadao; and the closely spaced Jiefang and Haizhu bridges off Yanjiang Lu, which become Tongqing Lu and Jiangnan Dadao respectively. Metro line #2 runs along Jiangnan Dadao, with stations at Shiergong and Jiangnanxi, or you can just walk across the nearest bridge and explore on foot.

Prior to 1949, Honan was Guangzhou's red-light district, crawling with opium dens, brothels and gambling houses, none of which survived the Communist takeover. Indeed, in 1984 Honan was chosen as a model of **Hu Yaobang**'s "Civic Spirit" campaign, which called on residents to organize kindergartens, old folks' clubs, and to keep their communities clean and safe. It's still a surprisingly calm and quiet corner of the city, the small flagstoned alleys off Nanhua Lu and Tongfu Lu kept litter-free and lined with austere, wooden-gated homes. During the **spring flower festival** (a southern Chinese tradition originating in Guangzhou), however, florist stalls along riverfront Binjiang Lu attract crowds from all over the city to buy blooms of every colour and shape for good luck in the coming year. There's also another big Cantonese-style **market** here – a rather more spirited affair than Qingping – in the backstreets southwest off the Nanhua Lu/Tongqing Lu junction.

Honan's sole formal sight is in **Haizhuang Park** (daily 6.15am–9pm; ¥2), sandwiched between Nanhua Lu and Tongfu Lu, about ten minutes' walk from Renmin Bridge. The buildings here have been returned to their original purpose as **Qian Chu Si** (daily 8am–5pm), a sizeable Buddhist monastery. Renovations have spruced up the broad south hall, with its fine statuary and interlocked wooden-beam roof, so typical of south China's early Qing temple buildings – the flashing, coloured "haloes" surrounding several of the statues are less traditional touches.

Eastern Guangzhou and Baiyun Shan Park

Hemmed in on all other flanks by rivers and hills, Guangzhou inevitably expands east to accommodate its ever-growing population, and it's here you'll find the most "modern" parts of the city, shadowed by skyscrapers housing corporate headquarters and cut by several expressways. **Huanshi Lu** and **Dongfeng Lu** are the biggest of these, converging out in the northeastern suburbs at the vast open-plan district of **Tianhe**. Much of the city's **expat community** is based out this way, and there are numerous Western-oriented **restaurants and bars** – if few actual sights – to recommend a visit. One exception is **Baiyun Shan Park**, which lies immediately to the north and offers an unexpectedly thorough escape from the city.

Northeast off Huanshi Dong Lu along Xianlie Lu, **Huanghua Gang Park** (daily 8am–5pm; ¥10) recalls Sun Yatsen's abortive 1911 Canton Uprising in the **Mausoleum to the 72 Martyrs**, a very peculiar monument reflecting the nationalities of numerous donors who contributed to its construction – Buddhist iconography rubbing shoulders with a Statue of Liberty and Egyptian obelisk. **Guangzhou Zoo**, about 1km farther out along Xianlie Lu (daily 9am–4pm; ¥20; bus #6 from Dongfeng Lu, one block east of the Sun Yatsen Memorial Hall), is the third largest in the country, with the animals kept in relatively decent conditions – though far below what you'll probably consider pleasant. Among the rarities are clouded leopards, several species of wildfowl and, of course, pandas.

You'll most likely find yourself out at **Tianhe**, the area surrounding the train station 2km due east of the zoo, en route to Guangzhou East train station. A planned area of vast spaces of concrete paving, broad roads and glassy towers, where pedestrians are reduced to insignificant specks, Tianhe has as its showpiece a huge **sports stadium** built for the 1987 National Games (Tiyu Zhong Xin metro), all revamped when Guangzhou was the Games' host for the second time in 2001.

Baiyun Shan Park

Just 7km north of downtown, **Baiyun Shan** (White Cloud Mountain) is close enough to central Guangzhou to reach by city bus, but open enough to leave all the city's noise and bustle behind. Once covered with numerous monasteries, Baiyun's heavily reforested slopes now offer lush panoramas out over Guangzhou and the delta region. A **park** here encloses almost thirty square kilometres (¥18), its entrance a thirty-minute ride on bus #24 from the south side of Renmin Park, immediately northeast of the Jiefang Lu/Zhongshan Lu crossroads.

It's a good three-hour walk from the entrance off Luhu Lu to **Moxing Ling** (Star-touching Summit), past strategically placed teahouses and pavilions offering views and refreshments. There's also a **cable car** (¥20) from the entrance as far as the **Cheng Precipice**, a ledge roughly halfway to the top, which earned its name when the Qin-dynasty minister **Cheng Ki** was ordered here by his emperor to find a herb of immortality. Having found the plant, Cheng nibbled a leaf only to see the remainder vanish; full of remorse, he flung himself off the mountain but was caught by a stork and taken to heaven. Sunset views from the precipice are spectacular.

Eating

Eating out is the main recreation in Guangzhou, something the city is famous for and caters to admirably. Guangzhou's restaurants, the best to be found in a province famed for its food, are justification enough to spend a few days in the city, and it would be a real shame to leave without having eaten in one of the more elaborate or famous **Cantonese** places – there's nothing to match the experience of tucking into a Cantonese spread while being surrounded by an enthusiastic horde of local diners. Locals are so proud of their cuisine that a few years ago it was hard to find anywhere serving anything else, though now you can also track down a good variety of **Asian**, **European** and even **Indian** food – not to mention **regional Chinese**. Some canteens open as early as 5am, and breakfast – including traditional **dim sum** – is usually served from 7 to 10am, later on Sundays or if the restuarant has a particularly good reputation. Lunch is on offer between 11am and 2pm, and dinner from 5 to 10pm, though most people eat early rather than late.

Guangzhou restaurants

1920s Café	一九二零餐厅	*yījiǔèr líng cāntīng*
Banana Leaf Curry House	蕉叶饮食	*jiāoyè yǐnshí*
Cow and Bridge Thai	泰国牛桥	*tàiguó niúqiáo*
Daiwo Sushi	大禾会日本饭店	*dàhéhuì rìběn fàndiàn*
Datong	大同大酒家	*dàtóng dàjiǔjiā*
Dongbei Ren	东北人	*dōngběi rén*
Fo Shijie Su Shishe	佛世界素食社	*fóshìjiè sùshíshè*
Guangzhou	广州酒家	*guǎngzhōu jiǔjiā*
Huimin Fandian	回民饭店	*huímín fàndiàn*
Hunan Girl	湘妹子	*xiāngmèi zi*
Jiangxi Ren	江西人	*jiāngxī rén*
Lan Kwai Fong	兰桂坊	*lán guì fǎng*
Lemon House	越茗苑	*yuèmíng yuàn*
Lian Xiang Lou	莲香楼	*liánxiāng lóu*
Liwan Mingshijia	荔湾名食家	*lìwān míngshíjiā*
Lucky Fellow	幸运楼酒家	*xìngyùnlóu jiǔjiā*
Lucy's Bar	露丝吧	*lùsī bā*
Nanyuan	南园酒店	*nányuán jiǔdiàn*
Panxi	泮溪酒家	*pànxī jiǔjiā*
Papa John's Pizza	棒约翰中信餐厅	*bàngyuēhàn zhōngxìn cāntīng*
Rose Garden of the Moon	玫瑰园西餐厅	*méiguìyuán xīcāntīng*
Samba	森巴西餐厅	*sēnbāxī cāntīng*
Station Western	车站西餐酒廊	*chēzhàn xīcān jiǔláng*
Tao Tao Ju	陶陶居	*táotáo jū*
Wanfu Lou	万福楼	*wanfú lóu*
Xin Lizhi Wan	新荔枝湾酒楼	*xīnlìzhīwān jiǔlóu*

Restaurants are pretty evenly spread across the city, though Dishifu Lu in the west, and Shamian Island, have a ridiculous quantity and variety between them. Ordering is a bit easier here than in the average Chinese city, as many restaurants have an **English menu** tucked away somewhere, even if these omit dishes that they believe won't appeal to foreigners. **Prices** have actually fallen somewhat in recent years, though the sociable Cantonese fashion of entertaining (and impressing) family or wealthy clients with food means that you'll pay upwards of ¥40 a head for a good Chinese meal, and ¥60 if you're after more exotic Asian or Western food.

You can, of course, eat for a fraction of this cost day or night at the city's numerous **food stalls** which, like the restaurants, are never far away (streets off Beijing Lu have the best selection). Here you can pick up a few slices of roast duck or pork on rice, meat and chicken dumplings, or noodle soups, usually for less than ¥10 a plate. Be sure to try a selection of **cakes** and the fresh tropical **fruits** too; local lychees are so good that the emperors once had them shipped direct to Beijing.

If Chinese dining just isn't for you, there are Western fast-food outlets throughout the city, though there's no need to resort to them – **bars** and **cafés** listed below serve grills, sandwiches, and counter meals as good as anything you'll get at home. Tourist **hotels** have restaurants used to dealing with foreign palates too, and some are worth checking for special sittings. The daily dessert buffet at the *China Marriott* (3–5pm; ¥46 per person), for example, features an unbelievable array of pastries and cakes served with tea or coffee; the *White Swan* does endless coffee refills (¥40) as well as a buffet breakfast (¥138) before 11am – and has the best riverside views in Guangzhou.

Central Guangzhou

1920s Café Yanjiang Lu. This refined German restaurant, with mains (¥50–130) including bratwürst, schnitzel, German noodles and sauerkraut, also has a pleasant, almost-riverside outdoor patio – perfect if you fancy knocking back a beer or two.

Datong 63 Yanjiang Xi Lu. If you're after an authentically noisy, crowded *dim sum* session with river views, head here to floors 2, 5 or 6 between 7am and noon. They pride themselves on their roast suckling pig. Window seats are in high demand, so arrive early.

Huimin Fandian (aka Five Rams) Southeast corner of the Renmin Lu/Zhongshan Lu crossroads. The city's biggest and most popular Muslim restaurant, serving lamb hotpots, roast duck, lemon chicken and spicy beef at reasonable prices.

Lemon House 507 Huifu Dong Lu. Recognized as the best Vietnamese in town, with queues every evening and lunchtime. *Tiger Prawn* across the road at no. 548 is another option, but is beginning to attract queues of its own.

Lucky Fellow Sixth floor of a shopping centre on the corner of Taikang Lu and Huilong Lu. This large, smart establishment serves up a range of Chinese cuisines, focusing on Cantonese – both the roast goose and fragrant chicken are excellent. Plus an extensive English menu. It's all reasonably priced, with main dishes starting at ¥18.

Wanfu Lou Corner of Beijing Lu and Yushan Lu. Full-on Cantonese restaurant, with a take-away roast-meat shop and canteen downstairs, and more formal arrangements above.

Northern and eastern Guangzhou

Banana Leaf Curry House Fifth floor, World Trade Centre, Huanshi Dong Lu. Good, eclectic mix of Thai, Malaysian and Indonesian fare, all authentically spiced. Not cheap, though; expect upwards of ¥70 a head.

Dongbei Ren Opposite Liuhua Park on Renmin Bei Lu. Nationwide chain serving Manchurian food in comfortable surroundings. The sautéed corn kernels with pine nuts, steamed chicken with mushrooms, or eggs and black fungus are all good. Portions from ¥20.

Hunan Girl Taojin Lu. Hunanese restaurant more popular with Guangzhou's expats than Chinese residents – the interior even looks like an average Chinese restaurant overseas – though the cooking is good and prices are reasonable.

Jiangxi Ren 475 Huanshi Dong Lu. It's easy to spot the huge earthenware jars outside this one, and the second-floor restaurant is decked out in Chinese "folksy" furnishings. The main thing to try

Guangdong cooking

Guangdong cooking is one of China's four major regional styles and, despite northern critics decrying it as too uncomplicated to warrant the term "cuisine", it's unmatched in the clarity of its flavours and its appealing presentation. The style subdivides into **Cantonese**, emanating from the Pearl River Delta region; **Chaozhou**, from the city of the same name in the far east of Guangdong; and **Hakka**, from the northeastern border with Fujian, named after the Han subgroup with whom it originated. Though certain Chaozhou and Hakka recipes have been incorporated into the main body of Guangdong cooking – sweet-and-sour pork with fruit, and salt-baked chicken, for instance – it's Cantonese food which has come to epitomize its principles. With many Chinese emigrants leaving through Guangzhou, it's also the most familiar to overseas visitors, though peruse a menu here and you'll soon realize that most dishes served abroad as "Cantonese" would be unrecognizable to a local.

Spoiled by good soil and a year-round growing season, the Cantonese demand absolutely **fresh ingredients**, kept alive and kicking in cages, tanks or buckets at the front of the restaurant for diners to select themselves. Westerners can be repulsed by this collection of wildlife, and even other Chinese comment that the Cantonese will eat anything with legs that isn't a piece of furniture, and anything with wings that isn't an aeroplane. The cooking itself is designed to keep **textures** distinct and **flavours** as close to the original as possible, using a minimum amount of mild and complementary seasonings to prevent dishes from being bland. **Fast stir-frying** in a wok is the best known of these procedures, but **slow-simmering** in soy sauce and wine and **roasting** are other methods of teasing out the essential characteristics of the food.

No full meal is really complete without a simple plate of rich green and bitter **choi sam** (*cai xin* in Mandarin), Chinese broccoli, blanched and dressed with oyster sauce. Also famous is **fish and seafood**, often simply steamed with ginger and spring onions – hairy crabs are a winter treat, sold everywhere – and nobody cooks **fowl** better than the Cantonese, always juicy and flavoursome, whether served crisp-skinned and roasted or fragrantly casseroled. Guangzhou's citizens are also compulsive snackers, and outside canteens you'll see **roast meats**, such as whole goose or strips of *cha siu* pork, waiting to be cut up and served with rice for a light lunch, or burners stacked with **sandpots** *(sai bo)*, a one-person dish of steamed rice served in the cooking vessel with vegetables and slices of sweet *lap cheung* sausage. **Cake shops** selling heavy Chinese pastries and filled buns are found everywhere across the region. Some items like **custard tartlets** are derived from foreign sources, while roast-pork buns and flaky-skinned **mooncakes** stuffed with sweet lotus seed paste are of domestic origin.

Perhaps it's this delight in little delicacies that led the tradition of **dim sum** (*dian xin* in Mandarin) to blossom in Guangdong, where it's become an elaborate form of breakfast most popular on Sundays, when entire households pack out restaurants. Also known in Cantonese as **yum cha** – literally, "drink tea" – *dim sum* involves little dishes of fried, boiled and steamed snacks being stuffed inside bamboo steamers or displayed on plates, then wheeled around the restaurant on trolleys, which you stop for inspection as they pass your table. On being seated, you're given a pot of tea, which is constantly topped up, and a card, which is marked for each dish you select and which is later surrendered to the cashier. Try *juk* (rice porridge), spring rolls, buns, cakes and plates of thinly sliced roast meats, and small servings of restaurant dishes like spareribs, stuffed capsicum, or squid with black beans. Save most room, however, for the myriad types of little fried and steamed **dumplings** which are the hallmark of a *dim sum* meal, such as *har gau*, juicy minced prawns wrapped in transparent rice-flour skins; and *siu mai*, a generic name for a host of delicately flavoured, open-topped packets.

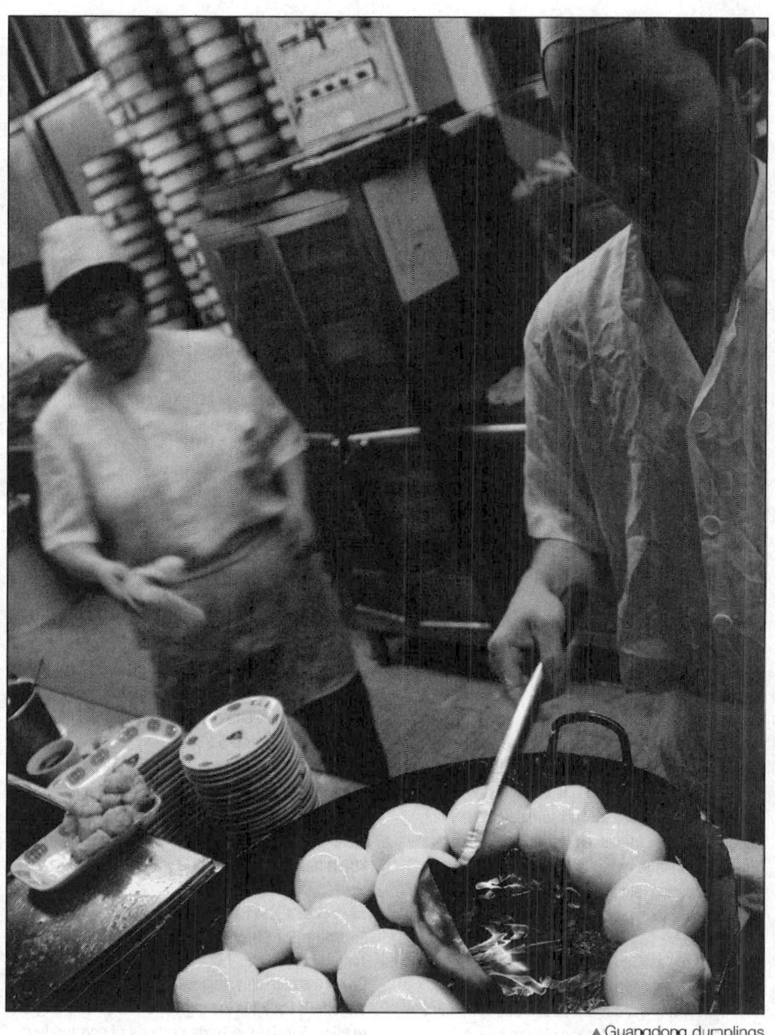

▲Guangdong dumplings

here is the Jiangxi-style giant soups, enough for three or four people, at around ¥35–60; the duck and pear variety is excellent.

Papa John's Pizza CITIC Plaza. Total American pizza experience housed on the second floor of a swish mall one metro stop from the eastern rail station. Everything much the same as you would expect at home, including the prices.

Samba Jianshe Lu. Excellent evening atmosphere here, with South American music (live, courtesy of the Brazilian staff), a colossal selection of imported booze, and various all-you-can-eat deals for about ¥50–70 – if you're not tempted by the juiciest beef ribs in town.

Western Guangzhou

City Kitchen 93 Dishifu Lu, a few doors down from *Liwan Mingshijia*, this modern restaurant offers a range of simple Cantonese meals, mostly under ¥30. Plenty of photographs help no end with the ordering.

Daiwo Sushi Shibafu Lu, just south of the *Guangzhou* restaurant. Conveyor-belt sushi; good fun and very popular. Plates are colour-coded according to a ¥5–15 pricing scheme, and staff tot up your empties at the end.

Guangzhou Corner of Wenchang Nan Lu and Xiajiu Lu; other branches citywide. The oldest, busiest and most famous restaurant in the city, with entrance calligraphy by the Qing emperor Kangxi and a rooftop neon sign flashing "Eating in Guangzhou". The menu is massive, and you won't find better crisp-skinned chicken or pork anywhere – bank on ¥80 a person for a decent feed. Service is offhand.

Lian Xiang Lou 67 Dishifu Lu. Established in 1889 and famous for its mooncakes, baked dough confections stuffed with sweet lotus paste and shaped as rabbits and peaches, which you can buy from the downstairs shop. The upstairs restaurant does commendable roast suckling pig, brown-sauced pigeon, and duck fried with lotus flowers for about ¥30 a portion.

Liwan Mingshijia 99 Dishifu Lu. Ming-style canteen and teahouse decked in heavy marble-and-wood furniture, crammed with diners wolfing down *dim-sum*-style snacks. Some of the finest *sheung fan* (stuffed rice rolls), *zongzi* (steamed packets of rice and meat) and *tangyuan* (glutinous riceballs filled with chopped nuts in a sweet soup) you'll find. No English and not much Mandarin spoken, but you can order by pointing to other people's dishes.

Panxi Longjin Xi Lu, Liwan Park. The best thing about this Cantonese restaurant – a teahouse of ill repute in the 1940s – is the lakeside location and interesting *dim sum* selection. Main meals are undistinguished, however, and the English-language menu is disappointingly perfunctory. Inexplicably popular with tour groups, who apparently haven't discovered the far superior *Tao Tao Ju*.

Tao Tao Ju Dishifu Lu. Looks upmarket, with huge chandeliers, wooden shutters and coloured leadlight windows, but prices are mid-range and very good value. Roast goose is the house speciality, and they also do cracking seafood – plain boiled prawns or fried crab are both excellent – along with crisp-skinned chicken, lily-bud and beef sandpots, and a host of Cantonese favourites. Comprehensive English menu; mains ¥18–80.

Shamian Island

Cow and Bridge Thai Shamian Bei Jie. Very formal place to dine on what is unquestionably the finest Thai food in Guangzhou, if not all China. The food is beautifully presented and the service impeccable. Main dishes are pricey, but turn to the back of the menu for cheaper options at ¥30 plus which are more than enough for one.

Darling Coffee Fort Shamian Nan Jie. Bizarrely named, *Darling* is actually a Thai and Vietnamese restaurant. It is not cheap by Guangzhou's standards, but at around ¥50 per head it shouldn't break the bank.

Lucy's Bar Shamian Nan Jie. Sit outside in the evening at this Westerner-oriented place and eat decent Mexican-, Thai- and Indian-style dishes, along with burgers, pizza and grills. Mains ¥25–70; cheap beer at ¥20 a pint; and afternoon tea for ¥20 per person.

Lan Kwai Fong Salon Shamian Nan Jie. Taking its name from Hong Kong's central bar and restaurant district, this slightly pricey Guangdong restaurant's two outlets – one overlooking the tennis courts and one at the eastern end of the park – are extremely popular with locals, especially at the weekend.

Rose Garden of the Moon Shamian Nan Jie. Generic bar/restaurant in the park. Nothing to cross town for but nice enough, with good river views.

Station Western Shamian Bei Jie. If you fancy a break from the usual, this mid-range place offers an assortment of cuisines (from Asian to BBQ to Italian), either served in the garden or, if you've got the cash to splash, in a private room aboard one of its two train carriages.

Victory Shamian Bei Jie. Worth a visit for good, if pricey, *dim sum* eaten among the usual cheerful throngs. Daily 7am–5.30pm.

Xin Lizhi Wan Shamian Nan Jie. One of the most highly regarded seafood restaurants in the city, always busy with a mostly upmarket clientele. Not too expensive, however; you can eat well here for ¥80 a head.

South of the river

Fo Shijie Su Shishe Niu Nai chang Jie, South off Tongfu Lu, just West of the Red Cross Hospital. Down a small alley, this is hard to find but worth the effort. Look for the sign in Chinese and English reading *Fut Sai Kai*. Huge portions of scrumptious vegetarian food; crispy chicken drumsticks in sweet-and-sour sauce, salt-fried prawns, chicken-ball casserole and the rest are all made from bean curd, with heaps of straightforward vegetable dishes too. Full English menu; most dishes under ¥30.

Nanyuan 142 Qianjin Lu. Possibly the best restaurant in Guangzhou, serving cheapish *dim sum* until about 10am, when it transforms into an upmarket establishment. Superb stewed Chaozhou-style goose, Maotai chicken (steamed in the famous sorghum spirit of that name) and fish with pine nuts. Metro Line #2 to Jiangnanxi or bus #35 from Haizhu Square on Yanjiang Zhong Lu.

Drinking, nightlife and entertainment

By Chinese standards, Guangzhou has good **nightlife**. A scattering of **clubs** in the central and eastern parts of the city ranges from warehouse-sized discos to obscure, almost garage-like affairs, aimed at a mostly Chinese student and yuppie crowd; some have a **cover charge** (usually around ¥30 including a beer) though most get their money through higher-than-average prices for drinks. Expats favour the bars located in Guangzhou's eastern reaches, where the booze is cheaper (around ¥25 a pint), pub-style meals can be had for ¥20–40, and the music is for listening to rather than dancing. Club hours are from 8pm to 2am, bars are open anytime from lunch to 2am, but don't expect much to be happening before 9pm at either. As usual, places open and close without notice, or swing in and out of popularity; one promising up-and-coming area is waterfront **Yanjiang Lu**. The places reviewed overleaf are good starting points, but check out ⓦwww.thatsgz.com for the latest.

Cantonese opera is superficially similar to Beijing's, but more rustic. Virtually extinct by the 1990s, it has recently bounced back in popularity, with Guangming, south of the river at the junction of Baogang Dadao and Nanhua Lu in Honan (ⓣ020/84499721), and Jiang Nan at 130 Chang Gang Zhong Lu (ⓣ020/84324187) hosting several performances monthly. You might also catch amateur groups performing in the parks at the weekends – Shamian Park on Shamian Island is a good place to look.

Clubs

Babyface 83 Chang Di Da Ma Lu (Yanjiang Lu). Offspring of the Beijing and Shanghai superclub, this far smaller version is expensive but, for the moment, the place to be seen.

Bonbon 358–364 Chang Di Da Ma Lu. Little brother of one of Shanghai's favourite clubs, this place is far more fun than the image-oriented *Babyface* just around the corner. Banging tunes, lively atmosphere and occasional big-name DJs.

Café Elle's Floor 2, *Huaxin Dasha*, northeast corner of Huanshi Lu and Shuiyin Lu. The best jazz and blues venue in the city, with regular international bands and nightly mixes of Latin and dance. It's not easy to find the right entrance, which is the small one on the eastern side of the building.

Cave Huanshi Dong Lu, west from the *Garden* hotel. Italian cantina and dance club, hidden down in a basement, with DJs or drummers playing to an ultraviolet-lit crowd.

Deep Anger Music Club 183 Yanjiang Lu. Vast, Gothic-style venue offering a range of entertainment from disco to live music and floor shows.

Guangzhou drinking and nightlife

Bars and clubs		
Baby Face	娃娃脸	*wá wá liǎn*
Café Elle's	木子吧	*mùzǐ bā*
Cave	墨西哥餐厅酒吧	*mòxīgē cāntīng jiǔbā*
City Bar	城市酒吧	*chéngshì jiǔbā*
Deep Anger Music Club	咆哮	*páoxiào*
Elephant and Castle	大象堡酒吧	*dàxiàngbǎo jiǔbā*
Gipsy Queen/King	万紫千红酒吧	*wànzǐ qiānhóng jiǔbā*
Gold Mango	金芒果酒吧	*jīnmángguǒ jiǔbā*
Hill Bar	小山吧	*xiǎoshān bā*
Peace	和平路西餐酒廊	*hépínglù xīcān jiǔláng*
Tang Club	塘俱乐部	*táng jùlèbù*
Yes	音乐工厂	*yīnyuè gōngchǎng*
Opera venue		
Guangming Theatre	光明剧院	*guāngmíng jùyuàn*

ET Space Yanjiang Lu. Next to *Deep Anger*, this place offers more of the same in a space-age setting.

Gipsy Queen/King 360 Huanshi Dong Lu, just west of *Cave*, this place is of a similar ilk, but has nightly shows around 10pm.

Peace Road Heping Lu. First in a string of bars along this street in the Overseas Chinese Village including *China Box*, *The Place*, *Wave* and *Chic*. Nightly live music on two floors – everything from Canto-pop to Chinese rock and more offbeat local bands.

Tang Club 1 Jianshe Liu Ma Lu. One of Guangzhou's more refined night spots with a resident band knocking out techno, reggae, pop and Latin hits.

Yes Liuhua Plaza, Dongfeng Xi Lu, south of Liuhua Park. Huge, popular, full-on house experience at maximum decibels.

Bars

City Bar City Plaza, Tianhe Lu, Tianhe. Relaxed place to spend an hour or two over a Heineken before your train goes from Guangzhou East. Hard to find, the building is east of the better-signed Teem Plaza.

Elephant and Castle 363 Huanshi Dong Lu. Dim corners and a cramped bar make this a favourite with barfly foreigners, though it has a good beer garden and typically gets loud and busy as the evening progresses. Variable happy hours. Opens late afternoon.

Gold Mango 361 Huanshi Dong Lu, next to *Elephant and Castle*. Bit of a pick-up joint, but cosy and laid-back atmosphere, welcoming staff and fine beer garden.

Hill Bar 367 Huanshi Dong Lu, across from the *Garden* hotel. Third choice in the trinity of adjacent expat bars, serving cheap beer (¥20 a pint) and bar meals, with occasional live music.

Soho Bar Yanjiang Lu, next to *Babyface*. Typical Chinese Western bar with Happy Hour deals. It's a good place to watch the crowds heading on their way into *Babyface*.

Shopping

Guangzhou's **shopping** ethos is very much towards the practical side of things. The **Changshou Lu** area in western Guangzhou is a mass of shopping plazas, designer clothes shops and boutiques, with **Beijing Lu** a similar, more central version; both have sections which are pedestrianized at weekends. To see where Guangzhou – and China – is heading, however, make your way over to the shockingly modern and upmarket **Friendship Store**, five floors of expensive imported designer gear and some good-value, domestic formal wear; it's on easterly Taojin Lu, just off Huanshi Dong Lu.

For souvenirs, the streets running east off the southern end of Renmin Lu might give you some ideas. Yide Lu has several huge wholesale warehouses stocking **dried foods** and **toys** – action figures from Chinese legends, rockets and all things that rattle and buzz. Other shops in the area deal in home decorations, such as colourful tiling or jigsawed decorative wooden dragons and phoenixes, and at New Year you can buy those red and gold good-luck posters put up outside businesses and homes. For out-and-out tourist souvenirs, head first to the *White Swan* hotel on Shamian Island. Their batiks and clothing, carved wooden screens and jade monstrosities are well worth a look, if only to make you realize what a good deal you're getting when you buy elsewhere – such as in the shops just outside on Shamian Si Jie. Wende Lu, running south from Zhongshan Lu, and various small shops in the streets between Dishifu Lu and Liuersan Lu, have varying selections of authenticated **antiques**, jade, lacquerwork, scrolls, chops and *cloisonné* artefacts, identical to what you'll find in the Yue Hua stores in Hong Kong, but at half the price. The **jade market** near Hualin Si (see p.576) is also worth a snoop.

For **Western groceries**, the Beatrice Supermarket, attached to the *Victory* on Shamian Si Jie, is a treasure trove of imported cheese, olives, pasta and biscuits – and there's also a coffee bar with hearty brews at ¥15 a cup.

Listings

Acupuncture Anyone interested in receiving cheap acupuncture preceded by massage should head for the clinic attached to the Zhongshan Medical College, Zhongshan Lu, where students practise. Alternatively, the more tourist-oriented Traditional Chinese Medicine Centre on Shamian offers foot massages, herbal baths, acupuncture and hot cupping from around ¥40.

Airlines China Southern Airlines, 181 Huanshi Dong Lu (ⓣ020/22272726), two doors east of the main train station; Japan Airlines *China Marriott* (ⓣ020/86696688); Malaysia Airlines (ⓣ020/83358868), Thai Airways (ⓣ020/38821818) and Vietnam Airlines (ⓣ020/83867093) all have offices at the *Garden*, Huanshi Dong Lu.

Banks and exchange Bank of China branches in the enormous office in the centre of the city on Dongfeng Zhong Lu and outside the *White Swan*, Shamian Island (both open for currency exchange Mon–Fri 9am–noon & 2–5pm). Counters at the *Liuhua*, *China Marriott*, *Landmark* and *Garden* hotels change currency for non-guests; the *White Swan* does not.

Bicycle hire If you want to try a different, if difficult, way of getting around Guangzhou, there's a tandem bike hire shop on Binjiang Zhong Lu, just east of the Haizhu Bridge (two-person bike ¥10/hr, three-person bike ¥15/hr).

Bookshops The Xinhua bookstore on Beijing Lu has an unexciting range of English literature and translated Chinese classics. The city's biggest bookstore, Guangzhou Books Centre, is at the southwest corner of Tianhe Square, Tianhe Lu – four storeys of technical manuals, computer texts and university tomes, but little in English. Otherwise, the main source of reading material is the comprehensive and expensive range of everything from potboilers to coffee-table works and contemporary Chinese fiction paperbacks – along with international newspapers and magazines – available at the *White Swan*.

Consulates Australia, Room 1509, *Guangdong International*, 339 Huanshi Dong Lu ⓣ020/83350909, ⓕ83350718; Canada, Room 801, *China* ⓣ020/86660569, ⓕ86672401; France, Room 803, *Guangdong International*, 339 Huanshi Dong Lu ⓣ020/83303405, ⓕ83303437; Germany, Floor 19, *Guangdong International*, 339 Huanshi Dong Lu ⓣ020/83306533, ⓕ83317033; Italy, Room 5207, CITIC Plaza, 233 Tianhe Bei Lu ⓣ020/38770556, ⓕ38770270; Japan, *Garden*, 368 Huanshi Dong Lu ⓣ020/83338972, ⓕ83878009; Malaysia, Floor 19, CITIC Plaza, 233 Tianhe Bei Lu ⓣ020/38770766, ⓕ38770769; Netherlands, Room 905, *Guangdong International*, 339 Huanshi Dong Lu ⓣ020/83302067, ⓕ83303601; Philippines, Room 709, *Guangdong International* 339 Huanshi Dong Lu ⓣ020/83311461, ⓕ83330573; Thailand, *Garden*, 368 Huanshi Dong Lu ⓣ020/83338989, ⓕ83889567; UK, Floor 2, *Guangdong International*, 339 Huanshi Dong Lu ⓣ020/83351354, ⓕ83327509; US, Shamian Nan Jie, Shamian Island ⓣ020/81218000 ⓕ81219001; Vietnam, Room 27, *Hua Xia*, Haizhu Square ⓣ020/83305910 ⓕ83305915. Note that consulates' visa sections are usually only open from around 9–11.30am, and getting served isn't always easy.

Hospitals Call ⓣ120 for emergency services. There's an English-speaking team at SOS, Guangdong Provincial Hospital of Traditional Chinese Medicine, 261 Datong Lu, Er Sha Island, Guangzhou (Mon–Fri 9am–6pm; ⓣ020/87351051). Other options include Guangdong Provincial People's Hospital, 106 Zhongshan Er Lu (ⓣ020/83827812) and the Red Cross Hospital, 396 Tongfu Zhong Lu (ⓣ020/84412233). There are English-speaking dentists at Sunshine Dental Clinic, 2 Tianhe Bei Lu (24hr English hotline; ⓣ020/33874278). For anything serious, though, you're better off heading to Hong Kong.

Internet access Places come and go very quickly, but can be found for as little as ¥2 an hour. The unnamed Internet café one block south of Chen Jia Ci metro is such a place. Many hotels offer Internet access, but this tends to be very expensive. *Starbucks* in the city also offer free Wi-Fi access for customers bringing their laptops. On Shamian Island, Michael's, at the south end of Shamian Er Jie, is principally a shop, but offers Internet access for ¥10 an hour (daily 9am–9pm); if you fancy a caffeine kick with your browsing, *Blenz Coffee* on Shamian Dajie provides free Internet use for its customers.

Interpreters The major hotels can organize interpreters for upwards of ¥600 per day – you're also expected to cover all additional incidental costs such as meals and transport.

Left luggage Offices at the train (24hr) and bus station (daily 8am–6pm).

Mail and telephones There are major post offices with IDD telephones, parcel post and poste restante, on the western side of the square outside

Guangzhou train station (daily 8am–8pm), and across from the Cultural Park entrance on Liuersan Lu (daily 8am–6pm). Shamian Island's post counter is open Mon–Sat 9am–5pm for stamps, envelopes and deliveries. All hotels have postal services and international call facilities.

Police For all police matters, such as reporting theft, head to the PSB.

PSB On the corner of Jiefang Lu and Dade Lu (Mon–Fri 8–11.30am & 2.20–5pm; ⓣ020/83115721).

Travel agents Try the following if hotels can't help with tours and transport reservations: CITS Travel, 618 Jie Fang Bei Lu, just north of Gongyuan Qian metro station (ⓣ020/22013539 or 22013546, ⓦwww.citsgd.com.cn), which can book tours, hotels and tickets within China, or CTS, next to the *Landmark* (ⓣ020/83336888, ⓦwww.chinatravelone.com).

The Pearl River Delta

The **Pearl River Delta** initially seems to be entirely a product of the modern age, dominated by industrial complexes and the glossy, high-profile cities of **Shenzhen**, east on the crossing to Hong Kong, and westerly **Zhuhai**, on the Macau border. Back in the 1980s these were marvels of Deng Xiaoping's reforms, rigidly contained **Special Economic Zones** of officially sanctioned free-market activities, which were anathema to Communist ideologies. Their incredible success inspired an invasion of the delta by foreign and domestic companies, obscuring an economic history dating back to the time of Song engineers who constructed irrigation canals through the delta's **five counties** – Nanhai, Panyu, Shunde, Dongguan and Zhongshan. From the Ming dynasty, local crafts and surplus food were exported across Guangdong, artisans flourished and funded elaborate guild temples, while gentlemen of leisure built gardens in which to wander and write poetry.

Today, it's easy to hop on high-speed transport and cut through the delta in a couple of hours, seeing little more than the unattractive urban mantle that surrounds the highways. But spend a little longer on your journey or dip into the region on short trips from Guangzhou, and there's a good deal to discover about China here, especially in the way that everything looks hastily built and temporary – development is clearly happening too fast for any unified planning. The past survives too. Don't miss **Foshan**'s splendid **Ancestral Temple**, or **Lianhua Shan**, a landscaped ancient quarry; historians might also wish to visit **Humen**, where the destruction of British opium in 1839 ignited the first Opium War, and **Cuiheng**, home village of China's revered revolutionary elder statesman, **Sun Yatsen**.

The delta has China's highest density of **expressways**, including the 175-kilometre **Guangshen Expressway**, which runs southeast from Guangzhou to Shenzhen. The delta's western side is covered by a mesh of roads which you can follow more or less directly south between sights to Zhuhai, 155km from Guangzhou. Buses from Guangzhou's Liuhua and Provincial bus stations cover all destinations in the locality. There's also the **Guangzhou–Shenzhen train**, though services don't tend to stop along the way, and a **metro link** to Foshan (from Kengkou metro station).

It's worth noting that both Shenzhen and Zhuhai SEZs are surrounded by electric fences and inspection posts to deter smugglers – one of the few times you're likely to see armed police in China – and you'll need to show **passports** to get through, whether you're coming in by bus or, to Shenzhen, by train. Don't confuse these checks with actual border formalities; you'll still have to fill out forms and get your passport inspected again to cross into Macau or Hong Kong from the SEZs.

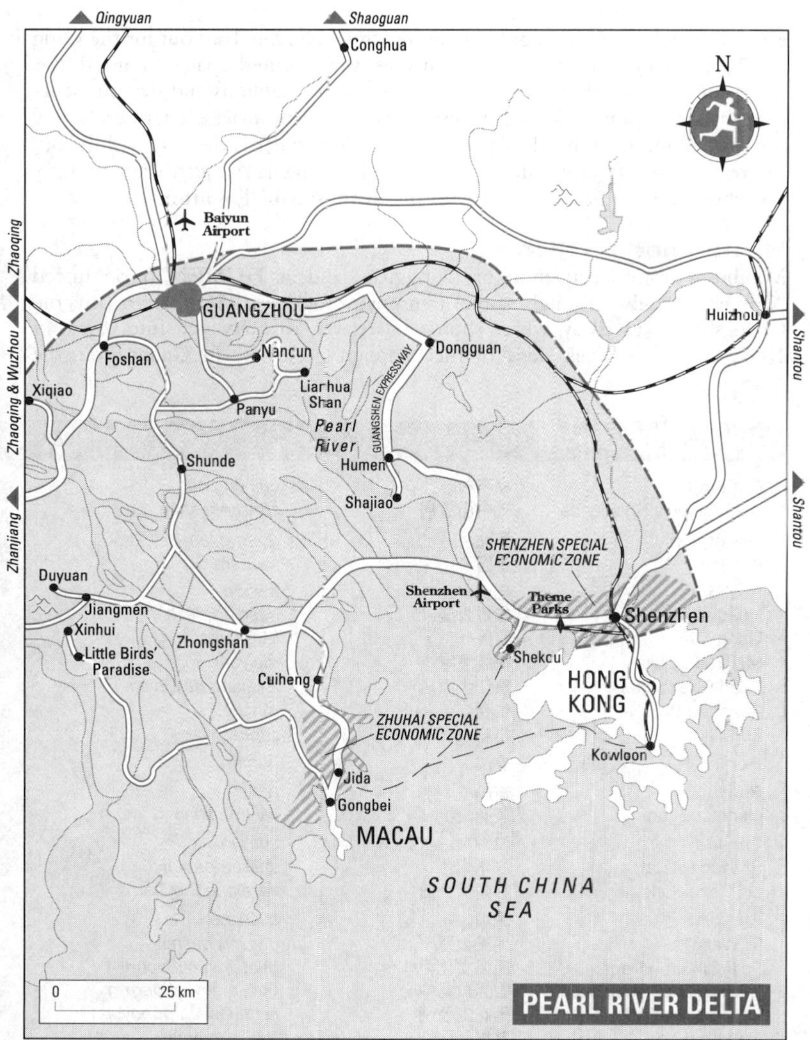

Southeast to Shenzhen

An hour southeast of Guangzhou down the expressway, **DONGGUAN** is the administrative seat of the delta's most productive county, its factories churning out textiles, electronic components and pirated VCDs and computer software – an industry which, controlled as it is by the military, Beijing has had no success in suppressing, despite periodic US threats of trade sanctions.

If you're heading to Dongguan's port, **Humen**, famous for its role in the nineteenth-century **Opium Wars**, you may need to stop in Dongguan to change buses, in which case you could take the time to have a look at **Keyuan** (daily 8am–4pm; ¥8), once one of Guangdong's "Four Famous Gardens". Walk north from the **bus station** up Wantai Dadao for 250 metres, turn west along

Keyuan Nan Lu, and it's about 1km away across the river. Laid out for the Qing minister, Zhang Jingxiu, Keyuan puts its very limited space to good use, cramming an unlikely number of passages, rooms, pavilions and devious staircases inside its walls, all built in distinctive, pale blue bricks. There are a few flowerbeds and trees, but Keyuan's most striking aspect is the way it shuts out the rest of the city at ground level – though Dongguan's motorways are only too obvious from the upper storey of the main **Yaoshi Pavilion**.

Humen and Shajiao

Minibuses from Guangzhou or Dongguan land at **HUMEN** (pronounced "Fumen" locally), though some transport drops you 5km short on the Guangshen Expressway, where shuttle buses wait to carry you into town. In 1839, after a six-week siege of the "Foreign Factories" in Guangzhou, the

The Pearl River Delta

Cuiheng	翠亨村	*cùihēng cūn*
Sun Yatsen's Residence	孙中山故居	*sūnzhōngshān gùjù*
Dongguan	东莞	*dōng guǎn*
Keyuan	可园	*kěyuán*
Foshan	佛山	*fóshān*
Huaqiao Dasha	华侨大厦	*huáqiáo dàshà*
Liang Yuan	梁园	*liángyuán*
Mei Yuan Jiujia	梅园酒家	*méiyuán jiǔjiā*
Pearl River Hotel	珠江大酒店	*zhūjiāng dàjiǔdiàn*
Renshou Si	仁受寺	*rénshòu sì*
Zu Miao	祖庙	*zǔmiào*
Humen	虎门	*hǔmén*
Panyu	番禺	*pānyú*
Lianhua Shan	莲花山	*liánhuā shān*
Shajiao	沙角	*shājiǎo*
Shajiao Paotai	沙角炮台	*shājiǎo pàotái*
Lin Zexu Park	林则徐公园	*línzéxú gōngyuán*
Shenzhen	深圳	*shēnzhèn*
Di Wang	地王大厦	*dìwáng dàshà*
Folk Culture Village	民俗文化村	*mínsú wénhuàcūn*
International Trade Centre	国际贸易中心	*guójìmàoyì zhōngxīn*
Linhuashan Park	莲花山公园	*liánhuāshān gōngyuán*
Lizhi Park	荔枝公园	*lìzhī gōngyuán*
Luo Hu Border Crossing	罗湖	*luóhú*
Minsk World	明思克航空世界	*míngsīkè hángkōng shìjiè*
Shekou	蛇口	*shékǒu*
Shenzhen Grand Theatre	深圳大剧院	*shēnzhèn dàjùyuàn*
Shenzhen Museum	深圳博物馆	*shēnzhèn bówùguǎn*
Splendid China	锦绣中华	*jǐnxiù zhōnghuá*
Window on the World	世界之窗	*shìjiè zhīchuāng*
Downtown metro stops		
Da Ju Yuan	大剧院	*dàjùyuàn*
Guo Mao	国贸	*guómào*
Ke Xue Guan	科学馆	*kēxuéguǎn*
Lao Jie	老街	*lǎojiē*
Luo Hu	罗湖	*luóhú*

British handed over 1200 tons of **opium** to **Lin Zexu**, the Qing official in charge of stopping the opium trade. Lin brought it to Humen, mixed it with quicklime, and dumped it in two 45-metre pits on the beach 4km south of Humen's centre at **Shajiao**; after three weeks, the remains were flushed out to sea. Incensed at this destruction of their opium, the British massacred the Chinese garrisons at Humen and on nearby **Weiyun Island**, and attacked Guangzhou. Lin got the blame and was exiled to the frontier province of Xinjiang, only to be replaced by the ineffectual Yi Shan, a nephew of the emperor, later a signatory to the humiliating Guangzhou Treaty.

These events are recounted in Chinese documents and heroic sculptures at the **Lin Zexu Park Museum** on Jiefang Lu (daily 9am–5pm; ¥20), a twenty-minute walk between the skyscrapers northwest of Humen's bus station. It's more rewarding, however, to catch a minibus to Shajiao, where the opium pits

Shijiezhichuang	世界之窗	*shìjiè zhīchuāng*
Accommodation and eating		
Airlines	航空大酒店	*hángkōng dàjiǔdiàn*
Café de Coral	香港大家乐	*xiānggǎng dàjiālè*
Days Inn	戴斯酒店	*dàisī jiǔdiàn*
Dengpin Vegetarian	登品素食府	*dēngpǐn sùshífǔ*
GS Railway	广深铁路大酒店	*guǎngshēn tiělù dàjiǔdiàn*
Guang Dong	粤海酒店	*yuèhǎi jiǔdiàn*
Landmark	深圳富苑酒店	*shēnzhèn fùyuán jiǔdiàn*
Laurel	丹桂轩酒楼	*dānguìxuān jiǔlóu*
Little Sheep Hotpot	小肥洋火锅	*xiǎoféiyáng huǒguō*
Loft Youth Hostel	侨城旅友国际青年旅舍	*qiáochéng lǚyǒu guójì qīnnián lǚshè*
Petrel	海燕大酒店	*hǎiyàn dàjiǔdiàn*
Shunde	顺德	*shùndé*
Feng Cheng Jiudian	凤城酒店	*fèngchéng jiǔdiàn*
Feng Ling Park	凤岭公园	*fēnglǐng gōngyuán*
Marriott Courtyard	顺德新世界万怡酒店	*shùndé xīnshìjiè wànyí jiǔdiàn*
Qinghui Gardens	清晖园	*qīnghuī yuán*
Xishan Gumiao	西山古庙	*xīshān gǔmiào*
Xiqiao	西樵	*xīqiáo*
Zhongshan	中山	*zhōngshān*
Zhuhai	珠海	*zhūhǎi*
Changan Jiudian	昌安酒店	*chāngān jiǔdiàn*
Gongbei	拱北	*gǒngběi*
Huasha Shijie	华夏食街	*huáxià shíjiē*
Jida	吉大	*jídà*
Min'an Jiudian	民安酒店	*mín'ān jiǔdiàn*
Shen Jing Canteen	深井烧鹅拱北分店	*shēnjǐng shāo'é gǒngběi fēndiàn*
Taida Jiudian	泰达酒店	*tàidá jiǔdiàn*
Xiangzhou	香州珠海度假村	*xiāngzhōu zhūhǎi dùjiàcūn*
You Yi Jiudian	友谊酒店	*yǒuyí jiǔdiàn*
Yuehai Jiudian	粤海酒店	*yuèhǎi jiǔdiàn*

remain, along with a fortress, **Shajio Paotai** (daily 8am–5.30pm; ¥15). The whole place is thick with poinsettias, banyans and butterflies, all making for a nice couple of hours on the beach.

Shenzhen

Incredibly, in 1979 **SHENZHEN** was a simple rural hamlet and train station called **Bao'an**, the first office foundations yet to be dug in its alluvial plains on the Hong Kong border. Within six years, delegations from all over China were pouring in to learn how to remodel their own businesses, cities and provinces on Shenzhen's incentives-based economy. By 1990 the city had four harbours and its manufacturing industries alone were turning over US$2 billion a year, necessitating the construction of a nuclear power station to deal with local energy needs; today the city has more than a dozen buildings over 200 metres tall and produces almost all the world's Ipods and Apple computers.

Shenzhen may not have been the cause of capitalism in the People's Republic, but it has been a glorious piece of propaganda for those who promoted its

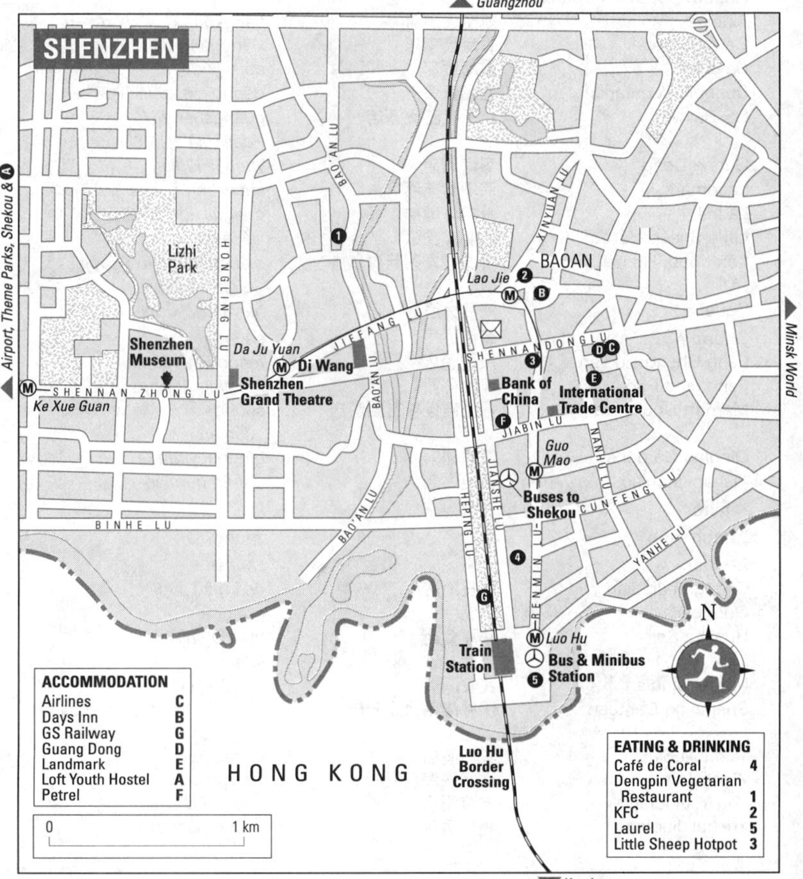

virtues. It's no coincidence that, on his landmark 1992 "**Southern Tour**", Deng Xiaoping chose Shenzhen as the place to make his memorable statement: "Poverty is not Socialism: to get rich is glorious", voicing the Party's shift from Communist dogma to a pragmatic, results-driven approach to economics – and opening the gate for the start of China's financial boom.

Having said all this, with similar skylines rearing up all over China, Shenzhen is no longer quite as amazing as it once was; the border area around the station in particular is a bit grubby, not to mention overrun with pushy hotel touts, beggars and pickpockets. The city is a useful transport hub, however – onward flights to the rest of the country are significantly cheaper from here than from Hong Kong's International airport, which is just an hour away by ferry – and is popular with Hong Kongers, many of whom make the short journey north to take advantage of their neighbours' cheap shopping, restaurants and spa treatments.

Arrival and information

A five-kilometre-wide semicircle immediately north of the Hong Kong border, central Shenzhen is evenly bisected by the **rail line** that descends straight down Jianshe Lu to the Luo Hu border crossing. The border area itself is defined by the massive Luo Hu **bus station** to the east and **train station** to the west.

Shuttle buses (30–40min; ¥20) operate between the **international airport**, 20km west of town, and the city centre; a taxi costs ¥120–150. The **port** lies 15km west of the centre, at **Shekou,** from where you can catch bus #204 into town, or take a taxi for around ¥75.

Taxis and minibuses roam everywhere, and the city has an enviably efficient bus service, as well as a **metro system**; line #1 runs from Luo Hu in the

Moving on from Shenzhen

The **Hong Kong border** is open daily, from 6.30am to midnight. There's a lack of directional signs in the vicinity; you need to get on to the overpass from upstairs at the train station and then head south past souvenir stalls, roasted meat vendors and pet shops. Border formalities on both sides are streamlined, and it shouldn't take more than an hour to find yourself on the other side, purchasing a ticket for the **KCR** (Kowloon–Canton Railway) train into Hong Kong.

Trains to Guangzhou East can take as little as an hour on the new high-speed track; they run between 6.25am and 10.30pm and tickets cost ¥70. There is a designated Guangzhou **ticket office**, at street level, and, next door, another sells tickets on direct services to dozens of destinations between Shenzhen and Beijing.

Buses leave regularly from the Luo Hu bus station for the delta, Guangzhou, the rest of Guangdong and many places in central China. **If you are catching a ferry, take** bus #204 from Jianshe Lu to the port at Shekou, where there are departures for Macau (4 daily; 8.15am–6.30pm; 90min; ¥125), Zhuhai (every 30min; 7.30am–8.30pm; 1hr; ¥80) Hong Kong (7 daily; 7.45am–9.30pm; 1hr; ¥110), Kowloon (6 daily; 8.30am–5.30pm; 1hr; ¥110) and Hong Kong Airport (hourly; 30min; ¥240).

For **flights** into the rest of China, contact CAAC on Shennan Zhong Lu or go through one of the many online booking agencies such as ⓦwww.elong.net (ⓣ400/8101119) or ⓦwww.ctrip com (ⓣ800/8206666) who should be able to deliver tickets to wherever you are in return for cash. To get to the airport you can either catch the metro to Shijiezhichuang and then take public bus #327, or get off the metro at Kexue Guan and catch the dedicated airport shuttle from outside the *Hualian* hotel (30–40min; ¥20). A taxi from the centre to the airport will cost ¥120–150.

southeast to Window on the World at Shijiezhichuang in the west of the city. The considerably shorter line #4 runs south from Shaoniangong to Huangang on the border with Lok Mau in Hong Kong. Fares are ¥2–5 and trains operate from 6.30am to 11pm.

A host of English-language information about Shenzhen is available **online**. Useful tourism/news sites and blogs include Ⓦwww.visitshenzhen.com, Ⓦwww.theszweb.com, Ⓦwww.sznews.com and Ⓦwww.shenzhenwindow.net.

There are **banks** at the border crossing, the airport, ferry terminal and some hotels, and a suitably oversized Bank of China on Jianshe Lu (Mon–Fri 9am–5pm).

Accommodation

A magnet for business travellers, Shenzhen has a glut of central two- and three-star **hotels**, almost all of which will offer around a 50-percent reduction from the advertised rates of ¥250–500. Many of them have good restaurants, too, along with karaoke bars, interpreters, conference facilities, postal services and the like. A host of cheap (¥100–180) if uninspiring options are to be found running north from the train station along Heping Lu, while more familiar, not to mention more expensive, names such as *Shangri-la*, *Novotel*, *Sheraton*, *Holiday Inn* and *Best Western* also all have a presence.

Airlines Shennan Zhong Lu Ⓣ0755/82237999, Ⓕ82237866. Good, comfortable rooms, a seafood restaurant and an expensive coffee shop. ❺

Days Inn 57 Yongxin Jie, Jiefang Lu Ⓣ0755/82203333, Ⓕ82259666, Ⓦwww.daysinn.cn. Close to the old town area, this chain hotel is a little shabby on the outside but perfectly presentable in. Handy for town-centre shopping and far enough from the train station to escape the worst of the city's less-desirable street life. ❻

GS Railway Heping Lu Ⓣ0755/68857218, Ⓦwww.25591911.com. A little way north of the railway underpass, this is the nearest to the train station of a string of budget hotels along this street. Cheap and handy for the station, what it makes up for in practicality it loses in cleanliness and comfort, but the staff are friendly. ❹

Guang Dong Shennan Zhong Lu Ⓣ0755/82228339, Ⓦwww.gdhhotels.com. A smart business hotel with three restaurants, including a Japanese option. ❼

Landmark Nanhu Lu, corner of Shennan Zhong Lu Ⓣ0755/82172288, Ⓕ82290473. One of Shenzhen's most upmarket venues, boasting a beautifully furnished neo-colonial interior and three restaurants, one of which is described as a "Banquet Hall". ❾

Loft Youth Hostel 3 Enping Lu Ⓣ0755/26949443/26601293, Ⓔloftyha@yahoo.com.cn. Newly refurbished hostel backing onto the "Loft," a former factory now housing art galleries, cafés, bars and trendy offices. Clean and modern with dorms, doubles, twins and triples, some en suite. Take Metro line #1 to Qiaocheng-dong and leave by exit A. Keep walking straight ahead for a couple of minutes, turn right at the petrol station and the hostel is straight ahead, just beyond the Loft complex. A bit out of the centre, but far more comfortable than options around the train station. Dorm beds ¥60, ❸

Petrel Jiabin Lu Ⓣ0755/82232828, Ⓕ82221398. Smart, friendly option with views of Shenzen's skyline. ❺

The City

For a bird's-eye view of what has become of this one-time fishing village take the lift to the observation platform on the 68th floor of the **Di Wang building** at the junction of Shennan Lu and Bao'an Nan Lu (¥60). A closer glimpse of the city's extremes of wealth and poverty can be had by strolling along Renmin Lu, which runs northeast from the train station and **Luo Hu border crossing** (you might see the Cantonese rendering, Lo Wu, on signs). The **International Trade Centre** is a three-storey block on the corner of Jiabin Lu, full of shoppers browsing upmarket jewellery and perfume. Push on over Jiefang Lu and you're in the tangle of narrow lanes which formed the **old town** of Bao'an;

now a pedestrianized warren of shops selling cheap clothes, shoes, gadgets and the ubiquitous knock-off DVDs. There is a historic monument of sorts here in a squat, blue-roofed diner on Qingyuan Lu – China's first *McDonald's* restaurant, since joined by a *KFC*, *Starbucks* and *Pizza Hut* a little further along the Lao Jie shopping street.

For a shot of greenery, try getting lost on the meandering paths of **Lianhuashan Park** north of the Shaoniangong northern terminus of metro line #4. After enjoying the day-glo marvels flying at Kite Square, head up the hill for a great view of the city where a giant bronze Deng Xiaoping gazes happily across the skyline – a sight for which he is largely responsible – towards Hong Kong.

If that sounds like too much effort, **Lizhi Park** by Da Ju Yuan metro station on Shennan Zhong Lu is more central and a surprisingly refreshing open space, with a nice lake. Across Hongling Lu on Shennan Zhong Lu, the **Shenzhen Museum** (Tues–Sun 9am–5pm; free) holds thousands of paintings and works of calligraphy – fascinating, even without English explanations.

For Shenzhen's biggest guilty pleasure, hop on metro line #1 to its terminus at Shijiezhichuang, or catch bus #204 from Jianshe Lu for the thirty-minute ride west to the city's three biggest **theme parks**, situated next to each other on the Guangshen Expressway – look for a miniaturized Golden Gate Bridge spanning the road. Amid limitless souvenir stalls, **Window on the World** (daily 9am–10pm; ¥120) is a collection of scale models of famous monuments such as the Eiffel Tower and Mount Rushmore, while **Splendid China** (daily 8am–5pm; ¥120) offers the same for China's sights. The latter's ticket also includes the **Folk Culture Village**, an enjoyably touristy introduction to the nation's ethnic groups – there are yurts, pavilions, huts, archways, rock paintings and mechanical goats, with colourful troupes performing different national dances every thirty minutes (¥35). A short walk north gets you to **Happy Valley** (daily 9am–10pm; ¥150), Shenzhen's answer to Disneyland. It's best avoided at weekends and national holidays when it can take several hours to queue for a single ride.

If you're after something completely different, jump aboard bus #202 or #205 from the bus depot by the border to **Minsk World** (¥110), a whole Russian aircraft carrier – complete with aircraft – moored up at the docks for your entertainment; allow at least half a day for a full exploration.

Eating, drinking and nightlife

The cheapest places to **eat** are in the streets immediately north of Jiefang Lu, where Chinese canteens can fill you up with good dumplings, soups and stir-fries. There are also dozens of smarter options all through the centre.

For up-to-date info on Shenzhen's (predominantly expat and overseas Chinese) **nightlife**, check out Ⓦwww.shenzhenparty.com. The ultramodern **Grand Theatre** (Ⓦwww.szdjy.com.cn) on Shennan Zhong Lu stages everything from traditional Chinese opera to Disney musicals, while the Shekou port area, popular with expats, is the current centre of Shenzhen's **bar** and **club** scene. You can get to the port on the #204 bus from Jianshe Lu – it's a little further out than the theme parks.

Restaurants

Café de Coral Jianshe Lu. This Macanese chain provides quality Chinese food with a Western influence in a handy order-by-pictures format. A main meal with drink should set you back around ¥40. It can be standing room only at lunchtime.

Dengpin Vegetarian Third floor of the Jun Ting Ming Yuan, north of Bao'an Nan Lu's junction with Hongbao Lu. Choose the all-you-can-eat vegetarian buffet for ¥50 or order from the menu for a little more. The buffet's a great way to try a bit of everything – "steak", "fish" and "duck" are all in evidence, as are plenty of greens, mushrooms, noodles and rice.

Laurel Fifth floor of Louhu Commercial City in Railway Station Square. Some of the best Cantonese food in town – you may recognize dishes such as sweet-and-sour prawns, but snake doesn't make it onto the English menu. Expect ¥50–100 per person.

Little Sheep Hotpot Renmin Lu at the junction with Shennan Zhong Lu. Seat yourself at a bubbling cauldron of the nationwide chain's signature spicy broth and order meat and vegetables to stew in it – best enjoyed by groups of three or more. Around ¥60 per person.

The western delta: Foshan

Twenty-five kilometres southwest of Guangzhou, and today a satellite suburb of the city, **FOSHAN** historically was very much a town in its own right, with a history dating back to the seventh century. Along with the nearby village of **Shiwan**, Foshan became famous for its ceramics, silk, metalwork and woodcarving – a reputation it still enjoys – and the splendour of its **temples**, two of which survive on **Zumiao Lu**, a kilometre-long street shaded by office buildings and set in the heart of what was once the old town centre. At the southern end, **Zu Miao** (Ancestral Temple; daily 8.30am–7.30pm; ¥20) is a masterpiece of southern architecture, founded in 1080 as a metallurgist's guild temple. Ahead and to the left of the entrance is an elevated garden fronted by some locally made Opium War **cannons** – sadly for the Chinese, poor casting techniques and a lack of rifling made these inaccurate and liable to explode. Nearby, magnificent glazed **roof tiles** of frolicking lions and characters from local tales were made in Shiwan for temple restorations in the 1830s. The temple's **main hall** is on the left past here, its interior crowded with minutely carved wooden screens, oversized guardian gods leaning threateningly out from the walls, and a three-tonne **statue of Beidi**, God of the North, who in local lore controlled low-lying Guangdong's flood-prone waters – hence this shrine to snare his goodwill.

Opposite the hall is the elaborate masonry of the **Lingying archway**, similar to those at Shexian in Anhui province (see p.465). Foshan is considered the birthplace of Cantonese opera, and beyond the archway you'll find the highly decorative **Wanfu stage**, built in 1685 for autumnal performances given to thank the Divine Emperor for his bountiful harvests. Foshan is also renowned as a **martial-arts centre**, and there are exhibitions dedicated to past masters Yip Man, Bruce Lee's instructor, and, in the north of the complex, another to Huang Fei Hong, a doctor and fighter who has been the subject of many a movie.

A few blocks north, **Renshou Si** (Benevolent Longevity Temple; daily 8am–5pm; free) is a former Ming monastery whose southern wing, graced by a short seven-storey pagoda, is still consecrated. The rest has been cleaned out and turned into the **Foshan Folk Arts Research Institute** (daily 9am–5pm; free), a good place to look for souvenirs including excellent **papercuts** with definite Cultural Revolution leanings, showing the modernizing of rural economies. At the time of the Spring Festival, side halls are also full of celebratory lions, fish and phoenixes constructed from wire and coloured crepe paper.

About 1km due north of here on Songfeng Lu – continue up Zumiao Lu to its end, turn right and then first left – **Liang Yuan** (¥10) is another of the delta's historic **gardens**, built between 1796 and 1850 by a family of famous poets and artists of the period. There are artfully arranged ponds, trees and rocks, and the tastefully furnished residential buildings are worth a look, but the real gem here is the **Risheng Study**, a perfectly proportioned retreat looking out over a tiny, exquisitely designed pond, fringed with willows.

Practicalities

Fenjiang Bei Lu forms the western boundary of the old town, running south for about 2km from the **train station**, over a canal, past the **long-distance bus station** and through to where the skyscrapers, which constitute Foshan's business centre, cluster around a broad roundabout. **Buses** from Guangzhou's Liuhua bus station (¥15; 1hr) deposit you at **Zumiao station**, just east of the roundabout on Chengmentou Lu; walk 50m east and you're at the bottom end of Zumiao Lu. When Foshan's delayed Guangzhou metro link will finally come into operation is unclear, but the smart money says, as with all other construction projects in the country, it will be open in time for the 2008 Olympics. To reach Zumiao Lu from the other stations, catch bus #1, #6, or #11, or walk down Fenjiang Bei Lu for about 700m, then east for a few minutes along tree-lined Qinren Lu to the intersection with Zumiao Lu. Foshan's main **Bank of China** (Mon–Fri 8.30am–5pm, Sat 9am–4pm) is between the two temples, as is a post office, whilst a branch of CTS can be found between the two hotels reviewed below.

Foshan is comfortably visited as a day-trip from Guangzhou; however, if you'd prefer to **stay**, try the former *Huaqiao Dasha*, now the *Carrianna* (ⓣ0757/82223828, ⓦwww.fshq-hotel.com; ⑥), across and a little north from Renshou Si at 14 Zumiao Lu, or the *Pearl River Hotel (Zhujiang Da Jiudian)* a few buildings north (ⓣ0757/82963638, ⓕ82292263; ④). Both have **restaurants** and bars, and there are Western-style fast-food outlets scattered through the centre; for something more authentic you could try the moderately priced *Mei Yuan Jiujia* just south of Zu Miao, which specializes in Cantonese hotpots.

Around Panyu: Lian Hua Shan

A couple of attractive sights surround the town of **PANYU**, about 50km east of Foshan. It's roughly the same distance by road from Guangzhou, with buses departing from the Liuhua station (¥10; 80min), and there are also direct **ferries** from Hong Kong.

Overlooking the Pearl River 15km east of Panyu, **Lian Hua Shan** (daily 8am–4pm; ¥35) is an odd phenomenon, a mountain quarried as long ago as the Han dynasty for its red stone, used in the tomb of the Nanyue king, Zhao Mo. After mining it in such a way as to leave a suspiciously deliberate arrangement of crags, pillars and caves, Ming officials planted the whole thing with trees and turned it into a pleasure garden laid with lotus pools, stone paths and pavilions. A fifty-metre-high pagoda was built in 1612, and the Qing emperor Kangxi added a fortress to defend the river. Still a popular excursion from Guangzhou, it's an interesting spot to while away a few hours, though frequently crowded.

Shunde

Yet another antique garden, **Qinghui Gardens** (daily 8am–5.30pm; ¥15), is one reason to pause in the county town of **SHUNDE**, also known as **Daliang Zhen**, 50km south of Guangzhou on the most direct route to Zhuhai (¥30 from Guangzhou's Liuhua bus station). In the middle of town on Qinghui Lu, the well-kept gardens contain a series of square fish ponds surrounded by osmanthus, mulberry bushes and bamboo. The other highlight here is the *Qinghui Yuan* **restaurant** (daily 7–9am, 11am–2pm & 5–7pm), in the grounds of the gardens, which is revered for serving the very best in classic Cantonese cuisine. It is expensive – count on at least ¥75 a person – but the dishes are superb, with mild, fresh flavours which have to be taken slowly to be properly appreciated; their braised sea carp with garlic and ginger melts in the mouth. After eating, you can walk off your meal in the restored colonial-style streets behind the gardens off Hua Lu, where the old town centre forms a miniature version of Guangzhou's back lanes, with flagstones, markets and a fully restored street of colonial-era architecture. Alternatively, it's about 1km north across a huge open square and Wenxiu Lu to wooded and hilly **Feng Ling Park**, with the old **Xishan Gumiao** temple on the east side. Shunde is also home to the world's first **Bruce Lee Museum**, situated in a teahouse that Bruce supposedly visited during his one and only visit to the town when he was five years old – Bruce's ancestral home was in nearby Shang village, Jun'an. Holding memorabilia from China, Hong Kong and the US, it's not really much of a museum – far more exciting is the rumoured prospect of a multi-million-dollar Bruce Lee theme park in the town.

Practicalities

Shunde's new **long-distance bus station** is about 3km south of the centre on the highway; catch bus #9 from here to Qinghui Lu and the gardens. For a **place to stay**, there's the plush *Marriott Courtyard* opposite the gardens on Qinghui Lu (Ⓣ0757/22218333, Ⓦwww.courtyard.com; ❽); a cheaper option, the *Feng Cheng Jiudian* (Ⓣ0757/22331688; ❸), lies between the river and the old town – bus #9 from the station runs here. **Moving on**, if you can't find necessary long-distance transport at the bus station, head to Guangzhou or Zhongshan and pick up services there.

Zhongshan and Cuiheng

Almost every town in China has a park or road named **Zhongshan**, a tribute to China's first Republican president, the remarkable **Dr Sun Yatsen**. Christened with the Cantonese name "Yatsen" (Yixian in Mandarin), while in exile in Japan he acquired the name Nakayama ("middle mountain"), the Chinese characters for which are pronounced "Zhongshan". Unless you need to change buses, there's no need to visit Zhongshan itself, a characterless county town 100km from Guangzhou, but 30km east of here on the coastal road to Zhuhai is the good doctor's home village of **CUIHENG**, now the site of a **memorial garden** (daily 8am–5pm; ¥20) celebrating his life and achievements. Transport from Zhongshan town and from Zhuhai (35km south) sets you down right outside, where there are also a few cheap **places to eat** and to buy ice creams;

Sun Yatsen

Born in 1866, **Sun Yatsen** grew up during a period when China laboured under the humiliation of colonial occupation, a situation justly blamed on the increasingly feeble Qing court. Having spent three years in Hawaii during the 1880s, Sun studied medicine in Guangzhou and Hong Kong, where he became inspired by that other famous Guangdong revolutionary, Hong Xiuquan (see p.419), and began to involve himself in covert anti-Qing activities. Back in Hawaii in 1894, he abandoned his previous notions of reforming the imperial system and founded the **Revive China Society** to "Expel the Manchus, restore China to the people and create a federal government". The following year he incited an uprising in Guangzhou under **Lu Haodong**, notable for being the first time that the green Nationalist flag, painted with a white, twelve-pointed sun (which still appears on the Taiwanese flag), was flown. But the uprising was quashed, Lu Haodong was captured and executed, and Sun fled overseas.

Orbiting between Hong Kong, Japan, Europe and the US, Sun spent the next fifteen years raising money to fund revolts in southern China, and in 1907 his new when you need to move on, you'll find that public transport heads in both directions along the highway until at least 6pm.

Along with a banyan tree supposedly brought back from Hawaii and planted by Sun, the grounds incorporate a comprehensive museum of photographs, relics (including the original Nationalist flag) and biographical accounts in English emphasizing the successful aspects of Sun Yatsen's career. There's also the solid, Portuguese-style family home where he lived between 1892 and 1895, "studying, treating patients and discussing national affairs with his friends". Out the back of Sun's home are some rather more typical period buildings belonging to the peasant and landlord classes, restored and furnished with wooden tables and authentic silk tapestries.

Zhuhai

ZHUHAI is an umbrella name for the Special Economic Zone encompassing three separate townships immediately north of **Macau** (Aomen): **Gongbei** on the border itself, and **Jida** and **Xiangzhou**, the port and residential districts 5–10km farther up along the coast. Full of new offices, immensely wide roads and tasty economic incentives, Zhuhai has yet to blossom in the way that Shenzhen has – probably because Zhuhai's neighbour is Macau, not Hong Kong. Sights are also few; the coastline hereabouts is pretty enough on a warm day, but there are few true beaches (Lingjiaozui, in Jida, is the best bet for swimming) and most people have come for the border crossing, or to take advantage of what amounts to a **duty-free enclave** aimed at Macanese day-trippers in Gongbei's backstreets. **Lianhua Lu** is Gongbei's liveliest street, a kilometre of hotels, restaurants, and shops selling cheap clothes, household goods and trinkets you never realized you needed. South across a paved square, the **crossing into Macau** is itself concealed inside a huge shopping plaza – labelled "Gongbei Port" in gold on the red roof – where you can buy more of the same.

Practicalities

If you've just **walked across the border** – which is open 7am to midnight – into Zhuhai from Macau, you exit the customs building at Gongbei with Lianhua Lu and the two adjacent **bus stations** 250m diagonally across to the right. Buses go from both stations to the delta, Guangzhou, and beyond, with

Alliance Society announced its famous **Three Principles of the People** – Nationalism, Democracy and Livelihood. He was in Colorado when the Manchus finally fell in October 1911; on returning to China he was made provisional president of the Republic of China on January 1, 1912, but was forced to resign in February in favour of the powerful warlord, **Yuan Shikai**. Yuan established a Republican Party, while Sun's supporters rallied to the Nationalist People's Party – **Guomindang** – led by **Song Jiaoren**. Song was assassinated by Yuan's henchmen following Guomindang successes in the 1913 parliamentary elections, and Sun again fled to Japan. Annulling parliament, Yuan tried to set himself up as emperor, but couldn't even control military factions within his own party, who plunged the north into civil war on his death in 1916. Sun, meanwhile, returned to his native Guangdong and established an independent Guomindang government, determined to unite the country eventually. Though unsuccessful, by the time of his death in 1925 he was greatly respected by both the Guomindang and the four-year-old Communist Party for his lifelong efforts to enfranchise the masses.

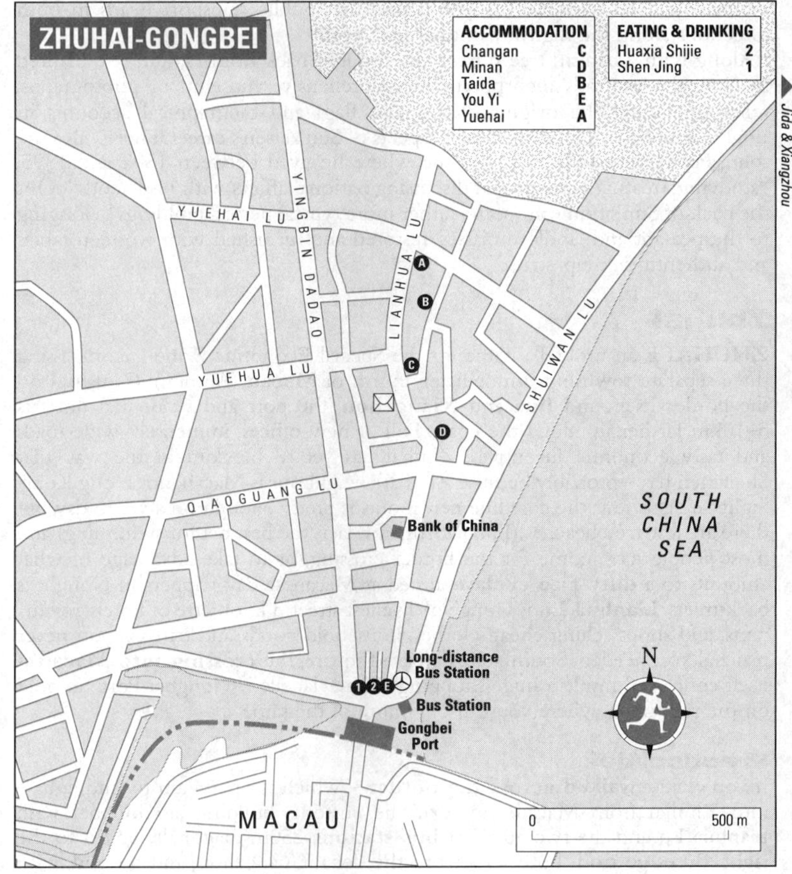

the last bus to Guangzhou leaving at 10pm (3hr; ¥70). **Jiuzhou ferry port** is 5km up the road at Jida, with twice-hourly services to Shenzhen between 8am and 6pm (1hr; ¥80), and ten daily departures to Hong Kong from 8am to 9.30pm (1hr; ¥180). Buses #2, #4 and #13 (daily 6.30am–9.30pm) run up to the port from Gongbei, or you can hail a taxi (around ¥20).

For **accommodation**, there are literally dozens of mid-range places in Gongbei with almost identical facilities and prices (which can plummet considerably during the week): on Lianhua Lu, *Min'an* (Ⓣ0756/8131168; ❻) is the pick of the moderate bunch, with large, comfortable rooms and attentive staff, whilst the *Changan* (Ⓣ0756/8118828; ❻) nearby is of a similar standard. Nearer the border crossing and bus stations, the *You Yi* (aka *Friendship Hotel*; Ⓣ0756/8131818; ❺) at 46 Youyi Lu is prone to more substantial discounts than the others. There's also the more upmarket *Yuehai* (aka *Guangdong Regency*; Ⓣ0756/8888128, Ⓦwww.gdhhotels.com; ❼) on Yuehai Dong Lu, whose exterior glass lift offers an ear-popping vantage of Macau. Unfortunately, though there are budget hotels around, most of them won't accept foreigners; try the *Taida* (Ⓣ0756/3821188; ❸) on Guangjia Bei Jie between Yuehai Dong

Lu and Lianhua Lu – inexplicably, your chances will improve if you have your name written in Chinese.

There are plenty of banks in Gongbei, and numerous **places to eat**, from bakeries to street vendors (the spicy beef and mutton skewers are delicious), to fast-food outlets and full-blown restaurants. *Huaxia Shijie*, which faces the border, has a dizzying choice of Chinese, Macanese, Indian and Southeast Asian food which you order direct from the chefs by pointing (try *jiuhua yu*, chrysanthemum fish) – portions are colossal and prices reasonable. The innocuous-looking *Shen Jing* canteen on the other side of the lane serves excellent salty chicken and Cantonese roast goose and duck.

Northern Guangdong

Guangdong's hilly northern reaches form a watershed between the Pearl River Valley and the Yangzi Basin, guarding the main route through which peoples, armies and culture flowed between central China and the south – there are even remains of the physical road, broad and paved, up near **Meiling** on the Jiangxi border. Its strategic position saw the region occupied as long ago as the Stone Age, and it was later used by the Taiping rebels and the nineteenth-century Wesleyan Church, who founded numerous missions in northern Guangdong. Today, **Qingyuan** and its pretty riverside temples lie only an hour northwest of Guangzhou by bus, while a host of offbeat attractions farther north around the

Northern Guangdong		
Liannan	连[illegible]	liánnán
Lianzhou	连州	liánzhōu
Qingyuan	清远	qīngyuǎn
Bei River	北江	běijiāng
Docks	水陆客运站	shuǐlù kèyùnzhàn
Feilai Si	飞来古寺	fēilái gǔsì
Feixia Si	飞霞古寺	fēilxiá gǔsì
Nandamen Jiudian	南大门酒店	nándàmén jiǔdiàn
Qing Xin Hot Springs Resort	清心温场	qingxin wenchang
Sun Hua Yuan	新花园酒店	xīnhuāyuán jiǔdiàn
Tai He Temple	太和古侗	tai he gudong
Tianhu Dajiudian	天湖大酒店	tiānhú dàjiǔdiàn
Yinglong Lüdian	迎龙旅店	yínglóng lǚguǎn
Zhiwei Guan	之味馆	zhīwèi guǎn
Shaoguan	韶关	sháoguān
Dajian Chan Si	大鉴禅寺	dàjiànchán sì
Danxia Shan	丹霞山	dānxiá shān
Fengcai Lou	风采楼	fēngcǎi lóu
Qujiang (Maba)	曲江（马坝）	qūjiāng (mǎbà)
Renhua	仁化	rénhuà
Royal Regent	丽晶酒店	lìjīng jiǔdiàn
Shaohua Jiudian	韶华酒店	sháohuá jiǔdiàn
Wu River	武江	wǔjiāng
Yixin	壹心宾馆	yìxīn bīnguǎn
Yuetong	粤通世纪酒店	yuètōng shìjì jiǔdiàn
Zhen River	浈江	zhēnjiāng

rail town of **Shaoguan** include **Danxia Shan**, a formalized mountain park. For those not continuing up into central China, Shaoguan is also a jumping-off point for a backwoods trip west **into Guangxi province** through ethnic Yao and Zhuang territories.

Qingyuan and around

Surrounded by countryside thick with rice fields and mud-brick villages, **QINGYUAN** is a busy back-road market town on the north bank of the **Bei River**, about 80km northwest of Guangzhou by bus from the Liuhua station (1hr; ¥35). Ringed by grimy manufacturing complexes, Qingyuan's centre is none too bad, but the town's true attraction lies in its position as a departure point for day-trips 20km upstream to the poetically isolated, elderly temple complexes of **Feilai** and **Feixia**.

Qingyuan's **bus station** is about 3km south of the river in an ugly residential area alongside the highway; from here there are several daily buses to Shaoguan, and masses to Guangzhou, Foshan and Shenzhen. Note, however, that there are unlikely to be any services after 8pm. Heading into the centre, orange bus #6 runs over the Beijiang Bridge and into town, whose kilometre-wide core is centred on the intersection of north–south **Shuguang Lu** and east–west **Xianfeng Lu**. Taxis cost around ¥10. To get to the ferry from the bus station, head south along **Sanggang Lu** and continue across the junction down **Beimen Jie,** at the end of which a quick left-right will take you onto **Nanmen Jie**, which runs down to the water. The **docks**, currently undergoing something of a facelift, run along Yanjiang Lu at the bottom end of Nanmen Jie.

If you miss the boat, you can kill time at the **Tai He Temple** (¥15), a series of Taoist pavilions dotting a path into the mountains north of town, complete with a crystal-clear swimming pool filled from the mountain stream, children's roller coaster and dodgems. The temple entrance is around ten minutes by motorbike taxi (¥10) from the #6 bus terminus. Further afield is the **Qing Xin Hot Springs Resort** (¥50), a favourite with locals and, apparently, also with some of China's best professional football teams. The resort can be reached in an hour from the bus station opposite where #6 terminates (¥10).

There's a collection of noisy, inexpensive **hotels** on the roundabout at the northern end of Beimen Jie: *Sun Hua Yuan* (Ⓣ0763/3311138; ❸) is the pick of the bunch, with friendly staff and clean, functional rooms – those on the third floor have pleasant, communal balconies, albeit overlooking the road. *Yinglong Lüdian* (Ⓣ0763/3313688; ❷), a couple of doors up along Sanggang Lu, is cheaper, with basic, worn rooms. There's also the plush and popular *Tianhu Dajiudian* (Ⓣ0763/3820126, Ⓕ3820333; ❺), on the Shuguang Lu/Xianfeng Lu intersection. Nanmen Jie and Beimen Jie have the best **places to eat**; options include river food at *Nandamen Jiudian*, a café and restaurant in various sections near the dock, as well as countless others to the west along Yanjiang Lu, and *Zhiwei Guan*, a Cantonese diner on Beimen Jie.

Feilai and Feixia

Ferries (¥50) to Feilai and Feixia supposedly depart daily at 8am from the Nanmen Jie dock and leave Feixia to return at about 3pm. However, vessels only leave if enough customers show, and other than in peak season and at weekends cannot be relied upon to actually be running. The alternative, a considerably faster but less robust six-person boat, can be chartered for the day for ¥300 from the waterfront.

The Bei River runs shallow in winter, and the boats oscillate from bank to bank along navigable channels. For the first hour it's a placid journey past a few brick pagodas, bamboo stands screening off villages, and wallowing water buffalo being herded by children. Hills rise up on the right, and then the river bends sharply east into a gorge and past the steps outside the ancient gates of **Feilai Gusi** (¥15), a charmingly positioned Buddhist temple whose ancestry can be traced back 1400 years. Wedged into the base of steep slopes, the current cramped halls date from the Ming dynasty, and manage to look extremely dignified. You'll only need about forty minutes to have a look at the lively ridge tiles and climb up through the thin pine forest to where a modern pavilion offers pretty views of the gorge scenery. If you have time to spare before your boat heads on, the temple gates are a good place to sit and watch the tame cormorants sunbathing on the prows of their owners' tiny sampans, or you can bargain with the local women for freshwater mussels and carp – you'll have a chance to get these cooked for you at Feixia.

Feixia

Some 3km farther upstream from Feilai at the far end of the gorge, **Feixia Gusi** (¥35) is far more recent and much more extensive in the scale and scope of its buildings. The name covers two entirely self-sufficient Taoist monasteries, founded in 1863 and expanded fifty years later, which were built up in the hills in the Feixia and Cangxia grottoes, with hermitages, pavilions and academies adorning the 8km of interlinking, flagstoned paths in between. Chinese visitors initially ignore all this, however, and head straight for the huge collection of **alfresco restaurant shacks** on the riverbank, where they buy and organize the preparation of river food with the numerous, eager wok-wielding cooks – a nice way to have lunch.

A couple of hours is plenty of time to have a look around. A broad and not very demanding set of steps runs up from the riverfront through a pleasant woodland where, after twenty minutes or so, you pass the minute Jinxia and Ligong temples, cross an ornamental bridge, and encounter **Feixia** itself. Hefty surrounding walls and passages connecting halls and courtyards, all built of stone, lend Feixia the atmosphere of a medieval European castle. There's nothing monumental to see – one of the rooms has been turned into a **museum** of holy relics, and you might catch a weekend performance of **traditional temple music** played on bells, gongs and zithers – but the gloom, low ceilings and staircases running off in all directions make it an interesting place to explore. If you walk up through the monastery and take any of the tracks heading uphill, in another ten minutes or so you'll come to the short **Changtian Pagoda** perched right on the top of the ridges, decorated with mouldings picked out in pastel colours, with views down over Feixia and the treetops. Another small temple next door offers food, drink and basic **accommodation** (❻).

Five minutes' walk east along the main track from Feixia brings you to the similar but smaller complex of **Cangxia**. Restorations began here in 1994, but Cangxia remains in a semi-ruinous state, though monks hounded out during the 1960s are back in attendance, and many of the statues and shrines are smudged with incense soot. Look for the garden with its fragrant white magnolia tree, an unusual, life-sized statue of the Monkey God, Sun Wu Kong, and some wonderful **frescoes** – one featuring an immortal crossing the sea on a fish, storm dragons and two golden pheasants.

Shaoguan

Many trains from the Guangzhou train station call in at **SHAOGUAN**, 200km north, and expresses take a mere two and a half hours – not a bad hard-seat experience (¥34). An ancient city, Shaoguan was unfortunately the target of

Japanese saturation bombing during the 1930s, which robbed the town of much of its heritage. Since the 1950s, textile mills and steelworks have ensured a moderate prosperity, if not a pretty skyline, but there's plenty to do in the immediate area.

Shaoguan's downtown area fills a south-pointing **peninsula** shaped by the **Zhen River** on the east side and the **Wu River** on the west, which merge at the peninsula's southern tip to form the Bei River. The pedestrianized main street, Fengdu Lu, crossed by Fengcai Lu at the north end of town, and Jiefang Lu in the south, runs vertically through the centre to the tree-lined **Zhongshan Park**. While there's plenty of activity in the clothing and trinket **markets** that fill the side streets off Fengdu Lu, and some crumbling colonial architecture, most of the town is functional and modern. The city sights, such as they are, comprise **Fengcai Lou**, a 1930s reconstruction of the old eastern city gate tower, up along Fengcai Lu; and **Dajian Chan Si**, an insubstantial monastery with ancient heritage – it was founded in 660 AD, and Huineng (see p.573 and p.619) taught here – just east off the bottom end of Fengdu Lu. The traditional **market** around the temple is worth a look, but is not for the squeamish, while the road running from the southeast corner of the train station square sees shops

West into Guangxi

Though the main transport routes run north and south from Shaoguan, if you're looking for an unusual way into Guangxi province, consider heading west through the mountainous strongholds of Guangdong's **Yao** and **Zhuang** population, a corner of the province virtually untouched by tourism. An early-morning bus leaves Shaoguan's long-distance station daily and takes about six hours to cover the 185km to **Lianzhou**, a Han town established by Emperor Wudi in 111 BC and containing an ancient **hexagonal pagoda** whose base is of Song vintage. Another 15km southwest from Lianzhou is **Liannan**, from where you can catch minibuses 10km out to **Sanpai**, a predominantly Yao village, and 35km beyond Liannan you'll find **Lianshan**, surrounded by Yao and Zhuang hamlets. Continuing through to Guangxi, the road from Lianshan runs a farther 100km over the mountains to **Hezhou**, a small town in Guangxi province from where you can get onward transport to Wuzhou or Guilin.

spill out onto the street selling everything from teacups to traffic cones, and ends with a faded fairground.

Practicalities

Both **arrival points** are immediately east of the centre over the Zhen River, linked to Jiefang Lu by the Qujiang Bridge: the **train station** sits at the back of a big square, while the **long-distance bus station** is just north of the bridge on the square's edge. Onward train tickets are in short supply, as this is the main line north out of Guangdong and, despite a continuous stream of trains passing through, it's perpetually overcrowded, as is the train station itself. Long-distance buses – heading north to Jiangxi and Hunan, east to Huizhou and Chaozhou, south to Guangzhou and west to Lianshan – leave throughout the day. There are a couple of morning buses to Qingyuan, but for more services you should head to the west station (Xi Zhan) over the Wujiang Bridge on the other side of town. **Taxis** cruise the streets (¥4 within town), with **minibuses** out to nearby attractions leaving from a depot just southwest of the train-station square. There's a **Bank of China** on Jiefang Lu (Mon–Fri 9am–5pm, Sat 10am–3pm), a **post office** on the south side of the train-station square, and several **Internet bars** just north of Fengcai Ta on Dongti Lu.

For accommodation, there are several options around the station square itself, including the cheap but basic *HPL* (ⓣ0751/8884095; ❷), and the mid-range *Yuetong* (ⓣ0751/8229944; ❹), all but next door to each other on the north side of the square, and the superior *Royal Regent* (ⓣ0751/8210218; ⓔsgregent@pub.shaoguang.gd.cn; ❺) at the southwest corner. In town, Jiefang Lu offers the most options, including the smart *Shachua* (ⓣ0751/8881870, ⓦwww.shaohuahotel.com; ❹) and the slightly pretentious *Juyaxuan* (ⓣ0751/8189333; ❹), which also has a vaguely Western restaurant on the first floor. Elsewhere, the *Yixin* (ⓣ0751/6990111❸), at the junction of Fuxing Lu and Xidi Lu, is probably the best deal in town.

Shaoguan has **restaurants** aplenty, with several upmarket *dim sum* joints along Fengdu Lu, such as *Bendao* at the junction with Heping Lu, and side streets packed with cheaper options. For the widest choice, head down the alley next to the *Yayuan Fandian*, where canteens serving up options from all over China rub shoulders. For Western food try the restaurant at the *Juyaxuan* or the *RBT* teahouse on Fengdu Lu, which has an English menu with a mix of Chinese and Western standards as well as countless kinds of tea.

Around Shaoguan: Danxia Shan

Buses and minibuses to various sights around Shaoguan leave from a depot just southwest of the train station square; just approach the area and touts will try to drag you on board. You will almost certainly be asked for at least double the correct fare – even Chinese tourists suffer this – and would be ill-advised to hand over any money without bargaining; nor should you get onto a partially empty vehicle unless you want a long wait. Alternatively, ask at the bus station to see if anything is heading your way.

The most interesting side trip is to **Danxia Shan**, a formation of vivid red sandstone cliffs lining the **Jin River**, 50km northeast of Shaoguan near the town of **Renhua**. Buses (¥12) drop you by the main road gates, where you pay the ¥70 **entry fee**, which includes all minibus rides into and around the park – note that these stop around 5pm, and that the **last bus** back to Shaoguan passes the gates in the late afternoon.

The first place to aim for is **Yuan Shan Jing**, 2km inside the gates across the Jin, famous for **Yangyuan Shi**, a rock that – though the description is less suitably applied to outcrops all over China – really does look like the male member. It's a tough climb to the summit of neighbouring (and less phallic) Yuan Shan, after which you can charter a **boat** (¥10 a person) or catch the bus for another couple of kilometres to Danxia Shan itself. The surrounding area is covered in 12km of paths, which rise steeply through woodland, past cliffside nunneries and rock formations, and up the various summits; Chinese tourists stay overnight in the handful of **hotels** here (upwards of ¥100) and rise early to catch the sunrise from the pavilion at the mountain's apex, **Changlao** – only an hour's climb – though the views are great all day long.

Eastern Guangdong

Taken in one go, it's an arduous six-hundred-kilometre journey east from Guangzhou to Xiamen in Fujian province, but there's a wealth of interesting territory to explore on the way. Only three hours away, **Huizhou**'s watery parkland makes it an excellent weekend bolt hole from Guangzhou, while over near the Fujian border, **Chaozhou** is famed for its own cooking style and Ming-era architecture. With enough time, you could spend a few days farther north in the hilly country around **Meizhou**, investigating ethnic **Hakka culture** in its heartland. Getting around is easy: **expressways** from Guangzhou or Shenzhen run via Huizhou along the coast to Shantou and on into Fujian, while the **rail line** from Guangzhou's East train station bends northeast from Huizhou to Meizhou – where a new extension runs up to Yongding in Fujian – then down to Chaozhou and Shantou.

Huizhou and Xi Hu

HUIZHOU, 160km from Guangzhou, is a place of water, caught between five lakes and the confluence of the Dong and Xizhi rivers. It was settled over two thousand years ago and later became capital of the Southern Han court. What saves Huizhou from being just another small, run-of-the-mill Chinese town is the genteel scenery surrounding the two-square-kilometre **Xi Hu** (West Lake). First laid out as a park by Song-dynasty engineers, the lakeside is a pleasant place to spend a day or a few hours strolling around the constructed landscapes and watching crowds of locals do the same.

Eastern Guangdong

Chaozhou	潮州	*cháozhōu*
Confucian Academy	海阳县儒学宫	*hǎiyángxiàn rúxuégōng*
Fenghuang Pagoda	凤凰塔	*fènghuáng tǎ*
Guangji Gate	广济门	*guǎngjì mén*
Hanwen Gong	韩文公	*hánwén gōng*
Kaiyuan Si	开元寺	*kāiyuán sì*
Xiangzi Qiao	湘子桥	*xiāngzǐ qiáo*
Xihu Park	西湖公园	*xīhú gōngyuán*
Xufuma Fu	许驸马府	*xǔfùmǎ fǔ*
Accommodation and eating		
Chaozhou Binguan	潮州宾馆	*cháozhōu bīnguǎn*
Chun Guang Dajiudian	春光大酒店	*chūnguāng dàjiǔdiàn*
Ciyuan Jiujia	瓷苑酒家	*cíyuàn jiǔjiā*
Feng Cheng Binguan	凤城宾馆	*fèngchéng bīnguǎn*
Hongyun Jiudian	鸿运酒家	*hóngyùn jiǔjiā*
Hu Rong Quan	胡荣泉	*húróng quán*
Jinlong Binguan	金龙宾馆	*jīnlóng bīnguǎn*
Yunhe Dajiudian	云和大酒店	*yúnhé dàjiǔdiàn*
Dapu	大埔	*dàpǔ*
Gongyuan Binguan	公园宾馆	*gōngyuán bīnguǎn*
Hu Shan	虎山	*hǔshā*
Huizhou	惠州	*huìzhōu*
Daxibei	大西北牛肉拉面	*dàxīběi niúròu lāmiàn*
Gui An Zhoudaxue	贵安州大学	*guìānzhōu dàxué*
Hui Hang Binguan	惠航宾馆	*huìháng bīnguǎn*
Huipinglou Lüye	惠平楼旅业	*huìpínglóu lǚyè*
Huizhou Binguan	惠州宾馆	*huìzhōu bīnguǎn*
Xi Hu	西湖	*xīhú*
Xi Hu Dajiudian	西湖大酒店	*xīhú dàjiǔdiàn*
Yuan Miao	元庙	*yuánmiào*
Meizhou	梅州	*méizhōu*
Dongshan Bridge	东山桥	*dōngshān qiáo*
Lingguang Si	灵光寺	*língguāng sì*
Meijiang Bridge	梅江桥	*méijiāng qiáo*
Mei River	梅江	*méijiāng*
Qianfo Si	千佛寺	*qiānfó sì*
Renjinglu	人境庐	*rénjìng lú*
Wenhua Park	文化公园	*wénhuà gōngyuán*
Yinna Shan	阴那山	*yīnnà shān*
Yuemei Bus Station	月梅汽车站	*yuèméi qìchēzhàn*
Accommodation and eating		
Huaqiao Dasha	华侨大厦	*huáqiáo dàshà*
Huihua Jiudian	晖华酒店	*huīhuá jiǔdiàn*
Hui Rui Zhu Su	辉瑞住宿	*huīruì zhùsù*
Kejia Fan	客家饭	*kèjiā fàn*
Meizhou Dajiudian	梅州大酒店	*méizhōu dàjiǔdiàn*
Shang's Meatball Store	尚记肉丸店	*shàngjì ròuwándiàn*
Tian Yuan Dajiudian	田园大酒店	*tiányuán dàjiǔdiàn*
Shantou	汕头	*shàntóu*

Huizhou isn't a large place, and Xi Hu covers about the same area as the centre of town. There are several **entrances** (daily 7.30am–9.30pm; ¥16; ¥5 after 6pm), but the main one is next to the *Huizhou Binguan* on Huangcheng Lu. If you want to enjoy the lake from the water, you can hire a boat here from upwards of ¥20 an hour, plus a deposit. From here, the path crosses the lake over a five-hundred-metre causeway, its two sections joined by a small humpbacked bridge made of white marble. It was built in 1096 by a monk named Xigu and funded by the Sichuanese poet-official **Su Dongpo**, then Huizhou's governor and composer of a famous verse extolling the beauty of the full moon seen from this spot. On the far shore there's a thirteen-storey brick pagoda from 1618, whose wobbly wooden stairs can be climbed for fine views north and south across the waters. Next door is a noble statue of Su Dongpo, with an adjacent museum displaying a battered inkstone said to have belonged to this ubiquitous man of letters.

The main path heads off across the lake again from here, this time via a zigzagging bridge and a series of strategically placed islets, thick with bamboo groves, to the northern shore forecourt of **Yuan Miao**, an old Taoist nunnery. It's a bizarre place, with an improbable number of tiny rooms and atriums decorated with Taoist symbols and auspicious carvings of bats, tigers and cranes; one hall at the back is dedicated to the Three Kingdoms hero and war god Guan Yu, and a side wing contains a pit full of live tortoises. Walking back down Huangcheng Lu from here, you will find a few more islands linked to the footpath, the favoured haunt of weekend street performers who keep crowds entertained with theatre and martial-arts displays.

Practicalities

Huizhou's town centre sits immediately below a kink in the 500-metre-wide Dong River, a proportionately thin strip of land hemmed in by the smaller Xizhi River to the east, and Xi Hu to the west. The **train** pulls in about 3km west, from where a taxi or bus #9 will take you past Huizhou's **long-distance bus station** to Huangcheng Lu. Arriving by bus, you will probably draw in to the long-distance station; however, some through services between Guangzhou and points further east may drop you near the expressway on Dongjiang Lu – it's best to take a cab to Xi Hu from here (around ¥10). The bus station is on a roundabout below several flyovers 1km south of the lake on Eling Bei Lu, which runs north, away from the roundabout, to Huangcheng Lu, which follows Xi Hu's eastern shore. Take any of the small side streets east off Huangcheng Lu and you'll end up on parallel Shuimen Lu, Huizhou's shopping precinct. The town's hotels can **change money**, and the Bank of China has branches opposite the bus station and on Huangcheng Lu (Mon–Fri 8.30am–noon & 2.30–5pm). For **Internet access** head for Neteasy on Huangcheng Lu.

There's inexpensive **accommodation** around the bus station; but these are mostly noisy places such as *Huipinglou Lüye* (Ⓣ0752/2662333; ❸) on Eling Bei Lu. For a little more, you can get a better room near Xi Hu at *Hui Hang Binguan* (Ⓣ0752/2180666; ❸) on Huangcheng Lu, where some rooms have side views of the lake. If you've got more cash to spare, the *Huizhou Binguan* is a very comfortable affair with spacious doubles (Ⓣ0752/2232333, Ⓕ2231439; ❺), right on Xi Hu's eastern shore, further south on Huangcheng Lu. The *Xi Hu Dajiudian* just across the road (Ⓣ0752/2226666, Ⓦwww.hzwestlakehtl.com; ❺) has plusher rooms, but only the more expensive ones have good views of the lake. For **food**, there are places near the bus station, including tasty and filling stretched beef noodles at spotless and friendly *Daxibei*, and inexpensive restaurants along

Huangcheng Lu and Shuicheng Lu. Try the hotels for more upmarket meals – the *Huizhou Binguan* and the *Xi Hu Dajudian's Japanese Teppanyaki* restaurant can both rustle up English menus.

Moving on, you can book train tickets through the *Huizhou Binguan*'s travel service (daily 8am–8pm); buses run back to Guangzhou and Shenzhen between 6am and 6pm, with several daily onwards at least as far as Chaozhou and Shantou.

Chaozhou

On the banks of the Han River, **CHAOZHOU** is one of Guangdong's most culturally significant towns, yet manages to be overlooked by tourist itineraries and government projects alike – principally through having had its limelight stolen during the nineteenth century by its noisy southern sister, **Shantou**, just 40km away. In response, Chaozhou has become staunchly traditional, proudly preserving the architecture, superstitions and local character which Shantou, a recent, foreign creation, never had, making it a far nicer place to spend some time. However, you may end up passing through Shantou to get to Chaozhou, as more transport finds its way there. There are frequent minibuses for the one-hour journey to Chaozhou from Shantou's long-distance bus station and express bus station. If you get to Shantou and have a few hours to spare, the crumbling **old quarter** around Anping Lu holds a certain seedy charm.

Chaozhou was founded back in antiquity, and by the time of the Ming dynasty had reached its zenith as a place of culture and refinement; the originals of many of the town's monuments date back to this time. A spate of tragedies followed, however. After an anti-Manchu uprising in 1656, only Chaozhou's monks and their temples were spared the imperial wrath – it's said that the ashes of the 100,000 slaughtered citizens formed several fair-sized hills. The town managed to recover somehow, but was brought down in the nineteenth century by famine and the Opium Wars, which culminated in Shantou's foundation. Half a million desperately impoverished locals fled Chaozhou and eastern Guangdong through the new port, many of them **emigrating** to European colonies all over Southeast Asia, where their descendants comprise a large proportion of Chinese communities in Thailand, Malaysia, Singapore and Indonesia. Humiliatingly, Shantou's rising importance saw Chaozhou placed under its administration until becoming an independent municipality in 1983, and there's still real rivalry between the two.

For the visitor, Chaozhou is a splendid place. In addition to some of the most active and manageable street life in southern China, there are some fine historic **monuments** to tour, excellent shopping for local **handicrafts**, and a nostalgically dated small-town ambience to soak up. Chinese speakers will find that Chaozhou's **language** is related to Fujian's *minnan* dialect, different from either Mandarin or Cantonese, though both of these are widely understood.

Arrival and information

Laid out on the western bank of the Han River, Chaozhou comprises an oval, 1500-metre-long **old town centre**, enclosed by Huangcheng Lu, which, divided into north, south, east and west sections, follows the line of the **Ming-dynasty stone walls**. A stretch of these still faces the river on the centre's eastern side, while Chaozhou's modern fringe spreads west of Huangcheng Lu. The old town's main thoroughfares are Taiping Lu, orientated north–south, crossed by shorter Zhongshan Lu, Xima Lu and Kaiyuan Lu, which all run east from Huangcheng Lu, through arched gates in the walls, and out to the river.

Chaozhou's **long-distance bus station** is just west of the centre on Chaofeng Lu; shuttles from Shantou wind up here too. The **train station** is about 5km northwest; from here, you can walk 100m to the main road and catch city bus #2 (daily 6.30am–8.30pm; ¥2) to Xinqiao Lu, a western extension of Kaiyuan Lu, or take a taxi (around ¥14). **Motor- and cycle-rickshaws** – the only vehicles able to negotiate the old town's backstreets – are abundant, though once in town everything is within walking distance, or you can go for the Chinese tourist option and hire a tandem bicycle for ¥4 an hour from just inside the Guanji Gate. There are branches of **Bank of China** (Mon–Fri 8.30–11.30am & 2–5pm) next to the Chaozhou Binguan and down the road on the southern side of Xihe Lu at the junction with Huangcheng Xi Lu. There are also a few cheap **Internet** places near here.

Moving on from Chaozhou, there are **buses** to Meizhou, Shantou, Guangzhou, Shenzhen and Fujian from the long-distance bus station, and **express coaches** east and west along the coastal road from a private station on Huangcheng Xi Lu. **Trains** (station ticket office open daily 6–11.30am & 1.30–5.30pm or try the travel office in the lobby of the Yunhe Jiudian) run down to Shantou or back to Guangzhou via Meizhou and Huizhou. Shantou is quickest reached by bus, Meizhou by the train.

Accommodation

There are plenty of **places to stay** clustered around the bus station, with a number of good budget options.

Chaozhou Binguan Opposite the long-distance bus station ⓣ0768/2333333, ⓦwww.chaozhouhotel.com. The smartest hotel in town, with large, clean rooms and many English-speaking staff. ❺

Chun Guang Dajiudian Xihe Lu ⓣ0768/2681288. A clear rung or two down from the nearby *Chaozhou*, but if you're not after huge lobbies and room service, the rooms are perfectly adequate. ❹

Feng Cheng Binguan Taiping Lu, near the junction with Zhongshan Lu ⓣ0768/2223211. Slightly shabby rooms, but a fair deal for the price considering its excellent location close to the old city. ❸

Jinlong Binguan Huangcheng Nan Lu ⓣ0768/2383888, ⓦwww.jinlong-hotel.com. Smart business hotel at the bottom of the old town. Clean, comfortable and handy for the town centre, but lacks the kudos of the *Chaozhou*. ❺

Yunhe Dajiudian Across the road from *Chun Guang Dajiudian* on Xihe Lu ⓣ0768/2136128. Worn but comfortable place that is very similar to the *Feng Cheng*. ❸

The Town

Chaozhou's old quarter may be past its heyday, but it has none of Shantou's decrepitude. Instead you'll find an endlessly engaging warren of narrow streets packed with a mixture of colonial and traditional buildings, far better maintained than in almost any comparable town in China. In the quieter residential back lanes, look for old wells, Ming-dynasty stone archways, and antique family mansions, protected from the outside world by thick walls and heavy wooden doors, and guarded by mouldings of gods and good luck symbols. Out on the main streets, motorbikes and cycle-rickshaws weave among the shoppers, who are forced off the pavement and into the roads by the piles of goods stacked up outside stores. If you need a target, **Xufu Mafu** is a decaying mansion on Zhongshan Lu, opposite the junction with Wenxing Lu. If you wander south down Wenxing Lu, you'll come to both a Ming-style memorial archway and a former **Confucian academy** – now a **museum** (daily 8am–5pm; ¥4), full of prewar photos of town. Down in the south of town, **Jiadi Xiang**, a lane west off Taiping Lu, is an immaculate Qing period piece, its flagstones, ornamental porticos and murals (including a life-sized rendition of a lion-like *qilin* opposite no. 16) restored for the benefit of residents, not tourists. For a bit of space, head up to **Xihu Park** (5am–midnight; ¥8), just north of the old town across a "moat" on Huangcheng Xi Lu, where there's a dwarf pagoda, hillocks, and some vegetated sections of the town walls.

If you bother with only one sight, however, make it **Kaiyuan Si** (daily 8am–5pm; ¥5) at the eastern end of Kaiyuan Lu. A lively Buddhist temple founded in 738 AD, it's still a magnet for pilgrims, but these days they're outnumbered by tourists and the inevitable beggars they attract. Three sets of solid wooden doors open onto courtyards planted with figs and red-flowered phoenix trees, where a pair of Tang-era **stone pillars**, topped with lotus buds, symbolically support the sky. The various halls are pleasantly proportioned, with brightly coloured lions, fish and dragons sporting along the sweeping, low-tiled roof ridges. Off to the west side is a **Guanyin pavilion** with a dozen or more statues of this popular Bodhisattva in all her forms. Another room on the east side is full of bearded Taoist saints holding a *yin-yang* wheel, while the interior of the **main hall** boasts a very intricate vaulted wooden ceiling and huge brocade banners almost obscuring a golden Buddhist trinity.

The town walls and the east bank

About 250m east past the temple down Kaiyuan Lu you'll pass the 300-year-old **Matsu Miao** set below the **old town walls**. Seven metres high and almost as thick, these were only ever breached twice in Chaozhou's history, and more than 1500m still stand in good condition. The walls run from the **North**

▲ Chaozhou's old quarter

Pavilion (daily 8.30am–5pm; ¥4), first constructed by the Song, past Guangji Gate and down as far as Huangcheng Nan Lu. There are access steps at several points along the wall, including above the main **Guangji Gate**, where there's also a guard tower which houses an exhibition (¥10) on the history of the adjacent **Xiangzi Qiao**, a 500m-long bridge whose piles were sunk in the twelfth century. Until the 1950s, when they were replaced by an ordinary concrete construction, the central section was spanned by a row of wooden punts. At the time of writing, renovations that had already lasted a couple of years were still ongoing, meaning a detour to the next bridge south or walking to the north end of Huangcheng Lu for a free ferry service. Crossing via the

Shopping

Chaozhou is a great place to buy **traditional arts and crafts**. For something a bit unusual, the **hardware market**, just inside the Guangji Gate along Shangdong Ping Lu, has razor-sharp cleavers, kitchenware and old-style brass door rings. **Temple trinkets**, from banners to brass bells, ceramic statues – made at the nearby hamlet of Fengxi – and massive iron incense burners, are sold at numerous stores in the vicinity of Kaiyuan Si, also a good area to find ceramic **tea sets** and **silk embroideries**.

For those who enjoy a bit of a haggle, an impromptu antiques market springs up most mornings along the pavement of Huangcheng Lu outside Xihu Park, and in the evenings a night market competes with motorcyclists and cars for road space along Kaiyuan Lu.

southern bridge, you'll see the shrub-covered shell of the ancient **Fenghuang Pagoda** and can head north to the gate of **Hanwen Gong** (¥10), a temple complex built in 999 in memory of Han Yu, a Confucian scholar who a century earlier had denounced Buddha as a barbarian and cleared the river of troublesome crocodiles. A flight of broad, steep granite stairs here leads up to three terraces, each with a hall; the uppermost one has numerous ancient stone proclamation tablets and a painted statue of Han Yu.

Eating, drinking and entertainment

Chaozhou's cooking style is becoming evermore popular in China, and thanks to emigrants from the region, it has long been unconsciously appreciated overseas. Seafood is a major feature, while local roast goose, flavoured here with sour plum – the use of fruit is a characteristic feature of the style, as is a garnish of fried garlic chips, a Southeast Asian influence – rivals a good Beijing duck. A good place to start looking is on Huangcheng Xi Lu, where a string of **restaurants** overlook Xihu Park, but wherever you are, and at pretty much any time of the day or night, you will never be far from **street stalls** doling out hotpots, noodles and other, less immediately recognizable dishes for just a few yuan.

Chaozhou's residents perform the local **tea** ritual, *gongfu cha*, on the slightest pretext – if nobody offers you a cup, most places to eat serve tea at a couple of yuan a session. First, the distinctive tiny pot and cups arrive on a deep ceramic tray with a grid on top for drainage; the pot is stuffed to the brim with large, coarse Oolong tea leaves, filled with boiling water, and immediately emptied – not into the cups, but the tray. Then the pot is topped up and left to steep for a moment before the cups are filled with a rapid movement that delivers an equal-strength brew to all. For all this effort you get a thimbleful of tea, which has to be swiftly downed before it goes cold.

For **entertainment**, try and track down a performance of *chaoju*, the indigenous **opera** style. It's quite listenable, with little of the warlike clanging and falsetto singing of Beijing's theatre; plots tend to involve witty cautionary tales about lax sexual morality. Your best bet is to catch one of the infrequent shows held during festivals in Xihu Park. For more modern evening entertainment, there are a few **bars and clubs** at the eastern end of Xihe Lu.

Restaurants

Ciyuan Jiujia Huangcheng Xi Lu Superb goose (around ¥100 for a whole bird), crispy-fried squid, steamed crab, fishball soup, fried spinach and a selection of *dim sum*.

Hu Rong Quan Taiping Lu. This bakery, specializing in mooncakes, makes the best spring rolls you'll ever eat, stuffed with spring onions, yellow beans, mushrooms and a little meat.

Lianhua Vegetarian Restaurant Opposite Kaiyuan Si. Good vegetarian restaurant, where a six-dish set meal, including sweet-and-sour ribs and kebabs will set you back about ¥20.

Turbo Café Xihe Lu. Western-style restaurant with steak set meals for around ¥30. It's hardly an inspired option, offering very much an interpretation of Western food rather than the real thing, but if you're desperate for a plate of chips, this is about the only place in town.

Meizhou and around

In the foothills of the Fujian border, 200km north of Chaozhou where rail lines from Guangzhou, Shantou and Fujian converge, **MEIZHOU** is the ancestral home of a huge number of Overseas Chinese, whose descendants have begun to pump an enormous quantity of money back into the region. While not a pretty city, Meizhou is ethnically **Hakka** (see p.532) and is thus a fine place to pick up local background before heading off into their Fujian heartlands, just up the train line around Yongding – if you can't make it out that far, a nearby mountain temple makes a good excuse for a quick trip.

Arrival and information

Meizhou lies on both sides of the Mei River, with the older **town centre** on the north bank, connected to the newer south-bank districts by the central Meijiang Bridge and the Dongshan Bridge 1km to the east. The **long-distance**

bus station is 1500m west of the centre on Meizhou Dadao and the number #3 bus route; while the Yuemei bus station is a similar distance north at the terminus of the #4 bus route near the university; the **train station** lies 5km south of the river at the end of Binfang Dadao – catch a taxi (around ¥14) or city bus #4 (¥1.5) to the centre via the Dongshan Bridge.

To **move on**, there are regular buses to Dapu, Longyan and Xiamen in the east, and everywhere west back to Guangzhou and Shenzhen. Where you've a choice, trains are generally faster, though Fujian-bound services (to Yongding, Longyan, Xiamen and Fuzhou) are surprisingly infrequent. It's easiest to buy train tickets through your hotel. The main **Bank of China** is south of the river on Meijiang Lu and there's another branch at the junction of Gongyuan Lu and Zhongyuan Lu (both Mon–Fri 8am–5pm). The **post office** is on Gingyuan Lu near the road off to the football stadium and there are a couple of **Internet** places next door and over the road.

Accommodation

Places to stay are distributed both sides of the river. There are plenty of low- and mid-range options, but as yet nothing really in the way of international-standard luxury.

Huaqiao Dasha Jiangbian Lu ☎0753/2232388. Newly refurbished place in a good central location. ④

Huihua Jiudian South of the Meijiang Bridge on Meijiang Lu ☎0753/2191888. Inexpensive option with clean, pleasant rooms. ③

Hui Rui Zhu Su Across the street from the Yuemei bus station, on Huanshi Bei Lu ☎0753/2356010. Cheap and basic, but clean, option, albeit one with intermittent hot water. ②

Meizhou Dajiudian Opposite the long-distance bus station ☎0753/2355700. With its basic, shabby doubles this place is good for early-morning departures, but little else. ②

Tian Yuan Dajiudian Across the road from *Huihua Jiudian* on Meijiang Lu ☎0753/2163888. Plush and modern affair, probably the most reliably comfortable option in town. ④

The Town and around

Meizhou is a lightly industrial town, producing handbags and clothing, surrounded by hills and set in the fertile bowl of a prehistoric lake bed through which flows the convoluted **Mei River**. The scruffy centre is a two-square-kilometre spread on the north bank, connected to the neat, newer southern suburbs by the **Meijiang** and **Dongshan bridges**. As in Chaozhou, almost everything is within walking distance or the range of cycle-rickshaws.

Meizhou's social focus and main shopping district surrounds the open **square** at the junction of various main roads immediately north of the **Meijiang Bridge**. The colonial-style shopfronts on Lingfeng Lu, which runs west along the riverfront, are worth a wander, but the tone is set by the Tian'anmen Square-like entrance to the football stadium; you'll certainly know when a game is on, as the entire town descends on the park, the merry-making kept in order by police. At other times, the park is pleasant enough, and at night, older houses in nearby streets look very atmospheric, lit by tapers and red paper lanterns.

For more local culture, head northeast off the square up Shunfeng Lu, and then follow the lanes and Chinese signs five minutes east to some scummy ponds outside **Renjinglu** (daily 8am–5.30pm; ¥5), former home of Meizhou's nineteenth-century poet and diplomat, **Huang Zunxian**. You may have to knock on the door to get them to open up. It is the most ornate of several buildings around the ponds, the others being classically austere **Hakka town houses**, with high central gateways and square-sided walls and windows.

Somewhat more attractive, **Qianfo Si** (Thousand Buddha Temple; ¥5) overlooks Meizhou 1km east of the Meijiang Bridge – take Jiangbian Lu east along the river for 700m to the Dongshan Bridge, follow Dongshan Dadao north for another 200m, take a right onto the new road just after **Kejia Park** – easily recognizable by its distinctive new exhibition hall – and then turn left up the hill as the road bends right past the sparkling new middle school campus. There's an excellent vegetarian **restaurant** among the group of buildings at the temple gates (see below). Above on the hill, the original temple and pagoda were demolished in 1995 in order to be totally rebuilt with expatriate funding and an attention to detail that has to be seen to be believed. The stonework is particularly accomplished, the temple pillars carved in deep relief with heroes and coiling dragons, while the base of the pagoda has finely executed scenes from Buddha's life.

Lingguang Si

One good day-trip from Meizhou is to head 50km east to **Yinna Shan**, sanctified by the elderly temple of **Lingguang Si**, founded in 861, though the present buildings are restored Qing. There are two 1000-year-old trees either side of the gate (a third died 300 years ago), and an extremely unusual wooden spiral ceiling in the main hall, the only other example being in a temple on Wudang Shan in Hubei province.

The temple is easily reachable by direct bus (1hr; ¥12) from the Yuemei bus station. Be sure to check when the last bus is returning.

Eating and drinking

The vegetarian restaurant at **Qianfo Si** serves outstanding meals daily at noon, including imitation meat dishes which are virtually indistinguishable from the real thing – you'll pay ¥48 for four dishes, ¥78 for five, and so on. Also try the **Hakka specialities** sold at the smart *Kejia Fan* and numerous family-run restaurants east of the square on Shunfeng Lu – juicy salt-baked chicken, wrapped in greaseproof paper (around ¥40 for a whole bird); little doughy rissoles made with shredded cabbage; and quick-fried cubes of bean curd, stuffed with pork and served in a gluey, rich sauce. For a takeaway, hunt down *Shangi's Meatball Store* on Wenbao Lu in the western backstreets. **Hakka wine** is pretty nice by Chinese standards, similar to a sweet sherry and often served warm with ginger – most places to eat can provide a bottle.

Dapu and beyond

To learn more about the Hakka, you need to head out to settlements north and east of Meizhou, surrounded in summer by some very attractive countryside. The small, dishevelled town of **DAPU**, two hours and 100km east, is a good place to start. A fraction of the size of Meizhou, the town shares the same river valley setting and an unexciting centre, but in the fields just outside, next to a modern sports stadium (another gift from an expatriate investing in his homeland), there's a huge square-sided **weiwu**, a three-storeyed Hakka house with walls as solid as any castle's. The residents, amazed to see a foreign face, will come out to chat if you walk over for a look. Elsewhere are some very nicely constructed low-set family compounds, whose walls enclose several temple-like halls, all with decorated roofs, and at least two small, traditionally circular homesteads. The largest, most highly regarded Hakka mansions anywhere in China, however, are three hours away over the Fujian border around **Yongding** (see p.556) – there are daily buses from Dapu.

The **bus station** is on the northern edge of town at the corner of Renmin Lu and Hu Shan Lu, which runs south right through Dapu, terminating below steps ascending to the tidy parkland of **Hu Shan** (Tiger Hill). There's **accommodation** at the relatively garish *Gongyuan Binguan* (❸) near the park on Tongren Lu, and plain beds in the peeling **hostel** (❶) 50m west of Hushan Lu on Yanhua Lu.

Western Guangdong

While it's not an unpleasant area, there's very little to delay your passage across western Guangdong on the way to Guangxi or Hainan Island. Buses cover both routes quickly, but the rail line is the most convenient way to get to **Haikou**, although as there's currently only one service daily you may find yourself taking a bus to **Hai'an**, from where there are regular ferries to Hainan. Either way, consider stopping off for a day or two at **Zhaoqing**, a pleasant resort town also connected by a direct ferry to Hong Kong, whose scenery has been a tourist attraction for more than a thousand years.

Zhaoqing and Dinghu Shan

Road, rail and river converge 110km west of Guangzhou at **ZHAOQING**, a smart, modern city founded as a Qin garrison town to plug a gap in the line of a low mountain range. The first Europeans settled here as early as the sixteenth century, when the Jesuit priest **Matteo Ricci** spent six years in Zhaoqing, using Taoist and Buddhist parallels to make his Christian teachings palatable. Ricci was eventually invited to Beijing by Emperor Wanli, where he died in 1610, having published numerous religious tracts. Since the tenth century, however, the Chinese have known Zhaoqing for the limestone hills comprising the

Western Guangdong		
Zhaoqing	肇庆	*zhàoqìng*
Chongxi Ta	崇禧塔	*chóngxī tǎ*
Dinghu Shan	鼎湖山	*dǐnghú shān*
Mosque	清真寺	*qīngzhēn sì*
Plum Monastery	梅庵	*méiān*
Qingyun Si	清云寺	*qīngyún sì*
Qixing Yan Park	七星岩公园	*qīxīngyán gōngyuán*
Accommodation and eating		
Dinghu Shan Youth Hostel	鼎湖山国际青年旅馆	*dǐnghúshān guójì qīngnián lǚguǎn*
Dynasty Cake Shop	皇朝西饼	*huángcháo xībǐng*
Huaqiao Dasha	华侨大厦	*huáqiáo dàshà*
Jinye Dasha	金叶大厦	*jīnyè dàshà*
Muslims' Canteen	清真饭店	*qīngzhēn fàndiàn*
Ming Tien Inn	名典酒店	*míngdiǎn jiǔdiàn*
Star Lake Hotel	星湖大酒店	*xīnghú dà jiǔ diàn*
Wenming Lu	文明路	*wénmíng lù*
Yu Xiang Mi Fang	渔湘米坊	*yúxiāng mǐfāng*
Zhanjiang	湛江	*zhànjiāng*
Hai'an	海安	*hǎi'ān*

adjacent **Qixing Yan**, the Seven Star Crags. Swathed in mists and surrounded by lakes, they lack the scale of Guilin's peaks, but make for an enjoyable wander, as do the surprisingly thick forests at **Dinghu Shan**, just a short local bus ride away from town.

Arrival, information and accommodation

Set on the north bank of the Xi, Zhaoqing is squashed between the river and the northerly lakes bordering Qixing Yan Park. Jianshe Lu and Duanzhou Lu run right across town east to west in numbered sections, crossed by **Tianning Lu**, which is oriented north–south between Qixing Yan Park's boundaries and the river. Zhaoqing's **train station** lies 5km away to the northwest – the #1 bus from outside the station will take you into town; the **long-distance bus station** is on Duanzhou Lu, 100m east of the northern end of Tianning Lu; and the **ferry port** lies on the southeastern side of town at the junction of Jiangbin Lu and Gongnong Lu, near Chongxi Ta. **Taxis** can be hailed everywhere, but otherwise there isn't much in the way of public transport; Zhaoqing is, anyway, somewhere to get about on foot.

Moving on, there are onward buses to Qingyuan, Shaoguan, Zhanjiang and just about everywhere between Guilin and Guangzhou – check which of Guangzhou's bus stations you're headed for before you board. Trains go to Nanning, Haikou (8hr), Guangzhou (2hr) and through to Shenzhen (3hr 30min) and Hong Kong (4hr). A daily ferry for **Hong Kong** (4hr; ¥150) leaves every afternoon from near the ticket office (daily 8–11.30am & 2–5pm; ⓣ0758/2225736) on the corner of Gongnong Lu and Jiangbin Lu west of Chongxi Ta. If you need help booking any of the above, try the **CTS** (daily 8am–9pm; ⓣ0758/2229908), just west of the *Huaqiao Dasha* – the transport ticket office is on the ground floor and the tours section is upstairs. The main **Bank of China** is 500m to the west (Mon–Fri 9am–noon & 2.30–5pm), and there's a **post office** (daily 8am–9pm) on Jianshe Lu.

The town has abundant **accommodation**, and there are also places to stay out at Dinghu Shan. Reasonable options include the *Huaqiao Dasha* (ⓣ0758/2232650, ⓕ2231197; ⓦwww.zhaoqingtour.net.cn; ④) on Duanzhou

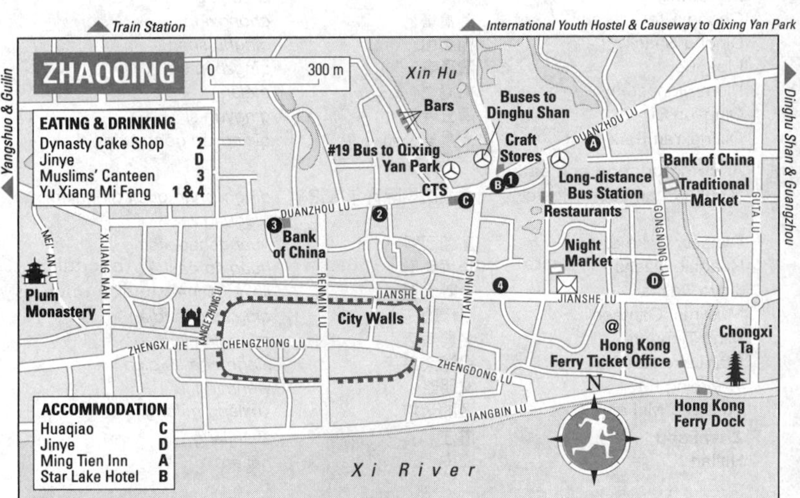

Lu; the excellent-value *Jinye Dasha* on Gongnong Lu (ⓣ0758/2221338, ⓕ2221368; ❸), which also has a good restaurant, and the modern *Ming Tien Inn* (ⓣ0758/2293333, ⓕ2293888; ❹) on Duanzhou Lu, east of the long-distance bus station, which has a passable café on the top floor serving Chinese and Western food. Probably Zhaoqing's most upmarket option, the central *Star Lake Hotel* (ⓣ0758/2211688; ⓦwww.starlakehotel.com ; ❻) on Duanzhou Lu has some rooms with a lake view, looking across towards the Seven Star Crags.

The Town

There's quite a bit to see in Zhaoqing itself, though the sights are widely scattered and not of great individual importance. Produced for more than a thousand years, Zhaoqing's **inkstones** are some of the finest in China – you can buy them at stationery and art stores around town, and at the souvenir market at the Duanzhou Lu/Tianning Lu intersection.

Overlooking the river, **Chongxi Ta** (daily 8.30–11.30am & 2.30–5pm; ¥5) is a Ming pagoda at the eastern end of riverfront Jiangbin Lu. Looking much like Guangzhou's Liurong Ta, at 57.5m this is the tallest pagoda in the province; views from the top take in sampans, cargo boats and red cliffs across the river surmounted by two more pagodas of similar vintage. A few aged buildings lurk in the backstreets west of here behind Jiangbin Lu – and there's an excellent **market** north off Zhengdong Lu – but Zhaoqing's most interesting quarter is a thirty-minute walk west beyond Renmin Lu. Solid sections of the **ancient city walls** stand here on Jianshe Lu, which you can climb and follow around to Chengzong Lu; head north from here along Kangle Zhong Lu and enter a tight knot of early-twentieth-century lanes, shops and homes – all typically busy and noisy – along with a brightly tiled **mosque**. Beyond the row of plant and bonsai stalls west of the mosque on Jianshe Lu, and a further kilometre out on the edge of town, the **Plum Monastery** (daily 8.30am–5pm; ¥10) on Mei'an Lu, was established in 996 and has close associations with **Huineng**, founder of Chan Buddhism (see p.573). He is remembered in various paintings and sculptures here.

Arranged in the shape of the Big Dipper and said to be fallen stars, the seven peaks that make up **Qixing Yan Park** (daily 7.30am–5.30pm; ¥50) rise 2km north of town on the far side of **Xin Hu**. To get here, go to the top end of Tianning Lu and cross over busy Duanzhou Lu to the paved area on the lakeshore, from where you can catch the #19 bus (15min; ¥1) along the **causeway** that continues north across Xin Hu. The crags themselves are quite modest, named after objects they resemble – **Chanchu** (Toad), **Tianzhu** (Heavenly Pillar), **Shizhang** (Stone Hand). An interlocking network of arched bridges, pathways, graffiti-embellished caves and willows makes for a pleasantly romantic two-hour stroll.

Eating and drinking

There's a shortfall of **restaurants** outside the hotels – where it's worth indulging in *dim sum* at the *Jinye Dasha*'s popular third-floor restaurant – though numerous places along eastern Jianshe Lu and all through the centre sell local *zongzi* (conical rice packets wrapped in a bamboo leaf), sandpots (stews served in earthenware pots) and light Cantonese meals. For something different try *Muslims' Canteen* on Duanzhou Lu, which serves typical Hui food such as lamb skewers and beef noodles at reasonable prices – note that it closes at 9pm. There are a couple of branches of the Guangdong *Yu Xiang Mi Fang* chain, on Duanzhou Lu and Jianshe Lu, which have a good selection of cheap staples and *dim sum*, and a string of canteens near the night market at the north end of Wenming Lu. As well as the usual Western fast-food contingent, the *Dynasty Cake Shop*, next to the hotel of the same name on Duanzhou Lu, sells good sandwiches. For **nightlife** there is a string of bars along Xin Hu's western shore.

Dinghu Shan

Twenty kilometres east of Zhaoqing, the thickly forested mountains at **Dinghu Shan** were declared China's first national park way back in 1956, and have since been incorporated into the UNESCO biosphere programme. With well-formed paths giving access to a waterfall, temple and plenty of trees, the small area open to the public gets crowded at the weekends, but at other times Dinghu Shan makes an excellent half-day out – particularly in summer, when the mountain is cooler than Zhaoqing. The one drawback is the steep **entry fee** (¥50); one way to get the most for your money is to take advantage of Dinghu Shan's fairly inexpensive accommodation and **stay overnight**.

To reach Dinghu Shan, catch public bus #21 from the bottom end of Xin Hu (¥3.6); the bus drops you off about 1km south of the reserve at Dinghu township, from where you can continue on foot or hire a motor-rickshaw uphill to the gates. A further kilometre brings you to a knot of restaurants and souvenir shops, where there's another *International Youth Hostel* (Ⓣ0758/2621668; dorm beds ¥50, ④). Beyond here, the forest proper and walking track start, dividing either to follow a stream or to climb a flight of stairs to **Qingyun Si**, a large temple with an expensive **vegetarian restaurant** open at lunchtime, and with restorations that have decked the exterior in awful green bathroom tiles while providing some accomplished statuary. The track along the stream takes you in ten minutes to a thirty-metre-high **waterfall**, whose plunge pool has been excavated and turned into a swimming hole. A lesser-used track continues up the side of the falls and eventually up to a vehicle road, which you can follow across to the temple. The round trip takes about two hours, and the last bus back to Zhaoqing leaves at 5pm.

Zhanjiang and Hai'an

The only reason to make the long haul to **HAI'AN**, 550km from Guangzhou at the province's southwestern tip, is to catch one of the regular ferries to Hainan Island. There is one direct train from Guangzhou to Haikou each day via Zhaoqing; however, if you haven't managed to get this, or are travelling by bus, you may have to change at **ZHANJIANG** en route to Hai'an; Zhanjiang's southern train station and bus station are next to one another on Jianshe Lu, and buses down to Hai'an take a little under three hours. From Hai'an's ramshackle bus station you can either walk (left out of the station and downhill) or take one of the free buses down to the ferry port. Ferries leave every couple of hours and it costs ¥37 for the ninety-minute journey.

Hainan Island

Rising out of the South China Sea between Guangdong and Vietnam, **Hainan Island** marks the southernmost undisputed limit of Chinese

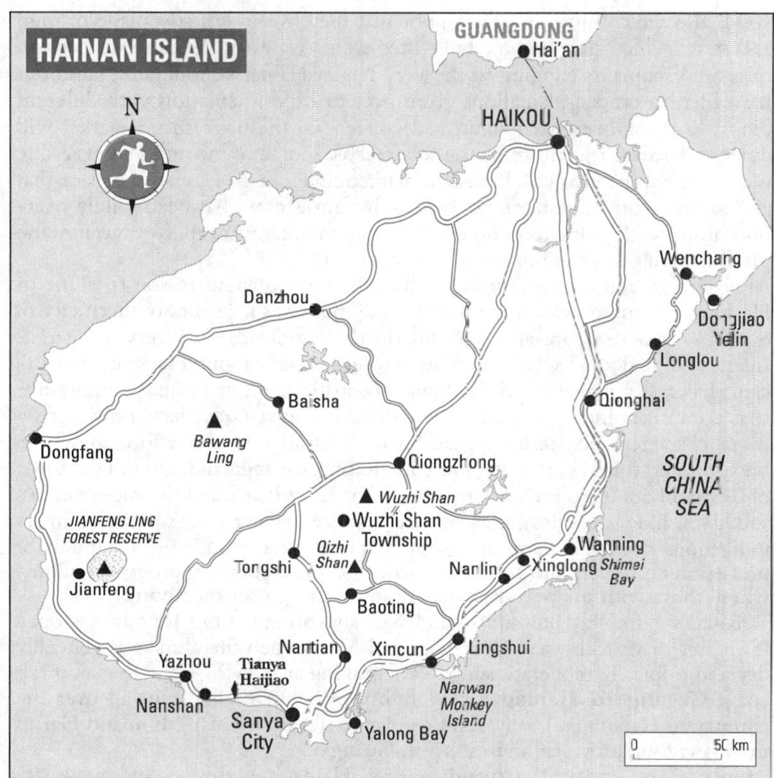

authority, a 300-kilometre-broad spread of beaches, mountain scenery, history, myth and – most of all – the effects of **exploitation**. Today a province in its own right, Hainan was historically the "Tail of the Dragon", an enigmatic full stop to the Han empire and – in the Han Chinese mind – an area inhabited by unspeakably backward races, only surfacing into popular consciousness when it could be of use. Han settlements were established around the coast in 200 AD, but for millennia the island was only seen fit to be a place of exile. So complete was Hainan's isolation that, as recently as the 1930s, ethnic **Li**, who first settled here more than two thousand years ago, still lived a hunter-gatherer existence in the interior highlands.

Modern Hainan is no primitive paradise, however. After two years of naval bombardments, the island was occupied by the Japanese in 1939, and by the end of the war they had executed a full third of Hainan's male population in retaliation for raids on their forces by Chinese guerrillas. **Ecological decline** began in the 1950s during the Great Leap Forward, and escalated through the 1960s when large numbers of Red Guards were sent over from the mainland to "learn from the peasants", and became involved in the first large-scale **clearing of Hainan's forests** to plant cash crops. Successive governments have continued the process of stripping the island's natural resources and abandoning the inhabitants to fend for themselves, in an appalling example of **economic mismanagement**: while there are skyscrapers and modern factories around the cities, you'll also see country people so poor that they live in lean-tos made of mud and straw, which have to be rebuilt after each wet season. With the exception of ragged remnants clinging to the very tips of Hainan's mountains, rainforest has ceded to eroded plantations given over to experimentation with different crops – rubber, mango, coconuts and coffee – in the hope that a market will emerge. **Tourism** seems to be the sole reliable source of income, and everyone is desperate to be involved. Persistent marketing has made Hainan the place that all Chinese want to come for a holiday, but investment has been wildly over-optimistic, with numerous hotels and entertainment complexes around the place standing empty, unfinished or never used.

For foreign and domestic tourists alike, the most obvious reason to come to Hainan is to flop down on the warm, sandy **beaches** near the southern city of **Sanya** – as a rest cure after months on the mainland, it's a very good one. Initially, there doesn't seem much more to get excited about. **Haikou**, Hainan's capital, bears evidence of brief colonial occupation, but its primary importance is as a transit point, while Han towns along the **east coast** have only slightly more character and scenic appeal. Spend a little time and effort elsewhere, however, and things start to get more interesting: the highlands around the town of **Tongshi** are the place to start looking for **Li culture**, and the mountainous southwest hides some forgotten **nature reserves**, where what's left of Hainan's indigenous flora and fauna hangs by a thread. There are even a handful of underwater sites off the southern coast, the only place in provincial China where those with the necessary qualifications can go **scuba diving**.

Hainan's extremely hot and humid **wet season** lasts from June to October. It's better to visit between December and April, when the climate is generally dry and tropically moderate, sunny days peaking around 25°C on the southern coast. **Getting to Hainan** is straightforward, with flights from all over the country to Haikou and Sanya, and regular ferries from Guangzhou and Hai'an in Guangdong province, and Beihai in Guangxi.

Once there, **getting around** is easy: Hainan's highways and roads are covered by a prolific quantity of **local transport**; high-speed buses link Haikou and Sanya in just three hours, while you can easily hop around the rest of the island by bus and minibus. As you move around you'll find that many of Hainan's towns have different local and Mandarin **names**; as the latter occur more frequently on maps and bus timetables, Chinese names are used below in the main text and character boxes, with local names indicated in brackets. Also note that, as a recognized tourist destination, Hainan is more **expensive** than the adjacent mainland – even Chinese tourists grumble about being constantly overcharged.

Haikou and the east coast

Haikou is Hainan's steamy capital, set at the north of the island and separated from Guangdong province by the thirty-kilometre-wide Qiongzhou Channel. For most visitors, Haikou is little more than a transit stop en route to Sanya, but the city and nearby coastal towns are looking more and more to get a piece of the tourist pie for themselves. If you can resist heading straight on to Sanya, it's worthwhile spending a couple of days around here and hopping between towns along Hainan's **east coast** – home to some of the few surfable beaches in China. This is the part of Hainan longest under Han dominion, and it's a good way to get the feel of the island.

Haikou and the east coast		
Haikou	海口	*hǎikǒu*
Central Bus Station	总站	*zǒngzhàn*
East Bus Station	汽车东站	*qìchē dōngzhàn*
Hai Rui Mu	海瑞墓	*hǎiruì mù*
Haikou Park	海口公园	*hǎikǒu gōngyuán*
New Port	海口新港	*hǎikǒu xīngǎng*
West Bus Station	汽车西站	*qìchē xīzhàn*
Wugong Ci	五公祠	*wǔgōng cí*
Xiuying Battery	秀英古炮台	*xiùyīng gǔpàotái*
Xiuying Wharf	秀英港	*xiùyīng gǎng*
Accommodation		
Banana Hostel	巴那那青年旅舍	*bānànà qīngnián lǚshè*
Civil Aviation	海南民航宾馆	*hǎinán mínháng bīnguǎn*
Haikou Binguan	海口宾馆	*hǎikǒu bīnguán*
Haikou Downtown	海口东堂	*hǎikǒu dōngtáng*
Huaqiao	华侨大厦	*huáqiáo dàshà*
Overseas	海外酒店	*hǎiwài jiǔdiàn*
Post and Telecommunications	邮电大厦	*yōudiàn dàshà*
Songtao	松涛大厦	*sōngtāo dàshà*
Eating		
Ganghai Canting	港海餐厅	*gǎnghǎi cāntīng*
Haikou Binguan	海口宾馆	*hǎikǒu bīnguǎn*
Hunan Ren	湖南人	*hùnán ren*
Japanese	香寿司	*xiāng shòusī*
Tailonghui Shifu	泰隆汇食府	*tàilónghuì shīfǔ*
Tong Shan Tang	同善堂全素餐厅	*tóngshàntāng quánsùcāntīng*
Xianzong Lin	仙踪林	*xiānzōng lín*
Yong He	永和	*yǒng hé*
Lingshui	陵水	*língshuǐ*
Puli Binguan	普利宾馆	*pǔlì bīnguǎn*
Yuyuan Binguan	怡园宾馆	*yíyuán bīnguán*
Longlou	龙楼	*lóng lóu*
Longlou Jiudian	龙楼酒店	*lónglóu jiǔdiàn*
Qishuiwan	其水湾	*qíshuǐwān*
Wenchang	文昌	*wénchāng*
Dongjiao Yelin	东郊椰林	*dōngjiāo yēlín*
Prima Resort	百莱玛度假村	*bǎiláimǎ dùjiàcūn*
Shimei Bay	石梅湾	*shíměi wān*

Haikou

Business centre, main port and first stop for newly arrived holidaymakers and hopeful migrants alike, **HAIKOU** has all the atmosphere of a typical Southeast Asian city. There's a smattering of French colonial architecture, a few parks and monuments, modern skyscrapers, broad streets choked with traffic and pedestrians, and the all-pervading spirit of wilfully glib commerce. An indication of the ethos driving Haikou is that nobody seems to be a local: officials, businessmen and tourists are all from the mainland, while Li, Miao and Hakka flock from southern Hainan to hawk trinkets, as do the Muslim Hui women selling betel nuts – all drawn by the opportunities that the city represents. More than anything, Haikou is a truly tropical city: humid, laid-back, pleasantly shabby, and complete with palm-lined streets, something particularly striking if you've just emerged from a miserable northern Chinese winter.

Arrival, city transport and information

Haikou's downtown area forms a compact block south of the waterfront Changti Dadao. The centre is marked by a busy circuit of wide one-way traffic flows and pedestrian overpasses surrounding **Haikou Park**, where much of the accommodation is located, with the most interesting shopping districts in the northerly **old colonial quarter** around Jiefang Lu and Bo'ai Bei Lu.

The **airport** is 2km south of town on Jichang Lu; bus #10 runs up to Haikou Park from outside, or catch the shuttle (¥15) to the CAAC/China Southern office on Haixiu Dong Lu. The **New Port** is north off Changti Dadao on Xingang Lu, where most ferries from Hong Kong and the mainland pull in; those from Beihai in Guangxi sometimes use the **Xiuying Wharf**, 5km farther west along Binhai Dadao – you can take bus #6 to the centre from either. Buses from the mainland wind up at the **central bus station** south of Haikou Park on Nanbao Lu; those from elsewhere on the island use the **east bus station** 2km down Haifu Dadao (bus #1 or minibus #217 to the Haifu Dadao/Haixiu Dong Lu junction), or the **west bus station** way out on Haixiu Xi Lu (bus #2 or minibus #217 go to Haixiu Dong Lu from here). The **train station** currently only offers one daily

Moving on from Haikou

Flying is the easiest way out of Haikou, with the city connected to Sanya and mainland locations between Harbin, Kunming and Hong Kong. Tickets for all airlines can be reserved at agents (see "Listings", p.627) or one of the numerous China Southern branches – the main office is in the CAAC (daily 8am–9.30pm; ⓣ0898/66525581, ⓕ6652580), next to the *Civil Aviation* hotel on Haixiu Dong Lu.

Ferries leave Haikou's New Port for Hai'an (¥37) at Guangdong's southernmost tip, where buses meet ferries for the 150-kilometre run to Zhanjiang. There are also ferries from the New Port (and sometimes from the Xiuying Wharf) for Beihai (seat ¥93; cabins from ¥123–333 per person, depending on the number of berths), on which it's worth paying for a cabin rather than spending the twelve-hour trip surrounded by seasick hordes watching nonstop kung fu flicks. Ticket offices at the ports open daily from 9am to 4pm, and there's usually no trouble getting a seat, though rough seas can suspend services. Your accommodation will be able to make bookings for boats and planes if you give them at least a day's notice.

The practicalities of getting out by **bus** depend on where you're heading. All **mainland traffic** leaves from the central bus station, where you'll find standard and luxury buses to destinations as far afield as Chongqing, Nanning, Jiujiang, Shenzhen and Guangzhou; tickets include ferry costs. **Sanya** and the **east coast** are served by the east bus station, from where there are also a few buses to Tongshi; a normal bus to Sanya is ¥50 and takes five hours, while an express is ¥80 and takes three. The west bus station deals mostly with **central and western** destinations, though you can also get to Sanya from here.

There's a **railway link** from Haikou to Guangzhou – unbelievably, the train goes onto a boat – which leaves daily at 7pm and takes twelve hours; you can book tickets, and for mainland trains departing from Zhanjiang, at the CTS office on Haixiu Lu (Mon–Sat 9am–5.30pm; ⓣ0898/66747268) or at another branch in the *Huaqiao* (same hours; ⓣ0898/66778455).

service to Guangzhou and is way out to the northwest – buses #28 and #40 head here from Haixiu Lu.

Haikou's **city bus service** is comprehensive and cheap, with more frequent and crowded private minibuses running the same routes. **Taxis** are so absurdly plentiful that you have only to pause on the street for one to pull up instantly. As an indication of fares, New Port to central Haikou costs around ¥20 – though if you negotiate prices beforehand you might pay only around two-thirds of the meter rate.

There's a total lack of **information** about the island in Haikou, with hotel tour agents only geared to getting you to Sanya as fast as possible. If you plan to explore Hainan's backwaters, pick up a **map** of the island from hawkers or kiosks (¥5); some include spreads of Haikou, Sanya and Tongshi, along with detailed road maps of the island including even minor sights marked in English.

Accommodation

There's plenty of central **accommodation** in Haikou, much of it conveniently located around Haikou Park. Room rates are always flexible; in summer, ensure that air conditioning is part of the bargain. Most hotels handle transport bookings and have their own restaurants.

Banana Hostel At junction of Renmin Lu/Sandong Lu, on Haidian Dao in the north of town ⓣ0898/66236780, ⓦwww.haikouhostel.com. This IYHA English-run establishment is the only accommodation in town geared towards budget travellers. Spacious, cheap rooms are supplemented with a lively bar serving cold beer and basic food, as well as Internet access and regular barbecues. Hidden down an alley, it's slightly hard to find – the best bet is to call beforehand and someone will come out to meet you. ❸

Civil Aviation Haixiu Dong Lu ⓣ0898/66506888, ⓕ66772610. Smart hotel with light and airy rooms, very central and not bad value. ❹

Haikou Binguan Daying Houlu ⓣ0898/65351234, ⓦwww.haikouhotel.com.cn. Formerly Haikou's most prestigious accommodation, now revamped with a more contemporary feel. Comfortable rooms and friendly staff. ❻

Haikou Downtown Datong Lu ⓣ0898/66796999, ⓦwww.hice.com. Luxury, international-standard business affair with all the trimmings. ❻

Huaqiao Datong Lu ⓣ0898/66773288, ⓕ66772094. A three-star business centre built in the early 1990s and beginning to look a bit threadbare, nevertheless comfortable enough and offering good discounts. ❸

Overseas Wuzhishan Lu ⓣ0898/65365999, ⓕ65365333. Fairly decent three-star venture, with tubs in each room taking advantage of a hot spring located 800m below the hotel. ❹

Post and Telecommunications Nanbao Lu ⓣ0898/66778340, ⓕ6778200. Hidden away in the backstreets, this hotel offers fair value, though the spruced-up lobby is not a reflection of the rooms. ❸

Songtao Wuzhishan Lu ⓣ0898/66729116, ⓕ66729006. One of Haikou's best deals, with cheap spacious tiled rooms and slightly more expensive newly renovated options. ❸

The City

The **old quarter**, boxed in by Bo'ai Bei Lu, Datong Lu and pedestrianized Deshengsha Lu, is the best area to stroll through, with its grid of restored colonial architecture housing stores and businesses. **Jiefang Lu** and **Xinhua Lu** are the main streets here, especially lively in the evening when they're brightly lit and bursting with people out shopping, eating and socializing; there's also a busy **market** west off Xinhua. Otherwise, **Haikou Park** and the adjacent lake are small but quite pleasant, the former a venue for extensive early-morning martial-art sessions, and with shrubberies concealing cracked stone statues, reputedly from a vanished Ming-dynasty temple.

Haikou has just three formal sights, any of which will fill you in on Hainan's position in Han Chinese history. Southeast of the centre along Haifu Lu, **Wugong Ci** (Five Officials' Memorial Temple; daily 8am–6pm; ¥20; bus #1 or minibus #217 down Haifu Lu) is a brightly decorated complex built in 1889 to honour Li Deyu, Li Gang, Li Guang, Hu Chuan and Zhao Ding, Tang men of letters who were banished here after criticizing their government. Another hall in the grounds commemorates Hainan's most famous exile, the poet **Su Dongpo**, who lived in the island's northwest between 1097 and 1100 and died on his way back to the imperial court the following year. A **museum** in a new building opposite has photos and Chinese-only captions of historical sites around the island, though a group of weathered Song-style **stone statues** of horses and scholars, almost lost in vegetation outside, is more interesting.

About 5km west of the centre, **Xiuying Battery** (daily 8am–7pm; ¥10) offers a different take on the island – to get there, catch minibus #32 from the south gate of Haikou Park. Built after the Chinese had apparently beaten off an attempted invasion by the French in the latter part of the nineteenth century, Xiuying was part of a string of coastal defences designed to deter foreign incursions along south China's coastline. A huge fortification, now maintained as a park, it's surrounded by basalt block walls concealing six twenty-centimetre naval cannons set in concrete bunkers, all connected by subterranean passageways. The bunkers are now camouflaged by fig trees and lit by bare bulbs, with the squat-barrelled, bezel-mounted guns pointing at high-rises to the north. It must be said that Xiuying's design and weaponry look suspiciously European – perhaps they were modernized in 1937 when the fort was dusted off to resist the Japanese.

A kilometre or so southwest of Xiuying on Qiuhai Avenue, a park and stone sculptures of lions surround **Hai Rui Mu**, tomb of the virtuous Ming-dynasty official Hai Rui (daily 8am–6pm; ¥10) – buses #28 and #40 from Haixiu Dong Lu stop near the junction of West Haixiu Lu and Qiuhai Avenue. Hai Rui's honesty, which earned him exile during his lifetime, caused a furore in the 1960s when historian **Wu Han** wrote a play called *The Dismissal of Hai Rui*, a parody of events surrounding the treatment of Marshal Peng Dehui, who had criticized Mao's Great Leap Forward. The play's suppression and the subsequent arrest of Wu Han, who happened to be a friend of Deng Xiaoping, are generally considered to be the opening events of the Cultural Revolution.

Eating

Perhaps because Haikou is essentially a mainland Chinese colony, **food** here is not as exotic as you'd hope. The ingredients on display at market stalls are promising: green, unhusked coconuts (sold as a drink, but seldom used in cooking); thick fish steaks, mussels, eels, crab and prawns; exotic fruits; and, everywhere, piles of seasonal green vegetables. But Hainan's most famous dishes – Wenchang "white-cut" chicken, steamed duck and glutinous rice, and Dongshan mutton – are nothing extraordinary, though tasty. Compounding this is a current craze for Cantonese and Western-style food, with hotel restaurants trying to out-compete each other in these lines.

The highest concentration of **restaurants** is in the old quarter along Jiefang Lu, with grilled chicken wings, kebabs and other snacks sold outside the cinema and in the market east off Xinhua Lu. A couple of palm-shaded cafés on the northern side of Haikou Park serve light snacks, fruit platters and endless teapots and make a good place to watch the world go by.

Coffee Time Jiefang Lu. Upmarket-looking Chinese interpretation of a Western restaurant. Despite appearances prices are reasonable, with mains including pizza and steak going for ¥20–50, and the menu also boasts a vast array of teas, fresh juices and cocktails. Open until 1am.

Ganghai Canting Jiefang Lu. Locals-oriented teahouse with tiled floor, dated wooden furniture and great *dim sum*.

Haikou Binguan Daying Houlu. With both Western and Chinese restaurants, this hotel is a good bet for local favourites, including steamed chicken in coconut milk and seafood rolls in coconut sauce. Not too expensive either – a whole chicken or duck costs around ¥60, with other dishes starting at ¥20.

Hunan Ren Nanbao Lu. Smart, ethnic-looking place serving up traditional Hunan dishes at reasonable prices. One of the better options in the town centre.

Japanese Floor 3, Tailongcheng building, Datong Lu. Sushi at ¥5–10 per plate, with set one-dish meals from ¥15.

Tailonghui Shifu 22 Haixiu Dong Lu. One of just a few places offering overseas food that isn't pizza or burgers, this first-floor Thai restaurant is a real find – the *tom yum* soup and green-curry mussels are to die for. Reckon on ¥20–30 per main dish.

Tong Shan Tang Vegetarian 33 Haidian Sandong Lu. Near the junction with Haihong Lu, this Buddhist gem has fake-meat versions of almost any Chinese dish you care to think of, and can even rustle up a "hamburger" if asked. A little hard to find, but worth the effort.

Xianzong Lin Nanbao Lu. Cute place with a Western/Chinese menu that includes pizza and some exotic cold drinks – black-sesame-seed milkshakes for one.

Yong He Dim Sum Wuzhishan Lu. *Dim sum* given the fast-food treatment. Order from the counter and in a couple of minutes fresh, cheap *dim sum* is brought direct to your table. No English menu, but plenty of photos to point to.

Listings

Banks and exchange There are numerous branches of the Bank of China including opposite the *Huaqiao*, and next to the *Haikou Downtown* on Datong Lu (Mon–Sat 8.30am–5.30pm).

Books The big Xinhua bookstore on Jiefang Lu, east of the post office, has a limited range of English classics on the third floor. For maps and guides to Hainan, mostly in Chinese, try the

discount bookstore upstairs at the Mingzhu Guangchang shopping centre on Haixiu Dong Lu, west of the bus station.
Cinema There's a popular screen and entertainment complex behind the snack stalls on Jiefang Lu.
Hospital Hainan Provincial People's Hospital, Longhua Lu ⓣ0898/6225933.
Internet access There's a Net bar on the second floor of the shopping centre at the junction of Jichang Dong Lu and Daying Lu, near the *Overseas*.
Mail and telephones The main post office, with parcel post service, is opposite the cinema on Jiefang Lu (24hr) and there are IDD phone places throughout the city.
PSB The Foreign Affairs Department is on Changti Dadao, just west of the junction with Longhua Lu.
Shopping Pearls are a good thing to buy while on Hainan, but Sanya is a much better place to find a bargain. Department stores along Haixiu Dong Lu such as Mingzhu Guangchang sell indigenous products such as coconut coffee, coconut powder, coconut wafers, coconut tea, palm sugar and betel nut; clothing sections also stock Hainan shirts, which differ from their Hawaiian counterparts in their use of dragons instead of palm trees on bright backgrounds. Whole shark skins – like sandpaper – dried jellyfish and other maritime curiosities in the shops along Jiefang Lu are also worth a look.
Travel agents China Travel Air Service, next to the *Huaqiao* (ⓣ0898/66781735, ⓕ66706281), are agents for a vast array of domestic and international carriers, including China Southern, Dragonair, Hainan Air, Cathay Pacific, Japan Airlines, Malaysia Airlines and Singapore Airlines. CTS in the *Huaqiao* (ⓣ0898/66778455) offers plane and train tickets and bus tours of the island.

The east coast

Most east-coast communities comprise small settlements of ethnic subgroups such as the Hakka, who were shuffled off the mainland by various turmoils, or returning Overseas Chinese deliberately settled here by the government, and many live by fishing, farming cash crops or pearl cultivation. Unless you plan to bask on the beaches at **Dongjiao Yelin** and **Longlou**, nowhere here takes more than half a day to look round, with the pick of the bunch being **Lingshui**, a hamlet with a long history, unexpected Communist connections and a nearby wildlife reserve. Everywhere has **accommodation** (often near the bus stations) and places to eat, and **minibuses** are the best way to get around, with shuttle services running between towns from sunrise until after dark. Bear in mind that there are **no banks** capable of foreign currency transactions along the way, so carry enough cash to last until Sanya.

Wenchang, Dongjiao Yelin and Longlou

WENCHANG, a decent-sized county town 70km southeast of Haikou, is known to the Chinese as the ancestral home of the sisters **Song Qingling** and **Song Meiling**, wives to Sun Yatsen and Chiang Kaishek respectively. Built up as a commercial centre in the nineteenth century by the French, it has now rather gone to seed, but you'll need to pass through to reach the beaches at **DONGJIAO YELIN**, Hainan's first **coconut plantation**, and the marginally less developed **LONGLOU**. Both are developing haphazardly, but are relaxing places to laze for a while, the palms forming a perfect backdrop to acres of white sands. Both places can be reached by direct bus from Wenchang, with the #13 bus to Dongjiao (1hr; ¥7.5) terminating directly outside the *Prima Resort* (ⓣ0898/6358222, ⓦwww.bailaima.com; ❹–❾), which has a range of comfortable wooden beachside bungalows and a few shabbier, cheaper rooms.

On arrival in Longlou (bus #9; 45min; ¥7), the best bet is to jump on a motor-taxi direct to the nearby Qishuiwan beach – the ten-minute journey should set you back about ¥5. Exposed to waves from the Pacific, Longlou is popular with Hainan's embryonic **surfing** community, some of whom run trips to this and other hidden surf spots, including Shimei Bay, which is fast becoming the focus of surfing in Hainan – for more details visit ⓦwww.surfinghainan.com or give Brendon, the brains of the outfit, a call on ⓣ1351/9800103 – he generally operates out of *Wave*

Bar on Sanya's Dadonghai beach. Longlou's sole hotel, the *Longlou Jiudian* (❷), has a rack rate of ¥150 that can be knocked down to less than half that. Next door is a basic but delicious and reasonably priced seafood restaurant.

Lingshui

An hour south of Wanning, **LINGSHUI** (Lingcheng) has been around for a long time. They were forging iron tools and making pottery here as far back as the Han dynasty, while uncovered silver tomb ornaments point to the town being an important commercial centre by the time of the Ming dynasty. Lingshui played a part in modern history when, having shifted south from Qionghai, China's **first Communist government** convened here in 1928; it was still functioning when the Japanese stormed Hainan in February 1939, whereupon its members retreated into the hills to wage guerrilla war on the invaders with the help of the local Li population (for more on the Li, see the box on p.638). The Communists never forgot this, and once in power granted the district nominal self-rule as **Lingshui Li Autonomous County**.

Today, Lingshui's dozen or so narrow streets are set back off the highway where it bends sharply past town near the bus station. Around town you'll see remains of a **Qing-dynasty monastery**, the interior still decorated with original frescoes, but now used to store video-game machines; a **Communist Museum** in another building of similar vintage (there's a cannon outside); and several fifty-year-old shops with what look like their original fittings. Wander off to Lingshui's fringes and you could be stepping back a hundred years, with lanes twisting into the countryside between walls surrounding family compounds, houses sporting decorative columns topped with lotus-bud motifs, and courtyards thickly planted with slender **areca palms**, often with conical buckets strapped around the trunks. These catch falling **betel nuts** (*binlang*), a crop cultivated as a stimulant by the Li since at least Ming times. Women are the biggest users, but just about everyone in Lingshui seems to have stained their lips and teeth from chewing slices of the palm seed, wrapped inside a heart-shaped pepper vine leaf.

Practicalities

Lingshui's main **bus station**, on a bend in the highway, is where most minibuses from Wanning drop off and where Sanya- and Haikou-bound vehicles depart. If you've arrived on an express bus, you may be dropped just off the expressway some 3km out of town from where you'll need to take a motorbike sidecar to the centre (¥5). Coming from the south, you might end up at the **minibus depot** about 1km down the road on the Sanya side of town. For **accommodation**, try the rooms at the *Puli Binguan* (Ⓣ0898/83325888; ❹) on the highway, five minutes north of the bus station, or smarter doubles at the *Yiyuan Binguan* (Ⓣ0898/83311000; ❹), nearby and just off the main road. The best places to **eat** are around here too, with numerous bustling **teahouses** along the highway and backstreets.

Sanya and the southern coast

Across the island from Haikou on Hainan's central southern coast (320km direct down the expressway), **SANYA** is, sooner or later, the destination of every visitor to the island. Though relics at the westerly town of **Yazhou** prove that the area has been settled for close on a thousand years, Sanya City itself is entirely modern, a scruffy fishing port and **naval base** maintained for monitoring events (and staking China's claims) in the South China Sea. These unexpectedly came to international attention in 2001, when a **US spyplane** made a forced landing here after colliding with a Chinese fighter jet. Sanya has also hosted two Miss World contests, which put the city in a different international spotlight and has certainly promoted outside investment. Generally, though, what pulls in the crowds – an increasing number of whom are Russian and Korean – are Sanya's surrounding sights, especially **Dadonghai beach**, one of the few places in China where you can unwind in public. The Chinese also flock to legendary landmarks atop the **Luhuitou Peninsula**, a huge granite headland rising immediately south of the city, and west at the scenic spot of **Tianya Haijiao**, while foreigners generally find beach life suffices.

Farther afield, the coastal arc between Sanya and the western industrial port of **Dongfang** sees few visitors. While Dongfang itself doesn't justify a trip, it's emphatically worth getting as far as **Jianfeng Ling**, the most accessible surviving fragment of Hainan's indigenous mountain **rainforest**. If this doesn't appeal, you can take advantage of plentiful transport north from Sanya to the Li stronghold of Tongshi, and on into the central highlands.

Sanya and the southern coast

Sanya	三亚	*sānyà*
Dadonghai	大东海	*dàdōng hǎi*
Diyi Shichang	第一市场	*dìyī shìchǎng*
Luhuitou Peninsula	鹿回头	*lùhuítóu*
Xinjian Jie	新建街	*xīnjiàn jiē*
Yalong Bay	亚龙湾	*yàlóng wān*
Accommodation and eating		
Blue Sky Hostel	蓝天国际青年旅舍	*lántiān guójì qīngnián lǚshè*
Cactus Resort	仙人掌度假酒店	*xiānrénzhǎng dùjiàjiǔdiàn*
Chatterbox Café	话匣子西餐厅	*huàxiázi xīcāntīng*
Chuanya	川亚宾馆	*chuānyà bīnguǎn*
Chunfeng Dajiudian	春丰大酒店	*chūnfēng dàjiǔdiàn*
Dongbei Wang	东北王	*dōngběi wáng*
Dongjiao Yelin Seafood	东郊椰林海鲜城	*dōngjiāoyēlín hǎixiānchéng*
Eagle Backpackers	背包客路馆	*bēibāokè lùguǎn*
Gloria Resort	凯莱度假酒店	*kǎilái dùjià jiǔdiàn*
Hawaii	夏威夷大酒店	*xiàwéiyí dàjiǔdiàn*
Holiday Inn	假日酒店	*jiàrì jiǔdiàn*
Landscape Beach	丽景海湾酒店	*lìjǐng hǎiwān jiǔdiàn*
Pearl Seaview	明珠海景酒店	*míngzhū hǎijǐng jiǔdiàn*
Rainbow	云博西餐酒吧	*yúnbó xīcān jiǔbā*
Sunny Sanya Family Inn	三亚红屋顶度假酒店	*sānyà hóngwūdǐng dùjià jiǔdiàn*
South China	南中国大酒店	*nánzhōngguó dàjiǔdiàn*
Sujingguong Haijing	水晶宫海景酒楼	*shuǐjīnggōng hǎijǐng jiǔlóu*
Xinghuayuan Seaview	兴华园海景酒店	*xīnghuáyuán hǎijǐng jiǔdiàn*
Yuhai Binguan	榆海宾馆	*yúhǎi bīnguǎn*
Dongfang	东方	*dōngfāng*
Jianfeng	尖峰	*jiān fēng*
Jiangfeng Ling Forest Reserve	尖峰岭热带原始森林自然保护区	*jiānfēnglǐng rèdài yuánshǐ sēnlín zìránbǎohùqū*
Nantian	南田	*nántián*
Nanshan	南山	*nánshān*
Tianya Haijiao	天涯海角	*tiānyá hǎijiǎo*
Yazhou	崖州	*yázhōu*

It must be said that though the beaches here are very pleasant, a trip to Sanya can also involve a few **irritations**, especially for those on a budget: at peak times rooms can be poor value; you'll have to watch for scams at cheaper restaurants; and foreign pedestrians are continually mobbed by taxi drivers and touts.

Arrival

The **Sanya area** comprises four sections: Sanya City, Dadonghai, the Luhuitou Peninsula – all fairly closely grouped – and Yalong Bay, a distant satellite tourist development. **Sanya City** occupies a three-kilometre-long peninsula bounded west by the Beibu Gulf and east by the Sanya River. Aligned north–south, Jiefang Lu is the main road, forking at its southern end to run briefly southwest to the cargo wharves as Jiangang Lu, and east to form busy Gangmen Lu. Changing its name several more times, this extends 4km out to **Dadonghai**, a kilometre-long spread of hotels, restaurants and shops backing on to Dadonghai beach, beyond which are the start of routes to Haikou and Tongshi. Accessible by road from Dadonghai, the **Luhuitou Peninsula** is separated from the cargo wharves by the harbour, while **Yalong Bay** is a cluster of insular resorts and nice beaches 20km east of town.

Phoenix **airport** is about 15km to the west, from where you'll need to catch a taxi into the city (¥40). Sanya's main **long-distance bus station** is at the northern end of Jiefang Lu and handles normal and luxury buses to Haikou, and normal services to just about everywhere on the island, including Dongfang, Tongshi and Wenchang. For **getting around**, there's the usual overload of taxi cabs (who may be reluctant to take you anywhere for less than ¥10) and some

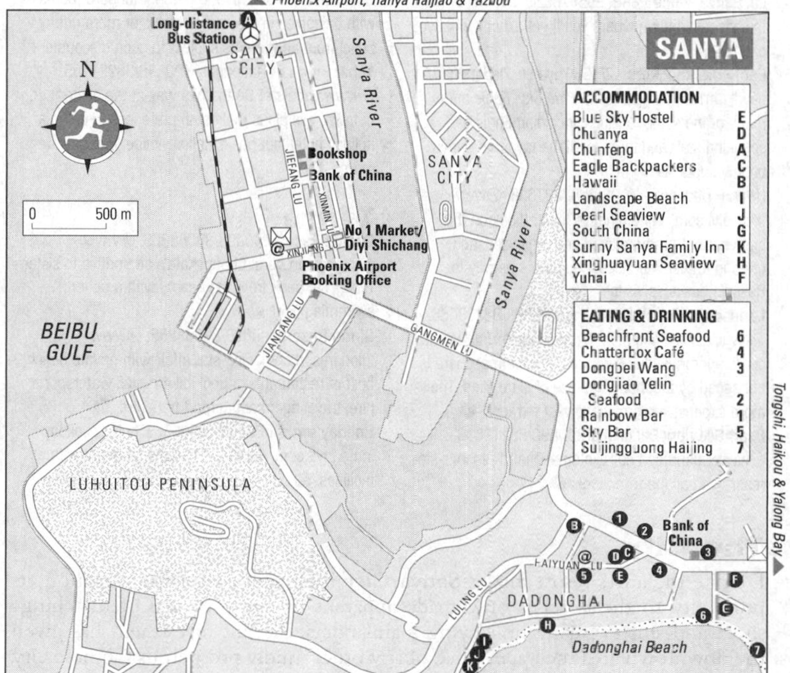

motorcycle-and-sidecar assemblies as well as **public buses** – #202 runs regularly from 6am until well after dark between the long-distance bus station and Dadonghai, while bus #102 runs every fifteen minutes (35min; ¥5) to Yalong Bay, via Jiefang Lu and the Summer Mall at Dadonghai. A faster double-decker bus runs the same route every forty-five minutes (25min; ¥5); get off at the giant stone totem pole, from where you can walk through to the beach.

Accommodation

Sanya's accommodation is constantly developing with increasing options across the board. The city itself is a pretty grotty place to stay, so most visitors head towards either the mostly cheap and cheerful **Dadonghai** or the more exclusive, and considerably pricier, **Yalong Bay**.

Sanya and Dadonghai

Blue Sky Hostel 29 Haiyuan Lu, Dadonghai ⓣ0898/88182320, ⓔsy.youthhostel@gmail.com. Backpacker central, this is not the cheapest option in town, but does have free wireless Internet, laundry facilities, a resident Taiwanese surf instructor and English-speaking staff who can arrange anything from dive trips to hiking in the rainforest. ❸

Chuanya Dadonghai ⓣ0898/38223000. A hastily cobbled-together apartment block, but amenable to bargaining and inexpensive for the area. ❸

Chunfeng Dajiudian Next to the bus station, Jiefang Lu, Sanya ⓣ0898/88276556. Basic, but one of the few places in town where you'll get exactly what you pay for. ❷

Eagle Backpackers 12F, 96 Yuya Lu, Dadonghai. A newly arrived competitor to *Blue Sky*, *Eagle* offers many of the same facilities, including English-speaking staff and tours to all the favourite Sanya beauty spots. ❸

Hawaii Dadonghai ⓣ0898/88227688, ⓦwww.xiaweiyi.com Unimaginative tower block on the highway, but pretty relaxed and organized, and offering immediate discounts. Caters heavily to Russian business visitors. ❺

Landscape Beach Dadonghai ⓣ0898/88228666, ⓦwww.sanyaliking.com. More characterful than its contemporaries, this low-rise place's atmosphere is enhanced by the thoughtful use of slate tiling. The more expensive rooms have vast terraces. ❼

Pearl Seaview Dadonghai ⓣ0898/88213838, ⓦwww.pearlresort.com. International-class four-star resort with all the trimmings. ❼

Sunny Sanya Family Inn Dadonghai ⓣ0898/88200128, ⓦwww.sunnysanya.com. A handful of low, tiled units in a slightly dishevelled courtyard beyond the *Pearl Seaview*; ask to see several rooms, as some are a bit tatty; nevertheless, it offers the cheapest accommodation right on the beach. ❹

South China Dadonghai ⓣ0898/88219888, ⓦwww.southchinahotel.com Comfortable, beachfront resort with all imaginable facilities, including computers with Internet access in the better rooms, a pool, gym and Western and Oriental restaurants. ❽

Xinghuayuan Seaview Dadonghai ⓣ0898/88677666, ⓕ88677488. Standard rooms with balconies in a concrete block, or more quirky beachfront apartments subject to good discounts. ❻

Yuhai Binguan Dadonghai ⓣ0898/38221105, ⓦwww.yuhai.net On the highway at the eastern edge of town, this place makes no pretences to being a holiday hotel, but has excellent-value, immaculate rooms. ❹

Yalong Bay

Cactus Resort ⓣ0898/88568866, ⓦwww.cactusresort.com. Cheapskate's alternative to sister *Gloria*, set back from the beach, with a better swimming pool. ❼

Gloria Resort ⓣ0898/88568855, ⓦwww.gloriaresort.com. Five-star affair with private beach, host of restaurants, a pool, bike rental, watersports hire, travel agent and airport transfers. ❾

Holiday Inn ⓣ0898/88565666, ⓔhotel@holiday-inn-sanya.com. Another international effort, with all facilities. ❾

The City

Despite the area's resort image, **Sanya City** itself is not a tourist attraction, its proximity to the beaches only made apparent by the presence of matching-short-and-shirt-wearing holidaying mainlanders. Recent investment has given the downtown area the appearance of any other mildly prosperous Chinese city, but it has atmosphere, and for seediness you can't beat the **wharf area** along Jiangang Lu, where dubious characters, scantily clad women and an air of lazy indifference fill the untidy teahouses and back alleys. Sanya's **No. 1 Market (Diyi Shichang)**, centred around Xinjian Jie running east off Jiefang Lu, is an interesting place to snack on local seafood and shop around the overstuffed open-fronted stores. Night or day, you can buy all manner of tropical fruits here, along with clothes, boiled sweets by the kilo, kitchen hardware from coconut graters to giant cleavers and woks, and expensive imported toiletries, cigarettes and spirits smuggled in through Vietnam.

Dadonghai and the Luhuitou Peninsula

Just 150m from the main road, often crowded and seasonally blistering hot, three-kilometre-long **Dadonghai** has pretty well everything you could ask for in a tropical beach: palm trees, white sands, and warm, blue water. Beachside bars and kiosks renting out beach umbrellas, jet skis, catamarans and rubber rings complete the scene, but on the whole the Chinese appear strangely bemused by beach life, as if they know it should be fun but are unsure of how to go about enjoying themselves. Swimming out farther than waist-deep water may draw disbelieving looks from holidaying mainlanders, many of whom seem uncomfortably self-conscious in swimwear and hardly dare get their ankles wet. While it's all very relaxed for China, don't mellow too much, as unattended valuables will vanish, and women going topless, or any nudity – other than at the far eastern end of the beach where there's a nudist colony, mainly consisting of Chinese men well past the first bloom of youth – could lead to arrests.

The **Luhuitou Peninsula** shouldn't take up much of your time. You can catch a motorcycle combi – or bus #101 – from outside the *Hawaii* at Dadonghai to the summit entrance, where ¥50 gains access to a ponderous granite statue depicting a Li legend about a deer transforming into a beautiful girl as it turned to face a young hunter – Luhuitou means "deer turns its head".

Eating and drinking

Given Sanya's tropical climate and location at China's southernmost point, there's something perverse about the bias towards northern and western Chinese food – probably explained by the fact that most of the restaurateurs are migrants from Sichuan and Dongbei. Like accommodation, eating here can be an expensive business, though the excellent **seafood** (almost all from Indonesia and the

▲ Dadonghai beach

Philippines – Sanya's marine fauna is long fished out) is reasonably priced. The stretch of **Haiyuan Lu** between the turn off to *Blue Sky* hostel and the junction with Haihua Lu is home to Dadonghai's best-value and most varied selection of food – including Japanese, Italian and Muslim restaurants, a couple of Western-style cafés and a string of small seafood canteens which spill out onto the street at night. Don't eat anywhere – especially cheaper spots – without getting solid confirmation of **prices**, or you could end up paying ¥30 for a bowl of noodles.

As far as **nightlife** is concerned, KTV's and Chinese interpretations of Western nightclubs abound, although smaller, more authentic Western bars, such as *Rainbow*, are slowly appearing.

Restaurants

Beachfront Seafood Just above the beach near the *South China* hotel, Dadonghai. A surprisingly romantic place to eat in the evening: select fish, crabs, lobster, prawns and other seafood from the live tanks and say how you want it cooked, order a couple of beers, and kick back at outdoor tables under the coconut trees. A *jin* of prawns is about ¥40.

Chatterbox Café On the ground floor of the Summer Mall on the opposite side of the highway to *Dongjiao Yelin*, Dadonghai. Tasty, if pricey, Asian and Western food in refined, modern surroundings. The square in the middle of the mall is home to a varied but overpriced open-air food court with cuisine from across China.

Dongbei Wang On the highway, Dadonghai. Lively, enjoyable Manchurian restaurant, with a menu illustrated with photos. Portions are huge and the service good. The fried whole fish with pine nuts is a treat, as are cold beef shreds with aniseed, and a stir-fried mix of peas, pine nuts and corn kernels. ¥60 will feed two.

Dongjiao Yelin Seafood Yayu Lu, Dadonghai. A warehouse of a restaurant, offering a glut of seafood and Hainanese dishes in an opulent setting. Expensive.

Suijingguong Haijing At the eastern end of the bay, Dadonghai. One of several waterfront restaurants predominantly catering to sunset groups, with good views and reasonably priced food. Good seafood and Hainan specialities such as sweet coconut rice.

Bars

Rainbow Opposite the *City Hotel* on Yayu Lu, Dadonghai. *Rainbow* would not be out of place in the bar districts of Shanghai or Beijing. Big screen sports, pool, table football and darts are all on offer alongside decent quality, if marginally too expensive, drinks and food.

Sky Bar Haiyuan Lu, Dadonghai. Inexplicably popular bar/nightclub home to banging Euro-techno and provocatively dressed, shape-throwing Russians.

Listings

Airlines Most hotels have airline agents on hand. The Phoenix airport booking office is at the junction of Gangmen Lu and Jiefang Lu, Sanya (Mon–Sat 9am–noon & 1.30–5pm; ⓣ0898/88278221 or 88277409). There's also a major Hainan Air booking office beside the bus station (ⓣ0898/88267988, ⓕ88252168).

Banks and exchange The main Bank of China, on Jiefang Lu in Sanya (Mon–Fri 9am–5pm), is excruciatingly understaffed and slow. There's another branch opposite the bus station (same hours) as well as a Dadonghai branch (same hours), but it has been known to refuse to cash traveller's cheques.

Internet access There's an Internet café on the third floor of the Haitian bookstore, near the Bank of China on Jiefang Lu, Sanya, and a few more west of the post office on Xinjiang Lu. In Dadonghai, the hostels have Internet access, as does Ultra Speed net café near the *Chuanya*.

Mail There are post offices on Xinjiang Lu, Sanya, and on the highway at Dadonghai (daily 7.30am–6pm).

Scuba diving Low visibility and maximum depths between 10m and 30m don't make Hainan the most exciting location for this, but it can be good fun and there's always the novelty of having dived in China. The three areas are at Yalong Bay, east of Sanya (best for its moderate coral growth, and a variety of fish and lobster); Tianya Haijiao, over to the west (good for molluscs, but extremely shallow); and the coral islands, also west (these are the deepest sites). Staff are NAUI/PADI qualified, hire gear is of reasonable quality, and you'll be expected to flash a C-card or make do with an introductory "resort" dive (¥260). Two shore dives cost ¥410, two boat dives ¥610, or a single dive at Yalong Bay will set you back ¥660.

Bookings can be made through virtually any hotel, but touts who are more amenable to bargaining often patrol the beachfront at Dadonghai. Prices at Yalong will typically be 50–100 percent more than at Dadonghai for what will very likely be a similar, if not identical, service.

Shopping Sanya is a good place to pick up pearls, white, pink, yellow or black. The best buys are from local hawkers on Dadonghai beach, who sell strings of "rejects" for ¥40 or less with hard bargaining. Most of these pearls are perfectly genuine, just not of good enough colour, shape or size for commercial jewellery. If in doubt, scratch the surface – flaking indicates a thinly coated plastic bead.

Travel agents Any of the hotels or hostels, even those without their own travel desks, will arrange scuba diving, climbing, coral island or fishing trips and, if not able to actually book air tickets themselves, will be more than happy to point you in the direction of one of the many travel agencies in the town that can.

Around Sanya

For a very Chinese tourist experience, any westbound bus from Sanya, or tourist bus #101 from the roundabout at the base of the Luhuitou Peninsula at Dadonghai, can cart you 20km out of the city to **Tianya Haijiao** (¥60), a long beach strewn with curiously shaped boulders, whose name roughly translates as the "ends of the earth". This isn't as fanciful as it sounds, as for Hainan's scholarly political exiles this was just about as far as you could possibly be from life's pinnacle at the imperial court. The modern world has unfortunately descended very heavily on the area, however, and a new township with expensive accommodation and restaurants, ever-escalating entry fees to the beach itself and overly persistent hawkers makes for an irritating experience. Chinese come in their thousands to have their photographs taken next to rocks inscribed with big red characters marking them as the "Sweetheart Stones", or "Limit of the Sky, Edge of the Sea". An overpriced and overexploited attraction, if nothing else Tianya Haijiao provides a wonderful opportunity for people-watching.

Another 15km west, beyond a luxurious golf course, is **YAZHOU**, formerly one of Hainan's biggest towns but now more of a bottleneck for through traffic. It's chiefly known as the place where the thirteenth-century weaver **Huang Daopo** fled from her native Shanghai to escape an arranged marriage. After forty years living with the coastal Li, she returned to northern China in 1295 and introduced

The South China Sea islands

Chinese maps of China always show a looped extension of the southern borders reaching 1500km down through the South China Sea to within spitting distance of Borneo, enclosing a host of reefs and minute islands. These sit over what might be major **oil and gas reserves**, and are consequently claimed by every nation in the region – China, Malaysia, the Philippines, Taiwan and Vietnam have all put in their bids, based on historical or geographic associations. Occupied by Japan during the 1940s but unclaimed after World War II, the **Spratly and Paracel islands** are perhaps the most contentious groups. Vietnam and China both declared ownership of the Paracels in the 1970s, coming to blows in 1988 when the Chinese navy sank two Vietnamese gunboats. Then the Philippines stepped in in 1995, destroying Chinese territorial markers erected over the most westerly reefs in the Spratly group and capturing a nearby Chinese trawler. Continuing minor brawls encouraged the nations of the region – including China – to hammer out a landmark agreement in November 2002, which basically allows access for all, while territorial disputes are settled one by one. This is likely to be a relief to companies such as the US conglomerate Exxon, who – despite the fact that guaranteed oil reserves have yet to be found – are already investing in the region their superior textile techniques to the mainland. Get off the bus when you see the reconstructed **Ming city gate**, and walk through it to a tiny **temple museum**, which includes traditional Li clothing and a **Hui** headstone and mosque oil lamp. The Hui have been on Hainan for centuries – some say they were originally Song-dynasty refugees from Vietnam, others that they're a relict of the old Maritime Silk Road – and the countryside hereabouts is peppered with their distinctive cylindrical graves. Walk back onto the main road and continue 1km or so west out of town, and you'll find a 400-year-old, seven-storey brick **pagoda** leaning at a rakish angle next to a school – one of the few genuinely old structures on the island. The last direct transport back to Sanya leaves in the late afternoon.

Nantian and Nanshan

Two popular day-trips from Sanya are to the hot spring resorts of **Nantian**, an hour northeast of the city, and **Nanshan**, a spectacularly upmarket Buddhist retreat 20km further along the coast beyond the Ends of the Earth. **NANTIAN**, a wholly secular affair, consists of a complex of pools sourced from natural hot springs and includes play pools with slides as well as more secluded hot tubs and a pool filled with kissing fish who provide a natural exfoliation service; happily, and ticklishly, nibbling away at any dead skin they can find. Most hotels in Dadonghai sell discounted tickets for Nantian (¥128) with a return shuttle bus from the Summer Mall included in the price. Male bathers should be warned that on the somewhat dubious grounds of hygiene they will be required to don a figure-hugging Chinese-style swimming costume before being allowed into the pools. Buying a pair of the lycra wonders will set you back around ¥20 at Dadonghai, or ¥60 at Nantian itself. For women a standard bikini is acceptably clean.

A similar distance in the opposite direction, **NANSHAN** is a Buddhist retreat-cum-luxury spa with a ¥150 entry fee. Centring on a 108m-high statue of Buddha rising up out of the sea, Nanshan also has a temple complex, hot springs, immaculate gardens, a highly regarded vegetarian restaurant and luxury accommodation (❾). The slightly overwhelming atmosphere of commerce detracts slightly from the experience of what is undoubtedly, a stunning location. To get there catch bus #102 or the tourist double-decker from Sanya to the Ends of the Earth, from where a taxi (¥30) is the only way to cover the remaining 20km to Nanshan itself.

West to Jianfeng and Dongfang

There are departures from Sanya's long-distance bus station for the 165-kilometre run to the western port of **Dongfang**, up the coast beyond Yazhou, or you could also travel there in stages by minibus. This side of the island is incredibly poor and undeveloped compared with the east, partly because it's too far remote to benefit from tourism, but also because the main sources of income here are various forms of **mining**, an industry that sees little financial returns for local communities.

The real reason to head out this way is to spend a day at **Jianfeng Ling Forest Reserve**, a small indication of what the whole of southwestern Hainan looked like before the 1960s. Head first for **JIANFENG** township, which lies at the base of the distinctively peaked Jianfeng range some 10km east of the coastal road, about 115km from Sanya. Dongfang-bound transport can drop you at the turning, from where you can walk or wait for the next passing vehicle to pick you up. A dusty little hollow where pigs and dogs roam the streets between the market, Jianfeng has two teahouses and around a hundred homes. The sole **guesthouse** (❸) is a friendly place with a fine **restaurant** (try the chicken with locally grown cashew nuts), functioning plumbing and electric power.

The reserve itself is in the mountains 18km beyond Jianfeng, reached daily by a single scheduled minibus (¥10), although it's possible to hire one (¥70 up, ¥50 down). **Jianfeng Ling** – the mountain range itself – was aggressively logged until 1992, when a UNESCO survey found 400 types of butterfly and 1700 plant species up here and persuaded the Chinese government to establish the reserve, leaving a sharp-edged forested crown above bare lowland slopes. Though commercial timber stands have since been planted, locals have been left without a livelihood for the time being, a problem slightly eased by aid packages from the Asian Development Bank. The dirt road to the summit ends on the forest's edge at a group of stores, a small restaurant, a botanical research station, and a little-frequented **hotel** (④), whose staff will be most surprised to see you. A tiled gateway marks the reserve entrance about 100m back up the road, from where partially paved paths lead off uphill for an hour-long circuit walk taking in some massive trees, vines, orchids, ferns, birds, butterflies and beautiful views from the 1056-metre ridge. After dark, if you're armed with a torch and some caution, it's a good place to look for small mammals and reptiles.

Tongshi and the highlands

Occupying the island's central core, **Hainan's highlands** get scant attention from visitors, despite evidence of long association with **Li and Miao** peoples. Just 100km north of Sanya and lying on the main inland route between Haikou and Sanya, **Tongshi**'s quiet pace and large concentration of Li make it the favoured place to start delving into the region.

Tongshi and around

Lacking heavy traffic or industry, pocket-sized **TONGSHI** (Tongza, also known as **Wuzhi Shan Shi**), two hours north of Sanya, is a pleasantly unpolluted spot to hang out for a day or two, surrounded by pretty countryside. Energetic hikers might want to go scrambling up nearby **Qizhi Shan** and **Wuzhi Shan**, whose summits are both steeped in local lore. Before 1987, Tongshi was also capital of Hainan's autonomous Li government, until it blew a billion-yuan road grant by importing luxury goods from Hong Kong and Vietnam, and building the literally palatial offices, now **Qiongzhou University**, on the hill above town. When

Tongshi and the highlands

Tongshi (Wuzhi Shan Shi)	通什(五指山市)	*tōngshì (wǔzhǐ shān shì)*
Jinyuan Dajiudian	金源大酒店	*jīnyuán dàjiǔdiàn*
Nationality Museum	民族博物馆	*mínzú bówùguǎn*
Qiongzhou University	琼州大学	*qióngzhōu dàxué*
Shang Cheng Chazhuang	山城茶庄	*shānchéng cházhuāng*
Tongshi Guolü Binguan	通什国旅宾馆	*tōngshíguólǚ bīnguǎn*
Tongza Resort Hotel	通什旅游山庄	*tōngshí lǚyóu shānzhuāng*
Baisha	白沙	*báishā*
Baoting	保亭	*bǎotíng*
Qizhi Shan	七指山	*qīzhǐ shān*
Qiongzhong	琼中	*qióngzhōng*
Wuzhi Shan	五指山	*wǔzhǐ shān*
Wuzhi Shan Binguan	五指山宾馆	*wǔzhǐ shān bīnguǎn*

Beijing caught up with what was going on, they sacked the government and put the region under their direct control, a move that, while entirely justified, was greatly resented by the Li.

Reached via a street running uphill just beyond the bus station, and then past the ostentatious green-tiled **university**, the **Nationality Museum** (daily 8am–5.30pm; ¥10) affords views across town to the aptly named **Nipple Mountain**, 5km away to the west, while the collection itself is excellent. **Historical exhibits** include prehistoric stone tools and a bronze drum decorated with sun and frog motifs, similar to those associated with Guangxi's Zhuang; Ming manuscripts about island life; Qing wine vessels with octopus and frog mouldings; and details of the various modern conflicts culminating in the last pocket of Guomindang resistance being overcome in 1950. Artefacts and photos illustrate Hainan's **cultural heritage**, too – Li looms and textiles, traditional weapons and housing, speckled pottery from Dongfang, and pictures of major festivals. Back across the river, you can tour the town centre's handful of streets and modern concrete-and-tile buildings in around thirty minutes. **Henan Lu** runs west along the waterfront from the bridge; two blocks back, Tongshi's **public square** is a sociable place to hang out after dark and meet people, full of tables serviced by drink and snack vendors, crowds watching open-air table-tennis tournaments and queuing for the cinema. Nearby, on

Li and Miao

Hainan's million-strong **Li** population take their name from the big topknot (*li*) which men once wore. Archeological finds and traditions shared with other southwestern Chinese peoples point to their arriving on Hainan from Guangxi about 200 BC, when they occupied the coast and displaced the aboriginal inhabitants. Driven inland themselves by later Han arrivals, the Li finally settled Hainan's central highlands (though a few remained on the coast) and spent the next two thousand years as rice farmers and hunters, living in villages with distinctive tunnel-shaped houses, evolving their own shamanistic religion, and using poisoned arrows to bring down game. **Li women** have long been known for their **weaving** skills, and the fact that, until very recently, many had their faces heavily **tattooed** with geometric patterns – apparently to make them undesirable to raiding parties of slavers from the coast, or rival **clans**. The latter form five major groups – Ha, Qi, Yun, Meifu and Cai – and they have never coexisted very well, quarrelling to this day over territorial boundaries and only really united in their dislike of external rulers.

Though actively supporting Communist guerrillas against the Japanese, the Li have no great affection for the Han as a whole, and there were fourteen major rebellions against their presence on the island during the Qing era alone. Superficially assimilated into modern China, the Li would probably revolt again if they felt they could get away with it. They are, however, pretty friendly towards outside visitors, and though traditional life has all but vanished over the last half-century, there are still a few special events to watch out for. Best is the **San Yue San festival** (held on the third day of the third lunar month), the most auspicious time of the year in which to choose a partner, while in more remote corners of the highlands, **funerals** are traditionally celebrated with gunfire and three days of hard drinking by male participants.

Touted as Hainan's second "native minority" by the tourist literature, the **Miao** are in fact comparatively recent arrivals, forcibly recruited from Guizhou province as **mercenaries** to put down a Li uprising during the Ming dynasty. When the money ran out, the Miao stopped fighting and settled in the western highlands, where today they form a fifty-thousand-strong community. Though they apparently now intermarry with the Li, the US adventurer, Leonard Clark, who traversed the highlands in 1937, reported them as living apart in the remotest of valleys (for more on the Miao, see p.761).

Jiefang Lu, there's a chance to see dark-dressed Miao and the occasional elder Li women with tattoos at the daily **market**, whose wares include sweet, milky-white spirit sold in plastic jerrycans, deer and dog meat, and also **rat**, split open like a French roll and grilled.

You can see more of the Li by catching a minibus 2km south to the tacky displays at **Fanmao Mountain Fortress Village**, but there's more to be said for just heading off into the countryside on foot. From the north side of the bridge, follow Hebei Xi Lu west along the river for 150m to a grossly patronizing **statue** of grinning Li, Miao and Han characters standing arm in arm. Take the road uphill from here past the *Tongzha Luyou Shanzhuang* and keep going along the dusty road as long as you want to, through vivid green fields and increasingly poor villages, ultimately built of mud and straw and surrounded by split bamboo pickets to keep livestock in. Among these you'll see more substantial barns with traditional tunnel shapes and carved wooden doors.

Practicalities

Set at the base of low hills, Tongshi's tiny centre sits on the southern bank of a horseshoe bend in the generally unimpressive **Nansheng River**. The main road comes up from the coast as **Haiyu Lu**, skirts the centre, crosses over the river and passes the **post office**, turns sharply left past the **bus station**, and bends off north through the island towards Qiongzhong and Haikou. Buses from the station head to Baoting, Baisha, Qiongzhong, Haikou and Sanya, as well as a couple of daily services to Wuzhi Shan. There are a couple of **Internet cafés** around the bus station, but there's no **Bank of China** in town.

Tongshi's very reasonable **accommodation** prices are a relief after Sanya. Directly opposite the bus station's main door, *Jinyuan Dajiudian* has clean, tiled rooms (Ⓣ0899/86622942; ❷), as does the slightly nicer *Tongshi Guolü Binguan* (Ⓣ0899/86633158; ❸), which can be reached by turning left out of the bus station and following the road round to the right as it turns towards the river. Easily the town's best accommodation is the bargainable *Tongza Resort Hotel* (Ⓣ0898/86623188, Ⓕ86622201; ❻) on the northeastern edge of town, whose characterful rooms have balconies looking out to the hills, and there's a swimming pool to cool down in after a hike.

Teahouses near the market fill with sociable crowds on most mornings, which is also a good time to eat *dim sum* in *Shan Cheng Chazhuang* on Jiefang Lu – an extraordinary institution whose men's-club atmosphere is compounded by a card-gaming hall out the back; *hainan gau* here are sticky rice packets with coconut and banana. The *Tongza Resort Hotel* has a reasonable **restaurant** with an English menu of sorts, and there are plenty of canteens around the bus station.

Wuzhi Shan and Qizhi Shan

Several Li myths explain the formation of **Wuzhi Shan** (Five-Finger Mountain), whose 1867-metre summit rises 30km northeast of Tongshi at Hainan's apex. In one tale, the mountain's five peaks are the fossilized fingers of a dying clan chieftain, while another holds that they represent the Li's five most powerful gods. Either way, Wuzhi Shan was once a holy site drawing thousands of people to animist festivals. Though the mountain is rarely a place of pilgrimage for the Li today, more remote villages in this part of Hainan maintain the old religion, raising archways over their gates, which are occasionally embellished with bull or chicken heads. It's still possible to climb the mountain – take a bus from Tongshi to **Wuzhi Shan township**, then local transport to the *Wuzhi Shan Binguan* (Ⓣ0898/86622981; ❸). From here it's a steep and slippery three-hour scramble to the peak, initially through jungly scrub, then pine forests. Although it's often clouded over, the summit offers further contorted pines, begonias and views.

Qizhi Shan (Seven-Finger Mountain), representing seven lesser Li immortals being vanquished by Wuzhi's five, lies about 40km by road southeast of Tongshi via **Baoting** (Baocheng). A sleepy place, Baoting is another good place from which to wander aimlessly off into the countryside, and you can get to the base of the mountain by catching available transport 10km east to **Shiling**, and thence 11km north to **Ba Cun**. The climb is said to be shorter than that at Wuzhi Shan, but much harder.

Travel details

Trains

Chaozhou to: Guangzhou (2 daily; 6hr 30min–8hr); Huizhou (3 daily; 4hr 30min–6hr 30min); Meizhou (3 daily; 2hr); Shantou (5 daily; 30min).
Fuzhou to: Beijing (1 daily; 35hr); Longyan (1 daily; 10hr 30min); Meizhou (1 daily; 13hr 30min); Nanchang (6 daily; 11hr 30min–13hr 30min); Shanghai (2 daily; 19hr); Shenzhen (1 daily; 20hr 30min); Wuyi Shan (4 daily; 5hr 30min–6hr); Yongding (1 daily; 12hr).
Guangzhou to: Beijing (2 daily; 24hr); Changsha (38 daily; 7–10hr 30min); Chaozhou (2 daily; 8hr); Chengdu (1 daily; 40hr 30min); Foshan (10 daily; 45min); Ganzhou (1 daily; 12hr); Guilin (2 daily; 11hr); Guiyang (6 daily; 21–27hr); Haikou (1 daily; 11hr); Huizhou (3 daily; 2hr); Kowloon (3 daily; 2hr); Kunming (1 daily; 23hr); Meizhou (2 daily; 6hr); Nanchang (1 daily; 12hr); Nanning (2 daily; 13hr 30min); Shanghai (2 daily; 23hr); Shantou (1 daily; 7hr 30min–9hr); Shaoguan (56 daily; 2–4hr); Shenzhen (2 hourly; 1–2hr 30min); Wuhan (25 daily; 10hr 30min–16hr 30min); Xiamen (1 daily; 12hr); Xian (1 daily; 24hr); Zhaoqing (4 daily; 2hr); Zhanjiang (1 daily; 8hr).
Haikou to: Guangzhou (1 daily; 12hr).
Huizhou to: Chaozhou (3 daily; 4hr 30min–6hr 30min); Guangzhou (10 daily; 2–3hr); Meizhou (6 daily; 4hr 30min); Nanchang (13 daily; 8hr 30min–12hr 30min); Shantou (3 daily; 5–7hr); Wuhan (1 daily; 14hr 30min).
Meizhou to: Chaozhou (3 daily; 2hr); Fuzhou (1 daily; 14hr); Guangzhou (3 daily; 6hr 30min); Huizhou (6 daily; 4hr 30min); Longyan (3 daily; 3hr); Shantou (3 daily; 3hr); Yongding (1 daily; 3hr).
Quanzhou to: Wuyi Shan (1 daily; 12hr).
Shantou to: Chaozhou (5 daily; 30min); Guangzhou (2 daily; 7–8hr 30min); Huizhou (3 daily; 5–7hr); Meizhou (3 daily; 2hr 30min).
Shaoguan to: Changsha (34 daily; 5–7hr 30min); Guangzhou (55 daily; 2–4hr); Hengyang (43 daily; 3hr 30min–5hr).
Shenzhen to: Changsha (7 daily; 9–11hr 30min); Fuzhou (1 daily; 20hr); Ganzhou (3 daily; 9hr); Guangzhou (71 daily; 50min–3hr); Shantou (1 daily; 8hr 30min); Shaoguan (9 daily; 4–5hr 30min); Wuhan (4 daily; 12hr 30min–16hr).
Wuyi Shan to: Fuzhou (5 daily; 6hr); Quanzhou (1 daily; 12hr); Shanghai (4 daily; 12hr); Xiamen (3 daily; 13–16hr).
Xiamen to: Guangzhou (2 daily; 14hr 30min); Nanchang (4 daily; 17hr); Nanjing (1 daily; 31hr); Shanghai (1 daily; 26hr 30min); Wuyi Shan (3 daily; 13–16hr); Xi'an (1 daily; 38hr).
Zhaoqing to: Guangzhou (20 daily; 2hr); Hong Kong (1 daily; 4hr); Shenzhen (10 daily; 3hr 30min).

Buses

Generally, there are countless services between the places listed below (see text for exceptions), though smaller towns may cease to see any traffic after 8pm.
Chaozhou to: Guangzhou (6hr); Huizhou (4hr); Meizhou (3hr); Shantou (1hr); Shenzhen (5hr); Xiamen (5hr 30min).
Fuzhou to: Guangzhou (12hr); Longyan (7hr); Ningbo (9hr); Quanzhou (2hr 30min); Shantou (7hr); Shenzhen (12hr); Wenzhou (7hr); Wuyi Shan (7hr); Xiamen (4hr).
Guangzhou to: Beihai (24hr); Changsha (20hr); Chaozhou (7–8hr); Dongguan (1hr); Foshan (1hr); Fuzhou (12hr); Ganzhou (11hr); Guilin (13hr); Haikou (12hr); Huizhou (2hr); Jiangmen (2hr); Kowloon (3hr); Meizhou (12hr); Nancun (1hr); Nanning (30hr); Panyu (1hr); Qingyuan (1hr); Shantou (6hr); Shaoguan (4hr); Shenzhen (3hr); Shunde (1hr 30min); Xiamen (9hr); Zhangjiang (5hr); Zhaoqing (2hr); Zhuhai (3hr).
Haikou to: Chongqing (28hr); Guangzhou (12hr); Guilin (12hr); Lingshui (3hr); Qionghai (2hr 30min); Sanya (3–5hr); Shenzhen (15hr); Tongshi (4hr); Wanning (3hr); Wenchang (1hr); Zhanjiang (5hr).
Huizhou to: Chaozhou (4hr); Guangzhou (2hr); Meizhou (5hr 30min); Shantou (4hr); Shenzhen (2hr).

Meizhou to: Chaozhou (3hr); Dapu (2hr); Guangzhou (12hr); Huizhou (5hr 30min); Longyan (4hr); Shaoguan (12hr); Shantou (4hr); Shenzhen (10hr); Xiamen (9hr); Yongding (4hr).
Quanzhou to: Fuzhou (2hr 30min); Guangzhou (10hr); Hangzhou (11hr); Longyan (5hr); Ningbo (11hr); Shenzen (10hr); Xiamen (1hr 30min).
Qingyuan to: Foshan (2hr); Guangzhou (1hr); Shaoguan (3hr); Shenzen (2hr 30min); Zhaoqing (5hr).
Sanya to: Dongfang (3hr); Haikou (3–5hr); Lingshui (2hr); Qionghai (4hr 30min); Tongshi (2hr); Wanning (3hr); Wenchang (4hr); Yazhou (1hr).
Shantou to: Chaozhou (1hr); Fuzhou (7hr); Guangzhou (6hr); Huizhou (4hr); Meizhou (4hr); Shenzhen (6hr); Xiamen (5hr).
Shaoguan to: Chaozhou (12hr); Ganzhou (4hr); Guangzhou (4hr); Huizhou (4hr); Lianshan (5hr); Meizhou (12hr); Pingshi (4hr); Qingyuan (3hr).
Shenzhen to: Chaozhou (7hr); Dongguan (2hr); Fuzhou (12hr); Guangzhou (3hr); Haikou (15hr); Hong Kong (2hr); Huizhou (2hr); Meizhou (10hr); Shantou (6hr); Zhanjiang (7hr).
Xiamen to: Chaozhou (5hr 30min); Fuzhou (4hr); Guangzhou (9hr); Longyan (5hr); Meizhou (9hr); Quanzhou (1hr 30min); Shantou (5hr 30min); Shenzhen (9hr); Wenzhou (18hr); Yongding (5hr).
Yongding to: Longyan (1hr); Meizhou (4hr); Xiamen (5hr); Zhiling (1hr).
Zhanjiang to: Guangzhou (5hr); Hai'an (3hr); Haikou (5hr); Shenzhen (7hr); Zhaoqing (7hr).
Zhaoqing to: Guangzhou (2hr); Guilin (10hr); Qingyuan (5hr); Yangshuo (8hr 30min); Zhanjiang (7hr).
Zhuhai to: Cuiheng (1hr); Foshan (3hr); Fuzhou (15hr); Guangzhou (3hr); Guilin (13hr); Haikou (15hr); Jiangmen (2hr); Shunde (2hr 30min); Zhongshan (1hr).

Ferries

Guangzhou to: Hong Kong (2 daily; 2hr 30min).
Hai'an to: Haikou (10 daily; 1hr 30min).
Haikou to: Beihai (3 daily; 11hr); Hai'an (10 daily; 1hr 30min); Hong Kong (2 weekly; 25hr).
Shenzhen to: Hong Kong (20 daily; 1hr); Macau (daily; 2hr); Zhuhai (20 daily; 1hr).
Xiamen to: Hong Kong (1 weekly; 18hr).
Zhaoqing to: Hong Kong (1 daily; 4hr).
Zhuhai to: Hong Kong (10 daily; 1hr); Macau (5 daily; 20min); Shenzhen (20 daily; 1hr).

Flights

Besides the domestic flights listed here, Guangzhou is linked by regular services to major Southeast Asian cities and increasingly more destinations worldwide.

Fuzhou to: Beijing (6 daily; 2hr 30min); Guangzhou (1 daily; 1hr 30min); Haikou (6 weekly; 2hr); Hong Kong (3 daily; 1hr 30min); Shanghai (7 daily; 1hr 10min); Shenzhen (2 daily; 1hr 20min); Wuyi Shan (5 weekly; 30min); Xiamen (1 daily; 30min).
Guangzhou to: Beihai (2 daily; 1hr 20min); Beijing (20 daily; 2hr 45min); Changsha (3 daily; 1hr); Chengdu (10 daily; 2hr); Chongqing (10 daily; 1hr 35min); Dalian (2 daily; 3hr); Fuzhou (1 daily; 1hr 30min); Guilin (4 daily; 1hr); Guiyang (5–6 daily; 1hr 15min); Haikou (7–10 daily; 1hr); Hangzhou (14 daily; 1hr 45min); Harbin (2 daily; 4hr 15min); Hefei (3 daily; 1hr 45min–3hr); Hohhot (3 weekly; 3hr 10min); Hong Kong (7 daily; 40min–1hr); Kunming (6 daily; 2hr); Lanzhou (2 daily; 3hr); Meizhou (1 daily; 50min); Nanchang (3 daily; 1hr); Nanjing (6 daily; 2hr); Nanning (4–5 daily; 1hr 20min); Qingdao (4 daily; 2hr 40min–3hr 20min); Sanya (10 daily; 1hr 20min); Shanghai (25 daily; 2hr); Shantou (2–4 daily; 40min); Tianjin (2 daily; 2hr 30min); Ürümqi (3 weekly; 5hr); Wuhan (5 daily; 1hr 30min); Xiamen (4 daily; 1hr); Xi'an (6 daily; 2hr 30min); Yichang (daily; 1hr 45min); Zhengzhou (4 daily; 2hr).
Haikou to: Beijing (6 daily; 3hr 30min); Beihai (1 daily; 40min); Changsha (1–2 daily; 1hr 40min); Chengdu (1 daily; 2hr); Guangzhou (9 daily; 1hr); Guilin (1 daily; 1hr 20min); Hong Kong (1 daily; 1hr); Kunming (2 daily; 1hr 40min); Nanjing (1 daily; 2hr); Shanghai (5 daily; 2hr 20min); Shenzhen (11 daily; 1hr); Wuhan (2–3 daily; 3hr 20min); Xiamen (1–2 daily; 1hr 30min); Xi'an (3 daily; 3hr–3hr 30min); Zhanjiang (2 daily; 30min); Zhuhai (1–2 daily; 1hr).
Sanya to: Beijing (5 daily; 3hr 30min); Guangzhou (10 daily; 1hr 10min); Hong Kong (6 weekly; 1hr 30min); Shanghai (4–5 daily; 2hr 30min–4hr); Shenzhen (3–4 daily; 1hr 15min).
Shenzhen to: Beihai (1daily; 1hr); Beijing (17–19 daily; 3hr); Changsha (5 daily; 1hr); Chengdu (9 daily; 2hr 15min); Chongqing (10 daily; 2hr 35min); Fuzhou (1–2 daily; 1hr); Guilin (3 daily; 1hr); Guiyang (4 daily; 1hr 30min); Haikou (13 daily; 1hr); Hangzhou (8 daily; 1hr 50min); Harbin (1 daily; 4hr); Hefei (2 daily; 2hr); Kunming (3–4 daily; 2hr); Nanchang (1–2 daily; 1hr); Nanjing (5 daily; 2hr); Sanya (3–4 daily; 1hr 15min); Shanghai (many daily; 2hr); Wuhan (5 daily; 1hr 30min); Xiamen (2 daily; 1hr); Xi'an (5 daily; 2hr 20min).
Wuyi Shan to: Fuzhou (5 weekly; 30min), Shanghai (5 weekly; 1hr); Xiamen (5 weekly; 40min).
Xiamen to: Beijing (4–5 daily; 2hr 30min); Fuzhou (1 daily; 30 min); Guangzhou (4 daily; 1hr); Hefei (1 daily; 1hr 35min); Hong Kong (2–3 daily; 1hr); Macau (1–2 daily; 1hr 20min); Shanghai (12–13 daily; 1hr 30min); Shenzhen (3–4 daily; 1hr 10min); Wuyi Shan (4 weekly; 40min).

CHAPTER 9 **Highlights**

* **Hong Kong Island trams** The best way to travel the north shore of Hong Kong Island is by rattling double-decker tram. Ride from North Point to Western, upstairs and at night for the full effect. See p.653

* **Star Ferry** The crossing from Tsim Sha Tsui to Hong Kong Island is the cheapest harbour tour on earth – and one of the most spectacular. See p.655

* **Harbour view from The Peak** At dusk, watch the city's dazzling lights brighten across Hong Kong, the harbour and Kowloon. See p.665

* **Sai Kung Peninsula** Get away from the crowds and concrete, amidst beautiful seascapes, beaches and wild countryside in this often overlooked corner of Hong Kong. See p.680

* **Ngong Ping 360** Amazing vistas of Lantau's coast, mountains and Big Buddha on this cable-car ride from Tung Chung to Po Lin Monastery. See p.683

* **Dim sum** Book in advance for an authentic *dim sum* lunch alongside enthusiastic families – try the chicken's feet and barbecue pork buns. See p.685

* **Old Macau** Hunt for bargain rosewood furniture and traditional clothing in central Macau's cobbled streets. See p.701

* **Coffee, tarts and port** Thanks to Macau's Portuguese heritage, most cafés and restaurants serve ink-black coffee, delicious custard tarts and port wine – almost unknown elsewhere in China. See p.708

▲The view from The Peak

Hong Kong and Macau

The handover of **Asia's last two European colonies**, Hong Kong in 1997 and Macau in 1999, opened new eras for both places. While evidence of colonial times remains obvious, the essentially Chinese heritage underlying everything is increasingly apparent, as these two **SAR**s, or "Special Administrative Regions of China", seek to establish new identities for themselves. After all, Hong Kong and Macau's population is 97 percent **Chinese**, the dominant language is Cantonese, and there have always been close ties – if often tinged with suspicion – with the mainlanders just over the border.

It is hard to overstate the symbolic importance that the handovers had for the Chinese as a whole, in sealing the end of centuries of foreign domination with the return of the last pieces of occupied soil to the motherland. The people of Hong Kong and Macau also widely supported the transfer of power – if only to see how much leeway they could garner under the new administration. Both entities now find themselves in the unique position of being capitalist enclaves subject to the ultimate control of an unaccountable communist state, under the relatively liberal "**One Country, Two Systems**" policy coined by the late Chinese leader Deng Xiaoping.

First under colonial and now mainland Chinese rule, Hong Kong and Macau's citizens have never had a say in their futures, so they have concentrated their efforts on other things – notably, **making money**. With its emphasis on economics and consumerism, **Hong Kong** offers the greatest variety and concentration of **shops and shopping** on earth, along with a colossal range of **cuisines**, and vistas of sea and island, green mountains and futuristic cityscapes. The excellent **infrastructure**, including the efficient public transit system, the helpful tourist offices and all the other facilities of a genuinely international city make this an extremely soft entry into the Chinese world.

While Hong Kong is a place to do business, **Macau** has leapt ahead in recent years as a Las Vegas of the East, a haven for **gambling** and other sins. The marks of its colonial past are more immediately obvious than they are in Hong Kong, in its Mediterranean-style architecture, cheap Portuguese wine, Macanese cooking, and comparatively mellow, faintly Latin lifestyle.

Visitors will spend more **money** here than elsewhere in China, though not necessarily as much as you might expect, considering the cheap public transport

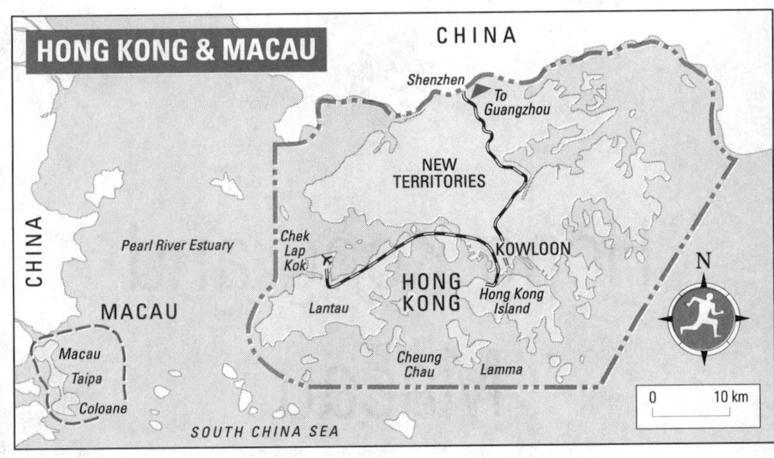

and higher quality of service compared to the mainland. Travellers on a tight **budget** who stay in dormitory accommodation can just about get by on HK$300 a day, though at the other end of the market in hotels, restaurants and shops, prices quickly rise to international levels.

Hong Kong

In its multifaceted role as one of the key economies of the Pacific Rim, a repository of traditional Chinese culture, and an experiment in governance with which the mainland authorities hope to win over a recalcitrant Taiwan, **HONG KONG** is East Asia's most extraordinary city. The territory's per capita GNP has now overtaken that of Britain, its former imperial master, and the **Hong Kong Special Administrative Region** (**HK SAR**) is currently the largest source of external investment in the People's Republic of China. Yet Hong Kong's famous addiction to money and brand names tends to mask the fact that most people work long hours and live in crowded, tiny apartments in one of the most densely populated cities on earth. On the other hand, it's hard not to enjoy the sheer energy of its street- and commercial life, and the population of seven million is sophisticated and well informed compared to their mainland cousins, the result of a relatively free press. The urban panorama of sky-scrapered Hong Kong Island, seen across the harbour from Kowloon, is stunning, and you'll find a surprising wealth of undeveloped rural areas within easy commuter range of the hectic centre and its perennial, massive engineering projects.

The Hong Kong SAR comprises an irregularly shaped peninsula abutting the Pearl River Delta to the west, and a number of offshore islands, which cover 1100 square kilometres in total. The bulk of this area, namely the north of the peninsula as well as most of the islands, forms the semi-rural **New Territories**, the land leased to Britain for 99 years in 1898. The southern part of the peninsula, known as **Kowloon**, and the island immediately south of here, **Hong Kong Island**, are the principal urban areas of Hong Kong. Though ceded to Britain in perpetuity, the British government in 1984 saw no alternative but to agree to hand back the entire territory as one piece, returning it to Chinese control from midnight of June 30, 1997.

Hong Kong Island's north shore offers not only traces of the **old colony** – from English place names to ancient, double-decker trams trundling along the shore – but also superb **modern cityscapes** of towering buildings teetering up impossible slopes, along with whole districts dedicated to selling Traditional Chinese Medicine and herbs. As a further contrast, the south of the island offers several decent **beaches**, a huge **amusement park**, and even **hiking** opportunities. North of the harbour, Kowloon – especially **Tsim Sha Tsui** – is the SAR's principal tourist trap, boasting a glut of accommodation, and shops offering an incredible variety of goods (not necessarily at reasonable prices, though). North of Tsim Sha Tsui, Kowloon stretches away into the New Territories, a varied area of **New Towns** and older villages, secluded beaches and undeveloped country parks. In addition, the **Outlying Islands** – particularly **Lamma** and **Lantau** – are well worth a visit for their seafood restaurants and further rural contrasts to the hubbub of downtown Hong Kong.

Some history

While the Chinese justifiably argue that Hong Kong was always Chinese territory, the development of the city only began with the **arrival of the British** in Guangzhou in the eighteenth century.

The Portuguese had already been based at Macau, on the other side of the Pearl River Delta, since the mid-sixteenth century, and as Britain's sea power grew, so its merchants began casting envious eyes over the Portuguese trade in tea and silk. The initial difficulty was to persuade the Chinese authorities that there was any reason to want to deal with them, but from the 1750s, British traders were allowed to set up their warehouses in Guangzhou, transactions being organized through a Guangzhou merchants' guild called the **Co Hong**.

However, the foreigners soon found that trade was one way only, and so started to offer **opium**, cheaply supplied by their Indian territories. An explosion of demand for the drug followed, despite edicts from Beijing banning the trade; Co Hong, which received commission on everything bought or sold, had no qualms about distributing opium to its fellow citizens. Before long the balance of trade had been reversed in favour of the British.

The scene for the **Opium Wars** was now set. Alarmed at the outflow of silver, the Chinese destroyed the opium stocks warehoused in Guangzhou in 1840. The British responded by sending gunboats to blockade Chinese ports and raid along the coast, forcing the Chinese government into signing the **Treaty of Nanking** (1842), which gave a small, thinly populated, offshore island – Hong Kong – to Britain. Following more gunboat diplomacy eighteen years later the **Treaty of Peking** granted Britain the Kowloon peninsula, too, and in 1898, Britain secured a 99-year lease on an additional one thousand square kilometres of land north of Kowloon, later known as the New Territories.

Originally a seedy merchants' colony, by 1907 Hong Kong had a large enough manufacturing base to voluntarily drop the drug trade. Up until World War II, the city prospered as turmoils in mainland China drove money and **refugees** south into the apparently safe confines of the British colony. This confidence proved misplaced in 1941 when **Japanese forces** seized Hong Kong along with the rest of eastern China, though after Japan's defeat in 1945, Britain swiftly reclaimed the colony, stifling putative attempts by the residents to garner some independence. As the mainland fell to the Communists in 1949, a new wave of refugees – many of the wealthier ones from Shanghai – swelled Hong Kong's population threefold to 2.5 million, causing a housing crisis that set in motion themes still current in the SAR: **land reclamation**, the need for efficient infrastructure, and a tendency to save space by building upwards.

The early **Communist era** saw Hong Kong leading a precarious existence. Had China wished, it could have rendered the existence of Hong Kong unviable by a naval blockade, by cutting off water supplies, by a military invasion – or by simply opening its border and inviting the Chinese masses to stream across in search of wealth. That it never wholeheartedly pursued any of these options, even at the height of the Cultural Revolution, was an indication of the huge **financial benefits** that Hong Kong's international trade links, direct investment and technology transfers brought – and still brings – to mainland China.

In the last twenty years of British rule, the spectre of **1997** loomed large. Negotiations on the future of the colony led in 1984 to the **Sino-British Joint Declaration**, paving the way for Britain to hand back sovereignty of the territory in return for Hong Kong maintaining its capitalist system for fifty years. However, it appeared to locals that Hong Kong's lack of democratic institutions – which had suited the British – would in future mean the Chinese could do what they liked. Fears grew that repression and the erosion of freedoms such as travel and speech would follow the handover. The constitutional framework provided by the **Basic Law** of 1988, in theory, answered some of those fears, illustrating how the "One Country, Two Systems" policy would work. But the next year's **crackdown in Tian'anmen Square** only seemed to confirm the most pessimistic views of what might happen following the handover, especially to members of Hong Kong's embryonic **democracy movement**. When **Chris Patten** arrived in 1992 to become the last governor, he cynically broadened the voting franchise for the **Legislative Council elections** (**Legco**) from around 200,000 to some 2.7 million people, infuriating Beijing and ensuring that the road to the handover would be a rough ride.

Post-1997

After the build-up, however, the **handover** was an anticlimax. The British sailed away on HMS *Britannia*, Beijing carried out its threat to disband the elected Legco and reduce the enfranchised population, and Tung Chee-hwa, a shipping billionaire, became the **first chief executive** of the Hong Kong SAR. But his highly unpopular tenure was doomed from the start: within days, the **Asian Financial Crisis** had begun, causing a recession and soaring unemployment as stock and property values crashed. Added to this were the recurrent outbreaks of **avian flu**, involving the huge slaughter of chickens amid fears that humans might also contract the potentially deadly virus. Meanwhile, Tung stood unopposed for a second term in 2002, despite his inability to propose or see through any effective policy, alter the public's perception of **increased government corruption**, or hinder a continuously sluggish economy – not helped by Shanghai's rising star as a place to do business. And the worst was yet to come. Previous fears of avian flu soon proved nothing next to the global panic wrought by southern China's **SARS outbreak** of 2003 – some 299 people died and Hong Kong's tourist industry collapsed. Tung still refused to step down, despite the fact that each June 4 (the

The Olympics in Hong Kong

Hong Kong is hosting the **Olympic equestrian events** between August 9 and August 20, 2008. Jumping and dressage will be held at Sha Tin Racecourse (p.677) and cross-country at Beas River near Fanling in the New Territories. For more information, see ⓦwww.beijing-2008.org.

anniversary of the Tian'anmen Square crackdown), about half a million people were turning out to **demonstrate** against him.

This public display of dissatisfaction annoyed the powers in Beijing, who wanted Hong Kong to showcase the benefits of the "One Country, Two Systems" approach to **Taiwan** – which, now that former colonial territories have been reclaimed, remains the last hurdle to China being reunited under one government. Having been publicly chastised by the Chinese leader Hu Jintao, Tung **stood down** in March 2005 to be replaced as chief executive by career civil servant **Donald Tsang**, who was re-elected for a second term in 2007. Despite being a product of the colonial administration (he was even knighted in 1997), Tsang has also promoted ties with the mainland post-handover, and is seen as a neutral character, capable of providing a period of stability and so regaining both investor and public confidence in Hong Kong in the face of the above setbacks.

Orientation, arrival and information

Orientation for new arrivals in the main urban areas is relatively easy: if you are "**Hong Kong-side**" – on the north shore of Hong Kong Island – **Victoria Harbour** lies to your north, while to your south the land slopes upwards steeply to **The Peak**. The heart of this built-up area on Hong Kong Island is known, rather mundanely, as **Central**. North across the harbour you are "**Kowloon-side**", and here all you really need to recognize is the colossal north–south artery, **Nathan Road**, full of shops and budget hotels, that leads down to the harbour, and to the view south over Hong Kong Island. Two more useful points for orientation on both sides of Victoria Harbour are the **Star Ferry terminals**, where the popular cross-harbour ferries dock, in Tsim Sha Tsui (a short walk west of the southern end of Nathan Road) and next to the Outer Islands Ferry Pier in Central.

Arrival

Currently, nationals of the US, Canada, South Africa, Australia and New Zealand receive a three-month tourist **visa** on arrival in Hong Kong; British nationals can stay for six months. For present information, contact your local HKTB office or check ⓦwww.immd.gov.hk/ehtml/hkvisas_4.htm.

Hong Kong has its own separate currency, the **Hong Kong dollar**, which is pegged at around $8 to the US dollar and so is currently worth a little less than

Hong Kong phone numbers have no area codes. From outside the territory, dial the normal international access code + ⓣ852 (the "country" code) + the number. However, **from Macau** you need only dial ⓣ01 + the number. To call Hong Kong from mainland China, dial ⓣ00 + 852 + the number.

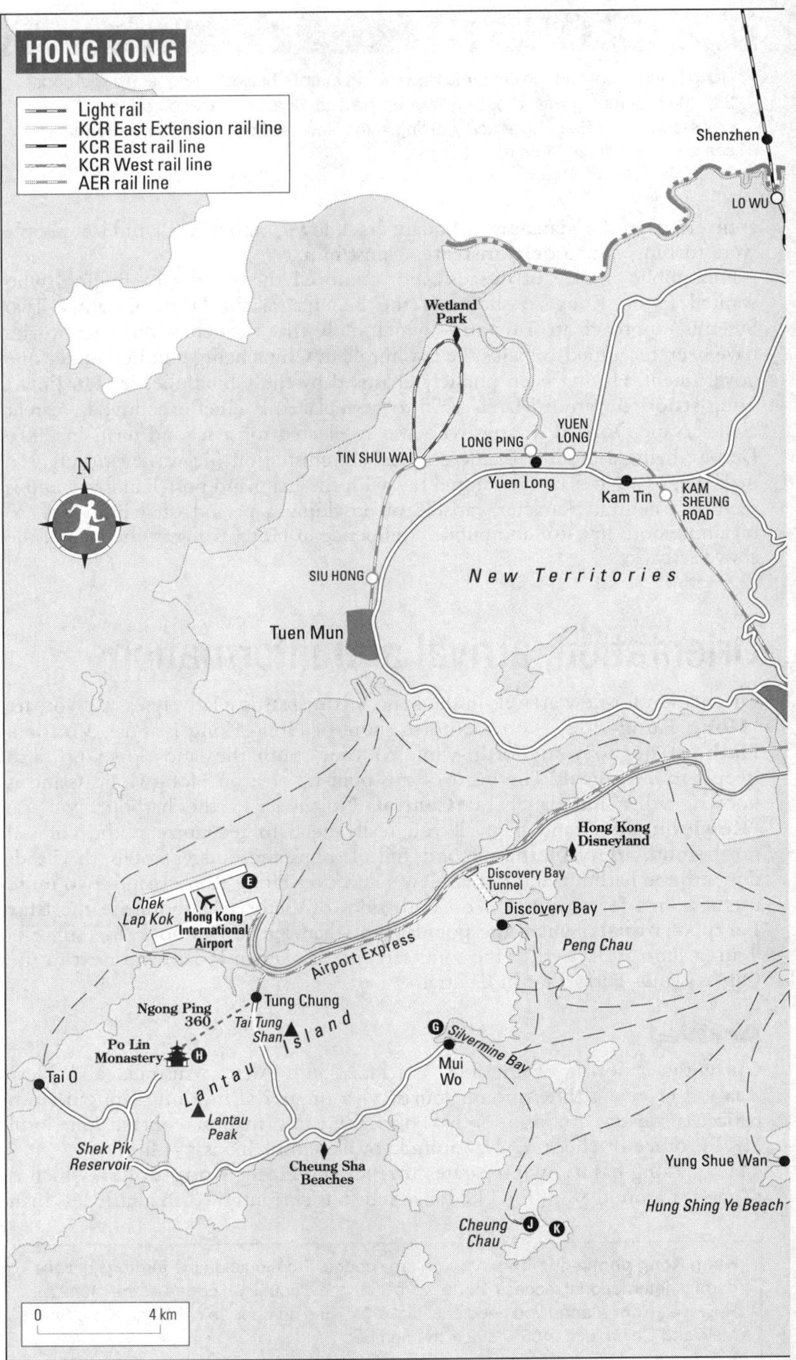
HONG KONG
Light rail
KCR East Extension rail line
KCR East rail line
KCR West rail line
AER rail line
Shenzhen
LO WU
Wetland Park
YUEN LONG
LONG PING
TIN SHUI WAI
Yuen Long
Kam Tin
KAM SHEUNG ROAD
N
SIU HONG
New Territories
Tuen Mun
Hong Kong Disneyland
Discovery Bay Tunnel
Discovery Bay
Chek Lap Kok
Hong Kong International Airport
E
Peng Chau
Airport Express
Tung Chung
Ngong Ping 360
Tai Tung Shan
Lantau Island
Po Lin Monastery
H
G
Silvermine Bay
Mui Wo
Tai O
Lantau Peak
Shek Pik Reservoir
Cheung Sha Beaches
Yung Shue Wan
Hung Shing Ye Beach
Cheung Chau
J
K
0
4 km

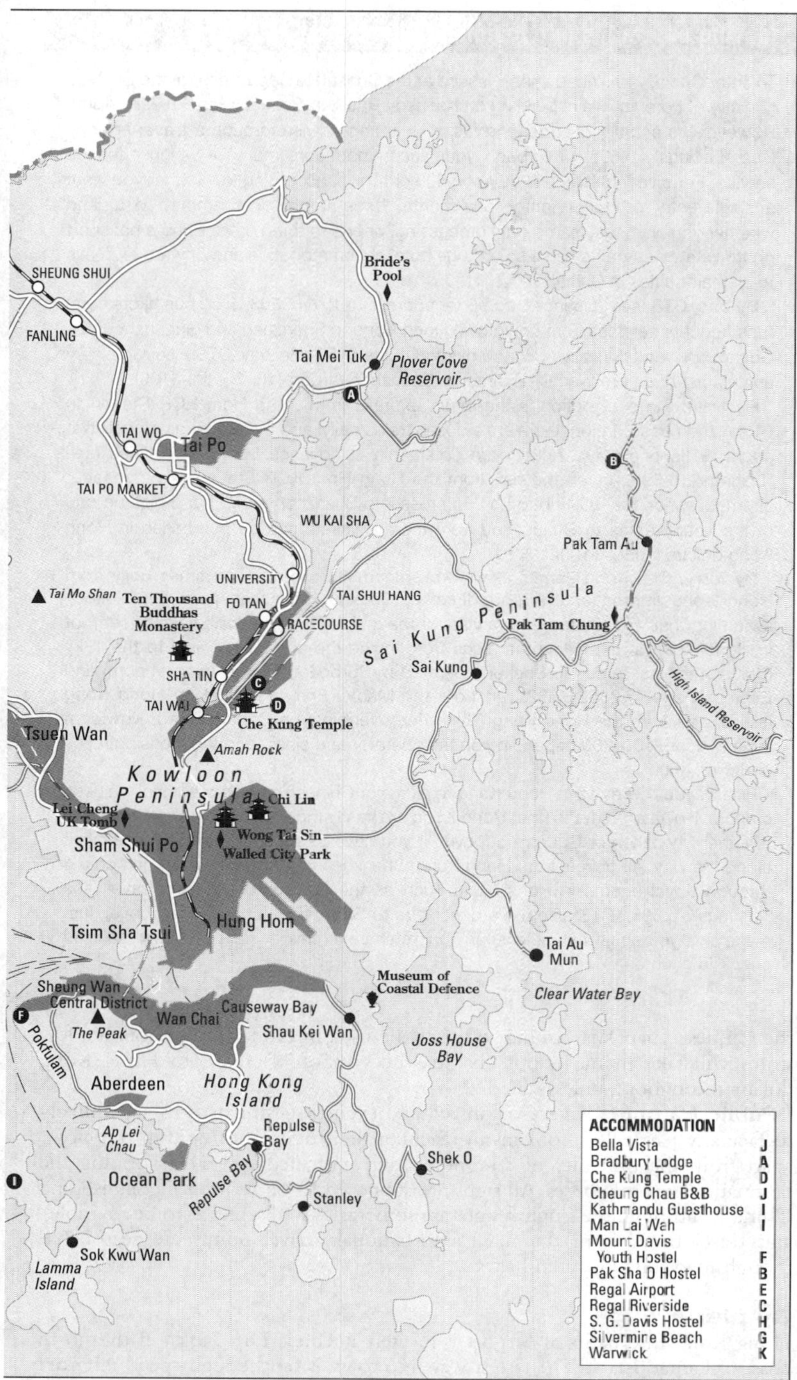
SHEUNG SHUI
FANLING
Bride's Pool
Tai Mei Tuk
Plover Cove Reservoir
A
TAI WO
Tai Po
TAI PO MARKET
B
WU KAI SHA
Pak Tam Au
UNIVERSITY
Tai Mo Shan
Ten Thousand Buddhas Monastery
FO TAN
TAI SHUI HANG
RACECOURSE
Sai Kung Peninsula
Pak Tam Chung
SHA TIN
Sai Kung
C
TAI WAI
D
Che Kung Temple
High Island Reservoir
Tsuen Wan
Amah Rock
Kowloon Peninsula
Chi Lin
Lei Cheng UK Tomb
Wong Tai Sin
Sham Shui Po
Walled City Park
Hung Hom
Tsim Sha Tsui
Tai Au Mun
Museum of Coastal Defence
Sheung Wan
Central District
Causeway Bay
Clear Water Bay
F
Wan Chai
The Peak
Shau Kei Wan
Pokfulam
Joss House Bay
Aberdeen
Hong Kong Island
Repulse Bay
Ap Lei Chau
Shek O
Ocean Park
Repulse Bay
I
Stanley
Sok Kwu Wan
Lamma Island
ACCOMMODATION
Bella Vista J
Bradbury Lodge A
Che Kung Temple D
Cheung Chau B&B J
Kathmandu Guesthouse I
Man Lai Wah I
Mount Davis Youth Hostel F
Pak Sha O Hostel B
Regal Airport E
Regal Riverside C
S. G. Davis Hostel H
Silvermine Beach G
Warwick K

Moving on: routes into mainland China

To enter China, you'll need a **visa**, issued at the Consulate Department of the Chinese Ministry of Foreign Affairs building on Kennedy Road, in Central (Mon–Fri 9am–4pm). However, it's actually cheaper and faster to arrange a visa through a **travel agency** (see "Listings", p.695) or through your accommodation, many of which offer the service. **Fees** vary between $200 and $600 or above, according to whether you want a single-entry or double-entry, one-month, three-month or six-month visa, and whether you want fast (same-day) processing, or two to three days. Bring a passport photo with you. Agents can also arrange hotel accommodation and onward journeys to all major cities in China.

By bus, CTS (see "Listings", p.695 for address; ⓣ2764 9803, ⓦctsbus.hkcts.com) runs frequent services from downtown Hong Kong to Shenzhen and Guangzhou; the Guangzhou run takes about 3hr 30min and costs $150 one way. CTS also run a very useful, fast bus from Wan Chai direct to Shenzhen Airport (2hr 30min; $100).

By train, the best option is the direct express from Hung Hom KCR Station to Guangzhou East Station; there are a dozen trains daily, and the trip takes around two hours ($185 one way). Tickets are obtainable in advance from CTS offices (see "Listings", p.695), or on the day from the Hung Hom KCR Station. As a cheaper alternative, ride the KCR up to Lo Wu, cross into Shenzhen on foot and pick up one of the hourly trains to Guangzhou from there – tickets can be purchased in Hong Kong dollars (about $100).

By ferry, Chu Kong Ferries (ⓦwww.cksp.com.hk) run a dozen times daily from Hong Kong International Airport direct to Shekou (Shenzhen port; $200), so – assuming that you already have a visa for the mainland – you don't have to set foot in Hong Kong at all; follow the signs from inside the arrivals terminal to the "Sky Pier". Other fast ferries to Shekou operated by TurboJet (ⓦwww.turbojet.com) and Express Ferry (ⓣ2852 7682) run from the Macau Ferry Terminal on Hong Kong Island, and from the Hong Kong China Ferry Terminal on Canton Road, Kowloon. Tickets cost $100–200 depending on the operator and class, and the crossing takes under an hour.

Finally, you can **fly** from Hong Kong to all major Chinese cities on regional Chinese carriers. However, airfares from Hong Kong are vastly more expensive than those out of either Shenzhen or Guangzhou, even if you have to spend a night in these cities along the way. Air tickets from Hong Kong, Shenzhen or Guangzhou can be booked through travel agents in Hong Kong such as the CTS or Shoestring Travel (see "Listings", p.695). CTS also run a direct **bus to Shenzhen Airport** (see above); just make sure you arrive with at least an hour to spare to clear the airport's disorganized check-in counter.

the Chinese yuan. Yuan cannot officially be used in Hong Kong, though a few stores will take them. In this chapter, the symbol "$" refers to Hong Kong dollars throughout, unless stated.

Public transport is very organized and even first-time arrivals are unlikely to face any particular problems in reaching their destination within the city – apart from the difficulty of communicating with taxi drivers or reading the destinations on minibuses. All signs are supposed to be written in English and Chinese (although the English signs are sometimes so discreet as to be invisible), and travel times from the main international arrival points are reasonable, though road traffic is often heavy.

By plane

Hong Kong International Airport is located at **Chek Lap Kok**, off the north coast of Lantau Island. The fastest way into town is on the high-speed **Airport**

Express (AEL) rail service, with platforms in both the arrival and departure halls. Trains whisk you to Hong Kong (Central) in 23 minutes ($100) with stops on the way at Tsing Yi (12min; $60) and Kowloon (19min; $90). Services operate daily every eight minutes between 5.50am and 1am. Once in town at either the Kowloon or Hong Kong AEL stations, you'll find taxi ranks and **free hotel shuttle buses** (coloured blue and marked with a "K"), which, even if you're not staying at one of the hotels they serve, can deliver to within a short walk of most accommodation.

A more complicated but cheaper rail option is to catch an #S1, #S56 or #S64 bus to **Tung Chung MTR Station** ($4), and then take the Tung Chung Line into town along a parallel route to the AEL (around $25). It's slower, with more stops, but the advantage here is that you can change trains at Lai King Station, and get on the Tsuen Wan Line via Mong Kok, Jordan and Tsim Sha Tsui – useful for reaching Kowloon's accommodation.

Cheaper again, but far slower, is to take one of the dozen **Airbus routes** into town – their departure points are clearly signposted in the terminal. The airport customer-service counters sell tickets and give change, while on the buses themselves you need to have the exact money. All routes have regular departures between 6am and midnight, and there's plenty of room for luggage. The most useful include the #A11 and #A12 to Causeway Bay on Hong Kong Island via Sheung Wan, Central, Admiralty and Wan Chai; and the #A21 to Hung Hom KCR Station via Tsim Sha Tsui, Jordan and Yau Ma Tei.

Taxis into the city are metered and reliable (see p.655 for more details). You might want to get the tourist office in the Buffer Hall to write down the name of your destination in Chinese characters for the driver, though they should know the names of the big hotels in English. It costs roughly $290 to get to Tsim Sha Tsui, about $350 for Hong Kong Island (and so is cheaper than the AEL for a group). There may be extra charges for luggage and for tunnel tolls – on some tunnel trips the passenger pays the return charge, too. **Rush-hour traffic** can slow down journey times considerably, particularly if you're using one of the cross-harbour tunnels to Hong Kong Island.

The airport is open 24hrs, but transport for **early or late flights** can be a problem, as between midnight and 5.50am, the rail connections are closed. **Night buses** include the #N11 to Central and the #N21 to Tsim Sha Tsui, but otherwise you'll have to take a taxi.

By train and bus

Express trains **from Guangzhou** arrive at **Hung Hom Railway Station** in Tsim Sha Tsui East, also known as the **Kowloon–Canton Railway** (or **KCR**) **Station** (Ⓣ2929 3399, Ⓦwww.kcrc.com). You'll also end up here if you crossed the border on foot **from Shenzhen** to Lo Wu, then caught the regular KCR train down through the New Territories. At Hung Hom, signposted walkways lead to a city bus terminal, taxi rank and – ten minutes around the harbour – the Hung Hom Ferry Pier to Wan Chai or Central (daily 7am–7pm, though this

In-town check-in

Leaving by air, many international airlines allow you to **check-in** for your flight, including checking through your in-hold luggage, up to 24hrs in advance at the Hong Kong and Kowloon AEL stations. This is useful if you have a late flight and don't want to drag your luggage around with you after checking out of your hotel, but also means you don't have to join the often lengthy check-in queues at the airport.

may close in the near future). For Tsim Sha Tsui, stay in the station and catch another KCR train for one stop south to its terminus at Tsim Sha Tsui East Station, which exits into Middle Road.

There are also regular daily **buses** from Guangzhou, Shenzhen and Shenzhen Airport operated by CTS and Citybus (tickets from $100); these take up to three hours thirty minutes and arrive in either Kowloon or Wan Chai.

By ferry

Two ferry terminals handle regular ferries from Macau and from Shekou (Shenzhen): the **Hong Kong–Macau Ferry Terminal** is in the Shun Tak Centre, on Hong Kong Island, from where the Sheung Wan MTR Station and numerous bus lines are directly accessible; while the **Hong Kong China Ferry Terminal**, which also handles ferries from the Pearl River Delta, is in downtown Tsim Sha Tsui, on Canton Road. For more on Macau and Shekou ferries, see p.650 & p.698. There is also a berth for international cruise liners at Ocean Terminal in Tsim Sha Tsui.

Information, maps and the media

The **Hong Kong Tourism Board** or **HKTB** (Ⓣ2508 1234 daily 8am–6pm; Ⓦwww.discoverhongkong.com) issues more leaflets, pamphlets, brochures and maps than the rest of China put together. Their two downtown **offices** (daily 8am–8pm) are in the Star Ferry Terminal in Tsim Sha Tsui and near Exit F, Causeway Bay MTR Station. English-speaking staff at both provide sound, useful advice on accommodation, shopping, restaurants, bus routes and hiking trails – or can tell you how to find out yourself. In addition, they run tours and organize short **free courses** on *tai ji*, Cantonese Opera, tea appreciation and more, for which you need to sign up a day in advance. They also sell the excellent-value **Museum Weekly Pass** ($30), which gets you unlimited entry to seven of the SAR's main museums (except special exhibitions).

Free HKTB **maps**, and the maps in this book, should be enough for most purposes, though street atlases such as the paperback *Hong Kong Guidebook*, which includes all bus routes, can be bought from bookstores (see "Listings", p.694). Free **listings magazines**, providing up-to-date information on restaurants, bars, clubs, concerts and exhibitions, include the trendy *HK Magazine* and acerbic *BC Magazine* (Ⓦwww.bcmagazine.net), both available in hotels, cafés and restaurants.

Hong Kong's two English-language **daily papers** are the *South China Morning Post*, whose bland coverage of regional news does its best to toe the party line, and the *Standard*, which is more business-oriented but can be outspoken about

Free things

Hong Kong might be an expensive place compared with the Chinese mainland, but there are a number of **free things** to take advantage of while you're here. These include entry to all downtown parks, plus the Zoological and Botanical Gardens (p.664); the Edward Youde Aviary and the Museum of Teaware in Hong Kong Park (p.664); all government-run museums on Wednesdays; martial-arts performances in Kowloon Park on Sunday afternoons (p.672); the ferry ride through Aberdeen Harbour to the *Jumbo* floating restaurant (p.668); Mong Kok's bird and goldfish markets (p.674); harbour views from Tsim Sha Tsui waterfront (p.670) and the Bank of China tower (p.663); and introductory cultural courses, plus a harbour cruise, offered by the HKTB (p.652).

politicians' failings. Other international papers, such as the local edition of the *Herald Tribune*, and journals such as *Time* and *Newsweek*, are widely available.

City transport

Hong Kong's public transport system is efficient, extensive and inexpensive – though best avoided during the weekday **rush hours**, which last about 7.30–9am and 5–7pm. If you plan to travel a good deal, get hold of an **Octopus Card** (Ⓣ2266 2222 for information), a rechargeable stored-value ticket that can be used for travel on the MTR, KCR, LRT, trams, the AEL, most buses, and most ferries (including the Star Ferry and main inter-island services). The card itself costs $50 (refundable only after a three-month period), and you add value to it by feeding it and your money into machines in the MTR. The fare is then electronically deducted each time you use the card by swiping it over yellow sensor pads at station turnstiles or, on a bus, beside the driver. Octopus cards can also be used to shop at *McDonald's*, Park'n'shop supermarkets, *Maxim's* restaurants and 7–11 stores.

Trains

Hong Kong's three train systems all operate on the same principles, and you buy single-journey **tickets** ($4–11) from easy-to-use dispensing machines at the stations, or use an Octopus Card.

The underground **MTR** (Mass Transit Railway) comprises five lines, operating from about 6am–1am. The **Island Line** (marked blue on maps) runs along the north shore of Hong Kong Island, from Sheung Wan in the west to Chai Wan in the east, taking in important stops such as Central, Wan Chai and Causeway Bay. The **Tsuen Wan Line** (red) runs from Central, under the harbour, through Tsim Sha Tsui and then northwest to the New Town of Tsuen Wan. The **Kwun Tong Line** (green) connects with the Tsuen Wan Line at Mong Kok in Kowloon, and then runs east to Yau Tong and Tiu Keng Leng on the Tseung Kwan O Line (see below). The **Tung Chung Line** (yellow) follows much of the same route as the AEL, linking Central and Tung Chung. Finally, the **Tseung Kwan O Line** (purple) links the Island Line stations of North Point and Quarry Bay under the harbour to Yau Tong and Tiu Keng Leng on the Kwun Tong Line, then continues northeast to Po Lam.

The other rail line is the overground **KCR** (Kowloon–Canton Railway), a commuter railway with two sections. The **KCR East Line** runs from Tsim Sha Tsui East KCR Station in Kowloon, via Hung Hom KCR Station, north through the New Territories to the border with mainland China at Lo Wu – though unless you have a visa for China, you can only go as far as the penultimate station of Sheung Shui. There is an interchange between the KCR East Line and MTR at Kowloon Tong Station, and a **KCR East Extension** northeast from Tai Wai, though this is of little interest to tourists. The **KCR West Line** connects with the Tsuen Wan MTR Line at Mei Foo, useful for bus connections to outlying attractions in the New Territories.

A third transport system, the **LRT** (Light Rail Transit) connects the New Territories towns of Tuen Mun and Yuen Long, though, again, tourists rarely use it except to reach the Hong Kong Wetland Park (see p.677).

Trams

Trams have been rattling along Hong Kong Island's north shore since 1904 and, despite being an anachronism in such a hi-tech city, they are as popular as

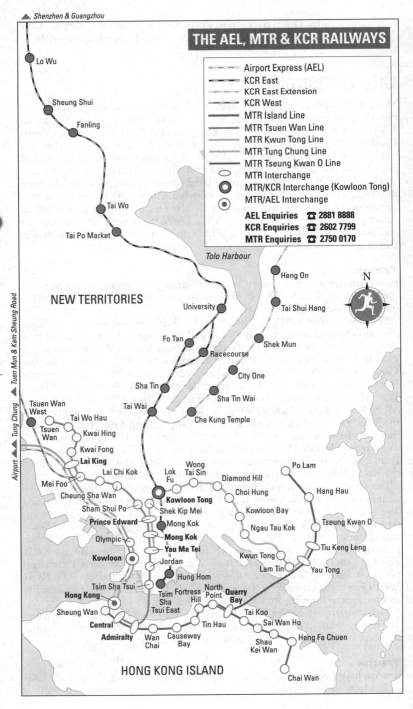

THE AEL, MTR & KCR RAILWAYS

Shenzhen & Guangzhou

Airport Express (AEL)
KCR East
KCR East Extension
KCR West
MTR Island Line
MTR Tsuen Wan Line
MTR Kwun Tong Line
MTR Tung Chung Line
MTR Tseung Kwan O Line
MTR Interchange
MTR/KCR Interchange (Kowloon Tong)
MTR/AEL Interchange

AEL Enquiries ☎ 2881 8888
KCR Enquiries ☎ 2602 7799
MTR Enquiries ☎ 2750 0170

Lo Wu
Sheung Shui
Fanling
Tai Wo
Tai Po Market
Tolo Harbour
Heng On
Tai Shui Hang
NEW TERRITORIES
University
Fo Tan
Racecourse
Shek Mun
City One
Sha Tin
Sha Tin Wai
Tai Wai
Che Kung Temple
Tuen Mun & Kam Sheung Road
Tung Chung
Airport
Tsuen Wan West
Tai Wo Hau
Tsuen Wan
Kwai Hing
Kwai Fong
Lai King
Lai Chi Kok
Mei Foo
Cheung Sha Wan
Sham Shui Po
Prince Edward
Olympic
Kowloon
Lok Fu
Wong Tai Sin
Diamond Hill
Choi Hung
Kowloon Tong
Shek Kip Mei
Mong Kok
Mong Kok
Yau Ma Tei
Jordan
Hung Hom
Kowloon Bay
Ngau Tau Kok
Kwun Tong
Lam Tin
Po Lam
Hang Hau
Tseung Kwan O
Tiu Keng Leng
Yau Tong
Tsim Sha Tsui
Tsim Sha Tsui East
Hong Kong
Sheung Wan
Central
Admiralty
Wan Chai
Causeway Bay
Tin Hau
Fortress Hill
North Point
Quarry Bay
Tai Koo
Sai Wan Ho
Shau Kei Wan
Heng Fa Chuen
Chai Wan
HONG KONG ISLAND

N

ever with locals and tourists alike, especially for the night-time view from the upstairs deck. The trams run between Kennedy Town in the west and Shau Kei Wan in the east, via Central, Wan Chai and Causeway Bay (some going via Happy Valley; check the front of the tram). You board the tram at the back, and swipe your Octopus Card or drop the money in the driver's box ($2; $1 for senior citizens and children; no change given) when you get off.

Buses, taxis and cars

The double-decker **buses** that run around town are comfortable and often air-conditioned, and are essential for reaching the south of Hong Kong Island and parts of the New Territories. You swipe your card or pay as you board (exact change is required); the amount is often posted up on the timetables at bus stops, and fares range from $1.20 to $45. The HKTB issues up-to-date information on bus routes, including the approximate length of journeys and cost. The **main bus terminal** in Central is at Exchange Square, though some services start from outside the Star Ferry Terminal/Outlying Islands Ferry Pier. In Tsim Sha Tsui, Kowloon, the main bus terminal is currently in front of the Star Ferry Terminal – though there is talk of shifting it elsewhere.

As well as the big buses, there are also ubiquitous sixteen-seater **minibuses** and **maxicabs**, which have set stops but can also be hailed (not on double yellow lines). They cost a little more than regular buses, and you pay the driver or swipe your card as you enter; change – in small amounts – is only given on the minibuses (which have a red rather than a green stripe). The drivers of either are unlikely to speak English.

Taxis in Hong Kong (red in the downtown areas and green in the New Territories) are not expensive, with a minimum fare of $15, although they can be hard to get hold of in rush hours and rainstorms. Note that there is a toll to be paid (around $5–15) on any trips through the cross-harbour tunnel between Kowloon and Hong Kong, and drivers often double this – as they are allowed to do – on the grounds that they have to get back again. Many taxi drivers do not speak English, so be prepared to show the driver the name of your destination written down in Chinese. If you get stuck, gesture to the driver to call his dispatch centre on the two-way radio; someone there will speak English. It is obligatory for all passengers to wear seat belts on Hong Kong Island and in Kowloon.

Car rental is theoretically possible, though unnecessary, given that taxis are far cheaper and more convenient.

Ferries

One of the most enjoyable things to do in Hong Kong is to spend ten minutes riding the humble **Star Ferry** between Tsim Sha Tsui in Kowloon and the pier in front of the IFC2 Tower on Hong Kong Island (daily 6.30am–11.30pm; upper deck $2.20, lower deck $1.70). The views of the island are superb, particularly at dusk when the lights begin to twinkle through the humidity and the spray. You'll also get a feel for the frenetic pace of life on Hong Kong's waterways, with ferries, junks, hydrofoils and larger ships looming up from all directions. Similarly fun ferries cross between Tsim Sha Tsui and Wan Chai, and Hung Hom and Wan Chai (both $5.30), though both operate at a loss and may not survive much longer

In addition, a large array of other boats runs between Hong Kong and the Outlying Islands, most of which use the **Outlying Islands Ferry Pier** in front of the International Finance Centre; details are given in the island accounts.

Accommodation

Hong Kong boasts a colossal range of **accommodation**, particularly in the Tsim Sha Tsui area of Kowloon, and – aside from during the Olympics – you will always find a room if you are prepared to do some traipsing around. At the upper end of the market are some of the best **hotels** in the world, costing several thousand dollars a night, though less renowned places offering motel-like facilities start around $500. You'll get the best **deals** on all hotels by **booking ahead**, either by phone or using a website such as the Hong Kong Hotels Association (Ⓦwww.hotels-in-hong-kong.com), which features deals, packages and offers for all HKHA properties.

The lower end of the market is served by **guesthouses and hostels**, the bulk of which are squeezed into blocks at the lower end of Nathan Road – though there are even a few on the Outlying Islands. Always check these rooms for size (many are minuscule), whether the shower is separate, whether it has a window, and whether you have to pay extra for the use of air-conditioning.

Even budget hotel accommodation is not that cheap, however – you'll be lucky to find a room for less than $250, though shared **dormitory accommodation** at one of the crowded travellers' hostels will get you down as low as $80–120 a night for a bed. The **Hong Kong Youth Hostels Association** (Ⓣ2788 1638, Ⓦwww.yha.org.hk) also operates seven hostels – mostly a long way from the centre – offering dormitory accommodation for IYHF members from $50.

Hong Kong Island

Accommodation on the island is mostly upmarket, though there's an emerging budget enclave in Causeway Bay (with prices a tad higher than Kowloon's), and the secluded but excellent *Mount Davis Youth Hostel*.

Bin Man Hotel 1/F, Central Building, 531 Jaffe Rd, Causeway Bay Ⓣ2833 2063, Ⓕ2838 5651. Worth staying here for the name alone, though this budget hotel is also quiet and well located for Causeway Bay's restaurants. ❸

Garden View International House 1 MacDonnell Rd, Mid-Levels Ⓣ2877 3737, Ⓦwww.ywca.org.hk. This comfortable YWCA-run hotel is off Garden Rd, south of the Zoological and Botanical Gardens. Maxicab #1A from outside the Star Ferry Terminal and Central MTR runs past. Prices change considerably depending on demand, but their cheaper rates are a very good deal. ❼

Hua Tai 30–32 New Market St, Sheung Wan Ⓣ2853 9488, Ⓕ2854 0921. Mainland Chinese-run budget hotel just west of Western Market, painted bright orange so you won't miss it. There's a faintly shambolic atmosphere to the place, and the cheaper rooms are the usual drab squeeze, but pricier ones are quite roomy. ❹–❺

Accommodation price codes

Hong Kong accommodation has been graded according to the following price codes, which represent the cheapest double room available to foreigners, except where the text refers specifically to dorm beds, when the actual price per person is given. Most places have a range of rooms, and staff will usually offer you the more expensive ones – it's always worth asking if they have anything cheaper. The more upmarket hotels will levy an additional ten-percent service charge on top of their quoted room rates. Our price codes are based on the pre-tax rates.

❶ Under $80
❷ $80–200
❸ $201–300
❹ $301–500
❺ $501–800
❻ $801–1200
❼ $1201–2000
❽ $2001–3000
❾ Over $3000

Jetvan 4A, Fairview Mansion, 51 Patterson St, Causeway Bay ⓣ2890 8133, ⓦwww.jetvan.com. Slightly tatty guesthouse, though staff are friendly, and if you stay a few days you can negotiate a better rate. ④

King's Hotel 303 Jaffe Rd, Wan Chai ⓣ3188 2277, ⓦwww.kingshotel.hk. Quirky boutique hotel with a "cyber" theme resulting in a sort of minimalist sci-fi decor. Rooms come with IDD computers and plasma-screen TVs, and deals can slash rates. ⑥, harbour view ⑦

Mandarin Oriental 5 Connaught Rd, Central ⓣ2522 0111, ⓦwww.mandarinoriental.com. Unassumingly set in a plain concrete box, this is one of the best hotels in the world, with unmatched service. The hotel lobby is also a great place to people-watch – anyone who's anyone in Hong Kong eats or drinks here. Internet rates begin at $2750. ⑨

Mount Davis Youth Hostel Mount Davis ⓣ2817 5715. Perched on the top of a mountain above Kennedy Town, this self-catering retreat has superb, peaceful views over the harbour. Getting here, however, is a major expedition, unless you catch the infrequent shuttle bus ($10) from the ground floor of the Shun Tak Centre (Hong Kong–Macau Ferry Terminal) – phone the hostel for times. Otherwise, catch bus #5 from Admiralty or minibus #3A from the Outlying Islands Ferry Pier in Central and get off near the junction of Victoria Rd and Mount Davis Path; walk back 100m from the bus stop and you'll see Mount Davis Path branching off up the hill – the hostel is a 35min walk. If you have much luggage, get off the bus in Kennedy Town and catch a taxi from there (around $50 plus $5 per item of luggage). Dorms $90, doubles/family rooms ③–⑤

National Guesthouse 22–32 Marsh St (reception on Gloucester Rd), Wan Chai ⓣ2834 9992, ⓕ2834 9991. The cheapest rooms here are barely larger than the bed, but the "hotel-style" rooms are more spacious, and some have harbour views. ③–⑤

Park Lane 310 Gloucester Rd, Causeway Bay ⓣ2293 8888, ⓦwww.parklane.com.hk. Located slap-bang on Victoria Park, this plush hotel is conveniently sited for the shopping and eating delights of Causeway Bay. ⑧

Kowloon

Most of the accommodation listed below is conveniently central, within fifteen minutes' walk of the Tsim Sha Tsui Star Ferry Terminal. For a less claustrophobic atmosphere, however, try locations in Jordan and Yau Ma Tei, which are all located near MTR stations. Places listed represent a fraction of the total on offer, and it is always worth having a look at several options.

Anne Black Guesthouse (YWCA) 5 Man Fuk Rd, Yau Ma Tei ⓣ2713 9211, ⓦwww.ywca.org.hk. Not far from the Yau Ma Tei MTR, this YWCA pension is surprisingly smart, light and airy. Check the website for massive discounts. ⑥

Louie Business Hotel 2/F, 49–50 Haiphong Rd, Tsim Sha Tsui ⓣ2311 1366, ⓔlouiebusinesshotel@hotmail.com. Expensive, but this guesthouse opposite Kowloon Park gives you more daylight and elbow room than most, along with cupboards, a microwave, kitchen sink and bathroom in each room. ④

Miramar 118–130 Nathan Rd, Tsim Sha Tsui ⓣ2368 1111, ⓦwww.miramarhk.com. The best upmarket deal in Tsim Sha Tsui, with very comfortable rooms and a good location across from Kowloon Park. ⑦

Nathan 378 Nathan Rd, Jordan ⓣ2388 5141, ⓦwww.nathanhotel.com. Smart, good-value hotel. Located in a slightly characterless area, though close to the night market and within easy reach of the MTR. ⑦

New King's Hotel 473–473A Nathan Rd, Yau Ma Tei ⓣ2780 1281, ⓕ2782 1833. Immediately south of the Yau Ma Tei MTR. More than a guesthouse – it occupies the whole building – this is probably the cheapest "real" hotel in town. ⑤

Peninsula Hotel Salisbury Rd, Tsim Sha Tsui ⓣ2920 2888, ⓦwww.peninsula.com. One of the classiest hotels in the world, which has been overlooking the harbour and Hong Kong Island for eighty years. Some upmarket package tours offer a good deal off standard rates. ⑨

The Salisbury (YMCA) 41 Salisbury Rd, Tsim Sha Tsui ⓣ2268 7888, ⓦwww.ymcahk.org.hk. Superb location next door to the *Peninsula Hotel* and with views over the harbour and Hong Kong Island; facilities include indoor pools, a fitness centre and squash court. For the price, the doubles are unbeatable value; relatively expensive four-bed dorms with attached shower are also available. Open to both men and women. Dorms $230, rooms ⑤

Star Guesthouse Flat B, 6/F, 21 Cameron Rd, Tsim Sha Tsui ⓣ2723 8951, ⓦwww.starguesthouse.com.hk. Very clean and friendly, with good English spoken. The rooms with windows and own bath are bright but slightly pricey for what they are; the cheaper rooms have shared bath. ③

Chungking Mansions

Set at the southern end of Nathan Road, Chungking Mansions is an ugly monster of a building, as deep and wide as it is tall. The lowest two floors form a warren of tiny shops and restaurants with a distinctly Central Asian flavour, while the remaining sixteen floors are crammed with budget guesthouses. Above the second floor, the building is divided into five blocks, lettered A to E, each served by two tiny lifts that are subject to long queues. Surprisingly, the guesthouses are pleasant and cheap, though overall the building is claustrophobic, and an undoubted safety hazard. The guesthouses listed below are just a handful of the total.

Kowloon Guesthouse Floor 10, Block B ⓣ2369 9802, ⓕ2739 6635. Fairly standard wooden furnishings, but under good management. ❸

Tai Wan Hotel Floor 3, Block A ⓣ2366 7468, ⓔtaiwan_hotel@hotmail.com. Bright place whose bigger rooms, savvy management and full-time door staff make it feel more comfortable than most. ❸

Tom's Guesthouse Flat 5, Floor 8, Block A ⓣ2722 4956. Under very friendly management, the double and triple rooms here are reasonably bright and very good value. *Tom's* has another branch at Flat 1, Floor 16, Block C (ⓣ2722 6035, ⓕ2366 6706), where the rooms are positively salubrious. ❸

Welcome Guesthouse Floor 7, Block A ⓣ2721 7793, ⓦwww.guesthousehk.net. A good choice, offering a/c doubles with and without shower. Nice clean rooms, luggage storage, laundry service and China visas available. ❷

Yan Yan Guesthouse Floor 8, Block E ⓣ2366 8930, ⓕ2721 0840. Helpful staff renting out doubles with all facilities; you could sleep three in some – at a squeeze – making them good value. ❷

Mirador Mansions

This is another block at 54–64 Nathan Rd, on the east side, in between Carnarvon Road and Mody Road, right next to the Tsim Sha Tsui MTR Station. Dotted about, in amongst the residential apartments, are large numbers of guesthouses. Mirador Mansions is cleaner and brighter than Chungking Mansions, and queues for the lifts are smaller.

Man Hing Lung Flat F2, Floor 14 ⓣ2722 0678 or 2311 8807. Run by a helpful, friendly man with good English, this is a clean place, offering both singles and doubles, although the rooms are very small. ❷

Mei Lam Guesthouse Flat D1, Floor 5 ⓣ2721 5278. Helpful, English-speaking owner and very presentable singles and doubles, all spick-and-span, with full facilities. Worth the higher-than-usual prices. ❸

New Garden Hostel Flat F4, Floor 3 ⓣ2311 1183. Recently refurbished, friendly travellers' hang-out, with washing machines, lockers and a patio garden. A *wing chun* martial-arts school is also based here, and you can arrange lessons with them. Mixed and women-only dorms; beds get cheaper if you pay by the week. Dorms $80, ❹

The New Territories and Outlying Islands

The New Territories and Outlying Islands offer an attractive escape from the city's congestion. You won't be the only one who is tempted by the idea, though – always book in advance, especially at weekends and during holidays. Most of Hong Kong's **youth hostels** are here; all are self-catering, require you to be a YHA member, and are too remote to be used as a base for exploring the rest of Hong Kong. Commuting from Lamma or Cheung Chau, however, is feasible – guesthouses here raise their rates at weekends but also offer package deals for a week or more. The HKTB can further advise about holiday flats on the islands.

New Territories

Bradbury Lodge 66 Tai Mei Tuk Rd, Tai Mei Tuk, Tai Po ⓣ2662 5123. Of all the hostels, this is about the easiest to get to. Take the KCR train to Tai Po, then bus #75K to Tai Mei Tuk Terminal. Walk south a few minutes, with the sea on your right. Lots of boating, walking and cycling opportunities right by the scenic Plover Cove Reservoir (see p.679). Two- to eight-bed rooms ❸–❺

Pak Sha O Hostel Pak Sha O, Hoi Ha Rd, Sai Kung ⓣ2328 2327. Take green minibus #7 going to Hoi Ha from Sai Kung (see p.680) and get off at the hostel. Great for access to Hong Kong's cleanest, most secluded snorkelling beaches. Dorms $50, camping $25.

Regal Riverside Hotel 34–36 Tai Chung Kiu Rd, Sha Tin ⓣ2649 7878, ⓦwww.regalhotel.com. The New Territories' best hotel – though there's not a lot of competition – right in the centre of Sha Tin. This comfortable place often appears in holiday packages; there's a fine Asian lunch buffet served here and a free shuttle bus to Tsim Sha Tsui, too. Check their website for discounted rates. ❻

S. G. Davis Hostel Ngong Ping, Lantau Island ⓣ2985 5610. From the Ngong Ping bus terminal (p.683) follow the paved footpath south, away from the Tian Tan Buddha and past the public toilets. It's a 10min walk and well signposted. This is a great base for hill walking on Lantau, and you can eat at the nearby Po Lin Monastery. It's cold on winter nights, though – bring a sleeping bag. Dorms $50, camping ¥25.

Outlying Islands

Bella Vista Miami Resort East Bay, Cheung Chau ⓣ2981 7299, ⓦwww.miamicheungchau.com.hk. One of several low-key guesthouses on the island; well located in a residential block near the east beach. Mon–Fri ❸, Sat & Sun ❹

Cheung Chau B&B Tung Wah Beach, Cheung Chau ⓣ2986 9990, ⓦwww.bbcheungchau.com.hk. Just back from the beach along the access Rd from the village, this is a cute, modern place with welcoming atmosphere. Mon–Fri & Sun ❹, Sat ❺

Kathmandu Guesthouse Yung Shue Wan, Lamma ⓣ2982 0028. Above Bubbles Laundry in Yung Shue Wan town, this hostel-like place has been going forever and offers dorm beds as well as doubles at some of the lowest rates on the island. Beds $100 weekdays, $130 at weekends; doubles ❷–❸

Man Lai Wah Hotel Yung Shue Wan, Lamma ⓣ2982 0220 or 0600. Right ahead from the ferry pier, this great low-key place has small, double-bed flats with balcony and harbour views. ❹

Regal Airport Hotel 9 Cheong Tat Rd, Hong Kong International Airport, Chek Lap Kok ⓣ2286 8888, ⓦwww.regalhotel.com. Over 1100 soundproofed rooms with a direct airbridge link to the airport express check-in, pools and a health club. The website often advertises inexpensive last-minute deals. ❼

Silvermine Beach Hotel 648 Silvermine Bay, Mui Wo, Lantau ⓣ2984 8295, ⓦwww.resort.com.hk. Superbly located right on the beachfront, a few minutes' walk from the Mui Wo Ferry Pier. The rooms here are comfortable and quiet, and good value during the week when they are discounted. The restaurant spilling out onto the terraces offers popular barbecues and Thai grub. ❻, sea view ❼

Warwick Hotel East Bay, Cheung Chau ⓣ2981 0081, ⓦwww.warwickhotel.com.hk. Overlooking Tung Wan Beach, this is the most upmarket and expensive of Cheung Chau's accommodation, with a swimming pool and restaurant. Rooms have balconies, private baths, cable TV, and good-value weekly rates. Mon–Fri ❺, Sat & Sun ❻

Hong Kong Island

As the oldest colonized part of Hong Kong, its administrative and business centre, and site of some of the most expensive real estate in the world, **Hong Kong Island** is naturally the heart of the whole territory. Despite this, it measures just 15km across, with development concentrated along its **north shore** – a frenetically crowded and entertaining area of shops, restaurants, bars and financial institutions – and the far greener, mellower **south coast**, which actually sports a few beaches. Hills between the two rise to **The Peak**, which offers some of the island's best scenery and its freshest air. **Transport** around the island is easy, with the MTR and trams covering the north shore, and plentiful buses elsewhere.

The north shore

The island's **north shore**, overlooking **Victoria Harbour** to Kowloon, focuses on a narrow six-kilometre-long financial, commercial and entertainment district. At its core, **Central** sprouts an astounding array of hi-tech towers, edged to the west by **Sheung Wan**'s smaller scale and traditional Chinese businesses. Behind this the land climbs steeply, past parks and knots of restaurants and bars, to **The Peak**, a superb escape from street-level claustrophobia with unequalled views over the city. Back along the harbour and moving east through **Wan Chai** towards **Causeway Bay**, the emphasis shifts from finance to wining, dining and shopping – not to mention gambling, with Hong Kong's main horse racetrack located nearby at **Happy Valley**. Further east again, it's worth heading out to **Shau Kei Wan** to visit the **Museum of Coastal Defence**, built inside an old fortification.

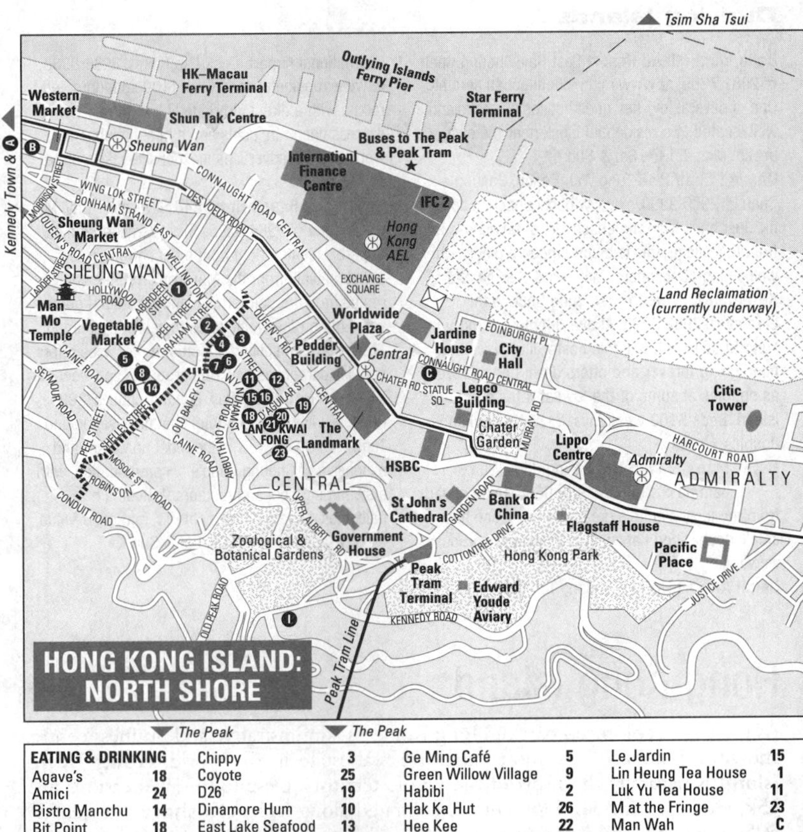

EATING & DRINKING							
Agave's	18	Chippy	3	Ge Ming Café	5	Le Jardin	15
Amici	24	Coyote	25	Green Willow Village	9	Lin Heung Tea House	1
Bistro Manchu	14	D26	19	Habibi	2	Luk Yu Tea House	11
Bit Point	18	Dinamore Hum	10	Hak Ka Hut	26	M at the Fringe	23
Blue Door	2	East Lake Seafood	13	Hee Kee	22	Man Wah	C
C-Bar/Calafornia	20	Fat Angelo's	14	IR 1968	29	Muyu Zigan	4
Carnegie's	27	Fook Lam Moon	31	Ivan the Kozak	7	Nha Trang	4
		Fringe Club	23	La Pampa	8	Old China Hand	30

The most obvious **arrival points** on the island are Central MTR Station, or via two of the vehicular **cross-harbour tunnels**, but it's far more romantic to reach Central aboard the **Star Ferry** from Tsim Sha Tsui, which docks immediately east of the Outlying Islands Ferry Pier. Aside from the MTR Island Line, buses and trams, you should make use, too, of the unique **Mid-Levels Escalator**, which runs uphill from Central, and the extensive system of **elevated walkways** that link many buildings between Sheung Wan and the Bank of China tower.

Note that the whole harbourside area between Central and Wan Chai is undergoing extensive **land reclamation** at present to provide space for a congestion-relieving expressway, plazas and parkland.

Central

Central takes in the densely crowded heart of Hong Kong's financial district, and extends for a few hundred metres in all directions from Central MTR Station. The main west–east roads here are Connaught Road, Des

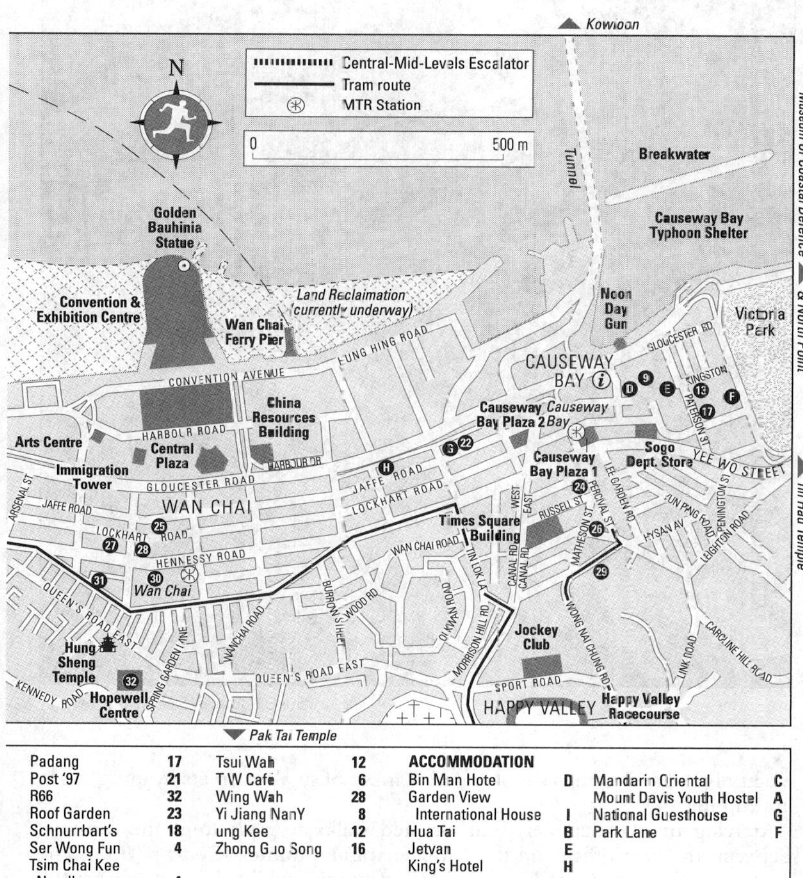

				ACCOMMODATION			
Padang	17	Tsui Wah	12	Bin Man Hotel	D	Mandarin Oriental	C
Post '97	21	TW Cafe	6	Garden View International House	I	Mount Davis Youth Hostel	A
R66	32	Wing Wah	28	Hua Tai	B	National Guesthouse	G
Roof Garden	23	Yi Jiang NanY	8	Jetvan	E	Park Lane	F
Schnurrbart's	18	ung Kee	12	King's Hotel	H		
Ser Wong Fun	4	Zhong Guo Song	16				
Tsim Chai Kee Noodle	4						

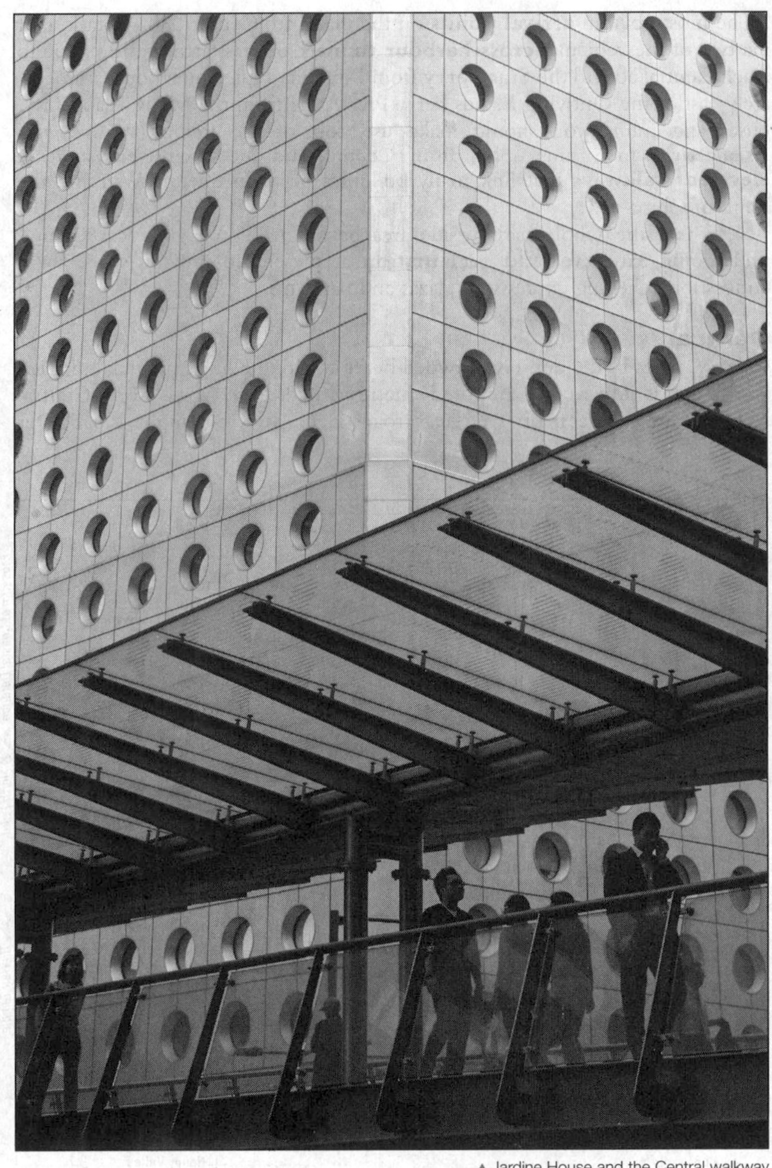

▲ Jardine House and the Central walkway

Voeux Road and Queen's Road, with a mesh of smaller streets heading south and uphill.

Arriving on the Star Ferry, an elevated walkway leads from the terminal between the post office and the **International Finance Centre** (**IFC**). The centre itself houses a **mall** and the AEL terminus, while above it sprouts the eighty-eight storey, 420-metre high **IFC2**, Hong Kong's tallest building. This is so beautifully proportioned that it's not until you see the top brushing the clouds that you realize the tower stands half as high again as anything else in the area. Sadly, you can't ride the lift up for views, though there's a virtual 360-degree version on the IFC website (Ⓦwww.ifc.com.hk/english).

Continue straight ahead on the walkway, and you pass between **Jardine House** (the tower full of portholes) and **Exchange Square**, before descending into the heart of an extremely upmarket shopping area along **Des Voeux Road** – easily recognizable from its tramlines. The smartest mall here is the **Landmark**, on the corner with Pedder Street, though the best-known shop is undoubtedly **Shanghai Tang** on tiny Theatre Lane between Des Voeux and Queens roads (next to Exit D2 from Central MTR), specializing in pricey designer garments in bright colours, recalling traditional Chinese wear.

South of Queen's Road, the land begins to slope seriously upwards, making walking laborious in hot weather. Head up D'Aguilar Street, and you'll enter the **Lan Kwai Fong** area, Central's barfly district, stuffed with theme bars and restaurants that now overflow into several neighbouring streets, including Wing Wah Lane (locally known as "Rat Alley"). Also of interest here is the **Luk Yu Tea House** on Stanley Street, a 1930s-style establishment (see p.686).

East of the Landmark along Queens Road lie two extraordinary buildings whose hi-tech appearance mask deeply traditional Chinese design beliefs. The **Hong Kong and Shanghai Bank (HSBC)** dates from 1985; designed by Sir Norman Foster, it reputedly cost over US$1 billion. The whole building is supported off the ground so that it's possible to walk right underneath – a necessity stipulated by the old *feng shui* belief that the centre of power on the island, Government House, which lies directly to the north of the bank, should be accessible in a straight line from the main point of arrival on the island, the Star Ferry. From underneath, the building's insides are transparent, and you can look up into its heart through the colossal glass atrium (and ride the escalators up to use the ATMs on the first floor).

Past the HSBC, the three-hundred-metre-high, blue-glass and steel **Bank of China** was designed by a team led by the renowned I.M. Pei. In *feng shui* terms, the bank's threatening, knife-like tower can be seen like a lightning conductor, drawing good luck down from the sky before any can reach its shorter rival next door. Many locals dislike it but there are exceptional **views** from long windows on the forty-third floor – you're allowed up during office hours. Below, **Statue Square** is an oddly empty space, sided to the east by the anachronistic, domed, granite **Legco Building**, century-old home of the Legislative Council, Hong Kong's equivalent of a parliament.

The Mid-Levels Escalator

Head east along Queens Road from the Central MTR – or follow walkways from the International Finance Centre – and you'll reach the covered **Mid-Levels Escalator**, which rises in sections 800m up the hill as far as Conduit Road and the expensive **Mid-Levels** residential area. During the morning (6–10am), when people are setting out to work, the escalators run downwards only; from 10.20am to midnight they run up. Places to get off and explore include the restaurant district between Wellington Street and Lyndhurst Terrace; the narrow lanes west of the escalator between Queens Road and Hollywood Road, full of crowded produce markets and small shops specializing in domestic goods; **Hollywood Road** itself, lined with antique shops and fine art galleries (see p.664); and the restaurant, bar and café district of **Soho**, laid out along Elgin and Staunton streets.

Sheung Wan

West of Central, **Sheung Wan**'s major landmark is the waterfront **Shun Tak** Centre, edged in red and housing both the Hong Kong–Macau Ferry Terminal and Sheung Wang MTR Station. The main road here, Connaught, is crammed with traffic and the area looks no different from Central, but venture inland and things begin to change rapidly.

First stop is **Western Market** (daily 10am–7pm), a brick Edwardian-era building featuring ground-floor tourist tack and excellent-value fabric shops upstairs. Follow **Morrison Street** uphill from here and you'll soon cross **Bonham Strand**; head west and you enter a web of lanes centred around **Bonham Strand West**, **Queens Road West** and **Wing Lok Street** whose shops specialize in dried foods and Traditional Chinese Medicine products such as birds' nests, ginseng, assorted marine creatures, deer antlers, edible fungus and aromatic fruits. There's a fine line between food and medicine in China, but the best way of telling the difference here is seeing what is displayed in tiny red- and -gold gift packages (rare medicines), and what is shifted by the sackful (usually food). Further up Morrison Street, **Sheung Wan Market** is a multi-storey maze of Chinese shoppers after fresh vegetables, fish and meat, with an inexpensive **cooked food** area up top.

Morrison Road dead-ends at Queens Road; turn east, and you'll soon see **Ladder Street**, a set of steep, broad stone steps heading uphill. This is one of many such stairways scattered between here and Central, a relic of the nineteenth-century sedan-chair carriers, who used them to get their loads up the hillsides. Halfway up Ladder Street, **Upper Lascar Row**, commonly known as **Cat Street**, is wall-to-wall with curio stalls loaded with coins, ornaments, jewellery, Chairman Mao badges and chops.

At the top of Ladder Street, the 150-year-old **Man Mo Temple** (daily 10am–6pm) on Hollywood Road is notable for its great hanging coils of incense suspended from the ceiling, filling the interior with eye-watering, aromatic smoke. The two figures on the main altar are the Taoist gods of Literature (*man* in Cantonese) and the Martial Arts (*mo*). Located as it is in a deeply traditional area, this is one of the most atmospheric temples to visit in Hong Kong. **Hollywood Road** itself is of interest for the slew of **antique shops and art galleries** running all the way east to the Mid-Levels Escalator, with goods and prices ranging from the touristy to the serious-art-collector-only brackets.

The Zoological and Botanical Gardens, Government House and Hong Kong Park

In a general southerly direction from Lan Kwai Fong – a short but steep walk along Glenealy Street and under the flyover – are the **Hong Kong Zoological and Botanical Gardens** (daily 6am–7pm; free); you can also get here on the #3B bus from Connaught Road, outside Exchange Square in Central. The gardens' two sections are connected by a walkway underneath Albany Street, and the modest collection of birds, monkeys and other beasts makes a pleasant refuge from the hubbub of Central. North of the gardens, just across Upper Albert Road, **Government House** was the official residence of fifteen Hong Kong governors, from 1855 until 1997. The house is closed to the public, and the gardens are only open one weekend a year – usually in March.

Exit the gardens via the walkway over Garden Road to the east, and it's fifteen minutes on foot along MacDonnell Road to **Hong Kong Park** (daily 6.30am–11pm; free). There are also entrances off Queens Road, east of the Bank of China tower, not far from Admiralty MTR (underneath the gleaming, bizarrely-shaped **Lippo Centre**). The park is a hilly but beautiful spot, full of greenery, lotus ponds and waterfalls, and a firm favourite with **brides** wanting wedding photographs. The highlight is the **Edward Youde Aviary** (daily 10am–5pm, free), where raised walkways lead you through a re-created rainforest canopy inside a giant meshed enclosure, with rare and colourful birds swooping about, nesting and breeding. Downhill near the Queen's Road entrance, the **Flagstaff House Museum of Tea Ware** (daily Wed–Mon 10am–5pm; free) is an elegant colonial structure built between 1844 and 1846, and houses three thousand Chinese artefacts related to tea making. You can sample quality brews next door – and buy good-value tea and reproduction antique teaware – at the pricey but pleasant *Lock Cha Teahouse* (daily 10am–10pm), which also serves *dim sum* snacks.

The Peak

Victoria Peak – usually known as just **The Peak** – rises 552m over Central and Victoria Harbour. Since the 1870s, The Peak has been the premier address for Hong Kong's elite – which these days usually means Chinese tycoons – and reasons to come up here include not just the superb vistas and forest walks, but also the ascent in the **Peak Tram** (daily 7am–midnight; $24 single, $30 return; you can also use Octopus cards). This is, in fact, a funicular railway, which runs from the **Peak Tram terminal** in Garden Road in Central, most easily reached aboard bus #15C from outside the Outlying Islands Ferry Pier (daily 10am–11.40pm; approximately every 30min; $3.50). The track is incredibly steep, climbing the 386 vertical metres to its upper terminus in about eight minutes.

You can also catch **bus** #15 (daily 6.15am–midnight; $9.20) to The Peak from Exchange Square bus station – the views are just as good, but it takes thirty minutes. Fitness fanatics can **walk** up, too, though for most people walking down is a more realistic option.

All ways up terminate around the ugly, wok-shaped **Peak Tower**, featuring lookout platforms and a branch of Madame Tussauds, with wax models ranging from Zhang Zemin to Jacky Chan. Opposite is the **Peak Galleria** mall, full of souvenir shops and cafés – the best value of which is the *Pacific Coffee Company*, which has a huge glass viewing window. Wherever you get them from, **views** from up here are stupendous, down over the Island's intensely crowded north shore (incredibly, you're not much higher here than the top of IFC2), across the busy harbour to a lower-rise, unspectacular Kowloon, and the green peaks of the New Territories.

To reach The Peak's very **summit** from this area, follow **Mount Austin Road** for twenty minutes to its end at the Victoria Peak Garden, formerly the site of the governor's residence. There's also an attractive, signposted hour-long **circuit walk** around The Peak, a shady stroll through forest with surprisingly large, old trees in places, plus more sweeping views down over the SAR.

An excellent way to **descend The Peak** is to walk down one of several tracks, the quickest being the **Old Peak Road**, a little hard to find around the side of the Peak Tower. A steep, twenty-minute hike lands you amongst high-rise residences southwest of the Zoological and Botanical Gardens, which you can reach by continuing down the road for a further fifteen minutes.

Wan Chai

East from Central, **Wan Chai** is a nondescript district of broad, busy main roads and more towers, though these mainly house commercial, rather than financial, institutions. Back in the 1950s, **Wan Chai** was a thriving red-light district, famed as the setting for Richard Mason's novel *The World of Suzy Wong*, and there's still a vaguely sleazy feel to its core of **bars** compared to those around

Central. The main arteries here are parallel **Hennessy Road**, **Lockhart Road** – both lined with shops, restaurants and businesses – and the waterfront expressway, **Gloucester Road**. Wanchai MTR Station is on Hennessy Road, while trams use Johnston Road, one block south; either are within walking distance of the sights.

Sights, however, are few. The most striking building is the **Hong Kong Convention and Exhibition Centre**, which juts out into the harbour and plausibly resembles a manta ray. This is where the British formally handed Hong Kong back to the Chinese in June 1997, and as such is a huge draw for mainland tourists, who pose beside the **Golden Bauhinia statue** behind, flanked by both the Chinese and Hong Kong SAR flags.

Immediately south across Gloucester Road soars the 78-storey **Central Plaza**, whose glowing cladding changes colour every fifteen minutes from 6pm to 6am. For splendid **360-degree views** over the city, catch the lift to the (free) public viewing area on the forty-sixth floor. If you like your views with afternoon tea, however, try *R66* on the sixty-sixth floor of the **Hopewell Centre**, further inland on Queens Road East (see p.689).

Elsewhere, Wan Chai's emphasis is more functional, though there are many backstreet **markets**, such as the flower and bird market down Tai Wong Street West, opposite the tiny **Hung Sheng Temple** on Queen's Road East. More imposing is the **Pak Tai Temple** (daily 8am–6pm), at the head of Stone Nullah Lane, dedicated to the flood-quelling God of the North. Craftsmen down the adjacent laneways make fantastic little **funeral offerings** out of bamboo and coloured paper, including cars, houses and aeroplanes.

Causeway Bay

East from Wan Chai, you can reach **Causeway Bay** by MTR or trams along **Yee Wo Street**, a continuation of Hennessy Road. The atmosphere here is lively, the streets loaded with restaurants and accommodation, and with scores of seething shopping and entertainment plazas dotted around. The biggest of these is **Times Square** (take Exit A from Causeway Bay MTR), two towers constructed in 1993 and packed with themed shopping over sixteen floors. These range from computers to haute couture, a cinema multiplex and four floors of eateries.

Wan Chai's sole tourist sight is the waterfront **Noon Day Gun** – immortalized in Noel Coward's song *Mad Dogs and Englishmen*. This small naval cannon is still fired off with a loud report every day at noon, a habit dating back to the early days of the colony; at other times, there's nothing to see, however, and the gun is difficult to reach across Gloucester Road's busy multi-lane layout (take the pedestrian bridge from the top of Percival Street and then walk east).

The eastern part of Causeway Bay is dominated by **Victoria Park**, an extensive, open space by Hong Kong's standards, which contains swimming pools and other sports facilities. This has become the location for the annual candlelit vigil held on June 4 to commemorate the victims of Tian'anmen Square, in addition to hosting Hong Kong's largest Chinese New Year fairs. Come early in the morning and you'll see dozens of people practising *tai ji*. Down at the southeastern corner of the park, right by Tin Hau MTR (Exit A), is the 200-year-old **Tin Hau Temple**, a rather dark, gloomy place surrounded unhappily by skyscrapers (daily 7am–7pm). Tin Hau is the name given locally to the Goddess of the Sea, and her temples can be found throughout Hong Kong, originally in prominent positions by the shore but often marooned by land reclamation far inland. You can also reach this Tin Hau Temple on any tram heading for North Point; get off immediately after passing Victoria Park on your left.

Happy Valley

Happy Valley is a mostly low-lying area south of Wan Chai and Causeway Bay, notable for its huge multi-ethnic **cemeteries**, which cover a hillside to the west. But – as its Cantonese name, *Pau Ma Dei* or "Horse Racetrack" makes clear – Happy Valley really means only one thing for the people of Hong Kong: horse racing, or, more precisely, gambling. The **Happy Valley Racecourse**, which dates back to 1846, is where you can witness Hong Kong at its rawest and most grasping: entrance to the public enclosure is just $10, with races almost every Wednesday during the racing season (Sept–June). Otherwise, enquire at HKTB about their "Come Horse-racing Tour" ($580 or more depending on the event; age and dress regulations apply), which includes transportation to and from the track, entry to the Members' Enclosure and a buffet meal at the official Jockey Club – and tips on how to pick a winner. Happy Valley can be reached from Central or Causeway Bay on a spur of the tramline, or on bus #1 from Central.

The Museum of Coastal Defence

Around 6km east of Causeway Bay, the splendid **Museum of Coastal Defence** (Fri–Wed 10am–5pm; $10) is located inside the 1887 Lei Yue Mui Fort, which itself is built into a hill overlooking the eastern end of the harbour. Aside from views on a sunny day from gun emplacements pointing seawards, the former barracks and ammunition rooms are now filled with artefacts, manneqins and photographs covering the period from the Ming dynasty to the handover. You can get here on the Island Line MTR to Shau Kei Wan; take Exit B1 and follow the signs for ten minutes via Shau Kei Wan Street East and busy Tun Hei Road.

Moving on from Shau Kei Wan, bus #9 runs from outside the MTR station to beaches at Shek O (see p.669).

The south coast

On its south side, Hong Kong Island straggles into the sea in a series of dangling peninsulas and inlets. The atmosphere is far quieter here than on the north shore, and the climate warmer and sunnier. You'll find not only separate towns such as **Aberdeen** and **Stanley**, with a flavour of their own, but also beaches, including those at popular **Repulse Bay** and, farther east, at the remoter outpost of **Shek O**. Especially if you're travelling with children, you should consider a visit to **Ocean Park**, a huge adventure theme park with a wonderful aquarium, just beyond Aberdeen.

Though there is no MTR line to the south coast, **buses** are plentiful to all destinations, and nowhere is more than an hour from Central.

Aberdeen

Aberdeen is the largest separate town on Hong Kong Island, with a population of more than sixty thousand living in garishly coloured tower blocks around the sheltered **harbour**. This is a thriving **fishing port**, its fleet of family-run trawlers providing around a third of Hong Kong's fish and prawn catch. You can appreciate the fleet's size during the fishing **moratorium** (June–July), when the harbour is packed to capacity with freshly cleaned vessels. The harbour is also the venue for the annual **Dragon Boat Festival** held on the fifth day of the fifth lunar month (usually in June), one of the biggest in Hong Kong.

To reach Aberdeen, catch **bus #70** from Exchange Square in Central (15min). From the bus stop, cross over or under Aberdeen Praya Road to reach the harbour, where there's a busy early-morning co-operative **fish market** and, through the day, women waiting to solicit your custom for a **sampan tour** (around $50 per head for a 30min ride, irrespective of the number of travellers). The trip offers photogenic views of houseboats complete with dogs, drying laundry and outdoor kitchens, as well as luxury yachts, boat yards and **floating restaurants**, which are especially spectacular lit up at night.

Cheapskates can, in fact, enjoy a ten-minute **free harbour trip** by catching a ferry to the garishly decorated three-floor *Jumbo Restaurant* (Mon–Sat 11am–11.30pm, Sun 7am–11.30pm; see p.687) from a signed dock with a red gateway near the fish market; there's no pressure to actually have a meal here if you just want to look around. You'll also pass through the harbour if you use the **Aberdeen–Lamma ferry** (see p.681), so again won't need to pay for a separate tour.

Moving on, bus #73 links Aberdeen to Repulse Bay, Deep Water Bay and Stanley; Ocean Park is better reached on the #48.

Ocean Park

Ocean Park, a gigantic theme and adventure park (daily 10am–6pm; $185, children aged 3–11 $93, children under 3 free; Ⓦwww.oceanpark.com.hk), covers an entire peninsula to the east of Aberdeen. The price of the ticket is all-inclusive, and once you're inside, all rides and shows are free. You could easily spend the best part of a day here, and at weekends in summer you may find yourself frustrated by queues at the popular attractions, so make sure you arrive early in order to enjoy yourself at a relaxed pace. **Bus #260** runs to the main eastern entrance from the Exchange Square station via Admiralty MTR (daily; approximately every 15min; 9am–6.30pm).

In the face of fierce **competition** from Disney over on Lantau, the park is busy repositioning itself, balancing its fairground rides with displays about wildlife and the natural world. Star attractions are four **giant pandas** (two of them presents from the mainland government to celebrate the tenth anniversary of the handover), for whom a special $80-million, 2000-square-metre complex was created, complete with kitchen, clinic, fake slopes and misting machines to mimic a mountain atmosphere.

The first area you'll see is the Lowland section, which includes some life-size moving dinosaur models and a butterfly house – from here, there's a peaceful 1.5-kilometre **cable-car ride** to the Headland section at the tip of the peninsula. This is where you'll find scary rides such as the Dragon roller coaster and Abyss Turbo Drop; a walk-through **aquarium**, where you can view sharks nose-to-nose through glass; the **Ocean Theatre**, where trained dolphins and sea lions perform; plus the **Atoll Reef**, a huge coral-reef aquarium that contains more than five thousand fish. Outdoor covered **escalators** take you back to ground level at the western gate, via the **Raging River** ride – expect to get soaked.

Moving on, bus #629 runs from Ocean Park's western entrance back to Admiralty MTR; from the eastern gate, bus #48 takes you to Aberdeen while #73 continues eastwards along the coastal beaches to Stanley.

Deep Water Bay, Repulse Bay and beyond

The seven-kilometre-long coastal strip east of Ocean Park forms several pleasant sandy **bays** linked to everywhere between Aberdeen and Stanley by **bus** #73, and to Ocean Park, Stanley and Central by bus #260. While the beaches offer a nice break from urban Hong Kong and there are plenty of good seafront **restaurants** out this way, note that the water is generally too polluted for swimming, the shoreline is increasingly built up, and the sand often packed to capacity through the summer and at weekends.

Deep Water Bay is small and enjoys excellent views of green islets offshore, though it drops straight off the coastal road so is hardly secluded. **Repulse Bay** is the most popular, partly because it contains a number of shops and restaurants, but also because of its **Tin Hau Temple**, which has a longevity bridge, the crossing of which is said to add three days to your life. The backdrop to Repulse Bay is slightly bizarre, with an enormous, garish tower silhouetted against verdant hills, focused around the *Repulse Bay Hotel* – actually a restaurant and shopping complex. South of Repulse Bay, you'll find **Middle Bay** and **South Bay**, fifteen and thirty minutes, respectively, farther along the coast. These offer more private but narrower beaches.

Stanley

Straddling the neck of Hong Kong's most southerly peninsula, **Stanley** is a residential town whose draws include a bustling tourist market, a clutch of expat-oriented restaurants, and Hong Kong's largest **Dragon Boat Races**, held on the fifth day of the fifth month of the lunar calendar. Get here on **bus** #6, #66 or #260 from Central, #73 from Aberdeen or Repulse Bay, or green minibus #40 from Times Square in Causeway Bay.

Stanley is a tiny place – walk downhill from the bus stop and you'll fall into covered **Stanley Market,** which sells a mishmash of tourist souvenirs including clothes, embroideries and trinkets. Out the other side of the market is **Stanley Beach**, which, although not suitable for swimming, is lined by a row of romantic – if pricey – seafront restaurants. North along the shore, Stanley Plaza faces one of Hong Kong's oldest colonial buildings, two-storey **Murray House**, which was dismantled and removed from its original site in Central to make way for the Bank of China. Today, its elegant stone colonnades house stores, bars and restaurants, as well as the **Hong Kong Maritime Museum** (Tues–Sun 10am–6pm; $20), a small collection of photos, paintings and models relating to the sea. Just across the square from Murray House is yet another **Tin Hau Temple**, built in 1767, and worth a look for the blackened tiger skin spread-eagled on one wall, the remains of an animal bagged near here in 1942 – the last ever shot in Hong Kong.

South of the market down Wong Ma Kok Road, it's about a ten-minute walk to the pleasant **St Stephen's Beach**, the best in the area, accessible by steps down to the right immediately after a playing field. Beyond here is **Stanley Military Cemetery**, on Wong Ma Kok Road, containing the graves of many of those killed fighting the Japanese in World War II, and also the top-security Stanley Prison. The southern part of the peninsula is a closed military zone.

Moving on, take any of the above buses westwards, though to continue east you need to take the #14 or #314 bus to the Stanley–Shek O junction, and then bus #9 or minibus #16 to Shek O – tell the #14 or #314 driver that you're heading to Shek O and they'll put you off at the right place. The whole journey takes some thirty minutes.

Shek O

In the far southeast of the island, **Shek O** is Hong Kong's most remote settlement, with an almost Mediterranean flavour in its stone houses, narrow lanes and seafront location. There's a strong surf beating on the wide, white **beach**, which has a shady area of vine trellises at one end for barbecues and, during the week, is more or less deserted. Come for sunbathing and lunch at one of the cheap local restaurants. The surrounding headlands are also popular for **hiking**;

the HKTB can provide you with information about walking part of the Hong Kong Trail along the D'Aguilar peninsula.

You can't miss the beach – it's just 50m from the bus stop, beyond a small roundabout; nearby shops such as the Tung Lok Beachside Store sell beachwear, inflatable floats, plastic buckets and so on, and have storage lockers for valuables. Most of the other businesses in the village are welcoming and fairly inexpensive restaurants, mostly Vietnamese, Thai or both.

On Sunday afternoons (2.10–6.10pm), **bus** #309 runs hourly from Exchange Square in Central to Shek O; otherwise, first catch the MTR Island Line to **Shau Kei Wan MTR Station** on Hong Kong's northeastern shore – from where you could detour to the Museum of Coastal Defence (see p.667) – and pick up bus #9 to Shek O. See the "Stanley" section on p.669 for details on how to get to there from Shek O.

Kowloon

A four-kilometre-long strip of the mainland ceded to Britain in perpetuity in 1860 to add to their offshore island, **Kowloon** was accordingly developed with gusto and confidence, not least in the still-ongoing **land reclamation**, which has more than doubled the width of the original peninsula. These days, it's not so clear-cut where Kowloon really ends: the original "border" with the New Territories to the north was **Boundary Street**, though now Kowloon district runs past here for a further 3km or so.

While Hong Kong Island has mountains and beaches to offset the effects of urban claustrophobia, Kowloon has just more shops, more restaurants and more hotels. Initially, it's hard to see how such an unmitigatedly built-up, commercial and intensely crowded place could possibly appeal to travellers. One reason is the staggering **view** across the harbour to Hong Kong Island's skyscrapers and peaks; another is the sheer density of shopping opportunities here – from high-end jewellery to cutting-edge electronic goods and outright tourist tack – especially in the couple of square kilometres at the tip of the peninsula that make up **Tsim Sha Tsui**. To the north, **Yau Ma Tei** and **Mong Kok** are less touristy – though no less crowded – districts teeming with soaring tenements and local **markets**, some of which sell modern daily necessities, others with a distinctly traditional Chinese twist.

Across Boundary Street, the commercial emphasis gradually shifts towards separate, towering **residential estates**, each clustered around shopping plazas, parks and other amenities. A scattering of sights here includes one of Hong Kong's busiest temples, the **Wong Tai Sin**, and its prettiest, the **Chi Lin Nunnery** with its Tang-style architecture and beautiful traditional garden.

The two main ways to reach Kowloon are by the **Star Ferry** from Central to Tsim Sha Tsui, or along the **MTR**'s **Tsuen Wan Line**, which runs from Central under the harbour and up through Kowloon, with stations dotted at regular intervals along Nathan Road.

Tsim Sha Tsui

The tourist heart of Hong Kong, **Tsim Sha Tsui**, is an easy place to find your way around. The prime arrival point, the **Star Ferry Terminal**, is right on the southwestern tip of the peninsula. East from here are a number of harbourside museums and galleries – not to mention outstanding views of Hong Kong Island. Hong Kong's most famous street, **Nathan Road**, runs north up

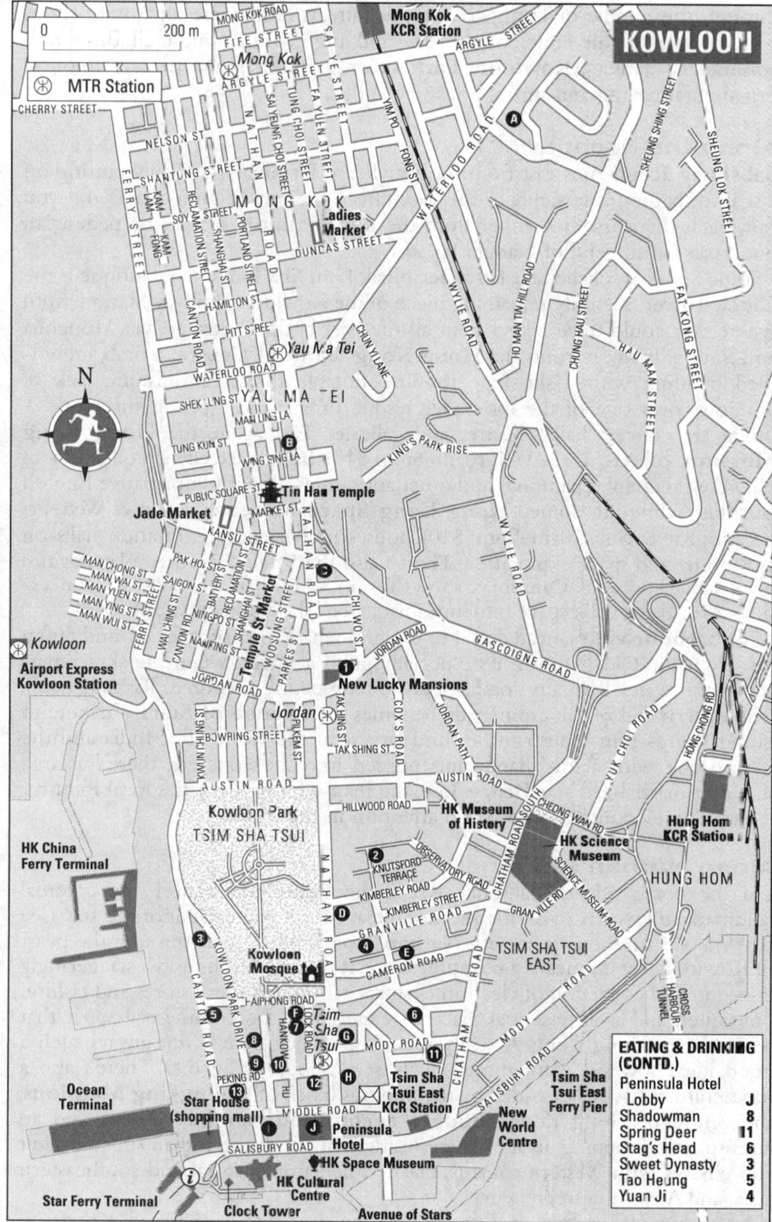

ACCOMMODATION				EATING & DRINKING			
Anne Black Guesthouse (YWCA)	A	Miramar	D	Aqua	13	Itamae Sushi	4
Chungking Mansions	H	Nathan	C	Bahama Mama's	2	Kakalok	10
Louie Business Hotel	F	New King's Hotel	B	Chao Inn	13	Light Vegetarian	1
Mirador Mansions	G	Peninsula Hotel	J	Delaney's	12	Macau Restaurant	7
		The Salisbury (YMCA)	I	Felix	J	Mrs Chan	12
		Star Guesthouse	E			Ned Kelly's Last Stand	9

through the middle of Tsim Sha Tsui, the streets either side alive with shops and shoppers at all hours of the day and night. In amongst all this brash commercial activity, **Kowloon Park** offers a bit of space to rest amongst ornamental paving and shrubberies.

Along the harbour

Salisbury Road runs east from the Star Ferry Terminal, physically cutting off a strip of harbourside sights to the south from the rest of Tsim Sha Tsui – you can reach them on foot either from the ferry terminal, or via the pedestrian underpass off the end of Nathan Road.

Some 50m east of the Star Ferry Terminal, Tsim Sha Tsui's main antique is the **Clock Tower**, the only remaining piece of the Kowloon Railway Station, from where you could once take a train all the way back to Europe, via Mongolia and Russia. Today, it fronts the **Hong Kong Cultural Centre,** a drab, brown-tiled building with a ski-slope roofline, notable for its astonishing lack of windows over one of the most picturesque urban landscapes in the world – inside are concert halls, theatres and galleries. East again, the **Hong Kong Museum of Art** (Fri–Wed 10am–6pm; $10) has an excellent collection of Chinese calligraphy, paintings and other antiquities, all with informative English labelling; while the domed **Hong Kong Space Museum** (Mon & Wed–Fri 1–9pm, Sat & Sun 10am–9pm; $10) houses user-friendly exhibition halls on astronomy and space exploration. There's also the **Space Theatre** planetarium here, which presents Omnimax shows for an additional fee ($24–32, concessions $16; Ⓦwww.hk.space.museum for current show information).

For **harbour views**, head down to the promenade that runs for around 500m east from the Clock Tower; it's especially good at night, when the skyscrapers across the water light up unashamedly in competing coloured, flashing neon. The eastern end of the promenade becomes the **Avenue of Stars**, a tribute to Hong Kong's film industry (the third largest in the world after India and the US). Along with actors' handprints pressed into the concrete, there's a large statue of martial-arts star **Bruce Lee**, the man who brought the local industry – and Chinese kung fu – to world attention in the 1970s.

Along Nathan Road

On the north side of Salisbury Road, the **Peninsula Hotel** – a colonial landmark still worth a visit for afternoon tea, even if you can't afford to stay (see p.689) – sits on the corner with **Nathan Road**, which cuts through the heart of Kowloon. By no means a beautiful street, it nonetheless houses a staggeringly concentrated collection of electronics shops, tailors, jewellery stores and fashion boutiques, and is an essential place to experience the commercial spirit that really drives Hong Kong. Actually spending money here is not always such a good idea, however – for more details, see "Shopping", p.690. There's also a multicultural flavour provided by the dubious block of **Chungking Mansions**, the centre of Hong Kong's **budget accommodation** (see p.658) and an atmospheric shopping arcade where immigrants from the Indian subcontinent rub elbows with Western tourists, businessmen from central and southeastern Asia, and African entrepreneurs.

A few hundred metres up past here on the west side of the road, **Kowloon Park** (daily 5am–midnight) is marked at its southeastern corner by the white-domed **Kowloon Mosque and Islamic Centre**, which caters to the substantial Muslim population of the area. The park itself provides welcome, green respite from the rest of Tsim Sha Tsui, though you can't see it from the street and have to climb steps up from Nathan Road. There's also an

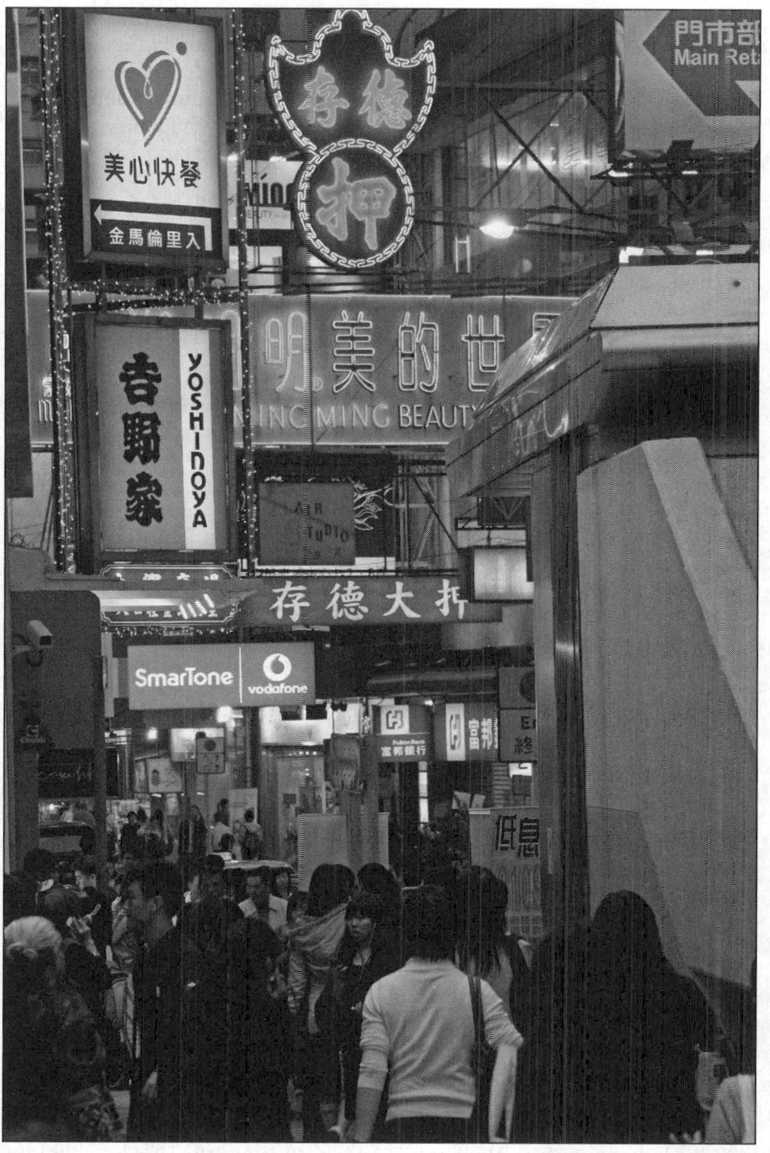

▲ Shopping off Nathan Road

Olympic-size indoor and outdoor **swimming pool complex** (daily 8am–noon, 1.30–6pm & 7.30–10pm; $21), plus an aviary, sculpture walk, and **Kung Fu Corner** (up behind the mosque), where experts in various martial arts give demonstrations every Sunday between 2.30 and 4.30pm.

Around 700m east of Kowloon Park and across busy Chatham Road South, a couple of informative but lifeless museums are perhaps best saved for a wet day.

The **Hong Kong Museum of History** (Mon & Wed–Sat 10am–6pm, Sun 10am–7pm; $10) features "the Hong Kong Story", a permanent history about the SAR's life and times, as well as numerous history-related, temporary exhibitions. Immediately south, the **Hong Kong Science Museum** (Mon–Wed & Fri 1–9pm, Sat & Sun 10am–9pm; $25) is of most fun for children, with a host of hands-on exhibits explaining the workings of everything from mobile phones to human perception.

Jordan to Mong Kok

North of Tsim Sha Tsui's boundary on Jordan Road, the neighbourhoods of **Jordan**, **Yau Ma Tei** and **Mong Kok** offer more of a Chinese flavour, plus some interesting markets. Nathan Road continues to be the main artery, dotted with **MTR stations** that you'll probably end up using to avoid the incredible crowds that clog the streets after about 10am and make walking tedious.

Running north off Jordan Road and within easy range of Jordan MTR (take Exit C2 and head west), **Temple Street** becomes a touristy but fun **night market** after 7pm every day. As well as shopping for cheap clothing, watches, DVDs and souvenirs, you can get your fortune told, eat some great seafood from street stalls, and sometimes listen in on impromptu performances of Chinese opera. A minute or two to the north of here is the local **Tin Hau Temple**, tucked away between Public Square Street and Market Street in a small, concreted park usually teeming with old men playing mahjong under the banyan trees. Just west, under the Gascoigne Road flyover at the junction of Kansu and Battery streets, the **Jade Market** (daily 9am–6pm) has 450 stalls in two different sections, offering everything from souvenir trinkets to family heirlooms in jade, crystal, quartz and other stones.

Near Yau Ma Tei MTR and running north off Dundas Street, Tung Choi Street hosts a **Ladies Market** (daily noon–10.30pm), flogging piles of cheap clothes, jewellery, toys and bags. Parallel streets – the heart of **Mong Kok** district – are thick with shops specializing in computers, cameras and mobile phones, a more reliable place to buy these things than Tsim Sha Tsui. Push on north over Argyle Street – you're close to Mong Kok MTR here – and Tung Choi transforms into a **Goldfish Market** lined with shops stocking aquaria, corals, exotic fish and even some dubiously exotic breeds of snake, lizard and turtle. Further north again, over Prince Edward Road (Prince Edward MTR), it's a short walk east – past the top of Fa Yuen Street and its discount **clothing stores** – to the **Flower Market** (daily from 10am), in Flower Market Road. This is best on Sundays and in the run-up to Chinese New Year, when people come to buy narcissi, orange trees and plum blossom to decorate their apartments in order to bring good luck. Flower Market Road runs east to the **Bird Garden** (daily 7am–8pm), where songbird stalls are set in a Chinese-style garden, with trees, seats and elegant carved marble panels showing birds in the wild. As well as the hundreds of birds on sale at the **market** here, along with their intricately designed bamboo cages, there are also live crickets – food for the birds. Local men bring their own songbirds here for an airing, and the place gives a real glimpse into a traditional area of Chinese life – spiritually, a thousand miles from the rest of Kowloon.

North of Boundary Street

The three-kilometre-deep area between Boundary Street and the first of the New Territories' mountains holds several places of interest, all accessible on the MTR from Kowloon. A couple of kilometres northwest of Boundary Street at

Cheung Sha Wan, the **Lei Cheng Uk Han Tomb Museum** on Tonkin Street (Mon–Wed, Fri & Sat 10am–1pm & 2–6pm, Sun 1–6pm; free) is constructed over a 2000-year-old Han-dynasty tomb that was unearthed by workmen in 1955. By far the oldest structure discovered in Hong Kong, the tomb offers some rare proof of the ancient presence of the Chinese in the area. What is really interesting, however, is to compare photos of the site from the 1950s (paddy fields and green hills) with the skyscrapers that surround the area today. Catch the Tsuen Wan Line to **Cheung Sha Wan MTR**, take exit A3, walk for five minutes along Tonkin Street and the museum is on your left.

Northeast along the Kwun Tong MTR Line

Northeast of Boundary Street are a string of attractions reached via successive stations on the **Kwun Tong MTR Line**. The first is **Kowloon Walled City Park** (daily 6.30am–11pm; free), the site of a Qing-dynasty fortified garrison post whose soldiers refused to cede sovereignty to Britain when it took over the New Territories in 1898. The extraordinary consequence was that for nearly a century it became a virtually self-governing enclave of criminals and vagrants, off-limits to the authorities until they negotiated its closure and demolition in 1994. It's now an attractive spread of lawns, trees and traditional buildings, including the "city's" reconstructed *yamen* (courthouse building). Get here by catching the MTR to Lok Fu, then taking bus #11D from near Exit A past the park entrance, a kilometre south on Junction Road.

East again from Lok Fu on the MTR, the next stop is Wong Tai Sin, for **Wong Tai Sin Temple** (daily 7am–5.30pm; small donation expected), a thriving Taoist, Buddhist and Confucian complex that's packed with more worshippers than any other in Hong Kong – from the MTR, take Exit B2 or B3 for the temple. Big, bright and colourful, it provides a good look at popular Chinese religion: vigorous kneeling, incense burning and the noisy rattling of joss sticks in canisters, as well as the presentation of food and drink to the deities. Large numbers of **fortune-tellers**, some of whom speak English, have stands to the right of the entrance and charge around $20 for palm-reading, about half that for a face-reading.

One stop further on at **Diamond Hill MTR** (Exit C2 and follow the signs for 5min), the modern **Chi Lin Nunnery** (daily 9am–3.30pm; free) is an elegant wooden temple built without nails in the Tang style, just about the only example of this type of architecture in all China. Opposite, the **Nan Lian Gardens** (daily 7am–9pm; free) continue the Tang theme in an exquisite reconstruction of a contemporary garden; there are contorted pine trees, artfully shaped hillocks, ornamental ponds populated by carp, wooden halls and brightly painted bridges and pavilions.

Moving on, buses from Diamond Hill run to Clear Water Bay or Sai Kung Town in the New Territories (see p.679 & p.680).

The New Territories

Many people fly in and out of Hong Kong without even realizing that the SAR comprises anything more than the city itself. However, the **New Territories**, a thirty-kilometre-deep swath between Kowloon and the Guangdong border, comes complete with country parks, beautiful coastlines, farming communities and craggy mountains – as well as booming **New Towns**, satellite settlements built from scratch in the last forty years to absorb the overflow from Hong Kong's burgeoning population. A whole series of designated **country parks** includes the unspoilt **Sai Kung Peninsula** to the east, offering excellent walking trails and secluded beaches. Less dedicated souls after birdlife should head northwest to the **Hong Kong Wetland Park**; while there's some architectural and cultural heritage to soak up around otherwise modern towns such as **Tsuen Wan** and **Sha Tin**. For serious extended hikes, the **MacLehose Trail** runs for 100km across the New Territories; contact the **Country and Marine Parks** (Ⓦwww.afcd.gov.hk/eindex.html) for information on trails and conditions.

Travelling around the New Territories is straightforward. Frequent **buses** connect all towns; the **KCR East** from Kowloon's Hung Hom KCR Station heads north via Sha Tin and Tai Po to the Chinese border; while the **KCR West** from the Mei Foo MTR Station gets you close to most of the northwestern sights.

The northwest

The recently opened **Hong Kong Wetland Park** is easily the main draw of the New Territories' northwest, offering a chance to see some genuinely wild wildlife – and how the Chinese like to organize nature. Also out this way, walled villages at **Tsuen Wan** and **Kam Tin** provide a glimpse of old Hong Kong, while hikers might want to get to grips with **Tai Mo Shan**, the SAR's tallest peak.

Tsuen Wan and Sam Tung Uk Museum

With over a million inhabitants, the New Town of **TSUEN WAN**, located at the end of the Tsuen Wan MTR Line, a thirty-minute ride from Tsim Sha Tsui, has all the amenities of a large, modern city in its own right. The only tourist sight, however, is the **Sam Tung Uk Museum** (Mon & Wed–Sun 9am–5pm; free), a restored 200-year-old **walled village** of a type typical of this part of southern China – take Exit E from the MTR and follow the signs for five minutes. The village was founded in 1786 by a **Hakka** clan named Chan, who continued to live here until the 1970s. Now, the houses have been restored with period furnishings, and there are various exhibitions on aspects of the lives of the Hakka people – for more on whom, see p.532.

Tai Mo Shan and Kam Tin

There's more old architecture north of Tsuen Wan at the small residential town of **Kam Tin**. To get here from Kowloon, catch a KCR West train to **Kam Sheung Road** station; from Tsuen Wan, hop on bus #51 to Kam Tin from an overpass just north of Tsuen Wan MTR. The train is fast but the bus ride spectacular, running past Hong Kong's 957-metre apex, **Tai Mo Shan**, which is nearly twice the height of Victoria Peak on Hong Kong Island. If you want to reach the summit, there's a bus stop on a pass below the peak – get off here and follow a signposted path up to the top, where you can link up with the MacLehose Trail.

Over on the far side of Tai Mo Shan, **KAM TIN** is the site of **Kat Hing Wai**, one of Hong Kong's last inhabited **walled settlements**. Dating back to the late seventeenth century when a clan named Tang settled here, the village ($3 donation to enter) still comprises thick, six-metre-high walls and guard towers. Note the gates, too – confiscated by the British in the late nineteenth century, they were eventually found in Ireland and returned. Inside the walls, there's a wide lane running down the middle of the village, with tiny alleys leading off it. Old Hakka ladies in traditional hats pester visitors with cameras for more donations, and most of the buildings are modern, but the atmosphere is as different from downtown Hong Kong as you can imagine. To get here from the #51 bus stop, walk a few minutes farther west (the same direction as the bus), and it's on your left, visible from the main road. From the Kam Sheung Road KCR Station, cross the bridge over the storm-water canal, and follow signs for 250m.

Hong Kong Wetland Park

Hong Kong Wetland Park (Wed–Mon 10am–5pm; $30) covers 61 hectares of saltwater marsh up along the Chinese border, part of a larger system of lagoons known as the **Mai Po Marshes** that draws wintering wildfowl between November and February, and a host of migrating birds from August to October. The park itself is carefully landscaped to be just as attractive to human visitors, with paths, bridges, bird hides and an excellent visitor centre, and makes a great half-day out. Highlights include the mangrove boardwalk, where you can watch mudskippers and fiddler crabs scooting over the mud; huge lotus ponds (look for the occasional swimming snake); and the visitor centre's aquarium stocked with gharial crocodiles and fish. There's a branch of *Café de Coral* here, serving inexpensive lunches and drinks.

To reach the park, take the Tsuen Wan MTR Line to Mei Foo, then the KCR West to Tin Shui Wai, then LRT (Light Rail) #705 or #706 to Wetland Park Station, from where the park is a signposted ten-minute walk past a surreal high-rise housing estate. This is actually a straightforward journey, and takes only around 1hr 15min from Tsim Sha Tsui.

North

The **KCR East** runs due north for 30km from Kowloon through the New Territories to the border with mainland China. The main points of interest here surround the New Town of **Sha Tin**, where's there's a good half-day's worth of museums, temples and short hikes to indulge, though if you're keen on getting out into some proper countryside, excellent walks further up around **Plover Cove Country Park** will need a day in themselves.

Sha Tin and around

The booming New Town of **Sha Tin** is best known to Hong Kongers as the site of the territory's second **racecourse**, which is packed with fanatical gamblers on race days. Tourist sights here are spread out either side of the **Shing Mun River**, and while it's possible to walk between, them they are better reached either on the KCR East from **Tai Wai** or **Sha Tin stations**, or by changing trains at Tai Wai and taking the KCR East extension one stop to **Che Kung Temple Station** – see the following accounts for the closest point

Get out at Tai Wai Station, take Exit C or D, and it's a five-minute ride aboard bus #80 up Hong Mui Kuk Road to trails ascending forested **Mong Fu Shek** (also known as **Amah Rock**). A steep but straightforward thirty-minute walk on a paved path brings you to the boulder-strewn top, with excellent views down over the Shing Mun River and Sha Tin's tower blocks and busy roadways.

Hong Kong's **Heritage Museum** (Mon & Wed–Sat 10am–6pm, Sun 10am–7pm; $10) is a well-signposted five-minute walk from Che Kung Temple KCR Station, just over the river – you can also walk in about thirty minutes from Tai Wai Station via the Che Kung Temple itself. The museum is packed with

▲Ten Thousand Buddhas Monastery

permanent and temporary exhibitions; one of the best covers life in the New Territories across the ages and features a mock-up of a traditional fishing village, while another focuses on Cantonese Opera, with theatre mock-ups, plot accounts and photos of famous performers. Also close to Che Kung Temple Station, **Che Kung Temple** (daily 7am–6pm; free) is a stark granite complex with oversized halls dedicated to a Song-dynasty general who became patron deity of a local village; it's notable for the numerous brass fans decorating the place, which are said to bring good luck.

Across town, Sha Tin's eccentric **Ten Thousand Buddhas Monastery** (daily 9am–5pm; free) dates only to the 1960s, but is one of the most interesting temples in the New Territories. Signs from Sha Tin KCR Station (itself a twenty-minute walk from the Heritage Museum along Tai Po Road), lead past Po Fook Ancestral Worship Halls to the temple path, which ascends a steep stairway flanked by five hundred gold-painted statues of Buddhist saints. The monastery comprises a garish collection of painted concrete statues and cheaply built halls, the main one of which houses some 13,000 miniature statues of Buddha. You can buy lunch here at the basic **vegetarian restaurant.**

Tai Mei Tuk and the Plover Cove Country Park

Northeast of Sha Tin, there are opportunities for escaping into some serious countryside at **Plover Cove Country Park**, which surrounds the massive Plover Cove Reservoir. To get here, take the KCR East to **Tai Po Market Station**, and then bus #75K to its terminus at the small village and service centre of **TAI MEI TUK**. There's a signposted circular walk here that takes about an hour, or a five-kilometre hike over the hills along the **Pat Sin Leng Nature Trail** to **Bride's Pool**, an attractively wooded picnic and camping site beside pools and waterfalls, which gets busy at weekends – you can also get here along a vehicle road from Tai Mei Tuk, though there are no buses. For more details about the many walks in this area, contact the HKTB (see p.652).

The east

The eastern part of the New Territories, around **Clear Water Bay** and the **Sai Kung Peninsula**, is where you'll find Hong Kong's prettiest beaches and walks. Things can get busy at weekends, however – it's best to come during the week and bring a picnic, though Sai Kung, at least, has plenty of good places to eat. The starting point for buses into both areas is **Diamond Hill MTR Station** on the Kwun Tong MTR Line; you'll need to put aside a whole day to visit either place.

Clear Water Bay

From Diamond Hill, catch **bus #91** for the forty-minute ride to Clear Water Bay. Around the terminus here are a couple of excellent, clean **beaches** – though with no nearby shops or facilities – and to the south is the start of a good three- to four-hour walk around the bay. First, follow the road to the **Clear Water Bay Golf and Country Club** (to use the tennis, swimming and golf facilities of this luxury club, visitors must join HKTB's "Sports and Recreation Tour", which costs $430 plus pay-as-you-play charges). From the car park outside the club entrance, follow signposts on to the wonderfully located **Tin Hau Temple** in **Joss House Bay**. There is thought to have been a temple to the Taoist Goddess of the Sea here for more than eight hundred years, and, as one of Hong Kong's few Tin Hau temples actually still commanding the sea, it's of immense significance: on the twenty-third day of the third lunar month each year (Tin Hau's birthday) a colossal seaborne celebration takes place on fishing boats in the bay.

Heading back up the slope, you can take another path that starts from the same car park outside the Golf and Country Club down past **Sheung Lau Wan**, a small village on the western shore of the peninsula. The path skirts the village, and continues on, forming a circular route around the headland back to the Clear Water Bay bus terminal.

Sai Kung Peninsula

Some way to the north of Clear Water Bay sits the irregularly shaped **Sai Kung Peninsula**, jagged with headlands, bluffs and tiny offshore islands. Though towns along the fringes are surprisingly upmarket and thick with harbours full of luxury yachts, the peninsula itself is Hong Kong's least developed area, and a haven for lovers of the great outdoors. Recommended **tour operators** specializing in the peninsula are NEI (Ⓣ2486 2112, Ⓦwww.kayak-and-hike.com), Asiatic Marine (Ⓦwww.asiaticmarine.com), and hiking specialists Explore Sai Kung (Ⓣ2243 1083, Ⓔjudy@accomasia.com).

The main access point is little **SAI KUNG TOWN**, which lies just south of the peninsula and is accessible on **bus #92** from Diamond Hill MTR. While developed in a laid-back way and with a large expat population, it's also obviously a Chinese fishing town, the promenade packed with seafood restaurants and fishermen offering their wares. Shops sell the usual run of swimming gear, sunscreen and bright inflatable floats; and there's a fruit market and supermarket if you're putting your own lunch together. The harbour is full of cruisers, small fishing boats and ad hoc ferries whose owners will offer rides out to various islands, the nearest and most popular of which is **Kiu Tsui Chau** (or Sharp Island), boasting a beach and a short hike to its highest point, although **Tai Long Wan** is also clean, quiet and beautiful.

The highlights of Sai Kung, however, are the **country parks** that cover the peninsula with virgin forest and grassland, leading to perfect sandy beaches, where you can go snorkelling. Although it is possible to see something of these on a day-trip, the best way really to appreciate them is to bring a tent or consider staying at the youth hostel on Sai Kung (see "Accommodation", p.659). Access to the parks is by **bus #94** from Sai Kung Town or **#96R** (Sun and public hols only) from Diamond Hill MTR, which pass through **Pak Tam Chung** on their way to Wong Shek pier in the north of the peninsula. Don't come to Pak Tam Chung expecting a town – all you'll find is a **visitors' centre** (daily Mon & Wed–Sun 9.30am–4.30pm), which supplies hikers with maps (some are free) and vital information about the trails.

Of the many possible hikes, the **MacLehose Trail**, liberally dotted with campsites, heads east from here, circumventing the **High Island Reservoir** before heading west into the rest of the New Territories. If you want to follow the trail just a part of the way, the **beaches** at Long Ke, south of the reservoir, and Tai Long, to the northeast, are Hong Kong's finest, though to walk out to them and back from Pak Tam Chung takes several hours. The last bus back from Pak Tam Chung is at 7.30pm.

The Outlying Islands

Officially part of the New Territories, Hong Kong's 260-odd **Outlying Islands** make up twenty percent of the SAR's land area but contain just two percent of the population. As such, they offer visitors a delightful mix of seascape, low-key fishing villages and rural calm, with not much high-density development. The islands of **Lamma** and **Cheung Chau** are fairly small and easy to day-trip around, while Lantau has a far greater range of sights and might even demand a couple of visits. You can also make use of local **accommodation** (see p.659) and base yourself on any one of the three, or just hop over for an evening out at one of the many **fish restaurants**. The main point of departure for all three islands is the **Outlying Islands Ferry Pier** in Central; Lamma can also be

Chinese cuisine

The principles of Chinese cuisine are based on a balance between the qualities of different ingredients. For the Chinese, this extends right down to considering the *yin* and *yang* attributes of various dishes, but is obvious even to foreigners in the use of contrasting textures and colour, designed to please the eye as well as the palate. Recipes and ingredients, however, are a response to more direct requirements. The chronic poverty of China's population is reflected in the traditionally scant quantity of meat used, while the need to minimize the use of firewood led to the invention of quick cooking techniques, such as stir-frying.

Taste

Taste in Chinese cuisine is sometimes something to be teased out of an ingredient, sometimes something to be suppressed. Sugar, soy sauce, rice wine and vinegar emphasize underlying fresh, sweet tastes; while heavier flavours are moderated – or occasionally created – by **marinating** using **spices** such as chilli, pickled vegetables, ginger, garlic and spring onion. Often, however, the object is to season without being too obvious, as any heavy-handedness could come across as an attempt to conceal a lack of **freshness**. This can be a major issue, especially in the south, where many restaurants keep live chickens, fish and seafood out the front so that diners can select the actual animal they want to eat.

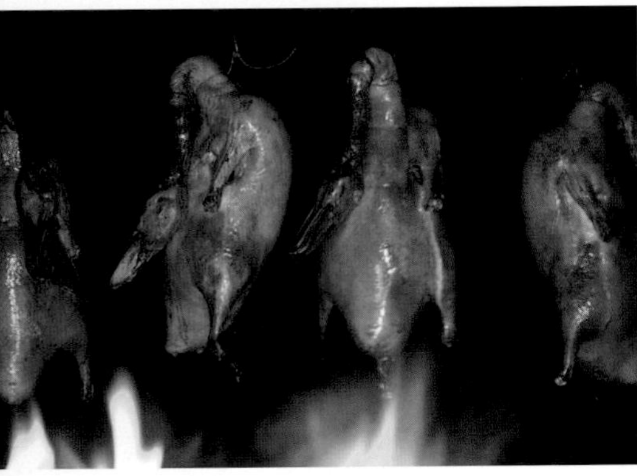

▲ Beijing duck

Texture

Texture is also an incredibly important part of a dish – indeed, ingredients such as birds' nests and sea cucumber are only used to provide texture, being completely flavourless themselves. Texture can be a natural attribute – such as the softness of tofu, or the crunchiness of bamboo shoots or lotus root – although usually it's the result of a specific cooking method: for example, deep-frying adds a layer of crispness to meats; while prolonged steaming or stewing renders fat and meat fibres butter-soft.

▲ Birds' nests for sale

Regional cooking

Not surprisingly, given China's scale, there are a number of **regional cooking styles**, divided into four major traditions. **Northern cookery** was epitomized by the imperial court and so also became known as Mandarin or Beijing cooking, though its influences are far wider than these names suggest. A solid diet of wheat and millet buns, noodles, pancakes and dumplings helps to face severe winters, accompanied by the savoury tastes of dark soy sauce and bean paste, white cabbage, onions and garlic. The north's cooking has also been influenced by neighbours and invaders: Mongols brought roast meats, and Muslims a taste for mutton, beef and chicken. Combined

Medicinal cooking

There's no boundary in Chinese cooking between food and medicine, as in **Traditional Chinese Medicine** (TCM; see p.1170) everything you eat or drink is believed to affect your health. This means that even ordinary dishes can be looked at in a medicinal way: chicken and beef, for example, are "warming" – they add *yang* energy to your system – while seafood such as crab is *yin* or "cooling". Along with specific medicinal herbs, culinary spices such as ginger, cinnamon, garlic, chillies and tangerine peel all have medicinal uses, too, which means that – if you know what your ailment is in TCM terms – you can actually create dishes to restore your health. Sadly, however, while there are abundant cookbooks based around medicinal cookery, there are very few restaurants in China specializing in the idea.

with exotic items imported by foreign merchants, imperial kitchens turned these rough ingredients and cooking styles into sophisticated marvels such as Beijing duck and birds' nest soup. Mongolian hotpot is another northern speciality, where you pay a set amount and are served with various raw meats and vegetables, which you cook at the table in a boiling stock.

The central coast provinces produced the **eastern style**, whose cooking delights in seasonal fresh seafood and river fish. Winters can still be cold and summers scorchingly hot, so dried and salted ingredients feature, too, pepping up a background of rice noodles and dumplings. Based around Shanghai, eastern cuisine (as opposed to daily fare) enjoys delicate forms and fresh, sweet flavours, though it tends towards being oily. Red-cooking, stewing meat in a sweetened wine and soy-sauce stock, is a characteristically eastern technique. **Western China** is dominated by the boisterous cooking of Sichuan and Hunan, the antithesis of the eastern style. Here, there's a heavy use of chillies and pungent, constructed flavours – vegetables are concealed with "fish-flavoured" sauce, and even normally bland tofu is given enough spices to lift the top off your head. Yet there are still subtleties to enjoy in a cuisine that uses dried orange peel, aniseed, ginger and spring onions, and the cooking methods themselves – such as dry frying and smoking – are refreshingly unusual. Sichuan is also home of the now-ubiquitous Sichuan hotpot (*huoguo*), like the Mongolian version but liberally laced with chillies. **Southern China** is fertile and subtropical, a land of year-round plenty. When people say that southerners – specifically the Cantonese – will eat anything, they really mean it: fish maw, snake, dog and cane rat are some of the more unusual dishes here, strange even to other Chinese, though there's also a huge consumption of fruit and vegetables, fish and shellfish.

Chillies pervade Western Chinese cooking ▶

Vegetarian food

Though Chinese meals anyway tend to feature a far greater quantity of vegetables than meat, vegetarianism has been practised for almost two thousand years in China for both health and philosophical reasons. The cooking takes several forms: plain vegetable dishes, commonly served at home or in ordinary restaurants; imitation meat dishes derived from Qing-dynasty court cuisine, which use gluten, bean curd and potato to mimic the natural attributes of meat, fowl and fish, and are still called by their usual name, such as honey pork; and Buddhist cooking, which often avoids onions, ginger, garlic and other spices considered stimulating.

Having said this, vegetarians visiting China will find their options limited, despite a growing interest in the cuisine. The Chinese believe that vegetables lack any physically fortifying properties, and strict vegetarian diets are unusual. There's also a stigma of poverty attached to not eating meat, and as a foreigner no one will understand why you don't want it when you could clearly afford to gorge yourself on meat on a regular basis. If you really want to be sure that you aren't being served anything of animal origin, tell your waiter that you are a Buddhist (see p.1220) – though be aware that cooking fat and stocks in the average dining room are of animal origins.

▲ Vegetable market stall in Hubei province

▲ Cantonese cuisine incorporates everything – including scorpion kebabs

Typically, the demand is for extremely fresh ingredients, quickly cooked and only lightly seasoned, though the south is also home to that famous mainstay of Chinese restaurants overseas, sweet-and-sour sauce. The tradition of *dim sum* – "little eats" – reached its pinnacle here, too, where a morning meal of tiny flavoured buns, filled dumplings and pancakes is washed down with copious tea, satisfying the Chinese liking for a varied assortment of small dishes (see p.582 for more details).

Ferries to the islands

The following is a selection of the most useful island ferry services – full timetables can be picked up at the Outlying Islands Ferry Pier in Central. **Lamma ferries** are operated by HKKF (www.hkkf.com.hk), while those **to Cheung Chau** and **Lantau** are run by First Ferry (www.nwff.com.hk). Schedules differ slightly on Saturdays and Sundays; where available, fast ferries cost more than normal ones.

To Cheung Chau

From Outlying Islands Ferry Pier 24hr departures (at least 2/hr 6.15am–11.45pm; 1hr; fast ferry 30min).

To Sok Kwu Wan, Lamma Island

From Outlying Islands Ferry Pier 11 daily 7.20am–10.30pm (50min; fast ferry 35 min).

To Yung Shue Wan, Lamma Island

From Outlying Islands Ferry Pier at least hourly 6.30am–12.30am (40min; fast ferry 25min).

From Aberdeen 10 daily 6.30am–8.15pm (25min).

To Mui Wo (Silvermine Bay), Lantau Island

From Outlying Islands Ferry Pier at least hourly 5.55am–11.30pm (1hr).

reached by ferry from Aberdeen, while the **MTR** links a couple of places along Lantau's north coast.

Lamma

Lying just to the southwest of Aberdeen, Y-shaped **Lamma** is the third largest island in the SAR – though at only around 7km in length, it's still pleasantly small. The island is identifiable from afar thanks to its **power station**, whose chimneys are unfortunately obvious; and a new **wind turbine** on the island's northeastern headland. Lamma's population of five thousand live mostly in west-coast **Yung Shue Wan**, and the rest of the island is covered in open, hilly country, with walking trails out past a couple of beaches to **Sok Kwu Wan**, a tiny knot of **seafood restaurants** on the upper east coast.

Ferries run from the Outlying Islands Ferry Pier to Yung Shue Wan, and from Aberdeen to Yung Shue Wan and Sok Kwu Wan. A nice way to appreciate the island is to take a boat to either Yung Shue Wan or Sok Kwu Wan, then walk to the other and catch the boat back from there.

Around the island

Yung Shue Wan is a pretty tree-shaded village with a large expat population, full of low-key modern buildings, which include several hotels, small stores and a **bank** with ATM. Of the **restaurants**, there are popular outdoor tables at the seafood-oriented *Man Fung*, between the ferry dock and the village; the *Sam Pan* does good *yum cha*; while the *Bookworm Café*, on the village main street, is a vegetarian place aimed at expats.

To walk to Sok Kwu Wan (1hr), follow the easy-to-find cement path that branches away from the shore past the grotty apartment buildings on the outskirts of the village, and you'll soon find yourself walking amid butterflies, long grass and trees. After about fifteen minutes you'll arrive at **Hung Shing Yeh Beach**, a nice place if you stick to its northern half; stray a few metres to the south, though, and you'll find your horizon rapidly filling up with power station. The *Concerto Inn* is a nice place to dine here, where you can sit on the outdoor terrace and eat relatively inexpensive sandwiches, noodles and rice dishes.

Continue on for another forty minutes or so and you'll reach **Sok Kwu Wan**, which comprises a row of seafood restaurants built out over the water. The food and the atmosphere are good, and the restaurants are often full of large parties of locals enjoying lavish and noisy meals; some – like the popular *Rainbow Seafood* (ⓣ2982 8100) – also operate **private boat services** for customers. If you're not taking a restaurant service, make sure you don't miss the last scheduled ferry back to Aberdeen around 10pm, because there's nowhere to stay here – your only other option would be to hire a sampan back.

Cheung Chau

Another great place to spend a couple of hours strolling around and then have dinner, hourglass-shaped **Cheung Chau** covers just 2.5 square kilometres but is the most crowded of all the outer islands, with a population of 23,000. Historically, the island is one of the oldest settled parts of Hong Kong, being notorious as an eighteenth-century base for **pirates** who enjoyed waylaying the ships that ran between Guangzhou and Macau. Today, it still gives the impression of being an economically independent little unit, the main streets jam-packed with shops (including another **bank** with ATM), markets and more **seafood restaurants**. If you can, visit during the extraordinary **Tai Chiu (Bun) Festival** in April/May, when the island fills to critical mass with raucous martial-arts displays, dragon dances, and a competition to climb vast conical towers made of steamed buns.

From the ferry dock, turn left (north) up main-street **Pak She Praya Road** and you'll soon reach a 200-year-old **Pak Tai Temple**. Fishermen come to the temple to pray for protection, and beside the statue of Pak Tai, the God of the Sea, is an ancient iron sword, discovered by fishermen and supposedly symbolizing good luck.

Ahead from the ferry, through the town and across the island's narrow waist, scenic but crowded **Tung Wan Beach** is a 700-metre-long strip of sand, with various places to rent windsurfing gear, have a snack, or just laze on the sand. At the south end of the beach, *Warwick Hotel* is the most upmarket place to stay on the island, though there are also plenty of more modest guesthouses (see p.659).

Turn right (south) from the ferry and follow the harbour road past the popular *Hoi Lung Wong* **seafood restaurant** and small places specializing in sweet and sticky desserts, and it's a half-hour walk to Cheung Chau's **southern headland**. You can circumnavigate this via a bit of scrabbling up and down rocks and through bays; there's also a nice picnic pavilion with sea views, and the **Cheung Po Tsai Cave**, named after Cheung Chau's most famous pirate, who used to hide here in the nineteenth century – it's tightly set into the base of some large granite boulders, and you'll need a torch.

Lantau

Mountainous **Lantau** is twice as big as Hong Kong Island but far less developed, despite the proximity of the International Airport just off the north coast. More than half is a designated **country park** and remains fairly wild, with trails linking monasteries, old fishing villages and secluded beaches. There are some major sights here, however, notably **Hong Kong Disneyland** on the northeast coast; the western fishing village of **Tai O**; and **Po Lin Monastery**, with its mighty Big Buddha and wonderful **Ngong Ping 360** cable-car ride. Roads and buses link everything, so getting around isn't difficult, though hikers can also tackle the seventy-kilometre **Lantau Trail** across the island – contact the Country Parks (Ⓦwww.afcd.gov.hk/eindex.html) for current information.

There are two ways to reach Lantau: by **ferry** from the Outlying Islands Ferry Pier to east-coast **Mui Wo** (Silvermine Bay); and on the **Tung Chung MTR Line**, which runs along the north coast to Disneyland and the town of **Tung Chung** – the latter terminus for the cable car, and close to the airport. Lantau is not necessarily somewhere to rush around, though to pack the island into one day you could arrive by ferry at Mui Wo, take buses across the island via a beach or two to Tai O and Po Lin, ride the cable car down to Tung Chung, and then catch the MTR back into town.

Mui Wo to Po Lin

MUI WO is just a clutch of restaurants grouped about the ferry pier, in front of which is a **bus stop** with departures around the rest of the island – though most of these only run every hour or so, so don't be in too much of a hurry. There's also a nice **beach** with a sprinkling of low-key hotels 500m to the north (see p.659), set in an attractive, curving, sandy bay.

The road west from Mui Wo passes along the southern shore, which is where Lantau's best beaches are located. **Cheung Sha Upper and Lower beaches** are the nicest: long, empty stretches of sand backed by a fringe of trees, with a couple of café-restaurants near the bus stops – buses #1, #2 and #4 all pass by. Beyond here, the road heads inland past the **Shek Pik Reservoir** – look north here and you'll glimpse the Big Buddha sitting up on the ridge – after which it divides: one fork and the #2 bus runs up to the Po Lin Monastery at Ngong Ping; the other and the #1 bus continues over to Tai O.

Located high up on the Ngong Ping Plateau, the **Po Lin Monastery** (daily 10am–6pm; free) is the largest temple in Hong Kong, though only established in 1927. A lively place of worship, the temple is overshadowed by the adjacent bronze **Tian Tan Buddha** (more often known as the Big Buddha), a 34-metre-high sculpture that depicts the Buddha sitting cross-legged in a lotus flower – climb the steps to the Buddha's feet for views over the temple. Po Lin's **vegetarian restaurant** serves set meals (daily 11.30am–5pm; meal tickets from $60), with an attached cheaper canteen. You can also stay the night nearby at the *S. G. Davis Youth Hostel* (see p.659), and then climb the 934-metre-high **Lantau Peak** – more properly known as Fung Wong Shan – which is a popular place to watch the sunrise. The steep, two-kilometre trail from Po Lin to the summit takes about an hour to complete, and on a clear day views reach as far as Macau. You can pick up the Lantau Trail here and continue 5km (2.5hr) east to the slightly lower **Tai Tung Shan**, or "Sunset Peak", from where it's a further five-hour hike to Mui Wo.

Moving on from Po Lin, bus #2 returns to Mui Wo, the #21 runs to Tai O, while the #23 goes to Tung Chung. A better way to reach Tung Chung, however, is on the **Ngong Ping 360 cable car** (Mon–Fri 10am–6pm; Sat & Sun 10am–6.30pm; $58 single, $88 return), a 5.7-kilometre ride that takes twenty-five minutes and provides fantastic panoramas of Lantau's steep north coast.

Tai O

Right on the far northwestern shore of Lantau, the fishing village of **TAI O** is home to two thousand people, and can be reached on bus #1 from Mui Wo, the #11 from Tung Chung or the #21 from Po Lin. There's plenty of interest in its old lanes, including shrines, temples, and a quarter full of tin-roofed stilt-houses built over the mud flats. The main street is lined by stalls selling dried and live seafood, and there's also a tiny **museum** (9am–5pm; free), displaying everyday artefacts such as washboards, vases, a threshing machine and a cutlass.

The pick of the village's temples is **Hau Wong Miu** on Kat Hing Back Street, about two minutes' walk from the bridge. Built in 1699, it contains the local boat used in the annual Dragon Boat Races (see p.52 for more about this festival), some shark bones, a whale head found by Tai O fishermen, and a carved roof-frieze displaying two roaring dragons.

The north coast: Hong Kong Disneyland and Tung Chung

The Tung Chung MTR Line can get you to two places along Lantau's north coast. Change at **Sunny Bay Station** for **Hong Kong Disneyland** (check Ⓦwww.hongkongdisneyland.com for times; $295), a tame place compared with their ten other franchises. It's split into four zones: **Main Street USA**, a recreated early twentieth-century mid-American shopping street (though the goods on sale are distinctly Chinese); **Adventureland**, home to Tarzan's treehouse and a jungle river cruise; **Tomorrowland**, whose excellent rides include a blacked-out roller coaster; and **Fantasyland**, populated by a host of Disney characters, and whose best feature is the PhilharMagic 3D film show.

At the end of the line, **TUNG CHUNG** is a burgeoning New Town near the airport. The only real reason to come here is for transport: there's the MTR; the Ngong Ping 360 cable car to Po Lin Monastery; and also a host of **buses**, including the #23 to Po Lin, the #3M to Mui Wo, and any service prefixed by "A" to the airport.

Eating, drinking and nightlife

Thanks to its cosmopolitan heritage and the incredible importance attached to eating in Chinese culture, Hong Kong boasts a superb range of **restaurants**. The native cooking – **Cantonese** – is the most prominent Chinese style, though you can also find places specializing in Chaozhou, Hakka, Beijing, Sichuanese and Shanghai food. International options include curry houses, sushi bars, sophisticated Southeast Asian cuisine, hotel lunchtime buffets, pizzerias, vegetarian, South American and Western **fast-food** chains. The choices listed below are a fraction of the total, with an emphasis on the less expensive end of the market. Free weeklies *BC* and *HK Magazine* review places of the moment, or you can fork out $120 or so for **restaurant guides** by *Hong Kong Tatler* (conservative and upmarket), *BC* (caustic and more adventurous), or *WOM* (less focused, but also covering low-key Chinese diners).

Hong Kong's **pubs** and **bars** sometimes host **live music**, but the clutch of restaurant-, bar- and pub-crammed streets known as **Lan Kwai Fong** remain the heart of Hong Kong's party scene and drinking-culture nightlife. Despite its image as a cultural desert, **classical concerts** appear increasingly frequently at several venues, and there are a number of art, jazz and other **festivals** year round (check the listings magazines detailed on p.652).

Popular English-language and regional films find their way to Hong Kong's **cinemas** soon after release, either shown in their original versions with Chinese subtitles, or dubbed into Cantonese. Some Chinese-language films are shown with English subtitles. There's also the two-week-long **Hong Kong**

International Film Festival, held each March, with good Southeast Asian representation – see ⓦwww.hkiff.org.hk for information.

Breakfast and snacks

The bigger hotels serve expensive Chinese and European buffet breakfasts with vast quantities of food. Cafés are cheaper for Western breakfasts; for Chinese *dim sum*, see "Restaurants" below. Western-style café chains include *DeliFrance*, *Oliver's Super Sandwiches*, *Pacific Coffee* (which has free Internet access for patrons), and *Prêt A Manger*, all of which offer muffins, breakfast dishes and sandwiches throughout the day and can be found, amongst other places, in most MTR concourses. Chinese fast-food chains include *Fairwood* and the surprisingly good *Café de Coral*, with noodles and rice dishes as their standbys.

Ge Ming Café 48 Staunton St, Soho. All-day breakfasts in a cosy, red-walled and tiled hang-out; fish and veggie dishes also served. Cheap and friendly.

Hui Lau Shan Locations all over the downtown – look for a red sign with gold characters, sometimes with English script, too. Great cold fruit drinks to take away – the mango, pearl milk and aloe mix is very soothing on a hot day.

Shadowman Up from *Ned Kelly's Last Stand* on Ashley Rd, Tsim Sha Tsui. Net bar, café, and light meals with a distinctly Indian flavour served in bright surrounds.

Taichong Bakery Lyndhurst Terrace, Central. Typical Cantonese take-away bakery specializing in roast pork buns and custard tarts, so popular that long queues form as each batch is removed from the oven.

TW Café Lyndhurst Terrace, Central. Not only fine coffee, but also large set breakfasts of egg and toast, fried fillet of sole, or chicken steaks for just $25. Window bar for people-watching.

Restaurants

The whole of **downtown Hong Kong** is thick with restaurants, and nowhere is a meal more than a few paces away. Cantonese places are ubiquitous, with the highest concentration of foreign cuisines found in Central, Soho, Wan Chai and Tsim Sha Tsui. The scene is, however, notoriously fickle, with places continually opening and withering away. Outside the centre, there are several popular Western-oriented restaurants along Hong Kong Island's **south coast**, while the **Outlying Islands** are famous for their seafood restaurants (see island accounts for these).

Menus in all but the cheapest places are in English as well as Chinese, although you many not get the full menu translated, and prices have been known to vary between the two versions. It's worth trying **seasonal dishes**: abalone, garoupa and dried seafood from March to May; melon greens, mushrooms and bean curd June to August; green, giant, soft-shell and hairy crabs between September

Medicinal tea

All through downtown Hong Kong you'll see open-fronted shops with large brass urns set out on a counter, offering cups or bowls full of dark brown **medicinal tea** at around $5 a drink. The Cantonese name for this is *lo cha* or "cool tea", because in Traditional Chinese Medicine tea is considered "cooling" to the body, though it can be served hot or cold. The teas are made from various ingredients and claim various benefits, but are almost always extremely bitter – ones to try include *ng fa cha* (five-flower tea) and *yat sei mei* (twenty-four-flavour tea). Two well-known medicinal tea- shops are the *Good Spring Company*, on Cochrane Street in Central; and *Lo Cha Da Yat Ga*, at the corner of Hennessy Road and Luard Road in Wan Chai – the latter is unusual for having all its brews named in English.

Curry houses in Chungking Mansions

It's not an attractive building, but Chungking Mansions on Nathan Road, Tsim Sha Tsui, is where you'll find some of Hong Kong's best-value curry houses, including:

Delhi Club Floor 3, Block C. A Nepali curry house par excellence, once you ignore the spartan surroundings and slap-down service. The ludicrously cheap set meal would feed an army.

Khyber Pass Floor 7, Block E. Consistently good Indian, Pakistani, Bangladeshi and Malay dishes; all *halal* and one of the best in Chungking Mansions.

Sher-E-Punjab Floor 3, Block B. Friendly service in clean surroundings, if slightly more expensive than some of its neighbours.

Taj Mahal Club Floor 3, Block B. Friendly place with excellent North Indian food. Good value if you avoid the relatively expensive drinks.

and November; and casseroles and hotpots from December to February. Please avoid **shark's fin**, which is harvested unethically.

The cheapest **restaurants** serve single-plate meals – wonton noodle soup, or rice with roast pork – from around $25. Having a *dim sum* breakfast (see p.582) is another inexpensive way to eat if you stay away from more famous establishments, though you'll need to get in early at the weekends when whole families pack out restaurants; here, you're looking at perhaps $50 a head, depending on how much you eat. For anything more formal, expect to pay upwards of $35 for a main dish, whatever the type of food being served – a full dinner won't cost less than $100 per head, with that figure climbing well above $500 in the plushest venues.

Restaurant opening hours are from around 11am to 3pm, and 6pm to late, though cheaper Chinese places open all day, winding down around 9pm. Don't worry too much about **tipping**: expensive restaurants add on a ten-percent service charge anyway, while in cheaper places it's customary to just leave the small change.

Central

Chippy 51A Wellington St, entrance down the steps on Pottinger St. Last authentic British fish 'n' chip shop in Hong Kong; tiny sit-down counter serving great fries, though fish is sometimes a bit mushy. A large plate of battered cod and chips costs $85.

Habibi 112–114 Wellington St ⓣ2544 3886. Great Egyptian place with main restaurant (featuring weekend belly dancing) and a cheaper café. Food is filling, tasty and not too expensive – you can gorge yourself for $100.

Lin Heung Tea House 160–164 Wellington St ⓣ2544 4556. This famous place relocated here from Guangzhou around 1950, and they've been so busy since, they haven't had time to change the furnishings or allow their ancient staff to retire. Fantastic atmosphere for *dim sum*, if you like crowded, lively venues with inexpensive food.

Luk Yu Tea House 24–26 Stanley St, just west of D'Aguilar St ⓣ2523 5464. A snapshot from the 1930s, with old wooden furniture and ceiling fans, this self-consciously traditional restaurant offers *dim sum* as the mainstay, though the quality is overrated and barely justifies the tourist-inflated prices. Upwards of $100 a head.

M at the Fringe 2 Lower Albert Rd ⓣ2877 4000. Stylish, high-priced restaurant much favoured by the glitterati for its boldly flavoured, internationally influenced, health-conscious meat, fish and veggie dishes.

Man Wah Floor 25, *Mandarin Oriental*, 5 Connaught Rd ⓣ2522 0111. Subtle and accomplished southern Chinese food at connoisseurs' prices, though the view outperforms the menu.

Muyu Zigan 26 Cochrane St. Small English sign over doorway reads "Between Wu Yue". Great inexpensive Shanghai-style snacks, including spicy noodles, stewed Dongpo pork, little dumplings and marinated cucumber slices. With the exception of the soups, portions are small, the idea being that you order a selection.

Nha Trang 88–90 Wellington St ☎2581 9992. First-rate Vietnamese food, whose crisp, clean and sharp flavours make a nice break from more muggy Chinese fare. The grilled prawn and pomelo salad, rice-skin rolls and lemongrass beef are excellent, and two can eat very well for $230.

Roof Garden Top floor at *The Fringe Club*, 2 Lower Albert Rd ☎2521 7251. Bar and buffet with rooftop tables, offering $65 vegetarian all-you-can-eat lunches, and evening tapas from $20. Drinks are cheaper here than in nearby Lan Kwai Fong, too.

Ser Wong Fun 30 Cochrane St (no English sign). Cantonese diner whose reputation rests on its snake soup, though it also does plenty of other straightforward dishes at low prices.

Tsim Chai Kee Noodle 98 Wellington St. No English sign, but easily located by the lunchtime queue tailing downhill; what makes it worth the wait and being jammed into the packed interior are the *wuntun* – jokingly known locally as "ping-pong wuntun" because of their huge size – served in soup for $14.

Tsui Wah 15–19 Wellington St. Warehouse-sized fast-food place with a big range of inexpensive single-dish meals – things to go for include the Hoi Nam chicken with rice, and their excellent fishball soups.

Yung Kee 32–40 Wellington St ☎2522 1624. An enormous place with bright lights, scurrying staff and seating for a thousand, this is one of Hong Kong's institutions. Their roast goose and pigeon are superb, and the *dim sum* is also good. Moderately expensive but highly recommended.

Zhong Guo Song 6 Wo On Lane ☎2810 4040. Tiny, with absolutely no decor, and no surprises on the Western-oriented Chinese menu. Portions are large and food prepared well, however. Mains from around $50 and set meals for two from $190.

Soho

Bistro Manchu 33 Elgin St ☎2536 9218 Moderately priced Manchurian food of the hearty stew and dumpling variety, laced with cumin – northern Chinese with a bit of Mongolian and Korean thrown in.

Fat Angelo's 49 Elgin St ☎2973 6808. Extremely popular, noisy Italian joint serving enormous pizzas and a range of pasta dishes. Two people can happily share one dish, making a fairly inexpensive night out.

Ivan the Kozak 46–48 Cochrane St ☎2851 1193. Portions of chicken kiev, lamb stew, cabbage and potatoes are good value and tasty, but the highlight is donning a fur coat and walking into the huge freezer for a shot of vodka and a photo.

La Pampa 32 Staunton St ☎2868 6959. Argentinian restaurant that does what it does – barbecued steak, mainly – exceedingly well. You order by weight, it's grilled just how you want it, and served with nominal quantities of vegetables.

Yi Jiang Nan 35 Staunton St ☎2136 0886. Chinese food from the Yangzi River region, incorporating both Shanghai and Sichuanese dishes – tiger-skin peppers, twice-cooked pork, crisp-skinned lamb and Longjing tea prawns. Good food but overpriced, with most mains over $80.

South Coast Hong Kong

Boathouse 86–88 Stanley Main St, Stanley ☎2813 4467. Popular hang-out, with waterfront views from the balcony of this stylish "Mediterranean" building. Food concentrates on fresh, unpretentiously cooked seafood. Booking essential.

Happy Garden Vietnamese Thai Shek O. On the way from the main bus stop to the seafront. One of several laid-back places with outdoor tables, luridly coloured drinks, and excellent food – try the morning glory with *blechan* beef, or huge Thai fish cakes. Mains around $60.

Jumbo Floating Restaurant Aberdeen Harbour ☎2553 9111, Ⓦwww.jumbokingdom.com. A Hong Kong institution, with several restaurants on three garishly decorated floors. While expensive and touristy, as a one-off trip for a *dim sum* session (served daily until 4pm) it can also be a lot of fun. Mon–Sat 11am–11pm, Sun 7am–11pm.

Spices *Repulse Bay Hotel*, 109 Repulse Bay Rd, Repulse Bay ☎2292 2821. Generic "Asian" dishes – from Japanese to Sri Lankan and Indonesian – are tasty but expensive. Sea views from outdoor tables compensate on a sunny day.

Verandah *Repulse Bay Hotel*, 109 Repulse Bay Rd, Repulse Bay ☎2812 2722. Pricey, romantic setting for dinner or indolent Sunday brunch. Jazz, candlelight and views across the bay in a mock-colonial retreat.

Tsim Sha Tsui

Aqua Floor 29 and Penthouse, 1 Peking Rd ☎3427 2288. Dark wooden floors and superlative harbour views through angled glass windows are the setting for consuming an unexpectedly successful blend of Italian and Japanese dishes. The atmosphere is informal, and the prices high. Reservations essential.

Chao Inn Floor 7, 1 Peking Rd ☎2369 8819. Need to book window tables for harbour views, and the moderately priced food – cuisine from Chaozhou in

▲ A Martini at Felix

Guangdong province – is also a cut above average, especially the roast goose.

Felix Floor 28, *Peninsula Hotel* ⓣ2315 3188. This restaurant was designed by Philippe Starck, and the incredible views of Hong Kong Island in themselves warrant a visit (not least from the gents' glass-walled urinals). The Eurasian menu averages over $600 a head, but you can just come for one of their famous Martinis.

Itamae Sushi 14 Granville Rd. Inexpensive, decent sushi served on a conveyer belt and priced according to colour-coded plates; you'll have to queue. Daily 11.30am–midnight.

Kakalok Corner of Ashley Rd and Ichang St. Fast-food counter with the sole distinction of serving the cheapest fried noodles, rice, and fish 'n' chips in Hong Kong. No seats, but Kowloon Park is 100m away.

Light Vegetarian 13 Jordan Rd ⓣ2384 2833. Comprehensive Chinese vegetarian menu, including taro fish, "bird's nest" basket filled with fried vegetables, pumpkin soup served in the shell, vegetarian duck, and a big *dim sum* selection. Dishes from $35.

Macau Restaurant 25–27 Lock Rd. Inexpensive Macanese cooking with set meals from $25; packed out at lunchtime with local workers and office staff downing baked rice dishes, pork cutlets and curried crab.

Mrs Chan Basement, 63 Peking Rd ⓣ2368 8706. Singapore-Malay restaurant with indifferent service but decent-sized portions of excellent saté, *otak-otak* (steamed fish parcels) and *rojak* (cucmber and pineapple salad). Mains around $30 each.

Peninsula Hotel Lobby *Peninsula Hotel* ☎2366 6251. The set tea served in the lobby from 2–7pm and accompanied by a string quartet, comes to around $185 a head – a good way to get a glimpse of a more elegant, civilized and relaxed Hong Kong. Dress is smart casual; no plastic or nylon footware, no sports-wear, and no sleeveless shirts for men.

Spring Deer 42 Mody Rd ☎2366 4012. Faded Beijing restaurant that must have been grand when they last redecorated in the 1960s. The mid-range food – especially the steamed lamb and Beijing duck – is worth it, though.

Sweet Dynasty 100 Canton Rd. Noodles and rice dishes are tasty but expensive; best stick to the Southeast Asian-style desserts, featuring sago, tofu, mango, lotus seeds and red beans. The pomelo pudding in coconut milk is exceptional.

Tao Heung Floor 3, Silvercord Complex, 30 Canton Rd (entrance on Haiphong Rd) ☎2375 9128. Opens for *dim sum* daily at 7.30am; come early for a window seat facing Kowloon Park. No trolleys, but they have an English menu and their selection is first rate and inexpensive.

Yuan Ji 16 Granville Rd. Cantonese fast-food joint serving noodle soups and rice dishes, whose major assets are that the food is tasty, portions are big, and prices are not geared to tourists. A plate of barbecued pork on rice costs $23.

Wan Chai and Causeway Bay

Amici Floor 2, 50–52 Russel St (Times Square), Causeway Bay ☎2577 2477. The tiny entrance of this homey Italian restaurant is easy to miss. Best known for its pizzas.

Coyote 114–120 Lockhart Rd, Wan Chai. Lively Tex-Mex bar and grill with good barbecued ribs, full of tequila-quaffing patrons digging into plates of nachos and spicy pizzas. Around $100 a head for a group.

East Lake Seafood Floor 4, Pearl City 22–36 Patterson St, Causeway Bay. Packed with cheerful, noisy Cantonese clientele eating *dim sum* from 7am.

Fook Lam Moon 35–45 Johnston Rd, Wan Chai ☎2866 0663. Very expensive Cantonese institution with astounding roast suckling pig, crispy-skinned chicken, abalone, and bird's-nest soup. Service is not good, however.

Green Willow Village Floor 4, World Trade Centre, Causeway Bay ☎2881 6669. Smart Shanghai restaurant featuring classic dishes such as soy-braised *dongpo* pork, lotus-leaf-wrapped pork, beggars' chicken (baked in mud) and braised stuffed duck. Mains upwards of $50.

Hak Ka Hut Floor 21, Lee Theatre Plaza, Causeway Bay ☎2881 8578. Moderately priced Hakka and Chaozhou dishes, including morning *dim sum* sessions – steamed stuffed bean curd, salt-baked chicken, *kourou* pork belly and baked turnip dumplings.

Hee Kee 379 Jaffe Rd, Causeway Bay ☎2893 7565. Drab strip lighting and heavy antique-style wooden tables are offset by excellent but pricey crab dishes; offerings change seasonally but chilli crab is always good.

IR 1968 28 Leighton Rd, Causeway Bay ☎2577 9981. The menu – offering spicy Indonesian staples – isn't particularly large, but top marks go to the chargrilled seafood or satays, along with curries and salad-like *gado gado*.

Padang JP Plaza, 22–36 Patterson St, Causeway Bay ☎2881 5075. A bit overpriced, but very authentic-tasting Indonesian grilled fish, mutton soup and noodle dishes – the highlight, however, is their cake and durian-flavoured dessert selection.

R66 Floor 62, Hopewell Centre, 183 Queens Rd East, Wan Chai ☎2862 6166. Revolving restaurant with views over Wan Chai, best visited for weekend buffet teas from 3 to 5pm ($88 a head) or daily high tea ($138 for two) from 2.30–6pm.

Wing Wah 89 Hennessy Rd, cnr of Luard Rd, Wan Chai (there's no English sign). Known for its *wuntun*, this locally famous noodle house also does mostly inexpensive. unusual medicinal soups, beef tendon noodles, and ground shrimps on pomelo skins.

Bars, pubs and clubs

The most concentrated collection of bars is in the **Lan Kwai Fong** area on Hong Kong Island, perennially popular for late-night carousing, with drinkers spilling out onto the street. Other locations include the long-established, slightly sleazy expat scene around **Wan Chai**, and a scattering of options aimed at travellers in **Tsim Sha Tsui**.

Opening times are from 10am at the earliest and often extend well into the small hours. Some venues charge a $50–200 entrance fee on certain nights (generally Fri & Sat), though almost everywhere also offers daily **happy hours** at some point between 3 and 9pm – worth catching, as drinks are otherwise pricey. **Live music**, and sometimes even **raves**, can be found if you look hard, though they are unlikely to match what you're used to back home – for details, consult free *HK* or *Beats* magazines. The **gay scene**, while hardly prominent, is at least more active than in other Chinese cities, given that laws on homosexuality are more liberal here than on the mainland.

Central

Agave's 33 D'Aguilar St, Lan Kwai Fong. Largest selection of tequilas in Hong Kong, so head here for frozen, fruit-flavoured margaritas.

Bit Point 31 D'Aguilar St, Lan Kwai Fong. German-theme bar, concentrating on meals until around 10pm, after which the bar starts selling industrial quantities of lager and schnapps as the juke box blares.

Blue Door 5th Floor, 37 Cochrane St. Hong Kong's main jazz venue, with top-quality live music Sat night 10.30pm–12.30am.

C-Bar/Calafornia 30–32 D'Aguilar St, Lan Kwai Fong. Basement bar boasting an in-house DJ, VIP zones, velvet and fur decoration, heaped-up cushions and a ground-floor bar dishing out shorts and long drinks.

D26 26 D'Aguilar St, Lan Kwai Fong. Small, low-key bar; a good place for a warm-up drink or if you actually want a conversation with your companions.

Dinamoe Hum 1st Floor, 28 Elgin St. Local and international artists play nightly at this tiny venue – there's room for an audience of just twenty. Variable cover charge depending on the band; food and drink available Tues–Sat.

Fringe Club 2 Lower Albert Rd Ⓦwww.hkfringeclub.com. Live acts, drinks, exhibitions and generally alternative culture in a rather bohemian hang-out in the red and white Fringe building. One of the cheaper places, with a regular Happy Hour.

Le Jardin Wing Wah Lane. Almost impossible to find unless you already know it's there, this comfortable bar has a covered terrace and is usually quieter than alternatives in nearby Lan Kwai Fong.

Post '97 9 Lan Kwai Fong. A disco downstairs and a vaguely arty, bohemian atmosphere in the bar upstairs, with a strong gay presence on Fri nights. Serves fry-ups, sandwiches and all-day breakfasts.

Schnurrbart's 27 D'Aguilar St, Lan Kwai Fong. Long-standing German bar with herring and sausage snacks, and some of the best beer around. Serious headaches are available courtesy of the 25 different kinds of schnapps – try the butterscotch.

Wan Chai

Carnegie's 53–55 Lockhart Rd. Noise level means conversation here is only possible by flash cards, and once it's packed, hordes of punters, keen to revel the night away, fight for dancing space on the bar. Regular live music.

Old China Hand Lockhart Rd. Great food and atmosphere in this dark, barfly hangout, full of embittered, seedy expats acting the part.

Tsim Sha Tsui

Bahama Mama's 4–5 Knutsford Terrace, just north of Kimberly Rd. A good atmosphere with a vibrant mix of nationalities, and plenty of space for pavement drinking. There's a beach-bar theme and outdoor terrace that prompts party-crowd antics. On club nights, there's a great range of mixed music.

Delaney's Basement, Mary Building, 71–77 Peking Rd. Friendly Irish pub with draught beers, including Guinness; features Irish folk music most nights.

Ned Kelly's Last Stand 11A Ashley Rd. Very popular, long-running venue, featuring a nightly performance from an excellent ragtime jazz band.

Stag's Head Hart Ave, Tsim Sha Tsui. Popular pub attracting expats and tourists alike; almost always has beer, spirit and wine promotions during happy hours.

Shopping

Many visitors come to Hong Kong to go **shopping**, drawn by the incredible range of goods packed into such a small area. While some things are good value for money – particularly **clothes, silk, jewellery, Chinese arts and crafts**, some **computer accessories** and **pirated software** – you should research prices and shop around before buying, especially in regard to electronic goods.

The farther you are from touristy Tsim Sha Tsui, the better value shopping becomes, and the less likely that you'll be **ripped off** by some scam.

Shops **open** daily; in downtown areas and shopping malls, 10am to 7pm or later is the norm. For more detailed listings, consult the HKTB shopping guide, or browse Ⓦwww.qtshk.com for shops and stores listed under the HKTB's Quality Tourism Services Scheme, or check their shopping guide (listed under "Things to do" at Ⓦwww.discoverhongkong.com).

Antiques, arts and crafts

Chinese collectors are too clued up to make it likely that you'll unearth bargain **antiques** in Hong Kong, but the quality is high and ranges from porcelain through to wooden screens and furniture, sculpture and embroidery. Hollywood Road (see p.664) is at the centre of the trade, a fun place to browse even if you don't intend to buy. "Antique" doesn't always mean more than 100 years old – ask to be sure. Hong Kong is also a reasonable place to pick up modern **arts and crafts**, with a couple of big chain stores dealing in Chinese products – prices are cheaper on the mainland, however. For **jade**, the Jade Market in Mong Kok (see p.674) is a good place to look, if you take everything the stallholders say with a pinch of salt.

Some more general stores include:

Eu Yan Sang Ground Floor, 152–156 Queen's Rd, Central Ⓣ2544 3308, Ⓦwww.euyansang.com. One of the most famous medicine shops in town, said to have been around for over ninety years, this is your source of teas, herbs and Chinese medicines, all carefully weighed and measured.

Karin Weber Gallery 20 Aberdeen St, Central Ⓣ2544 5004, Ⓦwww.karinwebergallery.com. Art gallery specializing in contemporary paintings from the mainland and Southeast Asia, plus antique Chinese furniture.

L&E Floor 21, Remex Centre, 42 Wong Chuk Hang Rd, east of Aberdeen Ⓣ2656 1220, Ⓦwww.lneco.com. Warehouse-sized store full of decorative porcelain and old Chinese furniture. Packing and shipping can be arranged.

Palette Collections Gallery Room 1103 Hing Wai Centre, 7 Tin Wan Praya Rd, Aberdeen Ⓣ2522 5928, Ⓦwww.palettecollections.com.hk. Paintings, porcelain and antique Chinese furniture; they prefer you phone in advance for viewings.

Shoeni Art Gallery 27 Hollywood Rd Ⓣ2869 8802, Ⓦwww.schoeni.com.hk. Agents for modern Chinese artists such as Chen Yu, who combines Chinese images with Renaissance-era scenery.

Teresa Coleman 79 Wyndham St Ⓣ2526 2450, Ⓔtcl@iohk.com. One of Hong Kong's best-known dealers, with an international reputation for Chinese textiles. In addition, they have a good selection of pictures and prints.

Yue Hwa China Products 301–309 Nathan Rd, Jordan; 1 Kowloon Park Drive, Tsim Sha Tsui; and elsewhere. Chinese medicines, clothing, sportswear, tea, books, spirits and every conceivable tourist knick-knack produced on the mainland.

Clothes

Clothes are good value in Hong Kong, particularly local fashion brand names such as Gordiano and Baleno, which have branches all over the city. Big-name foreign designer clothes are often more expensive than back home because of the cachet attached to foreign upmarket brands, but **sales** are worth checking out.

Another potentially cheap way to buy clothes (including designer clothes without the labels) is from **factory outlets**. These places open and close very quickly, so contact the HKTB for the latest information. Be sure to try things on before you buy – marked sizes mean nothing. For **markets** dealing in inexpensive clothes, try the Temple Street Night Market (p.674), Ladies Market (p.674) and stalls in lanes off **Ap Liu Street** in Kowloon (Sham Shui Po MTR).

If you just want to browse, good places to start include **Granville Road** in Tsim Sha Tsui, the **Pedder Building** on Pedder Street in Central and, just round the corner, **Wyndham** and **D'Aguilar streets**. Other places to look include:

Blanc De Chine Floor 2, Pedder Building, 12 Pedder St, Central. Elegant designs loosely based on traditional Chinese clothes, mostly in silk or cashmere.
Joyce Boutique 16 Queen's Rd, Central; Shop 226 & 344 Pacific Place, 88 Queensway, Admiralty. Hong Kong's most fashionable boutique offers its own range of clothing, as well as many top overseas designer brands.
Joyce Warehouse Hing Wai Centre, Aberdeen. Where the boutique sends last season's (or last month's) stuff that didn't sell, at discounts of up to eighty percent.
Shanghai Tang Ground Floor, Pedder Building, 12 Pedder St, Central. A must-visit store, beautifully done up in 1930s Shanghai style. It specializes in new versions of traditional Chinese styles like the *cheongsam* split-sided dress – often in vibrant colours – and they can also make to order, although items are far from cheap. The sales are regular and good.
Walter Ma Century Square, 1 D'Aguilar St, Lan Kwai Fong, Central. One of the best-known local designers, who designs for foreign figures as well as local people. He is particularly well known for his formal wear.

Tailor-made clothes

Tailor-made clothes are a speciality of the Hong Kong tourist trade, and wherever you go in Tsim Sha Tsui you'll be accosted by Indian tailors offering this service. But you may find better work elsewhere, in residential areas and locations such as hotels or shopping arcades where the tailors rely on regular clients. Western women in particular should look for someone who understands the Western body shape. Prices are relatively low, but not rock bottom; a cashmere man's suit, with a couple of shirts and ties, will cost upwards of $1500, more likely twice this. Sales techniques are fairly high-pressure, but don't commit yourself without knowing exactly what's included. Expect at least two or three fittings over several days if you want a good result. You'll need to pay about fifty percent of the price as deposit.

Johnson & Co 44 Hankow Rd, Kowloon. Does a lot of work for military and naval customers. Mostly male clientele.
Linva Tailor 38 Cochrane St, Central. Well-established ladies' tailor, popular with locals who want *cheongsams* for parties. They work a lot with embroidery.
Margaret Court Tailoress Floor 8, Winner Building, 27 D'Aguilar St, Lan Kwai Fong, Central. She has lots of local Western female clients, and a solid reputation for good work, although it doesn't come cheaply. A shirt costs around $300 plus fabric.
Pacific Custom Tailors Floor 3, 322 Pacific Place, 88 Queensway, Admiralty. Upmarket suits with a price to match, in one of Hong Kong's snazziest shopping malls.
Punjab House Shop J, Ground Floor, Golden Crown Court, 66–70 Nathan Rd, Tsim Sha Tsui. Former favourite of the British Forces and Fire Fighters; good-quality male and female formal wear.
Sam's Tailors 94 Nathan Rd, Tsim Sha Tsui ⓦwww.samstailor.biz. Probably the best-known tailor in Hong Kong, Sam is famous as much for his talent for self-publicity as for his clothes.

Electronic goods

With the advent of Internet shopping, prices in Hong Kong for **electronic goods** such as cameras, mp3 players, mobile phones and computers are often no longer the bargain they once were. Add the difficulty of getting any sort of **warranty**, the possibility of being ripped off and the impossibility of getting a refund, and it's not usually worth the risks. To take advantage of any possible bargains, make sure you know exactly what you want, and the price you'd pay for it at home or online. Your best bet is when new models of products are about to be launched, as shops try to ditch their old stock before it becomes unsalable to fashion-concious locals. **Chain stores** such as Fortress are good places to get a base price, though you'll do better at the three warehouse-sized computer centres listed below. For **second-hand** mobile phones and household appliances, try **Ap Liu Street** in Sham Shui Po, Kowloon (Exit A2 from Sham Shui Po MTR).

Pirated computer software is extremely cheap, though if it doesn't work, don't expect a refund – nor should you be surprised if it's taken off you at customs on your way home.

298 Computer Zone 298 Hennessy Rd, Wan Chai. Discounted computers and accessories, ranging from dodgy Chinese stuff to top-notch brands. You might also find pirated software here.

Golden Shopping Centre 156 Fuk Wah St, Sham Shui Po, Kowloon (Sham Shui Po MTR, exit D2). Lots of cheap computer goods.

Mong Kok Computer Centre Corner of Nelson St and Fa Yuen St, Mong Kok. More discounted goods; once also famous for pirated software, though this is much harder to find nowadays.

Malls and department stores

In summer, the air conditioning in Hong Kong's numerous, glossy shopping malls makes as good a reason as any to visit, and most have nice cafés to boot. Some of the best include Times Square (Causeway Bay MTR), IFC Mall (inside the International Finance Centre; Central MTR); Lee Gardens (Causeway Bay MTR) and Festival Walk (Kowloon Tong MTR). Department store chains include:

CRC Department Store Chiao Shang Building, 92 Queen's Rd, Central; Lok Sing Centre, 31 Yee Wo St, Causeway Bay. At the cheaper end of the spectrum, but a good supply of Chinese specialities such as medicines, foods, porcelain and handicrafts.

Lane Crawford 70 Queen's Rd, Central; One Pacific Place, 88 Queensway, Admiralty; Times Square, 1 Matheson St, Causeway Bay. Hong Kong's oldest Western-style department store.

SOGO East Point Centre, 555 Hennessy Rd, Causeway Bay. Another of the Japanese contingent. Immaculately presented goods inside one of the largest department stores in Hong Kong.

Wing On 26 Des Voeux Rd, Central (and other branches). Another long-established store, with branches throughout Hong Kong SAR. Standard, day-to-day goods rather than luxuries.

Jewellery

Hong Kongers – both men and women – love **jewellery**, and the city sports literally thousands of jewellers. Some offer pieces that look remarkably like the more popular designs of the famous international jewellery houses, but at much lower prices. As always, shop around, as different places may ask wildly different prices for the same design. The HKTB's free *Shopping Guide to Jewellery* is helpful for finding reputable stores.

Listings

Airlines Aeroflot, Rm 1606, Tower 2, Lippo Centre, 89 Queensway, Central ⓣ 2537 2637; Air Canada, Rm 1608–12, Tower 1, New World Tower, 18 Queen's Rd, Central ⓣ 2867 8111; Air India, Unit 01–02, 29/F Vicwood Plaza, 199 Des Voeux Rd, Central ⓣ 2522 1176; Air New Zealand, Suite 1701, Jardine House, 1 Connaught Place, Central ⓣ 2862 8988; British Airways, 24/F, Jardine House, 1 Connaught Place, Central ⓣ 2822 9000; Cathay Pacific, 10/F Peninsula Office Tower, 18 Middle Rd, Tsim Sha Tsui ⓣ 2747 1888; China Eastern, 4/F CNAC Building, 10 Queen's Rd, Central ⓣ 2861 0322; Dragonair, Rm 4611, COSCO Tower, 183 Queen's Rd, Central ⓣ 3193 3888; Japan Airlines, 30/F, Tower 6, The Gateway, Harbour City, 9 Canton Rd, Kowloon ⓣ 2523 0081; KLM, Rm 2201–03, World Trade Centre, 280 Gloucester Rd, Causeway Bay ⓣ 2808 2111; Malaysia Airlines, 1306, Princes Building, Chater Rd, Central ⓣ 2525 2321; Oasis Hong Kong ⓦ www.oasishongkong.com, ⓣ 3628 0628; Qantas, 24/F, Jardine House, 1 Connaught Place, Central ⓣ 2822 9000; Singapore Airlines, 17/F, United Centre, 95 Queensway, Admiralty ⓣ 2520 2233; Thai International Airlines,

24/F, United Centre, 95 Queensway, Admiralty ⓣ2876 6888; United Airlines, 29/F, Gloucester Tower, The Landmark, 11 Pedder St, Central ⓣ2810 4888.

Banks and exchange Banks generally open Mon–Fri 9am–4.30pm, Sat 9am–12.30pm; almost all have ATMs capable of accepting foreign cards. Banks also handle foreign exchange, though many levy hefty commissions on traveller's cheques. Licensed moneychangers, who open all hours including Sun, may not charge commission but usually give poor rates, especially in Tsim Sha Tsui – shop around and always establish the exact amount you will receive before handing any money over.

Bookshops The Swindon Book Company, 13–15 Lock Rd, Tsim Sha Tsui, is Hong Kong's best English-language bookstore, particularly good for books on Hong Kong, China and for glossy art books. Dymock's, in many locations including the IFC Mall, Central, also has a good range of popular fiction and local interest. Cosmos Books, at 30 Johnston Rd, Wan Chai, and 96 Nathan Rd, Tsim Sha Tsui, offers a range of both English- and Chinese-language books on all topics.

Embassies and consulates Australia, 23/F, Harbour Centre, 25 Harbour Rd, Wan Chai ⓣ2827 8881; Canada, 14/F, 1 Exchange Square, Central ⓣ2810 4321; China, 42 Kennedy Rd, Central ⓣ2106 6303; India, 16/F, United Centre, 95 Queensway, Admiralty ⓣ2528 4028; Ireland, 8/F, Princes Building, 10 Chater Rd, Central ⓣ2527 4897; Japan, 46/F, One Exchange Square, Central ⓣ2522 1184; Korea, 5/F, Far East Finance Centre, 16 Harcourt Rd, Central ⓣ2529 4141; Malaysia, 24/F, Malaysia Building, 50 Gloucester Rd, Wan Chai ⓣ2821 0800; New Zealand, 6501 Central Plaza, 18 Harbour Rd, Wan Chai ⓣ2525 5044; Philippines, 14/F, United Centre, 95 Queensway, Admiralty ⓣ2823 8500; Singapore, 901–2 Tower 1, Admiralty Centre, Admiralty ⓣ2527 2212; South Africa, 2706 Great Eagle Centre, 23 Harbour Rd, Wan Chai ⓣ2577 3279; Taiwan, 4/F, East Tower, Lippo Centre, 89 Queensway, Admiralty ⓣ2525 8315; Thailand, 8/F, Fairmont House, 8 Cotton Tree Drive, Central ⓣ2521 6481; UK, 1 Supreme Court Rd, Admiralty ⓣ2901 3000; US, 26 Garden Rd, Central ⓣ2523 9011; Vietnam, 15/F, Great Smart Tower, 230 Wan Chai Rd, Wan Chai ⓣ2591 4517.

Festivals Festivals specific to Hong Kong include the Tin Hau Festival, in late April or May, in honour of the Goddess of the Sea. Large seaborne festivities take place, most notably at Joss House Bay on the Sai Kung Peninsula (see p.680). Another is the Tai Chiu Festival (known in English as the Bun Festival), held on Cheung Chau Island during May. The Tuen Ng (Dragon Boat) Festival takes place in early June, with races in various places around the territory in long, narrow boats. Other Chinese festivals, such as New Year and Mid-Autumn, are celebrated in Hong Kong with as much, if not more, gusto than on the mainland.

Hospitals Government hospitals have 24hr casualty wards, where treatment is free. These include the Princess Margaret Hospital, Lai King Hill Rd, Lai Chi Kok, Kowloon ⓣ2990 1111; and the Queen Mary Hospital, Pokfulam Rd, Hong Kong Island ⓣ2855 3838. For an ambulance, dial ⓣ999.

Internet access Café chains such as *Pacific Coffee* provide 15 to 30 minutes' free use, provided you purchase something from them; some offer Wi-Fi, too. Libraries have free Internet, though you have to sign up for it in advance. There are also net bars in the lower two floors of Chungking Mansions, charging around $20 an hour.

Laundry There are many laundries in Hong Kong where you pay by dry weight of clothes ($10–20 per kilo) and then pick them up an hour or two later; ask at your accommodation for the nearest.

Left luggage There's an office in the departure lounge at the airport (daily 6.30am–1am), and at the Central and Kowloon stations for the Airport Express. There are also coin-operated lockers in the Hong Kong China Ferry Terminal in Tsim Sha Tsui. Costs are $20–80 depending on size of locker and time used. You can also negotiate to leave luggage at your guesthouse or hotel, but ensure you're happy with general security first.

Library The main English-language library is in the City Hall High Block, Edinburgh Place, Central (Mon–Fri 10am–9pm, Sat 10am–5pm, Sun 10am–1pm).

Mail The general post office is at 2 Connaught Place, Central (Mon–Sat 8am–6pm, Sun 9am–2pm), facing Jardine House. Poste restante mail is delivered here (you can pick it up Mon–Sat 8am–6pm), unless specifically addressed to "Kowloon". The Kowloon main post office is at 10 Middle Rd, Tsim Sha Tsui. Both have shops that sell boxes, string and tape, to pack any stuff you want to send home.

Martial arts You can see *tai ji* being practised alongside many other styles early in the morning at Kowloon Park and Victoria Park. If you're serious about studying, contact English-speaking C.S. Tang (ⓣ9426 9253, ⓔcstang.bagua@gmail.com), who besides teaching *bagua* and *tai ji*, can also put you in contact with good teachers of many other styles.

Police Crime hotline and taxi complaints ⓣ2527 7177. For general police enquiries, call ⓣ2860 2000.

Sport For horse racing, see "Happy Valley", p.667; for martial arts see above. Every Easter, Hong Kong is host to an international Rugby Sevens tournament (information from Hong Kong Rugby Football Union ⓦwww.hkrugby.com). The following activities are also available in the territory: sailing (Hong Kong Yachting Association ⓦwww.sailing.org.hk); windsurfing (try the Windsurf Centre on Kwun Yam Wan Beach, Cheung Chau Island, for rentals and instruction); marathon running (the Hong Kong Marathon takes place in Jan; ⓦwww.hkmarathon.com). For tennis courts, contact the Hong Kong Tennis Association (ⓦwww.tennishk.org), whose website lists clubs, facilities and events. The easiest way to get a round of golf on the crowded local links is by taking the HKTB's golfing tour, which provides transport and entry for around $500. Alternatively, check the Hong Kong Golfing Association's website (ⓦwww.hkga.com), which lists contact and access details for all of the SAR's driving ranges and clubs.

Swimming pools One of the most conveniently located public pools is in Kowloon Park on Nathan Rd, Tsim Sha Tsui (daily 6.30am–9pm; adults $19, children $8). Another is in Victoria Park, Causeway Bay (daily 6.30am–10pm; adults $19, children $8). All public pools tend to be very crowded, and the water is sometimes not that clean.

Telephones All local calls are free, and you can usually use any phones in hotel lobbies and restaurants for no charge. Payphones cost $1 for five minutes. The cheapest way to make IDD calls is by buying a prepaid discount phone card for the country you want to call; there are heaps of stores selling them inside the Pedder Building on Queen's Rd in Central, and in Chungking Mansions in Tsim Sha Tsui. For directory enquiries in English, call ⓣ1081, and for emergency services, call ⓣ999.

Tours The HKTB runs a series of interesting theme tours – horse racing, harbour cruises, city sights and the like – best suited for those in a hurry and with plenty of money; consult HKTB's brochures for details. Other tour operators include Star Ferry (ⓦwww.starferry.com.hk) for harbour cruises; Gray Line (ⓦwww.grayline.com.hk) for coach tours around the SAR; and Hong Kong Dolphinwatch (ⓦwww.hkdolphinwatch.com), who run boat trips out to see the renowned pink dolphins.

Travel agents Hong Kong is full of budget travel agents, all able to organize international flights as well as train tickets, tours, flights and visas to mainland China. These include Shoestring Travel Ltd, Flat A, 4/F, Alpha House, 27–33 Nathan Rd, Tsim Tsa Shui (ⓣ2723 2306, ⓕ2721 2085); Hong Kong Student Travel Ltd, Hang Lung Centre, Yee Wo St, Causeway Bay (ⓣ2833 9909); and CTS, 4/F, CTS House, 78–83 Connaught Rd, Central (ⓣ2789 5401, ⓦwww.ctshk.com), and 27–33 Nathan Rd (entrance on Peking Rd; ⓣ2315 7188). Cheaper hostels often have useful up-to-date information and contacts for budget travel as well.

TV English-language television channels include dull Pearl and ATV, although many hotels show satellite and cable TV channels.

Macau

Sixty kilometres west across the Pearl River Delta from Hong Kong lies the former Portuguese enclave of **MACAU**. Occupying a peninsula and a couple of islands of just thirty square kilometres in extent, Macau's unique atmosphere has been unmistakably shaped by a colonial past – predating Hong Kong's by nearly three hundred years – which has left old fortresses, Baroque churches, faded mansions, public squares, unusual food and Portuguese place names in its wake. But what draws in millions of big-spending tourists from Hong Kong, the mainland and neighbouring countries are Macau's **casinos**, the only place in China where they have been legalized. The income they generate – over five billion US dollars annually – now excedes that of Las Vegas, and has funded a **construction boom** for themed resorts, roads and large-scale **land reclamation**.

Considering that costs are a good deal lower here than in Hong Kong, and the ease of travel between Shenzhen, Hong Kong and Macau, it's a great pity

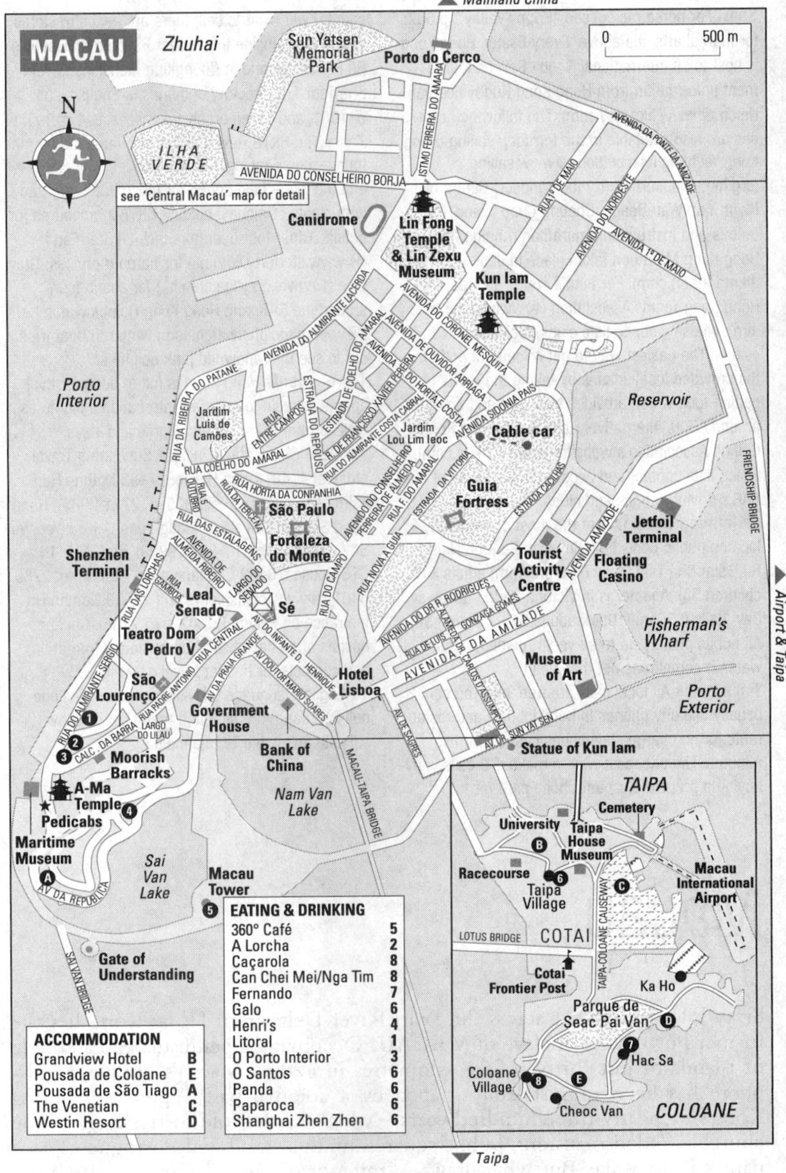

EATING & DRINKING	
360° Café	5
A Lorcha	2
Caçarola	8
Can Chei Mei/Nga Tim	8
Fernando	7
Galo	6
Henri's	4
Litoral	1
O Porto Interior	3
O Santos	6
Panda	6
Paparoca	6
Shanghai Zhen Zhen	6

ACCOMMODATION	
Grandview Hotel	B
Pousada de Coloane	E
Pousada de São Tiago	A
The Venetian	C
Westin Resort	D

not to drop in on Macau if you are in the region. A day-trip from Hong Kong is possible (tens of thousands do it every weekend), though you really need a couple of nights to do the place justice. Another reason to visit is the extremely **low airfares** to Singapore and Bangkok – what might be the first signs of Macau positioning itself as a bargain gateway to the rest of Asia, next to the expense of travelling from Hong Kong.

The Macau **currency** is the pataca (abbreviated to "MOP$" in this book; also written as "M$" and "ptca"), which is worth fractionally less than the HK dollar, and basically equivalent to the Chinese yuan. HK dollars (but not yuan) are freely accepted as currency in Macau, and a lot of visitors from Hong Kong don't bother changing money at all.

Some history

For more than a thousand years, all **trade** between China and the West had been indirectly carried out overland along the Silk Road through Central Asia. But from the fifteenth century onwards, seafaring European nations started making exploratory voyages around the globe, establishing garrisoned ports along the way and so creating new maritime trade routes over which they had direct control.

In 1557 – having already gained toeholds in India (Goa) and the Malay Peninsula (Malacca) – the **Portuguese** persuaded Chinese officials to rent them a strategically well-placed peninsula at the mouth of the Pearl River Delta, known as **Macao** (or "Aomen" in Mandarin). With their important trade links with Japan, as well as with India and Malaya, the Portuguese found themselves in the profitable position of being sole agents for merchants across a whole swath of East Asia. Given that the Chinese were forbidden from going abroad to trade themselves, and that other foreigners were not permitted to enter Chinese ports, their trade blossomed and Macau grew immensely wealthy. With the traders came **Christianity**, and among the luxurious homes and churches built during Macau's brief half-century of prosperity was the basilica of **São Paulo**, whose facade can still be seen today.

By the beginning of the seventeenth century, however, Macau's fortunes were waning alongside Portugal's decline as a maritime power. There was a brief respite when Macau became a base for European traders attempting to prise open the locked door of China during the eighteenth century, but following the British seizure of Hong Kong in 1841, Macau's status as a backwater was sealed. Despite the introduction of **licensed gambling** in 1847, as a means of securing some kind of income, virtually all trade was lost to Hong Kong.

As in Hong Kong, the twentieth century saw wave after wave of **immigrants** pouring into Macau to escape strife on the mainland – the territory's population today stands at 500,000 – but, unlike in Hong Kong, this growth was not accompanied by spectacular economic development. Indeed, when the Portuguese attempted unilaterally to hand Macau back to China during the 1960s and 1970s, they were rebuffed: the gambling, prostitution and organized crime that was Macau's lifeblood would only be an embarrassment to the Communist government if they had left it alone, yet cleaning it up would have proved too big a financial drain – after all, most of Macau's GDP and government revenue comes from gambling.

However, by the time China accepted the return of the colony – as the **Macau Special Administrative Region** (MSAR) – in 1999, the mainland had become both richer and more ideologically flexible. A pre-handover spree of violence by Triad gangs was dealt with, then the monopoly on casino licences – previously held by local billionaire **Dr Stanley Ho** – was ended in 2002, opening up this lucrative market to international competition. Response has been swift, and there are currently **28 casinos** in the territory, including the colossal *Venetian*, one of several US-owned properties. **Tourism** has increased alongside and the once-torpid economy is boiling, though an unforeseen embarrassment is that mainland officials have been accused of gambling away billions of yuan of government and public funds during holidays in the SAR.

Meanwhile, Macau's **government** operates along the "One Country, Two Systems" principle, with very little dissent – the reality is that, even more than Hong Kong, Macau desperately needs the mainland for its continuing existence, as it has no resources of its own. To this end, some giant infrastructure projects – including a tunnel to Hong Kong – are in the pipeline, as the SAR seeks to tie its economy closer to that of the booming Pearl River Delta area.

Arrival, information and transport

Macau comprises several distinct parts. The largest and most densely settled area is the **peninsula**, bordering the Chinese mainland to the north, where the original city was located and where most of the historic sights and facilities remain. Off to the southeast and linked to the peninsula by bridges are **Taipa** and **Coloane**, once separate islands but now joined by a low-lying area of reclaimed land known as **Cotai**, which is being developed as a new entertainment strip. It's all very compact, and it's possible to get around much of Macau on foot, with public transport available for longer stretches.

All boats and helicopters from Hong Kong arrive at Macau's **Jetfoil Terminal** (Nova Terminal in Portuguese) on the east of the peninsula, from where **Avenida**

Getting to Macau and moving on

Visa regulations are currently that citizens of Britain, Ireland and most European countries can stay 90 days on arrival; those of Australia, New Zealand, Canada, South Africa, the US and several others can stay 30 days on arrival – check Ⓦwww.macautourism.gov.mo for the latest. In Hong Kong, the Macau Government Tourist Office is in the Shun Tak Centre (Hong Kong–Macau Ferry Terminal), 200 Connaught Road, Central (Ⓣ2857 2287).

Ferries cross regularly to Macau from both Hong Kong and Shenzhen. **From Hong Kong**, First Ferry (Ⓦwww.nwff.com.hk) departs from the Hong Kong China Ferry Terminal on Canton Road, Tsim Sha Tsui around twice an hour between 7am and midnight; while Turbojet (Ⓦwww.turbojet.com.hk) runs between one and four times an hour, 6.40am to midnight, from the Hong Kong–Macau Ferry Terminal in the Shun Tak Centre, Central. Either service takes 55 minutes and costs about $140 one way, though discounts are often available. Usually you can buy a ticket immediately before departure, but at weekends and holidays – or if you're on a tight schedule – you should book the day before. Either way, turn up half an hour before sailing to clear customs. In Macau, both ferry services arrive and depart from the main Jetfoil Terminal. **From Shenzhen**, there are three ferries daily from Shekou port, currently departing at 10am, 2pm and 6.30pm. Tickets cost ¥90 one way, and the journey takes around eighty minutes; you arrive in Macau at the Shenzhen Terminal, on Rua Das Lorchas.

Macau has **air** links to Taiwan, Bangkok, Kuala Lumpur, Manila, Seoul and Singapore, as well as an expanding range of Chinese cities including Beijing, Shanghai, Guangzhou, Xiamen and Kunming. There's also a **helicopter service** from the Hong Kong–Macau Ferry Terminal in Central – contact East Asia Airlines (HKⓉ2108 9898, MCⓉ2872 7288).

By land, you can **walk** across the border (daily 7am–midnight) at the Porto do Cerco (Barrier Gate), into the Zhuhai Special Economic Zone. **By bus**, CTS (Rua de Nagasaki Ⓣ2798 0877) run daily services to and from Macau and Hong Kong, Guangzhou, and Zhaoqing in Guangdong province for MOP$50–120, and can also organize two-month **Chinese visas** overnight (MOP$217).

de Amizade runs past a strip of casinos to **Avenida Almeida Ribeiro**, which cuts westwards through the historic quarter and budget-hotel area to the **Porto Interior** (Inner Harbour), where ferries from Shenzhen (Shekou) dock. City buses #3, #3A and #10A cover this entire route between the two ports.

Macau International Airport is on Taipa, from where buses #21 and #26 run to Avenida Almeida Ribeiro, or catch #AP1 to the Jetfoil Terminal. If you've walked in **from Zhuhai** Special Economic Zone on mainland China through the Porto do Cerco (Barrier Gate), take bus #AP1 to the Jetfoil Terminal, or #2, #3A, #5 or #18 to Avenida Almeida Ribeiro.

Information

The **Macau Government Tourist Office**, or MGTO (tourist hotline ⓣ333000, ⓦwww.macautourism.gov.mo) provides helpful leaflets on Macau's fortresses, museums, parks, churches, self-guided walks and outlying islands as well as a good city **map**. The main office is at Largo do Senado 9, with counters at the airport, the Jetfoil Terminal, and the Zhuhai-border Porto do Cerco. All are open daily 9am–6pm.

In Hong Kong, MGTO have an office at the airport's arrivals hall, and in the Hong Kong–Macau Ferry Terminal, Room 1303, Shun Tak Centre (Mon–Fri 9am–6pm, Sat 9am–1pm; ⓣ2857 2287).

Transport

Macau's comprehensive **public bus** network costs a flat fare of MOP$2.50 on the peninsula, MOP$3.50 to Taipa, and MOP$4 to Coloane, except that Hac Sa beach is MOP$5; you need the exact fare, as change is not given. Important interchanges include the Jetfoil Terminal; outside the *Hotel Lisboa*; Almeida Ribeiro; Barra (near the A-Ma Temple); and the Porto do Cerco. Useful routes are indicated where necessary in the text.

Taxis charge MOP$10 to hire – including surcharges, the one-way fare from downtown to Coloane's Hac Sa beach (the longest trip you can possibly make) costs about MOP$80.

Accommodation

Accommodation is a good deal in Macau: the money that would get you a dingy box in Hong Kong here provides a clean room with private shower and a window. Note, however, that there are fewer real budget options, and that at weekends, holidays and during the Macau Grand Prix (third weekend in November), **prices** can more than double. Mid- and upper-range hotels often give discounted rates if you **book ahead**; while agents in Hong Kong such as the CTS offer good-value transport and accommodation **packages**.

The densest concentration and variety of hotels is found on the peninsula – especially in the vicinity of Avenida de Almirante Ribeiro – though Taipa, Cotai and Coloane also sport several upmarket resorts. Note that addresses in Macau are written with the number after the name of the street.

Macau phone numbers have no area codes. From outside the territory, dial the normal international access code + ⓣ853 (country code) + the number. **To call Hong Kong from Macau**, dial ⓣ01 + the number. To call Macau from mainland China, dial ⓣ00 + 853 + the number.

Accommodation price codes

All the accommodation in this book has been graded according to price codes, which represent the cheapest double room available. Accommodation in Macau has been given codes from the categories below. Note that accommodation is generally cheaper on weekdays, unless stated otherwise.

1 Under MOP$75
2 MOP$75–100
3 MOP$101–150
4 MOP$151–200
5 MOP$201–300
6 MOP$301–500
7 MOP$501–700
8 MOP$701–1000
9 Over MOP$1000

Western peninsula

Augusters Rua do Dr. Pedro Jose Lobo 24 ⓣ2871 3242, ⓔaugusters@augusta.usa.com. Tidy, if elderly dorms and double rooms in a downtown block; all have shared facilities. Dorms MOP$60, 4

East Asia Hotel Rua da Madeira 1 ⓣ2892 2433, ⓕ2430. One of Macau's oldest hotels – a little shabby, but comfortable, with friendly staff and good views from some of the upstairs windows. 6

Florida Beco do Pa Ralelo 2 ⓣ2892 3198, ⓕ3199. Don't be too put off by the density of lobby prostitutes; the rooms are a fair size, clean and reasonably furnished. 5

Hotel Central Avenida de Almeida Ribeiro 26–28 ⓣ2837 3888. Hundreds of budget rooms on seven floors in this elderly, gloomy block just around the corner from the Largo de Senado. Lower-priced rooms are generally good value, but ask to see a few. 5

Ka Va Calcada de Sao Joao 5 ⓣ2832 3063. On the left as you head uphill from Rua da Sé to the Sé church. A good budget choice if you stick to the tidy rear rooms, though those facing the St are windowless and prone to damp. 4

Ko Wah Rua da Felicidade 71 ⓣ2893 0755. Very pleasant hotel in one of Macau's most interesting quarters. Newly renovated and overall cheerful and welcoming. 5

Man Va Travessa da Caldeira 30 ⓣ2838 8655, ⓕ2834 2179. Clean and well-designed rooms with spacious bathrooms, spotless carpets and helpful management, though no English spoken. Top value. 5

San Va Rua da Felicidade 67 ⓣ8210 0193, ⓦwww.sanvahotel.com. Best budget deal in town, with elderly but spotless rooms and a friendly manager. 2

Sun Sun Praça Ponte e Horta 14–16 ⓣ2893 9393, ⓦwww.bestwestern.com. Slightly sleazy area but the hotel is well managed, organized and gives midweek discounts. 8

Universal Rua Felicidade 73 ⓣ2857 3247. South of Almeida Ribeiro, this is an older, fairly large place, tidy and with spacious rooms. 4

Southern and eastern peninsula

Hotel Lisboa Avenida de Lisboa 2–4 ⓣ2837 7666, HK reservations ⓣ800 969130, ⓦwww.hotelisboa.com. Once the most ostentatious building in Macau, tiled in orange and white and housing a casino, a shopping arcade and numerous restaurants. Double rooms around MOP$900 on weekdays and up to MOP$1400 at weekends; check the website for current offers. 8

Metropole Hotel Avenida Praia Grande 493–501 ⓣ2838 8166, ⓕ2833 0890. A few hundred metres west of the *Lisboa*; well located and smartly fitted out. 8

Pousada de São Tiago Avenida da República ⓣ378111, ⓦwww.saotiago.com.mo. Constructed from a seventeenth-century fortress on the southern tip of the peninsula, with walled stairways lined by gushing streams, huge stone archways, and 24 rooms with polished wooden furnishings. Prices upwards of MOP$3000.

Taipa, Cotai and Coloane

Grandview Hotel Estrada Governador Albano de Oliveria, Taipa ⓣ2883 7788, ⓦwww.grandview-hotel.com. Glitzy establishment, near the racecourse, which offers big discounts for advance bookings. Lots of facilities, and a shuttle bus to the piers. 8

Pousada de Coloane Praia de Cheoc Van, Coloane ⓣ2888 2143, ⓦwww.hotelpcoloane.com.mo. Great scenery, if somewhat remote, situated by Cheoc Van beach on Coloane's far south shore. All rooms have balconies overlooking the beach, there's a swimming pool and an Italian restaurant. If you want a relaxing holiday experience, this is the place for it. 8

Venetian Cotai ⓣ2883 7788, ⓦwww.venetianmacao.com. An incredible, full-scale replica of St Mark's Square in Venice fronts for a 3000-room resort, convention centre and casino complex: the convention space here alone is greater than the total available in Hong Kong. A sign of the wealth accruing in Macau – and where development is heading. Rates from MOP$1600. **Westin Resort** Estrada de Hac Sa, Coloane ⓣ2887 1111, ⓦwww.westin-macau.com. At the far end of Hac Sa's fine beach, this is good for a quiet day or two, midweek, although it fills up with Hong Kong families at the weekend. Three restaurants and excellent sports facilities, including an eighteen-hole golf course, two pools and a Jacuzzi. Often does good weekend special offers. Doubles from MOP$1625.

Macau peninsula

Macau's older core is centred around **Largo do Senado**, a large cobbled square north off Avenida Almeida Ribeiro and surrounded by unmistakeably European-influenced buildings, with their stucco mouldings, colonnades and shuttered windows. At Largo do Senado's southern side – across Avenida Ribeira – stands the **Leal Senado** (Mon–Sat 1–7pm; free), generally considered the finest Portuguese building in the city. The interior courtyard sports walls decorated with wonderful blue and white Portuguese tiles, while up the staircase from the courtyard is the richly decorated **senate chamber**, still used by the municipal government of Macau. In the late sixteenth century, the entire citizenry of the colony would gather here to debate issues of importance, and the senate's title *leal* (loyal) was earned during the period when Spain occupied the Portuguese throne and Macau became the final stronghold of loyalists to the true king. Adjacent to the chamber is the wood-carved **public library**, whose collection includes a repository of fifteenth- and sixteenth-century books, which you can still see on the shelves; you're free to go in and browse.

Across the road at Largo do Senado's northern end, the honey-and-cream-coloured, seventeenth-century Baroque church, **São Domingos**, is adjoined by Macau's **Religious Museum**, containing a treasury of sacred art under a timbered roof. Continue north from here along the cobbled lane and you'll soon find yourself flanked by *pastellarias* (biscuit shops) and stores selling reproduction antique furniture. The lane then opens up, a broad stone staircase rising in front to the richly carved facade of **São Paulo**, Macau's most famous landmark. The original church, built in 1602 and hailed as the greatest Christian monument in East Asia, was – the facade aside – completely destroyed by fire in 1835. The former crypt and nave have become a small religious **museum**, detailing the building and design of the church, and holding the bones of the followers of St Francis Xavier (daily Mon & Wed–Sun 9am–6pm; free). You'll also notice a small temple huddled by the side of São Paulo and built into a fragment of the **old town walls**.

The tree-covered slope immediately east of São Domingos is crowned by another colonial relic, the seventeenth-century fortress **Fortaleza do Monte**. For some great views, take a stroll round the old ramparts, whose huge cannons repelled a Dutch attack in 1622, when a lucky shot blew up the Dutch magazine. Up here you'll also find the **Museo de Macau** (Tues–Sun 10am–6pm; MOP$15), whose excellent collection focuses on the SAR's traditions, culture and habits. Highlights include video shows, a mock-up of a traditional Macanese street, and depictions of local arts and crafts, complete with evocative soundtracks of local sellers' cries.

A few hundred metres northwest of São Paulo, Rua de Santo Antonio winds up at a small square, to the north of which is **Jardim Luís de Camões** (daily 6am–10pm; free), a shady park full of large trees and granite boulders covered in ferns. A grotto in the park was built in honour of the great sixteenth-century Portuguese poet, Luís de Camões, who is thought to have been banished here for part of his life. Immediately east of the square, though, is the real gem, the

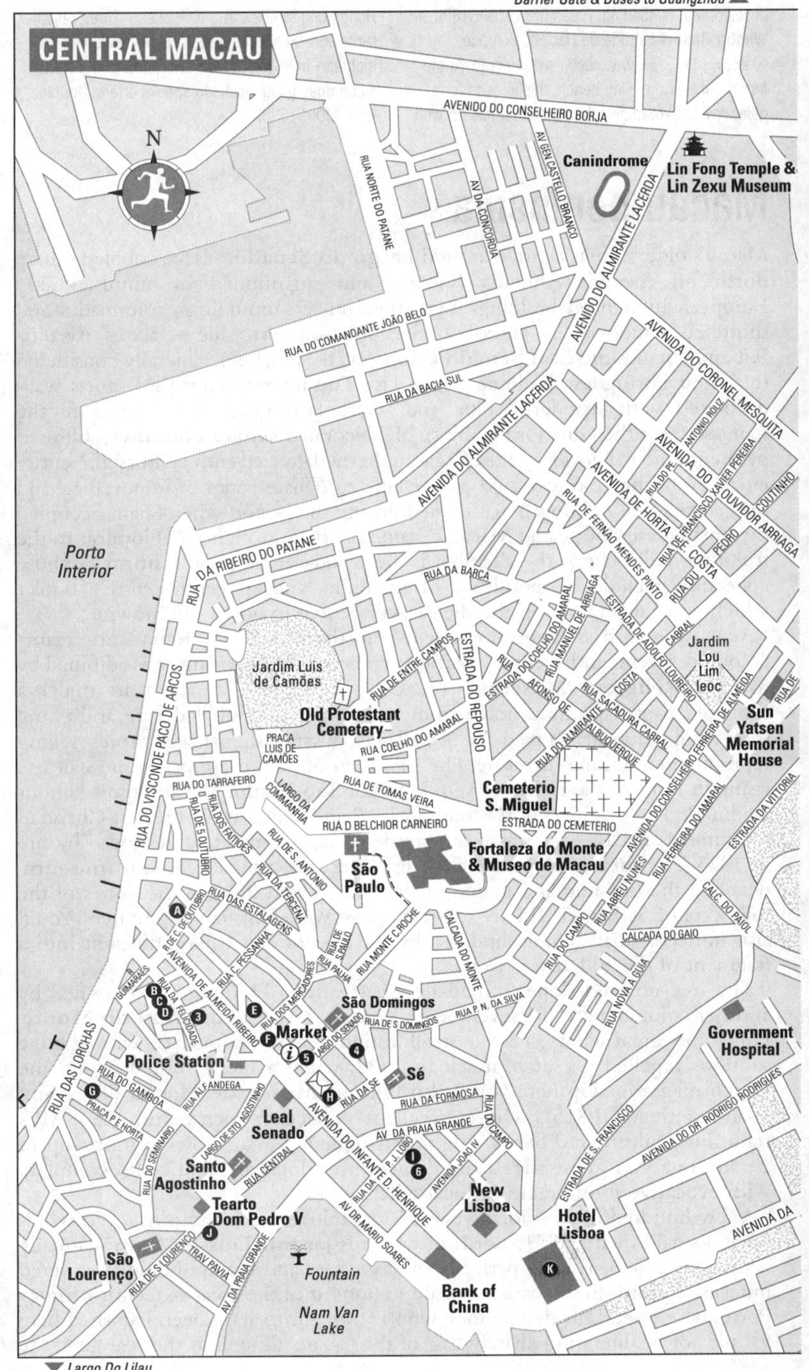

9 HONG KONG AND MACAU

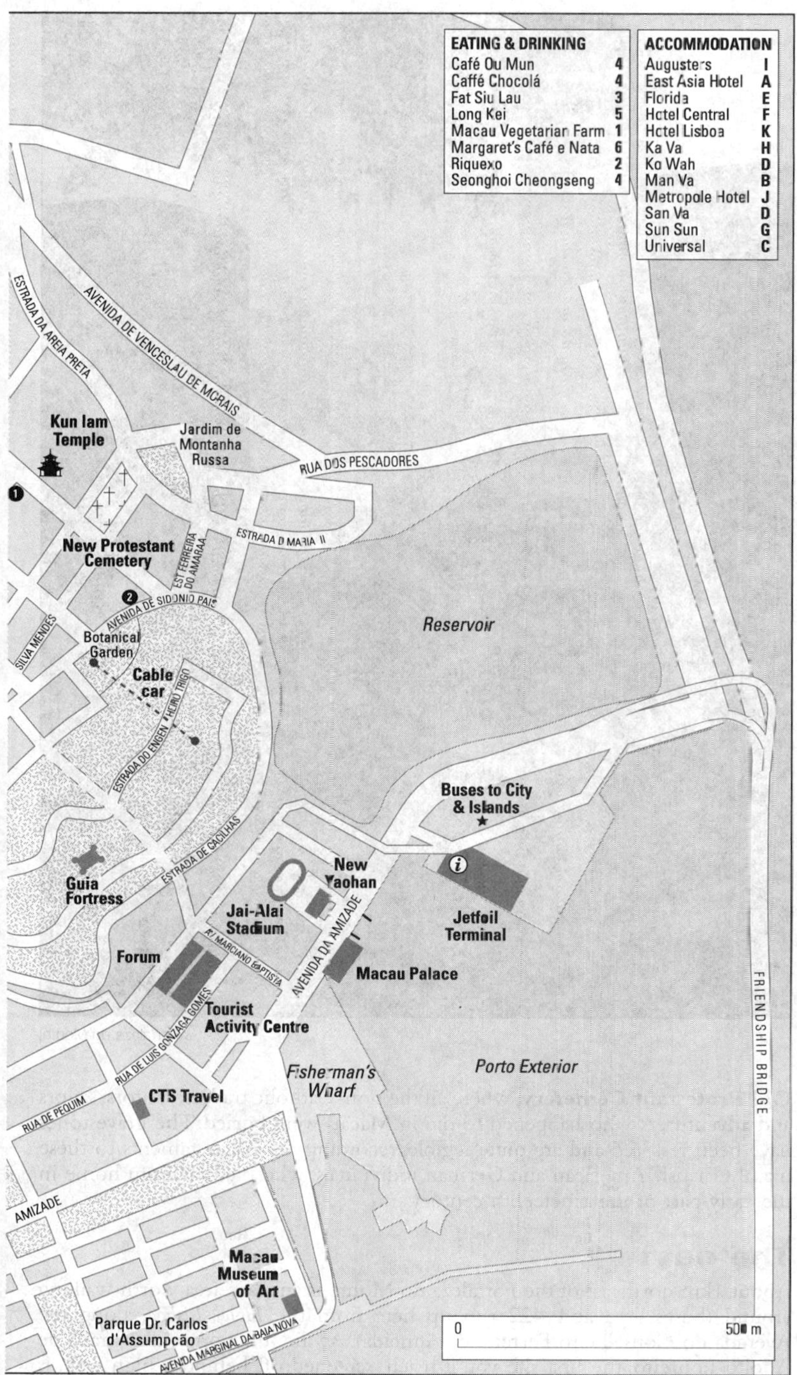
EATING & DRINKING
Café Ou Mun 4
Caffé Chocolá 4
Fat Siu Lau 3
Long Kei 5
Macau Vegetarian Farm 1
Margaret's Café e Nata 6
Riquexo 2
Seonghoi Cheongseng 4
ACCOMMODATION
Augusters I
East Asia Hotel A
Florida E
Hotel Central F
Hotel Lisboa K
Ka Va H
Ko Wah D
Man Va B
Metropole Hotel J
San Va D
Sun Sun G
Universal C
ESTRADA DA AREIA PRETA
AVENIDA DE VENCESLAU DE MORAIS
Kun Iam Temple
Jardim de Montanha Russa
RUA DOS PESCADORES
ESTRADA D MARIA II
New Protestant Cemetery
EST FERREIRA DO AMARAL
AVENIDA DE SIDONIO PAIS
SILVA MENDES
Botanical Garden
Cable car
ESTRADA DO ENGEN HEIRO TRIGO
Reservoir
Buses to City & Islands
ESTRADA DE CACILHAS
Guia Fortress
New Yaohan
Jai-Alai Stadium
Jetfoil Terminal
Forum
R/ MARCIANO BAPTISTA
AVENIDA DA AMIZADE
Macau Palace
Tourist Activity Centre
RUA DE LUIS GONZAGA GOMES
FRIENDSHIP BRIDGE
Fisherman's Wharf
Porto Exterior
CTS Travel
RUA DE PEQUIM
AMIZADE
Macau Museum of Art
Parque Dr. Carlos d'Assumpcão
AVENIDA MARGINAL DA BAIA NOVA
0
500 m
Airport, Taipa & Coloane

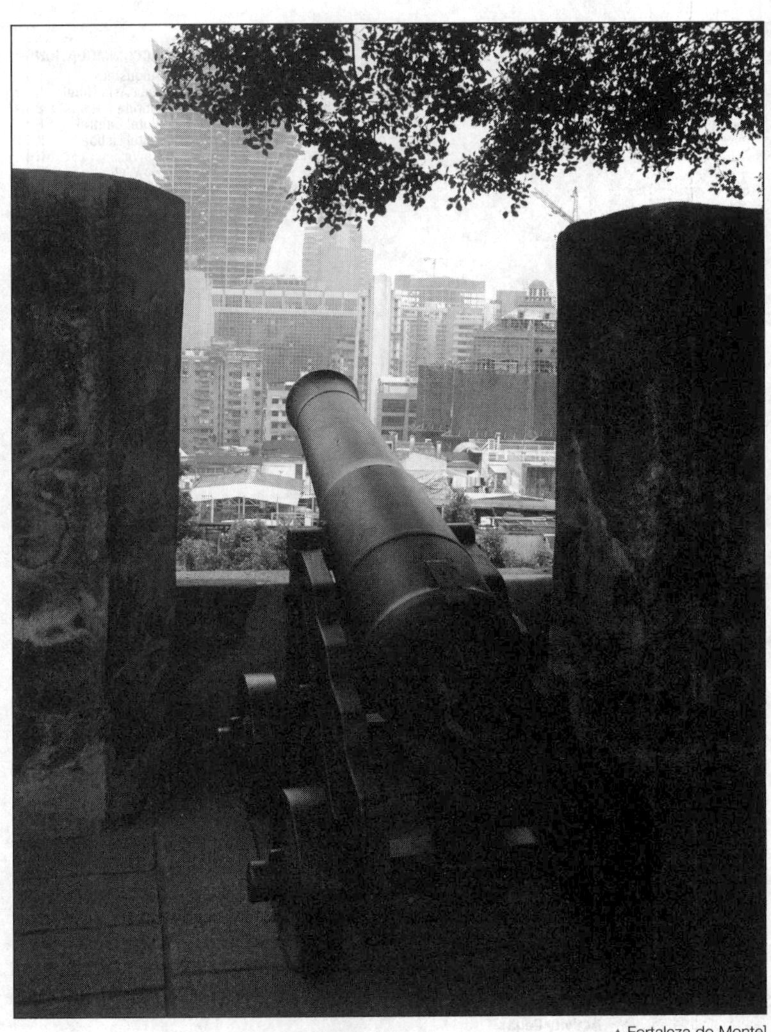

▲ Fortaleza do Monte]

Old Protestant Cemetery, where all the non-Catholic traders, visitors, sailors and adventurers who happened to die in Macau were buried. The gravestones have been restored and are quite legible, recording the last testaments to these mainly British, American and German individuals, who died far from home in the early part of the nineteenth century.

The east

About 1km northeast of the Fortaleza do Monte is another area worth walking around (buses #12 and #22 run up here from the *Hotel Lisboa*, along the Avenida do Conselheiro Ferreira de Almeida). At the junction with Estrada de Adolfo Loureiro, the first site you'll reach, screened off behind a high wall, is the scenic and calming **Jardim Lou Lim Ieoc** (daily 6am–9pm; free), a formal Chinese garden crowded with bamboos, pavilions, rocks and ancient trees arranged around a large pond.

East of here is **Guia Hill**, Macau's highest and steepest – if you don't want to walk up, catch a **cable car** (MOP$3 one way, MOP$5 return) from the **Botanical Garden** on Avenida de Sidonio Pais. The whole hilltop is one breezy park, planted with trees and shrubs, with outstanding views of the SAR and neighbouring parts of China; the summit is crowned by the seventeenth-century **Guia Fortress**, the dominant feature of which is a whitewashed lighthouse, added in the last century and reputed to be the oldest anywhere on the Chinese coast. The adjacent **Guia chapel** contains original Christian paintings featuring Chinese characters and dragons.

East of Guia Hill, the main thoroughfare is **Avenida da Amizade**, which runs parallel with the waterfront from the Jetfoil Terminal through a burgeoning **casino district**. Casinos aside, the most obvious nearby attractions are the **Tourist Activity Centre** (Mon & Wed–Sun 10am–6pm) on Rua de Luis Gonzaga Gomes, whose best feature is the entertaining **Wine Museum** (MOP$15); and **Fishermans' Wharf** (pay per ride), an open-air theme park with fairground rides, a Tang-style street, Roman ampitheatre and a forty-metre-high fake volcano that "erupts" daily at 5.40pm. South, the *Sands* casino conceals the waterfront **Macau Museum of Art** (Tues–Sun 9am–7pm, MOP$15; MOP$8 for children under 11, adults over 60 and students), housing exhibitions of Chinese calligraphy, China trade paintings, Shiwan ceramics and historical documents. Down on the waterfront behind the museum, a twenty-metre-high **bronze statue of Kun Iam** stands in front of views of the amazing, ribbon-like and hunchbacked **Taipa Bridge** and **Friendship Bridge**, both crossing to Taipa.

Casinos

Macau's 29 **casinos** (with several more under way) are all open around the clock and have no clothing restrictions, though you must be at least 18 years of age, are not allowed to bring in cameras, and often have to show your passport and go through a security check at the door. Once inside, many games have a **minimum bet** of MOP$10–100. For information on how to play the various games, ask MGTO for a leaflet; note, however, that signs in tiny print at the entrances to the casinos politely suggest that punters should engage in betting for fun only, and not as a means of making money.

Each casino has its own atmosphere and (almost exclusively Chinese) clientele, and a **casino crawl** will provide a wide scope for people-watching, even if you're not interested in gambling. The *Casino Jai Alai* on Avenida do Dr. Rodrigo Rodrigues is dark and verging on sleazy, with the feel of a hardcore den; the nearby floating casino, the *Macau Palace*, is surprisingly dull, though full of overblown, red good-luck signs and carved golden dragons; the gold-windowed *Sands* on Avenida de Amizade has a Las Vegas slickness and colossal, open interior; the *Wynn* offers a sophisticated and elegant atmosphere; while the *Galaxy* – despite a smart exterior and bright lighting – is another low-end deal specializing in tacky carpets and an ocean of slot machines (known here as "hungry tigers"). Save time, too, for a look around the old *Lisboa*, the orange- and white- tiled building at the junction of Avenida de Amizade and Avenida Infante D. Henrique, still Macau's best-known casino despite being upstaged by more modern counterparts – not to mention its own new incarnation over the road, whose soaring, gold-topped tower proves that Stanley Ho, despite losing his gaming monopoly, still has no peer when it comes to ostentation.

The north

The northern part of the peninsula up to the border with China is largely residential, though it has a couple of points of interest. It's possible to walk the 3km from Almeida Ribeiro to the border, but the streets at this end of town are not particularly atmospheric, so it makes sense to resort to the local buses.

On Avenida do Coronel Mesquita, which cuts the peninsula from east to west about 2km north of Almeida Ribeiro, is the enchanting **Kun Iam Temple** (daily 7am–6pm; free), accessible on bus #12 from the *Hotel Lisboa*. The complex of temples here, dedicated to the Goddess of Mercy, is around 400 years old, but the most interesting fact associated with the place is that here, in 1844, the United States and China signed their first treaty of trade and cooperation – you can still see the granite table they signed it on. Inside the complex, shaded by banyan trees, are a number of small shrines, with the main temple hall approached via a flight of steps. Around the central statue of Kun Iam herself, to the rear, is a crowd of statues representing eighteen *arhats*, or Buddhist saints. The worshippers you'll see here shaking bamboo sticks in cylinders are trying to find out their fortunes.

Bus #17 or a twenty-minute walk from here takes you northwest up Avenida do Almirante Lacerda to the **Canidrome** – Southeast Asia's only greyhound track, with races every Monday, Thursday, Saturday and Sunday from 7.45pm – and Lin Fung Temple, whose main point of interest is its accompanying **Lin Zexu Museum** (Tues–Sun 9am–5pm; MOP$10), a monument to the man who destroyed British opium stocks in Guangzhou and so precipitated the first Opium War (see p.1150). Stay on the bus and you'll wind up at the **Porto do Cerco**, or **Barrier Gate** (daily 7am–midnight), the nineteenth-century stuccoed archway marking the border with China. These days the old gate itself is redundant – people use the modern customs and immigration complex to one side or choose to cross at the new border gate on the Lotus Bridge. From here, bus #3 or #10 will get you back to Almeida Ribeiro and the *Hotel Lisboa*.

The south

The small but hilly tongue of land south of Almeida Ribeiro is a tight web of lanes, with colonial mansions and their gardens looming up round every corner. A good walk through this area begins by following **Rua Central** south past the peppermint-coloured **Teatro Dom Pedro V**, built in 1873 and still staging occasional performances, despite its main function as the members-only *Clube Macao*. Opposite is the early nineteenth-century church of **Santo Agostinho**, whose pastel walls are decorated with delicate piped icing. Further down on Rua de São Lourenço, the square-towered **São Lourenço** is a wonderfully tropical nineteenth-century church, with a mildewed exterior framed by palms and fig trees.

Another few minutes south and you arrive at **Largo do Lilau**, a tiny, pretty square with a shady fig tree and **spring**, whose waters are said to impart longevity. This is the site of Macau's original residential area, and almost all buildings here are over a century old, including the heavy-walled **Mandarin's House**, just off to one side at 10 Traversa da Silva. You're now in the **Barra district**, and Rua Central has mutated into **Calçada da Barra**, which you follow downhill past more elderly buildings – including the strikingly crenelated, yellow and white **Moorish Barracks** – to the seafront on the southwestern side of the peninsula. The celebrated **A-Ma Temple** here may be as old as 600 years in parts, and certainly predates the arrival of the

Portuguese on the peninsula. Dedicated to the goddess A-Ma (known in Hong Kong as Tin Hau), the temple is an attractive jumble of altars and little outhouses among the rocks.

Immediately across the road from here, the **Maritime Museum** (Mon & Wed–Fri 10am–5.30pm; MOP$10, MOP$5 at weekends) is excellently presented, covering old explorers, seafaring techniques, equipment, models and boats. A short walk south along the shore from the museum brings you to the very tip of the peninsula, which is today marked by the *Pousada de São Tiago*, a hotel built into the remains of the seventeenth-century Portuguese fortress, the **Fortaleza de Barra**. Enter the front door and you find yourself walking up a stone tunnel running with water – it's well worth climbing up to the *Pousada*'s veranda café for a drink overlooking the sea. The walk from here around the southern headland and back to the north again follows tree-lined Avenida da Republica, the old seafront promenade – today, its views take in **Sai Van Lake** and the 338-metre-high **Macau Tower** (daily 10am–9pm; various charges, up to MOP$70, depending on level of observation deck). At night, the waterfront promenade also offers Macau's version of Hong Kong's multicoloured harbourside skyline – except, of course, that here the financial institutions are casinos instead of banks.

The islands

Macau's two islands, **Taipa** and **Coloane**, were originally dots of land supporting a few small fishing villages; now, with the rapidly developing strip of reclaimed land, **Cotai**, joining the two, they look set to become part of a new entertainment district. Despite this, both retain quiet pockets of colonial architecture where you can just about imagine yourself in some European village, while Coloane also has a fine beach.

From Almeida Ribeiro, buses #11 and #33 go to Taipa Village; buses #21, #21A, #26 and #26A stop outside the *Hyatt Regency* on Taipa before going on to Coloane.

Taipa and Cotai

Taipa, site of Macau International Airport, racecourse, sports stadium, university and residential "suburbs", at first seems too developed to warrant a special stop. However, tiny **Taipa Village** on the island's east side, with its old colonial promenade, makes a pleasant place for an extended lunch. The bus drops you off by a modern market, where the hundred-metre-long **Rua do Cunha** (or "Food Street") leads down to the old covered **Feira do Carmo** market square, which is partly surrounded by a dragon wall and several restaurants (see p.710). On the far side of the square, turn right to more restaurants and a **Tin Hau Temple**, or left until you see a wavy set of tree-lined steps leading up to a small square and church above the old colonial promenade, **Avenida da Praia**. Five original, peppermint-green mansions with verandas here now form the **Taipa House Museum** (Tues–Sun 10am–6pm; MOP$5 allows entry to all five), which reveals details of early nineteenth-century domestic life for the resident Macanese families: high-ranking civil servants who were religious and well-to-do, but not enormously wealthy.

A few years ago, views south from the museum took in mud flats, reeds and the sea; now this has all been filled in to form **Cotai district**, and the scene is as incongrous as you could imagine. Right ahead is the extraordinary **Venetian**, a full-scale reproduction of Venice's St Mark's Square housing the world's largest casino resort, with 850 gaming tables, 4100 slot machines and its own permanent Cirque de Soleil troupe. This is only the first of several similar projects, with **Macau Studio City** – combining a further resort and casino complex with film-production facilities – also set to open in the near future. Further reclamation means that Cotai's western side now bumps up against the Chinese mainland, with the **Cotai Frontier Post** (not yet open to pedestrians) making access easy for coachloads of holidaying mainlanders.

Coloane

Coloane comprises nine square kilometres of hilly parkland, more colonial fragments and some decent **beaches**, making it a pleasant place to spend a few hours. After crossing Cotai, buses pass the **Parque de Seac Pai Van** (Tues–Sun 9am–7pm; free), a large park with paths leading uphill to a white marble statue of the goddess A-Ma – at 19.99m high, it is the tallest in the world. A short way on, all buses stop at the roundabout in pretty **Coloane Village** on the western shore, overlooking mainland China just across the water and home to a fair number of expats – *Lord Stow's Bakery*, at the sea end of the square, offers irresistible **natas**, Portuguese egg tarts. To the north of the village are a few junk-building sheds, while the street leading south from the village roundabout, one block back from the shore, contains a couple of shops selling dried marine products and the unexpected yellow and white **St Francis Xavier Chapel**, where a relic of the saint's arm bone is venerated. A couple of hundred metres beyond this is the **Tam Kung Temple**, housing a metre-long whale bone carved into the shape of a ship.

On the north side of the village roundabout there's a small shop where you can **rent bicycles** for MOP$12 an hour, a good way to travel the 3km farther round to **Hac Sa beach** (otherwise, take bus #21A, #26 or #26A), perhaps dropping in on **Cheoc Van beach** to the south on the way as well. The beach at Hac Sa, tree-lined and stretching far off round the bay, is without doubt the best in Macau, despite the black colour of its volcanic sand, and has cafés, bars, showers and toilets as well as some fine restaurants nearby (see p.710). There's also a sports and swimming pool complex (Mon–Fri 9am–9pm, Sat & Sun until midnight; MOP$15) although it all gets pretty crowded at weekends. Otherwise, try the **Parque Natural da Barragem de Hac Sa**; a short hop from Hac Sa beach, this features barbecue pits, a kids' playground and maze, boating on a small reservoir, and various short trails in the hills (Tues–Fri 2–7pm, Sat & Sun 10am–7pm; MOP$10–40 for boat rental).

Eating, drinking and nightlife

Macanese cuisine fuses Chinese with Portuguese elements, further overlaid with tastes from Portugal's Indian and African colonies. Fresh bread, wine and coffee all feature, as well as an array of dishes ranging from *caldo verde* (vegetable soup) to *bacalhau* (dried salted cod). Macau's most interesting Portuguese colonial dish is probably **African chicken**, a concoction of Goan and East African influences, comprising chicken grilled with peppers and spices. Other things worth trying include Portuguese baked **custard tarts** (*natas*), served in many cafés; **almond biscuits**, formed in a wooden mould and baked in a charcoal oven, which can be bought by weight in many *pastellarias*, such as Koi Kei, around São Paulo and Rua da Felicidade; and sheets of pressed **roast**

▲ Custard tarts, Lord Stow's Bakery, Coloane

meat, also sold in *pastellarias*. Straightforward **Cantonese restaurants**, often serving *dim sum* for breakfast and lunch, are also plentiful, though you'll find wine on the menus even here. Cafés tend to **open** around 8.30am, while restaurant times are about 11.30am to 2.30pm, and from 6 until 10pm. **Prices** for the typically generous portions are low compared to Hong Kong, with bills even in smart venues rarely exceeding MOP$250 per head, though watch out for little extras such as water, bread and so forth, which can really add to the cost of a meal. A bottle of house red will set you back around MOP$100 in a restaurant.

Macau's **nightlife** is surprisingly flat, if you don't count the casinos – drinking is done in restaurants or in the handful of bars in the "Macau Lan Kwai Fong", located along the waterfront facing the Porto Exterior, and offering live music and street-side tables.

Cafés

Café Ou Mun Fantastic breads, cakes and coffee, and light meals, very popular with Portuguese expats.

Caffé Chocolá Travessa de S. Domingos (off Largo do Senado at *McDonald's*). Difficult to choose between here and adjacent *Ou Mun* (see above) as to which might be best for breakfast or cake and coffee.

Leitaria I Son Largo do Senado 7. Virtually next door to *Long Kei*, this is an excellent milk bar, offering milk with everything – fruit, chocolate, eggs, ice creams, puddings and breakfasts.

Margaret's Café e Nata Rua Comandante Mata e Oliveira. Surrounded by gloomy apartment blocks, this is an excellent café with first-rate sandwiches and *natas*.

Restaurants

360° Café Level 60, Macau Tower ⓣ9888622. One of Macau's classiest places to dine, serving Indian and Macanese food in a revolving restaurant with unparalleled views. A good way not to bankrupt yourself is to opt for the set buffets at MOP$158 for lunch, and MOP$228 for supper.

A Lorcha Rua do Almirante Sérgio 289 ⓣ2831 3193. Genuine and excellent Spanish, Macanese and Portuguese food; the seafood rice or beer clams are outstanding.

Fat Siu Lau Rua da Felicidade 64 ⓣ2857 3585. A very popular, traditional old restaurant whose speciality is marinated roast pigeon, though they also do a great crab curry.

Henri's Avenida da Republica 4 ⓣ2855 6251. Order the grilled sardines or African chicken in the evening and kick back with a bottle of red at one of the pavement tables. Good food but tourist-inflated prices and irritating service.
Litoral Rua Almirante Sérgio 261-A ⓣ2896 7878. Reputedly the best place for Macanese food in Macau, with excellent charcoal-grilled chicken, fish or steak; *feijoada*; and stewed chicken rice at MOP$100 or more a dish. Their mango pudding is the business, too. If you can't get in, nearby *O Porto Interior* or *A Lorcha* are almost as good.
Long Kei Largo do Senado 7B. A 100-year-old, traditional, but inexpensive and excellent Cantonese restaurant, on the left side as you face the square from Almeida Ribeiro.
Macau Vegetarian Farm Opposite the Kun Iam Temple, Avenida do Coronel Mesquita 11 ⓣ752824 (no English sign). Warehouse-sized, characterless restaurant offering good-quality Chinese vegetarian cuisine at MOP$30–50 a dish; no English translations, but lots of photos of the food on menus.
O Porto Interior Rua da Almirante Sérgio 259-B ⓣ2896 7770. Just by the A-Ma Temple, this features antique Chinese screens, superb old Macanese cuisine such as African chicken or grilled sardines, plus a splendid wine cellar.
Riquexo Avenida Sidónio Pais 69-B. Self-service Portuguese canteen with no frills at all, though the food is hearty, and nearby office workers flock here for lunch. Menu changes daily but is likely to include *feijoada*, curry chicken, grilled lamb and *bacalhau* – at MOP$28–55 a serving.
Seonghoi Cheongseng Across from *Café Ou Mun* on Travessa de S. Domingos (no English sign). Inexpensive – hence perpetually full – Shanghai stir-fry restaurant. Good for noodles, steamed buns and seafood dishes.

Taipa

Galo In the square at Rua da Cunha 45, Taipa Village ⓣ2882 7423. Cute, blue-shuttered place with low prices and family-run feel. The crab is good.
O Santos Rua do Cunha, Taipa Village ⓣ2882 7508. Huge helpings of seafood rice, pork and bean stew, rabbit, roast suckling pig and other Portuguese mainstays from MOP$70.
Panda Rua Direita Carlos Eugenio 4–8 ⓣ2882 7338. On a tiny alley leading east from the southern end of Rua da Cunha in Taipa Village. Reasonably priced Portuguese place, with outdoor tables in good weather.
Paparoca Rua Correia da Silva 57, Taipa Village ⓣ2882 7636. Probably the most popular restaurant in Taipa Village, serving tasty Portuguese colonial food alongside various dishes from Goa and Africa.
Shanghai Zhen Zhen Rua do Cunha, Taipa Village (no English sign). Shanghai and Sichuanese food, including steamers of *xiao long bao* dumplings, cold sliced meats, "ants climbing the trees" (mince and chillies) and stir-fries. Mains MOP$35–50.

Coloane

Caçarola Rua das Gaivotas 8, Coloane Village ⓣ2888 2226. Welcoming and deservedly popular Portuguese restaurant with excellent daily specials, though becoming a little expensive. It's off the main village square.
Chan Chi Mei/Nga Tim Next to the St Francis Xavier Chapel, Coloane Village ⓣ2888 2086. A friendly Chinese place with outdoor tables under a colonnade, ideal for lunch or an evening drink; the best meals are crab or pork knuckle. Most mains under MOP$70.
Fernando Hac Sa beach ⓣ2888 2531. Not far from the bus stop. A casual, cheerful atmosphere and great Portuguese food make it a favourite with expats. You might need a taxi to get home, though. Advance booking recommended, and a must at weekends.
Lord Stow's Bakery Coloane Village Square. The best baked custard tarts in Macau, said to be made to a secret recipe without animal fat. Buy take-aways from the bakery itself, or sit down for coffee and a light meal at their café around the corner.

Listings

Airlines Air Asia ⓦwww.airasia.com; Air Macau ⓣ2836 5555; EVA Airways ⓣ2872 6866; Hainan Airlines ⓦwww.hnair.com; Tiger Airways ⓦwww.tigerairways.com; Xiamen Airlines ⓣ2878 0663.
Banks and exchange Most banks have branches around the junction of Avenida Almeida Ribeiro and Avenida Praia Grande, where you'll also find plenty of attached ATMs. Banks generally open Mon–Fri from 9am until 4 or 4.30pm, but close by lunchtime on Sat. There are also licensed moneychangers that exchange traveller's cheques (and that open seven days a week), including a 24hr one in the basement of the *Hotel Lisboa*, and one near the bottom of the steps leading up to São Paulo.

Bookshops The Portuguese Bookshop, Rua do São Domingos 18–22 (near São Domingos church), has a small English-language section with books on Macau's history, cooking and buildings.
Festivals The normal Chinese holidays are celebrated in Macau, plus some Catholic festivals introduced from Portugal, such as the Procession of Our Lady of Fatima from São Domingos church, annually on May 13.
Hospitals There's a 24hr emergency department at the Centro Hospitalar Conde São Januário, Calçada Visconde São Januário ⓣ2831 3731; English spoken.
Mail Macau's main post office is in Largo do Senado, on the east side (Mon–Fri 9am–6pm, Sat 9am–1pm); poste restante is delivered here. Small red booths all over the territory also dispense stamps from machines.
Police The main police station is at Avenida Dr Rodrigo Rodrigues ⓣ2857 3333. In an emergency, call ⓣ999.
Telephones Local calls are free from private phones, MOP$1 from payphones. Cardphones work with CTM cards, issued by the Macau State Telecommunication Company, on sale in hotels or at the back of the main post office (open 24hr), where you can also make direct calls.
Travel agencies CITS, Avenida da Praia Grande Trav. de Inacio de Carvalho 8–10 ⓣ2871 5451, ⓦwww.cits.net; CTS, Rua de Nagasaki ⓣ2870 6655, ⓕ2870 3789. Both can help organise flights, buses, accommodation, and visa for China.

Travel details

Trains

Hong Kong to: Guangzhou (12 daily; 2–3hr); Lo Wu (KCR East Line, for Shenzhen; frequent; 50min).

Buses

Hong Kong to: Guangzhou (frequent; 3hr 30min); Shenzhen (frequent; 2hr); Shenzhen Airport (5 daily; 2hr).
Macau to: Guangzhou (several daily; 4hr).

Ferries

Hong Kong to: Macau (frequent; 1hr); Shenzhen (12 daily; 45min).
Macau to: Hong Kong (frequent; 1hr); Shenzhen (3 daily; 1hr).

Flights

Hong Kong is a major international gateway for flights both within Asia and beyond. Macau offers international flights to and from Bangkok, Singapore and Taipei.
Hong Kong to: Beijing (many daily; 3hr); Chengdu (twice daily; 2hr 30min); Guangzhou (5 daily; 40min); Guilin (daily; 1hr 20min); Haikou (daily; 1hr 5min); Hangzhou (4 daily; 2hr); Kunming (twice daily; 2hr); Nanjing (3 daily; 2hr 20min); Ningbo (twice daily; 2hr); Shanghai (11 daily; 2hr); Shantou (daily; 45min); Tianjin (daily; 3hr); Wuhan (daily; 2hr); Xiamen (4 daily; 1hr).
Macau to: Bangkok (twice daily; 3hr); Beijing (daily; 3hr); Fuzhou (daily; 1hr 20min); Hangzhou (3 daily; 1hr 50min); Shanghai (7 daily; 2hr 15min); Shenzhen (twice daily; 30min); Xiamen (twice daily; 1hr); Xi'an (daily; 3hr 50min).

CHAPTER 10 Highlights

✱ **Li River** Cruise between Guilin and Yangshuo through a forest of tall, weirdly contorted karst peaks. See p.721

✱ **Dong villages** Communities of wooden houses, bridges and drum towers pepper remote rural highlands along the Guangxi–Guizhou border. See p.732

✱ **Hua Shan** Another boat trip to see a whole cliffside of mysterious rock art flanking Guangxi's Zuo River. See p.746

✱ **Sisters' Meal Festival** Exuberant showpiece of Miao culture, featuring three days of dancing, bull fighting and dragon-boat racing. See p.764

✱ **Zhijin Caves** The largest, most spectacular of China's subterranean limestone caverns, full of creatively named rock formations. See p.770

✱ **Caohai** Spend a day punting around this beautiful lake, a haven for ducks and rare black-necked cranes. See p.772

▲ Black-necked cranes, Caohai

10

Guangxi and Guizhou

If there's one thing that defines the subtropical southwestern provinces of **Guangxi** and **Guizhou**, it's **limestone**: most of the rivers here are coloured a vivid blue-green by it; everywhere you look are weathered karst hills worn into poetic collections of tall, sharp peaks; and the ground beneath is riddled with extensive **caverns**, some flooded, others large enough to fit a cathedral inside.

Though something of a tourist phenomenon today, historically this topography has proved an immense barrier to communications and, being porous, created some of China's least arable land, with agriculture often confined to the small alluvial plains in between peaks. So poor that it wasn't worth the trouble of invading, for a long while the region was pretty well ignored by Han China, and evolved into a stronghold for ethnic groups. But a period of social stability during the early Qing dynasty caused a population explosion in eastern China and an expansion westwards by the Han. Some of the ethnic minorities kept their nominal identity but more or less integrated with the Chinese, while others resisted assimilation by occupying isolated highlands; either way, the new settlers put pressure on available resources and only worsened the region's poverty, creating a hotbed of resentment against the government. This finally exploded in central Guangxi's **Taiping Uprising** of 1850 (see p.419), marking the start of a century of devastating civil conflict. Even today, while the minority groups have been enfranchised by the formation of several **autonomous prefectures**, industry and infrastructure remain underdeveloped and few of the cities – including **Nanning** and **Guiyang**, the provincial capitals – have much to offer except transport to more interesting locations.

Despite its bleak history, the region offers a huge range of diversions. The landscape is epitomized by the tall karst towers surrounding the city of **Guilin** in northeastern Guangxi, familiar to Chinese and Westerners alike through centuries of eulogistic poetry, paintings and photographs. Equally impressive are cave systems at **Longgong** and **Zhijin** in western Guizhou, while northern Guizhou has **Chishui**, a wild region of bamboo forests and waterfalls. Most rewarding, perhaps, is the chance of close contact with ethnic groups, particularly the **Miao**, **Dong** and **Zhuang**, whose wooden villages, exuberant festivals, and traces of a prehistoric past are all worth indulging. It's also one of the few places in the country where you can be fairly sure of encountering rare wildlife: notably monkeys at **Chongzuo** in southwestern Guangxi; and cranes at **Caohai** in Guizhou's far west.

While **travel** out to all this can be time-consuming, a reasonable quantity of buses and trains means that remoteness is not the barrier it once was. **Language** is another matter, as many rural people speak only their own dialects or local versions of Mandarin, which can be virtually incomprehensible. With geography

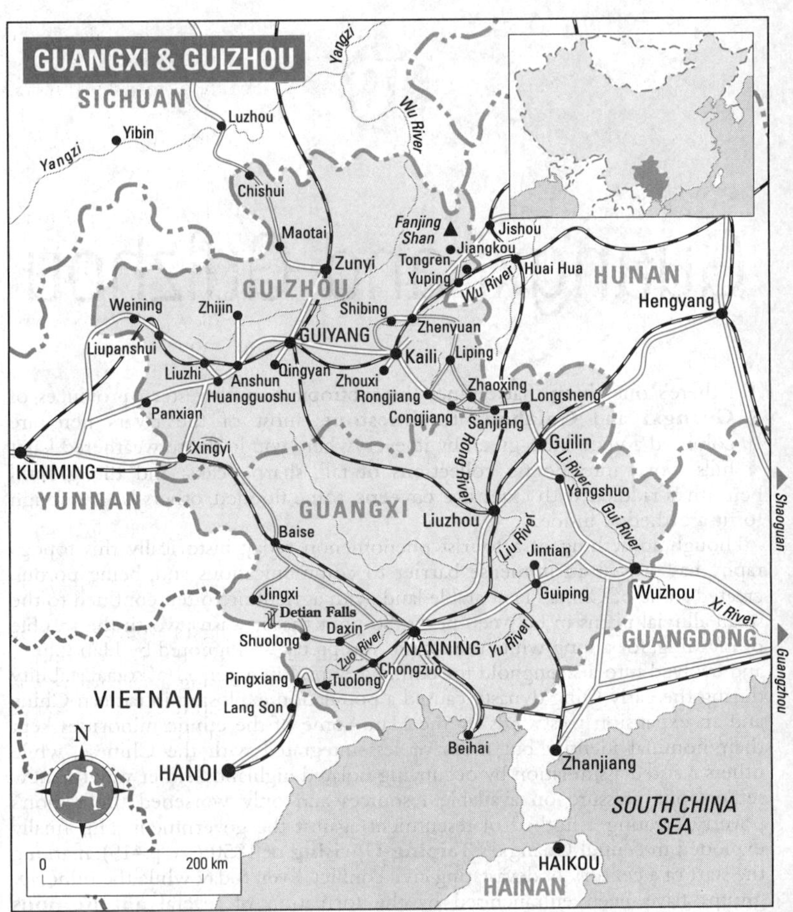

encompassing the South China Sea and some respectable mountains, **weather** is fairly localized, though you should expect warm, wet summers and surprisingly cold winters, especially up in the hills. April and May, and September and October are probably the driest, most pleasant months to visit the region.

Guangxi

Guangxi unfolds south from the cool highlands it shares with Guizhou to a tropical coast and border abutting Vietnam. Up in the northeast, the pick of the province's peak-and-paddy-field landscape is concentrated along the **Li River**, down which you can cruise between the city of **Guilin** and the travellers' haven of **Yangshuo**. Long famous and easily accessible, this has become a massive tourist draw, but just a few hours north the remoter hills around **Sanjiang** are home to the **Dong** ethnic group, whose architecture and way of life make for a fascinating trip up into Guizhou province, hopping between villages on public buses.

Diagonally across Guangxi, the tropically languid provincial capital **Nanning** has little of interest in itself but provides a base for exploring Guangxi's southwestern corner along the **open border with Vietnam**. Actually, since 1958 the province has not been a province at all but the Guangxi Zhuang Autonomous Region, heartland of China's thirteen-million-strong Zhuang nationality. They constitute about a third of the regional population and, although largely assimilated into Chinese life today, there's enough archeological evidence to link them with a Bronze Age culture spread throughout Southeast Asia, including **prehistoric rock friezes** west of Nanning. Nearby are two other major draws: the **Detian Waterfall**, which actually pours over the Vietnamese border; and **Chongzuo Ecology Park**, where it's possible to see the critically endangered white-headed langur, a cliff-dwelling monkey. **Guiping** – being central to the origins of the nineteenth-century Taiping Uprising – is the one place of interest east of Nanning, though you might also have to head down to **Behai**, the ferry port for Hainan Island (see p.620).

Though subject to fiercely hot, humid summers, Guangxi's **weather** can be deceptive – it actually snows in Guilin about once every ten years. Another thing of note is that the **Zhuang language**, instead of using *pinyin*, follows its own method of rendering Chinese characters into Roman text. This accounts for the novel spellings you'll encounter on street signs and elsewhere – "Minzu Dadao", for example, becomes "Minzcuzdadau".

Guilin

GUILIN has been famous since Tang times for its scenic location among a host of gnarled, two-hundred-metre-high rocky hills on the **Li River**, down which you can **cruise** to the village of Yangshuo (see p.724). The city rose from a rural backwater in 1372 when Emperor Hongwu decided to appoint **Zhou Shouqian**, a minor relative, to govern from here as the **Jinjiang Prince**, and this quasi-royal line ruled for fourteen generations, dying out in the 1650s when the entire city was razed in conflicts between Ming and Manchu forces. Guilin was later resurrected as de facto provincial capital until losing the position to Nanning in 1914; Sun Yatsen planned the Nationalists' "Northern Expedition" here in 1925; the Long Marchers were soundly trounced by Guomindang factions outside the city nine years later; and the war with Japan saw more than a million refugees hiding out here, until the city was occupied by the invaders – events harrowingly recounted in Amy Tan's *Joy Luck Club*. Wartime bombing spared the city's natural monuments but turned the centre into a shabby provincial shell, neatened up since the 1990s by plenty of well-designed landscaping, shady avenues and rocky parkland. Despite being prone to tourist-driven inflation and hard-sell irritations, the city is an attractive place to spend a day while organizing a cruise downstream.

Guilin

Guilin	桂林	*guìlín*
Duxiu Feng	独秀峰	*dúxiù fēng*
Elephant Trunk Hill	象鼻山	*xiàngbí shān*
Fubo Shan	伏波山	*fúbō shān*
Gu Nanmen	古南门	*gǔnánmén*
Jingjiang Princes' Palace	靖江王府	*jìngjiāng wángfǔ*
Li River	漓江	*líjiāng*
Lijiang Theatre	漓江剧院	*líjiāng jùyuàn*
Qixing Dong	七星洞	*qīxīngdòng*
Reed Flute Cave	芦笛岩	*lúdí yán*
Riyue Shuang Ta	日月双塔	*rìyuè shuāngtǎ*
Rong Hu	榕湖	*róng hú*
Seven Star Park	七星公园	*qīxīng gōngyuán*
Shan Hu	杉湖	*shān hú*
Xi Shan	西山公园	*xīshān gōngyuán*
Accommodation		
Backstreet Youth Hostel	后街国际青年旅馆	*hòujiē guójì qīngnián lǚguǎn*
Fengyuan	丰源酒店	*fēngyuán jiǔdiàn*
Flowers Youth Hostel	花满楼	*huāmǎnlóu*
Fubo Shan	伏波山大酒店	*fóbōshān dàjiǔdiàn*
Golden Elephant	金象大酒店	*jīnxiàng dàjiǔdiàn*
Home Inn	如家酒店	*rújiā jiǔdiàn*
Jingxiu	景秀大酒店	*jǐngxiù dàjiǔdiàn*
Lijiang Waterfall	漓江大瀑布饭店	*líjiāng dàpùbù fàndiàn*
Sheraton	大宇大饭店	*dàyǔ dàfàndiàn*
Eating		
Haodama	好大妈	*hǎodàmā*
Natural Café	闻莺阁	*wényīng gé*
Xiao Nan Guo	小南国菜馆	*xiǎonánguó càiguǎn*
Yaxu Nong Jia	雅叙农家菜馆	*yǎxù nóngjiācaì guǎn*
Yi Yuan	怡园饭店	*yíyuán fàndiàn*
Zhengyang	正阳汤城	*zhèngyáng tāngchéng*

Arrival

Central Guilin lies on the western bank of the Li, with a handful of small, isolated peaks hemming in the perimeter and riverbanks. Parallel with the river and about 500m west, **Zhongshan Lu** is the main street, running north for 4km or so from the train station past a knot of accommodation and services, the long-distance bus station and on through the centre. The main roads which cross it are Nanhuan Lu, Ronghu Lu and adjoining Shanhu Lu, and Jiefang Lu, all of which stretch for at least 1km west across town from **Binjiang Lu**, the riverside promenade.

Liangjiang International Airport is 20km west of the city, connected to the CAAC office on Shanghai Lu by airport bus (¥20) and taxi (about ¥75). The **train station** is centrally set at the back of a large square off Zhongshan Lu, within striking distance of accommodation and places of interest, with the **long-distance bus station** a couple of hundred metres further north. Buses from Yangshuo drop passengers in front of the train station. Most of Guilin's sights are close enough to walk to, others can be reached easily on public buses, or by taxi (which cost ¥8 to hire).

Moving on from Guilin

Buses to Yangshuo (¥14) leave the train station forecourt every few minutes through the day; watch out for bag-slashers and pickpockets who target foreigners getting on or off the bus. Buses from the long-distance station to elsewhere in the province and beyond are easy to book a day in advance: options include heading north to Longsheng, Sanjiang and Guizhou province (pp.730–748); east to the holy peaks at Heng Shan in Hunan; or southeast to Guangzhou – bear in mind you're likely to get a much better seat here than picking the service up at Yangshuo. **Flying** is similarly straightforward, with Guilin linked to cities right across the mainland, as well as to Hong Kong, Thailand, Korea and Japan. The airport bus leaves the CAAC office on Shanghai Lu every thirty minutes from 6.30am to 9pm, and costs ¥20.

Guilin also has good **rail links** to the rest of China, including direct services east to Shanghai and Beijing, southeast to Guangzhou, west to Chongqing and Kunming, and southeast to Nanning (on a double-decker express; 5hr). If you book a few days in advance you should get what you want; the ticket office opens daily (7.30–11.30am, 12.30–2.30pm, 3–7pm, & 7.30–9.30pm), and queues are not too bad. **Agents** in both Guilin and Yangshuo can also sort things out, though they still need three days' notice and charge steep mark-ups for each ticket.

Details for arranging **Li River cruises** to Yangshuo are covered on p.723.

Accommodation

Guilin's **hotels** are mostly mid-range and upmarket, with the choice of two **youth hostels** if you're after a budget bed. Competition is pretty stiff in town so always bargain at mid-range places, especially in winter, when discounted rates of fifty percent are not unusual. The nicest location is along the river, with lakeside options the next best thing. Everywhere will have a booking desk for cruises and local tours.

Backstreet Youth Hostel 3 Renmin Lu, near the Sheraton ⓣ0773/2819936, ⓔguilinhostel@hotmail.com. Excellent location in the centre of town and close to the river, with café, Internet and plain, comfortable doubles and triples – the one drawback being the persistent hawkers swarming outside. Dorms ¥30, ❸

Fengyuan 26 Zhongshan Zhong Lu, entrance on Yiren Lu ⓣ0773/2827262, ⓕ2827259. Just a clean, inner-city place with no outstanding features other than being reasonable value for money. ❺

Flowers Youth Hostel 6 Shangzhi Gang, Block 2, Zhongshan Lu ⓣ0773/3839625, ⓦwww.yhaguilin.com. A great option, hidden away behind the *Home Inn* opposite the train station: walk through a dreary alley to the back of the hotel, take the equally uninspiring stairs up a flight, and you'll find this delightfully warm, clean and friendly place, with a bar, café, Internet, dorms and doubles. Dorms ¥20, ❸

Fubo Shan 121 Binjiang Lu ⓣ0773/2569898, ⓕ2822328. An older but well-maintained hotel with good service and endless wings and corridors right next to Fubo Shan and the river. ❽

Golden Elephant 8 Binjiang Lu ⓣ0773/2808888, ⓕ2809999. Consistently smart and cosy three-star Korean-run affair overlooking Elephant Trunk Hill and the river; most of the rooms have views. Price-wise, this is an excellent deal if you're after something verging on upmarket. ❼

Home Inn Opposite the train station on Zhongshan Lu ⓣ0773/3877666, ⓕ3877555. Brand-new representative of this budget motel chain, offering excellent value for money – comfortable double rooms start at just ¥169. Book in advance. ❹

Jingxiu 8 Lingui Lu ⓣ0773/2869818, ⓕ2869918. Good service at this moderately upmarket place, located in a quiet, though stil pretty central, street. ❼

Lijiang Waterfall 1 Shanhu Lu ⓣ0773/2822881, ⓦwww.waterfallguilin.com. Huge tour-group and conference-delegate venue with all high-end frills. Doubles from ¥1320.

Sheraton 15 Binjiang Lu ⓣ0773/2825588, ⓦwww.sheraton.com/guilin. One of the nicest hotels in town, with the best rooms overlooking the river and across to Seven Star Park, though you pay for the privilege. Doubles from ¥1245.

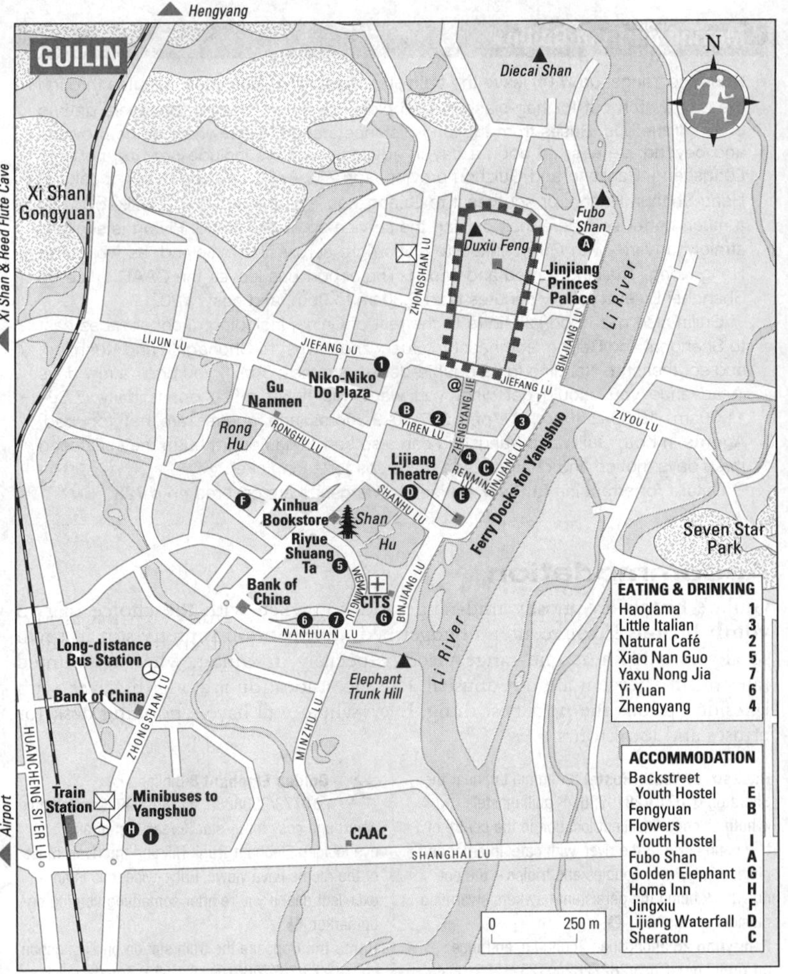

The City

Look at a map and Guilin's **medieval city layout** is still clearly visible, defined by the river to the east, Gui Hu to the west, Nanhuan Lu to the south, and protected from the north by Diecai Shan. Separated by Zhongshan Lu, **Rong Hu** and **Shan Hu** are two tree-lined lakes that originally formed a moat surrounding the inner city walls – the last remnant of which is **Gu Nanmen**, the tunnel-like Old South Gate on Ronghu Lu – and are now crossed by attractively hunchbacked stone bridges. Shan Hu is also overlooked by forty-metre-tall twin pagodas named **Riyue Shuang Ta**, one of which is painted gold, the other muted red and green, both attractively illuminated at night – you can climb to the top of both for ¥30.

Guilin's riverside promenade is Binjiang Lu, shaded from the summer sun by the fragrant **osmanthus trees** after which the city is named (Guilin means "osmanthus forest"). Down at the southern end, these also block views of **Elephant Trunk Hill** (daily 6.30am–10pm; ¥31; the entrance is off Minzhu Lu), said to be the body of a sick imperial baggage elephant who was cared for by locals and turned to stone rather than rejoin the emperor's army. For once the name is not poetically obscure; the jutting cliff with an arched hole at the base really does resemble an elephant taking a drink from the river. There's an easy walk to a podgy pagoda on top, and, at river level, you can have your photo taken holding a parasol while you sit next to a cormorant on a brightly coloured bamboo raft.

Two kilometres away at the opposite end of Binjiang Lu, **Fubo Shan** (daily 7am–7pm; ¥15) is a complementary peak, whose grottoes are carved with worn Tang- and Song-dynasty Buddha images. At the base is the "Sword-testing Stone", a stalactite hanging within ten centimetres of the ground, which indeed appears to have been hacked through. Steps to Fubo's summit (200m) provide smog-free views of Guilin's low rooftops.

West of Fubo Shan – the entrance is north off Jiefang Lu – **Jinjiang Princes' Palace** (daily 8.30am–5pm; ¥50 includes English-speaking tour guide) is where Guilin's Ming rulers lived between 1372 and 1650. Resembling a miniature Forbidden City in plan (and actually predating Beijing's by 34 years), it is still surrounded by five-metre-high stone walls, though the original buildings were destroyed at the end of the Ming dynasty, and those here today date from the late Qing and house Guangxi's Teachers' Training College. Some older fragments remain, notably a **stone slab** by the entrance embellished with clouds but no dragons, indicating the residence of a prince, not an emperor. The **museum** has abundant historical curios, modern portraits of the fourteen Jinjiang princes, and remains from one of their **tombs** (most of which lie unexcavated and overgrown about 6km northeast of the city). Out the back – and protecting the buildings from the "unlucky" north direction – is **Duxiu Feng**, another small, sharp pinnacle with 306 steep steps to the summit. Legend has it that the **cave** at the base of the hill was opened up by the tenth prince, thereby breaking Duxiu Feng's luck and seeding the dynasty's downfall. Get someone to point out the bland, eight-hundred-year-old **inscription** carved on Duxiu's side by the governor Wan Zhengong, which is apparently responsible for the city's fame: Guilin Shanshui Jia Tianxia – 'Guilin's Scenery is the Best Under Heaven'.

Outside the centre

Directly east over the river from the city, Guilin's most extensive limestone formations are at **Seven Star Park** (daily 7am–7pm; ¥25; bus #10 or #11 from Zhongshan Lu stops outside). With a handful of small wooded peaks arranged in the shape of the Great Bear (Big Dipper) constellation, a large cavern, and even a few semi-wild monkeys, it's a sort of Guangxi in miniature. The largest mass in the park, dotted with viewing pavilions, is **Putuo**, named after Zhejiang's famous Buddhist mountain, but the most striking formation is **Luotuo Shan**, which doesn't take much imagination to see as a kneeling dromedary. Some effort is required to find the entrance to **Qixing Dong**, however, which is a five-hundred-metre-long, thirty-metre-high introduction to the region's limestone caves (and China's romance with coloured lighting). Though a little tame, with most of the inner rock formations cleared to allow easy access, there's a small subterranean waterfall and the entranceway is liberally covered with carved inscriptions – some of which date back to the Tang dynasty.

Two other sights lie west of the centre on the #3 bus route from opposite the train station on Zhongshan Lu. Around 2km out, **Xi Shan** (¥20), the Western Hills, is an area of long Buddhist associations, whose peaks are named after

Buddhist deities. **Xiqinglin Si** here survives as one of Guangxi's major Buddhist temples, filled with hundreds of exquisitely executed statues ranging from 10cm to more than 2m in height. There's also a regional **museum** in the park (daily 9am–noon & 2.30–5pm; free) – a massive collection of ethnic clothing with few captions or explanations.

The #3 bus continues another 6km north to pass **Reed Flute Cave** (daily 8.30am–4.30pm; ¥80), a huge warren eaten into the south side of Guangming Shan which once provided a refuge from banditry and Japanese bombs before being turned into a tourist attraction in the 1950s. The caverns are not huge, but there are some interesting formations and one small underground lake, which makes for some nice reflections. You're meant to follow one of the tours that run every twenty minutes, but you can always linger inside and pick up a later group if you want to spend more time.

Eating, drinking and entertainment

Guilin's **restaurants** are famous for serving exotica, such as *pangolins*, snakes, turtles, cane rats, game birds, and deer (palm civets, a one-time favourite, are off the menu following their being blamed as the source of SARS). If you want to indulge, look for cages outside restaurants; otherwise, there are plenty of places to eat serving less confrontational fare. The best concentrations of restaurants are east off Zhongshan Lu along Nanhuan Lu, Wenming Lu, and Yiren Lu, and on pedestrianized Zhengyang Jie. Always check prices to avoid being overcharged. For cheap sandpots and stir-fries, try the side streets and canteens around the long-distance bus station.

Restaurants

Haodama Top floor of Niko-Niko Do Plaza, corner of Jiefang Lu and Zhongshan Lu. A busy place with a huge variety of snacks and light meals from all over China, laid out in front of the hard-working chefs. You get a card and wander round inspecting the food, hand your card over to be stamped when you find something you like, and wait for it to be delivered to your table. Dishes ¥5–20.

Little Italian Up past the *Sheraton* on Binjiang Lu. Small, friendly café (one of several nearby) with very good coffee, ginger and lemon tea, and light Western-style meals.

Natural Café Yiren Lu. Eclectic "foreign" menu including spaghetti, borscht, pizza and Southeast Asian coconut curries from ¥18, and steaks for around ¥50.

Xiao Nan Guo 3 Wenming Lu. Big, bright, cheerful and very popular local-style restaurant, without your menu choices languishing outside in cages. There's no English menu, so non-Chinese-speakers will need to do a round of tables and point. Mains from ¥18.

Yaxu Nong Jia 159 Nanhuan Lu. One of several smart, "country-style" restaurants along this street, with staff dressed in peasant garb and captive snakes, cane rats, crabs, pheasants and fish outside awaiting your delectation. Expect to pay around ¥60 for two.

Yi Yuan 106 Nanhuan Lu. Authentic Sichuanese food, comfortable surroundings and friendly, English-speaking staff make this a nice place to dine. Try the "strange-flavoured" chicken, green beans with garlic, sugared walnuts, or smoked duck. Two or three can eat well for ¥80.

Zhengyang Zhengyang Jie. Slow-simmered soups, plus Cantonese roast meats, sandpots and steamed greens, with popular pavement tables for when the weather is hot; not expensive at around ¥25 a head.

Drinking and entertainment

For **drinking**, there's a knot of foreigner-oriented pubs along pedestrianized Zhengyang Jie, at the junction with Renmin Lu; the street also hosts a string of souvenir stalls and is a popular place to stroll in the evening, though expect to be relentlessly harassed by hawkers and women offering "massages".

Lijiang Theatre holds daily performances of *A Dragon's Nationality* (8pm; ¥180), a contemporary take on local ethnic dances, incorporating ballet, acrobatics and amazing visuals; and *Liu San Jie* (4pm; ¥140), perhaps better experienced in the open at Yangshuo (see p.724). Other performances are sometimes laid on elsewhere at special occasions, such as **Spring Festival** – your accommodation will know the latest.

Finally, you can also make a circuit of downtown Guilin by **boat** via the lakes and river, best enjoyed at night when the bridges, pagodas and waterfront are lit up: cruises (1hr 30min; ¥120 without a/c, ¥155 with; no meal provided) can be booked through your accommodation or via English-speaking operators at ⓣ0773/2805098.

Listings

Airlines CAAC head office is on Shanghai Lu (daily 9am–5pm; ⓣ0773/3890000), with offices scattered all over the place. In addition, hotel tour desks can usually make bookings for you.

Banks and exchange There are several branches of the Bank of China with ATMs and foreign-exchange counters; the most useful lie between the bus and train stations on Zhongshan Lu, and on the corner of Zhongshan Lu and Nanhuan Lu.

Bookshops There's a subterranean Xinhua bookstore just west of Shan Hu on Zhongshan Lu, with a selection of translated Chinese classics, maps and stodgy Victorian potboilers, plus CDs, VCDs and DVDs.

Hospital Renmin Hospital, off Wenming Lu, is the best place to head if you get sick and your accommodation can't help out.

Internet access Several internet bars along Zhongshan Lu, and at the top end of pedestrianized Shazheng Yang Lu, charge ¥2 an hour.

Mail and telephones The most convenient post office (daily 8am–7pm) is just north of the train station on Zhongshan Nan Lu, with mail services and poste restante downstairs, telephones upstairs.

Shopping Zhongshan Lu is lined with well-stocked department stores, the best of which is the Niko-Niko Do Plaza on the corner with Jiefang Lu. For local flavour, try osmanthus tea (*guicha*) or osmanthus wine (*guijiu*), both of which are quite pleasant (though some brands of wine are pretty rough). For souvenirs – mostly outright tack and ethnicky textiles – try the shops and stalls on Binjiang Lu and Zhengyang Jie, but be prepared for some hard bargaining.

Travel agents Your hotel can sort out river cruises, book onward transport and organize day-trips to Longji Titian rice terraces (see p.730; ¥160 per person includes everything except the minibus up to the village gates; you get around 5hr on site). For more of the same, CITS are at 11 Binjiang Lu (ⓣ0773/2880319, ⓦwww.chinàseasons.com), with branches at many hotels.

The Li River and Yangshuo

The **Li River** meanders south for 85km from Guilin through the finest scenery that this part of the country can provide, the shallow green water flanked by a procession of jutting karst peaks that have been carved by the elements into a host of bizarre shapes, every one of them with a name and associated legend. In between are pretty rural scenes of grazing water buffalo, farmers working their fields in conical hats, locals poling themselves along on half-submerged bamboo rafts and fishing with cormorants, and a couple of small villages with a scattering of old architecture; the densest concentration of peaks is grouped around the middle reaches between the villages of **Caoping** and **Xingping**.

A **cruise** through all this is, for some, the highlight of their trip to China, and it would be hard not to be won over by the scenery, which is at its best during the wet, humid months between May and September, when the landscape is at its lushest and the river runs deepest – a serious consideration, as the water can be so shallow in winter that vessels can't complete their journey. At the far end,

The Li River and Yangshuo

Li River	漓江	*lijiāng*
Baxian Guojiang	八仙过江	*bāxiān guòjiāng*
Caoping	草坪	*cǎopíng*
Daxu	大圩	*dàxū*
Guan Yan	冠岩	*guànyán*
Jilong Shan	鸡笼山	*jīlóng shān*
Jiuma Hua Shan	九马画山	*jiǔmǎ huàshān*
River View Hotel	望江楼饭店	*wàngjiānglóu fàndiàn*
Wangfu Shi	望夫石	*wàngfū shí*
Xingping	兴坪	*xīngpíng*
Yangdi	杨堤	*yángdī*
Yellow Cloth Shoal	黄布滩	*huángbù tān*
Yu Cun	鱼村	*yúcūn*
Yuwei Ling	鱼尾岭	*yúwěi lǐng*
Yangshuo	阳朔	*yángshuò*
Green Lotus Peak	碧莲峰	*bìlián fēng*
Pantao Shan	蟠桃山	*pāntáo shān*
Produce market	农贸市场	*nóngmào shìchǎngxi*
Jie	西街	*xījiē*
Yangshuo Park	阳朔公园	*yángshuò gōngyuán*
Accommodation		
Backstreet Hostel	桂花街国际青年旅馆	*guìhuājiē guójì qīngnián lǚguǎn*
Bamboo House	竹林饭店	*zhúlín fàndiàn*
Double Moon	双月酒店	*shuāngyuè jiǔdiàn*
Giggling Tree Guesthouse	格格树饭店	*gégéshù fàndiàn*
Li River Retreat	水岸花园别墅	*shǔi'àn huāyuán biéshù*
Magnolia	白玉兰酒店	*báiyùlán jiǔdiàn*
Paradesa	百乐度假饭店	*bǎilèdùjià fàndian*
Peace	和平客栈	*hépíng kèzhàn*
River View	望江楼酒店	*wàngjiānglóu jiǔdiàn*
Sihai	四海饭店	*sìhǎi fàndiàn*
Snow Lion	雪狮岭度假饭店	*xuěshīlǐng dùjià fàndiàn*
Wanchang Xin	万昌鑫旅馆	*wanchāng xīn lǚguǎn*
Around Yangshuo		
Baisha	白沙	*báishā*
Black Buddha New Water Caves	黑佛新水洞	*hēifó xīnshuǐ dòng*
Black Dragon Caves	黑龙洞	*hēilóng dòng*
Camel Hill	骆驼山	*luòtuó shān*
Chaoyang	朝阳	*cháoyáng*
Gu Cheng	古城	*gǔ chéng*
Huang Tu	黄土	*huáng tǔ*
Moon Hill	月亮山	*yuèliàng shān*
XiaTang Zhai	下堂寨	*xiàtáng zhài*
Yulong River	玉龙河	*yùlóng hé*

the village of **Yangshuo** sits surrounded by more exquisite countryside, making it an attractive place to kick back for a couple of days and dig a little deeper into the region, though the village suffers from severe tourist overload during the peak season.

Cruising the Li River

The most popular **Li River cruise** covers the whole way between Guilin and Yangshuo, takes about six hours, and can be organized through the CITS or hotels in Guilin (see p.721). The cheapest fares – around ¥250 – get you a one-way ferry ticket to Yangshuo with a filling meal, while ¥450 should get you the cruise, more lavish food, an English-speaking guide, a return bus ticket, and possibly a quick tour of sights around Yangshuo. Either way, you'll have a comfortable seat on a flat-bottomed vessel – all have observation decks – that holds around a hundred people. In summer, boats depart from the **docks** on Binjiang Lu; when water levels are lower, alternative starting points downstream are used, with buses laid on to get you there. In really dry years, you start way down at Yangdi and only spend about an hour cruising around the middle peaks before catching a bus to Yangshuo, though you get charged the same amount and won't be told this beforehand.

Alternatively, you can do the stretch between Caoping (aka Guanyan) and Xingping (25km) in local boats for less money and and in less comfort, though the ninety-minute trip covers the most spectacular scenery and, in winter, may be the only way of seeing this part anyway. **Buses to Caoping** (¥7; 1hr) leave every thirty minutes from the depot just on the left inside Guilin's bus station gate, and terminate at the west bank resort village of **Guanyan**. Go down to the water, find a boat owner – they'll probably grab you anyway – and start bargaining; ¥100 per person is a fair deal, though they might insist on a minimum charge for the whole boat. These small vessels seat about ten people on wooden stools, and the roof peels back for views. Don't be too surprised if you get dropped off upstream from Xingping and have to walk the last kilometre to town – your boatman doesn't want to pay the tax for carrying you. From Xingping, there's heaps of transport through the day to Yangshuo. Operators in Yangshuo also offer a slightly shorter version of this trip, starting in Xingping and running upstream to **Yangdi**, for ¥60.

Downstream to Yangshuo

Aside from a few minor peaks, the first place of interest on the Li is around 25km along at the dishevelled west bank town of **DAXU**, which features a long, cobbled street, a few old wooden buildings, and a Ming-dynasty arched bridge – the Guilin–Caoping bus stops here. After this it's all rather flat until a grouping of peaks around **Wangfu Shi**, an east bank outcrop said to be a wife who turned to stone while waiting for her travelling husband to return home. Not far on, **CAOPING** is around 40km from Guilin, marked by **Guan Yan** (Crown Cliff; ¥40), a tiara-shaped rise whose naturally hollowed interior forms a twelve-kilometre-long cavern, garishly lit and complete with escalators and loudspeaker commentaries – access is from the shore (cruise boats don't pull in here). Just downstream on the opposite bank, a cliff jutting into the river obstructs footpaths, so that local travellers have to get around it by boat (named the **half-side ferry**, as it stays on the same bank).

South of here is the east bank settlement of **Yangdi**, where cruises from Guilin actually start in winter, and then you're into the best of the scenery, the hills suddenly tightly packed around the river. Three-pronged **Penholder Peak** drops down sheer into the water, followed by **Jilong Shan** (Chicken-coop Hill), **Yuwei Ling** (Fish-tail Peak), **Baxian Guojiang** (Eight Immortals Crossing the River), before the river squeezes past **Jiuma Hua Shan** (Nine Horses Fresco Hill) – the name referring to a one-hundred-metre-high cliff on whose weathered face you can pick out some horsey patterns. Look into the

▲ Cruising the Li River

water past here for **Yellow Cloth Shoal**, a flat, submerged rock at one of the shallowest spots on the river.

XINGPING, 70km from Guilin, is another scruffy, elderly west bank village of a half-dozen streets laid back from the water. The place is just starting to get its teeth into the tourist industry: down by the docks, the *River View Hotel* (☎0773/8702276; ¥30 per person) is the town's first backpacker joint. Opposite, *One World Café* and *Cottage Café* display English billboard menus. There's a **market** here, held on calendar dates ending in a 3, 6, or 9, and several old villages in the vicinity, including **Yu Cun**, dignified by several stone and wooden buildings. **Buses to Yangshuo** (¥5) leave through the day, while back on the water, the river broadens out for its final twenty-kilometre stretch to Yangshuo's docks beneath Green Lotus Peak.

Yangshuo

Nestled 70km south of Guilin in the thick of China's most spectacular karst scenery, **YANGSHUO**, meaning Bright Moon, rose to prominence during the mid-1980s, when foreign tourists on Li River cruises realized that beyond simply spending an hour here buying souvenirs, the village made a great place to settle down and get on intimate terms with the river and its peaks. Yangshuo has grown considerably since then and, despite retaining an outdated reputation as a mellow haven among Western travellers, has become a rowdy draw for domestic tourists, with the majority of its bars, restaurants and shops catering to their tastes. It remains, however, an easy place to spend a few days: hills surround everything, village lanes swarm with activity, and there are restaurants and accommodation everywhere. You can rent a bike and spend a day zipping between hamlets, hike around or go **rock climbing** on nearby peaks, or study cooking or martial arts.

Arrival and information

Ferries arrive a little upstream from Yangshuo, where tourists will face a 500m-long gauntlet of souvenir stalls as their introduction to the village. **Buses**

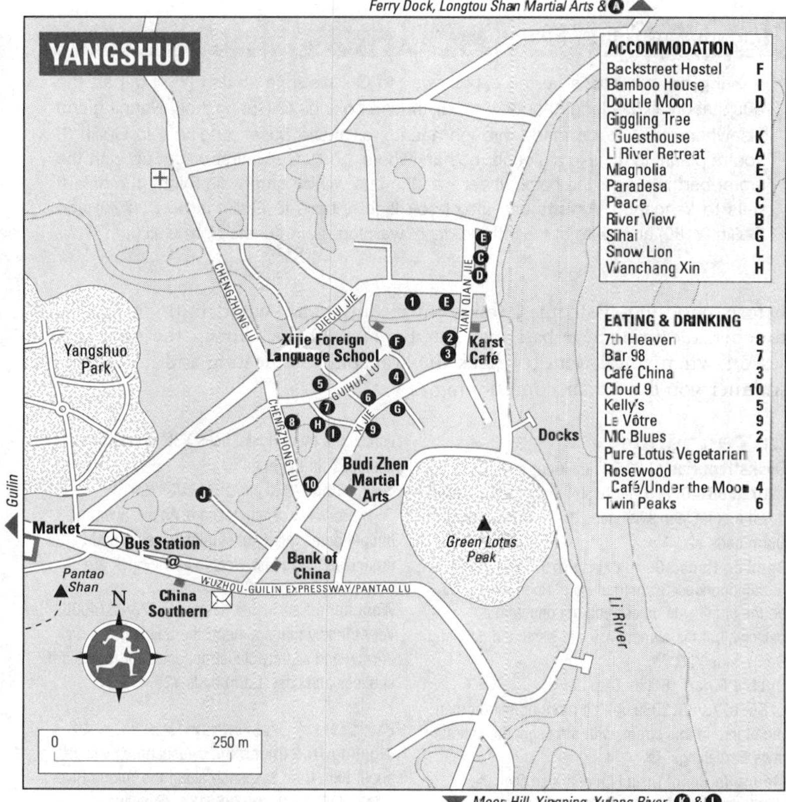

terminate at the station along the highway (also known as Pantao Lu), off which Yangshuo's two main streets run northeast to the river; **Diecui Jie** extends from the bus station through the village centre, while east and parallel is flagstoned, vehicle-free **Xi Jie** (or West Street), stretching down to the water past restaurants, bars, accommodation and shops.

There's a large quantity of **information** to be had in Yangshuo, either from the hotels – who all have tour desks – or foreigner-oriented cafés, most of which are located in the streets between Xi Jie and Diecui Jie. In addition, touts are everywhere, though with a couple of exceptions they're relatively low-pressure and easy enough to brush off if you're not interested. Some cafés also offer book exchanges (the best being at *Café Too* on Chengzhong Lu) and all have **Internet** access, usually free for customers. You can buy **maps** at many shops, most of which have plans of the river and surrounding area.

Accommodation

Stiff competition means that Yangshuo's **accommodation prices** are good value: options range from basic dorm beds at ¥15 and comfy doubles from ¥100 in town to relatively upmarket country retreats with river views in excess of ¥300 – worth the price if you want some quiet and scenic views. Note, however, that rooms can vary greatly in quality, even within individual establishments – Yangshuo's damp climate encourages mildew – so have a look at a few

Moving on from Yangshuo

Moving on, minibuses up the expressway to Guilin's train station (¥14) depart the bus station all day long, though long-distance bookings to Guangzhou, Nanning and elsewhere have to be made through agents, as these buses originate in Guilin. If you're planning to take a sleeper bus anywhere, go to Guilin first or put up with the worst berths – over the back wheel – as the bus will be otherwise full by the time it gets to Yangshuo. **Agents** can also book flights, taxis to Guilin airport (¥220) and Guilin (¥180) and, with at least three days' warning, train tickets from Guilin.

before choosing. Balconies, folksy furnishings and wooden floors are nice touches, locations near bars may not be. Rates halve during the winter low season, when you'll want to check the availability of heating and hot water; in summer you'll need air conditioning.

In Yangshuo

Backstreet Hostel 60 Guihua Xiang ⓣ0773/8814077. Sister hostel to the one in Guilin, down a quiet lane, with good dorms and doubles. Dorm beds ¥20, ❸

Bamboo House Guihua Xiang ⓣ0773/8823888, ⓔbamboohousé3@hotmail.com. Rooms are a bit on the small side unless you get one with a balcony, but the owners are laid-back and unpushy. Dorm beds ¥20, ❸

Double Moon 16 Xian Qian Jie ⓣ&ⓕ0773/8812989. A little more upmarket than the others in this street, with atmospheric, antique-style furnishings. ❺

Magnolia Cnr of Diecui Lu and Xian Qian Jie ⓣ0773/8819288, ⓕ8819218. Smart mid-range place with minimalist decor and huge rooms (though this and the tiling make it cold in winter); a popular choice with small-group tours. ❻

Paradesa Off Xi Jie ⓣ0773/8822109, ⓦwww.ys-paradesa.com. Yangshuo's longest-running upmarket affair, with a series of buildings set in a private garden complete with ornamental pond. ❼

Peace Xian Qian Jie ⓣ0773/8826262, ⓦwww.yangshuotour.org. One of the best deals in town: large rooms with a/c, bathroom and balconies in a quiet street just off Xi Jie. ❸

River View 11–15 Binjiang Lu ⓣ0773/8822688 (hotel) or 8829676 (hostel), ⓦwww.riverview.com.cn. The location is good – at least it is after 4pm, when the tourist stalls outside have cleared off. Pricier rooms with balconies overlook the river across the road. Hostel beds ¥35, doubles in the hostel ❸, in the hotel ❹

Sihai 73 Xi Jie ⓣ0773/8822013, ⓦwww.sihaihotel.com. Above-average budget hotel, more substantial, cleaner and better-organized than most. Rooms at the back are quieter. Dorm beds ¥20, doubles ❸

Wanchang Xin Guihua Xiang ⓣ0773/8814066. Very friendly management; the building is a bit narrow and slightly claustrophobic, but rooms are spotless and cosy. Dorm beds ¥25, ❸

Around Yangshuo

Giggling Tree Guesthouse Aishanmen village, about 5km from Yangshuo along the Yulong River (see p.729) ⓣ0136/67866154, ⓦwww.gigglingtree.com. Converted stone farmhouse buildings now forming an attractive hotel and restaurant, with courtyard, tiled roofs and a beautiful mountain backdrop. ❹

Li River Retreat About 1.5km upstream from Yangshuo along the Li River ⓣ0773/8735681, ⓦwww.li-river-retreat.com. Upmarket affair in very pleasant riverside setting, with rooms decked out in Chinese antique chic. ❼

Snow Lion Mushan village, about 2.5km downstream from Yangshuo ⓣ0773/8826689, ⓦwww.touryangshuo.com. Fantastic food and scenery coupled with comfortable and airy rooms make this a great place for a break. ❺

The village

Yangshuo has few formal attractions – it was a simple country marketplace before tourists arrived – but there's still plenty to explore. West off Diecui Jie is **Yangshuo Park** (¥6), a pleasant place in summer with its colourful formal garden and breezy vantages of town from pavilions lodged on the main rise. Squeezed between the highway and the river directly opposite is **Green Lotus**

Cormorant fishing

When you've had enough scenery for one day, do something unusual and spend an evening watching **cormorant fishing** (book through your hotel; ¥50 per person for a 90min trip). This involves heading out in a punt at dusk, closely following a tiny wooden fishing boat or bamboo raft from which a group of cormorants fish for their owner. Despite being turned into a tourist activity at Yangshuo, people still make their living from this age-old practice throughout central and southern China, raising young birds to dive into the water and swim back to the boat with full beaks. The birds are prevented from swallowing by rings or ties around their necks, but it's usual practice for the fisherman to slacken these off and let them eat every seventh fish – apparently, the cormorants refuse to work otherwise.

Peak, the largest in the immediate area – there's a track to the top off the highway east of the post office, but it involves some scrambling. An easier path (leading to better views) ascends **Pantao Shan** from behind the market. Otherwise, just walk upstream from Yangshuo for a kilometre or two and take your pick of the rough trails that scale many other slopes to summits covered in tangled undergrowth and sharp, eroded rocks – again, be prepared for some scrambling, and for safety reasons don't go alone.

The presence of tourists hasn't entirely altered the daily routine of villagers, who spend hours inspecting and buying wares in the **produce market**. It's an interesting place to hang out, especially on market days (held on dates ending in a 3, 6, or 9). There's a good selection of game, fruit (especially a winter glut of pomelos), nuts and mushrooms, laid out on sheets in the street here – look out for rats and pheasants, fresh straw and needle mushrooms, and spiky water caltrops, which contain a kernel similar to a Brazil nut.

Yangshuo's tourist drag, lined with shops selling a vast array of souvenirs, is **Xi Jie**. Trends change here all the time, but the current emphasis is towards clothes – from fake brand labels to Mao T-shirts, outdoor gear and even leatherwear – exorbitantly priced ethnic textiles, modern and traditional paintings, and a few stalls loaded with "new antiques". As always in China, check everything carefully before parting with your cash, don't forget to bargain – about a third of the asking price is recommended – and don't buy anything when tour boats from Guilin pull in unless you want to pay five times the going rate. In summer shops stay open late and at night the street is choked with crowds as they shop and orbit between the many restaurants and bars.

Yangshuo also offers a window into the more esoteric side of Chinese culture. For **martial arts**, you can study Chen-style *tai ji* at Longtou Shan Martial Arts School, about 2km upstream from Yangshuo at Shiban Qiao village (contact Mei on ⓣ0138/78376597, ⓦwww.longtoutaichi.com; accommodation available); or try the outstanding Budi Zhen martial-arts school (ⓣ1397/7350377, ⓦwww.budizhen.com.cn), run by the irrepressible Mr Gao and his twin sons. The more peacefully inclined should check out **cookery classes** – contact Linda at *Cloud 9* restaurant or William at *7th Heaven* (see "Eating" on below). It's also possible to find work in Yangshuo **teaching English** at the Xijie Foreign Language School on Guihua Lu (ⓣ0773/8860222).

Eating, drinking and nightlife

Yangshuo's numerous **restaurants** and cafés are split between those along Xi Jie, which mainly cater to Chinese tourists seeking exotic Western food; and those along Chengzhong Lu and Guihua Lu, which serve backpacker staples and Chinese and Western fare to a largely foreign crowd – though there's some crossover between the two. Both restaurants and cafés open early in the morning for Western breakfasts, and keep going well into the night; there are also plenty of inexpensive Chinese canteens and food stalls selling noodle soups and buns around the bus station.

Xi Jie has several **clubs and bars**, some of which host live music and all of which pump out raucous, high-decibel Chinese rock later on in the evenings. They come and go very quickly; the current picks are the perennially heaving *Stone Rose* and slightly more sedate *Meiyou's* and *Marco Polo*. If you're just after a drink and good atmosphere, head to *Bar 98* on Guihua Lu, which has outdoor seating and also does excellent coffee and light meals through the day.

Yangshuo's major after-dark event however, is **Liu San Jie**, an open-air song, dance and light spectacular put together by renowned film director Zhang Yimou. Featuring a cast of 600 local cormorant fishermen, minority women, singing children and the like, the whole affair lasts an hour, costs ¥150 to ¥200 and takes place about 2km downstream from town – book through your accommodation.

Restaurants

7th Heaven Chengzhong Lu. Well-above-average Western and Chinese food in pleasant surrounds; the outdoor terrace by the bridge is a nice place to sit on a hot evening. Their bar is well stocked too. Around ¥40 a head.

Café China Corner of Xi Jie and Xian Qian Jie. Good Shanghai food (claypot duck and "pearl meatballs") along with Mongolian-style grilled chicken, which you need to order in advance. Their coffee and cheesecake aren't bad either.

Cloud 9 Upstairs at the cnr of Chengzhong Lu and Xi Jie. Undoubtedly the best Chinese food in Yangshuo, juicy and flavourful; locals recommend any one of their slow-simmered medicinal soups (which sell out early), rural specialities such as taro and beef stew, or Sichuanese classics like crispy-skinned chicken. Around ¥40 a head.

Kelly's Guihua Lu. Friendly foreigners' café/restaurant, with Western food alongside good home-style Sichuan cooking – try their fiery hot boiled beef slices or cooling chicken salad.

Le Vôtre Xi Jie. Yangshuo's poshest dining, inside a Ming-era building complete with period furnishings. Food is French – snails, pâté, onion soup, steak *au poivre*, chocolate mousse – or Chinese seafood. Also, excellent coffee and croissants for breakfast. Expect to pay at least ¥50 a head.

MC Blues Xian Qian Jie. A long-running business catering to Western backpackers, serving toasted sandwiches, bamboo rats, vegetarian hotpots and much-lauded beer-battered fish.

Pure Lotus Vegetarian 7 Diecui Lu. Attractive place with attractive food; not cheap but perhaps worth a slight splurge. The almond rolls, vegetables cooked with rose petals, steamed winter melon and "steak" with XO sauce are all good. From ¥25 a dish.

Rosewood Café/Under the Moon Xi Jie. Café downstairs, restaurant upstairs with balcony seating. An extensive Western menu covering pizza, pasta, grills and salads, though perhaps pricey for what you get. Their ice cream is the best in Yangshuo. Two can eat well for ¥80.

Twin Peaks Xi Jie. The nice cosy café downstairs serves good breakfasts; upstairs things get slightly smarter with window seats for people-watching and a more comprehensive menu – and they keep the after-dark music down to conversational levels.

Listings

Airlines Book flights out of Guilin at China Southern, on the highway just west of the Post Office (ⓣ0773/8811651, ⓦwww.cs-air.com).

Bank There's a Bank of China with an ATM on Xi Jie (foreign currency transactions daily 9am–noon & 1–5pm).

Internet access Free at cafés if you have a meal too; otherwise, Net bars along the highway charge ¥2 an hour.

Medical For acupuncture or Chinese massage, contact Dr Lily Li at her clinic on Guihua Lu (ⓣ0773/8814625); if pain is any indication of quality, her therapeutic massage is the best you'll ever get, though you can also have blissfully mellow relaxation treatments.

Mail and telephones The Post Office (daily 8am–6pm; parcel and post restante services available) is on the highway. IDD telephones are all around Yangshuo, and at the bigger hotels.

Around Yangshuo

Getting to see the countryside around Yangshuo is easy enough, as the land between the hills is flat and perfect for **bicycles** – Xian Qian Jie is thick with rental touts if your accommodation can't help (¥10 a day for a standard bike; ¥30 for an electric one, up to 30km; and ¥50 for a scooter, up to 40km; plus at least ¥300 deposit). Various people offer informative **guided bike tours**, too, allowing close contact with villages and locals through an interpreter; costs are subject to negotiation.

Except in very dry winters, **boats** depart year round from the docks; there's a ticket office here and you'll also be mobbed by touts. While the entire reverse Li River cruise to Guilin is a tedious twelve-hour journey upstream, there are plenty of shorter options, though as Guilin operators have a monopoly on vessels, prices are still relatively high. One way around this is to catch a minibus to **Xingping**, and then hire a boat from there upstream to **Yangdi**, past the thickest, most contorted collection of peaks (2hr; ¥60); you can also do this on a two-seater bamboo raft for ¥200. From Yangdi, catch transport to either Guilin or Yangshuo along the highway. Agents in Yangshuo can arrange this for you – see p.724 for details of Xingpin and the river scenery.

If you just want to **swim**, take the road southeast of town to **Camel Hill**, turn right down a lane and follow the track to the river – about an hour's cycling time. Villagers turn up to wash at about 6.30pm, and there are clear views of Moon Hill from here.

The Yulong River and Moon Hill

There's nothing to stop you simply picking a distant hill and heading out there – cycling along the muddy paths between villages takes you through some wonderful scenery – but there are a couple of areas worth focusing on. Paralleling the highway to Guilin, the **Yulong River** west of Yangshuo offers a twelve-kilometre walk or cycle between small hamlets, with a couple of old stone bridges and at least two older-style villages with a few antique buildings. The road from Yangshuo leaves the highway east of the bus station – you might have to ask for directions to **Chaoyang**, the first large settlement along the way – and follows the east side of the Yulong via **Xia Tangzhai**, the old villages of **Huang Tu** and **Gu Cheng**, before rejoining the highway at **Baisha**, whose market runs on dates ending in a 1, 4, or 7 and where you can either cycle or catch a bus back to Yangshuo.

Climbing Yangshuo's peaks

Yangshuo is one of Asia's fastest-growing **rock-climbing** centres, with an estimated 70,000 pinnacles of up to 200m in height in the area. However, there are only about fifty established climbing routes, many of them under 30m in length – though those at Moon Hill are rated among the toughest in China – and, as most are within easy day-trips of Yangshuo, you won't need to plan any mighty expeditions (though camping out on site is fun).

The main **climbing season** lasts from October through to February, as the rest of the year can be uncomfortably hot or wet. There are several sources of local information along Xian Qian Jie in Yangshou, notably China Climb (ⓣ0773/8811033, ⓦwww.ChinaClimb.com), the *Karst Café* (ⓣ0773/8828482, ⓦwww.karstclimber.com), and Spiderman Climbing (ⓣ0773/8812339, ⓦwww.s-climbing.com) – they also sell copies of *Rock Climbing in Yangshuo* by Paul Collis, which gives invaluable information on routes, access, local conditions and grades. The above places can also organize **equipment**, **instruction** and **guides**.

Yangshuo's most famous peak is **Moon Hill**, which lies on the highway 10km southwest of town. Just before you get here, tracks off to the south lead to the **Black Buddha New Water Caves**, whose highlights include an underground river, fossils and bats. Another 3km along the same track are the equally imposing **Black Dragon Caves**, where you take a boat, then have to wade and stagger through the largest regional caverns yet discovered to a fifteen-metre subterranean waterfall and swimming holes inhabited by blind fish. Only open in summer, either system costs ¥130 for a three- or four-hour flashlight exploration – contact an agent in Yangshuo. Come prepared to get soaked, cold and very, very muddy.

Moon Hill itself (¥30) takes an easy thirty minutes to ascend, following stone steps through bamboo and brambles to the summit. A beautiful sight, the hill is named after a large crescent-shaped hole that pierces the peak. Views from the top take in the whole of the Li River valley spread out before you, fields cut into uneven chequers by rice and vegetable plots, and Tolkienesque peaks framed through the hole.

Longji, Sanjiang and on to Guizhou

A hundred kilometres northwest of Guilin the road winds steeply through some fine stands of mountain bamboo, and enters the southern limit of a fascinating ethnic **autonomous region**. With a rich landscape of mountains and terraced fields as a backdrop – best perhaps at **Longji** – it's possible to hop on local transport and tour a rural corner of China that remains relatively unaffected by the modern world. Day-trips abound, but, with five days or so to spare, you can push right through the mountainous **Dong** heartlands northwest of **Sanjiang** into Guizhou province, a fabulous journey which takes you to the area around **Kaili**, similarly central to the Miao people (p.761). Before starting, note that there are **no banks** capable of cashing travellers' cheques between Guilin and Kaili.

Longji

Around 90km north of Guilin, **Longji** is a range of hills whose name translates as "Dragon's Spine", where you'll find some of the most extraordinarily extreme **rice terracing** that exists in China: the steep-sided and closely packed valleys have been carved over centuries of backbreaking effort to resemble the literal form of a contour map. Most of the people up here are Zhuang, but there are also communities of **Yao**, some of whom still hunt for a living; more aspiring locals depict them as rustic savages, happy to own just a gun and a knife. Longji's villages are almost exclusively built of timber in traditional styles, and electricity and telephones are very recent introductions to the region.

Tourism is well established, however, with day-trips offered by most accommodation in Guilin (see p.721) – though you'll get a lot more out of the place if you stay a day or two and do some hiking. The access point is **Longsheng**, a highway town about two hours from Guilin, whose bus station has regular departures 20km southeast to the village of **PING AN.** You get dropped off in a car park pay the ¥50 **entry fee** and walk the last 500m up stone steps to Ping An itself, a beautiful Zhuang village of wooden homes and cobbled paths squeezed into a steep fold between the terraces. Many places offer **accommodation**, ranging from around ¥15 a person in a simple room with shared toilets and showers up to ¥100 for a double with a bathroom; the best atmosphere is at family-run businesses such as the *Liqing Guesthouse* or *Countryside Inn*, where

Longji, Sanjiang and on to Guizhou

Longji	龙脊梯田	*lóngjǐ tītián*
Liqing Guesthouse	丽晴旅社	*lìqíng lǚshè*
Longji Village	龙脊村	*lóngjǐ cūn*
Longsheng	龙胜	*lóngshèng*
Ping An	平安	*píng'ān*
Sanjiang	三江	*sānjiāng*
Chengyang Qiao Binguan	程阳桥宾馆	*chéngyángqiáo bīnguǎn*
Department Store Hostel	百货招待所	*bǎihuò zhāodàosuǒ*
Drum Tower	鼓楼	*gǔlóu*
Fulu Si	福禄寺	*fúlù sì*
Travellers' Home	行旅之家宾馆	*xínglǚzhījiā bīnguǎn*
Chengyang	程阳	*chéngyáng*
Wind-and-Rain Bridge	风雨桥	*fēngyǔ qiáo*
Guandong	关东	*guāndōng*
Mapang	马胖	*mǎpàng*
Bajiang	八江	*bājiāng*
Baxie	八协	*bāxié*
Dudong	独峒	*dútóng*
Gaoding	高定	*gāodìng*
Hualian	华联	*huálián*
Mengjiang	孟江	*mèngjiāng*
Tongle	同乐	*tónglè*
Diping	地坪	*dìpíng*
Jitang	纪堂	*jìtáng*
Longtu	龙图	*lóngtú*
Zhaoxing	肇兴	*zhàoxīng*
Dongjia Binguan	侗家宾馆	*dóngjiā bīnguǎn*
Potato Service Hotel	土豆旅官	*tǔdòu lǚguǎn*
Sanxiao Fanguan	三肖饭馆	*sānxiào fànguǎn*
Tang An	堂安	*táng'ān*
Zhaoxing Binguan	肇兴宾馆	*zhàoxīng bīnguán*
Liping	黎平	*lípíng*
Congjiang	从江	*cóngjiāng*
Basha	八沙	*bāshā*
Jianghu Lüguan	江湖旅馆	*jiānghú lǚguǎn*
Yueliang Shan Binguan	月亮山宾馆	*yuèliàng shān bīnguǎn*
Rongjiang	榕江	*róngjiāng*
Qingfeng Binguan	庆丰宾馆	*qìngfēng bīnguǎn*

some English is spoken, and meals are filling. Ask at your accommodation about the number of **walks** in the region – there's a four-hour round trip to lookouts, or across to the ancient village of **LONGJI** – some offer guides for about ¥25 per person including lunch. After hiking, you should try and find Mrs Pan, granddaughter of Ping An's last Traditional Chinese Medicine doctor, who runs a foot-soak and massage place. Ping An's two **stores** stock only absolute basics, so bring your own snacks or luxuries. **Leaving**, minibuses head back to Longsheng until about 5.30pm.

Sanjiang and the Dong

Two hours west of Longsheng the road crosses a high stone bridge over the Rongshui and lands you at **SANJIANG**, the small, desperately untidy capital of

Sanjiang Dong Autonomous County. The **Dong** people themselves are renowned for their wooden houses, towers and bridges which dot the countryside hereabouts, and it's well worth roving the region; there's a scattering of simple hostels and places to eat, and villagers will sometimes offer lodgings and sustenance – characteristically sour hotpots, *douxie cha* or **oil tea** (a bitter, salty soup made from fried tea leaves and puffed rice), and home-made rice wine. Just be aware that the only people who have any idea about **local bus departure times** are the drivers themselves – if you're staying the night somewhere remote, track yours down to confirm times or risk being stranded for a day.

Sanjiang is split in two by the river, with most of the town on the north bank, and a smaller, newer development on the south. The town's only two sights are also on the south bank, the easiest to locate being the huge **drum tower** (¥5) set on a rise overlooking the water. A special feature of Dong settlements, these towers were once used as lookout posts when the country was at war, the drums inside beaten to rouse the village; today people gather underneath them for meetings and entertainment. Built in 2003, this is the largest of its kind anywhere, at 47m high and with eleven internal levels, all built from pegged cedar and supported by four huge posts; you can climb to the top for views. Behind it, **Fulu Si** is a small Buddhist nunnery dedicated to Guanyin, with separate halls arranged up a slope behind the entrance gateway.

Sanjiang practicalities

Sanjiang's **long-distance bus station** lies south of the river on the main road – look for the speed barrier at the entrance on a curve in the road, as it's not otherwise marked – with connections south as far as Guilin and north to Liping and Congjiang. **Local buses** use the depot immediately north of the bridge in the main part of town. Sanjiang is also on the Huaihua–Liuzhou **rail line**; the train station is about 10km northwest of town with minibuses meeting arrivals and landing them immediately north of the bridge.

Places to stay north of the river include the budget *Department Store Hostel* (dorm beds ¥25) – look for the English sign near the local bus station – the *Chengyang Qiao Binguan* (☎0772/8613071; ❸), 100m west along the road; and, south of the river and about 100m back towards Longsheng from the long-distance station, the *Travellers' Home* (☎0772/8615584; ❸). For **food**, try the noodle and hotpot stalls north of the bridge, or your accommodation.

Chengyang

CHENGYANG, 18km north of Sanjiang on the Linxi River, is an attractive traditional Dong village reached over a splendid **wind-and-rain bridge**.

There are more than a hundred of these in the region, but Chengyang's is the finest and most elaborate. Raised in 1916, five solid stone piers support an equal number of pavilions (whose different roofs illustrate several regional building styles) linked by covered walkways, entirely built from wood – not one nail was used in the bridge's construction. Cool and airy in summer, and protected from downpours, these bridges – **fengyu qiao** in Chinese – make perfect places to sit around and gossip, though they once served a religious purpose, too, and other examples have little shrines grimed with incense smoke in their halfway alcoves. The shrine on Chengyang's is vacant as the bridge is a protected cultural relic and no fire is allowed. Women here hawk pieces of embroidery, cotton blankets boldly patterned in black and white, and the curiously shiny blue-black Dong jackets, dyed indigo and varnished in egg white as a protection against mosquitoes.

Across the bridge, Chengyang itself is a collection of warped, two- and three-storeyed traditional **wooden houses**, overlooked by a square-sided drum tower. By now you'll have noticed that the Dong are not great believers in stone or concrete buildings, as wooden structures can more easily be extended or even shifted as necessary. Fire is a major concern, though, and throughout the year each family takes turns to guard the village from this hazard. There's a trail from the main road up to two pavilions overlooking Chengyang, with some nice views of the dark, gloomy villages nestled among vivid green fields.

Wander out to the fields and you'll find a string of paths connecting Chengyang to visibly poorer hamlets, similar congregations of dark wood and cobbles, many with their own, less elaborate bridges and towers. On the way, look for creaky black **water wheels** made from plaited bamboo, somehow managing to supply irrigation canals despite dribbling out most of their water in the process.

The last **bus back to Sanjiang** passes by around 5pm, but Chengyang is a better place to stay overnight, with two **hostels**: the *Chengyang National Hostel* (dorm beds ¥15; meals extra); and the recommended ★ *Dong Village Hotel* (ⓣ0772/8582421, ⓔdvhcy@yahoo.com.cn; dorm beds ¥15), run by a local named Michael, who is very helpful and provides maps and advice on local **walking trails**. There's a good seven-hour circuit from Chenyang via Ping Tan, Gao Ma and Ji Chang, or you could hike from Chengyang to **Mapang** (see below), via the village of **Guandong**, in about six hours, and catch a bus back to Sanjiang from there – either way, you'll get plenty of views of more wooden hamlets, paddy fields and tea plantations.

Mapang and the upper Meng River

Feasible as a day-trip from Sanjiang, **MAPANG** lies some 30km north of town via a change of buses in **Bajiang**, and features a huge drum tower with an unusually broad rectangular base. The last buses back to Sanjiang leave late afternoon, though it's also possible to hike from here to Chengyang in about six hours.

The most interesting corner of this land, however, lies northwest across the mountains from Bajiang along the **Meng River**, which ultimately runs down from the north to Chankou on the Sanjiang road (see p.731). Morning buses from Sanjiang to **Dudong** from the local bus station cross these ranges, emerging 33km away above a deep valley containing the tiny, dark-roofed village of **ZHUOLONG**, where Deng Xiaoping rested up during the Long March. There are two drum towers here, but press on a couple of kilometres north to **BAXIE**, whose bright green and yellow bridge was built in 1980 (purists might notice a few nails in the decking). The cobbled village square in front of Baxie's drum tower also has a small stage carved with monkeys and lions for festival performances. The oldest surviving bridge, built in 1861, is in the next village north, **HUALIAN**, after which comes a unique two-tier example at the village of **BATUAN**, with one lane for people and another for animals. This bridge still has its shrine, a cupboard with a bearded god on a stone slab, and, at the far end, a path leads along the riverbank to where tall trees shade a small new temple.

At the end of the road, **DUDONG** was a centre for guerrilla action against the Japanese during the 1940s. There's a store and basic **guesthouse** (❶) here by the marketplace, which is the only place serving food – though not much of it, and only during daylight hours. An easy hike from here follows a broad, dusty road uphill to a stone bridge, where a smaller track leads to **GAODING**, an attractive Dong village of a hundred homes crammed into a deep fold in the hillside, with six towers, farm animals roaming the lanes, and nothing but wooden buildings (if you ignore the new school on the hill above). The walk takes about two hours each way, and it's best to ask directions from everyone you meet.

After a night in Dudong, either catch the bus back to Sanjiang (the first leaves around daybreak), or the **Tongle** bus as far as **MENGJIANG**, an interesting village just a few kilometres south of Zhuolong. Mengjiang is half Dong, half Miao – the name means "Miao River" – each community settled on opposite banks. After generations of fighting over land, their leaders became reconciled in the 1940s, and together built the traditionally designed **Nationality Union Bridge** across the divide. Today it's hard to distinguish between the two communities, as both dress similarly – women wearing heavy metal earrings or a piece of white cord through their lobes – though the drum tower is, naturally enough, on the Dong side. It's a great place to wander between the large houses and out into the fields, and tractors can be hired for the run down to **TONGLE**. Here you'll find a store, a hostel and an early-morning minibus for the ninety-minute ride back to Sanjiang.

Into Guizhou: Sanjiang to Kaili

The road west of Sanjiang cuts through Dong territory and up to the Miao stronghold of **Kaili** in Guizhou province, a 300km-long run of traditional rural villages, steeply terraced hillsides, lime-blue rivers and windy roads. Daily buses run from Sanjiang to **Zhaoxing** – itself a highlight – from where a couple of routes continue on to Kaili. Three days is a likely minimum for the trip, and it's not one that you'll get much out of by rushing in any case. Expect frugal facilities and food in villages, and cold, icy winters.

Sanjiang to Zhaoxing

The Sanjiang–Zhaoxing dirt road is slow-going until you reach the border with Guizhou, when it immediately becomes sealed and fast. Most buses travel via the scruffy villages of **Diping** and **Long E**, both with basic accommodation, drum towers and bridges; some, however, take a longer but better road via **Guandong**, **Jitang** and **Longtu**, with more of the same scenery – all make good places to get off the bus and explore.

ZHAOXING, around four hours by bus from Sanjiang, is set in a small valley with a generous smattering of old buildings – in fact, recent developments here have cleared away several ugly modern concrete boxes and replaced them with traditional structures. The town has five square-based **drum towers**, each differently styled and built by separate clans; accompanying wind-and-rain

▲ Drum tower, Zhaoxing

bridges and theatre stages are decorated with fragments of mirrors and mouldings of actors and animals. Miao and Dong women in town sell embroidery and silver, houses are hung with strings of drying radishes for sour hotpots, and the backstreets, teeming with roaming livestock, resound to the noise of freshly dyed cloth being pounded with wooden mallets to give it a shiny patina. Rice terraces and muddy tracks provide fine country walks, the best of which is 7km uphill from town to **Tang An**, another photogenic collection of wooden buildings.

Zhaoxing has many **places to stay,** from guesthouses such as the *Dongjia Binguan* (①), through basic hotels like the incredibly named *Potato Service Hotel* (Ⓣ0855/6130010; ②), to the expensive but scenic *Zhaoxing Binguan* (Ⓣ0855/6130558, Ⓦwww.zgzhaoxing.cn; ④). There are many places to **eat**, such as the *Sanxiao Fanguan*, which has a partially translated menu, decent food and welcome braziers on a cold day. **Moving on**, several buses run daily north to Liping, south to Sanjiang, and west to Congjiang.

Zhaoxing to Kaili

The fastest – though again, not the shortest – road to Kaili first heads north to **LIPING** (2hr), famous as the place where the Long Marchers made up their minds to storm Zunyi; it's a modern town with a single "old street" where buildings associated with the Long March days have been preserved. From here, it's another couple of hours southwest on a good road to **Rongjiang** (see below).

Alternatively, there's transport from Zhaoxing southwest to **CONGJIANG,** a drab, relatively large logging town on the Duliu River, with plenty of **accommodation** near the **bus station** – *Yueliang Shan Binguan* (Ⓣ0855/6418228; ③) is a bit dingy and poorly maintained, *Jianghu Lüguan* (②) much cleaner and less pretentious. In common with everywhere else in the region, there are precious few places to eat aside from stir-fry **canteens** around the station. The town is surrounded by picturesque villages, though – best known is **BASHA**, a Miao village 10km west whose inhabitants grow a long topknot and wear traditionally embroidered clothes, heavy metal jewellery and pleated skirts as a matter of course, not just for festivals.

Heading on, **RONGJIANG** is a reliable two hours away across the mountains, and has a frenetic Sunday **market** where you can watch villagers bargaining the last mao out of a deal. There are comfortable **rooms** at the *Qingfeng Binguan* (②), beside a small pavilion across from the bus station. From here it's five hours northwest on very twisty roads over beautifully green mountains to Leishan and Kaili. For more about Kaili and the Miao, see pp.758–764.

Nanning

Founded during the Yuan dynasty, **NANNING** was just a medium-sized market town until European traders opened a river route from neighbouring Guangdong in the early twentieth century, starting a period of rapid growth that saw the city supplanting Guilin as the provincial capital. Largely untouched by the civil war and Japanese invasion, it became a centre of supply and command first during the **Vietnam War**, and then a decade later when China and Vietnam came to blows in 1979. Following the resumption of cross-border traffic in the 1990s the city has capitalized on trade agreements with its neighbour, and today Nanning is a bright, easy-going place with a mild boom-town atmosphere and mix of leafy boulevards, modern architecture and a handful of narrow, colonial-era streets. There's good shopping, decent food, a **museum** strong on regional archeology, and both international and domestic transport connections – in particular, over the nearby **open border with Vietnam**.

Arrival and city transport

Well over 5km across, with its downtown area concentrated on the northern bank of the **Yong Jiang**, Nanning is a blandly user-friendly city, its streets dusty,

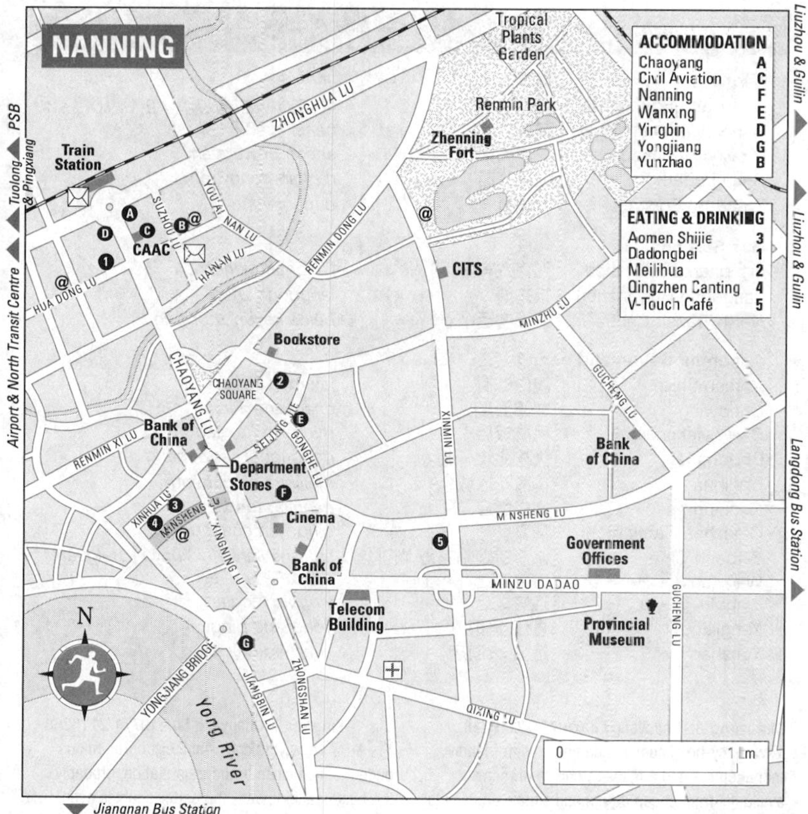

hot and planted with exotic trees. Most of the city's accommodation and attractions are in the vicinity of **Chaoyang Lu**, Nanning's main shoping precinct, which runs for 2km south from the **train station**, through the city centre and down to the river.

Coming from the north or east **by bus** will see you winding up at **Langdong station**, 10km east of the centre on Minzu Dadao – a #6 bus (50min) or a taxi (¥25) will get you to Chaoyang Lu. Approaching from the southwest will land you 7km south at **Jiangnan** station, forty minutes away from Chaoyang Lu on the #31 bus; a taxi will cost ¥20. From the northwest, you'll arrive just 2km from Chaoyang Lu at the **North Transit Centre**, also on the #31 bus route.

The **international airport** is 35km southwest of Nanning, with an **airport bus** (¥15) to the CAAC offices – taking a taxi costs around ¥100. In the city itself, a **taxi** costs ¥7 to hire, and you shouldn't have to pay much more than this to get anywhere central.

Accommodation

There's plenty of good-value, central **accommodation** in Nanning for all budgets, and most places also offer at least simple **meals**. Unusually for China, the train station area is by no means seedy or unpleasant.

Nanning

Nanning	南宁	*nánníng*
Chaoyang Square	朝阳广场	*cháoyáng guǎngchǎng*
Hanoi (Vietnam)	河内	*hénèi*
Provincial Museum	省博物馆	*shěng bówùguǎn*
Renmin Park	人民公园	*rénmín gōngyuán*
Zhenning Fort	古炮台	*gǔpàotái*
Bus Stations		
Jiangnan Bus Station	江南汽车站	*jiāngnán qìchēzhàn*
Langdong Bus Station	琅东站	*lángdōng zhàn*
North Transit Centre	北大客运中心	*běidà kèyùn zhōngxīn*
Accommodation and eating		
Aomen Shijie	澳门食街	*à omén shíjiē*
Chaoyang	朝阳酒店	*cháoyáng jiǔdiàn*
Civil Aviation	民航饭店	*mínháng fàndiàn*
Dadongbei	大东北饺子城	*dadōngběi jiǎozichéng*
Meilihua	美丽花冰城	*měilìhuā bīngchéng*
Nanning	南宁饭店	*nánníng fàndiàn*
Qingzhen Canting	清真餐厅	*qīngzhēn cāntīng*
V-Touch Café	水沙莲咖啡花语 咖啡馆	*shuǐshā liánkāfēi huāyú kāfēiguǎn*
Wanxing	万兴酒店	*wànxīng jiǔdiàn*
Yingbin	迎宾饭店	*yíngbīn fàndiàn*
Yongjiang	邕江 宾馆	*yōngjiāng bīnguǎn*
Yunzhao	运招 大酒店	*yùnzhāo dàjiǔdiàn*

Chaoyang 86 Chaoyang Lu ⓣ0771/2116388, ⓦwww.cy-hotel.com. A clean hotel with friendly management and a massive choice of rooms available, from cheap dorms and simple doubles to more comfy doubles with their own bathrooms. Dorm beds ¥25, ❷–❸

Civil Aviation 82 Chaoyang Lu ⓣ0771/2099000, ⓕ2099003. A decent mid-range option, with a very reasonably priced restaurant and negotable room rates. ❻

Nanning 38 Minsheng Lu ⓣ0771/2103888. A smart, central upmarket business venue, right across from the city's newest shopping plaza. ❽

Wanxing 42 Beining Jie ⓣ0771/2102888, ⓦwww.nnwxhotel.com. Small, boutique-style hotel, bright, new and friendly. Rates are very flexible. ❻

Yingbin 71Chaoyang Lu ⓣ0771/2116288, ⓦwww.ybfd.com. Another unpretentious budget option close to the train station, probably the best deal in town – the better doubles even come with free Internet. Some rooms have bathrooms. ❷–❸

Yongjiang Jiangbin Lu ⓣ0771/2180888, ⓦwww.yjhotel.cn. Set in a mighty 1950s Soviet-style edifice, the last in Nanning, this is now in the seriously upmarket league – their suites go for ¥9000 a night – with five-star service and copious restaurants. ❽

Yunzhao 67 Hua Dong Lu, on the corner with Suzhou Lu ⓣ0771/2191918, ⓕ2191919. Smart, small, almost guesthouse-like hotel; a cut above average for the price. ❹

The City

To get the feel of Nanning's bustle, wander around the crowded markets and lanes either west or southeast of Chaoyang Lu. Along with chickens, ducks, turtles and frogs, you'll see a variety of **tropical fruit**, including some of China's best **longan** (a bit like a spherical lychee). **Chaoyang Lu** itself is lined with modern shopping plazas, colourfully lit with fairy lights at night. Halfway along at the corner of Renmin Dong Lu, **Chaoyang Square** is an area of tidy paving, park benches and shady trees, popular with *tai ji* enthusiasts, chess

Moving on from Nanning

In addition to destinations within China, including Guilin, Guiyang, Kunming, Guangzhou and Hong Kong, there are also direct **flights** to Bangkok and Hanoi. CAAC (China Southwest) is up near the train station on Chaoyang Lu (☎0771/2095360 or 2431459, ®www.travelsky.com); you can also arrange flights through the CITS (see "Listings" p.740). The airport bus (¥15) leaves from the CAAC office and takes forty minutes.

There are three main **long-distance bus stations**. The biggest, with departures for east and northern destinations including Beihai, Guiping and Guilin, as well as Guiyang, is **Langdong station**, 10km out to the east at the end of the number #6 bus route – allow 50 minutes. You can buy tickets for Langdong departures from booths at the corner of Chaoyang Lu and Hua Dong Lu; they also have timetables. For destinations around the southwestern border area such as Chongzuo, Ningming and Pingxiang, as well as Beihai and Guilin, and inter-provincial buses to Haikou, Guangzhou and Shenzhen, head 7km south to **Jiangnan station**, on the #31 bus route (around 40min). Jiangnan tickets and timetables can be obtained from a booth on Zhonghua Lu, about 500m west of the train station on the corner with Huaqiang Lu. Much closer in, the **North Transit Centre** is about 2km northwest of the train station, also on the #31 bus route, and is of most use for traffic to Daxin (for Detian Waterfall) and Kunming.

Where available, you'll find **trains** are a faster option than the bus. Ticket windows are open from 9 to 11.50am and 12.20 to 5pm; queues here can be tiring. Services run at least daily northeast to Guilin and central China; southeast to Beihai; northwest to Kunming; and southwest via Chongzuo to Tuolong (Ningming) and the Vietnamese border at Pingxiang. The Nanning–Hanoi train also runs daily, though you still have to get out at Pingxiang, catch a minibus 15km to the border, walk across, and then catch further transport to the Vietnamese railhead at Lang Son – see p.747 for more.

players, amateur musicians, line dancers, and anyone after a breath of air. West from here and parallel with Chaoyang Lu, pedestrianized **Xingning Lu** and its offshoots sport the city's most attractive older facades, lit with red lanterns around the lunar New Year and always near critical mass with shoppers orbiting between clothing stores.

For a bit of space head to **Renmin Park** (¥2), a couple of square kilometres of waters and woodland about a twenty-minute walk east of the train station on Renmin Dong Lu. Stone causeways zigzag across the lake between islets inhabited by willows and chess players, while on the eastern side, steps ascend to **Zhenning Fort**, a defensive structure built in 1917 to house a six-inch German naval cannon – a serious piece of firepower in such a commanding position, with clear views of the whole city. The **tropical plants garden** (¥2) below has a medicinal herb plot and a carefully constructed undergrowth of philodendrons, palms, heliconias and giant "elephant-ear" taro, bird-nest ferns and cycads – its private recesses are popular with young couples.

The Provincial Museum

Essential viewing for anyone heading southwest to the Zuo River, the **Provincial Museum** on Gucheng Lu (bus #6 from Chaoyang Lu; daily 8.30am–5pm; ¥8) provides an insight into the enigmatic **Dongson culture**. Sophisticated metalworkers, the Dongson flourished over two thousand years ago in the Guangxi–Yunnan–Vietnam border area, and their works were ultimately traded as far afield as Burma, Thailand and Indonesia. The characteristic Dongson artefact is a squat, narrow-waisted **bronze drum**, finely chased with lively designs of birds, mythical animals, cattle, dancers and stars, sometimes incorporating dioramas on the lid or human and **frog** figurines sitting on the rim (suitably for a drum, frogs are associated with the thunder god in Zhuang mythology). They seem to have originated as storage vessels, though according to a Ming historian, the drums became a symbol of power: "Those who possess bronze drums are chieftains, and the masses obey them; those who have two or three drums can style themselves king." Drums appeared during the Warring States period and were cast locally right up until the late Qing dynasty; their ceremonial use survives among groups of Zhao, Yi, Miao and Yao in China, and on the eastern Indonesian island of Alor.

The museum has dozens of well-preserved varieties excavated in Guangxi and elsewhere across the region, including a rather gruesome example from Yunnan whose lid sports a diorama of crowds attending what appears to be a human sacrifice – note the "king" up on the platform, surrounded by drums. Check out the museum grounds too, with bamboo and palms growing between full-sized wooden buildings in regional architectural styles: a Zhuang rural theatre, Dong bridge and Miao houses, which are all put to use by Nanning's various communities during festivals.

Eating and drinking

Though there are plenty of places to **snack** in Nanning, real restaurants are a bit thin on the ground. The best place for inexpensive buns, dumplings, noodles, grilled chicken wings, steamed packets of lotus leaf-wrapped *zongzi* and basic stir-fries are at along the eastern end of Hua Dong Lu. Aside from the places below, hotels all have restaurants too, mostly serving Cantonese fare – including morning *dim sum* (see p.582). Western fast-food chains are grouped in the new plaza development north of the corner of Chaoyang Lu and Minzu Dadao.

Aomen Shijie Xinhua Lu. Popular place serving Cantonese-style snacks, including a host of dumplings, roast meats and quick-fried greens. You get a card, which is marked by the waitress according to what you order from the counter (or photographs). Dishes ¥5–25.

Dadongbei Cnr Chaoyang Lu and Hua Dong Lu. *Jiaozi* with big range of stuffings, ordered by the *liang* (50g), cold dishes such as spiced cucumber, spinach with peanuts, whole roasted aubergine, glass noodles, sliced beef with soy dressing, and preserved eggs, plus mammoth servings of mutton. A meal for two, plus beer, comes in around ¥35.

Meilihua (aka Mayflower) Cnr of Minzhu Lu and Chaoyang Square. The English-language menu, listing such things as noodle soups, fried rice, steak platters and florid desserts – including refreshing "snow ice", a Southeast Asian treat of shaved ice drizzled with luridly coloured syrups – and low prices make this a favourite with expats. There's another branch near the station on Zhonghua Lu. Most dishes are under ¥15.

Qingzhen Canting Xinhua Lu. Inexpensive Muslim restaurant on the ground floor of the pale green mosque. Their English menu is pretty comprehensive; the lemon duck, marinated cucumber and chicken soup with lily buds are tasty and well presented. Reckon on ¥25 a head.

V-Touch Cafe Xinmin Lu. Good coffee and set Chinese meals, wireless Internet and calm atmosphere make this a nice place to chill out on a hot day – there's also an "English Corner" here every Saturday from 9–11am for local Chinese and students who want to practise their English with any foreigners who turn up.

Listings

Banks and exchange The main Bank of China (foreign exchange Mon–Fri 8–11.30am & 2.30–5.30pm) is on Gucheng Lu, but there are smaller branches with ATMs all over town.

Books Nanning's Foreign Language Bookstore is on the ground floor of the elderly market complex overlooking Chaoyang Park on Minzhu Lu. The surprisingly large selection of pulp paperbacks, as well as English classics, some translated Chinese literature, magazines, maps and art books is above average. The top floors of the building are given over to CD and DVD shops.

CITS 40 Xinmin Lu (ⓣ0771/2612553, ⓦwww.citsgx.com; daily 8am–5.30pm) have extensive numbers of staff and offices but take little interest in independent travellers, with the exception of arranging Vietnamese visas (¥480, three working days in advance; you'll need to provide a passport and passport photo).

Hospital The City First Hospital (Shiyi Yiyuan) is southeast of the centre along Qixing Lu.

Internet access There are Net bars all over town charging ¥2 an hour.

Mail and telephones The most central post office is on Suzhou Lu (daily 8am–7pm); you can make overseas calls from the main telecom building on Minzu Dadao.

PSB About 1.5km north of the train station at 4 Xiuling Lu (ⓣ0771/2891264 or 2891303). Catch bus #14, #31, #71, #72, #84 or #85 and get off after the hospital.

Shopping Nanning is a great place to shop for clothes, either at the three department stores full of good-quality, low-price attire at the junction of Chaoyang Lu and Xinhua Lu or at the brand-label stores along Xingning Lu, such as Giordano, Baleno Meters/Bonwe and Yishion. The Nanning Antique Store, next to the museum, has a touristy and expensive selection of batiks, teapots, chops paintings and jade, set across two floors.

East of Nanning

East of Nanning, the country is unremittingly rural and the towns – such as the rail nexus of **Liuzhou**, or **Wuzhou**, right on the Guangdong border – hold little of interest to visitors. The main geographic feature here is, for once, not hills but the **Xi River**, a tiny section of a waterway which, under various names, runs from Yunnan, across central China, and finally flows into the Pearl River and so down to Guangzhou and Hong Kong. The surrounding countryside doesn't look too badly off today, but during the 1840s this corner of China was destitute, wracked by famine and the raising of new taxes to pay off indemnities levied by Britain following the Opium War. Rebellion flared across the region, culminating in the **Taiping Uprising**, a movement which started near the riverside town of **Guiping**, 150km east of Nanning, and ultimately involved millions of participants in the foundation of a rebel capital at Nanjing (see p.419). The other

East of Nanning

Guiping	桂平	*guìpíng*
Changtai Binguan	长泰宾馆	*chángtài bīnguǎn*
Dianzi Binguan	电子宾馆	*diànzǐ bīnguǎn*
Guiping Binguan	桂平宾馆	*guìpíng bīnguǎn*
Xi Shan	西山	*xīshān*
Xishi Si	西石寺	*xīshí sì*
Jintian	金田	*jīntián*
Taiping Museum	太平博物馆	*tàipíng bówùguǎn*
Taiping Tianguo	太平天国	*tàipíng tiānguó*
Beihai	北海	*běihǎi*
Beihai Sand Beach	北海银滩	*běihǎi yíntān*
Hainan Ferry Port	北海港客运站	*běihǎigǎng kèyùnzhàn*
Jiatianxia Dajiudian	甲天下大酒店	*jiǎtiānxià dàjiǔdiàn*
Liyuan Guoji Dajiudian	利源国际大酒店	*lìyuán guójì dàjiǔdiàn*
Waisha Harbour	外沙内港中山公园	*wàishā nèigǎng zhōngshān gōngyuán*

place of interest in the area lies 150km southeast of Nanning at **Beihai**, Guangxi's major coastal port and transit point for traffic to Hainan Island.

Guiping and Jintian

GUIPING is a poor, underdeveloped, but busy town at the junction of the Xi and Yu rivers, three hours by bus (¥50) from Nanning's Langdong station. The town centres around **Guangchang**, a public square at the intersection of east–west-oriented Renmin Lu and south-pointing Guinan Lu, where you'll also find the **long-distance bus station**.

The Chinese come to Guiping to see **Xi Shan** (¥15), a typical formalized sacred mountain right on the western outskirts – catch a bus (7am–4.30pm) from Guangchang square or simply walk for twenty minutes along Renmin Xi Lu to the gates. Far tamer than the country's great holy peaks, Xi Shan is a comfortable introduction to the Chinese obsession with landscaping natural phenomena to turn them into places of pilgrimage and weekend excursions. The two-hour hike to the top follows paved paths leading off into a forest of fish-tailed palms and huge pines, past the usual run of temples – near the entrance, **Xishi Si** has a **vegetarian restaurant** open for lunch – and up to a summit with hazy views of the two rivers snaking across a watery flatland to join at Guiping. **Tea** aficionados should sample the famous Xi Shan brand; rumour has it that temple-bought leaves are superior to anything you'll find in Guiping's shops.

Guiping's **accommodation** includes several hostels around the bus station, though they're not keen on foreign custom. Failing these, there are threadbare rooms with shower and, if you're lucky, functioning air conditioning at the *Dianzi Binguan* (dorm beds ¥30, ❷), on the west side of the square; a few hundred metres east along Renmin Lu, the elderly *Guiping Fandian* (Ⓣ0775/3369292, Ⓕ3380184; ❹) and newer *Changtai Binguan* (Ⓣ0775/3369988, Ⓕ3369000; ❺) are more expensive but better value – the only **restaurants** are here too, with sandpot and noodle stalls at the bus station as alternatives.

Jintian and Taiping Tianguo

For Taiping historians, Guiping is simply a stop on the way to **JINTIAN**, about 25km and thirty minutes to the north. Catch a minibus (which run whenever full; ¥3) from the western side of Guangchang square. You get dropped off at Jiantian's single, north-pointing street; look for a concrete archway to the west and follow this road for 4km to a small wooded hill and **Taiping Tianguo** (daily 9am–4.30pm; ¥15), the Taiping Uprising's first headquarters – a motorcycle-taxi costs around ¥5. A red sandstone statue of a very heroic-looking Hong Xiuquan, the Taiping leader, faces you as you enter; to the right are the three-metre-high, rammed earth defensive walls of their **barracks**, now a bit worn down and overgrown with pine trees. In the centre of this long rectangular enclosure is the rather ambiguous "pledge rock", supposedly where Hong declared his insurrection to be under way on 11 January 1851. There's also a **museum** here, to the left of the main entrance, though the blurred photos, old coins and rusty weapons throw little light on what became the world's largest civil revolt – as is often the case, it's the site associations, rather than tangible relics, that justify the journey. Buses run back to Guiping at least until 5pm.

Beihai

BEIHAI, a pleasant town on the Beibu Gulf, is Guangxi's sole seaport. A bland four-hour train ride from Nanning or an overnight ride on the **ferry from**

Hainan Island, it got going in the late nineteenth century after the Yantai Agreement allowed European traders to move in, and today the city remains a largely commercially oriented mesh of wide roads and modern high-rises. Housing prices here have rocketed recently, and there's a mild buzz to the place, though it's usually stifled by the tropical heat.

While the only reason to visit Beihai is in transit to Hainan, there's no problem filling in time between connections. The older part of town is along the seafront and on **Zhongshan Lu**, where mouldering colonial buildings add to the sleepily tropical atmosphere. It's best in the morning when the fresh catches arrive, and the fabulous **fish market** sells every type and part of sea life imaginable. Hop on a #2 bus heading west down **Haijiao Lu** from the end of Zhongshan Lu and you end up a couple of kilometres away at **Waisha harbour**, packed with scores of wooden-hulled junks, motorized and sailless, but otherwise traditionally designed. Most of the vessels here belong to the community of thirteen thousand refugee "**boat people**" living in the adjacent UN-sponsored village. They were victims of an attempt by the Vietnamese authorities to remove ethnic Chinese from their territory, a major cause of the 1979 war between China and Vietnam. China's reciprocal group are the **Jing**, ethnic Vietnamese who settled islands off Beihai in the sixteenth century.

Beihai Sand Beach (¥30) lies about 5km south of the centre at the end of the #3 bus route (¥3) from Sichuan Lu. It's a long, broad stretch of grey sand where you can organize a spin in a speedboat or a beach buggy, or just roam – swimming isn't perhaps such a great idea, given that the city lacks a sewage treatment plant. In all, Hainan's beaches are far better (and free to enter) so don't set aside an extra day for this one if you're in transit.

Practicalities

A hugely sprawling grid of right-angled streets, Beihai is so positioned on a broad peninsula that there is sea to the north and south of town. There's no real centre as such, though the busiest area is the kilometre-deep strip between east–west-oriented Beihai Dadao and the sea to the north. **Arrival points** are widely spread: the **train station** is south at the end of Beijing Lu; the **Hainan ferry port** and ticket office 5km away in the northwest of town along seafront Haijiao Lu; and the **long-distance bus station** 4km northeast on Beibuwan Lu. There's a comprehensive but slow **bus system**, so pick up a map on arrival or catch a **taxi** (¥7).

For **accommodation**, there are some cheap places around the bus station, which isn't a bad spot to stay; for something smarter, try the *Liyuan Guojia Dajidian*, at the corner of Beijing and Chongqing Lu, about halfway between the bus and train stations (Ⓣ0779/3220688; ❸); or the *Jiatian Xia Dajiudian*, about 1.5km southwest of the bus station at the junction of Beihai Dadao and Guizhou Lu (Ⓣ0779/3065666; ❸). **Places to eat** include the hotels, or the cheap, hole-in-the-wall restaurants beside the ferry and bus terminals.

Leaving, there are afternoon ferries to Hainan's capital, Haikou (10hr; seats ¥55; dorms ¥101, very basic private cabins ¥149 per person); all toilets are shared, and hot water urns and a snack shop are the only sources of refreshment. There are also daily trains to Nanning (3hr 15min; ¥55), and buses as far afield as Guilin, Nanning and Guangzhou.

Nanning to Vietnam

The region **west of Nanning** forms the Zhuang heartlands, consisting of scattered hills surrounded by seas of sugar cane and bananas up against the

Nanning to Vietnam

Chongzuo	崇左	*chóngzuǒ*
Chongzuo Ecology Park	崇左生态公园	*chóngzuǒ shēngtài gōngyuán*
White-headed Langur	白头叶猴	*báitóu yèhóu*
Detian Waterfall	得天瀑布	*détiān pùbù*
Daxin	大新	*dàxīn*
Detian Binguan	得天 宾馆	*détiān bīnguǎn*
Detian Lüguan	得天 旅馆	*détiān lǚguǎn*
Detian Shanzhuang	得天山庄	*détiān shānzhuāng*
Ningming	宁明	*níngmíng*
Pingxiang	凭祥	*píngxiáng*
Friendship Pass	友谊关	*yǒuyíguān*
Hanoi (Vietnam)	河内	*hénèi*
Jinxiangyu Dajiudian	金祥玉大酒店	*jīnxiángyù dàjiǔdiàn*
Shuolong	硕龙	*shuòlóng*
Hongle Lüguan	鸿乐旅馆	*hónglè lǚguǎn*
Tuolong	驮龙	*tuólóng*
Hua Shan	花山	*huāshān*
Zuo River	左江	*zuǒjiāng*

borders of Vietnam and Yunnan. Unlike many of southwestern China's ethnic groups, however, there's not much visible difference between the Zhuang and the Han, at least in terms of colourful clothing and festivals, and the towns here are poor and doggedly functional. It's an interesting area nonetheless, especially southwest towards the **Vietnamese border crossing** at **Pingxiang**, where extensive rock art at **Hua Shan** along the Zuo River proves that Zhuang culture goes back a long way; and where you can see the endangered white-headed langur at **Chongzuo Ecology Park**. North of here, there's outstanding scenery at the **Detian waterfall**, which actually pours across the border.

The area has good transport connections: Detian and Chongzuo Ecology Park are easiy reached by **bus**, while you can get within striking distance of the park, Hua Shan and the border crossing itself via the Pingxiang **train**.

Detian waterfall

Straddling the Vietnamese border 150km due west of Nanning, **Detian waterfall** is worth the trip not just for the falls themselves, but also because it draws you into the Zhuang heartlands – a world of dark karst hills, grubby towns, water buffalo wallowing in green paddy fields, and Zhuang farmers in broad-sleeved pyjamas and conical hats

Buses depart Nanning's North Transit Centre to **Daxin** (3hr; ¥15), from where there are regular minibuses to **Shuolong** (1hr; ¥6), the nearest settlement to the falls – and, if they get enough customers or you're willing to negotiate an extra fee, to Detian waterfall itself. **SHUOLONG** is a large village under a vertical cliff overhanging the marketplace where through traffic congregates; a motor-rickshaw for the last 15km to the falls from here costs around ¥10. If you get stuck at Shuolong for the night, *Hongle Lüguan* (❷, dorm beds ¥20) at the marketplace is the best **place to stay**, with a couple of basic restaurants opposite.

The falls

The **falls** repay the effort of reaching them in unexpected ways. The road there winds along a wide river valley to a small congregation of souvenir stalls and

▲ Detian waterfall

accommodation at the *Detian Binguan* and *Detian Lüguan*, both of which offer clean, comfortable rooms (❷). Just uphill is the **entrance** (¥30), and beyond here the upmarket *Detian Shanzhuang* (Ⓣ0771/3773570, Ⓦwww.detian.com; ❼) with views across the river into Vietnam. Then you're looking at the falls themselves, a delightful set of cataracts broader than their thirty-metre height and at their best after the spring rains, framed by peaks and fields. Paths lead down to the base of the falls past a series of pools and bamboo groves; at the bottom you can hire a **bamboo raft** and be punted over to straddle the mid-river borderline. The best part, however, is to follow the road along the top to its end in a field, where you'll find a **stone post** proclaiming the Sino-Vietnamese frontier in French and Chinese, along with a bizarre

border market – a clutch of trestle tables laden with Vietnamese sweets, cigarettes and stamps in the middle of nowhere. Despite locals crossing as they please, don't try to go any further: Chinese police will spring out from nowhere and stop you.

To Vietnam: Chongzuo, Hua Shan and Pingxiang

The **Vietnamese border crossing** lies about 170km southwest of Nanning beyond the town of **Pingxiang**. It's well worth spending time on the route, taking in the **Chongzuo Ecology Park**'s monkeys, and making the trip up the Zuo River to **Hua Shan**'s prehistoric **rock paintings**. Jumping-off points for these places lie along the Nanning–Pingxiang rail line, with two **trains** departing Nanning each morning to the border – though there are also plenty of buses through the day from the Jiangnan station.

Chongzuo Ecology Park

Chongzuo Ecology Park (¥40), a small spread of limestone hills and flat valleys, was created to protect the endangered and endemic **white-headed langur**, whose entire population numbers just 700 animals. The main reason for their decline, which has plummeted since the 1980s, is deforestation for new agricultural land. Their plight was first recognized by renowned panda specialist **Professor Pan** of Beijing University, who turned his attention here in 1996 and set up a permanent study programme, informing villagers of the monkeys' plight, and compensating them for the reserve's creation (which deprived them of potential farmland) by persuading local government to improve schools, water supplies and infrastructure in the area.

There are 250 monkeys in the reserve, and your chance of seeing some – albeit at a distance, as they spend much of their time bouncing around clifftops – is good. They form groups of around ten individuals, headed by a single adult male; the black-bodied adults have white heads and tail tips, and spend much of their time eating leaves (though they also like fruit and flowers). The babies, however, are golden all over, darkening during their first two years.

Before turning up, note that this is not a monkey theme park, but primarily a research base. They're happy to have visitors, but the park is fairly wild (cobras are common), and summers are exceedingly hot and wet. The reserve is 15km southeast of **CHONGZUO** city, which is a bit over halfway down the rail line between Nanning and Pingxiang. It's easier, however, to get here **by bus** from Nanning's Jiangnan station (90min; ¥35) – ask the driver to drop you at the park gates. Alternatively, minibuses (¥5) run from Chongzuo's bus station past the park until late afternoon. **Accommodation** at the park is in the former army barracks (❸), and they provide ample Chinese meals at around ¥50 per person a day – there's also room to **camp**, if you have the gear, but pack a **torch** either way. Staff act as guides, with best viewing times at dawn and dusk, and about 5km of walking trails to explore. For more **information**, contact Mr Qin, the park manager (Ⓣ0771/7930222, Ⓔbill@trax2.com). **Moving on**, flag down a minibus from outside the park to Chongzuo, from where there are buses through the day back to Nanning, or on to Tuolong or Ningming (for Hua Shan), and Pingxiang.

Hua Shan and the Zuo River

Set in a beautifully isolated spot where tall karst peaks flank the **Zuo**, the southwest's main river, **Hua Shan**'s waterfront cliffs are daubed with thousands of enigmatic figures believed to be connected with the local Zhuang culture of some 2000 years ago. The main access is by boat from **TUOLONG**, a single-street rail stop for the nearby town of **Ningming**, about two-thirds of the way to Pingxiang from Nanning. If nobody grabs you when you get off the train at Tuolong, walk out of the station and down the street to the river, where you'll find a bridge. Sampans moor up underneath here (there's also a small boatyard), and ask about ¥80 for the run upstream to Hua Shan – allow at least five hours for the return trip, including time to view the rock art.

It's a placid journey up the Zuo – buffalo wallow in the shallows, people fish from wooden rafts and tend family plots, and the banks are thick with spindly branched kapok trees, flowering red in April. Mountains spring up after a while, flat-faced and sheer by the river, and it's here you'll see the first painted figures: red, stick-like markings, though most are very faded or smeared with age. The boat docks just short of Hua Shan, where you pay the **entrance fee** (¥13) before walking along a track to the paintings. Nobody has worked out a definitive interpretation of the 1900 sharply posed figures, but they include drummers and dancers, dogs and cattle, a dragon-boat race, men with arms bent upwards, a "king" with a sword, and just two women, long-haired and pregnant. The designs are similar to those decorating the Dongson drums (see p.740), and there's little doubt that they were produced by the same culture, currently identified with the Zhuang people. A few Bronze Age weapons have also been found here.

Heading on, there are two morning trains a day in each direction from Tuolong, so you'll probably need to head 5km to **NINGMING** (¥1 by three-wheeler), a ghastly market town of cheap concrete construction drowned in exhaust fumes. Regular buses run from Ningming until around 4pm back to Nanning or on to Pingxiang – if you can't get out there are several cheap, nondescript places to stay around the bus station.

Pingxiang and the border crossing

Surrounded by jutting karst hills, **PINGXIANG** is a small, bustling trading town and railhead for the Vietnamese border crossing, 15km away. The **train station** lies about 3km outside town on the border road; the **bus station** is in the centre of town on the main street, Bei Da Lu. Gaggles of motor-rickshaws descend on new arrivals, the drivers engaging in Ben-Hur-like races down to the border – try for around ¥10.

You shouldn't really need to stay in Pingxiang, but almost every building within 100m of the bus station on Bei Da Lu offers **accommodation**: hostels ask ¥15–30 per person; while the *Jinxiangyu Dajiudian* (☎0771/8521303; ❸) is a typically clean, functional hotel, and gives massive discounts. There's a huge produce **market** behind the bus station, a **Bank of China** on Bei Da Lu, and cheap places to eat everywhere. Heading **back to Nanning**, the train currently leaves at 3.20pm – stopping at Tuolong and Chongzuo – with buses running the same route between 7am and 7pm.

The **border crossing**, known here as **Friendship Pass**, is worth a trip even if you're not heading to Vietnam. It's set in a natural gap through a series of steep cliffs and hills all wooded with conifers and bamboo; the Chinese side is marked by lines of imperious black cars with tinted windows, trucks loaded with vehicle chassis, a defunct French colonial Customs House built in 1914, and a huge Chinese **gate tower**. A Ming-era defensive **stone wall** runs off up into the hills to the north of here, which you can follow for a short way; just remember that this is a border area. Back down at the gate tower, walk under the arch and the **customs** are straight ahead. Assuming you have a valid visa, entering Vietnam shouldn't be too complicated, though the border guards examine all documents minutely. The Vietnamese town on the far side is **Dong Dang**, where there's further transport 5km south to **Lang Son**, the railhead for Hanoi.

Finally, be **warned** that, if crossing into China from Vietnam, you should keep this book buried deep in your bags – customs officials have been confiscating them recently because the maps colour Taiwan in differently, which is taken to imply support for the island's separatist cause (see p.1161).

Guizhou

A traditional saying describes **Guizhou** as a land where there are "no three days without rain, no three hectares without a mountain, and no three coins in any pocket". Superficially this is accurate: Guizhou records the highest rainfall in China and has a poverty ensured by more than eighty percent of its land being covered in untillable mountains or leached limestone soils. The province's recent history is none too happy either, though Guizhou's many **ethnic groups** were, for a long while, left pretty much to themselves. Chinese influence was established here around 100 BC, but it wasn't until the government began settling Han migrants in the province during the seventeenth century that the locals began to fight back, resistance culminating in the **Miao Uprising** of 1854–73, which rivalled the contemporary Taiping insurrection in terms of chaos and bloodshed. Sixty years later the region still hadn't recovered: Red Army soldiers passing through Guizhou in the 1930s found people working naked in the fields and an economy based on opium, and it's only in the last decade that Guizhou's population has exceeded numbers prior to the uprising.

This being said, ethnic identity and romantic landscapes have become marketable commodities in China, and Guizhou is beginning to capitalize on its two major assets. The province's most visible minority groups are the many branches of **Miao**, concentrated in the southeast around **Kaili**; and the **Bouyei**, who are based around the provincial capital, **Guiyang**, and the westerly town of **Anshun**. The Miao in particular indulge in a huge number of **festivals**, some of which attract tens of thousands of participants and are worth any effort to experience. There is also an accomplished artistic tradition to investigate, notably some unusual architecture and exquisite textiles. As for **scenery**, there are truly spectacular **limestone caverns** at **Longgong** and **Zhijin**, both accessed from Anshun; impressive **waterfalls** at **Huangguoshu** – again near Anshun – and **Chishui**, right up on the northern border with Sichuan; and everywhere terraced hills, dotted with small villages that tempt hikers. Naturalists will also want to clock up rare **black-necked cranes**, which winter along the northwestern border with Yunnan at **Caohai Lake**; and at least have a stab at seeing the reclusive **golden monkey**, which lives in the cloud forests atop Guizhou's single holy mountain, northeasterly **Fanjing Shan**.

While Guizhou's often shambolic towns are definitely not a high point of a trip to the region, Guiyang is comfortable enough, and conveniently central to the province. A couple of other places worth a visit in their own right are the historic northern city of **Zunyi**, which is steeped in Long March lore; and the atypically pleasant town of **Zhenyuan**, over on the eastern side of the province, which features some antique buildings squeezed along a beautiful stretch of river.

Guiyang and around

GUIYANG lies in a valley basin, encircled by a range of hills that hems in the city and concentrates its traffic pollution. Established as a capital during the

Guiyang and around

Guiyang	贵阳	*guìyáng*
Cuiwei Yuan	翠惟园	*cuìwéi yuán*
Hongfu Si	弘福寺	*hóngfú sì*
Jiaxiu Lou	甲秀楼	*jiǎxiù lóu*
Provincial Museum	省博物馆	*shěng bówùguǎn*
Qiangling Shan	黔灵山	*qiánlíng shān*
Qianming Si	黔明寺	*qiánmíng sì*
Renmin Plaza	人民广场	*rénmín guǎngcháng*
Wenchang Ge	文昌阁	*wénchāng gé*
Bus Stations		
Hebin Bus Depot	河滨客运站	*hébīn kèyùnzhàn*
Main Bus Station	贵阳客运站	*guìyáng kèyùnzhàn*
Tiyu Bus Station	体育馆客运站	*tǐyùguǎn kèyùnzhàn*
Accommodation		
Hebin	河滨饭店	*hébīn fàndiàn*
Jiaoyuan	教苑宾馆	*jiàoyuàn bīnguǎn*
Motel 168	莫泰连锁旅店	*mòtài liánsuǒ lǚdiàn*
Nenghui	能辉酒店	*nénghuī jiǔdiàn*
Post Office Hotel	贵州邮电宾馆	*guìzhōu yóudiàn bīnguǎn*
Sheraton	喜来登贵航酒店	*xǐláidēng guìháng jiǔdiàn*
Shunyuan	顺医宾馆	*shùnyuán binguǎn*
Trade Point Hotel	柏顿宾馆	*bódùn bīnguǎn*
Yidu/Youth Hostel	逸都酒店	*yìdūjiǔdiàn*
Eating		
Beijing Jiaoziguan	北京饺子馆	*běijīng jiǎoziguǎn*
Dongjia Shifu	侗家食府	*dóngjiā shífǔ*
Gangwei Tangguan	缸煨汤馆	*gāngwèi tāngguǎn*
Jue Yuan Sucaiguan	觉园素菜馆	*juéyuán sùcàiguǎn*
Laodong Zhouhuang	老东粥皇	*láodōng zhōuhuáng*
Nantianmen	南天门重庆火锅	*nántiānmén chóngqìng huǒguō*
Qiaowaipo	巧外婆	*qiǎowàipó*
Xinjiang Weiwu'er Tianshan	新疆维吾尔天山餐厅	*xīnjiāng weíwú'ěr tiānshān cāntīng*
Qingyan	青岩	*qīngyán*
Baisui Memorial Arch	百岁坊	*bǎisuì fǎng*
Guzhen Kezhan	古镇客站	*gǔzhèn kèzhàn*
Huaxi	花溪	*huāxī*
Old Town	古镇	*gǔzhèn*
South Gate	定广门	*dìngguǎng mén*

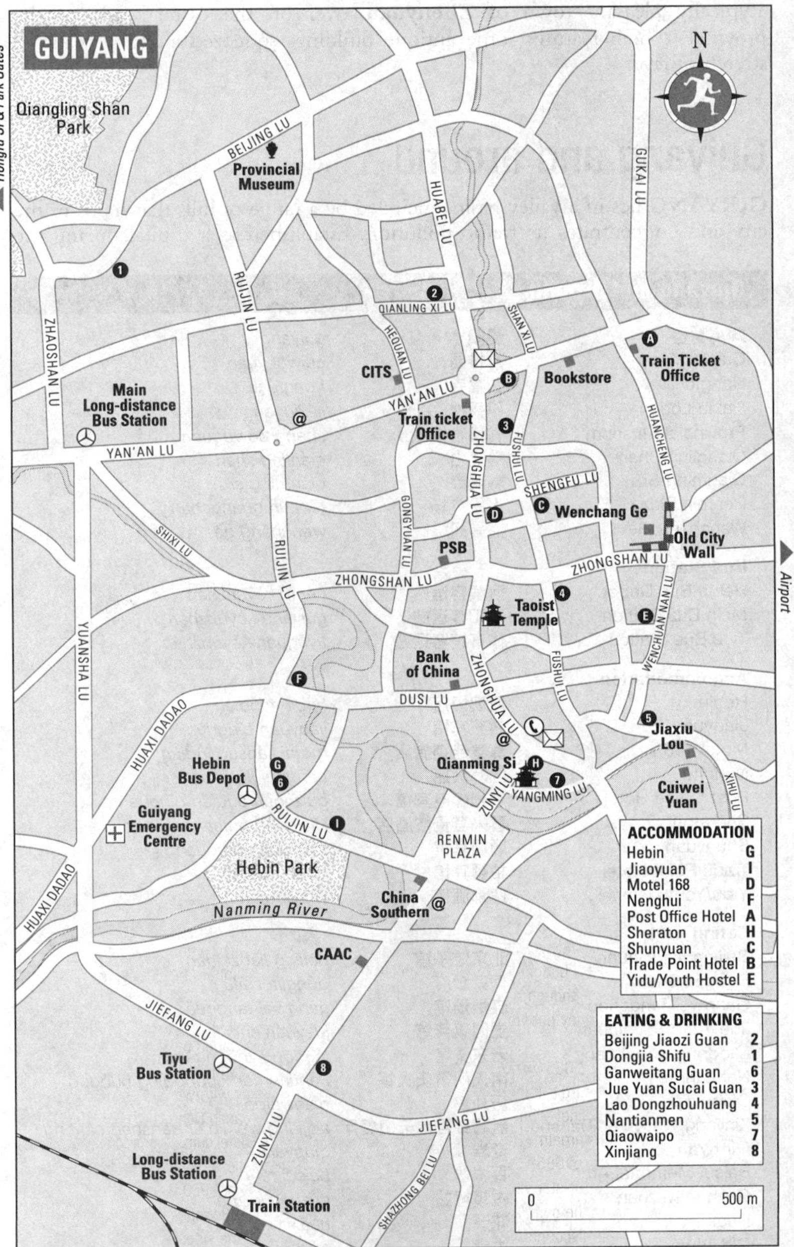
GUIYANG
Qiangling Shan Park
Hongfu Si & Park Gates
Provincial Museum
BEIJING LU
HUABEI LU
GUKAI LU
RUIJIN LU
QIANLING XI LU
SHAN XI LU
HEQUAN LU
ZHAOSHAN LU
CITS
Bookstore
Train Ticket Office
Main Long-distance Bus Station
YAN'AN LU
Train ticket Office
ZHONGHUA LU
FUSHUI LU
HUANCHENG LU
SHENGFU LU
Wenchang Ge
GONGYUAN LU
SHIXI LU
PSB
Old City Wall
ZHONGSHAN LU
Airport
Taoist Temple
WENCHUAN NAN LU
YUANSHA LU
Bank of China
DUSI LU
HUAXI DADAO
Jiaxiu Lou
Hebin Bus Depot
Qianming Si
YANGMING LU
ZUNYI LU
Cuiwei Yuan
XIHU LU
Guiyang Emergency Centre
RENMIN PLAZA
Hebin Park
China Southern
Nanming River
CAAC
JIEFANG LU
Tiyu Bus Station
Long-distance Bus Station
Train Station
SHAZHONG BEI LU
ACCOMMODATION
Hebin G
Jiaoyuan I
Motel 168 D
Nenghui F
Post Office Hotel A
Sheraton H
Shunyuan C
Trade Point Hotel B
Yidu/Youth Hostel E
EATING & DRINKING
Beijing Jiaozi Guan 2
Dongjia Shifu 1
Ganweitang Guan 6
Jue Yuan Sucai Guan 3
Lao Dongzhouhuang 4
Nantianmen 5
Qiaowaipo 7
Xinjiang 8
0
500 m

Ming dynasty, Guiyang received little attention until the early 1950s, when the Communist government brought in the rail line and filled the centre with heavy monuments and drab, rectangular apartment blocks. These are gradually being cleared, though enough remain to create something of a patchwork effect as they rub shoulders with glossy new high-rises and department stores, all intercut by a web of wide roads and flyovers. While the result may not be one of China's most beautiful cities – being also glaringly provincial in the cheap market stalls clogging the main streets every evening – it's a friendly place, whose unexpected few antique buildings and a surprisingly wild park lend a bit of character. There's enough in Guiyang to fill a day in transit, and it's worth making an easy side-trip to the ancient garrison town of **Qingyan**.

Arrival, city transport and accommodation

Central Guiyang comprises a concentrated couple of square kilometres around the narrow **Nanming River**, with the downtown area focused along Zhonghua Lu, which runs south through the centre into Zunyi Lu, crosses the river and continues for another kilometre before terminating at the **train station**. In the large square outside you'll find **taxis** (¥10), and a **city bus terminus** ahead to the east: #1, which goes along Zunyi Lu and Zhonghua Lu, turning west along Beijing Lu and back to the train station down Ruijin Lu; and bus #2, which does the same route in reverse, are the two best routes for getting you close to the hotels.

Guiyang's **airport** lies 15km east of town, ¥10 on the airport bus (every 30min) or a ¥50 taxi ride to the centre. There are several **long-distance bus stations**: coming from anywhere could see you arriving at the main long-distance bus station, west of the centre on Yan'an Lu; from Kaili, Anshun or Zunyi you'll probably arrive at or near the southerly Tiyu station on Jiefang Lu; while some fast buses from Zunyi wind up at the Hebin depot on Ruijin Lu.

Accommodation is not a problem, with a range of central places spanning budget to fairly upmarket brackets. Just don't waste your time trying to get in to one of the guesthouses surrounding the train station – they won't take foreigners, and are anyway no cheaper than the *Post Office Hotel, Yidu* or *Shunyuan*.

Accommodation

Hebin 118 Ruijin Nan Lu ⓣ0851/5841855, ⓕ5812988. A fairly new hotel on a busy road but quiet, close to a park, clean and cosy. Bargain and they'll give discounts, but are anyway fair value for a mid-range place. ❺

Jiaoyuan 130 Ruijin Lu ⓣ0851/8129519, ⓕ5814604. Bright, ordinary budget hotel with slightly overpriced doubles, though no dorms or lifts – a bit problematic if they put you in the upper floors. ❹

Motel 168 2 Shengfu Lu ⓣ0851/8168168. Not quite up to the usual standard – it looks like it was built in a rush and on a budget – but still a good deal if you get one of the bargain ¥168 rooms. ❹

Nenghui 38 Ruijin Nan Lu ⓣ0851/5898888, ⓦwww.gyspsb.com.cn. Four-star venture where all customers get free use of the gym, and executive suites garner many other discounts. ❼

Post Office Hotel 166 Yan'an Lu ⓣ0851/5585082, ⓕ5585086. One of the cheapest places in town – but even the dorms are tidy and comfortable. Triples ¥25 per person, doubles with or without bathroom ❷/❹

Sheraton 49 Zhonghua Nan Lu ⓣ0851/5888388, ⓦwww.sheraton.com/guiyang. Amazing marble construction full of restaurants, where rooms are priced according to square metreage, starting at ¥1580. ❾

Shunyuan 76 Fushui Lu ⓣ0851/5805022. Inexpensive, slightly faded budget hotel in the town centre, which, reluctantly, will take foreigners. Singles ¥40, doubles with/without bathroom ❷/❹

Trade Point Hotel Yanan Dong Lu ⓣ0851/5827888, ⓦwww.trade-pointhotel.com. Sharp, four-star option with local and Cantonese restaurants and all executive trimmings for ¥950 a night. ❾

Yidu/Youth Hostel 63 Wenchang Nan Lu; reception is around the side ⓣ0851/8649777, ⓦwww..gyyd08.51.com. Smart mid-range hotel also offering budget beds. Dorm beds ¥50, ❺

Moving on from Guiyang

CAAC (☎0851/5977777) and China Southern/Guizhou Airlines (☎0851/5828429) are near each other on Zunyi Lu (both daily 8.30am–5.30pm). The **airport bus** leaves CAAC every thirty minutes between 8.30am and 7pm and costs ¥10.

Guiyang's **main bus station**, handling departures to everywhere outside the province and cities within, is on the corner of Yan'an Lu and Zhaoshan Lu. The **Tiyu bus station**, down near the train station on Jiefang Lu, has frequent, fast departures to Kaili, Zunyi and Anshun from dawn to dusk. Outside on Zunyi Lu, a kerbside depot deals in more buses to Kaili, Zunyi, Anshun (the ticket office is a converted bus) and is the place to come if you are after **day-tours** of Longgong Caves and Huangguoshu waterfall. Tours leave in the early morning, and it's actually just as easy to reach these places yourself via Anshun.

Trains head east into central China and beyond via Kaili, Zhenyuan and Yuping (the jump-off point for Fanjing Shan); north to Zunyi and Chongqing; west to Kunming via Anshun and Liupanshui; and south into Guangxi. Buying tickets at the station is pretty easy, but you can also get them for a ¥5 mark-up at **advance-purchase offices** (8.30am–noon & 1–4pm) at a couple of branches of the Guiyang Commercial Bank – see the map on p.750 for locations.

The City

Guiyang's social focus is the large open space of **Renmin Plaza**, on the Nanming's south bank off Ruijin Lu, where early-morning crowds indulge in the local craze of spinning wooden tops – all overlooked to the east by a large but inconspicuous statue of Chairman Mao. Just across the river, **Qianming Si**, a recently renovated Ming-dynasty nunnery, marks the start of a 500m-long paved riverside promenade east to an arched stone bridge across to **Jiaxiu Lou** (¥4), a twenty-nine-metre-high, three-storeyed pavilion. This dates back to 1598, built to inspire students taking imperial examinations; it now. holds a teahouse and photos from the 1930s. Continue on across the bridge to the far bank, and you're outside **Cuiwei Yuan** (¥4), a Qing-dynasty ornamental garden whose buildings have served a variety of purposes over the years, and currently house tearooms and souvenir shops.

North of here up Wenchang Nan Lu is a restored fragment of Guiyang's **old city wall**, the seven-metre-high battlement capped by **Wenchang Ge**, a gate tower with flared eaves and wooden halls, built in 1596 and now yet another breezy teahouse.

For a final historical hit, catch northbound bus #1 from central **Zhonghua Lu** around to the **Provincial Museum** (Tues–Sun 9–11.30am & 1–4pm; ¥10), 2.5km north along Beijing Lu. It sits at the back of a car park; once you've woken up the surprised staff upstairs in the left wing, they'll unlock the place and turn the power on for you. **Ethnic groups** such as the Miao, Dong and Bouyei are represented through costumes, festival photos, and models of their architecture. There are also wooden **ground opera masks** (see p.769), a poster-sized manifesto and armour relating to the nineteenth-century Miao Uprising, and some lively glazed tomb figurines from the Ming dynasty, found near Zunyi.

Qiangling Shan Park and Hongfu Si

About 1km west of the Provincial Museum, **Qiangling Shan Park** (¥4) is a pleasant handful of hills right on the edge of town, thickly forested enough to harbour some colourful birdlife and noisy groups of monkeys. There's a series of ponds, bridges and ornamental undergrowth inside the entrance, but the highlight is **Hongfu Si**, an important Buddhist monastery up above – follow steps from the gates for thirty minutes to the top. You exit the woods into a courtyard containing the ornamental, four-metre-high **Fahua Pagoda** and a screen showing Buddha being washed at birth by nine dragons. On the right is a **bell tower** with a five-hundred-year-old bell, while bearing left brings you to a new Luohan hall inhabited by 500 glossy, chunky statues of Buddhist saints. The temple's main hall houses a 32-armed Guanyin, each palm displaying an eye, facing a rather benevolent-looking King of Hell.

Eating and drinking

With its predilection for dog meat, chillies and sour soups, Guizhou's cuisine comes under the Western Chinese cooking umbrella, though there's a wide variety of food available in town. Snack stalls are scattered through the centre; the block on Fushui Lu north off Zhongshan Lu has several long-established, inexpensive **duck canteens**, serving it crisp-fried in the local style. One local speciality is thin **crepes** – here called *tianwa*, or "stuffed dolls" – which you fill from a selection of pickled and fresh vegetables to resemble an uncooked spring roll. The best places to try them lie just outside Qiangling Shan Park. **Hotpots** are a Guizhou institution offered everywhere, with tables centred round a bubbling pot of slightly sour, spicy stock, in which you cook your own food. **Dog** is a winter dish, usually stir-fried with noodles, soya-braised or part of a hotpot – the southern end of Hequan Lu, opposite CITS, has the best. For **Western food**, there are dozens of **cafés** serving coffee and set meals of steak or burgers, and the *Trade Point Hotel* does a great all-you-can-eat buffet breakfast (7–10.30am; ¥75 a head).

Beijing Jiaozi Guan Qianling Xi Lu. *Jiaozi* with a bewildering array of stuffings – coriander with pork and tofu with egg are good – along with side dishes such as marinated spareribs, garlic cucumber and preserved eggs. You can bloat yourself for ¥15.

Dongjia Shifu Near Qianling Shan Park on Beijing Lu. Ethnic theme restaurant with staff dressed in colourful garb. Though realistically the menu shouldn't stretch far beyond dog hotpot, noodles and sour soup, there's actually a good range of meat, fish and vegetable dishes, and the place has some character. About ¥30 a head for two.

Gangweitang Guan Ruijin Lu, near the *Hebin* hotel. Shandong and Sichuanese food, with the speciality being slow-cooked soups (each enough for 2–3 people) served in an earthenware pot. The duck with white radish is worth a try, as is spare-ribs with fungus. Mains ¥15–40.

Jue Yuan Sucai Guan 51 Fushui Bei Lu. Vegetarian restaurant whose dishes tend to be liberally laced with chillies. Along with fairly inexpensive stir-fries, they also do elegant "Lion's Head" stewed rissoles, "Eight Treasure Duck" (stuffed with sweet beanpaste and sticky rice) "Lotus Fish", and Guizhou-style chicken – despite

Canine cuisine

Dog meat is widely appreciated not only in Guizhou, Guangxi and Guangdong, but also in nearby culturally connected countries such as Indonesia, the Philippines and Vietnam. Possibly the taste originated in China and was spread through Southeast Asia by tribal migrations. Wherever the practice of eating dog began, the meat is universally considered to be warming in cold weather and an aid to male virility. Chinese tourists to Guizhou generally make a point of trying a dog dish, but for Westerners, eating dog can be a touchy subject. Some find it almost akin to cannibalism, while others are discouraged by the way restaurants display bisected hindquarters in the window, or soaking in a bucket of water on the floor. If you're worried about being served dog by accident, say "*wo buchi gourou*" (I don't eat dog).

the names, all are made from meat substitutes. Photo menu. Dishes ¥10–35.
Lao Dongzhouhuang Fushui Lu, south of Zhongshan Lu. Cantonese-style fast-food chain, serving sandpots, steamed spare Ribs, stuffed bitter gourd slices, prawn dumplings, and even roast duck and pork. Lots of photos and displayed food help prevent language difficulties. Mains around ¥12–20.
Nantianmen Cnr Xihu Lu and Wenchuan Nan Lu. Very popular Sichuanese-style hotpot restaurant, with set selections starting at ¥35.
Qiaowaipo 6 Yangming Lu. Guizhou cuisine served in a smart, modern establishment with views of the river. ¥35 a head for two.
Xinjiang Zunyi Lu, set back off the street north of Jiefang Lu. Lively, slightly seedy place offering Muslim grills, stews, noodles and breads from just a few yuan up to around ¥35 for *dapan ji*, a huge plate of spicy chicken.

Listings

Banks and exchange The main Bank of China with an ATM is just west off Zhonghua Lu on Dusi Lu; foreign exchange is on the ground floor (Mon–Fri 9–11.30am & 1.30–5pm). There are other branches with ATMs at the eastern end of Yan'an Lu, and opposite the airline offices on Zunyi Lu.
Bookshops The Foreign Language Bookshop, on Yan'an Lu, is well stocked with classics, an eclectic range of children's books, maps of the city and province, and Chinese guidebooks on Guizhou.
Hospital Guiyang Emergency Centre (Guiyang Shi Jijiu Zhan) is on Huaxi Dadao on Guiyang's western side.
Internet access Two convenient places charging ¥2 an hour are on Yan'an Lu, just east of Ruijin Lu; and opposite China Southern on Zunyi Lu.
PSB The Foreign Affairs Department is in the city centre on Zhongshan Xi Lu.
Mail and telephones The main post office (daily 8am–7.30pm) is on the northeast corner of the Huabei Lu-Yan'an Lu intersection. There's a smaller branch, and international telephones, at the sprawling telecommunications building on Zhonghua Lu, facing Zunyi Lu.
Travel agents CITS are on Floor 7, Longquan Dasha, 1 Hequan Lu, near the corner with Yan'an Lu (Ⓣ0851/6901706, Ⓕ6901660, Ⓔgzcits @china.com). The 25-storey yellow tower is easy to find, but the entrance is not, especially as there is no CITS sign outside – you have to cut around to the back from Hequan Lu. Once there, you'll find the helpful staff speak English, though are not greatly aware of solo travellers' needs.

Qingyan

The remains of a Ming-dynasty fortified town 30km south of Guiyang at **QINGYAN** makes for an interesting few hours' excursion. Start by catching bus #201 from the Hebin depot on Ruijin Lu to **Huaxi** (40min; ¥1.7); at Huaxi, cross the road and pick up a minibus to Qingyan (20min; ¥2). On arrival, don't despair at the shabby main-road junction where the bus pulls up, but head west through the market area into the **old town**, which was founded in 1373 as a military outpost during the first major Han incursions into the region. The old town area forms a kilometre-long elipse, and while by no means comprising pristine period architecture (plenty of concrete and brick buildings put in an appearance), the original street plan is retained along with many temples, guildhalls, homes – even a couple of churches – and narrow, cobbled lanes, all built with skilful stonework and just beginning to be smartened up for tourism. The best area is at the southern end, where a flagstoned street lined with low wooden shops leads to the **Baisui memorial arch**, decorated with crouching lions, and out through the town wall into the fields via the solid stone **south gate**. There are plenty of places to **snack** as you wander – deep-fried balls of tofu are a local speciality – and even an atmospheric **hotel**, the *Guzhen Kezhan* (Ⓣ0851/3200031, ④), housed in an old guildhall next to the market. Transport connections back to Guiyang run until late afternoon.

Zunyi and the north

Northern Guizhou's mountainous reaches are famous for *baijiu* **distilleries**, with two interesting stops on the way up to Sichuan or Chongqing: the city of **Zunyi**, pivotal to modern Chinese history; and a wonderful spread of bamboo forests, waterfalls, and atypical red sandstone formations at **Chishui**. Zunyi is on the main road and rail routes, while Chishui lies off the beaten track, right up along the Sichuanese border in the northwestern corner of the province.

Zunyi and around

Some 170km north of Guiyang, **ZUNYI** is surrounded by heavy industry, but the city centre contains a pleasant older quarter surrounded by hilly parkland. It was here that the Communist army arrived on their **Long March** in January 1935, in disarray after months on the run and having suffered two defeats in their attempts to join up with sympathetic forces in Hunan. Having taken the city by surprise, the leadership convened the **Zunyi Conference**, a decision that was to alter China's history in that it saw Mao Zedong emerge as political head of the Communist Party. Previously, the party had been led by Russian Comintern advisors, who modelled their strategies on urban-based uprisings; Mao felt that China's revolution could only succeed by mobilizing the peasantry, and that the Communist forces should base themselves in the countryside to do this. His opinions carried the day, saving the Red Army from certain annihilation at the hands of the Guomindang and, though its conquest still lay fifteen years away, marking the Communists' first step towards Beijing. (For more on the Long March, see p.526.)

The City

The **Zunyi Conference Hall** (daily 8.30am–5pm; ¥40, includes nearby sites detailed below) is an attractive grey-brick, European-style house located in the older part of town on Ziyin Lu. It was upstairs, in a room barely big enough to hold the wooden table and chairs for the twenty delegates, that the conference was held from 15–17 January 1935, and where Mao, Zhu De, Zhou Enlai and Lu Shaoqi deposed the Russian Comintern's advisor Otto Braun (aka Li De)

Zunyi and the north

Zunyi	遵义	*zūnyì*
Fenghuang Shan Park	凤凰山公园	*fènghuángshān gōngyuán*
Monument to the Red Army Martyrs	红军烈士纪念埤	*hóngjūn lièshì jìniànbēi*
Zunyi Conference Hall	遵义会议址	*zūnyì huìyìzhǐ*
Accommodation		
Biyun Binguan	碧云宾馆	*bìyún bīnguǎn*
Xibu Dajiudian	西部大酒店	*xībù dàjiǔdiàn*
Youzheng Binguan	邮政宾馆	*yōuzhèng bīnguǎn*
Chishui	赤水	*chìshuǐ*
Bailong Falls	白龙瀑布	*báilóng pùbù*
Chishui Binguan	赤水宾馆	*chìshuǐ bīnguǎn*
Chishui Dajiudian	赤水大酒店	*chìshuǐ dàjiǔdiàn*
Sidong Gou	四洞沟	*sìdòng gōu*
Shizhangdong Falls	十丈洞瀑布	*shízhàngdòng pùbù*
Maotai	茅台	*máotái*

and his supporters, placing the course of the revolution in Chinese hands. Through the garden behind here is a small lane with a couple more contemporary buildings filled with period photos, maps and furniture: the former residence of **Bo Gu**, a Communist general criticized by Mao, who held that the marchers' military defeats were due to Bo's tactics; the **Site of the Red Army Political Department** in the grounds of a French Catholic Church, built in 1866 in an interesting compromise between Chinese and European Gothic styles; and the site of the **China Soviet Republic State Bank** – also known by the title of "Commission of Expropriation and Collection" – which funded the Communists by appropriating landlords' property, with cases of period banknotes stamped with the faces of Marx and Lenin displayed.

For a last taste of Red history, cross over the river and up into **Fenghuang Shan Park** (¥15) where the **Monument to the Red Army Martyrs** rises to the west, a reminder that only a quarter of the eighty thousand soldiers who started the Long March actually lived to finish it. However, it's grand rather than maudlin, with four huge red sandstone busts (vaguely resembling Lenin) supporting a floating, circular wall and a pillar topped with the Communist hammer and sickle.

Practicalities

Zunyi is awkwardly laid out around **Fenghuang Shan**, with arrival points and the newer part of town on the eastern side of the hill, and the older streets 2.5km away on the southern side, around the little **Xiang River**. The **bus and train stations** are within 100m of each other in a grimy area on **Beijing Lu**; from here, **Zhonghua Lu** and city buses #1, #6, #23 or #24 run southwest to the river, within walking distance of revolutionary sites – get off the bus at the big, open intersection by the river and cross to the huge **Bank of China** building, from where lanes lead up to the Conference Hall.

There's inexpensive **accommodation** up near the stations, which are surrounded by basic, noisy hostels (dorm beds ¥25) whose staff have no qualms about foreign custom. For something better, the *Xibu Dajiudian* (ⓣ0852/3191898; ❸), just around from the bus station on Waihuan Lu, is friendly and modern. Options in the nicer part of town include the post office-run *Youzheng Binguan* (ⓣ0852/8221244; ❺), across the intersection on the river; and the *Biyun Binguan* (ⓣ0852/8223671; ❻), a plusher place behind the Conference site on Yujin Lu. The station area has abundant places to get a bowl of noodles or plate of dumplings; otherwise, **eat** at your accommodation. **Leaving**, there are buses to Guiyang between 7am and 7pm (ordinary/express ¥25/40); three morning buses to Chishui (¥40) and trains through the day to Guiyang and Chongqing.

On to Sichuan: Maotai and Chishui

The rail line continues smoothly north of Zunyi to Chongqing, but there's also a roundabout route out of the province by road, taking in Guizhou's second most impressive waterfalls, near **Chishui**, up on the Sichuanese border some 350km and seven hours from Zunyi on local buses. The region you pass through, besides having some spectacular block-faulted limestone cliffs, positively reeks of brewing, with scores of large ceramic wine jars outside homes and businesses along the way, all sealed with red cloths and stamped with the character "*jiu*" (alcohol). The heart of this local industry is Renhuai County, more specifically the township of **MAOTAI**, nationally famous since travelling scholar Zheng Zhen declared it China's finest producer of sorghum spirits in 1704. There's nothing to see as such, but you'll know when you're close – roadside balustrades are shaped to resemble the Maotai brand's white porcelain bottle with its red diagonal stripe, and signs declare "Zhongguo Jiudu" (China's Spirit Capital). While no banquet would be complete without a bottle, Westerners tend to be of the opinion that Maotai is pretty indistinguishable from the contents of a cigarette lighter.

Chishui

CHISHUI is a small town on the south bank of the **Chishui River**, which marks the border with Sichuan. Geologically, this region belongs not to Guizhou but to Sichuan's **red sandstone** formations: *chishui* means "red water" and during the summer rains the river and its tributaries are coloured a vivid ochre with silt runoff from the surrounding hills. Being an undeveloped corner of the country, there are also some verdant pockets of subtropical **forests** featuring bamboos, three-metre-high *spinulosa* tree ferns, gingers, orchids and moss-covered rocks. The most accessible section is 14km away at **Sidonggou** – minibuses (¥5) run through the day from Renmin Lu to the **park gates** (¥30), from where 6km of flagstoned paths follow either side of a small, bright-red river, up through thick forest past three big **waterfalls** – including one split by a large boulder, and several water curtains to walk behind – to the trail's end at thirty-metre-high **Bailong Falls**. In addition to the scenery, there's plenty of local life: everywhere people are harvesting **bamboo**, weaving it into mats, and digging up fresh shoots; groups of farmers returning from market with pigs, horses laden with jerrycans of wine, and daily necessities; and several trackside **shrines**, carved with spirits' faces. After heavy rains, it's also worth heading 40km due south of Chishui to where the Fengxi River steps out at the **Shizhangdong Falls**, similar to the more famous Huangguoshu (see p.770) – buses run in summer.

Chishui is a quiet place, a kilometre broad, with no real centre; the **bus station** is on Renmin Lu, which runs downhill for 700m to the river. Along the way, there are cheap rooms at the *Chishui Dajiudian* (❷), the alternative being the upmarket *Chishui Binguan* (❻), east down Nanzheng Jie, and many places to **eat** scattered around. **Leaving**, three buses run daily to Zunyi; for Luzhou and connections to Yibin in Sichuan (see p.900), you might have to cross the bridge to the township of **Jiuzhi** and pick up services there.

Eastern Guizhou

The journey from Guiyang into **eastern Guizhou** passes through a quintessentially Southeast Asian landscape of high hills cut by rivers, and dotted with dark wooden houses with buffaloes plodding around rice terraces; women working in the fields have babies strapped to their backs under brightly quilted pads, and their long braided hair is coiled into buns secured by fluorescent plastic combs. They are Miao, and the scene marks the border of the **Miao and Dong Autonomous Prefecture**, arguably the best place in China to meet ethnic peoples on their own terms. Miao villages around the district capital, **Kaili**, are noted for their hundred or more annual **festivals**, which though increasingly touristed are such exuberant social occasions that – so far – there's little sign of their cultural integrity being undermined. Beyond Kaili, the adventurous can head southeast on public buses to the mountainous border with Guangxi province, where **Dong** hamlets sport their unique drum towers and bridges (see p.732), or push on northeast through the pretty countryside surrounding **Zhenyuan** to ascend **Fanjing Shan's tough steps and thick** cloud forests.

Even if you don't plan anything so energetic, the region is still enjoyable on a daily basis – the attractive home of a friendly people who take pride in their traditions. **Travelling around**, minibuses cover more destinations and leave more frequently than long-distance buses, but to reach more remote corners you'll probably have to aim for the nearest main-road settlement and take pot luck with tractor taxis or whatever else is available – there's also scope for some ad hoc **hiking**.

Kaili

KAILI, 170km east from Guiyang, is a moderately industrialized, easy-going focus for China's 7.5 million **Miao**, though the town is more a service centre than a sight in its own right. The most interesting **market area** is along the eastern end of Ximen Jie, a narrow street packed with village-like stalls selling vegetables, trinkets, meat and even livestock. Paths head up from here to **Dage Park**, a tiny hilltop area where old men gather to smoke and decorate the trees with their caged songbirds – there's also a wooden **pagoda** on the summit, home to a mix of incense-blackened Taoist statuary smeared with bloody chicken feathers. The town's only other diversion is the **museum** (¥10) at the far end of Zhaoshan Lu, two dusty floors of bright festival garments and silver jewellery, with more of the same on sale in the downstairs atrium.

Kaili and Miao villages

Kaili	凯里	*kǎilǐ*
Dage Park	大阁公园	*dàgé gōngyuán*
Dashizi	大十子	*dàshí zi*
Kaili Museum	民族博物馆	*mínzú bówùguǎn*
Accommodation		
Lidu Jiari Jiudian	丽都假日酒店	*lìdū jiàrì jiǔdiàn*
Petroleum Hotel	石油宾馆	*shíyóu bīnguǎn*
Xin Guotai Dajiudian	新国泰大酒店	*xīn guótài dàjiiǔdiàn*
Yingpanpo Binguan	营盘坡宾馆	*yíngpánpō bīnguǎn*
Chong An	重安	*chóng'ān*
Chong An Jiang Binguan	重安江宾馆	*chóngānjiāng bīnguǎn*
Xiao Jiangnan	小江南	*xiǎojiāng nán*
Huangping	黄平	*huángpíng*
Feiyun Dong	飞云洞	*fēiyún dòng*
Langde Shang	郎德上	*lángdé shàng*
Leishan	雷山	*léishān*
Matang	麻塘	*mátáng*
Xianglu Shan	香炉山	*xiānglú shān*
Nanhua	南花	*nánhuā*
Shibing	施秉	*shībǐng*
Shanhe Dajiudian	山河大酒店	*shānhé dàjiǔdiàn*
Shidong	施洞	*shīdòng*
Taijiang	台江	*táijiāng*
Lidu Lüguan	丽都 旅馆	*lìdū lǚguǎn*
Wenchang Ge	文场阁	*wénchǎng gé*
Xingguang Gongguang	星光公馆	*xīngguāng gōnggǔan*
Xijiang	西江	*xījiāng*

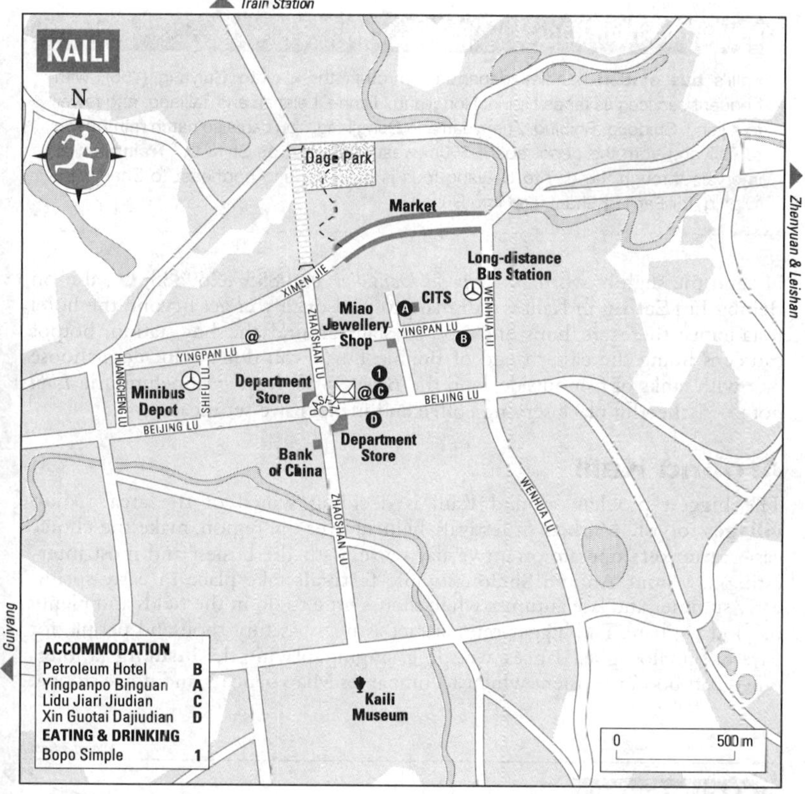

Practicalities

Kaili is oriented around the Beijing Lu–Zhaoshan Lu crossroads, known as **Dashizi**. The **train station** is 3km to the north, where taxis and buses #1 and #2 meet arrivals, while the **long-distance bus station** is central on Wenhua Bei Lu. The main **Bank of China** and ATM is on Zhaoshan Lu (foreign exchange Mon–Fri 8.30–11am & 2–5pm) – the last branch until you reach Guilin in Guangxi province, if you're heading that way – and the **post office** is right on Dashizi. There's also a convenient **Internet bar** just off the street near the *Lidu* hotel on Beijing Lu. For **information** about village festivals and market days, useful bilingual maps of Kaili and its environs, and guides who know the area backwards, call in on Kaili's superb **CITS**, just left inside the gates at the *Yingpanpo Binguan* (daily 8.30–11.30am & 2.30–5pm; ⓣ0855/8250665, ⓕ8222506 ⓦwww.crt118.com) – ask for Wu Zeng Ou (ⓔzengouwu@hotmail.com).

The cheapest foreigner-friendly **accommodation** is near the bus station on Yingpan Lu, where the under-maintained *Petroleum Hotel* (ⓣ0855/8234331; ③, dorm beds ¥40) has some doubles with air conditioning and bathroom. Otherwise your options are mid-range and include the *Yingpanpo Binguan* (ⓣ0855/3833333, ⓕ3837776; ⑤); *Lidu Jiari Jiudian* (ⓣ0855/8266662, ⓕ8266663; ⑤), a well-maintained business hotel offering discounts on Beijing

Moving on from Kaili

Kaili's **bus station** handles departures through the day to Guiyang (¥55), with frequent services as far as Liping, Rongjiang, Jianhe, Leishan and Taijiang, and fewer to Xijiang, Shidong, Shibing, Zhenyuan and Congjiang. You can also catch **minibuses** to Guiyang from the depot about 500m west of Dashizi on Shifu Lu. **Trains** run at intervals through the day to Guiyang (bus is quicker), and northeast to Zhenyuan, Yuping (for Fanjing Shan), and into Hunan.

Lu; and the slightly worn *Xin Guotai Dajiudian* (Ⓣ0855/8269888; ⑤), also on Beijing Lu. **Eating** in Kaili is a dismal prospect once you get beyond the hotel restaurants; there are buns and noodle stalls around the bus station, hotpot canteens lining the eastern end of Beijing Lu (if you don't want dog, choose one with tanks of fish outside), and the *Bopo Simple Restaurant* behind the *Lidu* hotel – a cheerful place serving coffee and inexpensive set meals.

Around Kaili

The biggest problem around Kaili is deciding which of the area's **Miao villages** to visit. Markets or festivals, held all over the region, make the choice easier: **markets** operate on a five-day cycle, with the busiest and most interesting at Chong An and Shidong; while **festivals** take place in early spring, early summer and late autumn, when there's little to do in the fields and plenty of food to share. The bigger ones attract as many as fifty thousand people for days of buffalo fights, dances, wrestling, singing, playing the **lusheng** (a long-piped bamboo instrument which accompanies Miao dances), and horse or boat

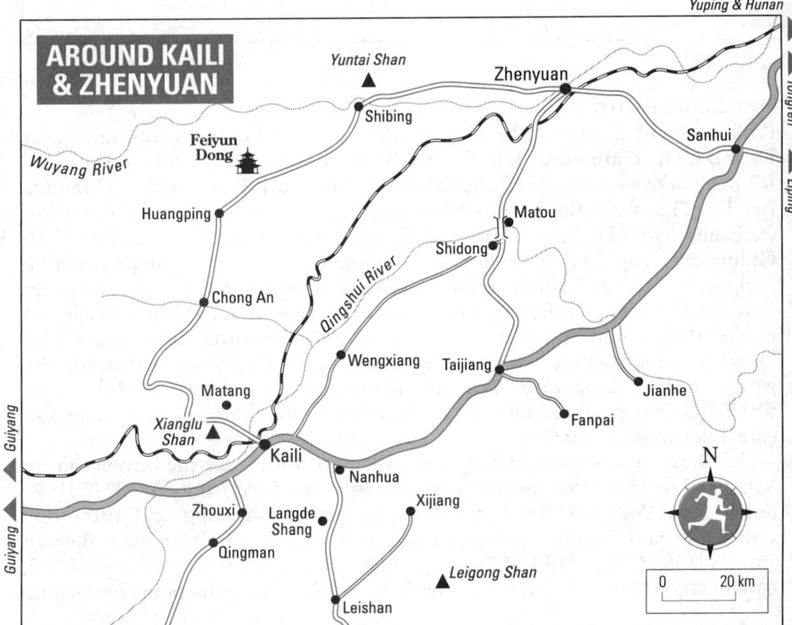

races. Participants dress in multicoloured finery, and the action often crosses over to the spectators. The biggest event of the year is the springtime **Sisters' Meal**, the traditional time for girls to choose a partner – see the box on p.764 – though smaller events, where tourists are less expected, can be that much more intimate. If planning a trip to coincide with particular events, be careful of **dates**, as Chinese information sometimes confuses lunar and Gregorian calendars – "9 February", for instance, might mean "the ninth day of the second lunar month".

If there's nothing special going on, the best area to concentrate on is the stretch south of Kaili down to Leishan and Xijiang, which has the most accessible and picturesque **villages**. While some of these are interesting in themselves, outside of the festival season people will be working in the fields, and smaller places may appear completely deserted. With luck, however, you'll be invited to tour the village, look around the distinctive wooden homes, fed – pickled vegetables and sour chicken hotpot, with copious amounts of **nomijiu**, a powerfully soporific rice wine, to wash things down – and asked if you'd like to see some antique wedding garments or have a young woman don full festival regalia for your camera. All this will cost, but its offered in good humour and worth the price; people often have embroidery or silver to sell, for which bargaining is essential.

CITS **tours** aside, all the villages below are connected by at least daily bus services from Kaili, and also make fine stopovers on the way into the Rongjiang or Zhenyuan regions. Return transport can leave quite early, however, so be prepared to stay the night or hitch back if you leave things too late.

The Miao

"Miao" is a Chinese word; Miao call themselves "Hmong", and their population, while centred in China and Guizhou in particular, is also spread through Vietnam, Laos and Burma. Treated with disdain and forced off their lands by the Qing-dynasty government, rebels in Guizhou such as local boy **Zhang Xiumei** took a lesson from the Taipings in adjacent Guangxi and seeded their own **uprising** in 1854, which – though involving the whole province, and not just ethnic minorities – was centred in the Miao heartlands. The uprising, which at its height saw Guiyang almost fall to the rebels, was only put down in late 1873 after troops were brought in from neighbouring Sichuan and Hunan provinces, and at the cost of a huge slaughter involving whole towns being obliterated – out of a provincial population of seven million, over half died during the revolt.

Outsiders have found it useful to identify separate Miao communities by their locally distinct ornamentation. Most eye-catching are the detailed **embroideries**: girls start practising with sashes and dress sleeves at an early age; the more accomplished their work, the higher their social standing. Dresses for festivals and weddings are so intricate that they take years to complete, and often become treasured heirlooms. Patterns are sometimes abstract, sometimes illustrative, incorporating plant designs, butterfly (the bringer of spring and indicating hoped-for change), dragon, fish – a China-wide good luck symbol – and buffalo motifs. Each region produces its own styles, such as the sequinned, curly green and red designs from the southerly **Leishan** district, **Chong'an**'s dark geometric work, and the bright, fiery lions and dragons of **Taijiang**. Some places supplement embroidery with other techniques – **batik** from the Gejia villages northwest of Kaili is the best known.

Many of the design themes recur in Miao **silverwork**, the most elaborate pieces being made for wedding assemblages. Women appear at some festivals weighed down with coil necklaces, spiral earrings and huge headpieces, all of which are embossed or shaped into flowers, bells and beasts.

Northwest of Kaili

The 110-kilometre-long road northwest from **Kaili to Shibing** passes a host of interesting villages and gets you much of the way to Zhenyuan (see p.764; note that buses direct from Kaili to Zhenyuan don't generally use this route). Buses leave from Kaili's main bus station, and the whole trip to Shibing costs ¥45 or so.

The first place to aim for is **MATANG**, a village 20km from Kaili, home of the **Gejia** (or Geyi), a Miao subgroup. Tell the bus driver where you're heading; the track to Matang heads off across the paddy fields from below square-topped **Xianglu Shan**, the mountain where rebel leader Zhang Xiumei met his end at the hands of imperial troops in 1873 – a big **festival** here each August commemorates the event. It's a twenty-minute walk from the main road to the village, a cluster of muddy fields and dark wooden houses, and you'll be mobbed on arrival to buy jewellery, swirly **batik** cloths and characteristic orange and yellow embroidery. To move onwards from Matang, return to the main road and flag down a passing vehicle.

Next stop is **CHONG AN**, a dishevelled riverside town about 50km north of Matang with the friendly, basic *Xiao Jiangnan* guesthouse (¥40 per person) or the plusher *Chong An Jiang Binguan* (❷), water-powered mills downstream, and a small **nunnery** just off the Kaili road, reached over a chain-and-plank bridge. Make sure you catch Chong An's fifth-day **market**, where you'll be battered and bruised by crowds of diminutive Miao grandmothers as they bargain for local crafts, or bring in clothes (everything from traditional pleated skirts to jeans) for dyeing in boiling vats of indigo. Children around here often wear bright blue "tiger hats", with tufted fabric ears and silver embellishments, which ward off bad luck. There are also some interesting villages near Chong An, and your accommodation may be able to organize guided **walks**.

Some 20km north again on the Shibing road, **HUANGPING**, known for its **silversmiths**, is a larger market town with a few old buildings. Between here and Shibing you pass **Feiyun Dong** (¥8), a quiet Taoist temple surrounded by trees and rocky outcrops, whose moss-covered main hall houses a **museum** of Miao crafts, a dragon-boat prow and a big bronze drum.

Set in a wide, humid valley 34km from Huangping, **SHIBING** is a busy, ordinary modern town laid out east–west along the south bank of the **Wuyang River**; the bus station is at the west end. If you get stuck between buses, the best bet for **accommodation** is the *Shan He Dajiudian* (❸), across the river by the bridge, or there are cheaper beds at the bus-station hostel (❶). **Moving on**, buses and minibuses set off when full back along the Kaili road, and east to Zhenyuan (2hr; ¥8) until late afternoon.

South of Kaili

The prettiest villages and scenery lie **south of Kaili** on the forty-five-kilometre road to **Leishan**, which follows a deep, winding river valley and is a rewarding route if you don't have much time. Buses run back and forth to Leishan through the day, and the best way to travel is simply to ask the driver to stop when you see somewhere you want to check out, then catch another vehicle when you've finished. At Leishan there's further transport northeast to the large village of **Xijiang**, surrounded by some easy walks. Irregular services also run to Xijiang from Kaili – though these often save time by taking entertaining but hair-raising cross-country diversions, avoiding the places below.

Around 13km from Kaili, **NANHUA** is the official "Miao Customs Performance Village", where hornfuls of *no mijiu*, dances and lusheng performances, and souvenirs are all laid on daily for tour buses. It's a nice setting, with a number of old wooden houses tucked into a fold in the hillside. Far better, however, is 12km further south at **LANGDE SHANG**, a rebel base during the Miao Uprising and still a tremendously photogenic collection of wooden houses, cobbles, fields and chickens set on a terraced hillside capped in pine trees, a twenty-minute walk from the main road. They are also used to tourists, with plenty of silverwork thrust at you as you wander – word gets around if you're not interested, however.

Twenty kilometres south of here, **LEISHAN** is a famous tea-growing region ninety minutes from Kaili. The formerly grubby town is currently being considerably rebuilt – once finished, **accommodation** here will range from basic to upmarket – though there are no sights as such. However, in a valley 40km (two hours) northeast of Leishan – there are direct buses from Kaili as well as Leishan – is **XIJIANG**, an incredible collection of closely packed wooden houses built on river stone foundations, all ranged up the side of two adjacent hills. When you've had enough of farmyard smells among the narrow, stepped, lanes, walk up through the village and onto the terraced fields above, where you could hike around for hours – views are tremendous. Xijiang has two basic **guesthouses** (❶) – the one above the post office, near where the buses pull up, is best – and a couple of early-closing shops selling rice noodles (boiled or fried). On market days, you can get transport back to Kaili or Leishan until dark; at other times, don't leave it this late, and confirm supposed departure times with bus drivers.

Southeast of Leishan are the fringes of a remote landscape of steep mountain terraces and dark wooden villages dominated by elaborately shaped towers and bridges that spill into Guangxi province: **Dong country**. Your first destination is the town of **Rongjiang**, 100km southeast of Leishan and connected to Kaili by direct buses: for more about the Dong, their architecture, and details of the trip, see pp.731–736.

Northeast of Kaili

The small town of **TAIJIANG** lies 55km northeast of Kaili on the junction of the Sansui and Shidong roads, its sports ground the venue for the big **Sisters' Meal Festival** held on the fifteenth day of the third lunar month (April/May – see p.764). A collection of cheap modern buildings centred on a crossroads about 700m from the main road, Taijiang features a daily **market** south of the crossroads, and **Wenchang Ge**, a recently restored Qing temple at the northern end of town, though it's often locked. Out on the highway, a paved area surrounds a **statue** of Zhang Xiumei (or "Zangb Xongt Mil" as it's written in Hmong), who was born at the nearby village of Bading Zhai in 1823. Though his role in the Miao Uprising is murky, there's no doubt that Taijiang was a major rebel base from 1855 until November 1870, when imperial troops are said to have killed 10,000 people and destroyed the town. Taijiang's **accommodation** is limited to guesthouses which surround the crossroads, such as *Lidu Lüguan* (❶), or the clean *Xingguang Gongguan* (Ⓣ0855/5328396; ❸), on the road between town and the highway.

Beyond Taijiang, there are two buses daily for the final two-hour, forty-kilometre leg to Shidong, through some of the most beautiful countryside this part of China can provide – there's also transport direct to Shidong from Kaili along a different road. **SHIDONG** itself is a tiny farming town set beside flat fields on a bend in the blue **Qingshui River**, with a single hotel (❷) and a great **market**, with splendid modern silverwork and embroideries for sale. The river is the setting of the region's biggest **dragon-boat festival**, which follows on from Taijiang's Sisters' Meal celebrations. This riotous occasion does not, as in

Sisters' Meal

Taijiang's **Sisters' Meal festival**, where Miao teenagers from all over the region meet to choose a partner, is the best one to catch. The town fills beyond capacity for the two-day event, crowds jostling between lottery stalls and markets, buying local produce and, of course, embroidery and silverwork. More of this is being worn by teenage girls from villages around Taijiang, who gamely tramp up and down the streets, sweltering under the weight of their decorated jackets and silver jewellery, jingling as they walk. By nine in the morning there's hardly standing room left in the sports ground, ready for the official opening an hour later; once the necessary speeches are out the way, things formally kick off with two hours of energetic **dancing and lusheng playing**, after which the party breaks up into smaller rings, dancers and musicians practising for bigger things later on in the festivities, or just flirting – this is a teenagers' festival, after all.

Discreet **cockfighting** (not to the death) and much drinking of *mijiu* carries on through the afternoon, then at dusk the **dragon-lantern dances** get under way, a half-dozen teams carrying their wire-and-crepe, twenty-metre-long hollow dragons and accompanying model birds and butterflies into the main street. Candles are lit and placed inside the animals before things begin in earnest, the dragons animated into chasing swirls by the dancers, who charge up and down the street battling with each other; the mayhem is increased by drummers, whooping crowds, and fireworks tossed at leisure into the throng.

Day two sees the action shifting a couple of kilometres west of town to a wide river valley, venue for mid-morning **buffalo fights**. Bloodless trials of strength between two bulls, these draw a good five thousand spectators who assemble around the ill-defined fighting grounds while competitors are paraded up and down, decked out with plaited caps, coloured flags and pheasant tail-feathers, and numbers painted in red on their flanks. The fights each last a few minutes, a skull-cracking charge ending in head-to-head wrestling with locked horns, bulls scrabbling for purchase; the crowds get as close as possible, scattering wildly when one bull suddenly turns tail and bolts, pursued by the victor. Back in town, the **Sisters' Meal** itself is under way, a largely personal affair where young men give parcels of multicoloured **sticky rice** to their prospective partner: a pair of chopsticks buried inside returned rice is an acceptance, a single chopstick or – even worse – a **chilli**, a firm refusal. The festival winds up that night back at the sports ground, the closing dances all held under floodlights, and followed again by much livelier, ad hoc dancing after which couples drift off into the dark.

the rest of China, commemorate the memory of Qu Yuan's suicide in 280 BC (see p.52), but celebrates a local hero who battled Han invaders. If you're here at this time then you'll be drunk, as a roadblock of young women in festival dress stops arrivals outside town, a draught of *mijiu* from a buffalo horn the price of passage – touch the horn with your hands and you have to drain it. Masses of transport is laid on for the festival, but at other times there are only a couple of buses a day back south from outside the hotel. To continue north **to Zhenyuan**, check with locals – at present, your best bet is to head north to the bridge and wait for the Kaili–Zhenyuan bus to pass.

Zhenyuan

A characterful place, **ZHENYUAN** was founded two thousand years ago, though today's town – occupying a straight, constricted valley 100km northeast of Kaili on the aquamarine **Wuyang River** – sprang up in the Ming dynasty to guard the trade route through to central China. The river runs westwards,

▲ Miao girls at the Sisters' Meal Festival

with Zhenyuan's tall houses piled together along two narrow, two-kilometre-long streets, one on either bank, the cliffs rising behind. The sole attraction on the south side is a fragment of the **old stone town wall** hidden between houses just west of the main bridge, which you can walk along for 100m. North of the river, **Tianhou Gong** (¥2) is a four-hundred-year-old Taoist complex housing Buddhist statuary at the west end of town, with a balcony overhanging the street. Continuing east, you pass the main bridge and enter Zhenyuan's **old quarter**, about 500m of wood and stone buildings in the Qing style, backed up against stony cliffs. The street eventually crosses the river via a multiple-arch, solid stone span leading to **Qinglong Dong** (¥30), a sixteenth-century temple currently being expanded, whose separate Taoist, Buddhist and Confucian halls appear to grow out of a cliff face, all dripping wet and hung with vines. If possible, catch the spectacular **dragon-boat races** here in the middle of June.

Both arrival points are at the west side of town, the **train station** on the south bank, and **bus station** on the north. The best **accommodation** lies on the south side of the river, where the *Jinfenghuang Zhoudaisuo* (❸), *Lidu Binguan* (Ⓣ0855/5726560; ❹) and *Rongfeng Binguan* (with/without bathroom ❸/❷) all offer clean, basic rooms and places to **eat**.

Zhenyuan

Zhenyuan	镇远	*zhènyuǎn*
Jinfenghuang Zhaodaisuo	金凤凰招待所	*jīnfènghuáng zhāodàisuǒ*
Lidu Binguan	丽都宾馆	*lìdū bīnguǎn*
Old Town Wall	卫城恒	*wèichénghéng*
Qinglong Dong	青龙洞	*qīnglóng dòng*
Rongfeng Binguan	容丰宾馆	*róngfēng bīnguǎn*
Tianhou Gong	天后宫	*tiānhòu gōng*
Wuyang River	舞阳河	*wǔyáng hé*

Moving on from Zhenyuan

There are several daily **trains** from Zhenyuan southwest to Kaili and Guiyang, and northwest via **Yuping** (1hr), jumping-off point for Fanjing Shan, to Huaihua (for connections to Zhangjiajie, p.505) and Changsha. Buy tickets from the station the day before travel if you don't want to stand. Plenty of **buses** through the day run west **to Shibing** (2hr), with a few direct services to Kaili, Shidong, Taijiang and Guiyang.

Fanjing Shan

Hidden away in Guizhou's northeastern corner, not far from the borders with Hunan and Chongqing, **Fanjing Shan** is the province's sole holy mountain. The temples today are in ruins, however, and the real reason to visit is to experience these remote, wild cloud forests and perhaps see rare *jinsi hou,* **golden monkeys**. Around 170 live on Fanjing Shan's upper reaches and it's easy to recognize their slight build, big lips, tiny nose and, in males, vivid orange-gold fur, should you be lucky enough to spot one. Just be aware that the ascent to the mountain's 2500m summit involves more than seven thousand stairs, which follow steep ridges with no regard for gradient. Take a torch and something warm for the top – it snows in winter – but don't bring up more than a day-pack.

The mountain is best reached via **Yuping**, a stop on the rail line running northeast from Guiyang via Kaili and Zhenyuan into Hunan. Exit left out of the station and you'll find **buses** through the day for the two-hour run to **Jiangkou**, from where there are further frequent departures for the final 30km to the **park gates** (¥50) at **Heiwan**, on the moutain's south side. Heiwan is a strangely despondent collection of food stalls, shops selling ponchos and walking sticks (both a good idea), with **accommodation** at the *Longfeng Binguan* (❸) and a **police station** where they might take down your details. **Maps** of the mountain seem unavailable. From Heiwan, it's a further 9km or so to the trailhead; minibuses ask ¥40 split between the passengers, but the road – which follows the river uphill through the forest – is so frequently cut by landslides that you might have to walk part of it anyway. At the end of the road, a covered food stall marks the start of Fanjing Shan's **steps**, which are numbered at intervals with red paint and carved inscriptions. The first section is probably the steepest, but there's little relief until you're well past the halfway point; further food and drink shacks provide sustenance until step 4500 (you can sleep at these places too) and then there's nothing until the top. The forest – hung with vines and old man's beard and with a dwarf bamboo understorey – is vibrantly green in summer, and also incredibly humid; each breath is like inhaling hot fog. Allow between three and five hours to reach the top, where there are two **places to stay** (dorm beds ¥20): the first in a concrete blockhouse just on the edge of the forest; the second in a wooden bunkhouse attached to **Zhenguo Si**, a tiny, barely functional temple 100m further up in the open – both provide cooked **meals**.

Give yourself a day to explore the summit area, which is a mix of open heath, woodland, rhododendron thickets and strangely piled rock formations such as **Mogu Shi**, "Mushroom Rocks". A short walk from Zhenguo Si, **Jinding**, the Golden Summit, is a steep, stocky peak capped by another small temple. Well-marked **paths** head north to more temple ruins and, ultimately, down off the back of the mountain via the **north gate**.

On from Fanjing Shan

While you can simply retrace your steps to Jinagkou and catch buses east **to Huaihua** in Hunan and then on to Zhangjiajie or Fenghuang (see pp.506–508),

Fanjing Shan		
Yuping	玉屏	*yùpíng*
Jiangkou	江口	*jiāngkǒu*
Fanjing Shan	梵净山	*fánjìng shān*
Golden Monkey	金丝猴	*jīnsī hóu*
Heiwan	黑湾	*hēiwān*
Jinding	金顶	*jīndǐng*
Longfeng Binguan	龙风宾馆	*lóngfēng bīnguǎn*
Mogu Shi	蘑菇石	*mógū shí*
Zhenguo Si	镇国寺	*zhènguó sì*
Xiyang	西阳镇	*xīyáng zhèn*
Longtan	龙潭	*lóngtán*
Gongtan	龚滩	*gōngtān*

there's also an interesting route **to Chongqing** from Fanjing Shan's north gate. From here, first catch a bus to the town of **Xiyang**, where you should stay the night and then day-trip by bus to either **Longtan** or **Gongtan**, two old towns each a couple of hours away with heaps of antique buildings. From Xiyang, there are also daily buses for the twelve-hour trip to Chongqing.

Western Guizhou

Extending for 350km between Guiyang and the border with Yunnan province, **Western Guizhou** is a desperately poor region of beautiful mountainous country and depressingly functional mining towns. **Anshun** is a transit hub for visiting **Bouyei villages**, the tourist magnets of **Longgong Caves** and **Huangguoshu Falls** and the remoter, more spectacular **Zhijin Caves**.

All routes west from Anshun ultimately lead to Yunnan's capital, Kunming (see p.779), whether you travel by bus along one of the three highways or – more comfortably – take the train. The only place worth a special stopover along the way is the northwesterly wildfowl sanctuary of **Caohai** – being poled around this shallow lake on a sunny day is one of Guizhou's highlights. Transport is straightforward, though note that the west has **no banks** capable of changing travellers' cheques.

Anshun

Some 100km west of Guiyang, **ANSHUN** was established as a garrisoned outpost in Ming times to keep an eye on the empire's unruly fringes. Today the town is a healthy but rough-around-the-edges marketplace, whose modern facade vanishes the moment you leave the main roads and find yourself among muddy alleys running between tumbledown shacks and wobbly wooden houses. The central crossroads is overlooked to the northwest by a hillock topped by **Bai Ta**, a short Ming-dynasty pagoda, with a park around the base containing some representative, restored antique buildings, including a long stone **church** with a Chinese-style bell tower. The other point of interest is **Wenhua Miao** (¥3), a Ming Confucian hall hidden away in the northeastern backstreets that, while somewhat neglected, has some superbly carved dragon pillars, which rival those at Qufu's Confucius Mansion (p.330).

Western Guizhou

Anshun	安顺	*ānshùn*
Bai Ta	白塔	*báitǎ*
Beimen Bus Station	北门客车站	*běimén kèchēzhàn*
Gourou Wang	狗肉王	*gǒuròu wáng*
Huayou Binguan	华油宾馆	*huáyóu bīnguǎn*
Main Bus Station	客车南站	*kèchē nánzhàn*
Ruofei Binguan	若飞宾馆	*ruòfēi bīnguǎn*
Wenhua Miao	文化庙	*wénhuà miào*
West Bus Station	客车西站	*kèchē xīzhàn*
Xixiu Shan Binguan	西秀山宾馆	*xīxiùshān bīnguǎn*
Youju Zhaodaisuo	邮局招待所	*yóujú zhāodàisuǒ*
Shitou Zhai	石头寨	*shítou zhài*
Zhenning	镇宁	*zhènníng*
Tianlong	天龙	*tiānlóng*
Wulong Si	伍龙寺	*wǔlóngsì*
Pingba	平坝	*píngbà*
Tiantai Shan	天台山	*tiāntái shān*
Longgong and Huangguoshu		
Guanling	关岭	*guānlǐng*
Guanyin Dong	观音洞	*guānyīng dòng*
Huangguoshu Falls	黄果树瀑布	*huángguǒshù pùbù*
Long Gong	龙宫	*lónggōng*
Longgong Caves	龙宫洞	*lónggōng dòng*
Yulong Dong	玉龙洞	*yùlóngdòng*
Liupanshui	六盘水	*liùpánshuǐ*
Weining	威宁	*wēiníng*
Black-necked Crane	黑颈鹤	*hēijǐng hè*
Caohai	草海	*cǎohǎi*
Heijing He Binguan	黑颈鹤宾馆	*hēijǐnghè bīnguǎn*
Jinye Binguan	金叶宾馆	*jīnyè bīnguǎn*
Juhongxuan Zhaodaisuo	聚弘轩招待所	*jùhóngxuān zhāodàisuǒ*
Zhijin	织金	*zhījīn*
Jinye Binguan	金叶宾馆	*jīnyè bīnguǎn*
Zhijin Caves	织金洞	*zhījīn dòng*

Practicalities

Anshun centres on **Xin Dashizi**, the large crossroads below Bai Ta (where you'll also find a **Bank of China** with an ATM). The **main bus station**, about 500m south of here on Zhonghua Nan Lu, handles traffic to Guiyang, Zhenning, Huangguoshu and Kunming; the **train station** (for everywhere between Guiyang and Kunming) is another 700m south again. North from Xin Dashizi, a strip of Zhonghua Lu forms the town's high street, running out of town a kilometre later past the **Beimen bus station** (for Zhijin). Finally, the small **west bus station**, 150m west of Xin Dashizi on Tashan Xi Lu, has further, frequent departures to Zhenning, Tianlong, Guiyang, Huangguoshu and Longgong – don't bother with the ticket office here, simply go around the back and shout your destination.

The cheapest **accommodation** likely to accept foreigners is the *Youju Zhaodaisuo* (❸) just north of the main bus station beside the Post Office; if they say no, there's the nearby *Ruofei Binguan* at 48 Zhonghua Nan Lu (☎0853/3320228; ❺); the upmarket *Xixiu Shan Binguan* opposite at 63 Zhonghua Nan Lu

(Ⓣ0853/2211888, Ⓕ2211801; ⑥); and cheaper *Huayou Binguan* (Ⓣ0853/3226021, Ⓕ3226020; ④), west of Xin Dashizi at 15 Tashan Xi Lu. In addition to the hotel **restaurants**, there are more north of Xin Dashizi on Zhonghua Lu, including a branch of *Dico's*, several hotpot places, and the *Gourou Wang*, a popular spot for dog.

Around Anshun

The land between the limestone hills **around Anshun** is intensely farmed by blue-skirted **Bouyei** busy planting rice or ploughing muddy flats with buffalo. The Bouyei number 2.5 million and range throughout southwestern Guizhou, though this is their heartland, their village buildings artfully constructed from split stone and roofed in large, irregularly laid slate tiles. Bouyei specialities include blue and white **batik work** and **Ground Opera** or *dixi*, in which performers wear brightly painted wooden masks; though native to the region and overlaid with animistic rituals, the current forms are said to have been imported along with Han troops in the Ming dynasty, and are based on Chinese tales such as the *Three Kingdoms*. The Spring Festival period is a good time to see a performance, held in many **villages** around Anshun – Guiyang's CITS can recommend likely locations.

The Anshun area's key draws, however, are **Longgong Caves** and **Huangguoshu Falls**, which can be fitted into a day-trip from either here or Guiyang. The caves are flooded and romantically require boats for some of the route, but Huangguoshu – while impressive on a good day – doesn't quite live up to its reputation. Finally, the trip north to the splendid **Zhijin Caves** requires an overnight stop, though it's well worth the effort.

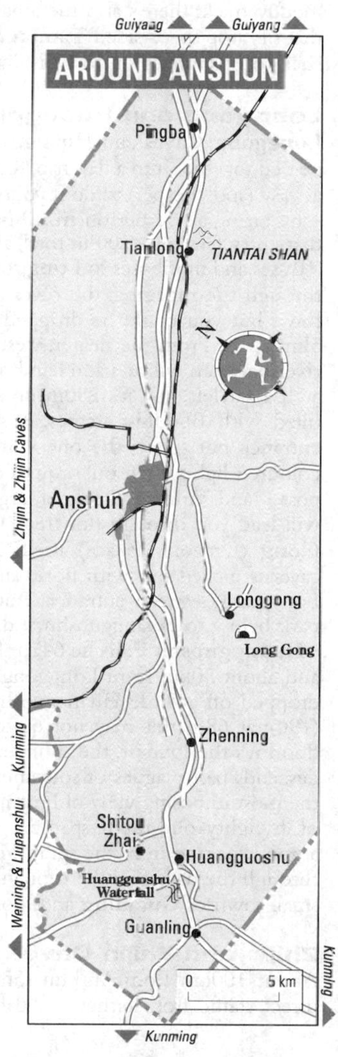

Shitou Zhai and Tianlong

While there are many Bouyei villages around Anshun, two are within easy striking distance. The first, six-hundred-year-old **SHITOU ZHAI**, lies 30km southwest off the Huangguoshu road past **Zhenning**; tell the driver, and Huangguoshu buses from the west station (40min; ¥6) will drop you at the junction, leaving a two-kilometre walk along a quiet road to the **village gates** (¥20). The fact that there's an entry fee betrays Shitou Zhai's popularity, but it's also a pretty spot, with forty or so stone houses grouped around a rocky hillock, all surrounded by vegetable plots. You'll be offered batik jackets, and might witness the whole process, from drawing the designs in wax, to dyeing in indigo and boiling the wax away to leave a white pattern. You could also walk out to similar surrounding villages, none of which charges admission. To return, walk back to the main road and flag down buses to Huangguoshu, Anshun or Zhenning (for transport to either).

An alternative lies 27km east of Anshun at **TIANLONG**, reached from the main bus station (30min; ¥5.5). The bus leaves you in a narrow, grubby main street choked with stalls, trucks and fumes, but duck south and you're immediately in the **old town**, a small maze of narrow lanes, antique stone and wood buildings with slit windows, running streams and errant livestock. Resemblances to old European villages are enhanced by the nineteenth-century **church-school** at the west end, built by French priests and now housing a collection of **ground opera masks** – Tianlong is a *dixi* centre. Three kilometres east down a muddy track, there's also the amazing **Wulong Si**, a fortress-like stone temple that sits atop sheer-sided **Tiantai Shan**. You can catch transport through the day back to Anshun, or on to Guiyang via **Pingba** town.

Longgong and Huangguoshu Falls

Longgong Caves and **Huangguoshu Falls** lie southwest of Anshun, and can be tied together into a day-trip. Tours run from Guiyang, but from Anshun it's just as easy (and cheaper) to do it yourself, either on public transport or – for a group – by hiring a five-person **minibus** (¥300 for the day) at the main station. Note that entry fees top ¥200 in total, and that Longgong requires a bit of walking.

Buses and minibuses to **Longgong** (1hr; ¥5–10) depart Anshun's west station through the morning; the caves are at the end of a country road 28km from town but you could be dropped at either **entrance** (¥120), which are about 5km apart. From the nearer, western gate, you begin by being ferried down a river between willows and bamboo, to a small knot of houses; walk through the arch, bear left, and it's 250m up some steps to **Guanyin Dong**, a broad cave filled with Buddhist statues. A seemingly minor path continues around the entrance but this is the one you want: it leads through a short cavern lit by coloured lights, then out around a hillside to **Jiujiu Tun** – site of an old guard post – and **Yulong Dong**, a large and spectacular cave system which a guide will lead you through (for free). Out the other side, a small river enters **Long Gong** (Dragon's Palace) itself, a two-stage boat ride through tall, flooded caverns picked out with florid lighting, exiting the caves into a broad pool at Longgong's eastern entrance. Transport until late afternoon runs from the car park below to Huangguoshu and, less frequently, back to Anshun.

Huangguoshu Falls lie 64km from Anshun's west or main bus stations (¥10), and about 30km from Longgong, along the Anshun–Yunnan highway. You get dropped off at little Huangguoshu township and walk down to the **entrance** (¥90); at 68m this may not quite rank as China's highest cataract, but in full flood it's the loudest, the thunder rolling way off into the distance. A staircase descends past plagues of souvenir stalls to the blue-green river below the falls; the most imposing view of Huangguoshu is off to the left where the full weight of its eighty-one-metre span drops into the **Rhino Pool** – prepare yourself for a good soaking from the spray. **Moving on**, buses run to Anshun and Guiyang through the day; if you're Yunnan-bound, first catch a minibus 7km west to the small town of **Guanling** and look for connections there.

Zhijin and Zhijin Caves

About 100km from Anshun (3hr) or 150km from Guiyang (4.5hr) – there's direct traffic from either – the dismal country town of **ZHIJIN** sits among

▲ Zhijin Caves

some gorgeous limestone pinnacles, beneath which are the astounding **Zhijin Caves**, which lie 25km northeast via the township of **Sanyou**. Buses from Zhijin to the caves (40min; ¥3) run through the day and leave you at the **visitors' centre** (daily 9am–5pm; ¥100) where you have to hook up with one of the **guided tours** that run whenever they have around ten people. The immensely impressive caves are absolutely worth the money (though commentary is in Chinese only); tours last a solid two hours and wind through untold numbers of caverns packed with grand and weighty rock formations. The inevitable coloured lighting is actually used creatively, picking out credibly named formations such as "Puxian Riding his Elephant" and "Hermit on Mountain". The last cavern, **Guanghang Dong**, is 240m long, 170m wide and 60m high. If you get here early enough you might not need to spend the night in Zhijin, as buses back to Guiyang or Anshun run until mid-afternoon; failing this, the *Jinye Binguan* (Ⓣ0857/7625327; ❸), downhill from the bus station near the market, has acceptable **rooms** and a decent **restaurant**.

The northwest: to Weining and Caohai

The land northwest of Anshun forms a tumultuous barrier of jagged peaks and deep valleys, all masterfully tamed by the Guiyang–Kunming road and rail line, both masterpieces of engineering. The reason to head up this way is to catch wintering birdlife at **Caohai**; the adjacent town of **Weining** can be reached directly from Anshun by road or rail (though trains stop very late in the day), but otherwise head first for **Liupanshui** – a mess of broken pavements and dilapidated buildings permanently mired in steel-plant fallout and coal dust – and pick up a minibus to Weining from there (around 3hr).

WEINING sits above the clouds on a two-thousand-metre-high plateau, and seems to enjoy a surprisingly mild microclimate. The town is another small, run-down shell of a place populated by a friendly mix of Muslim Hui, Yi and Dahua Miao, famous for its Yi torch festival in July/August, sheep farming and **potatoes** – skewers of chilli-dusted potato "kebabs" are sold everywhere. Exit the bus station, turn right, and you'll find Weining's most comfy **accommodation** 100m beyond the crossroads at the *Heijing He Binguan* (Ⓣ0857/6222048, Ⓕ6224438; ❷–❹), which has a mix of older doubles with or without bathroom and some newer rooms; exit the station, turn left for 50m, and take the street opposite, and you'll find several cheaper options, such as *Juhongxuan Zhaodaisuo* (Ⓣ0857/6223480; ❶), which is cleaner than most. **Restaurants** outside the *Heijing He* do inexpensive stir-fries and hotpots.

Immediately south of Weining – it's a ¥1.5 motor-rickshaw ride or a thirty-minute walk – **Caohai**, the "Grass Sea", fills about twenty-five square kilometres of a shallow lake basin, the core of a regional **nature reserve**. Wintering wildfowl shelter here in huge numbers, including 400 rare **black-necked cranes** along with golden eagles, white-tailed sea eagles, black storks, Eurasian cranes, spoonbills and assorted ducks. Walk down to the lake and you'll be approached by touts wanting to take you out on a **boat trip**: you pay about ¥60 for a three-hour tour, being poled around in a four-person punt. The Chinese head first for a meal at the hamlet of **Longjia** on the far shore, famed for its food. On a sunny day, Caohai's overall tranquillity is a complete break with daily life in China; wintering cranes often hang out in the shallows near the shore and are not too hard to catch on camera.

Moving on from Weining, there are buses to Liupanshui, Anshun, Guiyang, Zhaotong (for connections to Xichang in Sichuan) and Kunming (Yunnan); and a couple of trains daily to Kunming, Anshun and Guiyang.

Travel details

Trains

Anshun to: Guiyang (10 daily; 1hr 30min); Kunming (8 daily; 10hr); Liupanshui/Shuicheng (10 daily; 2hr).
Beihai to: Nanning (daily; 3hr 30min).
Guilin to: Beijing (3 daily; 28hr); Changsha (5 daily; 8hr); Guangzhou (twice daily; 14hr); Guiyang (twice daily; 15hr); Kunming (twice daily; 22hr); Nanning (7 daily; 5hr 30min–8hr); Shanghai (daily; 29hr); Shenzhen (daily; 16hr).
Guiyang to: Anshun (10 daily; 1hr 30min); Beijing (3 daily; 29hr); Changsha (3 daily; 14hr); Chengdu (3 daily; 19hr); Chongqing (9 daily; 11hr); Guangzhou (6 daily; 24hr); Guilin (twice daily; 15hr); Huaihua (5 daily; 7hr); Kaili (9 daily; 3hr); Kunming (8 daily; 13hr); Shanghai (3 daily; 30hr); Liupanshui/Shuicheng (10 daily; 4hr); Yuping (5 daily; 6hr); Zhenyuan (7 daily; 5hr); Zunyi (9 daily; 3hr).
Kaili to: Changsha (3 daily; 12hr); Guiyang (9 daily; 3hr); Huaihua (5 daily; 4hr); Yuping (5 daily; 3hr); Zhenyuan (7 daily; 1hr 30min).
Liupanshui to: Anshun (10 daily; 2hr); Guiyang (10 daily; 4hr); Kunming (8 daily; 8hr 30min).
Nanning to: Beihai (daily; 3hr 20min); Beijing (daily; 28hr); Chengdu (daily; 10hr 30min); Chongzuo (twice daily; 2hr); Guangzhou (twice daily; 14hr); Guilin (6 daily; 5–8hr); Kunming (7 daily; 14hr); Pingxiang (twice daily; 4hr); Tuolong/Ningming (twice daily; 3hr).
Pingxiang to: Chongzuo (twice daily; 2hr); Nanning (twice daily; 4hr); Tuolong/Ningming (twice daily; 1hr).
Zhenyuan to: Guiyang (7 daily; 5hr); Huaihua (7 daily; 3hr 20min); Kaili (7 daily; 1hr 30min); Yuping (7 daily; 1hr 10min).
Zunyi to: Chongqing (9 daily; 7hr); Guiyang (9 daily; 3hr).

Buses

Anshun to: Guiyang (2hr); Huangguoshu (1hr); Liupanshui (3hr); Longgong (1hr).
Beihai to: Nanning (3hr 30min).
Guilin to: Guangzhou (12hr); Hengyang (12hr); Longsheng (2hr); Nanning (6hr); Sanjiang (4hr); Yangshuo (1hr 30min).
Guiping to: Jintian (30min); Nanning (3hr).
Guiyang to: Anshun (2hr); Huangguoshu (3hr); Kaili (3hr); Kunming (19hr); Nanning (18hr); Rongjiang (8hr); Zunyi (2hr 30min).
Kaili to: Chong An (2hr); Guiyang (2hr 30min); Leishan (1hr 30min); Liping (6hr); Rongjiang (5hr); Shibing (3hr); Shidong (4hr); Taijiang (2hr); Xijiang (2hr); Zhenyuan (6hr).

Liupanshui to: Anshun (3hr); Guiyang (4hr); Weining (3hr).
Nanning to: Beihai (3hr 30min); Chongzuo (1hr 30min); Guangzhou (18hr); Guilin (6hr); Guiping (3hr); Ningming (4hr); Pingxiang (5hr); Yangshuo (6hr).
Pingxiang to: Chongzuo (5hr); Nanning (5hr); Ningming (1hr).
Sanjiang to: Baxie (1hr 30min); Chengyang (40min); Diping (2hr); Guilin (4hr); Liping (5hr); Longsheng (2hr); Mapang (2hr); Zhaoxing (4hr).
Weining to: Anshun (5hr); Guiyang (7hr); Liupanshui (3hr).
Yangshuo to: Guilin (1hr 30min); Nanning (6hr).
Zhaoxing to: Diping (2hr); Liping (1hr); Sanjiang (4hr).
Zunyi to: Chishui (7hr); Guiyang (2hr 30min).

Ferries

Beihai to: Haikou (twice daily; 10hr).

Flights

In addition to the domestic flights listed, there are international flights out of Guilin to Korea, Thailand and Japan, and from Nanning to Thailand and Vietnam.
Guilin to: Beijing (6 daily; 2hr 15min); Chengdu (3 daily; 1hr 20min); Guangzhou (6 daily; 50min); Guiyang (twice daily; 50min); Hong Kong (twice daily; 1hr); Kunming (twice daily; 1hr 15min); Shanghai (3 daily; 2hr); Shenzhen (twice daily; 1hr); Xi'an (twice daily; 1hr 30min).
Guiyang to: Beijing (twice daily; 2hr 30min); Chengdu (twice daily; 1hr); Guangzhou (5 daily; 1hr 30min); Guilin (twice daily; 50min); Hong Kong (daily; 1hr 30min); Kunming (daily; 55min); Nanning (daily; 1hr); Shanghai (daily; 2hr); Shenzhen (daily; 1hr 30min).
Nanning to: Beijing (4 daily; 3hr); Chengdu (twice daily; 1hr 30min); Chongqing (daily; 1hr 20min); Guangzhou (5 daily; 55min); Guiyang (daily; 1hr); Hanoi (twice weekly; 50min); Haikou (twice daily; 50min); Hong Kong (daily; 1hr); Kunming (at least 1 daily; 1hr); Shanghai (twice daily; 2hr 15min); Shenzhen (twice daily; 55min); Xi'an (daily; 2hr).

CHAPTER 11

Highlights

* **Kunming's bars** Check out the laid-back nightlife in one of China's most relaxed cities. See p.788

* **Yuanyang** Base yourself in this attractive town and visit nearby minority villages set in a landscape spectacularly sliced up by rice terraces. See p.796

* **Dali** An ancient town with an enjoyable, laid-back travellers' ghetto, offering café society and lush scenery. See p.800

* **Cycling around Lijiang** Take yourself out of the touristy town centre and cycle around the well-preserved villages at the heart of the Naxi Kingdom. See p.815

* **Tiger Leaping Gorge** Relax for a few days on the ridge of this dramatic gorge, trekking between farmstead homestays. See p.818

* **Meili Xue Shan** Dramatic jagged scenery in China's remote Shangri-la. See p.827

* **Ruili** A boisterous border town that has charming temples and countryside a short bike ride away. See p.836

* **Jungle trekking in Xishuangbanna** Explore a region populated by many different ethnic groups, each with their own distinctive dress and customs. See p.843

▲ Tiger Leaping Gorge

11

Yunnan

Yunnan has always stood apart from the rest of China, set high on the "barbarous and pestilential" southwestern frontiers of the empire, and shielded from the rest of the nation by the unruly, mountainous provinces of Sichuan and Guizhou. Within this single province, unmatched in the complexity and scope of its history, landscape and peoples, you'll find a mix of geography, climates and nationalities that elsewhere on Earth takes entire continents to express.

The fairly flat, productive northeast of the province is home to the attractive capital, **Kunming**, whose mild climate earned Yunnan its name, meaning literally "south of the Clouds'. Increasingly touristed, it's nonetheless a charming area, with enjoyable day-trips to nearby scenic marvels, and easy access to assorted little-visited sights southeast towards the border with **Vietnam**.

West of Kunming, the Yunnan plateau rises to serrated, snowbound peaks, extending north **to Tibet** and surrounding the ancient historic towns of **Dali** and **Lijiang**, while further west lies subtropical **Dehong**, a busy trading region that's an unlikely Chinese holiday destination on the central **border with Burma**. Yunnan's deep south comprises a further isolated stretch of the same frontier, which reaches down to the tropical forests and paddy fields of **Xishuangbanna**, a botanical, zoological and ethnic cornucopia abutting Burma and **Laos** – about as far from Han China as it's possible to be.

Dwelling in this stew of border markets, mountains, jungles, lakes, temples, modern political intrigue and remains of vanished kingdoms are 28 recognized **ethnic groups**, the greatest number in any province. Providing almost half the population and a prime reason to visit Yunnan in themselves, the indigenous list includes Dai and Bai, Wa, Lahu, Hani, Jingpo, Nu, Naxi and Lisu plus a host shared with other provinces (such as the Yi; p.896) or adjoining nations. Those in the south often have cultural ties with ethnic cousins in Laos, Burma and Vietnam, while the minorities in the north have strong links with Tibet. Each minority has its own spoken language, cuisine, distinctive form of dress for women, festivals and belief system. These cultures have survived decades of Han chauvinism; today, a more enlightened attitude prevails, and minority families are even allowed more children than their Han compatriots. Though much of what you'll initially glean of these cultures is put on for tourists, anyone with even a couple of days to spare in Xishuangbanna or Lijiang can begin to flesh out this image. With more time you can look for shyer, remoter groups whose lives are less influenced by the modern world. In all cases, the richest experiences of minority culture are offered by those projects that are run by or in partnership with local people, such as all the eco-lodges listed.

While all this diversity makes Yunnan as elusive a place for the modern traveller to come to grips with as it was for successive dynasties to govern, the province's obvious charms have in recent years spurred something of a tourist boom. Though much of this is associated with the domestic market, foreigners too will find plenty of resources geared to their needs, from backpacker cafés to companies offering cycling and trekking trips, which ensure that Yunnan is one of the easiest places to travel in China.

There are international flights into Kunming from Bangkok, Rangoon, Singapore and Vientiane, and to Jinghong – near the border with Burma and Laos – from Chiang Mai and Bangkok. Getting around can be time-consuming, thanks to Yunnan's sheer scale, but the province can boast of China's better airlines in Yunnan Air, and the state of country **buses and roads** is often surprisingly good; whatever their condition, it's an undeniable achievement that some routes exist at all. Be sure to travel at least briefly along the famous **Burma Road** between Kunming and the western border, built with incredible determination during the 1930s. At present there's only a limited **rail network** inside Yunnan, though Kunming itself is well linked to the rest of the country via Sichuan and Guizhou.

Yunnanese food

Yunnanese food splits broadly into three cooking styles. In the **north**, the cold, pastoral lifestyle produces dried meats and – very unusually for China – dairy products, fused with a Muslim cuisine, a vestige of the thirteenth-century Mongolian invasion. Typical dishes include wind-cured ham (*yuntui* or *huotui*), sweetened, steamed and served with slices of bread; toasted cheese and dried yoghurt wafers (*rushan* and *rubing*); the local version of crisp-skinned duck (*shaoya*), flavoured by basting it with honey and roasting over a pine-needle fire; and *shaguoyu*, a tasty fish claypot.

Southeastern Yunnan produces the most recognizably "Chinese" food. From here comes *qiguo ji*, chicken flavoured with medicinal herbs and stewed inside a specially shaped earthenware steamer, and **crossing-the-bridge noodles** (*guoqiao mian*), a sort of individualized hotpot that is probably the most famous dish in the province. The curious name comes from a tale of a Qing scholar who retired every day to a lakeside pavilion to compose poetry. His wife, an understanding soul, used to cook him lunch, but the food always cooled as she carried it from their home over the bridge to where he studied – until she hit on the idea of keeping the heat in with a layer of oil on top of his soup. It's best sampled in Kunming, where numerous places serve a huge bowl of oily, scalding chicken stock with a platter of noodles, shredded meats and vegetables, which you add along with chilli powder and spices to taste.

Not surprisingly, Yunnan's **southwestern borders** are strongly influenced by Burmese cooking methods, particularly in the use of such un-Chinese ingredients as coconut, palm sugar, cloves and turmeric. Here you'll find a vast range of soups and stews, roughly recognizable as **curries**, displayed in aluminium pots outside fast-turnover restaurants, and oddities such as purple rice-flour pancakes sold at street markets. As most of these aren't generally available outside the area, however, their description and a glossary of local names appears in the relevant section of this chapter (see p.837). The southwest also produces good **coffee** and red *pu'er cha*, Yunnan's best **tea**, both widely appreciated across the province.

In addition, each of Yunnan's minorities has its own culinary specialities, often quite distinctive from mainstream Chinese cuisine; these too are described in the relevant accounts.

Changes are afoot, however, as new multi-lane highways push through the mountainous and forested terrain from Kunming south to Jinghong – expected to cut journey times to Xishuangbanna down to a modest six hours when eventually completed around 2009 – and even more impressively west to Dali, Baoshan, Ruili and Burma. Survey work has also begun on a proposed rail link along the old Southern Silk Road, due to be finished around 2011.

The **weather** is generally moderate throughout the year, though northern Yunnan has cold winters and heavy snow up around the Tibetan border, while the south is always warm, with a torrential wet season in summer.

Roads in the more remote areas are regularly closed during the rainy season, usually because of landslides and bad weather, but sometimes thanks to the army looking for illegal cross-border traffic in cars, timber, gems and **opiates**. Much of Asia's illegal drug production originates in Burma and is funnelled through China to overseas markets. Officially, the Yunnanese government is tough on the drugs trade, executing traffickers and forcibly rehabilitating addicts. All this means that there are military **checkpoints** on many rural roads, where you'll have to show passports. It pays to be polite, and things are often easier if you avoid appearing fluent in Chinese in these circumstances.

Some history

Yunnan has been inhabited for a very long time, with evidence reaching back through galleries of Stone Age rock art to two 1.5-million-year-old teeth found near the northern town of Yuanmou. Records of civilization, however, are far more recent. According to the Han historian Sima Qian, the Chinese warrior prince **Zhuang Qiao** founded the pastoral **Dian Kingdom** in eastern Yunnan during the third century BC, though it's probable that he simply became chief of an existing nation. The Dian were a slave society, who vividly recorded their daily life and ceremonies involving human sacrifice in sometimes gruesome **bronze models**, which have been unearthed from their tombs. In 109 AD the kingdom was acknowledged by China: the emperor **Wu**, hoping to control the Southern Silk Road through to India, sent its ruler military aid and a golden seal. However, the collapse of the Han empire in 204 AD was followed by the dissolution of Dian into private statelets.

In the eighth century, an aspiring Yunnanese prince named **Piluoge**, favouring Dali for its location near the Silk Road, invited his rivals to dinner in the town, then set fire to the tent with them inside. Subsequently he established the **Nanzhao Kingdom** in Dali, which absorbed these private statelets and later expanded to include much of modern Burma, Thailand and Vietnam. In 937, the Bai warlord **Duan Siping** toppled the Nanzhao and set up a smaller **Dali**

The Muslim Uprising

Yunnan's Muslim Uprising of 1854–73 was unlike any of the other major popular revolts that plagued nineteenth-century China, in that it was racially motivated. Muslim Hui had first arrived in Yunnan with the Mongols in 1254 and settled as merchants. There were few problems with integration until China's eighteenth-century population explosion began to put pressure on resources. The Hui became targets for Han disaffection because, as shopkeepers, they controlled local economies, and because they ate lamb and beef, which disgusted the Chinese – lambs, which kneel to suckle, were seen as filial creatures, and cattle were companions in work, not food. Trouble erupted in 1854 when an anti-Hui riot broke out at a silver mine near Quxiong in Yunnan's north. Two years later, some Chinese who had taken part stopped at a village just outside Kunming. When local Muslims heard about it they torched the village, killed all its inhabitants, and held a victory march. Kunming's governor had the Hui ringleaders executed and issued a proclamation against rioting that was interpreted by Chinese vigilantes as an official sanction to get rid of the Hui.

On 19 May, 1856, the gates of Kunming were locked and the city's Muslim population slaughtered by the mob. Once word got out, Yunnan's entire Muslim community rose in revolt, led by the charismatic Ma Julong. His army laid siege to Kunming the next year, and butchered all the Chinese who lived outside the city walls – some seventy percent of the capital's population. This inspired Muslims in Dali to kick out the Chinese governor and set up an Islamic state.

The Qing government – already overstretched by the ongoing Taiping and Miao insurrections (see p.419 & 761) – was forced to negotiate. In return for ending his siege of Kunming, Ma Julong was given an official pardon, a government position and orders to pacify the rest of Yunnan. It was not an easy task. His first attempts against Dali backfired, and provoked local leader Du Wenxiu to storm eastwards and lay his own siege to Kunming in 1868, which was only defeated by the timely appointment of seasoned campaigner Chen Yuying as Yunnan's governor. Having chased Du back west, Chen posted Ma off to pacify southern Yunnan and sent his own men to take Dali. Government troops ransacked the city and massacred over ten thousand Muslims, effectively ending the uprising.

Kingdom, which survived until **Kublai Khan** and his Mongolian hordes descended in 1252, subduing the Bai. Directly controlled by China for the first time, Yunnan served for a while as a remote dumping ground for political trouble-makers, thereby escaping the population explosions, wars and migrations that plagued central China. However, the Mongol invasion had introduced a large **Muslim population** to the province, who, angered by their deteriorating status under the Chinese, staged a rebellion in 1856 (see box opposite). The rebellion was crushed with the wholesale massacre of Yunnan's Muslims, and a wasted Yunnan was left to local bandits and private armies for the following half-century.

Strangely, it was the **Japanese invasion** during the 1930s that sparked a resurgence of the province's fortunes. Blockaded into southwestern China, the **Guomindang government** initiated great programmes of rail and road building through the region, though they never really controlled Yunnan. Moreover, their poor treatment of minority groups made the Red Army's cause all the more attractive when civil war resumed in 1945. Liberation came smoothly, but the **Communists'** good intentions of coexistence with minorities, better hospitals, schools and communications were badly stalled during the Cultural Revolution and then, in the 1980s, by the war with Vietnam. Only recently has Yunnan finally benefited from its forced association with the rest of the country. Never agriculturally rich – only a tenth of the land is considered arable – the province looks to mineral resources, tourism and its potential as a future conduit between China and the much discussed, but as yet unformed, trading bloc of **Vietnam**, **Laos**, **Thailand** and **Burma**. Should these countries ever form an unrestricted economic alliance, the amount of trade passing through Yunnan would be immense – a resurrection of the old Silk Road – and highways, rail and air services have already been planned for the day the borders open freely.

Kunming and the southeast

All visitors to Yunnan find themselves at some point in **Kunming**, the province's comfortable capital and transport hub. The large population of young foreign expats, mostly students and teachers, testifies to Kunming's appeal as the Seattle of China – the most laid-back city in the country, and, with Chengdu, the most pleasant provincial capital. The city's immediate face is an ordinary blend of broad, monochrome main roads and glassy modern office blocks but its character is partly salvaged by the surrounding temples and fine lake-and-limestone-hill landscapes. From Kunming, both road and rail extend southeast all the way down to the **Vietnamese border**, taking you within striking distance of some fine scenery, old architecture, and a few offbeat sights to slow you down en route.

Kunming and around

Basking 2000m above sea level in the fertile heart of the Yunnan plateau, **KUNMING** does its best to live up to its traditional nickname, the City of

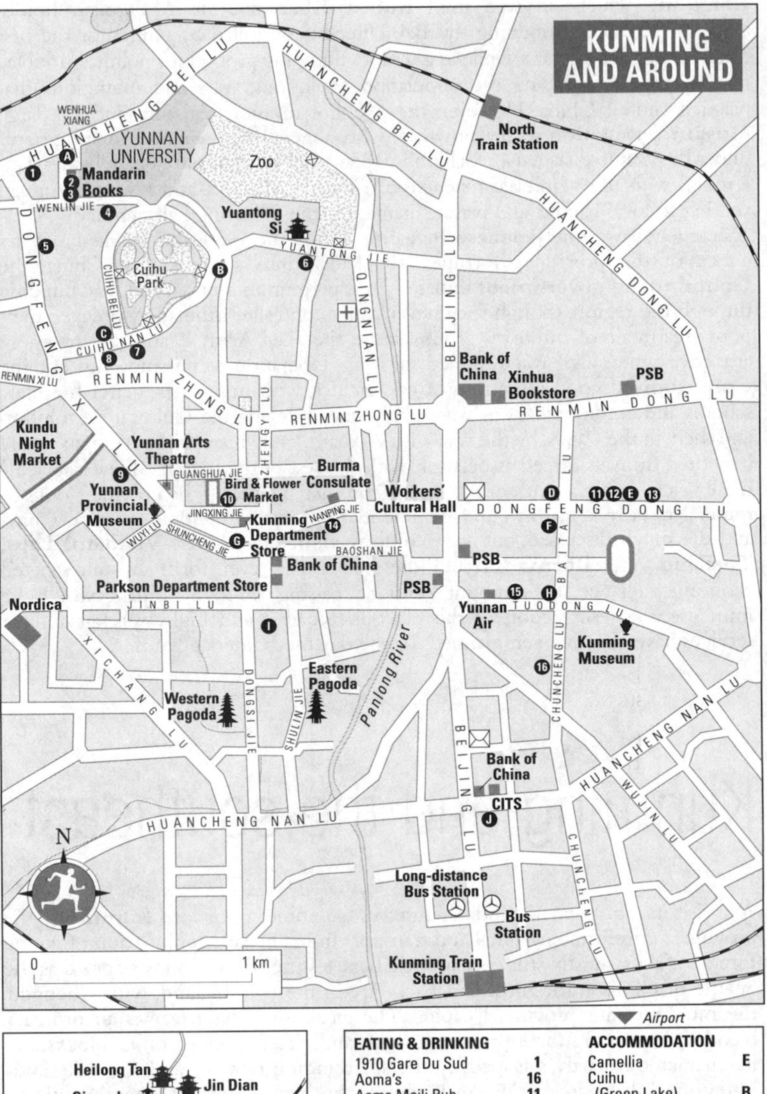

KUNMING AND AROUND

EATING & DRINKING

- 1910 Gare Du Sud 1
- Aoma's 16
- Aoma Meili Pub 11
- Blue Bird 8 & 9
- Camel Bar 15
- City Café 12
- French Café 3
- Fuhua Yuan 10
- Mamafu's 11
- Prague Café 4
- Salvadors 2
- Shiping Huiguan 7
- Speakeasy 5
- Vegetarian Restaurant 6
- Wei's Pizza 14
- Yunnan Flavour Restaurant 13

ACCOMMODATION

- Camellia E
- Cuihu (Green Lake) B
- Golden Dragon J
- Greenland H
- Hump Over The Himalayas I
- Kunming D
- Kunming Youth Hostel C
- New Era G
- Sakura F
- Yunnan University Centre for Chinese Studies A

Kunming and around

Kunming	昆明	*kūnmíng*
Bird and Flower Market	花鸟市场	*huā niǎo shìchǎng*
Cuihu Park	翠湖公园	*cuìhú gōngyuán*
Daguan Park	大观公园	*dàguān gōngyuán*
Eastern Pagoda	东寺塔	*dōngsì tǎ*
Kunming City Museum	昆明市博物馆	*kūnmíngshì bówùguǎn*
Mosque	南城清真寺	*nánchéng qīngzhēn sì*
Nordica	诺地卡	*nuòdì kǎ*
Western Pagoda	西寺塔	*xīsì tǎ*
Workers' Cultural Hall	工人文化宫	*gōngrén wénhuàgōng*
Yuantong Si	圆通寺	*yuántōng sì*
Yunnan Arts Theatre	艺术剧院	*yìshù jùyuàn*
Yunnan Provincial Museum	云南省博物馆	*yúnnánshěng bówùguǎn*
Zoo	动物园	*dòngwù yuán*
Accommodation		
Camellia	茶花宾馆	*cháhuā bīnguǎn*
Cuihu	翠湖宾馆	*cuìhú bīnguǎn*
Golden Dragon	金龙饭店	*jīnlóng fàndiàn*
Greenland	绿洲大酒店	*lǜzhōu dàjiǔdiàn*
Hump Over the Himalayas	金马碧鸡坊金	*jīnmǎ bìjī fāngjīn*
Kunming	昆明饭店	*kūnmíng fàndiàn*
Kunming Youth Hostel	昆明国际青年旅社	*kūnmíng guójì qīngnián lǚshè*
New Era	昆明新纪元酒店	*kūnmíng xīnjìyuán jiǔdiàn*
Sakura	樱花酒店	*yīnghuā jiǔdiàn*
Yunnan University Centre for Chinese Studies	云南大学国际学术教育交流中心	*yúnnán dàxué guójì xuéshù jiàoyù jiāoliú zhōngxīn*
Eating and drinking		
1910 Gare Du Sud	火车南站	*huǒchē nánzhàn*
Blue Bird	青鸟饭店	*qīngniǎo fàndiàn*
Camel Bar	骆驼酒吧	*luòtuó jiǔbā*
French Café	兰白红	*lánbáihóng*
Fuhua Yuan	福华园饭店	*fúhuáyuán fàndiàn*
Kundu Night Market	昆都夜市	*kūndū yèshì*
Mamafu's	妈妈付餐厅	*māmāfù cāntīng*
Prague Café	布拉格咖啡馆	*bùlāgé kāfēiguǎn*
Speakeasy	说吧	*shuōbā*
Vegetarian restaurant	玉泉斋	*yùquánzhāi*
Wenlin Jie	文林街	*wénlín jiē*
Around Kunming		
Dian Chi	滇池	*diānchí*
Heilong Tan	黑龙滩	*hēilóng tān*
Jin Dian	金殿	*jīndiàn*
Kunyang	昆阳	*kūnyáng*
Lunan	路南	*lùnán*
Qiongzhu Si	筇竹寺	*qióngzhúsì*
Shilin	石林	*shílín*
Tanhua Si	昙华寺	*tánhuásì*
Western Hills	西山	*xīshān*
Zhenghe Park	郑和公园	*zhènghé gōngyuán*

Eternal Spring. However, until recently it was considered a savage frontier settlement; the authorities only began to realize the city's promise when people exiled here during the Cultural Revolution refused offers to return home to eastern China, preferring Kunming's climate and more relaxed life. Today, its citizens remain mellow enough to mix typically Chinese garrulousness with introspective pleasures, such as quietly greeting the day with a stiff hit of Yunnanese tobacco from fat, brass-bound bamboo pipes. Other novelties – clean pavements enforced by on-the-spot fines, an orderly traffic system, and a low-profile but sizeable gay community – suggest that Kunming's four million or so residents enjoy a quality of life above that of most urban Chinese.

Though Kunming boasts few specific sights, the countryside around holds enough to keep visitors occupied for a good few days. Extraordinary sculptures make the westerly **Qiongzhu Si** the pick of local holy sites, while immediately south of Kunming is **Dian Chi**, a spectacular 270-square-kilometre spread of deep blue water dotted with the rectangular sails of fishing junks. You can boat across to the lakeside towns, but the lake's colourful sprawl is best absorbed from the nearby heights of Xi Shan, the **Western Hills**. Further afield, **Shilin**, the spectacular Stone Forest, is an enjoyable day-trip if you can accept the fairground atmosphere and the crowds dutifully tagging behind their cosmetically perfect tour guides.

Some history

Historically the domain of Yunnan's earliest inhabitants and first civilization, Kunming long profited from its position on the caravan roads through to Burma and Europe. It was visited in the thirteenth century by Marco Polo, who found the locals of **Yachi Fu** (Duck Pond Town) using cowries for cash, enjoying their meat raw, and inviting guests to sleep with their womenfolk. Little of the city's wealth survived the 1856 Muslim rebellion, when most Buddhist sites in the capital were razed, and the events some forty years later, when an uprising against working conditions on the **Kunming–Haiphong rail line** saw 300,000 labourers executed after France shipped in weapons to suppress the revolt. (Designed by the French so that they could tap Yunnan's mineral resources for their colonies in Indochina, the line was only completed in 1911.) Twenty-five years later, **war with Japan** brought a flock of wealthy east-coast refugees to the city, whose money helped establish Kunming as an industrial and manufacturing base for the wartime government in Chongqing. The allies provided essential support for this, importing materials along the Burma Road from British-held Burma and, when that was lost to the Japanese, through the volunteer US-piloted **Flying Tigers**, who flew in supplies over the Himalayas from British bases in India. The city consolidated its position as a supply depot during the Vietnam War and subsequent border clashes, though during the **Cultural Revolution** buildings that escaped the attentions of nineteenth-century vandals perished at the hands of the Red Guards.

Since the mid-1980s, Kunming has enjoyed snowballing tourism and foreign investment. Neighbouring nations such as Thailand trace their ancestries back to Yunnan and have proved particularly willing to channel funds into the city, which has become ever more accessible as a result.

Orientation, arrival and city transport

Though Kunming has few natural landmarks to help guide you around, its layout is uncomplicated. The city hangs off two main thoroughfares: **Beijing Lu** forms the north–south axis, passing just east of the centre as it runs for 5km between the city's two train stations, while **Dongfeng Lu** crosses it halfway

Moving on from Kunming

The **airport bus** (¥5) leaves from outside the Yunnan Air headquarters on Tuodong Lu – check inside for bus departure times, and be prepared to take a taxi (at ¥25–30, possibly the cheapest airport ride in China) if the bus doesn't materialize. The journey takes about forty minutes. Yunnan Air is very helpful and organized, and can also book you on other airlines out of Kunming, although agents around town sometimes have cheaper tickets.

At the **train station**, the booking office on the west side of the vast station square is open from 6.30am until midnight. When staffed, the ticket service desk here is pretty helpful and will fill you in on which queue to join. Trains run **north to Chengdu** via Xichang in southern Sichuan, **southeast** via Xingyi to Baise and Nanning in Guangxi, and **east through Guizhou**, via Liupanshui, Anshun and Guiyang, into the rest of the country. Tickets can be bought up to three days in advance of travel.

Trains no longer run to **Hekou and Vietnam**, so the 11-hour bus journey to the border crossing is the only option. There's one day bus to Hekou (¥119), and a night bus that takes slightly longer (¥109).

At Kunming's main **long-distance bus station**, the ticket office is computerized and staff are helpful, with standard, luxury, express and sleeper buses departing for all over Yunnan and neighbouring provinces. Tickets are also available from numerous ticket agencies around town. Keep a tight hold on your luggage at the bus station; plenty of people have something stolen either at the station or in transit. Tickets for luxury buses can be bought from an office just inside the entrance, on the right. If you're taking the long road to Jinghong, the new express bus takes 10 hours and costs ¥191. There's also a useful luxury service to Xiaguan (for Dali), which leaves hourly from 8am to 7.30pm (4hr; ¥120), while five buses daily run to Lijiang (7hr; ¥180). Most buses on these routes are new and feature hostesses and on-board toilets.

Leaving for **Laos by bus** is possible by heading for Mo Han, via Mengla, in Xishuangbanna (p.853). The only choice for foreigners entering **Burma** used to be to fly to Rangoon, but now you can cross overland, with a specific permit available through travel companies in Kunming (see p.789).

along. Most of the city's accommodation lies along Dongfeng Dong Lu and the southern half of Beijing Lu, while the majority of sights lie north and west of the centre around Dongfeng Xi Lu and **Cuihu Park**. Circling most of this is the first ring road, known for most of its length as **Huancheng Lu**.

Kunming's busy **airport** is out in the southeastern suburbs, with the international and domestic terminal buildings next to each other. At the south side of the square outside you'll find a **CAAC bus** which meets arrivals and runs via some of the downtown hotels to the Yunnan Air offices on Tuodong Lu (¥5). Alternatively, public bus #52 will take you into the centre of town for ¥1. **Taxis** should be caught from the rank opposite the entrance; a ride into town costs around ¥25–30 using the meter.

The **long-distance bus station** and **Kunming train station** are down at the seedy southern end of Beijing Lu. Bus #23 runs from here right up to the **North train station**, past hotels and the Dongfeng Lu intersection, where you can alight and head east for further accommodation prospects. You'll only arrive at the North train station if you're coming from the Vietnamese border or southeastern Yunnan. The **Western bus station** on Renmin Xi Lu is of most use for excursions around Kunming, though a few long-distance services also terminate here.

Kunming is not too large to walk around, while **bicycles** are readily rented from several of the hotels. In addition, plenty of **taxis** (¥8 standing charge) and

public buses cruise the main streets; stay up to date with the routes by picking up a bus **map** from street sellers.

Accommodation

Kunming has abundant accommodation, mostly mid-range, scattered throughout the city centre.

Camellia 96 Dongfeng Dong Lu ⓣ0871/3163000 or 3162918, ⓕ3147033, ⓦwww.kmcamelliahotel.com. This three-winged affair remains a budget traveller staple, offering dorms and private rooms, though these days it's never better than adequate. Situated on the third floor of an adjoining building, the four-bed dorms (¥35) represent better value than the rather cramped and overcrowded eight-bed alternative (¥30). The doubles are showing their age. The garden is a bonus, though watch out for rather predatory students of English. There's also a foreign-exchange counter, an expensive bar and restaurant, a number of ticket-booking services, Internet access (¥10/hr), luggage storage and bike rental. Take bus #2 or #23 from the main train station to Dongfeng Dong Lu, then any bus heading east for two stops. ❸

Cuihu (Green Lake) Cuihu Nan Lu ⓣ0871/5158888, ⓕ5153286, ⓦwww.greenlakehotel.com. A long-established and good-value upmarket hotel in pleasant surroundings by Cuihu Park, with a fancy lobby complete with palm trees, and an excellent restaurant. Airport transfers can be arranged; all major credit cards are accepted. ❾

Golden Dragon 575 Beijing Lu ⓣ0871/3133015, ⓕ3131082, ⓦwww.gdhotel.com.cn. Four-star comforts aimed at the upmarket business traveller, but still rather a tired atmosphere. ❼

Greenland 80 Tuodong Lu ⓣ0871/3189999, ⓕ3195888, ⓦwww.greenlandhotel.com.cn. Hefty discounts of up to fifty percent make this swanky place, on one of Kunming's more glamorous streets, worth investigating off season. Complimentary breakfast and late checkouts (3pm) are a nice touch. ❽

Hump Over The Himalayas Jinmabiji Fang, Jinbi Lu ⓣ0871/3640359, ⓦwww.thehumphostel.com. Three hundred police once raided this place to close it down. Now re-opened with a promise of good behaviour, it's basically a set of dingy dorms above a bar and disco complex, and is aimed squarely at the budget traveller for whom sleep is not a priority (though they'll give you earplugs if you ask). There's a bar, Internet access, a large common room and roof terrace. Dorms ¥25 including breakfast.

Kunming Dongfeng Dong Lu ⓣ0871/3162063, ⓕ3163784, ⓦwww.kmhotel.com.cn. A big, upmarket hotel with reasonable service and a Korean restaurant, which also offers bikes for rent. It's not cheap, though; the less expensive rooms are in the older, south wing. ❼

Kunming Youth Hostel Cuihu Nan Lu ⓣ0871/5175395. On a quiet street just around the corner from Cuihu Park, in an annexe of the provincial library, this might feel more like a standard two-star hotel than a youth hostel, and you wouldn't stay here for the atmosphere, but the rooms are very good value for the price. ❸.

New Era 99 Dongfeng Xi Lu ⓣ0871/3624999, ⓕ3636556, ⓦwww.erahotel.com. This smart, modern behemoth is slap bang in the city centre. It's smart, but not memorable. ❼

Sakura Dongfeng Dong Lu ⓣ0871/3165888, ⓕ3135189, ⓦwww.sakurahotel.cn. A tall, distinctive building with decent, mid-range rooms, though the lobby is rather poky. It's also home to a well-reputed Thai restaurant. Large discounts on the rack rate are sometimes available. ❼

Yunnan University Centre for Chinese Studies Wenhua Xiang ⓣ0871/5033624, ⓕ5148513. Aimed at long-stay foreign students but open to anyone. It's opposite the university's west gate, in one of the nicest parts of town, with plenty of cafés and bars around. The old wing, to the south, is musty but has a lovely garden and tiled patio, and some of the cheapest rooms in the city. Rooms in the bright new wing are a little more expensive; overall, this is one of the best budget options. ❷–❸

The City

The public focus of Kunming is the huge square outside the grandiose **Workers' Cultural Hall** at the Beijing Lu/Dongfeng Lu intersection, alive in the mornings with regimented crowds warming up on hip pivots and shuttlecock games. Later in the day you can consult a fortune-teller, or receive a shoulder and back massage from the hard-fingered blind practitioners who pounce on passers-by; you might catch weekend amateur theatre here, too. Rapidly being modernized, the city's true centre is west of here across the **Panlong River**, outside the modern Kunming Department Store at the Dongfeng Xi Lu/Zhengyi Lu crossroads, a densely crowded shopping precinct packed with clothing and hi-fi stores. The river itself, though black and oily, is at least nicely landscaped – the general impression is that time, trouble and planning has gone into these modernizations, unlike in many Chinese cities.

Running west off Zhengyi Jie, **Jingxing Jie** leads into one of the more bizarre corners of the city, with Kunming's huge **bird and flower market** – which sells a much greater range of creatures than its name suggests – convening daily in the streets that connect it with Guanghua Jie, parallel to the north. At least at weekends, this is no run-of-the-mill mix of kittens and grotesque goldfish: rare, multicoloured songbirds twitter and squawk to all sides, while furtive hawkers display geckos, monkey-like lorises and other endangered oddities illegally "liberated" from the forests of Xishuangbanna. There are plants here, too, along with **antique and curio** booths – where you'll find coins and Cultural Revolution mementos, bamboo pipes and prayer rugs – as well as plenty of opportunity to sample local snacks. At the time of writing, however, much of the surrounding area was being prepared for demolition; the market will undoubtedly continue in some form, but without its characterful backdrop of century-old buildings.

If the crowds get too much, head up the tiny alley on the right as you come in from Zhengyi Lu, and you'll find a peaceful **teahouse** built in traditional style around a courtyard.

The nearby **grounds of Wen Miao**, a vanished Confucian temple on Renmin Zhong Lu, are worth seeking out. This quiet spot, where old men play chess and drink tea, holds an avenue of pines, an ancient pond and pavilion, and beds of bamboo, azaleas and potted palms.

Yunnan Provincial Museum

About 500m west of the centre, along Dongfeng Xi Lu and the #5 bus route, the **Yunnan Provincial Museum** (daily 9.30am–5.30pm; last entry an hour before the museum closes; ¥10) has its moments, even if the building itself is dim, dusty and largely empty. Best are the **Dian bronzes** on the second floor, dating back more than two thousand years to the Warring States Period and excavated from tombs on the shores of Dian Chi, south of Kunming. The largest pieces include an ornamental plate of a tiger attacking an ox and a **coffin** in the shape of a bamboo house, but lids from **storage drums** used to hold cowries are the most impressive, decorated with dioramas of figurines fighting, sacrificing oxen and men and, rather more peacefully, posing with their families and farmyard animals outside their homes. A replica of the Chinese imperial **gold seal** given to the Dian king early in the second century implies that his aristocratic slave society had the tacit approval of the Han emperor. Upstairs again is a porcelain gallery and an exhibition of paintings by the Qing-dynasty artist Dan Dang.

Cuihu Park, Yuantong Si and the zoo

Cuihu Park (open from dawn until 10pm) is predominantly lake, a good place to join thousands of others exercising, singing, feeding wintering flocks of **gulls**, or just milling between the plum and magnolia gardens and over the maze of bridges. The park is a twenty-minute walk north of the museum via Dongfeng Xi Lu and Cuihu Nan Lu; alternatively, take bus #5 from the museum or bus #2 from the southern end of Beijing Lu. Immediately northwest, the **Yunnan**

University campus offers a glimpse of old Kunming, its partially overgrown 1920s exterior reached via a wide flight of stone steps. **Cafés** and cheap restaurants in the vicinity are the haunt of plenty of expats and students eager to practise their English – see opposite for details.

East from Cuihu Park along Yuantong Jie is the Qing-vintage **Yuantong Si** (daily 8am–6pm; ¥4), northern Yunnan's major Buddhist site, recently spruced up and an active place of pilgrimage. A bridge over the central pond crosses through an octagonal pavilion dedicated to a multi-armed Guanyin and white marble Sakyamuni, to the threshold of the **main hall**, where two huge central pillars wrapped in colourful, Manga-esque **dragons** support the ornate wooden ceiling. Faded frescoes on the back wall were painted in the thirteenth century, while a new annexe out the back houses a graceful gilded bronze Buddha flanked by peacocks, donated by the Thai government.

The temple sits on the southern slope of the large Kunming **zoo** (daily 8am–5pm; ¥10), with the entrance at the corner of Yuantong Jie and Qingnian Lu on the #4 bus route. It's not the worst in China, offering nice vignettes of children stroking and feeding the deer, along with views of the city from a hilltop planted with crab-apple groves.

Kunming City Museum

The highlight of the **Kunming City Museum** (daily except Mon 10am–5pm; ¥15), east of Beijing Lu along Tuodong Lu, is the **Dali Sutra Pillar**. In its own room on the ground floor, it's a 6.5-metre-high, pagoda-like Song-dynasty sculpture, in pink sandstone; an octagonal base supports seven tiers covered in Buddha images, statues of fierce guardian gods standing on subjugated demons, and a mix of Tibetan and Chinese script, part of which is the Dharani Mantra. The rest is a dedication, identifying the pillar as having been raised by the Dali regent, **Yuan Douguang**, in memory of his general **Gao Ming**. The whole thing is topped by a ring of Buddhas carrying a ball – the universe – above them. Formerly part of the defunct Dizang temple, the pillar is a powerful work, full of the energy that later seeped out of the mainstream of Chinese sculpture.

The other exhibits are a well-presented repeat of the Provincial Museum's collection. Enthusiasts for **bronze drums** can examine a range, from the oldest known example to relatively recent castings, to see how the typical decorations – sun and frog designs on top, long-plumed warriors in boats around the sides, tiger handles – became so stylized (for more on bronze drums, see p.740). There are cowrie-drum lids, too, and a host of other bronze pieces worth examining for nit-picking details of birds, animals and people. Other rooms contain two excellent **dioramas** of modern and Ming-dynasty Kunming, accounts (in Chinese) of the voyages of **Zheng He**, the famous Ming eunuch admiral, and five locally found **fossilized dinosaur skeletons** – including a tyrannosaurus-like allosaur, and the bulky *Yunnanosaurus robustus*.

Southern Kunming

Jinbi Lu runs roughly parallel to and south of Dongfeng Lu, and is reached on bus #3 from Beijing Lu. Two large Tang-dynasty **pagodas** rise in the vicinity, each a solid thirteen storeys of whitewashed brick crowned with four jolly iron cockerels. South down Dongsi Jie, past another **mosque**, the entrance to the **Western Pagoda** is along a narrow lane on the right. Paying a few jiao gains you admission to the tiny surrounding courtyard, where sociable idlers while away sunny afternoons playing cards and sipping tea in peaceful, ramshackle surroundings. The **Eastern Pagoda**, a few minutes' walk away on Shulin Jie, is a more cosmetic, slightly tilted duplicate standing in an ornamental garden. The temples associated with both pagodas are closed to the public.

For a change of atmosphere, ride bus #4 from Dongfeng Lu to the terminus at **Daguan Park** (daily 7am–8pm; ¥15) on Kunming's southwestern limits. Originally laid out by the energetic seventeenth-century Qing emperor Kangxi, it has been modified over the years to include a noisy funfair, snack stalls and souvenir emporiums, and is a favourite haunt of Kunming's youth. Among shady walks and pools, Daguan's focal point is **Daguan Ge**, a square, three-storeyed pavilion built to better Kangxi's enjoyment of the distant **Western Hills** and now a storehouse of calligraphy extolling the area's charms. The most famous poem here is a 118-character verse, carved into the gateposts by the Qing scholar Sun Ran; it's reputed to be the longest set of rhyming couplets in China. The park is set on Daguan Stream, which flows south into **Dian Chi** (see p.790), and there are frequent hour-long cruises down the waterway, lined with willows, to points along Dian's northern shore.

Eating

Eating out is the main pleasure in Kunming after dark; the city is stacked with Yunnanese specialities as well as more ordinary Chinese fare. While hotel restaurants have the most refined surroundings, independent restaurants tend to focus their efforts on the food, so don't be discouraged by the outward appearance of some venues.

The back lanes north of **Dongfeng Xi Lu** or **Jinbi Lu** hold some great stalls and cheap restaurants where you can battle with the locals over grilled cheese, hotpots, fried snacks rolled in chilli powder, loaves of excellent meat-stuffed soda bread, and rich duck and chicken casseroles. Two streets that run along the boundary of the university, **Wenlin Jie** and **Wenhua Xiang**, are packed with cafes, bars and restaurants (and clothing boutiques). Indian, Chinese, Korean, Japanese Thai and Western food can all be found here, as can a decent cup of coffee, in laid-back surroundings – several of the cafés even boast well-stocked book exchanges. For Western food and decent coffee, you can also visit the Nordica Art Gallery (see p.788). As well as the places below, the Kundu Night Market (see p.788) has a host of dining options, though none has an English menu.

1910 Gare Du Sud 8 Houxin Jie. ⓣ0871/3169486. Traditional Yunnan fare in a building that once served as a French colonial train station; there's a large balcony and courtyard and photos of colonial Kunming throughout. It's rather upscale, and a popular place for visitors to make their first experiments with local specialities. Going east along Huancheng Bei Lu from Dongfeng Xi Lu, it's in the first alley on the right.

Aoma's 20 Chuncheng Lu. Steaks, pasta, pizzas and some local dishes, in an urbane and relaxed atmosphere.

Blue Bird 127 Dongfeng Xi Lu ⓣ0871/3610478 and 132 Cuihu Nan Lu ⓣ0871/5315507. The larger branch at Dongfeng Xi Lu specializes in Thai and Burmese cuisine; fish with lemon sauce and chicken curry are recommended. The smaller branch on Cuihu Nan Lu serves Chinese and Thai cuisine and has a pleasant roof garden. A dinner for two should come to around ¥100.

City Café Dongfeng Dong Lu. Basic Western and Chinese meals at reasonable prices (¥15–); an adjoining ticket-agency booth also has a laundry service.

French Café Wenlin Jie. There's a large French contingent in Kunming, drawn perhaps by the colonial connection; this café, with its pastries, quiches and air of *hauteur*, must make them feel at home.

Fuhua Yuan Jingxing Jie. Airy, canteen-like affair in one of the most charismatic parts of town, serving crossing-the-bridge noodles and other light meals downstairs, full meals upstairs.

Mamafu's/Aoma Meili Pub Baita Lu and Dongfeng Dong Lu. Owned by the same people as *Aoma's*; of these interlinked premises, *Mamafu's* is a cultivated café while *Meili* focuses rather on evening drinks.

Prague Café 40 Wenlin Jie. This offshoot of a successful Lijiang enterprise offers very strong coffee and a decent breakfast (¥16), as well as Internet access and book exchange. One of the better cafés in this locality, it's a good place to while away an afternoon.

Salvadors Wenhua Xiang. The best of the foreign-run student cafés, with great home-made ice cream as well as such novelties as hummus and bagels.

Shiping Huiguan 24 Cuihu Nan Lu Ⓣ0871/3627444. This elegantly restored courtyard restaurant is a great place to sample Yunnan cuisine; it's rather well done but not expensive, and the nightly dance performances by Yi minority people are an added extra.

Vegetarian restaurant Opposite the Yuantong Si, Yuantong Jie. An excellent place, reasonably priced and with an English menu and pictures of the dishes on the wall. It serves a mix of straight vegetable and imitation-meat dishes – best of the latter are coconut-flavoured "Spareribs" (bamboo shoots, celery and fried bean-curd skin), "chicken" and fungus rolls (dried bean curd), and "fish" (deep fried mashed potato served in a rich garlic and vinegar sauce).

Wei's Pizza 27 Xiao Dong Jie off Nanping Jie Ⓣ0871/3166189. Long-standing popular restaurant with wood-fired pizzas, genuine Italian chefs and extremely reasonable prices. Also offered are some unusual Chinese dishes, including river moss with coriander and Hakka bean curd.

Yunnan Flavour Restaurant Dongfeng Dong Lu, next door to the *Camellia Hotel*. With (Han Chinese) hostesses in the traditional costume of Yunnan ethnic minorities welcoming you at the door, the atmosphere here is at best slightly tacky, but they do serve the full range of famous and not so well-known Yunnan dishes, including crossing-the-bridge noodles. Popular with tour groups.

Drinking, nightlife and entertainment

Thanks to rising incomes and a big expat population, Kunming makes a great place to go out, with plenty of friendly, reasonably priced **bars and clubs** patronized by a good mix of locals and foreigners. *Hump Over The Himalayas* on Jinbi Lu is a complex (or, after a few drinks, a maze) of interlinked bars – stumble out of one and you fall straight into another. The main foreign student hang-out is the underground dive, the *Speakeasy* at 445 Dongfeng Dong Lu; beers cost ¥6, and it holds a couple of pool tables. There's a Western DJ on Fridays, Thursday is hip-hop night, and there are occasional gigs. The *Camel Bar* on Tuodong Lu is slightly more upmarket, well established and polished, with a lively, predominantly Chinese clientele. Downstairs there's a dance floor, while the more laid-back upstairs area is ideal for sitting over a coffee during the day.

If you can't live without cheesy techno and flashing lights, join Kunming's silver-suited and platform-booted finest at the Kundu Night Market on Xinwen Lu, a street of bars and discos, with late-night restaurants and nail and tattoo parlours in between. Everywhere's free to get in, but drinks cost at least ¥25.

Kunming has several **operatic troupes** and indigenous entertainments that include *huadeng*, a lantern dance. For information on up-and-coming entertainment and cultural events, check out Ⓦwww.gokunming.com. Indoor performances are sadly infrequent, but there are often informal weekend shows outside the Workers' Cultural Hall and in Cuihu Park. Keep an eye on local newspapers (or ask at your hotel) for similar activities at the Yunnan Arts Theatre on Dongfeng Xi Lu. Gigs, club nights and talks take place frequently at the Scandinavian-run **Nordica**, 101 Xiba Lu (Ⓣ0871/4114692, Ⓦwww.tcgnordica.org), an old factory converted into a complex of galleries, café and studio spaces. Kunming attracts a lot of artists, and Nordica is also a good place to find them and their work.

Listings

Airlines Yunnan Air, Tuodong Lu (Ⓣ0871/3164270 or 3138562; daily 24hr), sells tickets for all Chinese airlines and has discounts on their own flights. Other Chinese airline offices include China Southern, 2 Xuefu Lu, Education Building (Ⓣ0871/5141240), and China Eastern, 1 Yongfeng Lu (Ⓣ0871/6176888). International airlines in Kunming include: Dragonair and Cathay Pacific in the *Golden Dragon Hotel* at 575 Beijing Dong Lu (☎0871/3138592); Thai Airways on the second floor of the *Jinhua Hotel* at 98 Beijing Lu (☎0871/3548655); Laos Aviation at the *Camellia Hotel*, 154 Dongfeng Dong Lu (☎0871/3125748); and Malaysian Airlines at 12 Yongping Yuan on Yongping Lu (☎0871/3570000).

Banks and exchange The main branch of the Bank of China is at the corner of Beijing Lu and Renmin Dong Lu (Mon–Fri 9–11.45am & 2.30–5.30pm). There are smaller branches on Huancheng Nan Lu and Dongfeng Xi Lu.

Bike rental The *Camellia Hotel*, the *Youth Hostel*, the *Hump* and the *Camel Bar* all rent bikes for ¥3/hr.

Bookshops The city's best English-language bookshop – in fact one of the best in the country – is Mandarin Books at 52 Wenhua Xiang, near the university, which has many imported novels, obscure academic texts, guidebooks and much that is published in English in China, all of it fairly pricey.

Cinema Kunming's main screen is on the south side of the Dongfeng Lu/Zhengyi Lu intersection. There's another good multiplex, the XJS, at the junction of Wenlin Jie and Dongfeng Xi Lu.

Consulates Burma (Myanmar): Rooms B503 & A504, Long Yuan Jewelery Centre Building, 166 Weiyuan Jie, behind the giant Carrefour on Dongfeng Xi Lu (☎0871/3641268 or 3603477; Mon–Fri 8.30am–noon & 1–4.30pm, closed during Burmese public holidays). Laos: ground floor, *Camellia* hotel, Dongfeng Dong Lu (☎0871/3176623; Mon–Fri 8.30–11.30am & 1.30–4.30pm); they take three working days to issue visas (costs depend on the applicant's nationality). Thailand: in a building in front of the *Kunming* hotel on Dongfeng Dong Lu (Mon–Fri 9–11.30am; ☎0871/3168916). Vietnam: in the *Zhaxing Hotel*, 157 Beijing Lu (☎0871/3515889; Mon–Fri 9–11.30am). Visas for these four countries can also be obtained through travel agents.

Hospital Yunnan Province Red Cross hospital and emergency centre is on Qingnian Lu.

Internet access You can get online in most hotels, and in the foreigner-oriented cafés up near the university, though it's considerably cheaper to do so at one of the many ordinary Internet cafés in the university district.

Mail and telephones The GPO is on the southern stretch of Beijing Lu (daily 8am–8pm). There are phones at the GPO, but the main Telecom building is north at the junction with Dongfeng Lu (Mon–Fri 8am–6.30pm, Sat & Sun 9am–5pm).

PSB The main office is on Beijing Lu, but the Foreign Affairs Department is in Jinxing Huayuan, Jinxing Xiao Lu (☎0871/5717030; daily 8–11am & 1–5pm) in the northeast of the city. They speak good English and are generally helpful with visa extensions.

Shopping. For items with a local flavour, try bamboo pipes, home-grown tobacco, and trinkets sold in backstreet markets, such as the curio stalls at the bird and flower market. Yunnan also has a reputation as a source of rare medicines, though prices in Kunming for many of these are grossly inflated – if you're curious, check out the handful of shops south of the Beijing Lu GPO for caterpillar fungus, dragon's blood and other weird items. A "gift pack" selection of these costs ¥680. For hiking gear and travellers' supplies, try On The Tourist's Way at 151 Baoshan Jie. Western culinary staples such as cheese and pasta can be bought at Paul's Shop on Wenhua Xiang, just east of Mandarin Books.

Travel agents Travel agents and ticket offices abound in Kunming, with virtually every hotel offering at least one travel service. CITS has counters at the *Holiday Inn* (☎0871/3165888), *King World Hotel* (☎0871/3138888), and at Yunnan Air (☎0871/3162214). The *Camellia Binguan's* agency (☎0871/3166388) is recommended for all independent travellers' needs. Both it and CITS can organize visas and private tours around the city and to Shilin, Dali and Xishuangbanna, and obtain train, plane and bus tickets. Expect to pay commissions of at least ¥20 for bus- or train- ticket reservations. Ko Wai Lin Travel, in room 221 of the *Camellia Binguan* (☎0871/3137555), specializes in overland travel into Burma from Ruili. For flights and overland jeep trips to Lhasa in Tibet, visit Mister Chen (room 3116, *Camellia Hotel*, 154 Dongfeng Dong Lu; ☎0871/3188114).

Heilong Tan, Jin Dian and Tanhua Si

Three pleasant temple parks can easily be visited from Kunming on public buses. Ten kilometres north on bus #9 from the North Bus station, **Heilong Tan** (Black Dragon Pool; daily 8am–6pm; ¥15) is set in a garden of ancient trees, full of plum blossoms in spring. The two Ming temple buildings are modest Taoist affairs dedicated to the Heavenly Emperor and other deities, while the pool itself is said to be inhabited by a dragon forced by the Immortal, Lu Dongbin, to provide a permanent source of water for the local people. It should also be haunted by a patriotic Ming scholar who zealously drowned himself and his family as a gesture of defiance in the face of invading Qing armies; his tomb stands nearby.

The same distance to the northeast, on bus #71 from the junction of Nanping Jie and Qingnian Lu, the **Jin Dian** (Golden Temple; daily 8am–5pm; ¥15) has a convoluted history. The original temple, built in 1602 as a copy of the Taihe Gong atop Wudang Shan (see p.490), was shifted to a monastery on Jizu Shan near Dali 35 years later, while the current double-eaved structure was founded by the Qing rebel general Wu Sangui in 1671. Again associated with the mystical Lu Dongbin, who apparently instigated its construction, the temple is supported on a marble base; the lattices, beams and statues in the main hall are made entirely of that thoroughly Yunnanese metal, **bronze**, and house two magical swords used by Taoist warriors. The gardens here are full of fragrant camellias and weekend picnickers, and a tower on the hill behind encloses a large Ming bell from Kunming's demolished southern gates.

Tanhua Si (¥10) is 4km east of the city at the base of the Jinma Hills, over the creek and can be reached on bus #145 from opposite the *Camellia Hotel*. There's little to see in the heavily restored Ming Buddhist temple, but the **ornamental gardens** are pleasant, with narrow paths winding around groves of exotic trees, bamboos, peonies and azaleas. *Tanhua* is a type of magnolia that grew here in profusion before the temple was built, but now only one slender, broad-leafed tree survives, in a small courtyard next to the scripture hall.

Qiongzhu Si

Facing Kunming from hills ten kilometres to the west, **Qiongzhu Si**, the Bamboo Temple (¥15), is an essential trip from town thanks to a fantastic array of over-the-top sculptures. No public bus comes all the way out here, but irregular **minibuses** (¥6) run from the Western bus station on Renmin Xi Lu, at the end of the #5 bus route, or you can charter a minibus in front of the Yunnan Arts Theatre on Dongfeng Xi Lu (¥80 for a seven-seater); alternatively an 8am **tour bus** runs from the same place, which also visits the Western Hills (see below), or you can charter a taxi – you should be able to secure a return trip for around ¥80.

The temple, a dignified building with black and red woodwork standing on Yuan-dynasty foundations, has been restored continually through the ages. Late in the nineteenth century, the eminent Sichuanese sculptor **Li Guangxiu** and his five assistants were engaged to embellish the main halls with five hundred clay statues of *arhats*. This they accomplished with inspired gusto, spending ten years creating the comical and grotesquely distorted crew of monks, goblins, scribes, emperors and beggars that crowd the interior – some sit rapt with holy contemplation, others smirk, roar with hysterical mirth or snarl grimly as they ride a foaming sea alive with sea monsters. Unfortunately it all proved too absurd for Li's conservative contemporaries and this was his final commission. A fourteenth-century **stone tablet** in the main hall records dealings between imperial China and Yunnan in Mongolian and Chinese script, while a good **vegetarian restaurant** is open at lunchtime.

Dian Chi and the Western Hills

Kunming has always owed much of its easy living to the well-watered lands surrounding **Dian Chi** (Dian Lake), which stretches for 50km south from the city. A road circles the shore, and you could spend a couple of days hopping

▲ Huating Si

around from Kunming's Western bus station, though the workers' sanatoriums and recently industrialized lakeside hamlets are not greatly appealing. One place to aim for is southerly **KUNYANG**, birthplace of China's only famous navigator, the Ming-dynasty Muslim eunuch **Zheng He**, who commanded an imperial fleet on fact-finding missions to Southeast Asia, India and Africa (and even, some claim, the Americas) – one of the few times in Chinese history that its rulers showed any interest in the outside world. A hill outside Kunyang has been set aside as a **park** in his memory, complete with a temple museum and the mausoleum of Zheng's pilgrim father, **Hadji Ma**.

Far better, however, are the views of the lake from the top of Xi Shan, the well-wooded **Western Hills**, which rise to 2500m above the shore, 16km southwest of Kunming. The easiest way to get here is by catching bus #5 from Dongfeng Dong Lu to its terminus on Renmin Xi Lu, then transferring to bus #6 for the township of **GAOYAO** (the last bus back to Kunming leaves around 6pm). From Gaoyao you can either slog up to the summit, 8km south, in about three hours, pausing for breath and refreshment in temples along the way, or catch a minibus up. There's also the 8am **tour bus** (¥15) to the top from outside the Yunnan Arts Theatre on Dongfeng Xi Lu, though walking up makes the trip far more worthwhile.

The first temple, **Huating Si** was originally designed as a country retreat for Gao Zhishen, Kunming's eleventh-century ruler, in the form of a pavilion surrounded by gardens and a small pond. Developed as a Buddhist temple from the fourteenth century, it was last rebuilt in the 1920s. Today, it holds some fine **statues** – especially the two gate guardians inside the entrance hall – and a moderately priced **Yunnanese restaurant**.

Winding on through groves of ancient trees, you next reach the halfway **Taihua Si**, a monastery set up by the roving Chan (Zen) sect monk **Xuan Jian** in 1306. It's best known for its carelessly arranged **botanical gardens**; a massive ginkgo tree near the entrance is claimed to be almost as old as the temple itself. A couple more kilometres bring you to the Taoist complex of **Sanqing Ge**, another former royal villa, set on the Western Hills' highest peak. The nine halls are stacked up the slopes in a fine display of Tao style and Qing architecture, each one dedicated to a particular patriarch.

Less than a kilometre beyond Sanqing Ge, the path runs into the **Dragon Gate Grotto**, a series of chambers and narrow tunnels through the hillside that took the late eighteenth-century monk **Wu Laiqing** and his successors more than seventy years to excavate, and which replaced a set of wooden stairs. It's incredible that anyone could conceive such a project, far less complete it with enough flair to incorporate the sculptures of Guanyin and the gods of study and righteousness that decorate niches along the way. At the end is **Grand Dragon Gate** (¥20), a precarious balcony offering magnificent views as it overhangs the wide expanse of Dian Chi.

Shilin and Lunan

Yunnan's premier natural wonder is **Shilin**, the **Stone Forest**, an exposed bed of limestone spires weathered and split into intriguing clusters, 60km east of Kunming near the town of **LUNAN**. There are many such "forests" in southwestern China, but here the black, house-sized rocks are embellished with trees and vines, steps, paths and pavilions. It's undeniably impressive but also touristy and expensive.

It takes about an hour to cover slowly the main circuit through the pinnacles to **Sword Peak Pond**, an ornamental pool surrounded by particularly sharp ridges, which you can climb along a narrow track leading right up across the top of the forest. This is the most frequented part of the park, with large red characters incised into famous rocks, and ethnic **Sani**, a Yi subgroup, in unnaturally clean dresses strategically placed for photographers. The busiest areas of the park can be intimidatingly crammed with Chinese tour groups, but the paths that head out towards the perimeter are much quieter, leading to smaller, separate stone groupings in the fields beyond where you could spend the whole day without seeing another visitor. You can see a bit more by staying the night, as Shilin is surrounded by Sani villages; furthermore, it's worth catching **market day** – Wednesday – in Lunan (a thirty-minute ride on a motorbike-taxi from outside the park gates), where Sani sell their wares and sport embroidered costumes.

Transport to Shilin is not a problem. Comfortable **day-tours** are run by hotels and travel agents in Kunming, but most convenient is the coach which runs every thirty minutes from outside the South Train Station (¥22). **Tour minibuses** (about ¥30) leave from the corner of Huancheng Nan Lu, next to the *King World Hotel* – look for the blue, bilingual sign – but these are largely Chinese-oriented and involve plenty of stops at souvenir shops along the way.

Entry to the park costs a steep ¥140, after which you cross the bridge and bear left up the hill for 50m to a basic hostel (❷) in the square. Continue round the lake and you'll find the ageing but comfortable *Stone Forest Hotel* (ⓣ0871/7711405; ❺) and the more modern *Shilin Summer Palace Hotel* (ⓣ0871/7711888; ❺), either side of steps which lead directly down into the forest itself. Keep going around the lake and uphill for the better-value *Yunlin Hotel* (ⓣ0871/7711409; ❸), which offers singles, doubles and triples. All these have decent **restaurants**, and host infrequent but surprisingly enthusiastic evenings of **Sani dancing**. At the park gates themselves, a mess of stalls sell pretty good, reasonably priced **food** – roast duck, pheasant, pigeon or fish – as well as poor souvenir embroideries.

Southeastern Yunnan

Off-limits until the early 1990s due to the Sino-Vietnamese War, the region between Kunming and Vietnam is a nicely unpackaged corner of the province, and there are plenty of reasons, besides the border, to head down this way. Amiable, old-fashioned **Jianshui** boasts a complement of Qing architecture, and an unusual attraction in nearby caves, while the surprisingly sophisticated **Gejiu** surrounds an artificial lake, an unintentional consequence of old mining methods. Visitors with more time should consider side-trips to **Malipo**, a remote Zhuang town reached via the rail town of **Kaiyuan**, or the impressive terraced landscapes of the **Hong He Valley**, best accessed from pretty **Yuanyang**.

There are two ways to cover the 350km between Kunming and the border town of **Hekou**: either on the daily, narrow-gauge **Kunming–Hanoi train**, which stops only at Kaiyuan along the way (see Kunming's "moving on" box, p.783); or by road, hopping between towns on **public buses** – the better option if you want to have a look around. There's a **Kunming–Hekou highway** too, reaching the border via Lunan and Kaiyuan, with a spur connecting it to Gejiu, but most of the sights lie on smaller roads. Note that if you plan to cross the border, you must obtain a Vietnam visa in advance.

The lakes

Surrounded by green farmland and russet, mud-block villages, **Fuxian Hu** is a thinner, smaller version of Dian Chi, its blue waters plied by long wooden fishing boats. Around 70km from Kunming along winding country roads, the county capital of **CHENGJIANG** marks Fuxian's northern end. This long-established market town holds a sixteenth-century Confucian temple that was

Southeastern Yunnan		
Chengjiang	澄江	*chéngjiāng*
Fuxian Hu	抚仙湖	*fǔiān hú*
Jiangchuan	江川	*jiāngchuān*
Gejiu	个旧	*gèjiù*
Baohua Park	宝华公园	*bǎohuá gōngyuán*
Liangyou Jiudian	良友酒店	*liángyǒu jiǔdiàn*
Shihaolou Binguan	十号楼宾馆	*shíhàolóu bīnguǎn*
Tin Capital Restaurant	锡城饭店	*xīchéng fàndiàn*
Hekou	河口	*hékǒu*
Jianshui	建水	*jiànshuǐ*
Chaoyang Lou	朝阳楼	*cháoyáng lóu*
Confucian Academy	文庙	*wénmiào*
Garden Hotel	花园招待所	*huāyuán zhāodàisuǒ*
Lin'an Jiudian	临安酒店	*lín'ān jiǔdiàn*
Yanzi Dong	燕子洞	*yànzidòng*
Zhujia Huayuan	朱家花园	*zhūjiā huāyuán*
Kaiyuan	开远	*kāiyuǎn*
Malipo	麻栗坡	*málìpō*
Wenshan	文山	*wénshān*
Xinmen	薪门	*xīnmén*
Yuanyang	元阳新街镇	*yuányáng xīnjiēzhèn*
Yunti Hotel	云梯大酒店	*yúntī dàjiǔdiàn*
Duoyishu	多依树	*duōyīshù*
Longshuba	龙树坝	*lóngshùbà*
Bada	坝达	*bàdá*
Nansha	南沙	*nánshā*
Jinzhuzhai	金竹寨	*jīnzhúzhài*
Mengping	勐平	*mèngpíng*

used by Guangdong province's Zhongshan University as its campus during the Japanese occupation. The main road from here follows the lake's western shore 50km south via smaller **Xingyun Hu** and **Jiangchuan**. Beyond is little **Qilu Hu**, on the west side of which lies **XINMEN**, home to a community of four thousand **Mongolians**; descendants of an army garrison left behind by Kublai Khan, they're now employed as fishermen and blacksmiths. It's hard to miss the place: by day you'll see Xinmen's huge **mosque**, while by night the town glows in the hellish light of its metal **foundries**, some factory-sized, others just backyard smithies.

Jianshui and Yanzi Dong

JIANSHUI lies 100km south of Fuxian Hu through some seriously eroded countryside full of short limestone fingers poking out of the soil – a stone forest beginning to sprout. An administrative centre for over a thousand years, the town is full of **historic old buildings**, most of which serve as schools and offices; the grandest are being restored and opened up to the public. The combination of architecture, the town's provincial, kitsch charm, and a friendly populace makes Jianshui a fascinating stopover. Get here sooner rather than later, though, as it's all being tarted up for tourists.

First impressions of a parochial Chinese town are dispelled as the huge red **Chaoyang Lou**, the former eastern gate tower in the city's Ming-dynasty walls, looms into view. Chaoyang Lou is locked and the surrounding grounds swarm with loungers, but there's a great **teahouse** at the top, done up in traditional style, where local musicians practise in the evening – a rare opportunity to observe folk traditions. Follow Jianzhong Lu, the main road, for 200m from the gate, then turn north up Jianxin Jie, and you'll arrive shortly at the grand **Zhujia Huayuan**, the Zhu Clan Gardens (¥60); it's a Chinese box of interlocking halls and courtyards, brightly painted and in good condition. Back on Jianzhong Lu, a few minutes' walk past more market activity and old shops brings you to the front of a **temple** – don't go in, it's used as a military base – followed shortly afterwards by another, grander, affair, the entrance to Jianshui's venerable **Confucian Academy**. The fee here (¥50) allows you to walk around a small **lake**, haunt of kingfishers and elderly musicians, to **Dacheng Men**, the actual gates of the complex. Behind are a school and a series of halls with accomplished interlocking wooden eaves (very good monkeys, as usual) and fine carved screen doors, while in the grounds stand some elderly stone statues of goats, lions and **elephants** – the latter a recurring theme in the academy's decorations.

Practicalities

Buses wind up 100m northwest of Chaoyang Lou on Chaoyang Bei Lu. There are regular departures to Kunming, Tonghai, Gejiu and Kaiyuan, and daily services to Hekou and Yuanyang.

From the bus station, heading back to the roundabout and following Jianzhong Lu, the town's main street, will bring you after 250m to the *Garden Hotel* (❶). Rooms with their own bathroom are the best bet as the communal ones, on the fourth floor, are pungent and unlit; the third-floor rooms have balconies and are pleasant enough. The *Lin'an Jiudian* (ⓣ0873/7651888; ❷) on Chaoyang Bei Lu is a little more classy but is also musty and in a dull part of town. Alternatively, and far more romantically, you can stay at the *Zhujia Huayuan's* hotel at 133 Jianxing Lu (ⓣ0873/7667988; ❺) – certainly one of China's more imaginative – in a room full of imitation Qing furniture; the four-poster beds are particularly fine.

In food circles, Jianshui's most famous product is the **qiguo**, a casserole whose inverted funnel design simultaneously poaches meat and creates a soup; unfortunately, it's hard to find a restaurant that serves the casserole, or a shop selling *qiguos*. The town's most atmospheric **restaurant** is the *Lin'an Fandian* on Jianzhong Lu, whose lower floor, with beam-and-flagstone decor, offers cheap soups and stir-fries; there are more formal arrangements in the balcony rooms upstairs. Otherwise, you'll fall over swarms of fruit sellers and cheap street kitchens, whose charcoal-grilled, skewered tofu, eggs, meat or veg with chilli relish are very popular locally.

Yanzi Dong

The karst formations along the forested Lu River valley, 30km east of Jianshui on the road to Kaiyuan or Gejiu, hold **Yanzi Dong**, the Swallows' Caves (¥60). Stone tools, animal bones and freshwater mussel middens prove the caves were used in Neolithic times, but for the last few centuries people have come to see the tens of thousands of swiftlets who nest here – the noise of wheeling birds is deafening during the early summer. Yangzi Dong has become an enjoyable Chinese-style tourist attraction, featuring wooden walkways and underground restaurants selling bird's-nest cakes – swiftlet nests, constructed out of hardened bird spit, are an expensive delicacy for the Chinese. If you can, catch the **Bird Nest Festival** on August 8, the only day of the year that collecting the then-vacant nests is allowed – a very profitable and dangerous task for local Yi men, who scale the sixty-metre-high cliffs as crowds look on. The caves are easy to reach on public buses heading this way from town, or by chartering a minibus or taxi (¥60) from either of the Chaoyang Bei Lu depots. Buses continue along the main road in both directions until mid-afternoon.

Kaiyuan, Malipo, Gejiu and Yuanyang

KAIYUAN, a major stop on the highway, is about 50km east of Jianshui and around the same distance north of **Gejiu** on the Hekou road. An interesting two-hundred-kilometre side trip by bus leads southeast of Kaiyuan, via the city of **Wenshan**, to **MALIPO**, a small town which the authorities may not want you to visit owing to its proximity to a remote section of the Vietnamese border. A number of ethnic groups inhabit the region hereabouts, and there's a collection of **rock paintings** on cliffs about 1km west of town near the Chaoyang River, apparently connected with local Zhuang mythology (for more on which, see p.747).

Gejiu

A more likely target, **GEJIU** is nothing like the towns further north, owing its character to the **tin mines** above which the city was founded during the late Qing dynasty. These collapsed during a flood in the 1950s, turning the town centre into the kilometre-long **Jin Hu**, a lake now fringed by a shiny and urbane new city whose main streets, along with remnants of the old town, are on the southern shore. There's not really anything to see, but it's a pleasant place to wander. Distant detonations and souvenir shops full of tin trinkets are reminders of the town's *raison d'être*, and you'll probably see village women in semi-traditional blue embroidered clothing in town to trade. There are brilliant vistas from the upper ridges of eastern **Baohua Park** (¥2 entry; cable car ¥20 one way, ¥30 return).

Gejiu's huge **bus station** is at the north of town, handling transport to neighbouring towns as well as Kunming and Tonghai. From here, **Jinhu Xi Lu** and bus #3, or **Jinhu Dong Lu** and bus #2, head down the west and east sides of the lake respectively, to either end of **Jinhu Nan Lu**, which follows the 300-metre-long southern shore. The town's older quarters, quickly being modernized, lie south of here. Gejiu's best-value **accommodation** is the *Shihaolou Binguan* (Ⓣ0873/2122514, Ⓕ2122830; ❺), at the southern end of Jinhu Dong Lu. Of the many places **to eat**, *Liangyou Jiudian*, halfway along Jinhu Nan Lu at the southwest corner of Zhongshan Lu, has excellent all-you-can-eat **hotpots** with sliced meat, fish, seafood and vegetables for ¥35, while the noisy, grubby *Tin Capital Restaurant* on Cailu Jie serves cheap steamers of filling dumplings. For street food, visit the covered market on the west side of the lake on Jinhu Xi Lu.

Yuanyang and around

Hong He, the **Red River**, starts life near Xiaguan in Yunnan's northwest and runs southeast across the province, entering Vietnam at Hekou and flowing through Hanoi before emptying its waters, laden with volcanic soil, into the Gulf of Tonkin. For much of its journey the river is straight, channelled by the **Ailao Shan range** into a series of fertile, steep-sided valleys. These have been **terraced** by resident **Hani**, whose mushroom-shaped adobe and thatch houses pepper the hills. The fields stretch as far as the eye can see, and make for one of the greatest sights of the province. In spring and autumn thick mists blanket the area, muting the violent contrast between red soil and brilliant green paddy fields. Though the best time to see them is between March and May, when the paddies are full of water, they are spectacular at any time.

To take in the scenery, the best base is **YUANYANG**, a small town 80km south of Jianshui and 110km southwest of Gejiu. Increasingly reliant on tourists for its income, but still remote enough to remain off the itinerary of tour groups, Yuanyang becomes a hive of activity on market days (every five days), when Hani, Miao, Yi and Yao minorities come into town from the villages around. Head out of town in any direction and you'll come across lovely **villages** precariously perched on hillsides.

Yuanyang town is split into two very distinct sections. **Nansha** is the new town, but don't get off here; stay on the bus for a further hour until it reaches **Xinjie**, the old town. For **information** on where to go, how to get there and how much to pay, the World Vision-sponsored Window on Yuanyang (Ⓣ1598/7374367; Ⓦwww.yuanyangwindow.cn) in the centre of town (down the steps to the right of the government guesthouse) is invaluable, with English-speaking staff, simple maps, and even a free English-speaking tour-guide service where guides accompany you if you charter a minibus. As the tourist information is all freely given, the Window funds itself and other local development projects through a café with a rooftop terrace and sales of "fairtrade" souvenirs – mostly colourful and intricate embroderies by local women.

Accommodation in Yuanyang is plentiful. The *Apartments of Terraced Fields*, directly opposite the bus station, have run-down budget rooms for ¥20, but there's a much nicer unnamed hotel 75m around the corner and up the hill (Ⓣ0873/5622903; ❸). The town's swishest accommodation is the three-star *Yunti Hotel* (Ⓣ0873/5624858; ❹) which can be found by heading downhill from the bus station, past the square where the main road goes through a short tunnel, and straight ahead up a flight of steps when the road bends left after the market. At the time of writing, the previously spartan *Government Guesthouse* in the central square was being rebuilt; views from some of the rooms will be jaw-droppingly good, but prices are likely to be high compared to the surrounding options (at least ❹).

Food in Yuanyang is nothing to write home about, but the *Donlin Fandian* between the bus station and the square has an English menu and a dapper chef, and can serve you up a main dish, a huge bowl of rice and a steaming mug of green tea for around ¥7.

Within easily walking range of Yuanyang are the hamlets of **Longshuba**, a Yi settlement, and **Jinzhuzhai**, peopled by the Hani minority, which nestle quietly amid trees, giant bamboo and paddy fields. A short minibus ride away, the village of **Bada** is a great place to see the famous terracing, while **Duoyishu** is renowned for its sunrise and **Mengping** for its sunset. Private minibuses ply popular routes from village to village for a few yuan per person (they display their destinations in their front windows), or you can charter a six-seater minibus for the day for around ¥200. The highly recommended *Sunny Guesthouse* in Duoyishu (¥30) can come in very handy, and allows an hour or so longer in bed if you plan to watch the sunrise.

Moving on from Yuanyang, the clear English bus timetable in the lobby of the *Yunti Hotel* can save a lot of confusion at the chaotic bus station. As well as plenty of services to nearby towns, there's a twice-daily bus to Kunming (8hr), and you can also ride down to Hekou near the Vietnam border (4hr). Unfortunately, however, the only option if you want to head to Jinghong and Xishuangbanna is the four-hour trip back up to Jianshui, from where you can catch a direct bus down the highway.

Hekou and the border

It's another 150km southeast from either Kaiyuan or Gejiu to the town of **HEKOU**, where the border post is only a few minutes' walk from the bus station. Across the border in Vietnam, **Lao Cai** has a huge game market, a few despondent hotels, and a **train station** 3km south that offers two services daily for the ten-hour run to Hanoi. Most travellers take a **bus** or motorbike-taxi (US$5) to the hill resort town of **Sa Pa**.

If you're **arriving from Vietnam**, head 50m up the main road and the bus station is on the left. Here you can catch sleeper buses to Kunming (11hr; ¥109), or ordinary buses to Gejiu, Yuanyang and Jianshui. To change money, walk up the main street from the border, turn right after 200m, and you'll arrive at the Bank of China (daily 8am–5.30pm; foreign exchange closed Sun).

Northwestern Yunnan

Vigorously uplifted during the last fifty million years as the Indian subcontinent buckled up against China, **northwestern Yunnan** is a geologically unsettled region of subtropical forests, thin pasture, alpine lakes and shattered peaks painted crisply in blue, white and grey. **Xiaguan**, an overnight trip from Kunming, is the regional hub, the start of roads north past the Bai town of **Dali**. Though Dali is firmly on the beaten track, **Er Hai** – the nearby lake – and mountains make a splendid backdrop, while a few hours beyond Dali lies the former **Naxi** kingdom of **Lijiang**. The Naxi are still resident, though the old town and surrounding villages endured major renovations following the terrible 1996 earthquake. Hikers can organize themselves here for a two-day trek through **Tiger Leaping Gorge**, where a youthful Yangzi cuts through the deepest chasm on Earth. East is **Lugu Hu**, lakeside home to the matrilineal **Mosuo**, while north again is the Tibetan town of **Shangri-La**, the beginning of trips up to the Tibetan borderlands at **Deqin**, or beyond into Sichuan province.

In a completely different direction, heading southwest from Xiaguan to the **Burmese border** brings you to the historic city of **Baoshan** and through the **Dehong region**, a subtropical pocket full of shady traders and ludicrous antics that revolves around the border towns of **Ruili** and **Wanding**. Finally, west of Xiaguan, the **Nu Jiang Valley** is one of China's intriguing backwaters, with pristine jungle and isolated minority communities.

Heading up through Dali to Lijiang and Shangri-La, you'll find mild, even warm **weather** from spring through to autumn, though winters are extremely cold, the likelihood of snow between November and April increasing as you move north. Southwest of Xiaguan, however, temperatures are warm year-round, with heavy summer rains and mild winter nights in the hills.

Transport is improving; rough roads – including the famous **Burma Road** between Kunming and Wanding – are being replaced or upgraded to highways, while Kunming is directly connected by **air** to Xiaguan, Lijiang, Shangri-La and **Mangshi** near Wanding, and by **train** to Xiaguan. As far as foreign travellers are concerned, the **Tibet road**, which follows the dramatic upper reaches of the Lancang River to Markam, then turns west towards Lhasa, is at the time of writing open only to groups travelling in a private vehicle, with a driver and a guide; agencies in Dali, Lijiang and Shangri-La can make the arrangements.

Chuxiong and Xiaguan

The first 390km of the **Burma Road** run west of Kunming to Xiaguan through a succession of valleys and mountain ranges that well repay a few days' exploration. For most visitors, however, the lure of Dali is too great, an all-too-easy trip from Kunming on a direct bus or train via Xiaguan.

Chuxiong

If leisurely travel suits you, the midpoint town of **CHUXIONG** makes a good base en route to Xiaguan. Inhabited since the Zhou dynasty (700 BC), it's now almost entirely modern and is home to a substantial Yi population, who celebrate their **Torch Festival** on the twenty-fourth day of the sixth lunar month with a fair and night-time revelries. The markets here are known for their silver jewellery, there are a few parks and temples nearby – most notably 20km away at **Zixi Shan**, a wooded mountain dedicated to Buddhism since the twelfth century – and, for historians and paleontologists especially, some interesting associations. In 1975 a huge Zhou mausoleum was discovered on Chuxiong's southern outskirts at **Wanjiaba**, containing farm tools and five of the oldest **bronze drums** yet discovered in Asia, now in the Provincial Museum in Kunming (for more on bronze-drum cultures, see p.740). Separate sites surrounding the town of **Lufeng**, 80km east, closer to Kunming, have yielded dinosaur bones and fragments of *ramapithecus* and *sivapithecus* fossils, possible hominid prototypes.

For **accommodation** in Chuxiong, try the *Chuxiong Binguan* on Xinshi Jie (❸) or the *Zixi Lüguan* on central Zhong Dalu (❸, dorm beds ¥15), both of which have fair restaurants.

Xiaguan

XIAGUAN, an increasingly industrialized transport hub, lies on the southern shore of Er Hai Lake. It's also confusingly known as **Dali Shi** (Dali City), and most "Dali" buses from Kunming actually terminate here – **for Dali** itself, you can either take bus #4, which passes along Jianshe Dong Lu every few minutes (¥2) and carries you all the way to Bo'ai Lu, or catch a taxi (¥30). The **train station** is 2km east on Dianyuan Lu along the #5 and #6 bus routes (for Dali, take bus #8). Xiaguan's main drag is **Jianshe Dong Lu**, a 500-metre-long street

Chuxiong and Xiaguan		
Chuxiong	楚雄	*chǔxióng*
Chuxiong Binguan	楚雄宾馆	*chǔxióng bīnguǎn*
Zixi Lüguan	紫溪旅馆	*zǐxī lǚguǎn*
Zixi Shan	紫溪山	*zǐxī shān*
Xiaguan	下关	*xiàguān*
Binchuan	宾川	*bīnchuān*
Xiaguan Binguan	下关宾馆	*xiàguān bīnguǎn*
Xiaguan Fandian	下关饭店	*xiàguān fàndiàn*

The Burma Road

More than two thousand years ago, merchants carrying goods between the Han empire and Rome along the Southern Silk Road established trade routes through northern Yunnan into **Burma** and beyond. Travelled by Marco Polo on one of his errands for the Mongol court, this became known as the "Tribute Road" following China's successful eighteenth-century annexation of eastern Burma, but later fell into disuse as the Qing court cut off ties with the outside world. When Japan invaded China during the 1930s they drove the Guomindang government to Sichuan, isolating them from their eastern economic and industrial power base. Turning west for help, the Guomindang found the **British**, who then held Burma and were none too keen to see China's resources in Japanese hands. In fact, there had been plans for a link through to Burma for forty years, and a road had already been built from Kunming to Xiaguan. Britain agreed to help extend this into a 1100-kilometre supply line connecting **Kunming** with the Burmese rail head at **Lashio**.

What became the **Burma Road** was swiftly completed by three hundred thousand labourers in 1938, an incredible feat considering the basic tools available and the number of mountains along the way. After the Japanese stormed French Indochina in 1940 and halted rail traffic between Vietnam and Kunming, the road became China's only line of communication with the allies, though it was always a tenuous one, cut frequently by landslides and summer monsoons. Lashio fell a year later, however, and the road became redundant once more, remaining so after the war ended thanks to Burma's self-imposed isolation and the chaos of the Cultural Revolution. Now partially sealed and open again as the Yunnan–Burma Highway, the 910-kilometre Chinese stretch between Kunming and the border crossing at **Wanding** remains – like the Great Wall – a triumph of stolid persistence over unfavourable logistics.

between Tai'an Lu in the east and Renmin Lu in the west. The **airport** is 15km east of here, for which you'll need a taxi (¥60 to Dali); the ticket office of Yunnan Air is on Jiangshe Lu, at the crossroads with Renmin Lu (Ⓣ0872/2166588). Long-distance buses stop at a number of depots along Jianshe Dong Lu, though the **main bus station** is down towards Renmin Lu. There are daily departures to, among other destinations, **Baoshan** and **Liuku** to the west, Jizu Shan and Lugu Hu to the northeast via **Binchuan**, and south to **Jinghong** in Xishuangbanna, a bumpy 27-hour journey. Plentiful minibuses shuttle between Xiaguan and the villages along the western shore of **Er Hai**.

There's a basic **hotel** at the bus station (❶), with the upmarket *Xiaguan Fandian* (Ⓣ8072/2125859; ❺), favoured by tour groups and with a CITS desk, about 100m east, and the mid-range *Xiaguan Binguan* (❹) on the Jianshe Dong Lu/Renmin Lu corner. Markets and cheap places to eat fill the backstreets. If you have time to kill, go for a stroll in **Erhai Gongyuan**, a green, hilly park a couple of kilometres northeast of the centre on the lakeshore. The PSB at 21 Tianbao Jie (Mon–Fri 8–11am, 2–5pm; Ⓣ0872/2142149) on the route of bus #8, offers same-day visa extensions.

Dali and around

A thirty-minute bus ride north of Xiaguan and almost a satellite suburb, **DALI** draws swarms of tourists: Chinese package groups come seeking some colourful history, while foreign backpackers experience China-lite in a Westerner-friendly theme park of beer gardens, massage parlours and hippified cafés. It

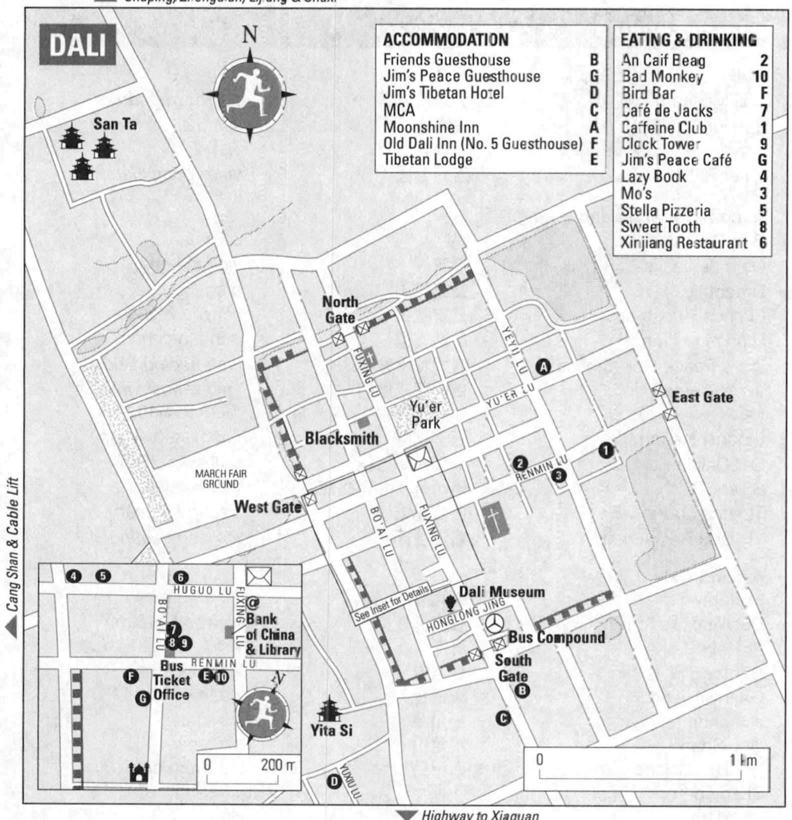

might sound like a blackspot, but so long as you avoid the over-commercialized central strip, the town is actually pretty, interesting and relaxed; if you had to choose between Dali and Lijiang, as plenty of foreign tourists do, Dali wins by a nose. Some, seduced by the lure of China's closest approximation to bohemia, and the local weed, forget to leave, and there are plenty of resident Westerners, some of whom run bars or cafés.

The town and surrounding villages are full of old houses, and hold an indigenous **Bai** population. To the east lies the great lake, **Er Hai**, while the invitingly green valleys and clouded peaks of the fifty-kilometre-long **Cang Shan range** rear up behind town, the perfect setting for a few days' walking or relaxation.

If you can, visit during the **Spring Fair**, held from the fifteenth day of the third lunar month (April or May). Originally a Buddhist festival, the event has grown into five hectic days of horse trading, wrestling, racing, dancing and singing, attracting thousands of people from all over the region to camp at the fairground just west of town. You'll probably have to follow suit at this time, as beds in Dali will be in short supply. In addition, an impressive but frankly rather scary **torch festival** is held on the 24th day of the sixth lunar month – flaming torches are paraded at night, and people even throw gunpowder at each other.

There's much more to Dali than its modern profile. Between the eighth and the thirteenth centuries, the town was at the centre of the Nanzhao and Dali

Dali and around

Dali	大理	*dàlǐ*
Dali Museum	大理博物馆	*dàlǐ bówùguǎn*
San Ta Si	三塔寺	*sāntǎ sì*
Yita Si	一塔寺	*yītǎ sì*
Yu'er Park	玉耳公园	*yù'ěr gōngyuán*
Accommodation and eating		
Bird Bar	鸟吧	*niǎobā*
Café de Jacks	樱花阁	*yīnghuā gé*
Dragonfly	蜻蜓花园	*qīngtíng huāyuán*
Friends Guesthouse	三友客栈	*sānyǒu kèzhàn*
Higherland Inn	高地宾馆	*gāodì bīnguǎn*
Jim's Peace Guesthouse	吉姆和平客楼	*jímǔ hépíng kèlóu*
Jim's Tibetan Hotel	吉姆藏式酒店	*jímǔ zàngshì jiǔdiàn*
MCA	MCA酒店	*MCA jiǔdiàn*
Moonshine Inn	苍岳别院	*cāngyuè biéyuàn*
Old Dali Inn	大理四季客栈	*dàlǐ sìjì kèzhàn*
Sweet Tooth	Sweet Tooth甜点屋	*tiándiǎn wū*
Tibetan Lodge	西藏宾馆	*xīzàng bīnguǎn*
Xinjiang Restaurant	新江餐厅	*xīnjiāng cāntīng*
Around Dali		
Butterfly Spring	蝴蝶泉	*húdié quán*
Du Wenxiu's tomb	杜文秀之墓	*dùwénxiù zhīmù*
Er Hai	洱海	*ěrhǎi*
Gantong Si	甘通寺	*gāntōng sì*
Guanyin Tang	观音堂	*guānyīn táng*
Jianchun	剑川	*jiànchuān*
Jizu Shan	鸡足山	*jīzú shān*
Nanzhao Island	南诏岛	*nánzhāo dǎo*
Shaping	沙坪	*shāpíng*
Shaxi	沙溪	*shāī*
Shegu Ta	蛇骨塔	*shégǔ tǎ*
Shibao Shan	石宝山	*shíbǎo shān*
Taihe	太河	*tàihé*
Tianzhuang Hotel	田庄宾馆	*tiánzhuāng bīnguǎn*
Wase	挖色	*wāsè*
Xiao Putuo Island	小普陀岛	*xiǎo pǔtuó dǎo*
Xizhou	喜洲	*xǐzhōu*
Zhonghe Peak	中和山	*zhōnghé shān*
Zhoucheng	周城	*zhōuchéng*

kingdoms, while in the mid-nineteenth century it briefly became capital of the state declared by **Du Wenxiu**, who led the Muslim rebellion against Chinese rule (see p.778). Millions died in the suppression of that revolt, and Dali was devastated, never to recover its former political position. An earthquake destroyed the town in 1925, but it was rebuilt in its former style. The majority of the regional population today are Bai, though Muslims and Han remain.

Arrival and transport

Dali covers only about four square kilometres, and much of the town is contained by what remains of its Ming-dynasty walls. The main axis of its grid-like street plan is **Fuxing Lu**, cobbled and planted with cherry trees, which runs between the old north and south gates. **Bo'ai Lu** runs parallel and to the west, while the centre hinges around **Huguo Lu**, cutting across both at right angles.

The #4 bus from Xiaguan drives through the town, but **long-distance buses** either drop off on the highway, which skirts Dali's western side, or deliver to the bus compound just inside the south gates on Fuxing Lu, where there's also a **ticket office**. There's another useful booking office on Bo'ai Lu, with more scattered around. **Leaving**, you might have to pick up long-distance services from the main road, or even proceed to Xiaguan first. **Minibuses** between Xiaguan and sites along Er Hai's western shore can be flagged down on the highway immediately west of Dali, and are a cheaper and more flexible way to get around the vicinity than the **tours** offered by agents – though the latter are convenient and reasonable value. Alternatively, you can rent a **bicycle** from hotels or foreigners' cafés for about ¥20 per day, plus deposit. Always check the condition of the bike, as you are fully responsible for any damage or loss.

Fuxing Lu is where to find the **Bank of China** (foreign exchange daily 8am–7pm), the only ATMs, and the **post office** (daily 8am–9pm), which contains Dali's international telephone counter. There's a telecom office with **Internet access** at the corner of Fuxing Lu and Huguo Lu, and a 24-hour Internet café at the top of Renmin Lu, near Bo'ai Lu (¥3). There's a branch of Kunming's excellent English-language bookshop, Mandarin Books, on Fuxing Lu.

Accommodation

Low-pressure touts meet the buses, hoping to escort arrivals to accommodation. During Chinese holidays, rates are at least double those indicated here.

Dragonfly Cai Cun Ma Tou ⓣ13529657680, ⓦwww.dragonflydali.com. This foreign-run hippyish hang-out down by Er Hai Lake has surprisingly comfortable rooms in a wooden lodge, all equipped with stand-alone showers and DVD players, though the walls are thin. There are cheaper cabins, and a tipi, in the garden. Call ahead for a free pick-up, or take bus #2 all the way to the terminus (10min ride). Their namecard invites you to roach it; it's that kind of place – expect yoga, fire jugglings, and genial befuddlement. Parties every Sat. ❶–❸

Friends Guesthouse 2 Wenxian Lu ⓣ0872/2662888, ⓦwww.friendsdali.com. This little compound, just east of the south gate, would be so much nicer withouth the metal ramp that despoils the garden and rattles noisily whenever a car runs over it. On the plus side, rooms are pretty good value, though some don't get enough light. Ask to see what's available before making your choice. ❷

Higherland Inn Cang Shan Daorendong ⓣ0872/2661599, ⓦwww.higherland.com. This small guesthouse retreat, located high in the Cang Shan range, allows guests to take full advantage of Dali's best feature, the mountains. The best way to get there is to take the cable car to the Zhonghe Temple (see p.806), from which it's a 10min walk west, uphill; otherwise it's a 2hr slog, which is no fun with luggage. Be sure to phone before you turn up. Rooms are simple but clean, and with a decent garden and restaurant on site, plenty of hiking all around, there's little reason to head back down to civilization. Dorms ¥40, ❷

Jim's Peace Guesthouse Bo'ai Lu ⓣ0872/2671822. Cosy rooms, though ask to see all those available and try to avoid the front of the building overlooking the road. The restaurant is a sociable place and Jim, the likeable half-Tibetan owner, runs plenty of tours. ❷

Jim's Tibetan Hotel 13 Yuxiu Lu ⓣ0872/2677824. Jim's second, larger and more luxurious venture is some way from the action, 10min walk west from the centre of town in a quiet suburb. Rooms, decorated in Tibetan style with plenty of old furniture, are characterful and spacious, with very soft beds, and the staff are helpful. There's a garden and rooftop terrace. Again, the excellent trips out of town are a useful bonus. ❹

MCA Just west off the road, 100m south of the south gate outside the town ⓣ0872/2673666. This old favourite offers rooms in a self-contained family compound arranged around a garden. There's a small library, even an art studio, and the eclectic furnishings include some sturdy antiques. Dorm beds ¥40, ❸

Moonshine Inn 16 Yu'er Lu, ☎0086/8722671319. This small guesthouse, run by a Bai lady and her German husband, looks like a boutique hotel, yet it's priced for backpackers, making it Dali's best place to stay. An old three-storey courtyard compound has been lovingly restored, with Teutonic attention to detail, in local wood, tile and stone – there's almost no metal anywhere, and the carved window frames and banisters are lovely. Rooms on the top floor, with access to a roof terrace, are the best. Note that all the loos are squat style. It's not easy to find at first, as it's twenty metres down a narrow, unnamed alley off Yu'er Lu; look for the red sign. ❸

Old Dali Inn (No. 5 Guesthouse) Bo'ai Lu ☎0872/2670382. Indifferent staff and basic toilets compensated for by very hot, powerful showers, and a courtyard surrounded by two tiers of wooden "traditional Bai" rooms – check a few out, as some are better than others. Free Internet access and nightly movies. Don't bother with the restaurant. Dorm beds ¥30, ❷

Tibetan Lodge 58 Renmin Lu ☎0872/2664177. A cosy place that's not Tibetan at all, but at least the Han owners run it competently. It's typical of the new breed of Chinese guesthouses that are popping up all over the province – faux ethnic, a bit chintzy, with a big TV in a little room. Rooms are poky with small bathrooms, but they rank among the best-value doubles in this price range. Free Internet access. ❷

The Town

Dali is small enough to walk around in a morning, though you may find yourself slowed by the crowds of hawkers, farmers and shoppers who descend for the Friday **market**. The main street, Fuxing Lu, is overrun with tourists at all hours, making it the least attractive part of town; chilled-out Renmin Lu is much more pleasant, while the many narrow stone side streets are great for wandering. Get your bearings on top of Dali's old **south gate** (¥2), where you can study Xiaguan, Er Hai, the town and mountains from the comfort of a teahouse. Dali's antique **pagodas** stand as landmarks above the roof lines, **Yita Si** due west, and the trinity of **San Ta** a few kilometres north. In the busy **artisans' quarter** below the gate, carpenters and masons turn out the heavy and uncomfortable-looking tables and chairs inlaid with streaky grey **Dali marble** that lurk in Chinese emporiums around the world. The marble is mined up in the hills, and smaller pieces of it are worked into all sorts of souvenirs – rolling pins, chopping boards, miniature pagodas – which you can buy from shops and stalls in town.

The **Dali Museum** (daily except Mon 9am–5pm; ¥5) opposite the bus compound, just 50m or so inside the gate, takes the form of a small Chinese palace with stone lions guarding the gate and cannons in the courtyard. It was built for the Qing governor and appropriated as Du Wenxiu's "Forbidden City" during Du's insurrection. Historic relics include a strange bronze model of two circling dragons, jaws clenched around what might be a tree; a few Buddhist figurines from the Nanzhao period; and some lively statues of an orchestra and serving maids from a Ming noblewoman's tomb – a nice addition to the usual cases of snarling gods and warrior busts. The gardens outside are pleasant, planted with lantana and bougainvillea, with the mountains behind.

North along Fuxing Lu, young and old socialize in the square outside the **library**, playing dominoes or video games. Huguo Lu's western arm, nicknamed "Foreigners' Street", forms the hub of the Western backpacker world, though it's rather too busy to be pleasant; a throng of **cafés**, cheap clothes shops, bilingual **travel agents** happy to book you on tours or long-distance buses (for a commission of ¥20 or so), and massage clinics advertising their services with couplets like "Painful In, Happy Out". It's also the best place to purchase beautiful jewellery and embroideries (many from Guizhou's Miao), and attractive Bai tie-dyes from hawkers – asking prices are ludicrously high, dropping swiftly once bargaining commences. Don't show any interest unless you really want to buy, or you'll be mercilessly hounded. The other ubiquitous touts are the middle-aged ladies hissing "ganja, ganja". You can escape all of this on the attractive eastern arm of Renmin Lu, where the hippy cafés do not yet outnumber the local businesses: don't miss the fantastic blue, multi-tiered Bai-style church in an alley off to the south.

Yita Si and San Ta Si

Built when the region was a major Buddhist centre, Dali's distinctively tall and elegant **pagodas** are still standing after a millennium of wars and earthquakes. Just west of Dali's south gate is the solitary **Yita Si**, a tenth-century tower and virtually abandoned Ming temple surrounded by ancient trees. Better presented is **San Ta Si**, the Three Pagodas, a twenty-minute walk north of town in the grounds of the now-vanished Chongsheng Monastery (daily 8am–5pm; ¥32). Built around 850, the 69-metre-tall, square-based **Qianxun tower** is a century older than the two smaller octagonal pagodas behind. As the structures are sealed, the stiff entrance fee gives access only to souvenir stalls and a hall at the back that contains religious relics discovered during renovations in the 1970s.

Eating and drinking

Two local **specialities** are based on fish from Er Hai: *shaguoyu*, where the fish is fried, then simmered with dried vegetables in a sour stock, and *youdeyu*, a casserole of small oily sprats and tofu. For breakfast, you could take your pick from the sweet buns and noodle soups sold by street stalls and cheap restaurants around the centre. Snacks include pickled vegetables wrapped in a fine pancake, and brittle "fans" of dried yoghurt, which are often fried and crumbled over other dishes – much nicer than it sounds.

Dali's tourist-oriented **cafés and restaurants** serve a mix of Western dishes, Chinese staples and even Bai specialities, and are good places to meet other foreigners and swap news. They're also places where you can use the **Internet** (around ¥5/hr) and get in touch with the latest martial-art, language or painting courses.

▲ San Ta Si

For nightlife, your best bet is to head to the bars of Renmin Lu. The long running *Bird Bar*, at the top of the hill, is the rather snobbish haunt of the Chinese arty set; much more fun is the raucous *Bad Monkey*, a little further down at number 74, run by a pair of English wide boys, who offer shepherds' pie, Lao and Belgian beer, and droll chat. There are plenty of smaller speakeasies further down, towards the east gate, best of which is the paint-spattered *Lazy Lizard* at no. 223, named after the owner's pet.

An Caif Beag 215 Renmin Lu. Low-key, Irish-run café with great burgers, whose outside seating is great for people-watching. Free Wi-Fi.
Cafe de Jacks Bo'ai Lu. Popular after dark for its bar and Chinese versions of curries, pizzas, apple pie and chocolate cake. The open fire makes it cosy on winter evenings.
Caffeine Club 370 Renmin Lu. A relaxed little hideaway with a pool table, offering a limited menu of pizza and pasta dishes.
Clock Tower In an alley off Bo'ai Lu. Slick new upscale venue offering the best full Western breakfasts in town (¥25), with a civilized bar upstairs.
Jim's Peace Café Bo'ai Lu. Restaurant underneath *Jim's Peace Guesthouse*, with comfy sofas, a well-stocked bar and a fine yak stew. Get four people together for a Tibetan banquet (¥30), cooked by the owner's mother.
Lazy Book Huguo Lu. A little detached from the main strip, and the better for it. It's well titled: a good library of books and DVDs makes this a prime venue for whiling away an afternoon.
Mo's Renmin Lu. Decent Indian curries for around ¥40. There's a real tandoori oven.
Stella Pizzeria Huguo Lu. The wood-fired clay oven delivers the best pizzas in town, and the laid-back decor is appealing too, with lots of nooks and crannies for privacy.
Sweet Tooth 52 Bo'ai Lu. A polished and pristine café, run by deaf-and-dumb staff, with great cheesecake.
Xinjiang Restaurant Huguo Lu. This family-run Xinjiang restaurant, just off the road in a narrow alley, is one of the best places around for a cheap meal. Try the pulled noodles or beef stew, and leave room for some skewers of mutton.

Around Dali

While Dali is nice, it can hardly claim to be the real China. Never mind though, you don't have to go far to find something a bit more authentic. Once you've settled in, consider investigating the largely undiscovered Bai town of **Shaxi**, or take a few days to cycle round the lake.

Zhonghe Peak

Due **west** of Dali, **Zhonghe Peak** is one of the tallest mountains in the Cang Shan range, its four-thousand-metre summit often remaining snowcapped until June. To make a partial ascent, start at the small bridge on the highway just north of town and walk through the graveyards to the **Shizu stele**, a four-metre-high inscribed tablet planted in 1304 to record Kublai Khan's conquest of Yunnan half a century earlier. An entrance fee of ¥30 is payable at the gate here. The easiest ascent is on the **chairlift** (¥30), but a fairly easy, two-hour path climbs up through the pine trees from here to **Zhonghe Si** – best handled on a windy day, when the chairlift is closed and the temple is therefore free of Chinese tour groups. Views of the lake and the mountains beyond are stupendous in any case. You'll also find the attractive *Higherland Inn* here (see p.803).

Heading south, at the base of the mountain, look out for the enormous Tianlongbabbu Film and TV City – a studio lot (daily 9am–6pm; ¥52) of fake Chinese temples, palaces, gatehouses, and so on, with excellent views. So long as they're not filming, you can wander the sets at will.

Er Hai

Half an hour's walk east out of Dali's east gate (or a short ride on bus #2) brings you to the shores of forty-kilometre-long **Er Hai**, so called because it's shaped like an ear ('*er*'). You can get out on the water by arranging a **fishing trip** or

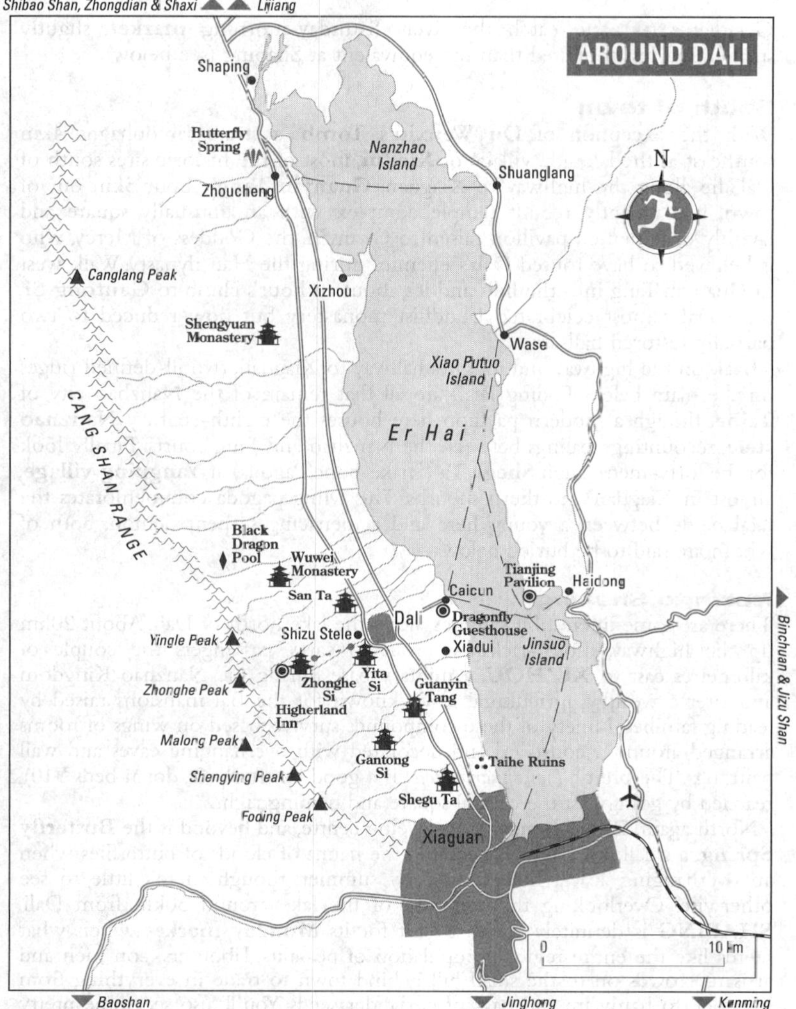

excursion out to the islets and villages around the lake's east shore (¥25–50), most easily done through an agent in Dali; boats have small cockpits and no canopies against sun and spray, so come prepared.

Besides fishing, there's really nothing to do on the lake beyond watching clouds forming over Cang Shan. Directly across from Dali, uninhabited **Jinsuo Island** was the summer retreat for Nanzhao royalty, while the more northerly **Xiao Putuo Island** is a tiny rock completely occupied by a temple whose withered guardian stumbles out after payment. **Nanzhao Island** at the lake's north end is a tourist trap with an overrated castle, but it does also have a pleasant guesthouse (❶).

The east-shore settlements of **HAIDONG** and **WASE** are full of narrow back lanes with crumbling adobe homes and family mansions, their waterfronts thick with fishing gear. You can stay the night in Wase at the *Government*

Guesthouse (❶) and catch the lively Saturday-morning **market**, slightly smaller and less touristed than the equivalent at Shaping (see below).

South of town

With the exception of **Du Wenxiu's Tomb**, a stone sarcophagus 4km southeast at the lakeside village of **Xiadui**, most of the historic sites south of Dali lie along the highway to Xiaguan. **Guanyin Tang**, about 5km out of town, is a recently rebuilt temple complex with an unusually square and lavishly ornamented pavilion raised to Guanyin, the Goddess of Mercy, who is believed to have routed Dali's enemies during the Han dynasty. Walk west of Guanyin Tang into the hills and it's about an hour's climb to **Gantong Si**, once Dali's most celebrated Buddhist monastery but now reduced to two partially restored halls.

Back on the highway and roughly halfway to Xiaguan, two ill-defined ridges on the plain below Foding Peak are all that remain of the Nanzhao city of **Taihe**, though a modern pavilion here houses the eighth-century **Nanzhao stele**, recounting dealings between the Nanzhao and Tang courts. Finally, look for the forty-metre-high **Shegu Ta** (Snake-bone Pagoda) at **Yangping village**, almost in Xiaguan's northern suburbs. This Ming pagoda commemorates the fatal battle between a young hero and a menacing serpent demon, both of whom are said to be buried below.

North to Shaping

There are some interesting **villages** along the lake north of Dali. About 20km up the highway, motor-rickshaws wait to carry passengers the couple of kilometres east to **XIZHOU**, a military base during the Nanzhao Kingdom and later a wealthy agricultural town known for the Bai mansions raised by leading families. Ninety of these compounds survive, based on wings of rooms arranged around a courtyard and decorated with overhanging eaves and wall paintings. The pretty *Tianzhuang Hotel* is a good example (❷, dorm beds ¥10), reached by going past the central square and turning right.

North again, **Zhoucheng** is a tie-dyeing centre, and beyond is the **Butterfly Spring**, a small pond which becomes the haunt of clouds of butterflies when an overhanging acacia flowers in early summer, though there's little to see otherwise. Overlooking the very top of the lake around 30km from Dali, **SHAPING** is definitely worth a visit for its **Monday market**, when what seems like the entire regional population of peasants, labourers, con men and artisans crowds on to the small hill behind town to trade in everything from livestock to hardware and bags of coriander seeds. You'll also see some pretty gruesome ad hoc dentistry taking place.

Shaxi and Shibao Shan

Shaxi, fifty kilometres north of Dali, is one of the best-preserved old towns in Yunnan, and looks like Dali might if no tourists ever went there. To reach it, take the bus from Xiaguan to Jianchuan and get off at Dianmen, about ten kilometres south of Jianchun, where the road forks. Here you can pick up minibuses for the short ride into town.

Shaxi was once a busy trading town on the southern Silk Road; Tibetans sold their sturdy horses and bought tea in return. Now listed as an endangered site by the World Monuments Fund, much of the town is being sympathetically restored, and it's just beginning to gear itself up for visitors. Certainly it has a lot to offer; as well as photogenic cobbled alleyways and wood and stone mansions, it serves as a base for trekking and mushroom hunting (the hills around are one of the few sources of the pine mushroom, a delicacy in Japan). Try to get here for the Sideng market, held every Friday, when Yi and Bai people come down from the remote mountain villages around. There's one very pleasant homestay guesthouse (❷) run by the helpful, English-speaking Wu Yunxing (Ⓔshaxi-travel@hotmail.com), who will also arrange trekking, tours and transport.

It's a two-hour hike, or a forty-minute taxi ride (¥50), from Shaxi to **Shibao Shan** (¥20), a nature reserve and religious sanctuary. There are plenty of temples here, many surprisingly well preserved; some date back to the Nanzhao era, with old-growth forest in between. Don't miss the remarkable Stone Bell temple, in caves in a steep cliff face, and its wonderful stone carvings of Nanzhao kings, Buddha and Guanyin. All the temples here have great frescoes; some show emissaries from India and the Middle East and everyday scenes from the Nanzhao court, while a few are graphically sexual.

Jizu Shan

Buses head 60km northeast from Xiaguan to **BINCHUAN**, from where it's a short hop to **SHAZHI** at the foot of **Jizu Shan** (Chicken-foot Mountain). This became one of western China's holiest peaks after the legendary monk **Jiaye** – who brought Buddhism from India to southern China – fought here with the wicked Jizu king. By the seventh century both Buddhist and Taoist pilgrims were arriving in their thousands to honour his memory. Although in its heyday a hundred or more monasteries graced the heights of Jizu, including the original Golden Temple transported here from Kunming, by 1980 all but half a dozen had decayed. Things are now picking up again, and the trip is worth it if you have the time to take in the stunning scenery and some charismatic temples, among them the **Zhusheng Si** and the ninth-century **Lengyan Pagoda** and accompanying **Jinding Si**, a temple splendidly positioned on a cliff edge at the summit. Entry is ¥40, while the steep ascent takes five hours or so, with – of course – a new cable car for the last and steepest section (¥30). There are some basic guesthouses at the halfway point and at the summit (❶), where people stay in order to get up and watch the dawn. Viewed from here, the spurs of the mountain resemble a bird's long toes – hence the name.

Lijiang

Some 150km north of Dali through numerous Bai and Yi hamlets, roads make their final descent from the ridges to a plain dominated by the inspiringly spiky and ice-bound massif of **Yulong Xue Shan**, the Jade Dragon Snow Mountain. **LIJIANG**, capital of the **Naxi Kingdom**, nestles southeast of the mountain, among green fields and dwindling pine forests – a centuries-old maze of winding lanes and clean streams, weeping willows and rustic stone bridges. In 1996, following a devastating earthquake, the government invested heavily in rebuilding and aimed to recap its investment through tourism. Now Lijiang is one of the most visited tourist destinations on the planet, and the old town, though undeniably pretty, has become a cultural theme park. Four-fifths of the thirty thousand Naxi who were here in 1995 have sold up and moved out, the houses they left behind converted into rank after rank of tacky souvenir shops. Even so, Lijiang is still worth visiting for the genuine culture that survives on its fringes, and offers plenty of potential **excursions** (see p.815).

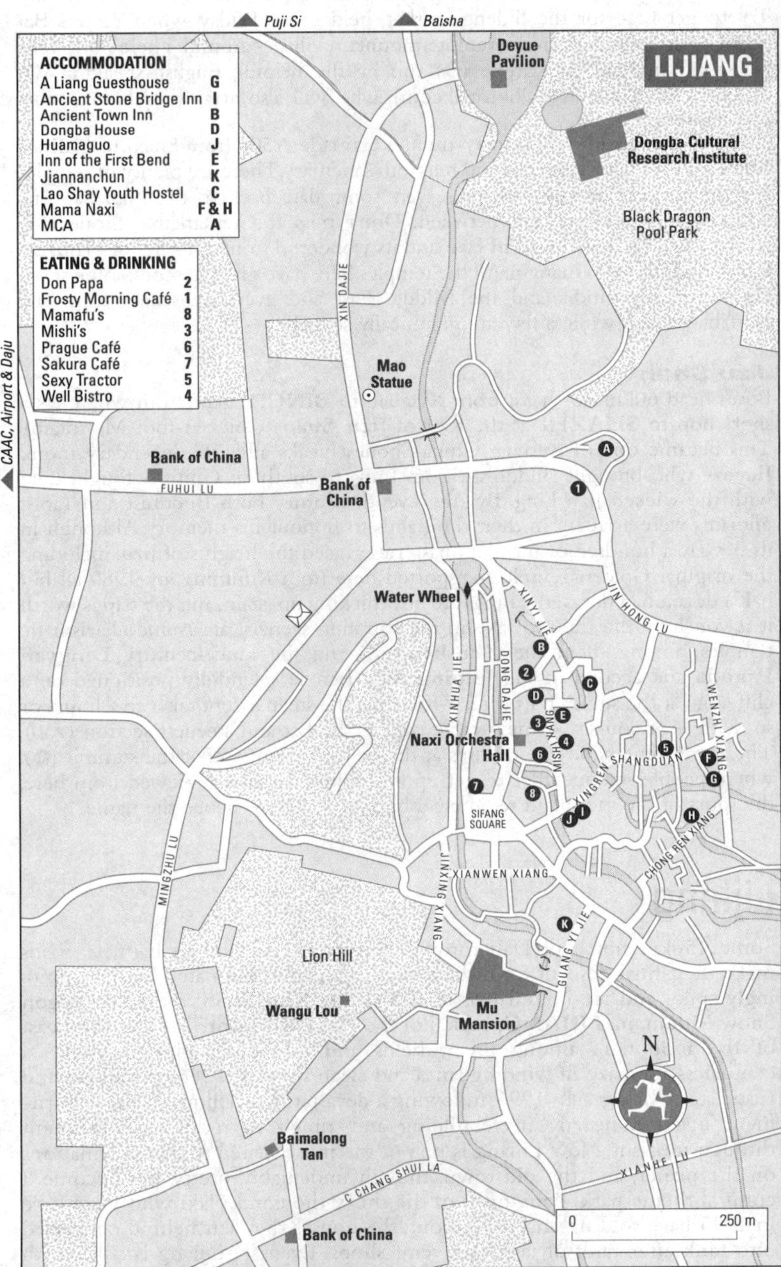
LIJIANG
ACCOMMODATION
A Liang Guesthouse G
Ancient Stone Bridge Inn I
Ancient Town Inn B
Dongba House D
Huamaguo J
Inn of the First Bend E
Jiannanchun K
Lao Shay Youth Hostel C
Mama Naxi F & H
MCA A
EATING & DRINKING
Don Papa 2
Frosty Morning Café 1
Mamafu's 8
Mishi's 3
Prague Café 6
Sakura Café 7
Sexy Tractor 5
Well Bistro 4
Puji Si
Baisha
Deyue Pavilion
Dongba Cultural Research Institute
Black Dragon Pool Park
XIN DAJIE
Mao Statue
Bank of China
FUHUI LU
Bank of China
CAAC, Airport & Daju
Water Wheel
XINYI JIE
JIN HONG LU
DONG DAJIE
XINHUA JIE
WENZHI XIANG
MISHI XIANG
Naxi Orchestra Hall
XINGREN SHANGDUAN
SIFANG SQUARE
CHONG REN XIANG
XIANWEN XIANG
JINXING XIANG
MINGZHU LU
GUANG YI JIE
Lion Hill
Wangu Lou
Mu Mansion
N
Baimalong Tan
C CHANG SHUI LA
XIANHE LU
0
250 m
Bank of China
Dali, Shigu, Qiaotou, Zhongdian & Main Bus Station

Lijiang

Lijiang	丽江	*lìjiāng*
Baimalong Tan	白马龙潭	*báimǎ lóngtán*
Black Dragon Pool Park	黑龙潭公园	*hēilóngtán gōngyuán*
Dayan	大研古城	*dàyán gǔchéng*
Dongba Cultural Research Institute	东巴文化研究室	*dōngbā wénhuà yánjiūshì*
Five Phoenix Hall	五凤楼	*wǔfèng lóu*
Lion Hill	狮子山	*shīzi shān*
Mu Family Mansion	木府	*mùfǔ*
Sifang	四方	*sìfāng*
Accommodation		
A Liang Guesthouse	阿亮客栈	*āliàng kèzhàn*
Ancient Stone Bridge Inn	古城大石桥客栈	*gǔchéng dàshíqiáo kèzhàn*
Ancient Town Inn	古城客栈	*gǔchéng kèzhàn*
Dongba House	东巴豪斯	*dōngbā háosī*
Huamaguo	花吗国客栈	*huāmaguó kèzhàn*
Inn of the First Bend	一湾酒店	*yīwān jiǔdiàn*
Jiannanchun	丽江剑南春文苑	*lìjiāng jiànnánchūn wényuàn*
Lao Shay Youth Hostel	老谢车马店	*lǎoxiè chēmǎdiàn*
Mama Naxi	古城香格韵客栈	*gǔchéng xiānggéyùn kèzhàn*
MCA Hotel	MCA酒店	*MCA jiǔdiàn*
Eating and drinking		
Don Papa	东巴爸	*dōngbābà*
Frosty Morning	雾都酒吧	*wùdū jiǔbā*
Mamafu's	妈妈付餐厅	*māmāfù cāntīng*
Mishi's	密士饭店	*mìshì fàndiàn*
Prague Café	布拉格咖啡馆	*bùlāgé kāfēiguǎn*
Sakura Café	樱花屋	*yīnghuā wū*
Sexy Tractor	翠竹临街	*cuìzhúlínjiē*
Tibetan Dance Centre	雪域风情藏吧	*xuěyù fēngqíng zàngbā*
Well Bistro	井浊餐馆	*jǐngzhuó cānguǎn*

Arrival and city transport

Lijiang is three hours from Dali on the expressway, or five hours if you take the older road (as is likely if you get a rattletrap country bus). The **airport** lies 20km south along the highway. As a rule of thumb, buses to or from northern destinations use the **North bus station**, while other directions are covered from the **main bus station**, at the southern edge of town. From the latter, a fifteen-minute walk uphill along Xin Dajie takes you past a shopping centre and the **post office**, then continues north to the **Bank of China**.

Walking and cycling are the main means of getting around – ask at your accommodation about bike rental. The old town is tough to find your way around – look out for prints of the hand-drawn English map, "Lijiang Old Town", sold in tourist stores (¥5). The best local **tourist agency** is run from the *Dongba House* (see p.812), which organizes hiking and jeep trips – they also hand out a good cycling map.

As for **moving on**, buses head in all directions: south as far as Kunming and Baoshan; west to Weixi; north to Qiaotou or Daju (for **Tiger Leaping Gorge**), and Shangri-La; and east to Lugu Hu and Panzhihua in Sichuan province. **CAAC** is in the western part of town on Fuhui Lu (the same road

The Naxi

The Naxi are descended from a race of Tibetan nomads who settled the region before the tenth century, bringing with them what are still considered some of the sturdiest horses in China and a shamanistic religion known as **Dongba**. A blend of Tibetan Bon, animist and Taoist tendencies, Dongba's scriptures are written in the only hieroglyphic writing system still in use, with 1400 pictograms. The Naxi deity Sanduo is a warrior god depicted dressed in white, riding a white horse and wielding a white spear. Murals depicting him and other deities still decorate temples around Lijiang, and are a good excuse to explore nearby villages by bicycle.

Strong matriarchal influences permeate Naxi society, particularly in the language. For example, nouns become weightier when the word female is added, so a female stone is a boulder, a male stone a pebble. Inheritance passes through the female line to the eldest daughter. Women do most of the work, and own most of the businesses; accordingly, the Naxi women's costume of caps, shawls and aprons is sturdy and practical, while retaining its symbolic meaning; the upper blue segment of the shawl represents night, a lower sheepskin band represents daylight, and those two circles around the shoulder depict the eyes of a frog deity. Naxi men often appear underemployed, though they have a reputation as good gardeners and musicians. You'll likely see a few falconers too. To learn more, try to find the exhaustive, two-volume *Ancient Nakhi Kingdom of Southwest China* by the eccentric botanist-anthropologist **Joseph Rock**, who lived here back in the 1930s.

as the **PSB**), or you can buy air tickets from the travel agents outside the bus station; as well as daily services to Kunming, there are daily flights to Jinghong in Xishuangbanna. All the foreigner-oriented cafés have **Internet access**, and many have Wi-Fi.

Accommodation

Lijiang has plenty of **accommodation**, ranking indeed as one of the very few places in China with characterful hotels, including some excellent small, family-run guesthouses in traditional houses in the old town. Mid-range hotels in the new town are legion, but there's no reason to stay there – even if you have an early bus, it's a very short taxi ride to the station from anywhere in town. All the hotels below are housed in Naxi-style buildings, some more authentic than others; recently, Han entrepeneurs have been buying up local houses and remodelling them in a faux-ethnic style for the domestic tourist market, whose main demand, it seems, is for a giant TV in the room. Facilities are usually shared in such places, as the plumbing is rudimentary. Though addresses are listed, they aren't much help – see the map for locations.

A Liang Guesthouse 110 Wenzhi Xiang ⓣ0888/5129923. One of the best places to stay in Lijiang, this is a snug old Naxi courtyard house – one of a hundred "specially protected" buildings in town – with rooms that the amiable resident family rent out at reasonable rates, though they are pushing things by turning more and more rooms into guestrooms. All facilities are shared. ❶

Ancient Stone Bridge Inn Xingren Shangduan ⓣ0888/5184001. Nice location at the heart of the old town, which, like many such places, has small attractive rooms arranged around a courtyard, with a common bathroom. ❷

Ancient Town Inn Xinyi Jie ⓣ0888/5189000, ⓕ5126618. Slightly more upmarket than most of the old-town guesthouses, this is a new, quiet, appealing place offering rooms with or without a bath. ❹

Dongba House Jishan Lane, 16 Xinyi Jie ⓣ0888/5187630; ⓦwww.shangrila-tour.com. One of the main centres for budget travellers, run by owners who understand their needs. The simple dorms and doubles are well kept, and the tour agency is the best in town. It's a good place to rent bikes (¥20 per day), as they also hand out a free map. Dorms ¥30, ❶

Huamaguo Xingren Shangduan ⓣ0888/5121688. The best of the new Chinese guesthouses, thanks to a superb location right beside the main canal, which you can appreciate from a charming courtyard. Rooms are a bit dark; bathrooms are communal. ❷

Inn of the First Bend 43 Mishi Xiang ⓣ0888/5181688. An old backpacker staple, with friendly, professional staff. Rooms surround a central courtyard, and all facilities are shared. Bike rental available. Dorm beds ¥30, ❷

Jiannanchun 8 Guanyi Xiang ⓣ0888/5102222. The upmarket option, an imitation Naxi building, in which the mostly Han staff wear Naxi costume all day. The location is good, but it's only worth considering if you absolutely must have your own bathroom. ❼

Lao Shay Youth Hostel 25 Jishan Alley, Xinyi Jie ⓣ0888/5116118; ⓦwww.laoshay.com. Well located at the heart of the old town; there's a wide range of rooms, though it's a little pricier than its competitors. Dorms ¥25, rooms ❷

Mama Naxi 78 Wenhua Jie, ⓣ0888/8881012, 70 Wenhua Jie ⓣ0888/5107713. The most popular backpacker guesthouse, thanks largely to its friendly staff and owner. All rooms, including three-bed dorms, are arranged around a courtyard. The second, larger, branch has a pleasant restaurant offering tasty breakfasts (¥20). Dorms ¥15–30, ❷–❸

MCA Hotel 44 Yueshangchang, ⓣ0888/5183699; ⓦwww.culture-week.cn. Good views and a convenient location make this worth considering. Rooms vary, so ask to see a few; the pricier ones have their own bathrooms. Dorms ¥20, rooms ❷–❸

The Town

Oriented north–south, **Xin Dajie** is Lijiang's three-kilometre-long main street. Just about everything west of this line is modern, but to the east, behind **Lion Hill**'s radio mast, you'll find the old town, known locally as **Dayan**. It's not easy to navigate around Dayan's backstreets, but as there are few specific sights this hardly matters. While you wander, try to peek in around the solid wooden gates of **Naxi houses**. These substantial two-storey homes are built around a central paved courtyard, eaves and screens carved with mythological figures and fish, representing good luck. Family houses are very important to the Naxi – Lijiang was formerly organized into clans – and many people spend a large proportion of their income maintaining and improving them.

Naxi music and dancing

The **Naxi Orchestra** is an established part of Lijiang's tourist scene. Using antique instruments, the orchestra performs Song-dynasty tunes derived from the Taoist Dong Jin scriptures, a tradition said to have arrived in Lijiang with Kublai Khan, who donated half his court orchestra to the town after the Naxi chieftain helped his army cross the Yangzi. Banned from performing for many years, the orchestra regrouped after the Cultural Revolution under the guidance of **Xuan Ke**, though the deaths of many older musicians have reduced their repertoire from over 60 to just 23 pieces. To counter this, the orchestra's scope has been broadened by including traditional **folk-singing** in their performances.

The orchestra now plays nightly in Lijiang in the well-marked hall just off Dong Dajie (8pm; ¥30–50). The music is haunting, but Xuan Ke's commentaries may seem too long; it's better to catch the orchestra practising in the afternoon in Black Dragon Pool Park, for free.

A little further north on Dong Dajie, another hall called the "Inheritance and Research Base of China" hosts a song-and-dance troupe who put on spirited nightly performances to a small audience (8–9.30pm; ¥20). Expect to be dragged on stage at the end. Similar audience participation is encouraged in the nightly dances that start around 7pm in Sifang Square.

All roads into Dayan lead to its core at **Sifang**, the main **marketplace**. Cheap **restaurants** around the square are well geared to the tourists who come to buy embroidery, hand-beaten copper pots, and wooden carvings of hawks and cockerels, and it is a fine place to stop and watch for older people wearing traditional dark tunics and capes patterned in cream and blue, representing the cosmos. North from here, Dong Dajie is lined with touristy, wooden-fronted souvenir shops; heading south instead takes you right into Dayan's maze, where you'll encounter more characterful streets. To the west, cobbled lanes lead up to views of tiled roofs from the fringes of **Lion Hill**, whose forested crown is topped by wooden **Wangu Lou** (¥15), an overbuilt, 22-metre-high pavilion. Below here, the southern part of Dayan didn't survive the earthquake and has been replaced by a complex of weighty Qing-style stone pavilions and ornamental arches, all emphatically Han Chinese and totally inappropriate for the town.

Less at odds with local character is the nearby **Mu Family Mansion** (daily 8.30am–6pm; ¥35). The centre of power for the influential Mu family, the mansion was destroyed in the 1870s but has been painstakingly rebuilt along the lines of the original, with an eclectic mix of Naxi, Bai and Tibetan architecture. The gardens are particularly impressive with their azaleas and orchids, and this is a good spot to retreat to if the crowds in the alleys outside become too wearying. The southern boundary of Dayan is marked by **Baimalong Tan**, an old, dragon-headed spring and washing pool in front of a small temple and tangled garden.

When you've had enough of strolling the streets, head up to **Black Dragon Pool Park** (daily from 7am until late evening; ¥60) on Lijiang's northern outskirts. The sizeable pool here is also known as **Yuquan** (Jade Spring) after the clear, pale green water that wells from the base of the surrounding hills. With Yulong Xue Shan behind, the elegant mid-pool **Deyue Pavilion** is outrageously photogenic. In the early afternoon, you can watch traditionally garbed musicians performing **Naxi music** in the western halls.

A path runs around the shore between a spread of trees and buildings, passing the cluster of compounds that comprise the **Dongba Cultural Research Institute**. The word *dongba* relates to the Naxi shamans, about thirty of whom are still alive and kept busy here translating twenty thousand rolls of the old Naxi scriptures – *dongba jing* – for posterity. Further around, almost at the top end of the pool, is a group of halls imported in the 1970s from the site of what was once Lijiang's major temple, **Fuguo Si**. The finest of these is Wufeng Lou, the **Five Phoenix Hall**, a grand Ming-dynasty palace with a triple roof and interior walls embellished with reproductions of the murals at Baisha (see opposite).

Eating and drinking

Lijiang's **restaurants** enjoy a good standard of cooking, though local treats are limited to *baba*, a rather stodgy deep-fried flour patty stuffed with meat or vegetables. The old town's **canteens** around Sifang marketplace are interesting places to wolf down claypots, pork stews and dried-ham dishes with locals. There are also plenty of **tourist restaurants** and foreigner-oriented **cafés** in the vicinity of Sifang. In winter, keep an eye open in the markets for the best **walnuts** in Yunnan, and bright orange **persimmons** growing on big, leafless trees around town – these have to be eaten very ripe and are an acquired taste.

Don Papa 3 Jinshanxiang Jie. Great cheesecake, pretty decent pizza and a friendly owner make this little French-style café worth a stopover.

Frosty Morning 13 Yuhe Xiang. Mellow pub with a helpful English owner, plus a pool table and satellite TV.

Mamafu's Xinyi Jie. Great outside seating by a stream, and tasty apple pie and Naxi staples such as *babas* (the local bread) and grilled noodles.

Mishi's Mishi Xiang. Chic modern establishment notable for decent approximations of Western dishes such as shepherds' pie.

Prague Cafe Xinyi Jie. Scores highly for its location, blueberry cake, DVD collection and menagerie of animals.

Sakura Cafe Off Sifang. Actually there are about five places with this name, all next to each other, and all claiming to be the first. All offer reasonably priced beers and coffees, Japanese and Korean food, and get lively in the evening.

Sexy Tractor 3 Wuyi Jie. The best bar in town, described as Irish meets Naxi; cosy, dark and friendly, it's a good late-night haunt.

The Tibetan Dance Centre 68–69 Guzuo Xiang, near the south gate; ⓦwww.thetibetandancecentre.org. Tibetan and vegetarian food, plus a nightly floor show of Tibetan dancing, starting at 9.30pm.

Well Bistro Mishi Xiang. Though this place wins universal approval for its pasta, apple cake and chocolate brownies, the service could be better.

Around Lijiang

Rich pickings surround Lijiang, with numerous **temples** and villages on the lower slopes of **Yulong Xue Shan** well within bicycle range. Single women should, however, be on their guard when visiting the more remote temples, as the past behaviour of some of the caretakers has been less than exemplary. To experience a less touristy Lijiang, the eco-lodge at Wenhai is recommended.

More ambitious trips are also possible from Lijiang: west to the small towns of **Shigu** and **Weixi**, south to **Shibao Shan** (see p.808), or the excellent two-day **hike** through **Tiger Leaping Gorge** along the Yangzi River (here called the **Jinsha**), due north of Lijiang. Anyone heading further afield, **east into Sichuan** via the rail head at Panzhihua or remote Lugu Lake, has the chance to delve deeper into regional cultures.

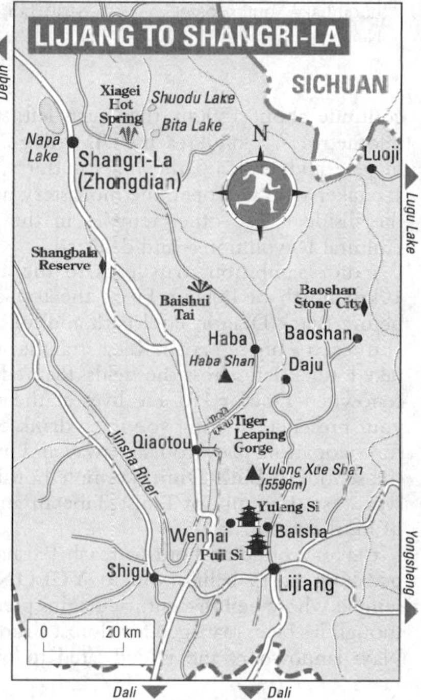

Puji Si, Baisha and beyond

Though the monastery of **Puji Si**, the closest religious site to Lijiang, may not be all that important, in summer the journey there takes you through a valley brimming with wild flowers of all descriptions. Head north past the Mao Statue, take the first left and

Around Lijiang

Baisha	白沙	*báishā*
Baoshan Stone City	宝山石头城	*bǎoshān shítouchéng*
Jinjiang	金江	*jīnjiāng*
Panzhihua	攀枝花	*pānzhīhuā*
Shigu	石鼓	*shígǔ*
Weixi	维西	*wéixī*
Wenhai	文海	*wénhǎi*
Yongsheng	永胜	*yǒngshèng*
Yuhu	玉湖村	*yùhúcūn*
Yufeng Si	玉峰寺	*yùfēng sì*
Yulong	玉龙	*yùlóng*
Yulong Xue Shan	玉龙雪山	*yùlóng xuěshān*
Tiger Leaping Gorge	虎跳峡	*hǔtiàoxiá*
Bendiwan	本地湾	*běndìwān*
Daju	大足	*dàzú*
Haba	哈巴村	*hābācūn*
Margo's Coffee House	玛佳咖啡屋	*mǎjiā kāfēiwū*
Naxi Family Guesthouse	纳西雅阁	*nāī yǎgé*
Sean's Guesthouse	山泉客栈	*shānquán kèzhàn*
Qiaotou	桥头	*qiáotóu*
Walnut Garden	核桃园	*hétáoyuán*
Lugu Hu	泸沽湖	*lúgū hú*
Dazu	大组	*dàzǔ*
La'ao	落凹	*luò'āo*
Lige Village	里格	*lǐgé*
Luoshui	落水	*luòshuǐ*
Lugu Lake Youth Hostel	泸沽湖国际青年旅舍	*lúgūhú guójì qīngnián lǚshè*
Ninglang	宁蒗	*nínglàng*

continue about 1500m, then turn left; snake around for a further couple of kilometres and you'll reach **PUJI village**. Ask here for a safe place to leave your bicycle and walk up the hill for thirty minutes or so, to find an eccentric caretaker who will open the monastery up for you. The temple itself is new on the inside – like other temples in the area, Puji was destroyed during the Cultural Revolution – and deserted.

A more ambitious trip leads to the attractive village of **BAISHA**, about 10km north of Lijiang. From the top of Xin Dajie, take the road left just before Black Dragon Pool Park and follow it for a couple of kilometres until you reach a big reservoir. Keep straight on up the main road for 8km and then take a track left across the fields. Planted with willows, Baisha is home to the renowned Doctor Ho. He lives at the north end and will doubtless detect your presence, inviting you in to drink one of his cure-all herb teas in return for a donation; prise yourself away and make for the alleyway leading up from the school to **Liuli Dian**, a temple housing wonderful Ming-dynasty **murals** whose strange mix of Taoist, Tibetan and Buddhist influences was the work of local *dongbas*.

It takes around an hour to reach Baisha by bike, and another ten minutes of pedalling north brings you to **YULONG village**. Nearby is **Beiyue Si**, a temple whose eighth-century origins predate the arrival of the Naxi in Lijiang, though it's been managed for almost a thousand years by descendants of the first Naxi landowners and is dedicated to one of their gods, **Sanduo**. There's a mighty statue of him inside, faced by the cringing, life-size image of a peasant – a very feudal tableau. From another village, a kilometre further north, a steep path climbs from the main road to **Yufeng Si**, the Jade Peak Temple (30min). It's not of great interest in itself, but there's an ancient, intertwined **camellia tree** in the top hall representing matrimonial harmony, and in spring the flower-filled courtyard with its mosaic floor is a nice spot for peaceful contemplation. Yufeng Si sits in the foothills of Yulong Xue Shan itself, and higher up there are villages of **Yi** herders and woodcutters, whose women wear oversized black bonnets and three-coloured skirts.

Two kilometres along the main road beyond Yufeng, **Yuhu** is the village where Joseph Rock (see p.812) based himself in the 1920s and 1930s. His house still stands, and an ever-dwindling number of locals can remember him.

Yulong Xue Shan

Though at 5596m, **Yulong Xue Shan** can't be climbed without proper equipment, you can ascend on any of three **cable cars**. A special tourist bus running from outside the Black Dragon Pool Park takes you to the base of each (or bus #7 terminates at the first cable car), where you'll pay an entrance fee of ¥85. The first cable car (¥160 one way) is an impressive 3km long and climbs to an altitude of over 4500m. A short trail leads to a glacier viewing point where tourists shelter from the wind before scuttling back to the relative safety of the cable car. The second cable car (¥40) continues for a kilometre to another glacier viewing point, and the third (¥60) to an alpine meadow. You'll be in the company of plenty of local tourists, but there are endless possibilities for careful and solitary wandering around the trails across the lower slopes – ask about routes at Lijiang's *Dongba House*.

A great place to base yourself for mountain treks is **WENHAI**, a beautiful village in the foothills that's a three-hour trek from Baisha, along the road leading northwest out of the village. Otherwise you can reach it by flagging down one of the passing tractors that serve as taxis, or arrange transport with Wenhai's excellent, locally run **eco-lodge** (ⓣ0139/08881817, ⓦwww.northwestyunnan.com, ❶). The converted courtyard house makes a pleasant retreat and has a library and gardens; the management can arrange homestays and guided treks.

Shigu and Weixi

Seventy kilometres west of Lijiang, **SHIGU** (Stone Drum) is a small place named after a tablet raised here in the eighteenth century by one of Lijiang's Mu clan to mark a particularly bloody victory over Han Chinese armies. The Yangzi River makes its first major bend here, deflected sharply to the northeast towards Tiger Leaping Gorge, having flowed uninterrupted in a thousand-kilometre arc from its source away on the Tibet/Qinghai border. Part of the Red Army chose this point to ford the river during the Long March in April 1936, breaking through Nationalist lines under the guidance of the spirited Communist general He Long. There's a small **guesthouse** in Shigu (❷), and it's a pretty area to spend a spring day walking around.

For the adventurous, buses run 100km northwest beyond Shigu through a beautiful, little-explored area which lacks any tourist infrastructure. The road follows the Yangzi to the halfway town of **Judian**, and then bears west past the slopes of **Hengduan Shan** and **Xinzhu Botanical Garden** – basically just a protected natural hillside boasting over three hundred species of trees, some of which are estimated to be a thousand years old. **WEIXI** town, marking the end of the road, is of interest for nearby villages inhabited by the **Pumi**, a Tibetan race forming one of China's smallest nationalities.

Baoshan Stone City

Ninety kilometres or so north of Lijiang, **Baoshan Stone City**, which gets its name from a karst formation resembling Kunming's stone forest, is beautiful and unspoilt, and clings to a hillside that invites exploration – though you should take a guide if you want to go far. A few local families offer accommodation and can arrange horse treks and guides. One direct morning bus to Baoshan Shitoucheng ("Stone City") from Lijiang leaves when full from outside Black Dragon Pool Park. The trip takes eight hours; don't get off at unremarkable Baoshan, but stay on for another hour and a half or so. Alternatively, take a morning bus from Lijiang bus station to Baoshan and then a local bus from there, or – by far the easiest option – take the three-day tour from Wenhai's eco-lodge (¥1600 for a jeep with guide and driver). Baoshan Stone City is the starting point for a four-day **trek to Lugu Hu** (see p.820), through some remote Naxi and Mosuo territory. The route calls at **Liuqin**, **Fengke**, **Gewa** and **Yongning**, each of which offers simple guesthouse accommodation. Much of the trail is along local footpaths, so a guide is essential.

Tiger Leaping Gorge

Around 70km north of Lijiang, and the same distance south of Shangri-La, the Yangzi channels violently through **Tiger Leaping Gorge**. The gorge is so narrow in places that legend has it a tiger once escaped pursuit by leaping across. The drama is heightened by this being the world's deepest canyon, set at an altitude of 2500m with the line of ash-grey mountains that form its southern wall rising for a further 3000m above the rapids. Statistics aside, what makes a **hike** through the gorge so compelling is that for once you're doing something entirely for its own sake: there are no temples to see, the villages along the way are quaint but minute, and the scenery is stark – the gorge's pastoral residents have long since stripped the land of trees and shrubs. Sadly, it looks as though the gorge may fall victim to yet another ill-conceived dam scheme: work had not started at the time of writing, but access roads and test bores had been built in preparation.

Two routes lead through the gorge between **Daju** in the east and westerly **Qiaotou**, on the Dali–Shangri-La road; both take at least two days of walking. No buses run between Qiaotou and Daju, though both are connected by daily services to Lijiang's North bus station. The routes are identical between Daju and the halfway point at the tiny village of **Hutao Yuan**, which has become known to foreign travellers as **Walnut Garden**. From here to Qiaotou, the forty-kilometre-long **low road** has better views of the river but follows a new vehicle track, especially built for Chinese tour buses; the fifty-kilometre **high road** – actually a trail – offers a rougher and more exciting detour.

Hostel **accommodation and meals** are available along the way, though you need to bring snacks, a solid pair of boots, a torch and a first-aid kit. Winter days are often warm enough to hike in a T-shirt and shorts, but nights are cold throughout the year. Plenty of people tackle the trek as if it were a competition, but you'll get more out of it if you take an extra day or two; there are few enough opportunities to stay in attractive villages in China, so take advantage here.

You can tackle the trail in either direction. If you want to head to Shangri-La afterwards, which has bus connections from Qiaotou, you might prefer to start at Daju – the way described below, which is mostly uphill. Alternatively, hike from Qiaotou (which makes for easier walking) as far as Walnut Garden, from where it's easy to hitch a lift back along the low road to Qiaotou; you can leave your luggage in Qiaotou at *Gorged Tiger Cafe* (see p.820). Yet another possibility is to trek into the gorge from the north, arriving at Walnut Garden from Baishui Tai via the Haba valley; see p.826 for details.

Try to pick up the home-made **maps** that float around cafés in Lijiang and at the stops on the route. It's best not to walk alone, in case something goes wrong along the way. The high road is marked by red and yellow arrows. Horses can be hired from villagers for around ¥80 per day. **Landslides** are a serious hazard and have been known to kill hikers, so do not attempt either route in bad weather or during the June–September **rainy season**. For the latest conditions, check ⓦwww.tigerleapinggorge.com, run by *Sean's Guesthouse* in Walnut Garden.

Daju to Walnut Garden

The early-morning bus from Lijiang takes an uncomfortable three hours, skirting the base of Yulong Xue Shan and climbing through patches of primeval forests and open pasture, before finally juddering to a halt at the dusty jumble of stone-walled houses that comprises **DAJU**. There are several restaurants and two simple guesthouses here (❶), along with similar outlying villages to explore; the **bus back to Lijiang** leaves at around 1.30pm.

All things considered, the hike to Walnut Garden is superb. From Daju, it's about an hour's walk, using a well-marked track across the open plateau, to the **ferry across the Yangzi**; the departure point is just short of a small pagoda. Make enough noise and the ferry will turn up, if it isn't there already; foreigners pay a hefty ¥30. Climb the bank on the far side and take any of the tracks towards the gorge, which is clearly visible away to the west. The next hour takes you past a couple of villages before a short, steep descent onto the main path. Head steadily uphill from here, around a huge, bowl-shaped depression to rejoin the river at the mouth of the gorge, which closes in abruptly, the path now running some 200m above a very fierce Yangzi. A further two hours should see you at the open valley surrounding **WALNUT GARDEN**, where you'll be charged a ¥50 entrance fee at a ticket office. Some people try to avoid this by coming through at night; they only end up getting lost in the dark. Keep the ticket, as you'll be asked to produce it at the other end.

Two establishments here provide good meals, beer and warm beds. The westerly one, *Sean's* (文; ⓣ0887/8806300; ❶), faces into the gorge and is a favourite for its English-speaking management and front porch, where you can sit after dark and watch an amazing number of satellites zipping through the clear night skies. There's a rare track down to the river here, and you can arrange a couple of **guided excursions**: a half-day round trip to a small **cave**, or a popular two-day trek to **Baishui**, on the way to Shangri-La. The other establishment, *Chateau de Woody* (ⓣ013988712705; ❶), is in an unattractive building but perfectly comfortable.

Turning northwest after Walnut Grove takes you out of the gorge into the **Haba valley**, for which you'll need a guide as far as **Haba village**, where there's accommodation. Another day's trek and you'll reach **Baishui Tai**, which has charmless guesthouses and a bus on to **Shangri-La**. You might prefer to tackle this trek southwards from Baishui Tai as an alternative route into Tiger Leaping Gorge, as this way you're heading downhill much of the time; for details, see p.826.

Walnut Garden to Qiaotou

The two routes diverge at Walnut Garden. The easier of the two, the **low road**, provides some splendid views: the gorge is tight and steep, the Yangzi fast and rough, and the road narrow. Formerly dangerous stretches now bore through a **tunnel**, but be aware, landslides do still occur along here. You are basically walking along a dusty road, however, and tourist buses will roar back and forth. Expect to take around eight hours to reach Qiaotou.

The **high road** – really a mountain path – is much more appealing. It's a long hike but there are a couple of excellent places to rest along the way, and it's worth taking your time. From Walnut Garden, a three-hour, mostly uphill hike leads to the *Halfway House* (❶) in **Bendiwan village**, where you can arrange horse-riding and guided walks. Another five hours bring you to the *Naxi Family Guesthouse* (Ⓣ0887/8806928; ❶), a homely farmhouse with tasty food. A couple more hours of light trekking takes you to **QIAOTOU**, an ordinary market town. English signs pick out the *Gorge Village Hotel* (❶) on the roadside, but the rooms at the *Youth Hostel* (❶), opposite on the main road, are better. The *Gorged Tiger Café*, just before the bridge, is good for information, and has a pleasant and helpful owner, but the food is pretty poor. Plenty of buses run from here to both Shangri-La and Lijiang, either of which is about three hours away; the last bus leaves at around 6pm.

To Sichuan: Panzhihua and Lugu Hu

An increasingly popular route into Sichuan heads 200km due east from Lijiang over the border to Panzhihua, a stop on the Kunming–Chengdu **rail line**. It's about a ten-hour trip – twelve coming the other way – and you're unlikely to forget the early stages of the journey, as the road traverses an almost sheer 1200-metre cliff on the way to the Yangzi crossing and the town of **Yongsheng**, where the bus will probably stop for lunch. It takes about five hours to reach Panzhihua from here, with most of the trip spent above the edges of broad irrigated valleys. **Dukou**'s barren hills and filthy industrial mess appear first, with **PANZHIHUA** – also known as **Jinjiang** – not far beyond. The bus stops right outside the station: try and get on one of the evening trains, as Panzhihua is no place to stay for long. There's a **hostel** (❷) opposite the train station if you get stuck, and a daybreak bus back to Lijiang.

Lugu Hu

Yongsheng marks the start of a three-hundred-kilometre trail north on public transport to Ninglang, and thence to **Lugu Hu**, a lake right on the provincial border, with transport links to **Xichang** in Sichuan. The shores, partially forested, are inhabited by groups of **Norzu** and **Mosuo**. The former are a branch of the Yi and were once **slave owners**: well into the 1950s, they would raid surrounding lowlands for captives. These were dragged off into the mountains and condemned to live in abject misery while their masters had the power of life and death over them (more of the story is told in Alan Winnington's excellent *Slaves of the Cool Mountains*). For their part, the Mosuo are a Naxi subgroup, still retaining the **matrilineal traditions** lost in Lijiang, such as *axia* marriage, sealed without a specific ceremony and freely broken by either party. Children are automatically adopted by the mother – men have no descendants or property rights. These days, Lugu Hu is being sold to Chinese tourists as the "Girl kingdom" and is much visited by single Chinese men looking for a bit of "Axia" action – they're inevitably disappointed, and seek solace in the arms of the resident Han prostitutes who wear Mosuo dress. Don't let this put you off, however: it's still a beautiful part of the world, and at least in the villages the locals are in charge of the tourist economy.

It takes five hours to get from Lijiang to **NINGLANG**, where the *Jiamei Binguan* (❷) is recommended as a place **to stay**, and another two hours in a shared taxi from there to lakeside **LUOSHUI**, where you'll be charged ¥30 for a "ticket" you never see. Alternatively, one direct bus to Luoshui leaves Lijiang at 9.30am daily, though buy the ticket at least a day in advance.

There's plenty of **accommodation** in Luoshui; best is the long-running, albeit fairly basic, *Husi Teahouse* (☎0888/5881170; dormitory ¥15, rooms ❷), which has good lake views. But Luoshui is a rather ordinary little settlement; much more romantically, you can head to one of the lakeside villages where many families rent out beds in their busy wooden farmhouses for around ¥20. At a couple of small guesthouses in Lige Village, you can arrange treks in appealing, hilly countryside, or boat rides on the lake. With no restaurants in the villages, you'll have to eat at your accommodation, but that's no hardship, as the food – lots of locally caught fish, of course – is pretty good. It's possible to hire a dugout and be ferried across into Sichuan, landing either at the north-shore village of **Dazu**, or eastern **Lawa** – nicely set at the foot of a 2800-metre peak. From either place, there's local transport east via **Muli** to **Xichang** (9hr), also on the Kunming–Chengdu line (see p.895); roads are pretty bad though.

Shangri-La and around

Three hours from Lijiang, the road northwest climbs out of a steadily narrowing gorge onto a high, barren plateau grazed by shaggy-tailed yaks and ringed by frosted mountains – the borderland between Yunnan, Sichuan and Tibet. The last major town before the high Himalayas is **SHANGRI-LA**. Don't get excited about the name, it's just a marketing ploy; the place was called **Zhongdian** a few years ago (Gyalthang in Tibetan). The provincial government renamed it after the fabled Buddhist paradise of James Hilton's classic novel, *Lost Horizon*, to try to stimulate a tourist boom, in the hope of restoring revenue lost now that logging is outlawed. It's a commonplace that all over China, traditional houses are being pulled down and ugly modern buildings going up; surely only in Shangri-La has this happened the other way around – a district of sturdy Tibetan houses and cobbled lanes has been built from scratch, to create what must be the newest "old town" in existence. It's undeniably pretty, with plenty of cafés, guesthouses and bars, though

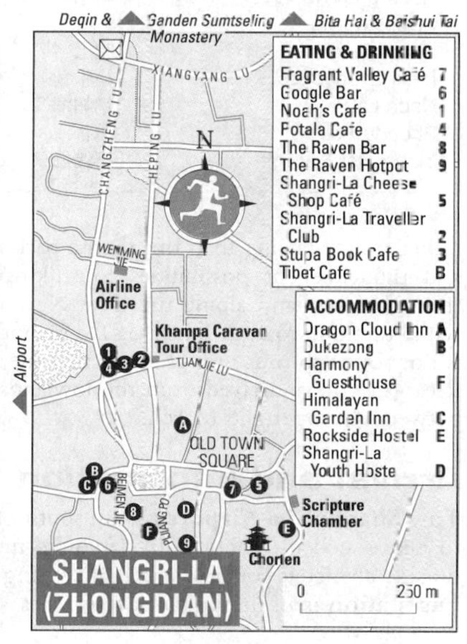

SHANGRI-LA (ZHONGDIAN)

Shangri-La and around

Shangri-La (Zhongdian)	香格里拉 (中甸)	*xiānggélǐlā (zhōngdiàn)*
Ganden Sumtseling (Songzanlin) Monastery	松赞林寺	*sōngzàn línsì*
Accommodation		
Dragon Cloud Inn	龙行客栈	*lóngxíng kèzhàn*
Dukezong	独克宗酒店	*dúkè zōng jiǔdiàn*
Gyalthang Dzong	建格宾馆	*jiàngé bīnguǎn*
Harmony Guesthouse	融聚客栈	róngjù kèzhàn
Himalayan Garden Inn	喜玛拉雅花园客栈	*xǐmǎlāyǎ* huāyuán kèzhàn
Khampa Caravan Eco Lodge	曲及社称尼	*qǔjí shè chēngní*
Rockside Hostel	滇藏驿站	*diānzàng yìzhàn*
Shangri-La Old Town Youth Hostel	古城国际青年旅店	*gǔchéng guójì qīngnián lǚdiàn*
Shangri-La Traveller Club	国际青年旅舍	*guójì qīngnián lǚshè*
Eating and drinking		
Fragrant Valley coffee	香谷咖啡	*xiānggǔ* kāfēi
Google Bar	格格吧	*gégé* bā
Potala Café	布达拉咖啡馆	*bùdálā kāfēiguǎn*
The Raven	乌鸦酒吧	*wūyā jiǔbā*
The Raven Hotpot	乌鸦火锅	wūyā *huǒguō*
Shangri-la Cheese Shop	香格里拉牦牛奶酪店	*xiānggélǐlā máoníunǎilào diàn*
Stupa Book Café	白塔书吧	*báitǎ shūbā*
Tibet Café	西藏咖啡馆	*xīzàng kāfēiguǎn*
Around Shangri-La		
Baishui Tai	白水台	*báishuǐ tái*
Bita Hai	碧塔海	*bìtǎ hǎi*
Haba Snow Mountain Guesthouse	哈巴雪山招待所	*hābā xuěshān zhāodàisuǒ*
Haba Village	哈巴村	*hābā cūn*
Little Zhongdian	小中甸	*xiǎozhōngdiàn*
Napa Lake	纳帕海	*nàpà hǎi*
Shuodu Hai	属都海	*shǔdū hǎi*
Xiagei Hot Springs	下给温泉	*xiàgěi wēnquán*

rather more alluring than this theme park is the monastery just north of town and the excellent possibilities for hiking and horse-riding in the vicinity, through forest and alpine meadow. New roads are opening up remote areas, while the long road to Tibet, via Deqin and the sublime Meili mountain range, is now open to tour groups. Note that the altitude is over 3000 metres, so take it easy if you've arrived from the lowlands, and be aware that's it's very chilly between October and March.

Arrival and information

Tiny **Shangri-La Airport** is 7km south of town; there's no bus, so you'll have to take a taxi in (about ¥20). If you're unlucky enough to be stranded – an outside chance if you arrive at night – ring a hotel and they'll pick you up. The **bus station** is in the north of town; bus #1 or #3 from here stop on Tuanjie

Moving on from Shangri-La

Daily **buses** head north from Shangri-La to Deqin (¥38), the last stop before the Tibetan border, between 7.20am and noon. Those taking the rough ride northeast into Sichuan can join the wild-looking guys who reek of yak butter on the 7.30am bus to Litang.

Some foreigners have been sold tickets for the daily 9.30am bus to Lhasa (three days; ¥550), but officially the road is closed to independent foreign travellers. There is no shortage of agencies that will arrange the journey in private transport, with the requisite guide and driver; recommended in Shangri-La are Khampa Caravan and Haiwei Trails. The Tibet Tourism Bureau in room 2206 of the *Shangbala Hotel* on Changzheng Lu (☎0887/8229028) is the government-approved organization, which means that they are able to organize trips when other agencies might not, for example around politically sensitive anniversaries. The standard price is around ¥4500 per person for a trip to Lhasa, which typically takes a week with stops in the forested Kham area of Tibet; longer trips are also available.

There's also a twice-weekly **flight** from Shangri-La to Lhasa, but it is often booked up by tour groups. The only way foreigners can get a ticket is through a tour agency, for around ¥2500, which includes the price of a permit that you'll never see. Flights to Kunming are relatively expensive at ¥700. There are also flights to Chengdu. Buy tickets at the airline office on Wenming Jie (daily 8.30am–noon & 2–6pm; ☎0887/8229555).

Lu, for the hotels, a couple of which rent out bikes. The **bank** and **post office** are in the north of town.

There is limitless **trekking** in the area, and a number of **travel agents** will help you out with routes and guides. Recommended is the Tibetan-run Khampa Caravan on Tuanjie Lu (☎0887/8288648, ⓦwww.khampacaravan.com), which works with local communities and offers trips and trekking not just locally but also in Tibet and western Sichuan. Another locally run agency that prioritizes sustainable development operates from the *Tibet Café* (☎0887/8230282; ⓦwww.tibetcafeinn.com). Foreign-owned Haiwei Trails (☎0887/8289239, ⓦwww.haiweitrails.com) offer plenty of imaginative treks and mountain-biking; their office is above their bar, the excellent *Raven*. If you are looking for other travellers to share a trip, check the noticeboards at the youth hostel and the *Harmony Guesthouse*. Tour agencies, cafés and hotels also provide information and can book you on **trips out** from Shangri-La – including the three-day hike via **Baishui** to **Tiger Leaping Gorge** (see p.818).

Accommodation

All Shangri-La's decent **accommodation** options are clustered in the far south of town. There are plenty of other Chinese hotels on or just off the main road, but none is very appealing; neither is the *Tibet Longlife Hotel* on Tuanjie Lu, once the only place for backpackers to stay, but now overtaken by the competition.

Dragon Cloud Inn 94 Beimen Jie. This backpacker hotel, at the edge of the old town, is looking a little worn, and staff are unenthusiastic at best. Dorm beds ¥20, ❷

Dukezong Changzheng Lu ☎0887/8230019, ⓦwww.shangbala.org. A new place behind the *Tibet Café* that's the best value in its price range. Dorms have their own bathrooms. Dorms ¥25, ❷

Gyalthang Dzong Hotel ☎0887/8223646, ⓦwww.coloursofangsana.com. This quiet designer hotel at the foot of a hill 3km from town, might, unusually for Chinese accommodation, be somewhere you reminisce about when you get home. The decor, all orange drapes, lacquer and longevity symbols, might best be described as Tibetan minimal. There's a spa and a bar, but no

TVs anywhere on site. Substantial discounts available online. ❻

Harmony Guesthouse 22 Beimen Jie ⓣ13988747739. Tibetan-style courtyard hotel that's the current backpacker favourite, thanks to cheap rooms and can-do, cheerful staff. Dorms ¥15, rooms ❶

Himalayan Garden Inn 28 Beimen Jie ⓣ0887/8230670, ⓦwww.himalayagardeninn.com. Huge courtyard-style hotel with a wide range of clean rooms. The attached restaurant has a good selection of Indian dishes. Dorms ¥25, rooms ❶–❸

Khampa Caravan Eco Lodge Trinyi Village ⓣ0887/8288648. A converted Tibetan house 6km southwest of town, just off the airport road, where each of the two rooms has seven beds. Call at the Khampa Caravan office when you arrive in town and they'll take you out here. You don't have much choice but to eat in, but the hotpots are delicious. Staff arrange trekking, homestays and horse-riding. Profits help build a school next door. ❶

Rockside Hostel 17 Changfang Jie ⓣ0887/8288036. A grand, two-storey Tibetan house in the old town, where rather too many beds have been crammed into the dingy rooms. There's a roofside patio. Definitely worth it if it's not busy, or if you're travelling in a large group. Dorms ¥20, ❷

Shangri-La Old Town Youth Hostel 177 Jinlo Jie, ⓣ0887/8227505. Clean, modern, well run and well located. Dorms ¥20, rooms ❷

Shangri-La Traveller Club 98 Heping Lu ⓣ0887/8228671. No-frills hostel with a nice bar that serves an inexpensive evening buffet. The affable owner arranges tours into Tibetan villages. Bike rental ¥20 per day; Internet access ¥5 per hour. There's a shared bathroom. Dorms ¥20, ❶

The Town

Shangri-La is orientated north–south, with most of the mundane business of a grimy frontier town going on in the north, where among cheap concrete and tile buildings you'll find plenty of grisly butchers and the like, and small shops selling knives or rancid yak butter. The tourist facilities and **old town** are all in the far south of town, which is rather more sanitized, and sanitary, and much more attractive. The cobbled alleyways of the old town are lined with sturdy two-storey wooden houses in traditional Tibetan style, mostly new and built with a great deal of skill and care; they look as though they'll stand for centuries, which you can't say about most contemporary Chinese buildings. Specific sights are few, though the **scripture chamber** (daily 8am–6pm; ¥10), a reconstructed temple with a couple of exhibition halls showing old photos of the town, is worth a poke around. The huge **chorten** at the centre of the old town makes a useful landmark, though it serves no religious function, and locals complain that it's tacky.

The star attraction is the splendid **Ganden Sumtseling Monastery** (Songzanlin in Chinese) just north of town (¥30); catch a northbound bus #3 from the main street. Destroyed during the 1960s but later reactivated, it now houses four hundred Tibetan monks. Among butter sculptures and a forest of pillars, the freshly painted murals in the claustrophobic, windowless main hall are typically gruesome and colourful. Don't forget that you should walk **clockwise** around both the monastery and each hall.

Eating and drinking

Don't be put off by the carcasses in the butchers' shops – the yak meat dishes which all the restaurants do are all pretty tasty. Be warned that addresses aren't much use in the old town, so it's easy to get lost. As there's no street lighting, mind those cobbles on the way home.

Fragrant Valley Coffee 22 Camfang Jie. Yunnan snacks such as fried goats' cheese and good Italian coffee in a quiet lane.

Google Bar 32 Beimen Jie. Popular local drinking hole with a good outdoor terrace; no doubt they'll soon be forced to change their name.

The Raven Hotpot Jinlong Jie. Backpacker friendly, barbecue and hotpot restaurant run by the same folk as the *Raven* bar.

The Raven 19 Beimen Jie ⓣ0887/8289239. Popular foreign-owned bar, friendly and atmospheric, and the best place to get the low-down on the local scene.

Potala Cafe Tuanjie Lu. This upstairs café is the most popular place to eat in town. There's a limited menu of Chinese staples but the ambience is pleasant, attracting a good mix of Chinese tourists, grizzly locals and foreigners.

Shangri-La Cheese Shop 22 Changfang Jie, ⓦwww.shangrilacheese.com. All the dishes at this little café use locally sourced yak cheese – rather like a creamy cheddar. Try cheese sticks for novelty value but a yak cheeseburger to fill up.

Stupa Book Cafe Tuanjie Lu. Specializes in Tibetan hotpots – pork soup stewed in a clay pot with ingredients such as yak meat, sausage, lotus root and wild mushroom thrown in. Best if you're in a group of four or more.

Tibet Café Changzheng Lu ⓣ0887/8238202. Hearty, if somewhat pricey, Western fried breakfasts. They also offer trekking advice and tours, and rent out bikes (¥20 a day).

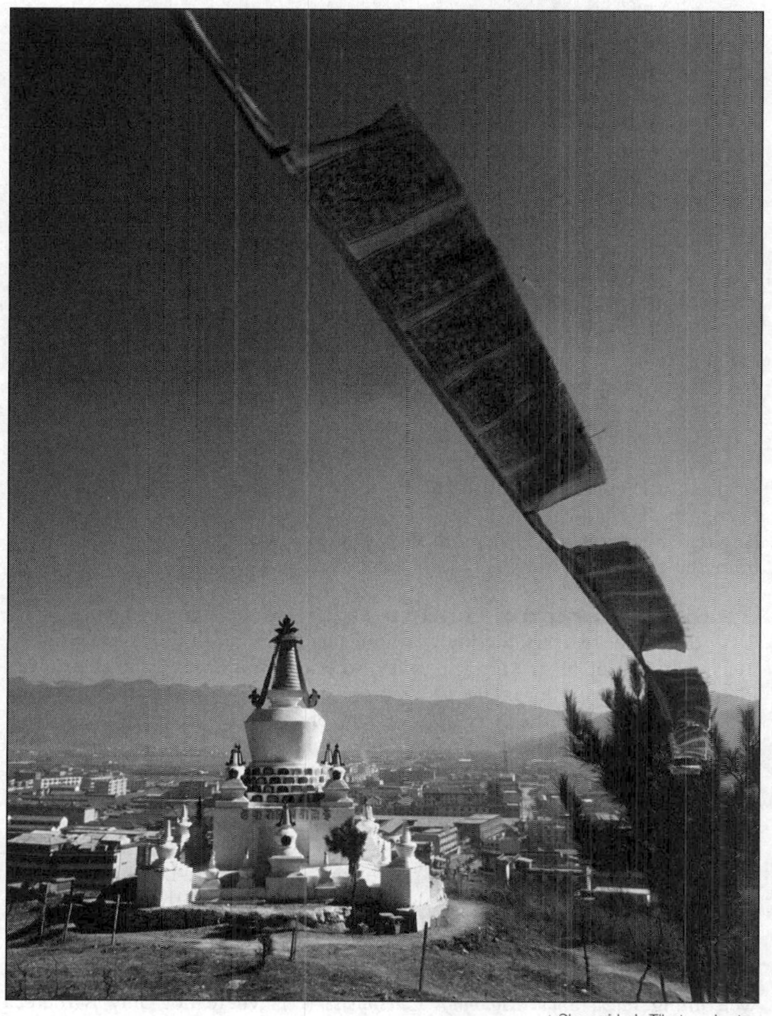

▲ Shangri-La's Tibetan chorten

Around Shangri-La

Several popular sights in the vicinity of Shangri-La are accessible by car: any taxi in town can be chartered for a day for ¥100 or so, depending on mileage and bargaining skills. **Napa Lake**, 7km north of town, is generally the first stop. Something of a tourist trap, it's only worth a visit in either autumn or, especially, winter, when it's home to a community of rare black-necked cranes. In summer it dries up almost completely.

Ten kilometres east of town, the **Xiagei Hot Springs** (¥10) are attractively situated beside a river and below a cave. Eschew the claustrophobic private rooms and swim in the small public pool (¥20); a shop on site sells swimming trunks (¥20). There's also a walking trail, and you can arrange rafting on the river with any tour agency in town (¥200 for an afternoon).

A further hour or so of driving brings you to **Shuodu Hai**, a lake inside the Three Rivers Nature Reserve that's renowned as a beauty spot. Although plenty of Chinese tour buses come here, the occupants don't seem to get much further than the restaurant and the huge shop in the car park that sells traditional medicines such as ginseng and dried ants. Turn right and follow the lakeshore for a pleasant, easy walk through old forest. Horses can carry you all the way around the lake for ¥80, which will take about two hours, or you can walk it in four.

Bita Hai, 25km northeast of Shangri-La, is an attractive alpine lake set at an altitude of 3500m and surrounded by lush meadows and unspoilt forest. The best way to explore the place is to ask to be dropped at either of its two entrances, south and west, and then picked up at the other. Most visitors arrive at the south entrance, from where it's an easy walk down to the lake. Take a rowboat across (a negotiable ¥30 per person) to the ferry quay, and you can then walk for around two hours along a well-marked trail to the west entrance. Horses can be rented at either entrance for ¥50 or so.

Thirty kilometres southeast of Shangri-La, the **Shangbala Nature Reserve** is a stretch of rugged foothills covered in old-growth forest. A lot of effort is going into keeping tourism sustainable here, and no tour buses turn up. The Shangbala Reserve Project (Ⓣ0887/8238202, Ⓔkangbaren@hotmail.com), based in Shangri-La's *Tibet Café*, will arrange a visit, and can also sort out homestays, camping, trekking and horse-riding.

Baishui Tai and the road to Tiger Leaping Gorge

Over thousands of years, the high carbonic acid content in the water sculpted steps, reminiscent of rice terraces, out of the limestone rocks at **Baishui Tai**. Plenty of less prosaic local legends account for their formation, and this is one of the holy sites of the Naxi. It's undeniably pretty, with wooden ladders allowing in-depth exploration of the milky-white tiers, which glow orange at sunset. The village at the foot of the site, **Sanba**, is busy transforming itself into a tourist town of guesthouses, all of which offer basic and fairly unattractive rooms.

The limestone terraces provide a scenic break on the trip down the back road to Tiger Leaping Gorge (see p.818). The trip from Shangri-La only takes two hours, and you can continue by bus all the way to Daju at the eastern end of the gorge. From Baishui Tai a good two-day trek leads to **Walnut Garden** via the pretty Haba valley and **HABA Village**, for which you'll need a local guide, best arranged in Shangri-La. **Accommodation** is available in Haba at the welcoming *Haba Snow Mountain Guesthouse* (❶), where not only is there a rudimentary shower, but the owner even serves coffee.

Deqin and Meili Xue Shan

Six hours north of Shangri-La across some permanently snowy ranges, and only 80km by road from Tibet, **DEQIN** has traditionally been one of Yunnan's remotest corners. What really makes the area exciting are the mouthwatering possibilities for hiking around the **Meili Xue mountain range**, whose highest peak, the Kawa Karpo (6740m), is of great religious significance to Tibetans. Some say it rivals the Annapurna circuit in Nepal for grandeur.

Deqin town itself is nothing special, with a couple of basic **accommodation** options. The *Deqin Lou* (Ⓣ0887/8412031; ❷, dorms ¥20), just north of the bus station, has tolerable rooms. More useful for budget travellers is the *Trekker's Home* (Ⓣ0887/8413966; dorms ¥20); walk north from the bus station for 200m, turn left, and the hostel is on the right. The helpful owner has a lot of information on local treks.

However, the most appealing prospect is to skip shabby Deqin town altogether, and, on arrival, jump in a taxi and head 15km north to the viewing point just below the **Feilai Si** (the trip should cost around ¥20), which has sublime views of the mountains and a cluster of guesthouses and cafés. Avoid the overpriced *Meili Hotel* (❷), and plump for the *Meili Shanzhuang* (❸, dorms ¥20) – but wherever you stay, try to get up to see the sunrise over Meili's thirteen peaks. The best place to eat, the *Migrating Bird Café*, also serves as an informal tourist agency and meeting point.

Meili Xue Shan

From the Feilai temple viewing point, it's a further 20km to the entrance to the **Meili Xue Shan reserve**, a trip that costs around ¥30 in a tractor. You could skip the ride, and the ¥63 **entrance fee** too, by walking for three hours along a local footpath to **Xidang village**, a couple of kilometres south of the hot springs (see below); pick up details of the route at the *Migrating Bird Café*.

Two trails set off from the main entrance. Most people head east for the three-hour ascent to the **Mingyong glacier**, one of the world's lowest at 2700m, and advancing relatively quickly at 500m a year. The road is relatively good for the area, and you'll find a fair few souvenir shops and guesthouses at the glacier viewing point.

Deqin and Meili Xue Shan		
Deqin	德钦	*déqīn*
Dexin Lou	德钦楼	*déqīn lóu*
Feilai Si	飞来寺	*fēilái sì*
Meili Hotel	梅里宾馆	*méilǐ bīnguǎn*
Meili Shanzhuang	梅里山庄	*méilǐ shānzhuāng*
Migrating Bird Café	季候鸟咖啡	*jìhòuniǎo kāfēi*
Meili Xue Shan	梅里雪山	*méilǐ xuěshān*
Hot springs	温泉	*wēnquán*
Kawa Karpa	卡瓦格博	*kǎwǎ gébó*
Lower Yubeng	雨崩下村	*yǔbēngxià cūn*
Mingyong glacier	明永冰川	*míngyǒng bīngchuān*
Ninong	尼农村	*nínóngcūn*
Upper Yubeng	雨崩上村	*yǔbēngshàng cūn*
Xidang	西当	*xīdāng*
Yubeng Shenpu	雨崩神瀑	*yǔbēng shénpù*

A more interesting option is to head west, into the old forest. Four hours' walk takes you to the **hot springs**, which have a couple of guesthouses, and are irregularly connected to Deqin by bus (officially at 8am and 3pm). The springs are nothing special, but might be the last hot water you'll see for a while. From here a gruelling three-hour ascent climbs to Nazongla Pass, or you can go up on a horse for ¥100. A well-marked path then takes you downhill to **Upper Yubeng village**, a Tibetan settlement of considerable charm. Though plenty of visitors stay here with local families (expect to pay ¥10 per night, plus ¥10 for a meal), it's worth persevering to the even prettier **Lower Yubeng village** – take the trail to the left as you come into Upper Yubeng and walk for a couple of hours, over a stream and then a bridge. At the end of Lower Yubeng you'll find *Aqinbu's Shenbu Lodge*, the best place to stay in the area, and a handy base for further treks, on which the helpful owner can advise. Be aware that the locals, as well as being fiercely traditional (Tibetan-style polyandrous marriages are common), are desperately poor – one of the few sources of income is picking rare mushrooms for export.

The most popular trip from Lower Yubeng is the straightforward two-hour walk to the dramatic **Yubeng Shenpu**, a sacred waterfall, with bears, snow leopards and the highly endangered Yunnan golden monkey lurking in the nearby forests. If you don't want to retrace your steps back to the reserve entrance, you can hike back via **Ninong**, which skips the Nazongla Pass, but you'll need a local guide.

More ambitious hikers can attempt the full Kawa Karpa pilgrimage trek, three circumnavigations of which are said to guarantee a beneficial reincarnation, according to Tibetan religious doctrine. The circuit takes twelve days or so, beginning in Deqin and ending in the village of Meili. Much of the route is above 4000m, and it's only possible with a local guide – travel agencies in Shangri-La can make the arrangements for you.

The Nu Jiang valley

The **Nu Jiang** (or **Salween River**) flows south through Yunnan from Tibet, skirting the Burmese border to the west. To the east towers the Gaoligong mountain range, a huge rock wall that has kept this area an isolated backwater; the only connection with the rest of the province is the road from Xiaguan, which peters out in the far north of the valley. Unless you're a very hardy trekker with a local guide, the culmination of any trip here is the bus ride back down again, as there is no public road from the north end into Deqin.

However, there are some fascinating attractions in this, Yunnan's last true wilderness. The river itself is narrow, fast, full of rapids and crisscrossed by precarious rope bridges, and the settlements clinging to the gorge's sides are

The Nu Jiang valley

Nu Jiang	怒江	*nùjiāng*
Bingzhongluo	丙中洛	*bǐngzhōngluò*
Cizhong	茨中	*cízhōng*
Dimaluo	迪麻洛	*dímáluò*
Fugong	福贡	*fúgòng*
Gongshan	贡山	*gòngshān*
Liuku	六库	*liùkù*

highly picturesque. Most of the population are Tibetan, Lisu or Dulong, and there are a surprising number of Catholics, the result of French missionary work in the nineteenth century. Tourism is starting to make inroads, with agencies based in Dali, Lijiang and Shangri-La offering **guided treks**, at present the best way to explore the area. While packages organized from Dali and Lijiang are likely to access the river valley via Xiaguan, agencies in Shangri-La may be able to organize a trek west towards the far north of the area, depending on the time of year. Be wary trekking in winter and spring, however, when high rainfall makes landslides common.

Liuku and Fugong

There's no hardship to spending a day or two in **LIUKU**, the ordinary, fairly laid-back capital of Nu Jiang prefecture – which is just as well, as it's an essential transport stop on the way up the valley. A seven-hour bus trip from Xiaguan, Liuku has a large minority population, but there's not much to do except wander the streets, and nothing to buy unless you're interested in illegally logged Burmese teak or crossbows of dubious efficacy. This sleepy place is at its liveliest around December 20, when the Lisu hold the **Kuoshijie festival**, at which, besides singing and dancing, you'll see local men showing off by climbing poles barefoot using swords as steps.

The town straddles both sides of the Nu, with the hotels and **bus station** on the east side. The best budget **place to stay** is the *Minzheng Binguan* (❷); from the bus station, head south back down the Xiaguan road, turn right after 200m and the hotel is a couple of minutes' walk away. Otherwise, try the *Government Guesthouse* (❶) on Renmin Lu, north of the bus station. The more upmarket *Nujiang Binguan* (❹) on Chuancheng Lu, the street east and parallel to this one, isn't that much better. The **bank** and **post office** are along Renmin Lu. For **food**, try the covered night market just south of the intersection of Renmin and Zhenxing Lu, where you'll see game from the surrounding forests as well as Yunnan staples.

Heading north from Liuku, you pass through some very scenic Lisu villages that cling to the steep sides of the gorge, and the river begins to reveal its fierce character, so it's a shame that the next big town, **FUGONG**, five hours from Liuku, is such a dump. Given its vistas of bleak concrete, it's basically a rest stop on the way to the more interesting Gongshan; the *Fugong Binguan* (❷) opposite the bus station is the best place to stay. Every five days there's a **market**, well attended by Lisu, Dulong and Nu people from nearby villages.

Gongshan, Bingzhong, Dimaluo and around

The far north of the Nu valley, being effectively a dead end, is Yunnan's most remote region, and with old forest, waterfalls and thatched-roofed villages, it's also one of the prettiest. But it's also very poor, and considerable degrees of malnutrition and alcoholism can be seen among the local minorities, who are nonetheless generally welcoming. Though tourism promises to be a lucrative new source of income, as yet there are fairly few facilities – the only people who get here are intrepid trekkers, most of whom arrive with an agency. Certainly it is not a good idea to venture too far alone, and a local guide is always advised for any ambitious walk.

First stop is the one-street town of **GONGSHAN**, a few hours' bus ride north of Fugong. You'll likely see plenty of Dulong people here: older women have tattooed faces, supposedly for beautification, though the practice seems to have started as a way to dissuade Tibetan slave-traders from kidnapping them. The bus-station **guesthouse** (❷) has hot water.

A bumpy two-hour journey north through dramatic gorge scenery brings you to **BINGZHONGLUO**, a lovely little village at the end of the road, with a couple of basic guesthouses (❶). This is the best place to base yourself for treks. One popular walk, simple enough to do alone, is to **Dimaluo**, a community of Catholic Tibetans. Board a bus heading south and get off at the footbridge that leads to Pengdang; cross the river and walk south until you reach a bridge and a dirt track, which you follow north to the village. The walk takes about two hours. At Dimaluo, there's accommodation and an intriguing Catholic church built in Tibetan style.

From Dimaluo it's a two-day hike across the Nushan range to **Cizhong**, a village with an impressive 100-year-old stone church; the locals even make their own red wine for communion, though Christianity in this region has been laid on top of much older, animist beliefs, and the result is something of an amalgam. A road of sorts leads from here to **Weixi** (see p.817), but it's treacherous between October and May. Outside these months there is an irregular, fair-weather bus service to Weixi (6hr), from where you can catch a bus to Deqin. Another popular three-day trek, over high passes and through thick forest, runs from Bingzhongluo to **Dulongjihan**. It's also possible to hire a four-wheel-drive vehicle for this, though again, the road is often closed in winter and spring.

Xiaguan to Burma

Southwest of Xiaguan, the last 500km of China's section of the Burma Road continues relentlessly through **Baoshan prefecture** and into the **Dehong Dai/Jingpo Autonomous Region**, cut by the deep watershed gorges of Southeast Asia's mighty **Mekong** and **Salween rivers** (in Chinese, the Lancang Jiang and Nu Jiang respectively). It's impressive country, almost entirely covered by tightly pinched extensions of the dark **Gaoligong Mountains**, and the road forever wobbles across high ridges or descends towards the green fields of rice and sugar cane that occupy the broad valleys in between. Settlements here have large populations of Dai, Burmese and Jingpo, among others, and until recently mainstream China never had a great presence. Even after Kublai Khan invaded and left his relatives to govern from inside walled towns, the region was largely left to the pleasure of local **saubwas**, hereditary landowners. Though they were deposed during the 1950s, it's still often unclear whether rules and regulations originate in Beijing or with the nearest officer in charge.

The Burma Road itself links the towns of **Baoshan**, **Mangshi** and the border crossing at **Wanding**, around which lie some of the most accessible of the Jinpgo settlements. From Wanding – and staying within China – it's only an hour west to the recently rehabilitated border town of **Ruili**. A rougher back road also connects Baoshan and Ruili, taking in **Tengchong** and some diminishing jungle, but these smaller roads tend to disintegrate during the subtropically humid **wet season** between May and October. Thanks to increased commerce between China and Burma a rejuvenated Southern Silk Road is emerging, with a new highway slicing its way west from Kunming through Baoshan to Ruili and into Burma, due for completion by 2009. Surveying is also already under way for an accompanying rail link, which, although not yet fully approved, is expected to see its first locomotive in 2011. However, neither route will be as quick as catching a plane to airports at Baoshan or Mangshi, both of which have almost hourly services from and to

Xiaguan to Burma

Baoshan	保山	*bǎoshān*
Longyang Hotel	隆阳大酒店	*lóngyáng dàjiǔdiàn*
Taibao Shan Park	太保山公园	*tàibǎoshān gōngyuán*
Wuhou Si	武候寺	*wǔhóu sì*
Yu Huang Si	玉皇寺	*yùhuáng sì*
Mangshi	芒市	*mángshì*
Dehong Binguan	德宏宾馆	*déhóng bīnguǎn*
Ruili	瑞丽	*ruìlì*
Huafeng market	华丰市场	*huáfēng shìchǎng*
Jingcheng Hotel	景成大酒店	*jǐngchéng dàjiǔdiàn*
Mandalay Garden Hotel	曼德丽花园	*màndélì huāyuán*
Nanyang Hotel	南洋宾馆	*nányáng bīnguǎn*
Ruili Hotel	瑞丽宾馆	*ruìlì bīnguǎn*
Ruili Jiang	瑞丽江	*ruìlì jiāng*
Zhong Rui Hotel	钟瑞宾馆	*zhōngruì bīnguǎn*
Around Ruili		
Denghannong Si	召尚弄寺	*zhāoshàngnòng sì*
Hansha Si	喊沙寺	*hǎnshā sì*
Jiegao	姐告	*jiěgào*
Jiele Jin Ta	姐勒金塔	*jiělè jīntǎ*
Jiexiang	姐相	*jiěxiàng*
Jinya Ta	金鸭塔	*jīnyā tǎ*
Leizhuang Xiang Buddhist Temple	雷奘相佛寺	*léizhuǎngxiāng fósì*
Tengchong	腾冲	*téngchōng*
Daying Shan	打应山	*dǎyìng shān*
Heshun Xiang	和顺乡	*héshùn xiāng*
Huoshankou	火山口	*huǒshān kǒu*
Laifeng Shan Park	来凤山公园	*láifèngshān gōngyuán*
Leihua Hotel	雷华酒店	*léihuá jiǔdiàn*
Mazhan	马站	*mǎzhàn*
Post Office Hotel	邮政宾馆	*yóuzhèng bīnguǎn*
Rehai	热海	*rèhǎi*
Tengchong Binguan	腾冲宾馆	*téngchōng bīnguǎn*
Tengyun Binguan	腾云宾馆	*téngyún bīnguǎn*
Tonglida Binguan	通利达宾馆	*tōnglìdá bīnguǎn*
Zhonghe	中和	*zhōnghé*
Wanding	畹町	*wǎndīng*
Longlong	弄弄	*nòngnòng*
Manbang	曼棒	*mànbàng*
Wanding Binguan	畹町宾馆	*wǎndīng bīnguǎn*
Wanding Forest Park	畹町国家森林公园	*wǎndīng guójiā sēnlín gōngyuán*
Yufeng Dajiudian	裕丰大酒店	*yùfēng dàjiǔdiàn*

Kunming, and are impervious to the regular landslides that often block roads during the rainy seasons.

Baoshan

BAOSHAN, 120km from Xiaguan, may be dull, but it has its share of history. The region was settled long before Emperor Wu's troops oversaw the paving of stretches of the Southern Silk Road nearby in 109 BC, and the third-century

Sichuanese minister **Zhuge Liang** later reached Baoshan in one of his invasive "expeditions" across southwestern China. Kublai Khan fought a massive battle with the Burmese king **Narathihapade** outside the town in 1277, won by the Khan after his archers managed to stampede Burmese elephants back through their own lines. Twenty years later the women and slaves of Marco Polo's "Pochan" (today's Baoshan) supported a tattooed, gold-toothed aristocracy – tooth-capping is still practised both here and in Xishuangbanna. Baoshan was again in the front line in the 1940s, when a quarter of a million Chinese troops fought to keep the Japanese from invading through Burma. Today it remains garrisoned, with young army recruits in poorly fitting green fatigues drilling around the parks and parade grounds.

The Town

The centre of Baoshan is boxed in by **Huancheng Lu**, the north, south, east and west sections of which follow the square lines of the now demolished Ming city walls. Ennobled as a city in 1983, Baoshan is nonetheless very much a provincial town, its streets grubby, half-modernized and full of activity. In the heyday of the Burma Road, the shops stocked Western goods siphoned off from supply convoys heading through to Kunming, and even now they seem abnormally well provisioned with locally grown "World Number One Arabica" coffee, tins and bottles of imported luxuries, smart suits and shoes. Rural produce gets an airing in the **main marketplace** on Qingzhen Jie, somewhere to browse among Baoshan's older buildings, but it's not especially exciting. A nicer spot to spend a few hours amid pine trees, butterflies and twittering birds is **Taibao Shan Park**, around 1500m west of the centre at the end of Baoxiu Lu. Near the entrance, the slanted pillars of **Yu Huang Si**, a Ming Taoist temple, support a small octagonal dome. It's no longer a place of worship – it's filled with photos and maps describing local engagements with the Japanese forces – but you'll have to remove your shoes to visit the five alabaster Buddhas in the tiny nunnery next door.

The path climbs higher to pavilions that offer views over town and the surrounding Baoshan Plain, before reaching **Wuhou Si** on the flattened, wooded summit. This temple commemorates Zhuge Liang, whose huge bearded statue sits between his ministers. Behind the hall are some respectably large trees, and fragments of stone tablets recording imperial proclamations.

Practicalities

Surrounded by dumpling, soup and noodle stalls, Baoshan's **main bus station** is on the corner of Huancheng Dong Lu and Baoxiu Lu, the latter of which runs due west straight through the city. Around 500m along, it's crossed by Zhengyang Lu, where there's a **Bank of China** (Mon–Fri 8am–6pm), a department store and a tiny, well-concealed **airline office**. Gradually narrowing in its final kilometre, Baoxiu Lu is further crossed by Qingzhen Jie and Huancheng Xi Lu before ending at a staircase that leads up to Taibao Shan Park.

Baoshan offers plenty of **accommodation and food**. At the top of the scale, the *Landu Hotel* (Ⓣ0875/2121888; ❺), at the top of Baoxiu Lu, is signed from the station, has an excellent restaurant upstairs on the first floor, and justifiably boasts a full three stars. As you head towards the *Landu*, you'll pass the considerably lower-budget, but still adequate, *Huatan Hotel* at 4 Lancheng Lu, just off Baoxiu Lu (Ⓣ0875/2160254; ❶). Probably the best option of all is the relatively new *Longyang* (Ⓣ0875/2148888; ❷/❸), 50 metres down Jiulong Road, directly south of the bus station, where the rooms are in reasonable condition and a shared twin room can cost as little as ¥40 per person.

As Baoshan undergoes rapid development, trendy clothes shops and malls are quickly taking over from the eateries that bunch along Baoxiu Lu towards the bus station. That said, this being China food is never too hard to find, and there are still a dozen or more restaurants between the bus station and the park including a couple of Muslim restaurants – look for the Arabic script.

Moving on, direct daily buses run to all destinations east and west, including Kunming, Tengchong and Ruili, and also two lengthy routes to Jinghong in Xishuangbanna (but see p.841 before you undertake that journey).

Tengchong and the back road to Ruili

The ghost of the former Southern Silk Road runs west of Baoshan, and the bus is slowed first by police roadblocks and crowded village markets, subsequently by steep hairpin bends, as it skirts the dense undergrowth of the **Gaoligong Shan Nature Reserve**. Two valleys along the way are fertilized by the Nu and **Shweli** rivers (the latter a tributary of the Irrawaddy), both of which ultimately empty into the sea several thousand kilometres away in southern Burma. Six hours from Baoshan the bus trundles to a halt at untidy, energetic **TENGCHONG**. A Han-dynasty settlement that originally grew wealthy on Silk Road trade, Tengchong is very prone to **earthquakes**, which have left it bereft of large historic monuments or tall buildings, but business still flourishes and there are some unusual geological sights nearby.

Tengchong's premier market, the **Frontier Trade Bazaar**, takes place every morning along western Guanghua Lu. With business revolving around household goods and food, things are not quite as romantic as they sound, but there's also a small **jewellery and gem market** on the main Fengshan Lu; both markets should whet your appetite for better affairs in Ruili.

For a stroll, head for **Laifeng Shan Park**, several square kilometres of hilly woodland immediately southwest of Tengchong. Paths ascend to **Laifeng Si**, a monastery-turned-museum, and a resurrected, thirteen-storey **pagoda** which will guide you to the park from town.

Practicalities

Tengchong has two **bus stations** – one in the eastern outskirts along Huancheng Dong Lu that serves destinations further south such as Ruili, and a new one in the far north of town, serving Kunming, Baoshan and Xiaguan. From the eastern bus station, continue south and then bear west down either Guanghua Lu or parallel Yingjiang Lu to where Tengchong's main street, **Fengshan Lu**, cuts across them at right angles. Continuing another kilometre south down Fengshan Lu takes you past a **post office** and **bank** to the junction with **Fangshou Lu**, the main road west out of town. Taxis wait at both bus stations, though a walk right across town takes only thirty minutes.

For **accommodation**, try the *Tonglida Binguan* (Ⓣ0875/5187787; ❷, dorm beds ¥20), which offers huge doubles with bathroom across from the old bus station; the *Post Office Hotel* (❸), next to the post office on Fengshan Lu; or the most traveller-friendly place, the *Linye Dasha* (Ⓣ0875/5144058; ❷), out in the southwest of town on Dongfang Lu, whose staff are friendly and endlessly helpful with tourist information. The only upmarket option is the reasonable-value *Leihua Binguan* in the south of town on Huancheng Nan Lu (❹), which could do with new carpets. Alternatively, take a taxi (¥10–15) to the pretty village of **Heshun Xiang** and stay with a family there (see below). Places to **eat** lurk along Yingjiang Lu and Guanghua Lu, where evening stalls also sell charcoal-grilled chicken and fish.

Around Tengchong

Five kilometres west of Tengchong along Fangshou Lu, **HESHUN XIANG** is a Qing-style village whose splendid memorial gateways, ornamental gardens and thousand or more houses are tightly packed within a whitewashed perimeter wall. It is trumpeted for the achievements of its former residents, many of whom have led profitable lives after emigrating overseas and have since ploughed money back into the village's upkeep, and you could easily spend half a day here with a camera. In particular, look for **Yuanlong Tan**, a delightful pond surrounded by pavilions and a creaky water mill. There's a nice place to stay too: go over the bridge, turn left, and on the main track that goes around the hill, look for the sign that says "*Inhabitant Hotel*". The family that live in this rather grand house rent out a few rooms (❶), sharing a bathroom.

Geological shuffles over the last fifty million years have opened up a couple of hotspots around Tengchong. The easiest to reach, **Rehai** ("Hot Sea"), is 11km southwest along the Ruili road, where the scalding **Liuhuang** and **Dagungguo** pools (each ¥30 entry; spa treatments up to ¥168) steam and bubble away, contained by incongruously neat stone paving and ornamental borders. Get there by minibus (¥5) from Huancheng Nan Lu, at the junction with the Ruili road.

Volcano hunters should ask around at the bus station or hotels for transport 10km northwest to **Zhonghe** village and the slopes of 2614-metre-high **Daying Shan**, or 30km north to **Huoshankou**, a large crater near the town of **Mazhan**. These two are the largest of many surrounding cones, dormant but covered in rubble from previous eruptions. Quite a few travellers do seek out these peaks, though the entrance fee (¥30) may seem a lot of money for the privilege of walking on a flat-topped hill.

On to Ruili

Although the most reliable route from Tengchong to Ruili, especially in view of the new Burma highway, is to backtrack to Baoshan and continue via Mangshi and Wanding (see below), there's also a direct road running west, towards and then along the Burmese border. A seven-hour trip on a good day, it takes considerably longer (if it's even possible) during the rainy season. The trip begins smoothly, cruising through a river valley where the scenery becomes less and less "Chinese" as the bus passes Dai villages with rounded wats, red-leaved poinsettias and huge, shady fig trees. Progress becomes unpredictable after a lunch stop and more officious police checks near **Yingjiang**, where the road turns south to cross the ranges above Ruili. You may well get a close look at the forests here – one downhill stretch is notorious for the house-sized boulders that crash down from the slopes above to block the road completely, causing extended delays. If this happens, go for a walk along the road, as there's birdlife hiding in patches of vegetation and villages that have seen few foreigners.

Mangshi

South of Baoshan, the Burma Road makes a grand descent into the Nu River Valley on the four-hour journey to **MANGSHI** (also known as **Luxi**), Dehong's little administrative capital and the site of its airport. Surrounded by Dai and Jingpo villages, the Mangshi region has a reputation for excellent pineapples and silverwork, though the town itself holds enough to occupy only a couple of hours between connections. Hot and grey, the highway runs through as **Tuanjie Dajie**, its eastern end marked by a large roundabout and its western end by a narrow, black canal. Just over this canal, **Yueyi Lu** points north into a jumble of quieter, older streets filled with markets and a fair complement of **Buddhist temples** raised on wooden piles in the ornate Dai style, many of which are being restored.

A sign on the main road outside town that hails Mangshi as one of China's top tourist cities is certainly more an aspiration than a reality; the only reason people come here at present is to pass through en route to the Burmese border. A giant Burmese-style temple – the **Da Jinta** – on a hill to the east of town is the biggest attraction for Chinese visitors. Impressive as it is, however, it was only completed in 2006, so it hardly comes steeped in history.

Incoming flights at the **airport**, 7km south off the main road, are met by taxis and minibuses to town, and also to Ruili and Wanding. A minibus to Ruili takes 2hr 30min, and should cost ¥25. Most Mangshi vehicles will set down at the eastern end of Tuanjie Dajie, either on the roundabout outside the **airline office** (daily 8.30–11.30am & 1.30–5pm) or 1km west at the cluster of depots where **long-distance buses** and **minibuses** stop. Note that there is transport southeast along the difficult route to Zhenkang and on to Xishuangbanna (see p.843).

Currently, there's little reason to stay in Mangshi longer than it takes to catch a bus or taxi somewhere else. However, the airline office has a clean and simple **hotel** attached (❷), while *Dehong Binguan* (❷), nicely located in large grounds at the top of backstreet Yueyi Lu, has some smart rooms, as well as a good **restaurant**. Countless shacks serve buns and curries in almost every lane through the town.

Wanding and around

Two hours south of Mangshi, the road crosses the **Long Jiang** (Shweli River), and then finally slaloms down the slopes of a narrow valley to the point where the shallow Wanding Stream separates Chinese **WANDING** from **Jiugu** over in Burma. Opened in 1938 as the purpose-built border crossing for the Burma Road, Wanding was immediately attacked by villagers who suspected that this customs post was connected with Guomindang units who were then busy trying to exterminate Mangshi's Jingpo hill tribes. The tension proved short-lived, but Wanding has never amounted to much – possibly because, aware of its showpiece status as China's official point of entry into Burma, authorities deter the illicit backroom dealings that make neighbouring Ruili such an attractive proposition for traders.

Not that Wanding is uninteresting: the **Wanding Bridge crossing** is a marvel, decked in customs houses, smartly uniformed military, barriers, barbed wire, flags and signs everywhere prohibiting unauthorized passage. The bridge itself – though ridiculously short – is a sturdy concrete span, and there's even a prominent red line painted across the road on the Chinese side. But it's all a sham; walk 100m downstream and you'll find people rolling up their trousers and wading across a ford almost within sight of patrolling soldiers, while further on some enterprising soul has even set up a bamboo raft (so long it's virtually a bridge) to punt customers over to the far bank. Naturally everyone knows what's happening, but this arrangement spares authorities and locals endless official bother.

Unfortunately, **foreigners** wanting to cross will find the situation very different. Westerners can only enter Burma either by flying to Rangoon or, if wanting to cross the border overland, by joining an authorized tour and obtaining a permit available through agencies in Kunming (see p.789). Though some have quietly snuck across – it would be easy enough to do – bear in mind that you'll be very conspicuous, there's nothing to see in Jiugu apart from a large wat on the hill above, and the repercussions if you're caught make this a seriously ill-advised photo opportunity.

Practicalities

Wanding stretches thinly for 1500m along the north bank of the Wanding Stream and Minzhu Jie, both of which run west towards Ruili, with Guofang Jie descending from the hills at Minzhu's eastern end to the border checkpoint and Wanding Bridge. While there's no **bus station** as such, local transport and vehicles shuttling between Mangshi (¥15) and Ruili (¥10) stop around the Minzhu Jie/Guofang Jie intersection. Here you'll also find a couple of fairly wholesome **restaurants**, with a **bank** (Mon–Fri 8.30–11.30am & 2–5pm) and **post office** (daily 8am–6pm) nearby on Minzhu Jie. **Accommodation** prospects are limited to the cavernous *Yufeng Dajiudian* (❶) on the northeast corner of the intersection, and the surprisingly good *Wanding Binguan* (❷) uphill off Minzhu Jie on Yingbin Lu. Despite the border, the backstreet **markets** along Wanding Stream are small affairs, except on Saturday mornings, when things get pretty enthusiastic. Street hawkers sell herbs and roots and you can pick up presentation packs of **Burmese coins** from shops near the bridge.

Around Wanding

One of the best ways to get a good look at Burma from the Chinese side is to spend an hour in **Wanding Forest Park** (¥5) – walk uphill along Guofang Jie, take the first lane on the left and follow it upwards to the park gates. From the amusement area a few minutes beyond, a dirt footpath leads into scrub and pine plantations behind the dodgems, eventually ending up at a recently built **temple**, bare inside except for prayer cushions and a large alabaster Buddha. The front entrance looks down across the border at Jiugu, undulating green hills and the red earth continuation of the Burma Road heading south of the crossing towards Lashio.

The **Jingpo** minority live a relatively secluded existence in the Dehong highlands. Always considered a primitive spirit-worshipping race by the Han government, they're so poor that in the early twentieth century they were forced to grow opium as a cash crop (hence the Guomindang campaign against them). A number of Jingpo villages are located around Wanding, including **LONGLONG**, 15km west via **Manbang** township. Longlong comes alive for the **Munao festival** on the last day of the lunar new year (usually some time in February), when hundreds of Jingpo take part in an ancient dance said to have been handed down to their ancestors by the children of the sun god. The *Wanding Binguan* sometimes organizes tours of the villages; otherwise, look for minibuses at the intersection in town.

Ruili and around

Once the capital of the Mengmao Dai Kingdom, the frontier boom town of Ruili revels in the possibilities of its proximity to Burma, 5km south over the Shweli River. So porous is the border between Jiegao in China and **Mu Se** on the Burmese side that locals quip, "Feed a chicken in China and you get an egg in Burma". Any trip to Jiegao will include the sight of groups of Burmese men scaling or squeezing between the bars of the less-than-intimidating border fence. This section of the border is still reckoned to be the main conduit for Burmese **drugs** entering China, and Ruili has one of the highest rates of drug addiction and HIV/AIDS in China.

Burmese glossary

Hello (polite)	*Min galaba jinbaya*	Pickled vegetables	*Lapatoh*
Thank you	*Jayzu tinbadé*	Rice	*Htamin*
I'd like to eat	*Htamin saa gyinbadé*	Sticky rice (in a bamboo tube)	*Kauk nyaimn paung (tauk)*
Beef	*Améda*	Sour sauce	*Achin*
Chicken	*Jeda*	Spoon	*Zone*
Curry	*Hin, tha*	Tea	*La pay-ee*
Cold drink	*A-ay*		
Crushed peanuts	*Nanthaung*	One	*Did*
		Two	*Nhid*
Dhal (split soup)	*Pey hin pea*	Three	*Dhong*
		Four	*Lay*
Fish	*Nga*	Five	*Ngar*
Fish soup with banana stem and noodles	*Moh hin gha*	Six	*Chauk*
		Seven	*Khunik*
		Eight	*Chind*
Fork	*Khayan*	Nine	*Cho*
Milk	*Nwa nou*	Ten	*Desay*
Noodles	*Kaukswe*	Eleven	*Say did*

Burmese, Pakistani and Bangladeshi nationals wander around in sarongs and thongs, clocks are often set to Rangoon time, and markets display foreign goods. Most Chinese in town are tourists, attracted by the chance to pick up cut-price trinkets and hop across the border to catch a Burmese transvestite show (see the pictures displayed in travel agency windows). The town's **markets** are unquestionably fascinating; many foreign traders speak good English and make interesting company. Additionally, the surrounding countryside, studded with Dai villages and temples, is only a bike ride away.

Arrival and information

Ruili's kilometre-long main street, **Nanmao Jie**, runs west from a tree-shaded roundabout, passing the Bank of China (foreign exchange Mon–Fri 9–11.30am & 2.30–4.30pm), and the **long-distance bus station**, before it crosses Renmin Lu. Turn north here and there's a **post office** 50m away on the corner of Xinjian Lu. The minibus station opposite the north end of Jiagang Lu sees hourly departures to Wanding and Mangshi (from where there's transport on to **Zhenkang**, first stop on the rough, three-day haul to Xishuangbanna; see p.841), while the long-distance station has at least daily services to everywhere along the highway between here and Kunming. Getting to and from the **airport** costs ¥25 in a minibus or ¥50 per person in a taxi. Most local travel agencies specialize in short group tours for Chinese tourists to Burma, but for flight tickets there are China Eastern offices (Ⓣ0692/4148777) in the *Jing Cheng Hotel* and on Renmin Lu, just north of Nanmao Jie; an Air China office (Ⓣ0692/8889955) directly opposite the *Jing Cheng Hotel* on Maohan Lu, and the independent Huaxin Agency in the lobby (Ⓣ0692/4141222) of the *Ruili Jiang Hotel* on Biancheng Lu.

Accommodation

Ruili has a reasonable selection of mid-range **hotels**, in the heart of town between the principal markets.

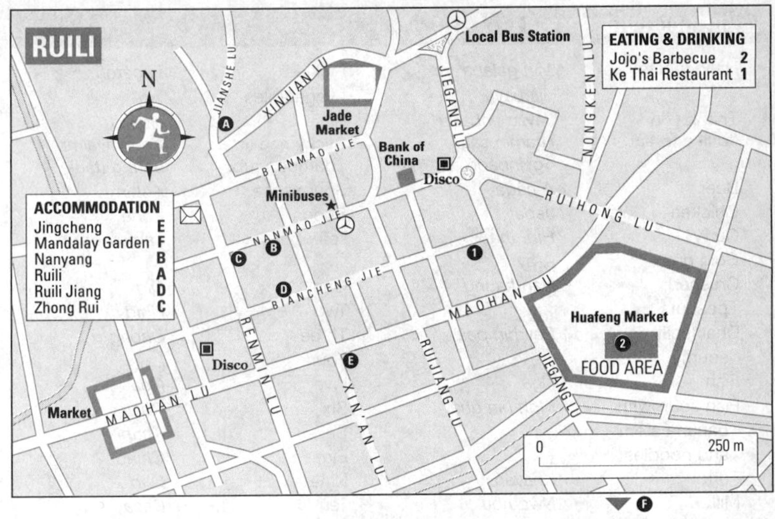

Jingcheng Maohan Lu ⓣ0692/4159666. A reliable four-star place on a street that's south of and parallel to Nanmao Jie, with decent rooms, swimming pool, tennis court and gym. ❺

Mandalay Garden Jiegang Lu and Sihao Lu ⓣ0692/4153924, ⓦwww.mandalaygarden.com. A ¥10 taxi ride south of the bus station, this laid-back backpacker hang-out is run by Burmese Moe, a mine of information about the area. Accommodation is simple – a bed on a floor, in dorms or private rooms – and facilities are shared. There's a very pleasant garden, a DVD lounge, and a restaurant with Western food. Dorms ¥25, ❷

Nanyang 32 XirAn Lu ⓣ0692/4141768. Take the first left, about 200m west of the bus station and this budget hotel is in a courtyard on the right-hand side. Rooms in the old building are cheaper but best left well alone; those in the new building are clean, en suite and count as absolute bargains. ❷

Ruili corner of Jianshe Lu and Xinjian Lu ⓣ0692/4100888. Set in pleasant grounds, the rooms here are bright and airy, even If the pine panelling installed during a recent renovation is more than slightly overdone ❸

Ruili Jiang Biancheng Lu ⓣ0692/4147888. A basic business hotel in the centre of town, where the rooms are tidy enough and those higher up have good views over the town. The Huaxin travel agency is in the lobby. ❸

Zhong Rui corner of Remin Lu and Nanmao Jie ⓣ0692/4100555. Smart new place with clean en-suite twins and doubles. Other facilities are lacking but as a comfortable option in the centre of town, it's more than adequate. ❸

The markets

By day Ruili's broad pavements and drab construction pin it down as a typical Chinese town. Fortunately, the **markets** and people are anything but typical. The **Burmese stallholders** in the market off Xinjian Lu can sell you everything from haberdashery and precious stones to birds, cigars, Mandalay rum and Western-brand toiletries; Dai girls powder their faces with yellow talc, young men ask if you'd like to be shown to a backstreet casino and street sellers skilfully assemble little pellets of stimulating **betel nut** dabbed in ash paste and wrapped in pepper-vine leaf, which stains lips red and teeth black.

The Burmese are very approachable, and some are refugees of a sort, as upheavals in Rangoon in 1988 and 1991 saw Muslims slipping over the border to enjoy China's relative religious freedom. Many peddle their wares at the Traveller Street **jade and gem market** on Bianmao Jie, a recently renovated part of town with a "Disneyland Burma" look. Chinese dealers come to stock up on ruinously expensive wafers of deep green jade, but most of the rubies, amethysts, sapphires, moonstones and garnets on show are flawed and poorly cut; dealers produce their better stones only for properly appreciative customers. Buying is a protracted process here, and for the newcomer it's safer just to watch the furtive huddles of serious merchants, or negotiate souvenir prices for coloured pieces of sparkling Russian glass "jewels', chunks of polished substandard jade, and heavy brass rings.

Dai and Jingpo haunt Ruili's huge **Huafeng market** on Jiegang Lu. Following recent renovations, Huafeng is now a well-ordered and slightly characterless affair, but comes alive at night when the stalls in a southeastern covered area start serving spicy Burmese barbecue and chilled, prize-winning Myanmar Beer.

For a more rough-and-ready shopping experience, try the morning market at the western end of Maohan Lu, where you'll find not only meat, fish, fruit and vegetables, but also locally made wood and cane furniture as well as shoes, clothes and even roadside jewellers selling "gold" rings and bracelets by the gram.

Eating and drinking

Stalls around the market on Xinjian Lu serve fine grilled meats, hotpots, soups and buns, and you'll also come across some Burmese delicacies. Try *moongsee joh*, a sandwich made from purple glutinous rice pancakes heated over a grill until they puff up, and spread with sugar and peanut powder. Another similar confection involves bamboo tubes stuffed with pleasantly bland, sweetened rice jelly, while *niezi binfang* is a thoroughly Southeast Asian drink made with sago, coconut jelly, condensed milk, sugar, crushed ice and water – quite refreshing on a hot day.

Hole-in-the-wall **Burmese cafés** scattered around town hold a dozen or so pots of curry lined up from which to choose – they may not look up to much, but can produce a tasty platter along with half-dozen small pots of tasty pickles for about ¥10. But the real treat is the covered food area in Huafeng market, which has seating for several hundred diners and comes alive from about 8pm onwards, especially at weekends. *Jojo's Barbecue* is highly recommended, particularly the fish encrusted with tandoori-esqe bright-orange spices (look for the sign in English, though not much English is spoken, and not much Chinese either). The food is all laid out on show so ordering by pointing is simple, and you can wash it down with Myanmar Beer, or any number of the fresh juices. Alternatively, the *Ke Thai Restaurant* at the end of Biancheng Lu in the town centre is also good value, and there are a string of more conventional Chinese restaurants on Ruijiang Lu immediately south of the long-distance bus station

Around Ruili

Villages and Buddhist monuments dot the plains around Ruili, easy enough to explore either by renting a bicycle from the *Nanyang Binguan*, or by minibus from the Nanmao Jie depot – just keep repeating the name of your destination and you'll be shepherded to the right vehicle. Hotels can also organize private transport for the day, but it tends to be expensive. Most of the destinations below are only of mild interest in themselves, really just excuses to get out into Ruili's attractive countryside. For more about the Dai, see the Xishuangbanna section (p.845).

A few sights lie within walking distance. About 5km east along the Mangshi road is the two-hundred-year-old **Jiele Jin Ta**, a group of seventeen portly **Dai pagodas** painted gold and said to house several of Buddha's bones. In some open-air hot springs nearby, you can wash away various ailments. Travelling the same distance south takes you past the less expansive **Jinya Ta** (Golden Duck Pagoda) to the busy **bridge over the Shweli River** into Burma, though apart from the volume of traffic, there's little to see.

Another 5km west along the road from Jinya Ta is a small bridge with the region's largest Buddhist temple, the nicely decorated **Hansha Si**, just off to the north. Ten kilometres further on, the town of **JIEXIANG** boasts the splendid Tang-era **Leizhuang Xiang**, where the low square hall of a nunnery is dominated by a huge central pagoda and four corner towers, all in white. Another fine temple with typical Dai touches, such as "fiery" wooden eave decorations, **Denghannong Si**, is further west again. The current halls only date from the Qing dynasty, but Buddha is said to have stopped here once to preach.

Finally, five minutes in a taxi is enough to get you to **Jiegao**, which has three official border crossings for motorbikes, cars and trucks respectively, and a hundred other unofficial crossing points where bars have been bent or removed completely from the fence that marks the frontier. It's surrounded on all sides by Burma, and the Burmese population outnumber the Chinese, but these days it's not so much a town as a giant trading estate, albeit one with an obvious and active red-light district. If you follow the border fence along to the west, you'll see the derelict shell of what was once a giant casino about 20 yards inside Burma. Pressure from the Chinese authorities saw it closed down and with good reason – locals say that anyone who won big ended up in the river.

Southwestern Yunnan

The culture and history of southwestern Yunnan are products of adjoining countries. **Transport** into the region has always been a problem for any external power seeking control; even the rivers – historically so important for inter-provincial communications in central China – here run out of the country, and long-promised highways were only completed in the 1990s. Most visitors find their attention fully occupied by the ethnically and environmentally diverse corner of **Xishuangbanna**, barely an hour from Kunming on the flight to the regional capital, **Jinghong**. Coming by road is not such a bad option either, with sleeper buses making the 24-hour incarceration as comfortable as possible, but watch that your luggage doesn't disappear while you slumber – chain bags securely or rest your legs over them. There's also some interesting territory **along the Burmese border** between northwest Yunnan and Xishuangbanna, though you'll need time and motivation to get the best from landscape and people along the way – and to be impervious to long, tortuous bus rides on extremely rough roads.

The emphatically tropical **weather** of the southwest divides into just two main seasons: a drier stretch between November and May, when warm days, cool nights and dense morning mists are the norm, after which high heat and torrential daily rains settle in for the June–October **wet season**. Given the climate, you'll need to take more than usual care of any cuts and abrasions, and to guard against mosquitoes (see "Health" in Basics, p.61). The busiest time of the year here is mid-April, when thousands of tourists flood to Jinghong for the Dai **Water-splashing Festival**; hotels and flights will be booked solid for a week beforehand. Once you're there, **getting around** Xishuangbanna is easy enough, with well-maintained roads connecting Jinghong to outlying districts. **Place names** can be confusing, though, as the words "meng-", designating a small town, or "man-", a village, prefix nearly every destination.

Along the Burmese border

Bear a few things in mind before you tackle any of the 500-kilometre-long roads that probe down **along the Burmese border** between Xiaguan, Baoshan or Ruili in northwestern Yunnan and Jinghong in Xishuangbanna. The new highway to Jinghong means journey times have been cut and the roads are smoother but, however you go, you're in for a tough two- to five-day trip. In fact the roads along the border itself are so poor that it can be quicker to travel via Kunming – which is what most tour companies will tell you to do if you ask. But if you do choose to penetrate China's untouristed backwaters and zigzag across the cold, thinly inhabited mountain folds between the **Nu** and **Lancang** river systems, you'll see some spellbinding scenery, glimpse at least three regional ethnic groups, and get the thrill of travelling through an area that sees virtually no foreigners.

The direct route

The most direct route along the border – though still an eighteen-hour bus journey – is to catch a Jinghong-bound sleeper bus from either **Xiaguan** (see p.799) or **Baoshan** (see p.831). These routes converge around 120km into the trip at **Yunxian**, from where there's now a main road all the way to Jinghong passing through Pu'er (known almost universally by its old name, **SIMAO**), briefly a French concession, where the road joins the final 150km of the main Kunming–Jinghong highway.

From Ruili

Beginning at **Ruili** is a much tougher prospect, though there's far more in the way of interest on this route, and the landscape is a spread of intensely cultivated, vastly scaled peaks and deep river valleys, dotted with tiny villages. Start by catching a bus to Mangshi and on to **ZHENKANG**, a small town right on the Burmese border, though there's a mountain in the way to stop you wandering

Along the Burmese border		
Cangyuan	沧原	*cāngyuán*
Gengma	耿马	*gěngmǎ*
Lancang	澜沧	*láncāng*
Shangye Binguan	商业宾馆	*shāngyè bīnguǎn*
Mengding	孟定	*mèngdìng*
Menglian	孟连	*mènglián*
Nansan	南伞	*nánsǎn*
Simao	思茅	*sīmáo*
Yunxian	云县	*yúnxiàn*

over. From Zhenkang, the road continues 90km southeast over a seemingly endless succession of serrated ranges to the far more animated market town of **MENGDING**, another possible stop with a range of accommodation options and a host of outlying thatched villages.

GENGMA, a further 30km along, is a small concrete-and-brick town in a broad valley. Minibuses from Zhenkang drop off at a depot on its northern edge; walk south down the 250-metre-long main street, past a **guesthouse** (❷), to a roundabout, where you'll find the **long-distance bus station** (with departures to Cangyuan, Lincang, Menghai, Menglian and Jinghong), and a **hotel** (❸) opposite. Call in at Gengma's large, every-fifth-day **market**, west of the main street, and you'll be eyeballed by disbelieving villagers from the hills. If you're travelling south, Gengma is the first place you'll encounter **Dai** in any quantity – there's even a five-spired Dai pagoda on a hill southeast of the roundabout.

A worthwhile detour from Gengma takes you 90km south towards the Burmese border at **CANGYUAN**, a trading centre that supplies everything from motorbikes to betel nut and mushrooms, and is surrounded by attractive villages whose population are mostly **Wa**. Though Buddhism was introduced from Burma at some point, several remote **rock-painting sites** associated with earlier religious rituals survive in the Awa Mountains northeast of the city. As recently as the 1960s the Wa were head-hunters, also known for their sacred drums, passion for smoking, and festivals involving the frenzied dismemberment of live bulls. Such things are rare today, however.

Lancang

Back on the main Jinghong road, it's 180km to **LANCANG**, the compact capital of **Lahu Autonomous County**. The main reason to pause in the area is to spend a day or two looking at nearby villages, some of which are **Lahu**. Hunters of legendary skill – both men and women hunt – whose name loosely implies "Tiger-eaters", the Lahu probably originated in the Dali area, perhaps driven into this southern refuge by the Mongols. Lahu men shave their heads and wear turbans.

Lancang's main streets form an inverted "T", the stem pointing north towards Gengma, the arms heading southeast to Jinghong and southwest to **Menglian**. Where they meet, at the centre of town, there are scores of places to eat and stay, while there's a good market at the north end, and separate **long-distance bus stations** on both arms. The best **accommodation** is on the southeastern arm, at the friendly *Shangye Binguan* (❷), right behind the Jinghong road bus depot. **From Lancang**, it's just four hours to Jinghong on buses from either station, descending into Xishuangbanna through the westerly town of Menghai (see p.855).

Menglian

Alternatively, try spending a few days 40km southwest of Lancang at **MENGLIAN**, a pleasant Dai and Lahu town reached on hourly minibuses from the Menglian road bus station. A drab, kilometre-long main street holds everything of use, including the **bus station**; head west from here and it's a five-minute walk to a **bank**, and nearby the comfortable *Menglian Binguan* (❸), next to a **bridge**. Over the road, a simple **restaurant** faces the water, while around 500m south along the river there's another gold-painted Dai **pagoda**. Cross the bridge from the *Menglian Binguan* and bear right (uphill) into the **old town**, where you'll find plenty of winding streets and some fine traditional wooden buildings, including two **temples** and the **Xuanfu Shishu museum**. Menglian also has a busy **market** every fifth day, this time patronized by **Hani** wearing porcupine quills and colourful beetles in their hair, and offers the chance to hitch rides out to Wa settlements, such as **Fu'ai**, 28km northwest.

Xishuangbanna

A lush tropical spread of virgin rainforests, plantations and paddy fields, nestled 750km southwest of Kunming along the Burmese and Laotian borders, **Xishuangbanna** has little in common with the rest of provincial China. Despite recent resettlement projects to affirm Han authority, thirteen of Yunnan's ethnic groups constitute a sizeable majority of Xishuangbanna's 500,000-strong population. Foremost are the **Dai**, northern cousins to the Thais, whose distinctive temples, bulbous pagodas and saffron-robed clergy are a common sight down on the plains, particularly around **Jinghong**, Xishuangbanna's sleepy capital. The region's remaining 19,000 square kilometres of hills, farms and forest are split between the administrative townships of **Mengla** in the east and **Menghai** in the west, peppered with villages of Hani, Bulang, Jinuo, Wa and Lahu; remoter tribes are still animistic, and all have distinctive dress and customs. Cultural tourism aside, there are a number of marginally developed **wildlife reserves** inhabited by elephants and other rare beasts, plenty of hiking trails, and China's **open border with Laos** to explore.

Flowing down from the northwest, the Lancang River neatly cuts Xishuangbanna into two regions on either side of Jinghong. To the **east**, there's a choice of roads through highland forests or more cultivated flatlands to the botanic gardens at **Menglun**, down beyond which lies **Mengla**, and the open **Laotian border**. Head **west** and your options are split between the **Damenglong** and **Menghai** regions – linked by a three-day hiking trail – with a more varied bag of ethnic groups and a crossing into Burma (permits to enter the country overland can be secured in Kunming). Direct public buses and tours run to most destinations from Jinghong, but in rural areas the mass of short-range minibuses is far more convenient, and tractors pick up where these won't go. **Cycling** is another possibility in the lowlands, though Xishuangbanna's hill roads are steep, twisted and long.

▲ Dai women at a market in Xishuangbanna

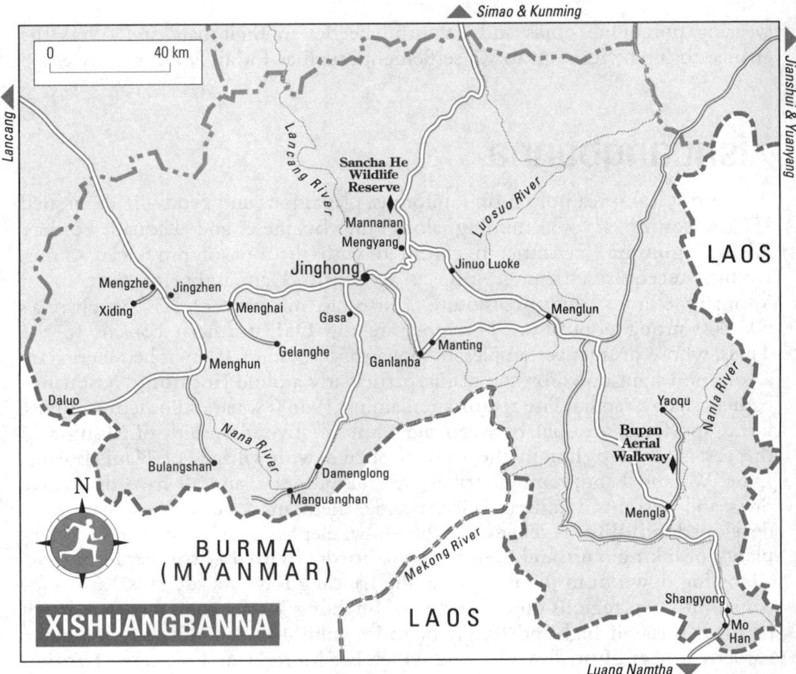

With the exception of Mengla, most main centres can be visited on day-trips from Jinghong, but you won't see more than the superficial highlights unless you stop overnight. The towns are seldom attractive or interesting in themselves, so you'll need to get out to surrounding villages, small temples and the countryside to experience Xishuangbanna's better side. Be prepared for basic accommodation and generally bland, if plentiful, food. Many people are friendly and some villagers may offer meals and a bed for the night in return for a small consideration – or yank you enthusiastically into the middle of a festival, if you're lucky enough to stumble across one – but elsewhere locals are wary of strangers, so don't force your presence while looking around. There have also been a couple of **muggings** in recent years along remoter stretches of the Burmese border – walking alone is ill-advised.

Some history

Historically, there was already a Dai state in Xishuangbanna two thousand years ago, important enough to send ambassadors to the Han court in 69 AD; it was subsequently incorporated into the Nanzhao and Dali kingdoms. A brief period of full independence ended with the Mongols' thirteenth-century conquest of Yunnan. For ease of administration, the Mongols governed Xishuangbanna through Dai chieftains whom they raised in status to **pianling**, hereditary rulers, and the region was later divided into **twelve rice-growing districts** or *sipsawng pa na*, rendered as "Xishuangbanna" in Chinese. The *pianling* wielded enormous power over their fiefdoms, suppressing other minorities and treating people, land and resources as their personal property. This virtual slave system survived well into the twentieth century, when Xishuangbanna came under the thumb of the tyrannical Han warlord, **Ke Shexun**.

The Dai

Although the Dai once spread as far north as the Yangzi Valley, they were driven south by the Mongol expansion in the thirteenth century. These days, they are found not only in southwest China but also throughout Thailand, Laos and Vietnam. Reputed as skilful farmers, they have always flourished in fertile river basins, growing rice, sugar cane, rubber trees and bananas. Accordingly, Dai cuisine is characterized by sweet flavours not found elsewhere in China – you'll encounter rice steamed inside bamboo or pineapple, for instance. Oddities such as fried moss and ant eggs appear on special occasions.

Dai women wear a sarong or long skirt, a bodice and a jacket, and keep their hair tied up and fixed with a comb, and often decorated with flowers. Married women wear silver wristbands. Dai men have traditional tattoos on their chests, though you're only likely to see this in rural areas. Their homes are raised on stilts, with the livestock kept underneath. Some of the most distinctive and ornate Dai architecture is well decoration, as the Dai regard water as sacred. They're Buddhists, but like their compatriots in Southeast Asia follow the Thervada, or lesser wheel school, rather than the Mahayana school seen throughout the rest of China. When visiting Dai temples, it's important to **remove your shoes**, as the Dai consider feet to be the most unclean part of the body.

Not surprisingly, the **Communists** found Xishuangbanna's populace extremely sceptical of their attempts at reconciliation after taking control of the region in 1950, an attitude eventually softened by the altruistic persistence of medical and educational teams sent by Beijing. But trust evaporated in the violence of the **Cultural Revolution**, and the current atmosphere of apparent cultural freedom is undercut by resentment at what verges on colonial assimilation. More contentious aspects of religion have been banned, and forests are logged to the detriment of semi-nomadic hunter groups, who then have to settle down and plant rice. Many minority people feel that the government would really like them to behave like Han Chinese, except in regard of dress – since the colourful traditional clothing attracts the tourists. It's certainly true that Xishuangbanna is a rather anaemic version of what lies across the border in Laos, though in fairness, Chinese administrators admit the "terrible mistakes" of the past, and argue that they are now developing the area as sensitively as possible.

Jinghong

It was under the Dai warlord **Bazhen** that **JINGHONG**, Xishuangbanna's small and easy-going "Dawn Capital" (as it's called in Dai), first became a seat of power. Ever since Bazhen drove the Bulang and Hani tribes off these fertile central flatlands, and founded the independent kingdom of Cheli in 1180, Jinghong has been maintained as an administrative centre. There was a moment of excitement in the late nineteenth century when a battalion of British soldiers marched in during a foray from Burma, but they soon decided that Jinghong was too remote to be worth defending.

Today the grey edifices of Jinghong's contemporary Han architecture make a suitably colonial backdrop for the Dai women in bright sarongs and straw hats who meander along the gently simmering, palm-lined streets, and for the most part the city is an undemanding place to spend a couple of days investigating Dai culture. Aside from energetic excesses during the water-splashing festivities, you'll find the pace of life is set by the tropical heat – though the centre is often full of people, nobody bothers rushing anywhere. Once you've tried the local food and poked around the temples and villages that encroach

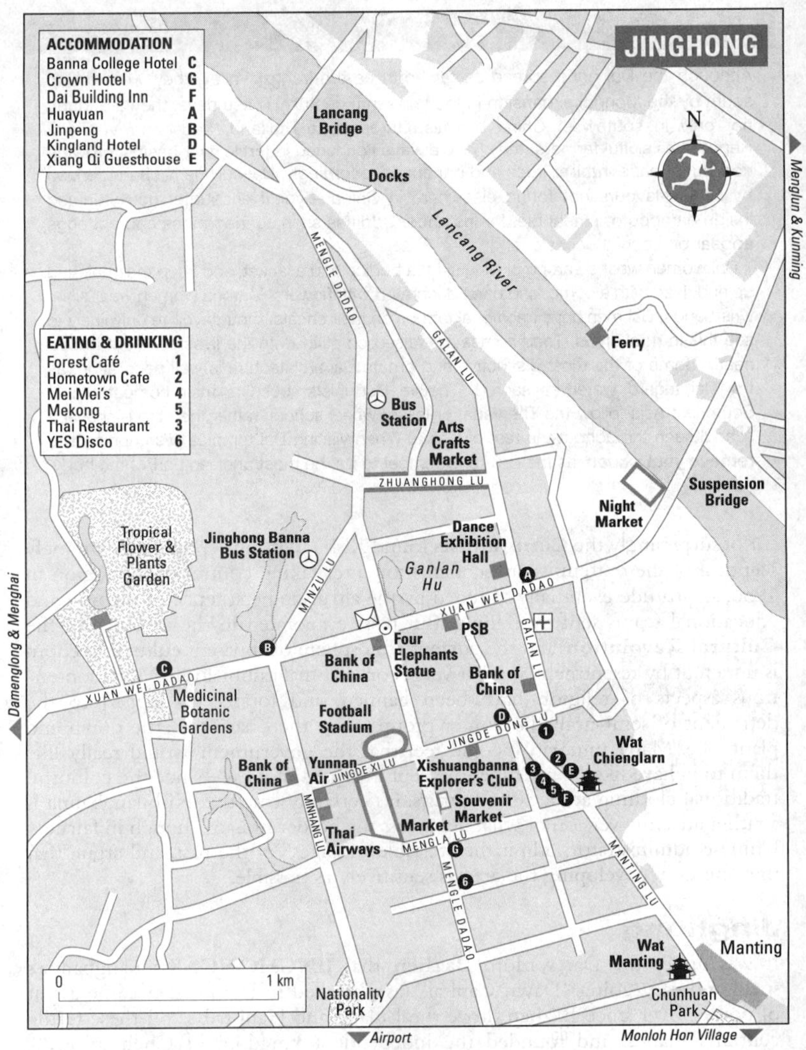

on the suburbs, there's plenty of transport into the rest of the region. **Menghan**, only 45 minutes away on the bus, makes a tempting first target (see p.852); indeed, as a place to soak up atmosphere for a few days, it's preferable to Jinghong in some respects.

Arrival and city transport

Jinghong sits on the southwestern bank of the **Lancang River**, which later winds downstream through Laos and Thailand as the Mekong. The city centre is marked by a sculpture of four elephants set where **Mengle Dadao** radiates north and south, and Xuan Wei Dadao east and west. A kilometre north along Mengle Dadao is the **Lancang Bridge** and the top of **Galan Lu**, which runs

Xishuangbanna (Jinghong)

Xishuangbanna	西双版纳	*xīshuāngbǎnnà*
Jinghong	景洪	*jǐnghóng*
Chunhuan Park	春欢公园	*chūnhuān gōngyuán*
Dance Exhibition Hall	勐巴拉娜西艺术宫	*mèngbālā nàxī yìshùgōng*
Manting	曼听	*màntīng*
Medicinal Botanic Gardens	药用植物园	*yàoyòng zhíwùyuán*
Tropical Flowers and Plants Garden	热带花卉园	*rèdài huāhuì yuán*
Wat Manting	曼听佛寺	*màntīng fósì*
Accommodation and eating		
Banna College Hotel	版纳学院	*bǎnà xuéyuàn*
Burmese Café	缅甸咖啡馆	*miǎndiàn kāfēiguǎn*
Crown Hotel	皇冠大酒店	*huángguān dàjiǔdiàn*
Dai Building Inn	傣家花苑小楼	*dǎijiā huāyuán xiǎolóu*
Forest Café	森林咖啡厅	*sēnlín kāfēitīng*
Huayuan	花园	*huāyuán*
Jinpeng	金鹏	*jīnpéng*
Mei Mei's	美美咖啡厅	*měiměi kāfēitīng*
Mengyuan	勐园宾馆	*měngyuán bīnguán*
Thai Restaurant	泰国风味	*tàiguó fēngwèi*
Xiang Qi Guesthouse	缃祁宾馆	*xiāngqí bīnguǎn*

parallel with Mengle Dadao and the river; there's also a **suspension bridge** over the river off the eastern end of Xuan Wei Dadao.

The **airport** lies about 10km southwest of the city, a ten-minute, ¥20–25 taxi ride into the centre along a new expressway, or ¥5 on the bus. Of the two **bus stations**, the main one, Jinghong Banna bus station on Minzu Lu, handles services from all over Xishuangbanna and beyond, including Xiaguan, Kunming and even the Vietnamese border at Hekou (see p.798); the other depot, 500m north on Jinghong Bei Lu, concentrates on minibuses from Menghan and other places around Xishuangbanna. Central Jinghong is too small for a public bus service – nothing is more than a twenty-minute walk away – but there are plenty of taxis, which have a ¥5 basic charge. Watch out for pickpockets at the post office and bus stations.

Accommodation

All but the smallest lodgings have restaurants and tour agencies.

Banna College Hotel Xuan Wei Dadao ⓣ0691/213865. This basic budget guesthouse, close to the botanical gardens in the grounds of the university, has clean twin rooms and 24-hr hot water courtesy solar power. It's great value, but lack of a/c can be a major issue during the summer months. ❶

Crown Hotel 70 Mengle Dadao ⓣ0691/2199888, ⓕ2127270. One of a number of upmarket places grouped around the Mengle/Mengla intersection, all aimed at the wealthy Chinese tourist. Unmemorable but clean and comfortable. ❹

Dai Building Inn Manting Lu. Run by a resident Dai family, this offers simple comforts in very popular, spotless bamboo stilt houses with separate toilets and solar-heated showers. Dorm beds ¥20, ❶

Huayuan Junction of Galan Lu and Xuan Wei Lu ⓣ0691/8985070. Well located on the river side of the town centre, this newly opened hotel has large, spotless (though oddly shaped) twin rooms. Try to get a room at the back, as those along the road can be noisy late into the night and in the early morning. ❷

Jinpeng Junction of Minzu Lu and Xuan Wei Lu ⓣ0691/2198812. Though hideous on the outside, once inside this is a fairly pleasant if generic business hotel. Clean, spacious and extremely handy for the bus station. ❺

Kingland Hotel 6 Jingde Dong Lu ⓣ0691/2129999, ⓕ2199198. The entrance to this luxury option – with gym, sauna, restaurants and business centre – is marked by two enormous elephant statues. The marble-clad lobby and ethnic staff uniforms create an impressive atmosphere, but one rather lacking genuine local flavour. ⑧

Xiang Qi Guesthouse 48 Manting Lu ⓣ0691/8985115. At ¥30 for a twin room, and ¥35 for one with a/c, if you've got someone to share with this place has to have the cheapest beds in town. And it's directly opposite *Mei Mei Café*, so you can spend what you're saving on a slap-up breakfast. ①

The City

Right in the centre of Jinghong, **Galan Hu** is an unexceptional flagstoned park and pond used for early-morning exercises. Much more interesting is the **Tropical Flower and Plants Garden**, 1500m west down Xuan Wei Dadao (daily 7.30am–6pm; ¥40), which holds palms, fruit trees and brightly flowering shrubs and vines, nicely arranged around a lake. The gardens – aerial flower subgarden, bougainvillea subgarden, and so on – are well worth a visit, and in the early afternoon local dancing is put on for tour groups. The street that leads to the gardens is lined with bars, which are dead in the daytime but can get lively during the evening, especially at weekends.

Across the road, the newly renovated **Medicinal Botanic Gardens** consist of quiet groves scattered among the shaded gloom of closely planted, rainforest trees (daily 8am–6pm; ¥20). They lead to a large **Traditional Medicine Clinic**, whose friendly staff may invite you in for a cup of tea and impromptu *qi gong* demonstration.

For some more greenery and an introduction to Dai life, head 1km southeast of the centre to **Manting**, once a separate village but now absorbed into Jinghong's lazy spread. Set off down Manting Lu (Jinghong's "Traveller Central"),

The Lancang River and New Year festivities

Despite its potential as a great river highway, the **Lancang River** has never seen much traffic, and today the docks in the north of town at the junction of Galan Lu and Jinghong Bei Lu are usually moribund. The only vessels you're likely to see are the tour boats to Thailand, which leave twice a week and take two days to reach Chiang Saen. Tickets cost between ¥400 and ¥600, depending on the boat. The easiest way to buy a ticket is to get a tourist agency, such as the one at the *Forest Café*, to sort it out for you; otherwise queue up at the booking office at the ferry port.

Where the river does come into its own, however, is during the highlights of the **Dai New Year celebrations**, of which the famous **Water-splashing Festival** is just a part. Once set by the unpredictable Dai calendar, the dates are now reliably fixed by the Han authorities for **April 13–16**. The first day sees a **dragon-boat race** on the river, held in honour of a good-natured dragon spirit who helped a local hero outwit an evil king. On the second day everybody in Jinghong gets a good soaking as water-splashing hysteria grips the town, and basinfuls are enthusiastically hurled over friends and strangers alike to wash away bad luck and, hopefully, encourage a good wet season. Manting Park also hosts cockfighting and dancing all day. The finale includes **Diu Bao** (Throwing Pouches) games, where prospective couples fling small, triangular beanbags at each other to indicate their affection, and there's a mammoth **firework display**, when hundreds of bamboo tubes stuffed with gunpowder and good-luck gifts are rocketed out over the river. Nightly carousing and dancing – during which generous quantities of *lajiu*, the local firewater, are consumed – take place in the parks and public spaces. Look out for the **Peacock dance**, a fluid performance said to imitate the movements of the bird, bringer of good fortune in Dai lore, and the **Elephant-drum dance**, named after the instrument used to thump out the rhythm.

and on the way you'll pass the temple school of **Wat Chienglarn**. Traditionally, all Dai boys spend three years at such institutions getting a grounding in Buddhism and learning to read and write – skills denied to Dai women. Manting itself is mostly modern, though Neolithic pottery has been dug up here and a few older, two-storey wooden Dai houses still lurk in the wings (you'll see entire villages of these elsewhere in the region).

Near the end of the road, **Wat Manting** is Jinghong's main **Buddhist monastery** and the largest in all Xishuangbanna. A simply furnished affair, it's currently being renovated – check out the glossy **jinghua murals**, an art form derived from India; the roof rafters, full of ceremonial bits and pieces; and a giant ceremonial canoe in the monastery grounds. Dai temples differ from others across the land both in their general shape and the almost exclusive use of wood in their construction, which necessitates their being raised off the ground on low piles to guard against termites and rot. Furthermore, unlike Buddhists elsewhere in China, whose Mahayana (Greater Vehicle) teachings filtered through from India, the Dai follow the **Theravada** (Hinayana, or Lesser Vehicle) school of thought, a sect common to Sri Lanka, Thailand, Laos and Burma.

Next to Wat Manting is the rather more secular **Chunhuan Park** (also known as Manting Park; daily 7.30am–6.30pm, ¥30), where the royal slaves were formerly kept. A giant gold statue of former premier Zhou Enlai welcomes visitors to the park, tour groups are treated to water-splashing displays every afternoon, and there's also a large pen bursting with **peacocks**, which you can feed. Corners of the park are very pleasant, with paths crossing over one of the Lancang River's tiny tributaries to full-scale copies of Jingzhen's Bajiao Ting (see p.855) and a portly, Dai-style pagoda. Continuing past the park, the road ends at **Manloh Hon village**, which gets its water through the efforts of a large bamboo water wheel, beyond which is a ferry across the Lancang to paddy fields, more villages and banana groves.

As with many of the main towns in Yunnan, Jinghong itself has comparatively little to offer – but it is a great base from which you can explore the jungly mountains and remote minority villages in the surrounding area. Some villages are close enough to cycle to independently, but to get right off the beaten track your best bet is to book a trek at one of the tourist cafés (such as Sarah and Stone at the *Forest Café*; Ⓣ0691/8985122, Ⓦwww.forest-cafe.org) or through Zhaoyao (English name "Joe"; Ⓣ13769146987), an independent tour guide who patrols Manting Lu looking for customers. Most trips include an overnight stay with a local host family and cost around ¥250 per person – prices fall as the number of people in your group goes up.

Eating, drinking and entertainment

Jinghong is the best place in Xishuangbanna to try **authentic Dai cooking**, either in restaurants or on the street. **Sticky rice** in various guises is the staple. One type is wrapped in banana leaves, rammed into a bamboo tube and grilled; a prized purple strain is used as the basis of pancakes, stuffed with sugar and chopped nuts. Formal menus often feature meat or fish courses flavoured with sour bamboo shoots or lemongrass, while oddities include **fried moss**, and **pineapple rice** for dessert – the fruit is hollowed out, stuffed with pineapple chunks and sweet glutinous rice, and steamed. Fresh **tropical fruit** is also sold around town year round – try jackfruit, physically weighty and heavily scented. Sit-down stalls sell bland curries, clay-pot casseroles, hotpots and huge bowls of noodle soup. Not surprisingly, **tourist cafés** are comparatively expensive, but they're good places to pick up local information, rent bikes and arrange tours. The pick of these are 𝕏 *Mei Mei's* on Manting Lu, and the *Forest Café* on Jingde Dong Lu, both of which also double as tour agencies. Sarah at the *Forest Café*, in particular, is a mine of information about local treks. Also on Manting Lu, the *Mekong*, just north of the *Dai Building Inn*, and *Thai Restaurant* at no. 193, are popular options. For vegetarians the *Hometown Café*, opposite *Mei Mei's*, should suffice.

Entertainment is unpredictable, but there's always something going on. For a kitsch extravaganza of dance routines with a connection to minority culture that's at best tenuous, visit the **Dance Exhibition Hall** on Ganlan Lu (Ⓣ0691/2120100). Their nightly performances begin at 8.30pm and go on for two hours (¥120–280). Alternatively, turn up around 6.30pm and you might catch (and even be encouraged to join) one of thee free open-air shows in front of the theatre via which they drum up custom.

For more raucous minority dancing, visit the *YES Disco* on Jinghong Nan Lu (open until 3am), which is packed every night with hard-drinking Dai kids. It's free to get in, and a beer costs ¥20.

A popular, and far more relaxing, evening activity is to stroll along the flood protection levee which stretches southeast along the river from the suspension bridge. As the sun goes down, path-side masseuses, complete with massage tables, spring up along the levee, while if you follow the path long enough you'll come to some of the last remaining traditional wooden buildings in town – farmhouses overlooking riverside banana plantations.

Listings

Airlines Yunnan Air, on the corner of Jingde Xi Lu and Minhang Lu (Ⓣ0691/2124774; daily 8am–8pm), sells tickets for their flights to Kunming and Lijiang. Bangkok Airways, just around the corner at 8 Minhang Lu (Ⓣ0691/2121881; Mon–Fri 9am–6pm), has flights to Chiang Mai and Bangkok.
Banks and exchange Three branches of the Bank of China, on Mengle Dadao, Jingde Xi Lu and Galan Lu, are open for foreign exchange (Mon–Fri 8am–6pm, Sat 8–11.30am & 3–6pm). Larger hotels cash traveller's cheques outside these hours.
Bike rental *Mei Mei's* , the *Forest Café*, Xishuangbanna Explorers Club at 6 Jingde Donglu, and the Youqi Bicycle Shop on Manting Lu all have bikes for rent at ¥20 per day, and will be able to sort you out with maps and advice on where to go.
Hospital The Provincial Hospital is at the lower end of Galan Lu.
Internet access There are plenty of Internet cafés along Manting Lu.
Laundry Foreigner cafés offer the least expensive laundry services in town.
Mail and telephones The GPO, with poste restante and international telephones, is on the corner of Jinghong Bei Lu and Jinghong Xi Lu (daily 8am–8.30pm).
PSB At Jinghong Dong Lu, across from Ganlan Hu Park (Ⓣ0691/2130366; Mon–Fri 7–11.30am & 3–5.30pm) – look for the English sign.
Shopping For everyday needs, there are plenty of well-stocked department stores around the centre. Zhuanghong Lu, a narrow street between Galan Lu and Jinghong Bei Lu, has a very regulated arts and crafts market run for the most part by Burmese selling gems, jade, colourful curios, elephant carvings and Thai and Burmese food. The most interesting shop, no.87 at the eastern end of the street, sells ethnic clothing and textiles. The City Produce Market is at the western end of Jingde Lu, near the Yunnan Air office, where there's a massive range of food and clothing. A night market appears along Mengla Lu, between Mengle Lu and Menglong Lu each evening between 6 and 11pm selling a mix of tourist trinkets, "antiques", clothes and a whole gamut of kitsch baubles. Another tourist market on Mengle Lu between Jingde Lu and Mengla Lu sells much the same range of T-shirts, jewellery and water-pipes as found at stalls on Zhuanghong Lu.
Tour agents Hotel travel services in Jinghong offer much the same range of day-trips to Daluo on the Burmese border, the Botanic Gardens at Menglun, Mandian Waterfall, the Menglong region, the Sun market at Menghun, and (very rarely) Sancha He Wildlife Reserve. These trips are priced at ¥200–300. Backpackers are better off looking at the guided tours offered by *Mei Mei's* and the *Forest Café*, which include boat trips to Menghan and Thailand.

The northern route to Menglun

The road to Menglun, 80km east of Jinghong, divides shortly after crossing the Lancang Bridge on the outskirts of town. The **northern route** initially follows the road to Kunming, winding up through forested hills for 35km before levelling out at **MENGYANG**, a market and transport stop that's surrounded by a host of **Huayao** villages. The Huayao (Flower Belt) form one of three Dai subgroups, though they differ greatly from the lowland "Water Dai', who scorn them for their overelaborate costumes – the women wear turbans draped with thin silver chains – and the fact that they are not Buddhists. Though you'll see plenty of Huayao at Mengyang, the village considered most typical is about 10km further north along the main road at **MANNANAN**.

On a completely different tack, a further 18km beyond Mannanan (still on the Kunming road), the **Sancha He Wildlife Reserve** (¥50) is a dense chunk of rainforest based around the Sancha Stream. Buses from the Banna bus station frequently make the 90-minute journey up to the large stone sign that marks the reserve entrance. The main attractions for visitors are the fifty or so **wild elephants** resident at Sancha He, which are most frequently seen at dawn from creaky wooden riverside hides. The jungle gets more interesting the further you venture along the overgrown, partially paved trails – you're sure to encounter elephantine footprints, along with brightly coloured birds, butterflies and snakes. Give the **elephant displays** here a wide berth, however, unless you enjoy watching captive animals perform circus tricks while being jabbed with a spear. In order not to miss the wild elephants' early morning appearance, many visitors opt to stay the night in the park's treehouse accommodation. If you simply turn up at the park, it'll cost almost ¥400, but if you book beforehand it's just ¥100 – any of the tourist cafés can help you with this free of charge. For those who don't fancy a night in the treetops, the reserve also has a hotel; once again, book the day before and you'll save at least a couple of hundred yuan.

The final 45km of the northern route to Menglun misses all this, however, diverging east off the Kunming road between Mengyang and Mannanan. Twenty kilometres along is **JINUO LUOKE** (Jinuo Shan), home to the independently minded **Jinuo**, who received official recognition of their

Eastern Xishuangbanna

Jinuo Luoke	基诺	*jīnuò*
Manna'nan	曼那囡	*mànnànān*
Sancha He Wildlife Reserve	三岔河自然保护区	*sānchàhé zìrán bǎohùqū*
Manting	曼听	*màntīng*
Dadu Pagoda	大独塔	*dàdútǎ*
Manting Buddhist Temple	曼听佛寺	*màntīng fósì*
Menghan	勐罕	*měnghǎn*
Ganlanba Hotel	橄榄坝宾馆	*gǎnlǎnbà bīnguǎn*
Mengla	勐腊	*měnglà*
Bronze Spire Pagoda	青铜尖顶塔	*qīngtóng jiāndǐngtǎ*
Menglun	勐仑	*měnglún*
Tropical Botanic Garden	热带植物园	*rèdài zhíwùyuán*
Mengyang	勐养	*měngyǎng*
Mo Han	边贸站	*biānmào zhàn*
Shangyong	尚勇	*shàngyǒng*
Yaoqu	瑶区	*yáoqū*
Bupan Aerial Walkway	补蚌望天树空中索道	*bǔbàng wàngtiānshù kōngzhōngsuǒdào*

ethnicity as recently as 1979. An enigmatic group whom some say are descended from the remnants of Zhuge Liang's third-century expedition to Yunnan, the Jinuo once lived by hunting and slash-and-burn farming, but now grow tea as a cash crop. Numbering around twenty thousand today, they never got on well with external rulers, describing their highland homeland as *youle* ("Hidden from the Han"), and were almost annihilated by Ke Shexun and the Dai ruling caste after they poisoned a government tax collector in 1942. Jinuo women wear a distinctive white-peaked hood, while both sexes pierce their ears and formerly practiced tattooing. Although Jinuo Luoke is not the most welcoming of places, there's a **guesthouse** that might let you stay, and local families can usually be persuaded to take in a guest for around ¥30. Alternatively there's plenty of through traffic for the final 25-kilometre run to Menglun, where a bed for the night is assured.

The southern route to Menglun

Because of the time it takes to climb the range to Mengyang, most buses between Jinghong and Menglun follow the **southern road**. This begins across the Lancang Bridge and follows the Lancang River valley downstream for 30km, between endless neat rows of rubber trees, to **MENGHAN**, the main settlement of the famously fertile "Olive-shaped Flatland", as its alternative name, "Ganlanba", translates. This is one of Xishuangbanna's three major agricultural areas, won by force of arms over the centuries and now vitally important to the Dai (the other two are west at Damenglong and Menghai). Farming hamlets throughout the vicinity sport **traditional wooden houses** completely covered by huge roofs, raised on stilts off the moist earth. However, under "modernization" orders from the regional government, this style is being replaced by absurdly humid brick structures. Menghan itself is pleasantly surrounded by paddy fields and low hills, and is a great place to stop over and sample regional life for a few days. In the northwest of town, the Dai Minority Park (daily; ¥50), a large and landscaped strip of land incorporating several villages, offers a sanitized version of minority life – and daily water-splashing festivals – to visiting tour groups. It holds several guesthouses and a few hotels, while many of the houses also rent out rooms for around ¥20–30 per bed – and you should only have to pay the entrance fee once. There are also plenty of day walks and cycle rides – any place you stay will be able to help you rent a bike. One popular ride is to take a bike across the Mekong on the local ferry, and then head left for Dai villages.

A couple of kilometres east, at **MANTING**, the excellent **Manting Buddhist Temple** and **Dadu Pagoda** are fine reconstructions of twelfth-century buildings destroyed during the 1960s. Paths lead further east from Manting along and across the river to more pagodas and villages, somewhere to spend a couple of days of easy exploration.

Menglun

Both routes from Jinghong meet at **MENGLUN**, a dusty couple of streets overlooking the broad flow of the **Luosuo River**. There's no bus station, so vehicles pull up wherever convenient on the main road, usually among the restaurants and stores on the eastern side of town. Take the side street downhill through the all-day market, and within a couple of minutes you'll find yourself by a large pedestrian **suspension bridge** over the river. Here you pay ¥60 to cross into Menglun's superb **Tropical Botanic Gardens**, founded in 1959 by the botanist **Cai Xitao** who, having carved the gardens out of the jungle, started investigating the lives and medicinal qualities of Xishuangbanna's many little-known plant species. One of his pet projects involved the effects of resin from the **dragon's blood tree**, used as a wound-healing agent in Chinese medicine. The tree itself, which looks like a thin-stemmed yucca with spiky leaves, was believed extinct in China since the Tang dynasty, but Cai located a wild population in Xishuangbanna in 1972 and transplanted some to the gardens. You could spend a good half-day here, as there's masses to see, from dragon's blood trees and rainforest species to a thousand-year-old cycad and groves of palms, bamboos, vines and shrubs. You might also encounter Chinese visitors serenading the undistinguished-looking "Singing Plant", which is supposed to nod in time to music.

A **guesthouse** inside the gardens (❹) at the side of the pool offers the chance of seeing the place at its most charismatic, early in the morning and in the evening. Plenty of cheap and unremarkable alternatives can be found in town. To catch onward transport you'll need to tramp back onto the main road or out to the rear of the gardens, near the accommodation, where an exit on to the Mengla road enables you to flag down buses heading southeast.

Mengla

Having been a patchy affair thus far, the jungle really sets in for the hundred-kilometre, four-hour trip from Menglun to Mengla. After an initial, slow-going, uphill climb, the bus suddenly turns along a ridge, giving early-morning passengers a clear view (best in winter) back down onto a "cloud sea" over the treetops below. Further on, rock outcrops and small roadside settlements are carved out of the forest, and though the trees begin to give way to rubber plantations and cultivated land once you're over the mountains, it's all pretty impressive. This is the largest of Xishuangbanna's five wildlife reserves, comprised of relatively untouched tracts that the government has set aside to be protected from development, and full of the plants you'll have seen at the Botanic Gardens up the road.

Doubtless anything would be a disappointment after this, but **MENGLA** seems a deliberately ugly town, quiet and grey. Its main point of interest lies 2km south near the river, at the **Bronze Spire Pagoda**, originally founded in antiquity by two Burmese monks as a shrine for Buddha relics. With a spire donated by heaven, according to local belief, the pagoda brought lasting peace to the land, but it eventually fell into disrepair and had to be rebuilt in 1759, when Jinghong's Dai ruler contributed thirty thousand silver pieces to cover the pagoda and temple columns in bronze. What happened next is a bit of a mystery, as Mengla was closed to foreign eyes for almost thirty years after the Cultural Revolution, but it's nowhere near this grand today. You'll see plenty of monks floating around Mengla itself, however, and there's a smaller temple pagoda on the hill to the west. **Plain-clothes police** too are everywhere – even among the Uyghur running the kebab stalls – as this is the last major town before the Laotian border, 60km southeast.

Mengla's northern end has a proper **bus station**, with services to Menglun throughout the day, as well as to Jinghong. From here Mengla's main street – which holds the last **bank** before Laos – runs south for 1500m to the far end of town, and a **depot** for southbound vehicles. The most comfortable place to stay is the *Tianyi Hotel* (❷) directly opposite the bus station, but there are plenty of other, cheaper options along the same street, as well as a host of noodle shops and restaurants.

Around Mengla: to Yaoqu and Laos

An afternoon bus runs from Mengla to the small town of **Yaoqu** (returning the following morning), 40km north through the beautiful farmland and forest

Into Laos

On the opposite side of the border from Mo Han lies the Laotian village of **Ban Boten**. Assuming you've already obtained a visa from the Laotian consulate in Kunming (see p.799), the border crossing itself should be free and uncomplicated. Yuan are accepted in Ban Boten, but there's nowhere to stay or change your Chinese currency for Laotian kip. The nearest banks and beds are a ¥10 truck ride away at the town of **Luang Namtha**, from where you can hitch out to the early-morning markets at Muong Sing to see local people in full tribal regalia. There's transport from Luang Namtha to **Nung Kie** via Muong Tai, and thence by boat down the Mekong to **Luang Phabang** (though you can also come the whole way from the border by road).

scenery that flanks the **Nanla He**. Not far off the road, just over halfway, look out for the **Bupan aerial walkway**, a very insecure-looking metal "Sky bridge" running across the forest canopy. **YAOQU** itself is a roadhead for remote highland villages, with two **hostels** (❶), and all sorts of people turning up to trade, including Yao, dressed in dark blue jackets and turbans, and possibly Kumu, one of Xishuangbanna's officially unrecognized nationalities.

Heading down from Mengla's south bus station **towards Laos**, it takes about ninety minutes to reach **SHANGYONG**, the last village before the border. Shangyong is a centre for Xishuangbanna's isolated **Miao** population, more closely allied here with their Hmong relatives in Laos than with other Miao groups in China. The Hmong made the mistake of supporting US forces during the Vietnam War and were savagely repressed in its aftermath, many fleeing into China from their native regions in northern Vietnam and, after the Vietnamese army swarmed into China in 1975, to Laos.

Not much further on, **MO HAN** township (also known as **Bian Mao Zhan**, literally "Frontier Trade Station") is just 6km from the **border crossing**. There's basic **accommodation** at Mo Han, and transport to the relaxed customs post (closes mid-afternoon).

Damenglong and the trail to Bulangshan

Several buses a day make the seventy-kilometre run south from Jinghong's Minzu Lu depot to **DAMENGLONG** (or **Menglong** as it's often marked on maps), one of the many western Xishuangbanna towns worth visiting for its **Sunday market**. The area boasts a rich Buddhist heritage, and just about every

Western Xishuangbanna

Bulangshan	布朗山	bùlǎng shān
Damenglong	大勐龙	dàměng lóng
Manfeilong Sun Ta	曼飞龙笋塔	mànfēilóng sǔntǎ
Manguanglong Si	曼光龙寺	mànguānglóng sì
Hei Ta	黑塔	hēitǎ
Gelanghe	格朗和	gélǎng hé
Jingzhen	景真	jǐngzhēn
Baijiao Ting	八角亭	bājiǎo tíng
Menghai	勐海	měnghǎi
Menghun	勐混	měnghún
Mengzhe	勐遮	měngzhē
Manlei Fo Si	曼佛寺	mànfó sì
Xiding	西定	xīdìng

village along the way has its own temple and pagoda. One worth closer inspection is **Manguanglong Si** near **Gasa** (15km from Jinghong), a monastery with a wonderful dragon stairway. The most impressive and famous structure in the region is **Manfeilong Sun Ta** (Bamboo Shoot Pagoda), on a hill thirty minutes' walk north of Damenglong. First built in the thirteenth century and now brightly adorned with fragments of evil-repelling mirrors and silver paint, it's a regular place of pilgrimage for Burmese monks, who come to meditate and to worship two footprints left by Sakyamuni in an alcove at the base. The pagoda's unusual name derives from its nine-spired design, which vaguely resembles an emerging cluster of bamboo tips. On a separate rise closer to town, Damenglong's other renowned Buddhist monument is the disappointingly shoddy **Hei Ta** (Black Pagoda), though it looks good from a distance.

Damenglong holds plenty of cheap places to **eat**, but high-volume karaoke at the new **bus-station guesthouse** (❶) doesn't always make for a relaxing stay. Head instead to the main crossroads, turn right, and you'll find an unmarked hotel (❷) 20m up on the right, where the rooms even have a VCD player.

The Bulangshan trail

Though most visitors come to this region for the hiking, the once-popular three-day, 40km trek along the Nana He and its tributaries to **Bulangshan** township, has recently fallen out of favour thanks to the asphalting of much of the path and deforestation along the route. A better option these days is the trail from Mengshuo to Bulangshan, and then from Bulanshang to Menghua. Each of the two legs requires an overnight stay in villages along the way – ¥30 should be enough to secure you hospitality, food and a place to sleep for the night with a local family. For hiking maps, information on the current state of the trail, and the best places to stay, ask at the *Forest* or *Mei Mei* cafés in Jinghong.

Menghai and the Hani

Western Xishuangbanna's principal town, **MENGHAI**, is centrally placed on the highland plains 55km from Jinghong. The usual grubby assemblage of kilometre-long high street and back lanes, Menghai was once a **Hani** (Aini) settlement until, as elsewhere, the Hani were defeated in battle by the Dai and withdrew into the surrounding hills. They remain there today as Xishuangbanna's second-largest ethnic group and long-time cultivators of **pu'er tea**, the local red, slightly musty brew that's esteemed from Hong Kong to Tibet for its fat-reducing and generally invigorating properties. Apart from a nice village temple about 2km east off the Jinghong road, and a tea-processing factory in Menghai that you can tour, the town is little more than a stop on the way towards outlying Dai and Hani settlements.

The **bus station** is at the eastern end of town along with a **mosque** and Muslim canteens, while the **bank**, **post office** and attached **hotel** (❹), and the basic *Banna Hotel* (❷), are grouped around the central crossroads. The **minibus depot** for western destinations is on the far outskirts.

Beyond Menghai to the Burmese border

The main routes **beyond Menghai** head southwest down to **Daluo and the Burmese border**, or northwest out of Xishuangbanna towards the Lancang region (see p.942). The most celebrated Buddhist sights around Menghai are within an hour's drive along this latter road, including the hilltop **Baijiao Ting** (Octagonal Pavilion), 20km away at **JINGZHEN** – a bizarre structure built in the eighteenth century to quell an angry horde of wasps – and **Manlei**

Buddhist Temple, 5km further on at **MENGZHE**. Both are inferior copies of older buildings, but have important collections of Buddhist manuscripts written on fan-palm fibre. There's plenty of **minibus** transport to Mengzhe throughout the day, plus a small **guesthouse** (❶) near the marketplace if you want to stay. Even better would be to overnight at similar lodgings 10km southwest at **XIDING**, whose busy Thursday **market** is less touristed than some in the region.

One of the best places to come to grips with the Hani is at **GELANGHE** township, 30km southeast of Menghai, which offers hostel accommodation (❶). In fact, many of the people here are Dai and **Akha**, a long-haired Hani subgroup that's spread as far afield as Menglian and Simao. In common with other Hani, unmarried women have elaborate head ornaments while wives wear cloth caps decorated with silver beads and coins. An excellent walk leads up into the hills above Gelanghe past a lake and plenty of traditional wooden Akha villages, though the inhabitants are very shy.

You can meet locals on more even terms at tiny **MENGHUN**, 25km out along the Daluo road, where the **Sunday market**, starting at daybreak and continuing until noon, does a good job of lowering ethnic barriers. If you stay in Menghun the night before, you'll already have seen plenty before the tour buses from Jinghong descend around 9am. It's up to you which of Menghun's shabby **guesthouses** (❶) gets your custom – there's one on the main street (look for the English sign), and another 75m on the left down the road leading south into the fields. However, the market is worth a night's discomfort to see Hani women under their silver-beaded headdresses, Bulang in heavy earrings and oversized black turbans, and remote hill-dwellers in plain dress, carrying ancient rifles. Most common of all are the Dai, who buy rolls of home-made paper and sarongs. Take a look around Menghun itself, too, as there's a dilapidated nineteenth-century **monastery** with a pavilion built in the style of Jingzhen's octagonal effort, and a **pagoda** hidden in the bamboo groves on the hills behind town. Another temple down on the flats to the south is linked to a legend that the stream here changed course at the bidding of Sakyamuni.

Beyond Menghun, the fifty-kilometre-long road takes you past the turning south to Bulangshan (see above) and through a stretch of forest inhabited by a nomadic group only "discovered" in the late 1980s. At the end of the bitumen, the town of **DALUO** (served by two daily buses to and from Menghai) is set just in from the Burmese border. Here there's a multi-trunked, giant **fig tree** whose descending mass of aerial roots form a "forest". You'll find **lodgings** at the newish, white hotel on the far side of the bridge (❶), and a daily **border trade market** is timed for the arrival of Chinese package tours between 11am and 1pm. Chinese nationals can also get a two-hour visa for Burma, ostensibly to shop for jade; in fact, many are really going over to catch transvestite stage shows held for their benefit – check out the photos in the windows of Jinghong's processing labs.

Travel details

Trains

Hekou to: Kaiyuan (2 daily; 8hr); Kunming (daily; 15hr).

Kunming to: Beijing (daily; 48hr); Chengdu (3 daily; 18–21hr); Chongqing (2 daily; 23hr); Hanoi (daily; 28hr); Hekou (daily; 16hr); Guangzhou (2 daily; 45hr); Guilin (2 daily; 30hr); Guiyang (5 daily; 12hr); Kaiyuan (2 daily; 8hr); Nanning (daily; 20hr); Panzhihua (3 daily; 6hr); Shanghai (2 daily; 60hr); Xiaguan (daily; 8hr); Xichang (3 daily; 12hr).

Buses

Baoshan to: Jinghong (23hr); Kunming (12hr); Lancang (12hr); Lijiang (8–12hr); Lincang (12hr); Mangshi (4hr); Ruili (6hr); Tengchong (5hr); Wanding (7hr); Xiaguan (6hr).
Dali to: Kunming (5hr); Lijiang (3hr); Shangri-La (6hr); Shaping (1hr); Xiaguan (30min); Xizhou (30min); Zhoucheng (45min).
Daluo to: Menghai (2 daily; 2hr).
Deqin to: Shangri-La (6hr), Weixi (daily; 10hr).
Gejiu to: Hekou (6hr); Jianshui (2hr); Kaiyuan (30min); Kunming (5hr); Tonghai (4hr); Yuanyang (6hr).
Hekou to: Gejiu (6hr); Jianshui (9hr); Kaiyuan (9hr 30min); Kunming (15hr); Tonghai (6hr).
Jianshui to: Gejiu (2hr); Hekou (8hr); Kaiyuan (2hr); Kunming (5hr); Tonghai (2hr); Yuanyang (4hr).
Jinghong to: Baoshan (23hr); Damenglong (4hr); Kunming (9hr); Lancang (5hr); Lincang (10hr); Menghai (1hr); Menghun (3hr); Mengla (7hr); Menglun (2hr); Xiaguan (18hr).
Kunming to: Anshun (24hr); Baoshan (12hr); Chengdu (36hr); Chuxiong (6hr); Dali (12hr); Gejiu (5hr); Guiyang (72hr); Hekou (11–15hr); Jianshui (5hr); Jinghong (16–21hr); Kaiyuan (5hr); Lijiang (9–11hr); Mangshi (22hr); Nanning (72hr); Panxian (12hr); Ruili (19hr); Shilin (3hr); Tonghai (2hr); Wanding (25hr); Xiaguan (5–7hr); Xichang (24hr); Xingyi (13hr); Yuanyang (13hr).
Lancang to: Gengma (7hr); Jinghong (8hr); Lincang (10hr); Menglian (2hr).
Lijiang to: Baoshan (8–12hr); Daju (4hr); Dali (3hr); Kunming (9–11hr); Ninglang (5hr); Panzhihua (10hr); Qiaotou (4hr); Shangri-La (3hr) Shigu (2hr); Weixi (5hr); Xiaguan (6hr); Yongsheng (5hr).
Ruili to: Baoshan (6hr); Kunming (19hr); Mangshi (hourly; 1–2hr); Nansan (12hr); Tengchong (6hr); Wanding (hourly; 30min–1hr); Xiaguan (14hr).
Shangri-La to: Deqin (6hr); Lijiang (3hr); Litang (9hr); Xiaguan (11hr).
Xiaguan to Baoshan (6hr); Binchuan (2hr); Dali (30min); Jinghong (27hr); Kunming (10hr); Lancang (24hr); Lijiang (6hr); Lincang (12hr); Liuku (7hr); Ruili (14hr); Shangri-La (11hr); Tengchong (14hr); Wanding (12hr).
Yuanyang to: Jianshui (4hr); Kunming (13hr).

Ferries

Jinghong to: Chiang Saen (Thailand; 2 weekly; 40hr).

Flights

Baoshan to: Kunming (3 weekly; 30min).
Dali (Xiaguan) to: Kunming (5 weekly; 30min).
Jinghong to: Kunming (3 daily; 55min); Lijiang (2 weekly; 1hr 20min).
Kunming to: Baoshan (3 weekly; 30min); Beijing (6 daily; 2hr 35min); Changsha (1 or 2 daily; 1hr 30min); Chengdu (6–9 daily; 1hr 5min); Chongqing (4–7 daily; 50min); Dali (5 weekly; 30min); Deqin (3 weekly; 2hr); Guangzhou (5 daily; 1hr 20min); Guilin (1 or 2 daily; 1hr 30min); Guiyang (1 or 2 daily; 1hr 10min); Hong Kong (1 or 2 daily; 2hr 45min); Jinghong (3 daily; 55min); Lijiang (4 weekly, 40min); Mangshi (2 daily; 45min); Nanning (2 daily; 50min); Shanghai (2–3 daily; 2hr 30min); Xi'an (2–4 daily; 1hr 40min).
Lijiang to: Jinghong (daily; 1hr 20min); Kunming (daily; 40min).
Shangri-La to: Chengdu (weekly; 2hr); Kunming (3 weekly; 2hr); Lhasa (2 weekly; 1hr 30min).

CHAPTER 12 **Highlights**

* **Teahouses** A central feature of Sichuanese social life. **See p.871**

* **Huanglongxi** Tidy village of authentic Qing-dynasty shops and temples. See p.879

* **Emei Shan** A tough climb is rewarded with gorgeous scenery and monasteries that make atmospheric places to stay. **See p.887**

* **Dafo, Leshan** You will never forget the first time you see this gargantuan statue of the Buddha. **See p.893**

* **Dazu** China's most exquisite collection of Buddhist rock art, illustrating religious parables and cartoon-like scenes from daily life. **See p.902**

* **Cruising the Yangzi** Relax as the magnificent scenery of the towering Three Gorges glides past your boat. **See p.912**

* **Wolong Giant Panda Research Base** The best place to see pandas in something resembling their natural habitat. **See p.918**

* **Horse-trekking, Songpan** A chance to get really out into the wild and give your feet – though not your seat – a rest. **See p.923**

* **Litang** Gritty Tibetan monastery town in the heart of Sichuan's wild west, where monks and cowboys tear around on motorbikes. **See p.938**

▲ Cruising the Yangzi River

12

Sichuan and Chongqing

Ringed by mountains that, according to the Tang poet Li Bai, made the journey here "harder than the road to heaven", **Sichuan** and **Chongqing** stretch for more than 1000km across China's southwest. Administratively divided in 1997, when **Chongqing** Shi was carved off the eastern end of Sichuan province, the region has long played the renegade, differing from the rest of China in everything from food to politics and inaccessible enough both to ignore central authority and to provide sanctuary for those fleeing it. Recent divisions aside, Sichuan and Chongqing share a common history, and the area splits more convincingly into very different geographic halves: a densely populated eastern plain, and a mountainous west, emphatically remote.

In the east, peaks surround one of the country's most densely settled areas, the fertile **Red Basin**, whose subtropical climate and rich soil conspire to produce endless green fields turning out three harvests a year. This bounty has created an air of easy affluence in **Chengdu**, Sichuan's relaxed capital, and the southern river towns of **Zigong** and **Yibin**. Elsewhere, visitors have the opportunity of joining pilgrims on **Emei Shan** in a hike up the holy mountain's forested slopes, or of sailing **down the Yangzi** from Chongqing, industrial powerhouse and terminus of one of the world's great river journeys. You'll also find that the influence of **Buddhism** has literally become part of the landscape, most notably at **Leshan**, where **Dafo**, a giant Buddha sculpted into riverside cliffs, provides one of the most evocative images of China; and farther east at **Dazu**, whose wooded hillsides conceal a marvellous procession of stone carvings.

In contrast, western Sichuan is dominated by densely buckled ranges overflowing from the heights of Tibet; this is a wild, thinly populated land of snowcapped peaks, where yaks roam the treeline and roads negotiate hair-raising gradients as they cross ridges or follow deep river valleys. Occupied but untamed by Han China, the west has its appeal in its **Tibetan heritage** – clearly visible in the many important **monasteries** – and raw, rugged alpine scenery. Nearest to Chengdu, there's a chance to see giant pandas at **Wolong Nature Reserve**, while travelling north towards Gansu takes you through ethnic Hui and Qiang heartlands past the vivid blue lakes and beautiful mountain scenery of **Songpan** and **Jiuzhaigou**, with the tranquil village of

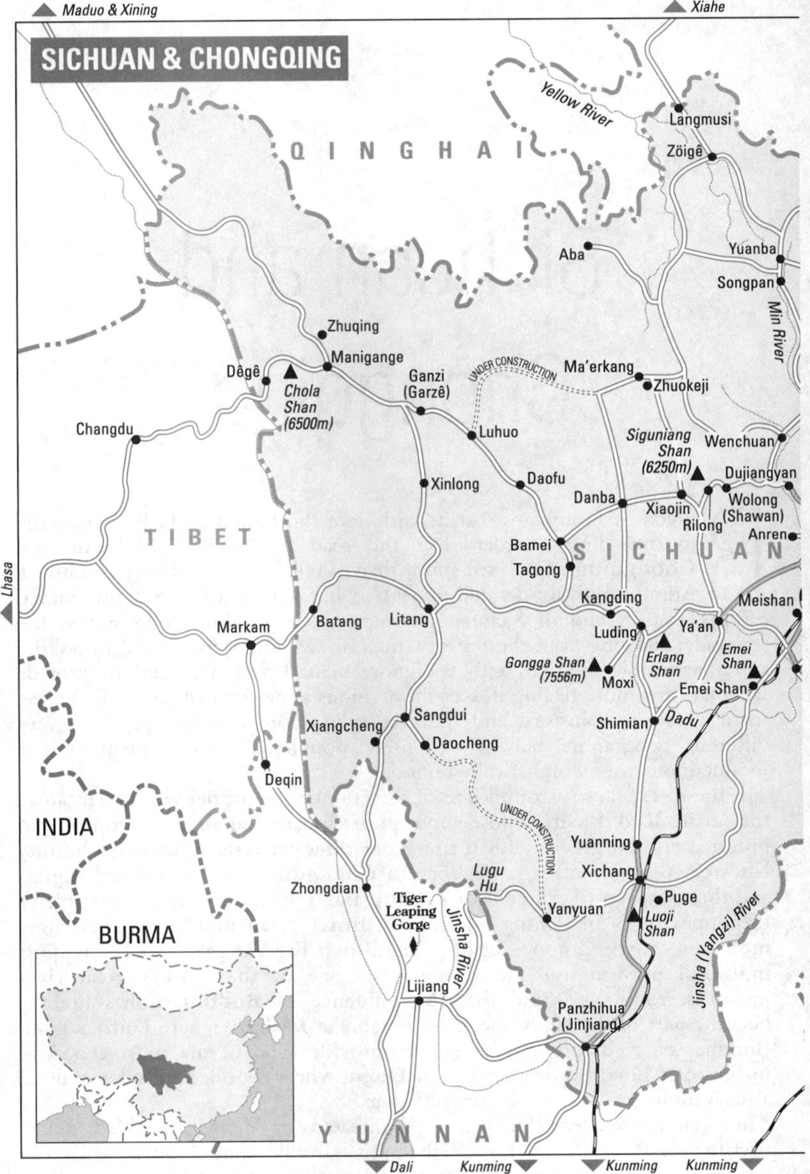

Langmusi the most remote of targets, right on the provincial border. Due west of Chengdu, the real wilds begin beyond **Kangding**, with the monastery towns of **Dêgê** and **Litang** the pick of destinations – not forgetting an exciting back-road **route to Yunnan**.

Getting around all this is fairly straightforward, though those heading westwards need to prepare for unpredictably long and uncomfortable

journeys. **Rail lines** are restricted by geography, and most people use the train only for travel beyond regional borders; the most useful internal route is along the Xi'an–Kunming line, which runs southwest from Chengdu via Emei Shan and Xichang. As for the **weather**, expect hot, humid summers and cold winters, with the north and west frequently buried under snow for three months of the year.

Sichuanese cooking

Dominating the southwestern China cooking school, **Sichuanese cooking** is noted for its heavy use of **chilli**, which locals explain as a result of climate – according to Traditional Chinese Medicine, chillies dispel "wet" illnesses caused by Sichuan's seasonally damp or humid weather. You'll also find that chillies don't simply blast the taste buds, they stimulate them as well, and flavours here are far more complex than they might appear at the initial, eye-watering, mouthful.

Sichuan cuisine's defining taste is described as **mala** – "numb and hot" – created by the potent mix of chillies and **huajiao** (Sichuan pepper), with its soapy perfume and mouth-tingling afterbuzz. One classic *mala* dish is **mapo doufu**, bean curd and minced pork; others include **strange-flavoured chicken** (dressed with sesame paste, soy sauce, sugar and green onions mixed in with the chillies and *huajiao*), and the innocently named **boiled beef slices**, which actually packs more chillies per spoonful than almost any other Sichuanese dish.

A cooking technique unique to Sichuan is **dry-frying**, which involves deep frying to dehydrate the ingredients, followed by sautéeing in a sweet-salty sauce until the liquid has evaporated. **Dry-fried pork shreds**, where the slivers of pork end up dark, chewy and aromatic, is a classic example using meat; a vegetarian counterpart is **dry-fried green beans**, salty and rich with garlic.

Other more general dishes include **hot and sour soup**, flavoured with pepper and

Eastern Sichuan and Chongqing

One of the most pleasant areas of China to explore randomly, eastern Sichuan is focused around **Chengdu**, the relaxed provincial capital. Famed not least for its fiery cuisine, the city offers a number of easy excursions to nearby sights, the most unusual of which is a two-thousand-year-old irrigation scheme at **Dujiangyan**. Northeast is the historically important **route to Shaanxi**, and also **Langzhong**, with its Qing-dynasty architecture; southwest, both road and rail run past Buddhist landmarks at **Emei Shan** and **Leshan** and down to the Yunnanese border via **Xichang**. Southeast of the capital, the historic towns of **Zigong** and **Yibin** offer access to picturesque bamboo forests, and traces of an obscure, long-vanished society. Further Buddhist sites surround the country town of **Dazu**, east of Chengdu; beyond, western China's largest city, **Chongqing**, marks the start of the **journey down the Yangzi** to Hubei province, with ferries exiting the region through the dramatic **Three Gorges**.

Some history

In prehistoric times, what is now eastern Sichuan and Chongqing was divided into the eastern **Ba** and western **Shu kingdoms**, which amalgamated during the Shang era (1600–1100 BC). Numerous sites across the region suggest the Ba–Shu was a slave society with highly developed metalworking skills and bizarre aesthetics. Agricultural innovations at the end of the third century BC opened up eastern Sichuan to intensive farming, and when the Qin armies vinegar; **double-cooked pork**, where a piece of fatty meat is boiled, sliced thinly and then stir-fried with green chillies; **fish-flavoured pork** (whose "seafood" sauce is made from vinegar, soy sauce, sugar, ginger and sesame oil); **gongbao chicken**, the local version of stir-fried chicken and peanuts; **smoked duck**, a chilli-free cold dish, aromatic and juicy; and **crackling rice**, where a meat soup is poured over a sizzling bed of deep-fried rice crusts. There's also a great number of Sichuanese **snacks** – *xiaochi* – which some restaurants specialize in: green beans with ginger, pork with puréed garlic, cucumber with chilli-oil and sesame seeds, **dandan mian** ("carry-pole" noodles, named after how street vendors used to carry them around), **tiger-skin peppers**, scorched then fried with salt and dark vinegar, five-spiced meat steamed in ground rice (served in the bamboo steamer), and a huge variety of sweet and savoury dumplings.

One Chongqing speciality now found all over Sichuan (and China) is **huoguo** (hotpot), a social dish eaten everywhere from streetside canteens to specialist restaurants. You get plates or skewers of meat, boiled eggs or vegetables, cooked – by you at the table – in a bubbling pot of stock liberally laced with chillies and cardamom pods. You then season the cooked food in oil spiced with MSG, salt and chilli powder. The effect is powerful, and during a cold winter you may well find that hotpots fast become your favourite food.

stormed through, they found an economic base that financed their unification of China in 221 BC – as did Genghis Khan's forces almost 1500 years later. In between, the area became the Three Kingdoms state of **Shu** – a name by which Sichuan is still sometimes known – and later twice provided refuge for deposed emperors.

Otherwise too distant to play a central role in China's history, the region leapt to prominence in 1911, when government interference in local rail industries sparked the nationwide rebellions that toppled the Qing empire. The next four decades saw rival warlords fighting for control, though some stability came when the **Nationalist government** made Chongqing their capital after the Japanese invaded China in 1937. The province suffered badly during the Cultural Revolution – **Jung Chang**'s autobiography, *Wild Swans*, gives a first-hand account of the vicious arbitrariness of the times in Sichuan. Typically, it was the first province to reject Maoist ideals, when party leader Zhao Ziyang allowed farmers to sell produce on the free market, spearheading the reforms of his fellow native Sichuanese, **Deng Xiaoping**. So effective were these reforms that by the 1990s Sichuan was competing vigorously with the east-coast economy, a situation for which Chongqing – the already heavily industrialized gateway river port between Sichuan and eastern China – claimed a large part of the credit; Chongqing's economic weight secured separate administrative status for the city and its surrounds. Meanwhile, development continues across the region, bringing all the problems of runaway growth: appalling industrial pollution, ecological devastation and an unbelievable scale of urban reconstruction.

Chengdu and around

Set on the western side of the Red Basin, **CHENGDU** is a determinedly modern city, full of traffic, high-rise department stores and residential blocks.

But it's also a cheerful place: seasonal floral displays and ubiquitous **ginkgo trees** lend colour to its many excellent **parks**, rubbish is scrupulously collected, and the formerly dire wastelands that flanked the central riverbanks have been landscaped with willows, lawns and wavy paths. The population is also nicely laid-back, enjoying its **teahouse culture** at every opportunity and unfazed by this being interpreted as laziness by other Chinese.

Chengdu was styled **Brocade City** in Han times, when the urban elite were buried in elegantly decorated tombs, and its silk travelled west along the caravan routes as far as imperial Rome. A refuge for the eighth-century Tang emperor Xuan Zong after his army mutinied over his infatuation with the beautiful concubine Yang Guifei, the city later became a **printing** centre, producing the world's first paper money. Sacked by the Mongols in 1271, Chengdu recovered soon enough to impress Marco Polo with its busy artisans and handsome bridges,

Chengdu and around

Chengdu	成都	*chéngdū*
Baihuatan Park	百花潭公园	*bǎihuātán gōngyuán*
Cultural Palace	文化宫	*wénhuà gōng*
Daci Si	大慈寺	*dàcí sì*
Du Fu Caotang	杜甫草堂	*dùfǔ cǎotáng*
Giant Panda Breeding Research Base	成都大熊猫繁育研究基地	*chéngdū dàxióngmāo fányù yánjiū jīdì*
Hospital of Traditional Chinese Medicine College	中医药大学	*zhōngyīyào dàxué*
Kuan Xiangzi	宽巷子	*kuānxiàngzi*
Qingyang Gong	青羊宫	*qīngyáng gōng*
Renmin Park	人民公园	*rénmín gōngyuán*
Shufeng Yayun	蜀风雅韵	*shǔfēng yǎyùn*
Shunxing Lao Chaguan	顺兴老茶馆	*shùnxīng lǎocháguǎn*
Sichuan University Museum	四川大学博物馆	*sìchuān dàxué bówùguǎn*
Tianfu Square	天府广场	*tiānfǔ guǎngchǎng*
Wangjiang Lou Park	望江楼公园	*wàngjiānglóu gōngyuán*
Wenshu Yuan	文殊院	*wénshū yuàn*
Wuhou Ci	武侯祠	*wǔhóu cí*
Yong Ling	永陵博物馆	*yǒnglíng bówùguǎn*
Bus Stations		
Beimen	北门汽车站	*běimén qìchēzhàn*
Chadianzi	茶店子客运站	*chádiànzi kèyùnzhàn*
Chengbei	城北客运中心	*chéngběi kèyùn zhōngxīn*
Wuguiqiao	五桂桥中心站	*wǔguìqiáo zhōngxīnzhàn*
Xinnanmen	新南汽车站	*xīnnán qìchēzhàn*
Zhaojue Si	照觉寺汽车站	*zhàojué sì qìchēzhàn*
Accommodation		
Binjiang	滨江饭店	*bīnjiāng fàndiàn*
Dragon Town	龙城宽巷子青年旅馆	*lóngchéng kuānxiàngzi qīngnián lǚguǎn*
Green Bamboo Homestay	新竹家居	*xīnzhú jiājū*
Holly's Hostel	九龙鼎青酒店	*jiǔlóng dǐngqīngjiǔdiàn*
Huanhua Shanzhuang	浣花山庄	*huànhuā shānzhuāng*
Jiaotong	交通饭店	*jiāotōng fàndiàn*

since when it has survived similar cycles of war and restoration to become a major industrial, educational and business centre. There are some **downsides** – the city's traffic congestion and pollution can be atrocious – but on the whole Chengdu is a characterful place to spend a few days, perhaps as a base for visiting Qing-dynasty Huanglongxi or the irrigation system at Dujiangyan, or while organizing a flight or train **to Tibet**. Aside from touring the remaining historical monuments, you can spike your taste buds on one of China's most outstanding cuisines, not to mention getting close-up views of locally bred **pandas**.

Arrival and city transport

Chengdu's five-kilometre-wide **downtown** area contains a warped grid of streets enclosed on three sides by the canal-like **Fu** and **Jin** rivers, themselves surrounded

Jinjiang	锦江宾馆	*jǐnjiāng bīnguǎn*
Sam's Backpacker House (Rongcheng)	荣城宾馆	*róngchéng bīnguǎn*
Sim's	观华青年旅舍	*guānhuá qīngnián lǚshè*
Youyi	友谊宾馆	*yǒuyí bīnguǎn*
Eating and drinking		
Banmuyuan	半亩苑	*bànmǔ yuàn*
Beijing Roast Duck	北京烤鸭饭店	*běijīng kǎoyā fàndiàn*
Cacaja Indian	印度菜菜	*yìndù càicài*
Chen Mapo Tofu	陈麻婆豆腐	*chénmápó dòufù*
Chengdu Xiaochi Cheng	成都小吃城	*chéngdū xiǎochīchéng*
Fiesta Thai	非常泰泰国风味餐厅	*fēichángtài tàiguófēngwèi cāntīng*
Grandma's Kitchen	祖母的厨房	*zǔmǔde chúfáng*
Highfly Café	高飞咖啡	*gāofēi kāfēi*
Lai Tang Yuan	来汤圆	*láitāngyuán*
Laochuzi Chuancanguan	老厨子川餐馆	*lǎochúzi chuāncàiguǎn*
Long Chaoshou	龙抄手饭店	*lóngchāoshǒu fàndiàn*
Yanfu Renjia	盐府人家	*yánfǔ rénjiā*
Zhang Kaoya Jiudian	张烤鸭酒店	*zhāngkǎoyā jiǔdiàn*
Dujiangyan	都江堰	*dūjiāngyàn*
Anlan Suspension Bridge	安澜索桥	*anlán suǒqiáo*
Erwang Miao	二王庙	*èrwáng miào*
Fulong Guan	伏龙观	*fúlóng guàn*
Lidui Park	离堆公园	*líduī gōngyuán*
Songmao Road	松茂古道	*sōngmào gǔdào*
Xishu Jiudian	西蜀酒店	*xīshǔ jiǔdiàn*
Guanghan	广汉	*guǎnghàn*
Sanxingdui Museum	三星堆博物馆	*sānxīngduī bówùguǎn*
Huanglongxi	黄龙溪	*huánglóng xī*
Gulong Si	古龙寺	*gǔlóng sì*
Qingcheng Shan	青城山	*qīngchéng shān*
Shangqing Gongsi	上青宫寺	*shàngqīnggōng sì*
Xindu	新都	*xīndū*
Baoguang Si	宝光寺	*bǎoguāng sì*

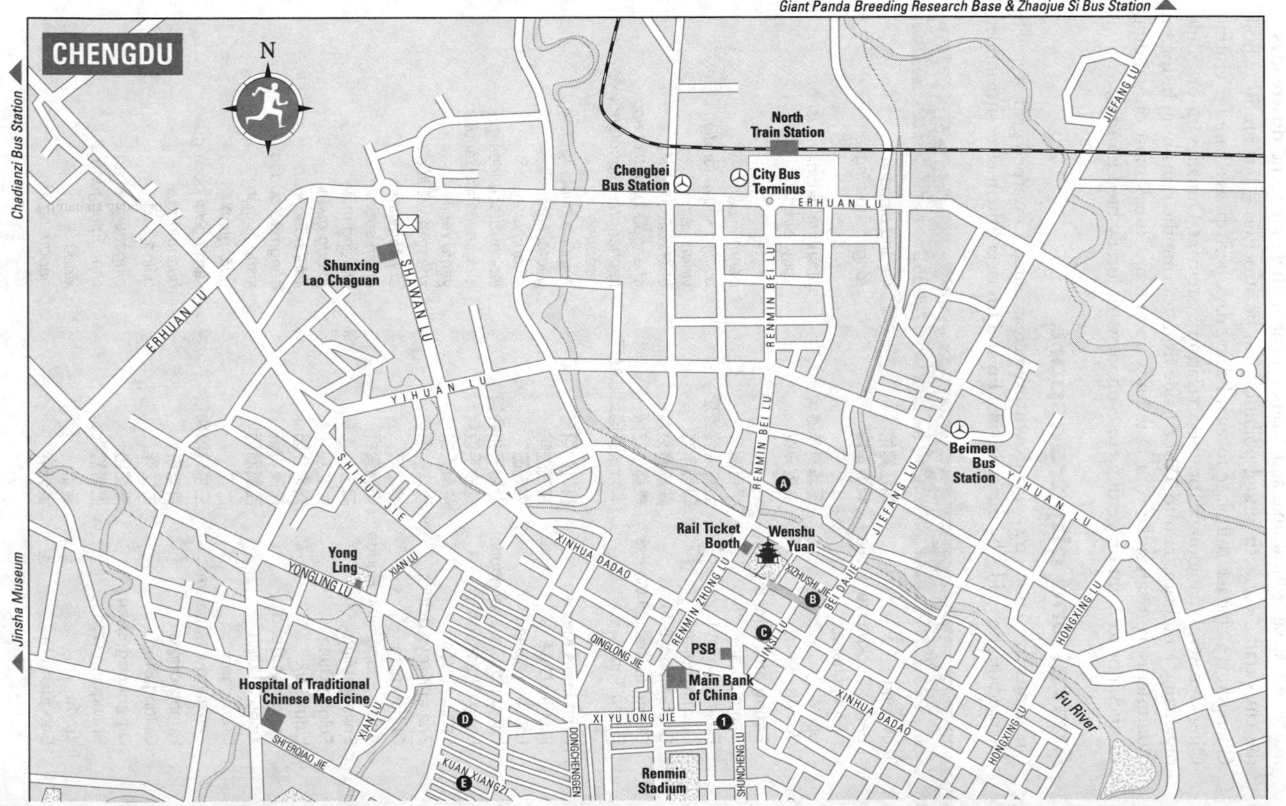
CHENGDU
N
Giant Panda Breeding Research Base & Zhaojue Si Bus Station
Chadianzi Bus Station
Jinsha Museum
North Train Station
Chengbei Bus Station
City Bus Terminus
ERHUAN LU
JIEFANG LU
Shunxing Lao Chaguan
SHAWAN LU
RENMIN BEI LU
YIHUAN LU
Beimen Bus Station
SHIHUI JIE
Rail Ticket Booth
Wenshu Yuan
XINHUA DADAO
Yong Ling
YONGLING LU
XIAN LU
RENMIN ZHONG LU
XIZHUSHI JIE
BEI DAJIE
HONGXING LU
INSI LU
QINGLONG JIE
PSB
Main Bank of China
Hospital of Traditional Chinese Medicine
XI YU LONG JIE
SHUNCHENG LU
DONGCHENGGEN
Fu River
SHI'EROIAO JIE
KUAN XIANGZI
Renmin Stadium
A
B
C
D
E
1

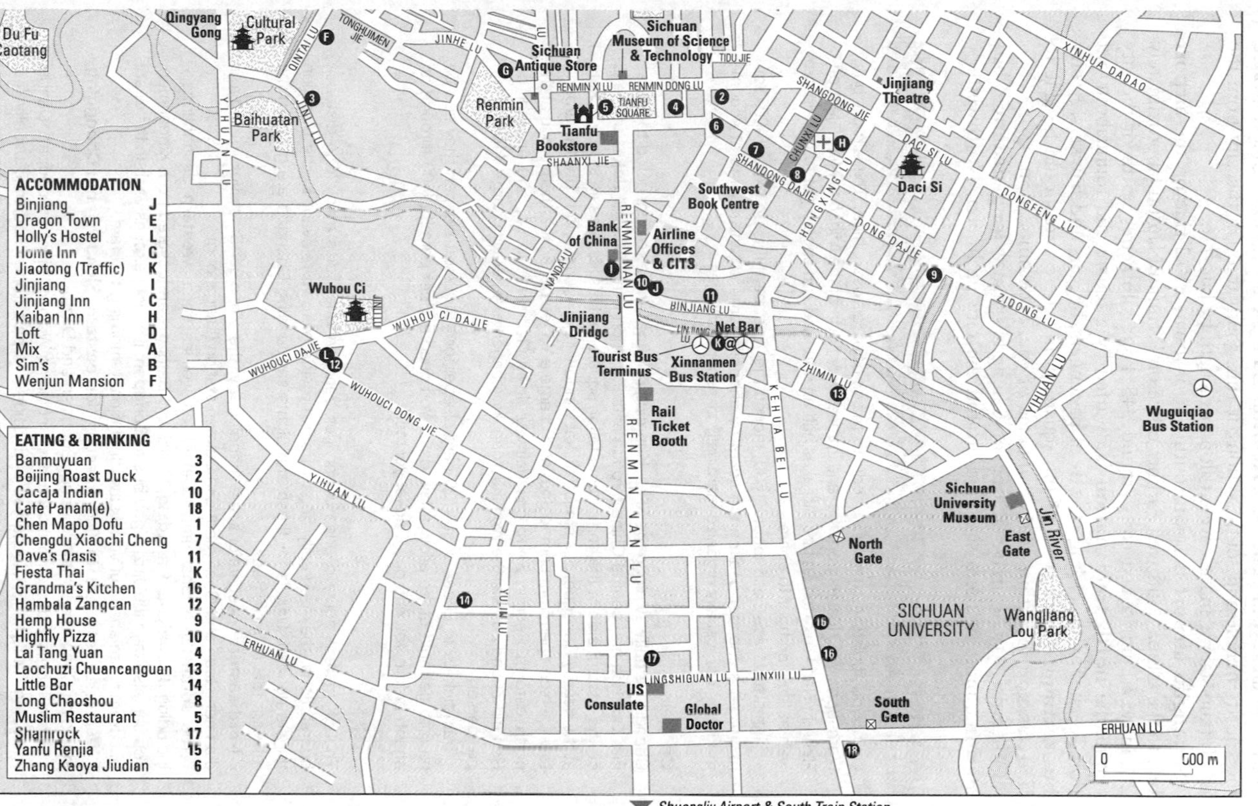

ACCOMMODATION
Binjiang J
Dragon Town E
Holly's Hostel L
Home Inn G
Jiaotong (Traffic) K
Jinjiang I
Jinjiang Inn C
Kaiban Inn H
Loft D
Mix A
Sim's B
Wenjun Mansion F
EATING & DRINKING
Banmuyuan 3
Beijing Roast Duck 2
Cacaja Indian 10
Cafe Panam(e) 18
Chen Mapo Dofu 1
Chengdu Xiaochi Cheng 7
Dave's Oasis 11
Fiesta Thai K
Grandma's Kitchen 16
Hambala Zangcan 12
Hemp House 9
Highfly Pizza 10
Lai Tang Yuan 4
Laochuzi Chuancanguan 13
Little Bar 14
Long Chaoshou 8
Muslim Restaurant 5
Shamrock 17
Yanfu Renjia 15
Zhang Kaoya Jiudian 6
Du Fu Caotang
Qingyang Gong
Cultural Park
Baihuatan Park
Renmin Park
Sichuan Antique Store
Sichuan Museum of Science & Technology
Tianfu Bookstore
Tianfu Square
Jinjiang Theatre
Daci Si
Southwest Book Centre
Bank of China
Airline Offices & CITS
Jinjiang Bridge
Net Bar
Tourist Bus Terminus
Xinnanmen Bus Station
Rail Ticket Booth
Wuhou Ci
Wuguiqiao Bus Station
Sichuan University Museum
East Gate
North Gate
Jin River
Sichuan University
Wangjiang Lou Park
South Gate
US Consulate
Global Doctor
Qintai Lu
Tonghuimen Jie
Jinhe Lu
Jinli Lu
Yihuan Lu
Renmin Xi Lu
Renmin Dong Lu
Tidu Jie
Shangdong Jie
Chunxi Lu
Shandong Dajie
Hongxing Lu
Daci Si Lu
Dongfeng Lu
Xinhua Dadao
Dong Dajie
Shaanxi Jie
Nanda Lu
Renmin Nan Lu
Binjiang Lu
Linjiang Lu
Ziqong Lu
Zhimin Lu
Kehua Bei Lu
Wuhou Ci Dajie
Wuhouci Dajie
Wuhouci Dong Jie
Yulin Lu
Erhuan Lu
Lingshiguan Lu
Jinxiu Lu
0 500 m
Shuangliu Airport & South Train Station

by three ring roads – the most important of which is innermost **Yihuan Lu**. Broad and lined with plane trees, **Renmin Lu** is the main thoroughfare, divided into north, middle and south sections; it runs south through the city from the north train station and is covered along its length by bus #16.

Shuangliu airport is 16km southwest of town, a ¥12 ride on the **airport bus** to the China Southwest Airlines office on Renmin Nan Lu (approximately 2 hourly; 30min); a taxi costs around ¥45. Four kilometres north of the city centre, the **north train station** is dwarfed by a square and roundabout out front, packed with jostling crowds of passengers, beggars and hawkers. A **city bus terminus** is just west off this square, from where you should be able to find transport to within striking distance of your accommodation.

Otherwise, you'll arrive at one of Chengdu's many **long-distance bus stations**, most of them scattered around the city perimeter. Northwesterly

Moving on from Chengdu

Outbound **flights** connect Chengdu to major cities across China. The airport bus (7am–8pm; ¥12) leaves from the lane immediately north of the *Minshan Hotel*, just off Renmin Nan Lu, twice an hour; it takes half an hour and you should get to the airport with at least an hour to spare.

Flights **to Lhasa** cost about ¥1630, though the Tibet permit is an extra ¥400. You might get a cheaper deal on the ticket by shopping around, and agents at accommodation can usually organize marginally cheaper packages.

By train

Chengdu is halfway along the Xi'an–Kunming **rail line**, and also connected to routes into Guizhou and central China through easterly Chongqing. The rail **ticket office** is on the eastern side of the north train-station square, but it's less hassle to buy tickets at the nearby Chengbei bus station (ticket window #9) or from various **booths** around town, which open from 8am to 8pm and charge a ¥5 fee per ticket: there's one at the north gate of Renmin Park; one halfway down Renmin Nan Lu; and another on Renmin Zhong Lu near the Wenshu Yuan. Hotel agents generally charge ¥40 or more per person.

Train tickets **to Lhasa** cost ¥720 hard sleeper, or ¥1100 soft sleeper; they can be hard to get hold of, so allow a few days. You need a Tibet permit (¥400 through an agent) before you can buy a ticket yourself.

By bus

Though there is some overlap of services between Chengdu's many long-distance bus stations, they generally depart from the side of town relevant to the direction they're headed. Details for these and sights surrounding Chengdu are given in the relevant text as indicated.

Northeastern destinations are handled by the Zhaojue Si station (Jiangyou, Jianmen Guan and Guanyuan) and Beimen station (Langzhong).

The **south** (Emei Shan and Leshan), as well as some **western** destinations – including **Jiuzhaigou, Kangding**, Ganzi and Batang – are covered from Xinnanmen. You can also take the Jiuzhaigou bus to **Songpan**; it's more expensive than the direct bus from Chadianzi, but you'll save on the early-morning taxi fare.

Wuguiqiao is where to find transport for **eastern Sichuan and Chongqing**, including Chongqing, Yibin, Zigong, Gongxian and Dazu.

Buses for most of **western Sichuan** – including Wolong, Xiaojin, Songpan, Danba, Kangding, Maerkang, Jiuzhaigou and Zöige - depart from Chadianzi, usually first thing in the morning. If you don't fancy an early haul out to Chadianzi, stay overnight at Chandianzi's **bus-station hotel** (Ⓣ028/87506615 or 87503312; dorms ¥20, ❸).

Tourist bus routes

Two useful **tourist buses** leave from outside the *Jiaotong* hotel on Linjiang Lu between about 8am and 6pm: **bus #901** (¥3) travels via Chunxi Lu, Wuhou Ci, Renmin Park, Qingyang Gong, Dufu Caotang and terminates at the Jinsha Museum; while **bus #902** (¥2) heads northeast to the Giant Panda Breeding Research Base.

Chadianzi is the most remote, set out on the third ring road; bus #82 goes from here to Wuhouci Dajie and Binjiang Lu (opposite the *Jiaotong* hotel). Northeast of the centre are **Zhaojue Si** (bus #1 or #302 to Renmin Nan Lu and Wuhouci Dajie) and **Beimen** stations; to the east is **Wuguiqiao** (bus #58 passes Renmin Park); while the most central is **Xinnanmen**, next to the *Jiaotong* hotel.

City transport

Chengdu's roads are approaching gridlock, so give yourself enough time to get around. Single- and double-decker **buses** run from about 6am until after dark, and charge ¥1 (¥2 for air-con coaches). Fares double after 8pm. **Taxis** are everywhere – though it can be hard to find a free one - and cost ¥5 to hire. Motorbikes are illegal in the downtown area, so **bicycles** (and electric mopeds) remain popular, with cycle lanes and guarded parking throughout the city – see p.876 for rentals.

A **subway** is also under construction, due for unveiling around 2009; this means that many central roads are being dug up, causing traffic delays and detours.

Accommodation

Chengdu has a great number of **places to stay**, with a choice for every budget; the following are all central. Everywhere can make transport bookings and **hostels** – as well as the *Jiaotong* hotel – also offer Internet access, bike rental, travellers' noticeboards and good-value **tours** (see "Listings", p.877, for details). Note that the motels are better value for money than hostels if you're after a double. There's also accommodation at Chadianzi bus station for early-morning departures – see "Moving on from Chengdu" box, opposite.

Hostels

Dragon Town 27 Kuan Xiangzi ⓣ028/86648408, ⓦwww.dragontown.com.cn. Atmospherically set in a reproduction period building in a quiet, old-style street. Staff are a bit slack, but otherwise this is a good budget choice. Dorms ¥35, ❹

Holly's 246 Wuhouci Dajie ⓣ028/85548131. Set in an interesting area of Tibetan shops and martial-art supply stores (there's a sports college nearby). In addition to tours, the hostel also has a book exchange, a roof-garden café and a highly recommended Sichuan cooking class. Beds ¥30 depending on dorm size, ❸

Loft 4 Tongren Lu (aka Xiangtong Xiang) ⓣ028/86265770, ⓦwww.lofthostel.com. A very sharp operation in slickly converted 1980s warehouse, with a smart café and great second-floor venue offering pool table, video lounge and bar. But rooms are a little expensive for what you get. Dorms ¥40, ❹

Mix 23 Xinghui Xi Lu ⓣ028/83222271, ⓦwww.donkey-pal.com. Nasty tiled building on the outside but cosy and homely place once you're through the door. There are two buildings, one a backpackers with all shared facilities, the other a hotel with en-suite bathrooms. Dorms ¥35, ❹

Sim's 42 Xizhushi Jie ⓣ028/86914422, ⓦwww.gogosc.com. East of Wenshu Yuan, near one of Chengdu's reconstructed old quarters, so an interesting place to hole up. The 1920s grey-brick Sichuanese/European building has a small courtyard garden and a slightly spartan atmosphere. Very friendly and helpful; they'll pick up from the airport for ¥50. Dorm beds ¥35, ❸

Wenjun Mansion 180 Qintai Lu ⓣ028/86138884, ⓕ86132224. In an old-style street near to

Qingyang Gong and Baihuatan Park, this is a tidy, multi-floored place based along traditional courtyard design, though rooms are standard and functional. Dorm beds ¥40, ❺

Motels

Home Inn 9 Shaocheng Lu ⓣ028/86253111, ⓦwww.homeinns.com. Right across from the north entrance to Renmin Park, this bright yellow building offers the best mid-range deal in town, with friendly staff, good facilities and low prices. ❹

Jinjiang Inn 3 Jinsi Lu ⓣ028/86917890, ⓦwww.jj-inn.com.cn. South of Wenshu Yuan and the "antique" district, though the street itself is a bit gloomy – for the price, though, this is an excellent place to stay. ❹

Kaibin Inn (aka Diyi Cheng) 1 Xiao Ke Jia Xiang ⓣ028/86672888 ⓕ86716600. Hard to find the entrance – it's in a walkthrough between Chunxi Lu and Hongxing Lu – but this is yet another well-priced mid-range place, close to the shopping district. ❸

Hotels

Binjiang 16 Binjiang Lu ⓣ028/86651565, ⓕ86673271. This pink-tiled hotel next to the huge *Sofitel* is in a renovated 1980s building. Prices are surprisingly low: all rooms have showers and toilets, and standards compare favourably with the *Jiaotong*'s, though there's no dormitory. ❺

Jiaotong (Traffic) 77 Linjiang Lu, near Xinnanmen bus station ⓣ028/85451017, ⓦwww.traffichotel.com. Well-maintained standby, featuring spotless doubles and three-bed dorms with TV and shared or private bathroom. They're a little flexible with doubles' rates in the face of motel competition. Dorm beds ¥30, ❺

Jinjiang 80 Renmin Nan Lu ⓣ028/85506666, ⓦwww.jjhotel.com. Chengdu's original tourist hotel, now revamped with some panache to make the International grade and featuring smart rooms (from around ¥1700), bilingual staff, conference and business facilities, and a host of restaurants. ❾

The City

Chengdu's centre is marked by **Tianfu Square**, a huge space with dancing fountains, a subterranean metro stop and a white statue of Mao Zedong to the north. Behind Mao, the **Sichuan Museum of Science and Technology** (daily 9.30am–4.30pm; ¥30) is a hi-tech, airy museum with heaps of interactive exhibits illustrating physics and natural resources. It's good rainy-day material (especially for children), though Chinese captions glorifying GM products and widescale damming of rivers for electricity are a worry.

East of Tianfu, roads run through the heart of the city's commercial precinct, at the core of which is pedestrianized **Chunxi Lu**, full of clothes shops and upmarket department stores. Past here along **Daci Si Lu** is **Daci Si**, a small temple founded in 644 and dedicated to the Tang-dynasty monk **Xuanzang** (see p.1040), who lived briefly in Chengdu before starting on his journey to India. The Qing-style buildings are recent reproductions after the complex was used as a factory during the Cultural Revolution. Of most interest is a side-wing museum, which houses a few pieces of original Tang stonework, along with accounts of Xuanzang's journeys, and a portrait of him carrying a bamboo backpack.

Just west of Tianfu Square, past the city's main **mosque**, is **Renmin Park** (free except during floral exhibitions), which offers an introduction to Chengdu's reputedly slack pace of life, comprising a few acres of trees, paved paths, ponds and ornamental gardens with seasonally varying displays. Near the north entrance there's an ever-busy **teahouse** shaded by wisteria (look for the large bronze teapot at the gate), and the tall **Monument to the Martyrs**, an obelisk commemorating the 1911 rail disputes that marked the beginning of the end for the Qing empire – hence the unusual motifs of trains and spanners. Otherwise, the park is just a good place to stroll; look for vendors with little burners and a slab of marble along the paths who execute skilful designs of Chinese zodiac animals in **toffee**; there's also a **canteen** next to the teahouse

Teahouses

The Sichuanese have a reputation for being particularly garrulous, best experienced at one of the province's many **teahouses**. These hold much the same place in Sichuanese life as a local bar or pub does in the West; some are formal establishments with illuminated signs spelling out *chadian*, *chaguan* or *dachadian* (all meaning "teahouse"); others are just a humble spread of bamboo or plastic chairs in the corner of a park, a temple or indeed any available public space. Whatever the establishment, just sit down to have a waiter come over and ask you what sort of tea you'd like – the standard jasmine-scented variety costs around ¥5 a cup, up to ¥40 or more for a really fine brew. Most are served in the three-piece Sichuanese *gaiwancha*, a squat, handleless cup with lid and saucer. **Refills** are unlimited – either the waiter will give you a top-up on passing your table, or you'll be left with a flask of boiling water. In a country where it's usually difficult to find somewhere to relax in public, teahouses are very welcome: idlers can spend the whole day chatting, playing mahjong, reading or just staring into space, without anyone interrupting – except cruising masseurs and ear-wax removers.

serving Sichuanese *xiaochi*. The park is crammed with martial-arts practitioners every morning.

After an uprising in Chengdu in 1789, a Manchu garrison was stationed in the city and built themselves a miniature version of Beijing's *hutongs* in the area directly north of Renmin Park. Though the street plan survives, the only "old" buildings left – in fact, modern reconstructions of them – are along tree-lined **Kuan Xiangzi**, the lane where the *Dragon Town Hostel* is located (see p.869), and two adjacent lanes. The reconstructions are well done, and show off local Sichuanese building styles, with whitewashed wattle-and-daub or grey bricks filling in between solid wooden frameworks and carved gateways. This is the most "authentic" of Chengdu's resurrected old areas, in that the buildings appear to still be residential, not tourist-oriented.

Wenshu Yuan and around

Wenshu Yuan (¥5), a bustling, atmospheric Chan (Zen) temple dedicated to **Wenshu**, the Buddhist incarnation of Wisdom, sits 1.5km north of Tianfu Square on the #16 bus route, just east off Renmin Zhong Lu. The temple's four elegant single-storey halls were last rebuilt around 1700, each with red-washed walls, wooden pillars and vaulting, and roof corners drawn out into long points. The **first hall** contains a small gilded trinity, not of the usual three aspects of Buddha but of Guanyin, seated on a tiger, flanked by the Bodhisattva Puxian (on an elephant) and Wenshu, riding a **lion**. Wenshu's lion reappears elsewhere throughout the complex, such as in the cast-iron statue outside the **third hall**, whose interior houses some antique wooden *arhat* statues. The **fourth hall** too has a lion, this time as a mural and looking more like a shaggy, red-haired dog.

If you bear east (right) immediately on entering the temple you'll encounter a narrow, eleven-storey **pagoda**. According to some, the gold-leafed object visible in the base includes **Xuanzang's skull**, though other temples in China also claim to own his mortal remains. Just past here under the ginkgo trees is a small open-air **teahouse** area, along with a fine **vegetarian restaurant** – both good reasons to visit Wenshu at lunchtime.

The district east of Wenshu Yuan has been rebuilt as an "antique" quarter of stone streets and brick and timber buildings. Though it's all very touristy, with shops selling fair-quality if pricey souvenirs, it's also quite atmospheric and there are some good places to **eat** local snacks – though check prices first.

Qingyang Gong and around

Sited about 2km west of Renmin Park – buses #19 and #35 stop nearby, as well as tourist bus #901 – **Qingyang Gong** (Green Goat Temple; ¥5) is dedicated to Taoism's mythical proponent, Laozi. The temple's unusual **Bagua Pavilion** is an eight-sided hall with supporting posts wreathed in golden dragons, which houses a statue of **Laozi** astride his buffalo. According to legend, Laozi lost interest in teaching and headed west into the sunset, first baffling posterity by saying that he could be found at the green goat market once his philosophy was understood – hence the temple's unusual name. The tale is again reflected at the main **Three Purities Hall**, built in 1669, where two **bronze goats**, overlooked by the looming bulks of the Three Purities themselves, have been worn smooth by the caresses of luck-seekers. The right-hand "goat" is weird, being the simultaneous incarnation of all twelve zodiacal animals. West of here is an excellent **vegetarian restaurant**, open at lunchtime, but for active entertainment head around the back of the next hall, where those after a blessing stumble with eyes shut and arms outstretched towards three large good-luck symbols painted on the bricks, hoping to make contact; onlookers laugh at their efforts before trying themselves.

East of Qingyang Gong, **Qintai Lu** is a broad street built in a Qing/Ming style to create a kitsch "Chinatown", full of expensive jewellery shops and restaurants. At the south end, the entrance to **Baihuatan Park** is marked by a wooden pagoda and an attractive covered bridge, which crosses over to a spread of ornamental trees shading a large waterside teahouse area – a very pleasant spot to settle into on a hot day.

One place north of Qingyang Gong that is well worth a look is Chengdu's **Hospital of Traditional Chinese Medicine** – one of China's best – on Shi'erqiao Lu, 100m east of the intersection with Yihuan Lu. The Foreign Affairs department is signed in English about 70m inside the entrance on the right; they charge ¥30 for an excellent tour with an English-speaking guide. You can also study TCM here.

Du Fu Caotang

The line of minibuses pulled up outside **Du Fu Caotang** (Du Fu's Thatched Cottage; daily 9am–5pm; ¥60), located 2km west of Qingyang Gong on the #901 bus route, attests to the respect the Chinese hold for the Tang-dynasty poet **Du Fu**. His works record the upheavals of his life and times with compassion and humour, and are considered, along with the more romantic imagery of his contemporary Li Bai (see p.882), to comprise the epitome of Chinese poetry. Born in 712, Du Fu struggled for years to obtain a position at the imperial court in Chang'an, succeeding only after one of his sons had died of starvation and just as the empire was struck by the An Lushan rebellion (see p.277). Fleeing the war-ravaged capital for Chengdu in 759, he spent the next five years in a simple grass-roofed dwelling outside the city's west wall, where he wrote some 240 of his 1400 surviving poems. Du Fu spent his later years wandering central China "like a lonely gull between the earth and the sky", dying on a boat in Hunan in 770.

Three centuries after Du Fu's death, a pleasant park was founded at the site of his cottage by fellow poet and admirer Wei Zhuang, and around 1800 it was expanded to its current layout of artfully arranged gardens, bamboo groves, pools, bridges and whitewashed halls. Besides antique and modern statues of Du Fu – depicted as sadly emaciated – there's a small, free **museum** illustrating his life.

Wuhou Ci and around

Wuhou Ci (¥60), southwest of the centre on Wuhouci Dajie (bus #1 from Renmin Nan Lu runs past, as does tourist bus #901), is a temple-like complex nominally dedicated to **Zhuge Liang**, the strategist of *Three Kingdoms* fame. As his emperor **Liu Bei** is also buried here, however, the whole site is really a big shrine to the Three Kingdoms era (see p.453).

The site dates to Liu Bei's funeral in 223, though most of the buildings are of early Qing design; as usual in Chengdu, everything is surrounded by gardens. To the left of the entrance, the **Three Kingdoms Culture Exhibition Hall** has contemporary sculptures, lacquered furniture, painted bricks showing daily life (picking mulberry leaves, herding camels, ploughing), and a few martial relics such as arrowheads and copper cavalry figurines. Elsewhere, halls and colonnaded galleries house brightly painted **statues** of the epic's heroes, notably a white-faced Liu Bei flanked by his oath-brothers Guan Yu and Zhang Fei; and Zhuge Liang (holding his feather fan) and his son and grandson. Over in the complex's northwestern corner, **Liu Bei's tomb** is a walled mound covered in trees and guarded by stone figures.

The lane immediately east of Wuhou Ci, **Jinli Lu**, is yet another of Chengdu's new "old" streets: this one is more of an alley, about 300m long, and jammed with wooden-fronted shops selling snacks. It winds up at an open-air **theatre** (also accessible through Wuhou Ci), where there are performances of Sichuanese Opera in the evening (see p.876) – buy tickets just inside Wuhou Ci's main entrance.

The district south of Wuhou Ci forms Chengdu's **Tibetan quarter**, full of shops stocked to their roofs with heavy clothes, amber and turquoise jewellery, knives and prayer wheels, conches and other temple accessories – not to mention heavy-duty blenders capable of whipping up a gallon of butter tea in one go. None of this is for tourists; most customers are Tibetan monks, cowboys, and Khampa women with braided hair, all looking decidedly tall and robust next to the local Chinese.

Yong Ling

Northwest of the centre on Yongling Lu and the #46 bus route, **Yong Ling** (daily 8.30am–5pm; ¥20) is the tomb of **Wang Jian**, a member of the Imperial Guard under the Tang who broke away from the disintegrating dynasty and, in 907 AD, set himself up here as emperor of Shu. After Wang Jian's death in 918, his "fatuous and self-indulgent son" Wang Yan was unable to hold onto the kingdom, which the Tang empire reclaimed in 925. Tomb robbers stripped the site of artefacts centuries before it was excavated during the 1940s, but the brick-lined chambers retain Wang Jian's stone **sarcophagus platform**, richly carved with musicians and twelve very Central Asian-looking bodyguards, and a simply styled, placid **statue**.

Jinsha Museum

Around 5km west from the centre, at the terminus of the #901 tourist bus, the **Jinsha Museum** (daily 8am–6pm; ¥80) sits over the site of one of western China's major prehistoric settlements. The museum, comprising two halls set amongst gardens, was newly opened at the time of writing and lacked explanatory captions as interpretation of the site – and the **Ba-Shu** culture that inhabited it – is still being pieced together.

Finds from around Chengdu show that the region was well settled as early as 2700 BC, though its first cultural flowering came a thousand years later at

Sanxingdui (see p.878), which itself went into a decline as the Jinsha settlement blossomed from 1200 to 600 BC. Covering five square kilometres in total, Jinsha has yielded house remains, tools and artefacts of all descriptions, thousands of graves, and scores of **sacrificial pits** filled with ornaments and animal bones, all dating back to the Shang dynasty. The **first hall** protects a collection of these pits, which were dug a couple of metres deep into the grey soil in a regular grid pattern; the glass-sided building is well lit, and wooden boardwalks allow a close look at unexcavated bones and ivory poking out of the ground. The **second hall** is confusing; make sure you first go upstairs where there are dioramas of the site, plus domestic tools and a reconstruction of what the settlement might have looked like around 1200 BC. The **ground floor** has the pick of the finds, including a bronze statuette of a figure with a feather headdress and oversized hands (a smaller version of the famous sculpture at Sangxingdui, see p.878); some beautifully coloured, transluscent jades; small statues of tigers and kneeling slaves with bound hands (perhaps representing human sacrifice); and a thin, serrated **gold disc** interpreted as depicting the Sun God.

Sichuan University Museum and Wangjiang Lou Park

Southeast of the centre, **Sichuan University** merits a visit for its excellent **museum** (daily 9am–4pm; ¥10), donated in the 1920s by American scholar D.S. Dye – take bus #19 or #335 to the university's **east gate** and walk back 50m to the entrance. Slightly dry **ethnology** exhibits include Qiang, Yi and Miao textiles, and a room devoted to Tibetan religious artefacts – silverwork, paintings and a human thigh-bone flute. Chengdu's once-famous **brocades** also feature, some made into wedding costumes and coverings for an elaborate Qing bridal sedan; there's also a model tearoom with **shadow-puppet theatre** (*piying shi*, "skin-moving theatre" in Chinese), the walls covered with heroes, villains and mythical beasts, all made of flat pieces of leather snipped and pierced like paper cutouts.

Continue along the river past the university gates, and you'll soon reach slightly scruffy **Wangjiang Lou Park** (9am–6pm; ¥5), dedicated to the famous Tang poetess **Xue Tao**, who was buried here in 834. She was particularly fond of bamboo as a symbol of virtue and dignity, and the park is planted with many varieties. There's also a **well** where she drew water used to make a special red paper, the small grass mound of her **tomb**, and a Ming-style **pagoda** looking out over the river.

The Giant Panda Breeding Research Base

Some 8km northeast of central Chengdu, the **Giant Panda Breeding Research Base** (daily 8am–6pm; ¥30) offers the best possible views of both giant and arboreal red pandas – housed here in semi-naturalistic, spacious pens – short of your heading off to Wolong (p.918). There's also a **museum**, with bits of panda anatomy in glass jars and, for reasons that remain unexplained, a diorama of a sabre-tooth tiger. Get to the base early, as the pandas slump into a stupor after munching their way through piles of bamboo at around 10am. If you feel flush, you can also have a photo taken with an adult panda for ¥400, or cuddling a baby panda (subject to availability; ¥1000). **Tours** to the base offered by hostels are convenient but stupidly expensive at ¥80 a person – it's far cheaper to catch tourist bus #902 (¥2) from outside the *Jiaotong* hotel.

Eating

Most of Chengdu's abundant **places to eat** are Sichuanese, including some famous premises whose ugly plastic furnishings disguise both their venerable histories and the quality of their food. **Regional Chinese** and **foreign restaurants** allow a break from chillies and oil, as do **cafés**, which serve a run of coffee, pizzas, sandwiches, burgers, pasta and desserts. Top of the list are *Highfly Pizza* on Binjiang Lu; the above-average and inexpensive *Grandma's Kitchen*, near the university on Kehua Bei Lu, a cosy joint favoured by expats and overseas students; and the shabbily hip *Dave's Oasis* on Binjiang Lu, popular with backpackers. **Hotpot** places are legion, and your accommodation can point you to the nearest. Sichuanese food tastes especially good with **beer** – try locally brewed Xuehua. There are also good, mid-range **vegetarian restaurants** at the two temples, open at lunchtime.

Banmuyuan 98 Jinli Xi Lu, near Baihuatan Park. Florid decor, bouncy staff, and rice-free, pickle-enhanced Dongbei fare, where even confirmed carnivores might be embarrassed by the quantity of meat you can order in a single serving. A selection of cold vegetable dishes, pork stew, a plate of *jiaozi* and beer for two comes in around ¥50.

Beijing Roast Duck Shandong Jie, just west of Chunxi Lu's top end. Famous duck served with all the trimmings; they also do Mongolian hotpot and palate-cleansing side dishes such as tofu-garlic spring rolls and bitter bamboo shoots. Count on ¥40 a head with beer, and be prepared to wait for a table.

Cacaja Indian 18 Binjiang Zhong Lu ⓣ028/86670399. Bollywood soundtracks and a cosy, orange-painted interior draped in saris and posters of deities. Curries, *bhajis*, fresh yoghurt *raitas*, *dal* and *biryanis*, and plenty of meat-free dishes for vegetarians. Need to book at weekends. Mains ¥15–30.

Chen Mapo Doufu Xi Yulong Jie, not far from the PSB. Founded in 1862, this is the home of Grandma Chen's bean curd, where ¥20 buys a large bowl of tofu glowing with minced meat, chilli oil and *huajiao* sauce. They also do a good range of Sichuanese favourites.

Chengdu Xiaochi Cheng 134 Shandong Dajie. Staff are brusque but the low wooden tables, courtyard fountain and ¥15–30 samplers of classic Sichuanese snacks can't be beaten. Dishes include dumplings, *dandan mian*, small crispy-fried fish, dry-fried beef, rabbit in black bean sauce, shaved rice-jelly noodles, and much more.

Fiesta Thai outside the *Jiaotong Fandian*, Linjiang Lu. Silk-clad staff greet you in Thai, and the food, from green curry chicken, mother-in-law eggs (deep-fried boiled eggs), and pork and glass-noodle salad, through to coconut custard-filled pumpkin and other desserts, is faultless. Worth the ¥50-a-head price.

Hambala Zangcan Wuhouci Dong Jie, near *Holly's Hostel*. One of many nearby Tibetan restaurants, authentic down to the DVDs of Tibetan pop, a cowboy clientele, and begging acolytes going round the tables. Expect butter tea in metal teapots, dumplings, fresh yoghurt, and fried, boiled or chopped yak; don't count on vegetables. Around ¥15 a head

Lai Tang Yuan Long Bin Jie, the small street along the east side of the Parkson Building. One of Chengdu's famous canteens, good for a snack or light lunch. The house speciality is *tangyuan*, little rice-flour dumplings served with sweet sesame paste – a small bowlful costs just ¥2.

Laochuzi Chuancanguan 31 Zhimin Lu, 500m east of Xinnanmen bus station. Four-storey mid-range Sichuanese restaurant with lively atmosphere and hospitable staff. They do excellent sliced steamed pork, eaten in delicate "cut" buns; spiced chicken wings packed in sticky rice; sweet taro rolls; and tiger-skin peppers. Around ¥35 a head.

Long Chaoshou Chunxi Lu. A renowned dumpling house specializing in *chaoshou*, Sichuanese wonton, and samplers of Sichuanese *xiaochi* for ¥18–28. Eat in the downstairs canteen; the upper floors have the same food and terrible service at ten times the price.

Muslim Restaurant At the mosque on Xitu Jie. Catering to Chengdu's large Muslim population, this serves everything from *lamian* soup to meat-and-potato stew and upmarket Sichuanese dishes. Uyghurs stand outside grilling kebabs and bread, if you fancy a take-away.

Yanfu Renjia Kehua Bei Lu. One of several local stylish Sichuanese restaurants near the university. They don't drown everything in chilli oil, and pay attention to subtle flavours: the steamed spare ribs with mung beans, "beanflower" tofu soup, pork belly slices, and various delicate dumplings have won awards, and the place is always busy. Dishes around ¥25.

Zhang Kaoya Jiudian Qingnian Lu. With a tiny stairway entrance, this comprises a canteen downstairs with horrendous plastic decor and a nicer restaurant above, both serving an array of Sichuanese snacks and dishes; the real treat is their marinated roast duck in an aromatic stock. A plate of garlic cucumber or shredded white-radish soup balances the richness of the duck; a meal for two costs around ¥30.

Drinking, nightlife and entertainment

Chengdu has a solid **nightlife**, but venues open and close rapidly; the following have been around a while and make good starting points, and you can check the latest in the **free magazine** *Chengdoo* (Ⓦwww.chengdoo.com). South of the centre, *Café Panam(e)* at 143 Kehua Bei Lu (on the second-floor balcony of a restaurant complex) is a popular expat watering hole with half-litres of beer for ¥20, a pool table, DJs on Friday and bands some other nights. The *Shamrock*, on Renmin Nan Lu, has perhaps had its day but still supplies loud, live music Wednesday and Sunday, with a DJ filling in Friday and Saturday. The Yulin district, southwest of the centre, has several bars, the best of which is the *Little Bar* at 55 Yulin Xi Lu (which can supply directions to the *New Little Bar*). The more central *Hemp House*, on the third floor of a complex at Dongmen Daqiao, has live music parties at weekends. As for **entertainment**, you should spend a couple of hours at the theatre, soaking up at least the atmosphere, if not the plots, of *chuanxi*, one of China's main **opera** styles.

Listings

Airlines China Southwest is opposite the *Jinjiang* hotel on Renmin Nan Lu (Ⓣ028/86661100).
Banks and exchange The main Bank of China (Mon–Fri 8.30am–5.30pm) is up on Renmin Zhong Lu; a useful branch, with ATM and able to change traveller's cheques, is next to the *Jinjiang* hotel on Renmin Nan Lu. Many other branches around town have ATMs accepting foreign cards, as will some branches of the Agricultural Bank.
Bike rental All hostels rent out bikes for around ¥15 per day, plus a ¥100 deposit.
Bookshops The Southwest Book Centre opposite the south end of Chunxi Lu, and the Tianfu Bookstore at the southwest corner of Tianfu Square, stock maps, guidebooks in Chinese, and English-language novels – not all of them Victorian potboilers either.
Camping supplies If you're heading to Tibet, western Sichuan or elsewhere in China's wilds, there's a clutch of outdoor stores selling good-quality gear at competitive prices (compared to what you'd pay at home) on Yihuan Lu, just west of the intersection with Renmin Nan Lu.
Consulate US, 4 Lingshiguan Lu, Renmin Nan Lu (Ⓣ028/85583992, Ⓕ85518277).

Sichuan Opera

Sichuan Opera – known here as **chuanxi** – is a rustic variant on Beijing's, based on everyday events and local legends. Most pieces are performed in Sichuanese, a rhythmic dialect well suited to theatre, which allows for humour and clever wordplay to shine through. As well as the usual bright costumes, stylized action and glass-cracking vocals, *chuanxi* has two specialities: **fire-breathing** and **rapid face-changing**, where the performers – apparently simply by turning around or waving their arms across their faces – completely change their make-up.

Today, *chuanxi* has gone into a decline as a form of popular entertainment, and most locals are not much interested. There are several places to catch a show around town, however, catering to tourists with nightly **variety shows** featuring short opera scenes, fire-breathing and face-changing, comedy skits, puppetry, shadow-lantern play and storytelling. These are pretty enjoyable and you might even catch occasional full-length operas. Venues include **Shunxing Lao Chaguan**, in the Chengdu International Convention Centre, Floor 3, 258 Shawan Lu, diagonally across from the post office – enter what looks like a cinema, take escalators up two levels, then bear around the balcony to your right; **Shufeng Yayun** in the **Cultural Park** (enter off Qintai Lu); the Ming-style open-air stage in **Wuhou Ci**; and the downtown **Jinjiang Theatre**, in a lane north of Shangdong Jie. Each of these charges around ¥120–180 for a seat, depending on the row; you'll get a better deal on **tickets** – from around ¥80 – by booking through one of the hostels.

Guides The best independent guide in Chengdu is Tray Lee, who can often be found in Renmin Park (ⓣ0139/08035353, ⓔlee@rt98.com – he's not good at answering emails, though). He speaks excellent English, knows Chengdu and Sichuan very well, and has been guiding foreigners around the province for twenty years. Another good option, especially for tours of Chengdu, Tibet and Qinghai, is Peptours (ⓦwww.peptours.com), run by a long-time resident Westerner.

Hospitals and medical centres People's No. 1 Hospital and Chengdu Municipal Chinese Medicine Research Institute, Chunxi Lu ⓣ028/86667223. There's also the English-speaking Global Doctor, Ground Floor, Bangkok Garden, cnr of Erhuan Lu and Renmin Nan Lu ⓣ028/85226058, 24hr emergency number ⓣ0139/82256966; ⓦwww.globaldoctor.com.au.

Internet access Hostels and the motels all have Internet access; there's also a huge Net bar above Xinnanmen bus station – enter from the river side, not the station.

Left luggage Accommodation will look after excess gear while you're off in the wilds for around ¥2 per item per day. The train and bus stations also have left-luggage facilities open to anyone who can produce an onward ticket, though you can't generally leave things overnight.

Mail Chengdu's main post office is inconveniently located 2km west of the north train station at 73 Shawan Lu; they open daily 8am–7pm and the poste restante counter (marked "International Mail"; the postal code for letters is Chengdu 610031) is ahead and on the right as you enter.

Martial arts The Renmin Gongyuan Taiji Chuan association, headed by teacher Xiao, meets near the monument in Renmin Park every Saturday and Sunday morning around 9am – you'll need to speak Chinese to take part.

Massage One of the best places in town is Fuqiao Baojian, 77 Zhengfu Jie, just south of the PSB. It's a restaurant downstairs; take the lift to floor 3 or 4. Two hours of having your body pulled apart costs ¥100.

PSB The branch dealing with visa extensions and foreigners' problems is on Shuncheng Lu (Mon–Fri 9am–noon and 1–5pm), just south of the intersection with Wenwu Lu on the west side of the street.

Shopping For clothing, head to Chunxi Lu, where all the Chinese designer brands (and a few Western ones) have stores. There's an interesting, touristy curio market – good for Maomorabilia, wooden screens and all sorts of "new antiques" – just by a small bridge on the north side of the road about halfway between Qingyang Gong and Du Fu Caotang. For genuine antique snuff bottles, jewellery, birdcages and porcelain, try the Sichuan Antique Store, corner of Dongchenggen Lu and Renmin Xi Lu.

Travel agents and tours Unless you're pushed for time or don't want to try out your Chinese, you'll save money by booking transport tickets yourself; otherwise, use desks at your accommodation. For tours, the best deals are with independent agents at Chengdu's hostels and the *Jiaotong* hotel, who all offer part- and multi-day packages – you don't have to be staying to make bookings. Two-hour Sichuan Opera trips cost ¥80–100; three hours at Chengdu's Giant Panda Breeding Research Base (¥80); a day-trip to Qingcheng Shan (¥80); four days at Jiuzhaigou and Huanglong (around ¥850); a three-day package to Siguniang Shan (¥480, excluding horse trekking). Tibet packages should come in below ¥2000 for flights, or ¥1600 for the train. Hostels also arrange five-seater minibuses with a driver for the day to tour local sights (plus Wolong, Leshan or Emei Shan) at ¥300–700 depending on distance.

Around Chengdu

Chengdu's surrounding diversions are mostly ignored by visitors, lured or sated by grander prospects elsewhere. But the following all make worthy day-trips from the capital, and most can be used as first stops on longer routes. Just to the northeast, **Xindu**'s important Buddhist monastery is just a short hop from the **Sanxingdui Museum**, stuffed with inscrutable prehistoric bronzes. Unpretentious Qing architecture graces the picturesque market town of **Huanglongxi** southwest of Chengdu, while northwest, **Dujiangyan** sports a still-functional two-thousand-year-old irrigation scheme surrounded by wooded parkland, and nearby **Qingcheng Shan** is forested and peppered with Taoist shrines.

Xindu and Baoguang Si

Some 16km northeast of Chengdu, the market town of **XINDU** sits at the start of Shudao, the ancient "Road to Sichuan" (see p.881), to which the cheerful

Luohan halls

Buddhism's original array of eighteen **luohans** – also known as *arhats*, or saints – has, since the religion's arrival in China 1900 years ago, grown to include over five hundred famous monks, emperors, folk heroes and even the occasional foreigner (look for big noses, curly hair and full beards). This has spawned **luohan halls**, where statues of the five hundred, often grotesquely caricatured, are arranged in a mandala pattern, with an isolated statue of Guanyin at the centre. For an idea of what fate has in store for you, pick any luohan, then count off your years of age to a new one (moving left for men, right for women). Note this new statue's number, then go to the front desk and receive a card with that luohan's advice on how to make the most of your future.

and tranquil Buddhist monastery Baoguang Si here owes its fame. **Bus #650** to Xindu (40min; ¥5) departs from the rear lot of Chengdu's northeastern Beimen station, out on the first ring road off Jiefang Lu; once at Xindu, take local bus #1 or #8 for a kilometre to the temple.

Hidden away behind a bright-red spirit wall at the rear of a large modern plaza, **Baoguang Si** (¥5) had its moment of glory when Emperor Xizong fled to Sichuan down Shudao during a rebellion in 880 AD and found sanctuary at the monastery, bestowing its current name (meaning "Bright Treasure"). He later funded rebuilding, but the temple was razed during Ming-dynasty turmoils, and was only restored during the 1830s. Tang traces survive in the thirteen-storey **Sheli Pagoda**, whose upper seven levels have sagged off the perpendicular, and some column supports decorated with imperial dragons at the **Qinfo Hall**. Baoguang's highlight, however, is its **luohan hall**, which houses 518 colourful, surreal statues of Buddhist saints, along with 59 Buddhas and Boddhidarma, founder of the Chan sect (for more on which, see p.579). For lunch, try the inexpensive **vegetarian restaurant**, which has an English menu with pictures (daily 10am–2pm).

Sanxingdui Museum

In 1986, an archeological team, investigating what appeared to be a Shang-dynasty town 16km northeast of Xindu at **Sanxingdui**, made an extraordinary discovery: a set of rectangular **sacrificial pits** containing a colossal trove of jade, ivory, gold and **bronze** artefacts, all of which had been deliberately broken up before burial. Subsequent excavation revealed a settlement that from 2700 BC is believed to have been a major centre for the shadowy **Ba-Shu culture**, until it was upstaged by Jinsha (see 873) and abandoned around 800 BC.

All this is covered at the excellent **Sanxingdui Museum** (daily 8.30am–5pm; ¥80), with two main halls and English captions. The thousands of artefacts on display are both startling and nightmarish, the products of a very alien view of the world: a two-metre-high bronze figure with a hook nose and oversized, grasping hands standing atop four elephants; metre-wide masks with obscene grins and eyes popping out on stalks; a four-metre-high "spirit tree" entwined by a dragon with knives and human hands instead of limbs; and finely detailed bronzes, jade tools and pottery pieces.

To reach Sanxingdui, first catch a bus to **Guanghan**, 8km short of the site, from either Xindu (¥5) or Chengdu's Zhaojue Si station (¥10; you can reach Zhaojue Si on city bus #1 or #45 from Renmin Nan Lu). From Guanghan's bus station, buses for **Xigao** (¥2) serve the museum, as does local bus #6 (¥1).

Huanglongxi

HUANGLONGXI, 40km south of Chengdu, is a charming riverside village whose half-dozen understated **Qing-dynasty streets** – all narrow, flagstoned and sided in rickety wooden shops – featured in the martial-arts epic *Crouching Tiger, Hidden Dragon*. The village is popular with Chinese visitors, in particular art students and groups of old ladies coming to pray for grandchildren to Guanyin, to whom all the village's **temples** are dedicated.

Buses (¥11.5) leave Chengdu's Xinnanmen bus station between 8.50 and 11am; return buses, which run until at least 3.30pm, are marked with the characters for "Xinnanmen". From the highway bus stop, it's 500m through the quiet new settlement to the old village gate; take the left-hand lane, which is almost narrow enough to touch either side as you walk down the middle. All businesses are either shops selling irrelevant souvenirs or restaurants displaying **grindstones** for making one of Huanglongxi's specialities, *douhua* (soft bean curd). You soon reach the five-hundred-metre-long main street; turn left for two tiny **nunneries** (one on the left, the other at the end of the street beside a beribboned banyan tree), both containing brightly painted statues of Guanyin, Puxian and Wenshu.

At the opposite end of town, larger **Gulong Si** (¥1) has two main halls with similar statuary in a wobbly state of repair. There's an ancient banyan supported by posts carved as dragons; the former **governor's court** with a dog-headed guillotine for executing criminals; and an unusually three-dimensional, fifty-armed Guanyin statue in the right-hand hall.

Wandering around will fill an hour, after which you'll want **lunch**; the river-front restaurants near the nunneries are best, serving *douhua*, fresh fish and crispy deep-fried prawns. You can also buy bamboo-leaf-wrapped packets of *huanglongxi douchi*, smoked salted soya beans, then sit munching them under willows at one of the outdoor **teahouses**.

Dujiangyan

There's enough to hold you for a day at **DUJIANGYAN**, a large town 60km northwest of Chengdu, where in 256 BC the provincial governor, **Li Bing**, set up the **Dujiangyan Irrigation Scheme** to harness the notoriously capricious Min River. Li designed a three-part engineering project using a central dam and artificial islands to split the Min into an inner flow for irrigation and an outer channel for flood control. A spillway directed and regulated the water, while an opening carved through the hillside controlled the flow rate. Completed by Li Bing's son, the scheme has been maintained ever since, the present system of dams, reservoirs and pumping stations irrigating 32,000 square kilometres – even though the project's flood-control aspects became redundant when the **Zipingpu Dam**, 9km upstream, began operation in 2006.

Buses (¥16) depart for Dujiangyan every few minutes from Chengdu's north-westerly Chadianzi station. You end up at Dujiangyan's bus station, south of the town centre on Yingbin Dadao; cross the road and catch local bus #4 to the irrigation scheme's **entrance** at **Lidui Park** (daily 8am–6pm; ¥80), which encloses the original heart of the project. An ancient, three-metre-high stone statue of Li Bing found on the riverbed in 1974 graces **Fulong Guan**, a 1600-year-old temple flanked with die-straight *nanmu* trees, which sits right at the tip of the first channel. From here the path crosses to the midstream artificial islands, before arriving at the **Anlan Suspension Bridge**, which spans the whole width of the river. European explorers looked on this bridge as marking the boundary between the settled Chengdu plains and the western wilds, and indeed mountains do rise very abruptly on the western bank. Crossing to the east side brings you to steps ascending to **Erwang Miao**, an ornate Taoist hall dedicated to Li Bing and his son; look for an alcove bust of **Ding Baozhen**, the nineteenth-century governor responsible for renovations, and after whom the Sichuanese dish *gongbao jiding* ("Governor's Chicken Cubes") is named; and also a Qing mural of the whole scheme. Heading back, follow signs for the wooded **Songmao Road**, a fragment of the ancient route from Dujiangyan to Songpan (p.923), which passes through two stone gateways and the old **Town God's Temple** at the park exit on Xingful Lu, about 500m east of Lidui Park.

Accommodation is problematic in Dujiangyan; most places don't seem to want foreign custom. There's a **tourist information desk** at the bus station, which might be able to help; look lost outside and touts for cheap places will approach you, though with plenty of transport back to Chengdu until the evening, you shouldn't need to stay anyway. **Restaurants** are everywhere, especially leading up to Lidui Park. **Leaving**, buses head back to Chengdu throughout the day.

Qingcheng Shan

Amazingly fresh after Chengdu's smog, **Qingcheng Shan** is a smaller, easier version of Emei Shan, and has been a Taoist site since the Han-dynasty monk **Zhang Ling**, founder of the important Tianshi sect, died here in 157 AD. Qingcheng's Taoist **shrines** are all set in courtyards with open-fronted halls, at the back of which are ornate, glassed-in cases containing painted statues of saints. None gives much protection from the weather (being Taoist, that's probably the point), so reflect the seasons, dripping wet and mossy on a rainy summer day, coated by winter snows, or carpeted in yellow ginkgo leaves in early November. Most have **restaurants**, and though the food isn't great, the mountain's *gong* **tea** is worth trying. There are two **sections** to the mountain (¥80 each): the front – an easy walk – and the stiffer rear section.

The **front section** can be reached directly on buses from Chengdu's Xinnanmen station (7.40am–2pm; 2hr; ¥22), or on city bus #101 from the front lot of Dujiangyan's bus station. From the gates, the return walk to the 1200-metre summit takes around three hours, following stone steps through the forest; there's also a **cable car** (¥50 return). Pick of the shrines are **Ci Hang Dian**, dedicated to Ci Hang, the Taoist version of Guanyin; **Tianshi Dong**, a complex surrounding a small cave where Zhang Ling lived before his death at the age of 122; and **Shangqing Gong**, whose attractions include gateway calligraphy by the Guomindang leader Chiang Kaishek, shrines to the Three Purities and **accommodation** (❸, dorms ¥15). At the top is a six-storey **tower** containing a twelve-metre-high golden statue of Laozi and his buffalo, with views off the balconies of back-sloping ridges and lower temples poking out of the forest.

Qingcheng's **rear section** is next to the old township of **Tai'an**, where there are many basic places to stay and eat – get here on buses from Dujiangyan's station. It's a good six-hour round-trip hike from here through thick forest to Yinghua Shan, Qingcheng's 2128-metre apex; along the way are more pavilions, a **plank road** – the wooden slats morticed straight into the cliffside – several waterfalls and, below the peak, **Baiyun Si**, another atmospheric temple. Again, you can short-cut with various cable cars along the way.

Northeastern Sichuan

The fertile river valleys of **northeastern Sichuan** wind through awkwardly hilly, heavily farmed countryside, all abruptly terminated around 400km from

Chengdu by severe escarpments marking the border with Shaanxi. Originally, the sole way through these ranges was provided by **Shudao**, the "Road to Sichuan" linking Chengdu with the former imperial capital Xi'an, along which culture and personalities flowed over the centuries. The region features in *Three Kingdoms* lore; contains the hometowns of **Li Bai**, one of China's greatest poets, and the country's only empress, **Wu Zetian**; and was the escape route down which the Tang emperor Xuan Zong fled the An Lushan rebellion of 756 AD (see p.277). A Song-dynasty wooden structure and some death-defying martial monks survive at **Doutuan Shan**, while Shudao itself breaks out of the region through a sheer cleft in the ranges known as **Jianmenguan**, the Sword Pass.

The towns of primary interest along Shudao are **Jiangyou** and **Guangyuan**, the latter just 60km short of the Shaanxi border. Both are on the Chengdu–Xi'an **rail line**, and also on a fast expressway – you can get to Guangyuan in around four hours – making the bus the more convenient option, with frequent departures along this route from Chengdu's Zhaojue Si station. Shudao can also serve as the first stage in a journey to **Jiuzhaigou** (see p.883) – in winter, it's sometimes the only viable route.

Well east from Shudao, a large grid of old streets at the pleasant riverside town of **Langzhong** is one of the few places in Sichuan where you can still see substantial areas of urban Qing-dynasty architecture – a welcome refuge from the country's frenzied demolition of its past. Fast buses to Langzhong from

Northeastern Sichuan		
Doutuan Shan	窦团山	*dòutuán shān*
Dongyue Hall	东岳殿	*dōngyuè diàn*
Feitian Scripture Store	飞天藏	*fēitiān cáng*
Qifeng International Hotel	奇峰国际酒店	*qífēng guójì jiǔdiàn*
Yunyan Si	云岩寺	*yúnyán sì*
Guangyuan	广元	*guǎngyuán*
Silian Dajiudian	四联大酒店	*sìlián dàjiǔdiàn*
Zetian Dian	武则天殿	*wǔzétiān diàn*
Zhongsan Binguan	众森鸿福宾馆	*zhòngsēn hóngfú bīnguǎn*
Jianmenguan	剑门关	*jiànmén guān*
Liangshan Si	凉山寺	*liángshān sì*
Jiangyou	江油	*jiāngyóu*
Jiangyou Binguan	江油宾馆	*jiāngyóu bīnguǎn*
Jinxin Binguan	金鑫宾馆	*jīnxīn bīnguǎn*
Libai Museum	李白纪念馆	*lǐbái jìniànguǎn*
Libai's Former Residence	李白故居	*lǐbái gùjū*
Qinglian	青莲	*qīnglián*
Taibai Park	太白公园	*tàibái gōngyuán*
Langzhong	阆中	*lǎngzhōng*
Dafo Si	大佛寺	*dàfó sì*
Daoxiang Cun Jiucian	稻香村酒家	*dàoxiāngcūn jiǔjiā*
Dujia Kezhan	杜家客栈	*dùjiā kèzhàn*
Dunhuang Binguan	敦煌宾馆	*dūnhuáng bīnguǎn*
Gongyuan	贡院	*gòngyuàn*
Huaguang Lou	华光楼	*huáguāng lóu*
Hu's Courtyard	胡家院	*hújiā yuàn*
Kong's Courtyard	孔家大院	*kǒngjiā dàyuàn*
Scholar's Cave	状元洞	*zhuàngyuán dòng*
Zhang Fei Miao	张飞庙	*zhāngfēi miào*
Zhuangyuan Ge	状元阁	*zhuàngyuán gé*

Chengdu depart Beimen station, northeast of the centre on the first ring road; you can also get here direct from Chongqing and Guangyuan.

Note that though there are plenty of **banks** with ATMs in the region, none can change traveller's cheques.

Jiangyou and Doutuan Shan

JIANGYOU is a modern, pleasantly leafy town on the north bank of the Fu Jiang some 170km from Chengdu, within sight of the steep line of hills slanting northeast towards the Shaanxi border. It's famed as the hometown of the Tang poet Li Bai, but what really justifies a visit is a side trip to quirky **Doutuan Shan** nearby, whose monks perform some bizarre acrobatic stunts.

Though he grew up near Jiangyou, **Li Bai** – also known as Li Po and Tai Bai – was born in China's far northwest during a period when the country's arts, stimulated by unparalleled contact with the outside world, reached their heights. A swordsman in his youth and famous during his own lifetime, Li Bai is China's most highly regarded romantic poet, his works masterpieces of Taoist, dream-like imagery, often clearly influenced by his notorious **drunkenness** – he drowned in the Yangzi in 762 AD, allegedly while trying to grasp the moon's reflection in the water.

Unsurprisingly perhaps, Jiangyou's Li Bai monuments – such as the dim **Li Bai Museum** (8am–5pm; ¥30), off Renmin Lu in central riverside **Taibai Park** – fail to capture the great man's spirit. Fans are best off catching bus #9 from near Jiangyou's bus station on Taiping Lu 10km south to **Qinglian** township, above which, on a hill, sits **Li Bai's Former Residence** (8am–5pm; ¥40). Rebuilt many times, the quiet Ming-era halls and courtyards are filled with statues and paintings illustrating his life, and a shrine to his ancestor, the Han-dynasty general Li Xin. An oversized modern **pagoda** marks the hilltop, with a garden below planted with steles of his poems, and the **tomb** of his sister, Li Yueyuan.

Practicalities

Jiangyou's kilometre-wide centre is focused on the north–south Jiefang Lu and its intersections with Renmin Lu and Jinlun Lu; the little **Changming River** flows west of and parallel to Jiefang Lu through town. The useful **south bus station** is south of the centre on Taiping Lu; the **train station** is 5km to the east, from where city bus #2 will carry you to Taiping Lu. There's **accommodation** near the bus station at the adjacent *Jinxin Binguan* (Ⓣ0816/3261716, Ⓕ3270371; ③) and *Jindu Binguan* (no phone; ②); or 500m north on Fujiang Nan Lu at the newer *Jiangyou Binguan* (Ⓣ0816/3261113, Ⓕ3272450; ⑥). Hotel **restaurants** are as good as anywhere to eat, though there are also cheap stalls outside Taibai Park on Renmin Lu. The main **Bank of China** and ATM is in the centre on the Jiefang Lu–Jinlun Lu crossroads. **Leaving**, buses to Chengdu, Guangyuan and Langzhong depart until late afternoon.

Doutuan Shan

Doutuan Shan (¥50) is a twin-peaked ridge easily accessible 26km northwest of Jiangyou. **Buses** (¥18 return) depart the little depot 150m west of Jiangyou's south bus station on Taiping Lu between 7am and 6pm; alternatively, the bus station's **tour agency** offers the return trip plus entry for a bargain ¥50.

The mountain's **bus stop** sits below *Qifeng International Hotel* (Ⓣ0816/3879999, Ⓕ3879333; ⑧), a four-star country retreat with grand views down towards Jiangyou. Take the path uphill past the hotel and it's a few minutes to ornate gates at **Yunyan Si**, the temple's charming eighteenth-century halls filled with cheerfully cohabiting Taoist and Buddhist statuary, with Doutuan Shan's two sheer-sided pinnacles behind. The temple's centrepiece is the **Feitian Scripture Store**, built in 1180 and Sichuan's oldest wooden structure; an octagonal, eight-metre-high revolving drum, it somewhat resembles a pagoda, painted black and embellished with eight golden dragons.

In a grove behind Yunyan Si, you'll find racks of spiky weapons and a forest of three-metre-high wooden posts, atop which you can watch **kung-fu** stylist Luo Kun performing his high-speed boxing routines five times daily. The reason for this balancing practice becomes clear if you continue uphill – a surprisingly short, easy ascent on stone steps – to the mountain's main **summit**, which forms a small terrace outside **Dongyue Hall**, dedicated to Taoism's supreme deity, the Yellow Emperor. Every twenty minutes, Taoist monks cross from here to a tiny pavilion on the adjacent peak, using a **chain bridge** slung over the fifty-metre-deep chasm and performing acrobatics as they go – you won't begrudge them their safety rope.

Jianmenguan

Jianmenguan, the Sword Pass (¥50), commands a strategic position along Shudao as the only break through a tall line of hills 100km from Jiangyou and 50km from Guangyuan. Zhuge Liang's forces defended Shu from invasion here during the Three Kingdoms period, and in one spot the main path runs through a crevice barely half a metre wide – said to be the origin of the Chinese phrase "One monkey stops a thousand men", applied nowadays to bureaucratic obstruction. **Buses** run here direct from Guangyuan (see below); coming from Jiangyou, you'll be dropped 14km short on the hard shoulder, and you'll have to walk down the sliproad for a kilometre to waiting minibuses (¥40 for the vehicle).

Jianmenguan forms a narrow slash in the surrounding five-hundred-metre-high cliffs, which even today present an obstacle to traffic. The pass itself is marked by a heavy stone **gateway** and watchtower, around which progress is further slowed by the number of **restaurants** catering to tourists' needs. A **cable car** (¥20) heads up to a viewing area and tea terrace, or you can get here from the gateway by following Shudao's original route – a very narrow, steep, and slippery stone path along the base of the cliffs – for a couple of kilometres, after which you'll appreciate the sentiment behind Li Bai's poem, *Hard is the Road to Shu*. Back at the gateway, buses on **to Guangyuan** (¥10) pass by until late afternoon.

Guangyuan

GUANGYUAN, on the Jialing River halfway between Chengdu and Xi'an, is an unattractive manufacturing town of use as a jumping-off point for **Jiuzhaigou** buses, but is also the birthplace of China's only acknowledged empress, the Tang-dynasty ruler **Wu Zetian** (see p.282). About 2km south along the river from the train station, Tang rock sculptures at **Huangze Si** (¥15) offer a reappraisal of her reign after centuries of censure caused by her overturning of Confucian values, in which women had little status. The entranceway is graced by a unique **phoenix tablet**, representing female imperial power, instead of the usual dragon. Built into the cliffside behind is a two-storey **Zetian Dian**, whose lower grotto contains a gilded, life-sized statue of Wu Zetian, fashionably portly in the Tang style, while the upper cliff has been carved into a four-metre-high trinity of Amidah Buddha flanked by Bodhisattvas, including a very feminine Guanyin (identifiable by her vase) showing a definite Indian influence.

Guangyuan's two-kilometre-wide core, traversed by the main street, **Shumen Bei Lu**, is bounded by the Jialing River to the west, and the smaller Nan He to the south. The **train station** and **main bus station** share a huge square next to each other over the Jialing, about 1.5km from the centre; buses #2 and #6 from here cross the bridge and run down Shumen Bei Lu. Alternatively, you might end up 2km away at the **south bus station** on Shumen Nan Lu and the #6 bus route. A taxi anywhere shouldn't cost more than ¥7.

The city's most upmarket **accommodation** is the *Guangyuan Binguan* at 466 Shumen Bei Lu (Ⓣ0839/3330999, Ⓕ3218818; ❻); otherwise, head to the train station where there are numerous hostels – touts will grab you – charging ¥30 a bed, and a few hotels including the serviceable *Jialong Binguan* (Ⓣ0839/3217499; ❸). For **meals**, hotpot stalls and restaurants fill the town's backstreets. The most convenient **Bank of China** with an ATM is at the corner of pedestrianized Shichang Jie and Bei Jie in the older part of town, west off Shumen Bei Lu.

Leaving, the main bus station has dawn departures for the 348-kilometre run **to Jiuzhaigou**, and buses through the day to Chengdu and Langzhong. For Jianmenguan and Jiangyou, buses go when full from the south station, while for Xi'an, trains are your best bet.

Langzhong

About 225km northeast of Chengdu, **LANGZHONG** is a small, unassuming town occupying a broad thumb of land around which the Jialing River loops on three sides. Yet Langzhong once played a pivotal role in provincial history, even becoming the **Sichuanese capital** for seventeen years at the start of the Qing. Notable people associated with the town include the Three Kingdoms general **Zhang Fei**, who is buried here; **Luo Xiahong**, the Han-dynasty inventor of the Chinese calendar and armillary sphere; and no less than four scholars who became officials during the Tang and Song dynasties. In addition, about a quarter of Langzhong comprises a protected **old town**, Sichuan's largest collection of antique architecture, whose streets, houses and temples provide a fascinating wander.

The Town

Langzhong's **old town** covers about a square kilometre southwest of the centre. Orient yourself near the river at **Huaguang Lou** (¥15), a three-storey, 36-metre-high Tang-style gate tower on Dadong Jie, last reconstructed in 1867. From the top, there are views south over the river, north to the modern town, and down over the grey-tiled roofs and atriums of Langzhong's classical *siheyuan*, or **courtyard houses**. Many of these are open to the public (approx 9am–6pm; ¥4–8) and house museums or even accommodation, but there's no need to see more than a couple to get the idea of a central hall divided up by wooden screens opening into a courtyard, decorated with potted flower gardens – check the map for locations. Aside from *siheyuan*, small industries survive alongside elderly canteens and teahouses, not to mention touristy shops selling antiques, locally produced Baoning vinegar and preserved Zhangfei beef.

An unusual target in the north of the old town is the seventeenth-century **Gongyuan** (¥20), one of only two surviving imperial examination halls in China. Single-storey cells surround a long courtyard where prospective candidates lived and elaborated on their knowledge of the Confucian classics, on which the exams were based and according to which the country was (in principle) governed. Langzhong's most popular sight, however, is the **Zhang Fei Miao** (¥30), at the end of Xi Jie. This is a shrine to **Zhang Fei**, Liu Bei's

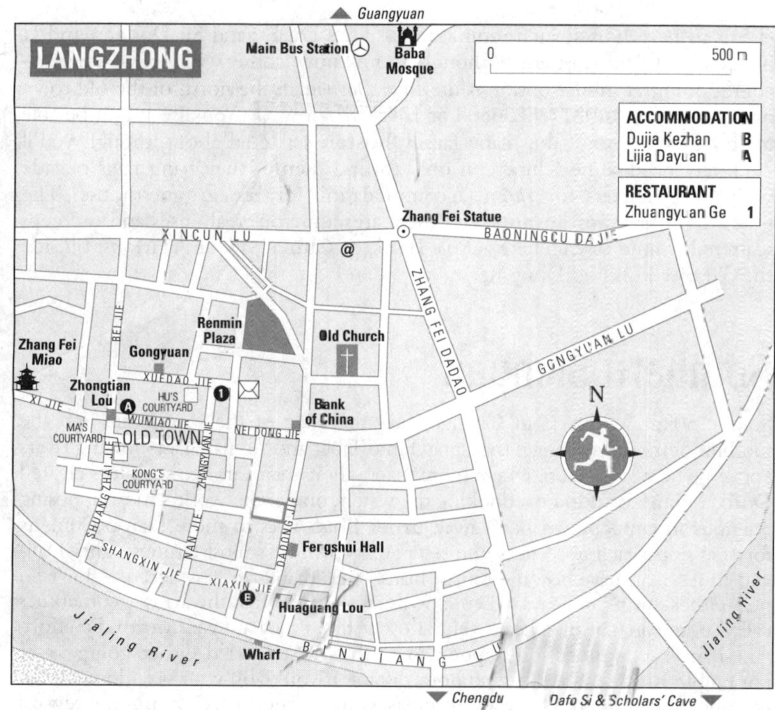

foremost general during the Three Kingdoms period (see box, p.453), a ferocious man who was murdered in 221 AD by his own troops while campaigning at Langzhong. Four courtyards of Ming halls, full of painted statuary and interlocking roof brackets, lead through to the grassy mound of his **tomb**, in front of which a finally triumphant Zhang Fei sits between two demons who are holding his cringing assassins **Zhang Da** and **Fan Qiang** by the hair.

As well as the old town, it's worth heading east across the river below a prominent Ming-dynasty pagoda – catch a taxi for ¥5 – to **Scholars' Cave** (¥40), a peaceful grotto laid with ponds and willows where two students, both later court officials, studied in their youth. Behind here, **Dafo Si** protects a ten-metre-high Buddha, which was carved into a rockface in Tang times and has survived more or less intact, along with thousands of smaller carvings and reliefs.

Practicalities

Langzhong's main road, **Zhang Fei Dadao**, runs south for a couple of kilometres to the river, its midpoint marked by a large **equestrian statue** of Zhang Fei; a further block south from here, Tianshanggong Jie leads west to **Nei Dong Lu** and into the heart of the old town.

Langzhong's main **bus station** is a block north of the statue along Zhang Fei Dadao, with buses to Chengdu, Guangyuan and Chongqing throughout the day. There are a number of **places to stay** in the area, but try and spend the night in the old town, whose antique buildings offer atmospheric lodgings. Pick of the **hotels** is *Dujia Kezhan* (Ⓣ0817/6224436, Ⓦwww.djkz.com.cn; ④), in the south of the old town at 63 Xiaxin Jie; founded during the Tang dynasty, it claims to have hosted such luminaries as poets Du Fu and Su Dongpo and is, incredibly, still in business – though rooms now come with toilets and air-conditioning. A similar option is the *Lijia Dayuan*, in the north of the old town on Wumiao Jie (☎0817/6236500 or 1345/8207599; ❸). You also might be able to stay in any one of the many family **hostels** scattered about, though you'll definitely need some Chinese, if only to find them – they hang flags outside with the characters for *zhusu* (accommodation) or *kezhan* (guesthouse). The hotels both have **restaurants**, and there are numerous teahouses and canteens scattered around town. There's also a **Bank of China** with an ATM just outside the old town on Nei Dong Jie.

Southern Sichuan

Some 150km southwest of Chengdu lies the edge of the Red Basin and the foothills of mountain ranges that sprawl into Tibet and Yunnan. Fast-flowing rivers converge here at **Leshan**, where more than a thousand years ago sculptors created **Dafo**, a **giant Buddha** overlooking the waters, one of the world's most imposing religious monuments; an hour away, **Emei Shan** rises to more than 3000m, its forested slopes rich in scenery and temples. As Sichuan's most famous sights, Dafo and Emei Shan have become tourist black holes thanks to easy access – don't go near either during holidays, when crowds are so awful that the army is sometimes called in to sort out the chaos – but at other times they are well worth the effort.

Leshan's accommodation is poor, so Dafo is best tackled either going to or coming from Emei Shan, just an hour distant. If you're on your way down south to Yunnan, you might also want to break your journey at **Xichang**, the reward

Southern Sichuan

Baoguo	报国	*bàoguó*
Baoguo Si	报国寺	*bàoguó sì*
Emei Shan Dajiudian	峨眉山大酒店	*éméishān dàjiǔdiàn*
Emei Shan Museum	峨眉山博物馆	*éméishān bówùguǎn*
Fuhu Si	伏虎寺	*fúhǔ sì*
Hongzhushan Binguan	红珠山宾馆	*hóngzhūshān bīnguǎn*
Emei Shan	峨眉山	*éméishān*
Chunyang Zhuang	纯阳殿	*chúnyáng diàn*
Hongchun Ping	洪椿坪	*hóngchūn píng*
Huazang Si	华藏寺	*huázàng sì*
Jieyin Hall	接引殿	*jiēyǐn diàn*
Jinding	金顶	*jīndǐng*
Jinding Dajiudian	金顶大酒店	*jīndǐng dàjiǔdiàn*
Niuxin Si	牛心寺	*niúxīn sì*
Qingyin Ge	清音阁	*qīngyīn gé*
Wanfoding	万佛顶	*wànfó dǐng*
Wannian Si	万年寺	*wànnián sì*
Woyun Nunnery	卧云庵	*wòyún ān*
Xianfeng Si	仙峰寺	*xiānfēng sì*
Xixiang Chi	洗象池	*xǐxiàng chí*
Leshan	乐山	*lèshān*
Dafo	大佛	*dàfó*
Lingyun Shan	凌云山	*língyún shān*

being the chance to visit villages of the **Yi minority**, as well as a research base from where China's Long March **space rocket** is launched (note that you'll need to apply a week in advance for a visitor's permit). Emei and Dafo are best reached on buses, but it's easier to get to Xichang via the Chengdu–Emei Shan–Kunming rail line.

Emei Shan

One of China's most enchanting mountains, **Emei Shan**'s thick forests and dozens of **temples**, all linked by exhausting flights of stone steps, have been pulling in pilgrims – and more recently, tourists – for two thousand years. Originally a Taoist retreat, Emei also hosted the sixth-century visit of Bodhisattva **Puxian** and his six-tusked elephant (images of whom you'll see everywhere), and extensive Ming-dynasty rebuilding on the mountain converted most of Emei's temples to Buddhism. Religion aside, the pristine natural environment is a major draw, and changes markedly through the year – lush, green and wet in the summer; brilliant with reds and yellows in autumn; or white, clear and very cold in winter.

You can see something of the mountain in a single day, but three would allow you to experience more of the forests, spend a night or two in a temple, and perhaps assault **Wanfoding**, the highest of Emei's three undulating peaks at 3099m. It's only worth climbing this high if the weather's good, however: for a richer bag of views, temples, streams and vegetation – everything, in fact, but the satisfaction of reaching the summit – you won't be disappointed with the lower paths.

Access is via **EMEI SHAN** town, a transit point 150km southwest of Chengdu and 7km short of the mountain. **Trains** pull into the station 3.5km

Lingyun Temple Museum	凌云神院博物馆	*língyún shényuàn bówùguǎn*
Taoyuan Binguan	桃园宾馆	*táoyuán bīnguǎn*
Wuyou Si	乌优寺	*wūyōu sì*
Xichang	西昌	*xīchāng*
Old quarter	古城	*gǔchéng*
Qianma Douhua Fanzhuang	千妈豆花饭庄	*qiānmā dòuhuā fànzhuāng*
South gate	南大门	*nándàmén*
Wumao Binguan	物贸宾馆	*wùmào bīnguǎn*
Xingye Binguan	兴业宾馆	*xīngyè bīnguǎn*
XITS	西昌国际旅行社	*xīchāng guójì lǚxíngshè*
Yuechang Plaza	月城广场	*yuèchéng guǎngchǎng*
Yuedu Jiari Jiudian	月都假日酒店	*yuèdū jiàrì jiǔdiàn*
Around Xichang		
Huang Shui	黄水	*huángshuǐ*
Liang Shan	凉山	*liángshān*
Lugu Hu	泸沽湖	*lúgū hú*
Luoji Shan	螺髻山	*luójì shān*
Panzhihua	攀枝花	*pānzhīhuā*
Puge	普格	*pǔgé*
Qionghai Hu	邛海湖	*qiónghǎi hú*
Space Flight Centre	航天发射中心	*hángtiān fāshè zhōngxīn*

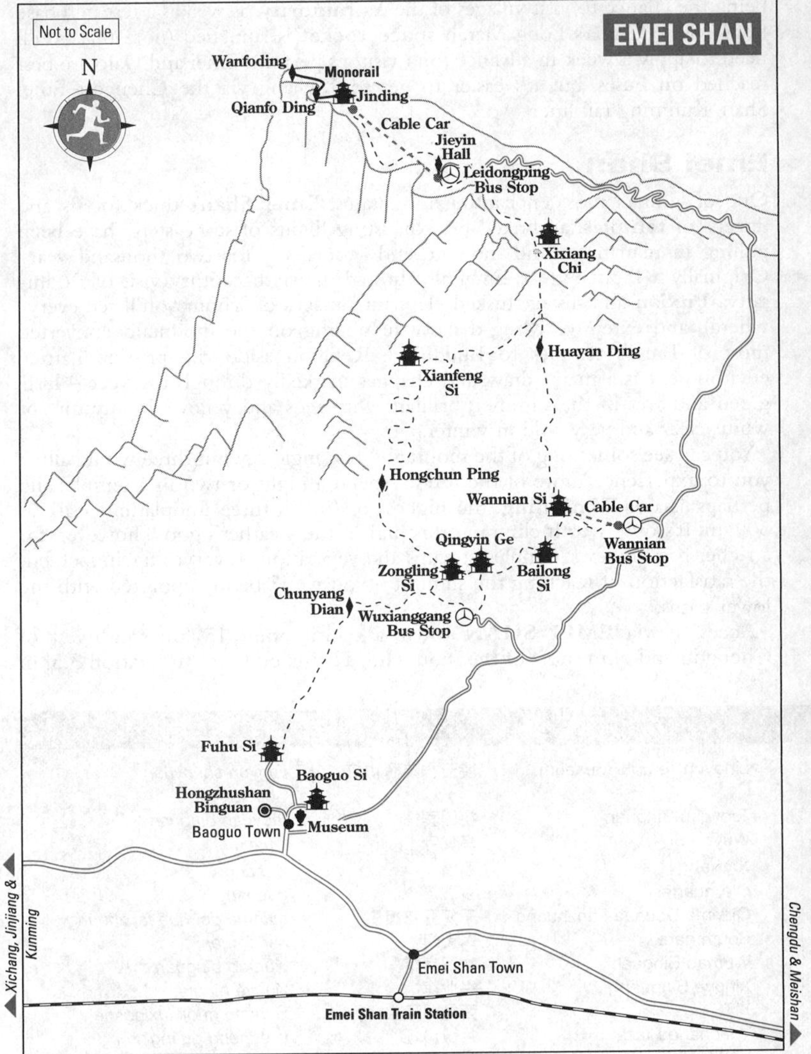

away from here, near to the **long-distance bus station** – catch blue city bus #1 from outside either to the terminus in town, then green bus #5 to the mountain's trailhead at **Baoguo**. Some buses actually terminate at Baoguo, so it's worth asking when buying your ticket. There are **hotels** at Baoguo and the summit area, but it can't be stressed enough that **temples** offer far more interesting lodgings, charging from ¥15 for a basic dorm bed to more than ¥80 per person for a double room with air-conditioning and toilet – reception offices display prices. Don't leave finding a room too late during the tourist season. **Food** on the mountain tends to be overpriced and

Emei Shan flora

Of Emei Shan's three thousand or so plant species, more than a hundred are Chinese endemics, including orchids, primulas, rhododendrons, camellias, cycads and tree ferns. Three unusual trees you'll see growing around temples are the **nanmu**, straight, tall and favoured for temple pillars; the **dove tree** (or handkerchief tree), which has hard spherical fruit, thin pale leaves and a white, two-petalled flower said to resemble a perching bird; and the **ginkgo**, identified by its lobed crescent leaves, which was saved from extinction by its popularity as an ornamental tree in monastery gardens, where it was perhaps grown for the medicinal qualities of its fruit – said to curb desire.

The ginkgo is not the only mountain plant to have benefited from cultivation. Most of Europe's ornamental **roses** are hybrids derived from wild Chinese stock two hundred years ago, and in summer you'll find bushes of their small pink and white ancestors blooming on Emei's lower slopes. The region is also famous for its **tea**, with excellent varieties such as *zhuye qing* (green "bamboo-leaf" tea) on offer at Baoguo. In addition, the mountain provides a huge range of fungi and **medicinal herbs**, such as gastrodia and fritillary, which you'll see for sale all over the place; make sure you know what you're buying and how to use it, as some are extremely poisonous.

ordinary; stir-fries and noodle soups are available either at roadside stalls or vegetarian temple restaurants.

Bring a **torch** in case you unexpectedly find yourself on a path after dark. **Footwear** needs to have a firm grip; in winter, when stone steps become dangerously icy, straw sandals and even iron cleats (sold for a few yuan and tied onto your soles) are an absolute necessity. Don't forget **warm clothing** for the top, which is around 15°C cooler than the plains and so liable to be below freezing between October and April; lower paths are very humid, though, during the summer. You'll also want an umbrella or other protection against the near certainty of **rain**. A **walking stick** is handy for easing the pressure on thigh muscles during descent – a range is sold along the way. One thing you don't want to take is a heavy backpack; store spare gear at Baoguo accommodation, or in Chengdu if you're contemplating a round trip.

If you need a **guide** for the mountain, contact Patrick Yang (ⓣ 0137/08131210, ⓔ patrickyanglong@yahoo.com.cn), who speaks good English and often takes tour groups up Emei Shan. He also arranges local "culture tours" for about ¥80 a person, touring a kung-fu school, noodle factory and kindergarten, with lunch in a farmer's house.

Baoguo

BAOGUO is basically one straight kilometre of hotels and restaurants running up past a **bus station** and an ornamental **waterfall** to a gilded pavilion, beyond which are some sights that you can visit without paying the mountain's entry fee. To the right, behind the waterfall, you'll find Emei's **museum** (daily 9am–5pm; free), which has accounts of the development of religion on the mountain, and photos of various rare **plants** found here. There are living examples of these in the surrounding **gardens**, beyond which is **Baoguo Si** (daily 7am–7pm ¥8), a large and serene temple featuring flagstoned courtyards decorated with potted magnolias and cycads, and high-roofed Ming-style halls. Besides the inevitable Puxian and Guanyin statues, look for the figures of the eight immortals carved into the rear hall's stone staircase, betraying Baoguo's Taoist origins. On a wooded hillock opposite Baoguo's entrance, the Ming-dynasty **Shengjishi bell**, encrusted with characters, can be heard 15km away.

If you bear left up the road past the waterfall, it's about 1km to overhanging *zhennan* and six-hundred-year-old **ginkgo trees** outside the charming **Fuhu Si** (Crouching Tiger Temple; daily 6.30am–8pm; ¥6). Emei's largest temple and once associated with the Taoist martial-arts master Zhang Sanfeng, today it's a Guanyin nunnery, with a new five-hundred-luohan hall and the bronze sixteenth-century **Huayan Pagoda**, engraved with 4700 Buddha images.

Practicalities

Baoguo's **bus station** has long-distance transport to Chengdu, Chongqing and Leshan until late afternoon. This is also where to catch buses **up the mountain** (every 30min; 6am–5pm) to Wuxianggang (for Qingyin Ge; ¥20 each way); Wannian (¥20 each way); and Leidongping (for Jieyin Hall and the summit; ¥40 up, ¥30 down).

Both Baoguo Si and Fuhu Si are wonderful **places to stay**, offering dorms from ¥15 up to doubles with TV, bathroom and air-conditioning (④), and vegetarian dinners in the monks' canteens. Otherwise, the *Teddy Bear Hotel* (☎0833/5590135, Ⓦwww.teddybear.com.cn; ④ dorms ¥30), in a side street just downhill from the bus station, has stuffy dorms, good doubles, Internet and a restaurant; while *Hongzhushan Binguan* (☎0833/5525777, Ⓦwww.hzshotel.com; ⑨) is a sprawling, four-star modern pile past the waterfall and sharp left; there's an adjacent **hot spring**, too, open to the public, for unkinking trail-weary muscles. The hotels can make transport bookings, though for a heavy fee.

The mountain

An ascent of Emei Shan can be tackled via two main **routes** from Baoguo: the sixty-kilometre, three-day "**long route**"; and the forty-kilometre, two-day "**short route**". Most people knock 15km or so off these by catching **buses** from Baoguo to alternative starting points near **Qingyin Ge** (Wuxianggang bus stop) or **Wannian Si**; leaving early enough, you could make it to the top in one day from either of these via the northern route, descending the next day – though your legs will be like jelly afterwards. If you're really pushed for time, you could get up and down in a single day by catching a minibus between Baoguo Si and **Jieyin Hall** (Leidongping bus stop), located a cable-car ride from the summit, but this way you'll miss out on what makes Emei Shan such a special place. Once past the temples around Baoguo, you'll have to pay Emei's **entry fee** (¥120 for a ticket valid for three days; students and over-65s-half price; trails open daily 7am–6pm).

The long route

From Fuhu Si, Emei's **long route** passes some minor sights to **Chunyang Dian** (5km from Fuhu Si), a nunnery founded in honour of the Taoist Immortal Lü Dongbin, spookily surrounded by mossy pine trees. It's a further easy 5km to **Qingyin Ge**, a pavilion built deep in the forest where two streams converge and tumble through a small gorge down **Niuxin Shi**, the ox-heart rock. It's a charming spot with a small **temple** (en-suite doubles ③, dorms ¥15), though being also just a short walk from the Wuxianggang bus stop, it can also get quite busy with guests.

Qingyin Ge is just 3km from Wannian Si (see p.892), but to continue the long route, follow the path up past the left side of Qingyin; this takes you along a river bed and past a **monkey-watching area**, before starting to climb pretty steeply through a series of gorges. About 6km further on, **Hongchun**

▲ Niuxin Shi

Ping (beds ¥40) is an eighteenth-century temple named after surrounding *hongchun* (toona) trees, and is about as far as you'd make it on the first day. Nearby, the unusually good *Hot Wok Café* is run by a chef who used to cook for Deng Xiaoping.

From here it's a very tough 15km of seemingly unending narrow stairs to **Xianfeng Si** (beds ¥40), a strangely unfriendly place, though well forested with pine and dove trees and planted with camellia and rhododendrons. The following 12.5km are slightly easier, heading partly downhill to a dragon-headed bridge, then up again to where the trail joins the north route near **Xixiang Chi** (see below), around 43km from Fuhu Si and two-thirds of the way to the summit.

The short route

Most people start their ascent by catching a bus from Baoguo to the Wannian Si bus stop at the start of Emei's **short route**. From here a three-kilometre path or cable car (¥40) leads to **Wannian Si** (daily 7.30am–7pm; ¥6; ❹, dorms ¥20), whose history goes back to the fourth century. Most of the halls burned down in 1945, however, leaving a squat brick **pavilion** out the back, built in 1601, as Emei's oldest structure. Its contents are stunning: three thousand tiny iron Buddhas surround a life-sized enamelled bronze **sculpture of Puxian**, riding a gilt lotus flower astride his great six-tusked white elephant. Weighing 62 tonnes and standing over 7m high, this masterwork was commissioned by the Song emperor Taizu and brought from Chengdu in pieces – note the gold spots on the elephant's knees, which people rub for good luck. Make sure you also visit Wannian's upper halls, which have great views over forested mountain folds.

From Wannian, a steady fourteen-kilometre hike through bamboo and pine groves – you'll pause every now and then to let **mules** ferrying up temple supplies get past – should see you beyond several smaller temples to where the two routes converge just south of **Xixiang Chi** (❸, beds ¥20). This eighteenth-century monastery sits on a ridge where Puxian's elephant stopped for a wash, and on cloudy days – being more or less open to the elements and prowled by monkeys – it's amazingly atmospheric, though somewhat run-down and frigid in winter. It's a popular place to rest up, however, so get in early to be sure of a bed.

On to the summit

Beyond Xixiang Chi the path gets easier, but you'll encounter gangs of aggressive **monkeys** who threaten you for food with teeth bared. They tend to pick on women; showing empty hands and calling their bluff by striding on seems to work, though you will probably feel safer with a stick in your hand and will need to keep a good grip on your bags. The path continues for 9km past some ancient, gnarled rhododendrons to **Jieyin Hall**, where the fifty-kilometre-long road from Baoguo, which has snaked its way round the back of the mountain, ends at **Leidongping bus stop** and a **cable car** to the summit (¥40 up, ¥30 down). The area is thick with minibus tour parties fired up for their one-day crack at the peak, and is also where to find buses back to Baoguo. **Hotels** around Jieyin are badly maintained and very expensive – they have been known to charge ¥200 for a mat on the floor – and you shouldn't plan to stay here.

Whether you take the cable car or spend the next couple of hours hoofing it (not to be attempted without cleats in winter), **Jinding**, the Golden Summit (3077m), is the next stop and, for many, the main reason to be up here at all. As it's bald and often shrouded in cloud, however, you may feel disappointed after the mountain's lower forests. There are two temples: the friendly **Woyun Nunnery** (❹, dorms ¥30) and the oversized **Huazang Si** (❹), whose Ming-dynasty bronze hall was destroyed by lightning in the 1890s. This has now been rebuilt, complete with a massive gilded statue of a multi-faced Puxian on four elephants, and makes a spectacular sight on sunny days. Also look for the thousands of **padlocks** engraved with couples' names affixed to handrails to symbolize eternal love; and make an effort to catch the **sunrise**, which is marvellous on a good day, as it lights up the sea of clouds below the peak. In the afternoon, these clouds sometimes catch rainbow-like rings known as **Buddha's Halo**, which surround and move with your shadow, while in clear conditions you can even make out Gongga Shan (see p.933), 150km to the west. You can also ride a **monorail** (¥60) along the ridge up to **Wanfoding**, Emei's true apex.

Leshan and Dafo

Set beside the wide convergence of the Qingyi, Min and Dadu rivers, 180km from Chengdu and 50km from Emei Shan, **LESHAN** is a spread-out market town with a modern northern fringe and older riverside core, a transit point for visiting **Dafo**, the Great Buddha, carved deep into a niche in the facing cliffs.

Leshan's main **bus station**, with regular connections to Chengdu, Emei Shan, Xichang, Zigong, Yibin and Chongqing, is 9km out on the town's northern reaches; a **taxi** to either Dafo's north entrance or the **ferry terminals** on Binjiang Lu shouldn't cost more than ¥10. Don't plan to stay at Leshan; the hotel situation is terrible and you're better off day-tripping from Emei or Chengdu.

Dafo

Impassive and gargantuan, **Dafo** (May–Sept 7.30am–7.30pm; Oct–April 8am–6pm; Dafo ¥70; entire site ¥110) peers out from under half-lidded eyes, oblivious to the sightseers swarming round his head, clambering over his toes and nearly capsizing their boats in their eagerness to photograph his bulk. Tang-dynasty Big Buddha carvings are pretty abundant in Sichuan, but none approaches Dafo's 71-metre height – this is the world's largest Buddhist sculpture. Statistics, however, can't convey the initial impression of this squat icon, comfortably seated with his hands on his knees, looming over you as the ferry nears.

The rough waters below the sandstone cliffs of **Lingyun Shan** had been a shipping hazard since before Qin times, but it wasn't until 713 AD that the monk **Haitong** came up with the idea of filling in the shoals with rubble produced by carving out a giant Buddha image. After Haitong blinded himself to convince corrupt officials to hand over funds, the project was overseen by

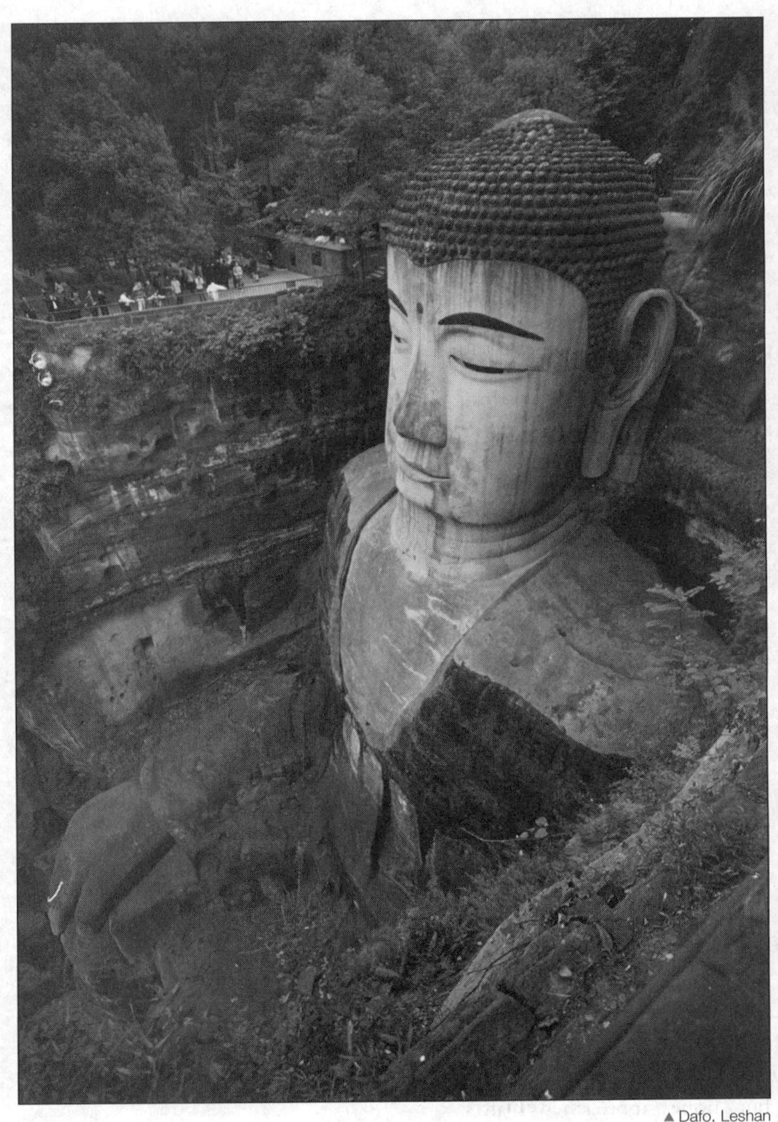

▲ Dafo, Leshan

various monks and finished by the local governor, Wei Gao, in 803. Once construction started, temples sprang up above the Buddha at Lingyun Shan and on adjacent **Wuyou Shan**, and today you can spend a good three hours walking between the sights.

The site can be accessed either from the **north entrance** or **by ferry** to Wuyou (¥30) – the route described below. From the north entrance, you can opt to just visit Dafo or buy a ticket for the whole site; landing by ferry you have to pay the full ticket price.

Wuyou Si to the Buddha

Crossing from Leshan jetty to Wuyou Shan, ferries turn in midstream so that both sides get a look at Dafo from beneath – the best view by far – and the vessel tilts alarmingly as people rush to the railings. Ashore, a steep staircase leads up to **Wuyou Si**, a warm pink-walled monastery founded in 742 AD, whose halls occupy the top of Wuyou Shan. The monastery **decorations** are particularly good; look for the splendid gate guardians as you enter, the animated scenes from *Journey to the West* on the second hall (Xuan Zang being carried off by demons, Monkey leaping to the rescue) and the grotesque sculptures inside the luohan hall.

Beyond, the path drops down through woodland to the water's edge, where a sturdy covered bridge links Wuyou with **Lingyun Shan**. The gully it crosses was cut in 250 BC on the orders of Li Bing (p.879) to reduce the rapids. On the far side, turn right and follow signs to where **Han-dynasty tomb** chambers at **Maohao Mu** indicate that this may have been a religious site long before the Buddha was carved. Stay on the main path, and you'll find a balustraded terrace offering good views of the river and town, beyond which the five-hundred-metre **Cliff Road**, dating in part to the eighth century, winds down towards the Great Buddha's toes. The upper track continues past minor sights to the terrace around the top of the **Dafo** himself. Elbowing your way through the throngs assembling for photos, you'll find yourself up against railings level with Dafo's ear, where you can watch lines descending the slippery **Staircase of Nine Turns** to his feet. You'll appreciate his scale here: Dafo's ears are 7m long, his eyes 10m wide, and around six people at once can stand on his big toenail. There's an insane-looking, modern **statue of Haitong** to one side of the terrace, while the **Lingyun Si** behind is a functioning temple, whose **Lingbao Pagoda** rises behind.

Past here, the path descends to the **north entrance**, from where you can catch bus #8 back to town. On the way down, have a good look at where the three rivers meet – despite Dafo's presence, there are still some vicious currents as brown and black waters mingle over low-lying shoals.

Xichang and around

The long train journey south from Emei Shan town to the Yunnanese border and ultimately Kunming is famous not for the scenery itself, splendid though it is, but for the fact that you rarely catch a glimpse of it. Estimates vary, but there are more than **two hundred tunnels** along the way, some lasting seconds, others several minutes, and you'll soon get fed up trying to get a long look at the peaks and gorges passing the window.

Given its otherwise remote setting in a very undernourished countryside seven hours from Emei Shan by train, **XICHANG**'s friendly bustle and almost prosperous air are surprising. Focus for southwestern China's **Yi community**, and a **satellite launching site** for China's Long March space programme (and also where China's controversial anti-satellite missile lifted off in 2007), Xichang is also a staging post for a back-roads trip to **Lugu Hu** on the Sichuan/Yunnan border, offering a more interesting alternative to continuing by train to Kunming. In town itself, Xichang's partially walled **old quarter** is just northeast of the centre, a fifteen-minute walk from the bus station via Yuechang Plaza. The old quarter's streets form a cross, of which the southern extension, **Nan Jie**, is the most interesting, running 150m through a busy market and past rickety wooden teahouses to the heavy stone **south gate** and attached battlements.

The Yi

Spread through the mountains of southwestern China, the **Yi** form the region's largest – and perhaps China's poorest and most neglected – ethnic group, with a population of around five million. Their shamanistic religion, language and unique, wavy script indicate that the Yi probably originated in northwestern China. Until the 1940s, they were farmers with a matriarchal **slave society** divided into a landowning "black" caste, and subordinate tenants and labourers who comprised a "white" caste. Officially, such divisions are gone, but shamanism is certainly still practised and there's a chance of at least a superficial view of the old ways during occasional **festivals**. These can be riotous occasions with heavy drinking sessions, bullfights and wrestling matches interspersed with music and archery displays. Traditionally everyone dressed up, though today this is largely left to the women who don finely embroidered jackets and sometimes twist their hair into bizarre horned shapes, the married women wearing wide, flat black turbans. Best is the **Torch Festival** at the end of the sixth lunar month, commemorating both an ancient victory over a heavenly insect plague, and the wife of Tang-dynasty chieftain Deng Shan, who starved to death rather than marry the warlord who had incinerated her husband. The Yi New Year arrives early, in the tenth lunar month.

Practicalities

Xichang's centre forms a kilometre-wide jumble of streets west of the often dry Dong He, with a focus of sorts provided by the open space of **Yuecheng Plaza**, not far from the river on the broad east–west **Chang'an Lu**. Xichang's main **bus station** is 500m west ofYuecheng Plaza on Chang'an Lu, the **train station** around 5km southwest at the end of the #6 bus route. For **accommodation**, turn east out of the bus station to either the *Xingye Binguan* at 60 Chang'an Dong Lu (Ⓣ0834/3225570; ④) or the *Wumao Binguan* opposite at no. 13 (Ⓣ0834/3223186; ②), or head 50m west to the corner of Shengli Lu and the *Yuedu Jiari Jiudian* (Ⓣ0834/3234888; ④). Inexpensive **restaurants** are concentrated around the bus station on Changan Dong Lu and just west of the old south gate on Shangshuncheng Jie, where you'll find excellent Sichuanese snacks at *Qianma Douhua Fanzhuang*.

For **information** on surrounding sights and to organize a space-centre visit, contact **XITS** (Ⓣ & Ⓕ0834/3240007 or Ⓣ0136/08148339). They're central but hidden away: head 50m west along Chang'an Lu from the bus station, then south down Shengli Lu to the first lane east; XITS are through the gates at the end.

Moving on, it's impossible to get reserved seats on trains here – you'll have to risk upgrading on board. Among the off-the-beaten-track possibilities, **Panzhihua** is five hours south by rail, and has connecting buses west to Lijiang (see p.809). There's also a bus west from Xichang to **Lugu Hu** (see p.920), from where you can take a boat across to the Yunnan side and then a bus to Lijiang; just don't confuse Lugu Hu with Lugu, a small town 50km east of Xichang.

Around Xichang

The area around Xichang, known as **Liang Shan** (the Cool Mountains), is heartland of the Yi community. Minibuses from the Chang'an Lu roundabout head 5km south to **Qionghai Hu**, a large lake where a **museum** exhibits Yi festival clothing and household items, and books written in the Yi script – you'll also see this on official signs around town. For more on the Yi, head 76km south to **PUGE** (buses daily 7am–5pm; 2hr; ¥15), marketplace for surrounding hamlets, where you're certain to see people in traditional dress; there's at least one **guesthouse** if you want to delve deeper, though the town is a dump.

To visit the **Space Flight Centre**, 65km north of Xichang, you need a week to arrange a permit and tour through the XITS (which requires your passport number, a photograph and ¥110), though they don't always accept foreigners and the centre closes if a launch is imminent.

To really get off the beaten track, ask XITS to organize a trip 40km south of Xichang to **Luoji Shan**, whose five main peaks rise above 4000m and whose lower slopes are thickly forested. There's some access from Luoji's east side from Puge, but also more adventurous routes around the base of the peaks – requiring horses and at least three days – from the town of **Huang Shui**, south from Xichang on the highway.

Southeastern Sichuan

Surrounding the fertile confluence of the Yangzi and Min rivers 250km from Chengdu, where Sichuan, Yunnan and Guizhou provinces meet, southeastern Sichuan has some intriguing attractions. The town of **Zigong** is a treat, with some well-preserved architecture, dinosaurs and salt mines, especially worth checking out during its Spring Festival lantern displays (though be warned that accommodation doubles in price at this time). Some 80km farther south, **Yibin** offers access to the aptly named **Shunan Bamboo Sea**, and some esoteric **hanging coffins**.

Both Zigong and Yibin are easily accessible **by bus** from Chengdu, Chongqing and Leshan. An interesting way out of the region is by bus east to **Luzhou** and then over to another bamboo forest at **Chishui** in Guizhou province (see p.755).

Zigong

ZIGONG, a thriving industrial centre, has long been an important source of **salt**, tapped for thousands of years from artesian basins below the city. In the fourth century, the Sichuanese were sinking three-hundred-metre-deep boreholes here using bamboo-fibre cables attached to massive stone bits. By the 1600s, bamboo buckets were drawing brine from wells bored almost a kilometre beneath Zigong, centuries before European technology (which borrowed Chinese techniques) could reach this deep. **Natural gas**, a by-product of drilling, was used from the second century to boil brine in evaporation tanks, and now also powers Zigong's buses and taxis.

Begin a city tour at the splendid **Xiqin Guildhall** on central Jiefang Lu, built in the Qing dynasty by merchants from Shaanxi and now an absorbing **salt museum** (daily 8.30am–5pm ¥20). Photos and relics chart Zigong's mining history, from pictorial Han-dynasty tomb bricks showing salt panning, to the bamboo piping, frightening metal drills and wooden derricks used until the 1980s. All this is slightly overshadowed by the building itself, whose curled roof corners, flagstone-and-beam halls and gilded woodwork – illustrating Confucian moral tales – were renovated in 1872 by master craftsman Yang Xuesan. Several similar contemporaneous structures survive nearby, most notably **Wangye Miao**, which sits high over the river on Binjiang Lu, and **Huanhou Gong**, whose beautifully carved stone gateway overlooks the junction of Jiefang Lu and Zhonghua Lu; both are now highly atmospheric **teahouses**.

Just west of the centre, **Lao Jie** – "Old Street" – is just that, a kilometre-long flagstoned riverside promenade lined with old trees and buildings, which passes

Southeastern Sichuan

Zigong	自贡	*zìgòng*
Caideng Park	彩灯公园	*cǎidēng gōngyuán*
Chenjia Citang	陈家祠堂	*chénjiā cítáng*
Dongfang Guangchang	东方广场	*dōngfāng guǎngchǎng*
Dinosaur Museum	恐龙博物馆	*kǒnglóng bówùguǎn*
Huanhou Gong	桓侯宫	*yuánhóu gōng*
Salt Museum	盐业历史博物馆	*yányèlìshǐ bówùguǎn*
Shenhai Well	海井	*shēnhǎi jǐng*
Wangye Miao	王爷庙	*wángyé miào*
Xianshi	仙市	*xiānshì*
Xiqin Guildhall	西亲会馆	*xīqīnhuìguǎn*
Accommodation and eating		
Hahu Jiaozi Wang	哈虎饺子王	*hāhǔ jiǎoziwáng*
Renxiyuan Jiulou	仁逸轩酒楼	*rényíxuān jiǔlóu*
Shawan Binguan	沙湾宾馆	*shāwān bīnguǎn*
Wenhua Gong Binguan	文化宫宾馆	*wénhuàgōng bīnguǎn*
Xiongfei Holiday Hotel	雄飞假日酒店	*xióngfēi jiàrì jiǔdiàn*
Zigong Lüguan	自贡旅馆	*zìgòng lǚguǎn*
Yibin	宜宾	*yíbīn*
Beimen bus station	北门汽车客运站	*běimén qìchē kèyùnzhàn*
Daguan Lou	大观楼	*dàguān lóu*
Nan'an bus station	南岸汽车客运站	*nán'àn qìchē kèyùnzhàn*
Ranmian Fandian	燃面饭店	*ránmiàn fàndiàn*
Renhe Binguan	仁和宾馆	*rénhé bīnguǎn*
Shengli Lüguan	胜利旅馆	*shènglì lǚguǎn*
Xufu Binguan	叙府宾馆	*xùfǔ bīnguǎn*
Around Yibin		
Changning	长宁	*chángníng*
Feicui Binguan	翡翠宾馆	*fěicuì bīnguǎn*
Gongxian	珙县	*gǒngxiàn*
Hanging coffins	悬棺	*xuánguān*
Luobiao	洛表	*luòbiǎo*
Shunan Bamboo Sea	蜀南竹海	*shǔnán zhúhǎi*
Wanli	万里	*wànlǐ*
Wanling	万岭	*wànlǐng*
West Gate	西大门	*xīdàmén*
Zhuhai Binguan	竹海宾馆	*zhúhǎi bīnguǎn*
Luzhou	泸州	*lúzhōu*
Rongxian	荣县	*róngxiàn*
Giant Buddha	荣县大佛	*róngxiàn dàfó*

several now-defunct wellheads. There are touristy waterside teahouses and canteens, but people still live here, hang up their washing across the street, play mahjong together and chat with the neighbours.

Bus #3 from opposite the *Shawan Fandian* on Binjiang Lu heads northeast to Zigong's suburbs and two other sights. First is **Shenhai Well** (daily 9am–5pm; ¥8), which in 1835 reached a fraction over 1000m, the deepest ever drilled using traditional methods. Operational until 1966, the twenty-metre-high wooden tripod minehead still overlooks the site, where you can inspect bamboo-fibre cables, stone engravings on the wall detailing the well's development (much of it using buffalo power), and the tiny well shaft itself, corked, reeking of gas, and barely 20cm across. Eight shallow vats in the building behind are evaporation pans, where the muddy brine is purified by mixing in tofu and skimming off the resultant scum as it rises, leaving a thick crust of pure salt when the liquid has been boiled off.

Back on the #3 bus, it's about 45 minutes from Binjiang Lu to the terminus at Zigong's **dinosaur museum** (daily 9am–5pm; ¥40), built over the site of excavations carried out during the 1980s. Near-perfect skeletal remains of dozens of Jurassic fish, amphibians and dinosaurs – including monumental thighbones, and Sichuan's own **Yangchuanosaurus**, a toothy, lightweight velociraptor – have been left partially excavated *in situ*, while others have been fully assembled for easy viewing, posed dramatically against painted backgrounds.

Practicalities

Zigong's compact, hilly centre lies on the north side of the narrow **Fuxi River**. The **long-distance bus station** is about 2km south of town on Dangui Dajie; turn right out of the station and it's 100m to the city bus stop (#33 will drop you outside the central *Shawan Fandian*) – while taxis charge about ¥7. Zigong's **train station** is on Jiaotong Lu, from where bus #34 heads to the *Shawan*. There's no main street in town – all the roads surrounding **Caideng Park** are equally busy, with markets, shops and facilities spread around.

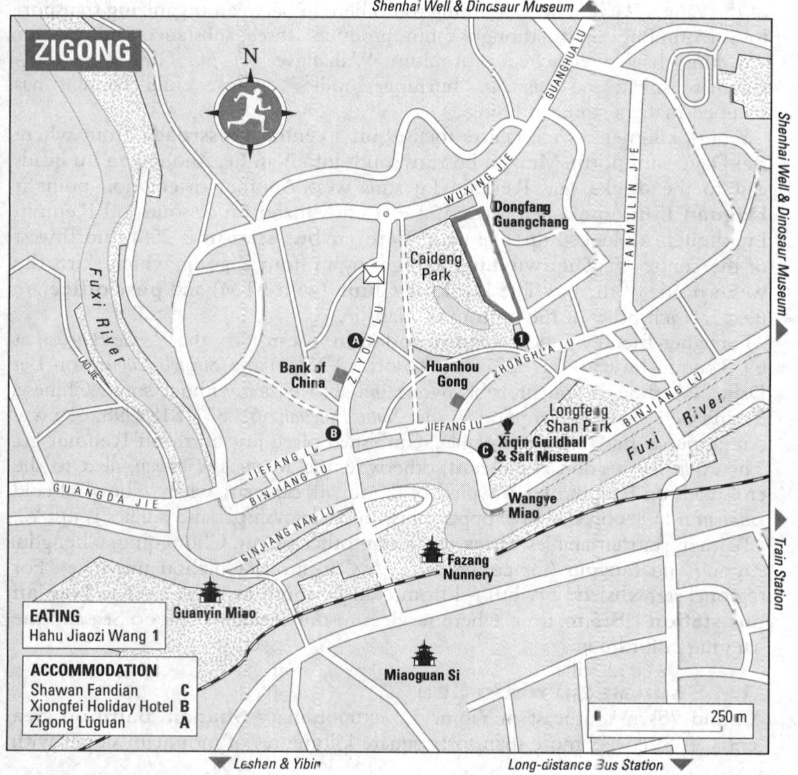

For bedrock **accommodation**, try the *Zigong Lüguan* (❷, dorm beds ¥25), which occupies two separate buildings on Ziyou Lu. Zigong's best mid-range option is the *Shawan Fandian* at 3 Binjiang Lu (Ⓣ0813/2218888, Ⓕ2201168; ❸), which has worn but well-priced rooms. A touch of luxury is provided by the smart *Xiongfei Holiday Hotel* at 193 Jiefang Lu (Ⓣ0813/2118888, Ⓦwww.sc-xf.com; ❼), whose **café** is the only one in town.

Zigong has an extraordinary density of **teahouses**, even for Sichuan; the most atmospheric are *Wangye Miao* and *Huanhou Gong*, with their century-old wood and stonework. Wonton and noodle vendors surround the southern entrance to Caideng Park in a pedestrianized area known as **Dongfang Guangchang**, where you'll also find *Hahu Jiaozi Wang*, which serves excellent *jiaozi* and Mongolian hotpot. Just east of here, Wangjiatang Lu hosts numerous Sichaunese hotpot restaurants.

Leaving, there are buses until mid-afternoon to Chengdu, Leshan, Emei Shan, Dazu, Luzhou and Chongqing; twice-hourly departures to Yibin; and daily buses each to Gongxian and Kunming. If you're heading to the Shunan Bamboo Sea (see below), a new expressway means that you can get there from Zigong in just two hours in a car – contact the *Xiongfei Holiday Hotel* about renting one with a driver.

Yibin and around

A crowded, grubby port with a modern veneer, the city of **YIBIN** sits where the Jinsha and Min rivers combine to form the **Chang Jiang**, the main body of the Yangzi River. There's nothing to do here in between organizing transport to surrounding sights, though Yibin produces three substances known for wreaking havoc: enriched plutonium; Wuliangye *bai jiu*, China's second-favourite spirit; and *ranmian*, "burning noodles", whose chilli content has stripped many a stomach lining.

Yibin's kilometre-wide centre focuses on a central **crossroads**, from where Bei Dajie runs north, Minzhu Lu runs south into Nan Jie, Zhongshan Lu heads east to the **docks**, and Renmin Lu runs west. Another orientation point is **Daguan Lou**, an old bell tower just east off Minzhu Lu or south off Renmin Lu, though it's locked up. The main **Beimen bus station** is 250m northwest of the centre off **Zhenwu Lu**, the highway in from Zigong, which skirts the western side of the city. The **Bank of China** (with ATM) and **post office** are next to each other at the bottom of Nan Jie.

Foreigner-friendly budget **accommodation** is scarce; try the *Renhe Binguan* at 69 Renmin Lu (Ⓣ0831/8227160; ❸, dorms ¥25), or the *Shengli Lüguan* on Bei Dajie (❸), though you probably won't get into either without some Chinese. Yibin's best mid-range option is the *Xufu Binguan* (Ⓣ0831/8189998, Ⓦwww.xufugroup.com; ❺), a comfortable, refurbished place just north off Renmin Lu. The *Xufu* has a good **restaurant**; otherwise, the *Ranmian Fandian*, next to the crossroads on Renmin Lu, is typical of the town's canteens, where a bowl of cold *ranmian* noodles dressed in chopped nuts, coriander, vinegar and chillies is just ¥2.

Beimen station handles **buses** to, among other places, Chongqing, Chengdu, Zigong and Luzhou (for connections to Chishui in Guizhou province). For regional sights, catch city bus #4 from Nan Jie south over the river to **Nan'an bus station** (15min), from where services to the Shunan Bamboo Sea and the hanging coffins depart.

The Shunan Bamboo Sea

Around 75km southeast of Yibin, the extraordinary **Shunan Bamboo Sea** (entry ¥68) covers more than forty square kilometres of mountain slopes with feathery green tufts, and makes for a refreshing few days' rural escape. It's a relatively **expensive** one, however – if you want to see similar scenery at budget rates you're better off heading to Chishui in Guizhou province. The main problem is simply **getting around** within the park; bus services are unpredictable and you'll probably end up having to charter taxis. Alternatively, you could rent a car and driver from Yibin or Zigong for the day – accommodation should be able to arrange this for around ¥400.

Having said all this, Shunan is an undeniably beautiful spot, if a bit spooky given the graceful ten-metre-high stems endlessly repeating into the distance. There's pleasure in just being driven around, but make sure you have at least one walk along any of the numerous paths – the trail paralleling the cable car is steep but superb, taking in a couple of waterfalls–and get a look down over the forest to see the bowed tips of bamboo ripple in waves as breezes sweep the slopes. The surreal atmosphere is enhanced by it being a favourite film location for martial-arts movies and TV series, so don't be too surprised if you encounter Song-dynasty warriors galloping along the roads.

Direct **buses to Shunan** are advertised as departing Yibin's Nan'an station, but these may not materialize and it's usually just as quick to catch one of the many buses to **Changning** (¥10), a small town 15km short of Shunan's main **West Gate**, which has bus connections to Chongqing, Chengdu and Luzhou, and minibuses into the park. These go to Shunan's two main settlements of **Wanling** (¥2), 1.5km inside the gate, and **Wanli** (¥8), 20km inside, where you'll find plenty of **hotels** – the cheapest charge about ¥50 a bed, though most are mid-range (❺). Other places to stay are scattered in between right at the park's centre, *Feicui Binguan* (Ⓣ0831/4970111, Ⓕ4970155; ❹) is a good two-star option. **Food** in the park is universally good and not too expensive, with lots of fresh bamboo shoots and mushrooms.

As for **park transport**, stand by the road and wait for the next bus – they seem to run most frequently in the morning and afternoon, when locals are going to and from their villages – and don't be too surprised if drivers try to overcharge you. Otherwise, ask accommodation to organize a motorbike- or minibus-**taxi**.

The hanging coffins

Nobody is too sure of the exact history of eastern Sichuan's several **hanging coffin** sites, but they're generally associated with the enigmatic **Bo people**, the ancestors of today's **Tujia** ethnic group, who are scattered through the Three Gorges area into western Hunan and Hubei. The Bo themselves were routed by imperial forces after their leader rashly declared himself emperor during a sixteenth-century rebellion against the local governor. They left behind scores of their cliff-face burials along the broad Dengjia River valley, some 90km south of Yibin near the dispiriting hilltop settlement of **Luobiao**, where transport terminates. Walk downhill for 2km, and you'll see the first wooden coffins above you on the right; **entry** to the site costs ¥20. The coffins are mortised into the cliffs on wooden frames, or placed in shallow caves, with the surrounding rocks daubed in simple ochre designs depicting the sun, people and horses. Locating the coffins high up in the open on wooden galleries, it's believed, was done to aid the return of spirits to the sky.

Buses to the coffins are advertised at Yibin's Nan'an station, but if you can't find direct transport, aim first for **Gongxian** (¥12; 68km), then change to a nearby depot to catch transport to Luobiao (¥8). As it can take up to five hours to make the journey, be aware that this is a very long day-trip from Yibin, and that you'll have to leave Luobiao by mid-afternoon to catch connecting services all the way back.

Dazu and around

About 200km east of Chengdu and 100km west of Chongqing, **Dazu** is the base for viewing some fifty thousand exquisite **Buddhist cliff sculptures** dating back to the Tang and Song dynasties, which are carved into caves and overhangs in the surrounding lush green hills. The two main sites are **Bei Shan**, just outside Dazu, and **Baoding Shan**, 16km to the northeast. What makes these sites so special is not their scale – they cover very small areas compared with more famous works at Datong, Luoyang and Dunhuang – but their quality, state of preservation, and variety of subject and style. Some are small, others huge, many are brightly painted and form comic-strip-like narratives, their characters portraying religious, moral and historical tales. While most are set fairly deeply into rockfaces or are protected by galleries, all can be viewed in natural light, and are connected by walkways and paths.

Dazu

DAZU is a small, quiet place whose centre forms a seven-hundred-metre-wide rectangle along the north bank of the mild Laixi River. The east side of the rectangle is Longzhong Lu, the north side Beihuan Zhong Lu, and the west side Bei Jie. The **bus station** overlooks the river down at the southeast corner. Right next door, there's **accommodation** at the *Xingyuan Lüguan* (❷, beds ¥30), or three-star comfort another 100m north up Longzhong Lu at the *Dazu Binguan* (Ⓣ023/43721888, Ⓕ43722967; ❺), which is either packed with tour groups or empty. A further 500m up Longzhong Lu, the *Jinye Binguan* (Ⓣ023/43775566; ❹) is a cosy alternative next to Dazu's tobacco factory. For **food**, cheap noodle and stir-fry places are all everywhere, with a string of inexpensive restaurants on Beihuan Zhong Lu, near the intersection with Bei Jie – *Panzhong Can* does great dry-fried green beans, double-cooked pork and stuffed aubergines. **Leaving**, there are buses until early afternoon to Chengdu, Zigong, Yibin and Chongqing.

Bei Shan

The carvings at **Bei Shan** (daily 8.30am–5pm; ¥60, students ¥25; joint ticket including Baoding Shan ¥120) include Dazu's earliest works, begun in 892 AD by the Military Governor **Wei Junjing**, who was posted here while campaigning against Sichuanese insurgents. Filling some 264 numbered recesses in two groups and protected by an awning, they are formal in execution, but offer a contrast to livelier work at Baoding Shan. They're easy to reach from town: take the road uphill for 150m from Dazu's northwestern corner at the junction of Bei Jie and Beihuan Zhong Lu, then follow the stone steps and paths ascending Bei Shan for a kilometre or so until you reach the site entrance.

Dazu and around

Dazu	大足	*dàzú*
Baoding Shan	宝顶山	*bǎodǐng shān*
Bei Shan	北山	*běishān*
Dazu Binguan	大足宾馆	*dàzú bīnguǎn*
Guangda Si	广大寺	*guǎngdà sì*
Jinye Binguan	金叶宾馆	*jīnyè bīnguǎn*
Panzhong Can	盘中餐	*pánzhōngcān*
Xingyuan Lüguan	兴源旅馆	*xīngyuán lǚguǎn*

The first, original, group of carvings surrounds a small grotto and features several military pieces – including, tucked away in **niche 1** beside the entrance – a life-sized Wei Junjing in armour. **Niche 10** here shows a gold-faced Sakyamuni on a lotus surrounded by attendant Bodhisattvas, one of the few examples at Bei Shan showing traces of paintwork.

Immediately beyond here, Bei Shan's second group of carvings dates from the twelfth century, and decorate a five-metre-high, five-hundred-metre-long overhang. They mostly feature the Bodhisattva **Guanyin** in various incarnations and styles, along with monks, nuns, and private donors who funded the project. **Niche 130** shows an atypically fierce Guanyin as a demon-slayer, each of her many hands holding a weapon (and one severed head); next door in **niche 131**, she's in a more usual form, languidly gazing at the moon's reflection. **Niche 136** contains a 4.5-metre-high **prayer wheel**, looking like an octagonal merry-go-round mounted on a coiled dragon, again surrounded by Guanyin images. The Bodhisattva returns seated on a giant peacock in **niche 155**, while the most impressive piece fills **niche 245** with a depiction of the Kingdom of Buddha, showing the trinity surrounded by clouds of Bodhisattvas, with heavenly palaces above and earthly toil below.

Baoding Shan

Don't miss **Baoding Shan** (daily 8.30am–6pm; ¥80, students ¥45; joint ticket including Bei Shan ¥120), whose carvings are exciting, comic and realistic by turns. The project was the life work of the monk **Zhao Zhifeng**, who raised the money and designed and oversaw the carving between 1179 and 1245, explaining the unusually cohesive nature of the ten thousand images depicted here. **Buses** (¥2) from Dazu's station leave twice an hour until around 4pm and take thirty minutes for the sixteen-kilometre run.

The bus drops you among a knot of souvenir stalls, with a path bearing right for a kilometre to the main site. **Dafowan**, whose 31 niches are naturally incorporated into the inner side of a broad, horseshoe-shaped gully. Packed with

▲ Cliff carving, Baoding Shan

scenes from Buddhist scriptures and intercut with asides on daily life, they're in amazing condition given that most are unprotected from the weather, and kick off with a lion guarding the **Cave of Full Enlightenment**, a deep grotto where twelve life-sized luohans surround the Buddhist trinity. Past here is a smaller work depicting **buffaloes** with their herders, both a symbol of meditation and a tranquil picture of pastoral life, followed by a jutting rock shaped into a spirited **Fierce Tiger Descending a Mountain**. Demonic guardian figures painted in blue, red and green greet you at the overhanging rockface beyond, which follows around to a six-metre-high sculpture of a demon holding the segmented **Wheel of Predestination** (look for the faint relief near his ankles of a cat stalking a mouse). Next comes a similarly scaled **trinity** of **Amidhaba**, **Puxian** (holding a stone pagoda) and **Wenshu**; and then the Dabei Pavilion, housing a magnificent gilded **Guanyin**, whose 1007 arms flicker out behind her like flames, each decorated with an eye and sacred symbol.

By now, you're midway around the site, and the cliff wall here is inset with a twenty-metre-long **Reclining Buddha**, fronted by some realistic portraits of important donors, oddly sunk up to their waists into the ground. The following two panels, depicting **Parental Kindness** and **Sakyamuni's Filial Piety**, use Buddhist themes to illustrate Confucian morals, and feature a mix of monumental busts looming out of the cliff surrounded by miniature figures dressed in Song-dynasty clothing. Next comes the memorable **Eighteen Layers of Hell**, a chamber-of-horrors scene interspersed with amusing cameos such as the Hen Wife and the Drunkard and his Mother. The final panel, illustrating the **Life of Liu Benzun**, a Tang-dynasty ascetic from Leshan, is a complete break from the rest, with the hermit surrounded by multi-faced Tantric figures, showing a very Indian influence.

Chongqing and around

Based around a hilly, comma-shaped peninsula at the junction of the Yangzi and Jialing rivers, **CHONGQING** is southwestern China's dynamo, its largest city both in scale and population. Formerly part of Sichuan province and now the heavily industrialized core of **Chongqing Shi**, the city is also a busy **port**, whose location 2400km upstream from Shanghai at the gateway between eastern and southwestern China has given Chongqing an enviable commercial acumen. While it's not such a bad spot to spend a day or two while arranging **Yangzi River cruises**, in many other respects the **Mountain City** (as locals refer to it) has little appeal. Overcrowded and fast-paced, the city is plagued by oppressive pollution, winter fogs and summer humidity. Nor is there much to illustrate Chongqing's history – as China's wartime capital, it was heavily bombed by the Japanese – though the nearby village of **Ciqi Kou** retains a glimmer of Qing times.

Chongqing has been settled since around 1000 BC, with its current name, meaning "Double Celebration", bestowed by former resident **Zhaodun** on his becoming emperor in 1189. The city has a long tradition as a place of defiance against hostile powers, despite being ceded as a nineteenth-century **treaty port** to Britain and Japan. From 1242, Song forces held Mongol invaders at bay for 36 years at nearby **Hechuan**, during the longest continuous campaign on Chinese soil, and it was to Chongqing that the Guomindang government withdrew in 1937, having been driven out of Nanjing by the Japanese. The US military also had a toehold here under **General Stilwell**, who worked alongside

Chongqing and around

Chongqing	重庆	*chóngqìng*
Chaotianmen docks	朝天门码头	*cháotiānmén mǎtóu*
Chongqing Museum	重庆市博物馆	*chóngqìngshì bówùguǎn*
Ciqi Kou	磁器口	*cíqìkǒu*
Hongyan	红岩村	*hóngyán cūn*
Jiefangbei	解放碑	*jiěfàng bēi*
Luohan Si	罗汉寺	*luóhàn sì*
Metropolitan Tower	大都会商厦	*dàdūhuì shāngshà*
People's Concert Hall	人民大礼堂	*rénmín dàlǐtáng*
Pipa Shan Park	枇杷山公园	*píbāshān gōngyuán*
Sanxia Museum	三峡博物馆	*sānxiá bówùguǎn*
Stilwell Museum	史迪威将军博物馆	*shǐdíwēi jiāngjūn bówùguǎn*
Zhongjia Yuan	钟家院	*zhōngjiā yuàn*
Accommodation		
Chongqing	重庆宾馆	*chóngqìng bīnguǎn*
Chung King	重庆饭店	*chóngqìng fàndiàn*
Huatie	华铁宾馆	*huátiě bīnguǎn*
Huixian Lou	会仙楼宾馆	*huìxiānlóu bīnguǎn*
Marriott	重庆JW万豪酒店	*chóngqìng JW wànháo jiǔdiàn*
Milky Way	银河大酒店	*yínhé dàjiǔdiàn*
Sanxia	三峡宾馆	*sānxiá bīnguǎn*
Eating and drinking		
Da Paidang	大排档	*dà páidang*
Lao Sichuan	老四川	*lǎosì chuān*
Pangzixian Huoguo Cheng	胖子鲜鳝火锅	*pàngzi xiānshàn huǒguō*
Shi Jie	食街	*shíjiē*
Xiaobin Lou	小滨楼	*xiǎobīn lóu*
Around Chongqing: Hechuan and Diaoyu Cheng		
Diaoyu Cheng	钓鱼城	*diàoyú chéng*
Diaoyu Tai	钓鱼台	*diàoyú tái*
Hechuan	合川	*héchuān*
Huguo Si	护国寺	*hùguó sì*
Pao Tai	炮台	*pàotái*

the Nationalists until falling out with Chiang Kaishek in 1944. Though still showing a few wartime scars, since the 1990s Chongqing has boomed; now over two million people rub elbows on the peninsula, with five times that number in the ever-expanding mantle of suburbs and industrial developments spreading away from the river.

Arrival and city transport

Chongqing centres on its four-kilometre-long **peninsula**, whose downtown area surrounds the eastern **Jiefangbei** commercial district; **Chaotianmen docks**, where Yangzi ferries (see p.907) pull in, are just a short walk away at the eastern tip of the peninsula.

The city's seething **main long-distance bus** and **train stations** are on a complex traffic flow near river level at the western end of the peninsula; to reach the eastern end, either hail a taxi or catch bus #102 from the north side

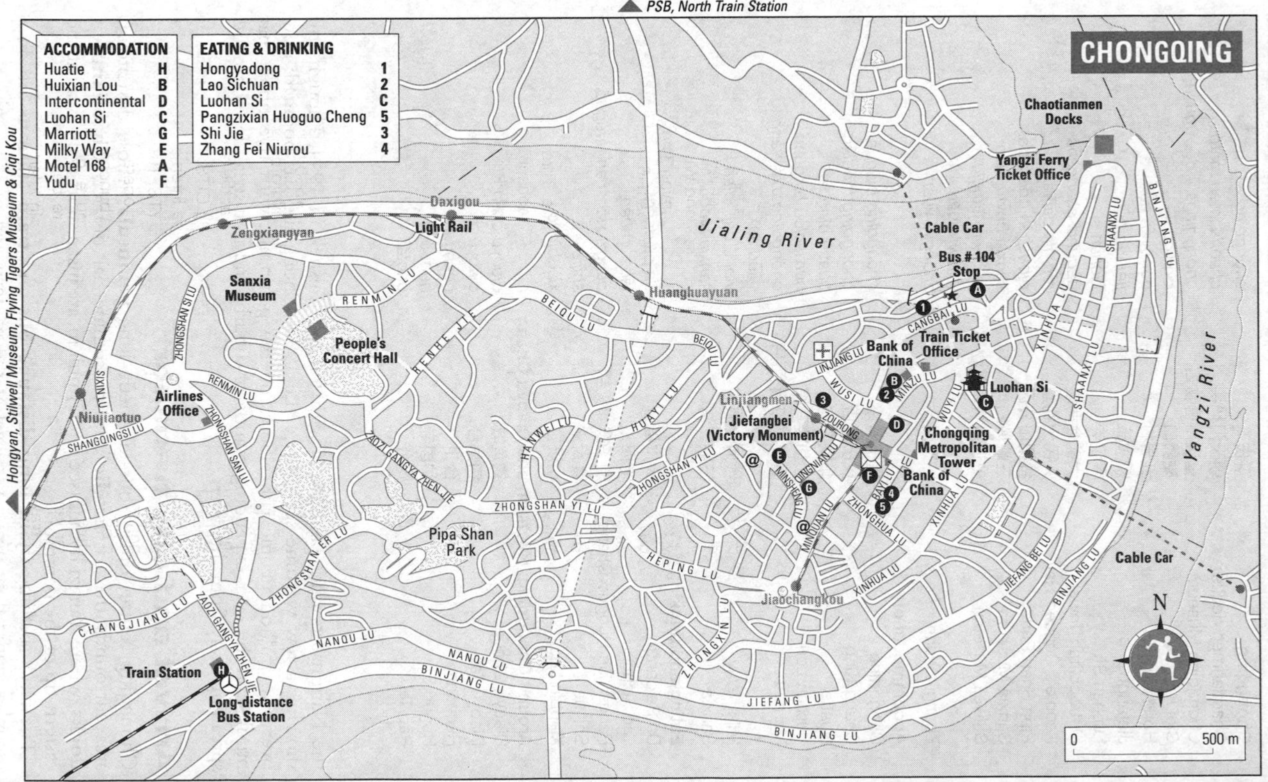
PSB, North Train Station
Hongyan, Stilwell Museum, Flying Tigers Museum & Ciqi Kou
CHONGQING
ACCOMMODATION
Huatie H
Huixian Lou B
Intercontinental D
Luohan Si C
Marriott G
Milky Way E
Motel 168 A
Yudu F
EATING & DRINKING
Hongyadong 1
Lao Sichuan 2
Luohan Si C
Pangzixian Huoguo Cheng 5
Shi Jie 3
Zhang Fei Niurou 4
Chaotianmen Docks
Yangzi Ferry Ticket Office
Cable Car
Bus # 104 Stop
Jialing River
Yangzi River
Daxigou
Light Rail
Zengxiangyan
Huanghuayuan
Sanxia Museum
People's Concert Hall
Airlines Office
Niujiaotuo
Train Ticket Office
Bank of China
Luohan Si
Linjiangmen
Jiefangbei (Victory Monument)
Chongqing Metropolitan Tower
Bank of China
Pipa Shan Park
Jiaochangkou
Cable Car
Train Station
Long-distance Bus Station
BINJIANG LU
SHAANXI LU
XINHUA LU
CANGBAI LU
LINJIANG LU
WUSI LU
MINZU LU
WUYI LU
ZOURONG
BAYI LU
MINSHENG LU
QINGNIAN LU
MINQUAN LU
ZHONGHUA LU
JIEFANG BEI LU
BEIQU LU
HUAYI LU
HANWEI LU
RENMIN LU
RENHE JIE
ZHONGSHAN YI LU
ZHONGSHAN ER LU
ZHONGSHAN SAN LU
ZHONGSHAN SI LU
ZAOZI GANGYA ZHEN JIE
SHANGQINGSI LU
SIXIN LU
HEPING LU
ZHONGXIN LU
CHANGJIANG LU
NANQU LU
JIEFANG LU
N
0
500 m

of the train-station square to Chaotianmen. There are other bus depots scattered far out in the suburbs, plus a **north train station** – cabs might be your only option. The **airport** is 30km away, connected to the airlines office on Zhongshan San Lu by a shuttle (daily 6am–6.30pm; ¥15), from where bus #103 runs via Jiefangbei to Chaotianmen.

Chongqing's gradients and horrendous road interchanges mean that nobody uses bicycles. **City buses** (¥1–2) are comprehensive if slow, though there's a nippy **light-rail** line from the Jiefangbei area, along the north side of the

Moving on from Chongqing

Buses to Chengdu, Langzhong, Hechuan, Leshan, Emei Shan, Dazu, Zigong, Yibin, Changning (for the Shunan Bamboo Sea) and beyond depart through the day from Chongqing's main long-distance bus station; it's a crowded place but buying tickets is easy enough. There's also transport from here to **Xiyang**, twelve hours southeast of the city near the Guizhou border, access point for Fajing Shan and the old towns of Longtan and Gongtan – see p.767.

The adjacent **train station** has a single, overnight service to Chengdu (slower than the bus, but you save the price of a hotel room) and useful links through to Kunming, Guiyang, Xi'an, Beijing, Shanghai and beyond, though note that northbound services may depart from the new **north train station**, 8km away. Aside from the station (which has Chinese-language electronic boards displaying seat and berth availability on all services for the next three days), you can buy **train tickets** for a ¥5 mark-up at the Yangzi Ferry Terminal, near the docks, and also through a street-level booth in the building housing the *Renren* restaurant on the corner of Minzu and Wusi Lu.

By air, there are daily departures to Chengdu, Guiyang, Kunming and provincial capitals across China; buy tickets and catch the **airport bus** (6am–6.30pm; ¥15) at the airlines office on Zhongshan Lu.

Yangzi ferries

Public ferries, a hydrofoil and luxury cruise-boats through the Three Gorges to Yichang depart daily year round from the **Ferry Terminal** at Chaotianmen's western tip. The main tourist season, when you might have trouble getting tickets for next-day departures, is May through to October.

Luxury cruisers cost upwards of ¥4000 and need to be booked through a reputable agent, preferably overseas, though you can also try out tour desks at upmarket hotels in Chongqing.

Buy tickets for **public ferries** and the **hydrofoil** either through an agent (see below) or at the Ferry Terminal at Chaotianmen (daily 8am–5pm), where electronic boards in Chinese show current timetables and prices. As a guide, ferry fares from Chongqing to Yichang cost ¥1062 per person for a double with bathroom, ¥530 for a bed in a quad, down to ¥130 for a bunk in a sixteen-berth dorm. The hydrofoil (which runs straight through to Yichang without stopping) costs ¥357.

Booking agents in Chongqing include the following, all located at the eastern end of the peninsula: CTS, 39 Wusi Lu (ⓣ023/63782666, ⓕ63803333); CITS, 151 Zourong Lu (ⓣ023/69093333, ⓦwww.citscq.com); Yangtze River Cruise International Travel Service, 99 Zhongshan Er Lu (ⓣ023/63522955, ⓕ63505789); CYTS, 109 Zourong Lu (ⓣ023/63709619, ⓕ63905408). Alternatively, a host of smaller operators surround the ferry ticket office, but be warned that, on the whole, they're a bunch of misleading hustlers. Make exhaustive enquiries about exactly what you're getting before handing any money over, and if you don't like the way you're being treated, go elsewhere. **Independent travellers** often book through hostels in Xi'an or Chengdu; in Chongqing, you could also try Jimmy Yin ⓣ13883305596, ⓦwww.yangtzedream.com, who speaks English and has had satisfied customers in the past.

peninsula and down to the city's southwest, which comes in handy for several sights. Trains run every six minutes from 7am to 7pm and cost under ¥3 a ride, depending on distance; the stations can be very hard to find, though. **Taxis** cost ¥5 to hire and, while drivers aren't too unscrupulous, it won't hurt to be seen studying a map along the way.

Accommodation

Given that the ferry is the main reason to come to Chongqing, it makes sense to stay up in the peninsula's eastern end around Jiefangbei and Chaotianmen. There's little budget accommodation, however; most places are mid-range or upmarket – though everywhere discounts during the winter, when few tourists are in town.

Huatie Between the bus and train stations. This is a well-run budget hotel managed by the railways, but the area is grotty. Dorm beds ¥25, ④

Huixian Lou 186 Minzu Lu ⓣ023/63845101, ⓕ63844234. Central, with tidy furnishings and a few English-speaking staff. Doubles are a good deal, though bathrooms can be a musty; the seven-bed dorms, with shared bathroom, are cheap for town. Dorm beds ¥50, ⑤

Intercontinental 101 Minzu Lu ⓣ023/89066888, ⓦwww.intercontinental.com. Business hotel with good-sized rooms, a Brazilian restaurant, and lobby café with cream cakes. ⑨

Luohan Si Xiao Shizi ⓣ023/63737144. The *Luohan Si* has rooms available, though these are meant for visiting clergy and they often stick tourists in the basic hostel next door. Dorm beds ¥20–30.

Marriott 77 Qingnian Lu ⓣ023/63888888, ⓦwww.marriotthotels.com. The best located of Chongqing's many upmarket international chains. Doubles from ¥1200. ⑨

Milky Way 49 Datong Lu ⓣ023/63808585, ⓦwww.cqyinhe.com. Smart and very friendly, a favourite with both foreign and domestic tour groups. ⑦

Motel 168 46 Cangbai Lu ⓣ023/63849999, ⓦwww.motel168.com. The usual friendly deal with spacious rooms at bargain rates (if you call ahead), though rooms are subterranean and only the pricier ones have windows. ④

Yudu 168 Bayi Lu ⓣ023/63828888, ⓕ63818168. Renovated older place and very comfortable; a cut above the *Huixian Lou*, though also a tad pricier. ⑤

The peninsula

During its Qing-dynasty heyday, the **peninsula** *was* Chongqing, described during the 1890s by the Australian journalist George Morrison (who became famous enough to have a Beijing street named after him) as an enormously rich port with mighty walls, temples, pagodas and public buildings. Civil war through the early twentieth century, the Japanese occupation of eastern China, and the subsequent flight to Chongqing of the Chinese government and millions of refugees brought an end to those days, however; after three years of Japanese bombers following the Yangzi upstream to the junction and unloading their cargoes, much of the peninsula was reduced to rubble. The peninsula as a whole remains grimy and shambolic – most development seems to be targeting Chongqing's newer, western suburbs – though it's being modernized to resemble a miniature Hong Kong, complete with skyscrapers, hills and a profit-hungry populace.

Jiefangbei and the east end of the peninsula

Isolated by a broad, paved pedestrian square and glassy modern tower blocks, **Jiefangbei**, the Victory Monument, marks the peninsula's social and commercial heart. The area is always packed to capacity with noisy, well-dressed crowds flitting between restaurants, cafés and the huge covered **market** on adjacent Bayi Lu, or shopping at the surrounding upmarket department stores.

The monument itself was a memorial to Sun Yatsen before being appropriated by the Communists in 1949 to celebrate their liberation of the city from seventy years of colonial and right-wing occupation – though you'd expect them to have chosen something more inspiring than this twenty-metre-high clock tower.

Heading northeast along Minzu Lu, you'll find **Luohan Si** (daily 8am–6pm; ¥5), hidden just off the street but given away by the incense sellers hanging around its ornate gates. Founded during the Tang dynasty and named for its luohan hall added in 1885, the temple unfortunately took a direct hit from a bomb in 1942 and is still being restored. The main sight here is the **luohan hall**, with a maze of 524 life-sized, grotesque statues of Buddhist saints to wander through – though the most lively, an isolated statue of the inebriated, authority-mocking **Ji Gong**, stands outside on his own. There's a good **vegetarian restaurant** here, too, open at lunchtime.

Across the road and around the corner from the temple, a **cable-car station** on Cangbai Lu offers rides high across the river to northern Chongqing (¥1.5); there's another cable car to the southern suburbs from Xinhua Lu. Views from either cable car take in river traffic, trucks collecting landfill in low-season mud, and distant hills – merely faint grey silhouettes behind the haze.

To spy on more waterfront activity, head down to **Chaotianmen docks**, a five-minute walk downhill from Luohan Si along Xinhua Lu. The paved **viewing area** on the high bank overlooking the tip of the peninsula makes a great perch to look down on **Yangzi ferries** and barges moored along the river; funicular trains ferry passengers and the inquisitive to water level from here. The viewing area is also somewhere to appreciate Chongqing's pollution – there are days when you can barely make out the centre of the river, let alone the far bank.

The west end

The peninsula's west end is mostly a business district, but there are a couple of sights to visit, both close to the Hongjiayan **light-rail** stop – catch the train from Linjiangmen station, just west of Jiefangbei. The mighty **Peoples' Concert Hall** on Renmin Lu was built in the 1950s along the lines of Beijing's Temple of Heaven, and accommodates four thousand opera-goers in the circular, green-tiled rotunda (where you can sit for ¥5 outside performance times). Facing it across a porphyry-paved plaza, the **Sanxia Museum** (daily 9am–5pm, last tickets 4pm; ¥40) commemorates Chongqing's regional history over four floors. Picks here include the Three Gorges Hall, with beautifully arranged dioramas of gorge scenery and a range of archeological finds; the Ba-Yu Hall, which covers everything from pre-human fossils to a marvellous array of Eastern Han tomb bricks; and the Li Chunli Hall, a donated collection of exquisite antique porcelain and paintings. You would, however, have to be very interested in period photos of Communist heroes to get much out of the "Anti Japanese Days (Savage Bombing in Chongqing)" Hall.

West along the Jialing River

Three worthwhile sights lie west of Chongqing's peninsula along a twelve-kilometre strip of the Jialing River: the wartime US command centre at the **Stilwell Museum**, the Communist headquarters at **Hongyan**, and antique streets at the one-time port town of **Ciqi Kou**. All can be tied together into a single trip using the light rail and city buses, but give yourself enough time – it can take well over an hour to get to Ciqi Kou from the centre.

The Stilwell and Flying Tigers museums

Just outside the peninsula on Jialingxin Lu, the **Stilwell Museum** (¥5) occupies the former home of General Joseph Stilwell, Chief Commander of the US forces' China, Burma and India operations from 1942 until 1944. Catch the light rail to Fotuguan station (¥3), then walk 250m downhill along the road to the museum.

Stilwell had served as a military attaché in China during the 1930s, and during the war had to coordinate the recapture of Burma and the re-establishment of overland supply lines into China from India. He was also caught up in keeping the shaky Nationalist–Communist alliance together, and his insistence that equal consideration be given to both the Guomindang and CCP caused him to fall out with Chiang Kaishek. The modernist 1930s building has been decked out in period furniture, with informative photo displays charting Stilwell's career.

Opposite the entrance to the Stilwell Museum, the little **Flying Tigers Museum** (March–Oct only; donation) is dedicated to the "American Volunteer Group of the Chinese Air Force", better known as the Flying Tigers, which formed under General Chennault in 1941 to protect supply flights over the "hump" of the Himalayas between Burma and China. T-shirts of a P-40 Tomahawk fighter plane with tiger's eyes and teeth are sold in the Stilwell Museum lobby (¥40).

Hongyan

From the Stilwell Museum, walk downhill to the main road and catch any bus heading 3km west to **HONGYAN** (daily 8.30am–5pm; ¥18), a scattering of European brick buildings set among pretty gardens, where China's wartime government set up in 1938 – wisely remote from the easily targeted peninsula. Mao was absent most of the time, but he visited under US auspices in August 1945 to negotiate a postwar coalition government with the Nationalists. Chiang's insistence that the Red Army disband led to nothing but a lukewarm agreement, however, described by Mao as mere "words on paper", and nobody was surprised at the subsequent resumption of civil war.

In truth, the Communists had little influence in national affairs during the course of the war, and so Hongyan's focus is on ideology rather than action: signs pick out the room used as the CCP propaganda department, the bed Mao slept in, buildings inhabited by Communist luminaries, without once mentioning the reasons behind their importance. As long as you're after atmosphere rather than information, however, it's interesting enough – and the heroic **waxworks** here of Mao and Zhou Enlai (who spent far more time here than Mao) are worth the entrance fee.

Ciqi Kou

Though well within the modern city's boundaries, **CIQI KOU**, a former porcelain production centre and port, incredibly retains a handful of flagstoned, one-hundred-year-old streets and wooden buildings, and offers an idea what the rest of Chongqing might once have looked like. Bus #808 from Hongyan drops you outside the village gates; on your right, **Zhongjia Yuan** (¥5) is a well-restored *siheyuan*, or courtyard house, built by a Qing official. The English-speaking caretaker provides knowledgeable accounts of the organization of a Chinese household of the time, and the relevance of the antique furniture, clothing and carvings in each room. This is Ciqi Kou's most interesting single structure, but you can spend an enjoyable hour roaming the half-kilometre-long main street and adjacent lanes, thronged with touristy crafts shops (selling local embroideries and romantic paintings of Ciqi Kou), old-style teahouses featuring traditional music recitals, and small restaurants. The #808 bus runs back to Hongyan until at least 5pm, from where – if you don't want to mess around with another bus and the light rail – you can catch bus #104 all the way back to Cangbai Lu, north of Jiefangbei.

Eating and drinking

Chongqing's centre is alive with canteens and food stalls, and at meal times already busy side streets and markets become obstacle courses of plastic chairs, low tables and wok-wielding cooks. Local tastes lean towards Sichuanese *xiaochi*; a local speciality is the use of puréed raw garlic as a dressing, which only the Sichuanese could get away with. **Hotpot** is believed to have originated here, with the basic ingredients arriving on plates, not skewers, so the pots are divided up into compartments to prevent everyone's portions getting mixed up.

The restaurants below provide a good introduction to Chongqing's culinary potential; around Jiefangbei, **café** chains such as *Shangdao*, and a *KFC*, are your best bets for non-Sichuanese fare. Chongqing Beer is the local brew, served in squat, brown-glass bottles.

Hongyadong Cangbai Lu. This bizarre, antique-style entertainment complex is built down the cliff from Cangbai Lu, with lifts and stairs connecting levels. Level 4 is a "food street", full of canteens serving snacks for a few yuan each, along with a couple of proper sit-down hotpot restaurants.

Lao Sichuan Minzu Lu, beside the *Huixian Lou* hotel. Do yourself a favour and eat at this Chongqing institution, featuring not only classic Sichuanese dishes, such as "wool" beef, *gongbao jiding*, and cold pork with garlic, but also more delicate options including chrysanthemum aubergine, and smoked duck with a steamed rice coating. The English menu is uninspired, so use the Chinese one (with photos). ¥40 a head.

Luohan Si Luohan Si Jie. A comfy vegetarian temple restaurant serving everything from humble *douhua*, soft tofu served with a chilli relish, to imitation spareribs or smoked goose. The menu has pictures, and some staff speak English. You can eat well here for ¥20 a head.

Pangzixian Huoguo Cheng Bayi Lu. An inexpensive, noisy hotpot place on the second floor – one of many on this street.

Shi Jie Zourong Lu. Easy to miss, the small entrance – with buns and snacks displayed – is next to a flight of stone steps. It's a good place to sample Chongqing's *xiaochi*, such as sticky rice dumplings, bitter gourd with sesame oil, "shadow-lantern" beef (very thinly sliced and wind-dried), and dry-fried beef in chilli oil. An English menu is available.

Zhang Fei Niurou Bayi Lu. Fun canteen specializing in dishes using Zhang Fei beef, a sort of chilli-enhanced, spiced silverside served thinly sliced and cold, or in a stew. An actor dressed as Zhang Fei himself (the fierce *Three Kingdoms* general; see p.453) accosts passers-by with a spear.

Listings

Airlines The China Airlines office is on Zhongshan San Lu ☎023/63862643 (daily 7.30am–6pm).

Banks and exchange Two useful branches of the Bank of China are located at the corner of Bayi Lu and Zuorong Lu, and next to the *Huixian Lou* hotel; both have ATMs and change traveller's cheques.

Bookshops The Xinhua Bookstore just west of Jiefangbei on Zourong Lu has Chinese-language maps and guides on the first floor, and a small, stock of English-language titles on the fourth floor.

Consulates The Chongqing Metropolitan Tower on Wuyi Lu has a British consulate in room 2801 (☎023/63691500) and a Canadian one in room 1705 (☎023/63738007).

Internet There are several Net bars scattered through the centre; a convenient option is above the small branch of the Xinhua Bookstore on Minsheng Lu.

Mail There's a post office behind all the mobile-phone sellers at 5 Minquan Lu 400010 (daily 8.30am–9.30pm).

PSB A long way north of the centre at 555 Huanglong Lu, Yubei District (☎023/63961916, Ⓕ63961917) – best go elsewhere if possible.

Hechuan and Diaoyu Cheng

In 1242, invading Mongol forces under Mengge Khan (Kublai's older brother) were brought up short by Song defences at **Diaoyu Cheng**, a fortified hilltop just outside the town of **HECHUAN**, some 60km north of Chongqing. Harried by generals Wang Jian and Zhang Yu, the Mongols needed 36 years and two hundred battles to defeat the Chinese, succeeding only after Mengge's death in 1259 – which cleared the way for Kublai to be elected khan. Set in pretty, rural surrounds, Diaoyu Cheng's fortifications are still visible, as is the battlefield. Buses to Hechuan (¥25) leave Chongqing's main bus station three times an hour from 8am and take ninety minutes; on arrival, walk across the plaza in front of Hechuan's bus station and you'll find battered minibuses for the eight-kilometre run to Diaoyu Cheng (¥3). Buses back to Chongqing depart until 5pm.

The minibuses from Hechuan drop you off at a short flight of steps leading up to **Diaoyu Cheng** (¥10); at the top, take the right-hand path until you see a small set of steps down to your right. These lead past some weatherbeaten Buddhist carvings to the remains of the Song observation post of **Diaoyu Tai**, the "Fishing Platform". Opposite is **Huguo Si**, now serving as a museum, with period stonework, paintings and maps illustrating key campaigns, and a useful diorama of the citadel – from which you'll realize that one of the reasons for Diaoyu's strength was the amount of fresh water available up here in ponds. Follow the escarpment from here and you'll come to crenellated **battlements**, parts of which are original. Immediately right is one of the old **gate towers**, from where a long flight of steps descends to the plain below; turning left, it's around 1.5km to **Pao Tai**, the cannon emplacement, below which is the 1259 battlefield, now a rather beautiful set of terraced fields hemmed in by the cliffs.

The Yangzi River: Chongqing to Yichang

Sichuan means "Four Rivers", and of these the most important is the **Yangzi**, once virtually the only route into the province and today still a major link between Sichuan and eastern China. Rising in the mountains above Tibet, the river defines the border with Tibet and Yunnan, and skirts Sichuan's western ranges before running up to Chongqing, from where it becomes navigable year round to all vessels as it continues east towards Shanghai and the coast. It receives seven hundred tributaries as it sweeps 6400km across the country to spill its muddy waters into the East China Sea, making it the third longest flow in the world. Appropriately, one of the Yangzi's Chinese names is **Chang Jiang**, the Long River, though above Yibin it's generally known as **Jinsha Jiang** (River of Golden Sands); the name applied by foreigners to the river as a whole, Yangzi, derives from a ford near Yangzhou in Jiangsu province.

Although people have travelled along the Yangzi since recorded history, it was not, until recently, an easy route – though it was still preferable to traversing Sichuan's difficult, bandit-ridden mountains. The river's most dangerous stretch was the two-hundred-kilometre-long **Three Gorges**, where the waters were squeezed between vertical limestone cliffs over fierce rapids, spread between **Baidicheng** and Yichang in Hubei province. Well into the twentieth century, nobody could negotiate this stretch of river alone; steamers couldn't pass at all, and small boats had to be hauled literally inch by inch through the rapids by teams of **trackers**, in a journey that could take several weeks, if the boat made it at all.

The Yangzi River: Chongqing to Yichang

Yangzi River	长江	*cháng jiāng*
Baidi temple	白帝庙	*báidì miào*
Baidicheng	白帝城	*báidì chéng*
Fengdu	丰都	*fēngdū*
Lanruo Dian	兰若殿	*lánruò miào*
Qutang gorge	瞿塘峡	*qútáng xiá*
Shibaozhai	石宝寨	*shíbǎo zhài*
Three Gorges	三峡	*sānxiá*
Three Little Gorges	小三峡	*xiǎo sānxiá*
Wanzhou	万州	*wànzhōu*
Wu Xia	巫峡	*wūxiá*
Wushan	巫山	*wūshān*
Xiling gorge	西陵峡	*xīlíng xiá*
Zhongxian	中县	*zhōngxiàn*
Zigui	秭归	*zǐguī*

All this is very much academic today, however, as the new **Three Gorges Dam** above Yichang (see p.484) has raised water levels through the gorges by over 100m, effectively turning the Chongqing–Yichang stretch into a huge lake and allowing **public ferries** and **cruise boats** easy access to this splendid scenery. While rising waters have submerged some of the landscape – not to mention entire towns – many settlements have been rebuilt on higher ground, and all the major historical sites have been relocated or preserved one way or the other.

Practicalities

Chongqing is the departure point for the two-day cruise downriver through the **Three Gorges** to Yichang. Thanks to numerous bridges, towns along the river are also accessible by **road** from Chongqing, so you can shorten the river trip by picking up the ferry along the way. There are two main **cruise options**, both of which run year round: relatively inexpensive public ferries, which stop along the way to pick up passengers; and upmarket cruise ships, which only stop at tour sites. **Prices** from Chongqing to Yichang, along with practical information on buying both ferry and cruise-ship tickets, are given in the "Moving on from Chongqing".

Public ferries are crowded and noisy, with berths starting at **first class** – a double cabin with bathroom – and descending in varying permutations through triples and quads with shared toilets, to a bed in sixteen-person cabins. Don't expect anything luxurious, as even first-class cabins are small and functional. If you're boarding anywhere except the endpoints, vessels are unlikely to arrive on time, so get to the dock early; once aboard, make haste for the purser's office on the mid-deck, where available beds are distributed. **Timing** is important: try to avoid leaving between 10am and noon, as you'll hit the first gorge too early and the third too late to see much. Not all ferries pull in at all ports, and schedules can change en route to compensate for delays, so it's possible that you'll miss some key sights. At each stop, departure times are announced in Chinese. **Meals** (buy tickets from the mid-deck office) are cheap, basic and only available for a short time at 7am, 10am and 6pm, though there's plenty available onshore at stops. Bring plenty of snacks, and in winter, **warm clothing**. Many tourists also complain of unhelpful or plain useless tour guides, and of being harassed by ferry staff to buy expensive on-board tickets for observation decks when access is, in fact, free or much cheaper than advertised.

Alternatively, you could travel in style on a **cruise ship**. These vessels verge on five-star luxury, with comfortable cabins, glassed-in observation decks, games rooms and real restaurants. They're usually booked out by tour parties during peak season, though at other times you can often wrangle discounts and get a berth at short notice.

Chongqing to Yichang

The cruise's initial 250km, before the first of the Three Gorges begins at Baidicheng, takes in hilly farmland along the riverbanks, with the first likely stop 172km from Chongqing at **FENGDU**, the "Ghost City". Behind rises **Ming Shan**, covered in shrines and absurdly huge sculptures dedicated to **Tianzi**, King of the Dead, all contained inside a **park** (¥100); the main temple here, **Tianzi Dian**, is crammed full of colourful demon statues and stern-faced judges of hell, as are cheaper fairground-style **sideshows** around town.

A further 70km downstream is **ZHONGXIAN**, famous for its fermented bean curd and, rather more venerably, the **Hall of Four Virtuous Men** where the poet Bai Juyi is commemorated. Next comes the midstream **Shibaozhai**, a 220-metre-high rocky buttress protected from new water levels by an embankment; grafted onto its side is the twelve-storey, bright-red **Lanruo Dian** (Orchid Hall), a pagoda built in 1819. The temple above dates to 1750, famed for a hole in its granary wall through which poured just enough rice to feed the monks; greedily, they tried to enlarge it, and the frugal supply stopped forever.

Ferries might pull in overnight 330km from Chongqing at the halfway point of **WANZHOU** (formerly Wanxian), an old city that has been extensively rebuilt above its original site. It's also on a main road, with **buses** running west to Chongqing and southeast to **Enshi** in Hubei, from where there are further services down to the Hunanese town of **Dayong**.

The Three Gorges

The **Three Gorges** themselves begin at **BAIDICHENG**, a town located strategically 450km from Chongqing at the mouth of the first gorge, and closely associated with events of the *Romance of the Three Kingdoms* (see box, p.453). It was here in 265 AD that **Liu Bei** died after failing to avenge his sworn brother Guan Yu in the war against Wu. These events are recalled at the **Baidi temple** (¥40), where there's a tableau of Liu Bei on his deathbed. The accompanying **Zhang Fei temple**, commemorating Liu's other oath brother, was recently relocated brick by brick to the nearby town of Yunyang.

Beyond Baidicheng, the river pours through a sheer slash in the cliffs and into the first gorge, **Qutang**, the shortest at just 8km long, but also the narrowest and fiercest, its once-angry waters described by the Song poet Su Dongpo as "a

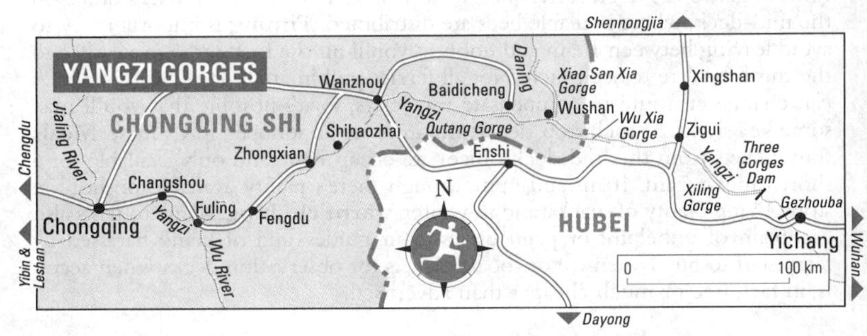

thousand seas in one cup". The vertical cliffs are pocked by **Meng Liang's staircase**, square holes chiselled into the rock as far as a platform halfway up, where legend has it that the Song general **Yang Jiye** was killed by traitors. When his bodyguard climbed the cliff to recover the headless corpse, he was deceived by a monk whom he later hung by the feet from the cliff face. Other man-made features include wooden scaffolds supporting four two-thousand-year-old **hanging coffins**, similar to those at Gongxian near Yibin (see p.901).

Through Qutang, the small town of **WUSHAN** serves as a likely half-day stopover to detour north up Xiao San Xia, the **Three Little Gorges**, lining the **Daning River**. On a good day, this five-hour, 33-kilometre excursion offers the best scenery of the entire Chongqing–Yichang trip: beautiful countryside fast, clear water; tiny villages; monkeys; remains of a Qin-era path cut into the cliffs; and the awesome **Longmen Gorge**. When you first arrive in Wushan, bargain with minibuses (¥15) for the ten-minute ride to the Xiao San Xia dock, where you pay ¥150 for a cruise up Xiao San Xia in a modern, open-topped canal boat.

Wushan also sits at the mouth of the second set of gorges, **Wu Xia**, 45km of fantastic precipices on the Yangzi where the goddess **Yao Ji** and her eleven sisters quelled some unruly river dragons and then turned themselves into mountains, thoughtfully positioned to help guide ships downriver. Nearby, a rock inscription attributed to Zhuge Liang proclaims: "Wu Xia's peaks rise higher and higher" – words that somehow so frightened an enemy general that on reading them he turned tail and fled with his army.

Farther downstream in Hubei, **ZIGUI** was the birthplace of the poet **Qu Yuan**, whose suicide a couple of millennia ago is commemorated throughout China by dragon-boat races. Zigui is also where 76-kilometre-long **Xiling** gorge begins. The Xiling stretch was the most dangerous: Westerners passing through in the nineteenth century described the shoals as forming weirs across the river, the boat fended away from threatening rocks by trackers armed with iron-shod bamboo poles, as it rocked through into the sunless, narrow chasm. The scenery hasn't changed a great deal since, but the rocks, rapids and trackers have gone and the boat passes with ease, sailing on to a number of smaller gorges, some with splendid names – Sword and Book, Ox Liver and Horse Lung – suggested by the rock formations. At the end, the monstrous **Three Gorges Dam** at **Sandouping** is another possible stopover, with regular minibuses running tourists from the dock to the dam site (see p.484).

Past here are the sheer cliffs and shifting currents of **Nanjin Pass**, and after that the broad gentle plain above **Gezhouba**, an enormous complex of dams, power plants, locks and floodgates. The boat squeezes through the lock, which can take some time, to dock in **Yichang**. Aside from catching fast buses from here to Wuhan, or trains to Xi'an, you could also visit the **Shennongjia Forest Reserve** in Hubei's mountainous north – for details, see Chapter 7.

Western Sichuan

Very much on the fringes of modern China despite recent infrastructure improvements, Sichuan's western half, extending north to Gansu, south to

Yunnan and west to Tibet, is in every respect an exciting place to travel. The countryside couldn't be farther from the mild Chengdu plains, with the western highlands forming some of China's most imposing scenery – broad grasslands grazed by yaks and horses, ravens tumbling over snowbound gullies and passes, and unforgettable views of mountain ranges rising up against crisp blue skies.

Though larger towns through the west have to a certain extent been settled by Han and Hui (Muslims) – the latter spread between their major populations in adjoining provinces – historically the region was not part of Sichuan at all but was known as **Kham**, a set of small states covering what is now western Sichuan, plus the fringes of Qinghai and Yunnan. The Tibetans who live here, called the **Khampas**, speak their own dialect, and see themselves as distinct from Tibetans further west – it wasn't until the seventeenth century, during the aggressive rule of the **Fifth Dalai Lama**, Lobsang Gyatso (see p.1097), that monasteries here were forcibly converted to the dominant Gelugpa sect and the people brought under Lhasa's thumb. The Khampas retain their tough, independent reputation today, and culturally the region remains emphatically Tibetan, containing not only some of the country's most important lamaseries, but also an overwhelmingly Tibetan population – indeed, statistically a far greater percentage than in Tibet proper. For details on Tibetan food, language and religious thought, see the relevant sections at the start of Chapter 14.

How you explore western Sichuan will depend on your long-term travel plans. For a brief dip into the region, the forested mountains at **Wolong Nature Reserve** are a short trip northwest of Chengdu, where you can see captive **pandas** and then do some hiking below the snowcapped peaks of **Siguniang Shan**. Alternatively, if you're heading north out of the province **to Gansu**, you first want to aim for the walled town of **Songpan**, horse-trekking centre and base for excursions to the nearby scenic reserves of **Huanglong** and **Jiuzhaigou**. Beyond Songpan, the road continues north via the monastery town of **Langmusi**, and so over into Gansu province.

Sichuan's immense **far west** is accessed from the administrative capital **Kangding** – itself worth a stopover for easy access to the nearby **Hailuogou glacier** and **Tagong grasslands**. Beyond here you can either weave northwest to Tibet via the monastery towns of **Ganzi** and **Dêgê**, with a faith-inducing mountain pass and Dêgê's **Scripture Printing Hall** as the pick of the sights along the way; or head due west to the high-altitude monastic seat of **Litang**, from where you can continue down into Yunnan, or press on to the Tibetan border at **Batang** (though at time of writing, crossing **into Tibet** from Sichuan was still forbidden for foreigners).

Travel in western Sichuan can be tough going, but better roads and buses mean that it's not always the severe endurance test that it used to be. You'll still need some stamina, however: journey times between towns remain long, roads twist interminably, breakdowns are far from uncommon, and landslides, ice or

Dog warning

Western Sichuan's wild, open countryside makes for good hiking, but you need to beware of **dogs**. Some of these are just the scrawny mongrels that roam around all Tibetan settlements, including monasteries; carry a pocketful of stones and a good stick, and you should be fine. Guard dogs, however, you need to keep well clear of: you don't want an encounter with a Tibetan mastiff. These are kept chained up as a rule, but don't go near isolated houses or, especially, **nomad tents** without calling out so that people know you're there and will check that their dogs are secure.

heavy snow can block roads for days at a time. It's worth noting that almost all the region rises above 2500m – one pass exceeds 5000m – and you'll probably experience the effects of altitude (see p.61). You'll need to carry enough **cash** to see you through, as there are no banks capable of dealing with traveller's cheques. Be aware, too, that **bus fares** are high – sometimes double what you'd expect – and in places you might need to charter **minibuses** to get to your destination. **Horse-trekking** is a popular pastime in the region, too, with well-established operations at Songpan, Siguniang Shan, Tagong and Langmusi, and plenty of ad hoc opportunities elsewhere. As for the **seasons**, the area looks fantastic from spring through to autumn – though warm, weatherproof clothing is essential whatever the time of year. Once the winter snows have set in, you'll need an infinitely flexible timetable.

Some history

As a buffer zone between Lhasa and China, control of the fractious states comprising Eastern Tibet, or **Kham** (a region that once included western Sichuan), was long disputed. Chinese claims to the region date back to the betrothal of the Tang **Princess Wenchang** to the Tibetan king Songtsen Gampo and the thirteenth-century Mongol invasions, though the first lasting external influence came when the Fifth Dalai Lama sent the Mongols in to enforce Lhasa's authority in the 1600s. Using the distraction provided by the Younghusband expedition's storming of Tibet in 1904 (see p.1097), China opportunistically invaded Kham, evicting the Dalai Lama who had fled the British. The Qing empire fell soon afterwards, however, and Tibet regained the disputed territory. In 1929, the Nationalists tried once again to claim the region for China by creating **Xikang province**, covering much of Kham. Xikang's presence on paper did little to alter the real situation: divided itself, China was hardly able to counter rival claims from Tibet or even control its own forces in the province. The whole issue was made redundant by China's annexation of Tibet in 1950; five years later, the local warlords whose private fief Xikang had become were finally subdued by Beijing.

The region's **monasteries** fared badly during the Cultural Revolution, and many are still being repaired. With the 2008 Olympics drawing world attention to China, the government desperately wants to be seen not to be oppressing its subjects, and there's no doubt that the last few years has seen a huge amount of cash pumped into the region for infrastructure improvements and some splendid temple restorations. However, it's also obvious that the monasteries today house a fraction of the number of monks that they once did, and many

Visiting monasteries

Among the draws of many towns in western Sichuan are their Tibetan Buddhist **monasteries**, most of which belong to the yellow-hat **Gelugpa sect** – though other sects are represented, as is **Bon**, Tibet's native religion (see p.925). Monasteries form huge medieval-looking complexes sprawling over hillsides, with a central core of large, red-walled, gold-roofed **temples** surrounded by a maze of smaller buildings housing monks and staff. Monasteries are **free to enter**, except where noted in the text; if there are no signs to the contrary, assume that **photography** is forbidden inside temples. **Monks** are generally friendly, encouraging you to explore, steering you firmly away from closed areas, and sometimes offering **food and accommodation** – though don't take these for granted. Most importantly, remember to orbit **clockwise** around both individual temples and the complex as a whole (the only exception to this rule being at the region's few Bon temples).

of the monastic living quarters – as opposed to the temple buildings – remain desperately poor.

As for ordinary Tibetans here, some are poor and a few have become very **rich** indeed: along with increasing tourism revenues and collecting valuable seasonal herbs used in Traditional Chinese Medicine, a good yak fetches perhaps ¥1500; horses three times this much; and a pure-bred Tibetan mastiff dog over ¥25,000.

Wolong, Siguniang Shan and beyond

Ideal for those with limited time, the round trip from Chengdu to **Wolong and Siguniang Shan** allows a quick sniff around western Sichuan's highlands, plus the chance to do some trekking and to see pandas in what approximates the wild; bear in mind it's also possible to push on from Siguniang Shan further into Sichuan's west. **Buses** to Wolong or **Rilong** (for Siguniang Shan) leave early in the morning from Chengdu's Chadianzi station, while three-day **tours** to Siguniang Shan are run by Chengdu's hostels (see Chengdu's "Listings", p.877).

Wolong

Covering a respectable two thousand square kilometres of high-altitude forest 140km northwest of Chengdu in the Qionglai Shan range, **Wolong Nature Reserve** was established in 1975 as the first region specifically protecting the

Wolong, Siguniang Shan and beyond		
Wolong Nature Reserve	卧龙自然保护区	*wòlóng zìrán bǎohùqū*
Giant panda	大熊猫	*dàxióngmāo*
Jiumei Jiujia	九妹酒家	*jiǔmèi jiǔjiā*
Panda Museum	大熊猫博物馆	*dàxióngmāo bówùguǎn*
Red panda	小熊猫	*xiǎoxióngmāo*
Shawan	沙湾	*shāwān*
Sitongyuan Binguan	四通源宾馆	*sìtōngyuán bīnguǎn*
Wolong Shanzhuang	卧龙山庄	*wòlóng shānzhuāng*
Wolong Zhen	卧龙镇	*wòlóng zhèn*
Xiongmao Shanzhuang	熊猫山庄	*xióngmāo shānzhuāng*
Yinchang Gou	银厂沟	*yínchǎng gōu*
Siguniang Shan	四姑娘山	*sìgūniang shān*
Changping Gou	长坪沟	*chángpíng gōu*
Haizi Gou	海子沟	*hǎizi gōu*
Qingnian Lüguan	青年旅馆	*qīngnián lǚguǎn*
Rilong	日隆	*rìlóng*
Shuangqiao Gou	双桥沟	*shuāng qiáogōu*
Siguniang Binguan	四姑娘宾馆	*sìgūniang bīnguǎn*
Xuequan Binguan	雪泉宾馆	*xuěquán bīnguǎn*
Danba	丹巴	*dānbā*
Ma'erkang	马尔康	*mǎ'ěr kāng*
Ma'erkang Binguan	马尔康宾馆	*mǎ'ěr kāng bīnguǎn*
Tusi Guanzhai	土司官寨	*tǔsì guānzhài*
Zhuokeji	桌克基	*zhuōkè jī*
Xiaojin	小金	*xiǎojīn*
Dianhua Binguan	电话宾馆	*diànhuà bīnguǎn*

▲ Giant panda

giant panda. Wolong's highland valley and steep mountains, green with undisturbed pine and bamboo forests, are home not just to the panda, but also white- and blue-eared pheasants and the unbelievably coloured, grouse-like Temminck's tragopan; there are also scattered groups of golden monkeys and near-mythical snow leopards. But don't expect to find these rarities ambling down local roads – you'll need to spend months getting worn out in Wolong's dense, wet, rough undergrowth for the chance of encountering any of these animals face to face.

Pandas

Two animals share the name panda: the **giant panda**, black-eyed symbol of endangered species worldwide; and the unrelated, racoon-like **red panda**, to which the Nepalese name "panda" was originally applied in the West. The Chinese call the giant panda *da xiongmao*, meaning big bear-cat.

News of giant pandas first reached Europe in the nineteenth century through the French zoologist and traveller **Père Armand David**, who came across a skin in China in 1869. They are decidedly odd creatures, bearlike, endowed with a carnivore's teeth and a digestive tract poorly adapted to their largely vegetarian diet. Though once widespread in southwestern China, they've probably never been very common, and today their endangered status is a result of human encroachment combined with the vagaries of their preferred food – **fountain bamboo** – which periodically flowers and dies off over huge areas, leaving the animals to make do with lesser shrubs and carrion, or starve. Half of Sichuan's panda habitat was lost to logging between 1974 and 1989, which, coupled with the results of a bamboo flowering during the 1980s, reduced the total wild population to a thousand animals, though a recent survey found that their numbers have bounced back to 1200. There are about a hundred at Wolong, with the remainder scattered through twelve other **reserves** in Sichuan, Yunnan and Guizhou.

In response to the international attention their plight garnered, the Chinese government set up a panda study programme at Wolong in association with the **World Wide Fund for Nature**, accompanied by successful **breeding programmes** here and in Chengdu. The government has also arrested (and sometimes executed) anyone found harming pandas. The most serious of the programmes' problems in the past have been that reserves were isolated from each other, leading to inbreeding, and were just too small to obviate the effects of the bamboo's cyclic lifestyle, though the formation of fourteen new interconnected reserves in 1995 was a step towards relieving the situation.

You can, however, see captive giant pandas easily enough at Wolong's modern **research base** (¥30), where they have been given spacious open-air pens to play or snooze the days away. Everything in China is a growth industry nowadays and pandas are no exception; the base's **breeding programme** has become so successful – reputedly by showing the notoriously indifferent bears "panda porn" to get them in the mood – that they're talking about setting up a business to sell them to foreign zoos. This means that there are often younger animals on show, which are far more boisterous creatures than their somnambulistic parents. You can do volunteer **work** here for about ¥200 a day – check out Ⓦwww.pandaclub.net for details.

Further west again, several marked **walking tracks** head a little way up into the hills, through some tight gorges. None is particularly remote or strenuous, but don't attempt them if the weather looks bad; the best is **Yinlong Gou** (Silver Dragon Gully) some 10km from Wolong Zhen.

Practicalities

Wolong consists of two parts: the research base itself, and a small cluster of buildings 7km further west along the main road at **WOLONG ZHEN**. Local **accommodation** is overpriced: outside the research base, there's the elderly but tidy *Xiongmao Shanzhuang* (Ⓣ0837/6243011, Ⓕ6243014; ❻); with *Wolong Shanzhuang*, up the road at Wolong Zhen (Ⓣ0837/624688, Ⓕ6246111; ❼) offering a plush conference-centre-type operation with huge rooms and soft beds. For anything resembling budget rooms, try the restaurants heading west (uphill) out of Wolong Zhen; *Jiumei Jiulou* (☎0837/6246737; ❷), where through-buses pull up for meals, is the best. **Minibus taxis** provide transport between Wolong Zhen and the research base or walking tracks – either will cost about ¥5–10 per person depending on bargaining skills. **Heading on**, ask at your accommodation about where to catch buses back to Dujiangyan and Chengdu or on to Rilong and Siguniang Shan.

Siguniang Shan

West of Wolong Zhen, there's a twenty-kilometre run up the ever-narrowing valley before you exit a gorge to face an abrupt mountain range blocking the view ahead. Rather than tackling this, the road slaloms northwest up less severe gradients to alpine pastures spotted with yak herds, edelweiss, gentian and daisies, and to a rocky, 4500-metre-high pass, typically draped in Tibetan prayer flags, where you might see **blue poppies** growing in August. On the other side you're out of Wolong Nature Reserve, and the hills are suddenly overgrazed and eroded, but just as you notice this, the snowy heights of **Siguniang Shan** pop into view. Siguniang means "Four Girls", and there is indeed a row of **four peaks**, the highest of which touches 6250m and looks most poetic lit by a low sun. The base for exploring the area is **RILONG**, a small and scruffy riverside tourist centre that hugs a bend in the road some 90km from Wolong. **Accommodation** possibilities here include the basic but friendly *Climbers and Travellers Hostel*, up at the bend (☎0837/2791869 or 13684392478; beds ¥20), which has pit toilets and only a tap to wash under; or further downhill, the cosy ✱ *Sunny Youth Hostel* (☎0837/2791585; ❸ beds ¥25,) and adjacent, similar *Longyun Shanzhuang* (☎0837/2791848 or 0138/82496631; ❸). The two hostels can organize **rental** of horses, camping and climbing gear, and **guides** if wanted. **Leaving**, book next-day bus tickets towards Chengdu or Rilong from booths either side of *Climbers and Travellers Hostel*; there are also infrequent **minibuses** to Xiaojin (¥30).

Rilong sits south of three valleys that run up below the snow-etched peaks; there are thick birch and pine forests draped in strings of "old man's beard", patches of meadow, and wildlife such as marmots, hares and plenty of birds. The closest valley to town is **Changping Gou** (¥70, plus ¥20 to use the bus), which starts 500m up along the river from the *Climbers and Travellers Hostel*. From the entrance, the road continues to **Lama Si** (6.5km) before winding up at **Kushu Tan** (another 3km); it's a sixteen-kilometre hike from here along the base of the four peaks to **Gou Wei**, literally the "Valley Tail". Come prepared for very changeable and potentially cold **weather**, even in summer.

Xiaojin, Danba and Ma'erkang

Beyond Siguniang Shan, public buses probe deeper into western Sichuan. Some 60km from Rilong, **XIAOJIN** is a gritty place of tiled-box design laid out along hairpin bends above a deep gorge; exit the bus station (which has morning services to Chengdu and Ma'erkang), turn right and it's 150m to a small **minibus depot** for transport to Danba or Rilong – they leave when full and cost about ¥30 to either place. If you get stuck, stay next to the bus station at the *Dianhua Binguan* (☎0837/2782888; ❷).

DANBA, 60km west from Xiaojin, is a transport nexus but also worth a stopover in its own right for some hikes out to nearby Tibetan hamlets. The town forms a two-kilometre stretch of shops along a deep river valley; the **bus station** – with daily runs to Ma'erkang, Kangding and Ganzi, plus additional Kangding minibuses through the day – is at the west end, while minibuses to

Xiaojin and Bamei (for Tagong) leave from a depot at Danba's eastern side. The best-value **accommodation** is down this way, too, namely the *Danba Dajiudian* (☎0836/352828; ❷) and nearby *Zaxi Zhoukang* (☎0836/3521806; beds ¥30), both of which can advise about walking trails. One easy trail heads to **Zhonglu**, a hillside district full of Tibetan houses about 10km back along the Xiaojin road.

If you're heading on towards Songpan or Zöigê, you need first to aim for the capital of Aba autonomous prefecture, **MA'ERKANG** (aka Barkam). This is a tidy government town of a dozen streets four hours north of Xiaojin or Danba; the **bus station** (with early departures to Chengdu, Xiaojin, Songpan, Zöigê and Danba) is about 3km east of town, connected by a town bus. There's standard **accommodation** next to the bus station at the *Yingbin Binguan* (❷), though it's lonely out here; and also in town at the riverside *Mingshan Binguan* (☎0837/2822918; ❷). Some 7km east (taxis charge ¥15), **Zhuokeji** is a stone-built Tibetan village of twenty tightly packed houses with brightly coloured window frames and flower gardens overlooking barley fields; the village gates are guarded by a wooden cannon. On the hill opposite, the sheer, stark walls and watchtower of the unoccupied **Tusi Guanzhai** (Landlord's Fortress) offer a bleak contrast – this was another site utilized by Mao during the Long March.

To Songpan and Gansu

The five-hundred-kilometre trip north from Chengdu via **Songpan** to the border with **Gansu** province hauls you through a region that's eminently Tibetan. The border village of **Langmusi** presents a vivid taste of monastic life, while the area's mountainous backdrop is enhanced by vivid blue waters at **Huanglong** and **Jiuzhaigou** reserves, both accessed from Songpan – just note that these are firmly on the Chinese tourist map, and are subject to severe visitor overload between spring and autumn. With this in mind, a few lesser-known reserves, rich in alpine grasslands, waterfalls and views, may be more appealing, and can be reached on **horseback** from Songpan.

You can get to Songpan by **bus** from Chengdu or Ma'erkang, and to Jiuzhaigou from Chengdu, Songpan, Jiangyou and Guangyuan. Arriving from Gansu, you'll enter the region via Langmusi; the Songpan–Zöigê–Langmusi–Gansu road is being turned into a **highway**, and when finished will make everything along this corridor easily accessible – though right now roadworks are prolonging travel times. Alternatively, **Jiuzhai airport**, 30km outside Songpan, has daily flights to and from Chengdu (at an absurd ¥700). **Tours** to Huanglong and Jiuzhaigou are offered by every travel agent in Sichuan, but avoid public holidays if you don't want to pay through the nose.

Wenchuan, Maoxian and the Qiang

Eastern Sichuan's plains end abruptly at Dujiangyan, from where the road twists up into the mountains as it follows the Min River valley past a succession of hydroelectric dams. The main towns along the route are **Wenchuan** and **Maoxian**, which don't offer much reason to stop unless you want to buy fresh *huajiao* (Sichuan pepper), which is cultivated on spiky bushes around here, or you started late in the day and are looking for a **bed** – Maoxian's *Fengyi Dajiudian* (☎0837/7427188; ❷), on the main road, is one of many offerings. Up in the surrounding stony hills, you'll see the flat-roofed, rectangular split-stone houses and twenty-metre-high watchtowers of the **Qiang**, who tend the apple

To Songpan and Gansu

Aba Autonomous Prefecture	阿坝自治州	*ābà zìzhì zhōu*
Huanglong	黄龙	*huánglóng*
Huanglong Gusi	黄龙古寺	*huánglóng hŭsì*
Huanglong Shanzhuang	黄龙山庄	*huánglóng shānzhuāng*
Middle Temple	中寺	*zhōngsì*
Jiuzhaigou	九寨沟	*jiŭzhài gōu*
Five-coloured Lake	五彩池	*wŭcăi chí*
Long Lake	长海	*chánghăi*
Nuorilang	诺日朗	*nuòrì lăng*
Pearl Beach Falls	珠滩瀑布	*zhū tān pùbù*
Primeval Forest	原始森林	*yuánshĭ sēnlín*
Shuzheng	树正	*shùzhèng*
Accommodation		
Jinde	金德宾馆	*jīndé bīnguăn*
Jiuzhaigou Binguan	九寨沟宾馆	*jiŭzhàigōu bīnguăn*
Jiuzhaigou Zhaodaisuo	九寨沟招待所	*jiŭzhàigōu zhāodàisuŏ*
Longtianyuan	龙天院宾馆	*lóngtiānyuàn bīnguăn*
Minzhu	民主饭店	*mínzhŭ fàndiàn*
Shenshan	神山宾馆	*shénshān bīnguăn*
Langmusi	郎木寺	*lángmùsì*
Maoxian	茂县	*màoxiàn*
Fengyi Dajiudian	风仪大酒店	*fēngyí dà jiŭdiàn*
Songpan	松潘	*sōngpān*
East Gate	东大门	*dōngdàmén*
Gusong Qiao	古松桥	*gŭsōngqiáo*
Mosque	古清真寺	*gŭ qīngzhēn sì*
North Gate	北门	*bĕimén*
South Gate	南门	*nánmén*
Accommodation		
Jiaotong	交通宾馆	*jiāotōng bīnguăn*
Gusong Qiao	古松桥宾馆	*gŭ sōngqiáo bīnguăn*
Shunjiang Horse Treks	顺江旅游马队	*shùnjiāng lǚyóu mădui*
Songpan	松潘宾馆	*sōngpān bīnguăn*
Wenchuan	汶川	*wènchuān*
Zöigê	诺尔盖	*nuòĕrgài*

and walnut groves lining the roadside. The Qiang themselves are easily identifiable: most rural Sichuanese wear white headscarves – in mourning, they say, for the popular Three Kingdoms minister Zhuge Liang – but the Qiang, who were persecuted by Zhuge, generally wear black turbans instead.

North of Maoxian, the valley narrows considerably while the hills become even starker and more prone to **landslides**. As the road continues to climb towards Songpan, you pass numerous small villages where white yaks, dressed in coloured ribbons and bridles, provide tour-bus photo opportunities.

Songpan

SONGPAN – also known as **Songzhou** – was founded 320km north of Chengdu in Qing times as a garrison town straddling both the Min River and the main road to Gansu. Strategically, it guards the neck of a valley, built up against a stony ridge to the west and surrounded on the remaining three sides by eight-metre-high stone **walls**. These have been partially restored, and you can walk between the north and east gates and above the south gate – if you're after views, the west gate stands alone high up on a hill above town. Though partly a tourist town, Songpan's **shops**, stocked with handmade woollen blankets (¥800–1200), fur-lined jackets (¥320), ornate knives, saddles, stirrups, bridles and all sorts of jewellery, cater primarily to local Tibetans and Qiang. In spring, Songpan – along with every town in western Sichuan – also becomes a marketplace for *chongcao*, the bizarre cordyceps or "**caterpillar fungus**" that grows in the mountains and is prized for use in Traditional Chinese Medicine. With luck, locals can find up to ten a day, worth here between ¥10 and ¥50 each (a fifth of their value in eastern China).

Songpan itself forms a small, easily navigated rectangle: the main road, partially pedestrianized, runs for about 750m from the **north gate** straight down to the **south gate** – both mighty stone constructions topped with brightly painted wooden pavilions. Around two-thirds of the way down, **Gusong Qiao** is a covered bridge over the Min whose roof, corners drawn out into long points, is embellished with painted dragon, bear and flower carvings. Side roads head off to the **east gate** – another monumental construction – and west into a small grid of market lanes surrounding the town's main **mosque**, an antique wooden affair painted in subdued yellows and greens, catering to the substantial Muslim population (there's another north of town). Just outside the south gate is a **second gateway**, with what would originally have been a walled courtyard between the two, where caravans were inspected for dangerous goods before entering the city proper.

The reason to stop in Songpan is to spend a few days **horse-trekking** through the surrounding hills, which harbour hot springs and waterfalls, grassland plateaus, and permanently icy mountains. Shunjiang Horse Treks (ⓣ0837/7231161 or 7231201, mob 013909043513), on the main road between the bus station and the north gate, charge around ¥450 a person for two- to four-day trips depending on destination, including everything except entry fees to reserves. Accommodation is in tents, and the guides are attentive, though prepare for extreme cold and tasteless food; some groups have bought and slaughtered a goat (¥400) to bolster rations. Note that the friendly veneer of Shunjiang's staff disappears rapidly if they're presented with a complaint, so be sure to agree beforehand on exactly what your money is buying.

Practicalities

Busy **Jiuzhai airport** is 30km to the northeast, with transport waiting for Songpan, Huanglong and Jiuzhaigou. Songpan's **bus station** is about 250m outside the north gate, with daily departures to Chengdu, Jiuzhaigou, Ma'erkang and Zöigê. **Minibuses** for Huanglong (¥80–100 per person) hang around between here and the north gate. For Langmusi, *Emma's Kitchen* (see below) might be able to set up a minibus transfer for about ¥100; otherwise, aim for Zöigê first.

Accommodation can be found at the bus station's tidy *Jiaotong Binguan* (ⓣ0837/7231818; ❸, dorms ¥30); opposite at *Guyun Kezhan* (0837/7231368; ❷), a basic but characterful Tibetan homestay; and above Shunjiang Horse Treks (beds ¥25), which has dusty rooms, a hot shower, and the most awkward squat toilet you will ever use. There are several tourist hotels outside the north and east gates, too, but they're very overpriced. Songpan's **water** – hot or otherwise – flows at unpredictable times, so use it when available. The Agricultural Bank of China, about 100m inside the north gate, has an **ATM** accepting credit cards.

Songpan's **places to eat** revolve around the numerous noodle joints between the north gate and the bus station; there's the slightly more lavish *Xingyue Lou* Muslim restaurant (with English sign and crisp roast duck) some 100m inside the north gate. South of the bus station, *Emma's Kitchen* (ⓣ0837/8802958, ⓔemmachina@hotmail.com) is a **foreigners' café** serving a tasty burger or barely soup, and providing **Internet** and **information** about local tours and bus times; there's a blind **masseur** next door if you're stiff after a tour in the saddle. *Maoniurou gan* (yak jerky) is sold in shops around town; you should also try *qingke jiu*, local **barley beer**.

Huanglong and Jiuzhaigou Scenic Reserve

Northeast of Songpan, the perpetually snow-clad Min Shan range encloses two separate valleys clothed in thick alpine forests and strung with hundreds of impossibly toned **blue lakes** – said to be the scattered shards of a mirror belonging to the Tibetan goddess **Semo**. Closest to Songpan, **Huanglong** a string of lakes and small ponds in a calcified valley, is relatively small and can be walked around in a few hours; further north on a separate road, **Jiuzhaigou Scenic Reserve** is grander in every respect and requires a couple of days to see properly. Both are targets of intense tourism – except in midwinter, don't come here expecting a quiet commune with nature, as the parks clock up a million or so visitors annually.

Jiuzhaigou can be reached direct on **buses** from Chengdu, Jiangyou and Guangyuan – from the latter, you might have to change at Jiuzhaigou town, 25km east of the reserve – while Huanglong is accessed by minibus from Songpan. In summer, there's also transport through the day between the two reserves, making it possible to travel from Songpan to Huanglong, spend a few hours there, and then go on to Jiuzhaigou.

Huanglong

Huanglong (¥110, students ¥80) lies 60km northeast of Songpan via the small town of **Chuanzhusi**, with its giant Long March memorial statue of a soldier with upraised arms, and the **Xuebaoding Pass** below the red rocks of Hongxing Yan. Xuebaoding itself is the Min Shan range's highest peak, a 5588-metre-high white triangle visible to the east on clear days. On the far side,

Bon

Scattered through Sichuan's northwestern reaches, the **Bonpa** represent the last adherents to Tibet's native religion, **Bon**, before it fused with Buddhist ideas to form Lamaism. A shamanist faith founded by **Gcen-rabs**, one of eighteen saints sent to clear the world of demons, Bon lost influence in Tibet after 755 AD, when the Tibetan royalty began to favour the more spiritual doctrines of Buddhism. As Yellow-hat Sect Lamaism developed and became the dominant faith, the Bonpa were forced out to the borders of Tibet, where the religion survives today.

Though to outsiders Bon is superficially similar to Lamaism – so much so that it's often considered a sub-sect – the two religions are, in many respects, directly opposed. Bonpa circuit their stupas anticlockwise, use black where Lamas would use white, and still have rituals reflecting **animal sacrifice**. Because of this last feature, both the Chinese government and Lamas tend to view Bon as a barbaric, backward belief, and Bonpa are often not keen to be approached or identified as such. Bon monasteries survive at Huanglong and several towns in the central Aba grasslands.

Huanglong reserve covers over a thousand square kilometres of rough terrain, though the accessible section that everyone comes to see is a four-kilometre-long trough at an average altitude of 3000m, carved out by a now-vanished glacier. Limestone-rich waters flowing down the valley have left yellow calcified deposits between hundreds of shallow blue ponds, and their scaly appearance gives Huanglong – "Yellow Dragon" – its name.

An eight-kilometre circuit track – much of it on well-made boardwalks over the fragile formations, but potentially tiring given the altitude – ascends east up the valley from the main-road **park gates**, through surprisingly thick deciduous woodland, pine forest and, finally, rhododendron thickets. On a good day, open stretches give broad views east to five-thousand-metre-high peaks. Pick of the scenery includes the broad **Golden Flying Waterfall** and the kilometre-long calcified slope **Golden Sand on Earth**, where the shallow flow tinkles over innumerable ridges and pockmarks. Around 3km along, the small **Middle Temple** (the lower one has long gone) was once an important **Bon** shrine; today, it seems inactive – even if signs do ask you to circuit to the right in the Bon manner. At the head of the valley, **Huanglong Gusi** is a slightly grander Qing building, featuring an atrium and two small Taoist halls, dedicated to the local guardian deity **Huanglong Zhenren**. Behind here, a three-hundred-metre-long bowl is filled with multi-hued blue pools, contrasting brilliantly with the drab olive vegetation; the best views are from a small platform on the slopes above.

Huanglong's only **accommodation** is the upmarket *Huanglong Shanzhuang* (☎0837/7249333; ❽) at the park gates. Hotel aside, food is available at a single **canteen** near the Middle Temple. There are **toilets** all along the trail, along with posts offering free **oxygen** should you find things tough going.

Jiuzhaigou Scenic Reserve

Around 100km from Songpan or Huanglong, **Jiuzhaigou Scenic Reserve** (¥220, students ¥170; unlimited bus use around the park ¥90; ticket valid for 2 days) was settled centuries ago by Tibetans, whose fenced villages gave Jiuzhaigou (Nine Stockades Gully) its name. Hemmed in by high, snowy peaks, the reserve's valleys form a south-orientated Y-shape, with **lakes** descending them in a series of broad steps, fringed in thick forests – spectacular in the autumn when the gold and red leaves contrast brilliantly with the water, or at the onset of winter in early December, when everything is dusted by snow (rather than frozen solid by the end of that month). The park gets incredibly busy, though – the best you can do is to get in when the gates **open** at 7am and try to stay one step ahead of the hordes. Gates **close** at 5.30pm, and there is no official accommodation inside (though locals sometimes offer beds).

JIUZHAIGOU KOU (also known as **Zhangzha**) is a kilometre-wide blob of services at the park gates comprising accommodation, places to eat, and a **bus station** with daily services to Chengdu, Songpan, Jiangyou and Guangyuan (buy tickets in advance). There is no direct bus from here to Zöigê; you'll have to return to Songpan first. There's also another bus station 25km east at **Jiuzhaigou town** (try the *Jinde Binguan*, ☎0837/7733168, ❸, if you get stuck here) for connections to Guangyuan or Jiangyou. **Accommodation** near the park gates with 24-hour hot water includes *Langjie's Home* (☎0837/7734818 or 7734616, Ⓦwww.gogojz.com; beds ¥30, ❷), a budget hostel with nice timber rooms and a bar; the attractive *You U Hostel*, Building 4, Kangba Manor (☎0837/7763111, Ⓦwww.youuhotel.com; ❷), also with a bar; the plush, Tibetan-style *New Jiuzhaigou Hotel* (☎0837/7734859; ❽); and the *Xingyu International Hotel* (☎0837/7766888; ❽), a resort-package complex with ten restaurants.

It's 14km from the park gates to the centre of the reserve around **Nuorilang**. You can use the bus, but it's a nice four-hour hike past little **Zharu Temple** – brightly decorated inside and out with murals and prayer flags – and the marshy complex of pools at the foot of imposing Dêgê Shan forming **Shuzheng lakes**, the largest group in the reserve and cut part-way along by the twenty-metre **Shuzheng Falls**. Here you'll find a tourist **village** featuring "typical" Tibetan dwellings on the lakeshore where you can don Tibetan garb and pose on horseback for photos.

Another 4km on is Jiuzhaigou's most famous cascades, the **Nuorilang Falls**. They look best from the road, framed by trees as water forks down over the strange, yellow crystalline rockfaces. The road forks east and west at Nuorilang, with both forks around 18km long. The **eastern branch** first passes **Pearl Beach Falls**, where a whole hillside has calcified into an ankle-deep cascade ending in a ten-metre waterfall similar to Nuorilang's, then the shallow **Panda-Arrow Bamboo Lake** and **Grass Lake**, before entering the **Primeval Forest**, a dense and very atmospheric belt of conifers. There's less to see along the **western branch** from Nuorilang, but don't miss the stunning **Five-coloured Lake** here, which, for sheer intensity, if not scale, is unequalled in the park. Superlatives continue at the road's end, where the mundanely named **Long Lake** is both exactly that and, at 3103m, Jiuzhaigou's highest body of water.

Zöigê, Langmusi and on to Gansu

Songpan sits just east of the vast, marshy **Aba autonomous prefecture**, which sprawls over the Sichuan, Gansu and Qinghai borders. Resting at around 3500m and draining directly into the convoluted headwaters of the Yellow River, the **Aba grasslands** are the domain of the independent-minded **Goloks**, a nomadic group of herders. It's also a **Bonpa** stronghold (see box, p.925), home to lots of **birdlife** – including black-necked cranes and golden eagles – and a corridor between Sichuan and **Gansu** province. Buses from Songpan run north to the grassland town of **Zöigê** and over the border, with Tibetan monasteries at **Langmusi** offering a prime reason to stop off along the way.

Around 150km northwest of Songpan at the grasslands' northernmost edge, **ZÖIGÊ (or Nuoergai)** is a tidy collection of markets and shops along Shuguang Lu and parallel Shangye Jie. Things perk up during the June/July **horse races**, when nomads set up tents outside the town and show off their riding skills to the crowds, and the town's low-key **Daza monastery** is worth a visit, especially for the small hall ahead and around to the right – look for paintings of skeletons on the door, and a terrace hung with animal skulls and stuffed, blood-spattered wolves. Transport connections mean you'll need **accommodation** here: on Shangye Jie, the *Ruoliang Binguan* (Ⓣ0837/2298081; ❷) and *Zangle Binguan* (Ⓣ0837/2298685; ❷) both advertise constant hot water and are clean and quiet; while the *Nuoergai Dajiudian* (Ⓣ0837/2291998; ❸) is the town's upmarket option. There are plenty of places to grab a simple meal, or you can just hang out at the *A-Lang* **teahouse** across from the post office on Shangye Jie. The **bus station** on Shuguang Lu has dawn departures for Songpan, Chengdu, Ma'erkang, Langmusi and Hezuo (in Gansu).

Langmusi

Just off the road to Hezuo, 90km from Zöigê, you'll find the scruffy village of **LANGMUSI**, whose surrounding forests, mountain scenery and **lamaseries** give an easy taster of Tibet. There's a direct **bus** from Zöigê, but coming from Hezuo you might get dropped at the main road intersection where jeeps wait

▲ Mountain scenery, Langmusi

to take you the 3km to the village itself (¥2–5). Either way, you end up on the single main street, with nearby **accommodation** at the *Langmusi Binguan* (Ⓣ0941/6671086 or 0138/93945886; beds ¥25, ❸), which has hot water in the evening, a rooftop terrace and a very helpful manager, though you need to bargain doubles down; the tidy, basic *Nomad's Youth Hostel* (Ⓣ0941/3380004, Ⓕ6671460; dorms ¥20); and the relatively smart *Langmusi Yuan Binguan* (Ⓣ0941/6671222 or 0138/93915888; ❸).

Langmusi's two small eighteenth-century **lamaseries** (¥16; ticket valid for two days) sit at the western end of the village. Walk up the main street and bear right over a bridge, and the road leads uphill to **Saizu Gompa**, whose main hall's walls are covered in pictures of meditating Buddhas and where you might see monks debating in the courtyard outside. For **Gaerdi Gompa**, bear left along the main road and then aim for the temple buildings in the back lanes; this is the larger complex with several sizeable, tin-roofed halls, but seems almost totally deserted. There's immense **hiking** potential up to ridges and peaks beyond, but make sure you're equipped for dogs and changeable weather. To arrange longer guided hikes or **horse-trekking**, contact Langmusi Tibetan Horse Trekking, near the bus stop (Ⓣ0941/6671504, Ⓦwww.langmusi.net), a very organized operation whose one- to four-day trips take in nomad camps and mountain scenery – the website has current schedules and costs.

For **food**, there are several simple Muslim and Chinese restaurants along the main street, though foreigners tend to gravitate towards *Leisha's*, a traveller-style **café** where portions of Chinese–Tibetan–Muslim dishes are huge and tasty. There's also a **Net bar** opposite the *Langmusi Binguan*, full of young, network-gaming monks. **Leaving**, buses assemble at dawn on the main street (ask at accommodation the night before for times) for daily runs to Zöigê, and Xiahe and Hezuo in Gansu. If enough people show, you might also score a minibus ride later in the day to Zöigê, which would save time there in limbo between buses. *Leisha's* can help charter minibuses to Jiuzhaigou and elsewhere (about ¥800 for a five-seater).

Sichuan's far west

Sichuan's **far west** begins some six hours over the mountains from Chengdu at **Kangding**, the regional capital. Yet it's only after you leave Kangding, bound northwest to **Ganzi** and **Dêgê** or southwest to **Litang** and **Yunnan**, that you enter what, geographically and ethnically, may as well be Tibet: lowland valleys chequered green and gold with barley fields; flowery grasslands grazed by yaks and dotted with black felt tents, each roped down against the weather and guarded by aggressive, curly-tailed mastiffs; hamlets of square, fortress-like stone or adobe houses; and stark mountain passes draped in coloured flags between wind-scoured peaks. The towns, with accompanying monastic complexes, pilgrims and red-robed clergy, reek of the Wild West, with their dusty, bustling streets roamed by livestock, beasts of burden, and cowboys in slouch hats – though like horsemen worldwide, Tibetans are ditching their trusty steeds for motorbikes and four-wheel-drives as fast as they become available.

Roads beyond Kangding are rough in places – mostly due to landslides or roadworks – but on the whole, journeys are exhausting due to length rather than physical discomfort. What makes them worthwhile are your fellow passengers, mostly monks and wild-looking Khampa youths, who every time the bus crosses a mountain pass cheer wildly and throw handfuls of paper prayer flags out of the windows. **Buying bus tickets** is frustrating, however – expect to find flexible schedules, early departures, ticket offices open at unpredictable times, and unhelpful station staff.

Though routes west of Dêgê and Litang press right through **to Lhasa**, for the present Westerners trying to cross the Tibetan border from Sichuan are almost certain to be pulled off the bus and booted back the way they came. Political considerations aside, these are some of the world's most dangerous roads, high, riven by gorges and permanently snowbound, and the Chinese government is not keen to have foreigners extend the list of people killed in bus crashes along the way. What might make the journey worth the risk is that it takes you within sight of the world's highest unclimbed mountain ranges, and even those hardened by stints in the Himalayas have reported the scenery as staggeringly beautiful. The situation is certain to change eventually, but for now, if you must attempt the crossing, it's better to do so from the Lhasa side – authorities are hardly likely to send you back into Tibet if you try to enter Sichuan here, though you may well be fined.

Kangding

KANGDING, 250km from Chengdu at the gateway to Sichuan's far west, is likely to be a bit of a disappointment. A crowded, artless collection of modern white-tiled blocks packed along the fast-flowing **Zheduo River**, visually this is a very Chinese town, and though Tibetans are certainly in evidence they are clearly outnumbered by the Hui and Han. But for all that, the deep gorge that Kangding is set in is overlooked by chortens and the frosted peaks of **Daxue Shan** (the Great Snowy Mountains), and, whatever the maps might say, this is where Tibet really begins.

The town was once an important marketplace for **tea**, portered over the mountains from Chengdu in compressed blocks to be exchanged for Tibetan wool, and is now the capital of huge **Ganzi prefecture**. Bus schedules mean that a **stopover** here is likely, but with a couple of temples to check out and huge, communal evening dancing in the central square it's not the worst of fates. In addition, Kangding is a stepping stone for day-trips to the

Sichuan's far west: Kangding and on to Tibet

Batang	巴塘	*bātáng*
Daocheng	稻城	*dàochéng*
Hot Springs	茹布查卡温泉	*rúbù chákǎ wēnquán*
Seaburay	喜波热藏庄	*xǐbōrè zàngzhuāng*
Xianggelila	香格里拉	*xiānggé lǐlā*
Yading	亚丁	*yàdīng*
Yading Jiudian	亚丁酒店	*yàdīng jiǔdiàn*
Dêgê	德格	*dégé*
Babang Monastery	八帮寺庙	*bābāng sìmiào*
Dêgê Binguan	德格宾馆	*dégé bīnguǎn*
Gangqing Monastery	篢庆寺庙	*gàngqìng sìmiào*
Scripture Printing Hall	印经院	*yìnjīng yuàn*
Shaquan Xiaochi	心泉小吃	*xīnquán xiǎochī*
Ganzi	甘孜	*gānzī*
Chengxin Binguan	诚信宾馆	*chéngxìn bīnguǎn*
Jinmaoniu Jiudian	金牦牛酒店	*jīnmáoniú jiǔdiàn*
Kandze Monastery	甘孜寺庙	*gānzī sìmiào*
Kangding	康定	*kāngdìng*
Anjue Si	安觉寺	*ānjué sì*
Nanmo Si	南甫寺	*nánfǔ sì*
Old Town Spring	水井子	*shuǐjǐngzi*
Paoma Shan	跑马山	*pǎomǎ shān*
Princess Wenchang Bridge	文成公主桥	*wénchéng gōngzhǔ qiáo*
Accommodation		
Kalaka'er Fandian	卡拉卡尔饭店	*kǎlā kǎ'ěr fàndiàn*
Sally's Knapsack Inn	背包客栈	*bēibāo kèzhàn*
Xiangbala Jiudian	香巴拉酒店	*xiāngbālā jiǔdiàn*
Litang	理瑭	*lǐtáng*
Changqingchun Ke'er monastery	理塘寺庙	*lǐtáng sìmiào*
Crane Guesthouse	仙鸿宾馆	*xiānhóng bīnguǎn*

Hailuogou Glacier Park, which descends **Gongga Shan**, western China's highest peak.

Kangding's most central temple is **Anjue Si** just off Yanhe Xi Lu; a small affair, it was built in 1654 at the prompting of the Fifth Dalai Lama. The main hall is unusual in being covered in miniature golden Buddha statues instead of the usual gory murals, and features some fine butter sculptures of animals and meditating sages. Following the main road southwest out of town brings you to the short stone arch of the **Princess Wenchang Bridge**; on the other side, a path runs uphill to **Nanmo Si**, built here in 1639 after the original site was sacked by the Mongols. Present renovations have reached two side halls containing a large gilded statue of Tsongkhapa and murals of Buddha in all his incarnations – images that, with their typically Tibetan iconography of skulls, demons and fierce expressions, paint a far less forgiving picture of Buddhism than the mainstream Chinese brand.

Kangding's **markets** – mostly selling clothing and household knick-knacks of all descriptions – surround the old town **spring** and a **mosque** off Yanhe Dong Lu. A lane opposite the mosque heads up to the entrance of pine-clad **Paoma Shan**, the mountain southeast of town, which hosts a **horse-race festival** in the middle of the fourth lunar month. It's a half-hour walk up stone steps to

Gaocheng Binguan	高城宾馆	gāochéng bīnguǎn
Litang Binguan	理塘宾馆	lǐtáng bīnguǎn
Safe and Life International Hotel	平安涉外旅馆	píng'ān shèwài lǚguǎn
Tianfu Chuancaiguan	天府川菜馆	tiānfǔ chuāncàiguǎn
Luding	泸定	lùdìng
Manigange	马尼干戈	mǎní gāngé
King Gesar	格萨尔王	gésà'ěr wáng
Manigange Pani Fandian	马尼干戈帕尼饭店	mǎní gāngé pàní fàndiàn
Xinlu Hai	新路海	xīnlùhǎi
Yulong Shenhai Binguan	玉龙神海宾馆	yùlóng shénhǎi bīnguǎn
Zhuqing Buddhist College	竹庆佛学院	zhúqìng fóxuéyuàn
Moxi	磨西	móxī
Gongga Shan	贡嘎山	gònggā shān
Hailuo Binguan	海螺宾馆	hǎiluó bīnguǎn
Hailuogou Glacier Park	海螺沟公园	hǎiluógōu gōngyuán
Minzhu Huayuan Jiudian	明珠花园酒店	míngzhū huāyuán jiǔdiàn
Xinfei Fandian	鑫飞饭店	xīnfēi fàndiàn
Sangdui	桑堆	sāngduī
Benbo Monastery	奔波寺	bēnbō sì
Haizi Shan	海子山	hǎizi shān
Zhujie Monastery	著杰寺	zhùjié sì
Tagong	塔公	tǎgōng
Mugecuo	木格措	mùgé cuò
Tagong Binguan	塔公宾馆	tǎgōng bīnguǎn
Tagong grasslands	塔公草原	tǎgōng cǎoyuán
Tagong Si	塔公寺	tǎgōng sì
Xiangcheng	乡城	xiāngchéng
Bamu Tibetan Guesthouse	巴姆藏庄	bāmǔ zàngzhuāng
Coffee Tea Hotel	象泉茶楼	xiàngquán chálóu
Chaktreng Gompa	桑披岭寺	sāngpīlíng sì

lookouts and the Roman-theatre-style racetrack, or you can catch a **cable car** (¥20 up, ¥30 return) from near the Princess Wenchang Bridge.

Practicalities

Kangding sits in a deep Y-shaped valley where the Zheduo River and a minor stream combine to form the Kangding River. The kilometre-long downtown area flanks the Zheduo as it flows northeast into the Kangding, with the two main streets – **Yanhe Dong Lu** on the southern side, **Yanhe Xi Lu** on the northern – joined by four bridges. Yanhe Dong Lu continues southwest out of town towards Ganzi and Litang over the Princess Wenchang Bridge.

The **bus station** is a run-down affair at Kangding's northeastern edge with atypically considerate, helpful staff; exit the building, turn right, and it's a five-minute walk to Yanhe Dong Lu. The bus station has departures until mid-afternoon to Chengdu and Danba, and early-morning runs to Tagong, Ganzi, Dêgê, Litang, Batang, Xiangcheng and Daocheng. **Minibuses** touting for Danba and Tagong, and **taxis** to Luding, cruise the streets outside.

Find **budget accommodation** at the *Black Tent Inn* (☎0836/8862907 or 8885368, beds ¥25) attached to Anjue Si; just up the hill from here at the sparkling, clean *Yongzhu Guesthouse* (☎0836/8888239 or 0139/90455863;

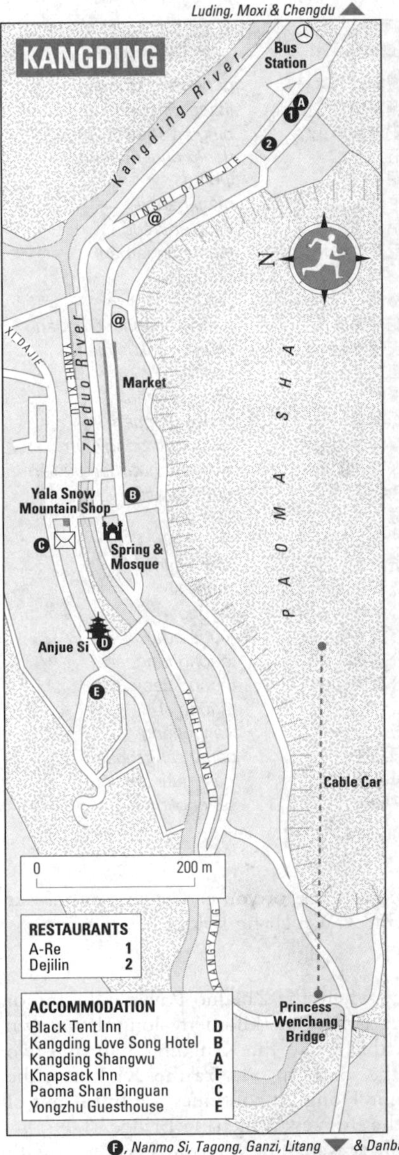

beds ¥30, ③); and 2.5km from the centre at the *Knapsack Inn* (Ⓣ0836/2838377; beds ¥20) – catch a taxi for ¥5 to the adjacent Jinggang Si. For something **mid-range**, try *Taining Shangwu Jiudian*, near the bus station (Ⓣ0836/6696888, Ⓕ6695210; ③) or the slightly weatherbeaten, central *Paoma Shan Binguan* (Ⓣ0836/2835888, Ⓕ2835898; ④). The town's **upmarket** option is the *Kangding Love Song Hotel* (Ⓣ0836/2813333, Ⓕ2813111; ⑦), which has its own cinema. **Eating**, the bus-station road has heaps of cheap restaurants, along with the *Dejilin*, a real Tibetan diner with murals and communal bench tables, and the *A-Re*, a fake Tibetan restaurant with waitress service next to the *Kangding Shangwu* hotel.

Finally, if you're after **guides** or advice for exploring the wilds around Gongga Shan, contact Yala Snow Mountain Shop (Ⓣ0836/2835798, Ⓕ2835777, mob 13330795696), next to the post office on Xi Dajie. Not only do they sell good-value outdoor gear, but you couldn't ask for a better bunch to arrange four- to eight-day hiking or horse-trekking expeditions to the mountain.

Luding, Moxi and Hailuogou Glacier Park

A fast road runs 100km from Kangding via Luding to the village of **Moxi**, at the Hailuogou Glacier Park gates; the journey takes two hours. It's possible to cram the trip to the glacier and back into one day if you start early, but better perhaps to overnight either in Moxi or the park itself. The easiest way to travel is to flag down a taxi outside Kangding bus station; they charge around ¥20 for a four-person cab to Luding, or ¥35 to Moxi. There's also a direct road from Kangding to Moxi, but at the time of writing, taxi drivers weren't using it.

Don't be surprised if you have to change vehicles an hour east of Kangding at the market town of **LUDING**, where a few minutes is enough to check out the **Luding Bridge** (¥10), one of the great icons of the Long March. In May 1935, the Red Army reached the Dadu River here to find that a nominal Nationalist force, baulking at destroying the only crossing for hundreds of kilometres, had pulled the decking off the Luding suspension bridge, but left the chains intact. Under heavy fire, 22 Communist soldiers climbed hand-over-hand across the chains and took Guomindang emplacements on the west bank. Official accounts say that only three Long Marchers were killed.

Though substantial by local standards, the bridge is simply a one-hundred-metre-long series of thirteen heavy-gauge chains spanned by planks. The Dadu flows roughly below, while temple-style gates and ornaments at either end lend the bridge an almost religious aspect; a pavilion on the far side houses a **museum** with period photos. For **moving on**, taxis cruise the main road through daylight hours for Kangding (¥20) or Moxi (¥15).

Moxi and Hailuogou Glacier Park

After the action at Luding, Mao and the Red Army recouped at the village of Moxi before heading off on a disastrous 56-kilometre trek north over the mountains to Xiaojin, in which Mao nearly joined the hundreds of victims of exposure and altitude sickness. Nobody here today is attempting anything so strenuous, most making an easy tour of **Hailuogou Glacier Park**, whose borders start immediately beyond Moxi. Set among an alpine backdrop of deep valleys forested in pine and rhododendron, Hailuogou is the lowest of four local **glaciers** descending **Gongga Shan** (Minya Konka in Tibetan), western China's highest point at 7556m – a stunning sight on the rare mornings when the near-constant cloud cover and haze of wind-driven snow above the peak suddenly clear. Warm, weatherproof **clothing** is advisable whatever time of year you visit.

The **park entrance** (¥110) is at **MOXI**, a group of hotels, restaurants and souvenir stalls centred around a crossroads where Luding and Kangding buses cluster. Downhill from the crossroads, it's 150m to Moxi's original single street of wooden shops and a small **Catholic church** built in the 1920s. Its colourful bell tower overlooks a European, box-like main building, its eaves pinched as a concession to local aesthetics. Top-notch **accommodation** is provided near the park gates by the *Mingzhu Huayuan Jiudian* (Ⓣ0836/3266166, Ⓦwww.sctrip.com; ❽), with cheaper options such as the tatty *Hailuo Binguan* (Ⓣ0836/3266297; ❸) and friendly *Xinfei Fandian* (Ⓣ0836/3266214; ❷) downhill from the crossroads. **Eat** either at your hotel or at any of the scores of stir-fry restaurants nearby.

The **Hailuogou Glacier Park** itself spreads westwards of Moxi, with a **road** running 25km from the gates to the glacier. Most visitors take a **tour bus** from the park gates (¥50 return), though you can also hike, resting up at the three **camps** along the way at the 8-, 15- and 22-kilometre marks. These were once humble campsites, but each now hosts a large hotel (❺), with **hot springs** (¥65) on hand at the first two – camp 2, near where the thicker pine forests begin, is the nicest spot to stay within the park. From camp 3, it's 3.5km to the glacier, from where you can reach a **viewing platform** by cable car (¥160 return) or by simply hiking up along a small path – allow two hours. From the platform, the glacier is revealed as a tongue of blue-white ice scattered with boulders and streaked in crevasses edged in black gravel, with – if you're lucky – Gongga Shan's peak rising in the distance.

To Ganzi and Dêgê

Northwest from Kangding, it's close on 600km across mountains and prairies to Tibet, and the main targets on the way are the people and monasteries around the highway towns of **Tagong**, **Ganzi** and **Dêgê**, the latter not far from the Tibetan border. The whole area hovers above 3500m, and the passes are considerably higher. **Buses** through the region run daily from Kangding via Tagong and take a full day to reach Ganzi, and two for Dêgê.

The Tagong grasslands

Starting 110km northwest of Kangding, the **Tagong grasslands** occupy a string of flat-bottomed valleys on a 3700-metre-high plateau, all surrounded by magnificent snowy peaks. Horse-riding, hiking, and a temple at the Tibetan township of **TAGONG** (**Lhagong**), are the attractions here; **buses** and minibuses connect

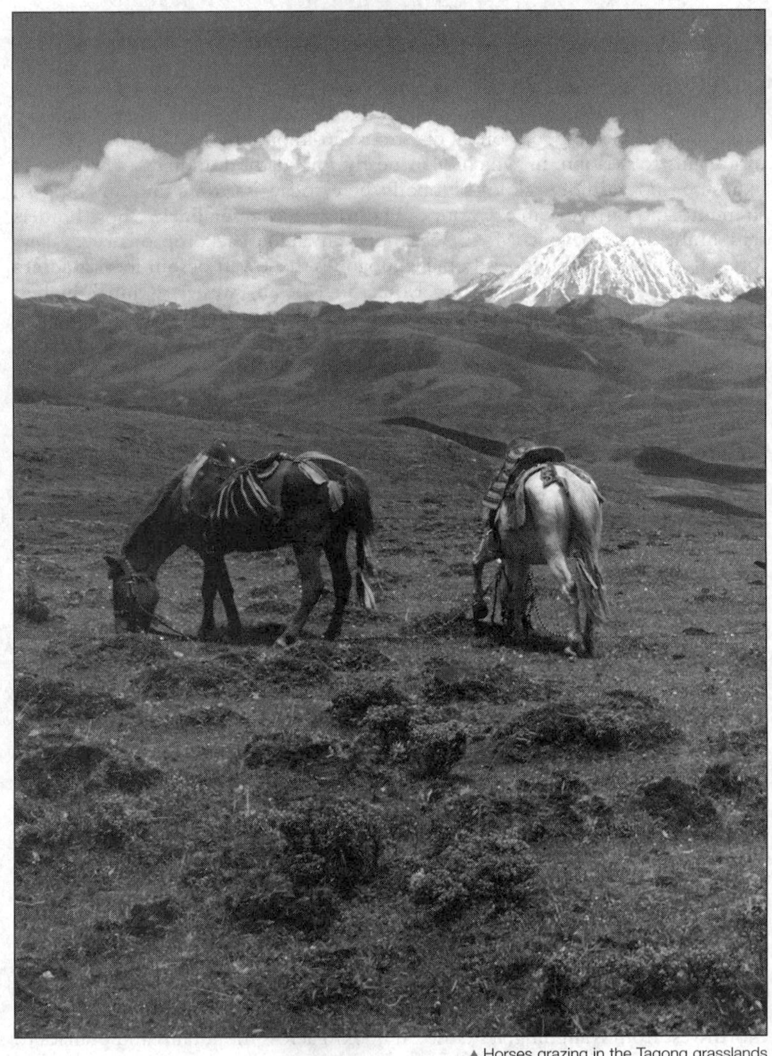

▲ Horses grazing in the Tagong grasslands

the village daily with Kangding, Danba, Bamei and Ganzi and drop you off on the single street next to the temple square. You'll probably be grabbed on arrival by the owner of *Jya Drolma & Gayla's Guesthouse* (☎0836/2866056; beds ¥20), whose hospitality and Tibetan home – not to mention hot showers – are almost worth the trip in themselves; facing the temple, it's the building behind you on the left. Otherwise, also beside the temple, *Snowland Hostel* (☎0836/2866098 or 0130/56457979; beds ¥20) is next to *Sally's Café* (closed Nov–March), a foreigners' restaurant with Tibetan, Chinese and Western staples. Over the road, the *Khampa Cultural Centre* (☎01355/8500741) has a similar café plus Internet, and organizes hikes for a bargain ¥85 a day including guides, accommodation with locals and food; horses cost about ¥120 a day.

Tagong's focus is the modest **Tagong Si** (¥10), a complex built to honour Princess Wenchang but now busy with monks chatting on their mobile phones during morning prayers. The seventeenth-century main hall houses a sculpture of Sakyamuni as a youth, said to have been brought here by the princess in Tang times. Behind the monastery is **Fotalin**, a forest of a hundred three-metre-high stupas, each built in memory of a monk. Follow the main road 500m past Tagong Si and you'll find the spectacular **golden stupa** (¥10), fully 20m tall and backed by snowy peaks, surrounded by a colonnade of prayer wheels – though according to the monks, this recent construction is less of a religious site than an excuse to collect tourist revenue.

The **grasslands** themselves begin at the golden stupa, a vast sprawl of pasture hemmed in by hillocks and peaks. Hiking and riding possibilities are legion: **Shedra Gompa**'s monastery and Buddhist college is only a couple of kilometres away; **Shamalong** village is two hours along a track from the stupa; while **Ani Gompa** is a valley nunnery with a sky-burial site some two hours hike cross-country. Get full directions for these routes from the *Khampa Cultural Centre* – and beware of dogs.

Tagong to Ganzi

Some 50km up the Ganzi road from Tagong, tiny **BAMEI** is where to catch a **minibus to Danba** (try the *Golden Sun* hotel, with beds for ¥30, if you get stuck); while a further 150km brings you to **DAOFU**, a fair-sized, orderly Tibetan settlement surrounded by hamlets. There are many places to stay here (beds start at ¥30), and also a private **homestay** out in the country (call in advance for prices on ☎0135/58514149) whose English-speaking owner arranges five-day **horse treks** for ¥350. A further 100km on again, **LUHUO** is where Kangding–Dêgê buses overnight, with well-stocked shops and the requisite gold-roofed monastery on a hill. Luhuo's best **accommodation** is near the bus station at the Tibetan-run *Kasa Dajiudian* (☎0836/7322368; ❷, dorm ¥30), whose warm, large rooms are most welcome if you've spent much time in the far west. From here, Ganzi is just three more hours up the road.

Ganzi

GANZI sits at 3500m in a broad, flat-bottomed river valley, with the long, serrated Que'er Shan range rising to the south. The dusty, noisy town owes its importance to the adjacent **Kandze monastery**, founded by the Mongols after they invaded in 1642 and once the largest Gelugpa monastery in the Kham region. A bit empty today, it nevertheless remains an important cultural centre, especially for the teaching of religious dances and musical instruments.

Ganzi acts as transport and social focus, with blue trucks rumbling through at all hours, wild crowds cruising the streets, and markets throughout the back lanes; the kilometre-long main road is lined with shops selling knives, rugs, silverware, all sorts of jewellery, saddles, religious accessories, copper and tin kitchenware. The **monastery** is 2km north of town – follow Jiefang Lu uphill from the bus station – and for such an obvious structure the entrance is not easy to find, being hidden behind mud-brick homes among medieval backstreets. The recently renovated buildings are splendid, and just wandering around fills in time, though there's little specific to seek out aside from the **main hall** – covered in gold, murals and prayer flags, and with an incredible view of the valley and town from its roof. The large adobe walls below the monastery are remains of the Mazur and Khangsar **forts**, built by the Mongols after they took the region.

Back in Ganzi, the highway runs east–west as main **Chuanzang Lu**, the **crossroads** with north-oriented **Jiefang Lu** marking the town centre. The **bus station** is on the crossroads, with daily departures to Bâtâng, Kangding and Chengdu. Staff here are helpful enough with information but you might have to buy tickets on the bus. If you're aiming for **Litang** and want to avoid going all the way back to Kangding, there's also a morning bus south **to Xinlong**, from where minubuses run to Litang if they get enough people (¥60–80 each, or about ¥300 for the whole van). Check with the Xinlong bus driver in Ganzi that the Xinlong–Litang stretch is open first, as it's subject to wash-outs and landslides.

Ganzi's **accommodation** prospects are not outstanding, and the best bet is probably the *Golden Yak Hotel* inside the bus-station compound (Ⓣ0836/7525288, Ⓕ7525188; ❹, beds from ¥15), which looks mildly upmarket but has both dorms and comfy doubles. Otherwise, the *Chengxin Binguan* opposite (Ⓣ0836/7525289; ❸, dorms ¥30) is typically functional. Almost every other business in town is a **restaurant**, though don't expect much beyond noodles and dumplings.

Manigange and around

Over a pass and out on the plains 95km northwest from Ganzi, **MANIGANGE** is a single-street township with at least two places to **stay and eat** – *Manigange Pani Fandian* and *Yulong Shenhai Binguan* – both offering dorms (¥20), doubles (❸) and hot water. There are two reasons to stop here: Tibetan **horse races** in late August, and the holy lake of **Xinlu Hai** (Yilhun Lhatso), 10km beyond Manigange on the Dêgê road. The kilometre-wide lake sits in a reserve for the elusive **white-lipped deer**, and is partially fed by dusty-brown glaciers descending the snow-tipped Qu'er Shan, whose slopes hem the shoreline; scores of boulders in the vicinity carved with "*om pani padme hum*" in Tibetan characters testify to spiritual importance. The area is beautiful and has limitless **hiking potential**, though you need to be fully equipped for the altitude and cold climate, even in summer.

Another possible reason to linger is the **Axu grasslands** north of Manigange, birthplace of the eleventh-century warrior-king **Gesar**, hero of Tibet's longest epic, whose fame for slaughtering his enemies extends from Mongolia to Yunnan. Images of him, inevitably depicted as a fiercely moustached horseman, can be found everywhere through Sichuan's far west. One place to aim for on the grasslands is **Zhuqing Buddhist College** (Dzongchen Gompa) 50km northwest of Manigange, which is in poor condition but remains the region's major Nyingmapa-sect monastery, established in 1684 and famous for originating an opera version of the Gesar epic. Note that, if you can find transport, the main road in this direction continues up to Maduo and ultimately Xining in **Qinghai** (see p.1019).

Dêgê and around

The road from Manigange to Dêgê is the most spectacular – and downright frightening – in the whole of Sichuan's far west. It first follows a rounded valley below the toothy, snowbound **Chola Shan**, then, at the valley's head, it zigzags back on itself and climbs to just below the peaks, crossing a razor-edged 5050-metre-high pass. As the road hairpins down the even more vertiginous far side, monks on the bus don't help raise expectations of survival by their furious chanting, but with luck you'll be pulling up at Dêgê four hours after leaving Manigange.

DÊGÊ initially appears to be no more than a small cluster of ageing concrete buildings squeezed into a narrow gorge, but was once the most powerful Kham state, and the only one to resist the seventeenth-century Mongol invasion – hence the absence of Gelugpa-sect monasteries in the region. The **bus stop** is on the main road, just where Dêgê's single street crosses a stream and rises uphill past shops, a **supermarket** and **Internet bar**, dozens of stir-fry **restaurants** – the *Xinquan Xiaochi* is good – to the monastery. The surly riverside *Dêgê Binguan* (❹, dorms ¥20) is the primary source of **beds**, with grubby dorms in an older wing and overpriced newer rooms in the main building; their comfortable tearoom, however, is a treat after the journey.

At the top of the main street is **Gangqing Si** (Gongchen Gompa), whose red-walled buildings form one of three hubs of Tibetan culture (the other two are Lhasa, and Xiahe in Gansu). The first building encountered is the famous **Bakong** (Scripture Printing Hall; ¥25; cameras forbidden), encircled by peregrinating pilgrims busy thumbing rosaries, who stick out their tongues in greeting if you join them. Built in 1729, the four-storey hall houses 290,000 **woodblocks** of Tibetan texts, stored in racks on the second floor like books in a library, and covering everything from scriptures to scientific treatises – some seventy percent of all Tibetan literary works. You can watch the **printing process** on the third floor: two printers sit facing each other, with the block in between on a sloping board; one printer inks the block with a pad and lays a fresh page over it; the other rubs a roller over the back of the page and then peels it off, placing it in a pile. Each page takes under six seconds to finish, and it's not unusual to watch ten pairs of printers going full pelt, turning out a hundred pages a minute between them.

The rest of the complex comprises a main hall and associated buildings, and there always seem to be ceremonies going on, which you may or may not be allowed to observe. For an easy walk, follow the stream up past the monastery and into barley fields for about forty minutes to a **swimming hole**.

Some 40km south of Dêgê, the eight-hundred-year-old **Babang Si** (Palpung Gompa) – also known as the "Little Potala" after its size and general design – is the largest and most important Kagyupa-sect monastery in Sichuan, currently undergoing much-needed repairs. The problem is getting here: there's no public transport, so you'll have to hike or ask at the hotel about chartering a jeep.

Leaving, you'll need to buy Ganzi or Kangding tickets a day in advance; the main-road bus-ticket booth opens at 7am and again at 2.30pm. There are also buses to Changdu (**Chamdo**) in Tibet – the border, marked by a youthful **Yangzi River** is about 15km west – if you want to try your luck with the border guards.

Kangding to Litang

From Kangding, it's 290km west to the monastery town of **Litang**, a major marketplace and transport hub from where you have two choices: to continue west to the Tibetan border (though this currently remains closed for foreigners); or head southwest to Yunnan.

The Kangding–Litang road is a real treat, steadily rising to a mountain pass at 4700m. The pass opens onto undulating highlands, whose soft green slopes drop to forests far below – look for **marmots** (prairie dogs) on the ground and wedge-tailed **lammergeiers** (bearded vultures) circling far above. Just as you're wondering whether the road goes on indefinitely, Litang appears below on a flat plain, ringed by mountains.

Litang

LITANG is a lively, outwardly gruff place with a large Tibetan population and an obvious Han presence in its businesses and army barracks. Wild West comparisons are inevitable – you'll soon get used to sharing the pavement with livestock, and watching monks and Khampa toughs with braided hair and boots tearing around the windy, dusty streets on ribboned motorbikes. It's also inescapably **high** – at 4014m above sea level, it actually beats Lhasa by over 300m – so don't be surprised if you find even gentle slopes strangely exhausting. As usual, the main distraction here is people-watching: the shops are packed with Tibetans bargaining for temple accessories, solar-power systems for tents, illegal furs, and practical paraphernalia for daily use; while smiths are busy turning out the town's renowned knives and jewellery in backstreet shacks.

Litang's **Changqingchun Ke'er monastery**, founded in 1580 at the behest of the Third Dalai Lama and one of the largest Gelugpa monasteries in China, is today somewhat dilapidated but still populated by over a thousand monks. From the main crossroads in town, head north up Tuanjie Lu to the intersection, turn left, and follow the road – it's a fifteen-minute walk, or a ¥3 taxi ride. For once, the approach gives a clear view of the complex, entirely encircled by a wall, the four main halls (two of them brand new) gleaming among an adobe township of monks' quarters. At the entrance is a large stupa and pile of brightly painted *mani* stones left by pilgrims for good luck, whose inscriptions have been carved to resemble yaks. The **upper temple** (Tsengyi Zhatsang) is the most interesting, its portico flanked by aggressively postured statues of guardians of the four directions, along with a typical, finely executed mural of a three-eyed demon wearing tiger skins and skulls, holding the Wheel Of Transmigration. Inside are statues of Tsongkhapa and the Third Dalai Lama, along with photos of the current Dalai Lama and tenth Panchen Lama. Side gates in the wall allow

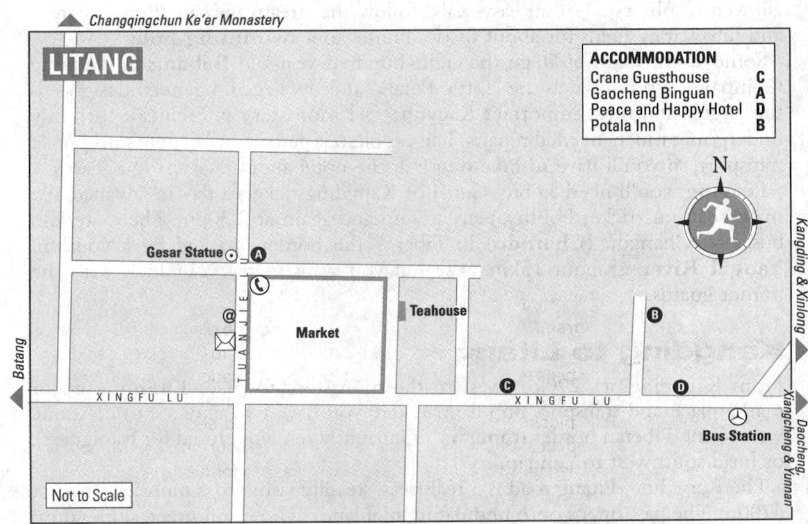

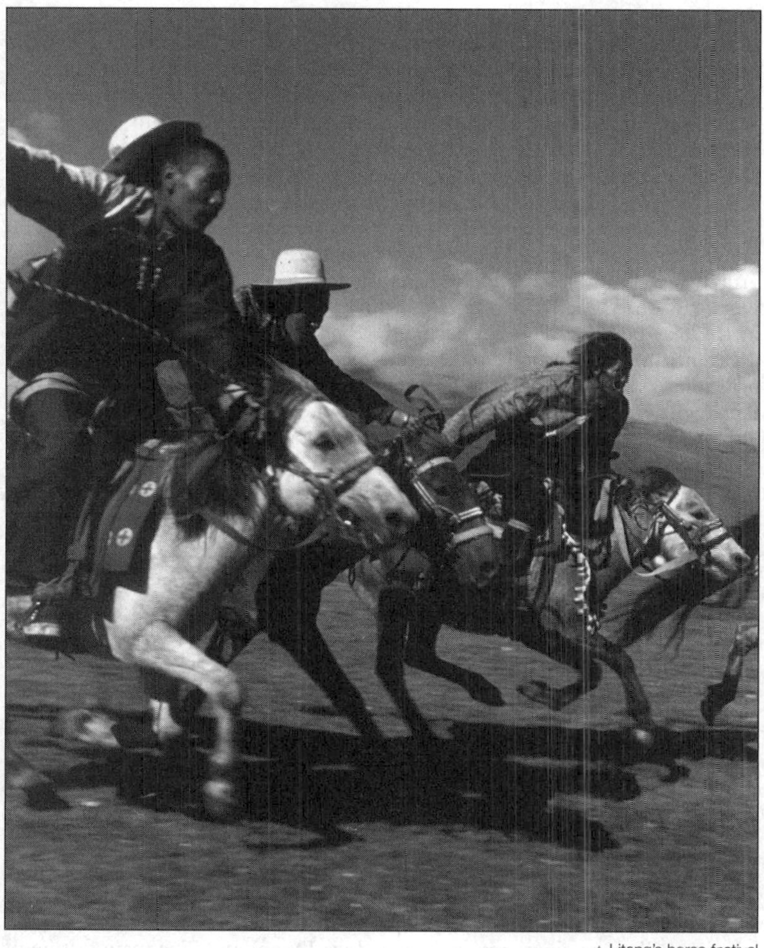

▲ Litang's horse festival

you to hike up onto the hills behind the monastery, sharing the flower-filled pasture with yaks, or join pilgrims circuiting the walls to the **sky-burial ground** to the right of the main gates.

Litang's horse festival

Litang's week-long **horse festival** kicks off each August 1 on the plains outside town. Thousands of Tibetan horsemen from all over Kham descend to compete, decking their stocky steeds in bells and brightly decorated bridles and saddles. As well as the four daily **races**, the festival features amazing demonstrations of horsemanship, including acrobatics, plucking silk scarves off the ground, and shooting (guns and bows) – all performed at full tilt. In between, you'll see plenty of **dancing**, both religious (the dancers wearing grotesque wooden masks) and for fun, with both men and women gorgeously dressed in heavily embroidered long-sleeved smocks.

Practicalities

Litang's main street is a 1.5-kilometre section of the highway known as **Xingfu Lu**, with the **bus station** at the eastern end. There are several buses daily to Kangding and at least one each to Batang, Xiangcheng and Daocheng, but the station staff probably won't sell you tickets and you may have to wait for the buses to turn up and see if seats are available. **Minibuses** and taxis to Batang, Daocheng, Xinlong (for Ganzi) and anywhere else they can get enough customers for hang around outside in the mornings.

The best budget **accommodation** options are across from the bus station on Xingfu Lu at the *Peace and Happy Hotel* (Ⓣ0836/5323861; beds ¥20), a friendly, grubby place with tiny rooms; or the efficient *Crane Guesthouse* 500m further west (Ⓣ0836/5323850; ❸, beds ¥20), with dorms at the front and good doubles in the rear building. The new and tidy *Potala Inn* (Ⓣ0836/5322533; ❸) is a Tibetan-run, Chinese-style place with spectacular views from its two front bedrooms; while the *Gaocheng Binguan* on Tuanjie Lu (Ⓣ0836/5322706; ❺) is the town's most upmarket joint, though located above a noisy teahouse-bar. Stir-fry **restaurants** run by migrants from Chengdu line the main street, some of which have English menus and all pretty much the same food. For **post**, **phones** and **Internet**, head to Tuanjie Lu.

Batang

Some 200km west of Litang across a boggy plateau ringed in peaks, **BATANG** is a small, orderly grid of shops, government offices and barracks in a wide valley just short of the **Tibetan border**. Although open to Chinese tourists, Westerners were not allowed across at the time of writing, so – as there are no sights in town – there's little point in visiting unless the situation changes. The **bus station** is 150m east on the highway, with daily departures to Lhasa, Kangding and Chengdu, with **accommodation** nearby at the *Jinlu Zhaodaisuo* (beds ¥25) or *W Binguan* (❷). The central square faces a **post office** and **phone bar** for international calls, with **Internet** available on the third floor of the main market.

Litang to Yunnan

The road south of Litang runs, via the valley settlement of **Xiangcheng**, right down to Zhongdian in Yunnan, though it's worth detouring along the way to take in **Yading**, an alpine reserve accessed via **Daocheng**. The main feature of the first stage of the journey is the bleak **Haizi Shan**, a former glacial cap and now a high, boulder-strewn moorland patterned by magenta flowers, small twisting streams, and pale blue tarns. You descend off this past the **Benbo monastery** to the valley settlement of **SANGDUI**, a scattered hamlet of Tibetan homes surrounding a junction where the routes to Xiangcheng and Daocheng diverge. The latter road follows the west side of a broad, long river valley 30km south to Daocheng; about 7km along, a bridge crosses to a track heading 5km over the valley to **Zhujie monastery**, famed for its meditating monks, and beautifully positioned halfway up the facing slope – a good excuse to get off the bus and explore.

Daocheng

DAOCHENG (or **Dabpa**) is a small, touristy T-intersection of low buildings and shops, the road from Sangdui running in past the **bus station** to the junction. Turn left (north) and the road runs out into the countryside, degenerating into a track that winds up 5km later at some **hot springs**, set among a tiny village at the head of a valley. **Bathhouses** here ask ¥3 for a soak, and you can cross the valley and hike along a ridge back into town – tiring, given the 3500-metre altitude.

Otherwise, the main point of interest lies a 76-kilometre ride south of Daocheng at **Yading**, a beautiful reserve of meadows, lakes and six-thousand-metre peaks – though serious **riots** here by local Tibetans against how the park was being developed shut the whole place down in 2007. If the **bus** is running, it charges ¥55 return to the reserve gates at **Long Ba** (also known as **Xianggelila**, or "Shangri-la"); otherwise, you'll have to arrange a five-person jeep or minibus through your accommodation (¥500). There's basic accommodation and places to eat in Yading – you'll be glad to take extra food, water and sleeping bags – but at present much of the reserve is only accessible on foot or horseback.

Daocheng's best **accommodation** option is the warmly hospitable **Tibetan guesthouses** such as the *Seaburay* (ⓣ0836/5728668; ¥30 per person; follow the English signs from near the bus station), where your ability to consume vast amounts of *tsampa*, dumplings and butter tea will be put to the test. Toilets are basic and you shower at the public bathhouse or, more enjoyably, at the hot springs. There's also the *Yading Youth Hostel* (ⓣ0836/5728994, ⓦwww.yading.net; beds ¥20, ❸), though it's a bit out of town over the bridge; and the similar *Tongfu Hostel* (ⓣ0836/5728667, ⓦwww.inoat.com; beds ¥20, ❸) – both have restaurants, bars and hot water. Daocheng has one tourist hotel, the *Yading Jiudian* (ⓣ0836/8674777; ❻) on the hot-springs road; it's comfortable, but characterless, though there's a useful **foreign-exchange** counter for guests.

Daily **buses** depart for Litang, Kangding, Xiangcheng and Zhongdian in Yunnan, all things being equal – but they often aren't. Note that the Zhongdian bus originates here, making it a better place to catch it than Xiangcheng (see below). Wherever you're headed, come to the ticket office around 2pm the day before and be prepared to fight for a place in the queue. You can also negotiate with **minibus** drivers outside for rides to Litang and Xiangcheng.

Xiangcheng and on to Yunnan

Some 80km over the steep ranges southwest of Sangdui and 200km from Litang, **XIANGCHENG**'s little core of shops and scattered spread of Tibetan farmhouses and red mud-brick **watchtowers** are set in a deep valley looking south to the mountains marking the Yunnan border. Once capital of a region romantically known as the "White Wolf State", today Xiangcheng is a functional few streets with the flat atmosphere of some long-abandoned outpost, but the small seventeenth-century **monastery** (Chaktreng Gompa; ¥10; photos allowed) is highly unusual and well worth the two-kilometre uphill hike from town. While you're in the portico gasping for breath, take a look at the wooden support pillars, deeply carved with painted hares, elephants, monkeys and tigers. Inside, the three-storey temple has extraordinary decorations, including murals of mandalas and warrior demons squashing European-looking figures, and a sculpture of a multi-headed, many-limbed Samvara in primary blues and reds cavorting in Tantric postures, fangs bared. Among all this is an eerie seated statue of Tsongkhapa, wreathed in gold filigree and draped in silk scarves.

Xiangcheng's semi-derelict **bus station** is a walled compound dotted with rubble and excrement; the town's short main street stretches beyond. If the owner doesn't meet you, take the small steps uphill from inside the bus station and it's 50m to *Bamu Tibetan Guesthouse* (there's a small English sign; ❶, dorm beds ¥18). This is Xiangcheng's highlight, a traditional three-storey Tibetan home decorated in murals, whose dormitory resembles the interior of a temple (the twin rooms are a bit poky, however). There are great views from the roof, and a basic outdoor shower and toilet – a torch is useful. Another decent option – though with none of *Bamu*'s character – lies just outside the bus-station gates at the *Coffee Tea Hotel* (☎0836/8659888; ❸), which also has a good **teahouse** and **bathhouse**.

There are usually daily buses to Litang, Daocheng and Zhongdian in Yunnan. You might be sold a ticket for Litang the day before departure at 2.30pm, but as Xiangcheng is only a brief stop on the Daocheng–Zhongdian run, you'll have to bargain with the driver for a seat to these destinations.

Travel details

Trains

Chengdu to: Beijing (3 daily; 25–30hr); Chongqing (1 daily; 12hr); Emei (10 daily; 2hr); Guangyuan (many daily; 5hr); Guangzhou (1 daily; 38hr); Guiyang (4 daily; 18hr); Jiangyou (many daily; 3hr 30min); Kunming (4 daily; 19hr); Panzhihua (8 daily; 13hr); Shanghai (4 daily; 40hr); Wuhan (3 daily; 17hr); Xi'an (8 daily; 16hr); Xichang (9 daily; 10hr).

Chongqing to: Beijing (2 daily; 25hr); Chengdu (1 daily; 12hr); Guangzhou (5 daily, 36hr); Guiyang (5 daily; 12hr); Shanghai (1 daily; 37hr); Wuhan (2 daily; 13hr); Xi'an (3 daily; 16hr).

Emei Shan to: Chengdu (10 daily; 2hr); Kunming (4 daily; 17hr); Panzhihua (8 daily; 11hr); Xichang (9 daily; 8hr).

Xichang to: Chengdu (9 daily; 10hr); Emei (9 daily; 8hr); Kunming (4 daily; 9hr); Panzhihua (8 daily; 3hr).

Buses

Chengdu to: Chongqing (6hr); Daocheng (2 days); Dazu (4hr); Dujiangyan (1hr); Emei Shan (2hr 30min); Ganzi (2 days); Guanghan (1hr); Guangyuan (4hr); Huanglongxi (1hr); Jiangyou (2hr); Jiuzhaigou (12hr); Kangding (6–8hr); Kunming (24hr); Langzhong (4hr 30min); Leshan (2hr 30min); Maoxian (5hr); Siguniang Shan (8hr); Songpan (8hr); Wenchuan (3hr 30min); Wolong (4hr); Xichang (8hr); Xindu (30min); Yibin (8hr); Zigong (6hr); Zöigê (14hr).

Changning to: Chongqing (6hr); Chengdu (10hr); Luzhou (3hr); Yibin (2hr).

Chongqing to: Chengdu (6hr); Dazu (3hr); Hechuan (2hr); Langzhong (5hr); Yibin (3hr 30min); Zigong (1hr 30min).

Dazu to: Chengdu (4hr); Chongqing (3hr); Leshan (3hr); Yibin (4hr); Zigong (2hr).

Daocheng to: Litang (5hr); Sangdui (2hr); Xiangcheng (3hr); Zhongdian (12hr).

Dujiangyan to: Chengdu (1hr); Guanghan (1hr 30min); Qingcheng Shan (45min); Songpan (7hr); Wolong (3hr).

Emei Shan to: Chengdu (2hr 30min); Leshan (1hr); Xichang (8hr).

Ganzi to: Chengdu (2 days); Dêgê (8hr); Kangding (12hr); Luhuo (3hr); Xinlong (3hr).

Guangyuan to: Chengdu (4hr); Jiangyou (2hr 30min); Jianmenguan (1hr); Jiuzhaigou (8hr); Langzhong (4hr).

Jiangyou to: Chengdu (2hr); Doutuan Shan (1hr); Guangyuan (2hr 30min); Jianmenguan (1hr 30min); Jiuzhaigou (8hr).

Kangding to: Bamei (4hr); Batang (2 days); Chengdu (6–8hr); Danba (4hr); Daocheng (14hr); Daofu (9hr); Dêgê (2 days); Ganzi (12hr); Litang (9hr); Luhuo (9hr); Manigange (15hr); Tagong (3hr); Xichang (8hr).

Langzhong to: Chengdu (5hr); Chongqing (5hr); Guanyuan (4hr).

Leshan to: Chengdu (2hr 30min); Chongqing (5hr); Dazu (3hr); Emei (1hr); Xichang (8hr); Yibin (5hr); Zigong (2hr 30min).

Litang to: Batang (4hr); Daocheng (5hr); Kangding (9hr); Sangdui (3hr); Xiangcheng (5hr); Zhongdian (12hr).

Songpan to: Chengdu (8hr); Huanglong (2hr); Jiuzhaigou (4hr); Langmusi (6-8hr); Ma'erkang (10hr); Zöigê (4–6hr).

Xiangcheng to: Daocheng (3hr); Litang (5hr); Zhongdian (8hr).

Xichang to: Chengdu (8hr); Kangding (8hr); Kunming (24hr); Panzhihua (3hr); Puge (2hr).

Yibin to: Changning (1hr 30min); Chengdu (4hr); Chongqing (3hr 30min); Dazu (4hr); Gongxian (2hr 15min); Luzhou (3hr); Zigong (1hr 30min).

Zigong to: Chengdu (4hr); Chongqing (4hr); Dazu (2hr); Emei (3hr); Leshan (2hr 30min); Luzhou (5hr); Yibin (1hr 30min).

Ferries

Chongqing to: Wanxian (daily; 12hr); Yichang (daily; 13hr by hydrofoil, 48hr conventional ferry).

Flights

Besides the domestic flights listed, there are flights from Chengdu to Bangkok and Singapore.

Chengdu to: Beijing (11 daily; 2hr); Changsha (2 daily; 1hr 30min); Chongqing (2 weekly; 45min); Guangzhou (4 daily; 2hr); Guilin (1 daily; 1hr 20min); Guiyang (2 daily; 1hr); Hong Kong (3 daily; 2hr); Jiuzhai (5 daily; 45min); Kunming (3 daily; 90min); Lhasa (2 daily; 1hr 50min); Shanghai (5 daily; 2hr 15min); Shenzhen (3 daily; 1hr 25min); Wuhan (2 daily; 1hr 20min); Wulumuqi (2 daily; 3hr 30min).

Chongqing to: Beijing (9 daily; 2hr); Chengdu (8 daily; 45min); Guangzhou (10 daily; 90min); Guilin (3 daily; 55min); Hong Kong (5 daily; 1hr 50min); Kunming (8 daily; 1hr 10min); Shanghai (9 daily; 2hr); Xi'an (3 daily; 1hr).

Songpan (Jiuzhai airport) to: Chengdu (daily; 1hr).

CHAPTER 13 Highlights

* **The grasslands** Explore the rolling green horizons of Inner Mongolia's "grass sea" – such as those near Hohhot – and sleep in a Mongol yurt. See p.959
* **Manzhouli** Bustling Sino-Russian border town, littered with century-old architecture from the Trans-Siberian Railway's glory days. See p.964
* **Labrang Monastery** The most imposing Lamaist monastery outside of Tibet, set in a beautiful mountain valley. See p.998
* **Jiayuguan Fort** Stronghold at the western end of the Great Wall, symbolically marking the end of China proper. See p.1006
* **Mogao Caves** Huge collection of Buddhist grottoes and sculptures, carved into a desert gorge a millennium ago. See p.1012
* **Qinghai Hu** China's largest salt lake is a magnet for birdwatchers and waterfowl, including the rare black-necked crane. See p.1027
* **Turpan** Relax under grape trellises or investigate Muslim Uyghur culture and ancient Silk Road relics, such as the intriguing ruins of Jiaohe. See p.1037
* **Tian Chi** An alpine lake surrounded by meadows and snow-covered mountains, home to a Kazakh population. See p.1049
* **Kashgar's Sunday Markets** Join crowds haggling for goats, carpets, knives and spices in China's most westerly and wild city. See p.1070

▲ Jiayuguan fort

13

The Northwest

Reaching across in a giant arc from the fringes of eastern Siberia to the borders of Turkic Central Asia, the provinces of **Inner Mongolia**, **Ningxia**, **Gansu**, **Qinghai** and **Xinjiang** account for an entire third of China's land area. Compressing so vast a region into a single chapter of a guidebook may seem something of a travesty – but at least it is based on a perception that originates from China itself, that these territories lie largely beyond the Great Wall. To ancient Chinese thinking the whole region was remote, subject to extremes of weather and populated by non-Chinese-speaking "barbarians" who were, quite literally, the peoples from beyond the pale – *sai wai ren*. It is here, thinly scattered through the vast areas of steppe and grassland, desert and mountain plateau, that the bulk of China's **ethnic minorities** still live. Out of deference to these, Inner Mongolia, Ningxia and Xinjiang are officially not provinces at all, but so-called **autonomous regions**, for the Mongol, Hui and Uyghur peoples respectively.

However, a **Chinese presence** in the area is not new. Imperial armies were already in control of virtually the whole northwest region by the time of the Han dynasty two thousand years ago, and since then Gansu, Ningxia and the eastern part of Qinghai have become Chinese almost to the core. The uncultivatable plains of Inner Mongolia have been intimately bound up with China since Genghis Khan created his great empire in the early thirteenth century, and even Xinjiang has always found itself drawn back into the Chinese sphere after repeatedly breaking free.

Today the relatively unrestricted use of **local languages and religions** in these areas could be taken as a sign of China's desire to **nurture patriotism** in the minority peoples, and regain some of the sympathy lost during disastrous repressions both under communism and in previous eras. Furthermore, in economic terms, there is a clear transfer of wealth, in the form of industrial and agricultural aid, from the richer areas of eastern China to the poorer, outer fringes of the country. On the other hand, the degree of actual autonomy in the "autonomous" regions is strictly controlled, and relations between Han China and these more remote corners of the Republic remain fractious in places.

Organized tourism across the Northwest has boomed in recent years, focusing particularly on the **Silk Road**, a series of historic towns and ruins running from Xi'an in Shaanxi province, through Ningxia, Gansu and Xinjiang, and eventually on into Central Asia. The Northwest also offers possibilities for enjoying the last great remaining **wildernesses** of China – the grasslands, mountains, lakes and deserts of the interior – far from the teeming population centres of the east. For this, there is perhaps no better place to start than **Inner Mongolia**'s famous **grasslands**, on which Genghis Khan trained his cavalry and

where nomads on horseback still live today. As well as visiting the supposed **tomb of Genghis Khan**, outside Dongsheng, it's also possible, in places, to catch a glimpse of the Mongols' ancient and unique way of life, packaged for tourists to a greater or lesser degree depending on how far off the beaten track you are willing to travel. You can sleep in a nomad's yurt, sample Mongol food and ride a horse across the grasslands, all within half a day's train journey from Beijing.

The other great natural feature of Inner Mongolia is the **Yellow River**, which detours north into the region from tiny, rural **Ningxia**. Here, at the resorts of **Shapotou** and **Sha Hu** you can witness mighty waters running between desert sand dunes. Rarely visited by foreign tourists, Ningxia also offers quiet, attractive cities and a variety of scenery ranging from terraced, abundantly fertile hillsides in the south to pure desert in the north. The train journey from Inner Mongolia to Ningxia's capital, **Yinchuan**, provides a fascinating tableau of industrial decay and human struggle in the face of creeping market exposure.

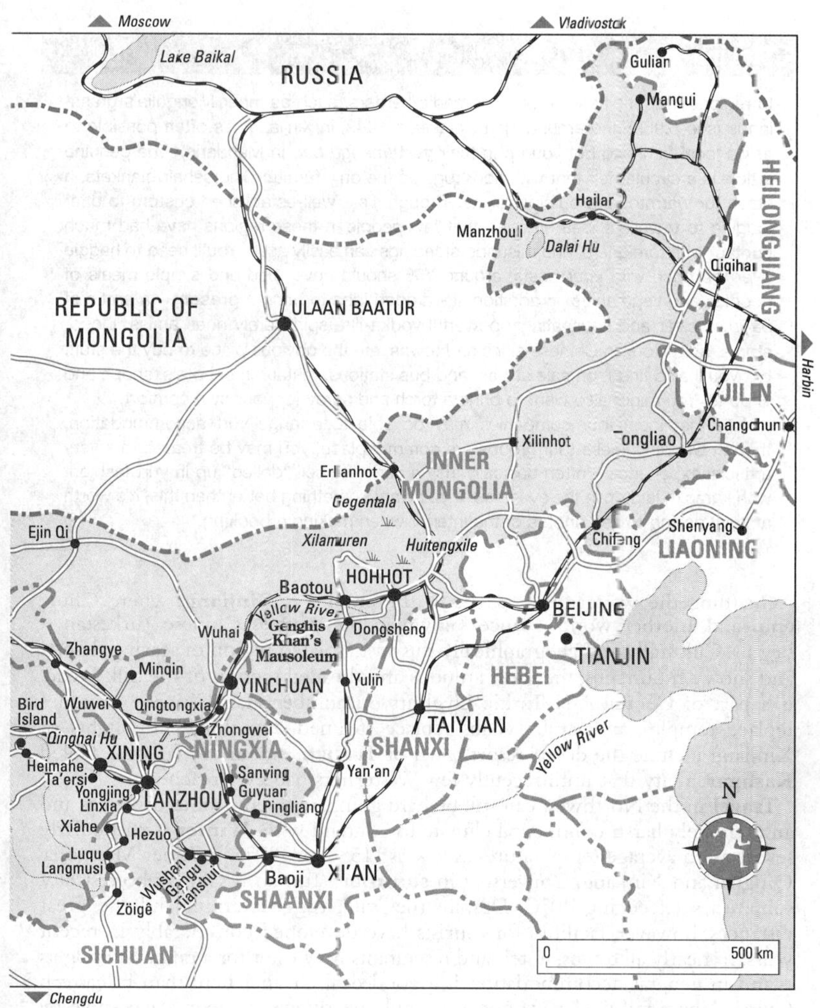

Extending west from Ningxia is **Gansu**, the historic periphery of ancient China. This rugged terrain of high peaks and desert is spliced from east to west by the **Hexi Corridor**, historically the only road from China to the West, and still marked along its length by the Great Wall – terminating magnificently at the fortress of **Jiayuguan** – and a string of Silk Road towns culminating in **Dunhuang**, with its fabulous Buddhist cave art.

The Kunlun Mountains rise to the south of the Hexi Corridor and continue beyond to the high-altitude plateau stretching all the way to India. The ancient borderland between Tibet and China proper is **Qinghai**, perhaps the least-explored province in the whole of the Northwest, which offers monasteries, mountains, the colossal lake of **Qinghai Hu** and, above all, **routes to Tibet** across one of the highest mountain ranges in the world. Originating in this province, too, are the Yellow and Yangzi rivers, the main transport arteries of China throughout recorded history.

Staying in a yurt

In regions that still harbour semi-nomadic herders, such as Inner Mongolia's grasslands (see p.959) and around Tian Chi (see p.1049) in Xinjiang, it's often possible to ask a local family to put you up in their **yurt** (*mengu bao* in Mandarin). The genuine article is a circular felt tent with floor rugs as the only furniture, horsehair blankets, a stove for warmth, and outside toilets. Though it's a well-established custom to offer lodging to travellers, bear in mind that few people in these regions have had much contact with foreigners, and misunderstandings can easily arise. You'll need to haggle over the price with your hosts; around ¥55 should cover bed and simple meals of noodles and vegetables. In addition, it's a good idea to bring a **present** – a bottle of *baijiu*, a clear and nauseatingly powerful vodka-like spirit rarely goes amiss. Liquor stores, ubiquitous in Chinese cities and towns, are the obvious place to buy the stuff, but you'll also find it on sale at train and bus stations, restaurants, hotels, shops and airports. You might also want to bring a torch and spray for your own comfort.

Note that local tour companies may be able to arrange yurt accommodation, though where Chinese tour groups are commonplace, you may be treated to a very artificial experience – often basically jusy a concrete cell "dolled" up in yurt fashion, with karaoke laid on in the evenings. If you want something better than this, it's worth at least asking to see photos of the interior when making a booking.

Guarding the westernmost passes of the empire is **Xinjiang**, where China ends and another world – once known in the West as Chinese Turkestan – begins. Culturally and geographically this vast, isolated region of searing deserts and snowy mountains, the most arduous and dreaded section of the Silk Road, is a part of Central Asia. Turkic Uyghurs outnumber Han Chinese, mosques replace temples, and lamb kebabs replace steamed dumplings. Highlights of Xinjiang include the desert resort town of **Turpan** and, in the far west, fabled **Kashgar**, a city that until recently few Westerners had ever reached.

Travel in the Northwest can still be hard going, with enormous distances and an extremely harsh continental climate to contend with. **Winter** is particularly severe, with average temperatures as low as -15°C or -30°C in Inner Mongolia, Qinghai and Xinjiang. Conversely, in **summer**, Turpan is China's hottest city, sometimes exceeding 40°C. Despite the wild, rugged terrain and the great distances, however, facilities for tourists have developed considerably in recent years. In nearly all towns, hotels and restaurants now cater for a range of budgets – and in general, accommodation is a good deal cheaper here than in eastern China. Where rail lines have not been built, nearly everywhere is accessible by bus, and more and more towns by plane as well. Finally there is the possibility of **onward travel** to or from China's Asian neighbours – the Republic of Mongolia, Kazakhstan, Kyrgyzstan and Pakistan can all be reached by road or rail from the provinces covered in this chapter.

Inner Mongolia

Mongolia is an almost total mystery to the outside world, its very name being synonymous with remoteness. For hundreds of years, landlocked between the two Asian giants Russia and China, it seems to have been doomed to eternal obscurity, trapped in a hopeless physical environment of fleeting summers and interminable, bitter winters. And yet, seven hundred years ago the people of this benighted land suddenly burst out of their frontiers and for a century subjugated and terrorized almost all of the Eurasian landmass.

Visitors to the **autonomous region of Inner Mongolia** will not necessarily find many signs of this today. The modern-day heirs of the Mongol hordes are not only placid – quietly going about their business of shepherding, herding horses and entertaining tourists – but, even in their own autonomous region, are vastly outnumbered by the Han Chinese (by seventeen million to two million). In addition, this is, and always has been, a sensitive border area, and there are still restrictions on the movements of tourists in some places, despite the demise of the Soviet Union.

Nevertheless, there are still traces of the "real" Mongolia out there, in terms of both landscape and people. Dotting the region are enormous areas of **grassland**, gently undulating plains stretching to the horizon and still used by nomadic peoples as pastureland for their horses. Tourists are able to visit the grasslands and even stay with the Mongols in their yurts, though the only simple way to do this is by **organized tour** out of the regional capital **Hohhot** – an experience rather short on authenticity. If you don't find what you are looking for in the Hohhot area, however, don't forget that there is a whole vast swath of Mongolia stretching up through northeastern China that remains virtually untouched by Western tourists, and here, especially in the areas around **Xilinhot** and **Hailar**, determined independent travellers can manage to glimpse something of the grasslands and their Mongol inhabitants. Finally, Inner Mongolia offers overland connections with China's two northern neighbours, the Republic of Mongolia (Outer Mongolia) and Russia, through the border towns of **Erlianhot** and **Manzhouli** respectively.

Some history

Genghis Khan (1162–1227) was born, ominously enough, with a clot of blood in his hand. Under his leadership, the Mongols erupted from their homeland to ravage the whole of Asia, butchering millions, razing cities and laying waste all the land from China to eastern Europe. It was his proud boast that his destruction of cities was so complete that he could ride across their ruins by night without the least fear of his horse stumbling.

Before Genghis exploded onto the scene, the nomadic Mongols had long been a thorn in the side of the city-dwelling Chinese. Construction of the **Great Wall** had been undertaken to keep these two fundamentally opposed societies apart. But it was always fortunate for the Chinese that the early nomadic tribes of Mongolia fought as much among themselves as they did against outsiders. Genghis Khan's achievement was to weld together the warring nomads into a fighting force the equal of which the world had never seen. Becoming Khan of Khans in 1206, he also introduced the Yasak, the first **code of laws** the Mongols had known. Few details of its draconian tenets survive today (though it was inscribed on iron tablets at Genghis' death), but Tamerlane, at Samarkand, and Baber the Great Mogul in India, were both later to use it as the basis for their authority.

The secret of Genghis Khan's success was skilful **cavalry tactics**, acquired from long practice in the saddle on the wide-open Mongolian plains. Frequently his armies would rout forces ten or twenty times their size. Each of his warriors would have light equipment and three or four horses. Food was taken from the surrounding country, the troops slept in the open, meat was

The Silk Road

The passes of Khunjerab and Torugut, linking China with western Asia – and ultimately with the whole of the Western world – have only in recent years reopened to a gradually increasing flow of cross-border traffic, mostly small-time traders. Yet a thousand years ago these were on crucial, well-trodden and incredibly long trade routes between eastern China and the Mediterranean. Starting from Chang'an (Xi'an), the **Silk Road** curved northwest through Gansu to the Yumen Pass, where it split. Leaving the protection of the Great Wall, travellers could follow one of two routes across the deserts of Lop Nor and Taklamakan, braving attacks from marauding bandits, to Kashgar. The **southern route** ran through Dunhuang, Lop Nor, Miran, Niya, Khotan and Yarkand; the **northern route** through Hami, Turpan, Kuqa and Aqsu. High in the Pamirs beyond Kashgar, the merchants traded their goods with the middlemen who carried them beyond the frontiers of China, either south to Kashmir, Bactria, Afghanistan and India, or north to Ferghana, Tashkent and Samarkand. Then, laden with Western goods, the Chinese merchants would turn back down the mountains for the three-thousand-kilometre journey home. **Oases** along the route inevitably prospered as staging posts and watering holes, becoming important and wealthy cities in their own right, with their own garrisons to protect the caravans. When Chinese domination periodically declined, many of these cities turned themselves into self-sufficient city-states, or **khanates**. Today, many of these once powerful cities lie buried In the sands.

The foundations for this famous **road to the West**, which was to become one of the most important arteries of **trade and culture** in world history, were laid over two millennia ago. In the second century BC nothing was known in China of the existence of people and lands beyond its borders, except by rumour. In 139 BC, the imperial court at Chang'an decided to despatch an emissary, a man called Zhang Qiang, to investigate the world to the west and to seek possible allies in the constant struggle against nomadic marauders from the north. Zhang set out with a party of a hundred men; thirteen years later he returned, with only two other members of his original expedition – and no alliances. But the news he brought nevertheless set Emperor Wu Di and his court aflame, including tales of Central Asia, Persia and even the Mediterranean world. Further **expeditions** were soon despatched, initially to purchase horses for military purposes, and from these beginnings trade soon developed.

By 100 BC a dozen immense caravans a year were heading into the desert. From the West came cucumbers, figs, chives, sesame, walnuts, grapes (and wine-making), wool, linen and ivory; from China, jade, porcelain, oranges, peaches, roses, chrysanthemums, cast iron, gunpowder, the crossbow, paper and printing, and **silk**. The silkworm had already been domesticated in China for hundreds of years, but in

cooked by being placed under the saddle; and when the going got tough they would slit a vein in the horse's neck and drink the blood while still on the move. There was no supply problem, no camp followers, no excess baggage, and no thought of administrative control – which would eventually contribute to the fall of the empire.

The onslaught that the Mongols unleashed on China in 1211 was on a massive scale. The Great Wall proved no obstacle to Genghis Khan, and with his two hundred thousand men he cut a swath across northwest China towards Beijing. It was not all easy progress, however – so great was the destruction wrought in northern China that **famine and plague** broke out, afflicting the invader as much as the invaded. Genghis Khan himself died (of injuries sustained in falling from his horse) before the **capture of Beijing** had been completed. His body was carried back to Mongolia by a funeral cortege of ten thousand, the West the means by which silk was manufactured remained a total mystery – people believed it was combed from the leaves of trees. The Chinese took great pains to protect their monopoly, punishing any attempt to export silkworms with death. It was only many centuries later that sericulture finally began to spread west, when silkworm larvae were smuggled out of China in hollow walking sticks by Nestorian monks. The first time the **Romans** saw silk, snaking in the wind as the banners of their Parthian enemies, it filled them with terror and resulted in a humiliating rout. They determined to acquire it for themselves, and soon Roman society became obsessed with the fabric that by the first century AD was coming west in such large quantities that the corresponding outflow of gold had begun to threaten the stability of the Roman economy.

As well as goods, the Silk Road carried new ideas in **art and religion**. Nestorian Christianity and Manichaeism trickled east across the mountains, but by far the most influential force was **Buddhism**. The first Buddhist missionaries appeared during the first century AD, crossing the High Pamirs from India, and their creed gained rapid acceptance among the nomads and oasis dwellers of what is now western China. By the fourth century, Buddhism had become the official religion of much of northern China, and by the eighth it was accepted throughout the empire. All along the road, monasteries, chapels, stupas and grottoes proliferated, often sponsored by wealthy traders. The remains of this early flowering of **Buddhist art** along the road are among the great attractions of the Northwest for modern-day travellers. Naturally, history has taken its toll – zealous Muslims, Western archeologists, Red Guards and the forces of nature have all played a destructive part – but some sites have survived intact, above all the cave art at **Mogao** outside Dunhuang.

The Silk Road continued to flourish for centuries, reaching its zenith under the Tang dynasty (618–907 AD) and bringing immense wealth to the Chinese nobility and merchants. But it remained a slow, dangerous and expensive route. Predatory tribes to the north and south harried the caravans despite garrisons and military escorts. Occasionally entire regions broke free of Chinese control, requiring years to be "re-pacified". The route was physically arduous, too, taking at least five months from Chang'an to Kashgar, and whole caravans could be lost in the deserts or in the high mountain passes.

There was a brief final flowering of trade in the thirteenth century, to which **Marco Polo** famously bore witness, when the whole Silk Road came temporarily under Mongol rule. But with the arrival of sericulture in Europe and the opening of sea routes between China and the West, the Silk Road had had its day. The road and its cities were slowly abandoned to the wind and the blowing sands.

who murdered every man and beast within ten miles of the road so that news of the Great Khan's death could not be reported before his sons and viceroys had been gathered from the farthest corners of his dominions. The whereabouts of his **tomb** is uncertain, though according to one of the best-known stories his ashes are in a mausoleum near Dongsheng (see p.969), south of Baotou.

In the years after Genghis Khan's death, the fate of both China and of distant Europe teetered together on the brink. Having conquered all of Russia, the Mongol forces were poised in 1241 to make the relatively short final push across Europe to the Atlantic, when a message came from deep inside Asia that the invasion was to be cancelled. The decision to spare Western Europe cleared the way for the **final conquest of China** instead, and by 1271 the Mongols had established their own dynasty – the **Yuan**. It was the first time the Chinese had come under foreign rule. The Yuan is still an era about which Chinese historians can find little good to say, though the boundaries of the empire were expanded considerably, to include Yunnan and Tibet for the first time. The magnificent zenith of the dynasty was achieved under **Kublai Khan**, as documented in Marco Polo's *Travels* (see box, below). Ironically, however, the Mongols were able to sustain their power only by becoming thoroughly Chinese, and abandoning the traditional nomadic Mongol way of life. Kublai Khan and his court soon forgot the warrior skills of their forefathers, and in 1368, less than a hundred years later, the Yuan, a shadow of their former selves, were **driven out of China** by the Ming. The Mongols returned to Mongolia, and reverted to their former ways, hunting, fighting among themselves and occasionally skirmishing with the Chinese down by the Wall. Astonishingly, history had come full circle.

Thereafter, Mongolian history moves gradually downhill, though right into the eighteenth century they maintained at least nominal control over many of

Kublai Khan

In Xanadu did Kubla Khan
A stately pleasure dome decree ...

Immortalized not only in the poetry of Samuel Coleridge but also in the memoirs of Marco Polo, **Kublai Khan** (1215–94) – known to the Chinese as Yuan Shizu – is the only emperor popularly known by name to the outside world. And little wonder: as well as mastering the subtle statecraft required to govern China as a foreigner, this grandson of Genghis Khan commanded an **empire** that encompassed the whole of China, Central Asia, southern Russia and Persia – a larger area of land than perhaps anyone in history has ruled over, before or since. And yet this king of kings had been born into a nomadic tribe which had never shown the slightest interest in political life, and which, until shortly before his birth, was almost entirely illiterate.

From the beginning, Kublai Khan had shown an unusual talent for politics and government. He managed to get himself elected **Khan of the Mongols** in 1260, after the death of his brother, despite considerable opposition from the so-called "steppe aristocracy" who feared his disdain for traditional Mongolian skills. He never learned to read or write Chinese, yet after audaciously establishing himself as **Emperor of China**, proclaiming the Yuan dynasty in 1271, he soon saw the value of surrounding himself with advisers steeped in Confucianism. This was what enabled him to set up one hundred thousand Mongols in power over perhaps two hundred million Chinese. As well as **reunifying China** after centuries of division under the Song, Kublai Khan's contributions include establishing **paper money** as the standard medium of exchange, and fostering the **development of religion**, Lamaist Buddhism in particular. Above all, under his rule China experienced a brief – and uncharacteristic – period of **cosmopolitanism** which saw not only foreigners such as Marco Polo promoted to high positions of responsibility, but also a final flowering of the old Silk Road trade, as well as large numbers of Arab and Persian traders settling in seaports around Quanzhou in southeastern China.

Ironically, however, it was his admiration for the culture, arts, religion and sophisticated bureaucracy of China – as documented so enthusiastically by Marco Polo – that aroused bitter hostility from his own people, the Mongols, who despised what they saw as a betrayal of the ways of Genghis Khan. Kublai Khan was troubled by skirmishing nomads along the Great Wall just as much as his more authentically Chinese predecessors, forcing the abandonment of **Xanadu** – in Inner Mongolia, near the modern city of Duolun – his legendary summer residence immortalized by Samuel Taylor Coleridge in his epic poem *The Ballard of Kublai Khan*. Today virtually nothing of the site remains.

the lands to the south and west originally won by Genghis Khan. These included **Tibet**, from where **Lamaist Buddhism** was imported to become the dominant religion in Mongolia. The few Tibetan-style monasteries in Mongolia that survive bear important testimony to this. Over the years, as well, came **settlers** from other parts of Asia: there is now a sizeable Muslim minority in the region, and under the Qing many Chinese settlers moved to Inner Mongolia, escaping overpopulation and famine at home, a trend that has continued under the Communists. The incoming settlers tried ploughing up the grassland with disastrous ecological results – wind and water swept the soil away – and the Mongols withdrew to the hills. Only recently has a serious programme of land stabilization and reclamation been established.

Sandwiched between two imperial powers, Mongolia found its independence constantly threatened. The Russians set up a protectorate over the north, while the rest came effectively under the control of China. In the 1930s, Japan occupied much of eastern Inner Mongolia as part of Manchuguo, and the Chinese Communists also maintained a strong presence. In 1945 Stalin persuaded Chiang Kaishek to recognize the independence of **Outer Mongolia** under Soviet protection as part of the Sino–Soviet anti-Japanese treaty, effectively sealing the fate of what then became the Mongolian People's Republic. In 1947, **Inner Mongolia** was designated the first autonomous region of the People's Republic of China.

Hohhot and around

There has been a settlement at **HOHHOT** (known to the Chinese as Huhehaote, or more commonly Hushi) since the time of the Ming dynasty four hundred years ago, though it did not become the capital of Inner Mongolia until 1952. Until relatively modern times, it was a small town centred on a number of **Buddhist temples**. The temples are still here, and although it's now a major city, Hohhot manages to be an interesting blend of the old and the new, and a relatively green and leafy place in summer – which is fitting, as the town's Mongolian name means "green city". As well as the shiny new banks and department stores downtown, there's an extensive area in the south of the town with old, narrow streets built of black bricks and heavy roof tiles. These days Hohhot is largely a Han city, though there is also a Hui and a Mongol presence; it's worthwhile tracking down the vanishing **Mongol** areas, not least to try some of their distinctive **food**. The other reason for visiting Hohhot is its proximity to some of the famous Mongolian **grasslands** within a hundred-kilometre radius of the city.

Arrival and accommodation

Hohhot is a fairly easy place to navigate. The heart of the modern commercial city, including most hotels, lies in the blocks to the south of the **train and bus stations**, while the old city and its flamboyant temples – in a seemingly permanent state of renovation – are southwest of the central Qingcheng Park. Hohhot's Baita **airport** lies 35km east of the city, and the airport bus (30min; ¥5) drops arriving passengers at the CAAC office on Xilin Guole Lu, the road running south from the bus station. A taxi will cost ¥20.

In summer, travellers arriving by train, in particular, are often subjected to furious and persistent harassment by travel agents' touts trying to sell them grassland tours. The only practical way to escape the melee is to get into a **taxi** – the minimum fare is ¥6, sufficient for most rides within the city.

Hohhot and around

Hohhot	呼和浩特	*hūhé hàotè*
Dazhao	大召	*dàzhào*
Great Mosque	清真大寺	*qīngzhēn dàsì*
Horse Racing Course	赛马场	*sàimǎ chǎng*
Inner Mongolia Museum	内蒙古博物馆	*nèiménggǔ bówùguǎn*
Jiangjun Yashu	将军衙署	*jiāngjūn yáshǔ*
Manduhai Park	满都海公园	*mǎndūhǎi gōngyuán*
Mongolian Consulate	蒙古共和国领事馆	*ménggǔ gònghéguó lǐngshìguǎn*
Nationalities Market	民族商场	*mínzú shāngchǎng*
Qingcheng Park	青城公园	*qīngchéng gōngyuán*
Wuta Si	五塔寺	*wǔtǎ sì*
Xilituzhao	席里图召	*xílǐtú zhào*
Xinhua Square	新华广场	*xīnhuá guǎngchǎng*
Accommodation		
Boyou Hotel	博友宾馆	*bóyǒu bīnguǎn*
Inner Mongolia Hotel	内蒙古饭店	*nèi ménggǔ fàndiàn*
Jia Xin Binguan	家馨宾馆	*jiāxīn bīnguǎn*
Railway Hotel	铁路宾馆	*tiělù bīnguǎn*
Shiyou Guesthouse	内蒙古石油招待所	*nèi ménggǔ shíyóu zhāodàisuǒ*
Zhaojun Hotel	昭君大酒店	*zhāojūn dàjiǔdiàn*
Eating		
A Le Kao Ba	阿乐烤吧	*ā lè kǎo bā*
Daxue Lu Market	大学路商场	*dàxuélù shāngchǎng*
Margaux Manor	玛歌庄园	*mǎgē zhuāng yuán*
Mr Li's Beef Noodles	美国加洲牛肉面大王	*měiguó jiāzhōu niúròumiàn dàwáng*
UBC Coffee	台湾牛肉面	*táiwān niúròumiàn*
Malaqin	马拉沁饭店	*mǎlāqìn fàndiàn*
Around Hohhot		
Bai Ta	百塔	*bǎi tǎ*
Erlianhot	二连浩特	*èrlián hàotè*
Gegentala	格根塔拉草原	*gégēntǎlā cǎoyuán*
Huitengxile	辉腾锡勒草原	*huīténgxīlè cǎoyuán*
Tomb of Wang Zhaojun	昭君墓	*zhāojūn mù*
Ulaan Baatur	乌兰巴托	*wūlán bātuō*
Wusutu Zhao	乌素图召	*wūsùtú zhào*
Xilamuren	希拉穆仁草原	*xīlāmùrén cǎoyuán*
Yurt	蒙古包	*ménggǔ bāo*
Zhaohe	召河	*zhàohé*

Accommodation

Hohhot's **accommodation scene** is changing rapidly, and as the old favourites by the train station fall prey to the wrecking ball demand is being met by more modern and central establishments.

Boyou Hotel 126 Xilin Guole Lu ⓣ0471/6293222. Just 300m south of the train station, this new venture is well looked after by staff who are happy to help. The doubles with shared bathroom are excellent value at ¥68, while standard doubles are still keen at ¥120. ❷

Inner Mongolia Hotel Wulunchabu Xi Lu ⓣ0471/6938888, ⓦwww.nmghotel.com. In the east of the city near the museum, this is a pretty plush affair, patronized by government and business types. The rear block provides cheaper accommodation with full use of hotel facilities

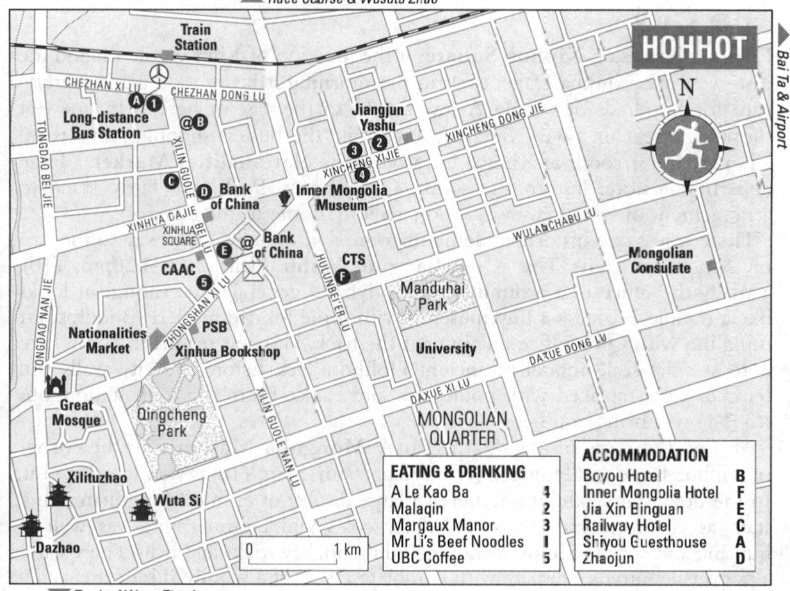

and a cracking view of a car park full of concrete yurts. 3–8

Jia Xin Binguan Malan Qiate Xi Jie ☎0471/6287766. Compact and bijou, this clean and nicely decorated family-run hotel has a good location and discounts to match. 3

Railway Hotel 131 Xilin Guole Lu ☎0471/6933377. Budget hotel with welcoming staff and clean facilities, far enough south of the train station to escape the attention of touts. They are also happy to book train tickets for guests. 3

Shiyou Guesthouse 14 Chezhan Xi Lu ☎0471/6962330. Cheap and near the train station, this guesthouse offers more than adequate facilities for budget travellers and has about the only dorm beds (¥20) in the city that you are going to brave. 2

Zhaojun 69 Xinhua Dajie ☎0471/6668888, www.zhaojunhotel.com.cn. A well-organized and comfortable place in the centre of town, diagonally across from Xinhua Square. The travel service in the lobby has information in English on their grassland and Genghis Khan Mausoleum tours. 6

Moving on from Hohhot

There are daily trains to the Mongolian border town of **Erlianhot** (see p.959), posted "Erlian" on schedules. Train #4602/3 departs Hohhot at 10.30pm, arriving at 7.18am the next day. Alternatively, train #5712/13 leaves Hohhot at 8.10am, pulling in at 7.32pm after rolling through the grasslands. Note that this view of the pastures will be far more relaxing, quiet and comfortable than joining one of many group tours.

To **Baotou**, buses run every ten minutes from 7am (1hr 30min; ¥30) from the long-distance bus station next to the train station. There are also buses every thirty minutes from 6.30am to 6.30pm to **Dongsheng** (3hr; ¥55) where there are no shortage of buses and tours to Genghis Khan's Mausoleum (see p.969).

Hohhot is linked by **train** to **Lanzhou** to the west, **Beijing** to the east and **Hailar** (a 38hr journey via Beijing) to the northeast. There are also trains to **Ulaan Baatur** in the Republic of Mongolia (see p.1077). Leaving Hohhot by train, you can seek the help of a travel agent to procure tickets for a small commission. You'll need to give them at least 36 hours' notice for a hard sleeper – or try your luck at the station ticket office, which is often hideously crowded with migrant workers.

The City

Hohhot focuses on **Xinhua Square**, at the junction of Xilin Guole Lu and the east–west axis Xinhua Dajie; early in the morning it becomes a giant exercise yard for hundreds of people. A few blocks to the east of here is the newest shopping street in town, Xincheng Lu, while the busiest shopping area is on Zhongshan Lu, south of Xinhua Lu, around the **Nationalities Market**, a huge department store. Just to the south, **Qingcheng Park** is a fairly standard arrangement of lakes, causeways and pavilions, home to the city zoo.

There is just one historic building marooned in the new city, away to the east on Xincheng Xi Jie. This is the **Jiangjun Yashu** (daily 8am–4.30pm; ¥10), actually the office of a prominent Qing-dynasty general, even though it looks like a temple. Now it's a tiny museum with some bizarre modern Buddhist art mingling with Qing office furniture at the back. The best reason to come here is to see the scale model of ancient Hohhot, back before the city walls and temples were replaced with boulevards and banks. From the train station, bus #3 (¥1) will bring you here.

Also on the route of bus #3, the **Inner Mongolia Museum** on the corner of Xinhua Dajie and Hulunbei'er Lu (daily 9am–5pm; ¥10) is well worth a visit. In the downstairs exhibition, there's a large display of ethnic Mongolian items, such as costumes, saddles, long leather coats and cummerbunds, as well as hunting and sporting implements, including hockey sticks and balls. There's also a good paleontology display, with complete fossils of a woolly rhinoceros and a sizeable dinosaur. Upstairs are interesting maps and objects detailing the exploits of Genghis Khan, and the huge Mongol empire of the thirteenth century. While there are some English explanations, if you're truly keen on grasping the significance of the display, check in at the main office behind the ticket desk, where the curator speaks English and may be willing to give you a tour. Be warned, the museum often closes for the first 20 days of April for work on exhibits.

A couple of kilometres north of the train station, and served by #13 bus from the centre of town, is the gigantic **Inner Mongolia horse racecourse**, the biggest in China, built in the shape of two circular Mongolian yurts, adjacent and connected to each other to form the elongated shape of a stadium. It's put to frenzied use during **Naadam**, the summer Mongolian festival that combines horsemanship with wrestling and other games. The dates vary, but Naadam usually falls between late July and early August. Outside the holiday, displays of Mongolian riding and dancing sometimes take place here. It's worth stopping by during the day to see what's scheduled, or try enquiring at hotels and travel agents.

Old Hohhot

Most of the historic buildings of Hohhot are crowded into the interesting – though fast-disappearing – old southwestern part of the city, where you can enjoyably spend half a day simply ambling around. From the train station, buses #6, #7 and #8 run here – get off at the Hui Middle School stop. You'll immediately see the Chinese-style minaret (topped with a pagoda roof) of the **Great Mosque**. This attractive black-brick building, situated at the southern end of Zhongshan Lu, blends traces of Chinese and Arabic style. Some of the Hui people who worship here are extremely friendly, and will probably be delighted if you ask to look round the mosque. The surrounding streets comprise the Muslim area of town, and besides a lot of old men with wispy beards and skullcaps, you'll find a good, if dwindling, array of noodle and kebab shops in the immediate area.

Walking south from the mosque for about fifteen minutes along the main road leads you to a couple of Buddhist temples. The biggest of these is the **Dazhao**, down a side street west of the main road (daily 8am–5.30pm; ¥30). Constructed in 1579, and recently the subject of a typically gaudy renovation, the structure was dedicated in the late seventeenth century to the famous Qing emperor Kangxi – a gold tablet with the words "Long Live the Emperor" was set before the silver statue of Sakyamuni, and in the main hall murals depicting the visit of the Emperor Kangxi can still be seen.

Just a few minutes from the Dazhao, over on the other side of the main road, is **Xilituzhao** (daily 8am–5.30pm; ¥10), another temple of similar scale and layout to the Dazhao, and dating from the same era, though it too has been restored since the destruction of the Cultural Revolution. The dagoba is interesting for featuring Sanskrit writing above Chinese dragons above Tibetan-style murals. Since 1735 this has been the official residence of the reincarnation of the Living Buddha, who is in charge of Buddhist affairs in the city.

Farther east, across what used to be the alleyways of the old city you'll come to Hohhot's most attractive piece of architecture, known as the **Wuta Si** (Five Towers Temple; daily 8am–5.30pm; ¥35). Built in 1727, in Indian style, this composite of five pagodas originally belonged to the Ci Deng Temple, which no longer exists. It's relatively small, but its walls are engraved with no fewer than 1563 Buddhas, all in slightly different postures. Currently stored inside the pagoda building is a rare, antique Mongolian cosmological map that marks the position of hundreds of stars.

Eating and drinking

The highlight of eating in Hohhot is dining on **Mongolian food**. Mongolian **hotpot**, or *shuan yangrou*, is best shared with friends and beer. It's a do-it-yourself meal: piles of thinly sliced mutton, ordered by the *jin*, are cooked by being dropped into a cauldron of boiling water at the table, then quickly removed and dipped into a spicy sesame sauce. Tofu, glass noodles, cabbage and mushrooms will often go into the pot too. Many restaurants in Hohhot serve *shuan yangrou* – the most famous being ★ *Malaqin Restaurant* on Xincheng Xi Jie, a few blocks east of Hulunbei'er Lu. Dinner with plenty of beer shouldn't cost more than ¥40 per head.

For an even more exotic meal, however, with the focus on Mongolian dairy products, head for the Mongolian quarter in the southeast of town. Bus #4 comes down here – get off at Daxue Xi Jie just south of the university. During term time, this area is packed with students eating and shopping; their increased spending power has seen many of the old eating places morph into clothing boutiques, but any restaurant with Mongolian letters above the door is worth trying. For an excellent breakfast or lunch, order a large bowl of sugary milk tea, and *chaomi* (buckwheat), *huangyou* (butter), *nailao* (hard white cheese), and *naipi* (a sweetish, biscuit-like substance formed from the skin of boiled milk). Toss everything into the tea, and eat it with chopsticks – it's surprisingly delicious. To make this into a substantial meal, eat it with *mengu baozi* or *jianbing* – dough stuffed with ground mutton, respectively steamed or fried.

Though many of the old favourite eating places near the train station have been or are about to be demolished, there's still a *Mr Li's Beef Noodle* branch on Chezhan Lu that serves up reasonable noodle staples. Over near Jiangjun Yashu you'll find *Margaux Manor*, where you can get an almost decent coffee and steak for upwards of ¥60. For more coffee, and Western-style food with Chinese accents, there's a *UBC Coffee* at the junction of Zhongshan Lu and Xilin Guole Lu. You can also have a lively **Korean BBQ** experience at *A Le Kao Ba*, opposite *Margaux Manor*, for around ¥30 per head, including beer, for a party of four. Finally, Zhongshan Xi Lu has two *McDonalds* and one *KFC*, where, at the very least you can get half-decent, cheap coffee.

Listings

Airlines CAAC, Xilinguole Lu, just south of Xinhua Square (Mon–Sat 8am–9pm; ⓣ0471/6963160).
Banks and exchange The easiest place to change money and traveller's cheques, is at the *Zhaojun Hotel*, which offers the same rates as the bank without the queuing and form filling. The head office of the Bank of China (daily 8am–5.30pm), across the road from the hotel, is equipped with ATMs, as is the branch opposite the post office at 19 Zhongshan Xi Lu.
Bookshops The Foreign Language Bookstore on Xilin Guole Lu, across the road from Xinhua Square has a poor selection of works in English.
Consulate The Consulate of the Republic of Mongolia is in the east of the city (Mon, Tues & Thurs 8.30am–noon; ⓣ0471/4303254), at 5 Wulanzaigu. Visas are fairly easy to obtain, though they cost ¥500 for a month and may take some time to be issued. US citizens do not need visas for stays up to thirty days.
Internet access The Green Net Café (9am–7pm) on the fourth floor of the tech goods centre on the corner of Zhongshan Xi Lu and Yingbin Xi Lu (opposite the post office) is about the only viable option, charging ¥3 an hour. Alternatively the *Zhaojun* offers access in its business centre at an extortionate ¥33 an hour.
Mail and telephones The main post office (daily 8am–6pm) is on the northeastern corner of the train staion square, and offers Western Union money transfer services should you find yourself in dire straits. There's another on the south side of Zhongshan Lu, just east of Xilin Guole Lu (Mon–Sat 8am–7pm). The Telecom Centre is adjacent (daily 8am–6pm), with a small 24hr office.
PSB In the government building to the south of the junction between Zhongshan Lu and Xilin Guole Lu.
Travel agents There are numerous travel agents in town, many of whom will find you before you find them. They nearly all have English-speaking employees, and deal in grassland tours as well as booking train tickets. CTS, on the third floor of a building behind the *Inner Mongolia Hotel* (ⓣ0471/6203448), has some pleasant, approachable staff. Or try the helpful desk in the lobby of the *Zhaojun Hotel*.

Around Hohhot

There are a few more sights scattered around the outer suburbs of Hohhot, some of which can be reached on city buses. The **Tomb of Wang Zhaojun** (daily 9am–5pm; ¥18) about 8km to the south of Hohhot, is the burial site of a Tang-dynasty princess sent from what is today Hubei to cement Han–Mongol relations by marrying the king of Mongolia. It isn't spectacular – a huge mound raised from the plain and planted with gardens, in the centre of which is a modern pavilion – but the romantic story it recalls has important implications for modern Chinese politics, signifying the harmonious marrying of the Han with the minority peoples. In the rose garden, among pergolas festooned with gourds, is a tiny museum devoted to Zhaojun, containing some of her clothes, including a tiny pair of shoes, plus jewels, books and a number of steles. You can reach the tomb by the #44 minibus (¥1.5), or by walking due south along the main road from the Great Mosque in the west of town.

Not accessible by bus, but well worth the effort to reach, is the **Wusutu Zhao** complex, the only temple in Mongolia to have been designed and built solely by Mongolians. Boasting buildings in Mongolian, Tibetan and Han styles, it lies 12km northwest of Hohhot, south of the Daqing Mountain and in attractive countryside separated from the city by the new expressway. Admission to each of the four neighbouring temples is ¥3, collected by an elderly monk who will probably be surprised to see you. There are still no souvenir stands, no gaudy refurbishments, so take the time to scour the Ming-era murals within and the ornate woodcuts attached to sticks at the base of the Buddhas. The surrounding grasslands and trails into the mountains make for a relaxing day out. To get here

On to Outer Mongolia

Should you require them, visas for the Republic of Mongolia, otherwise known as **Outer Mongolia**, are available in Hohhot and Beijing.

Currently, only MIAT (*Meng Hang,* the national airline of the Mongolian Republic) has flights **from Hohhot** to Ulan Bator; tickets can be bought at the office in the Mongolian consulate for around ¥3500. Air China and MIAT both fly three times weekly **from Beijing** to Ulaan Baatur; tickets for the two-hour flight cost around ¥2000 one way, while the **direct train**, which takes about 36 hours, is cheaper at ¥500.

Alternatively, you can do the journey in stages from Hohhot. The first leg is to get to the border at Erlianhot, shortened to Erlian on timetables. Two **direct trains** run daily (9–11hr; ¥73). Or you can break the trip and soak up more of the grasslands by stopping in Jining (2hr; ¥22), then change to the Erlianhot train (4 daily; 4–7hr; ¥46). If you want to take the **bus** from Hohhot to Erlianhot (9hr), check with the Hohhot PSB if you need a permit. The chances are you won't, but enforcement of permit requirements in China is changeable, to say the least.

Crossing the border at Erlianhot is still something of a hassle if you are not on a through train. Assuming you arrive in the evening you'll certainly have to spend one night here. In the morning there's one local bus that does the seven-kilometre trip across to the Mongolian town of **Zamen Uud**, though you may wait hours for it to leave. From there to Ulaan Baatur it's an eighteen-hour train journey.

Erlianhot itself is a curious border town in the middle of nowhere, catering mostly to Mongolian nomads and shepherds coming to do their shopping. It's also a famous centre for wool production. Twice a week its train station briefly fills with foreigners as the Trans-Mongolian Express comes through on its way to or from Moscow – there's even a disco and a bar here for their entertainment. Eat all you can in town, because the food in Outer Mongolia is notoriously poor.

from the train station, take bus #5 to its terminus and hire a taxi from there, a ride which shouldn't come to more than ¥20, though unless you're prepared to hire the taxi for a half day, you'll probably have to walk back to the bus stop later, about an hour's hike along a busy road.

Slightly farther out is one more site that you can reach only by taxi: the **Bai Ta**, or White Pagoda (daily dawn–dusk; ¥5), about 17km east of the city, is an attractive, 55-metre-high wood and brick construction, erected in the tenth century and covered in ornate carvings of coiling dragons, birds and flowers on the lower parts of the tower. You can reach it by following Xincheng Xi Jie east out of the city – it's a possible stopoff on the way to the airport.

The grasslands

Mongolia isn't all one giant steppe, but three areas in the vicinity of Hohhot are certainly large enough to give the illusion of endlessness. These are **Xilamuren** (which begins 80km north of Hohhot), **Gegentala** (150km north) and **Huitengxile** (120km northeast). It's hard to differentiate between them, save to say that Xilamuren – the only one of the three that can feasibly be reached independently – is probably the most visited and Gegentala the least. Bear in mind that your grassland experience in the immediate area of the regional capital is likely to be a rather packaged affair, and a visit to a grassland in another, remoter part of the region (such as Hailar – see p.962) may well give you a more authentic flavour of Mongolia.

The most convenient way to visit the grasslands is to take one of the **grassland tours**, which Westerners rarely enjoy but east Asian tourists seem to love – or at least put up with in good humour. The tours always follow a similar

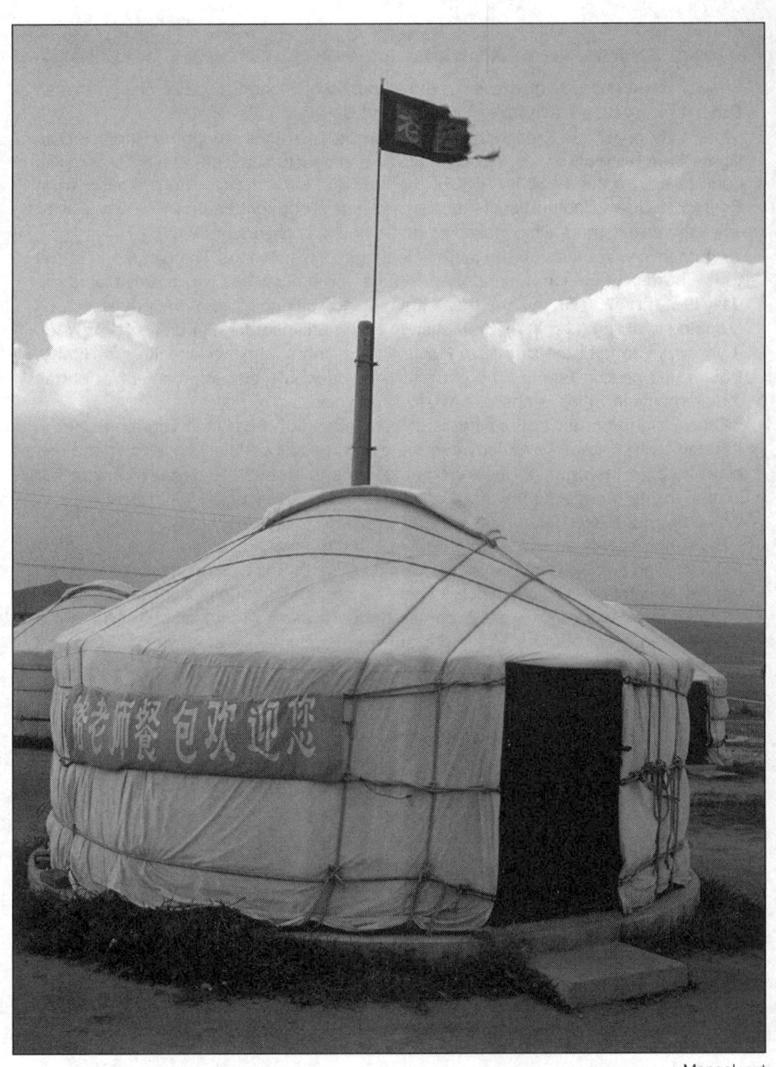

▲ Mongol yurt

pattern, with visitors based at a site comprising a number of **yurts**, plus a dining hall, kitchen and very primitive toilets. The larger sites, at Xilamuren, are the size of small villages. Transport, meals and accommodation are all included in the price, as are various unconvincing "Mongolian entertainments" – wrestling and horse-riding in particular – and visits to typical Mongol families in traditional dress. Only the food is consistently good, though watch out for the local firewater, *baijiu*, which you're more or less forced to drink when your Mongolian hosts bring silver bowls of the stuff round to every table during the evening banquet. The banquet is followed by a fairly degenerate evening of drinking, dancing and singing.

If you accept the idea that you are going on a tour of the grasslands primarily to participate in a bizarre social experience, then you'll get much more out of it. Besides, it is perfectly possible to escape from your group if you wish to do so. You can hire your own horse, or head off for a hike. If your stay happens to coincide with a bright moon, you could be in for the most hauntingly beautiful experience of your life.

Practicalities

A two-day **tour** (with one night in a yurt) is definitely enough – in a group of four or five people, this should come to around ¥450 each. Some travel services can tack smaller parties onto existing groups. Bear in mind that if you choose this option, you may find yourself sleeping crushed into a small yurt with six others who don't speak your language, and consequently the tour may not be in English, even if you've specifically requested that it should be.

Travelling independently to the Xilamuren grassland can work out a good deal cheaper than taking a tour. Store your luggage at your hotel in Hohhot, and catch a bus from the long-distance bus station (90min; ¥20) to the small settlement of **Zhaohe**, adjacent to the grassland. When you get off you will be accosted by people offering to take you to their yurts – try to negotiate an all-inclusive daily rate of about ¥50 per person, for food and accommodation, before you accept any offer. You aren't exactly in the wilderness here, but you can wander off into the grass and soon find it. Return buses to Hohot run regularly throughout the day.

The northeast of Inner Mongolia

The colossal area of land that comprises Inner Mongolia to the east and north of Hohhot is scarcely visited by tourists. As an area populated by nomadic sheep-herders since the beginning of history, its attractions lie not in old towns, but in the wilderness. The terrain is hilly, and the farther north you go the wetter it gets and the more trees there are. The grass on the **eastern grasslands** is accordingly longer and more lush, though for only a brief period each year. People are few and far between, the land outside the towns only occasionally punctuated by the sight of **muchang jia** – pastureland homes – comprising groups of yurts in the grass, surrounded by herds of sheep, cattle or horses. Visiting *muchang jia* is exclusively a summertime activity; during the long winters, temperatures can dip to an alarming -50°C.

For travellers the area is not easy to explore, given the paucity of **transport** connections. As the local authorities have in the past not been keen on foreign travellers crossing the region by **bus** (it's worth checking the current situation with the PSB), flying may turn out to be the only option if you don't want to spend ages on trains – though for rail enthusiasts, the epic train journeys are themselves a possible reason for coming here. The only rail lines are in the far north, offering access to **Hailar** and **Manzhouli** on the Russian border. Hailar lies 38 hours by train from Hohhot, the route first passing east through Datong to Beijing, then moving north back into Inner Mongolia, passing the towns of **Chifeng** and **Tongliao** – both of which are surrounded by their own grasslands which can also be visited. From here the train drifts east into Jilin province in Dongbei (see p.205). Much later the train cuts back into Inner Mongolia at Zhalantun from where it travels northwest to Hailar. For hour after hour there's barely a sign of sentient life, the train traversing hilly, grassy

The northeast of Inner Mongolia

Pastureland homes	牧场家	*mùchǎngjiā*
Chifeng	赤峰	*chìfēng*
Hailar	海拉尔	*hǎilā'ěr*
Bei'er Hotel	贝尔大酒店	*bèi'ěr dàjiǔdiàn*
Beiyuan Hotel	北苑宾馆	*běiyuán bīnguǎn*
Binzhou Fandian	滨州饭店	*bīnzhōu fàndiàn*
Hulunbeier Hotel	呼伦贝尔宾馆	*hūlúnbèi'ěr bīnguǎn*
Hulunbuir grasslands	呼伦贝尔草原	*hūlúnbèi'ěr cǎoyuán*
Japanese army tunnels	侵华日军海拉尔要塞遗址	*qīnhuá rìjūn hǎilā'ěr yàosài yízhǐ*
Laodong Hotel	劳动宾馆	*láodòng bīnguǎn*
Manzhouli	满洲里	*mǎnzhōulǐ*
Beifang Market	北方市场	*běifāng shìchǎng*
Century Square	世纪广场	*shìjì guǎngchǎng*
Dalai Hu	达赉湖	*dálài hú*
Dianli Hotel	电力商务大酒店	*diànlì shāngwù dàjiǔdiàn*
Friendship Hotel	友谊宾馆	*yǒuyí bīnguǎn*
International Hotel	国际大酒店	*guójì dàjiǔdiàn*
Jiaoyi Shichang	交易市场	*jiāoyì shìchǎng*
Meikuang	煤矿	*méi kuàng*
Mingzhu Hotel	明珠饭店	*míngzhū fàndiàn*
Shangmao Market	国际商贸中心	*guójì shāngmào zhōngxīn*
Wangquan Market	旺泉市场	*wàngquán shìchǎng*
Tongliao	通辽	*tōngliáo*

pastures, past mist-hung rivers and cool, wooded valleys during the last third of the journey.

Hailar

In the far northeast of Inner Mongolia, **HAILAR**, with rail connections as well as an airport, is the main transport hub of the region, and a centre for grassland visits. The town of Hailar itself is of minimal interest, a small, light-industrial and agricultural place on the banks of the Heilongjiang (Amur) River with a small Muslim population as well as the usual Mongol/Han mix. The main attraction in the town itself is the **network of tunnels** used by the Japanese army during World War II. Hailar was Japan's westernmost base during the war, the Japanese agreeing to halt their advance at Hailar in exchange for Russia's non-interference in Manchuria, which in turn allowed Russia to concentrate on battling Hitler in the West. The tunnel complex, wrought by Chinese prisoners of war, sits in Hailar's northwest, atop a ridge that affords an excellent vantage point of the river and grasslands. The site can only be reached by a bumpy taxi ride (¥30 return) from the train station via a rutted track in the grasslands. A plaque at the entrance explains, in English, the wartime history of the area. Enter the rebuilt bunker (¥20) to descend 40m underground into the tunnels themselves. A small Chinese-language exhibit greets you in the chilly depths, after which you're free to wander about with a torch amid the eerie echo of your footsteps. Back above ground, it's a pleasant thirty-minute walk among grasses and dunes back to the train station.

The chief reason most visitors come to Hailar, however, is to see the North Mongolian **Hulunbuir grasslands**, an apparently limitless rolling land of plains and low grassy mountains, traced by slow rivers teeming with fish.

Hundreds of thousands of sheep, cattle and horses graze this seemingly inexhaustible pasture, spread over hundreds of kilometres. In summer they occupy the higher pastures and in winter they come down to the lowlands still often deep in snow. Transport in the area is mostly by camel and pony. Not only is the grass scattered with a variety of flowers and huge fungi, but, as you soon discover, it's also alive with little black toads (which it's virtually impossible to avoid treading on), grasshoppers, birds and insects (**mosquito repellent** is essential).

As elsewhere in Inner Mongolia, there are the CITS-approved villages of Mongol herders, who earn part of their income from occasional groups of tourists, mostly from Japan. Though you could try to strike off independently, it's worth noting that the grassland **tours** here don't attract hordes of people. A day-trip from Hailar to eat a traditional mutton banquet on the grassland, for a group of four people, costs in the region of ¥250–300 each, but as the cost is mainly for transport, the more people you can squeeze into the minibus the cheaper it is per person. If you want to spend a night on the grasslands as well, reckon on around ¥600. Inclusion of an English-speaking guide sends the price soaring, so you'll need to be in a large group to make this worth your while. For bookings and more information, contact CITS (Ⓣ0470/8224017) at their office on the third floor of *Beiyuan Hotel* (see p.964).

Practicalities

A compact place, Hailar is divided into two by the Yimin River. The **train station** is on the west bank; to reach the city centre from here, turn left as you exit, continue on for a block and then turn left again to cross the tracks via a pedestrian bridge. Once across the footbridge, you'll find buses #1 and #3 running a little way south to Zhongyang Jie, the city's main artery, passing the **long-distance bus station**, at the junction of Huochezhan Jie and Shanghua Jie, on the way. The bus station is useful only for the frequent service to the Russian border at Manzhouli (3hr; ¥25). Zhongyang Jie turns into Qiaotou Jie at the *Bei'er Dajiudian*; the area between here and Zhongyang Qiao – the river bridge – is filled with shops selling everything from pirated CDs to Mongolian saddles. The district across the bridge, where the road becomes Shengli Dajie, is of minimal interest unless you're staying at one of its cavernous hotels. **CAAC** is off Qiaotou Jie (daily 8am–5pm; Ⓣ0470/8331010), on the small road leading east off the southwestern approach road to the bridge. There's a **bank** that will change money right next to the *Bei'er* hotel. The pedestrianized commercial district east of the *Bei'er Hotel* and north of Qiaotou Dajie has a bazaar atmosphere, and is worth wandering through its sprawl across both sides of Zhongyang Dajie. You'll find bookshops and **Internet cafés** here as well.

Hailar offers a range of **accommodation**, so be sure to bargain. One convenient place is the *Binzhou Fandian* (no phone), on the left-hand side of the train-station concourse as you exit the building. Rooms here are simple and clean, and the hot water works. Though it isn't close to the centre, its hourly (¥10) and half-day (¥30) rates make it a good pit stop if you've been out on the grasslands and want to wash up before heading out of town. In the centre, the best option is the *Bei'er Dajiudian* (Ⓣ0470/8358455; ❹), 36 Zhongyang Dajie, where the rate includes breakfast. The travel service here is helpful and its grassland tours cost less than those offered by CITS.

Lurking on the east bank of the river is Hailar's throwback to the bad old days of Chinese tourism, the enormous, impersonal *Hulunbeier Hotel* (Ⓣ0470/8211000, Ⓕ8221123; ❸–❺), with a large range of bland doubles in its many wings, as well as accommodation in cement "yurts" dotting its car park. For a better atmosphere at similar rates, head further east to the *Beiyuan Hotel* (Ⓣ0470/8235888; ❹), 22 Shengli San Lu, north off Shengli Dajie. Its major drawback is being surrounded by the district government and police offices, meaning street and nightlife congregate elsewhere.

The best area for **eating** is in the pedestrianized district east of the *Bei'er Hotel* and north of Qiaotou Dajie. Be sure to study the menu (or even better, the kitchen), as Hailarites have a taste for **dog**.

Manzhouli

A few hours to the west of Hailar is **MANZHOULI**, a bustling centre for cross-border commerce whose wholesale demolition, renovation and development – much of which has involved the surreal addition of Versailles-inspired facades to communist tower blocks – has left it with little atmosphere. Russian engineers on the Trans-Siberian Railway founded the town as Manchuria Station in 1903 and a few architectural remnants of their presence remain, most immediately outside the train station, where today's castle-like Railway Hospital was built as the czar's consulate. Other colonial-era buildings, including a few log cabins, still remain rotting away on this side of the tracks, so a walk along the dirt lanes is recommended.

Manzhouli's new town lies on the opposite side of the railyard, a colourful but largely soulless place, with migrants from all over China, attracted by the money to be made trading with Russia, now far outnumbering the few Mongolians. The town is compact, with five east–west roads (numbered *yi*, *er*, *san*, *si* and *wu dao jie*) crossed by five north–south avenues (*lu*). At the centre of town, **Century Square** at the intersection of Xi Wu Dao Jie and Xinhua Lu is testament to the origins of the town's new-found wealth; three indoor markets – **Beifang, Wangquan** and **Shangmao** – surround the square, each a warren of merchants selling everything from sink plungers to sexy nightdresses. All this and more is snapped up eagerly by Russian traders, who have been pouring in since the collapse of the Soviet Union and its manufacturing industry.

Practicalities

From the **train station**, a taxi across the tracks will cost ¥5 into town (few taxis have meters, so always make sure you set a fee before starting off), but if you've not too much luggage it is walkable. Long-distance **buses** drop off passengers from Hailar in the new town, whose bus station is tucked away in the west, amid wooden cottages and the original, now vacant and peeling, offices of the Trans-Siberian. **Bank of China** is at the junction of San Dao Jie and Xinhua Lu. The **post office** sits at the corner of Si Dao Jie and Haiguan Lu. **Internet cafés** are common; the one directly across from the *Friendship Hotel* is open 24hr. **PSB** is at 4 San Dao Jie.

Manzhouli's **hotels** mainly cater to overnight traders, but there are reasonable places to stay and most, like the rest of the town, are newly renovated. The *Friendship Hotel* at 26 Yi Dao Jie (Ⓣ0470/6248881; Ⓕ6223828; ❺) and the *International*, 35 Er Dao Jie (Ⓣ0470/6248188; ❻) are both smart three-star ventures, as is the much better value *Mingzhu*, at the junction of Xinhua Lu and Yi Dao Jie, (Ⓣ0470/6248977; Ⓕ6223261; ❹) a huge favourite with Russian visitors. The best budget option by far though is the *Dianli* at 1 San Dao Jie, at the junction with Shulin Lu (Ⓣ0470/3988887; ❸). Rooms may be worn, but they're a good size, staff are friendly and there's 24-hour hot water.

Eating is a treat if you love Russian food. At the east end of Yi Dao Jie, near the junction with Shulin Lu, a small group of the few remaining log cabins in town make up a string of lively restaurants. Elsewhere, the *Mingzhu* hotel has a smart restaurant upstairs (and a remarkably poor-value café/bar downstairs). The *Dianli* also has its own much cheaper restaurant focused on standard Chinese dishes. And if none of that tickles your fancy, there is always *KFC* on Century Square…

If you want to take an organized trip to the grasslands around Manzhouli (it's also possible to get there independently; see below), try **CITS** in the *International Hotel* (Ⓣ0470/6228319, Ⓦwww.mzlcits.com), who arrange trips for around ¥300 per person – double that if you want to stay overnight.

Around Manzhouli

The Trans-Siberian train from Beijing to Moscow passes through Manzhouli once a week in each direction. The tracks cross beneath the **Friendship Gate** on the Sino-Russian border. Aside from Chinese soldiers, guard dogs, and a very uninspiring cement arch that interrupts an otherwise interminable expanse of grassland, there's also a newly developed market, **Jiaoyi Shichang**, right on the border, for traders who decide Manzhouli is just too far to go for that cheap fur coat. A round-trip cab from town to the gate shouldn't cost more than ¥30.

Steam locomotive buffs can visit the opencast mine near **Jalainur**, 30km east of **Manzhouli** (¥30 in a taxi or ¥3 on the #2 bus from Wudao Jie). From Jalainur you'll pay ¥10 in a taxi to the site itself (as always, agree a price before setting off). Steam trains still operate in the huge open pit, though not during freezing months. There's not much to see, but the enormous hole in the ground is undeniably impressive, and Jailainur itself gives a flavour of how Manzhouli once was.

More appealing is the great lake **Dalai Hu** (Hulun Nur in Mongolian), a shallow expanse of water set in marshy grazing country where flocks of swans, geese, cranes and other migratory birds come to nest. In June and July, the grasslands in this region are said to be the greenest in all Mongolia, and coming here may be the most rewarding – and least expensive – way to see Inner Mongolia's grassland. A taxi from town will cost ¥150 round-trip, a ticket into the lake reserve only ¥10, and if you ask the driver nicely he might take you via Jalainur so you can see lake, birds and steam trains all in one trip. For a more organized visit, contact **CITS** in the *International Hotel* (see opposite).

The corner of China north of Hailar and Manzhouli is a **true wilderness**, China's final frontier. Here lie some of the last great areas of untouched primeval forest in the country, a natural habitat for the wolf and the much-threatened Manchurian tiger. A rail line meanders up as far north as Mangui, above the 52nd parallel, but before attempting to visit this area you should check with the Hailar PSB.

Baotou and beyond

Just three hours to the west of Hohhot by train or bus lies Inner Mongolia's biggest and bleakest city, **BAOTOU**. Its primary significance is as the chief iron- and steel-producing centre in China: if you're arriving at night from the direction of Yinchuan, your first glimpse of the city is likely to be of satanic fires burning in the great blast furnaces. The sky over the western half of Baotou glows a more or less permanent yellow, orange and purple. For visitors, there can be something magnificent about Soviet ugliness on such a

Baotou and beyond

Baotou	包头	*bāotóu*
Donghe	东河	*dōnghé*
Kundulun	昆都仑	*kūndū lún*
Qingshan	青山	*qīngshān*
Accommodation		
Bao Yuan	包院宾馆	*bāoyuàn bīnguǎn*
Baotou	包头宾馆	*bāotóu bīnguǎn*
Haide Binguan	海德酒店	*hǎidé jiǔdiàn*
Shenhua International	神华国际大酒店	*shénhuá guójì dàjiǔdiàn*
Eating and drinking		
Chinatown Bar	唐人街酒吧	*tángrénjiē jiǔbā*
Hanshifu Jiaroubing	韩师博夹肉饼	*hánshīfu jiāròubǐng*
Little Sheep Hotpot	小肥羊火锅	*xiǎoféiyáng huǒguō*
Tongxinyuan Zhoudaoguan	同心圆粥道馆	*tóngxīnyuán zhōudàoguǎn*
Dongsheng	东胜	*dōngshèng*
Dongsheng Hotel	东胜宾馆	*dōngshèng bīnguǎn*
Genghis Khan's Mausoleum	成吉思汗陵园	*chéngjísīhàn língyuán*
Jiaotong Hotel	交通宾馆	*jiāotōng bīnguǎn*
Tianjiao Hotel	天骄宾馆	*tiānjiāo bīnguǎn*
Wudangzhao	五当召	*wǔdāng zhào*
Yellow River	黄河	*huánghé*

scale, but otherwise, apart from a few minor sights, including **Wudangzhao**, an attractive Tibetan-style monastery nearby, the city does not have much to offer. One further site of interest, **Genghis Khan's Mausoleum** – which is unlikely to be the real thing – lies well to the south of Baotou near the town of **Dongsheng**.

The City

A colossal city stretching for miles in all directions, Baotou comprises three main areas: **Donghe**, the ramshackle, oldest part of town, to the east, and **Qingshan** and **Kundulun** to the west. Qingshan is a shopping and residential area, while Kundulun includes the iron and steel works on its western edge. The three parts of the city are well connected by frequent buses (#5 and #10; ¥2), which take thirty to forty minutes to travel between Donghe and Kundulun. Taxis begin at ¥6 for the first 3km, charging ¥1.2 per additional kilometre. Traversing Baotou, this can add up quickly.

Practicalities

There are two major **train stations**, one in West Baotou (Baotou Zhan), and one in Donghe (Baotou Dong Zhan). All through trains, including express trains from Beijing and Lanzhou, stop at both stations. Train tickets can be bought at the **booking office** on the east of A'Erding Square. The **bus station** is right opposite the Donghe train station; buy tickets for Hohhot here. For Dongsheng (every 30min), you also buy your ticket inside the bus station, though in warm months the touts will find you before you can say "Genghis Khan". The **airport** is just a couple of kilometres south of the Donghe train station. The **CAAC** office (Ⓣ0472/5135492) is on the south

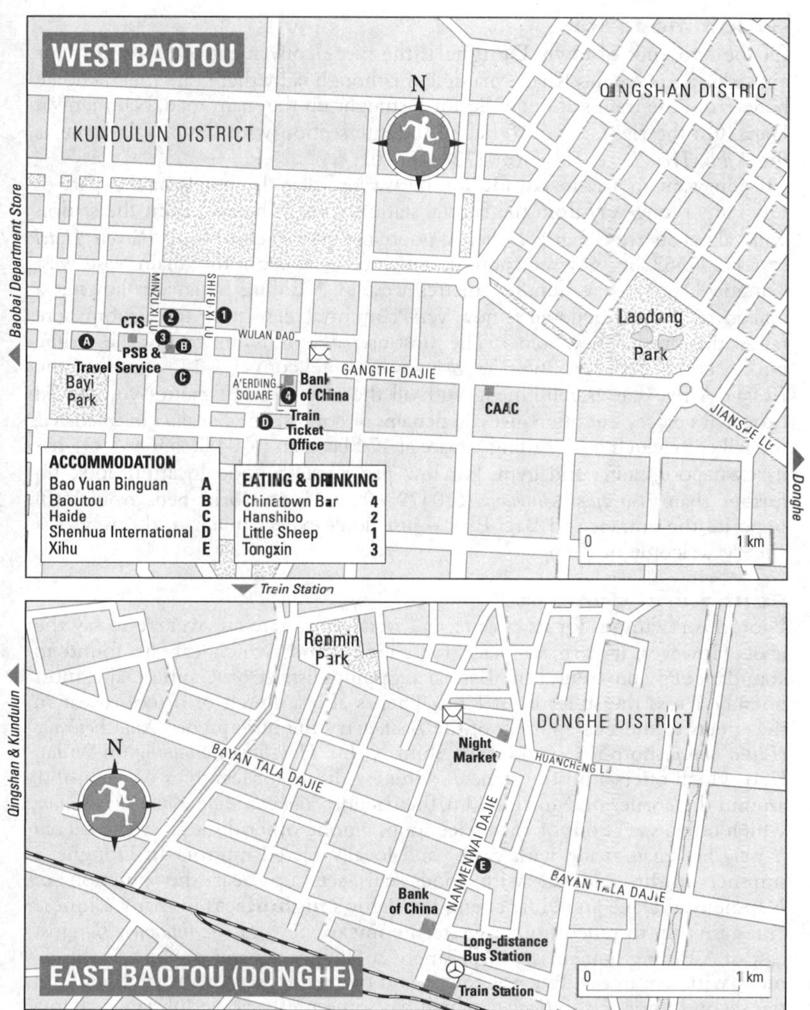

side of Gangtie Dajie, east of the post office, though the better hotels can also book for you.

There's a **CTS** office (ⓣ0472/2118966) just northwest of the *Baotou Hotel* on Wulan Dao. The **PSB** is in the *Baotou*, on the first floor. To change traveller's cheques, go to the main office of the **Bank of China** in Kundulun (daily 8am–6pm), on the main road just east of A'Erding Square. There are ATMs further up the street at the Baibao branch. In Donghe there's a branch 50m south of the train station on the western side of Nanmenwai Dajie; it has an ATM and also changes cash. The main **post and telecommunications office** is in Kundulun near the Bank of China, and there's also a post office in Donghe. You'll find an **Internet café** on the crossroads of Gangtie Dajie and Minzu Xi Lu, just west of the *Baotou Hotel*.

Accommodation

Of the two ends of town, **Donghe** is the more convenient place **to stay** for embarking to Genghis Khan's mausoleum, though sadly there isn't much choice here. From the train station, walk north straight up the main road, Nanmenwai Dajie. On the right, at no. 10 before the intersection with Bayan Tala Dajie, is the *Xihu (West Lake) Hotel* (Ⓣ0472/4187101; ❹).

If you want to stay in **Kundulun**, be warned that the hotels in this part of town are a long way from the central station, though bus #1 from the station will take you to Gangtie Dajie. A good bet is the enormous *Baotou Hotel* (Ⓣ0472/5362266, Ⓦwww.baotouhotel.com.cn; ❹), on the main east–west Gangtie Dajie, a few hundred metres west of A'Erding Square. Following a makeover, the old building is now very comfortable, so push for a room here rather than in the "new" block. The most upmarket hotel in town is the phallic pink *Haide* (Ⓣ0472/5365555, Ⓦwww.hd-hotel.com.cn; ❽) opposite the *Baotou*. A five-star establishment, with all the service and facilities you would expect, it's pricey but often gives 25 percent discounts. The *Shenhua International*, the tall edifice behind A'Erding Square at 17 Shaoxian (Ⓣ0472/536888; ❼), has its own pool, sauna and gym. For low prices *and* a good location, look no further than *Bao Yuan Binguan* (Ⓣ0472/6942628; ❷, dorm beds from ¥18) opposite the entrance to Bayi Park – just don't expect much in the way of a cheery welcome or decor.

Eating and drinking

Baotou isn't famous for its cuisine, and restaurants here are average to say the least. However, it's a great place for **snack food**, which can be found in abundance in and around the Baobai shopping district on Gantie Dajie, most notably across the street from *KFC*. There's also a clutch of places to eat in the streets to the side and rear of the *Baotou*: try the humungous *Xiao Fei Yang* (*Little Sheep*) hotpot restaurant on Shifu Xi Lu; *Hanshibo Jiaroubing* on Wulan Dao, which offers a host of standard Chinese dishes for less than ¥7 each; and, around the corner on Minzu Xi Lu, the friendly *Tongxin Yuan Zhou Dao Guan*, which offers variations of *zhou* (rice soup) among other dishes. Try the *ren can ji yang rou zhou*, made with carrot and locally reared mutton. In Donghe, a summer **night market** with food stalls sets up near the junction of Nanmenwai Dajie and Huancheng Lu. Batou's **nightlife**, as in many Chinese cities, isn't up to much from a Western point of view. *The Chinatown Bar*, just east of A'Erding Square, is a surprisingly cool, low-key and popular establishment with live music. Twice as rowdy and twice the price is the nightclub on the second floor of the *Baotou*, which has some pretty powerful dance-drama performances by an in-house troupe. You can also come here for karaoke and ten-pin bowling.

Wudangzhao and the Yellow River

The one definite attraction in the Baotou area, **Wudangzhao** (daily 8am–6pm; ¥35) is the best-preserved Lamaist monastery still functioning in Inner Mongolia, one of the results of the Mongolian conquest of Tibet in the thirteenth century. For centuries afterwards, the roads between Tibet and Mongolia were worn by countless pilgrims and wandering monks bringing Lamaist Buddhism to Mongolia. This particular monastery, of the Yellow Sect, was established in 1749 and at its height housed twelve hundred lamas; seven generations of Living Buddhas were based here, the ashes of whom are kept in one of the halls. Today, however, the few remaining monks are greatly

Chinese festivals

Whatever their origins, Chinese festivals are a time for family get-togethers and feasting. They're best experienced in the countryside – rural folk seem to observe them with more spirit than sophisticated city types – but wherever you are you're likely to enjoy dancing and a raucous sing-along, and you can generally bet on bright lights and pyrotechnics being involved somewhere. As well as the national events, every minority has its own celebrations, which are well worth seeking out. Just don't expect not to be invited to join in.

▲ Fake paper money

Qingming

The **Qingming** festival, or **Mourning Day**, held on April 5 each year, is a time to honour the dead by freshening up graves and burning fake paper money and incense. Yet, as a springtime festival, it's also regarded as a time of renewal – a propitious time to plant trees and go on outings. Its bittersweet character is captured by Tang-dynasty poet Du Mu:

A drizzling rain falls like tears on the Mourning Day;
The mourner's heart is breaking on his way.
Where can a hostel be found to drown his sadness?
A cowherd points to Xing Hua village in the distance.

Mid-Autumn Festival

The **Mid-Autumn Festival** falls on the fifteenth day of the eighth lunar month, when the moon is at its fullest and brightest. It's a celebration of abundance and togetherness – sweet mooncakes are eaten, lanterns lit, and the introspective pleasure of moon gazing indulged.

The Chinese say that the moon has a woman in it. Everyone knows a story about how she got there, though you'll rarely hear the same one twice. One of the more popular has it that she was the wife of the hero Hou Yi. The Mistress of Heaven gave him an elixir that would allow him to join her in the sky. Not wishing to part with his wife, he refused to drink it, and gave it to Chang E for safe-keeping. But villains heard about it and tried to steal it; to escape them, she drank it, and found herself carried up to heaven. Now, she's trapped on the moon, in the company (for no clear reason) of a rabbit; both are supposed to be visible as dark shadows on the moon's surface. Once a year, at the time of the Mid-Autumn Festival, she and Hou Yi are allowed to visit one another, meeting by means of a heavenly bridge – the Milky Way.

◀ Mooncakes

Chongyang

The ninth day of the ninth lunar month – usually in October – marks **Chongyang**, or the **Double Ninth Festival**. Traditionally, the number "9" was thought to be *yang*, meaning masculine or positive, and that made the ninth of the ninth a dangerous and powerful day; to ward off bad luck, people head for the heights – you'll see plenty of day-trippers climbing towers and holy mountains. The less energetic can make do with eating cakes – cake (*gao*) being a homonym for "height" – with the best Chongyang cakes, of course, having nine layers. Good luck is further courted with plants associated with cleanliness; chrysanthemum wine is drunk and *zhuyu*, dogwood, carried or worn.

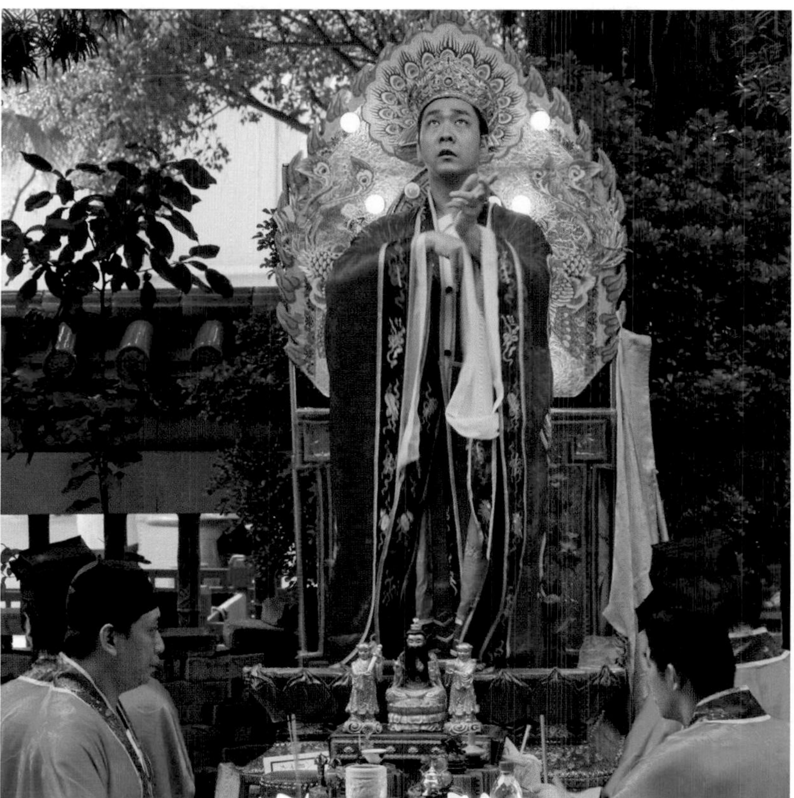

▼ Monks celebrating Chongyang in Kowloon

Double Ninth, Missing My Shandong Brothers

Such is Chongyang's prestige, schoolchildren learn Tang poet Wei Wei's popular composition, *Double Ninth, Missing My Shandong Brothers*:

As a lonely stranger in the strange land,
Every holiday the homesickness amplifies.
Knowing that my brothers have reached the peak,
All but one is present at the planting of zhuyu.

▲ Sisters' Meal Festival

▼ Tibetan Horse Racing Festival

Top five festivals

Dali Spring Fair The Bai people of Dali hold their spring fair every April. For once, locals outnumber the tourists as minority folk from surrounding villages flock into the town for five days of trading, singing and dancing. See p.801.

Water Splashing Festival Never mind those glorified wet T-shirt competitions put on for visiting tourists; the real Dai people's Water Splashing Festival is a riotous celebration – no one is going home dry. Get down to Jinghong in Xishuangbanna in April – and pack a towel. See p.848.

Sisters' Meal Festival This five-day Miao festival, held on the fifteenth day of the third lunar month (April/May), is like a Brueghel painting come to life: there's cockfighting, dragon dances, buffalo contests and, somewhere amongst the chaos, teenagers picking their partners. Head to Taijing to catch it in its full glory. See p.761.

Midi Music Festival For something completely different, check out the Midi in May; it's China's Glastonbury, when all of Beijing's indie bands strut their stuff, for once, in daylight. See p.131.

Tibetan Horse Racing Festival Only the Tibetans could mix gambling, drinking, horse racing and Buddhism. These equestrian events are held all over Tibet, at different times of the year, but the biggest is in Litang at the beginning of August. See p.939.

outnumbered by tourists from Baotou, and sadly their main duties now seem to involve hanging around at the hall entrances to check tourists' tickets.

Set in a pretty, narrow valley about 70km northeast of Baotou, the monastery can be reached by catching bus #7 (¥10) from outside the Donghe train station to the terminus at Shiguai. The monastery is another 25km on – if you arrive early enough there are one or two minibuses that go on to it from here, otherwise take a taxi from Shiguai (¥30). Once at the monastery, you can hike off into the surrounding hills and, if you're keen you should be able to **stay** in the pilgrims' hostel in the monastery as well. Returning to Baotou is fairly easy as there are various minibuses and other tour vehicles plying the route, up to around 5pm. Hiring a taxi for the round-trip to the temple should cost ¥150.

The Yellow River

The other main sight in the Baotou area is the **Yellow River**, worth having a look at, if only to ruminate on its historical significance. When the Chinese built the Great Wall far to the south, the area between the Inner Mongolian loop of the Yellow River and the Wall became known as the **Ordos** and remained the dominion of the nomad. However, to the Chinese the Yellow River seemed like the logical northern limit of China. The Qing eventually decided matters once and for all not only by seizing control of the Ordos, but also by moving north of the river into the heart of Mongolia. Today, the whole Yellow River region, from Yinchuan in Ningxia province up to Baotou and across to Hohhot, is thoroughly irrigated and productive land – without the river, it would be pure desert. You can take a stroll along the northern bank of the Yellow River by taking **bus** #18 (¥2) from in front of Donghe train station for about 6km to the new bridge. The river here is around a kilometre wide, shallow, sluggish and chocolate brown.

Genghis Khan's Mausoleum

The first thing to be said about **Genghis Khan's Mausoleum** (daily 24hr; ¥90) is that it's not all it's cracked up to be: it probably isn't the tomb of Genghis Khan, and it isn't a particularly attractive place anyway, but can nonetheless be fascinating as an insight into the modern cult of the famous warrior. Note that there are no English captions for the exhibits.

Genghis Khan is known to have died in northern China, but while his funeral cortege may have passed through this region on its way back to Mongolia, the story that the wheels of his funeral cart got stuck in the mud here, resulting in his burial on the spot, is almost certainly apocryphal. At best, scholars believe, the site contains a few of the warrior's relics – perhaps weapons. The real tomb is thought to be on the slopes of Burkhan Khaldun, in the Hentei Mountains, not far to the east of Ulaan Baatur in Outer Mongolia. The reason it came to be so strongly believed that the Khan was buried here in China appears to be that the tribe who were charged with guarding the real sepulchre eventually drifted down across the Yellow River to the Ordos – but continued to claim the honour of being the official guardians of the tomb.

The tomb's alleged **relics** have a murky political history. Several times they have been removed, and later returned, the most recent occasion being during World War II, when the Japanese seized them. Apparently the Japanese had plans to set up a puppet Mongol state, centred around a Genghis Khan shrine. They even drew up plans for an elaborate mausoleum to house them – plans that were then commandeered by the Chinese Communists who, having safely returned the relics from a hiding place in Qinghai, built the mausoleum for themselves in 1955 as a means of currying favour with the Mongolian people.

The site

The main part of the cement mausoleum is formed by three connecting halls, shaped like Mongolian yurts. The corridors connecting the halls are adorned with bizarre murals supposedly depicting the life of Genghis Khan – though note the women in Western dress (1890-style). In the middle of the main hall stands a five-metre-high marble **statue** of Genghis before a map of his empire. Whatever the truth about the location of his burial place, the popular view among Mongolians, both in China and in the Republic of Mongolia, is that this is a holy site: the side halls, all very pretty, have ceremonial yurts, altars, burning incense, hanging paintings and Mongolian calligraphy, and offerings as though to a god. Some bring offerings – not the usual apples and bread, but bottles of rotgut *baijiu* on sale in the souvenir shop – and bow in penitence. Others, including several of the female staff, get drunk early and keep sipping until they're surly – or extremely affectionate; be prepared for anything as the site attracts its fair share of dodgy characters, including about fifteen "hairdressers" just outside. There's a small, free **museum** by the ticket office with a few relics.

Special **sacrificial ceremonies** take place here four times a year on certain days of the lunar calendar – the fifteenth day of the third lunar month, the fifteenth day of the fifth lunar month, the twelfth day of the ninth month and the third day of the tenth month. On these occasions, Mongolian monks lead solemn rituals that involve piling up cooked sheep before the statue of the khan. The ceremonies are attended not only by local people, but also by pilgrims from the Republic of Mongolia itself.

Practicalities

The mausoleum is located in the Ordos, beside a road leading south into Shaanxi province, and is served by buses originating as far away as the historic walled city **Yulin**, some 200km north of Yan'an. At the time of writing, this route was being improved to an expressway. Presently, however, the most common approach to the site is from Baotou, taking a bus (1hr 20 min; ¥25) from outside the Donghe train station to the coal-mining town of **DONGSHENG**, 50km from the mausoleum. It would be possible, if you left Baotou very early in the morning, to reach the mausoleum and make it back the same evening – the last bus from Dongsheng to Baotou leaves at about 6pm. It's a tiring trip, though, and spending a night in up-and-coming Dongsheng is the most pleasant way to do it.

For **trains**, ask at the Baotou or Dongsheng (called Ordos) stations. At the time of writing, a service was planned to start between the two cities, with a connection to Xi'an made possible by transferring at Shenmu.

From Dongsheng to the mausoleum it takes a further hour on a new road by bus (¥7), and outside of summer there are only a few departures per day; if you don't want to spend the night, you should aim to catch a bus by 12.30pm. To return to Dongsheng from the mausoleum, simply stand in the road and flag down a passing minibus.

If you need a bed, you can **stay** either in Dongsheng or at the mausoleum itself. One of the cheapest places to stay **in Dongsheng** is the fading *Jiaotong* (Ⓣ0477/8321575; ❷), which is part of the bus station itself – turn right as you exit, then right again. A better bet is a few minutes' walk south down the main street, away from the bus station, to the *Dongsheng* (Ⓣ0477/8327333; ❸). Tour groups stay at the three-star *Tianjiao Hotel*, at 102 Dalate Nan Lu (☎0477/8533888; ❼). For **food**, Hangjin Bei Lu and Yijinhuoluo Xi Jie both have Chinese fast-food and Lanzhou-style hand-pulled noodle (*lamian*) restaurants; *Maikeni* and *Xin Xin* are popular.

You can also sleep **at the mausoleum** itself, in the (very) fake yurts on the grounds (¥40–50 per person). There are no showers.

Ningxia

Squeezed between Inner Mongolia, Gansu and Shanxi, **Ningxia Autonomous Hui Region** is the smallest of China's provinces. Historically, the area has never been a secure one for the Chinese: almost every dynasty built its section of **Great Wall** through here and, in the nineteenth century, the Hui people played an active part in the Muslim rebellions, which were subsequently put down with great ferocity by the Qing authorities. Until recent times, Ningxia's very existence as a separate zone remained an open question: having first appeared on the map in 1928, the region was temporarily subsumed by Gansu in the 1950s before finally reappearing again in 1958. It appears that the authorities of the People's Republic could not make up their minds whether the Hui population was substantial enough to deserve its own autonomous region, in the same way as the Uyghurs and the Mongols.

Hui is a vague term, applied to followers of the Muslim faith all over China who have no other obvious affiliation; Ningxia's Hui are descended from Middle Eastern traders who arrived here over a thousand years ago. In Ningxia, as with all the autonomous regions of the Northwest, the central government has steadily encouraged **Han immigration** – or colonization – as a way of tying the area to the Chinese nation, but the situation of the Hui people is not comparable with that of the disaffected Uyghurs or Tibetans. While remaining Muslim, the Hui have otherwise long since integrated with Han culture: barring a few Persian or Islamic words, they speak Chinese as their mother tongue and, at present, there is little concept of a Hui nation floating round the backstreets of the provincial capital, Yinchuan. Today, the Hui make up about thirty percent of Ningxia's tiny population of four million, the remainder comprising mainly Han. Indeed, most Hui do not live in Ningxia at all, but are scattered around neighbouring regions, to the point where they often seem strangely absent within what is supposed to be their homeland.

Despite a certain degree of industrialization since the Communists came to power, Ningxia remains an underdeveloped area. For visitors, the rural scenes provide the charm of the place, but this province is one of the poorest in the country. Geographically, the area is dominated by coalfields and the **Yellow River**, without which the hilly south of the province, green and extremely beautiful, would be barren and uninhabitable desert. Unsurprisingly, the science of **irrigation** is at its most advanced here: two thousand years ago, the great founding emperor of China, Qin Shi Huang, sent a hundred thousand men here to dig irrigation channels. To those ancient systems of irrigation, which are still used to farm cereal crops, have now been added ambitious reafforestation and desert reclamation projects. Some of these can be visited, particularly around the city of **Zhongwei**. Other sights include the capital **Yinchuan**, which makes a pleasant stopover, and one relic from an obscure northern branch of the Silk Road, the delightful **Xumi Shan Grottoes**, located well away from the Yellow River in the southern hills.

Yinchuan and around

The capital of Ningxia, **YINCHUAN** is a pleasantly unpolluted and leafy place to spend a couple of days, although the bland modern city possesses little of

Yinchuan and around		
Yinchuan	银川	*yínchuān*
Chengtiansi Ta	承天寺塔	*chéngtiānsì tǎ*
Dawu Kou	大武口	*dàwǔ kǒu*
Gulou	古楼	*gǔlóu*
Hai Bao Ta	海宝塔	*hǎibǎo tǎ*
Jinfeng	金凤区	*jīnfèng qū*
Nanguan Grand Mosque	南关清真寺	*nánguān qīngzhēn sì*
Nanmen	南门	*nánmén*
Regional Museum	宁夏博物馆	*níngxià bówùguǎn*
Xixia	西夏区	*xīxià qū*
Xixia Square	西夏广场	*xīxià guǎngchǎng*
Yuhuang Ge	玉皇阁	*yùhuáng gé*
Accommodation		
Gulou	古楼饭店	*gǔlóu fàndiàn*
Huatian	华天宾馆	*huátiān bīnguǎn*
Labour Union	宁夏工会大厦	*níngxià gōnghuì dàshà*
Longzhong	隆中大酒店	*lóngzhōng dàjiǔdiàn*
Ningfeng	宁丰宾馆	*níngfēng bīnguǎn*
Railway Station Hotel	银川铁道宾馆	*yínchuān tiědào bīnguǎn*
Rainbow Bridge Hotel	宁夏虹桥大酒店	*níngxià hóngqiáo dàjiǔdiàn*
Eating		
Dico's Burger	德克士汉堡	*dékèshì hànbǎo*
Hongyuan Shuai	红元帅	*hóngyuán shuài*
Xianhe Lou	仙鹤楼	*xiānhè lóu*
Xianhe Shuijiao	仙鹤水饺	*xiānhè shuǐjiǎo*
Yingbin Lou	迎宾楼	*yíngbīn lóu*
Around Yinchuan		
Baisikou Shuang Ta	拜寺口双塔	*bàisìkǒu shuāng tǎ*
Gunzhong Pass	滚钟口	*gǔnzhōng kǒu*
Helan Shan	贺兰山	*hèlán shān*
Qingtongxia 108 Dagobas	青铜峡一百零八塔	*qīngtóngxiá yībǎilíngbā tǎ*
Qingtongxia County	青铜峡镇	*qīngtóngxiá zhèn*
Sha Hu	沙湖	*shā hú*
Suyu Kou National Park	苏峪口国家公园	*sūyù kǒu guójiā gōngyuán*
Xixia Wangling	西夏王陵	*xīxià wánglíng*
Zhenbeibu China West Film Studio	镇北堡中国西部影视城	*zhènběi bǎo zhōngguó xībù yǐngshìchéng*

tourist interest. From 1038 Yinchuan (then Xingqing) was capital of the **Western Xia kingdom**, an independent state which survived for less than two hundred years (see box, p.977). It was virtually forgotten about until the early twentieth century, when the archeological remains of the kingdom started being recognized for what they were; you should definitely make a visit to their weathered **mausoleums**, some 20km outside the city.

Orientation, arrival and accommodation

Yinchuan is another of China's spread-out cities, divided into three parts from east to west: Xixia, Jinfeng and Xingqing. All the main sights and the main bus station are located in **Xingqing**. The train station, however, lies inconveniently in the west end of **Jinfeng**, some 12km away from Xingqing. Accommodation is adequate in both areas, though Xingqing is certainly the best place to stay. There is no particular reason to stay in **Xixia**, though it is sited close to the mausoleum.

Yinchuan's new **airport** lies 15km southeast of Xingqing. Airport buses (¥15) connect with the CAAC office on Shengli Jie, south of Nanmen Square. Buses from Xi'an, Lanzhou and Baotou arrive at the south long-distance **bus station** (aka Nanmen bus station) at the southeast corner of the square. The **train station** in Jinfeng serves Lanzhou to the west and Beijing (via Inner Mongolia) to the east. Bus #1 (¥1) leaves about every five minutes from the train station –

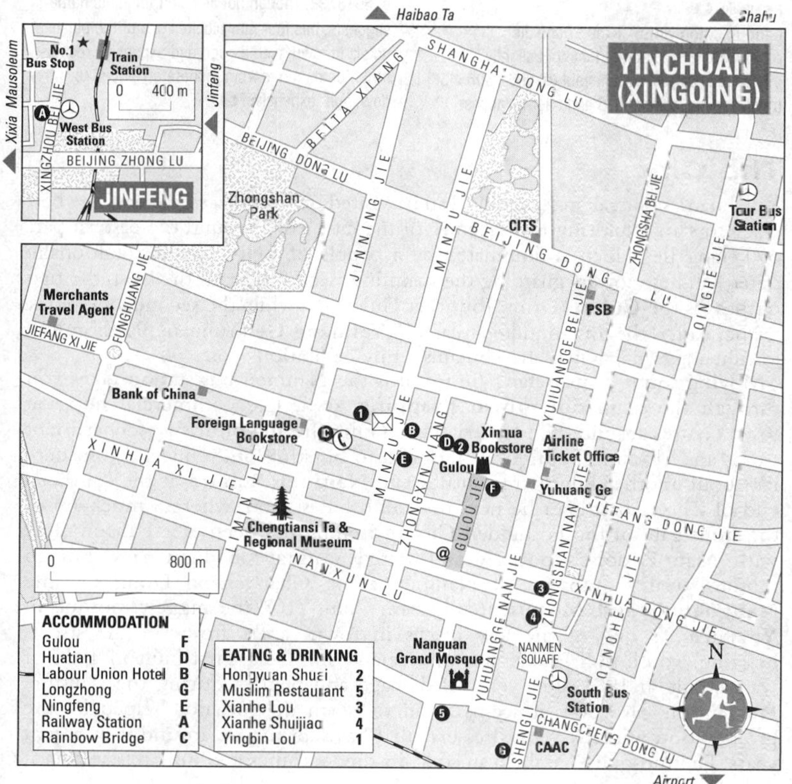

the stop is directly in front of the exit – into Jinfeng and on to the south long-distance bus station in Xingqing. Most of the hotels lie in the vicinity of this route – in Xingqing you can get off along Jiefang Jie, the main street that bisects the city. A taxi from the train station to Xingqing costs about ¥20.

Accommodation

Accommodation in Yinchuan can be amazingly tight in midsummer: Chinese tourists flock here and you may end up doing a lot of traipsing around to find a place. Fortunately, however, there are plenty of options in **Xingqing**. If you do have to stay in **Jinfeng**, though there is little, if anything of interest here, try the *Railway Hotel* (ⓣ0951/3962118; ❺) off Xinzhou Bei Jie, over to the left of the station exit. Rooms are spartan but adequate. There's also a clutch of guesthouses (❷–❹) directly left outside the station.

Xingqing

Gulou 26 Jiefang Dong Jie ⓣ0951/6028784. Well located beside the Gulou (Drum Tower), this little hotel has comfortable and affordable doubles, though they could do with a lick of paint and new bathrooms. ❸

Huatian West of the *Gulou*, on Jiefang Dong Jie ⓣ0951/6035555. Clean and friendly budget hotel. Considerable discounts are often available. ❸

Labour Union Hotel Jiefang Dong Jie ⓣ0951/6016898. Comfortable but slightly overpriced, with its own helpful (ⓣ0951/5055456) travel service, coffee shop and Internet access. ❻

Longzhong Shengli Bei Jie, opposite the CAAC building ⓣ0951/7864159. Good value and conveniently near the CAAC office. Generous discounts available off season. ❹

Ningfeng Jiefang Dong Jie, across the road from *Labour Union Hotel* ⓣ0951/6027224. Smart-looking place, with good doubles and flustered staff. ❹

Rainbow Bridge Jiefang Xi Jie ⓣ0951/6918888, ⓕ6918788. Though not as colourful as its name suggests, this four-star block is one of the plushest hotels in town, with a good and expensive restaurant. Rooms range from moderately priced to downright expensive. ❻

The City

Yinchuan's sights, all in Xingqing, can be visited on foot in a single day. The best place to start exploring is the centre of the city, based around the eastern part of Jiefang Jie, which is dominated by a couple of well-restored, traditionally tiered Chinese towers guarding the main intersections. From the west, the first of these is the **Gulou** (Drum Tower) at Gulou Jie, while the second, one block farther east, is the four-hundred-year-old **Yuhuang Ge** (Yuhuang Pavilion, ¥5), at Yuhuangge Jie, which also contains a tiny exhibition room.

Moving south from Jiefang Jie towards the Nanmen bus station takes you through the main **downtown shopping area**. The commercial heart of town centres around the pedestrianized Gulou Jie, full of massive department stores and clothing boutiques; crammed to bursting on Sundays. From here it's about another kilometre southeast to **Nanmen Square** at the southern end of Zhongshan Nan Jie near the south bus station, where a mock-up of the front gate of the Forbidden City in Beijing has been erected, complete with Mao Zedong's portrait and tiered seating for dignitaries. Fifteen minutes' walk southwest of Nanmen along Changcheng Dong Lu, the **Nanguan Grand Mosque** (daily 8am–7pm; ¥10), the biggest mosque in Yinchuan, is one of the few places in town (apart from on the streets begging) you'll find Hui in any appreciable numbers. First built in 1915, it was rebuilt in 1981 after years of damage and neglect during the Cultural Revolution. However, it seems again to be in decline, not helped by the proliferation of seedy "hair dressers" that have sprung up around it in recent years. The mosque is Arabian in style, its green domes and minarets setting it apart from the purely Chinese flying eaves and pagoda-style minarets of many mosques farther east.

At the junction of Jining Jie and Xinhua Xi Jie, a few blocks south of Jiefang Jie, are the **Regional Museum** and **Chengtiansi Ta** pagoda (also known as West Pagoda), on the same site (daily 8am–6pm; ¥20). The museum contains some interesting English-labelled exhibitions; relics from the Xixia Mausoleum include a nine-hundred-year-old Lishi pillar support (Lishi is shown as a squatting troll-like creature). Also presented are Helan Shan pictographs – drawings recording aspects of life and mysterious animals, presumably carved on rocks by nomads some thirty thousand years ago. Outside, the twelve-storey pagoda, in classic Chinese style, is a place of worship for Buddhists. It was built around 1050 during the time of the Western Xia with the top six storeys rebuilt during the Qing dynasty. You can climb the octagonal tower right to the top for excellent views.

Look north up Jining Jie from Jiefang Jie and you'll see another tower peering up from the horizon in the distance directly ahead – this is the 1500-year-old **Haibao Ta** (daily 8.30am–6pm; ¥10), otherwise known as the North Pagoda. Brick-built, 54m high and of an unusual, angular shape, with protruding ledges and niches at every level, it also offers fine views over the city. Walking there from Jiefang Jie takes an hour or bus #20 from Nanmen Square stops at the north end of Beita Xiang, from where it's a twenty-minute walk.

Eating and drinking

Xingqing has the best choice of **food**. In addition to the places reviewed below, there's a good **Muslim restaurant** in the backstreet behind the Nanguan Grand Mosque – look for the giant green dome, which is decorated with fancy neon lights at night. For Western-style eating, there are branches of *Dico's Burgers* on Gulou Nan Jie and Xinhua Jie, plus a *KFC* on Jiefang Xi Jie. The *Labour Union Hotel*'s coffee shop also does a decent brew.

Hongyuan Shuai Just west of the drum tower on Jiefang Dong Jie. A cheap noodle canteen with shared tables and tasty, Sichuan-style cold snacks and local noodle dishes; just point at the pictures.

Xianhe Lou On the west side of Zhongshan Jie. Inexpensive hotpots, casseroles and cold snacks. Be aware that their "vegetable dumplings" also contain meat.

Xianhe Shuijiao Near the bus station on Zhongshan Jie. *Xianhe Lou*'s sister restaurant deals in dumplings – vegetable or meat – which you order by the *jin* and watch being assembled by an army of cooks in the restaurant window. A half *jin* costs ¥20 and is plenty for one person.

Yingbin Lou On the east end of Jiefang Xi Jie. For real local delicacies, this smart, mid-range Muslim restaurant serves lamb hotpots, kebabs, noodles and eight-treasure tea.

Listings

Airlines The main CAAC office is at the Changcheng Dong Lu/Shengli Jie intersection (daily 8am–10.30pm; ⓣ0951/6913456). It also has a branch in the main post office of Xingqing, at window 8. Better domestic flight deals can be obtained at a private Airline Ticket office at the northeast corner of the Yuhuangge junction.

Banks and exchange The main Bank of China is in the western part of Xingqing, on Jiefang Xi Jie; the branch on Yuhuangge Bei Jie has an ATM.

Bookshops For English-language novels as well as local maps, the Foreign Language Bookstore (daily 9am–6.30pm) is at the corner of Jiefang Xi Jie and Jining Jie and is well stocked with classic titles.

Internet access At the time of writing foreign sites are not accessible in Yinchuan, due to the package sold by the local service provider, apparently. The business centre at the *Labour Union Hotel* is happy to help you log on for ¥6 per hour.

Mail and telephones The main post office (daily 8am–5.30pm) in Xingqing is at the junction of

Jiefang and Minzu Jie. There's another one on Beijing Zhong Lu, east of Tiedong Jie in Jinfeng. Long-distance calls can be made from the first floor of the China Telecom office (daily 8am–6pm) next to the *Rainbow Bridge* hotel or from the business centre in the *Labour Union Hotel*.

PSB At the corner of Beijing Dong Lu and Yuhuangge Bei Jie (Mon–Thurs 8am–noon & 2.30–6.30pm, Fri 2.30–6.30pm; ⓣ0951/6915080).

Travel agents The friendly Ningxia CITS is on the first floor of 375 Beijing Dong Lu (ⓣ0951/6732749, ⓦwww.nxcits.com). A good alternative is the Ningxia Merchants International Tour at 365 Jiefang Xi Jie (ⓣ0951/5064333, ⓦwww.cmitnx.com). Both travel agents can provide English-speaking tour guides and organize tours of areas outside the city.

Around Yinchuan

A few interesting spots outside Yinchuan can comfortably be visited as day trips. The best of these are the **Xixia Wangling** (Mausoleums of the Western Xia; daily 8am–6pm; ¥40) about 10km west of the new city. The mausoleums stand as monuments to the nine kings of Western Xia, whose kingdom was based at Yinchuan (see box opposite). The site is spectacular and atmospheric, with towering, haystack-shaped piles of brown mud bricks, slowly disintegrating and punctuating the view for miles around the Helan Shan range. The entrance fee includes transport within the complex to the museum, figure gallery and the biggest mausoleum of the nine. Interesting items in the museum include the original pieces of the Lishi pillar support and some terracotta bird ornaments with human faces. The cheapest way to reach the site is to take **minibus** #2 (¥2) from the west of Gulou Jie/Xinhua Dong Jie junction to Xixia Square. From here you can take a taxi (¥10) or hire a motor-rickshaw (¥5) for the last 10km.

The **Helan Shan** mountain ranges themselves are also of interest. The **Gunzhong Kou** (Rolling Bell Pass; ¥31), about 25km west of Xixia, where Li Yuanhao built his summer palace, is a pleasant resort with attractive, historic buildings and plenty of opportunities for hiking around the hills and admiring the views. Six or seven kilometres north of here are the **Baisikou Shuang Ta**, a couple of twelve-metre-high pagodas guarding another pass. A few more kilometres to the east is the **Zhenbeibu China West Film Studio** (daily 8am–6pm; ¥40) where the film *Red Sorghum*, directed by Zhang Yimou, was

▲ Qingtongxia 108 Dagobas

The Xi Xia kingdom

The ancient feudal **Xi Xia kingdom** (Western Xia Kingdom; 1038–1227 AD) encompassed a vast expanse of land, overlapping regions of what is now Ningxia, Gansu and Shaanxi provinces. Established by the nomadic Dangxiang clan of Qiang ancestry, the kingdom had twelve kings and developed its own **written language**, which combines influences from Mongolian, Tibetan and Chinese. The Xi Xia territory survived prior to independence by playing off the Song or Liao dynasties against each other. In 1038, **Li Yuanhao**, leader of Xi Xia, was militarily powerful enough to oppose Song jurisdiction and thus this third kingdom was created. A prosperous period ensued as the kingdom benefited from controlling the trade routes into central Asia. The new era saw a time of great **cultural development**, a state academy was erected, and future officials took Confucian examinations. Less emphasis, however, was placed on military matters, and in 1227 the Xi Xia were obliterated by the Mongol empire of **Genghis Khan**.

shot. The stunning film depicts village life in northwest China during the period leading up to World War II – in part a rural idyll, in part a brute struggle to survive. The scenes of dry, dusty hillsides alternating with the lush fields of sorghum are a fair record of how Ningxia still looks today. Get the #16 bus from Nanmen station. Fairly extensive galleries of engraved **rock art** have been found spread out near here at **Suyu Kou National Park** (¥40); you can also hike to the peak of Helan Shan. Merchants International Tour (see opposite) offers a tour of these places from Yinchuan for ¥350 including a car and an English tour guide; otherwise you can hire a taxi on the street for no more than ¥250.

Farther away from town, about 45km north of Yinchuan, is the beautiful **Sha Hu** (Sand Lake; summer ¥80; otherwise ¥60, includes a return trip by boat across the lake). This is a developing summer resort *par excellence*, with swimming, sand dunes, rafting and beautiful scenery. During winter the lake freezes over, making an ideal skating rink, though most tourists arrive in summer to view the expansive lily ponds. Camel rides and caravan trips are also offered in the desert nearby. **Accommodation** at the comfortable *Qingxin Fandian* (④) is available in summer. You can get there from the Tour Bus Station (also known as North Bus Station) on Qinghe Jie; an hourly direct bus (¥10) leaves from 10.30am till early evening (1hr). Return trips are easy in summer, but in winter the direct bus may stop running completely; if you get stuck, wait at the junction outside the lake entrance and flag down the minibus to Yaofu (¥3.5), where frequent transport back to Yinchuan is available into the late evening.

Finally, about 80km south of Yinchuan, are the **Qingtongxia 108 Dagobas** (¥60). These Buddhist stupas stand in a strange triangular pattern on a slope on the west bank of the Yellow River in Qingtongxia County. The white, bell-shaped dagobas are arranged in twelve rows, tapering from nineteen in the bottom row to a single one at the top. They are thought to have been built in the fourteenth century during the Yuan dynasty, though their exact significance is not known. Ticket price includes a boat ride around the site. To visit the dagobas, take a bus (3hr) from Yinchuan's South Bus Station to Qingtongxia Zhen. The first bus leaves at 11am. When you get off the bus a motor-rickshaw (around ¥15) can take you the remaining 7km east to the site. You won't be able to spend too long here if you want to get back the same day.

Zhongwei and Shapotou

A small country town, **ZHONGWEI** is 160km and three hours by bus to the southwest of Yinchuan. Historically, the old walled city was said to have had no north gate – simply because there was nothing more to the north of here. The city is still in a potentially awkward location, between the fickle **Yellow River** to the south and the sandy Tenger Desert to the north, but today Zhongwei is surrounded by a rich belt of irrigated fields, and the desert is kept at bay through reafforestation projects. The river outside the town, at **Shapotou**, is a splendid sight and should definitely be visited if you are in the area.

Zhongwei is based around a simple crossroads, with a traditional Gulou (Drum Tower) at the centre. It's small enough to walk everywhere, although there are cycle-rickshaws and taxis available to ferry you around. The town has one intriguing sight, the **Gao Miao** (daily 8am–6pm; ¥20), a quite extraordinary temple catering for a number of different religions, including Buddhism, Confucianism and Taoism. Originally constructed in the early fifteenth century, and rebuilt many times, the temple is now a magnificent jumble of buildings and styles. From the front entrance you can see dragon heads, columns, stairways and rooftops spiralling up in all directions. The left wing contains vivid sculptures of five hundred *arhats*. The right wing is a mock hell. Altogether, there are more than 250 temple rooms, towers and pavilions. You need a pretty expert eye to distinguish the saints of the various religions – they all look very much alike. There are even U.V. glow representations of hell in the basement, reached through a hall of mirrors of all things. To reach the Gao Miao, walk a few minutes north from the crossroads and you'll see the entrance on your left, opposite the *Zhongwei Da Jiudian*.

Practicalities

All trains on the main Lanzhou–Beijing (via Inner Mongolia) rail line call at Zhongwei. Branch lines also serve Wuwei in Gansu province and Baoji in Shaanxi. Zhongwei's **train station** is just off the north arm of the crossroads; the long-distance **bus station** is about 1km east of the Shapatou bus station, and has connections to Guyuan farther south and Wuwei in Gansu province. Buses to and from Yinchuan run frequently, but stop at around 5pm.

If you're arriving in Zhongwei by train, you'll find **accommodation** right outside the station at the *Railway Hotel* (Ⓣ0955/7031948; ❷), a nice, clean and friendly place offering double rooms with bath, though hot water is only available in the morning and evening. From the train station, it's a short walk into town – crossing Renmin Sqaure as you exit the station will lead you onto

Zhongwei and Shapotou		
Zhongwei	中卫	*zhōngwèi*
Gao Miao	高庙	*gāomiào*
Laomao Shouzhua Meishilou	老毛手抓美食楼	*lǎomáo shǒuzhuā měishíchéng*
Mou Wu Niurou Mian Guan	某五牛肉面馆	*mǒuwǔ niúròumiàn guǎn*
Railway Hotel	铁路宾馆	*tiělù bīnguǎn*
Xingtuo Fandian	兴拓饭店	*xīngtuò fàndiàn*
Zhongwei Binguan	中卫宾馆	*zhōngwèi bīnguǎn*
Zhongwei Dajiudian	中卫大酒店	*zhōngwèi dàjiǔdiàn*
Shapotou	沙坡头	*shāpōtóu*
Desert Research Institute	沙坡头沙漠研究所	*shāpōtóu shāmò yánjiūsuǒ*
Shapo Shanzhuang	沙坡山庄	*shāpō shānzhuāng*

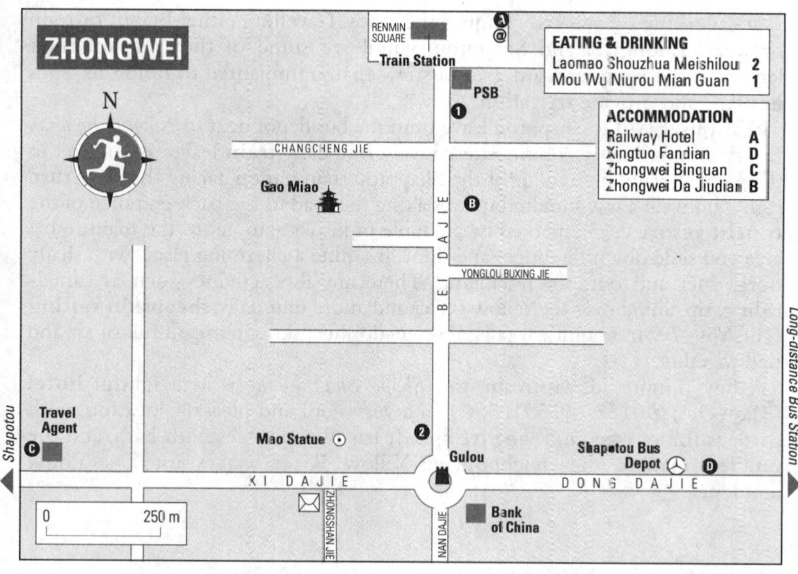

Bei Dajie and into the centre. Along Bei Dajie, you'll pass the plush – generous discounts out of season – *Zhongwei Da Jiudian* on the left (ⓣ0955/7025555; ❺), more or less opposite the entrance to the Gao Miao. An alternative is the faded *Zhongwei Binguan* (ⓣ0955/7012609, ⓕ7012350; ❹), ten minutes' walk west from the centre along Xi Dajie; the Peace Travel Service (ⓣ0955/7034880, ⓔxqnlzq@163.com) with friendly English-speaking staff is just outside and offers reasonably priced camel tours and Yellow River rafting trips. East from the centre, on Dong Dajie near the bus station, is the simple *Xingtuo Fandian* (ⓣ0955/7035761; ❹), which is nicely equidistant between the train and bus stations. The main **Bank of China** is immediately to the southeast of Gulou and there's a **post office** on Zhongshan Jie – a small lane several minutes' walk along Xi Dajie from the centre; you can also make long-distance phone calls from here. **Internet** access is available from a Net bar on the southeast corner of Renmin Square.

There are lots of cheap **noodle shops** along Bei Dajie near the Gao Miao. For real local flavour check out the ¥2.5 beef noodles at *Mou Wu Niurou Mian Guan*, between Changcheng Jie and Renmin Square. You'll also find a good-value Muslim restaurant *Laomao Shouzhua Meishilou* northwest of the Gulou (meals around ¥20 including beer). A string of smarter restaurants lies along pedestrianized **Yonglou Buxing Jie**, a few minutes south of the *Zhongwei Da Jiudian*.

Shapotou

SHAPOTOU, 16km west of Zhongwei, is a tourist resort of sorts by the banks of the Yellow River. Most people come on a day-trip, but you can easily spend an enjoyable night or two here. The main pleasure of the place is in the contrast between the leafy, shady banks of the river itself, and the harsh desert that lies just beyond. The **Shapotou Desert Research Institute** (entry free with tourist resort ticket) has been based here for forty years, working on ways to conquer the sands. Travelling either by bus or train between Zhongwei and Shapotou, you'll see some of the fruits of their labour in the chequerboard grid of straw thatch implanted to hold the sands in place and provide irrigation.

Minibuses (¥4) to Shapotou leave from the bus depot next to *Xingtuo Fandian* (every 30min 8am–5.30pm). Alternatively, one daily **train** leaves Zhongwei in the early afternoon. Arriving at the Shapotou train station, facing the river, turn right and walk a few hundred metres along the road to the back entrance of the **tourist resort** (¥65), marked by a couple of kiosks – to get to the main resort area you slide down the huge sand dune. It's quite a charming place, with shady trees, cafés and outdoor restaurants. There are also activities such as camel-riding, zip-lining over the Yellow River and, more unusually, **sheepskin rafting** (1hr; ¥50–70) in traditional rafts of sewn-up sheepskins, pumped full of air and tied together.

A few minutes downstream, the *Shapo Shanzhuang* is a delightful **hotel** (May–Oct; ⓣ0137/39559105; ❸) in a very cool and pleasant location, with gardens full of trees and vine trellises. It has nice doubles with bath, and the muffled roar of the neighbouring Yellow River makes for a soothing ambience.

Southern Ningxia

Located in the remote, impoverished southern part of Ningxia, the town of **Guyuan** has seen very little tourist traffic. Only in 1995 did it finally join the rail network, with the opening of the Zhongwei–Baoji line. Aside from a ruinous stretch of the **Great Wall**, built in the Qin dynasty, 5km north of town (you'll see it in passing), the main interest here is in the Buddhist grottoes at **Xumi Shan**, a major relic of the Silk Road, curiously marooned far to the north of the main route from Lanzhou to Xi'an. The great Taoist temple **Kongtang Shan** (see p.988) at Pingliang in Gansu is only two hours from Guyuan, another possible day-trip. The hills along the road from Gansu have been terraced for centuries; every inch of land in the vast landscape is under cultivation, with terraces laddering up the slopes and flowing round every tiny hillock and gully in fantastic swirls of colour.

The high pass on the border with Gansu, **Liupan Shan** (which you cross on the way to or from Tianshui), is also famous for the fact that the Long Marchers managed to elude pursuing Guomindang forces here in the 1930s; a commemorative stone marks the spot.

Southern Ningxia		
Liupan Shan	六盘山	*liùpán shān*
Xumi Shan	须弥山	*xūmí shān*
Dianli Fandian	电力饭店	*diànlì fàndiàn*
Haiyuan	海原	*huǎiyuán*
Sanying	三营	*sānyíng*
Guyuan	固原	*gùyuán*
Qingya Xuan	清雅轩	*qīngyǎ xuān*
Tiedao Binguan	铁道宾馆	*tiědào bīnguǎn*
Xiaochi Yitiaojie	小吃一条街	*xiǎochī yītiáojiē*
Xingyuan Binguan	兴源宾馆	*xīngyuán bīnguǎn*

Guyuan

A useful place to base yourself for a visit to the Xumi Shan grottoes, **GUYUAN** is itself of no special interest. Although trains now pass through on their way between Zhongwei and Baoji in Shaanxi province, the **train station** is inconveniently located several kilometres from town. It's easier to rely on long-distance **buses** connecting Guyuan with Xi'an to the east, Lanzhou and Ürümqi to the west. There are also frequent connections to Yinchuan (every 40min 8am–5.30pm; ¥50). Bus #1 (¥1) links the train station and the bus station in town; there is no signpost, so simply flag down the bus at the junction outside the train station. A taxi to anywhere in town costs ¥4.

Guyuan's **post office** is a short walk east from the bus station – it's on the right just past the roundabout. A **Xinhua Bookstore** lies 300m south from the roundabout on your left and there's also an **Internet** café (¥2/hour) down the lane across the way.

Accommodation is available at the *Xingyuan Binguan* (Ⓣ0954/2022558, Ⓕ2021556; ❺). Come out of the bus station, turn left, and the hotel is about 100m down the road, on the opposite side. The bathrooms are spacious and there's almost 24-hour hot water. If you arrive by train, your best option is *Tiedao Binguan* (❸). It's about 100m outside the train station to the right. Hot water is available twice a day and the price includes a simple breakfast, though the staff can be unhelpful.

You can find good and cheap Muslim **food** and cold snacks at the popular *Qingya Xuan*, 500m east of the bus station – look for the grey plate with green characters. Further east from here to the roundabout, turn right and walk a few minutes; an arch gate next to the Xinhua Bookstore on your left will lead you to the lively *Xiaochi Yitiaojie* (Snack Street), where kebabs, noodles and dumplings are all available from dozens of stands.

The Xumi Shan grottoes

The dramatic **Xumi Shan grottoes** (daily; ¥30) lie about 55km northwest of Guyuan. One hundred and thirty-eight caves have been carved out from the rusty red sandstone cliff face on five adjoining hillsides, and a large number of statues – primarily from Northern Wei, Sui and Tang dynasties – survive, in a somewhat diminished state. With a beautifully secluded natural backdrop, the grottoes occupy a huge site, the red cliffs and shining tree-covered slopes commanding panoramic views. The last stage of the journey there takes you through one of the remotest corners of rural China where, at the height of summer, you can see the golden wheat being cut by hand, then spread out over the road to be ground by passing vehicles.

The site takes at least two hours to walk around. After entering the cliffs area, bear left first for Cave no. 5 and the **Dafo Lou**, a statue of a giant twenty-metre-high Maitreya Buddha facing due east. Originally this Buddha was protected by a wall that has long since fallen away. Head back to the entrance and you'll see the five hillocks lined up along an approximate east–west axis, each with one key sight and a cluster of caves. After the Dafo Lou, the second major sight you come to is the **Yuanguang Si**, a temple housing caves 45, 46 and 48, where statues were built in North Zhou and Tang dynasties. You'll need to ask the nun to open the caves. Looking at their smoky coloured surface today, it is hard to imagine that all Buddha statues were once coated in gold. From here you have to cross a bridge and bear left to reach **Xiangguo Si**, centred around the magnificent Cave no. 51 with its five-metre-high Buddha seated around a central pillar. Returning to the bridge, walk underneath it and up the dry river bed towards the cliff, to reach **Taohua Dong** (Peach Blossom Cave).

Practicalities

There's no direct bus to Xumi Shan from Guyuan; the nearest you can get is the small town of **Sanying**, a stop on the Guyuan–Haiyuan bus route (hourly 7.30am–4.30pm; 1hr; ¥5). Tell the driver that you want to see the grottoes, and you will be dropped off at a junction. From Sanying, hire a minivan for the thirty-minute drive to the caves; a return trip (including 2hr wait while you look around) should cost about ¥50. There's a **drinks and snacks** kiosk at the grottoes' car park, plus a basic **hotel** in the unlikely event that you might need to stay the night. It's also possible to stay in Sanying at the respectable *Dianli Fandian* (❸).

Gansu

Traditionally, the Chinese have regarded **Gansu** as marking the outer limit of Chinese cultural influence. During the Han dynasty (206 BC–220 AD), the first serious effort was made to expand into the western deserts, primarily as a means to ensure control over the Silk Road trade. Prefectures were established and, although Gansu did not officially become a Chinese province until the Mongolian Yuan dynasty (1279–1368), it is unquestionably a part of the Chinese heartland. At various stages over the last two thousand years Chinese control has extended well beyond here into Xinjiang. Nevertheless, right into the nineteenth century the primarily Muslim inhabitants of this province were considered little better than the "barbarian" Uyghurs of Xinjiang by central government; the great Muslim revolts of that period were ruthlessly quashed.

A harsh and barren land, subject to frequent droughts, Gansu has always been a better place for travelling through than settling down in. The province's geography is remarkable – from the great **Yellow River**, dense with silt, surging through the provincial capital of **Lanzhou**, to the mountains and deserts of the **Hexi Corridor**, a thousand-kilometre route between mountain ranges that narrows at times to as little as sixteen-kilometre-wide bottlenecks. It's the Hexi Corridor that accounts for the curious dumbbell shape of the province: the Silk Road caravans funnelled this way, the Great Wall was built here, and today's trains chug along here as well, along what was – until the Qinghai–Lhasa railway was completed – the only link through Central Asia between China and the West. The towns along the Hexi Corridor are mere dots of life in the desert, sustained by irrigation using water from the mountains. Given that agriculture is barely sustainable here, central government has tried to import a certain amount of industry into the province, particularly in the east. The exploitation of mineral deposits, including oil and coal, was a tentative beginning, quickly followed by Mao's paranoid "Third Line" industrial development in the 1960s, when factories were built in remote areas to save them from possible Soviet attack. But still the population is relatively small, comprising just 26 million,

PICC insurance

Irrespective of any other insurance policies you may have, in many rural parts of China foreigners need to be covered by the state insurer, **PICC** (People's Insurance Company of China), in order to travel on buses. This has nothing to do with paying you in the event of an accident, but is a waiver to prevent the authorities from being sued. Generally, insurance for each journey is included in the ticket price, but in Gansu and Western Sichuan you're actually required to **buy** a separate PICC policy before anyone will even sell you a bus ticket. Certificates of two weeks' validity can be bought from PICC offices (in Gansu, all cities have them) for between ¥30 and ¥50, though some offices seem unaware of the regulations and can't understand what you're after. In this case, try hotels, CITS offices, or even bus stations, where you'll have to pay an additional commission.

As is always the case in China, the regulation is erratically enforced: sometimes flashing the policy at the right moment is the only way to get aboard a bus; sometimes nobody cares. If you can't get a policy and nobody will sell you a ticket, try flagging the bus down once it has left the station – often the drivers are happy to take you anyway.

who continue to display an extraordinary ethnic mix, with Hui, Kazakhs, Mongols and Tibetans all featuring prominently.

The province may be wild and remote by Chinese standards, but it's of enormous historical interest. The **Mogao Caves** at **Dunhuang** in the far west house the finest examples of Buddhist art in all China, and further Silk Road sights are scattered right along the length of the province, ranging from the country's largest reclining Buddha at **Zhangye** to the stunning Buddhist caves at **Bingling Si**, near Lanzhou, and **Maiji Shan**, near **Tianshui** in the far south. The Great Wall, snaking its way west, comes to a symbolic end at the great Ming fortress at **Jiayuguan**, and, in the southwest of the province, right on the edge of the Tibetan plateau, is the fascinating **Labrang Monastery** at the Tibetan town of **Xiahe**.

Eastern Gansu

West of the border with Shaanxi, the first significant Silk Road city is **Tianshui**, with the spectacular **Maiji Shan** complex just a few kilometres to the southeast. Maiji Shan – literally "Wheatstack Mountain", a name derived from its shape – is the fourth largest Buddhist cave complex in China, after Dunhuang, Datong and Luoyang. Set amid stunning wooded hills, the caves are easily accessed from Tianshui, which is about halfway along on the Lanzhou–Xi'an rail line. You will probably need to spend at least one night at Tianshui, the nearest transport hub to the caves, though in itself of limited interest to tourists. A little way to the west of Tianshui, towards Lanzhou, are some more fascinating Silk Road relics, in and around the towns of **Gangu** and **Wushan**.

Tianshui

The area around **TIANSHUI** was first settled back in Neolithic times, though today the city is an enormous industrial spread with two distinct centres, known as **Qincheng** (West Side) and **Beidao** (East Side), situated some 20km apart. Where you stay will probably be determined by whether you arrive at the

Eastern Gansu

Tianshui	天水	*tiānshuǐ*
Beidao	北道	*běidào*
Fuxi Miao	伏羲庙	*fúxī miào*
Qincheng	秦城	*qínchéng*
Yuquanguan Park	玉泉观公园	*yùquánguàn gōngyuán*
Yuquan Si	玉泉寺	*yùquán sì*
Accommodation and eating		
Golden Sun	阳光饭店	*yángguāng fàndiàn*
Jianxin	建新饭店	*jiànxīn fàndiàn*
Maiji	麦积大酒店	*màijī dàjiǔdiàn*
Tianhe	天和餐馆	*tiānhé cānguǎn*
Tianshui	天水宾馆	*tiānshuǐ bīnguǎn*
Yatai	天水亚太大酒店	*tiānshuǐ yàtài dàjiǔdiàn*
Zhoulin	舟林宾馆	*zhōulín bīnguǎn*
Gangu	甘谷	*gāngǔ*
Daxiang Shan	大像山	*dàxiàng shān*
Maiji Shan	麦积山	*màijī shān*
Pingliang	平凉	*píngliáng*
Kongtong Shan	崆峒山	*kōngtóng shān*
Kongtong Shanzhuang	崆峒山庄	*kōngtóng shānzhuāng*
Pingliang Hotel	平凉宾馆	*píngliáng bīnguǎn*
Pingliang Binguan Fenbu	平凉宾馆分部	*píngliáng bīnguǎn fēnbù*
Taihe Gong	太和宫	*tàihé gōng*
Wushan	武山	*wǔ shān*
Lashao Temple	拉稍寺	*lāshāo sì*
Shuilian Dong	水帘洞	*shuǐlián dòng*

Beidao train station or the Qincheng bus station. If your only interest is a trip to Maiji Shan and back, you should stay in Beidao, from where all the Maiji Shan minibuses depart, though this is the grottier of the two ends of town, with the feel of a rural backwater.

In slightly smarter Qincheng, head west from the main square (at the west end of Minzhu Lu) along Jiefang Lu and you'll almost immediately reach an area of crumbling, traditional architecture with low, upward-sweeping roof eaves and heavy tiles now gathering moss. Tiny alleyways lead off in all directions. About fifteen minutes' walk along Jiefang Lu is the Ming-dynasty complex of **Fuxi Miao** (daily 8am–11pm; ¥5) commemorating the mythological Fuxi, credited with introducing the Chinese to fishing, hunting and animal husbandry – there is a statue of him, clad in leaves, in the main hall. The temple is notable for its beautiful cypress trees; as you enter, you pass a thousand-year-old tree on the right. Another interesting temple complex, **Yuquan Si** (daily 8am–7pm; ¥10), in the western part of town, occupies **Yuquanguan Park**, up above Renmin Xi Lu. This is a 700-year-old active Taoist temple, on a hill about ten minutes' walk northwest of the main square. Surrounded by attractive cypress trees, it offers good views over the old city. Bus #24 (¥0.5) from Fuxi Miao will take you to the bottom of a path that leads to the entrance.

Practicalities

All trains stop at the **train station** in Beidao. **Buses**, including services to and from Lanzhou, Linxia, Pingliang, Guyuan (in Ningxia) and Xi'an, usually use

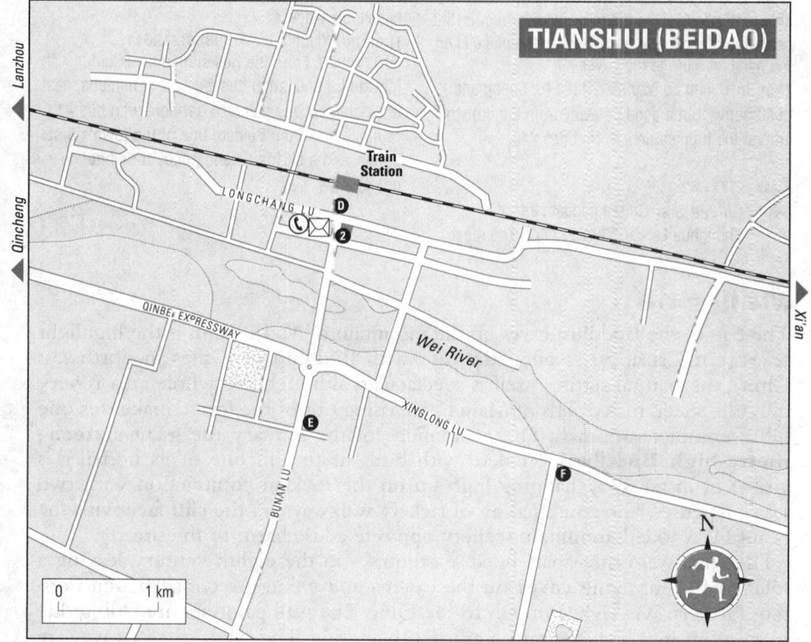

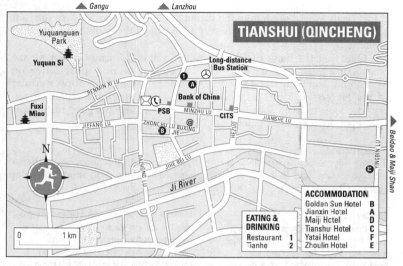

the long-distance **bus station** in Qincheng, or stop and start in front of the train station. **City transport** between the two centres is swift and efficient, with minibuses and bus #1 running between the two stations all day (6am–10pm; 30min; ¥2). A taxi between the two should cost around ¥20.

The Beidao **post office** is just southwest of the train station, the **Bank of China** just southeast. About the only decent place to get a **meal** in Beidao is at the *Tianhe* – head south from the station to the first crossroads, then turn left and it's on the corner. The staff are very friendly, and the cook makes an effort to impress.

In Qincheng, the **Bank of China** head office is on Minzhu Lu; look for the twin lions outside. To make long-distance calls, use the main **post office** on Minzhu Lu. The Tianshui **CITS** (Ⓣ0938/8287337) is on the northwest corner of the Hezuo Lu/Minzhu Lu intersection. English-speaking staff here can organize tours to Maiji Shan for a reasonable ¥200. There is a good **restaurant** right opposite the *Jianxin* hotel.

Accommodation

There's decent **accommodation** in both Beidao and Qincheng, but as there's little to detain you in town after a visit to Maiji Shan, you might consider getting a late train out.

Beidao

Maiji Opposite the train station Ⓣ0938/4920000, Ⓕ4929320. Not a bad choice, with elderly furnished rooms, and friendly staff. Dorm beds ¥40, ❹

Yatai Xinglong Lu Ⓣ0938/2727712. The lobby is a little pretentious given the fairly average rooms, but rates aren't expensive and, usefully, the place is on the minibus route to the caves. ❸

Zhoulin Bunan Lu Ⓣ0938/2738118. Cheap and unattractive, but a good getaway from the crowds around the train station. Dorm beds ¥45, ❷

Qincheng

Golden Sun On the pedestrianized Zhonghua Lu Ⓣ0938/8277777. The most upmarket option in town, with a bar and a restaurant. The staff can speak English. A taxi from the nearby bus station costs ¥3. ❻

Jianxin 5min walk west of the bus station Ⓣ0938/4985300. This aged hotel is a cheap and hospitable place. ❸

Tianshui Yingbin Lu Ⓣ0938/8212611, Ⓕ8213920. From the bus station, walk onto Minzhu Lu and catch bus #1, or any minibus, east to Yingbin Lu. You can also get here with bus #1 or minibuses from Beidao. One of the town's first hotels, and a bit frayed and pricey for what you get. ❺

Maiji Shan

The trip to the Buddhist caves on the mountain of **Maiji Shan** is the highlight of eastern Gansu. As is often the case with Buddhist cave sites in northwest China, the natural setting itself is spectacular: although the whole area is very hilly, the sheer, rocky cliffs of Maiji Shan, rising out of the forest, make this one hill a complete anomaly. The centrepiece of the statuary, the giant **sixteen-metre-high Buddha** (complete with birds nesting in one of its nostrils), is visible from far away, hanging high up on the rock in conjunction with two smaller figures. The combination of rickety walkways on the cliff face with the beautiful wooded, mountain scenery opposite adds charm to the site.

The cliffs were split apart by an earthquake in the eighth century, leaving a total of 194 surviving **caves** on the eastern and western sections, dating from the northern Wei right through to the Qing. The wall paintings are fading due to rain erosion, but the statues are worth visiting. The western cliff caves are particularly well preserved, and date mainly from the fourth to the sixth century AD: Cave no. 133 is considered to be the finest, containing sculptures and engraved stones. You are free to explore on your own, climbing higher and higher up the narrow stairways on the sheer face of the mountain. The caves are all locked, though, and you often find yourself peering into half-lit caverns through wire grilles, but for the non-specialist the view is probably adequate – at least some of the artwork and statuary shows up clearly. If you ask around at the site, you may be able to find an English-speaking guide to unlock the cave doors and explain the artwork Another option is to arrange a guide in advance with the pleasant Tianshui CITS before you set out.

Practicalities

Frequent **minibuses** run to the caves from the square outside Tianshui's train station (45min–1hr); the ride costs ¥10 each way, though foreigners are usually charged double. According to some local maps, bus #5 also goes to the caves from Qincheng, but in fact this route is only available on national holidays. When you reach Maiji Shan (daily 8am–6pm), there is a fee of ¥70 or ¥80 per person – depending on whether you want the bus ride up the mountain – to enter the mountain area.

Gangu, Wushan and Pingliang

West of Tianshui, on the road and rail line to Lanzhou, are a couple of little-known but fascinating reminders of the Silk Road era. The prime attraction at **GANGU**, 65km west of Tianshui, reached by either train or bus, is **Daxiang Shan** (Giant Statue; ¥10). It gets its name from the giant statue of an unusually moustached Sakyamuni Buddha which was carved out of a cliff during the Tang dynasty. The statue is more than 23m tall, and can be reached in about an hour by foot along a path leading uphill from the town, following a shrine-studded ridge all the way to the temple.

From **Wushan**, 45km west of Gangu, you can visit the **Shuilian Dong** (Water Curtain Grottoes; ¥10), which contain a number of important relics, including the **Lashao Temple** (Dafo Ya), as well as a Thousand Buddha Cave site. This extraordinary area is all the better preserved for being so inaccessible – the temple, set into a natural cave in a cliff, is not visible from the ground. Digging at the grottoes began during the Sixteen States period (304–439 AD) and continued through the dynasties. The Lashao Temple was built during the Northern Wei (386–534). There is a forty-metre-high statue of Sakyamuni on the mountain cliff, his feet surrounded by wild animals, including lions, deer and elephants. It is a rare design of Hinayana, a branch of Buddhism, in Chinese cave art. The grottoes, about 30km north of Wushan, can only be reached along a dried-up river bed – a new road is being built but it's worth asking about the situation before heading out.

All **buses** – and all **trains** except for express services – running between Tianshui and Lanzhou stop at both Gangu and Wushan. It's also possible to visit Gangu as a day-trip from Tianshui; minibuses run from the Qincheng bus station in the morning. If you want to visit both Gangu and the grottoes in one day from Tianshui you have to rent a vehicle; to handle the rough road from Wushan, it is better to get a small minibus (¥500) rather than a taxi (¥200). It is a long, tiring excursion and might be simpler to stay a night at either Wushan or Gangu, perhaps as a stopover on the way between Tianshui and Lanzhou. Note that access to the Water Curtain Grottoes is dependent on the weather – you won't be able to use the river bed if it has been wet recently.

Pingliang

About 200km northeast of Tianshui, an eight-hour bus journey, lies the modern city of **PINGLIANG**. The surrounding area, a mountainous and beautiful part of Gansu province near the border with Ningxia, is little known to foreigners. The chief local attraction is **Kongtong Shan**, originally a Taoist monastery now combining Buddhism. It is one of China's most venerated, perched precariously on a clifftop, with Guyuan in southern Ningxia a possible day-trip, two hours away by bus. The last bus to Guyuan is at 4pm, and there are trains leaving around midnight to Yinchuan and Xi'an.

If you arrive by bus, the most convenient **place to stay** is at the well-maintained *Tianxing* (Ⓣ0933/8713691; ❸, dorm beds ¥20,); come out of the bus station, turn left over a bridge and it's about 200m down on the left. Continue down the road and you come to a string of cheap **restaurants**; try the local *helao mian*, a noodle dish with vegetarian and meat choices (under ¥5). If you arrive at the train station, 2km out of town, the nearest hotel is the *Pingliang Binguan Fenbu* (Ⓣ0933/8623711; ❸, dorm beds ¥60), just south of the station, over the bridge and on the right. Continue down this road for 100m and you come to the **east bus station** with sleeper buses to Xi'an (¥50) and Lanzhou (¥63) leaving every thirty minutes. The plushest hotel in town is the *Pingliang* (Ⓣ0933/8253361; ❹) on Xi Dajie, where you can also change foreign currencies. Bus #1 from the train station will get you there. The **west bus station** on the other side of town, also reached by bus #1, is busier, serving destinations including Beijing, Ürümqi, Yinchuan, Guyuan, Lanzhou and Tianshui.

Kongtong Shan

Kongtong Shan lies 15km west of Pingliang; around ¥30 one way by taxi, or ¥5 on one of the summer-only tourist buses from the west bus station. You'll be dropped at the bottom of the mountain, from where you then walk 4km up a winding road to the top, buying a ticket (¥60) on the way. Alternatively, a shuttle bus can save you the effort for ¥15. On arrival you'll be rewarded with spectacular views over an azure lake, the surrounding ribbed landscape dotted with Taoist temples. Maps of the area are available from kiosks at the top, and you're free to hike off in any direction – head upwards for the best buildings, down towards the lake for the best scenery.

Getting to see everything Kongtong Shan has to offer takes at least three days; your ¥60 ticket allows you to stay as long as you want. It is certainly worth staying overnight if you want to avoid the day-tripping crowds; **accommodation** is available at the touristy *Kongtong Shanzhuang* (closed Nov–April; dorm beds ¥60) and a primitive Taoist hostel *Taihe Gong* (dorm beds ¥20) in the resort site.

Lanzhou and around

On the map, **LANZHOU** appears to lie very much in the middle of China, though this is a misleading impression. Culturally and politically it remains remote from the great cities of eastern China, despite being both the provincial capital and the largest industrial centre in the Northwest. At the head of the Hexi Corridor, it was a vital stronghold along the Silk Road and was the principal crossing point of the mighty Yellow River. For centuries it has been a transportation hub, first for caravans, then shallow boats and now rail lines. Not until the Communist era, however, did it become a large population centre as well, in response to the city's burgeoning industry. Now the city has nearly three million people, the vast majority of them Han Chinese.

Lanzhou is an ugly but friendly city with an excellent **museum**, tasty food and busy downtown **shopping** areas. The Yellow River, running thick and brown through the city against a backdrop of hills dim with mist, dust and industrial pollution, is seen by some as one of China's classic sights, while the

Lanzhou and around

Lanzhou	兰州	*lánzhōu*
Baita Shan Park	白塔山公园	*báitǎ shān gōngyuán*
Baiyun Guan	白云观	*báiyún guàn*
City Museum	市博物馆	*shì bówùguǎn*
Dongfanghong Square	东方红广场	*dōngfānghóng guǎngchǎng*
Gansu Provincial Museum	甘肃省博物馆	*gānsùshěng bówùguǎn*
Journey to the West statue	西游记塑像	*xīyóujì sùxiàng*
Lanshan Park	兰山公园	*lánshān gōngyuán*
Wuquan Park	五泉公园	*wǔquán gōngyuán*
Xiguan Shizi	西关十字	*xīguān shízì*
Yellow River	黄河	*huánghé*
Yufo Si	玉佛寺	*yùfó sì*
Bus Stations		
East Bus Station	汽车东站	*qìchē dōngzhàn*
Main Bus Station	市长途汽车站	*shì chángtú qìchēzhàn*
South Bus Station	汽车南站	*qìchē nánzhàn*
West Bus Station	汽车西站	*qìchē xīzhàn*
Accommodation		
Hualian Hotel	兰州华联宾馆	*lánzhōu huálián bīnguǎn*
Lanshan	兰山宾馆	*lánshān bīnguǎn*
Lanzhou Fandian	兰州饭店	*lánzhōu fàndiàn*
Lanzhou Legend	飞天大酒店	*fēitiān dàjiǔdiàn*
Longfei	龙飞宾馆	*lóngfēi bīnguǎn*
Shengli	胜利宾馆	*shènglì bīnguǎn*
Youyi	友谊宾馆	*yǒuyì bīnguǎn*
Eating and drinking		
Boston Coffee	伯顿餐厅	*bódùn cāntīng*
Hage Fadian	哈格饭店	*hāgé fàndiàn*
Huifeng Lou	惠丰楼	*huìfēng lóu*
Miandian Wang	面点王	*miàndiǎn wáng*
Yuxiangge Niurou Mian	玉香阁牛肉面	*yùxīanggé niúròu miàn*
Bingling Si Caves	炳灵寺千佛洞	*bǐnglíngsì qiānfódòng*
Liujiaxia Reservoir	刘家峡水库	*liújiāxiá shuǐkù*
Liujiaxia Hydroelectric Dam	刘家峡水电站	*liújiāxiá shuǐdiànzhàn*
Yongjing	永靖	*yǒngjìng*

major historical and artistic attraction lies just beyond the city at the **Bingling Si** Buddhist Caves. Nearly all travellers on their way to or from Xinjiang will end up stopping in Lanzhou; it's worth staying a day or so but no longer.

Arrival

Squeezed 1600m up into a narrow valley along the Yellow River, Lanzhou stretches out pencil-thin for nearly 30km east to west. The eastern part of the city starts at Tianshui Lu and spreads west to the Xiguan Shizi Lukou (crossroads) with Dongfanghong Square roughly at the centre; this is the oldest part of the town, most interesting for walking, eating and shopping. The western part is relatively quiet, with the provincial museum and the popular *Youyi Hotel*.

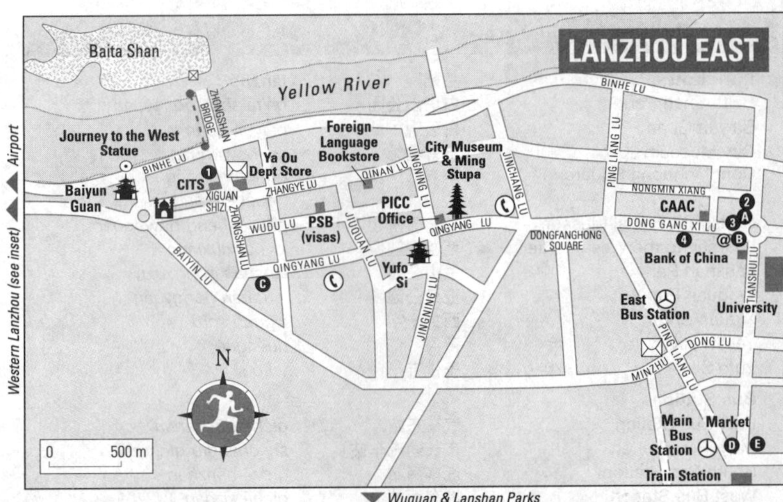

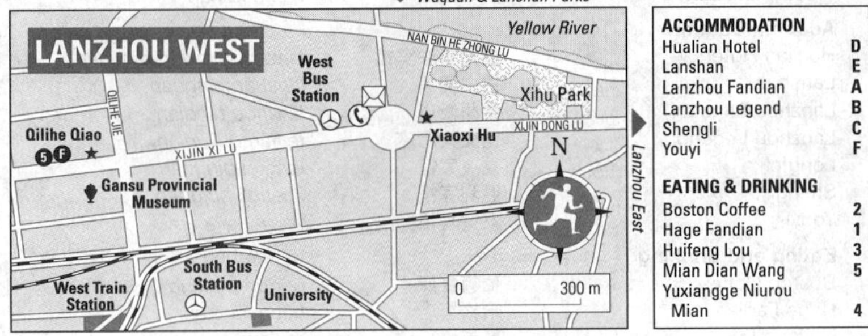

Lanzhou's **airport** lies about 70km north of the city, at least a ninety-minute journey, with connections to all major Chinese cities and Dunhuang and Jiayuguan within Gansu province. The airport buses (¥30) terminate conveniently in the eastern part of the city, outside the CAAC office on Dong Gang Xi Lu, a few minutes west of the *Lanzhou Fandian*.

As the main rail hub of northwest China, Lanzhou is an easy place to travel into or out of by train. Arriving this way, you will almost certainly be dropped off at the massive main **train station** in the far southeast of the city; there are a number of hotels nearby. Bus #7, #10 or #34 can take you the 2km north to Tianshui Lu, while western Lanzhou, more than a dozen kilometres away, can be reached on bus #1 and trolleybus #31. Should you arrive from Yinchuan, Jiayuguan, Wuwei or Xining by slow train, you can get off at the **west train station**, from where walking up Qilihe Jie will take you to the *Youyi Hotel*. **Taxi fares** start at ¥7 for 3km on the meter.

There are several **long-distance bus stations** in Lanzhou. Buses from **Xiahe** arrive at the **south bus station**; bus #111 outside can take you to Xiguan Shizi Lukou in the centre. Buses from the Hexi Corridor might wind up here too, or – along with traffic from everywhere else – terminate near the train station at the **main bus station** (well hidden on lower Ping Liang Lu), or at the larger **east bus station** 1km north.

Moving on from Lanzhou

Aside from the places mentioned below, plane and train tickets can also be booked through travel agents with 36 hours notice and around ¥30 commission – see "Listings", p.993.

There are **flights** to Dunhuang, Ürümqi, Beijing, Xi'an, Shanghai and plenty of other destinations China-wide. Lanzhou's CAAC office is on Donggang Xi Lu (daily 8am–9pm; ⓣ0931/8411606).

To buy **bus tickets**, you'll need a PICC Travel Insurance Certificate (see box, p.983), available at the bus stations, from travel agents at the *Lanzhou Fandian*, or direct from the PICC office on Qingyang Lu. The **west bus station** isn't of much use except to Liujia Xia, where you can get a boat to Bingling Si (see p.994). The earliest bus leaves at 7am, and takes about an hour (¥12). Be careful of touts here and buy the tickets only from the window – the station staff are very helpful. The **south bus station**, at the southwest end of the town, opposite the Lanzhou Science and Technology University, is more useful for tourists. There are three daily (7.30am, 8.30am & 2pm) luxury express buses to Xiahe and frequent buses to Linxia, with the earliest one leaving at 7am and only taking two and a half hours. There are also buses to Zhangye, Wuwei, Jiayuguan Dunhuang and Ürümqi. To get to the south bus station, take bus #111 (¥0.5) at Xiaoxi Hu on Xijin Dong Lu, heading west to the end. The **main bus station** on Ping Liang Lu is smaller and has frequent departures to Xining, Tianshui, Yinchuan, Guyuan and Pingliang, along with a sleeper to Ürümqi. The chaotic **east bus station**, twenty minutes north of the main station, handles basically the same destinations plus far more long-distance inter-province traffic.

Unless you're heading to Xiahe, Linxia or somewhere similarly remote, the **train** is probably the best way to leave Lanzhou – all main towns along the Hexi Corridor to the northwest have stations, and there are good connections east to Tianshui, north to Yinchuan in Ningxia, and west to Xining over in Qinghai. Even better, you won't need a PICC certificate. Buying train tickets is easy enough at the station, though you'll have to queue. It can be hard to get tickets around the beginning of the year and in summer; in this case, try a travel agent, allowing at least 48 hours notice.

Accommodation

Most accommodation in Lanzhou is in the vicinity of the train station – an inexpensive but grotty location.

Hualian Hotel Tianshui Lu ⓣ0931/4992102, ⓦwww.lzhlbg.com. As you emerge from the train station, you can't miss this tinted-windowed monster. It's pretty plush inside for the price. On-site spa, travel service beauty salon, *et al.* ❸

Lanshan Tianshui Lu ⓣ0931/8617211 ext 218. Near the station end of Tianshui Lu – look for the blue sign. The interior is pretty basic, but the rooms are cheap and the staff friendly. ❶

Lanzhou Fandian Dong Gang Xi Lu, northeast of the Panxuan Lu bus stop ⓣ0931/8416321, ⓕ8418608. From the train station take bus #1, #7 or #10 due north a couple of stops. The semi-luxurious interior belies the grim Communist-era exterior, and there's a branch of Western Travel Service on site. ❻

Lanzhou Legend Panxuan Lu, across the road from its ugly cousin the *Lanzhou Fandian* ⓣ0931/8532888, ⓦwww.lanzhoulegendhotel.com. The plushest hotel in town, with international-standard rooms, three restaurants and a quiet bar. ❼

Shengli (Victory Hotel) Qingyang Lu ⓣ0931/8465221. Between the eastern and western halves of the city, handily placed for the downtown eating areas. Rooms are good value; cheaper dorms are in the west wing, but they are reluctant to rent them to foreigners. To get here, take trolleybus #31 or bus #1 from the train station (heading west) or bus #111 from the south bus station (heading northeast). Dorm beds ¥46, ❺

Youyi (Friendship Hotel) Xijin Xi Lu ⓣ0931/2689999, ⓕ2330304. A good budget option, clean, quiet and with 24hr hot water. It's opposite the museum, a 15min walk from the West bus station – convenient for Bingling Si. If you're arriving by bus from any point in western Gansu you'll pass in front of the hotel and can ask the driver to let you off. From the train station take bus #1 or trolleybus #31 and get off at Qilihe Qiao; it's a couple of minutes' walk to your left. ❷–❹

The City

The best place to start a tour of Lanzhou is the main shopping district, roughly in the middle of the city, in the blocks that lie to the north and east of Xiguan Shizi, along the street of Zhongshan Lu (this street comes south from Zhongshan Bridge, then turns east at the *Shengli* hotel). There's a downtown feel to the place, with boutiques, Western music, fast food and smart department stores; the city's **Muslim quarter** and white-tiled mosque is also here, at the western end of Zhangye Lu.

Immediately north, the city's greatest sight is the **Yellow River**, already flowing thick and fast, although it still has some 1500km to go before it finally reaches the sea at Qingdao. In summer, the water is a rich, muddy-brown colour, a legacy of the huge quantities of silt it picks up, and the fast flow helps to create a wind corridor through the city, which both moderates the climate and removes some of the worst effects of the pollution. For boating on the river, try the area just west of Zhongshan Bridge (city side) – a few motorboats (¥20/10min) run short scenic trips. Binhe Lu on the south bank has a paved promenade from where you can watch the mud slide by, with large *Journey to the West* statues featuring Xuanzang, Monkey, Pigsy, Sandy and the horse (see p.1206); across the road, **Baiyun Guan** (daily 8am–8pm) is a small, semi-ruinous Taoist temple being extensively restored. Over the bridge, **Baita Shan Park** (daily 6am–6pm; ¥5) is ranged up a steep hillside with great views down over the river from stone terraces. A cable car (daily 9am–5pm; ¥25 return), a few minutes west of Zhongshan Lu on the south bank, can take you over the river and on to a viewpoint in the park among the hills.

Moving east from the central area takes you into the mainly modern part of the city, which has few attractions for tourists. One possible exception, a few minutes southwest of Qingyang Lu, is the **Yufo Si**. The temple is interesting more for the poignancy of its location than anything else; with high-rise buildings looming on all sides, it looks as alien as a spaceship. Nearby, a few hundred metres west of **Dong Fanghong Square** on Qingyang Lu, is an impressive wooden Ming-dynasty stupa, now housing the **City Museum**, which opens irregularly for Chinese art exhibitions.

The Gansu Provincial Museum

The west of the city comprises a comparatively upmarket shopping and residential area strung out along Xijin Xi Lu; from the centre of town take bus #1, #6 or trolleybus #31. The one sight worth visiting here, the **Gansu Provincial Museum** (Mon–Sat 9am–noon & 2.30–5.30pm; ¥30), occupies a boxy Stalinist edifice opposite the *Youyi* hotel. It has an interesting collection, divided between natural resources of Gansu (including a mammoth skeleton) and historical finds. There are some remarkable **ceramics** dating from the Neolithic age as well as a huge collection of **wooden tablets and carvings** from the Han dynasty – priceless sources for studying the politics, culture and economy of the period. The bronze **Flying Horse of Wuwei**, 2000 years old and still with its accompanying procession of horses and chariots, is the highlight, however – note the stylish chariots for top officials with round seats and sunshades. The fourteen-centimetre-tall horse, depicted with one front hoof stepping on the back of a flying swallow, was discovered in a Han-dynasty tomb in Wuwei some thirty years ago.

Wuquan and Lanshan parks

In the hills bordering the south of the city lie **Wuquan** (daily 6.30am–6.30pm; ¥5) and **Lanshan parks** (daily 6am–6pm; ¥5), just south of the terminus of bus #8 (which you can pick up anywhere on Jiuquan Lu in the centre of town). Wuquan Park is full of mainly Qing pavilions, convoluted stairways twirling up the mountainside interspersed with teahouses, art-exhibition halls and ponds. One of the oldest buildings, the **Jingang Palace**, is Ming and contains a five-metre-high bronze Buddha cast in 1370. The current Buddha was restored after being smashed into pieces in the late 1940s. It's a nice place to wander with the locals at weekends. From Wuquan Park, Lanshan Park can be reached by chair-lift (¥20) – it's about twenty minutes to the very top (600m from the city).

Eating and drinking

Lanzhou, famed around China for its *niu rou mian* (beef noodles) and delicious summer fruits, has plenty of good places to eat. Nongmin Xiang, north of *Lanzhou Fandian* off Tianshui Lu, is a good place to find inexpensive Chinese restaurants, as is the area around the west bus station, and there's a lively street food market behind the *Hualian Hotel*. There's a *KFC* at the entrance to the Zhong Ou Department Store and another on Dongfanghong Square.

Boston Coffee Tianshi Lu, next to the *Lanzhou Fandian*. Western-style food in a quiet, low-lit environment. Coffee for ¥25 a pot, pizza (¥30), sandwiches (¥20) and banana pancakes (¥16), as well as set meals and steaks (around ¥40).

Hage Fandian Opposite the post office on Zhongshan Lu. Small, family-run Muslim restaurant – try the *shaguo* (vegetables or meat with noodles in clay pots) displayed outside the door.

Huifeng Lou In the *Lanzhou Fandian* compound, Dong Gang Xi Lu. Bright, busy mid-range place serving local delicacies. Try *jincheng niangpi* (spiced glass noodles) or *suancai fentiao* (noodles flavoured with pickled vegetables, chillies and aniseed).

Mian Dian Wang Xijin Xi Lu, west of the *Youyi* hotel. Cheap Chinese-style breakfasts of steamed or fried dumplings, rice porridge and bowls of soya milk with dough sticks.

Yuxiangge Niurou Mian Opposite the CAAC offices on Dong Gang Xi Lu. No-nonsense restaurant popular with locals; eat your fill of *niu rou mian* for less than ¥5.

Listings

Banks and exchange The main Bank of China (daily 8.30am–6pm) is on Tianshui Lu, just south of the *Lanzhou Legend*; foreign exchange is on the second floor and closes between noon and 2.30pm. Other branches are scattered all over town.

Bookshops The Foreign Language Bookstore, on the south side of Qinan Lu has a pitiful selection of novels in English, in a shop that looks like it's been hit by a tornado.

Internet access There are several Net bars south of the university on Tianshui Lu, all charging about ¥2 an hour – or try upstairs through the snooker hall more or less next to the *Lanzhou Legend*.

Mail and telephones The Post and Telecommunications Office (daily 8.30am–7pm) stands at the junction of Ping Liang Lu and Minzhu Dong Lu. There's also a post office at the west bus station, and you can make collect calls at the China Telecom Building on the corner of Qingyang Lu and Jinchang Lu.

PSB Visas can be extended at an office on Wudu Lu, a couple of hundred metres west of Jiuquan Lu.

Shopping Good things to buy in Lanzhou include army surplus clothes – winter coats, waistcoats, hats and boots are all locally produced, tough and cheap. They're made at the 3512 Leather and Garment factory at the west end of Yanchang Lu, north of the river, the largest factory of its kind in China. You can even visit and buy direct (bus #7 from the train station; get off at Caochang Jie).

Travel agents Just about every business remotely connected with travel, from the bus stations and hotels to the Bank of China, seems to have a counter where you can arrange train and plane tickets. The *Lanzhou* hotel's Western Travel Service is highly recommended (daily 8am–noon & 2.30–6pm; ☎0931/8820529,

Ⓔ wtslzgschina@sina.com), with English-speaking staff. The less helpful CITS (daily 9am–6.30pm; ⓣ 0931/847018) has a small office on the first floor of the huge department store northwest of Xiguan Shizi.

Bingling Si Caves

The excursion from Lanzhou to the Buddhist caves of **Bingling Si** is one of the best you can make in all of Gansu province – enough in itself to merit a stay in Lanzhou. Not only does it offer a glimpse of the spectacular **Buddhist cave art** that filtered through to this region along the Silk Road, but also it's a powerful introduction to the **Yellow River**.

The caves are carved into a canyon southwest of the **Liujiaxia Reservoir** on the Yellow River, and can only be reached by boat (see below). From Lanzhou, the first stage of the expedition is a two-hour bus ride through impressively fertile fields to the massive **Liujiaxia Hydroelectric Dam**, a spectacular sight poised above the reservoir and surrounded by colourful mountains. At the dam you board a waiting ferry, which takes three hours to reach the caves and offers excellent views en route of fishermen busy at work and peasants cultivating wheat, sunflowers and rice on the dark, steep banks. During the trip, the ferry enters a tall **gorge** where the river froths and churns; you'll see sections of the bank being whipped away into the waters.

The ferry docks just below the Bingling Si Caves. Cut into sheer cliff, amid stunning scenery above a tributary of the river, the caves number 183 in all. They are among the earliest significant Buddhist monuments in China – started in the Western Jin and subsequently extended by the Northern Wei, the Tang, Song and Ming. Since their inaccessibility spared the caves the attentions of foreign "collectors" in the nineteenth century and the Red Guards in the twentieth, most of the cave sculpture is in good condition, and some impressive restoration work is in progress on the wall paintings. The centrepiece sculpture, approached along a dizzying network of stairs and ramps, is a huge 27-metre **seated Buddha** (Cave 172), probably carved under the Tang. The artwork at Bingling Si reached its peak under the Song and Ming dynasties, and though the wall paintings of this period have been virtually washed away, there remain a considerable number of small and exquisite carvings.

Practicalities

The most convenient way to see the caves is on a pre-booked **day-trip** from Lanzhou. There are different sets of caves, with entrance fees from ¥50 to ¥160, so day-trip rates will depend on which ones you wish to visit. Check with your agent how far your ticket will take you once there.

Most travel services in Lanzhou can arrange trips to the caves (see "Listings", p.993) though solo travellers may have to hunt around in order to tag along with another group. For a maximum car-load of three passengers, an all-inclusive price (car, boat, entry ticket and insurance) usually comes to ¥400–500. There may also be larger (and therefore cheaper) group tours operating out of the *Shengli*, and Lanzhou Western Travel Service (see p.993) offers a cheaper day-trip at ¥340 per person for three to four people. The standard trip takes up to twelve hours, which includes less than two hours at the caves, but the scenery en route makes it worthwhile. If you want a detailed guided tour, encompassing all the caves, it's worth asking about the possibility of a private trip.

Alternatively, you could consider travelling **independently** to the reservoir. From the west bus station, frequent **buses** (¥12) leave from 7am to Liujia Xia in **Yongjing**, 75km southwest of Lanzhou. At the bus stop there's an arch with a Chinese-only map; here you can pick up a speedboat for a return trip (about 2–3hr one way; ¥80 per person) or charter your own motorboat to the caves (around ¥400). On the way back you may end up staying the night in Yongjing, if the last public bus back to Lanzhou (around 5pm) leaves without you.

South from Lanzhou

This mountainous and verdant area to the south and southwest of Lanzhou, bordering on Qinghai to the west and Sichuan to the south, is one of enormous scenic beauty, relatively untouched by the scars of industry and overpopulation. The people who live here are not only few in number, but also display a fascinating cultural and ethnic diversity, with a very strong **Hui** and **Tibetan** presence in the towns of **Linxia** and **Xiahe** respectively. Xiahe, in particular, is a delightful place to visit, housing as it does one of the major Lamaist temples in China, and attracting monks and pilgrims from the whole Tibetan world. South of Xiahe, it's possible to follow an adventurous route into **Sichuan** province.

From Lanzhou to Xiahe

The road southeast from Lanzhou to Xiahe passes by first Yongjing and Liujiaxia, the jumping-off points for Bingling Si, before traversing **Dongxiang**

South from Lanzhou

Dongxiang Autonomous County	东乡自治县	*dōngxiāng zìzhìxiàn*
Linxia	临夏	*línxià*
Hehai Dasha	河海大厦	*héhǎi dàshà*
Nanguan Mosque	南关大寺	*nánguān dàsì*
Shuiquan Yibu	水泉一部	*shuǐquán yībù*
South Bus Station	汽车南站	*qìchē nánzhàn*
West Bus Station	汽车西站	*qìchē xīzhàn*
Xiahe	夏河	*xiàhé*
Gancha grassland	甘加草原	*gānjiā cǎoyuán*
Gongtang Pagoda	贡唐宝塔	*gòngtáng bǎotǎ*
Hongjiao Si	红交寺	*hóngjiāo sì*
Labrang Monastery	拉卜楞寺	*lābùléng sì*
Sangke grasslands	桑科草原	*sāngkē cǎoyuán*
Accommodation and eating		
Gangjian Longzhu	刚坚龙珠宾馆	*gāngjiān lóngzhū bīnguǎn*
Labrang	拉卜楞宾馆	*lābùléng bīnguǎn*
Labrang Baoma	拉卜楞宝马宾馆	*lābùléng bǎomǎ bīnguǎn*
Nomad	牧民饭店	*mùmín fàndiàn*
Overseas Tibetan Hotel	华侨宾馆	*huáqiáo bīnguǎn*
Tara Guesthouse	才让卓玛旅社	*cáiràng zhuómǎ lǚshè*
Hezuo	合作	*hézuò*
Mila'erba Monastery	米拉日巴佛楼阁	*mǐlā rìbā fólóugé*
Luqu	碌曲	*lùqǔ*
Qiaotou	桥头	*qiáotóu*
Langmusi	郎木寺	*lángmù sì*
Nonghang Zhaodaisuo	农行招待所	*nóngháng zhāodàisuǒ*

Autonomous County. The Dongxiang minority, numbering nearly two hundred thousand, are Muslims with Mongol origins. These days, to outsiders at least, they are indistinguishable from the Hui except at certain celebrations and festivals when ancient Mongol customs re-emerge. Beyond the pilgrimage centre of Linxia, 60km from Lanzhou, the climb up to Xiahe takes three or four hours (but only two coming down again). The route passes through a zone of cultural overlap between ancient communities of Islamic and Buddhist peoples. A couple of China's lesser-known minorities also live here, the **Bao'an** and the **Salar**. The Bao'an, who number barely eight thousand, are very similar to the Dongxiang people as they, too, are of Mongolian origins. The Salar are a Turkic-speaking people whose origins lie, it's thought, in Samarkand in Central Asia; they live primarily in Xunhua County in neighbouring Qinghai province.

Linxia

A three-hour bus journey from Lanzhou, **LINXIA** is a very **Muslim** town, full of mosques, most of which have been restored since the depredations of the Cultural Revolution. Nearly everybody here seems to wear a white skullcap, and the women additionally wear a square veil of fine lace, black if they are married and green if they are not. Linxia is also the place where all the oversized, tinted spectacles that old men wear throughout this region are made. There's not much to see in town; nevertheless, it's an interesting place to stroll around for a few hours if you feel like breaking up your journey from Lanzhou to Xiahe.

Linxia's main street, which runs north–south through town, is called **Tuanjie Lu** in the north and **Jiefang Lu** in the south, with a large central square between the two. The main mosque, **Nanguan Mosque**, is immediately south of the square. There is no train station, though there are **two bus stations**. If you're arriving from the west (Xining or Tongren), you may be deposited at the smaller staion in the far northwest of the city (known as the west bus station). In which case, you'll have to catch a cycle-rickshaw or a minivan (¥5) into town. If you arrive at the main (south) station, on Jiefang Nan Lu a couple of hundred metres south of the Jiefang Lu traffic circle, you'll be able to walk to a **hotel**. The nearest is almost immediately on the right as you come out of the station – the *Shuiquan Yibu* (Ⓣ0930/6314968; ❷, dorm beds ¥38). It's the cheapest place around, with doubles and three-bed dorms, but foreigners are sometimes charged double. Otherwise, *Hehai Dasha* is the best option, despite its filthy carpets – rooms have Western toilets (Ⓣ0930/6235455, Ⓕ6235476; ❸). It's five minutes' walk west of Hongyuan Lu, which intercepts Tuanjie Lu around 500m north of the central square. The staff can be rude and are often absent (you need to find them for door keys every time you come back to the room), but the restaurant serves very good food with generous portions. There's also a **travel service** (Ⓣ0930/6235156, Ⓕ6210001) just outside the hotel; they organize tours to Xiahe and can also provide English-speaking tour guides in summer. A pleasant **night market**, set around the central square starting from 6pm, is a good place to stuff yourself on heavy round bread rolls (*bing*) flavoured with curry powder; roast chicken and potatoes are also available, as well as noodles and soups. There are a couple of very pleasant teahouses on terraces overlooking the south side of the central square, where you can sit out and enjoy the night air.

When trying to **leave** Linxia, be aware that touts for the bus companies can be very aggressive; watch your bags carefully, or they might be grabbed and hurled through a minibus window in a bid to get your custom. Buses won't leave until the bus is absolutely overloaded with people and goods. There are frequent departures from the main bus station to Lanzhou (via Liujiaxia, for Bingling Si; see p.994) and several daily to Xiahe, leaving in the morning till 4.30pm. You can also get to Xining, Tianshui and Wuwei (via Lanzhou). Bus #4 from Haihe Dasha will take you to the main bus station, or a taxi costs ¥3. The **Bank of China** lies a few minutes south of the Nanguan Mosque, to the west.

Xiahe and around

A tiny, rural town tucked away 3000m up in the remote hills of southern Gansu, right on the edge of the Tibetan plateau, **XIAHE** is an unforgettable place. As well as offering glimpses into the life of **Tibetan people** – living and working in one of the most beautiful Tibetan monasteries you are likely to see – Xiahe also offers visitors the rare chance to spend some time in open countryside, sited as it is in a sunny, fresh valley surrounded by green hills.

Xiahe is the most important Tibetan monastery town outside Tibet itself, and the **Labrang Monastery** (Labuleng Si) is one of the six major centres of the Gelugpa, or Yellow Hat Sect (of the others, four are in Tibet and one, Ta'er Si, is just outside Xining in Qinghai province; see p.1019). Tibetans from Tibet itself come here on pilgrimage in traditional dress (equipped with mittens, kneepads, and even leather aprons to cushion themselves during their prostrations), and the constant flow of monks in bright purple, yellow and red, alongside semi-nomadic herdsmen wrapped in sheepskins, makes for an endlessly fascinating scene.

The town is essentially built along a single street that stretches 3–4km along the north bank of the Daxia River, from the bus station in the east, through the Labrang Monastery in the middle, to the old Tibetan town and finally the *Labrang Hotel* in the west. The **eastern end** of town, where the bus station lies, is predominantly Hui-and Han-populated. It's also the commercial and administrative part of town, with a couple of banks, a post office and plenty of shops and markets. The shops round here make interesting browsing, with lots of Tibetan religious objects for sale, including hand-printed sutras, prayer wheels, bells and jewellery. There's also lots of riding equipment – saddles and bridles – for the nomads from the nearby grasslands who come striding into town, spurs jangling.

Beyond the monastery, at the **western end** of town, is the local Tibetan area. West of the bridge that carries all motorized traffic to the south side of the river the road becomes a bumpy dirt track with homes built of mud and wood, and

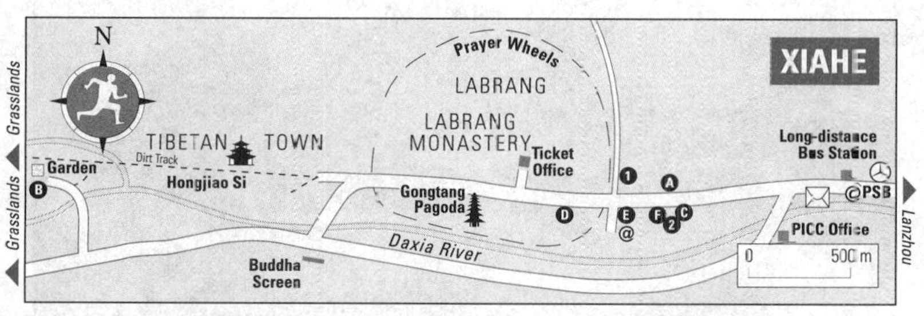

ACCOMMODATION						EATING	
Gangjian Longzhu	C	Labrang Baoma	A	Overseas Tibetan Hotel	F	Nomad	1
Labrang	B	Monastery Guesthouse	D	Tara Guesthouse	E	Tsewang's Café	2

pigs and cows ambling around. There is one more religious building up here, the **Hongjiao Si**, or Temple of the Red Hat sect, whose monks, clad in red robes with a large white band, live in the shadow of their rich and more numerous Yellow Hat brethren.

Labrang Monastery

About 1500m up from the bus station, the **monastery** area begins. There's no wall separating the town from the monastery – the two communities just merge together and the main road goes right through the middle of both. The only markers are the long lines of roofed **prayer wheels** stretching out to the right and left of the road, which together trace a complete circle around the monastery. To the south side in particular, along the north bank of the river, you can follow the prayer wheels almost to the other end of the monastery. It's a mesmerizing experience to walk alongside the pilgrims (clockwise around the monastery), who turn each prayer wheel they pass.

The monastery was founded in 1709 by a monk called E'Ang Zongzhe, who thereby became the first-generation Living Buddha, or **Jiemuyang**. Upon the death of each Jiemuyang, a new one is born, supposedly representing the reincarnation of the previous one. The present Jiemuyang, the sixth incarnation, is third in importance in the Tibetan Buddhist hierarchy after the Dalai Lama and Panchen Lama. Although Labrang may seem a peaceful haven today, it has not always been so. In the 1920s ferocious battles took place here between Muslim warlords and Tibetans, with atrocities being committed by both sides. Then in the Cultural Revolution came further disaster, with persecution for the monks and the virtual destruction (and closure) of the monastery. It was not until 1980 that it reopened, and although it is flourishing once again, it is nevertheless a smaller place today than it used to be. For an idea of its original extent, see the painting in the Exhibition Hall, on the wall at the far end from the entrance. There are now around nine hundred registered lamas, and two thousand unofficial monks, about half their former number.

▲ Labrang Monastery

The vast majority of the important **monastery buildings** are to the north of the main road. The buildings include six colleges, as well as temple halls, Jiemuyang residences and a mass of living quarters for the monks. The institutes, where monks study for degrees, are of Astronomy, Esoteric Buddhism, Law, Medicine and Theology (higher and lower). There are also schools for dance, music and painting. The **Gongtang Pagoda** (daily 7am–11pm; ¥10), built in 1805, is the only major monastery building to the south of the main road – you pass it when following the prayer wheels. You can buy tickets from the lamas inside the pagoda if the outside ticket office is closed. It's worth climbing to the top for a spectacular view over the shining golden roofs of the monastery.

Visiting the monastery

There is nothing to stop you, at any time of day or night, from wandering around the monastery site by yourself. You may even be allowed to wander into the temples – be sensitive and use your discretion, and walk clockwise. On the other hand, given the bewildering wealth of architecture, art and statuary, it's a good idea to take a **guided tour** at some stage during your stay in Xiahe. This can be arranged at the ticket office – take the only sizeable turn off the north side of the road within the monastery area (the right if coming from the station). The hour-long tours, including entrance to five buildings, led by English-speaking monks, cost ¥40, and start around 10am and 3.30pm, more frequently in peak season. You might also be approached by Tibetan students offering tours; settle a price (about ¥20) and route beforehand.

Labrang Monastery is the site of some spectacular **festivals** that, as with Chinese festivals, take place according to the lunar calendar. The largest is the **Monlam Festival**, three days after the Tibetan New Year (late Feb or early March). The opening of the festival is marked by the unfurling of a huge cloth adorned with a holy painting of the Buddha, measuring 20–30m, on the south side of the Daxia River. Subsequent days see processions, dances and the lighting of butter lamps.

Xiahe practicalities

Nearly all travellers arrive by **bus** at the station at the far eastern end of town, which is served by frequent buses from Linxia and Hezuo; there are also two buses a day to and from Lanzhou, and one morning departure for Tongren in Qinghai. For the route to Sichuan, you should take one of the two daily buses to Luqu and continue from there.

You can rent **bikes** from the *Overseas Tibetan* and *Labrang Baoma* hotels for ¥20 a day. There is no **Bank of China**, but the *Overseas Tibetan* can change cheques and cash (Euros and US dollars only). **Internet access** at ¥2.5/hour can be found at the Phoenix Internet café just south of *Tara's Guesthouse*, and at the *Labrang Baoma* at ¥5 per hour.

Accommodation

The east end of town has plenty of Chinese-style hotels. However, it's more fun to try one of the charismatic Tibetan-owned **guesthouses** farther up the road, which attract a mixed clientele of pilgrims and budget travellers.

Gangjian Longzhu 350m west of the bus station ⓣ0941/7123600. Corridors reminiscent of *The Shining* and an atmosphere to match. Hot water from 8–11pm. ④

Labrang In the fields to the west of the town ⓣ0941/7121849. It's 4km from the bus station and nearly 1km from the next nearest building; from the station, a cycle-rickshaw shouldn't cost more than about ¥5. Accommodation ranges from simple three-bed dorms with bath to rather damp concrete "Tibetan-style" cabins. Prices increase at the height of summer. Dorm beds ¥20, ⑥

Labrang Baoma In a courtyard opposite *Tsewang's Café* ⓣ0941/7121078, ⓦwww.labranghotel.com. New and very popular hotel sporting traditionally decorated rooms, Internet access, two small restaurants and 24-hour hot water. Dorm beds ¥30, ❸

Monastery Guesthouse In the heart of the monastery area. Run by monks who obviously have more important things on their minds than cleaning. Basic rooms with stoves, spartan as any monk's cell, are arranged around a scruffy courtyard. There's an 11pm curfew and no hot water. Dorm beds ¥40, ❶

Overseas Tibetan Hotel 50m east of the *Tara Guesthouse* ⓣ0941/7122642. A clean and well-maintained building offering the cheapest dorms in town. Well staffed with English-speaking employees, plus a wide range of services. Room rates include breakfast. Dorm beds ¥20, ❹

Tara Guesthouse Signed in English 50m west of the *Overseas Tibetan Hotel*, with its entrance a few doors down in the alley leading off to the south ⓣ0941/7121274. The Tibetan owners are eccentric, but it's a good place: the lovingly decorated rooms have stoves, some have *kangs*, and there's a stereo instead of a TV in most. 11pm curfew. Dorm beds ¥30, ❶

Eating

Whether you want to eat Tibetan food or banana pancakes, the eastern part of town has plenty of **restaurants**. The friendly *Tsewang's Café*, above street level, between the *Gangjian* and *Overseas Tibetan* hotels, offers the "best pizzas in town", which is a fair claim as it is about the only place you can get them, and they are in fact pretty good. The *Nomad Restaurant* (daily 8am–11pm), opposite the eastern entrance of the monastery, is also reliable, with rooftop views and a slightly overpriced English menu. They offer good breakfasts and decent Western, Chinese and Tibetan food. There's plenty more of the *Nomad*'s ilk on the same stretch. The *Overseas Tibetan* also offers set breakfasts at around ¥20 per person. For Chinese food, you can find a string of restaurants along the road west of the long-distance bus station.

Around Xiahe

Even without the monastery, Xiahe would be a delightful place to relax given its rural setting. The hills around the valley offer excellent hiking opportunities, and the views down to the monastery can be breathtaking. About 15km farther west up the valley are the **Sangke grasslands**, which can be reached by motor-rickshaw (about ¥30 return), or by bicycle. If you're cycling you can follow either the dirt track north of the river or the sealed road to the south. You'll know when you've arrived – a ticket booth (¥5) in the middle of nowhere marks the entrance, beyond which the valley opens out into a vast, grassy pasture, a lovely place to walk in summer. Nomads hang around offering rides on their horses for ¥20 an hour. From July to September you can also stay out here in yurts (¥40) affiliated to the *Labrang Hotel* – enquire at the hotel reception. Sadly, the associated garish pink casino is not an encouraging sign for the future development of this tranquil area. The **Gancha grasslands** (¥15), another 30km to the north, are less touristy and vaster, but harder to get to due to bad road conditions. A return trip by taxi costs around ¥200.

The road to Sichuan

South of Xiahe the roads are narrow and traffic irregular; nevertheless, there is a route you can follow by public bus that leads ultimately to Chengdu in Sichuan province. It's a rough trip, which requires several stopovers in remote towns, but a fascinating one – through one of the most beautiful parts of China. Some of the villages en route, notably **Langmusi** just inside Sichuan, are the most authentically **Tibetan** settlements most visitors are ever likely to see, given that it can be so hard to travel off the beaten track inside Tibet itself.

Hezuo

From Xiahe, the first stop is **HEZUO**, about 70km to the southeast. It's a trading post for Tibetan nomads and you'll see some fairly wild-looking types in the town. If you get the first morning bus (6.40am; ¥9) from Xiahe, you can move on to Luqu or Langmusi the same day – there's one bus daily from Hezuo at 9.30am. However, getting stuck here for a day is no trial.

Hezuo is centred on a crossroads with a sculpture of a Tibetan antelope in the middle, looking north. The **north bus station**, where you get off coming from Xiahe or Lanzhou, is on the northwest corner of the crossroads. Almost opposite, on the road leading north, is an adequate **hotel**, the *Gannan Binguan* (Ⓣ0931/8213186; ¥38, dorm beds ¥15), kept very clean by its Muslim staff. Look for the blue English sign. The Agricultural Bank, on the southwest corner, is the only place in town that will change **foreign currency**. Head east from the crossroads and you'll find a fascinating little street with a very good two-storey Muslim **restaurant** on the right. Buses heading south leave from the **south bus station**; a taxi there from the north bus station costs ¥2.

Hezuo also boasts one worthwhile attraction, the **Mila'erba Monastery** (¥20, negotiable), in the north of the city. From the crossroads, head west for 500m then turn north for another 1.5km – you'll see it on the left; you can hardly miss it as the impressive central temple is nine storeys high. The exterior may look stern and robust, but the interior is pure chocolate box, each room gaudy with paintings and sculpture. Provided you take your shoes off at the door, you are free to ascend every storey. From the roof you can gaze at hills dotted with prayer flags.

South of Hezuo

Beyond Hezuo, the road runs **south to Sichuan** via **LUQU**, 80km from Hezuo and served by four to five buses daily from the south bus station. The countryside around Luqu is beautiful and easily accessible for hiking; a stroll up or down the river is likely to turn up one or two monasteries. In **Luqu** itself you can stay at the *Nonghang Zhaodaisuo* (Ⓣ0941/6621085; ❷); there's no English sign, but turn right out of the bus station and it's less than five minutes' walk. From Luqu, it's a further 80km south to the charming **Langmusi**, just over the Sichuan border. Buses don't stop in Langmusi itself, but drop you off at **Qiaotou,** 4km away – it's easy to miss the stop, marked by an unobvious bridge – ask the driver to remind you beforehand. From Qiaotou jeeps or tractors will take you up the hill to the village for ¥3. For more on Langmusi, see p.927.

The Hexi Corridor

For reasons of simple geography, travellers leaving or entering China to or from Central Asia and the West have always been channelled through the narrow strip of land that runs 1000km northwest of Lanzhou. With the foothills of the Tibetan plateau, in the form of the Qilian Shan range, soaring up to the south, and a merciless combination of waterless desert and mountain to the north, the road known as the **Hexi Corridor** offers the only feasible way through the physical obstacles that crowd in west of Lanzhou.

Historically, whoever controlled the corridor could operate a stranglehold on the fabulous riches of the Silk Road trade (see box, p.950). Inevitably the Chinese took an interest from the earliest times, and a certain amount of Great Wall-building was already taking place along the Hexi Corridor under Emperor Qin Shi Huang in the third century BC. Subsequently, the powerful Han dynasty succeeded in incorporating the region into their empire, though the

The Hexi Corridor

Hexi Corridor	河西走廊	*héxī zǒuláng*
Jiayuguan	嘉峪关	*jiāyù guān*
First Beacon Tower	第一墩	*dìyī dūn*
Fort	城楼	*chénglóu*
Great Wall Museum	长城博物馆	*chángchéng bówùguǎn*
Heishan rock carvings	黑山岩画	*hēishān yánhuà*
Overhanging Wall	悬壁长城	*xuánbì chángchéng*
Qiyi Bingchuan	七一冰川	*qīyī bīngchuān*
Xincheng Dixia Hualang	新城地下画廊	*xīnchéng dìxià huàláng*
Accommodation and eating		
Jiaotong	交通宾馆	*jiāotōng bīnguǎn*
Jiayuguan Hotel	嘉峪关宾馆	*jiāyùguān bīnguǎn*
Jinhua Jiulou	金华酒搂	*jīnhuá jiǔlóu*
Jinye	金叶宾馆	*jīnyè bīnguǎn*
Linyuan Jiudian	林苑酒店	*línyuán jiǔdiàn*
Xiongguan	雄关宾馆	*xióngguān bīnguǎn*
Wuwei	武威	*wǔwēi*
Ancient Bell Tower	大云寺古钟楼	*dàyúnsì gǔzhōnglóu*
Leitai Si	雷台寺	*léitái sì*
Luoshi Pagoda	罗什塔	*luóshí tǎ*
South Gate	南门	*nánmén*
Wen Miao	文庙	*wénmiào*
Accommodation and eating		
Liangzhou	凉州宾馆	*liángzhōu bīnguǎn*
Tianma	天马宾馆	*tiānmǎ bīnguǎn*
Ya Ou	亚欧宾馆	*yà'ōu bīnguǎn*
Wanglaosan	王老三牛肉面	*wánglǎosān niúròu miàn*
Zhangye	张掖	*zhāngyè*
Dafo Si	大佛寺	*dàfó sì*
Daode Guan	道德观	*dàodé guàn*
Gulou	古楼	*gǔlóu*
Mu Ta	木塔	*mùtǎ*
Tu Ta	土塔	*tǔtǎ*
Xilai Si	西来寺	*xīlái sì*
Accommodation and eating		
Chengxin Binguan	诚信宾馆	*chéngxìn bīnguǎn*
Huachen International	华辰国际大酒店	*huáchén guójì dàjiǔdiàn*
Jindu	金都宾馆	*jīndū bīnguǎn*
Jin Xin	金鑫宾馆	*jīnxīn bīnguǎn*
Mingqing Jie	明清街	*míngqīng jiē*
Shibazhe Meishilin	十八褶美食林	*shíbāzhě měishílín*
Yi Jia e Chu	一家e厨	*yī jiā e chú*
Zhangye	张掖宾馆	*zhāngyè bīnguǎn*

influence of central government remained far from constant for many centuries afterwards, as Tibetans, Uyghurs and then Mongols vied for control. Not until the Mongol conquests of the thirteenth century did the corridor finally become a settled part of the Chinese empire, with the Ming consolidating the old Great Wall positions and building its magnificent last fort at **Jiayuguan**.

Two other towns along the corridor, **Wuwei** and **Zhangye**, offer convenient means of breaking the long journey from Lanzhou to Dunhuang, and have their own share of historic sights.

Wuwei and around

Lying approximately halfway between Lanzhou and Zhangye is the small city of **WUWEI**. Gansu's most famous historic relic, the Han-dynasty **Flying Horse of Wuwei**, was discovered here in 1969 underneath the Leitai Si, a temple just north of town. Now housed in the Lanzhou Museum (see p.992), the symbol of the horse, depicted in full gallop and stepping on the back of a swallow, can be seen everywhere in Wuwei.

The city is divided into four quadrants by the main north–south road (Bei Dajie and Nan Dajie) and the east–west road (Dong Dajie and Xi Dajie), with the centre of the city at the crossroads, marked by **Wenhua Square**. It is interesting just to wander about the square on a warm day, where people assemble to play traditional musical instruments with snack and trinkets stands peppered around. There's a trace of the old city near the bus station on Nan Dajie, where the original **south gate** has been impressively reconstructed. Ten minutes' walk north of here, if you take the first road on the right, you'll arrive at the Ming-dynasty-built **Wen Miao** (daily 8am–6pm; ¥31), a delightful museum in the grounds of an old temple with large gardens full of oleanders and singing birds. The most interesting item in the museum is a stone stele with Chinese and Xixia language on both sides (see box p.977).

About twenty minutes due north of here, through the last remains of the city's old adobe dwellings, the **Ancient Bell Tower** in **Dayun Si** (daily 8am–6pm; ¥10) is worth a visit mostly for its grounds, where old men play mahjong or cards and drink tea under vine trellises and enormous hollyhocks. Occasional Taoist ceremonies are undertaken outside the main hall in the temple, depending upon local demand. A further twenty minutes' walk west brings you to Bei Dajie, near the 1600-year-old brick **Luoshi Pagoda** from where you can catch bus #2 a few kilometres or walk twenty minutes north to **Leitai Si** (daily 8am–6pm; ¥50). The temple, built high up on impressive mud ramparts, is surrounded by modern construction projects, but its grounds remain pleasantly calm and shady. Beneath the site, through a separate entrance, a Chinese-speaking tour guide will lead you to the famous **Han-dynasty tomb** where the Flying Horse statue was discovered. There's not much to see – a

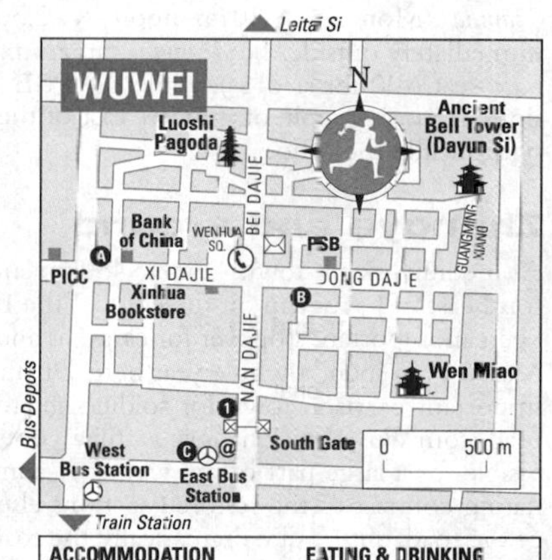

series of very low passageways, with a mock-up of the tomb contents at the back – but the 2000-year-old brickwork is still in perfect condition and amazingly modern in appearance. Ironically, the bronze Flying Horse, now a prized relic, remained in the tomb long after accompanying items of gold and silver had been stolen.

Practicalities

Wuwei's **east bus station** lies just outside the old south gates, with several freelance depots further west. There are frequent buses to Lanzhou (7am–8pm; 3hr). Five minutes' walk west from here is the newer **west bus station** with occasional luxury express buses to Lanzhou, Zhangye (4hr) and Zhongwei (5–6hr). The **train station** is 3km to the south, from where it costs a couple of Yuan to take a minibus into the centre. All trains between Ürümqi and the east stop at Wuwei, and there's also a slow train to Zhongwei in Ningxia. It's easy to buy hard-seat tickets at the station – fine for the short hops to Lanzhou or Zhangye – but sleepers are best arranged through a travel agent.

Accommodation, though increasing, is still scarce compared to elsewhere. Just a few minutes west of the bus station is the very good value *Ya Ou* (Ⓣ0935/2265700; ❶). The *Liangzhou* on Dong Dajie (Ⓣ0935/2265999; ❹), a couple of minutes east of the central crossroads, has nice doubles with 24-hour hot water, and good off-peak discounts. The dull *Tianma*, west on Xi Dajie (Ⓣ0935/2212356; ❸), is often stacked with Japanese tourist groups. Ask for rooms on the eighth or ninth floor, which are cleaner and quieter. For **food**, there are numerous noodle houses around the bus station and on Nan Dajie north of the south gate, serving soups and mutton dishes heavily laced with chilli. Immediately to you left as you pass north under the South Gate, *Wanglaosan Niuroumian* do a fantastic *chaomian* that serves up more or less like a huge spaghetti bolognese. The *Liangzhou* has a decent Chinese restaurant, and *Ya Ou*'s does passable one-person hotpots. There's also a *Dico's* just west of Renmin Square.

The huge China Telecom building (daily 8am–6.30pm), where you can make long-distance phone calls, is immediately east of Wenhua Square, and across Bei Dajie is the **post office**. There's an unusually clean and friendly **Internet café** to the southwest of the South Gate. The **Bank of China** is just east of the *Tianma* (Mon–Fri 8.30am–noon & 2.30–6pm). **CITS** (Ⓣ0935/2267239), immediately outside the *Tianma*, can arrange train tickets (commission ¥15 for hard seat, ¥30 for sleeper), while the **PSB** office, which deals with visa extensions, is just a couple of minutes east of the *Liangzhou* – there's a small English sign outside the office.

Zhangye and around

A medium-sized town, about 450km northwest of Lanzhou and 150km southeast of Jiayuguan on the edge of the Loess plateau, **ZHANGYE** has long been an important stopover for caravans and travellers on the Silk Road. Indeed, Marco Polo spent a whole year here. During the Ming period, Zhangye was an important garrison town for soldiers guarding the **Great Wall**, and today the road from Wuwei to Zhangye is still a good place from which to view the Wall, visible for a large part of the way as a crumbling line of mud ramparts, a fascinating contrast to the restored sections elsewhere. Initially it runs to the north of the road, until, quite dramatically, the road suddenly cuts right through a hole in the Wall and continues on the other side.

Although Zhangye is not especially attractive, there are a number of places that should fill at least a day of sightseeing. The centre of the town is marked, as in many Chinese towns, by a **Gulou** (Drum Tower) at the crossroads. The tower, built in 1507 during the Ming dynasty, has two tiers and houses a massive bronze bell. The four streets radiating out from here, Bei Jie, Dong Jie, Nan Jie and Xi Jie, are named after their respective compass points. Most places of interest are in the southwest of town near the *Zhangye Hotel*.

Just east of the *Zhangye*, a central smoke-grimed hall at **Dafo Si** (Big Buddha Temple; daily: summer 7.30am–6.30pm, winter 8am–6pm; ¥40) houses a 34-metre-long **reclining Buddha**, easily China's largest, whose calm expression and gentle form make a powerful impression. Immediately behind the Buddha are ten disciples and grotesque-looking luohans (saintly warriors) standing around in the gloom. Unusually, the hall itself, built in 1098 and restored in 1770, is almost entirely made of wood. In the same grounds the **Tu Ta** (Earth Tower; same ticket) is a former Buddhist monastery; now in use as a local culture centre, it features a single large stupa 20m in height. At the time of writing the whole complex is in complete disarray as restoration work is carried out.

On Xianfu Jie, a few hundred metres north of the *Zhangye*, looms the 31-metre-tall **Mu Ta** (Wooden Tower; daily 8am–6pm; ¥5), built in the sixth century, before being burnt down and then restored in 1925… in brick. The octagonal tower is now home to a number of jackdaws. A few hundred metres south of here, and one block to the west, the **Xilai Si** is a small Buddhist temple where you can see monks chanting at dusk and dawn.

Much farther away, about fifteen minutes' walk due east from Gulou on the road to the train station, is a charming Taoist monastery, the **Daode Guan**. It's a small, dishevelled place of Ming origins, containing a tiny garden, some vine trellises, and some well-maintained Taoist statues and wall paintings. Monks here are hospitable and seem completely detached from the modern world. The monastery is hidden in a jumble of narrow lanes on the north side of Dong Jie, and can be easily lost among the neighbouring shops – look for the sign with gold characters on a blue background.

Practicalities

Zhangye's so-called **main bus station** is south of the centre on Huancheng Nan Lu, but most traffic now goes through the newer and bigger **western bus station** about 1km west of Gulou off Xi Jie. There's also a smaller **eastern bus station** about 2km east of Gulou. The **train** station is some 7km away to the northeast; trains are met by waiting minibuses which take you into town for ¥1.5. You could also take a taxi (¥10). There's a **Bank of China** (Mon–Fri 8.30am–6pm, Sat & Sun 9am–5pm), with ATM, and **CITS** (Ⓣ0936/8243445) just north of the *Zhangye* hotel, and the mother of all **Internet cafés** on the second floor of the building south of the *Jin Xin*. The **PSB** is on the fourth floor of a building on Qingnian Xi Jie, east of Mu Ta.

Hotels in Zhangye have enjoyed a boom in recent years. The 🏃 *Jin Xin* just northwest of Gulou is a good-value option with clean, modern rooms and bathrooms of a standard you'll rarely see in this price range (Ⓣ & Ⓕ0936/8255058; ❸). Another budget option, on Dong Jie, is the *Jindu* (Ⓣ0936/8245088; ❸), with ordinary rooms. The *Chengxin Binguan* (Ⓣ0936/8245800; ❸) at 18 Xianfu Jie is a happily staffed affair with a handy on-site travel service that will book train and bus tickets for a small fee. All of the above offer generous discounts for most of the year. The most upmarket place is the *Huachen International* (Ⓣ0936/8257777, Ⓔzyhcdh@public.lz.gs.cn; ❻), a few minutes east of the Daode Guan; staff speak good English and rooms are good value. Finally, *Zhangye* (Ⓣ0936/8212601, Ⓕ8213806; ❺), is one of the oldest and most austere hotels in town. The northern end of Xianfu Jie leads onto Mingqing Jie – a mock Ming-dynasty **food street** with more restaurants than you can shake a chopstick at, serving noodle soups, kebabs, hotpots and the like. Several places here specialize in excellent *shuijiao*, stuffed with either vegetables, seafood, beef or more exotic meats, from about ¥10 a *jin*; or try the almost smart *Shibazhe Meishilin*, partway up the east side of the street, which serves an inexpensive range of casseroles, hotpots and local snacks. If you are craving Chinese staples try 🏃 *Yi Jia e Chu* at the T-junction at the top of Mingqing Jie, where you'll find all your favourites lavishly cooked at little cost.

Moving on by bus, the western station handles most of the business, but it's still worth checking at the *Chengxin*'s travel service to find out which station you need. No trains originate or terminate in Zhangye, but most of the passing trains will stop here. You can buy train tickets at the *Chengxin* or the rail office off Mingqing Jie – look for the Marco Polo statue – the office is to its southwest.

Jiayuguan and beyond

One more cup of wine for our remaining happiness. There will be chilling parting dreams tonight.

Ninth-century poet on a leave-taking at Jiayuguan

To some Chinese, the very name **JIAYUGUAN** is synonymous with sorrow and ghastly remoteness. The last **fortress** of the Great Wall was built here by the

Ming in 1372, over 5000km from the wall's easternmost point at Shanhaiguan, from which time the town made its living by supplying the needs of the fortress garrison. This was literally the final defence of the empire, the spot where China ended and beyond which lay a terrifying wilderness. The fort, just outside the town and perfectly restored, is one of the great sights of northwestern China, and there are also a number of other forts and beacons scattered around in the desert.

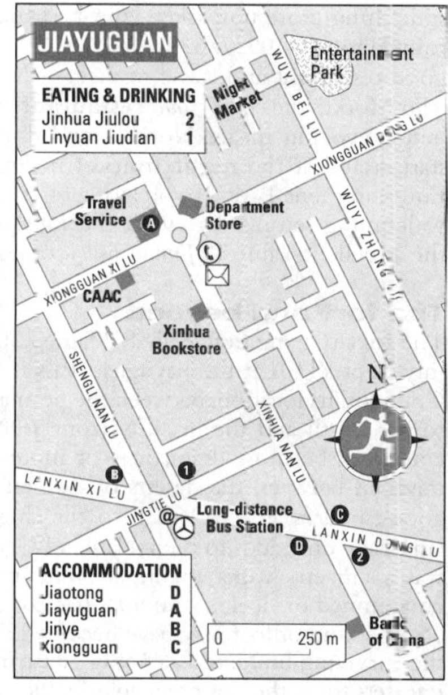

Apart from the great fort, Jiayuguan today is a bleak, lonely place. Despite this its inhabitants, on the whole, manage to be a cheerful bunch. The city, laid out in a regular grid pattern, is sliced through diagonally from east to west by Lanxin Dong Lu. The centre is a large traffic circle, overlooked by the *Jiayuguan* hotel and the post office; Xinhua Lu is the main street leading southeast from here. In the north of the town, the popular **Entertainment Park** (daily 8am–10pm) makes a good spot for an evening stroll among giant sculptures, pagodas, pleasure boats and dodgem cars. There's also an indoor swimming pool.

Practicalities

Jiayuguan's **train station** is in the far southwest of the city and linked by bus or minibus #1 (¥1) to the centre. All trains running between Ürümqi and eastern China stop here. The **bus station** has a much more convenient location on Lanxin Dong Lu, about 1km south of the central roundabout. The most useful buses are the connections with Dunhuang (5hr) or Zhangye (4hr). The **airport**, 10km from town, is connected by airport bus (¥10) to the *Jiayuguan* hotel, northwest of the central roundabout; a taxi costs (¥30).

The **travel agents** in both the *Jiayuguan* and *Xiongguan* hotels can supply train tickets for a ¥30 commission and organize local tours. **Train tickets** out of Jiayuguan are hard to come by in peak season – you will almost certainly need the help of a travel service, and may need to resort to a more expensive soft sleeper if you want to get your head down. The CAAC office (daily 8.30am–6.30pm; ⓣ0937/6266677) opposite the *Jiayuguan* to the west sells **flight tickets** to Lanzhou, Xi'an and Beijing. **Internet access** is available next to the bus station.

Accommodation is all fairly central if a little poor. Just north of the bus station, the terse staff of the *Jinye* (ⓣ0937/6201333; ❹), offer clean and tidy rooms with 24-hour hot water. The helpful *Xiongguan* (ⓣ0937/6201116; ❺) is slightly overpriced and has dubious plumbing, but is easy to find, with a handy travel service on the third floor. Over the road, the *Jiaotong* (ⓣ0937/6202260; ❸) provides smart rooms that belie its exterior, with hot water in the evenings from eight until late, and generous discounts. For something more upmarket, your best bet is the *Jiayuguan*, right on the central roundabout (Ⓣ0937/6226983, Ⓕ6227174; ❻), offering smart doubles and a good restaurant and travel service.

For food, the *Jiayuguan* **restaurant** serves bland Chinese breakfasts but better evening meals. Noodles and dumplings are available around the bus station and at the **night market** north of the *Jiayuguan* on the road to the Entertainment Park. If you want to sit down to standard Chinese food in a welcoming setting, try either the *Linyuan Jiudian* opposite the bus station or the excellent-value *Jinhua Jiulou* opposite the *Xiongguan*.

The fort and beyond

The **fort** (Cheng Lou; daily 8.30am–5.30pm; Oct–April ¥31, May & June ¥61, July–Sept ¥110) at the Jiayuguan Pass is the most important sight in the Hexi Corridor. Its location, between the permanently snowcapped Qilian Mountains to the north and the black Mazong (Horse's Mane) Mountains to the south, could not be more dramatic – or more strategically valuable. Everything that travelled between the deserts of Central Asia and the fertile lands of China – goods, traders, armies – had to file through this pass. The desolation of the landscape only adds to the melancholy – being forced to leave China altogether was a citizen's worst nightmare, and it was here that disgraced officials and condemned or fleeing criminals had to make their final, bitter farewells.

Some kind of fort may have occupied this site as early as the Han dynasty, but the surviving building is a Ming construction, completed in 1372. Sometimes referred to as the "Impregnable Defile under Heaven", it comprises an outer and an inner wall, the former more than 700m in circumference and about 10m high. At the east and the west of the inner wall stand symbolic gates, the Guanghua Men (Gate of Enlightenment) and the Rouyuan Men (Gate of Conciliation) respectively. Inside each gate are sloping walkways leading to the top of the wall, enabling horses to climb up and patrol the turrets. In between the Gate of Enlightenment and the outer wall stand a pavilion, a temple and a somewhat haunting open-air theatre that was once used to entertain troops. The entrance fee also covers the excellent **Great Wall Museum** (daily 9am–5pm), which reviews the history of the Wall from the Han to the last frenzied spurt of construction under the Ming. The highlights are photos and scale models of the Wall taken from points right across northern China, places that for the most part lie well away from tourist itineraries.

The so-called **Overhanging Wall** (daily 8am–7pm; ¥21), about 8km northwest of the fort, is a section of the Great Wall connecting the fort to the Mazong range, originally built in the sixteenth century and recently restored. The ramparts afford excellent views of the surrounding land; it was more atmospheric before they built a crassly environmentally insensitive tourist village nearby, but is still worth a visit so you can gaze out west and imagine what it was like when this place represented the end of China's civilized world.

Other desert sights

Several other desert attractions around Jiayuguan could also be combined with a trip to the fort and the Wall. About 6km south of Jiayuguan are the ruins of the **First Beacon Tower** (¥21). Built on the Great Wall in the sixteenth century, the long-abandoned tower is now crumbling on a clifftop on the northern bank of the Taolai River at the foot of the Qilian Mountains. The desert also harbours a couple of unusual collections of ancient Chinese art. One is the **Xincheng Dixia Hualang** (Underground Gallery; ¥31), about 20km northeast of Jiayuguan. Actually a burial site from the Wei and Jin periods, more than eighteen hundred years ago, the graves are brick-laid and contain vivid paintings depicting contemporary life on each brick. Not far beyond the fort, 9km northwest of Jiayuguan, are the **Heishan rock carvings**. These look more like classic "cave man" art: on the cliffs of the Heishan Mountain are carved more than a hundred pictures of hunting, horse-riding and dancing, all dating back to the Warring States Period (476–221 BC). Finally, one stupendous but rather inaccessible natural sight is the **Qiyi Bingchuan** (July 1st Glacier ¥51), located 4300m up in the Qilian Mountains, 120km from Jiayuguan – remarkably close considering what a hot place Jiayuguan is in summer.

Practicalities

The easiest way to reach both the fort and the Wall is to hire a **taxi** (around ¥100 for the whole trip); visiting the First Beacon Tower and the two art sites in conjunction with a tour of the fort and Overhanging Wall takes a day and costs ¥200. You can get to the fort by public transport in summer – take minibus #4 (¥1) from the roundabout outside the *Jiayuguan*. To **cycle** to the fort, follow Lanxin Xi Lu west from the bus station until you cross the bridge over the rail line. A blue sign pointing right indicates the way from here. From the fort to the Overhanging Wall, you go back 50m from the car park and follow the only road to your left with another blue sign not far ahead until reaching a junction, where you take a right, marked by an ugly grey concrete building. Ride straight down this road until you reach the ticket office. It's about thirty minutes to the fort, another thirty to the Overhanging Wall, and forty back into town.

A day-trip to the **glacier** by taxi costs at least ¥500. Travel agents (see p.1007) in town provide tours with an English guide for around ¥600. It's a long day, involving a three-hour drive, followed by five hours climbing up and down, and three hours driving back.

Dunhuang and the Mogao Caves

An oasis town perched right on the outer periphery of old Chinese Turkestan, **DUNHUANG** has always been literally on the edge of the desert – from downtown you can see giant, spectacular **sand dunes** at the bottom of the street, and winds can whip up abrasive yellow sandstorms. Dunhuang's fame rests on the astonishing artwork at the nearby **Mogao Caves**, and the town has become something of a desert resort for visiting them, with inexpensive hotels, lots of English-language menus in the restaurants and friendly people.

The town itself is made up of a few ordinary, appealing streets – the centre is marked by a traffic circle with streets radiating out to the north, east, south and west. On the main street east, Yangguan Dong Lu, there's the interesting **Shazhou night market** selling food and **souvenirs** every summer evening, where you can stroll with no pressure to buy. Coins, jade articles, Buddhas, Tibetan bells and horns, leather shadow puppets, scroll paintings and Chinese chops are all on sale. Nearby, the mediocre **Dunhuang City Museum** (daily 8am–6pm; closed Jan–March; ¥10) houses a few of the scrolls left behind after the depredations of the archeologist and adventurer Sir Aurel Stein (see box, p.1014). Next to the museum, the **Dunghuang Theatre** puts on three one-hour-long regional cultural dance performances every night from May 1 to September 31 (¥80–200).

Dunhuang and the Mogao Caves		
Dunhuang	敦煌	*dūnhuáng*
Baima Ta	白马塔	*báimǎ tǎ*
Dunhuang City Museum	敦煌市博物馆	*dūnhuángshì bówùguǎn*
Dunhuang Theatre	敦煌剧院	*dūnhuáng jùyuàn*
Mingsha Shan	鸣沙山	*míngshā shān*
Mogao Caves	莫高窟	*mògāo kū*
Research and Exhibition Centre	石窟文物研究陈列中心	*shíkū wénwù yánjiū chénliè zhōngxīn*
Shazhou Night Market	沙洲夜市	*shāzhōu yèshì*
Xi Qianfodong	西千佛洞	*xī qiānfódòng*
Yangguan	阳关	*yángguān*
Yueya Quan	月牙泉	*yuèyá quán*
Yumenguan	玉门关	*yùmén guān*
Accommodation		
Dunhuang Binguan	敦煌宾馆	*dūnhuáng bīnguǎn*
Dunhuang Fandian	敦煌饭店	*dūnhuáng fàndiàn*
Feitian	飞天宾馆	*fēitiān bīnguǎn*
Five Rings	五环宾馆	*wǔhuán bīnguǎn*
Guangyuan	广源大酒店	*guǎngyuán dàjiǔdiàn*
International	敦煌国际大酒店	*dūnhuáng guójì dàjiǔdiàn*
Liuyuan	柳园	*liǔyuán*

Practicalities

Until recently, there was no rail line directly to Dunhuang, with the nearest **train station** at Liuyuan about 130km away. However, at the time of writing the city's very own station was on the point of opening, with planned services to and from Ürümqi, Lanzhou and Yinchuan. Tickets are available at the offices next to the *Dunhuang* hotel and the entrance to the PSB. **Dunhuang bus station** lies south of town on Mingshan Lu, and the **airport** is about 13km southeast of town; the airport bus stops at the **CAAC** office (daily 8am–noon & 3–6pm; ⓣ0937/88222389) on Yangguan Dong Lu; minibuses cost ¥20 per person. In addition to the many hotel **travel agents**, *Charley Johng's Café* (ⓔdhzhzh@public.lz.gs.cn) on Mingshang comes especially recommended for organizing transport and tours, while *John's Information Café* in the *Feitian* hotel (ⓔjohncafé@hotmail.com) is also worth checking out. **CITS** are on the second floor in the building facing the *International* hotel (ⓣ0937/8835529) – an English-speaking guide from here costs ¥150 for the day, while a car will set you back upwards of ¥500. Both of the **Bank of China** branches (Mon–Fri 8am–noon & 3–6.30pm), one on either side of the post office roundabout on Yangguan Lu, have **ATMs**.

You can **rent bikes** from *Shirley's Café* or *Charley Johng's Café* for ¥2–4 an hour. *Charley Johng's* also offers a laundry service. **Internet access** is available for free for the first thirty minutes if you eat at *Shirley's*, and there is an Internet café on the first corner north of *Charley Johng's*. Surprisingly, for such a tourist-oriented town, nowhere has wireless connection.

Accommodation

There's a glut of **accommodation** in Dunhuang, especially at the lower end of the market. Prices rise in peak season (July and August), and are considerably discounted in low season, though you'll need to check on the availability of

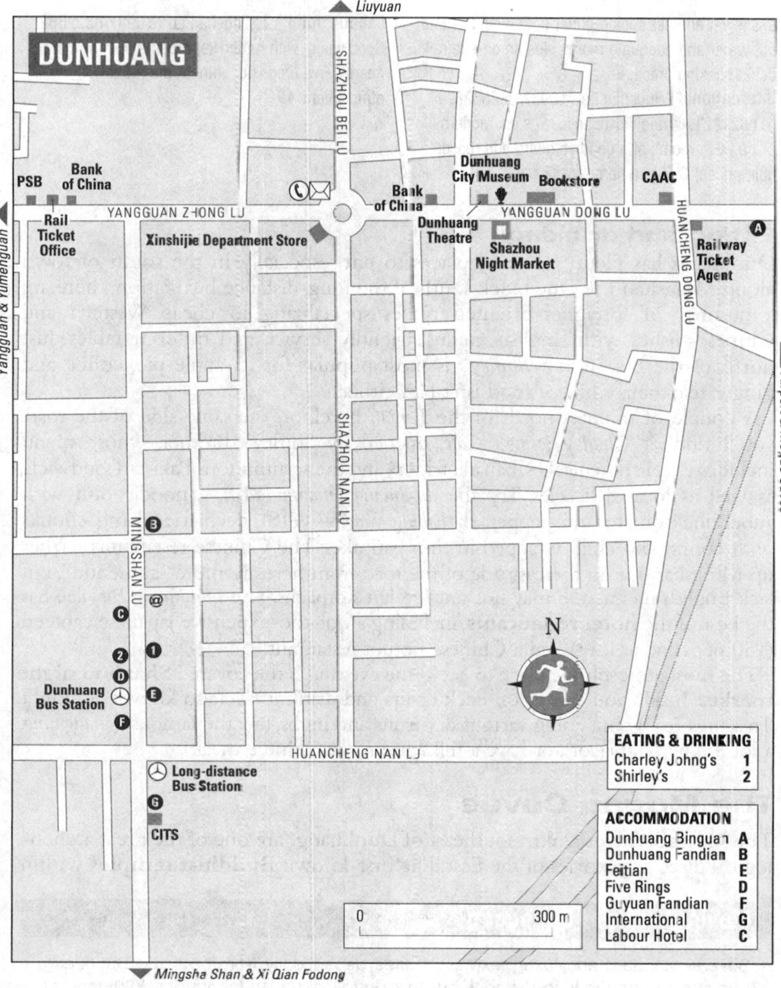

heating and hot water. A few places offer dorm beds; whether you'll get one depends on the management and how full the hotel is – they won't mix Chinese and Westerners in the same rooms.

Dunhuang Binguan Yangguan Dong Lu ⓣ0937/8859128. The drab 1980s concrete exterior betrays nice decor and a pretty stunning reception hall. Rooms are comfortable and you can usually get discounts. ❼

Dunhuang Fandian Mingshan Lu ⓣ0937/8822413, ⓔdhfd@public.lz.gs.cn. Mid-range comforts and dormitory beds available. Room rates include breakfast. ❻

Feitian Hotel Mingshan Lu ⓣ0937/8822337. Very conveniently located opposite the bus station, this place has decent doubles and inexpensive dorms – though the staff may refuse foreigners. *John's Information Café* has a branch here too. Credit cards are accepted and you can change foreign currency. Closed in winter. Dorm beds ¥40, ❻

Five Rings Mingshan Lu ⓣ0937/8822276. Just north of the bus station, this hotel is good value if you go for the four-bed dorms or cheaper doubles. Dorm beds ¥40–60, ❷

Guyuan Fandian 31 Mingshan Lu ⓣ0937/8853288. Convenient for the bus station, this is yet another cookie-cutter hotel with 24-hour hot water and adequate rooms plus an on-site rail ticket booking office. ❸

International Mingshan Lu ⓣ0937/8828638, ⓕ8821821, ⓔdhgjdid@public.lz.gs.cn. Modern place, with rooms of a good standard and reasonable prices; CITS are here too. ❼

Labour Hotel 19 Mingshan Lu ⓣ0937/8822582. Good value, with better-kept rooms than at the nearby *Five Rings* but without the friendly atmosphere. ❷

Eating and drinking

Dunhuang has plenty of good places to **eat**, especially in the south of town along Mingshan Lu. One block south of the long-distance bus station, there are a number of foreigner-oriented places specializing in cheap Western and Chinese dishes with English menus, friendly service and outdoor tables. Just north of the bus station *Shirley's* is most popular for its apple pie, coffee and ginger tea; their Chinese food isn't bad either.

A couple of minutes north of the *Feitian* hotel, on the same side of the road, you'll find *Charley Johng's Café*, opened by Shirley's brother, whose menu includes excellent pancakes, banana fritters and the scrumptious Pakistan sandwich, as well as local delicacies. Try the *dunhuang latiaozi* (¥10), a noodle dish with aubergine, tomato and pepper; or *bobing yangrou* (¥18), deep-fried lamb chunks with cumin and chilli wrapped in thin pancakes. The Chinese restaurants farther up Mingshan Lu on the east side of the road from here are more "authentic", but lack English menus and may not suit foreign stomachs. The *Dunhuang Binguan* has the best of the **hotel restaurants**, including a not-too-expensive Japanese canteen (¥50 per head at least) and a Chinese hotpot restaurant.

The most atmospheric place to eat in the evening is the covered **Shazhou night market**. Inside you can sit on deck chairs and drink *babao* (also known as "Eight Treasures Tea") containing various dry fruits and herbs, (try the famous *liguang qing*, a local type of apricot), or have a full Muslim or Chinese meal.

The Mogao Caves

The **Mogao Caves**, 25km southeast of Dunhuang, are one of the great archeological discovery stories of the East. The first-known **Buddhist temples** within

Moving on from Dunhuang

Several standard and luxury-express **buses** depart daily from both the Dunhuang bus station and the long-distance bus station to Jiayuguan (about 5hr; ¥90), and at least one daily to Lanzhou (24hr) and all points in between. There are also buses to Hami in Xinjiang (7hr). The eight-hour bus journey to **Golmud** in Qinghai province (on the road to Tibet) costs ¥78 for hard seat, ¥91 for sleeper bus. Wherever you're heading, nobody seems to be interested in seeing PICC certificates.

At the time of writing, there were **flights** twice a week to Lanzhou (Wed & Sun), and three times a week to Xi'an (Tues, Thurs & Sat). More frequent flights and more destinations (including Ürümqi and Beijing) occur in peak season, while in winter some flights may stop completely. Though other travel agents will insist this is impossible, **train tickets** (hard seat only) are most conveniently bought at a special window in the bus station, or at the rail office next to the **Bank of China**; a commission fee of ¥30 per ticket is charged. Frequent minibuses (¥15) for the **train station at Liuyuan** depart from outside the Dunhuang bus station; the journey takes two to three hours. A four-person taxi (¥30 per person) takes ninety minutes. Note that most **hotels** – and the local branch of *John's Information Café* inside the *Feitian*, as well as the CITS in the *International* – can organize plane and train tickets, for a commission of around ¥50 per person.

the boundaries of the Chinese empire, supposedly established in 366 AD by a monk called Lie Zun, they were a centre of culture on the Silk Road right up until the fourteenth century, and today contain religious artworks spanning a thousand years of history. Chinese Buddhism radiated out to the whole Han empire from these wild desert cliffs, and with it – gradually adapting to a Chinese context – came the artistic influences of Central Asia, India, Persia and the West.

Of the original thousand or more **caves**, over six hundred survive in recognizable form, but many are off limits, either no longer considered to be of significant interest or else containing Tantric murals which the Chinese reckon are too sexually explicit for visitors. Of the thirty main caves open to the public, you are likely to manage only around fifteen in a single day.

Visiting the caves

Getting to the caves (daily 8.30–11.30am & 2.30–5.30pm; ¥180 May–Sept, ¥100 Oct–April) from Dunhuang is easy in summer. Step on to the street between eight and nine in the morning and you will instantly be accosted by **minibus** drivers, who charge ¥10 for the one-way fare; the trip takes about thirty minutes. Choose a minibus that is nearly full – they won't leave until the last seat is occupied. In winter, when transport is much less frequent, you can arrange a return trip with any taxi driver in town (half day around ¥80–100, full day ¥200).

The entrance fee to the caves includes an English-speaking guide and admission to the museum and Research and Exhibition Centre. You need an extremely expensive permit to take a **camera**, and all bags must be left at an office at the gate (¥2). If you're caught taking photos without a permit you'll be made to delete them or have your negatives confiscated and you will be subjected to a large fine. There are only ever twenty or thirty caves open at any one time to reduce wear and tear, and they are not lit, to avoid damage to the murals; your guide will have a **flashlight**, but you are advised to bring one of your own.

Guides are well informed, though their English is not always great, and they will follow a set route. The **museum** gives insight into all the caves and has a history in English of the site, plus more scrolls, nineteenth- and twentieth-century photos of Mogao, and reproductions of some of the plundered frescoes, now in Europe.

Before or after your tour, visit the **Research and Exhibition Centre** (daily 9am–5pm), the giant modern building opposite the car park. Paid for by Japanese money, it holds eight replica caves – nos. 3, 45, 217, 220, 249, 275, 285 and 419. The big advantage here is that the lights are on, the colours are fresh and you can study the murals up close. The most impressive is the Bodhisattva statue of the one-thousand-hand and one-thousand-eye Guanyin – the original piece is no longer available for viewing due to the deteriorating conditions. A further cave is not from Mogao at all, but from the Yulin Caves (no. 25) in nearby Anxi County. Upstairs are a few surviving silk scrolls and manuscripts, and there's a film about the Mogao site.

Getting back to Dunhuang is simple in summer: go to the car park and wait for the next minibus; the last one leaves around 4pm. At other times you'll need to hire a taxi or prearrange transport.

The caves

What makes the caves so interesting is that you can trace the **development of Chinese art** over the centuries, from one dynasty to the next. Some grasp

The Mogao cave treasures

The story of Mogao's development, then subsequent abandonment and rediscovery, is an intriguing one. Before the arrival of Buddhism from India, the Chinese – Taoist and Confucian – temple tradition had been mainly of buildings in wood, a material well adapted to most Chinese conditions. The idea of cave temples came to China from India, where poverty, lack of building materials and the intense heat had necessitated alternative methods.

The emergence of the complex of cave temples at **Mogao** dominated early Chinese Buddhism, as pilgrims, monks and scholars passing along the Silk Road settled and worked here, translating sutras, or holy texts. Merchants and nobles stopped, too, endowing temples to ensure the success of their caravans or to benefit their souls, as they did in varying degrees all along the Silk Road. Huge numbers of **artists and craftsmen** were employed at Dunhuang, often lying on high scaffoldings in the dim light provided by oil lamps. The workers usually lived in tiny caves in the northern section of Mogao furnished with small brick beds, and were paid a pittance – in one collection of Buddhist scriptures, archeologists discovered a bill of indenture signed by one sculptor for the sale of his son.

Under the Tang, which saw the establishment of Buddhism throughout the Chinese empire, the monastic community reached its peak, with more than a thousand cave temples in operation. Thereafter, however, as the new ocean-going trading links slowly supplanted the Silk Road, Mogao (and Dunhuang) became increasingly provincial. At some point in the fourteenth century, the caves were **sealed and abandoned.**

Although Mogao's existence remained known to a few Buddhist scholars, it was only in 1900 that a wandering monk, **Wang Yuan Lu**, stumbled upon them by accident and decided to begin the work of excavation. He at once realized their significance, and made it his life's work to restore the site, excavating caves full of sand, touching up the murals, planting trees and gardens and building a guesthouse. This work he undertook with two acolytes and financed through begging expeditions.

The reconstructions might have gone on in relative obscurity were it not for the discovery of a bricked-up hidden chamber (cave no. 17), which Wang opened to reveal an enormous collection of **manuscripts**, **sutras** and **silk and paper paintings** – some 1000 years old and virtually undamaged. News of the cache soon reached the ears of the Dunhuang authorities, who, having appropriated a fair haul for themselves, decided to reseal them in the cave on the grounds that it would be too expensive to transport them. So it remained for a further seven years, until the arrival in 1907 of the Central Asian explorer and scholar **Aurel Stein**. Stein, a Hungarian

of the history of the caves is essential to appreciate them properly, but be warned, restorations and replacements in the modern era have complicated the picture, particularly where statuary is concerned – many of the statues are not original. You may hear your guide blaming the ugly replacements on the Qing dynasty – in other words on the monk Wang Yuan Lu – but some of them are a good deal newer than that. The caves are all clearly labelled with numbers above the doors.

Northern Wei

The earliest caves were hewn out in the fourth and fifth centuries AD during the **Northern Wei** (386–581). This dynasty was formed by Turkic-speaking people known as the Tobas, and as the centuries progressed there was constant friction between the forces of conservatism (who wanted to retain the ancient Toba customs) and those of change (who wanted to adapt Chinese customs).

working for the British and the Indian Survey (in other words, a secret agent), had heard rumours of the caves and been offered items for sale. In good Howard Carter tradition, he persuaded Wang to reopen the chamber. This is how Stein later described what he saw:

The sight the small room disclosed was one to make my eyes open; heaped up in layers, but without any order, there appeared in the dim light of the priest's little lamp a solid mass of manuscript bundles rising to a height of nearly 10 feet and filling, as subsequent measurement showed, close on 500 cubic feet – an unparalleled archeological scoop.

This was no understatement. Examining the manuscripts, Stein found original sutras brought from India by the Tang monk and traveller **Xuanzang**, along with other Buddhist texts written in Sanskrit, Sogdian, Tibetan, Runic-Turkic, Chinese, Uyghur and other languages unknown to the scholar. Amid the art finds, hardly less important were dozens of rare Tang-dynasty paintings on silk and paper – badly crushed but totally untouched by damp.

Eventually Stein, donating the equivalent of £130 to Wang's restoration fund, left Mogao for England with some seven thousand manuscripts and five hundred paintings. Later in the year a Frenchman, Paul Pelliot, negotiated a similar deal, shipping six thousand manuscripts and many paintings back to Paris. And so, virtually overnight, and before the Beijing authorities could put a stop to it, the British Museum and the Louvre had acquired the core of their Chinese manuscript and painting collections. Not all the caves were looted, however; a fresh batch of 248 was only located in 2001, though the scrolls and artefacts they contained have yet to be fully assessed.

Today, fuelled perhaps by Greek claims on the Elgin marbles, the Chinese are pressing for the **return** of all paintings and manuscripts in foreign collections. It is hard to dispute the legitimacy of these claims now, though it was only in 1961 that Mogao was declared a National Monument. Had the treasures not been removed, more would almost certainly have been lost in the chaotic years of the twentieth century. A large party of White Russians used the caves as a barracks in 1920, crawling their names over the frescoes. Fortunately, despite the massive loss in terms of manuscripts and scrolls, the artwork and statuary at the caves themselves are still fabulously preserved. The cave art was not damaged during the Cultural Revolution – protected, it is said, on a personal order from Premier Zhou Enlai.

The Wei caves are relatively small in size, and are often supported in the centre by a large column – a feature imported from India. A statue of the Buddha is usually central, surrounded in tiers on the walls by a **mass of tiny Buddhas** brilliantly painted in black, white, blue, red and green. The statues are in fact made of terracotta: the soft rock inside the caves was not suited to detailed carving, so the craftsmen would first carve a rough outline of the figure, then build it up with clay.

The style of the murals in these caves shows a great deal of **foreign influence**. Faces have long noses and curly hair, and women are large-breasted. **Cave no. 101**, decorated towards the end of the fifth century, provides a good example: the Buddha, enclosed by attendant Bodhisattvas, is essentially a Western figure, recognizably Christ-like, reminiscent of Greek Byzantine frescoes. In **cave 257** the Buddha seems to be dressed in a toga, while the beautiful **cave 428** shows a notably Indian influence in both content (note the peacocks on the ceiling) and style. There are, however, also the beginnings of Chinese influence in the wavy, flower-like angels sometimes seen fluttering above.

Though originally designed as a focus of devotional contemplation, the murals gradually acquired a **narrative purpose** as well, and the paintings soon move towards a wider subject matter, their story sequences arranged in long horizontal strips. **Cave 135** (early sixth century) illustrates a *jataka* story – concerning a former life of Buddha – in which he gave his own body to feed a starving tigress, unable to succour her cubs. The narrative, read from right to left, is broken up by simple landscapes, a frequently used device. **Cave 254** shows the story of Buddha defeating Mara, or Illusion.

Artistic changes, and a shift towards a more distinctive Chinese style, began to appear at the end of the Northern Wei period, around the middle of the sixth century. One of the most strikingly Chinese of the Wei murals is in **cave 120N** and shows, above the devotional niches, a series of battle scenes, interesting for their total lack of perspective. All the figures are drawn as though seen straight on, regardless of their relative positions, a favourite device throughout the history of Chinese painting.

Sui

With the founding of the short-lived but dynamic **Sui dynasty** in 581, Western influences began to decline rapidly. The Chinese empire had been torn apart by civil wars but now there followed a boom in Buddhism, and Buddhist art. In the four decades up to the emergence of the Tang, more than seventy caves were carved at Mogao.

Structurally, they dispense with the central column, while artistically, they show the replacement of the bold, slightly crude Wei brushwork with intricate, flowing lines and an increasingly extravagant use of colour that includes gilding and washes of silver. In **cave 150**, for example, painted in the last year of the Sui, narrative has been dispensed with altogether in favour of a repeated theme of throned Buddhas and Bodhisattvas. In terms of statuary, the Sui period also shows a change, with the figures becoming stiff and inflexible and dressed in Chinese robes. **Cave 427** contains some characteristic Sui figures – short legs, long bodies (indicating power and divinity) and big, square heads.

Tang

The **Tang-dynasty** artists (618–906), under whom the caves at Mogao reached their artistic zenith, drew both from past traditions and real life. The classic Tang cave has a square floor, tapering roof and a niche for worship set into the back wall. The statuary includes **warriors** – a new theme – and all figures are carefully detailed, the Bodhisattvas above all, with their pleats and folds clinging softly to undulating feminine figures.

For sheer size, their **Buddhas** are the most famous, notably in **caves 96 and 130**. The astonishing 34-metre-high seated Buddha in cave 96 – dressed in the traditional dragon robe of the emperor – is thought by some to have been designed deliberately to remind pilgrims of the famous Tang empress Wu Zetian. In **cave 148** there is another huge Buddha, this one reclining as though dead, and surrounded by disciples.

The **Tang paintings** range from huge murals depicting scenes from the sutras – now contained within one composition rather than the earlier cartoon-strip convention – to vivid paintings of individuals. One of the most popular and spectacular Tang mural themes was that of the *Visit of the Bodhisattva Manjusri to Vimalakirti*. **Cave 1** contains perhaps the greatest expression of this story. Vimalakirti, on the left, is attended by a great host of heavenly beings, eager to hear the discourse of the ailing old king. Above him the plane is tilted to take in a seemingly limitless landscape, with the Buddha surrounded by Bodhisattvas on an island in the middle. Another version can be seen in **cave 51E**, in a mural that is also especially notable for the subtle shading of its portraiture, which includes a magnificently depicted Central Asian retinue. Other superb Tang murals include a very free, fluid landscape in **cave 70** and, perhaps most developed of all, **cave 139A**'s depiction of the *Western Paradise of the Amitabha Buddha*. This last is a supremely confident painting, working in elaborate displays of architecture and figures within a coherent whole. The theme is the Buddha's promise of paradise: the souls of the reborn rise from lotus flowers in the foreground, with heavenly scenes enclosing the Buddha above.

The later caves

Later work, executed by the **Five Dynasties**, **Song**, **and Western Xia** (906–1227), shows little real progression from the Tang. Much, in any case, is simply restoration or repainting of existing murals. Song work is perhaps the most interesting, tending towards a heavy richness of colour, and with many of its figures displaying the features of minority races.

Towards the end of the Mongol **Yuan dynasty** (1260–1368), Mogao was abandoned, the standard niche in the back wall of the caves gave way to a central altar, creating fresh and uncluttered space for murals. Tibetan-style Lamaist (or Tantric) figures were introduced, and occult diagrams (mandalas) became fashionable. The most interesting Yuan art is in **cave 465**, slightly set apart from the main body of grottoes. You might try asking the guides if they will open this up for you, though they will probably only do so for a huge fee. In the fashion of Indian Buddhist painting, the murals include Tantric figures in the ultimate state of enlightenment, graphically represented by the state of sexual union.

Other sights around Dunhuang

A few kilometres to the south of town are the much-touted **Yueya Quan** (Crescent Moon Lake) and **Mingsha Shan** (Singing Sand Dune), set amid the most impressive sand-dune scenery anywhere in China, with dunes 200–300m high. The sands reportedly make a humming noise in windy weather, hence the name. The Crescent Moon Lake is not much to look at, but is curious for its

▲ Camel rides at Mingsha Shan

permanence, despite being surrounded by shifting sands – it was recorded in history at least two thousand years ago. A number of activities, including sand-tobogganing and paragliding, are on offer from the tops of the main dune. The paragliding is great fun and costs ¥30 – you get to try two or three times if your initial flight isn't successful. Tobogganing costs ¥10 and feels a little safer. Climbing the dune in the first place, however, is incredibly hot, exhausting work; you can ride up on a camel for ¥30 or use the wooden steps for ¥10.

In the summer heat the only sensible time to come is around 8 or 8.30am or in the evening after 5pm. **Minibus #3** (daily 8am–10pm; ¥1–3 per person) leaves from Mingshan Lu in Dunhuang and will drop you by the gate and **ticket office.** Otherwise you can walk here in about 45 minutes, or cycle in twenty – just head south out of town. Park your bike somewhere before the entrance or pay ¥5 to put it in the bike park. A one-way taxi should cost ¥10 on the meter, but your driver may ask for more.

Admission to the dune is ¥120 in peak season, ¥80 otherwise; factor in also ¥10 for the bus from the gate to the dune, ¥10 for gaiters to prevent sand getting up your nether regions, and additional costs if you want to ascend the dune by steps or camel.

About 4km west of town is the **Baima Ta** (White Horse Dagoba; ¥30). This attractive, nine-tiered dagoba was built in honour of the horse belonging to the monk Kumarajiva from Kuqa (see p.1056), which died on this spot in 384 AD. Lying amid cornfields, it's a pleasant spot to take a breather.

A number of other historical sites lie farther away from Dunhuang but within the scope of a day-trip. One is the **Xi Qianfodong** (Western Thousand Buddha Caves; ¥30; 35km west), another cave site along the lines of Mogao, if incomparably smaller and less significant. If you are a real Buddhist art buff, talk to a travel service about visiting this place: in the past it was open to groups only, and individuals were turned away. A taxi for the return trip costs ¥80.

There are also two Han-dynasty gates, **Yumenguan** (¥30) and **Yangguan** (¥40), which for periods of Chinese history marked the western border of China. They lie to the west of Dunhuang, 80km and 75km away respectively, and were originally joined together by a section of the Great Wall before being abandoned as long ago as the sixth century. Both sites are impressive for their historic resonance and total desolation as much as for anything else. The road to Yangguan is in good condition, but that to Yumenguan is relatively rough – to visit both gates by taxi would take all day and cost more than ¥200. One exciting option, however, is to visit them **by camel**; to see the two gates, and bits of the Han Great Wall (1km), takes around three to four days respectively or up to eight days for both, and in the mild months of the year – early or late summer – this can be an excellent expedition (¥200–300 per day including food and tent accommodation; contact *Charley Johng's Café* for more information).

Qinghai

Qinghai province is for the most part a huge, empty wilderness with a population of just 4.5 million. Geographically and culturally a part of the **Tibetan**

plateau, Qinghai has for centuries been a frontier zone, contested between Han Chinese, Tibetans and Muslims who originally dwelt in its pastures and thin snatches of agricultural land. Today, the **minority presence** in Qinghai can still be felt strongly – as well as Tibetans and Hui, there are Salar, Tu, Mongol and Kazakh people all living here.

Significant Han migration didn't occur until the late nineteenth century, when it was encouraged by the Qing dynasty. However, effective Han political control was not established until 1949 when the Communists defeated **Ma Bufang**, a Hui warlord who had controlled the area since 1931. The area is still perceived by the Han Chinese as a frontier land for pioneers and prospectors, and, on a more sinister note, a dumping ground for criminals and political opponents to the regime. The number of inmates held in Qinghai **prison and labour camps**, including those released but who must remain in the province because they cannot regain residency rights in their home towns, is estimated at 400,000 – almost a tenth of the population.

Only the eastern part of the province around **Xining** has a long-established Han presence. With its lush green valleys and plentiful annual rainfall, this is also the only part of Qinghai where sustainable agriculture takes place. To the west and south of here the land rises to a three-thousand-metre plateau which, bitterly cold for half the year, can at best be used as pastureland for cattle and sheep. To the northwest, on the other hand, towards the border with Xinjiang, the land sinks into an arid basin, which was good for little until the Communist era, when mineral deposits and oil were discovered. Now the area supports extensive mining.

For visitors, Qinghai's primary point of interest is as an access point **into Tibet**. To Lhasa you can fly from Xining, or take the road or train from **Golmud**. Qinghai is in many respects a part of Tibet, and in addition to the substantial Tibetan minority who live here, the splendid Kumbum, or **Ta'er Si**, one of the four great Tibetan lamaseries, is located just outside Xining.

The province has other attractions, too, chiefly as an unspoilt natural wilderness area incorporating the enormous **Qinghai Hu**, China's biggest lake, which offers opportunities for hikes and birdwatching. There are also possibilities for longer treks, rafting, and mountaineering. Such activities are best arranged by local travel agents, who can sometimes do so with just a few days' notice.

Xining and around

Qinghai's unassuming provincial capital, **XINING** contains few tourist sights in itself, and is usually regarded simply as a base from which to explore the nearby Tibetan monastery of **Ta'er Si**. Nevertheless, as the only sizeable city in Qinghai, Xining is an interesting place in its own right. Set in a rather extraordinary location, with imposing mountains rearing up right behind, the city has a cosy, reassuring feel. At a height of 2260m, on the outermost edge of the Tibetan plateau, Xining experiences pleasantly cool weather in summer and bitter cold in winter.

Although definitely a centre of Han population, Xining is also full of **minority nationalities**, in particular Hui and rather lost-looking Tibetans. It has quite an ancient history, having been established probably as early as the Han dynasty. It even served as a stopover on a minor southern route of the Silk Road and has been a fairly important trading city for the Han since at least the sixteenth century. It became the provincial capital when Qinghai became a province

Xining and around

Xining	西宁	*xīníng*
Beishan Si	北山寺	*běishān sì*
Dashizi	大十子	*dàshízì*
Dongguan Great Mosque	东关清真大寺	*dōngguān qīngzhēn dàsì*
Huangshui River	湟水河	*huángshuǐ hé*
Regional Museum	省博物馆	*shěng bówùguǎn*
Ximen	西门	*xīmén*
Accommodation and eating		
Daxinjie Night Market	大新街夜市	*dàxīnjiē yèshì*
Dico's	德克士汉堡	*dékèshì hànbǎo*
KFC	肯德基	*kěndéjī*
Mazhong Food Town	马忠美食城	*mǎzhōng měishíchéng*
Meining	美宁宾馆	*měiníng bīnguǎn*
Minzu	民族宾馆	*mínzú bīnguǎn*
Origus	好伦歌	*hǎolúngē*
Station Hotel	铁路宾馆	*tiělù bīnguǎn*
UBC Coffee	台湾上岛咖啡	*táiwān shàngdǎo kāfēi*
Xining Hotel	西宁宾馆	*xīníng bīnguǎn*
Xining Mansions	西宁大厦	*xīníng dàshà*
Xinshiji Binguan (next to the entrance of Daxinjie Night Market)	新世纪宾馆	*xīnshìjì bīnguǎn*
Ledu County	乐都县	*lèdū xiàn*
Nianbo Zhen	碾伯镇	*niǎnbó zhèn*
Qutan Si	瞿昙寺	*qútán sì*
Maduo	玛多	*mǎduō*
Ta'er Si	塔尔寺	*tǎ'ěr sì*
Kumbum Motel	千佛塔	*qiānfó tǎ*
Zongka Hotel	宗喀宾馆	*zōngkā bīnguǎn*
Tongren County	同仁县	*tóngrén xiàn*
Longwu Zhen	隆务镇	*lóngwù zhèn*
Longwu Si	隆务寺	*lóngwù sì*
Shangxia Wutun	上下五屯	*shàngxià wǔtún*
Xunhua County	循化	*xúnhuà*
Jishi Zhen	积石镇	*jīshí zhèn*
Mengda Nature Reserve	孟达自然保护区	*mèngdá zìrán bǎohùqū*

proper in 1928. Today, connected by fast trains to Lanzhou and other Chinese cities, Xining is a firmly established part of the network of Han China.

Arrival and information

Most of the city lies to the south of the river, though the **train station** lies immediately on the north bank, just across the bridge from the long-distance **bus station**. The centre of Xining is located about 3km to the west of here, along the main east–west streets Dong Dajie and then Xi Dajie, which connects **Da Shizi** (Big Crossroads) with the large **Ximen** intersection a few hundred metres farther west. Xining's **airport** is 26km east of town; a bus collects arrivals and drops them at the airline offices on Bayi Lu, about 1500m southeast of the train station – bus #2 runs west up Dongguan Dajie from Bayi Lu, or #28 will get you to the bus and train stations.

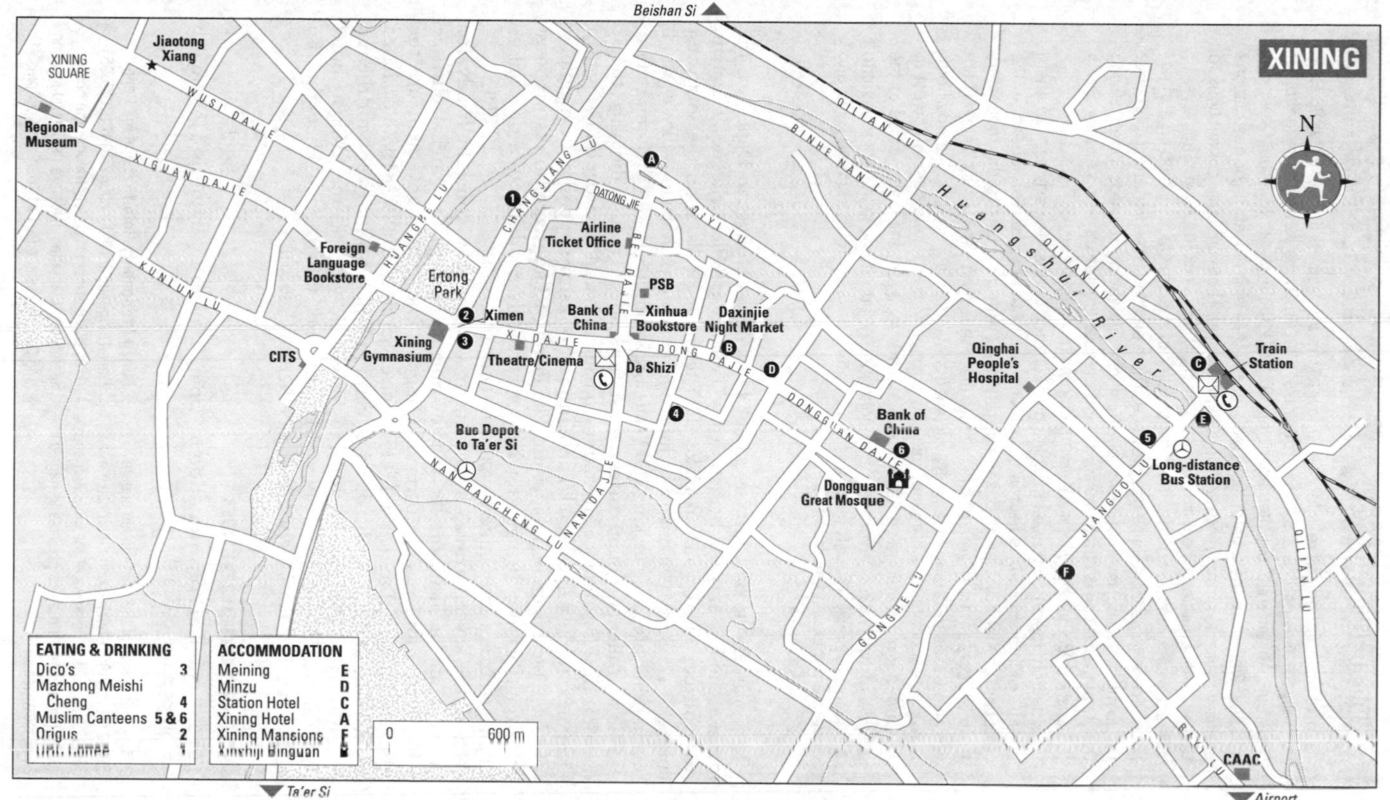
XINING
N
Beishan Si
Ta'er Si
Airport
XINING SQUARE
Jiaotong Xiang
Regional Museum
WUSI DAJIE
XIGUAN DAJIE
KUNLUN LU
HUANGHE LU
CHANGJIANG LU
DATONG JIE
BEI DAJIE
XI DAJIE
DONG DAJIE
DONGGUAN DAJIE
NAN DAJIE
NANDACHENG LU
GONGHE LU
JIANGUO LU
BAYI LU
QILIAN LU
BINHE NAN LU
QIYI LU
Huangshui River
Foreign Language Bookstore
Ertong Park
Ximen
Xining Gymnasium
CITS
Airline Ticket Office
PSB
Bank of China
Xinhua Bookstore
Daxinjie Night Market
Theatre/Cinema
Da Shizi
Bus Depot to Ta'er Si
Qinghai People's Hospital
Bank of China
Dongguan Great Mosque
Train Station
Long-distance Bus Station
CAAC
EATING & DRINKING
Dico's 3
Mazhong Meishi Cheng 4
Muslim Canteens 5 & 6
Origus 2
ACCOMMODATION
Meining E
Minzu D
Station Hotel C
Xining Hotel A
Xining Mansions
Xinshiji Binguan
0 600 m

Moving on from Xining

Xining's main **airline office** is located a few kilometres east of the centre at 85 Bayi Lu (daily 8.30am–noon & 2–5.30pm; ⓣ0971/8133333), on the #2 bus route (get off at Bayi Lu). An alternative ticket agent (ⓣ0971/8123555) is on Jianguo Dajie, ten minutes' walk from the train station; look for the IATA sign. Most major destinations are now available from Xining, and on a regular basis. There are daily connections to Beijing, Shanghai and Chengdu, but just one flight per week to Lhasa (Sat).

Direct **trains** run to and from most major cities in eastern China, including a three-hour service to Lanzhou in Gansu province. There are also three services (15hr) west to Golmud, leaving from late evening, for those gravitating towards Tibet; buying tickets at the station is straightforward – and Chinese timetables are on display. Seats to Lanzhou are generally available on the morning of departure.

Aside from the smooth rides to Golmud or Lanzhou on the new expressway, there are lots of interesting **bus routes** out of Xining, and **tickets** are very cheap. In the direction of **Xiahe**, frequent buses run to Linxia, with one daily to the monastery town of Tongren, from both of which there are connecting services to Xiahe. There are also buses to **Zhangye** (3 daily) in Gansu province, via a spectacular ride north across the mountains. An equally exciting possibility is to take a bus southwest to **Maduo**, a remote little town 4000m above sea level. From here, very close to the source of the Yellow River, you can continue by bus along a rough route into Sichuan province. Though this route is not officially open to foreigners, rules and drivers are increasingly relaxed.

The main **Bank of China** is a huge building on Dongguan Dajie near the mosque, and it is only this branch that will change traveller's cheques. The main **post office**, where you can make IDD telephone calls, is on the southwest corner of Da Shizi; you enter by climbing the raised pedestrian walkway. You'll find another office for making IDD calls a few minutes east of the train station, next to a smaller post office. **Internet** bars are scattered around the place; there's one near the long-distance bus station on Jianguo Lu, and another on Dongguan Dajie next to the *Minzu* hotel. The **Xinhua bookstore** opposite the main post office sells local maps of dubious use. The **Foreign Language bookstore**, west of Ertong Park on Huanghe Lu, has a surprisingly good selection of English-language classics and Chinese works in translation.

There are several **travel agents** in town that may come in handy for buying train or plane tickets, and for organizing trips to Qinghai Hu (see p.1027) or more remote parts of Qinghai. The most convenient are the Qinghai Jiaotong Lüxingshe (Traffic Travel Service; ⓣ0971/8133928), based at the front of the long-distance bus station on Jianguo Lu – look for the red English sign; Qinghai Nationality Travel Service at the *Minzu* hotel (ⓣ0971/8225247; closed Nov–March); and CITS, 156 Huanghe Lu (ⓣ0971/6133844, ⓦwww.Qinghai-Tibettravel.com).

Accommodation

The amount of **accommodation** in Xining is increasing as tourism in Qinghai becomes more established.

Meining East side of the train-station square ⓣ0971/8185380. Cheap, good-value place in a new building with fine views of the city. Staff speak a little English, and it may be possible to haggle. 24hr hot water. ❸

Minzu (Nationality Hotel) West of the Dong Dajie/Dongguan Dajie junction ⓣ0971/8225951, ⓕ8225892. Not particularly friendly, the best features of this faded place are its central location and 24hr hot water. Bus #1 (6.10am–6.40pm; ¥1) runs here (bus stop name: Huangguang) from the train station. ❸

Station Hotel On the west side of the station square ☎0971/81768888. The cheapest option in town, this shabby place has all the basics but little else. You might want to unplug your phone to avoid the torrent of calls offering "massages." ❶

Xining Hotel 348 Qiyi Lu ☎0971/8458701. About 1km north of Da Shizi, this monolith of Soviet architecture is surprisingly nice inside. Your fellow guests are likely to be businessmen and party apparatchiks. ❺

Xining Mansions On the corner of Dongguan Dajie and Jianguo Lu, ☎0971/8164800. The city's newest and swankiest hotel offers fantastic rooms at very reasonable rates, which can be knocked down. Staff speak adequate English and are more than helpful. ❺

Xinshiji Binguan 16 Dongguan Dajie, next to the entrance to Daxinjie night market ☎0971/8176888. A well-located alternative to the *Minzu*; the staff here are very enthusiastic and the rooms more than adequate. ❷

The City

The city is bordered by steep hills to the north, along the foot of which runs the Huangshui River. The major sight is the **Dongguan Great Mosque** (daily 8–10am & 2–8pm; ¥10), on Dongguan Dajie, one of the most attractive in northwest China. Originally built in 1380, it encloses a large public square where worshippers can congregate. The architecture is an interesting synthesis of Arabic and Chinese, its exterior adorned with the old Chinese favourite – the white tile.

The regional **museum** (daily: May–Sept 9am–5pm, Oct–April 9.30am–4pm; ¥15), southwest of Xining Square, is also worth a look, with artefacts from most dynasties and a display of ethnic minority clothing; the only shame is the lack of English captioning. To get to the museum, take bus #9 from the train station, and get off at Jiaotong Xiang along Wusi Dajie. It's a forty-minute walk west along Xiguan Dajie from Ximen.

To the north of the Huangshui River, a couple of kilometres west of the train station, it is possible to climb the mountain up to the 1700-year-old Taoist **Beishan Si** (North Mountain Temple; daily; ¥5). You climb hundreds of steps, then walk along a whole series of walkways and bridges connecting together little caves decorated with Taoist designs. At the very top a pagoda offers fine views over the city on a clear day. Unfortunately, much of it is closed off for safety reasons, but it is still worth a look. Bus #11 from the train station, or #10 from east of the Xining Gymnasium, will take you to Beishan Lu Kou on Qilian Lu, from where you walk under a railway bridge to the north and through an industrial estate to the temple entrance.

Eating

There's a power of food on offer in multi-ethnic Xining, especially at the **markets** downtown; staples include kebabs, bowls of spicy noodles, mutton hotpots, and *zasui* soup, made with ox and sheep entrails. *Shaguo* – earthenware hotpots full of tofu, mushrooms and meat cooked in broth – are excellent, as are *jiaozi*, *hundun* soup and other basic dishes prepared on the spot. Alternatively, you can head to the excellent **Daxinjie night market**, a lane off Dong Dajie near the *Minzu* hotel, or the nearby **Mazhong Meishi Cheng** food market, both of which turn into fresh-food bonanzas in the evenings, alive with sounds, sights and smells. Lunchtimes could be a lot worse spent than taking a walk down **Datong Jie**, where a panoply of ethnic cuisines are on offer. For Hui-style food, there's a canteen near the bus station, and a large and authentic Muslim place across from the mosque on Dongguan Dajie. If you're after Western food, head for *KFC*, *Origus* or *Dico's*, all on the Ximen intersection. Alternatively, try the *UBC Coffee* on Changjiang Lu – a

Taiwanese chain café also serving Western-style set meals – or *Xining Mansions'* Western-style restaurant.

Ta'er Si and beyond

Lying about 25km southeast from Xining, **Ta'er Si**, is one of the most important monasteries outside Tibet. Although not as attractive as Labrang in Xiahe, and often swamped by tourists, Ta'er Si is nevertheless a good introduction to Tibetan culture. Both as the birthplace of Tsongkhapa, the founder of the **Yellow Hat Sect**, and as the former home of the current Dalai Lama, the monastery attracts droves of pilgrims from Tibet, Qinghai and Mongolia, who present a startling picture with their rugged features, huge embroidered coats and chunky jewellery.

Aside from the hulking **military base** built right next to the monastery, the countryside around is beautiful. The views stretch away to distant mountains, and you can ramble over hills of wheat, pastures dotted with cattle and horses, and over ridges and passes dappled with wild flowers. Apart from the large numbers of Han Chinese tourists, the people you meet here are mainly Tibetan horsemen, workers in the fields who will offer an ear of roasted barley by way of hospitality, or pilgrims prostrating their way around the monastery walls.

The monastery

The monastery dates from 1560, when building was begun in honour of **Tsongkhapa**, founder of the reformist Yellow Hat Sect of Tibetan Buddhism, who was born on the Ta'er Si estates. Legend tells how, at Tsongkhapa's birth, drops of blood fell from his umbilical cord causing a tree with a thousand leaves to spring up; on each leaf was the face of the Buddha, and there was a Buddha image on the trunk (now preserved in one of the stupas). During his lifetime, Tsongkhapa's significance was subsequently borne out: his two major disciples were to become the two greatest living Buddhas, one the Dalai Lama, the other the Panchen Lama.

Set in the cleft of a valley, the **walled complex** (daily 8.30am–4.30pm; ¥80 provides access to nine temples) is an imposing sight, an active place of worship for about six hundred monks as well as the constant succession of pilgrims. Ignore the furtive hawkers offering Dalai Lama pendants at the gate – possession of them is illegal.

The most beautiful of the **temples** is perhaps the **Great Hall of Meditation** (Da Jingtang; temple no. 5 on your ticket), an enormous, very dimly lit prayer hall, colonnaded by dozens of carpeted pillars and hung with long silk tapestries (*thangkas*). Immediately adjacent to this is the **Great Hall of the Golden Roof**, with its gilded tiles, red-billed choughs nesting under the eaves, wall paintings of scenes from the Buddha's life and a brilliant silver stupa containing a statue of Tsongkhapa. The grooves on the wooden floor in front of the temple have been worn away by the hands of prostrating monks and pilgrims. This hall, built in 1560, is where the monastery began, on the site of the pipal tree that grew with its Buddha imprints. You will still see pilgrims studying fallen leaves here, apparently searching for the face of the Buddha.

Other noteworthy temples include the **Lesser Temple of the Golden Roof** (no. 1) and the **Hall of Butter Sculpture** (no. 7). The former is dedicated to animals, thought to manifest characteristics of certain deities – from the central courtyard you can see stuffed goats, cows and bears on the balcony, wrapped in scarves and flags. The Hall of Butter Sculpture contains a display of colourful painted yak-butter tableaux, depicting Tibetan and Buddhist legends. After touring the temples, you can climb the steep steps visible on one side of the monastery to get a general view over the temples and hills behind.

During the year, four major **festivals** are held at Ta'er Si, each fixed according to the lunar calendar. In January/February, at the end of the Chinese New Year festivities, there's a large ceremony centred around the lighting of yak-butter lamps. In April/May is the festival of Bathing Buddha, during which a giant *thangka* of Buddha is unfurled on a hillside facing the monastery. In July/August the birthday of Tsongkhapa is celebrated, and in September/October there's one more celebration commemorating the nirvana of Sakyamuni.

Practicalities

Buses from Xining to Ta'er Si (¥5) depart from a depot on Xiguan Dajie near the roundabout for Kunlun Bridge. Minibuses run frequently from around 7.20am until late afternoon; private tour buses start rolling up at Ta'er Si around 10am, after which the place gets crowded. Taxis from the rank at the roundabout should cost ¥6 for the same journey. The ride takes just over thirty minutes through summer scenery of wheat fields, green hills, lush woods and meadows of flowering yellow rape. On arrival, you may be dropped at the bus station 1km short of the monastery, or taken right up to the complex itself. From the bus station, it's a twenty-minute walk uphill past the trinket stalls and rug-sellers until you see the row of eight stupas at the monastery entrance. Returning to Xining, exit the monastery and hang around on the street until the bus arrives. Private taxis charge ¥10 per person back to Xining.

Most visitors just come up to Ta'er Si for a few hours, but it is also possible to stay the night and appreciate the monastery in more peace. **Accommodation** is available at the sixteenth-century pilgrims' hostel *Kumbum Motel* (dorm beds ¥20) just inside the monastery entrance, whose basic facilities include an ancient balcony and peeling murals; it's often full. For something smarter, there's also the large *Zongka Hotel* (Ⓣ0971/2236761; closed Dec–March; ❺) facing the monastery across a gully; the price includes a simple breakfast, but you should ask at the front desk for hot water. You can get **meals** at the *Pilgrim's Hostel* otherwise, try one of the Muslim restaurants on the road between the town and monastery. These are great value, providing huge, warming bowls of noodles with plenty of vegetables and tea for a few yuan.

Beyond Tai'er Si

Another monastery, **Qutan Si** (¥25), 85km to the east of Xining in Ledu County, is much less visited by tourists. Started in 1387 during the Ming dynasty, this was once among the most important Buddhist centres in China. Today, it is still impressive, with 51 rooms of murals, exceptionally fine examples of their type, illustrating the life story of Sakyamuni. You can reach the town of **Nianbo Zhen** in Ledu County by local train or bus (¥10) from Kunlun Bridge in Xining. From Nianbo Zhen you should be able to find minibuses (¥20 one way) for the 67-kilometre ride to Qutan Si, or you could take a taxi there and back for about ¥100 plus.

About 200km southeast of Xining lies an area of outstanding natural beauty, centred around **Mengda Nature Reserve** (¥35). This part of the province, **Xunhua County**, is the birthplace of the Panchen Lama and the homeland of the Salar people, a Muslim ethnic minority. Its wet, mild climate is conducive to the prolific growth of trees and vegetation, and the woods here are full of wild flowers and inhabited by deer and foxes – the highlight of the place is the Heaven Lake – a sacred spot for the Salar. Hardly any foreign tourists come this way, but if you want to try, take a bus from Xining's long-distance bus station to the town of **Jishi Zhen** (¥37) in Xunhua County, from where you can hop on the bus (¥25) to the reserve. **Accommodation** (dorm beds ¥30) is available at the reserve, and it is advisable that you bring along at least one day's food and water.

Approximately 180km south of Xining is the Qinghai Huangnan Tibetan autonomous region of **Tongren**, home to the Yuan-dynasty Tibetan lamasery **Longwu Si** (¥10) in the town of **Longwu Zhen**. *Thangka* painting reaches its peak at the intriguing **Shangxia Wutun** (upper and lower Wutun) villages, 8km northeast from Longwu Zhen along the Longwu River; you can see the colourful tapestries in and outside every household. There are three daily **buses** (¥30) to Longwu Zhen from the Xining long-distance bus station, or you can take a bus (2 daily) directly from Jishi Zhen in Xunhua. To head onto Shangxia Wutun, you can either walk or hire a taxi (¥10) as you come out of Longwu Zhen's Tongren Longwu bus station. It is about 1km between the two villages, which are marked by a monastery at the side of the road.

West of Xining

West of Xining, Qinghai for the most part comprises a great emptiness. The three-thousand-metre plateau is too high to support any farming, and population centres are almost nonexistent – the only people who traditionally have managed to eke out a living in this environment have been nomadic yak-herders. Not surprisingly, this is where China decided to site its **Nuclear Weapons Research and Design Academy** (daily; ¥70), where it developed its first atomic and hydrogen bombs in the 1960s and 70s. The centre is on a road and rail line 90km from Xining at **Haiyan** – known locally as "Atom Town".

The real highlight of the area, though, is about 150km west of Xining at the huge and virtually unspoilt saline lake of **Qinghai Hu**, the size of a small sea and home to thousands of birds. Beyond here, the solitary road and rail line wind their way slowly to **Golmud**, the only place of note for hundreds of kilometres, and then on to the Tibetan Plateau into Lhasa.

West of Xining		
Haiyan	海宴	*hǎiyàn*
Qinghai Hu	青海湖	*qīnghǎi hú*
Bird Island	鸟岛	*niǎodǎo*
Chaka Salt Lake	茶卡盐湖	*chákǎyán hú*
Chaka Zhen	茶卡镇	*chákǎ zhèn*
Dulan	都兰	*dūlán*
Heimahe	黑马河	*hēimǎ hé*
Wulan	乌兰	*wūlán*
Golmud	格尔木	*gé'ěr mù*
Cai Erhan Salt Lake	察尔汗盐湖	*cháěrhàn yán hú*
Golmud Hotel	格尔木宾馆	*gé'ěrmù bīnguǎn*
Golmud Mansion	格尔木大厦	*gé'ěrmù dàshà*
Kunlun Mountains	昆仑山	*kūnlún shān*
Qinggang Hotel	青冈饭店	*qīnggǎng fàndiàn*
Tibet Bus Station	西藏汽车站	*xīzàng qìchēzhàn*
Xiangsihai	香四海	*xiāngsìhǎi*
Yi Pin Baozi Guan	一品包子馆	*yīnpǐn bāoziguǎn*

Qinghai Hu and around

Situated 150km west of Xining, high up on the Tibetan plateau, is the extraordinarily remote **Qinghai Hu** (¥90, includes the ferry trip). The lake is China's largest, occupying an area of more than 4500 square kilometres, and, at 3200m above sea level, its waters are profoundly cold and salty. They are nevertheless teeming with fish and populated by nesting seabirds, particularly at **Bird Island**, which has long been the main attraction of the lake for visitors. If you don't have time to stop here, you can at least admire the view while travelling between Golmud and Xining: it's well worth scheduling your journey to pass the lake during daylight hours. The train spends some hours running along the northern shore; travelling by bus you will pass the southern shore.

Apart from a visit to Bird Island – which tends to be a rushed, hectic experience – you can also hike and camp in peaceful solitude around the lake. From the smooth, green, windy shores, grazed by yaks during the brief summer, the blue, icy waters stretch away as far as the eye can see. If you have a tent, and really want a wilderness experience in China, this may be the place to get it. Don't forget to bring warm clothes, sleeping bags and enough drinking water. To get to the lake, you can take any bus bound for Dulan or Wulan (both west of Xining), from Xining's long-distance bus station. Each route passes the lake – one possible place to get off is the **Qinghai Lake Tourist Centre**, where you can stay (❸, dorm beds ¥25) and enjoy boating, fishing and horse-riding.

Bird Island

This tiny rocky outcrop, situated at the far western side of the lake, is annually nested upon by literally thousands of birds. An immense variety of seasonal birds spend time here – gulls, cormorants, geese, swans and the rare **black-necked crane**. The main **bird-watching season** is from April to June, though the giant swans are best seen from November to February.

The best time to visit Bird Island is between June and August, when avian life is at its most dense. The easiest way to get there is on a **day-trip** from Xining, and your best bet is to take an excursion with one of Xining's **travel services** (see p.1022). Foreigners are charged ¥150 excluding food and **entrance fees** (¥58, including a tourist shuttle bus from the ticket office to the island). It's a very long day out, leaving at 7am and getting back at around 10pm: up to ten hours is spent driving. On the way up onto the plateau you will probably stop at the Riyue Pass, where you can see a Tibetan prayer-flag site and a couple of Chinese towers. One of the highlights is **lunch** – delicious and very cheap fried fish – which you have at a tiny settlement in a beautiful location just outside Bird Island.

Visiting Bird Island **independently** is something of a challenge, but it's possible, as a stopover between Xining and Golmud. Riding any bus between these two cities, make sure you get off at the right place by the lake – a grubby little Tibetan town called **Heimahe**, about four hours from Xining, which has a shop and a basic hotel (❶). From here you'll have to hitch a ride from a passing tractor or car. Fifty minutes' drive brings you to the *Bird Island Guesthouse*, which has clean, but very cold, double rooms with bath (❸). You'll be lucky if there's any hot water, but there's always plenty to eat (starting at around ¥20). You need to buy a **ticket** (¥58) at the guesthouse to continue the remaining 15km to the two **observation points**. The first of these is actually a beach, which you view from a hide; the second is Bird Island itself, which you observe from the opposite cliff.

Chaka Salt Lake

Not far beyond Qinghai Hu is the **Chaka Salt Lake** (¥35, ¥60 including cruise on the lake), which has recently become something of a tourist attraction. It's a potentially beautiful place, and from a distance its white gleaming salt crystals form a perfect mirror-like surface. At the site, you can ride a small freight train, visit a house of salt, walk on a sixty-kilometre salt bridge – and take a hunk of the stuff home with you afterwards. To visit the lake **independently**, catch a bus from the long-distance bus station heading to Dulan or Wulan and disembark at the small town of **Chaka Zhen**, near the lake – the earliest bus leaves at 8am. The *Yanhu Binguan* (❸) is the one hotel here. To return to Xining, flag down local buses to Heimahe, where there are more frequent buses back to Xining.

Alternatively, you can visit the lake on a **tour**, which will usually include a trip to Qinghai Hu. A hectic two-day visit to the two lakes (sleeping overnight at one of them) is run by Xining's Qinghai Jiaotong Lüxingshe (see p.1022) for ¥600 per person, inclusive of all food, tickets and accommodation. The tour runs only if there are enough people.

Golmud

Nearly 3000m up on the Tibetan plateau, **GOLMUD** is an incredibly isolated city, even by the standards of northwest China. An airport provides a link to Xining, but otherwise it lies at least fourteen hours away overland from the nearest sizeable population centre in Lhasa. In spite of this, it still manages to be the second-largest city in Qinghai, with around 130,000 mainly Han Chinese residents, most of whom work at the local potash plants. Recently, the city has suffered somewhat since the workers upped and left following the completion of the rail line to Lhasa. Many shops, and even a newly built hospital, now lie empty as occupants either returned home or set off to Lhasa to seek their fortunes; meanwhile, the city's newly constructed shopping centres and department stores long for customers who do more than just browse. For these reason Golmud is definitely worth a look purely for sociological reasons. Geographically, Golmud is located close to the massive **Kunlun Mountains** to the south, and to the **Cai Erhan Salt Lake** to the north. Both are very scenic in parts, though they remain as yet virtually unexplored by foreign tourists.

For travellers, the city is really only of interest as a transit point between Xining in the east, Dunhuang in the north and Lhasa in the south – Golmud used to be the only place in China where foreigners could officially cross by land to Tibet, but since the completion of the Lhasa rail link only a handful of travellers go by road to the plateau.

GOLMUD

EATING & DRINKING	
Qingshui Lou	1
Xiangsihai	3
Yi Pin Baozi Guan	2

ACCOMMODATION	
Golmud Hotel	A
Golmud Mansion	C
Qinggang Hotel	B

Practicalities

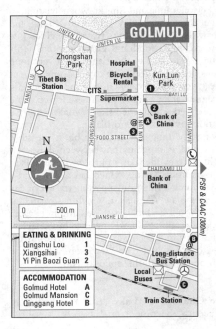

Golmud's **train and bus stations** sit facing each other in the south of the city. The scene as you disembark here is bleak almost beyond belief: a vast empty square, with a statue of the Flying Horse of Wuwei and a plaque defiantly proclaiming "Golmud Top Tourist City of China". A **taxi** to anywhere in town costs ¥5. Immediately to your right as you come out of the train station is the convenient but rapidly going downhill *Golmud Mansion* (ⓣ0979/8450876; ④). A smarter option is *Qinggang Hotel* (ⓣ0979/8456668, ⓕ8456666; ⑤; discounts available in off season) – a few minutes up Jiangyuan Lu from the long-distance bus station, it's the glassy building on the crossroads. The rooms are spacious and clean. You'll have to call in advance as it is often fully booked. Alternatively, take minibus #1 from the train station to the city's oldest hotel, the *Golmud* (ⓣ0979/412066, ⓕ8416484; ①–⑤, dorm beds ¥10). Permits (¥1700 to Tibet), tours and tickets can be obtained at the in-house CITS, when it is staffed.

There is a good range of **food** to be had in town. Across the road from the *Golmud*, and a few minutes to the south, is a reliable Sichuan restaurant *Xiangsihai*. Just around the corner, Shipin Jie (Food Street) has numerous restaurants serving hotpot, dumplings, noodles and Muslim food. For local delicacies, try the Muslim *Qingshui Lou* on Bayi Lu. *Yi Pin Baozi Guan*, near the *Golmud*, offers a welcome and cheap alternative to the usual dull breakfast fare. On weekend evenings **films** are shown at the Rail Workers' Cultural Hall, opposite the long-distance bus station. Although there are no English subtitles, it's worth going along just to experience some of the strange forlornness that swaddles much of the city that China forgot.

Though the main **CITS** branch is at 60 Bayi Zhong Lu (Mon–Fri 9am–noon & 2.30–6pm, Sat 10am–noon & 3–5pm; ⓣ0979/8412764), it's easier to use

The road to Tibet

Though the **road to Tibet** (The Qingzang Expressway, 1973km) itself is reasonable and sealed to within 50km or so of Lhasa, the fact that it crosses 5000-metre passes and almost continually runs above 4000m makes it one of the toughest in the world for passengers. The journey should take around thirty hours by bus but there are often long delays due to rock slides, and vehicles rarely have adequate heating so take plenty of warm clothing, food and drink.

The regulations concerning travel into Tibet **for foreigners** are constantly changing, but at the time of writing all arrangements must be made through Golmud's **CITS** (see above). There is no other official way of getting a bus ticket or of getting onto the bus into Tibet. The deal here is that you are buying a **"tour"** (¥1700) which covers a Tibet Entry Permit, two-month PICC insurance and one-way sleeper bus. On arrival you also get a guided tour in Lhasa for your money and three nights' dorm-bed accommodation. However, if – having arrived in Tibet – you are not enticed by the idea of a CITS tour, you are free to forfeit it and set off exploring on your own.

There are ways around this situation, though you'll need to be able to speak Chinese. Some people have managed to hook up with Chinese independent travellers renting **jeeps** for the journey; drivers have been known to reach Lhasa in a mere sixteen hours for a fraction of what it costs through CITS. The only other option is to try **hitching**, though note that this is a clandestine operation as drivers carrying foreigners can land themselves in big trouble; given the climate, you'll also have to decide whether you're up to possibly two days exposed to the elements in the back of a truck. Basically, if you hang around the Tibet bus station, you *may* be approached by a truck driver willing to take you. You'll still pay at least ¥800, and run the risk of being caught at police road blocks on the way. In reality, most drivers willing to risk taking you will usually only do so because they have an arrangement with the police – but you can never be sure. If you *are* caught, you will either be fined substantially, or have to pay a bribe, starting from another ¥500.

their branch at the *Golmud* hotel. As well as Tibet trips, CITS can arrange interesting local tours, in particular to **Cai Erhan Salt Lake**. **Internet** (¥2/hr) is available from a Net bar on Kun Lun Lu opposite and just south of the *Golmud* hotel, and next door to the *Qinggang Hotel*. There are **Bank of China** branches (Mon–Fri 8.30am–5.30pm, Sat & Sun 9.30am–4.30pm) on Kunlun Lu, north and south of the *Golmud* hotel. About 300m east from the junction along Chaidamu Lu is the **PSB** (Mon–Fri 8.30am–noon & 2.30–6pm) – look for the huge white complex with a red/gold badge on top. **Flight** tickets can be purchased through CITS at the *Golmud* or at the **CAAC** office (8.30am–noon & 1.30–5.30pm; ⓣ0979/8423333), another 100m east down Chaidamu Lu; airport buses leave from here (¥10). There are biweekly (Wed & Sun) flights to Xining, Xi'an and Qingdao.

Heading on to Xining is probably easiest by train: there are two fast trains daily (14hr) and one slow (16hr). You can only buy tickets from the station itself. The evening **bus** to Xining takes sixteen hours, while a **car service** takes half that (9am & 11am; ¥150). There are sleeper buses (9am & 6pm) to Dunhuang in Gansu province (8hr).

Xinjiang

Xinjiang Uyghur autonomous region is one of the most exciting parts of China, an extraordinary terrain, more than 3000km from any coast, which, despite all the historical upheavals since the collapse of the Silk Road trade, still comprises the same old oasis settlements strung out along the ancient routes, many still producing the silk and cotton for which they were famed in Roman times (see box, p.950).

Geographically, Xinjiang – literally "New Territories" – occupies an area slightly greater than Western Europe or Alaska, and yet its population is just thirteen million. And with the Han population probably comprising more than fifty percent of the whole, Xinjiang is perhaps the least "Chinese" of all parts of the People's Republic. By far the largest minority in Xinjiang is the **Uyghur**, though there are also some dozen other Central Asian minority populations.

The land of Xinjiang is among the least hospitable in all China, covered for the most part by arid **desert and mountain**. Essentially, it can be thought of as two giant basins, both surrounded on all sides by mountains. Between the two basins are the Tian Shan (Heavenly Mountains), which effectively bisect Xinjiang from west to east. The basin to the north is known as the **Junggar Basin**, or Jungaria. The capital of Xinjiang, and only major city, **Ürümqi**, is here, on the very southern edge of the basin, as is the heavily Kazakh town of **Yining**, right up against the border with Kazakhstan. The Junggar Basin has been subject to fairly substantial Han settlement over the past forty years, with a degree of industrial and agricultural development. It remains largely grassland, with large state farms in the centre and Kazakh and Mongol herdsmen (still partially nomadic) in the mountain pastures on the fringes. The climate is not particularly hot in summer, and virtually Siberian from October through to March. To the south is the **Tarim Basin**, dominated by

Xinjiang time

For travellers, the classic illustration of Xinjiang's remoteness from the rest of the country is in the fact that all parts of China set their clocks to Beijing time. The absurdity of this is at its most acute in Xinjiang, 3000–4000km distant from the capital – which means that in Kashgar, in the far west of the region, the summer sun rises at 9 or 10am and sets around midnight. Locally, there is such a thing as unofficial "**Xinjiang** time", a couple of hours behind Beijing time, which is used more frequently the further west you head towards Kashgar; when buying bus, train or plane tickets, you should be absolutely clear about which time is being used.

the scorching Taklamakan Desert, fiercely hot and dry in summer. This is where the bulk of the Uyghur population lives, in strings of oases (Turpan and Kashgar among them) scattered along the old routes of the Silk Road. Some of these oasis cities are buried in the desert and long forgotten; others survive on irrigation using water from the various rivers and streams that flow from surrounding mountains. As well as forgotten cities, these sands also cover another buried treasure – **oil**. Chinese estimates reckon that three times the proven US reserves of oil are under the Taklamakan alone, which is one reason that the government is firmly establishing a Han presence in the region.

Highlights of Xinjiang include the **Tian Shan** mountain pastures outside Ürümqi, where you can hike in rare solitude and stay beside Heaven Lake with Kazakhs in their yurts; but it is the old **Silk Road** that will attract most travellers. The most fascinating of the Silk Road oasis cities are **Turpan** and **Kashgar**. It is possible to follow not only the Northern Silk Road from Turpan to Kashgar via Aksu and Kuqa, but also the almost forgotten southern route via Khotan. The routes were established over two thousand years ago, but traffic reached its height during the Tang dynasty, when China's most famous Buddhist pilgrim, **Xuanzang**, used them on his seventeen-year voyage to India. There's still the possibility of continuing the Silk Road journey out beyond the borders of China itself – not only over the relatively well-established **Karakoram Highway** into Pakistan, but now also over the less well-known routes into Kazakhstan and Kyrgyzstan (see p.1068). Finally, there exists an exciting if perilous road from Kashgar into western Tibet, a route officially closed to tourists.

Some history

The region's history has been coloured by such personalities as Tamerlane, Genghis Khan, Attila the Hun and even Alexander the Great. More often, though, in counterpoint to the great movements of history, Xinjiang has been at the mercy of its isolation and the feudal warring between the rulers of its oasis kingdoms, or **khanates**.

The influence of China has been far from constant. The area – commonly referred to in the West as Eastern (or Chinese) Turkestan until 1949 – first passed under Han control in the second century BC, under Emperor Wu Di. But it was only during the **Tang dynasty** (650–850 AD) that this control amounted to more than a military presence. The Tang period for Xinjiang was something of a golden age, with the oases south of the Tian Shan largely populated by a mysterious but sophisticated Indo-European people, and the culture and Buddhist art of the oases at their zenith. Around the ninth century, however, came a change – the gradual rise to dominance of the **Uyghurs**, and their conversion to **Islam**.

Subsequent centuries saw the **conquests of the Mongols** under Genghis Khan and later, from the West, of Tamerlane. Both brought havoc and slaughter in their wake, though during the brief period of Mongol rule (1271–1368) the Silk Road trade was hugely facilitated by the fact that, for the first and only time in history, east and west Asia were under a single government.

After the fall of the Mongols, and the final disappearance of the Silk Road, Xinjiang began to split into khanates and suffered a succession of religious and factional wars. Nonetheless, it was an independence of a kind and Qing **reassertion** of Chinese domination in the eighteenth century was fiercely contested. A century later, in 1862, full-scale **Muslim rebellion** broke out, led by the ruler of Kashgaria, **Yakub Beg**, armed and supported by the British who were seeking influence in this buffer zone between India and Russia (for more on which, read Peter Hopkirk's excellent *The Great Game* – see p.1197). Ultimately the revolt failed – Beg became a hated tyrant – and the region remained part of the Chinese empire.

At the beginning of the twentieth century, Xinjiang was still a Chinese backwater controlled by a succession of brutal warlords who acted virtually independently of the central government. The last one of these before World War II, **Sheng Shizai**, seemed momentarily to be a reforming force, instituting religious and ethnic freedoms, and establishing trade with the newly emergent Soviet Union. However, he ended by abandoning his moderate positions. Slamming the door on the Soviets and on leftist influences within

The Uyghur

The Uyghur are the easternmost branch of the extended family of **Turkic peoples** who inhabit most of Central Asia. Around nine million Uyghurs live in Xinjiang with another 300,000 in Kazakhstan. Despite centuries of domination by China and some racial mingling along the way, the Uyghur remain culturally entirely distinct from the Han Chinese, and many Uyghurs look decidedly un-Chinese – stockily built, bearded, with brown hair and round eyes. Although originally Buddhists, the Uyghur have been **Muslim** for at least a thousand years and Islam remains the focus of their identity in the face of relentless Han penetration.

As the Uyghurs are for the most part unable to speak fluent Chinese and therefore unable to attend university or find well-paid work, their prospects for self-improvement within China are generally bleak. It is also true that many Han Chinese look down on the Uyghurs as unsophisticated ruffians, and are wary of their supposedly short tempers and love of knives. Perhaps as a consequence of this, Uyghurs seem at times to extend their mistrust of Han Chinese to all foreigners, tourists included. Nevertheless, gestures such as drinking tea with them, or trying a few words of their language, will help to break down the barriers, and invitations to Uyghur homes frequently follow.

Traveller's Uyghur

The **Uyghur language** is essentially an Eastern Turkish dialect, a branch of the Altaic languages from Central Asia (as well as Xinjiang, Uyghur is also spoken in parts of Kazakhstan, Kyrgyzstan and Uzbekistan). There are several dialects, of which the Central Uyghur (spoken from Ürümqi to Kashgar) is the most popular and hence given here. Unlike Chinese, Uyghur is not a tonal language. It involves eight vowels and 24 consonants and uses a slightly modified Arabic script. The only pronunciations you are likely to have difficulties with are **gh** and **kh**, but you can get away by rendering them as **g** and **k** with light **h** at the end.

Hello	*Yahximusiz*	Thank you	*Rhamat sizge*
Goodbye/Cheers	*Hosh*	Please/Sorry	*Kequrung*

Xinjiang itself in 1940, he began a reign of terror resulting in the deaths of more than two hundred thousand Communists, intellectuals, students and Muslim Nationalists.

The drive towards the defeat of the Guomindang in 1949 temporarily united the conflicting forces of Muslim nationalism and Chinese communism. After the Communist victory, however, there could be only one result. The principal Muslim Nationalist leaders were quietly murdered, allegedly killed in a plane crash, and the impetus towards a separate state was lost. The last Nationalist leader, a Kazakh named Osman, was executed in 1951.

Since 1949, the Chinese government has made strenuous attempts to stabilize the region by **settling Han Chinese** from the east, into Ürümqi in particular. The Uyghur population of Xinjiang, from being ninety percent of the total in 1949, slipped below fifty percent in the 1980s, and is still slipping, in spite of the minorities' exemption from the One Child Policy. Today, however, the Chinese government remains nervous about Xinjiang, especially given the enormous **economic potential** of the area, in terms of coal and now gold mining, oil exploration and tourism, plus its strategic value as a **nuclear test site**. There have been outbursts of **Uyghur dissent** in the region, most recently in 1997, when anti-Beijing demonstrations in Yining escalated into full-blown riots with many Uyghurs detained and some receiving the death penalty. The situation

Yes	*He'e*	Wednesday	*Qarxembe*
No	*Yakh*	Thursday	*Peyxembe*
Very	*Bek*	Friday	*Jume*
What is your name?	*Ismingiz nime?*	Saturday	*Xembe*
My name is...	*Mening ismim ...*		
How much is it?	*Bahasi khange?*	**Numbers**	
OK	*Bolidu*	1	*bir*
Good	*Yahxi*	2	*ikki*
Where is the ...?	*... nede?*	3	*uq*
toilet	*hajethana*	4	*tort*
hospital	*duhturhana*	5	*bash*
temple	*buthana*	6	*alte*
tomb	*khebre*	7	*yet'te*
I don't have enough money	*Yenimda yeterlik pul yokh*	8	*sekkiz*
		9	*tokh'khuz*
Please stop here	*Bu yerde tohtang*	10	*on*
		11	*on bir*
This is delicious	*Temlik/lezzetlik*	12	*on ikki*
Cold	*Soghukh*	etc	
Hot	*Issikh*	20	*yigrime*
Thirsty	*Ussitidighan*	30	*ottuz*
Hungry	*Ag khusakh*	40	*khirkh*
When?	*Vakhitta?*	50	*ellik*
Now	*Emdi/hazir*	60	*atmix*
Today	*Bugun*	70	*yetmix*
Yesterday	*Tunogun*	80	*seksen*
Tomorrow	*Ete*	90	*tokhsen*
Sunday	*Yekexembe*	100	*yuz*
Monday	*Doxembe*		
Tuesday	*Sixembe*		

appears to have calmed in recent years due to the increased presence of Chinese security forces; since the attacks of September 11, 2001 the Chinese government has equated Uyghur nationalism with global Islamic terrorism and indulged in its own "war on terror" by monitoring and arresting Uyghurs it claims are involved in separatist activities.

Eastern Xinjiang: the road to Turpan

The road from Dunhuang in western Gansu as far as **Hami** and then **Turpan** – the easternmost part of Xinjiang, east of the central area dominated by the Tian Shan – comprises some of the harshest terrain in the whole of China. Little water ever reaches this area of scorching depressions – geographically an extension of the Tarim Basin – which in summer is the hottest part of the country, and which was dreaded by the Silk Road traders as one of the most hazardous sections of the entire cross-Asia trip. Even today, crossing the area is most memorable for its suffocating heat and monotonous gravel and dune landscapes. Ironically Turpan – despite the heat – can be one of the most relaxing and enjoyable places in all China.

Hami

HAMI today is the eastern gateway to Xinjiang, a rich oasis in the midst of a seemingly endless desert, and famous throughout China for its **melons**, the

Eastern Xinjiang

Hami	哈密	*hāmì*
Bluebird Café	蓝鸟咖啡	*lánniǎo kāfēi*
Dianli Hotel	电力宾馆	*diànlì bīnguǎn*
Hami Hotel	哈密宾馆	*hāmì bīnguǎn*
Hui Wang Fen	回王坟	*huíwángfén*
Hui Wang Fu	回王府	*huíwángfǔ*
Jiageda Hotel	加格达宾馆	*jiāgédá bīnguǎn*
Tomb of Gess	盖斯墓	*gàisī mù*
Turpan	吐鲁番	*tùlǔfān*
Astana Graves	阿斯塔娜古墓区	*āsītǎnà gǔmùqū*
Bezeklik Caves	柏孜克里克石窟	*bózīkèlǐkè shíkū*
Daheyan	大河沿	*dàhéyàn*
Emin Minaret	苏公塔	*sūgōng tǎ*
Flaming Mountains	火焰山	*huǒyàn shān*
Gaochang	高昌	*gāochāng*
Grape Valley	葡萄沟	*pútáo gōu*
Iding Lake	艾丁湖	*àidīng hú*
Jiaohe	交河	*jiāohé*
Karez Irrigation Site	坎儿井	*kǎn'ér jǐng*
Accommodation and eating		
Best Food Burger	百富汉堡	*bǎifù hànbǎo*
Jiaohe Manor	交河庄园酒店	*jiāohé zhuāngyuán jiǔdiàn*
Jiaotong	交通宾馆	*jiāotōng bīnguǎn*
Turpan	吐鲁番宾馆	*tǔlǔfān bīnguǎn*
Xizhou Grand	西州大酒店	*xīzhōu dàjiǔdiàn*

hami gua. There's not much here to detain you; nevertheless, it's a convenient stopping point along the road between Dunhuang and Turpan – it lies more or less midway between the two.

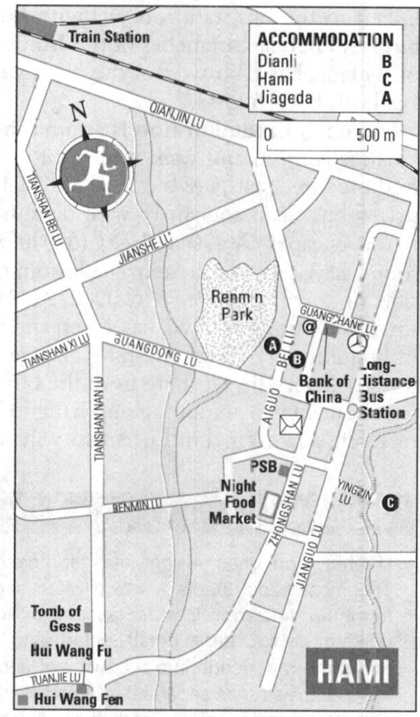

Historically, Hami has always been an important spot on the Silk Road, occupying one of the few fertile areas between Gansu province and Turpan. Xuanzang, the famous Buddhist pilgrim, nearly died of thirst on his way here, while Marco Polo noted with evident pleasure the locals' habit of not only supplying guests with food and shelter but also allowing them to sleep with their wives.

Kept small by the surrounding inhospitable desert, the town centres on the northern end of Zhongshan Lu. The bus station and hotels are in this area, while the train station is farther out to the north. There is just one historical site in Hami – the **Hui Wang Fen**, the Tombs of the Hami Kings (daily: May–Oct 10am–8pm, Nov–April 9am–7pm; ¥20), in the south of the city. From 1697 until 1930, Hami was nominally controlled by kings who for a time had obediently sent tribute to the Qing court, before becoming involved in the Muslim revolts that periodically engulfed Xinjiang. Although the kings ruled until 1930, Hami was virtually destroyed at least twice during these revolts. The entrance ticket covers three mausoleums, a mosque, a small museum and a Chinese-speaking tour guide. The main mausoleum is appealingly Arabic in style, and the two smaller pavilion-shaped mausoleums to the left combine Han, Hui, Mongol and Uyghur influences. The recently built reconstruction of the original Hami King's administration centre, **Hui Wang Fu** (daily 8am–6pm; ¥20), next to Hui Wang Fen, is rather crassly done. You can reach Hui Wang Fen and Fu by taking bus #10 along Zhongshan Lu or #1 from the train station south to its terminal, from where it is another few minutes' walk in the same direction. Alternatively, follow Zhongshan Lu south over the river and right along Tuanjie Lu to the end. It's an engrossing forty-minute walk through the dusty alleys of the disappearing Uyghur quarter. Nearby, the **Tomb of Gess** (daily 10am–6.30pm; ¥6), in a simple wooden structure with a green dome, is one of the earliest Islamic missionaries in China. To get here walk 200m east of Hui Wang Fen then turn left up Tianshan Nan Lu, and it's another 200m to the north. The area south of Hui Wang Fen takes you back in time, its old alleyways replete with donkeys, mud mosques and Uyghur cemeteries.

Practicalities

Most travellers get to Hami by **bus** from Dunhuang, Turpan or Ürümqi. There's also a daily bus link to Lanzhou from October to February. All **trains** running between Lanzhou and Ürümqi also stop at Hami. The train station is linked to the bus station on Jianguo Lu by bus #3 and to Zhongshan Lu by bus #1. There are branches of the **Bank of China** (daily 9am–1pm & 4–8pm) on Guangchang Lu west of the bus station and Guangdong Lu west of Aiguo Lu; both have **ATMs**.

There is a handful of **hotels** around the bus station. Exit the bus station onto Guangchang Lu and walk west until you come to Aiguo Bei Lu, where you'll find the three-star *Jiageda* (Ⓣ0902/2232140, Ⓦwww.xhjgd.com; ❻). Rooms are pricey but clean and smart, with discounts offered in winter. Directly opposite is the cheaper *Dianli Hotel* (Ⓣ0902/2260180; ❸), where the clean, basic rooms have fantastically retro bathroom suites. Set in leafy grounds on the other side of town, the *Hami* (Ⓣ0902/2233140, Ⓦwww.hmly.cn; ❹), one of the smartest options in town, has a gym and two restaurants (the cheapest rooms are in building #1). It's a refreshing change to wake to the sound of birdsong and not car horns. To get there from the bus station, walk south from the main exit for about fifteen minutes along Jianguo Lu, or take bus #3 for two stops, then turn left down Yingbin Lu. A taxi will cost ¥5.

Uyghur food

Uyghur food, unsurprisingly, has far more of a Central Asian than a Chinese flavour. The most basic staple – which often seems to be the only food available – is **laghman**, known in Chinese as *lamian*, literally "**pulled** noodles". Watching these being made to order is greatly entertaining: the speed at which a skilled cook transforms the raw dough into a bowlful of noodles, banging, pulling, and managing to keep all the strands separate, is incredible. In Xinjiang, *laghman* is served with a stew of mutton, tomatoes, chilli and other vegetables; rather different from the more soupy version sold elsewhere in China. For the same spicy sauce but without the noodles, try *tohogish* (known in Chinese as *dapan ji*), a chicken served chopped up in its entirety, head, feet and all; or *jerkob*, a beef stew – both are served in smarter restaurants. **Coriander leaf** is used as a garnish on everything.

In summer, apart from *laghman,* street vendors also offer endless cold noodle soup dishes, usually very spicy. **Rice** in Xinjiang appears mostly in **pilau** – a fried rice dish with hunks of mutton coloured with saffron. More familiar to foreigners are the skewers of **grilled mutton kebabs**, dusted with chilli and cumin powder – buy several of them at once, as one skewer does not add up to much more than a mouthful. They are often eaten with delicious glasses of ice-cold yoghurt (known in Chinese as *suannai*), which are available everywhere in Xinjiang. Big chunks of compressed **tea** (*zhuan cha* or literally "brick tea") are also sold everywhere – normally boiled with milk and salt – fancier ones come flavoured with cinnamon, cardamom and rosehips.

Oven-baked **breads** (*nang* in Chinese) are popular in markets: you'll see bakers apparently plunging their hands into live furnaces, to stick balls of dough on to the brick-lined walls; these are then withdrawn minutes later as bagel-like bread rolls, or simply flat – in villages local people bring their own flour to the bakery shop and make dozens of them – they last for a month. *Permuda* (known in Chinese as *kaobao)* are tasty baked dough packets stuffed with mutton and onions; they can also be fried (*samsa*) or steamed (*manta*); the latter are similar to Chinese dumplings.

A couple of other specialities are worth trying: **madang** is nougat thick with walnuts, raisins and dried fruit, sold by pedlars who carve the amount you want (or usually, more than you want – it's sold by weight) off massive slabs of the stuff. More refreshing is that characteristic Central Asian fruit, the **pomegranate**, known as *shiliu* in Chinese. You can find them whole at markets, or buy the juice from street vendors – look for the piles of skins and the juicing machines, which resemble a large, spiky torture implement.

For **eating**, you need go no farther than the excellent **night food market** which has a host of permanent outdoor canteens selling great kebabs, spicy grilled freshwater fish, noodles and *hundun* soup; it's on Zhongshan Lu just south of the PSB. For quasi-Western food, head for *Bluebird Café* or the usual suspects *KFC* and *Dico's*, all at the north of Zhongshan Lu.

Moving on by bus, there are frequent daily departures to Turpan and Jiuquan in Gansu province (via Jiayuguan), two daily to Dunhuang and three daily to Ürümqi – all leaving in the early morning – journey time to Dunhuang and Turpan is between six and eight hours, while to Ürümqi it's about eleven hours.

Turpan

The small and economically insignificant town of **TURPAN** (**Tulufan** to the Chinese) has in recent years turned itself into one of the major tourist destinations of Xinjiang. Credit for this must go largely to the residents, who have not only covered the main streets and walkways of the town with vine trellises, converting them into shady green tunnels (partly for the benefit of tourists), but have also managed to retain a relatively easy-going manner even in the heady economic climate of modern China.

Today, Turpan is a largely **Uyghur-populated** area, and, in Chinese terms, an obscure backwater, but it has not always been so. As early as the Han dynasty, the Turpan oasis was a crucial point along the Northern Silk Road, and the cities of **Jiaohe**, and later **Gaochang** (both of whose ruins can be visited from Turpan), were important and wealthy centres of power. On his way to India, Xuanzang spent more time than he had planned here, when the king virtually kidnapped him in order to have him preach to his subjects. This same king later turned his hand to robbing Silk Road traffic, and had his kingdom annexed by China in 640 as a result. From the ninth to the thirteenth century, a rich intellectual and artistic culture developed in Gaochang, resulting from a fusion between the original Indo-European inhabitants and the (pre-Islamic) Uyghurs. It was not until the fourteenth century that the Uyghurs of Turpan converted to Islam.

The town is located in a depression 80m below sea level, which accounts for its extreme climate – well above 40°C in summer and well below freezing in winter. In summer the **dry heat** is so soporific that there is little call to do anything but sleep or sip cool drinks in outdoor cafés with other tourists or the friendly locals. To ease the consciences of the indolent there are a number of **ruined cities** and **Buddhist caves** worth visiting in the countryside around the city, testimony to its past role as an important oasis on the Silk Road.

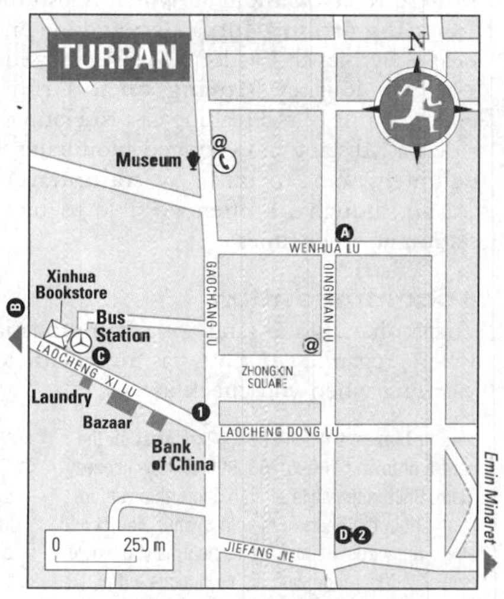

ACCOMMODATION		RESTAURANTS	
Jiaohe Manor	B	Best Food Burger	1
Jiaotong	C	John's Information Café	2
Turpan	D		
Xizhou Grand	A		

Turpan is also an agricultural oasis, famed above all for **grapes**. Today, virtually every household in the town has a hand in the grape business, both in cultivating the vines, and in drying the grapes at the end of the season (a Grape Festival is held at the end of August).

Note that Turpan is very much a **summer resort**; if you come out of season (Nov–March), the town itself is cold and uninspiring, with the vines cut back and most businesses closed – though the surrounding sights remain interesting, and devoid of other tourists.

Arrival, information and getting around

The only way to arrive in downtown Turpan is by **bus**. Frequent buses (9am–8pm; every 20min) run between Ürümqi and Turpan, and there's a daily bus service to and from Hami and Korla. If you're coming from Hami you'll probably be dropped at the north end of Gaochang Lu. Simply jump on a #202 bus heading south and ask to get off at *Laocheng Xizi Lukou*. Turpan's **train station** is 55km away at Daheyan (marked "Tulufan" on timetables) – from where it takes at least an hour to get into town by bus (summer 8am–11pm, winter 9am–8pm; ¥8). From Daheyan station, turn right and walk a few hundred metres to reach the bus station, or catch a minibus from the station concourse. If you miss the last bus, you'll either have to stay the night in Daheyan or get a taxi (¥50).

Turpan has two **travel agents** that can help out with transport bookings for around ¥30 commission (including, in the absence of an airport at Turpan, flights out of Ürümqi), as well as local tours. CITS have a branch on the first floor of the *Jiaotong* (Ⓣ0995/8535809), and there's also the independent *John's Information Café* (Ⓔjohncafé@hotmail.com) inside the *Turpan* hotel. **Internet access** is available at a café on the corner of Qingnian Lu and the park. On Laocheng Wi Lu you will find a **Bank of China**, a laundry, and a Xinhua Bookstore across the road which is also the **post office** (daily 9.30am–8pm).

Getting around Turpan is best done on foot, or – given the extreme summer heat – by bicycle or donkey cart, for which you should expect to pay around ¥4–5 per journey. **Moving on** to Ürümqi there's a good bus (8.10am–8pm; every 20min; 3hr). Heading east to Hami or west to Korla it's a bumpy five hour ride past distant snow-ridged mountains, and for anywhere more distant, you definitely want to travel by **train**; travel agents can make bookings in peak season, though it's often possible to buy your own train tickets at Daheyan station at other times.

Accommodation

Turpan has a good range of accommodation available to foreigners, and everywhere, regardless of cost, has **air conditioning** – just make sure that yours is working when you check in.

Jiaohe Manor 9 Jiaohe Dado, 2km west of the centre of town Ⓣ0995/7685999, Ⓦwww.jiaohezy.com. Built in the style of an old fort, this venture lies right in the heart of the old Uyghur district and all its vineyards. Rooms are as neat as you would expect in this range with big reductions out of season. ❼

Jiaotong 230 Laocheng Xi Lu, at the bus station Ⓣ0995/8535809. Inexpensive, with grubby corridors that house surprisingly sufficient rooms with 24-hour hot water. ❸

Turpan South of Qingnian Lu Ⓣ0995/8568898, Ⓕ8569299. An attractive out-of-the-way setting with standard rooms. In the hot summer evenings, there are cheerful displays of local singing and dancing in the gardens by the nearby *John's Café*. Ask about discounts. ❻

Xizhou Grand 8 Qingnian Lu Ⓣ0995/8554000, Ⓕ8554068. The plushest place in town, with comfortable, clean rooms and pleasant staff. ❺

The Town

For some travellers, the real draw of Turpan is its relaxing absence of sights. The downtown area doesn't amount to much, with most of the services near the bus station on Laocheng Lu; pedestrianized Qingnian Lu is protected from the baking summer sun by vine trellises. There is a **museum** on Gaochang Xi Lu (daily 10am–7.30pm; ¥20), with a smallish collection of dinosaur fossils as well as silk fragments, tools, manuscripts and preserved corpses recovered from the nearby Silk Road sites. Other than this, the **bazaars** off Laocheng Lu, almost opposite the bus station, are worth a casual look, and though they are not comparable to anything in Kashgar. You'll find knives, clothes, hats and boots on sale, while the most distinctively local products include delicious sweet raisins, as well as walnuts and almonds.

One of the nicest ways to spend an evening after the heat of the day has passed is to **rent a donkey cart** and take a tour of the countryside south of town, a world of dusty tracks, vineyards, wheat fields, shady poplars, running streams and incredibly friendly, smiling people. You are unlikely to encounter many more tranquil rural settings than this in China. Donkey-cart drivers gather outside the *Turpan* hotel; two or three people will pay around ¥10–15 each for a tour lasting an hour or more.

Eating and drinking

John's Information Café, situated at the back of the *Turpan* hotel, has an English menu and is not a bad place to drink beer in the evenings and listen in on the Uyghur singing and dancing in the gardens nearby. Alternatively for Western food try the *McDonald's* wannabe *Best Food Burger* on the Gaochang Lu/ Laocheng Lu intersection.

For **Chinese** cuisine, there's a whole series of touristy restaurants with English menus, to the west of the main crossroads north of the *Turpan* hotel on Laocheng Dong Lu. All have outdoor tables and chairs under the vines, and friendly service – though you should establish prices when ordering. Try *liang ban huang gua*, a delicious cold cucumber salad with garlic and soya sauce. The Bazaar next to the Xinhua Bookstore is an excellent place to sample **Uyghur cuisine** including kebabs, *laghman* and dry and fresh fruits; around 10am and 7pm are the best times to pick up fresh nan bread. For more upmarket Chinese and Uyghur food, try the restaurants in the *Oasis Hotel,* north of Qinggang Lu. It's also worth buying a bottle of the **local wine** (around ¥40–50 a bottle). The red is sweet and thick like port, the white fruity and very drinkable.

Uyghur music – muqam

Song and dance is at the core of Uyghur cultural identity and is commonly presented at all social gatherings. The most established form of Uyghur music, *muqam*, has developed since the sixth century into a unique collection of songs and instrumentals, quite separate from Arabic and Persian influence. A *muqam* must open with a flowing rhythm that complies with strict modal constraints, followed by a suite of pieces that tie into the opening. In the late sixteenth century scholars and folk musicians gathered to collate this music into a definitive collection of twelve *muqams*. The entire collection takes 24 hours to play and involves around fifteen traditional instruments such as the plucked mandolin-like *rawap*, metal-stringed sitar and large *dumbak* drums. Sadly, few people can play *muqam* nowadays, but recordings are popular and sold on CD and DVD throughout Xinjiang.

Xuanzang and the Journey to the West

Trade goods were not the only things to travel along the Silk Road; it was along this route that **Buddhism** first arrived in China at some point in the first century AD. Cities along the way became bastions of the religion (which in part explains their abandonment and desecration following the introduction of Islam after 1000), and from early on, Chinese pilgrims visited India and brought back a varied bag of Buddhist teachings. The most famous is the Tang-dynasty monk **Xuanzang**, unique for the depth of his learning and the exhaustive quantity of material with which he returned after a seventeen-year journey from the then capital of China, Chang'an (Xi'an), to India.

Born near Luoyang in 602, Xuanzang favoured **Mahayana** Buddhism, which depicts the world as an illusion produced by our senses. Having studied in Luoyang, Chengdu and Chang'an, he became confused by often contradictory teachings, and in 629 he decided to visit India to study Buddhism at its source. But China's new Tang rulers (the dynasty was established in 618) had forbidden foreign travel, so Xuanzang went without official permission, narrowly avoiding arrest in western Gansu. He almost died of thirst before reaching **Hami** and then **Turpan**, at the foot of the Flaming Mountains. Turpan's king detained him for a month to hear him preach but eventually provided a large retinue, money and passports for safe passage through other kingdoms. Despite bandits, Xuanzang reached **Kuqa** unharmed, where he spent two months waiting for the passes north over the Tian Shan to thaw – even so, a great number of his party died traversing the mountains. On the far side in modern Kyrgyzstan, Xuanzang's religious knowledge greatly impressed the Khan of the Western Turks, before he continued, via the great central Asian city of **Samarkand**, through modern-day Afghanistan, over the Hindu Kush and so down into **India**, arriving about a year after he set out. Xuanzang spent fifteen years in India, journeying from the northern mountains, through Assam down the east coast to around Madras, then crossing the centre of the country to north-western Nasik and Baroda. Everywhere he visited holy sites (including the Ganges and places from Buddha's life), studied major and esoteric forms of Buddhism, lectured, and entered debates – which he often won – with famous teachers on aspects of religious thought.

Around Turpan

Nearly all visitors to Turpan end up taking the customary **tour** of the historical and natural sights outside town. These are quite fun, as much for the chance to get out into the desert as for the sights in themselves, which usually include the two ancient cities of **Gaochang** and **Jiaohe**, the **Emin Minaret**, the **Karez irrigation site**, the **Bezeklik Caves** and **Astana Graves**. Sites are open daily, for most of the hours of daylight.

Assuming you can get together a group of five people – both CITS and the tourist hotels can organize this – a trip to all the above sites will take the best part of a day (with a break for lunch and siesta if you choose) and cost around ¥50 per person for the minibus. CITS also offer a car with driver for ¥200 per day. Alternatively, for places close to town, **cycling** is a good option. Be aware that, however you travel, you'll be in blistering heat for the whole of the day, so sun cream, a hat, water bottle and sunglasses are essential.

Entry fees, which are not included in the cost of a tour, range from ¥20 to ¥30 per site. Frankly, the only site which is unquestionably worth the money is Jiaohe: if you're looking to cut costs, the Bezeklik Caves can be skipped, and you can get good views of Gaocheng and the Emin Minaret without actually entering the sites.

If he hoped to find ultimate clarity he was probably disappointed, as the interpretation of Buddhist lore in India was even more varied than in China. However, he did manage to acquire a vast collection of Buddhist statues, relics and – especially – **texts**, and in 644 decided that it was his responsibility to return to China with this trove of knowledge. Given an **elephant** to carry his luggage by the powerful north Indian king Harsha, Xuanzang recrossed the Kush and turned east to travel over the Pamirs to **Tashkurgan** (near where the elephant unfortunately drowned) before heading up to **Kashgar**, then – as now – an outpost of the Chinese empire. From here he turned southeast to the silk and jade emporium of **Khotan**, whose king claimed Indian ancestry and where there were a hundred Buddhist monasteries. Xuanzang spent eight months here, waiting for replacements of Buddhist texts lost in northern India, and a reply from the Tang emperor **Taizong**, to whom he had written requesting permission to re-enter China. When it came, permission was enthusiastic, and Xuanzang lost little time in returning to Chang'an via Minfeng, Miran, Loulan and **Dunhuang**, arriving in the Chinese capital in 645. He had left unknown, alone, and almost as a fugitive; he returned to find tens of thousands of spectators crowding the road to Chang'an. The emperor became his patron, and he spent the last twenty years of his life translating part of the collection of Buddhist texts acquired on his travels.

Xuanzang wrote a biography, but highly coloured accounts of his travels also passed into folklore, becoming the subject of plays and the sixteenth-century novel **Journey to the West**, still a popular tale in China. In it, Xuanzang (known as **Tripitaka**) is depicted as terminally naïve, hopelessly dismayed by the various disasters which beset him. Fortunately, he's aided by the Bodhisattva of Mercy, **Guanyin**, who sends him spirits to protect him in his quest: the vague character of **Sandy**; the greedy and lecherous **Pigsy**; and **Sun Wu Kong**, the brilliant Monkey King. As many of the novel's episodes are similar, varying only in which particular demon has captured Tripitaka, the best parts are the lively exchanges between Pigsy and Monkey, as they endeavour to rescue their master. A good abridgement in English is Arthur Waley's *Monkey* – see "Books".

The Emin Minaret, Jiaohe and Karez irrigation site

You can walk to the eighteenth-century **Emin Minaret** (¥30), 2km southeast of the city, by following Jiefang Jie east out of town for about thirty minutes. Unlike other Islamic architecture, the minaret is built to a very simple style – slightly bulging and potbellied – and erected from sun-dried brown bricks arranged in differing patterns. The tower tapers its way 40m skyward to a rounded tip adjoining a mosque with an interesting latticework ceiling. You can see the complex without entering the site; otherwise you can ascend the tower to gain good views over the green oasis in the foreground and the distant snowy Tian Shan beyond.

About 11km west of Turpan is the ruined city of **Jiaohe** (¥40; signposted in English), just about within cycling range on a hot day. Although Jiaohe was for large parts of its history under the control of Gaochang (see p.1042), it became the regional administrative centre during the eighth century, and occupies a spectacular defensive setting on top of a two-kilometre-long, steep-sided plateau carved out by the two halves of a forking river. What sets Jiaohe apart from all other ruined cities along the Silk Road is that although most of the buildings comprise little more than crumbling, windswept mud walls, so many survive, and of such a variety – gates, temples, public buildings, graveyards and

▲ Harvesting grapes near Turpan

ordinary dwellings – that Jiaohe's **street plan** is still evident, and there's a real feeling of how great this city must once have been. As with Gaochang, a Buddhist monastery marked the town centre; its foundations – 50m on each side – can still be seen. Another feature is the presence of ancient wells still containing water. Make sure you walk to the far end of the site, where the base of a former tower, dated to around 360 AD, overlooks the river.

Returning from Jiaohe, minibus drivers usually drop you off at a dolled-up **Karez irrigation site** (¥40), an intrinsically interesting place unfortunately turned into an ethnic theme park, complete with regular Uyghur dance shows, presumably to justify the entry fee. Karez irrigation taps natural underground channels carrying water from source – in this case glaciers at the base of the Tian Shan – to the point of use. Strategically dug wells then bring water to small surface channels that run around the streets of the town. Many ancient Silk Road cities relied on this system, including those much farther to the west, in areas such as modern Iran, and Karez systems are still in use throughout Xinjiang – there are plenty of opportunities to see them for free on the way to Kashgar.

The Bezeklik Caves, Astana Graves and Gaochang ruins

For the other sites, you definitely need to take a minibus – they are too far to reach by bicycle. The first stop is usually the Bezeklik Caves, but on the way you'll pass the **Flaming Mountains**, made famous in the sixteenth-century Chinese novel *Journey to the West* (see p.1040). It's not hard to see why the novel depicts these sandstone mountains as walls of flame, the red sandstone hillsides, lined and creviced as though flickering with flame in the heat haze. The plains below are dotted with dozens of small "nodding donkey" **oil wells**, all tapping into Xinjiang's vast reserves.

The **Bezeklik Caves** (¥30), in a valley among the Flaming Mountains some 50km northeast of Turpan, are disappointing, offering mere fragments of the former wealth of Buddhist cave art here, dating back to 640 AD. The location is nonetheless strikingly beautiful, with stark orange dunes behind and a deep river gorge fringed in green below, but most of the murals were cut out and removed to Berlin by Albert Von Le Coq at the beginning of the twentieth century, and the remainder painstakingly defaced by Muslim Red Guards during the 1960s. (A good deal of the murals removed by Le Coq were subsequently destroyed by the Allied bombing of Germany in World War II.) Outside the site you can ride **camels** along the Flaming Mountains for ¥80 per person. Just before the caves is a bizarre **theme park** (¥25), featuring giant sculptures of characters from *Journey to the West* – a very surreal sight springing up out of the desiccated landscape.

South of here, the **Astana Graves** (¥20) mark the burial site of the imperial dead of Gaochang from the Tang dynasty. Unfortunately, the graves have had most of their interesting contents removed to museums in Ürümqi and Turpan, and little remains beyond a couple of preserved corpses and some murals. The adjacent ruins of **Gaochang** (¥40) are somewhat more impressive, however, especially for their huge scale and despite having suffered from the ravages of both Western archeologists and the local population, who for centuries have been carting off bits of the city's ten-metre-high adobe walls to use as soil for their fields. You can walk, or take a donkey cart (¥20 per person), from the entrance to the centre of the site, which is marked by a large square building, the remains of a monastery. Its outer walls are covered in niches, in each one of which a Buddha was originally seated; just a few bare, broken traces of these Buddhas remain, along with their painted haloes. If you have time you can strike off on your own and listen to the hot wind whistling through the mud-brick walls.

Grape Valley and Iding Lake

Thirteen kilometres north of Turpan, and at the western end of the Flaming Mountains, is the so-called **Grape Valley** (¥60). There's very little point visiting this place out of season, but from mid-July to September it's a pleasant little oasis in the middle of a stark desert, covered in shady trellises bulging with fruit (which you have to pay for if you want to eat). Your ticket covers a Uyghur dance performance and a museum – you can find the locations of both on the map of the valley as you enter. This could be included on your minibus tour, or you could reach it on a very hot bicycle ride, but bear in mind that the scenery here is not much different from that of downtown Turpan.

Finally, about 50km south of Turpan, though not included on any tours, is the bleak but dramatic **Iding Lake**. Located in a natural depression 154m below sea level, this is the second-lowest lake in the world after the Dead Sea, though you won't actually see any water here except in spring – the rest of the year the lake is a flat plain of dried salt deposits. The land around the lake is white with crusty salt and dotted with bright yellow-green pools of saturated water that feels like oil on the skin. Locals rub it over themselves enthusiastically, claiming that it's good for you. A car to the lake and back should cost around ¥150 – the road is very rough and expect the one-way trip to take at least two hours. At the time of writing there is talk of turning the area into a kind of resort with a ¥460 entry fee, so ask at Turpan's **CITS** first. The area around the lake is very muddy, so don't take your best shoes.

Ürümqi

ÜRÜMQI – **Wulumuqi** in Chinese – is the political, industrial and economic capital of Xinjiang, and by far the largest city in the region, with a population of around two million, the overwhelming majority of whom are Han Chinese. Its name means "Beautiful Pastures" and although that hardly applies these days, the west of the city around Renmin Park can be a pleasantly green place in the summer, while the skyline to the east is dominated by the snowy massif of the Tian Shan. Three hours east of the city, **Tian Chi** (Heavenly Lake) is a welcome oasis.

For travellers arriving from western China or Central Asia, Ürümqi will be the first truly Chinese city on your route, offering the first chance to witness the consumer boom that is sweeping the high streets of China, in the shape of smart department stores and designer boutiques. So vital has the city become as China's most westerly industrial outpost that in 1992 it was officially decreed a "port" to enable it to benefit from the special low rates of tax, normally permitted only in port cities such as Shanghai and Xiamen – an unusual distinction, to say the least, for a city located 2000km from the nearest bit of coastline.

If you're coming from eastern China, there are still surprises in store as East meets West both in terms of geography and population. There are also lively

Ürümqi and Tian Chi

Ürümqi	乌鲁木齐	*wūlǔ mùqí*
Erdaoqiao Market	二道桥市场	*èrdàoqiáo shìchǎng*
Hongshan Park	红山公园	*hóngshān gōngyuán*
Main Bus Station	客运站	*kèyùn zhàn*
Renmin Park	人民公园	*rénmín gōngyuán*
South Bus Station	南郊客运站	*nánjiāo kèyùnzhàn*
Xinjiang Museum	新疆博物馆	*xīnjiāng bówùguǎn*
Accommodation and eating		
Akka Inn	家快捷酒店	*jiākuàijié jiǔdiàn*
Cabana	卡吧娜	*kǎbānà*
Dadianyuan Binguan	大滇园宾馆	*dàdiānyuán bīnguǎn*
Fifth Avenue	第五大道	*dìwǔ dàdào*
Fubar	福吧	*fú bā*
Kranzlers	凯宾斯基酒店	*kǎibīnsījī jiǔdiàn*
Overseas Chinese	华侨宾馆	*huáqiáo bīnguǎn*
Ramada	屯河华美达酒店	*túnhé huáměidá jiǔdiàn*
Shahediya Yanhuiting	沙合迪亚宴会厅	*shāhédíyà yànhuìtīng*
Sumin Niuriumian	苏民牛肉面	*sūmín niúròumiàn*
Super 8	速8酒店	*sùbā jiǔdiàn*
Toshkent	塔什干餐厅	*tǎshígàn cāntīng*
Wuyi Night Market	五一夜市	*wǔyī yèshì*
Xibu	西部大酒店	*xībù dà jiǔdiàn*
Youth Hotel	青年旅社	*qīngnián lǚshè*
Moving on: foreign cities		
Almaty	阿拉木图	*ālā mùtú*
Bishkek	比什凯克	*bǐshí kǎikè*
Islamabad	伊斯兰堡	*yīsī lánbǎo*
Moscow	莫斯科	*mòsīkē*
Tashkent	塔什干	*tǎshí gàn*
Baiyang Gou	白杨沟	*báiyáng gōu*
Xi Baiyang Gou	西白杨沟	*xī báiyáng gōu*
Tian Chi	天池	*tiānchí*
Dawanzi	大弯子	*dàwānzi*

bazaars and food markets, and a vibrant nightlife, its business people, gold-, and oil-miners lending the place a certain pioneering feel.

Under the name of Dihua, Ürümqi became the capital of Xinjiang in the late nineteenth century. During the first half of the twentieth century the city was something of a battleground for feuding warlords – in 1916 Governor Yang Zengxin invited all his personal enemies to a dinner party here, and then had

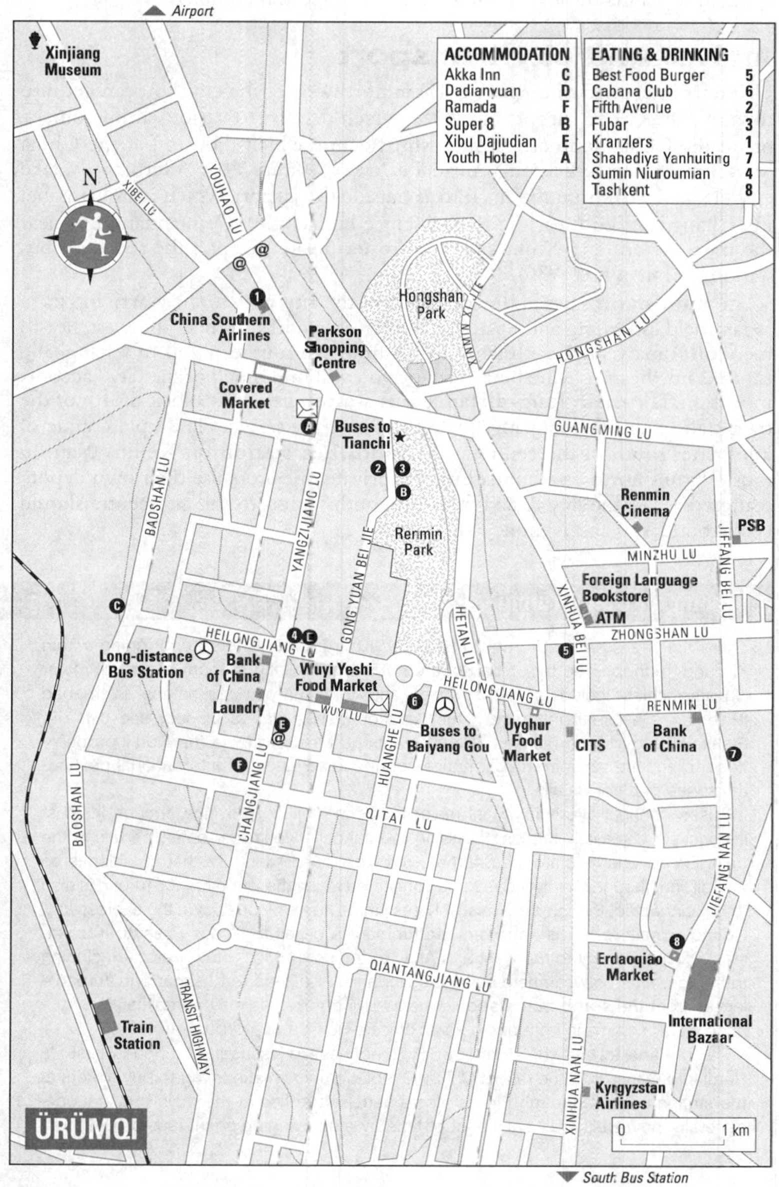

their heads cut off one by one during the course of the banquet. Later, shortly before the outbreak of World War II, **Soviet troops** entered the city to help quell a Muslim rebellion; they stayed until 1960. Ürümqi began to emerge from its extreme backwardness only with the completion of the Lanzhou–Ürümqi **rail line** in 1963. This more than anything helped to integrate the city, economically and psychologically, into the People's Republic. And with the opening of the Ürümqi–Almaty rail line in 1991, the final link in the long-heralded direct route from China through Central Asia to Europe was complete.

Arrival and city transport

Ürümqi's international **airport** is 15km northwest of the city; you can get into town on the CAAC airport bus (¥18), which delivers to various airline offices, or on the China Southern Airlines **shuttle bus** which drops off at the China Southern Airlines office on Youhao Lu (every 30min; ¥10). Alternatively, take city bus #51 (¥5) from the main road outside the airport, which runs via Xibei Lu, Changjiang Lu (near the long-distance bus station), Qiantanjiang Lu (near the train station) and Xinhua Nan Lu to terminate just past the southern bus station; or hire a taxi (¥36).

The **train station** lies in the southwest of the city, with services arriving from as far afield as Beijing and Shanghai in the east, and Kashgar in the west, not to mention Almaty in Kazakhstan. Bus #8 from the southern end of Changjiang Lu runs northeast to Minzhu Lu, where you will find much of the city's accommodation. The **main long-distance bus station** lies a few blocks north of the train station, on Heilongjiang Lu, but just as many services end up a couple of kilometres south of the centre at the **south bus station** on Xinhua Nan Lu (bus #1 runs north up Xinhua Lu), and private operators use their own depots, scattered across the city. A taxi from the south station to the city centre should cost around ¥10 and is money well spent.

Moving on from Ürümqi

There are **flights** from Ürümqi to Kashgar, Korla, Kuqa, Khotan and Yining within Xinjiang (monopolized by China Southern Airlines' Xinjiang branch) and to all major Chinese cities including Hong Kong, and to Almaty (Kazakhstan), Islamabad (Pakistan – a useful fall-back if the Karakoram Highway is closed; see p.1074), Bishkek (Kyrgyzstan), Tashkent (Uzbekistan) and Moscow. Note that you'll probably need to acquire visas from your native country in advance for international destinations; see p.32 for details.

Buses connect Ürümqi with all major towns in Xinjiang province, though in most instances – especially the long crossing to Kashgar – you're far better off taking the train. Exceptions here are the Southern Silk Road, and Yining, neither of which is on the rail line, though Yining is due to be connected to Jinghe in the future; Turpan is also to be connected, though it is a relatively easy three hours by bus down the expressway. Ürümqi's **main long-distance bus station** serves buses to Hoegs Pass (to Kazakhstan), Yining, Almaty to the west and Altay to the north. Most other traffic – including traffic to points between here along the Northern Silk Road to Kashgar and Turpan – leaves from the **south bus station**, where buying tickets is only complicated by the huge, noisy scrums in front of the ticket offices. Beware of pickpockets.

The **rail line** follows the Northern Silk Road west to Kashgar, and heads east via Hami into Gansu and the rest of China. Chaotic crowds make trying to buy tickets at the station difficult, though there's also a hard-seat office at the main bus station – generally, however, you'll save a lot of time by employing an agent (see p.1049).

It's easy enough to get around the city with **buses** #1, #2, #7, #101, #102 and #111 serving most areas of interest; **taxis** cost ¥6 for the first three kilometres.

Accommodation

Ürümqi's **accommodation** options are gratifyingly diverse, with a good choice between budget and luxury options.

Akka Inn 2 Baoshan Lu, near the north bus station ⓣ0991/4557866, ⓦwww.akkainn.com. This imposing modern structure provides grand vistas of Ürümqi and bright, up-to-date rooms. Discounts of more than 50 percent are often given. ❻

Dadianyuan 167 Heilongjian Lu ⓣ0991/5856611. Nicely located around the corner from the bustling Gongyuan Bei Ji and Wuyi Lu, this new venture has clean rooms, excellent service and a very popular in-house hotpot restaurant. ❸

Ramada 52 Changjiang Lu ⓣ0991/5876588, ⓦwww.ramadainternational.com. Upmarket yet reasonably priced place with all the usual four-star facilities. Reductions of more than 50 percent are available off season. Amiable staff speak good English. ❼

Super 8 140 Gong Yuan Bei Jie ⓣ0991/5590666, ⓦwww.super8.com.cn. Probably the most remote outpost of this chain of budget hotels, *Super 8* offers individually decorated rooms and suites, often at discounted rates. They are reluctant to book rooms in advance, so if you want a PC and a bath, call *Fubar* (see p.1049), who have an arrangement with them. ❻

Xibu Dajiudian 41 Changjiang Lu ⓣ0991/5566868. Formerly a favourite with foreign visitors, this budget option still provides comfortable, if somewhat worn, rooms. ❸

Youth Hotel 131 Yangzijiang Lu ⓣ0991/4509766. Surprisingly clean and comfortable budget option, well located for the nearby parks and bars, and with 24-hour water. ❷

The City

Ürümqi centres around the junction of Zhongshan Lu and Xinhua Lu, though visitors are more likely to find themselves gravitating towards the east of the

To Kazakhstan

The rail link between China and Kazakhstan connects the ports of eastern China with those of northwestern Europe – a route that offers a substantial saving of time over the Trans-Siberian route. However, the link is used by just two **trains** a week in both directions connecting Ürümqi and Almaty, departing on Saturday and Monday nights from both ends. In Ürümqi, tickets (sleepers only, from about ¥600) can be bought in the international departure lounge at the north end of the train-station building (daily 10am–1pm & 3.30–7.30pm). Bear in mind that you need to double-check the availability of these trains when planning the trip, since they sometimes stop running without notice.

Buses to Almaty run daily from Ürümqi's long-distance bus station for US$60 and take at least 24 hours; alternatively, you can pick up a bus from Yining every day except Sunday for only US$30; tickets are sold at a special office inside Yining bus station. The Hoegs Pass to Kazakhstan has a string of interesting souvenir shops selling Turkish chocolates, Russian binoculars and random foreign cigarettes including "American" cigars. Expect protracted delays at the border – upwards of four hours to sort out the paperwork and shift cargo around is usual. There is one **flight** every Wednesday between Ürümqi and Almaty, costing ¥2031 from China Southern Airlines, Xinjiang branch. Nationals of all countries (except Commonwealth of Independent States) require **visas** for Kazakhstan, which at the time of writing had to be obtained from their home country.

city near **Renmin Park** (daily 8am–10.15pm; free), which houses a boating pond and a funfair among other attractions. Clearly visible on a hill to the north across Guangming Lu is **Hongshan Park** (daily 7am–11pm; free), another pleasant place with boating, pavilions and pagodas, and a steep hill to climb. At the cool and shady summit you can sit and have a drink while watching the locals clambering about over the rocks; on clear days the view over the rapidly changing city skyline with desert and snowy mountains in the background is impressive.

A must-see sight in Ürümqi is the **Xinjiang Museum** (daily 9.30am–7.30pm; ¥30, free on Sun), on Xibei Lu in the north of the city. Exhibits focus on the lives, culture and history of the peoples of the region along with a number of ancient, desiccated **corpses** retrieved from their desert burial sites. Among them is the so-called "Loulan Beauty", a woman with long fair hair, allegedly 3800 years old, recovered from the city of Loulan on the Southern Silk Road (p.1061). Of a distinctly non-Chinese appearance, the Loulan Beauty has been taken to heart by some Uyghur Nationalists as a symbol of the antiquity (and validity) of their claims for sovereignty over these lands. To reach the museum, take bus #7 from Xinhua Bei Lu.

Shopping in Ürümqi can be quite an eye-opener – consumerism has reached China's final frontier, with boutiques with pseudo-French and Italian names springing up along Xinhua Bei Lu, the main shopping street. For a something with a more local flavour, head south of here, down Jiefang Nan Lu; the shops become steadily more Uyghur-oriented, until you reach the **Erdaoqiao market**, a great place for souvenir shopping, selling knives, handmade musical instruments, jade, carpets, clothes and various ornate crafts (be prepared to bargain prices down to about one third of the initial cost). The **International Bazaar** complex opposite sells similar items at a relatively cheaper price, in a more relaxed if less authentic atmosphere. A string of music shops here sell CDs of traditional Uyghur music (see box, p.1039). To get a real feel for the area, try slipping down some of the alleyways off Jiefang Nan Lu, where you can find blacksmiths fashioning axes amidst a plethora of other traditional cottage industries.

Eating

Ürümqi has a good variety of places to **eat**, whether you're after Uyghur specialties or Cantonese favourites, with a couple of exceptional food markets.

Kranzlers In the former *Kempinski* hotel attached to the China Southern offices, 576 Youhao Nan Lu ⓣ0991/6388888. Excellent food in mediocre surroundings. The hotel's flagship restaurant serves up a fantatstic-value Arabic and Asian all-you-can-eat lunch buffet for ¥98 for two, and a dinner buffet for ¥128 for two.

Shahediya Yanhuiting 262 Jiefang Nan Lu ⓣ0991/8872444. Locals flock to this traditional Uyghur restaurant with byzantine interior and nightly traditional song and dance shows. Ordering can be a problem with the lack of English and Chinese spoken.

Sumin Niuroumian Heilongjiang Lu, next to the *Dadianyuan* hotel. Cheap local place offering a range of noodles and a very popular ¥6–8 lunch buffet.

Toshkent 51 Xinhua Nan Lu ⓣ0991/88557798. Uzbek restaurant in the heart of the Erdaoqiao market, serving up Uyghur and Central Asian food at reasonable prices. The borscht and grilled lamb chops are especially popular with locals.

Wuyi Yeshi Wuyi Lu. This night food market launches an assault on the senses as crowds struggle through the fug of cooking smoke to gorge on cheap and plentiful delicacies from all over the country. Fires up daily from 8pm until late.

Drinking and nightlife

Though nightlife in Ürümqi is limited, it can be lively. Most people start out at *Fubar* and ask the owners about other options should they wish to move on.

Cabana Club Huanghe Lu, 200m south of Renmin Park south gate. Highly charged atmosphere generated by the young, mainly Uyghur, crowd, and the nightly live acts.

Fifth Avenue Gongyuan Bei Jie opposite *Fubar*. Unusually open gay club providing a break from the norm with drag and performance artistes strutting their stuff on stage.

Fubar 1 Gongyuan Bei Jie ⓣ0991/5844498, ⓦwww.fubar.com.cn. An oasis of travel information, wireless Internet, beers, spirits and Western food in the only foreign-owned bar in Xinjiang. Stylish interior and local regulars provide a welcoming and interesting environment and a magnet for travellers and expats alike.

Listings

Airlines China Southern's office is at 576 Youhao Nan Lu (ⓣ0991/2308788 or 2825368). Kyrgyzstan Airlines (ⓣ0991/2316638 or 2316333) is in the lobby of the *Overseas Chinese Hotel*, in the south of the city on Xinhua Nan Lu.

Banks and exchange The main Bank of China is at the junction of Renmin Lu and Jiefang Lu (Mon–Fri 9.30am–1.30pm & 4.30–7pm); its ATMs only accept charge cards. Any China Construction bank will take cards with Cirrus; try the one next to the Foreign Language Bookstore on Xinhua Bei Lu.

Bookshops The Foreign Language Bookstore (daily 9am–6pm) on Xinhua Bei Lu has English novels and a few Chinese classics In English on the third floor. Maps of Ürümuqi with English can also be found on the first floor.

Internet access There's a huge Internet café next to the Xibu Dajiudian on Changjiang Lu.

Mail and telephones The main post office (daily 10am–8pm) is west of the northern end of Renmin Park. For long-distance phone calls you can buy and use cards available in the lobbies of upmarket hotels, post offices or *Fubar*.

Travel agents Oriented towards Chinese travellers, Ürümqi CITS (ⓣ0991/2821426, ⓦwww.xinjiangtour.com), 38 Xinhua Nan Lu, is of limited use. You'll do better at Fubar Adventure Solutions (ⓣ0991/5844498, ⓦwww.fubar.com.cn), which can offer free travel advice and custom-designed trips (including trekking with packhorses, and horse-riding to an array of lesser-known destinations in and around Xinjiang).

Tian Chi and Baiyang Gou

Tian Chi means "Heaven Lake", and this unspoilt natural haven 110km east of Ürümqi – the starting point of Vikram Seth's book *From Heaven Lake* – does almost live up to its name, especially for travellers who have spent a long time in the deserts of northwest China. At the cool, refreshing height of 2000m, the lake is surrounded by grassy meadows, steep, dense pine forests and jagged snow-covered peaks, including the mighty **Bogda Feng**, which soars to over 6000m, and the nicest feature of the area is that you can wander at will (you are likely to see eagles flying overhead as you trek towards the far side of the lake). There are no restrictions on accommodation (most people stay in yurts, with the semi-nomadic Kazakh population), and there is virtually limitless hiking. You need only to watch the **weather** – bitterly cold in winter, the lake is really only accessible during the summer months, May to September.

The **Kazakhs**, who lead a semi-nomadic herding existence in these hills, are organized into communes, very loosely managed by the State, which in theory owns both their land and animals and lets them out on fifteen- or thirty-year "contracts". Their traditional livelihood is from sheep, selling lambs in spring if the winter spares them. But it's a hard, unpredictable business – the State sometimes has to bail them out if the winter is a disastrous one – and revenues come increasingly from tourism. As in Inner Mongolia, the Kazakhs have taken to performing at horse shows, mostly for tourists. The extra income from providing visitors with food and accommodation is also welcome.

If you have not pre-booked your accommodation, you can simply set off to find yourself a **yurt**. Staying in one is a well-established custom, and you'll soon find people eager to cater for you. Most tourists lodge by the near side of the lake, but you can climb right up into the remote valleys of the Tian Shan – choose the right-hand main road around the lake to several Kazakh catering points – or you can hire a guide and a horse for the trip (¥50–100 per day), a service which young Kazakhs at the lakeside are happy to provide. Once up at the snowfields, the valleys are yours. Each is dotted with Kazakh yurts, and there's nearly always somewhere you can spend the night. One nice Kazakh stopover is **Dawanzi**, close to the lake's edge and about an hour's walk from the main camps as you approach the lake (look for the map on the way). If you come in May – considered the most beautiful time – you may get to try the alcoholic *kumiss*, fermented mare's milk, a rare delicacy. The rest of the year the Kazakhs make do with an infusion of dried snow lily and sheep's milk.

Practicalities

To get to the lake take a **bus** (9am–3pm; ¥30–50 return) from the northern entrance of Renmin Park. The 120-kilometre journey takes around three hours, and the outward trip from Ürümqi is spectacular, initially taking you through flat desert, then climbing through green meadows, conifer forests and along a wild mountain river. There's a ¥100 **entrance fee** to the lake area, which you pay just before arriving at the small lakeside **village.** This comprises a bus park, some shops and souvenir stands and a guesthouse – the only place to supply you with fresh water if you stay in the yurts with the Kazakhs. If you come by private transport, you are expected to pay an extra ¥10 parking fee when buying entrance tickets. Expect to pay around ¥50 per person for a night in a **yurt**; if you want to leave early the next morning private cars can take you for a cost of around ¥30 per person. They will only leave when full.

One way to avoid any anxieties around communication with the Kazakhs is to join a **pre-booked tour**, which will include yurt accommodation as well as transport between Ürümqi and the lake. Agents such as CITS in Ürümqi offer these, but they are relatively expensive and can be of dubious quality; your best bet is to ask at *Fubar*.

Baiyang Gou

Seventy-five kilometres south of Ürümqi spreads another natural paradise, the **Baiyang Gou** in the Nan Shan area of Tian Shan. Basically, it's another green valley with a stream and a waterfall, and a backdrop of fir trees and snowy peaks. The Kazakhs and Uzbeks like to summer here and, accordingly, there are opportunities for tourists to join them. There's a ¥10 entrance fee on the road leading to the area. Horse-riding trips to the waterfall take about an hour and cost around ¥50 per person; you can also get here by **bus** (9.30am–4.30pm; 4 daily) from the depot well hidden in a lane off Heilongjiang Lu. Yurt accommodation is available on the pasture.

Yining and around

The pretty **Ili Valley** is centred around the city of **Yining** (known to the Uyghurs as Kulja), just 60km east of the border with Kazakhstan, and 400km northwest of Ürümqi. As it is right off the principal Silk Road routes, not many people make the detour to get here, but it's a worthwhile trip if you have the time, or you're travelling to Kazakhstan. Ili is one of the three so-called **Kazakh Autonomous Prefectures** within Xinjiang (the other two are Karamay and Altai), which form a block along the northwest frontier. Despite the nominal Kazakh preponderance, the Uyghurs are the more dominant minority group in the city, and there have been occasional protests against Beijing's rule. Today, however, after years of Han migration, the "frontier" character of Yining is fast disappearing.

The **climate** in the valley is relatively cool and fresh even at the height of summer (and very chilly sometimes – make sure you have warm clothes whatever the time of year), and the views of the Tian Shan – from all routes into Yining, especially if you're coming up from Kuqa to the south – are fabulous. The road climbs the harsh, rocky landscape of the northern Taklamakan, then enters pure alpine scenery with marching forests of pine, azure skies and the glorious blue waters of **Big Dragon Lake**, before drifting into a vast grassland ringed by snowy peaks. At the time of writing, however, a tunnel 130km north of Kuqa is officially closed following a collapse, forcing an inconvenient 400-kilometre detour in either direction, or a treacherous motorbike or jeep journey through the unlit remains of the tunnel. Another draw, north of Yining, is the beautiful **Sayram Lake**, where you can find accommodation in Kazakh yurts.

The **history** of the Ili Valley is one of intermittent Chinese control. At the time of the Han dynasty, two thousand years ago, the area was occupied by the **Wusun kingdom**. The Wusun people, ancestors of today's Kazakhs, kept diplomatic relations with the Han court and were responsible for introducing them to the horse. By the eighth century, however, a Tang-dynasty army had taken control of the region for China – its value as a staging post for a newly developing branch of the Silk Road was too great a temptation. In the thirteenth and fourteenth centuries, the area was controlled first by Genghis Khan from the east, then Tamerlane from the west. This east–west tug of war has gone on ever since, with the Qing seizing the area in the eighteenth century, only for the Russians to march in, in 1871, under the cover of Yakub Beg's Xinjiang rebellion (see p.1032). There remained a significant Russian presence in one form or another until 1949, and traces of this can still be seen in the architecture of Yining. During the 1960s there was a forced mass exodus

Yining and around

Yining	伊宁	*yīníng*
Chapucha'er	察布查尔	*chábù chá'ěr*
Hoegs Pass	霍尔果斯口岸	*huò'ěr guǒsī kǒu'àn*
Huiyuan	惠远	*huìyuǎn*
Sayram Lake	赛里木湖	*sàilǐmù hú*
Tomb of Telug Timur	吐虎鲁克铁木尔墓	*tǔhǔ lǔkè tiěmù'ěr mù*
Accommodation		
Ili	伊犁宾馆	*yīlí bīnguǎn*
Yaxiya	亚细亚宾馆	*yàxìyà bīnguǎn*
Yilite Dajiuiian	伊力特大酒店	*yīlìtè dàjiǔdiàn*
Youdian	邮电宾馆	*yóudiàn bīnguǎn*
Youyi	友谊宾馆	*yǒuyì bīnguǎn*
Ili	伊犁	*yīlí*

of sixty thousand Kazakhs and Uyghurs to the USSR, an event which has left behind much bitterness.

Yining

YINING today is a booming city and as such has changed almost unrecognizably from the remote backwater it once was. Nevertheless, it's a small, compact place, pleasant for walking, and with an extraordinary amount of food for sale from street vendors. The centre of town isn't readily obvious – most of the action seems to straddle the length of **Jiefang Lu**, though the old city is centred around **Qingnian Park** to the southeast. The **Uyghur bazaars**, just south of Qingnian Park, are well worth exploring.

Practicalities

The **bus station** is in the northwest of the city, well concealed on Jiefang Lu. Buses depart hourly to Ürümqi from 9am until late (¥120), and two daily buses serve Kashgar (3pm & 3.30pm; 48hr). A daily service to Kuqa also departs at 9am (¥145) – fierce competition between government and private operators drives down prices and ensures that service is good, though private buses leave only when full, despite any guarantees made by their drivers. If you stand still for more than a second at the station, a host of touts will invariably crowd around you, each shouting the name of the place to which his bus departs. Another interesting bus service out of Yining is the Monday to Saturday service, leaving at 9am, to Almaty (12hr; US$30) through the Hoegs Pass in China and into Kazakhstan, though Kazakhstan visas, now essential, are not available here (see p.1047). There is no train to Yining, though plans to connect it with the nearby rail stop in Qinghe are under way. The only **flights** are to and from Ürümqi. Yining's **CAAC** office (☎0999/8044000) is in the *Yilite Hotel*, where there's also a helpful **travel service** (☎0999/7829000).

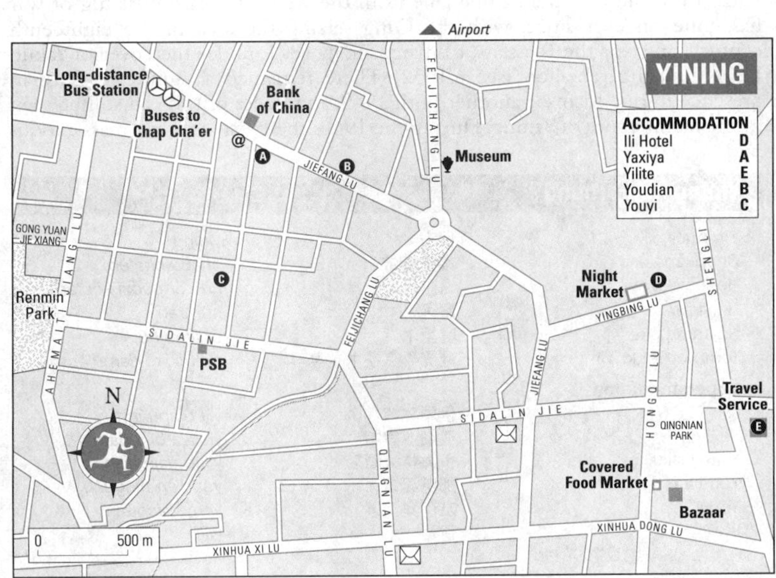

Accommodation

Ili Hotel Yingbing Lu ⓣ0999/8023126, ⓕ8024964. Old-fashioned place in huge leafy grounds, with a number of buildings offering varying degrees of comfort and different prices – building no. 4 has respectable, if small, doubles with bath. To reach the hotel from the bus station, take bus #1 heading east for three stops, cross the road and it's a few minutes' walk east along Yingbing Lu. ④

Yaxiya Jiefang Lu ⓣ0999/8031800. There's no English sign, but you can recognize it from the Greek columns outside; the doubles with bath are clean and modern and breakfast is included in the price. Dorm beds ¥50, ④

Yilite On the crossroads just east of Qingnian Park ⓣ0999/7829000. A range of sizeable and smart rooms at reasonable prices. ⑤

Youdian Jiefang Lu ⓣ0999/8223844. Mid-range doubles, slightly the worse for wear but not bad value. ③

Youyi (aka Friendship Hotel) ⓣ0999/8023901, ⓕ8024631. The hotel is far from any bus route; leaving the bus station, continue right along Jiefang Lu until you pass the Bank of China on the left-hand side of the road, take the next street on your right, passing the *Yaxiya*, and walk for a good 10min. Long-standing hotel with cheap doubles in the old wing and smarter singles and doubles in the new wing. Dorms do exist, though it may depend upon which member of staff you talk to as to whether these are available to foreigners. ④–⑤

Eating and drinking

Street food is particularly good in Yining. Bundles of **food stalls** appear on the city streets as the sun sets, though this can depend on the weather. Immediately south of Qingnian Park is a covered **food market** where you can get food from all over China, including *baozi*, hotpots and grilled fish. You can also buy the excellent and locally made *kurut* – hard, dry little **cheeses** – from street vendors. Just outside the *Ili* hotel is a busy **Uyghur night market**. Roast chickens, *samsa*, kebabs and noodles are all available, along with the local **beer**, which is made with honey. The distinctive bottles have a black rubber cork – but it is advisable to try no more than one bottle of this sticky and sweet concoction. The Ili Valley is also famous for its **fruit**, so look out for apricots in June, grapes and peaches in July.

As for **restaurants**, opposite the *Yaxiya* there is a nice Sichuan place where *tangcu liji*, a sweet-and-sour pork dish, both filling and satisfying, is highly popular. The *Ili* has a pleasant Chinese restaurant and an expensive Western restaurant, while on Hongqi Lu opposite the hotel, leading down to Qingnian Park, there are lots of **outdoor restaurants** where a whole *dapan ji* will set you back around ¥40.

Around Yining

There are a couple of obscure and unusual destinations within a day of Yining. About 20km south is the little town of **CHAPUCHA'ER**, home to the **Xibo** people, a tiny minority numbering just twenty-eight thousand. Of Manchu descent, despatched to Xinjiang in 1764 as warriors to guard and colonize the area, the Xibo still zealously preserve their own language, script and other customs, including a prowess in archery that is of Olympic standard. Chapucha'er is just thirty minutes by bus from outside Yining's long-distance bus station (¥30 by taxi). From the same bus station, there are also buses to **HUIYUAN**, 30km west of Yining, a small but historic town with a three-storey **drum tower** (¥10) dating from the nineteenth century. Another 20km north of here is the pretty Persian-style **tomb of Telug Timur** (¥10), a fourteenth-century Muslim leader, located just outside the small town of **Qingshui**. You can climb a staircase to the upper floor and even onto the roof to see the view. To visit Huiyuan and the tomb as a combined trip from Yining, rent a car from a travel service – a day with the car will cost about ¥350.

About 180km out of Yining, on the road east to Ürümqi, **Sayram Lake** occupies a fantastic location between mountains and grassy banks. More than 2000m above sea level and decidedly chilly for most of the year, Sayram is a great place to escape the urban hustle. Tourism here is still at a pioneering stage – there are simple **guesthouses** (❹) at the lakeside, and accommodation in Kazakh or Mongol **yurts**. Every year on July 13–15 thousands of Kazakhs and Mongolian nomads congregate here for traditional games and entertainment. Access to and from the lake is by bus from Yining (3hr) or Ürümqi (15hr); given the frequency of the buses on this route it should be easy to pick one up if you stand on the road.

Korla to Kashgar: the Northern Silk Road

Some 300km southwest of Ürümqi, and 400km southwest of Turpan, the wealthy but dull town of **Korla** marks the start of the most direct route to Kashgar, which follows the ancient Northern Silk Road (see box, p.950). Having crossed the Tian Shan and entered the Tarim Basin, this route skirts round the northern rim of the Taklamakan Desert for more than 1000km, flanked by snowy peaks. The region is largely a barren wilderness, though there are occasional transitions from parched desert to green pasture in the rare places where water from the Tian Shan has found its way down to the plain. The small oasis towns west of Korla usually comprise brown mud-built houses, perhaps a few vine trellises, and thick muddy water running in trenches beside the streets; **Kuqa**, about a third of the way to Kashgar, is worth a stopover for its traditional feel and a couple of low-key Silk Road relics in the surrounding deserts.

The Northern Silk Road

Korla	库尔勒	*kù'ěrlè*
Hualing Bus Station	华凌汽车站	*huálíng qìchēzhàn*
Jiaoyuan Binguan	教园宾馆	*jiàoyuán bīnguǎn*
Main Bus Station	汽车客运总站	*qìchē kèyùn zǒngzhàn*
Silverstar Hotel	银星大酒店	*yínxīng dàjiǔdiàn*
Tiemen Guan	铁门关	*tiěmén guān*
Yumizhixiang	渔米之湘	*yúmǐ zhīxiāng*
Bositun Hu	博斯腾湖	*bósīténg hú*
Bohu Xian	博湖县	*bóhú xiàn*
Yanqi Xian	焉耆县	*yānqí xiàn*
Kuqa	库车	*kùchē*
Kizil Thousand Buddha Caves	克孜尔千佛洞	*kèzī'ěr qiānfódòng*
Qiuci Ruined City	龟兹古城	*qiūcī gǔchéng*
Subashi Ancient Buddhist Complex	苏巴什佛寺遗址	*sūbāshí fósì yízhǐ*
Tomb of Molana Ashidinhan	默拉纳额什丁坟	*mòlānà'é shídīng fén*
Accommodation and eating		
Australian Style Noodles	澳大利亚风情面馆	*àodàlìyà fēngqíng miànguǎn*
Best Food Burger	百富汉堡	*bǎifù hànbǎo*
Kala Kuer Binguan	卡拉库尔宾馆	*kǎlākù'ěr bīnguǎn*
Kuqa Hotel	库车宾馆	*kùchē bīnguǎn*
Meile Chuancaiguan	美乐川菜馆	*měilè chuāncàiguǎn*
Minmao	民贸宾馆	*mínmào bīnguǎn*
Qiuci	龟兹宾馆	*qiūcī bīnguǎn*

The **road** is in fairly good condition, though given the vast distances involved, it makes much more sense to use the parallel **railway**, with two services daily running the full distance from Ürümqi, via Korla and Kuqa, to Kashgar; Ürümqi to Kashgar takes 24 hours in an air-conditioned train, instead of at least 36 hours of dust, baking heat and boredom in a bus seat. While epic bus journeys do have their attractions, die-hards will find more of interest in the three-day trip to Kashgar via the Southern Silk Road (see p.1059).

Korla

There's been a settlement at **KORLA** (**Kuerle** in Chinese) since at least Tang times, and today the city is capital of the **Bayangol Mongol Autonomous Prefecture**, a vast region that encompasses the eastern side of the Taklamakan as well as better-watered areas around the city itself. Despite all this, Mongols themselves are not much in evidence today in a Korla that is termed the "national clean city" and functions mostly as a base for companies – including the US conglomerate Exxon – tapping into the Taklamakan's **oil reserves**. It's also of inescapable interest as a transport nexus: the rail line and roads from Ürümqi and Turpan converge here; the Northern Silk Road heads due west; and the Southern Silk Road curves down around the eastern side of the Taklamakan via Ruoqiang. The town is also a terminus for buses shortcutting the Southern Silk Road by crossing diagonally southwest across the Taklamakan to Minfeng and Khotan. There isn't anything aside from transport connections to justify a stopover here, though the grey brickwork and red-tiled roof of the Ming-dynasty **Tiemen Guan** (¥6), the Iron Gateway, asserts Korla's age in the face of what is otherwise a relentlessly modern city – you'll see it from the bus to the north of town. In summer, locals spend all their spare time 67km east at **Bositun Hu** (¥30), a huge lake where you can cool off in the water, rent a beach umbrella, and kick back on the sand, admiring distant desert mountain ranges. For Bositun Hu, a taxi return including two hours waiting costs around ¥250. Alternatively, you can take a bus from Korla bus station to **Bohu Xian** or **Yanqi Xian**, which are both quite close to the lake. If you come with a tour, however, you will probably be dropped off at Lianhua Hu (Lotus Lake), a much more touristy resort, 25km from Korla.

Practicalities

Korla's **centre** is only about 1km across, bisected from west to east by the main street, Renmin Lu, home to a massive **Bank of China** (daily 9.30am–1.30pm & 4.30–7.30pm) and lined with upmarket **hotels** – including the four-star *Silverstar Hotel* (Ⓣ0996/2028888, Ⓕ2216868; ❽) – and oil-company and mining offices. One cheaper option is the clean and newly furnished *Jiaoyuan Binguan* (❸, dorm beds ¥30), a few minutes' walk north from the east end of Renmin Lu. The **main bus station** is on Beishan Lu, north off Jiaotong Dong Lu, and has frequent departures through the day to Ürümqi and Turpan. For Kashgar, Khotan via Minfeng, Kuqa and Ruoqiang on the Southern Silk Road, you'll need to go to the **Hualing Bus Station** at the north end of Beishan Lu, about 600m from the main bus station. The **train station**, on the Hami–Ürümqi–Kashgar line, is about 3km east at the end of the #1 bus route from Renmin Lu. Taxis cost ¥5 to anywhere in town. A good place for **food** is the moderately smart *Yumizhixiang*, on the street southeast of *Silverstar Hotel*. The food is in spicy Hunan style; try their *mutong fan* – steamed rice with flavoured vegetables and meat in a bamboo bucket.

Kuqa and around

KUQA (pronounced "ku-cher" and known to the Chinese as **Kuche**) was once a cosmopolitan town full of Silk Road traders and travellers, the "land of jewels" in Xuanzang's journal. It lies about 300km to the west of Korla, past one of the world's largest **wind farms** laid out across the desert. A good place to break the long journey to Kashgar, it's a small town with a long history, and a largely Uyghur population. The fourth-century linguist and scholar **Kumarajiva**, one of the most famous of all Chinese Buddhists, came from here. Having travelled to Kashmir for his education, he later returned to China as a teacher and translator of Buddhist documents from Sanskrit into Chinese. It was in large measure thanks to him that Buddhism came to be so widely understood in China and, by the early Tang, Kuqa was a major **centre of Buddhism** in China. The fantastic wealth of the trade caravans subsidized giant monasteries here, and Xuanzang, passing through the city in the sixth century, reported the existence of two huge Buddha statues, 27m high, guarding its entrances. The city even had its own Indo-European language. With the arrival of Islam in the ninth century, however, this era finally began to draw to a close, and today only a few traces of Kuqa's ancient past remain.

Arrival, information and moving on

Flights connect Kuqa with Ürümqi; the New City is a very short taxi ride west of the **airport** (¥10). The **bus station** is in the far southeast of the New City, while the **train station** is 5km further southeast (¥5 in a taxi).

For plane tickets out of Kuqa, and for **booking tours** of the sites outside the city, it's worth paying a call on the friendly Kuqa **CITS** (Mon–Sat 10am–1.30pm & 3.30–7.30pm; ⓣ0997/7136016, ⓕ7122524), in the upmarket *Qiuici Hotel* on Tianshan Lu. Commission fee on a plane ticket is ¥40. For train tickets, though, they are reluctant to help independent travellers. For visa extensions, the **PSB** (Mon–Fri 9.30am–7.30pm) is on Jiefang Lu, five minutes' walk north of *Minmao Hotel*. There's also a **Bank of China** (Mon–Fri 9.30am–8pm) south of here, and a **post office** on Wenhua Lu.

There are regular **buses** to Korla (10am–6pm; 3hr 30min), Ürümqi and Turpan (both 5am–8.30pm, 12hr & 15hr respectively); Kashgar buses don't originate in town – you'll need to take the bus to Aksu (11 daily; 10am–7.30pm)

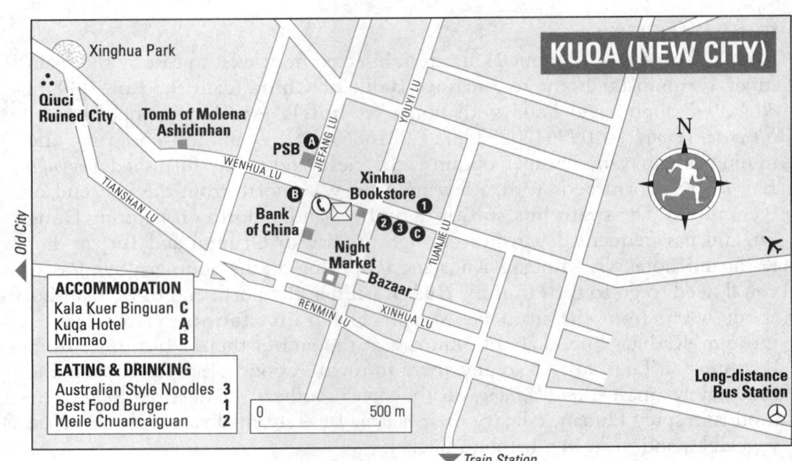

first and change from there. Two **trains** daily head west to Kashgar, and three east to Ürümqi (the other eastbound service stops in Korla). You can only buy hard-seat tickets, and only just before the train pulls in; go to carriage seven to upgrade on board, or try an agent to reserve you something better. Your hotel will be able to give you the current train timetable.

Accommodation

There are a couple of **hotels** right outside the bus station, but this is a rather distant corner of the town to stay in. To reach the more central hotels from here, catch bus #2 from just in front of the station, heading west. Get off at the second stop and take the next road north, **Jiefang Lu**. Motor-rickshaws also run from the station, or it's around a twenty-minute walk.

Kala Kuer Binguan One block east of the post office ⓣ0997/7122957. Clean and neat accommodation, with dorm beds available. Dorm beds ¥50, ③

Kuqa Hotel Jiefang Lu, north of the PSB ⓣ0997/7122901. The buildings have their own gardens, and the big and bright rooms have 24-hour hot water. ④

Minmao On the southwest side of the intersection between Jiefang Lu and Wenhua Lu ⓣ0997/7122888. A convenient place to stay, with reasonably priced rooms whose furniture has seen better days. ③

The City

There's little evidence now of Kuqa's past wealth; today the city is dusty and poor. It is effectively in two parts, the old (to the west) and the new (to the east), lying a few kilometres apart. The New City, largely Han-populated, is uninteresting but contains all the facilities you'll need, while the Old City, largely Uyghur, is peppered with mosques and bazaars and has a Central Asian atmosphere.

From the **New City**, a couple of sights are easily accessible. One is the remains of the ruined city of **Qiuci** (the old name for Kuqa), though there is nothing really to see beyond a solid, weatherbeaten mud wall. If you follow Tianshan Lu, the ruined city is about ten minutes' walk west of the *Qiuci Hotel*. Across the road from the old wall is the neglected **Xinghua Park** (¥3) – a peaceful place for a picnic. Slightly more interesting is the nearby **Tomb of Molena Ashidinhan**, built in 1867, a simple shrine made of wood, in honour of an Arab missionary who came to the city probably in the fourteenth century. It's on Wenhua Lu, about fifteen minutes' walk west of the *Minmao Hotel*. There's also a daily **bazaar** in the lane running east for several blocks from the Bank of China, north of and parallel with Xinhua Lu, containing Xinjiang's second-largest **goldsmiths' quarters** (after Kashgar's).

To reach the **Old City**, take any bus heading west along Renmin Lu, the main street on which the bus station is located, until you reach a bridge across the river – the Old City lies beyond the river. Right by the bridge, the **bazaar** is the main venue for a **Friday market**, where the Uyghur population are out in force in both sections of town, buying and selling leather jackets, carpets, knives, wooden boxes, goats and donkeys. Cattle and sheep are traded on the riverbanks below. It's not to be missed, though it's a much smaller affair than at Kashgar. Beyond the bridge, you can soon lose yourself in the labyrinth of narrow streets and mud-brick houses. Right in the heart of this area, fifteen minutes approximately northeast of the bridge, is the **Kuqa Mosque** (¥10), built in 1923. Delightfully neat and compact, with an attractive green-tiled dome, this mosque is of wholly arabesque design, displaying none of the Chinese characteristics of mosques in more eastern parts of the country. Beyond the mosque, on Linji Lu, the **museum** (daily: Nov–April 10am–9.30pm; May–Oct 9.30am–8.30pm; ¥15), houses interesting collections of Qiuci relics. The four rooms (labelled in English) exhibit pottery, coins, ancient clothes and a few frescoes – if you don't have time to visit the cave paintings around Kuqa, it's well worth a look. From the bridge, rusty blue English signs direct you to the mosque and the museum along the main road, or you can hire a donkey cart for less than ¥1 per person per trip.

Eating and drinking

Near the New Town's market area around the Renmin Lu/Youyi Lu intersection are numerous **food stands** – hugely busy on Fridays – where you can tuck into delicious baked *kaobao*, *samsa*, bowls of *laghman* and Uyghur tea, with great rough sticks and leaves floating in the cup. One thing definitely worth trying is the giant nan bread; served, unlike elsewhere in Xinjiang, thin and crispy and covered with onion, sesame and carrot. On Xinhua Lu, a little east of Jiefang Lu, is a busy, smoky **night market** full of the usual kebabs and roast chickens, as well as plenty of fresh fruit in season.

Outside the *Kala Kuer* hotel you will find a string of small **Uyghur restaurants** where you can sit outside among the locals. Try the canteen-like *Australian Style Noodles* (English sign outside), bizarrely decorated with fake bamboo. The food isn't Aussie – their *dingding chaomian* (¥5) is a cube-shaped noodle dish cooked with tomato sauces, meat and spring onion. A couple of minutes west is a family-run Chinese restaurant, *Meile Chuancaiguan*, serving cheap **Sichuan food**. If you want something Western, there's a *Best Food Burger* opposite the *Kala Kuer* hotel.

Around Kuqa

Around Kuqa, you can explore a whole series of ruined cities and Buddhist cave sites. Probably the two most significant of these are the **Subashi Ancient Buddhist Complex**, 30km north of Kuqa along a good paved road, and the **Kizil Thousand Buddha Caves**, 75km to the northwest. The Kizil Caves, in particular, were once a Central Asian treasure-trove, a mixture of Hellenistic, Indian and Persian styles with not even a suggestion of Chinese influence. Sadly, the caves suffered the ravages of the German archeologist and art thief Albert Von Le Coq (see p.1043) who, at the beginning of the twentieth century, cut out and carried away many of the best frescoes. However, it is still an interesting place to visit and even older than the more extensive Mogao caves in Gansu. Your ticket (¥35) covers eight caves but you can pay extra to be guided round others, including no. 38, the "cave of musicians" – which has Bodhisattvas playing musical instruments on the ceiling.

The **Subashi Ancient Buddhist Complex**, abandoned in the twelfth century, comprises fairly extensive ruins from east to west intercepted by a river. The entrance fee is ¥15 to each side – the west parts of the ruins are more interesting and contain various pagodas and temples, and the remains of some wall paintings. The entire site looks very atmospheric with the bald, pink and black mountain ranges rising up behind. Along the way there, look for the **irrigation channels** carrying runoff from the mountains to villages.

To visit either of these sites, you'll need to rent a car (Kuqa CITS can arrange this – their day-trip tour to both Subashi and Kizil costs ¥300) or simply stop a taxi and start negotiating – ¥1 per kilometre covered is a reasonable rate, so expect to pay ¥150 for the round trip to Kizil, and ¥60 for Subashi.

The Southern Silk Road

Originally, the **Southern Silk Road** split off from the northern route near Dunhuang in Gansu province, crossed to **Ruoqiang** on the eastern edge of the Taklamakan, then skirted the southern rim of the desert before rejoining the northern road at Kashgar. In modern times this route has fallen into almost total obscurity, lacking as it does any major city and connected by poor roads and minimal transport. Of the two branches, however, this route is actually the older and historically more important of the two. The most famous Silk Road travellers used it, including the Chinese Buddhist pilgrims Fa Xian and Xuanzang (see p.1040), as well as Marco Polo, and, in the 1930s, the British journalist and adventurer Peter Fleming. The ancient settlements along the way were oases in the desert, kept alive by streams flowing down from the snowy

The Southern Silk Road

Khotan	和田	*hétián*
Carpet Factory	地毯厂	*dìtǎn chǎng*
Jade Dragon Kashgar River	玉龙喀什河	*yùlóng kāshíhé*
Jiya Xiang	吉亚乡	*jíyà xiāng*
Melikawat	米力克瓦特古城	*mǐlìkèwǎtè gǔchéng*
Silk Factory	丝厂	*sīchǎng*
Accommodation and eating		
Hetian	和田宾馆	*hétián bīnguǎn*
Hetian Yingbinguan	和田迎宾馆	*hétián yíngbīnguǎn*
Huimin Fanguan	回民饭馆	*huímín fàndiàn*
Jiaotong	交通宾馆	*jiāotōng bīnguǎn*
Liangweitian Kuaican	粮为天快餐	*liángwéitiān kuàicān*
Maixiang Yuan Bakery	麦香园蛋糕坊	*màixiāngyuán dàngāofāng*
Weilimai Burgers	维利麦汉堡	*wéilìmài hànbǎo*
Xiangchuan Boziwang	湘川钵子王	*xiāngchuān bōziwáng*
Yurong	玉融宾馆	*yùróng bīnguǎn*
Minfeng	民丰	*mínfēng*
Tarim Desert Expressway	沙漠公路	*shāmò gōnglù*
Xiyu Binguan	西域宾馆	*xīyù bīnguǎn*
Qiemo	且末	*qiěmò*
Qiemo Gucheng	且末古城	*qiěmò gǔchéng*
Muzitage	木孜塔格宾馆	*mùzī tǎgé bīnguǎn*
Ruoqiang	若羌	*ruòqiāng*
Jiaotong Binguan	交通宾馆	*jiāotōng bīnguǎn*
Miran	米兰古城	*mǐlán gǔchéng*
Lop Nor	罗布泊	*luóbù bó*
Loulan	楼兰古城	*lóulán gǔchéng*
Yarkand	莎车	*shāchē*
Altunluq Mosque	阿勒屯清真寺	*ālètún qīngzhēnsì*
Amannisahan Tomb	阿曼尼莎汗纪念陵	*āmànníshāhàn jìniànlíng*
Meraj Restaurant	米热吉快餐	*mǐrèjí kuàicān*
Shanche Binguan	莎车宾馆	*shāchē bīnguǎn*
Yecheng	叶城	*yèchéng*
Jiaotong	交通宾馆	*jiāotōng bīnguǎn*
Yecheng Dianli	叶城电力宾馆	*yèchéng diànlì bīnguǎn*
Yengisar	英吉沙	*yīngjí shā*
Knife Factory	英吉沙县小刀厂	*yīngjíshā xiàn xiǎodāochǎng*

peaks of the Kunlun Shan, which constitute the outer rim of the Tibetan plateau to the south.

Following what remains of this southern route opens up the prospect of travelling overland from Turpan to Kashgar one way, and returning another way, thus circumnavigating the entire Taklamakan Desert. The southern route is not to everyone's taste, in that it chiefly comprises desert interspersed with extremely dusty oasis towns, with none of the green or the tourist facilities of the northern route; nor is there a rail line to fall back on if bus travel loses its appeal. Nevertheless, it represents the chance to visit an extremely little-known corner of China, where foreigners are still a rare sight.

Today, there is no sealed road covering the eastern section of the original route between Dunhuang and Ruoqiang, though there are other roads to Ruoqiang from Korla and, less reliably, from Gansu and Qinghai provinces. Once at Ruoqiang – itself 450km from Korla – a decent road runs 1400km around the southern perimeter of the Taklamakan to Kashgar, with the ancient city of **Khotan** the pick of places to get off the bus and explore. You can also reach Khotan more or less directly from Korla, via the splendid 522km-long Tarim Desert Expressway which traverses the very heart of the Taklamakan and is one of the longest desert roads in the world. For the truly intrepid, it's possible to leave the Southern Silk Road between Khotan and Kashgar and slip south **into Tibet** – for foreigners, an illegal (though regularly travelled) route to Lhasa which will severely test your abilities to travel rough.

From Korla to Khotan

The most painless way to deal with the southern route is to take the desert expressway southwest from Korla **across the Taklamakan** to **Minfeng** and Khotan. It's a very quick road, and the whole one-thousand-kilometre trip between Korla and Khotan takes a mere seventeen hours. Built by the oil companies in the late 1990s, the road gives you a close-up of why the Uyghurs call this desert the "Sea of Death". Unfortunately, most buses coming either way make the crossing at night, so you don't get a view of the impressive irrigation grid that provides water for shrubs to protect the road from the ever-shifting desert sands.

For a dustier, rougher, more rewarding trip to Khotan, you'll want to catch a bus southeast from Korla around the eastern edge of the Taklamakan to **Ruoqiang**. It's also theoretically possible to get here from Dunhuang or Golmud along routes that approximately parallel the original Silk Road. One possible route involves negotiating a jeep from Ruoqiang to Shimian Kuang (Mine of Asbestos), then taking a bus from the mine to Huatu Gou where you will find more regular buses into Gansu or Qinghai. Foreigners used to be pulled off buses by policemen and kicked back in the direction they came from, probably due to the proximity of **Lop Nur**, a huge salty marshland covering 3000 square kilometres northeast of Ruoqiang which happens to be China's **nuclear test site**.

Ruoqiang

A small, busy place, **RUOQIANG** (**Charkhlik** to the Uyghurs) is most notable for being the jumping-off point for treks by camel or jeep out to two little-known ruined cities of Silk Road vintage. **Accommodation** is available at the primitive *Jiaotong Binguan* (❸, dorm beds ¥30) just north of the bus station. The first ruined city, **Miran** (¥100) – subject of Christa Paula's book *Voyage to Miran* – is relatively accessible, approximately 75km northeast of Ruoqiang; a far more ambitious trip would be to **Loulan**, at least 250km from town on the western edge of Lop Nor. Loulan is particularly intriguing, as its very existence had been completely forgotten until the Swedish explorer **Sven Anders Hedin** rediscovered the site, which had been buried in sand, in the early twentieth century; it wasn't until the 1980s that the first Chinese archeological surveys were undertaken. Remains include traces of the city walls and huge numbers of collapsed wooden and adobe houses; the site was also littered with wooden bowls and plates. Foundations of a pagoda indicate a Buddhist population, graves yielded mummified corpses of non-Chinese appearance wrapped in silk and wool (see p.1048), and **Han-dynasty coins** reveal the city's age. What little is known about Loulan comes from contemporaneous records written in Chinese and a northern Indian language found here, which mention that large numbers of people were abandoning the city in the early fourth century – why is a mystery. Certainly by 399, when the Buddhist monk Fa Xian passed through this area, Loulan was depopulated. Unfortunately, the entrance fee to Loulan for foreigners is ¥3000 (compared to ¥1500 for Chinese), so unless you are an archeological expert this may not be the place for you.

Qiemo and Minfeng

Back on the Kashgar road, the next settlement of any size is **QIEMO** (Cherchen), another small, surprisingly modern town famed for the frequency of its sandstorms (especially in April), and lying some 360km southwest of Ruoqiang. There are more **ruins** about 10km to the northwest at **Qiemo Gucheng** – dated to at least 2000 years old. A taxi here and back shouldn't cost more than ¥30, though the entrance fee, depending upon how well your driver knows the site staff, will range from ¥15 to ¥300.

From here it's a further 300km west to **MINFENG**, where you meet up with the trans-Taklamakan expressway from Korla. You can stay at the simple *Xiyu Binguan* (❷, dorm beds ¥40), 50m north of Minfeng's bus station. Minfeng comes alive every evening, when long-distance buses converge and the main street becomes one long chaotic strip of kebab, bread and noodle vendors. On the final 300km between here and Khotan, you pass through some of the most vividly empty landscapes you will ever see, an indication of what the centre of the Taklamakan must be like: a formless expanse of sky and desert merging at a vague, dusty yellow horizon.

Khotan and around

KHOTAN (known in Chinese as **Hetian**) has for centuries been famed throughout the country for its **carpets, silk** and **white jade**. A bleak and dusty grid of wide streets, the town itself is pretty ordinary, but the substantial Uyghur population is hospitable, and there's ample opportunity to watch the materials for which Khotan is famed being worked in much the same way as they always have been.

Arrival, information and accommodation

Khotan's **airport**, with daily connections to Ürümqi, lies 10km west of town. You can reach the centre either by taxi (¥15–20) or by the airport bus that meets incoming flights. The **bus station** is on the south end of Taibei Xi Lu, north of the city, with six daily services to Korla and Ürümqi via the Taklamakan Desert, and to everywhere else along the Southern Silk Road between Kashgar and Qiemo. Other useful bus routes include Yining and Turpan in the east of Xinjiang. Taxis charge ¥5 to any hotel.

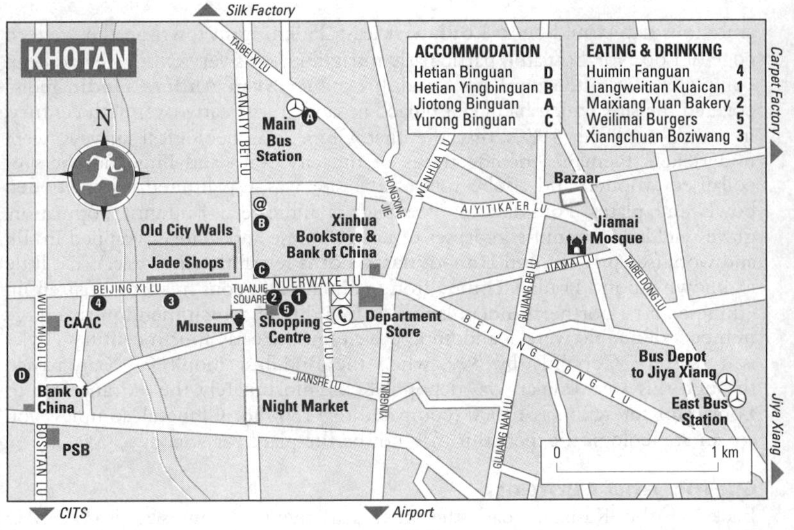

Right beside the bus-station entrance, the *Jiaotong* (☎0903/2032700; ❸) is the cleanest of several **hotels** in the station area, though that's not saying much; more central options include the rather gloomy but friendly *Hetian Yingbinguan* (☎0903/2022824; ❹ including breakfast), and the genial, unpretentious *Yurong Binguan* (☎0903/7829666; ❹), more or less on Tuanjie Square. Finally, the *Hetian Binguan* in the southwest of the city (☎0903/2029999; ❺ including breakfast) is comfortable and good value, despite the slightly aged furniture.

You can buy flight tickets at the **CAAC office** (daily 10am–8.30pm; ☎0903/2518999), 14 Wulumuqi Lu, a few minutes north of the *Hetian Binguan*. South from here, your visa can be extended at the **PSB** (Mon–Fri 10am–2pm & 3.30–7.30pm). All hotels have **travel services** for booking plane and bus tickets and arranging **tours**. Local excursions with a guide, taking in the carpet and silk factories should set you back ¥50–100, and it's possible to organize lengthier jeep or camel trips around the region, using routes not necessarily covered by public transport. Expect to pay ¥300 per day for a jeep, ¥100 for a camel; camping gear is around ¥50 per person, and a guide will cost ¥100 a day. If your hotel can't help, try **CITS** (☎0903/2516090), inconveniently located on the third floor of a building at the end of Bositan Lu.

The Town

Khotan centres on **Tuanjie Square**, from where the city is partitioned by two main roads – Beijing Lu (running east–west) and Tanaiyi Lu (north–south). The crenellated **old city walls** still dot along the west side of Tanaiyi Bei Lu, east of the river – surrounded by fences in a vain effort to protect them from development. The giant sculpture in the middle of the square shows Chairman Mao shaking hands with a local Uyghur old man, an actual person who went to Beijing to congratulate the Communist party's victory in the 1950s – the symbol still serves its function, though the hostility of the local Uyghurs towards Han Chinese is no secret.

The fascinating **bazaar** takes place every Friday and Sunday. Silk, carpets, leather jackets, fruit and spices are all on sale, with innumerable blacksmiths, tinsmiths, goldsmiths and carpenters hard at work among the stalls. The bazaar stretches across the whole of the northeast part of town; the easiest way to reach it is to head east along Aiyitika'er Lu, off Wenhua Lu near the centre. Follow the stalls south towards Jiamai Lu, along where you can see a pretty Jiamai mosque.

About 4km to the east of town, following Beijing Dong Lu, is the **Jade Dragon Kashgar River** from which, historically, so much jade has been recovered, and which still yields the odd stone for casual searchers. The river flows through a wide, stony plain; it's easy to get down here and forage, but you'll need to find one of the locals – who come with garden forks to rake the stones – to show you what you are looking for or you may end up with a pocketful of pretty but worthless quartz.

The town **carpet factory** stands just across the river to the left; it's particularly worth a visit if you are interested in buying. Prices here, and in the shop in town, are very cheap (around ¥3500 for a 5m x 2.5m handmade carpet). The atmosphere in the factory workshop is friendly, with the workers, mostly young women, exchanging banter as they weave with incredible dexterity. They encourage visitors to take pictures, and ask to be sent copies.

The Silk factory and Jiya Xiang

If you're interested in the secrets of **silk production**, catch bus #1 north to its last stop along Taibei Xi Lu, on the same road as the long-distance bus station. After you get off, walk back just a few hundred metres towards town and you'll come to the front entrance of the head office of the **silk factory**. The security man there should understand what you want. If you come during the week (avoid the 1–3pm lunch break), the chances are that you will be supplied with an English-speaking employee to show you round for free. You can see the whole process: the initial unpicking of the cocoons, the twisting together of the strands to form a thread (ten strands for each silk thread), the winding of the thread onto reels, and finally the weaving and dying. The women here have it hard compared to their sisters in the carpet factory: the noise in the workshops is immense, and they stand all day long. You can also buy silk designs at **Jiya Xiang**, northeast of the city, a small Uyghur village specializing in **atalas silk**. It is an idyllic place just to sample the rural life of locals and see silk being produced traditionally in small workshops. You can buy the silk at around ¥150 per length. To get here, take the minibus (9am–9pm; ¥2.5) from the small courtyard 150m northwest of East Bus Station on Taibei Dong Lu.

To see the nurturing of the **silkworms** themselves – only possible in the summer months – you'll need to explore some of the nearby country lanes in Jiya Xiang or in the vicinity of the silk factory. If you are able to explain your purpose to people (a drawing of a silkworm might do the trick), they will take you to see their silkworms munching away on rattan trays of fresh, cleaned mulberry leaves in cool, dark sheds. Eventually each worm should spin itself a cocoon of pure silk; each cocoon comprises a single strand about 1km in length. The farmers sell the cocoons to the factory, but hatching and rearing of silkworms is unreliable work, and for most farmers it's a sideline.

Melikawat

Finally, Silk Road specialists should visit the ruined city of **Melikawat** (¥20, plus ¥5 to take photos), out in the desert 30km to the south of town beside the Jade Dragon Kashgar River. This city, formerly an important Buddhist centre on the Silk Road, was abandoned well over a thousand years ago, and the arrival of Islam in the region did nothing to aid its preservation. The site is a fragmentary collection of crumbling walls set among the dunes and tamarisk bushes, thousands of wind-polished pot shards littering the ground – you might find odd fragments of glass or wood poking out of the ruins. For a visit to Melikawat, contact a travel service (see p.1062) or flag down a taxi and start some hard bargaining; ¥60 is a reasonable price for the return trip.

Eating and drinking

Eating in Khotan is pretty straightforward. *Huimin Fanguan*, just west of the river on Beijing Xi Lu, is a bustling **Muslim restaurant** popular with locals, serving *laghman*, beef noodle soups, kebabs and the like, with nothing over ¥8. There is also excellent Uyghur street food just south of Tuanjie Square. For **Chinese food**, head to the east of Tuanjie Square to the excellent Sichuan restaurant *Liangweitian Kuaican*, at 9 Nuerwake Lu, or try the just as good, but not as snazzy, Hunan/Sichuan restaurant *Xiangchuan Boziwang*, on Beijing Xi Lu, a few minutes' walk west of the square, set amidst a load of shops selling wellington boots and fishing nets. *Hetian Binguan* has two large restaurants serving Chinese and Muslim food. The *Maixiang Yuan Bakery* on the northeast corner of Tuanjie Square is a great place if you miss **Western food**, as is *Weilimai Burgers* just a few doors south.

Khotan to Kashgar

The last 500km of the Southern Silk Road runs northwest from Khotan to Kashgar through a dusty wasteland interspersed with dunes, camels, mountain ranges, and sudden patches of greenery marking irrigated settlements. Some 200km along, **YECHENG** (Karagilik) is a kind of giant Uyghur highway service station, with flashing lights, fires, bubbling cauldrons, overhead awnings and great hunks of mutton hanging from meat hooks. **Accommodation** is available just outside the bus station to the left, at the basic *Jiaotong* (❷, dorm beds ¥30). For a smarter option, try the *Yecheng Dianli* (*Yecheng Electricity Hotel*, ⓣ0998/7289800; ❹). Turn right as you come out of the bus station, to the main road, and walk east 500m. It's the light-coloured building with a shiny dome on

Yecheng to Tibet

The road southeast **from Yecheng** follows the Karakoram mountain ranges for about 1000km to the town of **Ali** in **western Tibet** (see p.1139). Though this route into Tibet is illegal for foreigners, a steady trickle seems to make it through each year. At the time of writing, hitching on trucks was not possible; instead, there are regular local buses whose drivers are willing to take foreigners. The dusty and rough Yecheng–Ali road is best tackled between July and October, but can be extremely **cold** even then – adequate water, food, sleeping bags, and warm, windproof clothing are essential. You'll be travelling at higher than 5000m for most of the duration, with no chance of a speedy descent if you develop **altitude sickness**. There are several **police checkpoints** along the way, and if detected you may be arrested, fined, and sent back. However drivers usually have an arrangement with the police or manage to avoid checkpoints by taking detours.

In Yecheng, you can find **local buses** to Ali in the Ali Banshichu (Ali Representative Office). Bus #2 from the Yecheng bus station stops right outside the gate to the office – you can see plenty of trucks docking outside. Walk through the gate about 50m to the yellow houses on your left; the buses are hidden away near here. The people here should understand what you are after, and bus drivers will sell you a ticket to Tibet for ¥1000 (you can bargain this down to ¥700–800). The 23-person buses leave for Ali twice a week at around 8 or 9pm, though you may need to wait for a few days if the demand is not sufficient; the trip takes around two days.

top to your left. Every Wednesday there's a fantastic **market** about 1km out of town towards Khotan. A lot more earthy and colourful than the Kashgar Sunday market, it's well worth your time if you are in the area.

The road divides at Yecheng, one fork running north towards Kashgar, the other southwest into **Tibet** (see box, opposite). Heading a further 60km north lands you at **Yarkand**, a miniature version of Kashgar but with minimal tourist infrastructure. That said, the backstreets are possibly the closest you'll come in China to the Central Asia of a hundred years ago.

Yarkand and Yengisar

A strategically important staging post for at least the last thousand years, **YARKAND** (also known as **Shache**) is – now that Kashgar is becoming ever more developed and sanitized – possibly the best place to soak up the character of Muslim Xinjiang. The town centres on a crossroads, from where Xincheng Lu runs west through the Han-dominated part of town towards Kashgar, while Laocheng Lu runs east into the older, Uyghur quarters. The best thing to do here is simply wander the northeastern backstreets, a warren of muddy lanes lined with willows and crowded by donkey carts, artisans' quarters, bazaars and traditional adobe homes with wooden-framed balconies. You'll find the town's major sights here too, close together on a road running north off Laocheng Lu: the **old fort** is opposite the **Altunluq mosque** and **Amannisahan tomb** (¥10), flanked by two narrow towers. The mosque itself is off limits to non-Muslims, but the tomb, built for Amannisahan, the wife of a sixteenth-century khan, is a beautiful white- and blue-tiled affair; Amannisahan was also the most influential contributor to *muqam* music (see box, p.1039). The adjacent **cemetery** contains the mausoleums of several of Yarkand's former rulers, including Amannisahan's husband, and is also crowded with more ordinary cylindrical Muslim tombs and truly ancient trees. Sunday would be the best time to visit Yarkand, when a huge rustic **market** along the same lines as the more famous one in Kashgar is held in the main bazaar behind the fort – though this area is pretty good most days.

The **bus station**, with frequent departures through the day to Kashgar and Khotan, is south off Xincheng Lu. You can find the **Bank of China**, post office and China Telecom around the crossroads. The only **hotel** that accepts foreigners, the *Shache Binguan* (Ⓣ0998/8512365; ④), is a ten-minute walk west along Xincheng Lu from the crossroads; it's a friendly place, but a little overpriced. The best place to **eat** is the *Meraj Restaurant* on the northeast corner of the crossroads. Extremely popular with local Uyghurs, they serve stuffed nan bread and large plates of noodle dishes of all kinds; the delicacy here is pigeon meat.

Some 120km further on up the Kashgar road, the town of **YENGISAR** has for centuries been supplying the Uyghur people with handcrafted knives. Most of the knives on sale in Xinjiang these days are factory-made, but here at the **Yengisar County Small Knife Factory**, a few craftsmen still ply their old skills, inlaying handles with horn or silver alloy. Some of the more decorative knives take nearly a fortnight to forge. From here it's a mere 70km or so to Kashgar.

Kashgar

A large part of the excitement of **KASHGAR** lies in the experience of reaching it. Set on the western edge of the Chinese empire astride overland routes to Pakistan and Kyrgyzstan, Kashgar is fantastically remote from eastern China: as the crow flies, it's more than 4000km from Beijing, of which the thousand-plus kilometres from Ürümqi are for the most part sheer desert. As recently as the 1930s, the journey time to and from Beijing ran to a number of months. And yet Kashgar today, an oasis 1200m above sea level, is a remarkably prosperous and pleasant place, despite being, in part, an essentially medieval city.

Kashgar remains a visible bastion of old Chinese Turkestan, though gradually the more "authentic" parts of the town are being cleaned up as tourist attractions, and its residents moved to modern high-rises on the city limits. Nonetheless, despite Han migration into the city, its population is still overwhelmingly Muslim, a fact you can hardly fail to notice with the great **Id Kah Mosque** dominating the central square, the Uyghur bazaars and teashops, the smell of grilled lamb and, above all, the faces of the Turkic people around you. If you can choose a time to be here, catch the Uyghur Corban **festival** at the end of the Muslim month of Ramadan, and again, exactly two months later, which involves activities such as dancing and goat-tussling. And don't miss Kashgar's **Sunday market**, for which half of Central Asia seems to converge on the city and which is as enchanting to the average Han Chinese as to the foreign tourist.

Kashgar

Kashgar	喀什	*kāshí*
Hanoi Ancient City	罕诺依古城	*hànnuòyī gǔchéng*
Id Kah Mosque	艾提尕尔清真寺	*àitígǎ'ěr qīngzhēnsì*
Id Kah Square	艾提尕尔广场	*àitígǎ'ěr guǎngchǎng*
Kashgar Silk Road Museum	喀什丝绸之路博物馆	*kāshí sīchóuzhīlù bówùguǎn*
Moor Pagodas	莫尔佛塔	*mò'ěr fótǎ*
Sunday Market	中西亚市场	*zhōngxīyà shìchǎng*
Tomb of Abakh Hoja	阿巴克霍加麻扎	*abākè huòjiā mázhā*
Tomb of Yusup Hazi Hajup	哈斯哈吉南墓	*hāsīhā jí nánmù*
Ulagh Bazaar	远方市场	*yuǎnfāng shìchǎng*
Yekshenba Bazaar	中细亚市场	*zhōngxìyà shǐchǎng*
Arrival and international destinations		
Ilkshtan Pass	伊尔克什坦口岸	*yī'ěrkè shítǎn kǒu'àn*
International Bus Station	国际汽车站	*guójì qìchēzhàn*
Bishkek	比什凯克	*bǐshí kǎikè*
Main Bus Station	客运站	*kèyùnzhàn*
Narin	那伦	*nàlún*
Torugut Pass	吐尔尕特口岸	*tù'ěr gātè kǒu'àn*
Wuqia County	乌恰县	*wūqià xiàn*
Accommodation, eating and drinking		
Barony	邦臣酒店	*bāngchén jiǔdiàn*
Laoding Niurou Mian	老鼎牛肉面	*lǎodǐng niúròumiàn*
Nanlin Jiucheng	南林酒城	*nánlín jiǔchéng*
Qiniwak	其尼瓦克宾馆	*qíní wǎkè bīnguǎn*
Pakistan Restaurant	巴克斯坦餐厅	*bākèsītǎn cāntīng*
Sahra	色哈乐宾馆	*sèhālè bīnguǎn*
Seman	色满宾馆	*sèmǎn bīnguǎn*
Tiannan	天南饭店	*tiānnán fàndiàn*
Tuman River	吐曼河大饭店	*tǔmànhé dàfàndiàn*

Some history

Kashgar's **history** is dominated by its strategic position. There was already a Chinese military governor here when Xuanzang passed through on his way back from India in 644. The city was Buddhist at the time, with hundreds of monasteries; Islam made inroads around 1000 and eventually became the state religion. More recently, the late nineteenth century saw Kashgar at the meeting point of three empires – **Chinese**, **Soviet and British**. Both Britain and the Soviet Union maintained consulates in Kashgar until 1949: the British with an eye to their interests across the frontier in India, the Soviets (so everyone assumed) with the long-term intention of absorbing Xinjiang into their Central Asian orbit. The conspiracies of this period are brilliantly evoked in Peter Fleming's *News from Tartary* and Ella Maillart's *Forbidden Journey*. At the time of Fleming's visit, in 1935, the city was in effect run by the Soviets, who had brought their rail line to within two days of Kashgar. During World War II, however, Kashgar swung back under Chinese control, and with the break in Sino-Soviet relations in the early 1960s, the Soviet border (and influence) firmly closed. In the wake of the break-up of the Soviet Union, however, it seemed that Kashgar would resume its status as one of the great travel crossroads of Asia, but this recovery sadly stalled after the events of September 11, 2001 and the ensuing conflict in Afghanistan. The town is still

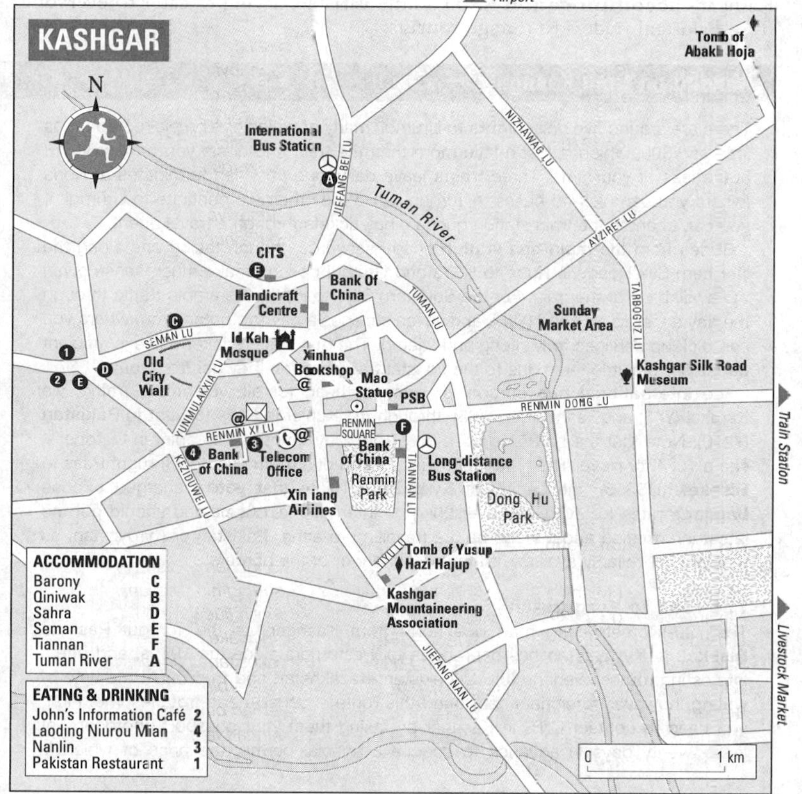

experiencing something of a downturn, with neither traders nor tourists as plentiful as they once were.

Orientation, arrival and accommodation

It's helpful to think of Kashgar as centred on a large cross, with a principal north–south axis, Jiefang Bei Lu and Jiefang Nan Lu, and an east–west axis, Renmin Dong Lu and Renmin Xi Lu. North of Renmin Lu lies the core of the **old town**, containing much of the accommodation, the Id Kah Mosque, former consulates, and interesting streets; south of Renmin Lu the prevailing cityscape is modern Chinese, with grey-fronted department stores and overly wide roads. The **train station** is 7km east of town, where bus #28 to Jiefang Bei Lu, minibuses and taxis await new arrivals. Just east of the centre on Tiannan Lu is the main **long-distance bus station**, handling connections from most parts of Xinjiang, including Ürümqi, Kuqa, Korla, Yarkand and Khotan. The **international bus station**, about 1500m north up Jiefang Bei Lu and just over the river beside the *Tuman River* hotel, is terminus for luxury buses from Ürümqi, as well as all traffic from Tashkurgan, Sust in Pakistan, and Bishkek in Kyrgyzstan – bus #2 runs down Jiefang Bei Lu from here. Kashgar's **airport** is 14km north of town; the airport bus (¥5) drives straight down Jiefang Lu to China Southern Airlines' Xinjiang office.

Accommodation

Kashgar's **accommodation** is still a little variable, having to cater to everyone from Pakistani traders to foreign tourists.

Moving on from Kashgar

There are around five daily **flights** to Ürümqi, many of which can be picked up for as little as ¥300, which is just a little more than the train and costs you a massive 18 hours less of your time. Three **trains** leave daily, one of which terminates at Korla (where you can pick up buses to Turpan) while the other two continue to Ürümqi; if you can't handle the train station queues, buy tickets through a travel agent.

Buses from the **main bus station** head eastwards, though taking one along the Northern Silk Road via Kuqa to Korla and Ürümqi doesn't make much sense given the availability of the train. For the Southern Silk Road, there's ample traffic through the day as far as Yarkand (¥25), and seven services a day to Khotan, from where you can pick up services to Minfeng and Qiemo. The bus station ticket office is efficient but staff are a little terse due to the constant aggravation they get from touts.

The **international bus station** is where to head for all westbound traffic, via Karakul (¥43) and Tashkurgan (¥63), through the Kunjerab Pass to **Sust in Pakistan** (¥270). Note that the border is open only from May 1 until some point in October – see p.1074 for more. The other option is to travel due north over the Torugut Pass to **Bishkek** (US$55), the capital of **Kyrgyzstan**. Note that you're charged **excess baggage** rates for every kilo over 20kg on international buses, and should get the latest information about **visas** before travelling to either Pakistan or Kyrgyzstan, as they are not reliably available either in Kashgar or at the borders.

The road to Kyrgyzstan

The 720-kilometre-long road due north from Kashgar via the Torugut Pass to **Bishkek** in **Kyrgyzstan** has been open to Westerners since the 1990s, and offers interesting routes overland into Uzbekistan, Kazakhstan and Russia. At the time of writing, however, foreigners had found this route expensive and troublesome. First, you need to contact CITS in Kashgar by faxing them your passport photocopy at least twenty days in advance to acquire a special permit, the price of which is

Barony 242 Seman Lu ⓣ0998/2586888, ⓦwww.baronytxnhotels.com. Kashgar's swankiest establishment, with a gym, three restaurants and a small but well-formed garden. ❾

Qiniwak (aka Chini Bagh) 144 Seman Lu ⓣ0998/2982103, ⓕ2982299. A pleasant place conveniently located near the Id Kah Mosque. A large variety of rooms is available with bath and a view over Kashgar. Cheaper rooms in the rear block. ❸–❻

Sahra Seman Lu opposite the *Seman* ⓣ0998/2581122. A low-budget option with 24-hour hot water, a roof and beds. It's not exactly the *Hilton* but it won't break the bank. ❷

Seman Seman Lu ⓣ0998/2822129. A popular choice, this rambling old complex has clean and comfortable rooms, and bike rental for ¥30 per day. Dorms ¥60, ❹–❻

Tiannan 272 Tianan Lu, opposite the long-distance bus station ⓣ0998/2824023. A cheap option with smelly basic rooms; if you are looking for class, keep walking. ❷

Tuman River 5 Jichang Lu, beside the international bus station ⓣ0998/2961352. A mid-range option popular with traders, though in a noisy area. ❷

The City

There are one or two monuments of note in Kashgar, but the main attractions of this city are the ordinary streets of the old town – principally the bazaars, the restaurants, the teahouses and the people in them. Roads radiate out from the centre of the original Uyghur city which is focused on **Id Kah Square** with its clock tower and huge mosque. A few hundred metres to the south is the modern, commercial centre, at the junction between Jiefang (Bei and Nan) Lu and Renmin (Xi and Dong) Lu. The other main landmark is the absurdly

included in the fee for the trip. You will then have to pay ¥1200 for a car and a tour guide, which will take you to the border (160km away), across which you'll need to sort out your own transport into Kyrgyzstan (CITS can arrange a US$100 bus to Narin). Going from China to Kyrgyzstan, vehicles are not allowed to **cross the border** until after 1pm; coming the other way, you must cross before 1pm. There are noodle shops on the Chinese side of the pass and you can also change small amounts of money here. The weather at the 3750-metre pass is very cold, with snow and hail showers frequent even in midsummer. **On the Kyrgyz side** you may be expected to offer **bribes** (try US$20 as a starter); if the guards are happy with you, you'll be through in minutes, though waiting for hours is not uncommon.

An alternative option is to use the southern **Ilkshtan Pass** in Wuqia County, part of the Kizilsu Kirgiz Autonomous Prefecture. The Ilkshtan Pass was officially opened to foreigners in 2002 and is 240km west of Kashgar along rough roads. From the pass to the Kyrgyzstan border, there is another 5km to hitch or walk, though tickets bought in Kashgar to Bishkek (US$55) will include this section. According to the CITS staff, few people choose this pass despite the apparent low costs. This may be due to the harsh road conditions, or simply because the Ilkshtan Pass is so little known – check the situation with local authorities before you go.

Kyrgyzstan visas currently cost US$50 and, in China, are only available through the Beijing consulate (see p.139) or from the Ürümqi consulate (ⓣ0991/3839117) at the Free Economic Zone High and New Technology centre on Beijing Lu. In theory, if you have a visa for any CIS country (for example, Kazakhstan, Uzbekistan or Russia) then you can obtain a three-day transit visa (US$25) through Kyrgyzstan at the border; in practice, you may not be able to do so. If you do not have any visa at all, you will not be allowed through the Chinese side.

Kazakhstan visas can be obtained from the Kazakhstan Embassy, 31 Kunming Lu (ⓣ0991/3815796), for around US$50.

colossal **statue of Mao Zedong** hailing a taxi on Renmin Dong Lu, a towering reminder of the ultimate authority of China over the region. Opposite the statue is the bald, stone expanse of **Renmin Square** with an attached park behind. Finally, scattered around the fringes of the city, are a number of **mausoleums** to Uyghur heroes of the past, best reached by bus or bicycle.

Id Kah Square and around

The main historical sight in central Kashgar is the **Id Kah Mosque**, occupying the western side of Id Kah Square, off Jiefang Bei Lu. Originally built in 1442, it has been restored many times, most recently after the Cultural Revolution. It is one of the biggest mosques, and almost certainly the most active, in the country; you can even hear the call to prayer booming around the city centre – a rare sound in China. Although visitors are theoretically allowed in (there is a entrance fee of ¥10 to the grounds), Western tourists are sometimes shooed away by zealous worshippers – note that visitors of either sex should have their arms and legs fully covered when entering this (or any other) mosque. You certainly won't be admitted on Fridays, the main Muslim prayer day, when some ten thousand people crowd the mosque and square; the quietest time, when your presence will cause least disturbance, is probably early to mid-morning on any other day. Inside are pleasant courtyards and tree-lined gardens where worshippers assemble.

The main Uyghur bazaars are in the neighbouring streets, and while you're in the area, keep an eye open for a couple of substantial fragments of Kashgar's **old city walls**, most easily viewed south of Seman Lu and west offYunmulakxia Lu. And don't miss out on the **old consulates** either: the British had theirs behind the *Qiniwak* hotel, while the Russian headquarters survive as a nicely preserved period piece in the courtyard behind the *Seman* hotel.

Kashgar's Sunday market

Known in Chinese as the **Zhongxiya Shichang** (Western-Central Asia Market), or in Uyghur as the **Yekshenba Bazaar** (Sunday Bazaar), what was once the mother of all markets attracts up to one hundred thousand villagers and nomads, all riding their donkey carts from the surrounding area and gathering in two sites to the east and the southeast of town. For the sheer scale of the occasion, it's the number one sight in Kashgar, if not all Xinjiang. Considering the large numbers of minority peoples who come to trade here, all sporting their own particular headwear, it is also an anthropologist's delight. Knives, hats, pots, carpets, and pans, fresh fruit and vegetables, clothes and boots and every kind of domestic and agricultural appliance – often handmade in wood and tin – are all on sale, and some produce, such as Iranian saffron, has come a very long way to be sold here. The market goes on all day and into the early evening, and food and drink are widely available on and around the site.

Due to the traffic chaos thousands of animals used to bring to the city centre every Sunday, the livestock market has been moved to an area a few kilometres south of town to **Ulagh Bazaar**, or **Yuanfang Shichang** in Chinese. Here you'll find traders haggling over everything from camels to cattle, while sheep turn a blind eye to the food stalls on the periphery.

To get to the Sunday market from Renmin Square, take bus #16 to its terminus; it heads on to Yekshenba Bazaar from there. From the Id Kah mosque you can take a fascinating forty-minute walk through the old city with its adobe lanes full of traders, coppersmiths and blacksmiths; buses #7, #8 and #28 all follow the same route. A taxi from the centre of town will cost around ¥13.

▲ Kashgar's Sunday livestock market

The bazaars

The street heading northeast from Id Kah Square is the main **carpet** area. The region's best carpets are handmade in Khotan, but some good bargains are to be had in the Kashgar bazaars. You should be able to get a nice felt of rolled coloured wool (1.5m x 2.5m) for less than ¥200. A larger hand-knotted carpet, approximately 2m x 3m, should cost around ¥800. The carpets are relatively rough in quality and have geometric designs only, but the prices are about a third of the equivalent in Turkey. Bear in mind, of course, that not everyone is an expert and there will be a few dubious traders looking to pocket your cash. Elvis Ablimit (see p.1073) is an antique carpet specialist and will be happy to help you should you wish to buy (ⓣ138/99136195). You can see people making carpets, musical instruments and jewellery at the Handicrafts Centre 200m north of Id Kah Square on Jiefang Lu; high-quality double-sided silk carpets cost around ¥1000 per square metre. Kashgar **kilims**, produced by nomads, are highly sought after and almost impossible to find locally. If you really want one, again, contact Elvis Ablimit.

A small road east of Id Kah Square, parallel to Jiefang Lu, is a big area for Central Asian **hats**. As well as the green and white square-shaped variety so beloved by old Uyghur men, there are prayer caps, skullcaps, furry winter hats and plain workmen's caps. Following this lane south, turn right, where a large semi-underground market occupies the space between the square and hat lane. Here you will find a large selection of **clothes**, carpets and **crockery** as well as Uyghur nuts, sweets and spice stands, and the occasional blacksmith hammering at his trade. Further south down hat lane, you will come to a **woodcraft** area.

North of the square you'll find **jewellery** and high-quality ornate **knives**, produced in Yengisar. The lane directly south of Id Kah Mosque, heading due west, sells a mixture of hats, jewellery, large **chests** overlain with brightly coloured tin (purpose-built for carrying gifts for brides-to-be), and handmade **musical instruments**. The two-stringed *dutah* is the most common. The *tanber* has an even longer stem and a round bowl shaped like half a gourd, while the *rawupu* has five strings and a snakeskin drum.

In the southern part of the square is the Kashgar **night market**, while to the west – the two roads to the north and south of the Id Kah Mosque – are a few **Uyghur teahouses** and small eating establishments, as well as daytime street food.

The outskirts

The historic architecture remaining in Kashgar today chiefly comprises a number of mausoleums to famous Uyghur personages. From May to October, a tourist minibus (¥1) runs through the city and covers most sites. At other times, they are accessible by public transport. The most central mausoleum is the **Tomb of Yusup Hazi Hajup** (daily 10am–7pm; ¥30), the eleventh-century Uyghur poet and philosopher. The mausoleum, of handsome blue and white wall tiles, was slightly shoddily reconstructed in 1986. It's about 1500m south of Renmin Lu, on Tiyu Lu, a small road located between Jiefang Nan Lu and Tiannan Lu – bus #8 down Jiefang Lu comes within striking distance.

Within a few kilometres east of the centre, on Tarbogue Lu, the **Kashgar Silk Road Museum** (daily 10am–8pm; ¥12), on the #10 bus route from Renmin Lu, holds an Iron Age **mummy** recovered from the desert hereabouts, still dressed in felt hat and fur-lined jacket, woollen trousers, leather boots, and a belt with herbs and a knife attached. There are also examples of various ancient **scripts** found at Silk Road sites, including Indian-derived Kharosthi (from Khotan), along with the usual run of pottery, wooden and metal artefacts, some of which date back to 1000 BC.

The most impressive of all Kashgar's tombs is the **Tomb of Abakh Hoja** (daily 10am–7.30pm; ¥30), 8km northeast of the centre on bus #20 from Renmin Square, or forty minutes by bike through wheat fields and poplar woods. From downtown, head past the Sunday Market site and the turning for the mausoleum is signposted in English after a few kilometres. The mausoleum itself is a large, mosque-like building of blue and white tiles with a green dome and tiled minarets. Built in the seventeenth century, it was the resting place for a large number of people – the most famous being Abakh Hoja and his granddaughter Ikparhan, who is known in Chinese as **Xiang Fei**, "Fragrant Concubine". Having led the Uyghurs in revolt against Beijing, she was subsequently seized and married to the Qing emperor Qian Long, later being ordered to commit suicide by the emperor's jealous mother. In both commemorating a local heroine and stirring anti-Qing propaganda in the cruelty she suffered, the story serves the convenient dual purpose of pleasing both the Uyghurs and the Han Chinese.

Outside Kashgar and accessible only by car are the **Moor Pagodas** (¥15) at the **ancient city of Hanoi** on a rough road about 30km east of the city. The pagodas have been worn down to rough stumps about a dozen metres high, but the remains of the ruined Tang city walls of Hanoi make quite a dramatic scene in what is a virtual desert. To reach this place, you'll need to rent a car from a travel service, costing around ¥350 through the Mountaineering Association (see below), or deal directly with a taxi yourself – try for ¥60 return.

Eating and drinking

Kashgar has **places to eat** for all budgets. Westerners tend to gravitate towards the foreigner-friendly restaurants on the roundabout outside the *Seman* hotel; the branch of *John's Information Café* here (see p.1038) offers its usual Sino-Western food and beer, but is quite expensive. The *Pakistan Restaurant* opposite the *Seman* hotel is a good option, with a simple English menu, friendly service and great food. Try the breakfast here of roti, nan and sweet tea. The best place to pick up **Uyghur food** is around Id Kah Square. Street vendors sell pilau, kebabs, cold spicy noodles, *kao bao* and *jiaozi*. *Laghman* is available almost everywhere. Other street food worth sampling is the vanilla ice cream, mixed up on the spot in containers encased in lumps of ice, which is delicious, though not obviously hygienic. For a more relaxed atmosphere, try *Laoding Niurou Mian*, a clean canteen on the corner of Renmin Xi Lu and Keziduwei Lu, selling huge bowls of beef noodle soup, along with buns, *laghman* and kebabs; clear noodles with spicy sauce accompany the meal for a mere ¥1 a bowl. For **Chinese food**, *Nanlin Jiucheng* is a well-established hotpot restaurant on Renmin Xi Lu with occasional music performances. A good place to go **drinking** is at the outdoor seating area at the north end of Jiefang Nan Lu, which is usually open until the small hours. The waitresses bring you beer and nibbles, including such staples as chickens' feet.

Listings

Airline China Southern, 152 Seman Lu (daily: May–Oct 9am–8pm; Nov–April 10am–7.30pm; ⓣ0998/2985118).

Banks and exchange The main Bank of China, in the northeast corner of Renmin Square (daily: summer 9.30am–1.30pm & 4–7.30pm; winter 10am–2pm & 3.30–7pm), can change foreign currency. You may have to show proof of purchase for cashing traveller's cheques. Their ATM does not accept Cirrus cards.

Bike rental By far the best, and most reliable, places to rent bikes are from the stall at the front gate of the *Qiniwak*, and from the *Seman* hotel; both charge ¥30 per day.

Bookshops Xinhua Bookshop is at 32 Jiefang Bei Lu, on the east side of the road and just north of the intersection with Renmin Lu.

Internet access There's an Internet café just southeast of the *Barony* in a well-marked basement (¥2/hr).

Mail The post office is at 40 Renmin Xi Lu, a short walk west of Jiefang Lu (Mon–Sat 9.30am–8pm).

PSB Renmin Dong Lu (Mon–Fri 10.30am–2pm and 4–9.30pm), just opposite the Bank of China.

Telephones Direct-dial long-distance calls can be made from an office opposite the post office on Renmin Xi Lu, at China Telecom (daily 9.30am–8pm), or from the *Qiniwak* and *Seman* hotel. Both charge by the minute.

Travel agents There are one- and two-day tours available to places such as Karakul Lake and the Taklamakan Desert. CITS (daily 9.30am–1.30pm & 4–8pm; ⓣ0998/2984836, ⓔnjt56789@hotmail.com) has a branch inside the *Qiniwak*. Staff are friendly and speak English. A freelance operator named Elvis Ablimit (ⓣ13899136195, ⓔElvisablimit@yahoo.com) provides guided camel safaris into the Taklamakan; his English is good, and he knows the surrounding terrain well. There's also the Kashgar Mountaineering Association (daily 9.30am–1.30pm & 4–8pm, ⓣ0998/2523660, ⓦwww.kashgaralpine.com), inside the Kashgar Gymnasium on Jiefang Nan Lu. They're a helpful, English-speaking bunch who can arrange private transport into Ali in Tibet as well as a range of adventure activities including climbing and rafting trips. It is advisable to contact them well in advance if you plan something ambitious, as most activities require some equipment and paperwork preparations.

The Karakoram Highway

For centuries the **Khunjerab Pass**, lying some 400km south of Kashgar, was the key Silk Road crossing point between the Chinese world and the Indian subcontinent – and thence to the whole of the Western world. Today the 4700-metre pass still marks the frontier between China and **Pakistan**, but, while crossing the mountains used to be a highly perilous journey undertaken on horse, camel or foot, modern engineering has blasted a highway right through the pass, opening the route to a seasonal stream of trucks and buses. The entire 1300-kilometre route from Kashgar over the mountains to Rawalpindi in northern Pakistan is known as the **Karakoram Highway**. The trip is still not without its perils, but it's hard to think of a more exciting route into or out of China. If the highway is closed for any reason, note that you can also **fly** twice weekly direct from Ürümqi to Islamabad (Wed & Sun; ¥1900).

En route from Kashgar, travellers have to spend a night in **Tashkurgan** on the Chinese side, before crossing over the pass to the Pakistani town of **Sust**. There is also the option of camping out for a night or two by the wintry but beautiful **Lake Karakul**, in the lee of glaciers. The road over the pass is open from the beginning of May until the end of October each year, though it can close without notice when the weather is bad, for days at a time, even in summer. The journey from Kashgar to Rawalpindi/Islamabad, or vice versa, takes a minimum of four days if there are no hold-ups. Most travellers need a **visa to enter Pakistan**; at the time of writing, you'll need to arrange this in your home country – neither Beijing nor Ürümqi supplies the service.

Lake Karakul

Southwest of Kashgar, the road soon leaves the valley, with its mud-brick buildings and irrigated wheat and rice plantations, behind. Climbing through river gorges strewn with giant boulders, it creeps into a land of treeless, bare dunes of sand and gravel, interspersed with pastures scattered with grazing yaks and camels. The sudden appearance of **Lake Karakul** (¥20) by the roadside, some 200km out of Kashgar, is dramatic. Right under the feet of the Pamir Mountains and the magnificent 7546-metre Mount Muztagata, whose vast snowy flanks have been split open by colossal glaciers, the waters of the lake are luminous blue. The opportunities for **hiking** over the surrounding green pasture are virtually limitless, especially if you are equipped with a tent and warm clothing; at 3800m, the weather can be extremely cold even in summer, with snow showers normal well into June. It's possible to walk round the lake in a day, in which case you will almost

The Karakoram Highway

Karakoram Highway	中巴公路	*zhōngbā gōnglù*
Khunjerab Pass	红其拉甫口岸	*hóngqí lāpǔ kǒu'àn*
Lake Karakul	喀拉湖	*kālā hú*
Sust	苏斯特	*sūsī tè*
Tashkurgan	塔什库尔干	*tǎshí kù'ěrgàn*
Ice Mountain	冰山旅店	*bīngshān lǚdiàn*
Jiaotong	交通宾馆	*jiāotōng bīnguǎn*
Pamir	帕米尔宾馆	*pàmǐ'ěr bīnguǎn*
Stone City	石头城	*shítou chéng*

certainly encounter some friendly Kyrgyz yurt-dwellers on the way – they may well invite you to stay with them if you can communicate your meaning (not easy). Otherwise, if you are without your own tent, you can stay at a rather dull and not particularly enticing **tour-group yurt site** just off the road, with its own restaurant and local attendants. This costs about ¥60 per head, on the basis of four people in a yurt, plus ¥70 per person per day for all meals. The food is good and the local people are friendly. There are very rudimentary washing and toilet facilities, and fresh drinking water originates from the lake, hence swimming is forbidden.

Transport to the lake is simple. From the Kashgar international bus station there are two daily **buses** (¥48) from May to October, leaving at 10am and 4pm. From Tashkurgan you can take the Kashgar bus and get off at the lake. Leaving the lake requires slightly more ingenuity – for either direction you will need to flag down the passing buses or taxis, which may involve standing assertively in the middle of the road; taxis back to Kashgar cost ¥60 or more per person. It's best to ask a local from the yurt for help, or at least check approximate expected times of buses with them. For travellers heading to Pakistan, it is perfectly feasible to travel to Tashkurgan via the lake, and then book yourself onto a bus to Sust from Tashkurgan (contrary to what you may be told in Kashgar).

Tashkurgan

The last town before the border, **TASHKURGAN**, lies 280km southeast of Kashgar, and about 220km north of the Pakistani town of Sust. Its primary importance for travellers is as a staging post between the two towns, and all travellers passing through, in either direction, must stay the night here. It's a tiny place, comprising a couple of tree-lined streets, with the bus station and several budget hotels in the northwestern part of town.

The town boasts a long history as well as fantastic mountain scenery. The Chinese Buddhist pilgrim and Silk Road traveller **Xuanzang** stopped here in the seventh century, a time when, as now, it was the last outpost of Chinese rule. Today, Tashkurgan has a peculiar atmosphere. The native population is mainly Tadjik, but there are also groups of melancholy Han Chinese, thousands of miles from home, as well as intrepid Pakistanis setting up shop outside their country – plus, incredibly, a minor entertainment industry involving sex and alcohol for Pakistani tourists. Few visitors bother to stop longer than necessary, but you could pleasantly rest up here for 24 hours or so. Worth a look, especially at sunset, is the 600-year-old, crumbling, mud-brick **Stone City** (¥10, negotiable). If you clamber to the top, the scenes of snowy mountains running parallel on both flanks, and woods and wetland dotted around, are more than picturesque. To reach it, walk east from the bus station right to the end of town passing the *Pamir* hotel, then strike off a few hundred metres to the left.

Practicalities

At the **bus station**, the *Jiaotong Hotel* (April–Nov; ⓣ0998/3421192; ❹, dorm beds in triples ¥20) is a simple **place to stay**; 24-hour hot water is available in the double rooms. Alternatively, you can try the primitive *Ice Mountain* (❸, dorm beds ¥15–20). As you exit the bus station, turn right and walk 100m to the east along Hongqilapu Lu; it's across the road. The *Pamir* at the east end of the same road is much more upmarket (April–Oct; ⓣ0998/3421085; ❹), with high ceilings and eclectic decor. Hot water is available all day, though you may need to double-check with the friendly staff.

The plentiful **beer** in Tashkurgan often comes as a relief to travellers arriving from Pakistan. For **food**, your best bet is to try one of the Chinese restaurants, like *Laochengdu Canting*, a couple of hundred metres east of the bus station. For delicious bread – excellent for breakfast and a snack on long bus journeys – try the bakery south from the east end of Hongqilapu Lu. Keep walking south from here and you will reach the central crossroads, marked by an eagle statue. The **post office** (daily 10am–2pm & 4–7pm) is at the southeast corner, where you can also make international phone calls. The **PSB office** is diagonally opposite the post office, while the only **bank** (Mon–Fri 10.30am–2pm & 4–7pm) lies 150m south of the eagle statue. Cash (and sometimes traveller's cheques) can be changed here at official exchange rates. If arriving from Pakistan, you can easily change your rupees with the locally resident Pakistanis if the banks are closed.

The **entry and exit formalities** for Western tourists are dealt with a few hundred metres south from the bank, and are straightforward to the point of being lax. You may or may not be issued with Currency and Valuables Declaration forms – but nobody seems to care what you put on them. If your bus arrives late in the evening, your passports are collected and formalities take place the next morning. Onward connections, in both directions, will wait until everyone is through customs, so there is no need to worry about being left behind.

Travellers heading to Pakistan do not need to buy onward bus tickets – the ticket from Kashgar covers the whole route right through to Sust. Coming from Pakistan, however, you'll find that the only onward transport is the bus to Kashgar (¥60). Buying your ticket requires standing in a long and heated queue, but don't worry – sufficient transport will be laid on for however many people need it. Whichever way you're heading, note that **cyclists** are not allowed to ride their bikes through the pass, but have to bus it between Tashkurgan and Sust. If you plan to get off at Lake Karakul (see p.1074) en route to Kashgar, you may be asked to pay the full Kashgar fare anyway. The alternative to catching buses is to **hitch a ride** on a truck. These often cruise around town in the evening looking for prospective customers to Kashgar (or Karakul) for the day after. You'll pay, but it will be cheaper than travelling by bus.

The Khunjerab Pass

Khunjerab means "River of Blood" in the local Tadjik language – which may refer to the rusty colour of local rivers, or to the long traditions of banditry in these areas. The trip across the border at the **Khunjerab Pass** is not a totally risk-free affair – people are killed almost every year by falling rocks on the highway and you should be aware that if your bus departs in rainy weather, you can almost certainly expect mud slides.

From Tashkurgan, the road climbs into a vast, bright plain, grazed by yaks and camels, with the mountains, clad in snow mantles hundreds of metres thick, pressing in all around. Emerging onto the **top of the pass**, you're greeted by a clear, silent, windswept space of frozen streams, protruding glaciers and glimpses of green pasture under the sunshine. The only creature that lives here is the chubby ginger Himalayan marmot; a kind of large squirrel or woodchuck, easily spotted from the bus. At these heights (the pass lies at some 4800m) a lot of travellers experience some form of **altitude sickness**, though most people will feel little more than faintly feverish or nauseous. The journey time between Tashkurgan and the small town of **Sust**, where Pakistani customs and immigration take place, takes about seven hours. Travellers in both directions have to spend a night here, and accommodation is plentiful. From Sust there are direct daily buses to Gilgit, from where frequent buses cover the sixteen-hour route to **Rawalpindi** and **Islamabad**.

Travel details

Trains

Baotou to: Beijing (10 daily; 12hr); Dongsheng (daily; 4hr 30min); Hailar (daily; 40hr); Hohhot (15 daily; 2hr); Lanzhou (twice daily; 14hr); Shanghai (daily; 31hr); Xi'an (daily; 25hr); Yinchuan (4 daily; 7hr).

Daheyan (for Turpan) to: Hami (13 daily; 5–6hr); Jiayuguan (12 daily; 11–16hr); Korla (5 daily; 8hr); Lanzhou (11 daily; 20–28hr); Liuyuan (10 daily; 10–12hr); Tianshui (10 daily; 25–34hr); Ürümqi (16 daily; 2–3hr); Wuwei (20 daily; 17–23hr); Zhangye (12 daily; 14–19hr).

Golmud to: Lhasa (4 daily; 12hr); Xining (4 daily; 17–19hr).

Guyuan to: Lanzhou (daily; 10hr); Yinchuan (3 daily; 7–9hr); Zhongwei (5 daily; 4hr).

Hailar to: Baotou (daily; 40hr); Beijing (daily; 26hr); Harbin (5 daily; 11hr); Hohhot (daily; 38hr) Manzhouli (5 daily; 2hr 30min); Qicihar (6 daily; 8hr).

Hami to: Daheyan (13 daily; 5hr); Lanzhou (14 daily; 10–13hr); Ürümqi (12 daily; 7–8hr).

Hohhot to: Baotou (15 daily; 2hr); Beijing (12 daily; 10hr); Erlianhot (twice daily; 9–11hr); Hailar (daily; 38hr); Shanghai (daily; 28hr); Taiyuan (twice daily; 12hr); Ulaan Baatur (daily; 25hr); Xi'an (daily; 22hr).

Jiayuguan to: Daheyan (12 daily; 12–17hr); Lanzhou (10 daily; 11–13hr); Liuyuan (12 daily; 4hr); Tianshui (10 daily; 14–19hr); Ürümqi (11 daily; 13–16hr); Wuwei (10 daily; 5–7hr); Zhangye (16 daily; 2hr 30min–4hr).

Kashgar to: Korla (twice daily; 13–15hr); Kuqa (twice daily; 9–11hr); Ürümqi (twice daily; 24hr or 30hr).

Korla to: Daheyan (5 daily; 8–13hr); Kashgar (twice daily; 13–15hr); Kuqa (3 daily; 3hr 30min–4hr 30min); Ürümqi (4 daily; 11–15hr).

Lanzhou to: Baotou (twice daily; 15hr); Beijing (4 daily; 22hr); Chengdu (3 daily; 22hr); Daheyan (10 daily; 22–28hr); Hami (10 daily; 17–23hr); Hohhot (twice daily; 17hr or 20hr); Guangzhou (daily; 35hr); Guyuan (daily; 10hr); Jiayuguan (13 daily; 10–14hr); Lhasa (4 daily; 29hr); Liuyuan (11 daily; 13–19hr); Shanghai (3 daily; 25hr); Tianshui (25 daily; 5hr); Ürümqi (10 daily; 24–30hr); Wuwei (13 daily; 5hr 30min–8hr); Xi'an (18 daily; 9–11hr); Xining (9 daily; 3hr); Yinchuan (3 daily; 8hr); Zhangye (12 daily; 8–11hr); Zhongwei (4 daily; 6hr).

Liuyuan (for Dunhuang) to: Beijing (daily; 35hr); Daheyan (13 daily; 8–9hr); Jiayuguan (12 daily; 4hr); Lanzhou (10 daily; 13–18hr); Tianshui (10 daily; 19hr); Ürümqi (9 daily; 12hr); Wuwei (9 daily; 3–5hr); Zhangye (12 daily; 5–8hr).

Manzhouli to: Beijing (twice daily; 29hr); Hailar (5 daily; 2hr 30min); Harbin (3 daily; 13hr); Qiqihar (daily; 11hr).

Tianshui to: Daheyan (10 daily; 28hr); Jiayuguan (10 daily; 14–19hr); Lanzhou (24 daily; 4hr); Liuyuan (10 daily; 17–24hr); Ürümqi (9 daily 27–36hr); Wuwei (10 daily; 8–12hr); Zhangye (10 daily; 12–16hr).

Ürümqi to: Almaty (Kazakhstan; 2 daily; 36hr); Beijing (daily; 46hr); Chengdu (daily; 54hr); Daheyan (16 daily; 2–3hr); Hami (12 daily; 7–8hr) Jiayuguan (11 daily; 13–16hr); Kashgar (twice daily; 23hr or 29hr); Korla (4 daily; 10–14hr) Lanzhou (10 daily; 23–30hr); Liuyuan (12 daily; 10–12hr); Shanghai (daily; 48hr); Tianshui (9 daily; 28–36hr); Xi'an (9 daily; 32–41hr); Wuwei (11 daily; 19–24hr); Zhangye (11 daily; 15–22hr).

Wuwei to: Daheyan (13 daily; 17–21hr); Jiayuguan (11 daily; 5–10hr); Lanzhou (15 daily; 5–7hr); Liuyuan (12 daily; 8hr 30min–12hr); Tianshui (10 daily; 9–12hr); Ürümqi (13 daily; 19–24hr); Zhangye (11 daily; 3–5hr); Zhongwei (3 daily; 4–6hr).

Xining to: Beijing (daily; 25hr); Golmud (4 daily; 14–44hr); Lanzhou (9 daily; 3–5hr); Lhasa (4 daily; 26hr); Shanghai (daily; 33hr); Xi'an (4 daily; 12–15hr).

Yinchuan to: Baotou (4 daily; 6hr 30min–9hr); Beijing (3 daily; 19hr); Guyuan (3 daily; 6–9hr); Hohhot (4 daily; 9–11hr); Lanzhou (3 daily; 8hr); Xi'an (twice daily; 14hr); Zhongwei (7 daily; 3–4hr).

Zhangye to: Daheyan (12 daily; 5–8hr); Jiayuguan (16 daily; 2–4hr); Lanzhou (13 daily; 8–10hr); Liuyuan (12 daily; 5hr 30min–8hr); Tianshui (9 daily; 12–15hr); Ürümqi (11 daily; 16–20hr); Wuwei (16 daily; 3–5hr); Xi'an (9 daily; 16–21hr).

Zhongwei to: Baotou (3 daily; 9–12hr); Guyuan (5 daily; 4hr); Hohhot (3 daily; 11–14hr); Lanzhou (5 daily; 6hr); Shapotou (daily; 30min); Yinchuan (7 daily; 3–5hr); Wuwei (3 daily; 4–6hr).

Buses

Baotou to: Dongsheng (hourly; 2hr 30min); Hohhot (every 30min; 2hr 30min).
Dongsheng to: Baotou (hourly; 2hr 30min); Hohhot (hourly in summer, daily in winter; 4hr).
Dunhuang to: Golmud (8hr); Hami (6hr 30min); Jiayuguan (6hr); Lanzhou (18hr); Liuyuan (2hr); Wuwei (15hr); Zhangye (13hr).
Golmud to: Dunhuang (15hr); Lhasa (36hr); Xining (16hr).
Guyuan to: Lanzhou (7hr); Luoyang (16hr); Pingliang (2hr); Sanying (40min); Tianshui (6hr); Xi'an (7hr); Yinchuan (4hr 30min).
Hailar to: Manzhouli (hourly; 3hr).
Hami to: Dunhuang (6hr 30min); Turpan (8hr); Ürümqi (11hr).
Hohhot to: Baotou (every 30min; 2hr 30min); Beijing (daily; 12hr); Dongsheng (hourly in summer, daily in winter; 5hr).
Jiayuguan to: Dunhuang (5hr); Lanzhou (16hr); Wuwei (12hr); Zhangye (5hr).
Kashgar to: Khotan (11hr); Korla (30hr); Kuqa (20hr); Lake Karakul (6hr); Sust (36hr); Tashkurgan (8hr); Ürümqi (35hr); Yarkand (2hr 30min); Yecheng (4hr); Yining (40hr).
Khotan to: Kashgar (11hr); Korla (17hr); Minfeng (5hr); Qiemo (12hr); Ürümqi (22hr); Yarkand (5hr).
Korla to: Kashgar (30hr); Khotan (17hr); Kuqa (12hr); Turpan (10hr); Ürümqi (5hr).
Kuqa to: Aksu (12hr); Korla (10hr); Turpan (14hr); Ürümqi (12hr); Yining (24hr).
Lanzhou to: Dunhuang (24hr); Guyuan (7hr); Hezuo (8hr); Jiayuguan (16hr); Linxia (3hr); Tianshui (8hr); Ürümqi (44hr); Wuwei (5hr); Xiahe (8hr); Xi'an (16hr); Xining (5hr); Yinchuan (14hr); Zhangye (11hr).
Linxia to: Lanzhou (3hr); Tianshui (9hr); Wuwei (9hr); Xiahe (5hr); Xining (11hr).
Manzhouli to: Hailar (hourly; 3hr).
Pingliang to: Guyuan (2hr); Lanzhou (5hr); Xi'an (5hr).
Tianshui to: Guyuan (daily; 10hr); Lanzhou (8hr); Linxia (9hr); Pingliang (6hr); Wushan (5hr); Xi'an (9hr).
Turpan to: Hami (6hr 30min); Korla (10hr); Kuqa (12hr); Ürümqi (3hr).
Ürümqi to: Almaty (Kazakhstan; 36hr); Altai (24hr); Hami (11hr); Kashgar (35hr); Khotan (22hr); Korla (10hr); Kuqa (15hr); Lanzhou (44hr); Liuyuan (daily; 23hr); Turpan (3hr); Yining (15hr).
Wuwei to: Dunhuang (14hr 30min); Jiayuguan (10hr); Lanzhou (4hr); Minqin (1hr 30min); Zhangye (4hr); Zhongwei (7hr).
Xiahe to: Hezuo (2hr); Lanzhou (6hr); Linxia (4hr); Tongren (6hr).
Xining to: Golmud (16hr); Lanzhou (5hr); Linxia (11hr); Maduo (24hr); Tongren (8hr); Zhangye (24hr).
Yecheng to: Ali (40–50hr); Kashgar (4hr); Ürümqi (24hr); Khotan (2hr 30min).
Yinchuan to: Guyuan (7hr); Lanzhou (14hr); Xi'an (12hr); Zhongwei (4hr).
Yining to: Almaty (Kazakhstan; Mon–Sat; 12hr); Kashgar (twice daily; 48hr); Kuqa (24hr); Ürümqi (13hr).
Zhangye to: Dunhuang (8hr); Jiayuguan (5hr); Lanzhou (11hr); Wuwei (6hr).
Zhongwei to: Guyuan (5hr); Shapotou (1hr); Wuwei (7hr); Yinchuan (3hr).

Flights

Besides the domestic services listed below, there are international flights linking Ürümqi with Almaty, Bishkek, Islamabad, Moscow, Novosibirsk and Sharjah.
Baotou to: Beijing (3 daily; 55min); Shanghai (twice daily; 2hr 25min).
Dunhuang to: Beijing (daily; 4hr); Lanzhou (daily; 2hr); Ürümqi (daily; 2hr); Xi'an (daily; 2hr 30min).
Hailar to: Beijing (6 weekly; 2hr); Hohhot (3 weekly; 2hr 25min).
Hohhot to: Beijing (5 daily; 1hr 10min); Chifeng (twice daily; 1hr 10min); Guangzhou (5 weekly; 3hr); Haikou (3 weekly; 6hr 45min); Hailar (3 weekly; 2hr 25min); Qingdao (2 weekly; 2hr 50min); Shanghai (twice daily; 2hr 30min); Shenyang (3 weekly; 1hr 30min); Shenzhen (3 weekly; 3hr); Taiyuan (5 daily; 50min); Tianjin (2 weekly; 1hr); Tongliao (daily; 1hr 40min); Ulanhot (daily; 1hr 40min); Wuhai (daily; 50min); Xi'an (3 weekly; 1hr 30min); Xilinhot (3 weekly; 1hr).
Jiayuguan to: Lanzhou (daily; 1hr 30min).
Kashgar to: Ürümqi (daily; 1hr 20min).
Khotan to: Ürümqi (daily; 1hr 45min).
Kuqa to: Ürümqi (2 weekly; 1hr 50min).
Lanzhou to: Beijing (3 daily; 2hr); Changsha (3 weekly; 2hr); Chengdu (daily; 1hr); Chongqing (1 weekly; 1hr 40min); Dunhuang (1 or 2 daily; 2hr); Guangzhou (daily; 3hr); Haikou (daily; 4hr); Jiayuguan (daily; 1hr 30min); Kunming (daily; 1hr 20min); Qingdao (daily; 3hr 30min); Shanghai (1 or 2 daily; 2hr 30min); Shenzhen (daily; 4hr); Ürümqi (daily; 2hr 30min); Xiamen (4 weekly; 4hr); Xi'an (1 or 2 daily; 1hr); Yinchuan (4 weekly; 50min).
Ürümqi to: Beijing (daily; 3hr 30min); Changsha (daily; 4hr); Chengdu (daily; 3hr 20min); Chongqing (daily; 3hr 30min); Dunhuang (daily; 2hr); Guangzhou (daily; 4hr 40min); Kashgar (daily; 1hr 20min); Khotan (daily; 1hr 45min); Korla (daily; 1hr); Lanzhou (daily; 2hr 30min); Shanghai (daily; 4hr); Xi'an (daily; 2hr 45min); Xining (daily;

2hr 20min); Yinchuan (daily; 3hr); Yining (twice daily; 2hr).
Xining to: Beijing (daily; 2hr 10min); Chengdu (daily; 1hr 20min); Guangzhou (daily; 3hr); Lhasa (2 weekly; 2hr 15min); Shanghai (daily; 2hr 40min); Ürümqi (daily; 2hr 20min); Xi'an (daily; 3hr).
Yinchuan to: Beijing (twice daily; 2hr); Chengdu (daily; 2hr); Guangzhou (daily; 4hr); Lanzhou (3 weekly; 50min); Nanjing (daily; 3hr 30min); Shanghai (daily; 3hr 30min); Ürümqi (daily; 3hr); Xi'an (daily; 50min).
Yining to: Ürümqi (twice daily; 2hr).

CHAPTER 14

Highlights

* **The Jokhang, Lhasa** Shrouded in juniper smoke and surrounded by prostrating pilgrims, it's hard not to be affected by this, one of the world's most venerated sites. See p.1104

* **Samye** Remote walled town encapsulating Tibet's first Buddhist monastery. See p.1116

* **Namtso Lake** Lies bright as a jewel beneath muscular peaks. See p.1123

* **The Friendship Highway** This undulating road connecting Lhasa and Nepal cuts through some of the region's best and certainly most accessible sights. See p.1133

* **Mount Everest Base Camp** Breathe deep and gaze up at the jagged, snow-blown peak of the world's highest mountain. See p.1136

* **Mount Kailash** The world's holiest mountain, its very remoteness an intrinsic part of its appeal. See p.1139

▲ Mount Kailash

14

Tibet

Tibet (Bod to Tibetans, Xizang to the Chinese), the "Roof of the World", has exerted a magnetic pull over travellers for centuries. The scenery has a majesty and grandeur that are spellbinding, the religious monuments and practices are overwhelmingly picturesque and moving, and the Tibetan people are welcoming and wonderful. But look just a little below the surface and it is all too apparent that Tibet's past has been tragic, its present is painful, and the future looks bleak. Tibet today is a sad, subjugated colony of China. While foreign visitors are perhaps more worldly than to expect a romantic Shangri-la, there is no doubt that many are surprised by the heavy military and civilian Chinese presence, the modern apartments and factories alongside traditional Tibetan rural homes and monasteries. All this doesn't mean you should stay away, however: though tourism provides legitimacy as well as foreign currency to the Chinese government, many people, the Dalai Lama included, believe that travellers should visit Tibet to learn all they can of the country and its people.

In reaching Tibet, you'll have entered one of the most isolated parts of the world. The massive **Tibetan plateau**, at an average height of 4500m above sea level, is guarded on all sides by towering **mountain ranges**: the Himalayas separate Tibet from India, Nepal and Bhutan to the south, the Karakoram from Pakistan to the west, and the Kunlun from Xinjiang to the north. To the east, dividing Tibet from Sichuan and Yunnan, an extensive series of subsidiary ranges covers almost a thousand kilometres. The plateau is also birthplace to some of the greatest **rivers** of Asia, with the Yangzi, Mekong, Yellow and Salween rising in the east, and the Indus, Brahmaputra, Sutlej and some feeder rivers of the Ganges in the west, near Mount Kailash.

Tibet's isolation has long stirred the imagination of the West, yet until a British expedition under the command of Colonel Francis Younghusband, invaded in 1904, only a trickle of bold eccentrics, adventurers and Jesuit missionaries had succeeded in getting close to Lhasa, and then only at serious risk to their lives, for it was Tibetan policy to repel all influence from the outside world. So great was the uncertainty about the geographical nature of the country even 150 years ago, that the British in India despatched carefully trained spies, known as *pundits*, to walk the length and breadth of the country, counting their footsteps with rosaries and mapping as they went. When Younghusband's invasion force finally reached Lhasa, they were, perhaps inevitably, disappointed. One journalist accompanying them wrote:

If one approached within a league of Lhasa, saw the glittering domes of the Potala and turned back without entering the precincts one might still imagine an enchanted city. It was in fact an unsanitary slum. In the pitted streets pools of rainwater and piles of refuse were everywhere: the houses were mean and filthy, the stench pervasive. Pigs and ravens competed for nameless delicacies in open sewers.

Since the Chinese **invasion** in 1950, Tibet has become much more accessible, with approaches eased by plane links with Chengdu and Kathmandu. There has subsequently been heavy Han migration into the region, and although it is impossible to know how many Chinese live here now, it is likely that they outnumber Tibetans. The situation is most marked in the cities, where the greatest opportunities exist: not only are the numbers of Han increasing all the time, but they are becoming economically dominant too, – a situation that will be further exacerbated by the Qinghai–Lhasa railway line that was completed in June, 2006.

Today's **Tibetan Autonomous Region** (TAR), though covering a massive 1.2 million square kilometres, is but a shadow of the former Tibetan lands. The old area, sometimes referred to as Greater Tibet or Ethnographic Tibet, was carved up by the Chinese following their invasion, when the Amdo and Kham regions were absorbed into Qinghai, Sichuan, Gansu and Yunnan provinces. The TAR consists only of the West and Central (U-Tsang) regions of Greater Tibet and divides into four geographical areas. The northern and largest portion is the almost uninhabited **Chang Tang**, a rocky desert at an average altitude of 4000m, where winter temperatures can fall to minus 44°C. South of this is the **mountainous grazing area**, land that cannot support settled agriculture, inhabited by the wide-ranging nomadic people with their herds of yaks, sheep and goats. **Eastern Tibet**, occupying around a quarter of the TAR, is heavily forested. The **southern valleys**, sandwiched between the nomad areas and the **Himalayas** along the southern border, are the most hospitable for human habitation. As such, this is the most populated area and where visitors spend the majority of their time, particularly in the extensive valley system of the Tsangpo River (Brahmaputra) and its tributaries.

Lhasa, **Shigatse** and **Gyantse** offer the most accessible **monasteries** and **temples** – the Jokhang, Tashilunpo and the Kumbum, respectively – and are also tourist-friendly cities with the biggest range of facilities in the region. The **Potala Palace** in Lhasa remains an enduring image of Tibet in the Western mind, and should on no account be missed, plus there are plenty of smaller sights in the city to keep anyone busy for several days. Farther afield, the **Yarlung** and **Chongye** valleys to the southeast boast temples and ancient monuments, and the ancient walled monastery of **Samye** is easily combined with these. The tourist corridor between Zhangmu on the Nepalese border and Lhasa is relatively well-trodden these days, although by no means overcrowded, and offers side-trips to the huge Mongolian-style monastery at **Sakya** and to **Everest Base Camp**.

While the Chinese prefer easily controlled, high-rolling tour parties to the less malleable, less lucrative budget travellers, they are for the moment, prepared to tolerate both – though the trip is likely to be expensive, as the Chinese authorities are keen to milk tourism by charging for permits to enter the region and restricting accommodation and transport options available to foreigners. **Tibetan organizations** abroad ask that visitors try, wherever possible, to buy from Tibetans and to hire Tibetan guides. At all times, you should avoid putting Tibetans – and yourself – at risk by bringing up **politically sensitive issues**;

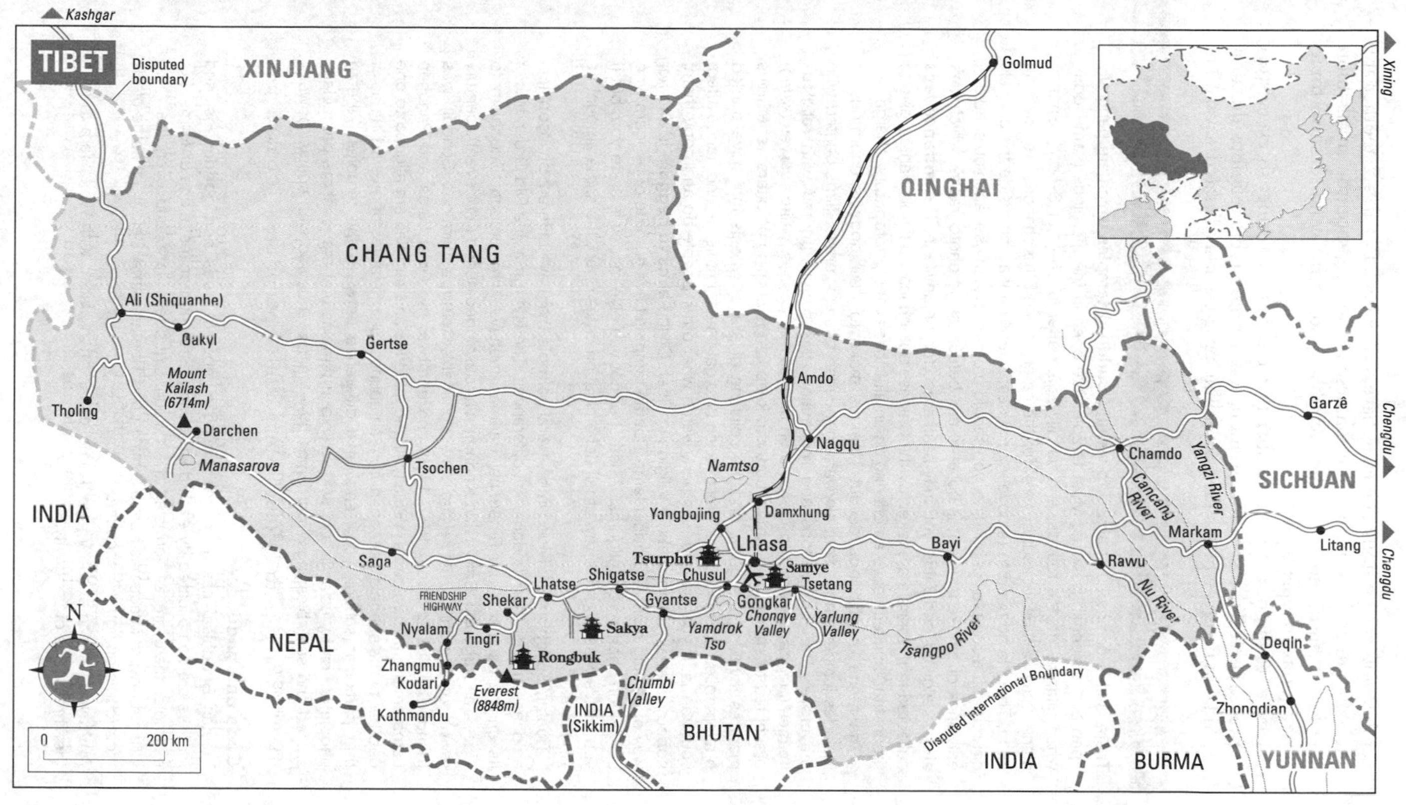
TIBET
Kashgar
Disputed boundary
XINJIANG
Golmud
Xining
QINGHAI
CHANG TANG
Ali (Shiquanhe)
Gakyl
Gertse
Mount Kailash (6714m)
Tholing
Darchen
Manasarova
Tsochen
Amdo
Nagqu
Namtso
Damxhung
Yangbajing
Lhasa
Tsurphu
Chusul
Samye
Tsetang
Gongkar
Chongye Valley
Yarlung Valley
Yamdrok Tso
Shigatse
Gyantse
Lhatse
Sakya
Saga
FRIENDSHIP HIGHWAY
Shekar
Nyalam
Tingri
Rongbuk
Zhangmu
Kodari
Kathmandu
Everest (8848m)
Chumbi Valley
INDIA (Sikkim)
BHUTAN
INDIA
NEPAL
0
200 km
N
Bayi
Tsangpo River
Disputed International Boundary
Chamdo
Cancang River
Yangzi River
Garzê
Chengdu
SICHUAN
Markam
Rawu
Nu River
Litang
Deqin
Zhongdian
INDIA
BURMA
YUNNAN

remember, you can go home, Tibetans have to live here. Emails are another area where you should be careful – the Chinese authorities monitor emails more strictly here than in the rest of the Republic – so, again, avoid sensitive topics and mentioning people by name.

However, it's important to remember that there are two sides to every story. The pre-Chinese Tibetan administration; was a xenophobic religious dictatorship, feudal in nature, which stifled economic progress and tolerated slavery. The

Living Buddhism

There is little ceremony attached to **visiting Buddhist temples** which are generally open and welcoming places. Most temples are open in the mornings (9am–noon), when pilgrims do the rounds, and usually again after lunch (2 or 3–5pm). Smaller places may well be locked, but ask for the caretaker and the chances are you'll be let in. There is no need to remove your shoes, but when walking inside the chapels or around the complex or building, you should proceed **clockwise**, and you shouldn't eat, drink or smoke inside. It is polite to ask before taking photographs, which isn't always allowed, and if it is, you may be charged for the privilege. The **entrance fees** collected from tourists are taken by the Chinese authorities, so if you want to give to the institution itself, leave an offering on an altar or pay the photography charge.

The range of **offerings** devout Tibetans make to their gods is enormous. It includes juniper smoke sent skyward in incense burners, prayer flags printed with prayers erected on rooftops and mountains, tiny papers printed with religious images (*lungda*) and cast to the wind on bridges and passes, white scarves (*katag*) presented to statues and lamas, butter to keep lamps burning on altars, repetitious mantras invoking the gods, and the spinning of prayer wheels that have printed prayers rolled up inside. The idea of each is to gain merit in this life and hence affect your karma. If you want to take part, watch what other people do and copy them; nobody is at all precious about religion in Tibet. Giving **alms to beggars** is another way of gaining merit, and most large Tibetan temples have a horde of beggars who survive on charity from pilgrims. Whether or not you give money is up to you, but if you do it's wise to give a few small denomination notes or so, the same amount as Tibetans.

Tibetan Buddhism is divided into several **schools** that have different philosophical emphases rather than fundamental differences. The **Nyingma**, the Old Order, traces its origins back to Guru Rinpoche, Padmasambhava, who brought Buddhism to Tibet. The **Kagyupa**, **Sakya** and **Kadampa** all developed during the eleventh-century revival of Buddhism, while the now dominant **Gelugpa** (Virtuous School) was founded by Tsongkhapa (1357–1419) and numbers the Dalai Lama and Panchen Lama among its adherents. Virtually all monasteries and temples are aligned to one or other of the schools, but, apart from an abundance of statues of revered lamas of that particular school, you'll spot little difference between the temples. Tibetan people are pretty eclectic and will worship in temples that they feel are particularly sacred and seek blessings from lamas they feel are endowed with special powers, regardless of the school they belong to.

Gods and goddesses

Tibetan Buddhism has an overwhelming number of **gods and goddesses**, and matters are complicated by each deity having different manifestations or forms. For example, there are 21 forms of the favourite goddess Tara, and even the most straightforward image has both a Sanskrit and Tibetan name. Below are some of the most common you will encounter:

Amitayus (Tsepame) and **Vijaya** (Namgyelma), often placed with White Tara to form the Three Gods of Longevity.

people who had the most to lose in Tibet when the Chinese arrived, the monied and the ruling classes, were the same people that fled to India and never returned. What they left behind was a working class so uneducated the people didn't even know they had been existing in a state of serfdom.

Today, the Tibetan people, for the first time, have a chance to make a better life for themselves, and ironically, strengthen their culture. However, this is often hindered by overfed monks, most notably in Lhasa, who can often be

Avalokiteshvara (Chenresi in Tibetan, Guanyin in Chinese temples), patron god of Tibet, with many forms, most noticeably with eleven faces and a thousand arms.

Maitreya (Jampa), the Buddha of the Future.

Manjusri (Jampelyang), the God of Wisdom.

Padmasambhava, with eight manifestations, most apparent as Guru Rinpoche. You may see him with his consorts, Yeshe Tsogyel and Mandarava.

Sakyamuni, Buddha of the Present.

Tara (Dolma), Goddess of Compassion. Green Tara is associated with protection and White Tara with long life.

Festivals

Festival dates are calculated using the Tibetan lunar calendar and thus correspond to different dates on the Western calendar each year. There is a list of festival dates in the Western calendar at www.kalachakranet.org/ta_tibetan_calendar.html.

February/March

Driving out of evil spirits. Twenty-ninth day of the twelfth lunar month, the last day of the year.

Losar, Tibetan New Year. First day of the first lunar month.

Monlam, Great Prayer Festival, Lhasa. Eighth day of the first lunar month.

Butter Lamp Festival, on the final day of Monlam. Fifteenth day of the first lunar month.

May/June

Birth of Buddha. Seventh day of the fourth lunar month.

Saga Dawa (Buddha's Enlightenment). Fifteenth day of the fourth lunar month.

Gyantse Horse Festival. Fifteenth day of the fourth lunar month.

July

Tashilunpo Festival, Shigatse. Fifteenth day of the fifth lunar month.

July/August

Buddha's First Sermon. Fourth day of the sixth lunar month.

Drepung Festival. Thirtieth day of the sixth lunar month.

August/September

Shotun (Yoghurt Festival), Lhasa. First to the seventh day of the seventh lunar month.

Bathing Festival, Lhasa. Twenty-seventh day of the seventh lunar month.

September

Damxhung Horse Festival. Thirtieth day of the seventh lunar month.

September/October

Harvest Festival. First to the seventh day of the eighth lunar month.

November

Lhabab (Buddha's descent from heaven). Twenty-second day of the ninth lunar month.

November/December

Peldon Lhama Festival, Lhasa. Fifteenth day of the tenth lunar month.

seen getting in and out of taxis, eating in good restaurants, talking in English into the latest mobile phones, and yet still taking money from uneducated and malnourished pilgrims who have spent months prostrating and begging their way to the capital.

Meanwhile, the Han Chinese in Tibet are not demons – most are people trying to make a life for themselves and their families, and they may have little knowledge or understanding of the wider political implications of their presence.

Some history

According to legend, the **earliest Tibetans** came from the union of the ogress, Sinmo, and a monkey, reincarnation of the god Chenresi, on the mountain of Gangpo Ri near Tsetang. Ethnographers, however, think it likely the Tibetans are descended from the nomadic Qiang who roamed eastern Central Asia, to the northwest of China, several thousand years ago. The first Tibetan king, Nyatri Tsenpo, believed to have come to earth via a magical "sky-cord", was the first of a long lineage of 27 kings who ruled in a pre-Buddhist era when the indigenous, shamanistic **Bon religion** held sway throughout the land (see p.925). Each of the **early kings** held power over a small area, the geographical isolation of Tibet making outside contact difficult. Nevertheless, it is apparent that as early as the seventh century there was considerable cultural exchange between Tibet and its neighbours. Pens, ink, silks, jewels and probably tea reached Tibet from China in the seventh century, and for many centuries Tibet looked to India for religious teaching.

It was in the time of **King Songtsen Gampo**, the thirty-third ruler in the dynasty, born in 617 AD, that expansionism began. Songtsen Gampo's twenty-year rule saw the unification of the country and the aggressive spread of his empire from northern India to China. To placate their assertive neighbour, China and Nepal each offered Songtsen Gampo a wife: in 632, he married Princess Bhrikuti (also known as Tritsun) of Nepal, and in 641 Princess Wencheng arrived from the Tang court, sent by her father, Emperor Taizong. They both brought their Buddhist faith and magnificent statues of the Buddha, which are now the centrepieces of Ramoche temple and the Jokhang in Lhasa. Songtsen Gampo himself embraced the **Buddhist faith** and established Buddhist temples throughout the country, although the indigenous Bon faith remained the religion of the ordinary people. Following his death in 650, his descendants strengthened the kingdom politically, and in 763, Tibetan armies even took the Chinese capital Chang'an (modern Xi'an). Trisong Detsen (742–797) was another champion of the new faith, who invited two Indian Buddhist teachers to Tibet, Shantarakshita and the charismatic and flamboyant **Padmasambhava**. The latter, who was also known as Guru Rinpoche, is regarded as responsible for overcoming the resistance of the Bon religion and ensuring the spread of Buddhism within Tibet. Although he is closely associated with the Nyingma school of Buddhism, you'll spot his image somewhere in most temples.

In 838, the infamous **Langdarma** came to the throne, having assassinated his brother. A fervent supporter of Bon, he set about annihilating the Buddhist faith. Temples and monasteries were destroyed, monks forced to flee and the previously unified Tibet broke up into a number of small principalities. A Buddhist revival involving monastery construction, the translation of scriptures into Tibetan and the establishment of several of the schools of Tibetan Buddhism was spearheaded by the arrival of **Atisha** (982–1054), the most famous Indian scholar of the time. Politically, the country was not united, but the various independent principalities lived largely in harmony and there was little contact with China.

Absorbed in internal events, the Tibetans had largely neglected the outside world, where the Muslim surge across India in the twelfth and thirteenth centuries resulted in the destruction of the great Buddhist centres of teaching to which the Tibetans had looked for generations. And to the north and east of Tibet, the **Mongol leader**, Genghis Khan, was beginning his assault on China. In 1207, Genghis Khan sent envoys to Tibet demanding submission, which was given without a fight, and the territory was largely ignored until Genghis Khan's grandson, Godan, sent raiding parties deep into the country. Hearing from his troops about the spirituality of the Tibetan lamas, Godan invited the head of the Sakya order, Sakya Pandita, to his court. In exchange for peace, Sakya Pandita again offered Tibetan submission and was created regent of Tibet at the Mongolian court, making the Sakya lamas the effective rulers of Tibet under the patronage of the emperor. This lasted through the generations, with Godan's son **Kublai Khan** deeply impressed by Sakya Pandita's nephew, Phagpa.

When the Chinese Ming dynasty overcame the Mongols in the fourteenth century, Tibet began a long period of independence, which ended in 1642 with the Mongols intervening directly in support of the Fifth Dalai Lama, Lobsang Gyatso (1617–82), of the **Gelugpa order**. Often referred to as "**the Great Fifth**", he united the country under Gelugpa rule and within fifteen years, largely neglected by Mongol rulers, established authority from Kham to Kailash – the first time that one religious and political leader had united and ruled the country. He invited scholars to Tibet, restored and expanded religious institutions and began work on the Potala in Lhasa.

One disadvantage of the **reincarnation system** of succession (in which a newborn child is identified as the next manifestation of the dead lama) is that an unstable period of fifteen or twenty years inevitably follows a death while the next reincarnation grows up. Initially, the death of the Fifth Dalai Lama in 1682 was concealed by his regent, Sangye Gyatso, who raised the Sixth Dalai Lama to adulthood while claiming the Fifth Dalai Lama had entered a period of solitary meditation. The following two centuries saw no strong leadership from the Dalai Lamas, and there were repeated incursions by Mongolian factions. The most influential figures in Tibet at this time were the regents and representatives of the Manchu rulers in China, the *ambans*. During the **nineteenth century**, Tibet became increasingly isolationist, fearing Russian plans to expand their empire south and British plans to expand their's north. Seeing themselves caught in the middle, Tibet simply banned foreigners from their land. But at their borders Tibetans continued trading with Indians, and in 1904, their one-sided trading arrangements exasperated the British, who determined to forge a fair treaty on the subject. The Tibetans refused to negotiate, so an expeditionary force was sent in 1904 under Colonel Younghusband. Meeting with obfuscation and hostility from Tibet's rulers, the invaders marched further and further into Tibet, and fought a couple of dispiriting battles against peasant soldiers armed with scythes and charms of invulnerability – gifts from their lamas, who stood at the back yelling encouragement. Patching up their poor opponents in improvised field hospitals along the way, the British marched up to Gyantse through the Chumbi Valley and eventually on to Lhasa. A series of British representatives in Lhasa forged good relationships with Tibet and became a window on the outside world.

The **Thirteenth Dalai Lama**, Tubten Gyatso (1876–1933), was an insightful and capable leader who realized that Tibet's political position needed urgent clarification, but he had a difficult rule, fleeing into exile twice, and was much occupied with border fighting against the Chinese and tensions with conservatives inside the country. Following his death, the **Fourteenth**

Dalai Lama was identified in Amdo in 1938 and was still a young man when world events began to close in on Tibet. The British left India in 1947, withdrawing their Representative from Lhasa. In 1949, the Communists, under Mao Zedong, created the People's Republic of China and the following year declared their intention "to liberate the oppressed and exploited Tibetans and reunite them with the great motherland". This probably had as much to do with Tibetan Khampa tribesmen attacking the bedraggled Red Army on the Long March as with Chinese notions of irredentism. In October 1950, the People's Liberation Army invaded the Kham region of eastern Tibet before proceeding to Lhasa the following year. Under considerable duress, Tibet signed a seventeen-point treaty in 1951, allowing for the "peaceful integration of Tibet".

The Chinese era

Initially, the Chinese offered goodwill and modernization. Tibet had made little headway into the twentieth century; there were few roads, no electricity, and glass windows, steel girders and concrete were all recent introductions. Hygiene and health care were patchy, and lay education was unavailable. While some Tibetans viewed modernization as necessary, the opposition was stiff, as many within the religious hierarchy saw changes within the country and overtures to the outside world as a threat to their influence. Throughout the 1950s, an underground resistance operated, which flared into a public confrontation in March 1959, fuelled by mounting distrust and hostility, as refugees from eastern Tibet fled to Lhasa and told of the brutality of Chinese rule, including the sexual humiliation of monks and nuns, arbitrary executions, and even crucifixions. In Lhasa, the Chinese invited the Dalai Lama to a theatrical performance at the Chinese military HQ. It was popularly perceived as a ploy to kidnap him, and huge numbers of Tibetans mounted demonstrations and surrounded the Norbulingka where the Dalai Lama was staying. On the night of March 17, the Dalai Lama and his entourage escaped, heading into **exile** in India where they were later joined (and still are today) by tens of thousands of refugees.

Meanwhile, the **uprising in Lhasa** was ferociously suppressed – 87,000 people were killed by the Chinese between March 1959 and September 1960. From that point on, all pretence of goodwill vanished, and a huge military force moved in, with a Chinese bureaucracy replacing Tibetan institutions. Temples and monasteries were destroyed and Chinese **agricultural policies** proved particularly disastrous. During the years of the Great Leap Forward (1959–60), it is estimated that ten percent of Tibetans starved, and it wasn't until the early 1980s that the food situation in Tibet began to improve. Harrowing accounts tell of parents mixing their own blood with hot water and *tsampa* to feed their children.

In September 1965, the U-Tsang and western areas of Tibet officially became the **Xizang Autonomous Region** of the People's Republic of China, but more significant was the **Cultural Revolution** (1966–76), during which mass eradication of religious monuments and practices took place under the orders of the Red Guards, many of them young Tibetans. In 1959, there were 2700 monasteries and temples in Tibet; by 1978, there were just eight monasteries and fewer than a thousand monks and nuns in the TAR. Liberalization followed Mao's death in 1976, leading to a period of relative openness and peace in the early 1980s when monasteries were rebuilt, religion revived and tourism introduced. However, by the end of the decade, martial law was again in place – thanks to China's current leader, Hu Jintao – following riots in Lhasa in 1988–9. In the early 1990s, foreigners were allowed back into the region. The current mood is one of apparent openness, with the encouragement of tourism against a background of increased internal control of the Tibetan population. Dissent is ruthlessly quashed and there are currently between six and seven hundred political detainees, more than at any time since 1990. Estimates of three hundred thousand to one million have been given for the number of Tibetans who have perished directly or indirectly at the hands of the Chinese or misguided policy-making.

Meanwhile, the profile of the **Tibetan Government in Exile**, led by the Dalai Lama, is again on the wane following a peak in the early 1990s when it was fashionable for the likes of Richard Gere and Steven Segal (who believes he is the reincarnation of a great lama), to be seen shaking hands with His Holiness. Based in Dharamsala in northern India, the organization represents some 130,000 Tibetan refugees, 100,000 of whom are in India. The world community has refused to take a stand for the Tibetans, yet the Dalai Lama, known to the Tibetans as Gyalwa Rinpoche and regarded as the earthly incarnation of the god Chenresi, has never faltered from advocating a peaceful solution for Tibet, a stance that led to his being awarded the 1989 Nobel Peace Prize. In recent years, relations have thawed, as the Dalai Lama wishes to return to his homeland before he dies, while the Chinese administration wants to improve its image before the Beijing Olympics in 2008. The two sides are increasingly in communication regarding the Dalai Lama's return. In the meantime, several thousand Tibetans every year make the one-month trek to India, an arduous and dangerous journey – evidence suggests that some pilgrims are picked off by Chinese snipers in the Himalayas; though increasingly these days they stay only for a few years before heading back home.

For the Tibetans who remain here, the reality of life in Tibet is harsh. China admits that the inhabitants of a quarter of the TAR counties cannot feed or clothe themselves, one third of children do not go to school, and Tibet's literacy rate is about thirty percent, the lowest in China. Between 1952 and 1998, it is estimated that China subsidized the TAR to the tune of ¥40 billion – yet Tibetans are among the poorest people in China and have the lowest life expectancy in the country. As Tibet provides the Chinese with land for their exploding population along with a wealth of yet to be exploited natural resources, the influx of Han Chinese settlers threatens to swamp the Tibetan population, culture and economy. However, the largest threat to the Tibetan way of life – and the biggest promise of modernization, and therefore rising living standards – comes from the **Qinghai–Lhasa Railway line** built at a cost of US$4 billion. It makes little economic sense in the short term but is proof to foreign investors of China's commitment to improving the infrastructure here to facilitate mining operations – uranium and copper are in particular abundance in the region. It also aids the immigrant Han population, who consume huge quantities of expensively imported food – the Tibetans, in contrast, are largely self-sufficient. The project was hugely ambitious, with more than 1200km of new track being built by 11,000 migrant workers, much of it at an attitude of over 4000m and on permafrost, with more than 30km of tunnels. It is claimed that the train carriages are pressurized, like an aircraft, so passengers will suffer the discomforts of altitude sickness on arrival rather than during their trip; however, open windows in toilets and symptoms of altitude sickness during the journey suggest otherwise.

Tibet practicalities

The **best time to visit** Tibet is April to October, outside the coldest months. June to September is the wettest period, when blocked roads and swollen rivers can make travel difficult, but the countryside will be at its greenest. However, health considerations should be taken seriously at any time of the year, and even in relatively balmy Lhasa, temperatures fall below freezing on a regular basis. In winter, as long as you come fully prepared for the cold (most hotels have no heating) and possible delays due to snow-covered passes, the lack of tourists and the preoccupation of the security forces with staying warm can make for a pleasant trip.

It's worth noting that the Chinese authorities are much pricklier around **festival times** (see box, p.1084) and the week before and after certain historically significant dates, when they'll be much more likely to **clamp down** on unregulated travel and demand permits for inspection. Dates to bear in mind include March 5 and 10 (the anniversaries of uprisings in 1988 and 1989), July 6 (the Dalai Lama's birthday), September 27 and October 1 (the anniversary of protests in 1987), and December 10 (International Human Rights Day, and the anniversary of the Dalai Lama's Nobel Peace Prize).

Getting there

Officially, you need only a **Chinese visa** to travel to Tibet. However, the authorities control entry into the country by insisting that independent travellers purchase a "**permit**" when they buy travel tickets for the region. You

Traveller's Tibetan

Although some people involved in the tourist industry are now conversant in several languages, including English, most Tibetans speak only their native tongue, with perhaps a smattering of Mandarin. A few words of Tibetan are not only greeted enthusiastically, but are nigh-on essential if you're heading off the beaten track or going trekking.

Tibetan belongs to the small Tibeto–Burmese group of languages and has no similarity at all to Mandarin or Hindi, despite what Chinese texts say. Tibetan script was developed in the seventh century and has thirty consonants and five vowels, which are placed either beside, above or below other letters when written down. There are obvious inaccuracies when trying to render this into the Roman alphabet and the situation is further complicated by the many dialects across the region; the Lhasa dialect is used in the vocabulary below. Word order is back-to-front relative to English, and verbs are placed at the ends of sentences – "this noodle soup is delicious" becomes "*tukpa dee shimbo doo*", literally "noodle soup this delicious is". The only sound you are likely to have trouble with is "**ng**" at the beginning of words – it is pronounced as in "sa**ng**".

Basic Phrases

Hello	*tashi delay*	Thirsty	*ka gom*
Goodbye, to someone staying	*kalay shu*	Tired	*galay ka*
Goodbye, to someone going	*kalay pay*	I don't understand	*nga ha ko ma-song*
Thank you	*tuk too jay*	What is your name?	*kayranggi mingla karay ray?*
Sorry	*gonda*	My name is ...	*ngeye mingla... sa*
Please	*coochee*	Where are you from?	*kayrang kanay ray?*
How are you?	*kusu debo yinbay?* or *kam sangbo dugay?*	I'm from ...	*nga ... nay yin*
		Britain	*Injee*
		Australia	*Otaleeya*
I'm ...	*nga ...*	America	*Amerika*
Fine	*debo yin*	How old are you?	*kayrang lo katsay ray?*
Cold	*kya*		
Hungry	*throko- doe*	I'm ...	*nga lo ... yin*

will probably not see this permit and once you are in Tibet nobody is interested in it. **Visa extensions** can be problematic in Tibet; you can apply for extensions at any PSB but, at best, they will ask to see proof that you are on your way out of the country and then only give you one week. Tour operators outside Tibet – notably those in Chengdu – will exaggerate the difficulty of independent travel in Tibet; don't believe what they say and talk to other travellers instead. Once in Tibet, you are fairly independent.

By air

Domestic flights operate daily to Lhasa from Chengdu (¥1700 including permit), and there are also services from Beijing (via Chengdu), Xining (see p.1019), Deqin Airport in Shangri-La (see p.821; ¥1430, but the permit will cost a further ¥1000 or so) and Kunming (via Shangri-La; ¥1750 for the ticket plus ¥1000 for the permit). There are also flights from Chongqing, but as the PSB there isn't geared up to handing out the required permits, the only time you might be using this route is when leaving.

The easiest and cheapest option is to fly from Chengdu, where plenty of tour operators, most of them grouped around the *Traffic Hotel*, offer tickets with

Where are you going?	*kaba drogee yin?*
I'm going to ...	*nga ... la drogee yin*
Where is the ...?	*... kaba doo?*
hospital	*menkang*
monastery	*gompa*
temple/chapel	*lhakhang*
restaurant	*sakang*
convent	*ani gompa*
caretaker	*konyer*
Is there ... ?	*... doo gay?*
hot water	*chu tsa-bo*
a candle	*yangla*
I don't have ...	*nga ... mindoo*
Is this OK/ can I do this?	*deegee rebay?*
It's (not) OK	*deegee (ma)ray*
(Not) Good	*yaggo (min)doo*
This is delicious	*dee shimbo doo*
Do you want ... ?	*kayrang ... gobay?*
I want tea	*nga cha go*
I don't want this	*dee me-go*
What is this/that?	*dee/day karray ray?*
When?	*kadoo?*
Now	*danta*
Today	*dering*
Yesterday	*kezang*
Tomorrow	*sangnyee*
Monday	*sa dowa*
Tuesday	*sa mingma*
Wednesday	*sa lagba*
Thursday	*sa purbur*
Friday	*sa pasang*
Saturday	*sa pemba*
Sunday	*sa nima*
How much is this?	*gong kadso ray?*

Numbers

1	*chee*
2	*nyee*
3	*soom*
4	*zhee*
5	*nga*
6	*droo*
7	*doon*
8	*gyay*
9	*goo*
10	*chew*
11	*chew chee*
12	*chew nyee*
20	*nyi shoo*
21	*nyi shoo chee* etc
30	*soom chew*
40	*shib chew*
50	*ngab chew*
60	*drook chew*
70	*doon chew*
80	*gyay chew*
90	*goop chew*
100	*gya*
200	*nyee gya*
1000	*dong*

Getting to Tibet on the Qinghai–Lhasa Railway

The **Golmud–Lhasa section** of the **Qinghai–Lhasa Railway** is the world's longest (1956km) and highest plateau railway, peaking at heights of over 5000m during the fourteen-and-a-half hour journey (¥160). Since its opening, ahead of schedule, in June 2006, the rail link has proved increasingly popular, and the once hectic bus station at Golmud is now a depressing shell of a place, with only the occasional passenger and disinterested staff. However, many travellers are using Golmud as their departure point by train due to ease of ticket purchase and lack of Tibet entry-permit requirements. Other train stations along the route can be a lot more capricious, asking to see your permit before selling you a ticket, while many will sell you the ticket only for you to be refused boarding on the day of departure.

Passengers who had hoped to be protected from the effects of altitude by the much-vaunted "**pressurized carriages**" will be disappointed – with toilet windows left open and some passengers experiencing altitude sickness, the carriages are not all they're cracked up to be, though they are comfortable. The journey itself, however, provides fantastic vistas of the plateau, with huge herds of yaks and fascinating glimpses of human life that exists – against the odds – in this thinly oxygenated environment.

There are numerous **departure points to Lhasa**, in addition to Golmud: Beijing (¥619); Chengdu (¥712); Chongqing (¥754); Guangzhou (¥809); Lanzhou (¥552); Shanghai (¥845); and Xining (¥523). Prices quoted are for a single in a hard-sleeper berth. Return journeys can be booked at the ticketing office at the Tibet Tourism Office on Luobulinka Lu.

permit (which you'll never see) for ¥1600–1850. They also sell tours, including flight, transport from Gongkar Airport into Lhasa, and a few days' accommodation at a budget hotel – a guide can be included, often for not much more; be warned, however, that guides play off hotels against each other for the best kickback, often leaving visitors tramping the streets of Lhasa looking for accommodation. Tickets are simple to arrange and are usually available for the next day. Once in Lhasa, you can buy flights back at the standard price of around ¥1500.

Flights from **Kathmandu** leave twice weekly (Tues & Sat) but not in winter (Oct–March) and can be booked only as part of a tour operated by a travel agent there; expect to pay upwards of US$360 for a flight and a three-day tour. If you don't already have a Chinese visa, you'll only get in as part of a group, on a group visa. You can change this to an individual visa in Lhasa, but the process is expensive (around ¥300) and its success depends on how well connected your travel agent is.

By land

Overland routes to Tibet are well established, although they can be physically taxing. From within China, **Golmud to Lhasa** (1160km; 30 jarring hours by bus) is the only officially permitted land route for foreigners (see p.1029), and, with the completion of the Qinghai–Lhasa Railway (see box, above), is more often done by train. CITS charge an outrageous ¥1700 for a return bus ticket (they won't sell singles). The return leg is dated three days from the date of the inbound trip; you can change your date of return at the bus station in Lhasa, though most people throw the ticket away and fly out – no one wants to do that trip twice. Some travellers have got around the CITS scam by standing on the road outside Golmud, waiting for the bus, and then making a deal with the driver; others make shady deals with characters who hang around the bus station. It's worth trying, if only to avoid enriching CITS.

It's also possible to go overland **from Yunnan** as part of a tour (¥5000 per person, one week to Lhasa – see p.823 for more details), or, as an increasing number of travellers are doing, by public bus – or jeep – from Zhongdian. By jeep (¥5000 per person), you'll take the road through Deqin, Markam and Bayi, though permits and a guide are required, as most of the towns on the way are **heavily policed and militarized**. Drivers tend to avoid Markam, as police there are prone to demand money off tourists, despite them having permits. At the time of writing, this journey was also being undertaken by independent travellers on public buses, but the activities of certain "pro-Tibet" groups in the run up to the Beijing Olympics has made it an increasingly difficult option.

The overland routes **from Sichuan** (over 2000km from Chengdu to Lhasa) and Kashgar (1100km to Ali) are officially closed to foreigners, and potentially dangerous, although a few intrepid travellers manage to get through. If you're caught by the authorities, you will be fined (around ¥300, after negotiation) and sent back in the direction you came from – so most travellers simply tell the authorities they came from where they're actually headed, and are sent on their way. At the time of writing, foreigners could buy tickets on sleeper buses from Yicheng in Xinjiang to Ali in Tibet for the local price, then in Ali they received a fine and a permit for Mount Kailash, from where it is possible to move on to Lhasa by – albeit infrequent – bus.

Entering Tibet overland **from Kathmandu** via Kodari on the Nepal side and Zhangmu on the Tibetan side is a popular option, but travellers on this route are vulnerable to snap changes in entry regulations, and also to landslides in summer and snow-blocked passes in winter. The situation in Nepal has quietened down somewhat since the people's uprising of 2006, and shouldn't present any particular dangers for travellers. Under no circumstances should you apply for a Chinese visa in Kathmandu if you want to travel independently to Tibet – the Chinese embassy will not issue these unless you are booked on an organized tour through a Kathmandu travel agent. Independent travellers must have their Chinese visa before arrival in Kathmandu, and even then, Foreigners' Travel Permits (see p.1090) for the route to Lhasa (which cost US$30 in Kathmandu) are issued only if an organized tour through to the capital is booked. Generally, the permits cannot be renewed in China, though some travellers have had success in Ürümqi. Expect to pay around US$500 for an organized seven-day overland trip to Lhasa, or around US$300 for a three-day trip. Make sure you get accommodation as part of the deal. An agency that will group individual travellers together is Nature Trail Trekking at Durbar Marg in Kathmandu (Ⓣ977 1470 1925, Ⓦwww.allnepal.com), which charges US$330 for a five-day overland "tour" to Lhasa. They will tell you that a ticket out of Tibet is necessary, but some people who don't have one still get in. The best advice is to spend some time in Kathmandu to get a feel for the current situation and check out your options. Beware of your guides offering money-changing services, citing a dearth of options in Tibet. This is untrue and once you're in Tibet you'll find plenty places to change cash at much more competitive rates.

At the time of writing, **cyclists** on this route were unable to persuade the authorities to issue a permit without being part of a tour, but this might change. If you're going to attempt cycling, bear in mind that some of the road between Zhangmu and Shigatse is unpaved and very rough. The altitude gain from Kodari to Zhangmu is 530m in about 9km, then 1450m in the 33km to Nyalam followed by a tough 1300m in the 57-kilometre climb to the Lalung Pass at 5050m. Allow around twenty days to cycle from Kathmandu to Lhasa. You'll need camping equipment, food (plus stove) and adequate warm-weather gear. Dogs are a particular hazard near villages.

Getting around

Foreigners' Travel Permits (¥150) are issued by the PSB, and give you permission to visit specified places within specified time limits – they were becoming increasingly irrelevant and there were even rumours that they were to be scrapped altogether until a rather ill-judged and poorly executed protest at Everest Base Camp by some American travellers in spring 2007. At the time of writing, the only parts of Tibet where you did not need a Foreigners' Travel Permit were Lhasa, Shigatse, Zhangmu, Tsetang and Namtso Lake. For all other areas you need to apply to the PSB for a permit; the best place to apply is at the comparatively lenient and friendly office in Shigatse. You'll be asked what places you want put on the document, and as the price is fixed you may as well fill it up. Independent travellers will be allowed a permit for all destinations on the Friendship Highway to Nepal, and sights nearby such as Everest, but only those travelling in tour groups with accredited agencies are allowed permits for western or eastern Tibet. There are some areas where a permit will not be given under any circumstances, such as the highly militarized Chumbi Valley. The status of other areas seems to change from one day to the next. Penalties for being caught somewhere without a permit can be fairly heavy: travellers have faced big fines, been harangued at length, and forced to write "confessions". If you are coming into Tibet from Xinjiang without a permit, you will be fined ¥300 at Ali by the PSB, who will then make you buy a permit for Ali (¥50). From here, most travellers continue to Lhasa and beyond unhindered.

The **public transport** system in Tibet, such as it is, consists of large public **buses** and the smaller, nippier **minibuses**. For Tibetans these are largely interchangeable, but for foreigners the difference is highly significant. There are, as yet, no problems with foreigners travelling on the public buses, but minibuses come under the label of "private vehicles" and foreigners are banned from travelling on these (although the minibuses that operate within Lhasa itself seem exempt from this), regardless of the fact that they are often the best – and sometimes only – public transport between two points.

Arranging private transport

For specific excursions, most travellers end up **hiring a jeep** with a driver and perhaps a guide as well (the latter may be obligatory, depending on your destination). There are many private **tour companies** in **Lhasa** who can arrange this: all the hotels have agencies for the purpose, and they adorn Beijing Dong Lu and Mentsikhang Lu. You'll need to decide your exact itinerary, get together five people to fill up the jeep, write a contract detailing timings and costs and pay the deposit (usually half the agreed fee) before you go. You should check that the quoted price includes the cost of permits (which the tour company should arrange), plus fees, lodging and food for the driver and guide, and the cost of fuel – in fact, everything except your own food and lodging and the cost of your admission to monasteries. It pays to be precise in your itinerary (so, for example, don't say Rongbuk Monastery if you mean Everest Base Camp), as well as to work out what the extra cost should be if one of your party falls ill and you are delayed (about ¥200 a day is reasonable). The most popular option, a five-day tour to the Nepalese border, taking in Gyantse, Shigatse and Everest Base Camp, should cost around ¥4400. The cheapest short tour is a trip to Namtso Lake and back (¥425 per person for four days). When rules become more strict, the official agency, FIT, will be able to do things the others won't (see Lhasa listings, p.1111). Hopefully you'll have no problems, but in the event of a misunderstanding, you may wish to **complain** to the Tour Service Inspection Office of Lhasa's **Tibet Tourism Bureau**, 208 Luobulingka Lu (☎0891/6333476 or 6334193).

Long-distance cycling is also technically illegal, but the authorities don't seem too bothered, certainly not by those attempting the popular route to Nepal, which takes two to three weeks. The first part of the trip, from Lhasa to Shigatse, is legal, then you'll have to apply for a permit – don't tell them you're on a bike – and hope for the best. Most of the route is level, but the road leaves a lot to be desired, dogs and weather can be a hazard, and there are five 5000-metre passes to contend with – but the last haul is a great three-day downhill. Most of the time, you'll have to camp and cook your own food. The route is covered by a few cycle tour companies, such as the UK-based Exodus (Ⓣ0870/ 240 5550, Ⓦwww.exodus.co.uk) and HMB Tours in Kathmandu (Ⓣ977 1470 0437, Ⓦwww.bikingnepal.com).

Of the **maps** available, recommended is the new *Tourist Map of Tibet* in English, Tibetan and Chinese, available in the souvenir shop next to the *Yak Hotel* for ¥8. The English-language *China Tibet Tour Map* and *Lhasa Tour Map* are a little dated but should be available in most hotels for less than ¥10. *On This Spot Lhasa Map*, published by the International Campaign for Tibet, shows another side to the city, marking the notorious Drapchi Prison, security facilities and army bases – needless to say, you shouldn't take it there with you.

Health

Tibet poses particular health hazards to travellers. Almost every visitor is affected by **altitude sickness**, as most of Tibet is over 3000m, with plenty of passes over 5000m. For your first two or three days rest as much as possible and drink plenty of water. You can buy oxygen canisters in most hotel receptions (¥20), though whether they're much use is debatable. A few painkillers should help to relieve any aches and pains and headaches, but more serious problems can develop; see "Basics", p.61 for more details. The prescription drug Diamox can help, but don't take it as a substitute for descent. Trekkers and anyone travelling long distances in the backs of trucks need also to be particularly aware of the dangers of **hypothermia**.

Travellers to Tibet should have a **rabies immunization** before they travel. The dogs here are very aggressive, bites are common and, if you get bitten, Kathmandu is the nearest place stocking rabies serum. A significant number of travellers to Tibet also suffer from **giardiasis**, an unpleasant and debilitating intestinal complaint (see p.60), although there is some controversy over whether it is endemic to the region or brought in from outside. The treatment is Tinadozol or Flagyl, neither or which is reliably available in Lhasa; bring a course along with you if you're planning an ambitious or lengthy trip. They can both be purchased cheaply and easily in big cities within China.

Accommodation

In most Tibetan towns, simple **guesthouses** offer accommodation to foreigners, pilgrims and truck drivers. You can expect dormitory accommodation, with bedding, of variable cleanliness, provided. The communal toilets are usually pit latrines and there are few washing facilities, although most places have bowls. You can expect hot water in vacuum flasks, for drinks and washing, everywhere. Lighting may be by lantern.

There is a greater choice of accommodation in the main tourist centres of Lhasa, Shigatse, Gyantse, Tsetang and Zhangmu, where international-standard hotels provide comfortable rooms with attached bathrooms and at least some hours of hot water. In the administrative centres of Lhasa and Shigatse, foreigners are allowed to stay at **mid-range hotels**, with rooms of a similar quality and generally offering very reasonable value for money.

If you are trekking, you can **camp** wherever the fancy takes you, although many trekkers find accommodation in village houses or with nomadic yak-herders. You should not expect them to feed you, and should pay ¥15 or so per night.

Eating, drinking and nightlife

The traditional **Tibetan diet** – constrained by what little will grow at over 4000m – consists in large part of **butter tea**, a unique mixture of yak butter, tea and salt, all churned into a blend that many Westerners find undrinkable, but which Tibetans consume in huge quantities. Into this is stirred **tsampa**, roasted barley flour, to make dough with the consistency of raw pastry and a not unpleasant nutty flavour. **Yak meat**, yoghurt and cheese (often dried into bite-sized cubes to preserve it) and sometimes a soup of a few vegetables supplement this. **Thukpa** (pronounced "tukpa") is a noodle soup with a few bits and pieces of whatever is available thrown in. If you're lucky, you'll find **momos**, tiny steamed or fried dough parcels containing meat or vegetables (a *thri momo* is a solid dough parcel without a filling). The local brew, Lhasa Beer, is widely available – and very drinkable.

Lhasa

Situated in a wide, mountain-fringed valley on the north bank of the Kyichu River, **LHASA** (Ground of the Gods), at 3700m, is a sprawling, rapidly expanding, modern Chinese city with a population of around 200,000. An important settlement for well over a thousand years, it was originally called Rasa, but was renamed by King Songtsen Gampo in the seventh century when

Lhasa

Lhasa	拉萨	*lāsà*
Barkhor	八角街	*bājiǎo jiē*
Jokhang	大昭寺	*dàzhāosì*
Norbulingka	罗布林卡	*luóbùlínkǎ*
Potala Palace	布达拉宫	*bùdálā gōng*
Tibet Museum	西藏博物馆	*xīzàng bówùguǎn*
Accommodation		
Banak Shol	八朗学旅馆	*bālángxué lǚguǎn*
Dong Cuan Cuo Youth Hostel	正昌东措国际青年旅馆	*zhèngchāng dōngcuò guójì qīngnián lǚguǎn*
Grand Hotel Tibet	西藏国际大酒店	*xīzàng guójì dàjiǔdiàn*
House of Shambala	香巴拉宫	*xiāngbālā gōng*
Hubei Hotel	湖北宾馆	*húběi bīnguǎn*
Kirey	吉日宾馆	*jírì bīnguǎn*
Kyichu	拉萨吉曲饭店	*lāsà jíqǔ fàndiàn*
Lhasa Hotel	拉萨饭店	*lāsà fàndiàn*
Mandala	满斋酒店	*mǎnzhāi jiǔdiàn*
Snowlands Hotel	雪域宾馆	*xuěyù bīnguǎn*
Yak Hotel	亚宾馆	*yà bīnguǎn*

he moved his capital here from the Yarlung Valley. Following the collapse of the Yarlung dynasty two centuries later, power dispersed among local chieftains, and the city lost its pre-eminence. It was not until the seventeenth century, with the installation of the Fifth Dalai Lama as ruler by the Mongolian emperor, Gushri Khan, that Lhasa once again became the seat of government. It continues now as the capital of the TAR, and while glorious sites from earlier times are spread throughout the area, it is this third period of growth, following the Chinese invasion, which has given the city its most obvious features – wide boulevards and concrete-and-glass blocks. The Chinese population of Lhasa is highly active economically, with two Chinese businesses to every Tibetan one, a ratio that reflects the city's population.

There are plenty of sights in and around Lhasa to keep most visitors occupied for at least a week: the **Potala**, **Jokhang** and **Barkhor** district are not to be missed, and at least one trip to an outlying monastery is a must. It's also worth taking time to see some of the smaller, less showy temples and simply to absorb the atmosphere of the "Forbidden City", which large numbers of explorers died in vain efforts to reach around a hundred years ago.

Offering tourists better **facilities**, with more choice of accommodation, restaurants and shopping than anywhere else in Tibet, Lhasa is the best place to arrange trips to other parts of the region (see p.1094). Whatever the comforts of Lhasa, remember that the city is just one face of Tibet – 88 percent of the population live in the countryside.

Moving on from Lhasa

Public buses depart mostly from the bus station, where it's advisable to buy tickets a day in advance. **Pilgrim buses** and **minibuses** leave from various points, but note the possible restrictions on your use of these (p.1094). Further details are given in the accounts of the destinations and in "Travel details" at the end of the chapter. For information on arranging **private transport** for a customized itinerary, see p.1094.

Leaving Tibet

You can buy **flight** tickets at CAAC in Lhasa or at the ticket agency in the *Grand Hotel Tibet*. Destinations served are: Kathmandu (Tues & Sat; ¥2190), Chengdu daily (¥1500) and Beijing (daily ¥2560 at peak periods). The price includes the departure tax. Airport buses leave from outside the CAAC office in Lhasa, at 1 and 5pm, and also on Tues at 6am, Thurs and Sat at 10am (¥35). An early-morning jeep-taxi from Lhasa to the airport costs ¥350 for five people plus luggage, or you can arrange a taxi in advance, through the *Pentoc Hotel* on Mentsikhang Lu (☎0891/632 2367) for only ¥200.

At the time of writing, **cycling out** of Tibet was a lot easier than cycling in – you just have to be wary of two checkpoints: one outside Lhatse and one outside Shekar. See "Getting there", p.1090, and "Getting around", p.1094. The only destination outside Tibet that you can reach **by bus** is Golmud, for which buses leave the main bus station daily at 8.30am. There's a choice between luxury buses with reclining seats (¥400) or more basic ones with upright seats (¥210). It's also possible to get to Zhongdian in Yunnan on one of the returning **jeep** tours (¥7000 for 4 people); you'll need to make regular trips to travel agents for information. There's no longer any public service to **Nepal** – most people heading to Nepal make their own arrangements through **tour companies** in Lhasa, hiring a jeep and driver plus guide. Expect to pay upwards of ¥4500 for a six-day, seven-night trip taking in Rongbuk Monastery. Alternatively, you could cadge a lift with one of the minibuses and jeeps that leave Lhasa regularly to collect tour parties at the Nepal border. They complete the trip in two days, and it will cost around ¥350 per person. You have to ask around a bit to arrange transport this way, as the companies would rather you took a more expensive tour.

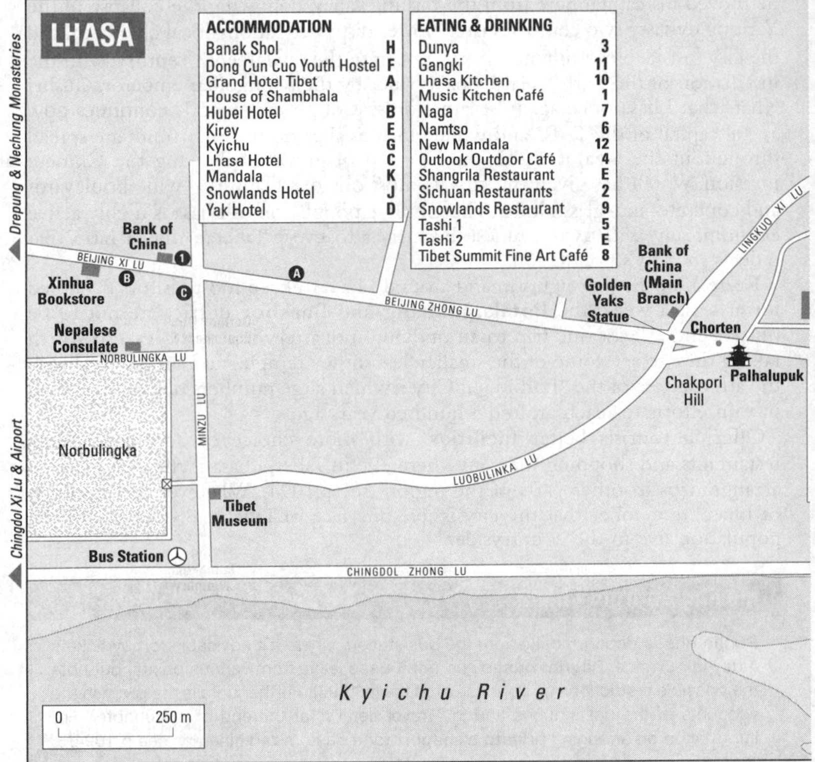

Orientation, arrival and city transport

The **central areas** of Lhasa are along and between three main roads that run east–west, parallel to and north of the Kyichu River: Chingdol Lu, Beijing Lu and Lingkuo Lu. Lhasa is at its most sprawling to the west, where there is very little countryside between the outskirts of the city and the monastery of Drepung, 8km west of town, and north, where the city virtually merges into the Sera monastery complex, 4km distant. So far, the river has prevented a spread south, while to the east the city peters out within a couple of kilometres, as the road towards Ganden deteriorates quickly. The Potala Palace, on Beijing Zhong Lu, is the major landmark visible throughout the city and, together with the Tibetan enclave around the Jokhang temple (known as the Barkhor), forms the centre of interest for most visitors. The Golden Yaks Statue, at the junction of Beijing Zhong Lu and Luobulingka Lu in the west of the city, erected in 1991 to celebrate the fortieth anniversary of the "liberation" of Tibet, is another useful landmark.

Arriving by air, you'll land at **Lhasa airport** at Gongkhar, a hefty 93km to the southeast of the city. CAAC buses (¥25) bring you to the CAAC office on Nyangrain Lu in less than two hours, while foreigners coming on tours will be met by guides with transport. A few minibuses and pilgrim buses (notably from Shigatse, Ganden and Tsurphu) ply into the middle of town, usually Barkhor Square, but you'll probably be dropped at the main **bus station**, west of the

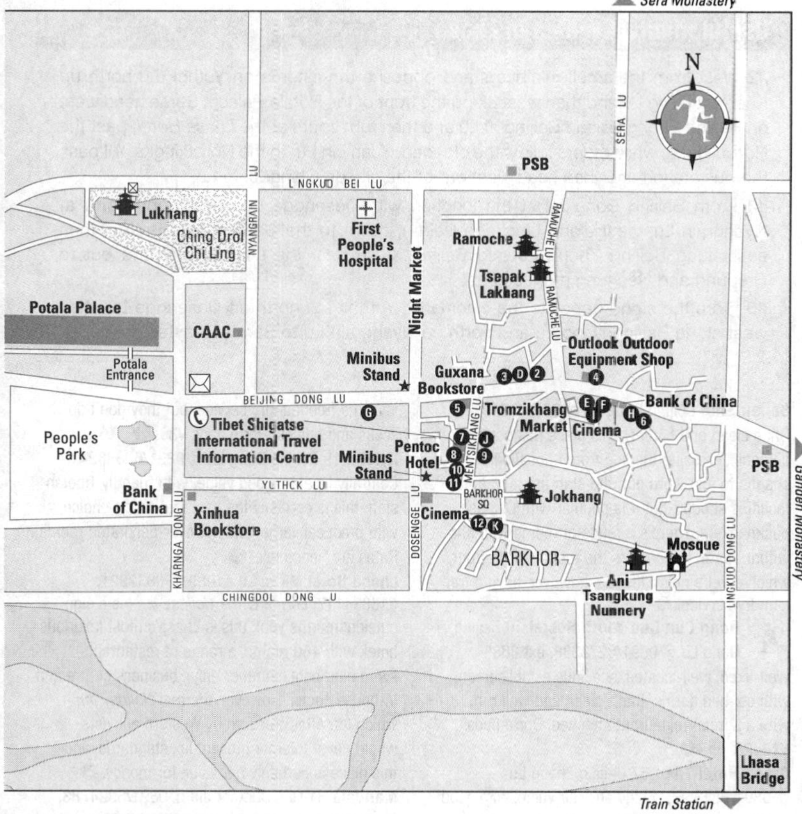

centre, at the junction of Chingdol Zhong Lu and Minzu Lu. From here, either take a taxi into town (¥10), or use the #2 minibus (¥2), which will take you most of the way (see "City transport", below). The **train station** is about 6km from the centre of Lhasa via Lhasa Bridge (¥30 into town by taxi).

City transport

The easiest way to get around the city and its environs is by **minibus** (daily 7am–10pm; ¥1-2 flat fare) or on a **cycle-rickshaw**; although you'll have to haggle a little for the latter, it should be around ¥3-4 for most trips. There are plenty of **taxis** around, which have a ¥10 basic rate, and although not as fun as rickshaws, they remove the bind of having to negotiate prices. **Bike rental** is available at some hotels, bike shops and travel agencies. Prices range anywhere from ¥15 a day to ¥60, as do deposits. Apart from the altitude, there are few problems with cycling in Lhasa; roads are wide, the traffic isn't overwhelming, though it's getting there, and there are traffic lights and traffic police at the main junctions to control the flow.

Accommodation

Most foreigners stay near the Barkhor in the long-standing **budget** stalwarts of the *Snowlands Hotel*, *Yak Hotel*, *Banak Shol*, *Youth Hostel* or *Kirey*. The **mid- and upper-range hotels** in the outskirts are mostly standard Chinese-style.

Useful minibus routes in Lhasa

#2 West from the small minibus stand opposite the cinema on Yuthok Lu north up Kharnga Dong Lu and then west along the front of the Potala Palace. Some head west on Beijing Zhong Lu and Beijing Xi Lu and then turn south at the *Lhasa Hotel*, past the Norbulingka, while others follow the old road, Yuan Lin Lu, to the Norbulingka. All pass the bus station and then head west out of the city on Chingdol Xi Lu.

#3 From Beijing Dong Lu at the junction with Dosengge Lu, then loops north at Nyangrain Lu, west along Lingkouo Bei Lu, down to the Golden Yaks Statue, then east along Beijing Zhong Lu and Beijing Xi Lu past the *Lhasa Hotel* and out to Drepung and Nechung monasteries.

#5 From the stand opposite the cinema on Yuthok Lu, north up Dosengge Lu, then west along Beijing Dong Lu and north up Nyangrain Lu to Sera Monastery.

Banak Shol Beijing Dong Lu ⓣ0891/6323829. Once clean and homely, this place has gone downhill, crossing the line from appealingly chaotic to just worn out; the staff are lazy, the facilities shoddy, but it is popular with Chinese backpackers. There's a range of rooms with and without bath, but beware the rooms at the front, which can be noisy. It does, however, have a free laundry service. ❷–❹

Dong Cun Cuo Youth Hostel 10 Beijing Dong Lu ⓣ0891/6273388, ext 8888. Well-liked, well-located, spacious establishment, with six-bed dorms, that's clean and well run, with a Korean restaurant attached. Dorm beds ¥15–25, ❶–❷

Grand Hotel Tibet 67 Beijing Zhong Lu ⓣ0891/6816666. Shiny and fair value, with good facilities and a surplus-to-requirements oxygen bar. Big discounts on standard doubles between the Oct and May national holidays. ❺

House of Shambhala 7 Jiri Erxiang ⓣ0891/6326533, ⓦwww.houseofshambhala.com. Newly built in traditional Tibetan style, this boutique hotel, run by the non-profit Shambhala organization, offers stylish suites and a great – if expensive – rooftop restaurant in the Barkhor district. All proceeds go towards development and cultural preservation projects in Tibet ❽

Hubei Hotel Beijing Xi Lu ⓣ0891/6820999. Chinese, business-oriented hotel, friendly, well run and offering better value than any of its nearby competitors; certainly a better bet than the *Lhasa Hotel*. Big discounts off season. ❻

Kirey Beijing Dong Lu ⓣ0891/6323462. Conveniently close to the Barkhor, and with the *Tashi 2* restaurant on the premises. Don't be deterred by the characterless, concrete compound; the rooms are pleasantly furnished, and overall this place represents very good value. As with the other budget places, staff take their duties lightly. There is also a free laundry service, but they don't do socks and undies. Dorm beds ¥30. ❷

Kyichu 19 Beijing Dong Lu ⓣ0891/6338824. Centrally located, good value, with friendly Tibetan staff, this is certainly the best mid-range choice, with practical, large, and not over-decorated rooms. Rates are negotiable. ❺

Lhasa Hotel Minzu Lu ⓣ0891/66832221, ⓕ6834117. Formerly the *Holiday Inn* (as a sign outside informs you), this is Lhasa's most luxurious hotel, with 460 rooms, a range of restaurants, swimming pool (summer only), business centre and in-house doctor. However, the real *Holiday Inn* – which left after pressure by Western activists – would never tolerate present lax standards, and this place is certainly not value for money. ❽

Mandala 31 Nan Barkhor Jie ⓣ0891/6324783. Well located, right on the edge of the Jokhang circuit, and a good mid-range option. It's quiet, and rooms are wood-panelled. No dorms means no backpackers, which could be considered an advantage. ❺

Snowlands Hotel Mentsikhang Lu ⓣ0891/6323687. Well situated near the Jokhang, and livelier than it used to be, thanks to a partial renovation. The new wing has standard doubles at an exorbitant ¥350, complete with nightmare-inducing furnishings and childlike attempts at Tibetan art on the walls and ceilings. In the old wing, the six-bed dorms are cramped, but not without character; doubles are better value at ¥80. Dorm beds ¥25–30.❷–❻

Yak Hotel 100 Beijing Dong Lu ⓣ0891/6323496. Following a massive overhaul, this hotel is no longer the budget favourite it once was. Common (double) rooms have replaced dorms. Standard rooms (¥350) offer all the same comforts – TV, tea-making facilities, private bathrooms – but come with some rather ugly, over-engineered Chinese-style furniture. ❶–❻

The City

With its mix of ascendant Chinese modernity set side by side with ancient Tibetan traditions, Lhasa is a vibrant, fast-changing city that throws up some bizarre paradoxes – witness the pilgrims on their rounds of prostrations passing the ATM machines of the Bank of China. Construction sites abound, but it is still easy to get around to all the major monuments, many of which are within walking distance of the two central landmarks, the **Potala Palace** and **Jokhang**.

The Potala Palace

Perched 130m above Lhasa atop Marpo Ri (Red Mountain), and named after India's Riwo Potala – holy mountain of the god Chenresi – the **Potala Palace** is dazzling both inside and out, an enduring landmark of the city of Lhasa. As you glory in the views from the roof, gaze at the glittering array of gold and jewels and wend your way from chapel to chapel, you'll rub shoulders with excited and awestruck pilgrims from all over ethnic Tibet, making offerings at each of the altars. But be aware that you're in a sad shell of a place: most of the rooms are off limits, part of a UNESCO World Heritage grant was spent on a CCTV system, and the caretaker monks are not allowed to wear their robes. And don't tackle the Potala on your first day at altitude – the palace is a long climb, and even the Tibetans huff and puff on the way up; you'll enjoy it more once you've acclimatized.

Rising thirteen dramatic storeys and consisting of over a thousand rooms, the palace complex took a workforce of at least seven thousand builders and fifteen hundred artists and craftsmen over fifty years to complete. The main mass of the Potala is the **White Palace** (Potrange Karpo), while the building rising from the centre of this is the **Red Palace** (Potrang Marpo). Built for several purposes, the Potala served as administrative centre, seat of government, monastery, fortress and the home of all the Dalai Lamas from the Fifth to the Fourteenth, although from the end of the eighteenth century, when the Norbulingka was built as the Summer Palace, they stayed here only in winter. It was King

▲ The Potala Palace

Songtsen Gampo who built the first palace on this site in the seventh century, though it was later destroyed by invaders. Today's White Palace (1645–1648) was built during the reign of the Fifth Dalai Lama, who took up residence in 1649, while the Red Palace, begun at the same time, was completed in 1693. Both survived the Cultural Revolution relatively unscathed; apparently Zhou Enlai ordered their protection.

There's a huge amount to take in on one visit and a second look helps to put it all in perspective, though the **entrance fee** is a painful ¥100, sometimes going up to ¥200 during peak periods. **Opening hours** are daily 8.30am to 3.30pm, but if you are already in you can hang about until 6pm. Tickets have to be bought one or two days in advance, depending on availability, although if you are on your own, they will often let you in on the spot as part of a group. Morning is certainly the best time to come, when the place bustles with excited pilgrims. **Photography** is banned inside, but there's no problem with taking pictures on the roof or on the balconies outside the chapels.

Into the palace

The #2 minibus passes the gate in the front wall of the massive compound. You enter here and walk through Shol village, once the red-light district of Lhasa, now lined with souvenir shops and vendors, then turn right through the gates and climb to the inner courtyard of the White Palace, the **Deyang Shar**, where you'll find the ticket office. Monks' rooms and stores surround the courtyard, with the **Quarters of the Dalai Lama** at its eastern end. The opulently carved and painted **Official Reception Hall** beyond is dominated by the bulk of the high throne and hung with fabulous brocade and *thangkas* (embroidered or painted religious scrolls) with a small doorway leading into the private quarters of the Fourteenth Dalai Lama next door. There's a small audience chamber, a chapel, a hallway and finally the bedroom, with an extremely well-painted mural of Tsongkhapa, founder of the Gelugpa school to which the Dalai Lama belongs, over the bed. On the other side of the Official Reception Hall are the private quarters of the previous Dalai Lamas, but these are closed to the public.

Stairs lead from the inner courtyard up into the **Red Palace** and continue straight to the roof, for fabulous views across Lhasa. You can then descend a floor at a time to tour the palace, moving clockwise all the way. The first room on the **upper floor** is the **Maitreya Chapel**, its huge number of fabulously ornate statues setting the tone for the remainder of the chapels. It's dominated by a seated statue of Maitreya, made at the time of the Eighth Dalai Lama and said to contain the brain of Atisha, the eleventh-century Indian scholar responsible for a Buddhist revival in Tibet (see p.1086). On the far left of the Dalai Lama's throne is a statue of the Fifth Dalai Lama, commissioned soon after his death and supposedly containing some of his hair.

The Red Palace is the final resting place of the Fifth to Thirteenth Dalai Lamas, except for the Sixth who died on his way to China and is said to be buried near Qinghai Hu in Qinghai province. However, not all the tombs are open. Although they vary in size, all are jewel-encrusted golden *chortens* (traditional multi-tiered Tibetan Buddhist monuments that usually contain sacred objects), supporting tier upon tier of fantastic engravings; encased deep within are the bodies of the Dalai Lamas, preserved in dry salt. You should at least be able to see either the Tomb of the Thirteenth Dalai Lama or Tomb of the Eighth Dalai Lama on the upper floor.

Considered the oldest and holiest shrines in the Potala, the **Lokeshvara Chapel**, on the upper floor, and the **Practice Chamber of the Dharma**

King, directly below on the **upper middle floor**, date back to Songtsen Gampo's original construction, and are the focus of all Potala pilgrims. It's easy to miss the Practice Chamber, entered from a small corridor from the balcony. King Songtsen Gampo supposedly meditated in this dark, dingy room now dominated by statues of the king and his ministers, Tonmi Sambhota and Gawa. At the base of the main pillar is a stove, apparently used by Songtsen Gampo himself.

Although you pass through the lower middle floor, the chapels here are all closed and the remainder of the open rooms are on the **lower floor** leading off the large, many-columned Assembly Hall. The highlight down here is the grand **Chapel of the Dalai Lamas' Tombs**, containing the awesome golden *chorten* of the Fifth Dalai Lama, which is three storeys high and consists of 3700kg of gold. To the left and right are smaller *chortens* with the remains of the Tenth and Twelfth Dalai Lamas, and the *chortens* on either side of these main ones are believed to contain relics of Buddha himself. Visitors leave the Red Palace by a door behind the altar in the **Chapel of the Holy Born**, from where the path winds down the west side of the hill to the western gate.

Around the Potala Palace

The area around the Potala Palace offers plenty of enjoyable sights. Opposite the front of the palace, on the south side of Beijing Dong Lu, **People's Park** is a mini Tian'anmen Square, built in an effort to reinforce China's claim to the region; there is a Chinese flag and a monument celebrating Tibet's "liberation". Farther west along Beijing Dong Lu, the new *chorten* in the middle of the road marks the site of the old West Gate to the city. South of here, **Chakpori Hill**, the previous site of the medical college, is now topped by a radio transmitter. For a scenic view of the Potala Palace, climb the hill using the path that goes in front of the public toilets just south of the *chorten*; you'll be able to go only as far as a massive tree, laden with prayer flags, before the guards at the transmitter start shouting.

From just east of the public toilets at the *chorten*, a path leads a couple of hundred metres to the fabulously atmospheric **Palhalupuk Temple**, built around an ancient cave. You'll spot the ochre and maroon, and far less interesting, Neten Temple on the cliff first; Palhalupuk is the smaller, white building below. Entered from an ante-chapel, the cave, about five square metres, was King Songtsen Gampo's retreat in the seventh century and is lined with rock carvings, many of which date from that time. The most important altar is in front of the huge rock pillar that supports the roof, the main image here being of Sakyamuni, flanked by his chief disciples. At the far right-hand corner stands a jewel- and *katag*-bedecked statue of Pelden Lhamo, the fierce protective deity of Tibet, on a tiny altar. The back wall has been left untouched, and it's said that the jewels of Songtsen Gampo's Nepalese wife, Princess Bhrikuti, are hidden behind. They don't get many tourists here, and the caretaker and monks are welcoming.

The main area of **rock carvings**, numbering around five thousand, is on the west and southern sides of Chakpori Hill. Back on the road continue west from the *chorten* along the left fork. Just as you get to the junction with Luobulinka Lu that leads down from the Golden Yaks statue, you'll find a rough track leading off to the left. Follow it beside a stream for a couple of hundred metres and you'll arrive at the start of the rock paintings and carvings that supposedly represent the visions seen by King Songtsen Gampo during his meditation. The carvers at work here copy ancient texts and prayers or sacred *mantras*; they work partly for alms but also produce work for sale.

North of the Potala Palace

Around the other side of the Potala Palace, but off limits at the time of writing due to reconstruction, the park of **Ching Drol Chi Ling** has fine views up to the north facade of the Potala and sports a large area of ill-kept trees and a boating lake formed by the removal of earth during the construction of the palace. The park is entered from the north side of the lake or via the entrance at the end of the Farmers Products Market. On an island in the lake is the small, pleasant **Lukhang**, built by the Sixth Dalai Lama in honour of the *naga* king and for use as a retreat. Legend tells of a pact between the builder of the Potala and the king of the *nagas*, subterranean creatures who resemble dragons – the earth could be used as long as a chapel was built in their honour. The temple is famed for the very old and detailed murals on the middle and top floors, but you'll need a torch if you want to study them in detail, and the protective wire in front doesn't help. The top-floor pictures showing the stages of human life, the journey of the soul after death, and various legends, are somewhat esoteric, but the middle-floor murals, depicting the construction of the great monasteries of Sera and Drepung among others, are far more comprehensible.

The Jokhang

The **Jokhang** (daily 8am–6pm; ¥70) – sometimes called Tshuglakhang (Cathedral), and which is the holiest temple in the Tibetan Buddhist world – can be somewhat unprepossessing from afar, but get closer and you'll be swept up by the anticipation of the pilgrims and the almost palpable air of veneration. Inside, you're in for one of the most unforgettable experiences in Tibet; many visitors end up returning day after day.

King Songtsen Gampo built the Jokhang in the seventh century to house the **dowry** brought by his Nepalese bride, Princess Bhrikuti, including the statue known as the *Akshobhya Buddha*. This later changed places with the *Jowo Sakyamuni* statue from Princess Wencheng's dowry, which was initially installed in Ramoche temple (see p.1106), and which is now regarded as Tibet's most sacred object. The **site** of the temple was decided by Princess Wencheng after consulting astrological charts, and confirmed by the king following a vision while meditating. However, construction was fraught with problems. Another vision revealed to the king and his queens was that beneath the land of Tibet lay a huge, sleeping demoness with her head in the east, feet to the west and heart beneath Lhasa. Only by building monasteries at suitable points to pin her to the earth, could construction of the Jokhang succeed. The king embarked on a scheme to construct twelve demon-suppressing temples: four around Lhasa, which included Trandruk (see p.1120), to pin her at hips and shoulders; a set of four farther away, to pin her at elbows and knees; and four even more distant, to pin her hands and feet. When these were finished, construction on the Jokhang began.

The Jokhang stands 1km or so east of the Potala Palace, in the centre of the only remaining Tibetan enclave in the city, the **Barkhor area**, a maze of cobbled alleyways between Beijing Dong Lu and Chingdol Dong Lu. If you're coming from the western side of town, the #2 or #3 minibus may come into Barkhor Square or – more likely – drop you about five minutes' walk away on Dosengge Lu or Beijing Dong Lu.

Pilgrims go in at the front, but the foreign visitors' entrance is on the southeast side, and **entry** – until quite recently free – is now a shocking ¥70. The best time to visit is in the morning, when most pilgrims do the rounds.

Inside the temple

The main entrance to the Jokhang is from **Barkhor Square**, which is to the west of the temple and full of stalls selling prayer flags, white scarves (*katag*) and incense. Two bulbous incense burners in front of the temple send out juniper smoke as an offering to the gods, and the two walled enclosures here contain three ancient engraved pillars. The tallest is inscribed with the Tibetan–Chinese agreement of 821 AD and reads: "Tibet and China shall abide by the frontiers of which they are now in occupation. All to the east is the country of Great China; and all to the west is, without question, the country of Great Tibet. Henceforth on neither side shall there be waging of war nor seizing of territory."

In front of the huge temple doors, a constant crowd of pilgrims prostrate themselves – you can hear the clack of the wooden protectors on their hands and the hiss as the wood moves along the flagstones when they lie flat on the ground. Head round the southern side to the visitor's entrance and you'll enter the main courtyard, where ceremonies and their preparations take place. Rows of tiny butter lamps burn on shelves along the far wall, and it's a bustling scene as monks make butter statues and dough offerings and tend the lamps. Through a corridor in the north wall, with small chapels to left and right, you pass into the inner area of the temple. The central section, **Kyilkhor Thil**, houses statues galore, six of them considered particularly important. The most dramatic are the six-metre-high Padmasambhava on the left, which dates from 1955, and the half-seated figure of Maitreya, the Buddha of the Future, to the right.

Devout pilgrims turn left to move clockwise and enter each chapel in turn to pray and make offerings. They don't hang around, though; stand still to admire the statues and you'll get trampled in the rush. Some of the wooden door frames and columns are original – in particular, the door frame of the Chapel of Chenresi, in the north, and the columns in front of the Chapel of Jowo Sakyamuni, in the east, were created by Niwari craftsmen from Nepal during the temple's early years. As with all temples in Tibet, it's often difficult to know exactly what you are looking at. Some of the statues are original, others were damaged during the Cultural Revolution and have been restored either slightly or extensively, and others are replicas – all are held in deep reverence by the pilgrims.

It's easy to feel overwhelmed, but if you manage only one chapel it should be the **Chapel of Jowo Sakyamuni** in the middle of the eastern, back wall of the temple. The 1.5-metre-high Sakyamuni is depicted at twelve years of age, with a sublimely beautiful golden face. Draped in heavy brocade and jewels, this is the most deeply venerated statue in Tibet. Although the Jokhang was originally built to house the statue the *Jowo Sakyamuni* first stood in the temple of Ramoche until rumours of a Tang invasion late in the seventh century led to its removal to a hiding place in the Jokhang. During the reign of Trisong Detsen, the Bon opponents of Buddhism removed the statue and buried it, but it was found and sent out of Lhasa for safety. The statue was again buried during King Langdarma's attempt to annihilate Buddhism, but eventually returned to the Jokhang, where it rests today. Although there is a rumour that the original was destroyed in the eighteenth century by Mongol invaders, neither it nor the chapel was harmed during the Cultural Revolution and the statue is widely regarded as the original. Monks here keep the butter lamps topped up while the pilgrims move around the altar, bowing their heads to Jowo Sakyamuni's right leg and then his left.

By the time you reach the **upper floor**, you'll probably be punch-drunk; fortunately perhaps, there is less to detain you up here than down below, although most of the chapels are now open after restoration. Of most interest here is the **Chapel of Songtsen Gampo**, directly above the main entrance in the west wall and featuring a large statue of the king flanked by his two queens. Continue up the stairs in the southwest corner of the chapel to one fierce and one peaceful image of **Pelden Lhamo**, who is regarded as the protective deity of Tibet and is particularly popular with pilgrims.

From the temple **roof**, the views down over Barkhor Square, into the temple courtyard and as far as the Potala Palace in the distance, are wonderful, the golden statues even more impressive. You can get up to the roof using any of a number of staircases, located just to the right of the main entrance, in the far southeast corner of the temple itself, or at the far end of the side courtyard to the right of the main entrance.

The Barkhor

Traditionally, pilgrims to Lhasa circled the city on two clockwise routes: an outer circuit called the Lingkhor, now vanished under two-lane highways and rebuilding, and the shorter **Barkhor** circuit through the alleyways a short distance from the Jokhang walls. This maze of picturesque streets, a world away from the rest of Lhasa, has survived. It's now lined with the stalls of an outdoor market selling all manner of goods – saddles and stirrups, Chinese army gear, *thangkas*, jewellery, blankets, cassette tapes, carpets, tin trunks and pictures of lamas, to mention a fraction only. The many trinkets and "antiques" are, of course, fakes, made in Nepal. The pilgrims are an amazing sight: statuesque Khampa men with their traditional knives and red-braided hair, decorated with huge chunks of turquoise; Amdo women dripping jewels with their hair in 108 plaits; and old ladies spinning their tiny prayer wheels and intoning *mantras*. The Barkhor circuit is at its most interesting in the early hours of the morning, before the sun has risen and stallholders have set up. It is at this time that the feeling of devotion is most prevalent as the constant mumble of prayer and shuffle of prostrations emit from the shadows cast by the lambent pre-dawn light.

The whole Barkhor area is worth exploring – with huge wooden doors set in long, white walls and leading into hidden courtyards – but try not to miss **Tromzikhang market** to the north of the Jokhang; take the main alleyway into the Barkhor that leads off Beijing Dong Lu just east of Ramoche Lu and it's just down on your left. The two-storey modern building is a bit soulless, but nowhere else in the world can you see (or smell) so much yak butter in one place.

One other sight to seek out here is the **Ani Tsangkung Nunnery** (¥6) to the southeast of the Jokhang; you'll probably need to ask the way (see "Language", p.1217). With over a hundred nuns in residence, several of whom speak good English, there is a lively but devout atmosphere here, especially around prayer time at 11am. A fabulous Chenresi in a glass case dominates the main chapel. From the back of the chapel, facing the main door, you can head right, round the outside, to visit the long, narrow room containing King Songtsen Gampo's meditation chamber in a pit at the end. Supposedly, his meditation here altered the course of the Kyichu River when it looked likely to flood the construction of the Jokhang.

Ramoche

The three-storey, robust **Ramoche** temple (daily 9am–4.30pm; ¥20, plus up to ¥50 per chapel for photographs) is small but intriguing, and second only in importance to the Jokhang. A short walk north of the Barkhor, on Ramoche Lu between Beijing Dong Lu and Lingkuo Bei Lu, it was built in the seventh century by Songtsen Gampo's Chinese wife, Princess Wencheng, to house the *Jowo Sakyamuni* statue that she brought to Tibet. The statue later ended up in the Jokhang and was replaced by the *Akshobhya Buddha*, a representation of Sakyamuni at the age of 8. This much-revered statue was broken in two during the Cultural Revolution, with one part taken to China and narrowly saved from being melted down, while the other was later discovered on a factory scrapheap in Tibet. The statue in position today in the main shrine, the **Tsangkhang** at the back of the temple, is likely to be a copy.

While you're in the area, call in on the tiny **Tsepak Lakhang** to the south of Ramoche. The little entrance is just beside a huge incense burner, and, once inside, you pass along a small alley lined with a row of prayer wheels. There are two small chapels in this hugely popular temple, and the 55 friendly monks in residence chant their daily prayers around noon. You can walk the small circuit around the walls of Tsepak Lakhang, where the murals have been newly painted.

Norbulingka and the Tibet Museum

Situated in the west of town, on the route of the #2 minibus, **Norbulingka** (Jewel Park), the Summer Palace of the Dalai Lamas (daily 9am–6.30pm; ¥60), is not in the top league of Lhasa sights, but is worth a look if you've time on your hands and don't object to the steep entrance fee. However, if you're in Lhasa during the festivals of the Worship of the Buddha (July) or during Shotun, the Yoghurt Festival (Aug/Sept), when crowds flock here for picnics and to see masked dances and traditional opera, you should definitely make the trip out here. The forty-hectare park has been used as a recreation area by the Dalai Lamas since the time of the Seventh incarnation. The first palace to be built was the **Palace of the Eighth Dalai Lama**, constructed towards the end of the eighteenth century, and the closest to the entrance. This palace became the official summer residence to which all Dalai Lamas moved, with due ceremony, on the eighteenth day of the third lunar month.

Other buildings open to the public are the **Palace of the Thirteenth Dalai Lama** in the far northwest corner – beyond the appalling zoo – and, the highlight of the visit, the **New Summer Palace**, built in 1956 by the Fourteenth Dalai Lama; it was from here that he fled Lhasa in 1959. Visitors pass through the audience chamber, via an anteroom, to the meditation chamber, on to his bedroom and then into the reception hall dominated by a fabulously carved golden throne, before passing through to the quarters of the Dalai Lama's mother. Western plumbing and a radio sit beside fabulous *thangkas* and religious murals. It's all very sad and amazingly evocative, the forlorn rooms bringing home the reality of exile.

Opposite the Norbulingka, the **Tibet Museum** (daily 9am–6pm; ¥30) offers curiosities to anyone who's had enough of religious iconography; there are some fascinating *thangkas*, illustrating theories from Tibetan medicine, as well as stuffed Tibetan wildlife, Neolithic tools and the like. Its primary purpose, however, is propaganda, so it's best to take the captions with a pinch of salt.

Eating, drinking and entertainment

Besides the vast number of restaurants in Lhasa, there are noodle places near Tromzikhang market, and bakeries outside the mosque in Barkhor selling tasty nan breads. For **trekking food** such as muesli and chocolate, try the counters at the *Kailash* or *Snowland* restaurants, or one of the **supermarkets** at the west end of Lingkuo Bei Lu. The *Dunya* restaurant does a good picnic lunchbox.

Restaurants and cafés

Dunya Beijing Dong Lu. Run by a Dutch couple, very civilized but not very Tibetan. A diverse range of specials, good Western, Indian and Nepali food, and even half-decent Australian wine. Expect to pay around ¥60 a head. The tasty breakfast buffet is ¥25. The upstairs bar is the liveliest place in the east end of Lhasa.

Gangki Corner of Mentsikhang Lu and Barkhor Square. This rooftop place is good value and has great views of the Jokhang. Very popular with Tibetans and often extremely busy. Main dishes cost ¥10–30; Tibetan tea and *tsampa* are also available. No toilets.

Lhasa Kitchen Mentsikhang Lu, opposite the *Snowlands Hotel*. Ignore the tacky lampshades and concentrate on the excellent Tibetan cuisine served in this upmarket but inexpensive place. Try soup with *shaphali* (meat and vegetable patties) followed by *deysee* (rice, raisins and yoghurt). Often overrun with parties of bloated Western tourists after 6pm.

Naga Mentsikhang Lu, just up from the *Lhasa Kitchen*. A cosy place that attempts a fusion of Nepalese and French food – *pot au feu de yak*, for example – with varying success.

Namtso In the *Banak Shol*, Beijing Dong Lu. This excellent eatery serves a set breakfast of sausage or bacon, plus eggs, toast, hash browns and tomatoes for ¥25. Other crowd-pleasers include the vegetable gratin, spinach patties and spaghetti bolognese.

New Mandala On the southwest corner of Barkhor Square, this two-level affair specializes in Nepali and Indian cuisine. The main draw is the rooftop seating area with a great view of the Jokhang. The *saag aloo* is fantastic, as is the ginger tea.

Outlook Outdoor Café Beijing Dong Lu, opposite the *Kirey*. Notable for a huge collection of *National Geographics*, and passable coffee.

Shangrila Restaurant In the courtyard of the *Kirey*. Pleasant Tibetan furnishings, with a large menu, though the food is designed not to tax the palate of any of the tour groups who invade en mass every evening to watch Tibetan singing and dancing (7pm).

Sichuan restaurants Beijing Dong Lu. Perhaps it's preferable to go Tibetan, but it has to be admitted that their Chinese counterparts make tastier food – the three little places here do inexpensive and delicious Sichuan food and hotpots.

Snowlands Restaurant Mentsikhang Lu. Tour group-friendly, long-established eatery with bland curries and standard Western and Tibetan dishes.

Tashi 1 and 2 Corner of Beijing Dong Lu and Mentsikhang Lu; in the *Kirey Hotel*. Sister restaurants – the *Tashi 2* is the rather more atmospheric of the two – that form the mainstay of budget travellers in Lhasa. Both offer the same small and inexpensive menu.

Tibet Summit Fine Art Café 1 Danjielin Lu, off Zangyi Lu. American-owned venture aiming to promote the arts in Tibet by serving up what are arguably the best cakes and coffee in the city amidst overpriced works by local artists.

Drinking and entertainment

There's a scattering of **bars** aimed at the well-off Chinese; most are on Beijing Zhong Lu, close to the *Lhasa Hotel*, and charges are comparable to those in the West. Best is the *Music Kitchen Café*, where beers are ¥20.

Sadly, there's not much chance to see **traditional Tibetan** music, dance and opera, unless you happen to be here during a festival. There are occasional shows put on for tourists; ask in your hotel or check for notices in the *Lhasa* or *Tibet* hotels, or look in on the *Shangrila Restaurant* (see above). In season, shows of Tibetan opera are sometimes held at the *Potala Hotel*, at the base of the Potala Palace in Shol village. Performances begin at 8 and 9.30pm and last one hour. Tickets cost ¥100, and should be bought in advance.

The **cinemas** on Yuthok Lu at the junction with Dosengge Lu, and on Beijing Dong Lu between the *Banak Shol* and *Kirey*, have some films from the West, but check whether they've been dubbed into Chinese before you bother.

Shopping

A major tourist activity in Lhasa is **shopping**. The main area for browsing is the **Barkhor**, where the better stuff is in the shops behind the stalls, but they're much more expensive than vendors outside. The vendors on the street outside the *Lhasa Hotel* have essentially the same range, but in smaller quantities, and they start off at even higher prices. The shop at the *Pentoc Hotel* has a good range of souvenirs, including **yak-wool jumpers** and socks. A string of gift shops on Mentsikhang Lu sells jewellery, handmade paper and the like. More handicrafts are available at Dropenling, at 11 Chaktsal Gang, just north of the mosque. Profits here go to local charities.

The search for **postcards** can be frustrating and expensive, as sets on offer at the main sights are generally pricey; those at the post office and the Xinhua Bookstores are the best value. For **film**, check out the photography shops on Kharnga Dong Lu, opposite People's Park. Most Internet cafés offer a **CD-burning** service for around ¥25, but it only costs around ¥15 at the photo-shops along Kharnga Dong Lu.

Some travellers buy **bikes** here and ride them to Nepal, where they can be sold, sometimes at a profit (see p.1095 for more on the practicalities of cycling the Freedom Highway). There is now a wealth of bikes on offer in Lhasa, mostly from the clutch of shops around the cinema on Beijing Dong Lu, and even in its entrance (see "Listings, p.1110, for more).

Finally, if you feel like doing some shopping *for* rather than *from* Tibetans, buy notebooks and pens to donate to an orphanage and give them to Neema at the *Snowlands Restaurant*. Alternatively, turn up at the orphanage itself, at 42 Beijing Xi Lu.

Books

If you're very lucky, you might find the odd, classic English novel in one of the two Xinhua Bookstores on Yuthok Lu and on Beijing Xi Lu, just east of the *Tibet Hotel*. The best on offer is the coffee-table paperback *Potala Palace*, with good pictures of many of the treasures in the Potala that either will be closed off when you're there or you'll fail to notice as you're too overwhelmed. The hardback glossies, *Tibet* and *Snowland Tibet*, are both pricey and heavy, but have evocative photographs taken throughout the country. If you're into Buddhist art, take a look at the even glossier and heavier *Precious True Word Picture Album of the Buddha, Images of Buddhism*.

For a Tibetan **novel**, get hold of *The Secret Tale of Tesur House*, sold in the *Banak Shol* and the shop at the *Pentoc Hotel*. The first fiction translated from Tibetan into English, it's not a bad read, with a plot centred on gory murders and business intrigue. It's full of fascinating descriptions of Tibetan life and customs – the kind of minutiae that you won't find described elsewhere.

The Guxuna Bookshop, at the junction of Beijing Dong Lu and Mentsikhang Lu, has a Tibetan phrasebook with tape, plus a plethora of Chinese- and English-language propaganda.

Carpets and paintings

If it's **carpets** you're after, visit Khawachen, at 103 Chingdol Xi Lu (Mon–Sat 9am–6.30pm; ⓣ0891/6333255), on the route of the #2 minibus. This government-affiliated and US-financed organization offers the best selection of carpets in Lhasa and the chance to watch them being produced, and can also arrange to ship the merchandise home for you. Available in muted, attractive, traditional designs, plus some with a modern slant, the carpets range from 50 square centimetres (US$25) to 2.7m x 3.6m (US$1300). The Lhasa Carpet Factory, out of town on Chingdol Dong Lu (Mon–Fri 9am–1pm & 3.30–6pm, Sat 9am–1pm; ⓣ0891/6323447), is a bigger operation, where you can watch huge carpets being woven; an extensive range of traditional and modern patterns is available here, costing from ¥140 to ¥32,000. Shipping can also be arranged. In town, the

Shambhala carpet shop on Jiri Erxiang (right out of the *Kirey* and first right) has a selection of on-site crafted rugs and carpets which again can be shipped back home for you after purchase.

Tibetan **thangkas** (religious scrolls) and religious and secular **paintings** would appear to be obvious souvenirs, but many are of poor quality – best to spend some time browsing before you buy. The least expensive *thangkas* – you'll find masses of these in the Barkhor – have a printed religious picture in the middle, while the better quality, higher-priced ones have a hand-painted image. Look carefully, though, at the quality of the painting itself: the best ones have finely drawn and highly detailed backgrounds; the less skilled artists leave larger areas of the canvas blank, with less meticulously painted details. The asking prices are high; bargain hard. An excellent range of good-quality, hand-painted *thangkas* is available at the **Tibet Traditional Art Gallery**, just a shop, despite the name, next door to the Ramoche – expect prices starting at ¥3000. Look also in the shops in Shol village just inside the entrance to the Potala Palace and in the *Lhasa Hotel* lobby shop (daily 9am–8pm), which has a range of paintings (¥500–2500) and will give you some idea of the top end of the scale.

Clothes

There are plenty of **tailors** in town, both Chinese and Tibetan, who can make traditional Tibetan or Western clothes; look on Beijing Dong Lu west of the *Yak Hotel*. A huge range of materials, from light, summer-weight stuff, to heavier, warmer textiles, is available. Prices depend on the material, but light jackets start around ¥100, while skirts, trousers or a floor-length Tibetan woman's dress (*chuba*) cost ¥80 and up. Many places have samples made up and you can simply shop around until you find the style and material you want. From first measuring to collecting the finished item, usually takes 24 hours.

Trekking equipment

For rucksacks, sleeping bags and serious **hiking gear**, check out Outlook Outdoor Equipment on Beijing Dong Lu, opposite the *Kirey* (Ⓦwww.ontheway.com.cn). Export-quality Chinese sleeping bags cost anywhere from ¥80 to ¥600 (¥20–30 a day to rent), and two- or three-person tents, rucksacks, Karrimats and stoves are ¥30–40 per day to rent. Nikko Outdoor Commodities on Mentsikhan Lu, opposite the *Naga*, also has a good selection of gear at some of the best prices in town, with very helpful English-speaking staff.

Listings

Airlines CAAC, Nyangrain Lu (open 24hr; Ⓣ0891/6833446).

Banks and exchange There are several branches of the Bank of China around town, but the main one on Lingkuo Bei Lu, north of the Golden Yaks Statue (Mon–Fri 9am–1pm & 3.30–6pm), is the only place in Tibet for cash advances on credit cards. The branch on Beijing Dong Lu is conveniently located close to the *Banak Shol* (Mon–Fri 9.30am–6pm, Sat & Sun 11am–3pm).

Bike rental The *Snowlands* and *Pentoc* offer a small range of clunky bikes for rent at ¥30 a day. Bikeshops on Beijing Dong Lu offer better bikes, often at better rates, but large deposits are required.

Consulates The Nepalese Consulate, 13 Norbulingka Lu (Mon–Fri 10am–noon; Ⓣ0891/6830609), has a next-day visa service, for which you'll need to submit one passport photograph. Single-entry visas cost ¥135 for fifteen days, ¥225 for thirty days; multiple-entry visas are ¥360 for thirty days, ¥540 for sixty days. You can get single-entry visas at Kodari (see p.1138), but payment there has to be in US dollars.

Hospital First People's Hospital, Lingkuo Bei Lu (Mon–Fri 10am–12.30pm & 4–6pm; at weekends, emergencies only). It's better to go in the morning when more staff are available, and you'll need to take a Chinese translator.

Internet access Cybercafés are not hard to find in Lhasa now. The most notable being next to the

Trekking Tibet

For the experienced hiker, Tibet offers plenty of enticing **trekking routes**. The popular Ganden–Samye trek (see box, p.1116) has the advantages that both the start and finish points are relatively accessible from Lhasa and that it takes only three to four days. Also worth considering are treks to the cave hermitage of **Drak Yerpa** from Lhasa (allow a full day and be prepared to camp), and the five-day trek from Tingri to **Everest Base Camp** via Rongbuk. You'd be advised to take a guide for this.

More challenging options include: the sixteen-day mammoth trek to the **Kangshung** face of Everest, exploring the valleys east of the mountain (the trip to second base camp and beyond on the mountain itself should only be tackled by experienced climbers); the 24-day circumnavigation of Namtso lake, including the arduous exploration of the Shang Valley to the southwest; and the great thirty-day circuit (a guide is highly recommended) from Lhatse to **Lake Dangra** up on the Chang Tang plateau.

Spring (April–June) and autumn (Sept–Nov) are the best **seasons** in which to trek, though cold-weather threats such as hypothermia and frostbite should be taken seriously even in these months. While trekking is possible at any time in the valleys, high altitudes become virtually impossible in the winter; anyone contemplating trekking at this time should be sure to get local information about the terrain and likely conditions. During the wettest months (June–Sept), rivers are in flood, and crossing them can be difficult, even impossible. Once you start trekking, you get off the beaten track extremely quickly and there is no infrastructure to support trekkers and no rescue service; you therefore need to be fit, acclimatized, totally self-reliant and prepared to do some research before you go. There are two essential books: *Tibet Handbook: a Pilgrimage Guide* by Victor Chan (Moon), and *Trekking in Tibet* by Gary McCue (Cordee), which is especially good for shorter day-treks that anyone can do without all the gear.

Dong Cun Cuo Youth Hostel, in the *Shangrila* bar, and in the *Banok Shol*, all on Beijing Dong Lu.

Mail and telephones The main post office is on Beijing Dong Lu, just east of the Potala Palace (daily 9am–8pm). Poste restante and international customs (Mon–Fri 9.30am–1pm & 3.30–6pm) is the counter facing you on the far left as you enter. Mail to be collected here should be addressed Poste Restante, Main Post Office, Lhasa, Tibet, China. Check both the book that lists mail received at the office and ask to see new mail. There's a charge of ¥1.5 per item received. EMS collection is next door to the post office opposite the Potala Palace, while over the road is a 24hr office with direct-dialling facilities and a fax service.

Pharmacies Most are along Yuthok Lu around the junction with Dosengge Lu. There is a pharmacy specializing in Tibetan medicine on the north side of Barkhor Square. Again, you'll need a translator.

PSB Lingkuo Bei Lu and also Beijing Dong Lu (both Mon–Fri 9.30am–1pm & 3.30–7pm). While PSB offices should be the place to go for factual information about closed and open areas, the information is rarely reliable and frequently inconsistent from one office to the next. The office on Beijing Dong Lu is larger and handles permits and visa extensions.

Tour Agencies These are all over town, and all offer much the same services, but the official agency FIT, in the courtyards of the *Banak Shol* and *Snowlands Hotel* is sometimes able to offer trips the others cannot. One of the most trusted agents in town is the Tibet Shigatse International Travel Information Centre, (Ⓣ0891/6912080, Ⓔb4melone@yahoo.com) on Mentisikhang Lu, on the right as you walk down to Borkhar Square. Ask for Tenzing, who can help you custom-design tours with a full breakdown of costs, and even join you up with other parties, space permitting.

Around Lhasa

Not only is Lhasa awash with enough sights to keep even the most energetic visitor busy for several days, but the major monasteries of **Sera**, **Drepung**,

Around Lhasa

Drepung Monastery	哲蚌寺	*zhébàng sì*
Ganden Monastery	甘丹寺	*gāndān sì*
Samye Monastery	桑木耶寺	*sāngmùyē sì*
Sera Monastery	色拉寺	*sèlā sì*

Nechung and **Ganden** are easily accessible from the city as half-day or day-trips. Indeed, Sera and Drepung have virtually been gobbled up in the urban sprawl that now characterizes Lhasa, while the trip to Ganden is a good chance to get out into the countryside. Morning visits to any of them are likely to be in the company of parties of devout pilgrims who'll scurry around the temples making their offerings before heading on to the next target. Follow on behind them and you'll visit all the main buildings; don't worry too much if you aren't sure what you are looking at – most of the pilgrims haven't a clue either. The monasteries are generally peaceful and atmospheric places where nobody minds you ambling at will, and sooner or later you're bound to come across some monks who want to practise their English. Nearby, the walled, combined village and monastery of **Samye** is not only the most ancient in Tibet, but also a lively and interesting place to spend a day or two.

Sera Monastery

To reach **Sera Monastery** (Mon–Sat 9am–4pm; ¥50), 4km north of Lhasa, by public transport, take a #5 **minibus** from the southern end of Nyangrain Lu, or from the small minibus stand opposite the cinema on Yuthok Lu. You'll either be dropped on the road, about 500m outside the white-walled monastery compound, or be taken along the track to the entrance. To get transport back, it's better to walk back out to the road. The last minibuses leave just after the end of the debating at about 5pm. Alternatively, you can cycle there – it's surprisingly close.

Founded in 1419 by Sakya Yeshe, one of the main disciples of Tsongkhapa, founder of the Gelugpa order, Sera is situated below a hermitage where the great man spent many years in retreat. Spared during the Cultural Revolution, the

Life in the great monasteries

Fifty years ago, there were still six great, functioning **Gelugpa monasteries**: Sera, Drepung and Ganden near Lhasa, plus Tashilunpo in Shigatse (see p.1130), Labrang (see p.998) and Kumbum (see p.1126). They each operated on a similar system to cope with the huge numbers of monks that were drawn to these major institutions from all over Tibet. In their heyday, Sera and Ganden had five thousand residents each and Drepung (possibly the largest monastery the world has ever known) had between eight and ten thousand.

Each monastery was divided into colleges, **dratsang**, which differed from each other in the type of studies undertaken. Each college was under the management of an abbot (*khenpo*), and a monk responsible for discipline (*ge-kor*). Attached to each college were a number of houses or *khangsten*, where the monks lived during their time at the monastery. Usually, these houses catered for students from different geographical regions, and admission to the monastery was controlled by the heads of the houses to whom aspirant monks would apply. Each college had its own assembly hall and chapels, but there was also a main assembly hall where the entire community could gather.

buildings are in good repair, although there is always a fair amount of ongoing building work. Pilgrims proceed on a clockwise circuit, visiting the three main **colleges** – Sera Me, Sera Ngag-Pa and Sera Je – and the main assembly hall, Tsokchen. All are constructed with chapels leading off a central hall and more chapels on an upper floor. They're great places to linger and watch the pilgrims rushing about their devotions. However, if you just want to catch the flavour of the most dramatic buildings, head straight up the hill from the main entrance. After a couple of hundred metres, you'll reach the **Tsokchen**, Sera's largest building, built in 1710. The hall is supported by over a hundred columns, and it's here, between statues of the Fifth and Thirteenth Dalai Lamas, that you'll find the main statue of Sakya Yeshe, the founder of the monastery. The *Sakya Yeshe* statue is a reproduction of the original one in Sera Ngag-Pa college. When there were plans to move the original to the Tsokchen, the story goes that the statue itself said that it wished to stay in the college, so a copy was made.

At the top of the path, the walled and shady **debating courtyard** is definitely worth a visit at 3.30pm, when the monks assemble in small animated groups to practise their highly stylized debating skills, involving much posturing, clapping and stamping. They're used to visitors – indeed, it's hard not to suspect the whole circus is put on for visitors – and there seems to be no problem about taking photographs.

To the left of the courtyard, the college of **Sera Je** is the best college to visit if you manage only one. Its spacious assembly hall is hung with fine *thangkas*, but the focus for pilgrims here is the Hayagriva Chapel (Hayagriva or Tamdrin, "the Horse-Headed One", is the protective deity of Sera), reached via an entrance in the left-hand wall.

If you're feeling energetic, take the path up the hillside, from behind the Tsokchen (follow the telegraph wires) to **Choding Khang** (Tsongkhapa's Hermitage), which is a reconstruction of the original – his meditation cave is a bit farther up. There are splendid views over Lhasa from here.

Drepung and Nechung monasteries

Once the largest monastery in the world, **Drepung Monastery** was an immediate success, and a year after opening, there were already two thousand

Not every member of the community spent their time in scholarly pursuits. Communities the size of these took huge amounts of organization, and the largest monasteries also maintained large estates worked by serfs. About half the monks might be engaged in academic study while the other half worked at administration, the supervision of the estate work and the day-to-day running of what was essentially a small town.

The most obvious feature of these **monasteries today** is their emptiness; hundreds of monks now rattle around in massive compounds built for thousands. Such has been the fate of religious establishments under the Chinese and the flow of lamas into exile that there are now questions about the quality of the Buddhist education available at the monasteries inside Tibet. Monks and nuns nowadays need to be vetted and receive Chinese-government approval before they can join a monastery or convent, and although there are persistent rumours of tourists being informed on by monks, it's also apparent that both monks and nuns have been, and continue to be, at the forefront of open political opposition to the Chinese inside Tibet.

monks in residence, and ten thousand by the time of the Fifth Dalai Lama (1617–82). To reach Drepung, 8km west of Lhasa, catch the #3 **minibus** from the stand at the junction of Dossenge Lu and Beijing Dong Lu. It may drop you on the main road (¥2), leaving you with a thirty-minute walk, or carry on up the hill to the entrance of the massive, walled monastery (¥3). Minibuses come back to Lhasa infrequently from the monastery itself, and it's better to walk down the hill to Nechung and then out to the main road to pick up transport there. Easily combined with a trip to Drepung is the eerie **Nechung Monastery**, less than 1km southeast of Drepung and reached by a well-trodden path.

Drepung Monastery

Drepung Monastery (daily 9am–6pm, chapels closed noon–3pm; ¥40) was founded in 1416 by Jamyang Choje, a leading disciple of Tsongkhapa. Although it has been sacked three times – in 1618 by the king of Tsang, in 1635 by the Mongols, and in the early eighteenth century by the Dzungars – there was relatively little damage during the Cultural Revolution.

Drepung is a huge place, and it's easy to attempt to see everything and get overloaded. One thing to make sure to do is to go up on to the **roofs** – the views across the Kyichu Valley are splendid – and it's definitely worth spending a bit of time just wandering the alleyways, through courtyards, and past ancient doorways.

The easiest way to find your way around is to follow the clockwise pilgrim circuit. This leads left from the entrance up to the grand and imposing **Ganden Palace**, built in 1530 by the Second Dalai Lama, and home to the Dalai Lamas until the Fifth incarnation moved to the Potala Palace. The private quarters of the Dalai Lama are behind the balcony at the top right-hand side of the building, but there's little to see inside.

The next stop is the **Tsokchen**, the main assembly hall, its entrance via a small door on the left-hand side, facing the building. Its roof supported by over 180 solid wooden columns, the hall is the highlight of Drepung, a space of awesome size and scale. The *thangkas* and brocade hangings add to the incredible ambience, with dust motes highlighted by the rays of the sun slanting down from the high windows. The main chapel at the rear of the hall is the **Buddha of the Three Ages Chapel**, the most impressive in Drepung, with statues crammed together in such profusion the mind reels. The central figures are Sakyamuni with his two main disciples, Shariputra and Maudgalyayana.

There are two upper storeys, both definitely worth a visit. On the next floor up, the **Maitreya Chapel** contains the head and shoulders of a massive statue of Maitreya at a young age, commissioned by Tsongkhapa himself, while the **Tara Chapel** contains a version of the *Kanjur*, sacred Buddhist scriptures, dating from the time of the Fifth Dalai Lama. In the middle of the volumes, which are loose leaves stored between wooden planks and wrapped in brocade, sits a statue of Prajnaparamita, the Mother of Buddhas; the amulet on her lap is said to contain a tooth of Tsongkhapa's. Of the three chapels on the top floor, the highlight is the stunning statue of the head of Maitreya, boasting exquisite gold ornamentation.

Behind the Tsokchen, there's a tiny **Manjusri Temple**, obligatory for the pilgrims who make offerings to the image of the Bodhisattva of Wisdom, carved out of a large rock. The remainder of the circuit is taken up with the **Ngag-Pa College**, to the northwest of the Tsokchen, and **Loseling**, **Gomang and Deyang colleges** to the southeast. They all have items of interest – the stuffed goat at the entrance to the Protector Chapel on the upper storey of Loseling, the cosy Deyang, and the wonderful array of statues in the central chapel of Gomang – but don't feel too bad if you've had enough by now. The main steps of the Tsokchen, looking across the huge courtyard in front of the building, are a good place to sit and admire the view and watch the comings and goings of the other visitors.

Nechung Monastery

Nechung Monastery (daily 9am–6pm, chapels closed noon–3pm; ¥10) was, until 1959, the seat of the **state oracle of Tibet**. By means of complex ritual and chanting, an oracle enters a trance and becomes the mouthpiece of a god, in this case Dorje Drakden, the chief minister of the main spiritual protector of Tibet, Pehar Gyalpo; no important decisions are made by the Dalai Lama or government without reference to Drakden. The original shrine on the site was built in the twelfth century, and the Fifth Dalai Lama built the temple later. It was much damaged during the Cultural Revolution, but restoration work is now proceeding quickly. The state oracle fled Tibet in the footsteps of the Dalai Lama in 1959, having questioned Dorje Drakden himself as to what he should do. He died in 1985 in Dharamsala, but a successor has been identified there.

Nechung's spookiness begins outside. The beggars are abject, the villagers seem sullen. Inside you are confronted by a panoply of gore – the doors are decorated with images of flayed human skins and the murals in the courtyard depict torture by devils and people drowning in a sea of blood. In the chapels, unusually subdued supplicants are more likely to offer booze than apples. Bloodshot eyes sunk into the sockets of grinning skulls seem to follow you around.

Upstairs, the main room is the audience chamber, where the Dalai Lama would come to consult the oracle. The inner chapel is dedicated to Tsongkhapa, whose statue is between those of his two main disciples, Gyeltsab Je and Khedrup Je. In the only chapel at roof level is the statue of Padmasambhava that, though it dates from the early 1980s, is gloriously bedecked in old Chinese brocade. It's worth the climb up here, if only to escape from the air of sinister corruption below.

Ganden Monastery

Situated farther from Lhasa than the other main temples, **Ganden Monastery** (daily 9am–4pm; ¥25) is 45km east of Lhasa, the final 6km of the journey being along a winding track off the Lhasa–Sichuan Highway. It is also the most dramatically situated, high up on the Gokpori Ridge, with excellent views over the surrounding countryside. To get here, take the **pilgrim bus**, which leaves Lhasa daily at 6.30am from the west side of Barkhor Square (3–4hr; ¥20) and returns at 2pm.

Founded by Tsongkhapa himself in 1410 on a site associated with King Songtsen Gampo and his queens, the main hall was not completed until 1417, two years before Tsongkhapa died after announcing his disciple, Gyeltsab Je, as the new **Ganden Tripa**, the leader of the Gelugpa order. The appointment is not based on reincarnation but on particular academic qualifications. The Chinese have always particularly targeted Ganden, possibly because it is the main seat of the Dalai Lama's order, and what you see today is all reconstruction.

While it is possible, as always, to follow the pilgrims through the various buildings on their circuit, the highlight is the imposing **Serdung Lhakhang**, on the left side as you follow the main path north from the car park. This temple contains a huge gold and silver *chorten*. The original contained the body of Tsongkhapa, who was said to have changed into a 16-year-old youth when he died. The body was embalmed and placed in the *chorten* and, when the Red Guards broke it open during the Cultural Revolution, they supposedly found the body perfectly preserved, with the hair and fingernails still growing. Only a few pieces of skull survived the destruction and they are in the reconstructed *chorten*. Up the hill and to the right, the **Sertrikhang** houses the golden throne of Tsongkhapa and all later Ganden Tripas; the bag on the throne contains the yellow hat of the present Dalai Lama.

Be sure to allow time to walk the **Ganden kora**, the path around the monastery. The views are startling and it takes about an hour to follow round. There is a basic **guesthouse** at the monastery, used mostly by people heading off on the Ganden–Samye **trek** (see below).

Samye

A visit to **SAMYE**, on the north bank of the Tsangpo River, is a highlight of Tibet. A unique monastery and walled village rolled into one, it's situated in wonderful scenery and, however you arrive, the journey is splendid. You can climb the sacred Hepo Ri to the east of the complex for excellent views (1hr); it was here that Padmasambhava is said to have subdued the local spirits and won them over to Buddhism.

The monastery

Tibet's first monastery, **Samye** was founded in the eighth century during King Trisong Detsen's reign, with the help of the Indian masters Padmasambhava and Shantarakshita, whom he had invited to Tibet to help spread the Buddhist faith. The first Tibetan Buddhist monks were ordained here after examination and are referred to as the "Seven Examined Men". Over the years, Samye has been associated with several of the schools of Tibetan Buddhism – Padmasambhava's involvement in the founding of the monastery makes it important in the Nyingma school, and later it was taken over by the Sakya and Gelugpa traditions. Nowadays, followers of all traditions worship here, and Samye is a popular destination for Tibetan pilgrims, some of whom travel for weeks to reach it.

The design of the extensive monastery complex, several hundred metres in diameter, is of a giant **mandala**, a representation of the Buddhist universe, styled after the Indian temple of Odantapuri in Bihar. The main temple, the **utse**, represents Buddha's palace on the summit of Mount Meru, the mythical mountain at the centre of the Buddhist universe. The four continents in the vast ocean around Mount Meru are represented by the *lingshi* temples, a couple of hundred metres away at the cardinal points, each flanked by two smaller temples, *lingtren*, representing islands in the ocean. The *utse* is surrounded by

The Ganden–Samye trek

Though popular, the **Ganden–Samye trek** is no less serious and demanding than other treks. The route, which takes four days to complete, crosses the mountains that divide the **Kyichu Valley** from that of the Tsangpo and travels through high mountain passes and alpine pasture to the dry, almost desert-like countryside around Samye. The trek goes by **Hebu** village (three hours south of Ganden and a good place to hire yaks and guides) and involves camping out or sleeping in caves or nomad encampments, long climbs to the Jooker La and Sukhe La passes, and some deep-river wading.

four giant *chortens*, each several storeys high, at the corners, and there are *nyima* (sun) and *dawa* (moon) temples to the north and south respectively. A renovated enclosing wall topped by 1008 tiny *chortens* with gates at the cardinal points flanks the whole complex. This sounds hugely ordered, but the reality is far more confusing and fun. Samye has suffered much damage and restoration over the years; today, you'll find the temples dotted among houses, barns and animal pens, with only a few of the original 108 buildings on the site remaining in their entirety.

The utse

The **utse** (daily 9am–12.30pm & 3–5pm; ¥40) is a grand, six-storey construction and needs a couple of hours to see thoroughly. Be sure to take a torch as there are some good murals tucked away in shadowy corners.

The grand, main assembly hall dominates the first floor, with fine, old *mandalas* on the high ceiling. On either side of the entrance to the main chapel are statues of historical figures associated with the monastery. Those on the left include Shantarakshita, Padmasambhava (said to be a good likeness of him), Trisong Detsen and Songtsen Gampo. The impressive main chapel, **Jowo Khang**, is reached through three tall doorways and is home to a Sakyamuni statue showing Buddha at the age of 38. To the left of the assembly hall is a small temple, **Chenresi Lhakhang**, housing a gorgeous statue of Chenresi with an eye meticulously painted on the palm of each of his thousand hands – if you look at nothing else in Samye, search this out. To the right of the main assembly hall is the **Gonkhang**, a protector chapel, with all the statues heavily and dramatically draped. Most of the deities here were established as the demons of the Bon religion and were adopted by Buddhism as the fierce protectors – the chapel is an eerie place, imbued with centuries' worth of fear.

Although the first floor is the most impressive, the upper storeys are also worth a look. The **second floor** is an open roof area, where monks and local people carry out the craftwork needed for the temple. The highlight of the **third floor** is the **Quarters of the Dalai Lama**, consisting of a small anteroom, a throne room and a bedroom. A securely barred, glass-fronted case in the bedroom is stuffed full of fantastic relics, including Padmasambhava's hair and walking stick, a Tara statue that is reputed to speak, and the skull of the Indian master Shantarakshita. The Tibetan pilgrims take this room very seriously and the crush of bodies may mean you can't linger as long as you would like. From the **fourth floor** up, you'll see only recent reconstruction, but the views from the balconies are extensive.

The surrounding buildings

The rest of the buildings in the complex are in varying stages of renovation. Unashamedly modern, the four coloured **chortens** are each slightly different, and visitors love or hate them. There are internal stairs and tiny interior chapels, but generally they are more dramatic from a distance. It's difficult to locate the outer temples accurately and many are still awaiting renovation – some serve as barns and stables, others show the effects of the Cultural Revolution. The most finely worked murals in Samye are in **Mani Lhakhang**, now a chapel in a house compound in the northwest of the complex, but the occupants are happy for visitors to look around.

Practicalities

Permits are needed for Samye, but the PSB in Tsetang will issue them only if you have arranged a tour. That said, the PSB rarely check up on foreigners except at festival times. The Lhasa–Tsetang road runs along the south bank of the Tsangpo and is served by public transport from both ends. To reach the monastery, you'll need to cross the river via the **Samye ferry**, 33km from Tsetang and 150km from Lhasa. Ferries leave when full and are more frequent in the morning, but run until mid-afternoon. The crossing (¥3, although foreigners are charged ¥10) is highly picturesque and takes an hour or more as the boats wind their way among the sandbanks inhabited by Brahmini ducks, grebes and plovers. On the other side, tractors (45min; ¥5) and trucks (30min; ¥3) ply the bumpy 8km to Samye through rolling, deforested sand dunes, newly planted here and there with willows. If you want to make life easier for yourself, just get the bus from Barkhor Square (¥40) between 6 and 8am, returning at 2pm. The small, white-painted *chortens* carved out of the hillside about halfway along mark the place where King Trisong Detsen met Padmasambhava when he came to Samye in the eighth century. **Leaving**, a very useful truck departs from the front of the *utse* each morning at 8am to connect with the ferry and a Lhasa-bound bus on the other side of the river. In addition, local tractors and trucks run until mid-afternoon, but you may well have to wait at the ferry and on the other side of the river for connections.

The only place to stay at Samye is the **guesthouse** next to the *utse*, which provides comfortable, cheap dorm accommodation (❶). The monastery **restaurant** is just north of the *utse*, but a better option is the newer establishment opposite the east reception office near the east gate. There's no menu in either place; you negotiate based on what they have. There are several small shops in the monastery complex that are well stocked with tinned goods, beer, confectionery and even Chinese wine.

Tsetang and around

The town of **Tsetang**, southeast of Lhasa and just south of the Tsangpo River, and the nearby valleys of **Yarlung** and **Chongye**, are steeped in ancient history. Legend claims the first Tibetans originated on the slopes of Gongpo Ri to the east of Tsetang, and that the Yarlung Valley was where the first king of Tibet descended from the heavens to earth upon a sky-cord. This king then fathered the first royal dynasty, many members of which are buried in the nearby **Chongye Valley**. The Yarlung Valley was also where, in the fourth century, the first Buddhist scriptures fell from the sky upon the first king's palace at **Yumbulakhang**.

Tsetang is easily accessible via a good road and public transport from Lhasa. However, there is no public transport in the Yarlung and Chongye valleys, although **getting around** by hitching lifts on tractors is feasible for the former. Transport out to Chongye is more limited. The best way to explore is to hire a vehicle and driver in Tsetang to take you to Chongye and Yumbulakhang on a day-trip. For vehicle rental, try the *Tsetang Hotel* first, then the *Gesar* restaurant opposite – after hard bargaining, expect to pay around ¥350 for the day.

Tsetang is also the starting point for a trip to **Lhamo Lhatso**, a sacred lake 115km northeast of Tsetang where visions on the surface of the water are believed to contain prophecies. Regents searching for the next incarnations of high lamas come here for clues, and Dalai Lamas have traditionally visited for hints about the future. Buses leave the main Tsetang intersection on Monday and Friday for **Gyatsa** (returning the next day), where you have to walk across

Tsetang and around		
Chongye	阱结	jǐngjié
Tsetang	泽当	zédāng
Yarlung Valley	雅鲁鲁流域	yǎlǔlǔ liúyù
Trandruk Si	昌珠寺	chāngzhū sì
Yumbulakhang	雍布拉康	yōngbùlākāng

the bridge and pick up another ride up to Chokorgye Monastery and then trek for around five hours up to the lake. You should bring your own food and be prepared to camp, unless you're intending a long day's walking.

Keep in mind that the **permit** situation here is unclear. The PSB in Tsetang should issue permits to Yarlung, Chongye, Samye and Lhamo Lhatso, but at the time of writing refused to do so unless you were on an organized tour with your own transport and guide – for which purpose, you'll be quoted ¥2000–2500 in Lhasa to rent a jeep and driver for three days and two nights.

Tsetang

There is little to recommend an extended stay in the town of **TSETANG**, administrative centre of Lhoka province, a region stretching from the Tsangpo down to the Bhutan border. However, Tsetang is largely unavoidable as a base for explorations of the area.

Heading south from the main traffic intersection along Naidong Lu, take a narrow left turn through the small, bustling market into the **Tibetan area** of town, a typical jumble of walled compounds swarming with unwelcoming dogs, and children scrapping in the dust. The largest monastery and the first you'll come to is **Ganden Chukorlin** (¥5), now bright and gleaming from restoration, having been used as a storeroom for many years. It was founded in the mid-eighteenth century on the site of an earlier monastery, and there are good views of the Tibetan quarter from the roof. At the nearby fourteenth-century **Narchu Monastery** (¥5), restoration is less complete, but it's worth stopping by for the three unusual, brown-painted Sakyamuni statues on the altar. A little farther up the hill, the **Sanarsensky Nunnery** (¥5) was one of the first of its kind in Tibet. It was founded in the fourteenth century in the Sakya tradition but later became a Gelugpa establishment.

Practicalities

Daily **public buses** leave Lhasa between 6 and 8am from Barkhor Square and run as far as the Samye ferry point (4hr; ¥26). You'll then need to pick up another bus or a minibus for the remaining 33km on to Tsetang (¥15) – it's a bit hit-and-miss, but you shouldn't have to wait more than an hour or so. Alternatively, direct **minibuses** leave the main bus station in Lhasa for Tsetang from 8am onwards (3hr; ¥35) – they may not be willing to take foreigners, although there are no checkpoints between Lhasa and Tsetang. Tsetang's **bus station** is about 500m west of the main traffic intersection in town.

Unfortunately, **accommodation** in Tsetang is not particularly good, and is terribly expensive (typically costing over ¥500 for a double room). Turn right at the intersection on to Naidong Lu past the post office and numerous restaurants and you'll come to the only comparatively cheap hotel that will take foreigners, the *Postal House* (❹), though with dingy rooms and sullied corridors, it's far from a bargain. Continue down the road and you'll come to the grossly overpriced *Tsetang Hotel* (Ⓣ0893/21899, Ⓕ21688; ❽). Naidong Lu itself is lined with bars and **restaurants**.

The Yarlung Valley

Though the **Yarlung Valley** is renowned as the seat of the first Tibetan kings, these days it is the dramatically sited and picturesque **Yumbulakhang**, the first Tibetan palace, which draws visitors to the area. The road due south from Naidong Lu in Tsetang to Yumbulakhang is fairly busy, and it's possible to hitch a lift without too much trouble (there's no public transport).

Trandruk Monastery

The small but significant **Trandruk Monastery** (¥70), 7km south of Tsetang, is a grand and imposing structure. One of the earliest Buddhist temples in Tibet, Trandruk was built in the seventh century during the reign of King Songtsen Gampo, and is one of the twelve Demon-Suppressing Temples (see p.1104) – Trandruk anchors the demoness's left shoulder to the earth. Legend tells how the site chosen for Trandruk was covered by a large lake containing a five-headed dragon. King Songtsen Gampo emerged from a period of meditation with such power that he was able to summon a supernatural falcon to defeat the dragon and drink the water of the lake, leaving the earth ready for Trandruk (meaning Falcon-Dragon). Damaged during the Bon reaction against Buddhism in the ninth century, and again by Dzungar invaders in the eighteenth century, the temple then suffered the loss of many highly prized religious relics and objects, following the Chinese invasion. Its remaining glory is the **Pearl Thangka**, an image of King Songtsen Gampo's wife, Princess Wencheng, as the White Tara, created from thousands of tiny pearls meticulously sewn onto a pink background. This is in the central chapel upstairs, which also houses an original statue of Padmasambhava at the age of 8.

Yumbulakhang

From afar, the fortress temple of **Yumbulakhang** (¥70), 12km south of Tsetang, appears dwarfed by the scale of the Yarlung Valley. But once you get close, and make the thirty-minute climb up the spur on which it is perched, the drama of the position and the airiness of the site are apparent. Widely regarded as the work of the first king of Tibet, Nyatri Tsenpo, when he arrived in Yarlung, the original Yumbulakhang would have been over two thousand years old and the oldest building in Tibet when it was almost totally destroyed during the Cultural Revolution. The present building is a 1982 reconstruction in two parts, with a small, two-storey chapel and an eleven-metre-high tower. The lower floor of the **chapel** is dedicated to the early Tibetan kings: Nyatri Tsenpo is to the left and Songtsen Gampo to the right of the central Buddha statue. The delightful and unusual upper-storey chapel, with Chenresi as the central image, is built on a balcony. Some of the modern murals up here show legendary events in Tibetan history; look out on the left for Nyatri Tsenpo and for the Buddhist scriptures descending from heaven. The energetic can ascend by ladders almost to the top of the tower where King Nyatri Tsenpo supposedly meditated. The deep, slit windows at knee level mean the views aren't that wonderful, however; for the best scenery, take a walk up to the ridge behind the temple.

The Chongye Valley

From Tsetang it's a bumpy 27km south along unsurfaced roads through the attractive **Chongye Valley** to the village of **CHONGYE**, a sleepy little place currently expanding with plenty of new buildings. There are a couple of restaurants and a basic guesthouse here, but you'll need to ask to find it. On the way, you'll pas the **Tangoboche Monastery**. However, the target for most visitors, the **Tombs of the Kings**, is around a kilometre farther south from the Chongye. The entire valley is an agricultural development area and the patchwork of fields is interspersed with irrigation work. Be warned, though, that there's no **public transport** out here from Tsetang, and very little traffic either.

Tangboche Monastery

On the east side of the valley, about 20km southeast of Tsetang, **Tangboche Monastery** is situated at the base of the hill and is somewhat difficult to spot among the village houses. It was founded in the eleventh century, and the great Tsongkhapa, founder of the Gelugpa tradition, is thought to have stayed here in the fourteenth century. Take a torch so you can really appreciate the most interesting features here – genuine old murals, commissioned in 1915 by the Thirteenth Dalai Lama, are too numerous to list. Look out in particular for Pelden Lhamo on the left as you enter, and, on the right-hand wall, Padmasambhava, Trisong Detsen and Shantarakshita. The artistry and detail of subject and background make an interesting comparison with some of the more modern painting you'll see in Tibet. A couple of hundred metres up the hill is the **hermitage** where the scholar Atisha spent some time in the eleventh century. It's small and recently renovated and, not surprisingly, dominated by rather lurid images of the Indian master. A much-revered statue of Atisha and a set of texts brought by him from India were lost in the Cultural Revolution.

The Tombs of the Kings

One kilometre south of Chongye, the **Tombs of the Kings** are scattered over a vast area on and around the slopes of Mura Ri. Some are huge, up to 200m in length and 30m high. The body of each king was buried along with statues, precious objects and, some sources suggest, live servants. Some of the greatest kings of the Yarlung dynasty were buried here, although there is disagreement over the precise number of tombs – some sources claim it's 21, but far fewer are visible, and there is uncertainty about which tomb belongs to which king.

For the best view of the entire area, climb the largest tomb, **Bangso Marpo** (Red Tomb), belonging to **Songtsen Gampo**, just beside the road that heads south along the valley; it's easily identifiable by the chapel on the top. Songtsen Gampo, supposedly embalmed and incarcerated in a silver coffin, was entombed with huge numbers of precious gems, gifts from neighbouring countries (India sent a golden suit of armour), his own jewelled robes, and objects of religious significance, all of which were looted long ago. The cosy chapel (¥10), originally built in the twelfth century, has central statues of Songtsen Gampo, his wives and principal ministers, Gar and Thonmi Sambhota.

If you look east from this viewpoint, the large tomb straight ahead belongs to Songtsen Gampo's grandson, Mangsong Mangtsen (646–676), who became king at the age of 4. The tomb some distance to the left is that of Tri Ralpachan (805–836), and the nearby enclosure contains an ancient pillar, recording the events of his reign, and constructed on top of a stone turtle symbolizing the foundation of the universe. Originally, every tomb had one of these pillars on top, but the others have long since disappeared.

The ruins of **Chingwa Tagste Dzong**, perched high on the mountainside to the west, give an idea of the scale of the fortress and capital of the early Yarlung kings before Songtsen Gampo moved to Lhasa. To the left, the monastery of

Riwo Dechen is visible, and a rough road means you can drive to within ten minutes' walk of this now thriving Gelugpa community of around eighty monks. Originally founded in the fifteenth century, it was later expanded by the Seventh Dalai Lama and restored in the mid-1980s. There are three main chapels, the central one dominated by a large Tsongkhapa figure.

Tsurphu and Namtso

One of the most rewarding and popular trips in Tibet is to **Namtso lake**, around 230km northwest of Lhasa, taking in Tsurphu Monastery on the way. All these sights can be combined into a two-night/three-day trip from Lhasa in a rented jeep, for which you can expect to pay around ¥1800. There are no checkpoints on the roads between Lhasa and Namtso, so you should be fine without a permit. If you don't have your own transport, Tsurphu and the town of Damxhung are still reachable, although you may find pilgrim-bus and minibus drivers unwilling to risk carrying you. There is only very infrequent transport (every day or two) from Damxhung across to Namtso Qu on the shores of Namtso.

Tsurphu Monastery

It takes two to three hours by jeep to travel the 70km or so northeast of Lhasa to **Tsurphu Monastery** (daily 9am–1pm; ¥10), at a height of 4480m. A **pilgrim bus** for the monastery leaves Lhasa daily between 7 and 8am (¥25) from the western end of Barkhor Square, returning at 2pm. The monastery is the seat of the **Karmapa Lama**, though it's a seat that's pretty cold these days as the present incumbent, the Seventeenth, Urgyen Trinley Dorge, fled to India in 1999. Identified in 1992 at the age of 7, Urgyen is the second holiest Tibetan after the Dalai Lama and seems charismatic and able, and is regarded by many in the government in exile as a natural successor for the role of leader when the Dalai Lama dies.

Founded in the twelfth century by Dusun Khenyapa, the Karmapa order is a branch of the Kagyupa tradition, where members are known as the **Black Hats** after the Second Karmapa was presented with one by Kublai Khan. Most powerful during the fifteenth century, when they were close to the ruling families of the time, they were eventually eclipsed in 1642 when the Fifth Dalai Lama and the Gelugpa order, aided by the Mongol army, gained the ascendancy. The Karmapa were the first order to institute the system of reincarnated lamas, *tulkus*, a tradition later adopted by the Gelugpa school.

Tsurphu is now undergoing reconstruction after being damaged in the years after the Chinese invasion. The solid **Zhiwa Tratsang** has a splendidly ornate gold roof and houses the main assembly hall, dominated by statues of Sakyamuni and a *chorten* containing the relics of the Sixteenth Karmapa Lama, who played a major part in establishing the order overseas and died in Chicago in 1981. The murals here depict the successive Karmapa lamas. The festival of **Saga Dawa**,

Tsurphu and Namtso		
Damxhung	当雄	*dāngxióng*
Namtso	纳木错	*nàmùcuò*
Tsurphu Si	楚布寺	*chǔbù sì*

on the full moon of the fourth lunar month, usually in May or June, is especially fine at Tsurphu, as the massive new *thangka*, completed in recent years, is displayed at this time.

A visit to the monastery can be exhausting, as it's at a considerably higher altitude than Lhasa. In addition, the clockwise path, the **kora**, climbs steeply up the hill behind the monastery from the left of the temple complex and circles around high above and behind the monastery before descending on the right. The views are great and the truly fit can even clamber to the top of the ridge, but you need to allow two to three hours for the walk.

There's little reason to stay at Tsurphu unless you're trekking in the area, although there is a basic monastery **guesthouse** (❶) – you'll need to take your own sleeping bag, food and candles.

Damxhung and Namtso

If you're heading up to Namtso, you'll need to continue on the main highway past the Yangbajing turning for another 80km to **DAMXHUNG** (4360m), a bleak truck-stop town. The road is good, and the awesome Nyanchen Tanglha mountain range to the north is dramatically topped by the peak of Nyanchen Tanglha itself (7117m). Minibuses bound for these two places leave Lhasa from just east of the *Yak Hotel* around 7am each morning (3–4hr; ¥30). The turning north to Namtso is about halfway through the town, where a large concrete bridge crosses the river towards the mountains. For **accommodation** in Damxhung, there are several unmemorable places, including the noisy and basic *Tang Shung Shey* (❶), opposite the new petrol station at the far end of town. In front stands the cavernous but atmospheric Muslim **restaurant**, *Ching Jeng*, and there are plenty of Chinese restaurants around.

Namtso

Set at 4700m and frozen over from November to May, **Namtso** (Sky Lake) is 70km long and 30km wide, the second largest saltwater lake in China (only Qinghai Hu is bigger; see p.1027). The scenery comes straight from a dream

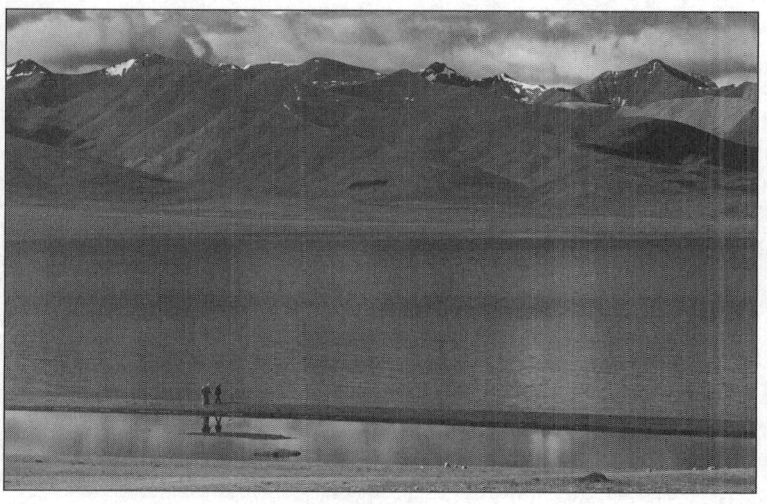

▲ Namtso lake

image of Tibet, with snowcapped mountains towering behind the massive lake and yaks grazing on the plains around nomadic herders' tents.

From Damxhung, it takes around two hours to pass through the Nyanchen Tanglha mountain range at Lhachen La (5150m) and descend to **Namtso Qu**, the district centre numbering just a couple of houses at the eastern end of the lake. Here you'll be charged the annoying "entrance fee" of ¥80. The target of most visitors is **Tashi Dor Monastery**, considerably farther west (a hefty 42km from Lhachen La), tucked away behind two massive red rocks on a promontory jutting into the lake. At Tashi Dor (¥10), a small Nyingma monastery is built around a cave and there's a dirt-floored **guesthouse** (❶) between the monastery and lake. It's a glorious site, but facilities are limited – bring your own food and torches. Although some bedding is provided, you'll be more comfortable in your own sleeping bag, and your own stove and fuel would be an advantage. You can walk around the rock at the end of the promontory and also climb to the top for even more startling views. For true devotees, a circuit of the lake can be attempted, though this takes twenty days and involves camping on the way.

The old southern road and Gyantse

The road west from Lhasa divides at the Chusul Bridge and most vehicles follow the paved Friendship Highway along the course of the Yarlung Tsangpo to Shigatse. However, there is an alternative route, the longer but extremely picturesque **old southern road** that heads southwest to the shores of **Yamdrok Tso**, before turning west to **Gyantse** and then northwest to Shigatse.

There is no public transport between Lhasa and Gyantse, and most people rent jeeps to explore the area or include it on a tour en route to or from the border with Nepal. Allow around six or seven hours' driving time from Lhasa to Gyantse in a good jeep. Alternatively, take the public bus to Shigatse, stay the night, then take one of the frequent minibuses from there to Gyantse. Day-trips to Yamdrok Tso from Lhasa are feasible; you'll start negotiating at about ¥1000 per jeep for these.

Yamdrok Tso

From Chusul Bridge, on the western outskirts of Lhasa, the southern road climbs steeply up to the Kampa La Pass (4794m) with stunning views of the turquoise waters of the sacred **Yamdrok Tso**, the third largest lake in Tibet. It is said that if it ever dries up then Tibet itself will no longer support life – a tale

The old southern road and Gyantse		
Gyantse	江孜	*jiāng zī*
Gyantse Dzong	江孜古堡	*jiāng zī gǔbǎo*
Gyantse Kumbum	江孜千佛塔	*jiāng zī qiānfó tǎ*
Accommodation		
Gyantse Hotel	江孜饭店	*jiāngzī fàndiàn*
Jianzang	建藏饭店	*jiànzàng fàndiàn*
Wutse	乌孜饭店	*wūzī fàndiàn*
Yamdrok Tso	羊卓雍错	*yángzhuó yōngcuò*

of heightened importance now that Yamdrok Tso, which has no inflowing rivers to help keep it topped up, is powering a controversial hydroelectric scheme. From the pass, the road descends to Yamtso village before skirting the northern and western shores amid wild scenery dotted with a few tiny hamlets, yaks by the lakeside and small boats on the water.

On the western side of the lake, 57km beyond the Kampa La Pass, the dusty village of **Nakartse** (4500m) is the birthplace of the mother of the Great Fifth Dalai Lama. There is basic **accommodation** in the village (ask for directions), but there have been instances of midnight awakenings here as the PSB move foreigners on. There are several Chinese **restaurants**, but the favourite with visitors is the Tibetan restaurant with tables in a tiny courtyard, hidden away in the middle of the village, where you can eat rice with potato and meat curry (they fish out the meat for vegetarians) under the eyes of the local dogs. Jeep drivers usually come here; otherwise, look for the tourist vehicles parked outside.

Yamdrok Tso has many picturesque islands and inlets visible from the road, and there's a seven-day circular **trek** from Nakartse exploring the major promontory into the lake. The climb up from Nakartse to the **Karo La Pass** (5045m) is long and dramatic, with towering peaks on either side as the road heads south and then west towards apparently impenetrable rock faces. From the pass, the road descends gradually, via the mineral mines at Chewang, to the broad, fertile and densely farmed **Nyang Chu Valley** leading to Gyantse.

Gyantse

On the eastern banks of the Nyang Chu at the base of a natural amphitheatre of rocky ridges, **GYANTSE** is an attractive, relaxed town, offering the splendid sights of the **Gyantse Kumbum** – famous among scholars of Tibetan art throughout the world – and the old **Gyantse Dzong**. Despite the rapidly expanding Chinese section of town, it has retained a pleasant, laid-back air. It lies 263km from Lhasa on the old southern road and 90km southeast of Shigatse.

Little is known about the history of any settlement at Gyantse before the fourteenth century, when it emerged as the capital of a small kingdom ruled by a lineage of princes claiming descent from the legendary Tibetan folk hero, King Gesar of Ling. Hailing originally from northeast Tibet, they allied themselves to the powerful Sakya order. Also at this time, Gyantse operated as a staging post in the **wool trade** between Tibet and India, thanks to its position between Lhasa and Shigatse. By the mid-fifteenth century, the Gyantse Dzong, Pelkor Chode Monastery and the Kumbum had been built, although decline followed as other local families increased their influence.

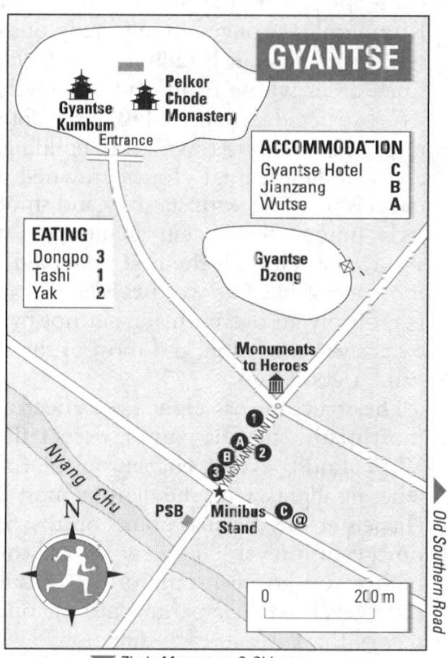

Gyantse rose to prominence again in 1904 when Younghusband's British expedition, equipped with modern firearms, approached the town via the trade route from Sikkim, routed 1500 Tibetans, killing over half of them, and then marched on Gyantse. In July 1904, the British took the Dzong with four casualties while three hundred Tibetans were killed. From here the British marched on to Lhasa. As part of the ensuing agreement between Tibet and Britain, a British Trade Agency was established in Gyantse and as relations between Tibet and the British in India thawed, the trade route from Calcutta up through Sikkim and on to Gyantse became an effective one.

The Town

The best way to get your bearings in Gyantse is to stand at the main traffic intersection, where, in lieu of a bus station, minibuses drop you off. Heading northeast from here takes you past the cheaper hotels and to the square at the base of the Gyantse Dzong, where a road leads off to the Gyantse Kumbum.

The original **Gyantse Dzong** (daily 7am–7pm; ¥55) dates from the mid-fourteenth century, though given the extensive damage caused by the British in 1904, today's remains are a lot more recent. Having climbed up to the fort, visitors are allowed into the **Meeting Hall**, which houses a waxworks tableau, and the **Anti-British Imperialist Museum**, where weapons, used by the defenders against the British, are on display. Climb higher and you reach the upper and lower chapels of the **Sampal Norbuling Monastery**. A few of the murals in the upper chapel probably date from the early fifteenth century, but most of the other artefacts are modern. The best views are from the top of the tallest tower in the north of the complex. You'll need to climb some very rickety ladders, but the scenery is well worth it.

Gyantse Kumbum and Pelkor Chode Monastery

At the northern edge of town, the rather barren monastic compound that now contains Pelkor Chode Monastery and the glorious Gyantse Kumbum (daily 9am–8pm; ¥45, additional ¥10 for photographs, includes admission to the Kumbum) was once home to religious colleges and temples belonging to three schools of Tibetan Buddhism: the Gelugpa, Sakya and Bu (the last of these is a small order whose main centre is at Zhalu; see p.1127).

Constructed around 1440 by Rabten Kunsang, the Gyantse prince most responsible for the town's fine buildings, the **Gyantse Kumbum** is a remarkable building, a huge *chorten* crowned with a golden dome and umbrella, with chapels bristling with statuary and smothered with paintings at each level. It's a style unique to Tibetan architecture and, while several such buildings have survived, Gyantse is the best preserved (despite some damage in the 1960s) and most accessible. The word *kumbum* means "a hundred thousand images" – which is probably an overestimate, but not by much. Many of the statues have needed extensive renovation, and most of the murals are very old – take a torch if you want a good look.

The structure has eight levels, decreasing in number and size as you ascend; most of the chapels within, except those on the uppermost floors, are open. With almost seventy chapels on the first four levels alone, there's plenty to see. The highlights, with the densest, most lavish decoration, include the two-storey chapels at the cardinal points on the first and third levels and the four chapels on the fifth level. The views of the town and surrounding area get better the higher you go, and some of the outside stucco work is especially fine. At the sixth level, you'll emerge onto an open platform, level with the eyes of the *chorten* that look in each direction.

The other main building in the compound is **Pelkor Chode Monastery**, also built by Rabten Kunsang, around twenty years earlier than the Kumbum and used for worship by monks from all the surrounding monasteries. Today, the main assembly hall contains two thrones, one for the Dalai Lama and one for the main Sakya Lama. The glitter and gold and the sunlight and flickering butter lamps in the chapels make a fine contrast to the gloom of much of the Kumbum. The main chapel, **Tsangkhang**, is at the back of the assembly hall and has a statue of Sakyamuni flanked by deities, amid some impressive wood carvings – look for the two peacocks perched on a beam. The second floor of the monastery contains five chapels, and the top level just one, **Shalyekhang** (Peak of the Celestial Mansion), with some very impressive, two-metre-wide *mandalas*.

Practicalities

A permit (¥50) is supposedly required to visit Gyantse, but no one ever seems to have one and the PSB and hotels never ask for them. Minibuses operate between the bus station in Shigatse and the main traffic intersection in Gyantse from around 8am to 4pm daily. Most tourists end up paying ¥30 for the two-hour trip.

Accommodation options are all within easy walking distance; north of the main crossroads on Yingxiong Nan Lu, the *Jianzang* (ⓣ0892/8173720) and the 🏅 *Wutse* (ⓣ0892/8172909) are the two best budget options. Both are built around old courtyards, and offer dorms (❶) and rooms (¥150–350) as well as food and laundry services. The *Gyantse Hotel*, a favourite with tour groups, situated east of the main crossroads, is the most comfortable place in town (ⓣ0892/8172222; ❽), with a spacious, Tibetan-style lobby and 24-hour hot water and satellite TV. Bike hire here costs ¥5 an hour.

The most obvious **restaurant** in Gyantse is the friendly *Tashi*, just north of the *Wutse*, which knocks up acceptable *momos*; everything here is ¥10–20. On the opposite side of the street, the *Yak*, aimed at tour groups, does decent Nepalese curries. As usual, the best food available is Chinese; in this case at the *Dongpo*, on the main crossroads. There are a couple more Chinese restaurants just west of the *Gyantse Hotel* and, just to the east, a smoke-filled Internet café.

Zhalu Monastery and Gyankhor Lhakhang

Accessible enough for a day-trip from Shigatse, or an easy side-trip between Gyantse and Shigatse, **Zhalu Monastery** is around 22km from Shigatse, 75km from Gyantse and 4km south of the village of Tsungdu between kilometre-markers 18 and 19 on the Gyantse–Shigatse road. Originally built in the eleventh century, Zhalu has a finely colonnaded courtyard decorated with luck symbols, but is most remarkable for the green-glazed tiles that line the roof. It rose to prominence as the seat of the Bu tradition of Tibetan Buddhism founded by Buton Rinchendrub in the fourteenth century. Buton's claim to fame is as the scholar who collected, organized and copied the Tengyur commentaries by hand into a coherent whole, comprising 227 thick volumes in all. However, his original work and pen were destroyed during the Cultural Revolution. Although there were once about 3500 monks living here, the tradition never had as many followers as the other schools. But it had a fair degree of influence – Tsongkhapa, among others, was inspired by Buton's teaching. Major renovations are currently under way and chapels have been closed and rearranged, but the monks are friendly and the village is a quiet and pleasant place. For the energetic, it's a one- to two-hour walk up in the hills southwest of Zhalu to the hermitage of **Riphuk**, where Atisha (see p.1086) is supposed to have meditated. You'll need directions or a guide from Zhalu, as you can't see it from the monastery.

About 1km north of Zhalu, **Gyankor Lhakhang** dates from 997. Sakya Pandita, who established the relationship between the Mongol Khans and the Sakya hierarchy in the thirteenth century (see p.1087), was ordained here as a monk, and the stone bowl over which he shaved his head prior to ordination is in the courtyard. Just inside the entrance is a conch shell, said to date from the time of Buton Rinchendrub and be able to sound without human assistance.

Shigatse

Traditionally the home of the Panchen Lamas – historically religious and political rivals to the Dalai Lamas - Tibet's second city, **SHIGATSE**, is often only used by travellers as an overnight stop on the way to or from Lhasa. While one day is long enough to see the two main sights, **Tashilunpo Monastery** and **Shigatse Dzong**, it's worth spending at least an extra night here simply to do everything at a more leisurely pace, take in the market and spend a bit of time absorbing the atmosphere and wandering the attractive, tree-lined streets. Basing yourself here also gives you the opportunity to explore some of the sights along the old southern road to Lhasa (see p.1124).

Arrival

From Lhasa, public **buses** run to Shigatse from the bus station (¥65), and there are also **minibuses** (¥40) from Beijing Dong Lu, just east of the *Yak Hotel*. Public buses terminate at the **bus station** on Shanghai Lu, returning to Lhasa from here early in the morning (8am & 9am). Minibuses to and from **Gyantse** run until around 4pm. Taxis are ¥10 for any destination in town or it's about a twenty-minute walk from the bus station to the *Tenzin Hotel*.

Conveniently situated on Xigezi Lu, Shigatse's **PSB** (Mon–Fri 9.30am–1pm & 3.30–7pm) is one of the more friendly offices; they'll send you to FIT for permits (see box, opposite), but may extend your visa if you say you are headed to the border and don't have enough time to make it before your existing visa runs out. The **Bank of China** (Mon–Sat 10am–4pm), just beyond the *Shigatse Hotel*, cashes travellers' cheques and gives advances on visa cards. If you're heading west, stock up here on local currency, as there are no more facilities until Zhangmu. At the **post office**, on the corner of Shandong Lu and Zhufeng Lu (daily 9am–7pm), you can send international letters and faxes, but not parcels, and they don't stock postcards – go to the *Shigatse Hotel* for those. There

Shigatse		
Shigatse		
Shigatse Dzong	日喀则宗	*rìkāzé zōng*
Tashilunpo Monastery	扎什伦布寺	*zhāshílúnbù sì*
Accommodation		
Orchard	刚坚宾馆	*gāngjiān bīnguǎn*
Shigatse Hotel	日喀则饭店	*rìkāzé fàndiàn*
Tenzin Hotel	旦增宾馆	*dànzēng bīnguǎn*
Zhufeng Youyi Binguan	珠峰友谊宾馆	*zhūfēng yǒuyí bīnguǎn*

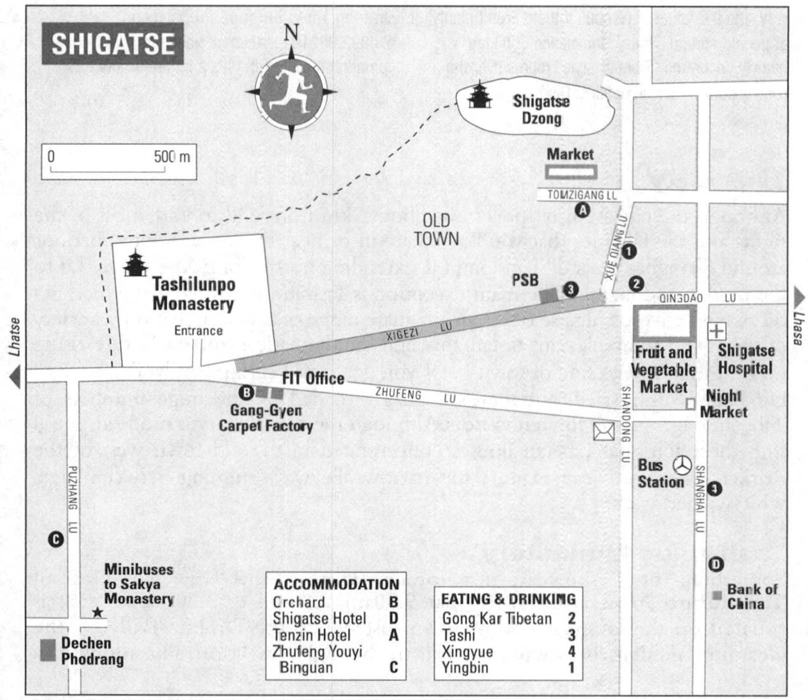

are also international **telephones** here (7am–noon), but no poste restante service. The Shigatse **hospital** on Shanghai Lu has a first-aid post (daily 10am–12.30pm & 4–6pm) – take a Chinese translator with you. There are a couple of Internet cafés just south of the post office and also opposite the *Shigatse Hotel*.

Accommodation

Tenzin Hotel Opposite the market on Bangchelling ☎0892/8822018. A long-standing travellers' haunt but renovation has removed its ramshackle charm; it now looks like everywhere else and charges twice as much. Six-bed dorms are ¥35. ❷

Orchard Hotel Zhufeng Lu ☎0892/8820234. The Orchard has possibly the plushest dorms in China for ¥40, as well as decent mid-range rooms. ❷–❸

Shigatse Hotel 13 Shanghai Zhonglu ☎0892/8822525. Tour-group hotel, a bit out of the

Moving on towards Nepal

If you are heading independently to the **border with Nepal**, you can get a minibus to Tingri (10hr) at 8am, and arrange onward transport from there. There is also a daily 8.30am bus service to Lhatse (4hr) buses for Sakya (4hr) leave from outside the Dechen Phodrang at 8.30am.

For every trip, you'll need a permit, a document that costs ¥150 and is easily obtained, with only half an hour's wait, at the FIT office on Zhufeng Lu (daily 9am–5.30pm, ☎0892/8991189). At the time of writing, permission was being granted for everywhere west of here, which means independent travel and hiking in, for example, the Sakya or Everest area is easier than it used to be.

way, and it's rather cavernous if there aren't plenty of people around. There's the choice of taking heavily decorated "Tibetan-style" rooms over the cookie-cutter Chinese options. Discounts often given. ❼

Zhufeng Youyi Binguan Puzhang Lu ☎0892/8821929. Another place offering slightly upmarket facilities, but it's a bit out of town. ❻

The City

Although the city is fairly spread out, about 2km from end to end, most of the sights and the facilities that you'll need are in or near the north–south corridor around Shanghai Lu and Shandong Lu, extending north along Xue Qiang Lu to the market and Dzong. The main exception is Tashilunpo Monastery, which is a bit of a hike west. Shigatse offers an adequate range of accommodation, a variety of shops and some pleasant restaurants, and the dramatic **Drolma Ridge** rising up on the northern side of town helps you get your bearings easily. The pace of life here is unhurried, but there's a buzz provided by the huge numbers of Tibetan pilgrims and foreign visitors. Although most of the city is modern, you'll find the traditional Tibetan houses concentrated in the old town west of the market, where you can explore the narrow alleyways running between high, whitewashed walls.

Tashilunpo Monastery

Something of a showcase for foreign visitors, the large complex of **Tashilunpo Monastery** (Mon–Sat 9.30am–2.30pm & 3.30–6pm; ¥55) is situated on the western side of town just below the Drolma Ridge – the gleaming, golden roofs will lead you in the right direction. The monastery

The Panchen Lama controversy

The life of the **Tenth Panchen Lama** (1938–89) was a tragic one. Identified at 11 years of age by the Nationalists in 1949 in Xining, without approval from Lhasa, he fell into Communist hands and was for many years the most high-profile collaborator of the People's Republic of China. His stance changed in 1959 when he openly referred to the Dalai Lama as the true ruler of Tibet. In 1961, in Beijing, the Panchen Lama informed Mao of the appalling conditions in Tibet at that time and pleaded for aid, religious freedom and an end to the huge numbers of arrests. Mao assured the Panchen Lama these would be granted, but nothing changed. Instructed to give a speech condemning the Dalai Lama, he refused and was prevented from speaking in public until the 1964 Monlam Great Prayer Festival in Lhasa. With an audience of ten thousand people, he again ignored instructions and spoke in the Dalai Lama's support, ending with the words, "Long live the Dalai Lama". He was immediately placed under house arrest and the Chinese instituted a campaign to "Thoroughly Smash the Panchen Reactionary Clique". The Panchen Lama's **trial** in August 1964 lasted seventeen days, following which he vanished into prison for fourteen years, where he was tortured and attempted suicide. He was released in 1978, following the death of Zhou Enlai two years earlier, and the Chinese used him as evidence that there was a thawing of their hard-line attitude towards Tibet. He never again criticized the Chinese in public and in private he argued that Tibetan culture must survive at all costs, even if it meant giving up claims for independence. Some Tibetans saw this as a sellout; others worshipped him as a hero when he returned on visits to Tibet. He died in 1989; the Chinese say from a heart attack, others say he was poisoned.

The search for the **Eleventh Panchen Lama** was always likely to be fraught. The central issue is whether the Dalai Lama or the Chinese government have the right to has some of the most fabulous chapels outside Lhasa, and it takes several hours to do it justice.

Tashilunpo was founded in 1447 by Gendun Drup, Tsongkhapa's nephew and disciple, who was later recognized as the First Dalai Lama. It rose to prominence in 1642 when the Fifth Dalai Lama declared that Losang Chokyi Gyeltsen, who was his teacher and the abbot of Tashilunpo, was a manifestation of the Amitabha Buddha and the Fourth reincarnation of the **Panchen Lama** (Great Precious Teacher) in what has proved to be an ill-fated lineage (see box below). The Chinese have consistently sought to use the Panchen Lama in opposition to the Dalai Lama, beginning in 1728 when they gave the Fifth Panchen Lama sovereignty over western Tibet.

The **temples** and shrines of most interest in Tashilunpo stand in a long line at the northern end of the compound. From the main gate, head uphill and left to the **Jamkhang Chenmo**. Several storeys high, this was built by the Ninth Panchen Lama in 1914 and is dominated by a 26-metre gold, brass and copper statue of Maitreya, the Buddha of the Future. Hundreds of small images of Maitreya and Tsongkhapa and his disciples are painted on the walls.

To the east, the next main building contains the gold and jewel-encrusted **Tomb of the Tenth Panchen Lama**, which was consecrated in 1994 and cost US$8 million. Near the top is a small window cut into a tiny niche, containing his picture. The next building, the **Palace of the Panchen Lamas**, built in the eighteenth century, is closed to the public, but the long building in front houses a series of small, first-floor chapels. The Yulo Drolma Lhakhang, farthest to the right, is worth a look and contains 21 small statues showing each of the 21 manifestations of Tara, the most popular goddess in Tibet.

determine the identity of the next incarnation. Stuck in the middle was the abbot of Tashilunpo, Chadrel Rinpoche, who initially led the search according to the normal pattern, with reports of "unusual" children checked out by high-ranking monks. On January 25, 1995, the Dalai Lama decided that Gendun Choekyi Nyima, the son of a doctor, was the reincarnation, but – concerned for the child's safety – he hesitated about a public announcement. The search committee headed by Chadrel Rinpoche supported the same child.

However, the Chinese decreed that the selection should take place by the drawing of lots from the Golden Urn, an eighteenth-century gold vase, one of a pair used by the Qing emperor Qianlong to resolve disputes in his lands. Chadrel Rinpoche argued against its use. In May, the Dalai Lama, concerned about the delay of an announcement from China, publicly recognized Gendun Choekyi Nyima, and the following day Chadrel Rinpoche was arrested while trying to return to Tibet from Beijing. Within days, Gendun Choekyi Nyima and his family were taken from their home by the authorities, put on a plane and disappeared. The Chinese will only admit they are holding them "for protection". Fifty Communist Party officials then moved into Tashilunpo to identify monks still loyal to the Dalai Lama and his choice of Panchen Lama. In July, an open revolt by the monks was quelled by riot police. By the end of 1995, they had re-established enough control to hold the Golden Urn ceremony in the Jokhang in Lhasa, where an elderly monk drew out the name of a boy, Gyaincain Norbu. He was enthroned at Tashilunpo and taken to Beijing for publicity appearances. Nearly a decade and a half and one awarding of the Olympics later, the whereabouts of Gendun Choekyi Nyima and his family are still unknown.

To the east again, the **Tomb of the Fourth Panchen Lama** contains his eleven-metre-high *chorten*, with statues of Amitayus, White Tara and Vijaya, the so-called Three Gods of Longevity, in front. His entire body was supposedly interred in the *chorten* in a standing position, together with an ancient manuscript and *thangkas* sent by the second Manchu emperor. Next comes the **Kelsang Lhakhang**, the largest, most intricate and confusing building in Tashilunpo, in front of the Tomb of the Fifth Panchen Lama. The Lhakhang consists of a courtyard, the fifteenth-century assembly hall and a whole maze of small chapels, often interconnecting, in the surrounding buildings. The flagged **courtyard** is the setting for all the major temple festivals; the surrounding three-level colonnaded cloisters are covered with murals, many recently renovated. Dominating the **assembly hall** are the huge throne of the Panchen Lama and the hanging *thangkas*, depicting all his incarnations. If you've got the energy, it's worth trying to find the **Thongwa Donden Lhakhang**, one of the most sacred chapels in the complex, containing burial *chortens*, including that of the founder of Tashilunpo, the First Dalai Lama, Gendun Drup, as well as early Panchen Lamas and abbots of Tashilunpo.

Spare an hour or so to walk the three-kilometre **kora**, the pilgrim circuit, which follows a clockwise path around the outside walls of the monastery. Turn right on the main road as you exit the monastery and continue around the walls; a stick is useful, as some of the dogs are aggressive. The highlight of the walk is the view of the glorious golden roofs from above the top wall. The massive, white-painted wall at the top northeast corner is where the forty-metre, giant, appliqued *thangka* is displayed annually at the festival on the fifteenth day of the fifth lunar month (usually in July). At this point, instead of returning downhill to the main road, you can follow the track that continues on around the hillside above the Tibetan part of town and leads eventually to the old Shigatse Dzong.

Shigatse Dzong

Shigatse Dzong is now a dramatic pile of ruins. It was built in the seventeenth century by Karma Phuntso Namgyel when he was king of the Tsang region and held sway over much of the country, and it's thought that its design was used as the basis for the later construction of the Potala Palace in Lhasa. The structure was initially ruined by the Dzungars in 1717, and further damage took place in the 1950s. Unlike at Gyantse, there has been no attempt at rebuilding, and the main reason to climb up is for the fantastic views. To get here from town, head west along Tomzigang Lu until the paved surface runs out. A little farther along, a motorable track heads up the hill between some houses to a small pass, from where you can climb right up to the Dzong.

The market and the Tibet Gang-Gyen Carpet Factory

The **market**, opposite the *Tenzin Hotel*, is worth a browse for souvenirs, jewellery, fake antiques and religious objects, and the scale of the place is a bit easier to manage than Lhasa's Barkhor. You'll need to brush up on your bargaining skills and be patient – the stallholders are used to hit-and-run tourists, so the first asking price can be sky-high.

If you're interested in **carpets**, drop into the **Tibet Gang-Gyen Carpet Factory** (Mon–Fri 9am–12.30pm & 2.30–7pm) on Zhufeng Lu, a few minutes' walk from the entrance of Tashilunpo. Their carpets are made from ninety-percent sheep's wool and ten-percent cotton, and you can watch the whole process, from the winding of the wool through to the weaving and finishing. They have a good range of traditional and modern designs, ranging in price from US$30 up to US$370, and can also arrange shipping.

Eating and drinking

There's no shortage of **restaurants** in Shigatse. Best is the ★ *Tashi* on pedestrianized Xigezi Lu, whose Nepalese cooks whip up great Chinese, Tibetan and Nepalese standards. It's where all the tour groups are herded to, so it's a little pricey. Of the Chinese places lining Xue Qiang Lu, head for the *Yingbin*, which has pretty decent Sichuan food that makes no concessions to wimpy Western palates. Slightly farther away, on Qingdao Lu, the ★ *Gong Kar Tibetan* restaurant has fabulously painted pillars outside and comfortable sofas within. Adventurous carnivores can try yak's heart salad, pig's trotters and ears here, although there are also more mainstream meat and vegetable dishes (¥12–20). Upmarket Chinese food can be had at the *Xingyue*, north of the *Shigatse Hotel*. There's a small **night market** on the corner of Zhufeng Lu and Shanghai Lu, where you can sit on sofas on the pavement and eat spicy kebabs and nourishing bowls of noodles. If you're getting a **picnic** together, visit the **fruit and vegetable market** off Shandong Lu.

The Friendship Highway

From Shigatse, the **Friendship Highway** west to Zhangmu on the Nepalese border is partly surfaced, but generally rough and quite slow. The only public buses in this direction are the Shigatse to Sakya, Lhatse and Tingri services. From the broad plain around Shigatse, the road gradually climbs to the pass of Tsuo La (4500m) before the steep descent to the Sakya Bridge and the turn-off to Sakya village. If you have time, a detour off the Friendship Highway to Sakya is worthwhile: the valleys are picturesque, the villages retain the rhythm of their rural life, and **Sakya Monastery** is a dramatic sight, unlike anything you'll encounter elsewhere in Tibet. Further south, the side-trip to Mount Everest Base Camp is a once-in-a-lifetime experience.

Sakya

The small but rapidly growing village of **SAKYA**, set in the midst of an attractive plain, straddles the small Trum River and is highly significant as the centre of the Sakya school of Tibetan Buddhism. The main reason to visit is to see the remaining monastery, a unique, Mongol-style construction dramatically visible from miles away. The village around is now a burgeoning Chinese community, full of ugly concrete, and has been corrupted by tourism; children everywhere will try to sell you quartz or fossils, or sometimes just rocks, and food is very expensive.

Sakya Monastery

Originally, there were two monasteries at the present-day **Sakya Monastery** site (Mon–Sat 9am–noon & 4–6pm; ¥50, photographs inside the chapels ¥80).

The Friendship Highway		
Everest Base Camp	珠峰大本营	*zhūfēng dàběnyíng*
Lhatse	拉孜	*lāzī*
Sakya	萨迦	*sàjiā*
Tingri	定日	*dìngrì*
Zhangmu	樟木	*zhāngmù*

The imposing, Mongol-style structure of the **Southern Monastery** that most visitors come to see today, and the **Northern Monastery** across the river, which was a more typical monastic complex containing 108 chapels; the latter was completely destroyed during the Cultural Revolution and has been largely replaced by housing. Prior to the Chinese occupation, there were around five hundred monks in the two monasteries; there are now about a hundred. The Northern Monastery was founded in 1073 by Kong Chogyal Pho, a member of the Khon family, whose son, Kunga Nyingpo, did much to establish Sakya as an important religious centre. He married and had four sons; three became monks but the fourth remained a layman and continued the family line. The Sakya order has remained something of a family affair, and, while the monks take vows of celibacy, their lay brothers ensure the leadership remains with their kin. One of the early leaders was a grandson of Kunga Nyingpo, known as Sakya Pandita. He began the most illustrious era of the order in the thirteenth century when he journeyed to the court of the Mongol emperor, Godan Khan, and established the Sakya lamas as religious advisers to subsequent emperors and effective rulers of Tibet. This state of affairs lasted until the overthrow of the Mongols in 1354.

The Southern Monastery

The **entrance** to the Southern Monastery is in its east wall. On the way there, note the unusual decoration of houses in the area – grey, with white and red vertical stripes; this dates back to a time when it denoted their taxable status within the Sakya principality.

A massive fortress, the Southern Monastery was built in the thirteenth century on the orders of Phagpa, nephew of Sakya Pandita. The five main temples in the complex are surrounded by a huge wall with turrets at each corner. On the left of the entrance is the tall, spacious chapel on the second floor of the **Puntsok Palace**, the traditional home of one of the two main Sakya lamas, who now lives in the US. It is lined with statues – White Tara is nearest to the door and Sakya Pandita farther along the same wall. The central figure of Kunga Nyingpo, the founder of the Northern Monastery, shows him as an old man. The *chortens* contain the remains of early Sakya lamas. As you move clockwise around the courtyard, the next chapel is the **Phurkhang**, with statues of Sakyamuni to the left and Manjusri to the right of Sakya Pandita. The whole temple is stuffed with thousands of small statues and editions of sacred texts with murals on the back wall.

Facing the entrance to the courtyard, the **Great Assembly Hall** is an imposing chapel, with walls 3.5m thick. Its roof is supported by forty solid wooden columns, one of which was said to be a personal gift from Kublai Khan and carried by hand from China; another was supposedly fetched from India on the back of a tiger, a third brought in the horns of a yak and yet another is said to weep the black blood of the *naga* water spirit that lived in the tree used for the column. The chapel is overwhelmingly full of brocade hangings, fine statues, butter lamps, thrones, murals and holy books. The grandest statues, of Buddha, are against a golden, carved background, and contain the remains of previous Sakya lamas.

Next along, the **Silver Chorten Chapel** houses eleven *chortens*, with more in the chapel behind. Completing the circuit, the **Drolma Lhakhang** is on the second floor of the building to the right of the entrance. This is the residence of the other principal Sakya lama, the Sakya Trizin, currently residing in India, where he has established his seat in exile in Rajpur. Be sure to take time to walk around the top of the walls for fine views, both into the monastery and over the surrounding area.

Practicalities

Situated 150km southwest of Shigatse, Sakya is an easy side-trip off the Friendship Highway if you've got your own transport. Public **buses** run here from Shigatse on weekdays (see box on p.1129), returning from Sakya at 11am the next morning; it's a surprisingly slow trip – allow six hours or more each way. If you want to continue from Sakya to Lhatse, get the bus to drop you at the Friendship Highway turn-off, which it reaches around 1pm. The bus from Shigatse to Lhatse passes here about 1.30pm, so you shouldn't have to wait for long. The **permit** situation is variable: there's a checkpoint just before the village, but some travellers without permits have been waved through by the lazy guards. Don't rely on this, however; if you haven't got a permit and you're trying to get to Nepal, it might be best to give Sakya a miss.

On arrival, avoid the miserable **accommodation** at the bus station turn right out of the bus-station entrance and walk straight ahead for 150m to the *Tibetan Hotel* opposite the north wall of the monastery; it is marginally better, though electricity is temperamental and pit latrines are the only facilities. The best **restaurant** in Sakya, the *Sichuan Flavour Restaurant*, is just west of the hotel entrance, next to a small shop sporting a "Simone Soda and Cigs" sign This tiny Chinese restaurant has a surprisingly lengthy menu, written in English, with the usual range of meat, vegetable, rice and noodle dishes (¥10–20) their pancakes make a good breakfast. Alternatively, there is basic accommodation on the Friendship Highway at the turn-off for Sakya (❶) – there's no sign, so ask in the compound there.

Sakya to Mount Everest

Just 24km west of Sakya Bridge (there's no checkpoint between the two), the truck-stop town of **Lhatse** (4050m) lines the Friendship Highway and has plenty of restaurants and basic accommodation. There's little to detain you, but most bus drivers stop here. Another 6km west from Lhatse, there's a checkpoint, after which the road divides: the Friendship Highway continues to the left, and the route to the far west of Tibet heads right.

The continuation of the Friendship Highway is rough going, though not as bad as it used to be thanks to infrastructure investment. Allow about four hours in a good jeep, up over the Lhakpa La Pass (5220m) to the checkpoint and turn-off to **Shekar** (also known as New Tingri). Avoid the much-advertised but overpriced *Chomolungma Hotel*, a couple of hundred metres towards Shekar off the Friendship Highway, and stay at the comfortable, if basic, *Pelbar Family Hotel* (❶), on the highway. There are a few cosy restaurants around here, too. The village itself is 7km farther on, with the Shekar Chode Monastery on the hillside above. There's basic accommodation (❶) in the village, but you'll have to ask, and there's little reason to hang around.

Shekar boasts another checkpoint on the highway about 5km from the *Pelbar Family Hotel* where some visitors have reported that the guards here are particularly assiduous in confiscating printed material specifically about Tibet from travellers entering the country (books on China that include Tibet seem to be fine). Just 7km west of this checkpoint, the small turning to **Rongbuk Monastery** and on up to **Mount Everest Base Camp** is on the south side of the road. It's a long, bumpy and spellbinding 90km to Rongbuk and worth every tortured minute of the three- or four-hour drive along the rough track. About 3km from the turning, the checkpoint at Chay will collect entrance fees (¥400 per jeep, ¥65 per person) for the Everest area.

From Chay, the road zigzags steeply up to the Pang La Pass (5150m), from where the glory of the Everest region is laid out before you – the earlier you go in the day the better the views, as it clouds over later. There's a **lookout** spot with a plan to help you identify individual peaks such as Cho Oyu (8153m), Lhotse (8501m) and Makalu (8463m), as well as the mighty Mount Everest (8848m; Chomolungma in Tibetan, Zhumulangma in Chinese). From here the road descends into a network of fertile valleys with small villages in a patchwork of fields. You'll gradually start climbing again and pass through Peruche (19km from Pang La), Passum (10km farther), where there is accommodation just beside the road at the *Passumpembah Teahouse* (❶), and Chodzom (another 12km), before the scenery becomes rockier and starker and you eventually reach Rongbuk Monastery, 22km farther on.

Rongbuk Monastery and Everest Base Camp

Rongbuk Monastery – at 4980m, the highest in the world – was founded in 1902 by the Nyingma Lama, Ngawang Tenzin Norbu, although a hardy community of nuns had used meditation huts on the site for about two hundred years before this. The chapels themselves are of limited interest; Padmasambhava is in pride of place and the new murals are attractive, but the position of the monastery, perched on the side of the Rongbuk Valley leading straight towards the north face of Everest, is stunning. Just to sit outside and watch the play of light on the face of the mountain is the experience of a lifetime.

Everest Base Camp (5150m) is a farther 8km due south. The road is driveable, but it's mostly flat, and the walk alongside the river through the boulder-strewn landscape past a small monastery on the cliff is glorious. Base camp is often a bit

▲ Everest Base Camp

of a surprise, especially during the climbing seasons (March–May, Sept & Oct), when you'll find a colourful and untidy tent city festooned with Calor gas bottles and satellite dishes. It's possible to camp near the monastery, where there's also a guesthouse offering dorm **accommodation** (❶). Grubby quilts are provided, but you'll be more comfortable with your own sleeping bag. Each room has a stove and pot to boil water (you collect it from up the valley) and the monks will provide fuel (although if you can manage to buy some in the villages on the way, this would be insurance against a shortage – a night here without heat would be grim). There's a small monastery shop selling mostly leftovers from mountaineering expeditions – take your own food. Don't be surprised if you suffer with the **altitude** here. However well you were acclimatized in Lhasa, base camp is around 1500m higher, so be sensible and don't contemplate a trip here soon after arrival up on the Tibetan plateau.

To the Nepalese border

From the Rongbuk and Mount Everest Base Camp turning on the Friendship Highway, it's a fast 50km south to **TINGRI** (4342m). The road is good and you should allow about an hour in a jeep. Tingri is the last stop on the public bus service, so if you're headed for Nepal you'll have to hitch from here. A convenient stop before the final day's drive to Zhangmu, Tingri has good views south towards Everest. To get the best of these, climb up to the old fort that stands sentinel over the main part of the village. The three **accommodation** options are on the northern side of the main road. The first, the *Snow Leopard*, is best avoided as it's twice as expensive as the others and has nothing they don't, except carpets. The *Himalaya Hotel* (❶) and *Everest Veo* (❶) are a little farther east, and both offer dorm accommodation, latrines with view, and seats in the sunshine. In both of these, the family's living room doubles as a restaurant, and they produce good, basic fare. For something fancier, try the Sichuan restaurant opposite – look for the red sign.

The road west of Tingri is good quality and lined with ruins of buildings destroyed in an eighteenth-century Gurkha incursion from Nepal. The road climbs gradually for 85km to the double-topped **Lalung La Pass** (5050m), from where the views of the Himalayas are great, especially looking west to the great slab of Shishapangma (8013m). The descent from the pass is steep and startling as the road drops off the edge of the Tibetan plateau and heads down the gorge of the Po Chu River. Vegetation appears and it becomes noticeably warmer as you near Nyalam, around four hours' drive by jeep from Tingri.

Although difficult to spot if you're coming from the north, **Milarepa's Cave** (10km north of Nyalam) is worth a halt – look out for a white *chorten*, to the left of the road on the edge of the gorge. Milarepa (1040–1123) was a much-revered Tibetan mystic who led an ascetic, itinerant life in caves and was loved for his religious songs. The Kagyu order of Tibetan Buddhism was founded by his followers, and the impressions in the walls and roof are believed to have been made by Milarepa himself. A temple has been built around the cave, the main statue being of Padmasambhava. Perched on the side of the Matsang Zangpo River gorge, **Nyalam** (3750m) is a small village with several Chinese restaurants and a variety of basic accommodation, although there is little to recommend staying the night here rather than continuing to Zhangmu.

The steep descent through the Himalayas continues on a twisty and dramatic road that winds in and out of the forested mountainsides and feels almost tropical as it descends the 33km to the border town of **ZHANGMU** (2300m). This Chinese–Tibetan–Nepalese hybrid clings gamely to the sheer mountain, a collection of tin shacks, construction sites, wooden huts, shops, brothels and offices. It's a great place, with a Wild-West-comes-to-Asia atmosphere, although good-quality **accommodation** is limited. The choice is between the *Zhangmu Hotel* (ⓣ08074/882272; ❻), at the bottom end of town, with no hot water in the private bathrooms (although there's a shower on the top floor of a building opposite), and the *Himalaya Hotel and Lodge* (❶), on the right heading down through town, offering clean dorms and great views down the valley. There are no washing facilities, but there's a shower operation just up the hill and putrid latrines across the street. The **PSB** is tucked away in an alley close to the *Zhangmu Hotel*. Zhangmu boasts two branches of the **Bank of China** (both Mon–Fri 10am–1pm & 3.30–6.30pm, Sat 10am–2pm), one near the border post at the bottom of town and one just above the *Himalaya Hotel and Lodge*. Even if you produce exchange certificates, they'll refuse to change Chinese money into either Nepalese or other hard currency, so if you've got excess, you'll be forced onto the thriving black market. Follow the music and flashing lights for the nightly disco/hostess/**karaoke bar** in the middle of town, where everyone dances the waltz.

Entering Nepal

Border formalities are fairly cursory if you're leaving Tibet for Nepal. The **border posts** (both open daily 9.30am–5pm Chinese time) on the Chinese and Nepalese side, at **Kodari** (1770m), are an extremely steep 9km apart. You can either rent a truck (¥300 for 4 people), hire a porter (about ¥10 per bag) or carry your own stuff for the ninety-minute walk down (either follow the road or take the short cuts that slice across the zigzags) to the Friendship Bridge, where there is another Chinese checkpoint before you cross the bridge into Kodari. The **Nepalese Immigration** post is a couple of hundred metres over the bridge on the left. You can get only single-entry visas here, and you have to pay in US dollars and produce one passport photograph (see p.1110 for details of Nepali visas available in Lhasa). Don't forget to put your watch back (2hr 15min) when you cross into Nepal.

To head to **Kathmandu**, either take the express bus there or the cheaper local service to Barabise and then change for Kathmandu. Alternatively, there are taxis in Kodari, or you can negotiate for space in a tourist bus that has just dropped its group at the border – bargain hard and you'll end up paying Rp400–600 (US$13 or so) per person for the four-hour trip.

Western Tibet

Travellers in Lhasa spend huge amounts of time and energy plotting and planning trips to the highlights of **western Tibet**: Mount Kailash, Lake Manasarova, and, less popular but just as enticing, the remains of the tenth-century Guge kingdom, its capital at Tsaparang and main monastery at Tholing. However, this is no guarantee of reaching any of these destinations, and it can be dangerous.

Regulations regarding visits to the west change frequently and you shouldn't underestimate the time it will take to set up a trip. Tour companies in Lhasa arrange journeys for trucks of travellers, generally quoting around ¥22,000 per truck for a two- to three-week return trip. Unless you have huge amounts of time and are willing to persevere, there is little realistic alternative to going on an organized tour; there is no public transport beyond Lhatse.

The **southern route** passes through Saga, Dongpa and Horpa, a stunningly picturesque journey, parallel to the Himalayas, but with rivers that become swollen and passes that get blocked by snow. This route is most reliable from May through to the beginning of July, and again in October and November, although luck plays a big part. The distance is around 1400km from Lhasa to Mount Kailash. The alternative **northern route** via Tsochen, Gertse and Gakyi is longer; Lhasa to Ali (Shiquanhe) is over 1700km and then it's another 300km or so southeast to Mount Kailash. It is also less scenic but it's more reliable and there's more traffic using it. Many tours plan to go on one route and return on the other – expect at least a week travelling time on either.

Mount Kailash and around

Top of most itineraries is **Mount Kailash** (6714m), Gang Rinpoche to the Tibetans, the sacred mountain at the centre of the universe for Buddhists, Hindus and Jains. Access is via **DARCHEN**, where there's a guesthouse used as a base by visiting pilgrims. The 58-kilometre tour around the mountain takes around three days; you might consider hiring a porter and/or yak (from about ¥45 per day each) as it's a tough walk and you need to carry all your gear, including a stove, fuel and food. On the first day you should aim to reach Drirapuk Monastery, on the second day you climb over the Dolma La Pass (5636m) to Zutrulpuk Monastery, and the third day you arrive back in Darchen.

After the exertions of Mount Kailash, most tours head south 30km to **Manasarova Lake** (Mapham Tso), the holiest lake in Asia for Hindus and Tibetan Buddhists alike. For the energetic, it's a four-day, ninety-kilometre trek to get around the lake, but plenty of travellers just relax by the lakeside for a day or two. Travel agencies in Lhasa charge around ¥22,000 for one jeep for a seventeen-day trip. Other agencies might be willing to go for a lot less, though allow plenty of time in Lhasa to sort this trip out.

The third major pilgrimage site in Western Tibet is **Tirthapuri Hot Springs**, which are closely associated with Padmasambhava; they're situated about 80km northwest of Mount Kailash and accessible by road. Pilgrims here immerse themselves in the pools, visit the monastery containing his footprint and the cave that he used, and dig for small, pearl-like stones that are believed to have healing properties.

The only remains of the tenth-century kingdom of **Guge**, where Buddhism survived while eclipsed in other parts of Tibet, are the main monastery of **Tholing**, 278km from Ali, and the old capital of **Tsaparang**, 26km west of Tholing. Both places are famous for their extensive ruins, some of which are around 1000 years old, and there are many well-preserved murals, but it's all even less accessible than Mount Kailash and Lake Manasarova.

The major town in the area, **ALI** (also known as Shiquanhe), is a modern Chinese-style settlement at the confluence of the Indus and Gar rivers. The only official foreigners' **accommodation** is the overpriced *Ali Hotel* (❸) west of the main crossroads. The PSB here are comparatively decent and, after fining independent travellers ¥300, will sell them permits to Mount Kailash for ¥50.

Travel details

Buses

Gyantse to: Shigatse (frequent minibuses; 2hr).
Lhasa to: Damxhung (daily minibus; 3–4hr); Ganden (daily pilgrim bus; 3hr); Golmud (daily bus; 30hr); Samye ferry crossing (daily bus; 4hr); Shigatse (daily bus; 8hr; frequent minibuses; 9hr); Tsetang (frequent minibuses; 3hr); Tsurphu (daily pilgrim bus; 2–3hr); Xining (daily bus; 40hr).
Sakya to: Shigatse (daily; 7hr).
Shigatse to: Gyantse (frequent minibuses; 2hr); Lhasa (daily bus; 8hr; frequent minibuses; 9hr); Sakya (daily; 5hr); Lhatse (daily; 4hr); Tingri (one daily; 10hr).
Tsetang to: Lhasa (frequent minibuses; 3hr).

Trains

Lhasa to: Beijing (daily; 48hr); Changsha (daily; 51hr); Chengdu (daily; 25hr); Chongqing (daily; 49hr); Golmud (4 daily; 12hr); Guangzhou (daily; 58hr); Lanzhou (4 daily; 29hr); Shijiazhuang (daily; 45hr); Xian (daily; 37hr); Xining (4 daily; 26 hr).

Flights

Lhasa to: Beijing (daily; 4hr 30min); Chengdu (daily; 2hr); Chongqing (4 weekly; 2hr); Kathmandu (Mar–Oct, 2 weekly; 1hr).

Contexts

Contexts

History

As modern archeology gradually confirms ancient records of China's earliest times, it seems that, however far back you go, Chinese history is essentially the saga of the country's autocratic **dynasties**. Although this generalized view is inevitable in the brief account below, bear in mind that, while the concept of being Chinese has been around for over two thousand years, the closer you look, the less "China" seems to exist as an entity – right from the start, **regionalism** played an important role. And while concentrating on the great events, it's easy to forget that life for the ordinary people wavered between periods of stability, when writers, poets and artisans were at their most creative, and dire times of heavy taxation, war and famine. While the Cultural Revolution, ingrained corruption and clampdowns on political dissent may not be a good track record for the People's Republic, it's also true that since the 1980s – only yesterday in China's immense timescale – the quality of life for ordinary citizens has vastly improved.

Prehistory and the Three Dynasties

Chinese legends relate that the creator, **Pan Ku**, was born from the egg of chaos and grew to fill the space between Yin, the earth, and Yang, the heavens. When he died his body became the soil, rivers and rain, and his eyes became the sun and moon, while his parasites transformed into human beings. A pantheon of semi-divine rulers known as the **Five Sovereigns** followed, inventing fire, the calendar, agriculture, silk-breeding and marriage. Later a famous triumvirate included **Yao the Benevolent** who abdicated in favour of **Shu**. Shu toiled in the sun until his skin turned black and then he abdicated in favour of **Yu the Great**, the tamer of floods. **Yu** was said to be the founder of China's first dynasty, the **Xia**, which was reputed to have lasted 439 years until its last degenerate and corrupt king was overthrown by the **Shang** dynasty. The **Shang** was in turn succeeded by the **Zhou**, whose written court histories put an end to this legendary era. Together, the Xia, Shang and Zhou are generally known as the **Three Dynasties**.

As far as archeology is concerned, **homo erectus** remains indicate that China was already broadly occupied by human ancestors well before modern mankind began to emerge 200,000 years ago. Excavations of more recent Stone Age sites show that agricultural communities based around the fertile Yellow River and Yangzi basins, such as **Banpo** in Shaanxi and **Homudu** in Zhejiang, were producing pottery and silk by 5000 BC. It was along the Yellow River, too, that solid evidence of the bronze-working Three Dynasties first came to light, with the discovery of a series of large rammed-earth palaces at **Erlitou** near Luoyang, now believed to have been the Xia capital in 2000 BC.

Little is known about the Xia, though their territory apparently encompassed Shaanxi, Henan and Hebei. The events of the subsequent Shang dynasty, however, were first documented just before the time of Christ by the historian **Sima Qian**. Shang society, based over much the same area as its predecessors and lasting from roughly 1750 BC to 1040 BC, had a king, a class system and a skilled **bronze technology** which permeated beyond the borders into Sichuan, and which produced the splendid vessels found in today's museums. Excavations on the site of Yin, the Shang capital, have found tombs stuffed with weapons, jade ornaments, traces of silk and sacrificial victims – indicating belief in **ancestor worship** and an afterlife. The Shang also practised divination by incising questions onto tortoiseshell or bone and then heating them to study the way in which the material cracked around the words. These **oracle bones** provide China's **earliest written records**, covering topics as diverse as rainfall, dreams and ancestral curses.

Around 1040 BC a northern tribe, the **Zhou**, overthrew the Shang, expanded their kingdom west of the Yellow River into Shaanxi and set up a capital at Xi'an. Adopting many Shang customs, the Zhou also introduced the doctrine of the **Mandate of Heaven**, a belief justifying successful rebellion by declaring that heaven grants ruling authority to leaders who are strong and wise, and takes it from those who aren't – a concept that remains integral to the Chinese political perspective. The Zhou consequently styled themselves "Sons of Heaven" and ruled through a hierarchy of vassal lords, whose growing independence led to the gradual dissolution of the Zhou kingdom from around 600 BC.

The decline of the Zhou dynasty

Driven to a new capital at Luoyang, later Zhou rulers exercised only a symbolic role; real power was fought over by some two hundred city states and kingdoms during the four hundred years known as the **Spring and Autumn** and the **Warring States** periods. This time of violence was also an era of vitality and change, with the rise of the ethics of **Confucianism** and **Taoism** (see pp.1164–1169). As the warring states rubbed up against one another, agriculture and irrigation, trade, transport and diplomacy were all galvanized; iron was first smelted for weapons and tools, and great discoveries were made in medicine, astronomy and mathematics. Three hundred years of war and annexation reduced the competitors to seven states, whose territories, collectively known as Zhong Guo, the **Middle Kingdom**, had now expanded west into Sichuan, south to Hunan and north to the Mongolian border.

The Qin dynasty

The Warring States Period came to an end in 221 BC, when the **Qin** armies overran the last opposition and united China as a single centralized state for the first time, introducing systems of currency and writing that were to last two millennia. The rule of China's first emperor, **Qin Shi Huang**, was absolute and harsh, his advisers favouring the philosophy of **Legalism** – the idea that mankind is inherently bad, and needs to be kept in line by draconian punishments. Ancient literature and historical records were destroyed to wipe out any ideas that conflicted with his own, and peasants were forced off their land to work as labourers on massive construction projects, including his tomb outside Xi'an (guarded by the famous **Terracotta Army**) and an early version of the **Great Wall**. Determined to rule the entire known world, Huang gradually pushed his armies beyond the Middle Kingdom, expanding Chinese rule, if not absolute control, west and southeast. When he died in 210 BC – ironically, during a search for mythical herbs of immortality – the provinces rose in revolt, and his heirs soon proved to lack the personal authority that had held his empire together.

The Han dynasty

In 206 BC the rebel warlord **Liu Bang** took Xi'an and founded the **Han dynasty**. Lasting some four hundred years and larger at its height than contemporary imperial Rome, the Han was the first great **Chinese** empire, one that experienced a flowering of culture and a major impetus to push out frontiers and open them to trade, people and new ideas. In doing so it defined the national identity to such an extent that the main body of the Chinese people still style themselves "**Han Chinese**".

While Liu Bang maintained the Qin model of local government, to prevent others from repeating his own military takeover, he strengthened his position by handing out large chunks of land to his relatives. This secured a period of stability, with effective taxation financing a growing civil service and the construction of a huge and cosmopolitan capital, **Chang'an**, at today's Xi'an. Growing revenue also refuelled the expansionist policies of a subsequent ruler, **Wu**. From 135 to 90 BC he extended his lines of defence well into Xinjiang and Yunnan, opening up the Silk Road for trade in tea, spices and silk with India, west Asia and Rome. At home Wu stressed the Confucian model for his growing civil service, beginning a two-thousand-year institution of Confucianism in government offices.

By 9 AD, however, the empire's resources and supply lines were stretched to breaking point. Increased taxation led to unrest, and the ruling house was split by political intrigue. Following fifteen years of civil war, the dynasty re-formed as the **Eastern Han** at a new capital, Luoyang, where the classical tradition was reimposed under Emperor **Liu Xiu**. But the Han had passed their peak, and were unable to stem the civil strife caused by local authorities setting themselves up as semi-independent rulers. Despite everything, Confucianism's ideology of a centralized universal order had crystallized imperial authority; and **Buddhism**, introduced into the country from India, began to enrich life and thought, especially in the fine arts and literature, while itself being absorbed and changed by native beliefs.

The Three Kingdoms

Nearly four hundred years separate the collapse of the Han in about 220 AD from the return of unity under the Sui in 589. However, although China was under a single government for only about fifty years of that time, the idea of a unified empire was never forgotten.

From 200 AD the three states of **Wei**, **Wu** and **Shu** struggled for supremacy in a protracted and complicated war (later immortalized in the saga *Romance of the Three Kingdoms*; see p.453) that ruined central China and encouraged mass migrations southwards. The following centuries saw China's regionalism becoming entrenched: the **Southern Empire** suffered weak and short-lived dynasties, but nevertheless saw prosperity and economic growth, with the capital at **Nanjing** becoming a thriving trading and cultural centre. Meanwhile, with the borders unprotected, the north was invaded in 386 by the **Tobas**, who established the northern **Wei dynasty** after their aristocracy adopted Chinese manners and customs – a pattern of assimilation that was to recur with other invaders. At their first capital, **Datong**, the **Tobas** created a wonderful series of Buddhist carvings, but in 534 their empire fell apart.

The Three Kingdoms period was a dark age of war, violence and genocide, but it was also a richly formative one, and when the dust had settled a very different society had emerged. For much of this time, many areas produced sufficient **food surpluses to** support a rich and leisured ruling class in the cities and the countryside, as well as large armies and burgeoning Buddhist communities. So culture developed, literature flourished, and calligraphy and sculpture – especially Buddhist carvings, all enriched by Indian and Central Asian elements – reached unsurpassed levels.

The Sui

After grabbing power from his regent in 581, general **Yang Jian** unified the fragmented northern states and then went on to conquer southern China by land and sea, founding the **Sui dynasty**. The Sui get short shrift in historical surveys, but – though they were soon eclipsed by their successors, the Tang – two of the dynasty's three emperors could claim considerable achievements. Until his death in 604, Yang Jian (Emperor **Wen)** was an active ruler who took the best from the past and built on it. He simplified and strengthened the bureaucracy, brought in a new legal code, recentralized civil and military authority and made tax collection more efficient. Near Xi'an his architects designed a new capital, **Da Xing Cheng** (City of Great Prosperity), with an outer wall over 35km round – the largest city in the world at that time.

Following Wen's death in 604, **Yang Di** elbowed his elder brother out to become emperor. Yang improved administration, encouraged a revival of Confucian learning and promoted a strong foreign policy. Universally, he is portrayed as a proverbially "Evil Emperor", thanks to the use of forced labour to complete engineering projects. Half the total workforce of 5,500,000 died during the construction of the two-thousand-kilometre **Grand Canal**, built to transport produce from the southern Yangzi to his capital at Xi'an. Yang was assassinated in 618 after popular hatred inspired a military revolt led by General **Li Yuan**.

Medieval China: Tang to Song

The seventh century marks the beginning of the medieval period of Chinese history. This was the age in which Chinese culture reached its peak, a time of experimentation in literature, art, music and agriculture, and one which unified seemingly incompatible elements.

Having changed his name to **Gao Zu**, Li Yuan consolidated his new **Tang dynasty** by spending the rest of his eight-year reign eliminating rivals. Under his son **Tai Zong**, Tang China broadened its horizons: the Turkic peoples of the Northwest were crushed, the Tibetans brought to heel and relations established with Byzantium. China kept open house for traders and travellers of all races and creeds, who settled in the mercantile cities of Yangzhou and Guangzhou, bringing with them their religions, especially **Islam**, and influencing the arts, cookery, fashion and entertainment. Chinese goods flowed out to India, Persia, the Near East and many other countries, and China's language and religion gained currency in Japan and Korea. At home, **Buddhism** remained the all-pervading foreign influence, with Chinese pilgrims travelling widely in India. The best known of these, **Xuan Zang** (see p.1040), set off in 629 and returned after sixteen years in India with a mass of Buddhist sutras, adding greatly to China's storehouse of knowledge.

As the population of Xi'an swelled to over a million, the city became one of the world's great cultural centres, at the heart of a centralized and powerful state. Within a decade after Tai Zong's death in 649, his short-lived son **Gao Zong** and China's only empress, **Wu Zetian**, had expanded the Tang empire's direct influence from Korea to Iran, and south into Vietnam. Though widely unpopular, Wu Zetian was a great patron of Buddhism, commissioning the famous Longmen carvings outside Luoyang; she also created a civil service selected on merit rather than birth. Her successor, **Xuan Zong**, began well in 712, but his later infatuation with the beautiful concubine **Yang Guifei** led to the **An Lushan rebellion** of 755, his flight to Sichuan and Yang's ignominious death at the hands of his mutinying army. Xuan Zong's son, **Su Zong**, enlisted the help of Tibetan and Uigur forces and recaptured Xi'an from the rebels; but though the court was re-established, it had lost its authority, and real power was once again shifting to the provinces.

The following two hundred years saw the country split into regional political and military alliances. From 907 to 960, all the successive **Five Dynasties** were too short-lived to be effective. China's northern defences were permanently weakened, while her economic dependence on the south increased and the dispersal of power brought social changes. The traditional elite whose fortunes were tied to the dynasty gave way to a military and merchant class who bought land to acquire status, alongside a professional ruling class selected by examination. In the south, the **Ten Kingdoms** (some existing side by side) managed to retain what was left of the Tang civilization, their greater stability and economic prosperity sustaining a relatively high cultural level.

Eventually, in 960, a disaffected army in the north put a successful general, **Song Tai Zu**, on the throne. His new ruling house, known as the **Northern Song**, made its capital at **Kaifeng** in the Yellow River basin, well placed at the head of the Grand Canal for transport to supply its million people with grain from the south. By skilled politicking rather than military might, the new dynasty consolidated authority over surrounding petty kingdoms and re-established civilian primacy. However, northern China was occupied by the **Jin** in 1115, who pushed the imperial court south to **Hangzhou** where, guarded by the Yangzi River, their culture continued to flourish from 1126 as the **Southern Song**. Developments during their 150-year dynasty included gunpowder, the magnetic compass, fine porcelain and movable type printing. In due course, however, the Song preoccupation with art and sophistication saw their military might decline and led them to underrate their aggressive "barbarian" neighbours, whose own expansionist policies culminated in the thirteenth-century **Mongol Invasion**.

The Yuan dynasty

In fact, Mongolian influence had first penetrated China in the eleventh century, when the Song emperors paid tribute to separate Mongolian states to keep their armies from invading. These individual fiefdoms were unified by **Genghis Khan** in 1206 to form an immensely powerful army, which swiftly embarked upon the conquest of northern China. Despite Chinese resistance and Mongol infighting, the **Yuan dynasty** was on the Chinese throne by 1278, with **Kublai Khan**, Genghis Khan's grandson, at the head of an empire that stretched way beyond the borders of China. The Yuan emperors' central control from their capital at Khanbalik – modern **Beijing** – boosted China's economy and helped repair five centuries of civil war. China was thrown wide open to foreign travellers, traders and missionaries; Arabs and Venetians were to be found in Chinese ports, and a Russian came top of the Imperial Civil Service exam of 1341. The Grand Canal was extended from Beijing to Hangzhou, while in Beijing the **Palace of All Tranquillities** was built inside a new city wall, later known as the **Forbidden City**. Descriptions of much of this were brought back to Europe by **Marco Polo**, who recorded his impressions of Yuan lifestyle and treasures after he'd lived in Beijing for several years and served in the government of Kublai Khan.

The Yuan only retained control over all China until 1368. Their power was ultimately sapped by the combination of becoming too Chinese for their northern brethren to tolerate, and too aloof from the Chinese to assimilate. After northern tribes had rebelled, and famine and disastrous floods brought a series of uprisings in China, a monk-turned-bandit leader from the south, **Zhu Yuanzhang**, seized the throne from the last boy emperor of the Yuan in 1368.

The Ming dynasty

Taking the name **Hong Wu,** Zhu Yuanzhang proclaimed himself the first emperor of the **Ming dynasty**, with Nanjing as his capital. Zhu's influences on China's history were far-reaching. His extreme despotism culminated in two appalling purges in which thousands of civil servants and literati died, and he initiated a course of **isolationism** from the outside world which lasted throughout the Ming and Qing eras. Consequently, Chinese culture became inward-looking, and the benefits of trade and connections with foreign powers were lost. Nowhere is this more apparent than in the Ming construction of the current Great Wall, a grandiose but futile attempt to stem the invasion of northern tribes into China, built in the fifteenth century as military might and diplomacy began to break down.

Yet the period also produced fine artistic accomplishments, particularly **porcelain** from the imperial kilns at Jingdezhen, which became famous worldwide. Nor were the Ming rulers entirely isolationist. During the reign of **Yongle**, Zhu's twenty-sixth son, the imperial navy (commanded by the Muslim eunuch, Admiral **Zheng He**) ranged right across the Indian Ocean as far as the east coast of Africa on a fact-finding mission. But stagnation set in after Yongle's death in 1424, and the maritime missions were cancelled as being incompatible with Confucian values, which held contempt for foreigners. Thus the initiative for world trade and exploration passed into the hands of the Europeans, with the great period of world voyages by Columbus, Magellan and Vasco da Gama. In 1514, **Portuguese** vessels appeared in the Pearl River at the southern port of Guangzhou (Canton), and though they were swiftly expelled, Portugal was allowed to colonize nearby **Macao** in 1557. Although all dealings with foreigners were officially despised by the imperial court, trade flourished as Chinese merchants and officials were eager to milk the profits.

In later years, a succession of less-able Ming rulers allowed power to slip into the hands of the seventy thousand inner court officials, who used it not to run the empire but in intriguing among the "eunuch bureaucracy". By the early seventeenth century, frontier defences had fallen into decay, and the **Manchu tribes** in the north were already across the Great Wall. A series of peasant and military uprisings against the Ming began in 1627, and when rebel forces led by **Li Zicheng** managed to break into the capital in 1644, the last Ming emperor fled from his palace and hanged himself – an ignoble end to a 300-year-old dynasty.

The Qing dynasty

The Manchus weren't slow to turn internal dissent to their advantage. Sweeping down on Beijing, they threw out Li Zicheng's army, claimed the capital as their own and founded the **Qing dynasty**. It took a further twenty years for the Manchus to capture the south of the country, but on its capitulation China was once again under foreign rule. Like the Mongol Yuan dynasty before them, the Qing initially did little to assimilate domestic culture, ruling as separate overlords. Manchu became the official language, the Chinese were obliged to wear the Manchu **pigtail**, and intermarriage between a Manchu and a Chinese was strictly forbidden. Under the Qing dynasty the distant areas of Inner and Outer Mongolia, Tibet and Turkestan were fully incorporated into the Chinese empire, uniting the Chinese world to a greater extent than during the Tang period.

Soon, however, the Manchus proved themselves susceptible to Chinese culture, and ultimately they became deeply influenced by it. Three outstanding early Qing emperors also brought an infusion of new blood and vigour to government. **Kangxi**, who began his 61-year reign in 1654 at the age of six, was a great patron of the arts, blotting countless scrolls of famous calligraphy and paintings with his seals as evidence that he had seen them. He assiduously cultivated his image as the Son of Heaven by making royal progresses throughout the country and by his personal style of leadership. His fourth son, the Emperor **Yungzheng** (1678–1735), ruled over what is considered one of the most efficient and least corrupt administrations ever enjoyed by China. This was inherited by **Qianlong** (1711–99), whose reign saw China's frontiers widely extended and the economy stimulated by peace and prosperity. In 1750 the nation was perhaps at its apex, one of the strongest, wealthiest and most powerful countries in the world.

During the latter half of the eighteenth century, however, economic problems began to increase. Settled society had produced a **population explosion**, putting pressure on food resources and causing a land shortage. This in turn saw trouble flaring as migrants from central China tried to settle the remoter western provinces, dispossessing the original inhabitants. Meanwhile, expanding European nations were looking for financial opportunities. From around 1660, Portuguese traders in Guangzhou had been joined by British merchants shopping for tea, silk and porcelain, and during the eighteenth century the British **East India Company** moved in, eager for a monopoly. Convinced of their own superiority, however, China's immensely rich and powerful rulers had no desire to deal directly with foreigners. When **Lord Macartney** arrived in 1793 to propose a political and trade treaty between Britain and China, he found that the emperor totally rejected any idea of alliance with one who, according to Chinese ideas, was a subordinate.

The Opium Wars and the Taiping Uprising

Foiled in their attempts at official negotiations with the Qing court, the East India Company decided to take matters into their own hands and create a clandestine market in China for Western goods. Instead of silver, they began to pay for tea and silk with **opium**, cheaply imported from India. As demand escalated during the early nineteenth century, China's trade surplus became a deficit, as silver drained out of the country to pay for the drug. The emperor intervened in 1840 by ordering the confiscation and destruction of over twenty thousand chests of opium – the start of the first **Opium War**. After two years of British gunboats shelling coastal ports, the Chinese were forced to sign the **Treaty of Nanjing**, whose humiliating terms included a huge indemnity, the opening up of new ports to foreign trade, and the **cession of Hong Kong**.

To be conquered by foreigners was a crushing blow for the Chinese, who now suffered major internal **rebellions** inspired by anti-Manchu feeling and economic hardship – themselves fuelled by rising taxes to pay off China's war indemnity. While serious unrest occurred in Guizhou and Yunnan, the most widespread revolt was the **Taiping Uprising**, which stormed through central China in the 1850s to occupy much of the rich Yangzi Valley. Having captured Nanjing as their "Heavenly Capital", the Taipings began to make military forays towards Beijing, and European powers decided to step in, worried that the Taiping's anti-foreign government might take control of the country. With their support, Qing troops defeated the Taipings in 1864, leaving twenty million people dead and five provinces in ruins.

It was during the uprising that the **Empress Dowager Wu Cixi** first took control of the country, ruling from behind various emperors from 1861 until 1908. Ignorant, vain and certain that reform would weaken the Qings' grasp on power, she pursued a deep conservatism at a time when China needed desperately to overhaul its political and economic structure. Her stance saw increased foreign ownership of industry, rising Christian missionary activity that undermined traditional society, and the disintegration of China's **colonial empire**. France took the former vassal states of Laos, Cambodia and Vietnam in 1883–85; Britain gained Burma; and **Tibet**, which had nominally been under China's control since Tang times, began to assert its independence. Even worse, a failed military foray into Korea in 1894 saw China lose control of **Taiwan** to Japan, while a Russian-built rail line into the northeast effectively gave Russia control of Manchuria.

The Boxer Movement – the end of imperial China

By the 1890s China was dissolving into chaos, and popular resentment against the authorities who had allowed the country to be humiliated by foreigners finally crystallized into the **Boxer Rebellion**. The Boxers suffered an initial defeat at the hands of Cixi's troops in 1899, but Cixi's government then decided that the Boxer army might in fact make a useful tool, and set them loose to slaughter missionaries and Christian converts. During the summer of 1900 the Boxers took control of Beijing, besieging the foreign legation compound, though they were routed when an international relief force arrived on August 14. In the massacre, looting and confusion which followed, Cixi and the emperor disguised themselves as peasants and fled to Xi'an in a cart, leaving her ministers to negotiate a peace.

Though they clung feebly on for another decade, this was the end of the Qing, and internal movements to dismantle the dynastic system and build a new China proliferated. The most influential of these was the **Tong Meng Hui** society, founded in 1905 in Japan by the exile **Sun Yatsen**, a doctor from a wealthy Guangdong family. Cixi died three years later, and, in 1911, opposition to the construction of railways by foreigners drew events to a head in Wuchang, Hubei province, igniting a popular uprising which finally toppled the dynasty. As two thousand years of dynastic succession ended, Sun Yatsen returned to China to take the lead in the provisional **Republican Government** at Nanjing.

From republic to communism

Almost immediately the new republic was in trouble. Though a **parliament** was duly elected in 1913, the reality was that northern China was controlled by the former leader of the Imperial Army, **Yuan Shikai** (who had forced the abdication of the last emperor, **Pu Yi**). Sun Yatsen, faced with a choice between probable civil war and relinquishing his presidency at the head of the newly formed Nationalist People's Party, the **Guomindang**, stepped down. Yuan promptly dismissed the government, forced Sun into renewed exile, and attempted to establish a new dynasty. But his plans were stalled by his generals, who wanted private fiefdoms of their own, and Yuan's sudden death in 1916 marked the last time in 34 years that China would be united under a single authority. As civil war erupted, Sun Yatsen returned once more, this time to found a southern Guomindang government.

Thus divided, China was unable to stem the increasingly bold territorial incursions made by Japan and other colonial powers as a result of **World War I**. Siding with the Allies, Japan had claimed the German port of Qingdao and all German shipping and industry in the Shangdong Peninsula on the outbreak of war, and in 1915 presented China with **Twenty-One Demands**, many of which Yuan Shikai, under threat of a Japanese invasion, was forced to accept. After the war, hopes that the 1919 **Treaty of Versailles** would end Japanese aggression (as well as the unequal treaties and foreign concessions) were dashed when the Western powers, who had already signed secret pacts with Japan, confirmed Japan's rights in China. This ignited what became known as the **May 4 Movement**, the first in a series of anti-foreign demonstrations and riots.

The rise of the CCP

As a reflection of these events, the **Chinese Communist Party** (CCP) was formed in Shanghai in 1921, its leadership including the young **Mao Zedong** and **Zhou Enlai**. Though the CCP initially listened to its Russian advisers and supported the Guomindang in its military campaigns against the northern warlords, this alliance began to look shaky after Sun Yatsen died in 1925. He was succeeded by his brother-in-law and military chief **Chiang Kaishek** (better known in China as Jiang Jieshe), a nationalist who had no time for the CCP or its plans to end China's class divisions. In 1927, Communist elements in Shanghai organized a general strike against Chiang, seizing the military arsenal and arming workers. Industry bosses and foreign owners quickly financed a militia for Chiang, which massacred around five thousand workers and Communists, including much of the original Communist hierarchy. Chiang was declared head of a national government in 1928.

Those Communists who had escaped Chiang's purge regrouped in remote areas across the country, principally at **Jinggang Shan** in Jiangxi province, under the leadership of Mao Zedong.

Mao Zedong, the Red Army and the Long March

Son of a well-off Hunanese farmer, **Mao** believed social reform lay in the hands of the peasants who, despite the overthrow of the emperors, still had few rights and no power base. Drawing upon the analyses of Karl Marx, Mao recognized the parallels between nineteenth-century Europe and twentieth-century China, and argued that a mass armed rising was the only way the old order could be replaced.

After events in Shanghai, Mao organized the first peasant-worker army in Changsha, in what was later to be called the **Autumn Harvest Uprising**. Moving with other Communist forces to the Hunan–Jiangxi border in 1927, the **Red Army** of peasants, miners and Guomindang deserters achieved unexpected successes against the Nationalist troops sent against them until **Li Lisan**, the overall Communist leader, ordered Mao out of his mountain base to attack the cities. After the ensuing open assaults against the vastly superior Guomindang forces proved disastrous, Chiang Kaishek mobilized half a million troops, and encircled Jinggang Shan with a ring of concrete block-houses and barbed-wire entanglements.

Forced to choose between fight or flight, in October 1934 Mao organized eighty thousand troops in an epic 9500-kilometre retreat which became known as the **Long March**. By the time they reached safety in **Yan'an** in Shaanxi province a year later, the Communists had lost three-quarters of their followers to the rigours of the trip, but had also started their path towards victory: Mao had become undisputed leader of the CCP at the **Zunyi Conference**, severing the Party from its Russian advisers.

Japanese invasion and the United Front

Meanwhile, **Japan** had taken over Chinese Manchuria in 1933 and installed Pu Yi (last emperor of the Qing dynasty) as puppet leader. The Japanese were obviously preparing to invade eastern China, and Mao wrote to Chiang Kaishek advocating an end to civil war and a **United Front** against the threat. Chiang's response was to move his Manchurian armies, under **Zhang Xueliang**, down to finish off the Reds in Shaanxi. Zhang, however, saw an alliance as the only way to evict the Japanese from his homeland, and so secretly entered into an agreement with the Communist forces. On December 12, 1936, Chiang was kidnapped by his own troops in what became known as the **Xi'an Incident**. With Zhou Enlai as a mediator, he reluctantly signed his assent to the United Front on Christmas Day. Briefly, the parties were united, though both sides knew that the alliance would last only as long as the Japanese threat.

Full-scale war broke out in July 1937 when the Japanese attacked Beijing. Inadequately armed or trained, the GMD were forced west and south. By the end of the year, the Japanese had taken most of eastern China between Beijing and Guangzhou. With a capital-in-occupation at Nanjing, the Japanese concentrated their efforts on routing the GMD, leaving a vacuum in the north that was filled by the Communists, establishing what amounted to stable government of a hundred million people across the North China Plain.

The outbreak of war in Europe in September 1939 soon had repercussions in China. Nazi Germany stopped supplying the weaponry upon which the GMD relied, while the bombing of Pearl Harbor two years later put an end to all military aid from the United States to Japan. With the country's heavy industry in Japanese hands, China's United Front government, having withdrawn to **Chongqing** in Sichuan province, became dependent on supplies flown over the Himalayas by the Americans and British. Chiang's true allegiances were never far below the surface, however, and after he failed to distribute the arms among the Red Army in 1941, the United Front effectively collapsed.

The end of the war ... and the Guomindang

By the time the two atom bombs ended the Japanese empire and World War II in 1945, the Red Army was close on a million strong, with a widespread following throughout the country; Communism in China was established. It was not, however, that secure. Predictably enough, the US sided with Chiang Kaishek and the GMD; more surprisingly, so did the Soviet Union – Stalin believed that with American aid, the GMD would easily destroy the CCP. All the same, **peace negotiations** between the Nationalist and Communist sides were brokered by the US in Chongqing, where Chiang refused to admit the CCP into government, knowing that its policies were uncontrollable while the Red Army still existed. For their part, it was evident to the CCP that without an army, they were nothing. The talks ended in stalemate.

However, buoyed by popular support in the wake of Chiang's mishandling of the economy, in 1948 the Communists' newly named **People's Liberation Army** (PLA) rose against the GMD, decisively trouncing them that winter at the massive battle of **Huai Hai** in Anhui province. With Shanghai about to fall before the PLA in early 1949, Chiang Kaishek packed the country's entire gold reserves into a plane and took off for **Taiwan** to form the **Republic of China**. Here he was to remain until his death in 1975, forlornly waiting to liberate the mainland with the two million troops and refugees who later joined him. Mopping-up operations against mainland pockets of GMD resistance would continue for several years, but in October 1949 Mao was able to proclaim the formation of the **People's Republic of China** in Beijing. The world's most populous nation was now Communist.

The People's Republic under Mao

With the country laid waste by over a century of economic mismanagement and war, massive problems faced the new republic. Though Russia offered its support, the US refused to recognize Mao's government, siding with Chiang Kaishek. China's infrastructure, industries and agriculture were wrecked, and there were no monetary reserves. By the mid-1950s, however, all industry had been nationalized and output was back at prewar levels, while, for the first time in Chinese history, land was handed over to the peasants as their own. A million former landlords were executed, while others were enrolled in "**criticism and self-criticism**" classes, a traumatic re-education designed to prevent elitism or bourgeois deviancy from contaminating the revolutionary spirit.

With all the difficulties on the home front, the government could well have done without the distraction of the **Korean War**. After Communist North Korea invaded the south in 1950, US forces intervened on behalf of the south and, despite warnings from Zhou Enlai, continued through to Chinese territory. China declared war in June, and sent a million troops to push the Americans back to the thirty-eighth parallel and force peace negotiations. As a boost for the morale of the new nation, the campaign could not have been better timed. Meanwhile, China's far western borders were seen to be threatened by an uprising in **Tibet**, and Chinese troops were sent there in 1951, swiftly occupying the entire country and instituting de facto Chinese rule. Eight years later, a failed coup against the occupation by Tibetan monks saw a massive clampdown on religion, and the flight of the **Dalai Lama** and his followers to Nepal.

The Hundred Flowers campaign and the Great Leap Forward

By 1956 China's economy was healthy, but there were signs that the euphoria driving the country was slowing. Mao – whose principles held that constant struggle was part of existence, and thus that acceptance of the status quo was in itself a bad thing – felt that both government and industry needed to be prodded back into gear. In 1957 he decided to loosen restrictions on public expression, and following the slogan "Let a hundred flowers bloom, and a hundred schools of thought contend", intellectuals were encouraged to voice their complaints. The plan backfired: instead of picking on inefficient officials as Mao had hoped, the **Hundred Flowers** campaign resulted in attacks on the Communist system itself. As Mao was never one to take personal criticism lightly, those who had spoken out found themselves victims of an **anti-rightist** campaign, confined to jail or undergoing heavy bouts of self-criticism. From this point on, intellectuals as a group were mistrusted and scrutinized.

Agriculture and industry were next to receive a shake-up. In August 1958 it was announced that all farmland was to be pooled into 24,000 self-governing **communes**, with the aim of turning small-scale farming units into hyper-efficient agricultural areas. Industry was to be fired into activity by the co-option of seasonally employed workers, who would construct heavy industrial plants, dig canals and drain marshes. Propaganda campaigns promised eternal well-being in return for initial austerity; in a single **Great Leap Forward,** China would match British industrial output in ten years, and overtake America in fifteen to twenty years.

From the outset, the Great Leap Forward was a disaster. Having been given their land, the peasants now found themselves losing it once more, and were not eager to work in huge units. This, combined with the problem of ill-trained commune management, led to a slump in agricultural and industrial production. In the face of a stream of ridiculous **quotas** supplied by Beijing – one campaign required that all communes must produce certain quantities of steel, regardless of the availability of raw materials – no one had time to tend the fields. The 1959 and 1960 harvests both failed, and millions starved. As if this wasn't enough, a thaw in US–USSR relations in 1960 saw the Soviet Union stopping all aid to China.

With the economy in tatters, the commune policy was abandoned, but the incident had ruined Mao's reputation and set members of the Communist Party Central Committee against his policies. One critic was **Deng Xiaoping**, who had diffused the effects of commune policy by creating a limited free-market economy among the country's traders. Behind this doctrine of material incentives for workers was a large bureaucracy over which Mao held little political sway.

The Cultural Revolution

Mao sought to regain his authority. Using a campaign created by Communist Party Vice-Chairman **Lin Biao**, he began in 1964 to orchestrate the youth of China against his moderate opponents in what became known as the **Great Proletarian Cultural Revolution**. Under Mao's guidance, the movement spread in 1966 to Beijing University, where the students organized themselves into a political militia – the **Red Guard** – and within weeks were moving out onto the streets.

The enemies of the Red Guard were the **Four Olds**: old ideas, old culture, old customs and old habits. Brandishing copies of the *Quotations of Chairman Mao Zedong* (the famous **Little Red Book**), the Red Guard attacked anything redolent of capitalism, the West or the Soviet Union. Academics were assaulted, books were burned, temples and ancient monuments desecrated. Shops selling anything remotely Western were destroyed along with the gardens of the "decadent bourgeoisie". As under the commune system, quotas were set, this time for unearthing and turning in the "Rightists", "Revisionists" and "Capitalist Roaders" corrupting Communist society. Officials who failed to fill their quotas were likely to fall victim themselves, as were those who failed to destroy property or denounce others enthusiastically enough. Offenders were paraded through the streets wearing placards carrying humiliating slogans; tens of thousands were ostracized, imprisoned, beaten to death or driven to suicide. On August 5, 1966, Mao proclaimed that reactionaries had reached the highest levels of the CCP: Deng Xiaoping and his followers were dismissed from their posts and imprisoned, condemned to wait on tables at a Party canteen, or given menial jobs.

Meanwhile, the violence was getting completely out of control, with Red Guard factions attacking foreign embassies and even turning on each other. In August 1967 Mao ordered the arrest of several Red Guard leaders and the surrender of all weapons to the army, but was too late to stop nationwide street fighting, which was halted only after the military stormed the Guard's university strongholds. To clear them out of the way, millions of Red Guards were rounded up and shipped off into the countryside, ostensibly to reinforce the Communist message among the rural community.

Ping-pong diplomacy and the rise of the radicals

The US, its foreign policy determined by business and political interests that stood to gain from the collapse of Communism, had continued to support Chiang Kaishek's Guomindang in the postwar period, while also stirring up paranoia over the possibility of a Sino–Soviet pact (despite the split between Khrushchev and Mao in 1960). After China exploded its first **atomic bomb** in 1964, however, and joined the league of nuclear powers not automatically friendly to Washington, the US began to tread a more pragmatic path. In 1970, envoy Henry Kissinger opened communications between the two countries, cultural and sporting links were formed (the latter gave rise to the phrase "**ping-pong diplomacy**"), and in 1971 the People's Republic became the official representative at the UN of the nation called China, invalidating claims of Chiang Kaishek for Taiwan. The following year US president **Richard Nixon** was walking on the Great Wall and holding talks with Mao, trade restrictions were lifted and China began commerce with the West. The "bamboo curtain" had parted, and the damage caused by the Cultural Revolution began slowly to be repaired.

This new attitude of realistic reform derived from the moderate wing of the Communist Party, headed by Premier Zhou Enlai – seen as a voice of reason – and his protégé Deng Xiaoping, now in control of the day-to-day running of the Communist Party Central Committee. Zhou's tact had given him a charmed political existence which for fifty years kept him at Mao's side despite policy disagreements; several holy sites were apparently saved from the Red Guards at Zhou's order. But with Zhou's death early in 1976, the reform movement immediately succumbed to the **Gang of Four**, who, led by Mao's third wife **Jiang Qing**, had become the radical mouthpiece of an increasingly absent Mao. In early April, at the time of the **Qing Ming** festival commemorating the dead, the Heroes Monument in Beijing's Tian'anmen Square was filled with wreaths in memory of Zhou. On April 5 radicals removed the wreaths and moderate supporters flooded into the square in protest; a riot broke out and hundreds were attacked and arrested. The obvious scapegoat for what became known as the **Tian'anmen Incident,** Deng Xiaoping, was publicly discredited and thrown out of office for a second time.

The death of Mao

In July 1976 a catastrophic **earthquake** centred on Hebei province killed half a million people. The Chinese hold that natural disasters always foreshadow great events, and no one was too surprised when Mao himself died on September 9. Deprived of their figurehead, and with memories of the Cultural Revolution clear in everyone's mind, his supporters in the Party lost ground to the Right. Just a month after Mao's death, Jiang Qing and the other members of the Gang of Four were arrested. Deng returned to the political scene for the third time and was granted a string of positions that included Vice-Chairman of the Communist Party, Vice-Premier and Chief of Staff to the PLA; titles aside, he was now running the country. The move away from Mao's policies was rapid: in 1978 anti-Maoist **dissidents** were allowed to display wall posters in Beijing and elsewhere, and by 1980 Deng and the moderates were secure enough to sanction officially a cautious condemnation of Mao's actions. His ubiquitous portraits and statues began to come down, and his cult was gradually undermined.

"One Party" capitalism

Under **Deng Xiaoping**, China became unrecognizable from the days when Western thought was automatically suspect and the Red Guards enforced ideological purity. Deng's legacy was the "open door" policy, which brought about new social freedoms as well as a huge rise in the trappings of Westernization, especially in the cities. The impetus for such sweeping changes was economic. Deng's statement, "I don't care whether the cat is black or white as long as it catches mice", illustrates the pragmatic approach that he took to the economy, one which has guided policy ever since. Deng **decentralized production**, allowing more rational decision-making based on local conditions, and the production and allocation of goods according to market forces; factories now contracted with each other instead of with the state. In agriculture, the collective economy was replaced, and farming households, after meeting government targets, were allowed to sell their surpluses on the free market. On the coast, **Special Economic Zones** (SEZs) were set up, where foreign investment was encouraged and Western management practices, such as the firing of unsatisfactory workers, were cautiously introduced.

Economic reform did not precipitate **political reform**, and was really a way of staving it off, with the Party hoping that allowing the populace the right to get rich would halt demands for political rights. However, dissatisfaction with corruption, rising inflation, low wages and the lack of freedom was vividly expressed in the demonstrations in **Tian'anmen Square** in 1989. These started as a mourning service for former Party General Secretary **Hu Yaobang**, who had been too liberal for Deng's liking and was dismissed in 1987; by mid-May there were nearly a million students, workers and even Party cadets around the square, demanding free speech and an end to corruption. On May 20, **martial law** was declared, and by the beginning of June, 350,000 troops were massed around Beijing. In the early hours of June 4 they moved in, crushing barriers with tanks and firing into the crowds, killing hundreds or possibly thousands of the demonstrators. Discussion of the event is still contentious in China, particularly as the issues the students identified have not been dealt with, but the Party's moral authority has been greatly reduced.

China in the twenty-first century

The spectacular **growth** of the Chinese economy was among the great success stories of the twentieth century and will be one of the most important factors in defining the character of the twenty-first. For a quarter of a century, China's GDP has grown at an average rate of nine percent per year, and the country has overtaken Germany to become the world's third largest economy. China is now the world's main producer of coal and steel and, among other things, makes two-thirds of the world's shoes, DVD players and photocopiers. Chinese production and US consumption together form the engines for global growth. But China is also a massive consumer; in 2004, for instance, the nation bought almost half of the world's cement. Some predict that the Chinese economy will overtake that of the US by 2040. The speed of this is astonishing: in the 1970s the "three big buys" – consumer goods to which families could realistically aspire– were a bicycle, a watch and a radio; in the 1980s they were a washing machine, a TV and a refrigerator; and the urban Chinese today can aspire to the same material comforts as their Western counterparts. No wonder the country comes across as confident and ambitious.

Under the faceless **Jiang Zemin**, who took power in 1993, China continued its course of controlled liberalization. Jiang's core idea was the doctrine of the "three represents" – basically, that the party should represent all aspects of society rather than just the workers – but he is more likely to be remembered for the shift at which this hints: the final abandonment of Marxist doctrine. In its pursuit of a "socialist market economy with Chinese characteristics", the state continued to retreat from whole areas of life. Mechanisms of control such as the household registration and work-unit systems have largely been abandoned. The private sector now accounts for almost half of the economy, and foreign-funded ventures represent more than half the country's exports.

Jiang officially stepped down in November 2002 – though he remains a significant force behind the scenes – passing power to his protégé **Hu Jintao**. Hu and his clique of **technocrats** (almost everyone in the politburo has an engineering degree) remain at the reins today. Alarmed at growing income inequality, they have begun to try to shift society away from unbridled capitalism towards a more socially responsible model of development.

Reform and repression: China's record on human rights

China's most serious **human-rights abuses** are being perpetrated in **Tibet**, where dissent is ruthlessly suppressed and Tibetan culture is being swamped by Han in-migration. In 1995, when the exiled Dalai Lama selected a new Panchen Lama following the death of the previous incumbent, the boy he chose, Gedhun Choekyi Nyima, was arrested, and became the world's youngest political prisoner, while the Chinese government enthroned their own representative. Another cause for concern is the Chinese **gulags** – most of them in Xinjiang and Qinghai – in which up to fourteen million prisoners, an estimated ten percent of them political, are kept in punishing conditions and used as slave labour.

Despite hopes for improvement, the government continues to lock up its critics and shows no sign of changing tactics. Recent sufferers have included prominent dissidents Xu Wenli and Qin Yongmin, leaders of the **Chinese Democratic Party**, the first organized opposition to CCP rule. In 2004 journalist Shi Tao wrote an email critical of government censorship; after it was handed to the authorities by Yahoo, he was sentenced to ten years in jail. Doctor Gao Yaojie exposed how blood collectors in the 1990s were spreading AIDS by re-using dirty needles, and has been under house arrest, on and off, ever since.

The most daring display of political activism since Tian'anmen came from a very unusual source; in 1999 ten thousand elderly members of **Falun Gong**, a

How China is governed

Since 1949 the Chinese state has been controlled by the **Communist Party**, which brooks no dissent or rival, and which, with 66 million members, is the biggest political party in the world. It has a pyramid structure resting on millions of local organizations, and whose apex is formed by a politburo of 24 members controlled by a nine-man standing committee. The Party's workings are opaque; personal relations count more than job titles, and a leader's influence rests on the relations he builds with superiors and protégé, with retired party elders often retaining a great deal of influence. Towards the end of his life, for example, Deng Xiaoping was virtually running the country when his only official title was head of a bridge club. The country's head of state is its president, while the head of government is the premier. Politburo members are supposedly chosen by the three thousand delegates of the National People's Congress, officially a parliament though it in fact serves largely as a rubber stamp for politburo decisions. In recent years, though, it has displayed a modicum of independence, for instance delaying an unpopular fuel tax in 1999.

The Party owes its success, of course, to the **military**, and links with the PLA remain close, though the army has lost power since Jiang Zemin stripped its huge business empire in the 1990s. There is no PLA representative on the standing committee, but the military has a strong influence on policy issues, particularly over Taiwan and relations with the US, and generally maintains a hard line.

The law in China is a mix of legislation based on party priorities and new statutes to haul the economy into line with those of major foreign investors. The National People's Congress is responsible for drafting laws covering taxation and human rights, among other subjects. In other areas, the State Council and local governments can legislate. Even after laws have been passed there is no guarantee they will be respected; provincial governments and state-owned enterprises view court decisions as negotiable, and for the party and the state, the rule of law is not allowed to supersede its own interests.

quasi-spiritual sect, sat cross-legged in Beijing on the pavement outside Zhongnanhai, the Communist Party headquarters, to protest perceived oppression. Their reward has been ruthless suppression.

Though most observers agree that the pace of political change is not fast enough, there have been improvements. The **National People's Congress** has begun to take its task of drafting laws and monitoring government seriously. Under Premier **Wen Jiabao**, central government has shrunk. More room has been made in government for talented thinkers, including former Tian'anmen protestors. One of the biggest political changes has come at grass roots, where "village" democracy is now practised by two-thirds of the rural population, who have taken with great gusto to their new right to oust incompetent village leaders. No one, though, has yet dared to apply this idea to positions higher up in government.

Stumbling blocks

Behind the talk of a wonder economy there are **problems**. Even now, more than half of China's citizens live on less than a dollar a day. Prosperity has been delivered unevenly – the east-coast cities have benefited most – **inflation** is rising, and there's little in the way of medical care or subsidized education for either urban or rural poor. One of the more visible results of rising living costs (exacerbated by increased agricultural mechanization) has been the **mass migration** of the working class from the country to the cities, where most remain unemployed or are hired by the day as labourers.

Fifteen million new jobs need to be created every year just to keep up with population growth. Bubbles are forming in property and the steel market. Power generation and water supplies are running up against capacity constraints. The banking system is inefficient, with US$500 billion of bad loans. Only a high domestic savings rate and uncontrolled exploitation of natural resources make China's growth possible, and neither is sustainable.

Short-term gain has become the overriding factor in Chinese planning, with the result that the future is mortgaged for present wealth. Too little thought is given to the environmental effects of modernization, and China now boasts eight of the top ten most **polluted cities** in the world. As success is largely dependent on *guanxi* (connections), the potential for **corruption** is enormous – indeed, graft is thought to be slicing at least a percentage point off growth figures. As in the past, a desperately poor peasantry is at the mercy of corrupt cadres who enrich themselves by setting and purloining local taxes.

Perhaps China's biggest problem is its massive **population** (1.3 billion in 2007), which could put unbearable pressure on resources if it continues to rise. Under the **one-child policy**, which began in 1979, couples who have a second child face a cut in wages and restricted access to health care and housing. The policy has been most successful in the cities, but given the heavy preference for male children, female infanticide, and the selling off of girls as brides, are not unusual, while there is a growing trend in the kidnapping of male children for ransom or, again, sale.

Despite all the gleaming high-rises, little progress has been made on the hallmarks of genuine modernity – investment in education, the rule of law, the freedom of the press and executive accountability. Every year, there are widespread demonstrations by industrial workers who are out of work or owed back pay, by villagers protesting at pollution or corruption, and by homeowners protesting at enforced demolitions. Such actions represent possibly the biggest internal threat to the state. The blame, as well as the credit for creating and managing an economic boom, lies squarely with the Communist Party; designed to change society, it is now incapable of adapting to it. That's fine, as long as economic growth continues apace. But without the safety valves provided by transparency and democracy, if the economy falters, China's political stability is far from assured.

China and the world

Historically, being surrounded by "barbarians" and inhospitable terrain has led China towards **insularity**. Accordingly, the government's tactic during China's stellar period of economic development has been not to intervene on the world stage. But its explosive expansion is now forcing engagement, and the country is coming under scrutiny as never before. As the world's biggest emitter of greenhouse gases, it is under increasing international pressure to start cleaning up its act. China's skewed **business environment** – lax enforcement of intellectual property and business laws, bullying of foreign companies in favour of local competition, unfair regulatory barriers and an artificially low currency – is now attracting plenty of criticism from its trading partners.

In order to fuel growth, China needs to look elsewhere for raw materials: in Africa, the Pacific and Southeast Asia, China has become the new **resource colonizer**, striking deals with all comers, including nations shunned by the West such as Zimbabwe and Sudan. China is well regarded by trading partners for its respect for national sovereignty: its deals come with few strings attached. But China's desire to use the 2008 **Olympic Games** as its coming-out party to the world opened it up to external pressure. The campaign to re-dub the games as the "genocide Olympics", thanks to China's support for the government of Sudan produced some small results, with China forced to stop blocking Security Council resolutions on the subject. China was faced with a similar dilemma when the ruling junta in Myanmar – another set of unsavoury allies – brutally suppressed an uprising of Buddhist monks in 2007. China stopped far short of sanctions but did sign up to a Security Council statement critical of the country. Finally, China has joined the US in putting pressure on its ally North Korea to shut down its nuclear programme.

How China handles its growing influence will determine whether east Asia remains stable enough to continue to prosper, or tumbles back into conflict and rivalry. China's willingness to bind itself to global rules, such as those of the World Trade Organization, has been a welcome way to assimilate it, but an authoritarian, anti-democratic China will never be easy for its neighbours to live with, and Chinese primacy in the Pacific is contested by both Japan and the US.

China's antipathy towards **Japan** stems from Japan's perceived failure to be properly contrite over its crimes in World War II, ongoing territorial disputes over some insignificant islands, and simple rivalry. In 2004, anti-Japanese riots followed Japan's soccer victory over China in the final of the Asia Cup, and in 2005, in protests against Japan's bid for a permanent seat at the United Nations, Japanese businesses in several Chinese cities were attacked by mobs. Such demonstrations are awkward for the government: patriotic demonstrations in the last century were often the precursor to pro-democracy unrest, but at the same time the Party would rather not crack down on expressions of nationalism, as such fervour is whipped up by the Party to justify its existence and right to rule.

China today embraces the outside world as never before; witness the passion with which the English language is studied and the fascination with foreign

Hong Kong and Taiwan

In 1997, China regained control of **Hong Kong**. In the handover agreement between China and the UK, Hong Kong was to retain a high degree of **autonomy** – part of China's avowed "one country, two systems" approach. In practice, the Chinese government quickly reneged on its promise by replacing LEGCO, the democratically elected legislative council, with a group of carefully selected Beijingers. It also interfered with the rule of law (regarded by Hong Kong's people as vital for prosperity) by overturning court judgements and preventing the establishment of a Court of Final Appeal.

Events in Hong Kong are keenly watched from **Taiwan**. In 1949, the defeated Guomindang fled to Taiwan and declared itself the legitimate government of China, in opposition to the Communists. Now Taiwan is one of the most successful, and certainly the most democratic, of the Asian tiger economies. Though both Taiwan and China want to be part of the same country, the affluent Taiwanese have no desire to be ruled by Beijing, certainly not after seeing what has happened in Hong Kong.

After years of martial law, Taiwanese politics came alive in 1996, when the country held **presidential elections** for the first time. The favourite, Lee Tenghui, displeased China by pushing for Taiwan's entry into the UN and the WTO, and by having the temerity, in China's view, to treat Taiwan as a separate country. In an attempt to influence the elections, China conducted intimidating missile tests over the island. The US government, as Taiwan's firm ally, responded by parking two aircraft carriers off Taiwan's coast. Lee won the election, despite China's bullying. Elections in 2003 brought even worse news for China, as they returned Chen Shuibian, the first non-GMD president of the island and an avowed supporter of Taiwanese independence. He remains a hate figure in China, where state news organs can hardly bring themselves to call him by name referring to him as the "arch-splittist".

In 2005, China passed an **anti-secession law**, authorizing the use of force against Taiwan should it assert its independence. The move brought international condemnation, and resulted in Europe delaying the lifting of a ban on arms sales to China. Conciliatory moves followed in a highly unusual fashion when Lien Chan, the head of the GMD, was invited to meet Hu Jintao in China. Rather cheekily, he took the opportunity to publicly call for democratic reform. Away from the sabre rattling, the two nations have increased their economic ties, with much of Taiwan's industrial production relocating to the mainland. Despite the scaremongering, war looks unlikely; more plausibly, China will continue trying to undermine the independence movement while building up its military power until it could realistically threaten to invade, at which point Taiwan and its allies will baulk at a potential conflict, and some form of reunification process will begin.

mores, goods, even football teams. Both China and the world have much to gain from Chinese openness. It would be a shame for both should political shakiness lead to a retreat from that.

Chronology

4800 BC ▸ First evidence of **human settlement**. **Banpo** in the Yellow River basin build Bronze Age town of **Erlitou** in Henan. **Yin** in Anyang boasts a rich and developed culture.

21C–16C BC ▸ **Xia dynasty**.

16C–11C BC ▸ **Shang dynasty**. First extant writing in China.

11C–771 BC ▸ **Zhou dynasty**. The concept of **Mandate from Heaven** introduced.

770 BC–476 BC ▸ **Spring and Autumn** period. Kong Fuzi or **Confucius** (c. 500 BC) teaches a philosophy of adherence to ritual and propriety.

457 BC–221 BC ▸ **Warring States** Period. The **Great Wall** "completed".

221 BC–207 BC ▸ **Qin dynasty**. Emperor **Qin Shi Huang** founds first centralized empire. **Terracotta Army** guard Qin's tomb.

206 BC–220 AD ▸ **Han dynasty**. Han emperors bring stability and great advances in trade; leave **Han tombs** near Xi'an. **Confucianism** and **Buddhism** ascendant. **Silk Road** opens up first trade with central Asia.

220–280 ▸ **Three Kingdoms** period; influence of Buddhist **India** and **Central Asia** enlivens a Dark Age.

265–420 ▸ **Jin dynasty**. Northern barbarians absorbed into Chinese culture.

420–581 ▸ **Southern dynasties and Northern dynasties**: rapid succession of short-lived dynasties brings disunity. Earliest **Longmen caves** near Luoyang.

581–618 ▸ **Sui dynasty**. Centralization and growth under **Wen Di**. Extension and strengthening of **Great Wall**; digging of **Grand Canal**.

618–907 ▸ **Tang dynasty**. Arts and literature reach their most developed stage. **Great Buddha** at Leshan completed.

907–960 ▸ **Five dynasties**. Decline of culture and the northern defences. **Cliff sculptures** of Dazu.

960–1271 ▸ **Song dynasties**. Consolidation of the lesser kingdoms.

1271–1368 ▸ **Yuan dynasty**. **Genghis Khan** invades. Trade with Europe develops under **Kublai Khan**. **Forbidden City** built. **Marco Polo** visits China 1273–92.

1368–1644 ▸ **Ming dynasty**. Imperial investigative fleet under **Admiral Zheng He** reaches Africa. Later isolationist policies restrict contact with rest of world.

1644 ▸ **Qing dynasty** begins. **Manchus** gain control over China and extend its boundaries.

Mid- to late 17C ▸ **Potala Palace** in Lhasa rebuilt by Fifth Dalai Lama.

Late 18C ▸ **East India Company** monopolizes trade with Britain. **Summer Palace** in Beijing completed.

1839–62 ▸ **Opium Wars**. As part of the surrender settlement, **Hong Kong** is ceded to Britain.

1851–64 ▸ **Taiping Uprising**. Conservative policies of Dowager Empress **Cixi** allow foreign powers to take control of China's industry.

1899 ▸ **Boxer Rebellion**.

1911 ▸ **End of imperial China**. **Sun Yatsen** becomes leader of the **Republic**.

1921 ▸ **Chinese Communist Party** founded in Beijing.

1927 ▸ **Chiang Kaishek** orders massacre of Communists in Shanghai. **Mao Zedong** organizes first peasant-worker army.

1932 ▸ Japan invades **Manchuria**.

1936–41 ▸ The Nationalist **Guomindang** and the **People's Liberation Army form the United Front** against the Japanese.

1945 ▸ Surrender of Japan. **Civil war** between the Guomindang and the People's Liberation Army.

1949 ▸ Communist takeover. Chiang Kaishek flees to **Taiwan**. The newly proclaimed **People's Republic of China** supports North Korea in the **Korean War**.

1956 ▸ The **Hundred Flowers** campaign unsuccessfully attempts liberalization.

1958 ▸ Agricultural and industrial reform in the shape of the **commune system** and the **Great Leap Forward**. Widespread famine results.

1964 ▸ China explodes its first atomic weapon.

1966–8 ▸ In the **Cultural Revolution**, Red Guards purge anti-Maoist elements along with "ideologically unsound" art and architecture.

1971 ▸ People's Republic replaces Taiwan at the **United Nations**.

1972 ▸ **US president Nixon** visits Beijing.

1976 ▸ The **Tian'anmen Incident** reveals public support for moderate **Deng Xiaoping**. **Mao Zedong dies**, and the **Gang of Four** are arrested shortly afterwards.

1977 ▸ Deng Xiaoping rises to become **Party Chairman**.

1980 ▸ Beginning of the "open door" policy.

1981 ▸ Trial of the **Gang of Four**.

1989 ▸ Suppression of the democracy movement in **Tian'anmen Square**.

1992 ▸ Major **cabinet reshuffle** puts Deng's men in power.

1995 ▸ Death of Chen Yun, last of the hardline Maoists in the Politburo. Work begins on the **Three Gorges Dam**.

1997 ▸ **Hong Kong** returns to the mainland. Death of **Deng Xiaoping**.

1999 ▸ **Macau** returns to the mainland. Persecution of **Falun Gong** begins.

2001 ▸ China admitted to the **World Trade Organization**. Beijing wins bid to host **2008 Olympics**.

2002 ▸ **Hu Jintao** becomes President.

2003 ▸ China puts a man into space.

2004 ▸ **SARS** epidemic; China's population reaches 1.3 billion.

2006 ▸ The **Three Gorges Dam** is finished, and the new railway line to **Tibet** opens.

Chinese beliefs

The resilience of ancient beliefs in China, and the ability of the Chinese people to absorb new streams of thought and eventually to dominate them, has been demonstrated again and again over the centuries. While China has been periodically dominated by foreign powers, her belief systems have never been overwhelmed. Instead, conquering invaders, such as the Mongolians in the thirteenth and the Manchus in the seventeenth centuries, have found themselves inexorably **sinicized**. On this strength rests the understandable Chinese confidence in the ultimate superiority of their beliefs, a confidence that has survived through the lowest periods in Chinese history.

That said, the visitor to modern China will find few obvious indications of the traditional beliefs that have underpinned the country's civilization for three thousand years. Certainly, the remains of religious buildings litter the cities and the countryside, yet they appear sadly incongruous amid the furious pace of change all around. The restored temples – now "cultural relics" with photo booths, concession stands, special foreign tourist shops and cheerful throngs of young Chinese on outings – are garish and evoke few mysteries.

This apparent lack of religion is hardly surprising, however: for decades, the old beliefs have been derided by the authorities as feudal **superstition**, and the oldest and most firmly rooted of them all, Confucianism, has been criticized and repudiated for nearly a century. In actual fact, however, the outward manifestations of the ancient beliefs are not essential: the traditions are expressed more clearly in how the Chinese think and act than in the symbols and rituals of overt worship.

The "Three Teachings"

The product of the oldest continuous civilization on earth, **Chinese religion** actually comprises a number of disparate and sometimes contradictory elements. At the heart of it all, **three basic philosophies** lie intermingled: Confucianism, Taoism and Buddhism. The way in which a harmonious balance has been created among these three is expressed in the often quoted maxim *san jiao fa yi* – "Three Teachings Flow into One".

Both **Confucianism** and **Taoism** are belief systems rooted in the Chinese soil, and they form as much a part of the Chinese collective unconscious as Platonic and Aristotelian thought does in the West. **Buddhism**, however, was brought to China from India along the Silk Road by itinerant monks and missionaries, from about the first century AD onwards. Just as the mutual contradictions of Confucianism and Taoism had been accommodated by the Chinese, Buddhism did not long eclipse other beliefs – as it established itself, its tenets transformed into something very different from what had originally come out of India.

Confucianism

China's oldest and greatest philosopher, Kong Zi, known in the West by his Latinized name **Confucius**, was in his lifetime an obscure and unsuccessful scholar. Born in 551 BC, during the so-called Warring States Period, he lived in an age of petty kingdoms where life was blighted by constant war, feuding and social disharmony. Confucius simply saw that society was something that could be improved if individuals behaved properly. Harking back to an earlier, mythic age of peace and social virtues, he preached adherence to **ritual and propriety** as the supreme answer to the horrifying disorder of the world as he found it. As he wandered from court to court attempting to teach rulers a better way to rule, he was, like his contemporary Socrates far away in Greece, largely ignored by men in power. In the centuries after his death, however, Confucianism, as reflected in the **Analects**, a collection of writings on his life and sayings compiled by his disciples, became the most influential and fundamental of Chinese philosophies.

Never a religion in the sense of postulating a higher deity, Confucianism is rather a set of **moral and social values** designed to bring the ways of citizens and governments into harmony with each other, and with their ancestors. Through proper training in the scholarly classics and rigid adherence to the rules of propriety, including ancestor-worship, the superior man could attain a level of moral righteousness that would, in turn, assure a stable and righteous social order. As a political theory, Confucianism called for the "**wisest sage**", the one whose moral sense was most refined, to be ruler. With a good ruler, one who practised the virtuous ways of his ancestors and was exemplary in terms of the **five Confucian virtues** – benevolence, righteousness, propriety, wisdom and trustworthiness – the world and society would naturally be in order. Force, the ultimate sanction, would be unnecessary. As Confucius said:

Just as the ruler genuinely desires the good, the people will be good. The virtue of the ruler may be compared to the wind and that of the common people to the grass. The grass under the force of the wind cannot but bend.

Gods play no part in this structure. Man is capable of perfection in his own right, given a superior ruler whose virtues are mirrored in the behaviour of his subjects. Instead of God, **five hierarchical relationships** are the prerequisites for a well-ordered society; given proper performance of the duties entailed in these, society should be "at ease with itself". The five relationships outline a strict structure of duty and obedience to authority: ruler to ruled, son to father, younger brother to older, wife to husband, and – the only relationship between equals – friend to friend. The intention is to create order and stability through rule by a moral elite, though in practice adherence to the unbending hierarchy of these relationships, as well as to the precepts of filial piety, has been used to justify a form of totalitarian rule throughout Chinese history. The supreme virtue of the well-cultivated man and woman was always **obedience**.

During the time of the Han dynasty (206 BC–220 AD), Confucianism became institutionalized as a **system of government** that was to prevail in China for two thousand years. With it, and with the notion of the scholar-official as the ideal administrator, came the notorious Chinese **bureaucracy**. Men would study half their lives in order to pass the imperial examinations and attain a government commission. These examinations were rigid tests of the scholar's knowledge of the Confucian classics. Right until the start of the twentieth century, power in China was wielded through a bureaucracy steeped in the classics of rites and rituals written five hundred years before Christ.

The Confucian ideal ruler, of course, never quite emerged (the emperor was not expected to sit the exams), and the scholar-officials often deteriorated into corrupt bureaucrats and exploitative landlords. Today, its rituals are no longer practised and its ideas have no currency. However, just as Protestantism is seen as having provided the underpinning to the advance of the West, so

Superstitions

Though the Chinese are not generally religious in the conventional sense, they are often very **superstitious**. You'll see evidence of this everywhere you go, especially in the form of wordplay. Thus the Chinese expression for "let luck come", *fudao*, happens to sound similar to "upside-down luck"; hence the inverted *fu* character pasted up outside homes and businesses at Spring Festival, encouraging good fortune to arrive on the premises. Other **lucky symbols** include peaches and cranes (for longevity), fish (prosperity), mandarin ducks (marital fidelity), dragons (male power), phoenixes (female power), and bats (happiness).

Colours are also important. **Red**, the colour of fire, and **gold**, the colour of money, are auspicious, and used extensively for decorations, packaging, weddings and festive occasions. **White** traditionally represents death or mourning, though traditional Western wedding dresses are becoming increasingly popular. **Yellow** is the colour of heaven, hence the yellow roof tiles used on temples; yellow clothing was formerly reserved for the emperor alone.

Confucianism, with its emphasis on order, harmony and co-operation, can be regarded as providing the ideological foundations for the recent successes of Asian culture.

Taoism

Tao translates literally as the "Way" and, in its purest form, Taoism is the study and pursuit of this ineffable Way, as outlined in the fundamental text, the **Daodejing** (often written as *Tao Te Ching*) or "The Way of Power". This obscure and mystical text essentially comprises a compilation of the wise sayings of a semi-mythical hermit by the name of **Lao Zi**, who is said to have been a contemporary of Confucius. The *Daodejing* was not compiled until at least three centuries after his death.

The *Tao* is never really defined – indeed by its very nature it is undefinable. To the despair of the rationalist, the first lines of the *Daodejing* read:

The Tao that can be told
is not the eternal Tao.
The name that can be named
is not the eternal name.

In essence, however, it might be thought of as the Way of Nature, the underlying principle and source of all being, the bond that unites man and nature. Its central principle, **Wu Wei**, can crudely be translated as "no action", though it is probably better understood as "no action which runs contrary to nature". Taoism was originally the creed of the recluse. Whereas Confucianism is concerned with repairing social order and social relationships, Taoism is interested in the relationship of the individual with the natural universe. It simply looks at human problems from another, higher plane: having good relations with one's neighbours is of no use if one is not in harmony with nature.

Taoism's second major text is a book of parables written by one ideal practitioner of the Way, **Zhuang Zi**, another semi-mythical figure. Acknowledged in his lifetime as a great sage, he rejected all offers of high rank in favour of a life of solitary reflection. His works – allegorical tales that have delighted Chinese readers for centuries – reveal humour as well as perception. In the famous butterfly parable, Zhuang Zi examines the many faces of reality:

Getting around a Chinese temple

Whether Buddhist or Taoist, Chinese temples share the same broad **features.** Like cities, they **face south** and are surrounded by walls. Gates are sealed by **heavy doors**, guarded by paintings or statues of warrior deities to chase away evil. Further protection is ensured by a **spirit wall** that blocks direct entry; although easy enough for the living to walk around, this foils spirits, who are unable to turn corners. Once inside, you'll find a succession of **halls** arranged in ornamental courtyards. In case evil influences should manage to get in, the area nearest the entrance contains the least important rooms or buildings, while those of greater significance – living quarters or main temple halls – are set deeper inside the complex.

One way to tell **Buddhist** and **Taoist** temples apart is by the colour of the **supporting pillars** – Buddhists use bright red, while Taoists favour black. **Animal carvings** are more popular with Taoists, who use decorative good-luck and longevity symbols such as bats and cranes; some Taoist halls also have distinctive raised octagonal cupolas sporting the black-and-white *yinyang* symbol.

Once upon a time Zhuang Zi dreamed he was a butterfly. A butterfly flying around and enjoying itself. It did not know it was Zhuang Zi again. We do not know whether it was Zhuang Zi dreaming that he was a butterfly, or a butterfly dreaming he was Zhuang Zi.

In its affirmation of the irrational and natural sources of life, Taoism has provided Chinese culture with a balance to the rigid social mores of Confucianism. In traditional China it was said that the perfect lifestyle was that of a man who was a Confucian during the day – a righteous and firm administrator, upholding the virtues of the gentleman/ruler – and a Taoist after the duties of the day had been fulfilled. The practice of Taoism affirms the virtues of withdrawing from public duties and giving oneself up to a life of **contemplation and meditation**. If Confucianism preaches duty to family and to society, Taoism champions the sublimity of withdrawal, non-committedness and "dropping out". The **art and literature** of China have been greatly enriched by Taoism's notions of contemplation, detachment and freedom from social entanglement, and the Tao has become embedded in the Chinese soul as a doctrine of yielding to the inevitable forces of nature.

Buddhism

The first organized religion to penetrate China, **Buddhism** enjoyed a glorious, if brief, period of ascendancy under the Tang dynasty (618–906 AD). In the eighth century there were over three hundred thousand Buddhist monks in China. This time saw the creation of much of the country's **great religious art** – above all the cave shrines at **Luoyang** (Henan), **Datong** (Shaanxi) and **Dunhuang** (Gansu), where thousands of carvings of the Buddha and paintings of holy figures attest to the powerful influence of Indian art and religion.

Gradually, though, Buddhism too was submerged into the native belief system. Most contemporary schools of Indian Buddhism taught that life on earth was essentially one of suffering, an endless cycle in which people were born, grew old and died, only to be born again in other bodies; the goal was to break out of this cycle by attaining nirvana, which could be done by losing all desire for things of the world. This essentially individualistic doctrine was not likely to appeal to the regimented Chinese, however, and so it was the relatively small **Mahayana School** of Buddhism came to dominate Chinese thinking. The Mahayana taught that perfection for the individual was not possible without perfection for all – and that those who had already attained enlightenment would remain active in the world as **Bodhisattvas**, to help others along the path. In time Bodhisattvas came to be ascribed miraculous powers, and were prayed to in a manner remarkably similar to conventional Confucian ancestor-worship. The mainstream of Chinese Buddhism came to be more about maintaining harmonious relations with Bodhisattvas than about attaining nirvana.

Another entirely new sect of Buddhism also arose in China through contact with Taoism. Known in China as **Chan** (and in Japan as Zen) Buddhism, it offered a less extreme path to enlightenment. For a Chan Buddhist, it was not necessary to become a monk or a recluse in order to achieve nirvana – instead this ultimate state of being could be reached through life in accord with, and in contemplation of, the Way.

In short, the Chinese managed to marry Buddhism to their pre-existing belief structures with very little difficulty at all. This was facilitated by the general absence of dogma within Buddhist thought. Like the Chinese, the **Tibetans**, too, found themselves able to adapt the new belief system to their old religion, **Bon** (see p.925), rather than simply replacing it. Over the centuries, they established their own schools of Buddhism, often referred to as Lamaist Buddhism or **Lamaism**, which differ from the Chinese versions in minor respects. The now dominant **Gelugpa** (or Yellow Hat) school, of which the Dalai and Panchen Lamas are members, dates back to the teachings of Tsongkhapa (1357–1419). For more on Buddhism in Tibet, see p.1084.

Minority faiths and popular beliefs

Though Buddhism was the only foreign religion to leave a substantial mark on China, it was not the only one to enter China via the Silk Road. Both **Islam** and **Christianity** also trickled into the country this way, and to this day a significant minority of Chinese, numbering possibly in the tens of millions, are Muslims. Unlike much of the rest of Asia, however, China did not yield wholesale to the tide of Islam, and thoroughly rejected it as a political doctrine.

When Jesuit missionaries first arrived in China in the sixteenth and seventeenth centuries, they were astounded and dismayed by the Chinese **flexibility of belief**. One frustrated Jesuit put it thus: "In China, the educated believe nothing and the uneducated believe everything." For those versed in the classics of Confucianism, Taoism and Buddhism, the normal belief was a healthy and tolerant scepticism. For the great majority of illiterate peasants, however, **popular religion** offered a plethora of ghosts, spirits, gods and ancestors who ruled over a capricious nature and protected humanity. If Christian missionaries handed out rice, perhaps Christ too deserved a place alongside them. In popular Buddhism the hope was to reach the "Pure Land", a kind of heaven for believers ruled over by a female deity known as the Mother Ruler. Popular Taoism shared this feminine deity, but its concerns were rather with the sorcerers, alchemists and martial-arts aficionados who sought solutions to the riddle of immortality; you may well see some of these figures depicted in Taoist temples.

Modern China

During the twentieth century, confronted by the superior military and technical power of the West, the Chinese have striven to break free from the shackles of superstition. Since the imperial examinations were abolished at the start of the century, Chinese intellectuals have been searching for a modern yet essentially Chinese philosophy. The **Cultural Revolution** can be seen as the culmination of these efforts to repudiate the past. Hundreds of thousands of temples, ancestral halls and religious objects were defaced and destroyed. Monasteries that had preserved their seclusion for centuries were burnt to the ground, and their monks imprisoned. The classics of literature and philosophy – the "residue of the reactionary feudal past" – were burned. In 1974, towards the end of the Cultural Revolution, a campaign was launched to "criticize Lin Biao and Confucius", pairing the general with the sage to imply that both were equally reactionary in their opposition to the government.

Yet the very fact that Confucius could still be held up as an object for derision in 1974 reveals the tenacity of traditional beliefs. With the Cultural Revolution now long gone, they are once again being accepted as an essential part of the cultural tradition that binds the Chinese people together. Despite a lifetime of commitment to the Marxist revolution, the older generation are comforted and strengthened by their knowledge of the national heritage, while the young are rediscovering the classics, the forbidden fruit of their school days. The welcome result is that Chinese temples of all descriptions are once more prosperous, busy places, teeming with people who have come to ask for grandchildren or simply for money. The atmosphere may not seem devout or religious, but then perhaps it never did.

Traditional Chinese Medicine

As an agricultural society, the Chinese have long been aware of the importance of the proper **balance** of natural, elemental forces: too much heat causes drought; too much rain, floods; while the correct measure of both encourages farmers' crops to grow. The ancient Chinese saw heaven, earth and humankind existing as an integral whole, such that if people lived in harmony with heaven and earth, then their collective health would be good. The medical treatise *Huang Di Neijing*, attributed to the semi-mythical Yellow Emperor (2500 BC), mentions the importance of spiritual balance, acupuncture and herbal medicine in treating illnesses, and attests to the venerable age of China's medical beliefs – it may well be a compilation of even earlier texts. Acupuncture was certainly in use by the Han period, as tombs in Hebei dated to 113 BC have yielded acupuncture needles made of gold and silver.

The belief in universal balance is known as **Dao** (or Tao) – literally "the Way", but implying "the Way of Nature". As an extension of Daoist principles, life is seen as consisting of opposites – man and woman, sun and moon, right and left, giving and receiving – whereby all things exist as a result of their interaction with their opposites. This is expressed in the black-and-white Daoist diagram which shows two interacting opposites, the **yin** ("female", passive energy) and the **yang** ("male", active energy). At the core of traditional Chinese medicine lies the belief that in order for a body to be healthy, its opposites must also be in a state of dynamic balance; there is a constant fluctuation, for example, between the body's heat, depending on its level of activity and the weather, and the amount of water needed to keep the body at the correct temperature. An excess of water in the system creates oedema, too little creates dehydration; too much heat will cause a temperature, and too little cause chills. Chinese medicine therefore views the body as an integrated whole, so that in sickness, the whole body – rather than just the "ill" part of it – requires treatment.

Qi and acupuncture

An underlying feature of Chinese medical philosophy, **qi** (or *chi*) is the energy of life: in the same way that electricity powers a light bulb, *qi*, so the theory goes, enables us to move, see and speak. *Qi* is said to flow along the body's network of **meridians**, or energy pathways, linking the surface tissues to specific internal **organs** that act as *qi* reservoirs; the twelve major meridians are named after the organ to which they are connected. The meridians are further classed as *yin* or *yang* depending on whether they are exposed or protected. In the limbs, for instance, the channels of the outer sides are *yang*, and important for resisting disease, while the channels of the inner sides are *yin*, and more involved with nourishing the body.

Mental and physical tensions, poor diet, anger or depression, even adverse weather, however, are said to inhibit *qi* flow, causing illness. Needles inserted (and then rotated as necessary) in the body's **acupuncture points**, most of which lie on meridians and so are connected to internal organs, reinforce or reduce the *qi* flow along a meridian, in turn influencing the activities of the organs. When the *qi* is balanced and flowing smoothly once more, good health is regained; acupuncture is specifically used to combat inflammation, to regenerate damaged tissue, and to improve the functional power of internal organs.

Despite the growing acceptance of acupuncture in the West, there remains no good evidence for its efficacy. Studies have found that patients treated by acupuncturists had the same recovery rate as patients poked with needles at random positions. Sceptics argue that the act of sticking needles in the body produces pain-killing endorphins, which, combined with the placebo effect, aids recovery.

Herbal medicine

In the 2200 years since the semi-mythical Xia king **Shennong** compiled his classic work on **medicinal herbs**, a vast amount of experience has been gained to help perfect their clinical use. Approximately seven thousand herbs, derived from roots, leaves, twigs and fruit, are today commonly used in Chinese medicine, with another thousand or so of animal or mineral origin (still nonetheless classified as "herbs"). Each is first processed by cleaning, soaking, slicing, drying or roasting, or even stir-frying with wine, ginger or vinegar, to influence its effects; the brew is then boiled down and drunk as a tea (typically very bitter and earthy tasting).

Herbs are used to prevent or combat a wide variety of diseases. Some are used to treat the underlying cause of the complaint, others to treat symptoms and help strengthen the body's own immune system, in turn helping it to combat the problem. An everyday example is in the treatment of flu: the herbal formula would include a "cold action" herb to reduce the fever, a herb to induce sweating and thus clear the body-ache, a purgative to clear the virus from the system, and a tonic herb to replenish the immune system. In all treatments the patient is re-examined each week, and as the condition improves the herbal formula is changed accordingly.

Just as Western aspirin is derived from willow bark, many Chinese drugs have been developed from herbs. One example is the anti-malarial herb *qinghacsu*, or artemisinin, which has proved effective in treating chloroquine-resistant strains of malaria with minimal side effects.

The martial arts of China

Given China's tumultuous history of warring clans, warring states and even warring dynasties, it's hardly surprising that so much energy has been invested in the development and fine-tuning of the **martial arts**. In a society unable to rely on the government for protection, being a capable martial artist was often an essential skill. Fighting techniques evolved in almost all isolated communities, from Buddhist and Daoist temples down to clan villages. Only in recent times have outsiders been able to learn these distinctive styles, though some are now so popular that the government has approved formal versions.

Styles and techniques

Thousands of martial arts have evolved in China, but all can be classed into two basic types. **External** or hard styles (*waijia*) concentrate on developing *li*, or physical strength, to literally overpower opponents; for example, conditioning hands by punching plate iron and slapping concrete blocks thousands of times until one is able, by sheer force, to break planks of wood and stones. **Internal** or soft styles (*neijia*) concentrate on developing the internal energy known as *qi*, which supposedly circulates around the body along acupuncture meridians and is also one of the central aspects of Chinese medicine (see p.1170). **Qigong** – which means "breath skills" – is used to build up an awareness of *qi* and an ability to move it around the body, eventually replacing excess muscular action and making all movements fluid and powerful.

In practice, however, such distinctions are blurred; many external styles also use *qigong* techniques, just as most internal styles rely on some brute force. From the outside, internal and external styles can look similar, as both use **forms** – prearranged sets of movements – to develop the necessary speed, power and timing; both use punches, kicks and open hand strikes as well as a wide variety of **weapons**; and both often incorporate **animal movements** – for instance, in monkey-style kung fu the practitioner behaves and moves like a monkey while fighting. The following brief accounts describe some of the better-known martial arts, which you may well see being performed in public parks in China.

Shaolin kung fu

One of the most influential figures in the development of Chinese external martial arts was the sixth-century Indian Buddhist monk **Boddhidarma**, who spent many years at the **Shaolin temple** (see p.299). Here he taught the monks movement and breathing exercises, which were later combined with indigenous martial arts to form **Shaolin kung fu**. "Shaolin" is a very nebulous term in China today, indiscriminately used to describe a host of fighting styles that probably have little historical connection with the temple. Nonetheless, it's a vigorous art best known for its powerful kicks and animal styles – especially eagle, mantis and monkey. The classic Shaolin weapon is the **staff**, and there's even a **drunken form**, where the practitioner behaves as if inebriated – an athletic and surprisingly effective technique.

Xingyi quan

Xingyi quan translates awkwardly as "shape through intent boxing", reflecting its guiding principle that the body should act directly from the mind. Believed to have been developed from Shaolin kung fu spear forms by the famous Song-dynasty general **Yue Fei**, *xingyi* is now an internal art, though using *qi* rather differently from either *bagua* or *tai ji*. *Xingyi* schools emphasize **linear** attacks, smashing straight through an opponent's defences and defeating them as directly and effectively as possible. In this uncluttered philosophy, and the use of relatively few techniques, *xingyi* is probably the easiest of the internal arts to learn and use for fighting.

Bagua zhang

Bagua zhang means "*bagua* palm", which refers both to the eight-sided symbol used in the Chinese book of divination, the *I Ching*, of which *bagua zhang* is a martial expression, and to the fact that strikes are almost invariably made with the **palm**. *Bagua* is among the most distinctive martial arts to watch being performed, employing fast footwork and characteristic **twisting movements** to simultaneously evade attacks and place the defender behind the aggressor, and thus in a position to strike back. An internal art, it nonetheless uses some physical force, and tends towards devastating overkill in its response to attacks. The various schools use **circle-walking forms** to develop *qi* – if you see somebody walking endlessly around a tree in a Chinese park, they're practising this – as well as less abstract linear forms to learn fighting skills. *Bagua*'s continuous twisting pumps *qi* from the spine around the body, and *bagua* practitioners are famous for their health and longevity.

Tai ji quan

Though Tai ji quan (*yinyang* boxing) is the world's most popular martial art, it's seldom taught as such. The original form, known as **Chen tai ji**, is closely related to Shaolin kung fu but emphasizes *qi* usage; a later form developed by **Yang Luchan** (1799–1872) is entirely internal, and the hardest of any style to learn for practical fighting. Despite this, these older forms are effective martial arts, relying on acute sensitivity to anticipate attacks and strike first; counter-strikes are made with the entire body in a state of **minimal tension**, creating *tai ji*'s characteristic "soft" appearance, and increasing *qi* flow and power. Strong *qi* flow means good health, and Yang Luchan's grandson, **Yang Chengfu** (1883–1936) slowed *tai ji* movements and stripped it of obvious martial content so the elderly or infirm could learn it and thus avoid illness – it's versions of this simplified form which are most widely taught today. A two-person sensitivity training technique common to all *tai ji* styles is *tui shou* (**push hands**), in which practitioners alternately attack and yield, learning to absorb and redirect their opponent's force.

Studying martial arts

There's been a considerable watering down of martial arts in China in recent years. Since the 1950s, the Chinese government has produced "official" versions of various fighting styles that are collectively known as **wushu** (literally, "martial

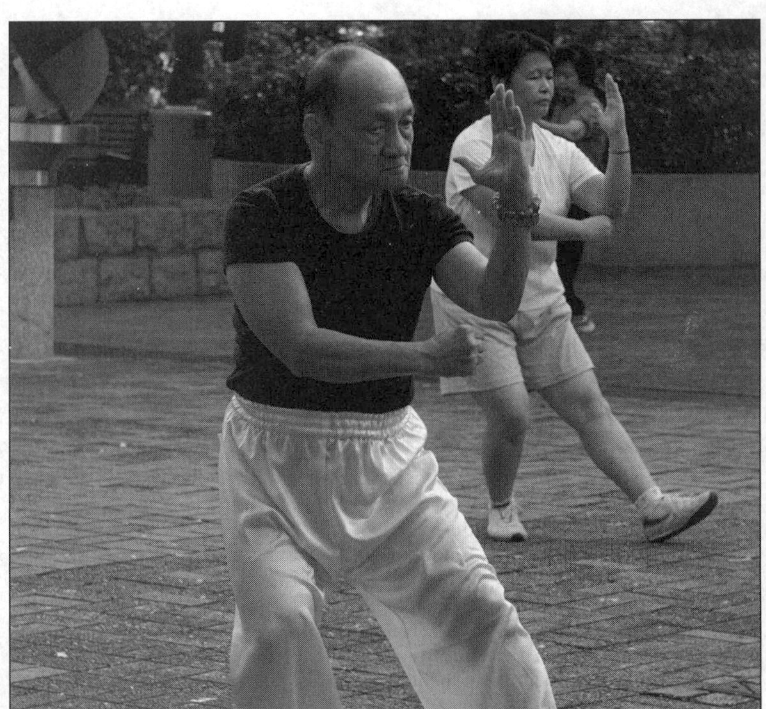

▲ Practising tai ji

arts"). The main intent with *wushu* styles is to promote health and fitness, not fighting ability, and they're taught mainly as competitive sports. In the process, much of what is openly taught today in China is – in martial terms – second-rate. Depending on what you're after, therefore, finding competent **instruction** can be difficult.

Famous martial-arts centres, such as Shaolin and the Taoist temples at **Wudang Shan** (see p.490), might seem like the obvious **places to study**, but in practice, their fame has been counter-productive. Shaolin, for example, is surrounded by martial-arts schools all claiming to be the only one to teach the "real" Shaolin techniques. Still, they're used to foreigners turning up, and courses at the schools are very organized; Wudang Shan has yet to become as commercialized, however, and they remain choosy in whom they teach. *Wushu* is widely taught at **sports institutes**, including Beijing University of Physical Education, but serious martial content is lacking. Otherwise, visiting the nearest **park** at dawn to see people practising is a good way of finding an instructor or – if you already know a style – meeting up with others to practise with, though outside of Hong Kong you'll need to speak some Chinese.

If you can't speak Chinese, you'll be better off considering the travellers' havens of Dali and Yangshuo, both of which have martial-arts teachers used to dealing with foreigners; Yangshuo's Budi Zhen school is particularly good (see p.727). For more information on Chinese martial arts, check out **China From Inside** (Ⓦwww.chinafrominside.com) – as well as interviews with martial artists, there's a message board and plenty of links.

Art

This very brief survey aims to reflect what you are likely to see most of in Chinese provincial and city museums and art galleries – and to an extent *in situ*. When you look at the art displayed in Chinese museums, bear in mind that while for more than two thousand years imperial China produced an incredible wealth of art objects, from the mid-nineteenth century onwards, many of these were acquired – more or less legitimately – by Westerners. Later, too, some of the great imperial collections were removed by the Nationalists to Taiwan, where they are now in the National Palace Museum; perhaps just as well, as most of what was left in the country was destroyed during the Cultural Revolution.

Pottery, bronzes and sculpture

The earliest Chinese objects date back to the Neolithic farmers of the **Yangshao** culture – well-made **pottery** vessels painted in red, black, brown and white with geometric designs. You'll notice that the decoration is usually from the shoulders of the pots upwards; this is because what has survived is mostly from graves and was designed to be seen from above when the pots were placed round the dead. From the same period come decorated clay heads, perhaps for magic or ritual, and pendants and small ornaments of polished stone or jade, with designs that are sometimes semi-abstract – a simplified sitting bird in polished jade is a very early example of the powerful Chinese tradition of animal sculpture. Rather later is the Neolithic **Longshan** pottery – black, very thin and fine, wheel-turned and often highly polished, with elegant, sharply defined shapes.

The subsequent era, from around 1500 BC, is dominated by **Shang and Zhou bronze vessels** that were used for preparing and serving food and wine, and for ceremonies and sacrifices. Each of the many distinct shapes has its own name and specific usage. One of the most common is the *ding*, a three- or four-legged vessel that harks back to the Neolithic pots used for cooking over open fires. As you'll see from the museums, these bronzes have survived in great numbers. The **Shang** bronze industry appears already fully developed, with advanced techniques and designs and no sign of a primitive stage. Casting methods were highly sophisticated, using moulds, while design was firm and assured and decoration often stylized and linear, featuring both geometric and animal motifs, as well as grinning masks of humans and fabulous beasts. There are some naturalistic animal forms among the vessels, too – fierce tigers, solid elephants and surly-looking rhinoceroses. Other bronze finds include weapons, decorated horse harnesses and sets of bells used in ritual music. Later, under the **Zhou**, the style of the bronzes becomes more varied and rich: some animal vessels are fantastically shaped and extravagantly decorated; others are simplified natural forms; others again seem to be depicting not so much a fierce tiger, for example, as utter ferocity itself. You'll also see from the Shang and Zhou small objects – ornaments, ritual pieces and jewellery pendants – bearing highly simplified but vivid forms of tortoises, salamanders and flying birds. Some painted clay funeral figures and a few carved wooden figures also survive from the end of this period.

Although the Shang produced a few small sculpted human figures and animals in marble, **sculptures** and works in stone begin to be found in great quantities in **Han-dynasty** tombs. The decorated bricks and tiles, the bas-reliefs and the terracotta figurines of acrobats, horsemen and ladies-in-waiting placed in the tombs to serve the dead, even the massive stone men and beasts set to guard the Spirit Way leading to the tomb, are all lifelike and reflect concern with everyday activities and material possessions. The scale models of houses with people looking out of the windows and of farmyards with their animals have a spontaneous gaiety and vigour; some of the watchdogs are the most realistic of all. Smaller objects like tiny statuettes and jewellery were also carved, from ivory, jade and wood.

It was the advent of **Buddhism** that encouraged stone carving on a large scale in the round, using mallet and chisel. **Religious sculpture** was introduced from India; in the fourth-century caves at **Datong** (see p.231), and the earlier caves at **Longmen**, near Luoyang (see p.294), the Indian influence is most strongly felt in the stylized Buddhas and attendants. Sometimes of huge size, these have an aloof grace and a rhythmic quality in their flowing robes, but also a smooth, bland and static quality. Not until the **Tang** do you get the full flowering of a native Chinese style, where the figures are rounder, with movement, and the positions, expressions and clothes are more natural and realistic. Some of the best examples are to be seen at **Dunhuang** (see p.1012) and in the later caves at Longmen. The **Song** continued to carve religious figures, and at **Dazu** in Sichuan (see p.902), you'll find good examples of a highly decorative style that had broadened its subject matter to include animals, ordinary people and scenes of everyday life; the treatment is down-to-earth, individual, sometimes even comic. As the Dazu carvings are very well preserved, they can still be seen painted, as they were meant to be. In later years, less statuary was produced until the **Ming** with their taste for massive and impressive tomb sculptures. You can see the best of these in **Nanjing** and **Beijing**.

Ceramics

From Neolithic painted pottery onwards, China developed a high level of excellence in **ceramics**, based on the availability of high-quality materials. Its pre-eminence was recognized by the fact that for more than four hundred years the English language has used the word "china" to mean fine-quality ceramic ware. In some of the early wares you can see the influence of shapes derived from bronzes, but soon the rise of regional potteries using different materials, and the development of special types for different uses, led to an enormous variety of shapes, textures and colours. This was noticeable by the **Tang dynasty**, when an increase in the production of pottery for daily use was partly stimulated by the spread of tea drinking and by the restriction of the use of copper and bronze to coinage. The Tang also saw major technical advances; the production of true **porcelain** was finally achieved, and Tang potters became very skilled in the use of polychrome glazing. You can see evidence of this in the *san cai* (three-colour) statuettes of horses and camels, jugglers, traders, polo players, grooms and court ladies, which have come in great numbers from imperial tombs, and which reflect in vivid, often humorous, detail and still-brilliant colours so many aspects of the life of the time. It was a cosmopolitan civilization open to foreign influences, and this is clearly seen in Tang art.

The **Song** dynasty witnessed a great refinement of ceramic techniques and of regional specialization, many wares being named after the area that produced them. The keynote was simplicity and quiet elegance, both in colour and form. There was a preference for using a **single pure colours**, and for incized wares made to resemble damask cloth. In the museums you'll see the famous green celadons, the thin white porcelain *ding* ware and the pale grey-green *ju* ware reserved for imperial use. The Mongol **Yuan** dynasty, in the early fourteenth century, enriched Chinese tradition with outside influences – notably the introduction of **cobalt blue underglaze**, early examples of the blue and white porcelain that was to become so famous. The **Ming** saw the flowering of great potteries under imperial patronage, especially **Jingdezhen**. Taste moved away from Song simplicity and returned to the liking for vivid colour previously displayed by the Tang – deep **red**, **yellow** and **orange** glazes, with a developing taste for pictorial representation. From the seventeenth century onwards, Chinese export wares flowed in great quantity and variety to the West to satisfy a growing demand for chinoiserie, and the efforts of the Chinese artists to follow what they saw as the tastes and techniques of the West produced a style of its own. The early **Qing** created delicate enamel wares and *famille rose* and *verte*. So precise were the craftsmen that some porcelain includes the instructions for the pattern in the glaze.

You can visit several potteries such as at **Jingdezhen** in Jiangxi province, where both early wares and modern trends are on display. Not so long ago they were turning out thousands of figurines of Mao and Lu Xun sitting in armchairs; now the emphasis is on table lamp bases in the shape of archaic maidens in flowing robes playing the lute, or creased and dimpled Laughing Buddhas.

Painting and calligraphy

While China's famous ceramics were made by craftsmen who remained anonymous, **painting and calligraphy** pieces were produced by famous scholars, officials and poets. It has been said that the four great treasures of Chinese painting are the brush, the ink, the inkstone and the paper or silk. The earliest **brush** to have been found dates from about 400 BC, and is made out of animal hairs glued to a hollow bamboo tube. **Ink** was made from pine soot, mixed with glue and hardened into a stick that would be rubbed with water on an **inkstone** made of non-porous, carved and decorated slate. **Silk** was used for painting as early as the third century BC, while **paper** was invented by **Cai Lun** in 106 AD. The first known painting on silk was found in a **Han** tomb; records show that a great deal of such painting was created, but in 190 AD the vast imperial collection was destroyed in a civil war, when soldiers used the silk to make tents and knapsacks. All we know of Han painting comes from decorated tiles, lacquer, painted pottery and a few painted tombs, enough to show a great sense of movement and energy. The British Museum holds a scroll in ink and colour on silk from around 400 AD, attributed to **Gu Kaizhi** and entitled *Admonitions of the Instructress to Court Ladies*, and we know that the theory of painting was already being discussed by then, as the treatise *The Six Principles of Painting* dates from about 500 AD.

The **Sui–Tang** period, with a powerful stable empire and a brilliant court, was the perfect moment for painting to develop. A great tradition of **figure painting** grew up, especially of court subjects – several portraits and pictures of the emperor receiving envoys, and of court ladies, can be seen in Beijing.

Although only a few of these survived, the walls of Tang tombs, such as those near Xi'an, are rich in vivid frescoes that provide a realistic portrayal of court life. Wang Wei in the mid-eighth century was an early exponent of monochrome **landscape painting**, but the great flowering of landscape painting came with the **Song dynasty**. An academy was set up under imperial patronage, and different schools of painting emerged which analysed the natural world with great concentration and intensity; their style has set a mark on Chinese landscape painting ever since. There was also lively **figure painting**, as epitomized by a famous horizontal scroll in Beijing that depicts the Qing Ming River Festival. That the last emperor of the Northern Song, **Hui Zong**, was himself a painter of some note indicates the status of painting in China at the time. The Southern Song preferred a more intimate style, and such subjects as flowers, birds and still life grew in popularity.

Under the **Mongols**, many officials found themselves unwanted or unwilling to serve the alien Yuan dynasty, and preferred to retire and paint. This produced the **"literati" school**, in which many painters harked back to the styles of the tenth century. One great master, **Ni Can**, also devoted himself, among many others, to the ink paintings of bamboo that became important at this time. In this school, of which many examples remain extant, the highest skills of techniques and composition were applied to the simplest of subjects, such as plum flowers. Both ink painting as well as more conventional media continued to be employed by painters during the next three or more centuries. From the **Yuan** onwards, a tremendous quantity of paintings has survived. The **Ming dynasty** saw a great interest in collecting the works of previous ages, and a linked willingness by painters to be influenced by tradition. There are plenty of examples of bamboo and plum blossom, and bird and flower paintings being brought to a high decorative pitch, as well as a number of schools of landscape painting firmly rooted in traditional techniques. The arrival of the Manchu **Qing dynasty** did not disrupt the continuity of Chinese painting, but the art became wide open to many influences. It included the Italian **Castiglione** (Lang Shi-ning in Chinese) who specialized in horses, dogs and flowers under imperial patronage; the Four Wangs who reinterpreted Song and Yuan styles in an orthodox manner; and the individualists such as the Eight Eccentrics of Yangzhou and certain Buddhist monks who objected to derivative art and sought a more distinctive approach to subject and style. But on the whole, the weight of tradition was powerful enough to maintain the old approach.

Calligraphy

Calligraphy – the word is derived from the Greek for "beautiful writing" – was crystallized into a high art form in China, where the use of the brush saw the development of handwriting of various styles, valued on a par with painting. Of the various different scripts, the **seal script** is the archaic form found on oracle bones; the **lishu** is the clerical style and was used in inscriptions on stone; the **kaishu** is the regular style closest to the modern printed form; and the cursive **cao shu** (grass script) is the most individual handwritten style. Emperors, poets and scholars over centuries have left examples of their calligraphy cut into stone at beauty spots, on mountains and in grottoes, tombs and temples all over China; you can see some early examples in the caves at Longmen (see p.294). At one stage during the Tang dynasty, calligraphy was so highly prized that it was the yardstick for the selection of high officials.

Other arts

Jade and lacquerware have also been constantly in use in China since earliest times. In Chinese eyes, **jade**, in white and shades of green or brown, is the most

Contemporary Art

Contemporary art is both flourishing and highly accessible in China. There are hundreds of private galleries and every major city has an arts centre, often an old factory converted into studios and exhibition spaces – 798 in Beijing and 50 Moganshan Lu in Shanghai are the biggest examples, but it's also worth noting Nordica in Kunming and OCT in Shenzhen, among others. Fairs such as the Shanghai Biennale and Guangzhou's triennal have become enormous events. Chinese art is seen as hot by investors, and there's plenty of money sloshing around; it helps that art is less easy to counterfeit than other cultural forms, and, because "meaning" in art can be nebulous, trickier for the government to censor.

However, the first crop of modern Chinese artists, who emerged in the 1990s, worked in obscurity with, it seemed, no prospects of exhibition. They banded together for survival in artists' villages most famously at the **"Yuanmingyuan Artists Community"** outside Beijing. The artists here developed a school of painting that expressed their individualism and their sceptical, often ironic and sometimes jaundiced view of contemporary China; this was, of course, the generation that had seen its dreams of change shot down at Tian'anmen Square. Nurtured by curator **Li Xianting**, known as the "Godfather of Chinese art", as well as sympathetic foreign collectors, they built the foundations of the art scene as it is today. The most famous of these so-called "cynical realists" is **Fang Lijun**, whose paintings of disembodied bald heads against desolate landscapes are now some of the most characteristic images of modern Chinese art. Look out too for **Yue Minjun**'s paintings of the Tian'anmen massacre that reference Goya, **Yang Shaobin**'s slickly painted sinister figures, and the bitingly satirical caricatures of **Wang Yinsong** and **Song Yonghong**.

Artists such as **Wang Guangyi** developed another school of distinctly Chinese contemporary art, "political pop". Here, a mocking twist is given to the iconography of the Cultural Revolution in order to critique a society that has become brashly commercial; Red guards are shown waving iPods instead of Little Red Books and so on. Of late this has become rather a hackneyed genre, though every artist seems to go through a phase of it, and it's enthusiastically collected in the West.

Although it's hard to pick out trends amid such a ferment of activity, artists these days are not surprisingly preoccupied with documenting the destruction of the Chinese urban landscape. and the gut-wrenching changes that have accompanied modernization. As spaces for viewing art have grown, artists have diversified into new media such as **performance and video**. Exciting new faces to look out for include **Chen Lingyang**, who makes disturbing photographs of flowers with her genitals, and **Qing Qing**, whose gossamer-thin clothes, made of straw, flowers and the like, are part of an investigation into the role of women in Chinese society. **Cui Xiuwen**'s videos of women in a toilet at a karaoke bar are shocking and memorable, as was **Xu Zhen**'s video *Rainbow*, in which his back is seen turning red from unseen slaps; it was one of the best works at the 2001 Venice Biennale. **Documentary photography** is also very popular at the moment; among its finest exponents is **Yang Fudong**, notable for his wistful images of city life. **Wu Gaozhong** first drew attention for a performance piece in which he climbed into the belly of a slaughtered cow, but his recent work, involving giant props implanted with boar hair, is more subtle, and has a creepy beauty. And it's always worth looking out for a show curated by *enfant terrible* **Gu Zhenqing**, who has a reputation for gleefully pushing the limits.

precious of stones. It was used to make the earliest ritual objects, such as the flat disc **Pi**, symbol of Heaven, which was found in Shang and Zhou graves. Jade was also used as a mark of rank and for ornament, in its most striking form in the jade burial suits to be seen in the country's museums.

Lacquer, made from the sap of the lac tree, is also found as early as the Zhou. Many layers of the stuff were painted on a wood or cloth base that was then carved and inlaid with gold, silver or tortoiseshell, or often most delicately painted. Numerous examples of painted lacquer boxes and baskets survive from the Han, and, as with jade, the use of this material has continued ever since.

Music

The casual visitor to China could be forgiven for thinking that the only traditional style of music to compete with bland pop is that of the kitsch folk troupes to be heard in hotels and concert halls. But an earthy traditional music still abounds throughout the countryside; it can be heard at weddings, funerals, temple fairs and New Year celebrations – and even downtown in teahouses. A very different, edgier sound can be heard in certain smoky city bars – the new Chinese rock, with its energetic expressions of urban angst.

Traditional music

Han music (like Irish music) is **heterophonic** – the musicians play differently decorated versions of a single melodic line. Percussion plays a major role, both in instrumental ensembles and as accompaniment to opera, narrative-singing, ritual music and dance.

Chinese musical roots date back millennia – archeological finds include a magnificent set of 65 bronze bells from the fifth century BC – and its forms can be directly traced to the Tang dynasty, a golden age of great poets such as Li Bai and Bai Juyi, who were also avid musicians. Several *qin* (zithers) from this period are still played today, and there's a good market in fake ones, too.

After China's humiliation at the hands of foreign imperial powers, and in the turbulent years after 1911, **Western ideas** gained ground, at least in the towns. Some intriguing **urban forms** sprang up from the meeting of East and West, such as the wonderfully sleazy Cantonese music of the 1920s and 1930s. As the movie industry developed, people in Shanghai, colonial Canton (Guangzhou) and nearby Hong Kong threw themselves into the craze for Western-style jazz and dance halls, fusing the local traditional music with jazz, and adding saxophone, violin and xylophone to Chinese instruments such as the *gaohu* (high-pitched fiddle) and the *yangqin* (dulcimer). Composers **Lü Wencheng** and **Qiu Hechou** (Yau Hokchau), the violinist **Yin Zizhong** (Yi Tzuchung), and **He Dasha** ("Thicko He"), guitarist and singer of clown roles in Cantonese opera, made many wonderful commercial 78s during this period. While these musicians kept their roots in Cantonese music, the more Westernized (and even more popular) compositions of **Li Jinhui** and his star singer **Zhou Xuan** subsequently earned severe disapproval from Maoist critics as decadent and pornographic.

New "**revolutionary**" music, composed from the 1930s onwards, was generally march-like and optimistic, while in the wake of the Communist victory of 1949, the whole ethos of traditional music was challenged. Anything "feudal" or "superstitious" – which included a lot of traditional folk customs and music – was severely restricted, while Chinese melodies were "cleaned up" with the addition of rudimentary harmonies and bass lines. The communist anthem "**The East is Red**", which began life as a folksong from the northern Shaanxi province (from where Mao's revolution also sprang), is symptomatic. Its local colour was ironed out as it was turned into a conventionally harmonized hymn-like tune. It was later adopted as the unofficial anthem of the Cultural Revolution, during which time musical life was driven underground, with only eight model operas and ballets permitted on stage.

The **conservatoire style** of **guoyue** (national music) was an artificial attempt to create a pan-Chinese style for the concert hall, with composed arrangements in a style akin to Western light music. There are still many conservatoire-style chamber groups – typically including *erhu* (fiddle), *dizi* (flute), *pipa* (lute) and *zheng* (zither) – playing evocatively titled pieces, some of which are newly composed. While the plaintive pieces for solo *erhu* by musicians such as **Liu Tianhua** and the blind beggar **Abing** (also a Daoist priest), or atmospheric tweetings on the *dizi*, have been much recorded by *guoyue* virtuosos like **Min Huifen** or **Lu Chunling** respectively, there is much more to Chinese music than this. Folk music has a life of its own, and tends to follow the Confucian ideals of moderation and harmony, in which showy virtuosity is out of place.

The qin and solo traditions

Instrumental music is not as popular as vocal music in China, and many of the short virtuosic pieces that you hear played on the *erhu* or *dizi* are in fact the product of modern composers writing in a pseudo-romantic Western style for the concert hall. The genuine solo traditions that date back to the scholar-literati of imperial times, and which live on in the conservatoires today, are for the *pipa*, *zheng* and *qin*.

The **qin** (also known as *guqin*) is the most exalted of these instruments. A seven-string plucked zither, it has been a favourite subject of poets and painters for over a thousand years, and is the most delicate and contemplative instrument in the Chinese palette. It's also the most accessible, producing expressive slides and ethereal harmonics. Though primarily associated with the moderation of the Confucian scholar, the *qin* is additionally steeped in the mystical Daoism of ancient philosophy – the contemplative union with nature, in which silence is as important as sound. The only instruments that may occasionally blend with the *qin* are the voice of the player, singing ancient poems in an utterly introverted style, or the *xiao* end-blown flute.

Modern traditions of the **pipa** (lute) and **zheng** (zither) also derive from regional styles, transmitted from master to pupil, although "national" repertoires developed during the twentieth century. For the *zheng*, the northern styles of Henan and Shandong, and the southern Chaozhou and Hakka schools, are best known. The *pipa*, on the other hand, has thrived in the Shanghai region. It makes riveting listening, with its contrast between intimate "civil" pieces and the startlingly modern-sounding martial style of traditional pieces such as "Ambush from All Sides" (*Shimian maifu*), with its frenetic percussive evocation of the sounds of battle.

The poetic titles of many so-called classical solo pieces – like "Autumn Moon in the Han Palace" or "Flowing Streams" – often relate to an identification with nature or to a famous historical scene. Correspondingly, the music is often pictorial, underlining the link with the artistic background of the educated classes of imperial times. The similar titles of the pieces played by folk ensembles, however, are rarely illustrative, serving only as identification for the musicians.

The North: Blowers and Drummers

What we might call classical traditions – derived from the elite of imperial times – live on today not just with solo instruments but more strongly in **folk**

ensembles, which are generally found in the north of the country. The most exciting examples are to be heard at **weddings and funerals**, known as "red and white business" – red being the auspicious colour of the living, white the colour of mourning.

These occasions usually feature raucous **shawm** (a ubiquitous instrument in China, rather like a crude clarinet) and percussion groups called **chuigushou** – "blowers and drummers". While wedding bands naturally tend to use more jolly music, funerals may also feature lively pieces to entertain the guests. The "blowers and drummers" play not only lengthy and solemn suites but also the latest pop hits and theme tunes from TV and films. They milk the audience by sustaining notes, using circular breathing, playing even while dismantling and reassembling their shawms, or by balancing plates on sticks on the end of their instruments while playing. Some shawm players also love to perform while successively inserting cigarettes into both nostrils, both ears, and both corners of the mouth. Some of the more virtuoso shawm bands are found in south-western Shandong around Heze county.

Mentioned as far back as the tenth century BC, the **sheng** ranks among the oldest Chinese instruments. It comprises a group of bamboo pipes of different lengths bound in a circle and set in a wooden or metal base into which the player blows. Frequently used for ceremonial music, it adds an incisive rhythmic bite. Long and deafening strings of firecrackers are another inescapable part of village ceremony. Some processions are led by a Western-style brass band with a shawm-and-percussion group behind, competing in volume, oblivious of key. In northern villages, apart from the blowers and drummers, ritual **shengguan** ensembles are also common, with their exquisite combination of mouth organs and oboes, as well as darting flutes and the shimmering halo of the *yunluo* gong-frame, accompanied by percussion. Apart from this haunting melodic music, they perform some spectacular ritual percussion – the intricate arm movements of the cymbal players almost resemble martial arts.

Around Xi'an, groups performing similar wind and percussion music, misleadingly dubbed **Xi'an Drum Music** (**Xi'an guyue**), are active for temple festivals not only in the villages but also in the towns, especially in the sixth moon, around July. If you remember the tough shawm bands and haunting folksong of Chen Kaige's film *Yellow Earth*, or the harsh falsetto narrative in Zhang Yimou's *The Story of Qiuju*, go for the real thing among the barren hills of northern Shaanxi. This area is home to fantastic folk singers, local opera (such as the Qinqiang and Meihu styles), puppeteers, shawm bands and folk ritual specialists. Even *yangge* dancing, which in the towns is often a geriatric form of conga dancing, has a wild power here, again accompanied by shawms and percussion.

The South: Silk and Bamboo

In southeast China, the best-known instrumental music is that of **sizhu** ("silk and bamboo") ensembles, using flutes (of bamboo) and plucked and bowed strings (until recently of silk). More mellifluous than the outdoor wind bands of the north, these provide perhaps the most accessible Chinese folk music.

The most famous of the many regional styles is that of **Shanghai**, where enthusiasts get together in the afternoons, sit round a table and take it in turns to play a set with Chinese fiddles, flutes and banjos. You can't help thinking of an Irish session, with Chinese tea replacing Guinness. The most celebrated meting place is the teahouse in the **Chenghuang Miao**

Discography

In China, it is easier to find good recordings of opera than instrumental music, but authentic recordings of Chinese instrumental and religious music are finally beginning to match the conservatoire-style recordings of souped-up arrangements that used to dominate the market. All the recordings listed are available on CD. If you're interested in finding recordings from rock bands, check the recommendations at Ⓦwww.niubi.com.

General traditional

Li Xiangting *Chine: L'Art du Qin* (Ocora, France).
Professor of *qin* at the Central Conservatoire in Beijing, Li is also a poet, painter and calligrapher. Though a fine introduction to the refined meditation of the *qin*, this album actually ends with the celebrated "Guangling san", a graphic depiction of the assassination of an evil tyrant, contrasting with the instrument's tranquil image.

Lin Shicheng *Chine: L'art du Pipa* (Ocora, France).
Includes not only favourites such as a version of the popular ensemble piece "Spring – River – Flowers – Moon – Night" and the martial piece "The Tyrant Removes his Armour" (also on the Wu Man CD below), but also some rarer intimate pieces.

The Uyghur Musicians from Xinjiang *Music From the Oasis Towns of Central Asia* (Globestyle, UK). An enjoyable introduction to the Uigur music of the Northwest, recorded on a spare day during a UK concert tour, and featuring some fine playing of the long-necked, lute-like *tambur* and *satar*, plus the *surnay*, a small twin-reeded shawm.

Wu Man *Traditional and Contemporary Music for Pipa and Ensemble* (Nimbus, UK).
From the southern town of Hangzhou, Wu studied with masters such as Lin Shicheng in Beijing. Since making her home in the US, she has championed new music for the *pipa*.

Wu Zhaoji *Wumen Qin Music* (Hugo, Hong Kong).
The late Wu Zhaoji's playing typified the contemplative ethos of the *qin*, eschewing mere technical display. "Wumen" refers here to the Wu style of the canal city of Suzhou.

Compilations

An Anthology of Chinese and Traditional Folk Music: A Collection of Music played on the Guqin (China Record Co., China; Cradle Records, Taiwan).
An eight-CD set for serious *qin* enthusiasts, featuring some fantastic reissues of the great masters of the 1950s.

China: Folk Instrumental Traditions (VDE-Gallo/AIMP, Switzerland).
A 2-CD set of archive and recent recordings of village ensembles from north and south compiled by Stephen Jones. Includes earthy shawm bands, mystical *shengguan* ritual ensembles, refined silk-and-bamboo, and some awesome percussion. Features some master musicians from before the Cultural Revolution, such as the Daoist priests An Laixu on *yunluo* and *Zhu Qinfu* on drums.

Chine: musique classique (Ocora, France).
A selection of solo and ensemble pieces featuring the *qin*, *pipa*, *sheng*, *guanzi* (oboe), *dizi*, *xiao*, *erhu* and *yangqin*, played by outstanding instrumentalists of the 1950s, including Guan Pinghu, Cao Zheng and Sun Yude.

Songs of the Land in China: Labour Songs and Love Songs (Wind Records, Taiwan).
Two CDs featuring beautiful archive recordings of folk singing, mostly unaccompanied, from different regions of China, including rhythmic songs of boatmen, Hua'er songs from the Northwest, and plaintive songs from northern Shaanxi. A surprisingly varied and captivating selection.

Special Collection of Contemporary Chinese Musicians (Wind Records, Taiwan).

A more comprehensive 2-CD set of archive recordings of some of the great 1950s instrumentalists, including masters of the *qin*, *zheng*, *pipa*, *suona* and *guanzi*.

Northern traditions

The Li Family Band *Shawms from Northeast China Vol. 2* (Musique du Monde, France).
Led by the senior Li Shiren, this band typifies northern shawm and percussion groups. The disc features a spectrum of music from doleful funereal music for large shawms to more popular festive pieces.

Compilations

Chine: Musique ancienne de Chang'an (Inédit, France).
The wind pieces on this conservatoire recording are impressive, though they lack the subtlety of tuning, complexity of tempi and sheer guts of the folk ensembles.

China: Music of the First Moon. Shawms from Northeast China Vol. 1 (Musique du Monde, France).
Ear-cleansing shawm and percussion, featuring various groups from the Dalian region playing music for New Year festivities. Earthy stuff with good notes.

Xi'an drums music (Hugo Hong Kong).
Majestic wind-and-percussion music performed for funerals and calendrical pilgrimages around Xi'an, including some rarely heard vocal hymns (weirdly translated as "rap music").

Southern traditions

Tsai Hsiao-Yueh *Nan-kouan: Chant courtois de la Chine du Sud Vol 1* (Ocora, France).
The senior *nanguan* singer Tsai Hsiao-yueh (Cai Xiaoyue), with her group based in Tainan, Taiwan, maintains the proud amateur tradition of this exalted genre that originated just across the strait in Fujian. This album features haunting chamber ballads, the female voice accompanied by end-blown flute and plucked and bowed lutes.

Compilations

China: Chuida Wind and Percussive Instrumental Ensembles (UNESCO/Auvidis, France).
Three traditional ensembles from southern China, including some unusual silk-and-bamboo from Shanghai and ceremonial music for weddings and funerals from Fujian and Zhejiang.

Rain Dropping on the Banana Tree (Rounder, US).
Taking its title from a popular Cantonese melody, this collection of reissued 78s from 1902 to 1930 features early masters of Cantonese music such as Yau Hokchau, as well as excerpts from Beijing and Cantonese opera.

Sizhu/Silk Bamboo: Chamber music of South China (Pan, Netherlands).
Several styles of chamber ensemble along the southeastern coast, from silk-and-bamboo from Shanghai to the refined instrumental *nanguan* music from Xiamen, plus Chaozhou and Hakka pieces featuring *zheng*, and also examples of the more modern Cantonese style. Excellent notes.

Temple music

Tianjin Buddhist Music Ensemble *Tianjin Buddhist Music Ensemble* (Nimbus, UK).
Buddhist ritual *shengguan* music played by a group of musicians in their 70s, with some wonderful *guanzi*. Good notes, too.

Compilations

China: Buddhist Music of the Ming Dynasty (JVC, Japan).
Exquisite music played by the monks of the Zhihua temple, Beijing, in collaboration with musicians from the Central Conservatoire. Features double-reed pipes, flutes, Chinese mouth organs, a frame of pitched gongs and percussion.

Discography *contd...*

Chinese opera

Compilations

⊙ *An Introduction to Chinese Opera* (Hong Kong Records, Hong Kong).
A series of four CDs illustrating the different styles, including Beijing, Cantonese, Shanghai, Huangmei, Henan, Pingju and Qinqiang operas.

⊙ *China: Ka-lé, Festival of Happiness* (VDE-Gallo/AIMP, Switzerland).
Mainly instrumental music from the operas of the Quanzhou Puppet Troupe.

⊙ *Chinese Classical Opera: Kunqu. The Peony Pavilion* (Inédit, France).
A two-CD set featuring excerpts from the great opera by the early seventeenth-century Tang Xianzu. The vocal sections give a better idea of the tradition than the kitsch harmonized orchestral arrangements.

⊙ *Opera du Sichuan: La Legende de Serpent Blanc* (Musique du Monde, France).
A double CD of traditional opera from Sichuan, featuring the distinctive female chorus and ending with the attractive bonus of a "bamboo ballad" on the same theme sung by a narrative-singer.

Contemporary/new wave

⊙ **Wu Man and the Kronos Quartet** *Ghost Opera* by Tan Dun (Nonesuch, US).
An extraordinary multimedia piece "with water, stones, paper and metal", and incorporating traditional shamanistic sounds of the composer's childhood in remote Hunan province, alongside Bach and Shakespeare. Totally original.

⊙ **Yo-Yo Ma** *Symphony 1997* by Tan Dun (Sony Classical).
Yo-Yo Ma's cello provides the narrative element here, blending his classical technique with gliding tones reminiscent of *erhu* music. The theatrical musical panorama includes the 2400-year-old bells, Cantonese opera recorded on the streets of Hong Kong, a dragon dance plus quotations from Beethoven's "Ode to Joy" and Puccini's *Turandot*. Naïve, yet sophisticated and certainly colourful.

(see p.374), a picturesque two-storey structure on an island in the old quarter, where there are Monday-afternoon gatherings. The contrasting textures of plucked, bowed and blown sounds are part of the attraction of this music, each offering individual decorations to the gradually unfolding melody. Many pieces consist of successive decorations of a theme, beginning with the most ornate and accelerating as the decorations are gradually stripped down to a fast and bare final statement of the theme itself. Above the chinking of tea bowls and subdued chatter of the teahouse, enjoy the gradual unravelling of a piece like "Sanliu", or feel the exhilarating dash to the finish of "Xingjie", with its breathless syncopations.

Amateur *sizhu* clubs can be found throughout the lower Yangzi area, including the cities of Nanjing and Hangzhou. Although this music is secular and recreational in its urban form, the *sizhu* instrumentation originated in ritual ensembles and is still so used in the villages and temples of southern Jiangsu. In fact, amateur ritual associations exist all over southern China, as far afield as Yunnan, punctuating their ceremonies with sedate music reminiscent of the Shanghai teahouses, albeit often featuring the *yunluo* gong-frame of northern China.

Another fantastic area for folk music is the coastal region of **southern Fujian**, notably the delightful cities of Quanzhou and Xiamen. Here you can find not only opera, ritual music and puppetry, but the haunting **nanguan**

ballads. Popular all along the coast of southern Fujian, as in Taiwan across the strait, *nanguan* features a female singer accompanied by end-blown flute and plucked and bowed lutes. The ancient texts depict the sorrows of love, particularly of women, while the music is mostly stately and the delivery restrained yet anguished.

Still further south, the coastal regions of **Chaozhou** and **Shantou**, and the **Hakka** area (inland around Meixian and Dabu), also boast celebrated string ensembles that feature a high-pitched *erxian* (bowed fiddle) and *zheng* (plucked zither), as well as large and imposing ceremonial percussion bands, sometimes accompanied by shrill flutes.

The temples

All over China, particularly on the great religious mountains such as **Wutai Shan**, **Tai Shan**, **Qingcheng Shan**, **Wudang Shan** and **Putuo Shan**, temples are not just historical monuments but living sites of worship. Morning and evening services are held daily, and larger rituals on special occasions. The priests mainly perform vocal liturgy accompanied by percussion – few now use melodic instruments. They intone sung hymns with long melismas, alternating with chanted sections accompanied by the relentless and hypnotic beat of the woodblock. Drum, bell, gongs and cymbals also punctuate the service.

Melodic instrumental music tends to be added when priests perform rituals outside the temples. These styles are more earthy and accessible even to ears unaccustomed to Chinese music. The Daoist priests from the Xuanmiao Guan in **Suzhou**, for example, perform wonderfully mellifluous pieces for silk-and-bamboo instruments, gutsy blasts on the shawm, music for spectacularly long trumpets, and a whole battery of percussion.

Opera and other vocal music

Chinese musical drama dates back at least two thousand years, and became overwhelmingly popular with both the elite and common people from the Yuan dynasty onwards. Of the several hundred types of regional opera, **Beijing Opera**, a rather late hybrid form dating from the eighteenth century, is the most widely known – now heard throughout China, it's the closest thing to a "national" theatre. The rigorous training the form demands – and the heavy hand of ideology that saw it as the most important of "the people's arts" – is graphically displayed in Chen Kaige's film *Farewell My Concubine*. Many librettos now performed date back to the seventeenth century and describe the intrigues of emperors and gods, as well as love stories and comedy. Northern "**clapper operas**" (*bangzi xi*), named after the high-pitched woodblock that insistently runs through them, are earthy in flavour – for example, the "Qinqiang" of Shaanxi province. **Sichuan opera** is remarkable for its female chorus. **Ritual masked opera** may be performed in the countryside of Yunnan, Anhui and Guizhou. Chaozhou and Fujian also have beautiful ancient styles of opera: **Pingju** and **Huangmei Xi** are genteel in style, while **Cantonese opera** is funkier. If you're looking for more music and less acrobatics, try to seek out the classical but now rare **Kunqu**, often accompanied by the sweet-toned *qudi* flute. There are also some beautiful **puppet operas**, often performed for ritual events; Quanzhou in Fujian boasts a celebrated marionette troupe, and other likely areas include northern Shaanxi and the Tangshan and Laoting areas of eastern Hebei.

While Chinese opera makes a great visual spectacle, musically it is frankly an acquired taste, resembling to the uninitiated the din of cats fighting in a blazing firework factory. The singing style is tense, guttural and high-pitched, while the music is dominated by the bowed string accompaniment of the *jinghu*, a sort of sawn-off *erhu*. It also features plucked lutes, flutes and – for transitional points – a piercing shawm. The action is driven by percussion, with drum and clappers leading an ensemble of gongs and cymbals in an assortment of set patterns. Professional opera troupes exist in the major towns, but rural opera performances, which are given for temple fairs and even weddings, tend to be livelier. Even in Beijing you may come across groups of old folk meeting in parks to go through their favourite Beijing Opera excerpts.

Narrative-singing, sadly neglected in recordings, also features long classical stories. You may find a teahouse full of old people following these story-songs avidly, particularly in Sichuan, where one popular style is accompanied by the *yangqin* (dulcimer). In Beijing, or more often in Tianjin, amateurs sing through traditional *jingyun dagu* ballads, accompanied by drum and *sanxian* banjo. In Suzhou, *pingtan*, also accompanied by a plucked lute, is a beautiful genre. Found in Beijing and elsewhere, *xiangsheng* is a comic dialogue with a know-all and a straight man, though its subtle parodies of traditional opera may elude the outsider.

Traditional **folk songs** (as opposed to sentimental bel canto arrangements warbled by ball-gowned divas) are more difficult for the casual visitor to find in Han Chinese areas than among the ethnic minorities, but the beautiful songs of areas like northern Shaanxi and Sichuan have thankfully been captured on disc.

Chinese rock

Although often connected to the Hong Kong/Taiwanese entertainment industry, China's indigenous **rock** is a different beast, one which has its traditions in passionate and fiery protest, and which still possesses a cultural and political self-awareness. The rock scene was nonexistent in China until the mid-1980s, when foreign students on cultural exchange brought tapes of their favourite rock and pop music (and their own electric guitars) to the Chinese mainland, and shared them with their fellow students. Their music quickly caught the imagination of Chinese university youth and the urban vanguard.

Chinese **protest-rock** really began with singer-trumpeter-guitarist **Cui Jian**, who was influenced by the Taiwanese singer **Teresa Teng** (known to the Chinese by her original name, Deng Lijun; 1953–95). Teng's singing style can be directly traced to Zhou Xuan and 1930s Shanghai. Probably the most popular Chinese singer of her time, her recordings were circulated in China on the black market from the late 1970s onwards, when such music was officially banned.

A Beijinger born of parents of Korean descent, **Cui Jian** studied the trumpet at an early age, trained as a classical musician and joined the Beijing Symphony Orchestra in 1981. After being introduced to Anglo-American rock in the mid-1980s, however, he forged an independent path and his gritty voice became the primary reference point of Chinese rock.

Ostensibly a love song, Cui's "Nothing To My Name" became an anthem of the democracy movement, thanks to lyrics that could be interpreted as a political monologue of the ruled about his ruler:

I used to endlessly ask
When will you go away with me?
You laugh at me always.
I have nothing to my name.
I want to give you my dreams
And also my freedom.
You laugh at me always.
I have nothing to my name.
I must tell you, I have waited too long.
I'll tell you my last request:
I'll hold your two hands
To take you away with me.

This song evoked a memorable complaint from General Wang Zhen, a veteran of the Long March: "What do you mean, you have nothing to your name? You've got the Communist Party, haven't you?"

Even though Cui's lyrics have always been ambiguous, his voice has occasionally been muffled. A nationwide tour was cancelled midway because of actions on stage (blindfolded in red cloth – the colour of Communism) that mesmerized his fans but enraged officials. He also upset the authorities with his recording of "*Nanni Wan*", a revolutionary song closely associated with the Communist Party and its ideals, glorifying Chinese peasants and their contribution to society. Cui's rock interpretation was understood by many as a challenge to (or mockery of) authority.

Like most of China's rockers, Cui turned more introspective as the Nineties progressed. His 1994 album *Hongqi Xiade Dan* (*Eggs Under the Red Flag*) reflected how the concerns of China's youth were shifting from politics to the realities of earning a living. Its powerful title track neatly encapsulated both:

Money floats in the air,
We have no ideals.
Although the air is fresh,
We cannot see into the distance.
Although the chance is here,
We are too timid.
We are wholly submissive,
Like eggs under the red flag.

Notable 1980s bands that followed in Cui Jian's wake include Black Panther *(Hei Bao)* and Tang Dynasty, though their long hair and leathers were perhaps more influential than their soft rock. They were followed by Cobra, China's first all-female rock band, folk-rocker Zhang Chu, bad boy He Yong, Compass, Overload, and Breathing, among others. Unsigned, these bands would perform for very little money as part of vaudeville shows, until 1990, when China's first domestic full-scale rock concert took place. Six bands, including Tang Dynasty and Cobra, played at the Beijing Exhibition Centre Arena and were immediately signed by Japanese and Taiwanese labels, who then brought their music to the mainstream. They paved the way for homegrown labels such as Modern Sky, Scream, New Bees Records, and Zhengda Guoji, which now specialize in Chinese rock, hip-hop and alternative music.

The rock scene these days is healthy, with hundreds of bands, though it does centre heavily on Beijing. For visitors, it's well worth exploring, and surprisingly accessible, as most bands sing at least half of their songs in English. Acts to look out for include Sex Pistols wannabes Joyside, who recently toured America; folk punk showmen Top Floor Circus; long running ska punk outfit Brain Failure; and Joy Divisionistas, the Retros. For dance and electronica you can't beat Queen Sea Big Shark, while Car Sick Cars are the up-and-coming indie shoegazers to watch out for. To fully immerse yourself in the scene, visit Beijing's annual three-day **Midi Festival** in July, or the irregular **Meili Xue Shan** festival held outside Lijiang in Yunnan. For free downloads, check out Ⓦwww.yuyintang.com.

Stephen Jones & Joanna Lee,
with additional contributions from Simon Lewis

Film

Film came early to China. The first moving picture was exhibited in 1896 at a "teahouse variety show" in Shanghai, where the country's first cinema was built just twelve years later. By the 1930s, cinema was playing an important role in the cultural life of Shanghai, though the huge number of resident foreigners ensured a largely Western diet of films. Nevertheless, local Chinese films were also being made, mainly by the so-called **May Fourth intellectuals** (middle-class liberals inspired by the uprising of May 4, 1919), who wanted to modernize China along Western lines. Naturally, Western influence on these films was strong, and they have little to do with the highly stylized, formal world of traditional performance arts such as Beijing Opera or shadow-puppet theatre. Early film showings often employed a "storyteller" who sat near the screen reading out the titles, for the benefit of those who could not read.

The Shanghai studios

Of the handful of important **studios** in Shanghai operating in the 1920s and 1930s, the most famous was the **Mingxing**, whose films were left-leaning and anti-imperialist. *Sister Flower* (1933) tells the story of twin sisters separated at birth, one of whom ends up a city girl living in Shanghai, while the other remains a poor villager. Another film from the same year, *Spring Silk Worm*, portrays economic decline and hardship in Zhejiang province, and levels the finger of accusation at Japanese imperialism. Finally, *The Goddess* (1934), from the **Lianhua** studio, depicts the struggle of a prostitute to have her son educated. The improbably glamorous prostitute was played by China's own Garbo, the languorous Ruan Lingyu. Despite the liberal pretensions of these films, it was inevitable – given that audiences comprised a tiny elite – that they would later be derided by the Communists as bourgeois.

When the **Japanese occupied** Shanghai in 1937, "subversive" studios such as the Mingxing and Lianhua were immediately closed, and much of the film-making talent fled into the interior. The experience of war put film-makers in touch with their potential future audiences, the Chinese masses. China's great wartime epic, **Spring River Flows East** (1947–48), was the cinematic result of this experience. The story spans the duration of the anti-Japanese war – and the ensuing civil war – through the lives of a single family torn apart by the conflict. The heroine, living in poverty, contrasts with her husband, who has abandoned his wife for a decadent existence in Shanghai. Traumatized by a decade of war, the Chinese who saw this film appreciated it as an authentic account of the sufferings through which the nation had lived. Over three-quarters of a million people saw the film at its release, a remarkable figure given that the country was still at war.

Communism and the cinema

The story of Chinese film-making under the **Communists** really dates back to 1938, when Mao Zedong and his fellow Long Marchers set up their base in

Yan'an. No world could have been further removed from the glamour of Shanghai than this dusty, poverty-stricken town, but it was the ideal location for the film-makers of the future People's Republic to learn their skills. Talent escaping through Japanese lines trickled through in search of employment, among them the actress **Jiang Qing**, later to become Mao's wife and self-appointed empress of Chinese culture. One thing upon which all the leading Communists in Yan'an were agreed was the importance of film as a **centralizing medium**, which could be used to unify the culture of the nation after the war had been won.

The immediate consequence of the Communist victory in 1949 was that the showing of foreign films was curtailed, and the private Shanghai studios wound down. A **Film Guidance committee** was set up to decide upon film output for the entire nation. The first major socialist epic, **Bridge**, appeared in 1949, depicting the mass mobilization of workers rushing enthusiastically to construct a bridge in record time. Although predictably dull in terms of character and plot, the cast still contained a number of prewar Shanghai actors to divert audiences. At the end of the film the entire cast gathers to shout "Long live Chairman Mao!", a scene that was to be re-enacted time and again in the coming years.

A year after *Bridge*, one of the very last non-government Shanghai studio films appeared, **The Life of Wu Xun**, a huge project that had started well before 1949, and, surprisingly, was allowed to run to completion. Its subject was the famous nineteenth-century entrepreneur, Wu Xun, who started out as a beggar and rose to enormous riches, whereupon he set out on his lifetime's ambition to educate the peasantry. Despite the addition of a narrator's voice at the end of the film, pointing out that it was revolution and not education that peasants needed, the film was a disaster for the Shanghai film industry. Mao wrote a damning critique of it for idolizing a "Qing landlord", and a campaign was launched against the legacy of the entire Shanghai film world – studios, actors, critics and audiences alike.

The remains of the May Fourth Movement struggled on. The consolation for the old guard was that newer generations of Chinese film-makers had not yet solved the problem of how to portray life in the contemporary era. The 1952 screen adaptation of Lao She's short story *Dragon's Beard Ditch*, for example, was supposed to contrast the miserable pre-1949 life of a poor district of Beijing with the prosperous life that was being lived under the Communists. The only problem, as audiences could immediately see, was that the supposedly miserable pre-1949 scenes actually looked a good deal more heart-warming than the later ones.

Nevertheless, the Communists did achieve some of their original targets during the **1950s**. The promotion of a universal culture and language was one of them. All characters in all films – from Tibetans to Mongolians to Cantonese – were depicted as speaking in flawless **Mandarin Chinese**. Above all, there was an explosion in audiences, from around 47 million tickets sold in 1949, to 600 million in 1956, to over 4 billion in 1959. The latter figure should be understood in the context of the madness surrounding the Great Leap Forward, a time of crazed overproduction in all fields, film included. Film studios sprouted in every town in China, though with a catastrophic loss of quality – a typical studio in Jiangxi province comprised one man, his bicycle and an antique stills camera. The colossal output of that year included uninspiring titles such as *Loving the Factory as One's Home*.

The conspicuous failure of the Great Leap Forward did, however, bring certain short-lived advantages to the film industry. While Mao was forced temporarily into the political sidelines during the late 1950s, the cultural bureaucrats signalled that in addition to "revolutionary realism", a certain degree of "**revolutionary romanticism**" was to be encouraged. Chinese themes and subjects, as opposed to pure Marxism, were looked upon with more favour. A slight blossoming occurred, with improbable films such as *Lin Zexu* (1959), which covered the life of the great Qing-dynasty official who stood up to the British at the time of the Opium Wars. There was even a tentative branching out into comedy, with the film *What's Eating You?* based on the relatively un-socialist antics of a Suzhou waiter. Unusually, the film featured local dialects, as well as a faintly detectable parody of the government's campaign to encourage greater sacrifices by promoting the mythical hero worker Lei Feng.

The Cultural Revolution

Sadly, this bright period came to a swift end in 1966 with the **Cultural Revolution**. No interesting work was done in China for nearly fifteen years – indeed, no film was produced anywhere in the whole country between 1966 and 1970. Of the few films that did subsequently appear before Mao's death were made under the personal supervision of Jiang Qing, all were on the revolutionary model, a kind of ballet with flag waving. Attendance at these dreadful films was virtually **compulsory** for people who did not wish to be denounced for a lack of revolutionary zeal. Ironically, Jiang Qing herself was a big fan of Hollywood productions, which she would watch in secret.

Recovery from the trauma of the Cultural Revolution was bound to take time, but the years 1979 and 1980 saw a small crop of films attempting to assess the horror through which the country had just lived. The best known, *The Legend of Tianyun Mountain*, made in Shanghai in 1980, featured two men, one of whom had denounced the other for "Rightism" in 1958. The subsequent story is one of guilt, love, emotions and human relationships, all subjects that had been banned during the Cultural Revolution. Understandably, the film was an enormous popular success, though before audiences had time to get too carried away, a subsequent film, *Unrequited Love* (1981), was officially criticized for blurring too many issues.

Modern cinema

In **1984** the Chinese film industry was suddenly brought to international attention for the first time by the arrival of the so-called "**Fifth Generation**" of Chinese film-makers. That year, director **Chen Kaige** and his cameraman **Zhang Yimou**, both graduates from the first post-Cultural Revolution class (1982) of the Beijing Film School, made the superb art-house film **Yellow Earth.** The story of *Yellow Earth* is a minor feature; the interest is in the images and the colours. Still shots predominate, recalling traditional Chinese scroll painting, with giant landscapes framed by hills and the distant Yellow River. The film was not particularly well received in China, either by audiences, who expected something more modern, or by the authorities, who expected something more optimistic. Nevertheless, it set the pattern for a series of increasingly foreign-funded (and foreign-watched) films comprising stunning images of a "traditional" China, irritating the censors at home and delighting audiences abroad.

Chen Kaige's protégé Zhang Yimou was soon stealing a march on his former boss with his first film **Red Sorghum** (1987), set in a remote wine-producing village of northern China at the time of the Japanese invasion. This film was not only beautiful, and reassuringly patriotic, but it also introduced the world to **Gong Li**, the actress who was to become China's first international heart-throb. The fact that Gong Li and Zhang Yimou were soon to be lovers added to the general media interest in their work, both in China and abroad. They worked together on a string of hits, including *Judou*, *The Story of Qiu Ju*, *Raise the Red Lantern*, *Shanghai Triad* and *To Live*. None of these could be described as art-house in the way that *Yellow Earth* had been, and the potent mix of Gong Li's sexuality with exotic, mysterious locations in 1930s China was clearly targeted at Western rather than Chinese audiences. Chinese like to point out that the figure-hugging Chinese dresses regularly worn by Gong Li are entirely unlike the period costume they purport to represent.

One of Zhang Yimou's most powerful films, **To Live** (1994), follows the fortunes of a family from "liberation" to the Great Leap Forward and the Cultural Revolution. The essence of the story is that life cannot be lived to prescription. Its power lies in the fact that it is a very real reflection of the experience of millions of Chinese people. Similarly, Chen Kaige's superb **Farewell My Concubine** (1994) incorporates the whole span of modern Chinese history, and although the main protagonist – a homosexual Chinese opera singer – is hardly typical of modern China, the tears aroused by the film are wept for the country as a whole.

Zhang Yimou has since been warmly embraced by the authorities and his films have got worse. **Not One Less** (1998) re-creates the true story of a country teacher who travels to the city to track down a pupil who has run away. All the characters are portrayed by themselves and give magnificent performances, but ultimately the film is sentimental. Zhang's most recent Hollywood-friendly martial-arts spectaculars **Hero** (2002), **The House of Flying Daggers** (2004), and **Curse of the Golden Flower** (2007) are commercial successes, and beautifully shot, but have been derided in some quarters for their shallowness.

Contemporary realism

The best Chinese films of the modern age are those that have turned their back on the frigid perfection on offer from Zhang Yimou and are raw, gritty reflections of Chinese life. Inevitably, the fifth generation was followed by a sixth, which produced **underground movies**, generally shot in black and white, depicting what they consider to be the true story of contemporary China – ugly cities, cold flats, broken and depressed people. One of these, **Beijing Bastards** (1993), had a role for the famous rock singer and rebel **Cui Jian**, who is depicted drinking, swearing and playing the guitar.

Many of the finest modern movies turn a baleful eye on the recent past. **Lei Feng is Gone** (1997) is based on the true story of the man who accidentally killed the iconic hero of Maoist China, the soldier Lei Feng. The potent personal story also works as a metaphor for the state of the nation. **In the Heat of the Sun** (1995), directed by Jiang Wen, chronicles the antics of a Beijing street gang in the 1970s. Written by Wang Shuo, the bad boy of contemporary Chinese literature, it displays his characteristic irreverence and earthy humour. Jiang Wen's next film, **Devils at the Doorstep** (2000) goes a little further back, and its eye is even more jaundiced. Set during the anti-Japanese war, it's a black farce concerning a group of peasants who get a couple of hostages dumped on their farm by the local Communists. Unwilling to execute them or release them, they decide to try and return them to the Japanese in return for food.

Many films are simply too controversial for domestic release, but if they garner attention abroad they then become available at home as illegal DVDs. The most notable film to become popular in this way is **Xiao Wu** (1997), the intimate portrayal of a pickpocket whose life is falling apart, directed by **Jia Zhangke**. Jia's other films revisit similar territory, depicting the moral wasteland of Chinese youth; **The World** (2004) is set in a world culture theme park in Beijing, where the workers squabble and fail to communicate against a backdrop of tiny replicas of the world's famous monuments. The protagonists of **Still Life** (2007) are just as lost, as they search for people who have gone missing in the mass displacements caused by the Three Gorges Dam project.

But the best of the banned genre is **Blind Shaft** (2003), directed by Yang Li, about two coal miners who kill colleagues, make it look like an accident, then collect the mine owner's hush money. As well as a telling indictment of runaway capitalism, it's a great piece of film noir. His latest, **Blind Mountain** (2007), is about a young girl who is kidnapped and sold as a bride. Again, it combines social critique with a sharp crime story; this is a young director to look out for.

Similar in its clever combination of genre and uncompromising realism is **Ke Ke Xi Li** (Chuan Lu; 2004), a hard-boiled true story about a volunteer gang fighting against ruthless antelope poachers on the high Tibetan plateau. It was filmed using non-professional local actors and has the feel of a western, but is entirely unsentimental. More non-professional actors and grand scenery were used to great effect in Wang Quan'an's documentary-style **Tuya's Marriage** (2006), the story of a Mongolian herdswomen's search for a new husband, which won first prize at the 2007 Berlin Film Festival. Like much good contemporary Chinese art of all genres, its subject is people struggling to cope with vast social change.

Hong Kong

The movies that have the least difficulty with the Chinese censors are those produced in **Hong Kong**, the world's third-largest movie producer, behind India and the US. Its popular appeal is made easier by the content: generally easy-to-digest romances, comedies, or high-speed action, with little interest in deeper meanings or the outside world – and certainly not in politics.

World interest in Hong Kong's film industry dates back to 1970s martial-arts legend **Bruce Lee**. Although Lee was better known overseas for the Hollywood-financed *Enter the Dragon*, the success in Hong Kong of his earlier films *Fist of Fury* and *The Big Boss* launched a domestic **kung-fu movie boom**, off the back of which sprung **Jackie Chan** and a much-needed element of slapstick comedy – best seen in Chan's early works, such as *Drunken Master*. As the genre faltered in the 1980s, directors mixed in a supernatural aspect, pioneered by **Tsui Hark** in *Zu: Warriors from the Magic Mountain* and *Chinese Ghost Story*. The kung-fu genre has been recently revived by director **Stephen Chow**, whose *Shaolin Soccer* and *Kung Fu Hustle* sport uniquely surreal humour and visuals.

Martial arts remain an inevitable component of Hong Kong's modern **action movies** and **police thrillers**. This genre can largely be attributed to **John Woo**'s influential 1980s hits *A Better Tomorrow* and *Hard Boiled*, which feature Chow Yun Fat shooting his way through relentless scenes of orchestrated violence. Woo's many imitators have mostly succeeded only in making pointless,

▲ Film poster, Hong Kong

bloody movies whose plots inevitably conclude with the massacre of the entire cast, though recent efforts such as *Infernal Affairs* (remade in the US as *The Departed*) at least add a little depth to the heroes' moody characters.

At present, Hong Kong's only director interested in anything but light entertainment is **Wong Karwai**, whose early works such as *Chungking Express* depict Hong Kong as a crowded, disjointed city where people, though forced together, seem unable to communicate. His more recent films have added a European sense of style, which worked in the sensuous *In the Mood for Love* but overwhelmed the plot in the obscure, self-referential *2046*. Look out for his upcoming dreamy spy story, *Lady of Shanghai*.

Books

The following is a personal selection of the books that have proved most useful during the preparation of this guide. The last few years has seen a glut of excellent writing coming out of China, from Western commentators' views on current economic and social upheavals, to translated journalism and popular novels, and often eccentric expat memoirs.

Classics aside, few of our chosen titles are available in China (though you might get lucky in Hong Kong), so it's best to locate them before your trip – we've listed publishers throughout. Titles marked 🏃 are particularly recommended, while those marked o/p are out of print.

History

Patricia Ebrey *Cambridge Illustrated History of China* (Cambridge University Press, UK). An up-to-date, easy-going historical overview, excellently illustrated and clearly written.

Peter Fleming *The Siege at Peking* (Oxford University Press, UK). An account of the events that led up to June 20, 1900, when the foreign legations in Beijing were attacked by the Boxers and Chinese imperial troops. Lasting 55 days, the siege marked a watershed in China's relations with the rest of the world.

Jacques Gernet *Daily Life in China on the Eve of the Mongol Invasion 1250–1276* (Allen and Unwin, UK; Stanford University Press, US). Based on assorted Chinese sources, this is a fascinating survey of southern China under the Song, focusing on the capital, Hangzhou, then the largest and richest city in the world Gernet also deals with the daily lives of a cross-section of society, from peasant to leisured gentry, covering everything from cookery to death.

🏃 **Larry Gonick** *The Cartoon History of the Universe vols II and III* (W.W. Norton, US). A masterwork setting world history in cartoon format, full of verve, great visuals and awful puns, but also accurate – the bibliography shows how much research has gone into this manic project. About the only textbook that seriously attempts to set Chinese history in a world context.

🏃 **Peter Hopkirk** *Foreign Devils on the Silk Road* and *The Great Game* (Oxford University Press, UK). *Foreign Devils* is the story of the machinations of the various international booty-hunters who operated in Turkestan and the Gobi Desert during the early twentieth century – essential for an appreciation of China's northwest regions. *The Great Game* is a hugely entertaining account of the nineteenth-century struggle between Britain and Russia for control of Central Asia. In tracing the roots of the Chinese occupations of Tibet and Xinjiang, and also detailing the invariable consequences to foreign powers who meddle with Afghanistan, it's also disturbingly topical.

Ann Paludan *Chronicle of the Chinese Emperors* (Thames and Hudson, UK). Lively stories on the lives of all 157 of those strangest of characters, the Chinese emperors. Well illustrated and a good starting point for getting to grips with Chinese history.

Sima Qian *Historical Records* aka *Records of the Historian* (Oxford Paperbacks, UK; Columbia University Press, US). Written by the Han-dynasty court historian, *Records* is a masterpiece, using contemporary court documents and oral tradition to illuminate key characters – everyone from emperors to famous con men – from Chinese history up to that point. Although long discredited, Sima Qian's accounts have now been partially corroborated by recent archeology.

Edgar Snow *Red Star Over China* (Penguin, UK; Grove Press, US). The definitive first-hand account of the early days of Mao and the Communist "bandits", written in 1936 after Snow, an American journalist, wriggled through the Guomindang blockade and spent months at the Red base in Yan'an.

Jonathan Spence *The Gate of Heavenly Peace* (Penguin, UK & US), *The Search for Modern China* (W.W. Norton, US). The first of these traces the history of twentieth-century China through the eyes of the men and women caught up in it – writers, revolutionaries, poets and politicians – and is among best books for getting to grips with China's complex modern history. Though quite hard for a straight-through read, *The Search for Modern China* is authoritative and probably the best overall history of China available.

Susan Whitfield *Life along the Silk Road* (John Murray, UK). Using archeological remains and historical sources, Whitfield creates ten fictional characters to illustrate life in north-western China during its tenth-century Buddhist heyday.

Tibet

John Avedon *In Exile From the Land of Snows* (HarperCollins, UK; Perennial, US). A detailed and moving account of modern Tibetan history, covering both those who remained in the country and those who fled into exile. Required reading for anyone contemplating a trip.

Victor Chan *Tibet Handbook: a Pilgrimage Guide* (Avalon Travel, US). A hugely detailed guide to Tibet's pilgrimage sites and treks, and how to reach them. Absolutely essential if you're considering a trek.

Graham Coleman (ed) *A Handbook of Tibetan Culture: a Guide to Tibetan Centres and Resources Throughout the World* (Shambhala, UK). The subtitle says it all; the book exhaustively documents cultural organizations, teaching centres and libraries across the globe that have a Tibetan focus. It also includes biographies of major Tibetan lamas, brief histories of the major schools of Tibetan Buddhism and an illustrated glossary.

Heinrich Harrer *Seven Years In Tibet* (Flamingo, UK; Jeremy P. Tarcher, US). A classic account of a remarkable journey to reach Lhasa and of the years there prior to the Chinese invasion, when Harrer was tutor to the Fourteenth Dalai Lama.

Isabel Hilton *The Search for the Panchen Lama* (Penguin, UK & US). The whole sorry story of the search for the Eleventh Panchen Lama, and how the Tibetans' choice ended up as the world's youngest political prisoner.

Peter Hopkirk *Trespassers on the Roof of the World: the Race for Lhasa* (Oxford University Press, UK). Around the start of the twentieth century, imperial Britain, with the help of a remarkable band of pundits and wallahs from the Indian Survey, was discreetly charting every nook of the most inaccessible part of the earth, the High Tibetan plateau. Peter Hopkirk researched his subject thoroughly and came up with a highly readable account of this fascinating backwater of history.

Thubten Jigme and Colin Turnbull *Tibet, Its History, Religion and People* (Penguin, UK & US). The best account around of the traditional everyday lives of the Tibetan people, co-authored by the brother of the Fourteenth Dalai Lama.

Culture and society

Ian Baruma *Bad Elements* (Orion, UK; Random House, US). Interviews with dissident exiles abroad tell an (inevitably anti-government) story of modern China.

Jasper Becker *The Chinese* (John Murray, UK). An incisive portrait of modern China at both government and individual level by one of the great sinologists. Becker draws intriguing parallels between modern rulers and ancient emperors.

David Bonavia *The Chinese: A Portrait* (Penguin, UK & US). A highly readable introduction to contemporary China, focusing on the human aspects as a balance to the socio-political trends.

Gordon Chang *The Coming Collapse of China* (Arrow, UK; Random House, US). A detailed and well-informed overview of what's wrong with contemporary Chinese society by an influential prophet of doom, though his thesis, that a popular revolution will eventually destroy the Communist Party, is overstretched; they've been saying this for years and it hasn't happened yet.

Chen Guidi and Wu Chuntao *Will the Boat Sink the Water?* (Public Affairs, UK). Modern China was founded to improve the lot of its peasant majority, but the journalist authors show how – and how badly – the country's officials are failing them. Banned in China, it has since sold ten million copies on the black market.

John Gittings *Real China* (Pocket Books, UK; Simon and Schuster, US). This series of essays on rural China may lack depth, but it gives a very different picture from the descriptions of the economic miracle on which most Western commentators have focused. His newer *The Changing Face of China* (OUP, UK), offers more analysis but is less unique.

Tim Glissold *Mr China* (Constable and Robinson, UK). The well-told and eye-opening story of how the author went to China to make a fortune and lost 400 million dollars. A great first-person account of the eccentric Chinese business environment, and a must for anyone thinking of investing there.

Duncan Hewitt *Getting Rich First* (Chatto & Windus). Written by a long-term foreign resident and journalist, this excellent book moves beyond commonplace Western views of China – all dynastic history, Cultural Revolution and economic boom – with an informed look at the major social themes shaping the nation.

Will Hutton *The Writing on the Wall* (Little, Brown). Unusually for a view on how modern China interacts with the world, this purely academic work considers the possibility of the West and China cooperating, rather than automatically behaving as implacable rivals.

Joe Studwell *The China Dream* (Profile, UK; Grove Press, US). Mandatory reading for foreign business people in China, this is a cautionary tale, written in layman's terms, debunking the myth that there's easy money to be made from China's vast markets. A great read for anyone interested in business, economics or human greed.

Robert Temple *The Genius of China* (Andre Deutsch, UK; Inner Traditions, US). Derived from Joseph Needham's epic work *Science and Civilization in China*, this thoroughly illustrated compendium covers hundreds of important Chinese inventions through the ages – though the text does labour over how little credit the West gives China's creative talent.

Xinran *The Good Women of China* (Chatto and Windus, UK; Anchor, US). Tales of the struggles of Chinese women; their stories are heartwarming though the editor, a Beijing journalist, seems smug and self-obsessed.

Lin Yutang *My Country and My People* (o/p). An expatriate Chinese scholar writes for Western audiences in the 1930s about what it means to be Chinese. Obviously dated in parts, but overall remarkably fresh and accessible.

Zhang Xinxin and Sang Ye *Chinese Lives* (Penguin, UK; Pan Macmillan, US). This Studs Terkel-like series of first-person narratives from interviews with a broad range of Chinese people is both readable and informative, full of fascinating details of day-to-day existence that you won't read anywhere else.

Travel writing

Charles Blackmore *The Worst Desert on Earth* (John Murray, UK; Trafalgar Square, US). Sergeant-majorly account of an arduous and possibly unique trip across the Taklamakan Desert in northwest China.

Mildred Cable with Francesca French *The Gobi Desert* (Virago Press, UK; Beacon Press, US). Cable and French were missionaries with the China Inland Mission in the early part of the twentieth century. *The Gobi Desert* is a poetic description of their life and travels in Gansu and Xinjiang, without the sanctimonious and patronizing tone adopted by some of their contemporary missionaries.

Austin Coates *Myself a Mandarin* (Oxford UP East Asia, UK). Despite dated views and the changing times, this humorous account of the author's time as a Hong Kong magistrate during the 1950s still rings true.

Rachel DeWoskin *Foreign Babes in Beijing* (Granta UK). Wry, witty snapshot of 1990s Beijing as a place of untested, unexpected opportunities: the author arrives to manage a PR firm and ends up as a bohemian soap-opera star.

Peter Fleming *One's Company: a Journey to China* (Pimlico, UK) and *News from Tartary* (Birlinn, UK; Tarcher, US). The former is an amusing account of a journey through Russia and Manchuria to China in the 1930s. En route, Peter Fleming (brother of Ian) encounters a wild assortment of Chinese and Japanese officials, and the puppet emperor Henry Pu Yi himself. *News from Tartary* records an epic journey of 3500 miles across the roof of the world to Kashmir in 1935.

Peter Hessler *River Town – Two Years on the Yangtze* (John Murray, UK; Perennial, US). One of the best of the mini-genre "how I taught English for a couple of years in China and survived". The book accepts China's positive aspects and avoids cynicism when dealing with social problems and contradictions. Especially worth a read if you're planning a lengthy stay in China.

Somerset Maugham *On a Chinese Screen* (Vintage, UK; Arno Press, US). Brief, sometimes humorous, and often biting sketches of the European missionaries, diplomats and businessmen whom Maugham encountered in China between 1919 and 1921; worth reading for background detail.

Matthew Polly *American Shaolin* (Abacus). A stereotypical weakling, Polly dropped out of a US college to spend two years studying kung fu at the legendary Shaolin Temple. Not just the macho romp you'd expect, the book is self-deprecating, funny and steers clear of cultural cringe.

Marco Polo *The Travels* (Penguin, UK & US). Said to have inspired Columbus, *The Travels* is a fantastic read, full of amazing details picked up during Polo's 26 years of wandering in Asia between Venice and the court of Kublai Khan. It's not, however, a coherent history, having been ghost-written by a novelist from Marco's notes.

Vikram Seth *From Heaven Lake: Travels through Sinkiang and Tibet* (Phoenix, UK; Random House, US). A student for two years at Nanjing University, Seth set out in 1982 to return home to Delhi via Tibet and Nepal. This account of how he hitched his way through four provinces, Xinjiang, Gansu, Qinghai and Tibet, is in the finest tradition of the early travel books.

Colin Thubron *Behind the Wall* (Vintage, UK; HarperCollins, US). A thoughtful and superbly poetic description of an extensive journey through China just after it opened up in the early 1980s. The single best piece of travel writing to have come out of modern China.

Guides and reference books

Kit Chow and Ione Kramer *All the Tea in China* (Sinolingua, UK; China Books, US). Everything you need to know about Chinese teas, from variations in growing and processing techniques to a rundown of fifty of the most famous brews. Good fun and nicely illustrated.

Mackinnon, Showler and Phillipps *A Field Guide to the Birds of China* (Oxford University Press, UK). By far the best book on the subject, with over 1300 species illustrated (mostly in colour), plus outline text descriptions and distribution maps.

Jessica Rawson *Ancient China: Art and Archaeology* (Icon, UK & US). By an oriental antiquities specialist at the British Museum, this scholarly introduction to Chinese art puts the subject in historical context. Beginning in Neolithic times, the book explores the technology and social organization that shaped its development up to the Han dynasty.

George Schaller *Wildlife of the Tibetan Steppe* (University of Chicago Press, US). Reference book on the mammals – especially the rare Tibetan antelope – that inhabit the inhospitable Chang Tang region, by a zoologist who has spent over thirty years studying China's wildlife.

Karen Smith *Nine Lives: Birth of Avant-Garde Art in New China* (Scalo, US). Explores the development of the Chinese contemporary art scene through dense studies of nine of its founders and key players.

Mary Tregear *Chinese Art* (Thames and Hudson, UK & US). An authoritative, clearly written, and well-illustrated summary of the main strands in Chinese art from Neolithic times, through the Bronze Age and up to the twentieth century.

Cookery

Fuchsia Dunlop *Sichuan Cookery* (Penguin, UK; W.W. Norton, US). The best available English-language cookbook on Chinese cuisine, from a talented writer who spent three years honing her skills at a Chengdu cookery school. Dishes smell, look and taste exactly as you find them in Sichuan.

Hsiang Ju Lin and Tsuifeng Lin *Chinese Gastronomy* (Tuttle, US). A classic work, relatively short on recipes but strong on cooking methods and philosophy – essential reading for anyone serious about learning the finer details of Chinese cooking. Wavers in and out of print, sometimes under different titles; look for Lin as the author name.

Kenneth Lo *Chinese Food* (Faber & Faber, US). Good general-purpose cookbook covering a wide range of methods and styles, from Westernized dishes to regional specialities.

Wei Chuan Cultural Education Foundation *Vegetarian Cooking* and *Chinese Dim Sum* (Wei Chuan, Taiwan). Two in a series of excellent, easy-to-follow cookbooks published by the Taiwanese Wei Chuan cooking school; simplified versions of classic dishes that produce good results. Not available in China, but easy enough to find in major bookstores in the West.

Martial arts

Paul Brecher *Principles of Tai Chi and Secrets of Energy Work* (HarperCollins, UK). Two excellent books by a long-time internal martial artist: the first maps out the fundamentals behind *tai ji*, whichever style you practise; the second is a manual on using *qigong* for health.

Kumar Frantzis *The Power of Internal Martial Arts* (North Atlantic Books, US). Trawl through Frantzis' forty years of experience studying the internal martial arts in Japan, China, Taiwan and the US, with personal accounts of different masters and their styles. Articulate and interesting even if you don't know your *li* from your *jing*, though fellow practitioners will find plenty of gems.

Erle Montaigue *Power Taiji* (Paladin Press, US). For those who think *tai ji* is just a series of pretty movements, this book – based on the Yang long form – lifts the lid on an infinitely subtle art that can be used for both healing and combat.

Religion and philosophy

Asiapac series (Asiapac Books, Singapore). These entertaining titles, available in Hong Kong and Beijing, present ancient Chinese philosophy in comic-book format, making it accessible without losing its complexity. They are all well written and well drawn. Particularly good are the *Book of Zen*, a collection of stories and parables, and the *Sayings of Confucius*.

Kenneth Chen *Buddhism in China* (Princeton University Press, US). Very helpful for tracing the origin of Buddhist thought in China, the development of its many different schools and the four-way traffic of influence between India, Tibet, Japan and China.

Chuang Tzu *The Book of Chuang Tzu* (Penguin, UK & US). Wonderful Taoist parables, written in antiquity by a philosopher who clearly had a keen sense of humour and a delight in life's very inexplicability.

Confucius *The Analects* (Penguin, UK & US). Good modern translation of this classic text, a collection of Confucius's teachings focusing on morality and the state.

Lao Zi *Tao Te Ching* (Penguin, UK & US). The collection of mystical thoughts and philosophical speculation that form the basis of Taoist philosophy.

Arthur Waley *Three Ways of Thought in Ancient China* (Routledge-Curzon UK; Stanford University Press US). Translated extracts from the writings of three of the early philosophers – Zhuang Zi, Mencius and Han Feizi. A useful introduction.

Biographies and autobiographies

Anchee Min *Red Azalea* (Orion, UK; Berkley, US). Half-autobiography, half-novel, this beautifully written book is an unusually personal and highly romantic account of surviving the Cultural Revolution.

Dalai Lama *Freedom in Exile* (Abacus, UK; HarperCollins, US). The autobiography of the charismatic, Nobel Prize-winning Fourteenth Dalai Lama.

Richard Evans *Deng Xiaoping* (Penguin, UK and US). The basic handbook if you want to understand the motives and inspirations that lay behind one of the most influential men in modern China.

Jung Chang *Wild Swans* (Perennial, UK; Touchstone, US). Enormously popular in the West, this three-generation family saga was banned in China for its honest account of the horrors of life in turbulent twentieth-century China. As well as being a good read, it serves as an excellent introduction to modern Chinese history.

Ma Jian *Red Dust* (Vintage, UK; Anchor, US). Facing arrest for spiritual pollution, writer and artist Ma Jian fled Beijing to travel around China's remotest corners in the 1980s, often in extreme poverty. This picaresque tale of China in the first phase of its opening up is told in lively prose and offers the kind of insights only an alienated insider could garner. His latest book, *The Noodle Maker*, is a satirical novel about a propagandist and a professional blood donor. An early travelogue, *Stick out Your Tongue,* set in a gritty and unromanticized Tibet, has recently been translated into English.

John Man *Genghis Khan* (Bantam, UK). Lively and readable biography of the illiterate nomad who built the biggest empire the world has ever seen, intercut with Man's travels to Mongolia and China to find his tomb.

Naisingoro Pu Yi *From Emperor to Citizen* (FLP). The autobiography of the young boy who was born into the Qing imperial family and chosen by the Japanese to become the puppet emperor of the state of Manchukuo in 1931.

Philip Short *Mao: A Life* (John Murray, UK; Owl Books, US). Despite its length, an extremely readable account of Mao and his times – even if the Great Helmsman's ideologies are becoming ever less relevant in contemporary China.

Hugh Trevor-Roper *Hermit of Peking: the Hidden Life of Sir Edmund Backhouse* (Eland, UK). Sparked by Backhouse's thoroughly obscene memoirs, *Hermit of Peking* uses external sources in an attempt to uncover the facts behind the extraordinarily convoluted life of Edmund Backhouse – Chinese scholar, eccentric recluse and phenomenal liar – who lived in Beijing from the late nineteenth century until his death in 1944.

Marina Warner *The Dragon Empress* (Vintage, UK; Atheneum, US). In this exploration of the life of Cixi, one of only two women rulers of China, Warner lays bare the complex personality whose conservatism, passion for power, vanity and greed had such a great impact on the events that culminated in the collapse of the imperial ruling house and the founding of the republic.

Literature

Modern writing

JG Ballard *Empire of the Sun* (Harper Perennial, UK, Simon & Schuster, USA). This, the best literary evocation of old Shanghai, is a compelling tale of how the gilded life of ex-pat Shanghai collapsed into chaos with the onset of war, based on the author's own experience growing up in a Japanese internment camp. It was made into a pretty decent film by Steven Spielberg.

Pearl S. Buck *The Good Earth* (Simon & Schuster, UK; Washington Square Press, US). The best story from a writer who grew up in China during the early twentieth century, *The Good Earth* follows the fortunes of the peasant Wang Lung from his wedding day to his dotage, as he struggles to hold onto his land for his family through a series of political upheavals.

Louis Cha *The Book & the Sword* (Oxford). Northwestern China becomes a battleground for secret societies, evil henchmen, Muslim warlords and sword-wielding Taoists as a quest to save a valuable copy of the Koran uncovers a secret that threatens to topple the Qing emperor. Written in the 1950s by China's foremost martial-arts novelist, it has inspired numerous films and TV shows.

Chen Yuanbin *The Story of Qiuju* (Panda Books, China). A collection of four tales, of which the title story, about a peasant woman pushing for justice after her husband is assaulted by the village chief, was made into a film by award-winning director Zhang Yimou.

Chun Sue *Beijing Doll* (Abacus Books, UK; Riverhead Books, US). A rambling *roman à clef* about a confused teenage girl who has unsatisfactory sexual encounters with preening rock and rollers – it has to be said, if it wasn't China it wouldn't be interesting.

Robert Van Gulik *The Judge Dee Mysteries* (Perennial, UK; University of Chicago Press, US). Sherlock Holmes-style detective stories set in the Tang dynasty and starring the wily Judge Dee, who gets tough on crime as detective, judge and jury. There are a lot of them; recommended are *The Red Pavilion*, *Murder in Canton* and *The Chinese Nail Murders*. Fun, informative and unusual.

Guo Xiaolu *The Village of Stone* (Chatto and Windus, UK). A sensitive study of a woman reflecting on her life as a modern metropolitan citizen, and her tough country childhood. Her recent *A Chinese English Dictionary for Lovers,* concerning a Chinese girl's journey of self-discovery when she comes to London, is a bright, lively book, daringly written in Chinglish.

James Hilton *Lost Horizon* (Summersdale, UK; Pocket, US). The classic 1930s novel of longevity in a secret Tibetan valley, which gave the world – and the Chinese tourist industry – the myth of Shangri-la.

Lao She *Rickshaw Boy* (FLP) Lao She was driven to suicide during the Cultural Revolution for his belief that all politics were inherently unjust. The story is a haunting account of a young rickshaw-puller in pre-1949 Beijing.

Lu Xun *The True Story of Ah Q* (FLP). Widely read in China today, Lu Xun is regarded as the father of modern Chinese writing. *Ah Q* is one of his best tales, short, allegorical and cynical, about a simpleton who is swept up in the 1911 revolution.

Mian Mian *Candy* (Back Bay Books). This louche tale of self-destruction, drugs, sex and navel-gazing garnered its colourful Shanghai authoress a reputation as China's foremost literary wild child – it helped, of course, that it was banned.

Mo Yan *The Garlic Ballads* (Penguin, UK & US). A hard-hitting novel of rural life by one of China's greatest modern writers, banned in China.

Qian Zhongshu *Fortress Besieged* (Penguin). Scathing satire, set in the 1930s, about a failed student who uses a fake degree to win a teaching post and a wife. Now highly influential, it was banned for years in both mainland China and Taiwan.

Qiu Xiaolong *When Red is Black, a Loyal Character Dancer, A Case of Two Cities.* Procedural detective stories set in Shanghai, featuring the poetry-loving Inspector Chen. Though sometimes Qiu seems more interested in examining society and morals than in weaving a mystery, his stories of corrupt officials, sharp operators and compromised cops are some of the best evocations of modern China in contemporary English fiction.

Neal Stephenson *The Diamond Age* (Penguin). An ambitious, flawed but brilliant science fiction novel set in China, in "Nu-Chusan" – a re-imagining of Shanghai's concession era in the age of nano-technology.

Wang Shuo *Playing For Thrills* (Penguin, UK & US) and *Please Don't Call Me Human* (No Exit Press, UK; Oldcastle, US). Wang Shuo writes in colourful Beijing dialect about the city's wide boys and chancers. *Playing For Thrills* is fairly representative – a mystery story whose boorish narrator spends most of his time drinking, gambling and chasing girls. *Please Don't Call Me Human* is a satire of modern China as a place where greed is everything, as the Party turns a dignified martial artist into a vacuous dancer in order to win an Olympic gold medal.

Wei Hui *Shanghai Baby* (Constable & Robinson, UK; Washington Square Press, US). Salacious chick-lit about a Chinese girl who can't decide between her Western lover and her drug-addled Chinese boyfriend (though her real love seems to be for designer labels). Notable for the Chinese authorities' attempts to ban it and for spawning a genre in modern Chinese writing, the urban girl's saucy confessional.

Classics

Asiapac series (Asiapac Books, Singapore). Chinese classics and folk tales entertainingly rendered into cartoon format. Titles include *Journey to the West*, *Tales of Laozhai* and *Chinese Eunuchs*.

Cyril Birch (ed) *Anthology of Chinese Literature* (Avalon Travel, US). Two volumes that cover three thousand years of poetry, philosophy, drama, biography and prose fiction, with interesting variations of translation.

Cao Xueqing and Gao E *Dream of Red Mansions/Story of the Stone* (FLP; Penguin, UK & US). This intricate eighteenth-century tale of manners follows the fortunes of the Jia Clan through the emotionally charged adolescent lives of Jia Baoyu and his two girl cousins, Lin Daiyu and Xue Baochai. The full translation fills five paperbacks, but there's also a much simplified English version available in China.

Li Bai and Du Fu *Li Po and Tu Fu* (Penguin, UK & US). Fine translations of China's greatest Tang-dynasty poets, with a detailed introduction that puts them in context. Li Bai was a drunken spiritualist, Du Fu a sharp-eyed realist, and their surprisingly accessible and complementary works form an apex of Chinese literature.

Luo Guanzhong *Romance of the Three Kingdoms* (FLP). Despite being written 1200 years after the events it portrays, this tale vividly evokes the battles, political schemings and myths surrounding China's turbulent Three Kingdoms Period. One of the world's great historical novels.

Pu Songling *Strange Tales from a Chinese Studio* (Penguin). Born during the early Qing dynasty, Pu Songling spent his life amassing these contemporary folk tales, which range from the almost believable to downright weird stories of spirits, ghosts and demons.

Shi Nai'an and Luo Guanzhong *Outlaws of the Marsh* aka *The Water Margin* (FLP). A heavy dose of popular legend as a group of Robin Hood-like outlaws takes on the government in feudal times. Wildly uneven, and hard to read right through, but some amazing characters and set pieces.

Sun Zi *The Art of War* (Penguin, UK; Running Press, US). "Lure them with the prospect of gain, then take them by confusion". This classic on strategy and warfare, told in pithy maxims, is as relevant today as when it was written around 500 BC. A favourite with the modern business community.

Wu Cheng'en *Journey to the West* (FLP). Absurd, lively rendering of the Buddhist monk Xuanzang's pilgrimage to India to collect sacred scriptures, aided by Sandy, Pigsy and the irrepressible Sun Wu Kong, the monkey king. Arthur Waley's version, *Monkey* (Penguin), retains the spirit of the tale while shortening the hundred-chapter opus to paperback length.

Language

Language

Chinese

As the **most widely spoken** language on earth, Chinese can hardly be overlooked. Chinese is, strictly speaking, a series of **dialects** spoken by the dominant ethnic group within China, the Han. Indeed, the term most commonly used by the Chinese themselves to refer to the language is **hanyu**, meaning "Han-language", though *zhongyu*, *zhongwen* and *zhongguohua* are frequently used as well. However, non-Han peoples such as Uyaphurs and Tibetans speak languages which have little or nothing to do with Chinese.

The dialects of *hanyu* are a complicated story in themselves. Some of them are mutually unintelligible and – where the spoken word is concerned – have about as much in common as, say, German and English. The better-known and most distinct dialects include those spoken around China's coastal fringes, such as **Shanghainese** (*shanghai hua*), **Fujianese** (*minnan hua*) and **Cantonese** (*guangdong hua* or *yueyu*), though even within the areas covered by these dialects you'll find huge local divergences. Cantonese and Fujianese are themselves languages of worldwide significance, being the dialects spoken by the people of Hong Kong and among Overseas Chinese communities, particularly those in Southeast Asia.

What enables Chinese from different parts of the country to converse with each other is **Mandarin Chinese**. Historically based on the language of Han officialdom in the Beijing area, Mandarin has been systematically promoted over the past hundred years to be the official, unifying language of the Chinese people, much as modern French, for example, is based on the original Parisian dialect. It is known in mainland China as **putonghua** – "common language" – and in Taiwan (and also remoter corners of China) as *guoyu* – "national language". As the language of education, government and the media, Mandarin is understood to a greater or lesser extent by the vast majority of Han Chinese, and by many non-Han as well, though there are two caveats to this generalization: first, that knowledge of Mandarin is far more common among the young, the educated and the urban-dwelling; and second, that many people who understand Mandarin cannot actually speak it. For example, the chances of the average Tibetan peasant being able to speak Mandarin are extremely small. In Hong Kong and Macau, likewise, there has been until recently very little Mandarin spoken, though this situation is now changing fast.

Another element tying the various dialects together is the Chinese **script**. No matter how different two dialects may sound when spoken, once they are written down in the form of Chinese characters they become mutually comprehensible again, as the different dialects use the same written characters. A sentence of Cantonese, for example, written down beside a sentence of the same meaning in Mandarin, will look broadly similar except for occasional unusual words or structures. Having said this, it should be added that some non-Han peoples use their own scripts, and apart from Cantonese it is unusual to see Chinese dialects written down at all. Most Chinese people, in fact, associate the written word inextricably with Mandarin.

From the point of view of foreigners, the main distinguishing characteristic of Chinese is that it is a **tonal** language: in order to pronounce a word correctly, it is necessary to know not only its sound but also its correct tone. Despite initial impressions, there is nothing too difficult about learning the basics of communication, however, and being able to speak even a few words of Chinese can mean the difference between a successful trip and a nightmare. Given the way tones affect meaning – and the fact that individual characters are monosyllabic – accuracy in **pronunciation** is particularly important in Chinese, for which an understanding of the **pinyin** phonetic system is vital (see opposite). For advanced **teach-yourself** grounding in spoken Mandarin, try *Hugo's Chinese in Three Months*, which includes *pinyin* transliteration and tapes and, while a bit dry, is wider in its approach than purely business- or travel-oriented alternatives. On the road, the Rough Guide *Mandarin Chinese Dictionary Phrasebook* provides useful words and phrases in both *pinyin* and characters, while Langenscheidt's *Pocket Dictionary Chinese* is – for its size – perhaps the best available **dictionary** of colloquial usage. Once you're in China, you'll find that any bookshop will have a huge range of inexpensive Chinese–English dictionaries, and perhaps livelier teach-yourself texts than are available overseas.

Chinese characters

There are tens of thousands of **Chinese characters**, in use since at least the Shang dynasty (1600–1100 BC), though the vast majority of these are obsolete – you need about 2500 to read a newspaper, and even educated Chinese are unlikely to know more than ten thousand. The characters themselves are **pictograms**, each representing a **concept** rather than a specific pronunciation. This is similar to the use of numerals: there is nothing in the figure "2" which spells out the pronunciation; having learned what the symbol means, we simply know how to say it – whether "two" in English, "deux" in French, and so on. Similarly, Chinese speakers have to memorize the sounds of individual characters, and the meanings attached to them. While the sounds might vary from region to region, the meanings themselves do not – which is how the written word cuts through regional variations in language.

Although to untrained eyes many Chinese characters seem impossibly complex, there is a logic behind their structure which helps in their memorization. Firstly, each character is written using an exact number of brush (or pen) **strokes**: thus the character for "mouth", which forms a square, is always written using only three strokes: first the left side, then the top and right side together, and finally the base. Secondly, characters can very broadly be broken up into two components, which often also exist as characters in their own right: a **main** part, which frequently gives a clue as to the pronunciation; and a **radical**, which usually appears on the left side of the character and which vaguely categorizes the meaning. As an example, the character for "mother" is made up of the character for "horse" (to which it sounds similar), combined with a radical which means "female". In a few cases, it's easy to see the connection between the pictogram and its meaning – the character *mu*, wood, resembles a tree – though others require some lateral thinking or have become so abstract or complex that the meaning is hidden.

Given the time and difficulty involved in **learning characters**, and the negative impact this has had on the general level of literacy, the government of the People's Republic announced in 1954 that a couple of thousand of the most common characters were to be, quite literally, **simplified**, making them not only easier to learn but also quicker to write, as the new characters often use far fewer pen strokes. This drastic measure was not without controversy.

Some argued that by interfering with the original structure of the characters, vital clues as to their meaning and pronunciation would be lost, making them harder than ever to learn. These simplified characters were eventually adopted not just in mainland China but also in Singapore; but Hong Kong and Taiwan, as well as many Overseas Chinese communities, continue to use the older, traditional forms.

Today, ironically, the traditional forms are also making a **comeback** on the mainland, where they are now seen as sophisticated. Note that some of these traditional forms differ considerably from the simplified forms provided in this book, though their meaning and pronunciation are identical.

Grammar

Chinese **grammar** is relatively simple. There is no need to conjugate verbs, decline nouns or make adjectives agree – being attached to immutable Chinese characters, Chinese words simply cannot have different "endings". Instead, context and fairly rigid rules about word order are relied on to make those distinctions of time, number and gender that Indo-European languages are so concerned with. Instead of cumbersome tenses, the Chinese make use of words such as "yesterday" or "tomorrow"; instead of plural endings they simply state how many things there are, or use quantifier words equivalent to "some" or "many".

Word formation is affected by the fact that the meanings of many Chinese characters have become diffuse over time. For instance, there is a single character, pronounced *ju* with the third tone in Mandarin, which is a verb meaning "to lift", "to start" or "to choose", an adjective meaning "whole" and a noun meaning "deed". In a very dim way we might perhaps see the underlying meaning of *ju* on its own, but to make things clear in practice, many concepts are referred to not by single characters but by combining two or more characters together like building blocks. In the case of *ju* above, the addition of character for "world" creates a word meaning "throughout the world"; and the addition of "eye" creates a word meaning "look".

For English-speakers, **Chinese word order** follows the familiar subject-verb-object pattern, and you'll find that by simply stringing words together you'll be producing fairly grammatical Chinese. Just note that adjectives, as well as all qualifying and describing phrases, precede nouns.

Pronunciation and pinyin

Back in the 1950s it was hoped eventually to replace Chinese characters altogether with a regular alphabet of Roman letters, and to this end the **pinyin** system was devised. Basically, *pinyin* is a way of using the Roman alphabet (except the letter "v") to write out the sounds of Mandarin Chinese, with Mandarin's four tones represented by **accents** above each syllable. Other dialects of Chinese, such as Cantonese – having nine tones – cannot be written in *pinyin*.

The aim of replacing Chinese characters with *pinyin* was abandoned long ago, but in the meantime *pinyin* has one very important function, that of helping foreigners to pronounce Chinese words. However, in *pinyin* the letters do not all have the sounds you would expect, and you'll need to spend an hour or two learning these. You'll often see *pinyin* in China, on street signs and shop displays, but only well-educated locals know the system well. Occasionally, you will come across **other systems** of rendering Mandarin into Roman letters, such as **Wade-Giles**, which writes Mao Zedong as Mao Tse-tung, and Deng Xiaoping as Teng Hsiao-p'ing. These forms are no longer used in mainland China, but you may see them in Western books about China, or in Taiwanese publications.

The Chinese terms in this book have been given both in characters and in *pinyin*; the pronunciation guide below is your first step to making yourself comprehensible. Don't get overly paranoid about your tones: with the help of context, intelligent listeners should be able to work out what you are trying to say. If you're just uttering a single word, however, for example a place name – without a context – you need to hit exactly the right tone, otherwise don't be surprised if nobody understands you.

The tones

There are **four tones** in Mandarin Chinese, and every syllable of every word is characterized by one of them, except for a few syllables which are considered toneless. This emphasis on tones does not make Chinese a particularly musical language – English, for example, uses all of the tones of Chinese and many more. The difference is that English uses tone for effect – exclaiming, questioning, listing, rebuking and so on. In English, to change the tone is to change the mood or the emphasis; in Chinese, to change the tone is to change the word itself.

First or "High" *ā ē ī ō ū*. In English this level tone is used when mimicking robotic or very boring, flat voices.

Second or "Rising" *á é í ó ú*. Used in English when asking a question showing surprise, for example "eh?".

Third or "Falling-rising" ǎ ě ǐ ǒ ǔ. Used in English when echoing someone's words with a measure of incredulity. For example, "John's dead." "De-ad?!".

Fourth or "Falling" *à è ì ò ù*. Often used in English when counting in a brusque manner – "One! Two! Three! Four!".

Toneless A few syllables do not have a tone accent. These are pronounced without emphasis, such as in the English **u**pon.

Note that if there are two consecutive characters with the third tone, the first character is pronounced as though it carries the second tone.

Consonants

Most consonants are pronounced in a similar way to their English equivalents, with the following exceptions:

c as in ha**ts**

g is hard as in **g**od (except when preceded by "n" when it sounds like sa**ng**)

q as in **ch**eese

x has no direct equivalent in English, but you can make the sound by sliding from an "s" sound to a "sh" sound and stopping midway between the two

z as in su**ds**

zh as in fud**ge**

Vowels and diphthongs

As in most languages, the vowel sounds are rather harder to quantify than the consonants. The examples here give a rough description of the sound of each vowel followed by related combination sounds.

a usually somewhere between **far** and **man**

ai as in **eye**

ao as in **cow**

e usually as in **fur**

ei as in **gay**

en is an unstressed sound as at the end of hyph**en**

eng as in **sung**

er as in **fur** (ie with a stressed "r")

i usually as in **tea**, except in *zi*, *ci*, *si*, *ri*, *zhi*, *chi* and *shi*, when it is a short clipped sound like the American military "**si**r"

ia as in **yak**

ian as in **yen**

ie as in **yeah**

o as in **bore**

ou as in **show**

ü as in the German ü (make an "ee" sound and glide slowly into an "oo"; at the mid-point between the two sounds you should hit the ü-sound)

u usually as in **fool** except where *u* follows *j*, *q*, *x or y*, when it is always pronounced **ü**

ua as in **suave**

uai as in **why**

ue as though contracting "you" and "air" together, **you'air**

ui as in **way**

uo as in **wore**

Useful words and phrases

Chinese put their **family names first** followed by their given names, exactly the reverse of Western convention. The vast majority of Chinese family names comprise a single character, while given names are either one or two characters long. So a man known as Zhang Dawei has the family name of Zhang, and the given name of Dawei.

When asked for their name the Chinese tend to provide either just their family name, or their whole name. In **formal situations**, you might come across the terms "Mr" (*xiansheng*), "Mrs" (*taitai*, though this is being replaced by the more neutral term *airen*) or "Miss" (*xiaojie*), which are attached after the family name: for example, Mr Zhang is *zhang xiansheng*. In more casual encounters, people use familiar terms such as "old" (*lao*) or "young" (*xiao*) attached in front of the family name, though "old" or "young" are more relative terms of status than indications of actual age in this case: Mr Zhang's friend might call him "Lao Zhang", for instance.

Basics

I	我	wǒ
You (singular)	你	nǐ
He	他	tā
She	她	tā
We	我们	wǒmén
You (plural)	你们	nǐmén
They	他们	tāmén
I want...	我要	wǒ yào...
No, I don't want...	我不要 ...	wǒ bú yào...
Is it possible...?	可不可以...?	kěbùkěyǐ...?
It is (not) possible.	(不)可以	(bù) kěyǐ
Is there any/Have you got any...?	有没有...?	yǒuméiyǒu...?
There is/I have	有	yǒu
There isn't/I haven't	没有	méiyǒu

Please help me	请帮我忙	qǐng bāng wǒ máng
Mr...	.....先生	xiānshēng
Mrs...	.....太太	tàitài
Miss...	.....小姐	xiǎojiě

Communicating

I don't speak Chinese	我不会说中文	wǒ bú huì shuō zhōngwén
My Chinese is terrible	我的中文很差	wǒ de zhōngwén hěn chà
Can you speak English?	你会说英语吗?	nǐ huì shuō yīngyǔ ma?
Can you get someone who speaks English?	请给我找一个会说英语的人	qǐng gěi wǒ zhǎo yí ge huì shuō yīngyǔ de rén?
Please speak slowly	请说得慢一点	qǐng shuōde màn yidiǎn
Please say that again	请再说一遍	qǐng zài shuō yí biàn
I understand	我听得懂	wǒ tīngdedǒng
I don't understand	我听不懂	wǒ tīngbùdǒng
I can't read Chinese characters	我看不懂汉字	wǒ kànbùdong hànzì
What does this mean?	这是什么意思?	zhè shì shénme yìsi?
How do you pronounce this character?	这个字怎么念?	zhè ge zì zěnme niàn?

Greetings and basic courtesies

Hello/How do you do?	你好	nǐ hǎo?
How are you?	你好吗?	nǐ hǎo ma?
I'm fine	我很好	wǒ hěn hǎo
Thank you	谢谢	xièxie
Don't mention it/You're welcome	不客气	búkèqi
Sorry to bother you...	麻烦你	máfan nǐ
Sorry/I apologize	对不起	duìbùqǐ
It's not important/No problem	没关系	méi guānxi
Goodbye	再见	zài jiàn
Chitchat	聊天	liáotiān
What country are you from?	你是哪个国家的?	nǐ shì nǎ ge guójiā de?
Britain	英国	yīngguó
Ireland	爱尔兰	ài'érlán
America	美国	měiguó
Canada	加拿大	jiā'nádà
Australia	澳大利亚	àodàlìyà
New Zealand	新西兰	xīnxīlán
China	中国	zhōngguó
Outside China	外国	wàiguó
What's your name?	你叫什么名字?	nǐ jiào shěnme míngzi?
My name is...	我叫....	wǒ jiào...
Are you married?	你结婚了吗?	nǐ jiéhūn le ma?
I am (not) married	我(没有)结婚(了)	wǒ (méiyǒu) jiéhūn (le)
Have you got (children)?	你有没有孩子?	nǐ yǒu méiyǒu háizi?
Do you like...?	你喜不喜欢.....?	nǐ xǐ bù xǐhuān....?

I (don't) like...	我不喜欢....	wǒ (bù) xǐhuān...
What's your job?	你干什么工作?	nǐ gàn shénme gōngzuò?
I'm a foreign student	我是留学生	wǒ shì liúxuéshēng
I'm a teacher	我是老师	wǒ shì laǒshī
I work in a company	我在一个公司工作	wǒ zài yí ge gōngsī gōngzuò
I don't work	我不工作	wǒ bù gōngzuò
Clean/dirty	干净/脏	gānjìng/zāng
Hot/cold	热/冷	rè/lěng
Fast/slow	快/慢	kuài/màn
Pretty	漂亮	piàoliàng
Interesting	有意思	yǒuyìsi

Numbers

Zero	零	líng
One	一	yī
Two	二/两	èr/liǎng*
Three	三	sān
Four	四	sì
Five	五	wǔ
Six	六	liù
Seven	七	qī
Eight	八	bā
Nine	九	jiǔ
Ten	十	shí
Eleven	十一	shíyī
Twelve	十二	shíèr
Twenty	二十	èrshí
Twenty-one	二十一	èrshíyī
One hundred	一百	yībǎi
Two hundred	二百	èrbǎi
One thousand	一千	yīqiān
Ten thousand	一万	yīwàn
One hundred thousand	十万	shíwàn
One million	一百万	yībǎiwàn
One hundred million	一亿	yīyì
One billion	十亿	shíyì

*liǎng is used when enumerating, for example "two people" liǎng ge rén. èr is used when counting.

Time

Now	现在	xiànzài
Today	今天	jīntiān
(In the) morning	早上	zǎoshàng
(In the) afternoon	下午	xiàwǔ
(In the) evening	晚上	wǎnshàng
Tomorrow	明天	míngtiān

The day after tomorrow	后天	hòutiān
Yesterday	昨天	zuótiān
Week/month/year	星期/月/年	xīngqī/yuè/nián
Monday	星期一	xīngqī yī
Tuesday	星期二	xīngqī èr
Wednesday	星期三	xīngqī sān
Thursday	星期四	xīngqī sì
Friday	星期五	xīngqī wǔ
Saturday	星期六	xīngqī liù
Sunday	星期天	xīngqī tiān
What's the time?	几点了?	jǐdiǎn le?
10 o'clock	十点钟	shídiǎn zhōng
10.20	十点二十	shídiǎn èrshí
10.30	十点半	shídiǎn bàn

Travelling and getting about town

North	北	běi
South	南	nán
East	东	dōng
West	西	xī
Airport	机场	jīchǎng
Ferry dock	船码头	chuánmǎtóu
Left-luggage office	寄存处	jìcún chù
Ticket office	售票处	shòupiào chù
Ticket	票	piào
Can you buy me a ticket to…?	可不可以给我买到.....的票?	kěbùkěyǐ gěi wǒ mǎi dào… de piào?
I want to go to…	我想到.....去	wǒ xiǎng dào … qù
I want to leave at (8 o'clock)	我想(八点钟)离开	wǒ xiǎng (bā diǎn zhōng) Líkāi
When does it leave?	什么时候出发?	shénme shíhòu chūfā?
When does it arrive?	什么时候到?	shénme shíhòu dào?
How long does it take?	路上得多长时间?	lùshàng děi duōcháng Shíjiān?
CAAC	中国民航	zhōngguó mínháng
CITS	中国国际旅行社	zhōngguó guójì lvxíngshè
Train	火车	huǒchē
(Main) Train station	主要火车站	(zhǔyào) huǒchēzhàn
Bus	公共汽车	gōnggòng qìchēzhàn
Bus station	汽车站	qìchēzhàn
Long-distance bus station	长途汽车站	chángtú qìchē
Express train/bus	特快车	tèkuài chē
Fast train/bus	快车	kuài chē
Ordinary train/bus	普通车	pǔtōng chē
Minibus	小车	xiǎo chē
Sleeper bus	卧铺车	wòpù chē
Lower bunk	下铺	xiàpù
Middle bunk	中铺	zhōngpù

Upper bunk	上铺	shàngpù
Hard seat	硬座	yìngzuò
Soft seat	软座	ruánzuò
Hard sleeper	硬卧	yìngwò
Soft sleeper	软卧	ruănwò
Soft-seat waiting room	软卧候车室	ruănwò hòuchēshì
Timetable	时间表	shíjiān biăo
Upgrade ticket	补票	bŭpiào
Unreserved ticket	无座	wúzuò
Returned ticket window	退票	tuìpiào
Platform	站台	zhàntái

Getting about town

Map	地图	dìtú
Where is…?	……在哪里?	…zài nălĭ?
Go straight on	往前走	wăng qián zŏu
Turn right	往右拐	wăng yòu guăi
Turn left	往左拐	wăng zuŏ guăi
Taxi	出租车	chūzū chē
Please use the meter	请打开记价器	qĭng dăkāi jìjiàqì
Underground/Subway station	地铁站	dìtiĕ zhàn
Rickshaw	三轮车	sānlún chē
Bicycle	自行车	zìxíngchē
I want to rent a bicycle	我想租自行车	wŏ xiăng zū zìxíngchē
How much is it per hour?	一个小时得多少钱?	yí gè xiăoshí déi duōshăo qián?
Can I borrow your bicycle?	能不能借你的自行车?	néng bùnéng jiè nĭ de zìxíngchē?
Bus	公共汽车	gōnggòngqìchē
Which bus goes to…?	几路车到……去?	jĭ lù chē dào … qù?
Number (10) bus	(十)路车	(shí) lù chē
Does this bus go to…?	这车到……去吗?	zhè chē dào … qù ma?
When is the next bus?	下一班车几点开?	xià yì bān chē jĭ diăn kāi?
The first bus	头班车	tóubān chē
The last bus	末班车	mòbān chē
Please tell me where to get off	请告诉我在哪里下车	qĭng gàosù wŏ zài nălĭ xià chē
Museum	博物馆	bówùguăn
Temple	寺院	sìyuàn
Church	教堂	jiàotáng
Mosque	清真寺	qīngzhēn sì
Toilet (men's)	男厕所	nán cèsuŏ
Toilet (women's)	女厕所	nǚ cèsuŏ

Accommodation

Accommodation	住宿	zhùsù
Hotel (upmarket)	宾馆	bīnguăn
Hotel (downmarket)	招待所，旅馆	zhāodàisuŏ, lǚguăn
Hostel	旅社	lǚshè

Foreigner's guesthouse (at a university)	外国专家楼	wàiguó zhuānjiā lóu
Is it possible to stay here?	能不能住在这里?	néng bù néng zhù zài zhèlǐ ?
Can I have a look at the room?	能不能看一下房间 ?	néng bù néng kàn yíxià fángjiān?
I want the cheapest bed you've got	我要你最便宜的床位	wǒ yào nǐ zuì piányi de chuángwèi
Single room	单人房	dānrénfáng
Twin room	双人房	shuāngrénfáng
Three-bed room	三人房	sānrénfáng
Dormitory	多人房	duōrénfáng
Suite	套房	tàofáng
(Large) bed	（大）床	(dà) chuáng
Passport	护照	hùzhào
Deposit	押金	yājīn
Key	钥匙	yàoshi
When is the hot water on?	什么时候有热水?	shénme shíhòu yǒu rèshuǐ?
I want to change my room	我想换一个房间	wǒ xiǎng huàn yí ge Fángjiān
laundry (the action)	洗衣服	xǐyīfu
laundry (the place)	洗衣店	xǐyīdiàn
washing powder	洗衣粉	xǐyīfěn

Shopping, money and banks, and the police

How much is it?	这是多少钱?	zhè shì duōshǎo qián?
That's too expensive	太贵了	tài guì le
I haven't got any cash	我没有现金	wǒ méiyǒu xiànjīn
Have you got anything cheaper?	有没有便宜一点的?	yǒu méiyǒu piányi yìdiǎn de?
Do you accept credit cards?	可不可以用信用卡?	kě bù kěyǐ yòng xìnyòngkǎ?
Department store	百货商店	báihuò shāngdiàn
Market	市场	shìchǎng
¥1 (RMB)	一块(人民币)	yí kuài (rénmínbì)
US$1	一块美金	yí kuài měijīn
£1	一个英磅	yí gè yīngbàng
HK$1	一块港币	yí kuài gǎngbì
Change money	换钱	huàn qián
Bank of China	中国银行	zhōngguó yínháng
Traveller's cheques	旅行支票	lǚxíngzhīpiào
PSB	公安局	gōng'ān jú

Communications

Post office	邮电局	yóudiànjú
Envelope	信封	xìnfēng
Stamp	邮票	yóupiào
Airmail	航空信	hángkōngxìn
Surface mail	平信	píngxìn
Poste restante	邮件侯领处	yóujiàn hòulǐngchù
Telephone	电话	diànhuà
International telephone call	国际电话	guójì diànhuà

Reverse charges/collect call	对方付钱电话	duìfāngfùqián diànhuà
Fax	传真	chuánzhēn
Telephone card	电话卡	diànhuàkǎ
I want to make a telephone call to (Britain)	我想给(英国)打电话	wǒ xiǎng gěi (yīngguó) dǎ diànhuà
I want to send a fax to (US)	我想给(美国)发一个传真	wǒ xiǎng gěi (měiguó) fā yí ge chuánzhēn
Can I receive a fax here?	能不能在这里收传真?	néng bù néng zài zhèlǐ shōu chuánzhēn?
Internet café	网吧	wǎngbā

Health

Hospital	医院	yīyuàn
Pharmacy	药店	yàodiàn
Medicine	药	yào
Chinese medicine	中药	zhōngyào
Diarrhoea	腹泻	fùxiè
Vomit	呕吐	ǒutù
Fever	发烧	fāshāo
I'm ill	我生病了	wǒ shēngbìng le
I've got flu	我感冒了	wǒ gǎnmào le
I'm (not) allergic to…	我对.....(不)过敏	wǒ duì … (bù) guòmǐn
Antibiotics	抗生素	kàngshēngsù
Quinine	奎宁	kuíníng
Condom	避孕套	bìyùntào
Mosquito coil	蚊香	wénxiāng
Mosquito netting	蚊帐纱	wénzhàngshā

A food and drink glossary

The following lists should help out in deciphering the characters on a Chinese menu – if they're written clearly. If you know what you're after, try sifting through the staples and cooking methods to create your order, or sample one of the everyday or regional suggestions, many of which are available all over the country. Don't forget to tailor your demands to the capabilities of where you're ordering, however – a street cook with a wok isn't going to be able to whip up anything more complicated than a basic stir-fry. Note that some items, such as seafood and *jiaozi*, are ordered by weight.

General

Restaurant	餐厅	cāntīng
House speciality	拿手好菜	náshǒuhaǒcài
How much is that?	多少钱?	duōshǎo qián?
I don't eat (meat)	我不吃(肉)	wǒ bù chi (ròu)
I'm Buddhist/I'm vegetarian	我是佛教徒/我只吃素	wǒ shì fójiàotú/wǒ zhǐ chī sù
I would like...	我想要....	wǒ xiǎng yào...
Local dishes	地方菜	dìfāng cài
Snacks	小吃	xiǎochī
Menu/set menu/English menu	菜单/套餐/英文菜单	càidān/tàocài/yīngwén càidān
Small portion	少量	shǎoliàng
Chopsticks	筷子	kuàizi
Knife and fork	刀叉	dāochā
Spoon	勺子	sháozi
Waiter/waitress	服务员/小姐	fúwùyuán/xiǎojiě
Bill/cheque	买单	mǎidān
Cook these ingredients together	一快儿做	yíkuàir zuò
Not spicy/no chilli please	请不要辣椒	qǐng búyào làjiāo
Only a little spice/chilli	一点辣椒	yìdiǎn làjiāo
50 grams	两	liáng
250 grams	半斤	bànjīn
500 grams	斤	jīn
1 kilo	公斤	gōngjīn

Drinks

Beer	啤酒	píjiǔ
Sweet fizzy drink	汽水	qìshuǐ
Coffee	咖啡	kāfēi
Milk	牛奶	niúnǎi
(Mineral) water	(矿泉)水	(kuàngquán) shuǐ
Wine	葡萄酒	pútáojiǔ
Spirits	白酒	báijiǔ
Soya milk	豆浆	dòujiāng
Yoghurt	酸奶	suānnǎi

Teas

Tea	茶	chá
Black tea	红茶	hóng chá
Chrysanthemum	菊花茶	júhuā chá
Eight treasures	八宝茶	bābǎo chá
Green tea	绿茶	lü`chá
Iron Buddha	铁观音	tiěguānyīn
Jasmine	茉莉花茶	mòlìhuā chá
Pu'er	普洱茶	pu'er chá

Staple foods

Aubergine	茄子	qiézi
Bamboo shoots	笋尖	sǔnjiān
Bean sprouts	豆芽	dòuyá
Beans	豆	dòu
Beef	牛肉	niúròu
Bitter gourd	葫芦	húlu
Black bean sauce	黑豆豉	hēidòuchǐ
Bread	面包	miànbāo
Buns (filled)	包子	bāozi
Buns (plain)	馒头	mántou
Carrot	胡萝卜	húluóbo
Cashew nuts	腰果	yāoguǒ
Cauliflower	菜花	càihuā
Chicken	鸡	jī
Chilli	辣椒	làjiāo
Chocolate	巧克力	qiǎokèlì
Coriander (leaves)	香菜	xiāngcài
Crab	蟹	xiè
Cucumber	黄瓜	huángguā
Dog	狗肉	gǒuròu
Duck	鸭	yā
Eel	鳝鱼	shànyú
Eggs (fried)	煎鸡蛋	jiānjīdàn
Fish	鱼	yú
Fried dough stick	油条	yóutiáo
Frog	田鸡	tiánjī
Garlic	大蒜	dàsuàn
Ginger	姜	jiāng
Green pepper (capsicum)	青椒	qīngjiāo
Green vegetables	绿叶素菜	lü`yè sùcài
Jiaozi (ravioli, steamed or boiled)	饺子	jiǎozi
Lamb	羊肉	yángròu
Lotus root	莲心	liánxīn
MSG	味精	wèijīng

Mushrooms	磨菇	mógu
Noodles	面条	miàntiáo
Omelette	摊鸡蛋	tānjīdàn
Onions	洋葱	yángcōng
Oyster sauce	蚝油	háoyóu
Pancake	摊饼	tānbǐng
Peanut	花生	huāshēng
Pork	猪肉	zhūròu
Potato (stir-fried)	(炒)土豆	(chao) tǔdòu
Prawns	虾	xiā
Preserved egg	皮蛋	pídàn
Rice, boiled	白饭	báifàn
Rice, fried	炒饭	chǎofàn
Rice noodles	河粉	héfěn
Rice porridge (aka "congee")	粥	zhōu
Salt	盐	yán
Sesame oil	芝麻油	zhīma yóu
Shuijiao (ravioli in soup)	水饺	shuǐjiǎo
Sichuan pepper	四川辣椒	sìchuān làjiao
Snails	蜗牛	wōniú
Snake	蛇肉	shéròu
Soup	汤	tāng
Soy sauce	酱油	jiàngyóu
Squid	鱿鱼	yóuyú
Star anise	茴香	huíxiāng
Straw mushrooms	草菇	cǎogū
Sugar	糖	táng
Tofu	豆腐	dòufu
Tomato	蕃茄	fānqié
Vinegar	醋	cù
Water chestnuts	马蹄	mǎtí
White radish	白萝卜	báiluóbo
Wood ear fungus	木耳	mùěr
Yam	芋头	yùtóu

Cooking methods

Boiled	煮	zhǔ
Casseroled (see also "Claypot" opposite)	焙	bèi
Deep-fried	油煎	yóujiān
Fried	炒	chǎo
Poached	白煮	báizhǔ
Red-cooked (stewed in soy sauce)	红烧	hóngshāo
Roast	烤	kǎo
Steamed	蒸	zhēng
Stir-fried	清炒	qīngchǎo

Everyday dishes

Braised duck with vegetables	炖鸭素菜	dùnyā sùcài
Cabbage rolls (stuffed with meat or vegetables)	卷心菜	juǎnxīn cài
Chicken and sweetcorn soup	玉米鸡丝汤	yùmǐ jīsī tāng
Chicken with bamboo shoots and babycorn	笋尖嫩玉米炒鸡片	sǔnjiān nènyùmǐ chǎojīpiàn
Chicken with cashew nuts	腰果鸡片	yāoguǒ jīpiàn
Claypot/sandpot (casserole)	沙锅	shāguō
Crispy aromatic duck	香酥鸭	xiāngsūyā
Egg flower soup with tomato	蕃茄蛋汤	fānqié dàn tāng
Egg-fried rice	蛋炒饭	dànchǎofàn
Fish-ball soup with white radish	萝卜鱼蛋汤	luóbo yúdàn tāng
Fish casserole	焙鱼	bèiyú
Fried shredded pork with garlic and chilli	大蒜辣椒炒肉片	dàsuàn làjiāo chǎoròupiàn
Hotpot	火锅	huǒguō
Kebab	串肉	chuànròu
Noodle soup	汤面	tāngmiàn
Pork and mustard greens	芥末肉片	jièmò ròupiàn
Pork and water chestnut	马蹄猪肉	mǎtí zhuròu
Pork and white radish pie	白萝卜肉馅饼	báiluóbo ròuxiànbǐng
Prawn with garlic sauce	大蒜炒虾	dàsuàn chǎoxiā
"Pulled" noodles	拉面	lāmiàn
Roast duck	烤鸭	kǎoyā
Scrambled egg with pork on rice	滑蛋猪肉饭	huádàn zhuròufàn
Sliced pork with yellow bean sauce	黄豆肉片	huángdòu ròupiàn
Squid with green pepper and black beans	豆豉青椒炒鱿鱼	dòuchǐ qīngjiāo chǎoyóuyú
Steamed eel with black beans	豆豉蒸鳝	dòuchǐ zhēngshàn
Steamed rice packets wrapped in lotus leaves	荷叶蒸饭	héyè zhēngfàn
Stewed pork belly with vegetables	回锅肉	huíguōròu
Stir-fried chicken and bamboo shoots	笋尖炒鸡片	sǔnjiān chǎojīpiàn
Stuffed bean-curd soup	豆腐汤	dòufutāng
Stuffed bean curd with aubergine and green pepper	茄子青椒煲	qiézi qīngjiāobǎo
Sweet-and-sour spareribs	糖醋排骨	tángcù páigǔ
Sweet bean paste pancakes	赤豆摊饼	chìdòu tānbǐng
White radish soup	白萝卜汤	báiluóbo tāng
Wonton soup	馄饨汤	húntun tāng

Vegetables and eggs

Aubergine with chilli and garlic sauce	大蒜辣椒炒茄子	dàsuàn làjiāo chǎoqiézi
Aubergine with sesame sauce	拌茄子片	bànqiézipiàn
Bean curd and spinach soup	菠菜豆腐汤	bōcài dòufu tāng
Bean-curd slivers	豆腐花	dòufuhuā
Bean curd with chestnuts	马蹄豆腐	mǎtí dòufu
Braised mountain fungus	炖香菇	dùnxiānggū
Egg fried with tomatoes	蕃茄炒蛋	fānqié chǎodàn
Fried bean curd with vegetables	豆腐素菜	dòufu sùcài
Fried bean sprouts	炒豆芽	chǎodòuyá
Monks' vegetarian dish (stir-fry of mixed vegetables and fungi)	罗汉斋	luóhànzhāi
Pressed bean curd with cabbage	卷心菜豆腐	juǎnxīncài dòufu
Spicy braised aubergine	香茄子条	xiāngqiézitiáo
Stir-fried bamboo shoots	炒冬笋	chǎodōngsǔn
Stir-fried mushrooms	炒鲜菇	chǎoxiān'gū
Vegetable soup	素菜汤	sùcài tāng

Regional dishes

Northern

Aromatic fried lamb	炒羊肉	chǎoyángròu
Beijing (Peking) duck	北京烤鸭	běijīng kǎoyā
Fish with ham and vegetables	火腿素菜鱼片	huǒtuǐ sùcài yúpiàn
Fried prawn balls	炒虾球	chǎoxiāqiú
Lion's head (pork rissoles casseroled with greens)	狮子头	shīzitóu
Mongolian hotpot	蒙古火锅	ménggǔ huǒguō
Red-cooked lamb	红烧羊肉	hóngshāo yángròu

Eastern

Beggars' chicken (baked)	叫花鸡	jiàohuājī
Brine duck	盐水鸭	yánshuǐ yā
Crab soup	蟹肉汤	xièròu tāng
Dongpo pork casserole (steamed in wine)	东坡焙肉	dōngpō bèiròu
Drunken prawns	醉虾	zuìxiā
Five flower pork (steamed in lotus leaves)	五花肉	wǔhuāròu
Fried crab with eggs	蟹肉鸡蛋	xièròu jīdàn
Pearl balls (rice-grain-coated, steamed rissoles)	珍珠球	zhēnzhūqiú
Shaoxing chicken	绍兴鸡	shàoxīng jī
Soup dumplings (steamed, containing jellied stock)	汤包	tāngbāo

Steamed sea bass	清蒸鲈鱼	qīngzhēnglúyú
Stuffed green peppers	馅青椒	xiànqīngjiāo
West Lake fish (braised in a sour sauce)	西湖醋鱼	xīhúcùyú
"White-cut" beef (spiced and steamed)	白切牛肉	báiqie niúròu
Yangzhou fried rice	杨州炒饭	yángzhōu chǎofàn

Sichuan and western China

Boiled beef slices (spicy)	水煮牛肉	shuǐzhǔ niúròu
Carry-pole noodles (with a chilli-vinegar-sesame sauce)	担担面	dàndànmiàn
Crackling-rice with pork	爆米肉片	bàomǐ ròupiàn
Crossing-the-bridge noodles	过桥面	guòqiáomiàn
Deep-fried green beans with garlic	大蒜刀豆	dàsuàn dāodòu
Dong'an chicken (poached in spicy sauce)	东安鸡子	dōng'ān jīzǐ
Doubled-cooked pork	回锅肉	huíguōròu
Dried yoghurt wafers	乳饼	rǔbǐng
Dry-fried pork shreds	油炸肉丝	yóuzhá ròusī
Fish-flavoured aubergine	鱼香茄子	yúxiāng qiézi
Gongbao chicken (with chillies and peanuts)	宫保鸡丁	gōngbǎo jīdīng
Green pepper with spring onion and black bean sauce	豆豉青椒	dòuchǐ qīngjiāo
Hot and sour soup (flavoured with vinegar and white pepper)	酸辣汤	suānlà tāng
Hot-spiced bean curd	麻婆豆腐	mápódòufu
Rice-flour balls, stuffed with sweet paste	汤圆	tāngyuán
Smoked duck	熏鸭	xūnyā
Strange flavoured chicken (with sesame-garlic-chilli)	怪味鸡	guàiwèijī
Stuffed aubergine slices	馅茄子	xiànqiézi
Tangerine chicken	桔子鸡	júzijī
"Tiger-skin" peppers (pan-fried with salt)	虎皮炒椒	hǔpí chǎojiāo
Wind-cured ham	火腿	huǒtuǐ

Southern Chinese/Cantonese

Baked crab with chilli and black beans	辣椒豆豉焙蟹	làjiāo dòuchǐ bèixiè
Barbecued pork ("char siew")	叉烧	chāshāo
Casseroled bean curd stuffed with pork mince	豆腐煲	dòufubǎo
Claypot rice with sweet sausage	香肠饭	xiāngchángfàn

Crisp-skinned pork on rice	脆皮肉饭	cuìpíròufàn
Fish-head casserole	焙鱼头	bèiyútóu
Fish steamed with ginger and spring onion	清蒸鱼	qīngzhēngyú
Fried chicken with yam	芋头炒鸡片	yùtóu chǎojīpiàn
Honey-roast pork	叉烧	chāshāo
Kale in oyster sauce	蚝油白菜	háoyóu báicài
Lemon chicken	柠檬鸡	níngméngjī
Litchi (lychee) pork	荔枝肉片	lìzhīròupiàn
Salt-baked chicken	盐鸡	yánjī
White fungus and wolfberry soup (sweet)	枸杞炖银耳	gǒuqi2 dùnyín'ěr

Dim sum

Dim sum	点心	diǎnxīn
Barbecued pork bun	叉烧包	chāshāo bāo
Chicken feet	凤爪	fèngzhuǎ
Crab and prawn dumpling	蟹肉虾饺	xièròu xiājiǎo
Custard tart	蛋挞	dàntà
Doughnut	炸面饼圈	zhá miànbǐngquān
Fried taro and mince dumpling	蕃薯糊饺	fānshǔ hújiǎo
Lotus paste bun	莲蓉糕	liánrónggāo
Moon cake (sweet bean paste in flaky pastry)	月饼	yuèbǐng
Paper-wrapped prawns	纸包虾	zhǐbāoxiā
Pork and prawn dumpling	烧麦	shāomài
Prawn crackers	虾片	xiāpiàn
Prawn dumpling	虾饺	xiājiǎo
Prawn paste on fried toast	芝麻虾	zhīmaxiā
Shanghai fried meat and vegetable dumpling ("potstickers")	锅贴	guōtiē
Spring roll	春卷	chūnjuǎn
Steamed spareribs and chilli	排骨	páigǔ
Stuffed rice-flour roll	肠粉	chángfěn
Stuffed green peppers with black bean sauce	豆豉馅青椒	dòuchǐ xiànqīngjiāo
Sweet sesame balls	芝麻球	zhīma qiú
Turnip-paste patty	萝卜糕	luóbo gāo

Fruit

Fruit	水果	shuǐguǒ
Apple	苹果	píngguǒ
Banana	香蕉	xiāngjiāo
Durian	榴莲	liúlián
Grape	葡萄	pútáo
Honeydew melon	哈密瓜	hāmì guā

Longan	龙眼	lóngyǎn
Lychee	荔枝	lìzhī
Mandarin orange	橘子	júzi
Mango	果	mángguǒ
Orange	橙子	chéngzi
Peach	桃子	táozi
Pear	梨	lí
Persimmon	柿子	shìzi
Plum	李子	lǐzi
Pomegranate	石榴	shíliu
Pomelo	柚子	yòuzi
Watermelon	西瓜	xīguā

Glossary

General terms

Arhat Buddhist saint.

Bei North.

Binguan Hotel; generally a large one, for tourists.

Bodhisattva A follower of Buddhism who has attained enlightenment, but has chosen to stay on earth to teach rather than enter nirvana; Buddhist god or goddess.

Boxers The name given to an anti-foreign organization which originated in Shandong in 1898. Encouraged by the Qing Empress Dowager Cixi, they roamed China attacking Westernized Chinese and foreigners in what became known as the Boxer Movement (see p.125).

Chorten Tibetan stupa.

CITS China International Travel Service. Tourist organization primarily interested in selling tours, though they can help with obtaining train tickets.

CTS China Travel Service. Tourist organization similar to CITS.

Concession Part of a town or city ceded to a foreign power in the nineteenth century.

Cultural Revolution Ten-year period beginning in 1966 and characterized by destruction, persecution and fanatical devotion to Mao (see p.1189).

Dagoba Another name for a stupa.

Dong East.

Dougong Large, carved wooden brackets, a common feature of temple design.

Fandian Restaurant or hotel.

Fen Smallest denomination of Chinese currency – there are one hundred fen to the yuan.

Feng Peak.

Feng shui A system of geomancy used to determine the positioning of buildings (see p.1191).

Gang of Four Mao's widow and her supporters who were put on trial immediately after Mao's death for their role in the Cultural Revolution, for which they were convenient scapegoats.

Ge Pavilion.

Gong Palace; usually indicates a Taoist temple.

Grassland Steppe; areas of land too high or cold to support anything other than grass, and agriculturally useful only as pastureland for sheep or cattle. Found especially in Inner Mongolia, Qinghai and Xinjiang.

Guan Pass; in temple names, usually denotes a Taoist shrine.

Guanxi Literally "connections": the reciprocal favours inherent in the process of official appointments and transactions.

Guanyin The ubiquitous Buddhist Goddess of Mercy, the most popular Bodhisattva in China, who postponed her entry into paradise in order to help ease human misery. Derived from the Indian deity Avalokiteshvara, she is often depicted with up to a thousand arms.

Gulou Drum tower; traditionally marking the centre of a town, this was where a drum was beaten at nightfall and in times of need.

Guomindang (GMD) The Nationalist Peoples' Party. Under Chiang Kaishek, the GMD fought Communist forces for 25 years before being defeated and moving to Taiwan in 1949, where it remains a major political party.

Hai Sea.

Han Chinese The main body of the Chinese people, as distinct from other ethnic groups such as Uyghur, Miao, Hui or Tibetan.

He River.

Hu Lake.

Hui Muslim minority, mainly based in Gansu and Ningxia. Visually they are often indistinguishable from Han Chinese.

Hutong A narrow alleyway.

I Ching The Book of Changes, an ancient handbook for divination that includes some of the fundamental concepts of Chinese thought, such as the duality *yin* and *yang*.

Inkstones Decoratively carved blocks traditionally used by artists and calligraphers as a palette for mixing ink powder with water. The most famous, smooth-grained varieties come from Anhui and Guangdong provinces.

Jiang River.

Jiao (or mao) Ten fen.

Jiaozi Crescent-shaped, ravioli-like dumpling, usually served fried by the plateful for breakfast.

Jie Street.

Kang A raised wooden platform in a Chinese home, heated by the stove, on which the residents eat and sleep.

Kazakh A minority, mostly nomadic, in Xinjiang.

Lamian "Pulled noodles", a Muslim speciality usually served in a spicy soup.

Legalism In the Chinese context, a belief that humans are intrinsically bad and that strict laws are need to rein in their behaviour.

Ling Tomb.

Little Red Book A selection of "Quotations from Chairman Mao Zedong", produced in 1966 as a philosophical treatise for Red Guards during the Cultural Revolution.

Long March The Communists' 9500-kilometre tactical retreat in 1934–35 from Guomindang troops advancing on their base in the Jinggan Shan ranges, Jiangxi, to Yan'an in Shaanxi province.

Lu Street.

Luohan Buddhist disciple.

Mandala Mystic diagram which forms an important part of Buddhist iconography, especially in Tibet.

Mantou Steamed bread bun (literally "bald head").

Men Gate/door.

Miao Temple, usually Confucian.

Middle Kingdom A literal translation of the Chinese words for China.

Nan South.

PLA The People's Liberation Army, the official name of the Communist military forces since 1949.

PSB Public Security Bureau, the branch of China's police force which deals directly with foreigners.

Pagoda Tower with distinctively tapering structure, often associated with pseudo-science of *feng shui*.

Pinyin The official system of transliterating Chinese script into Roman characters.

Putonghua Mandarin Chinese; literally "Common Language".

Qianfodong Literally, "Thousand Buddha Cave", the name given to any Buddhist cave site along the Chinese section of the Silk Road.

Qiao Bridge.

RMB Renminbi. Another name for Chinese currency literally meaning "the people's money".

Red Guards The unruly factional forces unleashed by Mao during the Cultural Revolution to find and destroy brutally any "reactionaries" among the populace.

Renmin The people.

SEZ Special Economic Zone. A region in which state controls on production have been loosened and Western techniques of economic management are experimented with.

Sakyamuni Name given to future incarnation of Buddha.

Shan Mountain.

Shi City or municipality.

Shui Water.

Shuijiao Similar to *jiaozi* but boiled or served in a thin soup.

Si Temple, usually Buddhist.

Siheyuan Traditional courtyard house.

Spirit wall Wall behind the main gateway to a house, designed to thwart evil spirits, which, it was believed, could move only in straight lines.

Spirit Way The straight road leading to a tomb, lined with guardian figures.

Stele Freestanding stone tablet carved with text.

Stupa Multi-tiered tower associated with Buddhist temples that usually contains sacred objects.

Sutra Buddhist texts, often illustrative doctrines arranged in prayer form.

Ta Tower or pagoda.

Taiping Uprising Peasant rebellion against Qing rule during the mid-nineteenth century, which saw over a million troops led by the Christian fanatic Hong Xiuquan establish a capital at Nanjing before their later annihilation at the hands of imperial forces.

Tian Heaven or the sky.

Treaty port A port in which foreigners were permitted to set up residence, for the purpose of trade, under nineteenth-century agreements between China and foreign powers.

Uyghur Substantial minority of Turkic people, living mainly in Xinjiang.

Waiguoren Foreigner.

Xi West.

Yuan China's unit of currency. Also a courtyard or garden (and the name of the Mongol dynasty).

Yurt Round, felt tent used by nomads. Also known as *ger*.

Zhan Station.

Zhao Temple; term used mainly in Inner Mongolia.

Zhong Middle; China is referred to as *zhongguo*, the Middle Kingdom.

Zhonglou Bell tower, usually twinned with a Gulou. The bell it contained was rung at dawn and in emergencies.

Zhou Place or region.

Travel store

ROUGH GUIDES Complete Listing

UK & Ireland
Britain
Devon & Cornwall
Dublin **D**
Edinburgh **D**
England
Ireland
The Lake District
London
London **D**
London Mini Guide
Scotland
Scottish Highlands & Islands
Wales

Europe
Algarve **D**
Amsterdam
Amsterdam **D**
Andalucía
Athens **D**
Austria
Baltic States
Barcelona
Barcelona **D**
Belgium & Luxembourg
Berlin
Brittany & Normandy
Bruges **D**
Brussels
Budapest
Bulgaria
Copenhagen
Corfu
Corsica
Costa Brava **D**
Crete
Croatia
Cyprus
Czech & Slovak Republics
Denmark
Dodecanese & East Aegean Islands
Dordogne & The Lot
Europe
Florence & Siena
Florence **D**
France
Germany
Gran Canaria **D**
Greece
Greek Islands
Hungary
Ibiza & Formentera **D**
Iceland
Ionian Islands
Italy
The Italian Lakes
Languedoc & Roussillon
Lanzarote & Fuerteventura **D**
Lisbon **D**
The Loire Valley
Madeira **D**
Madrid **D**
Mallorca **D**
Mallorca & Menorca
Malta & Gozo **D**
Menorca
Moscow
The Netherlands
Norway
Paris
Paris **D**
Paris Mini Guide
Poland
Portugal
Prague
Prague **D**
Provence & the Côte D'Azur
Pyrenees
Romania
Rome
Rome **D**
Sardinia
Scandinavia
Sicily
Slovenia
Spain
St Petersburg
Sweden
Switzerland
Tenerife & La Gomera **D**
Turkey
Tuscany & Umbria
Venice & The Veneto
Venice **D**
Vienna

Asia
Bali & Lombok
Bangkok
Beijing
Cambodia
China
Goa
Hong Kong & Macau
Hong Kong & Macau **D**
India
Indonesia
Japan
Kerala
Laos
Malaysia, Singapore & Brunei
Nepal
The Philippines
Rajasthan, Dehli & Agra
Singapore
Singapore **D**
South India
Southeast Asia
Sri Lanka
Taiwan
Thailand
Thailand's Beaches & Islands
Tokyo
Vietnam

Australasia
Australia
Melbourne
New Zealand
Sydney

North America
Alaska
Baja California
Boston
California
Canada
Chicago
Colorado
Florida
The Grand Canyon
Hawaii
Honolulu **D**
Las Vegas **D**
Los Angeles
Maui **D**
Miami & South Florida
Montréal
New England
New Orleans **D**
New York City
New York City **D**
New York City Mini Guide
Orlando & Walt Disney World® **D**
Pacific Northwest
San Francisco
San Francisco **D**
Seattle
Southwest USA
Toronto
USA
Vancouver
Washington DC
Washington DC **D**
Yellowstone & The Grand Tetons
Yosemite

Caribbean & Latin America
Antigua & Barbuda **D**
Argentina
Bahamas
Barbados **D**
Belize
Bolivia
Brazil
Cancùn & Cozumel **D**
Caribbean
Central America
Chile
Costa Rica
Cuba
Dominican Republic
Dominican Republic **D**
Ecuador
Guatemala
Jamaica
Mexico
Peru
St Lucia **D**
South America
Trinidad & Tobago
Yúcatan

Africa & Middle East
Cape Town & the Garden Route
Dubai **D**
Egypt
Gambia
Jordan

D: Rough Guide **DIRECTIONS** for short breaks

Kenya
Marrakesh D
Morocco
South Africa, Lesotho & Swaziland
Syria
Tanzania
Tunisia
West Africa
Zanzibar

Travel Specials
First-Time Africa
First-Time Around the World
First-Time Asia
First-Time Europe
First-Time Latin America
Travel Health
Travel Online
Travel Survival
Walks in London & SE England
Women Travel
World Party

Maps
Algarve
Amsterdam
Andalucia & Costa del Sol
Argentina
Athens
Australia
Barcelona
Berlin
Boston & Cambridge
Brittany
Brussels
California
Chicago
Chile
Corsica
Costa Rica & Panama
Crete
Croatia
Cuba
Cyprus
Czech Republic
Dominican Republic
Dubai & UAE
Dublin
Egypt
Florence & Siena
Florida
France
Frankfurt
Germany
Greece
Guatemala & Belize
Iceland
India
Ireland
Italy
Kenya & Northern Tanzania
Lisbon
London
Los Angeles
Madrid
Malaysia
Mallorca
Marrakesh
Mexico
Miami & Key West
Morocco
New England
New York City
New Zealand
Northern Spain
Paris
Peru
Portugal
Prague
Pyrenees & Andorra
Rome
San Francisco
Sicily
South Africa
South India
Spain & Portugal
Sri Lanka
Tenerife
Thailand
Toronto
Trinidad & Tobago
Tunisia
Turkey
Tuscany
Venice
Vietnam, Laos & Cambodia
Washington DC
Yucatán Peninsula

Dictionary Phrasebooks
Croatian
Czech
Dutch
Egyptian Arabic
French
German
Greek
Hindi & Urdu
Italian
Japanese
Latin American Spanish
Mandarin Chinese
Mexican Spanish
Polish
Portuguese
Russian
Spanish
Swahili
Thai
Turkish
Vietnamese

Computers
Blogging
eBay
iPhone
iPods, iTunes & music online
The Internet
Macs & OS X
MySpace
PCs and Windows
PlayStation Portable
Website Directory

Film & TV
American Independent Film
British Cult Comedy
Chick Flicks
Comedy Movies
Cult Movies
Film
Film Musicals
Film Noir
Gangster Movies
Horror Movies
Kids' Movies
Sci-Fi Movies
Westerns

Lifestyle
Babies
Ethical Living
Pregnancy & Birth
Running

Music Guides
The Beatles
Blues
Bob Dylan
Book of Playlists
Classical Music
Elvis
Frank Sinatra
Heavy Metal
Hip-Hop
Jazz
Led Zeppelin
Opera
Pink Floyd
Punk
Reggae
Rock
The Rolling Stones
Soul and R&B
Velvet Underground
World Music (2 vols)

Popular Culture
Books for Teenagers
Children's Books, 5-11
Conspiracy Theories
Crime Fiction
Cult Fiction
The Da Vinci Code
His Dark Materials
Lord of the Rings
Shakespeare
Superheroes
The Templars
Unexplained Phenomena

Science
The Brain
Climate Change
The Earth
Genes & Cloning
The Universe
Weather

Small print and

Index

A Rough Guide to Rough Guides

Published in 1982, the first Rough Guide – to Greece – was a student scheme that became a publishing phenomenon. Mark Ellingham, a recent graduate in English from Bristol University, had been travelling in Greece the previous summer and couldn't find the right guidebook. With a small group of friends he wrote his own guide, combining a highly contemporary, journalistic style with a thoroughly practical approach to travellers' needs.

The immediate success of the book spawned a series that rapidly covered dozens of destinations. And, in addition to impecunious backpackers, Rough Guides soon acquired a much broader and older readership that relished the guides' wit and inquisitiveness as much as their enthusiastic, critical approach and value-for-money ethos.

These days, Rough Guides include recommendations from shoestring to luxury and cover more than 200 destinations around the globe, including almost every country in the Americas and Europe, more than half of Africa and most of Asia and Australasia. Our ever-growing team of authors and photographers is spread all over the world, particularly in Europe, the USA and Australia.

In the early 1990s, Rough Guides branched out of travel, with the publication of Rough Guides to World Music, Classical Music and the Internet. All three have become benchmark titles in their fields, spearheading the publication of a wide range of books under the Rough Guide name.

Including the travel series, Rough Guides now number more than 350 titles, covering: phrasebooks, waterproof maps, music guides from Opera to Heavy Metal, reference works as diverse as Conspiracy Theories and Shakespeare, and popular culture books from iPods to Poker. Rough Guides also produce a series of more than 120 World Music CDs in partnership with World Music Network.

Visit www.roughguides.com to see our latest publications.

Rough Guide travel images are available for commercial licensing at www.roughguidespictures.com

Rough Guide credits

Text editor: Sam Cook, Gita Daneshjoo, Keith Drew & Greg Ward
Layout: Ajay Verma
Cartography: Karobi Gogoi
Picture editor: Mark Thomas
Production: Rebecca Short
Proofreader: Karen Parker
Proofreader (Chinese): Xiaoshan Sun
Cover design: Chloë Roberts
Editorial: **London** Kate Berens, Claire Saunders, Ruth Blackmore, Alison Murchie, Karoline Densley, Andy Turner, Edward Aves, Alice Park, Lucy White, Jo Kirby, James Smart, Natasha Foges, Róisín Cameron, Emma Traynor Emma Gibbs, Kathryn Lane, Christina Valhouli, Joe Staines, Peter Buckley, Matthew Milton, Tracy Hopkins, Ruth Tidball; **New York** Andrew Rosenberg, Steven Horak, AnneLise Sorensen, April Isaacs, Ella Steim, Anna Owens, Sean Mahoney; **Delhi** Madhavi Singh, Karen D'Souza
Design & Pictures: **London** Scott Stickland, Dan May, Diana Jarvis, Nicole Newman, Sarah Cummins, Emily Taylor; **Delhi** Umesh Aggarwal, Jessica Subramanian, Ankur Guha, Pradeep Thapliyal, Sachin Tanwar, Anita Singh, Nikhil Agarwal
Production: Vicky Baldwin
Cartography: **London** Maxine Repath, Ed Wright, Katie Lloyd-Jones; **Delhi** Jai Prakash Mishra, Rajesh Chhibber, Ashutosh Bharti, Rajesh Mishra, Animesh Pathak, Jasbir Sandhu, Amod Singh, Alakananda Bhattacharya, Swati Handoo
Online: Narender Kumar, Rakesh Kumar, Amit Verma, Rahul Kumar, Ganesh Sharma, Debojit Borah, Saurabh Sati
Marketing & Publicity: **London** Liz Statham, Niki Hanmer, Louise Maher, Jess Carter, Vanessa Godden, Vivienne Watton, Anna Paynton, Rachel Sprackett; **New York** Geoff Colquitt, Megan Kennedy, Katy Ball; **Delhi** Ragini Govind
Manager India: Punita Singh
Reference Director: Andrew Lockett
Publishing Coordinator: Helen Phillips
Publishing Director: Martin Dunford
Commercial Manager: Gino Magnotta
Managing Director: John Duhigg

Publishing information

This fifth edition published April 2008 by
Rough Guides Ltd,
80 Strand, London WC2R 0RL
345 Hudson St, 4th Floor,
New York, NY 10014, USA
14 Local Shopping Centre, Panchsheel Park,
New Delhi 110017, India
Distributed by the Penguin Group
Penguin Books Ltd,
80 Strand, London WC2R 0RL
Penguin Group (USA)
375 Hudson Street, NY 10014, USA
Penguin Group (Australia)
250 Camberwell Road, Camberwell,
Victoria 3124, Australia
Penguin Books Canada Ltd,
10 Alcorn Avenue, Toronto, Ontario,
Canada M4V 1E4
Penguin Group (NZ)
67 Apollo Drive, Mairangi Bay, Auckland 1310,
New Zealand
Cover concept by Peter Dyer.

Typeset in Bembo and Helvetica to an original design by Henry Iles.

Printed and bound in China

1256pp includes index

A catalogue record for this book is available from the British Library

ISBN: 978-1-84353-872-1

1 3 5 7 9 8 6 4 2

Help us update

We've gone to a lot of effort to ensure that the fifth edition of **The Rough Guide to China** is accurate and up to date. However, things change – places get "discovered", opening hours are notoriously fickle, restaurants and rooms raise prices or lower standards. If you feel we've got it wrong or left something out, we'd like to know, and if you can remember the address, the price, the hours, the phone number, so much the better.

Please send your comments with the subject line "**Rough Guide China Update**" to
© mail@roughguides.com. We'll credit all contributions and send a copy of the next edition (or any other Rough Guide if you prefer) for the very best emails.

Have your questions answered and tell others about your trip at
Ⓦ community.roughguides.com

Acknowledgements

This guide is dedicated to the memory of a wonderful travel writer, **Jeremy Atiyah**, who will be sorely missed.

Simon Farnham Thanks M, Steph, Yu Feixia, Si Lewis, Paul Pinder, Andy Heald, Fiona McNeil, Chen Qu, Liu Xin, Mr Chez, Mark South, and Keith Drew for his patience.

David Leffman As always, huge thanks to Narrell; also to Jim, Terry, Stuart and Dan; Xiao Laoshi and Li Laoshi; the Gaos; Mei; Jalal Afhim; Michael Udel; Leo; Seb; and Sam. Special thanks to CS Tang and CS Luck for enthusiastic help with food and martial investigations; and to Peter and Shelagh Hardy, who started me Chinawards twenty-five years ago.

Simon Lewis Thanks to Noe, Summer, Chris T, Xiao Song, Tim, Du, TieYing, Kat, ShenYe, Kai Yuen, Adrian, Anny, Ya Ou, and in memory of the great traveller Giles.

Mark South Thanks to Barbara Deniau, Ineke Williams, Tim Wild, Surfing Hainan, James Leung, David Niven and Club Football Beijing.

Martin Zatko Thanks to the staff at Leo Hostel in Beijing for their help with queries; Fanny at the Far East for her Chinese lessons and all-round cheeriness; Mullark for being an able partner in crime both in Beijing and beyond; Taiwan Penny for her assistance in Chengde, Maidstone and various other places; and Shanhaiguan for falling down just as I was about to review it.

Readers' letters

Thanks to all those readers of the fourth edition who took the trouble to write in with their amendments and additions. Apologies for any misspellings or omissions.

Katrina Abatis, Simon Allen, Edithe Aussedat, Andrea Bieder, Ted Bier, David Burnett, Martin Cabalzar, Pere Camps, Matthew Chance, Ken Chapman, Xenia Cherkaev, John and Maggie Coaton, Julie Collins, John & Ros Crossland, Mary Durran, Michael Engl, Nigel Gayner, Hadar Goshen, Emma Harradine, Porshia Ho, Robbie Ho, Andrea Hsu, Sophia Lambert, Larry D. Little, Sarah Lockwood, Leo Lacey, Maria Lahiffe, Barbara Leung, Elinor Lloyd-Philipps, Ukirsari Manggalani, Rodney Mantle, Stacey McDonald, Alison Middleton, C. A. Murray, Rick Ong, Andrew Pickett, Sarah Pritchard, Ni Qian, Maria Rivera, Roger Schlapbach, Tom Shortland, David Styles, David Thomas, Steven Tour, Sebastian Turner, Yael Weisz-Rind, Christian Williams, Diana Williams, Winnie Wong, Nan Wu.

Photo credits

All photos © Rough Guides except the following:

Introduction
Shanghai skyline © Timothy Allen/Axiom
Terraced rice paddies in Guangxi province © Karen Su/Getty Images
Temple detail © Ian Cumming/Axiom
Woman carrying piglet, Yunnan province © Karen Su/Getty Images
National Olympic Stadium © View Stock/Alamy
Incense spirals at the Man Mo Temple in Hong Kong © Mark Thomas
Shanghai metro system © Karen Su/Getty Images
Chinese script © Keith Drew
Temple in Lijiang, Yunnan province © Jim Holmes/Axiom
Cyclists in Xi'an © James Sparshatt/Axiom
Pollution in Tian'anmen Square © Lou Linwei/Alamy
Ya Long River © Rob Penn/Axiom

Things not to miss
01 Mount Everest © Dan Rafla/Getty Images
03 Meili Xue Shan © China Tourism Photo Library
06 The Silk Road © Karen Su
07 Tiger Leaping Gorge © Alan Copson/Alamy
09 The Jokhang © Getty Images
10 Bird-watching in Caohai © David Leffman
11 Mogao Caves © Panorama Media/Alamy
12 Kashgar Sunday Market © Iain Masterton/Alamy
13 Hong Kong's skyline © Mark Thomas
15 Sichuanese teahouses © Craig Lovell/Getty Images
16 Sisters' Meal Festival © Getty Images
17 Tai Shan © Hideaki Tanaka/Getty Images
18 Minority villages © Neil McAllister/Alamy
19 Jiayuguan fort © Karen Su/Getty Images
22 The Yungang Caves © Liu Xiaoyang/Alamy

23 Tiger in Changbai Shan Nature Reserve © Steve Bloom Images/Alamy
24 The Great Buddha © Keith Drew
27 The Terracotta Army © Getty Images
26 Chengde © AM Corporation/Alamy
29 Li River © Karen Su/Getty Images
30 Labrang Monastery © Robert Preston
31 The Yangzi River © Liu Liqun/Imaginechina
32 Beijing duck © Ludwig M Brinckmann/Alamy
33 Harbin Ice Festival © Iain Masterton/Alamy
34 Dali © Nicolas Lee/Getty Images

Chinese festival colour section

Dragon dance performance © Karen Su/Getty Images
Paper money © Purestock/Getty Images
Mid-Autumn Mooncake © Bon Appetit/Alamy
Double Ninth Festival © dbimages/Alamy
Sisters' Meal Festival © John Lund/Getty Images
Horse festival © Matthieu Ricard/Getty Images

Chinese cuisine colour section

Roast duck © Lou-foto/Alamy
Birds' nests © John Warburton Lee/Alamy
Dried chillies in Xinjiang © Ian Cumming/Axiom
Food stalls in Wuhan © Gordon Clements/Axiom
Scorpion snacks © Ron Yue/Alamy

Chinese architecture colour section

Xi'an Bell Tower © Keith Drew
Wind-and-Rain Bridge © Urbanmyth/Alamy
Xintiandi © Alamy

Black and whites

p.72 Forbidden City © Keith Drew
p.94 Tian'anmen Square © Keith Drew
p.134 Acrobats at Chaoyang Theatre © Keith Drew
p.145 The Great Wall © Keith Drew
p.152 The Bishu Shanzhuang © DK Images
p.160 Tianjin's old city © AAD Worldwide/Alamy
p.181 Putuozongcheng Miao © Liu Xiaoyang/Alamy
p.184 Tian Chi © Alex Fairweather/Alamy
p.192 Imperial Palace © Jon Bower/Alamy
p.204 New Yalu Bridge © JTB Communications/Alamy
p.219 Harbin Ice Festival © Robert Harding/Alamy
p.226 The Terracotta Army © Keith Drew
p.237 The Yungang Caves © DK Images
p.242 Ta Yuan Si © DK Images
p.254 Pingyao © Karen Su/Getty Images
p.267 Xi'an Bell Tower © Keith Drew
p.284 Famen Si © Eddie Gerald/Alamy
p.295 Fengxian Cave © Liu Xiaoyang/Alamy
p.323 The path up Tai Shen © Karen Su/Getty Images
p.338 The beach at Qingdao © Karen Su/Getty Images
p.396 Fragrant Isle, Zhuozheng Yuan © DK Images
p.408 Wumen Qiao © DK Images
p.411 Tongli © DK Images
p.433 Su Di Bridge © DK Images
p.440 Lu Xun's Former Residence © DK Images
p.447 Puji Si © DK Images
p.450 Wudan Shan © David Leffman
p.472 Huang Shan © DK Images
p.487 Three Gorges Dam © Liu Xiaoyang/Alamy
p.516 Tengwang Pavilion © Mediacolour's/Alamy
p.523 Jingdezhen porcelain © DK Images
p.530 Thirty-Six Peaks © Panarama Media/Alamy
p.556 Hakka tulou © DK Images
p.583 Guangdong dumplings © DBimages/Alamy
p.612 Chaozhou's old quarter © DK Images
p.633 Dadonghai Beach © JTB Communications/Alamy
p.662 Walkway in Central © Mark Thomas
p.673 Busy street in Kowloon © Mark Thomas
p.678 Ten Thousand Buddhas Monastery © Mark Thomas/Axiom
p.712 Black-necked cranes © David Leffman
p.724 The Li River © DK Images
p.735 Drum tower in Zhaoxing © Dbimages/Alamy
p.745 Detian waterfall © Panarama Media/Alamy
p.765 Sisters' Meal Festival © Getty Images
p.774 Tiger Leaping Gorge © Robert Preston/Alamy
p.791 Hauting Si © Alamy
p.805 San Ti Si © Neil McAllister/Alamy
p.825 Shangri-La © Neil McAllister/Alamy
p.843 Dai woman © DK Images
p.858 Yangtse River © View Stock/Alamy
p.891 Niuxin Shi © Keith Drew
p.894 The Great Buddha © DK Images
p.903 Cliff carving, Boding Shan © DK Images
p.918 Panda © DK Images
p.928 Langmusi © DK Images
p.934 Horses grazing © Victor Paul Borg/Alamy
p.939 Litang's horse festival © Bjorn Svensson/Alamy
p.944 Jiayuguan fort © DK Images
p.960 Mongol yurt © Eddie Gerald/Alamy
p.976 Qingtongxia 108 Dagobas © DK Images
p.998 Labrang Monastery © Simon Farnham
p.1017 Camel ride at Mingsha Shan © DK Images
p.1043 Harvesting grapes, Turpan © Cephas Picture Library/Alamy
p.1071 Kashgar market © Simon Farnham
p.1080 Mount Kailash © Craig Lovell/Alamy
p.1101 Potola Palace © Getty Images
p.1123 Namtso lake © Michele Falzone/Alamy
p.1136 Mount Everest © DK Images

Index

Map entries are in colour.

The following abbreviations are used throughout this index:

AH Anhui	**HEB** Hebei	**QH** Qinghai
BJ Beijing	**HEN** Henan	**SAX** Shaanxi
CQ Chongqing	**HN** Hainan	**SC** Sichuan
DB Dongbei	**HUB** Hubei	**SD** Shandong
FJ Fujian	**HUN** Hunan	**SX** Shanxi
GD Guangdong	**IM** Inner Mongolia	**T** Tibet
GS Gansu	**JS** Jiangsu	**XJ** Xinjiang
GX Guangxi	**JX** Jiangxi	**YN** Yunnan
GZ Guizhou	**NX** Ningxia	**ZJ** Zhejiang

INDEX

C

INDEX

I

J

N

O

P

Q

R

S

INDEX

T

I

INDEX

Map symbols

maps are listed in the full index using coloured text

International boundary
Provincial boundary
Chapter boundary
Disputed boundary
Expressway
Major road
Minor road
Pedestrianized road
Steps
Tunnel
Path
Railway
Metro station & line
Monorail
Funicular railway
Cable car
Ferry route
Waterway & dam
Canal
Wall
Gate
Bridge
Mountain range
Mountain peak
Cliffs
Gorge/cutting
Marshland
Waterfall
Spring
Tree
Caves
Viewpoint
Point of interest

Arch
Statue
Public gardens
Airport
Bus station/depot
Minibus stand/bus stop
Embassy/consulate
Hospital
Internet access
Telecom office
Information office
Post office
Hotel
Restaurant
Skiing area
Museum
Ruins
Tower
Monument
Border-crossing post
Temple/monastery
Pagoda
Mosque
Stupa
Building
Church/cathedral
Market
Stadium
Park
Beach
Forest
Cemetery